DATE DUE

DEMCO 38-296

WORLD WHO IS WHO AND DOES WHAT
IN
ENVIRONMENT & CONSERVATION

EDITED BY
NICHOLAS POLUNIN

COMPILED BY
LYNN M. CURME

St. Martin's Press
New York

THE FOUNDATION FOR ENVIRONMENTAL CONSERVATION, GENEVA

JANUARY 1997

Printed by Biddles Ltd, Guildford and King's Lynn, UK

ISBN 0–312–17448–9

Library of Congress Cataloging in Publication Data applied for

INTRODUCTION

With our 'civilized' world in its present, increasingly precarious state, there can scarcely be any subject more important for its survival than due action on the environmental movement's front towards implementation of the often substantial advances, at least in prospect, that are being made practically all over Planet Earth. These advances commonly depend on discoveries made, or campaigns led, by dedicated individuals: but how and where, and with what leadership — and real practical effect, even locally? Their overall potential for improvement of our world's state is great, especially if they 'all pull together', and the present work endeavours to make this the more possible and even practicable by offering details of leading concerned individuals' interests, activities, further capabilities, and ready means of contact and hence chances of concordant collaboration. To such ends this volume and its planned successors should prove uniquely helpful.

Rather many years ago we recognized this serious gap delaying effective execution in Mankind's holistic functioning — despite our species' increasing pandominance and despite the upgrowth of concerns that seemed bent on narrowing the gap — and started planning an *ad hoc* compilation as part of our very small Foundation for Environmental Conservation's attempt at global amelioration to however modest a degree. As a result we now come out with this initial edition of a pioneering *World Who Is Who and Does What in Environment & Conservation*, which we plan to follow with at least two more (cumulative) editions to surpass our original target of 3,000 up-to-date (including updated) biographies. Although this will depend on our continuing health, availability, and financial capability, the prospects just now look good and our dedicated resolve likely to prevail — as it has done in the past with such activities as our International Conferences on Environmental Future, our World Campaign (and subsequently World Council) For The Biosphere, our founding editorships of *Biological Conservation* and then of *Environmental Conservation* for the last 22 years, and our dedication to (some say leadership of) the environmental/conservational movement over the past 30 years.

The A–Z biographical listings form the main body of this work but particularly noteworthy and uniquely helpful are the major Appendixes dealing with biographees (I) by Country (*i.e.* in which each is mainly working, regardless of his or her nationality) and (II) by Speciality, so that users can readily identify, locate, and contact, experts in any geographical region or desired field of concern or endeavour. At the very end of the book is Appendix III of used Abbreviations, Acronyms, etc. The personal listings include information on each biographee's qualifications and affiliations, educational background and pertinent work experience, achievements and awards, and specialist interests and publications. Details are also given of biographees' pertinent capabilities and language abilities, their willingness to be consulted for advice or by 'the media' or to act as consultants or referees, and finally their contact addresses, with telephone and fax etc. numbers.

To vindicate the many years of hard work already spent on this project or expectably in future, we sincerely hope that government departments, universities and colleges, alert and alerting councils, environmental and conservational organizations, wisely forward-looking businesspeople and politicians, and all others seeking (or anyway needing) specialist advice on environment-related issues or due conservation of Nature's riches, will find this new kind of 'Who's Who' a valuable and unique source of reliable reference or guidance — no matter where they are centred or otherwise located, and regardless of their needs and general circumstances. This should be effective throughout the human-inhabited world, but always remembering that more than 70% of our globe's surface is currently occupied by oceans or ice-caps, concerning which situation we must always preserve a fully-global and holistic perspective.

As in the present work the Editor has permitted himself to insert details rather widely from personal knowledge, from his correspondence files dating back to his 1966 'vision' of our world being threatened by human pandominance, and from other sources, and in view of the surprising paucity of representation of our chosen biographees in such standard works as the *International Who's Who* and *Who's Who in the World*, our pertinent, recorded data in this compilation are almost entirely 'original'. Thus apart from the last 30 years of personal contacts and correspondence, the main source has been from returned Questionnaires which we have sent to chosen, seemingly-qualified individuals in recent years throughout the world. This policy *cum modus operandi* is being continued at least for the Second Edition, which it is hoped to publish before the end of 1999. But as it would be wasteful to send further Questionnaires to biographees who are already represented in this First Edition, they and other supportive users are asked to fax or write us about any necessary corrections or desired updatings, and likewise the names and addresses of, and a line or so of leading details concerning, anybody further whom they may feel we ought to consider for possible inclusion in the Second Edition. This procedure is likely to be continued for the Third and any possible further editions of what we hope will become recognized as the standard work of reference and often urgently-needed source of such details throughout the world.

CHOICE OF BIOGRAPHEES

The process of consideration for inclusion in our *World Who Is Who and Does What in Environment & Conservation* includes approval of each one of the initially-proposed individuals in the lists that are submitted periodically to the Foundation's international but strictly confidential *Awards Committee*, which has the right to blackball without question the name of anybody they consider unqualified or otherwise unsuitable for further consideration, and have done so on occasion.

As for the compilation of these lists of proposals, the sources are legion and further proposals always welcome though preferably in writing. Most notably and valuably they have been enriched in the past by their Commission members' and other Lists from IUCN (now the World Conservation Union), WWF International (now in most regions styled the World Wide Fund for Nature), and the United Nations Environment Programme (UNEP, particularly its Global 500 Roll of Honour). The often close collaboration of these three last-named 'world' bodies has been particularly valuable in preparing this First Edition and is now as ever most gratefully acknowledged.

Finally (if not foremost!) we wish to acclaim the generous help of the Nippon (then Sasakawa) Foundation, of Tokyo, Japan, and of our own Foundation for Environmental Conservation, of Geneva, Switzerland, which between them have made this work practicable by affording some hard-earned recompense to the Compiler and necessary facilities and overheads to the project, the Editor having been glad to give his services *con amore* in (mostly) better times. We also value the ever-helpful and most skilful collaboration of our Printer, Gilbert-E. Huguet, and the patient understanding of our chosen Publisher, Earthscan, in giving us the prospect of early publication in library-viable hardback form at a reasonable price which we hope will be conducive to the beneficial use world-wide of this result of our protracted labours — gladly given, we like to think, for the benefit of a beautiful but troubled world.

POINTS TO REMEMBER FOR FULLY BENEFICIAL USE

The following items should be borne in mind by users of this work, who should note also that the numbering of paragraphs corresponds to that used in the Questionnaires:

1. Hyphenated family **names** we have treated as if they were single, without cross-referencing, *i.e.* under the initial letter of the first (part of the) name, but multiple unhyphenated names and prefixes we have cross-referenced to their position under the initial letter of the last name, *e.g.* **BUMPER CROP, John**, *see* **CROP, John** BUMPER, and VAN **BREE, Peter J.H.**, *see* **BREE, Peter J.H.**VAN. (If, however, John had hyphenated his family names, he would have been listed and cited as **BUMPER-CROP, John**). Thus unaffixed 'prefixes' such as 'VAN', 'DE', 'VAN DER', and 'VON', and 'LA', 'LE', 'EL', and 'AL', are generally given (*sic*) in small capitals, and the earlier parts of the unhyphenated multiple names are given in large and small capitals in cross-referencing, but all in bold-face type.

2. **Titles** have been retained except for 'Mr', which may be understood for males if no other indication has been given. Mrs, Miss, or Ms, is used where seemingly necessary for clarity.

'Dr' is used for a 'first doctorate' such as a PhD or DPhil as well as for a 'full doctorate' such as DSc, ScD, SD, etc. 'Drs' and 'Da' are ignored as indicating only lower degrees, while degrees presented *honoris causa* are similarly ignored as titles because they do not *necessarily* indicate any academic or other professional qualification.

'Ms': we use this modern designation only where it seems to be needed, such as where a married woman uses a family name other than her husband's, as in the case of **Ute RECKERS** (*qv*).

We have attempted to maintain dignity and help bibliographers by not using 'pet' or contracted names or omitting initials of 'given' names despite the confusing modern 'lazy' tendency to do so.

Names commencing with 'Mac' or 'Mc' will be found entered separately, while punctuation etc. within names is ignored in determining sequences, thus maintaining strict alphabetical order.

In our endeavour to accommodate expressed wishes of biographees, and some other than a first given name has been indicated (or is known to us) as preferred and commonly used, we have placed brackets around any other given name or names, *e.g.* **AICKIN, (Robert) Malcolm**. Also, we have indicated any commonly-preferred cognomen in quotes after any relevant given name, *e.g.* **DASMANN, Raymond 'Ray' Frederic**.

3. The 'main *pertinent* field(s) of specialization &/or activity or activities' are used in compiling Appendix II [of Biographees] by **Speciality**, while Appendix I indicates each Biographee's **Country** or region of main activity (regardless of actual nationality) and chief pertinent interests and/or capabilities.*

4. If **Current positions** are held at the same institution, they are joined with an ampersand (&); otherwise a comma is used between them.

5. Date and place of birth are given before nationality, with parentage following if significant in choice of a pertinent vocation (*see also* 7).

---

* As indicated in the footnote to the third page of Appendix I, it is intended to exercise proper care henceforth in the use of semi-colons to indicate where necessary all major changes or groupings of subject when listing the (commonly multiple) pertinent interests of individual Biographees.

6. **Nationalities** are given in English, and usually in alphabetical order if more than one.

7. Names of father and/or mother are included only if they have environmental/conservational interests (or likely influence) which should then be indicated.

8. If a wife uses a different family name for professional or other reasons it is given, and likewise if spelling differs, *e.g.* Pavlova (wife of Pavlov). A cited daughter's married name will be given if customarily used and she qualifies subject-wise.

9. Close family members may be cited if they have pertinent interests which will then be indicated.

10. Higher **Education:** the name of the relevant institution is given first, then the course taken &/or degree or degrees awarded, with dates.

11. The request was to indicate pertinent **experience**, though sometimes this item has been confused with the next, and *vice versa*.

12. The request was to outline personal **career**.

13. Occasionally instead of **Achievements** we have indicated **'Endeavour(s)'** — probably at the Biographee's suggestion or implied choice while admiring his or her strict truthfulness when projects or missions have not been completed.

14. **Memberships:** during the protracted preparation of this work it has been found impracticable always to use recognized (or even regularly the same) abbreviations and contractions throughout. Our abbreviations etc. are explained in Appendix III — list of 'Abbreviations, Acronyms, Contractions, and Some Explanations' — ending this volume. Having had to decide on a system and keep to it throughout, we offer our apologies for any (wholly unintended) hurt feelings and inconsistencies.

When two or more acronyms and/or contractions are identical, it is usually left for the reader (user) to decide from the context which is applicable in a particular case; however, this being somewhat hazardous, in such cases we have sometimes indicated which of a choice of versions is involved. It is hoped that in future editions this and some other defects will be remedied.

Every effort has been made to give the correct meaning of all abbreviations and acronyms but if any errors of wrong use of conjunction (*e.g.* 'Association for...' rather than 'Association of ...' or the singular or plural *e.g.* 'Science' for 'Sciences' or *vice versa* are found, it is hoped that the Compiler will be informed — for remedy in the next Edition.

15. **Awards:** it has been the aim to indicate the awarding body and date of award in every at all major case where these   often very interesting   details are not obvious.

16. Of the titles of Biographees' **publications**, we have attempted to indicate (i) books and other 'separate' publications by printing them in *italic*, (ii) book chapters by using Roman (upright) type with upper-case initial letters of nouns, and (iii) journal papers all in lower-case after the initial letter (unless, of course, names of people, places, or identified species or genera of biota, are involved). However, this distinction has not usually been considered sufficiently important to ask about alone, and so should not be relied on in this widely pioneering First Edition.

17. Indication of each Biographee's attitude is requested regarding (a) personal publicity, and (b) support by news media, with future consultation possibilities in mind — for the benefit of the environmental movement and of specialist environmental or conservational consultants (*see also* 20).

18. **Languages** have been given in alphabetical order (in English). If no level of proficiency or fluency is stated, this should indicate that it is very good/fluent or is a biographee's mother tongue. However, users of this work ought to verify these matters of written and other proficiency in cases of importance — such as consultation or other employment.

19. It is our impression — and experience after many years' use and involvement — that, except in the case of the American *Who's Who in the World*, people usually survive in the main Who's Whos when once they get in. So we have commonly omitted dates indicating these sources from which '**further details** may be obtained'.

20. When '**consult. etc.**' is given, it denotes that the biographee is willing to act as a consultant and/or referee and to judge proposals in his or her pertinent field(s) of interest. Otherwise, that which a Biographee is willing to do is stated alone. Here we feel it incumbent on us to put in a plea for proper recompense for consultation etc. — such as members of the medical and legal professions would be expected to demand.

21. **Telephone** and **fax** numbers are usually given as submitted in the hope that the reporting subject (*i.e.* the Biographee) will be familiar with his or her method of presentation and any user know what the presented figures mean — without unexplained parentheses, zeros, or other single digits, and whether or not there is any joining by hyphens or separation by spaces etc. Numbers have been grouped (or sometimes left alone) to indicate country code, area/city code, then local number (without the zero [or zeros] or plus-signs used in front or elsewhere for a particular country).

Home telephone numbers are indicated as such, to prepare callers for family members' answering. For users of **e-mail**, a space has been inserted between the last digit of the 'number' and the final full-stop, thus indicating that the latter is not part of the former. Following this there is room to indicate details of any other system in use by a Biographee.

ADDITIONAL EXPLANATIONS ETC.

A. Although all possible care has been, and will continue to be, taken to ensure accuracy throughout this work (the Editor is accustomed to working, albeit slowly, for 12–14 hours daily) it is unthinkable that there will not be some **errors** or out-of-date statements among the hundreds of thousands of facts that are being crammed into this volume and its contemplated successors, and so users should not be too dismayed if they come across an occasional inaccuracy, inclarity, or misleadingly outdated statement. Warning us of any perceived errors or necessary updatings at any time (and by any effective means) would not only be a kindness 'all around' but also conducive to improvement of the subsequent edition, the same being true of omission of any worthy biographee or biographees — *see* page iii.

B. We have used **English spellings** etc. throughout (following the great Oxford English Dictionary, except in quotations or addresses etc.) and been gratified by the willingness of our many admirable American colleagues to follow suit in the interest of general clarity and conformity. Foreign words are given in full unless they are spelt the same as in English (often they were originally French words) in which case the abbreviation (if one has been used) has been doubly correct to use.

C. A stop ('full stop' or 'period') usually means (if not terminating a sentence or paragraph) that a word has been cut off before its end (in which case there will be no need of a subsequent space before the next word, whereas the absence of a stop indicates that the abbreviation ends with the last letter of what remains of the truncated word (*e.g.* geog.= geography, geogl = geographical).

D. Where a company or university or other name is given which is thought not to be generally known, the country or state is indicated for identification.

E. Where an asterisk is inserted at the beginning or end of an item in a biography, a further, second one will be found later in the same biography — thus linking the two items.

F. Rarely, some names (*e.g.* of companies) are given in full capital letters. If they have transpired not to be acronyms or contractions, no explanation is given. One can then safely assume that, if the name is given in full capitals and there is no explanation (*e.g.* of a presumed acronym), this is the way the name is to be written.

G. Except for Proper Names and habitually in special cases such as 'Nature' and 'Biosphere', strict consistency in the capitalization of initial letters of nouns has at times proved beyond us, though we have endeavoured to capitalize the initial letters of English or vernacular names of identified *species* (but not higher taxa), with insertion of the scientific ('Latin') names duly italicized in brackets immediately after them. Following the international rules, generic names are always 'capitalized' but those of lower taxa are not.

H. Despite attempting to follow Biographees' wishes in the rendering of their personal names, we found such variation in usage that we had in the end to abandon this attempt when dealing with such prefixes as 'DE', 'VON', 'VAN DER', and others mentioned in the first paragraph on page iv, that we decided to place them all in SMALL CAPITALS (*sic*) throughout our work, cross-referencing where necessary. Oriental 'given' names we generally retained as written by their owners as regards any hyphenation and internal capitalization, cross-referencing with their family names 'for safety'.

OUR CONFIDENT SEND-OFF

In the firm belief that so much *ad hoc* labour for years on our part, and on that of ultimately thousands of collaborating biographees throughout the world, can scarcely fail to help to bring environmentalists and conservationists together and thus support the environmental/conservational movement in many of its most needful aspects, we commend this hard-won First Edition of our compilation for widespread use. It will give included users (namely our chosen and collaborating Biographees) detailed knowledge about one another — their individual backgrounds and qualifications, specialist interests and achievements (including publications), as well as indications of availability for consultation etc. Commonly they are eminent men or women of foresight and dedication who have shown their worth to (and potentialities for) the world and ought to be more widely recognized in it.

This world-wide making available of details of qualified Biographees' pertinent actions and capabilities will surely help to bring them and others together for, we firmly believe, our needy Planet's alleviation of ills and ultimate positive benefit.

With its detailed Appendixes indicating (I) the Country (or State) of main activity of each potentially chosen, responding, and finally accepted, Biographee, (II) his or her pertinent speciality or specialities, and (III) list of used Abbreviations, Acronyms, Contractions, and some Explanations, the work is designed to be as helpful and handy as possible. The whole should also be of unique value to governmental and other leaders seeking the best obtainable advice and guidance in particular themes and regions in circumstances of need or, preferably, in good time to avoid environmental emergencies such as seem destined to increase immeasurably in frequency and intensity in future.

NICHOLAS POLUNIN, *Editor*
&
LYNN M. CURME, *Compiler*

Foundation for Environmental Conservation
7 Chemin Taverney (7th & 8th Floors)
1218 Grand-Saconnex
Geneva, Switzerland.

DEDICATION *IN MEMORIAM*

With often profound affection and/or due admiration, we dedicate this book to the memory of the following who would expectably have been in it more substantially if they had not died within the last 20 or so years. In a few cases it must be considerably longer since they left us; but in such instances our memory of them is so vivid, and/or their influence in the cause of the viable world for which we all strive has been so lasting, that we feel they should be included *e.g.* as pioneers of unusual perception and foresight. The order of presentation is merely that in which these paragons of the past returned to mind or were proposed by others.

Prof. Dr Victor A. KOVDA
Dr F. Raymond FOSBERG
HE Prof. Dr Jean-Paul HARROY
Mr Ryoichi SASAKAWA
Prof. Dr Donald J. KUENEN
HH Fatehsinghrao P. GAEKWAD
Prof. Dr Ma SHIJUN
Prof. Dr Linus PAULING
Mr Gerald Malcolm DURRELL
Prof. Dr A. Roy CLAPHAM
Prof. Dr Paul W. RICHARDS
Mr Charles S. ELTON
Prof. Dr Nikolaas TINBERGEN
Prof. Dr Jan TINBERGEN
Sir Peter M. SCOTT
Prof. Dr Konrad Z. LORENZ
Mr Harold J. COOLIDGE
Prof. Eilif DAHL
Prof. Dr Sir Harry GODWIN
Dr Sir Julian S. HUXLEY
Dr Fred M. PACKARD
Prof. J.P.M. 'Pat' BRENAN
Prof. Dr Gordon M.B. DOBSON
Acad. Prof. Vladimir Nikolaevich SUKACHEV
Dr E.F. SCHUMACHER
Prof. Dr William S. COOPER
Dr Rachel CARSON
HE Prof. Dr Gunnar K. MYRDAL
Lord (Eric) ASHBY
Prof. Dr G. Evelyn HUTCHINSON
Dr Barbara WARD
Mr Roger de CANDOLLE
Prof. Dr Charles BAEHNI
Dr Kai CURRY-LINDAHL
Mr Henry FIELD

Lord (Edward A.A.) SHACKLETON
Dr Brian B. ROBERTS
Mr Thomas HARRISSON
Mr Boonsong LEGAKUL
Sir Frank FRASER DARLING
Prof. Sir Harry G. CHAMPION
Mr Ian GRIMWOLD
HE Mrs Indira GANDHI
Mr Oleg POLUNIN
HE Prof. Dr Olav GJAEREVOLL
Ambassador Francis L. DALE
Mr Kailash SANKHALA
Prof. Dr François BOURLIÈRE
Sir Hugh ELLIOTT
Prof. Dr Erik HULTÉN
Dr Thorvald SØRENSEN
Dr Jacques ROUSSEAU
Prof. Dr Vladimir N. ANDREEV
Prof. Dr Roger REVELLE
Prof. Dr Jean BAER
Lord HURCOMB
Richard St Barbe BAKER
Prof. Sir Arthur G. TANSLEY
Prof. Dr René DUBOS
Dr Sir (David) A. DAVIES
Prof. Dr Stanley A. CAIN
Dr John Randal BAKER
Dr John PROCTER
Prof. Dr Sir Alister HARDY
HE Dr Friedrich T. WAHLEN
Mr (Stephen) Harold HART
Mr Gordon RATTRAY TAYLOR
Prof. Dr Kenneth MELLANBY
Prof. Dr Wladyslaw SZAFER
Prof. Constantinos A. DOXIADIS

CONTENTS

Introduction   iii

Dedication *In Memoriam*   vii

Biographies   1

Appendix I by Country   369

Appendix II by Speciality   409

Appendix III Abbreviations, Acronyms, Contractions, and Some Explanations   547

BIOGRAPHIES

ABBASI, Professor Dr Shahid Abbas. Environmental engineering, aquatic ecology, and alternative energy systems. Centre Director. *B*.6 June 1950, Khilchipur, India. Indian. *M*.Naseema (envl systems specialist): 3 *d*. **Education:** IIT PhD 1975, advanced training in Japan 1983, Cochin U.of Sci.& Tech. DSc 1987. **Experience:** 25 yrs' res.& teaching, 23 yrs' consult. to num. govtl agencies & industry; 14 yrs' admin.as Chairman, Bd of Studies in Ecol.and Memb.of Academic Council, Pondicherry U.& Pondicherry State Envt Cttee 1991–. **Career:** Lect./ Sci. Bhopal U. IIT & BITS 1970–9; Head, Water Qual.& Envt Div. Centre for Water Resources (Kozhikode) 1979–87; Vis.Prof. Calif.SU at Sonoma 1985–8; Prof.& Course Dir, Salim Ali Sch.of Ecol.1987–91 and Dir, Centre for Poll. Control & Biowaste Energy 1991–, Pondicherry U.; short-term vis.assignments for lectures, res. & consult. in Japan, Spain, & USA 1983–93. **Achievements:** conducted first-ever comp.studies on ecol.of man-made lakes, and on envl impact of major water resources projects, in S.India; first-ever exhaustive studies on utilization of aquatic weed *Salvinia molesta,* now regarded as one of the world's worst weeds; developed a novel hydroponic system for studying impact of water qual.on germination & early growth of angiosperms, a first-ever systems model & allied software package for benefit–cost analysis of high-rate anaerobic biowaste treatment systems, and new economically-viable methods for the recovery of lead from battery scrap and for trace analysis of heavy-metals in envl matrices; unveiled inadequacy of several existing water qual.standards and worked out rational 'safe concentrations' of several heavy-metals and pesticides for setting new standards; estab.the efficacy of *Eucalyptus* hybrid (*E.globulus x tereticornis*) as an ecolly-benign wasteland plant; currently conducting one of the first, and perhaps the most comp., multi-industry EIAs in India; dev.of eight software packages for use in EIA & risk assessment. **Memberships:** F.IE, F.IPHE, APO. **Awards:** F'ship APO, F.CSIR 1975–76. **Publications:** 12 books incl. *Envl Impact of Water Resources Projects* 1992, *Modelling & Simulation of Biogas Systems Econ.*1993, *World's Worst Weed — Control & Utilization* 1993, *Urbanization and its Envl Impacts — A Case Study of a Typical Indian Town* 1993, *The New Japanese Pesticide CARTAP — as Safe as Claimed?* 1993; 180 res.papers; Ed.Bd *Intl J.of Energy–Envt–Econ., J.of Industrial Poll.Control, Poll.Res., J.Mendale*. Favours pers.pub.& news media support. **Languages:** Arabic, Bengali, English, Gujarati, Hindi, Urdu. Further details may be obtained from var. Who's Whos. Willing to act as consult.etc. **Address:** Centre for Pollution Control & Biowaste Energy, University Campus, Kalapet, Pondicherry 605 014, Tamil Nadu, India. **Tel.** (office) 91 41 385567 & 62, (home) 91 41 385527 & 63; **fax** 91 41 385563 & 5.

ABBASPOUR, Professor Dr Madjid. Environmental safety, marine pollution, air pollution in cities, energy policy, renewable energy, solid waste, noise in transportation, ocean engineering. Professor, Chief Technical Adviser, Director, Adviser. *B*.14 Sept.1951, Iran. Iranian. Father Abbas Abbaspour (conservationist). *M*.Vahideh: 2 *s*., *d*. **Education:** Sharif U.of Tech. BSc 1973; MIT, MSc 1975, ME 1976; Cornell U. PhD 1981. **Experience:** res.on air poll.modelling, seawater poll.modelling in Persian Gulf, Caspian Sea, Sea of Oman; admin.re.posts of Chief Tech.Adv.of EPA of Iran and Tech.Adv.to Pres. **Career:** Prof. Sharif U.of Tech.1981–; Chief Tech.Adv. 1985–, Dir of Ocean Res.Studies 1987–, Iranian EPA; Adv.to Min.of Heavy Industry, 1988–. **Achievements:** writing a two-vols book* in Farsi; studying effect of 'Desert Storm' war on Persian Gulf. **Memberships:** ASCE, ASME, ASTM, High Consulate of Envt in Iran. **Award:** The Sea Man of the Year 1990 (Iran). **Publications:** *The Hydroelectric Power Plant,* Vol.I 1985, Vol. II 1986, **Envl Engg,* Vol.I 1992, Vol.II 1993 (in Farsi), Modelling of oil spills in Persian Gulf Area, Noise poll. problems of Tehran Metro. Indiff.to pers.pub.& news media support. **Languages:** Arabic (read), English, Farsi. Willing to act as consult.etc. **Address:** Department of Mechanical and Environmental Engineering, Sharif University of Technology, Azadi Avenue, Tehran, Iran. **Tel.**(office) 98 21 646 8549 or 98 21 918399, (home) 98 21 258 1789; **fax** 98 21 866504.

ABDEL NOUR, Professor Hassan O., *see* **NOUR, Professor Hassan O. ABDEL.**

ABDEL-GAWAAD, Professor Dr Ahmed Abdel-Wahab. Rural environmental pollution control. Professor of Environmental Pollution. *B*.16 June 1937, Cairo, Egypt. Egyptian. *M*.Kamilia: *s., d*. **Education:** Alexandria U. BSc (Agric.) 1959, MSc(Econ.Entomol.) 1964, PhD (Econ. Entomol.) 1968; Friedrich-Schiller U. DSc(Biochem.) 1975. **Experience:** 25 yrs' res. on eval.of impact of pesticides' residues on Egyptian & global envt incl.monitoring of such residues in fresh water, agricl soils, food, and the atmos.; lecturing, u. admin. **Career:** Dem., Asst Lect., Lect., High Inst.for Cotton Affairs 1960–73; Asst Prof. 1973–77, Prof.of Envl Poll. 1977–, Chairman 1982–6 and Head 1994– of Dept of Plant Prot. Zagazig U.; sometime Consult. for Egyptian Govt, Greenpeace, and Environmics (MD, USA). **Achievements:** brought benefits & risks of pesticides-use into the public eye with successful decrease in quantities of pesticides used; evolved a model village scheme for sust. dev.which is followed by nine small villages in Menofia & Ismailia Governorates; through pubns has brought attention to need for envl prot.in Egypt. **Memberships:** EST (VP), Nat.Soc.of Envt Prot. (Gen. Sec.), EES, MESAEP, Pugwash Soc., African Soc., var. nat.cttees. **Awards:** Alexander von Humboldt Fndn Scholarship 1975–7, State Academic Encouragement Award 1986, Global 500 Roll of Honour (UNEP) 1992. **Publications:** *Econ.Insects* 1977, *Econ.Acaricides* 1979, *Envl*

Enc. Series (23 booklets) 1990, *Econ.Pests in the Arab World* 1992, *Soil Poll.by Pesticide Residues* (in press); 150+ papers. Indiff.to pers.pub., favours news media support. **Languages:** Arabic, English, German. Willing to act as consult. etc. **Address:** Villa Nr 57, Street Nr 104, El-Maadi, or POB 613, El-Maadi, Cairo, Egypt. **Tel.** (office) 20 13 470306, (home) 20 2 350 3503; **fax** 20 2 349 6295.

ABDELHADY, Professor Dr Abdelaziz. National & international environmental law, legal aspects of wildlife protection & of natural protected areas. Professor of Environmental Law. *B.*27 June 1946, Mansura, Egypt. Egyptian. *M.*Sofia. **Education:** U.of Lyon, Doctorat d'Etat en Droit 1981. **Experience:** former legal adv.to Envl Affairs Agency, Nat.Council of Ministers, legal consult.to UNEP. **Career:** Judge in Council of State (Admin.Court) 1973–4; Prof.of Intl Law, Mansura U.1981–91 and Fac.of Law, Kuwait U.1991–. **Achievements:** drafting Egyptian Law Nr 103/1983 re.Natural Prot.Areas, and Project of Egyptian Law concerning Marine Envt which has been integrated as Part 3 into Envl Law Nr 104/1994. **Memberships:** ESIL, Egyptian Councils of Envl Law and Envl Res., IUCN CEL. **Award:** State Prize in Envl Educ.1986. **Publications:** num. Favours pers.pub.& news media support. **Languages:** Arabic, English, French. Willing to act as consult.etc. **Address:** in Kuwait — Faculty of Law, Kuwait University, POB 5476, 13055 Safat, Kuwait, **tel.**(office) 965 48 14346, (home) 965 48 30236; in Egypt — 13 Street 251, Maadi, Cairo, Egypt, **tel.**20 2 352 9905.

ABDUL AZIZ, Professor Panarambil K., *see* **AZIZ, Professor Panarambil K.** ABDUL.

ABDUL GAYOOM, HE President Maumoon, *see* **GAYOOM, HE Maumoon** ABDUL.

ABERNETHY, Professor Dr Virginia Deane Kendrick. Population–immigration–environment. Professor of Psychiatry. *B.*4 Oct.1934, Havana, Cuba. American. *M.*C.Gregory Smith: 2 *s.*, 2 *d.* **Education:** Wellesley Coll. BA 1955: Harvard U. MA 1968, PhD 1970; Vanderbilt U. MBA 1981. **Experience:** Teaching F. Harvard U.1967–9, Post-doctl Res.F. Harvard Med. Sch.1969–71, symp.direction, memb.of u.cttees & adv.bds.1981–, community participation 1976–. **Career:** Res.Assoc. Dept of Psychiatry 1971–2, Assoc.in Psychiatry (Anthrop.) 1972–5, Harvard Mcd.Sch.; Asst Prof.of Psychiatry (Anthrop.) & Dir of Div.of Human Behavior, Dept of Psychiatry, Vanderbilt Sch.of Med.1975–6 and Vanderbilt U.Sch.of Medicine 1976–80; Prof.of Psychiatry (Anthrop.), Dept of Psychiatry, Vanderbilt U.Sch.of Med.1980–; F.Vanderbilt Inst.for Public Policy Studies, Vanderbilt U.1985–. **Membership:** AAA, AAAS, Sigma Xi (Exec.Cttee, Vanderbilt U. Chapter 1986–8), HOLIS, Edl Bd *J.of Women's Health* 1992–4. **Awards:** Cert.of Commendation (co-, Amer. Psychiatric Assn Hosp.and

Community Psychiatry Service) 1975, Alumni Achievement Award (Riverdale Country Sch., NY) 1988; num.res. grants. **Publications:** num. books, monogrs, articles, invited book reviews, symp.and invited papers incl.*Pop.Politics: The Choices that Shape Our Future* 1993, Changing the USA's pop. signals for a sust.future 1994, Optimism and overpopulation 1994, Ed.-in-Chief *Pop.and Envt* 1988–. **Language:** English. Willing to act as a consult., etc. **Address:** School of Medicine, Vanderbilt University, Nashville, Tennessee 37240, USA. **Tel.** 1 615 322 6608; **fax** 1 615 343 8639.

ABROL, Dr Inder Pal. Natural resource management, ecosystem productivity, soil & water management, desertification, land degradation & rehabilitation, agroforestry, sustainable agriculture. Deputy Director-General, Agriculture Commissioner. *B.*13 March 1939, Lahore, Pakistan. Indian. *M.*Prem (info.dissemination on envl issues): *d.*Reena (active in envl issues). **Education:** Punjab U. (Chandigarh), BS 1957; IARI, MS 1959, PhD 1962; Hebrew U. Post-doctl F.1962–3; Texas A&M U. Vis.Sci.1972. **Experience:** teacher, researcher for nearly 25 yrs in soil sci., natural resource mgmt, problems of land degradation and their rehab.partic.due to salinity problems; mgmt of country-wide network res. progs in resource mgmt; consult.for nat.& intl orgns incl.FAO, UNEP, Ford Fndn. **Career:** Researcher, Assoc.Prof.of Soils, Punjab Agricl U.(Hisar) 1964–9; Head Div.of Soils & Agron. 1964–9, Dir.1981–6, C.Soil Salinity Res.Inst.; Dep.DG, ICAR 1986–. **Achievements:** Chairman, Sub.Comm.of Salt Affected Soils 1982–6, and of Soil Tech.1986–90, ISSS; Pres.Indian SSS 1990–92; Consult.Ed.*Soil Sci.*(USA); Pres.8th ISCO Conf.1994; scientific contribns in mgmt of salt-affected soils have formed basis for large-scale rehab.of degraded soils in India and elsewhere. **Memberships:** Indian SSS (Life), SWCS of India (Life), ASA, SWCS (USA), SSSA, ISSS. **Awards:** André Mayor Award (FAO) 1972, Rafi Ahmed Kidwai Mem.Prize (ICAR) 1972–3, Medal for service to community (GASA) 1980, VASVIK Res.Award 1985, Hari Om Ashram Trust Award 1989. **Publications:** *Tech. for Rehab.of Degraded Lands* 1989, *Agroclimatology and Sust.Agric.in Stressed Envts* 1994; 200+ papers in nat.& intl scientific journals; ed./authored FAO Bulletin Nr 39 on *Salt Affected Soils and Their Mgmt.* Indiff.to pers. pub., favours news media support. **Languages:** English, Hindi, Punjabi. Willing to act as consult.etc. **Address:** Indian Council of Agricultural Research, Krishi Bhavan, New Delhi 110001, Delhi, India. **Tel.**(office) 91 11 383762, (home) 91 11 675381; **fax** 91 11 387293.

ABROUGUI, Dr Mohamed Ali. Environment, biodiversity, conservation of Nature, ecotourism, environmental policy, climate change & energy. Association President. *B.*3 March 1938, Le Kef, Tunisia. Tunisian. *M.*Sylvia: 2 *s.* **Education:** U.of Liège, Dr Med.Vet., Vet.Surgeon 1970,

Dipl.in Mycology. **Experience:** resp.for animal safety & prod.for 25 yrs, admin. of many nat.socs. **Career:** Dir of Animal Prod. Office of Terres Domaniales 1972–6 & 1986–9; Pres. *Assn Tunisienne pour la Prot.de la Nature et de l'Environnement 1986–; Envt Officer, Municipality of Tunis 1991–5. **Achievements:** init. envl movement in Tunisia and N.Africa, Assn Pres.*, IUCN Counc. **Memberships:** IUCN (Regnl Counc.for Africa, Bur.1993–6), FoE, Nat. Comm.for Sust.Dev. **Publications:** num. and var. Favours pers.pub.& news media support. **Languages:** Arabic, French, English (good). Willing to act as a consult. **Address:** Association Tunisienne pour la Protection de la Nature et de l'Environnement, 43 Avenue Louis Braille, 1082 Tunis, Tunisia. **Tel.**(office) 216 1 288141, (home) 216 1 287603; **fax** 216 1 797295.

ABU-IZZEDDIN, Faisal, *see* **DEAN, Faisal.**

ABU-RUBEIHA', HE Ali Abdulla. Natural & mineral resources. Businessman. *B.*1 Jan.1941, Dheiban-Madaba, Jordan. Jordanian. *M.*Nuran: 3 *s.*, 2 *d.* **Education:** Istanbul U. BSc (Geol.& Geophys.) 1967; Camborne Sch.of Mines (UK), Dipl.in Mineral Tech.1977; Advanced Mgmt Sem.1985. **Experience:** res., admin., business, travel throughout most Arab and some Asian & Euro.countries and the USA, exploration of petroleum & mineral resources, geol.engg, Memb.of Upper House of Parliament (Nat. Council) in Jordan. **Career:** Sr Geol. Res. Center 1967–8; Supervisor, Yugoslavian petroleum co.1970–71; Sr Geol. UN Project for Dev.of Alphosphate Reservoir 1971–5; Geophysics Directorate 1977–9, Bd of Dirs 1986–9, Natural Resources Auth.; Asst Dir of Regnl Planning Dept, Min.of Municipalities 1979–80 and of Envt Dept, Min.of Municipal, Rural & Envl Affairs 1980–82; Memb. Consults Nat. Council 1982–4; VP Jordan Valley Auth.1984– 88; Dir/Adv. Admin.& Fin.Directorate, Min.of Water & Irrigation; Businessman 1989–. **Achievements:** controlling water poll.; forest prot., preserv., & planning. **Memberships:** RSCN, Jordan Envt Soc., Jordanian Geologists' Assn (Pres.1984–7), Arab Union of Geologists (VP 1984–87), Jordanian Engrs' Soc., Jordanian Geologists' Soc. **Awards:** title of Excellency conferred by HM K.of Jordan 1982. **Publications:** Govt Deptl Report re.water cons.& poll., local newspaper & magazine articles. **Languages:** Arabic, English, Turkish. Willing to act as consult. etc. **Address:** POB 950310, Amman 11195, Jordan. **Tel.**(office) 962 6 698531, (home) 962 6 712308; **fax** 962 6 698532.

ABUZINADA, Professor Dr Abdul Aziz Hamed. Conservation management & research. Secretary-General. *B.*1940, Jeddah, Kingdom of Saudi Arabia. Saudi Arabian. *M.*Ibtisam. **Education:** U.of Minnesota, MSc 1967; U.of Durham, PhD 1971. **Experience:** microbiol.res., teaching & cons.mgmt. **Career:** Asst Prof.of

Bot.1973–83, Prof.of Bot.1983–7, Chairman of Dept of Bot. 1976–87, Riyadh U.; Sec.-Gen. NCWCD 1987–. **Achievements:** played a key role in estab.of Kingdom's nat.cons.agency, successfully restored pops of endangered native ungulates, set up a network of prot.areas throughout the Kingdom. **Memberships:** num. regnl & intl bodies incl. IUCN Counc.& SSC VC, IUBS Exec.Cttee, several nat.govtl cttees. **Awards:** Fred M. Packard (IUCN CNPPA) 1992, Corres. Memb. (Senkenberg Mus., Frankfurt) 1993. **Publications:** six books incl. *Wildlife Cons.and Dev. in Saudi Arabia* (Ed.) 1989, *Biol.for Sec.Schools in the Arab World*; num.thematic books & j.papers, Chief Ed. *Arabian Wildlife* (UK). Favours news media support. **Languages:** Arabic, English. Further details may be obtained from *Who's Who in the World* 1994. Willing to act as consult.etc. **Address:** National Commission for Wildlife Conservation and Development, POB 61681, Riyadh 11575, Kingdom of Saudi Arabia. **Tel.**96 61 441 8700; **fax** 96 61 441 0797.

ADAMS, Aubrey. Environmental activist, writing. Public Relations Manager, Newspaper Columnist. *B.*21 Aug.1919, Trinidad & Tobago. Trinidadian. *M.*Jacqueline Elizabeth: *s.*, *d.* **Education:** St Mary's Coll. Camb.& London Sch.Cert., U.of the W.Indies, Health Educ.; IIM Treasury, training in orgn & methods; training in community dev.& theatre in Germany, England, and France; Columbia U. **Experience:** 33 yrs' govt admin., orgn & methods specialist, cultural adv.to PM, consult.to UN, dir of TV & tourist bds. **Career:** entered Trinidad & Tobago Govt Service 1943 — Orgn & Methods Officer 1950, Personnel Officer, Min.of Health 1957, Cultural Adv. to PM 1968, Community Dev.Cultural Adv.1969, Dir of Bd of Trinidad & Tobago TV 1983, Dir of Bd of Tourism 1985; Public Relations Mgr, Amar Group of Cos 1985–. **Achievement:** Chairman & org.of nat.envl prog. **Awards:** Trinidad & Tobago Nat.Awards, Bronze 1970, Silver 1989; awards received from German & Italian Govts, Shaw U.(NC), and City of Atlanta. **Publications:** papers presented to sems practically throughout the world. Favours pers.pub.& news media support. **Languages:** English, French (fair), Spanish (fair). Willing to act as consult. **Address:** Fields Cape Drive, Diego Martin, Trinidad, West Indies. **Tel.**(home) 1 809 63 21406.

ADAMS, Dr Lowell William. Urban wildlife, ecology, & management. Institute Vice-President. *B.*8 Aug.1946, Harrisonburg, VA, USA. American. *M.*Patricia Ann: *s.* **Education:** VPI, BS 1968; Ohio SU MS 1973, PhD(Wildlife Biol.) 1976. **Experience:** res. ranging from envl contaminants & effects of roads on wildlife to urban wildlife ecol.& human– wildlife relationships in the urban envt; consult.— num.projects re.wildlife & habitat; teaching wildlife ecol.& mgmt at BSc level. **Career:** Wildlife Biol., Res.Dir, then VP, Nat. Inst.for

Urban Wildlife 1976–; Instructor, Fac.Assoc., & Adjunct Prof. U.of Maryland and Johns Hopkins U. 1987–. **Achievements:** pioneering influence in furthering cons.of wildlife in urban, suburban, & urbanizing, areas. **Memberships:** AOU, ASM, Phi Sigma Soc., Sigma Xi, Wildlife Soc., WOS, Xi Sigma Pi. **Awards:** Chevron Cons. Award 1987, Daniel L.Leedy Urban Wildlife Cons.Award 1992. **Publications:** *Integrating Man & Nature in the Metropolitan Envt* (co-Ed.) 1987, *Wildlife Reserves & Corridors in the Urban Envt* (co-Author) 1989, *Wildlife Cons.in Metropolitan Envts* (co-Ed.) 1991, *Urban Wildlife Habitats: A Landscape Perspective* 1994. Favours pers.pub.& news media support. **Language:** English. Further details may be obtained from *Amer.Men & Women of Sci., Who's Who in the East, Who's Who in Sci.& Engg.* **Address:** National Institute for Urban Wildlife, POB 3015, Shepherdstown, West Virginia 25443, USA. **Tel.**1 304 274 0205; **fax** 1 304 274 0678.

ADIS, Professor Dr Joachim Ulrich. Holistic analysis of neotropical ecosystems. Senior Scientist, Accredited Professor (twice). *B.*4 March 1950, Stuttgart-Degerloch, (then) FRG. German. *M.*Irmgard: *d.* **Education:** U.of Göttingen, MSc(Biol.) and exam.for teachers of sec.schools in biol., chem., & pedagogics 1975; U.of Ulm, DSc(Natural Scis) 1979; U.of Kiel, Habil.& U.Lect.(PD) 1991. **Experience:** holistic analysis of ecosystems (*see* Achievements), Managing Ed.*Amazoniana,* j.ref., Ed.-in-Chief *Studies on Neotrop.Fauna and Envt* 1995–; cong.participation, 108 scientific lectures 1976–, postgrad.student supervision. **Career:** Postdoctl F. Smithsonian Instn 1979–80; scientific stay, INPA 1979; Sci.1980–91, Sr Sci.1992–, Trop.Ecol.WG, Max-Planck-Inst.for Limnol.; Sci.& Foreign Rep. German–Brazilian Project of INPA–Max-Planck 1980–88; Accredited Prof.in Entomol. Postgrad.Prog. INPA/U.of the Amazon 1980–; Accredited Prof.in Trop.Entomol. U. of Kiel, and Teaching Prof. U.of São Paulo 1989–; Accredited Prof.in Entomol. Escola Superior de Agricultura, U.of São Paulo 1991–5. **Achievements:** ecol., ethology, physiol., & morphol., of river.invertebrates in Amazonian wetlands (esp.inundation forests) and their adaptations as compared with invertebrates from non-flooded areas in & outside the tropics; needs for res., utilization, & prot., of Amazonian floodplains; postgrad.student supervision (eight Brazilian and one German MSc, three Brazilian and one German PhD, concluded). **Memberships:** CIDA, CIM, INTECOL, ISTE, ATB, DGT, DGE, DZG, Gesellschaft für Ökologie, Naturwissenschaftlicher Verein Wuppertal. **Publications:** 109 in English or German incl. Ecol.Res.on Arthropods in C.Amazonian Forest Ecosystems with Recommendations for Study Procedures (co-Author) 1984, Adaptation of an Amazonian pseudoscorpion (Arachnida) from dryland forests to inundation forests (co-Author) 1988, How to Survive Six Months in a Flooded

Soil: Strats in Chilopoda and Symphyla from C.Amazonian Floodplains 1992, Amazonian Floodplains: Needs for Res., Utilization and Prot.1992. **Languages:** English, French (better at spoken), German, Portuguese. Willing to act as consult.etc. **Address:** Max-Planck-Institute for Limnology, Tropical Ecology Working Group, Postfach 165, D-24302 Plön, Germany. **Tel.**49 4522 7630; **fax** 49 4522 763281; **e-mail** adis@mpil-ploen.mpg.d400.de.

AGARDY, Dr M. Tündi. Marine protected area planning, coastal management, tropical marine ecology; identification of critical marine ecological processes and areas, fisheries conservation. Senior Conservation Scientist. *B.*10 May 1957, NJ, USA. American. **Education:** Wellesley Coll./ Dartmouth Coll. BA 1980. U.of Rhode Is. M(Marine Affairs) 1985, PhD(Biol.Scis) 1989. **Experience:** developed & coordinated jt US FWS/USVI govt prog.in endangered species' cons.& recovery, early 1980s; res.on pop.dynamics & mgmt of migratory marine species & marine prot.area design as an Instn F.*; consult.to World Bank, IUCN, James Dobbin Assocs (coastal planners), and other instns; num.TV & radio appearances. **Career:** Endangered Species Prog.Coord. USVI 1980–82; *Woods Hole Oceanographic Inst F.1987–89; Spec.Consult./Adv.to IUCN on marine cons. 1987–. Researcher 1990; Cons.Sci.WWF 1990–91; Sr Cons.Sci.1992–; **Achievements:** working to promote functional, as opposed to conventional structurally-oriented, cons.of coastal ecosystems by targeting critical processes and identifying linkages between ecosystem components &/or habitats; extensive public outreach work. **Memberships:** AAAS, AFS, ASCB, MAPA, IUCN Comms on (formerly) Ecol.(VC), NPPA, & Species Survival (Marine Turtle SG). **Awards:** selected as 1993 sci.for 'Sci.for Cons.' prog., elected to scientific adv.bd, New England Aquarium 1992. **Publications:** *Using Sci.to Design & Implement Marine Prot.Areas* 1993; main chapter for *'Oceans: A Celebration'* 1993; 24+ scientific/policy pubns. Indifferent to pers.pub., favours news media support. **Languages:** English, French, German, Hungarian, Portuguese (read), Spanish (read & basic conversation). Willing to act as consult. etc. **Address:** WWF, 1250 24th Street NW, Washington, DC 20037, USA. **Tel.**(office) 1 202 861 8301, (home) 1 202 298 8481; **fax** 1 202 293 9211.

AGUIRRE GONZALEZ, Dr Juan Antonio, *see* **GONZALEZ, Dr Juan Antonio AGUIRRE.**

AHMAD, Yusuf J. Environmental economics & management. Senior Adviser. *B.*1 March 1927, Bangladesh. American, Bangladeshi. Father A.M. Ahmad (interest in possibility of an effective system of envl legis.). *M.*Dagmar (deceased): *s.* Nessim J.(resource econ.), *d.*Nermin K.(ecol.& envt). **Education:** LSE, BSc (Econ.) 1951; Fletcher Sch.of Law & Diplomacy, MA 1953. **Experience:** held nr of assignments in Pakistan Diplomatic Service (notably in Turkey, Perm. Mission to the UN in NY, Mission to Comm.of EEC in Brussels as Chargé d'Affaires, Min.of Foreign Affairs of Pakistan in Islamabad (twice), and in Paris rising from Third Sec.to Amb.); rep.of Pakistan at various UN confs & bodies. **Career:** Jt Sec.to Govt of Pakistan in charge of UN & Econ.Coordn, Min.of Foreign Affairs (with rank of Amb.) 1970–72; Econ.Consult.to OECD 1973–75; Dep.Asst Exec.Dir 1976–8, Acting Asst Exec.Dir 1980–81, Office of Envt Fund & Admin.and Dep.Asst Exec.Dir in Office of Envt Prog.1978–80, Dir for Spec.Assignments, Adv.to Exec.Dir 1984–88, Sr Adv.to Exec.Dir 1988–, all at UNEP. **Awards:** Clayton Res.F'ship (Fletcher Sch.of Law & Diplomacy) 1956, Tam– gha-a-Qaid-e-Azam (Govt of Pakistan) 1963, Parvin F'ship (Princeton U.) 1972, Global 500 Roll of Honour (UNEP) 1988. **Publications:** *Desert.: Fin.Support for the Biosphere* (co-Author) 1987, *Elements of Envl Mgmt* 1989, *Envl Accounting for Sust.Dev.* (co-Ed.) 1989; num. others. Indiff.to pers.pub., favours news media support. **Languages:** Bengali, English, Urdu; French & German (tech. competence). Willing to act as consult.etc. **Address:** 2141 Wisconsin Avenue NW, Apartment 204, Washington, District of Columbia 20007, USA. **Tel.**(home) & **fax** 1 202 338 7488.

AICKIN, Dr (Robert) Malcolm. Mechanisms of environmental degradation, environmental risk reduction, environment policy, social & cultural changes required by 'sustainable development', environmental insurance & security. Independent Environmental Consultant, Chairman. *B.*17 May 1949, London, England, UK. British. *M.* Catherine Margaret: *s., d.* **Education:** Cheltenham Coll., U.of St Andrews BSc(Hons)(Chem.) 1971, UCL, PhD 1974. **Experience:** fundamental academic res.on envl effects, commercial application of scientific knowledge and uncertainty within insurance, consulting, formation of public policy. **Career:** Teacher (part-time), Lycée Français de Londres 1971–3; post-doctl res. U.of Oxf. 1974–8; employee 1979–80, Mgr 1980–81, Dir.1981–5, Dir. in Charge 1985–6, Clarkson Puckle Group; employee 1983–6, Dir 1986–7, Sec.1987–8, Dep.Chairman 1988, Chairman 1988–, The Envt Council; Mgr, Toplis & Harding 1986–9; Prin. Dames & Moore Intl 1989–91; Ind.Envl Consult.1991–. **Achievements:** discovery of mechanism of accumulation of some heavy-metals by selected Bacteria, leading intl Envl Impairment Liability Insurance prog.Underwriter, early indicator of extent of insurance industry exposure to envl liabilities, early recognition & encouragement of the message 'envl sense is commercial sense', Chairmanship of dev.of UK's leading cross-sectoral orgn (The Envt Council) devoted to devising & implementing effective envl solutions. **Memberships:** CII (Assoc.), RSC (Chartered Chem. Memb.), BILA, UK ELA (Assoc.), SCI, F.RSA, past memb.of Envl Audit Panel of IEA, and Working Party on Poll.& Insurance of AIDA. **Award:** Territorial Decoration (Territorial Army). **Publications:** Insuring Envl Liabilities 1986, Hazards of biotech.real or imaginary: does it make any difference 1989, Risk Mgmt Techniques for Envl Liability 1989, Envl Info.for All: External Pressures in Industry 1990, Options for Funding Envl Risk 1991; num.conf.& j.papers. **Languages:** English, French (reasonable), German (adequate read). Willing to act as consult. etc. **Address:** 69 Lauriston Road, London E9 7HA, England, UK. **Tel.**(home) 44 181 985 2539; **fax** 44 181 985 1827.

AJAYI, Professor Dr Seth Sunday. Wildlife conservation. Professor of Wildlife Conservation. *B.*16 May 1944, Mopa, Kogi State, Nigeria. Nigerian. *M.*Christiana: 5 *s.*, 3 *d.* **Education:** Ahmadu Bello U. BSc(Hons) (Zool.) 1968; U.of Edinburgh (UK), MSc (Wildlife & Range Mgmt) 1971; Coll.of African Wildlife Mgmt (Tanzania), Cert.in Wildlife Mgmt 1971; U.of Ibadan, PhD(Wildlife Mgmt) 1974. **Experience:** curriculum dev., biodiv. survey & action plans, domestication of African wildlife; estab.of first Dept of Wildlife and Fisheries Mgmt at U.of Ibadan 1981–8; widespread res.in ecol.of African wildlife, wildlife utilization, wildlife farming with emphasis on African small game animals; moderator & consult. **Career:** Asst Lect.1969–72, Lect. 1972–5, Dept of For., Sr Lect. Dept of Forest Resources Mgmt 1975–8, Reader 1978–80, Prof.1980– then Head 1981–, Prof. of Wildlife Cons.1990–, Dept of Wildlife and Fisheries Mgmt, U.of Ibadan; Vis.Prof., Memb.of U. Council, & Dean of Coll.of Envl Resources' Mgmt, U.of Agric.(Abeokuta) 1988–90. **Achievements:** estab.of first Dept of Wildlife and Fisheries Mgmt at U.of Ibadan which produced first generation of resource mgrs & conservators and graduates who have since taken leadership positions in wildlife & fisheries cons., led team of scientists which has completed 35 nat.& eight intl assignments concerned with natural resources' cons. **Memberships:** F.ZSL, MIBiol., F.LS, F.RZSS. **Awards:** Intl Man of the Yr (Intl Biogl Centre) 1991–2, Global 500 Roll of Honour (UNEP) 1994. **Publications:** num.incl. *Wildlife Mgmt in Savanna Woodland: Recent Studies in African Wildlife* 1979, *Action Plan for the Dev.of All Natural Resources in Nigeria* 1991, *Ensuring Sust.Dev.of Wildlife Resources: The Case of Africa* 1993. Favours pers.pub.& news media support. **Languages:** English, Yoruba. Willing to act as consult.etc. **Address:** Department of Wildlife and Fisheries Management, University of Ibadan, Ibadan, Nigeria. **Tel.**& **fax** 234 2 810 1868.

AKHTAR, Dr Waseem. Solid-waste management research, environmental engineering. Associate Professor of Environmental Engineering. *B.*10 Nov.1945, Saharanpur, UP, India. Pakistani. *M.*Shama R.: *s.,* 2 *d.* **Education:** U.of Karachi, MSc(Organic Chem.) 1964; U.of Windsor (Ont.), MASc(Chem.Eng.) 1972, PhD

(Chem.Eng.) 1978. **Experience:** res., consult., & teaching, in envl engg. **Career:** Sr Chem. Dawood Industries (Karachi) 1964–7; Chem.& Consult. Warnock Hersey Intl Ltd (Toronto) 1967–8; Instructor & Teaching Asst. U.of Windsor 1973–8; Vis.Asst Prof. Dept of Chem.Engg, U.of Kentucky (Lexington) 1978–80; Res.Engr, Shell Dev.Co.(Houston) 1980–7; Assoc.Prof.of Envl Engg, Inst.of Envl Engg & Res. Nadirshaw Edelji Dinshaw U.(Karachi) 1987–. **Achievements:** involved in num.res.projects on solid waste mgmt, industrial & coastal poll., EIA. **Memberships:** IAIA, Pakistan Engg Council. **Awards:** Merit Scholarship (U.of Karachi) 1960–2, Pres.'s Roll of Scholars (U.of Windsor) 1968–70, F.& Res. Scholarship (NRC Canada) 1970–5. **Publications:** ten major papers in open, and 20 others in Shell Dev.Co., lit. Indiff.to pers.pub.& news media support. **Languages:** English, Urdu. Willing to act as consult.etc. **Address:** Institute of Environmental Engineering and Research, Nadirshaw Edelji Dinshaw University of Engineering and Technology, University Road, Karachi, Pakistan. **Tel.**92 21 496 9263–8 ext. 2271 or 92 21 663 7516; **fax** 92 21 496 1934.

AKSORNKOAE, Professor Dr Sanit. Mangrove ecology, coastal-zone management. Professor, Vice-President. *B.*9 Feb.1941, Pattani, Thailand. Thai. *M.*Srilak: *2 s.* **Education:** Michigan SU, PhD(Plant Ecol.) 1975. **Experience:** 20 yrs' res.on mangrove ecol., Sec.to Minister of Agric.& Cooperatives 1991–2, Consult.to FAO 1985 & ADB 1985–6. **Career:** Lect.on Mangroves & Coastal-zone Mgmt 1966–89, Prof. Fac.of For. 1989–, VP for Acad.Affairs 1992–4, Kasetsart U. **Achievement:** instrumental in achieving a nat. policy for mangrove mgmt & cons. **Memberships:** ISME, IUCN Comm.on Ecol. **Awards:** Outstanding Alumni (Kasetsart U.) 1991, Biwako Prize for Ecol.(Japan) 1993. **Publications:** *Mangroves — Ecol.& Mgmt* 1993, *Plants in Mangroves* 1992. Favours pers.pub.& news media support. **Languages:** English, Thai. Willing to act as consult.etc. **Address:** Faculty of Forestry, Kasetsart University, Bangkok, Thailand. **Tel.**(office) 66 2 579 7160, (home) 66 2 573 2963; **fax** 66 2 561 3721.

AL-ALAWNEH, Ziyad. Environmental issues, public environmental campaigns. Programme Manager, National Coordinator. *B.*1955, Zarga, Jordan. Jordanian. *M.*Huda: *s.*, 2 *d.* **Education:** Amer.U.of Beirut, BSc(Envl Health) 1982. **Experience:** promotion of public envl awareness, res., admin. **Career:** Envl Health Researcher, Min.of Envt 1982–4; Dir, Preventive Med.Dept & Sr Sanitarian, Armed Forces Hosp. King Abdul Aziz Air Base 1984–91; Extension Officer 1991–2, Mgr 1992–, Nat.Envl Info.& Educ.Prog.; Nat.Coord. Arab Network for Envt & Dev., Arab Office for Youth & Envt (Egypt) 1993–. **Achievements:** conducted 50+ sems in coopn with Nat.Envl Info.& Educ.Prog., prod.of envl exhibition, prep.of many papers on diff.local &

intl envl issues. **Memberships:** IUCN Comm.on Educ., RSCN, Jordan Desert.& Envt Socs. **Publications:** Human settlement & pop. growth in Jordan 1992, Jordanian Envl Laws, Instns, and Treaties Affecting the Gulf of Aqaba 1993; Ed./Sec.*Resalet Albia* (envl newsletter) 1991–4. **Languages:** Arabic, English. Willing to act as consult.etc. **Address:** POB 340 636, Amman 11134, Jordan. **Tel.**(office) 962 6 699844 or 601830, (home) 962 6 892208; **fax** 962 6 695857.

AL-HOUTY, Dr Wasmia. Protected areas, fauna & insect surveys. Associate Professor. *B.*1 Jan. 1954, Kuwait City, Kuwait. Kuwaiti. **Education:** U.of Kuwait BSc 1974, U.of Bath PhD 1979. **Experience:** res.on insect fauna and termite ecol., writer, admin. **Career:** Lect. 1974– 87, Assoc.Prof.1987–, Dir of Desert Studies 1990–, U.of Kuwait. **Achievements:** res.& pubns, participation in many confs. **Memberships:** RES, local Natural Hist.Mus.& Wild Life Cttees. **Publications:** *Insect Fauna of Kuwait 1989;* num.papers. **Languages:** Arabic, English. Willing to act as consult.etc. **Address:** Department of Zoology, Faculty of Science, University of Kuwait, POB 5969, Safat 13060, State of Kuwait. **Tel.**965 481 1188 ext. 5902; **fax** 965 481 6605.

ALI, Professor Dr Abd 'El moneim' Maher. Environment disinfection, 'social' insects & vertebrate pests, pesticides, conservation of Nature. Company President, Emeritus Professor of Plant Protection. *B.*9 March 1922, Dammanhour, Egypt, Egyptian. *M.*Fardos: *2 s.* **Education:** U.of Cairo BSc(Agric.) 1943, UCL PhD 1953, U.of London Fac.of Med. radio isotopes 1955. **Experience:** admin.as Head of plant prot. dept and Dir of Agric.Pesticide Lab.; consult. on plant prot.for FAO. **Career:** Head of Dept & Prof.of Plant Prot.(now Emer.) Assiut U.1970–, Pres. Aradis Co.1982–. **Memberships:** ERC, Egyptian AS, Hon.Consult.IUCN SSG and Wadi El Assiuty Prot.Area., EACNR (Gen.Sec.). **Awards:** Order of Merit Egypt 1964, State Prize in Agricl Scis 1964, Order of Rep.of Egypt 1984. **Publications:** num.scientific papers, Ed. Egyptian *J.for Wildlife & Natural Resources.* **Languages:** Arabic, English. Willing to act as consult.and/or ref. **Address:** Aradis Co., POB 318, Dokki, Giza, Egypt. **Tel.**(office) 20 3 462 029, (home) 20 2 703 988; **fax** 20 2 346 2029.

ALI, Professor Dr Iqbal. Environmental conservation, water resources' engineering, environmental quality standards. Institute Director & Professor of Environmental Engineering. *B.*1 Jan. 1937, Amrawati, Pakistan. Pakistani. *M.* Farhat Iqbal. **Education:** Jabalpur U. BE (Hons) 1958; IIT, M.Tech.1960; Res.F. AIT 1962; Leeds U.(UK) PhD 1969. **Experience:** 35 yrs' teaching, res.& consult., seven yrs' admin.as Inst.Dir, Adv.to NESPAK, Engg Assocs, Harvard Inst.for Intl Dev.etc. **Career:** Prof.of Civil Engg, U.of Engg & Tech.(Lahore) 1974–5; Assoc.Prof. King Fahd U.of Petroleum

& Minerals (Saudi Arabia) 1975–88; Dir & Prof.of Envl Engg, Inst.of Envl Engg & Res. 1988–. **Achievements:** estab.& dev.of Inst.of Envl Engg & Res.for awarding MSc & PhD degrees, framing of Envl Qual.Standards for EPA (Sindh) Pakistan. **Memberships:** F.IE (Pakistan), ASCE, IAIA, PEC. **Publications:** three books, 47 papers, Ed.-in-Chief *Envl News*, num.articles. Favours pers.pub.& news media support. **Languages:** Arabic, English, Urdu. Willing to act as consult.etc. **Address:** 276-B-Shabbirabad, Jauher Road, Karachi 75350, Pakistan. **Tel.**(office) 92 21 496 9261–8, (home) 92 21 442676; **fax** 92 21 496 1934.

ALIEU, Emmanuel Keifala. Forestry development, energy, environmental conservation. Assistant Chief Conservator of Forests. *B.*19 April 1951, Manowa, Kailahun Dist., SL. Sierra Leonean. **Education:** U.of SL BSc(Hons)(Bot.) 1976, U.of Wales BSc(Hons)(For.) 1982. **Experience:** wood-burning stove res.& ext.; reforestation of mined-out sites, envl mgmt & agrofor. **Career:** sec.sch.teacher 1976–7; Asst Conservator 1977–84, Sr Asst Conservator 1984–8, Conservator 1988–92, Asst Chief Conservator 1989–, of Forests, Dept of Agric.& For.; consult.for Wildlife Cons.Intl, CARE (SL), Sierra Rutile Mining Co. **Memberships:** ISTF, CFA, IUCN SSC Primate SG, Nitrogen Fixing Trees Assn, Sec.of NAC & Cons.Soc.of SL. Awards: Hon.VP (SL) (ISTF). **Publications:** Agrofor. dev.in the humid tropics: the ultimate goal 1983–4, Improved wood-burning stove prog.in Bo, SL 1986–7, The birth of the first village forest assn in SL 1989, The control of seasonal bush-fires in SL 1992. Favours pers. pub.& news media support. **Languages:** English, French (some read). Willing to act as consult. etc. **Address:** Forestry Division, Department of Agriculture and Forestry, Youyi Building, Brookfields, Freetown, Sierra Leone. **Tel.** (office) 232 22 3445, (home) c/o 232 23 2117 or 26 3320.

ALLAVENA, Stefano. Management of State natural reserves. Division Director & Service Head. *B.*26 Nov.1941, Milan, Italy. Italian. *M.* Mariarosa: *d.* **Education:** U.of Florence M (For.) 1967. **Experience:** res. on poplars, tech., consult. **Career:** Asst Dir, Abruzzi Nat.Park; Dir, Div.Nr 5 (control of health of forests) 1988–, Head of Service for Mgmt of Prot.Areas 1988–, Nat.Forest Service. **Achievements:** estab.& mgmt of prot.areas, orgn of CITES mgmt auth. **Publications:** several incl.The Birth of Circeo Nat.Park 1977. Favours pers.pub.& news media support. **Languages:** English, French (read), Italian, Spanish (read). Willing to judge proposals. **Address:** Via Carducci 5, 00187 Rome, Italy. **Tel.**(office) 39 6 482 4765, (home) 39 6 6615 5091; **fax** 39 6 482 0665.

ALLEN, Dr Irma. Environmental education (formal & non-formal), environmental management and sustainable community develop-

ment. Technical Adviser. *B.*12 July 1938, Mercedes, TX, USA. American. Father Prof. Alfonso Acosta, biol. *M.*Dale R.Allen (farmer & envlist): 3 *s.*Roger, Wayne, Keith (all engrs working in intl sust.dev.). **Education:** Trinity U.(San Antonio, Texas) BS 1960, U.of Rhodesia MA 1975, U.of Arizona PhD 1980. **Experience:** 30 yrs in educ., mgmt, cons., & dev.work in rural & urban envts esp.in Africa; res.in sci., educ., envl educ.& curriculum dev.; extensive admin.& managerial exp., and intl consulting work. **Career:** teaching at primary, sec., & tertiary, levels; moved to envl educ.specifically in curr.dev.& teacher educ.and to nonformal approaches *e.g.*radio, public campaigns, cons.clubs, women's groups; designed & involved in implementing & heading-up donor-funded projects; Dir.of In-service Educ.& Training and Coord.of Nat.Envl Educ.Prog., Min.of Educ., Swaziland –1993; Tech.Adv. Global Envl Educ. Res.& Communication Project, USAID 1994–. **Achievements:** developed & wrote books for envl educ.curr.course for Grades 1–7 in Zimbabwe, appointed Commissioner of NT Comm.of Swaziland and first chairperson of The Swaziland Envt Auth., Founder memb.& Exec.memb.of 'Yonge Nawe' (Cons.Clubs, NGO), Founder & Coord.of nat. campaign 'Clean & Beautiful Swaziland', Coord.of Nat.Envl Educ.Prog., Memb.of Swaziland Del.to UNCED; consult.to Baha'i Office of the Envt; EcoLink SA (Bd). **Memberships:** Global 500 Forum (Governing Council), WNWED (Founder Memb. Southern Africa Chapter), Council of EEASA, NAAEE, Envl Adv.Cttee for Min.of Natural Resources. **Awards:** Global 500 Roll of Honour (UNEP) 1988, 'Success story' at Global Assembly of Women and the Envt 1991, local. **Publications:** *Dev.of an Envl Sci.& Agric.Curriculum* (Grades 1–7) 1979, *Envl Sci.& Agric.*(texts, co-Author) 1980 & 1981, *Practical Arts: Gdn & Outdoors* 1984 (both teachers' & resource books), Envl Educ.for Nomads 1982, *Pre-school Teacher Training Manual* (co-Author) 1993; *Resources for Envl Educ.in The Gambia* 1994, *Nat.Envl Educ.Strat./Plan for The Gambia* 1994; Ed.& co-Author of four teachers' guides & four trainees' handbooks for sch.mgmt; 200+ papers. Indiff.to pers.pub., favours news media support. **Languages:** English; Portuguese & siSwati (fairly fluent); Spanish. Willing to act as consult.etc. **Address:** POB 135, Mbabane, Swaziland. **Tel.**(office) 268 84010, (home) 268 42376; **fax** 268 86284.

ALLEN, John Polk. Biospherics, closed life-systems; ecology of ecobiomes in relation to Biosphere. Consultant, Vice-President &/or Director of numerous enterprises, Institute Director. *B.*6 May 1929, Carnegie, OK, USA. American. **Education:** Northwestern, Stanford, & Oklahoma Univs, world hist., classics, writing, anthropol., culturology & human evol. 1946–50; Colorado Sch.of Mines, BS(Eng.), (Metallurgical Mining)(Hons) 1957; Harvard U.

MBA(Hons) 1962; Michigan U. Cert.in Advanced Physiol.Systems for Engrs 1971. **Experience:** factory worker, civil rights sec., march leader & org., res., self-financed 21-months' around-the-planet trip by land & sea, training *etc*.of US forces in Vietnam, co-Convenor of multi-disc.intl confs of scis & thinkers 1974–91, co-Founder/Consult./Dir of num.orgns intlly, extensive business exp. **Career:** Owner, Soft Fruit Farm 1950; Machinist, US Army Engr Corps 1952–3; Sr Metallurgist, Allegheny-Ludlum Steel Corpn 1957–9; Dept Head, Uravan Mill Nuclear Corpn 1959–60; Asst VP, Dev.and Resources Corpn (NYC) 1962–3; Pres. Connecticut Valley Chemicals Corpn 1962–6; Pres. Mtn and Manhattan Inc.1963–6; Mgmt Consult.1964–5; Adv.Bd and playwright/dramaturge, Theater of All Possibilities 1966–95; Chief Metallurgist, Meadow Gold Inc.1966–74; Gen.Mgr, Synergia Ranch (New Mexico) 1969–74; co-Founder, Project Tibet 1973–80; co-Founder & Dir, Inst.of Ecotechnics (London, UK) 1973–; co-Founder & Consult. Savannah Systems Pty (W.Australia) 1978–; co-Founder & Dir, Sarbid Ltd (now Biospheric Design Inc.) 1978–; Dir & New Projects Consult. Decisions Team (Ltd HK & Inc.USA) 1981–; Conceiver, Inventor, & Head of Dev. Biosphere 2 1984–94; VP, Ecol. (savanna, desert, rain-forest) Systems, Eco-Frontiers Inc.1994–; co-Founder & Dir, Planetary Coral Reef Fndn (Calif.) 1991–; co-Founder & Chairman, Cyberspheres Inc.(Calif.) 1994–. **Achievements:** promoting Biosphere 2 and its educl spin-offs worldwide to schools, univs, & gen.public, to show interrelatedness of life, humans, & technics; co-Convenor of *c*.20 scientific confs on ecol.issues; creation of eight eco-projects around the world. **Memberships:** F.LS, F.RGS. **Awards:** Tau Beta Pi (Colorado Sch.of Mines) 1956, Baker Scholar and High Dist.(Harvard Business Sch.) 1962, Hon.Citizen (Fort Worth, Texas) 1989. **Publications:** num. incl.*Space Biospheres* 1986, 1989, Biosphere 2 and the concept of the noosphere 1992, *The Human Experiment* 1991; Intl Edl Adv.Bd *Nanobiology*. Dislikes pers.pub., favours news media support. **Languages:** English, Spanish. Willing to act as consult.etc. **Address:** Cyberspheres Inc., 32038 Caminito Quieto, Bonsall, California 92003, USA. **Tel.**1 619 723 8566; **fax** 1 619 723 3326.

ALLOTTA, Dr Gaetano. Environmental & marine protection. Journalist, President. *B*.12 May 1930, Belmonte Mezzagno, Palermo, Italy. Italian. *M*.Prof.Rita: *s., d.* **Education:** U.of Palermo, Dottore in Giurisprudenza 1953. **Experience:** journalism, fin., admin. **Career:** *Procuratore* Legal 1953–6; Officer 1956–73 and Super.of Finance 1973–91, Fin.Admin.of Italian Rep.; Journalist 1970–; Pres. Agrigento Branch of Lega Navale Italiana 1981–. **Achievements:** nine published books concerning envl prot. **Memberships:** Order of Italian Journalists, Lions' Club Intl, Italian Assn of

Awarded or Chivalrous Hons, Nat.Cttee for Prot.of Biol.Marine Resources (Min.of Mercantile Marine of Italy) 1981–88. **Awards:** Culture Prize (PM of Italian Rep.) 1963, Global 500 Roll of Honour (UNEP) 1989, Cavaliere di Gran Croce della Repubblica Italiana 1990, Taormina Award for Arts & Scis 1993. **Publications:** nine books incl.*L'Azione Comunitaria per la Protezione dell'Ambiente nel Bacino del Mediterraneo* 1990, *Pescatori di Ieri* 1992, *Rupe Atenea* 1993. Indiff.to pers.pub.& news media support. **Languages:** French, Italian. Willing to act as consult.etc. **Address:** Via Diodoro Siculo 1, 92100 Agrigento, Italy. **Tel.**39 922 20831; **fax** 39 922 608163.

AL-MANDHRY, Abdullah Rashid. Policy development, monitoring. Director of Environmental Health & Malaria Eradication. *B*.15 May 1963, Kenya. Omani. *M*.Fawziya: 3 *s.,d.* **Education:** Indiana U. BSc(Envl Health) 1986; LSHTM, MSc(Occupational Health) 1990. **Experience:** res., tech., admin.; Temp.Adv. WHO Regnl Conf.on Dev.of Envt & Health (Dec.1988) and *ad hoc* WG on Needs Assessment for Training and Capacity Bldg (July 1995), Expert seconded to UNITAR July 1995. **Career:** Sr Sanitary Super.1986–8, Tech.Adv. & Supervisor, Directorate Gen.of Health Affairs 1988, Head of Occupational Health 1988–92, Dir of Envl Health 1992–3, Dir of Envl Health & Acting Dir of Malaria Eradication 1993, Dir of Envl Health & Malaria Eradication 1993–, Min.of Health, Sultanate of Oman. **Achievements:** designed, programmed, computerized, and implemented, envl monitoring, eval.and mgmt system in Oman (incl.info.systems). **Memberships:** num.nat.tech.cttees *e.g.*Cttee on Nat.Oil Spill Contingency Plan, Nat.Tech. Review Cttee on Regs for Solid (non-Hazardous) & Hazardous Wastes, Nat.Tech.- & Sub-Cttees on Supply of Equipment for Monitoring Radioactivity in Foodstuffs. **Publications:** *Occupational Health & Safety/Industrial Hygiene Survey Report* 1988, *Study of Degreasing Operations in Automobile Garages in Oman* 1990, *Cytotoxic Drug Prep.in Oman* 1991, *Health Effect of Air Poll.in Musandam Regn from the Kuwait Oil Fires* 1991. Indiff.to pers. pub., favours news media support. **Languages:** Arabic, English, Swahili. Willing to act as consult.etc. **Address:** Directorate General of Health Affairs, Ministry of Health, POB 393, Muscat 113, Sultanate of Oman. **Tel.** (office) 968 562 898, (home) 968 535 297; **fax** 968 563 121.

ALNASER, Dr Waheeb Essa. Environmental physics: estimating potential of solar, wind, tidal, water current, and wave, energy in Bahrain as these energies are pollution-free & non-depleting; correlating the climatical parameters with astronomical parameters such as cosmic radiation, ultraviolet solar radiation, and noise pollution. Associate Professor in Applied Physics. *B*.4 May 1959, Hidd Town, Bahrain. Bahraini. *M.*Annesa A.: 2 *s.* **Education:** King Saud U. BSc 1979, Coll.of Health Sci. Dipl.in Health Sci.Educ.1980, U.of Aston MSc(Phys.) 1982, U.of Kent PhD 1986. **Experience:** admin. — Conf.Chairman, Intl Conf.in Condensed Matter Phys.& Applications, Bahrain 1992, & Ed.of Conf.Proc.; consult.for sci.budget and perm.memb.of Renewable Energy Group, Arabic League for Educ., Culture & Sci.; supervision of several BSc projects in envl phys.; Rapp.1st Bahrain Intl Conf.on Envt 1992; daily Astronomical Forecasting on Bahrain Radio 1993–. **Career:** Supervisor, Directorate of Stats 1979, Instr.Coll.of Health Sci.1980, Counterpart of UNESCO Phys.Expert, UC of Bahrain 1981, Asst Prof.1986, Assoc.Prof. 1992–, Chairman Phys Dept 1989–, U.of Bahrain. **Achievements:** used solar radiation measurement to measure several envl parameters for Bahrain's sky such as turbidity, transparency, extinction coefficient, emissivity, transmittance, visibility, optical thickness, ground & sky albedo; working also on uses of renewable energy resources in Bahrain as they are poll.-free sources; since 1993 studied effect of cars' fuel consumption on visibility in Bahrain's sky; estab.of Envl Phys.course at Bahrain U. **Memberships:** Inst.of Phys., WREN UK (co-Founder), Bahrain Astronomical Soc., IEF (Chairman of Middle E.), ISES (Chairman, Arabic Section), Planetary Soc.UK; many cttees at deptl, coll.& u.levels. **Awards:** State Prize for Nat.Achievement 1992, Brit.Council Visitorship, UNESCO Scholarship. **Publications:** five books incl. *Your Guide to Bahrain's Sky* 1992, *Traffic Phys.* 1993; sch.textbooks & *c.*70 scientific papers; Ref.for *Urban Atmos.*and *J.of Alloys & Compounds.* Welcomes pers.pub.& news media support (also actively supports local news media). **Languages:** Arabic, English. Willing to act as consult.etc. **Address:** Physics Department, University of Bahrain, Isa Town, POB 32038, State of Bahrain. **Tel.**(office) 973 688398 & 381, (home) 973 713722; **fax** 973 682582.

ALON, Azaria. Nature conservation: writing, photography, editing. Society Chairman. *B.*15 Nov.1918, Vollodarsk, Ukraine. Israeli. *M.* Ruth: 2 *s., d.* **Education:** Teachers' Seminary (Tel-Aviv) 1950–51; Tel-Aviv U. BSc(Biol.) 1962–4. **Experience:** writing, lecturing, editing, & advising, on biol.& cons., Nature photography, public campaigns. **Career:** radio broadcasting, writing & editing, public campaigns for cons.& envt, dir.of Keep Israel Clean project, Nature photography. **Achievements:** co-Founder 1953, Gen.Sec.1969–77, Chairman 1977–89, Soc.for Prot.of Nature; writing, broadcasting, editing articles & books on Nature, cons.& envt; leading campaigns especially Saving the Wild Flowers of Israel; Author & photographer of 20+ books. **Memberships:** Israeli Planning & Bldg Govtl Council and Geogl Names Govtl Cttee, Botl Names Cttee of Hebrew Language Acad. **Awards:** Israel Radio Awards

1967, Govtl Awards for Nature & envt activities 1978 & 1984, Israel Prize for Soc.for Prot.of Nature and its leaders 1980, Global 500 Roll of Honour (UNEP) 1987, Hon.PhD *H.C.*(Weizman Inst.) 1991, Yigal Allon Prize. **Publications:** 22 books incl.*Enc.of Plants & Animals of the Land of Israel* (Ed.12 vols) 1982, 1992, *300 Wild Flowers in Colour* 1987 (in Hebrew), 1992 (in Arabic), 1993 (in English), *Trees & Bushes of Israel* 1991 (in Hebrew), 1993 (in Arabic), *Lexicon of Plants & Animals of Israel* (Ed.3 vols) 1992; num.booklets & brochures. **Languages:** Arabic, English, German, Hebrew, Yiddish. **Address:** Society for the Protection of Nature, 4 Hashfela Street, Tel-Aviv 66183, Israel, or Kibbutz Beit Hashitta, 18910 Israel. **Tel.**(office) 972 3 375063, (home) 972 6 536867; **fax** 972 3 377695 or 972 6 536577.

ALSTON, Dr Frank Henry. Genetics & breeding of apples & pears including the introduction of pest- & disease-resistance. Programme Leader. *B.*5 May 1936, Lancaster, England, UK. British. *M.*Jill: 2 *d.* Catrina Mary (envl health), Elizabeth Anne (landscape arch.). **Education:** Bentham Grammar Sch.; Sheffield U. BSc (Gen.Hons) (Bot.& Zool.) (1st Class) 1957, U.of Camb. post-grad.training in plant breeding, Reading U. PhD 1963. **Experience:** genetical res.in apples & pears incl.genome mapping, training postgrad.students, transferring pest & disease resistance from wild species, developing improved selection systems for plant breeding, managing breeding progs, integrating plant breeding into biological control systems. **Career:** Fruit Breeding Dept, E.Malling Res. Station (now Breeding & Genetics Dept, HRI) 1962–; Prog.Leader, Apple & Pear Breeding Prog. HRI 1980–. **Achievements:** intro.of high levels of disease & pest resistance into apple & pear breeding material as part of effort to reduce pesticide inputs in hort., training several workers in breeding & resistance selection techniques incl.postgrad.& postdoctl students. **Memberships:** AAB, Genetical Soc., EUCARPIA. **Award:** Jones-Bateman Cup (RHS) 1988–91. **Publications:** 80+ incl.reviews *e.g.* Breeding pome fruits with stable resistance to diseases 1989, Flavour improvement in apples & pears through plant breeding 1992. Favours pers.pub. & news media support. **Language:** English. Willing to act as consult.etc. **Address:** Horticulture Research International–East Malling, West Malling, Kent ME19 6BJ, England, UK. **Tel.**(office) 44 1732 843833, (home) 44 1622 738104; **fax** 44 1732 849067.

ALVARADO, Juan SKINNER. Management & development of protected areas. Field Director. *B.*31 Aug.1961, Washington, DC, USA. American, Guatemalan. **Education:** Coll.of San Mateo, Assoc.in Sci.(Biol.) 1984–9; UCD, BS(Intl Agricl Dev.& Natural Resource Mgmt) 1989–91. **Experience:** admin., u.studies focussed on envl sci.and applied anthrop. **Career:** farm dev.in rainforest area of Guatemala

1979–81; Info.Resource Dev. Stanford U. 1981–6; Dir, Sierra de las Minas Biosphere Reserve 1991–3; Exec.Dir, Asociación Amigos del Lago Atitlán 1993–. **Achievements:** estab.of Sierra de Las Minas Biosphere Reserve, envl mgmt of Atitlán Nat.Park. **Award:** Gold Piolet for climbing 15 volcanoes of Guatemala by the age of 12 yrs. Dislikes pers.pub., indiff.to news media support. **Languages:** English (good), Qeqchi (one of the 22 Mayan languages of Guatemala, spoken), Spanish. Willing to act as consult.etc. Address: 14 Avenida 1-45 Zona 14, interior 1-39, Guatemala City, Guatemala. Tel.(office) 502 2 374886, (home) 502 2 681764; fax 502 2 680843.

ALVAREZ, Juan Marco. Protected area management, environmental education, ecotourism. Executive Director. *B.*29 Oct.1963, San Salvador, El Salvador. Salvadorean. **Education:** (in Costa Rica) Universidad Autónoma de Centro Amer. BBA 1988; Instituto Centroamericano de Administración de Empresas, MBA (Natural Resources) 1995. **Experience:** business admin. re.coffee plantations & fin.instns, involvement in prot.areas & ecotourism. **Career:** Bank Exec. BANCORP (El Salvador) 1988–90; Exec.Dir, SalvaNatura Fndn 1990–3, 1995–. **Achievements:** Init./Founder of SalvaNatura in 1990 and launched land purchase campaign for Salvadorean Nat.Parks 1992, led govt to sign agreement for mgmt of El Salvador's premier nat.park. **Memberships:** SalvaNatura (VC 1990–2), Coatepeque Fndn of El Salvador (Bd 1993–5), Rotary Club of San Salvador (Hon.) 1993. **Award:** Cons.F'ship (The Nature Conservancy) 1992–3. **Publications:** Private support for the Salvadorean NPS: the case of El Imposible Nat.Park 1992; 10+ local newspaper articles. Favours pers.pub.& news media support. **Languages:** English, French (poor), Portuguese (poor), Spanish. Willing to act as consult.etc. **Address:** 3a Calle Poniente Nr 3647, San Salvador, El Salvador. **Tel.**(office) 503 223 3620, (home) 503 298 0455; **fax** 503 224 4848.

AMBASHT, Professor Radhey Shyam. Ecological research & writing. Professor of Botany. *B.*3 Dec.1936, Gyanpur, Varanasi, UP, India. Indian. *M.*Annpurna (co-Author of *Ecol.* (in Hindi) 1988): 2 *s.*Pravin K.(biochem.), Navin K.(ecol.). **Education:** BHU MSc(1st Class) 1957, PhD 1963. **Experience:** 36 yrs' res.— several projects on cons.& mgmt ecol.of wetlands, river corridors, grasslands & forests; teaching ecol.to BSc & MSc students and successfully supervising PhD students (27 to 1994); prog. coordn. **Career:** Lect.1960–70, Reader 1970–84, Prof.1984– & Head Dept of Bot.1988–90, Prog.Coord. Centre of Advanced Study in Bot.1989–, BHU. **Achievements:** originator of new Cons.value concept (Cv%) of plants for soil, water & nutrient cons.against erosion & runoff. **Memberships:** IBS, INTECOL (Bd 1995–8), ISTE (Sec.1989–94), SAB, NASc, NIE (Pres. 1994–6). **Awards:** F.of NASc, NIE & ISTE,

Prof. B.Sahni Gold Medal (IBS) 1995. **Publications:** *Plant Ecol.*(10 edns) 1969–1990, *Envt & Poll.*1990, 1992; 140+ papers. Indiff.to pers.pub.& news media support. **Languages:** English, German (a little), Hindi, Urdu. Willing to act as consult.etc. **Address:** Department of Botany, Banaras Hindu University, Varanasi 221 005, Uttar Pradesh, India. **Tel.**(office) 91 542 312989, (home) 91 542 312485; **fax** 91 542 312059.

AMIRKHANOV, Dr Amirkhan Magomed. Floristic research, taxonomic botany, biodiversity protection, Nature conservation. Deputy Minister of Environment. *B.*13 Nov.1952, Sutbuk, Dakhadaev Regn, Dhagestan. Dharginian. *M.*Epishina Lyudmila Vasilievna (soil chem.): *d.* **Education:** Dhagestan SU, MS *cum laude* 1974; Moscow SU, postgrad.BSc(Geobot.) 1977, Dr Biol.1978. **Experience:** res.— geobot., taxonomic studies of Campanulaceae species; admin.— natural prot.areas mgmt & res.; consult.— cons.of flora, wildlife prot. **Career:** Dep.Dir & Sr Researcher, N.-Ossetian State Nature Reserve 1978–83; Exec.Sec.& Dir, C. Scientific Res.Lab.on hunting game and Nature reserves, Chief Dept of Game 1983–92; Head, 'Chief Russia' Dept of Bioresources, and Dep.Minister of Envt 1992–. **Achievements:** fundamental description of n.Caucasus wildlife & Nature, assisting Russian Govt in wildlife prot. **Memberships:** Nat.Botl Soc.1974–, Moscow Naturalists' Soc.1974–. **Awards:** Hon.Dipl.(All-Russia Nature Conservationists' Soc.) 1984 and ('Chief Dept' of Game, Russia Council of Ministers) 1985 & 1990. **Publications:** Severo-Ossetinsky Zapovednik 1988; 100 scientific papers; Chief Ed. *Trans.of C.Scientific Res. Lab.* Favours pers.pub.& news media support. **Languages:** Dharginian, English (basic), German (basic), Russian. Further details may be obtained from *Biologists and Game Scientists of Russian Fedn* 1994. Willing to act as ref. **Address:** 8 Kedrova Street, Block 1, 117874 Moscow, Russia. **Tel.**7 095 124 0471; **fax** 7 095 125 6302.

ANADA, Tiega. Natural resource management. Country Representative. *B.*1949, Kalgo, Niger, W.Africa. Nigerien. **Education:** U.of Niamey BSc(Agric.) 1980, U.of Arizona MSc 1985. **Experience:** tech.— wildlife habitat & pop.in Niger, biodiv.assessment, envl law, prot.areas' mgmt, fisheries mgmt; admin. **Career:** Asst Dir of State Agency (Forest & Wildlife Dir of Wildlife & Fisheries), Govt of Niger 1980–90; Tech.Adv.1990–2, Country Rep.1992–, IUCN Niger. **Achievements:** prep.& implementation of over ten major projects in natural resource mgmt. **Memberships:** IUCN CNPPA & SSC, Wildlife Soc.(USA), six nat.assns. **Awards:** L'Ordre Nat.du Niger (Comm.for Major Acts), Chevalier de l'Ordre Nat.du Niger. **Publications:** *Biodiv.Assessment in Niger* 1990; num. articles. **Languages:** English, French, Haoussa. Willing to act as consult.&/or judge proposals.

Address: IUCN Niger Office, BP 10933, Niamey, Niger. **Tel.**(office) 227 753138, (home) 227 752710; **fax** 227 752215.

ANDALUZ WESTREICHER, Dr Antonio, *see* **WESTREICHER, Dr Antonio** ANDALUZ.

ANDERSON, Dr Edward Frederick. Systematics & ethnobotany of cacti, conservation of cacti. Senior Research Botanist. *B.*17 June 1932, Covina, CA, USA. American. *M.*Dr Adele Bowman: 4 *s.*, 3 *d.*incl.Erica R. (animal behaviour). **Education:** Pomona Coll. BA (Biol.) 1954, Claremont Grad.Sch. MA(Bot.) 1959, PhD(Bot.) 1961. **Experience:** extensive field-work in arid regns of New World, as well as ethnobotl work in SE Asia. **Career:** Asst Prof. 1962–67, Assoc.Prof.1967–76, Prof.1976– 92, of Biol. Whitman Coll.(Washington); Vis. Prof. of Bot.Chiang Mai U.(Thailand) 1976–77, 1983–4; Sr Res.Bot. Desert Botl Gdn (Arizona) 1992–. **Achievements:** Cactus cons.studies for WWF; Chairman IUCN SSC Cactus & Succulent SG. **Memberships:** IOSPS, LS, SEB. **Awards:** Paul Garrett F.1972–6, Walla Walla Town & Gown Award 1974, F.CSSA. **Publications:** *Peyote: The Divine Cactus* 1980, *Endangered Cacti of Mexico* (in press); *Plants & People of the Golden Triangle: Ethnobot.of the Hill Tribes of Northern Thailand* (in press); num.articles & reports. **Languages:** English, Spanish. Further details can be obtained from *Who's Who in Amer.*(48th edn). Willing to act as consult.etc. **Address:** Desert Botanical Garden, 1201 N. Galvin Parkway, Phoenix, Arizona 85008, USA. **Tel.**(office) 1 602 941 1225, (home) 1 602 759 3971; **fax** 1 602 481 8124.

ANDRIAMAMPIANINA, Joseph. Nature protection, management of protected areas; research on Malagasy primates. Director-General. *B.*26 March 1932, Antananarivo, Madagascar. Malagasy. *M.* Odette: *s.*, 2 *d.* **Education:** Ecole Nationale des Eaux et Forêts (France), Forest Engr 1962. **Experience:** res., teaching, admin. **Career:** Chief of Nature Prot. Antananarivo 1968–80; Chief of Forest Dept, U.of Antananarivo 1981–92; DG, Nat.Office of Envt 1992–. **Achievements:** policy, law & admin.for managing prot.areas, and for forestry. **Memberships:** IUCN SSC (past regnl memb.for Africa), IUCN CNPPA (past Consult.re.Madagascar). **Publications:** incl.Status of natural reserves in Madagascar 1987. Indiff.to pers.pub & news media support. **Languages:** English (fair written & spoken), French. Willing to act as a consult. **Address:** Office National de l'Environnement, Ambalavao-Isotry, Antananarivo, Madagascar. **Tel.** (office) 261 2 25999, (home) 261 2 29027; **fax** 261 2 30693.

ANDRIANARIVO, Dr Jonah A. Forestry in Madagascar, geographical information systems, journalism. Independent Consultant. *B.*2 Feb. 1951, Antsirabe, Madagascar. Malagasy. **Education:** U.of Madagascar, Engr(For.) 1976, Duke U. PhD(For.& Envl Studies) 1990. **Experience:** res.in forest sampling methods using GIS, consult.in USA, Kenya, Madagascar. **Career:** Mgr, Tsimbazaza Park 1978–81; Lect. U.of Madagascar 1981–3; Ind.Consult.1985–. **Achievements:** res., pubn of envl articles in nat. newspapers. **Membership:** NYAS. **Awards:** J.B. Duke F'ship 1983, Fulbright Scholarship 1988. **Publications:** Using GIS to evaluate the crowline intersect sampling method in forest survey 1993; several newspaper articles (in French & Malagasy). Favours pers.pub.& news media support. **Languages:** English, French, Malagasy. Willing to act as consult.etc. **Address:** POB 30709, Nairobi, Kenya. **Tel.**254 2 631075; **fax** 254 2 631499.

ANGEL, Dr Martin V. Ecology of deep oceanic communities, marine biodiversity, marine zoogeography, and taxonomy of pelagic Ostracods. Senior Research Biologist. *B.*14 April 1937, Harrow, Middlesex, England, UK. British. Mother Edna Laura, bot.teacher. *M.*Heather (Hon. DSc, wildlife photographer, Vis.Prof.in Biol. Illustration): *s.* **Education:** Wycliffe Coll., Magdalene Coll. Camb. Natural Sci.Tripos (Zool.) 1957–60, Bristol U. PhD(Zool.) 1967. **Experience:** student expedns to trop.rain-forest in Brit.Guiana, diving in Norwegian fjords, participation in Intl Indian Ocean Expedn 1963–4, res.admin. **Career:** Dem.in Zool. Bristol U.1960–65; 27 oceanogr.res.cruises (seven as Prin.Sci.) 1963–; Counc. Challenger Soc. 1972–92, Head of Biol.1982–93, Head Challenger Centre for Sea-floor Processes 1993–5, Deacon Lab. Inst.of Oceanogr.Scis 1965–95; co-Ed.*Progress in Oceanogr.*1979–; Chairman IUCN Comm.of Ecol.WG on Ocean Ecol. 1980–85; WWF(UK) Cons.Review Group 1985–. VP BES 1990–92; Steering Cttee of UK Biodiv.Strat.1994–; Sr Res.Biol. Southampton Oceanogr.Centre (UK) 1995–. **Achievements:** 105 res.papers, three books, Org. jt IUCN / SCAR symp.on Antarctic Cons.(Bonn 1985), UK SCOPE Cttee, RS Envt Cttee. **Memberships:** BES, ASLO, SCE, BANC, Challenger Soc.for Marine Sci., SCB. **Publications:** num.incl.Are there any potentially important routes whereby radionuclides can be transferred by biol. processes from the sea-bed towards the surface? 1983, *Marine Processes* (co-Author) 1987, Criteria for prot.areas and other cons.measures in the Antarctic Regn 1987, *Scientific Requirements for Antarctic Cons.*(co-Ed.) 1987, The deep-ocean option for the disposal of sewage sludge 1988, Variations in time & space: is biogeog.relevant to studies of long-time scale change? 1991, Deep abyssal plains, do they offer a viable option for disposal of large bulk low-toxicity waste? 1992, Managing biodiv.in the oceans 1992, Biodiv.of the pelagic ocean 1993, Monitoring the deep ocean for risk assessment: another role for GOOS 1994, Spatial distribn of marine organisms: pattern & process 1994. Favours pers.pub.& news media support. **Languages:** English, French (read). Willing to review res.proposals & papers.

Address: Southampton Oceanography Centre, Empress Dock, Southampton, Hampshire SO14 3ZH, England, UK. **Tel.**44 1703 596014; **fax** 44 1703 596247; **e-mail** Martin.V.Angel@soc. soton.ac.uk .

ANGELO, Professor Dr Homer Glenn. International law, communications, environmental protection. Professor of International Law. *B.*8 June 1916, Alameda, CA, USA. American. Father A.Heath Angelo, Founder of Coast Range Reserve (Eel River, Calif.). *M.*Ann B.(co-Founder, Foresta Inst.): *s.*Alex, 2 *d.*Christiane & Nancy (all participants in preserv.of Coast Range Reserve). **Education:** UCB, AB 1938, JD 1941; Columbia U. LLM 1947. **Experience:** co-Founder ICEL; Prof.of Intl Law, UCD 1968–; Prof.& Founder of one of the world's first courses on legal aspects of intl envl prot.at UCD 1971, and instnl & legal aspects of intl telecomms at UCD 1993 & UCB 1995; co-Founder of the Homer G.and Ann Borghill Angelo endowed prof.'ship and fund for intl legal & communications studies at UCD 1995. Dislikes & avoids pers.pub., favours news media support for a good cause. **Languages:** Dutch, English, French, Spanish. **Address:** 100 Thorndale Drive, San Rafael, California 94903, USA. **Tel.**(office & home) 1 415 492 2494; **fax** 1 415 499 1018.

ANI, Ambassador Olufemi. Environmental policies & legislation, urban environmental planning. Company Director & Group Principal Consultant. *B.*22 March 1941, Ado-Ekiti, Nigeria. Nigerian. *M.*Monisola (memb.of Nigerian Cons.Fndn): 2 *d.* Sister Prof.(Mrs) Afonja, Dir of Centre for Pop., Rural & Envl Studies. **Education:** Govt Coll.(Ibadan) 1953–8; Kingston-upon-Hull Coll.of Commerce (UK) 1958–9; Univs of Wales 1959–63, Geneva, & Montpellier, and Goethe Inst.(Arolsen, Germany) 1963–5. **Experience:** joined Diplomatic Service in 1963 and served at var.times in the Econ., Amer., OAU, Legal Affairs, and Intl Econ.Coopn, Depts, of Min.of Ext.Affairs (Lagos); at dir level and with rank of Amb.held top-level mgmt positions in govt and specialized in econ.& intl fin./industrial & commercial matters, UN — Leader of Nigerian Team on 2nd Cttee (for Econ.& Social Matters) of 38th UNGA 1983, and co-Chair of high-level Intergovtl Follow-up & Coordn Cttee on Econ.Coopn among Developing Countries, Manila 1982. **Career:** Desk Officer, Econ.Dept, Min.of Ext.Affairs 1963–4; Econ.& Commercial Affairs Officer (later appointed Nigerian Consul and Head of Post in Hamburg), Nigerian Embassy, Bonn 1965–8; In Charge, Min.of Ext. Affairs, OAU 1968–70; Head of Mission (Algiers) 1970–2; Couns., Minister-Couns., & Commissioner Gen.for Econ.Affairs, in Washington DC 1972–6; Minister Plenipotentiary & Dep.Dir, Dept of Intl Econ.Coopn (Lagos) 1976–8; Amb.& (served as) HC to SL 1978–82; Alternate Dir, Dept of Intl Econ.Coopn (Econ.

Affairs Dept) 1982–4 when retired from govt service; Dir & Bd Memb.of num.cos in Nigeria, UK, & W.Africa 1985–. **Achievements:** helped in conceiving envl policy and infant structure in Nigeria in the mid-1970s after study of US Fed.EPA system, set up a virile envl sector consult.practice based in Lagos, active in instn-building and in watchdog role re.maintenance of envl standards. **Memberships:** R.Africa Soc., Inst.of Dirs, Rotary Intl, Nigerian Inst.of Mgmt, and Econ.Soc.; memb.of num.Chambers of Commerce (Pres.of Nigeria–Belgian), and *ad hoc* of some fed.& state govt bodies (VP of Nigerian–Europe Assn). **Publications:** contribn to var.pubns incl.Energy & Dev.1975. Indiff.to pers.pub., favours news media support. **Languages:** English, French, German, Yoruba. Further details may be obtained from *Who's Who in Nigeria* [Newswatch] 1990. Willing to act as consult.etc. **Address:** Gothard Group, Ajebo House 6th Floor, 24–26 Macarthy Street, Onikan [or POB 72.816, Victoria Island], Lagos, Nigeria. **Tel.**(office) 234 1 263 1584, (home) 234 1 587 3351; **fax** 234 1 263 7855 or 587 3351.

ANISHETTY, Dr Narasimha Murthi. Conservation & utilization of plant genetic resources/biological diversity. Senior Officer. *B.* 12 Jan.1942, Hanamkonda, India. Indian. *M.* Anasuya: 2 *s., d.* **Education:** Karnataka U. BSc (Agric.) 1964, AP Agricl U. MSc(Agric.) 1966, U.of Georgia PhD 1973. **Experience:** exploration, collection, cons., documentation, eval.& utilization of crop genetic resources; bldg-up of nat.capacities & progs on genetic resources. **Career:** Oilseeds Officer, AP Agricl U. 1967–70; Res.Assoc. U.of Georgia 1970–73; Bot.Genetic Resources ICRISAT 1974–8; Asst Exec.Sec. IBPGR1978–87, Sr Officer, Plant Genetic Resources 1987–, FAO. **Achievements:** promoted & supported nat.efforts on collection & safe cons.of germplasm from diff.agro-ecol.regns of the world and estab.of nat.genetic resources progs. **Memberships:** ISGPB, ISPGR, several task forces re.plant genetic resources and biol diversity. **Award:** Silver Medal & Plaque (IBPGR) 1984. **Publications:** over 50 incl.*Genebanks and World Food* 1987. Indiff.to pers.pub. **Languages:** English, Hindi, Kannada, Telugu. Willing to act as consult.etc. **Address:** Food and Agriculture Organization, Via delle Terme di Caracalla, 00100 Rome, Italy. **Tel.**(office) 39 522 54652, (home) 39 503 6971; **fax** 39 522 56347.

APPLIN, Dr David Gerald. Insect biology, comparative neuroendocrinology, neurosecretory systems, evolution theory, conservation; wildlife photography. Head of Science, Author, Editor. *B.*12 March 1946, London, England, UK. British. *M.*Marjorie Anne: 2 *d.* **Education:** Leeds U. BSc(Zool.) 1969; IC, MSc 1970, DIC 1970; Birkbeck Coll. London PhD 1976. **Experience:** teaching, res., writing, editing, photography; reproductive biol.of sheep blowfly *Lucilia sericata*, pituitary thyroid relations in S.African Clawed Toad *Xenopus laevis* visualizing neuroendocrine system; co-Org. Conf.of BSC 1985, Consult.to US Food Admin.on control of moths in stored products, Vetting Panel for Key Stage 3 Sci.1994, Judge for Blake Shield Competition of BNA. **Career:** Head of Sci. Chigwell Sch.(Essex, UK) 1980–, Ed. *Country-Side* 1988–. **Achievements:** Ed.of *Country-Side* — heightening public awareness of cons.issues in UK & abroad. **Memberships:** F.RES, BNA (Council). **Publications:** num. sch.text-books, monogrs, & papers. Indiff.to pers.pub.& news media support. **Language:** English. Further details may be obtained from *Writers' and Artists' Yr Book* 1994. Willing to act as consult.etc. **Address:** POB 87, Cambridge CB1 3UP, England, UK. **Tel.& fax** 44 1933 314672.

ARAUJO, Joaquín. Ecology, environment, organic farming. Journalist, Lecturer, Adviser, Farmer. *B*.31 Dec.1947, Madrid, Spain. Spanish. *M*.Ana Clara: *s*. **Experience:** Pres./ Dir Centro Nacional de Educación Ambiental en la Naturaleza (first State Centre for Envl Educ.), film directing, geographer, writing, 27 yrs in envl socs, *c*.200 envl lectures in several cultural instns throughout Spain, organic farming. **Achievements:** founding of Asociación para el Estudio y Defensa de la Naturaleza, Coor dinadora de Organizaciónes de Defensa Ambiental, and Foro de debates sobre ecología y medio ambiente. **Awards:** Global 500 Roll of Honour (UNEP) 1991, some film awards. **Publications:** 21 books (in Spanish) incl. *Cultivar La Tierra, Los Parques Nacionales, Fauna Amiga, Los instantes del bosque* 1995, *Introducción al pensamiento ecológico* 1995, written &/or directed several documentary series for TV, three live from Kenya which were produced by BBC & TVE 1989; *c*.1,000 magazine & newspaper articles. Dislikes pers. pub.& news media support. **Languages:** English (read), Italian, Spanish. **Address:** Avenida de America 8, 5D, 28028 Madrid, Spain. **Tel.**(office & home) & **fax** 34 91 726 0343.

ARCEIVALA, Professor Soli J. (aka Jal Sorab). Water pollution control, environmental impact assessment, reuse of water, wastewater treatment. Chairman & Managing Director. *B*.17 Jan.1926, Madras, TN, India. Indian. *M*.Nergish: 2 *d*. **Education:** U.of Bombay BE(Civil) 1947, Harvard U. MS(Envl Eng.) 1955. **Experience:** res., consult. **Career:** Site Engr 1947–9, Engr 1949–53, Consult.Engr 1961–71, Bombay; Prof.& Head, Civil & Sanitary Engg Dept 1956–68, VP & Rector 1959–68, Vic. Jubilee Tech.Inst. U.of Bombay; Dir NEERI 1968–71; Expert WHO/UN (ultimately supervising WHO's Envl Health Progs in 11 countries in SE Asia) 1971–85; MD Associated Industrial Consults (India) Private Ltd 1985–. **Achievements:** estab.first envl consult.co.in India 1961, water cons.& reuse, wastewater treatment. **Memberships:** ASCE (Life), F.Instn of Engrs

(India), IWWA (Founder), IAEM. **Awards:** Nat.Design Award (Instn of Engrs) 1991. **Publications:** *Waste Water Treatment and Disposal* 1981, *Wastewater Treatment for Poll.Control* 1986, *Oxidation Ponds* (co-Author) 1970; 33 tech.papers (prizes awarded for three). Indiff.to pers.pub., favours news media support. **Language:** English. Willing to act as consult. etc. **Address:** Associated Industrial Consultants (India) Private Limited, Raheja Centre (13th Floor), Nariman Point, Bombay 400 021, Maharashtra, India. **Tel.**91 22 283 4052; **fax** 91 22 204 0398.

ARCHIBALD, Dr George. Preservation of cranes (Gruidae) & their habitats. Foundation Director. *B*.13 July 1946, New Glasgow, Canada. Canadian. *M*.Kyoko. **Education:** Dalhousie U. BS 1968, Cornell U. PhD 1976. **Experience:** doctl studies at Cornell U.addressed the comparative ethology of cranes & evol.relationships; since founding the Intl Crane Fndn have studied the ecol.of eight species of cranes in Australia, China, Iran, India, Japan, Korea, & USA; helped organize nine WGs on cranes incl.more than 900 researchers in 64 nations. **Career:** co-Founder, Intl Crane Fndn 1973–. **Achievements:** through the activities of the various WGs have stimulated actions that resulted in cons.of more than 5 m.ha of wetlands in Asia; under my direction the Intl Crane Fndn has established a 'species bank' of captive cranes and has been successful in breeding sig.nrs of several endangered species of cranes. **Memberships:** BNHS, CWS, Chicago AS, CAWC, IUCN, NYZS, Oriental Bird Club, OSC, WWF, US FWS, Yamashina Inst.for Ornith. **Awards:** Order of the Golden Ark 1983, MacArthur F.1984, Gold Medal (WWF) 1985, Global 500 Roll of Honour (UNEP) 1987, Disting.Conservationist Award (Nat.Audubon Soc.) 1993. **Publications:** *Comparative Ecol.and Behavior of Eastern Sarus Cranes and Brolgas in Australia* (co-Author) 1987, *Compendium of Crane Behaviour* Part I *Individual (non-social) Behavior* (co-Author) 1990. Favours news media support. **Language:** English. **Address:** International Crane Foundation, POB 447, E-11376 Shady Lane Road, Baraboo, Wisconsin 53913-0447, USA. **Tel.**1 608 356 9462; **fax** 1 608 356 9465.

ARGUS, Dr George William. Taxonomy of *Salix* in the New World, conservation of rare & endangered vascular plants in Canada. Research Scientist Emeritus. *B*.14 April 1929, Brooklyn, NY, USA. American, Canadian. *M*.Mary: 4 *s*. (one deceased), *d*. **Education:** Valparaiso U. (Indiana) 1947; U.of Alaska, BS(Geog.& Biol.) 1952; U.of Wyoming, MS(Bot.) 1957; Harvard U. MA 1961, PhD(Biol.) 1961. **Experience:** res.— n.Sask., Alaska, Rocky Mtns, n.Quebec, Se & Sw US; eight yrs' teaching at U.of Sask.; curation. **Career:** Surveyor, Juneau Icefield Res.Project (Alaska) 1952; Arctic Techniques Instructor, US Army 1953–5; Teaching F.

Harvard U.1957–60; emigrated to Canada 1961; Assoc.Prof. U.of Sask.1961–9; Assoc. Inst.for Northern Studies 1966–9; Assoc.Prof. U.of Oregon 1969–70; Res.Sci. Canadian For. Service (Ott.) 1970–2; Curator, Nat.Herbarium, Canadian Mus.of Nature 1972–95; Canadian Scientific Auth.for Flora, CITES 1974–95; Edl Cttee and Taxon Ed. *Flora of N.Amer.*1985–; Bot.& Canadian Del. Cons.of Arctic Flora and Fauna 1992–4. **Achievements:** basic res.on class.of New World *Salix*, contributing to many floras; ecol.& taxonomic studies in L.Athabasca sand-dune regn; conceived & directed the Canadian Rare and Endangered Plant Project. **Memberships:** IAPT, CBA, ASPT, Calif.Botl Soc., AAAS, AINA, Ott.Field Naturalists' Club, AIBS, New England Botl Club, Sigma Xi. **Awards:** Cons.Award (co-, Fedn of Ont. Naturalists) 1983, Gleason Award (NYBG) 1988, George Lawson Medal (CBA) 1991. **Publications:** incl.*The Genus Salix in Alaska and the Yukon* 1973, *The L.Athabasca Sand Dunes of Northern Sask.and Alb., Canada* (co-Author) 1982, *The Genus Salix* (Salicaceae) *in the Se US* 1986, *Rare Vascular Plants in Canada* (co-Author) 1990; Ed.series on Canadian rare vascular plants, num.scientific papers. Dislikes pers.pub.& news media support. **Language:** English. Further details may be obtained from *Who's Who in Sci.* Willing to act as consult.etc. **Address:** RR3, 310 Haskins Road, Merrickville, Ontario K0G 1N0, Canada. **Tel.**(office) 1 613 990 6441; (home) 1 613 269 4506; **fax** 1 613 990 6451; **e-mail** af150@freenet.carleton.ca .

ARIAS-CHAVEZ, Professor Jesus. Research in ecodevelopment (sustainable development & ecotechnologies) and applied physics, ecology, & biotechnology, re.recovery of refuse and under-utilized resources. Technical Secretary, Found-ation and Commission (twice) President, National & Regional Councillor. *B.*10 April 1944, Mexico City, Mexico. Mexican. *M.*Oso-rio S.Daisy: *d.*Margarita del C., *s.*Jose de J. (both students of agricl engg). **Education:** Superior Sch.of Phys.& Math.1966; teacher's course, UCB 1966; Nat.Poly.Inst., Nat.Autonomous U.& Mexican Petroleum Inst. MSc (Phys.) 1971. **Experience:** teaching, res., diverse academic responsibilities, inventor (1967) & inhabitant (1968–) of first Ecol.& Selfsufficient House (Xochiacalli), Presidential Adv.1974–6; Adv.to several Fed.Secretaries & academic instns in Mexico, to Latin Amer. Energy Orgn 1981–3 and German Appropriate Tech.Exchange 1984; creator of ecodev.prog.of Volcanoes Zone 1972–, training progs with UNICEF & many NGOs & govtl instns, conf.invitee world-wide (55 cities in Germany & The Netherlands), media exp. **Career:** Pres.of — Associated Techl Consults 1969–94, Xochiacalli Ecodev. Fndn 1980–, Comm.for Ecol.Mgmt of Re-sources, Chapingo Agricl U.1991–, Eval. Comm.for Productive Projects of NGOs for Sust.Dev.(after Rio Agenda XXI 1993–; Tech.

Sec. Council for Validation of Projects from NGOs in the State of Mexico & Adv.to Mexico City 1994–; Nat.& Regnl Counc. Secretariat of Envt 1995–. **Endeavours:** to improve eco-techl dev.and thus reach higher qual.of life through interdisc.& interinstitutional progs, using con-ventional & unconventional resources. **Mem-berships:** Bioconservation AC 1974, Appro-priate Tech.Assn 1978, Acad.of Med.Demo-graphy 1978, Pact of Ecologistic Groups 1985, Spaces Workshop 1992, Union of Envlist Groups 1992 — all in Mexico; RICCA 1994, Global Forum 1994. **Awards:** 1st Sr Prize in Ecol.(Dr Ruiz Castenada Assn) 1980, 1st Galardon 'Lacandonian Forest' (Mexican Assn of Journalists 1993), 1st Reward of Social Co-investment (Social Dev.Secretariat) 1993, Gold Medal Conservationist (Mexican NGOs) 1993, Global 500 Roll of Honour (UNEP) 1994, Hon.Pres. Scientific & Techl Comm.(Netzahual-coyotl City, Mexico) 1994. **Publications:** co-Author of several books incl.*Cattle Micro-biol.*1990, *The Dual Microplant to Recover Resources in Liquid & Solid Wastes of the Chapingo R.*1992, *Envl.Prot.Law for the State of Mexico* (co-Author) 1992, *Ecodev.& Qual. of Life* 1993, *Dual Microplant to Recover Resources in Wastes for the Urban Commu-nity of El Capulin* 1994; num.papers. Favours pers. pub.& news media support. **Languages:** English, Portuguese, Spanish; French & Italian (read). Willing to act as consult.etc. **Address:** Apartado Postal Nr 8, Ozumba 56800, State of Mexico, Mexico. **Tel.**(office) 52 5 579 7060 or 546 8827, (home & fax) 52 597 60100; **fax** 52 5 703 0106.

ARIFFIN, Ishak BIN. Natural resource & Nature park planning, strategies for sustainability, urban Nature conservation. Planning Adviser/Con-sultant, Executive Director. *B.*5 Sept.1960, Jitra, Malaysia. Malaysian. *M.*Fauziah M. Kaus. **Education:** U.of Wales, BSc(Hons) 1983, Dipl. in Town Planning 1986. **Experience:** tech.— planning for aborigine resettlement & rural settlements, regnl cons.strats, cons.strat.im-plementation, envl assessments, EIA reviews; admin.— mgmt of NGOs, clubs, & private cos; consult.— Nature reserves & recreational forest plans, strats for sust. **Career:** Asst Dir, Fed. Dept of Town Planning 1986–7; Project Officer & SSO, WWF Malaysia 1987–93; Exec.Dir, Dewan Perniagaan Melayu Malaysia (Malay Chamber of Commerce Malaysia) 1993–, Planning Adv./Consult. Via Natura (Malaysia) Sdn Bhd 1994–. **Achievements:** assisted Ma-laysia state govts in preparing & implementing cons.strats, advised city councils in estab.of Nature reserves, consult.for IUCN, ESCAP & Malaysian Forest Dept. **Memberships:** RTPI, Malaysian Inst.of Planners and Nature & Heritage Socs, ENSEARCH Malaysia. **Award:** Fed.Govt Scholar (under- & post-grad.). **Publications:** *Proposals for a Cons.Strat.for Selangor* (Report, co-Author) 1988, *Proposal for a Cons.Strat.for KL* (Report) 1989, *Bring Back* *the Birds* 1990; several reports & papers. Indiff.to pers.pub., favours news media support. **Languages:** English; French & German (poor spoken); Malay. Willing to act as consult.etc. **Address:** Via Natura (Malaysia) Sdn Bhd, 243M Jalan Tun Sambanthan, 50470 Kuala Lumpur, Malaysia. **Tel.**(office) 603 274 9861, (home) 603 255 5064; **fax** 603 273 4313.

ARMIJOS, Professor Mariano MONTAÑO. Natural resources' management, shrimp industry nutrition & management, coastal water quality, estuarine ecology, research management, technological applications. Professor & Researcher. *B.*18 Nov.1948, Loja, Ecuador. Ecuadorian. *M.*Nancy. **Education:** Escuela Politécnica Nacional, Chem.Engr 1977; ESPOL MBA 1987; Instituto de Acuacultura de Torre de la Sal (Spain) 1989; courses in Shrimp Nutrition Mgmt (Ghent U.) 1989, Coastal Water Mgmt (U.of Campeche) 1992, Estuarine Ecol. (U.of Sw Louisiana) 1992, Coastal Resources Mgmt, and Water Contamination Analysis (URI) 1992. **Experience:** gas chromatography technique applications on researching of fatty acid & nutrition of shrimp, and nitrogen cycle in estuarine envts; Res.Counc. ESPOL; consult.in coastal water qual.for Presidency of Rep.of Ecuador, and in water qual.and envl impacts for Comision de Estudios para el Desarrollo de la Cuenca del Rio Guayas. **Career:** Prof.of Chem. Escuela Politécnica Nacional 1974–7; Chief, Qual.Control & Process in TEXFIBRA (co. in Guayaquil) 1977–80; Prof.& Researcher, ESPOL 1980–. **Achievements:** basic charaterization of Ecuador's coastal water qual.to allow its cons. esp.in connection with shrimp pond aquaculture; lipid profile determination of shrimp larvae; proposal for settling lipid balance in shrimp ponds field in order to avoid overfertilization of water bodies and to conserve envt. **Memberships:** Coll.of Chem.Engrs of Litoral, Coll.of Consulters of Ecuador, Coll.of MBAs of Ecuador. **Awards:** EC Prize 1991, Hons (Coll. of Chem.Engrs) 1993. **Publications:** several incl.Biochem.& nutritional res.of *Penaeus vannamei* shrimp 1991, Lipid profile on plankton related with shrimp nutrition 1991, Perspectives of shrimp culture in Campeche, Mexico, and actual exp.in Ecuador 1992, Study of Ecuadorian coastal water qual.1993. Favours pers. pub.& news media support. **Languages:** English, Spanish. Willing to act as consult.etc. **Address:** Escuela Superior Politécnica del Litoral, Instituto de Ciencias Quimicas, Guayaquil, Ecuador. **Tel.**(office) 59 34 353368, (home) 59 34 237674; **fax** 59 34 354629; **e-mail** mmontanoe@espol.edu.ec .

ARMSTRONG, Geoffrey John. Forest/national-park recreation, voluntary involvement in conservation issues & organizations. Retired. *B.*10 July 1928, Newcastle, NSW, Australia. Australian. *M.*Isabel C.: 2 *s.*, *d.* **Education:** Sydney U. BSc(For.) 1950, AFS Canberra Dip.For.1950. **Experience:** field & forest mgmt,

admin., consult., attended intl sems & confs concerning NPPA. **Career:** Distr. Forester/ Regnl Forester (N.Coast and n.Tablelands hardwood forest areas) 1950–68, Hardwood Mgmt Officer 1968–71, For.Comm. of NSW; Chief Ops Officer 1971–7, Asst Dir (Mgmt) 1977–84, NPWS; dev.& mgmt of Wangat Lodge (own envl centre) 1984–90; consult.on forest rec.1990–4 (still co-owner of Wangat Lodge). **Achievements:** field involvement in planning & mgmt of NSW State Forest; as Asst Dir (Mgmt) in NSW NPWS, direction of planning & mgmt of NSW Nat.Parks; dev., bldg, & mgmt, of own private envl centre in NSW. **Memberships:** IFA IUCN CNPPA. Dislikes pers.pub., indiff.re.news media support. **Language:** English. **Address:** 7 Elanora Drive, Lake Cathie, New South Wales 2445, Australia. **Tel.**(home) 61 65 854412.

ASAVA, Wilfred W. Wildlife conservation. Resource Consultant. *B.*20 April 1940, Maragoli, Kenya. Kenyan. *M.*Mary A. Brother-in-law Dr Perez M.Olindo (African Wildlife Fund). **Education:** C.Missouri SU BSc(Wildlife Cons.) 1968. **Experience:** 23 yrs' working in wildlife cons., consult. **Career:** Warden of Marine Nat. Parks & Reserves 1969–76, Marine Res.Officer founding Marine Res.Station 1977–8, Sr Warden in Wildlife Cons.& Mgmt Dept 1976–88, Asst Dir 1988–91, Kenya Wildlife Service; Consult. in Natural Resources 1991–. **Achievements:** init.cons.areas in Kenya *viz.*Shimba Hills Nat.Reserve, and Marine Nat.Parks at Malindi & Shimoni. **Membership:** EAWS. **Publications:** num.presented papers & reports. Favours pers. pub.& news media support. **Languages:** English, Kiswahili, Luhya. Willing to act as consult. etc. **Address:** POB 439, Maragoli, Vihiga District, Kenya.

ASEM, Dr Samira OMAR. Range ecology, desertification control, wildlife conservation & management. Research Scientist. *B.*19 Dec. 1950, Kuwait City, Kuwait. Kuwaiti. *M.*Aziz A.Zaman: 2 *d.* **Education:** Kuwait U. BSc (Bot.& Chem.) 1972; UCB MSc 1979, PhD (Range Mgmt & Wildland Resource Sci.) 1990. **Experience:** advanced range mgmt res.in Kuwait & Gulf regn, integrated res.on range ecol., envt, soil, & mobile sand. **Career:** Lect. Kuwait U. 1973; Project Leader 1973–88 in & Mgr 1986–8 of Agro-Prod.Dept, Prog.Mgr 1992–, KISR; Res.F. UCB 1990–2; Sust.Dev. Adv. UNDP 1994–. **Achievements:** estab.of Range Mgmt Res.Unit at KISR and dev.of Range Enterprise (20 km^2) for cons.& mgmt of major plant communities, played major role in dev.of Kuwait Nat.Park (411 km^2) and other prot.areas. **Memberships:** Kuwait Envt Prot.Soc.(Bd), Women's Cultural and Social Soc.(Bd), Soc.of Range Mgmt, Once and Future Action Network, TWWAS. **Award:** Best Res.Achievement in Arabian Gulf Regn (Organizing Supreme Cttee, Intl Conf.on Range Mgmt in the Arabian Gulf Countries) 1990. **Publications:** Ed.of Proc.of Intl Confs on Range Mgmt (1st *Range Mgmt in*

Aridlands 1990, *2nd Range Mgmt in Arid Zones* 1995); several others.   Indiff.to pers.pub., favours news media support. **Languages:** Arabic, English. Further details may be obtained from *Who is Who in the West* 1994/5, Calif.Alumni Assn 1992 Membership Directory. Willing to act as consult.&/or ref. **Address:** Aridland Agriculture Department, Kuwait Institute for Scientific Research, POB 24885, Safat 13109, Kuwait. **Tel.**(office) 965 483 4198, (home) 965 257 2492; **fax** (office) 965 481 5194, (home) 965 252 0741.

ASFAW, Gedion. Policy & strategy development, monitoring, & evaluation, project preparation & appraisal. Vice-Minister. *B*.10 April 1948, Addis Ababa, Ethiopia. Ethiopian. **Education:** Fac.of Tech.(Ethiopia) BSc(Civil Eng.) 1973, U.of Stuttgart MSc(Infrastructure Planning) 1985, short courses on envl mgmt. **Experience:** nat.policy dev./cons.strats & envt action plans, admin., planning, negotiations, water resources' dev.master planning etc. **Career:** Dept Head, Rural Dev.Project, and Min.of Planning 1973–93, V.-Minister, Min. of Natural Resources & Envt Prot.1992–. **Achievements:** supervised over 60 rural water-supply systems, dev.of NCS and Disaster Preparedness Strat. **Memberships:** IUCN CESP. **Publications:** Envl prot.&dev.of subregional strat.to combat desert.in IGADD memb.countries 1990, Coordn & harmonization of strat.framework exercises 1991, Water resources & regnl dev.: impact of emerging govt policies 1993. Indiff./consenting re.pers.pub.& news media support. **Languages:** Amharic, English. Willing to act as consult.etc. **Address:** Ministry of Natural Resources Development & Environment Protection, POB 1034, Addis Ababa, Ethiopia. **Tel.**(office) 251 1 513906, (home) 251 1 513850; **fax** 251 1 513042.

ASHTON, Dr P. Mark S. Silviculture, regeneration ecology, forest restoration, agroforestry systems. Assistant Professor. *B*.23 Sept.1959, Sultanate of Brunei. American, British. Father Prof. Peter S.Ashton *qv*. **Education:** Rugby Sch.; U.of Maine BSc 1982, Yale U.Sch.of For.& Envl studies MF 1985, PhD 1990. **Experience:** res.in regeneration physiol.ecol.of complex natural forests, resto.of degraded forests, construction of agrofor.analogues to natural forests, and silviculture of natural forests. **Career:** Forest Mgr 1986–90; Lect.in Silviculture 1991–2, Asst Prof.of Silviculture 1992–, Yale U. **Achievements:** dev. of natural forest mgmt techniques for obtaining initiation, resto.of fernlands to forest. **Memberships:** ESA, BES, SAF. **Awards:** Teaching Excellence (Yale U.) 1994, Initiative (NPS) 1994. **Publications:** *Foresters' Field Guide to the Common Trees and Shrubs of Puerto Rico* (2nd edn) 1989; num.papers incl.A method for the eval.of advanced regeneration of forest types of S and SE Asia 1990, Leaf adaptations of some *Shorea* species to sun and shade (co-Author) 1992, A

comparison of leaf physiol.and anatomy of *Quercus* (section *Erythrobalanus*) species in diff.light envts (co-Author) 1994. Indiff.to pers. pub.& news media support. **Languages:** English, French, Sinhala (spoken). Willing to act as consult.etc. **Address:** School of Forestry & Environmental Studies, 360 Prospect Street, Yale University, New Haven, Connecticut 06511, USA. **Tel.**1 203 432 9835; **fax** 1 203 432 3809.

ASHTON, Professor Dr Peter Shaw. Understanding mechanisms by which plant diversity is maintained in tropical forests, and the impact of harvesting on biodiversity. Charles Bullard Professor of Forestry. *B*.27 June 1934, Boscombe, Hants, England, UK. British, Resident Alien USA. *M*.Helen Mary: *s*.P.Mark S. Ashton *qv*. **Education:** U.of Camb. BA 1956, MA 1961, PhD 1963. **Experience:** 37 yrs' ecol. & systematic res.in Asian trop.forests. **Career:** Forest Bot. Govts of Brunei & Sarawak 1957–67; Fac. U.of Aberdeen 1967–78; Dir Arnold Arboretum 1978–87, Charles Bullard Prof.of For.1987–, Harvard U. **Achievements:** assisted in planning the nat.parks' system now implemented in Sarawak, have advanced understanding of maintenance of biodiverse forest systems; niche specificity of trop.trees. **Memberships:** Amer.AAS, RSE, LS, BES. **Awards:** Envl Merit Award (EPA) 1987. **Publications:** Cons.of Biol.Diversity in Botl Gdns 1988, Species Richness in Plant Communities 1992, *Not by Timber Alone: Econ.& Ecol.for Sustaining Trop.Forests* (co-Author) 1992. Indiff. re.pers.pub.& news media support. **Languages:** English, French, Indonesian (spoken). Willing to act as consult.etc. **Address:** Arnold Arboretum, Harvard University, 22 Divinity Avenue, Cambridge, Massachusetts 01741, USA. **Tel.** (office) 1 617 495 2363, (home) 1 508 371 2669; **fax** 1 617 495 0527.

ASTLEY, Dr David 'Dave'. Genetic resources' conservation particularly horticultural crops & related taxa. Unit Head. *B*.8 Jan.1948, Solihull, England, UK. British. **Education:** Lanchester Poly. BSc(Biol. Geog.) 1971, U.of Birmingham MSc (Genetic Resources Cons.) 1972, PhD(Biosystematics) 1975. **Experience:** Chair, Euro. Cruciferous Crops WG –1991 and Euro.Cooperative Prog.Allium WG; Tech. Sec. UK Plant Genetic Resources Group; Hon. Teaching F. Coventry U.; Tech.Dir Overseas Dev.Prog.Genetic Resources. **Career:** U.of Birmingham Res.F.1975–80, RS F'ship in Leningrad 1977, Sec.EUCARPIA Genetic Resources Section 1978–94 and Head Genetic Resources Unit 1980–, HRI. **Membership:** EUCARPIA. **Language:** English. Willing to act as a consult. **Address:** Genetic Resources Unit, Horticulture Research International, Wellesbourne, Warwickshire CV35 9EF, England, UK. **Tel.** 44 1789 470382; **fax** 44 1789 470552.

ATAUR-RAHIM, Dr Mohammed. Freshwater fishery — biology, culture, pollution, conservation. Chief Scientific Officer. *B*.10 Sept.1936, Nagpur, CP, India. British, Pakistani. *M*.Jalees Fatima Rahim (Prof.of Zool.): *s*.Jahanzeb (keeper & breeder of ornamental fishes). **Education:** Karachi U. BSc 1959; Sindh U. MSc 1962, MEd.1965; Liverpool U. PhD 1975. **Experience:** widespread u.teaching, res., res. mgmt, admin. **Career:** Lect.in Zool. Govt Coll. (Hyderabad) 1962–6; Biol.Teacher, Wellington Sch.(UK) 1967–9; Head, Dept of Biol. Liverpool Inst. and part-time Lect.in Biol. Coll.of Further Educ.1972–7; Asst Prof.of Zool. U.of Riyadh 1977–9; Asst Prof.of Ecol.& Fish Biol. Inst.of Tech.(Brack, Libya) 1980–82; Dir.of Res.(Fish) 1983–8, Dir & Res.Coord. 1988–91, Chief SO (Fish) 1991–, PARC. **Achievements:** Chairman of Fishery Symp. (Saudi Arabia) 1979, PhD & MPhil.Examiner 1983–95 (U.of Karachi), Chairman FERRO mtg of PL-480 projects 1990, nat.rep.for Asian Fisheries Soc.(Pakistan) 1985, Corres.for Asian Agribusiness of England (Pakistan) 1985– and for US Intercoast Network, nominated memb.of Coastal Mgmt in Trop.Asia 1993, Convenor of Fish Cttee to Review Status 1993. **Memberships:** F.RES, ZSP (Life F.), Biol. Soc.of Pakistan (Life), Asian Fisheries Soc., FBA (Life), Salmon Trout Assn (UK, Life), Systematic Assn of Brit.Mus.(Life), IBiol., AIFRB, Inst.of Educ.(UK). **Awards:** cash awards for following books. **Publications:** *Contribn of Muslim Sci.during 13th & 14th Centuries: Hijri Indo–Pak.Subcontinent* 1983, *Agricl Bibl.*1989, and *Food & Nutrition of Muslim Ummah* 1991; Edl Bds *Proc.Parasitol., Sci.& Tech.in the Muslim World, Marine Res.;* Adv.Bd *Hamdard Medicus.* **Languages**: English, Urdu. Willing to act as consult.etc. **Address:** Pakistan Agricultural Research Council, POB 1031, Islamabad, Pakistan. **Tel.**(office) 92 51 820 05312, (home) 92 51 825325; **fax** 92 51 812968.

ATCHIA, Professor Dr Michael. Environmental education & management training. Unit Chief. *B*.14 Nov.1938, Mauritius. Mauritian. *M*.Paula. **Education:** Univs of Calcutta & London, BSc, MSc(Microbiol.) 1964; U.of Salford, MSc(Envl Resources) 1972, PhD(Envl Educ.) 1977. **Experience:** intl consult.1972– & civil servant, teaching, admin. **Career:** Teacher 1960–74; Prof.of Sci.Educ. Mauritius Inst.of Educ.1975–86; Chief, Envl Educ.& Training Unit, UNEP 1986–. **Achievements:** design & prod.of num.curr.courses & books in fields of envl educ.& mgmt training, sci.educ., low-cost equipment, design, family-life educ., & biol. **Membership:** IUBS Comm.for Educ. (Chair 1994–7) 1978–. **Award:** Tree of Learning (IUCN) 1990. **Publications:** 35 books incl. *Matter and Life* (textbook, co-Author) 1977, *Res.in Community-based Biol.Educ.*(IUBS) 1982, *Sea-Fishes of Mauritius & S.W.Indian Ocean* (IUCN/UNEP) 1990, *Envl Mgmt, Issues &*

Solutions (Ed.) 1995. Favours pers.pub.& news media support. **Languages:** English, French. Willing to act as consult.etc. **Address:** United Nations Environment Programme, POB 47074, Nairobi, Kenya. **Tel.**254 2 623462; **fax** 254 2 623917.

ATTENBOROUGH, Sir David Frederick. Nature, broadcasting, writing. *B*.8 May 1926, England, UK. British. *M*.Jane Elizabeth: *s*., *d*. **Education:** Wyggeston Grammar Sch.for Boys; Clare Coll.Camb. **Career:** R.Navy 1947–9; Edl Asst in educl publishing house 1949–52; Trainee Producer 1952 (undertook zool.& ethnographic filming expedns to SL 1954, Brit.Guiana 1955, Indonesia 1956, New Guinea 1957, Paraguay & Argentina 1958, SW Pacific 1959, Madagascar 1960, NT of Australia 1962, Zambesi 1964, Bali 1969, C.New Guinea 1971, Celebes, Borneo, Peru & Colombia 1973, Mali, BC, Iran & Solomon Islands 1974, Nigeria 1975), Controller BBC 2 1965–8, Dir of Progs TV and Memb.Bd of Mgmt 1969–72, Writer & Presenter BBC Series — *Tribal Eye* 1976, *Life on Earth* 1979, *The Living Planet* 1984, *The First Eden* 1987, *The Trials of Life* 1990, *The Private Life of Plants* 1995, all BBC TV Service. **Memberships:** NCC 1973–82; WWF UK (Trustee 1965–9, 1972–82, 1984–); Trustee WWF Intl 1979–86, Brit.Mus.1980, Sci.Mus. 1984–7 and R.Botanic Gdns 1986; Amer.Mus.of Natural Hist.(Corres.1985–). **Awards:** Spec. 1961 & Desmond Davis 1970 Awards (SFTA), Silver Medal (ZSL) 1966, Silver Medal 1966 & Huw Wheldon Mem.Lect.1987 (RTS), Cherry Kearton 1972 & Founder's Gold 1985 Medals (RGS), CBE 1974, Hon.F.(Clare Coll.Camb.) 1980, F.BAFTA 1980, Kalinga Prize (UNESCO) 1981, Washburn Award (Boston Mus.of Sci.) 1983, Hopper Day Medal (Philadelphia Acad.of Natural Scis) 1983, F.RS 1983, Commander of the Golden Ark 1983, Knighted 1985, Intl Emmy Award 1985, *Enc.Britannica* Award 1987, Hon.Freeman (City of Leicester, UK) 1990; num.hon.F'ships & degrees. **Publications:** num.incl.*Zoo Quest to Guiana* 1956, *Zoo Quest to Madagascar* 1961, *The Tribal Eye* 1976, *The Living Planet* 1984, 1985. **Language:** English. Favours pers.pub.& news media support. **Address:** 5 Park Road, Richmond, Surrey, England, UK.

AUGSTBURGER, Franz. Ecofarming, control of organic production. Company Director. *B*.27 Dec.1952, Berne, Switzerland. Swiss. *M*.: *2 s*. **Experience:** farm mgmt, conventional conversion to organic farming, res.in ecofarming in the tropics. **Career:** Dir, Ecotop 1992–. **Languages:** English, German, Portuguese, Quechua, Spanish. **Address:** Ecotop, Casilla 1836, Cochabamba, Bolivia. **Tel.**(office) 591 42 88820, (home) 591 42 88820; **fax** 591 42 88381.

AUSSEDAT, Nicole Marie. Island environments, protection of sites, marine conservation, plans for environmental management of human communities. Freelance Consultant. *B*.20 Oct. 1954, Annecy, France. French. **Education:** Grenoble Sch.of Pol. MA 1978. **Experience:** generalist in envt with detailed knowledge of diff.aspects of island or city envts incl. geol., biol., & prot., of sites (natural & cultural heritage), wastewaters and garbage treatment & disposal, and energy & transportation policy. **Career:** Campaigner, FoE (Paris) 1980–4; Consult.to local admin.and assns & fndns (NGOs) and to govtl orgns 1988–. **Achievements:** cons.of wetlands (salt ponds) in, and marine sanctuary in coastal waters of, St Barthélemy & St Martin, and envl mgmt plans for St Barthélemy & Terre-de-Haut (all French W.Indies). **Memberships:** JNE, IUCN. Indiff. to pers.pub.& news media support. **Languages:** English, French, German (spoken). **Address:** 13 rue Roger, 75014 Paris, France, *or* Gustavia, 97133 St Barthélemy, French West Indies. **Tel.**33 14 538 5978 (France) *or* 590 278149 (French W.Indies); **fax** 33 14 321 6149.

AWAD, Dr Adel R. Wastewater systems & treatment, submarine outfalls, solid waste management, urban hydrology, regional & urban planning, seismic zonation in land-use planning. Visiting Professor. *B*.28 March 1949, Lattakia, Syria. Syrian. *M*.Istiklal: 2 *s., d.* **Education:** Damascus U. BSc(Civil Eng.) 1973, Stuttgart U. PhD(Sanitary Eng.) 1983, PhD(Town Planning) 1983. **Experience:** res.— poll.& control, urban hydr., planning, envt & earthquakes; admin.— Chief, Envt Dept, Tishreen U.; consult.— UNEP (waste), ESCWA (energy), Arab League for Culture & Sci.(envt), Council of Arab Ministers for Housing (urban), Arab Center for Safety Studies (earthquakes); teaching envl engg to under- & post-grad.students. **Career:** military construction co. Damascus 1973–4, teaching/ res./admin. Tishreen U.1983–92, Vis.Prof. Jordan U.of Sci.& Tech.1992–5. **Achievements:** under- & post-grad.teaching & res.for over 10 yrs, contribn to estab.of an Envt Res.Higher Inst.at Tishreen U., determining curriculum of Envt Dept at Tishreen & Jordan Univs, Nominator for Swedish IDEA Award 1990, Stockholm Water Prize 1993 & 1994. **Memberships:** IAWPRC; Fed.Germany Cttee of Sewagewater Tech.and Cttee of Local, Regnl & Nat.Planning; Hypertext System, German Informatic Soc.; IEF. **Award:** Global 500 Roll of Honour (UNEP) 1990. **Publications:** nine books incl.*Select Researches in Envl Sci.*1989, *Fundamentals of Envl Engg* 1989, *Sewagewater Treatment: Housing–Industrial–Rainflow 1991*, *Earthquakes A Tragedy Shaking the World: Effect of Earthquakes on Urban Envt* 1992, *Women and Envt Prot.1995*, *Industrial Water Poll.Mgmt* 1995; *c*.140 scientific papers. Favours news media support. **Languages:** Arabic, English, German. Willing to act as consult.etc. **Address:** Faculty of Civil Engineering, Tishreen University, POB 1385, Lattakia, Syria. **Tel.**(office) 963 4 422201, (home) 963 41 470745; **fax** 963 41 418504 & 471250.

AZIS, Professor Dr Panaparambil Konthalam ABDUL. Ecology, biodiversity of aquatic ecosystems, environmental conservation and action plans. Professor of Ecology, Marine Ecologist. *B*.18 Jan.1947, Thodupuzha, Ker., India. Indian. *M*.P.A.Shyla Aziz: *s., d.* **Education:** U.of Ker. PhD 1978. **Experience:** 21 yrs' u.res.& teaching, admin.of several res.projects, consult.in prep.of envl cons.plans for coastal & inland systems, participated in *c*.200 cruises in diverse biotopes for scientific studies, memb.of several Indian govtl & non-govtl cttees and of exam.bds, and adjudicator of doctl theses from Indian & other Asian univs. **Career:** Res./Postdoctl F.1972–83, Asst Prof./Lect. Agricl U.(Ker.) 1983–7, Reader 1987–93, Prof.of Ecol.1993–, U.of Ker.; Marine Ecol. Saline Water Conversion Corpn R&D Center (Saudi Arabia) 1993–. **Achievements:** scientific data gathered during the past 21 yrs used to give sig.thrust to movement for the cons.of natural aquatic ecosystems in s.India; succeeded in getting the Shasthamcotta Fresh Water Lake and the Ashtamudi Estuary declared as prot.wetlands by Indian Govt and provided scientific support in formulating cons.plans for these systems; current involvement in study of Arabian Gulf with spec.ref.to envl impact of desalination plants. **Memberships:** MBA of India, IAM, SIL, INTECOL, IFSI, INRD (Sec.-cum-Exec.Dir 1978–). **Awards:** Res.Associateship (UGC, Govt of India) 1979, Jawaharlal Nehru Prize (for PhD thesis submitted under his guidance, ICAR) 1994. **Publications:** 58 papers incl.Ecol.of Indian estuaries (I–XIII) 1983–5, Ecol.of the coconut husk retting grounds in Ker.1986, Post-impoundment water qual.of the Kallada R.1989, Primary productivity of the retting zones in the Kodiramkalam estuary 1994; 12 popular scientific articles, five R&D papers, eight tech.reports. Favours reasonable pub.& news media support. **Languages:** English, Malayalam. Willing to act as consult.etc. **Address:** Research and Development Center, Saline Water Conversion Corporation, POB 8284, Al-Jubail 31951, Saudi Arabia. **Tel.**(office) 966 3 361 3713, (home) 966 3 361 0333 ext.33178; **fax** 966 3 361 1615.

BACKER, Professor Dr Inge Lorange. Environmental Law. Professor. *B*.19 March 1946, Oslo, Norway. Norwegian. *P*.Karin M. Bruzelius: *d.* **Education:** U.of Oslo, Cand. jur.1972, Dr Jur.1987; U.of Camb.Dipl.in Legal Studies 1978. **Experience:** res.& teaching in envl law, legal drafting & policy considerations concerning envl legis., admin.exp.at Govt Min.level, bd or cttee memb.of var.Norwegian vol.envl orgns. **Career:** Couns.Min.of Justice 1972–3, 1974–6; Dep.Judge 1973–4; Couns. Min.of Envt 1976–7; Lect., Res.F., Sr Lect., Fac.of Law 1977–84, Prof.1987– & Dir 1989–91 Dept of Public & Intl Law, U.of Oslo; Dep.DG, Min.of Envt (Nature Cons.& Mgmt) 1984–7; Chairman Norwegian Comms on Biotech. 1988–9 & Water Bill 1990–94; Memb. Norwegian Comm.on Disposal of Low & Middle

Radioactive Waste 1990–91; Consult.Nepal (water & energy legis.) 1989–91. **Achievements:** prep.of current Norwegian envl legis.notably Poll.Act 1981 & Gene Tech.Act 1993, estab.of envl law as teaching subject in U.of Oslo. **Membership:** ICEL 1990–. **Publications:** *Standing to Sue & to Appeal in Envl Matters* 1984, *Nature Cons.& Encroachments in Nature: Remedies in Admin. Law* 1986, *Intro.to the Law of Natural Resources and the Envt* 1990 (all in Norwegian). **Languages:** English, French, German (read), Norwegian. Willing to act as consult. **Address:** Department of Public and International Law, University of Oslo, Karl Johans gt.47, N-0162 Oslo, Norway. **Tel.** (office) 47 22 859458, (home) 47 22 149779; **fax** 47 22 859420.

BAEZ, Dr Albert Vinicio. Environmental education. Company President, Chairman Emeritus. *B.*15 Nov.1912, Puebla, Mexico. American. *D:* 3 *d.* **Education:** Drew U. BA(Maths & Phys.) 1933, Syracuse U. MA(Maths) 1935, Stanford U. PhD(Phys.) 1950. **Experience:** co-Inventor (with Paul Kirkpatrick) of X-ray microscope; Inventor of Zone Plate to focus X-rays. **Career:** teaching & res.in phys.at num. univs incl.Harvard & Stanford; Dir Div.of Sci.Teaching, UNESCO 1961–67; Pres. Vivamos Mejor/USA. **Achievements:** Chairman of IUCN Comm.on Educ.1979–83 and ICSU Cttee on Teaching of Sci.1974–76. **Memberships:** F.AAAS; past memb.of APS, AAPT & OSA; IUCN Comm.on Educ.(Chairman 1979–83, Emer.1983–). **Awards:** Hon.Dr of the U.(The Open U.of GB) 1974, Hon.Dr of Humane Letters (Drew U.) 1991, memb.Phi Beta Kappa (Drew U.) 1983, Dennis Gabor Award (SPIE — co-Awardee) 1991. **Publications:** *The Envt and Sci.& Tech.Educ.*(co-Ed.) 1987, *Innovation in Sci.Educ.World-wide* 1976, Teaching Youth about the Envl Impact of Sci. Tech.1991. Favours pers.pub.& news media support. **Languages:** English, French (read), Spanish. Willing to act as consult.etc. **Address:** 58 Greenbrae Boardwalk, Greenbrae, California 94902, USA. **Tel.& fax** 1 415 461 2082.

BAHRI, Ahmed. Population, environment, development. Division Chief. *B.*15 July 1938, Souk Naamane, Algeria. Algerian. *M.*Fatima (children, women, & social issues in Africa): 2 *d.*incl.Tarub (marine biol., ecol., cons.of biodiv.). **Education:** Ecole Nationale de la Statistique et de l'Admin.Economique (Paris), Statisticien–Economiste, Paris 1965; U.of Algiers, Diplôme d'Etude Supérieur (Econ.) 1969. **Experience:** exec.positions with govt (incl.res., mgmt, teaching). **Career:** Tech.Adv.& Dep. Dir, Stats & Census 1965–73, Dir Planning of Higher Educ.& Sci.Res.1973–5, Dir Planning of Human Resources 1975–6, all with Algerian Govt; Chief, Pop.Div.UNECA 1977–. **Achievements:** advocacy of relationship between pop. & envt, attendance at 18th IUCN GA 1990. **Memberships:** IUSSP, ISI, UAPS, SID. **Pu-**

blications: *Monographie de l'Algérie* 1974, *Pop.in African Dev.*(in English & French, co-Ed.) 1974, *Pop.et Sociétés en Afrique* (co-Author) 1988; several papers. Dislikes pers. pub., indiff.to news media support. **Languages:** Arabic, English, French, German (spoken), Italian & Spanish (some comp.). Willing to act as consult.etc. **Address:** United Nations Economic Commission for Africa, POB 3005, Addis Ababa, Ethiopia. **Tel.**(office) 251 1 510177, (home) 251 1 712707; **fax** 251 1 514416.

BAHUGUNA, Sunderlal. Social activism, propaganda for environmental awareness, initiator of Chipko Movement to save Himalayan Forests, opposition to construction of High Tehri Dam in mid-Himalayas. *B.*9 Jan.1927, Marora, Tehri-Garhwal, UP, India. Indian. Father Ambadatt Bahuguna, forester. *M.*Vimala: 2 *s.*Rajeev & Pradeep (all assist with envl activities). **Education:** Punjab U. grad.in Hist., Pol.Sci.& English 1949. **Experience:** worked among the common people to cultivate their envl awareness. **Career:** joined India's freedom movement at age 13 inspired by Mahatma Gandhi's ideas since when have endeavoured to educate & organize the Himalayan people re.envl awareness mostly by walking from village to village (to date have walked *c.*20,000 kms). **Achievements:** success of Chipko movement which established the truth that forests are not for timber but for soil, water, and oxygen; estab.of people's faith in non-violence by launching several non-violent campaigns. **Awards:** Singhvi Nat.Integration Award (Pres.of India) 1985, Jamna Lal Bajaj Award for Constructive Work 1986, Man of the Trees Award 1986, The Rt Livelihood Award (on behalf of Chipko Movement) 1987, Hon.DSc (Roorkee U.) 1989, Sher-I-Kashmir Award 1989, Rathindra Award (for popularizing sci. Vishwa Bharti U.) 1992, Pride of Doon 1995. **Publications:** incl.The crisis of civilization and the message of culture 1987, People's prog.for change 1992, Towards basic change in land use 1988, Toward a sust.soc.1994, Tehri Dam and high dams in Himalaya 1995. Favours pers.pub.& news media support. **Languages:** English, Hindi. **Address:** Ganga Himalaya Kuti, c/o River View Hotel, Tehri Garhwal, PIN 249001, Uttar Pradesh, India.

BAINES, Dr Graham Bruce Keith. Sustainable resource management of tropical land and marine ecosystems with special interest in customary land & marine tenure and indigenous knowledge. Independent Consultant. *B.*25 Dec. 1937, Brisbane, Australia. Fijian. *M.*Evelyn Miriam: *s., d.* **Education:** U.of Qld BAgrSc (Hons) 1961, U.of Saskatchewan MSc(Plant Ecol.) 1964, U.of Nottingham PhD(Envl Phys.) 1968. **Experience:** res.— 12 yrs' in four univs and Atomic Energy of Canada Ltd embracing soil fertility, plant ecol., radiation stress on fish, mangrove ecosystem mgmt, and atoll geomorph.; 18 yrs' residence in Fiji & Solomon

Islands from which emanated var.biodiv.mgmt & Nature cons.roles with Pacific Is.Govts and dev.agencies; consult.— ind.in envl mgmt, cons. of biodiv., working in Pacific Islands' regn & SE Asia for govts, aid donors, & dev.banks. **Career:** Nuffield Res.F. U.of Nottingham 1965–8, Lect.& Sr Lect. U.of the S.Pacific 1970–75, Envl Mgmt Adv.to Govt of Fiji 1976–8, Project Coord. Australian NPWS 1979–80, roles with Govt of Solomon Islands as Envl Mgmt Adv.and Sr Planning Officer 1981–8, Ind. Consult.1989–. **Achievements:** chaired Fiji-based NGO Atom Cttee (against tests on Moruroa), which was effective in developing Pacific Islander awareness of nuclear & other envl issues 1970–75, developed & taught innovative cross-disc.u.course in envl mgmt 1971–5, as Chairman of IUCN Trad.Ecol.Knowledge WG helped focus attention on subject of indigenous knowledge and provide a basis for subs.expansion of interest in this field 1982–90. **Memberships:** IUCN Comm.on Ecol.1979–, IASCP. **Publications:** Trad.resource mgmt in the Melanesian S.Pacific: a dev.dilemma 1989, *Trad.Ecol. Knowledge: Wisdom for Sust.Dev.*(co-Ed.) 1993. **Languages:** English, Melanesian Pidgin (fluent written & spoken). Willing to act as consult.etc. **Address:** 3 Pindari Street, The Gap, Brisbane, Queensland 4061, Australia. **Tel.** (office & home) 61 7 300 3304; **fax** 61 7 300 2693.

BAKER, Dr Frederick William George ('Mike'). Ecology generally with special interests in horticulture, mycology, & ornithology. Scientific Secretary. *B.*24 March 1928, Watlington, England, UK. British. *M.*Jacqueline: *s., d.* **Education:** U.of Manchester BSc 1952; Ecole des Hautes Etudes en Scis Sociales (Paris), Diplôme d'Etudes Avancées 1977, Doctorat 1981. **Experience:** res., admin., consult., editing, writing. **Career:** res.in biochem.of polluted water, sci.writer, admin.& editing Intl Geophys.Yr, ICSU, and CASAFA. **Achievements:** study of poll.of R.Thames 1953–5, Exec.Sec.IBP 1963–5 and ICSU 1965–89, Scientific Sec.CASAFA 1989–. **Memberships:** F.WAAS, F.LS, UIA (formerly memb. Exec. Council), ISWA, Brit.Sci.Writers. **Awards:** Marin Drynov Medal (Bulgarian AS), Medal of Honour (ICA). **Publications:** *Annals of Intl Geophys.Yr* (Gen.Ed.), 100+ articles in scientific journals, CASAFA Report Series (Gen.Ed.). Indiff.to pers.pub., favours news media support. **Languages:** English, French, Italian; German & Spanish (some). Further details may be obtained from *Who's Who in the World*, *Who's Who in Sci.*, *Intl Authors' & Writers' Who's Who*. Willing to act as consult. etc. **Address:** La Combe de Sauve, 26110 Venterol, France. **Tel.**(home) 33 7527 9112; **fax** 33 7527 9657.

BAKER, Professor Dr Joseph 'Joe' Thomas. Marine natural product chemistry, coastal zone management; total river catchment management; ecologically-sustainable development; inter-

disciplinary studies and their application to human needs. Senior Principal Research Scientist. *B.*19 June 1932, Warwick, Qld, Australia. Australian. *M.*Valerie Joy: 2 *s.*, 2 *d.* **Education:** U.of Qld BSc(Hons) 1957, MSc 1959, PhD 1966. **Experience:** widespread in u., govt agency, & industry, and on nat.& intl cttees; directed res.centres in academia, industry, & govt; has advised overseas univs on estab.of marine studies progs; member of intl adv.bds, UNESCO & SCOPE activities. **Career:** Lab. Asst CSIRO Brisbane 1950–55; Dem.& Sr Dem. U.of Qld 1956–60; Lect.in Chem.1961 then Sr Lect.in Chem.1962–9, UC of Townsville; Assoc.Prof.in Chem. James Cook U.of NQ (formerly UC of Townsville) 1970–73; Dir Roche Res.Inst.of Marine Pharm.1974–81; Dir of Res. Roche Australia 1976–81; Dir, Sir George Fisher Centre for Trop.Marine Studies, James Cook U.1981–5; Dir 1985–92, Sr Prin.Res. Sci.1992–, concurrently Sr F. AIMS; Commissioner for the Envt, ACT; Chairman Mgmt Cttee of Community Rainforest Reforestation Prog., Chairman Nat.Landcare Adv.Cttee & Nat.Cttee for Envt (Acad.of Scis). **Achievements:** fndn memb.of 3-persons GBRMPA 1975–88, Chairman Australian Heritage Comm.1984–5, Member Australian Spec.Prog.Cttee for World Heritage Conv.1981–4 (Chairman 1984), Chairman Australian Nat.Comm.for the Envt 1987–, Memb.& Pres. The Australian Mus.Trust 1975–84, Memb.Australian Marine Scis Assn 1964– (Pres.1982–4), Chairman Scientific Cttee & VP WWF(Australia) 1977–84; memb.many govtl & intergovtl WGs on envl issues. **Memberships:** above and F.RACI. **Awards:** F.ATSE 1989, OBE 1992, Leighton Medal 1993, Hon.Vis.F. ANU, Hon. Prof.James Cook U. **Publications:** *Compounds from Marine Organisms* (Vols I & II) 1976, 1981; num.papers in scientific journals and presented at major nat.& intl confs; Ed.Bds *Marine Chem., Asian Marine Biol.J., Advances in Marine Biotech.* Accepts pers.pub.in context of work being undertaken. **Languages:** English; French, German, & Italian (all read, written). Willing to act as consult.etc. **Address:** Australian Institute of Marine Science, PMB 3, Townsville MC, Queensland 4810, Australia. **Tel.** (office) 61 77 789241 or 61 6 207 2629, (home) 61 6 288 2816; **fax** 61 77 789285 or 61 6 207 2630.

BALČIAUSKAS, Dr Linas. Biodiversity, ecological diversity; ecology of hoofed, semi-aquatic, & small, mammals. Laboratory Head. *B.*30 Apr.1957, Birzai, Lithuania. Lithuanian. *M.* Laima (biol.). **Education:** Vilnius U. MS (Biol.) 1979; Moscow Inst.of Evol.Animal Morphology & Ethology, PhD(Biol.) 1988. **Experience:** res.in mammalogy & biodiv. **Career:** Researcher 1979–81, Jr Res.Assoc. 1981–9, Sr Res.Assoc. Lab.of Theriology 1988–93, Head of Lab.of Ecosystems' Biodiv.1993–, Inst.of Ecol. **Achievements:** leading the project Ecol. Diversity of Lithuania. **Memberships:** Lithuanian Theriological & Ornith.Socs, Edl Bd *Acta*

Ornithologica Lituanica. **Publications:** 40+. Indiff.to pers.pub.& news media support. **Languages:** English, Lithuanian, Polish, Russian. Willing to act as consult.etc. **Address:** Institute of Ecology, POB 2147, Vilnius 2017, Lithuania. **Tel.**370 2 359278; **fax** 370 2 359257.

BALDUS, Dr Rolf D. Wildlife conservation & management in eastern & southern Africa; hunting as a form of land-use; community involvement in sustainable wildlife use. Project Coordinator. *B.*2 Feb.1949, Gebhardshain, Germany. German. **Education:** Philipps U. Dipl. Volkswirt (Econ.) 1972, PhD 1975. **Experience:** mgmt of a major German tech.coopn project, Selous Game Reserve (Tanzania) incl. rehab.of Reserve and intro.of community wildlife mgmt in buffer zones; consults on wildlife projects in dev.coopn; hunting econ. **Career:** Govt Adv.1975–77, Consult.1977–82, Private Sec.to German Minister for Dev.Coopn 1982–86, Wildlife Adv. EEC Brussels 1986, Team Leader Selous GTZ 1987–93, Project Coord. German Min.for Econ.Coopn & Dev. 1994–. **Achievements:** assisting in rehab. of Selous; contribn towards developing community wildlife mgmt & its practical implementation. **Memberships:** IUCN CNPPA & Antelope SG. **Publications:** series of 18 'Selous Cons. Prog. Discussion Papers'; Wildlife — a forgotten resource 1987, The economics of safari hunting 1990, *Selous Game Reserve* (travel guide) 1989. Indiff.to pers.pub., favours news media support. **Languages:** English, German. Willing to act as a consult. **Address:** Lieberg 28, D57580 Gebhardshain, Germany. **Tel.**(home) 49 2747 1268 or 49 6428 4309.

BALICK, Dr Michael Jeffrey. Ethnobotany, economic botany, palm taxonomy, plant domestication. Director, Philecology Curator of Economic Botany. *B.*21 July 1952, Philadelphia, PA, USA. American. *M.*Daphne Allon: *s., d.* **Education:** U.of Delaware BSc(Hons) Agric. & Plant Sci.1975; Tel Aviv U. Jr Yr Abroad Prog. in Biol.& Humanities 1972–3; Harvard U. AM(Biol.)1976, PhD (Biol.)1980; Harvard Grad. Sch.of Business (three semesters of course-work), Harvard Intro.to Business Prog.for PhDs 1980, Harvard Sch.of Public Health (course-work). **Experience:** res.& fieldwork undertaken during 35 projects 1972–92; prin.investigator of some 20 intl projects; teaching at under- and post-grad.levels 1975–. **Career:** Intern, Winterthur Gdns (DE) 1970 and Henry Fndn for Bot.Res.(PA) 1974; Res.F.Trop. Hort. & Econ.Bot., Las Cruces Trop.Botl Gdn 1975; Curatorial Asst, Econ.Herbarium of Oakes Ames, Botl Mus.of Harvard U.1977; Res. Asst, Agribusiness Assocs Inc.(MA) 1979 and Botl Mus.of Harvard U.1979–80; Res.Assoc.in Plant Domestication, Botl Mus.of Harvard U.1980–86; Exec.Asst to Pres.1980–89, Asst Curator, Herbarium (1980–88) then Assoc. Curator (1988–90), NY Botl Gdn; Adjunct

Prof.CUNY 1982; Asst Dir 1984–8, Acting Dir 1988–90 Inst.of Econ. Bot.; Hon.Res.Assoc.La Salle Fndn (Caracas) 1990–. Adjunct Prof.Sch. of Forestry & Envl Studies, Yale U.1992– (Lect.in Trop.Studies 1983–92); Philecology Curator of Econ.Bot. 1989–; Dir, Inst.of Econ. Bot.1990–. **Memberships:** AABGA, AAM, ASP, ASPT, BSA, BSB, Gdn Writers' Assn of Amer., IAPT, F.LS, NEBC, Palm.Soc., Sigma XI, SEB, Soc.for Ethnobiology, SCB, Soc.for Ecol.Econ., Torrey Botl Club. **Awards:** Outstanding Young Horticulturist of 1970 (PA Hortl Soc.), Student Travel Award (AABGA) 1975, George H.M.Lawrence Mem.1979, Charles A.Lindbergh Fndn Grant 1980, F'ship (Metropolitan Life Ins.Co.) 1989–92, Oberly Award for Bibliographic Excellence (Agric.& Related Scis), ALA 1991. **Publications:** 12 books inc.*Useful Palms of the World* (co-Author) 1990, *The Subsidy from Nature, Palm Forests, Peasantry & Dev.on an Amazon Frontier* (co-Author) 1991, *Rainforest Remedies: 100 Healing Herbs of Belize* (co-Author) 1993, *Plants, People, and Culture* (co-Author) 1996, *Medicinal Resources of the Trop.Forest* (co-Ed.) 1996; 57 scientific papers, 25 hortl & gen. papers. **Language:** English. **Address:** The New York Botanical Garden, Bronx, New York 10458, USA. **Tel.**(office) 1 718 817 8763; **fax** 1 718 220 1029.

BÁNDI, Professor Dr Gyula. Environmental law & administration. Professor of Law. *B.*14 July 1955, Budapest, Hungary. Hungarian. *M.* Klara: *s., d.* **Education:** U. Eötvös Loránd, Law Degree 1973–8; Hungarian AS PhD(Envl Law) 1990. **Experience:** 15 yrs in envl law res.& educ.incl.ten yrs' mgmt practice in HLA (1980–92) partic.in envl law drafting processes, orgn & mgmt of postgrad.progs in envl mgmt & law, recently giving legal expert opinion in field of envl law. **Career:** Res.F.Dept of Law, Agricl U.(1978–82); Sec.1983–90 then Sec.Gen. 1991–92, HLA; Asst Prof.of Law 1990–91 then Prof.Fac.of Law 1991–, Eötvös Loránd U.; Pres.EMLA 1992–; Scientific Dir.Danube Envl Law Prog.of COPERNICUS. **Achievements:** extended res.in envl law & mgmt; consult.in envl law drafting processes, participating in then initiating & managing envl postgrad.progs; founder of envl law post-grad.course, Eötvös Loránd U., and of EMLA. **Memberships:** HLA (Sec.1983–90, Sec.Gen.1990–92), Hungarian AS (Comm.of Admin.Scis 1990–, Presidential Envl Scis Comm.1990–), ICEL 1991–, IUCN CEL 1991–. **Publications:** *Limited Growth?* (1987), *Envl Handbook* (in press), both in Hungarian; Right to envt 1990, Envl impact assessment — today & tomorrow 1989 (in Hungarian), Dev.of envl law in Hungary 1991, Envl enforcement in Hungary — today & tomorrow 1992, The right to envt in theory & practice — the Hungarian experience 1993. Favours pers.pub.& news media support. **Languages:** English, French (poor), Hungarian. Willing to act as consult.etc. **Address:** Faculty of Law,

Eötvös Loránd University, Egyetem ter 1–3n H-1053 Budapest, Hungary. **Tel.**(office) 36 1 266 4156; **fax** 36 1 4156 or 4091.

BANGURA, Kalie Ibrahim. Wildlife management & protection, antipoaching–protected areas. Game Superintendent. *B*.28 Jan.1952, Makoth, Kambia Distr., Sierra Leone. Sierra Leonean. Father Mr Kalie P.Bangura, farmer. *M*.Mabinty: 3 *s*., 2 *d*. **Education:** high sch.& in-service training; Coll.of African Wildlife Mgmt, Cert.1976 & Dipl.1983 in Wildlife Mgmt. **Experience:** ten yrs' fieldwork in antipoaching & prot.area mgmt, eight yrs' admin., prep.of mgmt progs and assignment of manpower for fieldwork in var.prot.areas in SL, has assisted num.researchers & consults. **Career:** Game Ranger-in-Training 1973–6, Game Ranger Grade III 1976–86, Asst Game Super.1986–95, Game Super.1994–, Wildlife Cons.Branch, For. Div. Govt of SL. **Achievements:** assisted in process to acquire land from local community for estab.of Outamba–Kilimi Nat.Park, now declared and constituted as SL's First Nat.Park. **Membership:** IUCN SSC. **Publications:** co-Author of *Zoonooz* on topic of Cornerstone for Cons.1981, num.articles in newsletters and local newspapers. Favours pers.pub. **Language:** English. Willing to act as consult.etc. **Address:** Wildlife Conservation Branch, Forestry Division, Tower Hill, Freetown, Sierra Leone. **Tel.**232 22 225352 or 223445.

BARAHONA-ISRAEL, Professor Dr Rodrigo. Environmental & natural-resource policy & law. Professor of Law, Centre President. *B*.28 Oct. 1945, San José, Costa Rica. Costa Rican. *M*.Mara (Attorney in Natural Resource Law): *s*.Rodrigo Gabriel, 2 *d*.Mariagauri, Ximena (all active in cons.clubs & projects). **Education:** U.of Costa Rica, Master's degree 1970; U. of Florence, Dr in Law 1993. **Experience:** res.; consult.to Earth Council, IDB, & IIAC; Presidential Adv. **Career:** Prof.of Law, U.of Costa Rica 1973–; Dir of Water and Irrigation Inst. 1980–82 and of C.Bank of Costa Rica 1984–6; Adv.to Pres.of Costa Rica 1982–6; V.Minister of Foreign Trade 1986–8; Pres. Envl and Natural Resources Law Centre 1989–. **Achievements:** writer of legal bills on envt & cons.for the Costa Rican Cong., author. **Memberships:** IUCN Envl Law Centre, Istituto Internazionale di Diritto Agrario. **Award:** Pres.of Natural Resources Law Assn (Costa Rica). **Publications:** Legal aspects of natural resource prot.in the agrarian reform laws of Latin Amer.(in Spanish) 1977, *Agrarian and Natural Resources Law* (textbook, in Spanish) 1980, The INbio (Instituto Nacional de Biodiversidad) contracts for biodiv.prospection (in Spanish, Legal Scis J.) 1993, A legal framework for the institutionalization of ecol.knowledge in land use planning in Costa Rica 1994. Favours pers.pub. & news media support. **Languages:** English, Italian, Spanish. Willing to act as consult.etc. **Address:** POB

1754-1000, San José, Costa Rica. **Tel.**(office) 506 223 8463, (home) 506 225 3357; **fax** 506 233 8256.

BARBARA, Dr Derek John. Plant virology, molecular plant pathology, mycology. Research Leader. *B*.31 July 1948, Somerset, England, UK. British. **Education:** U.of Birmingham BSc(Biol.Scis) 1969, PhD(Biol.Scis (Plant Virology)) 1972. **Experience:** full-time res. 1972–, edl. **Career:** Postdoctl F.Dept of Virology, U.of Birmingham 1972–6; Res.Sci.HRI 1976–; sabb.at Purdue U.1985–6. **Achievements:** wide-ranging res.in plant virology & molecular plant path.partic.concerning temperate fruit-crops. **Memberships:** AAB (Edl Bd), BSPP, BMS, SGM. **Publications:** many contribns to scientific lit., Edl Bd *Annals of Applied Biol.* Indiff.to pers.pub.& news media support. **Language:** English. Willing to act as consult. etc. **Address:** Plant Pathology and Weed Science Department, Horticulture Research International–East Malling, West Malling, Kent ME19 6BJ, England, UK. **Tel.**44 1732 843833; **fax** 44 1732 849067.

BARBIER, Dr Edward B. Economics of environment & development, environmental & natural resource economics. Senior Lecturer. *B*.22 July 1957, Washington, DC, USA. American. *M*.Joanne Catherine (envl economics): *d*. **Education:** Yale U. BA 1979, LSE MSc 1980, U.of London PhD 1986. **Experience:** econ.researcher, admin., teaching. **Career:** Lect.in Econ. Poly.of C.London, Poly.of the S.Bank, & Webster U.1980–86; Economist, IIED 1986–8; Assoc.Dir 1988–90, Dir 1990–93 LEEC/IIED; Sr Lect. Dept of Envl Econ.& Envl Mgmt, U.of York 1993–. **Achievements:** adv.& consult.for num.bilateral & multilateral aid agencies on econ.of envt & dev., author of many pubns in the field. **Memberships:** RSA, EAERE. **Publications:** seven books incl.*Econ., Natural Resource Scarcity, and Dev.*1989, *Econ.& Ecol.: The New Frontier* (Ed.) 1993; num.papers. Indiff.to pers.pub.& news media support; Assoc.Ed. *Envt and Dev.Econ.*1996–. **Languages:** English, French, Indonesian (some), Spanish (basic). Willing to act as consult.etc. **Address:** Department of Environmental Economics & Environmental Management, University of York, York, England, UK. **Tel.**44 1904 432 999; **fax** 44 1904 432 998.

BARCSAY, Dr László. Landscape protection, masterplanning for protected areas, tourism, & conservation, environmental impacts on Nature. Independent Environmental Expert. *B*.27 June 1930, Berettyóujfalu, Hungary. Hungarian. *D*. **Education:** U.of For. Forest Engr 1953, Dr Univ.1985; Tech.U. Civil Engg Coll. Civil Engr 1962. **Experience:** engg, Nature cons., consult. **Career:** Factory Engr in wood–chem.plant 1954–6; Structural Engr & Arch.in planning offices 1957–74; Conservationist, Head of first

Dept of Landscape Prot. Nat.Auth.of Nature Cons.1975–87; Counc. Min.for Envl & Regnl Policy 1988–91; Ind.Envl Expert 1991–. **Achievements:** orgn of Hungarian Nat.Parks' infrastructure 1975–81, creation & intro.of masterplanning system 1979, creation & estab.of survey and recording system 1985. **Endeavour:** solution of conflicts of envt with modern soc. **Publications:** *Nature Cons.Map of Hungary* 1991, Nature Cons.*(Enc.Hungarica)* 1992, and four vols on Hungarian prot.areas. Indiff.to pers.pub.& news media support. **Languages:** English (poor), French (poor), Hungarian. Willing to act as consult.etc. **Address:** Bürök u. 18.I.1, H-1124 Budapest, Hungary. Tel. (home) 36 1 155 48 86.

BARISHPOL, Dr Ivan F. Conservation of Nature, forestry. Society President. *B.*30 Dec. 1932, Kharkov Regn, Ukraine. Ukrainian. *M.* Nonna P.: *d.* **Education:** For.Dept, Kharkov Agricl Inst.1950–55; Crimea Corres.Agricl Inst. (Vine Prod.Dept) 1955–8; Kalmyk Agricl Inst. PhD(For.) 1963. **Experience:** res.& practical implementation & admin.in fields of for.& cons.of Nature. **Career:** Tech.Supervisor in For. Altay Regn (Siberia) 1955–8; Dir of For. Kalmykia 1959–66; Dep.Minister, Min.of For. (Tajikistan) 1967–78; VP 1978–90, Pres.1991–, All Russian Soc.for Cons.of Nature. **Achievements:** some advanced methods of walnut *(Juglans)* silviculture in new envts have been developed & introduced, with new approaches to manage Nature cons.movement under new social conditions. **Memberships:** Ecol.Council, Russian Min.for Cons.of Nature, Natural Resources Parliamentary Cttee of CIS (Envl Adv.). **Awards:** Order of Red Banner of Labour, Order of Friendship, Hon.Dipl.(Bulgarian Soc.for Cons.of Nature). **Publications:** over 60 books & papers incl.*For.in the Steppe Zone* 1975, *Walnut in Tajikistan* 1976, *Cons.of Nature in Russia* 1988. Indiff.to pers.pub., favours news media support. **Languages:** English (fair), Ukrainian. Willing to act as a consult. **Address:** All-Russian Society for Conservation of Nature, Bogoyavlensky Proezd 3, 103012 Moscow, Russia. **Tel.**7 095 921 78I2; **fax** 7 095 925 2864.

BARNES, Dr David John. Calcification & growth in scleractian corals, environmental records stored in coral skeletons. Senior Principal Research Scientist. *B.*18 Aug.1944, Lincoln, England, UK. Australian, British. *W.: s., d.* **Education:** U.of Manchester, BSc (Zool.) (1st Class) 1966; U.of Newcastle upon Tyne, PhD 1971. **Experience:** res.& field-work on coral reefs in Australia, Jamaica, Puerto Rico, Micronesia, Israel, & Japan; supervision of hons MSc & PhD students; admin. **Career:** Postdoctl F. NATO 1971–2; Queen's F.in Marine Sci.1973–5, Dep.Prin. John Flynn Coll.1974–9, James Cook U.; Res.Sci.1975, Sr Res.Sci.1977, Prin.Res.Sci.1982, Sr Prin.Res. Sci.1993–, AIMS; Vis.Prof.of Marine Biotech. U.of Tokyo

1991. **Achievements:** basic res.on coral calcification & growth, dev.of the $pH-O_2$ technique for measuring coral-reef productivity & calcification, res.into envl records stored in coral skeletons. **Memberships:** ACRS, ISRS. **Award:** Edl Bd *Coral Reefs.* **Publications:** *Perspectives on Coral Reefs* (Ed.) 1983; *c.*60 papers. Indiff.to pers.pub.& news media support. **Language:** English. Willing to act as consult.etc. **Address:** Australian Institute of Marine Science, PMB 3 MC, Townsville, Queensland 4810, Australia. **Tel.**(office) 61 77 534236, (home) 61 77 788147; **fax** 61 77 725852.

BARNEY, Dr Gerald O. Sustainable development, strategic planning, environment, future. Executive Director. *B.*1937, OR, USA. American. Father Richard D.& mother Gladys Hubbard both interested in cons.& envt. *M.*Carol Ann (cons., envl educ.): 2 *s.*William S. (atmos.chem.), Stephen E.(social ecol.); *d.*Kristen R.(envt, women, health). **Education:** U.of Wisconsin PhD(Fusion Phys.) 1967, Sloan Sch.of Mgmt Harvard/MIT Postdoctl res.1970. **Career:** CEQ 1971–2; Comm.on Critical Choices for Americans 1972–3; Chairman, Nat.Prog. Rockefeller Bros Fund 1973–7; Pres.Barney & Assocs 1977–84. Exec.Dir, Millennium Inst. 1983–. **Achievements,** promoted long-term integrated global thinking & analysis in over 40 countries; brought intl attention to critical issues of 21st century (such as envt) for over 20 yrs. **Memberships:** Balaton Group, Ecol.Econ., Congressional Clearinghouse/Futures, SID (Adv.Group). **Publications:** *Global 2000 Report to the Pres.*1980, *Managing a Nation: A Microcomputer Software Catalog* 1990, *Studies for the 21st Century* 1991, *Global 2000 Revisited: What Shall We Do?* 1993. Favours pers.pub.& news media support. **Languages:** English, German. Willing to act as consult.etc. **Address:** Millennium Institute, 1611 North Kent Street Suite 204, Arlington, Virginia 22209-2135, USA. **Tel.**1 703 841 0048; **fax** 1 703 841 0050; **e-mail** millennium@igc.apc.org .

BARRY, Dr James Michael. Mammalian ecology (Red Fox ecology, Otter conservation, Badger–bovine TB), non-vocal mammalian communication, diseases of the integument, hormonal influences on mood. Private Consultant. *B.*11 May 1925, Cork, Ireland. British, Irish. **Education:** Cork U. BSc 1953, PhD 1959, MB.BCh. & BAO 1963, Licence of Fac.of Occupational Medicine, R.Coll.of Physicians, and of Apothecaries' Hall, both Dublin. **Experience:** wildlife ecol.& communication, hormone-related skin diseases in human species. **Achievements:** Badger–bovine TB, Otter cons., Red Fox studies. **Memberships:** ZSL, Mammal Soc., RIAM. **Publications:** several pamphlets on badger, otter, and fox, ecol. Favours pers.pub.& news media support. **Languages:** English, Irish. Willing to act as consult. **Address:** 12 Sidney Place, Wellington Road, Cork, Ireland. **Tel.**(office) 353 21 502949, (home) 353 21 541498; **fax** 353 21 50012.

BASS, Stephen Michael John. Forest policy/environmental policy development especially in tropical regions. Director. *B*.6 May 1958, Reading, Berkshire, England, UK. British. *M. Christine Anne: 2 d.* **Education:** Oriel Coll. Oxf.U. BA(Hons) (Agricl & Forest Scis) 1979, Manchester U. BLD 1981; St Cross Coll. Oxf.U. MSc(Forestry) 1982. **Experience:** consult.— sr adv.to NCSs in Zambia & Nepal; num.other adv.posts re.nat.envl & forest policy dev. **Career:** Forestry and Landscape Arch.Consult. UK 1982–4; Consult.in Zambia, Nepal, Pakistan, & Carib., for IUCN 1984–7; Projects Mgr, s.Africa, IUCN 1987–9; Rockefeller Fndn F.NY 1989–90; Assoc.Dir (Forestry and Land Use) 1990–94, Dir 1994–, IIED. **Achievements:** assisting dev.of NCS and NEC Zambia; setting up major social forestry progs in N.Pakistan; formulating guidelines on preparing nat.cons.and sust.dev.strats. **Memberships:** IBiol., IUCN CESP. **Awards:** Triennial Coopers Hill Medal (Oxf.U.) 1982; Warren Weaver F'ship (Rockefeller Fndn) 1989–90. **Publications:** *Defending the Future: A Guide to Sust. Dev.*(co-Author) 1991, *Strats for Nat.Sust.Dev.: A Handbook for Their Planning & Implementation* (co-Author) 1994; Ed.of three NCS vols, several chapters, num.articles, instnl bulletins & unpublished reports & papers. **Languages:** English, French (read). Willing to act as consult.etc. **Address:** 6 Town Farm, Cheddington, Leighton Buzzard, Bedfordshire LU7 0RG, England UK. **Tel.**(office) 44 1071 388 2117; **fax** 44 1071 388 2826.

BASSOW, Dr Whitman. Industrial environmental management, environmental communications & policy, technical assistance & training. Company President, Contributing Editor. *B*.7 Jan.1921, New York City, NY, USA. American. *M.* Elizabeth: *d.* **Education:** City Coll.of NY, BS 1941; Columbia U. MA (Pol.Sci.) 1948; U.of Paris, Doct.in Hist.(highest hons). **Experience:** consult.on intl envt communications & mgmt 1990–. **Career:** taught Pol.Sci. (adjunct) at Hunter Coll.1946–48 and Brooklyn Coll.1969–70; Journalist in NY, Paris, & Moscow, for UPI, *Newsweek* 1954–66. **Achievements:** helped organize UN Conf.on Human Envt, Stockholm 1972 as Sr Public Affairs Officer; Founder/Pres. World Envt Center 1974–89; estab. first envl tech.assistance prog. based on industry volunteers; OPCA estab. Whitman Bassow Award for best envl reporting 1992. **Memberships:** CFR, OPCA. **Awards:** Fulbright F., Edward R.Murrow Press F., OPCA award for best book on foreign affairs 1988. **Publications:** num.articles in *Envl Prot.* Indiff. to pers.pub. **Languages:** English, French (spoken), Russian (spoken). Willing to act as consult.etc. **Address:** Whitman Bassow & Associates Inc.(Consultants), 655 Third Avenue, New York, New York 10017, USA. **Tel.**(office) 1 212 867 6365, (home) 1 212 876 0265; **fax** 1 212 697 6354.

BATANOUNY, Professor Dr Kamal H. Arid lands ecology, desert development, desertification, human life in deserts; salinity problems in arid regions, ethnobotany, conservation and ethics. Professor of Ecology, Head of Department, Centre Director. *B*.30 Jan.1936, Menoufiya, Egypt. Egyptian. *M*.Suzan M.: 2 *s*. **Education:** Cairo U. BSc(Hons) 1956, MSc 1960, PhD 1963, DSc 1985. **Experience:** res.in arid lands of the Middle East 1956–; teaching at Cairo, Baghdad, King Abdul Aziz, and Qatar, Univs. **Career:** Prof.of Ecol.at diff.univs in the Arab world; Dir, Centre for Envl Res.& Studies, Cairo U. **Achievements:** UNEP consult.for desert., and assessment of impact of war activities on terr.ecosystems in Kuwait, Iran, & Saudi Arabia; init.of cons.in Arab countries. **Memberships:** Pres. Int.Orgn for Human Ecol.and Egyptian Botl Soc., INTECOL, Chairman of many cttees in Egypt. **Awards:** State Prize for Envl Scis, and First Rank Decoration for Sci.and Arts, both in Egypt; Kuwait Fndn for the Advancement of Scis; Global 500 Roll of Honour (UNEP) 1989. **Publications:** 130+ incl.six books on ecol., envt of arid lands, Islam and the envt, bibliogs in natural hist., drugs and folk medicine in the Arab world, ecophysiological studies on desert plants and halophytes, adaptation of plants under dry & saline conditions in the Middle East. Favours pers.pub. & news media support. **Languages:** Arabic, English, French (read), German (written). Willing to act as consult.etc. **Address:** Faculty of Science, Cairo University, Giza, Egypt. **Tel.**(office) 20 2 571 5885, (home) 20 2 361 5883; **fax** 20 2 628884.

BATE, Professor Dr Guy Calder. Coastal ecophysiology — dunes, beaches & estuaries; environmental management. Professor & Head of Department. *B*.5 Mar.1933, Beaufort W., SA. S.African. *M*.Kerry Louise: *s.*, 2 *d.* **Education:** U.of Natal BSc(Agric.) 1958, Queen's U.(Ont.) PhD(Biol.)1966. **Experience:** 36 yrs in agric. (educ.& res., commercial), ecophysiol.of trop. savannas and temperate coastal envts. **Career:** Lect.in Agric. Gwebi Agricl Coll.(Zimbabwe) 1959–62; Sr Lect.in Agric.& Plant Physiol. U.of Zimbabwe 1971–6; Assoc.Prof. Dept of Bot. U.of the Witwatersrand 1976–80; Prof.& Head of Dept of Bot. Inst.for Coastal Res. U.of Port Elizabeth 1981–. **Achievements:** description & quantification of S.African surf/zone diatoms, freshwater requirements of S.African estuaries, Intl Coord./Org. Dunes' 94 (intl mtg on sci. & mgmt of coastal dunes). **Memberships:** SAAEES (Professional), IDA, RSSA, SAAB, PASA, IAIA. **Publications:** *c*.90 in intl journals. Indiff.to pers.pub.& news media support. **Language:** English. Willing to act as consult.etc. **Address:** Department of Botany, Institute for Coastal Research, University of Port Elizabeth, PB 1600, Port Elizabeth 6000, South Africa. **Tel.**(office) 27 41 504 2396, (home) 27 41 551614; **fax** 27 41 532317.

BATISSE, Dr Michel. Environment & development, Biosphere Reserves, MAB Programme, biodiversity, world heritage, future studies. President, Environmental Adviser. *B.*3 April 1923, Châteauroux, France. French. *M.*Claude (active in French envl NGO): 2 *d.* **Education:** Diplôme Ingénieur, Ecole Centrale (Paris) 1946; Docteur ès Scis (Physics), Sorbonne 1951. **Experience:** dev. of intgovtl res.progs; dev.& implementation of Biosphere Reserve concept; over 30 years' work in intl coopn on envt and natural resources. **Career:** Coord. Arid Lands Major Project 1957–62, Dir Natural Resources Res. Div.1961–72, Dir Dept of Envl Scis 1973–5, Dep.Asst DG for Sci.1976–83, Asst DG (Sci.) 1983–4, Pres. Medit.Blue Plan, and Envl Adv. 1984–, UNESCO; Envl Adv.UNEP. **Achievements:** org.Intl Hydrological Decade (1965– 74), Biosphere Conf.(1968) & MAB; promoter, Intl Network of Biosphere Reserves and World Heritage Conv. **Memberships:** Cons. Intl (WA, Bd), Office Intl de l'Eau (Paris, Scientific Bd), WAAS. **Awards:** French Legion of Honour (1989), John Phillips Medal for Intl Cons.(IUCN 1988), Global 500 Roll of Honour (UNEP) 1988. **Publications:** *Futures for the Medit.Basin: the Blue Plan* (Ed.) 1989, Envl problems and the scientist 1973, The relevance of MAB 1980, Developing and focussing the Biosphere Reserve concept 1986, The struggle to save our world heritage 1992. Indiff.to pers.pub., favours news media support. **Languages:** English, French. **Address:** 7 Rue de la Cavalerie, 75015 Paris, France. **Tel.**(office) 33 14 568 4051, (home) 33 14 734 1215; **fax** 33 14 065 9897.

BAYÓN GRUCZMACHER, Ricardo, *see* **GRUCZMACHER, Ricardo** BAYÓN.

BAZZAZ, Professor Dr Fakhri. Recovery & regeneration of ecosystems, biology of global change. H.H.Timken Professor of Science. *B.*16 June 1933, Baghdad, Iraq. American. *M.* Maarib: *s., d.* **Education:** U.of Baghdad, BS 1953; U.of Illinois, MS 1960, PhD 1963. **Experience:** res., admin., teaching. **Career:** Lect. (earlier Dem.) U. of Baghdad 1964–6; Asst Prof.1966–72, Assoc.Prof.1972–7, Prof.of Plant Biol.and of Forestry 1977–84, U.of Illinois; Prof.of Biol. 1984–8, H.H.Timken Prof. of Sci.1988–, Harvard U. **Memberships:** EDF (Sci.Adv. Panel 1990–), ESA/NSF Liaison Cttee 1990–91, Mus.of Natural Hist.& Envl Defense Fund Cttee 1991–3, Amer.AAS 1991–2, SCOPE 1993. **Awards:** F.Clare Hall Camb.(Life Memb.) 1981, Hon.AM (Harvard U.) 1984, Amer.AAS F'ship 1987, John Simon Guggenheim F'ship 1988, AAAS F'ship 1989. **Publications:** *The Ecol.of Plants in Successional Envts, Community Dynamics, Response of* *Plants to Varying Carbon Dioxide Levels* 1988, *Plants & Atmos.Carbon Dioxide* 1988, *Oldfield Ecosystems, Plant Strats* 1989, *Plant Exploitation of Envl Heterogeneity* 1990, *Species Responses to Disturbances in Nature* 1990; num.symp., conf., sem.& j.papers, and book reviews; Edl Bds of *Oecologia, Tree Physiol., Plants Today, Physiol.Ecol.Series, J.of Vegetation Sci., J.of the Fac.of Sci.*(UAE U.). **Language:** English. **Address:** Department of Organismic and Evolutionary Biology, Harvard University, The Biological Laboratories, 16 Divinity Avenue, Cambridge, Massachusetts 02138, USA. **Tel.**(office) 1 617 495 0916, (home) 1 617 862 1460; **fax** 1 617 496 5223.

BEARD, Dr John Stanley. Vegetation mapping, biogeography, ecological botany. Retired. *B.* 15 Feb.1916, Gerrards Cross, Bucks., England, UK. Australian, British. *M.*Pamela Evelyn: 3 *d.* **Education:** Marlborough Coll.; Pembroke Coll. Oxf. MA 1937, BSc 1941, DPhil.1945. **Experience:** num.pubns on veg.of trop.Amer. 1940– 53, silvicultural res.in SA 1947–61, botanic gdns admin.in Australia 1961–73, extensive fieldwork and veg.mapping in Western Australia 1964–81. **Career:** Asst Conservator of Forests, Trinidad 1937–46 (seconded as Adv.on For.in Windward & Leeward Islands 1943–7); Estates Res.Officer, Natal Tanning Extract Co.1947–61, Dir, King's Park & Botanic Gdn (Perth) 1961–70; Dir, R.Botanic Gdns (Sydney) 1970–73; Veg.Survey of Western Australia, in collab.with U.of Western Australia 1973–81. **Achievements:** veg.mapping of Western Australia, 2 1/2 m.km^2, at var.scales; class.of veg.types of trop.Amer.; taxonomy of genus *Protea.* **Memberships:** BSN (Pres. 1956–61), BES, ESA, IAVS, RSWA (Pres. 1983). **Award:** Medal (RSWA) 1983. **Publications:** incl. *Natural Veg.of Trinidad* 1946, *Natural Veg.of the Windward & Leeward Islands* 1949, *Descriptive Catalogue of W.Australian Plants* 1965, *Veg.Survey of Western Australia 1:1,000,000 Series* (seven vols with maps) and *1:250,000 Series* (21 vols with maps) 1974–81, *The Plant Life of Western Australia* 1990, *The Proteas of Trop.Africa* 1993. Favours pers. pub. & news media support. **Languages:** Afrikaans (read), Dutch (read), English, French (spoken), German (spoken), Italian (read), Portuguese (read), Spanish (spoken). Willing to act as consult.etc. **Address:** 6 Fraser Road, Applecross 6153, Western Australia, Australia. **Tel.**(home) 61 9 364 6644; **fax** 61 9 364 9972.

BEETON, Professor Robert James Sinclair. Protected area management, environmental problem-solving; training; environmental policy especially in context of managing fragmented landscapes. Associate Professor. *B.*19 Aug. 1946, Narrabri, Australia. Australian. *M.*Roslyn M.: 2 *s., d.* **Education:** U.of New England B(Rural Sci.) (Hons) 1970, M(Natural Resources) 1977. **Experience:** 22 yrs in prot.area mgmt. **Career:** Res.Ecol. bird pests in NW

Western Australia 1970–74; F.Zool.Dept, U.of New England, ecol.wildlife mgmt, animal behaviour 1975–8; dev.of prot.areas' training progs at all levels, 27 short courses for Australian agencies, consult.to industry, cons.agencies, and IUCN 1978–; Vis.Prof. Lincoln Coll.NZ 1980; Colorado SU, U.of Wisconsin–Green Bay, U.of Indiana Bloomington, Intl Sem.on Prot.Area Mgmt at U.of Michigan, 1985; Plenary speaker, George Wright Soc.1986; IUCN GA 1988–90; Convenor & Chair, Training Workshops at 4th World Cong.on NPPA, invited speaker at num.Australian confs 1992. **Achievements:** dev.of comp.prot.area mgmt prog. U.of Qld; current work on world prot.area mgmt training network & strat.; 26 short courses for prot.area mgrs 1982–. **Memberships:** George Wright Soc., RAIPR, EIA. **Publications:** The relationship between res.& mgmt in cons.agencies 1985, Tourism in prot.areas 1990; num.others. Favours pers.pub. & news media support. **Language:** English. Willing to act as consult.etc. **Address:** Department of Management Studies, University of Queensland, Gatton 4343, Queensland, Australia. **Tel.**(office) 61 74 601322, (home) 61 76 303407; **fax** 61 74 601324.

BEHRA, Olivier. Ecology of crocodiles, reptiles & amphibians; sustainable conservation & development in third-world countries, wildlife management. Director. *B*.6 Nov.1963, Casablanca, Morocco. French. *M*.Gillian: *s*. **Education:** Ecole Pratique des Hautes Etudes (Montpellier), Dipl.1995. **Experience:** wildlife in captivity (Paris Zoo) 1984–6; survey of crocodile pop.in Cameroon, Congo, Gabon, C.African Rep., French Guyana; consult.on wildlife mgmt & cons.for USAID, FAO, CITES, UNDP, GTZ, Swiss Govt etc.; direction of multidisc.team on cons.& sust.dev.; socio-econ., econ., & envl biol. **Career:** Researcher, Lab.of Reptiles & Amphibians Mus.(Paris) 1986–9; Head of UN Project in Madagascar 1989–91; Dir, BIODEV 1991–. **Achievements:** demn of sust.crocodile cons.prog.viability through local people implication, study & promotion of sust.use of wildlife for cons.concept. **Memberships:** IUCN SSC Crocodile (Dep. VC for Africa), Malagasy Reptiles & Amphibians, and Sust.Use of Wildspecies, SGs. **Publications:** *c*.20 incl.Status and distribn of crocodiles in Africa 1995. Favours pers.pub. & news media support. **Languages:** English, French, German (basic). Willing to act as consult.etc. **Address:** BIODEV, Lot VX 18, Andrefandrova, Antananarivo, Madagascar. **Tel.**(office) 261 2 34685, (home) & **fax** 261 2 28651.

BEL **KACEM, Slaheddine,** *see* **KACEM, Slaheddine** BEL.

BELANDRIA DE **REDAUD, Dr Maria Gladys,** *see* **REDAUD, Dr Maria Gladys** BELANDRIA DE.

BELL, Professor Dr (John) Nigel (Berridge). Research into effects of air pollution on plants & insects, pathways of radionuclides in the environment, and business & the environment. Professor of Environmental Pollution, Director, Section Head. *B*.26 April 1943, Derby, England, UK. British *D*.: 3 *s*. **Education:** U. of Manchester BSc(Bot.) 1964, PhD(Plant Ecol.) 1969; U.of Waterloo MSc(Biol.) 1965. **Experience:** occasional Specialist Adv.to House of Commons' Select Cttee on envl matters, Adv.on air poll.issues to UK DoE, extensive consult.exp.in UK & abroad. **Career:** Res.Asst, Bedford Coll.London 1968–70 & ICL 1970–72; Lect.1972–83, Sr Lect.1983–7, Reader in Envl Poll.1987–9, Prof.of Envl Poll.1989–, Dir Centre for Envl Tech.and Head Agricl & Envl Mgmt Section, Dept of Biol.1986–, ICL. **Achievements:** pioneering res.on low levels of sulphur dioxide on vegetation, first demn of evol.of tolerance by plants to SO_2, first identification in UK of ozone as a phytotoxic air pollutant. **Memberships:** BES, F.RSA, IUR. **Publications:** Depression of yield in ryegrass exposed to sulphur dioxide (co-Author) 1973, Air poll. increases *Aphis fabae* pest potential (co-Author) 1984, The role of ozone in global change (co-Author) 1991. Favours pers.pub.& news media support. **Languages:** English, French (limited), German (limited). **Address:** Imperial College Centre for Environmental Technology, 48 Prince's Gardens, London SW7 2PE, England, UK. **Tel.**(office) 44 171 589 5111 ext.7202, (home) 44 1734 580 653; **fax** 44 171 581 0245.

BELLAMY, Professor Dr David James. Botany, writing, broadcasting — evolution of ecosystems especially in wetlands and coral reefs, marine pollution, human–environment interaction, conservation, sustainable development, ecotourism, business–environment, arid lands in western Australia. Foundation Director, Trustee. *B*.18 Jan.1933, London, England, UK. British. *M*.Rosemary: 2 *s*., 3 *d*. **Education:** U.of London Chelsea Coll.of Sci.& Tech. BSc 1958 and Bedford Coll. PhD 1960. **Experience:** res., lecturing, presenter & scriptwriter for TV & radio progs, admin., has worked in all continents & climates and most major countries of the world. **Career:** Lect.then Sr Lect. Dept of Bot. U.of Durham 1960–80; Hon.Prof.of Adult & Continuing Educ. U.of Durham 1980–; Pres. WATCH 1982– & Living Landscape Trust 1985–; Spec.Prof. Nottingham U.1987; Founder Dir, Cons.Fndn (London), and Trustee, WWF 1985–. **Publications:** num.incl.*Peatlands* 1974, *The Gt Seasons* 1981, *The Vanishing Bogs of Ireland* (co-Author) 1986, *England's Last Wilderness* 1989; TV progs incl.*Longest Running Show on Earth* 1985, series incl.*Life in our Sea* 1970, *Bellamy on Bot.*1973, *Botanic Man* 1979, *Backyard Safari* 1981, *Bellamy's New World* 1983, *You Can't See the Wood* 1984, *Bellamy's Bugle* 1986. **Memberships:** LS, IBiol., YHA 1983–. **Awards:** F.LS, F.IBiol., Order of the Golden Ark 1988, Global 500 Roll of Honour (UNEP) 1990, OBE 1994.   Favours pers.pub.& news media support.   **Language:** English.   Further details may be obtained from Brit. *Who's Who* 1996.   **Address:** The Conservation Foundation, 1 Kensington Gore, London SW7 2AR, England, UK.   **Tel.**44 171 823 8842; **fax** 44 171 823 8791.

BENNETT, Dr Elizabeth Lesley.   Wildlife conservation field research in Southeast Asia, especially the Malaysian states of Sarawak & Sabah;   training local graduates & government staff.   Conservation Scientist.   *B*.6 April 1956, London, England, UK.   British.   **Education:** Nottingham U.   BSc(Hons)(Zool.) 1977, U.of Camb. PhD(Primate Ecol.) 1984.   **Experience:** 12 yrs' field res.in Malaysia, ten yrs as Tech Adv.to Sarawak Forest Dept on wildlife & parks matters, supervision of postgrad.students, Malaysia Coord.for WCS (then NYZS).   **Career:** SO WWF Malaysia and Res.F. WCS (NYZS) 1984–8;   Assoc.Res.Zool.1989–92, Cons.Sci.& Coord.for Malaysia 1993–, WCS (NYZS).   **Achievements:**   cons.res.on ecol.of banded langurs, first ecol.study of proboscis monkeys, surveys & prot.plans for Sarawak's coastal & inland forests, studies of effects of human disturbance (shifting cultivation, logging, hunting) on wildlife, and relevant mgmt recommendations.   **Memberships:** IPS, IUCN SSC Primate SG, PSGB.   **Publications:** *Envl Correlates of Ranging Behaviour in the Banded Lungur* (Presbytis melalophos) 1986, Social orgn & ecol.of Proboscis Monkeys in mixed coastal forest in Sarawak (co-Author) 1988, The value of a mangrove area in Sarawak (co-Author) 1993, *Proboscis Monkeys of Borneo* (co-Author) 1993.   Dislikes pers.pub.& news media support.   **Languages:** Bahasa Malaysia (good spoken), English, French (weak).   Willing to act as consult.etc.   **Address:** 7 Jalan Ridgeway, 93200 Kuching, Sarawak, Malaysia.

BENNETT, Dr Sara Louise.   Environmental aspects of international agriculture, water resources, transportation/navigation & sectoral/ regional planning projects;   preparation & management of project environmental components, field studies, impact assessments & EIA training;   wetland & biodiversity resource assessments & management strategies.   Environment Specialist.   *B*.14 April 1956, Lakewood, OH, USA.   American.   *M*.Herbert D.Wiebe: *d*.   **Education:** Colorado SU BSc (Chem.) 1977, MIT/WHOI Jt Prog.in Phys. Oceanogr. PhD 1988.   **Experience:** Envl Specialist based in Bangladesh 1989–94 involved in Bangladeshi projects incl.regnl water mgmt plan as part of Flood Action Plan;   missions & ind.res.in Vietnam, Nepal, & Indonesia;   phys. oceanographic field res.on N.Atlantic & S. Indian w.boundary currents, analysis of satellite ocean data.   **Career:** engg/scientific computing emphasizing climatology/solar energy engg & op.systems 1977–82, Grad.Res.Asst in Oceanogr.1982–88, Staff Specialist 1989–96, Envt

Specialist, Water Envt Intl 1996–, Northwest Hydraulic Consults.   **Achievements:** documented wetland resources of Sylhet Basin in NE regn of Bangladesh (*c*.one-fifth of the country);   findings incl.*i.a.*nine wetlands of intl sig.as defined by the Ramsar Conv., half-a-million migratory waterfowl,   & a nr of threatened habitats & species;   pioneer in EIA & EIA training in Bangladesh.   **Memberships:** AMS, ASEP (Life), BCAS, IUCN SSC SG Sust.Use of Wild Species.   **Award:** Carroll L.Wilson Award (MIT) 1988.   **Publications:** Relationship between vertical, diapycnal, and isopycnal velocity and mixing in the ocean gen.circulation 1986, Eastward flow through the mid-Atlantic Ridge at 11°N and its influence on the abyss of the e.basin 1991, *Bangladesh Wetland Resources Study* 1992, Potential initiatives for mgmt of wetland resources of Bangladesh 1993, Some uses of aquatic plants in NE Bangladesh 1993.   Favours pers.pub.& news media support.   **Languages:** Bengali (some spoken), English, French (read).   Willing to act as consult.etc.   **Address:** Water Environment International, Northwest Hydraulic Consultants, 4823 99th Street, Edmonton, Alberta T6E 4Y1, Canada.   **Tel.**(office) 1 403 431 0173 or 436 5868; **fax** 1 403 436 1645;   **e-mail** sbennett@tic.ab.ca; **URL:** http://www.tic.ab.ca/~sbennett .

BENSON, John Stuart.   Terrestrial plant ecology, vegetation survey & mapping, research on threatened plant species, environmental policy. Senior Plant Ecologist.   *B*.28 July 1954, Sydney, Australia.   Australian.   **Education:** Macquarie U. BSc 1976;   U.of Sydney, MSc(Prelim.) 1988. **Experience:**   public admin.of wildlife laws in NSW, surveys of native veg.(definition of plant communities), survey & res.of threatened Australian plant species, representation on nat.cttees on threatened plant species, translocation, & old growth forest prot., reserve estab., u.teaching. **Career:** Bot. Nat.Herbarium 1977–9, Sr Plant Ecol.1991–, R.Botanic Gdns (Sydney);   Resources Officer, NSW NPWS 1979–91. **Achievements:** estab.of many cons.reserves in NSW and res.on reserve design, ecol.surveys & standardizing methodologies, prot.of rare or threatened plants in Australia esp.NSW.   **Memberships:** IUCN SSC, Ecol.Soc.of Australia, ACF, NPA of NSW, Inst.of Wildlife Res.(U. of Sydney), Wilderness Soc.of USA.   **Publications:** *c*.40 incl.Australia's Threatened Plants 1990, The effects of 200 yrs of Euro.settlement on the veg.& flora of NSW 1991;   40 reports. Favours pers.pub.& news media support. **Languages:** English, French (basic).   Willing to act as consult.etc.   **Address:** Royal Botanic Gardens, Mrs Macquaries Road, Sydney, New South Wales 2000, Australia.   **Tel.**(office) 61 2 231 8149, (home) 61 2 810 4869;   **fax** 61 2 251 7231;   **e-mail** johnb@rbgsyd.gov.au .

BENTHEM, Roelof Jan.   Environmental planning.   Retired Chief of Landscape Planning.   *B*.2 Aug.1911, Hoogeveen, The Netherlands.   Dutch.

Education: originally trained in land-surveying problems and in later yrs involved in Nature cons., self-made career in envl planning. **Experience:** creating new, and reconstruction of existing old, landscapes in agricl areas; extensive travel & lecturing for envl purposes. **Career:** Landscape Consult.in s.part of The Netherlands 1943–46; memb.of staff & Bd of Dirs, The Netherlands State Forest Service 1946–76. **Achievements:** involved in many land consolidation schemes *e.g.* the rehab.of the war-damaged Is.of Walcheren, the Delta-project, & the Polders of the Zuiderzee 1943–76; in postwar period, launched & advocated idea of 'creative cons.' *i.e.* improvement of our natural surroundings as well as prot.of our valuable natural areas. **Memberships:** CCC (former Bd Memb.), NSLA (past-Pres.), IUCN CESP (then Comm.on Envl Planning, init.& past-Chairman). **Awards:** Euro.Prize, Nature Cons.& Landscape Dev.(Strasbourg) 1969; Officer, Order Oranje-Nassau (The Netherlands) 1970; first Keynote speaker, Euro.Cons.Yr Strasbourg 1970; Tamsaare Medal (IUCN E.Europe) 1988; IUCN Comm.on (then) Envl Planning (Hon.Memb.). **Publications:** *Spectrum-atlas van de Nederlandse Landschappen* (co-Ed.& -Author) 1979, *Veldgids Ecol.Landschappen* 1984; *c.*100 pubns & several papers for IUCN tech.mtgs on some of which was Rapp.-gen. Dislikes pers.pub., indiff. to news media support. **Languages:** Dutch, English, German. **Address:** Hoge Duin en Daalse Weg 13, 2061 AD Bloemendaal, The Netherlands. **Tel.**31 23 272458.

BERETEH, Mohamed A. Wildlife & forestry conservation & management. Game Superintendent & Divisional Head. *B.*2 Oct.1952, Kailahun, SL. Sierra Leonean. *M.*Babie: 2 *s., d.* **Education:** U.of Liberia, BSc(For.) 1983, res. studies in for.and MSc(Regnl Planning) 1984; U.of Michigan, Prot.Area Mgmt course 1986. **Experience:** cons.of wildlife & for., cons.& prot.area mgmt planning, cons.educ.& extension services, UN Vol.Specialist, consult.to UN WFP and Res.& Dev.Consults of SL. **Career:** Game Super.& Head of Wildlife Cons.Div.SL 1973–; Park Dir, Outamba–Kilimi Nat.Park (WWF Project) 1984; For.Res.& Mgmt Plan, Liberia 1985; Species Prot.& Site Mgmt Plans, Ghana 1987. **Achievements:** estab.of prot.area network, nat.park, and game reserves in SL, founder memb.of NGOs for envl awareness, produced videos & training manuals for UNDP and FAO Wildlife Project in Uganda. **Memberships:** EAWS, Cons.Soc.of SL, IUCN & UNDP/UN Vols. **Awards:** US NPS (Hon.), Cert.of Service (UNDP). **Publications:** *The SL Wildlife Legis., Excerpt of the African Wildlife Laws* 1976, *The People's Role in Wetland Mgmt* 1979, *Wildlife Cons.Strat.for the Uganda Nat.Parks & Game Dept* 1982, *Prot.Area Interpretation Manual* 1983, *The Sust.Econ.in Liberia: For.an Uncertain Potential* 1984. Favours pers.pub. & news media support. **Languages:** English, French & Kiswahili (some), Krio, Mende. Will-

ing to act as consult.etc. **Address:** World Food Programme, United Nations Development Programme, POB 1011, Freetown, Sierra Leone. **Tel.**(office) 232 22 2395, (home) 232 22 8220, **fax** 232 22 7094.

BERKES, Professor Dr Fikret. Common property resources. Professor & Director. *B.*17 Oct.1945, Istanbul, Turkey. Canadian, Turkish. **Education:** McGill U. BSc 1968, PhD 1973. **Experience:** worked on ecol.of Gulf of St Lawrence, human ecol.in James Bay; developed case-studies on the 'tragedy of the commons'; applied findings in num.intl settings. **Career:** Asst Prof.1974–6, Assoc.Prof. Prof./Dir of Envl Studies 1978–91, Brock U.; Adjunct Asst Prof.& Consult. Montreal 1977–8; Prof.& Dir, Natural Resources Inst. U.of Manitoba 1991–. **Achievements:** developed empirical & theoretical approaches to solution of the 'tragedy of the commons'; analysed interface between natural & social systems; helped implement co-mgmt in cons.–dev.projects. **Memberships:** ISSCP (Founding Bd memb.), INTECOL, AINA, ISEE, MAB Canada, var.IUCN Comms & WGs. **Awards:** NRC Canada Scholar, F. IHE. **Publications:** *Common Property Resources* 1989, *Ecol.and Envl Scis* (co-Author, in Turkish) 1990; *c.*58 chapters & j.papers; *c.*20 articles & professional reports. **Languages:** English, Turkish. Willing to act as consult.etc. **Address:** Natural Resources Institute, Winnipeg, Manitoba R3T 2N2, Canada. **Tel.**(office) 1 204 474 8375, (home) 1 204 489 7291; **fax** 1 204 261 0038.

BERRY, Professor Dr Robert James ('Sam'). Ecological & conservation genetics, environmental ethics. Professor of Genetics. *B.*26 Oct. 1934, Preston, Lancs., England, UK. British. *M.* Dr Caroline: *s.*Andrew (evol.genetics), 2 *d.* **Education:** U.of Camb. MA 1959; U.of London, PhD 1959, DSc 1974. **Experience:** mouse-catching in many parts of the world, participation in intl search for global ethic for sust.living. Chair of Envl Issues, Network of Council of Churches of Britain & Ireland; Trustee of Nat.Museums & Galleries on Merseyside 1985–94. **Career:** Lect., Reader, Prof. R.Free Hosp.Sch.of Medicine 1972–8; Prof.of Genetics, Dept of Biol. UCL 1978–. **Achievements:** demn of selection acting variably in natural pops of animals, stochastic changes in gene frequency through founder effect, reports on biol.recording, code of envl practice, etc. **Memberships:** NERC 1981–7, F.LS (Pres.1982–5), BES (Pres.1987–9), EEF (Pres.1990–92), MSBI (Pres.1995–2000). **Awards:** F.IBiol. 1974, F.RSE 1981. **Publications:** incl.Cons.Aspects of the Genetical Constn of Pops 1971, Conserving Genetic Variety 1974, *Inheritance & Natural Hist.*1977, *Natural Hist.of Shetland* 1980, *Evol.in the Galápagos* (Ed.) 1984, *Natural Hist.of Orkney* 1985. Indiff.to pers.pub.& news media support. **Language:** English. Further details may be obtained from Brit.*Who's Who* 1984–, *People of Today* 1992–, *Who's Who in Theology & Sci.* 1992. Willing to act as consult.etc. **Address:** Department of Biology, University College London, Gower Street, London WC1E 6BT, England, UK. **Tel.**(office) 44 171 380 7170, (home) 44 173 245190; **fax** 44 171 380 7096.

BERTRAM, Dr (George) Colin (Lawder). Seals, fisheries, Sirenia, and population problems. Retired, Life Fellow of St John's College Cambridge. *B.*27 April 1911, Worcester, England, UK. British. *M.*Cicely Kate (African fisheries, sirenia): *s.*Dr Brian Bertram (Formerly Curator of Mammals at London Zoo and Dir.of Wildfowl and Wetlands Trust). **Education:** Berkhamsted Sch., St John's Coll. Camb. MA 1937, PhD 1939. **Experience:** seal res.in Antarctica 1934–7 and res.on sirenia 1962– serving for several yrs on IUCN SSC Sirenia SG, Palestine fisheries & Middle E.1940–45. **Career:** zool. expedns to Bear Is.& E.Greenland 1932/3; coral reef res.in Red Sea 1933–4; British Graham Land Expedn to Antarctica 1934–7 incl.seal res.; Chief Fisheries Officer, Palestine 1940–44; Fisheries Consult. Middle E.Supply Centre 1944–5; Dir Scott Polar Res.Inst.1949–56; u.& coll.admin.1945–72. **Memberships:** F.RGS, FFPS, ZSL, IBiol., (Italian Inst. **Awards:** Polar Medal, Bruce Mem.Medal (SGS), Carter Medal (Galton Inst.). **Publications:** *Weddell & Crabeater Seals* 1940, Pop.trends & world's resources 1946, *Antarctica, Camb., Cons.& Pop.* 1987. **Language:** English. **Address:** Ricardo's, Graffham, Petworth, Sussex GU28 0PU, England, UK. **Tel.**(home) 44 17986 205.

BEZANSON, Dr Keith A. Environmental education & administration. President. *B.*12 May 1941, Kingston, Ont., Canada. Canadian. *M.* Monique. **Education:** Carleton U. BA 1964, Stanford U. PhD 1972. **Experience:** res., admin., consult., teaching. **Career:** Regnl Dir E.Africa Prog.1977–8, DG Multilateral Progs 1978–81, VP Americas Branch 1981–5, CIDA; Canadian Amb.to Peru & Bolivia 1985–8; Admin.Mgr Inter-Amer.Dev.Bank 1988–91; Pres.IDRC 1991–. **Publications:** *Maternal Health and Child Survival Issues: Lessons Learned* 1991, The collapsing vision of global dev.1992, Whither dev.? some perspectives and challenges 1992. **Award:** Medal of Bravery (Canada) 1981. **Languages:** English, French, Spanish. **Address:** International Development Research Centre, POB 8500, Ottawa, Ontario K1G 3H9, Canada. **Tel.**1 613 236 6163 ext. 2378; **fax** 1 613 235 6391.

BEZAURY-CREEL, Juan E. Protected areas management, integrated conservation & development projects. Executive Director. *B.*12 Jan.1954, Mexico City, Mexico. Mexican. *M.* Patricia: *d.* **Education:** Nat.U. B(Arch.) 1978. **Experience:** promotion for estab.of prot.areas in Mexico, strengthening of cons.NGOs, fund-

raising for cons.projects. **Career:** Arch.& Landscape Arch.1976–82; Chief, Office of Bldgs for Nat.Parks 1982–3; Chief Ops Dept of Nat. Parks 1983–5, Sub-Dir (Planning) Nat. Systems of Prot.Areas 1986–7, Exec.Dir Amigos de Sian Ka'an AC Biosphere Reserve. **Achievements:** orgn of Mexican system of prot.areas, instnl dev.of Biocenosis AC & Amigos de Sian Ka'an AC. **Membership:** Biocenosis AC (Bd). **Award:** Tinker F'ship. **Publications:** *Isla Contoy Reserve — Mgmt Plan* 1993, *Mgmt of the Coral Reefs, Sian Ka'an Biosphere Reserve* 1993, transl.IUCN's *Managing Prot.Areas in the Tropics* into Spanish. Indiff.to pers.pub., favours news media support. **Languages:** English, Spanish. Willing to act as a consult.&/or judge proposals. **Address:** Amigos de Sian Ka'an AC, Apartado Postal #818 Cancun, Quintana Roo 77500, Mexico. **Tel.**(office) 52 98 849583, (home) 52 98 873385; **fax** 52 98 873080.

BHARGAVA, Professor Dr Devendra Swaroop. Environmental engineering, water pollution control technology & strategies, advanced water & wastewater treatment, remote sensing of water quality surveys, Modelling & Indexes, river classification & zoning, dissolved oxygen sag analysis, adsorption, sedimentation, filtration, aerobic digestion, use-oriented impact assess-ment, research teacher index evaluation, consultancy & design. Professor (Environmental). *B.*14 March 1938, Alwar, Raj., India. Indian. *D.:* 2 *d.* **Education:** Rajasthan U. BE(Civil Eng.) 1959, U.of Roorkee Postgrad.Dipl.1960 & ME 1966 (both in Public Health Engg), IIT PhD(Envl Eng.) 1977. **Experience:** res.— envt related subjects to above-given interests; admin.— water poll.& mgmt at CBPCWP, coordn of projects & processing consent cases of var.types of industries in Delhi; consult.— design of water treatment plants, wastewater design systems, water poll. control-related problems etc.and design exp.in Tech.Consult. Bur.of NIDC; teaching BE to PhD levels 1960–. lecturing. **Career:** Lect. Birla Coll.of Engg (now BITS), Mugneeram Bangur Mem.Engg Coll.& Motilal Nehru Regnl Engg Coll.1960–67; Reader, Regnl Engg Coll. (Kurukshetra) 1971; Design Engr (Public Health) NIDC 1971; USSR Govt Scholarship, Moscow Engg & Construction Inst.1971–3; teaching & PhD work, IIT 1973–7; Envl Engr CBPCWP 1977–9; Reader (Poll.Control) 1979–85 & Prof. (Envl) 1985–, Roorkee U., Vis.Prof.(Envl) AIT 1986 & 1988. **Achievements:** single-handedly placed Roorkee U.on world's envl academic map and at top in Indian envl scenario in just one decade despite many fin., academic, & admin., constraints; scientifically-proved extraordinarily high self-purification & non-putrefaction of Ganga (Ganges) water; evolved rational models (replacing age-old Streeter-Phelps models) for biochem.oxygen-demand assimilation & dissolved oxygen sag by incorporating sediment-ation effects (questions related to his res.on

Ganga–Yamuna Rivers being asked by Indian Parliament); evolved rationally-integrated water qual.index for judging suitability of drinking water supplies and for classifying rivers, rational & scientific 'Teacher Index' for judging suitability of res.-level teaching fac.and new concepts in design of sedimentation tanks, filter components, low alt. remote-sensing of rivers etc.; pubns. **Memberships:** F.—ASCE, IE (India), IPHE (India), IWWA, & IS (India); IAWPC. **Awards:** 18 Gold Medals, Prizes, etc. (all non-pol.) mostly during last eight yrs. **Publications:** c.275 scientific res.papers in last ten yrs, sole author of about one-third. Favours pers.pub.& news media support if true scientific reporting is made. **Languages:** English, Hindi, Russian (poor spoken). Willing to act as consult.etc. **Address:** Department of Civil Engineering, University of Roorkee, Roorkee 247 667, Uttar Pradesh, India. **Tel.**(office) 91 1 332 72349 ext. 5429, (home) 91 1 332 72349 ext.943 (PP Room 17); **fax** 91 1 332 73560.

BHATT, HE Professor Dr Dibya Deo. Natural history, ethnobotany, mass communication & world affairs particularly regarding interaction between environment & development. Adviser. *B.*6 July 1930, Baitadi, W.Nepal. Nepali. *M.* Chandra Kala: 2 *s.*, 2 *d.* **Education:** Agra U. MSc(Bot.) 1951, Oregon SU PhD(Plant Path.) 1962, UCB post-doctl study in Dept of Bot.1962. **Experience:** res., admin., lecturing, diplomatic, good interaction with media, participation in num.intl confs & sems. **Career:** Asst Prof.& Prof. Dept of Bot. Tri-Chandra Coll.1951–65; UNESCO Consult. CASTASIA 1967; Sr Expert in Biol. U.of Lagos 1968–9; Prof.& Head of Dept of Bot.1972–7, Vis.Prof. Centre for Econ.Dev.& Admin.1980–81, Tribhuvan U. (Kirtipur) 1972–7; Acting Sec.1977–9, Sec. Cabinet Secretariat 1982–95, PM's Office; Sec. Min.of Communications 1979–80; Memb.Sec. Nat.Planning Comm.1981–2; R.Nepalese Amb. to Myanmar (concurrently accredited to Socialist Rep.of Vietnam and Laos PDR) 1985–90; currently Adv. Ecol.Soc. Dept of Bot. Tribhuvan U.& NHSN, Life Memb.& Adv. UN Assn of Nepal & Ex-Servicemen's Assn. **Achievements:** dev.& strengthening of ecol.teaching & res.at Tribhuvan U.and public awareness of need for envl cons. **Memberships:** NCSN (Founder), NHSN (Founder), Nepal Botl Soc.(Life), UN Assn of Nepal (past-Pres.), Nepal Coll.& U.Teachers' Assn (Founder & VP). **Awards:** Mahendra Vidya Bhushan 1964, Prabal Gorkha Dakshin Bahu 1984. **Publications:** num.incl. *Natural Hist.& Econ.Bot.of Nepal* 1977, *The Envt of Suklaphanta* 1977, Nepal Himalaya & Change 1981, *Nepal–Britain Relations* 1983. **Languages:** English, Hindi, Nepali. Willing to act as consult./resource person. **Address:** 3/477 Pulchowk, Lalitpur, Nepal. **Tel.**(home) 977 5 21790.

BILSBORROW, Professor Dr Richard E. Population processes; development & environment in developing countries. Professor of Biostatistics, Adjunct Professor of Ecology & Planning. *B.*3 Dec.1941, Evanston, IL, USA. American. *M.*Helen (demographer): 2 *s.* **Education:** Carleton Coll. BA(Econ.) 1963, U.of Michigan PhD(Econ.) 1968, Princeton U. Cert.(Demography) 1972. **Experience:** doctorate focused on econ.dev., taught econ.and became interested in pop.–dev.interrelationships so studied demography; res.on demographic & econ.data collection & analysis mainly in Latin Amer.; working on pop.& envt and dev.1986–. **Career:** Summer Intern, US AID 1964; Asst Prof. Dept of Econ. New York U.1968–71; Res.Staff, Office of Pop.Res. Princeton U. 1971–2; Asst Prof.then Prof. Dept of Biostats 1972–, Adjunct Prof. Ecol.Curr.and Dept of City & Regnl Planning 1989–, Carolina Pop.Center, U.of N.Carolina. **Achievements:** teaching, res. & pubns on envt, migration, & dev.; memb.of Cttee on Pop.& Envt of IUSSP 1991–, and of IUCN CESP; Founder, Center for World Envt & Sust.Dev.(NC) 1991–. **Memberships:** IUSSP, PAA (Bd), WCU. **Awards:** many res.grants, Fulbright F'ship at Universidad de los Andes (Bogotá) 1965–6. **Publications:** num.incl.Land Use, Migration, and Natural Resource Deterioration in the Third World: The Cases of Guatemala and Sudan (co-Author) 1991, Pop., Dev.and Deforestation 1993, Pop.Change and Agricl Intensification in Developing Countries (co-Author) 1993, Land Tenure and Land Use Systems, Deforestation, and Associated Demographic Factors: Farm-Level Evidence from Ecuador (in press). Favours pers.pub. **Languages:** English, French (limited), Spanish. Willing to act as consult.etc. **Address:** Carolina Population Center, University of North Carolina, 123 West Franklin Street, Chapel Hill, North Carolina 27516-3997, USA. **Tel.**1 919 966 2157; **fax** 1 919 966 6638; **e-mail** RICHARD_BILSBORROW@UNC.EDU .

BIN **ARIFFIN, Ishak,** *see* **ARIFFIN, Ishak** BIN.

BIRCH, Professor Dr L.Charles. Population ecology. Emeritus Professor. *B.*8 Feb.1918, Melbourne, Vic., Australia. Australian. **Education:** U.of Melbourne BAgrSci 1939, U.of Adelaide DSc 1948. **Experience:** res.on pop. ecol.and eval.of insects & application to human & other pops. **Career:** Res.Officer, Waite Agricl Res.Inst. 1939–45, Res.F. U.of Chicago 1946, Bureau of Animal Pop. U.of Oxford 1947; Sr Lect.in Biol. 1948–54, Reader 1954–60, Challis Prof.of Biol.1960–83, Emer.Prof.1984–, U.of Sydney. **Achievement:** theory of pop. ecol. of animals. **Memberships:** F.Australian AS, F.AAAS, BES (Hon.Life), IAEB (VP 1980–), Club of Rome, Ecol.Soc.of Amer.(Hon.Life). **Awards:** Gold Medal (Ecol.Soc.of Australia) 1988, Eminent Ecologist Award (Ecol.Soc.of Amer.) 1988, Templeton Prize 1990. **Publications:** incl.*The Distribn & Abundance of Animals* 1954, *The Ecol.Web* 1984. Accepts pers. pub.& news media support. **Language:** English. Further details may be obtained from *e.g. Who's Who in the World* (11th edn). **Address:** 5a/73 Yarranabbe Road, Darling Point, New South Wales 2027, Australia. **Tel.**(home) 61 2 362 3788.

BIRNIE, Dr Patricia Winifred. Public international law especially the Law of the Sea and international law & the environment. Visiting Professorial Fellow, Visiting Fellow. *B*.17 Nov. 1926, Lytham St Anne's, England, UK. British. *W.: s.,* 2 *d.* **Education:** U.of Oxf. BA(Hons) (Jurisprudence) 1947; Gray's Inn (London) Barrister-at-Law 1952; U.of Edinburgh PhD 1979. **Experience:** res.on all aspects of dev.of intl law pertaining to envl prot.incl.control of poll.from all sources and cons.of living resources; admin.— Admin.Asst HM Treasury, Dir of IMO Intl Maritime Law Inst.; consult.for IMO, FAO & var.NGOs, Spec.Adv.to House of Commons' Cttees on Fishing & Vessel-source poll. **Career:** Lect.in Public Intl Law, U.of Edinburgh 1968–83; Sr Lect.in Law, LSE 1983–9; Dir IMO Intl Maritime Law Inst.Malta 1989–92; Vis.Professorial F. QM&WC and Vis.F. LSE 1992–4. **Achievements:** educating students at all postgrad.levels in envl law esp.pertaining to marine envt & resources; advising many govtl & non-govtl bodies; publishing widely on these topics. **Memberships:** ILA, ICEL, UK ELA, ASIL. **Publications:** *The Maritime Dimension* (Ed.& co-Author) 1980, *Intl Regulation of Whaling* (2 vols) 1985, *Intl Law and the Envt* (co-Author) 1992; num.papers. Indiff.to pers. pub. & news media support. **Languages:** English, French. Willing to act as consult.etc. **Address:** 78 Windmill Street, Brill, Aylesbury, Buckinghamshire HP18 9TG, England, UK. **Tel.& fax** 44 1844 237880.

BISWAS, Dr Asit Kumar. Environmental policies (preparation of national environmental action plans), environmental impact assessment; irrigation management, management of international waters, sustainable agricultural development. President, Research Fellow. *B*.25 Feb.1939, Balasore, Orissa, India. Canadian. *M*.Margaret R.*qv.* **Education:** IIT BTech(1st Class Hons), MTech 1961; U.of Strathclyde PhD(Civ.Eng.) 1967. **Experience:** Lect. U.of Lund and Twente U.of Tech.; Sr Adv.to heads of four UN agencies, World Bank, ADB, CIDA, DANIDA, USAID, GTZ, AIT, NATO, and 17 govts on envl policy & water dev.; extensive consults with major UN agencies. **Career:** Lect. U.of Strathclyde 1963–67; Asst Prof. Queen's U.1967–8; Sr Sci. Dept of Energy, Mines & Res.(Ottawa) 1969–71; Dir, DoE Canada 1972–77; Sr Adv.& Exec.Dir. UNEP 1974–92; Sr Sci. IIASA 1978–79; Res.F. Intl Dev.Centre, U.of Oxf.1987–; Pres. ISEM, and Biswas & Assocs. **Achievements:** basic res.on water resources' mgmt, envl impact analysis; assisting 14 countries on developing their envt & water policies. **Memberships:** VP (1979–82) then Pres.(1989–91) IWRA, Pres.ISEM 1978–,

VP IACT 1988–93, ASCE, Chairman Middle E.Water Comm.1993–6, IWRS (Hon.), EEA. **Awards:** Walter L.Huber Prize (ASCE), F.in Intl Relations (Rockefeller Fndn), DSc*(h.c.)* (U.of Lund), Disting.Lect.(IWRA). **Publications:** 45 books incl.*Hist.of Hydr.*1970, *Systems Approach to Water Mgmt* 1976, *Models for Water Qual.Mgmt* 1984, *Earth & Us* 1990, *Envl Impact Analysis* 1992, *Climatic Fluctuations & Water Mgmt* 1992; over 500 papers etc.; Ed. *Intl J.of Water Res.Dev.,* member of Edl Bds of 14 intl scientific journals. Indiff.to pers.pub., strongly favours news media support. **Languages:** Bengali, English, Hindi, Urdu. Further details may be obtained from *Amer.Men of Sci., Engg Who's Who, Canadian Who's Who, Men of Achievement, Intl Who's Who.* Willing to act as consult.etc. **Address:** 76 Woodstock Close, Oxford OX2 8DD, England, UK. **Tel.**(office) 44 1865 57608, **fax** 44 1865 310905.

BISWAS, Professor Dilip. Pollution control, environmental impact assessment. Board Chairman. *B*.15 July 1941, Rangoon, Myanmar (Burma). Indian. *M*.Monimala: 2 *s.* **Education:** Jadvapur U. BE(Chem.Eng.) 1963, M.Tech. (Food Tech.& Biochem.Eng.) 1965; Louisiana SU MS(Agricl Eng.) 1969. **Experience:** more than 25 yrs in res., teaching, & admin., aspects re.envl mgmt and poll.control. **Career:** Assoc Prof.1969–75 and Prof.1975–6 in Agricl Engg, Div.of Agricl Engg, IARI; PSO & Sec.of NCEPC 1976–81, Dir 1981–7 and Adv.in Dept of Biotech.1987–8 and to Min.1988–93, Chairman of C.Poll.Control Bd 1993–, Min.of Envt & Forests, Govt of India. **Achievements:** prep.of Ganga Action Plan, and NCS & Policy Statement on Envt & Dev. **Award:** F'ship (Ford Fndn) 1967–9. **Publications:** *Air Poll. and Plants* 1983; *c.*50 papers. Favours news media support. **Languages:** Bengali, English, Hindi. Willing to act as consult.etc. **Address:** J-1878 Chittaranjan Park, New Delhi 110 019, Delhi, India. **Tel.**(office) 91 11 220 4948, (home) 91 11 646 3991; **fax** 91 11 220 4948.

BISWAS, Mrs Margaret Rose. Environmental policies, especially sustainable agricultural development; nutrition, environmental issues, and international relations. Company Director. *B*.5 March 1941, Beausejour, Canada. Canadian. *M*.Dr Asit K.Biswas *qv.* **Education:** U.of Manitoba BSc 1962, McGill U. MA 1964. **Experience:** res.on policy aspects of agric.& the envt; res.on other envl issues esp.energy, and on pol.& intl relations; advising nat.govts & UN agencies on envt & dev.issues esp.on food, agric.& energy. **Career:** Consult. DoE Ottawa 1973–4, Prog.Officer UNEP Nairobi 1974–5, Res.Scholar IIASA 1978–9, Balliol Coll.U. of Oxf.1979–89, Dir Biswas & Assocs 1976–. **Achievements:** memb.Adv.Cttee on Natural Resources, UNU Tokyo; consult.UNEP, UNU, OECD, UNIDO, IFAD, & FAO. **Memberships:** Chairman, Cttee on Nutrition and Dev. IUNS 1979–85, 1989–. **Publications:**

*Nutrition and Dev.*1985, *Food, Climate, and Man* (transl.into 5 languages) 1979, *Desertification* 1980, *New & Renewable Sources of Energy* 1982, *Nutrition in the Nineties* 1994; 45 major papers; Guest Ed.*S.Asia* and *Energy Policy*, Ed.of two book series on Envt and Natural Resources; Edl Bd of four major intl journals. Indiff.to pers.pub. favours news media support. **Languages:** English, German. Further details may be obtained from *World Who's Who of Women, Amer.Men & Women of Sci., Who's Who of Amer.Women.* Willing to act as consult.etc. **Address:** 76 Woodstock Close, Oxford OX2 8DD, England, UK. **Tel.**(office) 44 1865 57608; **fax** 44 1865 310905.

BJORNDAL, Dr Karen A. Biology & conservation of marine turtles. Director, Associate Professor. *B.*22 Feb.1951, Berkeley, CA, USA. American. **Education:** Occidental Coll.(CA) BA(Biol.) 1972, U.of Florida PhD(Zool.) 1979. **Experience:** res.— nutrition, productivity & movements of sea turtles, comparative nutrition of vertebrate herbivores; admin.as Center Dir; teaching basic biol., nutrition of herbivores, & sea turtle biol., to u.students. **Career:** WWF–US F.1979–80; Post-doctl F. U.of Florida 1980–87; Dir, Asst.& Assoc.Prof. Archie Carr Center for Sea Turtle Res.1987–. **Achievements:** work towards intl cons.of sea turtles, Chairman IUCN SSC Marine Turtle SG 1984–. **Memberships:** SAN, SCB, ASIH, HL, SSAR, ESA. **Publications:** *Biol.& Cons.of Sea Turtles* (Ed.) 1982; 40+ scientific papers. Favours pers. pub.& news media support re.sea turtle cons. **Language:** English. Willing to act as consult. **Address:** Center for Sea Turtle Research, Bartram Hall, University of Florida, Gainesville, Florida 32611, USA. **Tel.**(office) 1 904 392 5194; **fax** 1 904 392 9166.

BLAHNA, Dr Dale Jeffrey. Teaching & research in application of social science to natural resource management & planning issues. Assistant Professor of Forest Resources. *B.*3 July 1953, Milwaukee, WI, USA. American. **Education:** U.of Wisconsin–Milwaukee, BA (Biol. Aspects of Cons.) 1975; U.of Wisconsin–Stevens Point, MS(Natural Resources) 1978; U.of Michigan, PhD(Natural Resources) 1985. **Experience:** res., admin., lecturing, supervision of grad.students. **Career:** Natural Resource Sociologist, USDA Forest Service Office of Envl Coordn 1985 (Summer) and Office of Land & Resource Mgmt Planning 1986; Asst Prof. of Forest Resources, Northeastern Illinois U.1987–90 and Utah SU 1991–. **Achievements:** conducted in-depth analysis of public involvement methods used by USDA Forest Service in land mgmt planning, and several studies of use by ethnic minorities of nat. parks, nat.forests, etc. **Memberships:** SAF, Rural Sociological Assn, NPCA. **Awards:** Presidential Fac.Excellence Award (Northeastern Illinois U.) 1990, Xi Sigma Pi (For.Hon.Soc.). **Publications:** num.incl.Public involvement in resource planning: toward bridging the gap between policy and implementation (co-Author) 1989, Preservation or use? Confronting public issues in forest planning (co-Author) 1990, Envl reporting in ethnic magazines: implications for incorporating minority concerns in envl issues (co-Author) 1993, Expected and actual regnl econ. impacts of Ft Basin Nat.Park (co-Author) 1993. Indiff.re.pers.pub.& news media support. **Language:** English. Willing to act as consult. etc. **Address:** Department of Forest Resources, Utah State University, Logan, Utah 84322-5215, USA. **Tel.**(office) 1 801 797 2544, (home) 1 801 753 0754; **fax** 1 801 797 4040.

BLISS, Professor Dr Lawrence 'Larry' C. Arctic & alpine ecology; development, structure, & function, of arctic ecosystems, ecophysiology of plants in cold stressed environments, patterning of plant communities, role of soils in plant distribution, plant production, role of applied ecology in arctic development. Professor of Botany. *B.*29 Nov.1929, Cleveland, OH, USA. American. *M.* Gweneth J.: *s.*Dwight I.(geol.), *d.* **Education:** Kent State U. BS 1951, MS 1953; Duke U. PhD 1956. **Experience:** comparative study of microclimate & plant growth in arctic & alpine envts; plant growth & prod.in Presidential Range (NH), Olympic Mtns (WA), Rock & Pillar Range (NZ); structure & function of high-arctic ecosystems, soils, plant communities & prod., in Canadian Arctic; reorgn of ecosystems following eruption of Mt St Helena; ecophysiol.of num.alpine & arctic plant species. **Career:** Instr.in Biol. Bowling Green SU 1956; Instr.1957–8, Asst Prof.1958–61, Assoc.Prof. 1961–66, Prof.1966–8, in Bot. U.of Illinois; Prof.& Dir Controlled Envt Facility, Dept of Bot. U.of Alb. 1968–78; Chairman Dept of Bot. 1978–87, Prof.1978–, U.of Washington. **Achievements:** physiol.adaptations of arctic & alpine species, structure & function of high-arctic ecosystems, dev.of coastal & high-elevation arctic ecosystems, dev.of ecosystems after eruption of Mt St Helena. **Memberships:** AIBS, AINA, CBA, Ecol.Soc.of Amer.(VP 1876–7, Treas.1977–81, Pres.1982–3), Sigma Xi. **Awards:** Fulbright F.(NZ) 1963–4, Spec.Achievement Award (Kent State U.) 1986, F.AAAS, F.AINA. **Publications:** *Truelove Lowland, Devon Is., Canada: A High Arctic Ecosystem* (Ed.) 1977, *Tundra Ecosystems: A Comparative Analysis* (Ed.) 1981, *Lab.Manual for Gen.Bot.*(co-Author) 7th edn 1991. Indiff.to pers.pub., favours news media support. Willing to act as consult.etc. **Address:** Department of Botany, University of Washington, Seattle, Washington 98195, USA. **Tel.** (office) 1 206 543 8917, (home) 1 206 542 2612; **fax** 1 206 685 1728.

BLOOMFIELD, Michael I. Environmental education, sustainability, wildlife & wilderness, philanthropy, Caribou *(Rangifer tarandus* agg.) ecology, capture, and effects of human activity. Founder & Executive Director. *B.*1 Feb.1950,

Cleveland, OH, USA. Canadian. *M*.Christine D.(ethnobot., organic gardening, sust.agric.). **Education:** Merced Coll. Assoc.in Agric.1971, Ohio SU BSc 1974, U.of Alberta MSc 1979. **Experience:** wildlife biol., envl educ., assn exec. **Career:** Regnl Wildlife Biol.and provincial Caribou Specialist, Alberta Dept of Fish & Wildlife 1978–83; Founder & Exec.Dir, The Harmony Fndn of Canada 1985–; Founder of Green Works (workplace training for the envt), and Improv-Eco (youth envt prog.for community service). **Achievements:** res.& public awareness of land-use effects on climax species *e.g.* Caribou, envl educ.incl.Summer Inst.for Envl Values Educ., G500F (Governing Council). **Memberships:** Sigma Xi Fndn, Gamma Sigma Delta. **Awards:** Global 500 Roll of Honour (UNEP) 1992, Commonwealth Fndn F'ship 1994. **Publications:** var.professional & popular items incl. *Our Common Future: A Canadian Response to the Challenge of Sust.Dev.*1988, *Home & Family Guide: Practical Action for the Envt.*1989, *Community Workshops for the Envt* 1991, *Workplace Guide: Practical Action for the Envt* 1991, *Earthworms: Nature's Recyclers* 1992, *Discovering Your Community: a Co-operative Process for Planning Sust.*1994. Indifferent to pers.pub. **Language:** English. Further details can be obtained from *Canadian Who's Who.* Willing to act as consult.etc. **Address:** Harmony Foundation of Canada, 1183 Fort Street, Victoria, British Columbia V8V 3L1, Canada. **Tel.**1 604 380 3001; **fax** 1 604 380 0887.

BOA, Dr Eric. Tree health, forest pathology; Bamboos in rural development. Tree Health Specialist. *B*.9 July 1952, Edinburgh, Scotland, UK. British. *M*.Frances: 2 *s*. **Education:** U.of Aberdeen, BSc(Hons)(Bot.& Microbiol.) 1975, Dip.Ed.1976; U.of Leeds, PhD(Ash Canker) 1980. **Experience:** res., field surveys on wide var.of trop.tree diseases, surveys for FAO of neem diseases in W.Africa, project identification & formulation with bilateral & multilateral donors, consult.in agricl educ. **Career:** Tech. Coopn Officer, ODA 1981–90; Tree Crops Pathologist, NRI 1991–4; Tree Health Specialist, IMI 1994–. **Achievements:** applied res.on tree diseases in developing countries, training of counterparts in nat.res.instns, melding of natural & social scis in social for.overseas, bamboo res. **Memberships:** BSPP, BMS, SEB, TAA, RPS. **Award:** UK Membership Sec.(SEB). **Publications:** *c*.15 incl.*Diseases of Nitrogen Fixing Trees in Developing Countries — An Annotated List* (co-Author) 1994, *An Illustr.Guide to Pests and Diseases of Neem* 1995. Favours pers. pub. & news media support. **Languages:** English; French & Indonesian (fair spoken & written). Willing to act as consult.etc. **Address:** International Mycological Institute, Bakeham Lane, Egham, Surrey TW20 9TY, England, UK. **Tel.**(office) 44 1784 470111, (home) 44 181 336 0831; **fax** 44 1784 470909; **e-mail** E.BOA@ CABI.ORG .

BOARDMAN, Professor Dr Robert. Environmental policy & law, conservation of Nature. Professor of Political Science, Professor of Resource & Environmental Studies. *B*.3 March 1945, Manchester, England, UK. Canadian. *M*. Christine Elizabeth: *s., d*. **Education:** U.of London, BSc 1966, PhD 1970. **Experience:** extensive intl res.on envl policy, law & admin., teaching & res.supervision, collab.with EMDI project (Jakarta/Halifax) 1992–3. **Career:** Asst. Lect. U.of Surrey 1967–9; Lect.in Pol. U.of Leicester 1970–71; Asst.Prof.of Pol.Sci. 1971–6; Dir Centre for Foreign Policy Studies 1982–7 and Chair Dept of Pol.Sci.1988–92, Dalhousie U.; Vis.F. U.of Geneva 1977–8 and ANU 1984–5. **Achievements:** res.on Canadian envl policy and intl cons.instns; Ed./Adv.Bd *Intl J., Intl Insights, J.of Euro.Integration*; Co-Ed. *Canadian J.of Pol.Sci.*1984–7; Fac.adjunct Min.of Envt, Indonesia 1993; pesticides res.in Malaysia 1982. **Memberships:** CPSA, CNF, ISA. **Awards:** Assoc.Dipl. London Coll.of Music 1961, SSRC Doctl Award 1966–9, SSHRCC F'ship 1984–5. **Publications:** *Intl Orgn and the Cons.of Nature* 1981, *Nuclear Exports & World Pol.*(jt Ed.) 1983, *Pesticides in World Agric.*1986, *Global Regimes & Nation-states: Envl Issues in Australian Pol.*1990, *Canadian Envl Policy* (Ed.) 1992, *Post-socialist World Orders* 1994, num.papers. Favours pers.pub.& news media support. **Languages:** English, French, Indonesian (some), Russian (some). Willing to act as consult.etc. **Address:** Department of Political Science and School for Resource & Environmental Studies, Dalhousie University, Halifax, Nova Scotia B3H 4H6, Canada. **Tel.**(office) 1 902 494 6602, (home) 1 902 275 3426; **fax** 1 902 494 3825.

BOER, Professor Bernhard Willem. Environmental law. Professor of Environmental Law, Centre Director. *B*.9 Sept.1948, The Hague, The Netherlands. Australian, Dutch. *M*.Diane Beverley. **Education:** U.of Melbourne LLM 1978. **Experience:** extensive res.& consult.in envl law; teaching envl law at under- & post-grad.(15 yrs) levels. **Career:** Solicitor 1972–73; Tutor & Lect. La Trobe U.1974–8; Lect., Sr Lect., Assoc.Prof.of Law, Macquarie U.1979–91; Corrs Chambers Westgarth Prof.of Envl Law and Dir ACEL, U.of Sydney 1992–. **Achievements:** involved in estab.of Nat.& State Envl Law Assns and of Envl Defender's Office (public interest litigation law firm); widely published in envl law field; drafter Nepal envl legis.; Solomon Islands' legis. **Memberships:** IUCN CEL, ICEL, Barrister Supreme Court of NSW, Barrister & Solicitor Supreme Court of Vic. **Awards:** Best published article (NELA) 1989, Inaugural Res.Award (AMPLA) 1991. **Publications:** Solomon Islands review of envl law, Social ecol.& envl law 1984, Implementing sust.1992. Generally positive re.pers.pub., favours news media support. **Languages:** Dutch (good spoken & written), English, French (fair spoken & written). Willing to act as consult.etc. **Address:** Australian Centre for Environmental Law, Faculty of Law, University of Sydney, Sydney, New South Wales 2006, Australia. **Tel.**(office) 61 2 225 9317, (home) 61 2 692 9706; **fax** 61 2 225 9324.

BOJKOV, Professor Dr Rumen D. International atmospheric environment, particularly ozone studies. Scientist Emeritus, Special Adviser. *B.* 1 May 1931, Vellingrade, Bulgaria. Bulgarian, Canadian. *M.*Anneliese: *s.* **Education:** U.of Sofia MSc(Met.& Geophys.) 1955, U.of Moscow PhD(Phys.& Maths) 1964, U.of Rostock DSc(Atmos.Phys.) 1971. **Experience:** numerical data analysis & res., teaching of atmos.scis, intl negns on envl issues (*e.g.*ozone, climate change, poll.transport). **Career:** Synoptician, Bulgarian Met.Service 1955–9; Assoc.Prof. U.of Sofia 1960–64; Res.F. CMS 1960 & 1965–6 and US NCAR 1966–8; Prof.of Strat.Phys. SUNY (Albany) 1968–9; Sr Expert (Cairo) 1969–70, Chief Atmos.Scis Div.1970–83, Chief Envt Div.1988–93, WMO; Sr Sci.1983–8, Sci.Emer.for Ozone Res.1994–, Atmos.Envt Service of Canada; Spec.Adv.on Ozone & Global Envl Issues to Sec.-Gen. of WMO and Exec.Dir of UNEP 1991–. **Achievements:** init.& implemented coherent intl network for monitoring of ozone & other 'greenhouse' gases (WMO Global Atmos. Watch) and promulgated assessments of the precarious state of the stratospheric ozone layer or 'shield'. **Memberships:** AMS 1971, AGU 1973, Intl Ozone Comm.(Sec.1984–96). **Awards:** F.AMS 1986, citations from AGU and other nat.& intl agencies & socs. **Publications:** *Atmos.Phys.*(u.textbook) 1966; 100+ refereed scientific papers & num.assessment reports. Indiff.to pers.pub., favours news media support. **Languages:** Bulgarian, English, German (spoken), Russian. Further details may be obtained from *Who's Who in the World* 1995. Willing to act as consult.etc. **Address:** 63 Route de la Chapelle, 1212 Geneva, Switzerland. **Tel.** (office) 41 22 730 8455, (home) 41 22 343 7874; **fax** 41 22 740 0984.

BOLIN, Professor Dr Bert R. Global biogeochemical cycles, climate, climate change; global carbon cycle; interactions of environmental scientists and politicians. Ministry Expert, Chairman. *B.*15 May 1925, Nyköping, Sweden. Swedish. *D.*: 2 *s., d.* **Education:** Uppsala U. BS 1946; U.of Stockholm MS 1949, PhD 1956. **Experience:** res., teaching, intl coordn of res.in envl scis. **Career:** Asst Prof.1956–61, Prof.of Met.1961–90, U.of Stockholm; Head of Res. GARP 1965–71; Dir Intl Met.Inst.(Stockholm) 1956–91; Sci.Dir, Euro.Res.Orgn 1965–7; WCRP (prep.1974–7), IGBP (prep.1985–7, cttee 1987–92), Chairman IPCC 1988–, Expert to Swedish PM 1986–91. **Achievements:** res.in dynamic met., atmos.chem., global biogeochem.cycles; led nr of intl scientific initiatives. **Memberships:** RSAS, SAES, Norwegian AS, AMS (Hon.), EGS (Hon.). **Awards:** IMO Prize

(WMO) 1981, Tyler Prize (U.of Southern Calif.) 1988, Korber Prize (Korber Fndn) 1991, Rossby Prize (AMS), Rossby Prize (Swedish Geophys.Soc.) 1993, Milankowic Prize (EGS) 1993. **Publications:** *Intro.to Met.*1968, *We and the Weather* 1974, *The Threat of a Change of Climate* 1993 (all in Swedish); Ed.SCOPE Reports 13, 16, 21, & 29, overall charge of IPCC Assessments 1990, 1992, *c.*100 scientific papers. Indiff.to pers.pub.& news media support. **Languages:** English, German, Swedish. **Address:** Kvarnasvagen 6, 18451 Osterskar, Sweden. **Tel.**(home) 46 8 5406 9594; **fax** 46 8 157185.

Bo-Myeong WOO, Professor Dr, *see* **WOO, Professor Dr Bo-Myeong.**

Bong-Heang KIEW, Dr, *see* **KIEW, Dr Bong-Heang.**

BONINE, Professor John E. Environmental & public-interest law. Professor of Law, Attorney, Board Chair. *B.*14 March 1944, Lawton, OK, USA. American. *M.*Anne. **Education:** Stanford U. AB(Hist./Pol.Sci.) 1966, Yale Law Sch. LLB 1969. **Experience:** has handled 50+ envl law-court cases, first for US EPA then for envl groups, incl.nationwide court orders against pesticide spraying, freedom of info-lawsuits, EIA litigation; helps lead network of pro-envt lawyers in 30 countries. **Career:** Legislative Asst to US Senator –1972; Attorney, Air Qual., Noise and Radiation Div.1972–5, Dep.Assoc. Gen.Counsel for Pesticides (Legal Advice) 1975–6 & (Litigation) 1976, Assoc.Gen.Counsel for Air, Noise, and Solid Waste 1976–8, US EPA; Attorney, Western Envl Law Center and Prof.of Law, U.of Oregon 1978–; Chair, Bd of Dirs, E-LAW (US Office) 1991–. **Achievements:** co-Founder Envl Law Alliance Worldwide and Western Envl Law Center. **Memberships:** IUCN CEL, ICEL (elected). **Publications:** incl.*The Law of Envl Prot.*1992. **Address:** School of Law, University of Oregon, Eugene, Oregon 97403, USA. **Tel.**(office) 1 503 346 3876, (home) 1 503 345 2095; **fax** 1 503 346 3985.

BONNER, (William) Nigel. Marine mammals; Antarctic conservation. Consultant. *B.*15 Feb. 1928, London, England, UK. British. *M.*Jennifer Mary. **Education:** UCL BSc 1953. **Experience:** 40 yrs' Antarctic. **Career:** Falkland Islands Dependencies Survey 1953–61; Lect.Sir John Cass Coll. London 1961–7; Dir UK Seals Res.Unit 1967–74; Head, Life Scis Div.1974 to Dep.Dir 1986–8, Brit.Antarctic Survey; Consult.1988–. **Achievement:** Convener, SCAR Group of Specialists on Antarctic Cons.1974–92. **Memberships:** ZSL, IBiol. **Award:** F.IBiol. **Publications:** *The Fur Seal of S.Georgia* 1968, *Seals and Man, a Study of Interactions* 1982, *Cons.Areas in the Antarctic* 1985, *The Natural Hist.of Seals* 1989, *Whales of the World* 1989. Accepts pers.pub.& news media support. **Languages:** English, Norwegian. **Address:** 1

Laroc Close, Godmanchester, Huntingdon PE18 8AX, England, UK. **Tel.& fax** 44 1480 457300.

BOORMAN, Dr Laurie Allan. Salt marsh & sand-dune ecology; coastal-zone management. Senior Coastal Ecologist. *B.*8 May 1940, London, England, UK. British. *M.*Mary S. **Education:** U.of Oxf. BSc(Hons)(Bot.) 1962, DPhil (Salt-marsh Ecol.) 1966, MA 1986. **Experience:** 25 yrs in coastal res. **Career:** Seed Taxonomist & Asst Chief Officer, Official Seed Testing Station for Scotland 1966–71; Dune Ecol. Coastal Ecol.Res.Station (Norwich) 1971–9, Sr Coastal Ecol.1979–, ITE. **Achievements:** pioneered large-scale coastal impact surveys *e.g.*third London Airport at Maplin 1972, and work on use of veg.as civil engg material on steep waterways and sea walls; led work on the effects of climate change & sea-level rise on coastal ecosystems. **Memberships:** BES 1964–, ECSA (Counc.1988–91), Marine Forum 1988–, EUCC (Counc.1989–), Hydrographic Soc. **Awards:** Hon.Lect.(U.of E.Anglia) 1975– 91, Travelling F'ship (Sir Winston Churchill Mem.Trust) 1989. **Publications:** Salt Marsh and Sand Dune Stabilization 1990, Dry Coastal Ecosystems of Britain: Dunes and Shingle Beaches 1993, Comparative Relationships between Primary Productivity and Organic & Nutrient Fluxes in Four Salt Marshes (co Author) 1994. **Languages:** Dutch, English, French; German & Spanish (read and some spoken). **Address:** Institute of Terrestrial Ecology, Monks Wood, Abbots Ripton, Huntingdon, Cambridgeshire PE17 2LS, England, UK. **Tel.**44 1487 773381; **fax** 44 1487 773467.

BOOTE, Robert Edward. Environment, ageing society. Vice-President, Chairman. *B.*6 Feb.1920, Stoke-on-Trent, N.Staffs., England, UK. British. *M.*Vera (involved in envt & ageing soc.): *d., s.* **Education:** U.of London, BSc(Hons)(Econ.) 1953. **Experience:** econ.& ecol.applied to envl issues. **Career:** var.posts in NC 1954–80 (when retired); Dep.Sec.1963–5 and Sec.1965–71, HRH Prince Philip Duke of Edinburgh's Confs for 'The Countryside in 1970'; Memb.(with var.posts) Euro.Cttee for Cons.of Nature & Natural Resources 1963–71; Chairman, Euro.Cttee for Euro.Cons. Yr 1970, Council of Europe; DG NCC 1973–80; VP, WCU 1978–81, BTCV 1989–, The Wildlife Trusts 1980–95, and Age Concern 1990–; Chairman, Age Resource 1988–. **Achievements:** num.in pesticides, land-use planning & management, educ.& training, and in nat.& intl vol.& official orgns involved with the envt. **Memberships:** F.RGS, F.RSA, RTPI (Hon.), Landscape Inst.(Hon.). **Awards:** CVO 1971, Van Tienhoven Prize for Nature Cons.in Europe, 1980, Spec.Alfred Toepfer Prize for the Prot.of Nature in Europe (Goethe Fndn) 1995. **Publications:** incl.*Man and Envt: Crisis and the Strat.of Choice,* five edns 1967–87. Accepts pers.pub., fosters news media support for envt & Age Resource. **Languages:** English, French

(passable). Further details may be obtained from annual British *Who's Who, Who's Who in the World* 1980/81 *et seq.* Willing to act as a consult. **Address:** 3 Leeward Gardens, Wimbledon, London SW19 7QR, England, UK. **Tel.**(home) 44 181 946 1551; **fax** 44 181 944 1320.

Boping WEN, Professor, *see* **WEN, Professor Boping.**

BORGESE, Professor Elisabeth Mann. Law of the sea. Professor of Political Science. *B.*24 April 1918, Munich, Germany. *W.*: 2 *d.* **Education:** Conservatory of Music (Zürich), Dipl. 1937; Freies Gymnasium (Zürich), BA(Humanistic Studies) 1935. **Experience:** res., admin. **Career:** Founder & Chair, Intl Ocean Inst. 1972–; Chair, Intl Center for Ocean Dev. 1986–92; Sr F. Center for Study of Democratic Instns 1964–8; Prof.of Pol.Sci. Dalhousie U.1980–. **Achievements:** projects on envt & dev.in the Medit., bringing the Barcelona Conv.from Stockholm to Rio, Pacem in Maribus Conferences. **Memberships:** TWAS, WAAS. **Awards:** Order of Canada 1986, Intl Sasakawa Prize for the Environment (UN) 1987, St Francis Intl Envt Prize 1993, others. **Publications:** *The Ocean Regime* 1968, *Drama of the Ocean* 1976, *Sea Farm* 1981, *Mines of Neptune* 1986, *The Future of the Oceans* 1991, *Ocean Frontiers* (Ed.) 1992, *Chairworm and Supershark* 1992. Considers pers.pub.& news media support to be necessary evils. **Languages:** English, German, Italian. Willing to act as consult.etc.if time permits. **Address:** International Ocean Institute, Dalhousie University, 1226 Le Marchant Street, Halifax, Nova Scotia B3H 3P7, Canada. **Tel.**(office) 1 902 494 1737, (home) 1 902 868 2818; **fax** 1 902 868 2455.

BOS, Dr Luite. Plant virology, crop protection, ecology. Retired. *B.*22 March 1928, West-Stellingwerf, The Netherlands. Dutch. **Education:** Agricl U.Wageningen MSc 1953, PhD 1957. **Experience:** res.— plant morphology, plant virology, viruses & virus diseases of legume & vegetable crops (identification, ecol.& control), viruses & virus diseases of faba bean & other food legumes in Middle E.& N.Africa; admin.— Coord.Plant Virology, Res.Inst.for Plant Prot., Memb.& Chairman Bd of Eds, *Netherlands J. of Plant Path.*; Memb.& later Chairman Terminology Cttee, RNSPP; Sec.Intl WGs on Legume Viruses and on Vegetable Viruses; consult.to FAO, CGIAR Intl Agricl Res.Centres, ICRISAT, ICARDA, DGIS, EC, univs, private cos; teaching plant morphology & taxonomy at Agricl U. (evening courses for Fndn for Training of Lab.Technicians), and plant virology (courses for specialists of Agricl Ext. Services & Plant Prot.Service). **Career:** Sci. Asst, Dept of Plant Taxonomy, Agricl U. 1953–7; Res.Sci. Netherlands Min.of Agric., Fisheries & Nature Cons.1957–93; Founding father of Intl WGs on Legume Viruses 1962 and on Vegetable Viruses of ISHS 1970, Chairman, Terminology Cttee, RNSPP 1965–. **Achievements:** res.& publishing on ecol.of virus diseases of crops to develop preventive measures of control, emphasis on role of Man in creating ecol.niches for new problems to emerge *e.g.* by changing agro-ecosystems & intl transfer of plant propagation material; collab.with FAO & CGIAR Intl Agricl Res. Centres (*i.a.*IBPGR) for health improvement of intlly-distributed germ-plasm for storage in gene-banks (preserv.of genetic resources) and for genetic crop improvement; improvement of knowledge re.plant viruses and changing agricl envt; furthering of intl coopn in identification of, and res.on, viruses of legume & vegetable crops; standardization of crop prot.terminology. **Memberships:** RNSAS, RNSPP, NCPV. **Awards:** F. W.K.Kellogg Fndn 1960, F.Fulbright Orgn 1960, Officer Order Orange-Nassau 1992. **Publications:** some 250 incl.five books: *Symptoms of Virus Diseases in Plants* 1963 (3rd edn 1978), *Virussen en Planten* 1965, *Plantevirussen; Beknopte Inleiding tot de Plante-virologie* 1976 (4th edn 1983), *Intro.to Plant Virology* 1983, *Res.on Viruses of Legume Crops and the Intl WG on Legume Viruses: histl facts and pers.reminiscences* (in press). **Languages:** Dutch, English, French (spoken), German (spoken). Willing to act as consult.etc. **Address:** Research Institute for Plant Protection, POB 9060, 6700 GW Wageningen, The Netherlands. **Tel.**(home) 31 317 414682; **fax** 31 317 410113; **telex** 45888 intas-nl .

BOSWALL, Jeffery. Popularization & teaching of biology & conservation through media of film, video, & television; bird protection. Senior Lecturer. *B.*20 Mar.1931, Brighton, Sussex, England, UK. British. *M.*Pamela: *s.* Julian (envl law). **Education:** Taunton House Sch., Montpelier Coll.; Mons Officer Cadet Sch. Brit.Army –1949. **Experience:** teaching envl issues & ecotourism, natural hist.TV, film, video, & radio; visited 70 countries on all continents; lectured in 48 US States; three quals as underwater diver. **Career:** Asst Dir of Watchers and Sanctuaries 1951–4, Head of Film Unit 1987–92, RSPB; Radio & TV Producer, BBC 1957–87; Sr Lect. Derby U. 1992–. **Achievements:** co-Founder of Brit.Library of Wildlife Sounds 1968, memb.of IUCN SSC 1968– and of WWF Intl Pub.Cttee during 1970s. **Memberships:** ZSL (Scientific F.), Cornell Lab.of Ornith.(Res.Assoc.). **Awards:** Haile Selassie I Gold Medal (Govt of Ethiopia) 1968, Kearton Medal (RGS) 1977, num.for radio & TV progs. **Publications:** *Birds for All Seasons* 1986, *Field Guide to the Bird Songs of Britain & Europe* (recordings) 1981, annual update 1964– of 'Ornith.' entry in Enc.Britannica, 100+ papers. Favours pers.pub.& news media support. **Languages:** Amharic (a little spoken), English. Willing to act as consult.etc. **Address:** Birdswell, Stoney Steep, Wraxall, Bristol BS19 lJZ, England, UK. **Tel.**(office) 44 1332 622282, (home) 44 1275 853418; **fax** 44 1332 622296.

BOTCH, Professor Dr Marina Sergeevna. Wetland ecology, Nature protection esp.protected areas and peatland. Professor of Biology, Team Leader. *B.*28 Jan.1931, St Petersburg (then Leningrad), Russia. Father Sergei Botch, Quaternary geol. *W.: s., d.* **Education:** Leningrad SU, Bot. Dept 1953; Komarov Botl Inst. Russian AS PhD 1954–7. **Experience:** res.in peatland ecol., geog., class., cons.in arctic & boreal zones; consult.in peatland ecol., mgmt, & prot.; teaching peatland ecol.1972–3; admin. **Career:** Jr 1957–66 & Sr 1966–92 Researcher, Professor of Biol. & Team Leader 1992–, Komarov Botl Inst. **Achievements:** init.of peatland prot.in Russia 1969–, creation of mire prot.areas in Russia, orgn of Nature prot.in NW Russia. **Memberships:** IAVS, IMCG, RBS, Swedish Botl–Geogl Soc.(Foreign). **Awards:** Medal & Prize* (Govt of USSR) 1980, Prize (Soros Fndn) 1993. **Publications:** **Mire Ecosystems in the USSR* (co-Author) 1979, *Veg.of Nature Prot.Areas in Leningrad Regn* 1992, *Flora and Veg.of Mires in NW of Russia and Principles of their Prot.*(co-Author) 1993 (all in Russian); 200 others. Favours pers.pub.& news media support. **Languages:** English, German (read), Russian. Willing to act as consult. etc. **Address:** Komarov Botanical Institute, Russian Academy of Sciences, Popova Street 2, 197 376 St Petersburg, Russia. **Tel.**(office) 7 812 234 8426, (home) 7 812 246 7844; **fax** 7 812 234 4512.

BOTHE, Professor Dr Michael. International & comparative international law & policy. Professor of Public Law. *B.*11 June 1938, Berlin, Germany. German. *M.*Ursula. **Education:** studies in Law & Intl Relations at Univs of Heidelberg, Hamburg, & Geneva; Grad.Inst.of Intl Studies (Geneva) Dipl.1966; state exams in law 1961 & 1966, Dr jur.(Heidelberg) 1967, Dr jur.habil.1974. **Experience:** res., teaching & consult.in envl policy & law. **Career:** Res.F. Max-Planck-Inst.for Comparative Public Law & Intl Law 1964–79, Prof.of Public Law at Univs of Heidelberg 1977–, Hannover 1979–, & Frankfurt 1983–. **Achievements:** num.pubns. **Memberships:** GAEL, EELA (VP), IUCN CEPLA. **Award:** Elizabeth Haub Prize. **Publications:** num.books & articles. Indiff.to pers.pub.& news media support. **Languages:** English, French, German, Spanish. Willing to act as consult.etc. **Address:** Johann-Wolfgang-Goethe Universität Fachbereich Rechtswissenschaft, Institüt für Offentliches Recht, Senckenberganlage 31, D-60054 Frankfurt-am-Main, Germany. **Tel.**(office) 49 69 798 2264, (home) 49 6251 4345; **fax** (office) 49 69 798 8446, (home) 49 6251 65240.

BOUCHER, Dr Charles. Autecology, phytosociology, and restoration ecology, of Cape (South Africa) plants and vegetation. Senior Lecturer. *B.*14 Aug.1944, Stellenbosch, SA. S.African. Father Charles Boucher, nurseryman, and mother Eliza Mackay, agric. *M.*Dorothea Anna (co-worker in revision of genus *Pelargonium* and Flora of Namaqualand, SA): 2 *s., d.* Mother-in-law Dr M.C.Olivier (ecol.). **Education:** Hottentots-Holland High Sch.; U.of Stellenbosch, BSc(Hons)(Bot.) 1968, PhD 1987; U.of Cape Town, MSc 1972. **Experience:** res.— phytosoc.of Cape (SA) veg., autecology of endemic plants; consult.— EIA (botl), resto.ecol.; teaching gen.bot.& botl ecol.from BSc to PhD levels. **Career:** Agricl Researcher 1968, Officer-in-Charge 1983–5, Botl Res.Inst. Dept of Agric. (Stellenbosch) 1983–5; Lect.1986–7, Sr Lect. 1988–, Bot.Dept, U.of Stellenbosch. **Achievements:** basic res.on veg.in the Cape Province (SA), autecological studies of rare Cape plants *e.g.Orothamnus zeyheri* and *Audouinia capitata*. **Memberships:** SAAB, SAIEES, SACNAS (Registered Natural Sci.). **Awards:** Nat.Premium Award (co-awardee, Envl Planning Professions' Interdisc.Cttee) 1992, Best Res.Paper (co-awardee, SAAB) 1994. **Publications:** 70 refereed scientific papers (three in Ecosystems of the World series). Indiff.to pers.pub & news media support. **Languages:** Afrikaans, Dutch (basic), English. Further details may be obtained from *Botl Exploration of Southern Africa* (by M.Gunn & L.E.Codd) 1981. Willing to act as consult.etc. **Address:** Botany Department, University of Stellenbosch, PB X1, Matieland 7602, Republic of South Africa. **Tel.**(office) 27 21 808 3064, (home) 27 21 887 1421; **fax** 27 21 808 3607; **e-mail** cb@maties.sun.ac.za .

BOULTON, Mark N. Environmental education mainly in support of NGOs & governments in less-developed countries. Director. *B.*Nov. 1937, Cheltenham, Glos., England, UK. British. *M.* Sonia M.: *s.* Malcolm Andrew (cons.project, Zambia), 2 *d.*incl.Elisabeth Katherine (envl photo-researcher). **Education:** U.of Southampton BSc(Hons)(Zool.), U.of Nottingham Dip.Ed. 1959, Loughborough Coll.of Phys.Educ. Dipl.in Phys.Educ.(Hons) 1959. **Experience:** biol. teaching; teacher training overseas; tech. support for photography, audiovisual prod., desktop publishing & computing; consult.for UN, WWF, & IUCN, on educ. **Career:** Sr Biol. Hartlebury Grammar Sch.1960–63 and Solihull Grammar Sch.1963–67; Lect.Kenyatta Coll. 1967–71; Educ.Officer UN/FAO Zambia 1971–73; Educ. Consult.Nepal UN/FAO 1974; Cons. Educ.Consult.WWF/IUCN 1974–83. Dir ICCE 1984–. **Achievements:** practical (esp.tech.) support for cons.educ.in more than 50 developing countries; Founder Memb.of wild-life clubs in Zambia & Kenya; fndn of ICCE 1984 (UK-based charity). **Membership:** Steering Cttee IUCN CEC. **Award:** Order of the Golden Ark 1985. **Publications:** *Cons.Educ.in Zambia* 1972, *Cons. Educ.in Nepal* 1974, 100+ envl audiovisual presentations. Indiff.to pers.pub.& news media support. **Languages:** English, French (basic). Willing to act as consult.etc. **Address:** International Centre for Conservation Education, Greenfield House, Guiting Power, Cheltenham, Gloucestershire GL54 5TZ, England, UK. **Tel.**(office) 44 1451 850777, (home) 44 1242 674839; **fax** 44 1451 850705.

BOURDEAU, Professor Dr Philippe François. Ecology, environmental management. Professor of Environmental Sciences. *B.*25 Nov. 1926, Rabat, Morocco. Belgian. *M.*Flora Gorirossi (Acarology): 3 *d.* **Education:** U.of Gembloux, Ing. Agronome 1949; Duke U. PhD (Ecol.) 1954. **Experience:** res., consult., admin., teaching. **Career:** Prof.of Bot. SU of N.Carolina 1954–6 and Yale U.1956–62; Prof.of Envl Scis, Université Libre de Bruxelles 1977–; Head of Div.then Dir, Envl Res. Euro.Comm.1962–91; Dir, Euro.Envt Agency Task Force 1991–4. **Achievements:** res. in radioecology & ecotoxicology, mgmt of res. prog.in EU (Pres.of SCOPE 1995–). **Memberships:** Belgian Acad.of Applied Scis (Assoc.), var.scientific socs. **Award:** F.AAAS 1961. **Publications:** incl.*Europe's Envt* (co-Ed.) 1995, Ed. six SCOPE reports on ecotoxicology. Indiff.to pers. pub., favours news media support. **Languages:** Dutch (spoken), English, French, German (spoken), Italian (spoken). Further details may be obtained from *Intl Who's Who* 1994–5. Willing to act as consult.etc. **Address:** Université Libre de Bruxelles, CP 130-02, 50 Avenue F.D.Roosevelt, B-1050 Brussels, Belgium. **Tel.**(office) 32 2 650 4322, (home) 32 2 762 1098; **fax** 32 2 650 4324.

BOURNE, Dr William Richmond Postle. Birds especially of the sea & islands, petrels, marine pollution. Honorary Research Fellow. *B.*11 March 1930, Bedford, England, UK. British. *M.*Sheila: *d.* **Education:** Christ's Coll.Camb.& St Bartholomew's Hosp.London, MB BCh. Cantab.1954. **Experience:** started bird-watching at age 4 and when sent to Bermuda during WWII, Sec. Cambridge Bird Club (expedns to Scandinavia, Pyrenees, and Cape Verde Islands), Nat.Service in Cyprus & Jordan after which studied bird migration with radar and subs. studied seabirds in many countries. **Career:** Field Asst, Edward Grey Inst.1958–61; Res.F. (Hon.1979–) Zool.Dept, Aberdeen U. 1970–. **Achievements:** co-founder of Cyprus Ornithl Soc., founder first Seabird Group; investigated results of Torrey Canyon Oil poll. then incidence of toxic chemicals, distribn of birds at sea; past-Sec. Seabird Cttee of Intl Ornithl Cong.1966–78. **Memberships:** BOU (Council Memb.), Brit. Trust for Ornith.(past Council memb.), SOC (Council Memb.), AOU (Corres.F.). **Award:** Stamford Raffles Award (ZSL) 1993. **Publications:** *Seabirds of Britain & Ireland* (co-Author) 1974; many papers. Indiff.to pers.pub. & news media support. **Languages:** English, French (read). Further details may be obtained from *British Birds,* **17**, pp.123–5. Willing to act as consult.etc. **Address:** 3 Contlaw Place, Milltimber, Aberdeen AB1 0DS, Scotland, UK. **Tel.**(home) 44 1224 732348; **fax** 44 1224 272396.

BOXALL, John Edward. Environmental control, environmental services project management, cleaner production. Assistant Director. *B.*15 March 1945, Haslemere, Surrey, England, UK. British *M.*Fenella. **Education:** London U. BSc

1968, Chartered Civil Engr 1972. **Experience:** since 1980 have worked on waste mgmt strat.& strategic sewage disposal and recently on whole range of control activities incl.air, noise, waste, & water. **Career:** Civil Engr –1980; dev.of policy proposals for waste mgmt 1980–86, Project Mgr for waste facilities and major sewerage & sewage-treatment projects 1988–90, Asst Dir Envl Control, Envl Prot.Dept 1990– (dev.of envl control team), HK Govt. **Achievements:** dev.& implementation of waste disposal system for HK, dev.of proposals for disposal of sewage and of an effective control capability for air, noise, waste, & water, poll. **Memberships:** Instn of Civil Engrs, Inst.of Wastes Mgmt, BIM. Indiff. to pers. pub., favours news media support. **Language:** English. Willing to act as consult.etc. **Address:** Environmental Protection Department, 130 Hennessey Road 28th Floor, Wanchai, Hong Kong. **Tel.**(office) 852 835 1004, (home) 852 818 0755; **fax** 852 838 2155 or 834 5648.

BOYD, Dr John Morton. Conservation of Nature, island ecosystems, biology of pinnepeds, ecology of ungulates, environmental impacts of forest & electricity industries. Environmental Consultant, Hon.Conservation Consultant. *B.*31 Jan.1925, Darvel, Ayrshire, Scotland, UK. British. *M.*Winifred Isobel: 4 *s.*incl.Dr Ian Lamont Boyd (seal biologist, Brit.Antarctic Survey), Keith John Boyd (geol.). **Education:** Darvel Sch., Kilmarnock Acad.; Glasgow U. PhD 1957, DSc 1964, DLitt 1993. **Experience:** res.— pop.ecol.of earthworms, seals, feral sheep, sea birds; tech.— ecol survey of island ecosystems, mgmt planning & operational mgmt of nat.parks, game, forest, & Nature reserves; admin.— Dir NCC in Scotland, co-Chair (Area VI) Anglo-Soviet Jt Envl Comm.; consult.— cons.consult.in natural heritage, Nature cons.in for.& industry, scientific edl consultation. **Career:** Flight Lt Navigator, RAF 1943–47; Glasgow U. student & lect. 1947–57; Regnl Officer 1957–68, Asst Dir 1968–70, Dir (Scotland) 1971–85, NCC; Nuffield Travelling F.in Middle E.& E.Africa 1964–65; co-Chair, Anglo-Soviet Envl Jt Comm.(Area VI), 1974–75; Ecol.Consult. 1985–; Memb.Adv.Cttee on SSSIs in Scotland 1992–. **Achievements:** estab.govt side of Nature cons.& natural heritage in Scotland, Nat.Nature Reserves, & SSSI, natural hist.of the Hebrides esp.exploration of the outlying islands, biol.and protective legis.of Scottish flora & fauna. **Memberships:** F.RSE 1968, F.RSA 1985, F.IBiol.& CBiol.1985, BES 1953, IUCN Comm.on Ecol.1975–85. **Awards:** CBE 1987, Neill Prize (Natural Hist.) (RSE) 1983; Hon.F.RZSS 1985, Hon.F.RSGS 1985. **Publications:** *The Lumbricidae in the Hebrides* 1957, *St Kilda Summer* (co-Author) 1960, *Mosaic of Islands* (co-Author) 1963, *The Highlands & Islands* (co-Author) 1964, *Travels in the Mid-E.& E.Africa* 1966, *Island Survivors — The Ecol.of Soay Sheep* (co-Editor) 1974, *The Natural Envt of the Hebrides* (2 vols) 1979 & 1983, *Fraser Darling's Islands* 1986, *The Hebrides — A Natural Hist.*(co-Author) 1990,

Cons.Status of Sycamore in Britain 1991, *Fraser Darling in Africa* 1992. Indiff.to pers.pub.& news media support. **Language:** English. Willing to act as consult.etc. **Address:** 57 Hailes Gardens, Edinburgh EH13 0JH, Scotland, UK. **Tel.**(home) 44 131 441 3220.

BOYD, Dr William 'Bill' Edgar. Quaternary environmental science: environmental archaeology, cultural heritage management, Australian Aboriginal studies, archaeology. Senior Lecturer in Geography. *B.*12 Sept.1956, Totnes, Devon, England, UK. Australian, British. **Education:** U.of St Andrews BSc(Hons) (Geog.) 1979, Glasgow U. PhD(Geol.) 1982. **Experience:** u.— res.in above subjects, cttee admin.& course coordn, teaching in geol., geog.& engg. **Career:** Res. Asst 1972–5, Res.F.1985–6, Glasgow U.; Sr Teaching F. U.of Adelaide 1986–8; Lect.in Geog. U.of New England 1988–92; Sr Lect.in Geog. Southern Cross U.(was U.of New England until 1994) 1993–. **Achievements:** res.on wide range of envl hist.issues & past human–envt interaction; teaching geog./geol., envl hist., welfare & envt issue geog. **Memberships:** IBS, AEA, IAG, AAA, Australian Inst.for Aboriginal & Torres Strait Islander Studies (elected memb.). **Award:** Edwards Prize for Fieldwork (U.of St Andrews) 1979. **Publications:** 11 books & monogrs, 37 refereed j.articles, 7 peer-reviewed chapters, 22 non-refereed articles, 41 reports, incl.Quaternary pollen analysis in the arid zone of Australia: Dalhousie Springs, C.Australia 1990, Towards a conceptual framework for envl archaeology — envl archaeol.as a key to past geographies 1990, Proto-Swan Bay: A Palaeogeographical Model of the Late Holocene Eighteen Mile Swamp, N.Stradbroke Is., SE Qld 1993, Researches in Post-tertiary Geol.: the 19th Century Study of the Quaternary Coastal Envts of the Firth of Clyde Regn, SW Scotland 1993. Favours pers.pub. & news media support. **Languages:** English, French, German (fair spoken), Spanish (fair read). Willing to act as consult.etc. **Address:** Southern Cross University, POB 157, Lismore, New South Wales 1480, Australia. **Tel.**(office) 61 66 203 007, (home) 61 66 888 245; **fax** 61 66 212 669.

BOYLAND, Desmond Ernest. Conservation administration, organizational structures, wetlands, land-use. Branch Director. *B.*2 June 1941, Rockhampton, Qld, Australia. Australian. *M.*Judith Rose: *s., d.* **Education:** U.of Qld BSc 1966, MSc 1982. **Experience:** res.on botl & land-use studies and vegetation mapping 1966– 81; admin.— emphasis on strat.planning, prog.mgmt, prog. budgeting & staff mgmt in both envl & cons. progs 1981–. **Career:** Bot. 1966– 79; Supervising Dev.Planning Officer 1979–81; Asst Dir, Land Resources Branch 1981–4, Qld Dept of Primary Industries; Mgr, Mainland Estate 1984– 6; Acting Dir (Field Ops) 1986–8, Asst Dir (Policy) 1988–9, Acting Asst Dir (Exec.Services) 1989–91, Acting Dir 1991 (then Qld NPWS) then Regnl Dir, Se Regn 1991–4, Dir Cons. Strat.Branch 1994, (now) Qld Dept of Envt &

Heritage. **Achievements:** vegetation mapping of & land-use studies in Sw Qld, concessionaire mgmt in nat.parks and other prot. areas, mgmt & admin.of cons.progs. **Memberships:** WPSQ, IUCN CNPPA. **Award:** Public Service Medal 1994. **Publications:** A planned approach to Nature cons. mgmt 1992, Cons.— a legitimate land use 1992; Author or co-Author of 35 other pubns. Indiff.to pers.pub.& news media support. **Language:** English. Willing to act as consult.etc. **Address:** Conservation Strategy Branch, Department of Environment and Heritage, POB 155, Brisbane Albert Street, Queensland 4002, Australia. **Tel.**(office) 61 7 225 1506, (home) 61 7 808 3015; **fax** 61 7 227 6386.

BOYLE, Dr Terence P. Aquatic ecology, ecotoxicology; conservation biology, ecological risk analysis; protected area research. Research Ecologist. *B.*11 July 1943, Madison, WI, USA. American *M.*Susan (Historian, NPS). **Education:** U.of New Mexico, BS 1967, MS 1969; U.of Arizona PhD 1979. **Experience:** aquatic ecol.& ecotoxicology, developed lentic & lotic mesocosm for application to community and ecosystem study of toxic contaminants; ecol assessment in US prot.areas and dev.of monitoring systems in flowing waters; organized seven major symposia in intl mtgs in US & abroad; memb. of num.workshops, review panels, task forces, etc. **Career:** Res.Assoc. NSF– RANN 1973–74; leader, Ecosystems Res. Section, Columbia Nat.Fisheries Res.Lab. 1975– 84; Res.Ecol. NPS 1984–93; prog.for Ecol. Studies & Human Dimensions, Natural Resources Res.Unit, Colorado SU 1992–3; Res.Ecol. Nat.Biol.Survey 1993–. **Achievements:** Sr Ecol.Cert. ESA; Chairman, Bd of Professional Certification 1987–89, Intl Affairs Section 1990–91, and Intl Relations Cttce 1993–6, ESA; mcmb.IUCN CNPPA 1991–3; Temperate Ecosystem Directorate, US MAB Prog.1992–4. **Memberships:** ASLO, ISE, ESA, SECT, Assn for Ecosystem Res.Centers. **Award:** Sr Ecologist Cert.(ESA). **Publications:** *Validation & Predictability of Lab.Methods for Assessment of Envl Contaminants* 1982; *New Approaches for Monitoring Aquatic Ecosystems* 1984; 50+ papers. Indifferent to pers.pub.& news media support. **Languages:** English, Spanish. Willing to act as consult.etc. **Address:** National Park Service, Aylesworth NW, Colorado State University, Fort Collins, Colorado 80523, USA. **Tel.**(office) 1 303 491 1452, (home) 1 303 224 4167; **fax** 1 303 491 1511.

BRAMWELL, Dr David. Conservation of insular floras, biogeography & evolution of Canarian flora, conservation biology and conservation ecology of endangered species. Director. *B.*25 Nov.1942, Liverpool, England, UK. British. *M.*Zoe Irene (wildlife artist, authoress, landscape designer); *s.* **Education:** Old Hall Grammar Sch.; U.of Liverpool BSc(Hons) 1966, MSc 1967; Universidad de Sevilla 1968–69; U.of Reading PhD 1971. **Experience:** teaching plant taxonomy, biogeog.; res. in taxonomy, biogeog.,

cons.biol., envl and reserve planning & mgmt. **Career:** Curator, Herbarium of U.of Reading 1971–4; Dir, Jardin Botanico 'Viera y Clavijo' 1974–; Dir, Plan Especial de Protección de Espacios Naturales de Gran Canaria 1984–86. **Achievements:** creation of reserves and a new nat. park in Canary Islands, res.on cons.of endangered plant species, estab.of model botl garden for cons. **Memberships:** F.LS, F.El Museo Canario, IUCN SSC Island Plants SG, BGCI (Trustee). **Awards:** MBE, Sir Peter Scott Merit Award (IUCN SSC). **Publications:** *Wild Flowers of the Canary Islands* (co-Author) 1974, *Plants and Islands* 1979, *Botl Gdns and the WCS* 1987, *Historia Natural de Las Islas Canarias* (co-Author) 1987, *Flores Silvestres de Las Islas Canarias* 1990; 60 papers; Ed.*Botanica Macaronesica.* Dislikes pers.pub., favours news media support. **Languages:** English, French (poor), Spanish. Willing to act as consult. **Address:** Jardin Botanico 'Viera y Clavijo', Apto 14 Tafira Alta, Las Palmas de Gran Canaria, Canary Islands, Spain. **Tel.**(office) 34 28 355921, (home) 34 28 351491; **fax** 34 28 352250.

BRANDINI, Dr Frederico. Marine pelagic ecosystems of tropical and antarctic environments. Centre Director. *B.*18 March 1954, Florianopolis, SC, Brazil. Brazilian. *M.*Sada M.: *d.* **Education:** São Paulo U, D.(Biol.Scis) 1976, PhD(Biol. Oceanogr.) 1986; Tokyo U.of Fisheries, M.(Biol. Oceanogr.) 1981. **Experience:** primary prod.of marine phytoplankton, ecol.of pelagic microorganisms with emphasis on seasonal dynamics and spatial distribn; nutrients' dynamics in aquatic environments; teaching ecol.of phytoplankton & pelagic ecosystems. **Career:** Head of Phytoplankton Lab. 1981–, Dir 1994–, Center for Marine Studies, Fed.U.of Paraná; Chairman, Brazilian OSLR/ IOC/UNESCO 1993–; Brazilian Nominated Memb. SCOR 1994–. **Achievements:** dynamics in shelf & estuarine areas of phytoplankton pops re.hydrographic regime in Se Brazil. **Memberships:** BSPS, JOS (Foreign), Plankton Soc.of Japan (Foreign). **Publications:** c.35 scientific papers; Ed.*Neritica.* Indiff.to pers. pub.& news media support. **Languages:** English, French, Japanese (spoken), Italian (spoken), Portuguese, Spanish. Willing to act as consult.etc. **Address:** Centro de Estudos do Mar, Universidade Federal do Paraná, Pontal do Sul, Paranaguá, Paraná 83255-000, Brazil. **Tel.**(office) 55 41 455 1333, (home) 55 41 253 0358; **fax** 55 41 455 1105.

BREE, Dr Peter J.H.VAN. International Nature conservation, taxonomy of marine mammals. Curator Emeritus. *B.*17 Sept.1927, Tebing Tinggi, Indonesia. Dutch. Father the late Berend van Bree (forester). **Education:** U.of Amsterdam, BSc 1955, MSc 1958, DrSc 1973. **Experience:** res.on taxonomy of mainly marine mammals, field-work on carnivores and marine mammals abroad; admin.— mgmt of Nature cons.projects abroad, bd memb.of many Nature cons.orgns. **Career:** after u.studies appointed as Asst then

Curator, Dept of Mammals, Inst.of Taxonomic Zool. U.of Amsterdam 1959–. **Achievements:** Hon.Sec./Treas. Netherlands Comm. Intl Nature Cons.and Van Tienhoven Fndn, Memb.Steering Cttee IUCN SSC. **Award:** Officer of the Order of Orange Nassau. **Publications:** over 200. Dislikes pers.pub., indiff.to news media support. **Languages:** Dutch, English, French, German. Willing to act as consult.etc. **Address:** Institute of Taxonomic Zoology, Mauritskade 61, 1092 AD Amsterdam, The Netherlands. **Tel.**(office) 31 20 525 5437, (home) 31 20 632 4048; **fax** 31 20 525 7238.

BRENNAN, Mrs Ngairetta Joy. Environment, landcare. Association President, Association Vice-President. *B.*23 Sept.1929, Ulmarra, NSW, Australia. *M.*John Reginald Brennan (Sec. Men of the Trees Assn, Qld): *s.in-law* Ross D.Mc-Kinnon (Curator, Mt Coot-tha Botanic Gdns, Brisbane). **Education:** Methodist Ladies Coll. (Sydney); Sydney 1947–9 & Adelaide 1971–3 Univs Sci.Faculties; Qld U. BSc (Hons)(Envl Studies & Ethology) 1974–9. **Experience:** res. psych.— envl effect on human behaviour; admin. of vol.cons.body & community orgns. **Career:** Sec. St Lucia Garden Club (Qld) 1960–65; Pres. Men of the Trees 1981–; Memb.(First) Mgmt Cttee 1982–, VP 1994–, Greening Australia (Qld). **Achievements:** planting & maintaining trees/veg.(right tree in right place for right reason), raising awareness of value of above, promotion of urban for.values and ecolly sust.dev.through proper land mgmt. **Memberships:** WPSQ (Cttee 1960–68), Men of the Trees (UK) 1965–, ACF 1974–, Natural Resources & Cons.League 1974–, Save the Trees Campaign 1974–, Men of the Trees (Qld) 1981–, Greening Australia (Qld) 1982–. **Awards:** First Life Memb.(Men of the Trees, Qld) 1992, Life Memb.(Greening Australia Qld) 1995, AM 1995, Advance Australia Award 1995. Dislikes pers.pub., indiff.to news media support. **Language:** English. Further details may be obtained from *The First Decade Men of the Trees Qld* 1992. **Address:** 2 Florence Street, Clayfield, Queensland 4011, Australia. **Tel.**(home) 61 7 3262 1096.

BRERETON, Ms Vera Ann. Human resource development, ecotourism. Director of Education & Training. *B.*3 Feb.1949, St Vincent and The Grenadines, W.Indies. Vincentian. *D.: s.* **Education:** U.of W.Indies BA(Hons) (Econ.& Hist.) 1972, U.of Surrey Postgrad.Dipl.(Tourism Studies) 1978. **Experience:** tech.— training (design & facilitating); admin.— orgnl mgmt; consult.— needs assessments, product dev. (tourism), designing of training progs. **Career:** Dir of Tourism, St Vincent and The Grenadines 1979–85; Tourism Dev.Adv.for Brit.Virgin Islands, UNDP 1985–8; Dir of Educ.& Training, Carib.Tourism Orgn 1988–. **Achievement:** Coord.annual Carib.Tourism Orgn Conf.on Ecotourism. **Membership:** ASTD. **Publications:** Ed.of First Carib.Conf.on Educ.& Training for Tourism 1990 and Proc.of *Second & Third*

Annual Carib.Ecotourism Confs 1992 & 1993. Indiff.to pers.pub., favours news media support. **Language:** English. Willing to act as consult. etc. **Address:** Caribbean Tourism Organization, Sir Frank Walcott Building (2nd floor), Culloden Farm, St Michael, Barbados, West Indies. **Tel.** (office) 1 809 424 5242, (home) 1 809 424 4114; **fax** 1 809 424 3065.

BREWBAKER, Professor Dr James Lynn. Crop & tree improvement, agriculture of tropics. Professor of Horticulture, Genetics, and Agronomy. *B.*11 Oct.1926, St Paul, MN, USA. American. *M.*Kathryn B.(primary sch.envl educ.): *s.* **Education:** Colorado U. BS *cum laude* (Gen. Sci.) 1948, Cornell U. PhD(Plant Breeding & Biometry) 1952. **Experience:** res.— directed leucaena & corn improvement intlly, released num.cultivars with improved yield & pest-resistance; teaching — taught and published textbooks on agricl genetics, experimental design and quantitative genetics, supervised 45 PhD & MS graduates; consult.— founded & presided over Nitrogen Fixing Tree Assn, and intl on trop.agrofor. **Career:** NSF Postdoctl F'ship held at U.of Lund 1952; Asst Prof.of Agron. U.of Philippines 1953–5; Assoc.Geneticist, Biol.Dept Brookhaven Nat.Lab. USAEC 1956–61; Geneticist, Intl Agricl Exposition (Delhi) 1959; Assoc. Prof.1961, Prof.of Hort. Genetics & Agron. 1964–, Dept of Hort. U.of Hawaii; Geneticist, Maize Prog.(Bangkok) 1967, and Resident, Bellagio Study Center (Italy) 1993, Rockefeller Fndn; Consult. IAEA (Philippines) 1970; Vis. Prof. Dept of Plant Breeding, Cornell U.1974 & U.of Qld 1993; Vis.Sci. CIAT 1978, Taiwan Agricl & For.Res.Insts 1981, ANU 1985, & IITA 1989. **Achievements:** bred productive leguminous trees for trop.agrofor., founded Nitrogen Fixing Tree Assn 1980, bred disease- and pest-resistant maize. **Memberships:** ASA, ASHS, ASF, CSSA (F.1985), Hawaiian AS (Pres.1978), Hawaiian Botl Soc.(Pres.1967), Hawaii Crop Improvement Assn (Exec.Sec.1969–94), ISTF, Nat.Sweet Corn Breeders' Assn (Pres.1987), Nitrogen Fixing Tree Assn (Pres.1981–90), Sigma Xi (Hawaii, Pres.1990). **Awards:** Elected F.(ASA) 1975 & (CSSA) 1985, Outstanding Service Award (Office of Rural Dev. Korea) 1978, Excellence in Res.(U.of Hawaii) 1980, Disting.Service to Agric.(Gamma Sigma Delta) 1982, G.J.Watumull Disting.Achievement Award (Intl Agric.) 1982, Crop Sci.Res.Award (ASA) 1984, Recognition by Senate of State of Hawaii 1986, Intl Inventor's Award (For.)(Swedish Inventors' Assn) 1986, Sci.of the Yr (ARCS) 1988, Superior Service Award (USDA) 1990, Genetics and Plant Breeding Award (NCCPB) 1992, Crop Sci.Career Award (de Kalb) 1995. **Publications:** incl.*Agricl Genetics* (transl.into seven languages) 1964, *Experimental Design on a Spreadsheet* 1993, *Biometry on a Spreadsheet* 1994, *Quantitative Genetics on a Spreadsheet* 1995; *c.*206 scientific pubns (Author or co-Author) incl six chapters; Ed.*Nitrogen-Fixing Tree Res.Reports* 1983–92, *Leucaena Res.Re-*

ports 1980–, and 12 addit.documents. Indiff.to pers.pub.& news media support. **Language:** English. Further details may be obtained from num.pubns incl.*Amer.Men & Women in Sci.* 1960–, *Dict.of Intl Biog.*1969, *Intl Book of Honor* 1982, *Intl Who's Who of Contemporary Achievement* 1984, *Who's Who in Sci.& Engg* 1991. Willing to act as consult.etc. **Address:** Department of Horticulture, University of Hawaii, 3190 Maile Way, Honolulu, Hawaii 96822, USA. **Tel.**(office) 1 808 956 7985, (home) 1 808 262 4869; **fax** 1 808 956 3894.

BRIDGEWATER, Dr Peter. Landscape ecology and vegetation; seascape ecology; biodiversity conservation and management; conservation and management of mangrove and salt marsh. Chief Executive Officer. *B.*31 Dec. 1945, Bristol, England, UK. Australian, British. *M.*Gillian: *d.* **Education:** U.of Durham, BSc (Hons) 1967, PhD 1970. **Experience:** res., admin., field exp. on all continents. **Career:** var.u.positions in Australia 1970–82; Dir, Australian Bur.of Flora and Fauna 1982–8; First Asst Sec. Australian Dept of the Arts, Sport, the Envt, Tourism and Territories 1988–9; Chief Sci. NCC(UK) 1989–90; CEO, ANCA 1990–. **Achievements:** listing of the Wet Tropics of Qld World Heritage area; estab.of Southern Ocean Whale Sanctuary; dev.of indigenous involvement in prot.areas mgmt. **Memberships:** IWC (Australian Commissioner 1990–, VC 1991–4, Chairman 1994–), IUCN CNPPA (VC Australian Realm 1990–93) 1990– & SSC 1990–, ANC for UNESCO 1993–, Chairman UNESCO MAB Council 1994–, Standing Cttee for Conv.on Migratory Species (Bonn Conv., VC 1991–4, Chairman 1994–). **Awards:** Computerland Award (Smithsonian Instn) 1993 & Picasso Gold Medal (UNESCO) 1995 both awarded to ANCA. **Publications:** 100+ incl. Biodiv.and landscape 1988, NCS — or How to Arrive at the 21st Century in Good Shape 1993, Conspectus of major veg.units for Australia 1994, Prot.Areas in the Australian Realm — A Review (co-Author) 1994. Positive re.pers. pub. & news media support. **Languages:** English, French (read). Willing to act as consult.etc. **Address:** Australian Nature Conservation Agency, GPO Box 636, Canberra, Australian Capital Territory 2601, Australia. **Tel.**61 6 250 0222; **fax** 61 6 250 0228.

BRINCHUK, Dr Mikhail M. Environmental law, air pollution, toxic chemicals, solid & hazardous wastes, industrial safety. Director. *B.*4 Feb. 1945, Brest, Byelarus. Byelarussian (White Russian). *M.*Lydia: *d.* **Education:** Patrice Lumumba Peoples' Friendship U. LLB 1973; USSR AS PhD 1978. **Experience:** 20 yrs' res.in envl law. **Career:** Jr Researcher 1976–82, Sr Researcher 1982–91, Dir Sector of Ecol.Law 1991–2, Dir Center for Envl Legal Studies 1992–, Inst.of State & Law, Russian AS. **Achievements:** res. of legal problems of envl prot., air prot., toxic substances & waste control, elaboration of drafts of USSR & Russian laws in field of envl prot. **Memberships:**

IUCN CEL, Scientific Councils of Inst.of State & Law, Constitutional Court of Russia. **Awards:** Silver Medal 1982, Bronze Medal 1984, USSR Exhibition of Econ., DSc.Hon. (USSR AS) 1991, Achievements. **Publications:** *Legal Prot.of the Atmos. Air* 1985, *Legal Prot.of the Envt from Poll.by Toxic Substances* 1990; several chapters *e.g.* Mgmt in the Field of Envl Sci.in the Union Republics 1990; *c.*70 papers. **Languages:** Byelarussian, English, Russian, Ukrainian. Willing to act as consult.etc. **Address:** Znamenka str.10, Moscow 119841, Russia. **Tel.**(office) 7 95 291 3827, (home) 7 95 173 6288; **fax** 7 95 291 8574.

BRODEUR, Paul A. Journalism, writing. Staff Writer. *B.*16 May 1931, Boston, MA, USA. American. *M.*Milane: *s., d.* **Education:** Harvard Coll.1949–53. **Experience:** staff writer at *The New Yorker* for 35 years. **Career:** US Army Counterintelligence Corps 1953–56; Staff Writer, *The New Yorker* 1958–; Lect. Columbia U.Grad. Sch.of Journalism 1970–80. **Achievements:** alerted the nation to health & envl hazards posed by asbestos inhalation, CFC destruction of the ozone layer, microwave & radiofrequency radiation, and power-line magnetic fields. **Awards:** Nat.Magazine 1973, Sidney Hillman Fndn 1974, AAAS 1975, Silver Gavel (ABA) 1985, Global 500 Roll of Honour (UNEP) 1989. **Publications:** *Asbestos and Enzymes* 1972, *Expendable Americans* 1974, *The Zapping of Amer.*1977, *Outrageous Misconduct: The Asbestos Industry on Trial* 1985, *Currents of Death* 1989, *The Gt Power Line Cover-up* 1993. Favours pers.pub.& news media support. **Languages:** English, French (reasonable). **Address:** c/o The New Yorker, 20 West 43rd Street, New York, New York 10036, USA. **Tel.**(office) 1 212 840 3800; **fax** 1 212 536 5735.

BROOKS, Dr Peter Martin. Wildlife management, conservation of the African Rhinoceros. Head of Scientific Services. *B.*21 Feb.1946, Camb., England, UK. British. *M.*Elizabeth K.: 3 *s.* **Education:** U.of London BSc(Hons) (Zool.) 1967, U.of Durham MSc 1970, U.of Pretoria DSc 1974. **Experience:** wildlife mgmt res.on ungulate movements & census in Natal; strat. dev.& advice on cons.progs incl.mgmt planning, coordn of species and ecosystem cons.res. activities, and of dev.& land-use planning. **Career:** Ecol.& Regnl Ecol.for S.Zululand (incl.Hluhluwe-Umfolozi Park) 1972–81, Chief Ecol.1982–90, Head Scientific Services 1990–, Natal Parks Bd. **Achievements:** consolidation of res.role in mgmt ops; cons.mgmt advice to intl non-govt agencies & African cons.auths; formation of Rhino.Mgmt Group to coordinate plan for SA & Namibia. **Memberships:** IUCN African Rhino. SG (Chairman 1990–) & Rhino. Mgmt Group (Chairman 1989–), SAIE, Wildlife Mgmt Assn. **Publications:** *The Hluhluwe-Umfolozi Reserve: An Ecol.Case Hist.*1983, *Cons. Plan for the Black Rhino.in SA and Namibia* 1989, 90+ reports & papers. **Language:** English. Willing to judge proposals. **Address:** Natal Parks Board, POB 662, Pietermaritzburg

3200, Republic of South Africa. **Tel.**(office) 27 331 471961, (home) 27 331 471100; **fax** 27 331 471037.

BROUGH, Anthony Thomas. Financial management of the environment. Retired. *B.*25 Aug. 1932, Haywards Heath, W.Sussex, England, UK. British. *M.*Valerie Sibyl: *s., d.* **Education:** St Catharine's Coll.Camb. MA(Econ.) 1954. **Experience:** admin., consult. **Career:** Sr Economist Statistician 1961–3, Chief Economist Statistician 1963–70, Fin.Adv.1970–78, Govt of Kenya; Chief, Fund Prog.Mgmt Branch 1978–85, Asst Exec.Dir & subs.Dep.Exec.Dir 1985–93, UNEP. **Achievements:** intro.of fin. planning & programming techniques in field of envt, planning & programming Multilateral Fund estab.under Montreal Protocol and GEF. **Award:** CBE 1994. Indiff.to pers.pub.& news media support. **Language:** English. Willing to act as consult.etc. **Address:** POB 30181, Nairobi, Kenya. **Tel.**(home) 254 2 582338; **fax** 254 2 762178.

BROWN, Lester Russell. Analysis of global environmental & environmentally-related issues. President & Senior Researcher. *B.*28 March 1934, Bridgeton, NJ, USA. American. *D.*: *s., d.* **Education:** Rutgers U. BS(Agricl Sci.) 1955, U.of Maryland MS(Agricl Econ.) 1959, Harvard U. MPA 1962. **Experience:** farming, agric., public speaking, writing, editing, consult., admin. **Career:** Adv.to Sec.of Agric.1964–6; Admin. IADS 1966–9; co-founder ODC 1969– 74; Founder 1974, now Pres.& Sr Researcher 1974–, Worldwatch Inst. **Achievements:** founding of Worldwatch Inst., launching of *State of the World* reports & *World Watch* bimonthly magazine, estab.of *Envl Alert* (book series) 1991– (all pers.papers & MSs have been requested by The Library of Cong.). **Memberships:** Cosmos Club, Council on Foreign Relations, Northwest Envt Watch (Bd). **Awards:** 'Genius Award' (MacArthur Fndn), UN Envt Prize 1989, Gold Medal (WWF) 1990, Blue Planet Prize 1994; num.others & hon.degrees. **Publications:** 12 books incl.*Man, Land & Food* 1963, *World Without Borders* 1972, *By Bread Alone* (co-Author) 1974, *Bldg a Sust.Soc.*1981, *Saving the Planet: How to Shape an Envlly Sust.Global Econ.*(co-Author) 1991, *Vital Signs: The Trends That Are Shaping Our Future* (co-Author) 1992, *State of the World* (Project Dir & co-Author) 1984–, *World Watch* 1988–, *Worldwatch Papers* (monogr.series); num. others. Favours pers.pub. & news media support. **Language:** English. **Address:** Worldwatch Institute, 1776 Massachusetts Avenue NW, Washington, DC 20036, USA. **Tel.**(office) 1 202 452 1999, (home) 1 202 328 6256; **fax** 1 202 296 7365.

BROWN, Dr William Yancey. Natural history. Company Vice-President & Environmental Director. *B.*13 Aug.1948, Artesia, CA, USA. American. *M.*Mary Elizabeth: 2 *d.* **Education:** U.of Virginia, BA(Biol.) 1969; Johns Hopkins U. MAT 1970; U.of Hawaii, PhD(Zool.) 1973;

Harvard Law School, JD 1977. **Experience:** study of pop.biol.of sea birds during 1970s. Asst Prof. Biol.Scis, Mt.Holyoke Coll.1973–74; part-time with EPA 1973–77; headed Bd of Trustees, Envl Law Soc. Harvard Law Sch.1975–76. **Career:** Dir.Endangered Species Scientific Auth. 1977–79; Dir Intl Conv.Adv.Comm. 1979–81; Sr Sci., Attorney, & Acting Exec.Dir, EDF 1981–85; Envl Dir & VP, Waste Mgmt Inc.(now WMX Technologies Inc.) 1985–. **Memberships:** num.scientific professional & hon.socs, DC Bar, State Dept Antarctic Adv. Cttee, VC US Envl Training Inst., Bds of ANS & US Cttee for UNEP. **Publications:** extensive. **Address:** WMX Technologies Inc., 1155 Connecticut Avenue NW, Suite 800, Washington, DC 20036, USA. **Tel.**1 202 467 4480; **fax** 1 202 659 8752.

BRUNDTLAND, Dr Gro Harlem. Environment, conservation. *B.*20 April 1939, Oslo, Norway. Norwegian. *M.*Arne Olav Brundtland: 3 *s., d.* **Education:** U.of Oslo, MD 1963; Harvard U. M PH 1965. **Experience:** mostly pol., being leader of Cttee on Foreign & Constitutional Affairs 1980–81, 1981–86, 1989–90; has actively promoted equal rights & role of women in pol. **Career:** Med.Officer 1966–68; Asst Med.Dir 1968–74; Min.of Envt 1974–79; Dep.Leader, Norwegian Labour Party 1975– and Party Leader 1981–92; memb.of Storting for City of Oslo 1977–, Dep.Leader of Labour's Parliamentary Group 1979; Leader 1981–86, 1989–90; PM of Norway, Feb.–Oct.1981, 1986–89 & 1990–; after serving on Palme Comm.estab.& chaired WCED at request of UN Sec.-Gen. **Memberships:** first VP of the Socialist Intl 1992, Chairman WCED 1983, Independent Comm.on Disarmament & Security Issues (the Palme Comm.). **Awards:** Third World Prize 1988, Indira Gandhi Prize 1988, Onassis Fndn Delphi Prize 1992. **Publications:** WCED Report '*Our Common Future*' 1987 from which emanated the UNCED 1992; num. articles. **Languages:** English, Norwegian (mother tongue). **Address:** Prime Minister's Office, POB 8001, 0030 Oslo, Norway. **Tel.**47 22 349090; **fax** 47 22 349500.

BRYSON, Professor Dr Reid A. Climatology, interdisciplinary environmental studies, and climate change. Senior Scientist. *B.*7 June 1920, Detroit, MI, USA. American. *M.*Frances Edith: 3 *s., d.* **Education:** Denison U. AB (Geol.) 1941, U.of Chicago PhD(Met.) 1948. **Experience:** res.— PI, dynamics of Lake Mendota, Center for Climatic Res.& Climate/Food Res.Project; co-Investigator, Historical Climatology & Cultural Change; Cooperative Res.Prog.with India Met. Dept on Climatic Modification in Indian Desert; admin.— Dir Inst.for Envl Studies, U.of W–M; Pres.AQA, Chairman Interdisc.Studies Cttee on Future of Man, and Madison Campus Spec.Cttee on Envl Studies; consult.— Chairman NAS–NRC Cttee on Geog.Adv.to Office of Naval Res., NAS– NRC Cttee on Interdisc.Problems, NAS–NAE Envl Studies Bd., Memb.Council Smithsonian Instn, US Geol.Survey Geog.Section, UNEP, UNFAO, NSF, Envt Canada. **Career:** Asst Prof. Geol.& Met.1946–48, Met. 1948–50, Assoc.Prof.Met.1950–56, Prof.Met. 1957–86, Prof.Met.& Geog.1968–86, Emer. 1986–, Prof. 1970–86 & Dir 1970–85 Inst.for Envl Studies 1970–86, Emer.1986–, Sr Sci., Center for Climatic Res.1986, all at U.of W–M; Prof. Met.& Chairman 1956–57, U.of Arizona. **Achievements:** set up U.of Wisconsin Dept of Met.1948, built it into leading dept by 1960s; likewise Center for Climatic Res.1962 to emphasize interdisc.nature of climatology, and importance of climatic change; developed technique of airstream analysis in relation to climate & biota 1962, and evidence of nonstationary climatic series; in 1970s raised gen. awareness of importance of climatic change with respect to world food situation; estab.Inst.for Envl Studies 1970 and guided its growth for first 15 yrs. **Memberships:** Pres.AQA 1988–90, F.AMS, Pres.Wisconsin Phenological Soc.1961, SAA, F.AAAS, F.Wisconsin Acad.of Scis, Arts, and Letters (Pres.1984). **Awards:** Denison U. Hon.DSc 1971, Banta Medal for Lit.Achievement 1978, Hubert H.Humphrey Disting. Prof'ship in Intl Affairs, Macalester Coll.1979, Reid A.Bryson Disting.Prof'ship of Climate, Envt and People, founded at U.of Wisconsin, Global 500 Roll of Honour (UNEP) 1990, Best Paper Prize (*EC*) 1990, Sial Disting.Lectureship (Furman U.) 1990. **Publications:** over 220 incl.*Climates of Hunger* (co-Author) 1977, Synoptic climatology of the Arizona summer precipitation singularity (co-Author) 1955, Some aspects of the variance spectra of tree rings and varnes (co-Author) 1961, Radiocarbon & soils evidence of former forest in the s.Canadian tundra (co-Author) 1965, Airmasses, streamlines and the boreal forest 1966, An eval.of the thermal Rossby number in the Pleistocene (co-Author) 1968, The man–environment system approach 1970, On the climates of hist.(co-Author) 1980, Ancient climes and faraway times 1981, Year-in-advance forecasting of the Indian monsoon rainfall (co-Author) 1982, Milankovitch and global ice vol.simulation (co-Author) 1986, Civilization and rapid climatic change 1988, Late quaternary volcanic modulation of Milankovitch ultimate forcing 1988, Envl opportunities and limits for dev.1989, A macrophysical model of the Holocene intertropical convergence and jetstream positions and rainfall for the Saharan regn 1992, *Looking to the Future* 1993. Indiff.to pers.pub., willing to talk to news media. **Language:** English. Further details may be obtained from *Who's Who in Amer., Men of Achievement.* Willing to act as consult.etc.occasionally. **Address:** Center for Climatic Research, University of Wisconsin–Madison, 1225 West Dayton Street, Madison, Wisconsin 53706, USA. **Tel.**1 608 262 5814; **fax** 1 608 262 5964.

BUBLINEC, Professor Eduard. Soil science, ecology, monitoring. Institute Director. *B.*1 Feb. 1937 Komárno, Slovak Republic. Slovakian. *M.* Ana: *s.*, 3 *d.* **Education:** Fac.of For. U.of Zvolen,

Dipl.Ing.1960, CSc(Soil Sci.) 1969. **Experience:** teaching & res.in soil sci., acid precipitation & envl monitoring. **Career:** scientific worker, Forest Res.Inst. 1964–84; Head of Dept of Soil Sci.1984–90, Dir 1990–, Inst.of Forest Ecol.; Chair of Natural (Forest) Envt (Dept of Natural Envt), Fac.of For. Tech.U.1993–. **Achievements:** cycling of nutrients in forest ecosystems, acid precipitation, podsolization. **Memberships:** Slovak Ecol. Soc., Slovak SSS. **Award:** Silver Stage (Slovak AS) 1987. **Publications:** four books incl.*Podsolic Soil-forming Process under Pine Ecosystems in Temperate Zone* (in Slovak) 1974, *Output of Nutrients by Tree Harvesting from Spruce Ecosystems* (in Slovak) 1993; *c.*150 others. **Languages:** Czech, English, German (written), Russian (spoken), Slovak. Willing to act as consult.etc. **Address:** Faculty of Forestry, Technical University, Masarykova 24, 960 53 Zvolen, Slovak Republic. **Tel.**42 855 635 ext.499 or 855 24487; **fax** 42 855 27485.

BUCKLEY, Professor Dr Ralf Christopher. Ecology; environmental management, law, & economics; ecotourism; environment & trade. Professor of Ecotourism, Centre Director. *B.*13 April 1954, Bishops Castle, England, UK. Australian, British. **Education:** U.of Camb. BA(Hons) 1973, MA 1975; ANU, PhD 1978. **Experience:** envl sci.& mgmt res.& consult.in 40+ countries over 20 yrs, gave 30+ exec. training courses, sci.leader of expedns in Australia, Asia, & Africa, expert witness, govt & industrial enquiries in tourism, biodiv., overseas aid, & sust.dev., TV & radio progs on ecotourism and envl mgmt. **Career:** CSIRO F. AIMS 1979; Rothmans Res.F.1980–81, SRF 1988, ANU; Chief Envl Sci. AMDEL 1982–7; Professorial F. U.of New England 1987; Fndn Prof.of Envl Mgmt, Bond U.1989–90; Dir, Centre for Envl Mgmt (NGO) 1989–; Dir, Intl Centre for Ecotourism Res.1992–, Prof.of Engg and Applied Sci. 1991–5, Chair in Ecotourism 1995–, Griffith U. **Achievements:** early work on desert ecol.& geomorph., plant–insect interactions; pioneered dev.& intro.of envl planning & mgmt tools *e.g.*regnl envl planning, envl audit, corporate insurance, accounting, & mgmt, systems, and envl policy devs re.aid & trade; instrumental in improving Australian envl policy, legis., and practice. **Memberships:** IBiol., INTECOL, IAIA, AIB, Ecol.Soc.of Australia, EIA, NELA, Mineral Industry Consults' Assn, ATB. **Awards:** Program Leader (Japan–Australia Scientific Tech.Agreement) 1989–92, Emer.Prof.(China Nat.Envl Acad.), Scientific Adv.Cttee (AIMM), Inaugural Chair (Qld Wet Tropics World Heritage Mgmt Auth.), Sr Fulbright F.1994. **Publications:** seven books incl.*Ant–Plant Interactions in Australia* 1992, *Perspectives in Envl Mgmt* 1992, *Intl Trade, Investment & Envt* 1994; 100+ j.articles, 100+ major consult.reports, 300+ addit.; Edl Bds of var.journals. Indiff.to pers. pub., favours news media support. **Languages:** English, French (limited). Willing to act as consult.etc. **Address:** 22 Monaro Road, Mudgeeraba, Queensland 4213, Australia. **Tel.**(office) 61 7 5594 8668, (home) 61 7 55302 371; **fax** 61 7 5594 8679.

BUDOWSKI, Dr Gerardo. Conservation of tropical forests, ecotourism, appropriate land-use including agroforestry, management of protected areas and buffer zones. Director. *B*.10 June 1925, Berlin, Germany. Venezuelan. *M*.Thelma T.: 2 *d*. incl.Tamara Lea (Pres.of an ecotourism agency). **Education:** Universidad C.Caracas, Ingeniero Agrónomo 1948; IICA (Turrialba), MS 1954; Yale Sch.of For. PhD 1962. **Experience:** teaching at grad.level for several yrs, directed 15 intl short courses, managed UNESCO's progs on ecol.& cons.and involved in orgn of their 1968 'Biosphere Conf.', field-work in Latin Amer., Africa & Asia. **Career:** Forest Researcher 1947–52, Head 1951–2, Forest Service, Venezuela; Forester, OAS 1953–66; Vis.Prof. UCB 1967; Prog.Specialist for Ecol.& Cons. UNESCO 1967–70; DG IUCN 1970–76; Head Natural Resources, CATIE 1976–86; Dir Natural Resources, U.for Peace 1986–. **Achievements:** fieldwork in 16 countries in Latin Amer., five in Africa, and six in S & SE Asia; teaching at grad.level for over 35 yrs; six yrs as DG of IUCN, six as Bd Memb.of WWF Intl; 200+ pubns. **Memberships:** IUCN CEC, CNPPA, Comm.on Ecol., and one WG, ISTF, Organizing Cttee of Earth Council. **Awards:** Henri Pittier Award (Govt of Venezuela), Order of the Golden Ark, Hon.Memb.& Fred Packard Award (IUCN), 'Semper virens' (Govt of Nicaragua), Memb.of Honour (WWF), Hon Memb.(SAF), most outstanding IICA/CATIE grad.in past 50 yrs. **Publications:** *La conservacion como Instrumento para el Desarrollo* 1985, The Socioeconomic Effects of Forest Mgmt: The Case of C.Amer.and the Carib.1982, From Assisi to Costa Rica: What Have We Learned 1991; 200+ papers. Indiff.to pers.pub., favours news media support. **Languages:** English, French, German, Portuguese (good), Spanish. Further details may be obtained from *Intl Who's Who* 58th edn. Willing to act as consult. etc. **Address:** POB 198, 2300 Curridabat, San José, Costa Rica. **Tel.**(office) 506 2491 072, (home) 506 2253 008; **fax** 506 253 4227.

BUÉ, Dr Alain. Geopolitical aspects of environment and protection policies. Maître de Conférences in Geography. *B*.3 June 1946, Harrow, England, UK. French. **Education:** U.of Paris 8 Vincennes, Docteur IIIème Cycle (Geog.) 1982. **Experience:** res.& consult.in Africa & Europe for envt, prot., green spaces, & vol. work-camps in those fields. **Achievements:** nat.parks & other prot.areas, geopolitics. **Memberships:** IUCN CNPPA, JNE, French Assn of Journalistes et Ecrivains pour la Nature. **Publications:** 20 papers on geog.& human ecol., vol.work-camps in the fields on envt, nat.parks. Indiff.to pers. pub. **Languages:** English, French, German (spoken), Italian (spoken). Willing to act as consult. etc. **Address:** 17 Rue de Lappe, 75011 Paris, France. **Tel.**(home) 33 14 700 2363.

BURBIDGE, Dr Andrew Arnold. Conservation of threatened species & ecosystems, and of mammals & reptiles. Unit Director, Research Scientist. *B*.2 Feb.1942, Isle of Wight, Hampshire, England, UK. Australian. *M*.Merilyn: *s*., 2 *d*.incl.Frances Jean (marine biol.). **Education:** U.of Western Australia BSc (Hons) 1963, PhD 1967. **Experience:** res., admin., consult. **Career:** Asst Prof.of Zool. U. of Texas at Austin 1967–8; Res.Officer 1968–71, Sr Res.Officer 1971–8, Chief Res.Officer Wildlife 1978–85, Dept of Fisheries & Wildlife (originally Fisheries & Fauna); Vis.Sci. BC Ecol. Reserves Prog.1976; Sr Prin.Res. Sci. 1985–7, Dir of Res.1987–92, Dir Threatened Species & Communities Unit and Res.Sci. 1992–, Dept of Cons.& Land Mgmt, WA. **Achievements:** two vertebrate animals named in recognition of pioneering res.into status of Kimberley, Western Australia, fauna — the skink *Ctenotus burbidgei* Storr 1975 and the rock-wallaby *Petrogale burbidgei* Kitchener & Sanson 1978. **Memberships:** num. since 1972; Australian & NZ Envt & Cons. Council Task Forces, Endangered Fauna Network 1992– and Endangered Species & Communities Nat.Strat.(Chair) 1992–3; Endangered Species Adv.Cttee (Commonwealth Minister for the Envt) 1988–92; Endangered Species Adv. Cttee (Chair) and Endangered Species Scientific Subcttee (Chair), Commonwealth Endangered Species Prot.Act; IUCN SSC, Regnl Memb. 1991–, Australasian Marsupials & Monotremes SG 1978– (Chair 1991–), Tortoises & Freshwater Turtles SG 1981–. **Publications:** Ed.or co-Ed.of 12 books, conf. proc.or other major pubns incl.*The Status of Kangaroos and Wallabies in Australia* (Ed.) 1977, *Endangered Vertebrates of Australia and its Is.Territories* (co-Ed.) 1984, *Nature Cons.: the Role of Remnants of Native Veg.*(co-Ed.) 1987, Australian and NZ islands: nature cons.values and mgmt.(Ed.) 1989; Author or co-Author of 79 scientific papers & reports and 39 educl or other short articles. **Language:** English. Willing to act as consult.etc. **Address:** POB 51, Wanneroo, Western Australia 6065, Australia. **Tel.**61 9 405 5128; **fax** 61 9 306 1066.

BURBRIDGE, Dr Peter R. Environmental management & planning, coastal-zone management. Senior Lecturer. *B*.9 Nov. 1942, Gravesend, Kent, England, UK. British. *M*.Dr Veronica (envl planning, rural planning & mgmt). **Education:** Heriot-Watt U./Edinburgh Coll.of Art, Dipl.in Town & Country Planning 1968; Cornell U. MPS 1976, PhD 1978. **Experience:** 15 yrs' dev.planning & envl mgmt mainly in Asia as consult., extensive work with UN agencies, WWF, & IUCN, on envl mgmt & prog.dev. **Career:** res.into regnl planning, Min.of Housing & Local Govt 1966–7; res.& Lect. Econ.& Phys.Planning, Heriot-Watt U.1968–76; Project Specialist in Resources Mgmt, Ford Fndn Indonesia 1978–81; Consult.1981–92; Sr Lect. Dept of Envl Sci. Stirling U.1991–. **Achievement:** strengthening capacity of people from developing countries to plan & manage sust. resource dev. **Memberships:** RTPI, Phi Kappa Phi (Life), IUCN Comm.on Ecol., Eurocoast (UK). **Award:** Carnegie F.1974. **Publications:** Envl guidelines for resettlement in the humid tropics (co-Author) 1989, Integrated planning & mgmt of freshwater envts incl. wetlands (keynote address) 1992, Review of the experiences with integrated coastal mgmt by UNEP, IUCN & WWF (co-Author) 1992, Guidelines for oil & gas exploration and prod.in mangrove ecosystems 1993, Control & regulation of the envl impact of fish farming in Scotland (co-Author) 1993, Review of Scottish coastal planning issues (co-Author) 1993, Overview & guidelines for integrated planning & mgmt of tidal wetlands (co-Ed.) 1993. **Languages:** English, French (fair), Indonesian. Willing to act as consult. etc. **Address:** Department of Environmental Science, University of Stirling, Stirling FK9 4LA, Scotland, UK. **Tel.**(office) 44 1786 467849, (home) 44 1764 670900; **fax**(office) 44 1786 467853, (home) 44 1764 670981.

BURGER, Professor Dr Joanna. Behavioural ecology of vertebrates, biomonitoring, behavioural toxicology (particularly lead in birds); effects of incubation temperature on development and behaviour of snakes; population dynamics and effects of people on coastal birds (particularly endangered and threatened species). Professor of Biology. *B.*18 Jan.1941, Schenectady, NY, USA. American. *M.*Professor Dr Michael Gochfeld *qv: step-s., step-d.* **Education:** SUNY at Albany, BS 1963; Cornell U. MS 1964; U.of Minn. PhD 1972. **Experience:** res.— cons.and effects of people on coastal birds, partic. endangered & threatened species; biomonitoring of coastal species, partic.colonial species, to determine pop.status, possible declines, and possible role of people; biomonitoring of heavy-metals in birds and other vertebrates in several countries; behaviour & ecol.of coastal & marine birds in num.locations; landscape scale issues involving migrant shorebirds and strats for preserv.of migrant birds; effects of incubation temp.on dev.physiol., and behaviour of Pine Snakes *(Pituophis melanoleucus)*; admin.— Dir of Ecol.and Evol.Grad.Prog. and Assoc.Chair for Res.and Grad.Educ.in Biol.Scis, Rutgers U.; Dir of Elemental Analysis Lab., EOHSI 1990–; Bd of Dirs, Orgn for Trop.Studies; consult.— Bd of Envl Sci.& Toxicology, USNAS 1989–91; member of US SCOPE 1991–; US delegate to Intl SCOPE mtg in Sevilla 1992; Governor's Endangered and NonGame Species Council, State of NJ 1980–93; Port Auths of NY & NJ, FAA, US EPA, and private industry; teaching — undergrad.courses in ecol., evol., & animal behaviour, grad.courses in animal behaviour, ecol. risk; Dir grad.prog.in Ecol.& Evol., Rutgers U.1978–93; co-Dir, Envl Track for Toxicology Grad.Prog.1992–. **Career:** Instr. SUNY Coll.at Buffalo 1964–68; grad.student 1968–72, post-doctl 1972–4, Asst Prof.1973–76, Assoc.Prof. 1976–82, Prof.1982–93, Prof.II 1993–, all at

Rutgers U. **Achievements:** dev.of grad.prog.in Ecol.& Evol.; exam.of pop.dynamics and behavioural ecol.of Common Tern *(Sterna hirundo)*, Least Tern *(S. albitrons)*, & Black Skimmer *(Rhyncops nigra)*, over a 15-yrs' period; res.led to listing of Black Skimmers and Least Terns on the NJ Endangered Species List; similar work with Roseate Terns *(S. dougallii)* contributed to their listing and recovery plans in US; discovered that incubation temp.affects behaviour & physiol.in reptiles (as well as sex as was previously known); co-developed an avian model for study of effects of lead on behavioural dev.of young. **Memberships:** F.AOU, Soc.of Toxicology, ESA, WOS, STB. **Awards:** Palmer F.(Cornell U.), TriBeta (SUNY at Albany), F.AOU, Phi Beta Kappa (Cornell U.), F.AAUW. **Publications:** *Seabirds & Other Marine Vertebrates: Competition, Predation, & Other Interactions* (Ed.) 1988, *The Black Skimmer: Social Dynamics of a Colonial Species* (co-Author) 1990, *The Common Tern: Its Breeding Biol.& Behavior* (co-Author) 1991, *Threats to Seabirds on Islands* (co-Ed.in press); 200+ papers, several popular articles. Favours pers.pub.& news media support. **Languages:** English, Spanish (adequate). Further details can be obtained from *American Men & Women in Sci.* Willing to act as consult.etc. **Address:** Biological Sciences, Rutgers University, Piscataway, New Jersey 08855-1059, USA. **Tel.** (office) 1 908 932 4318, (home) 1 908 828 9390; **fax** 1 908 932 5870.

BURHENNE, Wolfgang E. Parliamentary and environmental law. Secretary-General. *B.*27 April 1924, Hannover, Germany. German. *M.* Dr Françoise Guilmin-Burhenne (envl law): *d.* **Education:** Acad.of Pol.Sci.(Munich) 1950–52. **Experience:** soldier until wounded in Russia (arrested at military hosp.in March 1942 for helping the resistance movement, imprisoned in var.camps incl.Dachau until 1945); assigned by occupation forces to Forest Police Service (Upper Bavaria), began parallel studies in for.at U.of Munich (self-financed by income from helping small cos to reconstruct premises & businesses after the war), assisted in prep.of var.bills of Fed.Parl.1950–52, prep.for founding of Interparliamentary Working Centre to encourage jt parliamentary initiatives and innovative legis.in major new policy areas, special assignment with staff of Fed.Parliament on financing of pol.parties & coopn with State Parliaments 1985–6. **Career:** Dep.to Chief of Wildlife Mgmt in Bavarian State Min.for Food, Agric.and For.1948–9; Edl Staff, BLV Publishing House (Munich) 1949–53; Legislative Adv. Bavarian Parliament 1950–52; Founder 1952, Sec.-Gen.(elected) 1953–85 (Hon.1985–), Interparliamentary Working Centre; vol.activities — First German Rep.to UNGA 1950, Fin.Adv.to Exec.Bd 1958–61, Chairman of Cttee & Comm. on Legis.1960–69, Chairman CEPLA (now CEL) 1977–90, Legal Adv.1990–93, IUCN, and Founding Memb.1969, Exec.Gov.1971–, resp. for Envl Notes for Parliamentarians (in English

& French) 1988–, ICEL; num.nat.& intl activities incl.co-founding of German Wildlife Prot. Assn (first German wildlife cons.group) 1949, Founding Memb.& Hon.Sec.1951–79 (co-Chairman –1979) and Bd Memb.–1985 of WWF Germany, Founding Memb.and first Sec.of CIPRA, invited expert for UN ECE and ECA 1961–, init.for elaboration of CITES 1963–73, Adv.to OAU 1965–, Memb.of AKUR WG for Envl Law (Chairman 1981 & 1991) 1972–, Dep.Chairman of Fund for Envl Studies (Tyrol) 1977–, Memb.of Law of the Sea Inst.(U.of Hawaii) 1976–, Memb.of Curatorium of Brehm Fonds for Intl Bird Prot.1976–, Invited Expert in UNEP Envl Law Expert Group 1979–, Chairman of German Fndn for Envl Policy 1980–, Dep. Chairman of Elizabeth Haub Fndn (Washington, DC) 1981, estab.of German UNEP Cttee 1986– and Coord.in Working Cttee, Obs.at Consult.Mtgs of Antarctic States 1987–, Contrib.to draft of Alpine Conv.1991 and eight protocols 1989–. **Achievements:** recognized effectiveness in drafting and influencing the adoption of nat.envl legis.and esp.intl agreements, and both initiating & participating in estab.of intl envl instns. **Awards:** Bundesverdienstkreuz am Bande 1973 and First Class 1978 (Pres.of FRG), Elizabeth Haub Prize & Gold Medal (VUB) 1976, Hon.LLD U.of Bhopal 1980 and Pace U.NY 1987, Madrid Bar Assn and Hon.Memb.of Assn Española de Derecho del Medio Ambiente 1984, Grosses Verdienstkreuz (Commander) (FRG) 1987, Hon.Memb.IUCN 1990 and CIPRA 1992, Envl Medal (The Better World Soc.NY) 1990, Intl Sasakawa Envl Prize (UN, co-awardee with Françoise Burhenne-Guilmin) 1991. **Publications:** num.incl.*Preliminary Comparative Study of Nature Cons.Legis.*(co-Author) 1964, a model waste oil disposal prog.in the FRG (co-Author) 1971, *The Importance of Intl Envl Law 1980, Demands for Improved Envl Policies* (co-Author) 1989, *Tourism and Envt — Need for Regulation Frameworks* 1992. **Languages:** English, French, German. Willing to act as consult.etc. **Address:** Commission on Environmental Law, IUCN–The World Conservation Union, Adenauerallee 214, D-53113 Bonn, Germany. **Tel.**49 228 2692 231; **fax** 49 228 2692 251 or 2.

BURKE, David Thomas 'Tom'. Politics of environment with special emphasis on business & environment and energy policy. Special Adviser. *B.*5 Jan.1947, Cork, Ireland. British., Irish. **Education:** St Boniface's 1965; U.of Liverpool BA(Hons) (Phil.) 1969. **Experience:** teaching, admin.up to Bd level, media contact. **Career:** Gt George's Arts Projects 1969–70; Lect. W. Cheshire Coll.1970–71 and Old Swan Tech. Coll. 1971–3; Local Groups Coord.1973–5, Exec.Dir 1975–9, Dir of Spec.Projects 1979–80, VC 1980–81n FoE; Bd of Dirs, Earth Resources Res.1975–87; Waste Mgmt Adv.Council 1976–81; Packaging Council 1978–82; Press Officer, Euro.Envt Bur.1979–87; Dir, The Green Alliance 1982–92; Contested (Social Democrats Party) Brighton Kemptown 1983, Surbiton 1987;

Exec.Cttee, NCVO 1984–9; UK Nat. Cttee, Euro.Yr of the Envt 1986–8; Exec.Cttee, Euro. Envt Bur.1987–91; Sec.Ecol.Studies Inst. 1987–92; Vis.F.Cranfield Sch.for Mgmt 1991–; Spec. Adv.to Sec.of State for the Envt 1991–; Overseas Adv.Cttee, Save the Children Fund 1992–; RSNC Counc.1993–; Intl Adv.Panel, WEC 1993–. **Membership:** F.RSA 1988– (Counc. 1990–92). **Awards:** R.Humane Soc. Testimonials — on Vellum 1966, on Parchment 1968; Hon.Vis.F. Manchester Business Sch. 1984, Global 500 Roll of Honour (UNEP) 1993. **Publications:** *Europe: Envt* 1981, *Pressure Groups in the Global System* (co-Author) 1982, *Ecol.2000* (co-Author) 1984, *The Green Capitalists* (co-Author) 1987, *Green Pages* (co-Author) 1988. **Languages:** English, French (some), Spanish (some). Further details may be obtained from British *Who's Who* 1994. Willing to act as consult. etc. **Address:** 36 Crewdson Road, London SW9 0LJ, England, UK. **Tel.**(office) 44 171 276 4299, (home) 44 171 735 9019; **fax** 44 171 276 3269.

BURLEY, Dr Jeffery. Tropical forestry — research, development, information & education; biodiversity; tree breeding. Institute Director. *B.*16 Oct.1936, Portsmouth, Hants., England, UK. British. *M.*Jean Shirley: 2 *s.*Jeremy Andrew (agricl engr), Timothy John (GIS). **Education:** Portsmouth Grammar Sch.; New Coll.& Dept of For. U.of Oxf. BA(Hons) (For.) 1961, MA 1964; Sch.of For. Yale U. MF 1962, PhD(Forest Genetics) 1965. **Experience:** admin.& tech.— ten yrs as Inst.Dir & four as Officer-in-Charge; 40 consults for intl agencies & UK Govt. **Career:** UNESCO Consult.& Expert in Forest Genetics, ARC of C.Africa 1965–8; Officer-in-Charge, Tree Improvement Res.Centre, ARC of Zambia 1968; Sr Res. Officer (Forest Genetics), Dept of For. Commonwealth For.Inst.1968–76, U.Lect. in For. 1976, Head of Dept of For.& Dir Commonwealth For.Inst.and Dir-Designate of Oxf. For. Inst.1983–5, Dir of Oxf.For.Inst.1985–, U.of Oxf. **Achievements:** exploration, eval., breeding & cons.of trop.tree species for planting. **Memberships:** CFA, ISTF. **Award:** CBE. **Publications:** c.250 (149 jt) incl.*Trop.Trees: Variation, Breeding & Cons.*(co-Ed.) 1976, *A Tree for ALL Reasons: the Intro.& Eval.of Multipurpose Trees for Agrofor.*(co-Author) 1991, *Managing Global Genetic Resources: Forest Trees* (co-Author) 1991; 56 reports, 50 reviews. Indiff.to pers.pub., favours news media support. **Languages:** English, French; German & Portuguese (read); Spanish (spoken & read). Further details may be obtained from British *Who's Who* 1993. Willing to act as consult.etc. **Address:** Oxford Forestry Institute, Department of Plant Sciences, University of Oxford, South Parks Road, Oxford OX1 3RB, England, UK. **Tel.**(office) 44 1865 275050, (home) 44 1865 390754; **fax** 44 1865 275074.

BURNETT, Professor Dr G. Wesley. Conservation in developing nations, historical geography of conservation; comparative philosophies of conservation, park planning & management; biogeography. Professor, Adjunct Professor of Geography. *B*.20 July 1944, St Louis, MO, USA. American. Father George W.Burnett (microbiol. & public health dentistry). *M*.Karen: *s., d*. **Education:** Southern Methodist U. AB (Geog.) 1966; U.of Oklahoma MA (Geog.) 1974, PhD(Geog.) 1976. **Experience:** field res.in Kenya, Cameroon, Dominica, Costa Rica, USA; admin.— Chair Geog.Dept (Kenyatta U.) and Bur.Chief; consult.& contracts with USFS, World Tourism Orgn & Montana Water Qual.Bur.; teaching at Clemson & Kenyatta Univs. **Career:** Chief, Planning & Project Admin.Bur. Montana Dept of Fish, Wildlife & Parks 1975–9; Prof. Parks, Rec.& Tourism Mgmt, Clemson U.1979–; Sr Lect.(on leave) Kenyatta U.1984–6; Adjunct Prof.of Geog. U.of Montana 1977–9 and Southern Illinois U.1986–; Coord. Clemson U. Archbold Trop.Res.Center, Commonwealth of Dominica 1989. **Achievements:** understanding of geogl, histl & phil.conditions resulting in cons. activity in less-developed countries. **Memberships:** F.RGS, Assn of Third World Studies. **Publications:** 80+ j.articles incl.Agric., res.& tourism in the landscape of L.Baringo, Kenya 1990, Nat.park & equivalent reserve creation in French & Brit.Africa 1990, Scientific vocabulary divergence among female primatologists working in E.Africa 1991, Wilderness and the Bantu Mind 1994; reviews, chapters & govt documents. Indiff.to pers.pub., favours news media support. **Languages:** English, French (read), Kiswahili (some spoken), Spanish (read & some spoken). Further details may be obtained from *Men of Achievement* 1993, *Dict.of Intl Biog*.1993. Willing to act as consult.etc. **Address:** Room 263 Lehosky Hall, Clemson University, Clemson, South Carolina 29631, USA. **Tel.**(office) 1 801 656 3400, (home) 1 801 639 4046; **fax** 1 801 656 2226.

BURNEY, M.Ilyas. Microbiology, public health, and environment. Scientist Emeritus. *B*.1 Jan. 1922, Simla, Punjab, India. Pakistani. *M*.Surraiya: 2 *s*. **Education:** Punjab U. MB BS 1948, Classified Specialist in Path.1951; U.of London MCP 1965, F.CPS Pakistan 1972, F.RCP London 1977. **Career:** Officer Incharge, Dept of Virology 1958–70, Officer Commanding 1970–73, Armed Forces Inst.of Path.(Rawalpindi); Dir Nat.Health Labs 1973– 80; Exec.Dir NIH 1980–87, Adv.(Fed.Sec.status) to Min.of Health 1988–9, Sci.Emer.NIH (Islamabad) 1989–. **Achievements:** estab.first Dept of Virology in Pakistan 1959, and Dept of Nat. Envl Control, NIH 1986; Nat.Coord.of Food Contamination Study and Control in Asia and Far E.for FAO 1984, and Pakistan Guinea Worm *(Dracunculus medinensis)* Eradication Prog. started in 1987; memb.Bd of Trustees, Cancer Res.Fndn of Pakistan, and Cttee on NCS of Pakistan; Nat.Org.of Sem.and Policy Briefings on Envl Poll.& Climate Change; ident.of a focus of Visceral Leishmaniasis in Baltistan in 1962, and discovery of new species of *Phlebotomus*

(named *P.burneyii,* specimen kept in Natural Hist.Mus. London, UK); isolated W.Nile Virus and Sandfly Fever Viruses from mosquitoes & human blood, Congo virus from human cases of Viral Haemorrhagic Fever, *Rickettsia tsutsugamushi* & *R.mooseri* strains from rodents, mites, & human blood, and *Chalamydia trachomatics,* and viruses EV-70 and Coxsackie-21 from cases of Acute Haemorrhagic Conjunctivitis; worked on viral causes of Acute Respiratory Illness and Diarrhoeas of children. **Memberships:** F.PAS 1983, F. PAMS 1990, F.PHA of Pakistan, F. PAP (Past Pres.), CRF of Pakistan; WHO Regnl Adv.Cttee on Health Res.1974–89, Regnl Tech. Adv.Group on Polio Eradication 1988–90, Tech. Adv.Group on Diarrhoeal Disease (1978–88), Global Adv. Group on Expanded Prog.on Immunization (EPI) 1985–7, and Expert Cttee on Viral Haemorrhagic Fever; Bd of Trustees PSF 1976–88, Chairman Expert Panel on Microbiol., Virology & Infectious Diseases (Pakistan MRC) 1978–87, Prof.Emer.(Hon.), Army Med. Coll.and Armed Forces Med.Coll. Rawalpindi. **Awards:** Hilal-i-Imtiaz (military) 1982, Shousha Award (WHO) 1984, Global 500 Roll of Honour (UNEP) 1988. **Publications:** *Health and Med.Profile of the Muslim World* (compiler) 1991; chapters, 70 res.papers in nat. & intl journals. **Languages:** English, Urdu. Willing to act as consult.etc. **Address:** 213/3 Ordnance Road, Rawalpindi, Pakistan. **Tel.** (office) 92 51 240110, (home) 92 51 568696, **fax** 92 51 583405.

BURNS, Professor Dr Carolyn Waugh. Freshwater ecology, Nature conservation. Professor of Zoology. *B*.3 Feb.1942, Lincoln, NZ. New Zealander. Father Sir Malcolm Burns, agric. *M*. John Ingram Hubbard. **Education:** U.of Canterbury, BSc(1st Class Hons) 1963; U.of Toronto, PhD 1966. **Experience:** res.— ecol.& productivity of lakes & wetlands, pop.biol.& behaviour of plankton; admin.— Edl Bds *Limnol.& Oceanogr.*1981–84, *Archiv für Hydrobiol.*1988–; teaching — limnol., cons.biol.at postgrad.level. **Career:** Res.Assoc.in Biol. Yale U. 1966–68; Lect. Sr Lect. Assoc.Prof. in Zool. 1969–92, Pers.Prof.in Zool.1993–, U.of Otago; Vis.Assoc.Prof. Kellogg Biol.Station, Michigan SU 1974–75; Vis.Res.Prof. Dartmouth Coll.1984– 85, 1991–92; Res.Sci. Max-Planck Inst.for Limnol.1992. **Achievements:** Nature Cons. Council 1975–83 (Chair 1978–83), member Nat. Parks & Reserves Auth.1981–90, Chair NZ Cttee IUCN Members 1986–90, Regnl Counc.IUCN 1984–90, memb.IUCN Comms on Ecol.1988– 90, Educ.1979–90, NPPA 1988–. **Memberships:** IATAL (VP), ASLO, ASL, FBA UK, NZLS, RSNZ, WAC. **Awards:** Sr Scholar (U.of Canterbury) 1962, Percival Mem. Prize in Zool.1962, Commonwealth Scholar (Canada) 1963–66, Member Sigma XI (Yale Chapter) 1967–, Hon.F.AAUW 1974–75, CBE 1984, 1990 Commem.Medal (NZ Govt). **Publications:** num.scientific papers on freshwater ecol., articles on nature cons. **Languages:** English,

French (basic). Willing to act as consult.etc. **Address:** Department of Zoology, University of Otago, Dunedin, New Zealand. **Tel.**(office) 64 3 479 7971, (home) 64 3 477 0590; **fax** 64 3 479 7584.

BURTON, John Andrew. Natural history, wildlife conservation, identification guides, history of natural history. Freelance Consultant, Chief Executive Officer. *B.*2 April 1944, London, England, UK. British. *M.*Vivien Gledhill (Mgr World Wide Land Cons.Trust, formerly Mgr FFPS, SSC Asst to the late Sir Peter Scott). **Education:** Alleyn's Sch., London. **Experience:** Consult.to CITES 1977–81, Kashmiri Govt re.fur trade 1985, DoE on plant identification manual for CITES 1987–93, and Envl Record Archive (wildlife films) 1990–91; Del.(Obs.) IWC 1971–80; extensive intl exp.partic.in N.Amer.& Belize; has attended many IUCN Confs and served on councils of num.natural hist.socs & cons.bodies. **Career:** Asst Info.Officer, Brit. Mus.(Natural Hist.) 1963–9; Freelance Consult.1969–; Asst Ed. Animals (now BBC Wildlife) Magazine 1971–3; Founder & CEO, World Wide Land Cons.Trust 1989–. **Achievements:** Natural Hist.Consult.to FoE 1971–5, Ed *Birds Intl* (ICBP) 1975–7, Asst Sec.FPS 1975–9, Exec.Sec. FFPS 1979–87, Chairman IUCN SSC Traffic Group 1976–81, Founder TRAFFIC Network 1978, Founder Chairman of Bat Cons.Trust 1990. **Memberships:** F.LS, F.RSA, F.RGS. **Award:** Memb. Emer.(IUCN SSC). **Publications:** several incl.*Owls of the World* (Ed.) 1973, *Field Guide to Amphibians and Reptiles of Europe* (co-Author) 1978, *Rare Mammals of the World* 1987, *Pocket Guide to Mammals of N.Amer.*1991, *Snakes — an Illustr.Guide* 1991; many children's books. Indiff.to pers.pub.& news media support. **Language:** English. Willing to act as consult.etc. **Address:** Old Mission Hall, Sibton Green, Saxmundham, Suffolk IP17 2JY, England, UK. **Tel.**44 1728 668619; **fax** 44 1986 874425.

BUSTAMANTE, Dr Georgina. Tropical marine fish life-history, ecology, & ecophysiology; conservation & management of coastal ecosystems & fishery resources. Visiting Research Associate. *B.*26 Jan.1952, Havana, Cuba. **Education:** U.of Havana, Lic.(Marine Biol.) 1973; Cuban AS PhD(Biol.) 1987. **Experience:** res.— marine fish cultivation, life-hist., ecol., ecophysiol., fisheries in the Carib.; admin.— Dep.Dir of Inst.of Oceanology; Adv.& Consult.on fishery & cultivation as well as coastal planning for Cuban agencies; grad.teaching — trop.marine fish ecol.in univs and centers of advanced studies & res.in Mexico, sems for grad.students & fac.in Florida Intl U.(Dept of Biol.) and Florida Marine Res.Inst.1994. **Career:** Jr Researcher 1973–82, Sr Researcher 1983–94, Asst Dir 1987–8, Dep.Dir for Dev. 1993–4, Inst.of Oceanology of Cuba; Vis. Res.Assoc.(TNC Florida/Carib.Marine Cons. Sci.Center) Dept of Biol. U.of Miami 1994–. **Achievements:** pubn of scientific papers & chapters, adv.on marine envt & resources in Cuba and other countries. **Membership:** Cuban Soc.of Marine Scis (Founder Memb.). **Award:** Tomas Romay (Cuban AS) 1985. **Publications:** *c.*25 papers & chapters. Favours pers.pub.& news media support. **Languages:** English, French (fair), Spanish, Russian. Willing to act as consult.etc. **Address:** Department of Biology, University of Miami, POB 249118, Coral Gables, Florida 33124-0421, USA. **Tel.**1 305 284 3013; **fax** 1 305 284 3039.

BUTLER, Professor Dr James 'Jim' Robert. Teaching & research in parks, wildlife, environmental conservation; ecotourism, conservation education, interpretation, parks & protected areas' management, endangered species' conservation, old-growth forest wildlife ecology. Professor of Parks, Wildlife & Conservation Biology, Company Director. *B.*24 Feb.1946, Wheeling, WV, USA. American, Canadian. *M.*Elaine Brooks (Ed.with *Borealis* magazine, author of *Attracting Birds*). **Education:** W.Virginia U. Wildlife Mgmt 1966; Ohio SU, Zool.1968; Manhattanville Coll.NY, MA in Humanities (Nature & Soc.) 1974; U.of Washington (Seattle), PhD(Interpretation/Outdoor Rec.) 1980. **Experience:** extensive overseas consult.incl.serving as memb.of master planning teams in Kenya; dev.of interpretive systems plan for all parks & reserves of Kenya, three nat.parks in Java, one each in Carib.& C.Amer.; Adv.Memb.for nat.parks & Nature reserves around L.Baikal (Russia); Head of WWF/IUCN Expedn to China 1986; directs own consult.co.; public speaking, occasional columnist on envl topics with CBC; grad.student supervision. **Career:** Park Naturalist, Oglebay Park 1964–7 and Dept of Natural Resources (Ohio) 1968; Chief State Naturalist, Dept of Parks (Kentucky) 1968–70; Resident Chief Naturalist & Admin.Dir, Corkscrew Swamp Sanctuary, Nat.Audubon Soc.1970–71; Envl Educ.Consult. & Field Programming Specialist, US Dept of Envl Educ.1971–4; Head, Educ.& Interpretation, Dept of Rec., Parks & Wildlife, Govt of Alberta 1976–9; Adjunct Prof.1977–9, Assoc. Prof.1979–87, Prof.of Parks, Wildlife & Cons. Biol.1987– and Envl Cons.Studies Prog. 1993–, Dir Intl Inst.for Prot.Areas Mgmt 1987–93, U.of Alberta; Dir, Peregrine Inst.of Res.& Planning Assocs 1985–. **Achievements:** breadth of exp. in planning, mgmt, ecol.& biol., terr.biodiv., cons. educ., interpretation, policy, envl econ., sociol.& psych.& intl diplomacy; being one of the foremost auths on subject of ecotourism, as a pioneer in its definitions & evol.and consulted on ecotourism throughout N.Amer.and overseas. **Memberships:** IUCN CNPPA, ICBP Cttee on Bird Ecotourism, CEAC (former), CPWS (past Nat.VP), Western Canada Wilderness Cttee (Sr Advising Sci.& Bd Dirs), ANSS (Bd Dirs), Heritage Interpretation Intl (co-Founder), USA– Venezuelan Tourism Task Force, Interpretation Canada (co-Founder & former Dir); Nat.Audubon Soc.(Chapter Pres.), Florida Audubon Soc.(Chief Consult.Naturalist); others. **Awards:** Annual Cons.Award (Edmonton Natural Hist.

Assn) 1990, Coll. Teaching Award (NACTA) 1991–2, Defender of the Wilderness (Western Canada Wilderness Cttee) 1993. **Publications:** *Fishing Canada's Mtn Parks* 1985, Arjin Mtns Nat.Reserve, China 1986, Ecotourism: its changing face & evolving phil.1992, Fostering the spiritual & affective (emotional) values of prot.areas 1992, The bird watchers of Point Pelee Nat.Park, Canada, applying res.findings toward improved park mgmt 1992, Econ.benefits associated with nat.parks' ecotourism 1992, Professional dev.of prot.area mgrs 1992, Interpretation as a Mgmt Tool 1993. Favours pers.pub. (generally handled by U.of Alberta), & news media support (works publicly & confidentially with press, radio & TV). **Language:** English. Further details may be obtained from *Canadian Who's Who* 1995. Willing to act as consult.etc. and as public speaker. **Address:** Environmental Conservation Program, Department of Renewable Resources, 7th Floor General Services Building, University of Alberta, Edmonton, Alberta T6G 2G6, Canada. **Tel.**(office) 1 403 492 2819 & 4413, (home) 1 403 439 2990; **fax** 1 403 492 4323.

BUTLER, Paul John. Conservation marketing, environmental education, & resource management. Director of Conservation Education. *B.*24 June 1956, London, England, UK. British, St Lucian. *M.*Magdalena: *d.* **Education:** N.-E.London Poly. BSc(Hons) 1st Class 1977. **Experience:** pop.studies of Carib.Parrots; admin.— adv.to Govt of St Lucia, project design & implementation throughout Carib.basin, EIA studies & fund-raising; consult.in envl educ.; teaching ecol.and implementation of cons. marketing/envl educ.progs; wide exp.of news media incl.TV. **Career:** Cons.Adv.1978–88, Acting Chief Forest Officer 1986, Forestry Dept, Govt of St Lucia; Consult.in St Vincent & Dominica 1988–9, Carib.Prog.Dir 1991–2, Dir of Cons.Educ.1992–, RARE Center for Trop. Cons. **Achievements:** played key role in saving endemic St Lucia Parrot from extinction, helped estab.Parks & Beaches Comm.on St Lucia, designed cons.marketing prog.that is currently being implemented in ten Carib.nations & S.Pacific. **Award:** Global 500 Roll of Honour (UNEP) 1989. **Publications:** *c.*10 incl.Parrots, Pressures, People & Pride 1991, Promoting Prot.Thru Pride — A Cons.Educ.Manual 1991, Marketing the Cons.Message 1994, Trails: cons. that makes dollars & sense 1994. Favours pers. pub.& news media support. **Language:** English. Willing to act as consult.etc. **Address:** POB GM 755, Gablewoods Mall, Castries, Saint Lucia, Windward Islands, West Indies. **Tel.**1 809 452 9424; **fax** 1 809 452 0864.

BÜTTIKER, Professor Dr William. Medical zoology, desert animal ecology, zoological survey of Arabia. Honorary Collaborator. *B.*5 Aug.1921, Olten, Switzerland. Swiss. *M.*Sonya (assisted with field & lab.work in Arabia 1975–88): *s.,* 2 *d.* **Education:** Swiss Fed.Inst.of Tech.(Zürich) BSc

1945, PhD 1948. **Experience:** Nature cons., muscology, applied zool., admin., consult., teaching. **Career:** Scientific Collab. J.R. Geigy AG 1948; Res.Entomol. Pest Control Ltd (UK) 1949–56; Adv.on Malaria Control, WHO 1956–8; Officer, Intl Liaison & Chief, Dev.of Pesticides, Ciba–Geigy AG 1959–75; Res.Biol. public health project, Ciba–Geigy AG (Riyadh) 1975–81; Envl Sci.Expert, Saudi Met.& Envl Prot.Admin.1982–5; participation in Oman Wahiba Sands Project, RGS 1986; Hon.Collab.Natural Hist.Mus. Basle 1986–, Consult. 1987–94 NCWCD. **Achievements:** working as consult. with Met.& Envl Prot.Admin.(Jeddah) 1982–5, proposing 40 cons.areas (terr.) now being estab. in Jeddah by NCWCD. **Memberships:** RGS, SES (VP & Pres. 1968–74), SZS, SSTMP, many others. **Awards:** Murchison Award (RGS) 1992, Pawlowski Medal (Russian AS) 1993, several other honours. **Publications:** *Fauna of Saudi Arabia* (Founder, Ed.& co-Author, 14 vols) 1979–94, *Die Lausfiegen der Schweiz* 1993. Indiff.to pers. pub.& news media support. **Languages:** Arabic (some); English, French, German, Italian (rusty). Willing to act as consult. etc. **Address:** Lanzenberg 21, 4312 Magden, Switzerland. **Tel.**(office & home) 41 61 841 1604; **fax** 41 61 831 4385.

BYE, Professor Dr Robert. Ethnobotany, economic botany, flora of Sierra Madre Occidental of Mexico, plant taxonomy (*Datura* & related genera), medicinal plants, edible plants, ornamental plants, history of botany & botanical exploration. Senior Researcher & Botanical Garden Director. *B.*13 Aug.1947, St Charles, MO, USA. American. *M.*Edelmira (ethnobot., medicinal plants, envl educ.). **Education:** SUNY at Syracuse U. Coll.of Envl Scis & For. BSc 1969; Harvard U. PhD 1976. **Experience:** res.— taxonomy & floristics (US & Mexico) 1976–, ethnobot.(US & Mexico) 1968–, archaeo-ethnobot.(US) 1968–81, hist.of bot.(US & Mexico) 1968 ; admin. botl gdn (Mexico) 1988 , biol. lect.& assoc.mus.curator (Colorado) 1976–87. **Career:** Prof.of Biol. U.of Colorado 1976–87; Vis.Researcher 1981–7, Sr Researcher 1987–, Dir Jardin Botánico 1991–, Universidad Nacional Autónoma de México (Instituto de Biología). **Achievements:** exploration, cultivation, cons. & dev.of useful plants of Mexico (with emphasis on pine–oak forests, dry trop.forests). **Memberships:** SBM, SE, SEB, AEM, Assn of Southwestern Naturalists. **Award:** Edward Fulling Award (SEB). **Publications:** *Tes Curativos de Mexico* (co-Author) 1984, 2nd edn 1990, *Seleccion de Plantas Medicinales de Mexico* (co-Author) 1988, *Biol. Diversity in Mexico: Origins & Distribn* (co-Ed.) 1993; 50 scientific papers. Indiff.to pers.pub.& news media support. **Languages:** English, Spanish. Willing to act as consult.etc. **Address:** Jardín Botánico, Instituto de Biología, Universidad Nacional Autónoma de México, Apdo Postal 70-614, 04510 México DF, Mexico. **Tel.**525 622 9046 or 616 1297; **fax** 525 622 9046 or 616 2326.

ČABOUN, Dr Vladimír. Ecological & ecophysiological relations in forest ecosystems and their dependence on dominant trees. Associate Professor & Head of Department. *B.*9 Aug. 1952, Zvolen, Slovak Republic. Slovak. *M.*Marta. **Education:** Tech.U.(Zvolen) PhD(Forest Scis) 1984. **Experience:** res.of allelopathy, forest ecol.& ecophysiol., Nat.Coord.of Strasbourg Resolutions S5 (EUROSILVA) & S6 (Euro. Network of Res. into Forest Ecosystems). **Career:** Lect.in Basic & Forest Ecol.1989–, Assoc. Prof.1993– and Head of Dept of Ecol.& Ecophysiol.of Forest Trees 1989–, Forest Res. Inst. **Achievement:** elaboration & realization of envl projects. **Awards:** several from Acad.of Agric., Slovak Lit.Fund Envt Cttee, etc. **Publications:** (all in Slovak) *Climatic Influence and Characteristics of Forests* 1989, *Allelopathy in Forest Ecosystems* 1990, *Ecol.& Ecophysiol. Res.in Forest Ecosystems* 1993, *Climatic Changes and Their Influences on Ecol.Stability of Slovak Forest Ecosystems* (report) 1994. Indiff. to pers.pub.& news media support. **Languages:** English, Russian, Slovak. Willing to act as consult.etc. **Address:** Forest Research Institute, Masaryka 22, 960 92 Zvolen, Slovak Republic. **Tel.**(office) 42 855 320316 to 8, (home) 42 855 20058; **fax** 42 855 23397.

CACCIA, Charles Luigi. Forestry, adult education. Member of Parliament. *B.*28 April 1930, Milan, Italy. Canadian, Italian. *M.* **Education:** U.of Vienna Liceo Scientifico Vittorio Veneto (For.Econ.) 1954. **Experience:** promoting adult educ., up-grading, skill dev.progs, and English language training for adults & youth in immigrant communities, admin.involved therewith; public speaking. **Career:** emigrated to Canada 1955; Fac.of For. U.of Toronto; Trade Analyst, Italian Trade Comm.; Memb.City of Toronto & Metro Council 1964 & 1966, Liberal MP for Davenport 1968–, Minister of Labour 1981–3 and of Envt 1983–. **Achievements:** founded publishing co. Caccia & Assocs 1958, and (co-) COSTI 1960; estab.of Parliamentary Centre for Envlly Sust.Dev.1989; num.Private Member's Bills & Motions. **Memberships:** Cttee on Sust.Dev.(Chair) and Priority & Planning Cttee, NLC; Standing Cttee on the Envt 1984–, Special Cttee on Acid Rain 1984– 88. **Award:** Global 500 Roll of Honour (UNEP) 1985. **Publications:** The OECD Nations & Sust.Dev. 1990, num.conf.& newspaper items. Favours pers. pub.& news media support. **Languages:** English, French, Italian. Willing to act as consult.etc. **Address:** House of Commons, Room 353S, Ottawa, Ontario K1A 0A6, Canada. **Tel.**1 613 992 2576; **fax** 1 613 995 8202.

CAEIRO PITTA, Prof. Luis, *see* **PITTA, Prof. Luis** C~AEIRO~.

CAHN, The Honorable Robert. Environmental writing. Freelance Writer, Environmental Consultant. *B.*9 March 1917, Seattle, WA, USA. American. *M.*Patricia Lovelady (envl educ.).

Education: U.of Washington, BA 1939. **Experience:** admin., consult., journalism. **Career:** Staff Corres. *Life Magazine* 1948– & *The Christian Sci.Monitor* 1965–70; Chief, Louisiana Bur. *Colliers Magazine* 1955–6; Midwest Ed. *Saturday Evening Post* 1961–2; White House Reporter 1963, 1964, US Info. Service; memb. CEQ (US Pres.'s) 1970–72; Field Ed. *Audubon* magazine 1978–82; Spec.Asst to Pres. of Nat.Audubon Soc.1982–5; Comm.on Res.& Res.Mgmt Policy for Nat.Park System, NPCA 1988–9. **Achievements:** one of the three original members of the Pres.'s CEQ (appointed by Pres.Nixon) 1970–72, recipient of Pulitzer Prize for Nat.News Reporting 1969. **Memberships:** IUCN CNPPA, Trust for Public Land (past Governing Bd), Envl Policy Inst.(now FoE, past Governing Bd), Inst.of Ecol.(past Acting-Chair, Bd of Trustees), Coastal Zone Mgmt Adv.Cttee (Dept of Commerce, past), Citizens Adv. Cttee on Envl Qual.(past), Governing Bds of Student Cons.Assn & Partners in Parks, Nat.Adv.Council of Trust for Public Land. **Awards:** Bronze Star Medal for Meritorious Service (US) 1945, Pulitzer Prize 1969, Cons. Service Award (USDI) 1969, Disting.Service Award (NWF) 1969, Horace M.Albright Lect. (U.of Calif.) 1980, Conrad L.Wirth Lect.(AILA) 1980, Marjorie Stoneman Douglas Award (NPCA) 1988, Hon.LLD (Allegheny Coll.) 1970. **Publications:** *Foot-prints on the Planet: A Search for an Envl Ethic* 1978, *Amer. Photographers and the Nat.Parks* 1981, *Birth of the NPS: The Founding Years* 1913–33 (co-Author) 1985; num.articles in many nat.periodicals. **Address:** 41942 Bald Hill Road, Leesburg, Virginia 22075, USA. **Tel.**(home) & **fax** 1 703 777 5410.

CALDWELL, Professor Dr Lynton Keith. Public law and policy for the environment, life sciences. Professor of Political Science, Emeritus, and of Public & Environmental Affairs. *B.*21 Nov.1913, Montezuma, IA, USA. American. *M.*Helen A.: *s., d.* **Education:** U.of Chicago, PhB(Hons)(English) 1934, PhD 1943; Harvard U. MA 1938. **Career:** Fac.appointments at U.of Chicago, Syracuse U., UCB, Indiana U., Dir of Res.& Pubns, Council of State Govs (USA), Bd of Govs of USA NC, Sci. Adv.Bd, Intl Joint Comm.(Canada & USA). **Achievements:** Consult.to US Senate for Nat. Envl Policy Act (originator of the Envl Impact Statement), service on num.US Fed.Adv.Bds and NRC. **Memberships:** IAIA, Nat.Acad.of Law & Social Sci.(Argentina), RSA, US NAPA. **Awards:** F.AAAS, William E.Mosher 1964, Burghfield 1972, Hon.LLD (Western Michigan U.) 1977, Dimock (ASPA) 1981, Rose Hulman (IAIA) 1989; Sprout (ISA), Order of Crown of Thailand, Global 500 Roll of Honour (UNEP) 1991. **Publications:** 12 books incl.*Envt: A Challenge to Modern Soc.*1970, *In Defense of Earth* 1972, *Intl Envl Policy* (2nd edn) 1990, *Between Two Worlds: Sci., The Envt and Policy Choice* 1990, *Policy for Land: Law & Ethics* (co-Author) 1993; 200+ articles & monogr., num.

reports. No objection to pers.pub., favours news media support. **Languages:** English, French (written), Spanish. Further details may be obtained from *Who's Who in America, Who's Who in Sci.& Engg, American Men & Women of Sci., Dict.of Intl Biog., Contemporary Authors, Men of Achievement.* Willing to act as consult.etc. **Address:** 4898 Heritage Woods Road, Bloomington, Indiana 47401, USA. **Tel.**(office) 1 812 855 7980, (home) 1 812 336 5961; **fax** 1 812 855 5678.

CÂMARA, Admiral Ibsen DE GUSMÃO. Conservation of natural ecosystems & protected areas. Society President. *B.*19 Dec.1923, RJ, Brazil. Brazilian. *M.*Gilda C.: 2 *d.* **Education:** Brazilian Naval Acad.(RJ), Naval Scis 1944; postgrad.courses at US Naval Postgrad.Sch. 1960, Brazilian Naval War Coll.(RJ) 1961, and Advanced War Coll.(RJ) 1969. **Experience:** for 20+ yrs, after retirement from the Navy, has fully dedicated time to cons. **Career:** Brazilian Navy — promoted to Rear Admiral 1972, Flag Officer to Navy Gen.Staff and Dir of Brazilian Naval War Coll., last active duty as V.-Chief of Armed Forces Gen.Staff 1977–81; Pres. Brazilian Soc.for Envl Prot.1988–. **Achievements:** one of leaders of successful campaign to stop whaling by Brazil, author of Atlantic Forest preserv.plan*. **Memberships:** 13 Brazilian cons. orgns. **Awards:** Ridder of the Order of the Golden Ark (Govt of The Netherlands) 1991, Fred M.Packard Award (IUCN) 1992. **Publications:** **Atlantic Forest Action Plan* 1991, co-Author of seven books concerning Brazilian ecosystems. Indiff.to pers.pub.& news media support. **Languages:** English, French, Portuguese, Spanish (read & understood). Willing to act as consult.etc. **Address:** Avenida das Americas 2300-Casa 40, Rio de Janeiro, RJ 22640 101, Brazil. **Tel.**(office) 55 21 537 7565, (home) 55 21 325 3696; **fax** 55 21 537 1343.

CAMINO, Dr Ronnie DE. Natural resources policy, economics, & management. Company Director & Chief Forestry Officer. *B.*5 March 1942, Santiago, Chile. Chilean. *M.*Maria Angelica: 2 *s.*incl.Tomas (biol.), *d.* **Education:** U.of Chile, Bacc.in Biol.1958, grad.studies in agricl econ.(hons) 1964, Forest Engr(Hons) 1965; U.of Freiburg, Dr Rer.Nat.(*magna cum laude*) 1972. **Experience:** wide in res., res. mgmt, instn mgmt & orgn; consult.for bilateral & multilateral agencies *e.g.*FAO, CATIE, GTZ, DEH, WRI, and private enterprise; teaching at grad.& postgrad.levels. **Career:** Dir, For.Sch. U.Astral de Chile 1967–74; Planning & Res. Mgr, Nat.Reforestation Co.(Venezuela) 1977– 84; Head, For.and Agrofor.Res.Area, CATIE 1985–90; Natural Resources Specialist, IICA/ GTZ Project 1991–5; Bd Dir 1992– & Chief For.Officer 1995–, Precious Woods Ltd (Costa Rica); Memb. Bd of Trustees, CIFOR 1992–. **Achievements:** contribns to reforestation of 500,000+ ha of forests in Venezuela, to vast res.network in C.Amer., and to creation of CIFOR. **Member-**

ships: TROPENBOS Fndn (Adv.Group), PROCI-TROPICOS (Scientific Cttee), IICA, IAEE, Centre for Our Common Future (Geneva, Switzerland), var.intl groups as Dir, Coord., or Memb. **Publications:** num.books incl.*Incentivos para la Participación de la Comunidad en Programas de Conservación* (transl.into English & French 1987) 1985, *Needs and Priorities for For.and Agrofor.Policy Res.in Latin Amer.*(co-Ed.) 1994; chapters incl. Consideraciónes Economicas Sobre las Plantaciónes Forestales en Amer. Latina 1989, Estrategias para el Uso & Manejo de Recursos Naturales 1995; num.papers. Indiff.to pers.pub.& news media support. **Languages:** English, French, German, Spanish; Italian & Portuguese (understood & a little spoken). Willing to act as consult.etc. **Address:** Precious Woods Limited, Apartado Postal 1180, 1250 Escazu, Costa Rica. **Tel.**(office) 506 231 1374, (home) & **fax** 506 282 6257; **fax** 506 231 1057.

CAMPBELL, Dr Kenneth L.I. Wildlife surveys, national park planning, geographic information systems, remote sensing, environmental impact assessment. Problem Area Manager. *B.*23 May 1953, Nairobi, Kenya. British. Father Ian L.I.Campbell, arch., botl illustrator; mother Anne Lise, ornith., bot. **Education:** U.of Aberdeen, BSc(Hons) 1976, U.of Exeter, PhD 1982. **Experience:** res.— fieldwork in Tanzania based in Serengeti Nat.Park, consult., admin. **Career:** Sr Consult. EcoSystems Ltd (Nairobi) 1983–6; Prog.Mgr, Serengeti Ecol. Monitoring Prog.1986–9 and Tanzania Wildlife Cons.Monitoring 1989–94, Serengeti Nat.Park; Problem Area Mgr (Wildlife, GIS, & Remote Sensing), Envl Scis Div. NRI 1994–. **Achievement:** estab.of long-term monitoring of wildlife nrs in Tanzanian Nat.Parks and Game Reserves 1986–93. **Memberships:** Companion of Inst.of Analysts & Programmers, LS, DIVERSITAS (Scientific Steering Cttee of 3rd theme [Inventory and Monitoring of Biodiv.]). **Publications:** 20 incl.Fishes of the genus *Sarotherodon* (Cichlidae) of springs along the n.Uaso Ngiro, Kenya 1981, People and Wildlife: Spatial Dynamics and Zones of Interaction (co-Author) 1995; 30 prog.& nine consult.reports. Indiff.to pers.pub.& news media support. **Languages:** English, French (poor written & spoken), Swahili (spoken). Willing to act as consult.etc. **Address:** Environmental Science Division, Natural Resources Institute, Chatham Maritime, Kent ME4 4TB, England, UK. **Tel.**(office) 44 1634 880088, (home) 44 1622 851264; **fax** 44 1634 880066 to 77.

CANADAY, Christopher. Conservation biology. Independent Consultant & Researcher. *B.*13 Aug.1961, Upland, CA, USA. American. **Education:** Humboldt SU BA/BS(Biol.& Wildlife Mgmt) *cum laude* 1985, U.of Florida, MA(Latin Amer.Studies esp.Trop.Cons.& Dev.) 1991. **Experience:** six yrs' res.& cons.projects in forests of trop.Latin Amer. **Career:** Cons. Biol. Fundación Ecuatoriana para la Conservación y

Desarrollo Sostenible 1991–2; Ind.Consult.& Researcher 1991– incl.dev.of land-use zoning within Cuyabeno Reserve (Ecuador) in coordn with Siona & Quichua indigenous communities, for Profors 1993–, and Ornith.in project measuring wildlife impacts of petroleum co.operating in Yasuni Nat.Park (Ecuador), Ecuambiente SA 1994–. **Achievements:** dev.of multivariate methods to describe & evaluate habitat effects within complex, speciose data-sets. **Membership:** CECIA. **Award:** Eagle Scout, Presidential Scholar (Humboldt SU). **Publications:** papers incl. Comparison of insect fauna captured in six diff.trap-types in a Douglas-fir [*Pseudo-tsuga douglasii*] forest 1987, Use of birds by Amazonian Indians 1990. Indiff.to pers.pub., feels news media support important but not always well-oriented. **Languages:** English; French & Portuguese (poor); Spanish. Willing to act as consult.etc. **Address:** Consejo Ecuatoriano para la Conservación e Investigación de las Aves, POB 17 17 906, Quito, Ecuador. **Tel.** (office) & **fax** 593 2 468 876, (home) 593 2 458 924; **e-mail** birdlife@cipa. org.ec .

CANNELL, Dr Melvin G.R.   Global environment, forestry & agroforestry, ecology. Head of Research Station. *B.*12 Aug.1944, Bungay, Suffolk, England, UK. British. *M.*Maria Femma: 2 *d.* **Education:** U.of Reading, BSc (Hons)(1st Class) 1966, PhD 1971, DSc 1986, all in Agricl Bot. **Experience:** res.& consult.in UK & tropics in for., tree biol.& agrofor.; res.in tree biol., biomass prod., envl impacts on forests, modelling, & plantation crops. **Career:** Res. Officer, Coffee Res.Fndn (Kenya) 1966–71; SSO Inst.of Tree Biol.1971–4, PSO 1974 & Project Leader 1979–85 ITE; Vis.Sci. Weyerhaeuser (For.) Co.1977–8; Dep.Head 1984–7 & Head 1987– of Edinburgh Res.Station ITE, NERC. **Memberships:** ICF, IBiol., IUFRO, BES, RSFS, AAB, Edinburgh Soc.of Organists. **Awards:** Silvicultural Prize (ICF) 1986, F.RSE 1991. **Publications:** five books incl.*Tree Physiol.and Yield Improvement* (co-Ed.) 1976, *World Forest Biomass and Primary Prod.Data* 1982, *Trees as Crop Plants* (co-Ed.) 1985; 107 papers. **Languages:** English, French (some), Swahili (some). Willing to act as a consult. **Address:** Edinburgh Research Station, Institute of Terrestrial Ecology, Bush Estate, Penicuik, Midlothian EH26 0QB, Scotland, UK. **Tel.** (office) 44 131 445 4343, (home) 44 1721 730355; **fax** 44 131 445 3943.

CANO , Dr Guillermo J.   Environmental law — national & international. Senior Consultant. *B.*14 Feb.1913, Mendoza, Argentina. Argentinian. *M.* Sara: 3 *d.* **Education:** U.of Cuyo, Dr Jur.1935, Dr *honoris causa* 1991. **Experience:** elaboration of Natural Resources Law since 1936, and of Envl Law since 1970. **Career:** Ed.-in-Chief *Ambiente y Recursos Naturales, Revista de Derecho, Política y Administración* 1984–91; Founder & Exec.Dir 1984–91, Sr Consult.1991–, Fundación Ambiente y Recursos Naturales. **Achievement:** quarterly pubn of above J. **Member**

ship: ICEL. **Award:** Elizabeth Haub Prize (VUB) 1978. **Publications:** incl.*Derecho, política y administración Ambientales* (three vols) 1979. Dislikes pers.pub.& news media support. **Languages:** English, French, Italian, Portuguese, Spanish. Willing to act as consult.& to judge proposals. **Address:** Arenales 2040 7-B, 1124 Buenos Aires, Argentina. **Tel.**(office) 54 1 781 9171, (home) 54 1 823 7292; **fax** 54 1 781 6115.

CAPPATO, Professor Jorge A.   Environmental journalism, communication, information, & education. Professor of Ecology, Executive Director, Environmental Consultant. *B.*8 June 1950, Santa Fe, Argentina. Argentinian. *M.* Rosa Gronda (envl journalism): 2 *d.*Betania & Albertina (both founding members of Sch.of Nature). **Education:** Nat.U.of Litoral, Tech.Chemist 1969. **Experience:** 20+ yrs in envl info., communication, & educ., coord.of progs re.cons. & sust.dev., adv.to Argentinian envl NGOs & intl bodies, media exp.1978–, coopn with IUCN's Argentine Cttee 1993–. **Career:** Lect.in Chem. (with envl orientation) 1973–85, Prof.of Ecol.(in social work/service) 1985–, Nat.U.of Entre Ríos and Superior Sch.of Social Service; Coord. The Sch.Litoral 1982–8; Presenter, Health for Everyone Prog. Nat.U.Radio of Litoral 1991–; Envl Consult. Santa Fe Municipal Govt 1989–; Exec.Dir, Fundación Proteger 1991–. **Achievements:** intro.of envl subjects to intermediate & tech.schools & univs 1973–, launched UNEP Campaign 'For Each Child a Tree' in Argentina 1982, congregated all Argentine envl NGOs in Santa Fe for first time 1983, wrote Ecol. Manifest of Santa Fe 1983, created Sem.of Ecol.at Superior Sch.of Social Service of Santa Fe 1985, founded Fndn Proteger for Sust. Dev.& Health 1991, launched 'Waste per Life' and 'More Trees' campaigns 1994. **Memberships:** G500F, IPPL, ATA, Council of Santa Fe Municipal Govt (Hon.Assessor). **Awards:** Preserving the Future (Argentine Admin.of Nat. Parks) 1988, Global 500 Roll of Honour (UNEP) 1992, St Claire of Assisi (Family Mothers' League of Argentina) 1992, Qual.of Life (Health Consult.) 1993, Fndn of Santa Fe 1993, Excellency Award (Argentinian Inst.of Excellency) 1994. **Publications:** incl. *Man and His Envt* 1987, Ecol.in Prov.of Santa Fe (enc.entry) 1991. Favours news media support. **Languages:** English, French, Italian & Portuguese (all written & read); Spanish. Willing to act as consult.etc. **Address:** Fundación Proteger para el Desarrollo Sostenible y la Salud, Casilla de Correo 550, 3000 Santa Fe, Argentina. **Tel.**& **fax** 54 42 970298; **e-mail** proteger@aamaisde. satlink.net .

CARDENAL SEVILLA, Lorenzo B., *see* **SEVILLA, Lorenzo B.** CARDENAL.

CARPENTER, Richard A.   Environmental impact assessment in developing countries; definition, measurement, & prediction, of sustainable development. Retired. *B.*22 August 1926, Kansas

City, MO, USA. American. *M*.Joanne F.: *s*.Prof. Stephen R.(ecol.), 2 *d*. **Education:** U.of Missouri BS(Chem.) 1948, MA(Organic Chem.) 1949. **Experience:** conceived & directed multinat., multidisc.studies of potentials & limitations of natural resources & envl systems for econ. dev., extensive travel in Asia & Pacific, admin.as Study Dir of Hawaii Envl Risk Ranking Project 1991–2, consult.with UN, World Bank, ADB, US CEQ, NRDC, US NC. **Career:** chem.res.& dev.1949–64; Founder & Chief of Envl Policy Div. Congressional Res.Service, Library of Cong.1964–72; Exec. Dir (First), CNR, NRC/NAS 1972–7; Sr F. E–W Center 1977–93. **Achievements:** training of envl professionals and assisting in prep.of envl laws & regs in developing countries, co-Founder Pacific Basin Consortium for Hazardous Waste Res. **Memberships:** ESA, Sigma Xi, NAEP, IUCN CESP, ACS, IAIA, ISEE. **Publications:** num.incl.*From Grave to Cradle: Trends in Hazardous Waste Mgmt* (co-Ed.) 1991, Can we measure sust.dev.? 1991, Envl Risks to Hawaii's Public Health and Ecosystems 1992, Keeping up with the dynamic hazardous waste business 1993, Monitoring & predicting sust.1994; Regnl Ed.for American *Land Degradation & Rehab.*, Edl Bd *EIA Rev., The Envl Professional*. Dislikes pers.pub., favours news media support. **Language:** English. Further details may be obtained from *Who's Who in America* 1992. Willing to act as consult.etc. **Address:** Route 5 Box 277, Charlottesville, Virginia 22901, USA. **Tel.**(home) & **fax** 1 804 974 6010.

CARRILLO, Dr Antonio MACHADO. Nature conservation: protected areas (inventories, planning, interpretation, management & legal aspects); species recovery plans (terrestrial); environmental policy (sustainable tourism etc.); entomology (Carabid beetles). Adviser for Protected Areas. *B*.19 Jan.1953, Madrid, Spain. Spanish. *M*.Chusy: *s*., 3 *d*. **Education:** U.of La Laguna, BSc(Hons.) 1975, PhD (honour dist.) 1991. **Experience:** teaching gen.ecol., taxonomic work (Coleoptera), field res.& resource inventories, park mgmt & interpretive planning, staff training, orgnl mgmt, law drafting, EIA studies, land-use planning, envl policy advising, ind.intl consults & intl coopn progs/convs (EEC, Council of Europe, US–Spain etc.) in Europe, Africa & S.Amer. **Career:** Res.F. Mus.of Natural Hist. Santa Cruz de Tenerife 1975–6; Lect.in Ecol. U.of La Laguna 1976–80; Res.Sci. ICONA and Dir Teide Nat.Park 1976–85; Spec.Adv. Cabinet of Presidency (Spanish Govt) 1987; Adv.for Envl Policy to Pres.1988–92 & to Min.of Finances 1991–3, Canary Islands Govt; Adv.for Prot.Areas, ICONA 1993–; Pres. ECNC 1994–. **Achievements:** founder/init. first park interpretive centre in Spain, devised & implemented master plans of several nat.parks, directs prot.areas network project in Canary Islands, init.recovery plan of Hierro giant lizard, Canarian law for prevention of ecol.impact.& of Nature symbols, trains conservationists, wrote descrip-

tion of several new genera & species of ground-beetles, promotes tourism–envl awareness in Canary Islands. **Memberships:** ICS, SAE, OBB, AFP (co-Founder), IUCN (Counc.). **Awards:** Spanish Agric.Medal from King Juan Carlos 1978, Teide Nat.Park Bd (Hon.Memb.). **Publications:** *Ecol., Envt & Tourism Dev.in the Canary Islands* 1990, *Monogr.of the Carabids of the Canary Islands (Coleoptera, Carabidae)* 1991, *Legal & Admin.Aspects of Nat.Parks* (co-Ed.) 1988; *c*.40 tech.& sci.papers. Favours pers.pub. & news media support. **Languages:** English, French (read), German, Portuguese (read), Spanish. Willing to act as consult.etc. **Address:** Urbanización Aguere 4, 38208 La Laguna, Tenerife, Canary Islands, Spain. **Tel.**(home) 34 22 253833; **fax** 34 22 632614.

CARROLL, Professor Dr John E. International environmental ethics & values; environmental diplomacy, ecology, religion. Professor of Environmental Conservation. *B*.19 May 1945, Brooklyn, NY, USA. American. *M*.Diana C.: 2 *d*. **Education:** Louisiana Tech.U. BA (Geog.) 1966, Western Michigan U. MA(Geog.) 1968, Michigan SU PhD(Resource Dev.) 1974. **Experience:** admin.of undergrad.& postgrad. degree progs in envl cons.; established res., writing, pubn, conf. organizing. **Career:** Dir Envl Studies, St John's U. 1967–74; Prof.& Coord.of Envl Cons.Prog. U.of New Hampshire 1974–; Vis.Prof.at U.of Edinburgh 1987–8 and Schumacher Coll.1992; Scholar-in-Residence, Monterey Inst.of Intl Studies 1994. **Achievements:** intl envl diplomacy, ethics, & values, and writing thereon; direction of under- & post-grad. envl cons.progs. **Membership:** ISEE. **Awards:** Kellogg Fndn Nat.F., Vis.Scholar at num.colls, memb.of various bds. **Publications:** *Acid Rain: An Issue in Canadian–Amer. Relations* 1982, *Envl Diplomacy* 1983, 1986, *Intl Envl Diplomacy* 1990; num.others. Favours pers.pub.& news media support. **Languages:** English, French (read). Willing to act as consult.etc. **Address:** Department of National Resources, University of New Hampshire, Durham, New Hampshire 03824-3589, USA. **Tel.**1 603 862 1020, (home) 1 603 868 2935; **fax** 1 603 862 4976.

CARVALHO, Emeritus Professor Dr G. SOARES DE. Evolution of coastal zones, Pleistocene–Holocene sedimentology & stratigraphy. Emeritus Professor of Geology. *B*.20 Mar.1920, Oliveira de Azamies (Aveiro), Portugal. Portuguese. *W*. **Education:** U.of Coimbra, PhD (Geol.) 1947. **Experience:** res., teaching, admin. **Career:** Asst Prof. Univs of Coimbra 1944–54 & Porto 1961–70; Head Geol.& Geol. Map Div. Angola Geol.Survey 1954–8; Res.F. Council of Overseas Res.(Lisbon) with geol. missions in Guinée-Bissau 1959 and India (Goa) & Angola 1960; Head, Dept of Earth Scis 1970–75, Dir 1975–6, Inst.for Scientific Res.of Mozambique; Prof.of Geol.& Head of Dept of Earth Scis 1976–88, Emer.1990–, U.of Minho. **Achievements:** coastal cons., envl geol. **Memberships:**

SGP, APG, SGL, SPAE, SGF, SEPM, IAS, SASQR, QRA, ASBPA, NAGT. **Publications:** num.since 1961 incl.*Quaternary Sea Level Changes in NW Portugal* (co-Author, in Portuguese) 1988, Dunes and Holocene Deposits of Coastal Zone of Portugal 1991, *Coastal Cons.and Prot.in NW Portugal* (co-Author) 1993. **Languages:** English (poor), French (good), Portuguese. Willing to act as consult.etc. **Address:** Rua Elísio do Moura 62 r/c, 4710 Braga, Portugal. **Tel.**(home) 351 53 7251; **fax** 351 53 610080.

CASTRO DELPIANO, José Pedro, *see* **DELPIANO, José Pedro** CASTRO.

CASWELL, Ms Patricia Joy. Environment, economy, management, equity. Executive Director. *B.*22 Aug.1948, Brisbane, Australia. Australian. *P.*Brian Boyd: *d.* **Education:** Qld U. BA(Hist. & English) 1970; U.of Western Australia, BA (Hons)(Theatre Arts) 1972, Dipl.of Educ.1973; Licentiate of Trinity Coll.London, Teacher's Dipl.(Speech & Drama) 1973; Latrobe U. B.Ed. 1974. **Experience:** given pa-pers/speeches based on ACF res.re.biodiv., water, coasts, forests, sust.agric.& industry, energy & transport, 'genethics', indigenous people, and green jobs; participation in all forms of media, public speaking, book interviews. **Career:** teaching & lecturing in NT, WA, & Vic. 1968–78; Industrial Officer 1979–81, Gen.Sec.1981–4 Tech.Teachers' Union of Vic.; Industrial Officer, Victorian Trades Hall Council 1984–92; Exec.Dir ACF 1992–. **Achievements:** pursuit of mainstreaming of envl issues around our major areas of work incl.biodiv., water, coasts, forests, sust.agric., sust.industry, energy & transport, 'genethics' indigenous people, and green jobs; estab.of comp.educ./schools prog. & curricula. **Memberships:** ANC for UNESCO 1984–90, 'Greenhouse Australia' Bd of Comm. for the Future 1989, Australia Council (Chairperson, Community, Art & Design Cttee) 1990–, Victorian Alcohol & Drug Council (Action Council) 1992–, RMIT Council 1993–, ICD 1993–. **Award:** Amer.Field Service Scholarship 1966–7. **Publications:** Will the Envt Movement Survive? 1994, Clean Prod.Must Also be Green Prod.1994, Keynote Address (Nat. Community Forum on Unemployment) 1994. Favours pers.pub.& news media support. **Language:** English. May be willing to act as consult. etc. **Address:** Australian Conservation Foundation, 340 Gore Street, Fitzroy, Victoria 3065, Australia. **Tel.**(office) 61 13 416 1166, (home) 61 13 348 1620; **fax** 61 13 416 2993.

CATANIA, Professor Dr Peter Joseph. Energy & environment and international exchanges, systems engineering education, renewable energy. Professor of Engineering, Foundation Chairman. *B.*6 Jan.1942, Newmarket, Ont., Canada. Canadian. *M.*Dr Josie: *s., d.* **Education:** U.of Alb. MASc(Chem.Eng.) 1969, PhD(Chem.Eng.) 1977. **Experience:** res., lect., invited speaker at num. intl energy confs, consults, 20+ yrs' exp.with news media. **Career:** Res.Asst, U.of Waterloo

1967; Res.Assoc. U.of Delaware 1969–71; NRC Res.Scholar, U.of Alb.1971–4; Prof.of Engg 1974–, Asst Dean, Fac.of Engg 1980–86, U.of Regina; Vis.Prof. U.of Paraíba (Brazil) 1977–9; Chairman, IEF 1989–. **Achievement:** estab.of IEF to enhance and strengthen intl communication among energy researchers worldwide. **Memberships:** ISES, AIChE, IPAC, CIIA, CSME, SESC, NYAS, Sask.Assn of Professional Engrs. **Awards:** selected as one of 2,000 outstanding engrs in Canada 1993, nominated for *Intl Directory of Disting.Leadership* (5th edn) 1994. **Publications:** 80 conf.& j. papers incl.Energy — the envt and econ.(presented at 5th Arabic Intl Solar Energy Conf.), Systems engg educ., res., and nat.policies 1995, *Horizontal and Vertical Well Ratio Analysis* 1995; 19 intl reports for CIDA. Favours pers.pub. & news media support. **Language:** English. Further details may be obtained from *Intl Who's Who of Intellectuals* 1985. Willing to act as consult.etc. **Address:** Faculty of Engineering, University of Regina, Regina, Saskatchewan S4S 0A2, Canada. **Tel.**(office) 1 306 585 4364, (home) 1 306 586 4993; **fax** 1 306 585 4855 or 781 8364.

CERDA, Professor Dr Alberto Mariano Vazquez DE LA. Research in physical oceanography in the Gulf of Mexico and protection of its reefs & islands. Professor of Oceanography. *B.*30 Aug.1943, DF, Mexico. Mexican. *M.*Olga: *s., d.* **Education:** Heroica Escuela Naval (Naval Acad.), B(Geogl Eng.) 1965, B(Mech.Naval Eng.) 1967; Texas A&M U. MSc(Oceanogr.) 1975, PhD(Phys.Oceanogr.) 1993. **Experience:** 25 yrs' oceanogr., three yrs as Commander aboard Oceanogr.Res.Vessel, 15 yrs' lecturing in oceanogr., thermodynamics, marine poll., & dredging; Dir of Oceanogr.Inst.and Naval Oceanographer; Mexican Del.at Workshop of Oceanogr.Atlantic Panel 1975 & 1978; Oceanogr.World Prog. (OCDE) 1993; Memb.CONACYT Earth Sci. Cttee 1992–5. **Career:** 37 yrs in Mexican Navy — Destroyer Navigation Officer 1965–6, Commander of Oceanogr.Res.Vessel H-02 1976–9, Dir of Naval Oceanogr.Inst.(Veracruz) 1980–86 & 1991, Gen.Dir of Naval Oceanogr.Office (Mexico City) 1992–4, retired as Vice-Admiral 1995; Prof.of Oceanogr. Inst.of Engg, Universidad Veracruzana. **Achievements:** res.in phys. oceanogr.& met.in Gulf of Mexico, prot.& cons.of reefs & islands in Mexico and the world. **Memberships:** AGU 1982–, The Oceanogr.Soc. 1990–. **Awards:** Naval 1961 & 1962, Honorific Mention in the Award of Oceanogr.in Mexico 1994. **Publications:** incl.*Currents and Waters of the Upper 1200 m.of the Southwestern Gulf of Mexico* (Master's thesis) 1975, *Bay of Campeche Cyclone* (doctl dissertation) 1993, The apparent erratic trajectory of hurricane Roxanne in the Gulf of Mexico 1995. Indiff.to pers.pub.& news media support. **Languages:** English, French (poor), Spanish. Willing to act as consult.etc. **Address:** Instituto de Ingenieria, Universidad Veracruzana, Boca del Rio, Veracruz 94294, Mexico.

Tel.(office) 52 29 217475 & 218718, (home) 52 29 216251; **fax** 52 29 217475; **e-mail** vazquez@sparc10-2.insting.uv.mx .

ČEŘOVSKÝ, Dr Jan. Plant ecology, biodiversity conservation (threatened species, protected areas), environmental education. Senior Scientist. *B*.2 Feb.1930, Prague, Czech Rep. Czech. *M*.Dr Jarmila (clinical anthrop.): 2 *s*. **Education:** Charles U. MSc 1954, PhD 1961, RNDr 1966. **Experience:** res., teaching, writing & editing; consult., intl coopn (cons., envl educ.). **Career:** Ed.-in-Chief, Czech popular-scientific Youth Magazine 'ABC' 1956–59; Res.Worker, State Inst.for Prot.of Monuments and Nature Cons.1959–69 & 1973–90; Educ.Exec.Officer, IUCN 1969–73; Sr Sci. Agency of Nature and Landscape Prot.of the Czech Rep.(before 1995 was Czech Inst.for Nature Cons.)1990–. **Achievements:** co-Founder of Intl Envl Educ.(with IUCN, UNESCO, UNEP), leader of several Czechoslovak progs & projects, *i.a.*Chief Coord. Czech & Slovak Red Data Book, co-Leader IUCN E.Euro.Prog.etc. **Memberships:** CBS; Pres.Bd of Dirs, Czech & Slovak Ecopoint Fndn; Bd of Trustees Czech EVA (Envl Educ.) Fndn; IUCN — Council 1988–94 (VP 1991–94), Comms on Survival, Nat.Parks, Educ.; ECNC (Bd.Chair of Steering Cttee of Planta Europe project). **Awards.** Merit Awards & Commem. Medals Krkonose (1983) & Tatra (1979, 1989) Nat.Parks, Meritorious Man of Czech Culture 1988, Merit Award (ABI) 1990, P.J. Lenne Medal (J.W.v.Goethe Fndn) 1993, H.Conwentz Medal (Arbeitsgemeinschaft Beruflicher und ehrenamtlicher Naturschutz) 1994; prizes for sci. dissemination among youth 1959–80. **Publications:** Author or co-Author of 15 books, *c*.300 scientific & tech.papers, and *c*.1,000 scientific popular articles, lectures, book reviews, interviews etc., Ed.*Newsletter, C.and Eastern Europe* (IUCN) 1991–. Indiff.to pers.pub. & support by news media. **Languages:** Czech, English, French, German, Russian, Slovak; can read Croatian, Dutch, Italian, Latin, Polish, Slovenian, Spanish. Willing to act as consult. etc. **Address:** Pernerova 50, CZ-18600 Praha 8, Czech Republic. **Tel.**(office) & **fax** 42 2 270417, (home) 42 2 232 1121.

CHADWICK, Professor Dr Michael John. Arid zone ecology, restoration of degraded land, quantitative measurement of comparative environmental risk. Institute Director. *B*.13 Sept. 1934, Leicester, England, UK. British. *M*.Josephine: *s*.Matthew Thomas (trop.land mgmt with ODA), 2 *d*. **Education:** U.of Wales BSc (Agricl Bot.) 1956, PhD 1959; Downing College Camb.MA 1962. **Experience:** res.— plant nutrition, desert ecol., land restoration & coordinated abatement strat.models related to acidic depositions; consult.— land mgmt in relation to arid zones & degraded land; teaching terr. ecol. from BSc to PhD levels. **Career:** Lect. U.of Khartoum 1959–62 and in Agricl Bot. U.of Camb.1962–6; Lect. Sr Lect. Reader & Prof.in

Plant Ecol. U.of York 1966–91; Dir Stockholm Envt Inst.1991–. **Achievements:** application of ecol.methods to land restoration and approaches to comparative envl risk studies. **Memberships:** BES (past-Sec.), F.IBiol. **Publications:** *c*.60 incl. The Restoration of Land (co-Author) 1980, Envl Impacts of Coal Mining & Utilization (co-Author) 1987. Mildly favours pers. pub., favours news media support. **Languages:** English, French (simple written & spoken). Willing to act as consult.etc.occasionally. **Address:** Stockholm Environment Institute, POB 2142, S-103 14 Stockholm, Sweden. **Tel.**46 8 723 0260; **fax** 46 8 723 0348.

Chae-Shik RHO, Dr, *see* **RHO, Dr Chae-Shik.**

CHALABI, Bouzid. Conservation of wetlands & waterbirds, conservation & management of national parks & protected areas, animal conservation, legislation re.conservation of Nature & environment. Assistant Chief Researcher, Head of Department. *B*.29 May 1954, Skikda, Algeria. Algerian. **Education:** Institut Nat. Agronomique d'Alger, Ing.d'Etat en Agronomie (for.& Nature cons.) 1980, Magister in Wetlands and Waterbirds Cons. 1990. **Experience:** res.in wetlands & waterbirds cons., NPPA mgmt, teaching at u.level 1987–, participation in num.confs & sems. **Career:** Dir of El Kala Nat.Park 1982–5; Chief of Lab, Institut Nat. Agronomique d'Alger 1987–92; Head, Dept of Agron.Institut Agrovétérinaire d'El Tarf 1992–. **Achievements:** supervision of many students' theses, discovery of new distribn site of Algerian nuthatch 1989, admin.of six nat.training courses in ornith.& wetlands cons. **Memberships:** PAOC 1992–6, IUCN CNPPA, Bird Life Intl (Algeria). **Publications:** Status of Algerian wetlands, past & present 1991, Situation passée et actuelle des Parcs Nationaux et des Aires protegées en Algérie 1992; several other papers. Indiff.to pers.pub.& news media support. **Languages:** Arabic, English, French. Willing to act as consult.etc. **Address:** BP 166, 36 000 El-Tarf, Algeria. **Tel.**(office) 213 8 61 0529 to 33.

CHALLINOR, Dr David. Forest soils & ecology, environmental conservation. Science Adviser. *B*.11 July 1920, New York, NY, USA. American. *M*.Dr Joan R. **Education:** Harvard Coll. BA 1943, Yale Sch.of For. MF 1959, Yale U. PhD 1966. **Experience:** cotton farmer in W.Texas following four yrs' active duty in US Navy during WWII, followed by five yrs in business, then grad.student at Yale U.; for. res.in New England, admin.of Yale's Natural Hist. Mus., trop.for. in C.Amer.& SE Asia, and finally resp. for all Smithsonian for. res.throughout the world. **Career:** Dep.Dir, Yale Peabody Mus.of Natural Hist.1960–66; Asst Sec. for Sci.1971–83 and for Res. 1983–7, Sci.Adv.to Sec.1988–, Smithsonian Instn. **Achievements:** directly involved in estab.of Smithsonian Envt Res.Center (MD), Smithsonian Cons.Res.Center (VA), K.Mahendra Trust for Nature Cons.in Nepal, & Seychelles Islands Fndn. **Memberships:** F. AAAS, SAF,

ESA, Sigma Xi, ATB, AIBS.   **Award:** Joseph Henry Medal (Smithsonian Instn).   **Publications:** Alteration of surface soil characteristics by four tree species 1968, Struggle for the survival of the Bermuda Cedar 1971, num.articles. Against pers. pub., indiff.to news media support. **Languages:** English; French & German (read, some conversation), Spanish. Further details may be obtained from *Who's Who in America* 1983–, *American Men & Women in Sci.*1983–. Willing to act as consult.etc. **Address:** Smithsonian Institution, National Zoo, Washington, District of Columbia 20008, USA. **Tel.**(office) 1 202 673 4705, (home) 1 202 965 9447; **fax** 1 202 673 4607.

CHANDAK, Surya Prakash. Air pollution control & energy management.   Director of Pollution Control.   *B.*14 March 1953, Allahabad, India. Indian. *M.*Sarla: *d.* **Education:** Calcutta U. BSc 1971, Kanpur U. BEng.(Chemical) 1975, Training Inst.for Productivity & Industrial Engg Postgrad.Cert.in Fuel Efficiency & Energy Mgmt 1978; AIT Industrial Poll.Control 1988; Centre for Envl Mgmt & Planning (Aberdeen), EIA 1991. **Experience:** 15 yrs' admin.& consult.in energy mgmt & industrial air poll.control. **Career:** Asst Dir 1978–83, Dep.Dir 1983–5, Sr Dep.Dir 1985–7 (all in Fuel Efficiency), Sr Dep.Dir 1987–91, Dir 1991– (both in Poll. Control), all at NPC. **Achievements:** dev. of cost-effective air poll.control systems, nat.team-leader for UNIDO & APO demn project in small & medium enterprises. **Membership:** Edl Panel, Envt Res.Cttee (Govt of India). **Award:** Chairman's Gold Medal 1978. **Publications:** incl. *Energy Envt Relationship* 1989. Favours pers.pub. & news media support. **Languages:** Bengali, English, Hindi, Italian (working knowledge). Willing to act as consult.etc. **Address:** National Productivity Council, Utpadakta Bhawan, Lodi Road, New Delhi 110003, Delhi, India. **Tel.**91 11 462 2359 or 61 1243; **fax** 91 11 461 5002.

Changdu CHEN, Professor, *see* **CHEN, Professor Changdu.**

CHAPMAN, Dean Professor Dr Joseph A. Mammalogy specifically of Lagomorpha. Professor of Wildlife Ecology, College Dean.   *B.*28 April 1941, Salem, OR, USA. American. *M.*Gale Willner: 2 *d.* **Education:** Oregon SU, BS 1965, MS 1967, PhD 1970 (all in Fisheries & Wildlife). **Experience:** 20 yrs at var.levels of admin.at two state univs incl.grad.student adv., dept head, lab.head, and coll.Dean. **Career:** Fac.Res.Asst 1969–70, Res.Asst Prof.1970–74, Assoc.Prof. 1974–8, Prof.1978–83 all in Wildlife Ecol., Head of Appalachian Envt Lab.1974–83, U.of Maryland; Prof.of Wildlife Ecol.1983–, Head of Dept of Fisheries & Wildlife 1983–9, Dean of Coll.of Natural Resources 1989–, Utah SU. **Achievement:** membership of IUCN Lagomorph SG 1982–91. **Memberships:** IBiol. (elected F.), F.Explorers' Club (NY), IUCN SSC (elected Emer.). **Awards:** Memb.Emer.(IUCN SSC) 1990–, Outstanding Book Awards (The

Wildlife Soc.) 1982 & 1984. **Publications:** incl. Systematics and biogeog.of the New England Cottontail (*[Sylvilagus transitionalis]* Bangs 1895) with description of a new species from the Appalachian Mtns (co-Author) 1992, Life hist. characteristics of insular *Peromyscus mariculatus* in the Bonneville Basin (co-Author) 1992. **Language:** English. **Address:** Office of the Dean, College of Natural Resources, Utah State University, UMC 5200, Logan, Utah 84322-5200, USA. **Tel.**(office) 1 801 797 2452, (home) 1 801 752 7019; **fax** 1 801 797 2443.

CHARLIER, Professor Dr Roger H.L. Coastal protection, coastal-zone management, alternative energies, environmental auditing. Vice-President, Scientific Adviser.   *B.*20 Nov.1923, Antwerp, Belgium. American, Belgian. *M.*Prof.Dr Patricia M.(envl educ.): *s.*Jean-Armand 'Jac' (politics & envt), *d.*Dr Constance C.P.Charlier-Keating (communications re envt). **Education:** VUB, BS (Geog.) 1940, Lic. (Pol.Sci.) 1941, Lic.(Earth Sci.) 1945; U.of Liège BS(Geol.) 1942; Friedrich-Alexander U. PhD(Geog.) 1947; U.of Paris Litt. D.(Geol.) 1956, DSc(Oceanogr.) 1958. **Experience:** –1983 mainly academic, 1984– mainly in private industry involved in envl projects incl. impact assessment, audits, *et al.* **Career:** Prof. of Geol. Geog.& Oceanogr. Northeastern Illinois U. 1961–87; Extraordinary Prof. VUB 1971–87; Vis Prof.(Oceanogr.), U.of Bordeaux I 1970–74, 1983–4; Exec.Dir Inst.for the Dev.of Riverine & Estuarine Systems 1974–76; Vis.Prof. U.of Maryland 1974–6, 1979–80, 1983; Exec.Adv. Dolmen Engg 1982–4; Adjunct Prof. Union Grad.Sch. 1980–; Memb. Euro.Community, XIIth Gen.Directorate, Comm.on Bioconversion 1985–; Prof. associé hon. U.of Bordeaux I 1986–, Prof. Emer.at Northeastern Illinois U. and Free U.of Brussels 1988–; Sci.Adv.Sopex NV 1988–89, Scientific Adv. Haecon NV 1989–; Memb. Bd of Dirs & VP for Euro.Ops, Envl Planning Group Inc., and Supervising Exec.Dir, Educl Centers, Houston (Texas, USA) & Moscow (Russian Fedn) 1992–. **Achievements:** launched educl prog.in 1970, pubns. **Memberships:** F.GSA, IAHO, RBSGS, AAUP, F.New Jersey AS (Pres. 1954–7, past-Pres.1957–8), Educ.Cttee of Marine Tech.Soc. **Awards:** Dolmen NV 1983; Project 'Utilization & Mgmt of the Coastal Zone' (Mins of Overseas Dev.and of Envt) 1984; Haecon NV 1985; Council of Europe 1986; UNESCO 1986; Paul-Henri Spaak Mem.Lect. Award 1992; num.others during 1953–80. **Publications:** Ocean Resources: An Intro.to Econ. Oceanogr.1978, Planning for Coastal Areas 1987, Ocean Non-living Resources: Histl Perspective on Exploitation, Econ.& Envl Impact 1990, Heavy-metals sediments poll.in estuarine & coastal waters: corrective measures for existing problems 1991, Water for the desert: a viewpoint 1991, Coastal engg: approaches to coastal defense & restoration 1993, *Ocean Energies: Envl, Econ.& Social Sig.*(co-Author) 1993; num.papers for presentation & pubn. Favours pers.pub.& news media support. **Languages:**

Dutch, English, Flemish, French, German; Italian & Spanish (spoken); Catalan & Romanian (comp.); Danish, Norwegian, Swedish & Swahili (read). Further details may be obtained from *Who's Who in the World* 1987–, *Who's Who in Amer.*1984–. Willing to act as consult.etc. **Address:** Haecon NV, Deinsesteenweg 110, B-9031 Gent, Belgium. **Tel.** (office) 32 92 27 6082 (Belgium) or 1 708 382 0020 (USA), (home) 32 2 649 0755 (Belgium) or 1 312 286 8024 (USA); **fax** 32 2 649 0755 (Belgium) or 1 708 382 0154 or 1 312 286 8024 (both USA).

CHATURVEDI, Amar Nath. Forestry, environment. Senior Fellow. *B.*5 Feb.1930, Chandrapur Village, Agra, UP, India. Indian. *M.*Manorama: *s.,* 2 *d.* **Education:** Agra U. MSc (Maths) 1951, Assoc.of Indian Forest Coll. (Dipl.) 1955. **Experience:** res.& tech., UP Forest Dept for 25 yrs, & admin.for ten yrs; consult.for six yrs. **Career:** UP For.Dept 1955–67; deputation to Forest Res.Inst.& Colls 1967–73, and to R.Govt of Bhutan 1976–79; Sr F. Tata Energy Res.Inst. 1986–; consult. FAO Philippines, Nov.–Dec. 1987. **Achievements:** rehab. of degraded sites at several places in UP and at Gwal Pahari in Haryana since 1987. **Memberships:** MAB Cttee, Dept of Envt, Govt of India; Soc.of Indian Foresters; IUCN SSC; Sr Sci. Panel of the Indo–US Prog.on Biomass, Govt of India. **Awards,** Hari Om Ashram (ICAR) 1986, Brandis 1988, Seth Mem.1990, Bochasanwasi Shri Akshar Purshottam Sanstha 1992. **Publications:** two books, 100+ res.papers/ articles. Dislikes pers. pub., favours news media support. **Languages:** English, Hindi. Further details can be obtained from *Who's Who* published in India. Willing to act as consult.etc. **Address:** Tata Energy Research Institute, 101 Jor Bagh, New Delhi 110003, Delhi, India. **Tel.**(office) 91 11 462 2189; **fax** 91 11 462 1770.

CHEEK, Dr Martin R. Taxonomic botany & conservation particularly of West & Central African forests; Malvales, Meliaceae, & carnivorous plants. Higher Scientific Officer. *B.*1 April 1960, Epping, Essex, England, UK. British. Father R.V. Cheek *qv.* **Education:** U.of Reading BSc(Hons) (Hort.Bot.) 1982, MSc(Pure & Applied Plant Taxonomy) 1983, Wadham Coll. Oxf. DPhil(Plant Taxonomy) 1989. **Experience:** res.— fieldwork in equatorial Africa 1984–, expedns to Madagascar 1985–9, cons.of plant biodiv.on Mt Cameroon, prod.of plant check-lists for forests in SW Cameroon mostly funded as consults by ODA (UK). **Career:** SO then Higher SO, R. Botanic Gdn 1987–. **Achievements:** The identification & mapping of cons.priorities on & around Mt Cameroon, and promotion of Mt Cameroon as a major centre of plant diversity; Founder of IUCN SSC Carnivorous Plants SG; prod.of articles drawing attention to need for cons.in carnivorous & other groups of plants. **Publications:** 55 incl.Conserving carnivorous plants 1990, *A Botl Inventory of the Mababa–Moliwe Forest* 1992. Indiff.to pers.pub.& news

media support. **Languages:** English; French, Latin & Malagasy (all poor). Willing to act as consult.etc. **Address:** Royal Botanic Gardens, Kew, Richmond, Surrey TW9 3AE, England, UK. **Tel.**44 181 332 5431; **fax** 44 181 332 5278.

CHEEK, Roy Victor. Conservation & cultivation of plants, planting design & management, tree surgery. Independent Plant Consultant, Visiting Professor. *B.*11 Nov.1934, Barnet, Herts., England, UK. British. *M.*Mary: 2 *s.*incl. Dr Martin R.Cheek *qv,* 3 *d.* **Education:** Sch.of Hort. (RHS), Dipl.in Hort.(Hons) 1958; Regent Street Poly. Dipl.in Park Admin.1965; S.Glamorgan Coll.of Higher Educ. M.Hort (RHS) 1963; U.of W.of England (formerly Bristol Poly.), B.Ed. (Mgmt) 1982. **Experience:** widespread exp.& consult.in tech., design, mgmt, educ.& training in plant cultivation, planting design, tree surgery and sports turf in var.regns of the world. **Career:** early yrs spent in commercial hort.; Nursery Mgr 1958–60; Sr Tech.Officer, Harlow New Town (Essex, UK) 1960–64; Divosnal Parks Super. 1964–7, Chief Parks Officer of Borough of Bebington 1967–9, City of Cardiff; Lect. Lancs Coll.of Agric.& Hort.1969–70; Sr Lect.& Curator, Somerset Coll.of Agric.& Hort.1970–91; Vis.Prof. Landscape Tech.U. Rep.of Uruguay 1993–; Ind.Plant Consult.1991–. **Achievements:** Founder Memb. NCCPG, Founder, Chairman & Pres.of Somerset & Avon Regn of NCCPG, created & managed ten nat.collections of diff.plant genera, created educl gdn with over 10,000 diff.species & cultivars, tree cons.by surgery in Uruguay & Argentina. **Memberships:** ILAM, F.IHort.1987, IDS, F.Inst.of Groundsmanship 1977; num. specialist plant socs. **Awards:** VC Floral Cttee (RHS) 1987, Assoc.of Honour (RHS) 1991, Judge (Hortl Exhibitions Assn) 1992, Gold & Silver Gilt Medals for major plant exhibits at Chelsea & Regnl Shows. **Publications:** *Complete Container Gardening* (co-Author) 1991, *RHS Enc.of Gardening* (co-Author) 1992; num.papers & articles. Favours pers.pub.& news media support. **Languages:** English, Spanish (poor). Further details may be obtained from the *Hortl Speakers Register* (RHS). Willing to act as consult.etc. **Address:** The Garden House, 35 Wembdon Rise, Bridgwater, Somerset TA6 7PN, England, UK. **Tel.**(home) 44 1278 451814.

CHEN, Professor Changdu. Ecology, conservation. Professor of Ecology, Scientific Consultant. *B.*18 Jan.1927, Hunan, PRC. Chinese. *M.* Wang Yinxuan: 2 *s.* **Education:** Qing-hua U. 1949, Botl Inst. Academia Sinica, postgrad. lab.study (= MS of Peking U.) 1953. **Experience:** mainly teaching in univs, conducted res.in Lab.of Geobot. Dept of Biol. Leningrad U. and Office of Arid Land Studies, U.of Arizona. **Career:** Lect. Assoc.Prof. Prof. of Ecol. Peking U.1953–, Scientific Consult. Nat.EPA 1991–. **Achievements:** res.on veg.of arid & semi-arid lands and their envl problems; Nature cons. (esp.biodiv.); main author of NCS of China and Action Plan for Cons.of Biodiv.of China.

Memberships: ESC (Pres.), GSC, INTECOL, IALE, IUCN CESP. **Awards:** Nat. Prizes of Natural Scis 1987 and for Advancement of Sci.& Tech.1990. **Publications:** *Plant Geog.*1980, *NCS of China* (prin.author) 1987, *Researches on Eco-envl Problems of Xinjian* (prin.author) 1989, *The Extremely Arid Deserts of China* 1988, *On Geoecol.*1986, *Key Regns for Biodiv.Cons.in China* 1993, *Action Plan of Biodiv.Cons.of China* (co-Author) 1994. Indiff. to pers.pub.& news media support. **Languages:** Chinese, English (written, some spoken). Willing to act as consult.etc. **Address:** Laboratory of Landscape Ecology, Department of Urban & Environmental Studies, Peking University, Beijing 100871, People's Republic of China. **Tel.**(office) 86 10 250 1179, (home) 86 10 256 1166/5283; **fax** 86 10 250 1187.

CHERIX, Dr Daniel. Biology, ecology, and protection, of Ants (mainly red wood ants [Formica rufa]). Curator, Suppleant Professor. *B.*8 June 1950, Lausanne, Switzerland. Swiss. *M.*Catherine (biol.teaching natural scis). **Education:** U.of Lausanne, BS 1973, PhD 1981. **Experience:** res.— biol.& ecol.of red wood ants and control of pest ants; teaching gen.& applied entomology at BS & MS levels. **Career:** travel res.grants, Hokkaidô U. Japan & U.of Georgia 1981–82; Curator, Mus.of Zool. Lausanne 1982–. **Achievement:** use of insect growth regulator (IGR) to control pest ants in Galápagos. **Memberships:** BES, RES, Scientific Cttee of Swiss Nat.Parks, IUSSI. **Awards:** Distinctions from Ameisenschutzwarte, Würzburg 1977 & Bayern 1982. **Publications:** *Les fourmis du bois ou fourmis rousses* 1986; *c.*80 papers. Favours pers. pub.& news media support. **Languages:** English, French, German, Spanish (basic). Willing to act as ref. **Address:** Musée de Zoologie, Place Riponne 6, 1000 Lausanne 17, Switzerland. **Tel.**(office) 41 21 312 8336; **fax** 41 21 323 6840.

CHERKASOVA, Dr Maria V. Ecology, protection of human rights for a healthy environment, ecology & children's health; public environmental movement, conservation of natural & cultural heritage; environmental education. Centre Director. *B.*13 March 1938, Moscow, Russia. Russian. *M.*Dr Alexander A. Dulov: *s., d.* **Education:** Moscow SU PhD (Biol.) 1962, Moscow Inst.of Nature Prot. PhD(Biol.) 1984. **Experience:** res.— birds of Altai High Mtns, rare & endangered species (Red Data Book of USSR); admin.— coord.of anti-dam prog.'Katun' (Altai), Ed.Red Data Book of USSR, Centre Dir; consult.— Mgr prog.on Intl Clearinghouse on the Envt (Moscow–Washington); journalistic — Head, Biol. Dept of popular sci.magazine '*Znaniye-Sila*'. **Career:** staff of Zool.Mus.of Moscow U. 1962–8 and of '*Znaniye-Sila*' 1970– 73; Scientific Worker, Res.Inst.for the Prot.of the Envt 1973–88; Dir, Centre for Ind.Ecol.Progs, Russian Socio-Ecol.Union 1988–. **Achievements:** estab.of Centre for Ind.Ecol.Progs and number of Nature prot.territories, organized

num.ecol.progs & projects (some intl), publishing in sphere of ecol., educ.& res.re.cons.of rare & endangered species. **Memberships:** Intl Socio-Ecol.Union (Counc.), MAB (Russian Cttee), WIPAC, IWA (Adv.Cttee), Inst.for Soviet–Amer. Relations (Envl Adv.). **Awards:** Global 500 Roll of Honour (UNEP) 1992, Overall Euro.Winner (Ford Euro.Cons.Awards) 1993. **Publications:** *They Must Live* (book series) 1983–7; *c.*150 books & articles incl.*Sounding the Alarm* (for UNESCO) 1992. Reserved & tolerant towards pers.pub.& news media support. **Languages:** English (basic), Russian. Willing to act as consult. etc. **Address:** Centre for Independent Ecological Programs, Malaya Bronnaya 12 apt 12, Moscow 103104, Russia. **Tel.**(office) & **fax** 7 095 118 8686, (home) 7 095 290 0809; **e-mail** cnep@glas.apc.org .

Chi Yung JIM, Dr, *see* **JIM, Dr Chi Yung.**

CHILD, Dr Graham Foster Tamplin. The institutions & economics essential to effective resource conservation. Independent Consultant. *B.*6 June 1936, Bulawayo, Zimbabwe. Zimbabwean. *M.*Diana: *s.*Brian (wildlife economist), 2 *d.* **Education:** U.of Cape Town PhD 1965. **Experience:** 17 1/2 yrs (1971–86) as Head of Parks and Wild Life Agency in Zimbabwe, adv.to 20 govts, prolific writing on wildlife biol. econ.& mgmt. **Career:** taught at U.of Cape Town 1959, Beit Res.F. L.Kariba 1959; Govt Ecol.1959–61; Keeper of Vertebrates, Nat.Mus.1961–5; FAO Expert advising Botswana Govt 1965–75; Chobi Nat.Park & NE of country (two yrs) and Dept of Wildlife & Nat.Parks (whole country, four yrs), Nat.Parks & Wildlife Mgmt 1971–86; IUCN Counc.for Africa 1984–90; Ind.Consult.1986–. **Achievements:** wildlife mgmt and instnl & econ.implications thereof. **Membership:** SASE. **Award:** Officer of the Legion of Merit, Civil Div. (Zimbabwe). **Publications:** 100+ scientific & phil.pubns incl.*Behaviour of Large Mammals during the Formation of L. Kariba* 1968, *Managing Prot.Areas in the Tropics* (co-Author) 1987. Indiff.to pers.pub.& news media support. **Languages:** Afrikaans (smattering), English, Shona (working knowledge), Sindebele (good spoken), Swazi & Zulu (fair–good spoken). Willing to act as consult.etc. **Address:** 11A Old Catton Road, Mount Pleasant, Harare, Zimbabwe. **Tel.**(office & home) & **fax** 263 4 304387.

CHITRAKAR, Anil. Education, communication, transfer of conservation skill and technology. Project Coordinator. *B.*21 March 1961, Nepal. Nepali. *M.*Rosha: *s.* **Education:** Rajasthan U. B.Mech.Eng.1987, U.of Penn. training in Energy Planning 1989. **Experience:** tech. transfer, cons.educ., NCS implementation. **Career:** Engr 1986, Coord.for ECCA 1987, prog. coord. NGO activities & NCS implementation. **Achievements:** educ.& communication, public action campaigns, tech.transfer to mitigate pressure on envt. **Memberships:** Nepal Heritage Soc. 1992, Nepal Engg Assn 1987; IUCN CEC 1990.

Awards: Citation (HM Govt of Nepal) 1991, Outstanding Achievement (U.of Penn.) 1989. **Publications:** *Envl Educ.Review* 1992, *Envl Law Review for Nepal* 1993. Indifferent to pers.pub., favours news media support. **Languages:** English, Nepali, Newari. Willing to act as consult. etc. **Address:** POB 3923, Kathmandu, Nepal. **Tel.**(office) 977 1 522712, (home) 977 1 271634; **fax** 977 1 521506.

CH'NG, Ms Kim-Looi. Management & conservation of marine ecosystems, integrated coastal-zone & marine pollution management. Division Director. *B.*19 Oct.1943, Penang, Malaysia. Malaysian. *M.*Joseph Au: *s., d.* **Education:** U.of Malaya, BSc 1967, BSc(Hons) 1978; U.of Wales, MSc(Econ.) 1978 **Experience:** admin., nat.& regnl project coordn, drafting of Fisheries 1985 & (co-) EEZ 1984 Acts both of Malaysia, prog.formulation. **Career:** Fisheries Officer (Fin.& Admin.) 1968–78, Dir of Training & Career Dev.(Capacity-bldg) 1979–81, Dir of Resource Mgmt & Dev.1981–91, Dept of Fisheries; Nat.Coord. ASEAN–US Coastal Resources Mgmt Project 1986–91; Dir, Intl Div. Min.of Sci., Tech.and the Envt 1991–4. **Achievements:** estab. of marine prot.areas in Malaysia 1986–91, ASEAN–US Nat.Coord., E.Asian Seas Coord.of four UNEP–COBSEA Projects on Coastal-zone and Marine Prot.Areas (produced training compendium for marine ecosystem mgmt & marine park mgr), WG Leader of IUCN/World Bank/GBRMPA initiative on global representatives of Marine Prot.Areas for E.Asian Seas (estab.document on status of current & potential marine prot.areas), drafting of above two Acts, formulated progs for estab.& mgmt of EEZ in Malaysia. **Memberships:** UNEP–COBSEA Experts WG for the E.Asian Seas, ASEAMS, IUCN CNPPA. **Publications:** Ed.of two intl pubns on coastal-zone mgmt, several intl conf.papers. Favours pers.pub.as long as it assists in the envl cause, and likewise news media support. **Languages:** Bahasa Malaysia (good), English, French (elementary). Willing to act as consult. etc. **Address:** 44 Jalan Setiaraya, Damansara Heights, 50490 Kuala Lumpur, Malaysia. **Tel.**(office) 603 293 6336, (home) 603 255 9728; **fax** 603 291 4345, 293 7981, or 735 5659.

CHOI, Professor Dr Yearn Hong. Environmental policy & management, waste management; Potomac River Basin drinking-water & waste water. Distinguished Professor. *B.*22 April 1941, Seoul, Korea. American. *M.*Jane Bong Hee: *s., d.* **Education:** Yonsei U. AB 1963, Indiana U. PhD 1972. **Experience:** Asst for Envl Quality in Office of US Sec.of Defense. **Career:** Asst Prof. U.of Wisconsin–Whitewater 1972–3; Assoc.Prof. Old Dominion U. 1973–8; Prof.1978–81, Disting.Prof.1981–, Jackson SU. **Achievements:** Dir of Envl Studies Prog.at Jackson SU and Prin.Project Dir of Water Resources Mgmt in Washington Metropolitan Area. **Memberships:** ASPA, APA, Chesapeake Bay Consortium. **Awards:** Fac.F. NASPAA,

NASA & NIH; Outstanding Fac.in Res.& Community Service (U.of Distr.of Columbia). **Publications:** *Readings in Public & Envl Affairs* 1987; 20 articles. **Languages:** Chinese (basic), English, German (basic), Korean. Willing to act as consult.etc. **Address:** 10255 Marshall Pond Road, Burke, Virginia 22015, USA. **Tel.**(office) 1 202 282 3718, (home) 1 703 250 4340; **fax** 1 202 282 3706.

CHRISTIAN, Dr Colmore Silas. Natural resource management, environmental impact assessment, conservation, reforestation, wildlife management (birds), environmental education. National Park Superintendent. *B.*Castle Bruce, Commonwealth of Dominica, W.Indies. Dominican. *M.*Yolanda: 3 *s.* **Education:** Cyprus Forestry Coll. Dipl.(Hons)(Forestry) 1975, U.of Michigan BSc(Natural Resources) 1985, Clemson U. MPRT(Resource Mgmt) 1991, PhD(Resource Mgmt) 1994. **Experience:** res. — parrot cons., nat.park dev.& mgmt in the Carib., outdoor rec.& tourism-related impacts in natural areas in the Carib.; tech.— Mgr./Coord. for many projects *e.g.* tourism site upgrading, reforestation; admin.— first & only nat.park Super.and mgmt positions in Forestry & Wildlife Div.; media. **Career:** Forest Cadet, Asst Forest Officer, Sr Asst Forest Officer (Acting), Park Super., Dep.Dir (Acting), & Dir (Acting), all with Dominica's Forestry & Wildlife Div. **Achievements:** one of pioneers of Dominica's nat.park prog., first host/producer of Forest & Wildlife Div.'s weekly radio prog., longest serving & most qualified sr officer of Dominica's Forest & Wildlife Div. **Memberships:** WNA, SCB, ISTF, CFA, CCA. **Award:** Best All-round Student (Cyprus Forestry Coll.) 1973–4. **Publications:** *The Parrot Cons. Efforts of the Islands of the Antilles (from Puerto Rico to Grenada)* (Master's thesis) 1991, Parrot cons. efforts in St Vincent and the Grenadines 1993. Indiff.to pers.pub., favours news media support. **Languages:** English, French (basic spoken & written), French Creole. Willing to act as consult.etc. **Address:** Forestry & Wildlife Division, Botanical Gardens, Roseau, Commonwealth of Dominica. **Tel.**(office) 809 448 2401 ext.418, (home) 809 448 4711.

Chung KIM, Professor Ke, *see* **KIM, Professor Ke Chung.**

CIFUENTES-ARIAS, Miguel. Planning & management of protected areas, teaching & technical assistance to protected areas. Regional Coordinator (Central America). *B.*29 May 1951, Baños, Tungurahua, Ecuador. Ecuadorian. *M.* Rosa Victoria: 2 *s.* **Education:** Catholic U. Lic. (Biol.) 1975, CATIE/U.of Costa Rica MSc(Natural Renewable Resources, Planning & Mgmt of Prot.Areas) 1983. **Experience:** consult.to nat.& intl agencies incl.tech.assistance & eval., teaching & course-planning involved with many workshops, sems, courses, symps etc. **Career:** Asst Lect. Catholic U. 1972–4; Asst to Dir, Charles Darwin Res.Station 1974–6 (Org.&

Prin.Instr.1974–80, 1983–6); Super. Galápagos Nat.Park 1976–81, 1983–86; PI Biosphere Reserves Project, MAB/UNESCO–CATIE 1982–3; Provincial Dir, Min.of Agric.& Livestock 1983–6; Assoc.Prof. Natural Resources Mgmt Prog. CATIE, and Regnl Coord. WWF C.Amer. 1986–. Lect. Postgrad.Sch. CATIE 1987–; Prin. Instr. Smithsonian Biodiv.Prog.(US)–MAB 1988–92; Instr. Galápagos NPS 1993. **Achievements:** consolidation of Galápagos Nat.Park. during almost 11 yrs as its Super., training & teaching more than 500 Latin Americans on prot.areas mgmt. **Memberships:** Ecotourism Soc., IUCN CNPPA & SSC (C.& S.Amer.), Charles Darwin Fndn for Galápagos Islands (Exec.Council); Bd of Dirs, Fundación Ecuatoriana de Conservación y Desarrollo, and Green Iguana Fndn. **Award:** WWF Cons.Merit 1986. **Publications:** Strat.planning of nat.or regnl systems of Biosphere Reserves: a methodology & case study from Costa Rica (co-Author) 1983, Galápagos, tierra de contrastes 1989, Conservación y manejo de la vegetación en Galápagos 1990, Determinación de capacidad de carga turistica en areas protegidas 1992; num.other papers. Indiff.to pers.pub., favours news media support. **Languages:** English (good written & spoken), French (fair read), Spanish. Willing to act as consult.etc. **Address:** 7170 Centro Agronómico Tropical de Investigación y Ensenanza, Turrialba, Costa Rica. **Tel.**(office) 506 556 1383, (home) 506 556 1634; **fax** 506 556 1421.

CIOCHIA, Dr Victor. Nature protection through biological control especially with entomophagous insects; artificial breeding of entomophagous insects (*Trichogramma, Prospaltella, Coccinellidae*); ornithology (structure, dynamics, bird protection); protection of mountainous zone and Danube Delta. Principal Scientific Researcher, Associate Professor. *B.*4 Nov.1932, Brasov, Romania. Romanian. Father (a hunter) & mother both passionate protectors of Nature, plants, & animals. *W.*: 2 *d.*Victorina-Gabriela (active in nature prot.), Elena-Gabriela Ularu (biol.teacher), *s.-in-law* Dr Biol. Pantelimon Ularu (flora & veg.prot.of Carpathian Mtns). **Education:** Alexandru Ioan Cuza U. Fac.four yrs (Biol.), Iasi U. PhD(Invertebrate Zool.) 1972, INRA (to specialize) 1969–70, 1982. **Experience:** biostation & half-industrial breeding tech.of entomophagous & *Trichogramma* spp., *Prospaltella* spp., and *Aphitis* spp., to mark with I.131 isotope of some Hymenoptera for study of dynamics. **Career:** Asst, Zool.Dept 1955–8, Scientific Researcher, Biol.Station 1970–74, Iasi U.; pol. prisoner 1958–63; Tech. Draughtsman, Bot.& Zool.Dept, Forest Fac. (Brasov), 1963–7; Prin. Scientific Researcher, Biol.Control & Nature Prot.Lab. Res.Inst.for Sugar-beet, ASAS 1974–; Assoc.Prof. Agric. Fac. Cluj-Nepoca 1982–. **Achievements:** Founder of Nature Prot.Lab. from Black Sea seaside (Agigea 1968), active participation in prot.of Danube Delta Biosphere Reserve, memb. (Founder) of Assn for Nature Prot.(Aristide Caradja-Piatra Neamt), and Soc.

for Ornithol.and Nature Prot., Founder of Natural Reservation 'Coada Lacului Techirghiol' (Dobrogea) 1969, and 'Lacul Agigea' Reservation (Dobrogea) 1969. **Memberships:** Romanian Soc. for Ornithol., Birds' Prot.& Nature Prot.(Pres.), Romanian Soc.for Entomol.(Cttee), Romanian Forestry & Agric.Acad.(Corres.1991), Euro. Ornithl Atlas Cttee (1972–80), ICBP (Fellowworker, 1985–90), IWRB (Fellow-worker for Romania, 1985–90), Romanian Photographic Artists' Assn, Romanian Amateur Fine Arts Assn. **Award:** Emil Racovita Prize (Romanian Acad.) 1981. **Publications:** 235 papers incl. Some aspects of the utilization of *Trichogramma* spp.in Romania 1991, Breeding birds in Romania–Atlas (in Romanian) 1992, Industrial breeding tech.for some auxiliary insects used in biol.control of pests (co-Author, in Romanian) 1993; 18 monogrs. Indiff.re.pers.pub.& news media support. **Languages:** English, German & Russian (tech.read), French, Romanian. Willing to act as consult.etc. **Address:** Romanian Academy of Forest and Agriculture, Str.Pavilioanele CFR Nr 30, 2200 Brasov, Romania. **Tel.**(office) 40 68 112620/1, (home) 40 68 129162, 160627 or 131406; **fax** 40 68 151508.

CLARK, Dr Colin. Effects of land-use change on hydrology & climate; rainfall frequency analysis & drainage-basin management; climatic effect of clouds; causes of low flows. Independent Research Worker. *B.*20 June 1952, Taunton, Somerset, England, UK. British. *M.*Linda Susan: *s., d.* **Education:** Sexey's Sch.Bruton; Southampton U. BSc(Hons)(Envl Geog.& Bot.) 1974, Exeter U. PhD(Hydr.) 1978. **Experience:** admin.as Head of Geog.at Poole Coll. and Chairman, Wyvern Rural Housing Assn; consult.to Wessex Water Auth., Porlock Parish Council, & The Porlock Soc. **Career:** teaching 1979–85, Lect. Poole Coll.1985–92, Ind.Res. Worker in Hydrology & Climate 1992–. **Achievements:** worked on flood hydr.of R. Brue; expert witness at Porlock Relief Road Inquiry, and witness at Somerset Structure Plan Inquiry & Hinkley Point 'C' Inquiry; advised Eds of *Area* & *EC.* **Memberships:** F.RMS, BHS. **Awards:** Rodwell Mem.Geog.Prize, Best Paper Prize (FEC) 1992. **Publications:** *Understanding Weather & Climate* 1984, *Floods at Bruton: Past, Present & Future* 1986; 25+ papers & reports; four-parameter model for rainfall frequency, trop.deforestation & climatic change. Favours pers.pub.& accurate news media support. **Language:** English. Willing to act as consult.etc. **Address:** Charldon Hill Research Station, 2 Shute Lane, Bruton, Somerset BA10 0BJ, England, UK. **Tel.**44 174 981 3513.

CLARK, John Russell. Environmental conservation particularly of coastal-zone resources. Senior Research Associate. *B.*11 April 1927, Seattle, Washington, USA. American. Father Prof.Donald H.Clark, for., Pres.of Northwest Hardwood Assn, author. *M.*Catherine: 3 *s.,* 3 *d.*; *s.-in-law* Dr Russell Vernon Clark (Scripps Instn of Oceanogr.). **Education:** U.of Washington BS(Fisheries Sci.) 1949, U.of Rhode Is.grad. studies, UCB & Gonzaga U. other courses. **Experience:** 20 yrs' res.& admin.; 1970– professional conservationist specializing in aquatic, coastal, & marine envts; tech.assistance given to many countries re.dev.of projects, training etc.; expertise & activities in planning, envl assessment, resource mgmt, prot.areas, biodiv.of marine habitats, teaching/training, facilitation, photography, maritime skills; consult., author; & critic. **Career:** military, commercial fisherman (seasonal) & student 1945–9; Dir & res.vessel Chief Sci. Woods Hole Fisheries Lab.1950–59; res., Asst Dir, Sandy Hook Marine Lab.& Dir Narragansett Marine Lab.1960–70, Coastal Resources Specialist 1982–7, USDI; Consult.(self-employed) to cons.groups 1971–; Sr Assoc.& Dir, Cons.Fndn 1972–81; Vis.Prof. (six months each) UCLA, Univs of Washington & N.Carolina 1972–81; sabbatical leave 1981–2; Sr Res.Assoc. Rosenstiel Sch.of Marine & Atmos.Scis, U.of Miami 1988–. **Achievements:** served as leading exponent of Integrated Coastal Zone Mgmt in US & abroad and wrote key lit.in the field; tested theories in case-studies globally. **Memberships:** Founder of — American Littoral Soc., Barrier Islands Coalition, Nat.Wetlands Tech.Council, Coastal Area Mgmt Network. **Awards:** Conservationist of the Yr (Amer.Motors) 1968, Meritorious Pubn Award (USDI) 1969, ALS Service Award, Outstanding Sci. Award (Hudson River Assn). **Publications:** 15 books incl.*Fish & Man* 1966, *Through the Fishes Eye* 1973, *Shark Watch* 1976, *Coastal Ecosystems Mgmt* 1978, *Wetland Functions & Values* 1979, *Marine & Coastal Prot.Areas* 1984, *Snorkeling* 1985, *Integrated Mgmt of Coastal Zones* 1992; 160 papers. Indiff.to pers. pub.& news media support. **Languages:** English, Spanish (fair written & spoken). Further details may be obtained from *Who's Who in America* 1981–. Willing to act as consult.etc. **Address:** Casa Mañana, 411 West Indies Drive, Ramrod Key, Florida 33042, USA; for mail use POB 313. **Tel.**(office & home) 1 305 872 4114; **fax** 1 305 872 3369.

CLARK, Dr Michael Frederick. Plant pathology, field & molecular plant virology, mycoplasma-like organisms, serology. Senior Research Scientist, Deputy Departmental Head. *B.*25 Sept.1938, Singapore. British. *M.*Rosemary Elisabeth (envl educ.consult.& author); *s.*, 3 *d.*incl.Kristen Alexandra Scott (landscape arch.). **Education:** U.of London, BSc(Agric.) (Hons) 1960; Cornell U. MS 1962; U.of Auckland PhD 1965. **Experience:** res.in USA, NZ, & UK, on disease detection & pathogen identification, involvement with res.on detection & identification of mycoplasma-like organism diseases in third-world countries; consult.to ACIAR re.overseas aid prog.to SE Asia 1986. **Career:** Res.Sci. DSIR NZ 1963–72; Postdoctl Res. Assoc. Purdue U. 1968–70; Sr Res.Sci. 1972–, Dep.Head Dept of Plant Path.& Weed Sci.1988–, HRI. **Achievements:** dev.of novel detection/

identification methods for obligate plant pathogens (viruses, mycoplasma-like organisms), introduced the technique of enzyme-linked immunosorbent assay (ELISA) into plant path.and have been involved with its dev.& application for disease detection & epidemiology in several countries. **Memberships:** SGM, AAB. **Award:** Lee M. Hutchins (APS) 1981. **Publications:** *c.*50 chapters & major refereed papers incl.Characteristics of the microplate method of enzyme-linked immunosorbent assay for the detection of plant viruses (co-Author) 1977, *Diagnosis and Control of Mycoplasma Diseases of Trop.& Subtrop.Plants with Particular Ref.to Thailand* 1992, Immunodiagnosis Methods Using Polyclonal and Monoclonal Antibodies 1994. Dislikes pers pub & news media support. **Languages:** English, French (basic). Willing to act as consult.&/or ref. **Address:** Department of Plant Pathology & Weed Science, Horticulture Research International–East Malling, West Malling, Kent ME19 6BJ, England, UK. **Tel.**44 1732 843833; **fax** 44 1732 849067.

CLARK, Professor Dr Robert Bernard. Marine pollution. Consultant, Emeritus Professor. *B.*13 Oct.1923, London, England, UK. British. *M.* Susan Diana: *s., d.* **Education:** U.of London BSc 1944, DSc 1964; U.of Glasgow PhD 1956. **Experience:** extensive teaching & res in marine invertebrate zool.and also birds, Head Zool.Dept & Dir Dove Marine Lab. consult.on marine envt mainly on shipping insurers. **Career:** Asst Lect. U.of Glasgow; Asst Prof. UCB 1953–5; Lect.in Zool. U.of Bristol 1956–65; Prof.of Zool., Head of Dept of Zool.and Dir of Dove Marine Lab. U.of Newcastle upon Tyne 1966–89. **Memberships:** F.RSE, F.IBiol., Council NERC 1971–77, 1982–5, RCEP 1978–82, RS Study Group on Marine Poll.1973–8, Adv.Cttee on Pesticides 1986–90, num.other nat.& intl adv.bodies. **Publications:** *Marine Poll.*1992 (3rd edn), Founder (1968) & Ed. *Marine Poll.Bull.;* sole or jt Author of six other books and Ed.of further three; 120+ res. papers. Indiff.to pers.pub.& news media support. **Languages:** English, French. Further details may be obtained from Brit. *Who's Who* 1990–. **Address:** Highbury House, Highbury, Newcastle upon Tyne NE2 3LN, England, UK. **Tel.**(office) 44 191 222 6661, (home) 44 191 281 4672.

CLARK, Professor William C., *see* p. 367.

CLARKE, Dr Andrew. Polar ecology, marine ecology, evolutionary history of polar regions, thermal ecology. Head of Marine Life Sciences. *B.*27 Jan.1949, London, England, UK. British. *M.*Gillian May. **Education:** Corpus Christi Coll.Camb. BA(1st Class) 1970, U.of Camb. PhD 1977. **Experience:** 25 yrs' biol.res.in polar regns (Arctic & Antarctic), eight yrs' mgmt of multidisc.res.team. **Career:** Marine Ecol. 1970–88, resp.(as Head of Marine Life Scis 1989–) for UK Marine Biol.Res.in Antarctica 1988–, Brit.Antarctic Survey. **Achievements:** basic res. on ecol.of polar regns, on physiol. adaptation to temp., and on evol.of Antarctic marine eco-systems. **Memberships:** MBA, BES, Challenger Soc.for Marine Sci. **Awards:** W.S.Bruce Medal (RSE) 1981, Polar Medal (UK) 1986, Hon.Prof. U.of St Andrews 1990. **Publications:** over 90 incl.the Origin of the Southern Ocean Marine Fauna (co-Author) 1989, What is cold adaptation and how should we measure it? 1991, Seasonal acclimatization and latitudinal compensation in metabolism: do they exist? 1993, Reproductive trade-offs in caridean shrimps 1993, Temperature and extinction in the sea: a physiologist's view 1993. Dislikes pers.pub., indiff.to news media support. **Language:** English. Willing to act as consult. etc. **Address:** British Antarctic Survey, High Cross, Madingley Road, Cambridge CB3 0ET, England, UK. **Tel.**44 1223 251400; **fax** 44 1223 62616; **e-mail/internet** a.clarke@bas.ac.uk .

CLEMENT, Dr Charles Roland. Plant genetic resources' conservation, crop origins, and biodiversity. Researcher in Fruit Crop Improvement. *B.*4 Aug.1950, Providence, RI, USA. American. Father Roland C.Clement, conservationist with Nat.Audubon Soc. *M.*Rosa N.S.: 2 *d.* **Education:** U.of Connecticut, BA 1973; U.of Costa Rica, MS 1986; U.of Hawaii at Manoa, PhD 1995. **Experience:** res.— fruit crop germ-plasm prospection, characterization, cons.1977–. **Career:** Asst Researcher 1976–86, Assoc.Researcher 1986–95, Researcher 1995–, INPA. **Achievements:** Coord. USAID-funded Pejibaye (*Bactris gasipaes* Kunth, Palmae) intl germ-plasm prospection in Amazonia to form or enrich four nat.(Brazil, Peru, Ecuador, and Colombia) germplasm banks; proposal of crop genetic diversity centre in NW Amazonia 1989. **Memberships:** Sociedades Brasileira de Fruticultura, Genetica, & para o Progresso da Ciencia, InterAmerican Soc.for Trop.Hort., IPS, SEB, AIBS. **Awards:** Gamma Sigma Delta (Honor Soc.of Agric.) 1994 and Achievement Rewards for Coll.Scis/George Orton Elmore Scholarship 1994 (both U.of Hawaii at Manoa). **Publications:** *c.*130 papers. Indiff.to pers.pub., favours news media support. **Languages:** English, Portuguese, Spanish. Willing to act as consult.etc. **Address:** Instituto Nacional de Pesquisas da Amazonia, CP 478, 69011-920 Manaus, Amazonas, Brazil. **Tel.** (home) 55 92 238 3838; **fax** 55 92 642 1845; **e-mail** cclement@cr-am.rnp.br .

CLEWELL, Dr André F. Ecological restoration. Company President. *B.*27 Mar.1934, Canton, OH, USA. American. **Education:** Indiana U. PhD(Bot.) 1963. **Experience:** resto. res.& practice primarily of bottomland forests on mined lands, ecol.description & assessment of plant communities, flora of Florida, taxonomy of selected legumes & composites, ecol.resto. consult. **Career:** Fac. Dept of Biol.Sci. Florida SU 1962–79, Ecol.Consult.1979–83, Pres. A.F. Clewell Inc.1984–. **Achievements:** dev.of ways to restore bottomland forests and of ecol.resto. policies, promotion of field of ecol. resto. **Mem-**

berships: SER (Pres.1993–5), others. **Award:** Fulbright Lectureship at Autonomous U.of Honduras 1971–2. **Publications:** *Guide to the Vascular Plants of the Florida Panhandle* 1985, *c.*45 papers. Favours pers.pub. & news media support when helping a greater cause. **Languages:** English, Spanish (moderate). Willing to act as consult.etc. **Address:** A.F.Clewell Inc., RT 7 Box 1195, Quincy, Florida 32351, USA. **Tel.**(office) 1 904 875 3868; **fax** 1 904 875 1848.

CLOUDSLEY, Timothy. Theories in the Sociology of the Environment (or 'Ecological Sociology'), Amazonian rain-forest particularly in Peru and in connection with indigenous native human societies. Lecturer in Sociology and the Environment. *B.*18 Sept.1948, Camb., England, UK. British. Father Prof.John L.Cloudsley-Thompson *qv*, Mother Ann Cloudsley (co-Ed.*J. of Arid Environments*). *M.*Rhona: 2 *s.* **Education:** Dulwich Coll.; Pembroke Coll. Camb. BA 1971, MA 1974; Durham U. post-grad.res. **Experience:** res.in theoretical work on society's relationship to natural envt, attitudes towards Nature in diff.socs, empirical studies of envl problems in the Peruvian rain-forest, and for Survival Intl (UK) & IWGIA. **Career:** Lect.in Sociol. Durham U., Newcastle Poly., Heriot Watt U.& Napier Coll.1973–7; Lect.in Sociol. and the Envt, Glasgow Caledonian U. 1977–. **Memberships:** PSA, IWGIA, Survival Intl, Greenpeace, WWF, FoE, Tourism Concern, Peru Support Group. **Publications:** num.incl. *Shell's Res.for Oil and its Effects on Natives in the Lower Urubamba Regn of the Peruvian Jungle* (res.document) 1987, Romanticism and the industrial revolution in Britain 1990. Favours pers. pub.& news media support. **Languages:** English, French, German, Spanish. Willing to act as consult.etc. **Address:** 31 Hamilton Drive, Glasgow G12 8DN, Scotland, UK. **Tel.**(office) 44 141 331 3545, (home) 44 141 334 8058.

CLOUDSLEY-THOMPSON, Professor Dr John Leonard. Temperature & water relations of Arthropods & Reptiles, diurnal rhythms, and desert adaptations. Emeritus Professor of Zoology. *B.*23 May 1921, Murree, India. British. *M.*J.Anne (Cloudsley): 3 *s.* incl.Timothy Cloudsley *qv*. **Education:** Marlborough Coll.; Pembroke Coll.Camb. MA 1948, PhD 1950; U.of Lond. DSc. **Experience:** widespread res., now Emer.Prof.of Zool. **Career:** 1939–45 War: commissioned into 4th Queen's Own Hussars 1941, transferred to 4th County of London Yeomanry (Sharpshooters); N.Africa until '41 when badly wounded, Instr.(Capt.) Sandhurst 1943 (hon.rank of Capt.on resignation), rejoined regiment for 'D'-day and invasion of Normandy 1944. Lect.in Zool. King's Coll.London 1950–60; Prof.of Zool. U.of Khartoum, and Keeper, Sudan Natural Hist.Mus.1960–71; NSF SRF, U.of New Mexico 1969; Vis.Prof.at U.of Kuwait 1978, U.of Nigeria at Nsukka 1981, U.of Qatar 1986, & Sultan Qaboos U. 1988; Vis.Res.F. ANU 1987 & Namib Desert Ecol. Res.Unit 1989; Hon.

Consult. U.of Malaya 1969, Arabian Gulf U.1986, & U.of Kuwait 1990; Camb.Iceland Expedn 1947, expedns to s. Tunisia 1954, (with wife) to parts of Africa 1960–73; trans-Sahara crossing 1967. **Achievements:** Liveryman of Worshipful Co.of Skinners 1952–, Chairman BNA 1974–83 (VP 1985–), Biol.Council 1977–82 (Medal 1985), Pres.BAS 1982–5 (VP 1985–6), BSC 1985–7, VP LS 1975–6, 1977–8, VP 1st World Cong.of Herpetol.1989, Hon.Memb.of RAS 1969 (Medal 1969) & BHS 1983 (Pres.1991–). **Memberships:** F.RES, F.LS, F.ZS, F.IBiol., F.WAAS. **Awards:** Silver Jubilee Gold Medal and Hon. DSc Khartoum 1981, KSS Charter Award (IBiol.)1981, J.H.Grundy Medal (RAMC) 1987, Best Paper Prize (FEC) 1989, Peter Scott Mem. Award (BNA) 1993. **Publications:** co-Founding Ed.*J.of Arid Envts* (assisted by Anne Cloudsley), Ed.book series *Adaptations of Desert Organisms*; 50+ major pubns incl. children's, some 400–500 addit. **Languages:** Arabic (some colloquial), English, French (better in written). Further details may be obtained from Brit. *Who's Who*, Debrett's *People of Today*, *The Writers' Directory*, etc. Willing to act as consult. etc. **Address:** Department of Biology, Darwin Building, University College London, Gower Street, London WC1E 6BT, England, UK. **Tel.**(office) 44 171 387 7050, (home) 44 171 359 7197; **fax** 44 171 380 7096.

CLOUTIER, Antoine. Park planning, regional integration. Acting Director (Development). *B.*3 June 1945, Quebec, Canada. Canadian. **Education:** Laval U. Bacc.(Geog.), M(Land Mgmt) 1970. **Experience:** nat.parks' planning in Canada incl.park dev., public consultation, regnl integration, programming & mgmt, systems plans; consult.in Ivory Coast, Cameroon, Niger, Congo, Ghana, Madagascar, Haiti, for IUCN, EEC, USAID, U.of Florida. **Career:** since 1971 with Parks Canada, Acting Dir (Dev.) 1994–. **Publications:** many in-house systems/ mgmt plans. **Languages:** English, French. Willing to act as consult.etc. **Address:** 3 Rue Buade, Québec G1R 4V7, Canada. **Tel.**(office) 1 418 648 4106, (home) 1 418 832 0271; **fax** 1 418 648 4234.

COBB, Dr Stephen Martin. Tropical protected areas and their conservation. Senior Associate, Group Director. *B.*28 Oct.1947, London, England, UK. British. *M.*Alison: 3 *step-d.* **Education:** U.of Oxf. DPhil.1976. **Experience:** more than 20 yrs of African wildlife cons.and envl policy activities. **Career:** Lect.in Cons. Biol. U.of Nairobi 1977–9, Dir of res.team, Jonglei Canal EIA (Sudan), EDF 1980–83, and Niger Delta (Mali), IUCN 1984–7; Consult.1988–9; SRF, Intl Dev.Centre 1988–92, Sr Assoc. Oxf.For.Inst. 1992–, U.of Oxf.; Dir, The Envt & Dev.Group 1990–. **Membership:** ZSL (Counc.1992–). **Publications:** incl.*The Jonglei Canal: Impact & Opportunity* (co-Ed.) 1987. Favours pers.pub. & news media support. **Languages:** English, French, German (rusty). Willing to act as a con-sult.and to judge proposals. **Address:** The Environment & Development Group, 13 St Giles, Oxford OX1 3JS, England, UK. **Tel.**44 1865 511455; **fax** 44 1865 511450.

COCKLIN, Dr Christopher Reid. Resources and environmental management & policy, environmental impact assessment, cumulative environmental change, Nature conservation, geographical information systems, business & the environment, environmental security & economics. Senior Lecturer in Geography, Director of Regional Research Unit. *B.*19 April 1958, Blenheim, NZ. New Zealander. Father Ralph Eugene Cocklin (biol./geneticist). *M.*Marjorie Lilian (Sr Planner, Nature cons.). **Education:** U.of Waikato BSc(Soc.Sci.) 1979, U.of Guelph MA 1982, McMaster U. PhD 1985. **Experience:** res.— natural resource analysis & mgmt, envl change, sust.dev., transportation planning, utilities' planning, energy resources, agric., forestry, indigenous forest ecosystems, and tourism; admin.— Dir Regnl Res.Unit, Planning Cttee for undergrad.degree in envl mgmt, Adv.Bd *Forestry Insights*, Founding Chair CAG Rural & Urban Fringe Study Group, Exec.Cttee Envt Auckland Regn, Project Dir several major res.progs; consult.— Envt Canada, CEARC, NZDC, NZ Mins of Envt, Energy, and Forestry, NZEC, private sector orgns, memb.EDGI; teaching — resources & envl mgmt at undergrad.& grad.levels. **Career:** Lect.in Geog.1985–91, Assoc.Staff Member Envl Sci.1987–91, and Sr Lect.in Geog. 1991–, U.of Auckland; Vis.Res.Scholar, CSRD 1992–, Vis.Assoc.Prof.in Geog.1992–, U.of Victoria. **Achievements:** extensive res.on dev.& application of methods for envl eval., dev.of concepts & methods re.cumulative envl change, application of GIS to envl analysis & mgmt, Corres. Memb.IGU CCESR, Full Memb.IGU Study Group on Sust.Rural Systems. **Memberships:** AAG, CAG, IGU, ACS. **Awards:** Energy Specialty Group Best Paper Award (AAG) 1985, Fac.Enrichment Award (Ext.Affairs of Govt of Canada) 1988, Intl Visitor Award (USIA) 1993. **Publications:** *Demands on Rural Lands: Planning for Resource Use* 1987; *c.*35 major papers, 38 addit.reports, 25 presentations to intl confs. Favours pers.pub.& news media support. **Language:** English. Further details may be obtained from *Orbus Geographicus* 1992/3. Willing to act as a consult. **Address:** Department of Geography, University of Auckland, PB 92019, Auckland, New Zealand. **Tel.**(office) 64 9 373 7599, (home) 64 9 817 5794; **fax** 64 9 373 7434.

COHEN, Professor Dr Joel E. Population biology, ecology, demography, epidemiology, population genetics. Professor of Populations & Head of Laboratory of Populations. *B.*10 Feb. 1944, Washington, DC, USA. American. *M.*Audrey J.: *d., s.* **Education:** Harvard U. PhD 1970, DrPH 1973. **Experience:** res., teaching. **Career:** Asst & Assoc.Prof. Harvard U. 1971–5, Prof.of Pops & Head, Lab.of Pops 1975–, Rockefeller U. **Memberships:** Amer.AAS, APS. **Publications:**

A Model of Simple Competition 1967, *Casual Groups of Monkeys and Men: Stochastic Models of Elemental Social Systems* 1971, *Food Webs and Niche Space* 1978, *Random Matrices and Their Applications* 1986, *Community Food Webs: Data and Theory* 1990, *How Many People Can the Earth Support?* 1995.   **Languages:** English, French, German, Spanish.   Further details may be obtained from *Who's Who in Amer.*1995.   **Address:** Rockefeller University, 1230 York Avenue, Box 20, New York, New York 10021-6399, USA.   **Tel.** 1 212 327 8883; **fax** 1 212 327 7974.

COHEN, Maria Luisa.   Environment, Nature conservation, environmental ethics & education. Council President.   *B*.10 Nov.1939, Gorizia, Italy. Italian.   *M*.Donald J.Cohen (Nature photographer, philanthropist): *d*.   **Education:** U.of Trieste, BA(Phil.) 1962;   St Martin Sch.of Art (UK), Dipl.in Art & Design 1967.   **Experience:** teaching & consult.in educ.(teacher training, curr.adv.), campaign org., incl.courses in envl ethics, plant ecol., organic gardening.   **Career:** art teacher, designer, comic-strip artist, children's pubns illustrator, journalist, envl activist, organic gardener, in-and-out-of-school envl educator.   **Achievements:** Org.of first World Children's Conf.on Future of the Envt, helped focus studies in envl ethics, Project Dir of envl awareness in rural areas, created Mediaeval Monastic Herb Gdn for preserv.of biodiv.and educ. **Memberships:** IUCN CEC & Ethics WG, Intl Sem.Terra Mater, BGCI.   **Awards:** Gabbiano d'Oro Prize (Comune di Ceraso) 1988, Tree of Learning (IUCN CEC) 1992.   **Publications:** Active Expressive Participatory Envl Educ.with Young Children 1987, Apology for an Aesthetic Approach to Nature's Cons.1991, Un Giardino dei Semplici 1994. **Languages:** English, French (spoken), Italian.   Willing to act as consult.etc.in envl educ.   **Address:** 3 Avenue de Jaman, Lausanne 1005, Switzerland.   **Tel.**41 21 320 7043; **fax** 41 21 323 0736.

COHEN, Professor Dr Michael R.   Children's concepts in science, technology, & the environment;   teacher education; experiential learning. Professor of Science & Environmental Education.   *B*.3 Dec.1938, Brooklyn, NY, USA. American.   *M*.Rochelle: *s*.Jeffrey H.(anthrop.), *d*.   **Education:** Brooklyn Coll. BS(Phys.Educ.) 1960, Columbia U. MA(Sci.Educ.) 1963, Cornell U. MST(Astronomy & Earth Scis) 1964, PhD(Sci.Educ.) 1968.   **Experience:** 25 yrs in sci.& envl educ., overseas teaching & res.in Israel, UK, Turkey, Costa Rica.   **Career:** Sci. Teacher, NY City Public Schools 1960–63; Grant Admin.at Cornell U.1966–8;   Dir Academic Affairs (Sch.of Educ.) 1985–9, Prof.of Sci.& Envl Educ.1968–, Indiana U.   **Achievements:** developed in 1990 a trop.rain-forest exp.for Indiana teachers in Costa Rica;   res.on envl attitudes. **Memberships:** NSTA, AAAS, AERA, NAAEE, Council for Elementary Sci.-Intl.   **Awards:** F.AAAS, Teaching & Service

Awards (Indiana U.).   **Publications:** two elementary sch.sci.textbook series incl.*Expanding Children's Thinking Through Sci.*(sourcebook) 1981, *Discover Sci.*(in Spanish 1991) 1989 & 1993;   num.j.articles.   **Languages:** English, Spanish (poor).   Willing to act as consult.etc.   **Address:** School of Education, Indiana University, 902 W.New York Street, Indianapolis, Indiana 46202-5155, USA.   **Tel.**1 317 274 6814;   **fax** 1 317 274 6864.

COHEN, Dr Yuval.   Marine pollution, environmental management, and policy.   Director-General.   *B*.11 Aug.1947, Tel-Aviv, Israel.   Israeli. *M*.Tamar: *s*., *d*.   **Education:** Hebrew U.of Jerusalem, BSc(Geol.) 1971, MSc(Oceanogr.) 1974; Oregon SU, PhD(Oceanogr.) 1978.   **Experience:** marine envl res., admin., consult. to UNEP. **Career:** Res.Assoc. Oregon SU 1978;   Head, Marine Poll.Section, EPS Israel 1978–87;   DG, IOLR Ltd 1987–.   **Achievements:** estab.& mgmt of Israel's nat.marine poll.control prog., coordn of marine envl res.& monitoring progs, scientific res., nat.& intl consult.   **Publications:** scientific papers & reports, policy documents.   Indiff.to pers.pub.& news media support.   **Languages:** English, Hebrew.   Willing to act as consult.etc. **Address:** Israel Oceanographic and Limnological Research Ltd, POB 8030, Haifa 31080, Israel. **Tel.**972 4 515202;   **fax** 972 4 511911.

COHN-SHERBOK, Rabbi Professor Dr Dan. Judaism and animals. Lecturer in Theology, Visiting Professor.   *B*.1 Feb.1945, Denver, CO, USA. American.   *M*.Lavinia.   **Education:** Williams Coll. BA 1966;   Hebrew Union Coll. (OH) BHL 1968, MAHL 1971, DD 1995;   U.of Camb.(UK) MLitt 1974, PhD 1990.   **Experience:** res.into Judaism and animal welfare.   **Career:** Lect.in Theol.1975–, Dir of Centre for the Study of Religion and Soc.1980–88, U.of Kent;   Vis.Prof. U.of Essex 1993-4, Univs of Mx, Wales, & St Andrews, 1995–.   **Achievements:** adv.on Judaism and animals to var.animal welfare groups. **Memberships:** AAR, LSSR, CCAR.   **Awards:** F. Hebrew Union Coll. 1972 and R.Asiatic Soc. 1985.   **Publications:** *On Earth as it is in Heaven: Judaism, Christianity and Liberation Theol.*1987, *World Religions and Human Liberation* 1994, *The Liberation Debate* 1996.   Favours pers.pub. & news media support.   **Language:** English. Further details may be obtained from *People of Today* 1995, *International Who's Who* 1995. Willing to act as consult.and judge proposals. **Address:** Darwin College, University of Kent, Canterbury, Kent, England, UK.   Tel.(office & home) 44 1227 764000.

COHON, Professor Dr Jared Leigh.   Environmental management, systems analysis & modelling. Dean & Professor of Environmental Systems Analysis.   *B*.7 Oct.1947, Cleveland, OH, USA. American.   *M*.Maureen B.: *d*.   **Education:** U.of Penn. BS(Civil Eng.) 1969;   MIT, PhD(Civil Eng.) 1973.   **Experience:** river basin planning in Argentina, India, & US;   energy-facility siting in US; res.& consult.for US State Govts & UN; Chairman of two US NAS cttees on floods and infrastructure systems. **Career:** Asst Prof.1973–7, Assoc.Prof.1977–81, Prof.of Envl Engg 1981–92, Asst Dean of Engg 1981–3, Assoc.Dean of Engg 1983–6, V.-Provost for Res.1986–92, Johns Hopkins U.; Legis.Asst for Energy & Envt to Hon.Daniel Moynihan 1977–8; Prof.of Envl Systems Analysis 1992–, Dean 1992–, Prof.of Mech.Engg 1995–, Sch.of For.& Envl Studies, Yale U. **Achievements:** res.— new methodologies & applications of multiple criteria decision-making for envl & natural-resources' mgmt; admin.— leadership in grad.educ.for envl & natural-resources' mgmt. **Memberships:** AGU, AWRA, ASCE, ORSA, Inst.for Mgmt Scis (the last two now merged and known as INFORMS). **Awards:** Resources for the Future Natural Resources F'ship (MIT) 1972, Tau Beta Pi (Nat.Engg Honor Soc.) 1984, Sigma Xi (Scientific Res.Soc.) 1986. **Publications:** books incl.*Multiobjective Programming and Planning* 1978; num.papers incl.Sequential explicitly stochastic linear programming models for design and mgmt of multipurpose multiple reservoir systems (co-Author) 1978, Reservoir mgmt in Potomac R.Basin (co-Author) 1982, Optimal water treatment plant design (co-Author) 1986. Indiff.to pers.pub.& news media support. **Language:** English Further details may be obtained from *Who's Who in Engg.* Willing to act as consult.etc. **Address:** School of Forestry and Environmental Studies, Yale University, 205 Prospect Street, New Haven, Connecticut 06511, USA. **Tel.**1 204 432 5109; **fax** 1 203 432 5942.

COLE, Professor Dr Norman Howard Ayodele. Research in tropical ecology; ecophysiology of plants; environmental sciences; environmental education, policies, legislation & training; conservation of biodiversity; environment & development (environmental impact assessment). Professor of Botany, Dean, Acting Vice-Principal. *B.*11 May 1931, Buhuru, n.Nigeria. Sierra Leonean. *M.*Edith Regina Eunice: 2 *s.*, 2 *d.* **Education:** Prince of Wales Sch.(Freetown); U.Coll. Leicester BSc(Hons)(Bot.) 1956; U.of Durham, Dip.Ed.1957, MSc(Bot.)(London Ext.) 1962; UCLA PhD(Plant Sci.) 1965. **Experience:** teaching undergrad.biol., plant taxonomy, ecol., envl sci., econ.bot.; post-grad.res. prog.in ecol.; admin.— Educ. Officer, Head of Dept of Bot., Dean of Fac.and Acting VP; consult.— Chief of Envt in Africa Prog.(UN ECA), co-team-leader for EIA of Bumbuna Hydroelectric Power by Electro-Watt Engg Consults (CH) and TECHSULT (SL). **Career:** Teacher then Educ. Officer, Dept of Educ. Govt of SL 1957–62; Lect. Njala U.Coll. U.of SL 1965–8; Sr Lect. Njala U.Coll.& Fourah Bay Coll.1968–75; Prof.of Bot. Fourah Bay Coll. 1975–8 & 1988–; Chief, Envt in Africa Prog. UN ECA 1978–88; Dean, Fac.of Pure & Applied Sci.1992–5, Acting VP 1993–5, VP 1995–6, Fourah Bay Coll. U.of SL. **Achievements:** creation of envl consciousness in

SL community as Chairman of SLENCA 1968–78, MAB 1975–, CHEC SL 1990–93, and govt adv.1990–; coordn of envt/ dev.activities with African govts as Chairman of SEPA 1970–78; local coord.of UNESCO/ICSU African Bio Sci.Prog.1989–93 and ICSU/IGBP on global climate change; whilst at UN ECA assisted memb.states to develop envt/dev.progs. **Memberships:** BES, AES, ATB, IUCN Comm. on Ecol., ISTE (India), F.LS, CBDC. **Awards:** UK Sec.of State Scholarship 1953–7, USA State Dept Exchange Scholar (IIE) 1962–3, Amer.– African Univs Prog.F'ship 1963–5, Summer F'ship (USA NSF) 1964, UK Academic Staff F.(IUC) 1972–3, U.of SL Res.Council 1990–. **Publications:** *Vegetation of SL* 1968, *Envl Legis.in the ECA Regn* 1980; 55 scientific pubns & conf.papers incl. Towards solving problems of envl stress in developing countries 1979, Conserving Africa's biodiv.: issues, impacts and priorities 1994; Ed.-in-Chief *J.of Pure and Applied Sci.*1990–. Favours pers.pub.& news media support, both in support of raising envl issues through the local press on NGO activities. **Languages:** English, French (read), Krio (competent). Willing to act as consult.etc. **Address:** Department of Botany, Fourah Bay College, University of Sierra Leone, Mount Aureol, Freetown, Sierra Leone. **Tel.**(home) 232 22 232648; **fax** 232 22 224439.

COLLIE, John Stuart. Conservation and natural history. Senior Conservation Officer. *B.*6 Oct. 1958, Seychelles. British, Seychellois. *M.* Thérèse: *d.* **Education:** Glasgow U. Marine Sci.1979. **Experience:** res., educ.mgmt, admin.in country parks & nat.parks in Scotland & Seychelles. **Career:** Ranger, Warden, Scottish Nat. Trust 1979–83 (incl.WHS); Sr Cons.Officer, Min.of Foreign Affairs, Planning & Envt (Seychelles) 1983–. Accepts pers.pub.& news media support. **Language:** English. Willing to act as consult.etc. **Address:** Ministry of Foreign Affairs, Planning and Environment, POB 445, Seychelles. **Tel.**(office) 248 224644, (home) 248 371671; **fax** 248 224500.

COLLIN, Dr Gérard. Man and Nature, heritage conservation. Head of Human Sciences Service. *B.*21 Dec.1945, Le Raincy, France. French. *M.* Florence. **Education:** U.of Paris Sorbonne PhD (Geog.) 1973. **Experience:** res.— habitat & envt on Mont Lozère, dynamics of chestnut grove in Cevennes; tech.— sem.for Euro.& N.African managers of prot.areas; consult.— eval.of Algerian nat.parks, Euro.plan for prot.areas. **Career:** Asst, U.of Paris 1970–73; Curator, Ecomuseum 1982–; Head of Service, Cevennes Nat.Park 1974–. **Achievements:** Consult.for UNESCO in N.Africa, c.Europe, & India, for prot.areas; Pres. French IUCN CNPPA. **Memberships:** IUCN, ICOM–UNESCO, French MAB Cttee. **Award:** Médaille du Patrimoine 1980. **Publications:** *The Cevennes Biosphere Reserve* 1985; *Rural Soc.& Prot.Area* 1989; *Ecomuseus & Ciencias de la Natura* 1991; *Conserver le Patrimoine Vivant* 1993. Indiff.to pers.pub.& news media support.

Languages: English, French, Italian (spoken), Spanish. Willing to act as consult.etc. **Address:** La Pecherie Bat.3, Av.du Mont St Clair Apt 19, 34280 Carnon, France. **Tel.**(office) 33 66 495 300, (home) 33 67 584798; **fax** 33 66 495302.

COOPER, Jeffrey 'Jeff.' Charles. Waste management, reduction, recycling, & planning. Waste Planner. *B.*10 Jan.1949, Twickenham, Middlesex, England, UK. British. **Education:** LSE, MSc 1971. **Experience:** res.& dev.of source separation recycling schemes in London 1982–6, prod.during 1982–95 of waste plan for Greater London covering period to AD 2015. **Career:** Sr Lect.in Geog. Kingston U.(UK) 1974–82; Recycling Coord., Greater London Council 1982–6; Waste Planner, London Waste Regulation Auth.1986–. **Achievements:** estab.of new recycling initiatives in the UK through Local Auth. Recycling Adv.Cttee (Chairman 1985–), Waste Watch (Chairman 1987–) 1986–, Nat.Recycling Forum 1990–. **Memberships:** RGS, IWM, ISWA. **Publications:** chapters in ref.works and readers, 200+ conf.papers 1987–. Dislikes pers.pub., favours news media support. **Languages:** English; French & German (passable). Willing to act as consult.etc. **Address:** London Waste Regulation Authority, 20 Albert Embankment, London SE1 7TJ, England, UK. **Tel.**(office) 44 171 587 3075, (home) 44 171 487 5865; **fax** 44 171 587 5258.

COPPINGER, Professor Dr Raymond. Nonlethal predator control, international agriculture & wildlife issues, canine behaviour & evolution. Professor of Biology. *B.*7 Feb.1937, Boston, MA, USA. American. *M.*Lorna (non-lethal predator control, behaviour of livestock-guarding dogs): *s.*Timothy (community-supported organic agric.), *d.*Karyn (envl scientist). **Education:** Boston U. AB(Amer.Lit.& Phil.), U.of Mass. MA(Zool.) 1964, PhD(Biol.) 1968. **Experience:** res.— behaviour of dogs, ecol.of monkeys, birds, & butterflies; admin.; consult.— behaviour of dogs, ecol.of landscaping, and sci.curricula; teaching. **Career:** postgrad. Res.Assoc.; Prof.of Biol. Hampshire Coll. 1969– incl.extensive summer res.projects. **Achievements:** teaching undergrads about critical issues in agric., estab.of Livestock Dog Project which introduced Old World guarding-dogs to N.& S.Amer. **Memberships:** ASM, Explorers' Club, Soc.of Sigma XI. **Awards:** Chevron Cons.Award 1990, grants in support of res.& teaching. **Publications:** *Interactions between Livestock Guarding Dogs & Wolves* (co-Author, in press), *The Evol.of Working Dog Behavior* (co-Author, in press). Favours pers. pub.& news media support. **Language:** English. Willing to act as consult.etc. **Address:** School of Natural Science, Hampshire College, Amherst, Massachusetts 01002, USA. **Tel.**1 413 582 5487; **fax** 1 413 256 1436; **e-mail** lcoppinger @hamp.hampshire.edu .

CORBET, Professor Dr Philip Steven. Medical entomology, wildlife conservation especially of dragonflies; energy use in agricultural systems, environmental education; carrying capacity, human population policies. Emeritus Professor of Zoology, Honorary Fellow. *B.*21 May 1929, KL, W.Malaysia. British, Canadian, New Zealander. Father Dr Alexander Steven Corbet (deceased), auth.on biol.processes in trop.soils and butterflies of W.Malaysia, sister Sarah Alexandra Corbet, envl consult., cons.of pollinators of agricl land. *D.*: *d.*Katarina Alexandra (cons., recycling). **Education:** Nelson Boys' Coll.(NZ), Dauntsey's Sch.(UK); U.of Reading, BSc(Hons)(Zool.)(1st Class) 1950, DSc 1962; U.of Camb. Gonville & Caius Coll. PhD(Entomol.) 1953, ScD 1976. **Experience:** res.— ecol.of insects (mainly) & fishes, behaviour & ecol.of mosquitoes & dragonflies, energy flow in agricl systems; admin.— dir, res.inst.for integrated control of agricl pests (Canada), head of two u.biol.depts (Canada & UK), dir of u.postgrad.prog.for training & res.in resource mgmt (NZ); consult.— integrated control of Yellow Fever Mosquito (Tanzania for WHO and Trinidad for EEC), dragonfly biol.& cons. **Career:** Zool. EAFFRO 1954–7; Entomol. EAVRO 1957–62; Res.Sci. (Entomol.) 1962–7, Dir 1967–71, Res.Inst. (Belleville), Canada Dept of Agric.; Prof.& Chairman, Dept of Biol. U.of Waterloo 1971–4; Prof.& Dir, Jt Centre for Envl Scis, U.of Canterbury & Lincoln Coll.1974–8; Prof. Dept of Zool. U.of Canterbury 1978–80; Commonwealth Vis.Prof. Dept of Applied Biol. U.of Camb. 1979–80; Prof.of Zool.(Emer.1990–) Dept of Biol.Scis (Head 1983–6), U.of Dundee 1980–90; Hon.F. Fac.of Sci. U.of Edinburgh 1990–. **Achievements:** in Canada — active on panels & adv.groups trying to gain recognition by fed.govt of need for nat.& global pop.policies; in NZ — (i) gaining recognition at govt level of need to incorporate principles of carrying capacity & energy balance into resource policies, based on res.init.& conducted at Centre for Resource Mgmt, (ii) producing and gaining acceptance of teaching materials (distributed to all sec.schools in NZ) explaining these principles, (iii) training postgrads who enter adv.or managerial posts connected with resource mgmt in govt & industry, (iv) Charter Memb.and service on first Council of NZDS, memb.first Exec.Cttee of NZ Club of Rome, membership of Envl Council of Govt Ind.Fact-finding Group on Nuclear Energy (MAB Cttee); in UK — membership of Cttee for Scotland NCC, Chairman of Cons.& Sci.Cttee, Scottish Wildlife Trust, and first Pres.of BDS. **Memberships:** AMCA (Life), ESC (Pres. 1971–2, F.1977), ESNZ, IBiol.(F.1967), IOS (Memb.of Honour 1985), RES, RSA (F.1991), RSE (F.1987), Soc.of Authors. **Awards:** Colin Morley Prize in Zool.(U.of Reading) 1949, Gold Medal for Outstanding Achievement (ESC) 1974, Hon.Memb.(BDS) 1991 (Pres.1983–92). **Publications:** *Dragonflies* (co-Author) 1960, *A Biol.of Dragonflies* 1962, *The Odonata of Canada & Alaska* Vol.3 (co-Author) 1975; c.200 res.& review papers and contributed chapters. Indiff.to pers.pub.& news media support. **Languages:**

English, French & German (modest), Kiswahili (simple spoken). Further details may be obtained from *Biog.Intl, Debrett's People of Today* 1995, *Dict.of Intl Biog., Intl Who's Who in Educ.,* Longman's *Who's Who in Sci., The Intl Authors' & Writers' Who's Who, VIP Scotland, Who's Who in Amer., Scotland* 1994, *The World Who's Who of Brit.Scientists* 1983. Willing to act as consult.etc. **Address:** Institute for Cell, Animal and Population Biology, Ashworth Laboratories, West Mains Road, Edinburgh EH9 3JT, Scotland, UK. **Tel.**(office) 44 131 650 5457, (home) 44 131 662 4696; **fax** 44 131 650 6564.

CORRAL, Thais. Women: health, environment, communication. Coordinator. *B.*2 Dec.1957, Rio de Janeiro, Brazil. Brazilian. **Education:** Public Admin.1980, Journalism 1984, Dev. Studies. **Experience:** consult.for UNDP and other intl instns such as GTZ on field of women & envt. **Career:** Prog.Officer, Dev.Alternatives with Women for New Era 1987–90; Ed.-in-Chief for Latin Amer. Women's Feature Service 1988–90; Coord. Network in Defense of Human Species 1990– and Centro de Projetos da Mulher 1990–. **Achievements:** work in field of women & envt giving shape & consistency to that issue. **Membership:** WEDO (co-Chair 1990–). **Publications:** *Terra Femina* (co-Ed.) 1992–, *Women Speak on Envt* 1992, Pop.control in Brazil: the failure of a success story (speech) 1994. Accepts pers.pub., favours news media support. **Languages:** English, French, Italian, Portuguese, Spanish. Willing to act as consult. etc. **Address:** Rua Julio Otoni 315/301, Rio de Janeiro 20241-400, Rio de Janeiro, Brazil. **Tel.**(office) 21 285 7510, (home) 21 265 8658; **fax** 21 556 3383.

COUSTEAU, Captain Jacques-Yves. Studying & addressing world environmental, economic, & social, issues, with the goal of protecting the rights of future generations. Society President, Council Chairman. *B.*11 June 1910, St André de Cubzac (Gironde), France. French. *M.*Francine: 3 *s., d.* **Education:** Stanislas Acad. Bachelier 1927; Midshipman, Brest Naval Acad. 1930. **Experience:** began experimenting with various prototypes of breathing apparatus 1936; coinvented aqualung (tm) 1943 and first underwater propellor system or scooter 1948; developed first decompression chamber for simulated dives to 300 m.1949 and first industrial equipment for undersea TV 1952; constructed first integrated undersea 35 mm camera 1955 and first integrated 16 mm underwater camera 1967; gave first undersea TV broadcast 1957; completed & operated first two-men diving saucer 1959; studied & constructed sensors to measure ultrasuperficial temp.of seawater 1979–83; constructed wind-propellor cylinder, turbosail (tm) system, & launching of experimental ship equipped with this system 1982. **Career:** Midshipman 1930–35, Chief French Naval Base in Shanghai 1935, began experimenting with var.prototypes of breathing apparatus 1936 and coinvented (with Emile Gagnan) the aqualung (tm) 1943; after WWII

(during which served in the French *Résistance*) co-created (with Commander Philippe Tailliez) an Experimental Diving Unit, acquired *Calypso* (retired minesweeper), and created Campagnes Océanographiques Françaises 1950; created Centre d'Etudes Marines Avancées 1952; Dir Musée Océanographique of Monaco 1957–88; retired from Navy with rank of Captain of Corvette 1957; continued saturation-diving experiments with estab.of 'Houses Under the Sea' 1959–65; accomplished long & complicated journeys with the *Calypso* team 1967–, incl. world's major river systems, documenting explored natural systems; created, and now Pres.of, The Cousteau Soc.1973; began study of new complementary wind-propellor system for ships 1980– which was finalized by launching experimental ship *Alcyone* fitted with a two-turbosail system for ocean trial, circumnavigating the earth in a 9-yrs Rediscovery of the World project aboard *Calypso* & *Alcyone* 1985–; Chairman newly-created Council for the Rights of Future Generations 1993–. **Achievements:** doing everything possible, through pers. diplomacy (*i.e.* mtg with world leaders, testifying before US Cong.and other govtl bodies), films, books, etc., to protect & preserve the qual.of life for present & future generations; in addition to planning & directing ongoing expedns, currently committed to strengthening role of UN in global stewardship & intl stability and to raising public awareness of the importance of addressing growing economic disparities between developed & other countries. **Memberships:** Académie Française, Council for the Rights of Future Generations, NAS (USA), Académie Royale du Maroc, others. **Awards:** Chevalier de la Légion d'Honneur, promotion to Officer & Commander, Intl Envl Prize (with Sir Peter Scott)(UN) 1977, Presidential Medal of Freedom (USA) 1985, TV Acad.Hall of Fame (USA) 1987, Founders Award (Intl Council of NATAS) 1987, Global 500 Roll of Honour (UNEP) 1988, Centennial Award (NGS) 1988, inducted into Académie Française 1989, Third Intl Catalan Prize 1991, Hon.PhD — UCB, Brandeis U., Rensselaer Poly.Inst., & Harvard U. **Publications:** 50+ books published world-wide in more than 12 languages incl.*The Cousteau Almanac* 1981, *Jacques Cousteau's Calypso* 1983, *Jacques Cousteau's Amazon Journey* 1984, *Jacques Cousteau/Whales* 1988; 100+ TV films of which some have won num.awards and incl.*The Silent World, World Without Sun, Voyage to the Edge of the World.* Prefers no pers.pub.but to focus on global issues, favours news media support where appropriate for his goals and activities of his orgns. **Languages:** English, French, German (fair), Russian (elementary). Further details may be obtained from The Cousteau Society Inc., 870 Greenbrier Circle Suite 402, Chesapeake, VA 23320, USA; also from the *International Who's Who* 1994–5 and *Who's Who in the World* 1996. **Address:** Equipe Cousteau, 7 Rue de l'Amiral d'Estaing, 75116 Paris, France. **Tel.**33 1 53 677777; **fax** 33 1 53 677771.

COUTANT, Dr Charles C. Aquatic ecology, thermal effects, Striped Bass (*Roccus saxatilis*) biology; Pacific salmon biology, energy–environment issues. Senior Research Ecologist. *B*.2 Aug.1938, Jamestown, NY, USA. American. *M*.Nancy Ann: 2 *d*. **Education:** Lehigh U. BA 1960, MS 1962, PhD 1965. **Experience:** wide-spread in freshwater & estuarine envts of the US Northeast, Gt Lakes, Pacific Northwest, c.Alaska, Calif.'s C.Valley & bay-delta, & Southeast; have conducted res.& envl assessments of temp.effects, thermal powerplants, hydropower facilities, and envl biol. of Pacific salmon & Striped Bass; has led res. teams & coordinated agency funding progs. **Career:** Battelle-Pacific Northwest Labs (B-PNL) 1965–70; Mgr Thermal Effects Prog.1970–79, Leader Multi-media Modelling Project 1979–82, Mgr Dept of Energy Global Carbon Cycle Prog.1985–6, Mgr Exploratory Studies Prog. 1989–91, Sr Res.Staff 1982–5, 1986–8, 1992–, ORNL. **Achievements:** field studies of thermal discharge effects on invertebrates of Delaware R.and, with lab. studies, of thermal effects of Hanford reactors on Columbia R.salmonids & other aquatic life; annual reviews of thermal effects pubns 1968–80; eval.of aquatic thermal effects info.to provide nat.water temp.criteria recommendations by NAS; participation in dev.of EPA guidelines for §316(a) thermal studies of power stations, and in estab.of Electric Power Res. Inst., memb.of its nat. Adv.Council; dev.of biol. data & criteria for EIAs of steam electric power plants; dev.of electronic temp.telemetry of fishes as res.tool for thermal behaviour studies; lead role in developing guidance for thermal power-plant impact assessment for UNESCO & IAEA; adv.on project eval.to Bonneville Power Admin.Fish & Wildlife Prog.& memb.of Scientific Review Group; elucidation of thermal ecol. of Striped Bass through lab.& field res.and its application to mgmt of species in fresh water & estuaries; eval.of impacts of hydropower on aquatic systems. **Memberships:** F.AAAS, F.AIFRB, AFS (Pres. Tennessee Chapter Southern Div.& Water Qual. Section, co-Ed.*Trans.*, Soc. 2nd VP to succeed to Pres.1885), ASLO, ASTM (Chair Envl Fate Models Task Group), ESA (VC Applied Ecol. Section), Sigma Xi (Southeast Regnl Lect., Pres. Oak Ridge Chapter); WPCF (Lit.Review Cttee — Thermal Effects). **Awards:** Darbaker Prize (Penn. AS), Dir's Award (Battelle-Pacific Northwest Labs), Excellence in Fisheries (Tennessee Chapter AFS), Outstanding Pubns (Martin Marietta Energy Systems), Disting.Pubn (ASIS). **Publications:** 26 chapters, 40 scientific j.papers, 19 non-refereed & 30 symp.articles, 53 lab.& agency reports, 8 book reviews & news items, 9 contribns to US NEPA Envl Impact Statements. Enjoys pers.pub.for the cause of envl cons.& news media support. **Languages:** English, French (poor). Willing to act as consult.etc. **Address:** Environmental Sciences Division, Oak Ridge National Laboratory, POB 2008, Mail Stop 6036, Oak Ridge, Tennessee 37831-6036, USA. **Tel.**(office) 1 615 576 6830, (home) 1 615 483 5976; **fax** 1 615 576 8646 or 8543; **e-mail** ccc@ornl.gov .

COVACEVICH, Ms Jeanette Adelaide. Taxonomy & zoogeography of extant and extinct Australian reptiles esp.those of rain-forests, heaths, & deserts; Aboriginal history, medicine (especially following envenomation), and adaptations to life in rain-forests & deserts. Senior Curator (Vertebrates). *B*.26 March 1945, Innisfail, Qld, Australia. Australian. **Education:** U.of Qld BA 1964, Griffith U. MSc 1977. **Experience:** curation, res., editing, and lecturing. **Career:** Asst Curator, Curator, Sr Curator, Qld Mus.1966–, Consult. R.Brisbane Hosp. 1977–. **Achievements:** description of many new species of reptiles, recognition of & much subs.res.on *Oxyuranus microlepidotus* (world's most venomous land-snake), increased knowledge of endemic, sometimes rare, species of the Wet Tropics rain-forests — a WHS. **Memberships:** RSQ (Sec. 1974–9, Council Memb. 1984– 7), ASH (Pres. 1988–90), Memb.Scientific Adv. Cttee for Qld Nature Cons.Act 1992–. **Award:** St John Priory Vote of Thanks 1991. **Publications:** six edited books incl.*Focus on Stradbroke* 1984, *Toxic Plants & Animals: A Guide for Australia* 1987, *Venoms & Victims* 1988; *c*.150 scientific papers. Dislikes pers.pub., favours news media support. **Languages:** English, French (some). Willing to act as consult.etc. **Address:** Queensland Museum, Box 3300, South Brisbane 4101, Queensland, Australia. **Tel.** (office) 61 7 840 7708, (home) 61 7 221 1918; **fax** 61 7 846 1918.

CRAIK, Dr Wendy. Marine areas and recreational tourism management, community involvement in planning. Executive Officer. *B*.5 Dec. 1949, Canberra, ACT, Australia. Australian. *M*.Grant Hawley. **Education:** ANU BSc(Hons) 1973, UBC PhD(Zool.) 1978, Capricornia Inst. of Advanced Educ. Grad.Dipl.of Mgmt 1986. **Experience:** res., teaching, and partic.marine park mgmt. **Career:** Teaching Asst, Simon Fraser U. 1976; Grad.Clerk DoE 1978; Dir Res.& Monitoring, Planning & Mgmt 1984–92, Exec.Officer 1992–, GBRMPA. **Achievements:** init.Reef Fisheries (esp.recreational) studies in GBR, dev.of GBRMPA Oil Spill Response capacity, dev.& implementation of contract res.prog.& coordn of GBR res., coordn of 25-yrs GBR World Heritage Area Strat.Plan. **Memberships:** ASFB (past Exec.memb.), AMSA (Pres.), ACRS, RAIPA, Zonta Club of Townsville (past memb.& Pres.), NQPS (past Exec.Memb.& past Pres.), Friends of the Palmetum (past Exec.memb.), EIA, IUCN CNPPA, QSOPC, QICMC (1991–2), QCMCC 1992–, GBRMAC (Chair 1992), Adv.Cttee on Res.on Effects of Fishing in GBR (Chair 1992–), NPAC 1993–, Tech.Adv.Cttee 1993–, Reefmac 1993–, E.Coast Tuna Mgmt Adv.Cttee 1987–92. **Awards:** Nat.Undergrad. Scholarship, Canberra Scholarship 1968–70 & 1972, U.Medal (ANU) 1973, Postgrad.Studentship (CSIRO) 1973–77. **Publications:** *c*.65 j., symp., workshop papers & reports incl. Monitoring in the GBR Marine Park 1986, Res.on GBR fishes 1989, Coral Reef Mgmt (co-Author) 1990, Oil Spills in the GBR Regn 1991, Current status of the GBR Marine Park: its estab., dev.& current status 1992. Favours pers.pub.& news media support. **Language:** English. Willing to act as consult. etc. **Address:** Great Barrier Reef Marine Park Authority, POB 1379, Townsville, Queensland 4810, Australia. **Tel.**(office) 61 7 7 81 8820, (home) 61 7 7 74 0206; **fax** 61 7 7 21 3445.

CRAMPTON, Professor Dr Colin Bassett. Geology, geomorphology, soils, palynology, archaeology, forestry, permafrost, land classification, toxicology and, recently, the ecological interactions of these earth sciences with *native* Canadian perceptions (oral traditions) of environmental conservation in western Canada related to *European* Canadian written traditions with their respect for organized science. Professor Emeritus in Geography. *B.*31 Dec. 1926, Gillingham, Kent, England, UK. British, Canadian. *W.*(Peggy): 2 *d.* **Education:** U.of Edinburgh, course in econ.1944 interrupted by RN service (radar & gen.electronics); U.of Bristol, BSc (Geol.) 1953, PhD 1956; memb. BC Assn of Professional Engrs & Geoscientists 1993. **Experience:** res.— 1956–67 extending into Yorks., s.Scotland, Bergen area of Norway & Eire, involving soils, land-use (agric.&/or for.), archaeology, geomorph.& palynology, with advice to Agricl Adv.Services, consults & municipalities re.preferred land use such as agric.or highways; 1967–70 soils & geomorph. and mapping of present worth of costs to break even with spruce-growing in diff.landscapes, 1970–73 determining sensitivity of land to pipeline construction in Mackenzie R.Valley NWT; 1973– interacting soil–biologic–geomorphic land class.in SW BC, n.BC & Alberta, Yukon and NWT; consult.— combined with res.into soils, compaction, veg., fluvial geomorph., permafrost, pipelines, pulp mills, aluminium smelting-plants & landscape-visual analysis as it affects use of land (which work has been extended into Alaska, Europe, and Russia); teaching — geol., soils, geomorph., natural hazards, Canadian N., field methods & terrain eval., supervision from BSc to PhD levels, u.corres.courses within regnl Colls and the prison service re.earth scis & envl issues; project reviewer Canadian ENSERC and USA NSF; for some yrs has been talking to schools across BC encouraging students to enter sci.with partic. emphasis upon evol.from geol.& biol.perspectives (with sympathetic attitude towards religious allegories), leading into current envl problems, and to school-parent & other assns re. earthquake preparedness. **Career:** PSO Rothamsted Experimental Station 1956–67; Res. Sci. Canadian For.Service 1967–70; spec.student in For.& Computing Sci. U.of New Brunswick 1968–70; Berger Comm.1970–73; Prof.in Geog. Simon Fraser U.1973– (Emer. 1992–); post-retirement contract for Geog.in Distance Educ. **Achievements:** three extensive maps of (i) soil distribn in S.& c.Wales, (ii) forest productivity in Maritimes of Canada, and (iii) terrain permafrost sensitivity to pipeline construction in Mackenzie R.Valley. **Member-**

ships: Canadian & Intl — Socs of Soil Sci., Assns of Geographers, Permafrost Assns, Socs for Ecol.Land Class., Quaternary Assns, Socs of Distance Educ.; CARC, WPRSA, AINA, PSA. **Awards:** recipient of Canadian ENSERC res. grants. **Publications:** The Potential Dev.of Northern Phys.& Biol.Resources 1986, Burnaby–Simon Fraser Mtn Landscapes 1994, Regnl Geographies of Major Resource Projects Affecting Euro.& Native Canadians in the Western Provincial N.1994; *c.*65 intl j.papers and as many conf. contribns; ms reviewer for *Can.J.of Soil Sci.* and *J.of Landscape Ecol.* Welcomes pers.pub. & news media support. **Languages:** English; French, German, Russian & Welsh (all limited). Willing to act as consult.etc.esp.within broad field of exp. **Address:** Department of Geography, Simon Fraser University, Burnaby, British Columbia V5A 1S6, Canada. **Tel.** (office) 1 604 291 3321, (home) 1 604 299 3021; **fax** 1 604 291 5841.

CRANBROOK, Earl of, *see* **GATHORNE-HARDY, Dr Gathorne** (formerly Lord Medway).

CROFTS, Roger. Natural heritage, conservation. Chief Executive. *B.*17 Jan.1944, Leicester, England, UK. British. *S.: s., d.* **Education:** Hinckley Grammar Sch., U.of Liverpool BA 1965, U.of Leicester Postgrad.Cert.of Educ. 1966, U.of Aberdeen M.Litt.1971. **Experience:** res.— sandy coastal systems in Scotland & Northern Ireland, raised shorelines in Canary Islands & Svalbard, dev.of geomorph.mapping techniques, effects of oil & gas dev.; consult.— commissioned var.res.progs. **Career:** Res.Asst U.of Aberdeen 1966–72, Res.F. UCL 1972–4, Res. Officer 1974–84 & Asst Sec.1984–91 The Scottish Office, Chief Exec. Scottish Natural Heritage 1991–. **Achievements:** developed coastal mgmt assessment methods, devised natural heritage areas system in Scotland and remit of Scottish Natural Heritage. **Memberships:** BGRG, QRA. **Award:** Vis.Prof. U.of London 1992. **Publications:** chapters incl.Self-catering Holiday Accommodation: the Role of Substitution 1977, Mapping Techniques in Geomorph. 1981, and papers incl.A method to determine shingle supply to the coast 1974, Geomorph. inputs into the planning process 1977. Favours pers.pub.& news media support. **Languages:** English, French (read). **Address:** 19 Manor Place, Edinburgh EH3 7DX, Scotland, UK. **Tel.**(office) 44 131 446 2201, (home) 44 131 225 1177; **fax** 44 131 446 2278.

CROKER, Professor Dr Robert A. History of ecology & conservation, coastal marine ecology, systematics–ecology of marine Amphipoda. Emeritus Professor of Natural Resources. *B.*4 Sept.1932, New York, NY, USA. American. *M.*Mary Ann Casey (urban for.): *d.*Jean Marie (hort.), *s.* **Education:** Adelphi Coll. AB*(cum laude)* 1958, U.of Miami MS 1960, Emory U. PhD(Biol.) 1966. **Experience:** res.— basic &

applied in marine envt (USA & overseas), on-site, oral, & archival hist.; admin.— Chair Inter-college Biol.Scis Orgn (NH) 1980–84; consult.— coastal ecol.& mgmt, natural preserves, envl educ.; teaching — zool., ecol., natural hist., envl biol.& hist., natural resources (all at BS/BA to PhD levels). **Career:** USAF 1951–5; Biol. NY State Cons.Dept. 1958; Res.Asst, Miami Marine Lab.& Rutgers Oyster Lab.1960; Biol. USDI 1960–64 & U.of Georgia Marine Inst.1964; Vis.Sci. Eniwetok (Micronesia) 1968–9 and W.Indies 1982 Marine Labs; NSF Pre-doctl F. Selection Cttee 1973–6; PhD Thesis Examiner, U.of Kerala 1975; Vis.Prof. Universidad Austral de Chile 1982; Prof.of Zool.1966–88, Prof.of Envl Hist.& Cons.1988–94, Emer.Prof.of Natural Resources 1994–, U.of New Hampshire. **Achievements:** ecol.& systematics of marine sand communities (Atlantic & Pacific Oceans, Carib.Sea); biogl work on early Amer.ecologists; advocacy for coastal wetlands in New England; integrated team teaching in undergrad. envl courses. **Memberships:** ASEH, ESA, NWF. **Awards:** F.AAAS, NSF F.at Miami U.1959– 60 & Duke U.1966. **Publications:** *Pioneer Ecologist* 1991; 40 papers. Favours pers.pub.& news media support. **Languages:** English, German (read), Spanish (fair). Further details may be obtained from *Amer.Men & Women of Sci.*1994– 5. Willing to act as consult.in Amer.envl hist. only. **Address:** 67 Wiswall Road, Durham, New Hampshire 03824, USA. **Tel.**(home) 1 603 659 5781.

CROSBY, Arturo. Environment — tourism, ecotourism & rural tourism; planning & design, training programmes, lecturing & advising. Lecturer, Director, Executive Director, Editor & Director, International Consultant. *B.*24 Sept. 1956, Madrid, Spain. American, Spanish. *M.* Margarita: *s.*, *d.* **Education:** Universidad Autonoma de Madrid, Envl Biol. 1980; courses on land-use mgmt, ecol.& econ. **Experience:** consult.for UNEP (Envt & Tourism Prog.in Medit.); dir of different projects in ecotourism, *e.g.* Banc d'Arguin Nat.Park; adv.on ecotourism to Cuba, World Tourism Orgn, Centre for Our Common Future, CEC etc.; lecturing world-wide, field trips to protected Nature and tourist areas of num.countries, tech.journalism & media exp. **Career:** Adv.to DG for Tourism (Regnl Govt of Madrid) 1985–6, Adv.to Spanish Min.of Tourism & Gen.Secretariat for the Envt 1985–8 & 1992–3, Dir & Lect.on Envt–Tourism 1985–, Exec.Dir *CEFAT 1987–, Ed & Dir *NaTour* 1988–, Intl Consult.1988. **Achievements:** init. of ecotourism in Spain and main supporter of cons.by using ecotourism planning & design; Founder of first NGO* concerning envt & tourism in Europe, and of first tech.magazine *NaTour;* promoter & Founder 1995 of lab.for designing Innovative Products based on natural resources to support local natural–rural areas. **Publications:** *Rural Tourism Self-employment Handbook* 1991, *Ecol.Improvements for your Hotel* 1992, *The Sust.Tourism Dev.in Rural*

Areas 1993, *Ecotourism–Rural Tourism: Manual for Training* 1995 (prin.Author, all in Spanish), *Interpretación Ambiental y Turísmo Rural* (co-Author) 1994; many magazine & newspaper articles. Favours pers.pub.& news media support. **Languages:** English; French, Italian & Portuguese (all understood); Spanish. Willing to act as consult.etc. **Address:** European Centre for Professional Training in Environment & Tourism (CEFAT), Viriato-20, 28010 Madrid, Spain. **Tel.**34 1 593 0831; **fax** 34 1 593 0980.

CROSS, Jeremy Vincent. Horticultural entomology, crop & environment protection, horticulture and pesticide application. Entomologist. *B.*15 Feb.1955, Stourport-on-Severn, Worcs, England, UK. British. *M.*Linda Ann (landscape mgmt consult., ecol.). **Education:** Trinity Coll. Camb. MA 1986. **Experience:** res.& consult.in hortl & agricl crop prot. **Career:** Agricl Sci. Specialist (Entomol.) 1976–8, Entomol. (Hort.& Agric.) 1979–82, Dep.Regnl Entomol.1982–3, ADAS; Sr Res.Entomol. HRI–E. Malling 1993–. **Achievements:** devising/testing & implementing integrated pest mgmt progs for hortl crops with view to reducing pesticide use & undesirable envl effects, and safer/more efficient spray application for tree & bush fruit crops. **Memberships:** F.RES, AAB (Convener of Pesticide Application Group), Scientific Sec. Intl Orgn of Biol.Control Group for Integrated Fruit Prod., Tech Cttee of GRO-ACT Ltd., E.Kent Fruit Soc., Register of Practitioners for Pesticide Advice, ISHS, Convener of Orchard Spraying Study & Discussion Group (UK). **Publications:** *c.*50 scientific papers incl.An overview of the second ISHS Intl Symp.on integrated fruit prod.1993, Apple enemy nr one 1994. Indiff.to pers.pub.& news media support. **Language:** English. Willing to act as consult.etc. **Address:** Horticulture Research International–East Malling, West Malling, Kent ME19 6BJ, England, UK. **Tel.**(office) 44 1732 843833, (home) 44 1233 813360; **fax** 44 1732 849067.

CROXALL, Dr John Patrick. Marine ecology especially of seabirds & seals and of polar regions. Deputy Chief Scientific Officer & Section Head. *B.*19 Jan.1946, Birmingham, England, UK. British. Father Dr Harold E.Croxall, mycology, plant pathol.; mother Marjorie, hort. **Education:** Queen's Coll.Oxf. BA(Zool.)(1st Class Hons) 1968, MA 1987; U.of Auckland, PhD (Zool.) 1971. **Experience:** rcs.in many fields of marine & terr.ecol., ecol.& pop. dynamics of Antarctic & Subantarctic seabirds & seals with particular emphasis on envl & cons.aspects 1985–; extensive admin.exp., Chairman of num. socs & cttees, Rapp.at many workshops & confs; scientific adv.to FCO on Antarctic envl affairs. **Career:** Sr Res.Assoc.& Dir, Oiled Seabird Res.Unit, Dept of Zool. U.of Newcastle upon Tyne 1971–5; Head of Birds and Mammals (now Higher Predators) Section 1976– (SSO 1976–9, PSO 1979–85, Sr PSO

1985–92, Dep.Chief Scientific Officer 1992–), Brit.Antarctic Survey. **Achievements:** post-doctl res.on trop.rainforest insectivorous birds, subs.Dir of res.group investigating seabirds–oil poll.relationships; estab.of leading res.group investigating foraging ecol.& pop.dynamics of Antarctic vertebrates which group pioneered many new tech., practical, & theoretical, devs; init.first comp.monitoring scheme in Antarctic (subs.intl standard); promoted first rigorous overview of cons.requirements for Antarctic vertebrates; org.of global reviews of cons.needs & priorities for seabirds *via* ICBP; developed use of data for predators in mgmt of commercial fisheries; coord.res.into action on seabirds–fisheries interactions, esp.mortality caused by longlines. **Memberships:** IUCN Birdlife Sea-bird SG (Exec Cttee 1982–), CCAMLR (UK Del.1987–), IOC (Standing Cttee for Coordn of Seabird Res. Memb.1978– & Sec.1982–94), IOC 1990–, BOU (Counc.1974–8 & 1992–5, Chairman Mtgs Cttee 1979–85, VP 1987–91, Chairman Ornithl Affairs Cttee 1993–5, Pres.1995–), RS Interdisc.Cttee on Antarctic Res.1990–93; RSPB (Counc.1989–, Chairman Cons.Cttee 1993–), Seabird Group (Counc.1975–9 & 1982–3, Chairman 1984–7); SCAR (Bird Biol.Subcttee Memb.1978–, Sec.1981–2 & Chairman 1986–94), BIOMASS Working Party on Bird Ecol. Sec.1980–85, Groups of Specialists on Seals 1984–90 & Southern Ocean Ecol.1986–, WG on Biol.1986–); Edl Bds *J.Applied Ecol.*1983–, *Marine Ornith.*1984–, *J.of Zool.*1989–94, *Bird Cons Intl* 1991–. **Awards:** Scientific Medal (ZSL) 1984, Polar Medal 1993. **Publications:** *Status and Cons.of the World's Seabirds* (co-Ed.) 1984, *Seabirds: Feeding Ecol.and Role in Marine Ecosystems* (Ed.) 1987, *Seabird Status and Cons.: A Supplement* (Ed.) 1991; 75 papers in refereed journals, 50 in books & conf.proc., 30 others & 50 published reports, num.book reviews etc. Indiff.to pers.pub., favours news media support. **Languages:** English, French (spoken). Further details may be obtained in *Who's Who in Ornith.*1994, *Who's Who in Sci.*(US) 1995. Willing to act as consult.etc. **Address:** British Antarctic Survey, High Cross, Madingley Road, Cambridge CB3 0ET, England, UK. **Tel.**(office) 44 1223 251608, (home) 44 1223 234287; **fax** 44 1223 62616.

CRUTE, Dr Ian. Genetics of plant–pathogen interactions in crop & natural ecosystems. Head of Department. *B.*3 June 1949, Sunderland, Co. Durham, England, UK. British. **Education:** U.of Newcastle upon Tyne PhD 1973. **Experience:** 20 yrs' res.on plant–pathogen interactions and the deployment of genetic resistance for the control of hortl crop diseases. **Career:** Res.Sci. 1973–87, Head of Plant Path.and Weed Sci.Dept 1992–, HRI Wellesbourne (Warks); Head, Crop and Envt Prot.Dept, HRI E.Malling (Kent) 1986–92. **Achievements:** elucidation of genetics of several host–pathogen interactions as an aid to breeding for disease resistance and as components in integrated disease mgmt strats.

Memberships: BSPP (Pres.-elect), AAB, IBiol., BMS. **Awards:** Res.Medal (RASEW) 1992. **Publications:** num.chapters & papers incl.the Contribn of Genetic Studies to Understanding Fungicide Resistance 1992, Phenotypic & genotypic characterization of interactions between isolates of *Peronospora parasitica* and accessions of *Arabidopsis thaliana* (co-Author) 1994. Indiff.to pers.pub.& news media support. **Languages:** English, French (basic). Willing to act as consult.etc. **Address:** Department of Plant Pathology and Weed Science, Horticulture Research International, Wellesbourne, Warwickshire CV35 9EF, England, UK. **Tel.**(office) 44 1789 470382, (home) 44 1926 651888; **fax** 44 1789 470552.

CULLEN, Dr James. Plant taxonomy especially of plants of horticultural interest. Trust Director. *B.*2 April 1936, Liverpool, England, UK. British. **Education:** U.of Liverpool BSc 1958, PhD 1962, DSc 1980. **Experience:** taxonomic res.on *Rhododendron*, prep.of The Euro.Gdn Flora. **Career:** Res.Asst, U.of Edinburgh 1961–6; Asst Dir, U.of Liverpool Botl Gdn 1966–72; Asst Keeper, R.Botanic Gdn (Edinburgh) 1972–89; Dir, Stanley Smith Hortl Trust 1989–. **Achievements:** plant taxonomy; recording systems for living plants. **Membership:** BGCI (Bd of Trustees). **Publications:** *The Identification of Flowering Plant Families* (co-Author) 1965–, Revision of the genus *Rhododendron* I 1980, *The Orchid Book* 1992. Dislikes pers.pub., indiff. to news media support. **Languages:** English; German, Latin & Spanish (all read). Willing to act as consult.etc. **Address:** Stanley Smith Horticultural Trust, Cory Lodge, POB 365, Cambridge CB2 1HR, England, UK. **Tel.**(office) 44 1223 336299, (home) 44 1223 360100; **fax** 44 1223 336278.

CULLEN, Professor Peter Wray. Eutrophication, state of environment reporting, public involvement, water quality and catchment planning. Professor of Resource & Environmental Science, Centre Director. *B.*28 May 1943, Melbourne, Victoria, Australia. Australian. *M.*Vicky: 2 *d.* **Education:** U.of Melbourne, M.Agr.Sci. 1968, Dip.Ed.1968. **Experience:** res., consult., and teaching. **Career:** Asst.Lect. U.of Melbourne 1969–71; Res.Officer, Port Phillip Auth. 1971–73; Lect.in Resource Mgmt 1973–88, Prof.of Resource & Envl Sci.and Dir Cooperative Res.Centre for Freshwater Ecol. 1988–, U.of Canberra (formerly Canberra Coll.of Advanced Education). **Memberships:** IUCN CNPPA, F.AATSE, AWRA, ANZAAS, ASL, AWWA, ESA, Higher Educ.Res.Dev.Soc.of Australasia, Hydrological Soc.(ACT), IAWPRC (now IAWQ), SIL, SWCAA. **Awards:** Jolly Award (ASL) 1988, U.Award for Innovative Teaching (U.of Canberra) 1993, others. **Publications:** 80+ scientific papers incl.Experiences with reducing point sources of phosphorus to lakes (co-Author) 1988, Bio-monitoring and envl mgmt 1990, The turbulent boundary between water sci.and water mgmt 1990. Positive re.pers. pub.& news media support. **Language:** English. Willing to act as consult.etc. **Address:** Co-operative Research Centre for Freshwater Ecology, University of Canberra, POB 1, Belconnen, Australian Capital Territory 2615, Australia. **Tel.**61 6 201 5168; **fax** 61 6 201 5038.

DA **FONSECA, Dr Ivan Claret Marques,** *see* **FONSECA, Dr Ivan Claret Marques** DA.

DA **SILVA, Ricardo** FREIRE, *see* **SILVA, Ricardo** FREIRE DA.

DAHL, Dr Arthur Lyon. Environmental assessment & monitoring environmental management & conservation of islands, coral-reef ecology, biodiversity, marine Algae. Deputy Coordinator. *B.*13 August 1942, Palo Alto, CA, USA. American. *M.*Martine: *s., d.* **Education:** Stanford U. AB (deptl hons, Biol.Scis) 1964, UCSB PhD (Biol.) 1969. **Experience:** res.— coral-reef ecol., marine Algae, island envts; admin.— planning, orgn & eval.of intl multidisc.progs; adv./consult.to govts & intl orgns in ecol., cons.& envl mgmt; prepared envl educ.and training materials for developing countries. **Career:** Assoc.Curator, Nat.Mus.of Natural Hist., Smithsonian Instn 1970–74; Regnl Ecol. Adv., S.Pacific Comm. 1974–82; consult.to govts & intl orgns (SPREP, UNEP, IUCN, UNESCO) 1982–9; Dep.Dir, Oceans & Coastal Areas Prog. UNEP 1989–91; Dep.Coord. Earthwatch, UNEP 1992–. **Achievements:** basic res. on coral-reef ecol.and monitoring; org.of S.Pacific Regnl Envt Prog.and other Regnl Seas Progs; contributed to UNCED Agenda 21, org.of UN system-wide Earthwatch. **Memberships:** BPS, IPS, ISRS, Pacific Sci. Assn, PSA, SID, IUCN Comms on Ecol.& NPPA. **Awards:** NDEA Title IV F'ship, Public Health Service Predoctl Res.F'ship (UCSB), Smithsonian Instn Postdoctl F'ship. **Publications:** *Regnl Ecosystems Survey of the S.Pacific Area* 1980, *Review of the Prot.Areas System in Oceania* 1986, *Unless and Until, A Baha'i Focus on the Envt* 1990, *Island Directory* 1991; c.60 papers and reports. Indiff. to pers.pub., favours news media support. **Language:** English, French. Willing to judge proposals or ref.papers. **Address:** UNEP Earthwatch, CP 356, CH 1219 Châtelaine, Geneva, Switzerland. **Tel.**(office) 41 22 979 9207, (home) 41 22 797 0211; **fax** 41 22 797 3471.

DAHL, Mrs (Rut) Birgitta. Environment & development, international affairs, social policy. Member of Parliament & Speaker. *B.*20 Sept. 1937, Råda, Sweden. Swedish. *M.*Enn Kokk: *s.,* 2 *d.* **Education:** U.of Uppsala BA(Scandinavian Languages, Hist., Pol.Sci.) 1960. **Experience:** res.in hist.& pol.sci., African & S.African affairs. **Career:** Teacher, Dag Hammarskjold Fndn 1960–64; Sr Admin.Officer, SIDA 1965–69; Minister of Energy 1982–6, of Envt & Energy 1986–90, and of Envt 1990–91, MP 1969–, Speaker 1994–, Swedish Parliament. **Achie-**

vement: orgn of new Min.of Envt which commenced 1 Jan.1987, intro.of new orgn & strat.for envt policy, concerned actively with UNEP, prep.for UNCED 1992, Baltic & Arctic Coopn, EFTA coopn, intro.of first plan to phase-out use of CFCs totally before 1995. **Publications:** *Guinea-Bissau — Rapport om ett Land och en Betnelserörelse* 1971; num.articles. Favours pers.pub.& news media support. **Languages:** English; French & German (good); Swedish. Willing to act as consult.etc. **Address:** Swedish Parliament, 10012 Stockholm, Sweden. **Tel.**(office) 46 18 786 4000, (home) 46 18 21 1793; **fax** (office) 46 18 201226, (home) 46 18 240305.

DALY, Ralph Hinshelwood. Conservation & development of the environment, habitat protection, management of Nature conservation areas & wildlife for the benefit of local people, re-introduction of Arabian Oryx (*Oryx leucoryx*) to the wild in Oman, conservation in wild & captive breeding of endangered species in Oman. Adviser for Conservation of the Environment. *B.*26 Jan. 1924, Glasgow, Scotland, UK. British. *M.*Elizabeth Anne. **Education:** Sherborne Sch. **Experience:** gained during 20 yrs working on cons.& dev.of the envt for Govt of Oman. **Career:** Army service 1943–7, Sudan Pol. Service 1948–55, HM Overseas Civil Service (Aden & Aden Protectorates) 1955–67, Shell Group (Petroleum Dev.[Oman] Ltd) 1969–74; Adv.for Cons.of Envt, HM The Sultan's Diwan of R.Court, Sultanate of Oman 1974–. **Achievements:** design (with help of IUCN, WWF & FFPS) and implementation by Govt of Oman of prog.for estab.of system to bring cons.of envt to support of rational dev.of Oman's natural & human resources, with main events being: 1974 legis.to protect certain mammal & bird species from over-hunting; 1975 & 1977 OFFS, pubn of scientific results in *J.of Oman Studies Spec. Reports;* 1975 Oman elected State Memb. IUCN; 1975–80 pubn in Arabic & English for educ.in Oman and gen.lay & scientific interest books on wildlife in Oman based on OFFS; 1976–8 scientific survey status of endangered relict endemic sp.*Hemitragus jayakari* (Arabian Tahr) and estab.of reserve for prot.in wild and prog. captive breeding; 1977–9 scientific status survey marine turtles & legis.for prot.; 1979– re.intro.of Arabian Oryx to native habitat in Oman having become extinct in the wild in 1972; 1982 estab.of HM Sultan's Captive Breeding Centre for Omani endangered mammals; 1984 estab.of Min.of Envt (now Min.of Regnl Municipalities & Envt [MRME]) with legislative powers to conserve envt, take measures to prevent poll., and require dev. projects to have envl impact statements for approval; 1985–8 field studies for & pubn of *Plants of Dhofar* (*s.regn of Oman*) *Trad. Economic & Medicinal Uses* (co-Author); 1984–93 ecol. survey (with IUCN under contract) of Oman's entire coastal zone, developing mgmt options for preserv.of qual.resources for rec., fisheries, culture, aesthetics, wildlife, & scenery, action now with MRME; 1984 estab.Planning Cttee for Dev.& Envt to protect & maintain productivity of unique natural resources in s.regn (Dhofar), 1994 jurisdiction with Min.of Dev.; 1984–7 survey (with IUCN under contract) for system Nature cons.areas, action now with MRME; 1985–7 RGS multi-disc.scientific survey of unique Wahiba Sands desert, pubn of scientific results in *J.of Oman Studies Spec.Reports* 3, action now with var.Govt depts; 1992–3 Action Plan and draft NCS, action with MRME; 1993 legis.(by MRME) protecting all wildlife in Oman and (by R.Decree) designating area of re-intro.as Arabian Oryx Sanctuary prior to acceptance as World Natural Heritage Zone. **Memberships:** RSAA, F.RGS, FFPS (VP), IUCN SSC. **Awards:** OBE 1965, Order of Oman (Civil) 2nd Class 1980, Officer of Order of Golden Ark 1985, FFPS Roll of Honour 1986, Hon.Degree (U.of Durham) 1986, Busk Medal (RGS) 1989. Indiff.to pers.pub., favours news media support concerning projects for cons.in Oman. **Languages:** Arabic, English. **Address:** POB 246, Muscat 113, Sultanate of Oman. **Tel.**(office) 968 736207, (home) 968 601454; **fax** 968 740550.

DAMERDJI, (Mohamed) Amine. Soil physics & improvement, combatting desertification; afforestation & soil preservation against erosion; water problems essentially in arid & semiarid countries; traditional irrigation in oases and their rehabilitation, water harvesting & supply; leguminous, rhizobium, & mycorrhization, systems approaches for agricultural development in the Sahara. Chargé de Cours (Lecturer). *B.*15 Oct. 1934, Tlemcen, Algeria. Algerian. *M.*Leïla: 2 *d.* **Education:** Lomonossov U.of Moscow, MBS(Soil Sci.) 1965; courses on isotopes, Nuclear Centre (Teheran) 1969 & microbiol., Pasteur Inst.(Paris) 1970. **Experience:** res.— soil microbiol.at Centre de Pédologie Biologique, CNRS (Nancy), and solar energy & water desalinization at Centre d'Etudes Nucléaires de Grenoble; Consult.Engr to NCIS re.prod.of Maize, starch & antibiotics 1975–7; has headed a soil analysis lab.and delivered many courses; militant for many yrs re.a better conscience about envl problems. **Career:** Engr, Service des Etudes Scientifiques (Algiers) 1965–6, Chargé de Cours, Institut Nat.Agronomique 1966–. **Achievement:** planned Integrated Solar Village 'Bou Saada' (Algeria) 1980–83. **Memberships:** ISSS, IWRA, IRCSA, Founding Memb.of num. ecol. assns such as Les Amis du Tassili and Société Algérienne pour l'Energie Solaire. **Publications:** num.articles & communications. Indiff. to pers.pub.& news media support. **Languages:** Arabic, English (scientific), French, Russian. Willing to act as consult.etc. **Address:** 21 rue Nr 5, Parc Paradou Hydra, Algiers 16035, Algeria. **Tel.**213 2 602957; **fax** 213 2 747655.

DAMMANN, Erik. Conflict between free trade and competition for economic growth on one side and the need for a just distribution of the world's resources on the other. Author, Permanent Government Scholar. *B.*9 May 1931, Oslo, Norway. Norwegian. *M.*Ragnhild: 4 *s.*, 3 *d.* (two adopted), all active in envl connections. **Education:** Norwegian Art & Handicraft Sch. 1955, Norwegian Inst.for Marketing 1961. **Experience:** envl consult.& writing. **Career:** author of books on other cultures, global justice & solidarity, pol.& ideology, lifestyles & views of life, popular sci.& free will, envt/ecol., children's books; former account exec.in marketing & advertising; Founder 1974 & Leader –1978 'The Future in Our Hands' (now intl); Init.1982 res.prog.'Alternative Future' which has since been financed by Norwegian govt. **Achievements:** founding 'The Future in Our Hands' movement — 25,000 members in Norway, sister orgns in 12 countries and dev.aid orgn with projects in 20 countries. **Awards:** perm. State stipend 1988–, The Rt Livelihood Hon. Citation 1992. **Publications:** 14 in six languages incl.*The Future in Our Hands* 1972 (English edn 1979), *Revolution in the Affluent Soc.*1979 (English edn 1984), *Money or Life* 1989. Indiff.to pers.pub., favours news media support for books & initiatives. **Languages:** English (good), Norwegian. May be willing to act as consult. **Address:** Loftuveien 48, 1450 Nesoddtangen, Norway. **Tel.**(office) 47 22 201045.

DANIELS, Professor Dr Frederikus J.A. Vegetation ecology of Greenland, lichens, species diversity. Professor of Geobotany. *B.*3 April 1943, Arnhem, The Netherlands. Dutch. **Education:** U. of Utrecht, PhD 1980. **Experience:** phytosociol.in Greenland, arctic veg.class., lichen ecol., European heathlands & dry grasslands. **Career:** Asst & Docent, Dept of Bot. U.of Utrecht 1960–87; Prof.in Geobot. Westfalische Wilhelms U. 1987–. **Achievements:** veg.survey in s.Greenland, succession studies in terricolous lichens. **Memberships:** IAVS, BLS. **Publications:** *c.*50 incl.Veg.of the Angmagssalik Distr. SE Greenland 1982. **Languages:** Danish, Dutch, English, French, German. Willing to act as consult.etc. **Address:** Institut für Ökologie der Pflanzen, Hindenburgplatz 55, 48143 Münster, Germany. **Tel.**49 251 833830; **fax** 49 251 838371.

DANIELS, Dr R.J.Ranjit. Conservation biology — birds, amphibians, biodiversity. Principal Scientific Officer. *B.*5 June 1959, Nagercoil, S.India. Indian. *M.*Vinetha: *d.* **Education:** Tamil Nadu Agricl U. BSc(Agric.) 1980, MSc(Agric.) 1983; IISc PhD 1990. **Experience:** started res. career in 1983 on bird cons.in Western Ghats. **Career:** Post-doct.F. Smithsonian Trop. Res.Inst. 1989 and IISc 1990–92, Res.Sci.Madras Crocodile Bank 1992–3, PSO M.S.Swaminathan Res.Fndn 1993–. **Achievements:** cons.of birds, amphibians, & biodiv.; invited to give plenary lect.on cons.of birds at 21st Ornithl Cong.1994. **Memberships:** IUCN SSC Amphibian & Reptile SGs, Captive Breeding SG, IOS (Regnl Sec.). **Publications:** *Of Feathers & Colours — Birds of Urban*

S.India 1992, *Field Guide to Birds of Sw India* (in press); 12 papers. Favours pers. pub.& news media support. **Languages:** English, Kannada, Tamil. Willing to act as consult.etc. **Address:** M.S. Swaminathan Research Foundation, 3rd Cross Street, Taramani Institutional Area, Madras 600 113, Tamil Nadu, India. **Fax** 91 44 235 1319.

DANKELMAN, Irene. Environment–development, gender–environment–development. Environment & Development Adviser. *B*.9 July 1953, Haarlem, The Netherlands. Dutch. **Education:** U.of Nymegen & Agricl U.Wageningen, MSc Biol.1978. **Experience:** Coord. nat.envt & dev.NGOs (Netherlands IUCN Comm./WCS Steering Group/Both Ends [envt & dev.service for NGOs]); Researcher/Lect. U.of Wageningen & Free U.of Amsterdam; consult.UNIFEM & Min.Foreign Affairs, The Netherlands; Sr Adv. NOVIB 1992–. **Career:** started in 1978 as jr consult.on envt & dev., since 1979 in coord. function; Lect./Researcher 1986 & 1989–92; Consult./Spec.Adv.to UNIFEM 1991–92; Sr Adv.to co-financing agency NOVIB 1992–, several consults. **Achievements:** lobbying and organizing activities which resulted in more and better envl integration in dev.policies (*e.g.* Dutch policies, NGOs); linking gender and envt & dev. issues. **Memberships:** IUCN CESP, WEDO, SID. **Award:** Van Nieuwenhoven Prize for Biol. 1978. **Publications:** *Women & Envt in the Third World: Alliance for the Future* (co-Author) 1988, *Women & Children First* 1991; others. Indiff.to pers.pub.& news media support. **Languages:** Dutch (mother tongue), English, French (mainly written), German (read & spoken). Willing to act as consult.etc. **Address:** Jonckherenhof 58, 6581 GD Malden, The Netherlands. **Tel.**(office) 31 70 3421 781, (home) 31 80 585580; **fax** (office) 31 70 3614 461, (home) 31 80 585580.

DARBY, Dr Peter. Hybridization & genetics of Hops (*Humulus lupulus*) with attention to resistance to pests & diseases. Head of Hop Research Unit. *B*.4 March 1956, Plymouth, Devon, England, UK. British. *M*.Margaret: 2 *d*. **Education:** U.of E.Anglia BSc(1st Class Hons) 1977, U.of E.Anglia/John Innes Inst. PhD 1982. **Experience:** u.teaching, hortl res. **Career:** Postdoctl Dem.in Plant Biol.& Genetics, U.of Keele 1980–81; Res.Sci. Hop Res.Dept 1981–4, Project Leader, Hop Breeding 1984–93, Head of Hop Res.Unit HRI 1993–, Wye Coll. **Achievements:** discovery of strong, heritable resistance to aphids in hop breeding material, dev.of dwarf hop plants to facilitate reduction in pesticide usage. **Membership:** Scientific Comm.of Intl Hop Growers' Cong. **Award:** Chevalier of the Order of the Hop 1991. **Publications:** *c*.40 on hop res.in scientific, tech.& trade journals. Dislikes pers.pub., indiff.to news media support. **Language:** English. Willing to act as consult. etc. **Address:** Hop Research Unit, Horticulture Research International, Wye College, Ashford, Kent TN25 5AH, England, UK. **Tel.**44 1233 812179; **fax** 44 1233 813126.

DAS, Dr Indraneil. Herpetology, biodiversity assessment, and conservation. Postdoctoral Fellow. *B*.18 Dec.1964, Calcutta, India. Indian. **Education:** U.of Calcutta BSc 1985, U.of Bhopal MSc 1988, U.of Oxf. DPhil 1992. **Experience:** field & museum res.in Asia & Europe. **Career:** SO, Madras Crocodile Bank 1988–91, 1993–; Postdoctl F. U.Brunei Darussalam 1991–3. **Achievements:** envl educ.in India, helping create (as Founding co-Chairman) the IUCN/SSC Indian Subcontinent Reptile & Amphibian SG. **Memberships:** BNHS, IUCN. **Publications:** *Indian Turtles: A Field Guide* 1985, *Colour Guide to the Turtles & Tortoises of the Indian Subcontinent* 1991; res.& review papers. Indiff.to pers.pub.& news media support. **Languages:** Bengali, English, Hindi. Willing to act as consult.etc. **Address:** Centre for Herpetology, Madras Crocodile Bank Trust, POB 4, Mamallapuram, Tamil Nadu 603 104, India. **Tel.**(home) 91 33 440 6972; **fax** 91 44 491 0910.

DASMANN, Professor Dr Raymond 'Ray' Fredric. Conservation biology and ecodevelopment. Emeritus Professor of Ecology. *B*.27 May 1919, San Francisco, CA, USA. American. *M*.Elizabeth: 3 *d*. **Education:** UCB BA 1948, MA 1951, PhD 1954 all in Zool. **Experience:** res., teaching, & admin., in the areas of cons. biol.and ecodev.since 1948 in many parts of the world. **Career:** res.in Californian & African wildlife; Prof.of Wildlife Biol.& Ecol.1953–58, 1962–66, and at UCSC 1977–; Dir Intl Progs, Cons.Fndn 1966–70; Sr Ecol. Acting DG, IUCN 1970–77; Consult.to UNESCO on developing MAB prog.and to UN ECOSOC on planning UNCHE 1972. **Achievements:** 13 books & several hundred papers & articles. **Memberships:** Wildlife Soc.(Pres. 1970); Hon. SCB & IUCN Comms; Sigma Xi, ASM, ESA. **Awards:** Memb.of Hon.(IUCN), Officer of Order of the Golden Ark, Leopold Medal (Wildlife Soc.), Browning Medal (Smithsonian Instn), F.AAAS. **Publications:** *Envl Cons.*(five edns) 1959–84, *Wildlife Biol.*(two edns) 1964–81, *Ecol.Principles for Econ.Dev.*(co-Author) 1973, *African Game Ranching* 1964, *Planet in Peril?* 1972, *A Diff.Kind of Country* 1968, *The Last Horizon* 1963, *The Destruction of California* 1965, *The Cons.Alternative* 1975. Indiff.to pers.pub.& news media support. **Languages:** English, French (limited written & spoken), Spanish (more limited). Further details may be obtained from *Who's Who in Amer., Amer.Men of Sci., Contemporary Authors.* Willing to act as consult.etc. **Address:** 116 Meadow Road, Santa Cruz, California 95060, USA. **Tel.**(office & home) 1 408 426 5261.

DAVE, Professor Dr Jaydev M. Environmental pollution: control & management. Professor Emeritus of Environmental Management. *B*.29 Nov. 1927, Gwalior, MP, India. Indian. *M*.Arun J.: 2 *s*. **Education:** Gujarati U. BE(Civil) 1968; U. of Minneapolis MS(San.Eng.) 1955, MPH 1957; U.of NC, PhD 1968. **Experience:** 37 yrs in professional res. admin. & postgrad.teaching in

India & USA, consult.to WHO, UNIDO, UNDP, World Bank. **Career:** Field Engr, Patel & Motichand 1953–4, Chief Design Engr, Hitchcock & Estabrook 1955–6, Design Engr, Tolt King Duvall & Assoc.1956–8, San.Engr 1958–9; Dep. Dir, C.Public Health Engg Res.Inst.1961–71; Adv. Public Health & Envl Engg, Govt of India 1971–3; Dir, NEERI 1976–7; Dean & Prof.of Envl Mgmt & Monitoring, Sch.of Envl Scis 1977–88, Emer.1989–, JNU. **Achievements:** helped develop envt policies & laws, estab.envt sci.sch.& res.progs, NEERI — all in India; Project Officer & Coord. NEERI 1962–8, Sec. Nat.Cttee on Air Poll. Control 1968–73, Chair Nat.Task Forces on Integrated Steel Plants 1986–93 and on Lead Industries 1993–, all Govt of India; Chair Taj Mahal Envt Prot.Cttee 1981–2, assisted Govts of Brazil, India, Indonesia, Bangladesh, & Syria, on drafting & enacting laws, rules & regs on Chairman Rules & Regs Cttee, Govt of India for Air Act 1981, 1984–6. **Memberships:** F.IE India (Life, Counc.1970–76), F.IAAPC (Life, Pres.1983–7), IPHA, IWAPCA (Pres.1983–5, 1985–7), F.IWWA (Life), founder memb.IACT, C.Poll.Control Bd.1981–6, Expert Panel WHO 1968–, Rules & Regs Cttee on Hazardous Industries Liability Act 1991–2 (Govt of India). **Publications:** *Energy Policy & Air Poll.*1985, *Mining Envt Mgmt* 1987; c.70 papers; Edl Adv. Bd *Excerpta Medica*, Edl Bds of *Envl Health* (1965–78) & *Indian J.of Air Poll.Control.* Favours pers.pub. **Language:** English. **Address:** 1347/B-I Vasant Kunj, New Delhi 110 070, Delhi, India. **Tel.**(office & home) 91 11 689 3952.

DAVIDAR, Ephraim Reginald 'Reggie' Chandrasekaran. Wildlife conservation and biology. Member Emeritus. *B.*1922, Trichy, TN, India. Indian. *M.*Margaret: 2 *s.*Mark, Peter (both wildlife biol.), *d.*Priya (forest ecol.). **Education:** U.of Madras BA 1942, LLB 1946. **Experience:** admin.— for several yrs associated with Nilgiri Wildlife & Envt Assn. **Career:** naturalist and wildlife photographer, writer of articles, and of books for children, on natural hist.subjects. **Achievements:** conducted status & distribn survey of the Nilgiri Tahr (*Hemitragus hylocrius*) over its entire range, and elephant migration pats' study in Nilgiri & Anamallai Hills. **Memberships:** IUCN SSC Asian Elephant (1971–90), Wild Cattle (1985–8) & Hyaena (1987–) SGs. **Award:** Kerala Agricl U.for elephant studies. **Publications:** incl.Distribn & status of the Nilgiri Tahr 1975. Indiff.to news media support. **Languages:** English, Tamil. **Address:** David Nagar, Padappai, Madras 601301, Tamil Nadu, India.

DAVIDSON, Professor Dr Donald Allen. Pedology, impact of ancient agriculture on soils; soil assessment for crops, geoarchaeology. Professor of Environmental Science & Head of Department. *B.*27 April 1945, Lumphanan, Aberdeenshire, Scotland, UK. British. *M.*Caroline E.: *s.*, 2 *d.* **Education:** U.of Aberdeen BSc 1967, U.of Sheffield PhD 1972. **Experience:** res.on land

resource assessment in UK & Greece; application of soil analysis to archaeol., currently image analysis & micromorphology; memb.of sci.based archaeol. cttee of SERC. **Career:** Lect. U.of Sheffield, St David's U.Coll. & U.of Strathclyde 1971–86, Prof.of Envl Sci.and Head Dept of Envl Sci. U.of Stirling 1993–. **Endeavour:** current main concern is to persuade agencies/ govt depts that there is a soil erosion problem in Scotland. **Memberships:** Brit.SSS, SAS. **Award:** John MacFarlane Prize (Aberdeen U.). **Publications:** Author or Ed.of ten books incl. *The Eval.of Land Resources* 1992; wide range of papers in scientific journals. Favours pers.pub. & news media support. **Languages:** English, French (basic). Willing to act as consult.etc. **Address:** Department of Environmental Science, University of Stirling, Stirling FK9 4LA, Scotland, UK. **Tel.**(office) 44 1786 467840, (home) 44 1786 823599; **fax** 44 1786 467843.

DAVIE, Dr James David Spencer. Conservation science, planning and management in tropical coastal environments especially concerning issues of human use, development, application of law, environmental decision-making, ethics. Senior Lecturer in Natural Systems Management. *B.*6 April 1950, Mackay, Qld, Australia. Australian. *M.*Fiona Jane (Sr Cons.Officer): *d.*, *s.* **Education:** Brisbane Grammar Sch., U.of Qld BSc(Hons)(Bot.& Zool.)(First Class) 1975, PhD(Bot.)(Coastal Ecol.) 1981. **Experience:** ecological & applied envl res.into coastal wetland & coral reef ecosystems in Australia & Indonesia; cons. planning & mgmt for Australian and Qld govt agencies in tidal wetlands, coral reefs, and trop.semi-arid envts, requiring multiple-use approaches; extensive exp.leading govt & u.res. teams involved in cons.sci. **Career:** post-doctl appointments at Dalhousie U.& ANU, Visitor to James Cook U.& Oxford U., teaching at all Brisbane univs, Sr Sci. Qld NPWS, short- & long-term adv.to Envl Studies Centres (Indonesia) and Indonesian Govt, Team Leader of World Bank/Indonesian Govt project on mangrove cons., Res.Assoc.at Communication Centre QUT, Australian Housing & Urban Studies Inst., & Centre for Cons.Biol. **Achievements:** convened & co-authored books on mangrove mgmt, contrib.to dev.& implementation of prot.area designation & mgmt in coastal Qld esp.the GBR Marine Park and in Indonesia. **Memberships:** AIB, RSQ, IUCN Comm.on Ecol.(Chairman, Mangrove WG 1987–94). **Awards:** Commonwealth Undergrad.Scholarship 1972–5, Australian Postgrad.Res.Scholar 1978–81, Foreign & Commonwealth F.1990. **Publications:** c.50 j.articles, edited conf.& workshop reports incl.*Global Status of Mangrove Ecosystems* 1983, *Coasts and Tidal Wetlands of the Australian Monsoon Regn* 1985, *Mangrove Ecosystems in Australia* 1987, *Planning for Nature Cons.in Rural Envts* 1994. Indiff. to pers.pub.but favours news media support. **Languages:** English, Indonesian. Willing to act as consult.etc. **Address:** Department of Management Studies, University of Queensland, Gatton College, Lawes, Queensland 4343, Australia. **Tel.**(office) 61 74 601027, (home) 61 74 622904; **fax** 61 74 601324.

DAVIS, Professor Dr Bruce W. Natural resources policy, environmental management. Deputy Director. *B.*30 Jan.1931, Hobart, Tasmania, Australia. *M.*Rosalie Jean. **Education:** U.of Tasmania, Dip.Str.Eng.1954, BEc(Hons) 1969, PhD 1982; U.of Tech. Dip.P.Admin.1965. **Experience:** intl & nat.consult.with sr exec.exp. in govt at State & Commonwealth levels. **Career:** Civil Engr & Project Mgr 1956–65; Intl Consult.1966–9; Academic, U.of Tasmania 1970–87 and Murdoch U.1987–9; Dep.Dir, Antarctic Cooperative Res.Centre, U.of Tasmania 1990–. **Achievement:** Chairman of Australian Heritage Comm.and Rural Industries R&D Corpn. **Memberships:** RAIPA, ACSANZ, APSA. **Award:** Order of Australia 1991. **Publications:** *c.*65 incl.The regulation of Antarctic tourism: a study of régime effectiveness (co-Author) 1993, *Asia In Antarctica* (co-Ed.) 1994. Dislikes pers. pub., accepts news media support. **Language:** English. Willing to act as consult.etc. **Address:** Antarctic Cooperative Research Centre, University of Tasmania, Hobart, Tasmania, Australia. **Tel.**61 02 202972; **fax** 61 02 202973.

DAWSON SHEPHERD, Dr Alexander Robert, *see* **SHEPHERD, Dr Alexander Robert DAWSON.**

DAYSH, Mrs Zena. Global interest in developing due understanding of human ecology. Executive Vice-Chairman. British, New Zealander. **Experience:** 30+ yrs involved in res.and applied res.& dev.of CHEC in 22 countries. **Career:** physiotherapist by training, Founder Memb.& Chief Admin. CHEC 1953–93. **Achievements:** has played a leading role in asserting estab.of foremost intl human ecol.NGO orgns. **Memberships:** F.RSA, F.RCS, BAPT (Assoc.) 1958, RSH 1963. **Awards:** Most Disting.F'ship (Delhi Sch.of Non-Violence) 1992, Scholarly Achievement Award (IOP) 1992. **Publications:** *Human Ecol.— An Indian Perspective* (co-Ed.) 1985, *Human Ecol., Envl Educ.& Sust.Dev.*(co-Ed.) 1991, *Human Ecol., Envl Mgmt & Educ., Regnl Sems — Carib.& Asian* (two companion vols, co-Ed.) 1991; *CHEC J.* (occasional). Favours pers.pub.& news media support if not overdone. **Languages:** English, French (limited). Willing to act as consult.etc. **Address:** 57 Stanhope Gardens, London SW7 5RF, England, UK. **Tel.** (office) 44 171 373 6761; **fax** 44 171 244 7470.

DE **CAMINO, Dr Ronnie,** *see* **CAMINO, Dr Ronnie** DE.

DE **CARVALHO, Professor Dr G.SOARES,** *see* **CARVALHO, Professor Dr G. SOARES** DE.

DE **GROOT, Professor Dr Wouter T.,** *see* **GROOT, Professor Dr Wouter T.** DE.

DE **GUSMAÕ CÃMARA, Admiral Ibsen,** *see* **CÃMARA, Admiral Ibsen** DE **GUSMAÕ.**

DE **KLEMM, Cyrille,** *see* **KLEMM, Cyrille** DE.

DE LA **CERDA, Professor Dr Alberto Mariano VASQUEZ,** *see* **CERDA, Professor Dr Alberto Mariano VASQUEZ** DE LA.

DE **LACY, Professor Dr Terry Peter,** *see* **LACY, Professor Dr Terry Peter** DE.

DE **REDAUD, Dr Maria G. BELANDRIA,** *see* **REDAUD, Dr Maria G. BELANDRIA** DE.

DE **SILVA, Allenisheo Lalanath Mark,** *see* **SILVA, Allenisheo Lalanath Mark** DE.

DE **SOUZA MARTINS, Eduardo,** *see* **MARTINS, Eduardo** DE **SOUZA.**

DE **THOMAS, Mrs Anamaria A.,** *see* **THOMAS, Mrs Anamaria A.** DE.

DE **VANTIER, Dr Lyndon Mark,** *see* **VANTIER, Dr Lyndon Mark** DE.

DE **YOUNG, Dr Raymond,** *see* **YOUNG, Dr Raymond** DE.

DE **ZSÖGÖN, Dr Silvia JAQUENOD,** *see* **ZSÖGÖN, Dr Silvia JAQUENOD** DE.

DEAN (aka **ABU-IZZEDDIN**), **Faisal.** Wildlife conservation, protected areas' management, and sustainable development, in the Middle East. Independent Environmental Consultant & Researcher. *B.*18 Jan.1942, Abadiye, Lebanon. American, Lebanese. *M.*Majd Muakassa: *d., s.* **Education:** Amer.U.of Beirut, BS(Agric.) 1964, MS(Livestock) 1969; U.of Michigan, Dipl.in Prot. Area Mgmt 1979. **Experience:** 25 yrs' proposing, implementing, and evaluating, projects in wildlife cons., prot.area mgmt, and sust.agric.; adv.to Govts of Bahrain, Oman, Jordan, Saudi Arabia, Egypt, UAE, Qatar, Syria, and Lebanon; consult. to intl agencies & funds incl.FAO, UNDP, GEF, UNEP, UNICEF, ESCWA, & IUCN; researcher with Smithsonian Instn's Cons.& Res.Center. **Career:** Asst Farm Mgr, Housh Sneid Farm (Lebanon) 1968–9; Farm Mgr, Arabian Horse Assn 1969–70; Sr Staff Memb. Office of Animal Prod. Min.of Agric.1970–73; Consult.in Agric.& Rural Dev. 1973–6; Regnl Adv.for Cons.of Nature in Middle E. UNEP 1976–8; Team Leader, Al-Areen Wildlife Park Project (Bahrain) 1978–83; Ind.Consult.& Researcher, Smithsonian Instn 1983–. **Achievements:** advocate of Nature cons. in Middle E.1970– alerting Arab officials to urgent need to protect endangered wild flora & fauna in regn, estab.of Al-Areen Wildlife Park (first educ.-oriented wildlife cons.park in Arabian Gulf), promoted the strong links between sust.agricl prod.and effective wildlife cons.in arid regns. **Memberships:** Smithsonian Instn, Audubon Soc., Bahrain Natural Hist.Soc. (Founder). **Publications:**

num.reports incl. *Mgmt of Nat.Wildlife Res.Center in Saudi Arabia* 1992, *Prot.Areas for Lebanon* 1993, *Training for Wildlife and Prot.Area Mgmt* 1994, *Wildlife Cons.for Sust.Dev.in Arab Countries* 1994. Favours pers.pub.& news media support. **Languages:** Arabic, English. Willing to act as consult.etc. **Address:** 552 Milldale Hollow Road, Front Royal, Virginia 22630, USA. **Tel.**(office & home) 1 703 837 1132; **fax** 1 703 636 8700.

DEARDEN, Professor Dr Philip. National parks, ecotourism; poverty, biodiversity, & development, in Highland South-East Asia; watershed management. Professor of Geography. *B.*9 Feb.1952, Todmorden, England, UK. British, Canadian. *M.*Jittiya (envl policy consult.). **Education:** U.of Birmingham BA(Hons) 1973, Mem. U. MSc 1975, Vic.U. PhD 1978. **Experience:** extensive res.in envt/resource mgmt/ nat.parks in n.Thailand; directed res. teams examining interaction between whales & whale-watching boats in BC, and several park-related projects. **Career:** Asst Prof.at Univs of Winnipeg 1978–9 and BC 1979–81, Asst to Prof.1981–93, Prof. 1993– Dept of Geog. U.of Victoria; Leader, Watershed Mgmt Team (U.of Vic./Chiang Mai U.) n.Thailand; Chairman (1981–6) BC Chapter, Canadian Parks & Wilderness Soc. **Achievements:** involved with many parks & wilderness issues in Canada esp.S.Moresby campaign, also with attempts to protect killer whales at Robson Bight. **Memberships:** CAG (Pres.Western Div. 1983), Regis. Professional Biol.(BC), IUCN CNPPA, Regnl Sci.Assn, AAG. **Awards:** Award for Grad. Res.(CAG) 1976, many res.grants, travel F'ships etc. **Publications:** *Landscape Evol.* 1989, *Watershed Mgmt Planning in n.Thailand* 1992, *Parks & Prot.Areas in Canada* 1993, *Wilderness Past, Present & Future* 1989, Tourism & sust. dev.in n.Thailand 1989, and other papers. Favours pers.pub.& news media support. **Languages:** English, Thai (spoken). Willing to act as consult.etc. **Address:** Department of Geography, University of Victoria, POB 3050, Victoria, British Columbia V8W 3P5, Canada. **Tel.**(office) 1 604 721 7335, (home) 1 604 477 8977; **fax** 1 604 721 6216.

DÉCAMPS, Dr Henri. Landscape ecology of river floodplains. Director of Research. *B.*18 Dec.1935, Paris, France. French. *M.*Dr Odile (bot.): 2 *s.* **Education:** U.of Toulouse, Doctorate of Sci.1968. **Experience:** res. **Career:** Researcher 1968–81, Dir of Res. Centre d'Ecologie des Systèmes Fluviaux 1981–, CNRS. **Achievement:** basic res.on stream & floodplain ecol. **Memberships:** SIL, IALE (Pres.1991–5). **Award:** Corres.Memb. (French AS). **Publications:** two books — *La Vie dans les Cours d'Eau* 1971, *Ecol.and Mgmt of Aquatic Terr. Ecotones* (co-Author) 1990; *c.*90 res. papers. **Languages:** English, French, Spanish. Willing to act as consult.etc. **Address:** Centre d'Ecologie des Systèmes Fluviaux, Centre National de la Recherche Scientifique, 29 Rue Jeanne-Marvig, 31055 Toulouse Cedex, France. **Tel.**(office) 33 62 269960, (home) 33 62 17 1118; **fax** 33 62 269999.

DEETES, Mrs Tuenjai. Hill people in Thailand. Secretary-General. *B.*8 April 1952, Bangkok, Thailand. Thai. *D.* **Education:** Chulalongkorn U. (Bangkok) BA(Pol.Sci.) 1974. **Experience:** teacher, dev.worker & admin., consult.re.Thai hill people. **Career:** teacher/dev. worker with Thai hill people 1974–76, consult. Adult Educ.Dept.1977–8, consult. Nonformal Educ.Dept developing curriculum for hill people 1979–83, continued dev.work 1984–5, Founder of Hill Area Dev.Fndn (community dev., sust.agric., envt) 1986–. **Achievements:** assisting communities in the Mae Chan–Mae Salong watersheds to coop.with each other & govt agencies in an integrated watershed mgmt prog.involving forest cons., sust.agric., & forest-fire prevention; facilitating involvement of women as well as men in prog.activities, assisting women to gain confidence & pride in their role and to participate in envl cons.activities; a successful example of people and the envt living in harmony, as an alternative to envlly-destructive modes of life. **Awards:** Ashoka F.1990–92, Khon Dee Sri Sungkhom (Good People of Soc.) 1991, Global 500 Roll of Honour (UNEP) 1992, Outstanding Alumnus (Chulalongkorn U.) 1992. **Publications:** *Mae Chan: The Changing Stream* 1981, *Tools for Working with Lisu Hill Tribes* (in Thai) 1992, *Tools for Working with Akha Hill Tribes* 1984: num. articles & papers. Favours pers.pub.& news media support. **Languages:** Akha (some), English, Lisu, Thai, Usu (spoken), Yunnanese Chinese (spoken). Willing to act as consult. **Address:** Hill Area Development Foundation, POB 11, Amphur Mae Chan, Chiangrai 57110, Thailand. **Tel.**(office) 66 53 715696, (home) 66 53 713988; **fax** 66 53 715696.

DEI MARCOVALDI, Guy Marie Fabio Guagni, *see* MARCOVALDI, Guy Marie Fabio Guagni dei.

DEI MARCOVALDI, Maria Ângela Guagni, *see* MARCOVALDI, Maria Ângela Guagni dei.

DEJMAL, Ivan. Landscape ecology, territorial systems of ecological stability. Section Chief, Ecologist, Landscape Architect. *B.*17 Oct.1946, Ústí nad Labem, Czechoslovakia. Czech. *M.* Katerina Dejmalová. **Education:** U.of Agric. (Prague), Ing.1969. **Experience:** admin., ministerial. **Career:** pol.dissident (& prisoner four yrs) 1970–89, Official of Min.of Envt 1990, Minister of Envt 1991–2, Chief of Strategic Studies Section, Czech Envl Inst. 1992–. **Achievements:** progs of revival of country (its formulation, enforcement, & realization) and territorial system of ecol.stability. **Memberships:** Corpn for Revival Country, Soc.for Sust. Living, League for Energetical Alternatives, Ecol.Soc., Green Circle, Charles U.Fac.of Phil. (Pol.Sci.Dept). **Award:** Nat.Award 1992. **Publications:** 30+. Indiff.to pers.pub.& news media support. **Languages:** Czech, French (written), Russian. Further details may be obtained from *Who's Who in Czechoslovakia* 1991–

2. Willing to act as a consult. **Address:** Kamenická 45, 170 00 Praha 7, Czech Republic. Tel.(office) 42 2 793 6635, (home) 42 2 371154; fax 42 2 793 6648.

DELGADO MENDEZ, Jesus Manuel, *see* **MENDEZ, Jesus Manuel DELGADO.**

DELOGU, Professor Dr Orlando E. Environmental land-use law. Professor of Law. *B.*4 Feb. 1937, New York, NY, USA. American. *M.*Judy: 2 *s.*, 2 *d.* **Education:** U.of Utah BS(Econ.) 1960; U.of Wisconsin MS(Econ.) 1963, JD Law 1966. **Experience:** consult.— Nat.Water Comm., Nat. Assn of Planners, State of Maine Depts of Planning, Cons.; 27 yrs' teaching, res.work with govt agencies on envl & land-use issues. **Career:** Economist, Wisconsin Dept of Resource Dev. 1962–63; Economist & Legal Researcher, Southeastern Wisconsin Regnl Planning Comm. 1964–65; Prof.of Law, U.of Maine Sch. of Law 1966–; consult.to fed., state, & local govtl agencies, land-use planning firms etc. 1966–. **Achievements:** Bd of Envl Prot. State of Maine 1968–73; author of envl legis. **Awards:** Res.F. ICEL 1973–74; Vis.Scholar, UC Galway 1981 & U.of Essex 1989; Libra Prof'ship, U.of Southern Maine 1991–2. **Publications:** *Fed.Envt Regulation* (2 vols, co-Author) 1990; *Maine Land Use and Zoning Control* 1992. Indiff.to pers.pub., will discuss issues with media. Willing to act as consult.etc. **Address:** University of Maine School of Law, 246 Deering Avenue, Portland, Maine 04102, USA. **Tel.**(office) 1 207 780 4368, (home) 1 207 773 8917; **fax** 1 207 780 4913.

DELPIANO, José Pedro CASTRO. Farming, cattle production, conservation & protection of natural resources. Farmer. *B.*14 Aug.1928, Florida, Uruguay. Uruguayan. *M.*Sonia: 3 *s.*incl. José Carlos (farmer). **Education:** Sagrada Familia Sch. **Experience:** 40 yrs' farming incl. prod. & cons.of ranch's resources, ranch admin. **Career:** Farmer, El Tapado Farm 1955–. **Achievements:** continuing endeavour to protect & conserve pampas deer during last 30 yrs and achieving a herd of 400. **Awards:** Global 500 Roll of Honour (UNEP) 1994, Nat.Envl Prize (Uruguayan Govt) 1994. Indiff.to news media support. **Languages:** Italian (spoken), Portuguese, Spanish. **Address:** El Tapado Ranch/Farm, 25 de Mayo 260 apto 1, 45000 Tucuarembó, Uruguay. **Tel.**(office & home) 598 2 632 3064; **fax** 598 2 493384 c/o Traffic Southamerica Office.

DEMPSEY, Dr Stanley. Management of environmental impacts of mining operations and of environmental conflict. Chairman & Chief Executive Officer. *B.*12 Aug.1939, La Porte, IN, USA. American. *M.*Judith R.: 4 *s.*, *d.* **Education:** U.of Colorado, BA(Geol.) 1960, JD(Law) 1964, Harvard Business Sch. Certified Prog.for Mgmt Dev.1969. **Experience:** managed siting of major mining & industrial plants, primary aluminium plants, envl compliance of molybdenum roasters, and envl conflict resolution projects; res.into

land-use planning mechanisms that will accommodate mining ops; mgmt of board-level envl oversight activities for many cos. **Career:** Gen. Counsel, VP Western Area, Chairman AMAX Australia, AMAX Inc.1960–83; Partner, Arnold & Porter 1983–7; Chairman & CEO, Denver Mining Finance Co.1987–, R.Gold Inc.1987– & Envl Strats Inc.1989–. **Achievements:** developed collabn mechanism to involve citizen envl activists in design & construction of a major ($500 m.) molybdenum mine in Colorado; cooperated with Gov.& Nat.Resource Dir of State of Colorado to adopt Colorado Joint Revue Process to envl permitting for major mining dev.insuring full citizen participation. **Memberships:** SME, ABA, CBA, Rocky Mtn Mineral Law Fndn, AUSIMM. **Award:** Disting.Alumnus (U.of Colorado Sch.of Law). Favours pers.pub.& news media support. **Language:** English. Further details may be obtained from *Who's Who in Amer.* 1992–3. Willing to act as consult.etc. **Address:** 10899 W.30th Avenue, Lakewood, Colorado 80215, USA. **Tel.**1 303 573 1660.

DER MEULEN, Frank VAN, *see* **MEULEN, Frank VAN DER.**

DER WALT, Dr Pieter T.VAN, *see* **WALT, Dr Pieter T.VAN DER.**

DESAI, Dr Bhagirath Navinkant. Marine sciences, pollution, outfalls, & resources; environmental conservation & management of marine environment; ocean policy; environmental impact assessment. Director. *B.*9 March 1934, Baroda, Gujarat, India. Indian. M.Asha. **Education:** U.of Bombay, BSc(Hons)(Zool.& Bot.) 1952; U.of Baroda, MSc(Zool.) 1954; U.of Wales, PhD(Marine Sci.) 1959; UNESCO/ SIDA course on Prot.of Marine Envt 1973. **Experience:** res.in marine sci.; admin.— R&D and personnel mgmt as Res.Officer, then Sci.-in-Charge; consult.on marine envl problems; teaching. **Career:** Dem.1952–54, Jr Lect.1954–56 Maharaja Sayajirao U.; SRF CSIR 1959–60; Res.Officer, Govt of Gujarat 1961–63 and Cellulose Products India 1963–65; Pool Officer, IIOE 1965–67; Sci.-in-Charge, Regnl Centre of NIO, Bombay 1976–81; Dir, Dept of Ocean Dev. Govt of India 1981–83; Dep.Dir 1984–86 then Dir.1986–, NIO India. **Achievements:** res.in marine ecol., marine envl studies along the Indian Coast, mgmt of nat.& intl R&D progs in marine scis, particle flux studies in Northern Indian Ocean, consult.for Envl Problems to Industries and other orgns, coastal zone mgmt, polymetallic nodules from Indian Ocean, mgmt of res.vessels, assistance for developing countries. **Memberships:** F.NAS, F.IGU, F.Gujarat Sci. Acad. **Awards:** Narottam Morarjee (Scindia) Silver Medal 1979, The Great Son of the Soil Award 1991. **Publications:** *Oceanogr.of the Indian Ocean* (Ed.) 1992, 110 papers, 40 tech. reports. Favours pers.pub.& news media support. **Languages:** English, Gujarati, Hindi; Marathi (written & spoken). Willing to act as consult.etc. **Address:** National Institute of Oceanography, Dona Paula, Goa 403 004, Goa, India. **Tel.**(office) 91 832 53352, (home) 91 832 53324; **fax** 91 832 53361.

DEY, HE Subhash Chandra. Conservation of wildlife, environment, & biodiversity. Additional Inspector-General. *B*.4 Aug.1939, Bagdogra, W. Bengal, India. Indian. *M*.Rubi: *s*. **Education:** Calcutta U. BSc(Hons) 1958, Dehradun U. Assocs of Indian Forest Coll. Hons* 1962; Oxf.For.Inst. Summer Course in Agrofor.** 1989. **Experience:** forest & wildlife mgmt incl. forest survey & inventory. **Career:** Divl Forest Officer 1964–82, Conservator of Forests 1982– 9, Chief Conservator of Forests 1989–92, Addit. Inspector-Gen.of Forests (Wildlife) 1992–, Min. of Envt & Forests, Govt of India. **Achievements:** dev.of public opinion towards cons.of living resources, combatting poaching & smuggling etc. **Memberships:** IUCN SSC Asian Rhino (Dep. Chairman) & Asian Elephant SGs. **Awards:** *Currie Scholarship (Forest Coll. Dehradun) 1962, **Schlich's Mem.Prize (Oxf.For. Inst.) 1989. **Publications:** incl.*Cons.of Rhino in N.Bengal* 1989, *Cons.of Elephant in W.Bengal* 1991 & 1993, *Reintro.of Siberian Crane in Bharatpur* 1993. Dislikes pers.pub., favours news media support. **Language:** English. Willing to act as consult.etc. **Address:** Ministry of Environment & Forests, Paryavaran Bhawan, CGO Complex, Room 126, Lodhi Road, New Delhi 110 003, Delhi, India. **Tel.**(office) 91 11 436 2785, (home) 91 11 301 1604; **fax** 91 11 436 0678.

DHINDSA, Dr Manjit S. Research & teaching in ornithology, behavioural ecology, wildlife conservation, bird management. Ornithologist. *B*.10 Sept.1953, Darawan, Punjab, India. Indian. *M*. Manpreet (MSc & MPhil.in Zool., postgrad. teacher); *s*, *d*. **Education:** Punjabi U. MSc (Zool.) 1976, PAU PhD(Zool.) 1980. **Experience:** 17 yrs' res.in ornith., behavioural ecol., & bird mgmt, in India & Canada; 12 yrs' teaching in ecol., wildlife cons., ornith., animal behaviour, & zool. **Career:** Teacher in Ecol. 1981–2, Asst. Prof.(Wildlife) 1982–85, (Ornith.) 1985–6 & 1988–, PAU; Lect.in Zool.Kurukshetra U.1982; Postdoctl F. U.of Alberta 1986–88. **Achievements:** assisted Punjab Govt on matters concerning wildlife cons.1989–, rep.of India on Intl Ornithl Cttee 1990–, compiled Punjabi names of birds of Punjab in 1992, studied avian fauna of major wetlands of Punjab, Sci.-in-Charge of Ludhiana Centre of all-India network project on agricl ornith., many pubns & j.Ed. **Memberships:** BNHS 1984–5, BOU 1987–, IES(Life), ISNE (Couns.), OSI (Exec.Cttee), Punjab State Wildlife Adv.Bd (PSWAB) 1989–. **Awards:** Gold Medal & Zoo-Taff Medal of Punjabi U.1976, Nat.Scholarship for Study Abroad 1985, election to IOC 1990 & PSWAB 1989–92 & 1992–5. **Publications:** *A Checklist of Birds of Punjab & Chandigarh* 1982, *Status of Wildlife in Punjab* (Ed.) 1984; *Indian J.Ecol.*(co-Ed.) 1983–8, *Ann.Biol.*(Ed.-in-Chief 1985–6 & co-Ed.

1987–), *Pavo–Indian J.Ornithol.*(co-Ed.1992–7); 7 book chapters, 3 reviews, & 61 res.papers. Favours news media support. **Languages:** English, Hindi, Punjabi. Further details may be obtained from *Who's Who in World Agric.*1985, *Ref.Asia* 1989, *Biog.Intl* 1990–91. Willing to act as consult.etc. **Address:** Department of Zoology, Punjab Agricultural University, Ludhiana 141 004, Punjab, India. **Tel.**91 161 401960 ext. 382; **fax** 91 161 401794.

DHUNGEL, Dr Surya P.S. Policy issues, legislation formulation, environmental management. Practising Lawyer, Associate Professor of Law, Founder President & Executive Member, General Secretary, President. *B*.4 March 1949, Sindhuli, Nepal. Nepali. *M*.Ms Kamala (Pres. of Women in Envt): 2 *d*. **Education:** U.of Poona, LLM(Constnl & Admin.Law) 1980, U.of Delhi, PhD(Constnl Law) 1990. **Experience:** legal consult.on legal drafting, constnl lawyer, envt & for.legis., res.on legal & constnl matters & envl issues; organized & participated in many nat.& intl confs/sems/training courses/workshops; Dir of Asia–Pacific NGO Envl Council; Sr Adv.to TREE Fndn (NGO); widely travelled. **Career:** Practising Lawyer, Supreme Court of Nepal, and Partner, Lawyers Inc. 1977–; Assoc. Prof.of Law, Tribhuvan U. 1977–; Founder Pres.& Exec. Memb LEADERS–Nepal (legal & envl NGO) 1987–; Gen.Sec.for Constnl & Parliamentary Exercises 1990–; Pres. Nepal Council of Envl Lawyers 1994–. **Achievements:** founded LEADERS 1987, improvement & reforms in for.- and natural resources-related legis., init. public interest litigation at Supreme Court of Nepal, pubns on envl issues. **Memberships:** ICEL, IUCN CEL, Asia Soc. (Intl Council), ASHOKA Fndn, SAARC Law Assn, Nepal Law Soc., Nepal Bar Assn. **Publications:** *Readings in the Legal System of Nepal* (Chief Ed.) 1986, *J.of Constnl and Parliamentary Exercises* (co-Ed.); num.papers. Indiff.to pers. pub., favours news media support. **Languages:** English, Hindi, Nepali. Willing to act as consult.etc. **Address:** POB 8721, New Plaza, Ramshah Path, Kathmandu, Nepal. **Tel.**(office) 977 1 410624, (home) & **fax** 977 1 415619.

DIAB, Professor Dr Roseanne Denise. Atmospheric science, particularly meteorology, ozone, & wind energy. Professor & Head of Department, Group Director. *B*.11 Nov.1949, Durban, SA. S.African. *M*.Richard M.Diab: *s*., 2 *d*. **Education:** U.of Natal, BSc(Hons) 1973, MSc 1975; U.of Virginia PhD 1983. **Experience:** ozone & wind energy res., undergrad.& postgrad.(envl sci.) teaching, EIA & urban air poll., consult. **Career:** Lect.1974–91, Head 1989–, Prof.1991–, Dept of Geogl & Envl Scis, and Dir of Atmos.Res.Group 1993–, U.of Natal. **Achievements:** being Counc.of SASAS and Memb.of CACGP, fostering interdisc.res.in atmos.sci.& networking in Africa. **Memberships:** IAIA, BWEA, SASAS, CACGP. **Publications:** *c*.50. Favours pers.pub.& news media support. **Lan-**

guages: Afrikaans, English. Willing to act as consult.etc. **Address:** Department of Geographical and Environmental Sciences, University of Natal, PB 10, Dalbridge 4014, South Africa. **Tel.**(office) 27 31 260 2300, (home) 27 31 814796; **fax** 27 31 260 1391.

DIAZ, Professor Dr José VALENCIA. Ecology of feeding & reproduction of Chilean birds, reptiles, & amphibians and their conservation; Antarctic Penguins. Professor of Zoology, Director. *B.*6 March 1935, Antofagasta, Chile. Chilean. *M.* Olga Lucia: 3 *d.*, 2 *s.*incl.Juan Pablo (for.engg & mgmt). **Education:** U.of Chile BSc 1954, UCR MA(Biol.) 1970, UCLA PhD(Biol.) 1973. **Experience:** extensive field-work in Chile, high Andes, valleys, deserts, coasts, river, and lakes; more than ten spring & summer seasons in Antarctica; expedns & faunal surveys to — Argentine north coastal & Chaco, high Andes Jujuy, Tierra del Fuego, Falkland Islands; Paraguay, Chaco & rivers; Brazil, south Sierra do Mar, Matto Grosso; Veneuela, high Andes Rancho Grande; USA, Calif., Arizona, N. Mexico deserts & mtns; Ecuador, Galápagos; perm. u.teaching, training of graduates, sci.& academic admin., participation in cttees for progs & res.grants awards; Adv.to Min.of Foreign Affairs 1975–93 on Antarctica — attended 12 Antarctic Treaty mtgs. **Career:** State Teacher in Biol.& Chem.1954–9; Instr.in Zool.1956–9 and in Biol.1963–7, Prof.of Biol. 1973– and Dir Sch.of Scis 1992–, U.of Chile; Instr.in Biol. Catholic U.of Chile 1959– 63; Teaching Assoc. Dept of Biol. UCLA 1969–72; Adv./Consult.to govt agencies & private cos. **Achievements:** memb.of Cons.Subcttee 1975–88 and of SG on Envl Affairs & Cons.1988–93, Chairman WG on Biol.1991–4, SCAR. **Memberships:** BOU, CSB, COU, ICSU, SCAR. **Awards:** F.BSSFF 1962, F.Ford Fndn 1968–72, A.Faivovich Fndn Nat.Award 1982, Disting.Vis.Prof.SUNY 1988. **Publications:** seven books incl.*Constraints for Life at High Alt.in n.Chile* (co-Author) 1983, *La fauna de vertebrados terrestres de Chile* (co-Author) 1982; *c.*60 scientific papers & monogrs. Would cooperate re.pers.pub.committed to scientific diffusion. **Languages:** English (good command), French (fair), German (fair), Spanish. Willing to act as consult.etc. **Address:** Department of Ecological Sciences, Faculty of Sciences, University of Chile, Las Palmeras 3425, Santiago, Chile. **Tel.**(office) 56 2 271 2865 ext. 212 & 312, (home) 56 2 211 1360; **fax** 56 2 271 7363; **e-mail** jvalenci@abello.seci. uchile.cl .

DIAZ-MARTIN, Diego. Conservation, environmental education, planning & management of natural protected areas; training personnel, communications, scientific research. General Project Coordinator. *B.*24 May 1961, Caracas, Venezuela. Venezuelan. *M.*Ana Maria. **Education:** Universidad C.de Venezuela, Licenciado en Biologia 1985; Instituto Universitario Politecnico de las Fuerzas Armadas Nacionales,

Magister Scientarium (Envl Admin.) 1993; specialization courses in Wildlife Cons.& Mgmt (Front R.) 1990, Mgmt of Natural Resources in Latin Amer. (Costa Rica OTS & U.of Costa Rica) 1992. **Experience:** sci.res., tech.mgmt of prot. areas, envl educ., community participation, project coordn, consult.on rec.& ecotourism activities, conceptual design of mgmt info. systems, u.teacher, radio commentator on envl matters, press media. **Career:** Consult. Inst.of Educative Rec.1978–83; Planner 1985–6, Scientific Project Coord.1986–88, NIHS; Gen.Project Coord.FUDENA 1988–. **Achievements:** action plans, training courses for journalists & other professionals, models of mgmt systems, coordn of activities at nat.& intl levels. **Memberships:** IUCN CNPPA, Asociación Venezolana para el Estudio de los Mamíferos, Red Latinoamericana de Bosques, Sociedad Venezolana de Ecología, FUDENA, Sociedad de Amigos del Árbol. **Awards:** Emer.Cross of Honour (Honorific Bd, Venezuelan Scout Assn) 1989, Recognition by Pres.of Venezuelan Rep.as one of the 100 Venezuelan Vigilant Vols of the Envt 1989. **Publications:** *Resultados del Dia Mundial de las Playas 1993* 1993, *Plan de Accion para la Supervivencia del Caiman del Orinoco* (co-Author) 1993, Cuanto vale la vida silvestre 1993. Favours pers.pub.& news media support. **Languages:** English, Spanish. Willing to act as consult.etc. **Address:** Apdo Postal 14635, Caracas 1001-A, Venezuela. **Tel.**(office) 58 2 238 1761, 1793, 1720 or 2930, (home) 58 2 266 7580, 941 7268, or 573 5850; **fax** 58 2 239 6547; **e-mail** fudena@dino.conicit.ve .

DICK, Dr Janet McPherson. Domestication of tropical trees, tree physiology. Higher Scientific Officer. *B.*5 March 1957, Peebles, Scotland, UK. British. *M.*Andrew George Coulter. **Education:** Napier U. HND 1977, Open U. BA 1985, U.of Edinburgh PhD 1989. **Experience:** res.flower induction of temperate trees, res.& consult.in vegetative propagation and clonal selections. **Career:** Asst SO 1977–82, SO 1982–9, Higher SO 1989–, being memb.of Temperate For.Group 1977–88 and of Trop. Forests Group 1988–, ITE. **Achievements:** basic res.in flower initiation and adventitious root formation of trop.& temperate trees, consults to implement res.& dev.projects in developing countries. **Publications:** 20 scientific & ten conf.papers, 15 contract reports. Indiff.to pers. pub.& news media support. **Languages:** English, French, Spanish (basic). Willing to act as consult.etc. **Address:** Institute of Terrestrial Ecology, Bush Estate, Penicuik, Midlothian EH26 0QB, Scotland, UK. **Tel.**44 131 445 4343; **fax** 44 131 445 3943.

DICKSON, Dr James Holms. Flora of Britain (especially Glasgow area), oceanic islands (Tristan da Cunha, St Helena, Canary Islands), Papua New Guinea; quaternary botany, archaeobotany. Reader in Botany. *B.*29 April 1937, Glasgow, Scotland, UK. British. *M.*Camilla Ada (archaeobot.): *s.*, *d.* **Education:** Glasgow U. BSc 1959, Clare Coll.Camb. MA 1963, PhD 1965. **Experience:** res.— decades of study of present & past flora, consult.— cons.of flora & veg.of Glasgow area, bot.of Scottish archl layers. **Career:** Asst in Res., Sr Asst in Quaternary Res. U.of Cambridge 1961–70, Leader of Trades House of Glasgow Expedn to PNG 1987, Lect., Sr Lect., Reader, in Bot. U.of Glasgow. **Achievements:** studies of flora of Tristan da Cunha & Canary Islands, flora of Glasgow area. **Memberships:** F.RSE, BES, LS, BBS, BSBI, BSS (Pres.1990–92), GNHS (Pres.1976–9, 1986–9). **Publications:** *Wild Plants of Glasgow: Cons. in the City & Countryside* 1991; *c.*110 other. Favours pers. pub.& news media support. **Languages:** English, French (poor). Willing to act as consult.etc. **Address:** Department of Botany, University of Glasgow, Glasgow G12 8QQ, Scotland, UK. **Tel.**(office) 44 141 229 8855 ext. 4364, (home) 44 141 956 4103; **fax** 44 141 330 4447.

DIDI, N.T.Hasen. Nature & fauna of Maldives especially the turtles. Retired Government Officer. *B.*13 Sept.1924, Malé, Maldives. Maldivian. **Education:** Madrasatul Majeediya (Malé), 1945. **Experience:** turtle res.in Maldives. **Career:** var. admin.positions in Mins of Health, Educ., Fisheries, & Agric.1948–92; Commissioner, Anti-Corruption Comm.1992–4 when retired. **Achievement:** work on turtle cons. **Membership:** IUCN SSC SG on Reptiles and Amphibians of the Indian Subcontinent. **Publications:** incl.*Sea Turtles of the Maldives* (in Divehi) 1993. Indiff.to pers.pub. & news media support. **Languages:** Divehi, English (fair), Urdu (fair). **Address:** Manel, Mafanu, Aburuzu Higun, Malé, Maldives. **Tel.**(home) 960 320558 or 322298.

DIEGUES, Dr Antonio Carlos S. Wetlands studies, coastal planning, maritime anthropology, wetland inventories. Director, Lecturer. *B.*14 June 1943, Santos, Brazil. Brazilian. **Education:** Ecole Pratique des Hautes Etudes en Sciences Sociales, Paris 1973; U.of São Paulo PhD(Social Scis) 1979. **Experience:** over 10 yrs' field exp. in Asia, Africa, & Latin Amer. working in UNHCR(Geneva) on rural & coastal human settlements, envl aspects of new rural settlements funded by UN; several yrs' coastal & fisheries dev.planning in FAO(Rome) and partic.in Latin Amer.; resp.for orgn & implementation of MS course on Envl Scis, U.of São Paulo. **Career:** Chief of Dept, Rural Settlement Planning, UN Geneva 1977–82; Sr Prog.Officer, Fisheries Planning, FAO 1982–4; Dir NUPAUB (Center for Research on Human Population and Wetlands in Brazil) 1987–. **Memberships:** IUCN Comms on Ecol. & NPPA, U.of São Paulo Comm.on Grad. Courses on Envl Scis. **Publications:** *Pescadores, Camponeses e Trabalhadores do Mar* 1983, *Inventory of Brazilian Wetlands* 1991, *Social Dynamics of Deforestation in Brazil, an Overview* (UNRISD) 1992, *Tradition & Change in the Coastal Communities*

*of Brazil — a Reader of Maritime Anthrop.*1992, *Trad.Communities & Prot.Areas — the Modern Myth of Untamed Wilderness in Brazil* 1993. **Languages:** English, French, Portuguese, Spanish (written & spoken); German, Italian (read). Willing to act as consult.etc. **Address:** NUPAUB, Rua do Amfiteatro 181, Colméia Favo 6, CEP 05508 Cidade Universidade, São Paulo, Brazil. **Tel.**(office) 55 11 211 0011 ext.3307, (home) 55 11 212 4057; **fax** 55 11 813 5819.

DMITRIEVA, Mrs Vera A. Conservation of Nature, environmental policy and education. Executive Director. *B.*1 Jan.1947, Minsk, Byelorussia. Russian. *M.*Dr Vladimir V.Dmitriev (microbiol.): *s.* **Education:** Inst.for Foreign Languages (Irkutsk), training as scientific transl. in fields of biol.and intl relations 1970–75 culminating in Bachelor's degree. **Experience:** scientific transl. incl.several books on biol. (Russian into English & *vice versa),* language teaching, admin. **Career:** Language Teacher, Teachers' Training Inst.(Khabarovsk) 1970–72; Scientific Transl. USSR AS (Biol.Centre of Pushchino) 1972–88; Asst in 'Sulphur' Unit, SCOPE–UNEP (Pushchino) 1982–7; V.-Dir on Intl Relations, Inst.of Soil Sci.and Photosynthesis, Russian AS 1988–93; Exec.Dir, Vernadsky Intl Centre for Biosphere Studies 1989–. **Achievements:** init.of NGO activity and educ.in Biol.Centre, Pushchino; assisting govtl agencies in Nature cons. **Awards:** Hon.Dipl.& Vernadsky Mem.Medal (USSR AS) 1989. **Publications:** incl.*Russian–English Dict.on Microbiol.*(co-Author) 1991, Background statement of global project: human-caused soil-ecol.changes and their effect on the Biosphere 1991. Favours pers. pub.& news media support. **Languages:** English, German (good), Russian. Willing to act as consult.etc. **Address:** Vernadsky International Centre for Biosphere Studies, POB 156, Pushchino 142292, Russia. **Tel.**(office) 7 095 925 9448; **fax** 7 095 923 3602; **e-mail** Dmitriev @ibpm.serpukhov.su .

DODDS, Professor Dr Donald Gilbert. Wildlife policy & management, forest–wildlife relationships, integrated resource management, mammalian reproduction & behaviour. Independent Consultant. *B.*4 Oct.1925, N.Rose, NY, USA. American. *M.*Pearl Frances: *s.*, *d.* **Education:** Coll. of For. Syracuse U. 1949–51; Coll. of Agric. Cornell U. BSc(Sci.Educ.) 1953, MSc(Wildlife Mgmt, minor soils) 1955; PhD (Wildlife Mgmt, minor soils & parasitology) 1960. **Experience:** res.— repro.& productivity of Snowshoe Hare *(Lepus americanus),* mammalian parasites, forest–wildlife relationships, moose *(Alces alces)* & deer ecol.; admin.— Asst & Acting Dir Wildlife, u. Dean, co.Pres.; consult.— UNDP &/or FAO and other var.wildlife & related resource dev.& training evaluations in Zambia, Botswana, Kenya, Ethiopia, Tanzania, & Trinidad, var.Canadian fed.& provincial agencies re.forest–wildlife, envl impacts, resource inventory, biophysical land class., for.industry re.forest–wildlife relationships; teaching mammalogy, wildlife ecol. & mgmt, human ecol., field biol. **Career:** Biol.1954, Wildlife Biol.1955–8, Newfoundland Dept of Mines & Resources; Teaching/Res. Assoc. Cornell U.1953–5 & 1958–60; Large Mammal Biol.1960–63, Asst 1963–4, Acting then Dir 1964, Nova Scotia Lands & Forests; Vis.Prof.1961–4, Assoc.Prof. 1964–70 & Prof. 1970–87 of Biol.(Wildlife), Dean of Sci.1975–9, Acadia U.(NS); Ecol./ Team Leader, FAO 1966–7; Pres. Eastern Ecol. Res.Ltd 1973–8; Ind.Consult.1987–. **Achievements:** assisting African govt agencies in developing wildlife training & dev.progs providing social & economic benefits to local people, developing & overseeing undergrad.& grad. wildlife progs at Acadia U.over 26 yrs, assisting govt & industry in adopting approaches to integrated forest/wildlife mgmt & sust.for.practices. **Memberships:** The Wildlife Soc.; many others in past years. **Awards:** Phi Kappa Phi 1955 & Sigma Xi 1960 (both Cornell U.), John Pearce Mem.(Wildlife Soc., NE Section) 1991, Professional Envl Award (NS) 1993, 125 Award (Canada) 1992. **Publications:** five books incl. *Wild Captives* 1965, *A Long Night in Codroy* 1992, *The Phil. and Practice of Wildlife Mgmt* (co-Author) 1987, 1992; 36 res.& mgmt pubns, num.reports, popular articles, & stories. Believes the media prefer emotionalism to facts relative to res. findings & envl issues. **Language:** English. Willing to act as consult.etc. **Address:** 2922 Borden Street, Coldbrook, Nova Scotia B4R 1A3, Canada. **Tel.**(home) 1 902 679 3398 or (summer only) 1 902 756 2299.

DONOSO, Professor Claudio. Forest ecology & dynamics; variation, genecology; plantations with native Chilean species. Professor of Forest Ecology. *B.*27 June 1933, Santiago de Chile, Chile. Chilean. *W:* 2 *s.*incl.Pablo (for., silviculture), *d.*Magdalena (cons.). **Education:** U.of Chile, Forest Engr 1969, UCB MSc(Forest Ecol.) 1977. **Experience:** u.admin.; teaching forest bot., forest ecol. & silviculture; work on plantations and application of silvicultural methods in native forests of Chile. **Career:** Army Officer 1954–64, Asst.Prof.of For. U.of Chile 1968–78, Prof.of Forest Ecol.1978– and Dir Inst.of Silviculture 1983–5 & 1989, U.Austral de Chile. **Endeavour:** during 25 yrs has fought for defence of native forests mainly through confs & the media. **Memberships:** Sociedads de Biología de Chile, de Ecología, de Botaníca de Chile, y de Vida Silvestre de Chile; Colegio de Ingenieros Forestales, Comité Pro de Defensa de Flora y Fauna. **Publications:** *Ecologia Forestal — El Bosque y su Medioambiente* (textbook, three edns) to 1981, *Los Tipos Forestales de Chile* 1981, *Arboles Nativos de Chile* (manual, six edns) to 1983, *Arbustos nativos de Chile* (manual, two edns) to 1985, *Bosques Templados de Chile y Argentina: Variacion, Estructura y Dinamica* (textbook) 1993. Dislikes pers.pub., favours news media support. **Languages:** English (better at written), Spanish.

Willing to act as consult.& ref. **Address:** Casilla 567, Universidad Austral de Chile, Valdivia, Chile, or Eleodoro Yáñez 1688, Valdivia, Chile. **Tel.**(office) 56 63 221228, (home) 56 63 216597; **fax** 56 63 221227.

DONOVAN, Richard Zell. Natural forest ecology & conservation, forest management, forestry certification. Visiting Lecturer, Programme Director. *B.*6 Aug.1952, Englewood, NJ, USA. American. *M.*Karen Ann: *s., d.* **Education:** Antioch New England Grad.Sch. MS(Natural Resources Mgmt) 1981. **Experience:** consults throughout Americas (N., C.& S.), SE Asia, Africa, & Europe. **Career:** Backcountry Guide & Envl Activist, Maine 1974; Peace Corps Vol.in Paraguay 1975–7; Ind. Logger, Photographer & For.Consult.in Minn., Vermont, New Hampshire, and Dominican Rep. 1978–80; Natural Resources Consult. Assocs in Rural Dev.Inc.1981–7; Sr F. Osa Peninsula (Costa Rica), WWF 1987–91; Ind.Consult. 1990–92; Vis.Lect. U.of Vermont 1992–; Dir, Smart Wood Prog. Rainforest Alliance 1992–. **Achievements:** assisted Costa Rican govt & cons.orgns to develop nat.system for working with communities surrounding nat.parks and for econ.mgmt of natural forests. **Memberships:** ISTF, Forest Stewardship Council (Chair, Principles & Criteria WG). Indiff.to pers.pub.& news media support. **Languages:** English, Guarani (Paraguay), Portuguese, Spanish. Willing to act as consult. **Address:** 2 Kettle Creek Road, Jericho, Vermont 05465, USA. **Tel.**1 802 899 1383; **fax** 1 802 899 2018.

DOODY, Dr James Patrick. Coastal conservation management in Europe. Head, Coastal Conservation Branch. *B.*2 Jan.1948, Oldham, Lancs, England, UK. British. **Education:** U.of Sussex, BSc(Hons)(Biol.) 1969; U.of Durham, PhD(Plant Pop.Ecol.) 1975. **Experience:** res., admin., involvement in wide range of statutory & non-statutory cons.activities, carried out nr of studies on cons.of flora & fauna of the Magnesian Limestone of County Durham, became familiar with wide variety of coastal habitats & sites in UK and their veg.& mgmt, currently mgr of Coastal Review Unit's (JNCC) data & info.service. **Career:** Asst Regnl Officer (NE England Coastal Ecol.), Chief Scientist Directorate, NCC 1973–91; Head, Coastal Cons. Branch, JNCC 1991–; co-Founder UK Coastal Res.& Mgmt Group (which is also UK Branch of EUCC) 1989– (Chair 1991–); Chair, Sci.Comm. EUCC 1991–. **Achievements:** 20 yrs' work on cons.of natural habitats in UK & Europe, dev.of Coastal Cons.Branch (JNCC) as an info.& adv.service in UK & Europe. **Memberships:** BES, IEEM. **Publications:** num.incl.*Sand Dune Inventory of Europe* 1991, *Natural Values, Cons.& Wise Use of the Euro.Coastal Zone* 1992, *Directory of the N.Sea Coastal Margin* 1993. Favours pers.pub.& news media support. **Languages:** English, French (some spoken). Willing to act as consult.etc. **Address:** European Union for Coastal Conservation, POB 11059, NL 2301 EB Leiden, The Netherlands. **Tel.** (office) 31 733 62626, (home) 31 480 457624.

DORMAN, H.C.'John'. Nature conservation, environmental planning, catchment management. Retired. *B.*12 Aug.1925, Concord, NSW, Australia. Australian. *M.*Rona Patricia: 3 *s.* **Education:** Sydney Tech.Coll. Dipl.of Chem. 1948, Sydney U. Dipl.of Social Studies 1850. **Experience:** active in Nature cons.1960–: Pres. Newcastle Flora & Fauna Soc.1974–75, 1980–84 and Nat.Parks Assn of NSW Inc.1972–8 (Counc.1966–); Chairman Cons.Cttee, Hunter Branch Nat.Trust 1973–88 and Myall Lakes/ Tomaree Nat.Parks Adv.Cttee 1985–92; Counc. ACF 1973–7; Chairman, Biodiv./Ecosystems Sub-cttee, L.Macquarie (NSW) Total Catchment Mgmt Cttee 1993–. **Career:** six yrs in industrial organic chem., 35 yrs as social worker (Distr. Officer) in child & community welfare until retirement in 1984. **Achievements:** to establish community awareness in cons.& envl planning; secured prot.of wetlands in L.Macquarie 1968, proposed system of Nat.Parks & Reserves for Hunter Valley (now largely in place) 1968–72, involved in setting up satellite monitoring/ ecol.res.in suburban/rural catchment of L.Macquarie. **Memberships:** IUCN CNPPA 1989–, NPA of NSW Inc., Nat.Trust, ACF. **Awards:** Hon.Life Membership of Newcastle Flora & Fauna Soc.and of the NPA of NSW Inc., Award for Envl Achievement (U.of Newcastle) 1989. **Publications:** Hunter 2000 (co-Author) 1972, Proposal for major additions to Tomaree Nat. Park 1993; num.shorter papers. Indiff.to pers. pub.& news media support. **Language:** English. May be willing to act as consult.etc. **Address:** 12 Rodgers Street, Teralba, New South Wales 2284, Australia. **Tel.**(home) 61 49 581564.

DORST, Professor Dr Jean. Systematics & ecology of birds & mammals. Professor. *B.*7 Aug. 1924, Mulhouse, Haut-Rhin, France. French. *M.* Emmanuelle. **Education:** U.of Paris, Licence 1945, Dr Sci.1949. **Experience:** res., tech., admin., consult. **Career:** Asst 1947, Maître de Confs 1949, Prof.1964, Dir Lab.of Zool.(mammals & birds), DG 1975–85, Muséum Nat.d'Histoire Naturelle; Expert for UNESCO, FAO, IUCN. **Achievements:** advancing Nature Cons. in France & Africa, having been Pres. (1964–74) of Charles Darwin Fndn for the Galápagos Islands. **Memberships:** Académie des Scis de l'Institut de France, Académie des Scis d'Outremer, Académie des Scis et Belles Lettres de Bordeaux, hon.memb.of num.scientific socs world-wide. **Awards:** Commandeur, Ordre Nat. du Mérite; Officer, Légion d'Honneur; Officer of the Order of the Golden Ark; Gold Medal (Min.of Agric. Italy), Gold Medal (Société Royale de Zoologie of Antwerpen), Golden Medal P.J. Lenné (J.W.von Goethe Stiftung). **Publications:** *Before Nature Dies* (17 translations) 1965, *C.and S.Amer.*1967, *Field Guide to the Larger Mammals of Africa* (co-Author) 1978, *La*

Force du Vivant 1979; 600+ scientific papers. Favours pers.pub.& news media support. **Languages:** English, French, German, Spanish. Willing to act as consult.etc. **Address:** 14 quai d'Orléans, 75004 Paris, France. **Tel.**(office) 33 1 40 79 3062, (home) 33 1 43 29 5222; **fax** 33 1 40 79 3063.

DOUMENGE, Professor Dr François. Coastal & marine development, island ecology, tropical aquaculture, aquariology. Emeritus Professor, Museum Director. *B.*9 Oct.1926, Viane (Tarn), France. French. *M.*Kiyoko: 4 *s.*incl.Jean-Pierre (sr researcher [French NRC], geographer [S.Pacific islands], anthroposociologist); Charles (IUCN Forest Officer, trop.bot.). **Education:** Montpellier Coll.& U. PhD (Geog.) 1966. **Experience:** admin.— high sch.& u.teaching system and coastal & marine labs' mgmt for underdeveloped countries; shrimp farming aquaculture; natural parks, reserve, & prot. areas' mgmt; zoo & aquarium mgmt; teaching — Medit.& trop. coastal & marine ecol., trop. islands' cons.& dev., Japanese fisheries & aquaculture; trop.islands and Japan socio-economics. **Career:** Lect.1957–67, Prof.(trop.geog.& oceanogr.) 1968–76, Montpellier U.; Prof. Trop.Geog. Abidjan U. 1967–68; Dir. Educ. Service and Chancellor of U., French W.Indies and Guyana 1976–79; Prof. Paris Nat. Museum of Natural Hist.(Chairman, Cons.of Live Animal Species) and Dir. Paris Zoo 1979–88; Dir. Monaco Oceanogr.Museum 1989–. **Achievements:** S.Pacific Islands Coral Reefs Scientific Surveys 1960–65; Trop.Islands Coastal & Marine Cons.& Dev.as Project Manager, S.Pacific Islands fisheries dev.agency FAO/UNDP 1971–73; Founder & Dir, Montpellier Zoo 1963–77; Curator, French Nat.zoos with special care for breeding endangered animal species 1979–88; memb. spec.Comm.for rehab. of Arcachon basin 1980–83; ICSEM 1988–; Pres.IUCN Comm.of Ecol.1991–93; Memb. WWF/IUCN team of experts for cons.of Shiraho Reef 1989–91. **Memberships:** Polynesian Soc. (NZ); Soc.des Océanistes, Club des Explorateurs, Soc.de Biogéographie (all in Paris); Eurocoast France (Hon.Pres.); IUCN Comm.on Ecol.; Gen.Sec.ICSEM. **Award:** Officer of Ordre Nat.de la Légion d'Honneur. **Publications:** eight books, 100+ scientific papers. **Languages:** English, French, Italian, Spanish. Willing to act as consult.etc. **Address:** Oceanographic Museum of Monaco, Ave Saint-Martin, MC-98000, Principality of Monaco. **Tel.** (office) 33 93 153600, (home) 33 93 304044; **fax** 33 93 505297.

DOUROJEANNI, Professor Dr Marc J. Sustainable development in American humid tropics & tropical Andes, protected areas' management; Amazon wildlife & forest management, environmental institution-building. Chief of Division. *B.*2 Jan.1941, Paris, France. French, Peruvian. *M.*Graciela: 3 *s.* **Education:** Universidad Agraria La Molina BSc(Agric.) 1963, MSc(For.) 1965; Utah SU Animal Behaviour 1965; Faculté Scis

Agronomiques de Gembloux PhD(Entomol.) (Hons) 1972. **Experience:** res., admin., consult. **Career:** Asst Prof., Assoc. Prof.& Prof., Chief Dept of Forest Mgmt, Dean Fac.of For., Planning & Budget U.Dir., Universidad Nacional Agraria 1964–88; VP Universidad San Martin 1972–3; DG Forest, Wildlife & Nat.Parks of Peru (Min.of Agric.) 1973–9; Prof.of Ecol.& Nat.Defence, Centre for High Military Studies of Lima 1975–88; Disting.Vis.Prof. U.of Toronto 1984– 5; Sr Envl Officer, World Bank 1988–90; Consult.for FAO, OAS, IBRD, etc.1978–88; Chief Envl Prot.Dev. Inter-Amer.Dev.Bank 1990–. **Achievements:** first Peruvian Prof.& researcher in forest entomology, wildlife, & prot.areas' mgmt; estab.most NPPAs of Peru; founded PFNC; developed the Vicuña Mgmt Prog.of Peru; organized envl qual.control at Inter-Amer. Dev. Bank. **Memberships:** ESP (Pres.1973), PSF (VP 1972–3), PFNC (Pres.1984–8), IUCN (VP 1986–8), IUCN CNPPA (VC 1975–88), WRI (Bd 1981–8), OEP (Bd 1982–3). **Awards:** Gt Officer Order Mérito Agrícola, Officer of the Order of the Golden Ark, Commander of Order Mérito Guardia Civil del Perú, Member Order al Mérito Forestal, Guggenheim F.1985, Peruvian Envl Prize 1987; others. **Publications:** eight books incl.*Nat.Parks of Peru* 1978, *Natural Resources & Dev.in Latin Amer.*1980, *Natural Resources & Dev.in Peru* 1986, *Wildlife Mgmt in Peru* 1986, *Amazon: What To Do?* 1990; 200+ papers (in Spanish, English, French). Dislikes pers.pub., favours news media support. **Languages:** English, French, Portuguese, Spanish. Willing to act as ref. **Address:** 6450 Divine Street, McLean, Virginia 22101, USA. **Tel.** (office) 1 202 623 1795, (home) 1 703 821 9163.

DRAKE, Christopher Michael. Developing & promoting greater awareness of humanity's impact on the environment and each individual's potential for a constructive response to its present condition; identifying more appropriate forms of interaction & relationship with the environment; stressing the ethical & moral elements of humanity's relationship with the environment, and of judicious use of natural resources. INGO Representative, Coordinator, Writer. *B.*8 Sept. 1957, Harpenden, Herts, England, UK. British. Father The Hon.Sir Maurice Drake DFC (WWF), Mother Lady Drake (benefactress, Guardian of the Rain-forest). **Education:** Stowe Sch., Exeter Coll.Oxf. MA (Jurisprudence) 1978. **Experience:** admin., consult., edl & writing. **Career:** Solicitor, Denton, Hall, Burgin & Warrens (London, HK & Singapore) 1980–87, Group Legal Adv. Industrial Innovation Mgmt SA (Switzerland) 1988–9, Consult. UNEP 1992, Rep.to UN of Brahma Kumaris World Spiritual U.(Geneva & NY) 1988–. **Achievements:** Coord.of Youth Task Force for UNEP's Global Youth Forum, New York 1992; lectures & sems in UK, USA, Canada, on envt & dev.; author of statements to UNCED; pubns. **Publications:** Ed.*Earthrights Newsletter* 1991, *Visions of a Better World* 1993, Guest Edl (jt) *EC* 1990.

Indiff.to pers.pub.& news media support. **Languages:** English, French, Spanish; Cantonese & Mandarin (basic spoken). Willing to act as consult. **Address:** 11 Carlton Court, 2B Blenheim Gardens, London NW2 4NS, England, UK. **Tel.**(office) 44 181 459 1400, (home) 44 186 738551 or 181 450 5563; **fax** 44 181 451 6480.

DRDOŠ, Dr Ján. Landscape ecology, environmental studies, environmental planning in national parks. Senior Researcher. *B.*6 Jan.1934, Vígl'aš, Slovakia. Slovak. *M.*Oldřiška. **Education:** Comenius U. MA 1958, PhD 1967, DSc 1980. **Experience:** landscape — ecol.res.and envl eval.of mountainous areas of W.Carpathian range; envl planning in High Tatra Nat.Park and in Sagarmatha Nat.Park, Himalaya; envl eval.of critical envl zones in Slovakia. **Career:** Slovak Inst.for Nature Conservancy 1958–63; Inst.of Landscape Biol.1964–8, Chairman Dept of Landscape Ecol. Inst.of Experimental Biol.& Ecol.1971–6, Chairman Dept of Envl Geog. 1978–91, Inst.of Geog.1977–, Slovak AS; Inst.of Nature Conservancy, U.of Tech.Hannover, 1969– 70. **Achievements:** coordn of res.projects in Slovakia 1965–; memb.State Council of Nature Conservancy 1980–85, Scientific Council of High Tatra Nat.Park 1978–, IUCN Nat.Cttee 1990–; VC Nat.Cttee of Geog.1993–; Ed.Bds *Geograficky časopis, Geografia y Desarrollo* (Mexico), and *J.of High Tatra Nat.Park*. **Memberships:** Chairman SGS 1978–86, 1990–93, PGS (Hon.), IUCN CESP 1983–, Sec.IGU WG on Landscape Synthesis 1980–88, IGU Comm.on Critical Envl Zones 1990–, Future Generations 1991–. **Awards:** Silver Medal Dionyz Štúr 1984, Hon. Medal Matej Bel 1984, Best Paper Prize (LITA) 1980, Main Prize for scientific–popular film on Settlements & Landscape (Intl Slovak Festival EKO–FILM) 1981, Prize for popularizing sci. (Slovak AS) 1991, Prize of the City of Bratislava 1976, 1985. **Publications:** *Landscape Synthesis* (Ed.) 1983, *Sagarmatha Nat.Park* (Ed.& co-Author) 1987, 6 other books, 100 scientific & 100 popular papers. Favours pers.pub.& news media support. **Languages:** English, French, German, Russian. Willing to act as consult.etc. **Address:** Pupavova 26, SQ-84104 Bratislava, Slovak Republic. **Tel.**(office) 42 7 492751, (home) 42 7 724136; **fax** 42 7 491340.

DRIJVER, Carel Alexander. Conservation & development in Surinam, Cameroon, West African Sahel, & Indonesia. Manager of Development Cooperation. *B.*14 July 1952, Heemskerk, The Netherlands. Dutch. **Education:** Agricl U. Ir (Ecol., Veg.Sci., Envl Sci., Socio-economy) 1979. **Experience:** scientific res.; educ. of postgrad.students as well as training practitioners in fields mentioned above mainly in W.Africa but also in Indonesia, Philippines, & Sri Lanka; eval.missions as well as project dev.& mgmt; all activities are problem-oriented and often have participatory approach; close coopn with IUCN, WWF, Ramsar Bur., & African Study Centre. **Career:** Bur.of Foreign Affairs, Agricl

U.1979; Envl Sci. Centre of Envl Sci. Leyden U.1980–83, 1985–94; Mgr, Dev.Coopn, WWF-The Netherlands 1994–. **Achievements:** educ.in theory & field methods of large nr of Dutch & African students; conceptualization, setting up & supervision of a large cons.& dev.project in Cameroon, init.& co-mgmt of Envl Sci.Centres in The Netherlands & Cameroon. **Memberships:** Bd of Community Dev.J., var.scientific WGs. **Publications:** Taming the floods — envl aspects of floodplain dev.in Africa (co-Author) 1986, People's Participation in Envl Projects 1992. Favours pers. pub.& news media support esp.for WWF. **Languages:** Dutch, English. Willing to act as consult.etc. Address: WWF-The Netherlands, Boulevard 12, 3707 BM Zeist, The Netherlands. **Tel.**31 30 69 37333; **fax** 31 30 69 12064.

DROSTE ZU HÜLSHOFF, Dr Bernd VON, *see* **HÜLSHOFF, Dr Bernd VON DROSTE ZU.**

DU TOIT, Raoul Frederick, *see* **TOIT, Raoul Frederick DU.**

DUFF, Dr Keith L. Nature conservation, geological site protection, research into Jurassic palaeontology. Science Director. *B.*16 July 1949, London, England, UK. British. *M.*Janet: 2 *d.* **Education:** U.of Wales (Cardiff), DSc(Hons) (Geol.) 1970; U.of Leicester, PhD(Geol.) 1975. **Experience:** res.on palaeoecology of Lower Oxf. Clay of C.England, leader of many geol. field study tours incl.several to w.USA, Assessor on NERC Marine Scis Cttee 1988–91, Dir of Nat.Stone Centre (Derbys.) 1985–8. **Career:** Geol.1975–8, Dep.Head of Geol.& Physiography Section 1978–84, Head of Earth Sci. Cons.1984–7, Asst Chief Sci.1987–91, NCC; Chief Sci.1991–4, Sci. Dir 1994–, NCC for England. **Achievements:** prot.& safeguard of many nationally- & intlly-important geol.sites, dev.of res.prog.focusing English Nature resources onto practical Nature cons.problems, pubns, memb.of Edl Bd *Geol. Today.* **Memberships:** Chartered Geol., F.Geol. Soc.(Council 1994–), UK Geologists' Assn (Council 1976–85, Field Mtgs Sec.1978–82, VP 1982–5), Instn of Geologists (Sec.of Ext.Relations Cttee 1987–90), Euro.WG on Earth Sci. Cons.(Founder Memb.). **Award:** Foulerton Award (Geologists' Assn) 1987. *Publications: Bivalvia of the Lower Oxf.Clay of Southern England* 1978, *New Sites for Old* (Ed.) 1985, Bivalves 1991; num.papers. Indiff.to pers.pub., favours news media support. **Language:** English. Further details may be obtained from UK *People of Today* 1995. Willing to act as consult. etc. **Address:** English Nature, Northminster House, Peterborough PE1 1UA, Cambridgeshire, England, UK. **Tel.**44 1733 318318; **fax** 44 1733 68834.

DUFFEY, Dr Eric Arthur Gerald. Invertebrate ecology especially of Araneida. Editor-in-Chief. *B.*2 Jan.1922, Leicester, England, UK. British. *M.*Rita Carol: *s., d.* **Education:** U.of Leicester (then UC) BSc(Hons) 1950; Bur.of Animal Pop. (Oxf.), PhD(Lond.) 1953. **Experience:** Nature cons.mgmt & zool.res.in Britain and abroad. **Career:** Asst to Keeper (Natural Hist.), Leicester Mus.1938–40; for.training, Charnwood Forest (Leics, UK, private for.co.) 1940–42; Commissioned Naval Pilot, WWII 1942–6; Regnl Officer (the first), NC 1953–62; Head, Grassland Ecol. Team, NCC (Monks Wood Experimental Station) 1962–74; Adv.Officer & Invertebrate Zool. ITE 1974–92; Ed.-in-Chief (taking over from Founding Ed.), *Biol.Cons.*1974–. **Achievements:** past-Pres. BAS, past-Sec.and later VP of BES, past-Pres. Intl Arachnological Cong. **Memberships:** RS, BES, BAS, Ligue Suisse pour la Prot.de la Nature, Société Européenne d'Arachnologie, Centre Intl de Documentation Arachnologique, SCB. **Awards:** Sir Jonathan North Bronze Medal (Leicester Educ.Cttee) 1948, OBE 1962, F'ship (NATO Envl Cttee) 1968, F.RS 1974, Winston Churchill F.(Winston S. Churchill Trust) 1980. **Publications:** five books incl. *The Nat.Parks and Nature Reserves of Western Europe* 1982; num.papers. Dislikes pers.pub. & news media support. **Languages:** English, French (moderate). **Address:** Cergne House, Wadenhoe, Peterborough PE8 5ST, England, UK. **Tel.**(home) & **fax** 44 1832 720293.

DUFFY, Dr David Cameron Ecology, research on seabird–fish interactions, herbaceous biodiversity & forest harvesting, and medical entomology. Assistant Professor & Programme Manager. *B.*17 April 1953, Baltimore, MD, USA. American. *M.*Maria Jose: *s., d.* **Education:** Harvard Coll. AB 1975, Princeton U. PhD 1980. **Experience:** widespread res.on marine ecosystems esp.in upwellings, res.on primary forest in Se US mtns, and Lyme borreliosis in Ne US; mgmt of biodiv.inventory in Alaska; admin.of Darwin Station and INTECOL. **Career:** Researcher & Dir (*pro tem.*), Darwin Station (Galápagos) 1980–81; Chief Scientific Officer, U.of Cape Town 1981–6; Vis.Prof. Universidad Nacional (Costa Rica) 1986–8; Exec.Dir, INTECOL 1988–9; PI, Lyme Disease Res.Project (NY) 1989–94 and Adjunct Prof. SUNY 1989–94; Asst Prof.& Prog.Mgr, Alaska Natural Heritage Prog. U.of Alaska 1994–. **Achievements:** documented that clear-cut forests in Se US mtns do not recover biodiv., studies of El Niño and seabird–fishery interactions in upwelling ecosystems, res.and public health measures to control Lyme borreliosis. **Memberships:** AAAS, AOU, PSG, CWS. **Publications:** 100+ refereed pubns incl. Ecol.lit.for libraries in developing countries 1990, Do Appalachian herbaceous understories ever recover from clearcutting? (co-Author) 1992, Landscape patterns of abundance of *Ixodes scapularis* (Acar: Ixodidae) on Shelter Is. New York (co-Author) 1994, & chapters incl.Stalking the Southern Oscillation: Envl Uncertainty, Climate Change and N.Pacific Seabirds 1993, Seabird–fishery Interactions: A Mgr's Guide (co-Author) 1994; 30 popular articles. Avoids pers. pub.but favours news media support. **Langu-**

ages: English, Latin (read), Spanish. Further details may be obtained from *Who's Who in Sci.and Engg* 1992. Willing to act as consult.etc. **Address:** Alaska Natural Heritage Programme, University of Alaska at Anchorage, 707 A Street, Anchorage, Alaska 99501, USA. **Tel.**(office) 1 907 257 2703, (home) 1 907 561 0169; **fax** 1 907 276 6847; **e-mail** AFDCD1@ACAD2.ALAS-KA.EDU .

DUFOUR, Dr Jules. Resource management, establishment & management of protected areas, environmental & peace education. Professor of Geography, Director. *B.*6 July 1941, Quebec, Canada. Canadian. *M.*Danielle: 3 *d.* **Education:** Laval U. Licence ès Lettres (Geog.) 1966, MA (Geomorph.) 1969, PhD(Regnl Studies, Costa Rica) 1979. **Experience:** worked on Nat.Atlas of Canada, Dept of Resources, Mines & Tech. Surveys, Ottawa 1965–6; Land Use Survey in Quebec 1967–69; res.in Costa Rica 1969–71. **Career:** Lect. U.of Quebec at Chicoutimi 1971–93; Lect.at both Universidades Iberoamericana 1981–2 & Autonoma del Estado de San Luis Potosi 1983; Head of Human Scis Dept 1979, Dean of Undergrad.Studies 1983–7, Dir, Master's Prog.in Regnl Studies 1991–5, all at U.of Quebec at Chicoutimi. **Achievements:** co-Dir. Sem.on Identity in the Carib., World U.Service of Canada 1974; Dir. Sem.on Geog.of Mexico 1975; VP Comm.on Geog. Panamerican Inst.of Geog.& Hist.1978–80; VP CALACS 1979–81; Pres. QAPG 1983–7; Coord. Quebec Steering Cttee for Celebration of Centennial of Canadian Nat.Parks 1984–6; Pres. QWC 1985–6; Consult. UNESCO 1989–90; Pres. Canadian Nat.Cttee for IGU 1989–93; Expert, Quebec Comm.on Toxic Wastes 1990–91; VP ACUNS 1990–92; Dir. Sem.on Geog.and Natural Resources Cons. Costa Rica 1991; Commissioner, Citizens' Inquiry into Peace & Security in Canada 1991–2, and Fed.envl assessment review of the Great Whale Hydro Project 1992; Dir. Sem.on Trop. Ecosystems in Costa Rica, U.of Quebec at Montreal 1993. **Memberships:** Bd of Admin. Quebec Fndn for Endangered Species 1985–; World Comm.on Nat. Parks 1992–; Expert on the Fed./Provincial Comm.for Envl Review of the Sainte-Marguerite-3 Hydro project 1992–; Chairman, Canadian Nat.Cttee for IGU 1989–; Nat.Cttee of Canada/MAB 1987–; Commissioner, Quebec Comm.of Toponymy 1990–; Consult. Intl Peace Bur.1992–4. **Awards:** Centennial of Canadian Nat.Parks Dist.1985; Regnl Merit for Peace 1990; Cert.of Merit for prep.of & participation in the Earth Summit, Envt Canada 1992. **Publications:** Soil and air temps in the Costa Rican tropics 1977, Natural hazards & medium-size cities in volcanic c.Amer.1978, Parks in Quebec: spaces to be created 1979, Regnl profile of n.Quebec 1983, Envt, resources, & soc., a common challenge 1985, Atlas of envl stresses in Quebec 1987–92, Towards sust.dev.of Canada's forests 1991, Perspectives on envt in N.Amer.1992, Transformation moment: a Canadian vision of common security. The report of

the citizen's inquiry into peace & security 1992. **Languages:** English, French, Portuguese, Spanish. Willing to act as consult.etc. **Address:** 121 Fillion, Chicoutimi-Nord, Quebec G7G 4L7, Canada. **Tel.**(office) 1 418 545 5371, (home) 1 418 693 1503; **fax** 1 418 545 5012.

DUGAN, Dr Patrick Joseph. Integrated management of natural ecosystems, wetland conservation & management, environmental policy. Director, Regional Affairs. *B.*7 Dec. 1955, Bathgate, Scotland, UK. British. **Education:** U.of St Andrews BSc 1975, U.of Aberdeen BSc(Hons) (Zool.) 1977, U.of Durham PhD (Biol.) 1981. **Experience:** res.& tech.— behavioural ecol.of small mammals, feeding ecol., survival & migratory strats of shorebirds, ecol.& behaviour of colonial waterbirds, survival strats of trans-Saharan migrant waterbirds, ecol.& cons.of Medit.wetlands; admin.— direction of cons.res. & mgmt progs in Medit.& W.Africa, dev.& direction of cons.progs in Africa, Latin Amer., Asia & Eastern Europe; consult.— var.consult.services for multilateral & bilateral aid agencies notably World Bank, UNDP, FINNIDA, ODA & GTZ. **Career:** Leverhulme Res.F.& RS Euro.Res.F. Station Biologique de la Tour du Valat, Camargue 1981–4; Project Dir, Wetland Survey & Mgmt, Senegal River Valley 1983–4; Wetlands Officer 1984–8, Wetlands Prog.Coord. 1988–92, Dir Regnl Affairs 1993–, IUCN. **Achievements:** dev.of assessment methodology for habitat qual.of Medit.wetlands, estab.of IUCN Wetlands Prog.and increased intl profile of wetland mgmt needs. **Awards:** Leverhulme Studentship 1981–3, RS F'ship 1983–4. **Publications:** *Wetland Cons.*1990, *The Sust.Use of Wetland Resources* (co-Author) 1992, *Managing the Wetlands of Kafue Flats & Bangwenlu Basin* (co-Author) 1992, *Wetlands in Danger* 1993; 25 scientific papers. Reluctant re. pers. pub., favours news media support. **Languages:** English, French, Spanish (spoken). Willing to act as consult. **Address:** IUCN, Rue Mauverney 28, CH 1196 Gland, Switzerland. **Tel.**(office) 41 22 999 0211; **fax** 41 22 999 0020.

DUMONT, Professor Dr Henri Jean. Conservation of the main aquatic biotopes of the Sahara, Sahel & the Arabian peninsula; special interest in zooplankton and Odonata. Professor of Animal Ecology, Biogeography and Conservation. *B.*8 Feb.1942, Denderleeuw, Belgium. Belgian. **Education:** U.of Gent, Lic.(Biol.) 1964, Doctorate (Biol.) 1968, D.Sci(Limnol.) 1979. **Experience:** res.in basic lake limnol.& river poll.in Belgium, relict waters in n.Africa and Arabian peninsular, reservoirs & lakes in S.Amer.; prep.of Belgium's participation & Belgian del.to UN re.UNCED & follow-up cttee; consult.for WHO on surface water (plankton) in N.Africa. **Career:** Res.F. Natural Sci.Fndn 1980s, Asst Prof.& Assoc.Prof.then Prof.of Ecol.1987– U.of Gent, Belgian del.to UN for Cttee on Sust.Dev.1993–. **Achievements:** documenting the enormous value of relict surface waters, their fauna & flora, of the arid n.half of Africa; combatting construction of shallow dams in Amazon basin; insect prot.in Belgium. **Memberships:** ISL, ASLO, BZS, IOS, AOS. **Award:** Book* Prize (Belgian Govt) 1980. **Publications:** *Limnol.of the Sahara and Sahel 1979; Dev.in Hydrobiol.— Nrs 21 Limnol.& Marine Biol.in the Sudan 1984, 23 Trop.Zooplankton 1984, & 60 Intrazooplankton Predation 1990, 1992; Studies in Trop. Zooplankton 1994; The regulation of plant & animal species & communities in African shallows, lakes, & wetlands 1992. Indiff.to pers.pub., favours news media support. **Languages:** Dutch, English, French, German (spoken), Portuguese (spoken), Spanish. Willing to act as consult.etc. **Address:** Institute of Animal Ecology, University of Gent, Ledeganckstraat 35, 9000 Gent, Belgium. **Tel.**(office) 32 9 264 5253, (home) 32 53 668890; **fax** 32 9 264 5343; **internet** Henri.Dumont @rug.ac.be .

DUNCAN, Dr Patrick. Ecology of mammalian herbivores; conservation of biodiversity (wetlands, rangelands). Research Director. B.14 Feb. 1948, Maseru, Lesotho. British. Father Patrick Baker Duncan, author of Man and the Earth 1974. M.Alison Marjorie Phillips (Coord., Intl Service, LPO): s. **Education:** U.of Oxf. BA(Hons Zool.) 1970, U.of Nairobi PhD(Ecol.) 1975. **Experience:** res.— mammalian ecol.& behaviour (African insectivores, antelopes, cattle, equids, roc deer [Caprellus spp.]), wetland ecol.; cons.— equids, wetlands; consult.— African & Medit. regns, range ecol.and prot.area mgmt, res.mgmt & cons.of herbivore pops, rangelands & wetlands in Africa & Europe; teaching undergrad., Masters & PhD levels; admin.— direction of interdisc.res.teams and field stations on ecol.of herbivores & wetlands, eval.of res.progs, units for Institut Nat.de Recherche Agronomique, CNRS, & EC. **Career:** postgrad. Serengeti Res. Inst.1970–73; Station Biologique de la Tour du Valat, Camargue 1975–90 (Scientific Dir. 1985–90); consult.to UNEP/UNDP, World Bank, private cos; Res.Dir. CNRS France 1990–; Dep.Dir.Centre d'Etudes Biologiques de Chizé 1993–. **Achievements:** res.on ecol.& behaviour of equids, esp.free-living horses; surveys & basic res.on rangeland ecol.in Africa & Europe; interdisc.res.for cons.of wetlands; edl adv./reviewer for 10 scientific journals; dev.of mgmt strats for animal pops & prot.areas in rangelands & wetlands; scientific adv.to ten TV films on cons.; teaching ecol.& resource mgmt at BSc & MSc levels, supervision/exam.of students up to PhD level in ecol. **Memberships:** ASAB, BES, FPS, IEEM, SFE, SFECA, Comité de Direction, Centre d'Etudes Biologiques de Chizé (1985–90); Tech.Group 'Integrated Mgmt of Coastal Wetlands of Medit.Type', EC, DGXI 1988–90; IUCN SSC Equid SG (Chairman 1988–); Conseil Scientifique, Parc Naturel Regnl du Marais Poitevin, Sec.1993–. **Awards:** Minor Scholarship (Wadham Coll.Oxf.)1967; Leverhulme Scholarship (RS) 1970; Vis. Scholar

(Wolfson Coll.Camb.)1983–4. **Publications:** Horses & Grasses 1992, Action Plan for the Cons.of Wild Zebras, Asses & Horses 1992; c.50 scientific pubns & 10 major reports. Indiff.to pers.pub., favours news media support. **Languages:** English, French, Swahili (spoken). Willing to act as consult.etc. **Address:** CNRS– Centre d'Etudes Biologiques de Chizé, 79360 Beauvoir-sur-Niort, France. **Tel.**(office) 33 49 096111, (direct line) 33 49 097163; **fax** 33 49 096526.

DUNLOP, Nicholas James. Coordination of EarthAction Network. International Coordinator. B.7 Nov.1956, Wellington, New Zealand. Irish, New Zealander. S.: d. **Education:** pre-u.in Singapore, NZ, & India, Vic.U.of Wellington BA (Pol.Sci.) 1977. **Experience:** admin.— coordn world-wide (101 countries) of the 700 citizen groups which comprise EarthAction Network and which seek to apply public pressure on intl negotiations. **Career:** Sec.-Gen. Parliamentarians for Global Action 1978–88, Consult. UNDP 1982–5, Intl Coord. EarthAction Network 1989–. **Achievements:** empowerment of citizens & elected officials to work for a more just, peaceful, & sust.world community; init.& org.Six Nation Peace Initiative, a group of heads of govt working on nuclear disarmament 1984–8. **Award:** Indira Gandhi Prize 1987 Welcomes news media support. **Languages:** English, French. Further details may be obtained from Who's Who in the World 1993. **Address:** 9 White Lion Street, London N1 9PD, England, UK, **tel.**44 171 865 9009; **fax** 44 171 278 0345; and rue René Christaens 39, 1160 Brussels, Belgium, **tel.**(home) 32 2 675 3023; **fax** 32 2 673 4029.

DUNNET, Professor Dr George Mackenzie. Nature conservation, ecology of mammals & birds (especially seabirds), environmental management. Emeritus Regius Professor of Natural History. B.19 April 1928, Dunnet, Caithness, Scotland, UK. British. M.Margaret: s., 2 d.(one deceased), s.-in-law Dr Ronald W.Summers (res.biol.). **Education:** U.of Aberdeen, BSc (Zool.)(1st Class Hons) 1949, PhD 1952, DSc 1984. **Experience:** ecol.res.with CSIRO in NZ, Sri Lanka, Falkland Islands, Ghana, Egypt, and Britain; studied envl impacts of oil industry in Scotland esp.Shetland; carried out fundamental res.in ecol.of birds & mammals; consult. to oil industry & govt. **Career:** Res. Officer CSIRO 1953–8; Dir Culterty Field Station 1953–88, Prof.of Zool.1971–4, Regius Prof.of Natural Hist.1974–92, Dean Fac. Sci.1984–7, U.of Aberdeen; served on NERC 1975–7, NCC Cttees 1970–91, NCC 1991–2, SNH 1992–. **Achievements:** original ecol.res., chairing review group on Badgers (Meles taxus) and bovine tuberculosis, Shetland Oil Terminal Envl Adv. Group, Salmon (Salmo salar) Adv.Cttee. **Memberships:** BES (VP 1973–4, Pres.1979–81), BOU, BTO, IBiol., many nat.cons.cttees & councils. **Awards:** OBE 1986, CBE 1994, F.

RSE 1970, F.IBiol.1974, F.RSA 1981, Godman Salvin Medal (BOU) 1990, Neill Prize (RSE) 1990, Hon.F.RZSS 1992. **Publications:** *Monogr.of the Fleas of Australia* 1974, Pop.studies of the Fulmar *[Fulmarus glacialis]* on Eynhallow, Orkney Islands 1991. Favours pers.pub.& news media support. **Languages:** English, French (rudimentary & conversational). Further details may be obtained from *Debrett's People of Today* 1991, Brit. *Who's Who.* Willing to act as consult.etc. **Address:** Whinhill, Inverebrie, Ellon, Aberdeenshire AB41 8PT, Scotland, UK. **Tel.**(office) 44 1224 272861, (home) 44 1358 761215; **fax** 44 1358 761462.

DURRANI, Shakil. Developing projects & programmes relating to conservation of wildlife & environment, narcotic drugs control. Planning & Development Director. *B.*9 Sept.1947, Abbottabad, Pakistan. Pakistani. *M.*Sabrina: 3 *s.* **Education:** Edwardes Coll. (Peshawar), BA (English, Hist., Pol.Sci.) 1967; Punjab U. MA (Pol.Sci.) 1969; U.of Bradford, MSc(Nat. Dev. & Project Planning) 1980; further training in law, econ., admin., and mgmt. **Experience:** as Sr Admin.in Govt of Pakistan, has planned, developed, & implemented, three projects — Wilderness Park at Deosai Plains, community-sponsored Ibex Conservation Project, and (assisting WWF) dev.of Khunjerab Nat.Park (all in Northern Areas of Pakistan). **Career:** Asst Commissioner of Abbottabad & Hangu Sub-Divisions 1973–4, Pol.Agent of Orakzai & Mohmand Agencies 1974–5 & 1977–8 and of Khyber Agency 1982–4, Chief of Industries & Coordn Section of Planning & Dev.Dept 1978–9, Dep.Commissioner of Chitral Distr.1980–82, MD of Small Industries Dev.1984–5, Commissioner of Kohat & Malakand Divs 1986–91, Sec.of Info., Tourism, Sports, Culture, & Archaeol.1991, Chief Commissioner of Northern Areas 1993–4, Dir of Planning & Dev.and Consult.on Narcotics Drugs Control, Anti-Narcotics Force 1994–, all Govt of NWFP. **Achievements:** has planned and developed nr of community-sponsored projects to conserve ibexes, Markhors *(Capra falconeri* agg.*)*, and partridges. **Memberships:** WWF Pakistan (Dir 1992–4), IUCN Pakistan (Hon. Regnl Dir 1990–), NWFP Wildlife Bd 1980–, Envt Prot.Fndn (Peshawar), Kalash Envl Prot. Fndn; nat.cttees re.restructuring instns in Federally Administered Tribal Areas and for reorgn of the Wildlife & Forest Dept of NWFP. **Award:** First in nat.C.Superior Services Exams 1971. **Publications:** incl.*Proposals on Social Action Prog.*1993, *Community Involvement in Wildlife Cons.in Hunza and Nagar* 1994; Leader of team of consults to write *Pakistan Drug Abuse Masterplan (1995–2000).* Favours pers.pub.& news media support. **Languages:** English, Pushto, Urdu. Willing to act as consult.etc. **Address:** 32 Defence Colony, Khyber Road, Peshawar, North West Frontier Province, Pakistan. **Tel.** (office) 92 51 813894, (home) 92 521 273302 or 813017; **fax** 92 51 818459.

DURRELL, Dr Lee McGeorge. Endangered species' conservation. Trust Honorary Director. *B.*7 Sept.1949, Memphis, TN, USA. American. *W.*(of the late Gerald Malcolm Durrell, OBE, Founder of JWPT, author and TV presenter of num.works on animal cons.1979–95). **Education:** Bryn Mawr Coll.(Phil. PA), BA(Phil.) 1971; Duke U.(Durham, NC), PhD(Zool.) 1979. **Experience:** res.— lemur behaviour in the wild and in captivity, and animal vocalizations in Madagascar; tech./admin.— dir & fund-raiser for Ploughshare Tortoise recovery prog.; consult.— adv.on JWPT cons.progs; Chairman of Intl Adv.Group of Scis for Madagascar 1983–6 (disbanded); media (var.). **Career:** Asst 1975–6, Temp.Instr.1976–7, Gen.Biol. Duke U.; writer & TV Presenter 1979–; Chairman, Durrell Trust for Cons.Biol.1990–; Hon.Dir, JWPT 1995–. **Achievements:** operation of Ploughshare Tortoise recovery prog.1986–; studying & promoting value of interactive captive–wild mgmt strats for endangered species; promoting concept of good zoos; helping all zoos to serve their cons.role better. **Memberships:** JWPT (Counc.1983–95, Scientific Adv. Cttee 1984–, Madagascar Prog.co-Coord. 1991–); WPTC (Hon.Trustee, Scientific Adv.Bd); WPTI (Hon.Dir); FFI (Counc.1986–90, 1992–); IUCN Primates 1986–, Non-marine Chelonians, Re-intro.1989–, & Tortoise and Freshwater Turtle 1991–, SGs; HCT (Trustee 1989–93); DICE (Bd of Mgmt 1990–, Adv.Bd 1994–). **Publications:** incl.*The Amateur Naturalist* (co-Author) 1981, *The State of the Ark* 1986; num.chapters, papers, & TV progs. Favours pers.pub.& news media support. **Languages:** English, French. Willing to act as consult.etc. **Address:** Jersey Wildlife Preservation Trust (JWPT), Les Augrès Manor, Trinity, Jersey JE3 5BP, Channel Islands, UK. **Tel.** (office) 44 1534 864666; **fax** 44 1534 865161; **e-mail** ldexec@itl.net .

EARLL, Dr Robert Clifford. Marine conservation including benthos, sharks & rays; marine protected areas, coastal-zone management, environmental management systems. Environmental Consultant. *B.*9 June 1949, London, England, UK. British. *M.*Dr Mary Louise: *d.* **Education:** U.of Hull BSc(Zool.) 1970, U.of Manchester PhD 1975. **Experience:** marine & bivalve ecophysiology, sublittoral ecol., marine cons., marine prot.areas, coastal-zone mgmt, poll. **Career:** Lect. Leeds Poly.1976–8; Project Coord.& Head of Cons. MCS 1978–92; Envl Consult.1992–. **Achievements:** Founder Memb. & Admin. MCS, Founder Marine Forum, Founder Memb. Euro.Elasmobranch Soc. **Memberships:** Euro.Elasmobranch Soc., Eurocoast, Seas At Risk (Cttee Marine Forum), Underwater Assn (Cttee & Chair Wildlife Link Marine Group) 1975–80, Ref.*Marine Poll.Bull.*, Reviewer *ICES J.* **Publications:** *Sublittoral Ecol.*(co-Ed.) 1983, *Marine Envl Mgmt: Review & Future Trends* (Ed.) 1994; 50+ papers, num.popular articles, sublittoral surveys. Indiff.to pers.pub., favours news media support. **Language:** English. Willing to act as consult.etc. **Address:** Candle Cottage, Kempley, Gloucester-shire GL18 2BU, England, UK. **Tel.**(office & home) & **fax** 44 1531 890415.

EATON, Professor Dr Peter Price. Environmental management in Southeast Asia & South Pacific regions, national parks & protected areas. Professor. *B.*25 July 1935, Nuneaton, England, UK. British *M.*Mavis: *s.*, 3 *d.* **Education:** LSE BSc(Econ.) 1956, U.of London MSc (Econ.) 1967, U.of Hull PhD 1978. **Experience:** res.— nat.parks & prot.areas, envl mgmt in SE Asia & S.Pacific; consult.— SPREP ESCAP; teaching u.courses in envl mgmt. **Career:** Educ.Dept (Sarawak) 1962–72; PNG 1973–88 — Admin. Coll.& U.of PNG (Dir of Land Studies Centre); Assoc.Prof.1988–93, Prof.1993–, Dept of Public Policy, U.of Brunei Darussalam. **Achievements:** promotion & eval.of wildlife mgmt areas in PNG; dev.of envl mgmt progs at Univs of PNG & Brunei Darussalam. **Memberships:** IUCN CNPPA, F.RGS. **Awards:** Vivien Stewart Award as Vis. Scholar (Wolfson Coll. Camb.) 1984. **Publications:** *Land Tenure & Cons.: Prot. Areas in the S.Pacific* 1985, *Borneo: Change & Dev.*(co-Author) 1992; 50+ other various. Indiff.to pers.pub., favours news media support. **Languages:** English; French, Indonesian & Malay (all fair written & spoken). Willing to act as consult.etc. **Address:** University of Brunei Darussalam, Gadong 3186, Brunei. **Tel.**(office) 673 2 427 001, (home) 673 2 244 207; **fax** 673 2 427 003.

EDINBURGH, HRH The Prince Philip, Duke of. *B.*10 June 1921, Corfu, Greece. British. *M.*1947 HRH The Princess Elizabeth; from 1952 HM Queen Elizabeth II: 3 *s.*, *d.* **Education:** Cheam Sch., Salem Sch., Gordonstoun Sch., R.Naval Coll. Dartmouth. **Career:** Pres.of Brit. Nat. Appeal, WWF UK 1961–82, Pres.WWF Intl 1981–, Patron or Pres.of many other cons.& envl orgns, travelled extensively world-wide in connection with WWF & IUCN. **Publications:** *Birds from BRITANNIA* 1962, *Wildlife Crisis* 1970, *The Envl Revolution* 1978, *Down to Earth* 1988. **Awards:** many foreign orders & decorations and hon.degrees from num.univs; Chancellor of Univs of Camb.& Edinburgh (and formerly of Univs of Wales & Salford). Further information may be obtained from C.Office of Info., London, England, UK, or from the Brit.*Who's Who, Intl Who's Who,* etc. **Address:** Buckingham Palace, London SW1A 1AA, England, UK.

EDMUNDS, Professor Dr Malcolm. Anti-predator defences of animals; biology & taxonomy of opisthobranch molluscs. Professor of Zoology. *B.*24 July 1938, Harlow, Essex, England, UK. British. *M.*Dr Janet (orb-web spider ecol., cons.). **Education:** Leighton Park Sch., Queen's Coll.Oxf. BA(Zool.) 1960, DPhil (Zool.)(Seaslugs) 1963. **Experience:** u.teaching & res. **Career:** Lect., Sr Lect., Acting Head, Dept of Zool.

U.of Ghana 1963–73; Sr Res.F. U.of Exeter 1973–4; Sr Lect., Prin.Lect. Preston (later Lancs) Poly. (now U.of C.Lancs) 1974–; Head 1976–83, Pers.Chair 1987–, Dept of Applied Biol. U.of C.Lancs. **Achievement:** VC Lancs Wildlife Trust 1983–. **Memberships:** F.IBiol., F.LS, BES, MBA, Malacological Soc., BSBI. **Publications:** *Defence in Animals: A Survey of Anti-predator Defences* 1974; 60+ res.papers & chapters etc. Favours pers.pub.& news media support. **Language:** English. Willing to act as a ref.if requested. **Address:** Department of Applied Biology, University of Central Lancashire, Preston PR1 2HE, England, UK. **Tel.**44 1772 893518.

EDSALL, Professor Dr John Tileston. General continuing concern with environmental problems; emphasis on population problems. Professor of Biochemistry Emeritus. *B.*3 Nov. 1902, Philadelphia, PA, USA. American. Father David Linn Edsall (1869–1945, notable physician & pioneer in med.res., Dean of Harvard Med. Sch.1918–35; much concerned with industrial med.& hazards to workers). *W.*: 2 living *s.* **Education:** U.of Camb.(UK) 1924–6; Harvard Coll. BA *cum laude* 1923; Harvard U. MD 1928. **Experience:** major res.was on chem.of proteins, amino-acids etc.; during WWII worked on proteins of blood plasma, their purification & uses in med.& surgery. **Career:** Harvard U. 1928–72, Instr.to Prof.1928–51, Prof.of Biochem. Emer.1973–; Guggenheim F. Calif.Inst.of Tech. 1940–41; Fulbright Lect.in Camb.(UK) 1952 & Tokyo 1964. **Memberships:** US NAS, Amer. AAS, ASBMB, R.Danish & Swedish Acads of Sci.and Leopoldina Acad. (Germany). **Awards:** Passano Award (med. res.) 1966, Willard Gibbs Medal (ACS) 1972, Philip Abelson Award (AAAS) 1989. **Publications:** Hazards of nuclear fission power and the choice of alternatives 1975, Toxicity of plutonium and some other actinides 1976; *c.*200 papers on phys.chem.of amino-acids, proteins, etc.and later on problems of scientific freedom, resp., & trustworthincss. **Languages:** English; French & German (good read). Further details can be obtained from *Who's Who in Amer., Intl Who's Who.* **Address:** Department of Molecular and Cellular Biology, Harvard University, 7 Divinity Avenue, Cambridge, Massachusetts 02138, USA. **Tel.**(office) 1 617 495 2314, (home) 1 617 876 5007; **fax** 1 617 495 8308.

EDWARDS, Mark. Environmental photography. Photo Agency Proprietor. *B.*12 June 1947, Blackheath, London, England, UK. British. **Experience:** worked in 80 countries photographing envl issues 1969–. **Career:** Proprietor, Still Pictures Envl Photo Agency. **Achievements:** first photographer to specialize in envl photography; photographs published worldwide. **Awards:** Global 500 Roll of Honour (UNEP) 1990, Cherry Kearton Medal (RGS) 1991. **Publications:** Changing Consciousness (co-Author) 1990. Indiff.to pers.pub., favours news media support. **Language:** English. **Address:**

199 Shooters Hill Road, Blackheath, London SE3 8HL, England, UK. **Tel.**(office) 44 181 858 8307; **fax** 44 181 858 2049.

EDWARDS, Professor Dr Peter John. Plant ecology, agroecology, environmental management. Professor of Plant Ecology & Institute Director. *B*.29 July 1948, Durban, South Africa. British. *M*.Yvonne: *d*. **Education:** Purbrook Grammar Sch.; Queen's Coll.Camb. MA 1970, PhD 1973. **Experience:** acad.res., admin. **Career:** Lect.to Sr Lect.in Ecol.1973–93, Dep. Dir. of GeoData Inst.1988–93, U.of Southampton; Prof.of Plant Ecol.& Dir, Geobotanical Inst. ETH 1993–. **Achievements:** wide range of res. in plant–herbivore interactions and ecosystem ecol., co-Founder (1990) & first Sec.IEEM. **Memberships:** INTECOL, BES (Prog.Sec. 1985–92), IEEM (Sec.1990–93), Gesellschaft für Ökologie. **Publications:** incl.Mineral cycling in montane rain-forest in New Guinea (series of five papers) 1977–82, *Ecol.of Insect–Plant Interactions* (co-Author) 1981, *Large-Scale Ecol. and Cons.Biol.*(co-Author) 1994. Indiff.to pers. pub. & news media support. **Languages:** English; German & Spanish (fair spoken). Willing to act as consult.etc. **Address:** Geobotanisches Institut–Eidgenössische Technische Hochschule, Zürichbergstrasse 38, 8044 Zürich, Switzerland. **Tel.**(office) 41 1 632 4330, (home) 41 1 252 0716; **fax** 41 1 632 1215.

EGLER, Dr Frank Edwin. Ecology, environment, conservation, ecosystematics; right-of-way vegetation management, aesthetic landscape vegetation management, land preservation. Founder & Company Officer. *B*.26 April 1911, New York, NY, USA. American. *M*.Happy Kitchel (deceased) (Amer.cons.orgns, Nature photography world-wide). **Education:** U.of Minn. MS 1934, Yale U. PhD 1936. **Experience:** ecosystematics, land conservancy, res., envl educ. **Career:** Prof., Consult., Founder of Aton Forest Inc. **Achievements:** in academic 'ecol.', veg. sci.; right-of-way veg.mgmt (power lines, roadsides, railroad lines, pipelines); two-vols I.*Aesthetic Landscape Veg.Mgmt*, II *Phil.of Ecol.* 1975, original res.on selectively-used herbicides. **Memberships:** ESA (Life) F.AAAS, AGS, AMNH; num.others. **Awards:** Guggenheim F'ship 1956–8, sundry minor awards, hons & prizes. **Publications:** five addit.books incl.*The Nature of Veg.: Its Mgmt & Mismgmt* 1977; major res.papers on Berkshire Plateau (Massachusetts), Arid Oahu (Hawaii), Everglades (Florida), Sand Dunes (Virginia), Tidal marshes (Connecticut); 400+ papers, reports etc. **Languages:** Dutch, English, French, German, Italian, Spanish. Further details may be obtained from var.Who's Whos. **Address:** Aton Forest Inc., Norfolk, Connecticut 06058, USA. **Tel.**1 203 542 5125.

EGLI, Robert A. Chemistry of the atmosphere. Independent Consultant. *B*.6 Aug.1926, Rheineck, Oberuzwil, Switzerland. *M*.Verena: 2 *s*. incl.Dr

Bernhard Egli (biol.& ecol.). **Education:** HTL (Winterthur), Dipl.in Chem. 1948. **Experience:** res., admin. **Career:** Group Leader in Organic Synthesis Lab.1948–58, Head of Analytical Dev.Lab.1958–72, Qual.Control Dir 1972–85, Dir of Patents, Library & Lit.Services 1985–9, Cilag AG; Ind.Consult.1990–. **Achievements:** studying air poll.problems & climatology, dissemination of info.to journalists & the public by distribn of own articles & lit.(on a non-profit basis). **Membership:** Schweizerischer Bund für Naturschutz (Bd, Schaffhausen Branch). **Award:** Phil Hofmann Res.Award (Johnson & Johnson). **Publications:** *c*.20 incl. Nitrogen oxide emissions from air traffic 1990, Climatic effects of air traffic 1995. **Languages:** English (fair), German. Willing to act as consult.etc. **Address:** Etzelstrasse 15, 8200 Schaffhausen, Switzerland. **Tel.**(office & home) 41 53 257166.

EGZIABHER, Dr Tewolde Berhan GEBRE. Plant ecology & taxonomy, conservation, sustainable development, biodiversity, biosafety. General Manager, Associate Professor of Biology, Herbarium Keeper, Project Leader. *B*.19 Feb.1940, Adwa, Ethiopia. Ethiopian. *M*. Suzan Burnell Edwards (plant taxonomist, Ed. *Flora of Ethiopia*): 3 *d*.incl.Sara (forester). **Education:** Haile Selassie I U. BSc(Biol.) 1963; U.of Wales, PhD(Plant Ecol.) 1970. **Experience:** res.— plant ecol., cons., sust.dev., tech. generation & diffusion, trad.med.; consults in plant ecol., res.& dev.capacity-bldg; teaching plant ecol., cons., plant systematics, medicinal and other economic plants; co-Chair UNEP Panel.IV on Biosafety; started first Ethiopian j.of sci.*Sinet*. **Career:** Dean of Fac.of Sci. 1974–8, Assoc.Prof.of Biol.1978–, Addis Ababa U.; Project Leader, Res.& Dev.in Rural Settings Project, Ethiopian Sci.and Tech.Comm. 1978–82; Pres. Asmara U.1983–91; Dir, NCS Secretariat 1991–4; Gen.Mgr, Nat.EPA 1994–; Keeper, Nat.Herbarium 1989–; Leader, Ethiopia Flora Project, 1980–. **Achievements:** estab.of courses in plant ecol.& cons.at Addis Ababa U., supervision of num.res.students, launching and continuing to lead v.successful Ethiopia Flora Project. **Memberships:** LS, ICTAE (Scientific Council), BES, Ethiopian PGR Centre (Counc.) & Ecol.Soc., Svenska Vaxtegeografiska Sallskapet (Hon.). **Award:** Chancellor's Gold Medal (Addis Ababa U.) 1963. **Publications:** several chapters incl.Questions Ambientals Vistes des d'una Perspetiva del Sud 1995, The Impact of Modern Sci.and Tech.on Human Rights in Ethiopia 1995; num.articles & reports. Against pers.pub., indiff.to news media support. **Languages:** Amharic, English, French (better at spoken), Tigrinya (N.Ethiopia & highland Eritrea). Willing to act as consult.etc. **Address:** POB 30231, Addis Ababa, Ethiopia. **Tel.** (office) 251 1 114323 or 181658, (home) 251 1 204210; **fax** 251 1 552350.

EHRLICH, Anne Howland. Population biology & control; environmental protection, environmental consequences of nuclear war. Senior Research Associate, Associate Director/Policy Coordinator. *B*.17 Nov.1933, Des Moines, IA, USA. American. *M*.Paul R.Ehrlich *qv*: *d*. **Education:** U.of Kansas 1953–5. **Experience:** res. on insect morphology & repro., reef fishes; human pop.& envt and writing on same; vol. activity with NGOs; lecturing, admin. **Career:** Res.Asst 1962–70, Res.Assoc. 1970–75, Sr Res.Assoc.1975–, Dept of Biol.Scis, and Assoc. Dir for Policy, Center for Cons.Biol. 1990–, Stanford U.; Bds of Pacific Inst.for Studies in Envt, Dev.& Security 1977– (Chair 1992–), Rocky Mtn Biol.Lab.1989– (Treas.1992–), and Ploughshares Fund 1990–; Adv.Bds of NPA, Redefining Progress, and Winslow Fndn; Chair, Cttee on Military Impacts on the Envt, Sierra Club 1985–, Pres.'s Comm.on Sust.Dev.Task Group for Academics & Scis 1994–. **Achievements:** writing books & num.articles, teaching. **Awards:** Humanist Disting.Service Award (jt), Raymond B.Bragg Award, Hon.Life Memb. (AHA) 1985, Hon.F.(Calif.AS) 1988, Global 500 Roll of Honour (UNEP) 1989, Hon.Doct. (Bethany Coll.) 1990. **Publications:** 12 books incl.*The Pop.Explosion* (co-Author) 1990, *Hidden Dangers: The Envl Consequences of Preparing for War* (co-Ed.) 1990, *Healing the Planet* (co-Author) 1991; num.papers & chapters. **Languages:** English, French (rusty), Spanish (a little). Willing to act as consult. etc. within limits. **Address:** Department of Biological Sciences, Stanford University, Stanford, California 94305, USA. **Tel.**1 415 325 1853; **fax** 1 415 323 5920.

EHRLICH, Professor Paul R. Population studies, biological sciences. Professor of Biological Sciences & Bing Professor of Population Studies. *B*.29 May 1932, Philadelphia, PA, USA. American. *M*.Anne H.*qv*: *d*. **Education:** U.of Penn. AB 1953; U.of Kansas MA 1955, PhD 1957. **Career:** Field Officer (Canadian Arctic & sub-Arctic), Northern Insect Survey (Canadian Govt), Summers of 1951 & 1952; Res.Asst, DDT Resistance Project (Dept of Entomol. U.of Kansas) 1952–4; F. Kansas U.1954–6; Pre-doctl F.NSF 1955–7; Assoc.Investigator, USAF Res. Project 1956–7; NSF Sr Postdoctl F. U.of Sydney 1965–6; Assoc. Center for the Study of Democratic Instns (Calif.) 1969–72; Pres.1969– 70 (Hon.1970–) Zero Pop.Growth (Pres.of Fund 1972–3); Adv.Council, FoE 1970–; Pres. The Cons.Soc.1972–3; Bd of Dirs, Common Cause 1972; Trustee 1971–86 & co-Chairman of Pres. Cttee 1973–5, Rocky Mtn Biol.Lab.; Bd of Consults, Lizard Is.Res.Station 1975–8; Asst Prof.1959–62, Assoc.Prof.1962–6, Prof.1966–, of Biol.Scis, Dir of Grad.Studies of Dept of Biol.Scis 1966–9 & 1974–6, Bing Prof.of Pop. Studies 1977–, Stanford U. **Memberships:** Lepidopterists' Soc.(Sec.1957–63, Exec. Council 1968), Calif.AS (F.1961), AIBS (Governing Bd Memb.-at-Large 1969–70, Pres.1989), Soc.for the Study of Evol.(VP 1970), ISAE (Memb.& active Committeeman 1969–70), Sierra Club (Scientific

Adv.Cttee 1972–), SSE (Counc. 1974–6), AAAS (F.1978), Amer.AAS (F.1982), NAS 1985, SCB (Bd of Govs 1986–8), ESA (F.1987), AOU (Elective 1989), APS 1990, EASA 1992. **Awards:** Grant-in-Aid of Res. (Sigma Xi–RESA) 1955, First Prize (Mitchell Fndn) 1979, John Muir Award (Sierra Club) 1980, Humanist Disting. Service Award (AHA) 1985, First Disting. Achievement Award (SCB) 1987, Gold Medal (WWF Intl) 1987, Gerard Piel Award (AAAS/ Scientific Amer.) 1989, Global 500 Roll of Honour (UNEP) 1989, Crafoord Prize (RSAS) 1990, Disting.Service Citation (U.of Kansas) 1991, MacArthur Prize F'ship (MacArthur Fndn) 1990–95, Major Achievement Award (New York City Audubon Soc.) 1991, Volvo Envt Prize 1993, World Ecol.Medal (ICTE) 1993, Sasakawa Envt Prize (UNEP) 1994, Heinz Award for the Envt 1995; Hon.— Dr of Humane Letters (U.of the Pacific) 1970, Life Memb.(AHA) 1989, Membership (BES) 1989, Doctorates at Bethany Coll.and Ohio Wesleyan U. 1990, and Memb.(ISPE) 1991. **Publications:** 35 books incl.*How to Know the Butterflies* 1961, *Human Ecol.: Problems and Solutions* 1973, *Extinction: The Causes and Consequences of the Disappearance of Species* 1981, *New World/New Mind: Moving Toward Conscious Evol.*1989, *The Pop. Explosion* 1990 (all co-Authored); 700 papers & articles; Edl Bds *Systematic Zool.*1961–7, *Intl J.of Envl Scis* 1969–71 and *Amer.Naturalist* 1974–6 (Sr Assoc. Ed.1984), Adv.Ed.*EC* 1974–, *Human Nature* 1977–9. **Languages:** English, Spanish. **Address:** Department of Biological Sciences, Stanford University, Stanford, California 94305, USA. **Tel.**1 415 723 2413; **fax** 1 415 723 6132.

EICHBAUM, William M. Pollution prevention, marine & coastal governance; biodiversity in the former Soviet Union. Vice-President. *B*.24 Dec. 1941, Knoxville, TN, USA. American. **Education:** Grad.Inst.of Intl Studies (CH) 1961–2, Dartmouth Coll. BA 1963, Harvard Law School LLB 1966. **Experience:** govt admin., NGO policy advocacy, envl law dev. **Career:** Dep. Sec. Penn.Dept of Envl Res.1970–77; Assoc. Solicitor, USDI 1977–9; F.Woodrow Wilson Center 1979–80; Asst Sec. Office of Envl Progs 1980–87; Under-Sec. Mass. Ext.Office of Envl Affairs 1987–9; VP Intl Envl Qual. WWF–USA 1990–. **Achievements:** developed major elements of US envl law, and strat.for prot.of Chesapeake Bay and related estuaries; developed biodiv.strat.for Russia. **Memberships:** IUCN CNPPA, US NAS (Bds), Penn.Bar Assn. **Awards:** NAEP 1984, Chesapeake Bay Cons. Award (Izaak Walton League) 1988. **Publications:** *Turning the Tide* (co-Author) 1992, two book contribns 1993. Favours pers.pub.& news media support. **Languages:** English, French. Willing to act as consult.etc. **Address:** World Wildlife Fund, 1250 24th Street NW, Washington, District of Columbia 20037, USA. **Tel.** (office) 1 202 778 9645, (home) 1 301 229 1713; **fax** 1 202 293 9345.

EIDSVIK, Harold Kristian. National parks & protected areas, world heritage, policy, planning, management, biological diversity. Senior Programme Specialist. *B*.4 July 1932, Prince Rupert, Canada. Canadian. *M*.Malvina: *s*., 2 *d*. **Education:** UBC BSc(For.) 1957, U.of Michigan MSc(For.) 1964. **Experience:** 30 yrs' resource cons.& park planning, admin., policy direction. **Career:** Parks Canada 1960–90, IUCN 1977–80, World Heritage Centre (UNESCO) 1990–, Adjunct Prof.at Univs of Guelph 1972, Michigan 1983–93, & BC 1992. **Achievements:** planning ten nat.parks in Canada, prin.writer of Canadian Parks policy, designed zoning scheme & systems plans for Parks Canada, developed categories of prot. areas. **Membership:** IUCN CNPPA (Chair 1983–90). **Awards:** McMillan Lect.(UBC) 1986, Fred Packard Award (IUCN) 1990, Fed./ Provincial Park Directors' Award 1990. **Publications:** *Prot.Areas, Cons.& Dev.*(McMillan Lecture) 1986, *Canada in a Global Context, in Endangered Spaces* 1989, *Framework for Mgmt Class.of Prot.Areas* (CNPPA) 1990, Strengthening Prot.Areas Through Phil., Sci.& Mgmt 1992. Indiff.to pers.pub.& news media support. **Languages:** English, French. **Address:** World Heritage Centre, UNESCO, 7 Place de Fontenoy, 75352 Paris 07 SP, France. **Tel.**(office) 33 1 456 81433, (home) 33 1 456 79445; **fax** 33 1 405 69570.

EKARATH, Dr Raveendran. Environmental pollution monitoring; air, water, soil, and waste management; standards, legislation, laboratory management. Senior Chemist. *B*.1 Jan.1950, Ker., India. Indian. *M*.Sasikala: *s*., *d*. **Education:** U.of Ker. BSc 1970, U.of Stirling PhD 1992. **Experience:** res.in field of envt (air poll., solid waste mgmt, marine poll.monitoring, EIA); 20 yrs' lab.mgmt, eight yrs in petroleum refinery, ten yrs' envl prot. **Career:** Chemist 1970–77, Analyst 1977–83, Sr Chemist 1983–, EPC, Bahrain. **Achievements:** estab.of lab.for EPC, baseline res.on air, water, land qual., mangrove area cons. **Memberships:** C.Chem., MRSC, F. AIC, IWEM. **Publications:** ten papers. Favours pers.pub.& news media support. **Languages:** English, Hindi, Malayalam. Willing to act as consult.etc. **Address:** Environmental Protection Committee, POB 26909, Bahrain. **Tel.**(office) 973 29693, (home) 973 258520; **fax** 973 293694.

EKINS, Paul Whitfield. Ecological economics, ecologically-sustainable development. Research Fellow in Economics, Special Adviser. *B*.24 July 1950, Djakarta, Indonesia. British. *M*.Susan Anne: *s*. **Education:** U.of London MSc(Econ.) 1988, U.of Bradford MPhil(Peace Studies) 1990. **Experience:** res.in envl sust.& econ.growth. **Career:** Gen.Sec. Green Party 1979–82, Dir The Other Econ. Summit, New Economics Fndn 1985–7; Res.F. U.of Bradford 1979–90; Res.Dir 1987–92 & Spec.Adv. Rt Livelihood Award; Res.F. Birkbeck Coll.1990–. **Achievement:** dev.of sust.dev. thinking & policy. **Memberships:** ISEE, EAEPE, SID. **Publications:** *The Living Economy* (Ed.) 1986, *A New World Order* 1992, *Wealth Beyond*

Measure (co-Author) 1992, *Real-life Economics* (co-Ed.) 1992. Favours pers.pub.& news media support. **Languages:** English, French, Italian. Willing to act as consult.etc. **Address:** 42 Warriner Gardens, London SW11 4PU, England, UK. **Tel.**(office) 44 171 631 6526, (home) 44 171 720 4973; **fax** 44 171 498 8183.

EL-DEEN HAMED, Dr Safei, *see* HAMED, Dr Safei EL-DEEN.

EL KASSAS, Senator Professor Dr Mohamed, *see* KASSAS, Senator Professor Dr Mohamed EL.

EL MEHDI HAFIDI, Moulay, *see* HAFIDI, Moulay EL MEHDI.

EL MOGHRABY, Professor Dr Asim I., *see* MOGHRABY, Professor Dr Asim I. EL.

'El moneim' Maher ALI, Professor Dr Abd, *see* ALI, Professor Dr Abd 'El moneim' Maher.

ELKINGTON, John Brett. Environmental consultancy, sustainable development, new technology (particularly biotechnology). Director (twice), Editor. *B*.23 June 1949, Padworth, Berkshire, England, UK. British. *M*.Elaine M.: 2 *d*. **Education:** Bryanston Sch., U.of Essex BA (Hons)(Sociol.& Social Psych.) 1970; UCL MPhil (Urban & Regnl Planning) 1974. **Experience:** envl consult., assessment, auditing; corporate strat.; tech.assessment; product life-cycle mgmt. **Career:** appointments in industrial & market res.1970–72, Assoc.& Sr Planner, TEST 1974–8; Founder–Editor of ENDS Report, MD ENDS Ltd.1978–83; Ed.Biotech. Bull.1982–; Dir, John Elkington Assocs 1983–; Founder– Dir, SustainAbility Ltd.1987–. **Achievements:** Cttee Memb. BP Chairman's Envl Award, and ACCA Envl Reporting Awards; Council Memb. ELF, IEM, WRI; Patron NEF. **Memberships:** F.Inst.of Dirs, F.RSA, RTPI, Strat.Planning Soc. **Awards:** Winston Churchill F.1993, Global 500 Roll of Honour (UNEP) 1989. **Publications:** since 1987 incl.*The Green Capitalists* 1987, *Green Pages: The Business of Saving the World* 1988, *The Green Consumer Guide* 1988, *The Green Consumer's Supermarket Shopping Guide* 1989, *The Young Green Consumer Guide* 1990, *A Year in the Greenhouse* 1990, *The Green Business Guide* 1991, *Holidays That Don't Cost the Earth* 1992; reports (from 1987) incl.*The Shrinking Planet: US Info.Tech.& Sust.Dev.*1988, *Cleaning Up: US Waste Mgmt Tech.and Third World Dev.*1989, *The Envl Audit* 1990, *Automotive Polymers: Issues and Views in Europe* 1990, *The Green Wave* 1991, *The Corporate Envlists: Selling Sust.Dev., But Can They Deliver?* 1992, *Coming Clean: Corporate Envl Reporting — Opening Up for Sust.Dev.?* 1993, *The LCA Sourcebook: A Euro.Business Guide to Life-Cycle Assessment* 1993, *The Corporate Envt Report* 1993; + num.envl audit reports. Favours pers.pub.& news media support. **Languages:** English, French (reasonable). Willing to act as consult.etc. **Address:** 1 Cambridge Road, Barnes, London SW13 0PE, England, UK.

ELLIS, Dr Peter Robin. Breeding pest-resistant varieties of horticultural crops, insect–plant relationships; non-chemical & integrated pest control. Research Leader. *B*.13 Oct.1940, Sutton Coldfield, England, UK. British. *M*.Peggy Doreen: 2 *d*.incl.Katie Louise (envl sci.). **Education:** Bishop Vesey's Grammar Sch.; Aston U. BSc(Hons)(Zool.& Bot.) 1964; U.of London MSc 1967, PhD 1970. **Experience:** res.— 30 yrs on pest control in hort., lecturing, admin. **Career:** Res.Leader, HRI (Sussex) 1964–70 and Entomol.Dept HRI (Warks) 1970–; sabbs at Cornell U.1978 & Crop & Food Res.(NZ) 1993; Hon.Lect. U.of Birmingham 1980–, Vis.Lect. U.of Zaragoza 1989–; Convener IOBC WG on Breeding for Resistance to Insects & Mites. **Achievements:** Convener IOBC WG, dev.of moderately-resistant carrot variety to carrot fly. **Memberships:** F.RES, M.IHort., AAB, RHS, Alpine Gdn Soc. **Awards:** Clarence Elliott Mem. Prize (Alpine Gdn Soc.) 1988, Sr Scientist F'ship (NATO) 1978. **Publications:** *Pest[s] & Diseases of Alpine Plants* 1993, three chapters, 100 addit. **Languages:** English, French (poor). **Address:** Horticulture Research International, Wellesbourne, Warwickshire CV35 9EF, England, UK. **Tel.**44 1789 470382.

ELLISON, Gabriel. Conservation through art. Independent Artist. *B*.23 Sept.1930, Lusaka, Zambia (then Northern Rhodesia). Zambian. *M*.Anthony Ellison. **Education:** in Rhodesia & England. **Experience:** studied in private studios in UK as an artist. **Career:** Head of Graphic Art & Exhibition Section and Chief Graphic Artist, Northern Rhodesian/Zambian Govt 1960–74; Ind.Artist 1974–. **Achievements:** book illustrations, illustrator of most of Zambia's postage stamps since 1964, exhibitions of wildlife & envl paintings, murals, sculptures. **Memberships:** F. of RSA, Brit.Display Soc., and Chartered Soc.of Designers. **Awards:** MBE, Grand Officer of the Order of Distinguished Service (Zambian Govt). **Publications:** Zambian postage stamps since 1964; illustrations in books incl.*Common Birds of Zambia* 1990, *Common Mammals of Zambia* 1991, *Common Amphibians & Reptiles of Zambia* 1994, *Rare Birds of Zambia* 1995. Indiff.to pers. pub., favours news media support. **Language:** English. Further details may be obtained from *Who's Who in S.African Art* 1989, *d'Art Africain contem Porain* 1992–4. Willing to act as consult. etc. **Address:** Box 320122, Leopards Lane, Lusaka, Zambia. **Tel.**260 1 261378.

ELMES, Dr Graham Wakely. Social insect ecology, ant/butterfly interactions, population ecology, insect conservation, rare species conservation. Principal Scientific Officer. *B*.7 Nov.1943, Dorset, England, UK. British. *M*.Jennifer Elizabeth: 2 *d*. **Education:** U.of London BSc 1968,

PhD 1975, DSc 1993. **Experience:** 35 yrs' res., carried out full range of contract work & consulting undertaken by ITE, entire career has been spent with Brit.Public Service at res.& cons.instns. **Career:** Asst 1961–4, Jr Sci.1965–73, Brit.NC; Jr Sci. 1974–81, PSO 1982–, ITE. **Achievements:** IUCN Ant SG (Chairman), Founder of Social Insect SG, res.& cons.of the endangered species of Maculinea butterflies. **Memberships:** BES, F.RES, IUSSI. **Publications:** 50+ scientific papers incl.Queen nr as an adaptable trait: evidence from wild pops of two red ant species (genus *Myrmica*)(co-Author) 1990, Complexity of species cons.in managed habitats: interaction between Maculinea butterflies and their ant hosts (co-Author) 1992, Specialized searching and the hostile use of allomones by a parasitoid whose host, the butterfly *Maculinea rebeli*, inhabits ant nests (co-Author) 1993. Indiff.to pers.pub., favours news media support. **Languages:** English, French (spoken & written elementary, reading moderate). Willing to act as consult.etc. **Address:** Institute of Terrestrial Ecology, Furzebrook Research Station, Wareham, Dorset BH20 5AS, England, UK. **Tel.**(office) 44 1929 551518, (home) 44 1929 553651; **fax** 44 1929 551087.

ELTRINGHAM, Dr Stewart Keith. Wildlife conservation; ecology & conservation of large mammals in East Africa. Lecturer in Zoology. *B*.21 June 1929, Edgerton, Alb., Canada. British, Canadian. *M*.Susan: 2 *d*. **Education:** U.of Southampton BSc 1954, PhD 1957. **Experience:** wildlife res.in Africa, Canada, & UK. **Career:** Pilot/Biol.Wildfowl Trust 1957–61; Lect.in Zool. King's Coll.London 1962–7; Dir Nuffield Unit of Trop.Animal Ecol. Uganda, Dir Uganda Inst.of Ecol., and Chief Res.Officer, Uganda Nat.Parks 1967–73; Lect.in Applied Biol.(1972–89) and in Zool.1989–, U.of Camb. **Achievements:** dir of wildlife res.in Africa, Assoc.Ed.*African J.of Ecol.,* memb.of Edl Bds of several other socs' journals. **Memberships:** F. IBiol., EAWS, BES, Wildlife Soc.(USA), ZSL. **Publications:** *Life in Mud & Sand* 1971, *The Ecol.& Cons.of Large African Mammals* 1979, *Elephants* 1982, *Wildlife Resources & Econ. Dev.*1984, *The Illustr.Enc.of Elephants* (Ed.) 1991; num.scientific papers & articles. Dislikes pers.pub.& news media support. **Languages:** English, French (read), Swahili (fading). Further details may be obtained from *Who's Who in Brit.Sci.*, Writers' Directory. Willing to act as consult.etc. **Address:** Department of Zoology, University of Cambridge, Downing Street, Cambridge CB2 3EJ, England, UK. **Tel.**(office) 44 1223 334455, (home) 44 1223 27652; **fax** 44 1223 336676.

ENGELMAN, Robert. Environment, population, natural resources, sustainable development. Programme Director. *B*.22 Aug.1951, Washington, DC, USA. American. Father Dr Gerald Engelman, agricl economist with USDA.

M.Colleen Corder: *d*.   **Education:** U.of Chicago, BA(Phi Beta Kappa) 1973; Columbia U.Grad.Sch.of Journalism, MSc 1976. **Experience:** envl journalism. **Career:** Reporter, The *Kansas City Times* 1979–82; Legislative Asst to Senator Nancy Landon Kassebaum (Republican, Kansas) 1983; Reporter, Scripps Howard Newspapers 1983–91; Dir, Pop.& Envt Prog. Pop. Action Intl 1991–. **Achievement:** Founder of US Soc.of Envl Journalists. **Membership:** US Soc.of Envl Journalists (Hon.). **Award:** Pulitzer Travelling F'ship (Columbia U.) 1976. **Publications:** incl.*Sustaining Water: Pop.and the Future of Renewable Water Supplies* 1993, *Stabilizing the Atmos.: Pop., Consumption and Greenhouse Gases* 1994, *Conserving Land: Pop. and Sust.Food Prod.*1995 (reports), Pop.Prospects (in press). Favours pers.pub.& news media support. **Languages:** English, French (some), Portuguese (some), Spanish. Further details may be obtained from US *Who's Who in the E.* Willing to act as consult.etc. **Address:** Population Action International, 1120 19th Street NW, Suite 550, Washington, District of Columbia 20036, USA. **Tel.**1 202 659 1833; **fax** 1 202 293 1795.

ENTWISTLE, Dr Andrew Robert.   Plant pathology, epidemiology of soil-borne plant pathogens, ornamental horticulture. Project Leader. *B*.20 Oct.1944, Coventry, England, UK. British. Father Donald Entwistle, res.organic chem., uncle Philip Entwistle, res.entomol. **Education:** King Henry VIII Grammar Sch., U.of Manchester BSc(Bot.) 1966, Queen's U.Belfast PhD(Mycology & Plant Path.) 1970. **Experience:** res.in soil-borne diseases of plants; admin. as Sec.*Allium* White-rot Group 1979–, and prin.co-Org.of four intl workshops on *Allium* White-rot; consult.in Egypt 1979–80 & Mexico 1992, 1994; extramural teaching. **Career:** Project Leader, Dept of Plant Path.& Weed Sci.1970–, HRI; Lect. Sci.in Gardening, Univs of Birmingham & Warwick 1978–88. **Achievements:** dev.of quarantine field-unit to screen fungicides to control soil-borne diseases, discoveries of control of *Allium* White-rot by seed & stem-base treatments with fungicide, and loss of control of *Allium* White-rot by enhanced degradation of fungicide in soil. **Memberships:** AAB, BMS, BSPP. **Publications:** *Pests & Diseases of Alpine Plants* (co-Author) 1993, Root Diseases 1990; *c*.50 res. papers. **Languages:** English, French (some), Spanish (intermediate). Willing to act as consult.etc. **Address:** Department of Plant Pathology & Weed Science, Horticulture Research International, Wellesbourne, Warwickshire CV35 9 ET, England, UK. **Tel.**44 1789 472031; **fax** 44 1789 470552.

ESCOBAR RAMIREZ, José Jairo, *see* **RAMIREZ, José Jairo Escobar.**

ESTÁCIO, Antônio Júlio Emerenciano. Conservation and improvement of Macau Green Areas. Chief, Agrarian Department. *B*.3 May 1947, Bissau, Rep.of Guinea-Bissau. Portuguese.

M.Ilda Bela S.C.: 2 *d*.   **Education:** Escola Nacional de Agricultura, Curso de Regente Agrícola (Engenheiro Técnico Agrário) 1964–67. **Experience:** resp.for Green areas in Macau & in Câmara Municipal das Ilhas, and for the annual Macau Green Week (15–21 March, 1982–86). **Career:** Technic in Missão de Estudos Agronómicos do Ultramar 1972–76, and in Missão de Estudos Cartográficos de Macau 1976–79; Chief, Serviços Florestais e Agrícolas de Macau 1979–85; Dep.Mayor 1986–93, Chief Agrarian Dept.1993–, Câmara Municipal das Ilhas (Macau). **Achievements:** participated in IUCN XVth GA (1981), IIIrd World Park Cong.(Bali) 1982, Green Forum (Osaka) 1986, Seminary of Envl Educ.(Israel) 1988, and in some tech. training in Portugal. **Memberships:** Liga para a Protecção da Natureza, IUCN Comms.on Educ.& NPPA, SPNI. **Award:** Citation (Govt of Macau) 1991. **Publications:** *Flora da Ilha da Taipa, Monografia e Carta Temática 1978, Flora da Ilha de Coloane* 1982, *Dinâmica das Zonas Verdes na Cidade de Macau* 1982, *Arborização em Macau* 1985, *Jardins e Parques de Macau* 1993. Dislikes pers.pub.& news media support. **Languages:** English (fair), French (good), Guiné-Bissau dialect (good), Portuguese, Spanish (medium). Willing to act as consult.etc. **Address:** Av.Coronel Mesquita 2H, Macau, *via* Hong Kong. **Tel.**(office) 853 328278, (home) 853 383449; **fax** 853 328271.

Eung-Bai SHIN, Professor, *see* **SHIN, Professor Eung-Bai.**

EVERETT, Dr Rodney David.   Permaculture design & teaching, ecological farming and building consulting, living gently on the Earth, green living. Manager. *B*.22 Jan.1951, Blackpool, England, UK. British. *M*.Jane: *d*. **Education:** UCNW BSc(Zool.) 1973, U.of York DPhil(Cons.Eval.) 1978, Permaculture Inst. Dip.Perm.DES 1992. **Experience:** teaching — adult educ., zool., permaculture, living gently, native trees, ecol.bldgs; charity — admin.mgmt, & fund-raising; organic farming — sheep & vegetables to Soil Assn standards; farm design and urban permaculture design consult.; Nature Reserve mgmt plans; practical — design & bldg of passive solar envly-friendly bldgs, woodland mgmt, creating Nature trails, rec.survey. **Career:** taught zool.at La Trobe U. Australia 1974; var.short-term contracts 1978–79; mgmt plans, Cumbria Naturalist Trust 1980; organic farming in Lancs., founded/managed Middle Wood Charitable Trust, taught at Univs of Liverpool and Lancaster, founded & managed 'green' training courses at Middle Wood, consult.in permaculture and organic gardening 1981–. **Achievements:** founding Middle Wood Charitable Trust, with demn of organic farming & gardening, low energy & envlly-friendly bldg and native woodland mgmt. **Memberships:** BES, Permaculture Assn, Middle Wood Trust (Trustee). **Publications:** num.papers. Favours pers.pub.& news media support. **Language:**

English. Willing to act as consult.and run permaculture training courses. **Address:** Middle Wood, Roeburndale West, Lancaster LA2 8QX, England, UK. **Tel.**44 15242 21880.

FAEGRI, Professor Dr Knut. Ecology, palynology. Retired. *B*.17 July 1909, Norway. Norwegian. *M*.Nancy: *s., d.* **Education:** Univs of Oslo & Bergen, Dr Philos.; U.of Stockholm, guest student. **Experience:** academic, sci.& admin., nat.& intl. **Career:** Professor of Systematic Bot. U.of Bergen 1946–79. **Achievements:** Pres.of W. Norway's Nature Cons. Orgn, u.teaching. **Memberships:** among many others, Pres.IUBS. **Awards:** Knight Commander, R.Order of St Olaf; Dr Philos.*h.c.* (U.of Uppsala); *c*.25 nat.& intl awards, hon.& invited m'ships of scientific socs etc. **Publications:** *Norges Planter* (two vols) 1958–60, 2nd edn 1970, *Spices in the Kitchen and in World Hist.*(in Norwegian) 1966 (Swedish transl.1968), *Textbook of Pollen Analysis* (Polish transl.1978) (4th edn) 1989, *Principles of Pollination Ecol.* (3rd edn) 1979 (Russian transl.1982); 450 others. Positive attitude re.pers.pub.& news media support. **Languages:** English, French (some), German, Norwegian etc, Spanish (some). Further details may be obtained from num.works of ref.incl.*Who's Who in the World* 1991, *Dict.of Intl Biog.* Willing to act as consult.etc. **Address:** Botanisk Institutt, Allegt 41, 5007 Bergen, Norway. **Tel.**(office) 47 55 213345, (home) 47 55 256570.

FAIZI, Shahul. Biodiversity, international environmental policy. Consultant Ecologist. *B*.25 May 1960, Poruvazhy, Kerala, India. Indian. Father T.Shahul Hameed, rural dev. *M*.Nazeema Beevi (energy cons.). **Education:** U.of Madras, MSc(Bird Pop.Ecol.) 1984. **Experience:** intl envl policy, UN envl negns, prot.areas dev., intl NGO mgmt, field ornith. **Career:** Field Biol. BNHS 1981–2; ind.field studies 1985; World Sec. IYF for Envl Studies & Cons.1986 8; Consult.Ecol. NCWCD 1988–. **Achievements:** contribn towards formulating s.perspective on biodiv., catalysed formation/strengthening of several NGOs in Asia & Africa, policy advice on cons.issues to NCWCD, successful campaigns for prot.of some wetlands and Silent Valley rain-forest in India. **Memberships:** IUCN SSC, SID, ISWA, ESI, etc. **Awards:** Youth F'ship (UNESCO) 1987, Mother India Intl Award [Non-Resident Indian Inst. (New Delhi)] 1992. **Publications:** 30+ essays & res.papers. Does not appreciate pers.pub., favours objective news media support. **Languages:** Arabic (poor), English, Hindi (fair), Malayalam, Tamil (fair), Urdu (fair). Willing to act as consult.etc. **Address:** National Commission for Wildlife Conservation and Development, POB 61681, Riyadh 11575, Kingdom of Saudi Arabia. **Tel.**966 1 441 8700; **fax** 966 1 441 0797.

FARAGÓ, Dr Tibor. International environmental issues, societal problems of conservation & sustainability, environmental science–policy,

climate change, natural hazards. Counsellor & Head of Global Environment Office. *B*.9 Dec. 1948, Budapest, Hungary. Hungarian. *M*.Judit Szebenyi: 2 *s*. **Education:** Leningrad U. BSc (Math.) 1972, PhD(Geophys.) 1987; Eötvös Lórand U. MSc(Math.) 1979; Hungarian AS PhD(Geog./Met.) 1987. **Experience:** res.in climatology, applied math.& mathl stats, participation in intl envl coopn & interdisc.studies. **Career:** Researcher, Hungarian Res.Inst.of Telecomm. 1972–4; Researcher & Head of Climatological Dept then Dir of Met.Inst. Nat. Met.Service 1974–92; Couns.& Head of Global Envt Office, Hungarian Min.for Envt & Regnl Policy 1992–. **Achievements:** assisting dev.of climatological res.& applications, contribn to intl negns on climate change sci.and convs and their use at nat.level, assisting interdisc.coopn & public awareness in field of envl prot., its intl issues & societal aspects. **Memberships:** HMS (Bd 1975–); Met.Sci.Cttee of Hungarian AS — Sec. GARP Subcttee 1976–80 and Sec. Climate Subcttee 1990–93; Climate Inst.(USA)(Bd of Adv.1991–), Nat.Cttee for UNCED (Sec. Climate Subcttee 1991–2), UNEP (Sci.Adv.Cttee, World Climate Impacts & Response Strats Prog.1992–), NCAR (USA)(Adjunct Sci. Envl & Societal Impacts Group 1993–), INCFCCC (VC WG I 1993–), Hungarian Comm.on Sust. Dev. (Sec.1993–), Edl Bd *Idojaras* (Weather). **Awards:** Outstanding U.Studies (Hungarian Min.of Educ.) 1973, Farkas Gyula Award (Bolyai János Mathl Soc.) 1976, Róna Zsigmond Award 1985, and Scientific Pubn 1991 (HMS). **Publications:** 70 incl.*Conv.on Biol.Div.*(co-Ed.) 1992, *Energy Use and Carbon-dioxide Emissions in Hungary and in The Netherlands* (co-Author) 1994, *Common Future of Envt and Soc.*(co-Ed.) 1994, *Intl Convs on Envl Prot.*(co-Author) 1994. **Languages:** English, Hungarian, Russian. **Address:** Hungarian Ministry for Environment and Regional Policy, Fö utca 44–50, H-1011 Budapest, Hungary. **Tel.**& **fax** 36 1 201 4091.

FARID, Dr Mohyeddin A. Vector control programmes, malaria eradication. Retired. *B*.4 June 1912, Helwan, Egypt. Egyptian. *M*. Samira. **Education:** U.of Cairo MD 1936, Dipl. in Trop.Med.& Hygiene 1941; Johns Hopkins U. MPH 1947, DrPH 1948. **Experience:** res.in above subjects, teaching at u.level, consult.in malaria control. **Career:** Med.Officer 1936–7, Res.Asst 1938–40, Asst Deptl Head 1941–6, Min.of Health; Project Team Leader — Malariologist 1949 & Epidemiologist 1950–54 both in Lebanon, Regnl Adv.1955–61, 1964–5, 1966–8, Office Chief 1962–3 & 1969–72, WHO. **Achievements:** envl methods in malaria control incl.engg, biological & naturalistic methods; contributing papers to Arabic monthly magazine Dev.& Envt. **Memberships:** WHO Expert Panel in Malaria, STM. **Award:** Darling Intl Prize in Field of Malaria (WHO) 1980. **Publications:** The Malaria Prog.from euphoria to anarchy 1980, The Aswan High Dam Dev.

Project 1975, Irrigation & Malaria in Arid Lands 1976; 20+ other scientific papers. Favours news media support. **Languages:** Arabic, English, French (good). Willing to judge proposals &/or ref.papers. **Address:** 7 Chemin Taverney, 1218 Grand-Saconnex, Geneva, Switzerland. **Tel.** (home) 41 22 798 1821.

FAULKNER, Hon.James Hugh. Environment and development. Executive Director, Vineyard Owner. *B.*9 March 1933, Montreal, Canada. Canadian. *M.*Jane Ellen: 2 *s., d.* **Education:** McGill U. BA 1956, IMI MBA 1957. **Experience:** parliamentary (public policy & govt progs dealing with envt & dev.issues), new business dev., lecturing. **Career:** Memb.of Canadian Fed.Parliament (Chairman, Labour & Employment Cttee of House of Commons, Canadian delegation to UNGA, Dep.Speaker of the House of Commons) 1965–79; Memb.of PM Trudeau's Govt & Queen's Privy Counsellor (Sec.of State, Minister of State for Sci.& Tech., Minister of Indian Affairs & Northern Dev.) 1972–9; Vis.Lect. McGill Bronfman Sch.of Mgmt and Vis.Prof. U.of Ottawa 1979–81; VP for Envt, Occupational Health & Safety, Alcan Aluminium Ltd 1981–3; MD Indian Aluminium Co. 1983–7; Exec.-in-Residence, IMI 1987 & 1988; Pres. Alcan Aluminium SA 1987–90; Sec.-Gen. ICC 1989–90; Exec.-in-Residence, IMD 1990; Exec.Dir, Business Council for Sust.Dev. 1990–; Owner, Le Grand Cros 50-ha vineyard 1990–. **Awards:** PC (Govt of Canada), Medals from Paris & Macon (re.wine-prod.). **Languages:** English, French. **Address:** Business Council for Sustainable Development, Case Postale 365, 1215 Geneva 15, Switzerland. **Tel.**41 22 788 3202; **fax** 41 22 788 3211.

FAZAL, Anwar. Consumer protection, lifestyles, community organizing, networking, training, urban management, toxic chemicals' control. Regional Director. *B.*15 July 1941, Perak, Malaysia. Malaysian. *M.*Mahmuda: *s., d.* **Education:** U.of Malaya, BA(Hons)(Econ./Business Admin.) & Postgrad.Dipl.in Educ.1961–4. **Experience:** consulting, govt admin., teaching. **Career:** Asst City Mgr, City of Penang 1965–72; Dir, Penang Dev.Corpn 1973–4; Dir IOCU 1974–91; Regnl Dir, Asia Pacific 2000 (UNDP) 1992–. **Achievements:** estab.of Consumer Interpol and Pesticide Action Network. **Awards:** Global 500 Roll of Honour (UNEP) 1988, Rt Livelihood Award, Envl Hall of Fame (*Mother Earth News*), Activist of the Yr (*Multinat.Monitor*). **Publications:** *The A to Z of the Consumer Movement* 1990, *Consumer Lifelines* 1991, *Consumer Educ.* 1991, *Consumer Prot.* 1991. Indiff.to pers.pub.& news media support. **Language:** English. Willing to act as consult. etc. **Address:** POB 1117, 10840 Penang, Malaysia. **Tel.**604 658 4816; **fax** 604 657 2655.

FEARNSIDE, Professor Dr Philip Martin. Human carrying capacity; causes, rates, & impacts, of tropical deforestation; 'greenhouse' gas

emissions;   impacts of hydroelectric dams. Research Professor. *B.*25 May 1947, Berkeley, CA, USA. American (Perm.Resident of Brazil). *M.*Neusa Hamada (entomol.): 2 *d.* **Education:** Colorado Coll. BA(Biol.) 1969; U.of Michigan, MS(Zool.) 1973, PhD(Biol.Sci.) 1978. **Experience:** res.in Brazilian Amazonia 1974–6 & 1978–; Pres. Cons.Food & Health Fndn 1985–; Res.Assoc. Chicago AS 1983–; Edl Bds *Climatic Change, Global Envl Change, Environmental Conservation, Mitigation and Adaptation Strats for Global Change, Amazônia Brasileira em Foco.* **Career:** Vol.(fisheries mgmt, India) US Peace Corps 1969–71; Teaching Asst, U.of Michigan 1972–4; F. Resources for the Future 1975–6 & Inst.of Envl Qual.1976–8; Res.Prof. Dept of Ecol. INPA 1978–. **Achievements:** study of human pops & deforestation on Osa Peninsula, Costa Rica, which contributed to decree of Corcovado Nat.Park 1972, studies of human carrying capacity, deforestation, & dev., in Amazonia 1974–, Founder of Ecol.Res. Reserve, Ouro Preto do Oeste (Rondônia). **Memberships:** Brazilian NAS (Corres.) 1993–, Brazilian Soc.for the Progress of Sci.(Counc. 1990–95) 1978–. **Awards:** Phi Beta Kappa 1969; Nat.Ecol.Prize (Brazil) 2nd 1988, shared 1st 1989; Global 500 Roll of Honour (UNEP) 1991. **Publications:** incl.Human Carrying Capacity of the Brazilian Rainforest 1986, Human Occupation of Rondonia (in Portuguese) 1989, The Balbina Hydroelectric Dam (in Portuguese) 1990, Hydroelectric dams in the Brazilian Amazon as sources of 'greenhouse' gases 1995. Indiff.to pers.pub., favours news media support. **Languages:** English, French (spoken), Hindi (spoken), Portuguese, Spanish (spoken). Further details may be obtained from Pew Scholars in Envt & Cons.'Green Pages' 1984, *Marquis Who's Who,* Intl Biogl Center. Willing to act as consult.etc. **Address:** Instituto Nacional de Pesquisas da Amazonia, CP 478, 69.011-970 Manaus-Amazonas, Brazil. **Tel.**55 92 643 3314; **fax** 55 92 236 3822.

FEDOROV, Professor Dr Vadim D. Ecology, hydrobiology, physiology of microorganisms. Professor & Chair of Hydrobiology. *B.*30 April 1934, Volsk, Saratov Region, Russia. Russian. *M.*Alla M.: *s.*Vadim V.(Cand.of Sci.[Biol.], staff memb.Inst.of Oceanogr.Russian AS), *d.* **Education:** Moscow SU PhD(Biol.) 1957, DSc(Biol.) 1970. **Experience:** res.— var.incl.phyto-plankton, functioning of cell communities (prognosis & mgmt of their productivity), biol.monitoring as a system of controlling reaction of biotic component of ecosystem to poll.of envt; teaching gen.hydrobiol.& ecol.and aquatic microbiol.; annual expedns to White Sea. **Career:** Res.F. Chair of Hydrobiol.1957–62, Head Lab.of Physiol.& Biochem.of Algae 1962–73, Head (Prof.) & Chair of Hydrobiol.1973–, Moscow SU. **Achievements:** first to plan multiple-factor experiments in studies of natural pops of micro-Algae. **Memberships:** All-Russian Hydrobiol. Soc.; Scientific–Tech.Bd of Min.of Nature, Russian Fedn; Union of Writers, Russian Fedn. **Awards:** Order of Honour of USSR, Hon. Memb. Duke U., Hon.Citizen of Houston. **Publications:** *Man & Biosphere* (book series, Ed.) 1972–, *Manual of Educl Methods of Studies in Phytoplankton* 1978, *Ecol.Manual* 1980, Ed. *J.of Biol.Scis,* 200+ major papers, 5+ children's books. Indiff.to pers.pub.& news media support. **Languages:** English (better at written), Russian. Further details may be obtained from the *Biographical Dict.* Fac.of Moscow SU. Willing to judge proposals. **Address:** Department of Biology, Moscow State University, Lenin [formerly Sparrow] Hills, Moscow 119 899, Russia. **Tel.**7 095 939 4505 or 3326.

FEICK, Ms Jenny L. Environmental citizenship, practical applications of ecologically-sustainable development, ecosystem & protected areas' management, environmental education and heritage interpretation. Chief. *B.*29 Dec.1954, Kitchener, Ont., Canada. Canadian. Father Milton Feick, mother Annie Rebecca (Hall) both of whom ran a private business in landscaping/hort.; nephew Robert Feick, ecotourism in Carib. *M.*Chris Junck (Educ. Prog.Coord., Calgary Zoo). **Education:** Ont. Scholar 1972; U.of Calgary BSc(Hons) 1977, M.of Envl Design (Envl Sci.) 1994. **Experience:** vol.activities in envl, cons., & social justice, groups, field-level positions in nat.parks in Canada from Newfoundland to BC working in communications, planning, res.and mgmt, regnl office position incl.work on developing & implement-ing Canada's Green Plan for a Healthy Envt *plus* strat.planning efforts. **Career:** 16 yrs with Parks Canada in interpretation, communications, planning, & mgmt; Chief, Heritage Interpretation, Western Regn, Envt Canada, Parks & Service; currently on leave of absence conducting res.in social sci. related to links between attitudes, values & behaviour as they apply to principles of sust. living; leads eco-tours for WestCan Adventure Tours Ltd to w.Canada, E.Africa, and other overseas destinations. **Achievements:** init.& coordinated recycling prog.for paper, cardboard, tin cans, & bottles, in Kitchener, Ont., which became the Blue Box Prog.; worked on the 'Save Nose Hill' campaign which resulted in the estab.of the largest municipal park in Canada in Calgary, Alb.; init.the Gt Divide Trail Assn dedicated to the vol.construction & maintenance of a long-distance hiking/horseback trail in the Canadian Rockies; init.the Friends of Mt Revelstoke & Glacier (a cooperating assn supporting envl educ.& rec.in nat.parks); Green Plan implementation work; Prin.Investigator for Earthwatch Centre for Field Res.'Mtn Town with a Vision' project. **Memberships:** IUCN CEC, VC Secretariat of Heritage Interpretation Intl, CSEB, CPWS, FoE, NC Canada, WWF. **Awards:** Ont.Medal of Good Citizenship, Commonwealth Medal, Grad.Students' Award (Fac.of Envl Design). **Publications:** *The Great Divide Trail: Banff to Waterton, A Planning and Developmental Manual* 1976, Marine interpret-ation potential at Terra Nova Nat.Park 1985, Planning to improve service to visitors in Canada's Nat.Parks 1989, The Jolly Green Giant reaches out: delivering envl messages in Canada's Nat.Parks and Historic Sites 1992, Revelstoke's vision: will it help achieve sust.dev.? 1993. Favours pers.pub.& news media support. **Languages:** English, French, Spanish (basic). Willing to act as consult.etc. **Address:** 3123 47th Street SW, Calgary, Alberta T3E 3X2, Canada. **Tel.**(office) 1 403 249 8226, (home) & **fax** 1 403 249 8226.

FENGE, Dr Terence Alfred Edward. Industrial development and environmental planning & management in Yukon, Northwest Territories, Nunavut, and the Arctic circumpolar world; rights & interests of aboriginal peoples; political development in the circumpolar Arctic, aboriginal self-government in Canada; protected areas, marine policy. Executive Director. *B.*14 March 1950, London, England, UK. British, Canadian. *M.*Wendy Lee: *s.,* 2 *d.* **Education:** U.of Wales BSc(Hons) 1973, U.of Vic.MA 1976, U.of Waterloo PhD 1982. **Experience:** teaching envl studies, regnl geog., aboriginal rights & interests, to both undergrad.& grad.levels; tech.eval.of envl issues for Inuit (Eskimo) & Dene in n.Canada; directed res.for negotiation of Inuit Land-claim in the NWT, oversaw operation of CARC, incl.fundraising, issue definition, staff supervision, publishing prog.etc. **Career:** Lect. Capilano Coll. Vancouver 1976–7; Asst Prof. Brock U.1980–82; Res.Dir 1982–6, Exec.Dir 1992–, CARC; Res.Dir Tungavik Fedn of Nunavut 1986–92. **Achievements:** directed res.and assisted in negotiating the Inuit land-claim agreement through which a new territory (Nunavut) is to be created, three nat.parks are to be estab.and a new regime is to be put in place to manage nearly 1.5 m.sq.miles (2,413,950 sq.km) of land & ocean; assisted in defining the 136,000 sq.miles (218,865 sq.km) of land in the Arctic, by far the most biologically productive, that Inuit now own. **Membership:** Bd, Canadian Circumpolar Inst. U.of Alberta. **Publications:** *Hinterland or Homeland: Land Use Planning in Northern Canada* 1987; *Nunavut: Pol.Choices and Manifest Destiny* 1989; 20 major & 40 addit. Indifferent to pers.pub., favours news media support. **Languages:** English, French (poor), Inuktitut (little). Willing to act as consult.etc. **Address:** Canadian Arctic Resources Committee, Suite 412 1 Nicholas Street, Ottawa, Ontario K1N 7B7, Canada. **Tel.**(office) 1 613 236 7379, (home) 1 613 729 7009; **fax** 1 613 232 4665.

FENNER, Professor Dr Frank. Infectious diseases of humans and animals, biological control of animal pests, conservation of biodiversity. Visiting Fellow. *B.*21 Dec.1914, Ballarat, Victoria, Australia. Australian. Father Charles Albert Edward Fenner, geologist, geographer, educationalist. *M.*Ellen Margaret Bobbie: *d.* **Education:** U.of Adelaide MD 1942. **Experience:**

res.— virology, microbiol., biol.control; admin.— Dir of res. schools 1967–79, Chairman WHO Global Comm.for the Certification of Smallpox Eradication 1980; teaching — PhD, virology and envl studies. **Career:** Med.Officer, Australian Imperial Forces 1940–46; Res.F. Walter & Eliza Hall Inst.1946–8; Prof.of Microbiol.1949–67 and Dir 1967–73, John Curtin Sch.of Med.Res.; Prof.of Envl Studies and Dir Centre for Resource & Envl Studies, ANU 1973–9. **Achievements:** VP ACF 1971–3; Member SCOPE 1971–6; Ed.-in-Chief, SCOPE Pubns 1976–80; estab. Fenner Confs on the Envt (Australian AS) 1988–. **Memberships:** F.Australian AS 1954, F.RS 1958, US NAS (Foreign Assoc.) 1977. **Awards:** MBE(Military Div.) 1944, MD *(h.c.)* (Monash U.) 1964, Britannia Australia Prize 1967, CMG 1976, Stuart Mudd Award 1986, Japan Prize 1988, AC 1989, Dr *h.c.*(U.of Liège) 1992. **Publications:** 16 books incl.*Myxomatosis* (co-Author) 1965, *Human Monkeypox* (co-Author) 1988, *Smallpox and its Eradication* (co-Author) 1988, *Hist.of Microbiol.in Australia* (Ed.) 1990. Indiff.to pers.pub., favours news media support. **Language:** English. **Address:** John Curtin School of Medical Research, Australian National University, GPO Box 334, Canberra 2601, Australia. **Tel.**(office) 61 6 249 2526, (home) 61 6 295 9176; **fax** 61 6 247 4823.

FERMOR, Dr Terence Robert. Mushroom science, composting, microbial ecology, bioremediation. Senior Research Scientist. *B*.3 Aug. 1950, Pembury, England, UK. British. *M*. Catherine Margery: 2 *s.*, *d*. **Education:** Maidstone Grammar Sch.; U.of Aston in Birmingham BSc(Hons)(Biol.Scis) 1971, PhD 1975. **Experience:** 20 yrs' on mushroom sci.and composting. **Career:** Researcher, Intl Biodeterioration Inst. 1971–5; Sr Researcher in Mushroom Sci.and Bioremediation, HRI (Sussex) 1975–94 & HRI (Warks) 1994–. **Achievements:** basic res.on microbial ecol.of compost systems. **Memberships:** BMS, SGM. **Publications:** *c*.50 on mushroom sci.incl.Compost as a Substrate and its Preparation (co-Author) 1985, Bacteriolysis by *Agaricus bisporus* (co-Author) 1991, Applied aspects of composting and bioconversion of lignocellulosic materials: an overview 1993. Dislikes pers.pub.& news media support. **Languages:** English, French (basic), Spanish (basic). Willing to act as consult.etc. **Address:** Microbial Biotechnology Department, Horticulture Research International, Wellesbourne, Warwickshire CV35 9EF, England, UK. **Tel.**44 1789 470382; **fax** 44 1789 470552.

FERNANDO, Dr Ranjen Lalith. Conservation of natural habitats, tropical forests and their fauna & flora, and the Sri Lankan wild elephant; creating awareness of significance & necessity to protect ecosystems & biodiversity; educating & encouraging youth on environmental protection. President. *B*.7 April 1939, Colombo, Sri Lanka. Sri Lankan. *M*.Preethi (envl educ.for schoolchildren): *d*.Ranmali Waduge (Sec.Wildlife Soc.).

Education: U.of Ceylon, MD 1965; U.of London, Dipl.in Anaesthetics 1973; self-educated in fields of envl scis, biodiv., ecol., watershed mgmt, soil cons., trop.forestry. **Experience:** tech.— eval.of and successfully changing Forestry Master Plan (World Bank & FINNIDA) for Sri Lanka 1986, evaluated progress of US–AID-sponsored Envl Prot.Prog. in Sri Lanka, formulated/sponsored/participated in conducting biol.surveys in ecolly-sensitive nat.parks, wetlands, and forest reserves; admin.— Pres. WNPS of Sri Lanka 1984–, adv.& consult.to several statutory bodies & steering cttees; consult.— reorgn of admin. infrastructure of Dept of Wildlife Cons.Sri Lanka. **Career:** Colombo Gen.Hosp. Consult. Anaesthetist 1976– as well as devotion of all leisure and free time to Nature cons.in Sri Lanka; held num.hon.offices in WNPS since 1968 culminating as Pres.in 1984; served on var. statutory & steering cttees 1968–. **Achievements:** changing the For.Master Plan for Sri Lanka 1986; arresting dev.of coal-powered thermal generator plan 1987; organizing & sponsoring 300+ school Nature clubs in Sri Lanka to educate youth on sig.of envl prot. **Memberships:** IPPL (Hon.), F.RCA, FFPS (Hon.), Envl Fndn of Sri Lanka. **Award:** Global 500 Roll of Honour (UNEP) 1992. **Publications:** Forest Cons.& Forestry Master Plan for Sri Lanka — A Review 1989; several papers in *Bionews* and *Sri Lanka Wildlife*. Indifferent to pers.pub., favours news media support. **Languages:** English, Sinhala. Willing to judge proposals. **Address:** 10 Daniel Avenue, Colombo 5, Sri Lanka. **Tel.**(office) 94 1 325248, (home) 94 1 501842; **fax** 94 1 580721 attn Dr R.Fernando.

FÉRON, Dr Eric Maurice. Wildlife conservation, sustainable development, rural development; biodiversity, community-based conservation. Project Manager. *B*.11 April 1963, Fria-Kimbo, Republic of Guinea. French. **Education:** U.of Edinburgh, MSc 1988; U.of Lyons, Docteur Vétérinaire 1989. **Experience:** res.in epidemiology, admin., consult., humanitarian aid, dev.projects, work with NGOs. **Career:** co-Founder & Dir, Vetaid (UK & Mozambique) 1988–90; Asst Project Mgr, Communal Areas Goat Res.(Zimbabwe) 1989–90; Consult. Campfire and French Min.of Foreign Affairs (Zimbabwe) 1990–91; Country Rep.(Zambia), IUCN 1991–2; Wildlife and Livestock Project Mgr, Centre du Coopn Internationale en Recherche Agronomique pour le Développement–Elevage et Médecine Vétérinaire Tropicale (Zimbabwe) 1992–. **Memberships:** IUCN SSC and Vet.SG, SA & Zimbabwe Vet.Assns' Wildlife Groups, RCVS. **Awards:** Ordre des Vétérinaires 1987, 1988, Fondation pour la Vocation–Promotion (Pres.de la République de Guinée) 1989. **Publications:** incl.Current importance of trad.hunting and major contrasts in wild meat consumption in sub-Saharan Africa (co-Author) 1993, New food sources and sust.

dev.1994. Indiff.to pers.pub., favours news media support. **Languages:** English, French. Willing to act as consult.etc. **Address:** Centre du Coopération Internationale en Recherche Agronomique pour le Développement, Box 1378, Harare, Zimbabwe. **Tel.**(office) 263 4 722850, (home) 263 4 744618; **fax** 263 4 722850 or 744618.

FERRAR, Anthony 'Tony' A. Tropical (savanna) resource ecology, wildlife management, ecological research, environmental education, conservation organization administration. Executive Director. *B.*22 Jan.1942, Lechlade, Glos., England, UK. British, S.African. *M.* Susan Valerie: 2 *s.*, 2 *d.* **Education:** U.of Natal BSc (Agric.) 1965, U.of Rhodesia MSc(Ecol.) 1973. **Experience:** 18 yrs' field res.& mgmt, eight yrs' res.coordn & admin., three yrs' as CEO of major NGO, some consulting. **Career:** Rhodesian/ Zimbabwean NPS 1966–81; Mgr Ecosystems Progs CSIR SA 1981–9; Chief Ecologist, Bophuthatswana Nat.Parks 1989–91; Exec.Dir WSSA 1991–. **Achievements:** involved at leading edge of cons.& envl educ.in s.africa for last 20 yrs thereby contributing to local progress in this field. **Memberships:** FPS (UK, Life), SAIE & SAWMA (Founder). **Publications:** several SA Red Data Books (Ed.) 1981–8, *Ecol.& Mgmt of Biological Invasions in SA* (co-Ed.) 1986; num. other CSIR pubns. Indiff.to pers.pub.& news media support. **Language:** English. Willing to act as consult.etc. **Address:** The Wildlife Society of South Africa, POB 44189, Linden 2104, Republic of South Africa. **Tel.**(office) 27 11 482 1670, (home) 27 11 789 5181; **fax** 27 11 482 2436.

FIELD, Hermann Haviland. Architecture and environmental planning, historic preservation, managing own 200-acres' wildlife protected area; public service at global & local levels in environmental issues. Chairman. *B.*13 April 1910, Zürich, Switzerland. American. Father Dr Herbert Haviland Field (deceased, intl zool. and pacifist). *M.*Kate: 2 *s.*, *d.*Alison (Founder & Director of INITIATIVES, E.Africa's leading envl publishing house). **Education:** Harvard U. BA(Fine Arts) *cum laude* 1933; Harvard Grad. Sch.of Design 1932–4; Swiss Fed.Poly.Inst. (ETH), Dipl.Arch.1936. **Experience:** init.& admin.of u.grad.dept, dir of major dev.projects. **Career:** Resident Arch. Commonwealth HQ of Roche Products 1936–9; refugee admin.in Krakow, Poland, and in England, for Czech Refugee Trust Fund; Dir — project to develop new downtown centre for Western Reserve U., and Planning Office of Tufts U.New England Med. Center 1947–72; init.& administered Tufts U. Graduate Dept in Urban & Envl Policy 1972–8. **Achievements:** estab.of first truly interdisc., interdeptl, envl prog.at Tufts U.; service on IUCN CEP (now CESP); service in Histl Comm., Cons.Comm., Planning Board, all in Mass. **Memberships:** F.AIA, IUCN, Global Tomorrow, AICP, Boston Soc.of Arch., Mass Assn of Cons.Comms. **Awards:** Envl Leadership (New England Envl Network), Envl Service (Mass

Assn of Cons.Comms), Preservation (Mass Historical Comm.). **Publications:** incl.*Sustaining Tomorrow* (co-Author) 1984. Accepts pers. pub., favours news media support. **Languages:** English, German. Further details can be obtained from *Who's Who in Amer.*1996. Willing to act as consult.etc. **Address:** 110 Center Road, Shirley, Massachusetts 01464, USA. **Tel.**1 508 425 4587; **fax** 1 508 425 4332.

FILHO, Dr Walter Leal. Environmental education, environmental information in industrialized & developing countries. Head of Environmental Education & Centre Director. *B.*26 March 1965, Salvador, Bahia, Brazil. Brazilian, Portuguese. *M.*Kirsten: *s.*, 2 *d.* **Education:** U. of Bahia BSc(Biol.)(First Class) 1985, U.of Bras. Dipl.of Specialist Envl Educ.1986, U.of Bradford PhD 1990, U.of Hamburg Post-doct.in Envl Info.1991. **Experience:** res.— var.projects on envl educ.& dev. issues; admin.— coord.of Master's, doctl & post-doctl progs on envl educ.; teaching — intl envl educ. and Third World issues. **Career:** Lect. U.of Hamburg 1990–92; SRF 1992–, Chair, Res.Unit on Envl Educ.& Dev.1992–, Dir of Euro.Res.Centre on Envl Educ.& Dev. 1993–, U.of Bradford. **Achievements:** youngest doctl degree holder (25 yrs) at U.of Bradford, prep.of Nat.Envl Strat.for UNCED, init.envl educ.centre in Bangladesh, Fndn of Euro.Res.Unit on Envl Educ.& Dev. **Memberships:** Scientific F.ZSL, CBiol. IBiol.(UK), BES, NT, ADSTW, BSAS. **Award:** First Prize on Contemporary Lit. (Brazil) 1985. **Publications:** *Ecol.& Educ.* 1987, *Key Issues in Envl Educ.*1992, *Envl Educ. in the Commonwealth* 1993, *Trends in Envl Educ.Worldwide* 1993; num.refereed & conf. papers. Favours pers.pub.& news media support. **Languages:** English, French, German, Italian (basic), Portuguese, Spanish. Willing to act as consult.etc. **Address:** Department of Environmental Science, University of Bradford, Bradford, West Yorkshire BD7 1DP, England, UK. **Tel.**(office) 44 1274 733466, (home) 44 1274 385259; **fax** 44 1274 384231.

FISCHER, Dr Gert Roland. Environmental conservation, autochthonous tropical forest management & conservation; soil recovery agriculture and forestry biological pest control. Independent Consultant. *B.*24 May 1937, Joinville, SC, Brazil. Brazilian. *M.*Maria de Lourdes: 2 *s.*, *d.* **Education:** Nat.Agron. High Sch. Agron. 1959; Planzenschutzampt (Ahlem-Hannover) PhD 1961. **Experience:** res.& tech.— nine yrs in S.Brazil on Atlantic Forest species, soil recovery on 75 ha in Guaramirim, SC 1979–, and sponsor & planner for Fed.U.of SC and SC State Govt; consult.— USDA–FAO Forest Service, World Bank/Intl Fin.Corpn; teaching — Prof. invited by Universidad Nacional de Colombia 1990. **Career:** organized first Silviculture enterprise 1969; planning & plantation admin.of 1,200 ha using fed.taxes 1970; consult.& planning to produce 210 small projects totalling

2,200 ha and 5.5 m.trees, all in SC; consulting & planning to produce 89 projects in States of SC, Par.& RS, totalling 3,500 ha and 8.5 million trees 1972; organized forest enterprise using fed.taxes to manage 1,200 ha in Paraná and 1,700 ha in SC 1973, and another using fed.taxes whose biggest project of 600 ha was estab.in Guaraquecaba–Paraná in 1974; Consult.on envl & forestry contracts with 53 cos 1975–. **Achievements:** founded & was elected first Pres.of Aprem–SC (an envl NGO) 1977, joined in Pan-Pesticides Action Network 1982, represented Brazil at Pan-intl mtgs in The Netherlands 1984, Canada 1986, and Ecuador (2nd Latin-Amer.) 1989, init.& coord. Dirty Dozen Campaign, Brazil 1985, received title of Senator Jr Chamber Intl 1987, attended on invitation from CATIE a coordinated project on Sust.Forests' Mgmt covering Costa Rica, Panama, Honduras, Guatemala & Belize 1992, contracted by Pronatura as Adv.1993. **Memberships:** BTS, BSTA, Organic Growers Assn, Agronomist Assn of State of SC, ISTF Inc.(USA), Envt & Balance Preserv.Assn of State of SC (Founder 1977), Engineer Assn of SC, Greenpeace Brazil. **Awards:** Global 500 Roll of Honour (UNEP) 1989. **Publications:** *Mangrove — Can We Save It?* 1983, *Sust. Native Forests Mgmt* 1987, *Less Poison in the Dishes — Alternative to Pesticides* 1993; *Informativo Madeireiro e Florestal* 1982–5, monthly newsletter *INFOPAN* 1982–. **Languages:** English, German, Portuguese, Spanish. Willing to act as consult.etc. **Address:** POB 947, Joinville, Santa Catarina 89201-972, Brazil. **Tel.** (office & home) 55 474 360647; **fax** 55 474 260649.

FITTER, Mrs Alice Mary 'Maisie' S. Editing journals on wildlife conservation. Retired. *B.*5 Dec.1912, Abbey Town, Cumberland, England, UK. British. *M.*Richard S.R.Fitter *qv*: 2 *s.* Julian R.*qv*, Alastair H.(biol.), *d.* **Education:** Greenhead High Sch.; Bedford Coll.(U.of London) BA 1934. **Career:** Edl Staff, *The Countryman* 1946–53; Ed.*Oryx* 1964–82; Ed. *Species* 1983–9. **Awards:** Order of the Golden Ark 1978, Memb.of Honour (IUCN SSC) 1988. **Address:** Drifts, Chinnor Hill, Chinnor, Oxfordshire OX9 4BS, England, UK. **Tel.**(home) 44 1844 351223.

FITTER, Julian Richmond. Conservation of island & marine ecosystems and ecocomplexes. Independent Financial Adviser, Trust Chairman. *B.*5 April 1944, Huddersfield, Yorks., England, UK. British. Father Richard Fitter *qv*, mother Alice M.Fitter *qv*, brother Alastair Hugh Fitter (biol.). *M.*Anna Catriona (Hon.Sec. Galápagos Cons.Trust): 2 *s., d.* **Education:** Leighton Park Sch. 1957–62. **Experience:** resident of Galápagos Islands 1964–79, worked on Falkland Islands 1979–81. **Career:** Ind.Yacht Charterage, Galápagos Islands 1965–79; Dev.of tourism industry 1979–82, Trustee 1979–, First Sec. 1980–82, Falkland Cons., Falkland Islands; Ind. Fin.Adv.(UK) 1981–; Chairman, Galápagos

Cons.Trust 1995–. **Achievements:** assisting in estab.of Falklands Cons.1979– and its continuing dev., strong involvement in Penguin Appeal 1993–5; estab.of Galápagos Cons.Trust (first Chairman) 1995. **Publications:** two chapters re.Galápagos. Favours pers.pub.& news media support. **Languages:** English, French (halting spoken), Spanish. Willing to act as consult.etc. **Address:** Butt of Sherry, The Commons, Shaftesbury, Dorset SP7 8JU, England, UK. **Tel.**(office) 44 1747 853380, (home) 44 1258 472748; **fax** 44 1747 855131; **e-mail** 100427.3012@composerve.com .

FITTER, Miss Perin Savakshaw. Tree planting, catchment approach to soil conservation, promotion of tree nurseries in primary & secondary schools. Volunteer & Founder. *B.*24 Aug.1948, Eldoret, Kenya. British (Kenyan Residence). **Education:** U.of Poona, BSc 1969. **Experience:** teacher-cum-envl conservationist, sharing progs with Perm.Presidential Comm.on Soil Cons.& Afforestation, Soil & Water Cons. Branch, within the Mins of Agric., Envt & Natural Resources, and Educ. **Career:** Teacher-cum-Patron of Wildlife Clubs of Kenya 1969– 79; Western Kenya Regnl Coord. Wildlife Clubs of Kenya 1980–86; Founder, Envt Cons.Vols Project 1987–. **Achievement:** through soil cons.sems for teachers some schools have initiated successful projects *e.g.*Manywanda Primary Sch. Kisumu Dist. **Award:** Global 500 Roll of Honour (UNEP) 1992. Favours pers.pub.& news media support. **Language:** English. **Address:** Kenya Youth Environment Conservation Project, POB 1690, Kisumu, Kenya. **Tel.**(office) 254 35 21079, (home) 254 35 44240.

FITTER, Richard Sidney Richmond. Field identification and writing field guides on, especially, birds & vascular plants. Retired. *B.*1 March 1913, Streatham, London, England, UK. British. *M.*Alice Mary S.*qv*: 2 *s.*Julian R.*qv*, Alastair H.(biol.), *d.* **Education:** Eastbourne Coll., LSE BSc(Econ.) 1933. **Career:** Pol.& Econ.Planning 1936–40; Mass-Observation 1940–42; Operational Res.Section, Coastal Command 1940–45; Sec.Wildlife Cons. Spec. Cttee 1945–6; Asst Ed. *The Countryman* 1946– 59; Dir Intelligence Unit, Council for Nature 1959–63; Open Air Corres.*The Observer* 1958– 66. **Memberships:** LS, ZSL, FFPS (Hon.Sec., VC, Chairman, VP 1987–) 1964–, Falklands Cons.(Hon.Sec.1979–82, Trustee 1979–94), IUCN SSC (Chairman, Steering Cttee 1975–88), WWF-UK (Trustee 1977–83). **Awards:** Silver Jubilee Medal 1977, Order of the Golden Ark 1978, Roll of Honour (IUCN SSC) 1988. **Publications:** *London's Natural Hist.*1945, *Wildlife for Man* 1986; num.field guides on birds & wild flowers. Indiff.to pers. pub., favours news media support. Further details may be obtained from Brit.*Who's Who* 1973–. **Address:** Drifts, Chinnor Hill, Chinnor, Oxfordshire OX9 4BS, England, UK. **Tel.**(home) 44 1844 351223.

FLETCHER, Raúl E. Conservation, environmental planning in protected areas. Conservation Director. *B*.6 Mar.1955, Panamá City, Panama. Panamanian. *M*.Valentina (BA[Biol.], marine areas): *s., d*. **Education:** U.of Kharkow (Russia), MSc(Biol.) 1981. **Experience:** cons., res., admin. **Career:** Directorate of Nat.Parks, Nat. Inst.of Natural Resources 1982–6; Asst Dir Cons.& Sci.1986–92, Cons.Dir 1992–, ANCON. **Achievements:** harmonized the relationship between private & public sectors. **Membership:** Colegio de Biologos (Panamá). Favours pers. pub., indiff.to news media support. **Languages:** English, Russian, Spanish. Willing to act as consult.etc. **Address:** Asociación Nacional para la Conservación de la Naturaleza, Apartado 1387, Panamá 1, Republic of Panama. **Tel.**(office) 507 64 8100, (home) 507 60 8455; **fax** 507 64 5990.

FLINT, Professor Dr Vladimir E. Biology of birds & mammals, endangered species, wildlife conservation strategy, captive breeding, sustainable use of wildlife. Head of Department. *B*.14 March 1924, Moscow, Russia. Russian. *M*. Tatiana: 2 *s*. **Education:** Moscow SU, BSc (Biol.) 1953, PhD 1959, DSc 1972. **Experience:** 45 yrs' field-work in tundra & desert, taiga–forest & steppe in Siberia, C.Asia and other parts of the former USSR. **Career:** Jr Researcher, Dept of Transmissive Animal Diseases, Inst.of Epidemiology & Microbiol. 1953–69; Sr Researcher, Zool.Museum, Moscow SU 1969–75; Head, Dept of Wildlife Cons. Russian Res. Inst.of Nature Cons.1976–. **Achievements:** init. of prot., cons., & sust.use, of wild animals on modern level in Russia; Regnl Counc. IUCN 1991–4, Dep.Chairman IUCN SSC 1991–, IOC 1978–, VP USSR Ornithol. Soc.1983, Pres.of Russian Bird Cons.Union 1993 . **Memberships:** BOU 1985– (Hon.), Whooping Crane Cons.Assn 1987– (Life), RRF 1992–, RANS (Academician) 1991. **Awards:** Order of 'Friendship between Peoples' (USSR) 1981, Order of the Golden Ark 1985, Audubon Medal 1987, Global 500 Roll of Honour (UNEP) 1987. **Publications:** over 500 incl.*Die Zwerghamster der Palaarktischen Fauna* 1966, *The Structure of Pops of Small Mammals* (in Russian) 1977, *A Field Guide to Birds of the USSR* 1984, *Captive Breeding of Endangered Birds* (in Russian) 1986. Favours pers.pub.& news media support. **Languages:** English, German, Russian. Willing to act as a consult. **Address:** Research Institute of Nature Conservation, Znamenskoye-Sadki, Moscow 113628, Russia. **Tel.**(office) 7 095 423 0322, (home) 7 095 938 0656; **fax** 7 095 423 2322.

FOGG, Professor Dr Gordon Elliott. Phytoplankton ecology, polar biology. Emeritus Professor of Marine Biology. *B*.26 April 1919, Langar, Notts., England, UK. British. *M*.Elizabeth Beryl (memb.N.Wales Wildlife Trust): *d., s*. Timothy (karst cons.in Ireland). **Education:** Dulwich Coll.; QMC London, BSc 1939; St Johns Coll.Camb. PhD 1943, ScD 1966. **Experience:** res.in pest control, freshwater & marine biol., antarctic biol. **Career:** Asst, Seaweed Survey of Brit.Isles, MBA 1942; Plant Physiol. Pest Control Ltd (Camb. UK) 1943–4; Asst Lect., Lect. & Reader in Bot. UCL 1945–60; Prof. of Bot. Westfield Coll.London 1960–71; Prof.of Marine Biol.1971–85, Emer.1985–, UCNW. **Achievements:** basic res.on weed-killers, physiol. of Cyanobacteria, physiol.ecol.of phytoplankton, biol.of shallow-sea tidal fronts. **Memberships:** F.RS 1965, IBiol.(Pres. 1976– 7), FBA (Chairman of Council 1974–85), RCEP 1979–85, Trustee of Natural Hist.Mus.1976–85 and R.Botanic Gdns 1983–9. **Awards:** Hon. LLD (U.of Dundee) 1974, F.QMC (now QMWC) 1976, CBE 1983. **Publications:** incl. *Algal Cultures and Phytoplankton Ecol.*(3rd edn, co-Author) 1987, The Explorations of Antarctica (co-Author) 1990, *A Hist.of Antarctic Sci.1992, A Critical Appraisal of the Biomass Prog.*1994. Dislikes pers.pub.& news media support. **Language:** English. Further details may be obtained from Brit.*Who's Who* 1995, Debrett's *People of Today* 1995, The *Writers' Directory* 1995. Willing to act as consult.etc. **Address:** Bodolben, Llandegfan, Anglesey, Gwynedd LL59 5TA, Wales, UK. **Tel.** (home) 44 1248 712916; **fax** 44 1248 716367.

FONSECA, Professor Dr Gustavo A.B. Wildlife conservation & management, biodiversity conservation, interdisciplinary approaches to biodiversity conservation & sustainable development. Professor of Zoology. *B*.25 Oct. 1956, Belo Horizonte, MG, Brazil. Brazilian. **Education:** U.of Bras. BSc(Ecol.) 1978; U.of Florida MA(Latin Amer.Studies) 1983, PhD(Wildlife Mgmt & Range Scis) 1988. **Experience:** consult.to FAO, UNDP, World Bank, GEF; u.teaching, cons.-related activities. **Career:** Biol. Brazilian Inst.of Geog.& Stats 1979–85; Prof.of Zool. Fed.U.of MG 1985– (Dir of first grad.prog.in Ecol., Cons., & Wildlife Mgmt 1988–92); Dir Brazil Prog.Cons.Intl 1991–. **Achievements:** leader in grad.educ.in biodiv. cons.& mgmt in Brazil. **Memberships:** BSZ, BSAS, Bd of Curators of Biodiversitas Fndn, memb.of several high-level scientific & govtl cttees at home & abroad. **Awards:** Travel Award (IPS), Oliver Austin Award (U.of Florida), Rodolpho von Inheringer Award (BSZ), Envl Prot.Award (State of MG). **Publications:** *c*.50 books incl.*Livro Vermelho das Espécies de Mamíferos Brasileiros Ameaçados de Extinção* (co-Author) 1993, chapters incl.Biodiv.1992, scientific & popular papers incl.The vanishing Brazilian Atlantic forest 1985, Small mammal species diversity in Brazilian trop.primary & sec.forests of diff.sizes 1989. Indiff.to pers.pub., favours news media support. **Languages:** English, French (read), Italian (read), Portuguese, Spanish. Willing to act as consult.etc. **Address:** Conservation International, Avenida Antonio Abrahão Caram 820/302, Belo Horizonte, Minas Gerais 31275-000, Brazil. **Tel.**(office) 55 31 441 1795, (home) 55 31 484 2497; **fax** 55 31 441 2582.

FONSECA, Dr Ivan Claret Marques DA. Fighting for, and defending, the environment. Ecologist, Physician & Surgeon. *B*.11 July 1938, Santo Estêvão, Bahia, Brazil. Brazilian. *M*.Leonídia: 2 *s*., 2 *d*. **Education:** U.of Bahia PhD 1964, Baiana Sch.of Medicine Doctor–surgeon 1966. **Experience:** spontaneous reforestation of trop.forest on Atlantic Coast, ambient educ.for sec.schools & univs. **Career:** since 1973 has fought for the Atlantic Coast rain-forest, and ambient educ.in sec.schools & univs; writes for newspapers & Brazilian TV. **Achievements:** founded mus.1973, built regnl Envt Mus.1990, presented 3.5 ha of land for use as an ecol.park — all three estab.in Nanuque, MG. **Memberships:** BCS, Geog.& Hist.Inst.(MG). **Awards:** Global 500 Roll of Honour (UNEP) 1990. **Publications:** 19 *books incl.Gotas Ecologica* 1991, *Meditacoes Ambientais* 1993, *Sobre a Natureza* 1993; *c*.80 papers & 26 monthly newsletters. Favours pers.pub., indiff.to news media support. **Languages:** English (poor), Portuguese (spoken), Spanish. Willing to act as consult.etc. (provided in Portuguese or Spanish). **Address:** Poços de Caldas Street, 165 Nanuque, Minas Gerais, Brazil. **Tel.**(office) 55 33 621 1366, prefers (home) 55 33 621 1506.

FORBES, Dr Bruce Cameron. Arctic biogeography, disturbance ecology. Fulbright Scholar in Arctic and Environmental Studies. *B*.17 July 1961, Boston, MA, USA. American. **Education:** St Mark's Sch., U.of Vermont BA(Envl Studies) 1984, Center for Northern Studies & Vermont Coll. Norwich U. MA(Northern Studies) 1987, McGill U. PhD(Biogeog.) 1993. **Experience:** undergrad.& grad.teaching & advising in human–envt relationships, ecol.field methods in boreal & sub-Arctic regns, cartography/airphotographic interpretation, n.studies. **Career:** Envl Cons.F. NWF 1986–7; Post-doctl Res.F.in Ecosystem Health, U.of Guelph 1993–5; Fulbright Scholar in Arctic and Envl Studies, Arctic Centre, U.of Lapland 1995–. **Achievements:** applied res.on n.forest & arctic tundra ecol.with emphasis on anthropogenic & natural disturbance regimes (Interior Alaska, Canadian Arctic Archipelago, NW Siberia), assessment of health in Canadian agro-ecosystems. **Memberships:** AAG, AINA, BES, CAG, CARC, ESA, INTECOL, IAVS, IPA, SCB, SER, Sigma Xi, Friend of NC. **Awards:** Young Investigator Russian Exchange Prog.in Arctic Ecol.(US NAS), Best Paper Prize (FEC) 1992, J.William Fulbright Scholarship in Arctic & Envl Studies 1994. **Publications:** *c*.10 incl. *Tundra Disturbance Studies* (paper series) 1992–. Favours pers.pub.& news media support only re.envl concerns. **Languages:** English, French (basic), Russian. Willing to act as consult.etc. **Address:** Arctic Centre, University of Lapland, POB 122, FIN-96101 Rovaniemi, Finland. **Tel.** 358 60 324794; **fax** 358 60 324777.

FORERO, Professor Dr Enrique. Vascular plant taxonomy, floristics, neotropics, botanical gardens, plant conservation. Director. *B*.7 Dec. 1942, Bogotá, Colombia. Colombian. **Education:** Universidad Nacional BSc(Bot.) 1965, CUNY PhD 1972. **Experience:** 25 yrs' res., u.& inst.admin., student supervision, consult.to Nat.Center for Res.on Genetic Resources (Brazil). **Career:** Dir, Colombian Nat.Herbarium 1972; Asst Prof.1973, Chairman of Bot.1973, Dir of Grad.Prog.in Systematics 1980–84, Prof. 1982–, Inst.of Natural Scis, Nat.U.; Dir of Res. Missouri Botl Gdn 1986–91; Dir, Inst.of Systematic Bot. NY Botl Gdn 1992–. **Achievements:** many public lectures, past memb.of WWF/IUCN Plants Adv.Group. **Memberships:** F.LS, IUCN SSC Plants Task Force, 17 intl & nat.scientific orgns. **Award:** Nat.Merit Award in Life Scis (Colombia) 1990. **Publications:** 54 incl.Needs and Opportunities of S.Amer.Botanic Gdns for Cons.1991, Flora Cons.in Latin Amer. with Particular Ref.to Botanic Gdns 1994. Favours pers.pub.& news media support. **Languages:** English, Portuguese, Spanish. Willing to act as consult.etc. **Address:** The New York Botanical Garden, Bronx, New York 10458-5126, USA. **Tel.**1 718 817 8628; **fax** 1 718 562 6780; **e-mail** eforero@nybg.org .

FOSTER, John. Countryside, informal recreation. Environmental Policy Consultant. *B*.13 Aug.1920, Glasgow, Scotland, UK. British. *M*. Daphne (countryside cons.): *s*., *d*.Caroline Mary (farming). **Education:** R.Tech.Coll. Glasgow 1937–40. **Experience:** Chief Exec.of a nat.park bd and a nat.countryside cons.agency (managing a multidisc.staff of planners, landscape architects, land agents, ecologists & educationalists; Memb. CNPPA 1973– and VC Western Palearctic Regn 1981–7, IUCN. **Career:** trained as Surveyor, Arch.& Planner specializing in rural/cons.aspects; Dir. PDNP 1954–68; Dir. Countryside Comm.for Scotland 1968–85; Envl Policy Consult.1985–. **Achievements:** developing & implementing policies for cons.& sust.dev.through planning & mgmt of inhabited countryside as within the PDNP & Scottish Highlands (cultural landscapes); introducing interpretation techniques to UK from USA in 1960s, and developing these, first in PDNP, as a tool for improving understanding of cons. principles by urban visitors to the countryside. **Memberships:** F.RICS, F.RTPI, RIBA (Assoc.), RIAS (Assoc.), F.RSA. **Awards:** CBE 1985, Hon.F.RSGS, Hon.Memb.IUCN CNPPA (Fred Packard Award), Hon.Memb.FNNPE, Memb.Emer. Heritage Interpretation Intl. **Publications:** num.contribns to books, periodicals, & tech.journals. Indiff.to pers.pub., favours news media support. **Language:** English. Further details may be obtained from *Dict.of Intl Biog.* 1987. Willing to act as consult.etc. **Address:** Birchover, Ferntower Road, Crieff, Perthshire PH7 3DH, Scotland, UK. **Tel.**(home) 44 1764 652336.

FOWLER, Ms Sarah L. Marine ecology & conservation, marine protected areas, coastal-zone management, elasmobranch ecology & conservation. Company Director. *B*.26 Feb. 1958, London, England, UK. British. *M*.Jonathan W.Spencer *qv.: s*. **Education:** Benenden Sch. UCNW BSc (1st Class Jt Hons Zool./ Marine Zool.) 1979, UCL MSc (Cons. Studies) 1981. **Experience:** res.— marine ecol. littoral & sublittoral surveys, surveillance & monitoring; benthic impacts of marine fish farming, cons.of elasmobranchs; tech.— Health & Safety Exec. Part IV Diver Training, Brit.Sub-Aqua Club Advanced Diver; admin.— mgmt of personnel, office & finance; consult.— advice, policy, & res., on marine ecol., cons., & coastal-zone mgmt. **Career:** Marine Ecol.& Diving Officer, NCC 1981–9; Dir The NCB Ltd 1989–. **Achievement:** work on promotion of marine cons.& coastal-zone mgmt within a UK govt adv.body and through NGOs, incl.provision of advice to Parliamentary Select Cttees; progressing elasmobranch (sharks, skates, & rays) cons. **Memberships:** IEEM, BANC, BES, BPS, ECSA, EUCC, IUCN SSC (Dep.Chair, Shark SG 1991–), MBA, MCS (elected Counc.), SUT. **Publications:** sub-Ed. & contrib.to *Directory of the N.Sea Coastal Margin,* sub-Ed.of *Whales, Dolphins & Porpoises of the World Red Data Book; c.*12 tech. papers. Generally indiff.to pers.pub.& news media support. **Languages:** English; French & Spanish (conversational). Willing to act as consult.etc. **Address:** The Nature Conservation Bureau Ltd, 36 Kingfisher Court, Hambridge Road, Newbury, Berkshire RG14 5SJ, England, UK. **Tel.**44 1635 550380; **fax** 44 1635 550230.

FOX, Allan Maitland. Park & Nature reserve management & interpretation, environmental management plans for industrial projects, writing & illustrating guide & natural history books, training & education of Aboriginal & non-Aboriginal natural-resource managers, development of ecotourism programmes. Independent Consultant, Managing Director, Executive Manager. *B*.16 March 1931, Coonabarabran, NSW, Australia. Australian. Father Oliver Stanton Fox, sch.Prin.& envl educator. *M*.Marjorie Lorraine: 3 *s*.incl.Jeffrey (Collections Mgr, Nat.Mus.NZ), Steven (Australian Heritage Comm.). **Education:** Balmain Teachers' Coll. Teacher's Cert.1949, New England U. BA (Geog., Biol., Hist.) 1976. **Experience:** 16 yrs' sch.teaching in eight jr schools and Nat.Fitness Camp Schools (envl educ.), one-yr teacher exchange to Plymouth (UK) 1957–8; admin., consult., educl. **Career:** Prin. Nat.Fitness Camp Schools 1950–65; Educ.& Admin.Officer, NSW Fauna Prot.Panel 1966–8; Chief Wildlife Officer 1969–72, Officer-in-Charge, Envl Educ. & Interpretation 1972–6, NSW NPWS; Officer-in-Charge, Training, Educ.& Info. Australian NPWS 1977–81; Ind.Consult.in Envl Mgmt & Info.1981–; Exec.Mgr, Uluru Exp.1991–; MD, Allan Fox & Assocs 1982–. **Achievements:** co-estab.of NSW NPA and *Nat.Parks J.*; reorgn of Kangaroo harvesting industry in NSW, through

writing & illustrating have created much envl awareness and a climate in politics which led to formation of var.NPWSs, estab.of techniques for producing effective Interpretive Plants, creation of transparency library for use in envl educ. pubns. **Memberships:** ACF, Heritage Interpretation Intl. **Awards:** NSW Prize for best illustrated natural hist.(RZS) 1984, Best 'Man & Envt' film *Never Stay in One Place* shown at Banff Film Festival (ABC). **Publications:** num. books incl.*Together in Social Studies* (Parts 1 & 2, sch.textbook) 1969, *Of Birds and Billabongs* 1983, *Australia's Wilderness Experience* 1984, *Kakadu Man* (co-Author) 1985, *Centenary Field Guide to S.Australia's Nat.Parks* (co-Author) 1991, *Field Guide: Mungo Nat.Park and World Heritage Area* 1993, *Nature Lover's Guide to C.Australia* (in press); num.papers & reports. Indiff.to pers.pub., finds news media support to be helpful in controversial areas. **Language:** English. Willing to act as consult. etc. **Address:** RMB 35 Beaumont Crescent, The Ridgeway, Queanbeyan, New South Wales 2620, Australia. **Tel.**(office & home) 61 6 297 3434; **fax** 61 6 297 5974.

FRANGI, Professor Dr Jean-Pierre. Environmental physics, planetary boundary layer, surface energy balance, atmospheric turbidity, microclimatology, arid climates (Sahelian environment), solar energy. Professor of Physics. *B*.25 July 1952, Marseille, France. French. **Education:** U.of Paris 7, Doctorat (Energy & Poll.) 1979; U.of Toulouse 3, Doctorat d'Etat ès Sciences 1988. **Experience:** res.— experimental studies of turbulence structure of convecting Boundary Layer, humidity & turbidity in Sahel, ground-based monitoring of spectral extinction and dusty Sahelian atmospheres, energy budget of Sahelian surface layer, solar radiation in the Sahel (solar energy), isotope characteristics of meteoric water in Sahelo–Sudanese zone, surface of the ocean (fluxes & interaction within atmos.); teaching physics at u.level. **Career:** Prof.in Phys. U.of Niamey 1979–91; Prof.in Phys. U.of Paris 7 1991–. **Achievements:** basic res.& teaching on envl phys.in developing & developed countries, solar applications to fight against desert.in Sahel. **Memberships:** CNU, Institut Universitaire Professionalisé de Génie de l'Environnement. **Award:** Prix Norbert Gerbier–Mumm (WMO) 1989*. **Publications:** *c.*30 major incl.Humidity and turbidity parameters in Sahel: a case-study for Niamey (Niger) 1983, Contribn à l'étude de l'atmosphère au Sahel 1986, Results from ground-based monitoring of vertical and horizontal spectral extinction 1986, Some specific characteristics of dusty Sahelian atmospheres 1986, *Rôle du sol dans les échanges d'énergie dans la couche de surface sahélienne 1988, Characteristics of solar radiation in the Sahel: Case-study — Niamey, Niger, 1992, Energy budget of the Sahelian surface layer 1992, Isotope characteristics of meteoric water and groundwater in Sahelo–Sudanese Africa 1992. Indiff.to pers. pub.& news media support. **Languages:** English, French. Willing to act as consult.etc. **Address:** Institut Buffon 'Environnement' T44-43 3ème étage, 2 place Jussieu, 75251 Paris Cedex 05, France. **Tel.**(office) 33 144 27 5631, (home) 33 145 47 5928; **fax** 33 144 27 5751.

FRANKIE, Dr Gordon William. Tropical ecology, applied conservation biology. NGO President, Faculty Member. B.29 Mar.1940, Albany, CA, USA. American. M.Jutta (Exec.Dir, Friends of Lomas Barbudal*). **Education:** UCB PhD(Entomol.) 1968. **Experience:** res.& teaching in entomol., natural resource mgmt, and applied cons.biol.; admin.of envl educ.prog.in Costa Rica. **Career:** Memb. Fac.of Entomol. Texas A&M U.1970–76 & UCB 1976–, Memb. Fac.of Biol.UCB 1976–, Pres. *Friends of Lomas Barbudal Inc.(NGO). **Achievements:** teaching & field res.in entomol.and applied cons.biol. with spec.emphasis on envl educ. **Memberships:** AIBS, SCB, Entomol.and Ecol.Socs of Amer., ATB. **Award:** recognition of cons.work from Costa Rican Govt. **Languages:** English, Spanish (almost fluent). Further details may be obtained from *Who's Who in Amer.*1996. Willing to act as consult.etc. **Address:** Friends of Lomas Barbudal Inc., 691 Colusa Avenue, Berkeley, California 94707-1517, USA. **Tel.**(office) 510 642 0973, (home) 510 526 4115; **fax** 510 528 0346.

FRAZER, Dr John Francis Deryk. Wildlife conservation; animal populations especially mammals, reptiles, & butterflies. Retired. B.8 March 1916, London, England, UK. British. M.Ann Mildred: 4 d. incl.Jane (field bot.& teacher). **Education:** Lancing Coll.(Exhibition in Maths); Merton Coll.Oxf. Postmaster [scholar] in Maths; Oxf.& St Mary's Hosp. BA(Hons) (Physiol.) 1949, MA 1942, BM,BCh 1942; London U. PhD 1953; U.of Oxf. DM 1955. **Experience:** res.in foetal physiol., insect toxins, animal behaviour, butterfly & newt pops in the wild; admin.& consult.positions in NC where posts occupied included Cons.Officer (England) and Head of Intl & Interpretive Branches. **Career:** House Surgeon to Prof.C.A.Pannet, St Mary's Hosp.1942–3, Med.Officer RN 1943–6, Jr–Sr Lectureships in Physiol.at St Mary's and Charing Cross Hosp.Med.Schools 1946–59, sr posts at NCC/NC (HQ) 1959–77, Org. UK exhibit, World Hunting Exhibition (Budapest) 1970. **Achievements:** Founder Chairman, Kent Trust for Nature Cons.; Sec.to Teesdale Trust Cttee; Pres. BHS 1955–82; VP First World Herpetological Cong.1989; memb.UK del.at founding mtg of CITES conv. **Memberships:** F.RES, BES, F.ZSL, Mammal Soc. (former Treas.), BHS (Hon.). **Award:** Medal (Mammal Soc.). **Publications:** *Sexual Cycles of Vertebrates* 1959, *Amphibians* 1972, *Reptiles & Amphibians in Britain* 1983. Indiff. to pers.pub.& dislikes news media support. **Languages:** English, French (fair). Willing to act as consult.etc. **Address:** Warren Farm, Boxley, Maidstone, Kent, England, UK. **Tel.** (home) 44 1622 752524.

FRAZIER, Dr John 'Jack' Gordon. Specialized training in biological conservation focusing on people in the tropics and quality control of their training and ecological work; ethics & politics in conservation of biotic & environmental resources; human ecology (= relationship between *Homo sapiens* and environment); land tortoises, marine turtles, island & coastal ecosystems. Research Associate, Professor Titular. B.29 Jan.1944, Rochester, NY, USA. American. D. Uncle Dr Donald J.Hare, geneticist (retired). **Education:** Cornell U. BSc (Zool.) 1966, U.of Oxf. DPhil(Zool.) 1973. **Experience:** teaching & public educ., field res. practically world-wide, lect., grad.student adv., film-making; num.symp., conf., sem., & lecture, presentations given, scientific collections deposited in museums in var.parts of the world. **Career:** RS Expedn to Aldabra Atoll 1968–70; Marine Park Warden, Seychelles 1973–4; Ind.Researcher on w.Indian Ocean 1972–6; Res.Assoc. Nat.Zool.Park, Smithsonian Instn 1979–; Vis.Investigator, NAS Cttee on Scholarly Communication with PRC 1985; Fulbright Scholar, Indo-Amer.Prog.1986–7; Vis.Prof. Universidad Nacional (Costa Rica) 1988–90; Profesor Titular, Centro de Investigación y de Estudios Avanzados, Instituto Politécnico Nacional 1990–. **Achievements:** studies of marine turtles and coastal habitats in the w.Indian Ocean; collabn/coordn & inspiration of sea-turtle & field biologists in Latin Amer.& w.Indian Ocean; training & inspiration of young biologists & conservationists in var.intl settings. **Memberships:** ABS, BNHS (Life), BES, BHS, Explorers' Club (F.), Herpetologists' League, IHS, INTECOL, Sigma Xi, Sociedad Herpetológica Mexicana, Societas Europaea Herpetologica, SHE, STB, SSAR, Tanzanian Soc. (Life), The Wildlife Soc., Universitarios por la Conservación de la Tortuga Marina en México AC (Founding Memb.), Wildlife Cons.Soc.of Tanzania. **Awards:** num. grants & F'ships received, Investigator Nivel III (Sistema Nacional de Investigadores, Mexico) 1992, Regular Memb. (Académia de Investigación Cientifica, Mexico) 1994. **Publications:** 100+ scientific incl.Observations on Sea Turtles on Aldabra Atoll 1971, Marine Turtles in the Seychelles and Adjacent Territories 1984, Marine Turtles in the Comoro Archipelago 1985, Intl Resource Cons.: Thoughts on the Challenge 1990; c.30 popular & educl articles; num.published reports & mss. Indiff.to pers.pub., favours news media support. **Languages:** Creole (Seychelles), English (Amer.& Brit.), French (fair), Spanish (and Argentine, Costa Rican & Mexican dialects), Swahili (fair). Willing to act as consult.etc. **Address:** Centro de Investigación y de Estudios Avanzados, Instituto Politécnico Nacional, AP 73 'Cordemex', Mérida, CP 91730, Yucatán, Mexico. **Tel.**52 99 812 960 or 942; **fax** 52 99 812 917 or 919; **e-mail** frazier&kin.cieamer.conacyt.mx .

FREIBERG, Dr Horst. Tropical silviculture, Nature conservation, plant sociology. Network Coordinator. B.29 Dec.1954, Ludwigshafen, Germany. German. M.Eva-Maria (envl educ.):

d. **Education:** U.of Munich, Dr Rer.Silv.1984. **Experience:** res.in silviculture and plant sociol.; admin. **Career:** Memb.of Forest Projects — Trop.Silviculture (Paraguay/U.of Asuncion) 1985–6 and Forest Educ.and Social For. (Guatemala) 1988–90, Forest Adv.1990–92, GTZ; Coord. ETFRN 1992–. **Achievements:** implementation of ETFRN and working contacts with EC on Trop.Forest Res. **Membership:** ISTF. Favours pers.pub.& news media support. **Languages:** English (good), German, Spanish (good). Willing to act as consult.etc. **Address:** European Tropical Forest Research Network, Bisdorfer Weg 19A, D-53332 Bornheim, Germany. **Tel.**(office) 49 228 984616, (home) 49 2222 64304; **fax** 49 228 984699.

FREIRE DA SILVA, Ricardo, *see* **SILVA, Ricardo** FREIRE DA.

FRIDRIKSSON, Dr Sturla. Genetics, ecology; biotic colonization of the volcanic island Surtsey. Emeritus Director of Agronomy, Biological Scientist. *B.*27 Feb.1922, Copenhagen, Denmark. Icelandic. *M.*Sigrún: *d.*Sigrún (biol.). **Education:** Cornell U. BA 1944, MS 1946; U.of Sask. PhD 1961. **Experience:** plant breeding, ecol.studies, volcanic is.of Surtsey 1964, genetical studies of human pop.of Iceland 1965. **Career:** Plant Breeder, Reykjavik U.Res.Inst. 1951–64; Exec.Dir, Genetical Cttee of U.of Iceland 1965–92; Head of Dept of Agron. 1970–92, Emer.Dir 1992–, Agricl Res.Inst. **Achievements:** author of first book in Iceland on ecol., studied prod.of n.ecosystems, erosion and its control. **Memberships:** NATO (eco-sci. panel, Sci.Cttee 1984–92), Societas Scientiarum Islandica (Pres.1965–7, Pres.of Award Fund 1965–). **Awards:** Decorated Knight of Icelandic Order of the Falcon, Golden Star Award (Grad. Student Soc.Reykjavik), Hon.Memb.of Life and Land (ecol.soc.). **Publications:** incl. *Ecol.in Iceland* 1973, *Surtsey: Evol.of Life on a Volcanic Is.*1975, *The Cell* (translation) 1961, *Surtsey, Ecosystem in Dev.*(in Icelandic) 1994; two books of poems 1988, 1992. Favours pers. pub. and news media support. **Languages:** Danish, English, Icelandic. Further details may be obtained from *Intl Who's Who of Intellectuals* 1978, *Who's Who in the World* 1982–3. **Address:** Skildingatangi 2, 101 Reykjavik, Iceland. **Tel.**(office) 354 577 1010, (home) 354 551 3030; **fax** 354 577 1020.

FRIEDMAN, Professor Yona. Architecture, planning, self-help survival in developing countries. Coordinator (Director). *B.*5 June 1923, Budapest, Hungary. French. *M.*Denise: 2 *d.* **Education:** Technical U. Budapest, Technion Haifa. **Experience:** member of Consulting Panel, Habitat Conf. Vancouver 1976; consult.to UNESCO. **Career:** U.Prof.at *e.g.*UCLA, MIT. **Achievements:** urban self-reliance, subsistence farming adapted to present global context. **Memberships:** IUCN CEC, WFSF, WAAS, F.RAA (The Hague). **Awards:** Grand Prize, Golden Lion (Venice Festival) 1962, Architecture Award (Berlin Acad.) 1972, PM's Prize (Japan) 1991, Habitat Roll of Honour (UN) 1992. **Publications:** *L'Architecture de Survie, Alternatives Ecologiques,* eight other books & *c.*500 papers. Indiff.to pers.pub.& news media support. **Languages:** English, French, German, Hebrew, Hungarian. Further details may be obtained from *Who's Who in Arch., Intl Writer's Who's Who.* **Address:** 33 Boulevard Garibaldi, 75015 Paris, France. **Tel.**(office) 33 14 783 2024, (home) 33 14 566 0484; **fax** 33 14 734 6911.

FRY, Professor Dr (Charles) Hilary. African & Arabian ornithology, human biology, evolution, conservation. Professor of Biology. *B.*13 Feb. 1937, Skegness, Lincs, England, UK. British. *M.*Kathleen. **Education:** U.of Camb. BA (Hons) (Zool.) 1960, MA 1963; Ahmadu Bello U. PhD 1966; U.of Aberdeen, DSc 1985. **Experience:** EIA re.Bardawil Lagoon, Sinai 1984; widely travelled, num.expedns & confs, *c.*150 pubns. **Career:** Lect.in Zool. Ahmadu Bello U. 1962–7; Lect.in Zool.and Human Ecol. U.of Aberdeen 1967–86; Assoc.Prof.then full Prof.of Biol. Sultan Qaboos U. 1986–. **Achievements:** Ed. *The Birds of Africa**, papers on bird cons.in Nigeria (late 1960s), teaching undergrad.& postgrad.courses in cons.at Sultan Qaboos U. 1988–, **Memberships:** BOU, BTO, DES, AOU, COS, WOS, AFO. **Awards:** Corres. F.(AOU), best bird book of yr** (Brit.Birds) 1992. **Publications:** *The Bee-eaters* 1984, **The Birds of Africa* (co-Ed.) Vols 2 1986, 3 1989, 4 1992, & 5 in press, ***Kingfishers, Bee-eaters, and Rollers* 1992. Indiff.to pers.pub.& news media support. **Languages:** English, French. Willing to act as consult.etc. **Address:** Department of Biology, College of Science, Sultan Qaboos University, POB 36, Al-Khod 123, Sultanate of Oman. **Tel.**(office) 968 515450, (home) & **fax** 968 513184.

FRY, Ian William. Environmental law development, advocacy, & training, environment & development assistance issues. Political Liaison Officer. *B.*10 Aug.1953, Sydney, Australia. Australian. **Education:** Canberra Coll.of Adv. Educ. BAS(Biol.) 1979, Grad.Dipl.in Media 1980; Macquarie U. MES 1991. **Experience:** lect.in cons.advocacy, wildlife mgmt; vol.res.in wildlife mgmt, Ngorongoro cons.area, Tanzania; reviewed impact of tourism in Annapurna Sanctuary, Nepal; run workshops on envl advocacy & lobbying, coordinated Aboriginal Ranger Educ.Prog. **Career:** Ranger 1973–6, Info./Educ.Officer 1981–2, NSW NPWS; Envl Consult. ABC TV 1982–; Dir, Wildlife Survival (envl NGO) 1986–7; Lect./Coord. Aboriginal Ranger Educ.Prog. Charles Sturt U. 1990–92; Pol.Liaison Officer, Greenpeace Australia 1992–. **Achievements:** co-Author of Threatened Species Habitat Prot.Act, estab.of Aboriginal Educ.Centre at Charles Sturt U. Murray Campus. **Memberships:** ICEL, IUCN CEL & SSC, Adv./Bd ACEL, UN Assn of Australia.

Publications: numerous. Favours pers.pub.& news media support. **Language:** English. Willing to act as consult.etc. **Address:** 119 Donald Road, Queanbevan, New South Wales 2620, Australia. **Tel.**(office) 61 6 257 6516, (home) 61 6 297 9054; **fax** 61 6 257 6526.

FÜLEKY, Professor Dr György. Soil fertility research, sustainable land-use, reconstruction of former environmental conditions. Professor of Agricultural Chemistry. *B*.5 Feb.1945, Ekecs, Hungary. Hungarian. *M*.Cecilia: 3 *s*.incl.Csaba (agron., biodiv.). **Education:** Eötvös Loránd U. MSc(Chem.& Phys.) 1968; U.of Agricl Scis, Dr U.1974; Hungarian AS, PhD(Soil Fertility) 1978. **Experience:** res.— new methods in soil fertility res., soil phosphorus, potassium, nitrogen, carbon cycle, fertilizer use and soil quality, long-term field experiments; admin.as deptl head and PhD prog.leader; consult.at archl sites; teaching soil sci., agricl chem., soil chem., soil fertility, fertilizer use, soil & plant analysis, to MSc & PhD levels. **Career:** Res.F. Res.Inst.for Soil Sci.and Agricl Chem. Hungarian AS 1968–83; Prof.of Agricl Chem. Dept of Soil Science 1983–, Dep.Dean of Fac.of Agricl Sci. 1987–94, U.of Agricl Scis. **Achievements:** participation in res.projects in connection with sust.agric., dev.of new testing methods for soil poll., prep.of Hungarian envl law, new techniques for envl prot. **Memberships:** Hungarian AS (Sec. Cttee for Soil Sci., Agricl Chem.and Irrigation), ISSS, CIEC, SCOPE, IRRS, Euro. Soc.for Agron.(Nat.Rep.), Edl Bd *Agrokemia es Talajtan*, Ed.-in-Chief *Bull.of the U.of Agricl Scis.* **Awards:** Youth Award (Hungarian AS) 1975, Awards from Min.of Agric. 1978 & 1981, Youth Assn 1980, and U.of Agricl Scis 1987, Treitz Peter Award 1991. **Publications:** *c*.150 incl.(in Hungarian) *The Soil* 1988, *Envl Enc.* 1993, *Future of the Envt in Hungary* (Soils) 1994, *Agro-21* (*Soil Cons.*) 1994; num.papers. **Languages:** English, German (spoken), Hungarian, Russian (spoken). Willing to act as consult.etc. **Address:** Department of Soil Science, University of Agricultural Sciences, Pater Karoly u.1, H-2103 Gödöllö, Hungary. **Tel.** (office) 36 28 310200; **fax** 36 28 310804.

FULLER, Dr Kathryn Scott. World Wildlife Fund. Fund President & Chief Executive Officer. *B*.8 July 1946, New York, NY, USA. American. *M*.Stephen Doyle: 2 *s*., *d*. **Education:** Brown U.(RI), BA(English & Amer.Lit.) 1968; U.of Texas Sch.of Law, JD(Hons) 1976; U.of Maryland, MS(Marine, Estuarine, & Envl, Scis) 1980. **Experience:** fieldwork — wildebeest behavioural studies in Tanzania 1973 and coral-reef crustacean studies in USVI 1981, legal, admin. **Career:** Res.Asst at Yale U.1968–9, ACS 1970–71, & Harvard U.Mus.of Comparative Zool.1971–3; Law Clerk in New York & Texas 1974–6 and to Chief Judge Singleton (US Distr. Court for s.Distr.of Texas) 1976–7; Attorney/Adv. Office of Legal Counsel 1977–9, Attorney 1979–80 then Chief 1981–2 of Wildlife and Marine

Resources Section, US Dept of Justice; Pres.& CEO, WWF (US) 1989–. **Memberships:** ICEL, Earth Council (Prog.Adv.Bd), num.nat. Cttees & Councils, Brown U.(Trustee), Ford Fndn (Trustee). **Awards:** outstanding Woman Law Student in Texas Scholarship 1975, Global 500 Roll of Honour (UNEP) 1990, William Rogers Outstanding Grad.Award (Brown U.) 1990, Hon.Doct.of Sci. (Wheaton Coll. IL) 1990, of Laws (Knox Coll.) 1992, and of Humane Letters (Brown U.) 1992. **Publications:** articles on wildlife law incl.debt-for-Nature Swaps 1989, Women, poverty and the earth 1991, The vital alliance 1992. **Languages:** English, French (good), Portuguese (fair read & comp.), Spanish (fair). **Address:** World Wildlife Fund, 1250 Twenty-Fourth Street NW, Washington, District of Columbia 20037-1175, USA. **Tel.**1 202 293 4800; **fax** 1 202 293 9211.

FUREDY, Dr Christine. Waste management in developing countries; community-based environmental management in Asia (urban); ecology of cities, developing countries, waste recycling, Asia. Associate Professor in Urban Studies. *B*.9 Jan.1940, Colombo, Sri Lanka. Canadian. *M*.Dr John J.Furedy. **Education:** U.of Sydney, BA(double hons, Hist.& Social Anthrop.) 1964; U.of Sussex, DPhil.(Hist.) 1971. **Experience:** u.teaching, consult.on solid waste mgmt in Asian cities for World Bank, WHO, ESCAP, UNCRD, IDRC, CIDA. **Career:** Lect.in Social Services 1969–73, Assoc.Prof.in Urban Studies 1974–, York U. **Achievements:** pioneered interest in social aspects of solid-waste mgmt in Asian cities as corrective to techno-managerial approach; researched people's attitudes & behaviours re. garbage and roles of waste-pickers & -recyclers, waste minimization. **Awards:** NSW Anthrop. Assn Prize 1964, Citation for Outstanding Contribn to U.Teaching (Ont.Confederation of U.Fac.Assns). **Publications:** incl.Social aspects of solid waste recovery in Asian cities 1990, Social aspects of human excreta reuse: implications for aquaculture in Asia 1991, Garbage: exploring non-conventional options in Asian cities 1992. Favours pers.pub.& news media support. **Language:** English. Willing to act as consult.etc. **Address:** 24 Astley Avenue, Toronto, Ontario M4W 3B4, Canada. **Tel.** (home) 1 416 924 2484; **fax** 1 416 962 4253.

FUTRELL, Professor J. William. Environmental law. Institute President. *B*.6 July 1935, Alexandria, LA, USA. American. *M*.Iva: *s*., *d*. **Education:** Tulane U. BA 1957, Free U. Berlin postgrad.1958, Columbia U. LLB 1965, Louisiana Bar 1966. **Experience:** widespread lecturing on envl law. **Career:** Attorney, Lemle & Kelleher, New Orleans 1966–71; Prof.of Law, U.of Alabama 1971–4 & U.of Georgia 1974–80; Pres. Envl Law Inst.1980–. **Achievements:** envl educ.& teaching, drafting law. **Memberships:** AAAS, Phi Beta Kappa, Woodrow Wilson F. Smithsonian Instn DC 1978–80, Sierra Club San Francisco (Pres.1977–8, nat.Bd of Dirs

1971–81), ABA, ALI, Phi Beta Kappa, Order of Coif 1972, Cosmos Club. **Publications:** Sust. Envt Law 1993. Favours pers.pub. & news media support. **Languages:** English, German, Spanish (good). Willing to act as consult.etc. **Address:** Environmental Law Institute, 1616 P Street NW Suite 200, Washington, DC 20036, USA. **Tel.**(office) 1 202 328 5150, (home) 1 703 522 0247; **fax** 1 202 328 5002.

GADE, Professor Dr Daniel W. Past & present ecological relationships of peasant & folk societies, vegetation change especially deforestation through historic time; process of plant & animal domestication, ethnobiology, settlement & disease. Professor of Geography. *B*.28 Sept. 1936, Niagara Falls, NY, USA. American. *M* Mary· *s* **Education:** Valparaiso U. AB 1959, U.of Illinois AM 1960, U.of W–M MS 1961, PhD 1967. **Experience:** res. — fieldwork in Peruvian Highlands, Bolivia, Paraguay, Brazil, Argentina, Ethiopia, Madagascar, and Rodrigues; admin.— Overseas Dir, U.of Nice; consult.to Library of Cong. **Career:** Prof.of Geog. U.of Vermont 1966–; F. U.of Pittsburgh 1985, Cornell U.1987, & John Carter Brown Library 1988. **Achievements:** conceptualizing ways of understanding process of deforestation in the Andes & on Madagascar. **Memberships:** AAG, AGS, IMS, Soc.for Ethnobiol., SEB, Conf. of Latin Americanist Geographers. **Awards:** Fulbright Award 1983 & 1993, US– Spanish Jt Cttee for Cultural & Educ.Coopn 1988–9. **Publications:** *Plants, Man & the Land in the Vilcanota Valley of Peru* 1975, *Handbook of Latin Amer.Studies* (contributing Ed.) 1987–, Corres.(from USA), *Bibl.Géographique Internationale* and *Cahiers de Géographie du Québec* 1992–5, Bd of Eds The Camb.Hist.& Culture of Human Nutrition Project 1990–, *Annals of AAG* 1993–; 71 papers. Accepts pers.pub., favours news media support. **Languages:** English, French, German (read), Italian (read), Portuguese, Spanish. Further details may be obtained from *Who's Who in the East* 1992, *Amer.Men & Women of Sci.*1991. Willing to act as consult.etc. **Address:** Department of Geography, University of Vermont, 112 Old Mill Building, Burlington, Vermont 05405-0114, USA. **Tel.** (office) 1 802 656 3060, (home) 1 802 862 4751; **fax** 1 802 656 8429 attn Gade ext 63060.

GAKAHU, Dr Christopher Gatama. Conservation biology, ecotourism; research, application & policy development. Conservation Biologist. *B*.15 Sept.1951, Muran'ga, Kenya. Kenyan. *M*.Alice. **Education:** U.of Nairobi, BSc(Hons) (Ecol.& Animal Behaviour) 1976, PhD(Cons. Biol.) 1983. **Experience:** res.— ecosystem monitoring, structure, and dynamics, savanna ecosystems, ecotourism, visitor attitudes, impact mgmt & carrying capacities of parks; u.teaching; project dev.mgmt & fund-raising; consult.at nat. & intl levels; policy dev.& intl duties in cons. and linking envt to sust.dev. **Career:** Grad.Asst/ Lect. U.of Nairobi 1979–85; Sr Lect. & Head Dept of Wildlife Mgmt, Moi U. 1985–8, Cons.

Biol. Wildlife Cons.Intl 1988–. **Achievements:** init.u.training prog.in wildlife mgmt; pioneering all aspects of ecotourism in Kenya and founding ESK. **Memberships:** IUCN SSC, EAWS, NCST, ESK. **Publications:** Res.Needs for Sust.Wildlife Use 1991, African Rhino: Current Numbers & Distribn 1991, Visitor Dispersal Strats in Ecotourism Mgmt: The Case of Maasai Mara Nat. Reserve Kenya 1992. **Languages:** English, Swahili. Willing to act as consult.etc. **Address:** Wildlife Conservation International, POB 62844, Nairobi, Kenya. **Tel.** (office) 254 2 221699, (home) 254 2 721401; **fax** 254 2 215969.

GALAZY, Acad. Dr Grigory Ivan. Ecology of water & land communities, limnology, geobotany. Academician, Department Head, Consultant. co-Director. *B*.5 Mar.1922, Kharkovskaya Distr., Ukraine. Ukrainian. *M*.Alevtina Vasily: 2 *s*. **Education:** Irkutsk SU, Cand. 1952, Dr 1968, of Biol.Scis. **Experience:** orgn & direction of Limnol.Inst., admin., creation of Russian AS scientific fleet (ten ships) on L.Baikal. **Career:** Dir, Baikal Limnol.Station, USSR AS 1954–61; Dir, Limnol.Inst. Siberian Branch of USSR AS 1961–87; Dir 1987–93, Consult.1993–, Baikal Ecol Mus.; co-Dir, Intl Limnol.Inst. 'Tacho– Baikal' 1991–; Head, Pribaikal Dept of Ecol. Res.1993–. **Achievements:** basic res.— the estimation of poll impact on Baikal and its tributaries, negative results of anthro-pogenous impact; compilation of Baikal Atlas which contains landscape maps; monitoring of poll.in L.Baikal and impact of water level of Lake on growth of woody plants; determination of warming of climate in n.hemisphere which began more than 5,000 yrs ago. **Memberships:** SIL, Hydrobiol.Soc.of Russia (VP 1975–), Russian Geogl Soc., 'Tacho–Baikal' Inst. **Awards:** Award of Presidium (USSR AS) 1954, Humbelt 1964 & Lomonosov 1975 Medals, Globul 500 Roll of Honour (UNEP) 1987. **Publications:** c.290 incl.*Baikal Atlas* (c.400 maps) 1993. **Languages:** English (better as spoken), Russian, Ukrainian. Willing to act as consult.and/or discuss proposals. Further details may be obtained from *Large Soviet Enc.*1971, *Enc.Britannica* 1974. **Address:** Department of Ecological Research of Pribaikal, Lermontov Street 281, 664033 Irkutsk, Russia. **Tel.**(office) 7 395 2 460324, (home) 7 395 2 334483; **e-mail** galazy@bem.irkutsk.su .

GALLON, Gary T. Environmental policy development, environmental association– and organization–building, environmental assessment, public participation. Association President. *B*.1 Oct.1945, CA, USA. Canadian. *M*.Janine Ferretti (Exec.Dir Poll.Probe Canada): 2 *d*. **Education:** Bakersfield Coll. AA 1966, Calif.SU Northridge BA (Sociol.) 1968, Canadian Investment Dealers' Assn Courses I & II (Hons) 1970. **Experience:** co-authored one of Canada's first sch.primers & workbooks on poll.1970, estab.one of first series of vol.community recycling depots in N.Amer. (BC) 1971–5, analysed & developed policy on W.Coast oil-spills and arctic oil & gas exploration & pipelines, helped develop community envl progs in developing countries, co-created roundtables on envt & economy in Canada to meet requirements of Brundtland Comm., contributed to dev.of systems for adopting envl econ. **Career:** Memb.of Founding Bd of Dirs, Greenpeace Intl 1971–2; Exec.Dir SPEC (BC) 1973–7; co-Founder, FoE Canada 1976–7; Exec. Dir ELCI 1977–81; Chair, UN NGO Conf.on New & Renewable Sources of Energy 1981; co-Coord. Probe Intl Canada 1982; Sr Policy Adv.to Minister of Envt, Govt of Ont.1985–90; Pres. Envl Econ.Intl 1990–93; Chairman, Earthroots Canada 1992–3; Pres. Canadian Envt Industry Assn 1993–. **Achievements:** helped — to ban use of DDT and 2,4,5-T in Canada, to encourage Canada to create a Min.of Envt and the Canadian Envl Prot.Act, to create strong intl NGO network based in developing countries (with ELCI), to deliver & implement WCS 1981, and to create new green industry sector. **Memberships:** AWMA, Water Envt Fedn. **Award:** Canadian Envlist of the Yr 1977. **Publications:** *The Crude Crisis: Ship Oil Spills* 1972, *A Trip North: Views of An Envlist* 1973, Bhopal and Canadian Aid 1985, The role of green economics in Canada 1993; Ed.*ECOFORUM* (ECLI quarterly) 1977–80; 62 other papers & articles. Favours pers.pub.& news media support (high pub.and media participation are the keys to public educ.& awareness). **Languages:** English, Swahili. Further details may be obtained from *Envl Profiles: A Global Guide to Projects & People* 1993, *Canadian Who's Who* 1994. Willing to act as consult.etc. **Address:** Canadian Environment Industry Association, 63 Poulson Street, Toronto, Ontario, Canada. **Tel.**1 416 778 6590; **fax** 1 416 778 5702.

GALUSHIN, Professor Dr Vladimir M. Environmental education, study & conservation of birds, especially birds of prey. Professor. *B.*9 May 1932, Arkhangelsk, Russia. Russian. *M.* Tatiana: *d.* **Education:** Gorky U. MS Dipl. 1955, PhD(Biol.) 1966. **Experience:** res. in ecol. & cons.of birds of prey; admin.— teacher training, UNESCO; teaching cons.of Nature, social ecol.(human pop.etc.), zool. (ornith.in particular). **Career:** Asst then Lect. 1958–67, Assoc.Prof.1972–92, Prof.1992–, Dept of Zool. & Ecol. Moscow Pedagogical U., UNESCO Chief Tech.Adv.& Expert in Biol. Sec.Sch.Sci. Project in India 1967–71, UNESCO Coord. Afghanistan 1982–6. **Achievements:** study & effective prot.of birds of prey, dev.of envl courses, teaching and envl educ.in India & Afghanistan. **Memberships:** IUCN Comm.on Educ.1969–, World WG on Birds of Prey 1970– (VC 1990–), BNHS 1970–, All-Russian SCN 1955– (Council memb.1987–), Union for Bird Cons.in Russia 1993– (VP 1993–). **Awards:** graduated from school with Gold Medal 1950, First Prize of All-Russian SCN for prot.of birds of prey 1982. **Publications:** 17 books incl. *Birds of Prey* 1970, *Forest Birds of Prey* 1980, *Significance of Raptors in Ecosystems* 1982, *Red*

Data Book of Russia (co-Author) 1983, *Methods of Study and Prot.of Raptors* (co-Ed.) 1990, *Fauna of the World: Birds* (co-Author) 1991, *Cons.of Nature* (text book, co-Author) 1975, 1981, 1987; num.text books in India & Afghanistan; 170+ papers. Favours pers.pub., indiff.to news media support. **Languages:** English, French (fair read), Russian. Willing to act as consult. etc.and deliver lectures. **Address:** Tarusskaya 8, Apt.211, 117588 Moscow, Russia. **Tel.**(office) 7 095 283 1634, (home) 7 095 425 7452.

GAMMELL, Alistair. Organization & growth of a world bird conservation movement and the achievement of effective conservation. Director of International Operations. *B.*28 July 1949, London, England, UK. British. *M.*Elizabeth: *s.*, 2 *d.* **Education:** Clifton Coll.(Bristol, UK) 1963–6. **Experience:** 25 yrs in Nature cons., 15 being in intl work; consult.to DGXI of EC 1984–90. **Career:** joined RSPB (Pubns Dept) 1969 and became PA to the DG 1974, in 1976 started the Society's Intl & Parliamentary Progs, became Head 1979 and Dir 1993– of Intl Ops. **Achievements:** started RSPB's Intl Prog.; played a leading role in reviving BirdLife Intl's (formerly ICBP) Euro.Continental section, and in formation of BirdLife Intl; chaired Euro. Steering Cttees which produced *Important Bird Areas in Europe*, and *Birds in Europe — Their Cons.Status.* **Memberships:** Euro.Cttee (BirdLife Intl), FFPS. **Award:** De Gouden Lepelaar (Vogelbescherming, The Netherlands) 1989. **Publications:** A Review of the Birds Directive 1972, Implementation of EC Birds Directive and Resolution on the Cons.of Birds after 1972 1987, A Review of the Habitats Directive 1992. Indiff.to pers.pub., favours news media support. **Languages:** English, French (not quite fluent). Willing to act as a consult.etc. **Address:** Royal Society for the Protection of Birds, The Lodge, Sandy, Bedfordshire SG19 2DC, England, UK. **Tel.**(office) 44 1767 680551, (home) 44 1767 681883; **fax** 44 1767 692365.

GANDY, Dr Matthew. Urban environmental problems in developed economies, environmental philosophy & politics, interdisciplinary environmental research. Lecturer in Geography. *B.*4 May 1965, London, England, UK. British. **Education:** St Catharine's Coll.Camb. BA 1988, LSE PhD 1992. **Experience:** res.on envl issues, consult.on UK envl problems in fields of recycling & waste mgmt, under- & post-grad. teaching. **Career:** Lect.in Geog. U.of Sussex 1992–; Vis.Scholar, Grad.Sch.of Arch., Planning and Preserv., Columbia U.(NY) 1995. **Achievements:** communication of complex issues to non-specialist readers, dev.of innovative teaching methods in envl educ. **Memberships:** IBG, AAG. **Award:** Global Envl Change F.(ESRC) 1994. **Publications:** Recycling and the Politics of Urban Waste 1994; num. papers & articles. Accepts pers.pub.& news media support. **Languages:** English, German (basic). Willing to act as consult.etc. **Address:** School of European Studies, University of Sussex, Brighton BN1 9QN, Sussex, England, UK. **Tel.** (office) 44 1273 606755; **fax** 44 1273 623246.

Gaoming JIANG, Dr, *see* **JIANG, Dr Gaoming.**

GARDNER, Dr Andrew Somerville. Ecology & evolution of geckos, biogeography, desert biology, ecology of desert mountains. Assistant Professor. *B.*19 Sept.1956, Aberdeen, Scotland, UK. British. Father Thomas A.M.Gardner, forest cons.in Kenya & Mauritius. *M.*Catherine Anne Oakley (biochem.): *s., d.* **Education:** Dollar Acad.; U.of Edinburgh BSc(Hons)(Zool.) 1979, U.of Aberdeen PhD 1984. **Experience:** res.— gecko evol.& ecol.(Seychelles, Arabia), biogeog., seabird ecol., ecol.of montane Juniper forests (Oman); consult.— herpetology (Oman), IUCN Cons.Monitoring Centre; teaching undergrad. zool., cons., field biol. **Career:** Jacobsen F.in Evol.Biol. UCL 1984–6, Asst Prof. Dept of Biol. Sultan Qaboos U.1987–. **Achievements:** ecol. survey work for cons.(Mauritius, Seychelles, and Oman), teaching cons.& field biol. (Oman), distribn mapping of reptiles (Oman). **Memberships:** F.LS, BOU, BHS, SSAR, The Herpetologists' League, IGS. **Award:** Ashworth Prize (Zool.) (U.of Edinburgh) 1979. **Publications:** *c.*25 papers, Edl Bd *Herpetological J.*, Ed. *Natural Hist.Newsletter* (Histl Assn of Oman). Favours pers.pub.& news media support. **Languages:** English, French (poor). Willing to act as consult.etc. **Address:** College of Science, Sultan Qaboos University, POB 36, Al-Khod 123, Muscat, Sultanate of Oman. **Tel.**(office) 968 515445, (home) & **fax** 968 513049.

GARDNER, Dr Julia Elaine. Public participation in environmental decision-making, environmental planning and policy, environmental nongovernment organizations, sustainable development, adult environmental education. Consultant. *B.*21 June 1955, Halifax, NS, Canada. Canadian. *P.*R.Daniel Moore (hydr.). **Education:** Trent U. BA(Hons)(Geog.) 1978, U.of Waterloo MA(Geog.) 1980, U.of Canterbury (NZ) PhD(Geog.) 1984. **Experience:** res.— coastal cons., policy for n.parks & native peoples, vol.envl stewardship, envlism, sust.dev.; consult.— envl policy, public involvement in envl planning, training on techniques of public involvement; teaching — grad.level in perspectives on envl mgmt, citizen involvement in envl planning. **Career:** Adjunct Prof. McGill U.1985–6; Ind. Envl Consult.1986–91; Asst Prof. Sch.of Planning and Westwater Res.Centre, UBC 1986–91; Prin., Dovetail Consulting 1991–. **Achievements:** dev.of widely-cited 'Principles for Sust.Dev.' pubns on social equity & sust.dev., basic res.on vol.envl stewardship (Fraser R.Basin, Canada), implementation of creative approaches to public involvement in envl planning. **Memberships:** IAPPP, IUCN CESP (WG on Tools for Sust.Dev.). **Awards:** Commonwealth 1980–82 and other grad.scholarships, Hon.Res.Assoc.of Sust.Dev.Res.Inst.

UBC 1993. **Publications:** *c.*20 chapters & papers incl.Park system planning: limitations in the pursuit of rationality 1990, Decision-making for sust.dev.: potential in selected approaches to envl assessment & mgmt 1990, Envl Non-govtl Orgns & Mgmt of Water Resources in the Fraser R.Basin 1991, Envl Non-govtl Orgns & Sust. Dev.1993, Bldg Alliances to Protect S.Moresby Is.(in press). Indiff.to pers. pub.& news media support. **Languages:** English, French (basic). Willing to act as consult.etc. **Address:** 2208 Cypress Street, Vancouver, British Columbia V6J 3M5, Canada. **Tel.**(office) 1 604 737 6868, (home) 1 604 734 0734; **fax** 1 604 737 6868.

GARRATT, Keith James. Environmental management policies, strategies, legislation and institutional development; multidisciplinary environmental studies; environmental programme and project formulation & management, public participation & consultation procedures with particular emphasis on developing countries. Environmental Management Consultant. *B.*20 Aug.1940, Taurauga, New Zealand. New Zealander. *M.*Anna M.: *s., d.* **Education:** Registered Land Surveyor 1963; U.of Auckland, Postgrad.Dipl.in Town Planning 1972. **Experience:** tech.— prot.areas' mgmt planning & policy, envl/resource mgmt legis.& policy, multidisc.envl & land-use studies, member NZ NCS task force, contributed to formulation and review of NCS projects in other countries on behalf of IUCN, formulation & implementation of 'green' and 'brown' envl progs & projects for UNDP and World Bank, formulation of GEF projects; admin.— Asst Dir & Dir both in Planning, sig.involvement in restructuring nat.envl instns in NZ, Sr Envl Adv. UNDP Nepal. **Career:** Land survey training & practice 1957–66, and sr land & envl mgmt planning/policy positions 1973–87, NZ Dept of Lands & Survey; NZ Colombo Plan Expert (Sarawak, Malaysia) 1967–9; land survey practice 1970–71; postgrad.town & country planning study 1972; consult.1987– incl.one yr for World Bank in Nepal as tech.adv.for envl studies related to the Arun III hydro scheme, and in 1992–3 two yrs of consult.contracts as Sr Envl Adv.for UNDP Nepal, advising UNDP & Govt in all aspects of envl mgmt and its relationship to dev. **Achievements:** leadership of major & innovative multidisc.envl & land-use studies and new nat.park investigations; key role in formulation of NZ NCS; prep.of Sagarmatha (Mt Everest) Nat.Park Mgmt Plan; conceptualization, formulation, and coordn, of Arun III; mgmt of Basinwide Envl Impacts Study (an innovative envl/regnl dev.study to identify & mitigate broad-scale & long-term effects of major infrastructure dev.in a remote but populated valley in Nepal); estab.of GEF Small Grants Prog.in Nepal; assistance to UNDP in formulation & launching of var.major envl progs and projects in Nepal. **Memberships:** NZ Planning Inst., NZ Inst.of Surveyors, IUCN CESP. **Publications:** var.tech. papers & articles, Author or co-Author of num.major tech. reports incl.*Sagarmatha (Mt Everest) Nat.Park Mgmt Plan* 1981, *NZ NCS* 1981, *Envl Mgmt & Sust.Dev.in the Arun Basin* 1991. Indiff.to pers. pub.& news media support. **Languages:** English, French; Malay & Nepali (fragmentary). Willing to act as consult.etc. **Address:** 215 Katherine Mansfield Drive, RD1, Upper Hutt, New Zealand. **Tel.**(home) 64 4 528 0280; **fax** 64 4 528 0231.

GATES, Professor Dr David Murray. Biophysical (physiological) ecology, climate change. Professor Emeritus, Distinguished Visiting Scientist. *B.*27 May 1921, Manhattan, Kansas, USA. American. Father Frank Caleb Gates, plant ecol., Pres.ESA 1951–2. *M.*Marian Penley: *s.*, 3 *d.* **Education:** U.of Michigan, BS(Phys.) 1942, MS(Phys.) 1944, PhD(Phys.) 1948. **Experience:** res.in atmos. spectroscopy using high alt.balloons, and on energy & gas exchange for plants & animals; teaching in phys., ecol.& climatol.; admin.in govt, u.& private instns; consult. **Career:** Asst Prof.of Phys. U.of Denver 1947–55; Scientific Dir London Branch, Office of Naval Res. 1955–7; Res.Sci.& Asst Chief, Upper Atmos.& Space Phys.Div. NBS 1957–64; Prof.of Natural Hist. U.of Colorado 1964–5; Prof.of Bot. 1965–71 and Dir Missouri Bot.Gdn 1965–72, Washington U.; Prof.of Biol.1971–90, Dir Biol.Station 1972–87, & Prof.Emer.1990–, U.of Michigan, Disting.Vis.Sci. Jet Propulsion Lab. CIT 1987–; Bd of Dirs Detroit Edison Co.1980–92, Consult.to Gen.Motors 1971–92. **Achievements:** created a new field of study *viz.*biophys.ecol.; Bd of Dirs or Trustees of Nat.Audubon Soc., Cons.Fndn, WWF US, Acid Rain Fndn; res.on energy budgets of plants & animals and their climates. **Memberships:** ESA, F.OSA, BSA, AIBS (past-Pres.), F.AAAS. **Awards:** Disting.Fac.Award (U.of Michigan) 1982, Henry Shaw Medal 1990, Award for Outstanding Achievement in Biometeorology (AMS) 1971, Gold Medal for Ecol.(Nat.Council of State Gdn Clubs). **Publications:** *Energy Exchange in the Biosphere* 1963, *Man & His Envt — Climate* 1972, *Biophys.Ecol.*1980, *Energy & Ecol.*1985, *Climate Change & Its Biol.Consequences* 1993; *c.*100 res.papers. Indiff.to pers. pub.& news media support. **Languages:** English, German (poor read). Willing to act as consult.etc. **Address:** Department of Biology, University of Michigan, Ann Arbor, Michigan 48109-1048, USA. **Tel.**(home) 1 313 769 4847 (in winter), 1 616 537 2172 (in summer); **fax** 1 313 747 0884.

GATHORNE-HARDY, Dr Gathorne (Fifth) Earl of Cranbrook, aka Lord Medway. Nature conservation, South-East Asian rain-forests, world-wide sustainable development. Authorities Member, Non-Executive Director, Chairman. *B.*20 June 1933, London, England, UK. British. Father John David (Fourth) Earl of Cranbrook, prominent in Brit.Nature cons., Treasurer of LS. *M.*Caroline: 2 *s., d.* **Education:** Eton Coll., Corpus Christi Coll.Camb. BA 1956, MA 1960; U.of Birmingham PhD 1960. **Experience:** 40 yrs as

envl biol.initially in SE Asia and latterly in UK & Europe; expedns to PNG & SW Pacific; lecturing, admin. **Career:** Tech.Asst, Sarawak Mus. 1956–8; Res.F. Yayasan Siswa Lokanatara (Indonesia) 1960–61; Lect.then Sr Lect.in Zool. U.of Malaya 1961–70; US NSF-supported res. team in PNG 1969; Dep.Leader, RS Expedn to New Hebrides 1971; Memb.& Hon.Clerk, Gt Glemham Parish Council 1971–; Chairman, Long Shop Mus.Trust 1978–, IEEP 1990–, & Stichting voor Europees Milieubeleid (Netherlands) 1991–; Ed.*Ibis* (BOU) 1973–80; Elected Memb. Suffolk Coastal Distr.Council 1974–83; Leader, Natural Hist.Mus.(then Brit.Mus. [Natural Hist.]) Expedn to Mt Lawit (Malaysia) 1974; Dep.Leader, Sarawak Forest Dept/RGS Mulu Expedn 1977–8; Memb.Select Cttee on Sci.& Tech.and Envt Subcttee (Chairman 1980–84, 1987–90) of Select Cttee on the EC, House of Lords 1979–90; Consult. WWF (Malaysia) Cons.Strats 1981–7; Memb. R.Comm.for Envl Poll. 1981–92; Memb. NERC 1982–8 & Anglian Water Auth.1987–9; Chairman, ITTO Enquiry into Sust.For.in Sarawak 1988–9; Chairman, Cttee for England, NCC 1990–91; Jt Leader, Universiti Brunei Darussalam/RGS Rain Forest Project 1990–92; Appointed Memb. Broads Auth.1988– & Harwich Haven Auth. 1989– (UK); Non-exec.Dir, Anglian Water PLC 1989–; Chairman (part-time & non-exec.) English Nature, NCC for England 1990–. **Achievements:** helped estab.Ulu Gombak Field Studies Centre while at U.of Malaya 1965, recognized remains of an extinct giant pangolin, a tapir, Javan Rhinoceros *(Rhinoceros sendaicus),* & wild dog, from archl sites in Borneo; discovered Bronzed Tube-nosed Bat (a new species of *Harpiocephalus)* and described a new species each of shrew and pencil-tailed treemouse from Borneo; planted more than 1,000 oak trees over the yrs. **Memberships:** F.IBiol. (CBiol.), F.LS, F.ZSL, F.RGS, BOU, MSGBI, BHS (past-Pres.), Skinner & Freeman of London (UK). **Awards:** Officer of the Order of St John (UK), Hon.— DSc (U.of Aberdeen), Dep.Lt (Co.of Suffolk, UK), Pres.Emer.(Rainforest Club), Pres.(Suffolk Wildlife Trust), VP of IEEM, Nat.Soc.of Clean Air and Envt, & Inst.of Envl Health, Memb. Malaysian Nature Soc., Inst.of Waste Mgmt, & IWEM. **Publications:** num.books, chapters, reports & papers incl. *Mammals of Borneo* 1965, 1977, *The Wild Mammals of Malaya (Peninsular Malaysia) and Singapore* 1969, 1978 (reprint 1983), *Birds of the Malay Peninsula* (co-Author) 1976, *Riches of the Wild: Land Mammals of SE Asia* 1987, 1991, *Key Envts: Malaysia* (Gen.Ed.& Contrib.) 1988, *Belalong: a Trop.Rainforest* (co-Author) 1994. Indiff.to pers.pub., favours news media support. **Languages:** English, French (poor), Malay (fair). Further details may be obtained from *Burke's Peerage* 1990, Brit.*Who's Who* 1996. Willing to act as consult.etc. **Address:** Glemham House, Great Glemham, Saxmundham, Suffolk IP17 1LP, England, UK. **Fax** 44 1728 663339.

GAYOOM, HE President Maumoon ABDUL. Astronomy. President, Commander-in-Chief, Minister. *B*.29 Dec.1937, Malé, Maldives. Maldivian. *M*.Nasreena (Founder Member, Soc.for Health Educ.: 2 *s*., 2 *d*. **Education:** Al-Azhar U. BA(Islamic Studies) 1964, Dipl.of Educ. 1965, MA(Islamic Studies) 1966. **Experience:** diplomatic & admin. **Career:** Res.Asst, Amer. U.of Cairo 1967–9; Lect.in Islamic Studies & Phil. Ahmadu Bello U. 1969–71; Teacher 1971–2; Shipping Dept Mgr 1972–3; Undersec. Telecommunication Dept & Dir Telephone Dept 1974; Spec.Undersec. Office of the PM 1974–5; Dep.Amb.of Maldives to Sri Lanka 1975–6; Undersec. Min.of Ext.Affairs 1976; Dep.Minister of Transport 1976–7; Perm.Rep.of Maldives to UN 1976–7; Minister of Transport 1977–8; Pres.of Republic of Maldives 1978–. Commander-in-Chief of the Armed Forces 1978–; Minister of Defence & Nat.Security 1982–; Minister of Finance 1989–. **Achievements:** calling for intl action on issue of predicted global warming & sea-level rise emphasising the vulnerability of small island nations & coastal states at UNGA and Commonwealth Heads of Govt Mtg in Oct.1987; init.efforts by SAARC to minimize adverse effects of natural disasters and the impacts of greenhouse effect as a result of which two regnl studies were carried out on the subjects. **Membership:** Constituent Council of Rabitat Al-Alam Al-Islami (Muslim World League). **Awards:** Hon.Doct.in Llt. (Alligarh Muslim U.) 1983, Hon.PhD in Pol.Sci.(Marquis Guiseppe Sciluna Intl U.Fndn) 1988, Global 500 Roll of Honour (UNEP) 1988, Doctor of Letters *(H.C.)*(Jamia Millia Islamia of India) 1990, Man of the Sea Award 1990 (Lega Navale Italiana) 1991. Indiff.to pers.pub.& news media support. **Languages:** Arabic, Dhivehi (Maldivian nat. language), English. **Address:** The President's Office, Bodu Thakurufaanu Magu, Malé 20-05, Maldives. **Tel.**(office) 960 323701, (home) 960 322200; **fax** 960 325500.

GEBRE EGZIABHER, Dr Tewolde Berhan, *see* **EGZIABHER, Dr Tewolde Berhan** GEBRE.

GEBREMEDHIN, Naigzy. Environmental management, reconstruction, redevelopment, emergency response, architecture, urban planning. Principal Officer, Coordinator. *B*.11 Aug.1934, Addis Ababa, Ethiopia. Eritrean. *M*.Mihret Samuel: 2 *s*., *d*. **Education:** U.of Kansas, BSc(Civil Eng.) 1957; MIT, MCP(Arch.& City Planning) 1967. **Experience:** admin., consult., engg, planning, lecturing, assisted num.govts (Yemen, Brazil, China, Tanzania) as Sr Adv.on var.aspects of envl mgmt, resp.for initiating tech.assistance projects in 20 countries under auspices of UNEP, and for UNEP's progs in envl emergency response, energy, human settlements, envl security (peace & security), sci.& tech. **Career:** Assoc.Prof.& Dean, Fac.of Bldg and Arch. Haile Selassie U. 1957–75; Social Affairs Officer, UN (NY) 1969–73; Lect. Lund Inst.of

Tech. and Consult.Engr/Planner (Stockholm & Addis Ababa), Falck, Fogelvik, Nordstrom, Smass 1972–3; Consult.Arch.& Engr, Pan-African Housing Group 1972–6; Sr Prog.Officer 1979–87, Prin.Officer 1987–, Coord. Nat.Envt Mgmt Plan (Eritrea) 1994–, UNEP. **Achievements:** basic res.on vernacular arch.and popular health in Africa, estab.and expansion of Bldg Res.Inst.(Addis Ababa), teaching at higher levels in Fac.of Arch., Urban Planning, and Envl Mgmt, Founder Memb.of Mazingira Inst.1977. **Memberships:** ASCE, AAP, KAA, EAAE. Indiff.to pers.pub. **Languages:** Amharic, English, French, Italian, Swedish, Tigrigna (Eritrea). Willing to act as consult.etc. **Address:** United Nations Environment Programme, POB 47074, Nairobi, Kenya. **Tel.**(office) 254 2 623428 or 59, (home) 254 2 48114; **fax** 254 2 230278.

Geping, QU, Professor, *see* **QU, Professor Geping.**

GHABBOUR, Professor Dr Samir Ibrahim. Animal ecology (soil fauna), conservation of natural resources, desert ecology. Professor of Soil Biology. *B*.30 Oct.1933, Cairo, Egypt. Egyptian. *M*.Ragaa: *s*., *d*. **Education:** U.of Cairo BSc 1954, Dip.Ed.& Psych.1955, MSc 1964, PhD Zool.(Ecol.) 1971. **Experience:** three yrs' teaching & res in Sudan, consult.on envl projects ALECSO (1972–81) and to UN/ECOSOC, UNEP, UNDP, ACCT, Blue Plan etc. **Career:** teacher of biol.at govt sec.schools 1955–71, Lect.in Animal Ecol.1971–8, Asst Prof.1978–84, Prof.of Soil Biol.1984–93, Emer. 1993–, Inst.of African Res.& Studies, Cairo U. **Achievements:** memb.of sci.res.teams on desert ecosystems; Prin.Investigator of three other similar teams; Sec.-Gen. ESES; Ed.of several books. **Memberships:** BES, SEF, WFSF; Edl Bds var.scientific periodicals. **Awards:** State Prize for Biol.Scis (Egypt) 1980; Medal of Arts & Scis, First Order (Egypt) 1981; Kuwait Prize for Envt (shared) 1986; Charles Sauvage Prize (SEF) 1990; Membre Correspondant 1990 & Vis.Prof.1992, Mus.Nat.d'Histoire Naturelle, Paris; Memb.Desert Res.Unit, Namibia 1990. **Publications:** *The Nile and its Envt* (co-Author) 1980, *The State of the Rural Envt in Dev. Countries* (co-Ed.) 1990; 190 scientific papers etc. Dislikes pers.pub., indiff.to news media support. **Languages:** Arabic, English, French. Willing to act as consult.etc. **Address:** Department of Natural Resources, Institute of African Research & Studies, Cairo University, 12613 Giza (Cairo), Egypt. **Tel.**(home) 20 2 392 4804; **fax** 20 2 628884.

GIMENEZ-DIXON, Dr Mariano. Animal ecology, wildlife conservation, threatened species management, cervids. Programme Officer. *B*.9 Oct.1955, Corrientes, Prov.of Corrientes, Argentina. Argentinian, British. **Education:** Nat. U.of La Plata, Lic.(Ecol.& Cons.of Renewable Natural Resources) 1979, Dr in Natural Scis (Ecol.& Cons.of Renewable Natural Resources)

1991. **Experience:** u.lecturing, wildlife mgmt & admin, endangered species cons., advising and drafting of cons.-oriented legis.(wildlife and prot.areas), mgmt of cons.-oriented networks (IUCN SSC network of SGs). **Career:** Staff Memb. Directorate of Natural Resources, Sub-secretariat of Agrarian Affairs 1980–84 and Min.of Agrarian Affairs 1984–7, Memb.of Bd of Directive Council of the Professional Council of Natural Scis 1986–8, Chief of Fauna & Commercialization Dept of Directorate of Natural Resources & Ecol.of Min.of Agrarian Affairs 1986–8, Staff Memb.of Natural Envts Cons.Directorate, Min.of Agrarian Affairs & Fisheries 1987–8, Ecol.Consult.to the V.-Presidency of Natural Resources & Envt Comm.of the Chamber of Reps 1988–9, Sec.of Directive Council of Professional Council of Natural Scis 1988–90, Staff Memb.of Natural Envt Cons. Directorate, Min.of Agrarian Affairs & Fisheries 1988–91, Memb. Auditory Comm.of Professional Council of Natural Scis 1990–91, all Prov.of Buenos Aires; Prog.Officer, Species Survival Prog. IUCN 1991–. **Achievements:** basic res.and drafting of legal instruments leading to creation of a natural reserve and the declaration of the local Pampas Deer *(Ozotoceros* sp.) as living Natural Monument (as defined in the Washington Conv.of 1940), both in the Prov.of Buenos Aires; lead participant in drafting of current Buenos Aires provincial law on Nature Reserves and prot.areas (first of its kind in the Prov.); prin.researcher on Pampas Deer cons.in Argentina from 1981–91 which work is basis of many current activities re. the local species. **Memberships:** NGS 1976–93, The Wildlife Soc.(USA) 1982–, Asociación Argentina de Ecología 1984–94. **Publications:** num.in English & Spanish incl.Panorama en la Provincia de Buenos Aires 1987, Action plans for species mgmt, an eval.of their effectiveness (co-Author) 1993, The Ramsar Conv.and the Cons.of Non-Waterfowl Species (Conf.Proc.) 1993. Indiff.to pers.pub.& news media support. **Languages:** English, Spanish. Further details may be obtained from the Wildlife Soc.(USA) Membership Directory. Willing to act as consult.etc. **Address:** IUCN—The World Conservation Union, Rue Mauverney 28, 1196 Gland, Switzerland. **Tel.**(office) 41 22 999 0155, (home) 41 22 364 0961; **fax** 41 22 999 0015.

GIRARDET, Herbert Kurt. Cultural ecology research, writing, film-making. Director. *B.*28 May 1943, Essen, Germany, German. *M.*Barbara: 2 *s.* **Education:** art hist.& philos. Tuebingen & Berlin Univs, LSE BSc(Econ.)(Social Anthrop.) 1974. **Experience:** writing & filming on trop.forests, forest die-back, reforestation, agroforestry; ecol.agric.; urban metabolism, urban ecol.and sust. **Career:** range of envl activities with main emphasis on writing and film-making. **Achievements:** drawing attention to key envl issues, particularly trop.forest destruction, reforestation, and urban ecol.; co-

organizing The Earth Parliament at UNCED 1992; Chairman of Schumacher Soc.(UK); Patron of The Soil Assn and The Ecol.Centre (London, UK); Trustee of Earth Core Fund and Ecol.Design Assn; Vis.Prof.Middlesex U. **Memberships:** G500F, Balaton Group, Fndn for Agrofor. **Awards:** Global 500 Roll of Honour (UNEP) 1992, intl awards for two films*. **Publications:** *Land for the People* (Ed.) 1976, *Forest* (Ed.) 1979–86, *Far from Paradise* (co-Author) 1986 (also TV series), *Blueprint for a Green Planet* (co-Author) 1987, *Earthrise* 1992, *The Gaia Atlas of Cities* 1993; TV films — **Jungle Pharmacy* 1989, *The Altamira Gathering* 1990, **Halting the Fires* 1990, *Metropolis* (on London's metabolism) 1994. Accepts pers. pub.& news media support. **Languages:** English, German. Willing to act as consult.etc. **Address:** 93 Cambridge Gardens, London W10 6JE, England, UK. **Tel.**44 181 969 6375; **fax** 44 181 960 2202.

GITTINS, John William Edward Henry. Environmental education, community environmental action, education for sustainability, environmental values & philosophy through teaching, art & environment, research, and encouraging good practice both in Britain & overseas. Director, Consultant, Trustee. *B.*31 Aug.1938, S.Brent, Devon, England, UK. British. *M.*Susan Janet (sometime Sec.of State's Appointed Memb.of Brecon Beacon Nat.Park, Dir Council for Nat.Parks): *s.* **Education:** U.of London, BSc(Econ.)(Hons) 1965; U.of Birmingham, Dip.Ed.1964. **Experience:** teacher, researcher, consult.& practitioner in fields of envl cons., rec., envl/outdoor educ., working in Britain, France, Denmark & Greece; since 1985 work has been based on envl educ.and local community envl action. **Career:** Res.F. Snowdonia Nat.Park Survey 1967–70; Exec.Sec. Countryside in 1970 Cttee for Wales and Prince of Wales' Cttee 1970–71; Lect.in Envl Educ. St Mary's Coll.Bangor 1971–4; Sec.of State for Wales' Appointed Memb.of Snowdonia Nat. Park 1971–5; Memb.Prince of Wales' Cttee for Welsh Envt 1971–86; Res.F. U.of Exeter 1974–5; Prin.Rec.& Cons.Officer, Welsh Water 1975–85; Asst Dir (Rec.& Countryside Mgmt), Cheshire Co.Council 1985–9; Dir, Cheshire Landscape Trust 1989–; Trustee, Mersey Basin Trust 1992– and Cywaith Cymru/Art Works Wales 1994–. **Memberships:** F.RSA, F.RGS. **Awards:** Winston Churchill F'ship 1973, Award of Merit (Brit.Canoe Union) 1986. **Publications:** Recreational Geog.1972, Leisure & Envt 1993; *Snowdonia Nat.Park* (co-Author) 1970, *A Cons.& Rec.Strat.for Waterspace in Wales* 1979, *Outdoor Adventure & Envl Cons.* 1990. Indiff.to pers.pub.& news media support. **Language:** English. Willing to act as consult.etc. **Address:** Cheshire Landscape Trust, Fountains Building, Upper Northgate Street, Chester CH1 4EF, England, UK. **Tel.**(office) 44 1244 376333, (home) 44 1978 364357; **fax** 44 1244 376016.

GIVEN, Dr David R. Conservation biology, threatened species, vegetation & species recovery, arctic–alpine biology, island biology, ethnobotany, ethics. Private Consultant, Visiting Lecturer. *B*.8 Nov.1943, NZ. New Zealander. Father Bruce B. Given (envl entomologist, retired). *M*.Karina C. **Education:** Nelson Coll.; U.of Canterbury BSc(Hons.), PhD 1970; Moore Coll. C.Theol. **Experience:** chiefly as res.sci.& intl consult., also in mgmt issues, dev.& eco-tourism, book writing, TV presentation. **Career:** Dem. Bot.Dept. U.of Canterbury 1965; Sci. DSIR Bot.Div. Christchurch 1965–90; Dean of Students, Christchurch Coll. U.of Canterbury 1967; Postdoctl Res.F. CNRC 1973–4; Scientist, DSIR Land Resources 1990–92; Prin. David Given & Assocs 1992–; Vis.Lect. Dept of Hort., U.of Lincoln 1993–. **Achievements:** ecol.& cons.field-work and mapping in Canadian Gt Lakes, Antarctica, Subantarctic Islands, Chatham Islands, & NZ (incl. geothermal systems); contracted to IUCN; ITTO, & UNDP, on biodiv., threatened species, CITES & sust.dev.issues, and Commonwealth Sci. Council on ethnobot.; init.of plant cons. issues (esp.endangered species & *ex situ* cons.) in NZ & elsewhere; frequent intl conf.presenter. **Memberships:** NZES (Counc.1978–81), SANZ (Inaugural Counc.1979–8), RSNZ *ad hoc* Cttee on Nat.Collections 1979–83, IAP (Inaugural Counc.1981–84), N.Canterbury Nat. Parks & Reserves Bd 1983–90; N.Canterbury Cons.Bd 1990–93; Chairman Pteridophyte SG & Comm. member IUCN SSC 1983– and Steering Cttee thereof 1990–, PSA Bot.Cttee 1988–; Commonwealth Sci.Council, NZ WG on Ethnobot.1989–; IUCN Ethics, Culture & Cons.WG 1990–; WWF-NZ Scientific Adv.Cttee 1991–; NZBS Threatened Plants Cttee 1992–; NZ Govt Pacific Dev.& Cons.Trust Adv.Trustee 1992–. **Awards:** CNRC Postdoctl F'ship 1973–4, Commonwealth Sci.Council Travelling F'ships 1980 & 1983, Sir Joseph Banks Mem.Lect. 1986 & Assoc.of Hon. 1993 (RNZIH), Artiste (FIAP) 1990, Tennant Lect.(U.of Otago) 1991. **Publications:** *The NZ Red Data Book on Rare & Endangered Plants & Animals* (co-Author) 1981, *Rare & Endangered Plants of NZ* 1981, *The Arctic–Alpine Element of the Vascular Flora at L.Superior* (co-Author) 1983, *Cons.of Plant Species & Habitats* (Ed.) 1983, *Cons.of Chatham Is.Flora & Veg.*(co-Author) 1984, *Threatened Plants of NZ* (co-Author) 1989, *Principles & Practice of Plant Cons.*(in press); *c*.120 papers & 60 reports. Favours pers.pub.& news media support. **Languages:** English, Spanish (elementary). **Address:** David Given & Associates, 101 Jeffreys Road, Christchurch 5, New Zealand. **Tel.& fax** 64 3 351 6069.

GLANTZ, Dr Michael Howard. Climate–society interactions, third-world development. Programme Head. *B*.14 Dec.1939, Providence, RI, USA. American. *M*.Karen: *d*. **Education:** U. of Penn. BS(Metallurgical Eng.) 1961, MA (Pol.Sci.) 1963, PhD 1970. **Experience:** num. u.teaching assignments, admin., course & conf.

org., Vis.Prof. U.of Colorado 1975–6 & 1977 and McGill U. 1980. **Career:** Metallurgical Engr, Westinghouse Corpn 1961–2 and Ford Motor Co.1964–5; Senate Intern 1963; Ops Res.Consult, U.City Sci.Center (PA) 1967–70; Commissioned Study Author, IFIAS 1974–6; Sr Postdoctl F.1974–5, Sci.1976–83, Sr Sci.& Prog.Head 1983–, Envl & Societal Impacts Group, NCAR. **Achievements:** Global 500 Award 1990 (UNEP). **Awards:** Scholar–Diplomat Prog.(US Dept of State) 1973, Sr Postdoctl F'ship (NCAR) 1974–5, US Envt & Resources Council Award 1975, Tour Speaker (CMOS/Atmos.Envt Services) 1980, John Wesley Powell Lect.(47th, SW and Rocky Mtn/AAAS) 1980, World Hunger Media Award 1987, Global 500 Roll of Honour (UNEP) 1990, George & Cynthia Mitchell Intl Prize for Sust.Dev.1991, Bradford Morse Disting.Lect. (Boston U. African Studies Center) 1991. **Publications:** Ed.or co-Ed. of 17 vols incl.*The Role of Regnl Orgns in the Context of Climate Change* 1994, *Drought Follows the Plow: Cultivating Marginal Areas* 1994; *c*.79 chapters & papers. Favours pers.pub.& news media support. **Languages:** English; French, Portuguese & Spanish (written & spoken); Russian (functionally literate). Willing to act as consult. etc. **Address:** Environmental and Societal Impacts Group, National Center for Atmospheric Research, POB 3000, Boulder, Colorado 80307-3000, USA. **Tel.**(office) 1 303 497 8119, (home) 1 303 449 9212; **fax** 1 303 497 8125.

GŁOWACIŃSKI, Professor Dr Zbigniew Andrzej. Bird ecology, biodiversity, succession, species extinction, wildlife protection & management. Head of Species Protection Unit. *B*.5 Feb.1943, Dukla, SE Poland. Polish. *M*.Maria J.: 2 *s*. **Education:** Jagiellonian U. MSc(Biol.Scis) 1966, PhD 1973, Dr hab.(Ecol.) 1981; scholarships held in Academiya Nauk (USSR) 1978, CSIC (Spain) 1983, & DAAD (Germany) 1985. **Experience:** res.orgn, diversity, energetics, & succession, of bird communities; changes in Polish vertebrate fauna (idea of winner & loser species); principles of animal cons.in prot.areas. **Career:** Res.Sci.1966–, Dep.Dir of (then) Nature Cons.Res.Centre 1985–91, Head of Species Prot.Unit, (now) Inst.of Nature Cons.1991–, Polish AS; VP, State Council for the Cons.of Nature (Warsaw) 1990–. **Achievements:** basic res.on animal ecol.& cons., Ed.*Polish Red Data Book of Animals** (1992), Editorship/Adv.concerning j.*Studia Naturae* (1975–94), *Prot.of Nature* (annual, 1993–); monogrs of Tatra Nat.Park and some Nature reserves; coordn of some nat.faunistic & ecol. progs connected with Nature cons.; prin. author of cons.& mgmt plan for fauna of Bieszczady Nat.Park and Intl Biosphere Reserve 'E.Carpathians'. **Memberships:** State Council for Cons.of Nature, Polish AS (Sec.of Cttee of Nature Prot.1981–7, Cttee of Zool.1993–), scientific councils of some biol.insts & nat.parks. **Awards:** Euro.Prize for Nature Prot.(J.W. Goethe Fndn/EU) 1993, First Prize 1993 & Gold

Medal 1995 (Envt Min.); others. **Publications:** besides above*, two scientific and two popular/scientific books (with co-Authors); c.150 scientific & popular/ scientific papers incl.energy flow through a bird community in a deciduous forest (co-Author) 1975, Situation of all vertebrates and selected invertebrates in Poland — list of species, their occurrence, endangerment, and status of prot. (co-Author) 1980, Stability in bird communities 1981. **Languages:** English (poor), German & Latin (basic), Polish, Russian. Willing to act as consult.&/or ref. **Address:** Institute of Nature Conservation, Polish Academy of Sciences, 46 Lubicz Street, PL-3l-5l2 Kraków, Poland. **Tel.** (office) 48 12 219701, (home) 48 12 581048; **fax** 48 12 210348.

GOCHFELD, Professor Dr Michael. Occupational & environmental medicine, environmental toxicology, neurobehavioural toxicology of heavy-metals (particularly lead & mercury); medical surveillance & biomonitoring, environmental biomonitoring, habitat & nest-site selection, reproductive synchrony, growth & behavioural development; global population & sustainable development. Clinical Professor of Occupational & Environmental Medicine. *B.*1 Jan.1940, Philadelphia, PA, USA. American. *M.*Professor Dr Joanna Burger *qv: s., d.* **Education:** Oberlin Coll. BA in Bot.(Ecol.) 1961, Albert Einstein Coll.of Med. MD 1965, CUNY PhD(Envl Biol.& Ecol.) 1975, Colorado Med.Center, Internship in Paediatrics 1965–6, Rockefeller U. Postdoctl Animal Behaviour 1975–6. **Experience:** res.(world-wide) — effects of heavy-metals on natural ecosystems, vertebrate behaviour & human health; envl risk assessment; ecol.risk assessment; criteria & alternatives to med.screening & med. surveillance for worker & community exposure to hazardous waste; factors influencing normal growth, behavioural dev.& learning; neurobehavioural toxicology; avian behavioural ecol.: biomonitoring of heavy-metals in birds & other vertebrates in several countries incl.Pacific Rim; admin.as Div.Dir.; consult.& adv.to Fed.& State agencies etc.on occupational & envl health, incl.poll.& hazardous waste; teacher of envl med. **Career:** Assoc.in Envl Health, Columbia U.Sch.of Public Health 1969–75; Instr.in Biol. 1969–73, Adjunct Assoc.Prof.of Biol.1973–5, CUNY–Queens Coll., Adjunct Assoc.Prof.of Biol. SUNY–Purchase 1975–6, Clinical Assoc. Prof.1980–86 and Clinical Prof.1986– in Envl & Occupational Med. U.of Med.& Dentistry of NJ–Robert Wood Johnson Med.Sch.; Dir Occupational Med.Envl & Occupational Health Scis Inst.1986–. **Achievements:** res.on colonial marine birds such as terns & skimmers has contributed to understanding of pop.dynamics on resource limitation and effects of human disturbance; work with Roseate Terns *(Sterna dougallii)* contributed to listing & recovery plans for them in the US; co-developed an avian model for study of effects of lead on behavioural dev.of young. **Memberships:** F.ACOEM, APHA, F.AOU, COS, WOS.

Awards: Sigma Xi Hon.Scientific Soc., Alpha Omega Alpha Hon.Med.Soc., Elected Memb. Collegium Ramazzini. **Publications:** Med. Surveillance of Hazardous Waste Workers (Ed.) 1990, Envl Health Perspectives on Chromium (Ed.) 1992, Black Skimmers *[Rhyncops nigra]* (co-Author) 1991, Common Tern *[Sterna hirundo]* (co-Author) 1992; 200+ refereed papers. **Languages:** English, Spanish (limited). Willing to act as consult.etc. **Address:** Environmental and Occupational Health Sciences Institute, 681 Frelinghuysen Road, Piscataway, New Jersey 08855, USA. **Tel.**(office) 1 908 455 0180; **fax** 1 908 455 0130.

GOLDBERG, Professor Dr Edward Davidow. Marine chemistry, management of the coastal zone. Professor of Chemistry. *B.*2 Aug.1921, Sacramento, CA, USA. American. *M.*Kathe Bertine (qual.of coastal marine waters): *s.*, 3 *d.* **Education:** UCB BA 1942, U.of Chicago PhD 1949. **Experience:** since 1949 has been carrying out res.progs in marine chem.and involved with confs & workshops on marine water qual. **Career:** rising to Prof.of Chem. Scripps Instn of Oceanography, UCSD 1949–. **Achievements:** formulated Mussel Watch Technique, proposed Assimilative Capacity Concept for maintenance of qual.of coastal waters. **Memberships:** Sigma Xi, US NAS, AAAS, AGU. **Awards:** Bostwick H. Ketchum (WHOI) 1984, Tyler Prize for Envl Achievement 1989. **Publications:** *Health of the Oceans* 1976, *Black Carbon in the Envt* 1985, num.others. Favours pers.pub.& news media support. **Language:** English. Willing to act as consult.etc. **Address:** Scripps Institution of Oceanography, University of California at San Diego, La Jolla, California 92093-0220, USA. **Tel.**(office) 1 619 534 2407, (home) 1 619 756 1420; **fax** 1 619 534 0784.

GOLDEMBERG, HE Professor Dr José. Physics, energy technology and strategies, environmental degradation, environmental education. Professor of Physics. *B.*27 May 1928, Santo Angelo, RS, Brazil. Brazilian. *M.*Therezinha Maria: 3 *s.*, *d.* **Education:** U.of São Paulo, BSc 1950, PhD(Phys.Scis) 1954. **Experience:** res.in nuclear phys.until 1974, and continuing in energy; much exp.in u.admin.and Chief Exec.of large state-owned energy utility, has held positions in State Govt of São Paulo and Fed.Govt of Brazil at ministerial level. **Career:** up to Prof.of Phys.1950–, Chairman of Phys.Inst. 1970–78, Rector 1986–7, U.of São Paulo; Res. Assoc. High Energy Phys.Lab. Stanford U. 1962–3; Assoc.Prof. U.of Paris (Orsay) 1964; (full) Prof.of Phys. U.of Toronto 1972; Head, Nuclear Phys.Div. Atomic Energy Inst.(São Paulo) 1973; Pres.of Companhia Energética de São Paulo, Companhia Paulista de Forca e Luz, Eletricidade de São Paulo SA, and Companhia de Gas de São Paulo 1983–5; Sec.of Educ. State of São Paulo 1990; Sec.of Sci.& Tech.1990–91, Minister of Educ.1991–2, Interim Sec.of Envt 1992, Fed.Govt of Brazil. **Achievements:** organized Inst.of Phys., modernized by-laws, and expanded res.& teaching facilities at U.of São Paulo; contributed significantly to modernization of comp.industry in Brazil; helped estab. concept of 'techl leapfrogging' as preferred strat.of developing countries in order to develop compatibly with sust. **Memberships:** Brazilian AS 1955–, State of São Paulo AS 1956–, Brazilian Soc.of Phys.(Prcs.1975–9), BSAS (Pres. 1979–81), IEI (Bd Chairman 1993–), IAE Governing Council 1992–. **Awards:** Award for Outstanding Contribns to Profession of Energy Econ.and to its Lit.(IAEE) 1989, Mitchell Prize for Sust.Dev.(co-, USA) 1991, DSc *H.C.*(Technion–Israel Inst.of Tech.) 1991, estab.of 'José Goldemberg Chair in Atmos. Phys.' (Tel Aviv U.) 1994. **Publications:** six books on energy incl.*Energy for a Sust.World* (co-Author) 1987, and *Energy and Environment in Developing Countries* (in press), four phys. textbooks, num. tech.papers & popular articles. Indiff.to pers.pub., favours news media support. **Languages:** English, French (poor), Portuguese, Spanish (poor). Willing to act as a consult.&/or ref. **Address:** Rua Doutor Alceu de Assis, 64-apto 162, 01455-110 São Paulo, São Paulo, Brazil. **Tel.**(office) 55 11 818 5053/4, (home) 55 11 210 3985; **fax** 55 11 818 5031; **e-mail** goldemberg @nhi.lead.org.br .

GOLDMAN, Professor Dr Marshall I. Economics of Russia, environmental problems of the former Soviet Union. Kathryn W. Davis Professor of Russian Economics, Associate Director. *B.*27 July 1930, IL, USA. American. *M.*Merle: 2 *s.*; 2 *d.* **Education:** U.of Penn. BS (Econ.) 1952, Harvard U. MA(Russian Studies) 1956, PhD(Russian Studies) 1961. **Experience:** res.in Russian econ., admin., consult.to State Dept and other govt agencies & several corpns, Consulting or Adv.Ed.*Current Hist., EC, Problems of Econ.* **Career:** Wellesley Coll.1958–, being Kathryn W.Davis Prof.of Russian Econ.1989–; Assoc. Dir, Russian Res.Center, Harvard U. 1975–; Vis.Asst Prof. Brandeis U.1991. **Memberships:** Amer.AAS, AEA, CFR. **Awards:** Fulbright–Hayes Lect.(Moscow SU) 1977, Hon. LLD (U.of Mass.) 1985, elected memb.of Amer.AAS 1991. **Publications:** *The Spoils of Progress: Envl Poll.in the Soviet Union* 1972, *Ecol.& Econ.: Controlling Poll.in the '70s* 1972, Envl Poll.in the Soviet Union 1973, *The Enigma of Soviet Petroleum: Half Empty or Half Full* 1980. Favours pers.pub.& news media support. **Languages:** English, Russian. Further details may be obtained from *Who's Who in America* (47th edn.). Willing to act as consult.etc. **Address:** Davis Center of Russian Studies, Harvard University, Coolidge Hall, 1737 Cambridge Street, Cambridge, Massachusetts 02138, USA. **Tel.**1 617 495 4485; **fax** 1 617 495 8319.

GOLDSMITH, Edward. Ecology, anthropology, life sciences in general, environmental campaigning. Founding Editor, President. *B.*8 Nov.1928, Paris, France. British, French. *M.*

Katherine Victoria (envl campaigner): *s.* Alexander (Founder Envl Digest). **Education:** U.of Oxf. MA 1961. **Experience:** res.for 14 books & many articles, writing, publishing, campaigning, consulting, teaching. **Career:** Author, Publisher, Ed.; taught short courses at U.of Michigan 1975 and Sangamon SU (IL) 1982; set up global ecol.course for Intl Hons Prog.in conjunction with Bard Coll.(NY); Founding Ed.*The Ecologist* 1969–; Pres. ECOROPA (France) 1990–. **Memberships:** SEE, RGS, ECOROPA, Schumacher Soc.(Dir) ELF (Trustee), Fndn for Gaia (Trustee), Green Party. **Awards:** Chevalier de la Légion d'Honneur 1990, Hon.Rt Livelihood Award 1991. **Publications:** *A Blueprint for Survival* (co-Author) 1972, *The Social and Envl Effects of Large Dams* (co-Author & co-Ed.) Vol.1 1984, Vol.2 1986, Vol.3 1992, *The Way: An Ecol. World View* 1992. Indiff.to pers. pub., favours news media support. **Languages:** English, French. Further details may be obtained from Brit.*Who's Who* 1985–. Possibly willing to act as consult.etc. **Address:** Hogarth House, 32 Paradise Road, Richmond, Surrey TW9 1SE, England, UK. **Tel.**(office) 44 181 332 6963, (home) 44 181 948 1418; **fax** 44 181 948 5102.

GOLDSMITH, Dr Frank Barrie. Nature conservation especially monitoring, plant ecology. Senior Lecturer. *B.*31 May 1942, Sutton, Surrey, England, UK. British. *M.*Marilyn Marie: 2 *d.* **Education:** U.of Wales, BSc(Hons)(1st Class) 1964, PhD(Veg.of Sea-cliffs) 1967. **Experience:** NT and Countryside Comm.(habitat restoration), Canadian Forestry Service (Nova Scotia hardwoods), ODA (St Vincent), Forestry Comm.(UK), UN FAO (monitoring in India), Brit.Council (SL & India), Earthwatch (Mallorca), etc. **Career:** Lect.1967–76, Sr Lect.1979–, UCL; Assoc.Prof. Dalhousie U. 1976–9. **Achievements:** teaching MSc course in Cons., res., pubns. **Memberships:** BES, RSPB, Herts & Mx Trust for Cons. **Publications:** book series on Cons.Biol.1992–, *Cons.in Practice* 1974, *Cons.in Perspective* 1983, *Monitoring for Cons. & Ecol.*1991, BES Symp.vol.1991, *Cons. in Progress* 1993. Favours pers.pub.& news media support. **Languages:** English, French (good), Spanish (basic). Willing to act as consult.etc. **Address:** Department of Biology, University College London, Gower Street, London WC1E 6BT, England, UK. **Tel.**(office) 44 171 387 7050; **fax** 44 171 380 7026; **e-mail** ucbt196 @ucl.ac.uk .

GOLLEY, Professor Dr Frank B. Ecology, ecosystems, human ecology. Research Professor of Ecology. *B.*24 Sept.1930, Chicago, IL, USA. American. *M.*Priscilla McKinzie (coworker on books and edl asst of *Landscape Ecol.): s.* **Education:** Purdue U. BS in Agric. (Animal Sci.) 1952, Washington SU MS (Wildlife Biol.) 1954, Michigan SU PhD(Zool.) 1958. **Experience:** associated with U.of Georgia since 1958, founded Savannah River Ecol.Lab.as first

Dir, co-founded Inst.of Ecol.as Exec.Dir, directed the NSF Div.of Envl Biol.1979–81. **Career:** rising to Prof. Inst.of Ecol. U.of Georgia 1958–. **Achievements:** prod.of many students, leadership in intl orgns, served as Pres.of ISTE, ESA, & INTECOL. **Memberships:** ESA, IALE, num.others. **Publications:** 12+ books incl.*Human Pop.from an Ecol.Perspective* 1989, 200+ papers incl.Deep ecol.from the perspective of ecol.sci.1987, Envl consequences of salts' exports from an irrigated landscape in the Ebro R.Basin, Spain 1989, Intl dimensions of landscape ecol.1989. Dislikes pers.pub., very cautious about news media support. **Languages:** English (mother tongue), French (very poor), German (read), Spanish (poor). Willing to act as consult.etc. **Address:** Institute of Ecology, University of Georgia, Athens, Georgia 30602, USA. **Tel.**(office) 1 706 542 2968; **fax** 1 706 542 6040.

GOLUBEV, Professor Dr Genady Nikolaevich. Assessment & management of water resources; planning & coordination of global change research & environmental management worldwide; glaciology. Standing Committee Chairman, Vice-President. *B.*17 Dec.1935, Moscow, Russia. Russian. *M.*Dr Irina (geomorph.): 2 *d.* Svetlana (Sr Expert, Russian Min.of Envt Prot.), Tatiana (biol.). **Education:** Moscow SU, Dipl. of Hydrologist–Geographer 1958, PhD 1963, DSc 1974. **Experience:** res.on water resources & envt interaction, high mtn hydr.& glaciology, dev.& mgmt of envt progs world-wide. **Career:** res.& teaching 1958–75 and Prof.1975–6, 1981, 1989–92, Moscow SU; res.at IIASA 1976–81; Asst Exec.Dir UNEP and Asst Sec.-Gen.UN 1981–9; Asst DG IUCN 1992–93. **Achievements:** dev.& coordn of UN system-wide Envt Prog.; Author, co-Author, or co-Ed.12 books & 140 papers. **Memberships:** IGBP (Scientific Cttee), IAHS (VP), START/IGBP (Chairman, Standing Cttee). **Publications:** *c.*150 incl. *Hydr.of Glaciers* 1976, *Interregional Water Transfers: Problems & Prospects* (co-Ed.) 1978, *Envl Mgmt of Agricl Watersheds* (Ed.) 1983, *Large-scale Water Transfers: Emerging Envl & Social Experiences* (co-Ed.) 1985, *Envl Problems of Russia* (co-Author) 1993. Indiff.to pers.pub. & news media support. **Languages:** English, French (spoken & read), Russian, Spanish. **Address:** ul.Butlerov 10 Kv.72, Moscow 117485, Russia. **Tel.**(home) 7 095 336 2353.

GONZALEZ, Dr Juan Antonio AGUIRRE. Resource economics, environmental accounting, valuation, & pricing, economics of agroforestry, project analysis. Economist & Area Head. *B.*7 April 1940, Habana, Cuba. Hondurean by nationalization. *M.*Maria Margarita: 2 *s.*, 2 *d.* **Education:** U.of Florida BS 1962, MS 1964 both in Econ.& Agricl Econ.; Cornell U. PhD (Resources Econ., Econ.& Photo Interpretation) 1969. **Experience:** res., teaching, admin., consult.to World Bank, Interamerican Dev. Bank, IFAD, FAO, AID. **Career:** Teacher, Pan Amer.

Sch.of Agric.(Honduras) 1964–9; Prof.of Resource Econ. CATIE 1969–72; Regnl Econ. 1972–4, Country Rep.in Nicaragua 1974–8 and Honduras 1988–91, Dir Center for Project Investment 1980–87, IICA; Policy Adv. Min.of Agric.& Livestock (Costa Rica) 1991–3; Natural Resource Econ.& Head of Area of Prod.& Cons.Econ. CATIE 1993–. **Achievements:** Sr Agricl & Envl Adv.in all C.Amer.countries, actively promoting change in policy & legis.; work on prot.rates, pricing & envl accounting and its impact in Nat.Accounts. **Memberships:** Asociación Latinoamericana de Economistas Agrícolas, ISEE. **Awards:** Best Paper (ASHS), Best Paper (Latin Amer.Assn of Banking Instns), 2nd place Shell Intl World Essays Contest, Kellog Fndn/IICA Award on Rural Dev.; invited papers. **Publications:** *Econ.v. Fin.Pricing of Timber and its Probable Impact in Nat.Accounts* 1994. Indiff.to pers.pub. **Languages:** English, Spanish. Willing to act as consult.etc. **Address:** Apartado 598, 2200 Coronado, San José, Costa Rica. **Tel.**(offices) 506 556 1016 or 221 0122, (home) & **fax** 506 235 8915.

GOOD, Roger Bishop. Alpine ecology (plant distributions & origins), fire research (natural fire regimes and plant responses), biodiversity research & assessment, land-use planning & management. Botanist & Senior Research Officer. *B.*11 Dec.1944, Griffith, NSW, Australia. Australian. *M.*Rhana (native plant cons.): 2 *d.* **Education:** Hawkesbury Agricl Coll. Dipl.of Agric.1964; U.of New England, BA 1972, BLitt.1976; U.of NSW, MSc 1982. **Experience:** extensive res.in natural area mgmt & cons., alpine ecol.and alpine land rehab.& revegetation, bush-fire res.& modelling, field surveys and assessment of biodiv.in Se Australia, rare & threatened plant species' surveys, extensive consult.to industry & govts on these topics, res.exp.in Europe, USA, & NZ. **Career:** Soil Conservationist, NSW Soil Cons.Service 1964–74; Bot./Res.Sci. Nat.Parks and CSIRO 1974–95; Lect. ANU and U.of New England 1977–95; Bot.& Sr Res.Officer, NSW NPWS 1995–. **Achievements:** sound ecol.fire mgmt in nat.parks, ecol.sust.in natural areas (partic.alpine catchments), founding memb.of Australian Alps Interstate Liaison Cttee, init.tri-state Murray R.corridor cons.prog. **Memberships:** ANPC, IMS, E.Asia Pacific Mtn and Mtn Prot.Areas Networks, IGU, IUCN CNPPA Task Forces on Tourism and Prot.Areas and on Nat.Systems for Prot.Areas. **Awards:** F'ship (ARAS) 1966–7, Vis.F'ship (USA Govt) 1988, Res.F'ship (French Govt) 1992. **Publications:** *Scientific Sig.of the Australian Alps* (Ed.) 1988, *Kosciusko Heritage* 1992, *Alpes Australiènnes* (co-Ed., series vol.) 1992; *c.*75 papers. Favours pers.pub.& news media support. **Languages:** English, French (poor). Willing to act as consult.etc. **Address:** 16 Nott Street, Fraser, Australian Capital Territory 2615, Australia. **Tel.**(office) 61 6 298 9718, (home) 61 6 258 5571; **fax** 61 6 299 4281 or 297 4851.

GOODALL, R.Natalie PROSSER. Flora, marine mammals (especially cetaceans), and history, of southernmost South America. Independent Biologist, Author, Publisher. *B*.13 April 1935, Morrow Co., OH, USA. American. *M*. Thomas D.Goodall: 2 *d*. **Education:** Kent SU, BS *cum laude* 1957, MA 1959. **Experience:** self-directed res.on flora of Tierra del Fuego 1963–80 and on small cetaceans of southernmost S.Amer. 1976–, Teacher for Mobil Oil in Venezuela 1959–62, contracts with CADIC/ CONICET 1982–92, ecol.studies for Total Oil Co. 1990–94, Lect.on flora & fauna on tourist ships 1986–. **Career:** Teacher in USA 1957–9 & Venezuela 1959–62, Ind.Biol.on farm in Tierra del Fuego 1963–. **Achievements:** res.on small cetaceans & flora of Tierra del Fuego, lecturing & pubn of maps & books on the area. **Memberships:** MMS, Sociedad Argentina de Botanica. **Awards:** Scholarships (Kent SU) 1953–7, Premio Albatros (U.of Patagonia Don J.Bosco) 1983, Faro del Fin del Mundo (Govt of Tierra del Fuego) 1994. **Publications:** *Tierra del Fuego* (guide) 1970, 1975 & 1979, *Tierra del Fuego* (map) 1970 + many reprints; illustrs & *c*.40 papers. Dislikes pers.pub., accepts news media support if account is accurate. **Languages:** English, Spanish. Further details may be obtained from *Nat.Geographic* (Housewife at End of World) Jan 1971. Willing to act as consult.etc. **Address:** Sarmiento 44, 9410 Ushuaia, Tierra del Fuego, Argentina. **Tel.**(home) 54 901 22742 and 3.

GOODLAND, Dr Robert J.A. Tropical ecology, tropical forests; biodiversity conservation, environmental assessment of economic development projects; environmental sustainability, ecology/economics interface; environmental aspects of agriculture, transport, & energy — especially big dams. Environmental Adviser. *B*.26 Sept.1939, Lincs, England, UK. Canadian. *M*.Dr Jonmin W.: *s*. **Education:** McGill U. BSc (Hons)(Biol.) 1964, MSc 1965, PhD 1969. **Experience:** envl consult.(1968–78) for engg corpns and for Govts of Brazil, Bangladesh, Malaysia, Indonesia, etc.; taught applied trop. ecol.in Brasilia, Manaus, Costa Rica. **Career:** injecting envt into World Bank ops from Washington DC 1978–. **Achievements:** author of nearly all World Bank's envl policies, such as those on Tribal Peoples, Dams & Reservoirs, Cultural Property, Biodiv.& Wildlands, Envl Mgmt. **Memberships:** ESA (Pres., Metropolitan 1990), IAIA (Chairman 1991, Pres. 1994–5), ISEE (co-Founding Ed.). **Awards:** Logan Ecol.Prize 1963, Penhallow (Cons.) 1964, Best Paper Prize (FEC) 1991 & 1993, Rose–Hulman (Envl Assessment) Prize (IAIA) 1993, Boulding Award (ISEE). **Publications:** *The Amazon Jungle: Green Hell to Red Desert?* 1975, *Bldgs & the Envt* 1976, *Power Lines & the Envt* 1977, *Envl Mgmt in Trop.Agric.*1983, *Race to Save the Tropics* 1990, *Envl Assessment Sourcebook* (three vols) 1991, *Pop., Affluence, Tech.: The Transition to Sust.*1992; *c*.70 envl articles. Favours pers.pub.& news media support. **Languages:** English, Portuguese. Willing to act as a ref.or judge proposals. **Address:** The World Bank, 1818 H Street NW, Washington, District of Columbia 20433, USA. **Tel.**(office) 1 202 473 3203, (home) 1 703 534 2205; **fax** 1 202 477 0565; **Internet** RGOODLAND@WORLDBANK.ORG .

GOPAL, Dr Brij. Plant ecology, wetland ecology, limnology. Associate Professor. *B*.7 March 1944, Muzaffarnagar, UP, India. Indian. **Education:** Meerut Coll. BSc 1961, Christ Church Coll.(Kanpur) MSc(Bot.) 1964, BHU PhD(Bot.& Ecol.) 1968. **Experience:** postdoctl res.in forest ecol., u.teaching. **Career:** Lect.in Bot. Agra Coll.1970–71, Asst Prof.of Bot. Rajasthan U. 1972–85, Alexander von Humboldt F. Max-Planck-Institut für Limnologie 1982–3, Vis.Prof. Geobotl Inst. ETH 1984, Assoc.Prof.of Envl Sci. JNU 1986–. **Achievements:** contributed mainly to ecol.of aquatic macrophytes, esp.aquatic weeds, and to studies of wetlands and their cons. **Memberships:** INTECOL Wetland WG 1978–, Chairman SIL Cttee on Limnol.in Developing Countries 1989– and SIL Wetland WG 1983–, SIL Tonolli Fund Cttee & Cons. Cttee. **Award:** Young Scientists' Medal (INSA) 1974. **Publications:** Light regulated seed germination in *Typha angustata* Bory et C.haub (co-Author) 1983, Seasonal changes in the concentration of major nutrient elements in the rhizomes and leaves of *Typha elephantina* Rox.(co-Author) 1984, *Water Hyacinth [Eichhornia crassipes]* 1987, *Ecol.& Mgmt of Aquatic Veg.of the Indian Subcontinent* 1990, Competition & allelopathy in aquatic plant communities (co-Author) 1993. Indiff.to pers.pub.& news media support. **Languages:** English, German (read), Hindi. Willing to act as consult.etc. **Address:** School of Environmental Sciences, Jawaharlal Nehru University, New Delhi 110 067, India. **Tel.**91 11 652438; **fax** 91 11 686 5886.

GORDON, John Keith. Political & institutional aspects of sustainable development. Author & Independent Consultant. *B*.6 July 1940, Fleet, Hants., England, UK. British. *M*.Elizabeth: 2 *s*. **Education:** U.of Camb. BA(Hons)(Hist.)(1st Class) 1962, Yale U. 1963, LSE 1966. **Experience:** diplomatic service, res., admin., consult. **Career:** Diplomat serving in Budapest 1966–8, Geneva 1974–5, Yaounde 1975–7, and Moscow 1981–2; UK Mission to EC 1982–3, UN Perm.Mission to UNESCO — Perm.Del. (Amb.) 1984–5, Head of Nuclear Energy Dept, FCO 1986–8, Academic Visitor to IC Centre for Envl Tech.1988–90; Dep.& Policy Dir, Global Envt Res.Centre, IC 1990–94; Ind.Consult.& Author 1994–. **Achievements:** putting sust.on pol.agenda, analysing what it means in practice, promoting coopn between govts, NGOs & academics. **Memberships:** F.RSA, S–N Centre for Intl Envt Policy Studies (Governing Bd), UNED–UK Nat.Cttee, Ind.Security Info-Service (Adv.Bd), Nat.Cttee of Friends of UNESCO.

Publications: *Instns & Sust.Dev.: Meeting the Challenge* 1992, *2020 Vision: Britain, Germany and a New Envl Agenda 1994, Canadian Round Tables 1994.* Favours pers.pub.& news media support. **Languages:** English, French, German (elementary), Hungarian & Russian (rusty), Spanish (elementary). Further details may be obtained from Brit.*Who's Who* 1994, *Intl Who's Who* 1994, *Debrett's People of Today* 1994. Willing to act as consult.etc. **Address:** 68 Hornsey Lane, London N6 5LU, England, UK. **Tel.**(office) 44 171 225 1818, (home) 44 171 263 3725.

GORIUP, Paul David. Nature conservation planning, ornithological research especially of Bustards (Otididae). Managing Director, Executive Director (part-time), Secretary. *B.*8 July 1955, Reading, Berkshire, England, UK. British. *M.*Sue Everett (Dir The Nature Cons. Bureau Ltd, bot., cons.journalism). **Education:** U.of Reading BSc(Comb.Hons)(Bot./Zool.) 1976, UCL MSc(Cons.Sci.) 1978. **Experience:** res.on aquatic macrophytes, bustards, site mgmt planning, project mgmt, cons.of arid/steppe ecosystems; now mainly in business directing a Nature cons.consulting co. **Career:** Sci.Officer, NCC UK 1976–9; freelance researcher specializing in bustard cons.for WWF, IUCN, ICBP 1979–82; Asst Dir for Prog. ICBP (now Bird-Life Intl) 1982–6, Dir/Chairman, The Nature Cons.Bureau Ltd 1986– Sec. Steppe & Grassland Bird Group, Bird-Life Intl 1990–; Exec.Dir (part-time) IEEM 1991–. **Achievements:** instn & dev.of ICBP (now BirdLife Intl) Global Bird Cons.Prog.; maintenance of SG for cons.of bustards, and more recently steppe & grassland birds in gen.; design & prog.dev.for NARC Abu Dhabi. **Memberships:** F.ZSL, Res.F.DICE, IEEM, IUCN SSC & CNPPA. **Award:** Duke of Edinburgh Gold Award. **Publications:** Ed. *Parks Magazine* (IUCN) 1990–, *Bustard Studies* (BirdLife Intl) 1982–, and *Ecol.& Cons.of Grassland Birds* (ICBP) 1988. Indiff.to pers. pub., favours news media support. **Languages:** English, French (basic spoken). Willing to act as consult.etc. **Address:** The Nature Conservation Bureau Ltd, 26 Kingfisher Court, Hambridge Road, Newbury RG14 5SJ, Berkshire, England, UK. **Tel.**(office) 44 1635 550380; **fax** 44 1635 550230.

GORZULA, Dr Stefan 'Steve'. Social & environmental impact assessments of large dams; wildlife conservation & management particularly of Crocodilians, neotropical herpetology. Consultant Biologist. *B.*10 Aug.1948, Harrow, Middlesex, England, UK. British, Venezuelan. *M.*Laura Josephine: 2 *s.*, *d.* **Education:** St Joseph's Coll.(Lond.); U.of London, Bedford Coll.BSc(Hons)(Zool.) 1970; Univs of London & Glasgow, UMBSM, PhD(Marine Biol.) 1976. **Experience:** widespread applied res. ranging from temperate marine to trop.terr. ecosystems, extensive field-work in Guyana (19 trips), Brazil, & Vietnam, consult.to CITES Secretariat.

Career: Res.Asst, St Thomas' Hosp. (Lond.) 1970–71; Ecol. Instituto Venezolano de Investigaciones Cientificas 1974–7; Project Leader, Ministerio del Ambiente y de los Recursos Naturales Renovables 1978–9; Jobsite Inspector, Geosurveys 1979–80; Chief Planner, Corporación Venezolana de Guyana 1980–82; Ecol. Corporación Venezolana de Guyana Electrificación del Caroni Compañía Anómina 1982–8; VP, Sustained Mgmt Systems (USA/ Venezuela/Guyana) 1988–90; Assoc.Researcher, Fundacion La Salle de Ciencias Naturales (Venezuela) 1989–; Consult.Biol. Biosphere Consults (UK & USA) 1991. **Achievements:** major exploration of table mtns in s.Venezuela, co-Author of descriptions of 20+ new species of reptiles and amphibians as well as two new genera. **Memberships:** IUCN SSC Crocodile SG, IBiol., C.Biol. **Awards:** Dipl.for Recognition of Services (Armed Forces, Rep.of Venezuela) 1985, Hon.Res.F.(UMBSM) 1991. **Publications:** *c.*80 incl.eight major tech.reports. Favours pers.pub.& news media support. **Languages:** English, Spanish; French, German, Portuguese, & Vietnamese (basic). Willing to act as consult.etc. **Address:** 614 West Main Street, Newbern, Tennessee 38059, USA. **Tel.**& **fax** (office & home) 1 901 627 3133; **e-mail** gorzula@ecsis.net .

GOUDIE, Professor Dr Andrew Shaw. Climatic change, geomorphology, desert environments. Professor of Geography & Chairman. *B.* 21 Aug.1945, Cheltenham, England, UK. British. *M.*Heather (bldg-stone decay): 2 *d.* **Education:** U.of Cambridge, MA 1970, PhD 1971. **Experience:** extensive envl res.in world's drylands. **Career:** U.Lect.1970–84, U.Prof.1984–, Chairman Envl Change Unit Task Force, Sch.of Geog., U.of Oxf. **Achievements:** estab.of Oxford Envl Change Unit. **Memberships:** RGS (former VP), Pres.of Geographical Assn. **Awards:** Founder's Medal (RGS) 1991, Mungo Park Medal (RSGS) 1991. **Publications:** incl.*Techniques for Desert Reclamation* (Ed.) 1990, *Human Impact on the Envt* (4th edn) 1993, *Envl Change* (3rd edn) 1993. Favours pers.pub.& news media support. **Language:** English. Further details can be obtained from Brit.*Who's Who.* Willing to act as consult.etc. **Address:** School of Geography, University of Oxford, Mansfield Road, Oxford OX1 3TB, England, UK. **Tel.**(office) 44 1865 271921; **fax** 44 1865 271923.

GOULANDRIS, Mrs Niki. Environmental conservation & education. Vice-President, President. *B.*9 Jan.1925, Athens, Greece. Greek. *M.*Angelos Goulandris (Pres. Goulandris Natural Hist.Mus.). **Education:** U.of Athens BS (Pol.Sci. & Econ.) 1954, U.of Frankfurt postgrad.studies in pol.sci.& phil.1957–60. **Experience:** mgmt of Greece's only natural hist. mus. **Career:** co-Founder & VP, Goulandris Natural Hist.Mus. 1964–; Dep.Minister for Social Services 1974–5, Dep.Pres. Hellenic Radio & TV 1974–81 and Nat.Tourism Orgn of Greece 1989–91, Pres.Save the Children Assn in Greece 1980–. **Achie-**

vements: init.envl awareness in Greece, botl paintings & world-wide exhibitions. **Memberships:** LS, IDRC of Canada for the Third World (Bd of Govs), ICCD, WCCD. **Awards:** Hon. Doct. (Aristotelian U.), Global 500 Roll of Honour (UNEP) 1990, Woman of Europe (EC) 1991, Officier of Légion d'Honneur. **Publications:** illustrator of *Wild Flowers of Greece* 1968, *Peonies of Greece* 1984, and 600+ species of Greek plants. Indiff.to pers. pub., favours news media support. **Languages:** English, French, German, Greek. **Address:** The Goulandris Natural History Museum, 13 Levidou Street, 145 62 Kifissia, Greece. **Tel.**(office) 30 1 8014 813, (home) 30 1 8013 191; **fax** 30 1 8080 674.

GOULDMAN, (Myer) Dennis. Environmental & planning law. Lecturer, Partner. *B.*25 Feb. 1935, Manchester, England, UK. Israeli. *M.* Yvette Shalom: 2 *s.*incl.Daniel (natural farming & biol.pest control), 2 *d.* **Education:** U.of Manchester LLB 1955, Solicitor of Supreme Court (England) 1958, Advocate (Israel) 1963. **Experience:** res.& teaching at Hebrew U.of Jerusalem. **Career:** Sr Asst State Attorney 1970–76, Head of Intl Dept, State Attorney's Office 1977–87, Min.of Justice; Staff Memb. Inst.for Urban and Regnl Studies, Hebrew U.of Jerusalem 1974–; Partner, Laster & Gouldman 1989 . **Achievements:** pioneer in planning laws in Israel, partner in law firm which represents local authorities, river & drainage bds, town assns for the envt in planning & envl matters. **Memberships:** Law Soc.(England), Israel Bar. **Publications:** *Legal Aspects of Planning Law in Israel* 1966, *Israel Nationality Law* 1970; num.legal articles. Indiff.to pers.pub.& news media support. **Languages:** English, French (medium), Hebrew. Willing to act as consult.&/or judge proposals. **Address:** Laster & Gouldman Law Offices, 10 Hanassi Street, Jerusalem 92188, Israel. **Tel.**(office) 972 2 635224, (home) 972 2 618463; **fax** 972 2 636926.

GRACE, Professor Dr John. Environmental impacts on vegetation (wind, temperature, drought stress), climatic change, carbon & water relations of forest ecosystems; global carbon balance, tropical ecology. Professor of Environmental Biology. *B.*19 Sept.1945, Northampton, England, UK. British. *M.*Elizabeth (clinical geneticist): 2 *s.*, *d.* **Education:** Bletchley Grammar Sch., U.of Sheffield PhD 1970. **Experience:** res.& teaching at U.of Edinburgh; admin. — Convenor, Sch.of Ecol.Scis, U.of Edinburgh, member of cttees of NERC; consult.for ECTF; Ed.of text books & scientific journals. **Career:** Lect.1970, Reader 1985, Prof.1992–, U.of Edinburgh. **Achievements:** co-founding Ed.of j.*Functional Ecol.*1987, res.on impact of wind on plants (leading to book*) and on carbon balance of rain-forest, Counc.of BES. **Memberships:** BES, ISB, SEB, BSS. **Awards:** Pers.Chair, U.of Edinburgh, num.res.grants. **Publications:** *Plant Response to Wind* 1977, *Plants and their Atmos.Envt* (co-Ed.) 1981, *Plant–Atmos.Rela-*

tionships 1983, *Water Transport in Plants under Climatic Stress* (co-Ed.) 1993; Section Ed.of *Enc.of Envt and Resource Mgmt* 1995; 100+ pubns in refereed journals & proc.of scientific symposia. Dislikes pers.pub., favours news media support. **Languages:** English, French, Portuguese (weak). Further details may be obtained from *Who's Who in Scotland* 1994. Willing to act as consult.etc. **Address:** Institute of Ecology & Resource Management, The University of Edinburgh School of Ecological Sciences, Darwin Building, Mayfield Road, Edinburgh EH9 3JU, Scotland, UK. **Tel.**(office) 44 131 650 5400, (home) 44 131 447 3030; **fax** 44 131 662 0478; **e-mail** jgrace&ed.ac.uk .

GRAD, Professor Dr Frank P. Environmental & public health law. Chamberlain Professor of Legislation, Fund Director. *B.*2 May 1924, Vienna, Austria. American. *M.*Lisa Szilagyi: *s.*, *d.* **Education:** Brooklyn Coll. BA *magna cum laude* 1947, Columbia U.Sch.of Law JD 1949. **Experience:** u.teaching of envl law 1970–, substantial exp.in envl law res.incl. service as reporter for US Superfund Study Group estab.by Congress under §301(e) of the Comp.Envl Response, Compensation & Liability Act 1980, and res.exp.in projects re.public health law; teaching of public health law at Yale & Columbia Schools of Public Health 1965–. **Career:** Assoc.in Law 1949–50, Lect.in Law 1954–64, Adjunct Prof.of Legis.1964–9, Assoc. Dir, Legislative Drafting Res.Fund 1955–69, Prof.of Law 1961–, Joseph P.Chamberlain Prof. of Legis.1982–, Dir Legislative Drafting Res. Fund 1969–, all at Columbia Sch.of Law. **Achievements:** direction, a reporter of the Congressionally-sponsored study of 'Injuries & Damages from Hazardous Wastes — Analysis & Improvement of Legal Remedies Pursuant to §301(e) of the so-called Superfund Law'; authorship of six-vol.*Treatise on Envl Law* * and num.pubns on envl law incl.those given below, membership of Legal Adv.Cttce of US CEQ 1970–73. **Memberships:** ALI, ABA, Assn of the Bar of the City of NY, F.APHA, ELI (Assoc.), ICEL. **Publications:** *Envl Control: Priorities, Policies, and the Law* 1971, **Treatise on Envl Law* (six vols 1973–94), *The Automobile and the Regulation of its Impact on the Envt* (co-Author) 1979, *Envl Law: Sources & Problems* 1985, *Public Health Law Manual* 1990; num.law review & periodical pubns. Favours pers.pub.& news media support. **Languages:** English, German. Further details may be obtained from *Who's Who in Amer.*1994, *Who's Who in Amer.Law* 1994, *Who's Who in the E.*1994. Willing to act as consult.etc. **Address:** Columbia University School of Law, 435 West 116 Street, New York, New York 10027, USA. **Tel.**(office) 1 212 854 2685, (home) 1 212 362 9042; **fax** 1 212 854 7946.

GRANDTNER, Professor Dr Miroslav Marian. Forest ecology, dendrology, international forestry. Emeritus Professor of Forest Ecology &

Associate Professor of International Forestry. *B*.23 Aug.1928, Liptovska-Teplicka, Slovakia. Canadian. *D.: d*. **Education:** Louvain U.(Belgium), BSc(Water & Forests) 1955, DSc(Plant Ecol.) 1962; Laval U.(Quebec) MSc(Forest Ecol.) 1959. **Experience:** res., teaching, editing, and consult., in veg.class.& mapping, land mgmt, intl for., plant bioindicators, and dendrology. **Career:** Cartographer, IRSIA (Belgium) 1955–8; Res.Asst 1955–8, Prof.of Forest Ecol.1958–93 (Emer.1994–), Assoc.Prof.of Intl For.1993–, Laval U.; Consult. Bur.d'Aménagement (Mont-Joli) 1963–6. **Achievements:** class.& cartography of veg.in Belgium, Spain, Canada, Senegal, Mali, and Antilles; experimental study of plant bioindicators; editing of a World Dict.of Trees (in prep.). **Memberships:** Société de Géographie de Québec (Life), IAVS, Fedn Internationale de Phytosociologie (Nomenclatural Comm.). **Award:** Hon Memb.(Assn des Biologistes du Québec) 1987. **Publications:** books incl.*La veg.forestière du Québec méridional* 1966 (13th reprint 1990), *Veg.in e.N.Amer*.(co-Ed.) 1994; papers incl.*La forêt de Beausejour* 1960, Nature cons.in e.Canada 1994, 200 addit.; Ed., Invited Ed., co-Ed., Assoc.Ed., or memb.of Edl Bds, of *Etudes écologiques, Dossiers de forèsterie internationale, Vegetatio, Phytocoenologia, Naturaliste canadien, Documents phytosociologiques, Braun-Blanquetia, Excerpta Botanica, & Les (i.e.*Forest). Favours pers.pub.& news media support. **Languages:** English, French, Slovakian; Czech, German, Polish & Spanish (all poor written & oral). Further details may be obtained from *Who's Who in Sci.& Engg, Amer.Men & Women of Sci., Who's Who in the World* (formerly). Willing to judge proposals &/or ref.papers. **Address:** Department of Wood and Forest Sciences, Laval University, Ste-Foy, Quebec G1K 7P4, Canada. **Tel.**(office) 1 418 656 2838, (home) 1 418 654 0508; **fax** 1 418 656 3177; **e-mail** Miroslav. Grandtner@sbf.ulaval.ca .

GRANJA, Professor Dr Helena Maria. Sedimentology & geomorphology of coastal environments, impact study of anthropic processes in the coastal zone. Auxiliary Professor of Geology. *B*.14 May 1953, Porto, Portugal. Portuguese. **Education:** U.of Porto, BSc (Geol.) 1977; U.of Bordeaux I, 3ème Cycle in Oceanology 1984; U.of Minho (Braga), PhD (Geol.) 1990. **Experience:** res., tech., consult. **Career:** Sedimentologist, Envt State Secretariat (Lisbon) 1977–84; Prof.of Geol.& Researcher, U.of Minho 1984–. **Achievements:** intervention in nat.& intl mtgs re.envt & cons.of coastal zone, talks in schools & municipalities, written reports (CORINE-coastal erosion, EUCC), Portuguese del.of EUCC, EC projects in field of envt. **Memberships:** IAS, EUCC, EUROCOAST (Portugal), ASBPA, SEPM, APEQ, APG, SGP. **Publications:** num.incl.The recent evol.of Póvoa de Varzim coast (NW Portugal) 1991, *A Synthesis of the Researches about the Pleistocene–Holocene Evol.of the NW Coastal Zone of Portugal* (Proc., co-Author) 1993, Sea level rise and neotectonism in a Holocene coastal envt at Cortegaça beach (NW Portugal) — a case study (co-Author) 1995, *Coastal Cons.and Prot. in NW Portugal* (Proc., co-Author) 1995. Indiff. to pers.pub., favours news media support. **Languages:** English (good written, medium spoken), French, Portuguese. Willing to act as consult.etc. **Address:** Departamento de Ciencias da Terra, Universidade do Minho, Campus de Gualtar, 4700 Braga, Portugal. **Tel.**(office) 351 53 604303, (home) 351 2 982 2651; **fax** 351 53 604304.

GRASSL, Professor Dr Hartmut, *see* p. 367.

GREEN, Professor Dr Brynmor Hugh. Habitat restoration & management particularly on farmland, agri-environmental policy; landscape protection. Professor of Countryside Management. *B*.14 Jan.1941, Mountain Ash, S.Wales, UK. British. *M*.Jean: 2 *s*. **Education:** U.of Nottingham, BSc(Bot.) 1962, PhD(Plant Ecol.) 1965. **Experience:** Founder Chairman of Kent Farming and Wildlife Adv.Group 1977–, NCC for England Cttee 1983–90, Countryside Commissioner 1984–93, Chairman of White Cliffs Countryside Mgmt Project 1989–, Adv.Council of Plantlife 1989–, Chairman of IUCN CESP Landscape Cons.WG 1993–. **Career:** Lect.in Plant Ecol. Dept of Bot. U.of Manchester 1965–7; Dep.& Regnl Officer, NC 1967–74; Lect.& Sr Lect.1974–87, Head of Envt Section & Prof.of Countryside Mgmt 1987–, Wye Coll.(U.of London). **Achievements:** res., dev., teaching, & extension, re.principles & practice of amenity, farm, and cultural, landscape prot.& mgmt. **Memberships:** IUCN CESP, BES. **Award:** OBE 1995. **Publications:** *Countryside Cons.*(2nd edn) 1985, *The Diversion of Land* (co-Author) 1991, *The Changing Role of the Common Agricl Policy* (co-Author) 1991; num. scientific papers. **Languages:** English, French (some). Further details may be obtained from Brit.*Who's Who* 1996. Willing to act as consult.etc. **Address:** Environment Section, Wye College, University of London, Wye, Ashford, Kent TN25 5AH, England, UK. **Tel.**(office) 44 1233 812401, (home) 44 1233 812575; **fax** 44 1233 812855.

GREGOIRE, Felix W. Forest, national park, environmental, and natural resources, management. Permanent Secretary. *B*.16 Jan.1952, Scotts Head, Commonwealth of Dominica. Dominican. *M*.Charmaine: 3 *s*. **Education:** U.of New Brunswick BSc (Forest Resource Mgmt) 1977. **Experience:** public admin., resource mgmt, community leader. **Career:** Forest Officer, For.& Wildlife Div.1977–80, Dep Dir of For.& Wildlife 1980–86, Dir of For.& Wildlife 1986– 93, Perm.Sec.1993–, Min.of Agric. Govt of Dominica. **Achievements:** estab.of Parks & Reserves, formulation of Nat.Envl Prog. **Memberships:** CFA (Pres.1988– 90), CCA, other nat. bodies. **Publications:** several conf. papers & popular articles. Favours pers.pub.& news media support. **Languages:** French Creole (good spoken & written), English, French (comp.). Willing to act as consult.etc. **Address:** Ministry of Agriculture, Government Headquarters, Roseau, Commonwealth of Dominica. **Tel.** (office) 809 448 2401, (home) 809 448 4815; **fax** 809 448 7999.

GRIFFITHS, Dr Richard Alun. Population, community, and behavioural, ecology; reptile & amphibian biology & conservation. Research Ecologist. *B.*11 June 1957, London, England, UK. British. **Education:** Stationers' Company's Sch., Westfield Coll.London BSc(Hons)(Biol. Scis) 1978, Birkbeck Coll.London PhD(Zool.) 1983. **Experience:** res.on ecol.& behaviour of all native British amphibians; Nat.Exec.of First World Cong.of Herpetology; co-Dir, JWPT Summer Schools. **Career:** Res.F.in Ecol. U.of Wales 1983–6 & Leicester Poly.1986–7, Lect.in Biol. Sci. NE Surrey Coll.of Tech.1987–90; NERC Advanced Res.F. DICE 1990–. **Achievements:** determination of factors regulating endangered pops of amphibians, effects of acidification & climate change on ecol.communities. **Memberships:** F.ZSL, BHS (Counc.), BES, ASAB. **Publications:** *How to Begin the Study of Amphibians* 1987, 33 papers. Indiff.to pers. pub., favours news media support. **Language:** English. Willing to act as consult.etc. **Address:** Durrell Institute of Conservation & Ecology, University of Kent, Canterbury, Kent CT2 7PD, England, UK. **Tel.**44 1227 764000 ext.3434; **fax** 44 1227 475480.

GRINBERG, Professor Miguel. Education, social ecology. Director. *B.*18 Aug.1937, Buenos Aires, Argentina. Argentinian. *M.*Flavia N.: 3 *s., d.* **Education:** U.de Buenos Aires BSc 1963, U.of New York BSc 1970, U.of Texas at Houston MSc 1979. **Experience:** field res.on social & envl issues, founder of nat., regnl, & intl, envl networks, consult.for public envl policies. **Career:** co-Founder — Nat.Network for Eco-Action (Argentina) 1986, Latin Amer.Pact for Eco-Action (Chile) 1989, Citizens' Perm. Envl Assembly (Argentina) 1989, The Ya Wananchi Coalition (Brazil) 1992 and (also Dir) Promundo Internacional 1992–. **Achievements:** Founder & Prof.of Social Ecol. Multiversidad de Buenos Aires 1982–7. **Membership:** Envt Liaison Centre Intl (Kenya). **Awards:** Global 500 Roll of Honour (UNEP) 1988, DuPont Argentina Medal 1989, Albert Schweitzer Award 1991. **Publications:** *La Nueva Revolución Norteamericana* 1968, *La Generación de la Paz* 1985, *Ecología Vivencial* 1988, *Introducción a la ecología social* 1992, *Ecología cotidiana* 1994. Favours pers.pub.& news media support. **Languages:** English, Portuguese, Spanish. **Address:** Promundo Internacional, CC Central 1933, 1000 Buenos Aires, Argentina. **Tel.**541 343 3768; **fax** 541 334 7802.

GRINEVALD, Dr Jacques M.L. Environmental education & history of ecology, philosophy & history of global ecology especially the concept of The Biosphere. Chargé de Cours. *B.*14 Jan. 1946, Strasbourg, France. French. **Education:** U.of Geneva, Licence scis politiques (études internationales, IUHEI) 1970; U.of Paris, Doctorat de 3ème Cycle en philosophie 1979. **Experience:** num.lectures & teaching in many countries; consult.to UNESCO, UNITAR; Homme–Technique–Environnement prog. EPFL. **Career:** Chargé de Cours at EPFL 1981–, Institut universitaire d'études du développement 1982– and at Faculté des scis économiques et sociales 1987–, U.of Geneva. **Achievements:** several contribns to phil.& historiography of global ecol.esp.the idea of The Biosphere & Gaia. **Memberships:** AAAS, ISEE, ECOROPA. **Awards:** 1st Prize in Phil.(Facultés catholiques de Lyon) 1966; Humbert Prize of Phil. (U.of Geneva) 1968. **Publications:** On a holistic concept for deep & global ecol. The Biosphere 1987, Sketch for the Hist.of the Idea of the Biosphere 1988, Europe and the Biosphere's Global Ecol.1991. Indiff.to pers.pub., favours news media support. **Languages:** English (poor), French. Further details may be obtained from *Who's Who in the World* (1993–94). Willing to act as a ref. **Address:** 6 Chemin Rieu, CH-1208 Geneva, Switzerland. **Tel.** (office) 41 22 731 5940, (home) 41 22 735 7015; **fax** 41 22 738 4416.

GRITZNER, Professor Dr Jeffrey Allman. Environmental history, the reconciliation of en vironmental rehabilitation with rural livelihood systems. Institute Director & Research Professor of Geography. *B.*10 Jan.1941, Newaygo County, MI, USA. American. *M.*Yvonne: 2 *s., d.* **Education:** UCB AB 1966, U.of Chicago AM 1974, PhD(Geog.) 1986. **Experience:** res., admin., consult., teaching. **Career:** Agron. Peace Corps 1972–4; Tech.Dir, Agricola du Tchad 1974–5; teacher Trinidad State Jr Coll.1975–8; Sr Prog. Officer NAS 1978–88; Consult.to UN & IUCN 1981–; Sr Assoc. WRI 1988–9; Dir Public Policy Res.Inst.& Res.Prof.of Geog. U.of Montana 1989–. **Achievements:** dev.of strats linking histl envl analysis with large-scale rehab., focusing upon African & S.Amer. drylands. **Memberships:** AAAS, ASEH, AAG, Gamma Theta Upsilon, IASCP, IUCN CESP. **Awards:** Fulbright–Hays F., Ford Fndn F., NDEA F. **Publications:** *Envl Degradation in Mauritania* 1981, *The W.African Sahel: Human Agency & Envl Change* 1988, Failed paradigms, neglected wisdom, and envl reality: an approach to the rehab.of the W.African Sahel 1988; *c.*47 others. Indiff.to pers.pub., favours news media support. **Languages:** Chadian Arabic (spoken), English, French, German (read), Persian (spoken), Spanish (read). Further details may be obtained from *Who's Who in Sci.& Engg* (2nd edn). Willing to act as consult.etc. **Address:** 378 One Horse Creek Road, Florence, Montana 59833, USA. **Tel.**(office) 1 406 243 5626, (home) 1 406 273 0665; **fax** 1 406 243 4840.

GROOT, Professor Dr Wouter T.DE. Environment & development, theory for problem-oriented analysis & management, deforestation, desertification. Deputy Director, Guest Professor. Dutch. *M*.Lenie E.: *s.*, *d.* **Education:** Tech.U.of Delft, MSc(Civ.Eng.) 1974; U.of Leiden, PhD 1992. **Experience:** res.— hydr., biol., anthropl methodology, for envl problem analysis & explanation; tech.— road & bridge design & construction; admin.— Dep.Dir, Centre for Envl. Sci; teaching — 15 yrs' envl sci. **Career:** Engr, Kenya 1974–7; explorations & pubns in hydr., sociol., econ., biol.etc.as fields contributing to analysis, explanation, & solution, of envl problems 1977–85; developing envl sci.as an integrating disc. **Achievements:** fostering problem-oriented envl sci.as a practical but theory-rich disc.for developed/developing nations; bldg coopn structures with univs in Cameroon & the Philippines. **Publications:** *Envl Sci.Theory* 1992; *c.*60 papers. Indiff.to pers.pub.& news media support. **Languages:** Dutch, English; French & German (intermediate). Willing to act as consult.etc. **Address:** Centre of Environmental Science, University of Leiden, POB 9518, 2300 RA Leiden, The Netherlands. **Tel.**(office) 31 71 277487, (home) 31 71 141888; **fax** 31 71 277496.

GRUBB, Dr Peter John. Vegetational dynamics, competition, and coexistence; plant–soil relations, plants in relation to herbivores & dispersers; tropical rain-forests and communities on calcareous soils of Europe. Reader in Ecology. *B.*9 Aug.1935, Ilford, Essex, England, UK. British. *M*.Elizabeth Adelaide: *s.*, *d.* **Education:** R.Liberty Sch.; Magdalene Coll. Camb. BA 1957, MA 1961, PhD 1962. **Experience:** res.— began in plant physiol.(ion uptake) of mosses, parallel exp.on expedns (Balkans, Andes) ended in shift to ecol., extensive studies of montane & lowland rain-forests in tropics, also Medit.-climate systems & widespread exp.in Australia; teaching bot.& ecol. **Career:** F.1958–, Tutor 1963–74, Pres.1991–6, Magdalene Coll.Camb.; Lect.1964–92, Reader in Ecol. 1992–, Camb.U.; Nuffield–RS Bursary, U.of Adelaide 1963; Hon.Res.F. ANU 1970–71; Vis. Prof. Cornell U.1982 & 1987. **Achievements:** res.on maintenance of species-richness and on control of relative abundance in plant communities, also on plant–soil relations; generalizing ideas on succession, trends in species-richness, plant defences etc.; jt Ed. *J.of Ecol.* 1972–7. **Memberships:** BES (Pres.1990–91), Camb.Phil.Soc.(Pres.1990–91), SEB, BBS, BLS. **Awards:** Frank Smart Prize 1956 & Student 1957–8 (Camb.U.), Rolleston Mem.Essay Prize (Oxf.U.) 1962. **Publications:** *Forests of Mt Kerigomna, PNG* (co-Author) 1985, *Toward a More Exact Ecol.*(co-Ed.) 1989; var.papers. Indiff.to pers.pub.& news media support. **Languages:** English, German (poor), Spanish (poor). Further details may be obtained from Brit.*Who's Who* 1994. Willing to judge proposals. **Address:** Magdalene College, Camb-

ridge CB3 0AG, England, UK. **Tel.**(office) 44 1223 332144, (home) 44 1223 276576; **fax** 44 1223 462589.

GRUBER, Professor Dr Samuel H. Elasmobranch (sharks etc.) research, conservation, sensory physiology, & behaviour. Professor & Field Station Director. *B.*13 May 1938, Brooklyn, NY, USA. American. *M*.Mariko (Asst Dir, Bimini Biol.Field Station): 2 *d.* **Education:** U.of Miami BS(Zool.) 1960, MS(Marine Sci.) 1966, PhD(Marine Scis) 1969. **Experience:** res.& teaching, thesis & dissertation adv., community, professional & cttee service, exp.at sea as Chief Sci.on 34 UNOLS/NSF & other cruises since 1979, num.formal presentations & sems since 1965. **Career:** Res.Sci.1969–73, Res.Asst Prof. 1972–73, Assoc.Prof.1976–84, Prof.1985, Dir Bimini Biol.Field Station 1990–, Rosenstiel Sch.of Marine & Atmos.Sci. U.of Miami; Vis.Sci.— Max-Planck-Inst. für Verhaltenphysiologie Seewiesen 1971–2, Heinz Steinitz Marine Biol.Lab.1984, Al Ghardaqua Marine Station 1984; Asst Prof. U.of Miami 1973–6; Adjunct Prof. U.of NC 1986. **Achievements:** founding Amer.Elasmobranch Soc. 1983, and Bimini Biol.Field Station 1990; recipient of Ocean Expo Life-time Achievement Award, and US NSF, US Office of Naval Res.& US–Israel Binational Sci.Fndn grants; being Chairman of IUCN SSC Shark SG, Counc.BNT, Disting. Scholar of AES, reviewer for several scientific journals, and proposal reviewer for NSF. **Memberships:** AES (Founder) 1983–, AIFRB 1974, ASIH 1969–, AFS 1979–, ASZ 1983–, ARVO 1973–80, IAAAM 1971–4, IAMAT 1971–4, Oceanographic Soc.1988–90, OSA 1973–80, Sigma Xi Assn (full) 1976, Soc.for Neurosciences 1975–86. **Awards:** Lifetime Achievement Disting.F.(AES) 1988, *c.*25 res. grants from var.agencies. **Publications:** num.incl.Morphological & Electrophysiological Studies in the Olfactory Organ of the Lemon Shark 1986, Studying the Savage Shark 1986, *Discovering Sharks: A Vol. Honoring the Work of Stewart Springer* (Ed.) 1991, Elasmobranchs as Living Resources 1990; num.conf.& presentation papers, j.papers etc. Favours pers.pub.& news media support. **Languages:** English, Spanish (spoken). Willing to act as consult.etc. **Address:** 9300 SW 99th Street, Miami, Florida 33176, USA. **Tel.**(office) 1 305 361 4146, (home) 1 305 274 0628; **fax** 1 305 361 4600.

GRUCZMACHER, Ricardo BAYÓN. Evolutionary biology, environmental communications. Information & Media Relations Officer. *B.*11 July 1968, Bogotá, Colombia. Colombian. **Education:** Brown U. BA 1989. **Experience:** admin., editing. **Career:** Envl Ed.*Buenos Aires Herald* 1989–91, Ed.*Network '92* 1991–3, Info. & Media Relations Officer IUCN 1993–. Favours pers.pub.& news media support. **Languages:** English, French (conversational), Spanish. Willing to act as consult.etc. **Address:**

IUCN–World Conservation Union, Rue Mauverney 28, 1196 Gland, Switzerland. **Tel.** (office) 41 22 999 0115, (home) 41 22 312 0520; **fax** 41 22 991 0010.

GUAGNI DEI MARCOVALDI, Guy Marie Fabio, *see* **MARCOVALDI, Guy Marie Fabio GUAGNI DEI.**

GUAGNI DEI MARCOVALDI, Maria Ângela, *see* **MARCOVALDI, Maria Ângela GUAGNI DEI.**

GUBBAY, Dr Susan. Coastal-zone management, marine ecology, marine conservation with particular reference to marine protected areas. Freelance Environmental Specialist. *B.*8 Sept. 1957, Calcutta, India. British. *M.*Alan Davis (for. & woodland mgmt). **Education:** Lancaster U. BSc(Hons)(Ecol.) 1978, York U. DPhil (Marine Ecol.) 1984. **Experience:** ten yrs' working for non-govtl cons.charity; developed proposals for UK coastal-zone mgmt strat., policy & lobbying for estab.of marine prot.areas; training & public awareness campaigns on aspects of marine cons.; intl exp.in aspects of marine cons. **Career:** Sr Cons.Officer, Marine Cons.Soc.1984–94; Freelance Envl Specialist 1994–; Specialist Adv.to House of Commons' Envt Select Cttee Inquiry into coastal zone planning & prot. **Achievements:** promotion of coastal-zone mgmt in UK, pubn of first review of sites of marine cons. importance in UK, assisted with designation of vol.& statutory marine Nature reserves. **Memberships:** F.RICS, Biodiv. Action Planning Steering Group (UK). **Award:** Buckland Prof. (Marine Prot.Areas & Fisheries) 1993. **Publications:** 30+ incl.*A Coastal Directory for Marine Nature Cons.*1988, *A Future for the Coast? Proposals for UK Coastal Zone Mgmt Plan* 1990, *Recommendations for a Euro.Union Coastal Strat.*1994. Indiff.to pers.pub.& news media support. **Language:** English. Willing to act as consult.etc.in moderation. **Address:** 55 Verschoyle Gardens, Ross-on-Wye, Herefordshire HR9 7HH, England, UK. **Tel.**& **fax** 44 1989 566486.

GUNAWARDENE, Nalaka Jayampati. Environmental journalism & education; writing, editing & producing material for public awareness; video & audio productions. Communications Specialist. *B.*13 Feb.1966, Colombo, Sri Lanka. Sri Lankan. *M.*Dushyanthi (ed.& writer on envt & dev.issues). **Education:** Ananda Coll.Colombo, High Sch. Biol.1986; Open U.of Sri Lanka, Dipl.in Journalism 1992. **Experience:** studying trends & conditions of third-world envt & dev.issues, training journalists on envl journalism, managing small envtl NGOs, planning & mgmt of large envl NGO support project, writing, editing & producing video films on envl themes, lecturing. **Career:** Sci.& Envt Corres.1986–9, Sci.Ed.1989–93, *The Island* Newspaper, Colombo, Sri Lanka Corres. *Asia Tech.* Hong Kong 1989–90, Envl Project

Mgr, The Asia Fndn, Colombo 1992, Communications Specialist, IUCN 1992–. **Achievements:** in writing, as Author of two books, and as producer of 12 TV/video progs on envt. **Memberships:** ISWA, Soc.of Envl Journalists, IUCN CEC. **Awards:** Sci.Writer of the Yr (Sri Lanka AAS) 1988, 1989; Sci.Popularization Award (Sri Lanka NSF) 1989. **Publications:** *Educ.Calendar Book* 1991, *A Status Study on Envl Educ.in Sri Lanka* (co-Author & Ed.) 1992; *c.*1,700 popular articles & 15 papers in Sri Lankan & intl journals. Favours pers.pub.& news media support. **Languages:** English, Sinhalese. Willing to act as consult.etc. **Address:** IUCN Sri Lanka, 7 Vajira Lane, Colombo 5, Sri Lanka. **Tel.**(office) 94 1 580202, (home) 94 1 863068; **fax** 94 1 698730.

GÜNDLING, Dr Lothar. International environmental law, comparative environmental law, law of the sea. Attorney, Legal Consultant. *B.*23 July 1949, Leutershausen, Germany. German. **Education:** U.of Frankfurt am Main, First State Exam.in Law 1973, Dr iur.1981; U.of Heidelberg, Second State Exam.in Law 1976. **Experience:** specific background in intl & comparative law, Euro.Comm.law, law consult.in developing countries world-wide. **Career:** F. Max-Planck-Inst.for Comparative Public Law & Intl Law 1976 90, Lect. U.of Heidelberg 1984–7, Projects Coord. IUCN Envl Law Centre 1990–94, Attorney and Legal Consult.1994–. **Achievements:** pubns in intl & comparative envl law, op.of IUCN's Envl Law Service, cons.in envl law. **Memberships:** ASIL, German AEL, ILA. **Award:** Otto-Hahn-Medal (Max-Planck-Soc.) 1979. **Publications:** seven books incl.*Trends in Envl Law* 1978, 1990, *Forest Resource Mgmt: Legal & Policy Issues in India & Germany* 1984, Problems of Euro.Envl Policy (in German) 1988; 60 articles & essays, Assoc.Ed. *Yearbook of Intl Envl Law.* Favours pers.pub.& news media support. **Languages:** English, French, German. Willing to act as consult.etc. **Address:** Franz-Liszt-Strasse 11, D-69214 Eppelheim, Germany. **Tel.**(office) 49 6221 769297, (home) 49 6221 766645; **fax** 49 6221 766430.

GUNDIA NEEL, Dr James VAN, *see* **NEEL, Dr James VAN GUNDIA.**

GUPTA, Brij Kishor. Wildlife conservation, captive-breeding programmes, environmental education & awareness programmes. Development Officer. *B.*15 May 1968, Fatehabad, Agra Distr., UP, India. Indian. *M.*Seema: *d.* **Education:** U.of Dayalbagh, M(Envl Zool.) 1989; Cons.and Res.Centre, Nat.Zool Park (USA), training in Wildlife Mgmt & Cons.1991; NAAEE/Smithsonian Instn, training in Malaysia in Envl Educ.1992; JWPT, training in Endangered Species Mgmt 1992; Singapore Zool Gdns, training in Marketing and Fund-raising 1994. **Experience:** res.— surveys on endangered raptors in India and on trade in lizards in c.India, studies on Rhesus Macaques, on endangered Round Is.Gecko, and on identification of nest predators. **Career:** Res.F. BNHS 1991–2; Head, Animal Welfare Soc.of India 1992–3; Asst Project Officer, WWF India 1993–4; Dev. Officer, Coimbatore Zool.Park & Cons.Centre 1994–. **Achievements:** location of places of animal trade in diff.parts of UP, animal welfare awareness campaign in some parts of UP, successful techniques to identify nest predators of ground-nesting birds. **Memberships:** IUCN SSC Cons.Breeding, Pheasant, and Varanus, SGs, WWF India, BNHS, Zoo Outreach Orgn India. **Award:** Best Project Award (Smithsonian Instn) 1991. **Publications:** several incl.*Tactics for Species Mgmt — Using Zoo Records* (conf.paper) 1994. Indiff.to pers.pub., favours news media support. **Languages:** English, Hindi. Willing to act as consult.etc. **Address:** The Coimbatore Zoological Park and Conservation Centre, Pioneer House, Peelamedu, Coimbatore 641004, Tamil Nadu, India. **Tel.**91 422 571411 or 572240; **fax** 91 422 571833.

GUSMÃO CÂMARA, Admiral Ibsen DE, *see* **CÂMARA, Admiral Ibsen** DE **GUSMÃO.**

HABER, Professor Dr Wolfgang. Landscape ecology, ecosystem research, conservation ecology, landscape planning & 'management', land-use ecology. Professor Emeritus of Landscape Ecology. *B.*13 Sept.1925, Datteln, Germany. German. *M.*Barbara: *s., 2 d.* **Education:** U.of Hohenheim MA 1955, U.of Münster PhD Rer.Nat.(Soil Ecol.) 1957. **Experience:** res.in above interests, admin., pol.adv. **Career:** Asst, Botl Inst. U.of Münster 1956–7; Conservator & V.-Dir, Westphalian Mus.of Natural Hist.1958–66; Full Prof.of Landscape Ecol. 1966–93, Emer.1993–, Munich U.of Tech. **Achievements:** advancement of concept of differentiated land-use for mitigating land-use impacts; advancement of 10% Rule for Nature cons.areas as minimum; weighted cons.strat. dev., Dir MAB 6 res.project in Bavarian Alps. **Memberships:** GFCEA (Chairman 1985–90), GES (Pres.1979–90), INTECOL (Pres.1990–94), NCC of Fed.Govt 1974–. **Awards:** Brubo H.Schubert Prize 1986, Justus von Liebig Prize 1989, German Envl Prize 1993. **Publications:** *Naturschutz und Landesentwicklung* 1973, *Ökologische Grundlagen des Umweltschutzes* 1993; *c.*300 scientific papers. Indiff.to pers.pub., favours unbiassed news media support. **Languages:** English, French, German, Italian (spoken). Willing to act as consult.etc. **Address:** Landschaftsökologie, Technische Universitat München, Weihenstephan, D-85350 Freising, Germany. **Tel.**(office) 49 8161 713495, (home) 49 8167 478; **fax** 49 8161 714427.

HACKMAN, Arlin Clemens. Canadian protected areas' system. Campaign Director. *B.*5 Oct.1950, Didsbury, Alb., Canada. Canadian. *P.*Judith Wright (Asst Dep.Minister, Ont.Min.of Envt & Energy). **Education:** York U. BA (Hons)(Geog.) 1973, MES 1976. **Experience:** num.consults, admin., res. **Career:** Exec.Dir. 1978–83, Dir.1983–, Algonquin Wildlands League; Dir, Coalition on Niagara Escarpment 1979–83; Founding Dir, Canadian Coalition on Acid Rain 1980–82; Fedn of Ont.Naturalists (Staff Envlist) 1983–4; Dir, Ottawa Field Naturalists 1984–6; Prin.Researcher, Task Force on Nat.Park Estab.1985–6; Dir, Endangered Spaces Campaign, WWF Canada 1987–; CCEA (Treas.1990–93). **Achievements:** successfully lobbied for major expansion of parks system in Ont.1983 and for all provincial, territorial, and fed.govts to commit to completing a rep.prot. areas' system in Canada by the yr 2000, init.successful effort to remove tax disincentives on private land cons.in Ont.through new legis., catalysed first community-based marine prot. area proposal in Canadian Arctic. **Memberships:** IUCN CNPPA, Prot.Areas and Species of Spec.Concern Adv.Cttee (WWF Intl), Cons. Council of Ont. **Publications:** *Our Parks– Vision for the 21st Century* (co-Author) 1986, *Ontario's Park System Comes of Age* 1989, *The Job to Be Done* 1992, *Inuit Create a Whale Sanctuary* 1993; num.articles, weekly natural hist.column appearing in 100 Ont.community newspapers. Indiff.to pers.pub.& news media support. **Language:** English. Willing to act as consult.etc. **Address:** Endangered Spaces WWF-Canada, 504–90 Eglinton Avenue East, Toronto, Ontario M4P 2Z7, Canada. **Tel.** (office) 1 416 489 8800, (home) 1 416 536 7109; **fax** 1 416 489 3611.

HADDANE, Dr Brahim. Conservation of endangered species of fauna, education & public awareness with regard to cons.of Nature. Assistant Director. *B.*10 Nov.1952, Sidi Kacem, Morocco. Moroccan. *M.*Houria (MD). **Education:** Vet.Sch. DVM 1977; Prince Leopold U.(Antwerp) MSc(Biol.)(Parasitology) 1980; courses in trop.diseases & path.(in Antwerp) 1979, wildlife econ.& mgmt with some aspects of educ.& cons.(at Jersey Wildlife Trust, UK) and cons.of Nature (in London) 1982. **Experience:** res.on wildlife animals of NW Africa, nat.& regnl consult.on wildlife mgmt & cons.to local orgns. **Career:** Animal Collection 1980–82, Vet.Officer & Head of Animal Collection 1983–5, Asst Dir 1985–, Zool.Gdn of Rabat. **Memberships:** IUCN SSC Captive (now Cons.) Breeding SG, SPANA, Assn Marocaine pour la Prot.de l'Environnement, BirdLife Intl. **Publications:** Repro.& path.of *Ratidea* 1982, Distribn & behaviour of bustards in Morocco (Otididae) 1988, Disease of *Panthera pardus:* case report 1990, Diseases of *Macaca sylvana:* case report 1992. Favours news media support. **Languages:** Arabic, English, French, Spanish. Willing to act as consult.etc. **Address:** Parc Zoologique National de Rabat, BP 4142, Temara, Rabat, Morocco. **Tel.**(office) 212 7 741259, (home) 212 7 741331; **fax** 212 7 799131 & 741153.

HAFIDI, Moulay EL MEHDI. Wildlife protection, natural resource conservation, prevention of desertification. Chief of Forest Service. *B*.28 Oct.1956, Midelt, Morocco. Moroccan. *M.* Benlafqih: *s., d.* **Education:** Nat.Forestry Sch. of Engrs, Dipl.in Forestry Engg 1982. **Experience:** field-work in prevention of desert., prot. of wildlife, admin.of Provincial Forestry Office. **Career:** resp.for prevention of desert. 1983–5 and prot.of wildlife in Southeastern Morocco 1985–, creation of e.High Atlas Nat. Park 1985–, Chief 1991–, Forest Service, Errachidia. **Achievements:** creation of e.High Atlas Nat.Park, conducted cons.awareness campaign resulting in reduced poaching of endangered Barbary sheep. **Membership:** Global 500 Forum. **Awards:** Global 500 Roll of Honour (UNEP) 1993. Indiff. to pers.pub., favours news media support. **Languages:** Arabic, English (beginner), French. Willing to act as consult.etc. **Address:** Park National du Haut Atlas, Eaux et Forêts, Errachidia, Morocco. **Tel.**(office) 212 5 572147, (home) 212 5 573572; **fax** 212 5 572252.

HAIGH, Professor Dr Martin John. Land reclamation, erosion control on lands affected by coal mining; landslide research in central Himalaya. Professor of Geography, Vice-President. *B*.29 July 1950, Caerleon, S.Wales, UK. British. Father Jack Haigh, geographer, *M.*Marianne P.Kilmartin *qv: s.,* 3 *d.* **Education:** U.of Birmingham BSc(1st Class Hons) 1971, PhD 1976, CPESC 1983. **Experience:** 20 yrs' res.in land reclamation & landslides incl.field projects in Bulgaria, India, Pakistan, UK, & USA; cartography direction and course evaluater; teaching at u.level. **Career:** Dem. U.of Keele 1974–5; Asst Prof.of Geog. Univs of Oklahoma 1975–6 and Chicago 1976–9; Dir of Cartographic Services, U.of Chicago 1977–9; Res.F'ship, Amer.Inst.of Indian Studies 1978–9; Sr Lect./ Prin.Lect. Oxf.Poly.1980–92; Prin.Investigator, Earthwatch Orgn 1991–; Prof.of Geog. OBU 1993. **Achievements:** dev.of new strats for self-sust.recultivation of surface-coalmine-disturbed land, and for prediction of landslides on new highways in the Himalaya. **Memberships:** WASWC (VP 1988–), SWCS, Himalayan Res.Group, IBG, IMS, Brit.Assn for Better Land Husbandry. **Award:** Cert.of Appreciation (CPESC) 1990. **Publications:** *Evol.of Slopes on Artificial Landforms* 1978, *Intl Confs on Headwater Control* (co-Ed.) 1989, 1992. Indiff. to pers.pub.& news media support. **Languages:** English, French (some). Willing to act as consult.etc. **Address:** Geography Unit, School of Social Sciences, Oxford Brookes University, Headington, Oxford OX3 0BP, England, UK. **Tel.**44 1865 483750; **fax** 44 1865 483937.

HAIGH, Nigel. European environmental policies. Institute Director. *B*.23 Feb.1938, Tokyo, Japan. British. *M.*Dr Carola: 2 *d.* **Education:** U.of Camb. BA(Mech.Scis) 1961, MA(Mech. Scis) 1966. **Experience:** policy studies. **Career:** Chartered Patent Agent 1962–72; Civic Trust 1973–80; VP, Euro.Envl Bur. 1975–9; Dir, Inst.for Euro.Envl Policy 1980–. **Achievement:** advancing Euro.envl policy and its implementation. **Memberships:** Hon.Res.F. Fac. of Laws, UCL; Vis.Res.F. IC Centre for Envl Tech. **Award:** OBE. **Publication:** *Manual of Envl Policy: The EC and Britain* 1992. **Languages:** English, French (spoken). **Address:** Institute for European Environmental Policy London, 158 Buckingham Palace Road, London SW1W 9TR, England, UK. **Tel.**(office) 44 171 824 8787, (home) 44 171 703 2919; **fax** 44 171 824 8145.

HAILES, Ms Julia Persephone. Environmental management incl.green consumerism. Company Director. *B*.23 Sept.1961, Templecombe, Somerset, England, UK. British. *M.*Edward de Courcy Bryant: *s.* **Education:** St Mary's Sch. (Calne, Wilts.). **Experience:** envl consult., assessment & auditing, corporate envl strat., eco-labelling. **Career:** Leo Burnett Advertising 1981–3; Dir (co-Founder) & Co.Sec. Sustain-Ability Ltd.1987–95; Dir, Creative Consumer Cooperative Ltd.1994–. **Achievement:** bringing 'green' consumerism to a world-wide audience. **Memberships:** Eco-labelling Bd (UK), UNEP (UK). **Award:** Global 500 Roll of Honour (UNEP) 1989. **Publications:** *Green Consumer Guide* 1988, *Green Pages* 1988, *Green Consumers' Supermarket Shopping Guide* 1989, *Young Green Consumer Guide* 1990, *Green Business Guide* 1991, *Holidays that Don't Cost the Earth* 1992, *LCA Sourcebook* 1993. Favours pers.pub. & news media support. **Languages:** English, French. Willing to act as consult.etc. **Address:** Tintinhull House, Yeovil, Somerset, England, UK. **Tel.**44 1935 823972; **fax** 44 1935 826176.

HALIM, Professor Dr Youssef. Monitoring & management of coastal zones. Retired Professor of Marine Sciences. *B*.27 Jan.1925, Cairo, Egypt. Egyptian. *W.: d.*Hala (cons.of nat.heritage). **Education:** U.of Paris, Dr in Sci.(Natural Scis) 1956. **Experience:** 35 yrs' res.& teaching on monitoring marine envt, leader of UNESCO project on Aquatic Poll.around Alexandria, consult.to UNESCO on coastal-zone mgmt, admin. **Career:** Prof.of Marine Scis 1972–, V.-Dean for Grad.Studies 1975–81, Fac.of Sci. U.of Alexandria; VC Jt Panel IOC–UNEP 1992–. **Achievements:** num.studies on biodiv.and on impacts of Man's activities on marine envt. **Award:** Global 500 Roll of Honour (UNEP) 1989. **Publications:** Marine sci.in Yemen 1977, Marine sci.in Mozambique 1984, The impacts of Man's alterations of hydrological cycles on ocean margins 1991, Poll.Problems of the Medit.Sea (MedPol) 1992, The Nile and the Suez Canal and their effect on living resources 1995. Favours pers.pub.& news media support. **Languages:** Arabic, English, French. Willing to act as consult.etc. **Address:** Faculty of Science, University of Alexandria, Alexandria 21511, Egypt. **Tel.**(home) 20 3 586 9661; **fax** 20 3 545 7611.

HALLER, René Daniel. Building economically-viable integrated ecosystems. Managing Director. *B*.18 Dec.1933, Lenzburg/Aargau, Switzerland. Swiss. *M*.Christa: 2 *s*.incl.Daniel Thomas (aquaculture consult.). **Education:** hort., landscaping & planning in Brugg 1953, trop.agron. Swiss Trop.Inst.1955. **Career:** managing coffee plantation 1956–8 and working on pyrethrum, coffee, and dairy, farms 1958–9 (Tanzania); Agron., Bamburi Portland Cement Co.Ltd, (Kenya) 1959; MD, Baobab Farm Ltd 1982–. **Achievements:** creating self-sustaining ecosystems from quarry wastelands. **Memberships:** AAK (Corporate), IUCN SSC Crocodile SG, ICLARM. **Awards:** Global 500 Roll of Honour (UNEP) 1987, Branden Burger Prize (Switzerland) 1991, Hon.Dr Phil.II (U.of Basel). **Publications:** *c*.50 news articles & reports incl.The Intensive Culture of *Tilapia* in Tanks, Raceways and Cages (co-Author) 1982, *Turning the Desert into a Forest of a Million Trees* 1988, *A Fresh Approach to Farming in the Third World* 1990, *From Wasteland to Paradise — A Modern Day Success Story of Land Reclamation* 1991. Dislikes pers.pub., favours news media support. **Languages:** English, German, Swahili. Willing to act as consult.etc. **Address:** Baobab Farm Ltd, POB 81995, Mombasa, Kenya. **Tel.& fax** (office) 254 11 486157, (home) 254 11 485473.

HAMANN, Professor Dr Ole Jørgen. Botanic gardens, *in situ* and *ex situ* conservation of plants, Galápagos Islands, environmental conservation. Professor of Botany. *B*.4 Feb.1944, Frederiksberg, Denmark. Danish. *M*.Michelle: *d*. **Education:** U.of Copenhagen MSc 1970, Dr Sc.1981. **Experience:** field res.in Galápagos Islands 1971–; dev.& implementation of res.& cons. progs & projects, Galápagos and worldwide; governance & admin.of intl cons.orgns; teaching at U.of Copenhagen; directing Botanic Gdn, U. of Copenhagen. **Career:** Lect.1970–74, Sr Lect. 1974–89, Prof.of Bot.& Dir, Botanic Gdn 1989–, U.of Copenhagen; UNESCO Assoc. Expert in Plant Ecol. Charles Darwin Res. Station 1971–2; IUCN Plants Prog.Officer 1984–7. **Achievements:** res.on Galápagos Islands' veg.& ecosystems; pubns on cons.and guiding of cons. activities on the Islands; assisting in leading & developing the Charles Darwin Fndn for the Galápagos Isles; leading the intl IUCN/WWF Plants Cons.Prog.1984–7; assisting in mobilizing botanic gdns of the world for cons. partic.through BGCI; directing dev.of the Botanic Gdn, U.of Copenhagen, incl.estab.of modern gene-bank facilities for endangered species; estab.collaborative links & progs on res. and cons.between Copenhagen and other botanic gdns partic.in the tropics; advising Nordic & var.Danish Govt Agencies, incl.DANIDA, on cons.of plants & plant genetic resources and on the implementation of CITES. **Memberships:** Charles Darwin Fndn for the Galápagos Isles (VP Europe) 1984–; Bds of The Galápagos Darwin Trust (Europe) 1990–, BGCI 1990–, and WWF-Verdensnaturfonden 1990–; IUCN

CNPPA 1991– & SSC 1992–. **Awards:** Rasch's Legat (DBS) 1981, Top-Danmark-Prisen 1989. **Publications:** *Plant Communities of the Galápagos Islands* 1981, *Botanic Gdns and the WCS* (co-Ed.) 1987, *Botl Res.& Mgmt in the Galápagos* (co-Ed.) 1990; Ex-situ *Cons.in Botl Gdns* (Ed.) 1992; num.papers & contribns to books. Favours news media support. **Languages:** Danish, English, Spanish (spoken and read). Willing to act as consult.etc. **Address:** Botanic Garden, University of Copenhagen, Oester Farimagsgade 2B, 1353 Copenhagen K, Denmark. **Tel.**45 353 22222; **fax** 45 353 22221.

HAMBLER, Clive. Conservation & ecology esp.of islands; succession in tropical & temperate regions. Research Associate, Lecturer in Biology, Principal. *B*.28 Feb.1960, Ibadan, Nigeria. British. Father Dr D.J. Hambler *qv*. **Education:** Bradford Grammar Sch.; St Catherine's Coll.Oxf. BA(Hons)(Zool.) 1981. **Experience:** res.— succession on Aldabra (Seychelles), giant tortoise pop.dynamics & reintro., ornith.of Seychelles' endemics, marine turtle surveys, endemic plant surveys; succession in UK — grassland & woodland invertebrate assemblages & their response to mgmt (grazing, coppicing etc.), spider autecology & use as indicators; admin.— admissions & coursework for coll.undergrads in biol.scis, expedn officer-ships (incl.Leader, Med.Officer, Treasurer); teaching animal behaviour (Natural Sci. Tripos, U.of Camb.) and etol.& cons.at undergrad., MSc & doctl level (U.of Oxf.). **Career:** Res.Assoc. Dept of Zool. U.of Oxf. 1981–, Biol.Recorder in Oxfordshire Reserves 1984–7, Founder & Prin. Oxf.Envl Consultancy 1988–, Lect.in Biol. Oriel Coll.Oxf.1991–. **Achievements:** helped estab. goat eradication measures for Aldabra Atoll WHS, participated in four cons.expedns to Seychelles & one to Colombia, reported for Council of Europe on Human Pop.& Envt. **Memberships:** BAS, BirdLife Intl. **Award:** Open Exhibition at St Catherine's Coll.Oxf. **Publications:** seven j.papers incl. The envl consequences of uncontrolled pop. growth (co-Author) 1993, Biodiv.cons.in Britain: sci.replacing trad.(co-Author) in press, Giant tortoise translocation to Curieuse (Seychelles): success or failure? in press; 25 in popular or specialist periodicals. Indiff.to pers. pub.& news media support. **Language:** English. **Address:** 44 Beauchamp Place, Beauchamp Lane, Oxford OX4 3NE, England, UK. **Tel.**(office) 44 1865 271124, (home) 44 1865 776192; **fax** 44 1865 310447.

HAMBLER, Dr David John. Plant ecology; grazing effects. Honorary Senior Lecturer. *B*.9 Dec.1930, Warwick, England, UK. British. *M*.Jeanne Audrey: 2 *s*.Clive *qv*, Keith (animal ecol. Aldabra [Goat demography], Peru [Cayman Survey]). **Education:** U.of London BSc(Hons)(Bot.) 1952, PhD 1956. **Experience:** trop.& temperate ecol. esp.of inselbergs & quarries, supervision of res.in plant ecol., archaeobot., taxonomy, human cytogenetics, envl monitoring etc. **Career:** Lect.& Sr Lect.in Bot. Nigerian Coll.of Arts, Sci.& Tech. 1955–61, Prin.Lect.in Biol. Bradford Inst.of Tech.1961–6, Sr Lect.then Hon.Sr Lec.in Envl Biol. U.of Bradford 1966–. **Achievements:** main endeavour has been to increase gen.biol. understanding, and due recognition of envl consequences flowing from the gen.lack of such understanding; contribn through u.teaching & res.to the body of competent envl scis, and to add a little to biol. knowledge. **Memberships:** BES, BSBI, IBiol., F.RMS, F.LS, Chartered Biol. **Award:** QMC Exhibitioner 1949–52. **Publications:** The bearing of the sandwich course on the u.educ.of biologists 1968, An experimental approach to the reclamation of a limestone quarry floor: the fourth to seventh yrs 1986, The relative potentials of six grass cultivars for rehab.& stabilization of a limestone quarry spoilbank 1990, Wildlife & cons.: rabbit middens on seeded limestone quarry spoil 1993, Ten years in rehabilitation of spoil: appearance, plant colonists, and the dominant herbivore (co-Author) 1995. Dislikes pers.pub., indiff.to news media support. **Languages:** English; French & German (read, in biol.contexts). Willing to act as consult.etc. **Address:** 14 Yew Tree Avenue, Bradford, West Yorkshire BD8 0AD, England, UK. **Tel.**(home) 44 1274 542329.

HAMED, Dr Safei EL-DEEN. Environmental planning, assessments, and ethics, arid lands' development, landscape analysis, ecotourism; architecture and city planning in the Arab World. Independent Environmental Consultant. *B.*23 March 1946, Cairo, Egypt. American, Egyptian. Father Abdelhamid Hamed, agricl engr. *M.*Linda Mae: *s.* **Education:** U.of Cairo BArch. 1968; U.of Georgia, M(Landscape Arch.) 1973; Virginia Poly.Inst.and SU, PhD(Envl Planning)* 1988. **Experience:** res.— envlly sust.dev.issues in developing countries, arid lands studies, ecotourism, EIA, arch.and urban planning in Arab–Muslim culture; has taught at Univs of Guelph, (Tech.) Nova Scotia, Georgia, & Maryland, and at K.Faisal U.& Virginia Poly.Inst.and SU; consult.to several nat.& intl orgns incl.Parks Canada, US FWS, Arab Dev.Inst., Envt Dept at World Bank. **Career:** Acting Head, Dept of Landscape Arch. King Faisal U. 1976–7; Asst Prof.of Landscape Arch. Tech.U.of Nova Scotia 1977–84; Instructor, Coll.of Arch.and Planning, Virginia Poly.Inst.and SU 1984–6; Asst Prof.of Envl Planning, U.of Maryland 1986–94; Ind.Envl Consult.1994– (at present in Land, Water, and Natural Habitats Div. Envt Dept, World Bank). **Achievements:** in 1976 at K. Faisal U. founded first Dept of Landscape Arch.in the Arab World, *PhD on Envl Objectives for the Arid Middle E. **Memberships:** ASLA, APA, Assn of Egyptian–Amer.Scholars. **Publications:** Landscape Planning in the Arid Middle E.1990, Seeing the envt through Islamic eyes 1992; Ed.*Landscape Intl* 1990–93, and *Envl Assessments: A Training Manual.* Indiff.to pers.pub.& news media support. **Languages:** Arabic,

English, French (working knowledge). Willing to act as consult.etc. **Address:** 8456 Snowden Oaks Place, Laurel, Maryland 20708-2302, USA. **Tel.**(office) 1 202 473 3647, (home) & **fax** 1 301 953 2140.

HAMILTON, Dr Alan. Tropical forest conservation, plant conservation, ethnobotany. Plants' Conservation Officer. *B.*24 Jan.1945, Parkstone, England, UK. British. *M.*Naomi (bot.). **Education:** U.of E.Africa PhD 1970, U.of Camb.ScD 1993. **Experience:** res.in many aspects of trop.forests & envl hist. **Career:** Lect. U.of Ulster 1972–89 and Makerere U.1981–2; Consult.on Trop.Forests, IUCN 1986–7; Plants Cons.Officer, WWF Intl 1987–. **Achievements:** creation of multiple-use zones in trop. forest estab.plan for Bwindi Nat.Park, Uganda. **Memberships:** BES, BSBI. **Publications:** *Field Guide to Uganda Forest Trees* 1981, *Envl Hist.of E.Africa* 1982, *Deforestation in Uganda* 1984, *E.Usambaras — Cons.& Mgmt* 1987; 40 scientific papers. **Languages:** English; French & Spanish (broadly competent), Luganda & Swahili (simple spoken). Willing to act as consult.etc. **Address:** WWF, Panda House, Weyside Park, Godalming, Surrey GU7 1XR, England, UK. **Tel.**(office) 44 1483 426444, (home) 44 1483 414597; **fax** 44 1483 426409.

HAMILTON, Professor Dr Lawrence Stanley. Sustainable use of small island & mountain environments; protected area planning & management, forestry. Partner, Professor Emeritus. *B.*5 June 1925, Toronto, Canada. American. *M.*Linda S.Hamilton (Partner in consult., small is.agric.& agricl ext.): 2 *s.*incl.Bruce H.(Dir of Cons., Sierra Club). **Education:** U.of Toronto BScF 1948, NY State Coll.of For. MS 1951, U.of Michigan PhD 1963, U.of Calif. postdoctl study. **Experience:** u.res.in field (29 yrs), res.in landuse policy in Asia & Pacific (13 yrs), short-term consult.in Venezuela, Costa Rica, & Australia, 29 yrs' teaching. **Career:** Zone Forester, Ont. Dept of Lands & Forests 1948–51; Extension Forester 1951–4, Prof.1954–80, Prof.Emer. 1980–, Cornell U.; Res.Assoc.then Sr F. E–W Center 1980–93, Affiliate Fac.in Geog. U.of Hawaii 1983–93; Partner, Islands & Highlands Assocs 1993–. **Achievements:** supervised 48 outstanding grad.students for MS &/or PhD degrees, worked with govt professionals, u.researchers & NGOs in 21 countries to develop more sust.land-use strats, instrumental in having at least five areas declared as Nat.Parks. **Memberships:** SAF, IMS, IUCN Comms on Ecol.& NPPA, PSA, ISTF. **Awards:** NSF Sci. Fac. F'ship 1964–5, Forest Conservationist of the Yr (NY State Cons.Council) 1969, Fulbright-Hays' F'ships 1969–70, 1978, FUNEP 500 Global Achiever 1985, Raymond Sherwin Award (Sierra Club) 1990. **Publications:** *An Analysis of NY's Forest Practice Act* 1963, *Trop.Forested Watersheds* 1983, *Res.Needs & Applications to Reduce Erosion & Sediment in Trop.Steeplands* (Ed.) 1990, *Sandalwood in the*

Pacific 1990, *Parks, Peaks & People* 1993, *Ethics, Religion & Biodiv.*1993; *c.*240 articles. Indiff.to pers.pub. & news media support. **Languages:** English, French (fair), Spanish (fair). Willing to act as consult.etc. **Address:** Rural Route #I, Box 1685A, Hinesburg, Vermont 05461, USA. **Tel.**(office & home) & **fax** 1 802 425 6509.

HAMMERTON, Professor Desmond.   Water pollution control, water quality management & monitoring. Visiting Professor, Consultant. *B.*17 Nov.1929, Wakefield, England, UK.   British. Father Charles Hammerton, Chief Chem. Metropolitan Water Bd (London, UK). *M.*Jean: 2 *s.*, 2 *d.*   **Education:** Harrow Weald Co.Sch.; Birkbeck Coll.London BSc(Spec.)(Bot.) 1953.   **Experience:** biol.monitoring of rivers & reservoirs, res.into reservoir mgmt, academic res.on trop.rivers & lakes, admin.of water poll. control policies, consult.in many countries on water poll.control.   **Career:** Asst.Biol. Metropolitan Water Bd 1948–55; Res.Biol. Bristol Waterworks Co.1955–8; Prin.Asst, Lothians R.Bd 1958–62; Dir. Hydrobiol.Res. U.of Khartoum 1962–71; Dep.Dir.1971–5, Dir.1975–94, Clyde R.Purification Bd; Vis.Prof. U.of Paisley 1993–; Consult. WHO 1977–.   **Achievements:** as consult.to WHO have advised on water poll.control & monitoring in over 20 countries incl.India, Syria, Greece, Turkey, and all the Danube countries. **Memberships:**   F.IBiol.,   F.IWEM,   F.RSE. **Awards:** Gans Medal (Soc. for Water Treatment) 1960, Alexander Houston Medal (Inst.of Water Engrs) 1960.   **Publications:** *c.*40 papers & chapters; Ed.of *c.*30 Annual Reports for Clyde R.Purification Bd and U.of Khartoum. Favours pers.pub.& news media support.   **Languages:** Arabic (poor spoken), English, French. Further details may be obtained from *Who's Who in Scotland.* Willing to act as consult.etc. **Address:** 7 Fairfield Place, Bothwell, Glasgow G71 8RP, Scotland, UK.   **Tel.**(office) 44 1355 238181, (home) 44 1698 852261; **fax** 44 1355 264323.

HANBURY-TENISON,   (Airling)   Robin. Exploration, protection of indigenous peoples, conservation. President, Explorer, Author. *B.*7 May 1936, London, England, UK.   British. Father Major Gerald Tenison, soldier & big-game hunter, mother Ruth, wildlife artist & naturalist. *M.*Louella (expedn companion): 2 *s., d.* **Education:** Eton Coll.; Magdalen Coll. Oxf. MA 1957, R.Agricl Coll. 1959.   **Experience:** num.expedns for geogl res.& human rights investigations.   **Career:** self-employed as farmer, author, journalist & photographer; co-Founder 1969, Chairman 1969–82, Pres.1982–, Survival Intl.   **Achievements:** Leader of RGS Mulu Expedn to Borneo rain-forest 1977–8 which res. heightened intl concern for trop.rain-forests. **Memberships:** RGS (past Counc.& VP), Explorers' Club (Intl F.), Ecol.Fndn (Trustee), Cornwall Wildlife Trust (Pres.). **Awards:** OBE 1981, Gold Medal (RGS) 1979, Krug Award for Excellence 1980, Dr *h.c.*(U.of Mons-Hainaut)

1992.   **Publications:** 13 books incl.*Mulu: The Rain Forest* 1980, 1992, *Worlds Apart* 1984, 1991, *The Oxf.Book of Exploration* 1993; num.articles & reviews.   Indiff.to pers.pub., favours news media support re.Survival Intl. **Languages:** English; French, German, Indonesian, Malay, Portuguese & Spanish (all now rusty).   Further details may be obtained from Brit.*Who's Who c.*1975, *Writers' Directory.* **Address:** Cabilla Manor, Cardinham, Bodmin, Cornwall PL30 4DW, England, UK. **Tel.**(home) 44 1208 821224; **fax** 44 1208 821267.

HAQUE, Dr Mohammed Asrarul.   Environmental pollution by heavy-metals, environmental education & awareness, environmental communication through electronic & print media.   Additional Director. *B.*28 April 1950, Munger, Bihar, India.   Indian. *M.*Bilquis Jabin.   **Education:** U.of Bhagalpur, MSc(Bot.) 1971; JNU, MPhil(Envl Sci.) 1977, PhD(Envt Poll.) 1981.   **Experience:** 23 yrs' res.in field of envl poll., admin.   **Career:** Lect.& Reader, L.N. Mithila U.1974–81; Res.Assoc. JNU 1981 & Salahdeen U.(Iraq) 1981–5; Sci. C.Poll.Control Bd 1987–9, Addit.Dir 1989–, Min.of Envt & Forests, Govt of India.   **Achievements:** instrumental in substantial spread of envl awareness & educ., created large nr of communication progs re.envt & its poll., Ed.*Paryavaran* (Min.quarterly).   **Memberships:** several professional bodies and nominated expert to diff.cttees & progs. **Awards:** U.Gold Medals (Bhagalpur U.) 1969 & 1971, Prize for original writing in field of envt (Govt of India) 1989.   **Publications:** 100+ incl. Copper, lead, and zinc poll.of soil envt (co-Author) 1982, Lead content of household dust from a city in Iraq 1987.   Indiff.to pers.pub.& news media support.   **Languages:** Arabic (good written, average spoken), English, Hindi, Urdu. Willing to act as consult.etc.   **Address:** C-1713 Palam Vihar, Gurgaon District, PIN 122017, Haryana, India.   **Tel.**(office) 91 11 436 0667, (home) 91 124 360893; **fax** 91 11 436 0678.

HARA, Professor Takeshi.   Environment and resources, environmental news reporting. Editor, Professor. *B.*20 Jan.1938, Tokyo, Japan. Japanese. *M.*Reiko.   **Education:** Waseda U. B.of Laws 1961.   **Experience:** journalism, lecturing. **Career:**   Chief Ed. Sci.Dept, *The Mainichi* Newspaper 1990–; Prof.of Intl Studies; Bunkyo U. 1993–; Counc.on envl & agricl issues to PM 1994–.   **Achievements:** Ed.-in-Chief NCSJ, Presidency of JFEJ.   **Memberships:** NCSJ, JFEJ.   **Award:** Global 500 Roll of Honour (UNEP) 1993.   **Publications:** ten books incl. *The Whale — Counterargument against Japanese Commercial Whaling* 1983, *What is Happening to Global Envt — Message to 21st Century* 1992, *Agric.in Japan* 1994. **Languages:** English, Japanese.   **Address:** Editorial Section, *The Mainichi* Newspaper, 1-1-1 Hitotsubashi, Chiyoda-ku, Tokyo 100, Japan.   **Tel.** (office) 81 3 3212 0321, (home) & **fax** 81 425 365134.

HARDI, Professor Dr Peter. Sustainable development, measuring performance and indicators, sustainable development project design, central European environment. Senior Fellow. *B.*2 Jan. 1942, Budapest, Hungary. Hungarian. *M.*Cornelia M. **Education:** Eötvös Loránd Tudomàny Egyetem (U.of Sci.), MSc(Chem.) 1967, MA (Phil.) 1972, PhD(Pol.Sci.) 1974; Hungarian AS, Academic Degree 1989. **Experience:** res.—five yrs in both structural analytical chem.and E.Euro.envl affairs 1989–94; consult.to World Bank 1990, three yrs' Adv.Council Memb.to Pres.of EBRD; three yrs in Canada working on measuring performance in sust.dev.; 25 yrs' teaching at var.univs. **Career:** Asst Prof., Assoc.Prof., Prof. Budapest U.of Econ.Scis 1972–88; Dir, Hungarian Inst.for Intl Affairs 1988–90; Exec.Dir, Regnl Envl Cntcr (Budapest) 1990–93; Sr F. IISD 1993–. **Achievements:** appointment to Chair of Ind.Expert Cttee to investigate the Gabcikovo–Nagymaros hydroelectric power station; co-Author & Ed.*Hardi Report**, instrumental in stopping envlly-undesirable construction in Hungary; Founder Chairman, Envl Legislative Task Force for C.and Eastern Europe 1990–93. **Memberships:** IUCN CESP, Earth Council (Adv.Bd), Amer.& Hungarian Pol.Sci.Assns. **Awards:** F'ship at Yale U.(ACLS) 1978–9, F'ship at Bellagio (Rockefeller Fndn) 1984, Plaque for Outstanding Leadership 1992 and Tribute of Appreciation for Service 1993 (both EPA). **Publications:** **The Hardi Report* 1989, *Impediments on Envl Policy Making* 1992, *New Horizons?* (co-Ed.) 1993, *Envl Prot.in E.C.Europe: A Market Approach* 1994; *c.*60 others. Indiff.to pers.pub., favours news media support. **Languages:** English, German, Hungarian; French, Italian, & Russian (all spoken). Further details may be obtained from Hungarian *Who's Who* 1994. Willing to act as consult.etc. **Address:** International Institute for Sustainable Development, 161 Portage Avenue East, Winnipeg, Manitoba R3B 0Y4, Canada. **Tel.**(office) 1 204 958 7731, (home) 1 204 256 0753; **fax** 1 204 958 7710.

HARDIN, Professor Dr Garrett. Population & ethics. Emeritus Professor of Human Ecology. *B.*21 April 1915, Dallas, TX, USA. American. *M.*Jane Swanson (Treas.of CAPS): 2 *s.*, 2 *d.* **Education:** U.of Chicago ScB 1936, Stanford U. PhD(Biol.) 1941. **Experience:** experimentalist in microbial ecol., writer of text- and popular books. **Career:** Experimenter in Microbial Biol. Stanford U. 1938–52, Prof.of Biol.1946–78 (Emer.1978–) UCSB, Writer 1949–, Bd Memb. FAIR. **Achievements:** writing articles such as *'The Tragedy of the Commons'* 1968, and books such as *Filters Against Folly* 1985, *Living Within Limits* 1993. **Memberships:** AAAS, APS, ISEE. **Award:** Phi Beta Kappa 1993. **Publications:** in addition to above, *Nature & Man's Fate* 1959, *Exploring New Ethics for Survival* 1972, *Stalking the Wild Taboo* 1973, *Promethean Ethics* 1980, *Naked Emperors* 1982. Indiff.to pers.pub., favours

news media support. **Languages:** English; French, German, Italian & Spanish (all basic). **Address:** 399 Arboleda Road, Santa Barbara, California 93110, USA. **Tel.**(home) 1 805 967 1384; **fax** 1 805 967 2715.

HARE, Professor Dr F.Kenneth. Climatology (northern & arid climates, heat & water balances) and environmental matters; energy policy, and in particular all aspects of safety of nuclear power. Emeritus Professor of Geography, University Chancellor, Chair International Programs Board. *B.*5 Feb.1919, Wylye, Wiltshire, England, UK. Canadian. *M.*Helen Neilson Morrill: 2 *s.*, *d.* **Education:** King's Coll. London BSc(Spec.) (Geog.)(1st Class Hons) 1939, U.of Montreal PhD (Climatology) 1950. **Experience:** spent war yrs as operational meteorologist & climatologist, UK Met.Office; emigrated to Canada 1945 since when taught at McGill U., UBC, Univs of London & Toronto; has held sr admin.rank in each of these instns and chaired/presided over many scientific socs; widespread res. **Career:** Asst Lect. U.of Manchester; Meteorologist, UK Air Min.; Asst Prof., Assoc.Prof., Chairman, Geog.Dept, Prof. of Geog.& Met., Dean of Arts & Sci., all at McGill U.; Prof.of Geog. King's Coll.London; Master of Birkbeck Coll.London; Pres.UBC; Prof.of Geog.& Phys., Dir of Inst.for Envl Studies, U.Prof., Provost of Trinity Coll., U.of Toronto; Chancellor, Trent U.; Chairman, Climate Prog. Planning Bd; Commissioner, Ontario Nuclear Safety Review; Chairman, Canadian Global Change Prog. RSC. **Achievements:** mapping of n.Canada, chiefly Labrador–Ungava, in 1940s & early 1950s; worked on Thames Terraces, England, as geomorphologist during 1940s; chaired/participated in many official enquiries in Canada, England, US, Sweden, & France; worked actively with WMO & UNEP esp.on nuclear safety, nuclear waste disposal, acid deposition, the 'nuclear winter' hypothesis, lead in the envt, and land-use questions; Assoc.Ed.or Adv.concerning *Geog.Rev., J.of Applied Met., Transactions of IBG, Envl Res., Geografiska Annaler, J.of Envl Geol., J.of Biogeog., Geojournal, J.of Phys.Geog., Annals of AAG, EC.* **Memberships:** AINA (Bd Chairman 1963, Gov.1971–6), CAG (Pres.1963–4), RMS (Pres. 1967–8, VP 1968–70); Counc.of CAG, AAG, AMS, RGS, Glaciological Soc., Société de géographie de Montréal, & AGS; Sigma Xi (Treas. U.of Toronto Chapter 1983–4, Pres. 1986–7), AAAS (Chair Section W.1985–6). **Awards:** Officer 1978–87 & Companion 1987– Order of Canada, F.RSC 1968–, F.King's Coll. 1967–, 23 others. **Publications:** *The Restless Atmos.*1953, *The Experiment of Life* 1982; The boreal bioclimates 1972, The geomorph.of a part of the Middle Thames 1947, A photo-reconnaissance of Labrador–Ungava 1959; *c.*250 others. Favours news media support. **Languages:** English, French (poor). Further details may be obtained from Brit.*Who's Who* 1992, *Canadian Who's Who* 1995, *Debrett's*

People of Today 1992, *Dict.of Intl Biog.*1993/4, *Intl Who's Who* 1994/5, var.others. Willing to act as a consult. **Address:** 301 Lakeshore Road West, Oakville, Ontario L6K 1G2, Canada. **Tel.**(home) 1 905 849 1374; **fax** 1 905 849 4954.

HAREIDE, Dag. Relationship between life quality and material well-being, consumption growth in rich societies, ecological economy in the transition period towards a sustainable society. Secretary-General. *B.*24 Feb.1949, Oslo, Norway. Norwegian. *M.*Ellinor Brune: 3 *d.* **Education:** Agricl Coll.1974, MA in Sociol. (theology, intellectual hist.& mass media) 1990. **Experience:** res.— UNDP, OECD & Norwegian 'Alternative Future': educl issues, famine preparedness, life qual.measures; admin.— founder & leader of several orgns. **Career:** journalist & youth worker during 1960s, teacher & prin.in folk highschools during 1970s, pastor in the Church & leader in solidarity & trade-union work, also work with Namibian refugees and freedom fighters 1980–85, UN Rehab. Coord.in Ethiopia 1985–8, Researcher with UNDP & Alternative Future 1988–90, Sec.-Gen. NSCN 1990–. **Achievements:** founded & led NNA; Rehab.Coord.for UN re.Ethiopian famine 1985–8, Sec.-Gen.of Norway's largest envl orgn. **Publications:** *Chile* 1972, *Vulnerability to Famine* 1989, *The Good Norway* 1990. **Languages:** English, Norwegian. **Address:** Parelius-veich 5b, 1177 Oslo, Norway. **Tel.** (office) 47 227 15520, (home) 47 227 42604; **fax** (office) 47 227 15640, (home) 47 227 42614.

HARRIS, Dr Philip John Charles. Organic agriculture & horticulture, sustainable forestry & agroforestry, tropical crop development, plant biotechnology. Head of Overseas Department, Principal Research Fellow. *B.*18 April 1950, Liskeard, Cornwall, England, UK. British. *M.* Stephanie: 3 *d.* **Education:** U.of Bath BSc (Applied Biol.)(1st Class Hons) 1972, U.of Glasgow PhD(Plant Physiol.) 1977. **Experience:** res., consult., teaching. **Career:** Dem.in Bot. U.of Glasgow 1972–5; Lect.1975–83, Sr Lect.1983–7, Prin.Lect.1987–90, Prin.Res.F. 1990–, U.of Coventry; Lect. U.of Sierra Leone 1978–82; Head, Overseas Dept HDRA 1986–; Vis.Prof. Kurukshetra U.(India) 1993–. **Achievements:** res.in organic & trop.agric.& for.; estab.HDRA Overseas Dept and prog.of res.in sust.agric.& for. **Memberships:** Chairman Mgmt Cttee, Nat.Herbarium of Sierra Leone 1980–82; HDRA Exec.Council 1985–9; Nat. Advice & Approval Bd for Training & Educl Courses in Organic Agric.& Hort.1988–91; IBiol., SEB, NERC Tree Biotech.Liaison Group, IUFRO Project Group on Agrofor., IAPTC, SEB. **Publications:** *Prosopis cineraria:* a multipurpose tree for arid areas (co-Author) 1991, For.& agrofor.in the Cape Verde Islands (co-Author) 1992, *Tecomella undulata* (Rohira): a valuable tree of the Thar Desert (co-Author) 1992, Vegetative Propagation of *Prosopis* 1993. **Languages:** English; French & Spanish (basic).

Willing to act as consult.etc. Favours pers.pub. & news media support. **Address:** Overseas Department, Henry Doubleday Research Association, Ryton-on-Dunsmore, Coventry, Warwickshire CV8 3LG, England, UK. **Tel.**(office) 44 1203 303517, (home) 44 1203 545001; **fax** 44 1203 639229.

HARRISON, Paul Anthony. Population, agriculture, development, environment, Africa. Writer, Consultant. *B.*10 July 1945, Oldham, Lancs., England, UK. British. *M.*Alvina: 2 *s.* **Education:** U.of Camb. MA 1967, LSE MSc (Econ.) 1969. **Experience:** res., writing, consult. **Career:** as well as books (below), jt prin. Author of *Agric.: Toward 2000* (FAO 1982), *Land, Food & People* (FAO 1984), *Human Nrs, Human Needs* (IPPF 1984); Team Memb. *Africa: From Crisis to Sust.Growth*, World Bank 1989; Author *The Greening of Lesotho* 1989: Writer *State of World Pop.* UNFPA 1990 & 1992; Leader, EC study of population–envt linkages 1984. **Achievements:** author of five books & num.reports on dev., envt & pop. **Memberships:** F. Inst.of Community Studies, IUCN CESP, UK UNED Cttee. **Awards:** Global 500 Roll of Honour (UNEP) 1988, Global Media Award (Pop.Inst.) 1992. **Publications:** *Inside the Third World 1979, The Third World Tomorrow* 1980, *Inside the Inner City* 1983, *The Greening of Africa* 1987, *The Third Revolution* 1983. Favours pers. pub.& news media support. **Languages:** English, French, German, Italian, Portuguese (good), Spanish (good). Willing to act as consult.etc. **Address:** 29a Nassington Road, London NW3 2TX, England, UK. **Tel.**& **fax** 44 171 794 6921.

HASAN, Professor Dr Mohammed NORDIN Hj. Tropical zoology, conservation biology, effects of habitat change on wildlife ecology especially due to logging, environmental impact assessment, animal behaviour. Professor of Zoology & Institute Director. *B.*10 Feb.1947, Klang, Selangor, Malaysia. Malaysian. *M.*Zahrah: 2 *s.,* 3 *d.* **Education:** U.of Malaya, BAgr.Sc.(Hons) 1971; U.of London, PhD 1974. **Experience:** res.in lowland & hill dipterocarp rain-forests of Peninsular Malaysia, Sabah, and Sarawak, on effects of logging on wildlife and of hunting on wildlife behaviour, and in EIA process; teaching zool.from BSc to PhD levels esp.in fields of envl biol., physiol., ethology, and cons.biol.; admin. in num.sr positions; consult.in EIAs of hydro-electric dev.projects. **Career:** Lect. Dept of Biol.1974–8, Assoc.Prof. Unit of Zool.1979–82, Prof. Dept of Zool.1983–, Bd of Dirs of Centre of Envl Technologies 1993–4, Dir Inst.for Envt & Dev.1994–, Universiti Kebangsaan Malaysia. **Achievements:** developed cons.biol.curr.at undergrad.level and an intensive one-yr MSc course in cons.biol.; Chairman WWF Malaysia 1987– & Bd Memb.WWF Intl; memb.Comm.on Sci.& Tech.for Dev.and *ad hoc* WG on Tech.Transfer of Comm.on Sust.Dev., UN Econ.& Social Council; memb.of Malaysian Business Council

Working Cttee on Sci.& Tech., Envt & Sust. Dev.; Chairman Select Cttee on Cons. Universiti Kebangsaan. **Memberships:** MEA (Adv.& Hon.Memb.1992–), MSAB (Life, Pres.1986–90), EMRAM. **Award:** Officer of the Order of the Defender of the Realm (Malaysia) 1993. **Publications:** *Biodiv.and its Cons.* (in Malay) 1991, A review of the taxonomy and natural hist.of the Lesser Mouse Deer, *Tragulus javanicus,* of Malaysia 1994, Envl Mgmt as a Strat. for Sust.Dev.; 30 others. Indiff.to pers.pub.& news media support. **Languages:** English, French (written & spoken working knowledge), Malay. Willing to act as consult.etc. **Address:** Institute for Environment and Development, Universiti Kebangsaan Malaysia, 43600 Bangi, Selangor, Malaysia. **Tel.**(office) 603 825 0001, 0601 or 0701, (home) 603 825 0804; **fax** 603 825 6484.

HASBÚN ROSE, Carlos Roberto, *see* **ROSE, Carlos Roberto** HASBÚN.

HASLER, Professor Dr Arthur D. Migration of fishes especially role of sense of smell in orientation (olfactory landscape imprinting), experimental limnology; physiology of aquatic organisms, radioisotopes in lakes (under ice, and transported by insects). Professor Emeritus of Zoology. *B.*5 Jan.1908, Lehi, UT, USA. *M.* 1.Hanne (deceased), 2.Hatheway. **Education:** Brigham Young U. BA 1932, U.of Wisconsin PhD 1937. **Experience:** trained 52 doctl candidates; extensive u., state, nat.& intl, cttee & adv., work; res.& lect. **Career:** Aquatic Biol. US FWS 1935–7; Naturalist NPS, summers of 1937 & 8; Instr.1937–8, Chairman 1953 & 1955–7, Prof.Emer.1978–, Dept.of Zool., Dir Lab.of Limnol.1963–78, U.of Wisconsin; Res. Analyst, USAF Strat.Bombing Survey 1945; Dir, The Inst.of Ecol.1971–4. **Achievements:** identifying role of olfactory imprinting in the homing migrations of anadromous salmon, basic res.work forming basis for mgmt practices now operating globally; estab.of role of land–water interactions in nutrient budget of lakes and remedial actions necessary for reversal of cultural eutrophication; continuing efforts in both scientific & policy-making context resulted in dev.of successful progs for improvement of water qual.; creation of experimental paradigm for dealing with whole ecosystems, res.protocol established resulted in dev.of both rigorous scientific practices and network of sites of wide benefit to current & future generations. **Memberships:** AAAS, AFS, AIBS, AIFRB, ASIH, ASLO, ASN, ASZ, ABS, ESA, IAE, IAGLR, IASF, Sigma Xi, SIL, Inst.of Ecol., Wisconsin Acad.of Scis, Arts and Letters. **Awards:** num.incl.Elected Memb.(NAS) 1969, Elected F. AAAS 1960 & Amer.AAS 1972, Award of Excellence (AFS) 1977, Disting.Service Award (AIBS) 1980, Sea Grant Award (Sea Grant Assn) 1980, Naumann-Thienemann Medal (SIL) 1992, Hon.DSc (Mem.U.of Newfoundland) 1967 & (Miami U. OH) 1988. **Public-**

ations: seven books incl.*Underwater Guideposts — Homing of Salmon* 1966, *Olfactory Imprinting and Homing in Salmon* (co-Author) 1983; *c.*200 other pubns 1934–85. **Languages:** English, German. **Address:** Center for Limnology, University of Wisconsin, Madison, Wisconsin 53706, USA. **Tel.**1 608 262 1627; **fax** 1 608 265 2340.

HASSAN, Dr Parvez. Conservation of Nature and environmental matters, especially law. Senior Partner. *B.*30 Sept.1941, Pakistan. Pakistani. **Education:** Punjab U. BA 1959, LLB 1961; Yale U. LLM 1963, Harvard U. LLD 1969. **Experience:** consult.— ESCAP Expert Group Mtg on Envl & Socio-econ.Aspects of Trop.Deforestation, Bangkok 1986, and Study on Instnl & Legislative Framework for For.Mgmt in the ESCAP Regn (Bangkok) 1985. **Career:** Vis.Lect.in many colls & law schools; Member Expert WG on Mgmt & Productivity, Govt of Pakistan; Member UNEP Mission to Bangladesh 1978 & Pakistan 1981 (drafted Envl Prot.Ordinance for Bangladesh & Pakistan); Regnl Councillor for W.Asia 1984–7, Legal Adv.1994–, IUCN; Sr Partner, Hassan & Hassan. **Achievements:** articles, papers, and addresses; drafted proposed Nat.Envl Prot.Ordinance for Pakistan & Bangladesh; consult.to many intl bodies. **Memberships:** WWF (Pakistan) 1979–, ICEL 1979–, UNEP Mission to Pakistan 1981, Lahore Cons.Soc.1984–, ESCAP Envl Mission to China 1986, IUCN CEL (Dep.Chairman 1989–90, Chairman 1990–), EPSOP (Pres. 1989–), PEPC 1989–, Family Planning Assn of Pakistan (Nat.Council 1989–, Chairman Cttee on Women, Youth, & Envt 1990–), Sust.Dev.Policy Inst.(Pakistan) 1991–, LEAD Pakistan (Chair, Nat.Steering Cttee 1995–). **Awards:** F'ship (Harvard Law Sch.) 1967–9 and (Yale Law Sch.) 1962–4, Global 500 Roll of Honour (UNEP) 1991. **Publications:** num.books, articles, & reports incl.*Legis.for Pakistan* 1989. Favours pers.pub.& news media support. **Languages:** English, Urdu. Willing to act as consult.etc. Address: Hassan & Hassan (Advocates), 2nd Floor PAAF Building, 70 Kashmir Egerton Road, Lahore, Pakistan. **Tel.**(office) 92 42 636 0800 to 3; **fax** 92 42 636 0811 & 2.

HATOUGH-BOURAN, Dr Alia Mohammed Ali. Conservation of arid & semi-arid ecosystems in Jordan and coastal regions, role of reserves in ecological stability, reintroduction programmes of locally-extinct species. Associate Professor of Ecology. *B.*7 Sept.1955, Amman, Jordan. Jordanian. *M.*Ishaq Bouran: *s., d.* **Education:** Russian AS MSc(Ecol.) 1979, PhD(Ecol.) 1982. **Experience:** ten yrs' teaching & res.in ecol., res. into ecol.& behaviour of Arabian Oryx, Scientific Adv.to RSCN & JSCP. **Career:** Asst. Prof.1983–91, Assoc.Prof.in Ecol.1991–, U.of Jordan. **Achievements:** basic & applied res.on Arabian Oryx ecol., ecol.of desert rodents, effect of pop.growth & assessment of wild species' displacement, estab.of reserves & assessment of their value, assessment of biol.diversity indices and ways of prot. **Memberships:** RSCN, JSCP, TWOW. **Publications:** four books incl.*Birds of the Hashemite Kingdom of Jordan: an Ecol. Outlook* 1989, *Ecol.*1994; 16 scientific. Favours news media support. **Languages:** Arabic, English, Russian (written & spoken). Willing to act as a consult. **Address:** Department of Biological Sciences, Faculty of Science, University of Jordan, Amman, Jordan. **Tel.**(office) 962 6 843555 ext.2300 & 2311, (home) 962 6 846612; **fax** 962 6 696733.

HAWKES, Professor Dr John Gregory. Conservation of plant genetic resources, cropplant evolution; taxonomy & phylogeny of Solanaceae, taxonomy, evol.& uses in plant breeding of wild & cultivated potato species. Emeritus Professor. *B.*27 June 1915, Bristol, England, UK. British. *M.*Ellen Barbara: 2 *s.*, 2 *d.* **Education:** Cheltenham Grammar Sch.; Christ's Coll.Camb. BA 1937, MA 1938, PhD 1941, ScD 1957. **Experience:** eight plant-collecting expedns in Latin Amer.1939–81; Pres. EUCARPIA Genetic Resources section 1961–86; Memb.Panel of Experts in Genetic Resources of Crops, FAO 1964–74; Consult.to IPC 1972–84 and to UNDP, World Bank, GTZ. **Career:** Founder & Dir., Master's Course in Cons.& Utilization of PGR, CPRI 1948–51; Lect.in Bot.1952–61, Pers.Chair 1961–7, Head Dept of Plant Biol.1967–82, Emer.Prof.1982–, U.of Birmingham. **Achievements:** estab.(with Sir Otto Frankel) disc.of PGR Cons.with FAO & IBPGR; in 1969 estab.Master's course in PGR, still running and only one of its kind, training *c.*400 students from all over the world; first to promote computer-mapped Flora; leading world taxonomist of wild & cultivated potatoes. **Memberships:** F.LS (Pres.1991–4), ISC (Pres.), SEB, EUCARPIA, APA, EAPR, Systematics Assn. **Awards:** Frank Meyer Mem.Award (AGA) 1973, Gold Medal (LS) and Silver Medal (IBPGR) 1984, Bronze Medal (N.I.Vavilov Inst. of Plant Industry) 1987, OBE 1994, Hon.Life membership of PAA & EUCARPIA. **Publications:** *c.*14 books incl.*The Potatoes of Argentina, Brazil, Paraguay & Uruguay* (co-Author) 1969, *A Computer Mapped Flora* (co-Author) 1971, *Cons.& Agric.* 1978, *The Diversity of Crop Plants* 1983, *The Potatoes of Bolivia* (co-Author) 1989, *The Potato — Evol., Biodiv.& Genetic Resources* 1990; 190+ res.papers. Indiff.to pers. pub.& news media support. **Languages:** English, Spanish. Further details may be obtained from *Debrett's People of Today* 1993 and Brit.*Who's Who* 1996. Willing to act as consult. etc. **Address:** School of Continuing Studies, University of Birmingham, Edgbaston, Birmingham B15 2TT, England, UK. **Tel.** (office) 44 121 44 6170, (home) 44 121 427 2944; **fax** 44 121 414 5619.

HAYNES-SUTTON, Dr Ann Marilyn. Ecology, wildlife conservation, national parks & protected areas, wetlands, seabirds, environ-

mental education. Private Ecological Consultant. *B.*7 Nov.1951, London, England, UK. British. *M.*Robert L.Sutton (ornith.). **Education:** U.of the W.Indies (at Mona), PhD(Zool.) 1995. **Experience:** res.— study of seabird ecol.cons.& mgmt at Morant Cays (Jamaica) 1982–7, and of status, moults, & plumages, of endemic Jamaican birds 1989–; admin.— Chief of Ecol.Branch of Natural Resources' Cons. Dept 1987, Pres.of Natural Hist.Soc.of Jamaica 1986–8, Exec.Cttee Memb.of Soc.for Carib. Ornith.1987–90; consult.— extensive incl.ecol. team leader for NPPA system plan project 1991, seabird mgmt plan for Natural Resources' Cons.Auth.1995, wetlands consult for S.Coast Cons.Fndn 1995–, var.species' mgmt plans, educ., bird hazard mitigation, resource assessments. **Career:** Res.Asst & Ecol.Branch Chief, Natural Resources' Cons.Dept 1979–87; Private Ecol.Consult.1987–; Co.Sec.& Founder Memb. Jamaica Cons.& Dev.Trust 1988–90. **Achievements:** promoted dev.of prot.areas in Jamaica incl.estab of first seasonal reserve for seabirds at Morant Cays, and involvement of NGOs in cons.incl.founding the Jamaica Cons.& Dev. Trust, work on system plan. **Memberships:** IUCN SSC (Regnl Memb.), AOU, BOU, Soc.of Field Ornithologists, Jamaica Jr Naturalists (Chairman 1991–). **Publications:** The Value of Seabirds as a Socio-econ.Resource in Jamaica 1987, Human exploitation of seabirds in Jamaica 1987. Favours pers.pub.& news media support. **Language:** English. Willing to act as consult. etc. **Address:** Marshall's Pen, POB 48, Mandeville, Jamaica, West Indies. **Tel.**(office & home) 809 963 8569; **fax** 809 964 6383; **e-mail** asutton@uwimona.edu.jm .

HEATHCOTE, Dr Ronald Leslie. Environmental perception, historical geography, aridland management, natural hazards. Reader in Geography. *B.*28 Oct.1934, Whaley Bridge, England, UK. Australian. **Education:** U.of London BA 1955; U.of Nebraska, MA 1959; ANU, PhD 1963. **Experience:** res., lect. **Career:** Lect.in Geog. UCL 1963–6; Sr Lect.& Reader in Geog. Flinders U. 1966–; Vis.Lect. UCB 1968 and U.of Nebraska 1978. **Achievements:** pubns. **Memberships:** AAG, RGS, IAG. **Awards:** Fulbright Scholarship 1955–7, Honour Award for Arid Land Studies (AAG) 1989, F.ASSA. **Publications:** seven books incl. *The Arid Lands: Their Use and Abuse* 1983, *Land, Water and People* 1988, *Australia* 1975, 1994. Dislikes pers.pub., indiff.to news media support. **Languages:** English, German (written). Willing to act as consult.etc. **Address:** Department of Geography, Faculty of Social Sciences, Flinders University, GPO Box 2100, Adelaide, South Australia 5001, Australia. **Tel.**61 8 201 2107; **fax** 61 8 201 3521.

HEDBERG, Dr Inga M.M. Taxonomic botany (especially Africa), ethnobotany especially of tropical plants, conservation of biodiversity. Independent Researcher. *B.*18 Nov.1927, Sweden.

Swedish. *M*.Prof.K.Olov Hedberg *qv:* 4 *s*.incl.Per O.(Dir.of Uppsala Nature Study Sch.), *d*. **Education:** U.of Uppsala BSc 1952, PhD 1970. **Experience:** field-work in Egypt, Ethiopia, E. Africa, Lesotho, Venezuela, Scandinavia; taxonomic res.on African plants; co-Leader, Ethiopian Flora Project; consults. **Career:** Res.Asst, Dept of Systematic Bot.1969–80, Assoc.Prof. 1970–93, U.of Uppsala; Sec.SNCB & RSAS 1981–91. **Achievements:** co-Leader of Ethiopian Flora project 1989–, and of the Tanzanian Rainforest project 1983–93; pubns. **Membership:** LS. **Award:** 'Winning Example' prize (SISI). **Publications:** *Cons.of Vegetation in Africa south of the Sahara* (co-Ed.) 1968, *Systematic Bot., Plant Utilization & Biosphere Cons.* (Ed.) 1978, *Parasites as plant taxonomists* (Ed.) 1979, *Res.on the Ethiopian flora* (Ed.) 1986, *Systematic bot., a key sci.for trop.res.& documentation* (Ed.) 1989, *Flora of Ethiopia* (co-Ed.) 1989; *c*.30 scientific papers. **Languages:** English; French & German (basic); Swedish. Willing to act as consult.etc. Indiff.to pers. pub., favours news media support. **Address:** Department of Systematic Botany, Villavagen 6, S-752 36 Uppsala, Sweden. **Tel.**(office) 46 18 18 2773, (home) 46 18 51 6199; **fax** 46 18 55 4369.

HEDBERG, Professor Dr K.Olov. Plant taxonomy & ecology, particularly of tropical high mountains, ethnobotany, conservation of biodiversity. Emeritus Professor of Systematic Botany. *B*.19 Oct.1923, Vasteras, Sweden. Swedish. *M*.Dr Inga M.M.*qv:* 4 *s*.incl.Per O.(Dir. of Uppsala Nature Study Sch.), *d*. **Education:** U.of Uppsala BSc 1947, PhD 1957. **Experience:** field work in Scandinavian mtns, Arctic Canada, Ethiopia, E.Africa, Lesotho, Venezuela; teaching of systematic bot.to grad.Scandinavian & African students; consults; taxonomic & ecol.res.on African flora. **Career:** Lect.1957–69, Prof.1970–88 (Emer.1988–) in Systematic Bot, U.of Uppsala; Chairman, SNCB 1981–7. **Achievements:** described veg.zonation and plant ecol.of E.African high mtns, co-Org.of trop.high mtn veg.and cons.of veg.in Africa in gen. **Memberships:** LS, RSAS. **Award:** Linnaeus Medal for Bot.(LS) 1978. **Publications:** *Afroalpine Vascular Plants, A Taxonomic Revision* 1957, *Features of Afroalpine Plant Ecol.1964, Vaxter pa Jorden — var Viktigaste Naturresurs* (co-Author) 1990; *c*.80 scientific papers. Indiff.to pers.pub., favours news media support. **Languages:** English, French (basic), German, ki-Swahili (basic), Swedish. Further details may be obtained from *Who's Who in Sweden*. Willing to act as consult.etc. **Address:** Department of Systematic Botany, Villavagen 6, S-752 36 Uppsala, Sweden. **Tel.**(office) 46 18 18 2771, (home) 46 18 51 6199; **fax** 46 18 55 4369.

HEINEN, Dr Joel Thomas. Ecology and conservation of terrestrial vertebrates; management of protected areas. Adjunct Professor of Biology, Assistant Professor of Environmental Studies. *B*.9 March 1958, Buffalo, NY, USA. American. **Education:** U.of Michigan, BS (Dist.) 1979, PhD 1992; Virginia Poly.Inst.and SU, MS 1982. **Experience:** lecturing at Inst.of For.1984–6 and res.at Dept of Nat.Parks 1986–8, Nepal; some consult.for WWF US & USAID. **Career:** Adj.Prof.of Biol. Biol.Station 1990–, Lect.in Ecol.Issues, Sch.of Natural Resources 1992–3, U.of Michigan; Asst Prof.of Envl Studies, Florida Intl U.1993–. **Achievements:** memb.of IUCN SSC, pubns, hons. **Memberships:** Ecotourism Soc., AAAS, SCB, ESA, Wildlife Soc., ATB. **Awards:** Xi Sigma Pi 1978, Phi Sigma 1981, Sigma Xi 1990, Trop.Biol.1990 & Rackham Dissertation 1991–2 F'ships (both U.of Michigan), NYAS 1994. **Publications:** 60+ papers incl.Park–people relations in Kosi Tappu Wildlife Reserve, Nepal: a socio-econ.analysis 1993, A review of cons. issues and progs in Nepal (co-Author) 1994; 30+ peer-reviewed articles. Favours pers.pub.& news media support. **Languages:** English, French, Spanish (written working knowledge), Nepali. Further details may be obtained from *Amer. Men & Women of Sci.*1995, *Who's Who in Sci.& Engg* 1996. Willing to act as consult.etc. **Address:** Department of Environmental Studies, Florida International University, CP 315, Miami, Florida 33199, USA. **Tel.**(office) 1 305 348 3732, (home) 1 305 267 5973; **fax** 1 305 348 3772.

HEISS, Dr Gerhard. Forest & mountain ecology (boreal, temperate, & Mediterranean, regions of Europe), systems' planning for protected areas (particularly national parks), evaluation methods for selection of natural & semi-natural forests, national park planning. Independent Consultant. *B*.20 Feb.1956, Kempten, Bavaria, Germany. German. **Education:** Ludwig-Maximilians-Universität Munich, Dipl.-Forstwirt 1980, Dr rer.silv.1992. **Experience:** eval.by satellite imagery (LANDSAT) & computer-aided processing (ARC/INFO) for selection of forest reserves on large-scaled regns, perm.field-work in var.Euro.nat.parks. **Career:** Project Leader of old-growth forest inventory by Council of Europe within its member states 1984–7; resp. for nat.park inventory in Europe undertaken by the FNNPE and in coopn with EC/Brussels 1988–90, consult.for IUCN, WWF & EC 1990–. **Achievements:** Inventory of old-growth forests in Europe; nat.park inventory of Europe; review of IUCN's prot.area categories in context of Europe; selection of most important Euro.forest & mtn ecosystems for EC/Brussels. **Membership:** IUCN CNPPA. **Publications:** *Notwendigkeit und Bedeutung von Waldschutzgebieten für Arten- und Ökosystemschutz unter besonderer Berücksichtigung von Altholz- und Totholz-zönosen* 1990, *Sydeuropas alpina Nationalparker* 1990, *Nationalparke in Europa* 1991, *Selection & Eval.of Large Forests for Establishing a Systems Plan for Germany* (in German) 1992. Dislikes pers.pub.& news media support.

Languages: English, French, German, Italian; Danish, Dutch, Norwegian, Portuguese, Spanish, Swedish (all read). Willing to act as consult.etc. **Address:** Schwabenweg 2, D-87 435 Kempten, Germany. **Tel.**49 831 23804.

HELLIWELL, D.Rodney. Forestry, ecology, arboriculture, landscape management. Consultant. *B.*2 April 1940, Halifax, England, UK. British. *M.*Carole: 2 *s.* **Education:** U.of Wales MSc 1965. **Experience:** woodland mgmt, local govt, Nature cons., res.inst., consult. **Career:** woodland mgmt 1961–3, u.res.1963–4, local govt (landscape/forestry) 1964–7, NC/ITE 1967–78, Consult.1978–. **Achievements:** signatory to declaration which set up 'Pro Silva' 1989, Chairman Brit. 'Continuous Cover Forestry Group' formed in 1991. **Memberships:** F.ICF, F.AA, IBiol., IEEM. **Publications:** *Options in For.* 1982, *Econ.of Woodland Mgmt* 1984, *Planning for Nature Cons.*1985. Dislikes pers.pub.& news media support. **Languages:** English, French (poor), Welsh (v.poor). Willing to act as consult.etc. **Address:** Yokecliffe House, West End, Wirksworth, Derbyshire DE4 4EG, England, UK. **Tel.**(office) 44 1629 824676; **fax** 44 1629 825389.

HEMMING, Dr John H. All aspects of environmental conservation, with personal interest in Amazon region. Director. *B.*5 Jan.1935, Vancouver, Canada. Canadian (UK resident). *M.* Sukie (Head of Dev., NT): *s., d.* **Education:** Eton Coll.; McGill U. 1955–6; Magdalen Coll. Oxf.U. MA 1961, DLitt 1981. **Experience:** expdns in Peru & to Iriri R., Brazil; series of expedns & visits to Indian tribes in Brazil. **Career:** Dir, RGS 1975–96. **Achievements:** Leader of Maraca Rainforest Project, Brazil 1987–8, participation in expedns in Amazonia & elsewhere 1960–, making RGS more envlly aware, pubns. **Memberships:** Bd or Council Memb.of The Brit.Council, Lepra, Anglo–Brazilian Soc., Geogl Club, Margaret Mee Amazon Trust, Inst.of Latin Amer.Studies, Survival Intl, Earth Centre, OUEC (Sr VP). **Awards:** CMG, Ordén de Mérito (Perú), Robert Pitman Literary Prize, Christopher Award (NY), Washburn Medal (BMS), Mungo Park Medal (RSGS), Founder's Medal (RGS), Hon.Doct.Warwick & Stirling Univs. **Publications:** *The Conquest of the Incas* 1970, *Tribes of the Amazon Basin in Brazil* (co-Author) 1972, *Red Gold, The Conquest of the Brazilian Indians* 1978, *Amazon Frontier* 1985, *Change in the Amazon Basin* (Ed. 2 vols) 1987, *Maraca, Rainforest Is.*(co-Author) 1993, *Roraima, Brazil's n.most Frontier* 1991, *The Rainforest Edge* (Ed.) 1993. Indiff.to pers. pub., favours news media support of activities. **Languages:** English, French, German (some), Portuguese, Spanish (some). Further details may be obtained from *The Intl Who's Who* 1994–5 and the British *Who's Who* 1996. **Address:** Royal Geographical Society, 1 Kensington Gore, London SW7 2AR, England, UK. **Tel.**(office) 44 171 589 0648, (home) 44 171 602 6697; **fax** 44 171 584 4447.

HEMPEL, Professor Dr Gotthilf. Marine & polar sciences, research policy & management. Centre Director, Institute Director. *B.*8 March 1929, Göttingen, Germany. German. *M.*Dr Irmtraut. **Education:** U.of Mainz & Heidelberg, Dipl.Degree in Biol.1951, PhD(Zool.) 1952. **Experience:** res.— ecol.& pop.dynamics of fish, life-hist.of fish larvae & Antarctic krill, life-ecol.of Weddell Sea; admin.— incl.Prog. Officer UNESCO 1964–6, Chairman ESF Network Polar Res.1987–9, several nat.& intl scientific adv.bds; Consult.to FAO 1966–7; teaching — marine & fisheries biol., marine pop.ecol.& dynamics, comparative ecosystem res. **Career:** Prof.of Marine & Fisheries Biol. 1967–81, Dir of Inst.for Polar Ecol.1982–94 (Kiel); Dir, Alfred Wegener Inst.for Polar & Marine Res.(Bremerhaven) 1981–92; Dir, Center for Trop.Marine Ecol.(ZMT, Bremen) 1992–; Dir, Inst.for Baltic Res.(Warnemunde) 1992–. **Achievements:** estab.of res.in field of global change in Germany, integration of nat.& intl res.activities in ocean & polar sci., eval.& implementation of a new structure in envl res.in Germany after unification. **Memberships:** DWK, ICES (Pres.1979–82), SCAR (VP 1984– 8), IASC, ECOPS (Chairman 1990), German Sci.Council, Academia Europea, Leopoldina, R.AS of The Netherlands. **Awards:** Georg Neumayer Medal (govt Pfalz) 1984, Order of Merit (FRG) 1986 & 1993, Karl Weyprecht Medal (German Soc.for Polar Res.) 1991, Hon.Doct.(U.of Oldenburg) 1994. **Publications:** incl.*N.Sea Fish Stocks — Recent Changes and Their Causes* (Ed./co-Ed.) 1978, *The Canary Current: Studies of an Upwelling System* 1982, *Rückkehr in die internationale Forschergemeinschaft. 40 Jahre Forschung in der Bundesrepublik Deutschland* (co-Author) 1989, *Oceanogr.and Biol.of Arctic Seas* 1989, *Antarctic Ecosystems: Ecol.Change and Cons.*(co-Author) 1990, *Weddell Sea Ecol.*1993, *Biologie der Polarmeere* 1995; Ed.*Polar Biol.*1981–. Indiff. to pers.pub., favours news media support. **Languages:** English, French (basic), German. Willing to act as consult.etc. **Address:** Zentrum für Marine Tropenökologie, Klagenfurter Strasse GEO, D-28359 Bremen, Germany. **Tel.**49 421 218 5151; **fax** 49 421 218 5170.

HENNING, Professor Dr Daniel H. Asian tropical forests & national parks, biodiversity, interdisciplinary approaches, public participation, ecotourism, role of Buddhism in Nature protection. Environmental Consultant & Trainer, Professor Emeritus of Environmental Affairs. *B.*1 Aug.1931, Cleveland, OH, USA. American. **Education:** Bowling Green SU (Ohio), BS(Biol./ Social Sci.) 1957; U.of Michigan, MS(Cons.) 1959, Syracuse U. PhD(Public Admin./For.) 1965. **Experience:** since 1990 res., training, & consult.in Asia with UN assignments — for. trainer in Cambodia, country study of Laos, UNEP Envl Educ.Project on Ecol.Teachings of Buddhism; envl training and prot.areas' consult. in Cambodia — the latter for Cambodian Min.of

Envt & UNDP. **Career:** Prof.of Pol.Sci./Envt 1966–90, Emer.Prof.of Envl Affairs 1990–, Montana SU (Billings); Vis.Prof. U.of New Mexico and Chinese U.of HK 1973–5, U.of Montana Flathead Lake Biol.Res.Station; Sr Fulbright Res.Scholar, SE Asia 1988–9. **Achievements:** num.books, articles, & papers, presented on envl training, values, & interdisc. approaches; assisted Cambodian Min.of Envt in prot.areas' legis.(20% of Cambodia for King's Decree) and planned & conducted training prog.for new prot.area staff; conducted res.& workshops on how Buddhism and 'Deep Ecol.' can contribute to protecting trop.forests in Asia. **Memberships:** ISTF, ISTE, ISTB, ASPA, IUCN ICEL, RIPA, EROPA (Asia). **Awards:** V.-Chancellor's Fac.Award of Merit (Chinese U.of HK) 1977, Fulbright SE Asia Regnl Award 1988–9, Vis.Sci. Interacademy Exchange Prog. Czech.(envl admin.& training, NAS) 1986, Travel Award (India, Smithsonian Instn) 1987. **Publications:** *Envl Policy and Admin.*(co-Author) 1957, *Envl Policy: Concepts and Intl Implications* 1973, *Interdisc.Envl Approaches: Theory by Disciplines* (Ed.) 1974, *Managing the Envl Crisis* (co-Author) 1989, Trop.Forest Admin.and In-Service Training: Interdisc.Ecol. Approaches and Values 1992, Trop.forest training in Thailand 1992. Indiff.to pers.pub.& news media support. **Language:** English Further details may be obtained from *Amer.Men and Women of Sci.*1980, *World Envl Dir.*1990, *Outstanding Educators of Amer.* Willing to act as consult.etc. **Address:** 17001 East Lake Shore, Bigfork, Montana 59911, USA. **Tel.**(home) 1 406 982 3025; **fax** 1 406 982 3201.

HENS, Professor Dr Luc. Human ecology. Professor of Human Ecology & Departmental Director. *B.*5 Dec.1951, Mechelen, Belgium. Belgian. *M.*: Erna: *s., d.* **Education:** Vrije Universiteit Brussel, Lic.in Biol.(Zool.)(*cum laude*) 1974, Aggregation of Higher Sec. Sch.Teaching (*cum laude*) 1975, PhD(*magna cum laude*) 1981. **Experience:** teaching/lecturing, res., logistics, project promotion, training abroad, memb.u. policy and extra.u.councils, book review Ed. **Career:** trained as biol., specialized in human cytogenetics with partic.ref.to clinical cytogenetics & mutagenesis; Prof.of Human Ecol.& Dir, Dept of Human Ecol. Vrije Universiteit Brussel 1990–. **Memberships:** BSCB, DAS, ESHG, BSM, SHE (VP), ESHRE, IFMBE, DSMES, Soc.for Envt & Health (VP); Edl Bd *Envt & Poll.* **Awards:** First Winner of Scientific Travel Grant Contest (Belgian Min.of Nat.Educ.& Dutch Culture) 1978, Winner RASA of Belgium (partim scis) 1984. **Publications:** co-Ed.of five books incl.*Envl Mgmt* 1993, *Intl Conf.on Envl Poll.*(two-vols Proc.) 1993; 39 papers in intl journals, 44 in Belgian & Dutch journals, 78 cong.pubns. Favours limited pers. pub.and news media support. **Languages:** Dutch, English & French (written & spoken), German (basic). Willing to act as consult.etc. **Address:** Department of Human Ecology, Vrije

Universiteit Brussel, Laarbeeklaan 103, B-1090 Brussels, Belgium. **Tel.**(office) 32 2 477 4281, (home) 32 15 61 5175; **fax** 32 2 477 4964.

HERKOVITS, Professor Dr Jorge. Ecotoxicology, chemical safety. Scientist, Programme Director. *B.*31 May 1947, Cluj, Romania. Argentinian. *M.*Adriana A.Fernandez MD: 3 *s., d.* **Education:** U.of Buenos Aires, MD 1971, PhD 1978; postgrad.courses & training at IIDB 1976, U.of Köln 1982 and US EPA 1993. **Experience:** res.— multidisc.studies on reproductive & devl biol.incl.hazard assessment, antagonism & synergism phenomena among metals, acclimation to xenobiotics and ecotoxicological studies for focal & non-focal points of contamination; admin. 12 yrs as inst.dir.; consult.— Sec.of State for Res.& Tech., & Min.of Foreign Affairs (Argentina), UNEP. **Career:** F.1973–8, Sci.1988–, Nat.Council of Sci.& Tech.; Prof.of Anatomy & Physiol.1978–90, Dir of Inst.of Biol.of Repro.& Dev.1979–90, Nat.U.of Lomas de Zamora; Dir, Prog.on Chem.Safety, Nat.Council of Sci.& Tech.1991–4 and Inst.of Envl Scis & Health 1994–; Sr Expert Consult.on Toxic Chemicals and Chem.Waste Mgmt Activities UNEP 1994–5. **Achievements:** self-recovery phenomenon; hazard assessment of xenobiotics, interaction of chemicals, dev.of parameters & standard methods for hazard & risk assessment; envl studies for point & non-point sources of envl poll., envl services studies; org.ot nat.& intl mtgs on envl issues. **Memberships:** SETAC, AAAS, ASMA, SEES, Intl Res.Group on Very Low Dose and High Dilution Effects, Intl Assn of Bioinorganic Scientists, Argentinian Socs of Toxicology, Devl Biol., Ecol., Morphology, & Herpetology. **Publications:** 120 scientific papers incl.Are shape and morphogenesis ind.phenomena? 1977, *Amphibian Embryos as Bioassays to Evaluate Envl Pollutants and to Reduce their Toxic Effects* (co-Author, conf.Proc.) 1990, Stage dependent uptake of cadmium in *Bufo arenarum* embryos (co-Author) in press. **Languages:** English, Hungarian, Portuguese, Rumanian, Spanish. Willing to act as consult.etc.(interested in intl res.project proposals). **Address:** Instituto de Ciencias Ambientales y Salud, Nicasio Oroño 710 (1405), Buenos Aires, Argentina. **Tel.** (office) 54 1 431 2445; **fax** 54 1 431 4206.

HERRERO, Professor Dr Stephen Matthew. Conservation biology, planning & management of natural areas, special expertise regarding the ecology & management of carnivores, especially bears. Professor of Environmental Science & Biology, President. *B.*31 Dec.1939, San Francisco, CA, USA. Canadian. *M.*Linda Carol Wiggins (cons.educ., researcher & writer): *s.*, 2 *d.* **Education:** UCB BA(Psych.) *summa cum laude* 1962, PhD(Psych./Zool.) 1967; U.of Calgary Postdoctl res.in animal ecol.1967–9. **Experience:** long-term u.teaching & res., extensive field res.on carnivores incl.capture, immobilization & biotelemetry, some admin.

Career: Prof.of Envl Sci.& Biol. U.of Calgary 1970–, Pres. BIOS Envl Res.and Planning Assocs Ltd 1980–. **Achievements:** founding memb.of interdisc.Fac.of Envl Design, U.of Calgary; supervised 39 Master's &/or PhD students; co-init.& supervised reintro.of Swift Fox *(Vulpes velox)* to Canada 1976–90, ± 225 foxes now survive free-ranging. **Memberships:** IABRM (Pres.1986–7), WWF Canada Prairie Cons. Action Cttee 1986–9, AAAS, IUCN SSC Bear SG (Chair/co-Chair) 1988–. **Awards:** Outstanding Contribns to Wildlife & Wilderness Cons.Award (Alberta Govt) 1985, IABRM voted Bear Attacks ...* to be 'the most imp. scientific work on bears in the past 20 yrs', prin.scientific adv.to Minnesota Mus.of Sci.for design of their US$ 600,000 travelling exhibit on bears. **Publications:** *Bear Attacks: Their Causes & Avoidance* 1985, *Bears & Man* (multiple award-winning film, Prin.Scriptwriter & Scientific Ed.) 1977. Accepts pers.pub.& news media support. **Languages:** English, French (good written), Nepali (fair spoken), Spanish (good written, fair spoken), Swahili (fair spoken). Willing to act as consult.etc. **Address:** Faculty of Environmental Design, University of Calgary, Alberta T2N 1N4, Canada. **Tel.** (office) 1 403 220 6605, (home) 1 403 243 3614; **fax** 1 403 284 4399.

HESSELINK, Frederik Joost. National & international environmental education & communication. Managing Director. *B*.25 Aug.1945, Amersfoort, The Netherlands. Dutch. **Education:** studied law at Utrecht SU. **Experience:** res.& consult.on envl educ.& strat.communication for the Dutch Govt, EC, industry, NGOs, & intl orgns. **Career:** F.Inst.of Intl Law, Utrecht SU 1968–72, teaching, and developing a new curriculum for, solid studies at sec.level 1972–83; co-Founder 1975 & MD 1983–, Inst.for Envl Communication (SME). **Achievements:** VC 1987–93 & Chair 1994– IUCN CEC, consult.to Dutch Govt on nat.strats for formal & informal educ. **Membership:** Dutch Nat.Comm.on Envl Educ. Favours pers.pub.& news media support. **Languages:** Dutch, English, French, German. Willing to act as consult.etc. **Address:** Institute for Environmental Communication (SME), POB 13030, 3507 LA Utrecht, The Netherlands. **Tel.**(office) 31 30 802444, (home) 31 30 511948; **fax** 31 30 801345.

HEYERDAHL, Thor. Exploring, anthropology, writing. *B*.6 Oct.1914, Larvik, Norway. Norwegian. *M*.1.Liv: 2 *s*.; 2.Yvonne: 3 *d*.; 3.Jacqueline. **Education:** Oslo U. degree in biol.with field res.in Marquesas Islands 1933–9, changed to anthrop. **Experience:** res., admin., primitive watercraft, writing, cong.participation, expedns. **Career:** res.& writing in Europe, BC, & USA –1941, Parachute Lt in Free Norwegian Forces 1942–3, Org./Leader of Kon-Tiki Balsa Raft Expedn from Peru to Polynesia 1947, res.in Peru, Bolivia, Colombia, & Ecuador 1950–54 incl.Org./ Leader of Norwegian Archl Expedns to Galápagos Islands with experiments revealing tacking principles of balsa rafts 1952, Org./ Leader of Norwegian Archl Expedn to Easter Is.1955–6, res.& writing 1957–69, Org./Leader of transAtlantic voyages on papyrus ships *Ra* and *RaII* from Safi (Morocco) 1969–70 (*RaII* reaching Barbados, W.Indies), Org./Leader of voyage using Sumerian-type reed ship Tigris from Iraq to Djibouti *via* Indus Valley 1977–8, Org./Leader of three archl expedns to Maldive archipelago 1982–4, Kon-Tiki Mus.Norwegian/ Chilean Archl Expedns to Easter Is.1986–8, and Kon-Tiki Mus.Norwegian/Peruvian Archl Project in Tucume (Peru) 1988–94. **Achievements:** has demonstrated that world oceans were no absolute barriers to early pre-Euro.civilizations by personally crossing the open spans of Pacific, Atlantic, and Indian, Oceans in aboriginal types of raft-ships; first to send warning to UN that world oceans were threatened by oil poll. **Memberships:** NY Explorers' Club 1941, RNAS 1958–, WAWF (VP 1966), WWF (Trustee, Intl Bd 1977), United World Colls (Intl Patron 1980), Intl Green Cross (Trustee 1993). **Awards:** num.incl.Retzius 1950 and Vega 1962 Medals (SSAG), Gold Medal (RGS) 1965, Commander Knights of Malta 1970, Intl Pahlavi Envt Prize (UN) 1978, Bradford Washburn Award (Boston Mus.of Sci.) 1982; Decorations — Commander with Star of St Olav (Norway), highest nat.Orders from Presidents of Peru, Egypt, & Italy, and the K.of Morocco; Hon.— Memb.Geogl Socs of Peru 1953, Norway 1953, Brazil 1954 & USSR 1964, Dir of NY Explorers' Club 1982; Dr *h.c.* U.of Oslo 1961 & USSR AS 1980. **Publications:** num.incl.*The Kon-Tiki Expedn* 1948 (transl.into 67 languages), *Aku-Aku: The Secrets of Easter Is.*1957, *Sea Routes to Polynesia* 1968, *Early Man and the Ocean* 1978, *The Maldive Mystery* 1986, *The Pyramids of Tucume* 1995; contribns to such pubns as Nat.Geogl Magazine, Russian AS Yearbook. **Films:** incl.*The Kon-Tiki* Expedn (documentary Oscar Award 1952), Aku-Aku and subs.expedns. **Languages:** English, French, German, Spanish, Norwegian. Further details may be obtained from *Señor Kon-Tiki* 1965, *The Kon-Tiki Man* 1990, *Thor Heyerdahl the Explorer* 1994. **Address:** The Kon-Tiki Museum, Bygdöy, Oslo, Norway. **Tel.**47 22 438050; **fax** 47 22 445085.

HIBBERD, John K. Conservation resource assessment & planning; ecological survey; sustainable forest management; GIS & remote sensing. Director of Conservation & Environment, Senior Fellow. *B*.2 May 1945, Sydney, Australia. Australian. *M*.Sylvia: 2 *s*. **Education:** UCL BSc(Spec.)(Hons)(Geog.& Geol.) 1966. **Experience:** postgrad.res.on veg.communities & water chem.1968–70 and below-ground productivity & decomposition 1970–74; four yrs' Exec.Sec.of Cons.NGO and Inaugural Sec./ Treas.of Australian Cttee for IUCN; 15 yrs' resource assessment & mgmt; six yrs' ecol.& cons.consult.; country exp.in Vietnam, PNG, Solomon Islands, Thailand, Malaysia, W.Samoa, Laos, Cambodia, Indonesia, Philippines, Finland, Turkey, Vanuatu. **Career:** Res.Sci. IBP Meathop Wood 1970–74; Exec.Sec. NCC of NSW 1975–9, scientific survey and coordn, EIA, & admin., posts, NSW NPWS 1979–88; Envt & Cons.Consult. Kestel Res.and IFERM Pty Ltd.1988–; Sr F. Envt Res.Inst. U.of Wollongong 1994–. **Achievements:** prot.for peatlands in Somerset (UK) Levels; improved mgmt of biol.resources in NSW through EIA & envl planning; greater knowledge & understanding of non-wood forest resources in Pacific; training in sust.dev.of forested-land mgrs in SE Asia; major scientific input into listing of Fraser Is.on World Heritage Register. **Memberships:** IAG, AES, IUCN CESP. **Publications:** *The Harvesting & Rehab.of Jounama Pine Plantation, Kosciusko Nat.Park* (Envl Impact Statement, co-Author) 1983, *Resource Planning* (four-vols textbook) 1986, *Nat.Forest Inventory: Review of Veg. Class.Systems* (report, co-Author) 1990, Integration of Satellite Imagery & Geographic Info. Systems for Habitat Mapping and the Prediction of Fauna Distribns (co-Author) 1990, Ecoforestry for the Pacific: options for maintaining biol.diversity (co-Author) 1990, *Nat.Index of Ecosystems* (report) 1991, The Solomon Islands Nat.Forest Resources Inventory: an appropriate approach? (proc.paper, co-Author) 1993. Favours pers.pub.& news media support. **Languages:** English, French & Pidgin (fair), Russian & Vietnamese (basic). Willing to act as consult.etc. **Address:** International Forest Environment, Research & Management Pty Ltd, GPO Box 2546, Canberra City, ACT 2601, Australia. **Tel.**(office) 61 6 257 3404, (home) 61 6 257 5345; **fax** 61 6 257 5336.

HILL, Dr Mark O. Vegetation ecology, bryophyte distributions, multivariate analysis, modelling. Biological Scientist. *B.*13 July 1945, Edinburgh, Scotland, UK. British. *M.*Denise H.M.: *s., d.* **Education:** King's Coll.Camb. BA 1966, PhD(Biol.) 1982; ICL Dipl.(Stats) 1967. **Experience:** stats & math.modelling combined with field bot.& studies of ecol.succession. **Career:** Math.Technologist, BP 1967–9; Nature Conservancy Bangor 1972–3; Vis.Res.F. Cornell U. 1978–9; Biol.Sci.ITE 1974–. **Achievements:** application of numerical techniques to practical ecol.problems. **Memberships:** BES, BBS (VP 1988–9, Pres.1990–91), IAVS. **Publications:** *Atlas of the Bryophytes of Britain & Ireland* 1991–3, computer programmes TWIN-SPAN 1979, DECORANA 1979, TABLEFIT 1993. Indiff.to pers.pub., dislikes news media support. **Languages:** English, French, German (written). **Address:** Institute of Terrestrial Ecology, Monks Wood, Abbots Ripton, Huntingdon, Cambridgeshire PE17 2LS, England, UK. **Tel.**(office) 44 14873 381, (home) 44 1223 329819; **fax** 44 14873 467.

HOBBS, Dr Richard John. Conservation biology, restoration ecology; vegetation management; fragmented ecosystems; biological invasions. Senior Principal Research Scientist. *B.*18 April 1954, Hostert, Germany. Australian, British. *M. Gillian M.: s., d.* **Education:** U.of Edinburgh, BSc(Ecol.Sci.) summa cum laude 1976; UCSB, MA(Biol.) 1977; U.of Aberdeen, PhD 1982. **Experience:** res.— two yrs' postdoctl on grassland ecol., and to date on fragmented ecosystems; postgrad.student supervision. **Career:** NATO Postdoctl Res.F. Stanford U.1982–4; Res.Sci. 1984–7, Sr Res.Sci.1987–90, Prin.Res.Sci. 1990–95, Sr Prin.Res.Sci.1995–, Div.of Wildlife & Ecol. CSIRO. **Achievements:** res.into fragmented ecosystems, integrating prod.& cons., biol.invasions. **Memberships:** ESA, BES, IALE, IAVS, AAEE. **Awards:** F'ship (Fulbright-Hays) 1976–7, Postdoctl F'ship (NATO) 1982–4. **Publications:** eight books incl.*Biodiv.of Medit. Ecosystems in Australia* 1992, *Reintegrating Fragmented Landscapes: Towards Sust.Prod. and Nature Cons.*(co-Author) 1993; 100+ papers & chapters. Favours pers.pub.& news media support. **Languages:** English, French (moderate), German (read). Willing to act as consult.etc. **Address:** Division of Wildlife & Ecology, CSIRO, LMB 4, PO Midland, Western Australia 6056, Australia. **Tel.**(office) 61 9 290 8122, (home) 61 9 336 1295; **fax** 61 9 290 8132; **e-mail** RichardHobbs@per.dwe.csiro.au .

HOECK, Dr Hendrik N. Ecodevelopment & management of conservation areas, ecotourism, management of research institutions, wildlife management. Freelance Consultant. *B.*18 Jan. 1944, Bogotá, Colombia. Colombian, Swiss. *M.*Pia: 2 *s.* **Education:** Colegio Andino, Bachiller 1961; U.of Munich, Dr Rer.Nat.(Biol.) 1975. **Experience:** field res.in behavioural ecol. in Serengeti; mgmt & admin. Charles Darwin Res.Station; envl impact studies in Europe & S.Amer.; teaching at u.level in ecol., ethology, evol.& island biogeog. **Career:** res.projects & teaching at Serengeti Res.Inst 1970–76, Max-Planck-Inst. für Verhaltensphysiologie 1976–7, and Univs of Munich 1976–7 & Konstanz 1981–8; WHO malaria survey in N. Syria 1966–8; Dir, Charles Darwin Res.Station 1978–80; co-Partner, BiCon AG (Applied Envl Scis Corpn Ltd) 1989–. **Achievements:** social orgn & ecol.of *Hyrax* in Serengeti; assisting Ecuadorean auths in mgmt of Nat.Parks; creation of Fundación Encenillo in Colombia for the prot.of Andean forests. **Memberships:** Charles Darwin Fndn, AMS, DZG, ABS, SCB, EANHS, IUCN SSC, Fundación Encenillo. **Publications:** num.incl.Ecol.& behaviour of Hydracoidea and ecol.of inselbergs (kopjes) in Serengeti 1982, *Introduced Species in Galápagos* 1984, *Socio-econ.Dev.in Galápagos* 1991. Dislikes pers.pub., favours news media support. **Languages:** English, French (basic), German, Spanish. Willing to act as consult.etc. **Address:** BiCon AG, Bodanstrasse 19, CH-8280 Kreuzlingen, Switzerland. **Tel.**(office) 41 72 722868, (home) 41 72 752165; **fax** 41 72 722869.

HOF, Tom VAN'T. Marine sciences & conservation. Independent Consultant, Director. *B.*31

Oct.1944, The Netherlands. Dutch. *M*.Helena (artist, envl illustrator): *s., d.* **Education:** U.of Amsterdam, MSc(Biol.) 1971. **Experience:** coral reef ecol., admin.of large intl res.progs, marine park planning, implementation & mgmt, prod.of envl educ.& interpretation materials, consult.on coastal resources mgmt. **Career:** Ops Coord. CICAR (UNESCO) 1971–6, Coord. Nat.Oceanogr.Prog. RNAS 1976–9, Project Manager Bonaire Marine Park, Curaçao Underwater Park & Saba Marine Park 1979–89, Ind.Consult.& Dir of Marine & Coastal Resource Mgmt, Saba, Netherlands Antilles 1989–. **Achievements:** developing & managing first three marine parks in Netherlands Antilles, successful application of concept of self-financing marine parks, several contribns to coastal cons. & park dev.throughout the Carib., econ.of marine parks. **Memberships:** ISRS, IUCN CNPPA & Comm.on Ecol. Coral Reef WG, Tech.Adv. Group of Consortium of Carib.univs for Nat. Resource Mgmt, Bd of Dirs CNRI. **Award:** Fred M.Packard Intl Parks Merit Award 1992. **Publications:** 4 park guides, *c.*25 papers. Favours pers.pub.& news media support. **Languages:** Dutch, English, French (spoken), German (basic), Papiamentu (spoken), Spanish (basic). Willing to act as consult.etc. **Address:** The Bottom, Saba, Netherlands Antilles. **Tel.**(office & home) 599 4 63348; **fax** 599 4 63299.

HOFFMANN, Dr Luc. Ecology, ornithology, wetland conservation & management. Foundation President. *B.*23 Jan.1923, Basel, Switzerland. Swiss. *M*.Daria: 3 *d.*incl.Maja (Nature film-maker), *s.* **Education:** U.of Basel, Dr Phil. 1952. **Experience:** admin., campaigning, project & conf.orgn, participation in waterfowl counts (discovery on L.Karla of greatest waterfowl concentration watched in the Medit.on a single lake 1964), govtl negns. **Career:** creation of Station Biologique de la Tour du Valat 1954–, WWF (now World Wide Fund for Nature) 1961 (VP 1961–88, Exec.VP 1971–8), Doñana Nat.Park 1969, Fondation Tour du Valat 1974, and Fondation Internationale du Banc d'Arguin 1985 (Pres.); Hon.Dir IWRB 1962–8, VP IUCN 1966–9, VP Wildfowl Trust (now Wildfowl and Wetlands Trust) (UK) 1971–, Memb.Bd of Dirs Hoffmann-La Roche & Co. 1956– (VP 1990–), Memb.Governing Bd of FEC 1974–94. **Achievements:** active participation in creation & dev. of many prot. areas in Europe & Africa, and in running & developing IUCN, WWF, IWRB, Tour du Valat, etc. **Memberships:** BES, most Euro.Ornithol.Socs, WWF Intl Cons.Cttee (Chair 1984–8), ICBP Exec.Cttee 1984–90, WWF Memb.of Honour. **Awards:** Dr *h.c.* Univs of Basel & Thessaloniki, Commander of the Order of the Golden Ark, First Class Cross of Merit for Sci.& Arts (Rep.of Austria), Award Pro Natura (Rep.of Hungary). **Publications:** *c.*60 pubns incl.Forum und Entstehung des Zeichnungsmusters dunenjunger Flusseeschwalben (*Sterna hirundo*) 1953, Le

passage d'automne du Chevalier Sylvain (*Tringa glareola*) en France méditerranéenne 1957, An ecol.sketch of the Camargue 1968, Camargue (co-Author) 1970, Proposals for Nature cons.in n.Greece (IUCN Occasional Paper Nr 1 which led to estab.of Prespa Nat.Park and attracted attention on Evros). Indiff.to pers.pub.& news media support. **Languages:** English, French, German. **Address:** Station Biologique de la Tour du Valat, Le Sambuc, 13200 Arles, France. **Tel.**33 90 972013 or 972175; **fax** 33 90 972019.

HOLCÍK, Vladimír. Water management, river regulations, hydraulic research on flows. Institute Director. *B.*8 Oct.1944, Bratislava, Slovak Republik. Slovak. *M*.Marta Holcíková MD. **Education:** Slovak Tech.U. Fac.of Civil Engg, Ing. Water Bldgs 1968, and Fac.of Machinery, Ing. Water Turbines & Pumps 1978; Open U.(City U.Bratislava) Effective Mgr 1994. **Experience:** consult.& adv., project & maintenance engr, res., admin. **Career:** Project Engr, Hydroconsult (Bratislava) 1969–70; Hydrol.of Ground-water Engr, Slovak Hydrometeorological Inst.1970–73; Chief Engr of Maintenance for Danube R.1973–86, Engr on Gabčíkovo Water Plant 1987–91, Danube R.Basin Admin.; Project Engr (Water Power Plants) Hydroprojet-Est (Algeria) 1986–7; Dir, Water Res.Inst. 1991–. **Achievements:** author of envl river regs (Danube & Morava Rivers), init.of anti-erosion precautions in Algeria. **Membership:** Slovak Comm.on Large Dams (VP). **Publications:** incl.*Danube Bridges* (Slovak part of the River) 1986, num.project reports. Indiff.to pers.pub.& news media support. **Languages:** Czech, English, French, German, Russian, Slovak; Arabic & Hungarian (poor). Willing to act as consult. etc. **Address:** Water Research Institute, nábr Gèn.Svoboda 5, 812 49 Bratislava, Slovak Republic. **Tel.**(office) 42 7 343337, (home) 42 7 762018; **fax** 42 7 315743.

HOLDGATE, Sir Martin Wyatt. Ecology especially of polar regions & oceanic islands, pollution and its impacts, conservation & sustainable use of Nature & natural resources, environmental trends & related social policies. Society President, Chairman. *B.*14 Jan.1931, Horsham, Sussex, England, UK. British. *M*.Elizabeth Mary: 2 *s.* **Education:** Arnold Sch. (Blackpool, UK); Queen's Coll.Camb. (Entrance & Fndn Scholar) BA Cantab. 1952, MA 1956, PhD Cantab. 1955. **Experience:** res.in insect physiol., plant ecol.& antarctic biol. 1952–66, subs.Dir of Res.in Cons.& Ecol. 1966–70 & 1974–6; public admin.in UK Civil Service incl. sci.policy 1970–74 & 1976–88, and in intl & cons.1970–94 but esp.1988–94. **Career:** Res. F. Queen's Coll.1953–6; Jt Leader, Gough Is.Scientific Survey 1955–6; Lect.in Zool. Manchester U.1956–7 & Durham U.1957– 60; Leader, RS expedn to S.Chile 1958–9; Asst Dir of Res. Scott Polar Res.Inst.1960–63; Chief of Biol. Brit.Antarctic Survey 1963–6; Dep Dir

(Res.), UK NC 1966–70; Dir, UK C.Unit on Envl Poll. 1970–74; Dir, UK ITE 1974–6; Chief Sci. UK Dept of Envt 1976–81, Dep.Sec.& Chief Envt Sci. UK Dept of Envt & Chief Sci.Adv. Dept of Transport 1981–8; DG IUCN (The World Cons.Union) 1988–94 when retired; Pres.Global 500 Forum 1992–, Pres.ZSL 1994–, Chairman IUCN-UK 1993–, UK Adv.Panel on Energy 1994–, IIED Bd 1994–. **Achievements:** as Chairman, WG on Biol.of the Scientific Cttee on Antarctic Res., coordinated dev.of intl prog. on antarctic biol.1963–94, played part in dev.of intl action to safeguard envt esp.with UNEP (Pres.Governing Council 1983–4) and IUCN (DG 1988–94). **Memberships:** BES, F.ZSL, F.IBiol.(UK), F.RGS. **Awards:** created knight 1994, Patron's Medal (RGS), Bruce Medal (RSE & RSGS), Livingstone Medal (RSGS), Charter Award (IBiol.), Intl Conservationist Award (NWF), Silver Medal & Global 500 Roll of Honour (UNEP); CB 1979, Commander of Order of Golden Ark 1991, Hon.DSc of Univs of Durham 1991 & Sussex 1993. **Publications:** *Mtns in the Sea: The Story of the Gough Is. Expedn* 1958, *Antarctic Ecol.*(2 vols) (Ed.) 1970, *A Perspective of Envl Poll.*1979, *The World Envt 1972–82* (co-Ed.) 1982, *The World Envt 1972–92* (co-Ed.) 1992, *From Care to Action* 1996; num.papers on antarctic biol., poll., cons., & envl trends. Dislikes pers.pub., favours news media support concerning professional activities. **Languages:** English, French (some spoken), Spanish (little). Willing to act selectively as consult.etc. **Address:** 35 Wingate Way, Trumpington, Cambridge CB2 2HD, England, UK. **Tel.** (home) 44 1223 840086.

HOLDICH, Dr David Malcolm. Environmental biology of aquatic crustaceans — particularly isopods, tanaids, and freshwater crayfish. Reader in Zoology. *B.*14 Feb.1942, Oxf., England, UK. British. *M.*Kay: 2 s. **Education:** U.Coll. of Swansea, BSc(Hons) 1964, PhD(Zool.) 1968; U.of Nottingham, DSc(Zool.) 1989. **Experience:** res.— field-work in marine & freshwater ecosystems incl.GBR & deep sea; teaching marine biol.& ecotoxicology; admin.as V.Dean of Sci.Fac.1990–94; consult.in aquaculture & freshwater poll. **Career:** Lect.& Sr Lect. Dept of Zool.1967–89, Reader in Zool. Dept of Life Sci.1989–, U.of Nottingham. **Achievements:** res.in trop.Australia has resulted in a much better understanding of ecol.& systematics of marine isopods; formulation of cons.strat.for native crayfish in UK. **Memberships:** BES, IAA (Pres. 1990–92), FBA, MBA, Crustacean Soc., Edl Bd *Crustaceana.* **Award:** Nuffield F.in Trop. Marine Biol.1976. **Publications:** 100 incl.one book *Tanaids: Linnean Synopsis of the Brit. Fauna* 1983 and three co-edited vols *Biol.of Terr.Isopods* 1984, *Freshwater Crayfish: Biol., Mgmt & Exploitation* 1988, and *Freshwater Crayfish IX* 1992. Favours pers.pub.& news media support. **Languages:** English, French (read). Willing to act as consult.etc. **Address:** Department of Life Science, The University of

Nottingham, Nottingham NG7 2RD, England, UK. **Tel.**44 1115 951 3219; **fax** 44 1115 951 3251.

HOLLEMAN, Andrew David. Wetlands preservation, environmental education. Student. *B.*6 Dec.1974, Boston, MA, USA. American. **Education:** Chelmsford High Sch.(Mass.). **Experience:** has spoken to groups throughout USA & former USSR stressing importance of natural envt & envl prot., and that one person can make a real difference through envl activism. **Career:** student studying Computer & Cognitive Scis, Vassar Coll.1993–. **Achievements:** instrumental in preventing construction of 180 condominiums which threatened wetland habitats of many rare plants & animals, as well as an aquifer recharge area. **Memberships:** G500F, NPCA (past), Giraffe Project, Boy Scouts of Amer., Nat.Eagle Scout Assn. **Awards:** Global 500 Roll of Honour (UNEP) 1989, Regnl Merit Award (US EPA), Land Pres.(MACC), Giraffe, Eagle Scout. **Publication:** David meets Goliath at City Hall. Dislikes pers.pub., favours news media support. **Languages:** English, Spanish (good). Further details may be obtained from Kids With Courage 1992, It's Our World, Too 1993. Willing to act as consult.etc. **Address:** 26 Judith Road, Chelmsford, Massachusetts 01824-4743, USA. **Tel.**(home) 1 508 256 3032; **e-mail** AnHolleman@vaxsar.vassar.edu .

HOLLIS, Dr George Edward. Wetlands, hydrology, water management, sustainable development. Reader. *B.*15 July 1947, Scunthorpe, Lincolnshire, England, UK. British. *M.*Celia: 3 d. **Education:** U.of London, BSc (Spec.)(Geog.) 1968, PhD 1974. **Experience:** res.& num.res. students; admin.— num.deptl & Coll.responsibilities; consults with e.g.DGXI (Envt), IUCN, RSPB, World Bank. **Career:** Lect.1971–89 then Reader 1989– in Geog. UCL; seconded half-time to Station Biologique de la Tour du Valat 1991–92. **Achievements:** whilst 20 yrs have been spent trying to inject envlly-friendly water mgmt into wetland cons.only two concrete achievements are the almost total closure of Friars Wash Well, Ver Valley (Hertfordshire, UK), and a contribn to stimulating construction of a still incomplete & inoperative sluice at L.Ichkeul (Tunisia); growing nr of invitations to participate in wetland cons.efforts. **Memberships:** IWEM, IBG, RGS, IWRB (Exec.Bd), AWB (Council of Mgmt), Station Biologique de la Tour du Valat (Bd). **Awards:** Brodrick-Parry Prize for Geog.& Fac.of Sci. Medal (UCL) 1968; Jt Best Paper Prize (*EC*) 1989. **Publications:** *Man's Impact on the Hydrological Cycle in the UK* (Ed.) 1979, The effects of sea-level rise on sites of cons.value in Britain and NW Europe (co-Author) 1989, *Wetland Cons.: Review of Current Issues and Required Action* (contribn to) 1990, *Managing Medit.Wetlands and their Birds for the Year 2000 and Beyond* (co-Ed.) 1992; large nr of j.papers & reports. **Languages:** English, moderate FORTRAN, French (some).

Address: 90 The Park, Redbourn, Hertfordshire AL3 7LT, England, UK. **Tel.**(office) 44 171 387 7050 ext.5520, home & **fax** 44 158 279 2062.

HOLLO, Professor Dr Erkki Johannes. Environmental, real estate, & water, law, environmental impact assessment, comparative environmental law. Professor of Law. *B.*28 Nov.1940, Janakkala, Finland. Finnish. **Education:** U.of Helsinki Law Fac. M 1966, Lic.Iur.1971, Dr Iur.1976; U.of Tübingen Law Fac. Dr Iur.1982. **Experience:** legal res.projects 1970–, adv.to govtl bds & cttees, memb.Finnish Supreme Admin.Court 1983–6, 1993–. **Career:** Asst Prof. Helsinki Law Fac.1974–7, Prof.of Econ. Law, Helsinki U.of Tech.1977–. **Achievements:** Chairman, Finnish SEL 1980– and SRL 1987–; memb.Finnish Acad./Envl Comm. **Memberships:** Finnish AS, ICEL, IUCN CEL, Conseil Européen de Droit Rural, Unione Mondiale degli Agraristi Universitari, Deutsche Gesellschaft für Umweltrecht. **Publications:** several monogrs incl.*The Finnish Water Poll.Control* (doctl thesis) 1976, *Real Estate Law* (in Finnish) 1980 & 1984, *Planning & Bldg Law in Practice* (in Finnish) 1989, *Envl Law* (in Finnish) 1990. **Languages:** English, Finnish, French, German, Swedish; medium Italian & Russian. Willing to act as adv.& consult.etc. **Address:** Kiskontie 16 B 18, SF-00280 Helsinki, Finland. **Tel.** (office) 358 0 451 3860, (home) 358 0 411 992.

HOLOWESKO, Mrs Lynn Pyfrom. National parks, environmental law, sustainable development, conservation of natural resources, sea birds of the Bahamas. Attorney at Law, Partner, Ambassador. *B.*11 Oct.1935, CT, USA. Bahamian Citizen. *M.*William P.Holowesko (Chairman, Envl Systems Prot.Fund): *d.*Susan Larson (BNT), *s.-in-law* Gary Larson (BNT). **Education:** Albertus Magnus Coll.1951–3, Catholic U.of Amer.1953–5, called to the Bahamas Bar 1985. **Experience:** consult.to PM & Minister of Finance on envt & sust.dev.; dev.of nat.parks, sust.dev.of fisheries resources. **Career:** elected Hon.Sec. BNT 1974–6, Pres.1976–82 & 1984–92, VP 1982–4, Chairman 1984–93, The Heritage Fund (BNT); Partner, Higgs & Kelly 1985–; Amb.of the Bahamas for Envt & Sust. Dev.1994–. **Achievements:** instn of Standing Cttee structure resulting in unprecedented membership involvement in work of BNT; estab.of The Heritage Fund to ensure fin.security for BNT; submission to Bahamas Govt of 'The Dev.of a Nat.Park System for The Bahamas' to identify potential nat.park etc.areas in the country; acquisition of The Retreat (rare & exotic palm gdn) as BNT HQ; arranged acquisition of Lucayan Nat.Park. **Memberships:** IUCN CNPPA (Dep.Chaiman 1994–), IBA, BBA, Carib.Natural Resources Inst.(Bd of Dirs). **Awards:** Outstanding Businesswoman Award 1984, Hon.Life 1991 & Hon.VP 1991 (BNT). **Address:** Higgs & Kelly, POB N4406, Nassau, Bahamas. **Tel.**(office) 809 322 7511, (home) 809 324 1093; **fax** 809 325 0724.

HOLROYD, Dr Geoffrey L. Avian ecology, temperate & tropical conservation. Research Scientist, Adjunct Professor. *B.*26 May 1947, Halifax, England, UK. Canadian. *M.*Elisabeth (bot.). **Education:** U.of Western Ont. BA 1969, U.of Toronto MSc 1972, PhD 1983. **Experience:** 30 yrs' res.on migratory birds & ecol.land class.in Canada (temperate, forest, mtns, prairies & arctic); res.trips to Malawi, SA, Guatemala & Mexico. **Career:** Biol. Banff Nat. Park 1976–83, Head Endangered Species Section 1984–8, Res.Sci.(raptors) 1988–, CWS; Adjunct Prof. U.of Alb.1985–. **Achievements:** Chairman of Long Point Bird Obs.1970–73, study of bird & veg.succession of Long Point, conducted foraging ecol.study of five species of swallows, supervised ecol.wildlife inventory of Banff & Jasper Nat.Parks, organized prog.& edited Proc.of three Prairie Cons.& Endangered Species Workshops, founded & co-Chaired Beaverhill Bird Obs., Adv.to WWF re.two prairie cons.progs, Chair of WWF team which published Praire Cons.Action Plan, nat.Chair Peregrine Falcon Recovery Team, Chairman of five cons.groups 1970–. **Memberships:** AOU, COS, WOS. **Awards:** Conservationist of the Yr (NPPAC) 1985, Volunteer Award (CNF) 1989, Cons.Award (Edmonton Natural Hist. Club) 1991, Citation of Excellence (Envt Canada) 1993. **Publications:** *Birds of the Rockies* 1991, Breeding birds of Long Point, L.Erie 1981, *Wildlife Inventory, Ecol.Land Class.of Banff & Jasper Nat.Parks* 1983, *Prairie Cons.& Endangered Species* (Workshop Proc.) 1987, 1991, 1993; *c.*100 others. Favours pers.pub.& news media support re.promotion of cons. issues. **Languages:** English, French (poor), Spanish (beginner). Willing to act as consult. &/or ref. **Address:** Canadian Wildlife Service, 4999-98 Avenue (Room 210), Edmonton, Alberta T6B 2X3, Canada. **Tel.**(office) 1 403 468 8922, (home) 1 403 438 1462; **fax** 1 403 495 2615.

HOLTHUS, Paul F. Coastal/marine conservation & environmental management, focus on islands in Asia/Pacific region with emphasis on coral reefs, marine parks, ecosystem classification and inventory, biodiversity conservation, and sea-level rise impacts. Programme Scientist (Coastal/Marine). *B.*10 Nov.1956, Oceanside, CA, USA. American. *M.*Laura E. **Education:** UCSB BA(Hons) 1981, U.of Hawaii MA 1985. **Experience:** res.— field surveys of coral reefs & coastal areas in Asia/Pacific; admin.— prog.dev.of SPREP specifically in coastal/marine, EIA, climate change, marine poll.control; mgmt planning — marine parks, coastal/reef/lagoon areas throughout Asia/Pacific regn. **Career:** SO, SPREP 1986–92; Envl Consult.1993; Marine Cons.Sci. Asia/Pacific Prog. The Nature Conservancy 1994–. **Achievements:** dev.of SPREP progs in EIA, coastal/marine, marine poll.control, & climate change; co-dev.of SPREP as premier envt body in Pacific; effective coastal/marine cons. **Memberships:** Coastal

Area Mgmt Planning Network 1986–, PSA Coral Reef Cttee 1987–, IUCN CNPPA 1989–. **Publications:** *c.*40 incl.*Marine Biol.Diversity and Marine Prot.Areas in the S.Pacific Regn: Status & Prospects* (cong.report, co-Author) 1992, *Prelim.Class.and Inventory of Ecosystems of US Affiliated Islands of the Trop.Pacific* (Prog.Report, co-Author) 1993, Coastal and Marine Envts of Pacific Islands: Ecosystem Class., Ecol.Assessment, and Trad.Knowledge for Coastal Mgmt (in press). Indiff.to pers.pub. & news media support. **Languages:** English, French (good spoken, fair written), Spanish (poor). Willing to act as consult.etc. **Address:** The Nature Conservancy Asia/Pacific Regional Office, 1116 Smith Street (Suite 201), Honolulu, Hawaii 96817, USA. **Tel.**1 808 537 4508; **fax** 1 808 545 2019.

Hong CHOI, Yearn, Professor, *see* **CHOI, Professor Yearn Hong.**

HOOPER, Dr John Norman Ashby. Systematics, biogeography, ecology, and chemical ecology, of Porifera; tropical Porifera. Senior Curator. *B.*2 March 1955, Greensborough, Australia. Australian. *M.*Leonie Gay (biol.illustrations for scientific papers incl.Zool.Catalogue of Australia): 2 *s.* **Education:** U.of New England DSc(Hons) 1977, MSc 1980, U.of Qld PhD 1988. **Experience:** Curator — marine biol. collections, Australasia, partic.trop.sessile marine invertebrates; res.— taxonomy, systematics, pop.ecol., chemotaxonomy, biogeog.of Demospongiae Porifera, and taxonomy, pop. dynamics, community ecol.of helminth parasites; consult.— pharmacological & pharmaceutical investigations for marine natural products, coral-reef surveys; mgr of taxonomic sorting & identification services. **Career:** Dem. U.of New England, Teacher St Leonard's Coll., Lect. NTU 1979–85; Asst Curator, Curator, Sr Curator, Sessile Marine Invertebrates, Marine Biol.Lab. Northern Territory Mus., Qld Mus.1981–; Consult.for AIMS, US Nat.Cancer Inst., ANCA, Water Bd (Sydney, Illawarra & Blue Mtns), Astra Pharmaceuticals, NSW Envl Prot.Auth.& CSIRO Australia. **Achievements:** documentation of trop.benthos in Australasia, application of survey data to strategic planning on marine cons.& preserv.of biodiv.on coral reefs & in other trop.marine ecosystems, res.in higher systematics & phylogenetics of Porifera. **Memberships:** AMSA Inc., RZS of NSW, AIB Inc. **Awards:** Churchill F.1988, Maître de Conf.(Musée Nat. d'Histoire Naturelle, France) 1988. **Publications:** Zool.Catalogue of Australia, Porifera (co-Author) 1994, Sponges of the New Caledonia Lagoon (co-Author) 1995; 45 scientific papers, three monographic revisions, some popular articles. Dislikes pers.pub., favours news media support. **Languages:** English, French (written working only). Willing to act as consult.etc. **Address:** Marine Biology Laboratory, Queensland Museum, POB 3300, South Brisbane, Queensland 4101, Australia. **Tel.**

(office) 61 7 840 7722, (home) 61 7 351 4307; **fax** 61 7 846 1918; **e-mail** j.hooper@mailbox. uq.oz.au .

HOUÉROU, Dr Henry Noel LE. Arid lands' ecology, ecosystems' dynamics, bioclimatology. Coordinator of Research Programmes. *B.*25 Dec.1928, Plougonver, Côtes d'Armor, France. French. *M.*Micheline: *s.,* 2 *d.* **Education:** Ing. Ecole Supérieure d'Agric.de Tunis, BSc(Agron.) 1952; Dr de l'Université de Montpellier, Licencié ès-Scis 1961, Diplôme d'Etudes Supérieures de Géologie; Université de Marseille-Aix, Dr ès-Scis d'Etat 1969; Université Paul Valery, Dr ès-lettres d'Etat 1992. **Experience:** res.sci., vis.sci. & Prof., consult.to many private & public nat.& intl orgns. **Career:** Res.Sci. U.of Montpellier 1953 & CNRS 1957–62 & 1986–93; on release to var.intl orgns *e.g.*FAO 1962–75, ILCA 1975–80 (Dir, Dept of Plant & Envl Scis), and Texas A&I U.1983–5 (Sr Res.Sci.& Prof.of Range Synecology, Coll.of Agric.& Caesar Kleberg Wildlife Res.Inst.); Coord. Climate Change, Drought & Desert. IPCC 1993–. **Achievements:** analysis of arid land ecosystems, inventory & mapping of ecosystems in N., W., & E.Africa and France, res.in range mgmt and in drought-tolerant fodder shrubs, agrofor., bioclimatology. **Memberships:** Soc.of Range Mgmt, Société Botanique de France, Assn Française pour l'Etude du Sol. **Awards:** Chairman Continuing Cttee of Intl Rangeland Cong.1978–84, Pres.IVth Intl Rangeland Cong. 1991, Chevalier du Mérite Agricole 1991. **Publications:** *c.*350 incl.some 20 books *e.g. Browse in Africa: The Current State of Knowledge* (Ed.) 1980, *The Grazing Land Ecosystems of the African Sahel* 1989, *Agro-Bioclimatic Class.of Africa* (co-Author) 1993; Bd *J.of Arid Envts, Agrofor.Systems, Minerva Biologica, Tree Crops J.* Moderately favours pers.pub.& news media support. **Languages:** English (good), French, Gaelic (good), Italian (fair), Latin (fair), Spanish (fair). Further details may be obtained from *Who's Who in Sci.in Europe* 1975. Willing to act as consult.etc. **Address:** 327 Rue A.L.De Jussieu, F-34090 Montpellier, France. **Tel.**(office) 33 6761 3284, (home) 33 6754 7609; **fax** 33 6741 2138.

HOUGH, Dr John Laurence. Social dimensions of natural resource conservation & sustainable development; protected areas' policy & management. Consultant. *B.*21 May 1954, Preston, England, UK. British, USA Perm.Resident. *M.*Janet Cynthia: *s., d.* **Education:** U.of Durham BSc(Hons) 1975; U.of Michigan MS 1986, PhD 1989. **Experience:** res.— prot.area/local people relations; consult.— strats for prot.areas & biodiv.cons.; leadership — multidisc.team-planning & implementing integrated cons.& dev.projects in Africa & Madagascar; teaching — U.of Michigan grad.course in Wildland Mgmt for 2 yrs. **Career:** Project Officer and Regnl Officer, BTCV 1975–8; Envt Officer & Michiru Mtn Cons.Area Coord. Malawi 1978–84;

Doctoral student, teaching & res.asst, then Lect. U.of Michigan 1984–9; Project Leader, WWF Madagascar 1989–91; Chief Tech.Adv.to Serengeti Regnl Cons.Strat. then Consult.to IUCN 1991–. **Achievements:** developed extensive vol. participation in cons.in NW England; estab.& led successful integrated cons.& dev. projects in Malawi & Madagascar, and an envl educ.prog.in Malawi; dev.role in Serengeti Regnl Cons.Strat.; innovative res.on social dimensions of cons. **Memberships:** IUCN, IMS, SCB, SID. **Awards:** Ayers Brinser & Stanley Cain awards & grad.scholarship (U.of Michigan Sch.of Natural Resources); Res.Partnership award (jt) and F'ship (U.of Michigan Grad. Sch.); Hon.Life Memb. Tyne–Tees Cons. Volunteers. **Publications:** 30+ papers and num.reports, popular articles etc. Indiff.to pers.pub.& news media support. **Languages:** English, French, basic Swahili. Willing to act as consult.etc. **Address:** Box 219, Sandy Spring, Maryland 20860-0219, USA. **Tel.**(office) 1 301 774 7391, (home) 1 301 774 7391; **fax** 1 301 924 2265 attn Gibian.

HOUGHTON, Professor Dr Sir John Theodore. Climate science & policy, remote sensing from space. Commission Chairman, Working-group Chairman. *B*.30 Dec.1931, Dyserth, Wales, UK. British. *M*.Sheila: *s., d.* **Education:** Jesus Coll.Oxf. BA(Phys.) 1951, DPhil (Atmos. Phys.) 1955. **Experience:** res., mgmt, admin. **Career:** Res.F. R.Aircraft Estab.1954–8; Lect.1958–62, Reader 1962–76, Prof.1976–83, Atmos.Phys. U.of Oxf.; Dir Appleton and Dep.Dir Rutherford Appleton Labs 1979–83, SERC; DG & Chief Exec. UK Met.Office 1983–91; Chairman, R.Comm.on Envl Poll.1991–; co-Chairman, Scientific Assessment WG, IPCC 1991–. **Achievements:** designed & built instruments for NASA Space Prog.for atmos.obs. **Memberships:** F. RS, OSA & Inst.of Phys., RMS (Pres.1977–8). **Awards:** Symons Gold Metal (RMS), Bakerian Lect.(RS) 1990, Hon.DSc (Univs of Wales, E.Anglia, & Leeds), Hon.Doct. (U.of Stirling). **Publications:** *Infra-Red Phys.*(co-Author) 1964, *Phys.of Atmospheres* 1976, 1986, *Does God Play Dice?* 1988, *Global Warming, the Complete Briefing* 1994. **Languages:** English, French (read). Further details may be obtained from Brit.*Who's Who* 1995. **Address:** Royal Commission for Environmental Pollution, Church House, Great Smith Street, London SW1, England, UK. **Tel.**(office) 44 171 276 2026; **fax** 44 171 276 2098.

HOWELL, Calvin A. Environmental education, public awareness. Executive Director. *B*.Nevis, W.Indies. Citizen of St Kitts & Nevis. *M*. Patience Olivia: *s.,* 2 *d.* **Education:** Concordia U. MA(Dev.Educ.) 1984. **Experience:** dev. educ., res., writing. **Career:** Envl Educ.Officer 1986–91, Exec.Dir 1991–, Carib.Cons.Assn. **Achievements:** provides effective leadership to a regnl envl/cons.orgn. **Membership:** NAAEE. **Publications:** *Guidelines for Starting an Envl Educ.Prog.*1988, *A Teacher's Guide to Birds of*

Our Is.(Poster Series) 1992, *Trends in Envl Educ.in the English-speaking Carib.*1992, Envl Educ.in the English-speaking Carib.1994, *A Strat.for Envl Educ.and Communications for the Carib.*(co-Author) 1995. Favours pers.pub. & news media support. **Languages:** English. Willing to act as consult.etc. **Address:** Caribbean Conservation Association, Savannah Lodge, The Garrison, St Michael, Barbados, West Indies. **Tel.**(office) 1 809 426 9633, (home) 1 809 426 4321; **fax** 1 809 429 8483.

HOYT, Dr John Arthur. Environmental & animal protection. Chief Executive, President, Vice-President. *B*.30 March 1932, Marietta, OH, USA. American. *M*.Gertrude Mohnkern: 4 *d.* **Education:** Rio Grande Coll. BA(*magna cum laude*) 1954, DD 1968; Colgate Rochester Divinity Sch. MDiv.1958. **Experience:** Presbyterian Clergyman (1957–70), memb.Bd of Dirs of two private colls. **Career:** Pres.& CEO 1970–92, Chief Exec.& CEO 1992–, The Humane Soc.of the US; Pres.& Bd Chairman, Nat.Assn for Humane & Envl Educ.1973–; Memb.of Council 1981–, Pres.1986–90, VP 1990–, World Soc.for the Prot.of Animals; Pres.& Dir, Center for Respect of Life & Envt 1987–; Dir Earth Day 1990; Dir, Global Tomorrow Coalition, Memb.Hon.Cttee & Spec. Council on Sust.Dev.1989–; VP 1991–4, Pres. 1994–, EarthKind USA; Pres. Humane Soc.Intl 1991–; Pres.& Chairman of Bd 1991–4, VP 1994–, EarthKind Intl; Bd of Advisers, The Albert Schweitzer Inst.for the Humanities 1991–. **Awards:** Medals of the Cities of Paris & Versailles 1987, Swedish Medal of Honour 1990, Founder's Award for Humane Excellence (ASPCA) 1991, George T.Angell Humanitarian Award (Mass.Soc.for the Prevention of Cruelty to Animals) 1992. **Publications:** incl.*Animals in Peril: How 'Sust.Use' is Destroying the World's Wildlife* 1994. Favours pers.pub.& news media support. **Language:** English. Willing to act as consult.etc. **Address:** The Humane Society of the United States, 2100 L Street NW, Washington, DC 20037, USA. **Tel.**1 202 452 1100; **fax** 1 301 258 3077.

HSU, Dr Kuo-Shih. Nature conservation, national parks, rare & endangered plant species. Institute Head. *B*.26 June 1942, Hunan, PRC. Chinese. *M*.Dr H.J.Chang (bot., envl educ.): *d.* **Education:** Nat.Taiwan Normal U. BS(Biol.) 1966, Nat.Taiwan U. MS(Bot.) 1971, Purdue U. PhD(Forest & Nature Resources) 1978. **Experience:** res., admin. **Career:** Specialist, Taiwan Forest Res.Inst.1978–86; Super. Taroko Nat.Park 1986–92; Sr Specialist, Planning Office 1992–4, Head Inst.of Nature Resources 1994–, Tung-Hwa U. **Achievements:** pioneer of Nature cons.in Taiwan, frequent participation in or Chair of intl & local Nature cons.confs. **Memberships:** Chinese Botl, Biol., & For., Socs, Nat.Park Soc.(Pres.1978–), Envl Educ.Soc., Soc.for Wildlife & Nature. **Award:** Taiwan Forest Promoter (Taiwan Forest Res.Inst.). **Public-**

ations: *Commelinaceae, Callitrichaceae, Sparganiaceae in flora of Taiwan* 1978, *The Illustration of Taiwan Local Plants* (vols I–X) 1981–6, *The Rare and Endangered Plants of Taiwan* 1984, *Ecol.Study of Trop.Strand Forest in Hengchung Peninsula* 1990. Favours pers. pub., indiff.to news media support. **Languages:** Chinese, English. **Address:** Institute of Nature Resource Management, National Tung-Hwa University, Hualien, Taiwan. **Tel.**(office) 886 38 662500-142, (home) 886 38 529446; **fax** 886 38 539120.

HUBA, Dr Mikuláš. Environmental geography, risks & hazards, landscape planning, coordination of environmental NGO activities, implication of sustainable development concept. Scientific Worker. *B.*24 March 1954, Bratislava, Slovakia. Slovak. Father Assoc.Prof.Dr Alexander Huba, Dir Inst.of Entomol.& Phytopath. Slovak AS, mother Olga Hubová-Alewy, bot. *M.*Dr Olga Hubová: 2 *s., d.* **Education:** Comenius U. MSc 1978, RNDr 1980; Slovak AS PhD 1987. **Experience:** res.— landscape potential and stability in regns of Bratislava, Tatras, Kysuce with dispersal settlement; *ad hoc* teaching; govt adv.to Min.for Envt. **Career:** Scientific Worker, Geogl Inst. Slovak AS 1987–; Adv. Slovak Govt 1990–; MP & Memb.of Presidium, Chairman Cttee for Envt & Nature Prot. 1990–92, Memb.Slovak Comm.for Envt 1990–92, Slovak Parliament. **Achievements:** basic landscape ecol.res.in regns of Bratislava, Tatras, Kysuce; assessment of landscape stability, estab.of some prot.areas in Slovak Rep.; practical envl prot. **Memberships:** SZOPK 1976–, Chairman Town Comm.1987–9, C.Comm. 1989–; Chairman, Czech & Slovak Bd of Nature Protectors 1991– 2; SCOPE 1986–; IUCN CESP 1985–, VP Envl Liaison Centre for CSFR (Ecopoint); Slovak Nat.Cttee for IUCN 1993; Slovak Comm.for Coopn with UNESCO; CSFR Prep. Comm.for UNCED 1991–2; FOE-Slovakia 1990–; Soc.for Sust.Living, Slovak Rep. Chairman 1993–, CSFR VC 1992–; Slovak Geogl Soc.(Scientific Sec.1979–80); Slovak Assn Club of Rome; Fndn of Czech & Slovak Council for Nature Cons. **Awards:** Medals — SZOPK, Slovak AS, Tatras Nat.Park, & Town Ruzomberok; EKOFILM Ostrava Main Prize 1981, 1988. **Publications:** *Bratislava (Loudly)* (Ed.& co-Author) 1987–, *State of Slovakia Message for Rio and Message to Luzern* (Ed.& co-Author) 1993, *Slovak Forests* 1990, *Slovak Agric.*1990, *About Some Questions of the Genesis and Present-day State in the Dispersal Settlement in Slovak Rep.— 14 Steps to the Landscape Plan* 1982; Edl Bds of *c.*6 spec.& scientific–popular newsletters; *c.*20 scientific studies, *c.*300 scientific–popular articles & films. Favours news media support but often has ambivalent results. **Languages:** Czech, English, Russian. Willing to act as consult.etc. **Address:** Starotursky chodnik 1, 811 01 Bratislava, Slovak Republic. **Tel.**(office) 427 492751, (home) 427 314635; **fax** 427 313968.

HUGHES, Dr George Ritchie. Wildlife management, ecotourism and marine turtles, trout angling. Chief Executive. *B.*13 May 1939, Aberdeen, Scotland, UK. South African. *M.* Alethea Joy: *s., d.* **Education:** Estcourt High Sch.; U.of Natal BSc(Hons)(Zool.) 1968, PhD(Zool.) 1974. **Experience:** marine turtle res.1965–; 17 yrs' admin.on Natal Parks Bd; consult.— French Govt, IUCN, SA Dept of Foreign Affairs (incl.missions to Comores & Seychelles Islands). **Career:** employed in industry 1957–9; overseas travel 1959–61; Game Ranger Natal Parks Bd 1961–5; u.study 1965–8; turtle res. Oceanographic Res.Inst.1969–74; turtle & trout res.1974–5, Head Drakensberg Mtn Mgmt 1975 80, Head Admin.1980–82, Head Cons.1982–8, Chief Exec.1988–, Natal Parks Bd. **Achievements:** monogrs *Sea Turtles of SA**, creation of at least four new prot.areas and Natal Parks Bd Cons.Trust now worth millions of rands; restructuring of Natal Parks Bd ops systems. **Memberships:** WMA, SAIE. **Award:** Dr Edgar Brooks Award for Human Freedom & Endeavour. **Publications:** **Sea Turtles of SA* (two vols) 1974; 70 sci.papers, 55 popular pubns, 14 contribns to books. Favours pers.pub.& news media support. **Languages:** Afrikaans, English, French, Zulu (spoken). Willing to act as consult.etc. **Address:** Natal Parks Board, POB 662, 3200 Pietermaritzburg, South Africa. **Tel.**(office) 27 331 471961, (home) 27 331 966058; **fax** 27 331 472977.

HÜLSHOFF, Dr Bernd VON DROSTE ZU. Conservation, ecology, forestry, heritage, hydrology, regional planning. Director. *B.*17 Sept. 1938, Essen, Germany. German, Swiss. *M.* Beatrice: *s., d.* **Education:** U.of Göttingen BSc(For.) 1962; U.of Munich PhD(Forest Ecol.) *(summa cum laude)* 1969. **Experience:** Assoc. Prof.in Forest Policy, Sec.of intergovtl MAB prog. 1989–92, Sec.World Heritage Cttee 1993–. **Career:** Govtl Professional Forester 1966; Asst Prof. Inst.of Forest Yield Scis 1967–9, Assoc.Prof. Inst of Forest Policy & Econ., Lect. Regnl Planning 1969–73, all at U.of Munich; Prog.Specialist in ecol.scis 1973–82, Sr Prog.Specialist in ecol.scis 1978–83, Dir Div.of Ecol. Scis, and Sec. Intergovtl MAB prog.1984–92 (UNESCO). **Achievements:** Founding Dir.of UNESCO World Heritage Centre, launching and/or directing several pubn series in ecol. *e.g.* MAB Digest & book series, World Heritage Newsletter, quarterly Nature and Resources; estab.of Intl Biosphere Reserve network; implementation of World Heritage Conv. **Memberships:** INTECOL, Bd São Paulo di Torino Fndn, Jury Memb.of St Francis Prize for the Envt, Parks Board, IUCN CNPPA & SSC. **Awards:** U.of Munich Prize for best thesis of yr 1968; Sileno Envt Prize 1989. **Publications:** three books, *c.*125 other. Favours news media support. **Languages:** English, French, German, Spanish (working knowledge). **Address:** World Heritage Centre, UNESCO, 7 place de Fontenoy, 75352 Paris 07-SP, France. **Tel.**33 14 568 1572; **fax** 33 14 056 9570.

HUMMEL, Solon Lamont 'Monte'. Conservation. President. *B*.4 Dec.1946, Toronto, Ont., Canada. Canadian. *M*.Sherry: 2 *s*. **Education:** U.of Toronto BS(Hons)(Phil., Hist. & English) 1969, MA(Phil.) 1970, MScF 1979. **Career:** co-Founder, Poll.Probe 1969; Coord. Envl Studies Prog.1973–80, Assoc. Inst.for Envl Studies, U.of Toronto; Exec.Dir WWF Canada 1978–; Exec. Coord. Wildlife Toxicology Fund; Founding Dir CCAR & CCEA, Dir Arctic Intl Wildlife Range Soc. **Memberships:** WWF Intl Adv.Council, Coll.of Biol.Scis Adv.Council (U.of Guelph), U.of Guelph Arboretum, Hon.F. Innis Coll. (U.of Toronto), CCAR & CCEA (Exec. Cttees). **Award:** E.J. Sanford Gold Medal 1969. **Publications:** *Poll.Probe* (co-Author) 1972, *Arctic Wildlife* 1987, *Endangered Spaces* 1989, *Wild Hunters: Predators in Peril* 1991; 100+ j.& magazine articles. **Language:** English. **Address:** RR 3, Cookstown, Ontario L0L 1L0, Canada.

HUNKELER, Dr Pierre. Nature conservation; relationships between agriculture & conservation; activities of NGOs. Executive Secretary, Lecturer, Consultant. *B*.31 Dec.1943, Neuchâtel, Switzerland. Swiss. *M*.Claudine: *s., d.* **Education:** U.of Neuchâtel, Licence ès Scis (Biol.) 1966, PhD 1974. **Experience:** res.in parasitology, primate behaviour; admin.in industry, IUCN, NGOs, with project dev., mgmt & eval., general mgmt, fund-raising; consult.in EIA, implementation of intl convs, eval.of prot.areas, project dev., u.teaching. **Career:** field-work in W.Africa 1967–70; pharmaceutical industry 1971–4; var.positions at IUCN HQ 1974–81; Partner, ECONAT (Studies in Applied Ecol.) 1982–90; Consult. IUCN, CITES, FAO, Council of Europe, EEC, Swiss Govt 1981–; Exec.Sec. Ligue Vaudoise pour la Prot.de la Nature 1982–; Lect. EPFL 1986–. **Achievements:** constant commitment for cause of cons.at diff.levels and world-wide. **Memberships:** IUCN CESP, SVOO, SZG, var.natural scis socs, var.NGOs involved in Nature or envl prot. **Publications:** num.reports & mtg proc., Ed.*La Nature Vaudoise* (quarterly bull.) 1980–, *Ecol.& Behaviour of the Lowe's Guenon* (film, co-Producer) 1970. Indiff.to/dislikes pers.pub., indiff.to news media support. **Languages:** English, French, German (comp.). Willing to act as consult.etc. **Address:** Chemin Valmont 214, 1260 Nyon, Switzerland. **Tel.**(office & home) 41 22 361 7075; **fax** 41 22 361 9638.

HUNT, Professor Dr George L., Jr. Biological oceanography, marine ornithology. Professor of Biology. *B*.10 Aug.1942, Boston, MA, USA. American. *M*.Peggy. **Education:** Harvard Coll. AB 1965, Harvard U. PhD 1971. **Experience:** res.— reproductive behaviour & ecol.of colonial birds, foraging ecol.of marine birds, phys./biol.coupling in marine envt, studies of marine birds re.oil poll.; teaching — ecol., behavioural ecol., ocean ecol., ornith. **Career:** Asst Prof.1970–76 & Assoc.Prof.1976–82 of Biol.,

Chair of Dept of Ecol./Evol.Biol.1979–83, Prof.of Biol.1982–, UCI. **Achievements:** studies of seabird ecol.in Calif.& Alaska re.offshore oil dev.; served as an outside reviewer for the Exxon Valdez oil-spill (US Dept of Justice and for the Trustees); Sr Sci.& Ed. Marbled Murrelet *(Brachyramphus marmoratus)* Cons.Assessment USFS. **Memberships:** AAAS, AOU, ESA, BES, BOU; others. **Awards:** F.(AAAS) 1981, F.(AOU) 1991. **Publications:** *c*.100. Indiff.to pers.pub., favours news media support. **Languages:** English; French & Spanish (poor spoken). Willing to act as consult.etc. **Address:** Department of Ecology and Evolutionary Biology, University of California at Irvine, Irvine, California 92717, USA. **Tel.**1 714 824 6322 & 6006; **fax** 1 714 824 2181.

HUQ, Dr Saleemul. Climate change impacts, environmental planning & management. Executive Director. *B*.2 Oct.1952, Karachi, Pakistan. Bangladeshi. *M*.Kashana. **Education:** ICL BSc(Hons) 1975, PhD 1978. **Experience:** res., admin., consult.to such as World Bank, UNDP, & IIED, u.teaching. **Career:** Asst.Prof. Dept of Bot. Dhaka U. 1979–83; Exec.Dir 1984–6 & 1988–, Bangladesh Centre for Advanced Studies; McNamara F. Dept of Bot. ICL 1986–7. **Achievements:** setting-up & running the biggest and most effective res.& policy inst.on envt in the non-govt sector of Bangladesh. **Membership:** BBS. **Awards:** McNamara F'ship (World Bank) 1986–7, Stephen Duggan F'ship (NRDC) 1989. **Publications:** *Envt & Dev.in Bangladesh, Envl Aspects of Surface Water Systems.* Dislikes pers.pub., favours news media support. **Languages:** Bengali, English, French (fair), Hindi, Urdu. Willing to act as consult.etc. **Address:** Bangladesh Centre for Advanced Studies, House Nr 620, Road Nr 10 A (New), Dhanmondi, Dhaka, Bangladesh. **Tel.**(office) 880 2 815829, (home) 880 2 505512; **fax** 880 2 811344.

HURNI, Dr Hans. Geoecology, environment & development, sustainable use of natural resources, soil erosion & conservation, protection of Nature reserves and sustainable development of buffer zones. Director, Privatdozent (PD). *B*.21 Dec.1950, Erlenbach, Switzerland. Swiss. *M*.Marlies: 2 *s*. **Education:** U.of Berne MSc (Geog.) 1975, PhD(Natural Scis, Climate Change) 1980. **Experience:** res.in Ethiopia on soil erosion damages & process studies and on climate change in high alt.envts, and in Thailand on soil cons.experiments; tech.dev.of cons. measures in Ethiopia; admin.dev.of cons.res. instn in Ethiopia, and of Group for Dev.& Envt; major consults for progs in Ethiopia, Yemen, Kenya, Niger, Madagascar, Thailand, Sri Lanka & Switzerland. **Career:** Chief Warden, Simen Mtns Nat.Park 1975–7; Dir Soil Cons.Res. Project 1981–7; Asst Prof. Addis Ababa U. 1986; Lect.1989–91, Privatdozent (tenure) 1991–, Dir Group for Dev.& Envt, Inst.of Geog.1988–, U.of Berne. **Achievements:** prot. & dev.of

Simen Mtns WHS, Ethiopia, for UNESCO & IUCN; dev.of — guidelines for soil cons.in Ethiopia, land resource scenarios for Ethiopia 1990–2040, and explanatory model of ecol. contribn to famine vulnerability in rural Ethiopia; co-orgn of sev.intl congs & workshops; founder & init.of Ethiopian soil cons.res., init.of global res.prog.WOCAT 1992–8; reviewer/co-Ed.of intl journals. **Memberships:** IBSRAM (Bd), ISCO (Bd), WASWC (VP 1988–91, Pres.1991–), IUCN Comm.on Ecol. 1981–91. **Award:** First Award of Fac.of Natural Scis (Berne U.) 1981. **Publications:** *Simen Mtns, Ethiopia: Climate and the Dynamics of Altitudinal Belts from the Last Cold Period to the Present Day* 1982, *Guidelines for Dev.Agents on Soil Cons.in Ethiopia* (also in Amharic) 1986–7, *Mgmt Plan, Simen Mtns Nat.Park and Surrounding Buffer Zone* 1986, *Soil Erosion & Cons.in Agricl Envts* 1991; over 50 chapters & papers. Favours pers.pub.& news media sup-port. **Languages:** Amharic, English, French, German, Italian (spoken). Willing to obtain mandates & consults in envt & dev. **Address:** Group for Development and Environment, Hallerstrasse 12, 3012 Berne, Switzerland. **Tel.**41 31 631 8822; **fax** 41 31 631 8544.

HUSBAND, Ms Vicky. Temperate rain-forest survival, old-growth forests, wilderness & wildlife in British Columbia; educating federal & provincial governments and public. Chair. *B.* 1940, Victoria, BC, Canada. Canadian. **Education:** UBC BA(Fine Arts & Hist.) 1963. **Experience:** leading campaigns for prot.of envt & biol.diversity and completion of Canada's system of parks & prot.areas by the yr 2000, and for change in forest practices leading to ecosystem-based forest mgmt; public speaking & slide-shows for groups, professionals, schools, and community groups; past professional artist, painter, and film-maker; work with CBC, The Journal, and The Nature of Things, BC TV, CBC Radio, local media, TV Ontario; fund-raising; leading workshops. **Career:** Pres. Friends of Ecol.Reserves 1988–90; Chair, Sierra Club of Western Canada 1991–. **Achievements:** spearheaded raising of over $100,000 for wildlife & forestry res.in Khutzeymateen Valley, proposed as Canada's first Grizzly Bear sanctuary; deep involvement in successful struggle to save S.Moresby (Haida Gwaii), Queen Charlotte Islands, as a Nat.Park Reserve; involved in campaign to protect Clayoquot Sound; resource person for the media on forestry, wilderness & envt issues. **Memberships:** major Canadian and BC envt orgns, Amnesty Intl, and others. **Awards:** Fred M.Packard Award (IUCN) 1987, Global 500 Roll of Honour (UNEP) 1988. **Films:** Producer of *Offerings in White & Gold* 1981, *Ninstints* 1983, *Canada's Vanishing Grizzly* 1987. **Language:** English. **Address:** 1525 Amelia Street, Victoria, British Columbia V8W 2K1, Canada. **Tel.**(office) 1 604 386 5255, (home) 1 604 478 0388; **fax** 1 604 386 4453.

HUTTON, Dr Jonathan Michael. Wildlife management & conservation, Crocodylia in many areas of Africa. Trust Director. *B.*4 Aug.1956, Louth, Lincs., England, UK. Zimbabwean. *M.* Jill Diana. **Education:** Jesus Coll.Camb. BA (Applied Biol.) 1978; U.of Zimbabwe, DPhil (Crocodile Ecol.) 1984. **Experience:** two yrs' Curator of Mammalogy, three yrs' as Sr Ecol., and three yrs' as Exec.Mgr of Crocodile & Ostrich Producers' Assns of Zimbabwe; execution of one of the longest-running wild-pop.studies which continues to provide info.on policy & mgmt re.crocodiles in many areas of Africa. **Career:** Sr Ecol. Dept of Nat.Parks of Zimbabwe 1985–9; Dir, Consulting Services 1989–92; Dir, Africa Resources Trust 1992–. **Achievements:** helped establish crocodile ranching as a major cons.tool in E.& s.Africa and, using this experience, subs.has been in the vanguard of a movement to lead modern cons.in Africa away from failed models of preserv.to a human-centred approach based on sust.use of wildlife. **Memberships:** IUCN SSC Crocodile SG (VC), Zimbabwe Scientific Assn, NYAS. **Publications:** 24 papers & chapters incl.Growth and feeding ecol.of the Nile Crocodile *[Crocodilus niloticus]* at Ngezi, Zimbabwe 1987, Incubation temps, sex ratios and sex determination in a pop.of Nile Crocodiles 1987, Cons.and Dev.Compromised by Animal Welfare 1995. Indiff.to pers.pub., favours news media support. **Languages:** English, French (poor). Willing to act as consult.etc. **Address:** POB HG 690, Highlands, Harare, Zimbabwe. **Tel.**263 4 732625; **fax** 263 4 795150.

HUTTUNEN, Professor Dr (Mrs) Satu. Forest tree ecophysiology, environmental ecology/air pollution. Professor of Plant Ecophysiology & Environmental Ecology, President. *B.*27 Sept. 1945, Sotkamo, Finland. Finnish. *M.*Jouko Huttunen: *d.* **Education:** U.of Oulu, DPhil 1975. **Experience:** pioneer in questions of air poll.effects on forests, hence grant from Acad.of Finland to study on sabbatical leave in 1994. **Career:** F.1975–80, Sr F.1983–8, Res.Council for Envl Scis; Prof.of Plant Ecophysiol.& Envl Ecol., Dept of Bot. U.of Oulu 1989–. **Achievement:** evidence on long-term effects of acid deposition on boreal forest ecosystems. **Memberships:** IUFRO (Project Group Leader, air poll.effects on forests), Finnish Forest Res.Inst.(Counc.), Finnish Nature Cons.Union (Pres.). **Awards:** Woman of the Yr 1986, Global 500 Roll of Honour (UNEP) 1987. **Publications:** *Save the Forests* (in Finnish) 1988; over 100 papers. Favours news media support. **Languages:** English, Finnish, French (read), German (reasonable), Swedish. Willing to act as consult.etc. **Address:** Department of Botany, University of Oulu, POB 400, FIN-90571 Oulu, Finland. **Tel.**358 81 553 1527; **fax** 358 81 553 1500.

IBARRA, Professor Jorge Alfonso. Environment, palaeontology, zoology. Museum Director.

B.12 Dec.1920, Quezaltenango, Guatemala. Guatemalan. *M*.Amparo (Museum vol.): *s*., 2 *d*.incl. German (collector of nocturnal insects). **Experience:** admin.— founding Nat.Museum of Natural History (named 'Jorge A.Ibarra' in 1988) and two journals. **Career:** Charge, Zool. Mus. Fac.Natural Scis 1936–47; Founder & Dir Museo Nacional de Historia Natural 1948–52; Dir of same which is now named 'Jorge A.Ibarra' 1952–; ecol.& writer 1950–. **Achievements:** creating new ecol.genre to write short stories that belong to new lit.approach using scientific facts re.ecol.& envt to awaken interest of reader in wildlife. **Memberships:** Operación Quetzal (Hon.Pres.1994), Pres.Guatemalan Circle of Scientific Journalism. **Awards:** Order Quetzal of Guatemala 1964, Order Stella della Solidariete Italiana, Ordine al Mérito de Italia, John R.Reitemeyer Prize (IAPA) 1968, Emer. (Faculdad de Humanidades, San Carlos U.) 1979. **Publications:** *Apunted de Historia Natural* 1959, *Mamíferos de Guatemala* 1959, *El Hombre ante Natural* 1964, *Fábulas y Temas Pro Natura* 1973, *Apuntes Botanico* 1974, *True Stories & Fables* 1975, *Don Ulises Rojas* 1980, *Cons.in Guatemala* 1960, *Paleontología en Guatemala* 1980, *Los Museos de Historia Natural de Guatemala* 1988, *Narraciones Ecológicas* 1989, *Ecol.Tales* 1990, *La Fauna en la Fábula y el Cuento* 1992; Founder of journals *Historia Natural* 1964 and *Pro Natura* 1985. Favours pers.pub.& news media support. **Languages:** English, Spanish. Willing to act as consult.etc. **Address:** Apdo postal 987, Guatemala City, Guatemala. **Tel.& fax** 502 2 720468.

IBARRA-OBANDO, Dr Silvia. Habitat preservation in coastal lagoons. Division Head. *B*.31 Dec.1951, Mexico City, Mexico. Mexican. **Education:** U.of Aix-Marseille II PhD(Ecol.) 1992. **Experience:** 15 yrs' res.in marine bot. mainly seagrasses, interest in coastal lagoons & their ecol.role. **Career:** Researcher, Ecol.Dept. 1979–93, Head Oceanology Div.1993–, CICESE. **Achievements:** fight for preserv.of n.Baja California's coastal lagoons, mainly Punta Banda estuary. **Memberships:** ERS, PERS. **Publications:** num.incl.Industrial dev.effects on the ecol.of a Pacific Mexican estuary (co-Author) 1987, The effects of tidal exclusion on salt marsh vegetation in Baja Calif.Mexico (co-Author) 1991, The Salt Marsh Vegetation of Punta Banda Estuary, Baja Calif.Mexico (co-Author) 1992. Dislikes pers.pub., favours news media support. **Languages:** English, French, Spanish. Willing to judge proposals & ref. papers. **Address:** Centro de Investigación Cientifica y de Educación Superior de Ensenada Baja California, Km 107 Carretera Tijeda, Ensenada, Baja California, Mexico. **Tel.**52 617 4 4200; **fax** 52 617 4 5154.

IDECHONG, Noah. Resource management. Executive Director. *B*.23 Nov.1952, Ngiwal, Rep. of Palau. Palauan. *M*.Teory Sokau: 3 *s*. **Education:** Hawaii Pacific U. BSc(Bus.Admin.)

1976, Certs of Completion Courses in Ocean Resource Mgmt (Intl Ocean Inst. Dalhousie U.) 1986, Fisheries' Planning & Mgmt (U.of Hull) 1987, Ocean Resource Mgmt — S.Pacific Focus (ORMP/FFA) 1988. **Experience:** planning, coordinating & directing res. activities towards achieving specific mgmt objectives, forming teams of intl scientists and, with limited resources, successfully conducting needed studies to assist with mgmt, former Palau del. to S.Pacific Comm.'s Regnl Tech.Mtg on Fisheries and the S.Pacific Forum Fisheries Cttee Mtgs. **Career:** Teacher, Palau High Sch. 1976–8; Head Admin.Section, Micronesian Mariculture Demn Center 1978–83; Fisheries Dev./ Mgmt Officer 1983–90, Chief Div.of Marine Resources 1990–95, Palau Div.of Marine Resources; Exec.Dir, Palau Cons.Soc. **Achievements:** participation as co-team leader in natural & cultural resource surveys of Palau SW Islands, consult.& mgmt re.natural resource surveys of Palau Main Islands, init.& co-planner of Palau aerial photography as planning & mgmt tool, developed concept of reconnaissance and detailed survey of Ngermeduu Bay and Ngerukewid Islands, and provided direction & support, co-installation of mooring buoys in popular diving areas, co-authored Mgmt Plan of Ngerukewid Islands Wildlife Preserve*, co-Prin. Investigator of monitoring of grouper-fish aggregations in Palau, planned & coordinated pop. surveys of endangered marine species *e.g.* Dugongs *(Dugong dugong)* & crocodiles, init.& directed Marine Turtles Res.& Cons.Prog., estab.of work relationship with SPREP, U.of Guam Marine Lab. and TNC. **Membership:** Palau Cons. Soc.(Founding Bd Memb.). **Awards:** F'ship (FAO) 1987, Outstanding Performance 1987 and Exceptional Performance 1989 (both Govt of Palau), Goldman Envl Achievement Prize (Goldman Envt Fndn) 1995. **Publications:** **Ngerukewid Islands Wildlife Preserve Mgmt Plan* (co-Author) 1989, Natural and cultural resources survey of the SW Palau Islands (co-Author) 1992, Natural resources survey of Palau Main Islands (co-Author) 1993; assisted with an educl film for Palau divers and a public awareness film *'Conserve Our Precious Envt'*. Favours pers.pub.& news media support provided they are balanced and accurate. **Languages:** English, Palauan. Willing to act as consult.etc. **Address:** Palau Conservation Society, POB 1197, Koror, PW 96940, Republic of Palau. **Tel.**(office) & **fax** 680 488 3993, (home) 680 488 2801.

IGNACIMUTHU, Professor Rev.Dr Father Savarimuthu. Genetic resources, environmental awareness & conservation, botanical insecticides, genetics, biotechnology, mutation breeding. Project Director & Research Guide. *B*.9 Sept. 1948, Sindalacherry, Madurai Distr., TN, India. Indian. Father Savarimuthu, mother Salethammal & three bros involved in envl awareness & cons. **Education:** Loyola Coll. BSc(Gold Medal) 1972, St Joseph's Coll. MSc(Gold Medal)

1978, U.of Delhi MPhil.& PhD 1985, Inst.of Envt, Postgrad.Dipl.in Ecol.& Envt 1989. **Experience:** res.— wild pulse genetic resources, ethnobot., envt, mutation genetics, botl insecticides, biotech.; admin.— Mus.Curator, Hostel Dir, Club & Soc.Pres.; consult.to social work orgns, educl instns, & scientific socs; teaching envt, genetics, & biotech.from BSc to PhD levels. **Career:** Prof.& Res.Guide, Dept of Bot. St Joseph's Coll.1980–82; Prin., Prof.& Res.Guide, Dept of Bot. St Xavier's Coll. 1992–3; Project Dir & Res.Guide, Entomol. Res.Inst. Loyola Coll.1993–. **Achievements:** init.envl awareness educ.in areas & educl instns, writing books to popularize envl concerns, forming Nature & eco clubs, investigating botl pesticides. **Memberships:** ISC, ISGPB, SCG, ISNAB, AEB. **Awards:** Nat.Merit Scholar, F.of Socs of Genetics and Plant Breeding, Cytology and Genetics, Nuclear Techniques and Agricl Biol., and Indian Sci.Acad. **Publications:** 10 books incl.*Envl Awareness* (in Tamil) 1993, *Our Surroundings* (in Tamil) 1994; 40 papers & gen.articles. Favours pers.pub.& news media support. **Languages:** English, French (basic), German (basic), Tamil. Willing to act as consult.etc. **Address:** Entomology Research Institute, Loyola College, Madras 600 034, Tamil Nadu, India. **Tel.**(office) 91 44 82 65542, (home) 91 44 82 76749.

IMBODEN, Dr Christoph Niklaus. Conservation, biodiversity, ecologically-sustainable development, ornithology. Independent Consultant. *B.*28 April 1946, Zürich, Switzerland. British, Swiss. *M.* Eve: *s., d.* **Education:** U.of Basel, PhD 1972. **Experience:** res., res.mgmt, project dev. & implementation, strat.planning, admin.of intl NGO, consult. **Career:** Sci. 1973–4, Asst Dir 1977–9, NZWS; Cons.Officer, WWF Intl 1975–6; DG ICBP (restyled BirdLife Intl 1993) 1980–96; Ind.Consult.1996–. **Achievement:** bldg ICBP into large professional orgn with project activities world-wide & offices in four continents. **Memberships:** various ornithl & nat.cons. orgns. **Award:** RSPB Cons.Medal 1993. **Publications:** *Life on Water's Edge* (in German) 1976, Save the Birds (in German) 1987; series of scientific & popular articles. **Languages:** English, French, German. Willing to act as consult.etc. **Address:** 8 Church Lane, Girton, Cambridge CB3 0JP, England, UK. **Tel.**(home) 44 1223 276230; **fax** 44 1223 276060; **e-mail** chi@imboden.demon.co.uk .

INGRAM, Dr Glen Joseph. Systematics, biogeography, & evolution, of birds, reptiles, frogs, and slaters (wood-lice *etc.*). Section Head. *B.*22 April 1951, Rockhampton, Australia. Australian. **Education:** U.of Qld BSc 1975, PhD 1986. **Experience:** teaching evol.& biogeog.; consult.— rain-forests, heath, birds, reptiles, and frogs; field-work in Australia, Malaysia, Guam, New Caledonia, Fiji, Kenya, Zaire, Zimbabwe, Namibia; cons.— declining frog pops. **Career:** Curator & Sr Curator 1976–92, Head of Ver-

tebrate Section 1993–, Qld Mus. **Achievements:** discovery of new species of reptiles & frogs and preserv.of their habitats; fund-raising to support pol.campaigns and scientific res.for cons. **Memberships:** ASH, IUCN SSC, QOS (Sec.), WPSQ (Pres.), QCC (Counc.), Qld Frog Recovery Team, RANA (Patron), Scientific Adv.Cttee of Gt Sandy Regn World Heritage Area, AFT (Chief Trustee), Adv.Cttee of Threatened Species Network Qld, QCM (Chairman), Wildlife Res.Group (Counc.). **Publications:** *An Atlas of Qld's Frogs, Reptiles, Birds & Mammals* 1991, *Invertebrate Biodiv.& Cons.* 1994; 140 scientific & popular articles. Favours pers.pub.& news media support. **Languages:** English, French (basic), German (basic). Willing to act as consult.etc. **Address:** Queensland Museum, POB 3300, South Brisbane 4101, Queensland, Australia. **Tel.**(office) 61 7 840 7707, (home) 61 7 378 8644; **fax** 61 7 846 1918.

INNES, Dr John L. Forest health, biomonitoring, environmental change, environment–forestry interactions. Section Leader. *B.*3 Sept.1957, Kirkcaldy, Scotland, UK. British. **Education:** Trinity Coll. Glenalmond; Christ's Coll.Camb. BA 1979, PhD 1982. **Experience:** widespread res.in forestry & forest health, and arctic–alpine ecosystems. **Career:** NERC Res.F. U.Coll.Cardiff 1983–5, Lect. U.of Keele 1985–6, 33O Forestry Comm.1986–92, Section Leader, Swiss Fed.Inst.for Forest, Snow & Landscape Res. (WSL) 1992–. **Achievements:** eval.of effects of air poll.on Brit.forests, design & implementation of nat.forest monitoring system for Switzerland. **Memberships:** BES, IEEM, Swiss For.Soc. **Awards:** Holland Rose and William Vaughan Lewis Prizes (U.of Camb.). **Publications:** *Forest Health: Its Assessment & Status* 1993; 100+ papers. Indiff.to pers.pub.& news media support. **Languages:** English, French, German. Willing to act as consult.etc. **Address:** Eidgenössische Forschungsanstalt für Wald, Schnee, und Landschaft, Zürcherstrasse 111, CH-8903 Birmensdorf, Switzerland. **Tel.** 41 1 739 2216; **fax** 41 1 739 2215.

ISHI, Professor Hiroyuki. Rain-forest, desertification, Earth warming. Science Editor, Professor. *B.*28 May 1940, Tokyo, Japan. Japanese. *M.* Tokiko: 3 *d.* **Education:** U.of Tokyo BA(Ecol.) 1965. **Experience:** lect.& consult., news media. **Career:** Reporter, Asahi Shimbun Newspaper 1969–82; Staff Corres. NY Bur.1979–82; Dep. Sci.Ed.1982–83; Sr Staff Writer 1983–7; Chief Corres. Nairobi Bur.1985–7; Sci.Ed.1988–; Dir JNCS 1975–, Consult. UNEP Asian & Pacific Office 1983 and HQ 1985–9; Lect. U.of Tokyo 1989–; Min.of Trade and Industry Adv.Bd 1990–; Prof. Kokushikan U.1991–; Bd of Trustees, Regnl Envl Center for c.& e.Europe 1993–. **Achievements:** spread envl awareness through news columns & other pubns; support of E.Euro.countries to estab.new envl laws. **Memberships:** RSA, JDS, JANC, JWBS. **Awards:** Boerma Award (FAO) 1988, Mainichi Book

Award 1989, Global 500 Roll of Honour (UNEP) 1990. **Publications:** 13 books, 80 scientific papers. Favours pers.pub.& news media support. **Languages:** Chinese (read), English, German (basic), Japanese. Further details may be obtained from *Who's Who in Japan, Asahi Almanac*. Willing to act as consult.etc. **Address:** 2-20-9 Nozawa, Setagayaku, Tokyo 154, Japan. **Tel.**(office) 81 3 5541 8564, (home) & **fax** 81 3 3495 2277.

ISMAIL, Dr Sultan Ahmed. Vermiculture, vermicomposting, organic waste recycling using local species of earthworms, organic farming. Institute Director. *B*.9 Oct.1951, Pondicherry, Pondicherry State, India. Indian. *M*.Tasneem: *d*. **Education:** Madras U. MSc 1974, M.Phil. 1978, PhD 1984. **Experience:** res.in studies re.earthworms, vermiculture, vermicomposting, organic waste recycling, etc.1978–; deputation to Nat.Council of Educl Res.& Training 1987–90. **Career:** Lect.in Zool.1975–, Dir of Inst.of Res.in Soil Biol.& Biotech.1994–, The New Coll.(Madras). **Achievements:** dev.of simple tech.('VERMITECH') to recycle organic garbage into organic fertilizer, have trained several farmers and housewives to recycle wastes into fertilizers, promotion of organic farming. **Memberships:** NYAS, ISSBE, ESI. **Awards:** Friend of the Envt Award (EXNORA) 1993, Vocational Service Award (Rotary Club) 1992. **Publications:** 40 res.papers, several popular articles, educl software on BBC micro, books on envl studies for children. Favours news media support. **Languages:** English, French (fair spoken). Willing to act as consult.etc. **Address:** 136 Jani Jehan Khan Road, Royapettah, Madras 600014, Tamil Nadu, India. **Tel.**(office) 91 44 826 7269, (home) 91 44 844832; **fax** 91 44 852 4362.

IYER, C.P.Jayalakshmi. Environmental NGO networking, management, and campaigning; project formulation, management, and evaluation. Programme Officer, Editorial Director, Managing Director. *B*.1 Oct.1961, Secunderabad, AP, India. Indian. *B*.C.P.Krishnan, water resources' mgmt esp.in coastal areas. **Education:** U.of Delhi, BSc(Hons)(Bot.) 1980, MSc(Bot.) 1982; JNU, Dipl.of Proficiency in French 1979, Certs of Proficiency in Spanish 1981 and Italian 1983, MPhil(Envl Sci.) 1984. **Experience:** res., computer tech., admin.in govt, NGOs & business, consult.to govt funding agencies, NGOs and cos, edl consult.to four magazines in Hindi & English. **Career:** Researcher, JNU 1982–7; Sci.Admin. Govt of India 1987–9; Consult. Tech.Info. Forecasting & Assessment Council, and Dir, Energy Envt Group 1989–92; Prog. Officer, Energy Envt Group 1992–4; Edl Dir, SIPI Features 1994–; MD, Nature Resorts (Pvt.) Ltd.1990–; Subject Matter Specialist: Info., Documentation, Media, for the Nat.(India) Coordn Unit for Fourth World Conf.on Women (Beijing 1995) 1994–5. **Achievements:** launched several NGOs at grassroots level for increased

envl awareness, written & campaigned on many issues re.wildlife, large dams, consumer issues, etc. **Memberships:** Energy Envt Group (Life), Bamboo Soc.of India (Life), WWF India (Life), ISWA (Life), ISCA, Consumer Unity Trust Soc., ELCI, SID, IUCN, Sahaman (NGO). **Awards:** Jr 1982–4 & Sr 1987 Res.F. (CSIR India), Gold Medal (U.of Delhi) 1982. **Publications:** four books incl.[Reader's Guide] (illustr.book on Brundtland Comm.Recommendations, in Hindi) 1989; two monogrs, two tech.handbooks, 250+ popular sci.articles, eight tech.papers., Managing Ed.*Vikalp*. Favours pers.pub.& news media support. **Languages:** English, Hindi, Tamil; French, Italian, & Spanish (basic spoken). Willing to act as consult.etc. **Address:** Nature Resorts (Private) Ltd, 220B Una Apartments, Nr 3 Ipextin, Patparganj, New Delhi 110 092, Delhi, India. **Tel.**(office) 91 11 223 0297, (home) 91 11 666175; **fax** 91 11 220 9608.

IZRAEL, Academician Professor Dr Yuri. Scientific research in fields of anthropogenic and natural environmental sciences, ecology, geophysics, physics of the atmosphere, oceanology, geography. Academician, Institute Director. *B*. 15 May 1930, Tashkent, Uzbekistan (former USSR). Russian. Father Izrael Antonij and mother Shatalina Antonina both physiol.–ecol. *M*.Elena: *s., d.* **Education:** C.Asian SU (Tashkent), PhD (Phys.& Maths) 1969. **Experience:** scientific investigations, admin. **Career:** Researcher, Sr Sci. 1953–63; Dep.Dir, Dir, Inst.of Applied Geophys.1963–72; Dep.Chief 1970–74, Prof.1971, Chief 1974–8, USSR Hydrometeorological Service; Exec.Counc.1974–91, Second then First VP 1975–87, Chairman WG II then VC IPCC, WMO; Chairman, USSR State Cttee for Hydrometeorology and Control of Natural Envt (as Minister) 1978–91; USSR Supreme Soviet Dep.1979–88; Dir Natural Envt & Climate Monitoring Lab.1988–91; Dir Inst.of Global Climate & Ecol.1991–. **Achievements:** scientific investigations directed at reducing envl poll. (dev.of pollutant dispersion models, standards for atmos.& water poll.emissions); dev.& facilitation of envt monitoring system in former USSR as All-Union Obs.& Natural Envt Monitoring Service incl.satellite data; work in framework of World Weather Watch dev., global monitoring, orgn of control of radioactive products produced by nuclear explosions & accidents and continuous work on radioactive control and in natural envts after the Chernobyl nuclear power-plant accident; work in field of disaster control, scientific investigations in climate change and its impact on envt, ecol.implications, activity on scientific substitutions of UN Conv.on Climate Change. **Memberships:** Russian AS (Corres.1974–94, Full [Academician] 1994), IAA (Full 1991), EAR (Full, 1994), HMS (Hon.). **Awards:** State Premium 1981, Gold Medal (USSR AS) 1983, Gold Medal (Ettore Majarana, Italy) 1990, Sasakawa Envt Prize (UNEP) 1992, Premium & Gold Medal (WMO) 1992; Orders of former

USSR & other states. **Publications:** mostly in Russian — 200+ scientific articles, 23 monogrs incl.*Isotopes' Composition of the Radioactive Fallout* 1973, *Peaceful Nuclear Explosions and Envt* 1973, *Global Climatic Catastrophes* (co-Author) 1986, *Anthropogenic Climate Change* (co-Ed.) 1987, *Anthropogenic Ecol.of the Ocean* (co-Author) 1989, *Chernobyl: Radioactive Contamination of the Envt* (Ed.) 1990, *Earth's Ozone Shield and its Changes* (co-Author) 1992; 50+ intl conf.reports. Indiff.to pers.pub.& news media support. **Languages:** English (spoken), Russian. Willing to act as consult.etc. **Address:** Institute of Global Climate and Ecology, Glebovskaya 20B, Moscow 107 258, Russia. **Tel.**7 095 169 2430; **fax** 7 095 160 0831.

JACOBS, Professor Peter Daniel Alexander. Environmental assessment planning & management, sustainable urban development, landscape architecture, conservation & development of open-space systems. Professeur titulaire. *B.*3 Dec.1939, Montreal, Quebec, Canada. Canadian. Father Joseph Jacob Jacobs, envl engr. *M.*Ellen-Gail Vineberg: *d.*Merav Beth (business & envt), *s.*David Avrum (envl health). **Education:** Antioch Coll. AB(Engg & Creative Arts) 1961, Harvard U. MLArch.1968, MArch.1984. **Experience:** res — field-work in Arctic Canada & n.Quebec, cons.& dev.strats at the rural/urban interface with emphasis on participatory planning in France, Israel, Thailand, & Colombia; admin.— Dir of undergrad.& grad.progs in landscape planning & design; consult.— Canadian & provincial Govts on cons.& dev., memb.Quebec Round Table on Envt & Econ., num.comms on envl perception & impact analysis. **Career:** Professor titulaire, Faculté de l'Aménagement, Ecole d'Architecture de Paysage (Quebec) 1971–. **Achievements:** Chairman IUCN CEP 1973–90, Kativik Envl Qual. Comm. 1980–, Public Adv.Cttee on Canada's State on the Envt Report 1990–92, and public envt reviews of major projects in n.Canada (Lancaster Sound), n.Quebec (Great Whale Hydroelectric Project) and num.critical urban envts. **Memberships:** F.CSLA, F.ASLA, Quebec Order of Architects. **Awards:** Vis.Scholar, Harvard & UBC; Invited Prof.Technion U.Israel, Univs of Paris (La Villette) and Valle (Colombia); Gov.-Gen.'s Medal (Canada); Tamaare Cons.Prize (e.Europe); Zuni Puebla (New Mexico). **Publications:** *Envl Strat.& Action: The Challenge of the WCS* 1981, *Cons.with Equity: Strats for Sust.Dev.*1983, *Dev.& Envl Assessment: Perspectives on Planning for a Common Future* 1990; *c.*50 papers & reports; memb.of seven professional & Academic Edl Cttees, and Guest Ed.of num.spec.issues on cons.& envt. Neutral re.pers.pub.& news media support. **Languages:** English, French, Spanish (in progress). Further details may be obtained from *Who's Who in Amer.*1992 *(et seq.).* Willing to act as consult.etc. **Address:** Université de Montréal, Faculté de l'Aménagement, Ecole

d'Architecture de Paysage, CP 6128 succursale A, Montréal, Quebec H3C 3J7, Canada. **Tel.**1 514 343 7119; **fax** 1 514 343 6104.

JACOBSON, Robert John. Implementation of integrated pest-management strategies in protected crops. Research Entomologist. *B.*8 April 1953, Oundle, Northants, England, UK. British. *M.*Pauline: *d.* **Education:** U.of Bradford, BTech (Hons)(Applied Biol.) 1975. **Experience:** res. — dev.of new pest-control strats to minimize pesticide usage in prot.crops; consult.— provide guidance to UK growers on practical implementation of integrated pest-mgmt strats involving minimal pesticide use. **Career:** Consult.Entomol. Agricl Dev.& Adv. Service, Min. of Agric. Fisheries & Food (UK) 1976–90; Tech.Services Mgr, Bunting Biol.Control Ltd. 1990–92; Res.Entomol. HRI 1992–. **Achievements:** contribn to reduction of pesticide usage in protected cucumber, pepper, tomato, aubergine, and ornamental crops, in UK. **Membership:** AAB. **Publications:** 15 refereed & major conf.papers, num.articles in UK hortl press. Favours pers.pub.& news media support. Willing to act as consult.etc. **Address:** Horticulture Research International, Cawood, Selby, North Yorkshire, England, UK. **Tel.**(office) 44 1 757 268275, (home) 44 1 937 845699; **fax** 44 1 757 268996.

JAIN, Dr Sudhanshu Kumar. Ethnobotany, medicinal plants, conservation of endangered species & habitats, floristic survey, taxonomy of grasses & orchids, psychoactive plants, formulation & administration of large research programmes, plant resources, botanic gardens. Emeritus Scientist. *B.*30 June 1926, Amroha, Dist.of Moradabad, UP, India. Indian. Father the late Prakash Chandra Jain, agriculturist. *M.*Satya: 3 *s.* **Education:** Allahabad U. BSc 1943, MSc 1946; Pune U. PhD 1965; training in taxonomy at Indian Botanic Gdn and Forest Res.Inst.1949–51, and in econ.bot.in USSR 1969. **Experience:** floristic & ethnobotanical exploration in NW–E Himalaya, arid west to humid east & peninsular India 1949–; res.in taxonomy, econ.bot., endangered plants, threatened habitats 1949–70, orchids, grasses 1971–91; psychoactive plants 1991–; admin.of sci. dept 1971–84; consult.to Govt & industry; eval. of large res.proposals; directing training courses in taxonomy & ethnobotany. **Career:** Asst Prof. U.of Meerut 1947–49; Edl Asst, Wealth of India series 1951–3; Sr Scientific Asst, Nat. Botanic Gdn (Lucknow) 1953–6; Sci.1956–70, Dep.Dir 1971–7, Jt Dir 1977, Dir 1977–84, Botl Survey of India; Nat.Envt F.1984–6, Emer.Sci. CSIR, Dept of Sci.& Tech.1986–, Govt of India. **Achievements:** init.resurgence of ethnobotany, new Flora of India work, and awareness of endangered species & habitats, prot.areas movement; started Indian Plant Cons.Bull. and Red Data books; cultivated many rare plants in botanic gdns. **Memberships:** Pres.& F. Soc.of Ethnobotanists, F.NA, F.NASc, F.Botl Soc.,

F.ITE, VP IASTAM, Chairman Ethnobotany Comm. **Awards:** Nat.Envt F'ship (Govt of India), Gold Medal (NAS) 1966, Maheshwari Medal (IBS) 1982, Harshbeger Medal (Soc.of Ethnobotanists) 1992, citations & certs of num.orgns. **Publications:** 25 books incl.*Dict.of Indian Folk-Med.& Ethnobotany* 1991, *Medicinal Plants of India* (2 vols) 1991, *Notable Plants in Ethnomedicine of India* 1991, Ed. *Ethnobotany*, Edl Bd of Yale U.series on Psychoactive plants; *c.*250 res.papers. Indiff.to pers.pub., favours news media support. **Languages:** English, Hindi, Urdu (simple spoken). Willing to act as consult.etc. **Address:** A-26 Mall Avenue Colony, Lucknow 226 001, Uttar Pradesh, India. **Tel.**(office) 91 522 236431, (home) 91 522 244556; **fax** 91 522 244330 or 243111.

JAKOWSKA, Professor Dr Sophie. Environmental ethics & education, religion-motivated environmental action. Retired. *B.*12 Feb.1922, Warsaw, Poland. American. *W.* **Education:** Fordham U. PhD(Biol.) 1947. **Experience:** res.in cytology, comparative haematology & path.of cold-blooded vertebrates, toxicology, experimental studies with natural products from the sea; admin.— IUCN CEC & memb.of ethics WG, memb.of Adv.Bd of Global Harmony Fndn and collab.in Pastoral Juvenil Arquidiocesana; helped develop prog.of Licenciatura en Biologia, Autonomous U.of Santo Domingo 1968–. **Career:** worked with a health fndn and toxicology-related govt & industry instns, Prof.of Biol., City U.of NY 1970–77 when retired. **Achievements:** wrote first envl educ.books for children in the Dominican Rep.such as *Enuna isla como la nuestra, Hijos de la Tierra, Amigos del Cocodrilo, Amigos del Cocodrilo en el parque zoologico, La quiera libre, En un pais como el nuestro* (Costa Rica); developed religiously-motivated envl educ.progs for youth & the community. **Memberships:** F.AAAS, F.NYAS, F.NYZS, LOP, IUCN CEC, Comision Nacional de Bioética, num.scientific socs. **Awards:** Tree of Learning Award (IUCN), Gold Medal (LOP). **Publications:** num.res.articles, and on envl educ.& ethics. **Languages:** English, French, Italian, Polish, Portuguese, Spanish. Willing to act as consult.and to speak on religious motivation for envl prot. **Address:** Arz.Merino 154, Santo Domingo, Dominican Republic. **Tel.** (home) 809 687 3948; **fax** 809 688 7696.

JAMES, Brian. Natural resources' management. Chief Forest Officer. *B.*13 Feb.1955, Micoud, St Lucia. St Lucian. Father Thomas James, farmer. **Education:** U.of New Brunswick BSc (For.) 1988; Eastern Carib.Inst.of Agric.& For. (Trinidad & Tobago) Dipl.(Gen.For.) 1991. **Experience:** teaching, admin. **Career:** Teacher, Desruisseaux Combined Sch.1972–5; Dep.Chief Forest Officer 1983–9 (Forester I 1989–91, Sr Forester 1991–2), Chief Forest Officer 1989–, Dept of For. Min.of Agric. **Memberships:** STF, CFA. **Award:** L.P.Sebastien Prize (U.of New Brunswick) 1988.

Favours pers.pub.& news media support. **Language:** English. Willing to act as consult.etc. **Address:** Department of Forestry, Ministry of Agriculture, Castries, St Lucia, West Indies. **Tel.**(office) 809 450 2078, (home) 809 454 4126; **fax** 809 450 2287.

JAMES, Dr David John. Plant biotechnology, genetic transformation of temperate fruit. Principal Research Scientist. *B.*1 Oct.1943, London, England, UK. British. *M.*Jane Mary. **Education:** U.of Sheffield BSc(Hons) 1965, U.of London PhD(Biochem. Cell Biol.) 1974; **Experience:** cytogenetics, control of adventitious organogenesis and embryogenesis in plant tissues, auxin metabolism, genetic improvement of fruit plants by somatic methods, polyploidy, gene transfer *via* agrobacterium; consult.to IAEA. **Career:** Asst Cytogeneticist, Paediatric Path.Dept, United Cardiff Hospitals 1968–70; Res.F. U.of London 1974–6; Prin.Res.Sci. HRI 1976–. **Achievements:** world's first in transforming apple (1987) and strawberry (1990), demonstrating Mendelian segregation of transgenes. **Memberships:** SEB, IAPTC, ISPMB. **Publications:** 60+ pubns & chapters on biotech.of apple, pear, cherry, & strawberry. Indiff. to pers.pub., favours news media support. **Languages:** English, French (written, some spoken). Willing to act as consult.etc. **Address:** Horticulture Research International–East Malling, West Malling, Kent ME19 6BJ, England, UK. **Tel.**(office) 44 1732 843833, (home) 44 1622 763013; fax 44 1732 849067.

JAMES, Philmore A. Environmental studies, ecotourism. Chief of Visitor Services. *B.*31 Jan.1958, Antigua, West Indies. Antiguan. *M.* Carmen L. **Education:** U.of W.Indies BSc (Geog./Geol.) 1980, U.of W.Indies Distance Teaching Enterprise, Cert.in Energy Mgmt 1982. **Experience:** basic res.for Nat.Parks Auth. Antigua. **Career:** Grad.Asst Teacher, Sec.Sch. 1980–86; Lect. Antigua State Coll.1986–9; Asst Examiner (Geog.), Carib.Exam.Council 1981–9; Admin./Researcher 1989–, Chief of Visitor Services 1989–, Nat.Parks Auth. **Achievements:** coordn with var.envl/cons.orgns & envl awareness groups in Antigua. **Memberships:** IUCN CNPPA 1990. **Language:** English. Willing to act as consult.etc. **Address:** Swetes Village, Antigua, Leeward Islands, West Indies. **Tel.** (office) 809 460 1379/80, (home) 809 460 1654; **fax** 809 460 1516.

JAMES, Roger Derek. Environmental coverage on broadcast television. Controller of Factual Programmes. *B.*13 June 1944, London, England, UK. British. *M.*Johanna: *d.* **Career:** Film Ed., Dir, Producer, Head of Documentaries, Controller of Factual Progs, CIT. **Achievements:** helped found, and on IAC of, TVE; leads a team which continues to produce envl progs broadcast around the world; projects incl.*Decade of Destruction* (10-yrs series which chronicled envl consequences resulting from destruction of Brazilian rain-forest), Seeds of Hope (events in Ethiopia before, during, and after, the '84 famine), *The Last Show on Earth* (marked 1992 World Envt Day), *Growing Up* (UNICEF/TVE prod.looking at future of 12 children around the world born in yr of 'Rio Summit'). **Membership:** F.RSA. **Award:** Global 500 Roll of Honour (UNEP) 1989. Favours pers.pub.& news media support. Will ing to act as consult.etc. **Address:** Central Television, 46 Charlotte Street, London W1P 1LX, England, UK. **Tel.**44 171 637 4602; **fax** 44 171 323 9150.

JAMES, Dr (Winston) Clive. International agricultural research & development, transfer of agri-biotechnology applications which contribute to sustainability and a better environment. Private Consultant, Organization Chairman, Company Chairman & CEO. *B.*8 April 1940, Carmarthen, Wales, UK. British, Canadian, Perm. Resident of Cayman Islands (Brit.W.Indies). *M.*Glenys. **Education:** U.of Wales, BSc(Hons) (Agricl Bot.) 1961; U.of Camb. PhD(Plant Path./Epidemiology) 1964. **Experience:** res.— specn assessment of econ.losses due to diseases, selection of benchmark ref.papers published; res.admin., many consults in Africa, Asia, & Latin Amer., over last 20 yrs, lecture tours, workshop orgn, memb of intl missions to & consulting cttees in third-world countries. **Career:** Res.Officer, MAFF 1964–8; Res. Officer, Fed.Dept of Agric.(Canada) 1968 75; Plant Prot.Officer, UN FAO 1975–7; Resource Officer, CIDA 1977–81; Dep.DG, CIMMYT 1981–8; Chairman & CEO, ABDIL 1990–; Bd Chairman, ISAAA 1992–; Private Consult. 1990–. **Achievements:** assessment of econ. losses due to plant diseases in global context, facilitated more resp.use of fungicides, recent transfer of agri-biotech. applications to third world which can contribute to a safer envt & sust.through, for example, less dependency on conventional pesticides. **Memberships:** APS (Chairman, Cttee on Plant Disease Losses 1972–4) 1975–8, ISPP (Chairman, Comm.on Disease Loss Appraisal 1973–8). **Awards:** F'ship (Australian Wheat Industry Res.Council) 1976, Award of Dist.(IXth ICPP) 1979. **Publications:** 50+ incl.Role of the Private Sector 1991, Estimated Losses of Crops from Plant Pathogens 1991. Favours pers.pub.& news media support. **Languages:** English, French, Spanish, Welsh. Willing to act as consult.re.missions to third world involving tech.transfer. **Address:** International Service for the Acquisition of Agri-biotech Applications, POB 427 Savannah, Apt 3–5/8, Coral Bay Village, Spotts, Grand Cayman, Cayman Islands, British West Indies. **Tel.**1 809 947 1839; **fax** 1 809 947 7337; **e-mail** cjames@Server.CandW.Ky .

JANSEN, Malcolm A.B. Biodiversity conservation, protected area management, environmental impact assessment. Biodiversity Specialist. *B.*21 July 1949, Colombo, Sri Lanka. Sri Lankan. **Education:** U.of Colombo, BSc (Hons)(Bot.) 1976; Tech.U.of Dresden, Dipl.in Ecosystem Mgmt 1979. **Experience:** res.— ecol.of changing river basin habitats; consult.— envl assessment of river basin dev., roads, and transmission facilities; taught BSc bot.; prep.of envl strats and action plans, eval.of for.& biodiv.projects, design of envl projects. **Career:** Lect. Dept of Bot. U.of Colombo 1976–7; Researcher, NSC of Sri Lanka 1977–8; Sr Envl Officer, Mahaweli River Basin Project 1979–87; Envl Officer/Project Dev.Officer, USAID 1987–91; Biodiv.Specialist, World Bank 1991–. **Achievements:** design of Integrated Prot.Areas System for Mahaweli River Basin; design of Natural Resources and Envl Policy Project for Sri Lanka; prep.of Biodiv.Status Report for Sri Lanka; Envl Action Plan for Sri Lanka; prep.of biodiv.cons.projects for India, Sri Lanka, & Laos PDR; prep.of Biodiv.Action Plans, and Integrated Cons.& Dev.Projects; contributed to prep.of For.Sector Study for India. **Memberships:** Sri Lanka AAS & MAB, March for Cons.Colombo 1979–80. **Publications:** *Biol. Diversity and Trop.Forests — Sri Lanka* 1988, *Natural Resources of Sri Lanka — Conditions and Trends* 1991; num.others incl.checklists of ferns and liverworts of Sri Lanka etc. **Language:** English. Willing to act as consult.etc. **Address:** Environment and Natural Resources Division, Asia Technical Department, The World Bank, 1818 H Street NW, Washington, DC 20433, USA. **Tel.**(office) 1 202 458 2748; (home) 1 202 363 9462; **fax** 1 202 522 1664.

JAQUENOD DE **ZSÖGÖN, Dr Silvia,** *see* **ZSÖGÖN, Dr Silvia** JAQUENOD DE.

JARIWALA, Professor Dr C.M. Environmental law & education, constitutional law, law of education. Professor of Law. *B.*19 Oct.1937, Burhanpur, MP, India. Indian. *M.*Dr Savitri Jariwala *qv: s., d.* **Education:** BHU BCom. 1957, LLB 1961; U.of London LLM 1966, PhD 1969. **Experience:** res.— constitutional & envl law, law of educ.; admin.— Dean, Head of Dept of Law; teaching at U.of Delhi & BHU since 1970. **Career:** Lect.in Law 1970–71, Reader in Law 1974–84, Prof.of Law 1984–, BHU; Assoc. Prof. Indian Law Inst.1971–3; Reader in Law, U.of Delhi 1973–4. **Achievements:** first in India to offer a course on Law & Envt 1977, to prepare Envt Educ.Model for the 21st Century, and to start prog.in Law of Educ. **Memberships:** ILI, ELC, ICEL, Constitutional & Parliamentary Studies, New Delhi. **Publications:** Freedom of an Interstate Trade in India 1975; *c.*66 articles. Favours pers.pub.& news media support. **Languages:** English, Hindi. Willing to judge proposals & ref.papers. **Address:** G/12 Arvindo Colony, Banaras Hindu University, Varanasi 221005, Uttar Pradesh, India. **Tel.**91 542 311294.

JARIWALA, Dr (Mrs) Savitri. Research in biological control of some plant diseases through the antagonistic activity of microorganisms. Reader in Botany. *B*.2 May 1942, Varanasi, India. Indian. *M*.Prof.C.M. Jariwala *qv*: *s*., *d*. **Education:** BHU MSc(Bot.) 1963, PhD(Bot.) 1965. **Experience:** teaching BSc & MSc classes in bot., supervising res.students, conducting two projects in field of mycology & plant path., 10 yrs' res.exp. **Career:** Lect.1965–84 & Reader 1984– Dept of Bot. BHU. **Achievements:** envl educ.through mass media, envl res.(control of envl poll.through biol.control of plant diseases). **Memberships:** Acta Botanica, IBS. **Award:** Gold Medal (IBS) re.MSc. **Publications:** 15 papers incl.Dev.& formulation of antagonistic microbes against *Drechslera oryzae* and *Alternaria solani* 1992, Effect of some medicinal plant parts' extract on growth and spore germination of *Drechslera oryzae* 1993; review articles incl.Soil Pollutants and Their Effect on Soil Microflora 1993; 18 abstracts incl.Studies in antagonism between *Fusarium oxysporum* f.sp.*lini* and some root regn mycoflora of linseed 1993. Favours pers.pub.& news media support. **Languages:** English, Hindi. **Address:** Department of Botany, Banaras Hindu University, G/12 Arvindo Colony, Varanasi 221-055, Uttar Pradesh, India. **Tel.**(home) 91 542 311294.

JAYAL, Nalni Dhar. Conservation of natural heritage, 'Greening of the Himalaya' project. Trust Secretary. *B*.11 Feb.1927, Almora, UP, India. Indian. *M*.Amena. **Education:** The Doon Sch.; Delhi U. BA(Hons) 1947. **Experience:** as Mgmt Auth.administered CITES and led Indian del.to Conf.of Parties to CITES 1979 and to Conv.on Cons.of Migratory Species of Wild Animals (Bonn) 1979; elected Regnl Counc.for E.Asia at IUCN GAs 1978 & 1981 and to its Bur.1979; Asia Rep.on IUCN Cttee for reviewing & formulating WCS; negotiated several wildlife res.projects and set-up Bharatpur Hydrobiol.Station with US FWS; led Indian del.to high-level mtg of officials of S.Asian countries to init.SACEP 1981; Indian rep.and elected Chairman of Extraordinary Conf. of Contracting Parties to Ramsar Conv.1982; led Indian team at a Festival of India Jt Indo–German Envt Sem.of Vol.Orgns 1992. **Career:** Indian Air Force (Pilot's Branch) 1948–54; Indian Frontier Admin.Service 1954–60; Dep. Commissioner Kinnaur (HP) 1960–67 and appointed to Indian Admin.Service; Dep.Sec. Union Dept of Family Planning 1967–9, Dir in Min.of Educ.1969–72, Jt Sec.for Forestry & Wildlife in Min.of Agric.1975–80, Govt of India; Dev.& Hill Commissioner to Manipur Govt 1972–4; Memb.Sec.of High Level Cttee on Envt 1980; Jt Sec.to newly-created DoE 1980–83, Adv.for Envt & Water Resources, Planning Comm.1983–5 when retired from govt service; Dir for Natural Heritage 1985–90, Dir-Gen. 1990–95, Adv. 1995–6, INTACH; Sec. Himalaya Trust 1994–. **Achievements:** resp.for setting-up network of Nat.Parks & Biosphere Reserves in the Himalaya and other sanctuaries & marine parks; assisted in

estab.of Union DoE; brought about policy changes against clear-cutting natural forests, monoculture plantations, and imposition of moratorium against exploitation of w.Himalayan forests; drafted revised Forest Policy; init. Greening of Himalaya projects; campaigned for greater concern for saving trop.rain-forests of Ker., Ne India, & A&N Islands. **Memberships:** IUCN CESP & CNPPA, Himalayan Club (VP), WWF India, India Intl Centre, Indian Mountaineering Fndn (former VP). **Publications:** num.incl.*India's Envt: Crises & Responses* (Ed.) 1985, *Eliminating Poverty: An Ecol.Response* (INTACH envl series) 1986, *An Unseen Crisis* 1990, *Himalaya: Our Fragile Heritage* 1991, *Alternative Strats for Dev*.1992, *Ecol.and Human Rights* 1993. Indiff.to pers. pub.& news media support. **Languages:** English, Hindi. Further details may be obtained from *Who's Who in India* 1991–2. Willing to act as consult.etc. **Address:** Himalaya Trust, 274/II Vasant Vihar, Dehra Dun 248 006, Uttar Pradesh, India. **Tel.**(office) 91 135 683081.

JEFFERIES, Bruce Edward. Protected area & biodiversity conservation management. Chief Technical Adviser, Project Manager. *B*.13 Sept. 1943, Wellington, NZ. New Zealander. *M*. Margaret Jillian (adventure travel & natural hist.journalist). **Education:** Lincoln U. Dipl.in Nat.Park Mgmt 1978. **Experience:** 25 yrs' cons./ natural resource mgmt & planning in NZ & *e.g.* Nepal, Philippines, PNG. **Career:** Ranger 1966–9, Distr.Ranger 1969–72, Field Supervising Ranger (Asst) 1972–4, Park Super. 1980–86, Tongariro Nat.Park; Project Mgr, Sagarmatha Nat.Park 1974–9; Chief Tech.Adv. Nepal Nat.Park System 1986–90; Regnl Mgr, Dept of Cons.NZ 1990–91; IUCN Consult. re. Philippines 1990–; Adv.to PNG Dept of Envt & Cons.(World Bank/UNDP consult.) 1991–. **Achievements:** estab.Mgmt Planning Framework of Sagarmatha Nat.Park, contributed to sig.planning & implementation activities in NZ, Nepal, Philippines, and PNG. **Membership:** IUCN CNPPA for Oceania. Indiff.to pers. pub. & news media support. **Languages:** English, Nepali (poor), Tok Pigun (fair). Willing to act as consult.etc. **Address:** United Nations Development Programme, POB 1041, Port Moresby, Papua New Guinea. **Tel.**(office) 675 254900, (home) 675 254929; **fax** 675 259192.

JENKINS, Professor Dr David. Zoology, environmental conservation, conservation of national & international wildlife especially vertebrates. Retired, Honorary Professor of Zoology. *B*.1 Mar.1926, Birmingham, England, UK. British. *M*.Margaret W.: *s*., *d*. **Education:** Marlborough Coll.; R.Vet.Coll. MRCVS 1948; U.of Camb. MA 1952; U.of Oxf. DPhil 1956, DSc 1982. **Experience:** 30 yrs' res.in ecol.& supervision of res.in ecol.& animal pop.dynamics. **Career:** Res.F. Scottish Landowners' Fedn 1956–60; Head, Mtns & Moorlands Res. Team 1960–66, Asst Dir (Res.) 1966–72, NC

(Scotland); Head of Vertebrate Res.Section 1972–82, Sr Officer, Banchory Res.Station 1972–86 (when retired), ITE; Chair Scientific Adv.Cttee 1977–94, Counc.& Ed. WPA; Hon. Prof.of Zool. U.of Aberdeen 1986–; Memb. NE Regnl Bd, Scottish Natural Heritage 1992–6. **Achievements:** personal res.in most Brit.habitats leading to over 50 pubns & eight edited symp.vols; guidance & supervision nationally in ITE and intlly in Edinburgh & Aberdeen Univs and for WPA; Ed.WPA Symp.vols.& Annual Rev., and Scottish Birds. **Memberships:** BOU, BES (before retirement), SOC, F.RSE. **Publications:** many ecol.papers incl.Social behaviour in the Partridge *(Perdix perdix)* 1961, The present status of the Wildcat *(Felis catus)* in Scotland 1962, Pop.studies on Red Grouse *(Lagopus scoticus)* (co-Author) 1963, The status of Red Deer *(Cervus elaphus)* in Sardinia in 1967, 1972, Problems of integration of use of upland areas 1973, Structure and regulation of a Shelduck *(Tadorna tadorna)* pop.(co-Author) 1975, Ecol.of Otters *(Lutra lutra)* in n.Scotland 1980. Indiff. to pers.pub.& news media support. Further details may be obtained from Debrett's *People of Today* 1991. Willing to act as consult. **Address:** Whitewalls, Aboyne, Aberdeenshire AB34 5JB, Scotland, UK. **Tel.**(home) 44 13398 86526; **fax** c/o 44 13398 86922.

JEWELL, Professor Dr Peter Arundel. Ecology of large African mammals, conservation of rare breeds of British farm livestock. Emeritus Professor, Fellow. *B.*16 June 1925, Gwithian, Cornwall, England, UK. British. *M.*Juliet (archaeozoologist, expert in hist.of domesticated animals): 3 *d.*incl.Vanessa (researcher for Greenpeace), Rebecca (social anthrop.). **Education:** St John's Coll.Camb. MA 1950, PhD 1951. **Experience:** trop.field res., orgn of zool.confs, consult.on tourism & wildlife dev. **Career:** Res.F. ZSL 1960–66, Sr Lect. U.of London 1967–72, Prof.of Biol. Univs of Nigeria 1966–7, London 1972–7, and Camb.1977–92. **Achievements:** estab.of long-term experiments in archaeobiol., dev.of teaching in cons., saving London Zoo from closure. **Memberships:** F.ZSL (former VP), C.Biol., F.IBiol., Rare Breeds Survival Trust (VP). **Awards:** Scholar & Wright's Prizeman (St John's Coll.) 1947, Hon.Dean (U.of Biafra) 1966–7, Former Pres. Mammal Soc. **Publications:** Is.Survivors: the Ecol.of the Soay Sheep of St Kilda 1974; 100+ major scientific papers. Favours pers.pub.& news media support. **Languages:** English, French (poor). Further details may be obtained from Brit.*Who's Who* 1994–. Willing to act as consult.etc. **Address:** St John's College, Cambridge CB2 1TP, England, UK. **Tel.**(home) 44 1223 357977; **fax** 44 1223 336676.

JIANG, Dr Gaoming. Environmental, plant, & pollution, ecology, urban ecology & botany. Associate Research Professor in Environmental Ecology. *B.*16 Sept.1964, Shandong Province,

PRC. Chinese. *M.*Jianjie Lu: *d.* **Education:** Shandong U. BA(Bot.) 1985, Inst. of Bot. Academia Sinica MS(Bot.) 1988, PhD (Bot.) 1993, vis.study U.of Liverpool 1991–2. **Experience:** res.— eco-envl planning for middle cities (China), bioindicating & biomonitoring air poll.by plants, phosphorus cycling & chem.ecol., ecol.of colliery spoils, urban vegetation, elemental background in China; admin.— init.of 1st Conf.for the Young Chinese Botanists (Beijing 1987) and of the 1st Conf.on Envt & Plant Resource Exploring in China (Changbaishan 1988). **Career:** Res.Assoc.& Assoc. Res.Prof.in Envl Ecol. Academia Sinica 1988–. **Achievements:** basic res.on bioindicating & biomonitoring air poll., first one to find poll. hist.of Chengde City, N.China, and to find reasons for death of ancient pine trees in gdns; estab.of multi-models for monitoring SO_2 poll. of woody plants, eco-envl planning for Summer Villa estate, the largest existing imperial gdn in China. **Memberships:** CBS, Beijing Ecol.Soc. **Awards:** Scholarship (Shandong U.) 1983, Excellent res.paper writer (Inst.of Bot. Academia Sinica) 1990. **Publications:** *The Biol.of the 21st Century in China* (in Chinese, co-Ed.) 1992, *Eco-envl Planning for the Summer Villa Estate* (in Chinese, co-Ed.) 1993; *c.*20 papers, Edl Bd *Dict.of Envl Sci.*(in Chinese) 1992. Favours pers pub. **Languages:** Chinese, English, Japanese (read). Willing to act as consult.or ref. **Address:** 141 Xizhimenwai Tajie, 100 044 Beijing, People's Republic of China. **Tel.**86 10 835 3831/266; **fax** 86 10 831 2840.

Jia-Shun ZHANG, *see* **ZHANG, Jia-Shun.**

JIGJ, Professor Dr Sonom. Ecologically-ustainable development, geoecological approach for studying human influence on Nature, prognosis of environmental changes, management & creation of network of protected areas & national parks, study of geodynamic processes of landscape of dryland regions, development of travel & tourism (recreation potential), management & educational aspects of environment, the model 'Nature–economics–population', economic & ecological regionalizations. Institute Director. *B.*12 Oct. 1941, Zavkhan aimag, Mongolia. Mongolian. *M.*H.Lonjid: 4 *s.* **Education:** Moscow U. 1968; Russian AS Dr 1971, PhD (both Geogl Sci.) 1990; course in English at a Mongolian U.1977, training courses in mgmt of envt in developing countries (Germany) 1978, in ecol.(Russia) 1980, and mgmt of Biosphere Reserves (India) 1986. **Experience:** mgmt of geoecol.& natural resources, qualitative & quantitative analysis of human influence on natural envt, prot.areas, geodynamic processes of landscape of steppe & desert regns, sust.dev.of travel & ecotourism (rec.potential), geomorph.& engg geog., educl aspects of envt. **Career:** Scholar 1968–74, Dir 1987–, Inst.of Geog.& Geocryology, Mongolian AS; Chairman, Dept of Prot.of the Envt of State Cttee of Sci. & Tech.1974–80; Gen.Sec. MSNE 1980–86.

Achievements: Pres. (first) of MGS 1990–, Chairman Mongolian Nat.Cttee for UNESCO MAB Prog.1987–, Gen.Couns.of Perm.Cttee of Prot.of Nature of the People's Gt Khural of Mongolian Parliament, Couns.of intl biodiv. project in Min.of Envt of Mongolia, Memb. Scientists' Council of MME. **Memberships:** Pres.MGS, IUCN CNPPA, Scientific Council of Intl Centre for Prot.of L.Baikal (Russia). **Awards:** Medal of Glory for Labour (Govt of Mongolia). **Publications:** *Main Genetical Types of Relief of Territory of Mongolia* 1975, *The Remote Sensing Res.of Envt of Mongolia* 1989, *The Basic Problems of Engg Geog.& Envt of Mongolia* 1979, *Exp.of Envl Prot.of Foreign Countries* 1983, *Propaganda of Envl Prot.of Mongolia* 1983, *Glacial forms of Relief of Mongolia* 1986, 100 *Questions & Answers of Envt* 1987; 120+ articles. **Languages:** English, German, Russian. Willing to act as consult.etc. **Address:** Institute of Geography & Geocryology, Mongolian Academy of Sciences, Ulaanbaater 210 620, Mongolia. **Tel.**(office) 976 1 326172, (home) 976 1 342146.

Jilan SU, Dr, *see* **SU, Dr Jilan.**

JIM, Dr Chi Yung. Tropical biogeography & soils, urban vegetation, soil & ecology, urban environmental impacts. Senior Lecturer in Biogeography & Soil Science. *B*.23 Jan.1953, Hong Kong. British. *M*.Grace. **Education:** U.of HK, BA(Hons)(Geog.& Geol.) 1975; U.of Reading (UK), PhD(Soil Sci.) 1981; US Geol.Survey (Hydr.) 1982. **Experience:** res.— urban tree & soil studies, urban envl impacts, ecol.impacts of recreational activities & urban encroachment into the countryside, ecol.rehab.of degraded lands; adv.to HK Govt on urban tree planting & mgmt and country-park planning & mgmt; consult.in soil sci.arboriculture & EIA; extensive field exp.; supervision of MPhil & PhD res. students; teaching of soil & vegetation sci.to BA, BSc & M landscape arch.students. **Career:** Asst Lect.1981, Lect.1981–92, Sr Lect.1992–, all in Biogeog.& Soil Sci. U.of HK. **Achievements:** Dep.Project Leader in Urban For. IUFRO; Observer as envl scientist of Prince of Wales' Business Leaders' Forum, twice project leader of govt-commissioned city-wide tree survey in HK. **Memberships:** IPSS, AAGB, BSSS, ISSS, HK Country Parks Bd, HK Country Parks Planning & Mgmt Cttee (Chairman), founding memb.& hon.adv.of Friends of Country Parks (HK), HSHK (Hon.), Res.F. Centre of Urban Studies & Envl Mgmt, Centre of Asian Studies, and Kadoorie Agricl Res.Centre. **Awards:** Best Teacher Award 1986, Commonwealth Scholarship 1987–90, Shell Better Envt Award 1990. **Publications:** *Trees in HK: Species for Landscape Planting* 1990, *Champion Trees in Urban HK* 1993, Soil compaction & tree growth in trop.& subtrop.urban habitats 1993, Trees and landscape of a suburban residential neighbourhood 1993; 70+ others; Edl Bd, *Arboricultural J.,* Assoc.Ed.*Asian Geographer,*

Adv.Ed. *EC.* Indiff.to pers.pub.but favours news media support. **Languages:** Chinese, English. Willing to act as consult.etc. **Address:** Department of Geography & Geology, University of Hong Kong, Pokfulam Road, Hong Kong. **Tel.**(office) 852 859 7020, (home) 852 819 4834; **fax** 852 559 8994.

JOHANNES, Dr Robert Earl. Traditional marine ecological knowledge & resource management systems in the tropics and their practical value today. Private Consultant. *B*.26 Sept.1936, North Battleford, Canada. American, Australian. **Education:** U.of BC, BSc(Zool.) & MSc (Zool.) 1958; U.of Hawaii PhD 1963. **Experience:** res.— 30 yrs' in trop.marine ecol. & fisheries with special emphasis on artisanal fisheries & trad.ecol.knowledge; consult.— extensive during 1979–93 on trop.marine cons.& fisheries mgmt; considerable exp.re.marine ecol. impacts of pulp mills. **Career:** Dept of Zool. & Inst.of Ecol. U.of Georgia 1963–7; Vis. Researcher, U.of Hawaii 1977–9; var.positions then Sr Prin.Res.Sci., Div.of Fisheries, CSIRO 1979–93, Private Consult.1994–. **Achievements:** two books & num.papers on marine ecol. & resource mgmt. **Memberships:** IUCN Comm. on Ecol. and WG on Cons.& Trad.Life Styles. **Awards:** Guggenheim F'ship 1973, CSIRO Medal 1990, Pew Scholar in Cons.& the Envt 1993. **Publications:** *Words of the Lagoon: Fishing & Marine Lore in the Palau Distr.of Micronesia* 1981 & 1992, Trad.Fishing in the Torres Strait Islands (co-Author) 1991. Favours pers.pub.& news media support. **Language:** English. Willing to act as consult. etc. **Address:** 10 Tyndall Court, Bonnet Hill, Tasmania 7053, Australia. **Tel.& fax** 61 2 283235.

JOHNSON, Dr David W. International environmental law, policy, and philosophy. *B*.27 May 1958, Charlottesville, VA, USA. American. **Education:** Carleton Coll. AB(Intl Relations) 1980, U.of Miami JD(Intl Law) 1983. **Experience:** marine biol.res.on gastropod *Norissia* sp.in *Macrocystis* ecosystem, marine ecol. res., baseline study in inland water 'ecosystems'; res.for intl orgns; interdisc.res.of indigenous peoples in neotrop.bioreserves. **Career:** legal practice Miami (FL) 1983–90, res.& writing in envl & intl envl law at Stanford Law Sch. 1991–4. **Achievements:** Candidate for JSD in intl envl law. **Memberships:** ABA, ATLA, FL & CA Bars. **Awards:** Intl Order of Barristers, Soc.of Bar & Gavel. **Publications:** *Envlism, Pragmatism, and the Three Strange Angels: A Middle Way Towards Envl Wisdom* 1993, *Developing Adaptive & Reactive Policy & Instns through Fuzzy Systems Theory* (dissertation) 1994. Favours pers.pub.& news media support. **Language:** English. Further details may be obtained from *Who's Who in Amer.Law* 1993. Willing to act as consult.etc. **Address:** 1618 Sand Hill Road, Palo Alto, California 94304, USA. **Tel.**(office & home) & **fax** 1 415 328 5600.

JOHNSON, Stanley Patrick. European environmental policy, population. Special Adviser on the Environment. *B*.18 Aug.1940, Penzance, Cornwall, England, UK. British. *M*.Jennifer. **Education:** Exeter Coll. U.of Oxf. BA & MA 1963, Dip.Ag.Econ.1965. **Experience:** as intl & Euro. civil servant, as politician, and as writer of both fiction and non-fiction books. **Career:** Staff Memb. World Bank 1966–8; Commissioner, UK Countryside 1970–73, Euro.1973–9, and EC 1984–90 Comms; Memb. Euro.Parl.1979–84; Spec. Adv.on the Envt, Coopers & Lybrand (UK) 1990–. **Achievements:** dev.of curo.cnvl & pop.policies. **Memberships:** RGS, RSA. **Awards:** Newdigate Prize (U.of Oxf.) 1962, Prize (Greenpeace) 1984, Richard Martin Award (RSPCA) 1984. **Publications:** num.books incl.*The Politics of Envt* 1972, *The Green Rev.*1973, *The Earth Summit* 1993, *World Pop — Turning the Tide* 1994. Favours pers.pub.& news media support. **Languages:** English, French. Further details may be obtained from Brit.*Who's Who* 1996, Debrett's *Eminent Persons* 1994. Willing to act as consult. etc. **Address:** 60 Regent's Park Road, London NW1 7SX, England, UK. **Tel.**(office & home) 44 171 722 4258; **fax** 44 171 483 1390.

JOHNSTON, Professor Dr Douglas Millar. Law of the sea, international environmental law; marine & coastal management, Asia Pacific region, Arctic. Chair in Asia–Pacific Legal Relations. *B*.30 April 1931, Dundee, Scotland, UK. British. *M*.Judith Elizabeth. **Education:** St Andrews U. MA 1952, LLM 1955; McGill U. MCL 1958; Yale U. LLM 1959, JSD 1962. **Experience:** res.& scholarship, teaching. **Career:** Prof.of Law and Founder of Marine & Envl Law Prog. Dalhousie U.1972–87, Observer at Third UN Conf.on Law of the Sea 1976–81, Dir Northern Waters Project 1984–7; Chair, Asia–Pacific Legal Relations, Centre for Asia–Pacific Initiatives, U.of Victoria 1987–. **Achievements:** co-Founder Dalhousie Ocean Studies Prog. (now Oceans Institute of Canada) 1979 and of SEAPOL 1983. **Memberships:** IUCN CEL, Law of the Sea Inst., ASIL, ICEL, others. **Publications:** *Intl Law of Fisheries* 1964, 1989, *Envl Law of the Sea* 1981, *Theory & Hist.of Ocean Fisheries* 1964, 1989, Envl Law of the Sea 1981, *Theory & Hist.of Ocean Boundary Making* 1991; num.articles. Dislikes pers.pub., indiff.to news media support. **Language:** English. Willing to act as consult.etc. **Address:** Centre for Asia–Pacific Initiatives, Room 131 Begbie Building, University of Victoria, POB 1700, Victoria, British Columbia V8W 2Y2, Canada. **Tel.**(office) 1 604 721 7023, (home) 1 604 721 1010; **fax** 1 604 721 3107.

JOHNSTON, Professor Dr Harold S. Chemistry of the stratosphere & the troposphere; the natural global ozone balance and its plausible perturbation by stratospheric aircraft, nuclear bombs, and other human activities. Professor Emeritus of Chemistry. *B*.11 Oct.1920, Woodstock, GA, USA. American. *M*.Mary Ella Stay: *s*.,

3 *d.* **Education:** Emory U. AB 1941, CIT PhD 1948. **Experience:** lab.& field res.in chem.warfare and micrometeorology, u.teaching of gen.& phys.chem., u.res.in gas phase reactions & photochem., past memb. NASC on Motor Vehicle Emissions, Dept of Transportation Climatic Impact Assessment Prog., SAC of FAA High Alt.Poll.Prog., NASA Ozone Trends Panel; SAC of NASA Atmos.Effects of Stratospheric Aircraft 1988–. **Career:** Res.Asst NDRC projects 1942–5, Instr.to Assoc.Prof. Stanford U. 1948–56, Vis.Assoc.Prof. CIT 1956–7, Prof. 1957–91 then Emer.1991– and Dean Coll.of Chem.1966–70, U.of Calif. **Achievements:** some work on chem.of urban smog 1950–70; developed case that large fleet of Mach 3 supersonic aircraft would double global input of stratospheric nitrogen oxides and probably would reduce global ozone (1971), which led to first large stratospheric res.prog., Dept of Transportation 1972–5. **Memberships:** NAS, Amer. AAS, ACS, APS, AGU. **Awards:** Poll.Control (ACS) 1974, Tyler Prize 1983, NAS for Chem.in Service to Soc.1993, Hon.DSc (Emory U.) 1965, Disting.Alumni (CIT) 1985, Berkeley Citation 1991. **Publications:** *Gas Phase Reaction Rate Theory* 1966, *Reaction Rates of Neutral Oxygen Species* 1968; 150 res.papers 1949–, chapters in *The Natural Stratosphere of 1974*, and in WMO Global Ozone Res.Reports Nr 16 1986 & Nr 18 1990. **Languages:** English; French, German & Italian (poor). Willing to act as consult.etc. **Address:** 132 Highland Boulevard, Berkeley, California 94708, USA. **Tel.**(office) 1 510 642 3674, (home) 1 510 525 6810; **fax** 1 510 642 6911.

JOHNSTON, Dr Neil. Waste minimization; biotechnology, cleaner technology & farming. Project Leader. *B*.21 Aug.1954, Darwin, Australia. British. *M*.Sue: *s*., *d*. **Education:** U.of Newcastle upon Tyne BSc(Hons) 1977, Balliol Coll. DPhil (Oxon.) 1982, Newcastle Poly. Dip.M.1985. **Experience:** res.into utilization of sewage sludge as a fertilizer, investigation of tech.needs of water industry, processors, and farmers, in reducing envl impact. **Career:** Market Analyst, Mono Pumps 1982–4; Marketing Exec. Ferranti Engg 1984–5; Marketing Consult. TEK Mgmt Consults 1985–90; Project Leader, CEST 1990–. **Achievements:** estab.of UKs first major demn of waste minimization techniques on the Aire & Calder; identification of barriers to exploitation of plant biotech. **Memberships:** F.RSA, IWEM, CIM. **Publications:** incl.Water: Resource & Opportunity 1992, Cleaner Farming 1993 (both Reports available from CEST). Indiff.to pers.pub.& news media support. **Languages:** English, French (working). Willing to act as consult.etc. **Address:** Centre for Exploitation of Science and Technology, 5 Berners Road, London N1 0PW, England, UK. **Tel.**44 171 354 9942; **fax** 44 171 354 4301.

JONES, Professor Dr Hamlyn Gordon. Plant environmental physiology & micrometeorology, plant–water relations & ecology. Director of Crop Science Research, Special Professor in Environmental Science. *B*.7 Dec.1947, Kuala Lumpur, Malaysia. British. *M*.Amanda Jane: 2 *d*. **Education:** St John's Coll.Camb. BA(Hons) (Natural Sci.)(Class I) 1969, ANU PhD(Envl Biol.) 1972. **Experience:** res.on envl physiol. of nr of agricl & hortl crops in Australia, Philippines, India; undergrad.teaching; vis.Prof' ships. **Career:** Res.Sci., Plant Breeding Inst. Camb.1972–6; Lect.in Ecol.(Hon.1979–) U.of Glasgow 1977–8; Group Leader, E.Malling Res.Station 1978–88; Dir of Crop Sci.Res./Head of Station, Hort.Res.Intl 1988–; Spec.Prof.in Envl Sci. U.of Nottingham 1991–. **Achievements:** basic res.& understanding of plant adaptation to envl stress, undergrad.teaching of envl plant physiol. **Memberships:** BES, SEB (Council 1986–90), F.IHort., ISHS (Council). **Awards:** Lister Scholar, College Prize, Wright Prize, Henry Humphreys Prize (all St John's Coll.), ANU Scholarship. **Publications:** *Plants & Microclimate* 1983–92, *Plants under Stress* (co-Ed.) 1988; *c*.120 papers; Edl Bds of *e.g. Trees: Structure & Function, Agronomie*. **Languages:** English, French (read). Willing to act as consult.etc. **Address:** Horticulture Research International, Wellesbourne, Warwickshire CV35 9EF, England, UK. **Tel.**44 1789 470382, **fax** 44 1789 470552.

JOOSTING, Dr Peter E. Medical environmentology: epidemiology, criteria, applied toxicology, standard-setting. Retired Medical Doctor. *B*.14 March 1927, Heerde, The Netherlands. Dutch. **Experience:** res.& consulting, specialist on global level in applied envl scis. **Career:** Medical Res.Officer & Adv. Inst.for Envl Hygiene, Dutch Orgn for Applied Scientific Res. 1958–87. **Awards:** Christopher Barthel Jr (IUAPPA). **Languages:** Dutch, English. **Address:** Laan van Oostenburg 16, 2271 AP Voorburg, The Netherlands.

JORDAN III, Dr William R. Ecological restoration. Editor & Outreach Officer. *B*.30 April 1944, Denver, CO, USA. American. **Education:** U.of W–M, PhD 1971. **Experience:** res., admin., editing. **Career:** Postdoctl F. ORNL 1972–3; Writer ACS 1975–6, Ed.& Outreach Officer U.of W–M Arboretum 1977–. **Achievements:** developed plan for Earthkeeping prog.& Earthkeeping Acad.(progs of resto.-based envl educ.), Founding Ed.of J.*Resto.& Mgmt Notes*. **Membership:** Founding Memb.Bd of Dirs, Soc.for Ecol.Resto. **Award:** NSF Res.Prof. U.of N.Texas 1993–4. **Publications:** *Resto. Ecol.: A Synthetic Approach to Ecol.Res.*(co-Ed.) 1987, A double value: ecol.resto.and the cons.of biol.diversity 1988, The reentry of Nature 1990; num.others. Indiff.to pers.pub., favours news media support. **Language:** English. Willing to act as consult.etc. **Address:** University of Wisconsin–Madison Arboretum, 1207 Seminole Highway, Madison, Wisconsin 53711, USA. **Tel.**1 608 263 7889; **fax** 1 608 262 5209.

JOVANOVIĆ, Dr Petar. Satellite telemedicine, environmental diseases; desertification, ozone depletion, Man-made 'natural disasters'. Liaison Officer. *B*.19 Oct.1920, Simanovci, Yugoslavia. Yugoslavian. *M*.Jovanka: *s., d*. **Education:** U.of Belgrade MD 1954, U.of Pittsburgh MPH 1963. **Experience:** participant in many intergovtl mtgs, presented papers to many intl scientific confs. **Career:** Gen.Practitioner 1955–57; Head, Dept of Preventive Curative Services, Min.of Public Health 1958–80 when retired; Liaison Officer, IAF with WHO– UNESCO. **Achievements:** first global prog. for satellite med.1985, first modelling of relationship between Man-made & natural catastrophes 1982, devised an action plan for combating diseases linked to desert.and improved method of their diagnosis. **Memberships:** ASU, IAF Rep., AAS. **Awards:** Global 500 Roll of Honour (UNEP) 1987. **Publications:** Satellite Med.Advance in Space Res. COSPAR 1986, Satellite tech.and the control of envl diseases 1987, Modelling Man-made natural hazards 1988, Satellite med.: world health 1989, Satellite tech.in health res.1990. Favours pers.pub.& news media support. **Languages:** English, French, German, Russian. Willing to act as consult.etc. **Address:** 8 Omladinskih Brigada, Belgrade, Yugoslavia. **Tel.**(home) 38 11 676157.

JUDGE, Anthony John. Organization of interdisciplinary information. Assistant Secretary-General. *B*.21 Jan.1940, Port Said, UAE. Australian. *M*.Hannelore: *s*. **Education:** U.of Cape Town. **Experience:** resp.for info.& res.prog. UIA. **Career:** Asst Sec.-Gen. UIA 1970–. **Achievements:** editing *Enc.of World Problems & Human Potential** 1976, 1986, 1991, 1994. **Memberships:** IUCN CESP, WFSF, WAAS. **Publications:** *Ed.of above Enc.and *Yearbook of Intl Orgns; c*.200 papers. **Languages:** English, French; German, Italian & Spanish (some). Willing to act as consult.etc. sometimes. **Address:** Union of International Associations, 40 Rue Washington, B-1050 Brussels, Belgium. **Tel.**322 640 4109; **fax** 322 646 0525; **e-mail** judge@uia.be .

JUEL-JENSEN, Dr Bent Einer. Tropical medicine, third-world medicine & development. Emeritus University Medical Officer (Chief), Honorary Consultant Physician. President of Oxford University Exploration Club. *B*.11 Nov.1922, Odense, Denmark. British. Father G.Juel-Jensen, zool./bot. *M*.(Cicele) Mary (envt). **Education:** Univs of Copenhagen, Oslo, Oxf.& Harvard — MA Oxf.1953, BM, BCh Oxon.1953, DM Oxon.1972. **Experience:** in charge of Oxford's Trop.& Infectious Diseases Unit until retirement in 1987; worked in Thailand, Ethiopia, Sudan, Kenya. **Career:** Consult.Physician 1966–87, U.Med.Officer 1973–90, Emer.1990–, U.of Oxf.; Med.Adv.to RGS 1976–97, Hon. Consult. Physician, Oxf.Health Auth.1989–. **Achievements:** as co-Founder of Ethiopian Democratic Union (with Prince Ras Mangashia,

GCVO), tried to stem communist destruction of Ethiopia's ancient heritage; with Ras Mangashia founded Ethiopian Aid Chain for Ethiopian refugees. **Memberships:** RCEP 1956, RCP 1972, F. RCP 1977 & RNS, Emer.F. St Cross Coll.Oxf.& ACHA. **Awards:** Rockefeller Travelling F.(Harvard) 1962, Marc Fitch Gold Medal for Bibl.(U.of Leeds) 1976, Hon.F. Liverpool Sch.of Trop.Med.& RGS. **Publications:** *Herpes Simplex, Varicella & Zoster* (co-Author) 1972; *c.*200 papers on med.& bibl. subjects. Indiff.to pers.pub.& news media support. **Languages:** Amharic (some), Danish, English, French, German, Norwegian, Tigrinya (some). Willing to act as consult.etc. **Address:** Monckton Cottage, 56 Old High Street, Headington, Oxford OX3 9HW, England, UK. **Tel.**(home) 44 1865 62848.

JUSOFF, Dr Kamaruzaman. Forest conservation & management, rehabilitation of degraded forest & mining lands, application of satellite remote-sensing in forest management & conservation, ecoengineering. Lecturer, Researcher, and Consultant. *B.*28 March 1958, Kota Bharu, Kelantan, Malaysia. Malaysian. Father Jusoff Taib, Mother Che Wook Abdullah (both had an interest in Nature cons.). *M.*Rohaita: 3 *d.* **Education:** UPM Sarawak, Dipl.For.1976; UPM Serdang, BS(For.) 1981; U.of New Brunswick/ UPM MS(Forest Ops/Engg) 1988; UPM/ Cranfield Inst.of Tech. PhD(Applied Remote-sensing) 1991. **Experience:** res.— forest survey, rehab.of degraded lands, applied remote-sensing in forest mgmt & cons., impact of for.dev.on soils & veg.; admin.— coordn of Dipl.For.Prog.1993 and Applied Remote-sensing Prog.1993 UPM, Malaysian rep.to USAID cons.progs; teaching — tree harvesting, forest engg, forest survey, timber transportation, land-use planning. **Career:** Lect. UPM 1988–. **Achievements:** completion of PhD thesis, ORA. **Memberships:** CSPE (Student 1982–4), IAgrE (Student 1989 & Assoc.1992). **Awards:** Commonwealth Forestry Book Prize 1979–80, Canadian Commonwealth Scholarship & F'ship Award 1981–4, ORA 1989–92, UPM Excellence Service Achievement Award 1993. **Publications:** *c.*35 papers & *c.*10 consult.reports. Favours news media support. **Languages:** Arabic, English, Malay. Willing to act as consult.etc. **Address:** Faculty of Forestry, Universiti Pertanian Malaysia Serdang, 43400 Selangor, Malaysia. **Tel.**(office) 60 3 948 6101, (home) 60 3 942 4886; **fax** 60 3 948 3745.

KABRAJI, Mrs Aban Marker. Environment/ conservation & management issues. Country Representative. *B.*12 Mar.1953, Quetta, Pakistan. Pakistani. *M.*Kairas Kabraji. **Education:** U.of London, BSc(Hons.)(Biol.) 1975. **Experience:** dev.& implementation of NCS in Pakistan, in mgmt-related issues, and in fields of envt/cons.& sust.dev. **Career:** PI, Marine Turtle Cons.Project, WWF/IUCN 1980–85; Regnl Dir, WWF Pakistan, and Project Rep. IUCN

1985–7; Country Rep.for Pakistan, IUCN 1988–. **Achievements:** strat.planning, cons. progs, instnl dev., policy influence. **Memberships:** Shirkat Gah (NGO, Bd of Trustees), Women's Action Forum, SDPI (Bd of Govs), IDRC (Pres.'s Roundtable), IISD (Bd). **Publications:** *The Nature of Pakistan: A Guide to Cons.& Dev. Issues* 1986, *What Can IUCN Deliver?* 1993; num.articles & papers. Dislikes pers.pub., indiff. to news media support. **Languages:** English, Urdu (adequate). Willing to act as consult.etc. **Address:** 1 Bath Island Road, 75530 Karachi, Pakistan. **Tel.**(office) 92 21 573079 to 82, (home) 92 21 587 1110; **fax** 92 21 587 0287.

KACEM, Slaheddine BEL Hadj. Nature protection, wild flora & fauna conservation including application of international agreements. Forestry Engineer & Director of Forestry Conservation. *B.*6 Nov.1935, Dar Chaabane, Tunisia. Tunisian. *M.*Mouna: 2 *s., d.* **Education:** Forest Sch.of Barres (France), For.Engg Dipl.1959; further training in hunting and wild fauna (Germany) 1964–5 & (Switzerland) 1974, and in mgmt of nat.parks (USA) 1971. **Experience:** tech.& admin.in engg 1959–95, attended *c.*100 missions as rep.of Tunisia to intl confs & sems re.mgmt of wild fauna, nat.parks, & intl agreements, *e.g.*CITES, RAMSAR, CMS. **Career:** Forest Engr & Head of For.Distr.1959–64, Officer in Dept of Hunting and Nat.Parks of Directorate of For.1965–70, Chief Engr in For.& Dep.Dir of For.Cons.1984–90 and Gen.Engr in For.& Dir.of For.Cons.1990–, Gen.Directorate of For., all Min.of Agric. **Achievements:** setting up legislative texts re.hunting, Nature prot., wild fauna & flora, nat.parks & reserves and wetlands; creation & mgmt of higher cttee of hunting & game cons.in Tunisia incl.regnl & nat.socs of hunters; creation & planning of six nat.parks and 14 nat.reserves; reintro.of wild fauna species to Tunisia; prot.of wetlands & avifauna and of forests against fire & parasites, application of six intl agreements (CITES, RAMSAR, CMS, Biodiv., African, Berne). **Memberships:** ICHGC, IWRB, CMS (Scientific Council), Board of Hunting & Game Cons. in Tunisia (Gen.Sec.). **Publications:** incl.[Reintro.of wild fauna in Tunisia] 1992, [Mgmt of wild fauna and nat.parks in Tunisia] 1994 (both in French). **Languages:** Arabic, English (limited), French, German (limited). **Address:** Direction Générale des Forêts, 30 Rue Alain Savary, Tunis, Tunisia. **Tel.**(office) 216 1 891497, (home) 216 1 292814; **fax** 216 1 801992.

KADLEČÍK, Dr Ján. Wetlands' conservation & management, mammals, ecology & conservation of carnivores. Agency Specialist. *B.*24 Aug.1957, Nitra, Slovakia. Slovak. *M.*Dr Alexandra Menšíková: *s., d.* **Education:** Comenius U. Biol. 1981, RNDr 1982, postgrad.course in Envl Prot.1988–9. **Experience:** res.— Euro.Otter *[Lutra lutra]* distribn, ecol.& cons.in Slovakia, mammals of Fatra Mtns Reserves, ecol.& prot.of birds of prey; wetlands' mgmt — IWRB courses;

membership of Comm.of Presidentship of Slovak AS for Envt (Sub-Comm.for Biodiv.1993–5) and Comms for Envt of distr.& local govts. **Career:** Specialist, Admin.of Prot.Landscape Area, Slovak Envl Agency 1982–. **Achievements:** init. & promotion of Slovak activities in Ramsar Conv., wetlands' inventory, estab.of some wetland reserves, coordn of nat.Otter survey in Slovakia. **Memberships:** IUCN SSC Otter SG & Slovak Nat.Cttee, Slovak Zool.& Ornith.Socs, Soc.for Prot.of Birds of Slovakia, Slovak Ramsar Cttee (Sec.1991–), Slovak Union of Nature and Landscape Conservationists (Chairman, Distr. Cttee 1990–94). **Award:** Bronze Plaque (Slovak Union of Nature and Landscape Conservationists) 1989. **Publications:** Ed.*Bull.Vydra* (Otter), *Let's Conserve the Turiec R.1993*, & *The Turiec* 1994. Favours pers.pub., indiff.to news media support. **Languages:** Czech, English, Hungarian (basic), Russian (basic), Slovak. Willing to act as consult.etc. **Address:** The Velká Fatra Mountains Protected Landscape Area Administration, Čachovsky rad 7, 038 61 Vrútky, Slovak Republic. **Tel.**(office) 42 842 284503, (home) 42 842 289108; **fax** 42 842 33535.

KAKABADSE, Yolanda. Public participation in 'sustainable development' and environmental issues. President, Executive President. *B.*15 Sept.1948, Quito, Ecuador. Ecuadorian. *D.:* 2 *s.*Alonso (envl econ.), Ignacio (envl econ.). **Education:** Catholic U. Educl Psych.1970. **Experience:** Exec.Pres.of Creation*, promotion of several NGOs in Ecuador and memb.of several intl orgns dedicated to increase civil soc.participation in decision-making. **Career:** Exec.Dir 1979–80, Pres.1990–, Fundacion Natura; NGO Liaison Officer, UNCED 1990–92; Exec.Pres. *Fundacion Futuro Latinoamericano 1993–. **Achievements:** promoter of Fundacion Natura (first & larger envl NGO in Ecuador); resp.for execution of public awareness progs in Ecuador and therefore for several pol.decisions re.these issues. **Memberships:** WWF Intl Bd, Adv.Bd to VP of Sust.Dev.of World Bank, SID (Bd). **Awards:** co-decoration from Govt of Ecuador, Order of the Golden Ark, Global 500 Roll of Honour (UNEP) 1991. **Publications:** *Movers and Shapers — NGOs in Intl Dev.*1994. Indiff.to pers.pub.& news media support. **Languages:** English, Spanish. Willing to act as consult.etc. **Address:** Los Cabildos 137, Quito, Ecuador. **Tel.**593 2 435521 or 433677; **fax** 593 2 462204 or 433677.

KASHYAP, Dr Kant. Pesticide technology, occupational health. Director. *B.*10 Oct.1936, Jhansi, UP, India. Indian. *M.*Kusum: 2 *s., d.* **Education:** U.of Agra MD 1963, U.of Gujarat PhD 1982. **Experience:** res.(which has been published in many intl journals), consult., training (teacher), served as Temp.Adv., Chairman/VC on 40 task groups for WHO & IPCS. **Career:** Asst Dir 1972–8, Dep.Dir 1978–84, Dir Grade Sci.1984–7, Dir 1987–, Nat.Inst.of

Occupational Health. **Achievements:** minimized health hazards for some industrial workers exposed to adverse envl conditions. **Memberships:** ICOH, NCCP. **Awards:** F.(Fac.of Medicine) RCP, F.NCCP. **Publications:** over 130. Indiff.to pers.pub.& news media support. **Languages:** English, Gujarati, Hindi. Willing to act as consult.etc. **Address:** National Institute of Occupational Health, Meghani Nagar, Ahmedabad 380 016, Gujarat, India. **Tel.** (office) 91 79 866842, (home) 91 79 865142; **fax** 91 79 866630.

KASSAS, Senator Professor Dr Mohamed EL. Desert plant ecology, conservation of Nature. Emeritus Professor of Plant Ecology. *B.*6 July 1921, Borg-el-Borollos, Egypt. Egyptian. *M.*Freda K.: *s., d.* **Education:** U.of Cairo BSc(Hons) 1944, MSc 1947; U.of Camb. PhD 1950. **Experience:** 50 yrs' res.in Egypt–Sudan arid lands. **Career:** Dept of Bot.1944–81, Emer.1981–, U.of Cairo; Memb.of Shoura Council (Second House of Parliament) 1980–. **Achievements:** init.of envl movement in Egypt and later in Arab regn., Pres.IUCN 1978–4. **Memberships:** EAS, IAS, WAAS. **Awards:** Pahlavi Prize for the Envt (UN) 1978, Order of the Rep.(Egypt) 1978, Order of Merit (Egypt) 1980, State Prize in Sci.(Egypt) 1981, Roll of Honour (IUCN) 1984 & (WWF) 1985, Order of the Golden Ark 1985, John-Philip Medal (IUCN) 1990. **Publications:** num.incl.Ecological Consequences of Water Development Projects 1972, The Three Systems of Man 1989. **Languages:** Arabic, English. Willing to act as consult.etc. **Address:** Faculty of Science, Cairo University, Giza 12613, Egypt. **Tel.** (office) 20 2 572 7213, (home) 20 2 348 5742; **fax** 20 2 5688884.

KASSIOUMIS, Dr Konstantinos. Protected area management & planning, biotopes' & species' conservation, environmental forestry, outdoor recreation. Researcher. *B.*28 Nov. 1946, Ioannina, Greece. Greek. *M.*Vassiliki: *s., d.* **Education:** U.of Thessaloniki, Dipl.in Forestry 1969; U.of Reading PhD(Envl Forestry & Rec.) 1978. **Experience:** wide admin.& tech. exp.in Nature cons.landscape planning etc. as civil servant, consult.to NGOs & memb.of var.Cttees of Experts of Council of Europe & EEC. **Career:** Officer & Head, Forest Directorate of Samos Is.1977–80 and Officer 1980–85 & Head 1986–92 Section for Forest Envt, Nat.Parks & Forest Recreation, all Greek Min.of Agric.; Researcher, Inst.of Medit.Forest Ecosystems & Forest Products' Tech. (NARF) 1992–. **Achievements:** improvement of public awareness & pol.commitment and active coopn with intl orgns to help better cons.& mgmt of Greek prot.areas. **Memberships:** IUCN CNPPA & SSC. **Publications:** The recreationists' response to forests & the implications for forestry & rec.mgmt 1981, Nature cons.in Greece (legis.& admin.of parks & reserves) 1987, Cons.of natural heritage — prot.areas in Greece 1988, Mgmt of prot.areas & regnl dev.(in Greek) 1989, Greece (chapter)

1990, Nat.parks & prot.areas: their meaning, purpose & mgmt 1993. Favours pers.pub.& news media support. **Languages:** English, French (poor), Greek. Willing to act as consult. etc. **Address:** Institute of Mediterranean Forest Ecosystems and Forest Products Technology, Terma Alkmanos, Ilissia, 115 28 Athens, Greece. **Tel.**(office) 30 1 7797 875, (home) 30 1 8064 174; **fax** 30 1 7784 602.

KAWANABE, Professor Dr Hiroya. Community ecology and animal sociology in relation to biodiversity. Professor of Ecology & Centre Director; Network Chairman. *B.*10 May 1932, Kyoto, Japan. Japanese. *M.*Aya: *d.* **Education:** Kyoto U. BSc 1955, MSc 1957, DSc 1960. **Experience:** fieldwork esp.freshwater envts in Japan 1955–, in other Asian countries 1962–, in Africa esp.L.Tanganyika 1977–, & on other continents 1970–. **Career:** Instr.1960–61, Lect. in 1961–7 & Assoc.Prof.of 1976–7, Zool., Prof.of Zool.& Ecol.1977–, Dir.of Centre for Ecol. Res.1991–, Kyoto U.; Chairman, Intl Network of DIVERSITAS in W.Pacific & Asia, IUBS/SCOPE/UNESCO 1993–. **Achievements:** discovery in 1950s of alternative behaviours of Ayufish *(Plecoglossus altivelis)* and the resultant effects of its social structure on pop.& prod.dynamics, and competitive food & habitat segregation, establishing 1960s of guidelines for Japanese IBP; emphasized in 1970s the evol.significance of social structure and other ecol.characters; direction of intl res.project in L.Tanganyika & adjacent regns 1979–; after initial proposition in 1991, estab.of Intl Network of DIVERSITAS 1993. **Memberships:** ESJ 1953– (Sec.-Gen.1984–7, Pres.1988–91), ZSJ 1955– (Bd 1968–), LSJ (Bd 1968–), JSPE 1967– (Bd 1967–86), FBA 1969–, BES 1970–, ISTAL 1974– (Bd & Nat.Rep.1983–, Chairman of Biodiv.WG 1995–), JSI 1981 (Bd 1985–), ISACF 1982–, INTECOL 1982– (VP 1986–90, Treas.1990–94), Ethological Soc.of Japan 1982– (Bd 1982–6), JSTE 1990 (Bd 1990–), ESA 1992–; num.nat.cttees. **Publications:** 50+ books incl.*Fishes in Rivers and Lakes: a Consideration of Food-chain Relationships* (in Japanese) 1969, *Illustr.Enc.of Freshwater Fishes of Japan* (in Japanese) 1976, *Ecol.of Rivers and Lakes* (in Japanese) 1985, *Ecol.for Tomorrow* 1990, *Mutualism and Community Organization* 1993, *The Ecol.of Symbiosis* (eight vols, in Japanese) 1994–5; Ed.-in-Chief *Physiol.and Ecol.*1975–, Ed.*African Study Monogrs* 1981–, Edl Bds of *Biol.Scis, Tokyo* 1965–, *Aquaculture and Fisheries Mgmt* 1982–, *Envl Biol.of Fishes* 1988–, *Intl J.of Ecol.and Envl Scis* 1993–, and African *J.of Trop.Hydrobiol.and Fisheries* 1994–; 600+ papers and articles. **Languages:** Chinese (read), English, German (read), Japanese. **Address:** Centre for Ecological Research, Kyoto University, 4 Shimosakamoto, Otsu 520-01, Japan. **Tel.**81 775 78 8055; **fax** 81 775 78 1436.

Ke Chung KIM, Professor, *see* **KIM, Professor Ke Chung.**

KEAGE, Peter Lawson. Glaciology, polar & alpine environmental management, Antarctic conservation, natural resources management & impact assessment, ecotourism. General Manager. *B.*6 March 1953, Sydney, Australia. *M.* Dianne E.: 3 *d.* **Education:** ANU BA(Geomorph.) 1974, U.of Tasmania MES 1981, U.of Camb. Scott Polar Res.Inst. MPhil.(Polar Studies) 1985. **Experience:** 25 yrs' active involvement in Antarctic sci.& mgmt, co-Founder of Poles Apart (bipolar envl & logistics consult.group) 1987–, supervision of major infrastructure & skifield improvements 1988–93, currently resp.for tourism infrastructure investment, cruise ship and air negns for Vic. **Career:** Glaciologist 1975–7, Prin.Res.Officer 1980–84, Exec.Officer 1985 8, Antarctic Div.; Policy Officer, Dept of Sci.and Envt Canberra 1979–80; Exec.Officer, Antarctic Div.1985–8; co-Founder, Poles Apart 1987–; Mgr of Resort Ops, Alpine Resorts Comm.1988–93; Gen.Mgr, Infrastructure Dev. Tourism Vic.1993–. **Achievements:** improved envl prot.over Australian Antarctic Territory and (sub-Antarctic) Heard Is.& the MacDonald Islands, prominent author on polar & alpine cons.& mgmt, consult.to nat.Antarctic progs, mgmt of redev.of Victoria's skifields 1988–93, major involvement in tourism development and improved air servicing to Vic 1993–. **Memberships:** SCAR Sub-Cttee on Cons.1986–9 and Group of Specialists on Antarctic Envl Affairs & Cons.1988–9; Edl Bd *Polar Record* 1987–93; Assoc.Clare Coll. Camb., Res.Assoc. Scott Polar Res.Inst.; EIA (Founding) 1987–, IUCN CNPPA Commissioner 1991– & Eco-tourism Cttee 1994–, Intl Fedn of Skiing (Envl Cttee 1991–). **Publications:** Status of Heard and MacDonald Islands 1981, *Waste Disposal in Antarctica* (SCAR Report) 1989, Ecol.sust.dev.and ski resorts 1992. **Awards:** postgrad.scholarships. **Language:** English. **Address:** Tourism Victoria, Level 11, 55 Swanston Street, Melbourne, Victoria 3000, Australia. **Tel.**(of-fice) 61 3 653 9799, (home) 61 3 816 9875; **fax** 61 3 653 9722.

KEATING, Michael Irvine. Environment and conservation. Independent Writer and Consultant. *B.*27 Feb.1943, Toronto, Canada. Canadian. *M.* Nicole. **Education:** Sangeen Distr.High Sch. –1962, Ryerson Poly.Inst. Dipl.in Journalism 1965. **Experience:** envl journalism, literary res. **Career:** Journalist, *Owen Sound Sun–Times* 1965–7, *Windsor Star* 1967–71, *Globe & Mail* 1971–88 (all Canadian newspapers); F.Envl Studies, York U.1985–; Assoc. Inst.of Envt Studies, U.of Toronto 1987–; Ind.Writer and Consult.1988–. **Achievement:** founded course in Envl Issues for Journalists at U.of Western Ont., pubns. **Memberships:** IUCN CESP, Canadian Global Change Prog.(Dir), SEJ, CAJ, CSWA. **Awards:** Silver Medal for Leadership (UNEP) 1984, Citation (CMOS) 1984, Schlenz Medal (WPCF) 1987. **Publications:** incl.*To the Last Drop* 1986, *Toward A Common Future* 1989, *The Earth Summit's Agenda for Change*

1993, *Covering the Envt* 1993. Indiff.to pers. pub., favours news media support. **Languages:** English, French (spoken). Further details may be obtained from *Canadian Who's Who* 1985–. Willing to act as consult.etc. **Address:** 10 Astor Avenue, Toronto, Ontario M4G 3M2, Canada. **Tel.**(home) 1 416 425 0005.

KEAY, Dr Ronald William John. Environmental biology and plant taxonomy of tropical areas especially Nigeria. Retired, Treasurer of Linnean Society of London. *B.*20 May 1920, Richmond, Surrey, England, UK. British. *M.* Joan Mary: *s.*, 2 *d.* **Education:** King's Coll. Sch.; St John's Coll.Oxf. BA 1941, DPhil.1963. Experience: 20 yrs in NFS, num.links with scientific socs & trop. countries, extensive work for RS & NGOs. **Career:** NFS, incl.duties as Prin.of Forest Sch.and Dir Forest Res. 1942–62; Dep.Exec.Sec.1962–77, Exec. Sec. 1977–85, RS; Leverhulme Emer.F.1987–8; Vis.Prof. U.of Essex 1990–93. **Achievements:** trop.forest ecol. & plant taxonomy, admin.of nat.& intl scientific orgns. **Memberships:** Sci. Assn of Nigeria (Pres.1961–2), F.LS (VP 1965– 7, 1971–3, 1974–6, Treasurer 1989–), African Studies Assn of UK (Pres.1971–2), IBiol. (Hon.F.1985, Pres. 1988–90), RHS (Hon.F. 1986), Nigerian Field Soc. (VP 1987–). **Awards:** OBE 1966, CBE 1977. **Publications:** *Outline of Nigerian Veg.* 1949 (& subs.edns); *Flora of W.Trop.Africa* Vol.I 1954 & 1958, *Trees of Nigeria* 1989; num.papers. Tolerant of pers.pub.& news media support. **Languages:** English, some French & Hausa. Further details may be obtained from Brit.*Who's Who* 1993, *Debrett's Disting.People of Today* 1993. Willing to act as consult.etc. **Address:** 38 Birch Grove, Cobham, Surrey KT11 2HR, England, UK. **Tel.** (office) 44 171 434 4479, (home) 44 1932 865677; **fax** 44 171 287 9364.

KEFELI, Professor Dr Valentin. Environment & physiology of plants. Director. *B.*12 July 1937, Moscow, Russia. Russian. Mother Alisa Kefeli-Tongur, biochem. *M.*Galina: *d.* Maria (biol.). **Education:** Agricl Acad. Moscow, PhD 1985. **Experience:** Head of lab.of plant hormones & synthetic regulators 1986–. **Career:** Memb.of staff, K.A. Timiryazev Inst.1961–88; Prof.1971–, Dir 1988–, Inst. of Soil Sci.& Photosynthesis, Russian AS. **Achievement:** in res.in metabolism of endogenous growth regulators. **Memberships:** RPPS (Pres.). **Award:** Prize (Czech AS) 1978. **Publications:** Natural Growth Regulators & Growth Inhibitors 1978. **Languages:** English, French, German, Russian. **Address:** Institute of Soil Science & Photosynthesis, Academia Nauk, Pushchino, Moscow Region 142 292, Russia. **Tel.**(home) 7 095 31715.

KELCEY, John Gordon. Urban ecology, industrial ecology; ecological engineering (*e.g.* habitat creation), people, badgers, trees, urban landscape, paintings. Environmental Consultant.

*B.*2 Aug.1942, Macclesfield, Cheshire, England, UK. British. **Education:** U.of Man-chester BSc(Bot.& Geol.) 1972. **Experience:** studies of anatomy of *Carex* and taxonomy of *Ulmus*, res.on num.tropics incl.urban & industrial ecol. **Career:** amateur naturalist 1952–65, Sec.of var.cttees of Cheshire Cons.Trust 1965–70, Ecol.and Linear Park Mgr, Milton Keynes Dev.Corpn 1972–83, Envl Consult.1983–. **Achievements:** frustration with failure of ecologists to confront and solve the needs of people & Nature, and the failure of Britain to recognize ecol.& Nature cons.in Europe (incl.c.& e. Europe). **Memberships:** Landscape Inst., IBiol., BES, RFS, Insts of Highways & Transportation, Leisure & Amenity Mgmt, and Envl Assessment. **Publications:** 55 articles & scientific papers. Strong dislike of pers.pub., dislikes news media sup-port. **Language:** English. Willing to act as consult.etc. **Address:** 38 Church Street, Wolverton, Milton Keynes, England, UK. **Tel.**44 1908 322452; **fax** 44 1908 316359.

KELLER, Michael Christian. Systematics of plants & birds of western Europe, environmental campaigns & education. Project Officer. *B.*12 Aug.1958, Sankt Wendel, Germany. German. *M.*Gabi: 2 *d.* **Education:** U.of Saarbrücken, Dipl.in Biol.1988. **Experience:** res.— chem.of cyanogenic plants, teaching plant physiol. **Career:** Scientific Asst, U.of Saarbrücken 1986–92; Project Officer, Naturschutzbund Deutschland 1992–. **Achievements:** teaching young people about envl problems, dev.of envl educ.prog. **Memberships:** Naturschutzbund Deutschland. **Languages:** English, French (read), German. **Address:** Naturschutzbund Deutschland, Grabenstrasse 22, 66606 St Wendel, Germany. **Tel.**(office) 49 6851 4797, (home) 49 6851 4890. **fax** 49 6851 5704.

KELLERMANN, Dr Adolf K. Environmental monitoring & research, national parks, environmental protection, polar marine ecology, early life-history of fish (particularly Antarctic fish). Monitoring Programme & Research Coordinator. *B.*9 Mar.1953, Neumünster, Schleswig-Holstein, Germany. German. *M.*Silke (marine biol.): 2 *s.* **Education:** Christian Albrechts U. Zool.Inst. MSc(Biol.) 1981 & Inst.for Polar Ecol. PhD 1985. **Experience:** 12 yrs' res.in ecosystem ecol., fish ecol., early life-hist.of fish incl.feeding, growth & dev., larval rearing & taxonomy, fish otoliths; several major expedns to Antarctic Peninsula 1981–90; several yrs' professional travel in S.Amer.& Pacific incl.res., courses, lectures; professional mgmt of multi-disc.res.projects. **Career:** Asst Researcher, Inst.for Marine Res.(Kiel) 1981–2; Asst Lect. Inst.for Polar Ecol. Kiel U. 1982–5; Assoc. Researcher & Post-doctl Sci. Alfred Wegener Inst.for Polar and Marine Res.(Bremerhaven) 1986–8; Post-doctl F. Sch.of Ocean, Earth Sci. and Tech. U.of Hawaii at Manoa 1989–91; Head, Coordinating Office of Ecosystem Res.,

Fed.Envl Agency (Berlin) 1992–; Coord.of Eco-system Res.Project Wadden Sea and Office of Trilateral Monitoring and Assessment Prog. 1992–, Nat.Park Office. **Achievements:** BIO-MASS Prog.on Southern Ocean ecol., var.mtgs and invited presentations in Europe, N.& S.Americas, conceptual work on the US GLOBEC Southern Ocean prog., German del.in TMEG of Wadden Sea nations, implementation of envl Trilateral Monitoring and Assessment Prog.in Germany incl.Chair of trilateral steering cttee. **Memberships:** French Soc.of Ichthyologists, NYAS, TMAG. **Publications:** c.30 incl.*Antarctic Ocean and Resources Variability* 1988, *Midwater Fish Ecol. Fndns for Ecosystem Res.in the Western Antarctic Peninsula Regn* 1995. Dislikes pers.pub., favours news media support. **Languages:** English, French, German, Latin, Spanish (better written). Willing to act as consult. etc. **Address:** National Park Office Schleswig-Holstein Wadden Sea, Schlossgarten 1, 25832 Tönning, Germany. **Tel.**(office) 49 4861 61645, (home) 49 4881 610; **fax** 49 4861 459.

KELLOGG, Dr William Welch. Climate theory, atmospheric physics, meteorological satellites. Retired Senior Scientist. *B.*14 Feb.1917, New York Mills, NY, USA. American. *M.*Elizabeth: 3 *s.*incl.Karl S.(geol.), 2 *d.* **Education:** Yale U BA 1939, UCLA MA 1942, PhD 1949. **Experience:** life has been devoted to envl res.& admin.of res., active involvement in US scientific socs, WMO, COSPAR, IUGG/IAMAP (past Chair ICC). **Career:** Asst Prof. Inst.of Geophys. UCLA 1949–52; Head Planetary Scis Dept, The Rand Corpn 1952–64; Assoc.Dir, Lab.Head & Sr Sci.NCAR 1964–87; Adv.to Sec.-Gen. WMO & Org.of First WCC, Geneva 1978–9. **Achievements:** conceived & oversaw dev.of first met.satellite 'TIROS' 1; developed radioactive fallout prediction technique; studied dynamics of upper atmos.; deeply involved in res.on theory of climate change & human impact on climate. **Memberships:** F.AMS (past Pres.), F.AGU (past Pres. Met.Section), F.AAAS (past Chair Atmos.& Hydr.Section), Sigma Xi. **Awards:** Spec.Award (AMS) 1961, nat.Decoration for Exceptional Civilian Service 1966, Commem.Medal (Soviet Geophys.Cttee) 1985, Cert.of Appreciation (USDC) 1985, Spec. Citation (Gdn Club of Amer.) 1988. **Publications:** *The Atmospheres of Mars & Venus* (co-Author) 1961, *Climate Change & Soc.* (co-Author) 1981; 150+ papers & conf.proc. Indiff.to pers.pub., favours news media support. **Languages:** English, French (weak), German (read). Further details may be obtained from *Amer.Men & Women of Sci.* 1994. Willing to act as consult.etc. **Address:** 445 College Avenue, Boulder, Colorado 80302, USA. **Tel.**(home) 1 303 443 5086.

KENCHINGTON, Richard Ambrose. Marine & coastal resources' management & conservation, marine sciences. Senior Director of External Services. *B.*29 March 1943, Barton on Sea, Hampshire, England, UK. Australian, British. *M.*Carol Elizabeth: 2 *s.* **Education:** King's School Canterbury; QMC BSc(Spec.) (Hons) (Marine Ecol.) 1965, U.of Wales MSc(Marine Biol.) 1968. **Experience:** res.— reef ecol., Crown of Thorns Starfish, large-area reef survey; tech.— strat.planning & mgmt of GBRMPA, cons.& multiple use of marine envt & resources; consult.— coastal mgmt & instnl dev.in Ecuador/Galápagos, Maldives, SE Asia & Pacific Islands. **Career:** Sr Tutor in Marine Biol. James Cook U.of N.Qld 1968–72, Res.F. Crown of Thorns Starfish *(Acanthaster planci)* 1972–7, Dir of Planning, Mgmt & Res. GBRMPA 1977–90, Sec. Coastal Zone Inquiry, Resource Assessment Comm. 1990–93, Sr Dir Ext.Services, GBRMPA 1993–. **Achievements:** field distribn of Crown of Thorns Starfish, declaration, zoning & mgmt of GBRMPA, dev.of policy & guidelines for cons.& multiple-use mgmt of trop.marine envts. **Memberships:** IUCN CEL, ACRS, EIA, NELA. **Awards:** Marine Policy F'ship (WHOI), RAPI, Qld Bicentennial Award of Excellence in Envl Planning & Design. **Publications:** *Coral Reef Mgmt Handbook* (co-Author) 1987, *Managing Marine Envts* 1990, *Guidelines for Establishing Marine Prot.Areas* (co-Author) 1991. Indiff.to pers.pub., favours news media support. **Languages:** English; French & Spanish (functional). Willing to act as consult.etc. **Address:** Great Barrier Reef Marine Park Authority, POB 791, Canberra City, ACT 2601, Australia. **Tel.**(office) 61 6 247 0211, (home) 61 6 251 5597; **fax** 61 6 247 5761.

KENDREW, Sir John Cowdery. Molecular biology, national & international science policy. Retired, Officer of IUPAB & ICSU. *B.*24 March 1917, Oxf., England, UK. British. **Education:** Trinity Coll.Camb. BA 1939, MA 1942, PhD 1949, ScD 1962. **Experience:** res.in molecular biol., active in nat.& intl sci.policy. **Career:** Dep.Dir, MRC Lab.of Molecular Biol. Camb. 1946–75; DG Euro.Molecular Biol.Lab. 1975–82; Pres. St John's Coll.Oxf.1981–7; Pres. ICSU 1983–8. **Memberships:** F.RS, var.foreign & hon. **Awards:** Nobel Prize 1962, Hon.F. Trinity Coll.& Peterhouse (Camb.) and St John's Coll.(Oxf.), var.hon.degrees. **Languages:** English; French, German, & Italian (moderately-fluent spoken, hesitant written). Further details may be obtained from Brit.*Who's Who* 1996, *Intl Who's Who* 1995. Willing to act as a consult. **Address:** The Old Guildhall, 4 Church Lane, Linton, Cambridge CB1 6JX, England, UK. **Tel.**(home) & **fax** 44 1223 891545.

KENNEDY, Professor Dr James Joseph. Natural resources: environmental policy & administration. Assistant Dean. *B.*11 June 1940, Philadelphia, PA, USA. American. *M.*Kathleen. **Education:** Penn.SU BS(Forest Mgmt) 1962, MS(Natural Resource Econ.) 1966; VPI, PhD (Natural Resource Policy) 1971. **Experience:** teaching — natural resources' planning, policy, econ.& admin., urban & regnl planning, social for., human dimensions of natural resources' mgmt, orgnl behaviour; admin.— Asst Dean & Dept Head. **Career:** Field Forester, USDA Forest Service 1961–4; Asst.Prof.of Natural Resource Planning & Econ. VPI, 1969–71; Res.Prof. & Asst Dean, Utah SU 1971– (sabbs at NZ Forest Service 1977–8, Trinity Coll.Dublin 1982–3, Wageningen U.1986–7, USDI Bur.of Land Mgmt (as Asst to Dir) 1994–6). **Achievements:** initial basic res.on social values in natural resources' mgmt, on agency values & reward systems, on professional dev.and orgnl behaviour in natural resources agencies. **Awards:** Sr Fulbright Scholar (Trinity Coll. Dublin) 1982–3; Nat.NZ Res.F.1977–8; Sr Res.Scholar (Wageningen U.) 1986–7; selected Outstanding Educator (Utah SU) 1974, 1976, 1986. **Publications:** five chapters & c.40 articles on managing natural resources as of social value, orgnl values, and in reward systems, professional & career dev.in natural resource agencies, or for natural resource symbolism. **Languages:** English, Spanish. Willing to act as consult.etc. **Address:** College of Natural Resources, Utah State University, Logan, Utah 84332-5215, USA. **Tel.**(office) 1 801 750 2573, (home) 1 801 753 2589; **fax** 1 801 797 4040.

KENNEDY, Dr Robert. Epidemiology & control of foliar fungal pathogens of Brassicas, Alliums, *Citrus,* & Cashew; control of post-harvest molds and mycotoxin production in stored-grain systems. Senior Research Scientist. *B.*6 Oct.1958, Ballymena, NI. British. **Education:** Queen's U. (Belfast) BSc 1981, MSc 1983; U.of Sydney PhD 1988. **Experience:** Ed.*Annals of Applied Biol.*Supplement *Tests of Agrochemicals & Cultivars*, Brit.Council-funded Res.F.(U.of Rome) 1990, EEC Res.Con-sult.at U.of Mysore 1990–91, ODA Res.Con-sult.at Cashew Res.Prog.Tanzania 1993–4. **Career:** Postdoctl Res.F. Reading U. 1987–9 and Rothamsted Experimental Station (AFRC) 1984–92; Res.Leader, Dept of Plant Path.& Weed Sci. HRI 1992–. **Achievements:** res.on control of fungal diseases in agricl systems with emphasis on reductions in pesticide-use through disease forecasting, dev.of cultural techniques for control of root diseases, and post-harvest storage moulds in developing countries. **Memberships:** APPS, AAB, BSPP, BMS. **Awards:** NI Postgrad.Scholarship (Queen's U.) 1981, F.H.Loxton Postgrad.Scholarship (U.of Sydney) 1983. **Publications:** num.journal & conf.papers and abstracts. Indiff.to pers.pub. & news media support. **Languages:** English, French, Irish. Willing to act as consult. **Address:** Department of Plant Pathology and Weed Science, Horticulture Research International, Wellesbourne, Warwickshire CV35 9EF, England, UK. **Tel.**(office) 44 1789 470382, (home) 44 1926 408496; **fax** 44 1789 470552.

KENT, Dr Paul Welberry. Biochemistry research, higher education. University Governor.

*B.*19 April 1923, Doncaster, England, UK. British. *M.*Rosemary E.B.: 3 *s.*, *d.* **Education:** U.of Birmingham BSc 1944, PhD 1947; U.of Oxf. MA 1951, DPhil 1953, DSc 1966. **Experience:** consult.to var.pharmaceutical cos, memb.of Res. Adv.Cttee on Cystic Fibrosis (1971–82), JP. **Career:** Lect. Birmingham U. 1946–50; Student & Tutor of Christ Church Oxf.1956– (Emer.1972–) & Dr Lee's Reader in Chem. U.of Oxf.1956–72; Master, Van Mildert Coll. Durham 1972–82; Vis.Prof.(USA & Canada); Gov. OBU 1983–. **Achievements:** orgn of Oxf.Intl Symposia (1972–87) for interdisc. exchange between Scis & the Humanities with substantial envl content, contributing to preserv.of rural amenities in & around Oxf. esp.Christ Church Meadow. **Memberships:** F.RSC 1950, Biochem.Soc., Sigma Xi. **Awards:** Rolleston Prize 1952, Medal of Société de Chémie Biologique 1969, Bundesverdienstkreuz 1970, Hon.D.Litt (Drury Coll.) 1973, Hon.F. Canterbury Coll. (Ontario) 1976, Hon.DSc. (OBU) 1991. **Publications:** *Intl Aspects of the Provision of Med. Care* 1976, *Resources, Envt and the Future* (co-Author) 1982. Indiff.to pers. pub., cautious about news media support. **Languages:** English, French (fair), German (fair). Willing to act as consult.etc. **Address:** 18 Arnolds Way, Cumnor Hill, Oxford OX2 9JB, England, UK. **Tel.**(office) 44 1865 224808, (home) 44 1865 862087.

KERN, Berndt. Saving tropical forests, promoting environmental education, biological research, reforestation, local development & sustainable agroforestry, raising awareness for Nature at home and in the tropics. Network Executive Officer, Coordinator, & Treasurer. *B.*16 Aug.1935, Hamburg, Germany. Swedish. *M.* Eha Kern *qv*: 2 *d.* **Education:** Elen Volksdorf Sec.Sch., Nordendalskolan Sch.of Nursing. **Experience:** nursing, consult.to schools, coopn with local non-profit orgns. **Career:** ladies' hairdresser 1950–79, medical help 1979–82, Nurse 1982–92; co-Founder 1987, Officer 1992–, Barnens Regnskog; Exec.Officer, Coord. & Treasurer (in Sweden), Intl Children's Rainforest Network 1987–. **Achievements:** creation of Intl Children's Rainforests Network 1987, and first Children's Rain-forest (forest reserve in Monteverde, Costa Rica) 1989; bldg of bridge between two Nat.Parks in Costa Rica thus forming a 33-km chain of Nat.Parks; assisted to create a lowland rainforest reserve (Bilsa) in Ecuador, a high forest reserve (Guanderra) in the Andes, and to enlarge Jatun Sacha reserve on the Napo R., Upper Amazon; promotion of enlargement of Sierra de la Minas reserve, Guatemala. **Membership:** Intl Children's Rain-forests Network. **Awards:** Barnens Regnskog has received several awards from Swedish Envl Party 1990, Året Runt (Envl Prize) 1990, Svenska Dagbladets (for Social Innovation) 1990 & Elmias Fndn 1990, and a Goldman Envl Prize 1991. **Publications:** *Frog Chirps* (in Swedish) which appears six times a yr 1988–. Favours pers.pub.& news media support. **Languages:** English, German, Swedish. Further details may be obtained from *GEO* (March 1990) and *Anuario de los Hechos* (Spain) 1991. Willing to act as consult.etc. **Address:** The Children's Rain-forest of Sweden (Barnens Regnskog), PL 4471, 137 94 Västerhaninge, Sweden. **Tel.& fax** (office & home) 46 8 530 23173.

KERN, Mrs Eha. Saving tropical forests, promoting environmental education, biological research, reforestation, local development & sustainable agroforestry, raising awareness for Nature at home and in the tropics. Organization Chairman, School Teacher. *B.*1947, Hultsfred, Sweden. Swedish. *M.*Bernd Kern *qv:* 2 *d.* **Education:** Bandhagens Läroverk Sec.Sch. **Experience:** work concerned with Barnens Regnskog has been self-learned, consult.for schools, coopn with local non-profit orgns. **Career:** elementary sch.teacher 1977–; co-Founder & Chairman, Barnens Regnskog (The Children's Rain-forest of Sweden) 1987–. **Achievements:** creation of Intl Children's Rainforests Network 1987, and first Children's Rain-forest (forest reserve in Monteverde, Costa Rica) 1989; bldg of bridge between two Nat. Parks in Costa Rica thus forming a 33-km chain of Nat.Parks; assisted to create a lowland rainforest reserve (Bilsa) in Ecuador, a high forest reserve (Guanderra) in the Andes, and to enlarge Jatun Sacha reserve on the Napo R., Upper Amazon; promotion of enlargement of Sierra de la Minas reserve, Guatemala. **Membership:** Intl Children's Rainforests Network. **Awards:** Barnens Regnskog has received several awards from Swedish Envl Party 1990, Året Runt (Envl Prize) 1990, Svenska Dagbladets (Social Innovation) 1990 & Elmias Fndn 1990, and a Goldman Envl Prize 1991. **Publications:** *Frog Chirps* (in Swedish) which appears six times a yr 1988–. Favours pers.pub.& news media support. **Languages:** English (spoken), Estonian (spoken), Spanish (weak), Swedish. Furthers details may be obtained from *GEO* (March 1990) and *Anuario de los Hechos* (Spain) 1991. Willing to act as consult.etc. **Address:** The Children's Rain-forest of Sweden (Barnens Regnskog), PL 4471, 137 94 Västerhaninge, Sweden. **Tel.& fax** (office & home) 46 8 530 23173.

KESSLER, Dr Edwin. Meteorology, agriculture, environment. Consultant, Adjunct Professor of Geography & Meteorology. *B.*2 Dec. 1928, New York City, NY, USA. American. *M.*Lottie Catherine: 2 *s.* **Education:** Columbia U. AB 1950, MIT SM(Met.) 1952, MIT & Harvard U. ScD(Met.& Astron.) 1957. **Experience:** 40 yrs' res.& dev., 30 yrs' middle-mgmt admin., 20 yrs' farm ops, 30 yrs as envl activist, 250 reports & pubns. **Career:** Weather Radar Branch, Air Force Camb.Res.Labs 1954–61; Occasional Lect. Boston U. during 1950s; Sr Res.Sci.1961–2, Dir Atmos.Phys.Div.1962–4, Travelers Res.Center; Adjunct Prof. U.of Oklahoma 1964–; Vis.Prof. MIT 1975–6 & Vis.Lect.

McGill U. 1980; Dir Nat.Severe Storms Lab. NOAA 1964–86 when retired. **Achievements:** mgmt & op.of 220-acres organic farm, experiments with winter prod.of vegetables in cold frames & with digested sludge to restore eroded prairie; extensive experimental planting of Bald Cypress *(Taxodium distichum)* trees in stream bottoms to control erosion. **Memberships:** AMS (F., Nat.Counc., num.cttees), Γ.AAAS, AIAA, RMS, Space Shuttle Weather Forecasting Adv.Panel 1986, Scientific Progs Eval.Cttee NCAR 1989, Audubon Soc.(Cleveland County Chapter), Sierra Club (Red Earth Group), Oklahoma Acad.of Sci., Common Cause Oklahoma (Chair), Oklahoma Native Plant Soc., Oklahoma Wildlife Fedn, Norman Recycling Assn, Inst.for Alternative Agric., AFHVS, AWMA, ACLU. **Award:** Cleveland Abbe Award (AMS). **Publications:** *On the Distribn & Continuity of Water Substance in Atmos.Circulations* (Ed. AMS award-winning monogr.) 1969, Model of precipitation & vertical air currents 1974, Duststorms from the US high plains in late winter 1977 — search for cause and implications 1978, Documentation of a 2,4-D accident 1980, Low-level windshear alert systems and Doppler radar in aircraft terminal ops 1990, Carbon burning, the greenhouse effect, and public policy 1991; num.other j., proc., & conf., papers. Favours pers. pub.& news media support. **Languages:** English, Spanish (read). Willing to act as a consult. **Address:** 1510 Rosemont Drive, Norman, Oklahoma 73072, USA. **Tel.**(home) 1 405 360 2194; **fax** 1 405 360 3246.

KETCHUM, Robert Glenn. Environmental photography & writing. Curator of Photography, Conservancy Councillor. *B.*12 Jan.1947, Los Angeles, CA, USA. **Education:** UCLA BA *cum laude* 1970, Calif.Inst.of the Arts MFA (Photography) 1974. **Experience:** world-wide field res.for seven major pubns, num.museum exhibitions, direct lobbying efforts in US Cong., nationally-recognized lect. **Career:** Exec.Dir, Los Angeles Center for Photographic Studies 1975–81; Curator of Photography, Nat.Park Fndn 1980–, Bd of Councillors, Amer.Land Conservancy 1993–. **Achievements:** helped to pass largest timber reform legis.in US hist., awards (*see* below). **Memberships:** Explorer's Club (F.Nat. 1988), Alaska Cons.Fndn (Bd of Trustees 1994–). **Awards:** Global 500 Roll of Honour (UNEP) 1991, Alumni Award (UCLA) 1993, Ansel Adams Award for Cons.Photography 1989. **Publications:** *The Hudson R.and the Highlands* 1985, *The Tongass: Alaska's Vanishing Rainforest* 1987, *Overlooked in Amer.* 1991, *The Legacy of Wildness: The Photographs of Robert Glenn Ketchum* 1993. Favours pers. pub.& news media support. **Language:** English. **Address:** 696 Stone Canyon Road, Los Angeles, California 90077, USA. **Tel.**(office & home) 1 310 472 3681; **fax** 1 310 440 2654.

KETO, Dr Aila. Nature conservation especially of rain-forests, world heritage, ecologically-sustainable use of native forests. Society President, Director. *B*.14 Mar.1943, Tully, Australia. Australian. *M*.Dr Keith Scott (Dir, Rainforest Cons. Soc.): *s*. **Education:** U.of Qld BSc(Hons) 1966, MSc 1970, PhD 1980, all in biochem. **Experience:** res.& teaching in biochem., full-time involvement in vol.cons.movement 1981–, memb.of num.cttees, public speaking, Scientific Adv.& Consult. **Career:** Tutor in Biochem. U. of Qld –1979; Pres.Rainforest Cons.Soc.1982–; Dir, Wet Tropics Mgmt Auth.1990–; State Counc. 1983–9, Exec.Counc.1987–9, ACF; Exec.Memb. QCC 1982–4, 1993–. **Achievements:** Cons.Rep. on Commonwealth Govt WG on Rainforest Cons.that gained $22.5 m.for a nat.rainforest cons.prog.; compiled major reports on natural heritage values of trop.rainforests of NE Australia (Wet Tropics of Qld); led nat.campaign for prot.of Wet Tropics which led to logging ban in 1987 and World Heritage listing in 1988; led cons.grops in Comm.of Inquiry into Fraser Is.and Gt Sandy Regn that led to cessation of logging in area and World Heritage listing of Fraser Is., developed case against application of N.Qld 'selective harvesting' model to other trop.rain-forests, successfully campaigned to stop all rainforest logging in Qld (which contains the major proportion of Australia's rain-forests); prepared influential submission to govt on Nature cons.& energy issues, and a nat.park proposal for part of Cape York peninsula. **Memberships:** ACF, Fraser Is.Defenders' Orgn, QCC, Rainforest Cons.Soc. **Awards:** Global 500 Roll of Honour (UNEP) 1988, Bicentennial Award (Envt) (The Broken Hill Proprietary Co.Ltd) 1988, Fred M.Packer Intl Parks Merit Award (IUCN) 1992, Advance Australia Fndn Award 1988, Hon.Life Memb. ACF 1991, Spirit of Achievement (Avon) 1993, Officer of the Order of Australia 1994. **Publications:** *Trop. Rainforests of N.Qld: Their Cons. Sig*.1986, chapters & book contribns, num. papers, Ed. *Liane*. Favours pers.pub.& news media support as part of furthering the cons. cause. **Languages:** English, Finnish (spoken). Willing to act as consult.etc. **Address:** Rainforest Conservation Society, 19 Colorado Avenue, Bardon, Queensland 4065, Australia. **Tel.**61 7 368 1318; **fax** 61 7 368 3938.

KHAN, Niaz Ahmad. Industrial environmental pollution control, solid/hazardous waste evaluation, disposal, and management, environmental studies, noise assessment, industrial & sewage wastewater treatment & disposal. Senior Environmental Officer. *B*.24 April 1954, Gujranwala, Pakistan. Pakistani. *M*.Perveen: *s*., 2 *d*.; *B*.G.S.Khan (retired Chem.Engr). **Education:** U.of the Punjab (Lahore), BSc(Hons)(Chem.) (Dist.) 1976; UET, BS(Chem.Eng.)(Dist.) 1980; APTI, postgrad. courses 1989–90. **Experience:** 14+ yrs resolving envl problems of major primary industries with emphasis on air, water, solid & hazardous wastes, and noise consult.on tech.envl matters. **Career:** Envl Engr, Envl Resources Techs/ Amer.Arabian Techs (USA)

1982–7 and Al-Jubail Fertilizer Co.(Samad) 1987–9; Supervisor of Envl Prog.of Jubail Industrial City, Royal Comm.1989–95; Sr Envl Officer, Free Zone Industrial Ops Control Dept, Jebel Ali Free Zone/Dubai Ports Auths 1995–. **Achievements:** highest envl mgmt position in the City after ten yrs of obtaining quals; presented paper at intl envl conf.in Bahrain about Gulf oil-spill (Feb. 1992); was nominated for UNEP's Sasakawa Envt Prize 1993. **Memberships:** PEC (Life, Registered Professional Engr), AIChE, SEE, ACS, AWWA, ASSE, NGWA (USA), AWMA, Instn of Envl Engrs (UK), SETAC, NAEP, IAIA, CEP. **Awards:** Gold Medallist (UET Students' Union) 1980, Cert.of Appreciation from US Army during Gulf War. **Publications:** incl. Envl Noise Poll.Control in the Kingdom of Saudi Arabia 1989, *Industry & Envt* (vol.2) 1989. Favours pers.pub.& news media support. **Languages:** Arabic, English, Urdu. Willing to act as consult.etc. **Address:** Jebel Ali Free Zone Authority/Dubai Ports Authority, POB 17000, Dubai, United Arab Emirates. **Tel.**971 4 804 0292; **fax** 971 4 818857.

KHANDELWAL, Dr Kailash Chand. Biomethanation, biofertilizers, rural energy planning, improved cookstoves, animal energy, organic farming, rural sanitation. Director. *B*.1 Jan. 1947, Jaipur, Raj., India. Indian. *M*. Sushila. **Education:** U.of Udaipur BSc(Agric.) 1966, IARI MSc(Microbiol.) 1968, PhD (Microbiol.) 1972; U.of Qld, training on Microbial Culture Collection 1983; Chengdu Centre, Min.of Agric. (China), Biogas training 1985. **Experience:** res.— microbiol.decomposition of rural & city wastes, biogas prod.; consult.— biogas, improved cookstoves, training personnel in Afghanistan, Bhutan, Malta; teaching gen. microbiol.& soil microbiol.for five yrs. **Career:** Lect. Haryana Agricl U.1971–6; Asst & Dep.Commissioner 1976–82, PSO 1982–7 Min. of Agric.; Dir Min.of Non-conventional Energy Sources, Govt of India 1987–. **Achievements:** assisting Govt in formulating policies; implementing massive progs for biogas, animal energy, and rural sanitation; arranging tech.training and R&D support; coordn with nat.& intl NGOs. **Memberships:** SESI, VC Biogas Tech.Cttee of World Energy Conf.1987–9. **Awards:** Nat. F'ship of Min.of Human Resources' Dev., Gold Medal (IARI). **Publications:** *Biogas Tech. Practical Handbook* 1986, *Biogas Sci.& Utilization* 1992; 19 scientific papers, 44 popular articles, reports, bulletins. Favours pers.pub.& news media support. **Language:** English. Willing to act as consult.etc. to formulate & evaluate renewable energy schemes. **Address:** H-12 Andrewsganj Extension, New Delhi 110 049, Delhi, India. **Tel.**(office) 91 11 436 0359, (home) 91 11 646 7198; **fax** 91 11 436 1298.

KHANNA, Professor Dr Purushottam. Environmental science & technology. Director. *B*. 14 July 1947, Sagar, MP, India. Indian. *M*. Aparna: *d*. **Education:** Jabalpur U. BE (Hons)

1964; Roorkee U. ME(Civ.Eng.) 1966, PhD (Envl Eng.) 1972. **Experience:** 26 yrs' teaching, res.& consult.in envl sci.& engg incl.six yrs' res.admin. **Career:** Prof.in Envl Sci.& Engg and Director, NEERI. **Achievements:** substantial changes in policy & practices for envl rejuvenation & preserv.in India due to work carried out in envl systems design, modelling & optimization, envl biotech., envl impact & risk assessment, and envl policy analysis. **Memberships:** IAWQ, IAEM (Pres.), F.IAE, IIE (F.& Council Memb.). **Awards:** Engg Personality (IIE) 1992, Envl Preserv.& Poll.Control (FICCI) 1990, Envl Engg Design (IIE) 1989, Poddar Mem.for Envl Poll.Control (Bharat Chamber of Commerce) 1986, IAEC Golden Jubilee 1980; Res.Awards (Roorkee U.) 1974 & 1977, (IWWA) 1974, 1979, 1980. **Publications:** two chapters + over 150 consult.reports and 170+ res.& conf.papers. Dislikes pers.pub., favours news media support. **Languages:** English, German (basic), Hindi. Willing to act as consult.etc. **Address:** National Environmental Engineering Research Institute, Nehru Marg, Nagpur 440 020, Maharashtra, India. **Tel.** (office) 91 712 523893, (home) 91 712 525222; **fax** 91 712 522725.

KHARIN, Professor Dr Nikolai. Desert plant ecology, conservation of Nature. Centre Deputy Director, Chief Scientific Consultant. *B*.7 Sept. 1926, Dolisichi, Bryansk Prov., Russia. Russian. *M*.Aza Kiriltseva (M.Biol., forester). *d*. **Education:** Bryansk Forest Inst. Forest Engr 1951; Russian AS, M.Agric.1959; Turkmenistan AS (Ashgabat), Dr of Biol.1969. **Experience:** lecturing, expedns to Mongolia 1986–7 & African countries 1988–90, Memb. Intl Panel of Experts on Desert.(UN, Geneva) 1993–4. **Career:** Soldier in 318 Infantry Regiment 1943–5; Aerial Forest Surveyor, Forest Mgmt Expedn (Leningrad now St Petersburg) 1951–4; Lab.Head, Forest Cartography, Inst.of Forest and Wood (Krasnoyarsk) 1960–64; Lab.Head, Aerial Photo Interpretation 1964–78, Prof.of Bot.& Lab. Head, Remote Sensing 1980–87, Chief Scientific Consult.1995–, Desert Res.Inst. (Ashgabat); Head Plant Ecol. Soviet Soil and Ecol. Expedn (Libya) 1978–80; Dep.Dir, ESCAP/ UNEP Centre for Training & Res.1987–. **Achievements:** 40 yrs' basic res.in ecol.& Nature cons.in Siberia, c.Asia, Mongolia, and African countries. **Memberships:** Turkmenistan AS (Academician), Turkmenistan Botl & Geogl Socs. **Awards:** Medal of Bravery (USSR) 1945, Order of Gt Patriotic War (USSR) 1985. **Publications:** 20 books incl.*Glossary of Terms on Desert Envt and Land Reclamation* 1978, co-Ed.*Problems of Desert Dev.*1971–, 240 scientific papers. Favours pers.pub.& news media support. **Languages:** English, French, German, Russian; Spanish (basic). Willing to act as consult.etc. **Address:** Desert Research Institute, 15 Gogol Street, 744000 Ashgabat, Turkmenistan. **Tel.**(office) 7 363 2 296067, (home) 7 363 2 431294; **fax** 7 363 2 257364 or 253716.

KHOSHOO, Dr Triloki Nath. Biodiversity, biomass energy, wasteland development, environmental management. Jawaharlal Nehru Fellow. *B*.7 April 1927, Srinagar, Kashmir, India. Indian. *M*.Mohini: 2 *s*. **Education:** Punjab U.at Lahore BSc(Hons) 1945, MSc (Hons) 1947, and at Chandigarh, PhD 1958. **Experience:** 46 yrs' R&D in genetics, breeding, ecorestoration, and biodiv.cons.& utilization. **Career:** Sr Lect. Punjab U.Chandigarh 1948–62; Head, Postgrad. Dept of Bot. J&K U.Srinagar; Asst Dir 1964–74, Dep.Dir 1974–6, Nat.Botanic Gdn (CSIR) Lucknow; Dir, Nat. Botl Res.Inst.(CSIR) Lucknow 1976–82; Sec.to Govt of India Dept of Envt 1982–5; Disting. Sci.CSIR, New Delhi 1985–90; Jawaharlal Nehru F.1991–. **Memberships:** F.of INSA New Delhi, IAS Bangalore, NAS Allahabad (Hon.), Instn of Engrs, ISGPB, IBS, IAAS, & TWAS; Pres.of Bot.Section ISCA, Bio-energy Soc.of India, NAS, ISGPB, & ISTS; ISCA (Gen.-Pres.), IUFRO (past Dep.Chairman, WG on Cytogenetics), UNEP (VC & Governing Council), IUBS (Nat.Chairman), SCOPE (New Delhi); Chairman of Task Forces on Biomass Prod.and Biodiv.and of Scientific Adv.Cttee of Dept of Biotech. Govt of India, Memb.of Scientific Adv.Cttee to the Union Cabinet, Intl Task Force on Trop.For., WRI (Intl F., Council & Adv.Bd), IUCN (Plant Adv.Group), ILEC (Scientific Cttee), UNESCO (Adv.Cttee to DG), IGBP INSA (Nat.Cttee). **Awards:** Prince of Wales' Gold Medal in Biol.1942, Rafi Ahmad Kidwai Medal and Prize (ICAR) 1977, Birbal Sahni Gold Medal (IBS) 1982, Seth Mem.Medal (ISTS) 1983, Ramdeo Misra Medal (IES) 1984, Dayawati Vira Medal (Agri-hort.Soc.of India) 1985, Sanjay Gandhi Award 1986, Disting. Service Award (ISC) 1988, Om Prakash Bhasin Fndn Award 1989, Disting.Service Award (ISGPB) 1991, Felicitation by Bochasanwasi Shri Aksharpurushotam Sanstha 1992, Award by Pres.of India 1992. **Publications:** Author of six and Ed.of 11 books incl.*Mahatma Gandhi: An Apostle of Applied Human Ecol.1995*; *c*.209 res. papers. Dislikes pers.pub., favours good news media support. **Languages:** English, Hindi. Willing to act as consult.etc. **Address:** Tata Energy Research Institute, 9 Jor Bagh, New Delhi 110 003, Delhi, India. **Tel.**(office) 91 11 462 2246, (home) 91 11 684 9625; **fax** 91 11 462 1770.

KHOSLA, Dr Ashok. Development of innovative technologies for basic human needs, environment planning & management, impact assessment & community management institutions. President. *B*.31 March 1940, Lahore, India. Indian. *M*.Rekha. **Education:** U.of Camb. BA(Natural Scis) 1962, Harvard U. MA 1964, PhD(Experimental Phys.) 1970. **Experience:** estab.& headed first Office of Envt of Govt of India; admin.as one-time Dir of INFO-TERRA; adv./consult.to Brundtland Comm., World Bank, UN agencies etc. **Career:** Lect. Harvard U.1962–71, Govt Official (New Delhi) 1972–6, Intl Civil Servant 1976–82, Pres.

Dev.Alternatives 1982–. **Achievements:** setting-up a govt agency for envt subs.to become a Min., of Global Info.System on Envt (INFO-TERRA), of major sust.dev.NGO (Dev.Alternatives). **Memberships:** Governing bodies of IUCN, WWF Intl, TVE (London), Centre for Our Common Future (Geneva), UNEP/IETC, SATIS & UIA. **Awards:** UNEP Global 500 Roll of Honour 1992, Order of the Golden Ark. **Publications:** The Survival Equation (co-Ed.) 1971, Sci.& tech.for sust.dev.1982, Decision support systems for sust.dev.1987; 150 others. Indiff.to pers.pub.& news media support. **Languages:** English, French, Hindi, Punjabi. **Address:** Development Alternatives, B-32 Tara Crescent, Qutab Institutional Area, New Delhi 110 016, Delhi, India. **Tel.**(office) 91 11 66 5370 or 657938, (home) 91 11 605835; **fax** 91 11 686 6031.

KHUSH, Dr Gurdev S. Plant breeding, genetics, cytogenetics, biotechnology. Principal Plant Breeder & Division Head. *B.*22 Aug. 1935, Roorkee, Punjab, India. Indian. *M.*Harwant Kaur: *s.*Ranjiv S.(molecular biol.), 3 *d.* **Education:** Punjab U. BSc(Agric.) 1955, UCD PhD(Genetics) 1960. **Experience:** cytotaxonomy of genus *Secale*, cytogenetics of tomato, breeding & genetics of rice; developed 80 varieties of rice which are planted to more than 50 million ha and started the green revolution in rice farming; consult.on rice breeding progs to India, Indonesia, China, Thailand, Vietnam, Bangladesh & Sri Lanka. **Career:** Res.Asst, UCD 1960–67; Rice Breeder 1967–72, Prin. Plant Breeder & Head, Div.of Plant Breeding, Genetics & Biochem.1972–, IRRI. **Achievements:** developed (as leader) high-yielding, disease- & insect-resistant, varieties of rice which are widely planted in Asia, Africa, & Latin Amer., can be grown without insecticides & fungicides, and contribute markedly to envl prot. **Memberships:** US NAS (Foreign Assoc.), TWAS, INSA, IAS, IAAS, GSA, CSSA. **Awards:** Borlaug Award 1977, Japan Prize 1987, Intl Agron.Award 1989, Emil A. Mrak Award 1990, Hon.Doct.(PAU) 1987. **Publications:** *Cytogenetics of Aneuploids* 1973, Plant Breeding Lectures 1986, *Rice Biotech.*(Ed.) 1991; 120 res.papers. Indiff.to pers. pub., favours news media support. **Languages:** English, Punjabi. Willing to act as consult.etc. **Address:** International Rice Research Institute, POB 933, Manila, Philippines. **Tel.**63 2 818 1926; **fax** 63 2 818 2087.

KIEW, Dr Bong-Heang. Biological conservation in tropical Southeast Asia, environmental impact assessment. Associate Professor. *B.*3 Aug.1944, Kajang, Selangor, Malaysia. Malaysian. *M.*Dr Helen Margaret Ruth (plant taxonomy, cons.): *s., d.* **Education:** U.of Malaya, BSc(Hons)(Zool.) 1969, PhD(Zool.) 1974. **Experience:** res., lecturing, consults incl.Hon. Scientific Consult.to WWF Malaysia 1978–82 and to IUCN SSC 1982–5, 1987 & 1990.

Career: Tutor 1969–74, Lect.1974–84, Assoc. Prof.1984–, U.of Malaya. **Achievement:** involved in Malaysia's cons.effort. **Memberships:** F.LS, ATB, ISEE, FMNH(Field Assoc.). **Award:** Memb.Emer.IUCN SSC. **Publications:** *Malaysian Mammals* (co-Author) 1988, *Endau Rompin — a Malaysian Heritage* 1988, *Malaysian Frogs & Toads* 1989, Wildlife 1993, Endau Rompin 1993; num.papers, consult. reports, newspaper & magazine articles. Accepts pers.pub.& news media support. **Languages:** English, Malay. **Address:** Department of Zoology, University of Malaya, Kuala Lumpur 59106, Malaysia. **Tel.**603 755 5466 ext.368; **fax** 603 757 3661.

KILMARTIN, Marianne P. Hydrology & soil development of lands reclaimed after surface coal-mining in Wales. Tutor/Counsellor, Postgraduate Student & Occasional Lecturer in Geography. *B.*25 Aug.1946, Arundel, Sussex, England, UK. *M.*Martin J.Haigh *qv: s.*, 2 *d.* **Education:** Open U. BA(Social Sci.) 1980, Oxford Poly. Dip.Adv.Studies 1987. **Experience:** seven yrs' res.on hydr.& soils of reclaimed surface coal-mine lands, five yrs' teaching at u.level. **Career:** Res.Student, OBU 1986–; part-time Lect. U.of Maryland (Europe) 1990–91; Tutor 1991– & Admissions Couns., Open U.1993–. **Membership:** BGRG. **Publications:** Land Reclamation: Policies & Practices (co-Author) 1988, Hydr.of reclaimed opencast coal-mined land: a review 1989. Positive re.pers. pub.& news media support. **Language:** English. **Address:** Geography Unit, Oxford Brookes University, Oxford OX3 0BP, England, UK. **Tel.**44 1865 483750; **fax** 44 1865 483937.

KIM, Professor Dr Ke Chung. Systematic/evolutionary biology (taxonomy, coevolution of arthropods), biodiversity conservation. Professor of Entomology & Curator, Director. *B.*7 March 1934, Seoul, Korea. American. *M.* Young Hee (biol., microtomist): *s.*Stuart K. (dev.biol., parasitologist), *d.*Sally A. (biological psych.). **Education:** Seoul Nat.U. BS 1956, U.of Montana MA 1959, U.of Minn. PhD 1964. **Experience:** widespread res.& consult.in entomol., forensics, envl & cons.prog., systematics of lice (Anoplura), flies, coevol.of parasitic arthropods, community ecol.; chaired num. scientific mtgs & cttees. **Career:** Res.Assoc. U.of Minn.1964–8; Asst, Assoc.then full Prof.of Entomol.1968–, Dir Center for Biodiv.Res. 1989–, Penn.SU. **Achievements:** Chair, Intl Adv. Council for Biosystematic Services in Entomol.1985–92, Entomol. Collections Network 1989–90, and Bioreserves Tech.Cttee of Penn. Biol.Survey 1991–3; Vis. Prof. U.of Heidelberg & Seoul Nat.U. 1975–6; co-Chair, Steering Cttee, Penn.Biodiv.Cons. Strat.1992–4. **Memberships:** ESA (Chair, Section A), ESW, SSB, SCB, Sigma Xi, others. **Awards:** Fulbright Hays Lect./Researcher Award 1975, L.O. Howard Disting.Achievement Award (ESA e.branch) 1988, Fulbright Sr Scholar Award 1993–4. **Publications:** eight books incl.*Coevol.of Parasitic Arthropods & Mammals* 1985, *The Sucking Lice of N.Amer.* 1986, *Evol.of Insect Pests* 1993; 17 book chapters, 135 scientific papers. Favours pers.pub.& news media support. **Languages:** English, Korean, Japanese. Further details may be obtained from *Who's Who in Sci., Who's Who in Amer.*(recent edns). Willing to act as consult.etc. **Address:** Center for Biodiversity Research, Environmental Resources Research Institute, The Pennsylvania State University, Land & Water Research Building, University Park, Pennsylvania 16802, USA. **Tel.**(office) 1 814 863 0159, (home) 1 814 234 1718; **fax** 1 814 865 3378.

Kim-Looi CH'NG, Ms, *see* **CH'NG, Ms Kim-Looi.**

KING, Dr Graham John. Molecular genetics as a basis for crop improvement, structural & environmental constraints on DNA sequence variation, assessment of genetic diversity in crop plants. Research Leader. *B.*12 July 1958, Bromley, Kent, England, UK. British. *M.*Jo L. **Education:** King's Sch.(Rochester); U.of Manchester BSc(Hons) 1979, U.of London PhD 1986. **Experience:** res.in molecular biol.& molecular genetics, technician in microbiol.& biochem.for six yrs, extensive computer programming, init.& leads Euro.Apple Genome Mapping Poject. **Career:** Technician, U.of London 1980–86; Res.Leader in Molecular Genetics, HRI 1986–; Vis.Researcher, CSIRO Div.of Hort.(Sydney) 1992; Coord. 'Dev.of the Euro. Apple Crop' (CEC Project involving eight nations) 1992–. **Achievements:** developed DNA 'fingerprinting' system for identification of *Pseudomonas* pathovars, init.work for molecular ident.of incompatibility alleles in *Brassica*, comp.structural modelling of yeast chromosome III DNA sequence, coord.of multidisc.work linking breeding to econ.of prod.& consumer preferences. **Memberships:** ISHS Comm.for Biotech.1993 , Biochem.Soc., EUCARPIA Genetical Soc. **Publications:** Molecular genetics & breeding of vegetable brassicas 1990, The Euro.Apple Genome Mapping Project (co-Author) 1991, Stability, structure & complexity of yeast chromosome III 1993. Dislikes pers. pub., indiff.to news media support. **Languages:** English; French & Italian (intermediate read, basic spoken); Pascal (computer language, intuitive). Willing to act as consult.& to judge proposals. **Address:** Horticulture Research International, Wellesbourne, Warwickshire CV35 9EF, England, UK. **Tel.**44 1789 472011; **fax** 44 1789 470552.

KIRA, Professor Dr Tatuo. Forest ecosystem studies (carbon & nutrient cycling, primary production, geography), management of lake watersheds. Director, Professor Emeritus. *B.*27 Dec.1919, Osaka, Japan. Japanese. Father Tetsuaki Kira, conchology. *M.*Yasuko. **Education:** Kyoto U. MSc(Agron.) 1942, PhD 1956. **Experience:** ecol.expedns to Ponape Islands

(Micronesia) 1941, and Gt Khingan Mtns (NE China) 1942; surveys of trop.forest ecosystems in SE Asia 1961–78; project leader, Japanese IBP team for integrated ecosystem studies on rain-forests & freshwater lakes of Peninsular Malaysia 1970–74; ecol.surveys on lakes & their watersheds in Yunnan Province, China 1988–92. **Career:** Assoc.Prof.of Hort. Kyoto U.1948–9; Prof.of Plant Ecol.1949–81 then Emer., Dir Botl Gdn 1951–74, Dean Fac.of Sci.1970–73, Osaka City U.; Dir, Lake Biwa Res.Inst.1982–. **Achievements:** involved in Nature cons.activities since 1955; participation in action against global & local envl problems as one of first members of SCOPE/ICSU and var.domestic cttees of nat.& local govts; making efforts for cons.of world lake envts as Dir of Lake Biwa Res.Inst.and Scientific Cttee Chairperson of ILEC. **Memberships:** ESJ (Pres.1980–83), BSJ, JSTE, SESJ, IAE, BES (Hon.), IBP/Productivity of Terr.Ecosystems Intl Cttee 1966–74, SCOPE/ ICSU 1969–73, ILEC Fndn (Chairperson, Scientific Cttee 1986–), JNCS (Councillor), NCNEC, IUCN Comm.on Ecol. **Awards:** Purple Ribbon Medal 1984, Second Order of the Sacred Treasure 1990 (both Japanese Nat.Govt). **Publications:** *Nature & Life in SE Asia* (vols 1–7, Ed.) 1961–76, *Biol.Prod.in a Warm-temperate Evergreen Oak Forest of Japan* (Ed.) 1978, *Ecol.of Trop.Forests* (in Japanese) 1983, *Cons. of Water Resources — Problems of Lake Biwa Watershed* (Ed., in Japanese) 1987, *World Lakes* (Ed., in Japanese) 1993, *c.*50 major papers, *c.*100 other papers & *c.*200 essays. Tolerant re. pers.pub., favours news media support. **Languages:** English, German (read), Japanese. **Address:** Lake Biwa Research Institute, 1-10 Uchidehama, Otsu City, Shiga 520, Japan, or 2-21-9 Nango, Otsu City, Shiga 520, Japan. **Tel.**(office) 81 775 26 4800, (home) 81 775 34 8229; **fax** 81 775 26 4803.

KIRBY, Dr Keith James. Forestry & woodland conservation, dynamics of woodland ground vegetation, survey & monitoring of forests, developing policies & practice for maintaining the biodiversity of managed forests, extent of & changes in ancient woodland. Woodland Ecologist. *B.*19 Jan.1952, Stanford Rivers, Essex, England, UK. British. *P.*Dr Trudy A.Watt *qv.* **Education:** Brasenose Coll.Oxf. BA (1st Class) 1973, D.Phil.1977. **Experience:** res.on changes in ground veg.under diff.for.treatment; adv. to *e.g.*govt depts & gen.public on woodland cons.in Britain within English Nature*. **Career:** Res. Asst, Lake Distr.Nat.Park Spec. Planning Board 1977; Field Surveyor, NCC (Cumbria) 1978; Woodland Ecol. NCC (Huntington & Peterborough) 1979–91; Woodland Ecol. *English Nature 1991–. **Achievements:** developed widespread knowledge, and supervised & arranged pubn of inventories, of ancient woodland in Britain. **Memberships:** BES, ICF, IEEM, BSBI. **Publications:** *Woodland and Wildlife* 1992, *Woodland Survey Handbook* 1992, chapters, Ed.of two symp.vols, *c.*50 others.

Indiff.to pers.pub.& news media support. **Languages:** English, French (poor). Willing to act as consult.etc. **Address:** English Nature, Northminster House, Peterborough PE1 1UA, England, UK. **Tel.**44 1733 318450; **fax** 44 1733 68834.

KIRKHAM, Professor Dr M.B. Soil–plant–water relations. Professor. *B*.Cedar Rapids, IA, USA. American. **Education:** Wellesley Coll. BA(Biol.Scis); U.of W–M, MS(Bot.), PhD(Bot. & Soil Sci.). **Experience:** Guest Lect. Inst.of Water Res.& Conservancy and Hydroelectric Power Res., and Farm Irrigation Res. China; Insts of Experimental Agron.(Italy) and Soil Fertility (The Netherlands); Massey & Wageningen Univs; Edl Bds *Crop Sci., Agron. J., Field Crops Res., Plant Physiol., Plant & Soil.* **Career:** Plant Physiol.USEPA; Asst Prof. U.of Mass.at Amherst; Asst Prof. Oklahoma SU; Assoc.Prof., Prof., Dept of Agron. Kansas SU. **Achievements:** published num.papers on uptake of heavy-metals by plants grown on sludge-treated agricl soil, and effects of elevated levels of carbon dioxide on plants. **Memberships:** ASA, SSSA, CSSA, AAAS, ASPP, ASHS, AMS, BSA, RMS, ISSS, many others. **Awards:** F.of ASA, SSSA, CSSA, and AAAS, Vis.Scholar Harvard U., Vis.Sci.NZ DSIR. **Publications:** 150+ scientific articles incl. Streamlines for diffusive flow in vertical & surface tillage: a model study 1994, Trace Elements 1994, Sludge Disposal 1994. Dislikes pers.pub.& news media support. **Languages:** English, French (fair), German (read). Willing to act as consult.etc. **Address:** Evapotranspiration Laboratory, Dept of Agronomy, Kansas State University, Waters Annex, Manhattan, Kansas 66506, USA. **Tel.**(office) 1 913 532 5731, (home) 1 913 539 5498; **fax** (office) 1 913 532 6094, (home) 1 913 539 1850.

KLEE, Professor Dr Gary A. Coastal resource management, human ecology (cultural ecology). Professor of Environmental Studies. *B*.2 May 1943, Pomona, CA, USA. American. *M*.Helen: *d*.Laura (biol.). **Education:** San Francisco SU, BA(Geog.) 1966; Calif.Standard Teaching Credential 1967; U.of Oregon, MA(Geog.) & PhD (Geog.) 1972. **Experience:** res.— trad. forms of cons.& mgmt in Oceania, marine sanctuaries as a modern-day marine cons.strat.; admin.— Grad.Adv.for MS in Envl Studies; consult.— coastal resource mgmt, human ecol., envl studies; teaching in coastal resource mgmt & human ecol.from BS/BA to MS levels. **Career:** Peace Corps Vol.(Palau, Micronesia) 1967–9, Asst Prof. U.of Wisconsin 1972–4, Vis.Asst Prof. San Diego SU 1974–6 and Pennsylvania SU 1976–7, Assoc.Prof.1981–6 & Prof. of Envl Studies 1981–, San José SU. **Achievement:** estab.MS degree in Envl Sci.at San José SU. **Memberships:** SHE, IUCN, Centers for Marine Cons.& for Indigenous Knowledge for Sust.Agric. **Awards:** Beyond War Award (Peace Corps) 1987, invited participant Micronesian Islands Project (San José SU), Vis.Geogl

Sci.Award (AAG) 1983. **Publications:** *World Systems of Trad.Resource Mgmt* (Ed.) 1980, *Cons.of Natural Resources* 1991, 30+ j.articles, chapters, etc. **Language:** English. Willing to act as consult.etc. **Address:** Department of Environmental Studies, School of Social Sciences, San José State University, San José, California 95192, USA. **Tel.**(office) 1 408 924 5455, (home) 1 408 462 5829; **fax** 1 408 924 5477.

KLEIN, Professor Dr David Robert. Arctic ecology, northern herbivory, assessment of effects of northern development on wildlife & habitats. Professor & Senior Scientist. *B*.18 May 1927, Fitchburg, MA, USA. American. *M*.Lou Anne: *s.*, 2 *d*. **Education:** U.of Connecticut, BSc (Wildlife) 1951, U.of Alaska MSc (Wildlife) 1953, U.of BC PhD (Zool.) 1963. **Experience:** res. and grad.-level teaching in wildlife ecol., professional work has included res.on Arctic & n.ungulates in Canada, Denmark, Norway, Greenland, Soviet Union, and African ungulates in S.Africa. **Career:** Field Biol. US FWS 1955–9, Res.Supervisor for wildlife res. 1961–2, Professor 1962–, Alaska Dept of Fish & Game; Leader 1961–91, Sr Sci.1991–, Alaska Cooperative (U.of Alaska/Nat.Biol.Survey/Alaska Dept of Fish & Game/Wildlife Mgmt Inst.) Wildlife Res.Unit, Inst.of Arctic Biol. U.of Alaska Fairbanks 1991–. **Achievements:** developed theory of alpine & arctic ungulate foraging dynamics, worked for cons.of Alaskan & circumarctic wildlife & habitats, monitored effects of oil dev.on wildlife in arctic Alaska. **Memberships:** F.AAAS, F.AINA, ASM, Sigma Xi, The Wildlife Soc. **Awards:** Fulbright Grantee 1971–2, Special Recognition Service Award (Wildlife Soc.) 1991, Honor Award for Meritorious Service (Dept of the Interior) 1992. **Publications:** over 100 tech.papers incl.The intro., increase & crash of Reindeer *[Rangifer tarandus]* on St Matthew Is.1968, Food selection by N.Amer. deer and their response to over-utilization of preferred plant species (Symp. Proc.) 1970, Diet selection by vertebrate herbivores in the high Arctic of Greenland 1991, Resource partitioning by mammalian herbivores in the high Arctic 1994. Favourable attitude towards pers.pub.& news media support. **Language:** English. Willing to act as consult.etc. **Address:** Cooperative Fish & Wildlife Research Unit, University of Alaska, Fairbanks, Alaska 99775, USA. **Tel.**(office) 1 907 474 6674, (home) 1 907 479 3201; **fax** 1 907 474 6967.

KLEMM, Cyrille DE. Nature conservation law, international and comparative. Consultant. *B*. 17 July 1927, Lausanne, Switzerland. French. **Education:** Licence en Droit, Aix-en-Provence 1950; U.of Paris, Diplômes d'Études Supérieures de Droit Public 1951, de l'Institut d'Études Politiques 1953, and d'Études Supérieures de Droit Romain et d'Histoire du Droit 1956. **Experience:** res.into all aspects of cons.law; consult to IUCN, Council of Europe, UNESCO, other intl orgns. **Career:** Consult.to intl orgns

1969–; Lect in Cons.Law, U.of Lyon 1984–, and U.of Strasbourg 1990–. **Achievements:** participated in prelim.drafting in num.major cons. convs; dev.of comparative law approach to cons. law esp.in field of species cons.& prot.areas. **Memberships:** ICEL (Founding Memb. New Delhi 1969 and its Intl Governor since), IUCN CEL 1965–, FSEL (VP). **Awards:** Elizabeth Haub Prize (VUB) 1988, Euro.Prize for Prot.of Nature (Johann Wolfgang von Goethe Fndn) 1992. **Publications:** c.100 incl.Wild plant cons. and the law 1990, Guidelines for legis.to implement CITES 1993, Biol.diversity cons.and the law: legal mechanisms for conserving species & ecosystems (co-Author) 1994. **Languages:** English, French; Italian & Spanish (read). Willing to act as consult.etc. **Address:** 21 Rue de Dantzig, 75015 Paris, France. **Tel.** (home) 33 14 532 2672; **fax** 33 14 533 4884.

KLINGEL, Professor Dr Hans. Wildlife research, conservation. Professor of Zoology. *B.*29 March 1932, Ludwigshafen, Germany. German. *M.*Ute (long-term field asst). **Education:** Universität Mainz, Dr rer.nat.1958. **Experience:** wildlife res.in Africa, Australia, & Asia; radio telemetry, DNA-fingerprinting, counting animals, immobilization techniques, computer analyses. **Career:** Res.F. Deutsche Forschungsgemeinschaft 1958–32; SCI (Seregenti, Tanzania), FAO 1962–5; Memb.of Zool. Dept, U.of Braunschweig 1965–. **Achievements:** cons.of African Wild Ass (*Equus africanus*) in Ethiopia (Yangudi Rasa Nat.Park), and African Equids. **Memberships:** IUCN SSC, DZG, ASM, others. **Publications:** Das Verhalten der Pferde (Equidae) 1972, Communication in the Perissodactyla 1977, Odd-toed Ungulates: Horses, Hippopotamuses, Camels, 1989. Indiff.to pers.pub., favours news media support. **Languages:** English, French, German, Swahili (good). Willing to act as consult.etc. **Address:** Zoologisches Institut, Technische Universität, D-38092 Braunschweig, Germany. **Tel.** (office) 49 531 391 3234 or 31, (home) 49 5307 1705; **fax** 49 531 391 8136; **e-mail** h.klingel @tu-bs.de .

KNIGHT, Peter T. Environment–business. Freelance Writer. *B.*10 May 1957, Fort Beaufort, RSA. British. **Education:** Rhodes U. BA 1975. **Experience:** consult.for *Fin.Times,* Imperial Chem.Industries, Digital Computers, BP, WWF. **Career:** Freelance Writer & Consult. 1975–. **Award:** Non-Specialist Envl Journalist of the Yr (Media Natura, UK) 1994. **Publications:** incl.*The Green Business Guide* (co-Author) 1991, Ed.*Envt Strat.Europe* and *Envt Strat.Amer.*1992/3/4/5. **Language:** English. Willing to act as consult.etc. **Address:** 22 Doria Road, London SW6 4UG, England, UK. **Tel.**44 171 731 0040; **fax** 44 171 731 0384.

KNILL, Professor Dr Sir John. Construction & environmental geology, earth science conservation, natural hazard reduction. Committee Chairman, Committee Member, Company Director. *B.*22 Nov.1934, Wolverhampton, England, UK. British. Father William Cuthbert Knill, water engr. *M.*(Lady) Diane (geol.): *s.* Patrick John (Japanese heritage), *d.*Fiona Mary (herborist). **Education:** Whitgift Sch.; ICL, BSc (Geol.) 1955, PhD(Geol.) 1957, DSc (Dalradian & Engg Geol.) 1981. **Experience:** res.into metamorphic rocks, engg geol., natural hazards, waste disposal, envl impact; admin. exp.as Dept Head & Council Chairman; intl consult.1959–. **Career:** Geol. Sir Alexander Gibb & Partners 1957; Asst Lect., Lect., Reader, Prof.of Engg Geol. IC 1957–93; Chairman, Radioactive Waste Mgmt Adv.Cttee 1987– & NERC 1988–93; Memb. JNCC 1991–; Dir. Donaldson Assocs 1993–. **Achievements:** earth sci.cons.in UK, intl natural hazard prediction, dev.of global envl res. **Memberships:** F.ICE, F.HKIE, Chartered Geol., F.RAE. **Awards:** Prize (Brit.Geotechnical Soc.), Whitaker Medal (IWEM), Aberconway Medal (Instn of Geologists), Hon DSc (Kingston U.), Hon.F. (City & Guilds of London Inst.). **Publications:** *Industrial Geol.* 1978, *Geol.& Landscape Cons.*1994. Favours pers.pub.& news media support. **Languages:** English, Farsi (weak), French (poor). Further details may be obtained from the Brit.*Who's Who* 1995. Willing to act as consult. **Address:** Highwood Farm, Shaw-cum-Donnington, Newbury, Berkshire RG16 9IB, England, UK. **Tel.** (office) 44 1635 552300; **fax** 44 1635 36826.

KOBAYASHI, Osamu. Environmental management, especially emission control over powerplants. Company Director & Divisional General Manager. *B.*20 Nov.1927, Kyoto, Japan. Japanese. *M.*Miyo: *d.* **Education:** Kyoto U. B.Eng. (Civil) 1952. **Experience:** leading nat.del.on poll.problems in US & Euro.countries. **Career:** employee in var.depts 1952–79, Gen.Mgr 1979–87 & Dir 1983–87 of Envt Dept, Dir & Dep. Gen.Mgr of both Plant Siting & Envt 1987– and Engg Res.& Dev.1991– Divs, The Tokyo Electric Power Co.Inc. **Achievements:** contributed to make The Tokyo Electric Power Co.Inc.the world's first electricity utility to use a low-polluting fuel for power generation and to develop & introduce innovative techs towards the high-level emission control (*i.e.*high-grade electrostatic precipitators, flue-gas desulphurization & denitrification techs); playing decisive role in concluding vol. agreements with local govts on emission control over thermal power-plants which are more stringent than required by Japan's nat.laws & ordinances. **Memberships:** WRI (Counc.), Min.of Foreign Affairs (Japan–Germany Council for Hightech.& Envl Tech.), Min.of Finance (Cttee), Min.of Intl Trade & Industry (Cttee), Japan Fedn of Econ.Orgns (Cttee). **Awards:** Commendation (DG of Envt Agency, Japan), Appreciation (Gov.of Tokyo Metropolitan Govt). **Publications:** *Pocketbook of Civil Engg* 1982 (includes Nuclear Civil Engg), *Resonance in Nature* Vol.3 *Towards a Creative Relationship with the Earth* 1990 (includes From Poll.Control to Envl Mgmt).

Favours pers.pub. & news media support. **Languages:** English (better at written), Japanese. Willing to act as consult.etc. **Address:** Environment Division, The Tokyo Electric Power Co.Inc., 1-1-3 Uchisaiwaicho, Chiyoda-ku, Tokyo 100, Japan. **Tel.** 81 3 3501 8111 ext.6384; **fax** 81 3 3504 1570.

KOESTER, Veit. National & international environmental law. Head of Division. *B*.30 May 1934, Berlin, Germany. Danish. *M*.Winnie: *s*., *d*. **Education:** U.of Copenhagen, LLM 1957. **Experience:** more than 20 yrs' legal & admin.exp.as civil servant for Danish Govt. **Career:** Scholarship to Inst.des Scis Politiques, Paris 1959; admission to the Bar 1962; Min.for Cultural Affairs 1967, Min.of the Envt 1973–; Examiner, U.of Copenhagen and Roskilde U.Centre 1985–; Danish EC Rep. Brussels 1971. **Achievements:** active contrib.to the prep.of several intl legal instruments; head of Danish delegations to several intergovtl confs; elected chairman *i.a.*for Bern Conv.1987–9; Council of Europe Envt Cttee 1987–9; Extraordinary Conf. of Ramsar Conv.1987; Conf.of Bonn Conv. 1988, UNEP Group on Biodiv.1988–90, VP Intergovtl Negotiating Cttee for the Conv.on Biol.Diversity 1991–2 and Intergovtl Cttee on the Conv.on Biol.Diversity 1993–4; resp.for drafting intro.& implementation of *i.a.* Danish Nature prot.legis. **Memberships:** Danish Nat. Comm.for UNESCO, Council of IUCN 1988–93 and ICEL 1983–. **Award:** Danish Animal Welfare Soc. 1981. **Publications:** num.in Danish on envl law, and in English *e.g.Nordic Countries Legis. on the Envt, The Ramsar Conv.* Favours news media support. **Languages:** Danish, English, French (basic), German (basic), Norwegian, Swedish. Willing to act as consult. etc. **Address:** National Forest and Nature Agency, Haraldsgade 53, 2100 Copenhagen, Denmark. **Tel.**(office) 4539 472000, (home) 4531 633621; **fax** 4539 279899.

KOH, Ambassador Professor Tommy Thong-Bee. Environmental law, Nature conservation, sustainable development, negotiations. Ambassador-At-Large, Director, Chairman. *B*.12 Nov. 1937, Singapore. Singaporean. *M*.Dr Siew-Aing: 2 *s*. **Education:** Nat.U.Singapore LLB 1961, Harvard U. LLM 1964, Cambridge U. Dipl.in Criminology 1965. **Experience:** envl diplomacy, writing, res. **Career:** Asst Lect.then Lect.1962–71, Assoc.Prof.& Dean 1971–4, Prof.1977, Fac.of Law, U.of Singapore; Perm. Rep.to UN (NY), concurrently accredited as HC to Canada 1968–71 and 1974–84 when also Amb. to Mexico 1974–84; Pres.3rd UN Conf.on the Law of the Sea 1981–2; Amb.to USA 1984–90; Chairman Prep.& Main Cttees for UNCED 1990–92; Amb.-At-Large, Min.of Foreign Affairs, and Dir, Inst.of Policy Studies 1990–; Chairman Nat.Arts Council 1991–. **Achievements:** Chairman, Main & Prep. Cttees of UNCED at which helped to achieve consensus; Patron, Nature Soc.of Singapore. **Memberships:** UN Adv.Cttee on Sust.Dev., Earth Council. **Awards:** Public Service Star 1971, Meritorious Service Medal 1979, Disting. Service Order 1990 (all from Govt of Singapore); Wolfgang Friedman (Columbia U.) 1984, Hon.LLD (Yale U.) 1984; Jackson Ralston Prize (Stanford U.) 1985, Asia Soc.Annual Award (NY) 1985, Intl Service (Tufts U.) 1987, Jit Trainor for Dist.in Practice of Diplomacy (Georgetown U.) 1987, Commander, Order of the Golden Ark 1993, Arts Award & Culture Award (JCCI Singapore Fndn) 1993. **Publications:** num.articles & chapters incl.the Scene in Singapore 1988, A View from E.& SE Asia 1989, Singapore's Ext.Relations in 1990 1990. Favours news media support. **Languages:** Chinese (spoken), English. **Address:** Ministry of Foreign Affairs, 250 North Bridge Road, 39-00 Raffles City Tower, Singapore 0617, Singapore. **Tel.**65 3305 600; **fax** 65 3381 908.

KOHLI, Dr Ravinder Kumar. Environmental botany, allelopathy, forestry, chemical ecology. Reader & Principal Investigator. *B*.2 Dec.1953, Gurgaon, Har., India. Indian. *M*.Dr Kum Kum (entomol., envl zool.): 2 *s*. **Education:** Panjab U. BSc 1973, Cert.course in German 1984; Meerut U. MSc(Bot.) 1975; Guru Nanak Dev U.(Amritsar), PhD 1978; UNESCO–WHO Longterm Postgrad.Course 'Modern Problems in Biol.' 1979; AIU Cert., Dipl.& Professional Courses in Eval., Methodology & Exam.1984–7. **Experience:** res.& teaching 1975–, postgrad. student supervision incl.eight PhD & 20 M.Phil.theses 1981–, PI of seven envl res. projects, lecturing, organized nat.& intl symposia on envt & for. **Career:** UNESCO–WHO Participant, Inst.for Experimental Bot.(Prague) 1978–9; CSIR Pool Officer Class I, N.Eastern Hill U.(Shillong) 1979–80 & Punjab Agricl U.(Ludhiana) 1980; Lect.in Plant Biochem. 1980–89, Reader in Envl Bot.1989–, Panjab U. **Achievements:** worked extensively on the negative aspects esp.Allelopathy of *Eucalyptus* and *Populus* spp. Monoculture plantations on envt, biodiv., and crop yield; mgmt of *Parthenium hysterophorus* (Congress Grass) weed and of weeds through Allelopathy. **Memberships:** IUFRO (Assoc., Dep.Leader of Forest Weed Mgmt Group), ISCA (Life), Dayamand Nat. Acad.of Envl Scis (Life & Gen.Sec.), Soc.of Envl Scientists (Life & Sec.); var.bodies & cttees at nat.level. **Award:** Nanda Mem.Nat. Young Scientist (in for.) 1988, Indian Soc.of Tree Scientists 1989. **Publications:** books incl. *Social For.for Rural Dev.*1988, *Congress Grass* (P.hysterophorus) — *an Annotated Book of Abstracts* 1993, *Tree Directory of Chandigarh* 1994; *c.*60 res.papers & 40 abstracts. Indiff.to pers.pub., favours news media support. **Languages:** English, German (read), Hindi, Punjabi. Willing to act as consult.etc. **Address:** House Nr 1516, Sector 11-D, Chandigarh 160 011, Punjab, India. **Tel.**(office) 91 172 541960 ext. 1228, (home) 91 172 546666 & 7777; **fax** 91 172 541409; **e-mail** Pulib@puchd.ren.nic.in .

KOLBASOV, Professor Dr Oleg Stepanovich.
Environmental law & management. Counsel.
*B.*11 April 1927, Cheboksary City, Russia. Russian. *M.*Vera: *s.*, *d.*Inena (envl law). **Education:** Vilnius U.Sch.of Law grad.1952, Leningrad U.Sch.of Law, postgrad.1955, Cand.of Juridical Sci.1955, Doctor of Juridical Sci.1968. **Experience:** res., admin., consult. **Career:** Investigator, City of Kaliningrad (Baltic Regn) 1951–2; Sr Lect. Tomsk U.1956–8; Sr Expert, Inst.of Soviet Legis.1961–5; Head Envl Law Office 1965–88, V.-Dir. 1988–91 Moscow Inst. of State & Law; Prof.of Envl Law 1976–; Dep.Minister 1991–3 & Counsel to Minister 1993– for Envl Prot.& Natural Resources. **Achievements:** dev.of theory of envl law, and drafts of main envl laws; creation of Assn of Envl Law. **Memberships:** All-Russian Nature Cons. Soc., RSAP (VC), IUCN CEL (Pres.), ICEL (VC), IAWL, IICAL, ELNI, Russian AS (Corres.Memb.1991–). **Awards:** Gt Patriotic War Medals (1941–5), Intl Elizabeth Haub Prize 1979, Hon.Medal 1987 and Hon.LLD 1990 (both Pace U.). **Publications:** 300+ incl.books transl.into other languages — *Ecol.: Pol.Instns & Orgns* 1978 (in French), 1982 (in Japanese), 1983 (in English), *Sozialismus und Umweltrecht* 1982, *Umweltschutz nach Volkerrecht* 1985. Favours pers.pub.& news media support. **Languages:** English, German (written). **Address:** Mozhaiskoe Schosse 17–9, Moscow 121471, Russia. **Tel.**(office) 7 095 254 6044, (home) 7 095 444 1696; **fax** 7 095 254 8283.

KONDRATYEV, Professor Dr Kirill Yakovlevich. Global change [esp.of atmospheric–climatic phenomena]. Academician, Counsellor. *B.*14 June 1920, Rybinsk, Russia. Russian. *M.*Svetlana I.(atmos.phys.): *s.*, *d.* **Education:** U. of Leningrad, PhD 1956. **Experience:** res.in field of radiative transfer in upper atmospheric layers & troposphere, atmos.thermal regime, and in ecol.using rockets & satellites; teaching & admin.; consult.to many instns. **Career:** Lect. & Res.Sci.in Fac.of Phys.1946–63, Prof.of Phys., V.-Rector for Scientific Work, then Rector 1964–70, U.of Leningrad; Sr Sci.then Chief Dept of Radiation Studies 1969–82, Main Geophys.Obs.; Couns. Russian AS Res.Centre for Ecol.Safety 1982–. **Achievements:** theory of longwave radiation transfer on the atmos.with var.practical applications, statl analyses of satellite earth's radiation budget data. **Memberships:** Russian AS, IAA, IASL (Hon.), RMS, AMS. **Awards:** Gold Medal (WMO) 1968, Symons Medal (RMS) 1976, USSR State Prize 1987, Hon.Dr of Univs of Lille & Budapest. **Publications:** *Radiation in the Atmos.*1965, *Weather and Climate on Planets* (co-Author) 1982, *Climate Shocks: Natural and Anthropogenic* 1988, *Observing Global Climate Change* (co-Author, in press). **Languages:** English, German, Russian. Willing to act as consult.etc. **Address:** Scientific Research Center of Ecological Safety, St Petersburg Center of the Russian Academy of Sciences,

Korpusnaya Street 18, 197042 St Petersburg, Russia. **Tel.**(office) 7 812 230 7837, (home) 7 812 231 7773; **fax** 7 812 235 4361 & 314 3360.

Koonlin TAN, Dr, *see* **TAN, Dr Koonlin.**

KORNAŚ, Professor Dr Jan. Plant geography (Europe, tropical Africa), plant ecology (Man's impact on flora & vegetation), plant taxonomy (pteridophytes & phanerogams). Emeritus Professor of Botany. *B.*26 April 1923, Kraków, Poland. Polish. *M.*Prof.Anna Medwecka-Kornaś *qv.* **Education:** Jagiellonian U. MSc(Bot.) 1946, PhD(Bot.) 1949, Dr Habil.1955. **Experience:** 50 yrs' res.in plant geog., esp.floristics & veg.sci., in Europe, Africa & N.Amer.; teaching plant geog., taxonomy & ecol.in Poland, Zambia & Nigeria. **Career:** Asst 1946– 54, Prof.1955–93, Head of Dept of Bot.1965–93, Emer.1993–, Jagiellonian U.; Prof.& Head of Dept of Biol. U.of Zambia 1971–3; Prof.& Head of Dept of Bot. U.of Maiduguri (Nigeria) 1977–8. **Achievements:** basic res.on plant community distributional patterns (veg.mapping) & successions; mechanisms of extinction of indigenous plant species and of invasions of aliens. **Memberships:** Polish AS (Corres.1973, Full 1981), PBS (Hon.1986), IAPterid.(Hon.VP 1990). **Awards:** Polonia Restituta Order 1973 & 1985, W.Szafer Medal for Scientific Achievements (PBS) 1989. **Publications:** *Szata roślinna Polski* (co-Author) 1959 & 1979, *Veg.of Poland* (co-Author) 1966, *Geografia roślin* (co-Author) 1986; 165 monogrs & res.papers, c.450 others. Favours pers.pub.& news media support. **Languages:** English, French, German, Latin, Polish, Russian, Spanish. Further details may be obtained from *Fragmenta Floristica et Geobotanica* (Kraków), Suppl.2(1), pp.1–70, 1993. Willing to act as consult.etc. **Address:** Institute of Botany, ul.Lubicz 46, 31-512 Kraków, Poland. **Tel.**48 12 221033 ext.421, (home) 48 12 114325; **fax** 48 12 219790.

KOSTENKO, HE Dr Yuriy I. Development of laws on environmental protection in Ukraine; national ecological reform concept & Nature protection programme. Member of Parliament & Minister for Environmental Protection and Nuclear Safety. *B.*12 June 1951, Vinnitsa Regn, Ukraine. Ukrainian. *M.*Alina: *s.* **Education:** Inst.of Machinery, Engr 1973; Paton Electric Welding Inst. Ukrainian AS, PhD in Tech.Scis 1985. **Experience:** engg, admin. **Career:** Researcher, Paton Electric Welding Inst.1973–85; Dep.Chairman, Parliamentary Comm.on Ecol. 1990–92; Head, Parliamentary WG on Nuclear Disarmament 1993, MP 1990– & Minister, Min.for Envl Prot.of Ukraine 1992–, Min.for Envl Prot.and Nuclear Safety of Ukraine 1995–, Supreme Rada of Ukraine. **Achievements:** dev. of law on envl prot.of Ukraine, nat.ecol.reform concept, participation in Parliamentary Chernobyl Comm., prep.of concepts on nuclear disarmament & nat.security in Ukraine (co-Author).

Membership: Ukrainian Popular Movement (RUKH). **Awards:** Honorable Dipl.for Rescue Expedn to Armenia (City Hall) 1989, F. Amer.AAS. **Publications:** Kiev and the bomb: Ukrainians reply 1993, *Ukraine's Nuclear Weapons: a Pol., Legal & Econ.Analysis of Disarmament* (Report) 1993, Chernobyl 'sarcofag' and the problems of nuclear policy 1994. Favours news media support. **Languages:** English, Russian, Ukrainian. **Address:** Ministry for Environmental Protection and Nuclear Safety of Ukraine, 5 Khreshchatik Street, 252001 Kyiv, Ukraine. **Tel.**380 44 226 2428; **fax** 380 229 83883; **e-mail** envukraine@gluk.apc.org .

KOZLOV, Dr Mikhail Vasilievich. Taxonomy & ecology of Lepidoptera, response of insect populations to industrial pollution. Laboratory Researcher. *B.*31 Aug.1962, Leningrad (now again St Petersburg), Russia. Russian. *M.*Dr Elena Lvovna Zvereva (Tsyrlina): *stepson* Vitaly Evgenievich Zverev (for.), *s.* **Education:** Leningrad U.1984; Biol.Inst.(Novosibirsk), PhD 1986. **Experience:** res.in taxonomy & ecol.of Lepidoptera, chem.communication in moths, plant prot., insect responses to industrial poll. **Career:** Researcher, Plant Prot.Inst.(Leningrad–Pushkin) 1986–91 and Ecol.Zool.Lab. U.of Turku 1991–. **Achievements:** res.on insect response to pollutants incl.changes in biodiv. along severe poll.gradients; applied bioindication. **Memberships:** SEL, ATL, Russian Entomol.Soc., Finnish Lepidopterists' Soc. **Publications:** *Impact of Human-induced Envl Changes on Terr.Insect Pops* (in Russian) 1990, *Aerial Poll.in Kola Peninsula* (Proc., co-Ed.) 1993; *c.*80 scientific papers. Indiff.to pers. pub.& news media support. **Languages:** English, German (read), Russian. Willing to act as consult.&/or ref.papers occasionally. **Address:** Ecological Zoology Laboratory, University of Turku, FIN-20500 Turku, Finland. **Tel.**(office) 358 21 633 5492, (home) 358 21 253 9159; **fax** 358 21 633 6550; **e-mail** MIKOZ@SARA.UTU.FI .

KOZLOWSKI, Professor Dr Jerzy. Methodology of urban & environmental planning. Professor of Town & Regional Planning. *B.*25 Jan.1931, Kraków, Poland. Australian, Polish. *M.*Zofia: *s.*Marek (town planner, arch.). **Education:** Tech.U.(Kraków) B.Arch.1953, M.Arch. 1955, Dr(Tech.Scis) 1972, Dr Habil.1981; Ministère de la Construction (Paris), Diplôme d'Urbanisme et d'Architecture 1963; U.of Edinburgh, PhD 1971. **Experience:** res.at Univs of Edinburgh & Qld and Res.Inst.on Envl Dev. (Kraków); tech.at Voivodship Town Planning Office (Kraków); admin.as Inst.Dir, Head of Dept, and Prog.Dir; consult.to UN and Dept of Housing & Local Govt (Qld); u.teaching. **Career:** Arch. Krakow Design Office 1954–5; Planner, Sr Planner & Team Leader, Voivodship Town Planning Office, and Ind.Consult. 1955–65; Arch. Municipal Design 1959–60 and Rural Design 1960–65 Offices; part-time & short-term

teaching incl.Vis.Prof.at Oulu 1976, Wuhan 1988, & Colombo 1989 Univs 1964–89; Arch./Planner 1965–7, Res.F. SRF & Postdoctl F. 1967–71, Planning Res.Unit, U.of Edinburgh; SRF & Head 1972–4, Assoc.Prof.& Dir 1974–81, Res.Inst.of Town Planning & Arch. (Krakow Branch); Prof.1982–8 & Head of Dept 1984–8 Dept of Regnl & Town Planning, Prof.& Dir of Regnl & Town Planning Prog. Dept of Geogl Scis 1988–91, Prof.of Town & Regnl Planning, Dept of Geogl Scis & Planning 1991–, U.of Qld. **Achievements:** dev., application, & dissemination, of the Ultimate Envl Threshold method and the Buffer Zone Planning approach; prep.of Phys.Plan for Tatry Nat.Park (Poland); design, mgmt, & implementation, of overall & specific res.progs of Res.Inst.on Envl Dev.; main involvement in prep.of Brisbane R.strat.for the future; u.teaching & supervision; active membership of IUCN CEP 1978–86 & CESP 1992–. **Memberships:** SARP, TUP, RAPI, CHEC, IUCN CESP. **Awards:** Nat.Prize in Town Planning, 2nd degree 1959, 1961 & 1975, and 3rd degree 1977, one intl and four Polish awards in architectural competitions. **Publications:** 13 books incl.*Threshold Approach in Urban, Regnl and Envl Planning* 1986, *Towards Planning for Sust.Dev.*(co-Ed.) 1993; num.papers incl.Ultimate envl threshold: an alternative tool for planning sust.dev.1993, Buffer zones: an unresolved problem (co-Author) 1993. Indiff.to pers. pub., favours news media support. **Languages:** English, French (fair), German (limited spoken), Polish. Further details may be obtained from *Who's Who in the World* (10th edn), *Dict.of Intl Biog.*(22nd edn), *Australian Directory of Academics*. Willing to act as consult.etc. **Address:** 118 Mildura Drive, Helensvale, Queensland 4210, Australia *or* ul.Zakow Krakowskich 10, 30-438 Kraków, Poland. In Australia **tel.**(office) 61 7 3365 6525, (home) 61 7 5573 5977; **fax** 61 7 3365 6899. In Poland **tel.**48 12 660079; **fax** 48 12 215355.

KRAJČOVIČ, Dr Roman Stefan. Environmental management and regional development, landscape ecology, environmental impact assessment; revitalization of abandoned & derelict landscape, land readjustment. Branch Director. *B.*25 Apr.1958, Bratislava, Slovak Rep. Slovak. *M.*Jana Trenčianska *qv:* 2 *d.* **Education:** Comenius U. BSc(Nature & Envt Prot.) 1982, MSc (RNDr)(Envl Mgmt) 1983; UCL Cert.in Dev.& Planning 1993, Inst.of Landscape Ecol. Slovak AS PhD 1996. **Experience:** res.(geomorph., visitor-mgmt in Nat.Parks, cultural heritage), dev.of LANDEP methodology (adopted by UNCED 1992); admin.(adaptation to new pol./econ.circs & issues re.policymaking, planning & mgmt etc.); tech. **Career:** Res.Asst, Stiavnicke Vrchy Hills Nat.Park 1982–8, Dep.Dir 1985–8, State Centre of Nature Cons.; Sec.-Gen. Regnl Orgn of Slovak Union for Nature & Landscape Prot.1984–8; Consult./Adv. Envl Comm. Slovak Youth Union 1984–9; Sr Researcher, Inst.of Landscape Ecol. Slovak AS 1988–91; Dir, Distr.

Dept of Regnl Dev.& Arch.1991–3; Dir, Nitra Branch, Slovak Envl Agency 1993–. **Achievements:** provision of systematic instruction in a body of planning methods & techniques combined into the 'action planning' process directed at envl spatial & phys.dev. thus creating an integrated planning strat. **Memberships:** IALE, IAA, Slovak Geogl Soc.of Slovak AS. **Awards:** Bronze Medal 1986 (Slovak Union of Nature & Landscape Conservationists) and 1988 (Regnl Govt, Dept of Culture & Nature). **Publications:** *Envl Manual for Local Auths* in *C.& Eastern Europe* (co-Author), three papers, 25 communications to scientific mtgs. Favours pers.pub.& news media support. **Languages:** English, French (slight), German (written & spoken), Russian. Willing to act as consult.etc. **Address:** Stodolova 6, 94901 Nitra, Slovak Republic. **Tel.**(office) 42 87 524189, (home) 42 7 484304; **fax** 42 87 524189.

KRASNOV, Professor Dr Eugene V. Marine geoecology & biogeochemistry, palaeoecology of coral reefs. Head of Department. *B*.16 Aug. 1933, Uzzhum, Russia. Russian. *M*.Galina Z.: *d*.Elene E.Kostina (hydrobiol.). **Education:** Kishinev SU, Geol.Engr 1957, Cand.Sci.1964, Dr Sci.1973. **Experience:** widespread res.& expedns in field geol.& palaeoecology, admin. **Career.** Field Geol.on many Russian & Ukrainian geol expdns 1957–67; Chairman of Ecol. Depts & Labs, Inst.of Marine Biol., Geol Inst. and Far E.SU 1967–87; V.-Rector & Head of Nature Prot.Dept. Kaliningrad SU 1987–. **Achievements:** Chairman of Primary Banch of Soviet Geog.Soc.1975–85, Baltic Ecol.Parliament (VC 1994–). **Memberships:** PSA, WSN, ISRS, IASFCP, Baltic U., EUCC. **Awards:** State Medals 1970 & 1976, Bronze Medal (All-Union Nat.Exhibition) 1975. **Publications:** *Interaction Between Water and Living Matter* (Proc., Ed., two vols) 1979, *Corals in Reefal Faces of the USSR* 1983, *Ecol.and Nature Mgmt* (textbook) 1992. Favours pers.pub.& news media support. **Languages:** English; French, Polish & Romanian (poor); Russian. Willing to act as consult.etc. **Address:** Pionerskaja Street 70-26, 236016 Kaliningrad, Russia. **Tel.** (office) 7 0112 436254, (home) 7 0112 462700; **fax** 7 0112 465813.

KRATTIGER, Dr Anatole F. International development, biotechnology, biodiversity, technology transfer, institution-building. Executive Director, Adjunct Professor, Visiting Fellow. *B*.5 June 1960, Basel, Switzerland. Swiss. **Education:** Swiss Fed.— Dipl.in Farming 1978, Cert.of Capacity (Farm Mgmt) 1980, and Dipl.in Agric.1980; Swiss Agricl Coll. BSc(Agron.) 1983; U.of Camb.(UK), MPhil(Plant Breeding) 1985, PhD(Biochem.& Genetics) 1988. **Experience:** plant breeding res., biotech.applications to agric., res.on sust.biodiv.-use (instnl issues), intl instn-bldg partic.for benefit of developing countries; created & developed biodiv./biotech.res.& capacity-bldg prog.at Intl Acad.of the

Envt 1993–5; leader of intl biotech.transfer orgn 1995–. **Career:** Farmer in France & Switzerland 1974–80; Assoc.Sci.(Biotech.), CIMMYT 1988–91; Consult.to *e.g.* ISAAA, Resources Dev.Fndn, SEI, UNIDO, UNESCO, 1991–5; Exec.Dir 1995–, ISAAA; Adjunct Prof. Intl Acad.of the Envt (Geneva) 1995– and Cornell U. 1995–. **Achievements:** estab.of ISAAA, conceptualization & dev.of facilitating mechanism for sust.biodiv.-use. **Membership:** SID (Life). **Awards:** Middleton Prize (U.of Camb.) 1985, Overseas Dev.Student Award (U.of Camb.) 1986 & 1987. **Publications:** four books incl. *Integrating Biotech.into Plant Breeding Progs: Principles, Methods and Applications* 1989, *The Equitable and Sust.Use of Biodiv: Perspectives from Latin Amer.and the Carib.*(Ed.) 1995; num. chapters, papers, reports. Indiff.to pers.pub., favours news media support. **Languages:** English, French, German, Spanish. Willing to act as consult.etc. **Address:** International Service for the Acquisition of Agri-biotech Applications (ISAAA), 260 Emerson Hall, Cornell University, Ithaca, New York 14853-1902, USA. **Tel.**(office) 1 607 255 1724, (home) 1 607 277 2412; **fax** 1 607 255 1215; **e-mail** afk3@cornell.edu .

KRAUS, Daniel. Cheeta[h]/predator conservation research & education including wildlife & livestock management outside of protected reserves, non-lethal predator control methods. Research Fellow, co-Director. *B*.27 Aug. 1954, White Plains, NY, USA. American, Namibian. *M*. Laurie Marker-Kraus *qv*. **Education:** Utah SU 1967–9, Montana SU 1976–8. **Experience:** conducted res.on Cheetahs since 1987, have worked with variety of wildlife species at two wildlife parks in USA & Kenya with Lion *(Felis leo)* & Leopard *(Panthera pardus)* relocation progs, have broad background on sea fisheries, co-Founded Cheetah Cons.Fund 1990 (multi-disc.& integrated prog.in cons.res.& educ.to assist survival of free-ranging Cheetah and its ecosystems). **Career:** Curator/Foreman, Safari Country 1979–80; oceanic res.in NOAA Res. Ship through Pacific Ocean & China Sea to S.Pacific, Philippines, Japan & China 1980–81; Deck Boss as commercial fisherman 1981–3 & 1984–6; Res. Assoc. KORA Reserve (Kenya) 1983–4; Carnivore & Elephant Ranger, Wildlife Safari 1987–8; co-Dir 1988–91, Res.F.1991–, Center for New Opportunities in Animal Health Scis, Smithsonian Instn; co-Dir Cheetah Cons. Fund 1990–. **Achievements:** have spearheaded global mgmt progs for the Cheetah in the wild, co-founded first intl cons.prog.for free-ranging Cheetahs throughout their range. **Memberships:** IUCN SSC & SSC Captive Breeding SG, PAAZAB. **Award:** Conservationist of the Yr (African Safari Club) 1992. **Publications:** several incl.The Namibian free-ranging Cheetah 1994. Favours pers.pub.& news media support. **Language:** English. Willing to act as consult.etc. **Address:** Cheetah Conservation Fund, POB 247, Windhoek, Republic of Namibia, or International Wilderness Leadership (WILD) Foundation, 2162 Baldwin Road, Ojai, California 93023, USA. **Tel.**264 651 416 (or in USA 1 805 649 3535); **fax** 264 61 34021 (or in USA 1 805 649 1757.

KREBS, Professor Dr John R. Population ecology, behavioural ecology, conservation biology. Chief Executive. *B.*11 Apr.1945, Sheffield, England, UK. British. *M.*Dr Katherine A.: 2 *d.* **Education:** City of Oxf.Sch.: Pembroke Coll. Oxf. MA 1970, DPhil. 1970. **Experience:** extensive res., admin. **Career:** Deptl Dem.in Ornith. 1969–70, U.Lect.in Zool.1976–8, Edward Grey Inst.of Ornith.; Lect.in Zool. 1969–70, E.P. Abraham F.in Zool.1981–8, Official F.1988–, Pembroke Coll.Oxf.; Asst Prof. Inst.of Animal Resource Ecol. UBC 1970–73; Lect.in Zool. UCNW 1973–4; F.of Wolfson Coll.1976–81; RS Res.Prof. Oxf.U.1988–94; Memb.1988–94, Dir Unit of Ecol.1989–94, Sr Scientific Consult.& Chair Animals Res.Cttee 1991–94, AFRC; Dir Unit of Behavioural Ecol.1989–94, Chief Exec.1994–, NERC. **Achievements:** major contribns to study of behavioural ecol. **Memberships:** ISBE (Pres. 1988–90), ZSL (Counc.1991–2), ASAB (Pres. 1993–), Chair NERC Review of Evol., Taxonomy & Biodiv. 1991–2, Scientific Bd Konrad Lorenz Inst.1991–, BBC Sci.Consult.Group 1991–3. **Awards:** Sci. F'ship (Nuffield Fndn) 1981, Scientific Medal (ZSL) 1981, Bicentenary Medal (LS) 1983, F.RS 1984, Ext. Scientific Memb.(Max Planck Soc.) 1985, Hon. DSc (U.of Sheffield) 1993. **Publications:** *Behavioural Ecol.: An Evol. Approach* (co-Ed.) 1978, 1984, 1991, *An Intro.to Behavioural Ecol.*(co-Author) 1981, 1986, 1993, *Foraging Theory* (co-Author) 1987, *Foraging Behaviour* (co-Ed.) 1987, *Behavioural & Neural Aspects of Learning & Memory* (co-Ed.) 1991. Indiff.to pers.pub.& news media support. **Languages:** English, French (some), German (good). Further details may be obtained from Brit.*Who's Who* 1995, *People of Today* 1995, *Who's Who* in the World 1995. Willing to act as consult. **Address:** Natural Environment Research Council, Polaris House, North Star Avenue, Swindon SN2 1EU, Wiltshire, England, UK. **Tel.**44 1793 411599; **fax** 44 1793 411780.

KRIKIS, Dr Andris. Implementation of Helsinki Convention, hazardous waste management, environmentally-sound transport of dangerous goods. Government Commission Representative. *B.*16 Feb.1936, Livani, Latvia. Latvian. *M.*Dr Dagnija Snikere: *d.* **Education:** Agricl U.of Latvia, M(For.) 1959, Bachelor's degree 1962; Riga Techl U. M(Applied Chem.) 1970; Inst.of Organic Synthesis, PhD(Bioorganic Chem.) 1976. **Experience:** res.in peptide chem.; tech.— amelioration projects, large-scale peptide synthesis; admin.as Lab.Head; engg. **Career:** Sr Engr, Meliorprojekts (Riga) 1959–68; Scientific co-Worker 1968–78, Dep.Lab. Head 1980–90, Inst.of Organic Synthesis, Riga AS; Head of Lab.for Envl Prot., Res.Inst.of Amelioration 1978–80; Head of Dept, Envl Prot.

Cttee 1990–93; Head, Helsinki Comm.of Latvia Bur. Min.for Envt, Prot.& Regnl Dev.1993–. **Achievements:** prep.of Helsinki Comm.on Baltic Marine Envt Prot.1972 & 1992 for ratification in Latvian Parliament 1994, compilation of nat.UNCED Report 1992, data surveying for 'Envt for Europe '93'. **Publications:** *c.*50. Dislikes pers.pub., favours news media support. **Languages:** English, Latvian, Russian. Further details may be obtained from *The Envt Enc.and Directory* 1994. **Address:** Blaumana iela 12-33, Riga LV 1050, Latvia. **Tel.**(office) 371 2 325195, (home) 371 2 283991; **fax** 371 7 243077.

KRISHNAMURTHY, Professor Dr Kothandaraman. Mangroves, estuaries, biological oceanography, plankton, ecology, environmental conservation. Senior Professor, Chairman. *B.*9 Aug.1935, Adoni, AP, India. Indian. *M.*Rajalakshmi: 2 *s., d.* **Education:** Annamalai U. MSc 1957, MA 1958, PhD 1969. **Experience:** res., res.super., lecturing, consult., org. **Career:** Res. Assoc., Reader, Prof.Dir 1985–7, Sr Prof. 1988–, Centre of Advanced Study in Marine Biol. Annamalai U.; Chairman, Res.Cttee, Gulf of Mannar Marine Biosphere Reserve 1989–. **Achievements:** CSIR Res.Scholar, Indian UGC; Brit. Council Vis.Sci.1965–6, Alexander von Humboldt F.at U.of Kiel 1966–7. **Memberships:** F.NAS, MBA of India, Current Sci. Assn of India. **Award:** Pitambar Pant Nat. Envt F'ship (Govt of India) 1981. **Publications:** some chapters incl.The Apiary of the Mangroves 1990, Wetlands of S.Asia (co-Author) 1993; *c.*200 others. Indiff.to pers.pub.& news media support. **Languages:** English, German. Willing to act as consult.etc. **Address:** 25 (Upstairs) Kanakasabai Nagar, Chidambaram 608 001, Tamil Nadu, India. **Tel.**(office) 91 4144 83223, (home) 91 4144 20090.

KRISHNAYYA, Professor Jaswant G. Multidisciplinary management analysis, geographical information systems applied to sustainable development planning. Executive Director. *B.*12 Apr.1935, Kolhapur, Mah., India. Indian. *M.* Veronica. **Education:** U.of Poona BE(Telecomm.) 1955; MIT, SM(Elec.Eng.) 1960, Elec. Engr 1961; Harvard Business Sch. ITP 1966. **Experience:** teaching systems analysis, applied res. on tools of multidisc.analysis, consult. **Career:** Lect.in Elec.Engg, MIT 1957–63; Multidisc. Systems Analyst, Inforonics Inc.(Mass.) 1964–5; Prof.(Operational Res.& Mgmt Info.Systems), IIM 1965–74; Founder & Exec.Dir, Systems Res.Inst.1974–. **Achievements:** work on several projects for Dept of Tourism attempting to design ecolly- & envlly-sound dev.progs, estab. of Systems Res.Inst. **Memberships:** Computer Soc.of India (Life), ORSI (Life), IETE (Life), Balaton Group for Sust.Dev., Expert Group on Application of Computers to Rural & Social Dev.of Dept of Electronics, and Futurology Panel of Dept of Sci.& Tech., Govt of India. **Awards:** F.Computer Soc.of India, F.IETE.

Publications: num.reports incl.*India — Basic Needs* (series) 1983–94, *Urbanization in Search of Energy and Modernization & Search for Air Qual.*1991–3, *Applications of THEMAPS GIS* 1988–94. Indiff.to pers.pub., favours news media support. **Languages:** English, French, Hindi (spoken), Russian. Willing to act as consult.etc. **Address:** Systems Research Institute, 17A Gultekdi, Pune 411037, Maharashtra, India. **Tel.**(office) 91 212 420323 or 425432, (home) 91 212 673930; **fax** 91 212 444253; **e-mail** jgk@ soochak.ncst.ernet.in .

KUFORIJI-OLUBI, HH the Otunba Ayora, Bola. Environmentally-sound technology & cooperation in sub-Saharan Africa; demographic dynamics–environment; solid waste disposal management, toxic chemicals & hazardous waste, waste pollution purification & control, waste recycling in the plastics industry. Group Executive Chairman, Chairman & National Representative, Board Member, Government Minister. *B.*28 Sept.1936, Lagos, Nigeria. British/Nigerian. *M.*Chief Daniel Adeyanju Olubi: 2 *s., d.* **Education:** U.of London, BSc(Econ.) 1963; F.of — ACIS 1964, ICAN 1964, ACA 1967, and ICAEW 1977. **Experience:** envl surveys & appraisal, public speaking, charities, widely-travelled. **Career:** Sch.Teacher 1956–9; Chartered Accountancy Articles 1963–6, 3; Audit Mgr 1967–8, Pannell, Kerr & Forster; Group Finance Controller 1968–9, Group Finance Dir 1970–76, MD 1977–83, Vivian, Younger & Bond Nigeria Ltd; Group Exec. Chairman, Bewac PLC 1984–; Memb.of pre-UNCED BCSD 1991–2 then Chairman (Nigerian Chapter) 1991–, Nat.Rep.WBCSD (Geneva) 1991– (then BCSD); Memb. High Level Adv.Bd on Sust.Dev. UN 1993–; Minister for Commerce & Tourism, Interim Nat.Govt 1993–. **Achievements:** being first Chairman of Ogun Osun R.Basin Dev.Auth.1976–80, and first female Chairman of an intl bank (the United Bank for Africa PLC) which resulted in erosion control and provision of credit for marginalized groups, esp.women, for their empowerment and sust.econ.dev.respectively; positions held in WBCSD. **Memberships:** F.of Insts of Directors and of Mgmt, Soroptimist Intl of EKO (Chartered). **Awards:** Memb.of Order of the Niger (Fed.Govt of Nigeria) 1979, Cert.of Merit (UN) 1980, Skomit Award for Excellence (U.of Benin) 1988, Intl Woman of the Yr (Intl Biogl Centre) 1991–2, Men of Achievement (Nigeria) 1992. **Publications:** several incl.Tech.Educ.as a Catalyst for Tech.Coopn and Econ.Growth in Developing Countries (essay) 1992. Favours pers.pub.& news media support. **Languages:** English; Hausa, Ibo, and Yoruba (all major Nigerian languages). Further details may be obtained from *Intl Register of Profiles* (11th edn). Willing to act as consult.etc. **Address:** Corporate Headquarters, Bewac PLC, 13–15 Wharf Road, Apapa, Lagos, Nigeria. **Tel.** (office) 234 1 587 5260, (home) 234 1 587 7534; **fax** 234 1 587 7526 & 1407.

KUKHAR, Professor Dr Valery Pavlovich. Bioorganic chemistry of natural compounds, chemical & technological aspects of environment protection, problems created by the Chernobyl disaster. Institute Director & Head of Laboratory, Professor of Organic Chemistry. *B.*26 Jan.1942, Kiev, Ukraine. Ukrainian. *M.* Nataly: *s., d.* **Education:** Chem.-Tech.Inst. Chem.Ing.1963, Inst.of Organic Chem.(NAS of Ukraine), Cand.of Chem.Sci.1967, Dr of Sci. (Chem.) 1973. **Experience:** res.— organic & organoelement chem.1960–, chem.problems of envl prot.1984–; teaching organic chem.for 18 yrs; admin.as Inst.Dir, VP & Memb.of Presidium of AS* of Ukraine, Head of Chem.Div. **Career:** Res.Sci.& Sr Res.Sci.1966–74 and Head of Lab.Polyhalogen Organic Compounds 1974–83 (Inst.of Organic Chem.), Head of Chem.Div. and Academician–Sec.& Memb.of Presidium 1978–88, VP 1988–93, Head of Lab.of Fine Organic Synthesis 1983– & Dir 1987– Inst.of Bioorganic Chem.& Petrochemistry 1983–, Dir 1987–, Ukrainian AS*; Prof.of Organic Chem. Kiev SU 1976–; VP 1983–8, Pres.1988–93, Ukrainian MAB Cttee, Memb. Chernobyl Comm.of Ukrainian AS* 1986–, Pres.Ukrainian Chem.Soc.1992–. **Achievements:** migration of radionuclides & toxic chemicals, purification of natural & waste water, ecotechnology in chem.industry. **Memberships:** Ukrainian AS (*NAS of Ukraine since 1994) 1985–. **Awards:** A.Kiprianov Award (Ukrainian AS*) 1988, Global 500 Roll of Honour (UNEP) 1993. **Publications:** *Ecotech: The Optimization of Industrial Tech.*(co-Author, in Russian) 1989, *Chem.of Bioregulator Processes* (co-Author, in Russian) 1992, *Chem.of Fluorine-containing Amino Acids* (co-Ed.) 1994. **Languages:** English, Russian, Ukrainian. **Address:** Institute of Bioorganic Chemistry & Petrochemistry, National Academy of Sciences of Ukraine, 1 Murmanskaya Street, 253660 Kiev 94, Ukraine. **Tel.**(office) 7 44 558 5388, (home) 7 44 228 3428; **fax** 7 44 543 5152.

KULL, Professor Dr Kalevi. Ecology of meadow plants, community modelling, theoretical ecology, evolutionary ecology, history of green philosophy, biosemiotics, semiotic mechanisms of biodiversity, plant community diversity. Head of Department & Professor of Ecophysiology. *B.*12 Aug.1952, Tartu, Estonia. Estonian. *M.*Tiiu (Pres.of Estonian Orchid Prot.Soc., plant pop.ecol.). *B.*Dr Olevi Kull *qv.* **Education:** Tartu U. BA 1975, PhD 1987. **Experience:** res.— experimental field plant ecol., plant pop.dynamics, species-coexistence modelling, math.modelling, techniques in ecol.; teaching (BSc–PhD levels) — theoretical ecol., math. modelling in ecol., biosemiotics; admin.— Chair, Meadow Res.Station, coordn of amateurs' res.through a naturalists' soc.; consult.— prot.& mgmt of natural meadows, energy forestry. **Career:** Prof.of Ecophysiol. Tartu U.1992–; Head, Dept of Ecophysiol.1984–, Professor of Ecophysiol.1992–, Inst.of Zool.and Bot. Estonian AS. **Achievements:** co-Founder of Laelatu Biol.Station, orgn of res.& prot.of wooded meadows as most species-rich communities in n.Europe, Founder of Jakob von Uexkull Centre. **Memberships:** IAVS, Soc.for Math.Biol., Estonian Naturalists' Soc.(Pres.1991–4), Jakob von Uexkull Centre; Edl Bds *Estonian Nature* and *Horisont.* **Award:** The Patron of Estonian Life Sci.(Club Dukduk) 1984. **Publications:** *Perspectives in Theory of Phytocoenology* (co-Ed.) 1988, *Lectures in Theoretical Biol.*(co-Ed.) Vols I 1988, II 1993, *Dynamic Modelling of Tree Growth* (co-Author) 1989; *c.*50 scientific papers, num. articles. Indiff.to pers.pub.& news media support. **Languages:** English, Estonian, German (written), Russian. Further details may be obtained from *Estonia: A Ref.Book* 1993, *The Envt Enc.& Directory* 1994. Willing to act as consult.etc. **Address:** Institute of Zoology and Botany, Vanemuise Street 21, EE2400 Tartu, Estonia. **Tel.**(office) 372 7 428619, (home) 372 7 475862; **fax** 372 7 433472; **e-mail** kalevi-@park.tartu.ee .

KULL, Dr Olevi. Research on plant community ecology, pollution impact on plants & ecosystems. Head of Department. *B.*22 June 1955, Rakvere, Estonia. Estonian. *M.*Thea Kull (bot.): *s.*, 2 *d.* *B.*Prof.Kalevi Kull *qv.* **Education:** Estonian Agricl U. BA(For.) 1981, Tartu U. PhD(Plant Ecol.) 1987. **Experience:** res.— plant community ecol., ecophysiol.of photosynthesis and growth, math.modelling, ozone impact on plants, alkaline poll.impact on plant communities; admin.— coordn of res., fundraising, eval.of proposals at Estonian Scis Fndn; consult.— plant community ecol., for.; teaching — plant ecophysiol.& tree physiol.(BSc–PhD levels). **Career:** Res.Sci. Inst.of Zool.& Bot.1979–83, Head of Dept, Inst.of Ecol.1990–, Estonian AS; Res.Sci. Lab.of Ecosystems, Tartu U.1983–9. **Achievements:** basic res.on functional structure of multilayer plant communities and changes under human impact; ozone absorption mechanism in plant leaves. **Membership:** Estonian Soc.of Ecologists. **Awards:** Pfeil Prize Stipendium (FVS) 1990, State Award in Scis (Estonia) 1995. **Publications:** [*Dynamic Modelling of Tree Growth*] (co-Author, in Russian) 1989; 11 scientific articles in Russian, 13 in English. Indiff.to pers.pub.& news media support. **Languages:** English, Estonian, German (basic), Russian. Willing to act as consult. etc. **Address:** Institute of Ecology, Lai 40, EE 2400 Tartu, Estonia. **Tel.** (office) 372 7 428619, (home) 372 7 477764; **fax** 372 2 453748.

KÜLVIK, Mart. Nature conservation, landscape biology, environment. Research Centre Administrator. *B.*20 Dec.1960, Tallinn, Estonia. Estonian. Father Enn Külvik & Mother Helju both foresters. *M.*Maaris: 2 *s.*, *d.* **Education:** U.of Tartu BSc(Biol.& Ecol.) 1984. **Experience:** envl admin., grassroots orgn & sci.; regnl & urban planning and Nature cons.; landscape biol.res.; admin.& applied res.of Nature prot.

Career: Res.F. Tallinn Botl Gdns, Estonian AS 1984–5; Ecol.Adv. Tartu City Auth.& Depts 1985–91; Head Dept of Nature Cons.1991–2, Admin. Nature Cons.Res.Centre 1993–, Min.of Envt. **Achievements:** init.of post-socialist envt & cons., orgn of envl grassroots groups in Estonia, drafting cons.legis.incl.Act on Prot. Natural Objects 1993. **Memberships:** IUCN Prog.Adv.Group (E.Euro.Prog.) and CNPPA, Estonian Fund for Nature (Bd). **Awards:** Intl Man of the Yr (Intl Biogl Centre) 1992–3. **Publications:** *Envl Status Report: Estonia* (Ed.) 1993, *Practical Implementation of the Conv.on Biol.Diversity in the Baltic Countries* (UNEP Workshop report) 1994. **Languages:** English, Estonian, Russian. **Address:** Nature Conservation Research Centre, Ministry of Environment, POB 222, Tartu EE2400, Estonia. **Tel.**372 27 436385; **fax** 372 27 436375; **e-mail** LKU@-LKUK.TARTU.EE .

KUMAR, Prem. Forest resource planning, environmental impact assessment and foreign aid. Regional Resource Management Officer. *B.*11 March 1935, Lahore, Punjab, India. Canadian. *M.*Sunita. **Education:** Indian Forest Rangers' Coll. BSc(For.) 1957, Punjab U. MA (Pol.Econ.) 1963, U.of Guelph MSc(Agricl Ext./Dev.) 1965, U.of Toronto MScF 1967, num.envl mgmt courses taken in Canada. **Experience:** res.forestry, coll.instruction, provincial resource planning, for./resource admin., adv.to & advocacy role in Canadian NGOs. **Career:** res.forester (India); Sr Instr. For. Sch.1967–9; Instr. Concordia Coll. 1969–71; Sr Planner, Alberta Forest Service 1971–6, Regnl Resource Mgmt Officer/For.& Natural Resources Adv. Indian & Northern Affairs, Fed. Govt of Canada 1976–. **Achievements:** memb. of original team of biophysical planners who developed resource eval. methodology for Alberta's wealth of renewable resources; prepared first-ever simple forest mgmt plan for Alberta's Indian reserves; writing & speaking about making Canada's foreign aid more meaningful to the Third World and bringing out contradictions in Canada's bilateral aid in terms of equity employment & hardware approach to dev. **Memberships:** formerly of PFS, ATA, AAB, AIA, CIP & CIF. **Awards:** Ontario Res. Asstship, Forestry Scholarship (Punjab Govt). **Publications:** *c.*15 reports & articles incl.The trop.for.action plan (co-Author) 1989, Some assumptions underlying Canada's foreign aid in For.(co-Author) 1990. Indiff. re.pers.pub.& news media support. **Languages:** English, Hindi, Punjabi (spoken), Urdu. Willing to act as consult.etc. **Address:** 6207–144 Street, Edmonton, Alberta T6H 4H8, Canada. **Tel.** (office) 1 404 495 2779, (home) 1 403 434 0671.

Kuo-Shih HSU, Dr, *see* HSU, Dr Kuo-Shih.

KUPER, Dr Jaap H. Forestry, Nature conservation. Forest Director. *B.*6 Nov.1946, Amsterdam, The Netherlands. Dutch. *M.*Loes. **Education:** Wageningen Agricl U. PhD(Forestry)

1994. **Experience:** admin., res., mgmt., consult. **Career:** Wildlife Res.Officer, Dept of NPWS, Govt of Zambia 1974–6; Regnl Wildlife Officer, FAO Regnl Office Thailand 1976–8; Dir, Het Loo Royal Forest (The Netherlands) 1978–. **Publications:** incl.*Sust.Dev.of Scots Pine Forests* 1994. Indiff.to pers.pub.& news media support. **Languages:** Dutch, English, French, German. Willing to act as consult.etc. **Address:** Koninklijk Park 1, 7315 JA Apeldoorn, The Netherlands. **Tel.**(office) 31 55 219 709, (home) 31 55 552935; **fax** 31 55 224462.

KUSHLAN, Professor Dr James A. Wetland ecology & conservation, conservation of colonial waterbirds (herons, ibises, spoonbills, storks). Professor & Chair of Biology. *B.*11 Oct.1947, Cleveland, OH, USA. American. *M.*Paula Frohring (envl consult., ecol.): *s., d.* **Education:** U.of Miami BS 1969, MS 1972, PhD 1974. **Experience:** res., admin., u.teaching. **Career:** Supervisory Res.Biol. Everglades Nat.Park 1974–84; Prof.& Dir, Water Resources Center, E.Texas SU 1985–7; Prof.& Chair of Biol. U.of Mississippi 1987–. **Achievements:** studies of wetland ecol.& mgmt in Everglades, founding Dir of Water Resources Center, dev.of U.of Mississippi Biol.Field Station. **Memberships:** F.AOU, SWS (Assoc.Ed. *Wetlands)*, CWS (Pres. -elect, past Ed *Colonial Waterbirds)* **Award:** Paul Harris F.(Rotary Intl). **Publications:** *Herons Handbook* 1984, *Storks, Ibises, Spoonbills of the World* 1992; *c.*150 papers. **Language:** English. Willing to act as consult. etc. **Address:** Department of Biology, University of Mississippi, University, Mississippi 38677, USA. Tel.1 601 232 7203; fax 1 601 232 5144.

LaBASTILLE, Dr Anne. Ecology, extinction & endangered species, wilderness conservation, land-use planning. Agency Commissioner, Author, Consultant. *B.*New York City, USA. American. **Education:** Cornell U. BS 1955, MS 1961, PhD 1969. **Experience:** res.in field ecol.in Guatemala, teaching cert., consult.in C. Amer., Carib.& USA. **Career:** 25 yrs as freelance writer, lect.& consult.; Commissioner Adirondack Park Agency, NY 1976–93. **Achievements:** NY State Licenced Guide, certified SCUBA diver. **Memberships:** The Wildlife Soc., Outdoor Writers of Amer., The Explorers' Club, ATB, SWG, num.others. **Awards:** Gold Medal (WWF) 1974, Citation of Merit (Explorers' Club) 1987, Chevron Cons.Award 1988, Gold Medal (SWG) 1993. **Publications:** incl.*Women and Wilderness* 1980, *Beyond Black Bear Lake* 1987, *Mama Poc* 1990, *The Wilderness World of Anne LaBastille* 1992; num.chapters + 150 popular articles & scientific papers. Favours pers.pub.& news media support. **Languages:** English, French (read), Spanish (good). Willing to act as consult.etc. **Address:** West of the Wind Publications Inc., POB 36C, Eagle Bay, New York 13331, USA. **Fax** 1 518 962 8295.

LaBUDDE, Samuel Freeman. Wildlife & species' protection, prevention of illegal trading in wildlife and parts thereof. Executive Director. *B.*3 July 1956, Madison, WI, USA. American. Father Dr John Arthur LaBudde, biochem., mother Bessie Freeman, bot. **Education:** Indiana U. BA(Biol.) 1986 and grad.work in evol.of ecol. **Experience:** campaign orgn & participation, field investigation supervision, extensive work with US Cong., fed.agencies, CITES, IWC, the EC, and other intl fora, to promote wildlife & species prot. **Career:** Machinist, Marine Engr, Seismic Technician, Reforestation Contractor, all in US Pacific Northwest 1977–84; Fisheries Biol. NMFS 1987; Field Biol./Campaign Coord. Earthtrust 1989–90; Field Investigator, FOA 1990; Euro. Consult. HSI 1990–93; Staff Biol./Campaigner, Earth Island Inst.and Marine Mammal Fund 1987 94; Exec.Dir, Endangered Species Project 1991–5. **Achievements:** organized & led campaigns in US & EC to reduce dolphin kills by 95% and to establish a UN moratorium on driftnet fishing in intl waters (both as a result of personal undercover video work); conducted & coordinated intl efforts to expose slaughter & illegal trade of endangered species in Southeast Asia and worldwide which led to US Pelly sanctions re.illegal tiger/rhino trade and passage of wildlife prot. laws in China, Singapore, S. Korea, & Taiwan; co-leader of efforts resulting in passage of first small cetacean resolutions by IWC, and US & EC legis.to protect dolphins & whales; expert testimony given to US & EC legislative cttees & CITES; photographs & film footage have appeared on all major networks world-wide and in num.documentaries, and have been introduced as evidence at legislative hearings in US Cong., EC assemblies, and before the UN. **Awards:** Goldman Envl Prize (Goldman Envl Fndn) 1991, 'Fifty Future World Leaders' (*Time* Magazine) 1994. **Publications:** incl. *Crime Against Nature: Organized Crime and the Illegal Wildlife Trade* (co-Author) 1994. Favours both pers.pub.& news media support as occupational hazards. **Languages:** English, Spanish. Further details may be obtained from *Time,* Dec.5 1994. Willing to act as consult.etc. **Address:** Endangered Species Project, Fort Mason Center E-205, San Francisco, California 94123, USA. **Tel.**1 415 921 3140; **fax** 1 415 921 1302.

LA **CERDA, Professor Dr Alberto M.** VASQUEZ DE, *see* **CERDA, Professor Dr Alberto M.** VASQUEZ DE LA.

LACERDA, Professor Dr Luiz Drude. Biogeochemistry of coastal systems, heavy-metal contamination in tropical ecosystems with emphasis on Hg contamination in the Amazon Basin. Professor of Ecology, Titular Professor of Geochemistry, Researcher. *B.*28 June 1956, RJ, Brazil. Brazilian. *M.*W.Rozane Valente: 2 *d.* **Education:** Universidade Fed.do Rio de Janeiro, BSc(Ecol.) 1978, MSc(Biol.Scis) 1980, PhD(Biophysics) 1983. **Experience:** res.prog. coordn (Head.of Grad.Prog.in Envl Geochem.), lecturing, admin. **Career:** Lect.in Ecol. Universidade Fed.do Rio de Janeiro 1973–81, Universidade Fed.Fluminense 1983–, and Universidad de la Republica (Uruguay) 1994–; Titular Prof. of Geochem. Dept of Geochem. Universidade Fed.Fluminense 1983–; Researcher, Nat. Sci. Council 1983–. **Achievements:** bringing attention to the Hg contamination problem in the Amazon, coordn of an Africa–Latin Amer. Mangrove Prog. **Memberships:** ATB, ISME, Brazilian AAS. **Publications:** incl.*Metals in Coastal Envts of Latin Amer.*1988, *Mercury in the Amazon: A Chem.Time Bomb?* 1991, *Cons.and Sust.Utilization of Mangrove Forest in Latin Amer.*1993; 136 refereed papers. Indiff.to pers.pub., favours news media support. **Languages:** English, French (read), Italian (read), Portuguese, Spanish. Willing to act as consult. etc. **Address:** Department of Geochemistry, Universidade Federal Fluminense, Niteroi, Rio de Janeiro 24020-007, Brazil. **Tel.** (office) 55 21 717 1313, (home) 55 21 239 5912; **fax** 55 21 719 7025.

LACY, Professor Dr Terry Peter DE. Research on Nature conservation and protected area management; parks, tourism, and heritage education. Head, School of Environmental & Information Sciences, and Centre Director. *B*.1 Feb.1948, Charles Sturt U., Albury, Australia. Australian. *M*.Sandra: *s., d.* **Education:** U.of Qld, BSc(Hons) 1969, PhD 1972; U.of Adelaide Dipl.of Educ.1974. **Experience:** res.— envl policy analysis; educ.— developed & managed major prog.in Australia for educ.& training natural- & rec.- area mgrs. **Career:** Lect.in Envl Sci. Roseworthy Agric.Coll.1973 & Riverina Murray Inst.1980; Fndn Head, Sch.of Envl & Info.Scis 1990 and Johnstone Centre for Parks, Recreation, & Heritage 1991, Charles Sturt U. **Achievements:** estimating cons.& rec. values of Australia's nat.estate forests; policy implications of Aboriginal ownership of nat.parks; strats for linking prot.areas & local-level dev.in Asia & the Pacific. **Memberships:** IUCN CNPPA, IAIA, AERC. **Publications:** *Aboriginal Involvement in Parks & Prot.Areas* 1992, *Valuing Natural Areas* 1992, *Culture, Cons.& Biodiv.: the Social Dimension of Linking Dev.& Prot.Areas* 1994. *c*.50 j.articles. Favours pers.pub.& news media support. **Language:** English. Willing to act as consult.etc. **Address:** School of Environmental & Information Sciences, Charles Sturt University, POB 789, Albury, New South Wales 1640, Australia. **Tel.**(office) 61 60 418850, (home) 61 60 218387.

LÅG, Professor Dr Jul. Soil science, geomedicine. Emeritus Professor. *B*.13 Nov.1915, Flesberg, Norway. Norwegian. *M*.Ingrid (deceased): *d., s.*Torleiv (Cand.Agric.). **Education:** Agricl U.of Norway, Cand.Agric.1942, Dr Agric.1949; num.visits to univs in Europe & N.Amer. **Experience:** res.work & admin., teaching soil sci.& related subjects for 37 yrs. **Career:** Prof. 1949–85 and Head 1949–80 Dept of Soil Sci., Rector 1968–71, Agricl U.of Norway; Chairman,

ACN. **Achievements:** two books on soil cons. and Ed.of *Basis of Accounts for Norway's Natural Resources* 1982; active memb.or Chairman of many cttees on envt &/or cons. **Memberships:** NASL 1953– (Pres.1976–84), RNSSL, scientific academies in Denmark, Finland, Poland, and Sweden. **Awards:** Commander of the Cross of Icelandic Order, Copernicus Medal (Polish Acad.), SSS of USSR (Hon.), SSSG (Corres.). **Publications:** five books in Norwegian, Ed.of ten in English incl. *Geomedicine* 1990; *c*.200 scientific pubns; Edl Bds of six scientific journals. Indiff.to pers.pub.& news media support. **Languages:** English, German, Norwegian. Further details may be obtained from *Intl Who's Who* 1995 & earlier edns. Willing to act as consult.etc. **Address:** Norges Landbrukshøgskole, Institutt for Jordfag, Postboks 5028, 1432 Ås, Norway. **Tel.**(office) 47 64 948212, (home) 47 64 940089; **fax** 47 64 948211.

LAIRD, Professor Dr Marshall. Medical entomology and parasitology, especially integrated control technologies for the amelioration of vector-borne diseases. Honorary Research Fellow. *B*.26 Jan.1923, Wellington, NZ. Canadian, New Zealander. *M*.Elizabeth Anne (during 1950s helped greatly in med.entomol.field res.in many trop.S.Pacific islands): 2 *d.* **Education:** Victoria U.of Wellington (then Victoria UC of U.of NZ), MSc(Hons) 1947, PhD 1949, DSc 1954. **Experience:** med.entomol.with partic. ref.to ecol.& control of Culicidae (esp.biol. control), emphasizing intl aspects; avian malariology — taxonomy and geogl distribn notably in Asian Trop.Subregn & Oceania. **Career:** during World War II and until 1954 Med. Entomol.RNZAF (Squadron-Leader); Lect.on Parasitology, Nat. U.of Singapore (then U.of Malaya) 1954–7; Asst Prof.then Assoc.Prof.of Parasitology, McGill U.1957–61; Chief, Envl Biol.Unit, WHO 1961–7; Prof.of Biol.& Dir Res.Unit on Vector Path. Mem.U.of Newfoundland 1967–83; Memb. NRCC 1968–71; Hon. Res.F. Sch.of Biol.Scis, U.of Auckland 1985–. **Achievements:** res.into intl carriage of mosquito vectors of disease by aircraft, and relevant disinfection requirements 1946–61 (Chairman WHO Expert Cttee on Insecticides, 11th Session); pioneer estab.of Singapore-derived *Coelomomyces* protistan pathogen of *Aedes* (*Stegomyia*) spp. mosquitoes, in the Tokelau Islands, trop.Polynesia 1958–60; estab.during 1961–7 of WHO's global prog.on role of biocontrol procedures in the suppression of arthropod vectors of human disease; ten yrs' direction of *Simulium* biocontrol investigations, Newfoundland & W.Africa; dev.of successful integrated control methodology against *Aedes aegypti* to break chain of dengue/DHF transmission on atolls, Funafuti, Tuvalu 1981–3. **Memberships:** RSNZ Wellington Branch (Hon.) 1966–, F.AAAS 1965–, F.RSTMH 1953– (Local Sec.for NZ 1989–), AMCA, OSNZ, SIP (Emer.1984–), PSA (Emer.1986–). **Awards:** Hamilton Prize (RSNZ)

1951, Res.Medal (NZ AS) 1952, Lect. Disting. Franklin Lecture Series (Auburn U. Alabama) 1975. **Publications:** 255 to date incl. *Tsetse — The Future for Biol.Methods in Integrated Control* (Ed.) 1977, *Bibl.of the Natural Hist.of Newfoundland and Labrador* 1980, *Integrated Mosquito Control Methodologies* (co-Ed.) two vols 1983, 1985, *The Natural Hist.of Larval Mosquito Habitats* 1988, *Blackflies — The Future for Biol.Methods in Integrated Control* (Ed.) 1981, *Commerce and the Spread of Pests and Disease Vectors* (Ed.) 1983, *Safety of Microbial Insecticides* (co-Ed.) 1990. Indiff.to pers.pub., favours news media support. **Languages:** English, French (rusty). Willing to act as consult.etc. **Address:** 'Awawhare', Pahi Road, RD1, Paparoa 1240, Northland, New Zealand. **Tel.**(home) 64 9 431 7208.

LAKSHMANAN, Professor Dr Kalimedu Kaliyanna 'gounder'. Angiosperm embryology, ethnobotanical conservation, taxonomy of medicinal & biocidal plants, agroforestry, plant anatomy, *in vitro* studies; coastal ecosystems with mangroves, seagrasses, & seaweeds. Professor of Botany (retired). *B.*19 Feb.1932, Kalimedu, TN, India. Indian. *M.*Kamalam. **Education:** U.of Madras MA 1956, MSc 1961, PhD 1964. **Experience:** res.— 36 yrs' exploration of montane to marine veg., embryology, anatomy, ethnobot., tissue culture; admin.; teaching for 32 yrs. **Career:** Asst Prof.of Bot. Presidency Coll. 1954–8; Researcher, India 1958–64; Alexander V.Humboldt F. Germany 1964–6; Prof.of Bot. Pachaiyappa's Coll.1967–77; Prof.& Head, Dept of Bot. Bharathiar U. 1967–77 (incl. Postgrad.Centre, U.of Madras 1977–92); Indo–US Vis.Prof.1986; Alexander V.Humboldt Fndn Guest Prof.1989. **Achievements:** assisting var. orgns such as Nature Charitable Medicare Trust and envl orgns in cons., Pres.of SEEDS, supervising PhD & foreign students. **Memberships:** IBS, SEEDS (Pres.1993–), Edl Bds of *Phytomorphology, Current Sci.Assn, Acad.of Plant Sci., Acta Botanica, Ethnobot.* **Awards:** Prof.V.Puri Gold Medal (IBS), Best Indian Botanist (SAPS) 1992. **Publications:** two books, *c.*260 papers. **Languages:** English, French (basic), German, Tamil. Willing to act as consult.etc. **Address:** 11 Jalli Thottam, Vadavalli, Coimbatore 641 041, Tamil Nadu, India. **Tel.**91 422 422431.

LAL, Professor Dr Jugal Behari. Sustainable forest use, forest ecology, forest sector development planning. Secretary-General. *B.* 13 Sept.1936, Jais, UP, India. Indian. *M.*Kamini: *s.*, 2 *d.* **Education:** Acad.of Dehradun, AIFC 1959; U.of Manchester, PhD 1980. **Experience:** res.in forest ecol., sectoral planning, and application of remote sensing in forest cons.& mgmt; admin., consult. **Career:** Dir, Forest Survey of India, Indian Govt 1987–90; DG, ICFRE 1990–91; Dir, IIFM 1991–4; Sec.-Gen. Dev.and Cons.Res.Soc.1994–. **Achievements:** pioneering effort in application of remote

sensing to forest mgmt in India, attempt at integrating ecol., econ., and ethnology, in forest mgmt in MP, res.in instnl aspects of forest mgmt. **Memberships:** NEC, ISTF, SIF, Soc.for Mgmt and Dev.Studies (Bd of Govs). **Awards:** Honorarium (IUCN) 1989, Order of Merit with Honour of Samaj Shri (ICME) 1993. **Publications:** three books incl.*Forest Ecol.*1992. Indiff.to pers.pub.& news media support. **Languages:** English, German (good), Hindi, Persian (good), Urdu. Further details may be obtained from WWF–India's *Dir.of Envl Scis Experts* 1993. Willing to act as consult.etc. **Address:** E-16, Shankar Nagar, Bhopal 462 016, Madhya Pradesh, India. **Tel.**(office) 91 755 554997, (home) 91 755 551600; **fax** 91 755 551600 or 555751.

LAL, Piare. Research and development work on tree improvement and vegetative propagation; clonal technology applications for development of genetically superior, high-yielding, and disease-resistant, clones of Poplars *(Populus* spp.), Eucalypts *(Eucalyptus* spp.), and *Casuarina*; farm forestry & reforestation projects, raw materials for wood-based industries. Vice President. *B.*26 Nov. 1942, Jalandhar Distr., Punjab, India. Indian. *M.*Balwant Kaur: 2 *s.*, *d.*Amarjit Saroa (anthropol.). **Education:** Govt Agricl Coll.(Ludhiana, Punjab), BSc(Agric.) 1961; Indian Forest Coll.(Dehra Dun), Associateship & Postgrad.Dipl.in For.1965. **Experience:** tech.& admin.positions in govt depts and commerce. **Career:** Asst/Dep.Conservator of Forests, Forest Dept of A&N Islands 1965–8; Asst Conservator of Forests, Punjab Cadre, Indian Forest Service 1968–70; rose to Group Gen.Mgr, Agrofor.Div. Wimco Ltd (Bombay) 1970–89; VP (Plantations), ITC Bhadrachalam Paperboards Ltd 1989–. **Achievements:** successful implementation for Wimco Ltd of 4,000 ha/yr Poplar plantations under agrofor.in Punjab, Haryana, & Uttar Pradesh, States, and of Farm For.Project for *Eucalyptus* plantations in six districts of Andhra Pradesh; led the R&D team which successfully developed genetically-superior, high-yielding, and disease-resistant, clones of *Eucalyptus*; promotion of clonal farm for. plantations, estab.of gene-banks and clonal seed orchards of genetically-superior 'Bhadrachalam' clones of *Eucalyptus*; R&D work for selection of genetically-superior clones of *Casuarina* is now progressing. **Memberships:** ISF, IPPTA, IPMA (Chairman, Raw Material Sub-Cttee). **Award:** Best Techl Dev.in Res.& Dev.by an Industrial/Scientific Orgn in the State (awarded to ITC Bhadrachalam Paperboards Ltd R&D team by Fedn of AP Chambers of Commerce and Industry). **Publications:** 18 tech.papers incl. Improved package of practices for poplars under agrofor.1991, Vegetative propagation for improvement of *Eucalyptus* 1992, Tech.for improving productivity of plantations 1994, Potential applications of clonal tech.in for.in India 1995. Indiff.to pers.pub., favours news media support. **Languages:** English, Hindi, Nepalese, Punjabi, Urdu. Willing to act as consult.etc. **Address:** ITC Bhadrachalam Paperboards Ltd, 106 Sardar Patel Road, Secunderabad 500 003, Andhra Pradesh, India. **Tel.** (office) 91 40 846566 & 73, (home) 91 40 848732; **fax** 91 40 842997.

LAL, Professor Dr Rattan. Teaching & research in soil conservation, soil processes and 'greenhouse' gas emissions, ecological consequences of tropical deforestation & water management. Professor of Agronomy. *B*.5 Sept.1944, Karyal, Punjab, Pakistan. Indian. *M*.Sukhvarsha S.: 2 *d*., 2 *s*. **Education:** PAU BSc(Agric.) 1963, IARI MSc(Soils) 1965, Ohio State U. PhD (Agron.) 1968. **Experience:** 25 yrs' soil & water cons.and land resto.in India, Australia, Africa & Amer. **Career:** Sr Res.F. U.of Sydney 1968–9, Soil Physicist IITA 1970–87; Assoc. Prof.1987–9, Prof.1989–, Dept of Agron. Ohio SU. **Achievements:** res.on basic processes of soil erosion and its control, soil degradation; developed methods of resto.of degraded lands; quantified ecol.consequences of deforestation in the tropics; studied soil processes & 'greenhouse' gas emissions. **Memberships:** SSSA (F. 1986), ASA (F.1985), ISSS, ISTRO, WASWC, AAAS. **Awards:** F.TWAS 1991, Intl Soil Sci. Award 1988, Soil Sci.Applied Res.Award 1992. **Publications:** *Trop.Ecol.& Phys.Edaphology* 1987, *Soil Erosion in the Tropics: Principles & Mgmt* 1990; Ed.or co-Ed.of further 17 books, Author or co-Author of *c*.500 res. papers. Indiff.to pers.pub.& news media support. **Languages:** English, French (spoken), Hindi, Punjabi, Urdu (spoken). Willing to act as consult.etc. **Address:** Department of Agronomy, The Ohio State University, 2021 Coffey Road, Columbus, Ohio 43210, USA. **Tel.**(office) 1 614 292 9069, (home) 1 614 442 1287; **fax** 1 614 292 7162.

LAMB, Professor Dr Hubert Horace. Climate & weather, human affairs & politics. Emeritus Professor (retired). *B*.22 Sept.1913, Bedford, England, UK. British. *M*.Moirat: *s*., 2 *d*. **Education:** Oundle Sch.(Scholar); Trinity Coll.Camb. BA(Natural Scis & Geog.) 1935, MA(Natural Scis & Geog.) 1947, ScD 1983. **Experience:** memb.pioneer group in forecasting for transatlantic civil aviation, res.on climatic changes, causes thereof, and reconstruction of past climate & weather situations and their impact on human socs (past & present) 1958–. **Career:** Tech. Officer 1936–40, Sr PSO 1945–71 Met. Office; transferred to Irish Met.Service 1940–44; seconded to Antarctic whaling expedn 1946–7 to forecast weather for air whale-spotting over Antarctic waters; long-range weather forecasting & climate res.1948–93; Founder, Climatic Res.Unit, U.of E.Anglia 1971–2; Prof.1971–8 (Emer.1978–), U.of E.Anglia. **Achievements:** a better understanding of global weather & climate dev.& forecasting, and impacts on human hist.& soc.; forecast height & position of main crest of Antarctica from weather analysis 1947. **Memberships:** RMS (1936–), RGS (1947–), AMS (sometime Assoc.), DNHS

(Corres.1978–), BASA 1983–, active in UK Liberal Democrat party. **Awards:** Murchison Award (RGS) 1974, Vega Medal (RSGS) 1984, Symons Mem.Medal (RMS) 1987, Hon.DSc (U.of E.Anglia), Hon.LLD (U.of Dundee). **Publications:** *Climate: Present, Past & Future* (two vols) 1972, 1977, *Climate, Hist.& the Modern World* 1982, *Weather Climate & Human Affairs* 1988, *Historic Storms of the N.Sea, Brit.Isles & NW Europe* 1991. Modest about pers.pub., favours news media support if appropriate. **Languages:** Dutch (some read), English, French (some read), German, Norwegian, other Scandinavian languages (fair spoken). **Address:** Climatic Research Unit, University of East Anglia, Norwich NR4 7TJ, England, UK. **Tel.**& **fax** 44 1603 56161.

LAMB, Robert Paul. Environmental television. Director, Chairman. *B*.19 June 1952, Windsor, England, UK. British. *S*.: *s*. **Education:** Downing Coll.Camb. MA 1979. **Experience:** features editing, public affairs dir, adv.& consult.to UN, World Bank. **Career:** Producer, BBC 1975–6 & ATV 1977, Ed.Earthscan and Adv.to IUCN & UNEP 1977–84, Founder & Dir TVE 1984–. **Achievements:** prod.of *c*.120 envl films* since 1984, num.pubns in mass media & specialist journals. **Membership:** F.RGS. **Awards:** Global 500 Roll of Honour (UNEP) 1988, Officer of Order of Golden Ark 1991. ***Films:** *Seeds of Despair* 1985, *Can Polar Bears Tread Water?* 1988, *Rivers of Sand* 1991, *Developing Stories* 1992. Favours pers.pub. **Languages:** English, French. Willing to act as consult.etc. **Address:** Television Trust for the Environment, Prince Albert Road, London NW1 4RZ, England, UK. **Tel.**(office) 44 171 586 5526, (home) 44 171 221 8661; **fax** 44 171 586 4866.

LAMBERT, Dr Michael Roderick Kirby. Tortoise conservation & sustainable utilization; ecotoxicology in reptiles (especially lizards) and amphibians, and their use as bioindicators of habitat contamination; Saharan & Sahelian herpetofaunal biodiversity. Environmental Biologist. *B*.3 Nov.1941, Sutton, Surrey, England, UK. British. *M*.Marilyn Christina Carol: *d*. **Education:** Trinity Coll.Dublin BA(Bot.) 1965, BA(Zool.) 1966, MA 1970; Birkbeck Coll. London PhD 1975. **Experience:** applied ecol. res.— locust flight behaviour (e.Australia), cons. of terr.chelonians (*Testudo graeca* in e.& s.Medit., *Geochelone* species in Sahelian & sub-Saharan Africa), effects of insecticides on reptiles esp.lizards, and amphibians in sub-Saharan Africa, use of herpetofauna as bioindicators; admin.as past-Chairman of BHS; managerial in organizing & coordinating field projects overseas. **Career:** Leader, Trinity Coll.Dublin High Atlas & Sahara Expedn 1966; Envl Biol. Anti-Locust Res.Centre (later Centre for Overseas Pest Res.and Trop.Dev.& Res.Inst., London, UK) now NRI (Kent, UK) 1967–. Consult. to FAO re.Sahel (Niger, Mali, Burkina Faso) 1975 and W. Africa (Gambia, Ghana, Nigeria,

Guinea, SL) 1988, and Hargeisa (Somaliland) 1993. **Achievements:** Consult.to WWF/FFPS on effects of trade on tortoises in Morocco 1969, and to RSPCA in Algeria & Morocco 1978; Chairman BHS Cons.Cttee 1970–77; Jt Founder IUCN SSC Tortoise (later '& Freshwater Turtle') SG 1981. **Memberships:** F.ZS, IBiol., F.LS, F.RGS, BHS (Chair 1980–91), IUCN SSC Tortoise & Freshwater Turtle 1981– and African Reptile & Amphibian 1993– SGs, World Cong. of Herpetology Exec.Cttee 1982–93. **Awards:** Edge Prizeman (Trinity Coll.Dublin) 1964, RS travel awards to mtgs in Vienna 1981 and Leon (Spain) 1983, and C.Asian Rep. 1994, Brit. Council F'ship to mtg in Prague 1985. **Publications:** *Proc.A, 2nd Euro.Chelonian Symp.*1981 (Ed.), *Testudo graeca* 1982, *Amphibia–Reptilia* 1984, Saharan amphibians & reptiles 1984, On effects of DDT against tsetse flies on lizards in Zimbabwe 1993. Favours pers.pub.& news media support. **Languages:** English, French (fair), Spanish (basic). Willing to act as consult.etc. **Address:** Natural Resources Institute, Central Avenue, Chatham Maritime, Kent ME4 4TB, England, UK. **Tel.**(office) 44 1634 883201, (home) 44 171 589 3558; **fax** 44 1634 880066 & 77 or 883386.

LAMBERTINI, Dr Marco. NGO development, protected areas' organization, development, & management, education and awareness, species' action plans. Director General. *B.*14 Nov.1958, Livorno, Italy. Italian. **Education:** U.of Pisa, PhD(Pharmaceutical Scis) 1983. **Experience:** res.— bird censuses, seabird ecol., envl pollutants, attitudes of people towards wildlife; tech. — NGO mgmt & dev., conflict resolution on prot.areas and wildlife, objective and priority setting in cons.strat.; teaching — ecol.in sec. sch., popularizing courses & sems, tech.sems for Reserve wardens, biologists, NGO volunteers; consult. **Career:** Bird-watching Campaign Officer 1982–4, Head of Reserves 1984–6, Head of Cons.Dept 1986–90, DG 1991–, LIPU; Researcher, Ornithl Section, Natural Hist. Mus. (Livorno) 1983–7; Coord.of Action Plan for the Po Delta Nat.Park 1994–. **Achievements:** estab. of Nat.Park of Tuscan Archipelago, of L. Montepulciano Nature Reserve (Siena), and of Sea-bird Rescue Centre (Livorno); dev.and increase of LIPU reserves and cons.projects. **Memberships:** FFPS, SCB. **Awards:** Agenzia Italiana Petrozi for Young Scis 1977, Spec. Mention Gambrinus Prize on Italian Scientific Lit. 1985. **Publications:** 11 books in Italian incl. [*Handguide of Trop.Ecol.*] 1992, [*The Cons.of Birds in Italy*] (Ed.) 1995, [*Born Free*] 1995, [*Birdwatching for Everybody*] 1986; *c.*30 scientific papers, *c.*400 popular articles. Favours pers.pub.& news media support. **Languages:** English, Italian; French & Spanish (sufficient). Willing to act as consult.&/or ref. **Address:** Lega Italiana Protezione Uccelli, Vicolo San Tiburzio, 5-43100 Parma, Italy. **Tel.** (office) 39 521 289976, (home) 39 337 615292; **fax** 39 521 287116.

LAMPREY, Dr Hugh Francis. National parks & protected areas' establishment, management, and assessment; endangered natural ecosystems. Consultant. *B.*2 Aug.1928, Cairo, Egypt. British. *M.*Rosamond: *s.*Dr Richard Hugh (land-use monitoring, wildlife survey, prot.area planning, aerial and remote-sensing survey), *d.* **Education:** Oxford U. BA(Hons)(Zool.) 1952, MA 1957, DPhil.1962. **Experience:** res.— mammalian ecol., plant–animal interactions, directed Serengeti Res.Inst. Tanzania Nat.Parks 1966–73; tech.— desert encroachment control and related tech.& sociological res.; admin.— supervision of above Instns and Arid Lands Project, Kenya; consult.— prot.area estab., planning, & mgmt, Africa & Middle E.; teaching. **Career:** Military 1946–8; Biol. Game Dept Tanganyika 1953–62; Prin. Coll.of African Wildlife Mgmt 1962–6; Dir, Serengeti Res.Inst. Tanzania Nat.Parks 1966–73; Rep.of IUCN & WWF in E.Africa, and UNEP Consult. Sudan 1974–5; Sr Ecol./Coord. UNESCO integrated project in Arid Lands (Kenya) 1976–85; WWF Regnl Rep.in E.Africa 1986–9; Consult.in Ecol., Wildlife & Prot.Areas 1990–. **Achievements:** elucidated principles of ecol.separation in Savanna mammal communities; estab. Coll.of African Wildlife Mgmt (as first Prin.); first Dir. Serengeti Res.Inst.; init.several WWF cons. projects; studied desert encroachment. **Memberships:** IUCN CNPPA, Edl Bd *African J.of Ecol.* **Awards:** Order of the Golden Ark, Global 500 Roll of Honour (UNEP) 1989, OBE, Fred M.Packard Award (IUCN). **Publications:** *c.*50 incl. Ecol.separation of the large mammal species in the Tarangire Game Reserve, Tanganyika 1963, Estimation of the large mammal densities, biomass & energy exchange in the Tarangire Game Reserve, Tanganyika 1964, On the mgmt of flora & fauna in nat.parks 1974, Distribn of prot.areas in relation to the needs of biotic community cons.in eastern Africa 1975, Structure & functioning of the semi-arid grazing land ecosystem of the Serengeti regn 1979, Pastoralism and the Problem of Overgrazing 1982. Indiff.to pers.pub.& news media support. **Languages:** English, French (read), Kiswahili (spoken, written). Willing to act as consult.etc. **Address:** Little Widefield Farm, Inwardleigh, Okehampton, Devon EX20 3DA, England, UK. **Tel.**(home) 44 1837 52627.

LANDFRIED, Dr Steven Erling. Crane (Gruidae) migration & conservation satellite tracking, environmental education in rural areas. Alternative Learning Coordinator, Author. *B.*1 Nov.1944, Sturgeon Bay, WI, USA. American. **Education:** Lawrence U. BA(Hist.) 1966; U.of W–M, MA 1972, PhD 1978 (both in Curr.& Instruction); addit.training — 1966 NDEA Hist.Inst. Wabash Coll. (IN), 1969 NSF Sociol.Inst. Western Michigan U., 1976 Nat.Chengchi U., and 1981 Harvard U.(Japan Inst.). **Career:** Social Studies Teacher 1966–70; Mgr/Agent for musical groups 1973–5; Public Affairs Officer (part-time), ICF 1979–81; Radio talk show Producer/Host 1986–9; Chairman of Social Studies Dept 1975–90, Coord. Alternative Learning Prog. 1992–, Stoughton High Sch. (WI); Intl Educ.& Wildlife Consult., workshop leader, and Author 1980–; Vis.Assoc.Prof.of Educ. Ripon Coll. (WI) 1991–2. **Achievements:** dev.of pub., educ., & res., activities on behalf of critically endangered Indo–Russian flock of Siberian Cranes; leading advocate of application of satellite tracking tech.to cranes. **Memberships:** BNHS (Life), ICF, Tourism & Wildlife Soc. (Jaipur), and WWF-Pakistan; Nat.Press Photographers' Assn 1985–, IUCN CET 1988–90. **Awards:** Disting. Service Award (NAEE) 1983, Rolex Award for Enterprise 1987, Recognition Award (Inst.of World Affairs, U.of Wisconsin–Milwaukee) 1994. **Publications:** num. incl.Western flocks of Siberian Cranes at the brink of extinction 1991, *The Siberian Crane* (Proc., co-Author) 1992, *Integrated Crane Cons.Activities in Pakistan: Educ., Res.& Pub.*(1980–93) 1994. Accepts pers.pub.& news media support. **Languages:** English; French, German & Spanish (some exposure). **Address:** The Ash House, 21 Albion Street, Edgerton, Wisconsin 53534, USA. **Tel.**(home) 1 608 884 4466; **fax** 1 608 884 4477.

LANG, HE Professor Dr Winfried. International environmental law (protection of ozone layer, climate change, air pollution, nuclear accidents). Ambassador. *B.*16 Nov.1941, Vienna, Austria. Austrian. *M.*Dr Jutta: 2 *s., d.* **Education:** U.of Vienna LLD 1963; Vienna Diplomatic Acad. Dipl.1965–6; Acad.of Intl Law, The Hague 1966. **Experience:** Austrian Diplomatic Service 1966–; Prof.Intl Law & Intl Relations, U.of Vienna 1982–. **Career:** Min.of Foreign Affairs, Vienna 1966; Austrian Embassy, Paris 1968–71 & Tokyo 1971–4; Intl Law Office, Vienna 1974–9; Dep.Head, Austrian Mission, Geneva 1979–84; Dep.Chef de Cabinet, Min.of Foreign Affairs, Vienna 1987–91; Amb.of Austria to UN in Geneva 1991–. **Achievements:** Pres.Vienna Conf.on the Prot.of the Ozone Layer 1985; Pres.Montreal Conf.on Substances that Deplete the Ozone Layer 1987. **Memberships:** ASIL, Deutsche Gesellschaft fur Völkerrecht, ICEL. **Award:** Global 500 Roll of Honour (UNEP) 1990. **Publications:** *Die Verrechtlichung des internationalen Unweltschutzes, vom 'soft law' zum 'hard law'* 1984; *Internationaler Umweltschutz, Völkerrecht und Aussenpolitik zwischen Oekonomie und Oekologie,* 1989; *Negotiations on the Envt* 1991; Is the ozone depletion regime a model for an emerging regime on global warming? 1991; The Intl Waste Regime 1991, Diplomacy and Intl Envl Law-Making 1992; *Intl Envl Agreements and the GATT— the case of the Montreal Protocol* 1993. **Languages:** English, French, German. **Address:** Permanent Mission of Austria, 9–11 rue de Varembé, 1211 Geneva 20, Switzerland. **Tel.** (office) 41 22 733 7050, (home) 41 22 750 2250; **fax** 41 22 734 4591.

LANG-BEERMANN, Professor Dr Ernst M. Ornithology and mammalogy, behaviour of animals, Nature protection. Retired Zoo Director, Professor of Biology of Zoo Animals. *B.*16 Oct.1913, Luzern, Switzerland. Swiss. **Education:** U.of Berne, Dr med.vet.1939. **Experience:** construction of zool.parks and specialist in zoo med. **Career:** Zoo Vet.1939–53, Zoo Dir 1953–78, Basel; Prof.of Biol.of Zoo Animals, U.of Basel 1972–. **Membership:** IUCN Hippo SG. **Awards:** Hon.Memb.IUDZG & German Zoo Dirs. **Publications:** *Goma the Baby Gorilla* 1962, *Das Zwergflusspferd* 1975, *Zootierkrankheiten* (co-Author) 1976; *c.*100 scientific papers. **Languages:** English, French, German. Willing to act as consult. **Address:** Mattweid 22, 6204 Sempach, Switzerland. **Tel.**(home) 41 41 460 1787.

LANGSLOW, Dr Derek Robert. Nature conservation, ornithology, ecology. Chief Executive. *B.*7 Feb.1945, London, England, UK. British. *M.*Helen Katherine: *s., d.* **Education:** Queens' Coll.Camb. MA 1966, PhD 1969. **Experience:** res., lecturing, admin. **Career:** Res. F. Univs of Camb.1969–72 and Kansas 1971; Lect.in Biochem. U.of Edinburgh 1972–8. Sr Ornithol.1978–84, Head of Res.1984–7, Dir of Policy 1987–90, NCC; Chief Exec. English Nature 1990–. **Achievements:** directed wide range of res.progs on birds for Nature cons.and new work on biodiv.& cons.activities. **Memberships:** BES, BOU. **Publications:** 80+ papers. **Language:** English. Further details may be obtained from Brit.*Who's Who* 1994. **Address:** English Nature, Northminster House, Peterborough PE1 1UA, England, UK. **Tel.**44 1733 318364; **fax** 44 1733 898290.

LARSEN, Professor Dr Thor. Conservation & management of natural resources; population biology of large mammals. Professor of Ecology & Centre Director. *B.*26 Feb.1939, Trondheim, Norway. Norwegian. *M.*Soelvi: *s., d.* **Education:** U.of Oslo, Cand.real.1966, Dr Philos.1985. **Experience:** in Europe, N.Amer. & the Arctic (1962–85), in Africa, Asia & C. Amer.(1985–), focussing on ecol.res., mgmt of wildlife, and natural resources, also cons.; Sci.Adv.to Norwegian Govt, intl instns, and NGOs; participation in *e.g.*negns, drafting, and implementation, of res.& cons.projects & progs; Regnl Counc.(w.Europe) & IUCN Council Symp.Convener of 5th World Wilderness Cong. 1993–4; Memb. Final Jury, Intl Wildlife Film Festival 1995. **Career:** Res.F. Norwegian Res. Council 1966–72; Head of Biological Dept 1972–85, Dir of Res.1990–91, Norwegian Polar Res.Inst.; Consult. Norconsult.1985–6; Asst Resident Rep.(Zambia) 1988–90, Spec.Adv. Envt & Dev. Office of DG 1990–95, NORAD; Assoc.Prof.1986–8, Prof.of Ecol. Inst.of Biol. and Nature Cons.1990–, Dir of NORAGRIC 1995–, Agricl U.of Norway. **Achievements:** ind.expert re.prep.of intl agreements & treaties since 1968; has been/is bd memb./chairman of 12 nat.& intl orgns, SGs, & comms; has been invited guest speaker and session chairman at num.intl mtgs & congs; teaching & supervision of MSc & PhD students, refereeing for scientific journals. **Memberships:** IUCN SSC (Regnl Memb.Europe 1990–, Steering Cttee 1991–, SG on Sust. Use of Wild Species 1992–), EAER (Bd, Coord.Cttee 1990–), 5th World Wilderness Cong.(Adv.Bd & Prog.Cttee 1991–), Fridtjof Nansen Inst.(Counc.1991–), EBCD (Bd 1995–); num.past IUCN & WWF comm./cttee memberships. **Publications:** 110 scientific articles, eight books incl.*The World of the Polar Bear* 1978, *Arktis* (Arctic, in English, Norwegian, and Swedish) 1979, *Espen i isen* (in Norwegian, Swedish, Finnish, Icelandic, German, and Japanese) 1981, *The Polar Bear Family Book* (in English, German, and Norwegian) 1991; num. newspaper & magazine contribns; contribns to 19 film & TV productions. Indiff.to pers.pub., favours news media support. **Languages:** English, French (some), German (fair), Norwegian. Willing to act as consult.etc. **Address:** Centre for International Environment and Development Studies (NORAGRIC), POB 5001, N-1432 Aas, Norway. **Tel.**47 64 949794 & 949950; **fax** 47 64 940760; **e-mail** thor.s.larsen@noragric. nlh.no .

LARSON, Professor Dr Joseph S. Wetland ecology, functions & values; application of wetland science to policy & management. Beavers (*Castor fiber* and *C.canadensis*). Professor & Director. *B.*23 June 1933, Stoneham, MA, USA. American. *M.*Wendy Nichols (horticulturist): 2 *d.*incl.Marion Elizabeth (wildlife educ.). **Education:** U.of Mass. BS 1956, MS 1948; VPI PhD 1966. **Experience:** res.— Beaver behaviour, wetland ecol.; teaching — wildlife biol., wetland ecol. and intl cons. to BS & PhD levels; admin.— positions in private & State natural resource agencies in MD & MA; Chairman, Dept of For.& Wildlife Mgmt; Dir, The Envl Inst.; consult.— State & nat.agencies in US, IUCN, Govt of Hungary, WWF in PRC. **Career:** Exec.Sec. Wildlife Cons.Inc.1958–9; State Ornith. & Asst to Dir. Mass.Div. of Fisheries & Game 1959–60; Head, Cons.Educ.Div.1960–62, and Res. Asst, Prof.& Biol.-in-Charge, Western MD Lab. 1965–7, Natural Resources Inst. U.of Maryland; Res.Biol. USFWS 1967–9; Assoc.Prof.then Prof. 1969–, Prof.& Dir of The Envl Inst.1984–, U.of Mass. **Achievements:** conducted first studies of Beaver behaviour by sex & age-class.; dev.first models to predict functions of freshwater wetlands; delegate to conf.of the contracting parties under the Conv.on Wetland of Intl Importance (RAMSAR) (1987 IUCN, 1990 US, & 1993 IUCN, Delegations); IUCN Ecol.Comm., Chairman Nat.Wetlands Tech. Council (US); presented papers and organized sessions in confs in India, France, USSR, Canada, Finland, Sweden, US. **Memberships:** Sigma Xi, Xi Sigma Pi (Forestry), Phi Sigma (Biol.), ESA, The Wildlife Soc., ASM, AAAS, Cosmos Club of Washington DC. **Awards:** Design & Envt Magazine 1976, Public Service (U.of Mass.) 1988; Chevron Cons.Award 1990.

Publications: N.Amer.Wetlands (in *Wetlands)* 1991, (in *Wetland Atlas of the World)* 1993; 70+ res.papers, reviews & reports; 40+ popular papers & book reviews. Indiff.to pers.pub., favours news media support. **Languages:** English, French (poor). Further details may be obtained from *Amer.Men & Women in Sci., Directory of Intl Biog., Who's Who in Amer.* Willing to act as consult.etc. **Address:** The Environmental Institute, Blaisdell House, University of Massachusetts, Amherst, Massachusetts 01003-0040, USA. **Tel.**(office) 1 413 545 2842, (home) 1 413 256 8256; **fax** 1 413 545 2304.

LASH, Dr Jonathan. Environmental law & policy. Institute President. *B.*8 Dec.1945, NY, USA. American. *M.*Eleanor: *s.*, 2 *d.* **Education:** Harvard Coll. BA 1967; Catholic U.(DC) MA 1971, Columbus Sch.of Law thereat JD 1974. **Experience:** works with instns in 50+ countries to bring insights of scientific research, econ.analysis, & practical exp., to pol., business, & NGO, leaders world-wide. **Career:** Clerk to Judge Coffin, US Court of Appeals, First Circuit 1974–5; Asst US Attorney 1974–7; Sr Staff Attorney at NRDC 1978–85; Sec. Vermont Agency of Natural Resources 1987–90; Consult. US EPA Sci.Adv.Bd 1989–90 and Inst.for Sust.Communities 1991–2; Dir, Envl Law Centre, Vermont Law Sch.1990–93, Pres. WRI 1993–. **Achievements:** co-Chair of US Pres.'s Council on Sust.Dev., former Chair of Nat. Comm.on Superfund. **Memberships:** Earth Council, TERI (Adv.Bd), Keidanren Cttee on Nature Cons.(Japan, Intl Adv.), The Alliance to Save Energy (Bd), The Keystone Center (Bd), Putney Sch.(Bd), Vermont Law Sch.(Bd). **Publications:** incl.*A Season of Spoils* 1984, Integrating Science, Values and Democracy 1994. **Languages:** English, Spanish. **Address:** World Resources Institute, 1709 New York Avenue NW, Washington, District of Columbia 20006, USA. **Tel.**1 202 638 6300; **fax** 1 202 638 0036.

LAST, Professor Dr Frederick Thomas. Effects of atmospheric pollutants, integrated land-use & tree biology (particularly the role of mycorrhizas). Part-time Consultant. *B.*5 Feb. 1928, Wembley, Middlesex, England, UK. British. *M.*Pauline Mary: 2 *s.* **Education:** Haberdashers' Aske's Sch.; ICL Assoc.RCS (Bot.) 1948, U.of London PhD 1951, DSc(Plant Path.) 1966. **Experience:** agric., hort., for., ecol., atmos.poll.studies at diff. times in temperate & trop.regns working with EC and as consult.with Envl Resources Mgmt Ltd. **Career:** Asst.Lect. ICL 1948–51; Rothamsted Experimental Station 1951–61 (seconded to Sudan Govt as Chief Plant Pathologist 1956–8); Head Mycology & Bacteriology, Glasshouse Crops Res.Inst.1961–9; Vis.Prof. Penn. SU 1969–70 & U.of Newcastle 1986–; Dir Inst.of Tree Biol. 1970–74; Prof.of For.& Natural Resources, U.of Edinburgh 1972–; Directorate, ITE 1974– 86. **Achievements:** identification of environs of leaves as ecosystems in miniature, physiol. analyses of effects of biotic & abiotic agents of disease incl.atmos.pollutants, tree improvement focusing on role of mycorrhizas. **Memberships:** AAB (Pres.1977–8, Hon.1982–), F.LS 1984–, F.IBiol.1965–, F.IHort.1986, ICF 1970–, Commissioner Red Deer Comm.1981–6, Chairman Scottish Adv.Cttee on SSSI 1992–, Chairman Tree Advice Trust 1993–. **Awards:** F.RSE 1975– (Prog.Convenor 1993–), Scottish Hortl Medal 1992, Foreign Memb.(RNBS) 1968–. **Publications:** *Tree Physiol.& Yield Improvement* (co-Ed.) 1976, *Land & Its Uses: Actual & Potential* 1982, *Acidic Deposition, Its Nature & Impacts* 1991; *c.*150 papers. Indiff.to pers.pub., welcomes news media support. **Languages:** English, French (basic), Spanish (basic). Further details may be obtained from *Who's Who in Scotland* (4th edn), *VIP Scotland* (1st edn). Willing to act as consult.etc. **Address:** Furuly, Seton Mains, Longniddry, East Lothian EH32 0PG, Scotland, UK. **Tel.**(home) 44 1875 852 102; **fax** 44 1875 852800.

LASTER, Dr Richard E. Environmental law. Senior Partner, Lecturer. *B.*8 July 1944, Richmond, VA, USA. American, Israeli. *M.*Hana Atiya: 3 *s*. **Education:** U.of Virginia BA 1966, U.of Richmond Law Sch.JD 1969, Harvard Law Sch.LLM 1970, Hebrew U. Dr Jur.1975. **Experience:** teacher, author, consult.& practitioner in private practice of envl law and, in certain specific areas, occupational health law where these areas are connected to envl nuisances. **Career:** Raider, memb.of Ralph Nader's staff, Washington 1970; articled clerk, District Court, Jerusalem 1972; Legal Staff, US EPA, 1973; Lect.in Legal Writing, Boston U.Law Sch.1969; Legal Adv. EPS 1973–9; Coord. Workshop in Envl Problems 1975–9, Instr. Sem.in Envl Policy 1981–, Adv. Sch.of Public Health 1986–, Lect. Envl Law 1989– and Center for Envl Studies 1990–, all at Hebrew U. Jerusalem; Partner, Laster & Zisquit 1979–89 and Laster & Gouldman 1989–. **Achievements:** helped to create EPS and served as its first legal adv.1973; at the same time edited the first vol.of annotated envl laws for State of Israel*; commenced private practice in 1979 specializing in envl law and served as legal adv.to the Assn of Towns for Haifa, Hadera & Northern Galilee, Southern Judea, Ashkelon, & Ashdod; served as legal adv. to — Drainage Auths of Rivers Naman, Kishon, Harod, and Basor, the Yarkon R.Auth. (first to be created in Israel), Former Asbestos Workers' Assn, workers injured at the Tadiran nickel–cadmium factory, and nuclear workers in the Dimona Nuclear Res.Facility. **Memberships:** IELA (Chairman), Assn for Health Educ.in Israel (Chairman), ICA Cttee for Envl Law, ICEL, ISEEQS (Sec.). **Awards:** Moot Court (U.of Richmond), selected honor soc. **Publications:** *Ed.of first vol. of annotated envl laws for the State of Israel, Reading D: planning and bldg or bldg and then planning? 1973, *The Legal Framework for the Prevention & Control of

Water Poll.in Israel 1976, Quarrying in Israel: admin.roulette 1976, L.Kinneret and the law 1977, *Envl Prot.in Israel: Taming the Wild E.*(selected papers) 1977, Observations: public participation in envl problems 1983, Legal Aspects of Water Qual.Mgmt in Israel 1980, Remedies for Air Poll.Damage to Agric.1983, River Auths in Israel: A Comparison of Different Models 1989, Right to Know in Israel Envl Law 1992; *Intl Enc.of Laws: Envl Law in Israel* (monogr.) 1993. Favours pers. pub.& news media support. **Languages:** English (mother tongue), French (weak read & spoken), Hebrew. Willing to act as consult, etc. **Address:** 10 Hanassi Street, Jerusalem 92188, Israel. **Tel.**972 2 635224; **fax** 972 2 636926.

LAVIEREN, Lambartus Piet VAN. Protected areas' & wildlife management, tropical forest management, environmental impact assessment. Senior Consultant. *B.*4 March 1941, Echteld, The Netherlands. Dutch. *M.*Gerdina J.A.: 2 *d.* incl.Hanneke (marine biol.). **Education:** Agricl U. Wageningen MSc 1970. **Experience:** wildlife res., training of prot.area supervising personnel in French-speaking Africa & Indonesia–ASEAN regn; consult.in trop.for.& ecol.(Africa, S & SE Asia) for intl financing agencies; project formulation & appraisal; EIA; envl profile studies. **Career:** Res.F. Agricl U. 1967; wildlife res.in Zambia, FAO 1970–73; Team-leader, prot.area & wildlife mgmt training in Cameroon, FAO 1973–9; Min.of Foreign Affairs (The Netherlands), Indonesia 1979–95; Sr Consult.in Trop.Forest & Ecol. Euroconsult 1985–. **Achievements:** Founder of Sch.of Envl.Cons.in Ciawi (Bogor); Team-leader Ecole de Faune, Garoua, Cameroon; training prot.area personnel for 18 French-speaking African countries. **Memberships:** IUCN CNPPA, NILI. **Publications:** *Wildlife Mgmt in Savannah Woodlands* (Africa) (co-Ed.) 1978, *Wildlife Mgmt in the Tropics* (text book, three vols) 1983; num.papers. **Languages:** Bahasa (fair), Dutch, English, French, German (spoken). Willing to act as consult.etc. **Address:** Euroconsult, POB 441, 6800 AK Arnhem, The Netherlands. **Tel.**(office) 31 85 577111, (home) 31 8889 1447; **fax** 31 85 577577.

LAVRENTIADES, Professor Dr George. Systematic botany, plant identification, systematic microbiology, plant sociology, flora & vegetation. Emeritus Professor of Systematic Botany and Plant Geography. *B.*11 April 1921, Trabzon, Black Sea, Turkey. Greek. *M.*Chatiklia: *d.*Sophia (biol.). **Education:** Aristotle U. graduated as Agriculturist 1947, as Naturalist 1951, PhD(Natural Scis) 1956; U.of Camb. (UK), Lower Cert.in English 1952; Conservatory of the State of Thessaloniki, graduated as Violinist 1955. **Experience:** u.teaching, main memb.of c.Adv.Cttee for Envl Prot. Min.of N.Greece, memb.Adv.Bd of Mtn Flora of Greece, Sci.resp.for Intl Medit.Progs res.progs of EU and for Ramsar Contract for N.Greece.

Career: Violinist, Symphony Orchestra of Thessaloniki 1940–55; Prof.& Head of Dept of Bot., Dean of Fac.of Sci., sub-Pres. U.of Patras (S.Greece) 1967–71; Prof.& Head of Dept of Systematic Bot.and Plant Geog.1971–87, Pres. Dept of Athletics 1983–5 and of Biol.Sch.of Fac.of Sci.1984–6, Pres. Sch.of Musical Studies of Fac.of Arts 1986–7, Emer.1987–, Aristotle U.of Thessaloniki (N.Greece); Pres. Soc.of Teachers of Natural Sci.at Gymnasiums and Lyceums (Middle Sch.) 1975–84. **Achievements:** geobotl investigations of Ormos Archangelou on Rhodes Is.1969, *Coastal Veg.of Greece and Its Prot.— Veg.Ecol.and Creation of New Envts* (Proc.of Intl Symp.in Tokyo) 1984; other pubns*. **Memberships:** Soc.of Musicians of Thessaloniki, Greek Soc.of Biol. Scis, Greek Botl Soc.(Founder Memb.), Internationale Vereinigung für Vegetationskunde, OPTIMA, IPE. **Awards:** Hon.Memb.(Dept of Athletics, Aristotle U.of Thessaloniki) 1985, Hon.Dist. (Biol.Sch.of Fac.of Scis, Aristotle U.) 1989, Hon.Dist.(Soc.of Greek Lit.Men) 1995. **Publications:** *num.incl.*Excerpta Botanica Sectio B Sociologica* (co-Author) 1966, *Prodromus eutopaischen Pflanzengesellschaften* (co-Author) 1960–61, *O Pontos* (Greek Enc., vols I & II, co-Author) 1991, *Ecosystems of the World* 1993; chapters & papers incl.Dry Coastal Ecosystems of Greece 1993. Favours pers.pub. **Languages:** English, French (poor), German, Greek, Italian (poor). Further details may be obtained from *Who's Who in Western Europe* 1981, *Intl Directory of Distinguished Leadership* (4th edn), *Flora Hellenica Literature Database* (Botl Lab. of U.of Copenhagen). Willing to act as consult. etc. **Address:** 23 Thessaloniki Street, 570 13 OreoKastron, Thessaloniki, Greece. **Tel.**(home) 30 31 696251 & 697274.

LAYDOO, Richard Stanislaus. Coral-reef ecology/biology, marine parks & protected areas, coral-reef management/monitoring, resource management, environmental impact assessment, conservation. Research Officer. *B*.13 Feb.1955, San Fernando, Trinidad. Trinidadian. *M*.Elizabeth Michelle. **Education:** U.of the W. Indies BSc(Bot.Hon.) 1978. **Experience:** coral-reef res.& monitoring, EIA, tech.consult.to CCA's Marine Park Mgmt Network Prog. **Career:** teacher to ordinary & advanced levels, St Joseph's Convent, 1978–81; Jr Res.Officer 1981–8, Res. Officer 1988–, Inst.of Marine Affairs. **Achievements:** survey & description of reef systems in Tobago, participation in prep. of Reef Mgmt Plan, advising Regnl Marine Parks Mgmt Network Prog. CCA. **Memberships:** U. of the W.Indies Biol.Soc.(Hon.), Trinidad & Tobago Scientific Assn. **Award:** Best Tech. Paper (Geol Soc.of Trinidad & Tobago) 1988. **Publications:** *The Shallow-water Scleractinians (Stony Corals) of Tobago, W. Indies* 1990, *A Guide to the Coral Reefs of Tobago* 1991; num.tech.reports. Indiff.to pers.pub., favours news media support. **Language:** English. Willing to act as consult, etc. **Address:** Institute of Marine Affairs, POB 3160, Carenage Post Office, Republic of Trinidad and Tobago. **Tel.**(office) 809 634 4291 to 4, (home) 809 627 6319; **fax** 809 634 4433.

LE **HOUÉROU, Dr Henry Noël,** *see* **HOUÉROU, Dr Henry Noël** LE.

LEAKEY, Dr Roger Richard Bazett. Domestication of tropical trees for forestry/agroforestry in humid, semi-arid, & montane, tropics; vegetative propagation and clonal selection of trees; agroforestry systems especially multi-strata agroforests; weed biology. Director of Research. *B*.19 July 1946, Nairobi, Kenya. British. Father the late Douglas G.B.Leakey, forester in Kenya. *M*.Alison E.: 2 *s*. **Education:** Marlborough Coll.; Seale-Hayne Agricl Coll.(Devon, UK) NDA & CDA 1967, UCNW BSc(Hons) 1970, U.of Reading PhD 1974. **Experience:** res.on physiol.of regeneration from rhizomes, rooting of tropical tree stem cuttings, & branching processes and flowering, extensive res.in E.& W.Africa, C.Amer., & SE Asia; admin.of res.teams and supervision of postgrad.students, Sec.of NERC Tree Biotech. Liaison Group, Memb.& Chairman (1993) of Edinburgh Centre for Trop.Forests' Supervisory Cttee; consults for FAO, World Bank, CGIAR, EDF, ODA. **Career:** grad.student, Weed Res. Orgn (O.xf.) 1970–74, SSO, ITB (Edinburgh) 1974–85; PSO (Head of Trop.Forests and Mycorrhizas Group), ITE 1985–94; Dir of Res. ICRAF 1994–. **Achievements:** domestication of range of trop.trees to mitigate against deforestation, envl degradation and soil depletion, and create sust.land-use systems. **Memberships:** CFA, ISTF, AAB. **Awards:** Hon.F. Fac.of Sci. and Hon.Memb. IERM (both U.of Edinburgh). **Publications:** *Domestication and the Rebuilding of Forest Resources* (co-Author) 1994, *Domestication of Trop.Trees for Timber & Non-Timber Forest Products* (co-Author) 1994; 100+ res.papers. Indiff.to pers.pub., favours news media support. **Languages:** English, French (basic spoken), Spanish (poor spoken). Further details may be obtained from ICRAF Staff List. Willing to act as consult.etc. **Address:** International Centre for Research in Agroforestry, POB 30677, Nairobi, Kenya. **Tel.**254 2 521006; **fax** 254 2 521001.

LEATHERWOOD, Dr James Stephen. Ecology & conservation of marine mammals. Research Associate, Consultant, Foundation Director. *B*.12 Oct.1943, Ozark (Dale Co.), AL, USA. American. *D*.: *s*., *d*. **Education:** Calif. SU, BS(Lit.) 1966; UCSB & San Diego SU, grad.studies in ecol.1969–75; Texas A&M U. PhD 1995. **Experience:** res.— marine mammal biol.(studies of ecol.of free-ranging marine mammals leading to concern re.num.cons. problems facing them around the world; since late 1970s work has been directed towards cons.with focus broadening to intl activities); consult.— US Marine Mammal Comm., Nat. Marine Fisheries Service, Minerals' Mgmt Service, Nat.FWS, Nat.Marine Sanctuary Prog., NPS, Calif.AS, UNEP MMAP & SPREP, IWC, Sri Lankan Govt, IUCN, Philippine Govt, States of Alaska, Calif., & Florida, San Diego Natural Hist.Mus., private industry; Scientific Adv.Bd M'ships — CRIOMM, ACS, CSI, The Whale Center, Terra Marine Res.& Educ., Oceanic Soc.Expedns, Marine Mammal Center, Therapy for a Damaged Planet, The Mirage Dolphin Prog., Ocean Park Cons.Fndn. **Career:** Teacher in lit., maths, & natural scis in high sch. 1966–7, Laverne Coll.1969, var.field schools 1973– and U.of Calif. 1974–6; Admin. Officer 1967–70, Res.Biol.1970–78 US Navy's MMRP; Sr Staff Sci. Hubbs Marine Res.Inst. 1978–89; Dir, Ocean Park Cons.Fndn 1993. **Achievements:** helping to implement plans of action of UNEP & IUCN SSC through fund-raising & collabn with researchers in many countries, increasing awareness re.marine mammals & their cons.in Indian Ocean Cetacean Sanctuary & the Philippines, working to bring reason to mgmt of intl fisheries affecting marine mammals, and to consolidate the res.findings of many workers on var.topics by editing vols of collected papers. **Memberships:** SMM (Charter Memb.), ASM, Res.Assoc.& F. San Diego Natural Hist.Soc., Res.Assoc. Inst.of Bioacoustics (Texas A&M U.), UNEP MMAP (Acting Sec.1989), Chairman IUCN SSC Cetacean SG 1990–. **Awards:** Man of the Year (ACS) 1973, Cons.Award for Baiji Cons.(Chinese AS) 1993. **Publications:** *The Seal World Book of Dolphins* (co-Author) 1981, *The Sierra Club Handbook of Whales & Dolphins* (co-Author) 1982, *The Gray Whale [Eschrichiius glaucus]* (Ed.) 1986, *Dolphins & Porpoises of the Eastern N.Pacific: A Guide to Their Identification in the Water* (co-Author) 1988, *The Bottlenose Dolphin* (Ed.) 1990, *The Sierra Club Handbook of Seals & Sirenians* (co-Author) 1992; Ed.or co-Ed.of four spec.issues of scientific journals; Author or co-Author of 150+ sci.papers. Does not object to pers.pub.provided there has been prior discussion, favours news media *support*. **Languages:** English; French & Spanish (some read & written). Willing to act as consult.etc. **Address:** POB 1090, Solana Beach, California 92075, USA. **Tel.**1 619 546 7148; **fax** 1 619 546 7003 or 792 0352.

LEBLANC, Dr Hubert. Development and environment. Independent Consultant. *B*.3 Nov. 1942, Hull, Quebec, Canada. Canadian. *M*. Monique: 2 *s*., *d*. **Education:** U.of Tolouse, Doctorat de 3c Cycle (Droit et Développement) 1972. **Experience:** worked with native communities on envl issues in n.Quebec hydro projects, with & through IDRC on land-tenure issues in Senegal, in land mgmt in Mali & Burkina Faso, assisted in elaboration of Envl Action Plan of Guinea, drafted Benin's envl law, prepared draft law in Laos intended to protect the customary rights of (ordinary) citizens to use of forest land & products. **Career:** Agent/Mgr in Dev.Res. IDRC 1971–6; Diplomat Canadian Foreign Service 1976–80; Dev.Officer (with Quebec

Natives) James Bay Energy Corpn 1980–83; Info.Researcher on refugee issues, Canadian Immigration 1984–5; Project Mgr, CIDA 1985–9 and 1990–91; Ind.Consult.1991–. **Achievements:** contributed to bringing envl issues closer to the everyday preoccupations (and basic needs) of poor rural communities in a few Third World countries and N.Amer.native communities. **Memberships:** Quebec Bar, IUCN CESP. Accepts pers.pub.& news media support. **Languages:** English, French, Spanish (good basic). Willing to act as consult.etc. **Address:** 173 rue Dumas, Hull, Québec J8Y 2N8, Canada. **Tel.** (home) 1 819 778 2594; **fax** 1 819 776 9973.

LEBRETON, Professor Dr Philippe. Biodiversity & bioconservation, species' protection & natural areas. Professor of Biology & Environmental Sciences. *B*.25 Oct.1933, Saint-Etienne, France. French. *M*.Paulette. **Education:** U.of Lyon Docteur-Ing.(Chem.& Biochem.) 1956, Docteur ès Scis Naturelles 1962. **Experience:** res.in vegetable biochem., ornith., and ecol. **Career:** up to Prof.of Biol.& Envl Scis, U.of Lyon I 1958–94. **Achievements:** Parc Nat.Vanoise, Council & Admin.Council; Solem Reserve naturelle de Dombes 1970–94; Parc Natural Regn Vercors & Parc Natural Regn Pilat, Scientific Council 1988–. **Membership:** Conseiller Régnl (Ecologiste) Rhône–Alpes 1992–8. **Awards:** Officier du Mérite Agricole, Global 500 Roll of Honour (UNEP) 1990, Hon.Memb. Conseil de la Société Ornithologique de France. **Publications:** *Savoie Vivante* 1973, *Atlas Ornithologique Rhône–Alpes* 1977, *Eco-Logique* 1978, *La Nature en Crise* 1988, *Guide du Naturaliste en Dombes* 1991; *c*.200 other scientific papers. **Languages:** English (read), French, German (read). Willing to act as consult.etc. **Address:** 78 Route de Paris, 69751 Charbonnières les Bains, France. **Tel.**(home) 33 78 553666; **fax** 33 72 258529.

LEE, Dr Lawrence H.Y. Applied biology, Nature conservation. Departmental Director. *B*.28 May 1937, HK. British (HK). *M*.Eileen: 2 *s*. **Education:** U.of HK, BSc(Zool.& Bot.) 1962, PhD(Ecol.of *Brassica* Aphids) 1977; U.of Reading, MSc(Tech.of Crop Prot.) 1969. **Experience:** res.in agricl entomol.with particular emphasis on vegetable pests; admin.in agric., fisheries, country parks & Nature cons. **Career:** Biol.Tutor, Chinese U.1962–3; Pest Control Officer 1963–7, Entomol.1967–74, Sr Agricl Officer 1974–80, Asst Dir (Agric.) 1980–83, Dep.Dir 1983–6, Dir 1986–, Agric.& Fisheries Dept, Country Parks Auth.; JP 1980–. **Achievements:** non-chem.control of aphids, dev.& mgmt of country parks & Nature reserves, designation & mgmt of marine parks & reserves. Promotion of envlly-friendly husbandry techniques in agric.& mariculture. **Memberships:** IBiol., Entomol.Soc.of Amer. **Awards:** Imperial Service Order, Hon.VP (MBA HK). **Publications:** *Check List of Agricl Insects of HK* (co-Author) 1981. Indiff.to pers.pub.& news media support. **Languages:** Chinese, English. **Address:** Agriculture & Fisheries Department, Canton Road Government Offices, 14/F 393 Canton Road, Kowloon, Hong Kong. **Tel.**852 733 2100; **fax** 852 311 3731.

LEEFLANG, Sietz Arnold. Ecological techniques (and ways of working, living, & building, on a human scale). Director, President. *B.*29 May 1933, Haarlem, The Netherlands. Dutch. *M.* Anke Maria (co-Founder, De Twaalf Ambachten*/De Kleine Aarde**). **Education:** Inst.for Press Scis, U.of Amsterdam 1952. **Experience:** teaching progs for practical biol.husbandry at De Kleine Aarde** Fndn, and ecol.techniques & practices at De Twaalf Ambachten* Centre; guest lect. Dcpt of Arch. Tech. U.Eindhoven. **Career:** Foreign Desk Ed.(1952– 6) and Sci.Ed.(1956 69) for nat.daily newspaper *Algemeen Handelsblad*; Ed.of popular sci.progs for Dutch TV 1965–70; publicist for Philips phys.labs (Eindhoven) 1969–72; co-founded (with wife) the envl centre **De Klcinc Aarde (Small Earth) in 1972, and *De Twaalf Ambachten (The Twelve Trades) Centre & Fndn in 1977. **Achievements:** introduced new methods for biol.husbandry, ecol. bldg & heating systems, and systems for small-scale water saving & purification in The Netherlands. **Award:** Global 500 Roll of Honour (UNEP) 1990. **Publications:** *Politieke Wereldatlas* (An Atlas of Pol.Affairs) 1956, *Vandaag Beginnen* (Starting Today) 1979, Ed.of several magazines, *e.g.Goed Wonen, Bèta, De Kleine Aarde*, 1962–. Indiff.to pers.pub., favours news media support. **Languages:** Dutch, English, French (poor), German. Willing to act as consult. etc. **Address:** De Twaalf Ambachten, de Bleken 2, 5282 HB Boxtel, The Netherlands. **Tel.**31 4116 72621 (9–13 hrs daily).

LEEMANS, Dr Rik. Ecological theory, biodiversity, vegetation dynamics & structure at different temporal & spatial scales. Senior Scientist. *B.*14 April 1957, Wijchen, The Netherlands. Dutch. *M.* **Education:** U.of Nijmegen, BSc 1980, MSc 1983; U.of Uppsala, PhD 1989. **Experience:** res.— computer implementation of forest dynamics' models, large-scale integrated envl models, databases & geographic info.systems; consult.— Nature cons. orgns re. climate change & global change issues. **Career:** Res.Scholar, Biosphere Project, IIASA 1988–91; Sr Sci. Dept of Terr.Ecol.& Global Change, Nat. Inst.for Public Health and the Envt 1991–. **Achievements:** dev.of several dynamic models linking ecol.theory with envl drivers & projecting future veg.dev. **Memberships:** IAVS, IEU, ESA, DES. **Publications:** num.incl.*A Systems Analysis of the Global Boreal Forest* (co-Ed.) 1992, Climate change due to the greenhouse effect & its implications for China (co-Author) 1992, *Assessing Impacts of Climate Change on Veg.using Climate Class. Systems* (co-Author) 1993, Quantifying feedback processes in the response of the terr.carbon cycle to global change: the modelling approach of IMAGE-2.0

(co-Author) 1993. Indiff.to pers.pub.& news media support. **Languages:** Dutch, English, German (fair), Swedish. Willing to act as consult.etc. **Address:** Department of Terrestrial Ecology & Global Change, National Institute for Public Health and the Environment (RIVM), POB 1, 3720 BA Bilthoven, The Netherlands. **Tel.** (office) 31 30 2743377, (home) 31 30 282560; **fax** 31 30 2744435; **e-mail** rik.leemans@rivm.nl .

LEES, Ms Annette Mary. Protected areas, design and implementation in tropical forests incorporating local & indigenous concerns, sustainable logging of tropical forests. Deputy Chief Executive Officer, Regional Representative. *B.*11 Nov. 1959, Whakatane, NZ. New Zealander. *M.*Dr Shane D.T.Wright *qv.* **Education:** U.of Canterbury, BSc 1982. **Experience:** forest cons.in NZ, S.Amer.& S.Pacific through NGOs and consults; since 1989 managed trop.forest cons.prog.for the Maruia Soc., S.Pacific. **Career:** Wildlife Surveyor, Wildlife Service, NZ Govt 1982; Scientific Researcher, Native Forests Action Council (NZ) 1983–6; Cons. Consult. S.Amer. 1986–8; Mgr, S.Pacific Trop. Forests Prog.l988–92, Dep.CEO 1992–, Maruia Soc.; Regnl Rep. Cons.Intl 1992–. **Achievements:** team leader for first ecol surveys to establish prot.areas in Fiji & Solomon Islands; developed prot.area prog. that accommodates indigenous landownership systems, indigenous cultural & social needs, and village based income generation. **Memberships:** Trustee, Pacific Dev.and Cons.Trust 1989–92; IUCN CNPPA 1993–; Biodiv.Expert, Tech.& Mgmt Adv.Group, S.Pacific Biodiv. Cons.Prog.1993–; Selection Cttee Memb. Vol. Agency Support Scheme, NZ Min.of External Relations & Trade 1994–. **Publications:** num. papers. Favours pers.pub.& news media support. **Languages:** English, Spanish (reasonable), Tok Pijin. Willing to act as consult.etc. **Address:** 120 Bethells Road, RD 1, Henderson, Auckland 8, New Zealand. **Tel.** 64 9 810 9535; **fax** 64 9 810 9535.

LEFF, Dr Enrique. Theory on environment & sustainable development in underdeveloped regions, environmental education & training in Latin America & the Caribbean. Regional Coordinator. *B.*24 May 1946, Mexico DF, Mexico. Mexican. *M.*Jacqueline: *s., d.* **Education:** Nat. U.of Mexico, BA(Chem.Eng.) 1968; U.of Paris I, Doctorat de Troisième Cycle 1975. **Experience:** res., admin./coordn. **Career:** Researcher 1973–84, Dir of Programa Universitario 'Justo Sierra' (Interdisc.Res.Centre in Social Scis) 1985, UNAM; Regnl Coord. Envl Training Network, Regnl Office for Latin Amer.& Carib. UNEP 1986–. **Achievements:** contribn to critical theory on envt & dev., promoting & coordinating regnl prog.for envl training in Latin Amer.& Carib. **Memberships:** IUCN CESP, Edl Bds *Capitalism, Nature, Socialism* (NY) and *Ecologia Politica* (Barcelona). **Awards:** Nat. Res. (Nat.System for Scientific Res.) 1985. **Publications:** *Ecologia y Capital* 1986 & 1994,

Medio Ambiente y Desarrollo en Mexico 1990, Cultura y Manejo Sustentable de Recursos Naturales (co-Coord.) 1993, *Ciencias Sociales y Formacion Ambiental* (co-Coord.) 1994. Indiff. to pers.pub.& news media support. **Languages:** English, French, Italian (spoken), Spanish. Willing to act as consult.etc. **Address:** Boulevard de Los Virreyes Nr 155, Col.Lomas Virreyes, CP 11000, Mexico DF, Mexico. **Tel.**52 5 202 4841/ 6913; **fax** 52 5 202 0950 or 520 7768.

LEMONS, Professor Dr John D., Jr. Research & writing on nuclear waste, biological conservation, national parks' management, climate change, environmental ethics, environmental education. Professor of Biology & Environmental Science, Editor-in-Chief. *B.*6 May 1947, CA, USA. American. **Education:** Calif.SU (Long Beach) BS 1970 (Zool.); U.of Wyoming, MS (Zool.& Physiol.) 1972, PhD(Zool.& Physiol.) 1975. **Experience:** sr level res.& admin.in govt, industry & academia; reviewing for several journals. **Career:** Researcher & Naturalist, NPS 1968–75; Res.Sci. Allied Chemical Corpn 1974–6; Dir Sierra Nevada Inst.1977–8; Assoc. Prof.& Chair, Dept of Biol.& Envl Studies, New England Coll.1978–82; Fac.Memb. Deep Springs Coll.1982–4; Assoc.Prof.& Chair, Dept of Envl Studies, Sweet Briar Coll.1984–7; Prof. of Biol.& Envl Sci.and Chair Dept of Life Scis, U.of New England 1987–; Ed.-in-Chief, *The Envl Professional* 1990–; Consult.Ed. Envl Handbooks series, Blackwell Scientific Pubns 1993–. **Achievements:** pubn of 70 peer-reviewed articles/chapters, selection as Ed.-in-Chief of *Envl Professional,* sig.dev.of envl sci./ studies progs at colls & univs, recipient of grants to support work in nat.park mgmt, nuclear waste disposal, envl ethics. **Memberships:** AAAS, AIBS, NAEP, NAEE. **Awards:** F'ships from Amer.Univs & USAEC 1974 and Amer.Univs & USEDA 1975 & 1976, Best Paper Award (NIES) 1985. **Publications:** Carbon dioxide & the envt: a problem of uncertainty 1985, US Nat. Parks mgmt: values, policy, and possible hints for others 1987, Integrated Envl Mgmt and the Use of Sci.at the Proposed High-level Nuclear Waste Repository at Yucca Mtn, Nevada 1994. Indiff.to pers.pub.& news media support. **Language:** English. Willing to act as consult. etc. **Address:** Department of Life Sciences, University of New England, Biddeford, Maine 04005, USA. **Tel.**(office) 1 207 283 0171, (home) 1 207 871 8062; **fax** 1 207 282 6379.

LEWIS-SMITH, Dr Ronald Ian. Antarctic plant ecology, environment & conservation. Senior Research Scientist & Section Head. *B.*29 Jan.1942, Aberdeen, Scotland, UK. British. *M.* Elinor Margaret Miller: 2 *s.* **Education:** Aberdeen Grammar Sch.; U.of Aberdeen BSc 1964, PhD 1968, DSc 1988. **Experience:** formerly memb.of SCAR Subcttee on Cons.and later Group of Specialists on Envl Affairs & Cons. **Career:** Sr Res.Sci.1964–, Head Plant Ecol.& Envt Section 1974–, Brit.Antarctic Survey

(Camb.UK). **Achievements:** Antarctic prot. areas (SPAs, SSSIs etc.) — site designation, proposals & mgmt plans leading to contribns to dev.of Protocol on Envl Prot.to the Antarctic Treaty, several Antarctic EIAs. **Memberships:** SCAR, BES, ESA, FFPS. **Award:** Polar Medal (HM Govt, UK) 1977. **Publications:** *Antarctic Cons.Areas* 1985, *Developing the Antarctic Prot.Area System* 1994; 100+ scientific papers since 1970. Indiff.to pers.pub.& news media support. **Languages:** English, French (some spoken, fair written), Spanish (written). Further details may be obtained from *Who's Who in Sci.*(US). Willing to act as consult.etc. **Address:** British Antarctic Survey, Madingley Road, Cambridge CB3 0ET, England, UK. **Tel.**44 1223 61188; **fax** 44 1223 62616.

LI, Shuang Liang. Harnessing & utilization of waste. General Adviser & Consultant. *B.*29 Sept.1923, Xin Zhou County, Taiyuan City, Shanxi Province, PRC. Chinese. *M.*Wang You Deng: 3 *s.,* 2 *d.* **Education:** Sr Middle Sch. **Experience:** dump harnessing & utilization for improvement of envt, comp.application of waste slag & residue spread over more than 60 enterprises throughout China, explosion techniques. **Career:** Gen.Adv.& Consult. Taiyuan Iron & Steel (Group) Co. –1980. **Achievements:** mgmt of steel slag, 17 diff.sorts of mix products & refractories have been recovered & reclaimed from slag (scrap of 9.30 m.tons), elimination of source of envt poll. **Memberships:** Emer.Prof. (Shanxi Province Party Sch.), rep.of People's Cong. **Awards:** Global 500 Roll of Honour (UNEP) 1988, Labour Day Medal (PRC), Model Worker of China. **Publications:** 10+. Favours news media support. **Languages:** Chinese, English. Willing to act as consult.etc. **Address:** Taiyuan Iron and Steel (Group) Company, Taiyuan City, Shanxi Province, People's Republic of China. **Tel.**(office) 86 351 301 3941, (home) 86 351 304 3745; **fax** 86 351 304 4170.

LI, Professor Wenhua. Forest ecology, Nature conservation, agroforestry, sustainable development. Professor. *B.*15 Jan.1932, Guangrao County, Shandong Prov., PRC. Chinese. *M.*Songhua: 2 *d.* **Education:** Beijing For.U. BSc.1953, Forest Inst. USSR AS MSc.1961. **Experience:** 2 yrs' res.coordn and consult.in topics of forest ecol., agrofor., Nature cons., natural resources, and watershed mgmt in China & S.Asia. **Career:** teaching and head of Div.of Forest Ecol.1953–73; head of forest group in Tibetan plateau expedn 1973–8; Assoc.Prof.& Head of Div.of Biol.Resources; Exec.Dir, Comm. for Integrated Survey of Natural Resources, Chinese AS; Exec.Pres.& Sec.-Gen.of Chinese Nat.Comm.for MAB prog. (UNESCO) 1978–; Guest Prof. ETH, Chief Tech.Adv.& Consult.to FAO & UNDP 1990–. **Achievements:** study of distribution & structure of subalpine coniferous forest of Eurasia for over 30 yrs; coordn of several LTER stations; researcher & leader of multidisc.expedns in Tibetan plateau, and

Himalaya and Hengduan mtns; Chairman/Chief Tech.Adv.for several intl progs such as MAB (UNESCO) and Watershed Mgmt in S.Asia (FAO). **Memberships:** CANR (VP 1983–), CAE (Standing Cttee 1982–94), IUCN (Regnl Counc.1986–94), Standing Cttee of START, Global Change Prog.ICSU 1990–. **Awards:** Hon. Dr (Chinese AS) 1982, scientific from Chinese Govt & AS, and for Nature Reserves of China. **Publications:** six books, 50 papers, Ed.in charge of series of monogrs comprised of 68 vols & pubns; V.Chief Ed.*Forest Ecosystem Studies* and *Natural Resources Scis.* Favours pers.pub., indiff.to news media support. **Languages:** Chinese, English, Russian. Willing to act as consult. etc. **Address:** Commission for Integrated Survey of Natural Resources, Chinese Academy of Sciences, POB 767, Beijing 100101, People's Republic of China. **Tel.**(office) 86 10 491 3580, (home) 86 10 256 8062; **fax** 86 10 491 4230.

Liang LI, Shuang, *see* **LI, Shuang Liang.**

LIKENS, Professor Dr Gene Elden. Limnology; aquatic ecology, analysis of ecosystems; biogeochemistry, precipitation chemistry, land–water interactions. Adjunct Professor, Professor (twice), President & Director. *B.*6 Jan.1935, Pierceton, IN, USA. American. *M.*Phyllis Irene: *s.*, 2 *d.* **Education:** Manchester Coll.Indiana, BS 1957; U.of W–M, MS 1959, PhD 1962. **Experience:** 35 yrs' res.in ecol., 15 yrs' admin. **Career:** Instructor/Asst Prof./Assoc.Prof. Dartmouth Coll. 1961–9; Assoc.Prof./Prof./Chairman, Section of Ecol.& Systematics, Cornell U.1969–83; Adjunct Prof. Cornell U. 1983–; Prof.of Biol. Yale U.1984–; Prof. Grad.Field of Ecol. (grad.prog.) Rutgers U.1985–; VP NYBG and Dir.Mary Flagler Cary Arboretum 1983–93; Dir.1983– & Pres.1993–, Inst.of Ecosystem Studies. **Achievements:** 11 books, *c.*315 other pubns. **Memberships:** NAS (Temp.Nominating Group, Chair Section 27), Amer.AAS, F.AAAS, AIBS, Amer.Polar Soc., ESA (Pres.1981–2), ASL, FBA, Gamma Alpha, Hudson River Envl Soc., IASWS, IAGLR, IWRA, Phi Sigma, Sigma XI, SIL (US Nat.Rep. Sept.1972–Aug.1995), ASLO (Pres.1976–7). **Awards:** Amer.Motors Cons.(Professional Category) 1969, NATO Sr F'ship 1969, G.E. Hutchinson (first, ASLO) 1982, Regents Medal of Excellence 1984, NYAS 1986, first Intl Prize in Limnetic Ecol. (Ecol.Inst.Oldendorf/ Luke, Germany) 1989, AIBS Disting.Service 1990, Tyler Prize 1993, World Prize for Envl Achievement 1993; elected — Amer.AAS 1979, NAS 1981, RSAS 1988, Hon.Memb. BES & AWRA; Guggenheim F'ship 1972–3, USDA Forest Service 75th Anniv.1980; Hon.Degrees — DSc Manchester Coll.1979, Rutgers U.1985, Plymouth SU 1989, and Miami U.1990, D. Humane Letters Union Coll.1991, Doctl *H.C.* U.für Bodenkultur (Vienna) 1992, DSc Marist Coll. 1993. **Publications:** *Biogeochem.of a Forested Ecosystem* (co-Author) 1977, *Dry Deposition of Sulfur: a 23-yr Record for Hubbard Brook Forest*

Ecosystems (co-Author) 1990, *The Ecosystem Approach: Its Use & Abuse* 1992. **Languages:** English, French (read), German. **Address:** Institute of Ecosystem Studies, Box AB, Millbrook, New York 12545-0129, USA. **Tel.**1 914 677 5343; **fax** 1 914 677 5976.

Lin SUN, Professor, *see* **SUN, Professor Lin.**

LINDNER, Dr Warren Henry. Implementation of action on sustainable development. Senior Political Adviser. *B.*13 Oct.1942, MD, USA. American. **Education:** U.of Denver BA(Psych.& Intl Relations) 1965, Duke U.Law Sch. JD 1969. **Experience:** res., admin., legal. **Career:** Assoc. Attorney, Mayer, Brown & Platt 1969–71; Staff Memb.Marymont Intl Sch. France 1971–2; Partner, Vinson & Elkins 1972–80; Dep.DG, WWF Gland 1980–82; Dir Energy Dept, Société Générale pour l'Energie et les Ressources 1982–4; Sec. WCED Geneva 1984– 8; Intl Coord. The '92 Global Forum; Chief Exec. '94 Global Forum 1993–4; Exec.Dir, The Centre for Our Common Future 1988–96; Sr Pol.Adv. 12th World AIDS Conf. (Geneva) 1996–. **Memberships:** Bd of Trustees of N–S Roundtable and of Gaia Fndn, Hon.Treas. N–S Roundtable, Adv. Bd Gallup Intl, Intl Prog.Adv.Bd of Earth Council, Comm.on Sust.Dev., Adv.Bd of Intl Literacy Group; Edl Bd *Tomorrow Magazine.* Indiff to pers.pub.& news media support. **Languages:** English, French. **Address:** 18 ter Chemin de Pinchat, 1227 Carouge, Geneva, Switzerland. **Tel.**(in France) 33 50 903612 & **fax** 33 50 900321; **e-mail** 101376.3300@CompuServe.Com .

LINDSTRÖM, Professor Dr U.B. Sustainable development, particularly sustainable agriculture and energy politics; ecological balance sheets. Executive Secretary. *B.*26 Jan.1937, Helsinki, Finland. Finnish. *M.*Kerstin. **Education:** U.of Helsinki, Agron.1962, Dr(Agron.& For.) 1969; U.of Wisconsin, MSc 1966. **Experience:** extensive teaching & counselling in developing countries re.sust.agric.& for., advising industrialized & developing countries. **Career:** Dir Central Assn for Artificial Insemination Socs in Finland 1962–7, Specialist Researcher 1968–77, Dep.Head 1976–7 then Prof.& Head 1977–80 Animal Breeding Dept, Agric.Res. Centre; Vis.Lect. U.of Nairobi 1972–4; Prof.& Head of Dept of Animal Breeding, U.of Helsinki 1980–83; Exec.Sec. Finnish Nat.Cttee for UNICEF 1984–. **Achievements:** extensive writing on envt, ecol., & sust.dev., lectured on sust.econ. dev.at Sch.of Commerce, Helsinki; has lectured & written on developing country issues since 1962; init.village progs in W.Africa for sust. dev. **Memberships:** Chairman, section for Dev.Res. Finnish Acad.1981; Bd of Dirs, Dev.Inst. Helsinki 1981–2; Nominator for World Hunger Awards, Brown U.1986–, Edl Bd *Envt & Dev.*magazine 1993–. **Awards:** Finnish Agricl Journalists' Prize for info.activities 1977, Student Assn of Helsinki U.Award for activities benefitting developing countries 1980, Global

500 Roll of Honour (UNEP) 1992, Swedish Cultural Fndn Award 1992. **Publications:** *Intro.to Genetics & Animal Breeding* (lecture notes) 1973, Food prod.in the world and in Finland (in Swedish) 1978, *Growth or Sust.*(in Swedish) 1981, *The Land of Camels & Desert* (schools booklet, in Finnish & Swedish) 1988; *c.*360 scientific articles. Favours pers.pub.& news media support. **Languages:** English, Finnish, French (satisfactory spoken), Swedish. Willing to act as consult.etc. **Address:** Finnish National Committee for UNICEF, Box 148 1 SF, 00211 Helsinki, Finland. **Tel.**(office) 358 0 6927 500, (home) 358 0 385676; **fax** 358 0 6923 932.

LINET, Mrs Christiane. Conservation. President. *B.*29 April 1934, Etterbeek, Belgium. Belgian. *W.* **Education:** U.of Brussels, License 1956. **Experience:** admin., consult. **Career:** Vol.1966, Chief Ed.of WWF-Belgium Magazine 1967–93, Memb.of Bd 1970–, President 1992–, WWF-Belgium. **Memberships:** IUCN SSC Otter SG 1976–. **Award:** Order of the Golden Ark 1975. **Languages:** French, English; Italian & Russian (some); Spanish. **Address:** WWF-Belgium, Chaussée de Waterloo 608, B-1060 Brussels, Belgium. **Tel.**32 2 347 0111; **fax** 32 2 344 0511.

LINZEY, Professor Rev. Dr Andrew. Ethical and theological status of animals. Senior Research Fellow, Special Professor in Theology. *B.*7 Feb.1952, Oxf., England, UK. British. *M.* Josephine Ann: 2 *s.*, 2 *d.* **Education:** King's Coll.London, BD, AKC 1973; U.of Wales Coll. of Cardiff, Dipl.in Pastoral Studies 1974; St Augustine's Coll.(Canterbury, England, UK), theological training 1974–5; U.of London PhD 1986; U.of Oxf. MA Status 1992. **Experience:** lecturing, consult., author. **Career:** Chaplain 1981–92, Dir of Studies, Centre for the Study of Theol.1987–92, U.of Essex; SRF* Mansfield Coll. U.of Oxf.1992–; Vis.Lect.in Theol. U.of Prince Edward Is.(Canada) 1993; Vis.Prof. St Xavier U.(Chicago, USA) 1994; Spec.Prof.in Theol. U.of Nottingham (UK) 1992–. **Achievement:** *holder of world's first post in the Ethics and Theol.of Animal Welfare. **Memberships:** IUCN CESP 1994–, RSPCA (Nat.Council 1972–6, Theol.Consult.1989–), Centre for Respect of Life and the Envt 1989–, Earthkind (Religious Affairs Consult.) 1989–, The Genetics Forum 1994–, Edl Bd *J.of Soc.and Animals* 1991–. **Awards:** Peaceable Kingdom Medal (INRA) 1990, F.RSA (Council nominee) 1993. **Publications:** Author &/or Ed.or co-Ed.of 15 books incl.*Animals and Christianity* 1988, *Animal Theol.*1995, *Dict.of Ethics, Theol. and Soc.*(co-Ed.) 1995. Favours pers.pub. & news media support. **Language:** English. Further details may be obtained from *Dict.of Intl Biog.*1995. Willing to act as consult.etc. **Address:** Mansfield College, Mansfield Road, Oxford OX1 3TF, England, UK. **Tel.**(office) 44 1865 270983, (home) 44 1865 201565; **fax** 44 1865 270983.

LIONNET, Joseph Felix Guy. Agronomy, natural history, scientific bibliography. Technical Adviser. *B.*31 May 1922, Curepipe, Mauritius. Mauritian. *M.*Marie-Therese M.: 2 *d.*, 2 *s.* **Education:** Coll.of Agric.(Mauritius), Dipl.in Agric.1944; City & Guilds of London Inst.in Sugar Manufacture, Dipl.1944. **Experience:** control of qual.of essential oils prior to export, investigating rendzina soils, res.on vanilla, cinnamon, & coconut, prod., involvement in biol. control of insect pests, res.on biogeog.& ecol. and on prior scientific investigations. **Career:** Lab.Asst 1945–56, Agricl Chemist 1956–9, Dir of Agric.1960–69, Dept of Agric.(Seychelles); Dir of Culture 1978–92, Tech.Adv.1992–, Min. of Educ.& Culture (Seychelles). **Achievements:** resp.for Nature cons.as Dir of Agric.and Chairman Agricl Bd of Seychelles, Nat.Envt Comm.& Seychelles' Is.Fndn, resp.for mgmt of two Seychelles Natural reserves declared as WHSs by UNESCO — Vallée de Mai and Aldabra. **Memberships:** IPS, Soc.for Hist.of Natural Hist., ADELF (mer/outremer), RSAS (Mauritius), Assn Historique Internationale de l'Océan Indien. **Awards:** MBE (Memb.), Chevalier de l'Ordre des Arts et des Lettres de France, Global 500 Roll of Honour (UNEP) 1987. **Publications:** *The Seychelles* 1972, *C. Western Indian Ocean Bibl.*(co-Author) 1973, *Striking Plants of Seychelles* 1975, *Le Monde des Vertébrés des Seychelles* 1984, *The Romance of a Palm: Coco-de-mer* 1986, *L'Ile aux Images* 1986. Indiff.to pers.pub., favours news media support. **Languages:** English, French, Seychelles Creole. Willing to act as consult.etc. **Address:** Ministry of Education & Culture, POB 68, Mahe, Seychelles. **Tel.**(office) 248 224688, (home) 248 344030; **fax** 248 224845.

LISICKÝ, Dr Mikuláš Juraj. Ecosozology (conservation science), ecology of floodplains. Head of Department. *B.*9 May 1946, Trenčín, Slovak Republic. Slovak. *M.*Eva Lisická-Jelínková (lichenologist). **Education:** Comenius U. MSc 1968, PhD(Zool.) 1983; Charles U. postgrad.study in Envl Sci. 1980. **Experience:** coordn of biol.monitoring on R.Danube 1989–92 and resto.project on Morava R.1994–, lecturing, admin. **Career:** Sr Lect.in Cons.Biol.1976–85, Head, Dept of Ecosozology & Physiotactics 1990–93, Comenius U.; Head, Dept of Ecosozology & Monitoring, Slovak AS 1989– 90, 1993–. **Achievements:** Founder of the above-mentioned two Departments. **Memberships:** Slovak Ecol & Zool Socs, Slovak Soc.for Sust.Living. **Awards:** IX Premio Europeo di Letteratura giovanile 'Provincia di Trento' per la letteratura didattica (U.of Padua, for book*). **Publications:** incl.*Living Symmetry (in Slovakian) 1980, *Nature Cons.: Intro.to Ecosozology* 1987, *Mollusca of Slovakia* 1991. Indiff.to pers. pub., favours news media support. **Languages:** English, French (spoken), German, Polish (spoken), Russian (spoken), Slovak. Further details may be obtained from *Who is Who in Slovakia* 1990, *Envt Enc.& Directory* 1994. Willing to act as consult.etc. **Address:** Dlhá ulica 15, 900 31 Stupava, Slovak Republic. **Tel.**427 378 2221.

LISTER-KAYE, Sir John, Bt of Grange, Yorkshire. Conservation lecturing, writing. Regional Chairman, Executive Director. *B*.8 May 1946, Yorks., England, UK. British. *M*.Lucinda Anne (Lady Lister-Kaye JP, Dir & Trustee, Aigas Field Centre). **Education:** Allhallows Sch. **Experience:** landowning, farming, admin., lect. **Career:** Founder/Exec.Dir, Aigas Field Centre 1970–; Farmer (family farms) 1974; NW Regnl Chairman, Scottish Natural Heritage 1991–. **Achievements:** founded Britan's first private field studies centre (Aigas Field Centre), and the Aigas Trust for Envl Educ. (1970). **Memberships:** RSPB (Scottish Chairman 1986–91), NCCS (NW Chairman 1991–2). **Award:** Gold Award for Envl Educ.(Wilderness Soc.) 1983. **Publications:** *The White Island* 1972, *The Seeing Eye* 1979, *Seal Cull* 1980. Indiff.to pers. pub.& news media support. **Languages:** English, French, Gaelic (some). Willing to act as consult.etc. **Address:** Aigas House, Bealy, Inverness-shire IV4 7AD, Scotland, UK. **Tel.**44 1463 782443; **fax** 44 1463 782097.

LITVIN, Professor Dr Vladimir M. Ocean geology, geography, ecology, cartography. Head of Department. *B*.10 Feb 1932, Tinepropetrovsk, Ukraine. Ukrainian. *M*.Ludmila: 2 *d*. **Education:** Moscow U. Geographic Fac.1955, Inst.of Oceanology Cand.Sc.1964, PhD 1980. **Experience:** marine expedn investigations in Arctic, Atlantic, Indian, & Pacific, Oceans, and Barents, Greenland, Norwegian, Baltic, Black, Medit., Red, & Carib., Seas 1955–85; u.lect.in oceanology, marine geomorph., ecol.& landscapes 1984–. **Career:** Scientific Worker, Polar Inst.of Fishery & Oceanogr. (Murmansk) 1955–65; Scientific Worker & Head of Geomorph.& Geophys.Lab., Atlantic Branch, Inst.of Oceanology (Kaliningrad) 1966–86; Head, Ocean Geog.Dept, Kaliningrad U. 1984–. **Achievements:** ecol–geographic investigations in Atlantic Ocean & Baltic Sea, marine landscape study & mapping, geoecol.system modelling of Baltic Sea and its coasts, u.teaching. **Memberships:** EUCC, REA, Russian Geog.Soc., Russian Soc.for Nature Cons., Baltic Ecol.Parliament. **Awards:** Honour Diplomas (Russian Geog.Soc.) 1971 & 1994, Prizes from Inst.of Oceanology 1975, 1978 & 1981 and Kaliningrad U.1992–4. **Publications:** 250+ incl.(all in Russian) [*Morphostructure of the Atlantic Ocean Bottom*] 1980, [*Morphostructure of the Ocean Bottom*] 1987, [*Fundamentals of the Ocean Phys.Geog.*] 1988, [*Geoecol.of the Marine Landscapes*] (Ed.) 1992, [*World of the Submarine Landscapes*] 1994. **Languages:** English, German (poor), Polish, Russian. Willing to act as consult.etc. **Address:** Ocean Geography Department, Kaliningrad University, ul.A.Nevskogo 14, 236041 Kaliningrad, Russia. **Tel.** (office) 7 0112 432434, (home) 7 0112 462540; **fax** 7 0112 465813.

LIU, Professor Peitong. Interaction, coadaptation, & copromotion, between Man & environment seeking a virtuous cycle in an ecologically-sound, sustainable anthropocentric superecocomplex. Honorary Director. *B*.5 Dec.1916, Xun Co., Henan Prov., PRC. Chinese. **Education:** Beijing Normal U. BSc 1936–40, Moscow Nat.U. Vis.Scholar 1957–9. **Experience:** res.& teaching in chemicogeography & envl sci., geog., envl cancers; investigated envl resource in SE Tibet & NW Yunan and chemicogeography in Daihai Basin; consult.for sci.instns & economic auths. **Career:** Researcher, China Geog.Inst.1940–46, Lect.& Researcher, Beijing Normal U.1946–. **Achievements:** fndn of chemicogeography in China which opened new approach in envl sci., estab.of pedo-chemico geography lab., envl lab., & nat. lab.for envl simulation (supported by World Bank); EIA for several key nat.economical projects incl.energy, hydro, chemical, mining & urban devs. **Memberships:** Academic Cttee Memb.of Geog.Inst. of Chinese AS and of CAES, Dir of Chemicogeography Cttee of GSC, Dir Educ. Comm.of CAES, Sci.Memb.of IGU Geog.& Public Admin.Comm., IUCN Comm.on Educ. **Awards:** State Awards for Excellent Teaching Material Dev.(Envl) 1987 & Outstanding Contribns 1992. **Publications:** Hydrochemicogeography of Daihai Basin 1965, *System Analysis of Envl Problems* (symp.proc.) 1980, *Devs & Envts: Regnl Study & Dev.*1987, *Chemicogeography* 1994. **Languages:** Chinese, English, Russian. Further details may be obtained from *Knowledge of Geog.*1987 (pp.19–21 8th edn). Willing to act as consult.etc. **Address:** Institute of Environmental Sciences, Beijing Normal University, 100875 Beijing, People's Republic of China. **Tel.**(office) 86 10 201 2510, (home) 86 10 201 2288 or 2583.

LOCK, Dr John Michael. Taxonomy of African Zingiberaceae & Leguminosae, plant–animal interactions, classification of world vegetation. Principal Scientific Officer. *B*.25 Sept.1942, Guildford, Surrey, England, UK. British. *M*. Lesley Moira McGowan: *s*., *d*. **Education:** U. of Camb. BA 1963, MA 1967, PhD 1967. **Experience:** res.into Hippopotamus ecol.; taxonomy & biol.of African Zingiberaceae; African Leguminosae; class.of world veg., teaching of bot.& ecol.in Africa, consults in envl effects of Jonglei Canal (Sudan); ranching & veg.(Llanos of Venezuela); veg.in area of new Fed.Capital of Nigeria; poisonous plants & cattle in S.Tanzania; veg.change in Queen Elizabeth Nat.Park (Uganda) 1970–88. **Career:** Res.F. Makerere U.1967–70; Lect. U.of Legon 1970–77; Ind. Consult.1978–90; PSO, R.Botanic Gdns 1990–. **Achievements:** ecol.of veg.in Uganda & Sudan, cons.& mgmt of Wicken Fen (UK). **Memberships:** BES, BBS. **Publications:** *Legumes of Africa — a Check List* 1988, *The Jonglei Canal — Impact & Opportunity* (co-Author) 1988, *Legumes of W.Asia — a Check List* (co-Author) 1990, *Legumes of Indochina — a Check List* (co-

Author) 1994. Indiff.to pers.pub.& news media support. **Languages:** English, French (moderate spoken). Willing to act as consult.etc. **Address:** Royal Botanic Gardens, Kew, Richmond, Surrey TW9 3AE, England, UK. **Tel.**44 181 332 5299; **fax** 44 181 332 5278.

LOENING, Dr Ulrich Eduard. Organic agriculture and ecologically-sound forestry, ambient (renewable) energy technologies, landscape & environmental photography; academic studies on biological, ethical, & economic, features of humankind's place in The Biosphere. Company Director. *B.*18 June 1931, Berlin, Germany. British. *M.*Francesca M.(popular ecol.): *d.*, 2 *s.*Adrian Edward (envl engr), Nicolas Walter (Greenpeace). **Education:** Merchant Taylors' Sch.; Wadham Coll.Oxf. BA(Hons)(Biochem.) 1954, DPhil(Oxon.) 1958. **Experience:** res.in molecular biol.since 1955 always with an organic & 'appropriate technological' approach; teaching & public promotion of ecol issues since 1972; founded & co-direct an ecol local timber & forest co.; designed & built large domestic solar air-heating system. **Career:** SO, John Innes Instn 1957–9; Nuffield Res.F'ship 1959–62 & Lect.1965–9 Dept of Bot., Lect.1969–72 then Reader 1972–89 Dept of Zool., Dir, then Emer.Dir, Centre for Human Ecol.1984–96, all at U.of Edinburgh; ARC F'ship 1962–5; Vis. Assoc.Prof. Biol.Dept MIT 1966; Vis.Res.F. Max Planck Inst.for Biol.1969; sabb.1973, and 1981 at l'Institut d'Ecologie Européen (Metz, France); Dir, Lothian Trees & Timber Ltd. 1987–. **Achievements:** helping to init.Organic Farming Centre, jointly with Edinburgh Sch.of Agric.; co-founded Lothian & Edinburgh Envl Partnership, and Parliamentary Liaison Group on Alternative Energy Strats; re-established Centre for Human Ecol.and launched new MSc course in Human Ecol. **Memberships:** ISES, ISEE, UK Soil Assn, Council for the Greening of Higher Educ.(V.-Dir), HDRA, Balaton Group (Intl Network of Resource Info.Centers). **Publications:** Our ancestors stole their future from us — the implications of sust.for.in reforesting Scotland 1991, The ecol challenges to pop. growth 1993; num.others. **Award:** for Envl Educ. (Schumacher Soc.) 1994. Favours pers. pub.& news media support. **Languages:** English, French (poor), German (spoken, some read). Willing to act as consult.etc. **Address:** Lothian Trees and Timber, The Airfield Sawmill, Cousland, Dalkeith, Midlothian EH22 2PE, Scotland, UK. **Tel.**(office) 44 1875 320622, (home) 44 1875 340541; **e-mail** uel@ed.ac.uk .

LÖFGREN, Rolf. Forest conservation, planning & establishment of new national parks. Principal Administrative Officer. *B.*10 Aug.1944, Karlstad, Sweden. Swedish. **Education:** Uppsala U. BSc(Bot., Zool., Geol.) 1971. **Experience:** cons.work at Swedish EPA for 20 yrs incl.investigations, inventories, and practical cons.with spec.ref.to forest reserves & nat.parks. **Career:** Biol.concerned with diff.inventories &

county boards 1971–3, Cons.Officer 1973–83, Prin.Admin.Officer 1983–, Swedish EPA. **Achievements:** resp.for several EPA investigations, incl.that for broad-leafed forest, which led to spec.prot.act; inventory of virgin coniferous forests & prot.plan for virgin forests; investigations & plans for new nat.parks in Sweden. **Publications:** The Broadleaved Deciduous Forest Investigation Report 1982, The Mtn Forest Inventory Report 1984, Nat.Park Plan for Sweden 1989. Indiff.to pers.pub.& news media support. **Languages:** English, Swedish. Willing to act as consult.etc. **Address:** Naturvardsverket, 17185 Solna, Sweden. **Tel.**(office) 46 8 799 1000, (home) 46 8 768 3539; **fax** 46 8 799 1402.

LOHANI, Dr Bindu Nath. Integration of environmental elements in development projects using environmental impact assessment & other tools and techniques; environmental planning & management; environmental pollution control; regional & global environmental policies and concerns. Assistant Chief, Office of the Environment. *B.*2 April 1948, Kathmandu, Nepal. Nepali. *M.*Sumana: *d.*, *s.* **Education:** BITS BE(Hons)(Civ.Eng.)* 1970; NC SU, MCE(Envl Eng.minor Stats)** 1973; AIT, DE(Envl Tech./Systems Mgmt) 1977. **Experience:** tech., consult., policy analysis & formulation. **Career:** Exec.Engr, HM Govt of Nepal 1976–7; Consult.to UN agencies & intl consulting firms 1972–85; Assoc.Prof.& Chairman, Envl Engg Div. AIT 1982–5; Asst Chief, Office of the Envt, Asian Dev.Bank 1992–. **Achievements:** integration of envl considerations in multilateral dev.banks' ops at var.planning levels — projects & progs, sectoral, regnl & nat.levels; pioneered use of analytical tools & techniques in support of former efforts, those applied incl.initial envl exam., EIA, and social impact analysis of dev.projects & biodiv.impact assessment; spearheaded instn-bldg efforts for envl instns in Asia–Pacific regn; mgmt info.systems to envt field. **Memberships:** Phi Kappa Phi, ASCE, Nepal Engr's Assoc., AEEP, AWRA, IWRS, IWRA. **Awards:** Colombo Plan Scholarship 1965–70, *U.Gold Medal for First Rank 1970, Mahendra Educ.Gold Medal 1971 and Coronation Medal 1975 (both from King of Nepal), **Highest Academic Award (Phi Kappa Phi) MCE (NC SU) 1973, King's Scholarship (Govt of Thailand) 1975–7, Jackson Mem.Award/F'ship (Griffith U.) 1986, Global 500 Roll of Honour (UNEP) 1992. **Publications:** *Envl Qual.Mgmt* 1984, *Envl Tech.in Dev.Countries* 1988 + 18 other books, manuals etc.; *c.*70 papers, *c.*42 engg reports; memb.of *c.*14 edl bds or intl WGs. Indiff.to pers.pub.& news media support. **Languages:** English, Hindi, Nepali. **Address:** Office of the Environment, Asian Development Bank, POB 789, 1099 Manila, Philippines. **Tel.**(office) 63 2 632 6883; **fax** 63 2 742 7961, 632 6816, or 631 7961.

LOURENÇO, Dr Wilson Roberto. Phylogeny, evolutionary ecology, biogeography, & reproduction, of scorpions; applied biogeography = conservation; public health problems resulting from scorpion stings. Independent Research Fellow. *B*.31 Mar.1948, SP, Brazil. French. *M*.Sabine Jourdan, MD: *d*. **Education:** U.of Brasilia, BSc 1973; Université Pierre et Marie Curie (Paris) MSc 1976, PhD 1978, DSc 1985. **Experience:** widespread res.in biol.of scorpions and theoretical biogeog.& ecol., applications in cons.planning and public health problems, orgn of editions & mtgs at Société de Biogéographie (Paris). **Career:** Asst Prof.of Zool. U.of Brasilia 1974–5; Res.F.Nat.Hist.Mus.(Paris) 1976–88; Consult. Dept of Nat.Parks and Biol.Reserves (Brazil) 1978–9; Res.F.& Asst Prof. Université Pierre et Marie Curie 1989–94; Ind.Res.F. Société de Biogéographie 1994–. **Achievements:** consult.& resp.for sust.projects in several nat.parks & reserves in Brazil, Coord.of 1995 Symp.on the Biogeog.of Madagascar. **Memberships:** ATB, CIDA, Société de Biogéographie. **Award:** Strand Prize (ZSF) 1989. **Publications:** Ed.*Biogeographica, Mémoires de la Société de Biogéographie, c.*170 papers incl.Parthenogenesis in the scorpion *Tityus columbianus* (Thorell) (Scorpiones, Buthidae) 1991, Diversity and endemism in trop.*v.*temperate scorpion communities 1994, Biogeographic patterns of trop. S.Amer.scorpions 1994. Favours pers.pub.& news media support. **Languages:** English, French, Italian (read), Portuguese, Spanish. Willing to act as consult. etc. **Address:** Société de Biogéographie, 57 rue Cuvier, 75005 Paris, France. **Tel.**(home) 33 14 680 7333.

LOVARI, Professor Dr Sandro. Ethology, behavioural ecology, & conservation, of large mammals *(e.g.*Caprinae, Cervidae, Canidae). Professor of Animal Behaviour. *B.*11 Aug. 1946, Siena, Italy. Italian. **Education:** Siena U. Dr of Biol.*(cum laude)* 1972. **Experience:** res.— social behaviour, mating systems, cons.of mtn ungulates, ranging behaviour of carnivores, food habits of carnivores & herbivores; consult.— WWF Intl, NGS (USA), Italian Min.of Envt, mammal mgmt in prot.areas of Kenya, India, Italy, Nepal, & Thailand; teaching animal behaviour, zool., and ecol., to BSc & PhD levels. **Career:** Vis.Researcher, Cambridge U.1971–2, Gröningen U.1972–3, & Stockholm U.1977; mil.service 1973–4; F'ship from Italian NRC, Siena U.1974–7; Researcher, Inst.of Zool. Parma U.1977–86; Sr Vis.Researcher, Sub.Dept of Animal Behaviour, Cambridge U.1984–5; Chair in Zool. Camerino U.1987–90; Chair in Animal Behaviour, Siena U.1990–. **Achievements:** estab.of Maremma Natural Park, coastal Tuscany; scholar of effects of envl factors affecting ranging movements & activity of medium-sized & large mammals; basic res.on systematics & cons.biol.of mtn ungulates (Caprinae); effects of anthropogenic activities on large mammal biol., trophic niche assessment & eval. in carnivores (Red Fox *[Vulpes vulpes],* Badger *[Meles meles],* Wolf *[Canis lupus]* & Stone Marten *[Martes foina]).* **Memberships:** IUCN SSC

Caprinae SG (Chairman 1985–), IZS (Council Memb.) 1992–5, ICBP World WG on Birds of Prey 1977–83, ASM, ASAB, WWF, JES. **Award:** Glaxo Prize for Sci.Popularization 1984. **Publications:** *Handbook of Field Ethology Methods* (in Italian) 1980, *People of the Rocks* (in Italian) 1984, *The Biol.& Mgmt of Mtn Ungulates* (Ed.) 1985; 150+ papers. Indiff.to pers.pub.& news media support. **Languages:** English, French (poor), Italian, Spanish (poor). Willing to act as consult.etc. **Address:** Department of Evolutionary Biology, Ethology and Behavioural Ecology Group, Siena University, Via P.A.Mattioli 4, 53100 Siena, Italy. **Tel.** (office) 39 577 298901, (home) 39 577 280436; **fax** 39 577 298898.

LOVEJOY, Professor Derek. Landscape architecture, environmental consulting, town planning. Consultant, Visiting Professor of Landscape Architecture. *B.*16 Sept.1925, London, England, UK. British. *M.*June: *s.,* 2 *d.*incl.Vanessa (landscape arch.). **Education:** RIBA, Dipl.in Town Planning 1949; Harvard U. BA(Landscape Arch.) 1950, MA(Landscape Arch.) 1951. **Experience:** envl consult.for new capital cities of Pakistan, Tanzania, & Malawi; EIA; public enquiries; parliamentary bills; intl exp.— 97 countries, worked in 25; ext.examining; BBC radio & TV contributor. **Career:** Arch./Planner, London City Council 1952–4; Chief Asst Planner, W.Ham Borough Council 1954–6; Arch./Chief Landscape Arch. Crawley Dev. Corpn 1956–8; Founding Partner 1956–68, Sr Partner 1968–88, Derek Lovejoy & Partners; Appointed Consult. Derek Lovejoy Partnership 1988–; Vis.Prof.of Landscape Arch. U.of Sheffield 1986–; Ext.Examiner, Kingston U.1993–. **Achievements:** Landscape & Envl Consult.for new capital cities of Pakistan and Tanzania, worked in 25 countries throughout the world on envl projects, awarded over 80 prizes for design and competition wins. **Memberships:** IFLA (Memb.Grand Council 1956–83, Sec.-Gen. 1960–68, First VP 1980–83, Chair Intl Cttee 1990, Rep.at UNCED 1992 and UN NY 1994), UNEP (Envt Assessor) 1983, Euro.Architectural Heritage Yr (Counc.) 1975, RIBA (Occasional Regnl Chairman of Arch.Awards, Chief Assessor for Competitions 1975–); num.other nat.& intl. **Awards:** Fulbright F'ship 1949, Hunt Bursary Prizeman (RIBA) 1952, Memb.of the Worshipful Companies of Chartered Architects, and Constructors, Freeman of the City of London, Assoc.of RTPI 1950 and Inst.of Landscape Architects 1951; F.— ILA, RTPI, Insts of Architects and Town Planning (both Pakistan) 1966, RSA (nominated by Council) 1967, RIBA 1968, Instn of Highways & Transportation 1985; Pres. ILA 1971–3. **Publications:** several incl. *Land Use and Landscape Planning Techniques, Spons Landscape Handbooks, Reclamation of Derelict Land, Highway Envt.* No objection to pers.pub.or news media support. **Language:** English. Further details may be obtained from *Intl Who's Who* 1994. Willing to act as consult.etc. **Address:** Hobtye, Church Lane, Godstone, Surrey RH8 9BW, England, UK. **Tel.** (home) 44 1883 743331; **fax** 44 171 630 6958.

LOVELOCK, Dr James Ephraim. Gaia research. Independent Scientist. *B*.26 July 1919, Letchworth, Herts., England, UK. British. *M.* Sandra Jean (Treas. Gaia Charity): 2 *d.,* 2 *s.* **Education:** U.of Manchester BSc(Chem.) 1941; U.of London PhD(Med.) 1949, DSc(Biophys.) 1959. **Experience:** 52 yrs' full-time res. **Career:** Staff Sci. NIMR 1941–61; Prof. Baylor Coll.of Med.1961–4; Ind.Sci.1964–. **Achievements:** invented Electron Capture Detector (provision of data for Rachel Carson) 1957, and the Gaia Hypothesis (later Theory) 1971; found CFCs in global atmos.1972, and dimethyl-sulphide 1972; helped prove connection between climate, clouds, & marine Algae 1987. **Membership:** F.RS 1974–. **Awards:** Award for Electron Capture Detector (ACS) 1980, Amsterdam Prize 1990, Norbert Gerbier Medal (WMO) 1988, CBE 1989. **Publications:** *Gaia* 1979, *Ages on Gaia* 1989, *The Practical Sci.of Planetary Med.*1991; 200+ papers. **Language:** English. **Address:** Coombe Mill, St Giles on the Heath, Launceston, Cornwall PL15 9RY, England, UK. **Fax** 44 1566 784799.

LOVINS, Amory Bloch. Energy, resource efficiency, nuclear non-proliferation, hypercars, sustainability, electric utility policy. Institute Vice-President, Director of Research, & Chief Financial Officer; co-Founder & Principal Technical Consultant; Group Principal; Center Founder/Director. *B*.13 Nov.1947, Washington, DC, USA. American. *M*.L. Hunter Lovins *qv: d*.Nanuq (dogsbody, Rocky Mtn Inst.). **Education:** Harvard Coll.1964–7; U.of Oxf. MA (Spec.) 1967–71. **Experience:** active in energy policy in more than 25 countries in as many yrs, adv.to num.cos world-wide and to public-sector instns, has briefed nine heads of state and given expert testimony in eight countries and 20+ states, has addressed scores of leading US and many overseas energy, envt, security, & dev. groups. **Career:** Jr Res.F. Merton Coll. U.of Oxf.1969–71; Regents' Lect.in Energy & Resources 1978 and in Econ.1981, U.of Calif.; Luce Vis.Prof. Dartmouth Coll. 1982; Disting. Vis.Prof. U.of Colorado 1982; Energy Res.Adv. Bd, USDE 1980–81; co-Founder, VP, Dir of Res.& CFO 1982–, Rocky Mtn Inst.; co-Founder/Prin.Tech.Consult., E SOURCE 1992–; Founder/Dir, The Hypercar Center 1991–; Prin. The Lovins Group 1994–. **Achievements and Endeavours:** participated in laying of most of the conceptual & tech.fndns for modern energy (esp.electric) efficiency, resulting in large savings inexpensively, making markets on saved resources and hence abating poll.at a profit; invented 'end-use/least cost' approach, whole-system engg for advanced 'negawatts', and ultra-light-hybrid 'hypercars'; currently seeking to transform car, real-estate, & utility, industries. **Memberships:** F.Amer.AAS 1984, F.WAAS

1988. **Awards:** Mitchell Prize (co-, Mitchell Energy Fndn) 1982, Right Livelihood Award (co-) 1983, Delphi Prize (Onassis Fndn) 1989, MacArthur F.(MacArthur Fndn) 1993, Nissan Prize 1993, Award of Dist.(Rocky Mtn Chapter, AIA) 1994; six Hon. Doctorates at US univs. **Publications:** 23 books incl.*Eryri, the Mtns of Longing* 1971, *Soft Energy Paths* 1977, *Brittle Power: Energy Strat.for Nat.Security* (co-Author) 1982, *Least-Cost Energy: Solving the CO2 Problem* (co-Author) 1982, five first-edn Tech.Atlases on electric end-use efficiency (var. co-Authors) 1988–92, *Faktor Vien: Doppelter Wohlstand, Halbierter Naturverbrauch* (co-Author) 1995, *Hypercars: Materials, Manufacturing, & Policy Implications* (co-Author) 1996; several hundred papers; electronics patent. **Languages:** English; German (some). Willing to act as consult.etc. **Address:** Rocky Mountain Institute, 1739 Snowmass Creek Road, Snowmass, Colorado 81654-9199, USA. **Tel.**1 970 927 3851; **fax** 1 970 927 4178.

LOVINS, Dr L.Hunter. Resource efficiency, corporate management, sustainability, environment enhancement/restoration, horse training & sales, fire-fighting/rescue. President & Executive Director, President. *B*.26 Feb.1950, Middlebury, Vermont, USA. American. Father Dr Paul Millard Sheldon, urban sociol.& envlist, and mother Farley Hunter, JD, Dev.Dir., Rocky Mtn Inst. *M*.Amory B.Lovins *qv: d*.Nanuq (dogsbody, Rocky Mtn Inst.). **Education:** Pitzer Coll. BA(Sociol./Pol.Studies) 1972, Loyola U.Sch.of Law, JD (Envl & Admin.Law) 1975. **Experience:** Memb.1979 City of Los Angeles Energy Mgmt Adv.Bd.; co-Prin.Investigator, Energy Policies for Resilience & Nat.Security; Consult.for num.govts including American, Swedish & German, and num.corpns incl.R. Dutch Shell, Bank of Amer.; teacher at several univs and Dartmouth Coll., lectured widely at colls & confs; memb.Bd of Dirs of AEAC, Renew Amer., Telluride Inst., & Basalt & Rural Fire Prot. Distr.; serves on many adv.bds. **Career:** co-Founder & Asst Dir. Calif.Cons. Project (Tree People) 1973–9; Policy Adv. FoE 1979–82; co-Founder & Pres./Exec.Dir. Rocky Mtn Inst. 1982–; co-Founder & Pres. Nighthawk Horse Company 1993–; co-Founder & Pres. Lovins Group 1994–. **Achievements:** enabled popularization of end-use/least-cost approach to solving energy & resource policy issues; created & managed-to-stability one of the world's pre-eminent resource policy centres; conceived & managed-to-successful-spin-off the world's premier info.service on electric efficiency. **Awards:** Alumni Award for Outstanding Service 1975 & Mitchell Prize for Sust.Dev.1982 (Loyola U.), Rt Livelihood Award ('Alternative Nobel') 1983, Best of New Generation (Esquire) 1984, Hon.Doct.of Humane Letters (U.of Maine) 1985. **Publications:** *Energy/War: Breaking the Nuclear Link* (co-Author) 1980, *Nuclear Power & Nuclear Bombs* (co-Author) 1980, *Brittle Power* (co-Author) 1982, *Least Cost*

Energy, Solving the CO_2 *Problem* (co-Author) 1982, 1989, *The 3rd Nuclear World War* (co-Author) 1984, *Energy Unbound* (prin. Author) 1986, *Factor 4* (co-Author, Ed.) 1995. Favours pers.pub.& news media support. **Languages:** English, Spanish (minimal). Willing to act as consult.etc. **Address:** Rocky Mountain Institute, 1739 Snowmass Creek Road, Snowmass, Colorado 81654-9199, USA. **Tel.**(office) 303 927 3851, (home) 303 963 2804; **fax** 303 927 4178.

LOVRIC, Dr Andrija Zelimir. Mediterranean & coastal ecology, archaeo-ecology, palaeobiocenoses. Laboratory Head & Studies Coordinator. *B.*5 June 1943, Zagreb, Croatia. Croatian. Father Prof.Mihovil Lovric (biogeog.& palaeontology). *M.*Prof.Alina (envl journalism). **Education:** Classical Coll.of Zagreb; U.of Zagreb MSc 1971 (Fac.of Scis), DSc 1985 (Ruder Boskovic Inst.). **Experience:** 32 yrs' ecol res.in Medit., Balkans, & SW Asia; 11 yrs' teaching phytogeog. **Career:** Asst Prof. Botl Inst.1967–77, Head of Lab.of Coastal Ecol.and Biocenology and Coord. Karstic Ecol.Studies & Palaeoecology, Ruder Boskovic Inst.1978–, U.of Zagreb. **Achievements:** basic res.on sea-cliff ecol.and on Medit.biocenoses, reconstitution of palaeocenoses & palaeoenvts in Tethys area, karstic ecosystem models, natural reserves in Adriatic. **Memberships:** CASA, CIESM, AIPS. **Publications:** [*Ecol.Dev.of SE Krk Is.in Adriatic*] (in Croatian, co-Author) 1976, [*Prehistoric Devs of the Croats and Croatia*] 1st edn in Croatian 1993, 2nd in English 1995; 412 papers. Indiff.to pers.pub., favours news media support. **Languages:** Croatian, English, French, Latin (all written & spoken); Assyrian, German, Greek, Hurrian, Italian, Russian, Sumerian (all basic knowledge & read). Willing to act as consult. etc. **Address:** Selcina 10, Zagreb-Sesvete CRO 41260, Croatia. **Tel.**(office) 38 511 456 1075, (home) 38 511 200 1304; **fax** 38 511 425497.

LUCAS, Percy Hylton Craig ('Bing'). National parks, protected areas, cultural & protected landscapes, world heritage. Chairman. *B.*9 June 1925, Christchurch, NZ. New Zealander. *M.*Kura Joyce: *s., d.* **Education:** U.of Canterbury, Accountancy Professional 1949. **Experience:** admin.as Dir of Nat.Parks & Reserves and DG of Lands, NZ; consult.re.nat.parks & prot.areas, prot./cultural landscapes, World Heritage Conv. **Career:** Dir, Nat.Parks & Reserves, NZ 1969–74; Asst/Dep.DG 1975–80, DG 1981–6, Lands, NZ; consult.in Nepal, China, Indonesia, Solomon Islands, Australia, NZ, Peru 1974–; secretariat IUCN 1989; Chairman IUCN CNPPA 1990–94. **Achievements:** enhancing NZ's nat. parks' system & estab.of career structure for professional staff; assisting in estab.of Sagarmatha (Mt Everest) Nat.park and with organizing 3rd & 4th World Congs on NPPA; estab.of NZ's walkway system. **Memberships:** IFPRA, IUCN CNPPA. **Awards:** Winston Churchill F.1969, F.WCF 1984, A.O.Glasse Award (NZPI) 1986,

Ian Galloway Cup for Outstanding Achievement (NZIP) 1990, F.E–W Center 1990, F.ICPL 1992, Hon.Memb.IUCN 1994, Fred M.Packard Intl Parks Merit Award 1994. **Publications:** *Conserving NZ's Heritage* 1970, *Prot.Landscapes — A Guide for Policy Makers & Planners* 1992. Indiff.to pers.pub., favours news media support. **Language:** English. Further details may be obtained from *Who's Who in NZ.* Willing to act as consult.etc. **Address:** 1/268 Main Road, Tawa, Wellington 6006, New Zealand. **Tel.**(office & home) 64 4 232 5581; **fax** 64 4 232 9129.

LUK, Professor Dr Shiu-hung. Land degradation & management, soil erosion & conservation, management of envt in China. Professor of Geography. *B.*11 Jan.1947, Hong Kong. Canadian. *M.* **Education:** U.of HK BA(Hons) 1968, MPhil 1972; U.of Alb. PhD 1975. **Experience:** conducted field res.in Canada, China, HK, Tanzania, USA; dir of major soil erosion & land mgmt projects in China; consult.to CIDA, IDRC, NASA, UNDP, WMO. **Career:** Lect. Dept of Geog. U.of Dar es Salaam 1975–6; Asst Prof. Dept of Geog. Brock U.1976–7 & U.of Guelph 1977–8; Asst Prof. 1978–83, Assoc. Prof.with tenure 1983–92 & Prof. 1992 Dept of Geog. and Dir Inst.of Land Info. Mgmt 1995–, U.of Toronto. **Achievements:** basic res.in soil erosion processes, applied res.in land mgmt & application of GIS, Ed.*China Envt & Dev. Catena.* **Memberships:** CAG, AAG, ASSWC. **Publications:** *Megaproject: The Case of the Three Gorges in China,* 45 j.articles, 100 other pubns. Indiff.to pers.pub.& news media support. **Languages:** Chinese, English, French (working knowledge). Willing to act as consult. etc. **Address:** Department of Geography, University of Toronto, Erindale Campus, Mississauga, Ontario L5L 1C6, Canada. **Tel.**1 905 828 5465; **fax** 1 905 828 5273; **e-mail** SLUK@tuzo.erin.utoronto.ca .

LUSCOMBE, Bruce Anthony. Wildlife conservation, natural-resource management, landuse strategies, animal behaviour, birds of prey esp.falcons. Private Consultant. *B.*19 Oct. 1937, Holstein, IA, USA. American. *M.*Neti V. (field asst): 2 *s.* **Education:** U.of S.Dakota, BA(Pol.Sci.) 1966. **Experience:** res.on raptorial birds (Peregrine Falcon *[Falco peregrinus]*, Prairie Falcon *[F.mexicanus]*, Golden Eagle *[Aquila chrysaetos]*, & Red-tailed Hawk *[Buteo jamaicensis]*), migratory birds (Common Terns *[Sterna hirundo]* & Peregrine Falcons), primates & cetaceans. **Career:** Tech.Coord. APECO 1982–5; Exec.VP 1985–92, Pres.& Exec.Officer 1992–5, ECCO. **Achievements:** co-rediscoverer of Peruvian Yellow-tailed Woolly Monkey *(Lagothrix flavicauda),* discovered type specimen of beaked whale species new for sci., Peruvian Beaked Whale *(Mesoplodon peruvianus),* three new subspecies of butterfly (one called *Heliconius erato luscombei,* n.ssp.), led many campaigns that resulted in significant cons.victories which saved nat.parks, reserves & sanctuaries, discovered first specimens of Melon-Headed Whale *(Peponocephala electra)* and Risso's Dolphin *(Grampus griseus)* ever found in Peru, as well as new info.on many bird species. Accepts pers.pub.& news media support depending on how they are used. **Languages:** English, Spanish. Further details may be obtained from *Primate Conservation.* Willing to act as consult.etc. **Address:** 330 West 56th Street, Apt 20H, New York, New York 10019, USA. **Tel.**(office & home) & **fax** 1 212 586 6805.

LUSIGI, Dr Walter. Range ecology and natural resources' management. Senior Ecologist. *B.*22 March 1947, Kakamega, Kenya. Kenyan. *D.*: 3 *d., s.* **Education:** CSU BSc 1971, MSc 1972 (both in Range Ecol.), Tech.U.of Munich PhD (Landscape Ecol.). **Experience:** 20 yrs' res.& natural resources' mgmt. **Career:** Res.Coord. 1980–86, Chief Tech.Adv.1986–90, UNESCO; Sr Ecol. World Bank 1990–. **Achievements:** VP IUCN 1984–90, over 50 cons.pubns. **Membership:** NASL. **Award:** Alumni Award (CSU) 1991. **Publications:** *The Cons.Unit Approach to Natural Resources Mgmt* 1978, *Managing Prot.Areas in Africa* 1990; num. others. Favours pers.pub.& news media support. **Languages:** English, German, Swahili. Willing to act as consult.etc. **Address:** 13114 Pavillon Lane, Fairfax, Virginia 22033, USA. **Tel.**(office) 1 202 473 4798, (home) 1 703 803 3980; **fax** 1 202 473 7916.

LUTZENBERGER, José Antonio. Sustainable development, environmental activism, landscaping; recycling of industrial waste, alternative sanitary engineering; regenerative agriculture. Foundation President, Company Director. *B.*17 Dec.1926, Porto Alegre, RS, Brazil. Brazilian, German. *W.*: 2 *d.*Lilly Charlotte (biol.), Lara Josette (biol.). **Education:** Universidade Fed. do Rio Grande do Sul, Agron.1950; Louisiana SU, postgrad.work in soil sci.& agri-chem. 1951–2. **Experience:** regenerative agric., soft sanitary engg, writing, lect. **Career:** Tech.Adv. to Brazilian fertilizer cos 1952–7; Commercial & Tech.Del. BASF 1957–70; co-Founder & Hon.Pres. AGAPAN 1972–; Spec.Envt Sec. Nat.Renovation Govt 1990–92; Pres. Fundação GAIA 1992–; Dir. Vida Produtos Biologicos Ltda and Tecnologia Convivial Ltda 1992–. **Achievements:** vigorous & successful campaign against conventional chem.methods in agric.at the same time promoting regenerative organic agric., supported intro.in 1988 of envl awareness to World Bank, promotion of people's envl awareness all over the world. **Membership:** Conselho Regnl de Engenharia, Arquitetura e Agronomia. **Awards:** Mérito Agrônomico (FAEAB) 1980, Bodo-Manstein Medal (Liga Para o Meio Ambiente e Proteção da Natureza da Alemanha Ocidental) 1981, Rt Livelihood Award 1988, Premio Internacional 'Vida Sana' 1990, Dr *H.C.*(U.of San Francisco) 1991 &

(Universität für Bodenkultur, Vienna) 1995; others. **Publications:** *[Fin del Futuro?]* (transl. into English) 1976, *[Giftige Ernte — Tödlicher Irrweg der Agrarchemie]* 1988, 1990, *[GAIA — O Planeta Vivo (Por Um Caminho Suave)]* 1991, *Knowledge and Wisdom Must Come Back Together* 1994. Favours pers.pub.& news media support. **Languages:** English, French, German, Portuguese, Spanish. Willing to act as consult. etc. **Address:** Rua Jacinto Gomes 39, 90040-270 Porto Alegre, Rio Grande do Sul, Brazil. **Tel.**(office) 55 51 331 3105, (home) 55 51 331 3105; **fax** 55 51 330 3567.

LYNCH, James Robert. Community development and Nature conservation in the humid neotropics. Association President. *B.*3 June 1952, Chicago, IL, USA. American. *M.*Angela: 3 *s.* **Education:** Yale U. BS(Biol.) 1976, MS(Forest Sci.) 1978. **Experience:** dir.of grassroots dev., cons.& res.projects — agrofor., sust.for.mgmt, reforestation, Iguana-raising, envl educ., community credit funds, community orgn, organic agric., regnl training center, rural housing, prot. area mgmt (wildlife refuge), leadership training, coastal mgmt. **Career:** Founder & Pres. Asociación 'ANAI' 1983–. **Achievements:** pioneered field-work with community-based initiatives, reconciling dev.with cons. Indiff.to pers. pub., favours orgnl news media support. **Languages:** English, French (mediocre), Portuguese (good), Spanish. Willing to act as consult.etc. **Address:** Asociación 'ANAI', Apartado 170-2070, Sabanilla, Costa Rica. **Tel.**506 224 6090; **fax** 506 253 7524.

MACDONALD, Dr David Whyte. Mammalian conservation, carnivores, agroecology. Unit Head. *B.*30 Sept.1951, Oxford, England, UK. British. *M.*Jennifer M.: *s.*, 2 *d.* **Education:** Wadham Coll.Oxf. BA(Hons)(Zool.) 1972, MA 1974; Wadham & Balliol Colls Oxf. DPhil. (Behavioural Ecol.of the Red Fox *[Vulpes vulpes]*) 1977. **Experience:** 22 yrs' res., admin. **Career:** Jr Res. F. Balliol Coll.Oxf. 1976–9; Ernest Cook Res.F.1979–84 & Nuffield Res. F.1984–7, Dept of Zool., SRF Lady Margaret Hall 1986, Head Wildlife Cons.Res.Unit 1986–, U.of Oxf. **Achievements:** set up and manage Wildlife Cons.Res.Unit, devoted to scientific res.to promote cons., supervised over 20 doctl theses, written several books & made several TV progs to popularize sci.& cons., given many public lectures in UK and overseas. **Memberships:** IUCN Canid SG (Chairman 1983–), RSPCA WG on Welfare and Wildlife Mgmt (Chairman 1991–), Scientific Adv.Panel of The Game Conservancy 1985–, Animal Welfare & Cons. Cttee of ZSL 1990–. **Awards:** Huxley Award for Contribns to Zool.1978, Natural Hist.Book of the Yr *(Running with the Fox)* 1988, Runner-up Natural Hist.Book of the Yr *(Field Guide to Mammals of Britain & Europe)* 1993. **Publications:** *Enc.of Mammals* 1984 (transl.into ten languages), *The Velvet Claw: a Natural Hist.of the Carnivores* 1992, Cause of

Wild Dog Deaths (co-Author) 1992, Rabies & wildlife: a cons. problem? 1993, Cooperative breeding in mammals (co-Author) 1994, many other contribns. Indiff.to pers.pub.& news media support. **Languages:** English; French, Portuguese & Spanish (all survival). Willing to act as consult.etc. **Address:** Wildlife Conservation Research Unit, Department of Zoology, University of Oxford, South Parks Road, Oxford OX1 3PS, England, UK. **Tel.**(office) 44 865 271289; **fax** 44 865 310447.

MacDONALD, Professor Dr Gordon James Fraser. Climate change, predictability, energy policy, mathematical statistics, geophysics. Professor of International Relations and Director of Environmental Policy Program. *B.*30 July 1929, Mexico City, Mexico. American. *M.*Margaret: 3 *s., d.* **Education:** Harvard U. AB(*summa cum laude*) 1950, AM 1952, PhD 1954. **Experience:** extensive res.on tech.& policy aspects of climate change, acid rain, energy policy & issues of predictability; teaching on envl issues; negotiating treaties & developing policy as memb. of CEQ; adv.on envl issues. **Career:** Jr F. Harvard U.1952–4; Asst.then Assoc.Prof.of Geol. & Geophys. MIT 1954–8; Prof.of Geophys.1958–68, Assoc.Dir of Inst.of Geophys. and Planetary Phys.1960–68, UCLA; VP for Res.1966 7, Exec.VP 1967 8, Inst.for Defense Analyses; Prof.of Phys.& Geophys.& V.-Chancellor for Res.& Grad.Affairs UCSB 1968–70; Memb.CEQ, Exec.Office of the Pres.1970–72; Prof.of Envl Studies & Policy and Dir Envl Studies Prog. Dartmouth Coll.1972–9; VP & Chief Sci. The MITRE Corpn 1979–90, Prof.of Intl Relations and Dir Envl Policy Prog. UCSD 1990–. **Achievements:** Memb.first CEQ of Exec.Office of the US Pres.1970–72; founded Dartmouth Envl Studies Prog.1972–9 and *J.of Envt & Dev.*1992. **Memberships:** Amer.AAS, APS, NAS, RAS (Foreign Assoc.), num.others. **Awards:** Phi Beta Kappa (Harvard U.) 1950, Monogr.Prize (Amer.AAS) 1959, James B. Macelwane Award (AGU) 1965, Man of Sci. 1966. **Publications:** 150+ incl.*The Rotation of the Earth* (co-Author) 1959, *The Long-term Impacts of Increasing Carbon Dioxide Levels* 1982, *Sound & Light Phenomena — A Study of Histl & Modern Occurrences* (co-Author) 1978, Scientific basis for the greenhouse effect 1988, *Global Climate & Ecosystem Change* (co-Author) 1990. Indiff.to pers.pub.& news media support. **Languages:** English, French, German, Italian, Portuguese (good), Spanish. Further details may be obtained from *Who's Who in Amer., Sci.Yr* 1966. Willing to act as consult. etc. **Address:** 1221 Robinson (0518), University of California San Diego, 9500 Gilman Drive, La Jolla, California 92093-0518, USA. **Tel.**(office) 1 619 534 3254, (home) 1 619 558 6507; **fax** 1 619 534 7655.

MacFARLAND, Dr Craig G. Management of protected areas; garnering support of local people for conservation and management of natural resources in developing countries. Foundation President, Consultant. *B.*17 July 1943, Great Falls, MT, USA. American. *M.*Dr Marilyn A.Swanson (food safety specialist): *d., s.*, 3 *step-daughters.* **Education:** Austin Coll. BA(Biol.) 1965, U.of W–M MA(Ecol.[Zool.])) 1969, PhD(Ecol./Cons.Biol.[Zool.]) 1993. **Experience:** 20 yrs' res., training, tech.coopn, planning & eval.of biodiv., and cons.& sust.-use of natural resources, in Latin Amer., direct exp.in 14 Latin Amer.countries. **Career:** Dir, Charles Darwin Res.Station 1974–8; Head, Mesoamerican Wildlands & Watershed Mgmt Prog. CATIE 1978–85; Pres. Charles Darwin Fndn for the Galápagos Isles 1985–96; Consult.(continuing) in planning & mgmt of trop.natural resources. **Achievements:** cons.of the Galápagos Islands 1969–, major adv. & leader in selection, estab., & mgmt, of prot. areas in Latin Amer. **Memberships:** ISTF, ATB, SCB, ESA, Sigma Xi. **Awards:** Hon.DSc (Austin Coll.) 1978, Intl Cons.Medal (ZSSD) 1978, Order of the Golden Ark 1983. **Publications:** num.incl. The Galápagos giant tortoises, *Geochelone elephantopus*, Part I Status of surviving pops, and Part II Cons.methods (co-Author) 1974, The Neotropic Realm (keynote address, co-Author) 1984; parts of three books and 60+ major tech.papers; mgmt plans, regnl dev.plans, manuals, training documents etc. Indiff./dis likes pers.pub., indiff.to news media support. **Languages:** English, Spanish. Further details may be obtained from *Who's Who in Amer.*1996. Willing to act as consult.etc. **Address:** 836 Mabelle, Moscow, Idaho 83843, USA. **Tel.**(office & home) 1 208 883 4876; **fax** 1 208 883 0653.

MACHADO CARRILLO, Dr Antonio, *see* **CARRILLO, Dr Antonio MACHADO.**

MacKINNON, Dr John Ramsay. Conservation, biodiversity databases, primatology, ornithology. Bureau Director. *B.*22 Jan.1947, Leeds, England, UK. British. **Education:** Winchester Coll.; Oriel Coll.Oxf. BA(Hons) (Zool.), MA(Oxon.), DPhil(Ecol.)1973. **Experience:** field res.on primates, insects, birds (over 20 years) in Africa & Asia; dev.of Nature reserves, country reserve systems, regnl reviews, dev.of nat.and regnl biodiv.databases with GIS Consultancy Services in dev.of aid, incl.GEF, projects; managing cons.progs and agency. **Career:** WWF Project Leader 1977–9; FAO Expert 1979–82; FAO Project Mgr 1983; WWF/IUCN rep.to Indonesia 1983–4; Consult.1984–6; Sr Cons.Adv. WWF 1986–92; Dir, Asian Bureau for Cons.1992–. **Achievements:** dev.of field methods & manuals for implementing cons.; designing Prot.Area Systems Plans for Indonesia, Vietnam, Bhutan, and China, and Species Survival Plans for Kouprey *(Bos sauveli)* and Giant Panda *(Ailuropoda melanoleuca)*; dev.of computer tools for monitoring biodiv.; co-discovery of two new large mammals *(Pseudoryx nhgetinhensis,* and *Megamuntiacus vuquangensis)* in Vietnam.

Memberships: F.RZS, FFPS, Malay Nature Soc., IUCN Comms on Species Survival (Emer.), and NPPA. **Awards:** Open Scholarship (Oriel Coll. Oxf.), Phyllis Bentley Award for Lit., professional awards declined. **Publications:** ten books include *In Search of the Red Ape* 1974, *Ecol.of Asia* 1974, *The Ape Within Us* 1978, *Managing Prot.Areas in the Tropics* 1986, *A Field Guide to the Birds of Borneo, Sumatra, Java, and Bali* 1993; *c.*100 papers & articles. Dislikes pers.pub., favours news media support. **Languages:** English, French, Malay/Indonesian, Mandarin; Portuguese, Thai & Vietnamese (all basic). Willing to act as consult.etc. **Address:** Asian Bureau for Conservation, c/o WWF Hong Kong, 1 Tramway Path, Central Hong Kong, Hong Kong. **Tel.**852 2526 1011; **fax** 852 2845 2734.

MacNEILL, James William. Environment, sustainable development. Company President, Senior Adviser, Chairman. *B.*22 April 1928, Mazenod, Sask., Canada. Canadian. *M.*Phyllis Beryl: 2 *d.* **Education:** U.of Sask. BSc 1949, BSc(Eng.) 1958; U.of Stockholm, Grad.Cert in Econ.& Pol.Sci.1951. **Experience:** res., consult., author, lect., diplomat; provincial, nat.& intl public servant. **Career:** Dir, Sask. Water Resources Comm.1959–69; Spec.Adv.to PM 1969–71; Dep.Minister, Min.of State for Urban Affairs Canada 1973–6; Canadian Commissioner Gen.& Amb.Extraordinary, UNCHS 1975–6; Dir of Envt, OECD 1978–83; Sec.-Gen. WCED 1983–7; Pres. MacNeill & Assocs 1987–; Sr Adv. UNDP 1994–; Chairman, IISD 1994–. **Achievements:** wrote first book on envl mgmt in Canada 1970, Commissioner Gen.for UNCHS (Habitat I) 1976, led res.& negns resulting in OECD's landmark 1984 decision that 'the envt and the econ.can be made mutually reinforcing', arch.& prin.author of WCED's (Brundtland) Comm.1987 report which set out new global agenda for sus.dev.and recommended 1992 Earth Summit. **Memberships:** Assns of Professional Engrs of Sask.and of Ont. **Awards:** Prize (a Swedish co.), Climate Inst.Award, Highest Achievement Award (Sask.), Lifetime Achievement Award (Canada), Silver Medal (City of Paris); Hon.— LLD (U.of Sask.) 1988, DSc (McGill U.) 1992, Dr of Envl Studies (U.of Waterloo) 1993, & Hon.Dr of Humane Letters (Lakehead U.) 1994. **Publications:** resp.for num. books incl.*Envl Mgmt* 1970, *Our Common Future* 1987, *Beyond Interdependence* 1992; articles & reports. Favours pers.pub.& news media support. **Languages:** English, French, Swedish. Further details may be obtained from *Who's Who in Amer.*1995, *Canadian Who's Who* 1995. Willing to act as consult.etc. **Address:** 110 Rideau Terrace, Ottawa, Ontario K1M 0Z2, Canada. **Tel.**(office) 613 238 2296, (home) 613 749 8681; **fax** 613 749 9186.

MACRORY, Professor Richard Brabazon. Environmental law. Denton Hall Professor of Environmental Law, Barrister. *B.*30 March 1950, Headley, Surrey, England, UK. British. *M.*Sarah Margaret: 2 *s.* **Education:** Westminster Sch.; U.of Oxf. BA 1972, MA(Jurisprudence) 1976. **Experience:** res.— UK & EEC envl law, comparative analysis of c.& e.Euro. Systems; teaching envl law at MSc & LLM levels; admin.; legal practice specializing in questions of nat.& EEC envl law. **Career:** Legal Adv. FOE Ltd 1975–8; Lect.in Envl Law 1980–89, Reader 1989–91, Prof.1991–, ICL; Barrister, Brick Court Chambers, Temple 1990–; Specialist Adv.in Envl Law, House of Commons Select Cttee on the Envt 1990–, Memb. R.Comm. on Envl Poll.1991–. **Achievements:** promulgating disc.of envl law in both acad.& practitioner circles, first Ed. *J.of Envl Law* 1988–, first Chairman, UK ELA 1986–8. **Memberships:** UK ELA, Soc.of Public Teachers of Law, Bd Memb. Envl Change Unit, U.of Oxford. **Awards:** Gerald Moody Exhibitioner (Grays Inn) 1973, Hon.Standing Counsel CPRE 1981–92. **Publications:** *Water Law — Principles & Practice* 1985; 50+ chapters & articles. Indiff.to pers.pub.& news media support. **Languages:** English, French (read). Further details may be obtained from Brit.*Who's Who* 1996, *Debrett's People of Today* 1994. **Address:** Imperial College Centre for Environmental Technology, 48 Princes Gardens, London SW7 2PE, England, UK, **tel.**(office) 44 171 589 5111 ext.8945, **fax** 44 171 823 7892; *or* Brick Court Chambers, 15–19 Devereux Street, London, WC2 3JJ, England, UK, **tel.**44 171 583 0777, **fax** 44 171 583 9401.

MADAR, Professor Dr Zdeněk. European environmental law. Scientific worker, Adviser. *B.*18 April 1929, Prague, Czech Republic. Czech. *M.*Dr Ju Jana. **Education:** Charles U. LLD 1952; Czech.AS Cand.of Sci.1962, DSc 1984; Institut universitaire d'études européennes (Torino), Diplôme d'études supérieures européennes 1967. **Experience:** fully specialized in Czech envl law 1964– and comparative euro. envl law 1970–. **Career:** Inst.of Law 1956–, Head, Dept for Envl Law 1972–, Czech AS; Adv. Andersen Consult.1990–; short-term Expert, WHO. **Achievements:** author of scientific conception of Czech envl law; participation in drafting some Czech Acts on envl prot.; author of two drafts of Acts for Laos PDR. **Memberships:** ICEL 1973–; CEPLA (Bonn) 1976–; Scientific Council, Centre intl de droit comparé de l'environnement, Limoges 1980–. **Awards:** Silver Medal (1979) & Gold Medal (1989) of Czech AS; Elizabeth Haub Prize 1990. **Publications:** 58 books incl.*Enc.Envt* 1973, *Legal Regs of Human Envt in Czech.*1973, *Czech Law, State and Admin.and Envt.*1977, *Legal Aspects of Intl Prot.of Envt* 1980, *Legal Prot. of Envt* 1983, *Mgmt of Envt in Euro.States* 1990; Chief Ed. *Lawyers' Dict.*(five edns); *c.*187 articles & studies. **Languages:** Czech, English, French, German, Italian, Russian. Further details may be obtained from Czech *Who's Who* 1991, *Enc.Biog.*1993. Willing to act as consult. **Address:** CZ 190 12 Prague, 9-Dolni Pocernice, V cenku 361, Czech Republic. **Tel.**(home) & **fax** 42 2 728 123.

MADDURI, Dr V.B.N.Sastry. Energy, environmental education. Senior Faculty. *B.*1 Sept. 1946, Bhimavaram, AP, India. Indian. **Education:** Andhra U. MSc 1966; U.of Alb. MA 1971, PhD 1978. **Experience:** teaching, res., specialization in econometric forecasting models in energy and econ.–related areas. **Career:** Reader, Fac.of Econ., U.of Hyderabad 1985–. **Achievements:** impact assessment studies dealing with socio–economic factors due to major energy prod.activities. **Membership:** IAEE. **Awards:** res.awards during 1974. **Publications:** num. incl *Energy Resource Requirements for Alb.* (res.report) 1986, Impact of thermal power plants: an envl econ.study (co-Author) 1992, *AWARE and its Work with Tribals and Harijans in AP* (res.report) 1993. **Language:** English. Willing to act as consult. etc. **Address:** Faculty of Economics, University of Hyderabad, Hyderabad 500134, Andhra Pradesh, India. **Tel.**(office) 40 253901, (home) 40 253275; **fax** 40 253145.

MADHAVAN UNNI, Dr N.V., *see* **UNNI, Dr N.V. MADHAVAN.**

MADULID, Dr Domingo. Plant conservation, flora of the Philippines, botanical gardens. Herbarium Curator. *B.*4 Aug.1946, Laoag, Ilocos Norte, Philippines. Filipino. *M.*Rosie S. (biol.). **Education:** U.of the Philippines, BS (Bot.) 1969; U.of Santo Tomas (Philippines), MS(Bot.) 1973; U.of Reading (UK), MSc(Plant Taxon.) 1976, PhD(Bot.) 1980. **Experience:** consult.bot.re. Integrated Prot.Areas System and Manila Bay Resource & Ecol.Assessment projects, and co-PI of Flora of the Philippines project. **Career:** Bot. Parks and Wildlife Office (Diliman) 1968–9; Mus.Researcher 1969–84, Sr Mus.Researcher 1984–9, Curator 1989–93, Bot. Div., Sci.III & In-Charge 1993–, Philippine Nat. Herbarium. **Achievements:** recipient of several study & travel grants, res.project participation. **Membership:** Assn of Pacific Systematists, IUCN SSC Palm SG. **Award:** Study F.(Brit. Council) 1976–80. **Publications:** incl.*A Pictorial Cyclopaedia of Philippine Ornamental Plants* 1995, *A Dict.of Philippine Plant-Names* (two vols, in press). **Languages:** English, Filipino. Further details may be obtained from *Flora Malesiana* vol.8, *Cyclopaedia of Collectors* 1977. Willing to act as consult.etc. **Address:** National Museum, Executive House Building, Padré Burgos Street, POB 2659, Manila, Philippines. **Tel.**(office) 632 527 1218; **fax** 632 527 0267.

MAGARIÑOS-DE MELLO, Ambassador Dr Mateo Jorge, *see* **MELLO, Ambassador Dr Mateo Jorge** MAGARIÑOS-DE.

Maher ALI, Professor Dr Abd 'El moneim', *see* **ALI, Professor Dr Abd 'El moneim' Maher.**

MAKHDOUM, Professor Majid F. Environmental evaluation, land-use planning. Professor & Head of Department of Environmental Planning. *B.*5 June 1945, Rasht, Iran. Iranian. Father Gholamhosein (naturalist). **Education:** Tehran U. MSc(Eng.) 1967, ANU MSc(Envt) 1977, Macquarie U. PhD(Envt) 1980. **Experience:** 24 yrs' res.on land ecol.capability eval.& land-use planning in Iran & Australia. **Career:** Fac.of Natural Resources, U.of Tehran 1969–. **Achievement:** founder of Dept of Envt in U.of Tehran. **Memberships:** Iranian AS, ISE. **Publications:** num.incl.*Fundamentals of Land-Use Planning* 1993, three books in Persian, 17 res.papers incl.The first application of automated eval.in Iran 1993. Favours pers.pub.& news media support. **Languages:** English, French (written), Persian. Willing to act as consult.etc. **Address:** Faculty of Natural Resources, University of Tehran, Karaj, Iran. **Tel.**& **fax** 98 21 658111.

MALAMIDIS, George. Conservation of the natural environment, evaluation & selection of natural areas of Greece which need special protection. Head of Landscape & Management. *B.*15 Mar.1939, Thessaloniki, Greece. Greek. **Education:** U.of Thessaloniki, B.(For.& Natural Envt) 1964; U.of Manchester, course in Methodology of Public Admin.Training 1973; U.of Salford, MSc(Envl Resources) 1978, participation in Intl Parks Sem.(USA & Canada) 1985. **Experience:** admin., consult., res. **Career:** admin.& planning work 1966–81, Recreational & Envl Planning 1985–9, Greek For. Service; Chief of Nat.Parks Dept, Min.of Agric. 1982–5; Head, Landscape & Mgmt, Forest Res.Inst.of Thessaloniki 1988–; Envl Researcher, Forest Res.Inst. and Consult.to Min.of Macedonia–Thrace on natural cons. 1989–93; Consult. UNESCO 1990–94 and Cyprus Govt 1992. **Achievements:** participation & contribn through IUCN (CNPPA) to studies of var. problems facing Greece concerning Nat.Parks and other prot.areas, orgn of envl sector of Greek For.Service, conducted Master Plans for Olympus Nat.Park, Aesthetic Forest of Thessaloniki and Suburban Forest of Athens, project leader of landscape resto., after fire, of Mt Athos and Kassandra peninsula. **Memberships:** IUCN CNPPA, Adventure Travel Soc., Biodiv. Coalition, Hellenic Assns of Foresters, & Agricl Researchers, and For.Soc., Geotechnic Chamber of Greece. **Publications:** 30+ papers & books incl.*Natural Prot.Areas (spec.ref.to Greece)* 1994, Natural areas with ecol importance in Chalkidiki Prefecture 1993. Indiff.to pers.pub.& news media support. **Languages:** English, French, Greek. Willing to act as consult.etc. **Address:** Forest Research Institute, Vassilika, Thessaloniki, Greece. **Tel.**(office) 30 31 461171/2/3, (home) 30 31 836306 or 840584; **fax** 30 31 461341.

MALCOLM, Dr 'Jay' R. Ecology & conservation of mammals. Associate Scientist. *B.*4 Mar. 1956, Peterborough, Ont., Canada. Canadian. *M.* Dr Justina C.Ray *qv.* **Education:** U.of Guelph,

BSc(Hons) 1979, MSc (awarded with dist.) 1982; U.of Florida, PhD 1992. **Experience:** field res.in c.Amazon, Jurua R., Urucu R.& Balbina damsite (Brazil), and Dzanga-Sangha Reserve (C.African Rep.), focus on small-mammal community structure, arboreal trapping of small canopy mammals, forest & landscape ecol., climate-change consult., fragmented landscapes, analytical & simulation modelling. **Career:** res.& teaching assistantships, Univs of Guelph & Florida, and postdoctl at Queen's U.(Ont.) 1991–3; Assoc.Sci. Centre for Biol.Cons. U.of Florida 1993–. **Achievements:** intensive census of arboreal small-mammal fauna using canopy traps, basic res.in small-mammal taxonomy & community structure, res.on edge effects in fragmented landscapes, quantitative modelling in landscape ecol. **Memberships:** ATB, ASM. **Publications:** c.20 incl.Edge effects in Amazonian forest fragments 1994, Comparative abundances of neotropical small mammals by trap height 1995. Indiff.to pers. pub., favours news media support. **Languages:** English, Portuguese. Willing to act as consult.etc. **Address:** 75 Wynford Heights Crescent, Unit 1608, Don Mills, Ontario M3C 3H9, Canada. **Tel.**(home) 1 352 378 3019; **fax** 1 352 372 4614.

MALLOCH, Dr Andrew John Cadoux. Phytosociology particularly of coastal environments, ecophysiology of maritime plants, animal–plant interactions. Senior Lecturer & Director of Ecology. *B.*5 Feb.1945, Clevedon, Somerset, England, UK. British. *M.*Dr K.Rachel: *s., d.* **Education:** U.of Camb. BA(Bot.) 1967, PhD 1970. **Experience:** res.(1967–) & teaching (1972–) in plant ecol.incl.res.projects for NCC; consult.in veg.ecol., computer analysis for ecol.; admin. **Career:** Postdoctl Res.1970–72, Lect.1972–89, Sr Lect.& Dir of Ecol.1989–, U.of Lancaster. **Achievements:** estab.basis of res.& major contribn to Brit.Nat.Veg.Class., developed *VESPAN* & *MATCH* computer packages for veg.sci., a leader in coastal ecol. **Memberships:** BES (Sec.1985–), IEEM, BSBI, BBS. **Awards:** elected BES Counc.1984 & Council Sec.1985. **Publications:** VESPAN II (a package to handle & analyse multivariate species data and species distribn data) 1988, *Plant Communities of Brit.Sand Dunes* 1989, sand-dune & sea-cliff sections of vol.5 of *Brit.Plant Communities* 1991–. Indiff.to pers.pub.& news media support. **Languages:** English, French (some). Willing to act as consult.etc. **Address:** Institute of Environmental & Biological Sciences, University of Lancaster, Lancaster LA1 4YQ, England, UK. **Tel.**(office) 44 524 593839, (home) 44 524 67498; **fax** 44 524 843854.

MALMBERG, Dr Ole Vilhelm. Environmental & family medicine, human ecology. Registered Family Physician/General Practitioner. *B.*19 Feb. 1951, Lund, Sweden. Swedish. Father Professor Torsten Malmberg *qv*. **Education:** U.of Lund, courses in Chem.(20 weeks) 1969, Med.(220 weeks) 1970–76, Envl Sci.(ten weeks) 1973,

Pharmacology (ten weeks) 1974, MD 1976; Educl Comm.for Foreign Med.Graduates (USA) 1978; U.of Camb. First Cert.in English 1979; Nordic Sch.of Public Health, part-time studies in envl med., epidemiology & biostats, res.methods in public health & primary health-care 1988–93, Dipl.of Public Health 1992. **Experience:** res.& teaching in human ecol., envl med., and public health 1978–; WHO F'ship 1991, held in UK, to study envl med., public health, and computers in primary health-care; rep.of NSHE & ISDE at UNCED & Global Forum in Rio de Janeiro 1992; ecol.expedn to Amazon regn 1992; participated in G500F mtg & UNEP 20th anniv. (Nairobi) 1992 where presented Rich Wetlands of Kristianstad project which was adopted as a G500F Agenda 21-project. **Career:** Registered 1978–, & Family 1982–, Physician, Sweden; Chief Distr.Med.Officer, Co.of Kristianstad 1986–92. **Achievement:** init.implementation of Agenda 21-concept in Kristianstad community. **Memberships:** SSPN 1976, NSHE (Founder memb.1978), F.SSM, SMA, SHE, SDE (Bd 1993–), ISDE (Liaison with UNEP, Directing Cttee Memb.1992–). **Award:** First Prize for Best Municipal Public Health Project* in s.Sweden (U.of Lund) 1988. **Publications:** (in Swedish) [Family med.from a human ecol. view] 1986, *[Environmental profile — a pilot study of envl factors with potential effect on ecol systems and public health in the local community] (co-Author) 1988, [Ecol.& health] (English summary, co-Author) 1992. **Languages:** English, Norwegian, Swedish. **Address:** Handskmakaregatan 2C, S-291 54 Kristianstad, Sweden. **Tel.**(office & fax) 46 44 312086 & 311945, (home) 46 44 120728.

MALMBERG, Professor Dr Torsten. Human ecology & conservation. Professor of Human Ecology & Division Head. *B.*5 July 1923, Helsingborg, Sweden. Swedish. *M.*Aimée Birgit: *s.*Dr Ole Vilhelm Malmberg *qv*, *d.*Anna Birgitta (envl medicine). **Education:** U.of Lund BA 1945, MA 1951, DSc 1973. **Experience:** res.& teaching in ornith., human ecol., and cons.l941–. **Career:** teacher at diff.schools 1953–78; Asst, Mus.Keeper, Librarian, Dept of Zool.1946–55, Asst Prof. Dept of Geog.1978–83, Head Human Ecol.Div.1984–, Prof. of Human Ecol. 1991–, all U.of Lund. **Achievements:** founder of Falsterbo Bird Obs.in southwesternmost Sweden, fundamental for res.& cons.of migrating birds; dissertation in 1973 disclosed the reason for large Rook (*Corvus frugilegus*) pop.decrease in Sweden to be mainly mercury seed-dressing which affected prot.of the species in Spring. **Memberships:** SSNP, SOS (Founder 1945, Bd Memb. 1949– 62), NSHE (Founder 1978, Pres. 1980–90), ISHE (Dep.Chairman 1980–84), F.IHE. **Awards:** Bronze Medal (SOS), Silver Medal (SSNP), F.& Global 500 Roll of Honour (UNEP) 1992. **Publications:** *Pop.Fluctuations & Pesticide Influence in the Rook,* Corvus frugilegus L., in Scania, Sweden (dissertation 1970), *Human Territoriality — Survey of Behavioural Territories in Man with Prelim.Analysis & Dis-*

cussion of Meaning 1980; *c*.300 papers; Founder & Ed. *Acta Oecologiae Hominis* 1989. Mostly favours news media support. **Languages:** English (good), French, German, Swedish. Willing to act as consult.etc. **Address:** Human Ecology Division, University of Lund, Box 2015, 220 02 Lund 2, Sweden. **Tel.**(office) 46 46 109685, (home) 46 46 118207; **fax** 46 46 104207.

MALONE, Professor Dr Thomas Francis. Role of scientists in achieving sustainable human development world-wide while maintaining a healthy & biologically-productive global environment in perpetuity. Distinguished University Scholar, Director. *B*.3 May 1917, Sioux City, Iowa, USA. American. *M*.Rosalie Ann: 5 *s*., *d*. **Education:** S Dakota State Sch.of Mines & Tech. SB 1940, MIT ScD 1946. **Experience:** for four decades has exercised leadership in charting a course to develop a deeper understanding of envl issues. **Career:** Asst then Assoc. Prof. MIT 1941–55; Res.Dir–Sr VP, Travelers Insurance Co.; Prof.of Phys.& Dean of Grad. Sch. U.of Conn.1970–73; Dir Holcomb Res. Inst. Butler U.1973–83; Scholar in Residence, St Joseph Coll. 1983–91; Exec.Sci. Conn.Acad.of Sci.& Engg 1988–91; Disting. U.Scholar NC SU 1990–; Dir, Sigma Xi Center 1992–. **Memberships:** NAS 1968– (Foreign Sec.1978–82, num.Bds & Cttees thereof), ICSU (VP 1970–72, Treas.1978–84, num.Cttees & Panels thereof), F.AAAS, AGS, F.AGU, F. AMS, Inst.of Ecol., F.NYAS, Sigma Xi 1943–, IUGG, NSF (var. Panels etc.), NASA, Dept of State, num.others. **Awards:** Spec.Citation (War Dept) 1946, Spec. Citation (Acting Gov.of Conn.) 1956, Losey Award (IAS) 1960, Charles Franklin Brooks Award (AMS) 1964, Conn. Conservationist of the Yr 1966, Cleveland Abbe Award (AMS) 1968, Guy E.March Medal (S.Dakota State Sch.of Mines & Tech.) 1976, Intl Met.Prize (WMO) 1984, Waldo E.Smith Award (AGU) 1986, Intl St Francis Prize for the Envt (UN/ICSU) 1991, Award for Intl Coopn (AAAS) 1994. **Publications:** *Compendium of Met.*(Ed.) 1951, Application of statistical methods in weather prediction 1955, A nat.inst.for atmos. res. 1958, Intl coopn in met.and the atmos.scis 1964, IUGG Cttee on Atmos.Scis 1965, Weather modification: implication of the new horizons in res.1967, New dimensions of intl coopn in weather analysis & prediction 1968, *Global Change* (co-Ed.) 1985, Mission to Planet Earth 1985, Global change and the human prospect 1991, Global change — the human & intl dimensions of sci.: view of the possible 1992, Towards a gen. method for analysing the regnl impact of global change (co-Author) 1992; num.others. Indiff.to pers.pub., favours news media support. **Language:** English. Further details may be obtained from *Who's Who in the World* (13th edn) 1996. Willing to act as consult.etc. **Address:** Sigma Xi, The Scientific Research Society, 99 Alexander Drive, POB 13975, Research Triangle Park, North Carolina 27709, USA. **Tel.**(office) 1 919 549 4691, (home) 1 919 490 1752; **fax** 1 919 549 0090.

MALONE-JESSURUN, Mrs Heidi Yolande. Fisheries, environmental pollution. Acting Foundation Director. *B*.2 Jan.1960, Paramaribo, Surinam. Surinamese. *M*.Gerald H.Malone: 3 *s*. **Education:** U.of Surinam MO A (Biol.) 1986, MO B(Biol.) 1994. **Experience:** res.in coastal shrimp- & fish-stock assessment. **Career:** Res. Asst 1986–92, Head 1992–3, Fisheries Res. Dept; Acting Dir, Stichting voor Vissery-bevordering (Fndn for Fisheries Promotion) 1993–. **Membership:** Envl Bd, Min.of Agric. Animal Husbandry and Fisheries. **Languages:** Dutch, English (good). Willing to act as consult.etc. **Address:** Stichting voor Vissery-bevordering, Cornelis Jongbawstraat 50, Paramaribo, Surinam. **Tel.**(office) 597 471324, (home) 597 454409; **fax** 597 421119.

MALTBY, Professor Dr Edward. Wetlands, peatlands, moorland, soils; ecosystem functioning & management. Professor of Environmental & Physical Geography, Institute Director. *B*.26 March 1950, South Bank, Middlesbrough, England, UK. British. *M*.Rosemary Jean: 3 *s*., *d*. **Education:** Sir William Turner's Sch.; U.of Sheffield BSc(First Class) 1971, U.of Bristol PhD 1977. **Experience:** over 20 yrs' res.in soils', peatlands', wetlands', & ecosystem, mgmt; work on nutrient dynamics, moorland ecosystems, microbial ecol., effects of fire, mgmt techniques/envl impacts; wide intl exp.; current emphasis on river marginal wetlands in Europe incl.Romania & Danube Basin, and peatlands in the tropics. **Career:** Dem. U.of Bristol 1971–4; Lect.1974–87 & Sr Lect. 1987–93 in Geog., Reader in Phys. Geog.& Dir Wetland Ecosystem Res.Group 1993–4, all at U.of Exeter; Prof.of Envl & Phys.Geog.and Dir R.Holloway Inst.for Envl Res. R.Holloway Coll. U.of London 1994–. **Achievements:** Coord. EC DGXII Project Functional Analysis Euro. Wetland Ecosystems, Chairman IUCN Wetlands Sci.Adv.Cttee, VC IUCN Comm.on Ecol., dev.of sci.base of wetland ecosystem functioning. **Memberships:** BES, RGS, BSSS, SWC, IBG. **Award:** Alice Garnett Prize (Sheffield U.). **Publications:** *Waterlogged Wealth: Why Waste the World's Wet Places* 1986, *Soils and Their Mgmt* (co-Author) 1989, *Do Not Disturb — Peatlands and the Greenhouse Effect* (co-Author) 1992; 130+ papers, chapters, & conf. proc. Indiff.to pers.pub., favours news media support. **Languages:** English, French (basic conversation). Willing to act as consult.etc. **Address:** Royal Holloway Institute for Environmental Research, Royal Holloway College (University of London), Huntersdale, Callow Hill, Virginia Water, Surrey GU25 4LN, England, UK. **Tel.**(office) 44 1784 477404, (home) 44 1784 432181; **fax** 44 1784 477427.

MANNERS MOURA, Robert, *see* **MOURA, Robert MANNERS.**

MANSER, Bruno. Contemplation of Nature in Switzerland and in Sarawak especially flora & fauna, traditional cultivation, customs, Nature medicine (Naturheilkunde), exploration of caves. Foundation President. *B*.25 Aug.1954, Basel, Switzerland. Swiss. **Education:** Basel High Sch.1964–73. **Experience:** fieldwork in Graubünden (1973–84), and in Sarawak (1984–90) while living with the Penan (a nomadic tribe in the rain-forests of Borneo); intl engagement (confs, spreading info., media-coverage, contacts with auths & orgns, expositions) *via* Bruno Manser Fndn for native people of Malaysia and prot.of their rain-forests 1990–; peaceful Nature activist. **Career:** Alpine Herdsman in Switzerland 1973–84; ethnological fieldworker, 1984–90; peaceful Nature activist 1990–; Founder & Pres. Bruno Manser Fndn 1990–. **Achievements:** supporting native people of Malaysia (esp.in Sarawak) in their efforts to keep the rights for their land and to conserve their rain-forests, endeavouring to prevent the importing of trop.timber by industrialized nations. **Membership:** Bruno Manser Fndn. **Award:** Prize for Envl Prot.(Binding-Prize) 1994. **Publications:** *Stimmen aus dem Regenwald* 1992 (transl.into French 1994, English 1995); num.reports for intl magazines. Indiff.to pers.pub., favours news media support. **Languages:** English, French, German, Italian (poor), Penan. Willing to act as consult.etc. **Address:** Bruno-Manser-Fonds, Heuberg 25, CH 4051 Basel, Switzerland. **Tel.**41 61 261 9474; **fax** 41 61 261 9473.

MANSFIELD, Professor Dr Terence Arthur. Plant physiology, responses of plants to abiotic stress. Dean. *B*.18 Jan.1937, Ashby de la Zouch, England, UK. British. *M*.Margaret Mary: 2 *s*. **Education:** U.of Nottingham, BSc 1958; U.of Reading, PhD 1961. **Experience:** past memb. Councils of RS and SEB; memb. Agric.& Food Res.Council (UK); Ed.*New Phytologist* 1979–. **Career:** Res.Plant Physiol. U.of Reading 1961–5; Lect., Reader, Prof., U.of Lancaster 1965–. **Achievements:** pioneering work on combined effects on plants of low concentrations of SO_2 & NO_2 poll.was undertaken in the 1970s. More recently it has been shown that exposure to these pollutants and to O_3 reduces the ability of plants to withstand natural stresses such as frost and drought. **Memberships:** SEB, BES. **Awards:** F.IBiol. 1984, F.RS 1987. **Publications:** *Effects of Air Pollutants on Plants* 1976, *Stomatal Physiol.*(co-Author) 1981, *Plant Adaptation to Envl Stress* (co-Author) 1993. Dislikes pers.pub., indiff.to news media support. **Languages:** English, French (written). Willing to act as consult. etc.if asked in advance. **Address:** Institute of Environmental and Biological Sciences, University of Lancaster, Bailrigg, Lancaster LA1 4YQ, England, UK. **Tel.**(office) 44 1524 593779, (home) 44 1524 791338; **fax** 44 1524 843854.

MARAGOS, Dr James Evans. Environmental impact assessment, protected areas' planning, coastal-zone management, marine ecology of tropical islands & coastal areas in Pacific & Asia regions. Private Consultant, Senior Fellow. *B*. 22 June 1944, Brooklyn, NY, USA. American.

D.: d. **Education:** UCR BA(Zool.) 1966, UHH PhD(Oceanogr.) 1972. **Experience:** intl marine & coastal consult., applied & basic res.on corals, reefs, coastal zones, & marine water qual., instruction & training in coastal-zone mgmt, EIA, field ecol.methods, resource mgr for govtl & non-govtl orgns, admin.of envl branch office, vol.in envl community assistance, envl educ. **Career:** Coral Reef Ecol. Inst.of Marine Biol. 1968–72, coral-reef mgmt (post-doctl) in Dept of Oceanogr. 1973–5, Instr.in Oceanogr.at Windward Community Coll.& Kanton Atoll (Kiribati) 1972–3, U.of Hawaii; Private Consult.(Pacific & SE Asia) 1970–; Chief, Envl Branch, US Army Corps (Trop.Pacific) 1975–90; Chief Sci. TNC (Pacific) 1991–3; Sr F. Prog.on Envt, E–W Center 1993–. **Achievements:** methodologies for EIA & ecol risk assessment, monitoring poll.on coral reefs and recolonization rates of corals, marine prot. planning & implementation, rapid ecol assessments & atlases for coastal trop.islands. **Memberships:** ISRS, PSA, IUCN CNPPA, NAEP. **Awards:** Employee of the Yr (US Army Corps of Engrs, Pacific Ocean Div.) 1981, Civilian Service Award & Medal 1986. **Publications:** num.incl.Reef corals of Johnston Atoll, the world's most isolated reef 1986, Coral Reef Restoration with Emphasis on Pacific Reefs 1992, Impact of coastal construction on coral reefs in the US affiliated Pacific Islands 1993, *How to Assess Envl Impacts on Trop.Islands and Coastal Areas* (co-Author) 1994, A description of the reefs & corals of the n.Marshall Is.1995, Revised checklist of the extant shallow water stony corals of Hawaii 1995. **Language:** English. Willing to act as a consult. **Address:** Program on Environment, East–West Center, 1777 East–West Road, Honolulu, Hawaii 96848, USA. **Tel.**(office) 1 808 944 7271, (home) 1 808 236 2724; **fax** 1 808 944 7298.

MARCOVALDI, Guy Marie Fabio GUAGNI DEI. Conservation & management of Marine Turtles off the coast of Brazil. Centre Director. *B*.10 Jan.1954, RJ, Brazil. Brazilian. *M*.Maria Ângela *qv*: *d*. **Education:** Fed.U.of Rio Grande, BSc (Oceanogr.) 1979. **Experience:** prelim. res on marine turtles in Brazil 1980–82, estab.& coordn of first and only nat.prog.for sea-turtle cons.& mgmt in Brazil, affiliated to IBAMA, 1981–. **Career:** Researcher, IBDF 1980–82; Coord. Nat.Marine Turtle Prog.(Projeto TAMAR-IBDF) 1982–; Founder & Dir, Nat. Center for Cons.& Mgmt of Marine Turtles 1990–. **Achievements:** establishing, coordinating, and maintaining, the only nat.sea-turtle cons.& mgmt prog.in Brazil. **Membership:** IUCN SSC Marine Turtle SG 1984–. **Language:** Portuguese. **Address:** Fundação Pró-TAMAR, Caixa Postal 2219, Salvador, Bahia, CEP 40.210-970, Brazil. **Tel.**55 71 876 1045; **fax** 55 71 876 1067.

MARCOVALDI, Maria Ângela GUAGNI DEI. Conservation & management of Marine Turtles off the coast of Brazil. Foundation President. *B*.3 July 1958, Porto Alegre, RS, Brazil. Brazilian. *M*.Guy Marie Fabio Guagni dei Marco-valdi *qv*: *d*. **Education:** Fed.U.of Rio Grande, BSc(Oceanogr.) 1981. **Experience:** conducted first survey of sea-turtle nesting distribn in Brazil 1980–82, dev.of first Brazilian sea-turtle tagging prog.1981, coordn of field activities for Projeto TAMAR-IBAMA's (Nat.Center for Cons.& Mgmt of Marine Turtles) sea-turtle mgmt & cons.activities in State of Bahia 1982–92. **Career:** prior to 1988 concerned with var.matters re.marine turtles; Founder 1988 & Pres. 1988–, Fundação Pro-TAMAR; Nat.Coord. (elected), WIDECAST 1991–; Res.F. WWF US 1992; Stagiaire, WWF Intl 1993. **Achievements:** establishing, coordinating, and then maintaining, only nat.sea-turtle cons.& mgmt prog.in Brazil (Projeto TAMAR-IBAMA) 1981–. **Membership:** IUCN SSC Marine Turtle SG (Exec.Team). **Languages:** English, Portuguese. **Address:** Fundação Pró-TAMAR, Caixa Postal 2219, Salvador, Bahia, CEP 40.210-970, Brazil. **Tel.**55 71 876 1045; **fax** 55 71 876 1067.

MARGARIS, Professor Dr Nickolas Stefanos. Teaching, research, and dissemination of information to mass media, on ecological matters. Professor & Departmental Chairman. *B*.4 March 1943, Volos, Greece. Greek. **Education:** Athens U, Dipl.(Natural Scis & Geog.) 1966, PhD(Bot.) 1972, 'Habil.' in Plant Ecol. 1977. **Experience:** study of Medit.-type ecosystems' structure, function, & mgmt; res.& teaching as well as distribn of results to mass media in which works permanently. **Career:** Lect.in Bot. U.of Athens 1973–8; Prof.& Dir of Dept of Ecol. U.of Thessaloniki 1978–86; Prof.& Chairman, Dept of Envl Studies, U.of the Aegean 1986–. **Achievements:** fire behaviour of Medit.ecosystems, island ecol., and dev.of popular perm.columns in mass media. **Memberships:** F.RGS, INSULA (Pres.). **Award:** Global 500 Roll of Honour (UNEP) 1989. **Publications:** ten books incl. *Being Alive on Land* (co-Author) 1984, *Econ.of Ecosystem Mgmt* (co-Author) 1985, *Desert.in Europe* (co-Author) 1986; 70+ scientific papers. Favours pers. pub.& news media support. **Languages:** English, Greek. Willing to act as consult.etc. **Address:** Department of Environmental Studies, University of the Aegean, 17 Karadoni Street, Mytilini 81100, Greece. **Tel.**(office) 30 251 20073, (home) 30 251 41035; **fax** 30 251 23783.

MARGULIS, Professor Dr Lynn. Symbiosis, environmental & cell evolution, cell biology; microbiology; Gaia theory. Distinguished University Professor of Biology. *B*.5 March 1938, Chicago, IL, USA. American. *D*.: 3 *s*., *d*. **Education:** U.of Chicago, AB 1957; U.of Wisconsin, MS 1960; UCB, PhD 1965. **Experience:** teaching, res., writing; field-work in Baja Calif.Norte, Mexico, and Delta del Ebro, Spain. **Career:** Fac.Memb. Boston U.1966–88; Sherman Fairchild Disting.Scholar, CIT 1976–7; Vis.Prof. Autonomous U.of Barcelona 1986;

Disting.U.Prof. Bot.Dept 1988–92 & Biol.Dept 1992–, U.of Mass.at Amherst. **Achievements:** discoveries in area of symbiosis & cell evol., aid in developing Gaia hypothesis of James Lovelock *qv*. **Memberships:** NAS, AAAS, SEP (ISEP co-Founder), ISSOL, LS, Sigma Xi, Phi Beta Kappa, Phi Beta Phi, Catalan Soc.for Biol. **Awards:** Guggenheim Fndn F., Sherman Fairchild Disting.Scholarship, MacDonald Award for Excellence in Res.(Boston U.), NASA Public Service Award, Fac.F'ship Award & Chancellor's Medal for Disting.Fac.(U.of Mass.), Hon.DSc from Southeastern Mass.U.and Westfield & Plymouth State Colls. **Publications:** *Microcosmos: Four Billion Yrs of Evol.from our Microbial Ancestors* 1986, *Five Kingdoms: An Illustr.Guide to the Phyla of Life on Earth* (2nd edn) 1988, *What Happens to Trash & Garbage? An Intro.to the Carbon Cycle* (co-Author) 1992, *Symbiosis in Cell Ecol.*(2nd edn) 1993, *Illustr. Glossary of the Protista* 1993, *Garden of Microbial Delights* (children's book) 1993; num.others. Avoids pers.pub.& news media support. **Languages:** English, French, Italian, Spanish. **Address:** Biology Department, Morrill South, University of Massachusetts, Box 35810, Amherst, Massachusetts 01003-5810, USA. **Tel.**(office) 1 413 545 3244; **fax** 1 413 545 3243.

MARINOV, Dr Uri. Environmental management. Managing Director. *B*.15 Dec.1935, Jerusalem, Israel. Israeli. *M*.Ora: *d*., 2 *s*. **Education:** Iowa SU, DVM 1965, MSc 1966. **Experience:** admin.of envt in Israel, first DG of Min.of Envt, consult.& teaching. **Career:** res. in repro. 1966–9, Dir Life Scis Div. Nat.Council for R&D 1969–73, Dir EPS 1973–88, DG Min.of Envt 1989–92, MD Envl Engg Systems Intl 1992–. **Achievements:** estab.envl admin.in Israel, working with all Medit.countries, consult. in dev.countries. **Memberships:** Edl Adv.Bd, World Resources Report; Intl Adv.Bd, Envl Impact Assn; IUCN CEPLA. **Award:** Global 500 Roll of Honour (UNEP) 1987. **Publications:** 40+ book chapters incl.Israel Envl Policy (co-Author); Guest Ed. *Envl Sci.& Tech.*(July 1993), papers. Favours pers.pub.& news media support. **Languages:** English, Hebrew. Willing to act as a consult. **Address:** 36 Mevo Harari, Jerusalem 97886, Israel. **Tel.**(office) 972 3 5102507, (home) 972 2 811704; **fax** 972 2 323066.

MARKER-KRAUS, Ms Laurie. Cheeta[h]/predator conservation research & education including wildlife & livestock management outside of protected reserves and non-lethal predator control methods. Studbook Keeper, co-Director & Research Fellow, co-Director. *B*.20 Jan.1954, Detroit, MI, USA. American, Namibian. *M*. Daniel Kraus *qv*. **Education:** Eastern Oregon SU BSc 1991. **Experience:** conducted res.on Cheetahs since 1974 and developed the most successful captive Cheetah breeding prog.in N.Amer., coordinated dev.of Cheetah Species

Survival Plan in N.Amer in 1983 and developed the *Intl Cheetah Studbook* for captive cheetah mgmt in 1987; began res.on Cheetahs in Africa in 1977 and co-founded Cheetah Cons.Fund in 1990 (a multidisc.and integrated prog.in cons. res.& educ.to assist the free-ranging Cheetah & its ecosystem). **Career:** Curator of Cheetahs 1974–88, Vet. Clinic Supervisor 1975–81, Dir/Educ.& Marketing 1981–8, Wildlife Safari; Intl Cheetah Studbook Keeper 1987–; co-Dir 1988–91, Res.F. l991–, Center for New Opportunities in Animal Health Scis (Smithsonian Instn); co-Dir, Cheetah Cons.Fund (Namibia) 1990–. **Achievements:** have spearheaded regnl & global mgmt progs for the Cheetah in captivity and in the wild, conducted first res.with re-intro.of captive-born Cheetahs into the wild (1977), co-founded first intl cons.prog.for free-ranging Cheetahs throughout their range. **Memberships:** IUCN SSC Cat SG & Captive Breeding SG, AZA, PAAZAB, SWG, AAUW. **Awards:** Young Careerist of Oregon 1984, Outstanding Women of Amer.1985, White Rose Award (Oregon's Top Ten Women) 1988, Conservationist of the Yr (African Safari Club) 1992. **Publications:** *Intl Cheetah Studbook* (annually since 1987), num.scientific & popular articles. Favours pers. pub.& news media support. **Language:** English. Willing to act as consult.etc. **Address:** Cheetah Conservation Fund, POB 247, Windhoek, Republic of Namibia, *or* New Opportunities in Animal Health Sciences (NOAHS) Center, National Zoo, Smithsonian Institution, Washington, District of Columbia 20008, USA. **Tel.**(in Africa) 264 651 4216 *or* (in USA) 1 202 673 4689; **fax** (in Africa) 264 61 34021 *or* (in USA) 1 202 673 4733.

MARQUEZ-MILLAN, Dr René. Sea-turtles' management, conservation, and population assessment. National Coordinator, Consultant. *B.*19 May 1941, Jalapa, Veracruz, Mexico. Mexican. *M.*Mirna E.Cruz-Romero (biol., sub-Dir of Regnl Center for Fisheries Research–Manzanillo, coastal fisheries res.): 2 *s., d.* **Education:** IPN Sch.of Biol. BSc(Biol.)(Hons) 1964, MSc(Biol.) 1981, PhD(Biol.) 1994; Tokai Res.Inst.(Japan) courses in Pop.Dynamics 1972, Fisheries Dynamics 1973; IPN/Centro de Investigaciónes Avanzadas (Mexico), course in Fisheries Biol.1988. **Experience:** res.in herpetology (sea-turtles), stock assessment, cons., behaviour, ecol., pop.enhancement, fishing regs etc.; teaching fisheries' biol.& taxonomy from BSc to MSc levels; consult.in sea-turtles' cons. & mgmt in Mexico, Cuba, C.Amer., Solomon Islands, and Japan; undergrad.assessor, sea-turtles' cons.training. **Career:** Chief of Herpetological Section: Marine Turtles, Nat.Fisheries and Biol.Inst.1963–5; Dir, Tamaulipas Fisheries Station 1966–71; Coord. Nat.Sea-Turtle Res.& Cons.Prog.in Mexico City 1971–82 and in Manzanillo 1983–; Consult. Japan Bekko Assn 1990–. **Achievements:** recipient of four res. grants from Comisión Nacional de Ciencia y Tecnología 1985, 1988 (2), & 1989, and one

from US NMFS–MMS to write a book* 1992–3; fndn of Sea Turtle Prog.in Mexico; installation of Sea Turtle camps & cons.training; consult.in decree for 17 Sea Turtle Natural Reserves in Mexico, and assessor for official sea-turtles Total Ban 1971–3 and 1990–; Prog.UNDP–FAO, for Fisheries Dev.& Cons.: Hawksbill Sea Turtle *[Eretmochelys imbricata]* Res.& Mgmt Project in Cuba 1991–2. **Memberships:** IUCN SSC Sea Turtles WG, Amer.Pacific Comm.for Marine Turtles Res.& Mgmt (Costa Rica, Pres. *ad hoc* Exec.Cttee 1986–90), Kemp's Ridley Sea Turtle** Recovery Team (US FWS) 1988–95; Nat.Sea Turtle Comm.(Tech.Asst Sec.). **Awards:** Dipl.(WWF) 1983 and (UNAM-Facultad de Ciencias) 1989, First Prize (Nat.Fisheries and Biol.Inst.) 1991 & 1994, First Prize (Fisheries Secretariat) 1991 & 1994, Nat.Prize in First Degree of XII Nat.Public Admin.Award 1991. **Publications:** *FAO Species Catalogue — Sea Turtles of the World* 1990, **Sinopsis de Datos Biologicos Sobre la Tortuga Lora*, ***Lepidochelys kempii (German)* 1993, *FAO Sinopsis Sobre La Pesca* (also in English) 1994, *Las Tortugas Marinas y Nuestro Tiempo* 1995; 46 papers as Author, ten as co-Author, 69 conf. proc.etc. Indiff.to pers.pub.& news media support. **Languages:** English, Spanish. Willing to act as consult.etc. **Address:** Centro Regional de Investigación Pesquera, Playa Ventanas S/N, Manzanillo, Colima 28200, Mexico. **Tel.** (office) 52 333 23750, (home) & **fax** 52 333 32491; **fax** 52 333 23751.

MARSH, Dr Clive Wallis. Conservation management of tropical forests, environmental impacts of tropical forestry; ecotourism; primate ecology. Assistant General Manager. *B.*22 Jan. 1951, London, England, UK. British. *M.*Ignatia Valentina: *s.* **Education:** Oundle Sch., Suffield Acad.; Bristol U. BSc(Hons)(Zool.) 1971, PhD (Primate Ecol.) 1978. **Experience:** field res.— ecol.& cons.of primates along Tana R.(Kenya) 1972–6, effects of logging & forest clearance on Malaysian primates 1978–81; cons.& forestry mgmt. **Career:** Res.Assoc. U. of Cambridge (attached to Malaysian Nat.U.) 1978–81; Wildlife Officer then Envl Services Mgr 1981–, Asst Gen.Mgr, Innoprise Corpn (commercial arm of) Sabah Fndn 1992–. **Achievements:** assisted Kenya Govt to estab.Tana R.Primate Nat. Reserve 1978–; estab.& runs Danum Valley Field Centre 1986– as res.station, and nearby Borneo Rainforest Lodge 1993 as commercial ecotourism venture in Sabah, both projects contributed to cons.of Sabah's largest prot.area of unlogged lowland forest; helped launch Sabah Nature Club educl initiative in Sabah sec.schools 1987–; helped negotiate first two projects in Asia funded by power cos for sequestration of 'greenhouse' gases through improved trop.forest mgmt 1992–. **Memberships:** IPS, IUCN SSC Primate SG and CNPPA. **Awards:** English-speaking Union Scholarship to Suffield Acad. 1969, Res.Assoc (NYZS) 1972–8. **Publications:** *Primate Cons.in Trop. Rain Forest* (co-

Ed.) 1978; *c*.30 other. Indiff.to pers.pub.& news media support. **Languages:** Bahasa Malaysia (spoken), English, French, Swahili. Willing to act as consult.etc. **Address:** Innoprise Corporation, POB 11623, 88817 Kota Kinabalu, Sabah, Malaysia. **Tel.**(office) 60 88 243245, (home) 60 88 427969; **fax** 60 88 243244.

MARSH, Professor Dr Helene Denise. Wildlife management, coastal zone management, ecology of Dugongs & sea-turtles and their habitats. Head of Department. *B*.8 April 1945, Sydney, Australia. Australian. *M*.Lachlan McLeod Marsh: 2 *s*. **Education:** U.of Qld, BSc(Hons) (1st Class) 1968; James Cook U. PhD 1973. **Experience:** Chair of community consultative cttee for GBR, tertiary teaching, res. **Career:** Res.F. 1973–87, Sr Lect.& Assoc.Prof.in Zool. 1987–91, Dir Envl Studies 1991–, Head Dept of Trop.Envt Studies & Geog.1994–, James Cook U. **Achievements:** Chair IUCN Sirenia SG 1985–, GBR CC 1989–, Qld Marine Parks CC 1991–2, and Scientific Adv.Cttee for Qld Nature Cons.Act 1993–. **Memberships:** Wildlife Soc., AMS, ASM, ACRS, AES, SMM. **Award:** Pers. Chair in Envl Sci. James Cook U. **Publications:** num.incl.The distribn and abundance of Dugongs* in the n.GBR Marine Park (co-Author) 1989, Mgmt of the trad.hunting of Dugongs [**Dugong dugon* (Muller 1776)] in the GBR Marine Park (co-Author) 1990, Biases associated with the manta tow technique with particular ref.to the Crown-of-thorns Starfish [*Acanthaster planci*] (co-Author) 1990; 60+ chapters, and papers in professional journals. Indiff.to pers.pub.& news media support. **Language:** English. Willing to act as consult. etc. **Address:** Department of Tropical Environment Studies & Geography, James Cook University, Townsville, Queensland 4811, Australia. **Tel.**(office) 61 77 81 4325, (home) 61 77 27 7502; **fax** 61 77 81 5581.

MARSH, Professor Dr John. Parks, tourism, sustainable development. Professor of Geography & Centre Director. *B*.27 Mar.1942, England, UK. Canadian. **Education:** U.of Alb. MSc 1965, U.of Calgary PhD 1972. **Experience:** res.in cons., tourism and dev.as Dir.of Res.Centre and consult.for WWF, IUCN, Govt of Canada; admin.in u.depts, nat.NGOs, confs; teaching in geog., cons., tourism, at BSc and MA levels. **Career:** Prof.of Geog.and Dir.Frost Centre for Canadian Heritage & Dev.Studies, Trent U. 1971–; Vis.Prof.Brit.Columbia, Japan, China, Calif., NZ, Mexico; consult.for WWF, IUCN in China, Turkey, World Heritage Sites. **Achievements:** 30 yrs' teaching of cons.& tourism, envl educ.; res.on balancing prot.& tourism in parks; contrib.to envl NGOs; publishing. **Memberships:** IUCN CNPPA, CAG, Heritage Interpretation Intl, NPA of Canada (Pres.). **Awards:** Mackinder Prize in Geog.(Reading U.), Commonwealth and Leverhulme Scholarships. **Publications:** *c*.200 books, papers, proc. reports, articles most recently on tourism and cons.in Antarctica;

systems plan for Canadian Heritage Rivers, ecotourism, cultural resources, and ecosystem planning; Ed.*Parks News*. Accepts pers.pub.and news media support. **Languages:** English; French & Spanish (some). Willing to act as consult.etc. **Address:** Frost Centre for Canadian Heritage and Development Studies, Trent University, Peterborough, Ontario K9J 7B8, Canada. **Tel.**1 705 748 1749 (sec. 1750); **fax** 1 705 748 1801.

MARTIN, Dr Claude. Conservation, environmental policy, tropical forests. Director-General. *B*.20 July 1945, Zürich, Switzerland. Swiss. *M*.Judy: *s*., 3 *d*. **Education:** U.of Zürich, MSc(Zool.), PhD(Wildlife Ecol.). **Experience:** prot.area mgmt, forest cons., wildlife res., and envl policy, in *e.g.*India, Ghana, Tanzania, Madagascar. **Career:** Sr Game Warden, Dept of Game and Wildlife (Ghana) 1975–8; Dir, WWF–Switzerland 1979–90; Dep. DG 1990–93, DG 1993–, WWF Intl. **Publications:** incl. *The Rainforests of W.Africa* 1991. **Languages:** English, French, German. Address: WWF International, Avenue du Mont-Blanc, 1196 Gland, Switzerland. **Tel.**41 22 364 9292; **fax** 41 22 364 5468.

MARTIN, Vance Gregory. Conservation of wilderness & wildland values; cultural, social, and psychological, constructs & strategies for Nature conservation; indigenous knowledge & natural resource management; trees and social forestry. President, Executive Director, Trustee, Director. *B*.20 July 1949, Washington, DC, USA. American. *M*.Catherine ('Kate') Elizabeth (artist with envl emphasis): *s*.Farren D.(experimental wilderness prog.staff & enthusiast), *d*.Felicia G.(cons.volunteer). **Education:** W. Virginia U. BA(Eng.Lit.) *magna cum laude* 1971. **Experience:** extensive in 21 countries with most recent emphasis throughout SA; consult.in natural resource mgmt & land-use (orgnl specialist) to num.agencies and orgns incl. USAID. **Career:** Dir.(Envt & Hort.) Findhorn Fndn 1974–84; Exec.Dir, World Wilderness Cong.1983–; Pres. Intl Wilderness Leadership (WILD) Fndn 1984–; Trustee, African Wildlife Heritage Trust 1990–; Adv. Center for Indigenous Envt & Dev.1993–; Dir Fulcrum Inc.1993–; Dir. Cons.Endowment Fund 1993–. **Achievements:** as Exec.Dir of World Wilderness Cong. advanced wilderness & wildland objectives and achievements incl. designation of Nature prot.areas, prompting World Bank/GEF activities, facilitated further definition & legis.concerning wilderness prot., founded tree planting & social for.prog.in n.Scotland. **Membership:** F. Findhorn Fndn. **Publications:** Exec.Ed.: *Wilderness Mgmt, Wilderness, Wilderness — The Way Ahead, For The Cons.of Earth*; var.others. Indiff.to pers.pub., favours news media spport. **Languages:** English, Spanish (spoken). Willing to act as consult. etc. **Address:** The WILD Foundation, 211 W. Magnolia, Fort Collins, Colorado 80521, USA. **Tel.**(office) 1 303 498 0303, (home) 1 303 482 5068; **fax** 1 303 498 0403.

MARTINS, Eduardo DE SOUZA. Nature conservation; sustainable use of natural resources. Programme Coordinator. *B*.22 Oct.1956, São José do Rio Preto, Brazil. Brazilian. *M*.Maria: *s., d.* **Education:** U.of Brasilia BA(Biol.) 1979, MSc(Ecol.) 1992. **Experience:** res.in primatology and hunting for subsistence in the Amazon regn; decision-making at fed.level; tech.adv.in envt issues; admin., prog.coordn. **Career:** Scientific Dev.Technician 1980–82, Coord. Humid Tropic Prog.1982–3, Nat.Council for Scientific & Technologic Dev.; Adv.for Amazonian Issues to Presidency of Projeto Rondon 1983–5; Tech.Adv.1985–7, Researcher of Primatology Nucleus 1987–9, Museu Paraense 'Emilio Goeldi'; Sec.-Gen.of Fed.U.of Para 1985–7; Dir. of Studies & Res. Envt Inst.of Acre (State Govt of Acre) 1989–90; Pres. IBAMA 1990–92; Adjunct Sec.of the Envt (Brazilian Fed.Govt) 1990–92; Tech.Coord. Grup de Trabalho Amazônico 1992–3; Prog.Coord. WWF Brazil 1993–. **Achievements:** basic res.on forest peoples and ways of subsistence/ecol.impact, elaboration of demonstrative projects for Brazilian trop.forests, implementation of WWF–Brazil. **Membership:** SBB. **Publications:** num.incl.Distribn & cons.of *Ateles belzebuth marginatus* (co-Author) 1988, Biologia e Ecologia de Primatas Não-Humanos na Amazônia: Avaliação e Perspectivas (co-Author) 1990, On the Track of the Road: Changes in Subsistence Hunting in a Brazilian Amazonian Village (co-Author) 1991. Favours pers.pub.& news media support. **Languages:** English, Portuguese. Willing to act as consult.etc. **Address:** WWF–Fundo Mundial para a Natureza, SHIS EQ QL 6/8 Conjunto E 20 andar, 71620-430 Brasília DF, Brazil. **Tel.** (office) 55 61 248 2899, (home) 55 61 244 5838; **fax** 55 61 248 7176.

MARUSIK, Dr Yuri M. Spider taxonomy & zoogeography, principles of systematics, biogeography of Beringia & North Holarctic. Associate Professor of Zoology. *B*.13 May 1962, Sarny, Rovno Area, Ukraine. Russian. *M*.Lyudmila V.: *d.* *B*.Andrei M.Marusik (plant physiol.). **Education:** U.of St Petersburg (then Leningrad) BSc 1984, PhD 1988. **Experience:** expedns in NE Siberia, C.Asia, Caucasus, Alaska; taxonomic res.on diff.spider families and ecol & physiol.res.in cold-resistance; teaching arthropod zool.& comparative invertebrate zool. **Career:** Jr Res.Sci. 1988–91, Sr Res.Sci.1991–4, Head of Entomol.Group 1992–, Assoc.Prof.of Zool.1994–, Inst.for Biolocal Problems of the North. **Achievements:** res.& description of biodiv.of NE Siberia, Sakhalin Is.& Kurile Islands, Yakutia, Mongolia, NW Amer.; taxonomic works in Thomisidae of C.Asia. **Memberships:** Eurasian (VP 1992–), Euro., Amer., & Intl, Arach. Socs, Russian Entomol.Soc. **Awards:** Prize of Far E. Branch (Russian AS) 1993, Russian AS 1994–7. **Publications:** c.80, c.15 book reviews. Indiff.to news media support. **Languages:** English, Polish, Russian, Ukrainian; gen.comp. of other Slavic languages. Willing to act as consult.etc.

Address: Institute for Biolocal Problems of the North, Karl Marx Prospekt 24, Magadan 685010, Russia. **Tel.**7 41 322 25801; **fax** 7 41 322 20166; **e-mail** ibpn@ibpn. magadan.su .

MASCARENHAS, Dr Anthony Francis. Plant-tissue culture, conservation of endangered species, micropropagation, biotechnology. Emeritus Scientist. *B*.3 Oct.1931, Nairobi, Kenya. Indian. **Education:** Poona U. MSc(Chem.) 1976, PhD(Biochem.) 1981. **Experience:** 25 yrs' res. in all aspects of plant-tissue culture (micropropagation, protoplast isolation & fusion, cons., somaclonal, embryo rescue); headed Tissue Culture Div.at Nat.Chem.Lab.(Pune) consisting of 30+ scientists; conducted res.on cons.of several endangered, and rare, plant/tree species in India using tissue culture methods, data obtained being presented at nat./intl mtgs; used micropropagation methods in biotech.to enlarge pop.of genetically/phenotypically superior forest trees *viz.Eucalyptus* spp., Teak *(Tectona grandis)* & bamboos; pioneered res.in India in dev.of tissue culture processes for extension and direct application to agric./for.; Coord.for jt Indo-Bulgaria, –Sweden, & –US Sr Scientists' Panel, and Nat.Chemical Lab.(Pune, India)–Brit. Council progs on plant-tissue culture. **Career:** Bacteriologist, Kasturba Med.Coll.(Mangalore) 1955–6; Sci.1956–88, Head 1988–91, Emer. Sci.1991–, Nat.Chem.Lab. **Achievements:** worked in capacity of project leader in 'hi-tech.' envlly-friendly biotech.projects such as cons.of endangered plant species and prod.of high-qual.planting stock for afforestation progs, success in inducing bamboos to flower precociously which can have far-reaching potential in bamboo breeding. **Memberships:** IAPTC, Plant Tissue Culture Assn of India, NYAS, ISTS, Res.Adv.Cttees on Biotech.for several govt & private depts. **Awards:** VASVIK Award 1988, FIEF (Ichal karanji) Award 1990, Technology Award (CSIR India) 1991. **Publications:** 100+ res.pubns incl. *Modern Topics in Plant Tissue Culture* 1989, Test Tube Forests 1992, *Handbook of Plant Tissue Culture* 1993. Indiff.to pers. pub., favours news media support. **Languages:** English, French (written), Hindi. Further details may be obtained from *Ref.India*, p.257 1993. Willing to act as consult.etc. **Address:** Sunnymeade, Padamji Park, Pune 411 002, Maharashtra, India. **Tel.**(office) 91 212 339338, (home) 91 212 654977; **fax** 91 212 330233 & 334761; **e-mail** afm@ncl.ernet.in .

MASING, Professor Dr Viktor. Peatland science (telmatology), mire conservation, geobotany, biocoenology, biogeography. Emeritus Professor of Plant Ecology. *B*.11 April 1925, Tartu, Estonia. Estonian. *M*.Linda Poots (Chief Ed. *Estonian Nature): s*.Matti (conservationist, small mammals), *d.* **Education:** Tartu U. *cum laude* 1951, PhD 1959, DSc(Biol.) 1969. **Experience:** res.— bog investigation, expedns to var.parts of USSR (Wrangell Is., Taimyr Peninsula, Far E., Karakum Desert); teaching bot.& biogeog.for 35 yrs. **Career:** Lect.1956–60, Asst Prof. 1961–70, Prof.of Plant Ecol.1971–93, Emer. 1993–, Tartu U. **Achievements:** veg.mapping of Nature Reserves, co-init.of mire prot.in Estonia and later in USSR, Chairman of IBP Telma Project in USSR 1964–74, Participant in SCOPE–UNEP Project on Wetlands, Ed.*Estonian Enc.* **Memberships:** Estonian AS 1992–, six geogl & botl socs in Baltic Regn. **Awards:** State Prize in Sci.(Estonia) 1977 & 1982, Karl Ernst von Baer Medal (Estonian AS) 1992, five awards from Mins of Estonia. **Publications:** ten books in Estonian, one in Russian; Mire Ecosystems in the USSR (co-Author) 1983; *c*.300 scientific papers incl.Approaches, levels and elements of veg.res.1994. Indiff.to pers. pub.& news media support. **Languages:** English, Estonian, German, Russian. Willing to act as a consult. **Address:** Department of Botany & Ecology, Tartu University, 40 Lai Street, Tartu EE 2400, Estonia. **Tel.**(office) 372 7 435240, (home) 372 7 431145.

MASSEY STEWART, John, *see* **STEWART, John** MASSEY.

MATHUR, Professor Dr Harbansh Bahadur. Combustion-generated pollution — monitoring & control; environmental impact assessment; air pollution monitoring & control equipment design & development; vehicular emissions and their control; design of catalytic convertors for 2- and 4-stroke engine-powered two- and four-wheeled vehicles. Professor, Coordinator. *B.*18 Nov.1936, Mandsaur, MP, India. Indian. Mother Mrs Jagrani Devi Mathur, devoted envl cons.activist & ecologist. *M.*Rekha (envl cons. activist with spec.ref.to flora–fauna & wildlife: s., 3 *d.*incl.Roopa (envl psych.), Jyoti (pharmaceuticals — herbal plants, flora & fauna). **Education:** U.of Bombay BE(Hons.) 1957, U.of Roorkee ME(Hons) 1963, IIT PhD 1971. **Experience:** 36 yrs of res., industrial consult., and teaching — EIA studies, consult.to Govt of India and memb.of Govt of India Min.of Envt Res.Adv.Cttee, Adv.to UNDP, supervised 18 PhD students & 80 BTech./MTech.projects. **Career:** engr in industry 1958–68; Lect.& Asst Prof. Madhav Inst.of Tech.1958–67; Asst Prof.1967–73, Prof.1973–, Head 1978–81 Mech. Eng.Dept, Jt Prof.1978–, Coord.Air Poll.R&D Prog.1978–, Prof.in charge Fuels & Poll.Lab.and Unconventional Fuels Lab.1978–, Centre for Energy Studies, IIT. **Achievements:** res.in field of energy & envt with spec.ref.to fuels–combustion–poll., vehicular poll.control, EIA studies; set up Air Poll.Instruments Lab.at IIT; lodged three patents on air poll.monitoring/control equipment/instruments; designed & dev. of catalytic converters for exhaust poll.control of 2- and 4-stroke engine-powered vehicles using cheaper catalysts such as sponge iron with high species conversion efficiencies; envl mapping of Delhi; set up mass emission standards for vehicles as Chairman, Govt of India Min.of Envt Cttee. **Memberships:** F.INAE, F.IAE, IAAPC

(F.& VP), Combustion Inst., SOCLEEN (Life), ISTE, Envt Sub-Cttee FICCI. **Publications:** *Alcohols — The Bio-solar Fuels* (*Their Prod.& Utilization*) 1988, 200+ tech.papers, 25+ tech. reports *e.g.Impact of Surface Transport on the Envt of Major Metropolitan Cities of India* 1986, *EIA Studies on Setting up of* both *InterState Bus Terminuses* 1987, and *Super Thermal Power Stations* (2000 *MW Capacity*) *at Muradnagar and at Sungrauli, India* 1982, *Kathmandu Valley Vehicular Emission Control, Nepal* 1993; Ed.in Chief, *J.Indian Assn of Air Poll.Control.* Favours pers.pub.& news media support. **Languages:** English, Hindi, Urdu. Willing to act as consult.etc. **Address:** Department of Mechanical Engineering, Indian Institute of Technology, Hauz Khao, New Delhi 110 016, Delhi, India. **Tel.**(office) 91 11 666979 ext.2129, (home) 91 11 652521; **fax** 91 11 686 2037.

MATTHEW, Father (Dr) Koyapillil Mathai. Field botany of South India, taxonomic monography; generation of environmental awareness among students & tribals; *in situ* & *ex situ* conservation on Palni Hills. Director. *B.*16 Mar. 1930, Ramapuram, Ker, India. Indian. **Education:** U.of Madras, MSc(Bot.) 1958; U.of Bombay, PhD (Systematic Bot.) 1960; U.of Reading (UK), MSc(Advanced Plant Taxonomy) 1972. **Experience:** res. in systematic bot., consult.in field bot., j.ref., grad.& postgrad.teaching in bot.esp.systematic bot. **Career:** Dir of The Rapinat Herbarium 1967– and of The Anglade Inst.of Natural Hist.1980–; over four yrs' work in five instalments at R.Botanic Gdns, Kew; Latinization of new taxa 1967–. **Achievements:** massive envl awareness generation among students & tribals; Org.of The Rapinat Herbarium (100,000 specimens –1993) as res.base and The Anglade Inst.of Natural Hist.as envl base; *c.*25,000 trainees from *c.*600 centres (linked by envl newsletter *SHOLA*) in S.India have been handled (1984–1993) on a three-day, round-the-yr, innovative prog.; Guest Lect.in Germany, The Netherlands, UK, Indonesia; attended Rio Summit as Vatican Rep.; Founder/VP of local envl council. **Memberships:** LS(Life), IAPT, SEB, SSE, BNHS, IBS, IPS. **Awards:** ZWO, F'ship for Flora Malesiana (the only Indian to date), Best Teacher Award (TN Govt) 1984–5. **Publications:** *Floras* (nine vols, mainly of S. India), 50+ papers & book reviews. **Languages:** English, Malayalam, Tamil. Willing to act as consult.etc. **Address:** The Rapinat Herbarium, St Joseph's College, Tiruchirapalli, Tamil Nadu 620 002, India. **Tel.**(office) 91 431 29052, (home) 91 431 24070.

MATTHIESSEN, Peter. Environment, Nature. Writer, Social Activist, Zen Teacher. *B.*22 May 1927, New York, NY, USA. American. Father E.A.Matthiessen, former Bd member of Nat. Audubon Soc.& Nature Conservancy. *M.*Maria: 2 *s.*incl.Alex (Rain Forest Action Network), 2 *d.* **Education:** Yale U. BA 1950. **Experience:** has taken u.courses in biol., ornithol., zool., bot.

Career: lifelong naturalist, envlist, Nature writer. **Achievements:** many articles & books on wildlife & cons.all over the world. **Memberships:** AAAL, AAAS, NYZS (Trustee 1965–78, Adv.1978–). **Awards:** Nat.Book Award* 1978, Gold Medal (Philadelphia AS) 1985, John Burroughs Medal 1982, Medal (African Wildlife Leadership Fndn) 1982. **Publications:** over 20 books incl.*The Snow Leopard* 1978, *Shadows of Africa* 1992, and num.articles. Indiff.to pers. pub., favours news media support. **Languages:** English, French (proficient), Spanish (poor). **Address:** 527 Bridge Lane, Sagaponack, New York, New York 11962, USA. **Tel.**(office) 1 516 537 1348, (home) 1 516 537 0837; **fax** 1 516 537 5372.

MAUGHAN, Dr O.Eugene. Aquatic ecology & management. Research Unit Leader. *B.*3 Jan. 1943, Preston, Franklin, ID, USA. American. *M.* LuDean: 2 *s.*, 4 *d.* **Education:** Utah SU, BS (Zool.) 1966; U.of Kansas, MA(Zool.) 1968; Washington SU, PhD(Zool.) 1972. **Experience:** wilderness & highly-modified systems, game & non-game mgmt; has worked in arctic, alpine, Gt Plains, SW desert, and trop., systems; teaching, res., admin. **Career:** Biol. R.Basin Studies 1971–2, Asst Leader of Virginia Cooperative Fishery Res.Unit 1972–7, Leader of Oklahoma Cooperative Fish & Wildlife Res.Unit 1977–87, US FWS; Leader of Arizona Cooperative Fish & Wildlife Res.Unit, US FWS 1987–93/Nat. Biol. Service 1993–. **Achievement:** assisted state & fed.agencies in mgmt of natural resources. **Memberships:** AFS, ASIH. **Awards:** Most Significant Paper *(Trans.AFS,* co-Author) 1983, Meritorious Service (USDI) 1991, Spec.Achievement (US FWS) 1991–2. **Publications:** several chapters incl.Trophic Dynamics of a Freshwater Artificial Tire Reef (co-Author) 1979, Withdrawals (co-Author) 1994; 160+ papers & symposia proc. Dislikes pers.pub.& news media support. **Languages:** English; French, German & Spanish (all read). Further details may be obtained from *Personalities of Amer.*1983, *Amer.Men and Women of Sci.*1995. Willing to judge proposals and ref.papers. **Address:** Arizona Cooperative Fish and Wildlife Research Unit, National Biological Service, 210 Biological Sciences East, University of Arizona, Tucson, Arizona 85721, USA. **Tel.**l 602 621 1959; **fax** 1 602 621 8801.

MAXIMOV, Professor Dr Victor N. Marine ecology: ecological monitoring of coastal ecosystems, multidimensional statistics in ecology. Professor of General Ecology. *B.*27 July 1933, St Petersburg (then Leningrad), Russia. Russian. Father Academician Nicolas A.Maximov (1880–1952), plant physiol. *M.*Helene S.Leshchinskaya: *d.*Olga (marine macrophyte ecol.). **Education:** Moscow SU, Fac.of Chem. MSc 1955 & PhD 1963, Fac.of Biol. DSc 1971. **Experience:** res.— community structure & biol. diversity of plankton & periphyton in connection with anthropogenic impact, multidimensional statl

analysis of ecol.data, ecotoxicology; admin.— chief of expedns on White Sea 1971–4 and Atlantic (Soviet–Amer.) 1975 & Indian Oceans 1980, Scientific Curator of System Ecol.Lab. Fac.of Biol. Moscow SU; consult.— experimental design in microbiol.& ecol., statl analysis of ecol data; teaching — gen.ecol., ecol stats, & biol monitoring, from BSc to PhD & post-doctl levels. **Career:** Res.Worker, Inorganic Chem. Dept 1955–61, Asst Prof. Radiochemistry Dept, Fac.of Chem.1961–4, Sr Res.Worker, Hydrobiol.Dept 1965–81 and Prof.of Gen.Ecol.1981–, Fac.of Biol., all at Moscow SU. **Achievements:** dev.& popularization of Experimental Design & Response Surface methodology in microbiol., entomol., & ecol., extension of multidimensional approach to analysis of ecol monitoring data, dev.of concept of ecosystem tolerance (contrary to organismic concept) as a base of threshold limit determination of pollutants in aquatic ecosystems. **Memberships:** Moscow Naturalists' Soc., Russian Hydrobiol.Soc. **Award:** Bronze Medal (Nat.Economical Achievements Exhibition) 1984. **Publications:** *Multifactorial Experiment in Biol.*(in Russian) 1980, *Experimental Design in Biol.& Agricl Sci.*(Ed., in Russian) 1991; 170+ scientific papers, some in English. Favours pers.pub., indiff.to news media support. **Languages:** English (poor), French (read & written with dictionary), German, Russian. Willing to act as consult.etc. **Address:** Block 1 apt 56, Rijazanssky Prospekt 87, 109542 Moscow, Russia. **Tel.**(office) 7 095 939 5560, (home) 7 095 371 2154.

MAYSTRE, Professor Lucien Yves. Environmental engineering & management. Professor of Environmental Engineering. *B.*3 Feb.1933, Geneva, Switzerland. Swiss. **Education:** ETH, Dipl.Ing.1956, Johns Hopkins U. MSc (Envl Eng.) 1969. **Experience:** tech.& consult. in Europe & overseas. **Career:** Envl Engr, Dept of Public Works, Geneva, 1958–68; Consult. WHO 1968–71; Prof.of Envl Engg & Mgmt, EPFL 1971–. **Award:** Dr *h.c.*(Faculté des scis agronomiques de Gembloux). **Publications:** four books incl.*Méthodes Multicritères électre* 1994, *Déchets Urbains* 1994. **Languages:** English, French, German. **Address:** Institut de Génie de l'Environnement, Ecole polytechnique fédérale de Lausanne, Ecublens, 1015 Lausanne, Switzerland. **Tel.**41 21 693 2711; **fax** 41 21 693 2859.

McALLISTER, Dr Donald 'Don' E. Biodiversity, conservation, taxonomic ichthyology, conservation of coral reef ecosystems, environmental education. Senior Biodiversity Adviser & Scientific Editor, President, Editor. *B.*23 Aug.1934, Victoria, BC, Canada. Canadian. *M.*Elisabeth: *s.*, 4 *d.* **Education:** UBC BA 1955, MA 1957, PhD 1964; U.of Michigan 1957–8. **Experience:** field collection of fish specimens; collection mgmt & computerization; res.on taxonomy, evol., biogeog., biodiv.geographic info.systems incl.eco-taxa hotspots analysis; cons.of boreal & trop.aquatic species; involved in advising on negotiations for ICBD, dev.of a Canadian Biodiv.Strat.and prep.of Canada Country Study in Biodiv.; created & edits two cons.bulletins. **Career:** Asst Curator, Inst.of Fisheries, UNC 1956; Curatorial Asst, Div.of Fishes, U.of Michigan 1957–8; Curator, Ichthyology Section, Nat.Museum of Natural Scis 1958–86; Adjunct Prof. U.of Ottawa 1969–92 and Carleton U.1981–; Ichthyology Res.Curator, Canadian Mus.of Nature 1986–; Pres. Ocean Voice Intl 1989–, Ed. Ocean Voice Bull.*Sea Wind* 1987–; Sr Biodiv.Adv.& Ed. *Canadian Biodiv.*1991–. **Achievements:** pubns on ichthyofauna & fish cons.in Canada, co-Author of Atlas of N.Amer.Freshwater Fishes, Ed.of *Global Biodiv./La biodiversité mondiale,* and of *Sea Wind,* Author of *Save our Coral Reefs.* **Memberships:** ASIH, JIS, CSEB, IUCN SSC Coral Reef Fish SG. **Awards:** NRC Scholarship, Stoneman Marine Envl 1990. **Publications:** 160 incl.A computerized working world fish list (abstract) 1987, Fishes of N.Amer. endangered, threatened or of special concern (co-Author) 1989, Envl, econ.& social costs of coral reef destruction in the Philippines 1989, A list of the fishes of Canada 1990, *Canadian Biodiv.: a Census & an Appraisal* (co-Author) 1991, *[Save our Coral Reefs]* (Author, in Indonesian) 1991, Mapping & GIS analysis of global distribn of coral reef fishes on an equal-area grid (co-Author) 1993. Dislikes pers.pub., supports envl pub.of issues. **Languages:** English, French (spoken, some written). **Address:** Canadian Centre for Biodiversity, Canadian Museum of Nature, POB 3443, Station D, Ottawa, Ontario K1P 6P4, Canada, *or* Ocean Voice International, 2883 Otterson Drive, Ottawa, Ontario K1V 7B2, Canada. **Tel.**(office) 1 613 990 8819, (home) 1 613 731 4755; **fax** 1 613 990 8818 (Mus.), 1 613 521 4205 (Ocean Voice Intl).

McCALLA, Dr Winston. Environmental legislation & policy. Attorney-at-Law, Consultant. *B.*24 Jan.1941, Jamaica. Jamaican. **Education:** U.of London, LLB 1962; Melbourne U. LLM 1967; LSE PhD 1973. **Experience:** direction of legal reform in Jamaica. **Career:** Crown Counsel, Jamaica 1962–4; Resident Magistrate 1964–6, Chief Parliamentary Counsel 1967–8, Solicitor-Gen.1968–70, all Malawi; Asst.Attorney-Gen.1970–72, Sr Asst Attorney-Gen.1972–4, Legal Adv.to Nat.Bauxite Comm.1974–6, Dir.of Legal Reform 1976–80, Jamaica; Sessional Lect. U.of W.Indies 1973–6; Assoc.Prof. U.of Sask.1980–81; Attorney-at-Law in private practice, Consult.1981–. **Achievements:** prep.of legis.to estab.Natural Resources Cons.Auth.for Jamaica, and envl legis.for several Carib.countries. **Memberships:** IUCN CNPPA, JBA, IAIA, IASCP, ABA (Assoc.), ELI Washington (Assoc.), Nat.Envl Socs Trust (past Chairman, Bd of Dirs), Richmond F'ship (Dep.Chairman), Carib.Cons.Assn (Tech.Adv.Cttee), Eastern Carib. Adv.Bd. **Publications:** *Prospects for Legal Dev.in the Carib.*1976, *Envl Law Country Studies for all OECS States* 1990; num.papers.& conf.presentations. Favours pers.pub.& news media support. **Languages:** English, Spanish. Willing to act as consult.etc. **Address:** 3 Markway, Kingston 8, Jamaica. **Tel.**(office) 809 92 21217, (home) 809 92 55701; **fax** 809 92 25202.

McCAMMON, Antony L.T. Fostering the links between banking/finance and environment/development; application of financial experience and principles to 'The Commons'. Bank Representative. *B.*18 Sept.1939, Jersey, Channel Islands. British. *M.*Angelika: 4 *s.* **Education:** Marlborough Coll.(UK); U.of the Sorbonne, Dipl.in Cours de Civilisation française 1957–8; McGill U. course in Commerce 1959 61. **Experience:** 30 yrs' intl commercial banking, organized 'Banking and The Envt: Intl Workshop' 1991, contributed to World Clean Energy Conf.1991, attended UNCED (as FEC del.) 1992, Model UN Conf.on Indigenous Peoples 1994, Citizen Amb.Prog. Moscow, Kiev, & Chernobyl 1994, participated in num. banking/envt sems, private envl initiatives 1990–. **Career:** (prin.postings) Intl Trainee at Chartered Bank UK (London) 1962–3, Intl Trainee in UK (London) 1963–4, in Brazil — Santos, Manaus, Salvador, & São Paulo, Exec. Officer 1964–7; PA to Chairman in UK (London) 1967–8, Asst Rep.in Switzerland (Zurich) 1968–73, Mgr (Oporto) & Interim Mgr (Portugal) 1973–7, all with BOLSA; Asst Mgr then Mgr, Lloyds Bank Switzerland 1977–91; Zürich Rep. Cater Allen Bank 1994–. **Achievements:** envt & dev.— res.& dialogue with bankers, envlists, and scientists, in developed & developing countries on 1) banks' actual & potential involvement in the envt & dev.sector, 2) internal & ext.EIA, and 3) *local* funding initiatives partic.in developing countries with a view to their complementing and eventually substituting for bilateral & multilateral financial assistance. **Publications:** incl.Banking responsibility and liability for the environment: what are banks doing? 1995. Favours pers.pub.& news media support. **Languages:** English, French, German, Portuguese & Spanish; Russian (basic knowledge of written & spoken). Willing to act as consult.etc. **Address:** Minervastrasse 117, 8032 Zürich, Switzerland. **Tel.** (office) 41 1 382 1162, (home) 41 1 980 2818; **fax** 41 1 382 1836.

McCARTHY, Gerald Patrick. Environmental conservation, sustainable development, environmental philanthropy, environmental law & public policy, education. Executive Director, Vice-Chairman. *B.*23 March 1943, New York, NY, USA. American, Irish. *M.*Lucile J.: *s., d.* **Education:** Manhattan Coll. BE(Elec.Eng.) 1965, U.of Washington, MSE 1967. **Experience:** admin.as Dir and Chairman & Admin., u. teaching. **Career:** Project Engr (First Lt) 1966– 7, Program Mgr (Capt.) 1968–70, USAF; Exec. Dir, Governor's Council on the Envt 1970–74, Chairman & Admin. Council on the Envt 1974–7, Commonwealth of Virginia; Exec.Dir, VEE

1977–; VC Virginia Cons.& Rec.Fndn 1992–. **Achievements:** estab.first US philanthropic orgn devoted solely to envl cons.(VEE), founding org.of Envl Grantmakers' Assn, instituted use of 'roundtable' technique for resolving envl conflicts in VA, developed envl impact report law for VA, helped launch several new envl cons.instns in VA. **Memberships:** Adv.Bds of VWC & VTEE, Boone & Crockett Club. **Awards:** Conservationist of the Year (Chesapeake Bay Fndn) 1982, President's Award (NC) 1986. Indiff.to pers.pub., favours news media support. **Languages:** English, Italian (basic). Further details may be obtained from *Who's Who in Finance & Industry* 1993, *Who's Who in S & SW* (USA) 1993. **Address:** 1051 E.Cary Street, POB 790, Richmond, Virginia 23206-0790 USA. **Tel.**1 804 644 5000; **fax** 1 804 644 0603.

McCARTHY PETERSON, Mrs Claire, *see* **PETERSON, Mrs Claire McCARTHY.**

McCLOSKEY, Dr (John) Michael. Protection of the environment, particularly Nature. Chairman, Adjunct Professor. *B*.26 April 1934, Eugene, OR, USA. American. *M*.Maxine E.*qv.* **Education:** Harvard Coll. BA 1956, U.of Oregon JD 1961. **Experience:** envl mgmt & negn, admin. **Career:** Field Rep. Pacific Northwest 1961–5, Cons.Dir 1966–9, Exec.Dir 1969–85 (Acting 1986–7), Chairman 1985, Dir Natural Value Mapping Project, Chairman Mgmt Cttee of Center for Envl Innovation, all at the Sierra Club; Adjunct Prof.of Public Policy, Sch.of Natural Resources and the Envt, U.of Michigan; num.vol.positions. **Achievements:** under his direction Sierra Club's membership and net worth grew five-fold, originator of first inventories of world wilderness and of wild rivers of the north, key draftsman of UN Charter for Nature, prin.legislative advocate for estab.of Redwood Nat.Park, sustained contribns to lit.on wilderness. **Memberships:** IUCN CNPPA, Collegium Ramazzini, Sierra Club (Life), ICEL, Explorers' Club. **Awards:** John Muir Award 1979 and Spec.Commendation Award 1987 (both of Sierra Club), Global 500 Roll of Honour (UNEP) 1992. **Publications:** contribns to seven books, Forewords to four, Ed.of three; articles to num.professional journals & periodicals incl. What do you expect of EPA: an envlist? 1990, Envlism & tech.: changing attitudes 1991, Business, envlism, and the market-place: new currents and possibilities 1991. Accepts pers.pub. & news media support. **Language:** English. **Address:** The Sierra Club, 408 C Street NE, Washington, District of Columbia 20002, USA. **Tel.**1 202 675 6279; **fax** 1 202 547 6009.

McCLOSKEY, Mrs Maxine E. Marine protected areas especially in the high seas; whale policy formation, marine mammals; coral reefs; the Arctic. Working Group Leader, Committee Member. *B*.26 April 1927, Portland, OR, USA. American. *M*.Dr J.Michael McCloskey *qv*: *s*., 3 *d*. **Education:** Portland SU BS 1962, Reed Coll. MAT 1963. **Experience:** admin., campaigning, vol.work, teaching. **Career:** Coll.Instructor of US hist.& govt 1960s & '70s; Founder, Exec.Dir., Pres.of Bd of Dirs, Whale Center 1978–85; Bd Memb. Defenders of Wildlife 1984–93; Memb.Sierra Club Marine Cttee 1992– and Defenders of Wildlife Prog.Policy Cttee 1990–; Leader, IUCN CNPPA High Seas WG 1994–. **Achievements:** arranged two-days' symp.on endangered species sponsored by AAAS 1974, memb.Calif.Citizen Nongame Adv.Cttee to Calif. Fish & Game Dept 1975–86 (Chair 1975–9), memb.US del.to eight annual mtgs of IWC. **Memberships:** Sierra Club, Defenders of Wildlife, WorldWIDE Network. **Awards:** Envl Achiever (Friends of UNEP) 1987, Citation (CSI) 1991. **Publications:** *Wilderness and the Qual.of Life* (co-Ed.) 1969, *Wilderness, the Edge of Knowledge* (Ed.) 1970, Prot.Areas on the High Seas and the Case for Marine Wilderness (Proc.) 1993; num.articles. Accepts pers.pub.& news media support. **Language:** English. **Address:** 5101 Westbard Avenue, Bethesda, Maryland 20816, USA. **Tel.**(home) 1 301 229 4967; **fax** 1 301 229 2923

McDOWELL, David Keith. Conservation. Director-General. *B*.30 April 1937, Palmerston North, NZ. New Zealander. *M*.Janice R.: *s*., 3 *d*. **Education:** Victoria U.of Wellington, MA (Hons) (Hist.). **Experience:** diplomatic admin., adv. **Career:** joined NZ Min.of Foreign Affairs in 1959 — Head of UN and African & Middle E.Divs 1973, Dir of Ext.Aid 1973–6, Head of Econ.Div.1980–81, Spec.Asst to Sec.-Gen. Commonwealth Secretariat (UK) 1969–72; High Commissioner in Fiji 1977–80 and India, Nepal, & Bangladesh 1983–5; Asst Sec. Min.of Foreign Affairs for Asia, Australia, the Americas, and S.Pacific 1981–5; First Sec. Perm.Mission to UN 1964–8, Perm.Rep.1985–8, DG Dept of Cons.(NZ) 1988–9, CEO Dept of PM and Cabinet 1989–91; Amb.to Japan 1992–4; DG IUCN — The World Conservation Union 1994–. Indiff.to pers.pub., favours news media support. **Languages:** English, French (read). Further details may be obtained from *Intl Who's Who* 1995. **Address:** IUCN — The World Conservation Union, Rue Mauverney 28, 1196 Gland, Switzerland. **Tel.**(office) 41 22 999 0295, (home) 41 22 369 4012; **fax** 41 22 999 0029.

McEACHERN, John D. Field implementation of National Conservation Strategies (planning & implementation), coastal-zone management, and economic impacts of large-capital projects (dams, pipelines, oil, & gas, exploration). Project Manager. *B*.22 April 1940, Montreal, Canada. Canadian. *M*.Jean Menzies (marine biol., tech. ed.): 5 *s*.incl.Preston (limnol.), 2 *d*. **Education:** McGill U. BA(Hons.)(Geog.) 1964, MA 1966; Intl Training Center for Aerial Survey (now IIASES), airphoto-interpretation tech.training for five months 1967; Cornell U. MS(Resource Econ.) 1973. **Experience:** consult.& project mgmt for 28 yrs, 14 each in Canada & intl

(Carib., W.Africa, SE Asia, S.Asia, Middle E.), spanning industry, govt, & INGOs. **Career:** summer field employment in Canadian Arctic, FRB & DIAND 1960–64; Super.of Photointerpretation, Land-use Survey of W.Malaysia, Lockwood Survey Corpn 1967–9; Sr Assoc. Is. Resources Fndn (USVI) 1972–4; Canadian Socioecon.consult.for industry (mining, oil, & gas, power generation) 1974–8; Econ.Planner, Agric. Sector, SL Min.of Dev. CIDA 1978–80; Socioecon.Coord. Gulf Canada Resources (Calgary & Inuvik NWT) 1981–5; Intl Consult. Coastal Zone Mgmt 1986–8; Mgr NCS for Jordan 1989–91, Project Mgr NCS Implementation Nepal 1991–, IUCN. **Memberships:** (current) F.RGS, F.The Explorers' Club, IUCN CNPPA & CESP, ASPRS. **Awards:** F'ships — Bronfman (at Center for Developing-area Studies), McConnel Mem., Canada Council. **Publications:** *c*.30 tech.reports. Favours pers.pub.& news media support. **Languages:** English; French & Spanish (read). Willing to act as a consult.&/or judge proposals. **Address:** IUCN Nepal, POB 3923, Kathmandu, Nepal, **tel.**(office) 9771 522712 & **fax** 9771 521506, *or* c/o P.J.Usher Consulting Services, Box 4815, Station E, Ottawa, Ontario K1S 5H9, Canada, **tel.**1 613 238 8556.

McGREAL, Dr Shirley. Primate conservation & protection. Founder & Chairwoman. *B.*4 May 1934, Mobberly, Cheshire, England, UK. British. **Education:** U.of Cincinnati Ed.D.1971. **Experience:** coll.teaching, founding & bldg-up large cons.orgn. **Career:** coll.teaching –1973, Founder & Chairwoman IPPL 1973–. **Achievements:** supporting rescue centres & primate sanctuaries, working to end intl trade in primates, investigating primate smuggling. **Memberships:** F.ISN (now INSONA), WSB (Hon.Life). **Awards:** Marchig Award for Animal Prot.1988, Global 500 Roll of Honour (UNEP) 1992. **Publications:** Ed.of *IPPL News* 1973–. Favours pers. pub.& news media support. **Languages:** English, French; Hindi, Spanish & Thai (some spoken). Willing to act as consult.etc. **Address:** POB 766, Summervila, South Carolina 29484, USA. **Tel.**(office) 1 803 871 2280; **fax** 1 803 871 7988.

McINTYRE, Professor Dr Alasdair Duncan. Marine ecology, fisheries, pollution. Emeritus Professor of Fisheries & Oceanography. *B.*17 Nov.1926, Helensburgh, Scotland, UK. British. *M.*Catherine Helen: *d.* **Education:** Glasgow U. BSc 1st Class Hons(Zool.) 1948, DSc(Marine Ecol.) 1973. **Experience:** biol.oceanogr.in several parts of world incl.NE & NW Atlantic, Indian Ocean, & E. Pacific Ocean. **Career:** Sci. Marine Lab. Aberdeen 1949–82; Dir. Fisheries Res.Services for Scotland 1982–86; Coord. UK Fisheries Res.& Dev.1986; Emer.Prof.of Fisheries & Oceanogr. U.of Aberdeen 1987–. **Achievements:** memb.of NCC for Scotland and of its res.& dev.Bd; World Bank consult.on marine poll.to the Chinese Univ.Project II; memb.

of Intl Adv.Panel to Swedish Envl Prot.Bd on their monitoring progs; Chairman — Adv.Cttee on Marine Poll.of Intl Council for the Exploration of the Sea, UN Group of Experts on the Scientific Aspects of Marine Poll. and UN (GESAMP) WG on state of marine env. **Memberships:** F.RSE, F.RSA, F.IBiol. **Publications:** several hundreds in scientific journals. Favours pers.pub.& news media support. **Language:** English. Further details may be obtained from Brit. *Who's Who.* Willing to act as consult.etc. **Address:** 63 Hamilton Place, Aberdeen AB2 4BW, Scotland, UK. **Tel.**(office) 44 1224 645633; **fax** 44 1224 620656.

McNEELY, Jeffrey A. Conservation, anthropology, economics; biological diversity; mammals of Southeast Asia. Chief Scientist. *B.*30 May 1944, Santa Cruz, CA, USA. American. *M.* Pojanan S.: 2 *s.* **Education:** UCLA, BA (Anthrop.) 1967. **Experience:** field exp.in Asia incl. Thailand, Indonesia & Nepal 1968–80; tech. missions to over 50 countries incl.Burma, Sri Lanka, Philippines, Laos, Cambodia, Vietnam, & China. **Career:** Animal Keeper, Los Angeles Zoo 1960–68; Peace Corps Vol.in Thailand 1968–70; Staff Mammalogist, ACW 1970–77; private expedn to Himalayas of e.Nepal 1972–4; Consult.to Mekong Cttee, FAO 1975– 7; WWF Rep.in Indonesia 1977–80; Exec.Officer of CNPPA 1980–83, Dir. of Prog.& Policy Div.1983–7, Dep.DG (Cons.) 1987–8, Chief Cons.Officer 1988–92, Sec.-Gen. IVth World Cong.on NPPA 1990–92, Chief Biodiv.Officer 1992–5, Chief Sci.1995–, all at IUCN. **Achievements:** field-work in or professional missions to more than 65 countries, designed system of prot.areas for Laos, Cambodia, & Vietnam, and num.cons.progs in var.Asian countries; promoted new approaches to design mgmt of prot.areas; contributed to dev.of concept of biodiv.as new and more politically-effective approach to cons.; stimulated new thinking about people–Nature relations. **Memberships:** SCB (Intl Counc.), Smithsonian Instn (Res.Assoc.), ZSL (Scientific F.), RAS, RGS, ISEE, Edl Adv.Bds *EC, Biodiv.& Cons., Sust.Dev., Oryx,* & *PARKS.* **Award:** Order of the Golden Ark 1995. **Publications:** 20+ books incl.*Mammals of Thailand* (co-Author) 1977, *Soul of the Tiger* (co-Author) 1988, *Econ. and Biol.Diversity* 1988, *Protecting Nature: Regnl Reviews of Prot.Areas* 1994; 100 peer-reviewed papers, *c*.250 popular pubns. Indiff.to pers.pub., favours news media support. **Languages:** English, French, Indonesian Nepali, Spanish, Thai. Willing to act as consult.etc. **Address:** IUCN — The World Conservation Union, Rue Mauverney 28, 1196 Gland, Vaud, Switzerland. **Tel.**(office) 41 22 999 0284, (home) 41 22 776 7414; **fax** 41 22 999 0025.

MECH, Dr L.David. Wolf ecology & behaviour, predator–prey relations, population regulation, social ecology. Wildlife Research Biologist, Adjunct Professor. *B.*18 Jan.1937, Auburn, NY,

USA. American. *D.*: 2 *s.*, 2 *d.* **Education:**
Cornell U. BS(Cons.) 1958, Purdue U. PhD
(Wildlife Ecol.) 1962. **Experience:** res., admin.,
consult., j.reviewer, consult.ed., film-maker;
num.special assignments at home & abroad.
Career: Res.Asst, Purdue U.1958–62; Res.
Assoc. U.of Minn.1963–6; Asst Prof.& Res.
Assoc. Macalester Coll.1966–8; Wildlife Res.
Biol. Div.of Endangered Species Res., Patuxent
Envl Sci.Center, Nat.Biol.Survey 1969–; Ad-
junct Prof. Dept of Ecol.and Behavioral Ecol.
1979– and Dept of Fisheries and Wildlife 1981–,
U.of Minn. **Achievements:** Founder 1985 of
Intl Wolf Centre, co-Inventor of radio capture
collar. **Memberships:** ASM, ESA, IUCN SSC
Wolf SG (Chair) 1978–, Wildlife Soc., Sigma Xi,
Gamma Sigma Delta, MZS (Bd 1971–80), Intl
Wolf Centre (Founder, Bd, VC 1985–93, Chair
1993–). **Awards:** Spec. Achievement Awards
1970 & 1981 and Civil Servant of the Yr 1973
(US FWS); Terr.Wildlife Pubn Award 1972,
The Minn.Award 1986, Professional Award of
Merit 1988, Aldo Leopold Award 1993 (Wildlife
Soc.); Best Wildlife Book* Award 1974, Disting.
Service in Sci.Educ.and Sci.Res.(Minn.AS) 1981,
Gulf Oil Professional Conservationist 1984, Best
Book** by Minn.Author (Minn.Festival of the
Book) 1989, Outstanding Job Performance
(Nat.Biol.Survey) 1994. **Publications:** *Wolves
of Isle Royale* 1966, **The Wolf: Ecol.and
Behavior of an Endangered Species* 1970, 1981,
Handbook of Animal Radio-Tracking 1983,
***The Arctic Wolf : Living with the Pack* 1988,
The Way of the Wolf 1991, *Wolves of the High
Arctic* 1992; Ed.*Intl Wolf* (quarterly); *c.*260
scientific, semi-tech., & popular articles; six
films & audio-visual presentations. **Language:**
English. Further details may be obtained from
Amer.Men & Women of Sci., *Dict.of Intl Biog.*,
Intl Authors' & Writers' Who's Who, *Marquis
Who's Who*, *Intl Directory of Disting. Leader-
ship.* **Address:** 1704D Pleasant Street, St Paul,
Minnesota 55113, USA. **Tel.**1 612 649 5231;
fax 1 612 649 5233.

**MEDWECKA-KORNAŚ, Professor Dr Anna
Maria.** Ecology (including plant sociology &
vegetation mapping), Nature conservation (basic
research), plant geography (especially of Europe
& Africa). Emeritus Professor of Plant Ecology.
*B.*28 Aug.1923, Kraków, Poland. Polish.
Mother Dr Maria Bieganska (geog.). *M.*Prof.Jan
Kornaś *qv*: 2 *s.*, 2 *d.* **Education:** Jagiellonian U.
MSc(Bot.) 1946, PhD(Bot.) 1950, Dr Habil.
(Bot.) 1956. **Experience:** widespread res.in
ecol.& plant geog.(esp.veg.sci.); organizing &
directing team res.progs; teaching ecol.& plant
geog., init.& editing ten vols of *Studia Naturae,*
managing NCRC for ten yrs. **Career:** Asst
1947–55, Prof. 1956–63 & 1973–93, Emer.
1993–, Jagiellonian U.; Dir NCRC (Krakow)
1963–73. **Achievements:** basic res.in xero-
thermic grasslands' & forest communities' ecol.,
dynamics & cons.; studies of air poll.& forest
dieback; syntheses of team res.work on landscape ecol.& mgmt. **Memberships:** PBS, Na-

ture Cons.Cttee of Polish AS, Counc.for several
Polish Nat.Parks, IUCN Exec.Bd 1968–71, IBP
Cons. of Terr.Communities & Productivity of
Terr. Communities Sections 1968–73. **Awards:**
Polonia Restituta Order 1979, Van Tienhoven
Preis (FVS) 1982, W.Szafer Medal for Scientific
Achievements (PBS) 1989. **Publications:** co-
Author of 14 books incl.*Veg of Poland* 1966,
Geografia Roślin (in Polish) 1986; 94 monogrs
& res. papers and *c.*100 other pubns. Favours
pers.pub.& news media support. **Languages:**
English, French, German (poor), Polish, Russian.
Further details may be obtained from Bibl.
1946–86, *U.Jagielloński Varia* 248, pp.45–6,
1988. Willing to act as consult.etc. **Address:**
Institute of Botany, ul.Lubicz 46, 31-512 Kraków, Poland. **Tel.**(office) 48 12 221033 ext.
421, (home) 48 12 114325; **fax** 48 12 219790.

Mehdi HAFIDI Moulay EL, *see* **HAFIDI Moulay
EL Mehdi.**

MEHER-HOMJI, Dr Vispy Minocher. Plant
geography, ecology, vegetation mapping, biocli-
matology, arid zones, conservation. National
Environment Fellow. *B.*18 Jan.1932, Bombay,
Mah., India. Indian. *M.*Kashmira (Pres. Lioness
Club): *s.*, 2 *d.* **Education:** Bombay U. BSc
(Hons) 1953, MSc 1955, PhD 1962; U.of Tou-
louse DSc 1960. **Experience:** res., admin.
Career: Res.Asst, Inst.of Sci. Bombay 1955–6;
Res.Scholar, U.of Toulouse 1957–61; Sci. French
Inst.(Pondicherry) 1962–87; Dean, Salim Ali
Sch.of Ecol. Pondicherry U.1987–90; NEF*
1991–93. **Achievements:** study of veg.of
peninsular India and mapping same at scale of
1:1,000,000 within framework of veg.carto-
graphy project of French Inst., three sheets of
Forest Maps of Western Ghats at 1:250,000;
determination of percentage area under forest in
each veg.type and recommendation of areas to be
conserved on priority basis; phytosociology of
Rajasthan desert and phytogeog.of the semi-arid
zones of India; assessment of variability of
climate of Indian subcontinent and importance of
regime (season of occurrence of rains) as a
significant factor in plant distribn; estab.of
analogous types in world of bioclimates in India
incl.ethnobotl surveys to bring out rare medicinal
plants unknown to med.world; investigation
towards better understanding of the relationship
between deforestation & rainfall cycle; providing scientific info.for cons.of critical areas
e.g. the Silent Valley rain-forest, Mangroves of
Pichavaram & Vikhroli, and Scrub jungles of
Coromandel coast; consult.to Min.of Envt &
Forests, and Planning Comm.on Envl Problems.
Memberships: F.INSA, F.IAS, F.NAS India,
Palaeobot.Soc., F.IBS, F.NIE, F.ISTE, Société
de Biogéographie, Bombay NHS, VP IABS &
Geogl Soc.of India, APQS (Pres.1987). **Awards:**
Meldrum Mem.Prize (Bombay Inst.of Sci.),
Eduljee Dinshaw 'D' Scholarship (U.of Bombay);
Prix d'Honneur (Fondation L.Emberger–Ch.
Sauvage) 1983; *Pitambar Pant NEF, Min.of
Envt & Forests, Govt of India. **Publications:**

Forest Ecol.(two vols, co-Author) 1983, 1989, *Forest Resources: Crisis and Mgmt* (co-Ed.) 1993; 175 res.papers.etc. Indiff.to pers. pub.& news media support. **Languages:** English, French, Gujarati, Hindi. Further details may be obtained from *Who's Who in India, Ref.India, Ref.Asia, Biog.Intl, Eminent Educationalists of India.* Willing to act as consult.etc. **Address:** French Institute, 11 St Louis Street, PB Nr 33, Pondicherry 605001, Pondicherry, India. **Tel.** (office) 91 413 34168 or 70; **fax** 91 413 39534.

MEHTA, Mahesh Chander. Environmental law & jurisprudence, human rights issues, grassroots action. Advocate. *B.*12 Oct.1946, Rajouri Distr., J&K, India. Indian. *M.*Radha: *d.*Tarini (both involved in envl activities). **Education:** Jammu U. LLB 1974, MA 1978. **Experience:** keynote speaker at var.nat.& intl confs, drafting legis., rep.of India at Commonwealth mtg on envt in 1990. **Career:** Legal Practice, J&K High Court 1974–83; Advocate, Supreme Court of India 1983–. **Achievements:** init.legal action (more than 40 cases being successful) on wide-ranging envl issues from controlling poll.in R.Ganges to prot.of Taj Mahal, each case having wide ramifications on govtl policies & progs on envt *e.g.*envl educ.in schools, intro.of lead-free petrol *etc.;* pioneered envl litigation in India and obtained landmark judgements on envt from Supreme Court; envl legis.which came into existence as a result of cases filed are Amendments in Factories Act incorporating provisions on hazardous industries, hazardous wastes (mgmt & handling rules), Envt Prot.Rules for Location of Industries, Public Insurance Liability Act, and Envt Tribunals Bill. **Memberships:** NEC, High Powered Cttee on Vehicular Poll., Supreme Court Bar Assn, ICELA, ILI (Life), India Intl Centre. **Awards:** Global 500 Roll of Honour (UNEP) 1993, Gt Son of the Soil (All India Conf.of Intellectuals) 1993. **Publications:** num. papers & articles. Indiff.to pers.pub., favours news media support. **Languages:** Dogri, English, Hindi, Urdu. Willing to act as consult. etc. **Address:** 5 Anand Lok, Khel Gaon Marg, New Delhi 110 049, Delhi, India. **Tel.**(office) 91 11 644 5214, (home) 91 11 622 1549.

MEKOUAR, Professor Dr Mohamed Ali. Environmental law, forestry, wildlife legislation. Legal Officer. *B.*1 April 1950, Fes, Morocco. Moroccan. **Education:** Licence en Droit 1972, Diplôme d'Études Supérieures en Droit Privé 1975, Rabat U.; Diplôme de Droit Comparé de l'Envt 1978, Diplôme d'Études Supérieures en Droit Comparé 1978 Strasbourg; Doctorat d'État en Droit (PhD), Casablanca 1980. **Experience:** 20 years' res./teaching var. legal disciplines, notably envl law; 10 yrs' legal consult.on natural resources & envl law in num.countries. **Career:** Asst Prof.of Law, Univs of Rabat & Casablanca 1973–80; Prof.of Law, U.of Casablanca 1980–88; Legal Officer (For.& Envt), FAO Legal Office (Rome) 1989–. **Achievements:** init.Envl Law Course, Fac.of Law, U.of Casablanca 1981;

founded MSEL 1986; lect.at num.univs in Africa, N.& S.Amer., and Europe. **Memberships:** MSEL (Pres.), ICCEL (Sec.-Gen.), IUCN CEL, ICEL, FSEL. **Publications:** Études en droit de l'environnement 1988; Recueil d'études en droit écologique 1988, *The Envtl Impact of Econ. Incentives for Agricl Prod.: A Comparative Law Study* 1990; +50 articles & *c.*15 consult.reports. **Languages:** Arabic (mother tongue), English, French (working), Italian (fair), Spanish (fair). **Address:** FAO Legal Office, Via Terme di Caracalla, 00100 Rome, Italy. **Tel.**(office) 39 522 55612, (home) 39 575 0614; **fax** 39 522 54408.

MELKANIA, Professor Dr Niranjan Prakash. Ecosystem analysis, restoration & conservation ecology, forest management, valuation of Man Nature interrelationships, integrated resource management, ecodevelopment & biodiversity, mountain & tropical regions of India. Professor of Integrated Resource Management, Centre Coordinator. *B.*30 Sept.1955, Almora, Uttar Pradesh, India. Indian. Father the late A.D. Melkania, community forestry. *M.*Dr Uma (envl monitoring & impact assessment): *d.* **Education:** Kumaun U. MSc(Bot.) 1977, MSc(Forest Ecol.) 1979, PhD Bot.(Ecol.) 1985, courses on bioassay, instrumentation for envl studies, planning & monitoring for educl instns. **Experience:** teaching courses on EIA and waste treatment design, and for.courses from BSc to PhD levels; res.— tree–herb assn, allelopathy, grassland ecol., Man–Nature interrelations, ecodev., ecosystem analysis, resto.ecol., biodiv.monitoring, valuation of forests and natural envt; course org.re.watershed mgmt, ecol.aspects & for.; consult.on Indo–German Dhauladhar Project, and for Narmada Valley Dev.Auth.& World Bank; admin.re.training progs and coordn of MPhil.admissions, and coordn & mgmt of res.of Nat.Afforestation and Ecodev.Bd; j.ref. **Career:** Asst Prof.of Envl Scis, G.B.Pant U. 1985–7; Asst Prof.(Ecosystem Mgmt) 1987–92, Assoc.Prof.(Grassland Mgmt) 1992–4, Prof.of Integrated Resource Mgmt 1994–, IIFM; Coord. Regnl Centre, Nat.Afforestation & Ecodev.Bd, Govt of India 1993–. **Achievements:** res.re. forest–, grassland–, and human–, ecosystems in the mtn areas and tropics of India; estab.of high-alt.field station at Auli and envl sci.lab.at Pantnagar; pioneer in estab.of fac.of ecosystem mgmt & tech.for., and co-pioneer re.planning & launching of MPhil. course in Resource Mgmt, both at IIFM; developed tech.for both grassland improvement and wasteland dev.in Himalaya, and ecodev.plan for wildlife retrieval in Narmada Valley Dev.Project. **Memberships:** NIE (Life), Indian Soc.of Allelopathy (Life), Range Mgmt Soc.of India (Life), INTECOL, IASCP, CFA (India Unit), ISTS (Couns.), Indian Envl Soc., ISTE, IUFRO WG on Econ.& Social Aspects of For.in Developing Countries and Pastoral Networks; other nat.WGs & Comms; Edl Adv.Bd *Ecol., Envt & Cons.* **Awards:** Yogyata Praman Patra (Kumaun U.), Res.F. (UGC India), Young Scientists Award (IBC),

F.ISTE & NIE. **Publications:** five books incl. *Habitat Himalaya: Issues & Responses* (co-Ed.) 1994; five monogrs incl.*Readings in Ecosystem Resto.*1992; 27 chapters incl.Info.Gaps in Linking Degradation of Wastelands in Ecosystem-level Mgmt 1993; num.scientific papers & tech. reports.   Favours pers.pub.& news media support. **Languages:** English, Hindi. Willing to act as consult.etc. **Address:** Indian Institute of Forest Management, PB 357, Nehru Nagar, Bhopal 462 003, Madhya Pradesh, India. **Tel.**(office) 91 755 65125, 65716 & 65998, (home) 91 755 68055; **fax** 91 755 62878.

MELLO, Ambassador Dr Mateo Jorge MAGARIÑOS-DE. Environmental law & policy, environmental economy & education, environment in general. President, Adviser. *B.*14 March 1914, Montevideo, Uruguay. Uruguayan. *M.* Helen Norah: *s.*Mateo Alejandro (econ.& ecol.), *d.* **Education:** U.of Uruguay LLD 1945. **Experience:** rep.of Uruguay at UN World Conf.on Envt (Stockholm) 1972, and all UNEP confs; Govt Council for Desert.& Water 1977; Pres. IXth Period of Sessions of Govt Council on behalf of Latin Amer.(Nairobi 1981); active participation in many WGs & Cttees such as INFOTERRA. **Career:** Under-Sec.& Minister of Foreign Affairs 1959–62, Pres.LAFTA 1959–61 (Provisional Cttee 1959), Amb.Perm. Rep.to UN Geneva, GATT (now WTO), IMO, FAO, CIME 1963–7, UNEP Governing Council & Confs 1972–84, Pres.for Latin Amer.1981, Dir Depts of Envt & of Intl Orgn, Min.of Foreign Affairs, Adv.to Parliament, Mins of Envt & Foreign Affairs, Intl Consult.to UN & ECLA. **Achievements:** promotion of envl law & policy at nat.& intl levels, participation in num.cttees & WGs at intl level *e.g.*Biodiv.(The Netherlands), Intl Tribunal of the Envt (Rome). **Memberships:** ICEL, AUDA (Montevideo), CIDYAA (Montevideo 1989–92), IUCN, Assn Intl de Droit de l'Environnement. **Awards:** Elisabeth Haub Fndn Award 1982, Global 500 Roll of Honour (UNEP) 1992. **Publications:** num.books on hist.and law incl.*Gen.Theory of Envl Law 1975, Relations Between the Envl & Econ. Concepts* 1980, *Textile Industry Poll.*1978, *The Envl Impact of the Gt Dams* 1977, *Human Rights & Envt* 1987, *The Envl Impact on the Evol.of Intl Law & Intl Legis.*1975, *Global Vision of the XXI Century* 1988, *Intl Law & Envt* 1989, *The Codification of Envl Law* 1992, Law and the Envt: The Role of Law in the Problems of Envt 1992. Favours pers.pub.& news media support. **Languages:** English, French; Italian & Portuguese (fluent spoken), Spanish. Willing to act as consult.etc. **Address:** Eche-varriarza 3396, Montevideo 11300, Uruguay. **Tel.**(office & home) 598 2 62 1014; **fax** 598 2 62 1024; **e-mail** AUDA@ chasque.apc-org .

MENDEZ, Jesus Manuel DELGADO. Resource policy & planning, training park personnel, environmental education. Independent Consultant. *B.*30 May 1952, Caracas, Venezuela. Ve-

nezuelan. *M.*Sonia Torri: *s.*, 2 *d.* **Education:** Cornell U. MSc 1981. **Experience:** res.in evaluating economical impacts of cons.and mangroves; training, parks admin.; consult.for UNEP, GTZ, IUCN, WWF, & For.Insts of SP and MG States; community orgn, pedagogy, EIA; envl educ.& interpretation. **Career:** Ind.Consult. 1987–; Pres. Sociedade Educativa Gaia de Baura 1992–4; Consult.1992–5 & Coord. Ecodev.Plan for Itirapina Regn (SP) 1994–, For.Inst.of São Paulo. **Achievements:** intro.of new philos.for For.Inst. of São Paulo, to have found efficient ways to develop prot.areas' mgmt plans, training hundreds of people in parks' mgmt, increasing local envl awareness, influencing formal & informal educl system. **Memberships:** IUCN CNPPA & CEC. **Awards:** Scholarships from Funda/Ayacucho & Min.of Agric., financial help from Sierra Club for thesis res.on mangroves, Hon.Memb. AGAPAN. **Publications:** num.incl. extension bulletins & training manuals, radio progs. Open minded re.pers.pub.& news media support. **Languages:** English, Portuguese, Spanish. Willing to act as consult.etc. **Address:** Joaquim da Silva Martha 13–27, Bauru 17040-012, São Paulo, Brazil. **Tel.** (office) 55 142 232023, (home) 55 142 239780; **fax** 55 142 232023.

MERZ, Mrs Anna H. Rhinoceros. Sanctuary Director. *B.*17 Nov.1931, Radlett, England, UK. British, Swiss. *W.* **Education:** Nottingham U. BA(Hons) 1954. **Experience:** running rhino sanctuary and studying their social behaviour. **Career:** Dir, Kumasi Engg Co.Ltd. 1960–75; Dir. Ngare Sergoi Rhino Sanctuary 1984–. **Achievements:** helped estab.Bia Nat.Park (Ghana) and Ngare Sergoi Rhino Sanctuary (Kenya). **Awards:** Global 500 Roll of Honour (UNEP) 1990, Hon.Game Warden (Ghana). **Publications:** *Rhino at the Brink of Extinction* 1991, Intelligence with Horns (article) 1993, Golden dunes and desert mtns 1993. Indiff.to pers.pub., favours news media support provided accurate. **Language:** English. Willing to help anyone who wants to help Rhinos. **Address:** Ngare Sergoi Rhino Sanctuary, c/o Chris Flatt, POB 56923 Nairobi, Kenya. **Tel.**(office) 254 2 506139; **fax** 254 2 502739.

MESSEL, Professor Dr Harry. Australian (northern) tidal waterways and their crocodile populations. Emeritus Professor of Physics, Executive Chancellor. *B.*3 Mar.1922, Levine Siding, Man., Canada. Canadian. *M.*Patricia Iona: 3 *d.* **Education:** R.Military Coll. Gov.-Gen.'s Silver Medal 1942; Queen's U. BA (Hons) 1948, BSc(Eng.Phys.) 1948; Inst.for Advanced Studies (Dublin) PhD 1951. **Experience:** field res.on crocodiles; admin., educ., lecturing, fund-raising ($100 m.in cash & kind for Sci.Fndn for Phys.of which Founder), worldwide traveller (100+ lecture tours). **Career:** Canadian Armed Forces 1942–6; Sr Lect. U.of Adelaide 1951; Chair of Phys.& Head of Sch.of Phys.1952–87, Emer.Prof.of Phys.1987–, U.of Sydney; Scientific Adv.to Attorney-Gen.and to

Minister for Customs & Excise, also in Nuclear Test case against French Govt in Intl Court of Justice 1973–5; Scientific Adv.to Minister for Minerals & Energy 1975; memb.of Australian Atomic Energy Comm.1974–81; Chancellor 1992, Exec.Chancellor (CEO) 1993–, Bond U. **Achievements:** built-up the Sch.of Phys.in U.of Sydney from a single-professorial Sch.to one of the leading undergrad.& postgrad.Schools of Phys.in the Brit.Commonwealth; pioneer of electronic computing in Australia with construction in 1954 of Australia's first u.computer; estab.& direction in 1954 of Sci.Fndn for Phys.(U.of Sydney); major force in pioneering u.–industrial coopn within the U.of Sydney; Founder of Intl Sci.Schools 1958–; pubn of series of 20 monogrs on results of n.Australian exploration & survey work. **Memberships:** IUCN SSC Crocodile SG 1974– (Chairman 1989–), IUCN SSC 1978–90 (VC [Australia] Steering Cttee 1978–91, Sr VC 1991–). **Awards:** Overseas Exchange F.in Maths 1948–9, CBE 1979, Hon.DSc (U.of Sydney) 1992, B.Mil.Sc (R.Military Coll.) 1994 (52 yrs late!). **Publications:** num.books incl.series of 20 monogrs on *Surveys of Tidal Waterways in Northern Australia and their Crocodile Populations* (co-Author) 1979–87; *The Study of Pop.* (Ed.& part-Author) 1985, *Highlights in Sci.* (Ed.& part-Author) 1987; c.95 scientific papers. **Language:** English. Favours pers. pub.& news media support. Further details may be obtained from *Who's Who in Australia* 1994, British *Who's Who* 1994. **Address:** Bond University, Gold Coast, Queensland 4229, Australia. **Tel.**61 75 951044; **fax** 61 75 951046.

MESSERLI, Professor Dr Bruno. Geoecology, mountain areas (Africa, Himalaya, Andes); climate change. Professor of Geography. *B.*17 Sept.1931, Lengenbuhl, Berne, Switzerland. Swiss. **Education:** U.of Berne PhD 1962, Habil.1965. **Experience:** res., consult. **Career:** Prof.1969 and Dir 1978–83, Inst.of Geog., Rector 1986–7, U.of Berne. **Achievements:** Dir UNESCO MAB-6 (Mtn) Res.Prog.in Swiss Alps 1979–86, Coord.UNU Mtn Ecol.& Sust. Dev. Prog. **Memberships:** IGU (VP 1992–), IUCN Comm.on Ecol.(past), Swiss Sci.Fndn (Counc.). **Awards:** Global 500 Roll of Honour (UNEP) 1988, Marcel Benoist Preis 1991. **Publications:** *The Himalayan Dilemma: Reconciling Dev.& Cons.*(co-Author) 1989, Climate, envl change & resources of the African mtns from the Medit.to the Equator (co-Author) 1992, Climate change & natural resource dynamics of the Atacama altiplano during the last 18,000 yrs: a prelim.synthesis (co-Author) 1993. Indiff.to pers. pub.& news media support. **Languages:** English, French, German. Willing to act as consult. **Address:** Brunnweid, 3086 Zimmerwald, Switzerland. **Tel.**(office) 41 31 631 8019, (home) 41 31 819 3381; **fax** 41 31 631 8511.

MEULEN, Dr Frank VAN DER. Landscape ecology, Nature conservation, geobotany; integrated coastal-zone management. Assistant Professor in Landscape Ecology. *B.*23 April 1948, Arnhem, The Netherlands. Dutch. *M.*Ida: 3 *d.* **Education:** U.of Utrecht, Drs(Biol.)(veg.ecol., soil sci., plant path.) 1972; U.of Nijmegen–Botl Res.Inst.(Pretoria, RSA), Dr(Land Ecol.& Landuse of Semi-arid Savannas) 1978. **Experience:** res.— landscape ecol., sust.land utilization & coastal-zone mgmt, veg.of coastal dunes; remote sensing & land–mgmt eval., survey & monitoring of coastal ecosystems; coord.several landscape mgmt projects along Dutch coast; consult. on coastal-zone mgmt in Europe. **Career:** Researcher, Botl Res.Inst. Min.of Agric.(RSA) 1972–9; Head of Res. Dune Water Works Co. (The Netherlands) 1980–88; Asst Prof.in Landscape Ecol. Landscape & Envl Res.Group, U.of Amsterdam 1988–. **Achievements:** tested use of Braun-Blanquet phytosociol.method in RSA for purposes of reconnaissance survey and Nature cons., reintroduced natural dynamics in Dutch coastal dunes; memb.of several adv.cttees to study sust.dev.of coastal envts. **Memberships:** Tech.Adv.Cttee of Dutch Min.of Roads & Public Transport, EUCC (VP), LICC–LERM (Chairman of Steering Cttee), Edl Bd *J.of Coastal Res.*(USA). **Publications:** *Perspectives in Coastal Dune Mgmt* (co-Ed.) 1987, *Thematic Issue Landscape Ecol.: Impact of Climate Change on Coastal Dune Landscapes of Europe* (co-Ed.) 1991; Ed.in Chief *J.of Coastal Cons.*(with R.Paskoff, France, 1995–); c.80 papers. Favours pers.pub.& news media support. **Languages:** English, French (reasonable), German. Willing to act as consult.etc. **Address:** Landscape and Environmental Research Group, University of Amsterdam, Nieuuse Prinsengracht 130, 1018 VZ Amsterdam, The Netherlands. **Tel.**(office) 31 20 525 7422 or 7451, (home) 31 71 720413; **fax** 31 20 525 7431; **e-mail** FM@FGB.FRW.UVA.NL.

MIKLÓS, Professor Dr Ladislav. Landscape ecology, ecological planning & politics. UNESCO Chair for Ecological Awareness and Sustainable Development, Head of Department. *B.*24 Jan.1949, Tornala, Slovak Republic. Slovak. **Education:** Comaenius U. MSc 1973, RNDr 1975; U.of J.E.Purkyne (Brno) CSc (Geog.); Tech.U.(Zvolen), Habil.for Assoc. Prof. 1993; Slovak AS, Dissertation for DrSc 1994; City U.(Bratislava), Open U.Business Sch.(UK) Courses 'Effective Mgr' 1994 & 'Envt' 1994. **Experience:** res.— at ecol.insts of Slovak AS in diff.positions; tech.— territorial & agricl planning in diff.projecting orgns in Slovakia, Coord.& co-Author of more than 30 ecol.projects; admin.— V.-Minister for Envt, Head & Dep.Head of del.of CSFR for all Prep. Cttees for UNCED 1992 and memb.of CSFR del.to Rio; num.teaching positions throughout e.Europe; media interviews. **Career:** Jr Sci. Inst.of Landscape Biol.1973–5, Sr Sci. Inst.of Experimental Biol.& Ecol.1975–90, Head of Dept of Landscape Ecol.Syntheses 1985–90, Chairman of Scientific Bd, Inst.for Landscape

Ecol.1993–4, Slovak AS; Specialist for Ecol Planning (part-time), Stavoprojekt Banska Bystrica, Inst.for Urbanism & Territorial Planning, and Agricl Projecting Inst.1979–89; V.-Minister, Min.for Envt, Slovak Rep.1990–92; Rep.for Slovakia (part-time) Agiplan Gruppe 1993–4; Guest Prof. Roskilde U.(Denmark) 1994–5; UNESCO Chair for Ecol.Awareness & Sust. Dev. Tech.U.1994–; Head, Dept of Regnl Landscape Ecol. Inst.of Landscape Ecol. Slovak AS 1994–. **Achievements:** one of main authors of methodics of LANDEP (listed in Agenda 21); as V.-Minister of Envt was resp.for ecol politics of Slovakia and developed & realized the policy called 'ecologization of dev.' based on scientific landscape–ecol.principles; conception of TSES and its relation to envl, agricl & territorial planning legis.in Slovakia; also involved with other important ecol projects — Ecol Gen. Model of CSFR & Slovak Rep., Ecol Plan of C. Slovak Regn. **Memberships:** IALE (Chairman LANDEP WG), IUCN CESP. **Awards:** Gold Medal (State Comm.for Envl Prot.of Bulgaria) 1984, Tribute of Appreciation (Admin.USEPA) 1993. **Publications:** Author or co-Author of 20 res.reports, eight books, nine chapters, three edited Proc.vols, 16 textbooks, 150+ scientific articles, 130 lectures (incl.abroad), 50+ expertises; in English are Spatial arrangement of landscape in landscape ecol.planning (LANDEP) 1986, Systematization & automatization of decision-making process in LANDEP method (co-Author) 1986, Basic Premises & Methods in Landscape–ecol. Planning & Optimization (co-Author) 1990, Protecting the Envt during Regnl Dev.1992. Indiff.to pers.pub., favours more than dislikes news media support. **Languages:** Czech.(read, some spoken), English, German (good), Hungarian, Polish (read, some spoken), Slovak, Russian, Ukrainian (read, some spoken). **Address:** Dobrovského ul.1, 81108 Bratislava, Slovak Republic. **Tel.& fax** 42 7 326705.

MILBRATH, Professor Dr Lester Walter. Sustainability of society, social change, environmental beliefs & values, environmental policy. Emeritus Professor of Political Science and Sociology, Research Programme Director. *B.*29 Oct.1925, Bertha, MN, USA. American. *M.* Kirsten M.: *s., d.* **Education:** U.of Minn. BA 1951, MA 1952; U.of N.Carolina, PhD 1956. **Experience:** was mainstream pol.sci.until *c.* 1970 when exposure to envl thinking resulted in shifting of teaching & res.to field of envt; admin.; sometime Vis.Res.Scholar at Aarhus U., ANU, and U.of Mannheim; Fulbright Scholar in Norway 1961–2 & 1972–3. **Career:** Assoc. Provost for Social Sci.and Dir of Social Sci. Res.Inst.1969–76, Dir of Envl Studies Center 1976–87, Dir of Res.Prog.in Envt & Soc.1987–, Prof.Emer.of Pol.Sci.1991–, and Sociol.1991–, SUNY at Buffalo; Vis.Prof. Aarhus U.1972 and UCI 1993/4/5; Fulbright Prof. Nat.Taiwan U. 1988. **Achievements:** pubns. **Memberships:** HOLIS: the Soc.for a Sust.Future (Founding Chair), IUCN, Global Info.and Action Network

(Adv.Bd), Sierra Club, The Balaton Group, NRDC, EDF, NWF, Wilderness Soc., Earth Is.Inst., F.IHE; several others. **Publications:** *Envlists: Vanguard for a New Soc.1984, Envisioning a Sust.Soc.: Learning Our Way Out* 1989, *Learning to Think Envlly: While There is Still Time* 1995; *c.*90 papers. Would accept pers.pub., favours media support. **Languages:** English, Norwegian (fair spoken). Further details may be obtained from *Who's Who in the E.*1993, *Who's Who in Sci.& Tech.*1994. Willing to act as consult.etc.to a small extent. **Address:** 21 Charming Lane, Williamsville, New York 14221, USA. **Tel.**(office) 1 716 645 2417 ext.470, (home) 1 716 634 7349; **fax** 1 716 645 2166.

MILIMO, Dr Patrick Baraza Wamalwa. Plant physiology, genetics, molecular biology. Research Extension Officer. *B.*2 July 1956, Bungoma, Kenya. Kenyan. Mother Juliana Masicha Nawire, farming. *S.: d.* **Education:** U.of Nairobi, BSc(For.) 1981; U.of Alb. MSc(For.) 1986; ANU, PhD(For.) 1994. **Experience:** plant stress physiol., animal nutrition and range mgmt, plant selection and matching of genotypes to specific sites, plant seed germination physiol. **Career:** Sr Res.Sci.1986–90, Prin.Sci.1994–5, Kenya For.Res.Inst.; Part-time Experimental Sci. CSIRO Div.of For.1990–94; Res.Ext. Officer, GTZ 1995–. **Achievements:** initiated dryland for.res.in Kenya, pioneered res.(15 yrs) on less-known *Melia volkensii.* **Memberships:** CFA, ATF. **Awards:** Scholarship (CIDA), F'ship (ACIAR). **Publications:** 28 scientific papers incl.Chem.composition of *Melia volkensii* Gurke: an unrealised browse potential for semi-arid agrofor.systems 1994. Indiff.to pers. pub.& news media support. **Languages:** English, Kiswahili. Willing to act as consult.etc. **Address:** GTZ House, POB 47051, Lenana Road, Nairobi, Kenya. **Tel.**254 2 562820/1/2 & 3; **fax** 254 2 562670 & 1.

MILLS, Dr Derek Henry. Ecology & conservation of Atlantic Salmon *(Salmo salar);* effects of hydroelectric developments on fish & aquatic environment; effects of afforestation & agriculture on fisheries. Fellow, Board Member, Environmental Adviser. *B.*19 March 1928, Bristol, England, UK. British. *M.*Florence Edith: *s., d.* **Education:** Harrogate Grammar Sch.; QMC London, BSc (Hons)(Zool.) 1953, MSc 1957, PhD 1963. **Experience:** res.on var.aspects of Salmon & Brown Trout ecol., effects of hydroelectric devs on freshwater ecol; resp.for undergrad.courses in fisheries mgmt & freshwater ecol. at U.of Edinburgh; consult.for Brit.Gas, Scottish Hydroelectric, C.Scotland Water Dev. Bd, and Welsh Water Auth. **Career:** Asst Experimental Officer, Marine Lab.(Aberdeen) 1953; SO Oceanographic Lab.(Edinburgh) 1954–6; Asst Sci. Fisheries Res.Bd of Canada 1956; SSO, Salmon Res.Lab.(Scotland) 1957–65; Lect. Sr Lect.& F. Dept of For.& Natural Resources (now Inst.of Ecol.& Resource Mgmt), U.of

Edinburgh 1965–; Envl Adv. Scottish Hydro-electric 1985–. **Achievements:** basic res.on juvenile Salmon survival, fish predators, effects of hydroelectric devs & afforestation on Salmon ecol. **Memberships:** F.LS, F.IFM, Tweed Fndn Trustee, Chairman Scientific Adv.Panel of Atlantic Salmon Trust, Scottish Natural Heritage (Bd). **Publications:** *Salmon & Trout: A Resource, its Ecol., Cons.& Mgmt* 1971, *Ecol.& Mgmt of Atlantic Salmon* 1989, *Salmon Rivers of Scotland* 1981 & (co-Author) 1992, *Freshwater Ecol.: Principles & Applications* (co-Author) 1990; *c.*100 others; Ed.*Fisheries Mgmt,* Jt Ed. *Aquaculture & Fisheries Mgmt, and Fisheries Mgmt & Ecol.* Indiff.to pers.pub.& news media support. **Languages:** English, French (written), German (basic). Willing to act as consult.etc. **Address:** Institute of Ecology & Resource Management, University of Edinburgh, Darwin Building, Edinburgh EH9 3JU, Scotland, UK. **Tel.**(office) 44 131 650 5422, (home) 44 1896 82 2719; **fax** 44 131 662 0478.

MILLS, Dr M.G.L. ('Gus'). Conservation & research of arid & savanna ecosystems; mammalian predator–prey relationships; carnivore behavioural ecology & conservation biology. Specialist Scientist. *B.*26 May 1946, Purley, Surrey, England, UK. S.African. *M.*Margaret: *s., d.* **Education:** St John's Coll. Johannesburg; U.of Cape Town BA/BSc 1970; U.of Pretoria BSc(Hons) 1971, MSc 1977, DSc 1981 all in Wildlife Mgmt. **Experience:** full-time field work in s.Kalahari (1972–84) & Kruger Nat.Park (1984–); co-Supervisor to postgrad.studies in these areas; fund-raising & handling of res. budgets; consult.in carnivore cons. **Career:** Res. Officer 1972–86, Specialist Sci.1986–, Nat. Parks Bd of SA. Res.F. U.of Aberdeen 1981; Lect. U.of Cape Town's Summer Sch. 1985, 1988. **Achievements:** co-Compiler of Mgmt Plan for s.Kalahari ecocomplex; IUCN SSC SGs on Hyaena *[Hyaenidae]* (1982–), Cat (1988–), & Canid (1993–), Chairman of first 1991– and Coord.of last's Lycaon Working Party 1993–. **Memberships:** ZSSA (Life), SAWMA, SAOS, WSSA. **Publications:** *A Guide to the Kalahari Gemsbok Nat.Park* 1989, *Kalahari Hyaenas* 1990; 55+ scientific papers. Indiff.to pers.pub., usually favours news media support. **Languages:** Afrikaans, English. Willing to act as consult. **Address:** Private Bag X402, Skukuza 1250, South Africa. **Tel.**(office) 27 1311 65611, (home) 27 1311 65550; **fax** 27 1311 65467.

MILNE, Mrs Christine. Green politics. Party Leader, Member of House of Assembly. *B.*14 May 1953, Latrobe, Tasmania, Australia. Australian. *M.*Neville H.Milne: 2 *s.* **Education:** U.of Tasmania, BA(Hons) 1974. **Experience:** teaching, involvement in Franklin R. 1982–3 and other campaigning, media, conf. addressee. **Career:** teaching English & Social Sci. Parklands High Sch.1975, Don Coll.1976, and Devonport High Sch.1976–84; Field Officer, Australian BiCentennial Auth. 1987–8; Cam-

paigner 1987–9; Green Ind. Memb.for Lyons 1989; re-elected to now-called Tasmanian Greens 1992–. **Achievements:** successful campaigns saving huts behind Waldheim Chalets at Cradle Mtn L. St Clair Nat.Park 1987, and opposing multi-million dollar Kraft Chlorine Pulp Mill siting, Wesley Vale 1988–9. **Awards:** Award for Educ.(Japan Fndn) 1982, Women '88 Award (Australian BiCentennial Auth.) 1988, Global 500 Roll of Honour (UNEP) 1990. Dislikes pers. pub., favours news media support. **Language:** English. **Address:** RSD 402, Castra Road, Ulverstone, Tasmania, Australia. **Tel.**(office) 61 04 217841, (home) 61 04 255655; **fax** 61 04 217844.

MIRANDA, Rui. Sustainable human development. Local National Officer & Sustainable Development Adviser. *B.*12 Nov.1950, Binar, Guinea-Bissau. Guinean. *M.*Isabel: *s.* **Education:** U.of Panama, Lic.in Agron.(animal husbandry) 1982. **Experience:** tech.& managerial as head of directions & tech.depts, consult.to FAO, IUCN, CILSS, & ILCA adv. **Career:** Chief, Res.Dept, Gen.Direction of Animal Husbandry 1982–9; Head of Wildlife Dept 1989–90, Dir of Nature Cons.Service 1990–92, Direcçao-Geral das Florestas e Caça (Gen.Direction of For.& Hunting)/MDRA; Nat.Dir of Coastal Zone Mgmt Project/Unit, IUCN/MDRA 1990–94; Local Nat.Officer & Sust.Dev.Adv. UNDP/ Bissau 1994–. **Memberships:** Associaçáo Guineense de Estudoes e Alternativos (Assn for Studies & Alternatives), Acçáo para o Desenvolvimento (Action for Dev.) (nat.NGOs). **Publications:** participation on papers written by coastal-zone mgmt team. Indiff.to pers.pub., favours news media support. **Languages:** English (fair), French, Portuguese (good), Spanish (good). Willing to act as consult.etc. **Address:** United Nations Development Programme, CP 179, POB 1011, Bissau Codex, Guinea-Bissau. **Tel.**(office) 245 201362, (home) 245 211314; **fax** 245 201753.

MISRA, Professor Dr Ramdeo. Balancing conservation and consumption. Professor Emeritus. *B.*26 Aug.1908, Dobhi Village, Khetasari, Jaunpur Distr., UP, India. Indian. *M.*Sunanda: *s.,* 4 *d.*incl.Gopa Pandey (Divl Forest Officer). **Education:** BHU, MSc(Bot.) 1931; U.of Leeds (UK), PhD(Ecol.) 1937. **Experience:** teaching & res.since 1931. **Career:** Lect.in Bot.1931–46; Reader & Head of Dept of Bot. Saugar U.(MP) 1946–55; Prof.& Head of Dept of Bot. 1955–71, Emer.Prof.1971–, BHU. **Memberships:** WAAS, ISTE, INSA. **Awards:** F.of WAAS, ISTE, & INSA, Sanjay Gandhi Award in Envt (Govt of India) 1993, Swami Pranavanand Award in Envt (UGC India) 1986. **Publications:** *c.*six books incl.*The Indian Manual of Plant Ecol.*(co-Author) 1954, *Envl Sci.& Soc.* 1995; *c.*150 papers & chapters incl.Edaphic factors in the distribn of aquatic plants in the English Lakes 1938, Comparison of Productivity of Dry Deciduous Forests and Grasslands of Varanasi 1971. Indiff.to pers.pub.& news media support.

Languages: English, Hindi. **Address:** Centre of Advanced Study in Ecology, Department of Botany, Banaras Hindu University, Varanasi 221 005, Uttar Pradesh, India. **Tel.**91 542 310290 ext.352; **fax** 91 542 312059.

MITTERMEIER, Dr Russell Alan. Biological diversity conservation; primates; herpetology. Foundation President. *B*.8 Nov.1949, New York, NY, USA. American. *M*.Cristina S.: 2 *s*. **Education:** Dartmouth Coll. AB 1971 *(Summa Cum Laude,* Phi Beta Kappa); Harvard U. MA(Biol. Anthrop.) 1973, PhD(Biol.Anthrop.) 1977. **Experience:** extensive field res., lecturing, fundraising, pubns, in pursuit of furthering primate cons.; concurrently practising herpetologist studying esp. side-backed Turtles *(Podocnemis* spp.) of S.Amer. **Career:** Cons.Assoc. NYZS 1976–7, Cons.F.in Primate Ecol. NYZS/WWF 1978–9, Head Primate Prog. WWF 1978–89, Pres. Cons.Intl Fndn 1989–. **Memberships:** LS (1987–), IUCN (Adv.Panel of Mammalogists 1976–7, SSC Primate SG 1977–), Edl Bd *J.of Med.Primatology,* IPSCC, ASPCC. **Awards:** Gold Medal (SDZS) 1987, Dipl.of Merit for Nature Prot.(MG Brazil) 1985. **Publications:** *Conserving the World's Biol.Diversity* 1990, *The GEF & Biodiv.: Lessons to Date & Recommendations for Future Action* 1994, *Ecol.& Behavior of Neotrop.Primates* Vol.1 1981, Vol.2 1988, *Primate Cons.*(Newsletter, Vols 1-11) 1981–90. Favours pers.pub.& news media support. **Languages:** English, French, German, Portuguese, Spanish. Willing to act as consult. etc. **Address:** Conservation International Foundation, 1015 18th Street NW, Suite 1000, Washington, DC 10036, USA. **Tel.**(office) 1 202 429 5660, (home) 1 202 387 7874; **fax** 1 202 887 0192.

MKANDA, Francis Xavier. Wildlife ecology, community involvement in wildlife management; research on vulnerability of wildlife to impacts of climate change. Senior Parks & Wildlife Research Officer. *B*.3 Nov.1957, Likoma Is. Malawi. Citizen of Malawi. *M*.Simwaka E.T.L.: 2 *s.*, *d.* **Education:** U.of Malawi, BSc (Agric.) 1982; U.of Edinburgh, MSc(Natural Resources' Mgmt) 1988. **Experience:** ecol.res. in nat.parks and wildlife reserve ecosystems, admin.of Wildlife Res.Unit. **Career:** Parks & Wildlife Officer 1984–93, Sr Parks & Wildlife Res.Officer 1994–, Dept of Nat.Parks and Wildlife. **Achievements:** res.on mortality of Nyala*, effects of fire, public attitudes towards prot. areas, and ecol.of Hippopotamus; pubns. **Publications:** several incl.*Causes of mortality of Nyala *(Tragelaphus angasi* G.) in Lengwe Nat.Park, Malawi 1991, Conflicts between Hippopotamus *(Hippopotamus amphibius* L.) and Man in Malawi 1994, Public attitudes and needs around Kasungu Nat.Park 1994. Indiff.to pers.pub.& news media support. **Language:** English. Willing to act as consult.etc. **Address:** Department of National Parks and Wildlife, POB 30131, Lilongwe 3, Malawi. **Tel.**(office) 265 723566 or 676; **fax** 265 723089.

MOESTRUP, Søren. Tree improvement, seed procurement, and genetic conservation, in developing countries. Centre Deputy Director. *B.* 14 Dec.1956, Copenhagen, Denmark. Danish. *M*.Rikke: *s.* **Education:** R.Vet.U. (Copenhagen), MSc(For.) 1983. **Experience:** consult.— within tech.fields given above in Costa Rica*, Nicaragua*, Mauritania, Burkina Faso*, Senegal, Sudan*, Somalia, Kenya, Tanzania*, Ethiopia*, Uganda*, Madagascar, Pakistan, Nepal*, Thailand*, India, & Indonesia*. **Career:** Assoc.Expert, Watershed Mgmt Project (Nepal), FAO 1983–6; Agrofor.Officer 1987–9, Dep.Dir 1990–, DANIDA Forest Seed Centre. **Achievements:** *profound assistance in suggesting estab.of nat. tree-seed progs in the ten above countries. **Memberships:** Danish Assn of Professional Foresters. Favours pers.pub.& news media support. **Languages:** Danish, English, Finnish (read). Willing to act as consult.etc. **Address:** DANIDA Forest Seed Centre, Krogerupvej 3A, DK 3050 Humlebaek, Denmark. **Tel.**(office) 45 42 190500, (home) 45 33 122776; **fax** 45 49 160258.

MOFFATT, Dr Ian. Environmental modelling including GIS; sustainable development in tropical & temperate environments. Lecturer in Environmental Science. *B*.10 Feb.1947, Newcastle upon Tyne, England, UK. British. *M.* **Education:** U.of London BSc 1969, U.of Newcastle upon Tyne MSc 1974, PhD 1980. **Experience:** widespread res.into envl systems' modelling, consult.for UK R.Comm.on Envl Poll., memb. Northern Territory Adv.Cttee on the Greenhouse Effect. **Career:** Lect.in Geog. U.of Liverpool 1977–8, Lect.in Envl Sci. 1978–90 & 1993– U.of Stirling, Sr Res.F. ANU 1990–93. **Achievements:** coordinated res.into cons.& dev.in N.Australia; contributed to envl policy on 'greenhouse effect ' & coastal mgmt in Australia and to eval.of econ.incentives for envl poll.in mgmt in UK; actively encouraged use of computers in envl sci.& mgmt. **Membership:** IBG. **Awards:** Sir Robert Menzies Vis.F. (ANU) 1989, F.NTU, Disting.Vis.Scholar U.of Adelaide 1993. **Publications:** *Cons.& Dev. Issues in N.Australia* (co-Author) 1992, *Greenhouse Effect Sci.& Policy in the Northern Territory, Australia* 1992; two other books, 60 papers. Dislikes pers.pub., favours news media support. **Languages:** English, French (written). Willing to act as consult. etc. **Address:** Department of Environmental Science, University of Stirling, Stirling, Scotland, UK. **Tel.**44 1786 467842 or 40 ext.7854; **fax** 44 1786 467843.

MOGHRABY, Professor Dr Asim I. EL. Freshwater ecology, ecosystems' management & protection, desertification and wildlife. Emeritus Professor of Ecology. *B*.10 Oct.1943, Khartoum, Sudan. Sudanese. *M*.Alawiyya (ecol., Women Envl Network [nat.NGO]): 2 *s.*, 2 *d.* **Education:** U.of Khartoum BSc(Hons) 1966, PhD 1972; U.of Dresden Dipl.in Ecosystems' Mgmt & Prot.1980. **Experience:** 27 yrs' teaching & res.from BSc to PhD levels in freshwater ecosystems & large dev.projects in arid lands, Dir of Hydrobiol.Res.Unit for eight yrs, first Acting Dir of Inst.of Envl Studies, widespread exp.in NGO activities in envl mgmt. **Career:** Fac.of Sci.1966–, Emer.Prof.of Ecol., U.of Khartoum. **Achievements:** pioneered in multi- & inter-disc.long-term teamwork & envl awareness in the regn as well as NGO work. **Memberships:** SIL, SWCS (Sec.& Founder Memb.), SECS (Founder Memb.), SMCS, Wildlife Club, Ornith. Soc., Edl Bds of *SIENT*, the Ethiopian *J.of Sci.*, and the Sudanese *J.of Sci.* **Awards:** a species of plankton, *Tropodiaptomus asimi*, was named (Dumont 1987) after him. **Publications:** *Limnol. and Marine Biol.in the Sudan* (co-Ed.) 1984, The energy crisis in the Sudan: alternative supplies of biomass (co-Author) 1985, Desert.in Western Sudan and strats for rehab.(co-Author) 1987. Dislikes pers. pub., indiff.to news media support. **Languages:** Arabic, English. Willing to act as consult.etc. **Address:** POB 1100, Khartoum, Sudan. **Tel.** (office) 249 11 76920 or 80589, (home) 249 11 443628; **fax** 249 11 81176/70735.

MOLDAN, HE Professor Dr Bedřich. Analytical chemistry, biogeochemistry; environmental policy; environment in general. Director, Associate Professor of Geochemistry. *B.*15 August 1935, Prague, Czech Republic. Czech. *M.* Dobrava Moldanova; 2 s incl Filip (hydr.), *d.* **Education:** Charles U. RNDr (Analytical Chem.) 1958, PhD 1964. **Experience:** res.in analytical chem.to PhD level (envt, geochem., biogeochem., small catchments res.up to SCOPE project 'Biogeochem.of Small Catchments'; memb.Czech Govt; active in green NGOs up to Chairmanship of CUNC (largest Czech NGO). **Career:** Chemist–Head, Biogeochem.Dept., Geol.Inst.of Prague 1959–89; Lect.on Envl Geochem. Charles U. 1978–; Minister for Envt (first in Czechoslo-vakia) 1989–91; MP 1990–92; Head, Czech Nat.Climate Prog.1991–; Chairman CUNC 1991–; Chairman, PrepCom WG III and VC & Rapp. Main Cttee UNCED 1991–2; Treas. SCOPE 1992; VC UN Comm. on Sust.Dev.1993–; Adv.to Min.of Foreign Affairs 1993–; Chairman of Bd, Regnl Envl Center 1993–; Dir, Charles U.Centre for Envl Scholarship 1992–. **Achievements:** estab.first Envl Min.in Czech Rep., u.teaching on ecol subjects, serving UNCED, creation of Charles U.Centre for Envl Scholarship. **Membership:** Ecol.Circle (Chairman 1992–). **Publications:** *Atomic Absorption Spectroscopy* (co-Author) 1969, *The Envt as Seen by a Sci.*(co-Author, in Czech) 1979, 1989, *The End of the Wasteful Age* (co-Author, in Czech) 1984, *Atmos.Deposition, A Biogeochem.Process* 1991, *Rainbow Prog., Envl Recovery Prog.for Czech Rep.*(co-Author) 1991; num.book & monogr.chapters, papers, and articles. Favours pers.pub.& news media support. **Languages:** Czech, English, German (spoken), Russian (spoken). Willing to act as consult.etc. **Address:** Na Kuthence 8, 160 00 Praha 6, Czech Republic. **Tel.**(office) 42 2 231 5334, (home) 42 2 311 3805; **fax** 42 2 231 5324.

MOLTKE, Dr Konrad VON. International environmental relations; environmental policy. Consultant, Senior Fellow, Adjunct Professor. *B.*23 Sept.1941, Kreisau Kreis, Schweidnitz, Germany. German. *M.*Ulrike: 3 *s.*, *d.* **Education:** Dartmouth Coll. BA(Maths) 1964, U.of Munich, U.of Gottingen PhD(Hist.) 1967. **Experience:** non-govtl intl envl relations. **Career:** Asst Prof.of Hist.1968–72, Assoc.Prof. of Hist. 1972–74, SUNY; Dir, Amerika Gesellschaft 1973–6; Dir, IEEP, Euro.Cultural Fndn 1976–84; Consult.on Intl Envl Relations 1984–; Sr F. WWF (WA) 1984– and Inst.for Intl Envl Governance 1992–; Adjunct Prof.of Envl Studies, Dartmouth Coll. 1984–. **Achievements:** developed Euro. envl policy studies and debt-for-Nature swaps; active on intl ccon.policy and its relationship to envl mgmt. **Memberships:** IUCN CEPLA, US EPA Nat.Adv.Cttee on Tech.Transfer, Trade & Envt, Global Tomorrow Coalition (Bd, Chair 1993–). **Publications:** 12 books incl.*Siegmund von Dietrichstein* 1970, *Public Policy for Chemicals* 1982, *Rolle der Umwelt-schutzverbande in den Niederlanden* 1982; num.tech.reports & papers; Ed.*Intl Envl Affairs;* others. **Languages:** Dutch, English, French, German, Italian. Willing to act as consult.etc. **Address:** RR2, Box 37A, Norwich, Vermont 05055, USA. **Tel.** (office) 1 603 646 3701, (home) 1 802 649 2823; **fax** 1 802 649 3539; **e-mail** Konrad.vonMoltke@ Dartmouth.edu .

moneim' Maher ALI, Professor Dr Abd 'El, *see* **ALI, Professor Dr Abd 'El moneim' Maher.**

MONOD, Professor Théodore André. Zoology, field natural history. *B.*9 April 1902, Rouen, France. French. *W.*(Olga): 2 *s.*, *d.* **Education:** Ecole Alsacienne, U.of Paris. **Career:** Asst 1922–42, Prof. 1942–74, Hon.Prof.1974–, Musée Nat.d'Histoire Naturelle; Dir, Institut Français d'Afrique Noire 1938–65; Dean, Fac.of Scis, Dakar U.1957–8. **Memberships:** Institut de France (Académie des Scis) 1963–, Académie des Scis d'Outremer 1949–, Académie de Marine 1957–. **Awards:** Dr *h.c.*(Univs of Cologne & Neuchâtel), Gold Medal (Société de Géographie, RGS & AGS), Haile Selassie Prize for African Res., Commandeur of Légion d'Honneur, Order des Palmes Académiques, Order of the Golden Ark, Commander of Order of Christ, Mérite Saharien, Mérite Nat. (Mauritania), Ordre Nat. (Senegal). **Publications:** num.incl.*Méharées, Explorations au vrai Sahara* 1937, 1947, new edn 1989, *L'Hippopotame et le Philosophe* 1946, 1993, *Bathyfolages, Plongées Profondes* 1954, new edn 1991, *Les Déserts* 1973, *L'Emeraude des Garamantes: Souvenirs d'un Saharien* 1984, new edn 1992. **Address:** 14 quai d'Orléans, 75004 Paris, France. **Tel.**(office) 33 14 079 3750, (home) 33 14 326 7950.

MONTAÑO ARMIJOS, Professor Mariano, *see* **ARMIJOS, Professor Mariano** MONTAÑO.

MONTESINOS, Dr José Luis VIEJO. Ecology & conservation of insects, mainly Lepidoptera.

Lecturer in Entomology. *B*.22 Oct.1954, Puertollano, Ciudad Real, Spain. Spanish. *M*.Consuelo: 2 *s*., *d*. **Education:** Universidad Complutense de Madrid, graduated in biol.scis 1977, Dr(Biol.Scis) 1981. **Experience:** 17 yrs devoted to study of Spanish butterflies. **Career:** Lect.& Head of Dept of Biol. Universidad Autónoma de Madrid 1977–. **Achievements:** estab.of relationships between butterfly fauna & plant formations, finding patterns of distribn of these insects; 60+ pubns on butterflies incl. Equatorial Guinean species. **Memberships:** SEL, Sociedad Hispano-Luso-Americana de Lepidopterologia, AEE, Systematics Assn. **Publications:** The importance of woodlands in the cons.of Butterflies in the centre of the Iberian Peninsula (co-Author) 1989, Selection of lepidopterologically interesting areas in c.Spain using UTM distribn maps (co-Author) 1991. Indiff.to pers.pub., favours news media support. **Languages:** English, French, Spanish. Willing to act as consult.etc. **Address:** Departamento de Biologia, Universidad Autónoma de Madrid, 28049 Madrid, Spain. **Tel.**(office) 34 1 397 8296, (home) 34 1 474 4259; **fax** 34 1 397 8344.

MOORE, Alan William. Protected area planning & management; training of protected area personnel. Freelance Consultant. *B*.9 March 1947, Nashua, NH, USA. American. *M*.Carol (geomorph. & soil erosion expert). **Education:** Middlebury Coll. BA(Hist.) 1969; U.of Mich., MS(Natural Resource Mgmt) 1975. **Experience:** field-oriented consult.for 20 yrs specializing in prot.area mgmt, planning, & training; ecotourism. **Career:** Peace Corps vol.with Costa Rican Park system 1970–73, Adv. Galápagos Nat.Park 1975–6, Freelance Consult.in Latin Amer.working with local & intl cons.orgns 1977–. **Achievements:** estab.tourism mgmt prog.in Galápagos Islands 1975, helped prepare first organized training prog.for prot.area personnel in Latin Amer. (Ecuador) 1989. **Membership:** IUCN CNPPA. **Publications:** *Manual para la Capacitacion de Personal de Areas Protegidas* 1993; several FAO cons.manuals. Indiff.to pers.pub. & news media support. **Languages:** English, Spanish. Willing to act as consult.etc. **Address:** 5425 Neubert Springs Road, Knoxville, Tennessee 37920, USA. **Tel.**1 615 573 7295; **fax** 1 615 974 6025.

MOORE, Dr James Walter. Aquatic ecology particularly of arctic & subarctic waters; chemical contaminants of surface water; large dams, regulatory toxicology; environmental management. Head of Aquatic Ecology Branch, Instructor. *B*.20 Nov.1947, Toronto, Ont., Canada. Canadian. **Education:** U.of Guelph BSc(Zool.) 1970, MSc(Zool.) 1972; U.of Bath PhD(Marine Biol.) 1975. **Experience:** res.— aquatic ecol.in Canadian arctic & subarctic waters (both coastal & freshwater), phycological & zooplankton studies of large lakes, feeding habits of freshwater & coastal fish, regulation of chem. contaminants in fresh water, envl effects of large dams, regulatory toxicology in support of envl legis., maintenance & use of herbivorous grass carp *(Ctenopharyngodon idella* spp.) to control weeds; adv.— expert court witness, transfer of lab.tech. to private sector, public interest groups, scientific ref.for num. journals; Instr.in Ecol. & Field Biol. to coll.students & schoolchildren. **Career:** Marine Biol. Govt of NWT, Fisheries & Oceans Canada 1972–3, Project Biol.then Sr Water Poll.Control Biol. Envt Canada 1975–9; Head, Aquatic Ecol.Branch, Alb.Envl Centre 1979–; Instr., Envl Sci. Lakeland Coll.1994–. **Achievements:** surveys of flora & fauna of remote arctic & subarctic waters, effects & mitigation of construction of large dams, extensive teaching to coll.students & schoolchildren on envl cons. **Memberships:** num.provincial & nat.cttees, Assoc.Ed. *Water Poll.Res.J. Canada.* **Awards:** Brit.Commonwealth Scholar. **Publications:** *Heavy Metals in Natural Waters — Applied Monitoring & Impact Assessment* (transl.into Russian) 1984, *Organic Chemicals in Natural Waters — Applied Impact & Monitoring Assessment* 1984, *The Changing Envt* 1986, *Balancing the Needs of Water Use* 1989, *Inorganic Contaminants of Surface Water — Res.& Monitoring Priorities* 1991; *c*.75 papers. Welcomes pers. pub.& news media support — has taken part in num.TV, radio & newspaper interviews. **Languages:** English, French (poor), German (poor). Willing to act as consult.etc. **Address:** Lakeland College, Vermilion, Alberta T0B 4M0, Canada. **Tel.**(office) 1 403 853 8519, (home) 1 403 853 4970; **fax** 1 403 853 7355.

MOORE, Dr [Sir*] Norman Winfrid. Wildlife conservation — research & policymaking especially in fields of pollution control and conservation of Odonata. Retired. *B*.24 Feb.1923, London, England, UK. British. *M*.Dr Janet (biol., retired): *s*., 2 *d*. **Education:** U.of Camb. BA 1943, MA 1960; U.of Bristol PhD 1954. **Experience:** res.during career and in retirement; admin.as Regnl Officer and Head of Toxic Chemicals & Wildlife Div.of Monks Wood Experimental Station, NC, and as Chief Adv. Officer of NCC. **Career:** served with R.Artillery 1942–7; Asst Lect.& Lect. Bristol U. 1949–53; Regnl Officer for SW England, NC 1953–60; Head of Toxic Chemicals & Wildlife Div.of Monks Wood Experimental Station 1960–74; Chief Adv.Officer, NCC 1974–83; Vis.Prof. Wye Coll. U.of London 1979–83. **Achievements:** achieving improved control of pesticides through res., orgn of res.& admin., rationalization of system for selecting sites of spec. scientific importance, identifying hazards of farming methods, and realizing constructive dialogue between farmers & conservationists; Founding Memb.FWAG; pioneer on studies of dragonfly behaviour & ecol. **Memberships:** BOU (VP 1977–81), RES, BES (VP 1984–6), BTO, BDS, IEEM (Patron), IBiol.(F.), IUCN Odonata SG (Chairman 1980–). [*Does not use his hereditory title of Sir.] **Awards:** Union Medal (BOU) 1972, Hon.F.LS, Cons.Book of the Yr Award** (RSNC) 1987. **Publications:** *Dragonflies* (co-Author) 1960, *Hedges* (co-Author) 1974,

The Bird of Time* 1987, *A Synopsis of the Pesticide Problem in Advances in Ecol Res.* 1967; 100+ scientific papers & articles. Favours supportive pers.pub. & news media reporting. **Languages: English, French (reasonable). **Address:** The Farm House, 117 Boxworth End, Swavesey, Cambridge CB4 5RA, England, UK. **Tel.**(home) 44 1954 230233.

MOORE, Professor Dr Peter Geoffrey. Marine biology, systematics & ecology, Amphipod Crustacea, conservation. Personal Chair in Marine Biology. *B.*7 Feb.1947, Bromsgrove, Worcs., England, UK. British. *M.*Judith Susan: 2 *s., d.* **Education:** U.of Leeds BSc(1st Class Hons) (Zool.) 1968, PhD 1972, DSc 1986. **Experience:** author of 110+ res.papers & books; consult.to MCS, Occidental Oil Co., Britannia Steamship Assurance Soc. **Career:** Lect.on Marine Biol. 1971–86, Sr Lect.1986–9, Reader 1989–93, Personal Chair 1993–, U.Marine Biol. Station Millport (Univs of London & Glasgow). **Achievements:** Ed.*J.of Natural Hist.*1988–, Invited Memb.SNH Marine Cons.Steering Group. **Memberships:** MBA (UK), F.LS, C.Biol., F.IBiol., Crustacean Soc., Queen's English Soc. **Award:** T.H.Huxley Prize (ZSL) 1972. **Publications:** incl.*The Ecol.of Rocky Coasts* (co-Ed.) 1985, On the feeding and comparative biol.of iron in coelenterate-associated gammaridean Amphipoda (Crustacea) from N.Norway (co-Author) 1994. Indiff.to pers.pub.& news media support save for our Lab. **Languages:** English, French. Willing to act as consult.etc. **Address:** University Marine Biological Station Millport, Isle of Cumbrae KA28 0EG, Scotland, UK. **Tel.**(office) 44 1475 530581, (home) 44 1475 530761; **fax** 44 1475 530601.

MORAN, Ms Katy. Applied anthropology, ethnobiology, economic botany; biocultural diversity; debt-for-Nature swaps; environmental policy. Executive Director. *B.*20 May 1940, Minneapolis, MN, USA. American. *D.: d., s.* **Education:** Amer.U.(Washington, DC) MA (Applied Anthrop.) 1987. **Experience:** res., adv., public speaking, admin., consult., conf. orgn, public policy. **Career:** Researcher (in Kenya) for UNESCO 1982; Res.Coord.incl. Dept Head & Instr. Audubon Zoo 1982–4; PI Nat.Zoo 1985–7 and Prog.Analyst, Ext.Affairs 1990–92, Smithsonian Instn; Legislative Aide (Envt) to Rep.John Porter 1987–9 and Press Sec.to Rep.James H.Scheuer 1989, US House of Representatives; Exec.Dir, The Healing Forest Conservancy 1992–. **Achievements:** drafted & passed first US legis.on debt-for-Nature swaps, linked envl & indigenous peoples' human rights issues. **Memberships:** IUCN SSC (Medicinal Plants SG 1994–6), ISE (Officer & Bd 1992–4), SAA, WorldWIDE (Bd 1990–94), Intl Dev. Conf.(Bd of Trustees 1992–), BioNet Steering Cttee. **Awards:** Phi Kappa Phi, Deptl Hons (Amer.U.& U.of New Orleans), Disting.Service in Anthrop.(U.of New Orleans), F'ship (Asia Fndn) 1994. **Publications:** num.incl.Debt for Nature swaps: US policy issues and options

1991, Ethnobiol.and US Policy 1992, Cons.of Biocultural Diversity through the Healing Forest Conservancy 1994, *Can Nuts Save the Rainforest? The Promise of Ethnobiol.and Nontimber Forest Products* (Ed.) in press. Favours pers.pub.& news media support. **Languages:** English, French (read). Willing to act as consult.etc. **Address:** The Healing Forest Conservancy, 3521 S Street NW, Washington, District of Columbia 20007, USA. **Tel.**(office) & **fax** 1 202 333 3438, (home) 1 202 337 3211.

MORELL, Merilio G. Natural resources' policy analysis, strategic planning for sustainable development, institutional development; management of national parks & protected areas, public administration. Forestry Institutions Officer. *B.* 17 Nov.1947, San Pedro Macoris, Dominican Republic. Dominican. *M.*Mercedes: 2 *s.* **Education:** Universidad Austral de Chile, For.Eng. (Hons.) 1975; Harvard U. MPA 1985. **Experience:** teaching — natural resources' mgmt, envl educ.; nat.park planning & mgmt, project formulation & eval., instnl aspects of natural resources' mgmt & sust.dev., policy formulation & analysis. **Career:** Dir, NPS 1978–83; Assoc. Dir. (For.) Peace Corps 1982; Natural Resources Researcher, Instituto Superior de Agricultura 1985–6; Exec.Dir, Fundación Progressio 1986–8, all in Dominican Rep.; Consult.for FAO, IIED, OAS, WWF, in Latin Amer.& Africa. **Achievements:** assisting the Dominican Rep. Govt in creating three nat.parks & six prot.areas; from 1976–83 estab.basic system for mgmt of Dominican Rep.Nat.Park system and developed successful nat.campaign for cons.of nat.parks and the country's natural resources. **Membership:** IUCN WG on Strats for Sustainability. **Publications:** *Situacion Forestal en Republica Dominicana* 1986, *Rentabilidad e Incentivos Forestales* 1988, *Grassroots Forest Mgmt Initiatives in Central Amer.: the Role of Local People's Orgns* 1992; num.working papers, projects, & case studies. Indiff.to pers.pub.& news media support. **Languages:** English (written, spoken), French (read), Italian, Portuguese (spoken, read), Spanish. Further details may be obtained from *Who's Who in Dominican Republic.* Willing to act as consult.etc. **Address:** UN Food and Agriculture Organization, Forestry Department, Via delle Terme di Caracalla, Rome 00100, Italy. **Tel.**(office) 39 6 522 54140, (home) 39 6 509 0424; **fax** 39 6 522 55137.

MORELLO, Professor Dr Jorge. Ecological consequences of land-use changes in Latin America. Emeritus Professor of Ecology, Programme Head. *B.*12 Oct.1923, Santa Fe, Argentina. Argentinian. **Education:** U.of La Plata, Dr in Biol.Scis 1949. **Experience:** res.& consult. in applied ecol.— land-use changes in rural & peri-urban areas and their envl consequences. **Career:** Prof.of Ecol.1959–95 (Emer. 1995–), Head of Land-use Prog. Center for Advanced Studies 1989–, U.of Buenos Aires; Dir, Nat. Parks 1983–9; Spec.Adv. InterAmerican Dev.

Bank 1992; Vis.Prof.* Harvard U.1994. **Achievements:** dev.of sch.of applied ecol.res.in Chaco regn (Paraguay, Argentina, Bolivia) devoted to study of ecol.consequences of cattle-raising in natural forest; improvement of network of prot. areas in Argentina. **Memberships:** ISE, IIED (Bd), Société de Biogéographie, Socieded Argentina de Ecologia. **Awards:** Premio Nacional Argentino a las Ciencias de la Tierra 1972, *Robert F.Kennedy Vis. Prof.(Harvard U.) 1994. **Publications:** incl.*Perfil Ecologico de Sudamerica* 1984, *Las Uto-pias del Medio Ambiente: Desarrollo sustentable en la Argentina* (co-Author) 1992. Favours pers.pub. & news media support. **Languages:** English, Spanish. Willing to act as consult. etc. **Address:** Centro de Estudios Avanzados, Universidad de Buenos Aires, Avenida del Libertador 4748, 1426 Buenos Aires, Argentina. **Tel.** (home) 541 772 6749; **fax** 541 963 6962.

MOREY, Professor Dr Miguel. Vegetation dynamics; Mediterranean ecosystems, island ecosystems; landscape ecology. Professor of Ecology. *B.*27 Nov.1934, Son Servera, Balearic Islands, Spain. Spanish. *M.*Isabel (Prof.of Marine Biol.): 2 *s*. **Education:** U.of Madrid, Licenciado in Biol.1958, PhD 1963. **Experience:** widespread teaching in ecol.in Spanish univs & Medit.Agronomic Insts of Chania & Zaragoza; res.on veg.dynamics & applied ecol.; direction of envl planning projects; envl assessment. **Career:** Prof.of Biol. U.of Madrid 1958–64, Consejo Superior Investigaciones Cientificas, Madrid & Canary Islands 1964–71; Prof.of Ecol. U.of Navarra 1967–8, U.of Oviedo 1971–7, U.of Santiago 1977–9, U.of Illes Balears (Centre for Advanced Studies, 1983–) 1980–. **Achievements:** direction of project for prot.of natural areas in Balearics which gave rise to actual 'Law for Prot.of Natural Areas'; direction of MAB project for eco-dev.for Formentera Is. and project for cons.of n.Majorca. **Memberships:** IUCN CESP, BES, ESA, Collab.MAB Prog., Real Soc.Española Historia Natural, Asociacion Española de Ecologia Terrestre, ADENA (WWF, Scientific Cttee), INSULA (MAB). **Award:** Europa-Preis für Landespflege (Johann Wolfgang von Goethe Fndn) 1989. **Publications:** contributions to *Culture & Cons.*1985, *Caring for the Earth* 1990, *Les Iles en Méditerranée: Enjeux et Perspectives* 1991, *Integrated Study of the Is.of Formentera* (main Author, in Spanish) 1992, *Natural Areas in the BI: Assessment of 73 Areas for Prot.*(in Spanish) 1987*; White Book on Tourism in the Balearic Islands* (in Catalonian) 1987; Diversity measurements in shrubland communities of Galicia (NW Spain)(co-Author) 1989, Change in envl stab.and the use of resources on small islands: the case of Formentera, Balearic Islands, Spain (co-Author) 1992. Indiff.to pers.pub.& news media support. **Languages:** Catalonian, English, French, Spanish. Willing to act as consult. etc. **Address:** Department of Environmental Biology, Universitat de les Iles Balears, E-07071 Palma de Mallorca, Spain. **Tel.**(office) 34 71 173177, (home) 34 71 200308; **fax** 34 71 173184.

MORRIS, Dr Michael George. Effects of conservation management on grassland invertebrates, conservation of British & European invertebrates; conservation & utilization of third-world insect resources especially butterflies. Head, Visiting Professor. *B.*18 April 1934, Bromley, Kent, England, UK. British. *M.*Judith: 3 *s*. **Education:** Christ's Hosp.and Selwyn Coll. U.of Camb. MA 1962, U.of London PhD 1962. **Experience:** cons.res.full- & part-time since 1961; entomol.& ecol.res.& mgmt. **Career:** Res. Monks Wood (Abbots Ripton, Cambs) 1961–75, Head of Furzebrook Res.Station (NERC ITE) 1975–. **Achievements:** estab.of principles for scientific mgmt of grasslands for invertebrate cons.; integration of invertebrate cons.with mainstream cons.in UK; estab.of utilization as essential for cons.of insects in Third World. **Memberships:** F.IBiol., F.RES, F.LS, BES, FBA. **Publications:** *Grassland Ecol. & Wildlife Mgmt* (co-Author) 1974, *Threatened Swallowtail Butterflies of the World* (co-Author) 1991, *The Scientific Mgmt of Temperate Communities for Cons.*(co-Ed.) 1991; *c.*200 papers/notes. Indiff.to pers.pub.& news media support. **Languages:** English, French (rudimentary), German, Spanish. Willing to act as consult.etc. **Address:** Institute of Terrestrial Ecology, Furzebrook Research Station, Wareham, Dorset BH20 5AS, England, UK. **Tel.**(office) 44 1929 551518, (home) 44 1305 267337; **fax** 44 1929 551087.

MORTON, Professor Dr Brian. All aspects of marine science especially malacology, coastal ecology, pollution, conservation, & coastal-zone management. Professor of Zoology & Director. *B.*10 Aug.1942, Cheshunt, Herts., England, UK. British. *M.*Janice Elizabeth: 2 *s*., 2 *d*. **Education:** U.of London, BSc 1966, PhD 1969. **Experience:** res.into fields of malacology, feeding, symbioses, coastal ecol.; teaching invertebrates, coastal ecol., poll., cons., fisheries & mariculture; supervision of MPhil & PhD students. **Career:** Res.Assoc. Portsmouth Poly.1969–70; Lect.1970–75, Reader 1975–82, Prof.1982–, Dept of Zool., Dir.The Swire Marine Lab.1989–, all at U.of Hong Kong. **Achievements:** bldg The Swire Marine Lab., founding MBA of HK, founding *Asian Marine Biol.* **Memberships:** MBA UK (Life), F.ZSL, F.LS, MBA HK (Chairman), UNITAS Malacologia. **Awards:** Global 500 Roll of Honour (UNEP) 1989, MS London (Hon.Life) 1992, PSA (Hon.Life F.) 1993. **Publications:** The Future of the HK Sea Shore (HK's first cons.book) 1979, *The Sea Shore Ecol.of HK* (co-Author) 1983, *Partnerships in the Sea* 1988; *Shore Ecol.of the Gulf of Mexico* (co-Author) 1989, *A Bibl.of HK Marine Sci.: 1842–1990* 1990, *Catalogue of the Marine Bivalve Molluscs of China* (co-Author) 1993; Founding Ed. *Asian Marine Biol.*1984–; *c.*300 papers, articles & edited vols. **Language:** English. Willing to act as ref. **Address:** The Swire Marine Laboratory, University of Hong Kong, Cape d'Aguilar, Hong Kong. **Tel.**& **fax** 852 809 2197.

MOSLEY, Dr John Geoffrey. Nature conservation, national parks; Antarctica; landscape protection; national self-sufficiency. Environmental Consultant. *B.*14 Sept.1931, Youlgrave, Derbys., England, UK. Australian, British. *M.* Jeanette: 2 *s.*, 2 *d.*; *P.*Elizabeth: *s.* **Education:** U.of Nottingham, BA(Hons) 1953, MA 1955; ANU PhD 1963. **Experience:** res., teaching, admin. & advocacy. **Career:** Postdoctl Res.F. U.of Newcastle 1965–6; Lect. ANU 1966–8; Asst Dir.1968–72, Dir. 1973–86, ACF; Envl Consult.1986–. **Achievements:** at ANU gave first yr-long course in Australia on cons.of natural resources, Regnl Counc.IUCN 1981–8, led NGO campaign for full prot.against minerals activity in Antarctica (Madrid Protocol). **Membership:** IAG. **Awards:** Nuffield F'ship 1967, Hon.Life Memb. ACF. **Publications:** seven books incl. *Antarctica, Our Last Great Wilderness* 1986, *Australia's Wilderness Heritage: World Heritage Areas* (co-Author) 1988, *Blue Mtns for World Heritage* 1989, *World Heritage Values and Their Prot.*(co-Author) 1992; *c.*60 papers. Favours pers.pub.& news media support. **Language:** English. Further details may be obtained from *Who's Who in Australia* 1985/6. Willing to act as consult.etc. **Address:** 113 Boyds Road, Hurstbridge, Victoria 3099, Australia. **Tel.**(office & home) 61 3 718 2998.

MOUDUD, Hasna Jasimuddin. Marine environment, coastal ecology, mangrove & coastal afforestation, policy and planning environmental guidelines; Law of the Sea, sharing common river water between countries; women & environment and cultural ecology. Association President. *B.*11 Nov.1946, Faridpur, Bangladesh. Bangladeshi. *M.*Moudud Ahmed MP. **Education:** Dhaka U. BA 1966, U.of Dayton MA(English) 1989, U.of Iowa Intl Writing Prog. 1989. **Experience:** involved in formulating first guidelines for coastal area cons.of Bangladesh, dev.& envt; lobbying for ratifying & implementing all UN Convs incl.Law of the Sea, Oil Spill; organized nat.confs on coastal mgmt & intl conf.on greenhouse effect; init.Govt policy towards distribn of free land jointly to husband & wife and to female heads of households; conducted parliamentary hearing on oil-spill in Bay of Bengal; promoted transl.of Agenda 21 into Bengali; init.Coastal Green Belt movement as prot.from sea-level rise, Save the R.Bengal Tiger and the Sundarbans mangroves; formulated guidelines towards sharing of Ganges water between India & Bangladesh; dev.of integrated coastal village dev.model using cons.measures. **Career:** Lect. Dhaka U.1972– 3; Alternative Rep.to UNGA 1983, MP 1986– 90; Founder Pres. Nat.Assn for Resource Improvement 1986– and Coastal Area Resource Dev.& Mgmt Assn 1987–; Memb.Intl Election Obs. Team, Nat.Democratic Inst.for Intl Affairs (USA) to Philippines 1988; UN Conv.on Elimination of Discrimination Against Women 1988; Chairman Spec.Parliamentary Cttee on Envt and Coastal Dev.1989–90; VP Global 500 Forum 1992–4;

Vis.Res.F. Queen Elizabeth House, U.of Oxf. 1994–6. **Achievements:** Rapp. Partnerships for Change Conf.1993, VP Global 500 Forum 1992–4. **Memberships:** IUCN (Assoc.), Asiatic Soc.Bangladesh. **Award:** Global 500 Roll of Honour (UNEP) 1992. **Publications:** *Women in China* 1980, *Bangladesh Coastal Area Resource Dev.& Mgmt* (co-Ed.) Vols I & II 1988, *The Greenhouse Effect & Coastal Area of Bangladesh* (co-Ed.) 1989, *A Thousand Yr Old Bengali Mystic Poetry* 1992. Indiff.to pers. pub., favours news media support. **Languages:** Bengali, English; French & German (little); Hindi & Urdu (spoken). Willing to act as consult.etc. **Address:** 159 Gulshan Avenue, Gulshan, Dhaka, Bangladesh. **Tel.**(office) 880 2 600076, (home) 880 2 882676; **fax** 880 2 865547.

MOURA, Robert MANNERS. Landscape ecology, design, & maintenance; protected areas' planning, management, & monitoring; voluntary work in protected areas; ecological education. Director. *B.*18 Nov.1942, Lourenço Marques (now Maputo), Mozambique. Portuguese. *M.*Maria Luisa: *s.*, *d.*Judite Luisa dos Santos (anthrop.). **Education:** first U.degree in Agric.(Tech. Educ.) now U.of Coimbra 1963, Landscape Arch.Dipl. Tech.U.of Lisbon 1974. **Experience:** res.connected with current postgrad. thesis, direction of prot.areas; support of IUCN CNPPA, and FNNPE both on matters concerning Portugal; teaching Parks, Reserves & Nature Cons. Polytech.of Bragança 1991–2. **Career:** undergrad.on probation, and grad., Lisbon Municipality 1971–6; Officer, Portuguese Service for Parks, Reserves & Nature Cons. 1976; Pres. Bd for Settlement of Arrabida Nature Park 1977; commissioned to estab.first regnl structures in NE Portugal* 1979; Pres. Bd for the settlement of Alvão Nature Park 1983; Dir of Alvão and Montesinho Nature Parks 1986–. **Achievements:** co-init.of Portuguese govtl main commitment towards prot. areas 1976; *commissioned to estab.& create first structures & prot.areas in NE Portugal (Montesinho 1979 and Alvão 1983 Nature Parks); Dir of the two latter Parks 1986–; prod.of Alvão Nature Park magazine *Erica.* **Memberships:** PLNP (NGO), PALA, IUCN CNPPA. **Publications:** *Contribn towards Landscape Planning* (in Portuguese) 1973, *Parks, Reserves & Nature Cons.*1992, *Alvão Nature Park on View* 1993; some papers & num.articles. Dislikes pers.pub.& news media support. **Languages:** English (better at written), French (poor), Portuguese, Spanish (spoken & written). Willing to act as consult.etc. **Address:** Quinta das Botelhas, Lote 6A, 5000 Vila Real, Portugal (home) or Parque Natural do Alvão, Rua Alves Torgo 22-3-Dto, 5000 Vila Real, Portugal. **Tel.**(office) 351 59 24138, (home) 351 59 73491; **fax** 351 59 73869.

MOYER, Dr Jack Thomson. Conservation of biodiversity, marine wildlife, & coral reefs. Adviser on Environmental Education & Marine

Wildlife. *B.*7 March 1929, Topeka, KS, USA. American. *M.*Lorna Paragsa. **Education:** Colgate U. BA 1952, U.of Michigan MA 1961, U.of Tokyo PhD 1984. **Experience:** admin.as Dir of a biol station, on Bd of Dirs JIS, and as j.Ed.; consult.to WWF–Japan, Toba Aquarium (envl cons.), & Amer.Sch.in Japan (envl educ.), and adv.to Govt of Miyake–Mura, Miyake–Jima, Japan. **Career:** Teacher/Admin. Amer.Sch.in Japan 1963–84; Dir Tatsuo Tanaka Mem.Biol Station 1970–; Consult. WWF–Japan 1985–, Japan Underwater Films Ltd 1987–, & Toba Aquarium 1988–; ind.envl columnist 1989–; Adv.in Envl Educ.& Marine Wildlife, Miyake–Jima Nature Center 1993–. **Achievements:** stopped US practice-bombing-site on Onohara-Jima, Izu Islands, thus protecting Crested Murrelet's major nesting-site; contributed to stopping airport construction on Shiraho coral-reef; major contributor to stopping military airport construction at Miyake-Jima, to stopping firing-range construction on Mikura-Jima, and to halting intro.of weasels for rat control on Miyake-Jima (though later introduced illegally) — all in Japan. **Memberships:** ISJ, ASIH, WCRPS. **Awards:** Cons.Award — Japan Wild Bird Soc.1953, Govt of Miyahe-Jima 1959 & Japan Envt Agency 1974; Hon.Citizen, Miyake-Jima. **Publications:** Pop.structure, reproductive behaviour, & protogynous hermaphroditism, in the Angel *Fish Centropyge interruptus* at Miyake-Jima, Japan (co-Author) 1978, Massive destruction of scleractinian corals by the murilid gastropod *Drupella* in Japan & the Philippines (co-Author) 1982, Threat to unique terr.& marine envts & biota in a Japanese Nat.Park (co-Author) 1985, Reef channels as spawning sites on the Shiraho Coral Reef, Ishigaki Is. Japan 1989, *Comparative Reproductive Strats of Labrid Fishes* (monogr.) 1991, *Miyake-jima Naturalist* (in Japanese) 1993, *Discoveries of an Underwater Naturalist* (in Japanese) 1994, *The Joy of the Ocean* (in Japanese) 1994; 100+ papers; Ed.*Japanese J.of Ichthyology.* Not opposed to pers.pub., favours news media support (both as a means of gaining attention for cons.efforts). **Languages:** English, Japanese. Willing to act as consult. **Address:** Miyake-Jima Nature Center, Tsubota, Miyake-Mura, Miyake-Jima, Tokyo 100-12, Japan. **Tel.**(office) 81 4994 6 0410, (home) 81 3 5982 2652; **fax** 81 4994 6 0458.

MUMBA, Mrs Wanga. Environment & population issucs; natural-resource use & management. Executive Director. *B.*25 July 1954, Chipata, Zambia. Zambian. *M.*Philip Mumba (family planning assn [PPAZ] vol.): 2 *s., d.* **Education:** U.of London, Postgrad.Dipl.in Social Scis specializing in Community Dev. Planning 1986–7. **Experience:** 16 yrs' in pop. & envt; res., tech., admin., consult. **Career:** Head, Lusaka Province Family Planning Prog. 1980–84; Head of Admin. PPAZ 1984–8; Founder & Exec.Dir, Envt & Pop.Centre 1989–. **Achievements:** memb.of UNCED Drafting Cttee (Agenda 21), ICPD Drafting Cttee & Nat.Planning Cttee for UN Confs. **Memberships:** IUCN, Global Fund for Women, World Public Radio. **Award:** Spec.Achievement Cons. Award (NWF) 1992. **Publications:** ICPD Nat.& Regnl Prep.Conf.Reports 1993 & 1994, *Post-UNCED Report for Zambia* 1994, Newsletter on Pop.& Envt for students & media. **Language:** English. Willing to act as consult. etc. **Address:** Environment and Population Centre, POB 35614, Lusaka, Zambia. **Tel.** (office) 260 1 220156/222679, (home) 260 1 251870; **fax** 260 1 224325.

MUNASINGHE, Dr Mohan. Sustainable development, energy, water resources, environmental economics. Distinguished Visiting Professor of Environmental Management. *B.*July 1945, Colombo, Sri Lanka. Sri Lankan. *M.*Sria (envl consultant): *s., d.* **Education:** Clare Coll. U.of Camb. BA(Hons)(Eng.) & MA 1967; MIT, SM(Elec.Eng.) & Professional Elec.Engr (Solid State Phys.) 1969; McGill U. PhD(Solid State Phys./Elec.Eng.) 1973; Concordia U. MA(Dev. Econ.) 1975. **Experience:** Adv. US Pres.'s CEQ 1990–92, several Vis.Prof'ships, SRFs & Bd memberships, memb.Edl Bds incl. (current) *The Energy J.*1983–, *Pacific and Asian J.of Energy* 1985–, *Intl J.of Electric Power Systems* 1987–, *Utilities Policy* 1990–, *Open Economies Review* 1992–, *Envt and Dev.Econ.* 1995–. **Career:** Sr Economist Engr 1975–81, Div.Chief for Energy and Infrastructure 1987–90 and for Envt Policy 1991–5, World Bank; Sr Energy Adv.to Pres.of Sri Lanka and Chairman of Computer and Info.Tech.Council of Sri Lanka 1982–7; F. Beijer Inst. RSAS 1990–; Dist-ing.Vis.Prof.of Envl Mgmt, U.of Colombo 1995–. **Achievements:** author of 50+ books & 200 tech.papers. **Memberships:** IAEE, ISEE, Amer.Phys.Soc., AEA, Sri Lanka AAS (Life), IEEE (Sr), Global Energy Soc.(Hon.Life), Sigma Xi. **Awards:** F.of — TWAS, NAS (Sri Lanka), RSA, Instn of Elec.Engrs (UK), & Inst.of Engrs (Sri Lanka), Sinha Gold Medal (Lions Intl Orgn) 1984–5, Energy Economist of the Yr Award (IAEE) 1987, Intl Prize (Fifth Latin Amer. Energy Conf.) 1988, Twin Commem.Vols of Selected Papers 1990, Best Treatise Award & Gold Medal (IFWST) 1995; num.others. **Publications:** num.incl.*Computers and Informatics in Developing Countries* (Ed.) 1989, Energy Analysis and Policy 1990, *Water Supply and Envl Mgmt* 1992, *Envl Econ.and Sust.Dev.*1993, *Economywide Policies and the Envt* 1994, *Property Rights in a Social and Ecol.Context* (co-Ed.) 1995, *Valuing Trop. Forests* 1995. Favours pers.pub.& news media support. **Languages:** English, French, Sinhala, Spanish (spoken). Further details may be obtained from *Who's Who in Amer.*1996, *Dict.of Intl Biography.* Willing to act as consult.etc. **Address:** 10 De Fonseka Place, Colombo 5, Sri Lanka. **Tel.**(office) 94 1 580822, (home) 94 1 500289; **fax** 94 1 580822; **e-mail** mohanm@ sri.lanka. net .

MUTTAMARA, Mrs Samorn. Water & wastewater treatment, water supply and sanitation; solid & hazardous waste management; environmental impact assessment. Associate Professor. *B*.6 Sept.1941, Nakhonsrithammarat, Thailand. Thai. *M*.Mr Niwat Muttamara: 2 *d.* **Education:** Chulalongkorn U. BSc 1964, Oregon SU MSc 1968. **Experience:** res.— supervised 90+ M.& Doctl theses; consult.— 20+ rcs.projects dealing with wastewater treatment, air/noise poll., EIA (airport, deep-sea port, dam, industry). **Career:** Lect. Env.Engg Div. AIT 1968–. **Achievements:** prepared & reviewed course curriculum (envl prog.) for num.univs in Thailand; formed Interdisc. Training Groups among the divs of AIT; chaired several Cttees in AIT and elsewhere; organized num.intl/nat.confs, sems, workshops, training courses; served as Prin./co-PI of many projects. **Memberships:** AEEP, Nat. Envt Bd, Thai Envl Engineers' Assn, WorldWIDE (women in envt), Fndn for Life-long Educ. **Award:** 25-yr Service Diamond Pin (AIT) 1993. **Publications:** three books, 11 journal papers, 70 conf. & other papers, 42 reports. Indiff.to pers.pub.and news media support. **Languages:** Chinese (spoken), English (written, spoken), Thai. Willing to act as consult.etc. **Address:** Environmental Engineering Program, Asian Institute of Technology, GPO Box 2754, Bangkok 10501, Thailand. **Tel.**66 2 524 5626; **fax** 66 2 524 5625.

MWALYOSI, Dr Raphael B.B. Ecology, environmental impact assessment, integrated resource management; conservation biology, limnology; environmental management. Senior Research Fellow. *B*.3 Dec.1946, Ludewa, Tanzania. Tanzanian. *M*.Rustica A. **Education:** U.of Dar es Salaam, BSc(Bot.& Chem.) 1974, MSc(Wildlife Ecol.) 1979; Agricl U.of Norway, PhD(Cons. Biol.) 1990. **Experience:** res.— animal–habitat interaction, EIA, integrated resource mgmt in semi-arid areas; consult.— extensive, both nat.& intl; admin.— head of several consults, project coordn. **Career:** Res. Officer, Manyara Nat.Park 1974–9; Ecol./Sr Ecol. Rufiji Basin Dev.Auth.1979–84; Researcher/SRF, U.of Dar es Salaam 1984–. **Achievement:** developed an integrated resource mgmt strat.for L.Manyara Catchment Basin. **Publications:** *c*.15 incl.Ecol eval.for wildlife corridors and buffer zones for L.Manyara Nat. Park, Tanzania, and its immediate envt 1991, Pop.growth, carrying capacity and sust.dev.in SW Masailand, Tanzania 1991, Land use/cover changes and resource degradation in SW Masailand, Tanzania 1992, The influence of livestock grazing on range condition in semi-arid Masailand, Tanzania 1992. **Languages:** English, Swahili. Willing to act as consult.etc. **Address:** Institute of Resource Assessment, University of Dar es Salaam, POB 35097, Dar es Salaam, Tanzania. **Tel.**& **fax** 255 51 43393.

MWASAGA, Belekebajobege. Conservation, wildlife ecology; ecotourism. Chief Park Warden. *B*.13 July 1948, Tukuyu, Tanzania. Tanzanian. *M*.Florida T. **Education:** Coll.of African Wildlife Mgmt Dipl.1974; U.of Dar es Salaam, BSc(Hons)(For.) 1979, MSc(Forest Ecol.) 1983. **Experience:** admin.— preparing many project proposals for funding incl.estab.of Corpn's Planning Unit, gen.admin.& reorgn of the orgnl structure of TANAPA. **Career:** Sr Park Asst, Arusha & Mikumi Nat.Parks 1971–3; Park Warden & PRO, TANAPA Head Office 1973–6; Park Warden-in-Charge, Mt Kilimanjaro 1979–81 and Arusha 1981–2 Nat.Parks; Sr Planning Officer & Acting Manpower Dev.& Admin.Mgr 1983–7, Chief Ecol.& Planning Officer, Acting Dep.Dir., several times Acting DG, TANAPA 1987–93; Chief Park Warden, Lake Manyara Nat.Park 1993–. **Achievements:** working on behalf of and for DG of Serengeti & Mt Kilimanjaro Nat.Parks to acquire status of WHS, and Lake Manyara Nat.Park & Biosphere Reserve; acquisition & gazetting of Udzungwa Mtns Nat.Park; extension of Lake Manyara Nat.Park; estab.of Ecol.Monitoring Unit; pioneered initial stages for gazetting marine parks in Tanzania. **Memberships:** EAWS, WST, IUCN CNPPA, ICA (Italy). **Awards:** Best Worker (TANAPA) 1980/'84/'89/'90/'92. **Publications:** regular contrib.to local & intl periodicals & magazines. Favours pers.pub.& news media support. **Languages:** English, Swahili. Willing to act as consult.etc. **Address:** Tanzania National Parks, POD 3134, Arusha, Tanzania. **Tel.**255 57 3471; **fax** 255 57 3472.

MYERS, Professor Dr Norman. Environment & development including forests, biodiversity, agriculture, water, energy, climate, and population, all within a context of environmentally-sustainable development & North–South relations. Visiting Fellow and Professor. *B*.24 Aug.1934, Whitewell, Yorks., England, UK. British. Father John Myers (farmer). *D.*: 2 *d.*incl. Malindi Elizabeth (envl econ.). **Education:** Clitheroe R.Grammar Sch.; U.of Oxf. MA 1958; UCB PhD 1973. **Experience:** fieldwork & res. in more than 40 countries, and working visits to a further 50; consult.to RS, US NAS, RSAS, former Soviet AS, and similar scientific bodies in many parts of the world, and consult. assignments for World Bank, UN agencies, Rockefeller and MacArthur Fndns, EC, and OECD; Sr Adv.to the Brundtland Comm.and UNCED. **Career:** colonial admin., professional photographer, TV film-maker, & popular writer, based in Kenya 1958–69; Ind.Sci.& Consult.based in Kenya & UK 1973; Vis.Prof.at var.univs. **Achievements:** originator in mid-1970s of the thesis that we are in the opening phase of a mass extinction of species, and of a series of innovative insights *e.g.*the 'hamburger connection', triage strat.for save-species planning, envl security; documented, in late 1970s/late 1980s, that trop.deforestation has been occurring twice as fast as has been officially supposed. **Memberships:** Foreign F.AAAS, WAAS. **Awards:** Volvo Envt Prize 1992, Gold Medal & Order of the Golden Ark (WWF Intl) 1973, Gold Medal (NYZS) 1986 & (SDZS) 1990, First Disting.

Achievement Award (SCB) 1988, Spec.Achievement in Intl Envt (The Sierra Club) 1983, Global 500 Roll of Honour (UNEP) 1989. **Publications:** 12 books incl.*The Gaia Atlas of Planet Mgmt* 1986; 200+ scientific papers; several hundred magazine & newspaper articles. Favours pers.pub.& news media support. **Languages:** English; French, German, and Swahili (all basic). Further details can be found in Debrett's *Disting.People of Today.* Willing to act as consult.etc. **Address:** Upper Meadow, Old Road, Headington, Oxford OX3 8SZ, England, UK. **Tel.**44 1865 750387; **fax** 44 1865 741538.

NANAYAKKARA, Vitarana Rajasingha. Forestry, agroforestry, wood-based energy development; ecology; Nature conservation. Visiting Fellow & Consultant. *B.*10 Nov.1931, Ratnapura, Sri Lanka. Sri Lankan. **Education:** R. Coll.; U.of Ceylon BSc(Spec.)(Hons)(Zool.) 1955; U.of Oxf. BA(Hons)(For.) 1959, MA 1962; U.of Idaho, cert.course in Land-use Planning in Natural Resource Mgmt 1982. **Experience:** 35 yrs' service in Sri Lanka Forest Dept, 12 yrs as Head; countrywide exp.in forest admin, orgn, plantations, nurseries, agrofor., res.mgmt, fuelwood, and watershed for., for.in river-valley dev., woodland mgmt, participatory community for.; extensive regnl exp.for FAO; Consult.to FAO, ADB, UNDP, UNESCO, WWF, in Myanmar (Burma), Thailand, and Sri Lanka. **Career:** Dem.in Zool. U.of Ceylon 1955; Asst Conservator 1956–67, Dep.Conservator 1967–78 & Conservator 1979–91, of Forests, Forest Dept, Sri Lanka; Consult.in For.& Envt, and Vis.F. ARTI 1991–, For.& Cons.Activist 1993–. **Achievements:** introduced participatory for.& forest extension for first time to Forest Dept., and concept of for. into integrated district rural dev.; increased nr of Forest Divs from seven to 18 when Conservator of Forests. **Memberships:** SLAAS (Life), UNASL (Life), Wadham Coll.Soc. Oxf.(Life), I.Biol.of Sri Lanka (F.& Memb.of Council), ISTF (VP), WLNPS (Sri Lanka). **Publications:** 29 incl.*Nat. Forest Policy Dev.in Sri Lanka* 1982, *Mgmt of Fuelwood Resources as a Source of Domestic Energy & Wood Energy Supply in Asia* 1983, *For.Res.Needs of Developing Countries* 1984, *Cons. Prot.& Mgmt of the Sinharaja Forest* 1985, *Wood Energy Systems for Rural & Other Industries in Sri Lanka* 1986, *Forest Hist.of Sri Lanka* 1987, *Cons.of the Knuckles Range of Forests* 1988, *Agrofor.Systems in Sri Lanka* 1990, *Forest Plantations in 22 Countries of the Asia Pacific Regn* 1992, *The Role of For.in Envl Dev.*1992; num.articles. No objection to pers.pub., favours news media support. **Languages:** English, French (read & understood), Sinhala. Willing to act as consult.etc. **Address:** 1/1 Mahindarama, Mawatha, Colombo 10, Sri Lanka. **Tel.**(office) 94 1 696 743, (home) 94 1 694882; **fax** 94 1 692423.

NASH, Nancy. Wildlife conservation; environmental ethics; public awareness. Consultant. *B.*7 May 1943, USA. American. **Experience:** cons. reporting in intl journals; res.into religious perceptions of Nature; co-Founder of and full-time consult.to WWF Hong Kong 1981–5; founded Buddhist Perception of Nature 1985. **Career:** advertising, public relations & marketing for commercial clients, hotels, airlines, etc. 1965–75; journalism specializing in envt 1975–; Consult. WWF Intl 1979–81 & WWF HK 1985–; Founder, Buddhist Perception of Nature 1985–; Consult. re.public awareness, UNEP 1991–. **Achievements:** designed & carried out first NGO official contact with China 1979, estab.of Buddhist Perception of Nature 1985. **Memberships:** SWG, Assisi Nature Council, Earth Ethics Res.Group, Wildfowl & Wetlands Trust, WorldWIDE (Women for Nature), Global Network on Responsibilities to Future Generations. **Awards:** Rolex 1987, Mermaid of Ecol.1987, Global 500 Roll of Honour (UNEP) 1993. **Publications:** *Tree of Life: Buddhism and Prot. of Nature* 1987, *The Man with the Key is Not Here: A Key to What they Really Mean in China* (co-Author) 1991; several travel guides on Asia. Indiff.to pers.pub., favours news media support. **Language:** English. Willing to act as consult. etc. **Address:** 5H Bowen Road, First Floor, Hong Kong. **Tel.**(office & home) 852 523 3464; **fax** 852 869 1619.

NAVEH, Professor Dr Zev. Landscape ecology, management, conservation, and restoration. Professor Emeritus of Landscape Ecology. *B.*2 Dec.1919, Amsterdam, The Netherlands. Israeli. *M.*Ziona: 2 *s.* **Education:** Hebrew U. MSc(Agron.) 1950, PhD(Range Ecol.) 1960. **Experience:** long-term in range res., mgmt, and dev., in Medit.plant ecol., and in landscape ecol.& cons.mgmt; guest lect.at many univs world-wide, participant in & invited lect.to num. confs., symp. & workshops. **Career:** Range Res.Sci. Vulcani Agricl Res.Inst.(Nev Yaar) 1950–62; Vis.Res.F. Sch.of For. UCB 1958–60; Range & Pasture Res.Sci. Agricl Res.Station of Northern Tanzania 1962–5; Consult. FAO 1969, Scientific Adv.1979, Vis.Prof.— UCB 1979 & 1989, Rutgers U.1986, San Diego SU 1988, and La Sapiense (U.of Rome) 1990; Sr Lect., Assoc.Prof.& Prof.1965–88, Prof.Emer.1988–, Israel Inst.of Tech. **Achievements:** pioneering res.in range mgmt & improvement, in reclamation of limestone quarries, in fire ecol.& landscape ecol., and in phototoxic effects of air pollutants in Israel & the Medit.; Memb. Adv. Cttee on Veg.Engg (Israel Min.of Agric.) 1966–70, co-Founder & -Chairman of ISEEQS 1970–72, Scientific Adv. to first Israel Parliamentary Cttee on Envt 1973–5, Adv.& Contrib.to high-sch.envl educ. teaching prog.(Israel Min.of Educ.) 1972–7, Memb.of Adv.Bd on Envl Qual.(Haifa Municipality) 1979–82, co-Founder & Scientific Dir of Envl Educ.Teacher Training & High Sch. Project (Desert Res.Inst.of Ben Gurion U.of the Negev at Sdeh Boker) 1976–9, Founder & Dir of Ecol Gdn (Israel Inst.of Tech.) 1981–88; Memb. of Adv. Edl Bds of *Agric.& Envt* 1979–82, *Agric., Ecosystems & Envt* 1981–4, *Forest Ecol.& Mgmt* 1981–90, *Landscape Ecol.*1987–,

*Restoration Ecol.*1992–, *Intl J.of Envl Mgmt* 1994–. **Memberships:** IUCN Comm.on Ecol. 1982–91 & CESP 1991– (Founder & Chairman, Landscape Cons.& Ecol.WG 1991–3), ISEEQS (co-Founder & co-Chairman 1970–72), ESA, IALE, ISOMED, Israel SNP, SRE. **Awards:** Henrietta Szold Prize (Hebrew U.) 1946, Bursary (Brit.Council) 1958, Vis.Res.Sci.F'ship (USA AS/NRC) 1958–60, Henri Gutwirth Fund for Promotion of Res.(Israel Inst.of Tech.) 1985, Disting.Memb.(ISOMED) 1987. **Publications:** four books incl.*Landscape Ecol.*(first English textbook) 1984, *Landscape Ecol., Theory & Applications* 1993 (second edn of former). Favours pers.pub.& news media support. **Languages:** English, French (read), German, Hebrew. **Address:** Faculty of Agricultural Engineering, Technion — Israel Institute of Technology, Haifa 3200, Israel. **Tel.**(office) 972 4 292620, (home) 972 4 245029; **fax** 972 4 221581.

NAYAR, Dr M.Param. Conservation; taxonomic botany, endangered plant species, endemism; biodiversity, phytogeography; mangroves, wetlands. National Environment Fellow, Emeritus Scientist. *B.*27 Jan.1932, Nagercoil, TN, India. Indian. *M.*Lakshmi: *d.* **Education:** U.of Kerala MSc 1955; U.of London PhD 1966. **Experience:** res.— flora of Western Ghats 1957–61, at Herbarium at R.Botanic Gdns Kew 1961–7, and survey & admin.for Botl Survey of India 1967–90. **Career:** Bot. R.Botanic Gdns Kew 1961–7, Keeper, C.Nat.Herbarium (Calcutta) 1968–77; Dep.Dir, Jt Dir, Dir, 1977–90, Emer.Sci.1990–, Botl Survey of India; Pitamber Pant Nat.Envt F. Trop.Botanic Gdns & Res. Inst.1994–. **Achievements:** pubns on endemic & endangered plants, taxonomy, keystone species in prot.areas, biodiv., flora of Western Ghats. **Memberships:** Envt Resources Rcs. Centre (Pres.1991–), ISCB (Pres.1994–), Life Memb.of IAAT, IBS, Zoo Out Reach Orgn, & INSONA. **Awards:** Sci.Emer.(Botl Survey of India) 1990–, Pitamber Pant Nat.Envt F.1994–, F.Indian NAS. **Publications:** 18 books incl. *Key Works to the Taxonomy of Flowering Plants* (five vols) 1984–6, *The Endemic Flora of Indian Regn* 1986, *Mangroves in India* 1990, *Econ. Plants of India* 1989, 1994, *Network of Botl Gdns* (Ed.) 1987, *Red Data Book of Indian Plants* (three vols) 1987, 1988, 1990; *c.*250 papers. Favours pers.pub.if it helps cons.cause. **Languages:** English, Hindi, Malayalam. Further details may be obtained from *India's Personages* (Vol.I) 1986. Willing to act as consult.&/or ref. **Address:** Tropical Botanic Garden & Research Institute, Palode PO, Trivandrum 695 562, Kerala, India. **Tel.**(office) 91 472 84226, (home) 91 471 340185; **fax** 91 471 437230.

NAYVE-ROSSI, Dr Portia A. Ecology, sustainable agriculture, health, bionutrition. Research Director & Lecturer. *B.*18 Oct.1936, Naga City, Camarines Sur, Bicol Bioregion, Philippines. Filipino. *M.*Basil A.Rossi (partner in ecol activities). **Education:** Ateneo de Manila, M(Eng.

Lit.) 1959; Philippine Women's U. M(Educ.) 1961, M(Envl Mgmt) 1980; U.of the Philippines, M(Comparative Lit.) 1969; Life Sci.Inst. (TX), Dr of Nutritional & Health Scis 1980; Emerson Coll.of Herbology, M.Herbology 1983; U.of Nueva Caceres (Naga City), currently studying for Dr of Educ. **Experience:** waste mgmt, vermicomposting, sheep-raising, humane animal husbandry, on-the-job training, lecturing, consulting. **Career:** Teacher of Lit. –1976; Res.Dir of Ecol Learning Centre & Lect.at Inst.of Sust.Rural Dev.Fndn Inc. 1976–. **Achievements:** introduced first recycling conf.in Philippines 1976, made first Nat.Waste Study of Philippine recyclable wastes, put up first integrated farm on humane & sust.agric., founded Ecology Learning Centre. **Memberships:** num. incl.IWM, ISTF, IWF, Nat.Audubon Soc., Theosophical Soc.of the Philippines, Global Educ. Assocs, Asian Recycling Assn. **Awards:** World Ecologism Award (USA) 1989, Woman of the Envt (Nat.Fedn of Women's Clubs of the Philippines) 1993. **Publications:** *Recycling and Non Waste Tech.*1979, *Enc.of Alternative Crops for the Tropics & Subtropics* (ten vols). Favours pers.pub. **Language:** English. Willing to act as consult.etc. **Address:** Progresong Samahan ng Pilipino (Prosamapi), Isarog Farms, Palestina, Pili, Camarines Sur, Bicol Bioregion, Philippines.

NDINGA, Dr Assitou. Conservation of fauna; forest policy. Programme Officer. *B.*29 July 1952, Brazzaville, Congo. Congolese. *M.*Irina. 3 *s.* **Education:** U.of Leningrad, M(Biol.) 1979, PhD(Biol.) 1982. **Experience:** res., admin., consult.to GTZ, WWF, ACCT. **Career:** Asst in Biol. U.of Congo 1982–; Adv.1984–8, Dir 1988–91, Fauna Cons. Ministère des Eaux et Forêts (Congo); Prog.Officer, IUCN (Congo) 1991–. **Memberships:** IUCN CNPPA & CESP. **Award:** Order of Merit (Congo). **Publications:** several, in French. Dislikes pers. pub., indiff.to news media support. **Languages:** English (good), French, Russian. Willing to act as consult.etc. **Address:** 50 bis Rue Dongou Ouenze, Brazzaville, Congo. **Tel.**(office & home) 242 820237; **fax** 242 821448.

NDUKU, Dr Willie Kusezwani. National parks and wildlife management. Department Director. *B.*2 June 1939, Chipinge, Zimbabwe. Zimbabwean. *M.*Stella: 4 *s., d.* **Education:** U.of London, BSc(Zool.& Chem.) 1964; U.of Waterloo MSc(Biol.) 1970, PhD(Biol.) 1973; U.of Michigan, Cert.in Resource Mgmt & Econ. Dev.1982; grad.courses at U.of Waterloo in limnol., physiol., & parasitology, 1969–73. **Experience:** res., admin., lecturing. **Career:** Grad. Asst, Snail Ecol.Unit, UC of Rhodesia & Nyasaland 1965; Professional Officer, ARC of C.Africa 1966–8 and Dept of Res.& Specialist Services, Min.of Agric.1968; SRF U.of Rhodesia 1973–6; Dir of Hydrobiol.Res.Unit, U.of Zimbabwe 1977–80; Dep.Dir 1981–7, Dir 1987–, Dept of Nat.Parks & Wild Life Mgmt. **Memberships:** ASLO 1969–; SIL 1976–, UNESCO MAB Nat.Cttee 1982– & MAB

Bur.(also Rapp.) 1989–92 and Standing Cttee on Sci.& Tech.(Chairman) 1989–, Nat.Parks Bd 1978–, Envl Assn (Zimbabwe) 1978–81, Scientific Assn 1974– & Council 1987– of Zimbabwe, Cttee for Agrofor.Res.& Ext.1986–, Focal Point: African Lake and R.Basin Cttee (of SADC) 1987–; Edl Cttee *Zimbabwe J.of Agricl Res.* 1982–. **Awards:** three nat.— Appreciation & Merit 1990, Cons.1990, Rhino & Elephant Fndn 1990. **Publications:** num.incl.*Wildlife and Human Welfare* (co-Author) 1985, Wildlife Mgmt and the Role of Nat.Parks in Zimbabwe 1987, Dev.of the Zimbabwe NCS for Black Rhinoceros *[Diceros bicornis]* (co-Author) 1991. Indiff.to pers. pub.& news media support. **Languages:** English, Shona (Zimbabwe). Further details may be obtained from *Who is Who in Zimbabwe* 1992. Willing to act as consult.etc. **Address:** 29 Twickenham Drive, PO Mount Pleasant, Harare, Zimbabwe. **Tel.**(office) 263 4 724027, (home) 263 4 301766; **fax** 263 4 724914.

NDYAKIRA, Ntamuhiira Amooti. Environmental journalism. Senior Writer. *B.*25 Oct.1956, Uganda. Ugandan. *M.*Beatrace: 2 *s.*, 2 *d.* **Education:** Makerere U. BA(Hons) 1981; IIMC Postgrad.Dipl.in Journalism 1990. **Experience:** journalism, writing. **Career:** Reporter, *Uganda Times* 1982–3; Chief Reporter, *The People* 1983–5; Sr Writer, *Weekly Topic* 1985–7; Sr Writer for *Envl Health, The New Vision* 1987–; contrib.*WWF Features* 1994–. **Achievements:** fought wildlife traffickers of endangered species etc.*e.g.*Gorilla *(Gorilla gorilla)*, Chimpanzee *(Anthropopithecus troglodytes)*, ivory; exposed mismgmt of cons.areas & caused change in policy & practice; exposed bureaucratic & pol. corruptions in wildlife mgmt. **Memberships:** Uganda Journalists' Assn, Health Press Assn of Uganda, Wildlife Clubs of Uganda (Trustee). **Awards:** Journalist of the Yr 1992, Investigative Journalist of the Yr 1992, Global 500 Roll of Honour (UNEP) 1993. **Publications:** num.press articles, nat.& intl. Favours pers.pub.& news media support. Willing to act as consult.etc. **Address:** The New Vision Newspapers, POB 9815, Kampala, Uganda. **Tel.**256 41 235209, 870, or 872 or 251101; **fax** 256 41 235843 or 221.

NEEL, Dr James VAN GUNDIA. Population genetics. Lee R.Dice Distinguished Professor of Human Genetics, Emeritus, and Professor of Internal Medicine, Emeritus. *B.*22 March 1915, Hamilton, OH, USA. American. *M.*Priscilla: 2 *s., d.* **Education:** U.of Rochester PhD 1939, MD 1944. **Experience:** 50 yrs' teaching, res., & consult., re.var.aspects of human genetics. **Career:** academic in teaching & res. punctuated by extensive field-work in Japan, Africa, & S.Amer. **Achievements:** prin.pertinent pers. endeavours such as 47-yrs' involvement in study of genetic effects of atomic bombs, leading to conclusion that humans are not as sensitive to the genetic effects of radiation as projected from murine experiments. **Memberships:** NAS, Inst.of Medicine, Amer.AAS, APS, AAP, RSM,

ASHG (Pres.1952–3), IGES (Pres.1992–3). **Awards:** Pres.ICHG 1981, US Nat.Medal of Sci.1975, Lasker Award (APHA) 1960, Allan Award (ASHG) 1965, Conte Award (Conte Inst.for Envl Health) 1991. **Publications:** *Human Heredity* (co-Author) 1954, *The Effects of Inbreeding on Japanese Children* (co-Author) 1965, *The Children of Atomic Bomb Survivors: A Genetic Study* (co-Ed.) 1991, *Physician to the Gene Pool* 1994. Selective re.pers.pub.& news media support. **Language:** English. Further details may be obtained from *Who's Who in Amer.*1994. Willing to act as consult.etc. **Address:** Department of Human Genetics, M4708 Medical Science II Building 0618, 1137 Catherine, University of Michigan, Ann Arbor, Michigan 48109-0618, USA. **Tel.**(office) 1 313 763 9312, (home) 1 313 994 5933; **fax** 1 313 763 3784.

NELSON, Professor Dr James Gordon. Research & education re.land-use resources, environment; special interest in parks & protected areas, coastal areas; assessment of human ecological perspective. Professor of Geography & Planning, & Centre Chairman. *B.*3 April 1932, Hamilton, Canada. Canadian. *M.*Shirley Ann Hutton: 2 *s., d.* **Education:** McMaster U. BA(Hons) 1955, U.of Colorado MHA 1957, Johns Hopkins U. PhD 1959. **Experience:** 35 yrs as teacher, researcher, educator, consult.; educl & res.admin.; citizen participation in public affairs esp.re.land-use cons. **Career:** Asst, Assoc., & Prof., Calgary 1960–71 & Western 1971 –5 Univs and U.of Waterloo 1975–; Consult.to govt, NGOs & private groups re.land-use, resources, envt 1964–; var.admin.posts incl. Dean of Faculty of Envl Studies 1975–83, Chairman of Heritage Resources Centre 1986–, U.of Waterloo. **Achievements:** 200+ pubns, supervision of 55 MA & PhD students, contribn to dev.of cons./res./envt as a field of study in Canadian univs and to land-use, resource & envt, heritage policy/practice in Canada and other countries. **Memberships:** CAG, AAG, F.RGS. **Awards:** Natural Heritage Award (DoE) 1978, Disting. Scholarship Award (CAG) 1983, Massey Medal (RCGS) 1993, F.RCGS 1993, Waterloo Regn Envl Award 1994. **Publications:** over 200 incl. *Man's Impact on the Western Canadian Landscape* 1976, *Tourism and Sust. Dev., Monitoring, Planning, Managing* 1993, *Public Issues: A Geogl Perspective* (co-Ed.) 1994; monogrs, edited papers & reports. Dislikes pers.pub., opinion of news media support depends on topic. **Languages:** English, French (fair). Further details may be obtained from *Canadian Who's Who* 1995. Willing to act as consult.etc.as time & resources permit. **Address:** Department of Geography, University of Waterloo, Waterloo, Ontario N2L 3G1, Canada. **Tel.**(office) 1 519 885 1211 ext.4555, (home) 1 519 888 7043; **fax** 1 519 746 2031.

NEPAL, Sanjay Kumar. Parks and protected areas, wildlife & heritage conservation; ecotourism, community-based tourism; rural development planning, regional environmental planning. Research Specialist. *B*.18 Nov.1962, Kathmandu, Nepal. Nepalese. *M*.Stella Amor F.: *s*. **Education:** Tribhuvan U. MA(Geog.) 1984; AIT, MSc (Rural Regnl Dev.Planning) 1991. **Experience:** over two yrs of involvement in res.re.ground-water resource dev., one yr in study of small market centres, six yrs in parks & prot. areas and wildlife cons., recently in sust.tourism; attended several intl workshops, confs, & training courses, on ecolly sust.dev., tourism, envl conflict resolution, and envt & dev. **Career:** Field Super.& Coord. Nissaku Co.Ltd 1984–6; Res.Asst, CEDA 1987–8; Rural Dev. Officer, Rastriya Banijya Bank 1988–90; Res. Assoc.1992–4, Res.Specialist 1994–5, AIT; Researcher, Swiss Fndn for Alpine Res.1995–. **Achievements:** several scholarly articles on hydropower dev., wildlife cons., and conflict resolution; intl workshop & conf.papers re.ecol tourism, tourism impacts, and conflict resolution. **Memberships:** NGS (ISA & Nepal), AIT Alumni Assn. **Awards:** Scholarship (CIDA) 1990–91. **Publications:** incl.*Struggle for Existence: Park–People Conflict in the R.Chitwan Nat.Park, Nepal* (co-Author) 1993, *Mgmt of Prot.Areas Under Conditions of Conflict* (co-Ed.) 1995; num.j.articles. **Languages:** English, Hindi, Nepalese. **Address:** Swiss Foundation for Alpine Research, Binzstrasse 23, CH-8045 Zürich, Switzerland. **Tel.**41 1 461 0147; **fax** 41 1 287 1368.

NEWMAN, Dr Edward Irvine. Research on sustainability of ecosystems especially agricultural systems. Senior Research Fellow. *B*.20 Oct.1935, Camb., England, UK. British. *M*.: *s*., 2 *d*. **Education:** U.of Camb. MA 1962, PhD 1962; U.of Bristol DSc 1979. **Experience:** res. & u.teaching on many aspects of ecol. **Career:** Lect.in Bot. U.Coll.of Wales (Aberystwyth) 1960–69 & U.of Bristol 1969–79; Reader in Ecol.1979–93, Sr Res.F.1993–, U.of Bristol. **Achievements:** training & enthusing students; res.on control of diversity; nutrient cycling, soil water, etc. **Memberships:** IEEM, BES. **Publications:** *Applied Ecol.*1993, more than 50 res.& review papers. Indiff.to pers.pub.& news media support. **Language:** English. Willing to act as consult.etc. **Address:** School of Biological Sciences, University of Bristol, Bristol BS8 1UG, England, UK. **Tel.**(office) 44 1272 303755; **fax** 44 1272 257374.

NEWTON, Dr Adrian Christopher. Forest conservation, genetic resources, resource ecology. Lecturer in Forest Resource Ecology. *B*. 13 June 1964, Manchester, England, UK. British. *M*. Lynn. **Education:** Clare Coll.Camb. BA 1985, PhD(Cantab.) 1989. **Experience:** res.& lecturing. **Career:** Higher to Sr Scientific Officer, ITE 1989–94; Lect.in Forest Resource Ecol. Inst.of Ecol.& Resource Mgmt, U.of Edinburgh 1994–. **Achievements:** pubns, co-Ed.of *Trop.Trees: ...**. **Memberships:** F.LS, BES. **Publications:**

over 30 res.incl.Genetic variation in mahoganies: its importance, capture & utilization (co-Author) 1993, **Trop.Trees: The Potential for Domestication* (co-Ed.) 1994. Dislikes pers.pub., favours news media support. **Languages:** English, Spanish (spoken). Willing to act as consult.etc. **Address:** Institute of Ecology & Resource Management, University of Edinburgh, Darwin Building, Mayfield Road, Edinburgh EH9 3JH, Scotland, UK. **Tel.**44 131 650 5419; **fax** 44 131 662 0478; **e-mail** A.NEWTON@ED.AC.UK .

NICHOLLS, Frank Gordon. Environmental law. Managing Director. *B*.1 Jan.1916, Melbourne, Australia. Australian. *M*.Yvonne Isabel. **Education:** Melbourne Boys' High Sch.; U.of Melbourne MSc 1936. **Experience:** res. into upper atmos., ecol surveys; admin.as Res. Sec. CSIRO, estab.of ASRCT, & Dep.DG IUCN. **Career:** Radio Res.Bd 1936–40, Australian & NZ Sci.Liaison (London) 1940–44, Asst.Sec.to Res.Sec. CSIRO 1945–70, Spec. Gov. ASRCT 1960–70, Dep.DG IUCN 1970–76, Managing Dir Trans Knowledge Assocs Pty Ltd 1977–. **Achievements:** in-depth study of dry sclerophyl forest (Thailand), prin.draftsman for nr of intl cons.treaties. **Memberships:** F.IESANZ, RACI, AIP, ICEL, Chartered Chemist. **Award:** Commander, Most Noble Order of the Crown of Thailand. **Publications:** num scientific papers. **Languages:** English, French, Thai; German, Italian, & Spanish (all read). Further details may be obtained from *Who's Who in Australia* 1995. Willing to judge proposals &/or ref.papers. **Address:** 61/4 Sydney Street, Prahran, Victoria 3181, Australia. **Tel.**(office) 61 3 9510 6611, (home) 61 3 9510 6339.

NIEMITZ, Professor Dr Carsten. Primatology; Nature conservation; evolution of communication. Professor of Human Biology and Anthropology & Institute Head. *B*.29 Sept.1945, Dessau, Germany. German. **Education:** U.of Freiburg, BSc(Biol.) 1968; U.of Giessen, MSc 1970, PhD 1974; U.of Göttingen, MB 1975, first part of final exam.in human med.1978. **Experience:** res.— primatology (captive & field, over two yrs in Sarawak, several expedns to Indonesia) and anatomy; tech.— professional filming, Visual Flight Rules pilot licence, radio features; admin.— Inst.Head and Insts' Acting Dir; teaching — human biol., anatomy, zool., human ecol., & Nature cons., from BSc to Habil.level; cons.— prot.of captive primates. **Career:** Researcher, Max-Planck Inst.for Brain Res.1968–71; Scientific Asst in Anatomy, U.of Göttingen 1971–4; Prof.of Human Biol.& Anthrop.and Head of Inst.for Anthrop.& Human Biol. Freie Universität Berlin 1978–. **Achievements:** primate prot.campaigns, campaigns for cons.of trop rain-forests; public educ.on cons. issues, radio progs; transl.& revision of *The Human Impact on the Natural Envt* by A.Goudie. **Memberships:** Deutsche Gesellschaft für Tropenökologie, Humboldt Gesellschaft (Presidential Bd), IPS, IUCN SSC Primates & Captive

Breeding SGs, Primatologische Gesellschaft, Intl F.Explorers' Club, F.Borneo Res.Council. **Awards:** several f'ships and memberships of presidential bds of scientific assns, Pres.of Gesellschaft für Anthropologie 1994–. **Publications:** books incl.*The Rainforest Book* (in German) 1990; other pubns, films, scientific papers. **Languages:** English, French, German; Indonesian, Italian, & Spanish (basic knowledge). Further details may be obtained from *Who's Who in the World* 1991. Willing to act as consult.etc. **Address:** Institut für Humanbiologie, Freie Universität Berlin, Fabeckstrasse 15, 14195 Berlin, Germany. **Tel.**49 30 838 2900; **fax** 49 30 838 6556.

NIKULIN, Professor Dr Valery Alexander. Hydroaerodynamics; ecology & resource conservation; applied mathematics. Director-General. *B.*1 Jan.1951, Izhevsk, Russia. Russian. *M.*Carolina: 2 *d.* **Education:** Moscow Higher Tech.Sch. Dipl.in Mech.Eng.1972; Moscow SU CSc 1979, Mech.Engg Inst. DSc 1989. **Experience:** res.— hydroaerodynamics, theory of turbulence, ecol.& resource cons.; applied maths; admin.— DG of Joint-stock Ecol.Russian Assn & of ISAR AERO, Pres. Regnl Centre of Ecol.Insurance 'Sapsan-AERO', consult.on hydroaerodynamics, phys., applied maths, ecol., & resource cons. **Career:** Soviet Army Officer 1972–4; Researcher, U.of Donetsk 1974–80; Docent, Applied Maths Dept, Donetsk Poly.Inst.1980–84; Head, Dept of Hydraulics & Heat Tech. Izhevsk State Tech.U. 1984–; DG, ISAR AERO 1989–; Prof.& Pres.of Higher Coll. AEROMech 1992–. **Achievements:** improvement of air in cities & towns of Udmurtia on basis of math.modelling of wind regime & turbulent transfer of polluting impurities; purification of sewage from heavy-metals' salts; ecol monitoring. **Memberships:** REA (Corres.Memb.1993, Chairman, Udmurt Branch), Chairman ISC on Phys.Problems of Ecol Nature Mgmt & Resources Cons. **Publications:** *c.*100 papers. Indiff.to pers.pub., favours news media support. **Languages:** English, German (better at written), Russian. Willing to act as consult.etc. **Address:** POB 3011, Izhevsk 426008, Russia. **Tel.**(office) 8 3412 238797 or 728, (home) 8 3412 255702; **fax** 8 3412 787010.

NILSSON, Professor Dr Sten. Natural resources, exploitation of natural resources; environment (forest sector); sustainability economics, systems analysis, policies. Professor in Economic Planning, Project Leader. *B.*15 July 1944, Lund, Sweden. Swedish. **Education:** Coll.of For. M(For.) 1971, Swedish U.of Agricl Scis D(For.) 1975. **Experience:** res.since 1971 in Sweden, Canada, & Austria; admin.as Prof. and Project Leader; consult.since 1975 with Euro.& N.Amer.forest industries, ECE, FAO, EC, OECD, World Bank. **Career:** Project Leader 1971–5, Prof.in Econ.Planning 1975–, Swedish U.of Agricl Scis; Scientific Leader

FEPA Inst., UBC 1983–4; Leader, For.& Climate Change Projects, IIASA 1986–. **Achievements:** assisting Swedish Govt on forest & sci.policies, and intl orgns on forest policies & sust. **Memberships:** RSAAS, SCAI. **Award:** Scientific Achievement Award (IUFRO) 1986. **Publications:** Euro.forest decline: the effects of air pollutants & suggested remedial policies 1991, Mtn world in danger: climate change in the mtns & forests of Europe 1991, *The Forest Resources of the Former Euro.USSR* 1992, *Future Forest Resources of Western & Eastern Europe* 1992, Envl impacts of waste paper recycling 1993. Favours pers.pub.& news media support. **Languages:** English, German (written & spoken), Swedish. Willing to act as consult.etc. **Address:** Forestry & Climate Change Project, International Institute for Applied Systems Analysis, A-2361 Laxenburg, Austria. **Tel.**43 2236 71521 ext.220; **fax** 43 2236 71313.

NISHIOKA, Dr Shuzo. Global & regional environmental management, environmental systems analysis. Centre Director. *B.*8 Dec.1939, Tokyo, Japan. Japanese. *M.*Reiko Sato: 2 *s.* **Education:** Tokyo U. B.(Mech.Eng.) 1962, M.Eng.1964, Dr Eng. 1967. **Experience:** res. — control engr, systems analysis, urban envl mgmt; tech.— chem.plant construction; admin.— res.team, mgmt for Nat.Inst.for Envl Studies; consult.for UNDP, UNEP, Govt of Japan. **Career:** Systems Engr, Asahi Chem.Co. 1967–74; Corporate Planner, Asahi Res.Center 1975–9; Sr Researcher 1979–, Dir of Center for Global Envl Res.1990–, Nat.Inst.for Envl Studies. **Achievements:** envl planning info.systems for local govt, modelling for urban traffic control, IPCC Report editing & chairing and prep.of IPCC impact assessment guidelines. **Memberships:** JSC (IGBP Cttee), JSES, JSCE. **Publications:** more than ten books and 300 articles incl.*Envl Indicators* I 1986, II 1995, *Impact Assessment for Energy* (IPCC Report) 1990, *Potential Inpact of Climate Change in Japan* 1992, *IPCC Tech.Guidelines for Assessing Climate Change Impact and Adaptation* 1994. Favours pers.pub.& news media support. **Languages:** English, Japanese. Willing to act as consult.etc. **Address:** Center for Global Environmental Research, National Institute for Environmental Studies, Onogawa 16-2, Tsukuba 305, Japan. **Tel.**(office) 81 298 502345, (home) 81 298 517277; **fax** 81 298 582645.

NJE, Dr Ngog. Terrestrial animal ecology. Director. *B.*14 June 1948, Kikot, Cameroon. Cameroonian. *M.*Ngo Mbei (biol.): 5 *s.*, 2 *d.* **Education:** U.of Paris VI, PhD(Animal Ecol.) 1981. **Experience:** res., admin., consult. **Career:** Lect., Asst Dir then Dir, Ecole de Faune, Garoua 1981–. **Achievement:** training technicians in mgmt of prot.areas. **Memberships:** IUCN CNPPA & SSC, Conv.on the Cons.of Migratory Species of Wild Animals, Conseil Intl de la Chasse et de la Cons.du Gibier. **Public-**

ations: *The Ecol.of Giraffe* [Giraffa camelopardalis] *in Waza Nat. Park* 1981, contribn to *The Biol.of Hippopotamus in the Benoue Nat.Park, Cameroon* 1988. Indiff.to pers.pub.& news media support. **Languages:** English, French. Willing to act as consult.etc. **Address:** Ecole de Faune, BP 271, Garoua, Cameroon. **Tel.**(office) 237 27 1135, (home) 237 27 1424.

NOBLE, Dr Ralph. Prevention of odour & water pollution from composting, controlled environment composting for mushroom cultivation, cultivation of different *Agaricus* spp.mushrooms. Senior Scientific Officer. *B.*12 Dec. 1958, Liverpool, England, UK. British. *M.* Lidia. **Education:** Reading U. BSc(Hons.) 1980, Cranfield Inst.of Tech. PhD 1984. **Experience:** 14 yrs' res.in agron., composting of organic wastes for mushroom cultivation, poll.-free composting; culture of *Agaricus* mushrooms. **Career:** Researcher, Cranfield Inst. of Tech.1980–84 and Bonn U.1984; Adv. Officer, MAFF (UK) 1984–9; SSO, HRI 1989–. **Achievements:** dev.of controlled composting system for mushroom cultivation; determining cultural & substrate requirements of wild *Agaricus* mushroom species. **Membership:** IHort. **Publications:** 30+ major. Favours pers. pub., indiff.to news media support. **Languages:** Dutch (read), English, German, Polish (read). Willing to act as consult.etc. **Address:** Department of Microbial Biotechnology, Horticulture Research International, Wellesbourne, Warwickshire CV35 9EF, England, UK. **Tel.**(office) 44 1789 470382, (home) 44 1903 691232; **fax** 44 1789 470552.

NORDERHAÜG, Magnar. Ornithology; ecology; global environmental trends. Executive Director. *B.*21 July 1939, Tönsberg, Norway. Norwegian. *M.*Ann Cecile: *d., s.*Kjell Magnus (biol.). **Education:** U.of Oslo, BSc(Ecol.) 1967. **Experience:** arctic wildlife res.(Norwegian Polar Res.Inst.), planning, estab., & mgmt, of cons.areas (Norwegian Min.of Envt); ecol.in foreign aid (NORAD). **Career:** Wildlife Biol. Norwegian Res.Inst.1967–72; Cons.Inspector, Norwegian Min.of Envt 1973–85; Ecol Adv. Norwegian Min.of Dev.Coopn 1985–9; Exec. Dir, Worldwatch Inst.Norden 1989–. **Achievements:** resp.for planning of nat.parks & Nature reserves in Svalbard during which ten yrs estab.35,000 sq.km of cons.area, and for estab.of system for Nature reserves in Norway. **Awards:** var.nat. cons.awards. **Publications:** 15 books incl.[The Birds of Svalbard] 1988, [Envl Frontlines] 1992, [Too Many?] 1994 (all in Norwegian); num.scientific pubns. Dislikes pers.pub., favours news media support. **Languages:** English, French (some), German (some), Norwegian. **Address:** Worldwatch Institute, POB 588, 3101 Tönsberg, Norway. **Tel.**47 333 10544; **fax** 47 333 10566.

NORDIN Hj. HASAN, Prof.Mohammed, *see* **HASAN, Prof.Mohammed NORDIN Hj.**

NORTON, Professor Dr Bryan G. Sustainability theory and obligations to future generations; valuation methodologies for policy analysis, analysis of biodiversity policy. Professor of Philosophy, Associated Scientist. *B.*19 July 1944, Marshall, MI, USA. American. **Education:** U.of Michigan, BA(Pol.Sci.) 1966, PhD(Phil.) 1970. **Experience:** res.— endangered species and biodiv.policy, eval.methods and sust.metrics. **Career:** Lect.in Phil. U.of Florida 1970–88; Res.Assoc. Inst.for Phil.and Public Policy, U.of Maryland 1981–2; Gilbert White F., Resources for the Future (Washington, DC) 1985–6; Prof.of Phil.of Sci.and Tech. Sch.of Social Scis 1988–91 and Sch.of Public Policy 1991–, Georgia Inst.of Tech.; Associated Sci. Zoo Atlanta 1989–. **Achievements:** formed WGs on preserv.of species and on ethical issues in captive breeding progs, pubns. **Memberships:** Amer.Phil.Assn, SCB, Intl Socs for Ecol Econ.and Envl Ethics. **Awards:** F'ship (Resources for the Future) 1985, res.support from num.nat.instns *e.g.*NSF, USEPA, USFS. **Publications:** five books incl.*Ecosystems Health: New Goals for Envl Mgmt* (Ed.) 1992, *Ethics on the Ark: Zoos, Animal Welfare, and Wildlife Cons.*(co-Ed.) 1995; num.j.articles incl.Scale and biodiv.policy: a hierarchical approach (co-Author) 1992, Evaluating ecosystem states: two competing paradigms 1995. Indiff.to pers.pub & news media support. **Languages:** English, French (some read). May be willing to act as consult.etc. **Address:** School of Public Policy, Georgia Institute of Technology, Atlanta, Georgia 30332, USA. **Tel.**1 404 853 9305; **fax** 1 404 853 0535.

NOSEL, José. Protected areas, natural park development. Park Director. *B.*3 Jan.1947, Martinique. French. **Education:** U.of Martinique, Diplôme de Scis Economiques 1973; U.of Bordeaux, Diplôme de Scis Politiques 1974; training courses in business mgmt, envt, ornith., renewable energy, museology, & computer-use. **Experience:** orgnl, mgmt, teaching, admin., public fin., & law. **Career:** Lect. Univs Fort-de-France & Bordeaux; Gen.Sec. Community of Sainte Marie (Martinique); Dir, Regnl Natural Park. **Achievements:** creation of Natural Reserve of Presqu'Ile of the Caravelle, the Ornithology Reserve of Sainte Anne, and the Park for Intl Flower Show of Martinique; dev.of base for Nature leisure activities. **Memberships:** ACE, Assns for the Dev.of Renewable Energy & Alternative Tech.(Pres.), Dev.of Aquaculture in Martinique (VP), Training in Envt (Pres.), and Popular Arts & Traditions in Martinique (VP). **Awards:** Chevalier de l'Ordre Nat.du Mérite. **Publications:** *La Planification aux Antilles* 1974, *Développement et Environnement* 1984. **Languages:** Creole, English, French, Spanish. Willing to act as consult.etc. **Address:** Parc Naturel Régional, BP 437, Domaine de Tivoli, 97200 Fort-de-France Cedex, Martinique. **Tel.**(office) 19 596 644259; **fax** 19 596 647227.

NOUR, Professor Dr Hassan Osman ABDEL. Forestry, environmental conservation & rehabilitation; natural resource surveys; biomass energy, gums, ethnobotany, forest entomology; termites in forestry & buildings. General Manager, Board Member. *B*.1 Jan.1944, Abu Usher, Sudan. Sudanese. *M*.Shane: 3 *s*. **Education:** Hantoub Sec.Sch.; Aberdeen U. BSc (For.) 1967; Khartoum U. MSc(Entomol.) 1972, PhD 1978. **Experience:** res.on termites 1972–; admin., lecturing; consult.to FAO, ILO, UNDP, US AID. **Career:** Utilization Officer, Sudanese For.Dept 1967–72; Lect.in For. Sudan Coll.of For.1972–81; Sr Forest Officer, Blue Nile Province (Sudan) 1981–3; Dean, Coll.of Agricl Studies, Khartoum Poly.1985–9; Gen.Mgr, Forests Nat.Corpn 1989–; Chairman, Gum Arabic Dev.Corpn 1994; Bd Memb. Gum Arabic Co.1990–. **Achievements:** streamlining Sudanese forest admin., estab.of Forests Nat.Corpn leading to improvements in forest preservation, afforestation, popular participation, & raising nat., individual, & official, envl awareness; politicization of forestry. **Memberships:** ISTF, Inst.of Envl Studies (U.of Khartoum). **Publications:** co-Author of many monogrs incl.*The Effect of Water Absorbing Synthetic Polymers on Stomatal Conductance, Growth and Survival of Transplanted* E[ucalyptus] microtheca *Seedlings in Sudan* 1982, *Convincing Sudanese Decisionmakers to Adopt an Integrated Land-use Policy* 1983; num.papers. Favours pers.pub.& news media support. **Languages:** Arabic, English. Willing to act as consult.etc. **Address:** Forests National Corporation, POB 658, Khartoum, Sudan. **Tel.**(office) 249 11 451575 & 6.

NOVOA, Laura. Environmental law, sustainable development, implementation of Agenda 21, human rights, education for democracy, women, governability, poverty, partnerships with civil society organizations. Advisory Board Member. *B*.14 Nov.1930, Chuquicamata, Chile. Chilean. *M*.Gastón Anriquez (prot.of forests): 2 *s*. **Education:** U.of Chile, Lawyer 1953; U.of New York, Anglo-Amer.Law 1958–9. **Experience:** broad exp.in private practice mainly mining projects; activities for promotion of social values 1973–. **Career:** Lawyer in Chile of large US copper co.1954–69; Gen. Counsel 1970–78 & 1990–93 Corporación Nacional del Cobre de Chile; Private Practice 1979–89 & 1994–. **Achievements:** one of the eight members of Comm.for Truth and Reconciliation designated by Pres.Aylwin to investigate cases of death and disappearance during dictatorship of Pinochet; worked in resto.of democracy and in forging alliances of civil soc.orgns with UN system through questionnaire discussed with about 70 orgns; participation in innumerable events, seminars, workshops, on matters of public interest. **Memberships:** UN High Level Adv. Bd, Participa (Pres.of Bd), Comm.of Experts of Chilean Govt for Implementation in Chile of Agenda 21. **Award:** Keogh Award (U.of New York) 1991. Dislikes pers.pub.& news media support. **Languages:** English (good), Spanish. Willing to act as consult.etc. **Address:** Moneda 970 12th Floor, Santiago, Chile. **Tel.**(office) 562 698 2523, (home) 562 211 8565; **fax** 562 698 1484.

N'SOSSO, Dominique. Parks' and protected areas' management; environmental conservation. Project Manager. *B*.1949, Brazzaville, Congo. Congolese. *M*.Louise: 2 *s.*, *d*. **Education:** Forest Inst.of Cap Esterias, sec.tech. degree 1970; Garoua Wildlife Sch. (Cameroon), higher degree in mgmt of parks & prot.areas 1983. **Experience:** parks' & prot.areas' mgmt; envl cons.; monitoring wildlife study projects; wildlife law. **Career:** Second Chief, Wildlife Dept (For.& Water) 1970–76; Chief, Nature Cons.Dept (For.& Water) 1976–80, Dir of Parks & Prot. Areas 1983–8, Counc. For.& Water Min.1987–9, Dir of Parks & Prot.Areas 1989– 91, Project Mgr in charge of African Elephants 1991–, all at Direction Faune et Flore. **Achievements:** estab. of terr.prot.areas in the Congo and assessment of their values, writer of Congolese Wildlife Law 1983. **Memberships:** IUCN CNPPA & SSC, Forest Inst.of Cap Esterias. **Award:** Congolese Order of Merit 1986. **Publications:** *Etude Ecologique* [of Mont Fouari Prot.Areas] 1982, *Comportement du Lion en Captivité* 1982, *Etude de la Relation entre les Intérêts de la Cons.et de l'Exploitation Forestière* 1989, *Prot.Areas in Regnl Dev.*1993. Favours pers.pub.& news media support. **Languages:** English (poor), French, Spanish (poor). **Address:** Direction Faune et Flore, BP 2153, Brazzaville, Congo. **Tel.**242 831718; **fax** 242 832903 or 837363.

NTAHUGA, Dr Laurent. Protection of wildlife; environment & development; biodiversity issues. Associate Professor. *B*.10 Jan.1951, Gisigi, Burundi. Burundian. *M*.Marie-Thérèse: *s.*, 3 *d*. **Education:** U.of Marburg/Lahn, Staatsexamen in Biol.& Sport 1978; U.of Kassel, PhD(Biol.& Zool.) 1984. **Experience:** res.on inventory of vertebrates of Burundian nat.parks & natural reserves; teaching gen.zool., ornith., mammalogy. **Career:** Assoc.Prof. Dept of Biol.1984–91, 1993–, Dean Fac.Sci.1989–91, U.of Burundi; DG Institut Nat.pour l'Environnement et la Cons.de la Nature 1991–3. **Achievements:** acquired legal status of Burundian nat.parks & natural reserves. **Membership:** Burundi Nature (VP). **Awards:** Scholarship from Deutscher Akademischer Austauschdienst 1988. **Publications:** *Phénomène Migratoire des Oiseaux et son Impact sur l'Avifaune au Burundi* 1988, *Prot.de la Nature au Burundi* 1989, *Fauna protected in the plain of L. Tanganyika* 1991. Favours pers.pub.& news media support. **Languages:** English, French, German. Willing to act as consult. **Address:** Université du Burundi, Faculté des Sciences, BP 2700 Bujumbura, Burundi. **Tel.**(office) 257 22 5556, (home) 257 22 8312.

NUMATA, Professor Dr Makoto. Vegetation dynamics; grassland & bambooland ecology;

Nature conservaton and urban ecology. President, Director. *B.*27 Nov.1917, Tsuchiura City, Japan. Japanese. *M.*Sakado: 2 *d.* **Education:** Tokyo U.of Lit.& Sci.1942, Kyoto U. DSc 1953. **Experience:** coefficient of homogeneity; degree of succession, rate of succession; buried-seed pop. **Career:** Assoc.Prof. Chiba Normal Coll. 1945–50 and Chiba U.1950–83; Prof. Chiba U.and concurrently Tohoku U.Sendai 1964–75; Leader of Himalayan Expedns to E.Nepal 1963, 1971, 1975, 1981, 1985; Dean Fac.Sci.1968–80, Prof.Emer.1983–, Chiba U. **Achievements:** pubns; Pres.BSJ 1983 & NCSJ 1988, Dir Nat. Hist.Mus.& Inst.1989, Pres.EESJ 1990. **Memberships:** BSJ, ESJ (Pres.1979), HCS, NCSJ, WSSJ, ESA (Hon.1986), IAVS (Hon.1988). **Awards:** Prize for Nature Cons. (Govt of Japan) 1970, Purple Ribbon Medal for Ecol Res.(Emperor of Japan) 1983; Prince Chichibu Mem. Prize on Mtn Res.1984; Duke of Edinburgh Prize (Japan Acad.) 1988. **Publications:** *Methodology of Ecol.*1953, *The Biol Flora of Japan* (two vols) 1970, *Nature Cons.& Ecol.*1973, *The Flora & Veg.of Japan* 1974, *Dict.of Ecol.*1974, *The Naturalized Plants* 1975, *Ecol Studies in Japanese Grasslands* 1975, *Studies in Cons.of Natural Terr.Ecosystems in Japan* 1975, *Handbook of Nature Cons.*1976, *Ecol Grassland & Bamboolands in the World* 1979, *Biol.& Ecol.of Weeds* 1981, *Biota & Ecol.of Nepal* 1983, *Ecol.& Cons.*1990. Favours pers.pub.& news media support. **Languages:** English, German, Japanese. **Address:** 74–13 Benten-cho, Chuo-ku, Chiba 260, Japan. **Tel.**(office) 81 43 265 3111, (home) & **fax** 81 43 251 7664.

NUORTEVA, Professor Dr Pekka Olavi. Holistic aspects of environmental conservation (in a historical perspective of four thousand million years); the role of metals in forest decline; bioaccumulation of metals in biota, effects of methyl mercury on health; environmental & forensic entomology; subarctic biology. Professor Emeritus of Environmental Protection. *B.*24 Nov.1926, Helsinki, Finland. Finnish. *M.*Sirkka-Liisa MSc. (biol., rock-pool plankton): *s.*, 2 *d.* **Education:** Helsinki U. Dr Sci.(Ecol.& Physiol.Zool.) 1955, officially stated competences for professorships of physiol., med., & ecol, zool. **Experience:** res.on phytopath., salivary physiol. in insects, subarctic ecol., metal bioaccumulation in biota, forest death, med.& forensic entomol., blowfly biol.; admin.being chief of entomol. mus.and prof.of envl prot.; lecturing on entomol., parasitology (global), & med.zool.; attendee of num.intl congs; good rapport with radio & TV having given 100 speeches/interviews. **Career:** Res.Worker, Agricl Entomol. (salivary secretions of Hemiptera as degraders of baking qual.of wheat 1952–3; Asst on Animal Morphology & Ecol.1954–7 (oat damage by planthoppers); Custodian, Entomol.Mus.(synanthropic flies, med.& forensic entomol., subarctic biol.) 1958–72; Chief 1972–5, Prof.of Envl Cons.1974–93, Prof.Emer.1993–, U.of Helsinki. **Achievements:** dissertation on host-plant selection of Homoptera

1952, Pres.of Finnish Envl League at time when modern envlism was becoming known to Finnish soc., first Prof.of Envl Prot.at U.of Helsinki. **Memberships:** many nat.comms. **Awards:** some Finnish govtl awards, many chairmanships of intl congs & confs. **Publications:** many books in Finnish incl.[*Atlas of Finnish Animals*] I–II 1955 & 1957, [*Outlines of Zool.*] (co-Author) 1966, [*Zool.*] I–II for high-sch.children (co-Author) 1968–9, [*Mercury in Finnish Nature & Admin.*] 1976, Sarcosaprophagous insects as forensic indicators 1977, [*Mercury Rain*] (co-Author) 1979, For.in the field of envl prot.(co-Author) 1984, Metal distribn patterns and forest decline 1990, [*Christian Life with Nature*] (co-Author) 1991; *c.*260 scientific papers, *c.*520 newspaper items. Strongly favours pers.pub.& news media support. **Languages:** English, Finnish, German, Latin (weak), Swedish. Further details may be obtained from *Environmentalica Fennica, 16, 1993.* Willing to act as consult.etc. **Address:** Caloniuksen k.6 C 64, FIN-00100 Helsinki, Finland. **Tel.**(home) 358 0 442228; **fax** 358 0 708 5462.

NYE, Peter Hague. Soil–plant nutrient interactions, solute movement in soil; simulation modelling. Emeritus Reader. *B.*16 Sept.1921, Hove, Sussex, England, UK. British. *M.*Phyllis Mary: *s.*, 2 *d.* **Education:** Charterhouse; Balliol Coll.Oxf. MSc(Oxon) 1944. **Experience:** res. on above subjects. **Career:** Agricl Chemist, Gold Coast 1947–50; Lect.in Soil Sci. U.of Ibadan 1950–52, Sr Lect. U.of Ghana 1952–60; Res.Officer, IAEA 1960–61; Reader in Soil Sci.1961–88, Emer.1988–, U.of Oxf.; F.1965–88, Emer.1988–, St Cross Coll. Oxf. **Achievements:** an understanding of shifting cultivation and the way plants obtain nutrients from soil. **Memberships:** F.RS, BSSS (former Pres.), F.IPSS, SCI, BES. **Awards:** F.RS, Institut Mondiale du Phosphat Award. **Publications:** *The Soil under Shifting Cultivation* 1960, *Solute Movement in the Soil–Root Zone* 1975; 160 res.papers. Dislikes pers.pub.& news media support. **Languages:** English, French (indiff.), German (poor). Further details may be obtained from Brit.*Who's Who* 1996. Willing to act as consult.etc. **Address:** Department of Plant Sciences, University of Oxford, Parks Road, Oxford OX1 3PF, England, UK. **Tel.**(home) & **fax** 44 1865 351607.

OBARA, Professor Hideo. General mammalogy; evolutionary ecology and comparative ethology; evolutionary etho-ecology of Man. Professor of Zoology and Humanology. *B.*2 July 1927, Tokyo, Japan. Japanese. *W.: foster-d.* **Education:** Hosei U. Histl Sci.1955. **Career:** Asst, Dept of Zool. Natural Sci.Mus. 1946–9; Full Prof.of Zool.& Humanology, Kagawa Nutrition U. **Achievements:** Bd Memb. 1971–93 and Chairman of Scientific Cttee 1981–93, WWF Japan; Chairman, TRAFFIC Japan Spec.Cttee 1982–3; Steering Cttee, Intl Theriological Cong.(UNESCO/IUBS) 1985–;

DG, NCSJ 1988–94; Rep.Dir, JEC 1991–; Pres. Japan Wildlife Cons.Phil.SG; Bd Memb.& Japanese Rep., African Elephant Fndn Intl. **Memberships:** INTECOL, IUCN SSC, Japan Ecol.Soc., NCSJ, JEC, The Wildlife Soc., Australian Mammal Soc., SSE, ASM, FAO Regnl Office for Asia and Pacific; Edl Bds *African J.of Ecol., Natural Hist., Wildlife Australia, Mammal Review, Intl Zoo News, Zeitschrift für Sangetierkude.* **Awards:** Cons.Merit (WWF Intl) 1982, Global 500 Roll of Honour (UNEP) 1988. **Publications:** 60+ books incl. *Changing Fauna of the World* 1965, *Man and his Envt* 1978, *History of Bio-natural Community in Tokyo* 1982, *Endangered Animals of the World* 1987; 80+ papers. Favours pers.pub.& news media support if concerned with Nature cons. **Languages:** English, Japanese. Willing to act as consult.etc. **Address:** Department of Zoology and Humanology, Kagawa Nutrition University, 3-9-21 Chiyoda, Sakado, Saitama 350 02, Japan. **Tel.**(office) 81 492 82 3603, (home) 81 3 3999 0361; **fax** 81 492 89 0458.

OBASI, Professor Dr Godwin Olu Patrick. Global environmental issues such as climate change, ozone-layer depletion, and ecologically sustainable development (especially role of meteorology, operational hydrology, and related fields). Secretary-General. *B.*24 Dec.1933, Ogori, Nigeria. Nigerian. *M.*Winifred: *s.*, 5 *d.* **Education:** McGill U. BSc(Hons)(Maths & Phys.) 1959, MIT MSc(Dist.)(Met.) 1960, DSc(Met.) 1963; Inst.of Statisticians 1971. **Experience:** leadership in intl coopn in met., operational hydr.& related fields; sr posts in teaching, res., and admin.; res.in dynamics of the atmos. (esp.tropics); res.supervision, scientific paper reviews. **Career:** Dem. Dept of Phys. McGill U.1958–9; Res.Asst, Dept of Met. MIT 1959– 63; Sr Meteorologist, Nigerian Met.Dept. 1963–7 (Chairman, WMO WG in Trop.Met. 1965–7) and Lagos Airport (incl.res.& training) 1964–5; WMO/UNDP Expert & Sr Lect. 1967–74, Acting Head Dept of Met.1972–3, Prof.of Met.and Chairman of Dept of Met. then Dean Fac.Sci.1974–6, U.of Nairobi; Adv. (Res. & Training) in Met.& Asst Dir, Nigerian Govt 1976–8 (VP & memb.Adv.Group, WMO Comm.for Atmos.Scis 1978); Dir Educ.& Training Dept 1978–83, Sec.-Gen.1984–, WMO. **Achievements:** promotion of scientific info.& assessment esp.re.policy-formulation & response to global envl issues such as climate change and ozone-layer depletion; leadership in envt & related activities special to WMO; encouragement of nat.participation, esp.developing countries, in addressing envl issues; training of scientists in developing countries now in sr positions in their respective countries; studies in trop.met.esp.through leading role in GATE. **Memberships:** F.of NMS, CMS, DRMS, EMS, RMS, AMS, and RSS; BIS, AMS, Cuban MS (Foreign). **Awards:** num.incl.Ogori Merit Award 1990, Doctor of Phys.*(H.C.)* U.of Bucharest 1991, Doctor of Law *(H.C.)* U.of Philippines 1992,

Doctor of Sci.*(H.C.)* Fed.U.of Tech.(Akure) 1992, Commander of the Nat. Order (Ivory Coast) 1992, DINAC Hon. Merit Award for Met.& Hydr.(Paraguay) 1992, Gold Medal (African MS) 1993, Hon.Doctor of Sci.(Alpine Geophys.Res.Inst., Russian Fedn) 1993, Recognition of Merit (Nat.U.of Asuncion) 1993, Hon.Memb. (Romanian MS), Commander of Nat.Order of Niger 1994. **Publications:** over 70 scientific & tech.papers. No objection to pers.pub., favours news media support. **Languages:** English, French (read), Igbirra, Ogori, Yoruba. **Address:** World Meteorological Organization, 41 Avenue Giuseppe-Motta, POB 2300, CH 1211 Geneva 2, Switzerland. **Tel.** (office) 41 22 730 8200, (home) 41 22 776 2825; **fax** 41 22 734 2326.

ODULA, Michael A.N. Environmental conservation, protection, & restoration, of the Earth; environmental education training; creation of public awareness. Executive Director. *B.*20 Oct.1947, Rusina Is., L.Victoria, Kenya. Kenyan. *M.*Jane A.P. **Education:** Kenyatta U. BEd.1974; envl educ.training at Danish For. Sch.(Copenhagen) 1986, U.of Vaasa (Finland) 1988, Colombia Teachers' Coll.(NY) 1990, SPNI 1994 & U.of Bradford (taken in Ghana) 1994. **Experience:** res., consult., admin., educationist; human rights activist; envl journalism. **Career:** Prin. Tom Mboya High Sch., L.Victoria 1974–93; Founder & Exec.Dir, Children's Alliance for the Prot.of the Envt (CAPE-KENYA) 1993–. **Achievements:** founding of CAPE-KENYA, launched envl prog.covering above-given interests. **Memberships:** Wildlife Clubs of Kenya (Assoc.), Friends of L.Victoria, KEEO, African Biodiv.Inst.& Earth Care– Africa. **Awards:** F.UNESCO 1988, Global 500 Roll of Honour (UNEP) 1990, Amb.(Cape Inc.Texas) 1993. **Publications:** incl.*Envl Guide Book for Schools* 1993. Favours pers.pub.& news media support. **Language:** English. Further details may be obtained from *Who is Who* (Vision Link Fndn, DC USA) 1991, Rhinoman Global Edn NC 1991. Willing to act as consult. etc. **Address:** CAPE-KENYA, POB 132, Homa Bay, Kenya. **Tel.**& **fax** 254 2 226831.

ODUOL, Dr Peter Allan. Wildlife management; arid ecosystems of Africa. Database Coordinator. *B.*30 Nov.1958, Kisumu, Kenya. Kenyan. **Education:** U.of Nairobi, BSc(For.) 1980; Texas A&M U. MSc(For.) 1985; U.of Edinburgh, PhD 1994. **Experience:** res.in for. & agrofor.; consult.— for., agrofor.; natural resource mgmt; envl cons.; biodiv. **Career:** Lect. Kenya For.Coll.(Londiani) 1981–2; Asst Conservator of Forests, Kenya Forest Dept 1981–5; Assoc.Res.Officer, ICRAF (Nairobi) 1985–93; Database Coord. Centre for Biodiv. Nat.Museums of Kenya 1993–. **Achievements:** res.on multipurpose tree improvement (basic & applied), dev.of database on biodiv.for Kenya, Uganda, & Tanzania. **Memberships:** KFA, Xi Sigma Pi 1985, AABNF 1988–90. **Award:** Xi

Sigma Pi (Texas A&M U.) 1985. **Publications:** *c.*30 incl.Variation among selected *Prosopis* families for pod sugar and pod protein contents (co-Author) 1986, The Banana *(Musa* spp.) — Coffee robusta: trad.agrofor.system of Uganda (co-Author) 1990. Favours news media support. **Languages:** English, French (basic). Further details may be obtained from *Who is Who in Tree Improvement* 1994. Willing to act as consult.etc. **Address:** Centre for Biodiversity, National Museums of Kenya, POB 40658, Nairobi, Kenya. **Tel.**(office) 254 2 740060, (home) 254 2 561331; **fax** 254 2 219550 or 741414; **e-mail** Biodive@tt.gn.apc.org .

OGUNDERE, Hon.Justice Joseph Diekola. Drafting of municipal & international environmental law or legislation. Retired Presiding Justice. *B.*31 Dec.1929, Ibadan, Oyo State, Nigeria. Nigerian. *W.:* 2 *s.* **Education:** U.of Lond. LLB 1957; Council of Legal Educ.(UK) BL 1957; Trinity Coll.Camb. LLB(Hons) and postgrad.studies in Intl Law 1961. **Experience:** res.in envl law, both municipal & intl, incl.Law of the Sea and Treaties; Perm.Sec.& Solicitor-Gen.of Fedn 1974–6; Chairman, Governing Bd of Ibadan Poly.1980–84. **Career:** private legal practice 1958; Law Officer 1958–76, Solicitor-Gen.& Perm.Sec.1974–6, Fed.Min.of Justice (Lagos), Judge, High Court, Oyo State 1977–8, Justice, Court of Appeal, Benin City 1985–94. **Achievements:** drafted legis.on deposit of toxic and other harmful wastes in Nigerian land-mass, territorial sea, and EEZ: Harmful Waste (Spec. Criminal Provisions) Act 1988. **Memberships:** NSIL, UNIDROIT 1968–78, IUCN 1968–. **Award:** Life Memb.*ad Honorem* (UNIDROIT) 1980. **Publications:** The Nigerian Judge and His Court 1994; articles incl.The dev.of intl envl law and policy in Africa 1972. Favours pers.pub. & news media support. **Languages:** English, Yoruba. Further details may be obtained from *Africa's Who's Who* 1981, *Who's Who in Nigeria* 1990. Willing to act as consult.etc. **Address:** Main POB 4964, Ibadan, Oyo State, Nigeria. **Tel.**(home) 234 2 810 0100.

OHN, U (= Mr). Restoration ecology; wildlife conservation; resources' planning and socio-economic survey; forestry. Retired. *B.*10 Aug. 1928, Sagaing, Myanmar (Burma). Burmese. *M.*(Daw = Mrs) Khin Mya: 2 *s.* **Education:** U.of Rangoon BSc 1951; UCNW BSc(Hons) (For.) 1956; Postmaster-General's Cert.on Electronic Data Processing 1971. **Experience:** res.— resto.ecol.and structural analysis of forest types; tech.— thinning control for Teak *(Tectona grandis)* plantations; admin.— resources' planning and watershed mgmt; consult.— NPPP for Feasibility Study on Mangrove Reforestation project 1992. **Career:** Admin.Officer 1979–82, Park Warden of Popa Mtn Park (c.Myanmar) 1982–6, Dir Planning & Stats and Project Dir (Kinda Watershed) 1986–7, Project Dir (Nat.Forest Mgmt & Inventory) 1987–8, Forest Dept, Myanmar. **Achievement:** restored ecol

status and successfully estab.Popa Mtn Park (Nature Cons.and Nat.Parks Project) in arid but pleasant rolling volcanic hills of c.Myanmar 1982–6. **Memberships:** IUCN SSC Regnl Memb., ISME (Life), Forest Consult.Group (Myanmar). **Publications:** Control in thinning of teak plantations 1968, The structure of Bago Yoma forests 1990, Mangrove forest prod.and utilization of the Ayeyarwady Delta 1992, Data collection, compilation and use in forest sector planning in Myanmar 1993, *Plantation For.on a Par with the Natural Forests* 1994. Favours pers.pub.& news media support. **Languages:** Burmese, English (good), Japanese (a little written & spoken). Willing to act as consult.etc. **Address:** D-35, Kyaikwine Pagoda Road, Mayangone, PO 11061, Yangon, Myanmar. **Tel.**(office) 95 1 64405, (home) 95 1 63681.

OJEDA, Professor Dr Ricardo Alberto. Ecology, biogeography & conservation of mammals; biodiversity; ecological management of watersheds; field biology. Researcher. *B.*22 April 1950, Tucuman Province, Argentina. Argentinian. *M.*Susana (biol.): 2 *d.* **Education:** U.of Tucuman, Lic.Biol.Sci.1975; U.of Pittsburgh, PhD 1985. **Experience:** res.& tech.— ecol. biogeog. & cons.of neotrop.mammals, biodiv.of arid lands of Argentina, and of Yungas subtrop. forests of northwestern Argentina; tech.& consult.— ecol mgmt of watersheds (Programa Manejo Ecologico del Piedemonte–IANIGLA–CRICYT). **Career:** Wildlife Biol. FWS of Argentina 1975–9; Prof.of Zool.& Gen.Biol. NPS and prof.of undergrad.& grad.courses in desert ecol., biodiv.of northwestern Argentina & Monte Desert, field biol.& wildlife planification 1976–; postdoctl, U.of Oklahoma 1988–9; Researcher, IADIZA 1983–. **Achievements:** diagnosis of wildlife cons.in Argentina with emphasis on faunal commercialization and its impact on biodiv.; ecol.& biogeog.of mammals of the trop.–temperate regn of Argentina; biodiv.of the Yungas forests, desert ecol. **Memberships:** Chairman, IUCN New World Marsupial SG 1990–; Pres.SAREM 1991–. **Awards:** F.Carnegie Mus.of Natural Hist. 1974–5, Tinker F. Center for Latin Amer. Studies (U.of Pittsburgh) 1989. **Publications:** *Cons.of S.Amer.Mammals* 1982, *Diversity of Caviomorphs* 1982, *Biogeog.of the Mammals of Salta* 1989, *Guide to the Mammals of Salta Province, Argentina* 1989, *Biodiv.& Latin Amer.*1989, *The Mammals of Tucuman* 1991. Favours news media support. **Languages:** English, Spanish. Willing to act as consult.etc. **Address:** Instituto Argentino de Investigaciones de las Zonas Aridas, Unidad Zoologia & Ecologia Animal, CC 507, 5500 Mendoza, Argentina. **Tel.& fax** 54 61 287995; **fax** 54 61 380370; **e-mail** ntcricyt@criba.edu.ar .

OJHA, Dr Ek Raj. Conservation of highland ecosystems. Agriculture Officer, Researcher. *B.*23 Sept.1957, Mauwa Village, Doti Distr., Seti Zone, Nepal. Nepalese. **Education:** U.of

Agricl Scis (Bangalore), BSc(Agric.) 1984; Tribhuvan U.(Nepal), BA(English) 1986; AIT, MSc 1990, PhD 1995 (both in Rural–Regnl Dev.Planning). **Experience:** res., teaching, project planning, conf.participation, was Resource Person for Centre for Language and Educl Tech.at AIT 1994, and Memb.of Adv. Cttees of WFSF for courses on Futures of Ecol.1993 and Futures of Peace: Civilizations, Structures, and Visions, 1994. **Career:** Sci. Teacher, Sec. Sch. 1977–80; Asst Agric.Officer, Dept of Agric. Kathmandu 1985–6; Agric. Officer, Nepal Rastra Bank 1986–; Res.Assoc. Human Settlements Dev. Prog. AIT 1990–95; Researcher under UN F'ship, UNCRD 1995–. **Achievements:** scholarships received for grad. & postgrad.studies. **Membership:** Natural Health Centre (Life). **Award:** Hon.Life Memb.(Pakistan Futurists' Fndn & Inst.). **Publications:** twelve incl.*Prod.Credit for Rural Women: An Impact Eval.of the PCRW Project around Gajuri, Nepal* (monogr., co-Author) 1993. **Languages:** English, Hindi, Kannada, Nepalese. Pub.favoured for coopn & dev. Willing to act as consult.etc. **Address:** United Nations Centre for Regional Development, Nagono 1-47-1, Nakamura-ku, Nagoya 450, Japan. **Fax** 81 52 561 9375; **cable** UNCENTRE NAGOYA; **telex** 359620 UNCENTRE .

OKAJIMA, Shigeyuki. Journalist, writer; alpinist. Deputy Editor. *B.*18 Jan.1944, Tokyo, Japan. Japanese. *M.*Reiko. **Education:** Sophia U. (Tokyo) BA 1967; Vis.Scholar, U.of Washington 1983. **Career:** Journalist, The Yomiuri Shimbun 1969 since when has specialized in envl matters. **Achievements:** envl ethics; climbed in Andes 1965 & Himalaya 1968, 1979, 1988. **Memberships:** VP Japanese Envl Journalists' Forum. **Awards:** Global 500 Roll of Honour (UNEP) 1988. **Publications:** [Cons.Movements in the US] 1990, [Discussion on Global Envts] 1992 (both in Japanese). Favours news media support. **Languages:** English, Japanese. **Address:** 1-5-5-204 Komatsugawa Edogawaku, Tokyo 132, Japan. **Tel.**(office) 81 3 3217 8268, (home) 81 3 3638 7305; **fax** 81 3 3217 8165.

OKE, Professor Dr Timothy R. Urban climates & microclimates. Professor of Geography & Head of Department. *B.*22 Nov.1941, Kingsbridge, S.Devon, England, UK. Canadian. *M.* Margaret Lorraine: *s., d.* **Education:** U.of Bristol BSc(Spec.)(Hons)(Geog.) 1963; McMaster U. MA 1964, PhD 1967. **Experience:** undergrad.teaching — climatology esp.microclimatology, boundary layer met.and phys.envt of city; consult.to WMO re.urban climates; Edl Bds of *Atmosphere–Ocean, Boundary-layer Met., Atmos.Envt, Progress in Phys.Geog., Intl J.of Climatology.* **Career:** Asst Prof. McGill U.1967–70; Asst, Assoc., Prof.& Head of Geog. UBC 1970–; Vis.F. Keble Coll.Oxf.1990–91. **Achievements:** res.into Nature & phys.basis of urban climates esp.energy & water balance of cities & urban heat-islands. **Memberships:** CAG, CMOS, AGU, AAG, AMS, EGS, RMS, RSC.

Awards: F. RSC & RCGS, Guggenheim F., Killam Res.Prize (Killam Fndn), Pres.'s Prize (CMOS), Award for Scholarly Dist.(CAG), Resident Scholar (Rockefeller Fndn). **Publications:** *Climate of Vancouver* 1975, 1994, *Boundary Layer Climates* 1978, 1987, *Vancouver and Its Regn* 1992, *Surface Climates of Canada*, in press; *c.*100 papers. Favours resp. news media support. **Language:** English. Further details may be obtained from *Canadian Who's Who* 1995, *Amer.Men & Women of Sci.,* and others. Willing to act as consult.etc. **Address:** Department of Geography, University of British Columbia, 1984 West Mall, Vancouver, British Columbia V6T 1Z2, Canada. **Tel.**(office) 1 604 822 2900, (home) 1 604 263 7394; **fax** 1 604 822 6150.

OKIDI, Professor Dr Charles Odidi. Environmental law (comparative & international), international water law, Law of the Sea. Task Manager. *B.*20 Nov.1942, Homa Bay Distr., Kenya. Kenyan. *M.* Doreen Akinyo: *s., d.* **Education:** Maseno High Sch.; Alaska Pacific (then Methodist) U. BA *Magna Cum Laude* 1971; The Fletcher Sch.of Law & Diplomacy, MA(Law & Diplomacy) 1973, PhD 1975. **Experience:** extensive scholarly res., consults, u.teaching. **Career:** Res.F. MIT 1974–6; Res. F. Inst.for Dev.Studies & Lect. Fac.of Law 1976–80, SRF Inst.of Dev.Studies & Sr Lect. Fac.of Law 1980–87, Assoc.Res.Prof. Inst.of Dev.Studies 1987–8, U.of Nairobi; Prof.of Envl Law & Dean (Founder) *Sch.of Envl Studies, Moi U.1988–94; Task Mgr, ELI in Africa, UNEP/UNDP 1995–. **Achievements:** Founding Dean of Sch.of Envl Studies*. **Memberships:** ASIL 1971–, ICEL 1978–, IAWL 1979–, IUCN CEL 1981–. **Awards:** James P.Warburg Award (UCWOS) 1973, Elizabeth Haub Prize 1984. **Publications:** 12 books & pamphlets; *c.*30 j.articles. Dislikes pers.pub.& news media support. **Languages:** Dho-Luo (vernacular), English, Swahili. Willing to act as consult.etc. **Address:** UNEP, POB 45891, Nairobi, Kenya. **Tel.**254 2 623815; **fax** 254 2 623859; **e-mail** charles.okidi@UNEP.no .

OKOŁÓW, Dr Czeslaw. Nature conservation; national parks education; ecology of bark beetles (Scolytidae). Director. *B.*21 Dec.1935, Biala, Poland. Polish. *M.*Helena: 2 *s.* **Education:** Agricl Acad.Warsaw, MSc(For.) 1958, DSc (For.) 1967; Agricl Acad.Kraków, postgrad. course in Nature Prot.1975; U.of Michigan Sem.on Nat. Parks & Preserves 1984. **Experience:** res.in entomology, museology; nat.parks' admin. **Career:** Dep.Chief of For.Distr. 1958– 60; Curator of Mus.1960–88, Chief of Scientific Lab.1988–9, Dep.Dir 1989–93, Dir 1993–, all at Bialowieźa Nat.Park. **Achievements:** plan of educl centre in Bialowieźa, scenery of exhibition held in Mus.of Bialowieźa Nat.Park; collection of bibl.of Bialowieźa Forest; training of tourist guides; consult.re.educl films. **Memberships:** PES, PFS, PZS, LNP, IUCN CNPPA, Nature

Cons.Comm.(Polish AS), Voivodship Council of Nature Prot.at Bialystok. **Awards:** Voivodship Award 1972, Voivodship Scientific Award and Silver Cross 1976, Golden Merit Cross 1980, Kluk Medal on Envt 1975, Golden Award for Envt 1989. **Publications:** *Bibl.of Bialowieźa Primeval Forest* (four vols) 1969, 1976, 1983, 1991; *c.*220 papers. **Languages:** English (written & spoken), German (spoken), Polish, Russian. Willing to act as a consult. **Address:** Bialowieźa Park Narodowy, 17–230 Bialowieźa, Poland. **Tel.**(office) 48 835 12306, (home) 48 835 12538; **fax** 48 835 12323.

OKOTH-OGENDO, Professor Dr H.Wilfred O. Public law. Professor of Public Law, Centre Director, Council Chairman. *B.*1 July 1944, Kisumu, Kenya. Kenyan. *M.*Ruth W.: 3 *s.*, 2 *d.* **Education:** U.of E.Africa LLB(Hons) 1970, Wadham Coll.Oxf. BCL (Hons) 1972, Yale U. JSD(Agrarian Law) 1978. **Experience:** res.— agrarian systems in Africa, Asia & Latin Amer.; envl policy & progs re.water, wildlife, and arid & semi-arid lands in Kenya, Lesotho, Swaziland, & Guyana; pop.-driven land-use changes in third-world countries; admin.re.positions held as Dean, Chairman, Dir etc.; teaching envl law for four yrs, agrarian law & policy for ten yrs, and law of property in land for 21 yrs. **Career:** Lect. 1970–78, Sr Lect 1978–84, Assoc Prof 1984–8, Prof.1988– in Public Law, Dean Fac.of Law & Chairman Dept of Public Law 1978–86, Dir Pop.Studies & Res.Inst.1986–90, all at U.of Nairobi; Vis.Assoc.Prof.of Law, Boston U.Law Sch.1986; Vis.Prof.of Law, U.of Florida at Gainesville 1987; Dir Centre for African Family Studies, Nairobi & Lome 1990–; Chairman Nat.Council for Pop.& Dev. Kenya 1993–. **Achievements:** assisting Govts of Kenya, Guyana, Lesotho, & Swaziland, to formulate envl policy & progs. **Memberships:** ILA, ICLPS, IUCN CEL, IGBP HDP Core Project Planning Cttee on Land-use/Land-cover Change. **Awards:** Winter Williams Scholarship (U.of Oxf.), Law & Modernization F'ship (Yale U.). **Publications:** ten monogrs & 61 papers incl. *Agrarian Reform Legis.for Guyana* 1984, *Tenants of the Crown: The Evol.of Agrarian Law & Instns in Kenya* 1990, Agrarian Reform in Sub-Saharan Africa 1993. Accepts pers.pub.& news media support. **Languages:** Dholuo, English, Kiswahili. Willing to act as consult.etc. **Address:** Department of Public Law, University of Nairobi, POB 30197, Nairobi, Kenya. **Tel.**(office) 254 2 443161, (home) 254 2 721818; **fax** 254 2 448621.

OKUN, Professor Dr Daniel A. Water-quality management. Emeritus Professor of Environmental Engineering, Consultant. *B.*19 June 1917, New York, NY, USA. American. *M.*Beth. **Education:** Cooper Union BS(Civ.Eng.) 1937, CIT MS(Civ.Eng.) 1938, Harvard U. ScD(Sanitary Eng.) 1948. **Experience:** res., tech., admin., consult. **Career:** Asst Sanitary Engr (Res.), US PHS 1940–42; First Lt–Major, US Army Sanitary

Corps 1942–6; Teaching F. Harvard U.1946–8; Assoc.Engr, Malcolm Pirnie Inc.1948–52; Vis.Prof. Tech U.(Netherlands) 1960–61 & UCL 1966–7 & 1973–4; Assoc. Prof.1952–5, Prof.& Head, Dept of Envl Sci.& Engg 1955–73, Kenan Prof.of Envl Engg 1973–82, Emeritus 1982–, U.of NC (Chapel Hill); num.offices held at U.of NC, other & hon. positions. **Achievements:** built up educl prog. at U.of NC in envl scis & engg from three to 30 fac.members; impacted on policies in protecting drinking-water qual.; promoting water reclamation & re-use, and studying regionalization; active in developing progs & policy for developing countries. **Memberships:** F.ASCE, AWWA, WEF, AAEE, APWA, IWEM (UK, Corporate F.), AIDIS, IWSA, F.AAAS, IWRA, IWQA, NAE, IOM. **Awards:** num.incl.Harrison Prescott Eddy Medal (WPCF) 1950, Gordon Maskew Fair Award (AAEE) 1972, Gordon Y.Billard Award (NYAS) 1975, Friendship Award (IWEM) 1984, Best Paper Award 1985, Abel Wolman Award 1991 (AWWA), Donald R.Boyd Award (AMWA) 1993. **Publications:** 12 books incl. *Regionalization & Water Mgmt: A Revolution in England and Wales* 1971, *Community Piped Water Supply Systems in Developing Countries: A Planning Manual* (co-Author) 1987, *Surface Water Treatment for Communities in Developing Countries* (co-Author) 1992, *Guidelines for Water Reuse* (co-Author) 1992; very many refereed papers, printed presentations, reports, chapters etc. Indiff.to pers.pub. & news media support. **Language:** English. Willing to act as consult.etc. **Address:** School of Public Health, Department of Environmental Sciences & Engineering, University of North Carolina at Chapel Hill, CB #8060, 210 North Columbia, Page Building, Chapel Hill, North Carolina 27599-8060, USA. **Tel.**(office) 1 919 966 4898, (home) 1 919 933 7903; **fax** 1 919 966 7646.

OLA-ADAMS, Dr Bunyamin Alao. Establishment & management of Nature Reserves, bioproductivity and nutrient cycling studies; fire ecology in natural forests & managed plantations. Senior Lecturer, Acting Head of Department. *B.*5 May 1944, Lagos, Nigeria. Nigerian. **Education:** U.of Ife BSc(Hons)(Bot.) 1969, U.of Birmingham MSc 1975, U.of Ibadan PhD 1987. **Experience:** has served as resource person & consult.to nat.& intl orgns on problems of cons., mgmt, & utilization, of forest genetic resources; has carried out impact assessment studies for multinat.cos, nat.& intl orgns, on some aspects of activities in for.& oil industries on the envt. **Career:** Res.Officer (Ecol.) to Chief Res. Officer, For.Res.Inst.of Nigeria 1969–90; Sr Lect.& Acting Head, Dept of For., Fisheries & Wildlife Mgmt, U.of Agric.(Abeokuta) 1990–. **Achievements:** Ext.Examiner to U.of Ibadan, Nat. Coord. UNESCO–MAB Project on Cons.of Natural Areas and the genetic material they contain; memb.Governing Council, U.of Agric. and IUCN Comms on NPPA & Ecol.; Chairman,

IUFRO Working Party on Cons.of Gene Resources 1991–. **Memberships:** F.LS, For.& Sci.Assns of Nigeria, Ecol.Soc.of Nigeria (VP). **Publications:** *c.*40 in scientific journals & conf. proc. Indiff.to both pers.pub.& news media support. **Languages:** English, Yoruba. Willing to act as consult.etc. **Address:** Department of Forestry, Fisheries, and Wildlife Management, University of Agriculture, PMB 2240, Abeokuta, Ogun State, Nigeria. **Tel.**234 39 233386; **fax** 234 39 234650.

OLI, Krishna Prasad. Coordinating governmental & nongovernmental organizations, planning of local areas; legal aspects of environmental management; community-based action research; preparation of environmental action plans. Programme Chief. *B.*28 Feb. 1950, Hoda, Athrai, Nepal. Nepali. *M.*Renuka D.: 2 *s., d.* **Education:** Edinburgh U. MSc 1983; FAO, course in Agric.Project Planning (Kathmandu) 1986; Tribhuvan U. LLB 1990; Washington SU, course in Econ.of Agrofor.1993. **Experience:** res.re.hills & mtn agricl systems & subsystems, prep.of envl planning guidelines, regs; nat.consult.on Nepal Envl Policy & Action Plan, and agric.& envl planning; admin.of rural dev. projects. **Career:** Asst Headmaster, Bhagawati Sec.High Sch.1975; Livestock Officer, ODA-funded projects 1976– 85; Chief Livestock Officer, Res.& Rural Dev.1986–8; Res.Specialist, Winrock Intl (Nepal) 1988–90; Sr Envl Planner 1990–92, Chief of Envl Planning Prog.1993–, IUCN (Nepal). **Achievements:** made sig.progress in revegetation res.on crop–livestock interaction, effective water-use, and grazing mgmt projects; dev.of envl planning guidelines at local & nat.levels; res.on legal instruments for sust.envl mgmt and spec.area planning. **Memberships:** Nepal Bar Assn, Nepal Agricl Soc. **Publications:** 30 incl. *Livestock in the Hills of Nepal* (co-Ed.) 1985, *Res.Needs in Nepal* (co-Ed.) 1989, *Planning by the People* (community study) 1992, *Indigenous People Decision-making Structure in Managing Natural Resources* (resource-based study) 1993, *Legal Instruments for Sust.Envl Mgmt in Nepal* (legal study) 1995. Favours pers.pub.& news media support. **Languages:** English, Hindi, Nepali, Urdu. Willing to act as a consult. **Address:** IUCN Nepal, POB 3923, Kathmandu, Nepal. **Tel.**(office) 977 1 522712, (home) 977 1 411970; **fax** 977 1 521506 or 9.

OLOJEDE, Ayodele Adekunle. Environment and public administration; environmental strategies & planning; natural resource management. Chief Environmental Scientist/Special Assistant. *B.*15 May 1956, Ile-Ife, Nigeria. Nigerian. *M.*Stella A.: *s.*, 3 *d.* **Education:** U.of Ife, BSc (Hons)(Agric.) 1978; U.of Edinburgh, MSc (Hons) (Resource Mgmt) 1984. **Experience:** tech.— mgr of forest nurseries, wildlife domestication projects, monitoring & eval.of for.projects, planning & policy analysis in envl & natural resources' mgmt; admin.— Head of

For.Regnl Offices, policy mtgs, report writing, staff supervision etc.; consult.— natural resources' info.planning & strat., mgmt consult.(orgn & reviews). **Career:** Monitoring & Eval.Specialist (Industrial For.) 1979–85, For. Regnl Admin.1985–90, Envl and Natural Resources Officer 1991–3, Fed.Public Service of Nigeria; Chief Envl Sci.& Spec.Asst to Chief Exec. Fed.EPA 1994–. **Achievements:** assisting Nigerian Govt in estab.of cons.agencies and their integration with envl prot.bodies. **Memberships:** IUCN CESP, For.Assn of Nigeria, Nigerian Field Soc. **Award:** United African Co.(Unilever Group) Scholar (U.of Ife) 1975–8. **Publications:** *c.*12 incl.Dev.and Implementation of Envl Strats and Action Plans in Nigeria (report) 1995. Indiff.to pers.pub.& news media support. **Languages:** English, Yoruba. Willing to act as consult.etc. **Address:** Federal Environmental Protection Agency, PMB 265, Abuja, Nigeria. **Tel.**(office) 234 9 523 3371, (home) 234 9 234 2264; **fax** 234 9 523 3373 & 5510.

OMAR ASEM, Dr Samira, *see* **ASEM, Dr Samira OMAR.**

ONAYEMI, Olarotimi Olakunle. Alleviating environment-related poverty in developing world, fighting for respect of human & animal rights; forest conservation in the tropics; creating sustainable development awareness & economies in the developing world. Founder & Director, Credit & Mortgages Manager. *B.*25 Nov.1968, Ijebu-Ode, Ogun State, Nigeria. Nigerian. **Education:** The Poly.(Ibadan), OND (Fin.& Banking) 1987; The Poly.(Onerti), HND (Fin.& Banking) 1991. **Experience:** res.in envt, poverty, & third-world underdev.; lect.in accounts, business law, econ., & envl auditing; consult.in founding a youth envt fndn and NEN; involvement in envl issues to help correct some of Africa's envl ills. **Career:** Founder & Dir NEN 1989–, Mgr(Credit & Mortgages), KSL Savings and Loans (Mortgage Bankers) 1992–. **Endeavours:** to create a common African NGO Forum, presenting some of African NGOs' views to UNCED (Feb.1992), assisting in alleviation of poverty caused by envl degradation in rural areas. **Memberships:** NED-Net, Chartered Inst.of Bankers (Nigeria). **Publications:** *The UN System Summits, Confs & African NGOs* 1989, *Fin.for Envt Mgmt & Sust.Dev.*1990, *Poor Citizens' Views on Envl Degradation* 1991, *Deforestation: One Advantage, Many Disadvantages* 1993, *Human Poverty & Rights in the Developing World* 1993. Indiff.to pers.pub., favours news media support. **Languages:** English, French (beginner), Yoruba. Willing to act as consult.etc. **Address:** 27a Ibadan Road, Ijebu-Ode, Nigeria. **Tel.**234 37 430329.

OPDAM, Dr Paul. Landscape ecology; conservation biology. Department Head. *B.*25 Oct. 1949, Amsterdam, Holland. Dutch. **Education:** U.of Nijmegen MSc(Biol.) 1975, PhD (Biol.)

1980. **Experience:** res.mgmt & consult. mainly in landscape ecol.(effects of landscape structure changes on animal & plant biodiv.in cultural landscapes). **Career:** Jr Researcher, U. of Nijmegen 1975; Researcher in Dept of Landscape Ecol.1976–86, Head of Dept of Landscape Ecol.Res.1986–, IFNR (then Inst.for Nature Mgmt). **Achievements:** basic res.in ecol.of birds-of-prey, basic & applied res.in ornith.& landscape ecol.; res.mgmt; j.Ed. **Memberships:** IALE, DOLE, DOS, INTECOL. **Publications:** *Landscape Ecol.of a Stressed Envt* (Ed.) 1993, 20+ others. Dislikes pers.pub., favours news media support. **Languages:** Dutch, English, French (basic), German, Spanish (basic). Willing to act as consult.etc. **Address:** Institute of Forestry & Nature Research, POB 23, NL-6700 AA Wageningen, The Netherlands. **Tel.** (office) 31 8370 95111, (home) 31 30 899450; **fax** 31 8370 24988.

OPSCHOOR, Professor Dr Johannes Baptist. Research on economic instruments, sustainable development, industrial metabolism, delinking growth from environment, environment & equity; research planning in environmental field. Professor of Environmental Economics, Council Chairman. *B.*22 May 1944, Zwyndrecht, The Netherlands. Dutch. *M.*Irene. **Education:** Erasmus U. MA(Econ.) *(cum laude)* 1968, Free U.(Amsterdam) PhD(Econ.) 1974. **Experience:** res.& res.mgmt; consult.for UNEP, EC, OECD, var.govts. **Career:** Researcher 1968–78, Res.F. Netherlands Inst.of Advanced Studies 1976–7; Sr Res.F. U.of Botswana 1978–81; Dir Inst.of Envl Studies (Amsterdam) 1982–90, Prof.of Envl Econ. Free U.1987–, Chairman Adv. Council on Nature & Envl Res.1990–. **Achievements:** dev.of Inst.of Envl Studies; co-init.of Ecoforum for Peace; pubns. **Memberships:** EAERE, AEE, ISEE, AAERE. **Awards:** Scientific Adv. Academia Sinica, Pers.Award (NCEP Bulgaria), Instnl Award (UN Peace Messenger, for Ecoforum). **Publications:** 11 books incl. *Econ.Instruments for Envl Prot.*(co-Author, transl.into Polish) 1989, *Persistent Pollutants: Econ.& Policy* (co-Ed.) 1991, *Envt, Economy & Sust.Dev.*(Ed.) 1992, *Econ.Incentives & Envl Policies: Principles & Practice* (co-Ed. in press); *c.*24 chapters & articles. Indiff.to pers.pub.& news media support. **Languages:** Dutch, English, French (spoken), German (spoken). Willing to act occasionally as consult.etc. **Address:** Raad Milieu en Natuur Onderzoek (Advisory Council on Nature and Environmental Research), PB 5306, Ryswyk 2280HH, The Netherlands. **Fax** 31 70 336 4310.

ORGLE, Dr Tetey Kwesi. Research in forest disturbance & recovery, tropical forest management. Unit Head & Forest Conservator. *B.*10 Mar.1963, Accra, Ghana. Ghanaian. *M.*Jennifer N.(active memb.of Ghana Assn for Cons.of Nature): *s.*, 2 *d.* **Education:** U.of Ghana (Legon), BSc(Hons)(Bot.with Zool.) 1985; U.of Aberdeen, PhD(Trop.Forest Ecol.) 1995. **Ex-**

perience: supervised field activities of Ghana forest inventory 1986–9; dev.of guidelines for species' use in degraded forests 1995; assisted with prep.of forest reserve mgmt plans 1989–90; acted as facilitator in promoting results and implications of forest ecol.res.for forest mgmt in Ghana. **Career:** Forest Botanist, Ghana Forest Inventory Project (Kumasi) 1987–8; Asst Conservator of Forests & Head of Bot.Unit 1988–90; Conservator of Forests & Head of Ecol.Unit, Planning Branch 1994–, Ghana For.Dept. **Achievement:** Pres.of Ghana Assn for the Cons. of Nature 1988–90. **Memberships:** INTECOL, Ghana Sci.Assn, Ghana Insts of Professional Foresters, and Biologists. **Award:** Tech.Training Coopn Award (Brit.Council) 1990–94. **Publications:** Effects of fire exclusion on savanna veg.at Kpong, Ghana (co-Author) 1992, *Ecol.of Burnt Forests in Ghana* (doctl thesis) 1994, *Drought and Fires in Ghana* (newsletter item, co-Author) 1995. Indiff.to pers.pub., favours news media support. **Languages:** English, French; Ga & Twi (spoken) (both Ghanaian). Willing to act as consult.etc. **Address:** Planning Branch, Forestry Department, POB 1457, Kumasi, Ghana. **Tel.**(office) 233 51 22376, (home) 233 21 226497; **fax** 233 51 22687.

ORHUN-HEWSON, Mrs Canan. Environmental education, field research in ornithology, oceanographic sampling (plankton tows, salinity, etc.); humpback whale (*Megaptera* spp.) identification work. Assistant Faculty Recruiter & Programme Coordinator. *B.*4 Dec.1960, Istanbul, Turkey. American. **Education:** Heidelberg Coll.(OH), BS(Envl Biol.) 1983, U.of Southern Illinois MS(Envl Studies) 1986. **Experience:** extensive travel/res.exp.in the field during coll.& grad.yrs, envl educ.& outreach in later yrs; ocean res.in N&S Amer., Greenland, Pacific Islands; consult. **Career:** Envl Educator for Breakthrough Inc., Sci.aboard res.vessel *Ramble*, Envl Consult., –1994; Asst Fac.Recruiter & Prog.Coord. Sch.for Field Studies (Massachusetts) 1994–. **Membership:** Sigma Xi. **Languages:** English, Turkish. Willing to act as consult.etc. **Address:** Red Gate Road, Essex, Massachusetts 01929, USA. **Tel.**(home) 1 508 768 6051; **fax** 1 508 768 6051 (call first).

ORIANS, Dr Gordon H. Ecology, conservation biology; science & environmental policy. Professor of Zoology and Environmental Studies. *B.*10 July 1932, EauClaire, WI, USA. American. *M.*Elizabeth N.: *s.*Colin Mark (entomol./plant chem.), 2 *d.*Carlyn Elizabeth (geog.), Kristin J.(marine chem.). **Education:** U.of Wisconsin–Madison BS(Zool.) 1954, UCB PhD (Zool.) 1960. **Experience:** ecol res.on all continents; admin.as Dir, Inst.for Envl Studies, U.of Washington 1976–86, and Pres. Orgn for Trop.Studies 1988–94. **Career:** Asst Prof.of Zool.1960–64, Assoc.Prof.of Zool.1964–9, Prof. of Zool.1968–, U.of Washington at Seattle. **Achievements:** init.cons.biol.courses at U.of Washington; pubns. **Memberships:** AAAS,

AIBS, ASN, ABS, COS, ESA, FAS, ISTE, SCB. **Awards:** elected to NAS 1989 and to Amer. AAS 1990. **Publications:** *Some Adaptations of Marsh-nesting Blackbirds* 1980, *Blackbirds of the Americas* 1985, *Life: The Sci.of Biol.*1983, 1987, 1992; 100+ scientific papers. Favours pers.pub.& news media support. **Languages:** English, Spanish. Willing to act as consult.etc. **Address:** Dept of Zoology, NJ-15, University of Washington, Seattle, Washington 98195, USA. **Tel.**(office) 1 206 543 1658, (home) 1 206 364 5743; **fax** 1 206 543 3041.

O'RIORDAN, Professor Dr Timothy. Environmental politics & management; environmental impact assessment; international environmental politics & law; interdisciplinary science and its role in policymaking. Professor of Environmental Sciences. *B.*21 Feb.1942, Edinburgh, Scotland, UK. British, Canadian. *W.*: 2 *d.* **Education:** U.of Edinburgh, MA(Geog.) 1963; Cornell U. MSc(Water Res.) 1965; U.of Camb. PhD 1967. **Experience:** consult.on major project mgmt and industrial envl auditing; res.into pol.structures for integrating envl sust.into all aspects of policymaking & implementation; Chair, Euro.Sci.Fndn Envt Sci.and Society res. prog.; Assoc.Dir, Centre for Social and Econ. Res.into the Global Envt. **Career:** Asst & Assoc.Prof. Dept of Geog. Simon Fraser U. 1967–74; Reader & Prof. Sch.of Envl Scis, U.of E.Anglia 1974–; Vis.Prof. U.of Canterbury (NZ) 1970 and Grad.Sch.of Geog. Clark U.(Worcester, MA) 1972. **Achievements:** two books, on theory & practice of envlism, and on legitimacy of a major UK public inquiry into a new nuclear power prog.; chaired num.intl social sci.networks in Europe, and recently, the pol.cttee overseeing the most important remaining wetland in the UK (Broads Auth.). **Award:** McGill Mem.(RGS) 1983. **Publications:** *Envlism* 1981, *Sizewell B: An Anatomy of the Enquiry* 1987, *The Greening of UK Govt* 1991. Modestly favours pers.pub., more-so newsmedia support. **Language:** English. Willing to act as consult.etc. **Address:** School of Environmental Sciences, University of East Anglia, Norwich NR4 7TJ, England, UK. **Tel.**(office) 44 1603 592840, (home) 44 1603 810534; fax 44 1603 250558.

OSEMEOBO, Dr Gbadebo Jonathan. Landuse planning & policy; species', habitats', & ecosystems', conservation; species' diversity and their utilization by human societies. Chief Park Conservation/Planning Officer. *B.*23 July 1952, Iruoke-Owan E., Edo State, Nigeria. Nigerian. *M.O.*Suzanna: *s.*, 4 *d.* **Education:** U. of Ibadan BSc(Hons)(For.) 1976, MSc(Forest Resources' Mgmt) 1982, PhD(Forest Land-use/Cons.) 1985. **Experience:** widespread in Nigeria's forest land-use planning, policy & wild biotic cons.; monitoring & supervising Fed. For.assisted projects in W.Nigeria. **Career:** Prin. Forest Officer, Field Office Benin 1977–8 & Field Office Abeokuta 1979–89; Consult.in Land-

use/Cons.1990–93, Chief Park Planning Officer 1993–, Nigeria Trop.For.Action Plan. **Achievements:** assisting in nat.policy formulation & execution for natural resources' cons.; mgmt & dev.of Zuguma Game Reserve to Nat.Park status. **Memberships:** NFA, RFDN, PDN. **Publications:** 48+ papers. Indiff.to pers. pub., favours news media support. **Languages:** English, Yoruba. Willing to act as consult.etc. **Address:** POB 2495, Garki-Abuja, Nigeria. **Tel.**234 9 523 0429; **fax** 234 9 523 0409.

OSMAN, Salih Mohamed. Environmental management & economics. Regional Office Director. *B.*1939, Sudan. Sudanese. *M.*Noura: 2 *s.*, 2 *d.* **Education:** U.of Beirut BA 1962, New York U. MA(Econ.) 1967, St John's U.(NY) PhD prog.1972–5. **Experience:** econ.policy and instnl adv.; envl policy res.& consult.; intl civil servant. **Career:** academic, Khartoum Tech. Inst.1962–3; diplomatic, Min.of Foreign Affairs, Sudan 1963–71; Asst Exec.Dir 1971– 95, Dir, Regnl Office for W.Asia 1995–, UNEP. **Achievements:** estab.of UN Habitat and Human Settlement Fndn in 1976 for low-cost housing finance; envl nat.instns & legis.in countries of W.Asia; estab.of Council of Arab Ministers resp.for Envt. **Memberships:** Sudan Phil.Soc., Arab Economists' Assn. **Award:** 20 yrs of Outstanding Service to UNEP and its Cause (UNEP). **Publications:** several UNEP reports, now instnl documents. **Languages:** Arabic, English, French (working knowledge). Willing to act as consult.etc. **Address:** Regional Office for West Asia, United Nations Environment Programme, POB 10880, Manama, Bahrain. **Tel.**973 276072; **fax** 973 276075.

OUEDRAOGO, Dr (Ouendkouni) Dieudonné. Population, environment & development; migrations; natural resources' management. Research Director. *B.*14 July 1947, Nodin, Burkina Faso, W. Africa. Burkinabe. *M.*Korotoumou. **Education:** U.of Bordeaux III, Doctorat 3e cycle 1976, Doctorat d'Etat 1986. **Experience:** res., admin., consult. **Career:** Researcher 1972–86, Dir.Social Scis Inst.1979–82, Nat.Centre of Res.; Lect. U.of Ouagadougou 1977–86; Dir of Res.1986–, Chief of Studies & Res.Div.1989–, Centre d'Etudes et de Recherche sur la Pop.pour le Développement. **Achievements:** memb.of Burkina team of MAB prog.1976–80; IUCN Task Force on Pop.& Natural Resources 1989–90; consult.to Comité Inter-états de Lutte contre la Sécheresse dans le Sahel, Institut Panafricain pour le Développement/Afrique de l'Ouest et Sahel. **Membership:** Union pour l'Etude de la Pop.Africaine. **Publications:** Drought & Pop. 1991, Démographie et développement durable au Sahel 1992; num.minor pubns. **Languages:** English (good spoken but mediocre written), French. Willing to act as consult.etc. **Address:** Centre d'Etudes et de Recherche sur la Population pour le Développement, BP 1530, Bamako, Mali, West Africa. **Tel.**(office) 223 223043, (home) 223 229136; **fax** 223 227831.

Ouyong XU, Professor, *see* **XU, Professor Ouyong.**

OVINGTON, Professor Dr John Derrick. Sustained natural-resource use; forest ecology; international aid, environmental programmes; environmental assessment; aboriginal interests. Company Director. *B.*14 May 1925, Spennymoor, Co.Durham, England, UK. Australian, British. *M.*Joyce: *s., d.* **Education:** U.of Sheffield, BSc(Hons) 1945, PhD 1947, DSc 1964. **Experience:** res.into ecosystem dynamics and forest succession; nat.park mgmt; liaison with aboriginal people re.resource use, tourism in outdoor situations; admin.of govt agencies; implementation of intl treaties; consult. **Career:** SO, Macaulay Inst.of Soil Res.1947–9; Sr PSO, NC (UK) 1949–65; Prof.and Head of Dept of For., Dean of Fac.of Sci. ANU 1965–74; Dir, Australian NPWS 1974–90; Dir, Ovid Pty Ltd 1990–. **Achievements:** res.into nutrient cycling, prot.of whales (as Australian Whaling Commissioner), involving aboriginal people in nat.park mgmt, prep.of mgmt plans, dev.of world heritage concept, prot.of endangered species. **Awards:** AO 1986, Order of the Golden Ark 1986. **Publications:** *Australian Endangered Species* 1978, *Temperate Broad-leaved Evergreen Forests* 1983, *Kakadu* 1986; 150+ res. papers. Indiff.to pers.pub.& news media support. **Languages:** English, French (intermediate). Further details may be obtained from *Who's Who in Australia* 1995. Willing to act as consult.etc. **Address:** 18 Downes Place, Hughes, Canberra, Australian Capital Territory 1605, Australia. **Tel.**(office & home) 61 6 281 2032.

OWEN, Professor Dr Denis Frank. Ecology, evolution & genetics; field studies on population genetics of lepidoptera & mollusca. Visiting Research Fellow. *B.*4 April 1931, London, England, UK. British. **Education:** U.of Oxf. MA 1958, U.of Michigan PhD 1961. **Experience:** extensive res.& teaching in univs esp.in Africa, US, Sweden, & England. **Career:** Lect.in Zool. Makerere U. 1962–6; Prof.of Zool. U.of Sierra Leone 1966–70; Dir UNESCO Biol. Teaching for Africa, U.of Cape Coast 1967–8; Vis.Prof. U.of Lund 1971–3 & U.of Bergen 1990–91; Disting.Vis.Prof. U.of Mass. 1974; Acad.Post Above Reader 1973–, Vis.Res.F. 1996–, OBU. **Achievements:** understanding (1) sig.of genetic variation in wild pops, (2) species diversity, (3) impact of agric.and of dogs. **Membership:** F.LS. **Award:** Hon.DSc (OBU) 1996. **Publications:** ten books incl.*Trop.Butterflies* 1971, *Man's Envl Predicament* 1973, *What is Ecol.?* 1974, *Camouflage & Mimicry* 1980; *c.*300 papers. Favours pers.pub.& news media support. **Language:** English. Willing to act as consult.etc. **Address:** 42 Little Wittenham Road, Long Wittenham, Abingdon, Oxfordshire OX14 4QS, England, UK. **Tel.**(office) 44 1865 819244, (home) 44 1865 407654; **fax** 44 1865 483242.

OZA, Professor Dr Gunavant Maneklal. Environmental and conservation movement, saving disappearing species; stressing Biosphere. Professor of Botany, Society General Secretary, Foundation President. *B.*24 Nov.1933, Baroda, Gujarat, India. Indian. *M.*Premlata *qv*: *s.*Mihir (recipient of Fatehsinghrao Gaekwad Cons. Award), 2 *d.*Nandini, Rudrani (all help INSONA and crusade for The Biosphere). **Education:** Baroda U. MSc 1956, PhD(Plant Taxonomy) 1962. **Experience:** more than three decades of res.& teaching at U.of Baroda and of field endeavours which have ultimately helped to stimulate the preserv.of pops of native plants & animals, and consequently to prevent extinction of world's unique wildlife; consult.for Putranjiva (Parks, Gdns, Envt & Dev.). **Career:** SO & Systematic Bot., Botl Survey of India 1962–4; Lect.1967–83, Reader 1984–92, Prof.1992–, Maharaja Sayajirao U.of Baroda; Founder & Gen.Sec. INSONA 1975–; Founding Ed. *Envl Awareness* 1977–, Founder & Pres. Fndn for Envl Awareness 1993–. **Achievements:** paramount contribn to save gravely endangered Kashmir Deer (Hangul) *[Cervus elaphus hanglu]* from extinction and to determine its food habits & migration route; determined habitats of at least 17 mammals threatened with extinction in hilly areas of Indian subcontinent; contribn towards estab.of a 'Living Museum' of trees typical to India; bio-archaeological preserv.of Indian monuments at Champaner; determined desertic habitat of endangered Arabian Oryx *[Oryx leucoryx]*; saved habitat for Indian Antelope (Blackbuck) *[Antilope cervicapra]*, highlighted plight of Himalayan Musk Deer *[Moschus moschiferus]*; contributed to improving deteriorating habitat & prospects of Asiatic Lion *[Panthera leo persica]* and Gt Indian Bustard *[Choriotis nigriceps]*, and to Silent Valley being declared a WHS. **Memberships:** F.LS, Scientific F.ZSL, F.INSONA, IUCN SSC (Emer.Memb.) & Comms on Ecol., Educ.& Communication, and NPPA. **Award:** Global 500 Roll of Honour (UNEP) 1990. **Publications:** *Flora of Pavagadh, Gujarat State, India* 1966; two books in Gujarati, *c.*300 res.etc.papers. Favours pers.pub.& news media support. **Languages:** English, Gujarati, Hindi, Marathi. Willing to act as consult.etc. **Address:** Oza Building, Salatwada, Baroda 390 001, Gujarat, India. **Tel.**(home) 91 265 428703; **fax** c/o 91 265 424799; **telex** c/o 175 6272 PCO IN; **telegrams** INSONA, Baroda, India.

OZA, Mrs Premlata. Environment & conservation movement, saving disappearing species; stressing Biosphere. Managing Editor, Foundation Trustee & Joint Secretary. *B.*9 March 1938, Basi Purani, Dist.Hoshiarpur, Punjab, India. Indian. *M.*Professor G.M.Oza *qv*: *s.*Mihir (recipient of Fatehsinghrao Gaekwad Cons.Award), 2 *d.* **Education:** J&K U. BSc 1962, B.Ed.1967; Maharaja Sayajirao U. M.Ed.1969. **Experience:** devoted to envt & wildlife cons.with a view to attaining human well-being, linking schoolchildren & women with envt in India in a manner that should set a worthy example for other countries at a global level. **Career:** taught sci.in num.schools in Kashmir Valley, Dem.in Bot. Govt Women's Coll.(Srinagar) 1962–3, Res. Asst, Pfizer Co.1964–; Managing Ed.*Envl Awareness* 1975–. Consult.on Parks, Gardens, Envt & Dev. Putranjiva 1992–; Jt Sec. Fndn for Envl Awareness 1993–. **Achievements:** jointly resp.for estab.of INSONA, and in promoting its quarterly J.*Envl Awareness* since 1975. **Memberships:** INSONA (Patron & Life), IUCN CNPPA & CET, Life Memb.of num.women's orgns, Fndn for Envl Awareness (Trustee 1993–). **Publications:** Every day a Biosphere day: path for sust.1994, two conf.reports. Favours pers.pub.and news media support. **Languages:** English, Gujarati, Hindi, Punjabi, Sanskrit, Urdu. Willing to act as consult.etc. **Address:** Oza Building, Salatwada, Baroda 390001, Gujarat, India. **Tel.**(home) 91 265 428703 & 421009; **fax** c/o 91 265 424799 (please mention name & address).

ÖZTÜRK, Professor Dr Münir. Plant ecology; pollution problems. Director. *B.*6 Dec.1943, Kashmir, India. Turkish. Father Mehmet Sultan, mulberry cultivation re.silk prod. *M.: s.* Bugrahan (memb.of student envl group), *d.* **Education:** Kashmir U. BSc 1962, MSc 1964; Ege U. PhD 1970, DSc 1975; Alexander von Humboldt F.1977–8, 1979, 1987. **Experience:** 30 yrs' res.on plant ecol.& Medit.ecosystems, eight yrs' admin., 12 yrs' consult. **Career:** Lect. in Biol. Govt of Unani Coll.(Kashmir) 1964; UGC F.1965–7; Res.Assoc.1967–75, Assoc. Prof. 1975–80, Prof.1980–, Dir 1990–, Envl Centre, Bot.Dept, Ege U. **Achievements:** init. autecol.work in Turkey, first pubns. **Memberships:** INTECOL, FEES, TNCS, FESPP (Turkish del.), TBS, TEPA. **Awards:** F.JSPS 1984–5, Certs.of Honour from TBS, TEPA Izmir, & Mayor Municipality Kusadasi. **Publications:** 16 books incl.*Plant Ecol.*(course book for undergrads) 1992, *Ecol.of Aegean Grasslands* 1993; 140 papers incl.Cement dust 1976, Poll.effects on plants 1986, Use of domestic waste water in the growth of plants 1988, Coastal Medit.plant cover & pollutants — a case study from Izmir 1993. Indiff.to pers.pub.& news media support. **Languages:** English, German (spoken), Turkish, Urdu. Willing to act as consult.etc. **Address:** Botany Dept E-Blok, Science Faculty, Ege University, 35100 Bornova-Izmir, Turkey. **Tel.**(office) 232 388 0110, 2445, or 2560, (home) 232 339 6874; **fax** 232 388 1036.

PACHAURI, Dr Rajendra K. Energy; environment, ecologically sustainable development. Director. *B.*20 Aug.1940, Nainital, UP, India. Indian. **Education:** NC SU MS(Industrial Eng./ Econ.) 1972, PhD(Industrial Eng.) 1973, PhD (Econ.) 1974; grad.of Instns of Prod.Engrs and Mech.Engrs (UK). **Experience:** practical engg, lecturing, admin. **Career:** Asst Works Mgr 1965–7, Govt of India Deputation to Montreal 1967–8, Works Mgr (Engine Div.) 1968–71, Diesel Locomotive Works; Asst Prof. NC SU

1974–5; Sr Fac. Memb.1974–9, Dir Consult.& Applied Res.Div.1979–81, Admin.Staff Coll.of India; Vis.Fac.Memb. NC SU 1976 & 1977, Vis.Prof. W.Virginia U. 1981–2, Sr Vis.F. E–W Center 1982, Vis.F. World Bank 1990; Dir, Tata Energy Res.Inst.1981–. **Achievements:** as its Dir, has built up the Tata Energy Res.Inst.into a premier think-tank & res.inst.on energy & envt-related policy & tech.; contribns to energy–envt field have helped to shape nat. & global policies. **Memberships:** WRI Council 1992, WEC, IAEE (Pres.1988, Chair 1989–90), Pres. Governing Council AEI, Phi Kappa Phi, UNU Task Force on Energy Planning & Modelling, Founder Memb. Coord.Cttee (past-Chairman 1980–83), Cooperative Intl Network for Training & Res.in Energy Planning UNESCO 1980–87, NAS (Life F.), SESI (Pres.1990–92), IEES (VC 1988–), num.other nat.bodies & instns. **Publications:** *Global Warming: Collaborative Study on Strats to Limit* CO_2 *Emissions in Asia & Brazil* (co-Ed.) 1992, *Global Partnerships for Sust.Dev.*(co-Ed.) 1994; num.others. Dislikes pers.pub., indiff.to news media support. **Languages:** English, Hindi. Further details can be obtained from *Intl Who's Who* 1994–5. Willing to act as consult. etc. **Address:** Tata Energy Research Institute, Darbari Seth Block, Habitat Place, Lodhi Road, New Delhi 110 003, Delhi, India. **Tel.**(office) 91 11 462 7651, (home) 91 11 463 4663; **fax** 91 11 462 1770.

PAGE, Dr Christopher N. Earth sciences; environmental evolution; taxonomy, evolution, & phytogeography, of Gymnosperms & Pteridophytes. Principal Scientific Officer. *B.*11 Nov. 1942, Gloucester, England, UK. British. *M.*Jane Clare: *s.*, 3 *d.* **Education:** Cheltenham Grammar Sch.; U.of Durham BSc(Hons)(Bot.) 1964, U.of Newcastle upon Tyne PhD(Fern Cytology) 1967. **Experience:** res.in gymnosperm (esp.conifer) and pteridophyte (esp.fern & horsetail) taxonomy, evol., & biogeog.; initially a geol. decided early on that more could be learned about the envt of post-plant-life by study of their living survivors; occasional broadcaster; leader of num. overseas expedns 1963–. **Career:** Post-doctl F. U.of Qld 1967–9; NATO Overseas Res.F. U.of Oxf.1970–71; PSO, R.Botanic Gdn Edinburgh 1971–; Hon.Lect. U.of Edinburgh 1980–. **Achievements:** founded IUCN SSC Conifer SG 1988–; Dir.of R.Botanic Gdn Edinburgh Conifer Cons. Prog.(funded by Sainsbury Family Charitable Trusts); uses accumulating biol data as basis for construction of forward cons.progs for both conifers & pteridophytes on a sound biol basis, involving integration of *in* & *ex situ* aspects. **Memberships:** F.LS & Tutor Scottish Field Studies Council, IUCN SSC Conifer SG (Founder & Chair), BSBI, Geol.Soc.of Edinburgh. **Award:** Hon.Life VP, Brit.Pteridological Soc. **Publications:** Ed.*The Fern Gazette* 1975–85, *The Ferns of Britain & Ireland* 1982, *Biol.of Pteridophytes* (co-Ed.) 1984; *Ferns, their Habitats in the Brit.and Irish Landscape* 1988; *c.*75 papers on pteridophyte & conifer ecol., evol., envl aspects, & taxonomy. Has helpful interactions with news media. **Language:** English. Further details can be obtained from *Who's Who in Scotland.* Willing to act as consult.etc.esp.for fern & conifer cons.issues and topics re.Bracken *(Pteridium aquilinum)* in Britain. **Address:** Royal Botanic Garden, Edinburgh EH3 5LR, Scotland, UK. **Tel.** (office) 44 131 552 7171; **fax** 44 131 552 0382.

PALMBERG-LERCHE, Christel Margareta. Technical assistance to developing countries, development assistance; conservation of genetic resources, forest tree improvement, forest genetic resources; forestry & the environment, deforestation; reforestation, biological diversity. Chief, Forest Resources Development. *B.*26 Aug. 1946, Mäntyharju, Finland. Finnish. *M.* Cai Leo Lerche (forest econ./mgmt). **Education:** U.of Helsinki, BSc/Academic For.Engr 1970, MSc(For.& Gen.Genetics) 1970. **Experience:** for.res.; tech.assistance to developing countries with emphasis on fields of for., forest genetic resource cons.& mgmt, deforestation/ reforestation, forest reproductive materials; gen.questions re.for.& envt, and for.& biol diversity; travel & assistance to countries in all trop.regns. **Career:** Researcher, Forest Genetics, Genetic Resources & Tree Improvement; Finnish Forest Res.Inst.1970–71 & 1977–8; Assoc.Expert, Seed Procurement & Tree Improvement 1971–4; Researcher, Tree Improvement, Genetics & Genetic Resources, CSIRO 1974–7; For. Officer, Forest Genetic Resources & Tree Improvement 1978–85, Chief Forest Resources Dev.Branch, Forest Resources Div.1985–, FAO. **Achievements:** involvement in tech.assistance projects in developing countries in temperate, high alt., sub-trop., trop., & arid/semi-arid, zones. **Memberships:** FAF, IFA, DSF (Treas.1970–71), SFSF (elected memb.), SID (Rome Chapter 1978–85), memb.of num.UN orgns' Panels, Task Forces, WGs, etc. **Publications:** some 60 incl. Res.needs in forest tree breeding and improvement in developing countries 1989, *Cons.of Genetic Resources as an Integral Part of Forest Mgmt & Tree Improvement* (Symp.Proc.Ed.) 1992, *Intl Progs for the Cons.of Forest Genetic Resources* (Symp.Proc.Ed.) 1993, *Present Status of Forest Plantations & Tree Improvement in the Americas, with Spec.Ref.to Trop.Amer.* (Cong. Proc.Ed.) 1993, The cons.of forest genetic resources: issues & progs 1993; Edl Bd *Unasylva,* Ed.*Forest Genetic Resources Info.*(FAO's annual Newsletter). **Languages:** Bahasa Indonesia (read/understood), English, Finnish, French (good), German (good), Italian (good), Portuguese (read/understood), Spanish, Swedish. Further details may be obtained from *Intl Who's Who of Intellectuals, Intl Directory of Disting.Leadership and Outstanding Service to the Profession* 1990. **Address:** Forestry Department, Food and Agriculture Organization, Via delle Terme di Caracalla, I-00100 Rome, Italy. **Tel.**(office) 39 6 522 53841, (home) 39 6 596 03753; **fax** 39 6 522 55137.

PALMER, Professor Sir Geoffrey. International environmental law. Professor of Law. *B.*21 April 1942, Nelson, NZ. New Zealander. *M.*Margaret Eleanor: *s., d.* **Education:** Victoria U.of Wellington BA 1965, LLB 1966; U.of Chicago JD 1967. **Experience:** extensive exp. in intl envl issues both as a Minister and an academic. **Career:** Prof.of Law 1969–79; MP Christchurch C.1979–1990, NZ Minister for the Envt 1987–90, Dep.PM 1984–9, PM 1989–90; Prof.of Law, Vic.U.(NZ) & U.of Iowa (USA) 1990–. **Achievements:** pol.decisions and academic legal writing; fashioned NZ policies on ozone layer prot., climate change, sust.mgmt, and drift-net fishing. **Memberships:** Barrister & Solicitor, High Court of NZ. **Awards:** Global 500 Roll of Honour (UNEP) 1991, Intl Adv. Council WWF, KCMG 1991, AC 1991. **Publications:** *Envl Politics — A Greenprint for NZ* 1990, New Ways to Make Envl Law 1992. Favours pers.pub.& news media support. **Languages:** English, French (read). Willing to act as consult.etc. **Address:** Unit 7, 85 Elizabeth Street, Wellington, New Zealand. **Tel.**(office) 64 4 715340, (home) 64 4 801 5185.

PALMER, [Mr] Prince Dowu. Forest conservation, advocating equitable forest policies which can satisfy the great majority of the resource users. Deputy Chief Conservator of Forests, Plan & Programme Coordinator. *B.*7 June 1942, Freetown, SL. Sierra Leonean. *M.*Gloria: 2 *d.* **Education:** U.of Montana BSc(Forest Mgmt) 1968. **Experience:** widespread in forest admin.& cons.in SL incl.init.& planning of many for.dev.projects such as TFAP & Gola Rain Forest Cons.Prog., took part in Gola Forest Inventory, consult.(short-term) for Economic Dev.Inst., World Bank Energy Dept, and Nat. Envl Action Plan. **Career:** Instr. For. Dept Training Sch.(Bambawo) 1969–70; Counterpart FAO Inventory Expert, Gola Forest Inventory 1970–72, Divl Forest Officer 1972–5, and Conservator of Forests 1975–9 (both Eastern Regn), Conservator of Forests in charge of Sector Planning & Project Prep.1979–81, Asst Chief Conservator of Forests 1981–5, Dep.Chief Conservator of Forests 1985–, Dept of Agric.& For., Govt Forest Service; Consult.& Resource Person, World Bank Energy Assessment & Planning Sems 1987–9; Mission Memb.for Africa, FAO Eval.of Multi-donor Trust Fund in Support of TFAP 1992. **Achievements:** contributed or init.some of the major devs in for. sector of SL incl.making exceptional advancement in TFAP process; commencement of sust.forest mgmt in Gola Forest under Gola Rain Forest Cons.Prog.; dev.of coopn between Govt Forest Service & NGOs; contribn to forest law reforms and revision of For.Act & Regs. **Membership:** SL Commonwealth For.Assn. **Publications:** incl. Issues and Options in Fuelwood Cons.1990. Indiff.to pers.pub.& news media support. **Languages:** English, French (rudimentary written). Willing to act as consult.etc. **Address:** Forestry Division, Department of Agriculture and Forestry, Youyi Building, Freetown, Sierra Leone. **Tel.** 232 223445; **fax** 232 242206.

PANDEYA, Professor Dr Satish Chandra.
Ecology: structure & functions of grazing land and forest ecosystems including production ecology & bioenergetics; process of desertification; systems analysis & holistic environmental management. Emeritus Professor of Environmental Science. *B*.1 Jan.1929, Kanpur, UP, India. Indian. *M*.Sheela: *s*., 3 *d*.incl.Dr Anjali Bahuguna (marine resources). **Education:** Saugar U. MSc(Bot.specn Ecol.) 1949, PhD(Grazing Land Ecol.) 1953; U.of Perugia, Perfetta di Ecologia Agraria 1955; Agra U. DSc(Desert.) 1992. **Experience:** res.—structure & functions, incl. productivity, of grazing lands of w.India; ecol.& productivity of forests in R.Narmada Catchment Area; envt of w.india and genecology & autecology of *Cenchrus ciliaris* (25 ecotypes) and *C.setigerus* (nine ecotypes), which two fodder grasses are now grown successfully in USA; impact of human activities on organic matter productivity of grazing lands from arid to drysubhumid envt; dynamics of desert.; holistic envl mgmt; cons.of Taj Mahal against air poll.in system context; running India's Envt Awareness Soc; envl educ.; consult.to Govt of India 1970–; served as memb. of or del.to num.intl specialist cttees, confs, etc. **Career:** Lect.1953– 60 then Reader 1960–69 in Bot. Gujarat U.; Prof.& Founder Head, First Integrated Dept of Bioscience, Saurashtra U. 1969–89; Nat.Lect. Govt of India, 1978–9 & 1986–7; Vis.Prof. Jiwaji U.(Gwalior, MP) 1988–9; Nat.Envt F. 1988–92; Emer. Prof.of Envl Sci. Dayalbagh Deemed U.& Raja Balwant Singh Coll.(Agra) 1992–. **Achievements:** estab.of climo–edapho–vegetational relationship in w.India's natural ecosystem by multivariate math.models and by simulation predictive modelling in system context; quantification of human activities on fodder prod.in arid to subhumid ecoclimates; investigation on dynamics of desert. and estab.of the syndrome and methods to cope with people's involvement; discovery of high forage-yielding ecotypes of two species complexes (viz.*Cenchrus ciliaris* and *C.setigerus*) and estab.of distribn & growth conditions; integrated concept of holistic envl mgmt, finding optimum sust.mgmt and use of natural resources; currently working on status of air poll.at Agra and cons.of Taj Mahal. **Memberships:** F.INSA, LS, INAS, IBS, ISTE, Nat. Inst.of Ecol., IRS. **Award:** Birbal Sahni Medal (IBS) 1990. **Publications:** *Res.Methods in Plant Ecol.*1968, *Ecol.of* Cenchrus *Grass Complex — Envl Conditions & Pop.Differences in Western India* 1993; 300+ res. papers. Indiff.to pers.pub., favours news media support. **Languages:** English, Gujarati, Hindi, Italian. Further details may be obtained from *Life Sketches of Fellows* (INSA). Willing to act as consult.etc. **Address:** 13/14 Pragatipuram, PO Dayalbagh, Agra 282005, Uttar Pradesh, India. **Tel.**(home) 91 562 350667.

PANDIT, Dr Ashok Kumar. Wetland ecology, limnology, Himalayan lake ecology; algology, plankton & benthic ecology; fish & wildlife ecology, trophic ecology, production ecology; ecosystem analysis & conservation of Himalayan ecosystems & natural resources. Ecologist (Scientist). *B*.20 Feb.1952, Hawal, Pulwama, Kashmir, J&K, India. Indian. Father Jia Lal Pandit, forester. *M*.Anita: 2 *s*. **Education:** U.of Kashmir MSc(Zool.)(First Class, Dist.in Ichthyology) 1974, PhD in Wetland Ecol.(Zool.) 1981; training course in chem.analysis of aquatic plants & animals, Health Phys.Div. Bhabha Atomic Res.Centre 1981. **Experience:** 20 yrs' res.in aquatic ecol.; consult.to diff.govt depts & private enterprises. **Career:** Jr then Sr Res.F. UGC Project 1975–80; Ecol.(Sci.), Centre of Res.for Dev., U.of Kashmir 1980–. **Achievements:** pioneering res.work on Kashmir Himalayan wetlands, tracing of food-chains & food-webs in aquatic ecosystems; estab.of poll. indicators; ecol.of snails, insects, fishes, & waterfowl; plant–animal relationships & cons.of natural resources. **Memberships:** NIE, IES, IAPCB, ISTE, ISN, World Wetlands Partnership (team memb.). **Awards:** F.J&K AS, Nat.Scholarshipholder throughout academic career, Merit Scholarship-holder at sec.sch.& MSc levels. **Publications:** *Wetland Ecosystems in Kashmir Himalaya* (in press), *Dal L.Ecosystem in Kashmir Himalaya* (in press); *c*.45 papers incl. Cons.of wildlife resources in wetland ecosystems 1991, Ecol.of wetland fishes with emphasis on their mgmt 1992, Eutrophication & cons.of Kashmir Himalayan lakes 1994. Favours news media support. **Languages:** English, Hindi, Kashmiri, Urdu. Willing to act as consult.etc. **Address:** Centre of Research for Development, University of Kashmir, Srinagar 190 006, Jammu & Kashmir, India.

PANDURANGAN, Dr Alagramam Govindasamy. Natural resource management for sustainable development; conservation biology; plant systematics and morphological studies. Scientist & Division Head. *B*.10 May 1958, Alagramam, TN, India. Indian. *M*.Revathi: *s*. **Education:** Madras U. MSc(Bot.) 1982; Bharathiyar U. (Coimbatore), PhD(Bot.) 1991; advanced training at Kerala Agricl U.in Spices Prod.Tech.1986 & 1992 and Ext.Methods & Public Relations 1988, at ICAR in Soil Cons.1986 and Pest & Disease Mgmt 1988, and at Indian Cardamom Res.Inst.in Shade Mgmt in Cardamom Plantations 1990; Inst.of Mgmt in Govt (Trivandrum), short prog.on Ecol., Envt, & Sust.Dev.1994. **Experience:** 12 yrs' in res., tech.& admin., currently res.guide to five PhD students at Kerala U. **Career:** Jr Res.F./SRF, Botl Survey of India 1982–5; Field Officer, Spices Bd 1985–92, Govt of India; Sci.& Head, Div.of Herbarium, Museum & Eco-Educ.; Trop. Botanic Gdn and Res.Inst.(Kerala) 1992–. **Membership:** SAB. **Awards:** Award (for popularizing spice cultivation, Spices Bd) 1992, Shields (three, for sci. exhibn stall on eco-educ.progs, Agri-Horti Soc.) 1993/4/5. **Publications:** 24 original res.papers, contributed 42 Red Data sheets to Red Data Book of Indian Plants. Dislikes pers.pub., favours news media support. **Languages:** English, Kannada (spoken), Malayalam (spoken), Tamil. Further details may be obtained from *Bot.2000 Taxonomists' Directory* (UNESCO, India). Willing to act as consult.etc. **Address:** Tropical Botanic Garden and Research Institute, Palode, Pacha PO, Thiruvananthapuram District, PIN 695 562, Kerala, India. **Tel.**91 47 284236; **fax** 91 47 143 7230.

PANGETI, George Nhamo. Design & implementation of wildlife management and environmental conservation projects. Independent Consultant, Project Coordinator. *B.*15 June 1947, Penhalonga, Zimbabwe. Zimbabwean. *M.*Dr Evelyn. **Education:** U.of Zimbabwe, BSc(Hons) (Biol.Scis) 1970, Grad.Cert.in Educ. 1977; Dalhousie U.Cert.in Project Mgmt 1983. **Experience:** extensive admin.in wildlife mgmt and community participation in cons.& mgmt of natural resources; contributed towards initiation of CAMPFIRE prog.in Zimbabwe and assisted neighbouring states; coordn of consult.studies. **Career:** Head of Sci.Educ. St. Augustine's Sch. and part-time Lect. U.of Zimbabwe 1970–82; Head of Admin.1983–8, Dep.Dir 1988–95, Zimbabwe Nat.Parks; Coord. Wildlife Mgmt & Envl Cons.Projects 1995–, Ind.Consult.1996–. **Achievements:** contributed towards CAMPFIRE prog.in Zimbabwe and initiated projects towards prot.of Rhino & Elephant, among other such activities. **Membership:** Zimbabwe Scientific Assn. Favours pers.pub.& news media support. **Language:** English. Willing to act as consult. **Address:** 32 Airdric Road, Eastlea, Harare, Zimbabwe. **Tel.**(office) 263 4 790593, (home) 263 4 490405; **fax** 263 4 733338.

PAPANASTASIS, Professor Dr Vasilios P. Ecology & management of Mediterranean rangelands; agroforestry; landscape ecology. Professor of Range Management (Ecology). *B.*21 June 1942, Kozani, Greece. Greek. *M.*Olympia (forest geneticist). **Education:** Aristotle U.of Thessaloniki, BS(For.) 1965; UCB, MSc(Range Mgmt) 1971, PhD(Range Mgmt) 1973. **Experience:** in the army served as topographic engr in artillery 1965–8, in 1968 hired by Min.of Agric.of Greece where worked in forest mgmt & cons.and later in for.res.as range researcher, besides conducting res.on improvement & mgmt of rangelands; became involved in several legislative, admin., & tech., cttees, after moving to u.spent time teaching and carrying out res.while visiting several countries. **Career:** Distr. Forester, Min.of Agric.1968–9; Asst Range Researcher 1969–70, Prin.Range Researcher 1973–86, Assoc.Prof.1986–91, Prof.of Range Mgmt (Ecol.) 1992–, Aristotle U.of Thessaloniki; Chairman, Working Party, IUFRO 1982– 6; Memb. Exec. Cttee of EGF 1988–92; Memb. Continuing Cttee, Intl Rangeland Cong.1991–9. **Achievements:** inventory of rangelands in Greece; writing-up plans on mgmt and improvement of rangelands, setting up standards for proper grazing of rangelands; promoting range cons.through FAO

in several Medit. countries. **Memberships:** SRM, Assn Française de Pastoralisme, Hellenic For. and Range & Pasture Socs. **Awards:** E.Benakis Award (Acad.of Athens) 1977, 1989. **Publications:** four books incl. *Threatened Medit.Landscapes, W.Crete* 1993, *Fodder Trees and Shrubs* 1994; papers incl. Rangelands and envt 1994, Seeding and sheep grazing in pine plantations 1995, Grazing and desert.in Crete 1995. Indiff. to pers.pub.& news media support. **Languages:** English, French (better at spoken), Greek. Further details may be obtained from Citation Index, *Herbage and For.Abstracts.* Willing to act as consult.etc. **Address:** 19 Gregoriou E' (Fifth) Street, 54248 Thessaloniki, Greece. **Tel.**(office) 30 31 998933, (home) 30 31 317179; **fax** 30 31 998886.

PARKIN, Mrs Sara Lamb. Green political campaigner. Writer & Campaigner, NGO Director. *B.*9 April 1946, Aberdeen, Scotland, UK. British. *M.*Donald Maxwell Parkin: 2 *s.* **Education:** R. Infirmary of Edinburgh, RGN 1970. **Experience:** Nursing Res.Unit (U.of Edinburgh), and Staff Nurse & Ward Sister (R.Infirmary of Edinburgh) 1970–74; var.posts in family planning & relationship counselling 1974–81. **Career:** self-employed writer & campaigner on green issues 1981–; Intl Liaison Sec.1983–90, Speaker Intl Affairs then Chair 1989–92, UK Green Party; co-Sec. Euro-Greens 1985–90; Adv. Engg Council (UK); Dir, Forum for The Future 1992–. **Achievements:** bldg-up green pol.parties in UK & Europe; advocacy for envl policy esp.re.security & econ.; dev.by Forum for The Future of young persons' Green Scholarship scheme. **Memberships:** New Econ.Fndn (Trustee), Finlaggan Trust. **Awards:** F.Schumacher Coll., Hon.HHD (Ball SU). **Publications:** include *Green Parties: an Intl Guide* 1989, *Green Futures* 1990, *The Life and Death of Petra Kelly* 1994. **Languages:** 18 Boulevard Pinel, 69003 Lyon, France. **Tel.**33 72 336597; **fax** 33 72 341331.

PARRY, Professor Dr Martin L. Impacts of climate change. Institute Director & Professor of Environmental Management. *B.*12 Dec.1945, England, UK. British. *M.*Cynthia Jane: 2 *d.* **Education:** U.of Durham, BS 1967; U.of W. Indies, MSc 1969; U.of Edinburgh, PhD 1973. **Experience:** 25 yrs of res. **Career:** Lect. U.of Edinburgh 1972–3; Vis.Lect. Punjab & Kurukshetra Univs 1973; Lect. 1973–85, Sr Lect.1986–8, Reader in Resource Mgmt 1988–89, Prof.of Envl Mgmt 1989–91 all in Dept of Geog. U.of Birmingham; Vis.Prof. U.of Manitoba 1975 and U.of W–M 1977; Vis.Res.Sci.Clark U. 1981; Dir Climate Impacts Project IIASA 1983–7 (Project Dir 1983–5 in Austria); IBM Dir, Prof.of Envl Mgmt, Professorial F.of Linacre Coll., Envl Change Unit, U.of Oxf.1991–4; Dir, Jackson Envt Inst.& Prof. of Envl Mgmt, Dept of Geog. UCL 1994–. **Achievements:** basic res.on impacts of climate change, two large vols of edited work on impacts of climate change. **Member-**

ships: Intl Study on Improving the Sci.of Climate Impact Assessment (ICSU/SCOPE) 1982–3; Scientific Adv.Cttee of World Climate Impacts Prog. (UNEP) 1987–; Project Steering Cttee, Intl Study of Impacts of Climate Change in SE Asia (UNEP) 1987–; UK Rep.to World Climate Impacts Network (UNEP) 1987–; Chair UK Climate Change Impacts Review Group, DoE 1989–, Chair WG IV (Impacts), NERC TIGER Prog. 1990–, Sr Author IPCC WG II 1990–, Adv.Bd on Global Change (IUCN) 1991–, Cttee on Global Envl Change (ESRC) 1991–, VC & Treas. Human Dimensions of Global Envl Change Prog.1992–, Scientific Adv. Cttee to Business in the Envt 1992–, UK Cttee for IGBP 1993–, Governing Body Inst.of Grassland & Envl Res. 1993–, Landscape Res.Group (Ltd) UK (Dir 1976–90), IBG (Rural Geog.1976–90 & Histl Geog.1976–90 Study Groups), RGS, AAG, RMS. **Awards:** Cuthbert Peek Grant (RGS) 1991, Norbert Gerbier-Mumm Intl Award (WMO) 1993. **Publications:** *The Impact of Climatic Variations on Agric.* Vol.1 *Assessments in Cool Temperate & Cold Regions* (co-Ed.) 1988, Vol.2 *Assessments in Semi-arid Regns* (co-Ed.) 1988, *Climatic Change & World Agric.* 1990, *Econ. Implications of Climate Change in Britain* 1995; 100+ papers, reports etc. Indiff.to pers.pub.& news media support. **Languages:** English, French. Willing to act as consult.etc. **Address:** Jackson Environment Institute, Department of Geography, University College London, 26 Bedford Way, London WC1H 0AP, England, UK. **Tel.**44 171 380 7577; **fax** 44 171 916 0379.

PARSONS, Dr David Jerome. Plant ecology; ecosystem management, wilderness ecosystems; fire ecology; global change. Research Biologist. *B.*18 May 1947, Berkeley, CA, USA. Father James J.Parsons (retired geographer, UCB). American. *M.*M.Susan: *s.* **Education:** UCD BS(Biol.Scis)(highest hons) 1969, Stanford U. PhD(Ecol.) 1973. **Experience:** res.— fire ecol., natural area mgmt, disturbance ecol.; admin.— developed & coordinated significant interdisc. res.progs on fire ecol.of Giant Sequoia *(Sequoiadendron giganteum)*, acid deposition, and global change effects on forests. **Career:** Res.Biol. USDI NPS (Sequoia & King's Canyon Nat. Parks) 1973–94; Dir Aldo Leopold Wilderness Res.Inst. USDA Forest Service 1994–. **Achievements:** developed & professionalized NPS res.prog., sig.influence on bringing credibility to this prog.through involving academic scientists. **Memberships:** ESA, CBS, Natural Areas Assn. **Awards:** Phi Beta Kappa, Phi Kappa Phi, Sci.of the Yr (NPS). **Publications:** *c.*100. Indiff.to pers. pub.& news media support. **Languages:** English, Spanish (good). Willing to act as consult.etc. **Address:** Aldo Leopold Wilderness Research Institute, POB 8089, Missoula, Montana 59807, USA. **Tel.**1 406 721 5697; **fax** 1 406 543 2663.

PARYSKI, Paul Edward. Environmental protection & rehabilitation; biodiversity conservation;

ecologically sustainable development. Chief Technical Adviser. *B.*16 Aug.1943, Toledo, OH, USA. American. *D.: d.* **Education:** Williams Coll. BA(Hons)(Hist.) 1965; Columbia U. MA (Hist./Educ.) 1967; Sems at U.of Florida on Farming Systems' Res.1989 and Intro.to Integrated Pest Mgmt 1990, on Sust.Dev. (WWF–US AID, in Haiti) 1985, and Parks & Prot.Areas (Intl, US NPS–Parks Canada–U.of Michigan) 1985. **Experience:** dev.of nat.envl policies & plans, envl strats, networks & coordn, community participation, cons.of biodiv., envl monitoring. **Career:** 2nd Sec. US Foreign Service, Casablanca 1968–72; co-Founder & -Dir. Third Eye Design Studio 1972–86; Consult.to Le Musée d'Art Haitien 1972–4; co-Founder & Asst Dir, Institut de Sauvegarde du Patrimoine Nat.1979–87; Field Coord.& Asst Prof. U.of Florida 1987–92; Envl Consult. UNDP 1992–. **Achievements:** organized sems on Amer.culture & politics in London for US Embassy 1968–70; estab.Haiti's first graphic design studio 1973 and assisted in estab.of Institut de Sauvegarde du Patrimoine Nat.1979; restored Fort Jacques 1979; init.Puerto Real archl project 1980; init./created two nat.parks in Haiti 1983; instrumental in starting envl movement in Haiti; creation of Haiti's first Biosphere Reserve 1988, and special UN Cttee to coordinate nat.envl progs, policies, & strats, for donor orgns, NGOs, & private sector, in Haiti 1992; estab.& manage model envl coordinating & monitoring unit for UNDP in Haiti to coordinate envl policies & strats, monitor the envt, fund envl microprojects, promote envl educ., and implement Agenda 21; helped design a regnl UNDP network (ECONET) as well as assisting UNDP in the Dominican Rep.and Nepal with their envl progs. **Memberships:** IUCN CNPPA 1986–, ICPB 1985–91, Société Haitiènne Audubon pour la Prot.de l'Environnement (Founding Memb.) 1985–, Orgn for the Rehab.of the Envt (Trustee & Dir), Fedn des Amis de la Nature (Founding Memb.& Tech.Consult.), Florida Mus.of Natural Hist.(Field Assoc. 1982–), USAID Team 1985–6, Govt of Haiti Task Forces 1986–7. **Awards:** var. local. **Publications:** The Macaya Biosphere Reserve project: report of observations, conclusions & recommendations (co-Author) 1989, Farmer participation in developing sust.agricl systems in the proposed Macaya Biosphere Reserve of Haiti 1990, The Macaya Biosphere Reserve project 1992; num.articles in Haitian media and participation in televised debates. Indiff.to pers.pub., favours news media support. **Languages:** Creole, English, French. Willing to judge proposals & ref.papers. **Address:** United Nations Development Programme, 18 Avenue Ducoste, Port-au-Prince, Haiti. **Tel.** (office) 509 234705 or 231401, (home) 509 452728; **fax** 509 239340 or 452728.

PATIL, Dr Rashmi S. Environmental impact assessment, air quality monitoring & modelling; air pollution meteorology. Associate Professor. *B.*26 March 1946, Kanpur, UP, India. Indian.

M.S.H.Patil. **Education:** Rajasthan U. first MSc (Phys.) 1967, Delhi U. PhD 1971. **Experience:** res.— developed air qual.dispersion models; fieldwork in envl monitoring, acid rain, receptor modelling; consult.to several industries & govt bodies on air qual.modelling & mgmt; teaching — grad.& undergrad.courses in envl sci.& engg for ten yrs. **Career:** Fac.Memb. IIT 1977–. **Achievements:** consults as described above, Convener of Intl Workshop in Envl Sci.& Engg Educ.sponsored by GTZ, invited lect.to several confs. **Memberships:** Govt of India Cttee on Envl Planning, Tech.Cttee of Maharashtra Poll. Control Bd, IASTA. **Publications:** 40+ j.&/or conf.papers. Dislikes pers.pub., favours news media support. **Languages:** English, Hindi. Willing to act as consult.etc. **Address:** Centre for Environmental Science and Engineering, Indian Institute of Technology, Powai, Bombay 400 076, Maharashtra, India. **Tel.**(office) 91 22 578 2545 ext.3251, (home) 91 22 578 5411; **fax** 91 22 578 3480.

PAYNE, Dr Junaidi aka **John Brian.** Conservation & management of Southeast Asian forests; mammals of Borneo. Project Director. *B*.15 Feb.1954, Cuckfield, Sussex, England, UK. British. *M*.Hajijah: *s., d.* **Education:** King's Coll.London BSc(Zool.) (1st Class Hons) 1975; Sidney Sussex Coll.Camb. PhD 1980. **Experience:** field res.surveys & liaison with Malaysian govt. **Career:** Project Dir, WWF Malaysia 1979–, team leader in prep.of Sabah Cons. Strat.1990–92. **Achievement:** assisting Sabah govt in furthering creation of biol.preserves. **Memberships:** MNS, BRC, Sabah Soc. **Publications:** *A Field Guide to the Mammals of Borneo* (co-Author) 1985, *Orang-utan, Malaysia's Mascot* (co-Author) 1989, *Wild Malaysia* 1990. Dislikes pers.pub., favours news media support. **Languages:** Bahasa Indonesia, Bahasa Malaysia, English. Willing to act as consult.etc. **Address:** Window Delivery Ticket Nr 40, 89400 Likas, Sabah, Malaysia. **Tel.**(office) 60 88 52170, (home) 60 88 248552; **fax** 60 88 236005/248552.

PAYNE, Dr Roger S. Whale conservation, ocean toxicology. Institute President. *B*.29 Jan.1935, New York City, NY, USA. American. *M*.1.Katharine: 2 *s*.incl.John and 2 *d*.Laura & Holly (all active envlists); 2.Lisa: *s.* **Education:** Harvard U. AB(Biol.) 1956, Cornell U. PhD (Animal Behaviour & Neurophysiology) 1961. **Experience:** res., lecturing, admin., cons. writing & filming. **Career:** Founder & Inst.Pres. Whale Cons.Inst.(then Long Term Res.Inst.) 1971–. **Achievements:** init.res.on directional sensitivity of bats, owls, & moths, leading to study of whale song; co-discovery that sounds of humpback whales (*Megaptera* spp.) were actually repetitive, rhythmic songs — ensuing attention led to estab.of Save the Whales movement and acceptance of whales as intelligent creatures; co-leader of campaigns to end world-wide commercial whaling and to create whale sactuaries; continuance of res.using now-accepted benign res.techniques that do not require death of the whale. **Memberships:** Bd on 11 cons.orgns, scientific adv.-consult.-at-large. **Awards:** James Duggan Mem.(ALS) 1976, Order of the Golden Ark 1978, Memb.of Honour (WWF) 1980, Albert Schweitzer Medal (co-awardee) 1980, MacArthur F'ship 1984, Joseph Krutch Wood Medal (HSUS) 1989, Global 500 Roll of Honour (UNEP) 1989, Lyndhurst Fndn Award 1994. **Publications:** two books incl.*Among Whales* 1995, 52 articles 1958–, three recordings of whale song, many documentaries, film work resulting in two Cable Ace Awards, an Emmy, and a Golden Eagle Award. Favours pers.pub.& news media support. **Languages:** English, Spanish (poor). **Address:** 88 Crescent Lane, London SW4 9PL, England, UK. **Tel.**44 171 498 7720; **fax** 44 171 498 3184.

PEARCE, Professor David William. Environmental economics. Professor of Economics, Centre Director. *B*.11 Oct.1941, Harrow, Mx, England, UK. British. *M*.Susan Mary: 2 *s.* **Education:** U.of Oxf. BA 1963, MA 1967. **Experience:** u.lect.; Adv.to UK & overseas govts, cos, intl orgns; Consult.to World Bank, OECD, GEF, UNIDO, UNDP, UNEP. **Career:** Lect.in Econ. U.of Lancaster 1964–7; Lect.& Sr Lect. U.of Southampton 1967–74; Dir, Public Sector Res. Centre, U.of Leicester 1974–7; Prof.of Econ, U.of Aberdeen 1977–83; Prof.of Econ.1983–, Dir of Centre for Social & Econ. Res.on the Global Envt 1990–, UCL. **Achievements:** author/ coord.of many documents for intl orgns, author of 20+ books on envl econ., lead author IPCC, memb.adv.panel of GEF. **Memberships:** EAEE, USAEE. **Awards:** Global 500 Roll of Honour (UNEP) 1989, Giuseppe Mazzotti Prize for Lit. **Publications:** 40+ books incl. *Blueprint for a Green Economy* 1989, *Blueprint 2* 1991, *Blueprint 3* 1993, *World Without End* 1993, *Econ. Values and the Natural World* 1993, *Causes of Deforestation* 1994. Indiff.to pers. pub.& news media support. **Language:** English. **Address:** Centre for Social & Economic Research on the Global Environment, University College London, Gower Street, London WC1E 6BT, England, UK. **Tel.**44 171 380 7874; **fax** 44 171 916 2772.

PEARLMAN, Miss Nancy. Environmental broadcasting. Executive Producer. *B*.17 April 1948, Huntington, W.Virginia, USA. American. **Education:** UCLA BA(Anthrop.) *cum laude* 1971, Community Coll.& Adult Educ. Credentials 1976–8; Antioch U. MA(Urban Studies & Planning) 1979; USC Secondary Teaching Credential 1979. **Experience:** consult.& media dir, freelance journalism; coll. instr.; travel & study in over 50 countries & 50 states. **Career:** Host/ Producer/Dir of weekly intl radio series Envl Directions 1977–; Exec. Producer & Host of 'ECONEWS' (a nationwide envl news, interview, & documentary TV series) 1984–; Exec. Producer, Educl Communications 1972–; Host, Envl Viewpoints radio series 1988–. **Achievements:** Founder, Ecol Center of Southern Calif.

1972–; has reached over 15 m.people weekly with the envl message; first to document critical ecol issues for nat.radio & TV; creator of Envl Directions (radio series) & 'ECONEWS'; Founding co-Coord. Earth Day 1970. **Memberships:** ATAS, Bd of Dirs & Adv.Council of num.envl, cons., & ecol, orgns *e.g.* Universal Pantheist Soc., Calif.Wilderness Coalition, Judge for Chevron-Time Cons. Awards. **Awards:** Chevron Cons.Award 1987, Diamond Award (Southern Calif.Cable Assn) 1989, Global 500 Roll of Honour (UNEP) 1989, Earth Harmony Achievement Award 1991, Renew Amer.Award (NEAC) 1992. **Productions:** *c*.300 TV shows, 850 radio progs, 127 issues of the *Compendium Newsletter*, 19th edn of *Directory of Envl Orgns*. Favours pers.pub.& news media support. **Language:** English. Further details may be obtained from *Who's Who of Amer.Women, The World Who's Who of Women, Outstanding Amer. Community Leaders* (all in 1970s). Willing to act as consult.etc. **Address:** POB 351419, Los Angeles, California 90035-9119, USA. **Tel.** (office) 1 310 202 7553 or 559 9160.

PEARMAN, Dr Peter Bretton. Ecology & conservation biology, tropical ecology, experimental field biology, amphibian ecology; evolution, development of science in developing countries. Postdoctoral Fellow. *B*.3 April 1959, Michigan City, IN, USA. American. **Education:** Duke U. MA 1988, PhD 1991. **Experience:** res.on effects of habitat subdivision & fragmentation on animal pops & communities 1987–95, Coord.of field courses in pop.& cons.biol.in Ecuador 1991–2. **Career:** Postdoctl F. Center for Cons.Biol. Stanford U.1993–; Scientific Adv. Ecuadorian Cons.Fndn (Jatun Sacha) 1994–5. **Achievements:** directed 'Jt Prog.for Biodiv.Res.' (Jatun Sacha Fndn & Center for Cons.Biol.), biodiv.mapping in Upper Amazon Basin. **Memberships:** ASIH, AAAS, Ecol.Soc.of Amer., SCB, Sigma Xi. **Publications:** *c*.ten papers incl.An agenda for cons. res.and its application, with a case-study from Amazonian Ecuador 1995. Indiff.to pers.pub.& news media support. **Languages:** English, Spanish. Willing to act as consult.etc. **Address:** Center for Conservation Biology, Department of Biological Sciences, Stanford University, Stanford, California 94305-5020, USA. **Tel.**(office) 1 415 723 7684; **fax** 1 415 723 5920.

PEGLER, Dr David N. Mycology: tropical macrofungi. Assistant Keeper (Mycology). *B*.2 Nov.1938, London, England, UK. British. **Education:** U.of London, BSc 1960, MSc 1969, PhD 1974, DSc 1989. **Career:** Mycologist 1960–65, Experimental Officer 1965–72, SSO 1972–6, PSO 1976–87, Head of Mycology & Asst Keeper 1987–, R.Botanic Gdns; Vis.Prof. Inst.of Bot. U.of São Paulo 1987 & U.of Slovenia 1987; Sr Ed. *The Mycologist* 1987–93; Edl Bds *Trans.BMS, Mycological Res.*, *Cryptography–Mycology, Mycology Helvetica,* & *Micologia Neotropical Applicada*; Sec.-Gen. 11th Cong.of

Euro.Mycologists 1992. **Achievements:** Chairman IUCN SSC (Fungi) 1988–, Euro.Council for Cons.of Fungi 1989–92, IMA Council for Fungi in Europe 1989–92, ICTF 1994–. **Memberships:** BMS, SMF, MSA, F.LS. **Awards:** RS & Nuffield Fndn Bursary to E.Africa 1968, Brit. Council Exchange to India 1974, Prix Leonard 'Services to African Bot.' 1977. **Publications:** several incl.*Agaric Flora of E.Africa* 1977, *Agaric Flora of Lesser Antilles* 1983, *Agaric Flora of Sri Lanka* 1986, *Brit. Truffles* 1993, *Fungi of Europe — Investigation, Recording & Cons.*(Ed.) 1993. Favours pers. pub.& news media support. **Languages:** English, French (written). Willing to act as consult.etc. **Address:** The Herbarium, Royal Botanic Gardens, Kew, Richmond, Surrey TW9 3AE, England, UK. **Tel.**(office) 44 181 332 5257, (home) 44 181 287 6067; **fax** 44 181 332 5284.

PEINE, Dr John Douglas. National park management; Man and The Biosphere Programme; research in parks; strategies for ecologically sustainable development. Research Scientist. *B*.21 Jan. 1944, Dallas, TX, USA. American. *M*. Marie Elaine: 2 *d*.Mary Anne, Emelie Kaye (both u.students in envl sci.). **Education:** Purdue U. BS(For.) 1967, U.of Arizona MS(Watershed Mgmt) 1969, PhD(Watershed Mgmt) 1972. **Experience:** air poll.res.& monitoring, human resources' monitoring in parks; designing resource monitoring prog.and climate change res.prog.; devising strats to protect cultural resources; developing strats for sust.dev.for bufferzones around parks; consult.with IUCN. **Career:** Outdoor Rec.Planner 1972–; Social Sci.conducting Nat.Rec.Surveys 1977–; Chief Sci. Gt Smoky Mtns Nat.Park, NPS 1982–92; NPS–MAB Coord.for SE US 1991–3; Sci., U.of Tennessee 1993–. **Achievements:** created the concept of Nat.Heritage Corridor, instigated regnl planning for air poll.control. **Memberships:** Sigma Xi, IUCN, WHII. **Awards:** Spec.Achievement Award (NPS), Sigma Xi. **Publications:** *Mgmt of Biosphere Reserves* (Conf.Proc., Ed.) 1985, The role of interpretation in the Nat.Heritage Corridor concept 1988, Managing the Gt Smoky Mtns Nat.Park Biosphere Reserve for biol diversity 1989, Gt Smoky Mtns Nat.Park Biosphere Reserve air qual.prog.1990, *Ecosystem Mgmt for Sust.: Principles and Practices Illustrated by a Regnl Biosphere Cooperative* (Ed.) 1995; num.others. Favours pers.pub.& news media support. **Language:** English. Willing to act as consult.etc. **Address:** Cooperative Park Studies Unit, Forestry, Wildlife, and Fisheries, 274 Ellington Hall, University of Tennessee, Knoxville, Tennessee 37996, USA. **Tel.**(office) 1 615 974 4056, (home) 1 615 428 0538; **fax** 1 615 974 5229.

Peitong LIU, Professor, *see* **LIU, Professor Peitong.**

PELL, Senator Claiborne. Legislation & treaties dealing with oceans & environmental protection. Senator. *B*.22 Nov.1918, New York, NY, USA. American. *M*.Nuala: 2 *s*., 2 *d*. **Education:** St George's Sch.RI; Princeton U. AB *cum laude* 1940; Columbia U. AM 1946. **Experience:** US Coast Guard Officer in charge of rebuilding Sicilian fisheries 1943–4; participated in SF Conf.that set groundwork for forming UN; Foreign Service Officer. **Career:** US Coast Guard veteran of WWII, Foreign Service Officer 1945–52, businessman 1952– 60, US Senator 1960– and Chairman US Senate Foreign Relations Cttee 1982–94. **Achievements:** efforts to curb nuclear arms race (incl.writing treaties to prohibit emplacement of weapons of mass destruction on the seabed and a treaty prohibiting the use of envl modification techniques as weapons of war); only US Senator to participate in UN's first envl conf.in Stockholm 1972, participated in UNCED Rio 1992; guided Montreal Protocol on Substances that Deplete the Ozone Shield through Senate Foreign Relations Cttee and full Senate in 100th Cong.; pioneering work on Section 119 of Foreign Assistance Act has resulted in a multimillion-dollar effort to assist countries in prot.of world's priceless biol diversity; originator of drive in 1972 for intl treaty which led to 1976 UN Envl Modification Conv.prohibiting alteration of envt as technique of warfare; Senate father of Sea Grant College Prog.Act 1965; co-Founder Sub cttee on Oceans & Envt 1971; co-Sponsor of Oil Spill Liability Act 1989; led Congressional efforts which eventually created Bur.of Oceans, Envt & Sci.; co-Author and jt introducer of Nat.Energy Policy Act 1990; advocate of negotiation of comp.treaty to govern usage of world oceans; co-Author (of Senate-adopted) measure calling for negotiation of EIA treaty; co-Author of legis.promoting support for debt-for-Nature swaps. **Awards:** Red Cross of Merit 1941, Grand Cross of Order of Christ 1980, Grand Cross of Order of Henry The Navigator 1987, Grand Cross of Order of Merit 1994 (all from Portugal); Caritas Elizabeth Medal (Cardinal Franz Koenig) 1957; Grand Cross of Merit (Knights of Malta) 1966; Grand Cross Order of Merit (Italy) 1972 and (Liechtenstein) 1973; Commander Order of Phoenix 1978 and Grand Cross of Order of Phoenix 1988 (both from Greece); Grand Cross of N.Star (Sweden) 1976; Gold Medal of St Barnabas (Cyprus) 1979; Grand Officer Order of Merit (Luxembourg) 1979; Grand Decoration of Honour in Silver with Sash (Austria) 1980; Knight, and Officer, Legion of Honour (France) 1982; Hugo Grotius Commem. Medal 1987 and Grand Officer in Order of Orange Nassau 1994 (both from The Netherlands); Global 500 Roll of Honour (UNEP) 1987; Medal of Nat.Order of Cedar, Grade of Commander (Lebanon) 1988; Sitara-I-Quaid-I-Azam (Pakistan) 1990; Presidential Citizen's Medal (USA) 1994; 46 hon. degrees. **Publications:** *Megalopolis Unbound* 1966, The *Challenge of the Seven Seas* (co-Author) 1966, *Power and Policy* 1972; legis. such as Nat.Sea Grant Coll.Prog.Act, and consideration of ratification of Law of the Sea Treaty. Favours pers.pub.& news media support. **Languages:** English; French, Italian & Potuguese (all minimal). **Address:** US Senate, 335 Russell Building, Washington, District of Columbia 20510, USA. **Tel.**1 202 224 4642.

PELUSO, Dr Nancy Lee. Sociology of forestry, political ecology, social forestry; environment, development. Associate Professor. *B*.15 Oct. 1952, Bridgeport, CT, USA. American. *M*. William D.Langbein: 2 *s*. **Education:** Friend's World Coll.(NY) BA(Anthrop.) 1977; Cornell U. MSc(Rural Sociol.) 1983, PhD(Rural Sociol.) 1988. **Experience:** 20 yrs' res.in Indonesia, 15 on forests & for.and indigenous/local mgmt of natural resources; teaching, consult. **Career:** Vis.Lect. Natural Resource Sociol. UCB 1988 & 1988–90; Asst Prof.1992–4, Assoc.Prof.(non-tenured) 1994–, of Resource Policy, Yale Sch.of For.and Envl Studies. **Achievements:** conducted baseline res.and helped estab.first social for.prog.in Java, conducted training for Chinese foresters & biologists in social sci.theory & methods, trained SE Asian social scis in theory & methods in pol.ecol.and resource tenure; res.in Java & Indonesia 1975– on people's interaction with trop.forests; Assoc.Ed.*Soc.and Natural Resources* 1988–94, Ed.*Common Property Resource Digest* 1995 , **Memberships** AAG, IASCP, Assn for Asian Studies, AAA, Rural Sociol.Soc. **Awards:** Lauriston Sharp Award for Scholarship & Community (Cornell U.) 1988, Award of Merit (Natural Resources Section, Rural Sociol.Soc.) 1994, Award for Outstanding Scholarly Achievement (Rural Sociol.Soc.) 1995. **Publications:** four monogrs incl.*Rich Forests, Poor People: Resource Control and Resistance in Java* 1992 (paperback 1994); num.refereed j.articles and chapters incl. Non-timber Forest Products in E.Kalimanatan, Indonesia: Can Extraction be Reserved? 1992, The rock, the beach, and the tidal pool: people and poverty in natural resource-dependent areas of the US (co-Author) 1994, Social aspects of for.in SE Asia: a review of the trends in the scholarly lit.(co-Author) 1995. **Languages:** Dutch (read), English, French, Indonesian, Javanese (spoken). Willing to act as consult.etc. **Address:** Yale School of Forestry and Environmental Studies, 205 Prospect Street, New Haven, Connecticut 06511, USA. **Tel.**1 203 432 8930; **fax** 1 203 458 8927.

PENNY, Dr Stella Frances. Conservation management. Regional Conservator. *B*.9 Jan.1948, Tavistock, Devon, England, UK. New Zealander. *M*.Evan Penny (Regnl Counc.& Envl Consult.): 3 *s*. **Education:** Victoria U.of Wellington, PhD(Zool.) 1976. **Experience:** ten yrs as envl consult.in freshwater biol., seven yrs as elected rep.in local govt, past memb. NZCA. **Career:** Chair & Bd Memb. Greenpeace NZ and Counc. Waikato Regnl Council 1989–93; Memb. NZCA 1990–93; Regnl Conservator, Waikato Dept of Cons.1993–. **Achievements:**

first woman in NZ appointed Regnl Conservator, improved admin.& policy dev.in envt/cons.orgns. **Membership:** NZLS. **Award:** Women's Suffrage Centenary Medal (NZ) 1993. Favours pers.pub. & news media support. **Language:** English. Willing to act as consult.etc. **Address:** 37 Albert Street, Hamilton, New Zealand. **Tel.**(office) 64 7 838 3363, (home) 64 7 856 0134; **fax** 64 7 838 1004.

PEREIRA, Dr Sir (Herbert) Charles. Management of tropical watersheds, research in hydrological effects of land-use; research organization. Independent Consultant. *B.*12 May 1913, London, England, UK. British. *M.*(Lady) Irene B.Sloan (conduct of maternity clinics in Africa). **Education:** U.of London BSc 1934, PhD(Soil Phys.) 1939, DSc 1961. **Experience:** military, admin., res. extensively in Africa, consult.to World Bank, FAO, UNDP, ODA, IDRC, WRI, and in 56 countries. **Career:** served to Major, R.Engrs (Mentioned in Dispatches) 1940–46; Kenya Coffee Res.(Colonial Service) 1946–52; Dep.Dir, EAAFRO 1952–61; Dir, ARC of C.Africa (Rhodesia, Zambia & Malawi) 1961–9; Dir, E.Malling Res.Station (UK) 1969–72; Chief Sci.(Dep.Sec.), MAFF 1972–7; Ind.Consult. 1978–. **Achievements:** trop.soil phys.& water-use res., estab.of long-term watershed studies of land-use changes in Kenya, Uganda, Tanganyika; in UK, as Chief Sci.of MAFF, introduced contract funding for res. **Memberships:** F.RS 1969, BSSS, RoyMetS, BHyd.S, WASWC, F.IBiol., TAA (Pres.). **Awards:** Haile Selassie Award for African Res.1966, Hon.F.(RASE) 1975, Hon.DSc (Cranfield U.) 1977, Knight Bachelor 1977. **Publications:** incl.*Land Use and Water Resources* 1973, *Policy & Practice in the Mgmt of Trop.Watersheds* 1989. **Languages:** English, French (read). Further details may be obtained from *Intl Who's Who* 1994–5, British *Who's Who* 1996. **Address:** Pear Trees, Nestor Court, Teston, Maidstone, Kent ME18 5AD, England, UK. **Tel.**(home) 44 1622 813333; **fax** 44 1622 764508.

PERES, Dr Carlos Augusto. Conservation biology, tropical ecology. Research Fellow, Visiting Professor. *B.*5 May 1963, Belém, Pará, Brazil. Brazilian. *M.*Anina Carkeek (social anthrop.): *d.* **Education:** U.of Florida, MSc 1986; U.of Camb. PhD 1991. **Experience:** res. — field-work in Amazonia and Atlantic forest 1983–; admin. — mgmt of three field projects in Brazilian Amazonia on biodiv.surveys, primate community structure, cons.of indigenous reserves; consultant to WWF, USAID. **Career:** Center for Trop. Cons. Duke U.1992–3; Vis.Prof. U.of São Paulo 1993–6; Res.F. Centre for Social and Econ.Res. on the Global Envt, U.of E.Anglia 1996. **Achievements:** helped secure, by negns with controlling Brazilian oil co. (Petrobra), large area (Urucu R.Basin, Amaz., 1 m.ha) for Nature cons.; revised guidelines for implementation of systems of Nature Reserves in Amazonia. **Memberships:** SCB, ATB, IUCN SSC. **Awards:**

Res.Awards (NGS & WCS) 1991, Biodiv.Leadership Award (Bay Fndn) 1995. **Publications:** 40+ incl. Amazonian Nature reserves: an analysis of the defensibility status of existing cons.units and design criteria for the future (co-Author) 1995. Indiff.to pers. pub.& news media support. **Languages:** English, Portuguese. Willing to act as consult.etc. **Address:** Department of Ecología, University of São Paulo, São Paulo CP 11.461, 05422-970, Brazil *or* Centre for Social and Economic Research into The Global Environment, University of East Anglia, Norwich NR4 7TJ, England, UK. **Tel.**(UK) 44 1603 593173; **fax** (Brazil) 55 11 813 4151, (UK) 44 1603 250588.

PERNETTA, Dr John Christopher. Environmental and climate change impact assessment, cross-sectoral integrated coastal-zone management. Project Director. *B.*7 April 1947, Surbiton, Surrey, England, UK. British. *M.*Mary Theresa: *s., d.* **Education:** Bolton County Grammar Sch.; St John's Coll. U.of Oxf. MA, D.Phil 1973. **Experience:** res. — boreal, temperate, and trop., ecol.with emphasis on Indo–West Pacific; archaeology, anthrop., subsistence use of wildlife; admin.— Chairman Trop. Marine Res.Station, Dean Fac.of Sci; consult. — EIA and climate change impacts; teaching — 20 yrs' pre-u./undergrad./postgrad./& adult educ. levels. **Career:** Lect. U.of S. Pacific 1975–6, Univs of Manitoba & Winnipeg 1976–8; Lect., Sr Lect., Assoc.Prof. Dean of Sci. U. of PNG 1978–90; self-employed envl consult.1990–93; Dir, LOICZ Core Project, IGBP 1993–. **Achievements:** sci.policy adv.to Minister of Sci.& Educ. PNG 1984–6, envl adv.to PNG Dept of Envt & Cons.1989–90, envt adv. Govt of Rep.of Maldives 1988–; adv.to IOC–UNEP–WMO on dev.of global coastal monitoring component of GOOS, and to IUCN Marine and Global Change progs 1990–93. **Memberships:** Founder Chairman, Assn of S.Pacific Envl Instns 1986–90; expert memb.of GESAMP; IUCN SSC & Comm.on Ecol. **Awards:** Trevelyan Scholar 1966–9 and Christopher Welch Biol. Scholar 1969–73 (U.of Oxf.); highly commended runner-up, Sir Peter Kent Cons.Book Prize 1992. **Publications:** *Oceans — A World Cons. Atlas* 1991, *Philips Atlas of the Oceans* 1994; 20 other books, eight monogrs, *c.*40 sci. papers, *c.*40 articles and consult.reports. Indiff.to pers.pub., favours news media support. **Languages:** English, French (moderate), Italian & Spanish (comp.& written), Tokpigin. Willing to act as consult.etc. **Address:** Land–Ocean Interactions in the Coastal Zone Core Project Office, Netherlands Institute for Sea Research, POB 59, 1790 AB Den Burg, Texel, The Netherlands. **Tel.**(office) 31 222 369404, (home) 44 1553 636833 (UK); **fax** 31 222 369430.

PERRY, Dr John S. Atmospheric sciences, climatology; computer applications; environmental policy; international science. Board Director. *B.*18 Oct.1931, Lynbrook, NY, USA.

American. *M*.Barbara: 2 *s*. **Education:** Queens Coll.NY BS(Maths) 1953; U.of Washington (Seattle), BS(Met.& Climatology) 1954, MS (Met.& Climatology) 1960, PhD (Met.) 1966. **Experience:** weather forecasting, res. mgmt 1953–74; consult.on intl scientific planning for WMO, ICSU, IIASA; admin. re.NRC, mgmt of scientific adv.activities. **Career:** USAF 1953–74; Exec.Sci. US Cttee for GARP 1974–80; Scientific Officer Jt Planning Staff for GARP, WMO–ICSU 1976–8; Staff Dir, Bd on Atmos. Scis & Climate 1979–91; Dir, Bd on Global Change (US Nat.Cttee for IGBP) 1983– 94; Dir, Bd on Sust.Dev.1994–. **Achievement:** support for US & Intl planning on envl res.progs. **Memberships:** F.AMS, F.AAAS, AGU, Sigma XI. **Awards:** Staff Award (NRC), Legion of Merit & Disting. Service Medal (USAF). **Publications:** *The US Global Change Res. Prog.*1992, *Understanding our Own Planet* (ICSU) 1993, Intl instns for the global envt. Favours pers.pub.& news media support. **Languages:** English, French (fair spoken, poor written); German & Russian (some familiarity); Spanish (good). Willing to act as consult.etc. **Address:** 6205 Tally Ho Lane, Alexandria, Virginia 22307, USA. **Tel.**(office) 1 202 334 3517, (home) 1 703 329 1646; **fax** 1 202 334 2530; **internet** JPERRY@NAS.EDU .

PERTET, Fred Ole. Game watching, lecturing. Institute Principal. *B*.16 Aug.1944, Kajiado, Kenya. Kenyan. *M*.Dr Anne: *s*., *d*. **Education:** Mweka Coll.(Tanzania), Dipl.in Wildlife Mgmt 1967; U.of Nairobi BSc(Zool.) 1970, MSc(Vet. Anatomy) 1973; paramilitary training. **Experience:** admin.— managing training function, budgeting, project planning & design, logistical support and staff supervision, memb. Moi U. Council, Bd of Govs NWFTI; consult.to CNPPA, EAWS, curr.& short course design; training the trainer; lect.— natural hist.of mammals from Cert.to Dipl.level; big-game hunting, game farming, park admin.& mgmt. **Career:** Game Warden, Min.of Tourism & Wildlife 1967–72; Game Biol. Kenya Game Dept 1972–7; Sec. Kenya Wildlife Fund Trust 1977–8; Systems Analyst, Kenya Rangeland Monitoring Unit 1978–9; Asst Dir Projects 1979–80, co-Head Wildlife Planning Unit CIDA, Game Dept 1980–82, Asst Dir Res. Game Dept 1982–4, Prin. 1984–, NWFTI. **Achievements:** basic res.on functional anatomy of Gazelle stomach (MSc thesis); estab.of NWFTI in 1984 (first in Kenya), dev.of its syllabus, and training scheme. **Memberships:** Moi U.Council (Presidential appointment), EAWS, OBMS (Mt Kenya Sch.of Adventure). **Award:** Field Prize (Mweka Coll.). **Publications:** num.incl.Tourism and its impact of wildlife cons.in Kenya (co-Author) 1984, Degradation and predation problems (conf.paper) 1985, Marine biosphere reserves in Kenya 1994. Indiff.to pers.pub.& news media support. **Languages:** English, Masai, Swahili (written). Willing to act as consult.etc. **Address:** Ministry of Tourism and Wildlife,

POB 30027, Nairobi, Kenya. **Tel.**(office) 254 2 331030, (home) 254 2 564138; **fax** 254 2 567577.

PETER, Ian W. Information, information technology, computer communications as applied to environmental research; rain-forest, sustainable development. Consultant. *B*.9 June 1948, Sydney, Australia. Australian. **Education:** N. Sydney Boys' High Sch. Higher Sch.Cert.1967. **Experience:** res.& consult.on application of info.technologies to sust.dev.; global communications; consult.to UNEP, UNCED, UNDP, on networking & communications initiatives. **Career:** Mgr, radio station 1980–83; Dir Rainforest Info.Centre, and co-Ed.*World Rainforest Report* 1983–8; Chairman, Pegasus Networks, & Intl Dir, Assn for Progressive Communications 1988–92; Consult.1992–. **Achievements:** promotion of rain-forest issues 1980–88, bldg of intl envl communications networks & linkages. **Membership:** IUCN CEC. **Publications:** *Australian Non-Buyers' Guide* 1985, *The Problem Solving Debate* 1986, *World Rainforest Report* (co-Ed.) 1980–88, Networks, *NGOs and New Possibilities in the Asian/Pacific Regn* 1993, *Sust.Dev.Networks — Concepts & Practice in Australia* 1993. Favours pers.pub.& news media support. **Languages:** English; limited French, German, Portuguese, & Spanish. Willing to act as consult.etc. **Address:** c/o Pegasus Networks, POB 284, Broadway, Queensland 4006, Australia. **Tel.**61 7 257 1111; **fax** 61 7 257 1087; **e-mail** ianp@peg.apc.org .

PETERKEN, Dr George Frederick. Forest ecology and Nature conservation particularly in relation to ancient woodlands in Britain and the rest of Europe. Independent Consultant, Special Professor. *B*.21 Oct.1940, Hillingdon, Mx, England, UK. British. *M*.Susan Mary: 2 *s*.incl. Andrew (Co.Officer, Countryside Council for Wales). **Education:** Haberdashers Aske's Sch.; King's Coll.London, BSc & AKC 1961; UCL PhD 1965; U.of London DSc 1989. **Experience:** initial posts in res., teaching, admin., & data processing, thereafter primarily as woodland ecol.involved in advising & resolving issues at all scales from individual sites to nat.policies; specialist in developing & applying res.directly related to cons.issues; wide exp.of Euro., N. Amer., & Australasian, native woodlands; frequent involvement in training of both ecologists & foresters. **Career:** Res.Dem. Bot.Dept, UC of Wales (Aberystwyth); Scientific Coord.for IBP section on Cons.of Terr.Communities 1965–7; SO in Biol.Records Centre, Monks Wood Experimental Station (NC) 1967–9; Woodland Ecol.with NC, NCC, JNCC 1969–93; sabb. Bullard F.in Forest Res. Harvard U. and Leverhulme Res.F'ship 1989–90; Ind.Consult.1993–; Ecol.Consult. Forestry Comm.(UK) 1993–; Spec. Prof. U.of Nottingham 1994–. **Achievements:** histl studies and long-term perm.plot studies of Brit.woodlands, helped pioneer histl approach to woodland cons.in Britain, developed concept of ancient woodland indicators and applied this to cons.issues, devised class.of semi-natural woodlands in Britain; helped develop cons.elements of 1985 Broadleaves Policy in UK and subs. detailed guidance on mgmt of ancient woods; contributed to re-design of plantation forests; promoted floodplain forest restoration; founded Cons.Ecol.Group in BES. **Memberships:** BES, BSBI, Inst.of Chartered Foresters, Natural Areas Assn, Home-grown Timber Adv.Cttee (UK) (Envt Sub-Cttee). **Awards:** James Cup (RFS) 1975, OBE 1994. **Publications:** *Guide to the Check Sheet for IBP Areas* (Compiler) 1967, *Woodland Cons.& Mgmt* 1981 & 1993, Forestry Auth.Guides — *Mgmt of Semi-natural Woodlands* (main Contrib.) 1994, *Natural Woodlands* (in press); *c.*70 papers. Indiff.to pers.pub.& news media support. **Language:** English. Willing to act as consult.etc. **Address:** Beechwood House, St Briavels Common, Lydney, Gloucestershire GL15 6SL, England, UK. **Tel.& fax** 44 1594 530452.

PETERSON, Mrs Claire McCARTHY. Land-use law and zoning especially respecting impacts of tourism on environmental & legal systems. Researcher, Author, Consultant. *B.*30 April 1944, New York, NY, USA. American. *M.*Prof.Craig A.Peterson *qv: s., d.* **Education:** Wellesley Coll. BA 1965, Harvard Grad.Sch.of Arts & Scis. **Experience:** num.res.& writing projects, researcher for num.legal cases in USA; lecturing in USA & abroad. **Career:** res.& writing in connection with consult.practice 1975–, Asst Legis.Dev.Ed. *Land Use & Zoning Digest* (APA) 1979–86. **Achievements:** studies concerning impact of tourism on envl & land-use patterns in Greece, and cultural tourism in Oaxaca (Mexico); res.& drafting of brief for major envl US Supreme Court case; lectured to Greek Min.of Envt & Planning; memb. Disability Rights Adv.Council (Office of the Attorney Gen.of State of IL) Zoning & Envl Barriers Cttees. **Membership:** APA. **Awards:** Durant Scholar (highest hons) & Phi Beta Kappa (Wellesley Coll.). **Publications:** *Handling Zoning & Land Use Litigation* (co-Author) 1982, *Arbitration, Strat.& Technique* (co-Author) 1986; num.academic articles. Indiff.to pers.pub.& news media support. **Languages:** English, French. Willing to act as consult.etc. **Address:** 2745 Woodbine Avenue, Evanston, Illinois 60201, USA. **Tel.**(office & home) 1 708 475 2409; **fax** 1 708 475 2438; **e-mail** clairemcp@aol.com .

PETERSON, Professor Dr Craig A. Land-use law especially re.impacts of tourism on environmental & legal systems. Professor of Law, Consultant. *B.*15 Nov.1941, Chicago, IL, USA. American. *M.*Claire McCarthy Peterson *qv: s., d.* **Education:** Cornell U. BA(Govt) 1963, Harvard Law Sch. JD 1966. **Experience:** PI on num. res.& writing projects; consult.attorney in num.legal cases in the US; lecturing in US & abroad. **Career:** Military Attorney 1967–71; Assoc.Attorney, Lord, Bissell & Brook 1971–3; Researcher & Consult.1973–; Prof.of Law, John

Marshall Law Sch.1974–. **Achievements:** studies concerning impact of tourism on envt & land-use patterns in Greece, and cultural tourism in Oaxaca, Mexico; Full Memb. *Land Use Reporter* panel which selects best academic articles in the land-use & envl fields; co-Counsel for num. US envl NGOs in important US Supreme Court envl case; educ.leader of study tours for attorneys, profs, and judges, to former Soviet Union and to PRC incl.lectures on envl topics; lectured to Greek Min.of Envt & Planning; former Legis. Dev.Ed.*Land Use & Zoning Digest* (APA). **Membership:** ABA. **Publications:** *Handling Zoning & Land Use Litigation* (co-Author) 1982, *Arbitration, Strat.& Technique* (co-Author) 1986, num.academic papers. Indiff.to newspaper pub. **Language:** English. Willing to act as consult.etc. **Address:** The John Marshall Law School, 315 South Plymouth Court, Chicago, Illinois 60604, USA. **Tel.** (office) 1 312 987 1439, (home) 1 708 475 2409; **fax** 1 708 475 2438; **e-mail/Internet** 7PETERSO@JMLS.EDU .

PETERSON, Dr Russell Wilbur. Influencing decision-makers (in & out of government) to face up to critical global issues such as population growth, environmental degradation, and depletion of resources. President Emeritus, Adviser. *B.*3 Oct.1916, Portage, WI, USA. American. *M.* Lillian J. **Education:** U.of Wisconsin BS 1938, PhD 1942. **Experience:** teaching, adv.to many envl orgns. **Career:** Res.Chemist to Dir R&D, E.I. du Pont de Nemours 1942–68; Gov.of Delaware 1969–73; Chairman & Pres. CEQ 1973–6; Dir Office of Tech.Assessment of US Cong. 1978–9; Pres. Nat.Audubon Soc. 1979–85; VP WCU (IUCN) 1984–8; Pres.ICBP 1982–90; VP Better World Soc.1985–90; Vis.Prof.at Dartmouth, Carlton Coll., & U.of W-M. **Achievements:** as Gov.authored & insured passage of Delaware Coastal Zone Act 1972 (first time in the world such prot.of coastal zone was enacted prohibiting further heavy industry along Delaware coast); as Chairman of Pres.'s CEQ led effort to implement Envl Impact Statement process throughout govt and estab.of Envl Industry Council, and over 15 yrs successfully led battle with nat.& intl orgns to include such variables as pop.growth, resource consumption, energy risk, and growth in tech., as critical factors in work to protect global envt; built Nat. Audubon Soc.into a potent broad-based instn. **Memberships:** ACS, AAAS, F.WCU, BirdLife Intl (Pres.Emer.), Sigma Xi. **Awards:** 14 Hon. Doctorates, Commercial Dev.Assn 1971, NWF 1971, Gold Medal (WWF) 1971, NAS 1977, The Wilderness Soc.1984, Envl Law Inst.1990, num. others, Procter Prize (Sigma Xi), Parsons Award (ACS). **Publications:** over 400. Favours pers. pub.& news media support. **Language:** English. **Address:** 1613 North Broom Street, Wilmington, Delaware 19806, USA. **Tel.**(home) 1 302 428 0736.

PETR, Dr Tomislav O. Inland fisheries and interactions with environment. Retired. *B.*11

Aug.1935, Nachod, Czechoslovakia. Australian. *M*.Mary Catherine. **Education:** Charles U. MSc 1960, U.of Ghana PhD 1970. **Experience:** res., tech., admin., & consult., in inland fisheries mgmt: design, execution, & eval., of projects in Africa, Europe, Asia, & Pacific; interactions among inland fisheries & watersheds; impact of devs *(e.g.* dams, irrigation, mining) on fish stocks; trop.& temperate, arid & humid, envts. **Career:** SRF, Volta Basin R. Project, U.of Ghana 1964–70; Reader, Dept of Zool. Makerere U. 1970–73; Sr Tutor, Zool.Dept, Monash U.1974–7; Envl Mgr, Office of Envt & Cons. PNG 1977–80; Sr Fishery Officer, Dept of Fisheries, FAO 1980–95. **Achievements:** studies on impacts of major dams of Africa, Asia, & Pacific, on envt esp.fish stocks; designing projects to harmonize multi-use of aquatic resources. **Memberships:** FBA, ASFB, SIL. **Publications:** *The Purari* 1983, *Regnl Symp.on Sust.Dev.of Inland Fisheries under Envl Constraints* (Ed.) 1995; *c.*120 papers incl.Inland fisheries in multiple use of resources 1985, Expert consultation in inland fisheries of the larger Indo–Pacific islands 1987, Intensification of reservoir fisheries in trop.and subtropical countries 1994, Fisheries in arid countries of C.Asia and in Kazakhstan under the impact of irrigated agric.1995 — all tech. Indiff.to pers.pub. & news media support. **Languages:** Czech, English, German, Russian. Willing to act as consult.etc. **Address:** 27 McLeod Street, Toowoomba, Queensland 4350, Australia. **Tel.** & **fax** 61 76 358058.

PETRETTI, Dr Francesco. Ornithology (grassland & steppe birds); conservation biology of Mediterranean & agricultural ecosystems; environmental restoration. Independent Consultant & Natural History Journalist. *B*.6 Dec. 1959, Rome, Italy. Italian. *M*.Maria Michela: *s.* **Education:** U.of Rome PhD(Biol.) 1983. **Experience:** res.on status of endangered birds and pop.ecol.of raptors & bustards; under contract to Italian cos to assess envl impact of dams, highways, railways, artificial basins, chem.industries; consult. re.estab.of prot.areas, envl restoration, EIA, and to IEEP re.analysis of extensive agric.in Italy; has directed num.films re.wildlife in Italy. **Career:** Head of Field Progs 1983–92 & Nature Reserve Network 1983–5, Scientific Consult. 1993–, WWF Italy; Ind.Consult.& Natural Hist. Journalist 1993–. **Achievements:** promoted & implemented many cons.projects to assess status of endangered species, to reintroduce & manage bird & mammal pops in Nature reserves of WWF Italy. **Memberships:** Albo Nazionale dei Biologi, NCB (Corres.), WGs on raptors & bustards (former ICBP), Inst.for the Relationship between Italy and the Arab World. **Publications:** num. incl.Breeding biol.of the Short-toed Eagle (*Circaetus gallicus*) 1978, *A Field Guide to the Birds of Italy* 1984, *Enc.on Vanishing Animals* 1986, Ecol.and status of the Little Bustard (*Tetrax tetrax*) in Italy 1985, 1992. Favours news media support. **Languages:** English, French

(spoken), Italian. Willing to act as consult.etc. **Address:** Via degli Scipioni 268/a, 00192 Rome, Italy. **Tel.**39 6 683 08306; **fax** 39 6 321 1683.

PETTS, Professor Dr Geoffrey. River regulation, environmental impacts of dams & water resource schemes. Director, Professor of Physical Geography. *B*.28 March 1953, Folkestone, England, UK. British. *M*.Judith (hazardous waste mgmt). **Education:** U.of Liverpool BSc 1974, U.of Southampton PhD 1978. **Experience:** Sec.BHS 1988–90, Dir IWRA; memb. Scientific Adv.Panels of UNESCO, MAB, Mgmt of Land –Water Ecotones, and USDI FWS, Long-term Monitoring Prog.for the Upper Mississippi R. **Career:** Lect.in Geog. Dorset Inst.of Higher Educ.1977; Lect.in Geog.1979 then Prof.of Phys.Geog.1989, Loughborough U.; Dir, Envl Res.& Mgmt, and Prof.of Phys.Geog. U.of Birmingham 1993–. **Achievement:** founding Ed.*Regulated Rivers* 1987–. **Memberships:** SIL, IFM, BGS, BHS, IBG, RGS, IWRA. **Publications:** *Impounded Rivers* 1984, *Alternatives in River Regulation* 1989, *Histl Analysis of Large Alluvial Rivers* 1989, *Water Engg & Landscape* 1990, *Lowland Floodplain Rivers* 1992, *R.Cons.& Mgmt* 1992, *Rivers Handbook* (vols 1 1992 and 2 1993); Ed.*Regulated Rivers* 1987–, 60+ major papers. Favours pers.pub.& news media support. **Languages:** English, French (reading good, speaking fair). Willing to act as consult.etc. **Address:** School of Geography, The University of Birmingham, Edgbaston, Birmingham B15 2TT, England, UK. **Tel.** 44 121 414 5544; **fax** 44 121 414 5528.

PFADENHAUER, Professor Dr Jörg. Vegetation sciences; restoration ecology. Professor & Head of Department of Landscape Ecology, Centre Coordinator. *B*.1 Feb.1945, Munich, Germany. German. **Education:** Ludwig-Maximilians-U.(Munich), State Scientific Exam.in biol., chem., & geog.1969, Dr rer. nat.1969, Habil. (Landscape Ecol.) 1975. **Experience:** res.— resto.of disturbed ecosystems (agro-ecosystems, semi-terr.wetlands), pop.biol.of plants, landscape ecol.& planning; teaching — veg.& landscape ecol., Nature cons., pop.biol.of plants. **Career:** Res.F'ship, ETH 1970–71; Res.Asst, Dept of For. U.of Munich 1971–4 and Dept of Plant Ecol. U.of Hohenheim 1974–82; Prof. Universidade Fed.do Rio Grande do Sul 1976–8; Prof.& Head, Dept of Landscape Ecol.II, Tech. U.of Munich 1982–; Coord.of Ecosystem Res.Centre (Agroecosystems, Munich) 1994–. **Achievements:** assisting German Govt to create strats for Nature cons.; assessment of Nature reserves; creation & valuation of dev.measures. **Memberships:** BES, IAVS, Gesellschaft für Ökologie, etc.; Edl Bds *J.Veg.Sci., Zeitschrift Ökologie Naturschutz,* & *J.Rural Dev.,* Ed.*Verhandlungen der Gesellschaft für Ökologie.* **Publications:** books incl.*Edellaubholzreiche Wälder im Jungmoränengebiet des Bayerischen Alpenvorlandes und in den Bayerischen Alpen* 1969, *Vegetationsökologie — ein*

Skriptum 1993; *c*.100 scientific papers. Favours news media support. **Languages:** English, German, Portuguese. Willing to act as consult.&/or judge proposals. **Address:** Department of Landscape Ecology II, Technical University of Munich, D-85350 Freising-Weihenstephan, Germany. **Tel.**(office) 49 8161 713498, (home) 49 8161 44244; fax 49 8161 714143.

PFEIFFER, Professor Dr Egbert W. Environmental problems of third world, especially those related to war; environmental physiology of mammals (adaptations to cold, *e.g.* hibernation). Professor Emeritus of Zoology. *B*.23 May 1915, New York, NY, USA. American. *M*.Jean (gardener with Montana Native Plant Soc.): 2 *s.* incl.James (anthrop.), *d.* **Education:** Cornell U. AB 1937; UBC MA 1948; UCB PhD 1954. **Experience:** renal physiol.during hibernation in ground squirrels & prairie dogs *(Cynomys* spp.); ecol.effects of war in SE Asia & Nicaragua. **Career:** First Asst, NGS expedn to SA 1937–8; Victoria Rifles of Canada & US Marine Corps (WWII) 1940–45; Prof.of Biol. U.of Idaho 1954–5; Prof.of Zool. Utah SU 1955–7; Prof.of Anatomy, U.of N.Dakota Sch.of Med.1957–9; Prof. Zool.& Envl Studies 1959–87, Prof.Emer.of Zool.1987–, U.of Montana. **Achievements:** assisting AAAS & US NAS in studying effects of herbicides in Vietnam during second Indochina War (1961– 75). **Memberships:** AAAS, APS, ASZ, Sigma Xi (past). **Awards:** Spec.F.(US PHS) 1965–6, Inuvik Prize for 'Ecocide: A Strat.of War' (First Intl Film Festival on Human Envt) 1973, *Reconocimiento* (ABEN) 1987, Charter Bd Memb.(SIPI). **Publications:** Urea and the Kidney 1970, Harvest of Death 1972; *c*.50 scientific papers. Strong desire to work with news media on scientific matters. **Languages:** English, French, German, Spanish (read). **Address:** 855 Beverly Avenue, Missoula, Montana 59801, USA. **Tel.**(office) 1 406 243 6273, (home) 1 406 549 0570. **fax** 1 406 243 2648.

Philip, HRH The Prince, Duke of EDINBURGH, *see* **EDINBURGH, HRH The Prince Philip, Duke of.**

PHILLIPS, Professor Adrian. Conservation, especially of protected areas; environmental protection. Professor of Countryside & Environmental Planning, Environmental Consultant. *B*.11 Jan.1940, Exmouth, Devon, England, UK. British. *M*.Cassandra F.E. *qv*: 2 *s*.incl.Dr Oliver L.B. Phillips *qv*. **Education:** Christ Church Oxf. MA(Geog.) 1962; UCL, Dipl.(Town & Country Planning) 1965. **Experience:** envl & cons.policy & practice (nat.& intl), consult.in same fields. **Career:** Planning Officer, Planning Services, UK Govt 1962–8; Asst Dir, Countryside Comm. 1968–74; Head Prog.Coordn Unit, UNEP Nairobi 1974–8; Prog.Dir, IUCN 1978–81; DG Countryside Comm.1981–92; Prof.of Countryside & Envl Planning (part-time), U.of Wales 1992–; Envl Consult.(part-time) 1992–. **Achievement:** managed Countryside Comm.for 11 yrs

and oversaw major growth in its prog.& resources. **Memberships:** RTPI, ILA, IUCN CNPPA (Dep.Chair). **Award:** F. Landscape Inst.1992. **Publications:** The Countryside Comm.in the Thatcher Yrs 1993; num.papers & articles. **Languages:** English, French (limited). Willing to act as consult.etc. with prior notice. **Address:** 2 The Old Rectory, Dumbleton, near Evesham, Worcestershire WR11 6TG, England, UK. **Tel.**44 1386 882094; **fax** 44 1386 882094.

PHILLIPS, Mrs Cassandra F.E. Antarctic conservation, whale conservation; advocacy in international conventions. Antarctic & Cetacean Officer. *B*.10 Dec.1940, Newbury, Berks., England, UK. British. *M*.Prof.Adrian Phillips *qv*: 2 *s*.incl.Dr Oliver L.B.Phillips *qv*. **Education:** N.London Collegiate Sch.; Somerville Coll.Oxf. BA(Hons)(Pol., Phil.& Econ.) 1962. **Experience:** attendance at annual mtgs of IWC 1982–, and Antarctic Treaty mtgs 1989–; coordn & dev.of WWF policy on Antarctica & whaling, two visits to Antarctica as NGO observer for Brit.Antarctic Survey. **Career:** Econ.Adv. NEDO (UK) 1962–5; Geog.Teacher in Nairobi 1974–8; Res.Officer 1979–81, Antarctic & Cetacean Officer 1989–, WWF Intl; Cons.Asst to Sir Peter Scott 1981–9. **Achievements:** helped secure & maintain IWC moratorium on commercial whaling, IWC Southern Ocean Whale Sanctuary, and overturn Antarctic Mining Conv.and secure Antarctic Treaty Envl Protocol, making Antarctica a natural reserve free of all minerals' exploitation. **Memberships:** ECS, FFPS, The Antarctica Project (Bd, USA). **Award:** Sch.Exhibition to Somerville Coll.Oxf. **Publications:** *WWF Cons.Yearbook* 1985–6 (Ed.), assorted papers, lectures etc. Favours pers. pub.& news media support. **Languages:** English, French (spoken good, written fair), Swahili (some). Willing to act as consult.etc. **Address:** World Wide Fund for Nature, 2 The Old Rectory, Dumbleton, Evesham WR11 6TG, England, UK. **Tel.**(office) 44 1386 882055, (home) 44 1386 881973; **fax** 44 1386 882055.

PHILLIPS, Dr Oliver L.B. Tropical forest ecology; ethnobotany. Researcher. *B*.28 Nov. 1965, London, England, UK. British. Father Professor Adrian Phillips *qv*, mother Cassandra F.E. Phillips *qv*. *M*.Kate. **Education:** U.of Camb. BA 1987, Washington U.(St Louis) PhD 1993. **Experience:** res.— ethnobot. esp.quantitative ethnobot.in Amazonian Peru, and trop.forest ecol. esp.species-richness, turnover, & productivity estimates, in neotropics; consults — ethnobot.& econ.bot. **Career:** consults for Center for Plant Cons.& Shaman Pharmaceuticals PLC 1991–4; Researcher, Missouri Botl Gdn 1993–. **Achievements:** modelling biodiv.patterns in trop.forest biomes; discovery of changing tree pop.dynamics in trop.forests; developing quantitative approach to ethnobot. **Memberships:** AAAS, SCB, ISTF, SEB. **Awards:** Fulling Award (SEB) 1992, Michaux Award (APS) 1994, doctl res.awards from NSF,

WWF–US/Gdn Club of Amer., & Cons.Intl. **Publications:** Increasing turnover through time in trop.forests (co-Author) 1994, Dynamics and species richness of trop.rainforests (co-Author) 1994, Quantitative ethnobot.and Amazonian cons. (co-Author) 1994. Favours pers.pub.& news media support. **Languages:** English, French (read), Spanish. Willing to act as consult.etc. **Address:** Box 299, Missouri Botanical Garden, St Louis, Missouri 63166, USA. **Tel.**1 314 577 9570.

PHORNPRAPHA, Dr Phornthep. Business & social activities. Company President. *B.*27 Dec. 1948, Bangkok, Thailand. Thai. *M.*Mayuree: 2 s., d. **Education:** Cerritos Jr Coll.(CA) 1967; Calif.Coll.of Commerce, B(Business Admin.) 1969. **Experience:** prod.of direction analysis documents on participation of private sectors namely private dev.orgns (non-profit) and private business to endeavour to solve envl problems; thesis on 'Think Earth Project', a new mechanism to protect envt & natural resources. **Career:** Pres. Siam Motors Co.Ltd & Siam Motors Group of Cos 1993–. **Achievement:** 'Think Earth Project'. **Membership:** Senator of Parliament. **Awards:** Global 500 Roll of Honour (UNEP) 1993, ASEAN Achievement Award 1993; Hon.Doctorates in Geog.(Srinakharinwiroj U.) 1993 and in Agricl Tech. (Landscape Tech., Mae Jo Agricl Tech.Inst.) 1994. **Publications:** *Private Dev.Orgn and Private Business on Solving the Envl Problem* 1993, *'Think Earth Project'* (thesis) 1993. Favours news media support. **Languages:** English, Thai. **Address:** 1200 Paholyothin Road, Lardyao, Chatuchak, Bangkok, Thailand. **Tel.**(office) 66 2 513 0310–9, (home) 66 2 318 0778; **fax** 66 2 513 3279.

PIANKA, Professor Dr Eric R. Evolutionary biology; evolutionary landscape; community & lizard ecology; remote sensing; phylogenetic systematics; biogeography. Professor of Zoology. *B.*23 Jan.1939, Hilt, CA, USA. American. *D.:* 2 d. **Education:** Carleton Coll. BA 1960; U.of Washington at Seattle PhD 1965; U.of Western Australia at Nedlands DSc 1990. **Experience:** lecturing (100+ invited), admin., res.— diversity & ecol.of desert lizards, intercontinental comparisons in N.Amer., Kalahari, & Australia. **Career:** NIH Postdoctl at Princeton U.(R.H. MacArthur) & U.of Western Australia (A.R. Main) 1965–8; Asst Prof. 1968–72, Assoc.Prof.1972–7, Prof.1977– 86, Denton A.Cooley Centennial Prof.of Zool. (endowed for life) 1986–, U.of Texas at Austin; Vis.Prof. Univs of Kansas 1978 & Puerto Rico 1981. **Achievements:** memb.of IUCN SSC Australasian Reptile & Amphibian SG, pubns urging people to adopt an equilibrium steady-state economy & pop.control; raising Amer. Bison *(Bison bison)*. **Memberships:** Herpetologists' League, ASN, ESA, SSE, WANC, SSAR, ASIH (Bd of Govs). **Awards:** Guggenheim F., F. AAAS, lifetime Endowed Prof'ship, Fulbright Sr Res. Scholar to Australia, grants from NASA,

NSF & NGS. **Publications:** *Evolutionary Ecol.* (five edns, transl into Japanese, Polish, Spanish & Russian) 1974/78/83/88/94, *Lizard Ecol.: Studies of a Model Organism* (co-Ed.) 1983, *Ecol.& Natural Hist.of Desert Lizards* 1986, *The Lizard Man Speaks* 1994, *Lizard Ecol.: The Third Generation* (co-Ed.) 1994; Managing Ed.*The Amer.Naturalist, BioSci., Nat.Geographic Res., Res.& Exploration, & Enc.of Envl Biol.*; num.chapters & 100+ scientific res.papers incl.four 'citation classics'. Indiff.to pers.pub.& news media support. **Languages:** English; French & German (little), Spanish (some). Further details may be obtained from *Who's Who in Amer.*1980–89. Willing to act as consult.etc.if contacted in time. **Address:** Department of Zoology, University of Texas, Austin, Texas 78712–1064, USA. **Tel.**(office) 1 512 471 7472, (home) 1 210 868 7516; **fax** 1 512 471 9651.

PICOUET, Michel René. Dynamics of demography, migration, & environment, in developing countries. Research Director. *B.*25 Feb.1940, Sousse, Tunisia. French. *M.* **Education:** U.of Paris, Diplôme d'Etudes Supérieures Spécialités (Econométrie) 1967, Expert Démographe 1968. **Experience:** res.in Tunisia 1968– 74, Venezuela 1975–81, France 1982–; consult. **Career:** Researcher 1957–85, Dir of Res. Laboratoire Pop.–Environnement 1985–, ORSTOM. **Achievements:** work on demographic dynamics & natural surroundings in Tunisia 1988–, demographic growth & envt in rural areas from theoretical approach to measurements. **Memberships:** IUSSP, Société d'Ecologie Humaine. **Publications:** *Dinamica de la Poblacion: Caso de Venezuela* 1979, *Des Villes et du Pétrole au Venezuela* 1984, *La Dimension Migratotre des Antilles* 1993; articles. Favours pers.pub.& news media support. **Languages:** French, Spanish. Willing to act as ref. **Address:** Laboratoire Population Environnement, Université de Provence (ORSTOM), 25 Rue de la Providence, 13710 Fuveay, France. **Tel.**(office) 33 42 580316, (home) 33 42 585559; **fax** 33 42 680161; **e-mail** Picouet@orstom.orstom.fr .

PIELKE, Professor Dr Roger Alvin. Climate change & variability, mesoscale meteorology; atmospheric–ecological interactions; air pollution modelling. Professor of Atmospheric Science. *B.*22 Oct.1946, Baltimore, MD, USA. American. *M.* **Education:** Towson State Coll. BS(Met.) 1968; Penn.SU MS(Met.) 1969, PhD (Met.) 1973. **Experience:** res.studies of regnl & local climate & weather for over 25 yrs, Pres.of ASTeR Inc.which has resp.for transferring res.into beneficial societal products. **Career:** Res. Meteorologist, NOAA Experimental Lab.1971– 3; Asst Prof.1974–7, Assoc. Prof.1978–81, Dept of Envl Scis, U.of VA; Assoc.Prof.1982–5, Prof.1985–, Dept of Atmos. Sci. Colorado SU. **Achievements:** directed dev.of new techniques to represent more accurately met.flow on local & regnl scale which provides improved weather prediction & air qual.assessments; helped identify important linkages 'between Biosphere & atmos.' which is being shown to exert major control on weather & climate. **Memberships:** F.AMS, AGU. **Awards:** Disting.Authorship Award (NOAA) 1974, Leroy Meisinger Award (AMS) 1977, Abell Res.Fac.Award (Colorado SU) 1987–8, Res.of the Yr Award (Colorado SU Res.Fndn) 1993. **Publications:** *Mesoscale Met. Modelling* 1984 (transl.into Chinese 1990), *The Hurricane* 1990, *Human Impacts on Weather & Climate* (co-Author) 1992, Nonlinear influence of mesoscale land use on weather and climate (co-Author) 1991, Atmos.–terr.ecosystem interactions: implications for coupled modelling (co-Author) 1993, Effects of Mesoscale Veg. Distribns in Mountainous Terrain on Local Climate (co-Author) 1993; num.others. Indiff. to pers.pub.& news media support. **Languages:** Chinese (poor spoken), English, French (poor written & spoken), German (fair written & spoken), Spanish. Willing to act as consult.etc. **Address:** Department of Atmospheric Science, Colorado State University, Fort Collins, Colorado 80523, USA. **Tel.**(office) 1 303 491 8293; **fax** 1 303 491 8449.

PIIROLA, Dr Jouko. Landscape evolution; cartography; wildlife management, Nature reserves; popularizing biological & geographical knowledge & information. Docent. *B*.23 Feb.1935, Pukkila, Finland. Finnish. *M*. Irma. **Education:** U.of Helsinki BSc 1958, MSc 1959, PhD 1967. **Experience:** consultancies in Zambia involving air photographic interpretation, envl investigations, cartography; lecturing on envl problems, cons.& wildlife mgmt; non-fiction writer. **Career:** Assoc.Prof. U.of Joensuu 1970–71; Docent U.of Helsinki 1972–; Sr Lect.in Biol. & Geog. U.of Lapland 1979–91; Assoc.Prof. U.of Zambia 1991–3; Consult.to Foreign Min.of Finland 1975–7 and to SIDA 1991–3, both in Zambia. **Achievements:** assisting by investigation the Nat.Bd of For.of Finland in the expansion of the Lemmenjoki Nat.Park, res.with reports & recommendations on wilderness cons.and on landscape & forest degradation in & around Lusaka. **Memberships:** Non-fiction Writers' Union of Finland, Biol.& Geog.Teachers' Union of Finland, U.Lecturers' Union of Finland, Lapin Sivistysseura (Soc.for Lap Culture, Life), Valamo Soc.(Life). **Award:** Lt (Armed Forces of Finland). **Publications:** *The Inari Regn of Finnish Lapland* 1972, Deglaciation of the main water divide Saariselkä, Finland 1982; two chapters 1983 & 1988 and feature articles in Finnish press. Favours pertinent press releases & news media support. **Languages:** English, Finnish, German (read), Swedish. Willing to act as consult. **Address:** Myllarintie 38 B9, 96400 Rovaniemi, Finland. **Tel.**(office) 960 324 427, (home) 960 182 150; **fax** 960 324 401.

Ping, Mrs ZHANG, *see* ZHANG, Mrs Ping.

PINK, Dr David Anthony Child. Genetics of host–pathogen interactions in plant diseases;

plant genetics; utilization of wild species in plant breeding. Principal Research Scientist. *B*.24 Feb.1956, Shamley Green, Surrey, England, UK. British. *M*.Barbara Patricia: *s., d.* **Education:** King's Sch.(Tynemouth); U.of Birmingham BSc 1978, PhD 1982. **Experience:** res.— use of wild species & genetic resources in plant breeding. **Career:** Higher SO, Plant Breeding Inst. (Camb.) 1981–2 and Nat.Vegetable Res.Station 1982–7; SSO, Inst.of Hortl Res.1987–91; Prin. Res.Sci. HRI 1991–. **Achievement:** Memb.of Council of AAB 1990–93. **Memberships:** BSPP, AAB. **Publications:** 30+ papers incl. Recent trends in the breeding of minor field-vegetable crops for the UK (Plant Breeding Abstracts) 1984, Novel pathotypes of lettuce mosaic virus — breakdown of a durable resistance? 1992, five chapters in *Genetic Improvement of Vegetable Crops* 1993. Indiff.to pers. pub.& news media support. **Language:** English. Willing to act as consult.etc. **Address:** Horticulture Research International, Wellesbourne, Warwickshire CV35 9EF, England, UK. **Tel.**44 1789 470381; **fax** 44 1789 470552.

PINOWSKI, Professor Dr Jan Krystyn. Ecology of birds *(Passer* spp.); applied ornithology; suburban ecosystems' management. Head of Department. *B*.15 Oct.1930, Kraków, Poland. Polish. Mother Jadwiga Przybylowska (biol.). *M*.Barbara (ecol.of *Passer* spp.): 2 *d*.incl. Agnieszka (hydrobiol.). **Education:** Jagiellonian U. B(Biol.) 1952; Warsaw U. M(Zool.) 1954, PhD 1959, Habil.1968. **Experience:** coordn of four interdisc.progs; ecol.of birds and mgmt of suburban ecosystems; admin.as Head of Ornithl Station (Gdansk) 1970–73 and Head of Dept of Vertebrate Ecol.(Poland & Caracas) 1978–9; org.of eight intl symposia. **Career:** Asst 1953–4 & 1957–60, Adjunct 1960–68, Docent 1969, Extraordinary Prof.1975, Prof.1989, Head of Dept of Vertebrate Ecol.1980–, Inst.of Ecol. Polish AS. **Achievements:** init.& co-org.of WG on Granivorous Birds (IBP/INTECOL) within which coordinated investigation on ecol. of granivorous birds esp.*Passer* spp.carried out in 25 countries; coordn of suburban mgmt studies. **Memberships:** INTECOL (Bd 1986–90), AOU, Polish Ecol.Soc., Kampinos Nat.Park (Scientific Council), Nature Prot.Comms in Poland. **Awards:** Hon.F.(AOU) 1977, VP of 20th IOC (1990, NZ). **Publications:** ten books incl.*Productivity Pop.Dynamics and Systematics of Granivorous Birds* (co-Author) 1973, *Granivorous Birds in Ecosystems* (co-Author) 1977, *Nestling Mortality of Granivorous Birds due to Microorganisms and Toxic Substances* (co-Author) 1991, and (of earlier works) *Synthesis* (co-Author) 1995; *c*.250 scientific pubns. Favours news media support. **Languages:** Czech, English, Polish, Slovak, Russian (basic). Further details may be obtained from *Intl Who's Who of Intellectuals* 1992, *Who's Who in the World* 1995, *Who's Who in Amer.*1996. Willing to act as a consult.&/or ref. **Address:** Institute of Ecology, Polish Academy of Sciences, 05-092

Lomianki, Poland. **Tel.**(office) 48 22 751 3046, (home) 48 22 352881 or 751 2676; **fax** 48 22 751 3100.

PITT, Professor Dr David. Mountain ecosystems; environmental security, ecodevelopment; health, islands, anthropology. Chargé de Recherches. *B.*15 Aug.1938, Wellington, NZ. New Zealander. *M.*Carol: 3 *s.*Jerome (agric.), Joshua (agricl engg), Joseph (hort.), 4 *d.* **Education:** U.of NZ BA 1961; Balliol Coll. Oxf. B.Litt, M.Litt 1963, DPhil.1966. **Experience:** taught at Univs of Oxf.(extra-mural studies), Victoria (BC), Auckland, and Waikato, before going to Geneva as consult.to UN and related NGOs. **Career:** Lect. Extra Mural Studies, U.of Oxf.1962–3; Asst Prof. Anthrop.& Sociol. U.of Vic.1966–9; Prof. Sch.of Social Scis, Waikato U.1969–72; Prof.& Head, Dept of Sociology, U.of Auckland 1972–80; Consult.UN 1980–86; Chargé de Recherches, GIPRI 1986–. **Achievements:** promoted mtn ecol.as Chairman IUCN Mtn Cttee 1985–9, and Sec. Alp Action, Bellerive Fndn 1989–. **Membership:** F.RAI. **Awards:** Sr Scholar (U.of NZ) 1961, Horniman Scholar (RAI) 1963–6, Vernadsky Medal (former USSR AS) 1989. **Publications:** 20 books incl. *Trad.& Econ.Progress in Samoa* 1970, *Culture & Cons.*1984, *Mtn World in Danger* 1991. **Languages:** English, French. Further details can be found in *Who's Who* (NZ), *Intl Biog.of Writers*. Willing to act as consult.etc. **Address:** 1265 La Cure, Switzerland. **Tel.** (home) 41 22 360 1452.

PITTA, Professor Luis CAEIRO. Environmental legislation; public participation; right to information; access to justice. Legal Consultant, Professor of EEC Environmental Law. *B.*24 July 1956, Montijo, Portugal. Portuguese. *D.: s.* **Education:** U.of Aix-en-Provence, Licence en Droit 1978, Maîtrise en Droit Intl & Commu nautaire 1979. **Experience:** consult.with EEC Comm. (DGXI), prep.for doctl degree on 'Public Participation in Envl Policies in Portugal', spec.attention to public participation & envl educ.in Portugal as well as EEC envl law implementation. **Career:** Legal Consult. Min. of Justice 1980–86, Min.of Envt & Natural Resources 1986–89, Min.of Foreign Affairs 1989–; Prof.of EEC Envl Law, Catholic U.of Portugal 1989–. **Achievement:** res.projects for EEC Comm.concerning implementation of envl law in Portugal. **Memberships:** IUCN CEL, CIEL. **Publications:** several articles. Favours pers.pub.& news media support. **Languages:** English, French, Italian, Portuguese, Spanish. Willing to act as consult.etc. **Address:** AMBIFORUM, Centro de Estudos Ambientais Lda, Praca José Fontana Nr 25–1°Dt°, 1000 Lisboa, Portugal. **Tel.**(office) 351 1 54 5219 or 315 2691; **fax** 351 1 315 2692.

PLAYER, Ian Cedric. Conservation issues, particularly wilderness. Foundation Vice-Chairman. *B.*15 March 1927, Johannesburg, RSA. S.African. *M.*Ann: 2 *s., d.* **Education:** St John's Coll. 1936–43. **Experience:** 40 yrs in cons. issues — govt advising, fund-raising, extensive lecture tours world-wide. **Career:** served with 6th S.African Armoured Div.attached to Amer.5th Army in Italy 1944–6, gold-mine worker 1946–52, Natal Parks Bd 1952–74, VC of The Wilderness Leadership Sch.1972–83, Founder 1974 & VC 1993– The Wilderness Fndn. **Achievements:** 1952–74 initiated prog. and led capture team that translocated 'White' Rhinoceros (*Ceratotherium simus*) thus saving it from extinction, introduced Wilderness Trails, estab.extensive anti-poaching network, raised funds for & assisted in prod.of many documentary films, founded Wilderness Leadership Sch.; 1974–90 founded Intl Wilderness Leadership Fndn (US) and Wilderness Fndn (UK), estab.World Wilderness Cong.and to 1993 four have been held, Adv.to Philippine Govt on endangered Tamarou *(Anoa mindorensis,* a diminutive buffalo), successful fund-raising for cons.& wilderness progs; initiated Pietermaritzburg–Durban Canoe Marathon (Dusi) which has won 3 times. **Memberships:** SAWH, NYSC, Game Rangers' Assn, Explorer Club of the US, Trustee of Cape of Good Hope Centre for Jungian Studies. **Awards:** Knight in Order of Golden Ark, Decoration for Meritorious Service (RSA), Gold Medal for Cons.(SDZS & WSSA), Conservationist of the Yr (Game Cons.Intl, and Mzuri Wildlife Fndn), Paul Harris F.(Rotary Intl), Cons.Statesman Award (Endangered Wildlife Trust), PhD *h.c.* (Natal U.), Disting. 'Wilderness Resource' Lect. (U.of Idaho). **Publications:** *Men, Rivers & Canoes* 1963, *Big Game* 1972, *White Rhino Saga* 1973, *Voice from the Wilderness* 1981, *More from the Wilderness* 1984, *Man and the Wilderness* 1986. Disfavours pers.pub.& news media support. **Language:** English. Willing to act as a consult. **Address:** Wilderness Foundation, POB 53269, Yellowwood Park 4011, Natal, Republic of South Africa. **Tel.**(office) 27 31 422808, (home) 27 332 302727; **fax** 27 31 428675.

POLOVINA, Dr Jeffrey Joseph. Tropical marine population dynamics; marine ecosystems and climate. Chief, Senior Fellow, Affiliate Graduate. *B.*30 Sept.1948, Troy, NY, USA. American. *M.* Cathy: *s., d.* **Education:** UCB PhD(Math.Stats) 1974. **Experience:** marine sci. res., res.direction; teaching pop.dynamics to grad.level; consult.on marine pop.dynamics (ADB, FAO, FFA). **Career:** Res.Sci.then Chief, Insular Resources Investigations, Southwest Fisheries Center, Honolulu Lab. NMFS 1979–; Sr F. Jt Inst.for Marine & Atmos. Res.1989–, Affiliate Grad. Fac.Dept of Oceanogr.1990–, U.of Hawaii. **Achievements:** dev.of ecosystem model (ECOPATH); res.on artificial reefs, climate, and ecosystems; trop.marine resources' pop.dynamics. **Membership:** F.AIFRB. **Award:** Fulbright Scholar (Kenya) 1992. **Publications:** 50+ in refereed journals. Favours pers.pub.& news media support. **Languages:** English, French (weak). Willing to act as consult.etc. **Address:** 2570

Dole Street, Honolulu, Hawaii 96822-2396, USA. **Tel.** (office) 1 808 943 1218, (home) 1 808 261 1895; **fax** 1 808 943 1290.

POLUNIN, Dr Ivan Vladimirovich. Research into general biology and synchronous displays by *Pteroptyx* fireflies; floral conservation*. *B.* 12 Dec.1920, Chiswick Mall, Chiswick, London, England, UK. British. Father the late Vladimir Polunin, graduate forester turned artist, whose vivid portrayals of *e.g.* birch and fir trees in his Russian Ballet sets and other designs widely influenced 'western' art towards realistic portrayal of natural features in theatrical art. *M.*Fam Siew Yin: 2 *d.* Brother Professor Nicholas Polunin *qv*, nephew Dr Nicholas V.C.Polunin *qv*. **Education:** St Paul's Sch.; U.of Oxf. BM & BCh 1945, BSc 1947, DM 1952. **Experience:** studies of epidemiology of tribal peoples of the Malay Peninsular, Sabah (n.Borneo), & Laos; relationship between health–envt–way of life. **Career:** Res.F. 1950–51, Lect.1952–60, Reader 1960–70, Assoc.Prof.of Social Med.and Public Health 1970–80 (when retired), at (now) Nat.U. of Singapore. **Achievements:** var.medical; in Kampung Kuantan (Selangor, Malaysia) instrumental in dev.of Synchronous Firefly Watching as a tourist attraction. **Awards:** incl.Open Scholarship at Queen's Coll.Oxf., and subs.Shorestein Res.F'ship of U.of Oxf. **Publications:** The med.natural hist.of Malayan Aborigines 1951–2, **Plants and Flowers of Singapore* 1987, *Plants and Flowers of Malaysia* 1988. Favours pers.pub. & news media support provided accurate. **Languages:** English, French, Malay. Willing to act as consult.etc. **Address:** 72 Jalan Dermawan, Singapore 669023, Republic of Singapore. **Tel.**(office) 65 760 6683, (home) 65 760 5296; **fax** 65 760 6683.

POLUNIN, Professor Dr Nicholas. Holistic ecological conservation, plant ecology/geography; ecocomplex realism; public appreciation and maintenance of The Biosphere; Noosphere and esp.Homosphere potentialities. Foundation President, Books' Series Convener etc. and Founding Editor of this work following leading intl quarterly journals for nearly 30 years. *B.*Hammonds Farm, Checkendon, Oxon., England, UK. British, Swiss domicile from 1959 by invitation. Father the late Vladimir Polunin (grad. forester turned artist); early influenced by Uncle the late Harold Hart (Camb.grad. farmer with deep appreciation of Nature, sometime Pres.of BOU). *M.*Helen Eugenie: 2 *s.*incl.Dr Nicholas V.C.Polunin *qv*, *d.*April Xenia (Ven. Mujin, founder & co-Dir of Intl Buddhist Inst.with due envl emphasis). *Brothers* the late Oleg Polunin, Author or co-Author of num. illustr.books on flowers and/or veg.of var. countries or regns, and Dr Ivan V.Polunin, *qv*. **Education:** Christ Church Oxf. BA(Bot.& Ecol.)(1st Class Hons) 1932, MS(Yale) 1934, MA (Oxon.) 1935, DPhil. (Oxon.) 1935, DSc(Oxon.) 1942, Res.Assoc., F. etc.at Harvard U. **Experience:** res.on arctic & subarctic flora, plant ecol.and veg.1930–38 (Spitsbergen, Lapland,

Greenland, Iceland, Labrador, Hudson Bay & Strait, and Akpatok, Baffin, Southampton, Devon, & Ellesmere, islands in Canadian Arctic (collections mainly in Nat.Mus.of Canada, Gray Herbarium of Harvard U., Brit.Mus., Fielding Herbarium Oxf.) and further in 1946–9; participation in estab.of Univs of Baghdad 1955–9 & Ife (where planned campus) 1962–6; admin.as Dean Fac.Sci., Deptl Head/ Chairman, Botl/Plant Ecol. Professorial Chairs on four continents, Fndn Pres., Founding Ed.or promoter of pioneering journals. **Achievements:** discovery in 1936 of plants in SW Greenland introduced by Vikings from N.Amer. and, in 1946, of last major islands (later named Prince Charles Is.& Air Force Is.) to be added to the world map; demn of existence of living microbial spores & pollen grains in atmos.high over N.Pole in Summer but not Winter 1948–9; discovered and described new species of arctic plants; orgn of four Intl Confs on Envl Future (ICEFs) extending from 1971 to 1990; founding & continued presiding over FEC & WCB; founding & editing of *Biological Conservation* 1968–74 & *Environmental Conservation* 1974–95; initiation of Biosphere Day 1991, and of Biosphere Clubs. **Memberships:** F.LS (Life), F.RGS (Life), F.RHS (Life), F.AAAS, F.AINA, ASEP (Life), NAAEE (Life), INSONA (VP), Ottawa Field Naturalists' (Life), INTECOL, others; memb.of Sr Common Rooms of Christ Church & New Colls Oxf., Assoc.F. Pierson Coll.(Yale). **Awards:** Open Scholar of Christ Church Oxf.(only one of yr for Natural Sci.) 1928–32, Goldsmiths' Sr Studentship 1932–3, Sigma Xi 1934, Henry F.(Yale U.) 1933–4, Sr Scholar to SRF (New Coll.Oxf.) 1934–47 (while latterly Demonstrator then U.Lect., Fielding Curator & Keeper of U.Herbaria), Rolleston Mem.Prize (jt, Oxf.U.) 1942, Guggenheim Mem. F.1950–52, CBE 1976, Order of Polaris (US) (twice), Ramdeo Medal (India) 1986, Marie-Victorin Medal (Canada), Intl Sasakawa Envt Prize (jt) 1987, President Quo Mo-Jo Medal (Chinese AS) 1987, Vernadsky Medal (USSR AS) 1988, 1989, Founder's (Zechenyi) Medal (Hungarian AS) 1990, Officer of the Order of the Golden Ark 1990, Global 500 Roll of Honour (UNEP) 1991, IAE (Governing Council) 1991– 6; several geogl features in Canadian Eastern Arctic named after him and likewise Canadian Arctic & Greenlandic plants. **Publications:** travel books from undergrad.days, num.vols convened & commonly edited in series of *Plant Sci.Monogrs* 1954–78, *World Crops Books* 1954– 76, *Envl Monogrs & Symp.*1979–88, Camb. *Studies in Envl Policy* (1988–), *Envl Challenges* (co-Ed.) 1993–; *Bot.of the Canadian Eastern Arctic* (three vols, Author & Ed.) 1940–48, *Circumpolar Arctic Flora* 1959, *Intro.to Plant Geog.& Some Related Scis* (with subs. otherlanguage edns) 1960, *Eléments de Géographie botanique* 1967, *Ecosystem Theory & Application* (Ed.) 1986, Ed.of four ICEF Proc.vols — *The Envl Future* 1972, *Growth Without Ecodisasters?* 1980, *Maintenance of The Biosphere* (co-Ed.) 1990, and *Surviving With The Biosphere* (co-Ed.) 1993; *Pop.and Global Security* (co-Ed) 1994 and (Ed.) in press; *c.*550 other pubns. Embarrassed by pers.pub.but welcomes news media support provided it is accurate & dignified. **Languages:** English, French (fading); German & Norwegian (some, formerly); Russian (only residual). Further details may be obtained from British *Who's Who, Who's Who in Amer., Canadian Who's Who, Euro.Biogl Directory, Intl Who's Who, Who's Who in the World* (all chronically), *Who's Who in Sci.from Antiquity to the Present* 1968, *Who's Who in Intl Affairs* 1990, *Envt Enc.& Directory* 1994, etc. Willing to act as consult.etc.on behalf of FEC. **Address:** Foundation for Environmental Conservation, 7 Chemin Taverney (7th & 8th Floors), 1218 Grand-Saconnex, Geneva, Switzerland. **Tel.**(office & home) 41 22 798 2383 and 4; **fax** 41 22 798 2344.

POLUNIN, Dr Nicholas Vladimir Campbell. Marine and coastal ecology. Research Coordinator & Lecturer. *B.*26 June 1951, Boston, MA, USA. American, British. Father Prof.Nicholas Polunin *qv*, father-in-law Prof.Garry W.Trompf *qv,* uncle Dr Ivan Polunin *qv*. *M.*Carolyn Lea: 2 *s*. **Education:** Eton Coll.; Christ Church Oxf. BA (Hons)(Zool.) 1972, MA(Oxon.) 1977; Trinity Coll.Camb. PhD(Freshwater Ecol.) 1980. **Experience:** res.— pop.biol.of coral-reef fishes; ecol.of freshwater marshes; material cycling in aquatic systems; admin.— coordn of undergrad.Marine Biol.degree, chairmanship of trop. coastal res.station, fund-raising for overseas students; consult.— coastal mgmt & ecol.; teaching aquatic ecol.& fish biol. BSc–PhD levels. **Career:** Marine Parks Warden (first) of Seychelles 1972–4; consults for IUCN/WWF in Indonesia then Camb.1979–82; Lect.in Marine Biol. U.of PNG 1982–6; Dem.then Lect.in Marine Biol.1986 & Coord. Coastal Mgmt Studies 1986–, U.of Newcastle upon Tyne. **Achievements:** basic res., estab.of marine prot.areas (Seychelles, Indonesia) and assessment of their values; higher educ.teaching of ecol.subjects with applied slant at undergrad., postgrad., & doctl levels, in developing & developed countries. **Memberships:** BES, ISRS, FSBI, Camb.Phil. Soc. **Award:** King's Scholar (Eton Coll.). **Publicatons:** *c.*40 incl.*Reef Fisheries* (co-Ed.) 1996, Edl Bd *J.of Experimental Marine Biol.& Ecol.,* Ed. *EC* 1996–. **Languages:** English, French. Willing to act as consult.etc. **Address:** Department of Marine Sciences and Coastal Management, The University, Newcastle upon Tyne NE1 7RU, England, UK. **Tel.**(office) 44 191 222 6675, (home) 44 191 281 6624; **fax** 44 191 222 7891; **e-mail** npolunin@ncl.ac.uk .

PONCE, Professor Carlos F. Protected areas' management. Field Vice-President for Andean Countries. *B.*20 Aug.1942, Lima, Peru. Peruvian. **Education:** Nat.Agrarian U. MSc 1985. **Experience:** former Dir for Cons.of Min.of Agric.and former Pres.of Peruvian Fndn for Cons.of Nature. **Career:** Chief of Nat.Parks 1967–73, Dir of Cons.1974–9, Peruvian Min.of

Agric.; Prof.of Wildlife Mgmt, Agrarian U. 1979–92; Field VP for Andean Countries, Cons.Intl 1992–. **Achievements:** co-Author of many books re.Nat. Parks and many projects to establish Nat.Parks in Peru. **Memberships:** RBZS (Life), PEA, PFEA, NGS. **Publications:** *Nat.Parks of Perú* 1978, *Mgmt of the Wild Vicuña* 1983, *Decade of Progress for S.Amer. Nat.Parks* 1985. Indiff.to pers.pub., favours news media support. **Languages:** English (working knowledge), French, Portuguese (working knowledge), Spanish. Willing to act as consult.&/or ref. **Address:** Conservation International, Chinchon 858-A, San Isidro, Lima 27, Peru. **Tel.**(office) 51 14 408967, (home) 51 14 374614; **fax** 51 14 408967.

PONCIANO, Ismael. Policy, planification, & management, of protected areas; environmental impact assessment; environment legislation. Researcher. *B.*30 April 1949, Guatemala. Guatemalan. *M.*Gladys: 2 *d*. **Education:** U.of San Carlos, BSc(Biol.) 1980. **Experience:** prot. areas' mgmt; natural resources' policies; EIA consult. **Career:** Researcher in Cons.Instn Dev. U.of San Carlos 1985–. **Achievements:** author & promoter of Prot.Areas' Law; studied & promoted the actual 'Maya Biosphere' (15,000 km^2 of trop.forest). **Membership:** Fundación Mario Dary Rivera (NGO). Indiff.to pers.pub., favours news media support. **Languages:** English (fair written & spoken), Spanish. Willing to act as consult. **Address:** 40 C 'B' S-11 Zona 8, CP 001-008 Guatemala, Central America. **Tel.**(office) 502 2 347662, (home) 502 2 721571; **fax** 502 2 347664.

POORE, Professor Dr (Martin Edward) Duncan. Science, philosophy, & policies, of environmental conservation; ecology of land-use especially in the tropics, mountains, and arid regions; Nature (biodiversity) conservation; sustainable forestry; principles of vegetational classification. Senior Research Fellow, Partner. *B.*25 May 1925, Dunkeld, Scotland, UK. British. *M.*Judith Ursula (zool.): 2 *s*. Father-in-law Lt-Gen.Sir Treffry Thompson, KCSI, concerned with envl med.in India. **Education:** Clare Coll. Camb. BA(Natural Scis) 1950, MA & PhD 1953; MA Oxon.(by incorporation) 1965. **Experience:** sci., practice, & admin., of Nature cons.in Britain & intlly; u.teaching & admin in KL & Oxf.; field exp.in envl aspects of land-use planning on all continents, ecol.res.; consults on cons., envl impact, for.& land-use policy; Biosphere Reserves, and the World Heritage Conv. with Countryside Comm.(UK), FAO, For. Comm. (UK), Hunting Tech.Services, IBDF (Brazil), IIED, ITTO, IUCN, ODA (UK), UNEP, UNESCO, World Bank, & WWF, in Bangladesh, Belize, Brazil, Cameroon, China, India, Indonesia, Madeira, Malaysia, Nigeria, N.Korea, Pakistan, Paraguay, Philippines, S.Korea, Sri Lanka, & Zaire. **Career:** Translator (Japanese), Brit.Foreign Office 1944–5; Staff Sci. NC Scotland 1953–6; Ecol.(in Jordan, Cyprus, Iraq, Italy, & Pakistan), Hunting Tech.Services 1956–9;

Prof.of Bot.& Dean of Sci. U.of Malaya 1959–65; Lect.in Forest Ecol.CFI 1965–6; Dir, NC GB 1966–73; Chairman of Drafting Cttee, CITES 1973; Scientific Dir (Acting DG 1976–7) IUCN 1974–8; Moderator, 8th World For. Cong.1978; Specialist Adv. House of Lords Select Cttee on Sci.& Tech.1980; Prof.of Forest Sci.& Dir CFI and F.St John's Coll.Oxf.1980–83; Memb.NCC and Chairman of its Adv.Cttee on Sci.1982–4; Memb. Thames Water Auth. 1982– 4; Memb. Cons.& Wildlife Adv.Group to the Duchy of Cornwall 1982–90; SRF (Sr Dir & Consult.), For.and Land Use Prog. IIED 1984–; Partner, Duncan & Judy Poore Assocs 1978–80, 1984–. **Achievements:** intro.of Euro.continental methods of veg.description to Brit.ecol., starting the veg. survey of the Scottish Highlands; bldg-up first U.Bot.Dept in Peninsular Malaysia; init.Nature Cons.Review (GB) and WCS (IUCN); changing the For.MSc at Oxf.to an MSc in For.and Land Use; dev.of For.and Land Use Prog.in IIED; coordinating for ITTO the first comp.survey of sust.mgmt of trop.forests. **Memberships:** F. RSA, F.RGS, F.IBiol., ICF, IEEM, CFA (VP), BANC (VP, Pres.1984–93). **Awards:** Memb.of Honour, Hon.Memb. (CNPPA), & Fred M. Packard Award (all IUCN). **Publications:** *Ecol Guidelines for Dev.in Trop.Rain Forests* 1976, *Ecol Guidelines for Balanced Land Use, Cons. and Dev.in High Mtns* (co-Author) 1977, *Nature Cons.in Northern and Western Europe* (co-Author) 1980, *The Ecol Effects of* Eucalyptus (co-Author) 1985, *Deforestation — Humanitarian Aspects* (co-Author) 1986, *Prot.Landscapes: The UK Exp.*(co-Author) 1986, 1992, *No Timber Without Trees: Sust.in the Trop.Forest* (with collaborators) 1989, *The Mgmt of Trop.Moist Forest Lands: Ecol Guidelines* (co-Author) 1991, *Guidelines for Mtn Prot.Areas* 1993; num.other pubns. Sympathetic to media but does not court publicity. **Languages:** English, French (fair), Japanese (rusty); has read Dutch, German, Norwegian, & Spanish. Further details may be obtained from British *Who's Who* 1996, Debrett's *People of Today* 1996. Willing to act as consult.etc. **Address:** Balnacarn, Glenmoriston, Inverness-shire IV3 6YJ, Scotland, UK. **Tel.**44 1320 340261; **fax** 44 1320 340248.

POPESCU, Professor Dr Dumitra. Environmental policy & law. Director of Research & Professor. *B*.24 Oct.1936, Margineni, Romania. Romanian. *M*.Emil Popescu. **Education:** Bucharest U. LLB 1958, LLD 1972; McGill U. LLM 1970; Hague Acad.of Intl Law, regular session 1973; Center of Res. The Hague Acad. 1974. **Experience:** res.— public intl law & envl law at nat.& intl levels; lect.in the Ecol.U. and acting as govtl expert in envl legislative process; consult.& res.for Envl Resources Ltd (UK) and CIEL (US). **Career:** First Asst Researcher 1958–63, Researcher, Public Intl Law & Envl Law 1961–70, Sr Researcher, River Law and the Law of the Sea 1970–78, Dir of Res.& Lect. Public Intl Law & Envl Law 1978–89, Dir of Res.& Prof.1990–, all at Inst.of Legal Res.

Romanian Acad. **Achievements:** basic res.on role of legal norms in envl prot.& cons.(poll.control of air, rivers, sea, prot.areas etc.); prevention, polluters pay, liability, state coopn in controlling poll.and waste mgmt. **Memberships:** Envl Law Centre (Bonn), IUCN CEL, Intl Envl Negotiation Network (Harvard Law Sch.), Envl Law Network Intl, Romanian Comm.of Envt & Ecol., RSEL (Pres.). **Publications:** *Investors' Envl Guidelines* (co-Author & Coord.) 1993; 40+ papers & 60 other studies, books, & monogrs. **Languages:** English, French (poor), Romanian. Willing to act as consult.etc. **Address:** Institute of Legal Research, Strada 13 Septembrie nr 13, Casa Academiei, Bucuresti, Romania. **Tel.** (home) 40 1 621 1625.

POR, Professor Dr Francis Dov. Taxonomy of copepods; meiobenthos; mangrove & salt lagoon ecology; limnology (Israel & Brazil); aquatic biogeography; macroevolution. Professor of Zoology. *B*.25 May 1927, Timishoara, Romania. Israeli. *M*.Dr Maria Scintila de Almeida Prado (planktologist): *d*.Noemi (biol.lect.). **Education:** U.of Bucarest MSc 1955; Hebrew U.of Jerusalem PhD 1963. **Experience:** teaching zool., hydrobiol., evol., & systematics for 34 yrs at Hebrew U.& 17 yrs at U.of São Paulo; fieldwork in Red Sea, Indian Ocean, Sinai, Atlantic Rain-forest, & mangroves the world over; admin.as Dept Chairman, Mus.Dir, Collection Chairman. **Career:** Prof. Hebrew U. 1975–; Vis.Prof. U.of São Paulo 1977–; Vis.Prof.at U.of Tokyo & USC San Diego; Scientific Sec. Fauna et Flora Palaestina (IAS), Memb.Israel State Comm.of Oceanogr.& Poll. 1971–4. **Achievements:** Founder of hydrobiol.& marine biol. teaching in Israel; Founder Adjunct Dir & Dir Heinz Steinitz Marine Biol.Lab. Eilat 1966–72; org.of scientific collections & fauna projects in Israel; init.of res.on Lessepsian Migration, co-Prin.Investigator of Hebrew U.–Smithsonian Instn project Biota of the Red Sea & Eastern Medit.1967–72; co-init.of Atlantic Rain-forest Res.1980–. **Memberships:** IZS (Chairman 1977–9), ESI (Bd 1972–4), WAC (Founding Memb.), SIL, Crustacean Soc. **Award:** Foreign Memb. R.Soc.of Liège. **Publications:** *Lessepsian Migration* 1978, *Hydrobiol.of the Mangal* 1984, *Que e a Zoologia?* 1985, *The Legacy of Tethys* 1989, *Lake Hula* 1992, *Sooretama — the Atlantic Rain Forest* 1992; num.scientific papers, Edl Bds (past or present) *Oceanologica Acta, Experimental Marine Biol., Marine Ecol.*(PSZN), Israel *J.of Zool., Fauna et Flora Palaestina* (Series Ed.). Indiff.to pers.pub.& news media support. **Languages:** English, French, German, Hebrew, Hungarian (spoken), Italian (read), Portuguese, Romanian, Russian. Willing to act as consult. etc. **Address:** Department of Evolution Systematics and Ecology, Hebrew University, 91404 Jerusalem, Israel. **Tel.**(office) 972 2 584574, (home & **fax**) 972 2 410421.

POTTER, Louis. Regulaton development, development planning; project review. Chief Physical Planner. *B*.20 March 1953, Tortola, BVI. British Virgin Islander. *M*.Susan E. **Education:** Pratt Inst.(NY), B.of Fine Arts 1980; U.of W.Indies, Grad.Dipl.in Natural Resource Mgmt & Envl Studies 1988. **Experience:** regulation of dev.by enforcing dev.control legis.; coastal-zone projects requiring EIA, participation in training workshops, planner for BVI Parks & Prot.Areas project 1982–7; dev.of mgmt plans for the Baths & Awgada Prot.Area. **Career:** Planning Asst 1975–81, Phys.Planner 1981–8, Chief Phys.Planner 1988–, Town and Country Planning Dept. **Memberships:** IAIA, CCA, BVI Nat.Parks Trust, IUCN CNPPA 1987–. **Publications:** Nat.mechanisms for project approval (workshop report) 1989, Comparing experiences in the Brit.and US Virgin Islands in implementing GIS for envl problemsolving 1994. Indiff.to pers.pub., favours news media support. **Language:** English. **Address:** Town and Country Planning Department, POB 468, Kingstown, Tortola, British Virgin Islands. **Tel.**(office) 809 494 3701, (home) 809 495 2793; **fax** 809 494 5794.

PRANCE, Professor Dr Sir Ghillean Tolmie. Plant systematics, Amazonian flora & conservation; economic botany; ethnobotany. Director. *B*.13 July 1937, Brandeston, Suffolk, England, UK. British. *M*.Anne E.: 2 d. **Education:** Malvern Coll.; Keble Coll. U.of Oxf. BA 1960, DPhil.1963, MA 1965. **Experience:** extensive field-work in Amazonia leading many botl expedns; res.on cons.and sust.use of Amazon rain-forest; extensive admin. **Career:** Res. Asst 1963–6, Assoc.Curator 1966–8, Krukoff Curator of Amazonian Bot.1968–75, Dir of Botl Res.1975–81, Sr VP & Dir Inst.of Econ.Bot. 1981–8, all at NYBG; Dir R.Botanic Gdns Kew 1988–. **Achievements:** contributed to theoretical basis for reserves in Amazonia; work on sust.use of forest; many papers on its cons. **Memberships:** F.RS, F.LS, F.Amer.AAS, F. IBiol., F.RGS; Pres.of ASPT 1984–5, ATB 1979–80, Systematics Assn 1988–91, and Leatherhead & Distr.Countryside Prot.Soc. 1992–; Bd Rainforest Alliance 1988–, Bd of Trustees Au Sable Inst.of Envl Studies 1984– and WWF Intl 1989–, Trustee Margaret Mee Amazon Trust 1988–. **Awards:** Fil.Dr.*(Hon.Causa)*(Göteborgs U.) 1983, Disting.Service (NYBG) 1986, Henry Shaw Medal (Missouri Botl Gdn) 1988, Linnean Medal 1990, Intl Cosmos Prize 1993. **Publications:** 12 books incl. *Leaves* 1986, *Out of the Amazon* 1992, *Bark* 1993; Ed.of 10 books incl. *Extinction is Forever* 1977, *Biol.Diversification in the Tropics* 1981, *Amazonia, Key Envts* 1985; 179 scientific papers & 94 gen.articles. Favours pers.pub.& news media support. **Languages:** English, Portuguese. Willing to act as consult. etc. **Address:** The Royal Botanic Gardens, Kew, Richmond, Surrey TW9 3AB, England, UK. **Tel.**44 181 332 5111; **fax** 44 181 948 4237.

PRASAD, Basudeo. Research & development of environmental monitoring instruments; air, wa-

ter, gas, noise, & consultation programmes. Head of Division. *B*.9 June 1946, Bahr, Patna, Bihar, India. Indian. *M*.Uma: *s., d.* **Education:** Bihar Inst.of Tech. B.Tech.(Electronics & Communication) 1966; Panjab Engg Coll. M.Tech. (Electronics) 1986. **Experience:** 5 yrs' res.& dev.and servicing & maintenance of instruments; 8 yrs' admin.; 15 yrs' teaching. **Career:** Asst Prof.1967, Sr Instr.1971; Sci.-in-Charge of Service & Maintenance Centre 1984, Sci.-in-Charge & Project Leader, Automobile Exhaust & Stack Opacity Monitor 1993–; Head of Envl Monitoring Instruments Div. C.Scientific Instruments Orgn 1993–. **Achievements:** set up Electronics & Communication Lab.; developed troposcatter propagation project; developed & released know-how of smoke opacity monitor & automobile exhaust monitor; developed & worked on many envl monitoring projects and instrument dev.in envl sci. **Memberships:** Envl Engg Soc., F.IETE, Instruments Soc.of India. **Awards:** Merit-cum-Means Scholarship 1963, V.Chancellor grants, certs, & prizes, for essay competition in envl scis. **Publications:** *Binary Arithmetic, Electronic Devices & Circuits* (compilation) 1994, *[Poll.& Safety]* (in Hindi) 1994; tech. reports. Dislikes pers.pub., favours news media support. **Languages:** English, Hindi, Sanskrit. Willing to act as consult.&/or ref. **Address:** Environmental Monitoring Instruments Division, Central Scientific Instruments Organization, Chandigarh 160020, East Punjab, India. **Tel.**(office) 91 172 42811, (home) 91 172 563813; **fax** 91 172 544533.

PRASAD, Manaparambil Koru. Informal environmental education; conservation; environmental campaigning. Centre Director. *B*.24 Jan.1933, Cherai, Ernakulam Distr., Ker., India. Indian. *M*.Shirley. **Education:** U.of Rajasthan, M(Bot.) 1955. **Experience:** guiding res.projects in rural tech.; admin.; consult.in legal matters re.envt. **Career:** Lect.in Bot. Ker. Govt Service 1955– 85; Prin.& Dep.Dir, Collegiate Educ.1985–7; Pro-V.-Chancellor, Calicut U. 1987–91; Dir, Integrated Rural Tech.Centre (Ker.) 1992–5 and Ker.Sastra Sahitya Parishat Envt Centre 1995–. **Achievement:** spearheaded campaign to save Silent Valley forests from destruction by proposed hydro project. **Memberships:** WWF India, IUCN CEC, Centre for Sci.& Envt (Delhi), BNHS, CHEC India. **Publications:** incl.*Man & Envt* 1969, *Birds that Stopped Singing* 1979, *Nature Cons.*1987 (all children's books). Indiff. to pers.pub., favours news media support. **Languages:** English, Malayalam. Willing to act as consult.etc. **Address:** Nr 62, 5th Cross, Girinagar, Cochin 682020, Kerala, India. **Tel.** (office) 91 487 24084, (home) 91 484 314861; **fax** 91 484 311393.

PRAVDIĆ, Professor Dr Velimir. Marine environmental research; environmental management, strategies for environmental management. Professor of Chemistry & Laboratory Chief. *B*.11 Aug.1931, Zagreb, Croatia. Croatian. *M*.

Dr Nevenka: s. **Education:** U.of Zagreb, PhD (Phys.Chem.) 1959. **Experience:** res.; teaching; expert service to intl orgns. **Career:** Center for Marine Res. Ruder Bošković Inst. U.of Zagreb 1956–64, 1967–; Lehigh U.1964–7, 1976–7. **Achievements:** mgmt of marine envts based on envl capacity; drafting of comp.strat.of envl prot.in former state of Yugoslavia. **Memberships:** CSNS, CCS, IACIS. **Publications:** 100+ papers in 'open lit.'. Dislikes pers.pub., favours news media support. **Languages:** Croatian, English, German. Willing to act as consult.etc. **Address:** Ruder Bošković Institute, POB 1016, Zagreb, Croatia. **Tel.**(office) 38 41 425384, (home) 38 41 279399; **fax** 38 41 425497.

PRAWIROATMODJO, Dr Suryo Wardhoyo. Environmental education & protection; conservation *in situ*. Director. *B.*22 June 1956, Surabaya, Indonesia. Indonesian. Uncle the late R. Soehoed Prawiroatmodjo (leader in eco-agrotourism). **Education:** Airlangga U. Drh. (Wildlife Cons.) 1982, Smithsonian Inst.1986 and ICCE 1987 for envt & cons.educ.courses. **Experience:** planning, implementing, developing, & bldg, envl educ.progs and an envl educ. centre. **Career:** Vet. Sarabaya Zoo 1980–82; Vet.Supervisor at a vet.product co.1983–4; In-charge of educ.materials on envl topics for Green Indonesia Fndn 1984–8; Founder/Dir PPLH 1988–. **Achievements:** estab.of PPLH, the first Indonesian envl educ.centre, which has concrete direct (outdoor) activities for the gen.public. **Memberships:** UNEP G500F, Caretakers of the Envt Intl, ASHOKA, SASEANEE, IUCN CEC. **Awards:** Award for Enterprise (Rolex) 1990, Innovators for the Public (ASHOKA) 1990, Global 500 Roll of Honour (UNEP) 1992. **Publications:** [*Cons.of the Maleo Bird*] 1981/2, [*Play with Indonesia's Nature & Animals*] (art book for children) 1986, [Tree Obs.] 1992 (all in Indonesian); Dev.of envl educ.in E.Java 1993. Indiff.to pers.pub., favours news media support. **Languages:** Dutch (fair), English (good), French, Indonesian. Willing to act as consult.etc. **Address:** Pusat Pendidikan Lingkungan Hidup, POB 03, Trawas, Mojokerto 61375, East Java, Indonesia. **Tel.**(home) 62 31 849 2313; **fax** 62 31 839616.

PRESCOTT, Jacques. Zoobiology, biodiversity; wildlife conservation; animal behaviour; mammalogy. General Curator, Training Programme Instructor. *B.*22 March 1953, Montreal, Canada. Canadian. *M.*Louise: *d.* **Education:** U.of Montreal BSc(Spec.)(Biol.) 1974, MSc (Biol.) 1976. **Experience:** res.— animal behaviour, zoobiol.; tech.— mgmt & dev.of zoos, biodiv.cons.; admin.— as Gen.Curator, Chairman & Bd Memb.of var.NGOs, coordn of undergrad.& grad.students, fund-raising & orgn of var.symposia; consult.— mus.exhibits, zoo dev. & tech.training, wildlife cons.policies; expedns — to Galápagos Islands, Mexico, Cameroon; Scientific Adv.to spec.exhibitions for Sher-

brooke Mus.of Natural Hist., Montreal Biodome, and Canadian Mus.of Nature; zoo dev.consult.to var.instns; lectured in zoos, museums &/or univs. at home & abroad. **Career:** Lab.& Res. Asst, Univs of Montreal & Edmonton 1974–6; Curator of Educ.& Res.1976–89, Gen. Curator 1989–, Jardin zoologique du Québec; Res.Assoc. Musée nat.d'Histoire naturelle (Paris) 1985; Instr. Smithsonian Instn Intl Zoobiol. Training Prog.1988–. **Achievements:** Memb.Exec.Cttee, Canadian Global Change Prog. RSC; Chairman Canadian Cttee for IUCN; Scientific Adv. WWF Canada Endangered Species Recovery Fund; VP & Pres. ABQ 1983–4; Pres. CNF 1989–91; Chairman Urban Dev. Symp.1986, Intl Forum for Future of Beluga 1988, Quebec Energy Policy & Hydroelectrical Dev.Symp.1989 & ICOM Natural Hist.Cttee Mtg 1992; Memb. Quebec Caucus, Parks Canada Heritage for Tomorrow Centennial 1984–5; Quebec Coord.of Wildlife 1987. **Memberships:** AZA & CAZPA (Professional F.), BAZ & FHGO (Hon.), Monarca AC (Mexico, Bd); ZCOG, ABQ, CNF, CWF, ASM, ABS. **Publications:** [*Mammals of Eastern Canada*] (in French) 1982, *For the Future of the Beluga* (co-Ed.) 1989; 135+ scientific & popular articles. Favours news media support. **Languages:** English, French, Spanish (basic). Willing to act as consult.etc. **Address:** Jardin zoologique du Québec, 8191 avenue du Zoo, Charlesbourg, Québec G1G 4G4, Canada. **Tel.**(office) 1 418 622 0313, (home) 1 418 652 1453; **fax** 1 418 646 9239.

PRESS, Professor Dr Frank. Science policy; geophysics; education. Senior Research Fellow. *B.*4 Dec.1924, Brooklyn, NY, USA. American. *M.*Billie: *s., d.* **Education:** CCNY BS 1944; Columbia U. MA 1946, PhD 1949. **Experience:** Sci.Adv.to Pres.and Dir, Office of Sci.& Tech. Policy 1977–80; Pres.NAS 1981–93; Memb.of Corpn, MIT 1982–. **Career:** Res. Assoc.1946–9, Asst.& Assoc.Prof.1951–5, Columbia U.; Prof.of Geophys.1955–65, Dir Seismological Lab.1957–65, CIT; Prof.of Geophys.& Chairman Dept of Earth & Planetary Scis, MIT 1965–77; Sci.Adv.to Pres.of US 1977–81; Pres. NAS 1981–94; Cecil & Ida Green Sr Res.F., Carnegie Instn of Washington 1993–. **Achievements:** promoted scientific basis for govt regs, increased support of scientific res.; discovered new methods for studying Earth's interior. **Memberships:** NAS, Amer. AAS, GSA, SSA, AGU, APS, AFAS, AAUP. **Awards:** Legion of Honour (Rep.of France) 1989, Cross of Merit (FRG) 1993, Japan Prize 1993, Pupin Medal 1993. **Publications:** incl.Earth (co-Author) 1986, Understanding Earth (co-Author) 1994. **Languages:** English, French. Further details may be obtained from *Who's Who in Amer.*, *Who's Who in Sci.& Engg, Amer.Men & Women in Sci.*, *Who's Who in the E., Intl Who's Who* 1994–5. **Address:** Carnegie Institution of Washington, 5241 Broad Branch Road NW, Washington, District of Columbia 20015, USA. **Tel.**1 202 686 4411; **fax** 1 202 364 8726.

PRESTON-WHYTE, Professor Dr Robert Arthur. Atmospheric systems (southern Africa); environmental management policy issues. Dean of Social Science. *B*.15 July 1939, Benoni, SA. S.African. *M*.Eleanor Mary: *s*., *d*. **Education:** U.of Natal BA(Hons) 1963, MA(1966), PhD 1971. **Experience:** res.— local circulation, air poll.climatology, synoptic met.; admin.— Deptl Chairman, Fac.Dean; consult.— air qual.; teaching — atmos.sci. **Career:** Lect., Sr Lect., Prof. & Chairman, Dept of Geogl & Envl Scis 1963–; Dean of Social Sci.1982–94, U.of Natal. **Achievements:** basic res.on local circulations, air poll.climatology, urban climatology, and synoptic met.in s.Africa. **Memberships:** SAGS, SAAAS, SASAS. **Publications:** The Atmos.& Weather of Southern Africa (co-Author) 1988; 26 papers. Indiff.to pers.pub.; favours news media support. **Languages:** Afrikaans, English. Willing to act as consult.etc. **Address:** Department of Geographical and Environmental Sciences, University of Natal, King George V Avenue, Durban 4001, South Africa. **Tel.**(office) 27 31 816 2283, (home) 27 31 259701; **fax** 27 31 260 1391; **e-mail** preston@mtb.und.ac.za .

PRESTRUD, Dr Pål. Polar research; protection of the arctic environment; arctic mammals & birds, Arctic Foxes *(Alopex lagopus)*, international environmental cooperation. Director of Research. *B*.18 Nov. 1953, Oslo, Norway. Norwegian. **Education:** U.of Oslo, Cand.real.1982, PhD 1992. **Experience:** res., admin. **Career:** Consult.in Arctic Wildlife Mgmt and Gov.of Svalbard 1982–5; Head of Polar Section, Min.of Envt 1988–94; Res.Dir, Norwegian Polar Inst. 1994–. **Publications:** 20 papers in refereed journals. Dislikes pers.pub., indiff.to news media support. **Languages:** English, Norwegian. Willing to act as consult.etc. **Address:** Norwegian Polar Institute, Middelthuns Gate 29, POB 5072, Majorstua, N-0301 Oslo, Norway. **Tel.**47 22 959500; **fax** 47 22 959501; **e-mail** Pal.Prestrud@npolar. no .

PRICE, Dr Mark Rangeley STANLEY. African conservation: reintroductions of plants & animals, planned and in practice; wildlife utilization in all forms; conservation & management of small biotic populations; involvement of rural human populations in conservation. Vice-President & Director of African Operations. *B*.26 Nov.1947, York, England, UK. British. *M*. Karen Olivia: 2 *d*. **Education:** U.of Oxf. MA 1969, DPhil.1974. **Experience:** field res.& mgmt; consult. **Career:** Field Researcher, Galana Game Ranch Res.Project 1974–8; Consult. Ecosystems Ltd 1978–9; Field Mgr, White Oryx *(Oryx leucoryx)* Project, Oman 1979–87; Dir of African Ops 1987–, VP 1991–, African Wildlife Fndn. **Achievements:** res.into physiol.& behavioural basis of domestication of Fringe-eared Oryx *(Oryx beisa callotis)* in Kenya; res. showing competition between Hartebeest *(Alcelaphus buselaphus)* & cattle; resp.for design &

mgmt of successful reintro.of White/Arabian Oryx into Oman; direction of African Wildlife Fndn through period of sustained growth & diversity of prog. **Memberships:** F.ZSL, F.RGS, FFPS, EAWS, SCB, IUCN SSC Reintroductions (Chairman), Antelopes, and Captive Breeding SGs; Edl Bd *Biodiv.and Cons.* **Awards:** Domus Scholarship (Pembroke Coll.Oxf.) 1958, Order of Oman 1987, Order of Golden Ark 1987. **Publications:** incl.*Animal Reintroductions: the Arabian Oryx in Oman* 1989. Indiff.to pers.pub., favours news media support. **Languages:** English; Arabic, French & Swahili (rudimentary spoken). Willing to act as consult.etc. **Address:** African Wildlife Foundation, POB 48177, Nairobi, Kenya. **Tel.**254 2 710367; **fax** 254 2 710372.

PRICE, Dr Martin Francis. Mountain peoples and their environments; human dimensions of global environmental change. Research Scientist. *B*.26 April 1957, London, England, UK. British, Canadian. **Education:** St Paul's Sch.; U.of Sheffield BSc(Spec.Hons) 1978; U.of Calgary MSc 1981; U.of Colorado at Boulder PhD 1988. **Experience:** res.& consult.on various aspects of envl sci.& policy, and interdisc.sci. **Career:** Envl Analyst, Bercha & Assoc. 1981–2; Tech.Writer CWNG 1983–4; Scientific Assoc.U.of Bern 1985–6; Postdoctl F. NCAR 1988–91; Scientific Dir, ICALPE 1991; Res. Sci. Envl Change Unit, U.of Oxf. 1992–. **Achievements:** Sec.ISSC Standing Cttee on Human Dimensions of Global Envl Change 1989–90; review of activities in Euro.mtns, UNESCO's MAB prog.1992–4; contrib.to *Mtn Agenda* UNCED 1992. **Publications:** *Mtn Forests as Common-property Resources* 1990, *Mtn Envts & Geographic Info.Systems* 1994, *Biosphere Reserves on the Crossroads of C.Europe* 1994, *Mtn Res.in Europe* 1994; *c*.35 papers. Indiff.to pers.pub.; favours news media support. **Languages:** English, French, German. Willing to act as consult.etc. **Address:** Environmental Change Unit, University of Oxford, 1a Mansfield Road, Oxford OX1 3TB, England, UK. **Tel.**44 1865 281180; **fax** 44 1865 281181.

PRIEUR, Dr Michel. Environmental law. Teacher of Law. *B*.26 Dec.1940, Boulogne, France. French. **Education:** Pol.Sci.Inst.(Paris), Doct. of Law, Aggregation, 1964. **Experience:** teaching envl law, Pres.of ICCEL & EAEL. **Career:** Dean, Law Sch., Limoges 1988–92; Dir CNRS Res.Centre 1984 and French Envl Law Review 1976; intl consult. **Award:** Elizabeth Haub Envl Law Prize 1976. **Publication:** *Envl Law* 1991. **Languages:** English, French, Spanish. Willing to act as consult.etc. **Address:** 5 rue du Général Cèrez, 87 Limoges, France. **Tel.**(office) 33 55 505421, (home) 33 55 794493; **fax** 33 55 505783.

PRINS, Professor Dr Herbert Henri Théodore. Large mammal ecology, population dynamics; savanna & steppe ecology; buffer-zone management; economic relation between Nature conservation and (local) human population; nomadism & pastoral ecology. Professor of Tropical Nature Conservation. *B*.9 June 1953, Gröningen, The Netherlands. Dutch. Father Emer. Prof.Adriaan H.J.Prins, ecol.anthrop., brother Prof.Harold E.L.Prins, ecol.anthrop. (native & land rights). **Education:** U.of Gröningen, Drs 1978, PhD 1987 (both *cum laude);* Darwin Coll.Camb. MA 1981. **Experience:** ecol field-work on geese (The Netherlands 1976–8 & Spitsbergen 1979); field-work on esp.buffalo (Tanzania 1981–7 & Gabon 1988); consult.in Indonesia on buffer-zone & res.mgmt 1989–90 and in Canada, Gabon, Zambia, Mozambique; field-work in Tanzania on bush encroachment & elephant ecol.1991; teaching at all levels. **Career:** Res.F. WOTRO 1981–5; Sr Sci. Zool. Lab. U.of Gröningen 1986–9; Consult. DHV Consults 1989; Res.F. KNAW 1989–91; Chair, Dept of Terr.Ecol.& Nature Cons. Wageningen Agricl U.1991–; Consult.to R.Shell, World Bank, WWF, The Netherlands' Govt. **Achievements:** basic res.on E.African large mammals & savanna ecol., tourist planning in Tanzania; buffer-zone mgmt in Indonesia; determining ecol res.priorities in Indonesia & Mozambique; ecol impact assessment, higher educ.& teaching of cons.biol.& Nature mgmt at undergrad.level, teaching at doctl level on trop.ecol.& large mammal ecol.; supervision of field-work of PhD students from such countries as Tanzania, Kenya, Indonesia, Cameroon, Mali, and Netherlands' Antilles; co-Founder of World Tree Fund 1991. **Memberships:** NOU, BOU, EAWS, NZS, ETBA (Educl Cttee). **Awards:** Netherlands Zool.Prize (NZS) 1992, Best Paper Prize (FEC) 1993. **Publications:** *c*.60 incl.E. African Grazing Lands: Overgrazed or Stably Degraded? 1989, Stability in a multi-species assemblage of large herbivores in E.Africa 1990, The pastoral road to extinction: competition between wildlife and trad.pastoralism in E.Africa 1992, Woodland structure and herbivore pop.crashes in E.Africa 1993. Favours pers. pub.& news media support. **Languages:** Dutch, English; French, German & Indonesian (basic). Willing to act as consult.etc. **Address:** Department of Terrestrial Ecology and Nature Conservation, Wageningen Agricultural University, Wageningen, The Netherlands. **Tel.** (office) 31 317 483174; (home) 31 317 423773; **fax** 31 317 484845; **e-mail** HERBERT.PRINS@-STAF.TON.WAU.NL .

PRITCHARD, Paul C. National Parks. President. *B*.17 August 1944, Huntington, W.Virginia, USA. American. *M*.Susan: *d*., 3 *s*. **Education:** Harvard U. Business Mgmt; U.of Missouri BA(Hons) 1966; U.of Tennessee MSP (Natural Resources & Econ.) 1970. **Experience:** directed Presidential Nat.Heritage Trust & Task Force; helped create nation's Coastal Zone Mgmt Act, fathering State Heritage Inventory, and generating Washington State coastal zone mgmt prog.(nation's first). **Career:** Gov. of Georgia's Task Force for State Govt

Reorgn 1971–2; Chief of Planning, Georgia Dept of Natural Resources 1972–4; Pacific Regn Coord. for coastal zone mgmt, NOAA 1974–5; Exec. Dir, Appalachian Trail Conf.1974–5; Dep.Dir, Bur.of Outdoor Rec.Heritage Cons. USDI 1977–80; Pres. NPCA 1980–. **Achievements:** as given for 'Experience'. **Awards:** Spec. F. US Dept of Housing & Urban Dev.1973; Outstanding Service Award (NOAA) 1975; Meritorious Service Award (USDI) 1980; Cons. Award (Gulf Oil) 1982; recognized as one of USA's ten most influential cons.leaders *(Fortune Magazine),* selected by *Nat.Geographic* to write article on Nat.Park Service 75th Anniv. Favours appropriate pers.pub.& news media support. **Languages:** English, French (spoken). Willing to act as consult.etc. **Address:** National Parks and Conservation Association, 1776 Massachusetts Avenue NW, Washington, District of Columbia 20036, USA. **Tel.**1 202 223 6722; **fax** 1 202 659 8183.

PROSSER   GOODALL,   R.Natalie,   *see* **GOODALL, R.Natalie** PROSSER.

PUCEK, Professor Dr Zdzislaw Kazimierz. Population biology of shrews; fauna and conservation of mammals. Director. *B*.2 April 1930, Radzyń-Podlaski, Poland. Polish. *M*.Michalina (Dr biol.): *s*.Tomasz Remigiusz (envl biol.). **Education:** Maria Curie-Sklodowska U. Dipl.in Biol.1952, PhD(Zool.) 1961; Warsaw U. MSc(Biol.) 1954; Jagiellonian U. Dr hab.1966. **Experience:** res.in mammalogy, editing scientific j., admin. **Career:** Jr Sci.Worker 1954–66, Sr Sci.Worker 1966–, Dir.1962–, Mammal Res.Inst.Bialowieźa; Ed.-in-Chief *Acta Theriologica* 1963–. **Achievements:** basic res.on seasonal & age changes in shrews; mapping distribn of Polish mammals; consult.— animal prot.in Poland esp.cons.strat.for Euro.bison. **Memberships:** Polish AS, ASM (Hon.), Teriological Soc., Russian AS(Hon.), PNCNC, IUCN Rodent SG (Coord. Europe) 1982–9, and Bison SG (Chairman) 1985–. **Publications:** *Atlas of Polish Mammals* (co-Ed.& co-Author) 1983, *Key to Polish Mammals* (Ed.& co-Author) 1984, *Polish Red Data Book of Animals* (co-Author) 1992; 150 j.pubns. Dislikes pers.pub.& news media support. **Languages:** English, Polish, Russian. Further details can be obtained from *Who's Who in the World, Who's Who in Amer., Dict.of Intl Biog.* Willing to act as consult.etc. **Address:** Mammal Research Institute, Polish Academy of Sciences, 17-230 Bialowieźa, Poland. **Tel.**48 835 12278; **fax** 48 835 12289.

PULIDO, Professor Victor. Wildlife conservation & protected areas. Executive Director. *B*. 26 Jan.1954, Lima, Peru. Peruvian. Father Fines Pulido Montejo (trop.& exotic flowers), Mother Luzmila Capurro Ramos (agric.). *M*. Joyce Del Pino (biol., genetics): *s*. **Education:** Universidad Nacional Mayor de San Marcos, BS 1979, Biol.& Zool.1980; Universidad Nacional Agraria La Molina, MS(For.Resources' Cons.)

1987. **Experience:** admin.— 16 yrs' in govt and private sector; consultant for such orgns as FAO, World Bank, Nat.Park of Peru; u.lecturing, edl. **Career:** Wildlife Biol.1979–81, Dir of Wildlife 1981–8, Dir of Nat.Park 1988–9, Min.of Agric.; Dir of Wildlife Res. Nat.Agrarian Res. Inst.1990–94; Exec.Dir, Wetlands of Peru Prog. 1992–; Prof.Postgrad.in Ecol.at Garcilaso de la Vega Private U.1993–5 and in Wildlife Mgmt and Envl Planification at San Marcos Nat. U.1995. **Achievements:** direction of wildlife, nat.parks, and other, depts of Peruvian Govt for last 14 yrs; worked on proposals for Peruvian prot.areas incl.Santuarios Nacional Pampas del Heath, de Calipuy, and las Lagunas de Mejia, pubns. **Memberships:** IUCN SSC & CNPPA 1990–, FAO (Nat.Coord.for Prot.Areas and Wildlife Network) 1989, IWRB (Nat. Coord.for Neotrop.Wetlands Inventory Project, and Nat. Del.) 1985–96, WHSRN (Nat.Rep.) 1985– 95, Acad.of Natural Scis of Philadelphia (Adjunct Researcher) 1983–6, Colegio de Biólogos del Perú (Council Directive 1991–3), Grupo de Aves Acuáticas del Perú (Gen.Coord.1992–4). **Award:** The World's Most Important Man (*Amer. Birds*) 1990. **Publications:** incl.*Red Data Book of Peru* 1991, some chapters, 45+ scientific & popular pubns; Ed.& Founder *El Volante Migratorio* 1983–94. Indiff.to pers.pub., favours news media support. **Languages:** English, Spanish. Further details may be obtained from *Who is Who in Peru* 1992. Willing to act as consult.etc. **Address:** Paseo los Eucaliptos, 285 Camacho, La Molina, Lima 12, Perú. **Tel.**(home) & **fax** 51 1 437 5567.

PULINKUNNEL, Dr P.S.Easa. Research, Nature education. Division Scientist & Head. *B.*25 Nov.1954, Chandiroor, Alleppey Distr., Ker., India. Indian. *M.*Saheeda Melethodika: *s., d.* **Education:** Calicut U. MSc(Zool.) 1977; Smithsonian Instn, wildlife training 1986; Kerala U. PhD(Zool.) 1990. On Elephant Ecol.1990. **Experience:** 18 yrs' res.on animals in trop. forests, admin.; lecturing to MSc forestry students. **Career:** Sci.(in diff.categories) & Head, Div.of Wildlife Biol. Ker.Forest Res.Inst.1978–. **Achievements:** num.papers on wildlife mgmt & biodiv.; training of personnel. **Memberships:** IUCN Asian Elephant (*Elephas maximus*) SG, Ker.State Wildlife Adv.Bd. **Award:** Wildlife Cons.Award (Rotary Club of Cochin). **Publications:** num.papers & chapters. Favours pers.pub.& news media support. **Languages:** English, Hindi, Malayalam. Willing to act as consult.etc. **Address:** Division of Wildlife Biology, Kerala Forest Research Institute, Peechi 680653, Kerala, India. **Tel.** (office) 91 487 782037 or 061-4, (home) 91 487 782334; **fax** 91 487 782249.

PUNNING, Professor Dr Jaan-Mati. Palaeogeography, palaeoecology; environmental management. Institute Director, Professor of Geography. *B.*13 March 1940, Rasina, Estonia. Estonian. *M.*Karin: *d.* **Education:** Tartu U. graduated 1963, PhD 1968, Dr Sci.(Geog.) 1981. **Experience:** res.palaeogeography of n.Hemisphere & Baltic Sea; admin.as Inst.Dir; consult.in envl mgmt & ecol.; teaching palaeoecology, glaciology & isotope geol.from BSc to PhD levels. **Career:** Sr Researcher, Inst.of Geol. 1970–87; V.-Dir 1989–92, Dir 1992–, Inst.of Ecol.& Marine Res. Estonian AS; Prof.of Geog. Tartu U.1989–93 and Prof.of Geog. Tallinn Pedagogical U.1993–. **Achievements:** estab.of isotope geol.lab.and Inst.of Ecol.; expedns to glaciers on mtn areas of Svalhard, Kamtchatka. **Memberships:** Estonian Geogl Soc.(Pres.), Steering Cttee of Intl Assn of 14C (Radiocarbon) Lab., Counc. Min.of Envt. **Awards:** N.Vavilov (All-Union Sci.Council) 1988 & K.E.Baer (Estonian AS) 1990 Medals. **Publications:** three books incl.[*Late Quaternary Paleogeography of Northern Europe*] (co-Author, in Russian) 1985, *The Influence of Natural and Anthropogenic Factors on the Dev.of Landscapes* 1994; 300+ scientific papers. **Languages:** English, Estonian, German (better at written), Russian. Further details may be obtained from *Who's Who in the World* 1996. Willing to act as consult.&/ or ref. **Address:** Institute of Ecology, Kevade 2, EE0001 Tallinn, Estonia. **Tel.**(office) 372 2 451634, (home) 372 2 538411; **fax** 372 2 453748.

PURCELL, Dr Arthur H. Preventive environmental management. Director, Adjunct Associate Professor of Environmental Management, Associate Professorial Lecturer in Environmental Engineering, Consultant, Author. *B.*11 Aug.1944, Evanston, IL, USA. American. Father Edward Purcell (planning engineer). *M.* Deborah: *d.* **Education:** Inst.of Euro.Studies, Cert.1965; Cornell U. BS 1966, Northwestern U. MS 1972, PhD 1973, all in Materials Sci. **Experience:** res., consult., lect.& writing, on envl & resource issues. **Career:** Dep. Dir, Office of Sci.& Govt, Amer.AAS 1973–4; Founder & Dir, Resource Policy Inst.1975 ; appointed to US Pres.'s Sci.Policy Task Force 1976; Sr Staff, US Pres.'s Comm.on the Accident at Three Mile Is.1979; named on Reagan admin.'Hit List' of influential envlists to be boycotted 1983; Special Consult. Envt & Human Settlements Div. ECE 1982–5; US Info. Agency Lect.1982, 1990; Vis. Sci. Hazardous Substances Control Res.Center, UCLA 1989; Chair, Geneva Conf.on Waste Minimization and Clean Tech.: Moving Toward the 21st Century 1989; Lect. Euro.-sponsored course on Setting Envl Priorities; Plenary Speaker, First Intl Symp.on Ceramics and the Envt 1994; Adjunct Assoc.Prof.in Envl Mgmt, W.Coast U.1994–; Assoc.Professorial Lect.in Envl Engg, USC 1995–. **Achievements:** developing & enhancing concepts in preventive approaches to envl problem-solving. **Memberships:** US Pres's Sci. Policy Task Force 1976 & Comm.on Scholars 1977–8, WCB 1988–93, Sigma Xi. **Awards:** Friends of UNEP, Alumni Merit (Northwestern U.). **Publications:** 135 papers & monogrs incl.*The Waste Watchers*

1980, *Resource Optimization & World Peace* 1982, *Indoor Air Poll.*1988, *Preventive Envl Mgmt* (in press).   Favours pers.pub.& news media support.   **Languages:** English, French (fair written & spoken), Spanish (spoken, read). Further details can be found in *Who's Who in Amer.* Willing to act as consult.etc.   **Address:** Resource Policy Institute, 1745 Selby Avenue Nr 11, Los Angeles, California 90024, USA.   **Tel.**1 310 475 1684;   **fax** 1 310 441 9170.

PUSHPANGADAN, Dr Palpu.   Ethnobiology, conservation biology and economic evaluation of biodiversity, conservation and sustainable utilization of biodiversity.   Tropical Botanic Garden & Research Institute Director.   *B.*23 Jan.1944, Prakkulam, Quilon, Kerala, India. Indian. *M.*Dr P.Sreedevi: 2 *s.*   **Education:** U.of Kerala BSc 1965; Aligarh Muslim U. MSc 1968, MPhil 1972, PhD 1975.   **Experience:** 25 yrs in survey inventory documentation and eval.of medicinal & aromatic plants of India, cons. biol.of rare & endangered species, ethnopharmacology and economic prospecting for wild medicinal plants etc.   **Career:** Res.Sci. Regnl Res.Lab. CSIR (J&K) 1969–83;   Chief Coord. All India Coordinated Res.Project on Ethnobiol. Min.of Envt & Forests, Govt of India 1983–90; Vis.Prof. R.Danish Sch.of Pharmacy 1991 and Dept of Pharmacy, Govt of Norway 1995; Dir, Trop.Botanic Gdn & Res.Inst.1990–.   **Achievements:**   successful in cons.of some rare and endangered wild medicinal plants by *ex situ* methods incl.by tissue culture techniques. **Memberships:**   UNESCO Bot.2000 Exec.Bd, ISCA (Life), Nat.MAB Cttee (Life), Intl Assn of Ayurveda and Naturopathy, ISE, ISEE, Nat. Acad.of Envl Scis; num.nat.assns, cttees, expert groups, etc.   **Awards:** Disting.Intl Award (ABI) 1994;   several nat.cash & others.   **Publications:** six books incl.*[Promising Medicinal Plants for Cultivation in Ker.and Their Cultural Practices]* (co-Author, in Malayalam) 1991, *Glimpses of Indian Ethnopharmacology* (co-Ed.) 1994; 125+ res.papers & *c.*30 review articles.   Indiff.to pers.pub., favours news media support.   **Languages:** English, Hindi, Malayalam, Sanskrit (read & written); Dogri, Punjabi, Tamil, Urdu, and some tribal dialects (spoken).   Willing to act as consult.etc.   **Address:** Tropical Botanic Garden & Research Institute, Pacha-Palode, Thiruvananthapuram 695562, Kerala, India.   **Tel.** (office) 91 472 84236, (home) 91 471 437698; **fax** 91 471 431178 & 437230.

PYROVETSI, Dr Myrto D.   Wildlife ecology & management, wetland ecology;   ornithology; Nature conservation.   Assistant Professor in Ecology.   *B.*4 Sept.1947, Florina, Macedonia, Greece. Greek. *D.: s., d.* **Education:** Aristotle U.of Thessaloniki, BSc(Natural Sci.) 1971; Michigan SU, MSc(Wildlife Ecol.) 1980, PhD(Wetland Ecol.& Mgmt) 1984.   **Experience:** res.— wetland ecol.& mgmt, bird biol.& ecol., cons.biol., envl educ., socio-ecol studies, wildlife mgmt; teaching — ecol.and Nature cons.

& mgmt from BSc- to PhD-level students. **Career:** Asst 1971–8, Teaching Asst 1982–8, Asst Prof.1989–, U.of Thessaloniki.   **Achievements:**   14 yrs leading projects on wetland cons.& mgmt;   init.of wetland cons., Nature cons.awareness, & envl educ., progs, and first mgmt project on wetlands — all in Greece. **Memberships:**   Greek Ornithol., Zool & Ecol Socs, CWS, Wetlands Soc.(USA), Greek Soc.for Nature Cons.and Cultural Heritage.   **Awards:** Scholarships from Nat.Fndn, Fulbright Fndn, Brit.Council.   **Publications:** num.papers & project reports.   Favours pers.pub.& news media support.   **Languages:** English, French (poor), Greek. Willing to act as consult.etc.   **Address:** 89 Tsimiski Street, 54622 Thessaloniki, Greece. **Tel.**(office & **fax**) 30 31 998284, (home) 30 31 236889 or 673959.

QU, Geping.   Environmental protection.   Committee Chairman.   *B.*14 June 1930, Shandong, PRC. Chinese. *M.*Zhang Kun: *d.* **Education:** Shandong U. BA 1952.   **Experience:** envl mgmt, envt & economy, pop.& dev.   **Career:** China's Chief Rep.to UNEP 1975–6;   Admin. NEPA 1982–93;   Chairman, Envl & Resources Prot.Cttee, Nat.People's Cong.of China 1993–. **Achievement:** being appointed Pres.of following organizations. **Memberships:** Chinese Soc. for Envl Scis (Pres.), Chinese Envl Prot. Fndn (Pres.), Chinese Assn for Envl Industries (Pres.), High-Level Adv.Bd on Sust.Dev.1993–.   **Awards:** Hon.PhD (U.of Bradford, UK) 1988, Intl Sasakawa Envl Prize (UNEP) 1992.   **Publications:** *Envl Mgmt in China* 1989, *Pop.& Dev.in China* 1992, *Envt & Dev.in China* 1993 (all in Chinese and English).   **Languages:** Chinese, English. **Address:** 23 Xijiaominxiang, Beijing 100805, People's Republic of China.   **Tel.**(office) 86 10 309 8121, (home) & **fax** 86 10 851 0537.

QURESHI, Mohummad Tahir.   Management of Mangrove ecosystems.   Unit Director.   *B.*1 Sept. 1944, Ajmer, Raj., India.   Pakistani.   *M.* Naheeda.   **Education:** Sindh U. MSc(Hons) 1968; Peshawar U. MSc(For.) 1976.   **Experience:** served as Forest Mgr for *c.*20 yrs in Sindh Province, conducted res.in Mangrove for.in Indus delta.   **Career:** Divl Forest Officer 1976– 92, Project Dir 1993–4, Sindh For.Dept;   Dir, Coastal Ecosystem Unit, IUCN Pakistan 1994–. **Achievement:** pubns*, established over 1,000 ha of Mangrove plantations along coast of Pakistan.   **Memberships:** ISME (Counc.), ZSP. **Publications:** **Mgmt Plan of Indus Delta* 1983– 4, *Experimental Plantations of Mangroves in Indus Delta* 1990; 12 papers. Favours pers. pub. & news media support.   **Languages:** English, Urdu.   Willing to act as consult.etc.   **Address:** IUCN–Pakistan, 1 Bathisland, Karachi, Pakistan.   **Tel.**(office) 92 21 473082, (home) 92 21 497 9637;   **fax** 92 21 587 0287.

QUTUB, Syed Ayub.   Conservations strategies; mobilizing rural communities for better common-property management. President & Chief Executive Officer. *B*.24 Sept.1949, Karachi, Pakistan. Pakistani. *M*.Attia (envl educ.): *s*., 2 *d*. **Education:** Queens' Coll.Camb. BA(Hons) 1971, MA 1975. **Experience:** team leader, field res.in mobilization of village communities for improved irrigation mgmt. **Career:** Gen.Mgr, Pakistan Envl Planning and Architectural Consults 1975–88; Coord. NCS Secretariat 1988– 91; Pres.& CEO, PIEDAR 1991–. **Achievement:** prin.writer of Pakistan NCS. **Memberships:** IUCN CESP & Cttee on Strats for Sustainability, EPSOP, IGSAC. **Publications:** Rapid pop.growth and urban problems in Pakistan 1992, *Climate Change in Asia: Pakistan* 1994. Indiff.to pers.pub., favours news media support. **Languages:** English; Punjabi & Urdu (good). **Address:** Pakistan Institute for Environment–Development Action Research, 2nd Floor Yasin Plaza, 74-W, Blue Area, Islamabad, Pakistan. **Tel.**(office) 92 51 211015, (home) 92 51 823790; **fax** 92 51 216507.

Quy, Professor VO, *see* **VO, Professor Quy.**

RACEY, Professor Dr Paul Adrian. Biology, ecology, and conservation of bats & other mammals. Regius Professor of Natural History. *B*.7 May 1944, Wisbech, Cambs., England, UK. British. *M*.Anna Priscilla: 3 *s*. **Education:** Ratcliffe Coll.; Downing Coll.Camb. MA 1967; U. of London PhD 1972; U.of Aberdeen DSc 1983. **Experience:** res.in mammalian reproductive biol., ecol., & ecophysiol.; teaching mammalogy, reproductive biol., and ecol.; admin. **Career:** EO Rothamsted Experimental Station 1965– 6; Res.Asst ZSL 1966–71; Ford Fndn Res.F. U.of Liverpool 1971–3; Lect., Sr Lect., Prof. U.of Aberdeen 1973–93. **Achievements:** Founding Chairman of Bat Cons.Trust, co-Chairman IUCN SSC Chiroptera SG, Chairman Cons.Cttee FFPS, Res.Bd Scottish Natural Heritage, Bd of Govs Macaulay Land Use Res.Inst., Terr.& Freshwater Scis Cttee of NERC, res.on residual effects of remedial timber treatment on bats. **Memberships:** BES, MS(UK, Council), ASM, SMM, FFPS (Council). **Award:** F'ship of RSE. **Publications:** *Old World Fruit Bats — An Action Plan for their Cons.* (co-Author) 1993; 100 primary res.papers + invited chapters & symp.papers. Dislikes pers.pub.; favours news media support. **Languages:** English, French (fair written). Further details may be obtained from Brit.*Who's Who* 1996. Willing to act as consult.etc. **Address:** Department of Zoology, University of Aberdeen, Tillydrone Avenue, Aberdeen AB9 2TN, Scotland, UK. **Tel.**(office) 44 1224 272858, (home) 44 1651 872769; **fax** 44 1224 272396.

RADICELLA, Professor Sandro M. Research and training for research in upper atmosphere physics & atmospheric system interactions, and radiowaves environment; planning & organization of research & development projects & units, particularly for developing countries.

Staff Associate & Head. *B*.7 May 1937, Messina, Italy. Argentinian, Italian. *M*.Marina. **Education:** Nat.U.of Tucumán, Licenciado en Física 1960. **Experience:** res.in atmos.phys.& radiopropagation; admin.— planning, orgn, and direction, of R&D projects & units, and training for res.activities in envt–related areas; consult.in non-conventional energy phys. **Career:** Researcher, Nat.Univs of Tucumán & La Plata 1958–68; Vis.Res.Assoc. US NBS Labs (CO) 1961, GSFC 1962, and U.of Illinois 1968–9; Full Prof. Nat.Univs of La Plata & San Juan 1969–76; Dir, Nat.Prog.of Radiopropagation of Argentina (NPRA) 1971–94; Exec.Sec. Nat. Prog.of Non-conventional Energies of the Sec. for Sci.& Tech. Argentine Govt, and Consult. for Non-conventional Energies, UNESCO 1979 80; Dir, Center for Regnl Res.of San Juan, NCSTRA 1980–87; Staff Assoc.& Head, Atmos.Phys.& Radiopropagation Lab. ICTP 1988–. **Achievements:** init.res.in ionospheric phys.in Argentina; founded, organizes & directs NPRA (forerunner of Nat.Progs of Sci.& Tech.in the country); organizes & directs Center for Regnl Res.of San Juan, organized cooperative efforts in Latin-Amer.in fields of aeronomy [sci.of the upper atmos.], climatology, & radiopropagation, and several training activities in envl topics as well as the APRL at ICTP. **Memberships:** AAGG, Panamerican Cttee on Solar–Terr.Phys. (Chairman), IURS Standing Cttee on Developing Countries (Chairman), ICTP (Sr Assoc.). **Award:** Golden Badge (Bulgarian Astronautical Soc.). **Publications:** 60+ papers. Indiff.to pers. pub.; favours news media support. **Languages:** English, French (spoken), Italian, Spanish. Willing to act as consult.etc. **Address:** International Centre for Theoretical Physics, POB 586, 34100 Trieste, Italy. **Tel.**(office) 39 40 224 0331, (home) 39 40 830094; **fax** 39 40 224604.

RAHMANI, Dr Asad Rafi. Conservation; ornithology — bustards, cranes, storks, francolins; deserts. Centre Chairman. *B*.30 July 1950, Mainpuri, UP, India. Indian. **Education:** U.of Agra, BSc 1971; Aligarh Muslim U. MSc(Zool.) 1974, PhD(Zool., Fisheries) 1979, Dipl.in Journalism 1977. **Experience:** 20 yrs' res.on fishes, birds, & mammals; extensive travel over India & 20 other countries; work on Indian bustards & other endangered birds, gazelles, & antelopes; consult. **Career:** Sr Sci. BNHS 1984–91; Reader 1991–4, Chairman 1994–, Centre of Wildlife & Ornith. Aligarh Muslim U.; Edl Bd *J.of BNHS, Bird Cons.Intl.* **Achievements:** work towards cons.of Bustards in India and highlighting plight of other endangered birds; init.res.on rare francolins, storks, bustards, & whinchats, rediscovery of Arabian Bustard *(Ardeotis arabs)* in Saudi Arabia 1987. **Memberships:** BNHS (Life), WWF–India, BirdLife Intl, Oriental Bird Club. **Publications:** ten tech.reports 1981–, 60 res.papers, 250 popular scientific articles. Favours pers.pub.& news media support. **Languages:** English, Hindi, Urdu. Willing to act as consult.etc. **Address:** Centre of Wildlife & Ornithology, Aligarh Muslim University, Aligarh 202002, Uttar Pradesh, India. **Tel.**91 571 401052; **fax** 91 571 400637.

RAI, Leghu Dhan. Conservation of Himalayan ecology & environment. Chairman. *B*.25 July 1958, Nepal. Nepali. *M*.Nanda Kumari: *s., d.* **Education:** Tribhuvan U. Dip.P.Admin.1986, BCom.1988, B.Ed.1989, MPA 1991, MA 1993, LLB 1994, postgrad.student in ecol.& envt. **Experience:** res.on Himalayan ecol.& envt. **Career:** politics; Chairman, Mt Everest Envt Cons.Fndn 1992–. **Endeavours:** to keep Mt Everest, and the affected parts of the Himalayan range of mtns in Nepal, free from the solid-wastes & garbage left behind by mountaineers, tourists, & trekkers. **Languages:** English, Hindi, Nepali, Rai (mother tongue). Willing to act as consult.etc. **Address:** The Mount Everest Environment Conservation Foundation, POB 3508, Kathmandu, Nepal.

RAI, Dr Suresh Chand. Land & water resource management; integrated rural area development; micro-level planning. Scientist. *B*.12 July 1958, Jahaniapur, Ajamgarh, UP, India. Indian. *M*. Kulwanti: 2 *s*. **Education:** BHU BSc(Hons) (Geog.) 1977, MSc(Geog.) 1979, PhD(Geog.) 1984; NRSA, training on Remote Sensing Techniques 1993; ICIMOD, training on GIS Techniques 1993. **Experience:** res.— land & water resource mgmt, watershed mgmt, micro-level planning, sust.dev.of rural ecosystems. **Career:** Res.Assoc. U.of Delhi 1987–9 & GBPIHED 1989–92; Sci.'A' 1992–3, Sci.'B' 1993–, GBPIHED. **Achievements:** basic res. on watershed mgmt, tech.dev.for rain-water harvesting, and degraded land mgmt in Sikkim (India). **Memberships:** Regnl Sci.Assn of India, IEMS, IGA. **Publications:** *Spatial Orgn of Rural Dev*.1988, *Integrated Watershed Mgmt* 1992; *c*.25 papers. Favours pers.pub.& news media support. **Languages:** English, Hindi. Willing to act as a ref. **Address:** G.B.Pant Institute of Himalayan Environment & Development, PO Tadong, Gangtok, Sikkim 737102, India. **Tel.& fax** 91 3592 23335.

RAJAGOPAL, Professor Dr Rangaswamy. Environmental information systems; risk assessment; water pollution control & monitoring; cost-effective regulation & policy. Professor of Geography & Departmental Chairman. *B*.20 July 1944, Bombay, Mah., India. American. *M*. Carol Ann: *d*. **Education:** U.of Bombay BSc (Maths/Phys.) 1964; U.of Florida ME(Systems Engg) 1969; U.of Michigan PhD(Resource Mgmt) 1974. **Experience:** extensive res.sponsored by public & private sources, teaching, founding Ed.*The Envl Professional.* **Career:** Asst Prof. U.of Washington 1973–4 and Duke U.1974–9; Assoc.Prof.1979–87, Prof. 1987–, Chairman 1993–, Dept of Geog. U.of Iowa; Vis.Sci.at USFS 1974, Admin.Staff Coll.of India 1984 & US EPA 1986–8. **Achievements:** supervised 45+ grad.student theses & dissertations;

directed 50+ workshops & sems on envl prot., risk assessment, info.integration, problem-solving, creativity, & innovation, to 2,000+ professionals in academia, govt, and industry. **Memberships:** Nominator annual Japan Prize 1985–, Health Effects Adv.Cttee (Gt Lakes Prot.Fund) 1992–, Bd of Trustees (Envl Careers Orgn) 1988–. **Awards:** Disting.Service Award (NAEP & US EPA), num.awards & res.contracts from public & private orgns & fndns. **Publications:** incl. *Water Resources of the US* (co-Author) 1992, *An Approach for Assessing the Utility of Large Databases in Envl Monitoring & Assessment* (co-Author) 1992; 100+ articles & reports. Favours pers.pub.to a modest extent, and news media support. **Language:** English. Further details may be obtained from *Who's Who in the Midwest* 1985, *Directory of Disting. Americans* (3rd edn), *Who's Who in Sci.& Engg* 1994–5. Willing to act as consult.etc. **Address:** 308 Jessup Hall, Department of Geography, University of Iowa, Iowa City, Iowa 52242, USA. **Tel.**(office) 1 319 335 0160, (home) 1 319 351 6585; **fax** 1 319 335 2725.

RAMAKRISHNAN, Professor P.S. ('Ram'). Ecol-ogy, environmental sciences & ecologically sustainable development: population ecology, ecosystem dynamics, agroecology, linkages between ecological & social processes, ecology of traditional societies. Professor of Ecology. *B*.24 Dec.1936, Palayanoor, India. Indian. Mother Lakshmi (practising agriculturalist). *M*.Sudha Mehndiratta (MAB-related activities, UNESCO): *s., d*.Poonam (envt & health, employment generation & sust.dev.). **Education:** Madras U. BSc 1955; BHU MSc 1957, PhD 1960. **Experience:** widespread in both nat.& intl teaching, res., and sci.mgmt. **Career:** post–doctl res.at BHU & U.of Western Ont.1960–67, Lect.in Bot. Agra U.&Panjab U. 1960–67, Reader in Ecol. Panjab U. 1967–74, Prof.of Bot.& of Eco-Dev.N.-Eastern Hill U.1974–85, Vis.F. Yale Sch.of For.& Envl Scis 1976–7, AVCC Vis.Prof.at Australian univs & res.instns 1979, Founding Dir GBPIHED 1988–9, Prof.of Ecol. Sch.of Envl Scis JNU 1985–, Consult./Adv. UNESCO, UNDP, World Bank, IUCN, ICSU, SCOPE APDC and num.nat.& intl scientific bodies, memb.Edl Bds of num.intl journals & pubns. **Achievements:** init.in 1957 studies in tropics on pop.differentiation & adaptation at the subspecific level related to soil factors and coexistence of species and pops in the same area; the multidisc.study of shifting agric.& sust. dev.in N.-Eastern India is recognized as a unique one linking up natural & social scis, through community-based participatory res., for sust. dev.of trad.hill socs; through a network approach, involved in bldg instnl linkages, and linkages between scientists, NGOs, govtl agencies, and local people, in the area of cons.& sust.dev. **Memberships:** elected F.of INSA, IAS & NAS India; BES, INTECOL, ISTE, ISWF, IBS, CSA, ISC. **Awards:** Pitamber Pant Nat.Envt Award (Govt of India); Disting.Sci.

Award in Envt Scis (NAS India); Swami Pranavananda Award in Envt Scis (UGC India); UGC Nat.Lect.in Envl Scis. **Publications:** *Ecol. of Biol Invasion in the Tropics* 1991, *Shifting Agric.& Sust.Dev.: An Interdisc.Case Study from N.-Eastern India* 1992; Edl Bds *Forest Ecol.& Mgmt, J.Trop.Ecol., Vegetatio, Intl J.of Wildland Fire* (USA); *c.*275 res.papers in refereed journals. Indiff.to pers.pub., favours news media support. **Languages:** English, Hindi; Malayalam, Punjabi & Tamil (all spoken); Sanskrit (working knowledge). Willing to act as consult. etc. **Address:** School of Environmental Sciences, Jawaharlal Nehru University, New Delhi 110 067, India. **Tel.**(office) 91 11 652438, (home) 91 11 663571; **fax** 91 11 686 5886; **e-mail** psrama@jnuniv.ernet.in .

RAMIREZ, Jose Jairo Escobar. Marine & coastal environment. Chief of International Affairs. *B.*13 Dec.1942, Santa Fé de Bogotá, Colombia. Colombian. *M.*Ligia Elena. **Education:** Expert in Gen.Biol.& Chem.1959, graduated in Marine Biol.1962, Universidad Jorge Tadeo Lozano; Expert in Bioassay & Testing Biol Material against Marine Poll.1965. **Experience:** res.in assessment of fishes' stocks in Colombian, Pacific, & Carib.seas, fishes' pop. dynamics in Magdalena R.Basin & marine coastal poll.in Colombia incl.mercury poll. studies in Cartagena Bay (inventories of sources of coastal poll.in Colombia); intro.of EIAs in Colombia, assessment & monitoring marine & coastal envt in SE Pacific Regn. **Career:** Asst to Gen.Sec. 1993–, Chief of Intl Affairs 1993–, Colombian Oceanographic Comm. **Achievements:** intro.of EIA studies in Colombia and Coastal Envt Mgmt Plan for SE Pacific coastal areas, founding first Bioassay & Biol.Testing Labs for marine studies in Colombia, formulated a marine integrated policy based on sust.dev. concept. **Memberships:** ALA, ACBM, CES. **Awards:** Global 500 Roll of Honour (UNEP) 1991. **Publications:** several tech.reports & other papers. Indiff.to pers.pub. **Languages:** English (fair spoken), Spanish. Willing to act as a consult. **Address:** Calle 41 Nr 46–20 Piso 4 can, Santa Fé de Bogotá DC, Colombia. **Tel.**57 91 222 0449; **fax** 57 91 222 0416.

RAMPHAL, The Hon.Sir Shridath S. International affairs with a special interest in international policy on the environment and sustainable development. Chairman, President, co-Chairman. *B.*3 Oct.1928, Berbice, Guyana. British, Guyanese. *M.*Lois Winifred: 2 *s.*, 2 *d.* **Education:** Queen's Coll.Guyana, Inter BA, Inter BSc 1947; King's Coll.London, LLM 1952; Harvard Law Sch.1962. **Experience:** an intlist with roots in the Carib.and a commitment to the advancement of the Third World; service as Sec.Gen.of Commonwealth was associated with strong championing of cause of freedom & justice in SA and efforts at bridgebuilding to advance global understanding on issues of econ.& social dev.; current endeavours are aimed

at promoting intl understanding, peace, and progress. **Career:** served Govt of Guyana & Fedn of W.Indies 1953–75 (Minister of Foreign Affairs & Justice, Guyana, 1966–75); Commonwealth Sec.Gen.1975–90; Chairman, W.Indian Comm.1989–92; Chancellor, Univs of The W. Indies 1989, Guyana 1988–92, & Warwick 1989; Chairman, Intl Steering Cttee, Rockefeller Fndn's Prog.for Leadership in Envt & Dev. 1991–; Pres.IUCN 1991–3; co-Chairman, Comm. on Global Governance 1992–. **Achievements:** memb.of Brundtland Comm.on Envt & Dev., Spec.Adv.to Sec.-Gen.of UNCED 1992. **Memberships:** RSA, Bencher of Gray's Inn, several ind.intl comms. **Awards:** Queen's Counsel, GCMG, Order of Excellence (Guyana), Order of the Carib.Community, Albert Prize, OM, René Dubos Envl Award, several hon.degrees. **Publications:** *Our Country, The Planet* 1992, *Our Global Neighbourhood* 1995 (co-Chair); num. articles. Favours pers.pub.& news media support. **Language:** English. Further details may be obtained from British *Who's Who* 1994, *Intl Who's Who* 1994–5, *Who's Who in the World* 1996. **Address:** The Sutherlands, 188 Sutherland Avenue, London W9 1HR, England, UK. **Tel.**(office) 44 171 266 3409, (home) 44 171 387 2019; **fax** 44 171 286 2302.

RAMPRASAD, Dr (Mrs) Vanaja. Women, health, environmental conservation. Associate Director & Regional Coordinator. *B.*28 Sept. 1943, Pollachi, TN, S.India. Indian. *M.*Mr Ramprasad: *d.*Jaya (atmos.scis). *B.*Dr Dev Mani, energy. **Education:** U.of Mysore, PhD(Human Nutrition) 1984. **Experience:** consult. — women & health, natural curing, study of herbal cure in primary health-care; consultation — envl impact study, biodiv.cons.(a grass-roots level prog.*); resource-person for UNDP mtgs in Nairobi & Geneva on desert., NGO participant at UNCED. **Career:** Nutrition Consult. community health progs 1972–8; Dev.Consult.to Ox-Fam, NOVIB, FAO, & ActionAid (funding partners) 1984–7; res.study on impact of green rev.in s.States of India 1988–90; Assoc.Dir & Regnl Coord. *Navdanya 1990–. **Achievement:** estab.of a nat.community-oriented seedbank & -network. **Awards:** Res.Awards (Ford & Rockefeller Fndns). **Publications:** *Ecol.& Pol.of Survival* (co-Author) 1991, *Cultivating & Sustaining Diversity* (Reports) 1993 & 1994; num.critiques. Dislikes pers.pub.& news media support. **Languages:** English, Tamil, able to converse in many S.Indian languages. Willing to act as consult.etc. **Address:** 839 23rd Main Road, 10th Cross, Jaya Prakash Nagar Phase II, Bangalore 560 078, Karnataka, India. **Tel.** (office & home) 91 80 663 5963; **fax** 91 80 663 1565.

RANDALL, Professor Dr John 'Jack'. Classification of Indo–Pacific reef fishes in particular Acanthurid and Labroid fishes; marine conservation through parks & preserves, underwater guides to reef fishes. Senior Ichthyologist, L.

Allen Bishop Distinguished Chair in Zoology, Researcher. *B*.22 May 1924, Los Angeles, CA, USA. American. *M*.Helen Au (Managing Ed.of series *Indo–Pacific Fishes*): *s.*, *d*. **Education:** UCLA BA(Zool.) 1950, U.of Hawaii–Manoa PhD(Marine Zool.) with Hons.1955. **Experience:** res.— fish class.& behaviour, biol.of fishes, marine preserves, shark behaviour & taxonomy, underwater photography, coral reef pop.and other ecol.problems; admin.— Dir of marine lab., chairman grad.student thesis res.for doctl degree; consult.for prep.of books on fishes; teaching systematics of fishes at all coll.levels. **Career:** Teaching Asst UCLA 1950; Grad.Asst 1950–53, Res.F.1953–5, U.of Hawaii; Res.F. Yale U.and Bishop Mus.1955–7; Res.Asst then Prof. U.of Miami Marine Lab. 1957–61; Prof. 1961–5, Dir 1962–5, U.of Puerto Rico Inst.of Marine Biol.; Dir Oceanic Inst. Waimanalo, Hawaii 1965–6; Ichthyologist 1965–75, Chairman Zool.Dept 1975–9, Sr Ichthyologist 1979–, Bishop Mus. Hawaii Inst.of Marine Biol. U. of Hawaii. **Achievements:** estab.of Buck Is. Reef Nat.Monument 29 Dec.1961 by Pres. Kennedy through film and other presentations; memb.Adv.Group for estab.of Bahamian land–sea park, marine parks & preserves in Hawaii (Monokini, Hanauma Bay, etc.). **Memberships:** State Adv.Cttee on Plants & Animals and Adv.Subcttee on Invertebrates & Aquatic Biota, IUCN SSC, GBR Cttee, ASIH, JIS, EUI, Explorer's Club, Biol. Soc.(WA), SFI, ISRS. **Awards:** Phi Beta Kappa, Sigma Xi; Stoye Award in Ichthyology, Disting.F., & Robert Gibbs Award (all ASIH). **Publications:** Monarch of the grass flats 1963, Contribns to the biol.of the Queen Conch (*Strombus gigas*) 1964, Food habits of reef fishes of the W.Indies 1967, *Carib.Reef Fishes* 1968, 1983, *Underwater Guide to Hawaiian Reef Fishes* 1981 and *The Diver's Guide to Red Sea Reef Fishes* 1982 (both waterproof on plastic pages), *Red Sea Reef Fishes* 1983, *Guide to Hawaiian Reef Fishes* 1985, *Sharks of Arabia* 1986, *Fishes of the GBR and Coral Sea* (co-Author) 1990, *Diver's Guide to Fishes of Maldives* 1992, 400+ others; Edl Bds of *Micronesia*, *Revue Française d'Aquariologie*, *Freshwater & Marine Aquarium*, *Indo–Pacific Fishes*, *Fauna of Saudi Arabia*. Indiff.to pers. pub.& news media support — prefers to see articles before pubn, will do TV interviews. **Languages:** English; French & Spanish (limited spoken). Further details may be obtained from *e.g. Who's Who in Amer.* Willing to act as consult.etc. **Address:** Dept of Ichthyology, Bishop Museum, POB 1900–A, Honolulu, Hawaii 96817–0916, USA. **Tel.**(office) 1 808 848 4130, (home) 1 808 235 1652; **fax** 1 808 841 8968.

RANDALL, Dr Roland E. Coastal plant ecology; Nature conservation, environmental management. Lecturer, Director of Studies, Staff Tutor. *B*.21 Sept.1943, Colchester, Essex, England, UK. British. *M*.Dreda Margaret (farmer): 2 *d*. **Education:** St Catharine's Coll.Camb.

BA(Geog.)(1st Class Hons) 1966; McGill U. MSc(Biogeog.) 1968; U.of Camb. PhD(Biogeog.) 1972. **Experience:** res.—field-work in UK, Medit., Carib., & NZ; admin.—held sr admin.rank in U.of Camb.Continuing Educ.Bd & Girton Coll.; consult.— private cos, NGOs, NCC; teaching — 25 yrs in ecol.& cons. **Career:** Lect. Dept of Biol.& Envl Studies, U.of Ulster 1970–72; Staff Tutor in Biol Scis & Cons., F.& Lect. 1977–, Bd of Continuing Educ.1972–, Girton Coll.; Dir.of Studies (Geog.) at Wolfson 1984–, Churchill 1990–, & Girton 1994–, Colls, U.of Camb. **Achievements:** furthering public awareness re.plant sci.& ecol., showing importance of ecol.& cons.of veg.of coastal shingle. **Memberships:** BES, IEEM, EUCC, IBG (Biogeog.Res. Group). **Award:** St Catharine's Scholar (U.of Camb.). **Publications:** *c*.60 scientific papers incl.The shingle veg.of the coastline of NZ 1992, *Dry Coastal Ecosystems of the Eastern Medit*.1993, *Coastal Vegetated Shingle Structures of GB* (four vols) 1994. Indiff.to pers.pub., favours news media support. **Languages:** English, French (poor). Further details may be obtained from current IEEM *Directory*. Willing to act as consult.etc. **Address:** Girton College, Cambridge CB3 0JG, England, UK. **Tel.**(office) 44 1223 338949, (home) 44 1480 830426; **fax** 44 1223 338896.

RANJITSINH, Dr M.K. Nature conservation, biodiversity; management of ecosystems, protected areas, wildlife & natural resources, conservation of endangered species; wildlife trade & tourism. Authority Chairman. *B*.19 Feb.1938, Wankaner, Gujarat, India. Indian. *M*.Kalpana: 2 *d*. **Education:** U.of Delhi BA (Hist.) 1957, MA(Hist.) 1959; Saurashtra U. PhD(Wildlife Ecol.) 1983. **Experience:** ecol.: cons.of endangered species, wildlife & natural resources' mgmt, catchment area cons.& land-use, wildlife trade, legis.on Nature cons., abatement of poll. incl.implementation of major river action-plan for poll.control, eval.of EIA & envl res.projects; Nature cons.& biodiv.: mgmt of ecosystems & prot.areas incl.nat. parks & Biosphere Reserves; admin.pertaining to forests & wildlife, finance, planning, and agric.& rural dev. **Career:** Sub-Divl Officer & Distr.Collector 1962–70, Sec. (Forests, Tourism & Sports) and Commissioner of Bhopal Div.1981–5, State Govt of MP; Dep.Sec.& Dir (Forests & Wildlife) and Dir, Wildlife Preserv. State Govt of MP & Govt of India 1970–75; Sr Regnl Adv.on Nature Cons. UNEP 1975–80; Jt Sec.(Forests & Wildlife) 1985–9, Addit.Sec.& Project Dir Ganga Project 1989–90, Addit.Sec. Min.of Envt & Forests 1990–92, Govt of India; Chairman, Narmada Valley Dev.Auth. MP 1993–. **Achievements:** instrumental in helping save endangered s.Barasingha *(Cervus duvauceli branderi)* from extinction; drafted & updated Indian Wildlife (Prot.) Act 1972, init.C.Assistance Schemes to assist nat.parks & sanctuaries and Project Tiger, assisted in formulation of SACEP and gave advice on Nature cons.to countries of the Asia &

Pacific Regn; helped create nine new nat.parks and 14 new sanctuaries, and in formulation of new Forest Policy and R.Valleys Action Plan for India. **Memberships:** IUCN SSC Regnl Rep. for Asia & memb.of Deer, Cat, Rhino, & Crocodile, SGs; BNHS, WPSI, RPS (Assoc.) 1985. **Awards:** Order of the Golden Ark 1979, Global 500 Roll of Honour (UNEP) 1991. **Publications:** *The Indian Blackbuck* 1990; 26 papers & reports. Indiff.to pers.pub., favours news media support. **Languages:** English, Gujarati, Hindi (good), Nepali & Swahili (comp.). Willing to act as consult.etc. **Address:** The Palace, Wankaner, Saurashtra, Gujarat, India. **Tel.**(office) 91 755 557326, (home) 91 755 550322; **fax** 91 755 557168.

RAPPOLE, Dr John Hilton. Ecology of Nearctic migratory birds that winter in the Neotropics; effects of tropical habitat loss on vertebrate populations. Research Coordinator. *B.*10 Nov. 1946, Jamestown, NY, USA. American. **Education:** Colgate U. AB 1968; U.of Minn. MS 1972, PhD 1976. **Experience:** res.— fieldwork in Mexico, Belize, Costa Rica, Minn., Texas & Virginia, on migratory bird ecol.(46 grants); consult to World Bank, Nat.Marine Fisheries; teaching ornith., vertebrate ecol., gen. biol., animal behaviour, biopolitics, gen.ecol., wildlife habitat mgmt. **Career:** Regular Army Comm.as 2nd Lt (1st on resignation) 1969–72; Sci.Dept Chairman, Breck Sch.1976–8; Postdoctl F. U.of Minn.1978–9; Curator of Birds, U.of Georgia Mus.of Natural Hist.1979–81; Curator of Natural Hist.Connor Mus.1981–3 & Res.Sci. Caesar Kleberg Wildlife Res.Inst. 1983–9, Texas A&I U.; Res.Coord. Cons.& Res. Centre, Nat.Zool.Park (Smithsonian Instn) 1989–. **Achievements:** elucidation of ecol.requirements of migratory birds partic.during transient & winter periods; dev.of 's.home' theory for evol.of many migratory bird species, focusing on importance of non-breeding habitat requirements for cons. **Awards:** Regent's Scholarship (NY State), Colgate Hon.Soc., Disting.Res.Award (Texas A&I U.). **Publications:** *Nearctic Avian Migrants in the Neotropics, A Field Guide to the Birds of Texas* 1994, four other books, 70 other pubns. Indiff.to pers.pub. & news media support. **Languages:** English, French (fair read), Spanish (fair). Further details may be obtained from *Contemporary Authors* 1987, *Who's Who in Intl Authors* 1990. Willing to act as consult. etc. **Address:** Conservation & Research Center, National Zoological Park (Smithsonian Institution), 1500 Remount Road, Front Royal, Virginia 22630, USA. **Tel.**1 703 635 6516; **fax** 1 703 635 6551.

RAUKAS, Professor Dr Anto. Quaternary geology, environment. Head of Department, Scientific Adviser, Professor of Geology. *B.*17 Feb. 1935, Tartu, Estonia. Estonian. Father Prof. Viktor Raukas, Estonian Agricl Academy. *M.* Sirje: *d.* **Education:** Tartu U. –1958; Estonian AS, MSc 1962, DSc 1973 (confirmed by Moscow Higher Attestation Comm.1973); U.of Western Ont. Postdoctl F. 1973. **Experience:** widespread res.in fields of Quaternary geol.& envl policy in former Soviet Union; memb.of coordinating bodies of USSR AS in fields of geol., geochem.& geophys., and geog., climatology, oceanology, & Nature cons.1981–90; Head, Estonian Marine and Lake Res.Comm. 1988–90; Scientific Tech.Expert, Min.of Envt of Estonian Rep. **Career:** Researcher & Sr Researcher 1958–64, Head of Dept of Quaternary Geol.1965–, Inst.of Geol., Academician–Sec. Div.of Chemical, Geol, & Biol, Scis 1981–9, Estonian AS; Scientific Adv.to PM 1992–; Prof.of Geol.& Envl Studies, Estonian Maritime Acad.1993–. **Achievements:** expedns in Estonia and to diff.parts of former Soviet Union; Memb.of Council of Envt of Estonian Govt 1979–84; Chairman of Edl Bds *Proc.of the Estonian AS, Geol.* 1982–, Assoc.Ed.*Oil Shale* 1983–. **Memberships:** Estonian AS 1977– (Memb.of Presidium 1977–89), Estonian Geogl Soc.(VP 1980–), Geogl Soc.of former USSR (Scientific Counc.1985–90), Assn of Baltic States' Geologists (Pres.1991–4), NYAS 1993–, Head of Estonian Comm.of Meteoritics, Estonian Natural Soc., Republican Soc.of Nature Cons., NGS, IFS, IAG (Estonian Rep.). **Awards:** Premium (Karl Baer Acad.) 1980 & (Luha Acad.) 1982, Academician Vavilov's Medal (All-Union Soc.'Sci.') 1984, Orden 'Sign of Honour' (Presidium of USSR Supreme Court) 1985, Hon.Sci.(Presidium of Estonian Supreme Council) 1987, Republican Premium of Sci. (Estonian Govt) 1991, several from Geogl Socs of Estonia & former USSR, First Class Award (Estonian Soc.of Naturalists) 1985, Corres. Memb. (Geol Soc.of Finland) 1990, Foreign Memb. (Societas Scientiarum Gedanensis, Poland) 1987–, Silver Medal (All-Union Exhibition of Nat.Economy) 1989. **Publications:** Author or co-Author of more than 400 books or scientific papers incl.*Marginal Glacial Formations in N.Estonia* (co-Author, in Russian) 1971, *Pleistocene Deposits in Estonian SSR* (in Russian) 1978, *Estonia During the Last Million Years* (in Estonian) 1988, published in 23 countries. **Languages:** English, Estonian, Finnish (poor), German (poor), Russian. Willing to act as consult.etc. **Address:** Institute of Geology, Estonian Academy of Sciences, 7 Estonia Avenue, Tallinn EE0100, Estonia. **Tel.**(office) 372 2 454 659, (home) 372 2 538 502; **fax** 372 6 312 074; **e-mail** Raukas@pzgeol.gi.ee .

RAVEN, Professor Dr Peter Hamilton. Plant systematics & evolution (evolutionary theory & biogeography); biodiversity assessment & conservation especially relating to tropical forests & human population growth; botanical gardens & scientific education. Director, Engelmann Professor of Botany, Adjunct Professor of Biology. *B.*13 June 1936, Shanghai, China. American. *M.*Tamra: *s.*, 3 *d.* **Education:** UCB AB(Bot.) 1957, UCLA PhD(Plant Scis) 1960. **Experience:** res.— widespread field-work esp.in W.N.

Amer.& Latin Amer.; admin.— Dir, Missouri Botl Gdn; Home Sec. US NAS; Chair, Report Review Cttee NRC, NSB; teaching plant systematics & evol.biol.to BS & PhD levels. **Career:** NSF F.at Brit.Mus.1960–61; Taxonomist & Curator, Rancho Santa Ana Botanic Gdn 1962; Asst then Assoc.Prof. Stanford U.1962–71; Sr Res.F. NZ DSIR, and John Simon Guggenheim Mem.F.1969–70; Dir Missouri Botl Gdn 1971–, Engelmann Prof.of Bot. Washington U.1976–, Adjunct Prof.of Biol. St Louis U.1973– and U.of Missouri–St Louis 1976–. **Achievements:** developed Missouri Botl Gdn as major trop.res.instn, influenced increased US fed.spending for envl res.& educ., facilitating dev.of biodiv.surveys in US, Mexico, China, Taiwan, Russia, etc. **Memberships:** US NAS, Accademia Nazionale delle Scienze detta dei XL (Foreign Memb.), USSR AS (Foreign Memb.), APhS, Russian AS, Australian AS (Corres.Memb.), Pontifical AS, LS. **Awards:** num.incl.Sigma Xi 1957, DeCandolle Prize 1970, Willdenow Medal 1979, Disting.Service Award (AIBS) 1981, Intl Envl Leadership Medal (UNEP) 1982, John D.& Catherine T.MacArthur F.1985–90, Intl Prize for Biol.(Japan) 1986, Archie F.Carr Medal 1987, Global 500 Roll of Honour (UNEP) 1987, Fellows' Medal (Calif. AS) 1988, Envl Prize of Institut de la Vie (jt) 1990, Order of the Golden Ark 1990 (Officer), Volvo Envt Prize (jt) 1992. **Publications:** 17 books incl.coll.textbooks: *Biol.of Plants* (5th edn 1992, transl.into 6 languages), *Biol.*(3rd edn 1992), *Understanding Biol.*(2nd 1991), & *Envt* 1993; 450+ other pubns. Favours pers.pub.& news media support. **Languages:** English; Latin & Spanish (read). Willing to act as consult.etc.upon availability. **Address:** Missouri Botanical Garden, POB 299, St Louis, Missouri 63166–0299, USA. **Tel.**(office) 1 314 577 5111, (home) 1 314 772 8409; **fax** 1 314 577 9595.

RAVEN, Dr Robert John. Role of spiders, especially Mygalomorphae, in questions of biodiversity, conservation, phylogeny, biogeography, & human envenomation. Senior Curator (Chelicerata). *B.*17 Feb.1953, Calcutta, W.Bengal, India. Australian. *M.*Debbie M.: 2 *s.*, *d.* **Education:** U.of Qld (St Lucia) BSc 1976, PhD 1982. **Experience:** founded Australasian Arach. Soc.; pioneered computerization of collections of Qld Mus.and subs.pubns; auth.on Mygalomorphae (taxonomy & phylogeny) — trapdoor, funnelweb, & tarantula, spiders. **Career:** Tech. Asst, Qld Mus.1973–82; Postdoctl F. Amer.Mus. of Natural Hist.1983–4; Asst Curator 1985, Curator 1986–7, Sr Curator 1989–, Qld Mus. **Achievements:** named over 300 new species of spiders; reports on wet tropics of Qld, and atlas of Qld's vertebrates; Chairman XII Intl Cong.of Arach.; host & co-Ed.of First Australian Conf.on Invertebrate Cons.& Biodiv. **Memberships:** Hennig Soc., Australian Entomol.Soc., ESQ, CIDA, BAS, Australian Arach.Soc. (Founder). **Awards:** Postdoctl Award (CSIRO) 1983–4. **Publications:** *An Atlas of Qld's Frogs,*

Reptiles, Birds & Mammals (co-Ed.) 1991, Mygalomorph spiders of the Barychelidae in Australia & the Western Pacific 1994, The Spider Infraorder Mygalomorphae (Araneae): Cladistics & Systematics 1985, *Proc.of XII Intl Cong.of Arach.* (co-Ed.) 1993, Invertebrate biodiv. & cons.1994. Favours pers.pub.& news media support. **Languages:** English, French. Willing to act as consult.etc. **Address:** Department of Arachnology, Queensland Museum, POB 3300, South Brisbane, Queensland 4101, Australia. **Tel.** (office) 61 7 840 7698, (mobile) 61 18 748467, (home) 61 7 288 4188; **fax** 61 7 846 1918; **e-mail** R.Raven@mailbox.uq.oz.au .

RAY, Professor Dr G.Carleton. Polar region & marine ecology with respective emphases on marine mammals especially Walrus and land–sea interactions in coastal zone, marine parks, and protected areas. Research Professor of Environmental Sciences (Ecology). *B.*15 Aug. 1928, New York City, NY, USA. American. *M.*Geraldine McCormick (res.sci.in marine cons.with expertise in molluscan biol.& ecol. (oyster reefs): *s.*, *d.* **Education:** Yale U. BS 1950, UCB MS 1953, Columbia U. PhD 1960. **Experience:** res.— polar regn ecol.with emphasis on marine mammals esp.Walrus, marine ecol.with emphasis on land–sea interactions in coastal zone; consult.to — incl.US NAS, ICES, IUCN, WWF (US); cons. — marine parks & prot.areas, scientific basis for marine & coastal cons., emphasis on fishes. **Career:** Curator, Field Assoc., Asst Curator, Assoc.Curator, Asst to Dir, NYZS (NY Aquarium) 1957–67; Assoc. Prof. Johns Hopkins U.1967–9; Prof.& Res. Prof.of Envl Scis (Ecol.) 1979–, U.of Virginia. **Achievements:** Founder BNT and Exuma Cays Land-and-Sea Park (the first of its kind) 1958; set stage for dev.of principles & practices in marine parks; helped draft marine mammal legis., leader in coastal concepts in cons. **Memberships:** incl.ESA, ASN, AIBS, ASLO; Edl Bds of *EC* 1974–95, *Aquatic Cons.*1993–. **Awards:** James Howard McGregor Award (Columbia U.) 1959, F.AAAS 1964, num.grants & contracts. **Publications:** Author or co-Author of nine books (two for children) and envl data atlases, 100+ scientific papers & reports, *c.*75 papers & reports in cons., *c.*50 popular articles; taken part in prod.of educl films. **Languages:** English; French (moderately good); German, Italian, & Spanish (passing knowledge). Willing to act as consult.etc. **Address:** Department of Environmental Sciences, Clark Hall, University of Virginia, Charlottesville, Virginia 22903, USA. **Tel.**(office) 1 804 924 0551, (home) 1 804 823 4939; **fax** 1 804 982 2137; **e-mail** cr@virginia.edu .

RAY, Dr Justina Coste. Ecology & conservation of African (and other tropical forest) carnivores & small mammals (rodents & shrews). Research Student. *B.*20 Mar.1965, London, England, UK. American. *M.*Dr 'Jay' R.Malcolm *qv.* **Education:** Stanford U. BS/MS 1987, U.of Florida,

PhD 1996. **Experience:** res.in C.African Rep. on ecol.& cons.of a small carnivore community 1992–4; admin.— cons.intern in NY office of WCS. **Career:** grad.student, U.of Florida 1989–96. **Achievements:** undertook first ecol study on small carnivore community in an African rainforest, membership of IUCN Small Carnivore Cons.Group. **Memberships:** IUCN Small Carnivore Cons.Group, ASM, SCB. **Awards:** Foreign Language and Area Studies (Title VI) F'ship (US Govt) 1989–91, Fulbright Scholarship 1991, Res.F'ship (WCS) 1991, 1993. **Publications:** *Civettictis civetta* 1995, Structure of a shrew community in the C.African Rep.based on the analysis of carnivore scats with the description of a new *Sylvisorex* (co-Author) 1996. Favours pers. pub.& news media support. **Languages:** English, French, German, Sangho (C.African Rep., spoken). Willing to act as consult.etc. **Address:** 1420 NW 43rd Avenue, Gainesville, Florida 32605, USA. **Tel.**(office & home) 1 352 378 3019; **fax** 1 352 372 4614.

RAY, Dr Prasanta K. Environmental research especially in toxicology, immunology, & cancer; water & air pollution. Institute Director. *B.*29 Sept.1941, Narrottampur, India. Indian. *M.* Khanna: 2 *s.* **Education:** U.of Calcutta BS 1962, MS 1964, PhD 1968, DSc 1974; U.of Minn. post-doctl res. **Experience:** 26 yrs' teaching, 30 yrs' res., 26 yrs' admin; tumour & transplantation immunology, microbiol., envl toxicology & cancer, planning, guiding, & administering, lab.res.& res.instns. **Career:** SSO Administering & Head of Cancer, Immunobiology Group, Bhabha Atomic Res.Centre 1973–6; Chittaranjan Nat.Cancer Res.Centre 1977–8; Dir & Head of Res., Bengal Immunity Res.Inst. 1978–9; Dir, Alma Dea Morani Lab.of Surgical Immunobiology (USA) 1979–84; Dir, ITRC (Lucknow) 1984–92; Dir, Bose Inst.1992–. **Achievements:** served as Dir ITRC for over eight yrs and has five patents for — portable water analysis kit, mobile water analysis lab. solar power, low-cost bacterial filter, sophisticated electronic device for Bacteria-free drinking water, kit for detection of food adulterants. **Memberships:** F.NAS, F.IBiol., F.ICAAI, F.STI, NYAS, AACR, SBCI, MSI. **Awards:** Nat.Award (ICMR) 1977, Ranbaxy Nat.Res. Award and Gold Medal (STI) 1985, Prof.S.C. Roy Commem.Medal 1986, Dr N.L.Ramanathan Mem.Oration 1992, Dr A.K.Banerjee Mem. Oration 1993. **Publications:** include *Disaster Preparedness in Chem.Industry* 1986, *Toxicity Data Handbook* vols I & II 1986, *Toxicology Map of India* vol.I 1989, *Aquatic Ecotoxicology* (manual) 1988, *Safety Eval.of Chemicals* (manual) 1989, *Bacteriological Map of India* 1989, *Poll.& Health* 1992, *Toxicology Atlas of India: Pesticides* 1990. **Languages:** Bengali, English, Hindi. Willing to act as consult.etc. **Address:** Bose Institute, P-1/12, CIT Scheme VII-M, Calcutta 700 054, West Bengal, India. **Tel.** (office) 91 33 379219 or 350 7073, (home) 91 33 321 7827; **fax** 91 33 343886.

RECKERS, Ms Ute. Sustainable land-use management, arid & semi-arid lands' projects, desertification, nomads, human & tropical ecology; range management & monitoring. Junior Professional Officer. *B.*11 March 1963, Flensburg, Germany. German. *M.*Heinz Müller. **Education:** U.of Bonn, Dipl.(Master's)(Geog. Anthrop. & Bot.) 1992. **Experience:** eight months' field study on human–ecol.aspects of E. Pokot (Baringo Distr.Kenya) within an NGO project; five months' consult.on range-mgmt for GTZ/Min.of Livestock Dev.and six-months' with GTZ on Pilot Prog.for trop.forest in Brazil and on desert.control activities in drylands. **Career:** Internship in Venezuela on envt 1987–8, field study in Kenya 1989–90, consult.to GTZ 1990–92, Jr Professional Officer, DC/PAC, UNEP 1993–. **Membership:** Info.Centre for Low External Input & Sust.Dev. **Publications:** *Nomadic Pastoralists in Kenya: Human–Ecol. Aspects of E.Pokot* 1992, *Migration Patterns & Envl Behaviour of the E.Pokot in Baringo Distr.* 1993. Favours pers.pub.& news media support. **Languages:** English, French (read), German, Portuguese (good spoken), Spanish (good). Willing to act as consult.etc. **Address:** Desertification Control Programme Activity Centre, United Nations Environment Programme, POB 47074, Nairobi, Kenya. **Tel.**(office) 254 2 623265, (home) & **fax** 254 2 582921.

REDAUD, Dr Louis Hubert Marie. Tropical ecology, protected area management; Nature conservation, Caribbean region. Scientific Adviser. *B.*25 Oct.1960, Tahiti, French Polynesia. French. *M.*Dr Maria Gladys Belandria de *qv*: 2 *d.* **Education:** U.de Lyon I Maîtrise (Biologie des Organismes et des Pops) 1983, U.de Grenoble Doctorat (Ecologie Appliquée) 1986. **Experience:** field exp.in c.Nepal 1984–6 and Andes of Venezuela 1987–9; prot.area mgmt since 1990. **Career:** Res.Assoc. U.de Los Andes 1987–89, Sci.Adv. Parc Nat.de la Guadeloupe 1989–. **Achievements:** record dev.for prot.areas in Guadeloupe (French W.Indies), Biosphere Reserve, Nature Reserve, RAMSAR Sites. **Memberships:** IUCN CNPPA. **Publications:** num.incl.L'Analyse des Ressources Naturelles et de leur Utilisation comme Méthode d'Etude du Fonctionnement d'une Société Rurale: Exemple du Nepal C.1990, Caracterización del Sistema de Producción Agricola de Los Nevados, Sierra Nevada de Merida, Venezuela (co-Author) 1991, *Recueil Bibliographique: 1 Les Milieux Naturels, La Faune et La Flore de l'Archipel de la Guadeloupe* (co-Author) 1994. Indiff.to pers.pub.& news media support. **Languages:** English (read), French, Spanish. Willing to act as consult.etc. **Address:** Parc National de la Guadeloupe, Habitation Beausoleil BP 93, F-97120 Saint-Claude, Guadeloupe, West Indies. **Tel.** (office) 590 802425, (home) 590 802177; **fax** 590 800546.

REDAUD, Dr Maria Gladys BELANDRIA DE. Lichens, bioindicators, heavy-metal pollution;

environmental education. Chargée d'Etude. *B.* 20 Mar.1956, Merida, Venezuela. Venezuelan. *M.*Dr Louis H.M.Redaud *qv*: 2 *d*. **Education:** Lycée Libertador (Merida), Bacc.Scientifique 1974; Université des Andes, 'Maîtrise' en Educ. (Biologie) 1979; Université de Grenoble, Diplôme d'Etudes Approfondies (Ecologie Appliquée)('mention AB') 1983, Doctorat (Ecologie Appliquée) 1986. **Experience:** res.— fieldwork in France (Lyon area and valleys of the Alps) & Venezuela (Merida) on lichens as bioindicators of heavy-metal poll.; teaching biol.at primary sch.and gen.ecol.at u.levels. **Career:** Contract in Dept of Envl Educ. Min.of the Envt 1979; Lect.in Biol. Lycée Libertador 1980–82 & 1986–91; Lect.(under contract) in Biol.& Natural Scis, Fac.of Humanity, U.of the Andes 1988–91; Chargée d'Etude, Direction Régionale de l'Environnement 1994– and Parc National de la Guadeloupe 1995–. **Achievements:** lichen inventory of Merida, atmos.poll. map of suburbs of Lyon, expositions on lichens as bioindicators of poll. **Membership:** AFL. **Awards:** Bursary (Govt of Venezuela) 1982–6 at Fondation Gran Mariscal de Ayacucho & 1987–8 at CONICIT. **Publications:** five incl. *Les lichens bioindicateurs: la poll.acide dans la régn lyonnaise* (co-Author) 1986, *Effect of sulphur dioxide and fluorine on ascospore germination of several lichens* (co-Author) 1989. **Languages:** English (poor), French, Spanish. **Address:** Rue Gaston Ramassamy, F-97120 Saint-Claude, Guadeloupe, West Indies. **Tel.** (home) 590 802177.

REEVES, Dr Randall Robert. Wild places & wildlife, preservation of such places & such creatures. Director of Research. *B.*18 Dec.1947, Scottsbluff, Nebr. , USA. American. *M.*Randi Roe: 2 *s*. **Education:** U.of Nebr.BA 1970, Princeton U. MPA 1973, McGill U. PhD 1993. **Experience:** field res.centred in N.Amer.Arctic & Greenland, W.Asia, & Peru; recent work has been in eval.& planning of hydroelectric project impacts & mitigation (Canada & Asia) with respect to aquatic or marine mammals; admin.& writing. **Career:** Admin. Woodrow Wilson Sch.of Public & Intl Affairs, Princeton U. 1973–5; Dir of Res. Okapi Wildlife Assocs 1981–. **Achievements:** PhD thesis, work on monodontid, platanistoid, & sirenian, cons. **Memberships:** SMM (Bd of Govs), IUCN SSC Cetacean SG (Dep.Chairman). **Award:** L. Byrne Waterman Award (co-Recipient, Kendall Whaling Mus.). **Publications:** Sierra Club Handbooks of *Whales & Dolphins* (co-Author) 1983 and *Seals & Sirenians* (co-Author) 1992, *The Bottlenose Dolphin* (co-Ed.) 1990; *c.*150 addit.books, chapters, etc. **Languages:** English, French, Italian (slight), Spanish. Willing to act as consult.etc. **Address:** Okapi Wildlife Associates, Hudson, Quebec, Canada. **Tel.** (office & home) and **fax** 1 514 458 7383.

REHBINDER, Professor Dr Eckard. National & comparative environmental law & policy.

Professor of Trade Regulation and Environmental & Comparative Law, Institute Director. *B.*15 Dec.1936, Potsdam, Germany. German. *M.* Heike (lawyer specializing in bldg & envl law). **Education:** U.of Frankfurt, first State exam.in Law 1960, LLD 1965, Privatdozent 1968; U.of Wiesbaden, second State exam.in Law 1964. **Experience:** comparative res.in envl law; consult.for Fed.& State govts, IUCN, & GTZ. **Career:** Prof.of Law at U.of Bielefeld 1969–72 and U.of Frankfurt 1972–, Dir Inst.for Foreign & Intl Trade Law, Frankfurt 1975–. **Achievements:** proposed reforms in envl law, esp.assn standing and intro.of resp.officer for envl prot.within firms (both partially or fully adopted by law). **Memberships:** German WG on Envl Law, ICEL, IUCN CEL, Fed.Council of Envl Advisers. **Award:** Elizabeth Haub Prize 1978. **Publications:** *Politische und rechtliche Probleme des Verursachaerprinzips* 1973, *Bürgerklage im Umweltrecht* (co-Author) 1973, *Chemikaliengesetz* (co-Author) 1985, *Envl Prot. Policy* (co-Author) 1985, *Das Vorsorgeprinzip im internationalen Vergleich* 1991. Indiff.to pers.pub.& news media support. **Languages:** English, French, German, Spanish. Willing to act as consult.etc. **Address:** Speckerhohlweg 3, 61462 Königstein, Germany. **Tel.**(office) 49 69 798 3390, (home) 49 6174 21587; **fax** (office) 49 6174 798 8383, (home) 49 6174 24065.

REHMAN, Syed Ziaur. Water & wastewater treatment, hazardous & solid waste management, air pollution. Assistant Professor. *B.*10 Jan.1945, Gonda, UP, India. Pakistani. *M.*Rooh Bano: 3 *d*. **Education:** U.of Karachi, BE (Civil Eng.) 1966; Nadirshaw Edelji Dinshaw (NED) U.of Engg & Tech.(Karachi) MSc(Envl Eng.) 1990. **Experience:** envl engg, teaching & res.in water & wastewater treatment, air poll., and solid waste mgmt. **Career:** Site Engr, Messrs.Syed Ali & Assocs (Karachi) 1966–70; Captain, Corps of Engrs, Pakistan Army 1970–77; Contract Mgr, Messrs Sazin London Ltd.(Saudi Arabia) 1977–86; Sr Lect. Jinnah Poly.Inst. (Karachi) 1986–92; Asst Prof. Inst.of Envl Engg & Res. Nadirshaw Edelji Dinshaw U.of Engg & Tech. 1992–. **Achievements:** involvment in res. projects on solid waste, air poll., & EIA. **Memberships:** Pakistan Engg Council, Pakistan Inst. of Engrs. **Award:** Tamgai Jang Quaid-e-Azam (Corps of Engrs, Pakistan Army) 1972. **Publications:** incl.Planning and Dev.Strat.for Ecotourism (conf.proc.) 1995. Indiff.to pers. pub. & news media support. **Languages:** English, Urdu. Willing to act as consult.etc. **Address:** Institute of Environmental Engineering and Research, Nadirshaw Edelji Dinshaw University of Engineering and Technology, University Road, Karachi 75270, Pakistan. **Tel.**92 21 496 9264/5/6 ext.2211; **fax** 92 21 496 1934.

REID, Dr Walter V. Biological diversity, conservation, sustainable agriculture, biotechnology. Institute Vice-President. *B.*13 July 1956, Berkeley, California, USA. American. *M.*Cheryl Cort. **Education:** UCB BA(Zool.) 1978, U.of Washington PhD(Zool.specializing in Pop.& Community Ecol.) 1987. **Experience:** policy res.on cons.of biol resources, sust.agric.& biotech.; study of pop.of Magellanic Penguin, Argentina; study of reproductive ecol.of marine birds, Gulf of Alaska. **Career:** Instr. U.of Washington 1987; Gilbert White F. Resources for the Future 1987–8; Sr Assoc.1988–92, VP for Prog.1992–, WRI. **Achievements:** policy res. on cons.of biol resources & dev.of prog.leading to formulation of Global Strat.for Conserving Biodiv. **Memberships:** AAAS, AIBS, DFC, ESA, SCB. **Awards:** Phi Beta Kappa, Sigma Xi, Cert.of Dist., Deptl Award in Zool.(all UCB); Predoctl F'ship (NSF), ARCS F'ship (U.of Washington). **Publications:** Global Biodiv.Strat. (prin.Author) 1992; co-Author of num.reports & articles incl.keeping options alive: the scientific basis for conserving biodiv.1989, Conserving the world's biodiv.1990, Drowning the nat.heritage: climate change & US coastal biodiv.1991, Biodiv.prospecting: using genetic resources for sust.dev.1993. **Language:** English. Willing to act as consult.etc. **Address:** World Resources Institute, 1709 New York Avenue NW, Washington, DC 20006, USA. **Tel.**(office) 1 202 662 2579; **fax** 1 202 638 0036.

REIJNDERS, Professor Dr Lucas. Pollution; natural resources. NGO Staff Member, Professor of Environmental Science. *B.*4 Feb.1946, Amsterdam, The Netherlands. Dutch. **Education:** U.of Amsterdam, PhD(Molecular Biol.) 1973. **Experience:** res., consult., adv.(govtl). **Career:** Staff Memb. Centre of Envl Studies, Gröningen U. 1974–80 & Fndn for Nature and Envt 1980–; Prof.of Envl Sci. U.of Amsterdam 1988–. **Achievements:** activities mainly in field of poll.prevention; improved use of natural resources. **Awards:** Golden Feather (Dutch Assn of Publishers) 1989, Spec.Award (Dutch Soc.for Consulting Engrs) 1992. **Publications:** *Plea for a Sust.Relationship with the Envt* (in Dutch) 1984, *Envlly-improved Prod.and Products* 1995. Indiff.to pers.pub.& news media support. **Languages:** Dutch, English, German. Further details may be obtained from *Intl Who's Who* 1994–5. Willing to act as consult.etc. **Address:** Stichting Natuur en Milieu, Donkerstraat 17, 3511 KB Utrecht, The Netherlands. **Tel.**31 20 525 6206 (Amsterdam) or 31 30 331328 (Utrecht); **fax** 31 20 525 6272 (Amsterdam) or 31 30 331311 (Utrecht).

REIJNDERS, Dr Peter J.H. Marine mammals (pinnipeds). Senior Scientist. *B.*29 May 1944, Siebengewald, The Netherlands. *M.*Majella: 2 *s*. **Education:** Agricl U.Wageningen, MSc 1973, PhD (Nature Mgmt & Wildlife Ecol.) 1980. **Experience:** res.on pop.dynamics, ecotoxicology, physiol.endocrinology, reproductive physiol., ethology, cons.and mgmt, EIA, and husbandry, of marine mammals (pinnipeds); admin. at IFNR. **Career:** Jr Sci. Dept of Animal Ecol. 1980–83, Sr Sci. Dept of Estuarine Ecol., Res.Inst.

for Nature Mgmt 1983– (renamed Dept of Aquatic Ecol. IFNR 1991). **Achievement:** compilation of IUCN Pinniped Action Plan (for cons.of all pinniped species). **Memberships:** Marine Mammals Cttee of ICES (former Chairman), Scientific Cttee of IWC, Netherlands Council for Sea Res.Comm.on Antarctic Res., UNEP Emergency Response Team for Marine Mammals, Cons.& Scientific Adv.Cttees of Marine Mammal Soc.; Chairman of both IUCN SSC Seals SG and Scientific Steering Cttee Jt Intl Cons.and Mgmt Plan for the Wadden Sea Seal Pop.; Consulting Expert on Seals for EC; Expert Memb.NERC (UK) Spec.Cttee on Seals. **Publications:** *c.*110 papers & reports. Favours pers.pub.and news media support. **Languages:** Dutch, English, French (moderate), German. Willing to act as consult.etc. **Address:** Institute for Forestry and Nature Research, Postbus 167, 1790 AD Den Burg, The Netherlands. **Tel.**31 2220 69700; **fax** 31 2220 19235; **e-mail** P.J.H. REIJNDERS @IBN.AGRO.NL .

REYNOLDS, Ms Fiona Claire. Environmental policy at UK & European levels — especially its impact on the countryside. Council Director. *B.* 29 March 1958, Alston, Cumbria, UK. British. *M.*Robert W.T.Merrill: 2 *d*. **Education:** U.of Camb. MA(Geog., Land Economy) 1979, MPhil (Land Economy) 1980. **Experience:** lobbying, campaigning in vol.sector. **Career:** Sec. Council for Nat.Parks 1980–87; Asst Dir 1987–92, Dir 1992–, CPRE. **Endeavours:** raising the profile of domestic cons.issues, promoting a more resp. policy framework. **Memberships:** Nat.Parks Review Panel 1990–, F.RGS. **Award:** Global 500 Roll of Honour (UNEP) 1990. **Language:** English. **Address:** Council for the Protection of Rural England, 25 Buckingham Palace Road, London SW1W 0PP, England, UK. **Tel.**44 171 976 6433; **fax** 44 171 976 6373.

RHO, Dr Chae-Shik. Environmental sciences, atmospheric sciences. Presidential Council Adviser. *B.*2 Dec.1930, Seoul, Republic of Korea. Korean. *M.*Jong Nam: *s*. **Education:** Seoul Nat.U. BSc(Phys.) 1957, DSc(Phys.) 1967; ICL DIC 1960. **Experience:** res.for 32 yrs in field of Site & Envt. **Career:** Weather Officer (Capt.) & Head of Ops Div., 50th Weather Group, Rep.of Korea Air Force 1953–8; Lect. Nat.Aviation Coll.1958–9; Dir Health Phys.Div.1960–73, Directorate Envt Dept 1973–81 & Sr Adv. Nuclear Safety Center 1981–90, KAERI; Sec.-Gen. Admin.Bureau, Office of Atomic Energy 1967–8; Sr Adv. KINS 1990–92; Pres.KETRI 1992–4; Adv. Presidential Council on Sci.& Tech.1993–. **Achievements:** Org.of 1975 Nat. Conf.on Human Envt, played important role in Nat.Data Center for Envl Poll.and Envl Affairs Forum; some recommendations made have been adopted in Korean Envl Preservation Law; Leader of drafting cttee of Presidential Declaration on Envt 1991 and Chairman of KORCES (comprising 25 academic envl sci.& engg socs). **Memberships:** AGU, IUAPPA, KPS, KMS,

KNS, KARP, KAPRA, KORCES. **Awards:** Presidential Citation (Rep.of Korea) 1977, Order of Merit (Camellia) (Rep.of Korea) 1982, Global 500 Roll of Honour (UNEP) 1990. **Publications:** *Intro.to Envl Scis* 1985, *Envl Degradation & Prot.*1993; four papers, the last being Size distribn of atmos. aerosols in Seoul 1986. Indiff.to pers.pub., favours news media support. **Languages:** English (written), German, Japanese, Korean. Further details may be obtained from *Who's Who in the World* 1980–81, *Community Leaders in the World* 1984. Willing to act as consult.etc. **Address:** 89-2 Neungdong, Seongdong-gu, Seoul 133-180, Republic of Korea. **Tel.& fax** (both home) 82 2 466 7002.

RICHARDSON, Paul Nigel. Biological control of insects, achieving reductions in pesticide usage; conservation of insect fauna. Principal Research Scientist. *B.*29 Sept.1946, Rustington, W.Sussex, England, UK. British. *M.*Heather: 3 *s.* **Education:** U.of London BSc(Spec.)(Zool.) 1969; ICL MSc, DIC 1970. **Experience:** 24 yrs' res.into biol.& control of mushroom & glasshouse pests, ecol.of predatory Coleoptera in cereals, persistence & infectivity of insect-parasitic Nematoda. **Career:** HRI (Sussex) 1971–95; Prin.Res.Sci. Entomol.Dept, HRI (Warks) 1995–. **Achievement:** provided growers of ornamental plants & mushrooms with safe, biol alternatives to use of toxic chemicals for insect pest control. **Memberships:** F.RES, AAB, ESN, SIP. **Awards:** Brit.Growers' Look Ahead Award 1990, Queen's Award for Envl Achievement 1993. **Publications:** 60 incl.Nematode pests of glasshouse crops and mushrooms 1993, Entomopathogenic nematodes and the soil envt 1994. Indiff.to pers.pub., favours news media support. **Languages:** English, French (read). Willing to act as consult.etc. **Address:** Entomology Department, Horticulture Research International, Wellesbourne, Warwickshire CV35 9EF, England, UK. **Tel.**44 1789 470382; **fax** 44 1789 470552.

RICHEZ, Dr Gérard. Protection of Nature in the context of tourism. Maître de Conférences. *B.*20 April 1940, Marseille, France. French. *M.*Josy: *d.* **Education:** U.of Aix-en-Provence, Diplôme d'Etudes Supérieures 1965, Docteur d'Etat ès Lettres et Scis humaines 1986. **Experience:** consult.concerned with Regnl Natural Park & Reserves of Corsica, and Nat.Park of Port-Cros. **Career:** Asst, U.of Avignon 1968–9; Maître Asst, U.of Aix-Marseille II 1969–90; Maître de Conférences, U.of Provence 1990–; Vis.Prof. U.of Ottawa 1993 & 1994. **Memberships:** IUCN CNPPA, MAB France, Assn Nat. (Paris) d'Assn Internationale (St Gall, Switzerland) d'Experts Scientifiques du Tourisme. **Publications:** *Parcs Nationaux et Tourisme en Europe* 1992; *c.*60 articles, reports. **Languages:** English, French, Italian, Spanish. Willing to act as consult.etc. **Address:** Université de Provence, 29 Avenue R.Schuman, 13621 Aix-en-Provence, France. **Tel.**(office) 33 42 592900, (home) 33 42 234430; **fax** 33 42 640158.

RICHTER, Robert. Documentary television/ educational productions on environmental subjects. Film Producer & Distributor. *B.*1929, USA. American. *M.:* *d.*Rowena (bot.). **Education:** Telluride Assn Jr Coll. AA 1949, Reed Coll. BA(Lit.) 1952, Columbia U. MA(Public Law & Govt) 1964. **Experience:** producer of documentary films, consult.for documentaries produced by others for PBS telecast. **Career:** Reporter *NY Times* 1962–3; Producer CBS News 1963–8, ind.Documentary Producer 1968–. **Achievements:** prod.of many documentaries on wide variety of envl subjects shown throughout the world on TV, in univs and by interest groups. **Memberships:** AIVF (Pres. 1981–), IDA (Bd of Dirs), CARE/USA, NATAS, Writers' Guild, IOJ. **Awards:** DuPont Columbia Broadcast Journalism (3), National EMMY (2), AAAS–Westinghouse Sci.Journalism, Global 500 Roll of Honour (UNEP) 1989, many Euro.& Amer. festival awards. **Documentaries:** *Incident at Brown's Ferry* 1977, *A Plague on Our Children* 1979, *For Export Only — Pesticides & Pills* 1981, *Hungry for Profit* 1985, *Increase and Multiply?* 1987, *Can Trop.Rain Forests be Saved?* 1992, *The Moneylenders* 1992, *Backlash in the Wild* 1993. Favours pers. pub.& news media support. **Languages:** English; French & Spanish (some). Willing to act as consult. **Address:** Richter Productions, 330 West 42nd Street, New York, New York 10036, USA. **Tel.**(office) 1 212 947 1395; **fax** 1 212 643 1208.

RIGGS, Dr Timothy John. Plant breeding and genetics of horticultural crops. Department Head. *B.*26 July 1941, Weymouth, Dorset, England, UK. British. **Education:** U.of Hull, BSc (Hons)(Bot.) 1963; U.of Edinburgh, PhD (Plant Breeding & Genetics) 1973. **Experience:** cotton breeding in Uganda 1964–8 and barley breeding 1968–84; res.on genetics and selection methods, statl & biometrical analysis; mgmt, overseas consults. **Career:** Res.Officer, Empire Cotton Growing Corpn (later Cotton Res.Corpn, Uganda) 1964–8; Barley Breeder, Scottish Plant Breeding Station 1968–73 and Plant Breeding Inst.(Camb.) 1973–84; Head, Plant Breeding Section, Nat.Vegetable Res.Station 1984–7; Head, Breeding & Genetics Dept, HRI 1987–. **Membership:** F.IHort. **Publications:** *c.*40 papers & chapters. Dislikes pers. pub., indiff.to news media support. **Languages:** English, French (written). Willing to act as consult.etc. **Address:** Breeding & Genetics Department, Horticulture Research International, Wellesbourne, Warwickshire CV35 9EF, England, UK. **Tel.**44 1789 472044; **fax** 44 1789 470552.

RITCHIE, Dr Jerry Carlyle. Ecology, soil science, remote sensing. Soil scientist. *B.*13 Dec.1937, Richfield, NC, USA. American. *M.* Carole (bot.): *s., d.* **Education:** Pfeiffer Coll. BA(Biol.) 1960, U.of Tennessee MS(Bot./Ecol.) 1962, U.of Georgia PhD(Ecol./Bot.) 1967. **Experience:** studied & developed techniques &

methodologies for understanding & managing agricl & natural resources on the landscape. **Career:** post-doctl res. U.of Georgia 1967–8; Soil Sci. Sedimentation Lab.1968–78, Ecol. Nat.Prog.Staff 1978–83, Soil Sci. Hydr.Lab. 1983–, USDA ARS. **Achievements:** developed techniques to use Caesium-137 to measure erosion & sedimentation, and remote sensing to study surface water qual. **Memberships:** ESA, IAHS, SSSA, AGU. **Award:** Nat.Envl Res. Award (USDA ARS) 1992. Favours pers.pub.& news media support. **Language:** English. **Address:** United States Department of Agriculture, Agricultural Research Service, Hydrology Laboratory, Beltsville Agricultural Research Center–West (Building 007), Beltsville, Maryland 20705, USA. **Tel.**1 301 504 7490; **fax** 1 301 504 8931.

ROBARTS, Dr Richard Denis. Freshwater & marine microbial ecology; microbial biogeochemical cycles and impacts of UV-radiation in prairie saline lakes & wetlands. Division Chief, Adjunct Professor. *B.*18 Dec.1944, Croydon, Surrey, England, UK. Canadian. *M.*Toba: 2 *s.* **Education:** U.of Victoria (Canada), BSc(Zool. & Ecol.) 1968; U.of Waterloo, MSc(Microbiol.) 1970; Rhodes U. PhD(Microbial Ecol.) 1974. **Experience:** res.— factors regulating bacterial growth and prod.in African reservoirs, subantarctic lakes, prairie wetlands, & saline lakes; phosphorus & organic carbon cycles in prairie lakes & wetlands; admin.— res.mgr of envl res.in aquatic ecol.and groundwater studies mainly in W.Canada; consult.— water qual. monitoring and aquatic ecol.teaching in developing countries; teaching MSc & PhD students in aquatic microbial ecol.; Chairman of Intl Cttee of Group for Aquatic Primary Productivity (SIL/INTECOL WG) 1993–. **Career:** Res.F.& Lect. U.of Zimbabwe 1973 6; Envl Consult. Toronto & Vancouver 1976–80; Sr Researcher 1980–87, Prog.Mgr (Microbial Fouling) 1987–8, CSIR (SA); Res.Sci.1988–90, Chief of Envl Scis Div.1990–, Nat.Hydr.Res.Inst. Envt Canada; Adjunct Prof. Dept of Applied Microbiol. U.of Sask.1990– and Dept of Biol Scis, U.of Alb. 1995–. **Achievements:** provided new info.on success of bloom-forming Cyanobacteria in African reservoirs; init.unique res.prog.on microbial biogeochem.cycles in prairie wetlands & saline lakes; made significant advances in use of labelled thymidine to determine bacterial growth and prod.in natural systems. **Memberships:** ASLO, SIL, CSL. **Awards:** Achievement Award (CSIR, SA) 1986/7/8. **Publications:** 120 papers and books incl.Applied and envl microbiol.(co-Author) 1986, *Inland Waters of Southern Africa: An Ecol Perspective* (co-Author) 1990, Limnol. and oceanogr.(co-Author) 1993, Advances in microbial ecol.(co-Author) 1993. Indiff.to pers. pub., favours news media support. **Language:** English. Willing to act as consult.etc. **Address:** National Hydrology Research Institute, Environment Canada, 11 Innovation Boulevard, Saskatoon, Saskatchewan S7N 3H5, Canada.

Tel.(office) 1 306 975 6047, (home) 1 306 249 4448; **fax** 1 306 975 5143; **e-mail** robartsr@ nhrisv.nhrc.sk.doe.ca .

ROBERTS, Professor Dr Thomas Michael. Applied ecology, air pollution impacts, derelict land reclamation; research management. Institute Director & Deputy Centre Director. *B.*12 May 1948, St Asaph, Wales, UK. British. *M.* Ann (Map Curator Sec., Antarctic Place-names Cttee, Brit.Antarctic Survey). **Education:** St Asaph Grammar Sch.; U.of Wales BSc(Hons) (Zool./Bot.) 1969, PhD (Applied Ecol.) 1972. **Experience:** res.at C.Elec.Res.Labs & ITE on effects of air poll.on veg.& soils, global envl change, derelict land reclamation, envl assessment; teaching applied ecol.to BSc & PhD levels at Univs of Toronto & Liverpool; integrated mgmt of interdisc.res.teams. **Career:** Vis.Prof. U.of Toronto 1972–4; Lect. U.of Liverpool 1974–8; Res.Mgr CEGB 1978–88; Dir 1989–, Dep.Dir of Centre for Ecol.& Hydr.1994–, ITE, NERC. **Achievements:** papers in *Sci.*and *Nature* on food-chain transport for heavy-metals; contribn of acid deposition to forest decline; dev.of integrated mgmt of interdisc.res.in ITE. **Memberships:** F.IBiol., BES, IEA. **Awards:** Vis. Prof. (U.of York & King's Coll.London), Ext. Examiner (U.of Manchester & ICL). **Publications:** *Envl Planning* (co-Author) 1982; *c.*40 j.papers & 20 chapters incl.Long-term effects of SO_2 on crops 1984, New perspectives on forest decline (co-Author) 1988, Case Study — Air Qual.(co-Author) 1992, Ed. *J.of Applied Ecol.*, several edl bds. **Languages:** English, French (read). Willing to act as consult.etc. **Address:** Institute of Terrestrial Ecology, Administrative HQ, Monks Wood, Abbots Ripton, Huntingdon PE17 2LS, Cambridgeshire, England, UK. **Tel.**(office) 44 1487 773381, (home) 44 1223 845662; **fax** 44 1487 773590; **e-mail** JANET .

RODHOUSE, Dr Paul Gregory Kenneth. Evolutionary biology, ecology, & fisheries, of marine molluscs; southern ocean Cephalopoda. Marine Ecologist. *B.*13 Feb.1951, Bromley, Kent, England, UK. British. Father Kenneth Frederick Rodhouse (salmonids). *M.*Laura: 2 *s., d.* **Education:** St Mary's Coll.; U.of Lond.(Westfield), BSc(Hons)(Biol.Scis) 1972; U.of Southampton, MSc(Oceanogr.) 1973, PhD(Oceanogr.) 1977, DSc 1994. **Experience:** fieldwork on Galápagos Islands 1972, scientific diving 1972–82; res.— marine bivalve physiol.& genetics 1973–82, marine ecosystem carbon budgets 1979–82, s.ocean cephalopod ecol.& fisheries 1985–, oceanic res.cruises and at sea on commercial fishing vessels 1985–, commissioned res.on s.ocean fisheries 1987–. **Career:** Res.Sci. Shellfish Res.Lab. UC Galway 1977–82; Res. Assoc.& Lect. Dept of Ecol.and Evol. SUNY Stony Brook 1982–4; Marine Ecol.(incl.one yr Detached Duty at MBA), Brit.Antarctic Survey 1985–. **Achievements:** basic res.on marine mollusc physiol., ecol. & genetics; assessment of carrying capacity of coastal marine sites for shellfish aquaculture; elucidation of role of cephalopods in s.ocean ecosystems. **Memberships:** F.LS, MBA, MSL (Counc.). **Publications:** *The Yachtsman's Naturalist* (co-Author) 1980; 80 scientific papers. Indiff.to pers.pub., favours news media support. **Languages:** English; French & Spanish (some reading knowledge). Willing to act as consult.etc. **Address:** British Antarctic Survey, High Cross, Madingley Road, Cambridge CB3 0ET, England, UK. **Tel.**(office) 44 1223 251612, (home) 44 1223 812785; **fax** 44 1223 362616; **e-mail** p.rodhouse @bas.ac.uk .

RODRIGUEZ, Andrés Roberto RODRIGUEZ. Ichthyology, ecology, marine sciences; environmental education; journalism, writing. Researcher. *B.* 13 May 1952, Santa Clara, Cuba. Cuban. *M.* Mylene Gonzalez: *d.* **Education:** U.of Havana, Lic.(Biol Scis) 1975. **Experience:** res. in marine scis; ecol. **Career:** Researcher 1975–80 & 1987–91, Center for Fisheries Res.(Havana, Cuba); Adv. Cuban Tuna Fleet (Havana) 1981– 6; Researcher, Estación de Investigaciones Marinas de Margarita, La Salle Fndn for Natural Scis 1994–. **Achievements:** co-estab.of CSBS 1980; active collabn with mass media (30 papers), pubns. **Memberships:** CSBS (Founder Memb.) 1980–. **Awards:** Young Sci.Prize 1981/ 3/5 and Fernando Ortiz Prize 1990 (both nat.). **Publications:** three books and two in press incl.*Peces Marionis Importantes de Cuba* 1987, *Lista de Nombres Cientificos y Comunes de Peces marinos Cubanos (Nomenclator)* 1984, *ECOCRISIS: El hombre en la naturaleza 1996*; Author or co-Author of 30+ papers. Favours pers.pub.& news media support. **Languages:** English, French, Spanish. Willing to act as consult.etc. **Address:** Estación de Investigaciones Marinas de Margarita, Fundación La Salle de Ciencias Naturales, Punta de Piedras, Apartado 144, Portlamar 6301, Estado Nueva Esparta, Venezuela. **Tel.**58 95 98051 or 98236 to 41; **fax** 58 95 98061; **e-mail** edimar@dino.conicit.ve .

RODRIGUEZ RODRIGUEZ, Andrés Roberto, *see above.*

ROMULUS, Giles. Environmental planning & management (in particular protected areas' planning) and co-management approaches to the environment. Director of Natural Heritage. *B.*1 Sept.1961, St Lucia, W.Indies. French, St Lucian. *M.*Nicole Marie E. **Education:** U.of W.Indies, BA(Hons)(Geog.) 1985, Dipl.(Resource Mgmt & Envl Studies)(Dist.) 1987; York U. MES(Envl Planning & Mgmt) 1995, Dipl. (Latin Amer.& Carib.Studies) 1995. **Experience:** part-time lecturing on climatology, work with WWF (Canada), and internship with TNC; consult.to CANARI & OECS Natural Resources' Mgmt Unit, project admin., Chairman of Educ. Cttee for Yr of Envt in St Lucia 1989. **Career:** Ed. Govt Census Office 1980; Teller, R.Bank of Canada 1980–81; Teacher, St Mary's Coll. 1981–82, 1985–6, 1987–8; Projects Coord./Planner 1988–

94, Dir of Natural Heritage 1994–, St Lucia NT. **Achievements:** planning & mgmt of the process for dev.of St Lucia's first Prot. Areas' Systems Plan, prep.of strategic plan for communities of Praslin & Mamiku (St Lucia). **Memberships:** St Lucia Naturalists' Soc.(past PRO), Bougainvillea Youth Club of Marchand (past PRO). **Awards:** Euro.Dev.Fund Scholarship, Commonwealth Scholarship. **Publications:** The value of the Mankote Mangrove within the St Lucia Prot.Areas System 1990, *A Gen.Profile of Costa Rica with an Emphasis on Parks and Prot.Areas* 1992, *The Need for Integrated Rural Dev.— a Case Study of the Cacao-Vigie Communities (Vieux Fort, St Lucia)* 1994; Ed. St Lucia Naturalists Soc.*Newsletter* 1987–9; several newspaper articles, editorials. Indiff.to pers.pub.& news media support. **Languages:** English, French (fair spoken). Willing to act as consult. etc. **Address:** St Lucia National Trust, POB 595, Castries, St Lucia, West Indies. **Tel.** (office) 809 452 1495, (home) 809 452 4258; **fax** 809 453 2791.

ROOM, Dr Peter Michael. Insect/plant interactions; biological control of weeds; plant responses to damage. Chief Research Scientist. *B.* 3 July 1947, York, England, UK. Australian, British. *M.*Sandra Elizabeth: 2 *s.* **Education:** ICL BSc 1968, Univs of Ghana/Lond. PhD 1971. **Experience:** res.— ant ecol., pests of cocoa, coconuts, oil-palm, cotton; biol control of weeds; simulation of plant growth; consults re. biol control of aquatic weeds in Africa, Asia, PNG; mgmt — cooperative res.centre for trop. pest mgmt. **Career:** Entomol. DoA PNG 1971–3; Res.Sci. CSIRO Cotton Res.Unit 1974–8; Sr to Chief Res.Sci. CSIRO Entomol. 1978–, Hon. Res.F. U.of Qld 1991–. **Achievements:** basic res.on ecol.of ants & mistletoes; first computer system for cotton pest mgmt in Australia (SIRATAC); led team which achieved biocontrol of *Salvinia* in many countries; init. estab.of Centre for Trop.Pest Mgmt. **Memberships:** BES, AES, RES, Australian Entomol. Soc. **Awards:** Sci.Prize (UNESCO) 1985, Best Didactic Values (Intl Festival of Sci.Films) 1985, Rivett Medal 1986 & Chairman's Medal 1991 (CSIRO), Award for Excellence (AIDAB) 1988, Rolex Hon.Mention 1990, Poleureka Prize 1990. **Publications:** *Insects & Spiders of Australian Cotton Fields* 1979, *Assault on the Sepik* (film) 1984, *c.*80 papers. Indiff.to pers.pub., favours news media support. **Languages:** English, French (limited), German (limited), Pidgin English. Willing to act as consult.etc. **Address:** Commonwealth Scientific and Industrial Research Organization — Entomology, PB Nr 3, Indooroopilly, Queensland 4068, Australia. **Tel.**(office) 61 7 214 2700, (home) 61 7 378 7251; **fax** 61 7 871 0819.

ROSE, Carlos Roberto HASBÚN. Sea-turtle conservation efforts with local communities, wildlife rescue & rehabilitation programmes, protection of wildlands. Service Head, Programme Director. *B*.17 May 1963, El Salvador, C.Amer. American, Salvadorean. **Education:** U.of Minn. BSc(Animal Sci., Biol.) 1986. **Experience:** sea-turtle cons.& res.studies in Mexico, Costa Rica, El Salvador; admin. **Career:** Dir, Nat.Zool Park 1989–91, Head, NPWS of El Salvador 1991–; Sea-turtle Prog.Dir, Admin. Auth.of CITES Conv.in El Salvador 1991–. **Achievement:** involvement of local poor communities of fishermen in sea-turtle cons.activities. **Membership:** IUCN SSC Marine Turtle SG. **Reward:** The smile of the children when they see that the sea-turtle eggs which they planted are hatching. **Publications:** *Sea-turtle Cons.Tech.Reports of El Salvador* (in Spanish) 1989–, *La Vida de la Tortages Marinas* (colouring book) 1991, *Morphometric Descriptions of Sea Turtles of El Salvador* (in Spanish) 1994, *Marine Mammals of El Salvador* (in Spanish) 1994. Indiff.to pers.pub., favours news media support. **Languages:** English, Spanish. Willing to act as consult.etc. **Address:** 7a Calle Pnt., # 5150 Col.Escalón, San Salvador, El Salvador. **Tel.**(office) 503 770622, (home) 503 986387; **fax** 503 770490.

ROSSI, Patrizia. Protected areas' management; mountain environment. Director. *B*.13 April 1953, Cuneo, Italy. Italian. *M*.Claudio Bruna: *d*. **Education:** Cuneo High Sch. Maturità Classica Liceo Classico 1972; U.of Turin, Laurea in Scienze Biologiche 1976, Specializzazione in Microbiologia 1979. **Experience:** admin. prot. areas' mgmt; consult.— mtn envt prot., wildlife mgmt; sec.sch. teaching. **Career:** teacher of scis & maths in sec.sch.1976–80, Dir Alta Valle Pesio Nature Park 1981–3, Dir Argentera Nature Park 1984 . **Achievements:** prot.of Maritime Alps, studies on alpine Ibex (*Capra ibex* L.), reintro.of Bearded Vulture (*Gypaetus barbatus* L.) in Maritime Alps; coopn & twinning with French Mercantour Nat.Park; Council of Europe Euro.Dipl.awarded to Argentera Nature Park; estab.of 'Valderia' alpine botl gdn. **Memberships:** EFNNP (Council), IAABG (Council), IBS, IBA. **Award:** Premio ITAS letteratura di Montagna 1988. **Publications:** *Parco Naturale Argentera, Itinerari Natura*, *c*.30 articles & papers. Indiff.to pers.pub.& news media support. **Languages:** English, French, Italian, Spanish (basic). Willing to act as consult.etc. **Address:** Parco Naturale Argentera, Corso Dante Livio Bianco 5, 12010 Valdieri, Cuneo, Italy. **Tel.** (office) 39 171 97397, (home) 39 171 699674; **fax** 39 171 97542.

ROSSWALL, Professor Thomas. Microbial ecology, biogeochemical cycles; global environmental change. Executive Director, Professor of Environmental Sciences. *B*.20 Dec.1941, Stockholm, Sweden. Swedish. **Education:** U. of Uppsala MSc 1966. **Experience:** res.— field & lab.res.in areas of interest incl.field-work in Sri Lanka & Brazil; teaching of microbial ecol.& biogeochem.primarily at grad.levels. **Career:** Res.Asst, Asst Prof., Assoc.Prof. Swedish U.of

Agricl Scis 1970–76 & 1980–84; Swedish Council for Planning & Coordn of Res.1976 8; Dir of SCOPE/UNEP Intl Nitrogen Unit, R.Swedish AS 1978–80; Prof. Dept of Water & Envl Res. U.of Linköping 1984–7; Exec.Dir IGBP 1987–; Prof.of Envl Scis, U.of Stockholm 1992–. **Achievements:** basic res.in microbial ecol.& biogeochem.cycling of carbon & nitrogen; resp. for planning & coordn of major intl res.prog.on global change. **Memberships:** Swedish Soc. Oikos; Swedish, French, Amer.& Brit.Socs of Microbiol.; ISSS, ICRO, AGU, others. **Awards:** F.R.Swedish AS, F.Academia European. **Publications:** Ed.of 15 scientific books incl.*Modern Methods in the Study of Microbial Ecol.*1973, *Terr.Nitrogen Cycles: Processes, Ecosystems Strats & Mgmt Impacts* (co-Ed.) 1981, *Scales & Global Change. Spatial & Temporal Variability of Biospheric & Geospheric Processes* (co-Ed.) 1988, *Ecol.of Arable Land. The Role of Organisms in Carbon & Nitrogen Cycling* (co-Ed.) 1989; 100+ papers. **Languages:** English, French (fair), Swedish. Willing to act as consult.etc. **Address:** International Geosphere-Biosphere Programme Secretariat, Royal Swedish Academy of Sciences, Box 50005, S-10405 Stockholm, Sweden. **Tel.**46 8 166448; **fax** 46 8 166405.

ROWLAND, Professor Dr Frank Sherwood 'Sherry'. Chemistry of the atmosphere especially ozone and chlorofluorocarbons. Research Professor of Chemistry & Professor of Chemistry. *B*.28 June 1927, Delaware, OH, USA. American. *M*.Joan Lundberg: *d., s*. **Education:** Ohio Wesleyan U. BA 1948; U.of Chicago, MS 1951, PhD 1952. **Experience:** lecturing, public speaking, res. **Career:** Instr.in Chem. Princeton U. 1952–6; Asst Prof.1956–8, Assoc.Prof. 1958–63, Prof.1963–4, of Chem. U.of Kansas; Prof.of Chem.& Dept Chairman 1964–70, Prof.of Chem.1964–, Daniel G.Aldrich Jr Prof.of Chem.1985–9, Donald Bren Prof.of Chem. 1989–94, Donald Bren Res.Prof.of Chem.1994–, UCI. **Achievements:** co-discovery that CFC gases deplete the ozone layer of the stratosphere, num.professional accomplishments. **Memberships:** US NAS 1978 (Foreign Sec.1994–), Amer.AAS 1977, AAAS (F., Pres.-elect 1991, Pres.1992, Chairman of Bd 1993–), F.AGU, F.APS. **Awards:** Tyler Prize for Envl Achievement 1983, Global 500 Roll of Honour (UNEP) 1989, num.nat.awards incl.Vis.Sci. (JSPS) 1980, Humboldt Sr F'ship (W.Germany) 1981, Silver Medal, John Jeyes Lect.(R.Inst.of Chem. UK) 1989, Robertson Mem.Lect.(NAS) 1993; Hon.DSc (U.of Chicago, Duke U., & Whittier Coll. 1989, Princeton U. 1990 and Haverford Coll. 1992), LLD (Ohio Wesleyan U. 1989 and Simon Fraser U. 1991); num. others incl.shared Nobel Prize for Chem.1995. **Publications:** more than 300 scientific incl. Chlorofluoromethanes in the envt (co-Author) 1975, Estimated future atmos.concentrations of CCl_3F (Fluorocarbon-11) for var.hypothetical tropospheric removal rates (co-Author) 1976,

The hydrolysis of chlorine nitrate, and its possible atmospheric significance 1986 (co-Author), CFCs, stratospheric ozone, and the Antarctic 'Ozone Hole' 1988. **Language:** English. Further details may be obtained from *Who's Who in Amer.*1996. **Address:** Department of Chemistry, University of California, Irvine, California 92717, USA. **Tel.**(office) 1 714 856 6016, (home) 1 714 760 1333; **fax** 1 714 725 2905.

ROWLEY, Mrs Diana Mary Rustat. Arctic science especially geography & history. Officially retired. *B.*21 June 1918, Khartoum, Sudan. Canadian. *M.*Graham W.Rowley *qv*: 3 *d*. **Education:** U.of Oxf. BA 1940, MA 1948. **Experience:** knowledge of Canadian Arctic esp. post-war dev.of sci.there, prehist.of the area, and hist.of exploration; scientific editing. **Career:** Ed.of *Geogl J., Arctic, Arctic Circular.* **Memberships:** AINA (past-Gov.), Glaciological Soc., RGS. Indiff.to pers.pub.& news media support. **Languages:** English, French. Willing to act as consult.etc. **Address:** 245 Sylvan Avenue, Ottawa, Ontario K1M 0X1, Canada. **Tel.** (home) 1 613 749 8114.

ROWLEY, Graham Westbrook. Arctic regions, circumpolar peoples especially Eskimos (Inuit & Yuit). Officially Retired. *B.*31 Oct. 1912, Manchester, England, UK. Canadian. *M.* Diana M.R.Rowley *qv*: 3 *d*. **Education:** U.of Camb. MA 1936, Staff Coll.Camberley (UK) 1941–2, Nat.Defence Coll.Kingston (UK) 1959–60. **Experience:** archaeol.excavation & geogl exploration in e.Canadian Arctic 1936–9; resp. for arctic res.in Canadian Defence Res.Bd 1946–53, involved in dev.of scientific policies & facilities in arctic Canada; travelled extensively in polar regns; studied impact of dev.on n.native peoples. **Career:** Sec. Adv.Cttee on Northern Devs (Canada) 1953–67, Scientific Adv. Dept of Northern Affairs & Nat.Resources (Canada) 1968–74, Vis.F. Clare Hall Camb.1968–9, Res. Prof. Carleton U.1981–6. **Memberships:** AINA (past-Chairman Bd of Govs), Arctic Circle (past-Pres.), F.RGS, Glaciol.Soc., Hakluyt Soc., Prehistoric Soc. **Awards:** Hon.LLD (U.of Sask.) 1975, Massey Medal (RCGS), OC, MBE, major is.in Canadian Eastern Arctic named after him. **Publications:** incl.*The Circumpolar N.*(co-Author) 1978. Indiff.to pers.pub.& news media support. **Languages:** English, Eskimo (some spoken), French (some read). Further details may be obtained from *Canadian Who's Who.* Willing to act as consult.etc. **Address:** 245 Sylvan Avenue, Ottawa, Ontario K1M 0X1, Canada. **Tel.** (home) 1 613 749 8114.

ROWLEY, John Richard. Editor of international magazine dealing with population, environment, & ecologically-sustainable development. Director, Editor. *B.*25 June 1931, Tipton, Staffordshire, England, UK. British. *M.*Rajamani (Dir of Pop.Concern). **Education:** Vic. Coll.; LSE BSc(Econ.) 1949. **Experience:** Ed./ News Ed. of UN conf.newspapers 1974–80,

Rapp./Recommendations Ed.at other intl mtgs; Leader IPPF delegation to UNCED 1992, reporting assignments in Asia, Africa, & Latin Amer.; Producer of & script-writer for film & video productions, Vis.Lect., Edl Bd Memb.of var.pubns. **Career:** Corres.& foreign news exec. for British newspapers incl.*The Guardian* and *The Times* 1952–73, Pubns Dir IPPF & Founder/Ed. *People* magazine 1972–92, Dir Planet 21 (Brit.NGO) & Ed.*People & The Planet* 1992–. **Achievements:** founded & edited *Earthwatch* (newsletter of UNFPA/IUCN/IPPF) to explore & promote awareness of interrelated issues of pop.& envt 1980–92. **Memberships:** RGS, Foreign Press Club, Commonwealth Journalists' Assn. **Awards:** Brit.Press Award, Pop.Inst.Award. **Publications:** *Human Numbers, Human Needs* (co-Author) 1984; num.newspaper/ magazine articles, reports, & book contribns. Willing to act as consult.etc. **Address:** 60 Twisden Road, London NW5 1DN, England, UK. **Tel.**(office) 44 171 487 7911, (home) 44 171 485 3136; **fax** 44 171 267 0874.

ROWNTREE, Matthew James William. Protected area management, particularly regarding subsistence community integration with protected area authorities. Programme Leader & Lecturer. *B.*13 Mar.1969, London, England, UK. British. **Education:** Coventry U. BSc (Hons)(Envl Sci.) 1992. **Experience:** res.for IUCN (Nepal) & Nat.Parks Bd (SA), consult.for Eastern Euro.Prog.(UK), specialist in community integration with prot.areas. **Career:** studying at Middlesex U.for MA(Cons.Policy) degree 1992–; Cons.Prog.Leader, and Lect.in Leisure & Tourism, N.Herts Coll. 1995–. **Endeavours:** to reduce unsustainable local subsistence community impacts on prot.areas thus contributing to enhancement & cons.of prot.areas & community values. **Membership:** IUCN CNPPA. **Publication:** Moldova (chapter, 1995). Indiff.to pers. pub., favours news media support. **Languages:** English, French (poor), Spanish (poor). Willing to act as a consult. **Address:** Ash Cottage, Ashwell, Near Baldock, Hertfordshire SG7 5LZ, England, UK. **Tel.**44 1462 742715; **fax** 44 1487 740464.

ROYES, Dr Veronica Irene Joy. Waste management particularly recycling activities, and organic farming using natural pesticides & manure. Retired science teacher. *B.*20 Feb. 1930, St Mary, Jamaica, W.Indies. Jamaican. *W.*(husband was Dr Vernon Royes, Geneticist, *Cajanus cajan* cultivar Royes of U.of Qld). **Education:** UC of W.Indies BSc(Bot.Zool. Chem.) 1957, (renamed) U.of W.Indies PhD 1971, Dipl.in Educ.1976; Edinburgh U. MSc (Genetics) 1962. **Experience:** res.in genetics (mutation in *Neurospora crassa)* and survey on air spora; taught sci.for 21 yrs and worked on projects such as Composting and Natural Pesticides; promoted safety awareness. **Career:** Teacher 1973–93; Head Sci.Dept. 1989–91, St Andrew's High Sch.for Girls. **Achievements:**

recycling kitchen waste to make compost; extracting natural pesticides to kill cattle ticks; sust.chicken farming; safety exhibitions on natural & Man-made disasters. **Memberships:** AST (Chairman Nat.Exec. 1989–91), NEST (VC 1991–2), Action Plan Cttees for Sci.& Tech., and Organic Farming. **Awards:** Esso Plaque 1984, Insurance Co.of the W.Indies STAR Scholar 1990, Guest of Global Assembly of Women and the Envt 1991, Global 500 Roll of Honour (UNEP) 1992. **Publications:** incl.Some components of the air spora in Jamaica & their possible med.application 1987. Favours pers.pub.& news media support. **Language:** English. Willing to act as consult.etc. **Address:** 4 Charlemont Avenue, Kingston 6, Jamaica. **Tel.**(home) 809 927 5949; **fax** 809 960 3909 c/o NEST.

Ru ZHANG, Professor Wan, *see* **ZHANG, Professor Wan Ru.**

RUGE, Dr Tiahoga. Environmental education & communication. Centre Director. *B.*23 Sept. 1952, Mexico City, Mexico. Mexican. *M.*Fernando Ortiz Monasterio (envl consult.): 2 *d.* **Education:** U.of Houston, BA(Social Anthrop.) and MS(Biol.) 1976, UNAM PhD(Anthrop.) 1984. **Experience:** producing & directing films & documentaries on envl issues, specialist in envl communication through videos & pubns, media exp., org.of nationwide contests on envt within the sch.system. **Career:** Lect.in Envt and Anthrop. UNAM 1981–4; Sci.& Culture Couns. Embassy of Mexico in India 1984–8; Dir of Envt & Culture, Min.of Culture (Mexico) 1988–90; Pres. Friends of The Biosphere 1991–6; Dir, Center of Info.and Communication on the Envt of N.Amer. 1995–. **Achievements:** promoting envl educ.through nationwide progs shown *via* TV, videos, comic books, etc. **Memberships:** G500F (Couns.for Latin Amer.), NAAEE. **Award:** Global 500 Roll of Honour (UNEP) 1991. **Publications:** articles on envl communication published intlly, several films. Indiff.to pers.pub., favours news media support. **Languages:** Dutch, English, French, German, Hindi (spoken), Italian, Spanish. Willing to act as consult.etc. **Address:** Jaime Nunó 77, Mexico 01020 Distrito Federal, Mexico. **Tel.**(office) 525 662 2783, (home) 525 663 0006; **fax** 525 661 9754.

RUIZ-MURRIETA, Dr Julio. Conservation, sustainable use of forest species & ecosystems; indigenous peoples. Programme Officer & Coordinator. *B.*25 Nov.1949, Iquitos, Peru. French, Peruvian. *M.*Jeanine Levistre: *s.* **Education:** U.of Toronto, BSc(For.) 1978, U.of La Sorbonne, Doct.1982. **Experience:** 20 yrs' res., educ., training, info., cons.& dev.of trop.forest ecosystems, all esp.in Latin Amer. **Career:** Forest Officer, Min.of Agric.(Peru) 1970–79; Sr Sci.& DG, Inst.of Amazon Res.& Dev.1982–9; Consult. UNESCO (Paris) 1990–93; Prog.Officer & Coord. World Forest Cons.Prog. IUCN 1994–. **Achievements:** assisting Latin Amer.orgns in

establishing Alliances for Nature Cons.and Sust.Dev.; Pres.of Amazon Dev.Plan 1985–8. **Memberships:** IUFRO, MAB, ISTF, ISE. **Awards:** Scholarships (CIDA) 1973 & (Min.of Coopn, The Netherlands) 1986. **Publications:** *Alternatives to Deforestation in the Humid Tropics* 1993, *Extractives Reserves* 1995; 40+ papers. Favours pers.pub.& news media support. **Languages:** English, French, Portuguese, Spanish. Willing to act as consult.etc. **Address:** IUCN — The World Conservation Union, Rue Mauverney 28, 1196 Gland, Switzerland. **Tel.** (office) 41 22 999 0260, (home) 41 22 364 5456; **fax** 41 22 999 0025.

RUMMEL-BULSKA, Dr Iwona. Environmental law. Secretariat Coordinator. *B.*30 April 1948, Warsaw, Poland. Polish. *M.*Dr Wojceich Bulski. **Education:** U.of Warsaw, LLB 1968, LLM 1969, PhD(Pol.Scis & Intl Law)(*cum laude*) 1978; Judge Exam.*(cum laude),* Court of Justice (Warsaw) 1971. **Experience:** Exec.Sec. and drafter of documentation for negns and Confs of Plenipotentiaries for Vienna Conv.on Ozone and Montreal Protocol, Basel Conv.on Hazardous Wastes, Biodiv. Conv., Climate Conv., etc.; lecturing at Warsaw U. –1982, Amer.U.(Nairobi) 1988–92 & U.of Geneva 1993–4; resp.for dev.of London Guidelines on Trade in Chemicals, and on Principles of EIA. **Career:** Chief of Envl Law & Instns Unit 1986–91, Coord. Secretariat of the Basel Conv. 1991–, UNEP. **Achievements:** dev.of Montreal Protocol, Basel Conv., Conv.on Biodiv. **Memberships:** ICEL, Global Assn of Lawyers (Poland). **Awards:** for negn of Ozone-Layer-related legal acts (Vienna Conv.& Montreal Protocol) 1987. **Publications:** several incl.Non-navigational Use of Intl Waterways 1981, Selected Multilateral Treaties in the Field of Envt 1981. Accepts pers.pub., favours news media support. **Languages:** English, French, Polish, Russian. **Address:** 17 chemin W.Barbey, 1292 Chambésy, Geneva, Switzerland. **Tel.**(office) 41 22 979 9213, (home) 41 22 758 2626; **fax** 41 22 797 3454.

RYAN, Dr Peter G. Biology & conservation of oceanic islands; marine debris, evolutionary ecology, ornithology. Lecturer in Zoology. *B.* 31 Aug.1962, Yorkshire, England, UK. S.African. *M.*Dr Coleen L.Moloney (zool., modeller). **Education:** U.of Cape Town BSc 1982, BSc(Hons) 1983, MSc 1986, PhD 1992, all in Zool. **Experience:** res.— extensive field-work at Southern Ocean Islands, in Antarctica and throughout s.Africa; taught courses at UCD & U.of Cape Town; admin.— Coord. MSc prog.in Cons.Biol. FitzPatrick Inst. **Career:** Cons.Officer of Tristan da Cunha (mounted three expedns to uninhabited Inaccessible Is.), FitzPatrick Inst. U.of Cape Town 1987–90; Postdoctl Assoc. UCD 1992; Lect. Dept of Zool. U.of Cape Town 1993–. **Achievements:** leading auth.on marine debris problem in s.Africa & adjacent seas, promotes public awareness of cons.value of oceanic islands. **Memberships:** Gough Is. Wildlife Reserve Adv.Cttee (Sec.); Res.& Rarities Cttees of SAOS. **Awards:** Medal (SAAAS) 1986, Purcell Mem.Prize 1986 & 1992. **Publications:** *Atlas of the Birds of the southwestern Cape* (co-Author) 1989; *c*.50 papers. Favours pers.pub.& news media support inasmuch as any pub. increasing public awareness of envl concerns is beneficial. **Languages:** Afrikaans, English. Willing to act as consult.etc. **Address:** FitzPatrick Institute, University of Cape Town, Rondebosch 7700, South Africa. **Tel.**(office) 27 21 650 2966, (home) 27 21 696 9402; **fax** 27 21 650 3295; **e-mail** PRYAN@ZOO.UCT.AC.ZA.

RYCHNOVSKÁ, Professor Dr Milena. Plant ecophysiology, grassland ecosystems, ecological function of grassland in landscape. Professor of Ecology. *B*.17 Oct.1928, Brno, Czech Rep. Czech. Father Dr Stephan Soudek, zool., ant & honey-bee studies, soil fauna ecol., first Prof.of Applied Entomol.in (then) Czech. *M*.Otomar Rychnovsky MD: 2 *s*. **Education:** Masaryk U. MSc(Plant Physiol.) 1952; Czech.AS PhD 1959, DrSc(Plant Ecol.) 1982. **Experience:** leader of ecosystem res.projects on grasslands for IBP 1965–72, Earthwatch Project 1993; bldg-up & heading Ecol.Dept of Botl Inst. Czech.AS 1960–85 and Head Dept of Ecol. Palacky U.1991–4; PI for EARTHWATCH expedn 1993; consult.; edl bd of two intl ecol journals; govtl evaluating bd for Czech.univs (biol. branches), c.Cttee for eval.of Insts of Czech AS; field exp.on savanna ecosystems in Cuba. **Career:** Lect.in Plant Physiol. Masaryk U.1952–5; Res.Asst to Head of Ecol.Dept, Botl Inst. Czech. AS 1956–85; Inst.of Landscape Ecol. Slovak AS 1986–90; Prof.in Ecol. Palacky U.1991–. **Achievements:** leader of team res.on ecosystem functioning (alluvial & highland meadows) in Czech.; invited to synthetize IBP res.on grasslands of temperate zone; introduced ecol eval.of grassland and its role in the landscape of Czech.; invited speaker at Intl Botl Cong.1969, Intl Grassland Cong.1977, & Euro.Grassland Fedn Congresses 1986 & 1994; Coord.of postgrad. educ.in ecol.in Czech Rep. **Memberships:** INTECOL, Czech. Nat.Cttees of IBP, IUBS (Scientific Sec. 1980–87) and MAB, Czech.Botl, Ecol, & Biol, Socs, Slovak Botl Soc., Czech.Soc.for Sust.Dev. **Awards:** Czech.AS Prize (team memb.) 1972. **Publications:** five books incl.*Structure and Functioning of Grassland Ecosystems* 1993; chapters incl.Semi-natural Temperate Meadows and Pastures 1979, Yield Formation in Grasslands 1988, *Ecosystems of the World* 1993; *c*.100 papers. Indiff.to pers.pub.& news media support. **Languages:** Czech, English, German, Russian; French & Spanish (less fluent); Latin & Polish (passive knowledge). Further details may be obtained from *Handbook of Contemporary Devs in World Ecol.* 1981, *Czech.Biographic Dict.*1992. Willing to act as consult.etc. **Address:** Department of Ecology, Palacky University, Svobody 26, Olomouc CZ 771 46, Czech Republic. **Tel.**(office) 42 68 522 2451, (home) 42 5 577049; **fax** 42 68 522 5737.

RYDÉN, Per Axel. Rural development, natural resource management. Acting Assistant Director-General. *B*.21 Jan.1945, Orebro, Sweden. Swedish. *M*.Vassula: *step-s*. **Education:** U.of Lund, Quaternary Geol.1965–6; Agricl Coll.of Sweden (Uppsala), MSc(Agron.)(Intl Crop Husbandry — Business Admin.& Marketing) 1972. **Experience:** two months' field-work in Ethiopia undertaking investigation of oil crops 1971; participation in Sem.on Shifting Cultivation & Soil Cons.in Africa (Nigeria), in mid-term review of Spec.Rural Dev.Prog.Migori (Kenya) both in 1973, and as Sec.to jt Nordic/ Tanzanian Eval.Team re.Agricl Res.and Training Inst.(Mbeya) 1976; consult.for SIDA to Guinea-Bissau to undertake analysis of rural sector in that country and present proposals for projects to be financed by SIDA, and further planning of Rural Dev. Project for SIDA-financing as proposed in the sector analysis 1979; participation in jt UNDP/ FAO team to study in depth an instn-bldg project in Min.of Cooperatives and Rural Dev.in Lesotho 1981, and in several visits to developing countries as official of SIDA & IUCN; acted as adv.to Mozambique Del.in 1977 FAO Conf. **Career:** Prog.Officer 1971–7 & 1979–80 (Stockholm), Acting Aid Prog.Coord./Planning Adv./Dep.Aid Prog.Coord./Prog.Coord.1977–81 (Mozambique), Sr Prog.Adv. Intensive Rural Works Prog.1984–7 (Bangladesh), SIDA; Rural Dev. Mgmt Adv.(Lesotho), FAO 1981–3; Sahel Prog. Coord.then Africa Coord.1987–91, Intl Prog. Coord.1991–3, Dir of Prog.1993–4, Acting Asst DG — Cons.Policy 1994–, IUCN. **Achievements:** through eight yrs of exp.with IUCN in increasingly resp.positions have gained extensive exp.in rural dev.and natural resource mgmt, 11 yrs' field exp.in the former being of considerable advantage. **Publications:** incl.*The IUCN Sahel Studies* (co-Ed.) vol.I 1989, vol.II 1991, *Deserts: The Encroaching Wilderness* (Consult. Ed.) 1993. Indiff.to pers.pub.& news media support. **Languages:** English, French, Portuguese, Swedish. Willing to act as consult. etc. **Address:** IUCN — The World Conservation Union, 28 Rue Mauverney, 1196 Gland, Switzerland. **Tel.**(office) 41 22 999 0293, (home) 41 21 728 7610; **fax** 41 22 999 0025.

SABOGAL, Dr Cesar A. Tropical silviculture, natural forest management; training activities. Senior Scientist. *B*.19 Dec.1954, Callao, Peru. Peruvian. *M*.Hannelore: *s*., *d*. **Education:** Nat. Agrarian U. BSc(For.) 1977, Forest Engr 1980; U.of Göttingen Inst.of Trop.& Subtrop. Silviculture, PhD(Forest Scis) 1987. **Experience:** res. — silviculture & mgmt of natural trop. forests; consult.— forest inventory, silviculture, mgmt plans; training — courses, workshops, in-service training. **Career:** Teaching Asst, Nat. Agrarian U.1978–82; Forest Researcher & Lect. 1987–90, Prin.For.Adv.(Nicaragua) 1990–92, Project Leader 1992–4, CATIE; Sr Sci. — Silviculture, CIFOR 1994–. **Memberships:** ISTF, CFA. **Publications:** *c*.14 incl.Regeneration of trop.dry forests in C.Amer.with examples from Nicaragua

1992, Sust.mgmt of trop.rain-forests in C.Amer.; the tech.component and results of its application (co-Author, in Spanish) 1993, Authorship and expectations of timber certification standards: a view from the S.(co-Author) 1994. Indiff.to pers. pub.& news media support. **Languages:** English, German, Portuguese, Spanish (mother tongue). Willing to act as consult.etc. **Address:** Center for International Forestry Research, Jalan Gunung Batu 5, 16001 Bogor, Indonesia. **Tel.** (office) 62 251 323018, (home) 62 251 323766; **fax** 62 251 326433.

SACKS, Professor Dr Arthur Bruce. International environmental information, education, & training; environmental problems & policies in the former Soviet Union. Professor of Liberal Arts & International Studies & Director, Professor of Environmental Science, Adjunct Professor. *B*.21 April 1946, New York City, NY, USA. American. *M*.Normandy L.: 2 *d*. **Education:** Brooklyn Coll. BA(Eng.Lit.) 1967, U.of W.–M. MA(Eng. Lit.) 1968, PhD(Eng. Lit.) 1976. **Experience:** admin.as Inst.Dir and Dir & Lect.in Envl Studies; US Chairman Area XII– Envl Info., Educ.& Training (US–Russian Agreement on Envl Prot.); lect.in USSR, China, Indonesia, w.Europe. **Career:** memb.acad.staff of Inst.for Envl Studies of U.of W.–M.1976–93; Adjunct Prof.of Natural Resources, Ohio SU 1990–; Prof.of Envl Sci. Intl U.(Moscow) 1992–; Prof.of Liberal Arts & Intl Studies & Dir Div.of Liberal Arts & Intl Studies, Colorado Sch.of Mines 1993–. **Achievements:** developed & managed diverse res.& educ.progs in envl studies; developed Area XII of the USA– Russian Agreement on Envl Prot.; assisted developing countries in estab.of envl studies' progs. **Memberships:** NAAEE (Pres.1985), IUCN CEC, ISEE. **Publications:** Ed.of *Current Issues in Envl Educ.*(vols IV–VIII) and *Monogrs in Envl Educ.* (vol.I); 20+ articles. Favours pers.pub.& news media support. **Languages:** English, French. Willing to act as consult.etc. **Address:** Division of Liberal Arts & International Studies, Colorado School of Mines, Golden, Colorado 80401-1887, USA. **Tel.**1 303 273 3570; **fax** 1 303 273 3751.

SAENGER, Professor Dr Peter. Mangrove & coral-reef ecology; wetlands' & coastal-zone management; environmental law. Centre Head & Director, Director of Postgraduate Studies. *B*.18 July 1943, Kiel, Germany. Australian. *M*. Helen: 2 *s*. **Education:** U.of Melbourne BSc (Hons)(Marine Bot.) 1967, PhD(Bot.) 1970. **Experience:** mangrove ecol.& mgmt; envl law; extensive consult. **Career:** Researcher, U.of Melbourne 1966–70; Lect.in Ecol. Rhodes U. 1970–71; Postdoctl F. U.of Uppsala 1972; Envl Researcher & Consult.1973–85; Head & Dir (Consult.) of Centre for Coastal Mgmt 1985–, Dir of Postgrad.Studies 1989–, Southern Cross U. **Achievements:** Consult.to estab.GBR Marine Park 1978–88; Adv. Bangladesh Mangrove Afforestation Project 1985–91; estab.of Centre for Coastal Mgmt 1985. **Memberships:** ESA,

ASABP, AMSA, LS, RSQ, ACRS. **Publications:** num.incl. *Envl Mgmt of Tourism in Coastal Areas*, vols.I & II (co-Ed.) 1990, Physiol., Temp. Tolerance and Behavioral Differences between Trop.and Temperate Organisms 1991, Pantropical trends in mangrove above-ground biomass and annual litter fall (co-Author) 1993, Cleaning up the Arabian Gulf: aftermath of an oil spill 1994. Indiff.to pers. pub., favours news media support. **Languages:** English, French (adequate), German. Willing to act as consult.etc. **Address:** Centre for Coastal Management, Southern Cross University, POB 157, Lismore, New South Wales 2480, Australia. **Tel.**61 66 203650; **fax** 61 66 212669; **e-mail** psaenger@ scu.edu.au .

SAKSHAUG, Professor Dr Egil. Marine phytoplankton ecology, polar ecology. Professor in Marine Botany. *B*.18 May 1942, Trondheim, Norway. Norwegian. *M*.Vibeke: *s*., *d*. **Education:** U.of Trondheim D.Sci.1978. **Experience:** res.in phytoplankton ecol.; Chairman of Barents Sea Res. Prog.'ProMare' 1984–9. **Career:** IBP Stipend 1969–70, Assoc.Prof. 1970–84, Prof.in Marine Bot.1985–, Trondhjem Biol Station. **Achievements:** evolving tools for diagnosing limiting factors for algal growth; marine photosynthesis — modelling & physiol. **Memberships:** NSMR, SSMR, ASLO, RNSSL, NATS. **Publications:** Ecosystem Barents Sea (in Norwegian, Ed.) 1992, *c*.50 intl & 50 popular articles, the latter mainly in Norwegian. Dislikes pers.pub., favours news media support. **Languages:** English, Norwegian. Willing to act as consult.etc. **Address:** Trondhjem Biological Station, Bynesveien 46, N-7018 Trondheim, Norway. **Tel.**(office) 47 73 591583, (home) 47 73 917423; **fax** 47 73 591597.

SALIM, H.E. Professor Dr Emil. Economics, population, environment & development. Professor of Economics, Adviser to United Nations. *B*.8 June 1930, Lahat, S.Sumatra, Indonesia. Indonesian. *M*.Roosminnie (Chair, Yayasan Bina Putera Sejahtera Fndn — dev.of children's welfare): *d*. **Education:** U.of Indonesia, Sarjana Ekonomi 1958; UCB MA 1962, PhD 1964. **Experience:** teaching, ministerial. **Career:** State Minister of Admin.Reform 1970–73, Minister of Transportation, Communication & Tourism 1973–8, Minister of Pop.& Envt 1978–93, Pres.Governing Council of UNEP 1984–7, WCED 1984–7, Prof.of Econ. U.of Indonesia 1976–, UN High-level Adv.Bd on Sust.Dev. 1993–. **Achievements:** setting up Indonesian Envl Impact Body (1990) and laying down laws on envt & pop.(1992). **Memberships:** Indonesian AS, CCED, IISD, IIED, IBF. **Awards:** Mahaputra Adipradana (Rep.of Indonesia) 1988, Paul Getty Award 1990. **Publications:** *Masalah Lingkungan Hidup* 1982, *Masalah Dan Kebijakan Pembangunan* 1986, *Pembangunan Berwawasan Lingkungan* 1989. **Languages:** Dutch (read), English, Indonesian. Willing to act as consult.etc. **Address:** Bona Indah C II/1, Lebak

Bulus, Jakarta Selatan 12440, Indonesia. **Tel.**(office) 62 21 380 0295, (home) 62 21 750 3115; **fax** (office) 62 21 380 6210, (home) 62 21 769 0199.

SALINAS, Professor Dr Pedro José. Animal ecology, wildlife management; insect ecology & behaviour; protected areas' planning & management; environmental law & education. Professor. *B.*23 June 1939, Caracas, Venezuela. Venezuelan. Mother Catalina (Nature cons.). *D.: s.*, 3 *d.*incl.Orquidea Catalina (landscape arch.of nat.parks). **Education:** C.U.of Venezuela, Agron. Engr 1962; ICL Dipl.1966, U.of London MSc 1966, PhD 1972. **Experience:** res.— pest control, insect ecol.& behaviour, wildlife mgmt, prot.areas' planning & mgmt, cloud forest & paramos ecol., envl law & educ.; admin.— Head, Dept of Cons. U.of the Andes; consult.— IUCN IV World Cong. on NPPA, EIA; teaching — ecol. (gen.& applied), animal ecol., wildlife mgmt, prot. areas' planning & mgmt, forest prot., res.methodology. **Career:** Researcher Shell Fndn 1963–8; Aggregate Prof. 1972– 80, Head of Dept of Cons.1978–83, Assoc. Prof. 1981–9, Titular Prof.1989–, U.of the Andes. **Achievements:** founder ecol movement in Venezuela (1960s); advocate of ecodev.& sust.dev., co-author of several envl laws & by-laws incl.Gen.Envl Law & Ecol Crimes Law; adv.on envl matters to other Latin Amer. countries; special Guest Lect. to num.scientific confs & mtgs world-wide; founder–teacher of many themes in Depts of Biol., For., Pharmacy, Med., Arch. **Memberships:** Venezuelan AAS, VSE, VSL (Spec.Hon.), VSEcol., Merida Cons.Soc. (Pres. 1974–), Venezuela's Rep.on Cttee of Latin Amer.Congresses 1974– (Pres.1977–80, Sec. 1980–83), Intl Jury re.'Prize to Nature Cons.in Iberoamerica' 1992. **Awards:** Henri Pittier Order 2nd Class 1982, 1st Class 1987; City of Merida Prize for Cons.1983; The Golden Book (U.of the Andes) 1986, 1987; First Prize, Best Res.Paper (Nat.Symp.of Family Med.) 1990. **Publications:** *Practical Initiation to Scientific Res.*(two edns) 1985, 1991, *Neotrop. Zool.* (Ed.) 1982, *Interamer.Sem.on Prot.Areas* (Ed.) 1992, Ed.-in-Chief *Med-Ula*; 50+ major papers & *c.* 100 others. Favours pers.pub.& news media support. **Languages:** English, French (poor written & spoken, good read), Italian, Portuguese, Spanish. Willing to act as consult. etc. **Address:** Apartado 241, Universidad de Los Andes, Merida, Venezuela. **Tel.**(office) 58 74 401556, (home) 58 74 446409; **fax** 58 74 441461.

SALLEH, Dr Mohamed Nor. Forestry and the environment. Director-General. *B.*20 Oct.1940, Negeri Sembilan, Malaysia. Malaysian. *M.*Habibah Alias. **Education:** U.of Adelaide, BSc (For.) 1964; U.of Michigan, MS 1973, PhD 1977. **Experience:** forest inventory 1964–73; res.mgmt. **Career:** DG, Forest Res.Inst. Malaysia 1985–; Pres.IUFRO 1990–95. **Achievement:** Inaugural Winner of Langkawi Award for contribn to cons. & envt 1991. **Memberships:** Malaysian Busin-

ess Council, Malaysian AS, Envl Qual.Council (Malaysia), Malaysian Nature Soc.(Pres.1978–). **Awards:** Kesatria Mangku Negara 1981, Darjah Setia Negeri Sembilan 1989, Langkawi Award 1991, Nat.Sci. Award 1993 (all Govt of Malaysia), Hon.DSc U.Kebangsaan 1992 & U.of Aberdeen 1993. **Publications:** *Trop.Gdn City* (co-Author) 1990, *Marine Heritage of Malaysia* (Ed.) 1992. Open-minded re.pers.pub.& news media support. **Languages:** English, Malay. Willing to act as consult.etc. **Address:** 13 Jalan Harmonis 6, Taman Harmonis, 53100 Gombak, Selangor Darul Ehsan, Malaysia. **Tel.**(office) 603 634 2152, (home) 603 688 0716; **fax** 603 634 2825.

SALM, Dr Rodney Victor. Marine & coastal conservation & protected areas. Marine & Coastal Conservation Activities' Coordinator. *B.*26 July 1947, Durban, SA. Dutch. *M.*Susan Talbot Walker (envl educ.): 2 *d.* **Education:** Natal U. BSc(Hons) 1971, Johns Hopkins U. PhD 1980. **Experience:** res.— coral-reef ecol., coral taxonomy, marine turtles, Walrus; tech.— resource & use-surveys of coastal and marine habitats in SE Asia, Indian Ocean, Carib.; integrated coastal-zone mgmt planning, marine park/reserve planning; admin.— project & prog. mgmt; num.consults. **Career:** leader of underwater natural hist.safaris (ecotourism) world-wide 1971–4; num.IUCN/ WWF consults 1974–92; Project Leader (Indonesia) IUCN/WWF 1980–84; Project Leader (Sultanate of Oman) 1984–92, Marine Prog.Coord. Eastern Africa Regnl Office 1992–, IUCN. **Achievements:** raising awareness of need for marine cons., design & dev.of marine/coastal cons.prog.in Indonesia; identification of marine parks & reserves and cons.priorities in Mauritius, Seychelles, Indonesia, Sri Lanka, India, Oman, & BVI. **Memberships:** IUCN CNPPA and Marine Turtle, Sirenian, & Cetacean, SGs; Sigma Xi The Scientific Res.Soc., ISRS, EAWS. **Publications:** six books incl.*Marine Parks & Prot. Areas: A Guide for Planners & Mgrs* (world first on marine prot. areas) 1984, Marine Cons.Data Atlas. Planning for the Survival of Indonesia's Seas and Coasts (co-Author) 1984, *Snorkelling and Diving in Oman* (co-Author) 1991, *Whales and Dolphins along the Coast of Oman* (co-Author) 1994; *c.* 180 scientific, tech., & popular, pubns. Indiff.to pers.pub.& news media support. **Languages:** Arabic (basic), English, Indonesian, Portuguese. Willing to act as consult.etc. **Address:** IUCN– The World Conservation Union, Eastern Africa Regional Office, POB 68200, Nairobi, Kenya. **Tel.**(office) 254 2 890605 to 12, (home) 254 2 732668; **fax** 254 2 890615.

SALMAN, Albert H.P.M. Nature conservation in coastal zones, sand-dune ecology & management, integrated coastal-zone management. Secretary-General, Director. *B.*8 Oct.1954, Noordwijk, The Netherlands. Dutch. *M.*Joke M.: *s.* **Education:** U.of Leiden, Drs(Biol.) 1982. **Experience:** res.— dune ecol.& mgmt; teaching — sand-dune mgmt; admin.— direction of nat.&

intl projects on coastal mgmt; consult.— coastal mgmt & cons. **Career:** Asst State Herbarium and Dept of Ecol. U.of Leiden 1975–9; Coord.& Dir, Dutch Inst.for Dune Cons.1980–; Sec.-Gen. EUCC 1991. **Achievements:** analysis of main steering processes in N.Sea dune and transl.into mgmt policies at a nat.level, and of coastal destruction in Europe with inculcation of due warnings into EC pol. agendas. **Memberships:** EUCC (Sec.-Gen.), Euro.Habitats Forum (Sec.). **Award:** Landscape Award S.Holland (received on behalf of Dune Cons.Inst.) 1992. **Publications:** *The Nat. Netherlands Strat.on Dune Mgmt* 1992, *Coastal Mgmt and Habitat Cons.* (Ed., in press); 30+ papers. Dislikes pers.pub., favour news media support for EUCC. **Languages:** Dutch, English, French, German, Spanish; Greek, Italian, Latin, & Portuguese (all read). Willing to act as a consult. **Address:** European Union for Coastal Conservation, POB 11059, NL-2301 EB Leiden, The Netherlands. **Tel.**(office) 31 71 122900, (home) 31 1711 12590; **fax** 31 71 124069.

SAMAD, Dr Syed Abdus. Development, sustainable development, information technology, economic reforms, public finance, planning, privatization, community development, urban & regional economics. Officer on Special Duty (Environment). *B.*23 Dec.1944, Dhaka, Bangladesh. Bangladeshi. **Education:** Civil Service Training Acad.(Pakistan), Dipl.in Econ.& Admin. 1966; U.of Boston, MEcon. 1977, PhD (Econ.) 1979. **Experience:** res., training, consult., admin. **Career:** Sr Lect.in Econ. Dhaka U. 1967–8; diff.Civil Service positions in Govts of Pakistan & Bangladesh 1969–73; Vis.Lect.in Econ. Boston State Coll.1977–9; Coord. APDC 1990–; Exec.Sec. ADIPA 1991–6; Officer on Spec.Duty (Envt), Min.of Estab., Govt of Bangladesh 1996–. **Achievements:** prep.of EIA document for public sector dev.projects of Bangladesh, Coord.of sust.dev.prog.of APDC (author/ed.of two books on sust.dev.). **Memberships:** Bangladesh Econ.Assn (Life), Malaysian Assn of Sust.Dev. **Awards:** Sr Scholarship (Govt of Pakistan) 1962, F'ship (Ford Fndn) 1974–6, Grad.Student Award (Boston U.) 1976–8. **Publications:** eight books incl.*Real Wages in Labour Surplus Economies* 1981, *Info.Tech.for Decentralized Dev.in Asia* 1992, *People's Initiatives for Sust.Dev.*1994; 50+ res.reports, 40+ articles & monogrs. Favours pers.pub. **Languages:** English, French (working knowledge). Willing to act as consult.etc. **Address:** Ministry of Establishment, Government of Bangladesh, Dhaka, Bangladesh. **Tel.** 880 2 956 8097; **fax** 880 2 863646 or 883528.

SAMWAYS, Professor Dr Michael John. Insect conservation biology, invertebrate conservation; landscape ecology, ecological landscaping. Professor of Entomology, Director, Fellow. *B.*22 Oct.1949, Hillingdon, England, UK. British. *S., d.* **Education:** U.of Nottingham BSc(Hons) 1971, U.of London PhD 1975.

Experience: mostly res., adv.on biol.control, insect behavioural ecol., insect cons.biol.; world traveller & entomol.explorer. **Career:** Inner London Educ.Auth.Res.F. Animal Acoustics Unit (formerly Sir John Cass Coll.London) 1975–7; Chief Entomol. Perifleur Ltd 1977–8; Vis.Prof. ESAL Brazil 1978; Sr Res.Entomol. CSFRI Outspan Citrus Centre 1979–86; Prof.of Entomol.& Dir Invertebrate Cons.Res.Centre, U.of Natal 1987–. **Achievements:** 100 res. papers, three books, many active res.progs; dev. of an Invertebrate Cons.Res.Centre. **Memberships:** RES, SCB, SAZS, SAES. **Awards:** F.U. of Natal, three Vis.Scholarships to France. **Publications:** *Biol Control of Pests & Weeds* 1981, *Insect Cons.Biol.*1993, *Perspectives on Insect Cons.*(co-Author) 1993; num.res.papers. Favours pers.pub.& news media support. **Language:** English. Willing to act as consult. **Address:** Department of Zoology & Entomology, University of Natal, Pietermaritzburg 3200, South Africa. **Tel.** (office) 27 331 260 5328, (home) 27 331 473964; **fax** 27 331 260 5105; **e-mail** samways@zoology. unp.ac.za .

SANCHEZ, Heliodoro. National parks and protected areas; conservation of biodiversity. Professional Specialist. *B.*4 July 1941, Bucaramanga, Colombia. Colombian. *M.*Maria Gladys de: 2 *s.* **Education:** U.Distrital, Forest Engr 1966. **Experience:** with Colombian govt for 26 yrs incl.nat.parks' and wildlife mgmt. **Career:** Chief of Regnl Nat.Park Prog.1970–74, Asst of Div.of Nat.Parks 1974–7, Chief of Div.of Nat.Parks 1977–85 then Professional Specialist 1985– of Instituto Nacional de Los Recursos Naturales Renovables y del Ambiente, all Min.of Agric. **Achievements:** contributed to the estab. of most of the nat.parks of Colombia and encouraged their correct mgmt. **Membership:** ACIF. **Publications:** *Colombian Nat.Parks* (co-Author) 1986, *New Nat.Park of Colombia* (co-Author) 1990, Colombian Natural Savannas (co-Author) 1994, all in Spanish. Indiff.to pers.pub. & news media support. **Languages:** English, Spanish. Willing to act as consult.etc. **Address:** Transversal 33 Nr 147-38, Santafe de Bogotá, Colombia, South America. **Tel.**57 1 243 8396; **fax** 57 1 432774 or 243 3776.

SANCHEZ, Professor Dr Pedro A. Agroforestry, sustainable alternatives to slash-and-burn agriculture; tropical deforestation, nutrient cycling, soil science. Director-General, Professor Emeritus. *B.*7 Oct.1940, Havana, Cuba. American. *M.*Cheryl Palm: 2 *d.*incl.Jennifer (envl lawyer), *s.* **Education:** Cornell U. BS (Agron.) 1962, MS(Soil Sci.) 1964, PhD(Soil Sci.) 1968. **Experience:** res.& teaching on, and mgmt of, trop.soils for sust.food prod.while protecting the natural resource-base. **Career:** Grad.Asst in Soil Sci. U.of the Philippines–Cornell Grad.Educ.Prog. 1965–8; Asst Prof.of Soil Sci. 1968 & co-Leader, Nat. Rice Prog.of Peru 1968–71; Leader 1971–6 & Coord.1979–82 & 1984–91 Trop.Soils Prog.; Assoc.Prof.of Soil Sci.1973,

Prof.of Soil.Sci. 1979, Prof.Emer.of Soil Sci.& For.1991–, all at NC SU; Coord. Beef–Trop. Pastures Prog. CIAT 1977–9; Chief NC SU Mission to Peru, Tech.Chief INIPA and Sr Adv. World Bank Project 1982–3; Dir Centre for World Envt & Sust.Dev. (Duke U./NC SU/U.of NC at Chapel Hill); DG ICRAF 1991–. **Achievement:** dedication of career to improving mgmt of trop.soils for sustained food prod.& prot.of the natural resource-base. **Memberships:** ASA (F.1983), SSSA (F.1983), ISSS, SSS of NC, AAAS, ALCA, ALCPP, AIAPP, SLCS, Gamma Sigma Delta, Sigma Xi, Sigma Iota Rho. **Awards:** ten various before 1990, Adjunct Prof.of Trop. Cons.(Duke U) 1990, ISSS Award 1993, Intl Service in Agron.Award 1993, Hon.Memb. SCCS & SPCS. **Publications:** ten books incl. *Properties & Mgmt of Soils in the Tropics* (also in Spanish 1981) 1976, *Suelos Acidos: Estrategia para su Manejo con Bajos Insumos en Amer.Trop.* (co-Author) 1983, *Mgmt of Acid Trop.Soils for Sust.Agric.* (co-Ed.) 1987, *Myths & Sci.of Soils of the Tropics* (co-Ed.) 1992; *c.*100 tech.papers. Favours pers.pub. & news media support. **Languages:** English, Portuguese, Spanish. Further details may be obtained from *Amer.Men & Women in Sci., Who's Who in the S.and Southwest.* **Address:** International Centre for Research in Agroforestry, POB 30677, Nairobi, Kenya. **Tel.**254 2 521003; **fax** 254 2 520023.

SANDBROOK, J.Richard. Sustainable development (environment–development). Executive Director. *B.*13 Aug.1946, Bath, England, UK. British. *M.*Mary: 2 *s.* **Education:** U.of E.Anglia BSc(Bioscis) 1969, Arther Andersen & Co. Chartered Accountant 1970. **Experience:** 23 yrs in envt & dev. **Career:** accountancy 1970–74; co-Founder 1971, joined as Dir 1974–6, FOE UK; concerned with marine issues 1976–80, admin.1980–85, Dep.Dir 1985–9, Exec.Dir 1989–, IIED. **Achievements:** bldg-up FOE & IIED. **Memberships:** BES, ICA. **Awards:** OBE, Blue Planet Prize (Asahi Glass Fndn), Global 500 Roll of Honour (UNEP) 1989. Dislikes pers. pub.& news media support. **Language:** English. **Address:** International Institute for Environment & Development, 3 Endsleigh Street, London WC1H 0DD, England, UK. **Tel.**44 171 388 2117; **fax** 44 171 388 2826.

SAOUMA, Edouard Victor. Sustainable development esp.agriculture, forestry, & fisheries. International Consultant. *B.*6 Nov.1926, Beirut, Lebanon. Lebanese. *M.*Ines Forero Ramos: *s.*, 2 *d.* **Education:** Ecole Nationale Supérieure Agronomique (Montpellier), Ing.Agronome 1952. **Experience:** agricl res., Chief Exec.of Res.& Agric.Dev.Orgns, sust.dev. **Career:** Founder & DG, Lebanese Agric.Res.Inst. 1952–62; Dep. Regnl Rep.for Asia and Far E.(New Delhi) 1962–5, Dir of Land and Water Dev.Div.(Rome) 1965–70; DG (and re-election for two more terms of six yrs each) 1976–93, FAO; Minister of Agric., Forest & Fisheries (Lebanon) 1970–

75; Consult.1993–. **Achievements:** as Officer of FAO (1965–75) directed prep.& pubn of The World Maps of Soil Resources (with UNESCO) and on Desert.(with UNEP), many irrigation dev.and soil cons. projects; as Chairman of FAO's Inter-deptl WG on Natural Resources and Envt was resp.for prep.of FAO's contribn, and led FAO's del.to 1972 Stockholm UNCHE; as DG of FAO (1976–93) led orgn of World Confs on Agrarian Reform & Rural Dev.1979, Mgmt & Dev.of Fisheries 1984, and Envt & Agric.('den Bosch' — The Netherlands) 1991, the Intl Yr of For.1985 and three world for.congs in 1978, 1985 & 1991, and the Intl Conf.on Nutrition 1992 (with WHO); direction of accomplishment of many major studies re.envt & sust.incl.200+ tech.pubns, and estab.of an Intl Declaration on Fisheries responsibilities 1992, and of launching many progs for rational utilization of natural resources & envl prot. **Memberships:** UN High Level Adv.Bd on Sust.Dev.1994–, UN Intl Task Force for prep.of UN Summit on Social Dev., Sponsoring Cttee Rencontres Internationales du Mémorial de Caen — Prévention de Conflits. **Awards:** Dr *H.C.*from 18 univs, Corres.of Nat. Acad.of Agric.of Italy, Hon. Prof. (Beijing Agricl U.). **Publications:** *FAO in the Front Line* 1993; hundreds of articles & papers. Favours pers.pub. & news media support. **Languages:** Arabic, English, French, Italian (spoken), Spanish (spoken). Willing to act as a consult.&/or judge proposals. **Address:** POB 40210, Baabda, Lebanon. **Tel.**(office & home) 961 1 423900 and 455122; **fax** 961 1 423901.

SARMA, Kalavakolanu Madhava. Public administration, development & environment issues. Coordinator. *B.*8 July 1938, Chiriwada, AP, India. Indian. *M.*Ramalakshmi: 2 *d.* **Education:** Andhra U. MA(Maths) 1957, Indian Statl Inst. Dipl.in Stats 1960. **Experience:** 30 yrs as memb. of Indian Admin.Service at sr levels in public admin., water, power, & envt; four yrs with UNEP. **Career:** Sec.for Irrigation and Power, Govt of TN, and Addit.Sec. Min.of Envt & For.–1991, Govt of India; Coord. Secretariat for Vienna Conv.and Montreal Protocol 1991–. **Achievements:** as Leader of the Indian Del., at official level, assisted Parties to Montreal Protocol (on substances that deplete the ozone layer) to amend the Protocol to suit the needs of developing countries; as Coord.of the Ozone Secretariat of UNEP, have assisted the Parties in implementing the Protocol in what has become an acknowledged, highly successful, manner. Dislikes pers.pub., favours sober, factual, news media support. **Languages:** English, Tamil, Telugu. **Address:** Ozone Secretariat, United Nations Environment Programme, POB 47074, Nairobi, Kenya. **Tel.**(office) 251 2 623885, (home) & **fax** 251 2 521183.

SARMIENTO, Professor Dr Fausto Oswaldo. Landscape ecology and environmental planning; restoration of 'tropandean' landscapes; sustainability, conservation ecology, monitoring of environmental impacts on infrastructure development. Research Associate, Centre Director. *B*.28 Sept.1958, Quito, Ecuador. Ecuadorian. Father C.Alberto Sarmiento, expert on Ecuadorian Amazonia. *M*.Elena Viteri-Sarmiento (psych.of the industry of Nature-oriented tourism): *s., d.* **Education:** Catholic U.of Ecuador, BSc(Biol Scis) 1988; Ohio SU, MSc(Trop.Ecol.) 1991; U.of Georgia, PhD(Landscape Resto.Ecol.) 1995. **Experience:** PI of several ecol res.projects on 'tropandean' landscapes; tech.exp.in dispersal ecol.for forest regeneration, consult. **Career:** Biol.Teacher, Colegio San Gabriel 1977–82; Asst Prof.of Ecol. Dept of Anthrop.1983–5, Prof.of Ecuadorian Ecol. Dept of Geog.1988, Catholic U.of Ecuador; Dir, Ecuadorian Mus.of Natural Scis 1986–8; Res. Assoc. Inst.of Ecol. U.of Georgia, 1991–; Dir, Center for Tropandean Studies, Illinois SU 1996–. **Achievements:** pubns on Ecuadorian ecol.and envl educ.; memb.& founder of several NGOs working on cons.& dev. **Memberships:** ESA, SCB, IALE. **Awards:** Students' Odum Award (Inst.of Ecol. U.of Georgia) 1994, Scott Neotropic Fund (Lincoln Park Zool Soc.) 1995. **Publications:** several books incl.*Ecologia y Sus Leyes* 1982, *Diccionario Ecologico Energetico Ecuatoriano* 1986, *Antologia Ecologica del Ecuador* 1987; num.papers incl.Human impacts on the Upper Guayllabamba R.1994, Naming and knowing a tropandean landscape 1995, The birthplace of ecol.: tropandean landscapes 1995. Favours pers. pub.& news media support. **Languages:** English, Portuguese (basic), Spanish. Willing to act as consult.etc. **Address:** Institute of Ecology, University of Georgia, 106 College Station Road #G-205, Athens, Georgia 30605-0089, USA. **Tel.**(office) 1 706 542 2968, (home) & **fax** 1 706 548 0089.

SATOO, Professor Dr Taisitiroo. Resource management. President. *B*.18 July 1923, Choju, Korea. Japanese. *M.* **Education:** U.of Tokyo BSc(For.) 1941, PhD 1960. **Experience:** res.in forest sci.; admin.as Pres.of res.-orientated Fndn; teaching forest sci.at u.level. **Career:** military service 1942–6; Assoc.Prof.1950, Prof.of For. 1962–79, Prof.Emer.1979–, U.of Tokyo; Pres. JWRC 1978–; Pres. Nagao (donor-family) Natural Envt Fndn 1989–. **Achievement:** cons. of biodiv.by sust.use through resources' mgmt tech. **Memberships:** JFS, ESJ, JSTE. **Awards:** Scientific Achievement Award (JFS), Global 500 Roll of Honour (UNEP) 1992, Disting. Achievement Award (Japan Min.of Envt). **Publications:** *Silviculture* 1982, *Biomass Prod.of Forest Ecosystems* 1975, *Silviculture of Larch* 1981. Indiff.to pers.pub.& news media support. **Languages:** English, French, German, Japanese, Spanish. **Address:** Japan Wildlife Research Center, 2-29-3 Yusima, Tokyo 113, Japan. **Tel.**(office) 81 3 3813 8806, (home) 81 489 22 4505; **fax** 81 3 3813 8958.

SATTLER, Paul Stephen. Nature conservation planning, selection & establishment of National Park & Protected Area systems; use of native wildlife (Kangaroos) to achieve ecologically-sustainable use of semi-arid lands; conservation policy development. Manager, Nature Conservation Planning. *B*.16 July 1950, Nambour, Qld, Australia. Australian. *D.*: 2 *d.* **Education:** U. of Qld BAS(Rural Tech.) 1972, U.of New England M(Nat.Res.) 1977. **Experience:** 21 yrs in Nature cons.and envl planning & policy dev. **Career:** EIA & policy, Qld Coord.-Gen.'s Dept 1972–4; metalliferous mining rehab.res.& admin. Dept of Mines 1974–5; veg.mapping, Qld Herbarium 1976; Nature cons.planning, Dept of Envt & Heritage (then Qld NPWS) 1976–. **Achievements:** expansion of rep.Nat. Park system for Qld on a systematic bioregnl basis; integrated land-use planning for prot.of biodiv.& ecol.sust.dev.; promotion of sust.wildlife utilization (kangaroos) to achieve cons.of semi-arid lands. **Memberships:** RSQ (Pres. 1986), IUCN CNPPA 1991–. **Publications:** *Nature Cons.in Qld: Planning the Matrix* (Presidential Address) 1986, *The Mulga Lands* (Ed.) 1986, Planning towards Consolidation of Qld's Nat.Park Estate 1992, Towards a Nationwide Biodiv.Strat.: the Qld Contribn 1994, num. others; Assoc.Ed. *Pacific Cons.Biol.*1992–. Favours news media support. **Language:** English. Willing to act as consult.etc. **Address:** Queensland Department of Environment & Heritage, POB 155, Albert Street, Brisbane, Queensland 4002, Australia. **Tel.**(office) 61 7 227 7810; **fax** 61 7 227 6386.

SAUNIER, Dr Richard E. Environmental management policy & planning, identification & management of resource-use conflicts; Biosphere reserves, *in situ* biodiversity conservation. Environmental Management Adviser. *B*.6 March 1936, Fort Morgan, Colorado, USA. American. **Education:** CSU BS(For.& Range Mgmt) 1961; U.of Arizona MS 1964, PhD 1967 (both in Watershed Mgmt & Range Ecol.). **Experience:** res.— range mgmt, distribn of Shrub Live-oak (*Quercus turbinella* Greene), physiol.ecol.of Creosote Bush (*Larrea tridentata* [D.C.] Cov.); use of herbicides on desert shrubs; tech.— support to US Peace Corps vols in for.& agric.in Paraguay, and in for., fisheries, nat.park planning, wildlife mgmt, & envl educ., in Latin Amer. & Carib.; Asst to 35 govts in Latin Amer.& Carib.in over 60 projects of integrated dev.planning, mgmt & planning of Biosphere Reserves, envl policy, EIA: OAS rep.at intl mtgs on envl policy: fac.memb.on short courses & sems in Latin Amer.; admin./consult.— Nat.Watershed Mgmt Plan, K.of Jordan: eval.of Watershed Mgmt Training Prog.for C.Amer.; envl mgmt component of Intl Watershed Mgmt short course: tech.adv.service to Sierra Club, UNEP, UNDP, USAID, World Bank, & Inter-Amer.Dev.Bank: Bd of Dirs of Planning Assistance (specialists in strat.planning in health, nutrition, & family planning, in Africa & Latin Amer.); taught forest ecol., silviculture, & plant physiol., in Chile. **Career:** Res.Assoc. U.of Arizona 1962–6 and US ARS 1967; Guest Prof. Universidad Austral de Chile 1967–9; Dep.Dir. Paraguay 1970–71 and Envl Progs Specialist (Latin Amer./Carib.) 1972–5, US Peace Corps; Sr Envl Mgmt Adv. OAS 1975–. **Achievements:** identification & mgmt of resource-use conflicts at prefeasibility level of dev.planning, formulation of methods for rapid assessment of resource-use conflicts, advising on nat.& local-level envl policies. **Memberships:** AIBS 1964–, ESA 1963–, Soc.of Sigma Xi 1966–, IUCN CESP 1985–. **Award:** Global 500 Roll of Honour (UNEP) 1989. **Publications:** *Envl Qual. & River Basin Planning: A Method for Integrated Analysis & Planning* (Ed.& co-Contrib.) 1978, *Integrated Regnl Dev.Planning: Guidelines & Case Studies from OAS Experience* (major Contrib.) 1984, *Minimum Conflict: Guidelines for Planning the Use of the Amer.Humid Tropics* (Ed.& major Contrib.) 1987. Indiff.to pers.pub., favours news media support. **Languages:** English, Portuguese (comp.), Spanish. Willing to act as consult.& ref. **Address:** 10266 Wilde Lake Terrace, Columbia, Maryland 21044, USA. **Tel.**(office) 1 202 458 3228, (home) 1 410 730 5138; **fax** 1 202 458 3560.

SAVAS, Mehmet Nizam. National parks, Nature conservation & environmental matters. Director. *B.*7 Jan.1948, Eskisehir, Turkey. Turkish. *M.*Inci: *s., d.* **Education:** U.of Istanbul Dip. Eng.1972, Tokyo Agric.& Tech.U. MS 1982. **Experience:** 22 yrs in nat.parks & Nature cons., res., admin., consult. **Career:** Nat.Park Ranger, Seven Lakes Nat.Park 1982–5; Dir, Termessos & Olimpos Nat.Parks 1985–8; Dir Coordn & Eval. Gen.Directorate of Nat.Parks & Wildlife 1988–. **Achievement:** coordn & eval. leading to identification & designation of nat. parks & prot.areas. **Memberships:** ANCT, WFT, ECFT. **Awards:** Hons from Mins of Interior & For. **Publications:** *c.*20 papers incl. Wildlife inventory of Anatolia 1971, Effects influencing the actuality of envl problems 1978, Veg.mgmt of Mt Takao Nat.Park 1982, Nat.parks & tourism 1991, Rec.activities in Nature prot.areas 1992, Nature trail & trekking 1993. **Languages:** Arabic (basic), English, German (basic), Japanese, Turkish. Further details may be obtained from *Who's Who in Turkey* 1996. Willing to act as consult. etc. **Address:** General Directorate of National Parks & Wildlife, Gazi, Ankara 06560, Turkey. **Tel.**(office) 90 312 221 3314, (home) 90 312 212 6300 or 2107; **fax** 90 312 222 5140.

SAXENA, Anil Kumar. Hazardous waste management; pollution monitoring, analysis, and control. Senior Deputy Director. *B.*25 Sept.1951, Tonk, Raj., India. Indian. *M.* Madhu. **Education:** Vikram U. MSc(Zool.) 1975, U.of Raj. PhD(Zool.) 1978; Advanced Training on Hazardous Waste Mgmt 1986; Loughborough U.of Tech. Postgrad Dipl.in Water Analysis & Qual. 1992. **Experience:** six yrs' res.on pesticides & toxicity, 12 yrs' consult.in hazardous waste mgmt & water poll.control. **Career:** CSIR Res. F. U.of Raj.(Jaipur) 1975– 81; Sci.1982, Asst Dir 1983–7, Dep.Dir 1988–9, Sr Dep.Dir 1990–,

all in Poll.Control, Nat. Productivity Council. **Achievements:** dev.of hazardous waste mgmt system for industrial estates; design of secured landfill for disposal of hazardous wastes, site identification for disposal of hazardous wastes; nat.expert on monitoring & analysis for UNIDO demn project in small & medium enterprises. **Publications:** *Toxic Waste Mgmt in India* (handbook) 1986, Hazardous wastes: identification, packaging, labelling & tracking 1993, Hazardous waste systems & regs in India 1993. Favours pers.pub.& news media support. **Languages:** English, German (working knowledge), Hindi. Willing to act as consult.etc. **Address:** National Productivity Council, Utpadakta Bhawan 5–6, Institutional Area, Lodi Road, New Delhi 110003, Delhi, India. **Tel.**91 11 461 1243, or 462 2359; **fax** 91 11 461 5002.

SAYER, Jeffrey Arthur. Terrestrial ecology & conservation; tropical forest conservation & management. Director-General, Professor of International Nature Conservation. *B.*22 May 1946, Wanstead, Essex, England, UK. British. *M.* Mireille: 2 *s.* **Education:** U.of Hull BSc (Bot.& Zool.) 1988, UCL MSc(Cons.) 1989. **Experience:** res.on forest & woodland ecol. oriented towards cons.planning in var.countries in Africa & Asia; planning & mgmt of prot.areas & nat.cons.progs; studies of major intl cons. policy issues with intl cons.& dev.agencies. **Career:** Res.Officer, Zambia Nat.Parks 1969–72; Adv. on Nature Cons. FAO/UNDP (Mali 1972–4, Rep.of Benin 1974–8, Afghanistan 1978–80, Thailand 1980–81, Burma 1981–3); Sr Cons.Officer, WWF Intl 1983–5; Head of Forest Cons. Prog. IUCN 1983–92; Sr Forest Ecol. World Bank 1992–3; DG CIFOR 1993–. **Achievements:** co-Author & active participant in many major intl cons.initiatives, notably the WCS and several NCSs; the Trop.For.Action Plan & several nat.for.plans, Author of IUCN & WWF position statements on intl cons. issues, coord.of major study of forest cons.issues in W.& c.Arica, founding DG of CIFOR. **Memberships:** BES, FFPS, Trop.Forest Fndn (Dir). **Awards:** Prof. Intl Nature Cons.(U.of Utrecht). **Publications:** *Mgmt of Trop.Moist Forest Lands* 1987 (co-Author 2nd edn 1991), *Rain Forest Buffer Zones* 1991, *Trop. Deforestation & Species Extinction* 1992, *Cons.Atlas of Trop.Forests: Africa* (co-Author) 1992 & *Asia* (co-Author) 1993; num. major papers, *c.*80 addit. Indiff.to pers.pub., favours news media support. **Languages:** English, French, Spanish (poor). Willing to act as consult.etc. **Address:** Centre for International Forestry Research (CIFOR), POB 6596, JKPWB Jakarta 10065, Indonesia. **Tel.**62 251 31 9423; **fax** 62 251 32 6433. **e-mail** cifor@cgnet.com .

SAYIGH, Professor Dr Ali M. Renewable energy. Secretary-General, Professor of Renewable Energy. *B.*20 Sept.1939, Kufa, Iraq. British. **Education:** ICL BSc 1963, DIC 1964, PhD 1966. **Experience:** worked with several consultants in Middle E. re.air-conditioning. **Career:**

Sec.-Gen. WREN 1992–, Chairman of World Renewable Energy Cong.1990/92/94, Prof.of Renewable Energy, U.of Reading 1986– 94 & U.of Herts 1995–. **Achievement:** setting-up WREN under UNESCO. **Memberships:** F.Inst. of Energy, IEE. **Publications:** 20 books, *c.*150 tech.papers. Favours news media support. **Languages:** Arabic, English. Willing to act as consult.etc. **Address:** 147 Hilmanton, Lower Earley, Reading, Berkshire RG6 4HN, England, UK. **Tel.**(office) 44 1734 611364, (home) 44 1734 874080; **fax** 44 1734 611365.

SCANNELL, Dr Yvonne. Land-use controls, pollution control; liability for environmental damage, mineral exploitation & development. Consultant, University Lecturer. *B.*5 July 1948, Tralee, Ireland. Irish. *M.*Sean O'Hegarty: *s., d.* **Education:** Trinity Coll.Dublin, MA 1971, PhD 1981; King's Inns (Dublin), Barrister 1973; Darwin Coll. U.of Camb. LLM 1972. **Experience:** consult.on envl law & policy; former Chairwoman, Envl Awareness Bur.; memb.adv. body to EPA. **Career:** Lect. U.of Dublin 1974–, Consult.in envl law & policy 1978–, Founder Memb.and first Chairwoman of Irish Assn.of Envl Lawyers. **Achievements:** author of four books, Founder Memb.IAEL, Counsel in many planning enquiries. **Memberships:** Edl Dds *Irish Law Reports Monthly* and *J.of Envl Law,* IAEL, Dir — Centre for Envl Law & Policy, Law Sch. Trinity Coll., Tara Mines Ltd, & Irish Nat.Petroleum Corpn. **Award:** F.(Trinity Coll.Dublin) 1989. **Publications:** *The Law & Practice relating to Poll.Control* 1974 revised 1982, *Envl Law in Ireland* 1993. Reservation re.pers.pub., welcomes news media support. **Languages:** English, French (read). Willing to act as consult.etc. **Address:** Law School, Trinity College, Dublin 2, Ireland. **Tel.**(office) 353 1 6702 1125, (home) 353 1 964163; **fax** 353 1 6770 449.

SCHALLER, Dr George B. Field studies of vertebrates, particularly large mammals (carnivores & ungulates) and conservation of such species. Director for Science. *B.*26 May 1933, Berlin, Germany. American. *M.*Kay M.: 2 *s.* **Education:** U.of Alaska BA, BS 1955; U.of Wisconsin PhD 1962. **Experience:** ecol.& behavioural studies in Zaire, India, Pakistan, Tanzania, Nepal, Brazil, China, Mongolia. **Career:** Res. Assoc. Dept of Pathobiology, Johns Hopkins U.1963–6; Dir for Sci. The Wildlife Cons. Soc. (formerly NYZS) 1966–. **Awards:** Gold Medal (WWF), Explorer's Medal (Explorers' Club). **Publications:** ten books incl.*The Mtn Gorilla* 1963, *The Serengeti Lion* 1972, *The Last Panda* 1993; 100+ papers. Indiff.to pers.pub., accepts news media support for cons.initiatives. **Languages:** English, German. Further details may be obtained from Brit.*Who's Who* 1996 & *Who's Who in America* 1996. **Address:** The Wildlife Conservation Society, Bronx, New York 10460-1099, USA. **Tel.**1 718 220 6807; **fax** 1 718 364 4275.

SCHARMER, Dr Klaus. Biomass as energy resource, engine fuels from vegetable oils; solar energy (cooling & water disinfection, medical applications); global warming, feeding 6,000 m.people. Managing Director. *B.*17 May 1938, Heidelberg, Germany. German. Father Dr Johannes Scharmer (biol.), Mother Ilse (zool.). **Education:** Karlsruhe Tech.U. Eng.Dipl.1965, Dr.Ing.1971. **Experience:** res.on energy tech., chem.engg, renewable energies (solar & biomass); consult.in Europe, India, Indonesia, S. Amer., Africa; large-scale project mgmt. **Career:** 16 yrs' res.in nat.centres in Germany & France and govtl R&D prog.mgmt, and 12 yrs' industrial res.& technological dev.; MD Gesellschaft für Entwicklungstechnologie mbH 1982–. **Achievements:** dev.of economically-viable methods to use biomass as modern energy carriers. **Memberships:** Verein Deutscher Ingenieure, Kerntechnisches Gesellschaft, ISES (Germany). **Award:** Global 500 Roll of Honour (UNEP) 1991. **Publications:** 50+ and four patents. Indiff. to pers.pub., favours news media support. **Languages:** English, French, German, Portuguese, Spanish. Willing to act as consult.etc. **Address:** Gesellschaft für Entwicklungstechnologie mbH, POB 1461, D-52446 Aldenhoven, Germany. **Tel.**(office) 49 2464 58127, (home) 49 2461 1323; **fax** 49 2464 58136.

SCHLAEPFER, Professor Rodolphe. Forest biometry, forest management in tropical forests, forest decline; climate change & forests; experimental design. Institute Director, Professor of Forestry Sciences. *B.*22 June 1940, Sainte-Croix, Switzerland. Swiss. *M.*Marianne: 3 *d.*, 3 *s.* **Education:** Swiss Fed.Inst.of Tech. Dipl.in For. 1964; Laval U.(Quebec) M(For.) 1966; U.of Edinburgh, Dipl.in Stats 1968. **Experience:** statl consult.(biol., pharm., agron., for.); teaching & res.in forest inventory, mgmt, growth, & stats; res.mgmt as Head of Res.Inst.of 300 employees. **Career:** Statistician, Ciba–Geigy 1969–75; Lect.& Statl Consult. Engg Sch.in Agron. 1975–82; Prof.of Forest Mgmt 1982–7, Prof.of For.Scis, ETH 1987–; Dir FSL 1987–. **Achievement:** res.in forest decline. **Membership:** IBS. **Publications:** incl. Long-term Implications of Climate Change and Air Poll.on Forest Ecosystems (Ed.) 1993. Dislikes pers. pub., favours news media support. **Languages:** English, French (mother tongue), German. Willing to act as consult.etc. **Address:** Swiss Federal Institute for Forest, Snow, and Landscape Research (FSL), CH-8903 Birmensdorf, Switzerland. **Tel.**(office) 41 1 739 2225, (home) 41 1 844 1289; **fax** 41 1 739 2575.

SCHRAM, Professor Gunnar G. International environmental law, Law of the Sea and Human Rights; promoting effectiveness of the UN in these fields. Professor of International & Constitutional Law, Legal Adviser. *B.*20 Feb.1931, Akureyri, Iceland. Icelandic. *M.*Elisa: 3 *s., d.* **Education:** U.of Iceland, Cand.Jur.1956; Max Planck Inst.for Public & Private Intl Law

1957–8; Sidney Sussex Coll.Camb. PhD 1962. **Experience:** rep.of Iceland in Nordic Council's envl coopn 1972–80, intro.of courses in envl law at U.of Iceland, Chairman of Icelandic Prep. Cttee for UNCED 1990–92, Adv.in Envt & Law to Reykjavik Min.for Envt 1990–92. **Career:** Head of Dept & Legal Adv.1966–9, Legal Adv.1992–, Min.for Foreign Affairs; Dep. Perm.Rep.of Iceland to UN NY 1971–4; Prof.of Intl & Constnl Law 1974–, Dean of Sch.of Law 1992–4, U.of Iceland; MP 1983–7. **Achievements:** assisting Icelandic Mins in estab.of intl coopn, active work in protecting the oceans from poll., drafting a nr of laws for prot.of envt. **Memberships:** IUCN CEL, ASIL (Envl Chapter), Centre for Intl Studies (Pres.) of U.of Iceland. **Publications:** *Cases on Constnl Law* 1976, *Envl Law* 1985, *Outline of Intl Law* 1986, *Protecting the Oceans* 1988, *The Future of Our Planet — The Road from Rio* 1993; 23 scientific papers, jt edl in *EC The high seas 'commons': imperative regulation of half our Planet's surface.* Favours pers.pub.& news media support. **Languages:** Danish, English, French (basic), German, Icelandic, Norwegian, Swedish. Willing to act as consult.etc. **Address:** Frostaskjol 5, 107 Reykjavik, Iceland. **Tel.**(office) 354 55 694385 to 7, (home) 354 55 28212; **fax** (office) 354 55 694388, (home) 354 55 13803.

SCHRIJVER, Nico J. Public international law, law of international institutions, international environmental law; peace research, North–South issues. Senior Lecturer in International Law and International Institutions. *B.*21 May 1954, Warmenhuizen, The Netherlands. Dutch. Father Cornelis Schrijver, farmer incl.organic farming. *M.*Yuwen Li (law of the sea issues). **Education:** U.of Gröningen LLB 1974, LLM 1978; U.of Thessaloniki, Dipl.*magna cum laude* (Intl Law & Intl Relations) 1981. **Experience:** sr researcher on intl-law aspects of peace & security, N–S coopn; envt & dev.both for academic purposes and for consult.; practical exp.in UN system; policy adv.to Netherlands Govt. **Career:** Dutch youth rep.in Netherlands' delegation to UNGA 1978; Lect.in Intl Law & Peace Res. U.of Gröningen 1979–85; Sr Lect.in Intl Law & Intl Instns, Inst.of Social Studies, The Hague 1986–; Legal Officer, Office of the Legal Counsel, UN (NY) 1990–91. **Achievements:** publicist and consult.on intl instnl & legal aspects of envt & dev., Gen.Rapp.(1993–) of Cttee on Legal Aspects of Sust.Dev.of the ILA. **Memberships:** ASIL, ILA, Academic Council of the UN system, Amnesty Intl, Netherlands Adv.Council for Intl Dev.Coopn, Adv.body of Dutch Minister for Dev.Coopn. **Publications:** Right to Dev.in Intl Law 1988, Intl Orgn for Envl Security 1989, Sovereignty and Sharing of Natural Resources 1993; co-authored & -edited books on UN 1988, *Solidarity Against Poverty* 1990, *Jt Implementation to Curb Climate Change* 1994. Favours pers.pub.if functional, welcomes news media support. **Languages:** Chinese (poor), Dutch, English, French (good), German (good).

Willing to act as consult.etc. **Address:** Institute of Social Studies, POB 29776, 2502 LT The Hague, The Netherlands. **Tel.**(office) 31 70 426 0561, (home) 31 70 352 0603; **fax** 31 70 426 0799.

SCHULTES, Professor Dr Richard Evans. Taxonomic botany, economic botany; ethnobotany of western Amazonia especially of medicinal, hallucinogenic, & toxic, plants and rubber-yielding plants; ethnobotanical conservation. Emeritus Professor of Biology and Museum Director. *B.*12 Jan.1915, Boston, MA, USA. American. *M.*Dorothy: 2 *s.*incl.Neil Parker (molecular biol.), *d.* **Education:** Harvard U. AB *(cum laude)* 1937, AM 1938, PhD 1941. **Experience:** res.— fieldwork in Colombian Amazonia incl.residence in the field 1941–54 with short visits annually since; teaching Harvard's course in Econ.Bot.for 27 yrs; admin. as Dir, Harvard Botl Mus.1967–85. **Career:** Plant Explorer, NRC F. 1941–2, Bur.of Plant Industry, USDA 1944–53; Field Agent, US Govt 1943–4; Res. Assoc.1941–53, Curator Orchid Herbarium of Oakes Ames 1953–8, Econ.Bot.1958–85, Exec. Dir 1967–70, Dir 1970–85, Emer.1985–, Harvard Botl Mus.; Prof.of Biol.1970–72; Paul C. Mangelsdorf Prof. of Natural Scis 1973–80; Edward C.Jeffrey Prof.of Biol.1980–85, Emer. 1985–, Harvard U.; Cecil & Ida H.Green Vis. Lect. UBC 1974; Adjunct Prof.of Pharmacognosy, Coll.of Pharmacy, U.of Illinois 1975–; Hubert Humphrey Vis.Prof. Macalister Coll. 1979, Vis.Scholar Rockefeller Fndn Study & Conf.Centre 1980 & 1988; Hon.positions — Prof. Universidad Nacional de Colombia 1953–, Memb.John Simon Guggenheim Mem.Fndn Selection Cttee for Latin Amer.1964–86, Assoc. in Ethnobot. Museo del Oro, Bogotá 1974–, Memb. Asociación Argentina de Antropología Medica 1977–, Memb. Sociedad Mexicana de Microbiologia 1978–. **Achievements:** assisting Colombian govtl agencies in furthering creation of biol preserves and areas in their Amazonia for prot.indigenous flora; co-Ed.*Psychoactive Plants of the World* (book series), Ed.*Econ.Bot.*1962–79 and *Botl Mus.Leaflets* 1957–85; Edl Bds *Lloydia* 1965–76, *J.Psychodelic Drugs* 1974–, *Hort.*1976–8, *Ethnopharmacology* 1978–, *Flora of Ecuador* 1976–, *Bol Mus'Goeld* (Brazil) 1987–, *EC* 1987–, *Envl Awareness* (India) 1988–, *Elaies* (Malaysia) 1988–, *Ethnobot.*(India) 1989–. **Memberships:** NAS, AAAS, F.LS, Colombian & Argentinian Acads of Sci., Ecuadorean Inst.of Scis, Sociedad Antonio Alzate de Mexico; F.of TWAS, NAS India, & Amer.Coll.of Neuropsychology. **Awards:** Phi Beta Kappa (Harvard U.), Gold Medal (WWF), Tyler Prize, Lindberg Award, Harvard Medal, Cross of Boyaca and Order of the Victoria Regia (Colombia), Scientific Medal of Commonwealth of Mass., MH (Universidad Nacional de Colombia) 1953, Hon.DSc (Mass.Coll.of Pharmacy) 1987; has large area of Amazonia named after him. **Publications:** eight books incl.*Generic Names of Orchids: Their Origin & Meaning* (co-Author)

1963, *Plants of the Gods: Origins of Hallu-cenogenic Use* (co-Author) 1979, *The Bot. & Chem.of Hallucinogens* (co-Author) 1973, 1980, *Where the Gods Reign: Plants & Peoples of the Colombian Amazon* 1988, *The Healing Forest; Medicinal & Toxic Plants of the Northwest Amazonia* (co-Author) 1990; *c.*440 scientific papers. Questionable attitude towards news-media support. **Languages:** English, French, German, Latin, Portuguese, Spanish, Swedish (read); English, Latin, Portuguese, Spanish (written); two native Amerindian languages of Colombian Amazonia (understood). Further details may be obtained from *Who's Who in Amer.*(48th edn). Willing to act as consult.etc. **Address:** The Village of Clark Pond Nr 105, 501 Lexington Street, Waltham, Massachusetts 02154, USA. **Tel.**(office) 1 617 495 2326.

SCHWAB, Professor Dr Klaus. Sustainable development. Forum President, Professor of Business Policy. *B.*30 March 1938, Ravensburg, Germany. German. *M.*Hilde: *s.,d.* **Education:** Swiss Fed.Inst.of Tech. Dr(Mech. Eng.) 1965; Univs of Zürich and Fribourg, Dr(Econ.) 1967; Kennedy Sch.of Govt, Harvard U. MPA 1967. **Experience:** high-level adv.& admin., business background. **Career:** Asst to MD, German Machine Bldg Assn 1963–6; Memb.of Gen. Mgmt, Escher Wyss (Zürich) 1967–70; Founder & Pres. World Econ.Forum 1971–; Prof.of Business Policy, U.of Geneva 1972–; Official Adv. to Sec.-Gen.of UNCED 1990–92, Memb. Eminent Person's Mtg on Financing Global Envt & Dev.1992–. **Memberships:** WFARP, ICG (Steering Cttee), UN High Level Adv.Bd for Sust.Dev., Earth Council, several intl cos' bds. **Awards:** num.incl.The Grand Cross of the Order of Merit (FRG) 1995, Hon.Doct. (Bishop's U. Canada) 1992 and (Universidad Autonoma de Guadalajara, Mexico) 1992. **Publications:** six books incl.*Overcoming Indifference* 1994; num. articles. **Languages:** English, French, German. **Address:** World Economic Forum, 53 chemin des Hauts-Crets, CH-1223 Cologny, Geneva, Switzerland. **Tel.**41 22 736 0243; **fax** 41 22 786 2744.

SCHWARZSCHILD, 'B' Shimon. Environmental & Nature conservation; sustainable development; travel/exploration. Development Adviser, Consultant, Editor, Writer. *B.*19 Dec. 1925, Wertheim, Germany. American. **Education:** NJ Inst.of Tech. BSc(Elec.Eng.) 1950, grad.courses in mgmt engg 1952–4. **Experience:** admin., media, editing, writing, engg. **Career:** spent war yrs as electronic specialist & tech.officer on US Navy vessels; Qual.control Mgr, Blonder-Tongue Labs 1952–6; VP Western Div. Decker Corpn 1956–62; Owner, Schwarzsch Assocs, and VP, RDX Corpn 1962–78; Exec.Dir, Amer-Youth Hostels, Golden Gate Council 1978–82; Nat.Dir, The Whale Center 1983–4; Tech.Pubns Ed in Biol.Scis, USDA Forest Service 1988–; Project Admin.& Proc.co-Ed. Intl Yew Resources Conf.1992–; Assoc. Producer–Dev. Green

TV 1992–. **Achievements:** improved urban liveability in San Francisco, launched Assisi Bird Campaign resulting in moratorium on hunting songbirds in Assisi, spearheaded successful USA effort to halt destructive logging of Yew trees and convert to sust.harvesting in Pacific NW to tap anti-cancer drug Taxol. **Memberships:** IUCN CEC, Action for Nature Inc.(Founder, past-Pres.& Bd). **Publications:** *No Birds Sing on Saint Francis' Mtn* 1983, *Pacific Yew: A Facultative Riparian Conifer with an Uncertain Future* (co-Ed.) 1988, *The Calif.Spotted Owl: A Tech. Assessment of its Current Status* (Ed.) 1992, *Proc.of Calif. Riparian Systems Conf.*(Ed.) 1988, *The Forest through the Trees — the Battle for Calif.'s Redwoods* 1991, *Proc.of Intl Yew Resources Conf.*(co-Ed.) 1994, *Sierra Meltdown* (TV documentaries, Assoc.Producer) 1994. Favours pers. pub.& news media support. **Languages:** English, German, Spanish (some spoken). Willing to act as consult.etc. **Address:** POB 1813, Sutter Creek, California 95685, USA. **Tel.**(office & home) & **fax** 1 209 296 1357.

SCLAVO, Jean-Pierre. Botany (taxonomy of cycads), entomology. Company Director. *B.*28 Nov.1937, Nice, France. French. *D.*: 2 *s.* **Education:** to sec.sch.level. **Experience:** res.— num.trips abroad for study of plants, and expedns world-wide from 1981–90; consult.— expert in agricl insurance. **Career:** Co.Dir (own construction co.) 1970–. **Achievements:** discovery of new species of plants and of important new localities for known species, creator of an intl conf.on Cycads (CYCAD) the first of which took place in 1987 (France), the second 1990 (Australia), the third 1993 (SA), the fourth being planned for 1996 in China. **Memberships:** IUCN SSC Cycad SG 1988–, Fairchild Trop.Gdn, BSSA, PCSA, Lepidopterists' Soc. **Awards:** Hon.Bot.(Naples Botl Gdn) 1990, Hon.PhD (Natural Scis.)(U.of Naples) 1994. **Publications:** *Encephalartos voiensis* (Zamiaceae), a new E.C.African species in the *E.hildebrandtii* complex 1989, Zamiaceae, a New Family for Zambia 1990, Recherches sur les *Encephalartos* Lehm.(Zamiaceae) d'Afrique Centrale (co-Author) 1992. Favours pers.pub.& news media support. **Languages:** English (spoken), French, Italian (spoken), Spanish (spoken). Further details may be obtained from *Envl Profiles: a Global Guide to Projects and People* (Garland Publishing) 1993. Willing to act as consult.etc. **Address:** Villa 'La Finca', Plateau du Mont Boron, 06300 Nice, France. **Tel.** (office) 33 4 93 546790, (home) 33 4 93 260091; **fax** 33 4 93 541044.

SEELY, Dr Mary Kathryn. Ecology of arid lands, conservation; environmental education & research training. Foundation Director. *B.*13 Dec.1939, San Carlos, California, USA. Namibian. **Education:** UCD BA(Phys.Sci.) 1961, PhD(Biochem.) 1965. **Experience:** res.— 27 yrs mainly in Namib desert; admin.— 24 yrs as res.unit Dir; consult.— four yrs in Namibia; 20 yrs as co-Super.of post-grad.field res.and four yrs establishing u.field courses. **Career:** Assoc. Researcher then Dir 1970–, Desert Ecol. Res.Unit of Namibia; Adjunct Prof. U.of New Mexico 1989–90 & 1994; Dir, Desert Res.Fndn of Namibia 1990–. **Achievements:** basic res.in desert ecol.and application of it to cons.of the Namib Desert at the same time making this Desert known in the scientific lit.; envl educ.& res.training in Namibia. **Memberships:** F.RES, F.RSSA, AAAS, ESA, BES. **Awards:** John Wesley Powell Mem.Lecture (AAAS) 1984, Hon.Doct.(U.of Natal) 1994, CSIR Res.& Travel Grants, Hon.Prof. Univs of Witwatersrand 1990– & Namibia 1994–. **Publications:** *Ecol. of Desert Organisms* (co-Author) 1982, *The Namib* 1987, *Namib Ecol.*(Ed.) 1990, *Drought & Desert.*1991, *Oshanas* (co-Author) 1992, *Deserts* (Ed.) 1994; *c.*80 papers (many co-Authored), *c.*15 envl educ.pubns (written or edited), *c.*60 popular articles. Indiff.to pers.pub., favours news media support on behalf of Desert Res.Fndn. **Language:** English. Willing to act as consult.etc. **Address:** Desert Ecological Research Unit, POB 1592, Swakopmund, Namibia. **Tel.**264 61 229855; **fax** 264 61 230172.

SEIBOLD, Professor Dr Eugen. Marine geology. Professor Emeritus. *B.*11 May 1918, Stuttgart, Germany. German. *M.*Dr Ilse: *d.* **Education:** U.of Tübingen, Doct.1948, Habil.1951; Univs of Tübingen & Bonn, geol.& palaeontology. **Experience:** marine geol.incl.many cruises on res.vessels in the Baltic, N., & Atlantic, Seas, and Indian Ocean, coastal res.around N.& Baltic Seas, and India; sci.mgmt as former Pres.of Deutsche Forschungsgemeinschat* and as Pres. of ESF; envl aspects of mineral resources & poll.as Pres.of IUGS 1980–86. **Career:** Asst Prof. Geol.Insts of U.of Tübingen 1949–51 and Tech.U.of Karlsruhe 1951–4; Assoc.Prof. U.of Tübingen 1954–8; Prof.of Geol.& Palaeontology and Dir of Dept of Geol.& Palaeontology 1958–80, Emer.1980–, U.of Kiel; Pres. *German Res.Council 1980–85 and ESF 1985–91. **Achievements:** coastal mgmt, hydrography, and poll., in such adjacent seas as Baltic, Persian–Arabian Gulf, & Medit.; offshore oil. **Memberships:** Leopoldina, Halle, Akademie der Wissenschaften uder Literatur Mainz, Academia Europaea, AS (Paris), Corres.Memb.of academies of science of München (Munich), Heidelberg, Dusseldorf, Göttingen, Zagreb. **Awards:** Palme académique (Paris) 1974, Medal Albert I (Monaco) 1980, Grosses Bundesve-dienstkreuz (Bonn) 1983, mit Stern 1985, Hon.Memb. (Geol. Socs of France, London, Amer., & Africa), Hon.Doct.(U.of E.Anglia) 1983 and (U.of Paris 6) 1986, Hon.Prof.(U.of Freiburg) 1986, Blue Planet Prize (Asahi Glass Fndn) 1994. **Publications:** several books incl.*The Sea Floor* (co-Author) 1982 (Russian & Japanese edns), 2nd edn 1993, 3rd 1995, *Geol.of the NW African Continental Margin* (co-Author) 1982, *Das Gedachtnis des Meeres* 1991; 300+ other in

German & intl journals. Considers news media support to be important. **Languages:** English, French, German, Italian (poor). Further details may be obtained from several *Who's Whos.* **Address:** Richard Wagnerstrasse 56, D-79104 Freiburg/Breisgau, Germany. **Tel.**(office) 49 761 203 6471, (home) 49 761 553368; **fax** 49 761 203 6483.

SEPP, Kalev. Landscape ecology, Nature conservation; landscape management in Nature conservation areas. Scientific Researcher, Lecturer. *B.*17 May 1961, Tallinn, Estonia. Estonian. **Education:** U.of Tartu BSc(Geog.) 1984, MSc(Landscape Ecol.) 1993; C.Euro.U. course in envl sci.& policy 1994. **Experience:** res.— air poll.influence on forest communities and soils, landscape diversity, landscape monitoring, envl educ.& policy; teaching landscape ecol.& Nature cons.at MSc level. **Career:** Scientific Researcher, Nature Cons.Res.Centre, Min.of Envt 1991–; Teaching Asst, C.Euro.U. 1994; Lect.in Nature Cons., Envl Prot. and Landscape Ecol. U.of Tartu 1994–. **Achievements:** res.in ecol.— soil alkanization influence on forest communities; landscape monitoring & diversity measures. **Memberships:** Estonian Geogl Soc. (VP 1991–5), Estonian Fund for Nature (Bd), IALE. **Publications:** *c.*30 incl.*Human Impact on Envt in NE Estonia* (Ed.) 1991, *Envl Guide Book to NE Estonia* (co-Author) 1993. Favours pers.pub.& news media support. **Languages:** Estonian, English (good), French & German (read), Russian. Willing to act as consult.etc. **Address:** Institute of Geography, University of Tartu, 46 Vanemuise Street, Tartu EE2400, Estonia. **Tel.**(office) 372 7 436385, (home) 372 7 483131; **fax** 372 7 436375.

SERAFIN, Dr Rafal Krzysztof. Heritage economics, environmental assessment, parks and protected areas; business and the environment, regional & landscape planning, green tourism; economic restructuring and environmental change in Poland. Research Assistant, Research Associate, Programme Director. *B.*21 July 1959, Huddersfield, England, UK. British, Canadian, Polish. **Education:** U.of E.Anglia, BSc (Hons) (Envl Scis) 1981; U.of Toronto, MA (Geog. (Envl Studies)) 1985; U.of Waterloo, PhD 1991. **Experience:** res.— heritage assessment, mgmt, & planning, in Canada, Poland, UK, & EU; res.& consult.— heritage & envt in context of econ.restructuring in Poland & *c.*Europe, partnerships for sus.dev.; consult.— industry & envt in Poland; tech.& admin.— dev.of a Heritage Res.Prog.in Poland. **Career:** Res.Assoc. IIASA 1985–7; Res.Coord.1990–92, Res.Asst/Lect.1992–, Res.Assoc.1992– Heritage Resources Centre, U.of Waterloo; Dir, Heritage Res. Prog. Polish Fndn for Nature Cons.1995–. **Achievements:** dev.of Heritage Res.Prog.in Poland, promotion & implementation of IUCN's Parks for Life (Poland); heritage & envl assessment in Canada; promoting a 'Baltic Europe' as a basis for sust.dev. **Memberships:**

IUCN CNPPA & CESP, CAG, AAG, Polish Ecol Club, Polish Nat.Assn for Prot.of Birds. **Awards:** George Langford Prize (U.of Toronto) 1985, Peccei Scholar (IIASA) 1986, Robert Dorney Award 1990 & Disting. Academic Achievement 1991 (both U.of Waterloo). **Publications:** Baltic Europe, Gt Lakes Amer. and ecosystem redev.(co-Author) 1988, Assessing biodiv: a human ecol approach (co Author) 1992, *Assessing and Monitoring Changes in Wetland Parks and Prot.Areas* (co-Ed.) 1993. Indiff.to pers.pub., favours news media support. **Languages:** English, French, Polish. Willing to act as consult.etc. **Address:** Heritage Research Programme, Polish Foundation for Nature Conservation, 9 Sebastiana Street, 31 049 Kraków, Poland. **Tel.**(office) 48 12 228937 or 217011, (home) 48 12 378929; **fax** 48 12 217411.

SERHAL, Assad. Protected areas & wildlife, in particular birds & mammals. Secretary-General, Manager. *B.*5 May 1958, Keyfoun, Lebanon. Lebanese. *M.*Zeina (producer of envl documentaries, Lebanese nat.TV): 2 *s.* **Education:** Oklahoma SU BSc(Spec.)(Wildlife Ecol. Mgmt) 1982, training with NAAEE 1992. **Experience:** res.on wild birds & mammals, consult.on envl affairs 1984–. **Career:** Consult. Min.of Agric. 1983–8 & IUCN 1982–, captive breeding of game birds 1984, Mgr Lebanese Hunting Council, Sec.-Gen. SPNL 1986–. **Achievements:** in Lebanon — init.of envl movement 1983, founder & Chairman of first bird sanctuary 1992 and helped estab.first marine reserve 1992, init. SPNL/IUCN/UNDP project to estab.Lebanese dept for wildlife & prot.areas (Min.of Envt) (1993), preparing Biodiv.& Prot.Areas' Action Plan (init.1993–4), and resp.for Lebanon Chapter of Important Bird Areas (init.& conducted by BirdLife Intl for Important Bird Areas of the Middle E.1993–4). **Memberships:** ICBP 1986–, IUCN CNPPA, Lebanese Network for Envt Educ.Clubs (Founder), Lebanese Envl Assembly (Founder & Treas.). **Publications:** *Wild Mammals of Lebanon* 1985, *Game Birds of the Arab Countries* 1986, *Field Guide to Birds of Prey of the Middle E.*1988, *Common Birds of Lebanon and the Middle E.*(nr 1 in series) 1993, all in Arabic; four TV documentaries on envt. Favours news media support. **Languages:** Arabic, English. Willing to act as consult.and/or ref. **Address:** Society for Protection of Nature in Lebanon, POB 11-5665, Beirut, Lebanon. **Tel.**(office) 961 1 342701 or 343740, (home) 961 1 807764 or 802097; **fax** 961 1 603208.

SEVILLA, Lorenzo B.CARDENAL. Planning & management of national parks & other protected wildlands, and of *in situ* conservation systems; design & planning of biological corridors, buffer zones, extractive and multiple-use reserves; land-use planning; geographical information systems; methodologies & techniques for strategic planning; sustainable development policy issues. Private Consultant, Governmental Scientific Adviser, Executive Director. *B.*25 May 1960, Mana-

gua, Nicaragua. Nicaraguan. *M.*Maria Auxiliadora: *s., d.* **Education:** Universidad Centroamericana, Licenciatura(Ecol.& Natural Resources Mgmt) 1982; postgrad.studies on envl interpretation (US) 1982, Nat.Park Planning & Mgmt (Costa Rica) 1983, EIA (Spain) 1984, Land-use Planning & Regnl Dev.(Venezuela) 1985, and GIS for Land-use Planning Studies (Nicaragua) 1991. **Experience:** in govt and public instns — project direction & coordn, admin., adv.; in NGOs — project coordn & mgmt, admin.; lecturing, invited conferee, consult.to such orgns as World Bank, UNDP, FAO, WWF, IUCN. **Career:** Officer/Technician 1982–5, Dir 1985–8, NPS, Nicaraguan Inst.of Natural Resources; Project Dir, Masaya Volcano Nat.Park's Envl Educ. Centre 1986–8; Adv.to Gen.Dir 1989, Dep.Dir of Planning and Project Coordn 1990, Gen. Directorate of Natural Resources; Vis.Prof. Latin Amer.Fac.of Social Scis 1991; Adv.to DG, Nicaraguan co-Coord.of Nicaragua–Costa Rica Intl System of Prot.Areas for Peace project, and memb.of Binational Tech.Comm.–1992; Adv. Biodiv.Cons.Policies, Min.of Envt and Natural Resources of Nicaragua 1992–4; Consult.in Policy and Strat.Planning, GreenPeace Latin Amer.1994; Interim, then Exec., Dir, Greenpeace C.Amer. 1994–. **Memberships:** Nicaraguan Coll.of Biologists & Ecologists (co-Founder, former Dir), Nicaraguan Envl Movement (co-Founder, former Exec.Dir). **Award:** Commem.Medal (Govt of Nicaragua) 1989. **Publications:** num.incl.Opportunities for Sust.Dev. in C.Amer.: the Envlist Perspective (in Spanish) 1992, *Nat.Study of Biodiv.and Nat.Prog.for Biodiv.Cons.*(in Spanish) 1993. Accepts pers.pub., considers news media support necessary for all envl & sust.dev.matters. **Languages:** English, Portuguese, Spanish. **Address:** Km 12.5 Carretera a Masaya, Managua, Nicaragua, **tel.**& **fax** 505 2 444696; *or* Greenpeace Central America, Avenida Reforma 1–50 Zona 9, Edificio Reformador, Oficina 602 6to. Nivel, Guatemala City 01009, Guatemala. **Tel.**502 334 5467; **fax** 502 360 1563.

SEVILLA, Rogue. Urban environment, national parks. City Councillor. *B.*16 July 1947, Quito, Ecuador. Ecuadorian. *M.*Pilar (sociologist, pesticides): 2 *d., s.* **Education:** Universidad Católica, Econ.1980; Harvard U. MPA 1991. **Experience:** pol.& admin. **Career:** Founder & Pres. Fundación Natura 1978–88, Dir Nat.For. 1985, WWF Intl Council Memb.1985– & US Bd Memb.1990–, Pres.Marina Area of Galápagos Comm.1985–6; Bd Memb. Charles Darwin Fndn 1985–90 and of sev.fin.instns in Ecuador; Quito City Counc.1992–6. **Achievements:** creation of Fundación Natura, Ecuador, 1978; ' promotion of $10 m. debt-for-Nature swap. **Memberships:** Bd Memb.of Quito Chamber of Commerce, Amer.–Ecuadorian Chamber of Commerce, and Fundación Natura Ecuador. **Awards:** Order of the Golden Ark 1988, Global 500 Roll of Honour (UNEP) 1989, Order of Isabel La Católica 1990. **Publications:** Mas alla de una advertencia (co-Author) 1983, Porque cambiar Deuda por Naturaleza (co-Author) 1989. Favours news media support. **Languages:** English, German, Spanish. **Address:** Whymper 1210, Casilla Nr 21-443, Quito, Ecuador. **Tel.** (office) 593 2 505660; **fax** 593 2 564773.

SHAPIRO, Professor Harvey Allan. Ecological planning in the Asia–Pacific region; coastal area management & planning; impacts & policies of sea-level rise in Pacific Basin. Professor of Environmental Planning. *B.*21 April 1941, Toledo, Ohio, USA. American. *M.*Fujiko N.: 2 *d.* **Education:** U.of Detroit B.Arch.1965, U.of Penn. MRP 1970. **Experience:** res.in Japanese urban ecol.; tech.— Adv.to City of Taishi (Japan); consult.— Assoc.in Japanese planning consult.firm. **Career:** US Army Lt 1966–8 (Vietnam 1966–7); Regnl Planner, WMRT Inc. (planners) 1968; Prof. Osaka Geijutsu U.1971–; Assoc. RPT Assocs Inc.(planners) 1974–. **Achievements:** helped estab.field of ecol planning and educated over 5,000 students 1971– (both in Japan), introduced Japanese coastal citizen movements to intl community. **Memberships:** PSA, Sierra Club, World Future Soc., Ecol Econ.Soc., IALE, JGA, JEA, IUCN. **Award:** ABI 1992. **Publications:** 100+ monogr.in var.intl & Japanese journals, conf.procs and books *e.g. Japan's Coastal Envt and Responses to its Recent Changes* 1988. Favours pers.pub.(if good), and good news media support. **Languages:** Chinese (basic), English, Japanese. Further details may be obtained from *Who's Who in the World* 1989. Willing to act as consult.etc. **Address:** Kyoto Grand Heights Apt 612, Entomicho 47-5, Shogoin, Sakyo-ku, Kyoto 606, Japan. **Tel.** (office) 81 721 933781, (home) 81 75 761 4792; **fax** 81 721 935380.

SHARMA, Professor Dr Archana. Environmental mutagenesis. Professor Emeritus of Genetics. *B.*16 Feb.1932, Poona, Mah., India. Indian. *M.*Prof.Arun Kumar Sharma *qv.* **Education:** U.of Raj. BSc 1949; U.of Calcutta MSc 1951, PhD(Bot.) 1955, DSc(Genetics) 1960. **Experience:** teaching at Master's degree & doctl levels for 25 yrs+ & res.1951–, adv.to 50+ doctl & post-doctl candidates; admin.as Treasurer, Sec.-Gen. then Gen.Pres. ISCA, memb.of UGC, Mins of Sci.& Tech., Educ., and Nat.Cttee on Women. **Career:** Res.F., Reader, then Prof., Dept of Bot. U.of Calcutta 1966–. **Achievements:** furthering focal theme of Sci.& Human Well-being as Gen.Pres.of ISCA, and formulating its policies, decision-making. **Memberships:** F.INSA (Delhi), IAS (Bangalore), NAS (Allahabad, Pres.of Biol.Scis.1985), IBS (Pres.). **Awards:** Padma Bhusan (Govt of India) 1984, J.C.Bose Award in Life Scis (UGC) 1974, S.S.Bhatnagar Prize in Biol Scis (CSIR) 1976, Award in Biomed.Scis (FICCI) & Sahni Medal (IBS) 1984. **Publications:** seven books incl. *Chromosome Techniques — Theory and Practice* (3rd edn) 1980, *The Chromosomes* (3rd edn) 1990; Ed.of 11 books, 300+ res.pubns. Indiff.to pers.pub.& news media support. **Languages:**

English, several Indian. Further details may be obtained from *Intl Who's Who of Women* (3rd edn). Willing to act as consult.etc. **Address:** Department of Botany, University of Calcutta, 35 Ballygunge Circular Road, Calcutta 700 019, West Bengal, India. **Tel.**(home) 91 33 440 5802.

SHARMA, Professor Dr Arun Kumar. Cytogenetics, cytochemistry, cell biology. Honorary Professor. *B.*31 Dec.1924, Calcutta, W.Bengal, India. Indian. *M.*Prof.(Mrs) Archana Sharma *qv.* **Education:** U.of Calcutta, Matriculation 1939, Intermediate in Sci.1941, BSc 1943, MSc 1945, DSc 1955. **Experience:** res., admin., res. supervision, cttee exp. **Career:** Asst Lect.1948, Lect.1952, Reader 1962, Prof.1970, Ghosh Prof.& Prog.Coord.of Centre of Advanced Study on Cell & Chromosome Res. Dept of Bot. 1972–90, Golden Jubilee Prof.(INSA) 1985–90, Hon.Prof.1991–, U.of Calcutta. **Achievements:** num.res.contribns incl.invention of new techniques for study of phys.& chem.nature of chromosomes adopted in all centres of the world; repeat DNA analysis, estab.of new concept of speciation in asexual organisms; clarification of chem.nature of plant chromosomes, induction of div.in adult nuclei; reorientation of angiosperm taxonomy; estab.of new concept of dynamism of structure & behaviour of chromosomes; embryo irradiation and *in vitro* cultures; functioning of repeat DNA sequences; Presidential Address to Sci.Cong.1981, former Chairman MAB Cttee (Govt of India), Memb.of Comm.on Bioindicators (IUBS) 1984–. **Memberships:** FASAS (Founding Pres.1984–, Chair Comm.on Sci.& Tech.for Dev.in Asia 1990–), TWAS (F.1988, Chair Biol Scis F'ship Cttee 1991–8), IUBS 1982–5, IFS (Bd of Trustees 1984–7), INSA (Pres.1983–4, Chair Indian Nat.Cttee –1978, VP 1977–8), ISCA (Pres.Bot.Section 1973, Gen. Sec.1975–8, Gen.Pres.1981), ISCG (Pres.1976– 8), Botl Soc.of Bengal (Pres.1977–9), Asiatic Soc. (Biol.Sec.–1977), ISNA (Sec.1979), Genetic Assn of India (Pres.), Soc.of Cell Biol. (Pres.1979–80), IBS (Pres.1980), F.& Counc.of INSA, IAS, INAS; num.adv.cttees of Govt of India; Chief Ed. *The Nucleus*, Edl Bds of num. journals. **Awards:** Shanti Swarup Bhatnagar Prize in Biol.(CSIR, Govt of India) 1967, Jawaharlal Nehru F'ship 1972, Paul Bruhl Mem.Medal (Asiatic Soc.) 1972, Birbal Sahni Medal (IBS) 1974, J.C.Bose Award in Life Scis (first, jt winner, UGC) 1976, Silver Jubilee Medal (INSA) 1976, FICCI 1979, Padma Bhusan (Pres.of India) 1983, Golden Jubilee Prof'ship (INSA) 1985–90, Om Prakash Bhasin Fndn for Biotech.1993, G.M.Modi Award 1994, J.C.Bose Mem.Award 1994, Sir Ashutosh Mukherjee Mem.Award (ISCA) 1995. **Publications:** *Chromosome Techniques — Theory & Practice* (co-Author) 1965/7, 1972, 1980, *Chromosome in Evol.of Eukaryotic Groups* (multivolume series, co-Ed.) 1986–7, *Chromosomes and Cell Genetics* vol.I 1989, vol.II 1990, *Chromosome Techniques — A Manual* 1994, Cell Biol. Techniques; num.others. **Languages:** Bengali,

English, Hindi. **Address:** Centre of Advanced Study, Department of Botany, University of Calcutta, 35 Ballygunge Circular Road, Calcutta 700 019, West Bengal, India. **Tel.**(office) 91 33 475 3681, (home) 91 33 440 5802; **fax** 91 33 475 4772.

SHARMA, Dr Subrat. Agroecology, forest ecology, human ecology. Technician. *B*.13 Mar. 1963, Khatima, Nainital, UP, India. Indian. *M*. Dr Smita (forest ecol.). **Education:** Kumaun U. MSc 1984, PhD 1990; ICIMOD, GIS training 1993. **Experience:** res.— PhD work and involvement in three projects; tech.— involved in UNICEF-sponsored project on soil iodine deficiency. **Career:** Jr 1988–9 & Sr 1989–91 Project F. Bot.Dept, Kumaun U.; Technician, GBPIHED 1991–. **Achievements:** energetics of agric.in Himalaya; linkages between Man & envt. **Membership:** Ecol.Res.Circle. **Publications:** four incl.Energy budget and efficiency of some multiple cropping systems in Sikkim Himalaya (co-Author) 1992, Energy use pattern & sust.dev.: a case-study in rural landscape of the C.Himalaya (co-Author) 1994. Indiff.to pers. pub., favours news media support. **Languages:** English, Hindi. Willing to judge proposals &/or act as ref. **Address:** G.B.Pant Institute of Himalayan Environment & Development, Kosi, Almora 163 643, Uttar Pradesh, India. Tel.91 5962 81144; **fax** 91 5962 22100.

SHARMA, Dr Sudhirendar. Environmental journalism, consulting. NGO Director. *B*.16 Nov. 1956, Kasauli, HP, India. Indian. *M*.Shalini (Trustee, The Ecol Fndn, Delhi): *s.* **Education:** HP U. MSc(Agric.) 1978, JNU PhD (Envl Sci.) 1984. **Experience:** res., admin., consult.to govtl agencies and Oxfam. **Career:** F.Centre for Policy Res.1984–5; Founder & Dir 1986–8, Dir 1989– Energy Envt Group; Envl Corres.*India Today* 1988–9. **Achievements:** leading envl journalist. **Memberships:** Indian SSS, ELC, ISWA, ACFOD. **Awards:** Award for best writing in Hindi (FAO) 1988, Ashoka Fndn F'ship 1986–8. **Publications:** several incl.*Our Common Future* (transl.into Hindi), Ed.*Vikalp* (Hindi bimonthly on sust.dev.etc.). Accepts pers.pub., favours news media support. **Languages:** English, Hindi. Willing to act as consult.etc. **Address:** POB 3627, New Delhi 110 024, Delhi, India. **Tel.**(home) 91 11 643 7479; **fax** 91 11 641 9042.

SHAW, Dr R.Paul. Sustainable development through investments in human resources; links between rapid population growth & environmental degradation; national sovereignty–warfaring propensities–and environmental degradation. Senior Economist. *B*.23 May 1944, Vancouver, BC, Canada. Canadian. *M*.Lori Ann Lothian: *s.* **Education:** UBC MA(Econ./Sociol.) 1968, U.of Penn. PhD(Econ./Demography) 1972. **Experience:** res.— links between pop.& envl degradation, and origins of the state, warfaring propensities, and impacts on envt, and

prospects for sust.dev.; UNFPA focal point on envt, and del.on UN Designated Officials for Envl Mgmt; policy analysis of pop., agricl, and envl, interface (NEXUS project) at World Bank. **Career:** Memb.of Secretariat, UN (NY) 1972–5; Regnl Labour Policy & Pop.Adv.(in Middle E.& N.Africa), ILO 1978–81; Sr Author, Stats Canada, and Vis.Prof. Norman Patterson Sch.of Intl Affairs, Carleton U.1982–6; Sr Pop.Economist, UNFPA 1987–91; Sr Economist, World Bank 1991–. **Endeavours:** to combine policy analysis of sust. dev.and envl cons.with implementation of multi- & bi-lateral progs aimed at producing more optimal outcomes, also to shed light on 'shackles' on intl envl dev.and cons.with specific focus on origins of intra- & inter-state conflict, and on negative impact of warfaring propensities on the envt and prospects for sust.dev. **Achievements:** res., pubns, and preparatory work, in advance of both UNCED & ICPD. **Award:** Best Paper* Prize (FEC) 1993. **Publications:** eight books and 30+ addit.articles incl.*Pop.and The Envt: The Challenges Ahead* (Ed.) 1991, *Pop., Resources and the Envt: The Critical Challenges* (Ed.) 1991, Shackles on intl envl dev.and coopn 1991, Intl dimensions of pop.policy and envt 1992, The impact of pop.growth on envt: the debate heats up 1992, *Warfare, nat.sovereignty, and the envt 1993. Indiff.to pers.pub.& news media support. **Languages:** English, French (working ability). Further details may be obtained from *Dict.of Demography Biographies* 1985. Willing to act as consult.etc. **Address:** Africa Technical Department, Human Resources and Poverty Division, Room J-2-073, The World Bank Group, 1818 H Street NW, Washington, District of Columbia 20433, USA. **Tel.**(office) 1 202 473 3441, (home) 1 202 537 5035; **fax** 1 202 473 7932.

SHAW, Professor Dr William W. Conservation biology, socio-political aspects of wildlife conservation, national parks & protected areas; conservation in metropolitan environments. Professor & Programme Chairman. *B*.12 May 1946, Pittsburgh, PA, USA. American. *M*.Darcy K.: 2 *s.* **Education:** UCB MA(Biol Sci.) 1968; Utah SU, MS(Wildlife Ecol.) 1970; U.of Michigan, PhD(Natural Resources) 1974. **Experience:** res.& consult.activities in many countries incl. Costa Rica, Argentina, Australia, Kuwait, Nepal, Mexico, & US; studies have focussed on integrating cons.into metropolitan envts, and on mgmt, planning, & design, of prot.areas. **Career:** Asst, Assoc., & Full, Prof.of Wildlife & Fisheries Sci.(Chairman 1982–), U.of Arizona 1974–; var.consults throughout the world and for USDI. **Achievements:** leadership in integrating biol. with social & pol. scis to address cons.biol.issues incl.relationships between prot.areas & adjacent human pops, integration of cons.into metropolitan planning, improved public attitudes towards wildlife & natural resources. **Memberships:** SCB, Wildlife Soc. **Awards:** Daniel Leedy Award for Urban Wildlife Cons.1988, F'ship (OAS) 1989, NRC Cttee on Fed.Acquisition of

Lands for Cons.1992. **Publications:** *c*.40 scientific & popular articles & papers. Indiff.to pers. pub.& news media support. **Languages:** English, Spanish. Willing to act as consult.& review papers. **Address:** School of Renewable Natural Resources, 325 Biological Sciences East, University of Arizona, Tucson, Arizona 85721, USA. **Tel.**1 602 621 7165; **fax** 1 602 621 8801.

SHEIKH, Muhammad Abdur Rashid. Wildlife conservation, wetland management, environmental education, research. Wetland Ecologist. *B*.21 Oct.1956, Kohat, Pakistan. Bangladeshi. Father Sheikh Mohammad Ain-ud-Din, cons. ethics; mother Shamsun Nahar Begum, envl educ. *M*.Umme Farhana Zarif. Father-in-law A.K.M.Anwar Husain (deceased), envl econ.; brother Group Captain M.A.Mateen (retired), cons. **Education:** U.of Dhaka MSc (Wildlife Biol.) 1982, U.of Kent MSc(Ecol.) 1992. **Experience:** res.— herpetofauna of Bangladesh, wetland mgmt, captive breeding of cranes and marine turtles; consult.in wildlife & wetland mgmt and coastal mgmt & ecol.to many intl bodies. **Career:** Res.F. IUCN/WWF 1982–3; Jt Sec, Wildlife Soc.of Bangladesh 1983–6; Sch.Teacher in Biol. 1986–7; Wetland Ecol. Nature Cons.Movement 1992–; Consult.to World Bank 1991, CIDA 1992. **Achievements:** taxonomic res.on herpetofauna of Bangladesh, res.on wetland resources; mgmt of wild elephants; arresting illegal trade in endangered turtle species. **Memberships:** IUCN SSC, BNHS, Bangladesh AAS, Nature Cons.Movement, Wildlife, Asiatic, & Zool., Socs of Bangladesh. **Awards:** Charles-Wallace (Bangladesh) Trust Award 1988, Brit.Council Scholar 1988–9. **Publications:** *Wetlands of Bangladesh* (Ed.) 1994, *c*.30 others. Indiff.to pers.pub., favours news media support. **Languages:** Bangla, English, Urdu; Hindi, Punjabi, Pushto (basic knowledge), Spanish (beginner). Willing to act as consult.etc. **Address:** Nature Conservation Movement, House 153/A, Flat 8, East Rajabazar, Dhaka 1215, Bangladesh. **Tel.** (office) 880 2 882823, (home) 880 2 813280; **fax** 880 2 883097.

SHELDRICK, Mrs Daphne Marjorie. Wildlife — raising & rehabilitating orphaned animals back into the wild; animal psychology. Chairman. *B*.4 June 1934, Nakuru, Kenya. British. *W*.(Husband the late David Leslie William Sheldrick MBE, Founder Warden of Kenya's Tsavo E.Nat.Park): 2 *d*.incl.Gillian Sala Ellen Woodley (assists mother). **Education:** Kenya Girls High Sch., Sr Camb.Sch.Cert.with Matriculation exemption and hons in English. **Experience:** over 40 yrs' practical field exp.; first to perfect the milk formulae for many milk-dependent infant wild orphans notably Elephants *(Loxodonta africana)* & Black Rhinos *(Diceros bicornis)*. **Career:** a lifetime of work for and with wild animals incl.30 years working with husband in Tsavo E.Nat.Park, Kenya; Chairman, David Sheldrick Wildlife Trust. **Achievements:** hand-reared 15 Elephants over 2 yrs of age

(1958–76) and eight infants from newborn (1987–93), eight Black Rhinos over the yrs as well as 23 Cape Buffalo, five Zebras, three Kudu, one Impala, six Duiker, three Dikzliks, three Elands, and other smaller species such as Mongooses, Civets, Reedbucks, Warthogs, and Bushpigs; intl recognition as specialist in subject of wildlife. **Membership:** Game Rangers' Assn of Africa (Hon.). **Awards:** MBE 1989, Global 500 Roll of Honour (UNEP) 1992. **Publications:** *The Orphans of Tsavo* 1963, *The Tsavo Story* 1973, *An Elephant called Eleanor* 1980, *Four-footed Family* 1982. Favours pers. pub.& news media support. **Languages:** English, Swahili (read & spoken). Willing to act as consult.etc. **Address:** David Sheldrick Wildlife Trust, Box 15555, Nairobi, Kenya. **Tel.**254 2 891996; **fax** 254 2 891307 (indirect).

SHEMSHUCHENKO, Professor Dr Yuri Sergueevich. Environmental law & management. Institute Director. *B*.14 Dec.1935, Glukhov, Ukraine. Ukrainian. *M*.Inna: 2 *s*. **Education:** Kiev U. LLB 1962, LLD 1970, DSc 1979. **Experience:** servant of admin.bodies 1962–6. **Career:** Public Prosecutor 1962–6; Scientific Researcher 1970–80, Chief of Dept 1980–88, Dir 1988–, Inst.of State & Law, Ukrainian AS. **Achievements:** scientific conception of juridical envl prot.in Ukraine; dev.of envl law & mgmt. **Memberships:** Head AUL, Biosphere Council of Ukrainian AS, IUCN CEL. **Award:** Prize for series of works concerning envl law (Ukrainian AS) 1991. **Publications:** *c*.250 incl.ten monogrs. Favours news media support. **Languages:** English, Russian. Willing to act as a consult. **Address:** 29 Turguenievskaya Str. Apt 14, 252054 Kiev, Ukraine. **Tel.**(office) 7 44 228 5155, (home) 7 44 216 2616; **fax** 7 44 228 5474.

SHEPHERD, Dr Alexander Robert DAWSON. Environmental education; coastal resource management, resource assessment (inventory & monitoring); reef fisheries, coastal-zone management; management audit & information systems. Consultant, Coastal Resources' Expert, Director. *B*.21 June 1954, Nicosia, Cyprus. British. **Education:** Cranleigh Sch.; UCNW BSc 1976; U.of York PhD (Reproductive Strats of a Coral-reef Wrasse) 1982. **Experience:** res.in reef fisheries' mgmt, coastal erosion & tourism; coastal-zone mgmt, adv.to developing country govts. **Career:** Consult.in coastal-zone mgmt for Govts & NGOs in Saudi Arabia, Yemen, Rep.of Maldives, and Sultanate of Oman 1982–; Postdoctl Res.F. Univs of York 1982–6 & Newcastle-upon-Tyne 1986–9; Dir, Trop.Marine Res.Unit 1986–; Tech.Coopn Officer, ODA (seconded to Govt of Rep.of Maldives) 1989–93; Coastal Resources Expert, Hunting Aquatic Resources 1993–. **Aspirations:** retention of integrity whilst remaining employable — to grow wiser through exp.with a view to using, with humility, the wisdom gained to help fellow Humankind. **Publications:** co-Author of five refereed papers incl.An analysis of fish community responses to coral mining in the Maldives (co-Author) 1992; primary Author of 60+ consult.reports; Ed.& primary Author *Crown of Thorns Starfish News-letter* (Marine Res.Section, Min.of Fisheries & Agric. Maldives). Indiff.to pers.pub.& news media support. **Languages:** English, French (poor). Willing to act as consult.etc. **Address:** Hunting Aquatic Resources, Department of Biology, University of York, POB 373, York YO1 5YW, England, UK. **Tel.**44 1904 432928; **fax** 44 1904 416611.

SHIN, Professor Dr Eung-Bai. Water & wastewater management. Professor of Environmental Engineering & Institute Director. *B*.17 April 1938, Hesan, Rep.of Korea. S.Korean. *M*.Kyung Sook Kim: *s., d*. **Education:** Han yang U. BE(Civ.Eng.)(*summa cum laude*) 1961; Seoul Nat.U. MS 1965; Vanderbilt U. PhD 1973. **Experience:** res.& res.direction in envl engg, consult. **Career:** Res.Assoc. Vanderbilt U. 1970–73; Res.Dir (Envl Engg) KIST 1974–90; Vis.Scholar, Harvard U.1983–4; consult. WHO 1989; Prof.of Envl Engg 1991–, Dir Envl Engg Res.Inst.1994–6, Hanyang U. **Achievements:** during last 20 yrs has been pioneer researcher in envl cons.& mgmt activities, helped estab.of nat.strat.for 'Cleaner and Greener Prog.' at fed.govt level; dedication to nr of diff.aspects of vitally-important envl qual.enhancements & sust.dev.for well-balanced social welfare. **Memberships:** Tau Beta Pi, ASCE, Pacific Basin Consortium for Hazardous Waste Res.(Chair 1990–92), WEF, IAWQ, AWMA, AWWA, KSEE (Pres.1988–92), KSCE, KAWPRC, KAPRA, KWWA, KIChE. **Awards:** Tau Beta Pi 1973, Nat.Presidential Cert.of Honour for Sci.Day 1981, Academic Achievement Medal (KSCE) 1982, Service Award (WEF) 1985, Nat.Cert.of Honour 1988, Green Medal 1988, Global 500 Roll of Honour (UNEP) 1992, Cert.of Appreciation (UNICEF) 1992, Arthur Sidney Bedell Award (WEF) 1992, Cert.of Contribn (KIST) & (KSEE) 1992 and (KAPRA) 1993, Cert.of Appreciation (Chung Buk Nat.U.) 1993. **Publications:** num.incl.Dose-response Relationship between Rice Plant and Atmos. Poll.(proc. contribn, co-Author) 1989, An Approach to Septic Tank Improvement (proc. contribn, co-Author) 1989, Start-up and op.of anaerobic biofilters with packing alternatives (co-Author) 1989, Effect of sulfur dioxide and hydrogen fluoride on yield of rice plant in industrial areas (co-Author) 1994. Favours pers.pub.& news media support. **Languages:** English, Korean. Willing to act as consult.etc. **Address:** Department of Civil and Environmental Engineering, Hanyang University, Seoul 133 791, South Korea. **Tel.**(office) 82 2 290 1506, (home) 82 2 967 0770; **fax** 82 2 291 8089.

Shiu-hung LUK, Professor Dr, *see* **LUK, Professor Dr Shiu-hung.**

SHORES, John Nelson. Biodiversity, ecotourism; NGO development, sustainable development,

resource conservation & planning; protected areas, wildland management; community participation, national parks, information systems. Senior Biodiversity Adviser. *B*.4 April 1950, Washington, DC, USA. American. **Education:** U.of Michigan BS(Natural Resource Planning) 1972, MS (Resource Policy & Mgmt) 1983. **Experience:** adv.to public & private sector orgns in more than 50 countries (mostly developing) on park & prot.area estab.& mgmt; consult.involving needs assessment, project designs & mgmt, training designs & workshops, monitoring progs, tech.eval. **Career:** Colombian Nat.Parks & Wildlife 1972–6, Directorate of Nat.Parks of Dominican Rep. 1976–8, RARE 1984–5, WWF-US 1985–6, TNC 1987–9, Sr Biodiv.Adv. US Peace Corps 1989– . **Achievement:** strengthening prot.area mgmt & nat.park systems in developing countries. **Publication:** The challenge of ecotourism: a call for higher standards (cong. paper) 1992. Favours pers.pub.& news media support. **Languages:** English, Spanish. Willing to act as consult.etc. **Address:** RR1 Box 4986, Camden, Maine 04843, USA. **Tel.**(home) 1 202 667 5307; **e-mail** jshores@capaccess.edu .

SHREEVE, David. Public relations. Foundation Director. *B*.9 March 1946, Plymouth, Devon, England, UK. British. *M*.Jacqui: *s., d*. **Education:** Devonport High Sch. **Experience:** admin. & consulting. **Career:** from social work, theatre, & broadcasting, into public relations; Dir, The Cons.Fndn 1982–. **Achievement:** founded The Cons.Fndn in a similar manner to that of Archimedes and his Principle. **Membership:** F.RGS. **Publications:** var.related to cons.interests. Favours pers.pub.& news media support. **Languages:** English, French (written). Willing to act as consult.etc. **Address:** The Conservation Foundation, 1 Kensington Gore, London SW7 2AR, England, UK. **Tel.**(office) 44 171 823 8842, (home) 44 181 994 5506; **fax** 44 171 823 8791.

SHRESTHA, Aditya Man. Environmental communications. President. *B*.15 March 1937, Ridi, Nepal. Nepali. *M*.Shobha: *s*. **Education:** Saugor U.(Madhya Pradesh) MA 1960. **Experience:** journalism, dev.& mgmt of NGOs. **Career:** Journalist (Nepalese & Saudi Arabian newspapers) 1963–85; Contrib.to news feature service of Manila 1985–8; Chairman, Asian Forum of Envl Journalists 1988–90; Pres. Cons.Asia 1990–. **Achievements:** dev.of envl journalism in Nepal & Asia. **Memberships:** Nepal Forum of Envl Journalists, Worldview Nepal, Cons.Asia. **Award:** Mitsubishi Award (Press Fndn of Asia) 1980. **Publications:** incl. *Ten Questions about Nepal's Forests* 1989, *Cons.Communications in Nepal* 1989, *Cons. Educ.in R.Chitwan Nat.Park* 1990. Favours pers. pub.& news media support. **Languages:** Enlish, French (read), German (spoken), Hindi, Nepalese. Willing to act as consult.etc. **Adress:** Conservation Asia, POB 3094, Kathmandu, Nepal. **Tel.**(office) 977 1 414190, (home) 977 1 470419; **fax** 977 1 417628.

Shuang Liang LI, *see* **LI, Shuang Liang.**

SHYAM, Dr Murari. Biomass utilization for rural energy supply, biomass-based fuels for internal combustion engines; energy conservation in production agriculture. Principal Scientist. *B.*14 April 1948, Pilibhit, UP, India. Indian. **Education:** G.B.Pant U.of Agric.& Tech. BSc(Eng.) 1968, MTech(Agric.Eng.) 1970; Punjab Agricl U. PhD(Farm Power & Machinery) 1984. **Experience:** more than 22 yrs' res.in energy cons.in mechanized farming, efficient application of agricl chemicals, utilization of agro-biomass for energy & manure. **Career:** Asst Prof. Haryana Agricl U.1971–3; Asst Eng. Punjab Agricl U.1973–5; Agricl Engr, C.Potato Res.Inst. 1975–86; Prin.Sci. Agricl Energy & Power Div. CIAE Bhopal 1986–. **Achievements:** cons.of petroleum fuels in mechanized Potato cultivation, dev.of tech.for use of farm residues & weeds for energy & manure, energy cons.in crop prod.through energy audit. **Memberships:** ISAE (Dir Energy & Envt), IPA (VP). **Awards:** Chapter Award (ISAE), Sr F'ship (ICAR). **Publications:** 26 papers in reputed journals; *c.*50 popular articles & bulletins. Indiff.to pers.pub., favours news media support. **Languages:** English, Hindi. Willing to act as consult.etc. **Address:** 106 (Ashoka) E-7, Arera Colony, Bhopal, Madhya Pradesh 462016, India. **Tel.**(office) 91 755 530980 to 7, (home) 91 755 565433.

SILVA, Allenisheo Lalanath Mark DE. Environmental law, land tenure; environmental impact assessment; public interest litigation, air–water pollution law; human rights. Attorney-at-Law, Executive Director. *B.*28 April 1959, Colombo, Sri Lanka. Sri Lankan. *M.*Lishanthi. **Education:** Trinity Coll.Kandy, R.Coll.Colombo, graduated from Sri Lanka Law Coll.1982, U.of Washington Law Sch. LLM(Marine Affairs) 1990. **Experience:** res.on land tenure & local communities, EIA in developing countries; admin.as Chairman, Envl Fndn Ltd for ten yrs, serving on num.govtl, non-govtl, & inter-govtl, bodies incl.NWSC, MAB Cttee, Envt Cttees of the Industrialization Comm.and of Bar Assn of Sri Lanka; consult.to World Bank, Govt of Sri Lanka (incl.Min.of Justice), Natural Resources & Envl Policy Project/Intl Resources Group Ltd, and private cos. **Career:** Attorney-at-Law in private practice 1982–; co-Founder & Chairman 1981–91, Exec.Dir 1992–, Envl Fndn Ltd. **Achievements:** pioneered public interest envl litigation in Sri Lanka, ensured that access to info.& public hearing rights were included in new legis.(1988); estab.course in Envl Law (U.of Colombo) 1993; co-Founded ELAW 1990 and first envl Public Interest Law firm in the developing world 1981. **Memberships:** BASL, ELAW, Law Asia, IASCP, SAARC LAW. **Awards:** Hector Jayawardena Gold Medal for Best Address to the Jury 1980, A.B.Cooray Mem.Prize for Civil Procedure & Pleading 1981, Duggan F.(NRDC) 1989, Hubert Humphrey

F.1989–90. **Publications:** num.papers & articles incl.Coast cons.Act 1981, The law & the envt 1987. Indiff.to pers.pub., favours news media support. **Languages:** English, Sinhala. Willing to act as consult.etc. **Address:** 18/216 M.E.D.Dabare Mawatha Street, Colombo 5, Sri Lanka. **Tel.**(office) 94 1 697226, (home) 94 1 502099; **fax** 94 1 697226; **e-mail** lalanath @af.org.oc.lk .

SILVA, Ricardo FREIRE DA. Sustainable utilization of wildlife. Executive Director. *B.*11 Sept.1954, São Paulo, Brazil. Brazilian. **Education:** U.of São Paulo, BSc(Phys.) 1977. **Experience:** several res.projects on wildlife; 15 yrs in charge of finances, admin., & scientific issues, of Brazilian Hunting & Cons.Assn; memb.of several comms on envt & wildlife. **Career:** Teacher of Phys.at several diff.schools & colls 1977–, chem.industry 1978–86, Exec. Dir Brazilian Hunting & Cons.Assn 1985–. **Achievements:** bringing into light the wildlife utilization subject in Brazil with some victories in court against envl malfactors and problems. **Publications:** *Hunting & Cons.*1985, Wildlife mgmt — a proposal for Amazonas State 1992, Some reflections on envl educ.in Brazil 1992. Indiff.to pers.pub., favours news media support. **Languages:** English, Italian (spoken), Portuguese (mother tongue), Spanish. Willing to act as consult.etc. **Address:** Rua Mourato Coelho 1372, São Paulo, São Paulo 05417-002, Brazil. **Tel.**(office) 55 11 813 8238, (home) 55 11 819 3032; **fax** 55 11 813 8238.

SIMMONS, Professor Dr Ian. Environmental history, books on environment, teaching. Professor of Geography. *B.*22 Jan.1937, Ilford, Essex, England, UK. British. *M.*Carol Mary: *s.*David (MSc, cons.biol.), *d.* **Education:** U.of London, BSc 1959, PhD 1962; U.of Durham, D.Litt 1990. **Experience:** res.into ecol hist.& its relevance for cons.& envl mgmt; running large dept.(budget > £1 m.); teaching non-specialized students in all these matters. **Career:** ACLS F. U.of Calif.1974–5, Churchill F.1971, Prof.of Geog. Univs of Bristol 1977–81 and Durham 1981–. **Achievements:** well-regarded papers & books on envl hist.& envl mgmt. **Memberships:** IBG, BES, AEEH. **Awards:** F.SAL, Best Paper Prize *(EC)* 1990. **Publications:** *Changing the Face of the Earth* 1989, *Earth, Air & Water* 1991, *Interpreting Nature* 1993, *Envl Hist.*1993; num.others. Dislikes pers.pub., indiff.to news media support. **Languages:** English, French, German (adequate), Japanese (some spoken), Spanish (adequate). Willing to act as consult.etc. **Address:** Department of Geography, Science Laboratories, South Road, Durham DH1 3LE, England, UK. **Tel.**44 191 374 2464; **fax** 44 191 374 2456.

SIMONIS, Professor Dr Udo E. Environmental policy studies. Research Professor of Environmental Policy. *B.*11 Oct.1937, Hilgert, Germany. German. *M.*Heide. **Education:** U.of

Freiburg, MA(Econ.) 1963; U.of Kiel, PhD 1967. **Experience:** res., adv., organizing NGOs such as German Envl Fndn. **Career:** Pers. Adv. to Pres.of Zambia 1967–9; Res.F. U.of Tokyo 1970–71 & German Sci.Orgn 1972–3; Prof.of Econ. Tech.U.of Berlin 1974–88; Vis.Prof. Chinese U.of HK 1976 & 1989; Dir, Intl Inst.for Envt and Soc.1981–7; Prof.of Envl Policy, Sci. Center Berlin 1988–. **Achievement:** orgn of comparative interdisc.& intl social sci.res.on envl problems. **Memberships:** UN Cttee for Dev.Planning 1988–94, German Council on Global Change 1992–, German Envl Fndn (Bd) 1978–; Edl Bds of several intl journals 1972–, Ed.*Jahrbuch Ökologie* 1991–. **Awards:** Best PhD dissertation of the yr (U.of Kiel) 1967, Book Prize* (German Employment Agency) 1985. **Publications:** Author or Ed.of 35 books incl. *More Tech. — Less Work?* (in German) 1985, *Beyond Growth* 1990, *Sust.and Envl Policy* 1992, *Industrial Metabolism* 1994; 175 book contribns, 220 academic j.articles. **Languages:** English, German. Willing to act as mediator and/or ref. **Address:** Science Center Berlin, Reichpietschufer 50, D-10785 Berlin, Germany. **Tel.**49 30 25491 245; **fax** 49 30 25491 247.

SIMPSON, Dr Philip George. Natural history of monocotyledons with secondary growth; restoration ecology; ethnobotany, environmental education. Botanist. *B.*9 Feb.1946, Motupipi (Nelson), NZ. New Zealander. **Education:** U.of Canterbury BSc(Hons) 1968; UCSB PhD 1975. **Experience:** 25 yrs' veg.survey in USA (Mojave Desert), Mexico, Australia, & NZ; 3 yrs in local govt (high-country erosion studies); 15 yrs in c.govt (public service, tech.advice, advocacy, policy formulation, phil.& res.in envl/ cons. mgmt; ten yrs' on intl cttees & working parties on advocacy for sust.land mgmt. **Career:** Soil Conservator, Marlborough Catchment Bd 1977– 80; Envl Educationist, Comm.for the Envt 1980–87; Bot., Dept.of Cons. 1987–. **Achievements:** aims to restore ecol viability to NZ, init. 'Tu Kakariki' (NZ tree prog.). **Memberships:** IUCN CEC, NZES, NZAEE, NZ MAB Cttee. **Awards:** Saywell Prize (Nelson Coll., NZ) 1963, Grad.Intern F'ship (UCSB) 1968, Prince & Princess of Wales Award 1992. **Publications:** incl.*Anatomy and Morphol.of the Joshua Tree (*Yucca brevifolia*)* (PhD thesis) 1975. Indiff.to pers.pub., favours news media support. **Language:** English. **Address:** Science and Research Division, Department of Conservation, POB 10420, Wellington, New Zealand. **Tel.**64 4 471 0726; **fax** 64 4 471 3279.

SINCLAIR, John. Conservation of Fraser Island; ecotourism, environmental strategies, ecotactics. Chief Executive Officer & Honorary Project Officer, Managing Director. *B.*13 July 1939, Maryborough, Qld, Australia. Australian. *M.*Sharan. **Education:** Qld Agricl Coll. Dipl.in Agric.1959; U.of Qld BE(Econ.& Govt) 1974; U.of New England, Dipl.in Continuing Educ.(Ext.) 1980. **Experience:** 26 yrs in envl

educ.; involved in vol.cons.movement from local to intl levels in hon.capacity; del.& organizing cttee for first Nat.Cons.Study Conf.1973; org.of seven-wks' study tour of vol.cons.movements in US, Canada, France, Switzerland, & Britain 1977; del.to 13th IUCN GA 1981, Third World Parks Cong.1982, and 18th IUCN GA 1990. **Career:** Qld Educ.Dept 1960–86, Prin. Parramatta Evening Coll.1987–8, Gen.Mgr *Go Bush* Safaris 1988–. **Achievements:** has led campaign to protect Fraser Is.since 1971 (stopping sand-mining in 1976 and logging in 1991) which was listed as a WHS in 1992. **Memberships:** WPSQ (Hon.Sec. Maryborough Moonaboola Branch 1967–78, Pres.1978–85), Fraser Is. Defenders' Orgn (Pres.& CEO 1971–83, Hon. Project Officer & CEO 1983–), ACF (Counc.) 1975–89, Pres.Australian Cttee IUCN 1982–3, IUCN CEP 1978–, Consult.Cttee NCS 1983–, Commonwealth Govt's Rain-forest WG 1984– 5, Mgmt Cttee Total Envt Centre 1987–91. **Awards:** Australian of the Yr 1976, Global 500 Roll of Honour (UNEP) 1990, Hon.Life M'ship (ACF), Goldman Envl Prize for Australia & Oceania 1993. **Publications:** *Discovering Fraser Is.*(three edns) 1977–87, *Gt Sandy Regn — World Heritage Nomination* (co-Author) 1984, *Mgmt Strat.for Fraser Is.*1987, *Mgmt Strat.for Lord Howe Is.*1988, *Fraser Is.& Cooloola* 1990, other books; memb & convenor, ACF & WPSQ Pubns Cttees; Comm.submissions; 50+ j.etc. articles. **Language:** English. **Address:** Fraser Island Defenders' Organization, POB 71, Gladesville, New South Wales 2111, Australia. **Tel.**(office & home) 61 2 817 4660; **fax** 61 2 816 1642.

SINGAL, Dr Sangar P. Acoustic sounding (SODAR), studies of atmospheric boundary layer, air pollution modelling; noise measurements, acoustic metrology, building acoustics; environmental pollution. Deputy Director. *B.* 15 March 1934, Moga, Punjab, India. Indian. *M.*Sudesh: 2 *s.* **Education:** BHU MSc(Phys.) 1957, PhD(Phys.) 1964. **Experience:** 35 yrs working in phys.acoustics/ultrasonics, 22 yrs in acoustic sounding (SODAR), 20 yrs' admin., 16 yrs' consult.on noise, bldg acoustics & air poll.-related met. **Career:** Asst to Dep.Dir, NPL 1958–; post-doctl assignment, John Carroll U. 1966–8; Vis.Sci. NZ Met.Dept 1987–8. **Achievement:** info.derived from acoustic remote sounding of lower atmos.has been used to determine met.parameters relevant to air poll. monitoring & modelling. **Memberships:** ISARS (Founder F.& Exec.Sec.), F.ASI (VP), F.USI, F.MSI. **Awards:** Award for developing SODAR (NPL) 1975, Cert.of Merit (Instn of Engrs) 1982, Raman Award (ASI) 1987. **Publications:** *Acoustic Remote Sensing* (Ed.) 1990; 100+ res.papers. Indiff.to pers.pub.& news media support. **Languages:** English, Hindi, Punjabi (spoken), Urdu. Willing to act as consult.etc. **Address:** National Physical Laboratory, New Delhi 110 012, Delhi, India. **Tel.**(office) 91 11 578 6592, (home) 91 11 574 7185; **fax** 91 11 575 2678.

SINGER, Professor Dr (Siegfried) Fred. Environmental science & policy, energy economics & policy; atmospheric physics & chemistry; global warming: stratospheric ozone; space pollution: orbiting debris. President, Professor of Environmental Science. *B.*27 Sept.1924, Vienna, Austria. American. *M.*Candace (envl communications & policy). **Education:** Ohio SU BEE 1943; Princeton U. AM 1944, PhD(Phys.) 1948. **Experience:** atmos.& space res., dir of weather satellite service (US Govt), chief sci. US Dept of Transportation; policy positions in USEPA & USDI; currently Pres. Sci.& Envl Policy Project, Prof.of Envl Sci.(Emer.) U.of Virginia; Disting.Res.Prof. George Mason U. **Career:** academic: Univs of Maryland, Miami, Virginia, interspersed with govt service and with short visits in public policy insts such as Brookings, Heritage, Woodrow Wilson C., & Hoover Instn. **Achievements:** devised technique for ozone measurement from satellites; predicted growth of atmos.methane and effects on stratosphere & ozone (*Nature* 1971). **Memberships:** AAAS, AGU. **Awards:** DSc (Ohio SU) 1970, IAA (Paris), White House Award, Gold Medal (USDC). **Publications:** incl.*Is There an Optimum Level of Pop.?* 1971, *The Changing Global Envt* 1975, *Arid Zone Dev.*1977, *The Price of World Oil* 1983, *Free Market Energy* 1984, *Global Climate Change* 1989. Favours news media support. **Languages:** Dutch (spoken), English, French (spoken), German, Spanish (spoken), Swedish (spoken). Further details may be obtained from *Who's Who in America* 1996. Willing to act as consult.etc. **Address:** 4084 University Drive, Suite 101, Fairfax, Virginia 22030, USA. **Tel.**(office) 1 703 934 6940, (home) 1 703 503 5064; **fax** 1 703 352 7535.

SINGH, Birandra Balbir. Conservation of sanctuaries & ecotourism projects, preservation of cultural & historic sites & buildings. Director. *B.*9 Oct.1951, Lautoka, Fiji. Fijian. Father Mr Balram Singh (contribn to estab.of quarantine legis.in Fiji). *M.*Shiu Kuari. **Education:** U.of Bombay BSc(Hons) 1978. **Experience:** cons.& preserv.as above, teaching, EIA auditing. **Career:** Cons.Officer 1978–88, First Dir 1989–, Nat.Trust for Fiji. **Achievements:** estab.& mgmt of Fiji's first animal sanctuary, Founder Memb.of Fiji's Envl Cttee which led to estab.of Dept of Envt. **Memberships:** IUCN CNPPA (VC Oceania Realm 1981–7), IUCN Comm.on Educ.1981–. **Publications:** *Plan for a System of Nat.Parks & Reserves for Fiji* (co-Author) 1980, keynote address on Prot.Areas in Oceania Realm for Third World Nat.Parks Cong. Indiff.to pers.pub., favours news media support. **Languages:** English, Fijian, Hindi. Willing to act as a consult. **Address:** National Trust for Fiji, POB 2089, Government Buildings, Suva, Fiji. **Tel.** (office) 679 301807, (home) 679 362203; **fax** 679 305092.

SINGH, Hari Bansh. Ecodevelopment programmes, environmental awareness through print media, environmental conservation activism. Centre Secretary, Scientist. *B.*15 Nov. 1959, Nema, Deoria, UP, India. Indian. *M.* Neeta: *s.* **Education:** U.of Gorakhpur, MSc (Plant Sci.) 1982; higher studies in envl health, Centre for Biochem.Tech.1995. **Experience:** six yrs' res., tech., and admin. **Career:** Sec. Eco-Transformation Centre 1988–, Sci. Dept of Sci.& Tech. 1990–, Govt of India. **Achievements:** orgn of ecodev.camps, promoting envl cons. awareness through sci.writing. **Memberships:** ISWA, Soc. of Envl Scientists, Soc.of Nature Photographers, Indian Aerobiological Soc. **Publications:** 22 scientific & four res.papers. Indiff.to pers.pub. & news media support. **Languages:** English, Hindi, Sanskrit. Willing to act as consult.etc. **Address:** Science & Engineering Research Council Division, Department of Science & Technology, Technology Bhawan, New Mehrauli Road, New Delhi 110 016, Delhi, India. **Tel.**(office) 91 11 667373 or 662135, (home) 91 11 729 5870; **fax** 91 11 696 3695 or 686 2418 or 3847.

SINGH, Harjit. Environmental information & education, natural resources' management. Government Adviser. *B.*26 Nov.1943, Lahore, (now in) Pakistan. Indian. *M.*Narinder: *d.*Ramanpreet (bot.). **Education:** Agra U. BSc 1963, MSc 1965; Indian Statistical Inst. M(Info.Sci.) 1969; Delhi U. Advanced Dipl.in Russian 1970; McGill U. postgrad.res.1980–82. **Experience:** over 27 yrs of res., tech.eval.of project proposals, grants-in-aid to NGOs etc. **Career:** Jr/ Sr Scientific Asst. Min.of Defence 1966–70; Librarian, IDSA 1970–73; SSO Min.of Defence 1973–5; Sr Documentation Officer, Min.of Sci.& Tech.1975–82; Dir 1985–90, Adv.1990–, Envl Info.System & Envl Educ. Min.of Envt & Forests, Govt of India. **Achievements:** looking after the Nat.Envl Info.System 1985–, envl educ., NGOs, & Nat.Natural Resources' Mgmt System. **Memberships:** INFOTERRA: Adv. Cttee 1989–90 & 1991–2, Mgr Indian Nat.Focal Point 1985–, Chairman Info.Mgmt Mtg of Regnl Service Centre, Rapp. Regnl Service Centre's 1987 mtg and 1989 World Conf., Mgr Regnl Service Centre for S.Asia Sub-regn 1985–; Resource Person & Chairman, S. Asia Coopn Envt Prog. RENRIC; ENVIS Adv.Cttee (Memb. Sec.); Adv.Cttee NISSAT & NMIS; num. others. **Awards:** Res.Assoc. (IDRC) 1980–82. **Publications:** 40+ incl.Role of NGOs in envl educ.1991, Info.on Envt 1992, Envt info.system in India (with spec.ref.to mtn dev.) 1992. Favours pers.pub. **Languages:** English, French, Hindi, Punjabi, Russian. Willing to act as consult.etc. **Address:** Ministry of Environment & Forests, Paryavaran Bhawan, Central Government Offices Complex, Lodi Road, New Delhi 110003, Delhi, India. **Tel.**(office) 91 11 436 0740, (home) 91 11 462 0769; **fax** 91 11 436 0748.

SINGH, Professor Dr Jamuna Sharan. Ecology of forests (Himalayan, dry & wet tropical) and savannas, ecophysiology, restoration ecology. Professor of Botany. *B.*26 Dec.1941, Allahabad, UP, India. Indian. *M*.Tripura: 2 *s*., 2 *d*. **Education:** Ewing Christian Coll. BSc 1957, Allahabad U. MSc(Bot.) 1959, BHU PhD(Plant Ecol.) 1967. **Experience:** res.— analysis of structural & functional attributes of trop., temperate, & alpine, grasslands and of Himalayan & dry trop.forest ecosystems; study of soil biol processes which influence ecosystem productivity, and of nutrient cycling & flux of radiatively important biogenic gases in var.habitats in dry trop.regns; resto.of drastically-disturbed ecosystems; teaching BSc–MSc level for 25 yrs. **Career:** Lect.in Bot. Kurukshetra U.1968–75; Reader in Ecol. Sch.of Planning & Arch.(New Delhi) 1975–6 and in Bot. Kumaun U.1976–84; Prof.of Botany, BHU 1984–; Spec.Grad.Fac. 1973–4 and Vis.Sci.1971–4, 1981–2 CSU. **Achievements:** served on several ecol.& envt-oriented cttees incl.Spec.Cttee of IGBP (ICSU), Nat.IGBP, SCOPE, & MAB, and Steering Group of Planning Comm.on Envt, Forests & Wastelands Dev.; assisted Min.of Envt & Forests of Indian Govt in launching MAB Prog.; integrated Action-oriented Ecodev.Res.Prog.in Himalayan regn. **Memberships:** F.INSA (Council 1989–91), IAS, NAS, ESA, IAVS (Sweden), CSA (India), ISCA (Nomenclature Cttee 1985–6), IBS, Nat.Cttee for Geosphere-Biosphere Prog. 1987–91, Jt Sec.CHEA India 1983–5, WII, GBPIHED. **Awards:** Dr Ram Saran Tiass Mem Silver Medal 1957, Shanti Swarup Bhatnagar Prize 1980, Pitamber Pant Nat.Envt F'ship 1984, Swami Pranavanand Saraswati Award 1985. **Publications:** 12 books incl.*Res.Methods in Plant Ecol.*(co-Author) 1968, *Grassland Veg.: Its Structure, Function, Utilization & Mgmt* (co-Author) 1977, *Sci.& Rural Dev.in Mtns* (co-Ed.) 1981, *Envl Regeneration in Himalaya: Concepts & Strats* (Ed.) 1985, *Perspectives in Ecol.*(co-Ed.) 1989, *Trop.Ecosystems: Ecol.& Mgmt* (co-Ed.) 1992, *Resto.of Degraded Land: Concepts & Strats* (Ed.) 1992, *Forests of Himalaya: Structure, Functioning & Impact of Man* (co-Author) 1992; Chief Ed.*Trop.Ecol.* 1984–90; Member Bd of Eds — *J.of BNHS* 1993–, *Oecologia Montana* 1991–, *J.of Veg.Sci.* 1990–, *Reclamation & Revegetation Res.*1984–7, *Proc. of IAS* (Plant Scis) 1986–91, *Proc.of INSA* 1986–90, *Himalayan J.of Envt & Zool.*1990–; *c*.260 res.& review papers. Favours news media support. **Languages:** English, Hindi. Further details may be obtained from *Who's Who in India* 1986, *Who's Who in the World* 9th edn, *Ref.India* 1992, *India Who's Who* 1990–91. Willing to judge proposals &/or ref.papers. **Address:** Dept of Botany, Banaras Hindu University, Varanasi 221005, Uttar Pradesh, India. **Tel.**(office) 91 542 310290 to 99 ext.352, (home) 91 542 312593; **fax** 91 542 312059.

SINGH, HE Dr Karan. Environmental conservation and sustainable development strategies; wildlife preservation, advocacy of nexus between religion and Nature; study of comparative religions and philosophy. Commission President, Foundation Chairman, Temple Chairman. *B*.9 March 1931, Cannes, France. Indian. *M*.Princess Yasho Rajya Lakshmi of Nepal: 2 *s*., *d*. **Education:** U.of J&K, BA 1954; U.of Delhi, MA (Pol.Sci.) 1957, PhD(Pol.Thought of Sri Aurobindo) 1961. **Experience:** Statesman, former Cabinet Minister, former Amb.to the US. **Career:** Regent 1949, Head of State 1964, Gov.1967, State of J&K; Minister of: Civil Aviation & Tourism 1967–73, Health & Family Planning 1973–7, and Educ.& Culture 1979, Govt of India; Memb. Lower House of Parliament (India) 1967–84; Pres. People's Comm.on Envt & Dev.(India) 1990–; Chairman (with rank of Minister of Indian Cabinet), Auroville Fndn 1990–; Chairman, Temple of Understanding 1989–. **Achievements:** as Govt of India Minister laid fndn of modern aviation in the country and gave new orientation and thrust to country's tourism sector, announced Nat.Pop.Policy, and steered successful Project Tiger during its formative yrs as Chairman of its Steering Cttee 1972–7. **Memberships:** Club of Rome (Exec. Council), Club of Budapest, UNESCO Intl Comm.on Educ.for 21st Century, Global Forum of Parliamentarians & Spiritual Leaders on Human Survival Intl Steering Cttee, Green Cross Intl (Bd of Trustees). **Awards:** Hon.D.Phil. from BHU, Aligarh Muslim U., & Soka U. (Japan). **Publications:** 15 books incl.*One Man's World* 1986, *Humanity at the Crossroads* 1988, *Essays on Hinduism* 1990. Favours pers. pub.& news media support. **Languages:** Dogri (Jammu), English, Hindi, Sanskrit. Further details may be obtained from *e.g. Indo–Amer. Who's Who* 1993, *International Who's Who* 1994–5. **Address:** 3 Nyaya Marg, Chanakyapuri, New Delhi 110 021, Delhi, India. **Tel.** (home) 91 11 301 1744; **fax** 91 11 301 3171.

SINGH, Professor Dr Kaushalendra Pratap. Ecology of tropical forests, savannas, & agro ecosystems. Professor of Botany. *B*.28 Dec. 1940, Jhansi, UP, India. Indian. Father V.R. Singh, Agric.Officer. *M*.Dr Sushila: 2 *s*. **Education:** BHU BSc 1958, MSc(Bot.) 1960, PhD (Ecol.) 1967. **Experience:** 25 yrs' teaching ecol.courses at postgrad.level, supervising doctl & postdoctl res.progs on analysis of trop. ecosystems. **Career:** Ecol.Res.Assoc.1964–9, Lect.1970–84, Reader 1984–9, Prof.1989–, Dept of Bot. BHU; Lect.in Plant Scis, Meerut U. 1969–70; served on deputation as Sr Envl Analyst, Dept of Sci.& Tech. Govt of India 1972–4. **Achievements:** Exec.Ed.1977– & elected Chief Ed.1990– of *Trop.Ecol.* **Memberships:** ISTE, BES, IBS, NIE. **Awards:** F.NAS, F.NIE. **Publications:** *Perspectives on Ecol.*(Ed.) 1987, *Trop. Ecosystems: Ecol.& Mgmt* (Ed.) 1992; 100+ res. papers & reports. Indiff.to pers.pub., favours news media support. **Languages:** English, Hindi. Further details may be obtained from *Year Book,* NAS, India. Willing to act as consult.&/or ref. **Address:** Department of Botany, Banaras Hindu University, Varanasi 221005, Uttar Pradesh, India. **Tel.**(office) 91 542 312989, (home) 91 542 311600; **fax** 91 542 312059.

SINGH, Dr Naresh. Sustainable development, poverty and sustainable livelihoods; ecosystem health. Visiting Professor, Programme Director. *B.*11 Feb.1951, Demerara, Guyana. Canadian, Guyanese. *M.*Sarojnee: *s.* **Education:** IARI, MSc 1979; U.of W.Indies, PhD(Chem.) 1985. **Experience:** instnl: prog.& project dev.& mgmt; res.; policy advice at govt ministerial level on envt & dev.issues. **Career:** Head, Industrial & Analytical Services Div., Scientific Res.Council of Jamaica 1985–6; Sr Sci. UNEP Project on Prot.of Coastal & Marine Envt of Carib.Islands 1986–9; Exec.Dir, Carib.Envl Health Inst.1990–93; Vis.Prof. U.of Boston Sch.of Public Health 1992–; Dir, Poverty & Empowerment Prog. IISD 1993–. **Achievements:** set up Carib.Envl Health Inst.owned by & servicing 15 Carib. countries, pubns incl.contribns to five books. **Memberships:** RSC, IUCN CESP, ISEE (Founding Cttee of Canadian Chapter). **Awards:** Commonwealth Scholar 1977, Pilgrim Mem. Fund Scholarship (Amer. Fndn) 1983, Adjunct Prof.(U.of Waterloo) 1991–2 & (U.of Manitoba) 1995, F.Lester Pearson Inst.for Intl Dev.1993. **Publications:** 70+ incl.*Sust.Dev.— An Imperative for Envl Prot.*(co-Author) 1992, *Role of Regnl Orgns in Climate Change* 1993, *Designing Work for Sust.*1994. Favours pers.pub.& news media support. **Languages:** English; French, Hindi & Spanish (working knowledge). Further details may be obtained from the *Membership Directory* (RS of Chem., UK), *Directory of Envl Orgns of the Carib.* Willing to act as consult.etc. **Address:** 161 Portage Avenue E. 6th Floor, Winnipeg, Manitoba R3B 0Y4, Canada. **Tel.** (office) 1 204 958 7748, (home) 1 204 489 1772; **fax** 1 204 958 7710.

SINGH, Professor Dr O.N. Atmospheric chemistry particularly stratospheric pollution; spectroscopy & fibre optics. Professor of Applied Physics. *B.*8 Nov.1943, Pureon, Jaunpur, UP, India. Indian. *M.*Savitri. **Education:** BHU MSc 1963, PhD 1967. **Experience:** *c.*30 yrs' teaching & res.; admin.— Incharge, Applied Phys. Section and Head, Dept of Applied Phys.; Exec.Ed.*The Yoga Review* 1985–7. **Career:** Lect.1963–4 & 1967–75, CSIR Res.F.1965–7, Reader 1975–86, Prof.of Applied Phys.1986–, all Dept of Applied Phys. BHU; Res.Sci.at ICTP 1973 & 1985, FOM IAMP 1974–5 & 1985, and Max-Planck Inst.of Aeronomy 1987–8, 1991 & 1992. **Achievements:** authored & co-authored 15 res.papers & articles on tropospheric & stratospheric poll., invited contrib.of chapter in *Enc.of Earth System Sci.*1992, first Indian nat.rep.on Comm.VI–4 of IUPAC since 1989. **Membership:** F.ICS. **Publications:** 60+ res. papers & articles. Favours pers.pub.& news media support. **Languages:** English, German (poor), Hindi. Willing to act as consult.etc. **Address:** Department of Applied Physics, Institute of Technology, Banaras Hindu University, Varanasi 221005, Uttar Pradesh, India. **Tel.** (office) 91 542 310291, (home) 91 542 311401; **fax** 91 542 312059 & 311693.

SINGH, Shekhar. Environmental planning & policy, biodiversity conservation, wildlife management. Coordinator. *B.*14 Aug.1950, Lucknow, UP, India. Indian. *M.*Uma: *d.* **Education:** U.of Delhi BA(Hons) 1970, MA 1972. **Experience:** res.— team leader for studies in biodiv., prot.area mgmt, nat.envl action plans; admin.— former Adv.to Planning Comm.and Chairman Envl Appraisal Cttee for Thermal Power Stations, both for Govt of India; consult.to UN & DANIDA. **Career:** Lect. U.of Delhi 1972–3 & N.-Eastern Hill U.1974–80, Fac.1980–90 and Coord. Centre for Public Policy Planning & Envl Studies 1992– IIPA, Adv. Planning Comm. Govt of India 1990–1. **Achievements:** helped finalize chapter on envt & forests in the nat.plan document, and allocations for eighth five-yr plan of India; prepared the Biodiv.Status Report for India. **Membership:** IUCN CNPPA & SSC Asia Pacific Regnl Rep. **Publications:** *Envl Policy in India* 1984, *Mgmt of Nat.Parks & Sanctuaries in India* 1989, *Directory of Nat.Parks in HP* 1990, *Directory of Nat.Parks in A&N Islands* 1991; num.papers. Indiff.to pers.pub.& news media support. **Languages:** English, Hindi. Willing to act as consult.etc. **Address:** C-17A Munirka, New Delhi 110067, Delhi, India. **Tel.**(office) 91 11 331 7309, (home) 91 11 652831.

SINHA, Dr Akhauri R.Prasad. Genecology & conservation of rare, endangered, & endemic, flora of Andaman & Nicobar Islands; environment & conservation. Postgraduate Department Head. *B.*7 July 1946, Bihar, Bihar State, India. Indian. *M.*Kumud: 3 *d.* **Education:** Bihar U. MSc(Bot.) 1967, LLB 1970, PhD(Weed Cytogenetics with ref.to Gene Ecol.) 1980. **Experience:** 18 yrs' res.on pop.genetics, gene ecol.& cons.of rare, endangered, & endemic, flora of A&N Islands; 25 yrs' teaching cytogenetics, biotech., & plant physiol., at BSc & PhD levels. **Career:** Head, Postgrad.Dept of Bot. Jawaharlal Nehru Govt Coll. 1971–. **Achievements:** basic res.covering ecol.& cytogenetical aspects of cons.of rare, endangered, & endemic, forest flora of Andaman & Nicobar Islands; has currently made cytological studies of *c.*120 plants, mostly rare, endemic, or endangered, of Andaman & Nicobar forest and reported the chromosome nr of 115 species for the first time; has broadcast num.talks on cons.& poll.of envt through All India Radio to make the public aware of their envt and share resp.for its cons.; estab.of a Gene Garden at Jawaharlal Nehru Rajkeeya Maharidyalaya to conserve the rare, endemic, & endangered, flora of the regn. **Memberships:** IBS, APSI, Botl Soc.(Patna U., Life), Andamans Sci.Assn (Counc.). **Publications:** *c.*35 res.papers, ref.for *Intl J.of Plant Scis.* Favours pers.pub. **Languages:** English, Hindi. Willing to act as consult.etc. **Address:** Postgraduate Department of Botany, Jawaharlal Nehru Government College, Port Blair 744104, Andaman & Nicobar Islands, India. **Tel.**91 3192 20503.

SINITSINA, Professor Dr Irene Eugene. Civil engineering, aerohydrodynamics; environmental problems. Docent, Vice-President, Laboratory Head. *B*.9 May 1953, Alatir, Russia. Russian. *M*.Alexander Sinitsin (envl cons.): *d*. **Education:** Civil Engg Inst. Dipl.in Civil Eng.1975; Continuous Medium Mechanics Inst. CSc 1990; CSRI of Water Resources Mgmt DSc 1993. **Experience:** res.— aerohydrodynamics of city areas, ecol monitoring, math.modelling of wind microclimate; turbulent diffusion of impurities in near-Earth layer of atmos.; admin.— Head of Engg Ecol.Lab., Sci.Dir of ISAR AERO, VP AEROMech High Coll., Sci.Sec. Intl Scientific Cttee (Physics); consult.in civil engg & air prot. **Career:** designer of heating & ventilation systems, Design Inst.1975–81; Docent, Hydraulics & Heat Engg Dept, Izhesvk State Tech.U. 1981–; Head of Lab.ISAR & Sci.Dir AERO 1989–; VP AEROMech Coll.1992–. **Achievements:** improvement of air in cities & towns of Udmurtia on basis of math.modelling of wind regime & turbulent transfer of polluting impurities. **Memberships:** ISC, Scientific Council of Izhevsk State Tech.U.& Civil Engg Fac., RAE (Udmurtia Branch). **Award:** bonus for achievement in ecol.1988. **Publications:** 60+ scientific papers & abstracts. Indiff.to pers.pub., favours news media support. **Languages:** English (better at written), Russian. Willing to act as consult.etc. **Address:** POB 3905, Izhevsk 426000, Russia. **Tel.**(office) 8 3412 238828, (home) 8 3412 251638; **fax** 8 3412 787010.

SINNER, Jean-Marie. Nature conservation & protection. Service Head. *B*.25 Dec.1945, Mersch, Luxembourg. Luxemburger. *M*.Nicole. **Education:** Albert-Ludwig U.(Freiburg), Diplom Forstwirt 1972; envl studies, Yale U. 1974. **Experience:** admin. **Career:** Forest Mgmt & Planning 1972–86, Head of Nature Cons. Service, Admin.des Eaux et Forêts 1986–, Luxemburg Forest Service. **Memberships:** Conseil Supérieur pour la prot.de la Nature. Dislikes pers.pub., indiff.to news media support. **Languages:** English, French, German. **Address:** Administration des Eaux et Forêts, Luxemburg Forest Service, 67 rue Michel Welter, L-2730 Luxemburg. **Tel.**352 402201; **fax** 352 485985.

SIOLI, Professor Dr Harald Felix Ludwig. Tropical ecology mainly of the Amazon region, cultures & fates of Amazonian Indians. Emeritus Director. *B*.25 Aug.1910, Köthen, Germany. German. *D*.: *d*., *s*. **Education:** U.of Heidelberg 1928–30; U.of Göttingen 1931; U.of Kiel, Dr phil.(Zool. Bot. Limnol.) 1934. **Experience:** res.— fieldwork in limnol.in arid NE Brazil (1934–5), in comparative physiol.1938–40 and in limnol.& landscape ecol.in Brazilian Amazon regn 1940–57; teaching — 1951–2 zool.and 1958–78 limnol.& trop.ecol., courses on Amazonian limnol.& ecol.in 1977 & 1980 at INPA & UCB. **Career:** Scholarship from German Res. Community 1936–7; Scientific Asst, Biol. Dept of Gen.Inst.against Tumor Diseases, Rudolf-Virchow-Hosp.1937–8; GRC Exchange Asst, Instituto Biologico, São Paulo 1938–40; Scholarship from GRC for limnol.res.in Brazilian Amazon regn 1940–42; civil internee, Brazilian internment camp 'Tomé-assú' 1942–5 (only physician in the regn, Head of Hosp.& Pharmacy 1942–4); Scientific Asst, later Head of Dept of Limnol. Instituto Agronómico do Norte (Belém-Pará) 1945–53 (during this period of three yrs [1948–50] at [formerly Ford] Rubber Plantations of Belterra & Fordlândia at Rio Tapajós); Researcher, Spec.Service of Public Health, Belo Horizonte 1954; Head, Dept of Limnol., Instituto Nacional de Pesquisas da Amazonia, Manaus-Amazonas 1955–67; Exec. Dir & Head of Ind.Dept of Hydrobiol.Anstalt, Max-Planck Soc.1957–66; Dir Dept of Trop. Ecol.1966–78, Emer.1978–, Max-Planck-Inst.of Limnol.; Vis.Prof. UCB 1977. **Achievements:** demonstrating rivers as renal systems of landscapes; clarifying relations of river (creek) waters & soils of headwater regns & functioning of forest-ecocomplex in case of extreme nutrient poorness as in most of Amazonia. **Memberships:** DZG, SIL, ATB (Pres.1971–3), ISTE. **Awards:** Scientific Consult. INPA 1957, Hon. Prof. U.of Kiel 1958, Brazilian Order of the Southern Cross 1967, Medal 'Ciencia para a Amazonia' (INPA) 1977, Medal 1st Class of Fundación La Salle de Ciencias Naturales (Venezuela) 1990, 'Prêmio Harald Sioli' founded by BSL for outstanding achievement by young Brazilian limnologists 1990. **Publications:** *Amazonien — Grundlagen der Ökologie des Grössten Tropischen Waldlandes* 1983, *The Amazon — Limnol.& Landscape Ecol.of a Mighty Trop. R.and its Basin* (Ed.) 1984, *Amazônia — Fundamentos da Ecologia da maior Região de Florestas tropicais* 1990; *c*.150 papers. **Languages:** English, French (read), German, Portuguese, Spanish (read). **Address:** Rautenbergstrasse 56, 24306 Plön, Germany. **Tel.**(home) 49 4522 802204; **fax** 49 4522 802281.

SISMAN, Richard 'Dick'. Travel and the environment, sustainable tourism policies, economics of rural tourism; coastal processes. Chairman & Managing Director, Adviser. *B*.13 June 1944, Doncaster, England, UK. British. *M*. Valerie: 3 *d*.incl.Katherine (BSc[Hons] [Geog.], author of review of sust.tourism policies for Seychelles) and Helen (BSc[Hons][Envl Sci.], Co.Sec.of Green Flag Intl). **Education:** Open U. BA 1978. **Experience:** carried out envl reviews of tourism industry for govts & businesses in UK, Cyprus, Malta, Tunisia, France, Portugal, Jersey; founded Green Flag Intl 1990; major contribn to tourism & envt policy dev. **Career:** local govt finance to position of deptl head 1960–76, c.govt, road planning policies 1976–9; sr planning positions with Countryside Comm. incl.dev.of coastal planning policies 1979–94; Envl Adv.to Assn of Ind.Tour Operators 1990–; Adv.to Pacific Asia Travel Assn 1991– and to World Travel & Tourism Council's Green Globe Prog.1993–; Chairman & MD Green Flag Intl

1989–. **Achievements:** developing open access policies for UK Nature reserves, and operational progs for envl improvements in Malta, Tunisia, Portugal, Jersey, & UK; helping tourism industry to understand and to contribute to environmentally sust.dev. **Publications:** *The Laona Project, Proposals for an Integrated Approach to Green Tourism in the Akamas Regn of Cyprus* 1989, *Sust.Tourism: The Way Forward* (EC Report) 1991, *A Green Flag Intl Guide to Sust.*1991, *Envl Review and Green Tourism Plan for Jersey* 1993; *c.*30 other papers & reports for tourism destinations & industry policy issues. No interest in pers.pub., prepared to provide info.about issues to media. **Languages:** English; French, Greek, Portuguese & Spanish (pleasantries). Prepared to act as consult.&/or judge proposals. **Address:** Green Flag International, POB 396, Linton, Cambridge CB1 6UL, England, UK. **Tel.**(office) 44 1223 890250, (home & **fax**) 44 1223 893587; **fax** 44 1223 890258.

SIVADAS, Dr Ponathil. Ecophysiology; natural history, environmental conservation; managing personal agriculture & aquaculture farms; promoting public awareness in social forestry; environmental health hazards; HIV/AIDS eradication & biodiversity protection programmes. Senior Principal Scientist. *B.*10 April 1939, Ernakulam, Cochin, Kerala, India. Indian. Father HH the late Rama Varma of Cochin R.family, ornith. *M.*Geetha (active campaigner against envl poll.& use of pesticides in agric.; aquaculture, agric.): *s., d.* **Education:** Annamali U. MSc(Limnol.& Fisheries Biol.) 1961, PhD(Endocrinology) 1968. **Experience:** substantial scientific exposure to fields of endocrinology, physiol., ecol., eco-physiol., poll., aquaculture, envl mgmt & cons.; project leader, consult., coord./mgr, supervisor & res.guide. **Career:** SRF Indian Nat.Council for Oceanic Res.1966–9, Res.Assoc. INSA 1969– 73, Sr Prin.Sci. NIO 1990–. **Achievements:** by assn with admin.body of Lakshadweep (Laccadive Islands), has been resp.for mooting & implementing num.envl cons.measures incl. declaring Pitti Is.as sanctuary for seagulls, terns, & noddies (*Sterna fuscata,* & *Anous stolidus*), submitting proposal for developing a Nat.Marine Park and Marine Reserve at Lakshadweep, requesting auths to stop cutting stones and/or using coral boulders from the reefs for house-construction (subs.implemented), reporting for first time presence of *Acanthaster planci* in Lakshadweep waters, and making the public aware of dangers. **Memberships:** MBA (India, Life), NAS (Life), Soc.for Reproductive Biol.& Comparative Endocrinology. **Award:** RS Grant for participation in IBP 1970. **Publications:** *c.*34 papers incl.Report on the occurrence of *Acanthaster* sp.in Lakshadweep waters 1978, An account of veg.of Kararatti Is. (Laccadives) 1982, Possible threats to the marine envt of Lakshadweep (Laccadive Islands) 1987; seven scientific & three tech.reports. Favours pers.pub.& news

media support. **Languages:** English, French (weak), German (weak), Hindi, Malayalam, Tamil. Further details may be obtained from *Intl Directory of Marine Scientists* (UNESCO) 1983, *Indian Nat.Directory of Marine Scientists* (NIO) 1993. Willing to act as consult.etc. **Address:** 1 Lal Bagh Apartments, Dewan's Road, Ernakulam, Cochin 16, Kerala, India. **Tel.**(office) 91 484 351814, (home) 91 484 362727; **fax** 91 484 372666.

SJÖGREN, Dr Erik Alex. Bryophyte ecology & sociology, 'Macaronesian' vegetation; epiphyllous bryophytes, protection of natural forest vegetation; bryophytes as indicators of pollution. Assistant Professor in Ecological Botany & Herbarium Tutor. *B.*5 Oct.1933, Kalmar, Sweden. Swedish. *M.*Berit (field-work asst): *s.* Jonas (copywriter of botl mss), *d.* **Education:** U.of Uppsala, Doct.in Ecol.Bot.1964. **Experience:** res.— three yrs' fieldwork in the Azores Islands and on Madeira, and in Scandinavia 1952–; admin.— Tutor in Bryophyte Herbarium (Uppsala) 1987– and Chairman of Swedish Phytogeogl Soc.; teaching in ecol bot.1965–. **Career:** Project Leader, Nat.Dept of Nature Cons.1965–83; Asst Prof.in Ecol Bot.1965–, Tutor in Bryophyte Herbarium 1987–, Dept of Ecol Bot. U.of Uppsala. **Achievements:** init.of prot.of calcareous Alvar heath on Oland (Sweden), and of work on prot.of Nature in the Azores and on Madeira; selection of indicator species for prot. **Memberships:** Swedish Phytogeogl Soc.(Chairman 1980–), Macaronesian Botl Soc., Ed. *Acta Phytogeographica Suecica* and *Studies in Plant Ecol.*(both from 1978). **Awards:** Linnaeus Prize (R.Soc.of Sci.) 1964, Economical Reward (Gulbenkian Fndn) 1982. **Publications:** seven books incl.*Epilithische und epigäische Moosvegetation in Laubwäldern der Insel Öland, Schweden* (English summary) 1964, *Bryophyte Veg.in the Azores Islands* 1978, *Changes in the Epilithic and Epiphytic Moss Cover in Two Deciduous Forest Areas on the Is.of Öland (Sweden) — A Comparison between 1958–1962 and 1988–90* 1995; 30 papers. **Languages:** English, French, German, Latin (read), Portuguese, Spanish (read). Willing to act as consult.etc. **Address:** Department of Ecological Botany, University of Uppsala, Villavägen 14, S-752 36 Uppsala, Sweden. **Tel.**(office) 46 18 182850 or 78, (home) 46 18 301720; **fax** 46 18 553419.

SKINNER ALVARADO, Juan, *see* **ALVARADO, Juan SKINNER.**

SKOLIMOWSKI, Professor Henryk. Ecophilosophy, eco-ethics, ecotheology. Professor Emeritus, Chair of Ecological Philosophy, Director. *B.*4 May 1930, Warsaw, Poland. American. Polish. **Education:** Tech.U.of Warsaw MSc 1956, Warsaw U. MA(Phil.) 1959, New Coll.Oxf. DPhil 1964. **Experience:** teaching ecophil., evol.epistemology, sci., & civilization in the USA, Europe, & India. **Career:** Lect.

Warsaw U.1958–62, Assoc.Prof.of Phil. U.of Southern Calif. 1964–70, Prof.of Phil. U.of Michigan 1971–93; Vis.Prof. Univs of Madras, Camb., Warsaw, and others; estab.first-ever Chair of Ecol Phil.at Tech.U.of Lodz (Poland) which held since 1991; Dir, Eco-Phil.Center, U.of Michigan 1981–. **Achievements:** creating new fields of inquiry called Ecol Phil.and then Ecotheology, pubn of seven books & num.articles in the field. **Memberships:** Teilhard Soc.(VP 1989–), IUCN Comm.on Ecol., Pres.Council on Ecol.(Warsaw); var.Bds publishing journals re. broadly-conceived ecophil. **Publications:** 18 books incl.*Living Phil.: Ecophilosophy as a Tree of Life* 1992, *A Sacred Place to Dwell, Living with Reverence upon the Earth* 1993, *Walking in Beauty* 1994, *The Participatory Mind* 1994; over 300 articles. **Languages:** English, Polish, Russian. Willing to act as consult.etc. **Address:** Sienna 89 M 39, 00-815 Warsaw, Poland. **Tel.& fax** 48 22 207782.

SKOULIKIDIS, Professor Dr Theodore. Corrosion & protection of metal, marbles, & monuments; liquid crystals; kinetics & catalysis. Professor of Physical Chemistry and Applied Electrochemistry. *B.*2 Sept.1925, Athens, Greece. Greek. *M.*Aliki: *s., d.* **Education:** Nat. Tech.U.of Athens, Dipl.in Chem.Eng. 1948, PhD(Eng.) 1950, two-yrs' Scholarship (Nat.Tech. U.of Athens) 1952–4, ten-months' Scholarship (Alexander von Humbolt Stiftung) 1956 and one-yr Deutsche Forchungsgemainschaft 1957–8, all held at U.of Munich. **Experience:** res., tech., admin., consult., educ. **Career:** Asst Prof. 1954–60, Assoc.Prof.1960–68, Prof.of Phys.Chem. and Applied Electro-chem.1968, V.-Rector 1981–5, Dean of Chem.Engg 1976–8 & 1985–9, all at Nat.Tech.U.of Athens. **Achievements:** developed new non-destructive *in situ* gypsum thickness measurements; method of inversion of gypsum back into calcite to consolidate surfaces and preserve details of statues; revelation of mechanism of sulphuration; new methods for distinguishing sulphurated surfaces from non-sulphurated ones using liquid crystals; cleaning marble surface; increasing mech. properties of calcite originating from lime, and prot.by using n-semiconductor pigments in polymers. **Memberships:** ICPM, Cttee for Preserv.of the Akropolis Monuments, ICOMOS team for Stone, EEC Cttee F2:Corrosion. **Awards:** Gold Medal (Inst.of Valorization of Greek Raw Materials) 1952, Gold Cross of K.George II and Taxiarch of K.George II (Greek Govt) 1961, Medal (ICPAM) 1988, Global 500 Roll of Honour (UNEP) 1989, Leonardo da Vinci Award of Arts (with all members of the Acropolis Preserv.Cttee) 1989. **Publications:** *Phys.Chem.and Applied Electrochemistry* (12 vols in Greek, one vol.trans.into German), Corrosion and Prot.of an Aluminium Alloy and Steel (in press); 150 scientific papers. Indiff.to pers. pub.& news media support. **Languages:** English, French, German, Greek. Willing to act as consult.etc. **Address:** National Technical University of Athens, Irron Polytechniou 9, Zographou 157 80, Athens, Greece. **Tel.**(office) 30 31 779 2438, (home) 30 31 622 0712; **fax** 30 31 770 0989 & 779 2438.

SLOCOMBE, Dr D.Scott. Ecosystem science, environmental planning & management, sustainability, nonequilibrium systems' theory. Assistant Professor & Director. *B.*15 April 1961, Halifax, NS, Canada. Canadian. *M.*Anna C. **Education:** U.of Waterloo BIS 1983, PhD 1990; UBC MSc 1986. **Experience:** res.— nonequilibrium systems' theory in envl planning & mgmt, hinterland prot.areas' mgmt, planning & mgmt tools for sust., ecosystem approaches, integrity, & mgmt; admin.re.res.centre; consult.— Canadian Parks Service, CARC, Envt Canada, & others; teaching resource & envl planning & mgmt from BSc to PhD level. **Career:** Lect.in Geog.1989–90, Asst.Prof. 1990–94, co-Dir 1990–93, Dir 1993– Cold Regns Res.Centre, all at Wilfred Laurier U.; PI, U.of Waterloo Sust.Soc. Project 1991–3. **Achievements:** innovative res.in non-equilibrium systems approaches in envl mgmt and ecosystem integrity & management; writings on sust.dev.& envl educ.; founding memb.of Exec.Cttee of CNEEC. **Memberships:** CAG, AAG, SWCS, FFPS, CSEB, NAAEE, IUCN CESP. **Publications:** *Managing Resources for Sust.*(in press), c.60 papers & reports. Dislikes pers.pub., but favours news media support. **Languages:** English, French (read); German & Spanish (basic spoken/written). Willing to act as consult.etc. **Address:** Department of Geography, Wilfrid Laurier University, Waterloo, Ontario, Canada. **Tel.**(office) 1 519 884 1970, (home) 1 519 746 7504; **fax** 1 519 725 1342.

SMIL, Professor Dr Václav. Interdisciplinary studies of environment–energy–food–economy interactions. Professor of Geography, Consultant. *B.*9 Dec.1943, Plzen (Pilsen), Czech Rep. Canadian. *M.*Eva: *s.* **Education:** Carolinum U. RNDr 1965, Penn.SU PhD 1972. **Experience:** res.1962–, consult.1966–, teaching 1972–. **Career:** consult.in Energy & Envl Affairs 1966–9; Res.Asst 1969–72, Prof.of Geog.1972–, U.of Manitoba; Consult.to *e.g.* World Bank, WRI, ODRC, USAID, CIDA, 1980–. **Achievements:** interdisc.studies of energy & envt interactions, work on global biogeochem.cycles, pioneering studies of China's envl degradation. **Memberships:** AAAS, NYAS. **Publications:** 13 books incl.*Carbon Nitrogen Sulfur* 1985, *Energy Food Envt* 1987, *Gen.Energetics* 1991, *China's Envl Crisis* 1993; *c.*160 papers. Indiff.to pers. pub.& news media support. **Languages:** Arabic (read), Chinese (spoken), Czech, English, French (read), German, Japanese (spoken), Latin (read), Polish, Russian. Willing to act as consult. **Address:** Department of Geography, University of Manitoba, Winnipeg R3T 2N2, Canada. **Tel.**(office) 1 204 474 9256, (home) 1 204 256 9916; **fax** 1 204 257 8281; **e-mail** vsmil@ ccv.vmanitoba.ca .

SMIRNOV, Professor Dr Nikolai Nikolaevich.
Ecology of catastrophic situations; limnology;
morphology & taxonomy of the Cladocera
(Crustacea). Professor & Laboratory Head. *B*.7
Jan.1928, Moscow, Russia. Russian. *M*.Dr La-
risa (ecol appraisal of hydraulic constructions on
freshwater zooplankton): 2 *s*.incl.Alexey (spore-
bearing plants; phytopath.). **Education:** Inst.for
Fisheries Mgmt (*cum laude*) 1950, PhD 1953;
Inst.for Foreign Languages (English Dept) 1955;
Zool.Inst. Russian AS DSc 1969. **Experience:**
teaching (1952–7) & res.(1957–90) in limnol.,
worked on IBP (memb.of Nat.Cttee) 1965–71
and at SIPRI 1977, 1978; served on SCOPE
Spec.Cttee on Monitoring 1971 and from 1965–
90 on var.nat.cttees on problems of envt.
Career: Asst, Asst Prof.1952–7, Sr Sci.1957–
90, Prof.& Head of Ecol.of Freshwater Communities Lab.& Hydrobiological station 'L.Glu-
bokoe' 1990–, Inst.for Animal Evol.Morphol.&
Ecol. Russian AS. **Achievements:** participation
in initial formulation of monitoring concept;
editing of several vols on envl appraisal (in
Russian); leadership in long-term limnol.prog.on
L.Glubokoe. **Publications:** *c*.200 books &
articles incl.vols of collected papers on ecol
appraisal (Ed.& co-Author) and The impact of
conventional war on natural areas of the USSR
1989, The Volga — A regn of ecol disaster 1992.
Indiff.to pers.pub.& news media support. **Languages:** English, Russian. Willing to act as con-
sult.etc. **Address:** Severodvinskaya 9–434,
Moscow 129224, Russia. **Tel.**(home) 7 095 476
5333; **fax** 7 095 954 5534.

SMITH, Professor Dr Keith. Hydroclimate variability, environmental hazards. Head, School
of Natural Sciences & Professor of Environmental Science. *B*.9 Jan.1938, Marple, England,
UK. British. *M*.Muriel Doris: *s*., *d*. **Education:** U.of Hull PhD 1964. **Experience:** academic. **Career:** Tutor of Geog. U.of Liverpool
1963–5; Lect.in Geog. U.of Durham 1965–70;
Sr Lect.in Geog.1971–5, Reader in Geog.
1975–82, Prof.of Geog.1982–6, U.of Strathclyde; Prof.of Envl Sci.1986–, Head of Sch.of Natural Scis 1994–, U.of Stirling. **Awards:** F.RSE,
Drapers' Co.Lect. (Australia). **Publications:**
Water in Britain 1972, *Principles of Applied
Climatology* 1975, *Human Adjustment to the
Flood Hazard* 1979, *Envl Hazards* 1992. Dislikes pers.pub.& news media support. **Language:** English. Willing to act as consult.etc.
Address: Department of Environmental Science, University of Stirling, Stirling FK9 4LA,
Scotland, UK. **Tel.**(office) 44 1786 467750.

SMITH, Kevin David. Nature conservation particularly forest, grassland, marine, & threatened,
species. Conservation Director. *B*.21 Nov.1953,
Taumarunui, NZ. New Zealander. *M*. Tania: *s*.,
2 *d*. **Education:** Canterbury U.(Christchurch,
NZ) BSc(Hons) 1973. **Experience:** forest ecol.;
publicist/advocate for Nature cons.; dev.& implementation of reserve proposals; negn of cons./
industry accords. **Career:** Asst in Indigenous

Forest Res., Forest Res.Inst. (Rotorua) 1974–5;
postgrad.work on indigenous forest ecol.
S.Westland 1976–8; Fur Trapper & Contract
Ecol.1979–84; W.Coast Field Officer 1984–9,
Cons.Dir 1989–, R.Forest & Bird Prot.Soc.of
NZ. **Achievements:** played leading role since
mid-1970s in NZ's cons.campaigns, highlights
include c.role in estab.of SW NZ World Heritage
Area, formation of Dept of Cons., and negn of
Forest Accord with industry. **Memberships:**
Native Forests Action Council (Chair of S.
Westland Branch 1979–83, Nat. Exec.
1980–84). **Award:** NZ Award (NZ Govt) 1990.
Publications: Rainforests of the South-West
1987, var.j.articles, num.scientific proposals for
estab.of specific reserves. Favours pers. pub.&
news media support. **Language:** English.
Further details may be obtained from *NZ Who's
Who* 1991. **Address:** Royal Forest & Bird
Protection Society of New Zealand, Box 631,
Wellington, New Zealand. **Tel.**(office) 64 4 385
7374, (home) 64 4 387 7711; **fax** 64 4 385 7373.

SMITH, Professor Dr Nigel John Harwood.
Conservation & management of natural re-
sources in the humid tropics, especially agri-
cultural resources; ethnobiology. Professor of
Geography. *B*.4 May 1949, Maracaibo, Vene-
zuela. American (naturalized). *M*.Lisa: 2 *d*., *s*.
Education: Eastbourne Coll.; UCB BA(Hons)
(Geog.) 1971, PhD(Geog.) 1976. **Experience:**
consult.on resource mgmt & cons.issues to
World Bank, USAID, CIAT Colombia, &
EMBRAPA. **Career:** Researcher in Cultural
Ecol. INPA 1976–80; Sr Researcher on renew-
able energy, Worldwatch Inst.1980; Assoc.Prof.
1981–6 & Prof.1986– Dept of Geog. U.of
Florida (Gainesville); Land-use Specialist, Latin
Amer.–Envt Div. World Bank 1993–4. **Achie-
vements:** Adv.to World Bank on land-use issues
& resource mgmt partic.in Amazonia. **Mem-
berships:** AAG, AIBS, AAAS. **Awards:** elec-
ted to membership of Cosmos Club 1985,
Guggenheim F.1986, F.LS 1991. **Publications:**
Man, Fishes and the Amazon 1981, *Rainforest
Corridors* 1982, *Genebanks and the World's
Food* (co-Author) 1987, *Networking in Intl
Agricl Res.*(co-Author) 1990, *Trop.Forests and
their Crops* (Sr Author) 1992. Favours pers.pub.
& news media support. **Languages:** English,
French (modest ability), Portuguese, Spanish
(fairly fluent). Willing to act as consult.etc.
Address: Department of Geography, University
of Florida, POB 117315, Gainesville, Florida
32611-7315, USA. **Tel.**1 904 392 0494; **fax** 1
904 392 8855.

SMITS, Dr Sir Willie. Tropical rain forests, Nature conservation, mycorrhizae, Orang-utans,
Dipterocarpaceae. Team Leader, Personal Ministerial Adviser. *B*.22 Feb.1957, Weurt, The
Netherlands. Dutch. *M*.Syennie: 3 *s*. **Education:** Agricl U.Wageningen, MSc 1981, PhD
1994. **Experience:** res., admin., consult.,
mgmt. **Career:** Team Leader, Intl Tropenbos-
Kalimantan Project, Min.of For.1987–; Pers.

Adv.to HE the Indonesian Minister of For. 1993–. **Achievements:** set up mass propagation & reforestation prog.with Dipterocarpaceae in SE Asia, developed largest-ever Orang-utan Cons.Prog. **Award:** Knighted by HRH Prince Bernhard of The Netherlands for cons.work 1984. **Publications:** Dipterocarpaceae: mycorrhyzae and regeneration 1994; 100+ others. Dislikes pers.pub., indiff.to news media support. **Languages:** Dayak (E.Kalimantan), Dutch, English, French, German, Indonesian, Spanish, Tombulu (N.Sulawesi). Willing to act as consult. etc. **Address:** Ministry of Forestry, c/o POB 319, Balikpapan 76103, Indonesia. **Tel.**(office) 62 542 22668, (home) 62 542 21404; **fax** 62 542 22640.

SMYTH, Professor Dr John Crocket. Environmental education particularly the development of national & local strategies. Emeritus Professor of Biology. *B.*21 March 1924, Edinburgh, Scotland, UK. British. *M.*Elizabeth Wallace: *s., d.* **Education:** George Watson's Coll.; U.of Edinburgh BSc(Zool.)(1st Class Hons) 1945, PhD 1948, Dip.Ed.1949. **Experience:** res.in coastal marine & estuarine ecol.; teaching & admin.in higher educ., curriculum dev.in biol educ. at sec.& tertiary levels, promotion & dev.of envl educ.; consult.to UNESCO–UNEP, UNCED Secretariat, & IUCN. **Career:** Vans Dunlop Scholar 1945–8, Asst.Lect.in Zool. 1949–53, U.of Edinburgh; Lect., Head of Dept & Prof.of Biol.1955–88, Emer.1988–, U.of Paisley (formerly Paisley Coll.). **Achievements:** Founding Memb.1977, Chairman 1983–91, Pres.1991–, SEEC; Chairman, Sec.of State for Scotland's WG on Envl Educ.1990–93; VP RZSS 1989–; Chairman, NW Europe Cttee of IUCN Comm.on Educ.1980–85; Countryside Commissioner for Scotland 1990–92. **Memberships:** F.IBiol., F.LS, F.RSA, BES, ZSL, MBA UK, SAMS. **Awards:** OBE 1985, Charter Award (I.Biol) 1989, Tree of Learning (IUCN) 1990, Hon.Prof. Dept of Envl Sci.(U.of Stirling). **Publications:** num.papers incl.The place of the envt in gen.educ.1983, Structuring envl educ.— a Strathclyde model (co-Author) 1984, What makes educ.envl? 1988; Learning to Survive with the Biosphere (co-Author) 1993. Indiff.to pers.pub.& news media support. **Languages:** English, French (read). Willing to act as consult.etc. **Address:** Glenpark, Johnstone PA5 0SP, Scotland, UK. **Tel.**(home) & **fax** 44 1505 320219.

SOARES DE CARVALHO, Prof. Dr G., *see* **CARVALHO, Prof. Dr G. SOARES DE.**

SOKOLOV, Professor Dr Vladimir. Biosphere reserves, Nature conservation; protection of endangered & disappearing species of mammals; biodiversity. Academician Secretary, Institute Director. *B.*1 Feb.1928, Moscow, Russia. Russian. *M.*Svetlana (bot.): *d.*Natalia (microbiol.). **Education:** Moscow SU 1945–50; Moscow Fur Inst. Cand.Sci.(Biol.) 1953, Dr Sci.(Biol.) 1964. **Experience:** res., teaching, admin., scientific leader of biol.expedns in Mongolia, Ethiopia,

Bolivia. **Career:** Asst Prof.1953–6, Lect.1956–7, Moscow Fishery Inst.; Sr Lect.1957–60, Docent 1960–65, Fac.of Biol. Moscow SU; Professor & Head of Vertebrate Zool.& Ecol.1965–, Dir Inst.of Ecol.& Evolutionary Problems 1967–, Head Dept of Gen.Biol.1985–, Head Trop.Dept 1988–, all Russian AS. **Achievements:** estab.of prot.areas, basic res.on Nature prot.; ecol.of endangered & disappearing animal species, biodiv. of animals; educ.in gen.zool.& ecol. **Memberships:** Mongolian AS, Polish AS, Acad.of Sci.& Arts of Bosnia & Herzogovina, IAZ, Indian NAS, Russian AS (Corres.Memb. 1970–74 & Full Memb.1974–), Russian MAB Cttee (Pres.), IUBS (VP), Theriological Soc. (Pres.1974–), Nat.Cttee on Russian Biol.(Pres. 1985–). **Awards:** Silver Medal (Cuban AS) 1972, Purkinje Medal (Czech.) 1978, Nord Star Orden (Mongolia) 1983, Karpinsky Preis (Germany) 1985, Ramdeo Medal (IES) 1988, Thomasius Medal (Germany) 1986, Pavlovsky Golden Medal (USSR AS) 1990. **Publications:** *c.*900 incl.books & monogrs — *Systematics of Mammalia* (3 vols) 1972, 1977, 1979, *Mammal Skin* 1973, 1982, *Dict.of Animal Names in Five Languages* 1984, *Rare & Endangered Mammals of the World* 1987, *Fauna of the World: Mammals* 1990, *Natural Reserves of C.Asia & Kasachstan* 1991, *Vertebrate Ecol.in Arid Zones* 1992, *Vertebrates of Caucasus* 1992, 1993, *At the Sources of Russian Theriology* 1993, *Mammal Fauna of Russia & Contiguous Countries* 1994. Favours pers.pub.& news media support. **Languages:** English, German (read), Russian. Willing to act as a consultant. **Address:** Leninskij Prospekt 33, 117071 Moscow, or Fersman Street 13, 117312 Moscow, Russia. **Tel.**(office) 7 095 952 7283 or 124 6000, (home) 7 095 202 0708; **fax** 7 095 954 5534; **e-mail** SEVIN@SOVAMSU SOVUSA.OOM .

SOLOMON, Professor Dr Allen M. Global ecology; Quaternary palaeoecology, palynology, plant ecology; vegetation geography, bioclimatology. Senior Research Global Ecologist. *B.*29 April 1943, Mt Clemens, Michigan, USA. American. *M.*Jean Marie Adamson (marine algal biol.). **Education:** U.of Michigan (Ann Arbor) BA(Biol.) 1965, Rutgers U. PhD(Bot.) 1970. **Experience:** admin.— lab.dir, project leader, & res.centre co-dir; teaching Quaternary palynology & biogeog., forest ecol.& forest biogeog. **Career:** Asst Prof. Geosci.& Dir Pollen Extraction Lab. U.of Arizona (Tucson) 1970–76; Res.Staff Ecol. ORNL 1976–87; Project Leader, Ecolly-sust.Dev.of The Biosphere, IIASA 1987–90; Prof.of Forest Ecol. Sch.of For. & co-Dir L.Superior Ecosystems Res.Center, Michigan Tech.U.1989–92; Sr Res.Global Ecol.& Project Leader of Global Veg.Redistribn Project, USEPA 1992–. **Achievements:** developed, tested, & applied, models of long-term climate–forest interactions at regnl & global scales at ORNL, assembled res.team and created global veg.models which are now IGBP departurepoint; created L.Superior Ecosystems Res.

Center; defined health constraints to ornamental plantings in desert areas. **Memberships:** ESA (Life), AMQUA, AAAS, AIBS, IAVS. **Publications:** *Toward Ecol Sust.in Europe* 1990, *Veg. Dynamics & Global Change* 1993; *c.*65 papers. Indiff.to pers.pub.& news media support. **Languages:** English, German (understood), Spanish (spoken). **Address:** Environmental Research Laboratory, United States Environmental Protection Agency, 200 SW 35th Street, Corvallis, Oregon 97333, USA. **Tel.**1 503 754 4772; **fax** 1 503 754 4799; **e-mail** solomon@heart.cor.epa.gov .

Song WANG, Professor, *see* **WANG, Professor Sung.**

SOPHONPANICH, Khunying* (Mrs) Chodchoy. Waste management, water pollution control; tree-planting directed at mass community level; anti-litter campaigning. Association President. *B.*7 Jan.1944, Bangkok, Thailand. Thai. *D.*: 3 *s., d.* **Education:** U.of Sydney BA(Econ.) 1965. **Career:** pioneered credit card industry in Thailand by way of founding & managing Diners' Club (Thailand) Ltd (the first credit card co.in Thailand) 1969; Founder & Pres. Thai Envl & Community Dev.Assn 1984–. **Achievements:** introduced 'Magic Eyes' campaign to create envl awareness of the masses by using advertising– marketing concept, together with educ.& community activities. **Awards:** Global 500 Roll of Honour (UNEP) 1987, *Royal Decoration (carrying title of 'Khunying'), 'Woman of the Year' 1991, many nat.awards for envt & admin. Favours continued news media support. **Languages:** English, Thai. **Address:** Thai Environmental & Community Development Association, 1508 Bangkok Bank Building (15th Floor), 333 Silom Road, Bangkok 10500, Thailand. **Tel.**66 2 231 4257; **fax** 66 2 236 8984.

SOTIRIADOU, Dr Victoria. Physical & urban environment protection and improvement; regional development policies at national & EEC levels. Secretary-General. *B.*8 Feb.1955, Greece. Greek. *M.*Stelios Kokkalas: 2 *d.* **Education:** Tech.U.of Athens, Arch.–Engr Dipl. 1979; Centre for Urban Res.(Paris), two postgrad.diplomas for res.on Urban Planning 1981 & 1983; U.of Sorbonne, M.(Regnl Planning & Urban Geog.) 1981, PhD(Urban & Regnl Planning 1986. **Experience:** res.on cons.policies for historic city centres & rundown c.urban areas, regnl dev.policies; admin.— nat.del.of Greece to OECD for envl affairs, participation in policymaking; spec.adv.to PM on envl affairs & regnl policies. **Career:** Memb.of Cttee for Cons.of Recent Monuments, Greek Min.of Culture & Civilization 1979 and of Greek Delegation to OECD 1981–6; Spec.Adv.to PM on envl affairs, regnl dev.policies, urban cons., & EEC regnl dev.fin.progs 1986–9; teaching urban & regnl policies at Public Admin.Nat.Sch. 1987–9; Dir, Direction for Regnl Dev.of Attica (Athens regn) 1989–90; Head of Div.for EEC Regnl Dev.Progs in Attica 1990–93; Sec.-Gen.for

Employment and the Mgmt of Euro.Funds Resources, Min.of Labour 1993–. **Achievements:** contributed to promoting coopn on envl affairs and to adopting OECD Decisions & Guidelines on var.specific envl aspects; influencing envl & urban cons.policies as well as reinforcing the awareness over the improvement & cons.of physical & man-made envt. **Memberships:** Tech.Chamber of Greece, Greek Urban & Regnl Planners' Assn, and Arch.s'– Engrs' Assn. **Awards:** Global 500 Roll of Honour (UNEP) 1988, Team Europe (CEEC). **Publications:** *Urban Renewal for Lasting Prosperity* (in Swedish) 1984, *Citizen Participation in Housing Cons.& Rehab.*1985, *An Intl Perspective on Urban Rehab.Partnerships* 1987, *Econ. Instruments: their Value & Complementarity as to Envl Prot.Regs* (Ed.) 1992, *Integrating Envl Concerns in Regnl Dev.Policies for 2000* 1995. Favours pers.pub.& news media support. **Languages:** English, French, Greek. Willing to act as consult.etc. **Address:** 73 Davaki Street, 156 69 Papagou, Athens, Greece. **Tel.**(office) 30 1 52 33146 or 49863, (home) 30 1 65 36741; **fax** 30 1 52 41977.

SOUTHWOOD, Professor Dr Sir (Thomas) Richard (Edmund). Ecology, entomology, environmental sciences & policy. Chairman, Pro-Vice-Chancellor & Professor of Zoology. *B.*20 June 1931, Northfleet, Kent, England, UK. British. *M.*Alison: *s.*Mark (Envl Consult.to Brit. Rail). **Education:** ICL BSc(1st Class), ARCS 1952; U.of London PhD 1955, DSc 1963; U.of Oxf. DSc 1987. **Experience:** res.in agricl envts & on natural succession, work with envl policy; teaching biol.& envl scis at under- & postgrad.levels. **Career:** ARC Res.Scholar, Rothamsted Experimental Station 1952–5; Res.Asst & Lect. ICL 1955–64; Reader in Insect Ecol. 1964–7, Prof.of Zool.& Applied Entomol 1967–9, U.of London; Linacre Prof.of Zool.1979–93, Prof.of Zool.1993–, V.-Chancellor-elect & Pro-V.-Chancellor 1987–9, V.-Chancellor 1989–93, Pro-V.-Chancellor 1993–, U.of Oxf.; num.addit. academic, vis., & public, appointments. **Achievements:** R.Comm.on Envl Poll.(Memb.1974– 86, Chairman 1981–6 [Reports 9, 10, 11]); NRPB (Memb.1980–, Chairman 1985–); Trustee, Brit. Mus.(Natural Hist.) 1974–83 (Chairman of Bd 1980–83), A.D.White Prof.-at-Large, Cornell U.1985–91. **Memberships:** RS (F.1977), Pontifical AS 1992, Acadamea Europaea, US NAS (Foreign 1988), AAAS 1981, NASL 1987, BES (Pres.1976–8, Hon.Memb.1988) Edl Bds *Entomologists' Monthly, Biol J.of the LS, J.Envl Law.* **Awards:** KB 1984, Cavaliere Ufficiale (Rep.of Italy) 1991, Ordem de Merito (II) (Rep. of Portugal) 1993, Forbes Medal 1952, and Huxley Medal 1962 (both ICL), Scientific Medal (ZSL) 1969, Gold Medal Zool.(LS) 1988, Hon. Degrees at Griffith, Lund, E.Anglia, McGill, Warwick, London, Liverpool, Oxf.Brookes, Bristol, Durham, Sussex, & Victoria, Univs. **Publications:** *Land & Water Bugs of the Brit. Isles* (co-Author) 1959, *Life of the Wayside & Woodland* 1963,

Ecol Methods (transl.into Chinese & Hungarian) 1966, 1978, *Insects of Plants* (co-Author) 1984, *Insect Abundance* (co-Ed.) 1968, *Insects & Plant Surfaces* (co-Ed.) 1986, *Radiation & Health: The Biol Effects of Low-Level Exposure to Ionizing Radiation* (co-Ed.) 1987; num.public lectures, papers & reports. Generally dislikes pers.pub., indiff.to news media support. **Languages:** English, French (moderate). **Address:** Animal Behaviour Research Group, Department of Zoology, The University, Oxford OX1 2JD, England, UK. **Tel.**44 1865 271280 or 271234; **fax** 44 1865 310447.

SPATE, Andrew 'Andy' Philip. Conservation & management of caves, karst & cave biota; antarctic geomorphology & limnology; impacts of human use of antarctic & alpine environments. Senior Scientific Officer. *B.*12 Dec.1946, London, England, UK. Australian. Father O.H.K.Spate, Fndn Prof.of Geog.and Dir of Res.Sch.of Pacific Studies, ANU 1951–79. *M.*Janet A.: 2 *s.*, 2 *d.* **Education:** U.of Canberra, B.(Applied Sci.) 1971. **Experience:** res. in many areas of Australia, and the Antarctic (austral summers of 1986–7, 1988–9, & 1992– 3); consult.in Australia, NZ, & SE Asia; admin.& land mgmt of nat.parks & other natural lands in Australia & NZ. **Career:** Res.Officer, Div.of Land Use Res. CSIRO 1971–81; SO 1981–5, SSO 1985– NSW NPWS. **Achievements:** founding of ACKMA 1987, estab.of professional Cave & Karst Mgmt Standards in Australia & NZ; baseline estab.of envl data to assess human impacts on antarctic envts. **Memberships:** ACKMA, ASF, BCI, BCRA, SRC. **Awards:** F.(ASF) 1977, F. (ACKMA) 1992. **Publications:** *c.*120 papers, consultative & other reports, incl.The micro-erosion meter: use and limitations (co-Author) 1985, Envl impacts of station dev.in the Larsemann Hills, Princess Elizabeth Land, Antarctica (co-Author) 1992, Do cavers have an impact? (co-Author) 1992, Cavers' impacts — some theoretical and applied considerations (co-Author) 1993. Indiff.to pers.pub., favours news media support. **Language:** English. Willing to act as consult., etc. **Address:** New South Wales National Parks & Wildlife Service, POB 452, Queanbeyan, New South Wales 1620, Australia. **Tel.**(office) 61 6 297 6144, (home) 61 6 230 2322; **fax** 61 6 299 6858.

SPECHT, Professor Dr Raymond Louis. Plant ecology, biogeography, conservation; history of Australian ecology; ethnobotany. Emeritus Professor of Botany, Honorary Research Fellow. *B.*19 July 1924, Adelaide, S.Australia, Australia. Australian. *M.*Marion Mary (mangrove & soil zool., Field Officer for Matriculation Biol.in Qld for Australian AS 1969–82): *d.*Dr Alison (growth dynamics and cons.of plant communities in Australia). Grandfather Carl Specht, hort.of *Gladiolus* in S.Australia (*Brit.Gladiolus Annual* 1933–9). **Education:** U.of Adelaide, BSc(Hons) 1946, MSc 1949, PhD 1953, DSc 1974. **Experience:** community-physiol.res.in

growth dynamics and biodiv.(per ha) 1946– and cons.survey 1965– of Australian plant communities; convergent evol.of structure and biodiv. (per ha) in Medit.-climate ecosystems, and heathlands (and related shrublands) on nutrient-poor soils, both throughout the world; Gondwanan origin of veg.of Australia and biogeog.; ethnobot.of Australian aborigines. **Career:** Grassland Ecol. Wait Agricl Res.Inst.(Adelaide) 1947; Bot./Plant Ecol. Amer.–Australian Scientific Expedn to Arnhem Land Aboriginal Reserve (NT) 1948; Lect./Sr Lect.in Bot. U.of Adelaide 1949–60; Reader in Plant Ecol. U.of Melbourne 1961–5; Prof.of Bot.1966–89, Emer. 1989–, U.of Qld; Hon.Res.F. Southern Cross U.1991–. **Achievements:** Australian veg. (1946–) — the community-physiol.processes controlling growth, structure, and biodiv.(per ha and per 1° latitude–longitude grid), and cons. survey of plant communities and rare & endangered species; Cons.Atlas of Australian Plant Communities 1995; eco-physiol.of Medit.-climate ecosystems of the world 1981, 1988; heathlands (and related shrublands) of the world — ecol.and dynamics 1979, 1981; hist.of ecol res.in Australia 1981. **Memberships:** ANZAAS, AIAS, AES, APPS, ACF, WWF Australia, R.Socs of Qld, S.Australia, & Vic., ISME. **Awards:** Fulbright, Smith-Mundt, & Carnegie, grants to USA 1956, Verco Medal (RS of S.Australia) 1961, Nuffield Fndn Commonwealth Bursary (RS) 1964, Res.Medal (RS of Vic.) 1976, Fulbright Sr Scholar Award 1983, Disting.Memb.Award (ISME) 1987, Australian–Greek Travel Award 1991. **Publications:** incl. *Plant Ecol., Bot.& Zool.of Arnhem Land* 1958, 1964, *Veg.of S.Australia* 1972, *Cons.Survey of Australia* 1974, 1995, Plant Biogeog.of Australia (Coord.) 1981, *Hist.of Ecol.in Australia* 1981, *Heathlands of the World* 1979, 1981, *Medit.-climate Ecosystems of the World* 1981, 1988, Biodiv.in Australia (1988–95) of plant species (per ha), plant communities (per 1° latitude–longitude grid), and of vertebrates (per plant community), *Late Cretaceous Veg.of Se Australia* 1992, Biogeogl *Regns in Australia* 1994, 1995. Indiff.to pers.pub.& news media support. **Languages:** English, French (read). Further details may be obtained from *Who's Who in Australia* 1994. **Address:** 107 Central Avenue, St Lucia, Queensland 4067, Australia. **Tel.&** **fax** (home) 61 7 870 2240.

SPENCER, Jonathan William. Nature conservation; forest ecology, silviculture; conservation of rare plants; historical ecology and landscape history. Conservation Officer. *B.*11 Aug.1956, Wokingham, Berks., England, UK. British. *M.* Sarah L.Fowler *qv: s.* **Education:** Forest Grammar Sch.; E.Berks Coll.of Further Educ.1972–4, U.of Nottingham BSc(Zool.& Bot.) 1977. **Experience:** writing, consult., promotion of Nature cons., teaching, training. **Career:** Res. Asst, Genetics Dept, U.of Camb.1979–81; Woodland Ecol. NCC Huntingdon 1981–9; Cons. Officer, Thames and Chilterns Team, English

Nature (formerly NCC for England). **Achievement:** compilation of Inventory*. **Memberships:** BSBI, BES, RFS, MCS, NSWA, OSME, Sail Training Assn, Wash Wader Ringing Group, var.Co.Naturalists' Trusts, Plantlife (Bd). **Publications:** *An Inventory of Ancient Woodland for England and Wales 1992, *Tilia cordata* Miller [the] Small-leaved Lime 1993, The rehab.of storm-damaged woods (co-Ed.) 1994, To What Extent Can We Recreate Woodland? 1995. **Languages:** English, Spanish (spoken). Willing to act as consult.etc. **Address:** 123 Greenham Road, Newbury, Berkshire RG14 7JE, England, UK. **Tel.**(office) 44 1635 268881, (home) 44 1635 580632.

SPETH, Professor James Gustave. Environmental sustainability and sustainable human development. Administrator. *B.*4 March 1942, Orangeburg, SC, USA. American. *M.* Caroline Cameron Council: *d.*, 2 *s.* **Education:** Yale U. BA *summa cum laude* 1964, LLB 1969; U.of Oxf. MLitt(Econ.) 1966; DC Bar 1969. **Experience:** Memb.then Chairman, CEQ in Exec.Office of Pres.1977–81; Founding Pres. WRI 1982–; organized Western Hemisphere Dialogue on Envt & Dev.which led to agreement on seminal 'Compact for a New World'; Chaired US Task Force on Intl Dev.& Envl Security 1991. **Career:** Law Clerk, US Supreme Court 1969–70; Sr Staff Attorney, NRDC 1970–77; Memb.CEQ 1977–9, Chairman 1979–81; Prof. of Law, Georgetown U.Law Center 1981–2; Pres.WRI 1982–93; Admin.UNDP and Under-Sec.Gen. UN 1993–. **Achievements:** Bd of Dirs of Cttee for Envt & Energy Study Inst., Envt Law Inst.NRDC, SC Coastal Cons.League, Global Envt Forum (Japan), Woods Hole Res. Centre. **Memberships:** Council on Foreign Relations (NYC), China Council for Intl Coopn on Envt & Dev. **Awards:** Rhodes Scholar at Oxf.1964–6, Resources Defence Award (NWF) 1976, Global 500 Roll of Honour (UNEP) 1988, Barbara Swain Award of Honour (Amer.NRC) 1992. **Publications:** Coming to terms: toward a north–south compact 1990, Envl security for the 1990s 1990, A post-Rio compact 1992, A new US prog.for intl dev.& the global envt 1992. **Language:** English. **Address:** The Administrator, United Nations Development Programme, 1 UN Plaza, New York, NY 10017, USA. **Tel.**1 212 906 5791; **fax** 1 212 906 5778.

SPINAGE, Dr Clive Alfred. African mammal ecology; planning & development of national parks & game reserves; wildlife legislation. Retired. *B.*24 June 1933, Carshalton, Surrey, England, UK. British. **Education:** U.of London, BSc (Spec.)(Zool.)(1st Class) 1963, PhD(Ecol.) 1968, DSc 1989. **Experience:** field & lab.res. mainly in Africa; dev.project planning & implementation of nat.parks & game reserves in Africa; botl & mammal surveys; teaching Wardens. **Career:** Scientific Asst UKAEA 1949–50 & EAAFRO 1956–60; NATO Res.F'ship, Uganda 1964–7; Ecol.to Rwanda Nat.Parks,

ODA 1968–9; FAO — Lect. Coll.of African Wildlife Mgmt 1971–5, Sr Wildlife Adv. C. African Rep.1975–82 & Burkina Faso 1982–4, Tech.Expert, Dept of Wildlife & Nat.Parks, Botswana 1986–91. **Achievements:** teaching of many present Wardens in African parks & reserves; background dev.of nat.parks in C. African Rep.; revision of Botswana wildlife legis.; recognized auth.on large African mammals. **Memberships:** F.ZS, F.IBiol., BES. **Publications:** *A Territorial Antelope: The Uganda Waterbuck* 1982, *Natural Hist.Antelopes* 1986, *Hist.& Evol.of the Fauna Cons.Laws of Botswana* 1991, *Elephants* 1994; 40 major papers. **Languages:** English, French (poor written, fair spoken), Kiswahili (poor). Willing to act as consult.etc. **Address:** Wickwood House, Stanford Road, Faringdon, Oxfordshire SN7 8EZ, England, UK. **Tel.**(home) & **fax** 44 1367 242338.

SPRINGUEL, Professor Dr Irina. Desert plant ecology, desert environment; conservation of Nature. Professor of Botany. *B.*2 April 1944, St Petersburg (then Leningrad), Russia. Egyptian, Russian. *M.*Prof.Belal Ahmed (physics, envt, cons.): 2 *s.* **Education:** Leningrad SU BSc 1964; Assiut U. MSc 1976, PhD 1981. **Experience:** preparing soil maps of s.part of Siberia (Russia) and veg.maps of Euro. part of Russia; class.of Nile Valley and desert veg.of Upper Egypt; cons.of desert & riparian ecosystems, sust.dev.of arid lands. **Career:** Asst Lect. Leningrad SU 1964–8; Researcher, Lab.of Air Methods, USSR AS 1969–70; Lect.1981–6, Prof.& Head 1986–, Bot.Dept Assiut U.at Aswan. **Achievements:** init.envl movement in Upper Egypt, estab.of two cons.areas in Aswan Governate and project on sust.dev.in W.Allagi (L.Nasser area). **Memberships:** EBS, BES, IGU (Corres.). **Award:** Global 500 Roll of Honour (UNEP) 1988. **Publications:** incl. Strat. analysis of submerged lake macrophyte communities: an intl example 1990, Plant communities in s.part of Eastern Desert (Arabian Desert) of Egypt 1991, Sust.dev.& resource mgmt in marginal envts: natural resources and their use in the Wadi Allaqui regn of Egypt 1993. Indiff.to pers.pub.& news media support. **Languages:** Arabic (spoken), English, Russian. Willing to act as consult.&/or ref. **Address:** Department of Botany, Faculty of Science, The University, Aswan, Egypt. **Tel.**(office) 20 97 480446 or 7, (home) 20 97 324442; **fax** 20 97 312760.

SRINIVASAN, Dr Kandadai. Research & teaching in environmentally-acceptable refrigeration and air-conditioning. Associate Professor. *B.*1 July 1947, Anantapur, Kar., India. Indian. *M.*Dr Bhavani: *s.*, *d.* **Education:** Sri Venkateswara U. BE 1968, IIT MS 1974, U.of London DIC 1980, ANU PhD 1982. **Experience:** 14 yrs' teaching & res., four yrs' engg. **Career:** Trainee, Atomic Energy Centre 1968–9; Engr, ISRO 1969–75; Pool Officer 1980–82, Asst Prof. 1982–7, IIT; Asst then Assoc.Prof. IISc 1987–. **Achievement:** res.on envlly-acceptable refrigerants. **Memberships:** F.IEAust., ASME, IIR (Assoc.). **Publications:** 47 j.pubns incl.11 single-authored. Indiff.to pers.pub., favours news media support. **Languages:** English, several Indian languages, Russian (working knowledge). Willing to act as consult.etc. **Address:** Department of Mechanical Engineering, Indian Institute of Science, Bangalore 560 012, Karnataka, India. **Tel.**91 80 334 4411 ext.2589; **fax** 91 80 334 1683.

STALTER, Professor Dr Richard. Research in plant ecology. Professor of Biology. *B.*16 Jan. 1942, Montvale, NJ, USA. American. *D.*: *d.* **Education:** Rutgers U. BS 1963, U.of S.Carolina, PhD 1968. **Experience:** res.— plant ecol., physiol.ecol., floristic inventories; consult.to Cabot Corpn (MA) & Southern Engg (GA). **Career:** Asst Prof.of Biol. High Point Coll.(NC) 1968–9 & Pfeiffer Coll.(NC) 1969–70; S.Carolina Poll.Control Auth.1970–71; Lect.in Biol. 1971–83, Prof.of Biol.1983–, St John's U.(NY). **Achievement:** pubn*. **Memberships:** Southern Appalachian Botl Club, Torrey Botl Club, Long Is.Botl Soc., Northeastern Weed Sci.Soc., Assn of Se Biologists, S.Carolina AS. **Award:** Sigma Xi. **Publications:** **Barrier Is.Bot.*1993, 100+ chapters & articles. **Language:** English. Further details may be obtained from *Who's Who in Amer.Sci.& Engg* 1995. **Address:** Department of Biology, St John's University, Jamaica, New York 11439, USA. **Tel.**1 718 990 6269; **fax** 1 718 380 8543.

STANFORD, Professor Dr Jack Arthur. Limnology; ground-water ecology; river ecology & life-histories of aquatic insects. Professor of Ecology & Biological Station Director. *B.*18 Feb.1947, Delta, CO, USA. American. Father LeRoy Sunderland Stanford, farmer & ecologist. *M.*Bonnie K.Ellis (microbial ecol.): 2 *s.* **Education:** CSU, BS(Fisheries Sci.) 1969, MS (Limnol.) 1971; U.of Utah, PhD(Limnol.) 1975. **Experience:** extensive res.& teaching, for 20+ yrs emphasis on former has been on 22,241 km² Flathead River–Lake ecocomplexes in Montana & BC; supervision of 25 grad.students. **Career:** Fisheries Biol. Alaska Dept of Fish & Game 1968–9; Res.Biol.& Instructor, U.of Montana 1973–4; Asst & Assoc.Prof. Dept of Biol Sci. N.Texas SU 1974–80; Dir, Flathead Lake Biol Station 1980– & Jessie M.Bierman Prof.of Ecol. U.of Montana 1986–. **Achievements:** helped cons.efforts on w.lakes & streams; contributed to recovery of endangered aquatic fauna; provided principles for stream resto. **Memberships:** ISTAL, ASLO, ESA, NABS, AAAS, AIBS, Sigma Xi. **Awards:** F'ship (Nordic Council for Ecol.) 1980, Disting.& Endowed Prof'ship (U.of Montana) 1986, F'ship (Fndn for Res.Dev. RSA) 1989, Golden Trout Award for Professional Service (W.Slope Chapter, Trout Unlimited) 1991. **Publications:** *Freshwater Imperative: A Res.Agenda* (co-Ed.) 1995, Ecol connectivity in alluvial river ecosystems & its disruption by flow regulation (co-Author) 1995, Freshwater ecosystems & their mgmt: a nat.initiative 1995.

Indiff.to pers.pub.& news media support. **Languages:** English, German (read). Further details may be obtained from *Groundwater Ecol.*1994. Willing to act as consultant.etc. **Address:** Flathead Lake Biological Station, The University of Montana, 311 Bio Station Lane, Polson, Montana 59860-9659, USA. **Tel.**1 406 982 3301; **fax** 1 406 982 3201.

STANLEY PRICE, Dr Mark Rangeley, *see* PRICE, Dr Mark Rangeley STANLEY.

STANTON, James Peter. Habitat management in protected areas, surveys for the assessment of natural resources. Principal Conservation Officer. *B.*23 April 1940, Brisbane, Qld, Australia. Australian. *M.*Karen. **Education:** U.of Qld BS (Agric.) 1962, Australian For.Sch. Dipl.of For. 1962. **Experience:** tech.& admin.— involved in nat.park mgmt as part of Dept of For.duties since 1964 and currently longest-serving Nat. Parks officer still working in Qld. **Career:** tech. & admin.posts, Qld Dept of For.incl.seven yrs in Nat.Parks Branch (second professional person appointed) 1963–74; private consult.1975–6; Regnl Dir, Qld NPWS 1981–9; Prin.Cons. Officer, Qld Dept of Envt & Cons.1989–. **Achievements:** carried out alone systematic resource surveys that led to creation of large area of nat.parks in Qld, first person to put assessment of potential nat.park areas over large part of the State on a systematic basis; first Regnl Dir apponted to Qld NPWS. **Membership:** IFA. **Award:** Fred M.Packard Intl Parks Merit Award (IUCN) 1982. **Publications:** *A Prelim.Assessment of Wetlands in Qld* 1975, *Nat.Parks for Cape York Peninsula* 1976, *The Rapid Selection & Appraisal of Key & Endangered Sites: The Qld Case Study* 1977. Indiff.to pers.pub.& news media support. **Languages:** English, high-sch. French. Willing to act as consult.etc. **Address:** PO Redlynch, Queensland 4879, Australia. **Tel.** (office) 61 70 534310, (home) 61 70 391022.

STANTON, Professor Dr W.Robert. Tropical Southeast Asian wetlands agroforestry for staple foods, particularly starches; fermentation — in tropical food & by-product recovery, nutritional improvement, waste treatment, and pollution control. Private Consultant. *B.*24 Feb.1923, Hampstead, London, England, UK. British. *M.*Dr Tan Koonlin *qv*: 2 *s.* (1 deceased), *d.* **Education:** U.of Reading BSc(Agric.spec. Hort.) 1944, U.of London PhD 1952. **Experience:** over 50 yrs in pursuit of applied plant sci., mainly food & microbiol., 30 yrs of which have been connected with the tropics, mainly W.Africa & SE Asia. **Career:** Adv.Officer, E.Riding of Yorks. 1944–5; SO (ARC Scholar), Long Ashton Res.Station 1945–8, and John Innes Inst.1948–52; SSO (HMOCS), W.African Maize Res.Unit 1952–7; PSO (Sr Bot. HMOCS) Min.of Agric.(N.Nigeria) 1957–62; Lect.in Biol. U.of London 1962; Sr Lect. Head of Plant Sci.& sometime Dean, 1963–4, Prof.of Bot. 1970–78, U.of Malaya; FAO Contract resulting in book*

1964–5, Head of Dept of Microbiol.(PSO) 1965–70, Trop.Products Inst.London (now NRI, Min.of Overseas Dev.); Guest Prof. Technische Universität (Graz) 1976–7; Private Consult.to Agro-industry, Malaysia 1978–83; Private Consult.& Author 1983–. **Achievements:** *promoted* (i) study of diverse indigenous coarse grains & grain legumes in W.Africa, (ii) over the course of two decades, the revival of ancient sago industry of SE Asia — using sago culture as a supreme example of a sust.form of trop.agro-for., supplying food & other needs of local people in many parts of the regn, (iii) study of applied microbiol.to cons.of foods, recovery of food wastes, and exploitation of these systems to reduce food industry poll.in SE Asia, after founding the continuing series of workshops throughout the regn under auspices of UNEP, UNESCO, ICRO, (iv) since 1972 the concept that 'good prod.& process design in trop.agro-industry' may help in both care for envt & profitability of enterprise; *founded & developed* the 50 ha Botanic Gdns of U.of Malaya and promoted the cons., cataloguing, study, & partic. use, of rainforest plants & trees, thus saving a bot.dept from extinction; *holder* of patents & process know-how on thermophilic fermentation treatment in vegetable-oil recovery from process lines partic.with application to palm & other vegetable oils, and on microbial methods for treatment of starchy wastes for recovery & enrichment of products for use as animal feed. **Memberships:** F.IBiol.(Life), CBiol., F.IFST (Life), Edl Bd *Bioresource Tech.* **Awards:** travelled in Europe (e.& Russia), Africa, Latin & N.Amer., India & Far E. under UN, Brit.Council, RS, FAO, ODA, EC, with Japanese & other funding. **Publications:** **Grain Legumes in Africa 1966* (French edn 1967), *Waste Recovery by Microorganisms* 1974, *Synthesis, Progress, Policy & Regnl Collab.*(Closing Address) 1977, *The Equatorial Swamp as a Natural Resource* (co-Author) 1980, *Global Impacts of Applied Microbiol.*(co-Author) 1981; Trop.fermented foods 1993, Have your trees and eat them 1993, Tableaux for conf.on *Food: Now and in the Next Fifty Years* 1993. Favours pers.pub.as necessary evil to attract funds and the critical reaction of other people, dislikes news media support as one is normally mis-reported. **Languages:** English, French, German (limited written), Malay/Indonesian (limited written). Willing to act as consult.etc. **Address:** 73 Stanbury, Keighley, West Yorkshire BD22 0HA, England, UK. **Tel.** (home) 44 1535 643482; **fax** 44 1535 643748.

STAPP, Professor Dr William B. Environmental education. Programme Director. *B.*17 June 1929, Cleveland, OH, USA. American. *M.*Gloria Lou: 2 *s., d.* **Education:** U.of Michigan, BA(Educ.) 1951, MA(Biol.) 1958, PhD(Natural Resources) 1963. **Experience:** project direction, teaching, and consults, during career appointments; membership of num.cttees and bds of dirs. **Career:** several Instr./Adv. posts 1951–63; Lect. Dept of Cons. U.of Michi-

gan 1963–4; co-Founder, Citizens' Assn for Area Planning 1968–70; Dir of Envl Educ. UNESCO 1974–6; Vis.Prof. Huxley Coll.of Envl Studies 1978; Prof.of Natural Resources, Sch.of Natural Resources and Envt 1963–94; Dir, Global Rivers Envl Educ.Prog.1989–, U.of Michigan. **Achievements:** first Dir of UNESCO's Envl Educ.Prog.; Founder of GREEN 1989. **Memberships:** NAAEE, ANSA, IUCN. **Awards:** Global 500 Roll of Honour 1992 and Outstanding Leadership 1993 (UNEP), Spec. Recognition (IUCN) 1993, Bronze Medal (US EPA) 1994; num.nat. **Publications:** 15 books incl.*An Action Curriculum Toward Resolving Hazardous Materials Issues* (co-Author) 1988, *Field Manual for Water Qual.Monitoring: an Envl Educ.Prog.for Schools* seventh edn 1993; num. chapters incl.A Creative Way of Educating Children: A Watershed Prog.Designed to Improve Water Qual., Educ.and Lives of People 1992; much audio-visual material 1967– incl. What is Envl Educ.(video) 1990; *c.*190 articles. Fervently favours news media support on envl matters. **Languages:** English, French. Further details may be obtained from *Who's Who in Amer.*1990. Willing to act as consult.etc. **Address:** School of Natural Resources and Environment, University of Michigan, Ann Arbor, Michigan 48109-1115, USA. **Tel.**1 313 761 4845; **fax** 1 313 936 2195; **e-mail** bstapp-@umich.edu .

STAWICKI, Dr Henryk. Natural & cultural landscape conservation in spatial planning. Studio Chief. *B.*17 April 1926, Turek, Poland. Polish. *M.*Alina: *d.* **Education:** Acad.of Fine Arts 1948–52, Wrocklaw U.of Tech. MSc (Eng.Arch.) 1955; Warsaw U.of Tech. PhD 1984. **Experience:** res.on buffer zones & nat. parks' cons.strat.; planning cultural & natural heritage cons.in c.Poland; design of plans for cultural areas. **Career:** Town Planner, Kielce Town Council 1955–64; Head, Natural Cons. Office, Voievodship Council 1964–84; Chief, Studio for Cultural Landscape (Kielce) 1984–. **Achievements:** project & realization of mgmt plans of quarries; strat.model of Świ⊤ókrzyski Nat.Park cons.(incl.realization in the buffer zone), cons.plans for natural & cultural heritage in the Kamienna R.valley. **Memberships:** Polish Town Planners' Soc., IUCN CESP, Intl Cttee for Regnl Arch.1992, Comm.of Świ⊤ó-krzyski Nat.Park. **Awards:** Press Award, four Min.awards of 1st & 2nd degree. **Publications:** three books incl.*Synthesis of Cultural Values of Heritage of Sandomierz Province* 1991, *From Saratoga to Raclawice — Studies of the Landscape of Battlefields* (in Polish & English) 1994; 35 papers incl.Landscape of battlefields of Saratoga (co-Author) 1993. Indiff.to pers.pub., favours news media support. **Languages:** English (fair), German, Polish. Willing to act as consult. **Address:** Pracownia Krajobrazu Kulturowego (Studio for Cultural Landscape), ul.Sienkiewicza 59, 25-002 Kielce, Poland. **Tel.** (office) 48 41 683086, (home) 48 41 614585; **fax** 48 41 622087.

STEINNES, Professor Dr Eiliv. Behaviour of trace-elements in the natural environment; long-range atmospheric transport of metals & other pollutants; soil chemistry, radioecology, chemical speciation. Professor of Environmental Science. *B*.21 Sept.1938, Elverum, Norway. Norwegian. *M*.Randi: 3 *d*. **Education:** U.of Oslo, Cand.real.(Nuclear Chem.) 1963, Dr Philos. (Analytical Chem.) 1972. **Experience:** widespread res., teaching, res.supervision, lab. mgmt, u.leadership. **Career:** Res.Sci.1964, Section Head 1969, Div.Head 1978, Norwegian Inst.of Atomic Energy; Prof.of Envl Sci.1980–, Assoc. Dean 1981–4, Rector 1984–90, Coll.of Arts & Sci. U.of Trondheim. **Achievements:** scientific contribns in neutron activation analysis; trace element speciation in natural waters; heavy-metals in terr.systems; organized large-scale studies of envl contamination. **Memberships:** NASL, RNSSL, NATS, NSSS (Pres. 1982–6), IUPAC Comm.V–7 (Memb.1971–85, Chairman 1981–3, Nat.Rep.1985–). **Publications:** Activation Analysis in Geochem.& Cosmochemistry (co-Ed.) 1970, Trace Elements in Natural Waters (co-Ed.) 1994; *c*.350 scientific papers. **Languages:** English, Danish (basic), French (limited), German (basic), Norwegian, Swedish (basic). Willing to act as consult.etc. **Address:** Department of Chemistry, College of Arts & Science, University of Trondheim, N-7055 Dragvoll, Norway. **Tel.**(office) 47 73 596237, (home) 47 73 529990; **fax** 47 73 596240.

STEPHENSON, Dr Peter J. Management of conservation & development projects, conservation management planning; conservation biology of tropical mammals. Programme Officer. *B*.27 Oct.1965, Abingdon, Berks., England, UK. British. **Education:** R.Holloway & Bedford New Coll. BSc(Zool.)(1st Class Hons) 1987, U.of Aberdeen PhD 1992. **Experience:** res.— published extensively on mammals (esp.Insectivora) in Madagascar; consult.— prod.of mgmt plan* for WWF Intl; tech.— managing & planning cons.& dev.projects in Africa. **Career:** Area SO, Scottish Natural Heritage 1992; Cons.Consult. WWF Africa & Madagascar Prog. 1993–4; Prog.Officer, WWF Country Office for Tanzania 1994–. **Achievements:** studied effects of human disturbance on rainforest ecosystems in Madagascar; veg.mapping in Cairngorms Nat.Nature Reserve, Scotland; author of first mgmt plan* for a Zaire Nature reserve. **Membership:** BES, IUCN SSC Insectivore, Tree-Shrew & Elephant-Shrew SG (Sec.). **Awards:** Prize for academic achievement (R. Holloway & Bedford New Coll.) 1987, Hon. Postdoctl Res.F. (U.of Aberdeen) 1991–3. **Publications:** *Okapi Wildlife Reserve, Zaire: Mgmt Guidelines* 1994 & *Operational Guidelines* 1994; *c*.20 scientific papers. Favours pers.pub.& news media support. **Languages:** English, French, KiSwahili (conversation). Willing to act as consult.etc. **Address:** WWF Country Office for Tanzania, POB 63117, Dar es Salaam, Tanzania. **Tel.**255 51 22664/28468; **fax** 255 51 46232.

STEWART, John MASSEY. Russian, particularly Siberian, environment. Freelance Writer, Lecturer, Consultant, Environmental Activist, Photographer. *B*.16 Dec.1932, Nottingham, England, UK. British. *M*.Penelope Norah Lynex: *d*., *s*. **Education:** Stowe Sch.; Trinity Coll. Camb. BA 1956, MA 1967. **Experience:** IUCN rep.: envl problems of W.Siberian indigenous peoples field trip 1992, USSR State Dept (Goskompriroda) project proposals prep.(Moscow) 1992, World Bank ecotourism project, L.Baikal watershed 1994, Organizing Cttee of NATO Advanced Res.Workshop on Baikal Regn Sust.Dev.(Ulan-Ude) 1994; Specialist Adv.to House of Commons Envt Cttee 'Poll.in Eastern Europe' (UK envl aid progs to c.& e. Europe incl.former Soviet Union) 1995; num. articles, lecturing world-wide, writing, consults. **Career:** freelance writing, journalism; Founder, London Initiative on the Russian Envt 1993–. **Memberships:** LS (formerly on Bicentenary Cttee), RIIA, RSAA (former Hon.Librarian), RGS, FFPS, ZSL, GB–USSR Assn (former, Exec. Council) now Britain–Russia Centre (Counc.), Intl Centre for Socio-Ecol Problems in the Baikal Basin (Founding), Edl Bd *Siberian Ecol J.* (*Novosibirsk*). **Publications:** incl. *Across The Russias* (travel book) 1969, *Baikal: On the Brink?* (booklet) 1991, *The Soviet Envt: Problems, Policies & Politics* (Ed.) 1992, *The Nature of Russia* 1992. Dislikes pers.pub., favours news media support. **Languages:** English, French (fair), German (some), Italian (some), Russian (good). Willing to act as consult.etc. **Address:** 20 Hillway, London N6 6QA, England, UK. **Tel.**(office) 44 181 341 3544, (home) 44 181 341 35544; **fax** 44 181 341 5292.

STEWART, Professor John Wray Black. Interrelationships between C/N/S/P biogeochemical cycles as influenced by anthropogenic activities. Professor of Soil Science, College Dean. *B*.16 Jan.1936, Coleraine, Northern Ireland, UK. Canadian. Father John Wray Stewart, farmer. *M*.F.Ann P.: *s*., *d*.Hannah Louise (marine biol.). **Education:** Queen's U.(Belfast, NI), BSc(Hons)(Chem.) 1958, BAgr(Hons) (Agricl Chem.) 1959, PhD(Soil Sci.) 1963, DSc 1988. **Experience:** res., teaching, & extension, in soil fertility, nutrient cycling, envl & sust. agric.; coordn of activities of fac.& res.scis (*c*.400) and progs of *c*.1,000 under- & post-grad.students. **Career:** Asst Prof.1966–70, Assoc.Prof.1970–76, & Prof. (tenured) 1976–81 in Dept of Soil Sci., Prof.& Head of Dept of Soil Sci.and Dir of Sask.Inst.of Pedology 1981–9, Dean of Coll.of Agric.1989–, U.of Sask.; Grant Selection Cttee of Food & Agric. NSERC Canada 1985–9, Chair of Canada Cttee on Land Resource Services 1986–9, Cttee Memb.of Terr. Atmos.Cttee of Canadian IGBP 1989–91, Canadian Global Change Prog.(RSC) 1991– and Canadian Global Change Res./Policy Cttee 1994–; VC of Cttee III of ISSS 1986–90, Pres.of SCOPE 1992–, Memb.of Bd of Trustees (Ibadan) 1991 and Chair of Prog.Cttee 1993–, of

IITA, Memb.of Scientific Adv.Cttee of Inter-Amer.Inst.for Global Change Res.1994–. **Achievements:** early studies in P and S cycling in agroecosystems led to documentation & dev. of conceptual and predictive mathl simulation models of P and S cycling in soil–plant systems and have progressed to exam.of sust.of land in trop.& temperate regns under diff.systems of mgmt; use of this info.in predicting effects of climatic & land-use changes on ecosystem properties; current work ranges from exam.of controls on trace-gas emission in n.wetlands to exam.of soil qual.in tropics using key elements as indicators. **Memberships:** Canadian (Pres. 1984–5), British, Brazilian, & Intl, Socs of Soil Sci., Agric.Inst.of Canada, ASA, AAAS, SCOPE. **Awards:** F.of — Canadian Soc.of Soil Sci.1987, Berlin Inst.for Advanced Study 1989–90, ASA 1990, & SSSA 1990. **Publications:** three books, 25 chapters incl.Interrelation of Carbon, Nitrogen, Sulphur, and Phosphorus, Cycles during Decomposition Processes in Soil 1984, Grasslands into Deserts? (co-Author) 1990, Global Cycles (co-Author) 1992, Innovative Phosphorus Availability Indices: Assessing Organic Phosphorus (co-Author) 1994; 145+ others. Dislikes pers.pub., favours news media support. **Languages:** English, French, Portuguese. Willing to act as consult.etc. **Address:** College of Agriculture, University of Saskatchewan, Saskatoon S7N 0W0, Canada. **Tel.** (office) 1 306 966 4050, (home) 1 306 653 3437; **fax** 1 306 966 8894.

STEWART, Philip J. Ecology of meaning & religion. Lecturer in Human Ecology. *B.*8 Jan. 1939, London, England, UK. British. *M. Lucile:* 3 *s.*incl.Christopher (zool.), 2 *d.* **Education:** U.Coll.Oxf. BA(Arabic) 1961, MA(For.) 1965. **Experience:** eight yrs in Islamic countries in forest cons.& rural dev.; res.into effect of Islam on land use; subs.study of other religions. **Career:** Statistical Officer, FAO Geneva & Rome 1965–6; Res.Officer, Algerian Forest Service 1967–71; Lect.in For. Instituts de Technologie Agricole, & Nat.Agronomique, Algeria, 1971–4; Vis.F. Inst.of Dev.Studies, U.of Sussex 1974–5; Lect.in Human Ecol. Pauling Human Scis Centre, U.of Oxf.1975–. **Endeavour:** attempt to construct a unified theory of phys.& mental ecol. **Membership:** CHEC. **Award:** Brunel Lect.(BA) 1983. **Publications:** *Islamic Law as a Factor of Grazing Mgmt: the Pilgrimage Sacrifice* (Cong.Proc.) 1978, Towards a new world pattern of land-use 1984, Life Between Greenhouse & Icebox 1990. Would tolerate pers.pub.& news media support. **Languages:** Arabic, English, French, German. Willing to act as consult.etc. **Address:** Pauling Human Sciences Centre, 58 Banbury Road, Oxford OX2 6QS, England, UK. **Tel.**44 1865 274704; **fax** 44 1865 274699.

STIRTON, Dr Charles H. Plant systematics especially of Leguminosae, Verbenaceae, and petaloid monocotyledons; biology of weeds,

evolutionary biology of plants and plant biogeography & conservation. Deputy Director (Science), Freelance Journalist. *B.*25 Nov.1946, Pietermaritzburg, Rep.of SA. British. *M.*Jana (phytochem., flavonoids of Commeliaceae): *d.* **Education:** U.of Natal BSc 1972, BSc(Hons) 1973, MSc*(cum laude)* 1975; U.of Cape Town PhD* 1989. **Experience:** widespread res.in systematics of legumes, weeds (*Lantana camara, Rubus* spp.), breeding systems, hybridization & cons.; consult.on plant biodiv.& hortl taxonomy; teaching microevol., pollination biol., legume biol., communications in sci., plant cons.biol., data analysis in systematics, macroevol., plant diversity; admin. **Career:** Res. Botl Res.Inst.(SA) 1975–82; S.African Liaison Bot. 1978–80, B.A.Krukoff Botanist for Legume Res.1982–7, Econ.Bot.(Shell F'ship) 1990–92, Dep.Dir, Science 1992–, R.Botanic Gdns, Kew; Chief Professional Officer, Botl Res.Inst. Dept of Agric.(SA) 1979–82; Assoc.Prof.& Head of Systematic Bot. U.of Natal 1988–90; Freelance Journalist 1990–. **Achievements:** Chairman & Founder ENVIRAC (Envl Action Cttee, U.of Natal), Pres.& Founder Natal Evol.Biol.Soc., gave probable first course in Africa on Plant Cons.Biol., cons.analysis of 110 African 'Psoraleoid' legumes, identification of invasive plants as major threat to biodiv. **Memberships:** Systematics Assn, Rainforest Club, BSB, SBNH, LS, Anglo–Brazilian Soc., SAAB, IAPT, ESSA. **Awards:** MIMgmt, CBiol., M.IBiol., F.LS, B.A.Krukoff Legume Res.F'ship, Hon.Life Memb.of Natal Evol.Biol.Soc., Shell Econ. Bot.F'ship, *SAAB Jr Medal for best PhD thesis in SA 1989, Hon.SRF (U.of Birmingham). **Publications:** *Plant Invaders — Beautiful but Dangerous* (Ed.) 1978, *Advances in Legume Systematics* Part 3 (Ed.) 1987, *Advances in Legume Biol.*(Ed.) 1990, *A Catalogue of Problem Plants in S.Africa* (co-Author) 1986; 83 papers. Indiff.to but recognizes need for pers. pub., favours news media support if it promotes bot.& Kew Gdns. **Languages:** Afrikaans, English; Dutch, Flemish, Portuguese & Spanish (read, some spoken); Latin (read); Czech & Zulu (some). Willing to act as consult.etc. **Address:** Directorate, Royal Botanic Gardens, Kew, Richmond, Surrey TW9 3AB, England, UK. **Tel.**(office) 44 181 332 5120, (home) 44 181 940 8428; **fax** 44 181 948 4237.

STOBAUGH, Professor Dr Robert Blair. Business education. Business Executive. *B.*15 Oct. 1927, McGehee, AR, USA. American. *M.*1.Beverly P.(deceased): 3 *s., d.*; 2.June M. **Education:** Louisiana SU, BS(Chem.Eng.) 1947; Harvard U.Bus.Sch. Doct.in Bus.Admin. 1968. **Experience:** Adv.Bd Instituto de Estudios Superiores de la Empresa 1973–80, co-Chairman The Dumbarton Oaks Symp.on Energy Efficiency 1979, Dir Alliance to Save Energy 1979–94, Expert Testifier (Cong.), Adv.to cabinet-level depts of White House & UN. **Career:** Refinery Engr, Exxon Corpn 1947–52; Engg Mgr, Caltex Oil Co.1952–9; Mgr Econ.Eval. Monsanto Co.

1959–65; Lect.1967–70, Assoc.Prof.1970–71, Prof.1972–83, Charles E.Wilson Prof.1984–, Chairman Doctl Progs 1984–9, Dir Energy Project 1972–83, Chairman Prod.& Ops Mgmt Area 1981–3, Harvard Business Sch.; Dir Ashland Oil Inc., Nat.Convenience Stores & Amer.Intl Petroleum, Chairman of Adv.Bd to Pres. Montedison 1981–7. **Achievements:** directed Energy Project at Harvard Bus.Sch.which produced first nat.best-seller book by that School's fac.namely *Energy Future: The Report of the Energy Project at the Harvard Bus.Sch.* **Memberships:** F.Acad. of Intl Bus.(Pres.1979–80), Council on Foreign Relations, AEA. **Award:** Hall of Dist. (Louisiana SU). **Publications:** *Money in the Multinat.Enterprise* (co-Author) 1973, *Nine Investments Abroad and Their Impact at Home* 1976, *Energy Future* (co-Author) 1979, *Tech. Crossing Borders* (co-Ed.) 1984, *Innovation & Competition* 1988. **Language:** English. Willing to act as consult.etc. **Address:** Harvard Business School, Soldiers Field Road, Boston, Massachusetts 02163, USA. **Tel.**1 617 495 6296; **fax** 1 617 496 4059.

STOIBER, Dr Hans Helmut. Nature conservation; description & evaluation of protected areas. Owning Managing Director. *B.*11 Oct. 1918, Zell am See, Salzburg, Austria. Austrian. *M.*Dr Ingrid Stoiber-Adler: 3 s. **Education:** U. of Vienna, Doctor juris 1949. **Experience:** Nature cons., nat.park planning esp.legal aspects. **Career:** Judge 1950–53, 1965–70; Lawyer 1953–65; Public Attorney 1965–70; 'Consulary' of the Nat.Park Hohe Tauern Comm.1971 & 1973; Professor by title (*H.C.*), Nat.Economy Dept, U.of Salzburg 1975–95. **Achievements:** estab. of Hohe Tauern Nat.Park, integration of Austria into the intl NPPA Network. **Memberships:** IUCN CNPPA, FNNPE. **Awards:** Prof.*H.C.* (Pres.of Rep.of Austria) 1992, Consulary on Envl Questions (Govt of Upper Austria) 1994. **Publications:** booklets on *Flowers of Salzburg* 1970 and *Slovenia* 1985, *Index of Upper Austrian Cons.Law* 1965, Problems of establishing alpine nat.parks in Austria (esp.Alm = alpine pasture) 1992. Indiff.to pers.pub.& news media support. **Languages:** English (good), German, Italian (poor). Willing to act as consult.etc. **Address:** Mailbox 132, A-5010 Salzburg, Austria. **Tel.**43 662 841389; **fax** 43 6432 8723.

STONE, Peter Bennet. Environment — international affairs & communication; mountain conservation. Editor-in-Chief. *B.*6 July 1933, Chadderton, Lancs., England, UK. British. *M.* Jennifer J.: 2 *d.* **Education:** Chadderton Grammar Sch.; Balliol Coll. Oxf.(Open Scholar) BA(Hons Geol.) & MA 1951. **Experience:** communications — BBC TV producer, sci.corres., Sr Info.Adv.& Ed.-in-Chief in UN; writing — articles, books, scripts. **Career:** Seaman Officer, RN 1955–7; Producer, BBC TV 1957–64; Sci.Corres.1964–70; Sr Info.Adv. UN Conf.on Envt 1972; Founder & Ed.-in-Chief, UN *Dev.Forum* 1972–83; Info.Dir, Brundtland Comm.1986; Ed.-

in-Chief *Mtn Agenda* 1990–. **Achievements:** worked to communicate envt & sust.dev. concerns at intl level 1968–; media work with scientific bias, popularizer. **Memberships:** F. RGS, F.GS, IMS, Alpine Club. **Publications:** *Japan Surges Ahead* 1967, *The Gt Ocean Business* 1971, *Did We Save the Earth at Stockholm?* 1973, *The State of the World's Mtns* 1992. Likes pers.pub., and favours news media support. **Languages:** English, French. Willing to act as consult. etc. **Address:** 6 Eyot Green, Chiswick Mall, London W4 2GT, England, UK. **Tel.**44 181 994 7342.

STRAHM, Dr Wendy Ann. Conservation; Mascarene Island botany, invasive species. Plants' Officer. *B.*3 March 1959, NY, USA. American, Swiss. **Education:** Oberlin Coll.(Ohio), BSc (Hons)(Biol.) 1981; U.of Reading, PhD(Bot.) 1994. **Experience:** res.in forest dynamics and taxonomy, forest mgmt, plant cons.in Mauritius & Rodrigues (Indian Ocean). **Career:** Project Leader, WWF 1983–93; Plants' Officer, Species' Survival Prog. IUCN 1993–. **Achievements:** dev.of plant cons.prog.in Mauritius & Rodrigues, strengthening global plant cons.network. **Membership:** IUCN Reintro.SG. **Award:** Watson F'ship (Watson Fndn) 1981. **Publications:** incl.*Plant Red Data Book for Rodrigues* 1989. Indiff.to pers.pub.& news media support. **Languages:** Creole (spoken), English, French, German (read). May be willing to act as consult.etc. **Address:** IUCN-World Conservation Union, Rue Mauverney 28, 1196 Gland, Switzerland. **Tel.**41 22 999 0157, (home) 41 21 808 7645; **fax** 41 22 999 0015.

STRASBERG, Dr Dominique. Conservation biology of rare plants, plant ecology, alien plants' invasion. Scientific Coordinator. *B.*6 Oct.1965, Autur, France. French. **Education:** U.of Dijon, Agricl Engr 1987; U.of Montpellier, PhD 1994. **Experience:** res.in plant ecol.& reproductive biol., teaching plant biol.and community & pop.biol. **Career:** Lect.in Biol.& Ecol. Université de La Réunion 1988–94; Scientific Coord. Conservatoire et Jardin Botanique de Mascarin 1994–. **Achievements:** setting-up WWF-project of cons.of plant species & their habitats on La Réunion Is., monitoring biodiv. plots in La Réunion rain-forests. **Memberships:** ESA, ATB. **Publications:** five papers. Dislikes pers.pub., cautious re.news media support. **Languages:** English, French. Willing to ref.papers. **Address:** Conservatoire et Jardin Botanique de Mascarin, Les Colimaçons, 97436 Saint-Leu, La Réunion, France. **Tel.**(office) 262 249227, (home) 262 411322; **fax** 262 248563.

STRONACH, Dr Neil Richard Hemsworth. Wildlife, wildlands and protected-area conservation management; management of vegetation fire. Freelance Ecological Consultant. *B.*9 Nov.1956, Tabora, Tanzania. British, Irish. Father late Brian Stronach (former Tsetse Officer, Game Warden, & Wildlife Coll.Instr., in

Tanzania; waterfowl res., Dir Wildlife Res. Ireland). *M*.Rosemary: 2 *d*. **Education:** St Columba's Coll.(entrance exhibitioner); Trinity Coll. Dublin BA(Mod.)(Zool.)(1st Class) 1979, St John's Coll.Camb. PhD(Fire Ecol.) 1990. **Experience:** res.— fire ecol., mammalian pops, bird biogeog.; tech.— project leader in cons. mgmt: fire mgmt in prot.areas; large mammal cons., Man–wildlife conflicts, mgmt planning, game ranching; admin.— project mgmt & planning, running own consult.business; consult.— fire mgmt, large mammal cons., range mgmt, prot.area mgmt, Man–wildlife conflict, project planning & eval.; teaching — on-the-job training of prot.areas' field staff, undergrad./ postgrad./wildlife wardens' courses in fire & wildlife mgmt. **Career:** Deer Farm Mgr, Dept of Primary Industry, PNG 1979–82; self-employed Wildlife Consult.in Ireland 1982–4; Fire Ecol. Serengeti Nat.Park 1985–7; WWF Consult. Selous Game Reserve 1990–93; self-employed Consult.1993–. **Achievements:** implementing & advising on wildlife cons.mgmt in developing countries esp.prot.areas, intro.of practical fire mgmt to several prot.areas in E.Africa, promotion of benefits from wildlife to local people, reduction in Man–wildlife conflict, basic res.in fire ecol., sig.contribns to knowledge of local avifaunas in Africa & New Guinea. **Memberships:** BOU, BOC. **Awards:** Exhibitioner (St Columba's Coll.) 1970, Bronze Medal (R. Dublin Soc., Texaco Award) 1967, Fndn Scholar (Trinity Coll.Dublin) 1977, Robert Gardiner Mem.Scholar (Camb.U.) 1984–7. **Publications:** num.papers and four wildlife TV films *e.g.The Long Shoreline* 1983, *Wild Ireland* 1984. Indiff. to pers.pub., favours news media support. **Languages:** English, French (basic), Irish Gaelic (basic written), Kiswahili (fluent spoken, basic written). Willing to act as consult.etc. **Address:** c/o Mrs S.Piggins, Clogher, Westport, County Mayo, Ireland. **Tel.**(office & home) 353 98 27590.

STRONG, Maurice F. Environmental administration; farming. Federation & Corporation President, Society Director, Council Chairman, Senior Adviser. *B*.29 April 1929, Oak Lake, Man., Canada. Canadian. *D*.: 2 *s*., 2 *d*.; *M*.Hanne: *foster-d.* **Education:** Oak Lake (Man.) High Sch. **Experience:** Memb. Intl Adv.Bd of Unisystems Corpn; Bd of Bretton Woods Cttee; Dir of Massey Ferguson (Canada); Chairman & Spec. Adv. Intl Energy Dev.Corpn (Geneva, Switzerland) 1980–83; Chairman of Canada Dev.Investment Corpn 1982–4; Memb. WCED; co-Chairman of Interaction Policy Bd (Vienna, Austria); Alternate Governor of IBRD, ADB & Carib.Dev.Bank; Chairman of North–South Energy Roundtable, Washington (DC) & Rome; Adv.Cttee of UNU; Dir, Memb.of Exec.Cttee, & VC, of Canada Dev.Corpn, Lindisfarne Assoc.; dir or memb.of num.business & cons.groups in Canada & intlly. **Career:** served in UN Secretariat 1947; worked in industry and Pres.or Dir of var.Canadian & intl corpns 1948–66; DG,

External Aid Office (later CIDA), Canadian Govt 1966–71; Chief Exec. Intl Conf.on Human Envt (Stockholm, Sweden) 1971–2; Chairman, Centre for Intl Mgmt Studies (Geneva, Switzerland) 1971–8; Exec.Dir, UNEP 1973–5; Pres., Chairman of Bd & of Exec.Cttee, Petro-Canada 1976–8; Pres. Stronat Investments Ltd 1976–80; Bd of Govs, IDRC 1977–8; Chairman of Bd, Strouest Holdings Inc., Procor Inc.1978–9 & AZL Resources Inc.(USA) 1978–83; VC & Dir, Société Générale pour l'Energie et les Ressources (Geneva, Switzerland) 1980–86; Under-Sec.-Gen. UN & Exec.Coord. UN Office for Emergency Ops in Africa 1985–7 & 1989; Chairman, Amer.Water Dev.Inc.1986–9; Pres. World Fedn of UN Assns 1987– & Baca Corpn; Dir, Better World Soc.1988–; Chairman, World Economic Forum Council 1988–; Sec.–Gen. UNCED 1990–92; Chairman, Ont.Hydro 1992–5; Sr Adv.to Pres.of World Bank 1996–. **Memberships:** F.RSA, Intl Asia Soc.(NY), Rockefeller Fndn (Trustee 1971–8), Aspen Inst. (Trustee 1971–), IFDA (Trustee); num.hon. degrees from univs & colls in Canada, USA, and UK. **Awards:** OC 1976, F.RSC 1987, Intl Award (Onassis Fndn) 1993, F.RS, Memb.of Queen's Privy Council for Canada. **Publications:** articles in var.journals. **Languages:** English, French. Further details may be obtained from Canadian *Who's Who* 1995, *Intl Who's Who* 1994–5. **Address:** Environmental Capital Corporation, 207 Queen's Quay West Suite 510, Toronto, Ontario M5J 1A7, Canada. **Tel.**1 416 203 8535; **fax** 1 416 203 7837.

STUTZIN, Godofredo. Environmental law; conservation of fauna & flora. Retired writer & conservation worker. *B*.21 Sept.1917, Darmstadt, Germany. Chilean. *M*.Nora: 2 *s*.incl. Miguel (vet., VP CODEFF). **Education:** U.of Chile, Attorney-at-Law 1946. **Experience/Career:** 45 yrs' law practice (retired 1986), 40 yrs' writing about, talking on, & working for, Nature cons., Pres.of Honour CODEFF 1968–. **Achievements:** Founder Chilean Nature cons. movement, Org.of CODEFF (the main cons. instn in Chile). **Memberships:** IUCN CEL & SSC, ICEL, APROFA (Chilean Branch of IPPF), IUCN Exec.Council (former memb.). **Award:** Global 500 Roll of Honour (UNEP) 1990. **Publications:** *Presencia San Francisco* I & II, *Ausencia San Francisco* 1974, 1979, 1990, *Es war einmal eine schone Welt* (poetry) 1992, Die Natur der Rechte und die Rechte der Natur 1980, Un inperativo ecológico: reconocer los derechos de la naturaleza 1984, A task for the law: re-establishing the ecol balance 1993. Indiff.to pers.pub., favours news media support. **Languages:** English, French, German, Spanish. **Address:** Camino El Alto 17220, Arrayán, Santiago 52, Chile. **Tel.** 562 217 1643; **fax** 562 696 8562.

SU, Professor Dr Jilan. Coastal oceanography, marine environmental science. Professor. *B*.31 Dec.1935, Hunan, PRC. Chinese. *M*.Lily: *s*., *d*. **Education:** Nat.Taiwan U. BSc 1957, VPI MSc

1961, UCB PhD 1967. **Experience:** res., teaching. **Career:** Acting Instr. Mech.Engg Dept, U. of Calif.1967; Asst Prof.& Assoc.Prof. Engg Sci. Dept, SUNY 1967–74; Jt Tsunami Res.Effort (vis.) Hawaii Inst.of Geophys.1971–2; Assoc. Prof. Ocean Engg Dept, Florida Atlantic U. 1974–80 (tenured in 1977); Vis.1979–80, Assoc. Prof.& Prof. Estuarine & Coastal Scis Div. 1980–, Second Inst.of Oceanogr., State Oceanic Admin. **Achievements:** basic res.on coastal circulation, estuarine circulation, & suspended matter transport; memb. var.IOC-sponsored cttees & groups of experts; co-opted memb.Exec.Cttee ICSU/SCOR 1988–92; Acting Chairman 1991–2, Chairman 1993–, IOC/WESTPAC; VC IOC 1993–; Memb.Chinese AS; Memb.Edl Bd 1982–8, Ed. in Chief 1989 *Acta Oceanologica Sinica*; Memb.Edl Bd *Oceanologia et Limnologia* 1989– and *Marine Geodesy* 1993–. **Memberships:** AGU, CSO. **Awards:** Tau Beta Phi, Sigma Xi. **Publications:** 80+ refereed papers (50+ in English). Dislikes pers. pub., indiff.to news media support. **Languages:** Chinese, English. Willing to act as consult.etc. **Address:** Second Institute of Oceanography, State Oceanic Administration, Hangzhou, Zhejiang 310012, People's Republic of China. **Tel.** (office) 86 571 807 6924; **fax** 86 571 807 1539.

SUBRAMANIAN, Professor Dr Tarakad Viswanathan. Environmental engineering, environment (bio)technology, clean technology, detoxification of hazardous wastes, environmental preservation using biotechnology. Professor of Chemical Engineering. *B.*4 Aug.1941, Madras, TN, India. Indian. **Education:** Madras U. BSc(Tech.)(Chem.Eng.) 1963, M.Tech. (Plant Design Stream) 1968, PhD(Chem.Eng.) 1974; Max Mueller Bhawan, Dipl.in French (Dist.) 1959, Cert.in German 1960. **Experience:** training in statl methods on chem.tcch. res., chem.reaction, bioengg, detoxification techniques monitoring & developments, polymer sci.& tech., biol & biogeochemical engg for resource recovery; 32 yrs' res.& teaching; attendance at several intl confs with invited & active participation, num.contacts with industry, res.& dev.projects; many academic positions held incl.Academic Counc.(Anna U.) and Evaluator for Scientific Projects for Govt of India. **Career:** Shift Engr, Min.of Defence, Govt of India 1963–4; Reader in Chem.Engg & Tech.1976–84, Professor of Chem.Engg for Related Developments, Dept of Chem.Engg & Related Studies 1985–, Anna U; Vis.F. Univs of Camb., Birmingham, Manchester, & Surrey 1986; Vis.Prof. Dept of Chem.Engg Scis, U.of Alcala (Spain) 1995–6. **Achievements:** co-dev. of biochem.sensors, res. in chem.& biodegradative approaches. **Memberships:** IICE (Assoc.), Task Force in Biochem. Engg (Govt of India), C.Alert Group (Govt of India). **Award:** Exchange Prog.F.(INSA–RS) 1986. **Publications:** num.papers incl.Waste recycling and reuse (co-Author) 1982, Poll.control and envirohygiene (co-Author) 1991, Hazard assessment and prevention methodologies 1992,

Chernobyl five years and later 1993, Conservation of aquatic environment by treating polluted wastes and waters 1995. Not averse to constructive pub. **Languages:** English, French, German, Hindi, Tamil. Willing to act as consult.etc. **Address:** Department of Chemical Engineering & Related Studies, Alagappa Chettiar College of Technology, Anna University, Madras 600 020, Tamil Nadu, India. **Tel.**91 44 235 1323; **fax** 91 44 415856.

SUETT, David L. Analytical & environmental chemistry; applied entomology. Principal Research Scientist. *B.*18 April 1937, Birkenhead, England, UK. British. *M.*Shelagh M.: *s., d.* **Education:** Lic.R.Inst.Chem.(by exam.) 1964, C.Chem., MRSC 1976. **Experience:** res.— insecticide behaviour in soils & plants, correlation with biol.efficacy, residue analysis; tech.— pesticide application tech.(treatment of seeds, of plant propagation modules); admin.— coordn of CEC-funded projects (concerted action and shared cost); consult.to IAEA. **Career:** Analytical Chemist, Chemical Microbiol.Dept, Nat.Inst.for Res.in Dairying 1963–6; Res.Sci. (Res. Leader in envl & analytical chem.) 1966– 77, Sr Res.Sci.1977–89, Prin.Res.Sci.1989–, Dept of Entomol. HRI. **Achievement:** fundamental res. on behaviour & efficacy of insecticides in soils & plants and on pesticide application to seeds & soils. **Memberships:** RSC, IBiol., AAB. **Award:** Churchill F.1986. **Publications:** *c.*30 major incl.Fate, distribn and biol performance of insecticide residues in vegetable crops following seedling treatment 1986, Enhanced insecticide degradation in soil — implications for effective pest control 1991, Stability of accelerated degradation of soil-applied insecticides: lab.behaviour ... in relation to their efficacy ... in previously-treated field soils 1993; *c.*40 others. Indiff.to pers.pub., favours news media support. **Languages:** English, French (indiff.). Willing to act as consult.etc. **Address:** Department of Entomology, Horticulture Research International, Wellesbourne, Warwickshire, England, UK. **Tel.**(office) 44 1789 470382, (home) 44 1926 493138; **fax** 44 1789 470552.

SUGIMURA, Dr Ken. Forest landscape management particularly for conservation of ecosystems; wildlife conservation & ecology. Head, Landscape Management Laboratory. *B.*9 May 1953, Tokyo, Japan. Japanese. *M.*Kumiko: 2 *s.* **Education:** Kyoto U. BSc 1978, Washington SU MS 1980, UCD MS 1982, U.of Hawaii PhD 1987. **Experience:** res.— public survey of forest envl cons., wildlife ecol.& cons.on southeastern Islands of Japan; consult. on riparian ecosystem mgmt; teaching biol.at BSc-level. **Career:** Researcher, JWRC 1980; consult.to Japan Bureau of Construction 1988–9; Lect. Kanagawa U. 1989–90; Researcher & Head, Landscape Mgmt Lab. JNIFS 1990–. **Achievements:** res.on methodologies of zoning forest landscapes for ecosystem mgmt, and on cons.of endangered species of wildlife. **Mem-**

berships: JFS, MSJ, CEIS (Japan), IUCN Lagomorph SG. **Awards:** Foreign Student Award (Washington SU & U.of Calif.), Student Grant (E–W Center). **Publications:** *c.*30 incl.Upsurge of envl concern and the current attitude towards cons.in Japan 1990, Landscape mgmt of the Arashiyama Nat.Forest, Kyoto, Japan: an eval.of alternatives 1992, Eval.of forest functions by local people: dev.of a res.method 1993. Favours pers.pub.& news media support. **Languages:** English, Japanese. Willing to act as consult.& judge proposals. **Address:** Forestry & Forest Products Research Institute, Kansai Research Centre, National Institute of Forest Sciences, Momoyama, Fushimi, Kyoto 612, Japan. **Tel.**(office) 81 75 711 1201, (home) 81 75 612 8928; **fax** 81 75 611 1207.

SULAYEM, Mohammad Saud Abdulaziz. Protected areas' planning & management; biodiversity conservation & management; conservation planning. Department Director. *B.* 23 Feb. 1954, Riyadh, Saudi Arabia. Saudi Arabian. *M.* Zakyah Shalhoub (geog.): *d.* **Education:** Calif. SU, BA(Spec.)(Envl Studies) 1984. **Experience:** orgn & supervision of survey field teams, co-org.& leader of two expedns to N.Africa to study Houbara Bustard *(Chlamydotis undulata)* habitat & breeding, co-coord.of work which led to estab.of System Plan for Prot.Areas in Saudi Arabia, working with NCWCD on estab.of its first prot.area followed by 14 others, and further such areas. **Career:** Researcher, Dept of Natural Resources, Met.and Envl Prot.Admin.(Jeddah) 1984– 6; Dir, Dept of Areas Planning, NCWCD 1986–. **Achievements:** participation in estab.of NCWCD in 1986 and exp.gained therefrom, rep. of NCWCD at many nat.& intl events. **Memberships:** IUCN CNPPA (Regnl VC for N. Africa and Middle E.1991–) and Regnl Counc. for W.Asia 1993–; Saudi Arabian Del.to Kenya & Bahamas Biodiv.Convs, both 1994. **Publications:** num.papers for nat.& intl journals & confs. Favours news media support. **Languages:** Arabic, English. Willing to act as consult. etc. **Address:** National Commission for Wildlife Conservation and Development, POB 1141, Riyadh 11431, Saudi Arabia. **Tel.**(office) & **fax** 966 1 441 8413, (home) 966 1 421 3012.

SULLIVAN, Francis. Forest conservation & certification, sustainable forest management. Forest Conservation Officer. *B.*6 March 1963, London, England, UK. British. *M.*Jackie. **Education:** U.of Oxf. BA(Hons)(Agric.& Forest Scis) 1985, MSc(For.and Its Relation to Land Use) 1986. **Experience:** seven yrs working on forest cons.field projects and policy role, WWF 1995 Group. **Career:** Forest Cons.Officer, WWF (UK) 1988–. **Achievements:** estab. of WWF 1995 Group and Forest Stewardship Council. **Membership:** RGS. **Publications:** incl.The Earth Summit Agreement 1993. Favours pers.pub.& news media support. **Languages:** English, French (spoken). Willing to act as consult.etc. **Address:** World Wide Fund for

Nature (UK), Weyside Park, Godalming, Surrey GU7 1XR, England, UK. **Tel.**44 1483 426444; **fax** 44 1483 426409.

SULTANA, Joe. Ornithology; Nature conservation. Environment Department Manager. *B.*11 Nov.1939, Gozo, Malta. Maltese. *M.*Lucy: *d.* Ruth (Council Memb. Malta Ornithl Soc.), *s.* **Education:** Lyceum Sec.Sch.(Gozo), St Michael's Teachers' Training Coll.1959–61. **Experience:** res.in ornith., govt & non-govt admin., envl educ., conf orgn. **Career:** Primary Sch.Teacher 1961–9; Sec.Sch. Sci.Teacher 1969– 77; Mgr of Field Studies Centre, Dept of Educ. 1977–80; Envt Officer (Cons.) 1981–92, Bd Memb.of Planning Auth.1992– and Envt Mgr (Reserves, Sites, & Habitats) of Envt Prot. Dept. 1993–, Govt of Malta. **Achievements:** co-creator of bird prot.laws 1980 & 1993, setting-up of first Maltese Nature reserve 1980, BTO bird-ringing scheme, pubns. **Memberships:** Bird-Life Intl (World Council Memb. 1994– when ICBP, Chairman of Malta Branch and Euro. Continental Section 1985–92), BOU, Malta Ornithl Soc.(Sec.1967–75, Pres. 1976–87). **Publications:** several books incl. *l'Aghsafar* (sr Author, in Maltese) 1976, *A New Guide to the Birds of Malta* (sr Author) 1982, *Important Sea Birds Sites in the Medit.*1993, *Flora u Fawna ta'Malta* (Ed.& co-Author) 1995. Indiff.to pers. pub., favours news media support re.believed principles. **Languages:** English, Maltese. Further details may be obtained from *Profiles in Action* (ICBP), Winter 1986. Willing to act as consult.etc. **Address:** 3 Sciberras Flats, Fleur-de-Lys Junction, B'kara Bkr 02, Malta. **Tel.** (office) 356 231782 or 895 or 232022, (home) 356 440278 or 561267; **fax** 356 241378 or 225665.

SUN, Professor Lin. Earth's climate. Centre Director. *B.*4 March 1934, Hubei, China. Chinese. *M.*Tongwein Li. **Education:** Shanghai Inst.of Foreign Languages 1953, Beijing Inst.for Intl Studies (equivalent to PhD[Intl Studies]) 1975. **Experience:** exp.& convictions in fields of cons.& envt are with regard to care of the Earth's envt for the benefit of present & future generations; this has become and will continue to be an increasingly pressing challenge for the World to face through the next century; intl law & global partnerships are two factors which are of crucial importance in mtg this challenge; as an intl lawyer & negotiator, has contributed and will continue to contribute to the further dev.& effective implementation of intl envl law through legal knowledge, practical exp., and diplomatic skills, to further global partnerships which address these pressing envl issues. **Career:** Assoc.Res.F.(1975–81), Dep.Dir Dept of Intl Law (1981–3), Beijing Inst.for Intl Studies; Legal Adv. Chinese Perm.Mission to the UN in NY 1983–8; Dep.Dir then Dir, Treaty & Law Dept, Min.of Foreign Affairs 1988–92; Prof.of Intl Law at China U.of Pol.Sci.& Law 1988–, Law Sch.of Wuhan U.1988–, and Foreign Affairs Coll.1988–; Dir.ELI/PAC, UNEP 1992–.

Achievements: Chief Negotiator, Head of Chinese Del., Chinese Govt, during sessions of Intergovtl Negotiating Cttee for a Framework Conv.on Climate Change 1991–2; Head, Chinese Del.to sessions of Antarctic Treaty Consult.Mtg leading to adoption of protocol in Prot.of the Antarctic Envt 1990, 1991, signing Protocol on behalf of Chinese Govt; Legal Adv. Chinese Govt Del.to UNCED; Chairman, Beijing Symp.on Developing Countries and Intl Envl Law 1991; participated actively in mtg of UNEP Group of Legal Experts to examine the implications of the Common Concern of Mankind Concept on Global Envl Issues 1991, and the Second Mtg of Sr Govt Officials Expert in Envl Law to review the implementation and further dev.of UNEP's 1981 Montevideo Prog. for the further dev.and periodic review of Envl Law; Experts' Mtg on Legal Aspects of a Conv. on Desert.sponsored by IAE (Geneva) 1993. **Memberships:** Chinese Soc.of Intl Law (VC); Exec.Memb. Chinese Soc of Law & China Assn of Envl Prot.Industry; Arbitration Cttee of PRC; Chinese Cttee of Polar Res. **Publications:** Retrospect & Prospect of Intl Court of Justice 1986, Four Decades of Intl Law Comm.1988, Study on the Strengthening of the Role of Intl Court of Justices: Reality and Expectation 1989, Envl Diplomacy 1992, Ed.–in–Chief *New Way Forward: Envl Law & Sust Dev* (UNEP's) 1993. **Languages:** Chinese (mother tongue), English, French (working knowledge), Russian. **Address:** Environmental Law and Institutions Programme Activity Centre, UNEP, POB 30552, Nairobi, Kenya. **Tel.**(office) 254 2 230800, (home & **fax**) 254 2 226886 or 90.

SUNDARESAN, Professor Dr Bommaya Bala. Environmental protection, environmental impact assessment of development projects. State Planning Commission Member. *B.*19 Feb.1929, Kombai, Madurai Distr., TN, India. Indian. *M.*Vijaya. **Education:** Madras U. BE(Civil) 1951, MSc (Public Health Eng.) 1957; U.of Florida PhD(Envl Eng.) 1963. **Experience:** industrial waste treatment, EIA, res.guide to postgrad.& doctl students, consult. **Career:** Lect. Guindy Engg Coll.1953–61, V.-Chancellor 1984–7, Madras U.; PhD Scholar & Postdoctl F. U.of Florida 1961–6; Prof.of Envl Engg, Anna U. 1966–77; Dir, NEERI 1977–84; Consult.to WHO 1977–87; EIA (coalmining, industrial, and irrigation, projects) 1988–94; Memb. TN State Planning Comm.1991–. **Achievements:** R&D in industrial poll.control systems in 300+ diff.industries, EIA of 40+ projects. **Memberships:** F.ASCE, INAE, IIE. **Award:** Engg Personality (IIE) 1988. **Publications:** five books incl.*Solid Waste Mgmt in Developing Countries* (co-Author) 1983; *c.*100 others incl.Envl impact assessment (co-Author) 1990, Water Resource Dev.: Econ.& Sociol.Perspective 1977–94. Favours news media support. **Languages:** English, Tamil. Willing to act as consult.etc. **Address:** 76 1st Avenue, Indira Nagar, Adyar, Madras 600 020, Tamil Nadu, India. **Tel.** (office) 91 44 842489, (home) 91 44 411799; **fax** 91 44 491 0746.

SUNDERLAND, Dr Keith David. Arachnology; agroecology; biological control. Research Leader. *B.*17 Nov.1947, Waterloo, Liverpool, England, UK. British. **Education:** Leeds U. BSc(Zool.)(1st Class Hons) 1973, PhD 1977. **Experience:** res.— pop.dynamics of Isopoda in coastal grassland, serological study of predation on woodlice, studies on ecol.of generalist invertebrate predators in n.temperate agroecosystems, devs of techniques for quantification of predation in the field: pop.dynamics of spiders in agroecosystems; admin.— deptl head for three yrs. **Career:** Higher SO, Dept of Entomol. 1976–9, SSO Dept of Entomol.& Insect Path. 1979–86, GCRI; PSO & Head of Entomol. Section, Dept of Entomol.& Insect Path. Inst.of Hortl Res. 1986–7; Head of Entomol.& Insect Path.Dept 1987–90, Res.Leader 1992–, HRI (Sussex, UK). **Achievements:** elucidation of beneficial role of invertebrate predatory fauna as pest control agents in cereals, dev.of novel techniques in pop.biol.and quantification of invertebrate predation. **Memberships:** BES, F.RES, BAS, AAB, Edl Panel *Annals of Applied Biol.* **Publications:** *c.*60 incl.A serological study of arthropod predation in a dune grassland ecosystem (co-Author) 1980, A study of feeding by polyphagous predators on cereal aphids using ELISA and gut dissection (co-Author) 1987, Density estimation for invertebrate predators in agroecosystems (co-Author) 1994. **Language:** English. Willing to act as consult.etc. **Address:** Entomology Department, Horticulture Research International, Littlehampton, West Sussex BN17 6LP, England, UK. **Tel.**(office) 44 1903 716123, (home) 44 1903 262405; **fax** 44 1903 726780; **e-mail** Keith.Sunderland@AFRC.AC. UK .

Sung WANG, Professor, *see* **WANG, Professor Sung.**

SUZUKI, Professor Kunio. Tropical ecology, environmental management. Professor of Environment. *B.*12 Jan.1948, Miyagi, Japan. Japanese. **Education:** Tohoku U.(Sendai), BSc 1970. **Experience:** res.staff of MAB project in trop.Asia 1978–. **Career:** Res.Assoc.1973–81, Assoc.Prof.of Envl Mgmt 1981–91, Prof.of Envt, Fac.of Business Admin.1991, Yokohama Nat.U. **Achievement:** worked actively with UNESCO/MAB esp.on resto.of trop.swamp ecosystems. **Membership:** INTECOL. **Publications:** *Ecol Mgmt* 1991; *c.*30 others. **Languages:** English, Japanese. **Address:** Institute of Environmental Science, Faculty of Business Administration, Yokohama National University, 156 Tokiwadai, Hodogaya, Yokohama, Japan. **Tel.**(office) 81 45 335 1451, (home) 81 45 333 2265; **fax** 81 45 335 2596.

SVOBODA, Professor Dr Josef. Arctic ecology: primary productivity, primary succession following deglaciation, colonization & revegetation of polar deserts, ecosystems of polar oases; toxic fallout. Emeritus Professor of Botany. *B.*16 July 1929, Prague, Czech Rep. Canadian, Czech. *M.*Miu-Yin: 2 *s.* **Education:** Masaryk U.1948–

9, Charles U.1966–8, U.of Western Ont. BSc (Hons) 1970, U.of Alb. PhD(Bot.) 1974. **Experience:** asst to Prof.Jan Calabek in lab.for time-lapse film; as pol. prisoner 1949–58 worked in uranium mines at Jachymov; on release became zoo inspector followed by technologist at hydr.survey, res.asst at Inst.of Bot. Czech.AS; emigrated to Canada 1968. **Career:** Asst Prof. 1973, Assoc.Prof. 1978, Prof.1985, Assoc.Chair 1990–92, Emer. 1994–, Dept of Bot., Erindale Coll., U.of Toronto. **Achievements:** primary productivity studies of a regenerated Cretaceous lake in S.Moravia in late 1960s and of raised-beach ridges at Devon Is.(75°N, Canada) in early 1970s (both IBP projects); long-term ecosystem team res.of polar oases at Alexandra Fiord (1979–85) and Sverdrup Pass (1986–94) Ellesmere Is.; estab.of experimental farms at Rankin Inlet (64°N) & Alexandra Fiord (79°N) with pioneer res.in arctic agric.1978–85; studies in initial succession and revegetation processes following deglaciation of polar desert landscapes, plant communities, herbivory, radio-active fallout, etc.; jt res.with German, Japanese, Russian, & Czech., scis; Assoc.Ed. *Arctic & Alpine Res., Ultimate Reality and Meaning*; reviewer of res.proposals, papers, & books; media interviews. **Memberships:** ITEX (Canadian Steering Cttee Chairman and Intl Exec.Cttee 1990–93), Long-term Ecosystem Res.& Monitoring Panel (Canadian Global Change Prog.) 1992–, ESA, CBA, CSAS, Soc.for the Study of Ultimate Reality & Meaning. **Awards:** Sr F'ship (NATO) 1979, F. AINA, Northern Sci.Award & Centenary Medal (Canada), Hon.Recognition (CGS) 1993, Hon. Memb.(CBS) 1994; others. **Publications:** *Arctic Ecosystems in a Changing Climate* (co-Author & -Ed.) 1992, *Ecol.of a Polar Oasis: Alexandra Fiord, Ellesmere Is.*(co-Author & -Ed.) 1994; *c.*85 papers incl.Ecol.and primary prod.of raised beach communities, Truelove Lowland 1977, The Canadian High N.: resource of renewal 1981, Succession in marginal arctic envts 1987, The reality of the phytosphere and (ultimate) values involved 1989, The Canadian Arctic realm and global change 1994. Indiff.to pers.pub., favours news media support. **Languages:** Czech, English (spoken), German (limited). Further details may be obtained from *Canadians Who Made a Difference* (Queen's Quarterly, Sesquicentennial Issue, 1991), *Canadian Who's Who* 1995. Willing to act as consult.etc. **Address:** Department of Botany, Erindale College, University of Toronto, Mississauga, Ontario L5L 1C6, Canada. **Tel.**(office) 1 905 828 5368, (home) 1 905 634 5443; **fax** 1 905 828 3792.

SWAMINATHAN, Dr Monkombu Sambasivan. Plant breeding, genetics, cytogenetics; conservation of biodiversity; ecological agriculture, economic ecology. Director. *B.*7 Aug. 1925, Tamil Nadu, India. Indian. *M.* **Education:** Travancore U. BSc 1944, Madras U. BSc(Agric.) 1947, Associateship of IARI in Genetics 1949, U.of Camb.Sch.of Agric. PhD 1952, UNESCO F.in Genetics, Agricl U.

Wageningen 1949–50, Res.Assoc.in Genetics, U.of Wisconsin 1952–3. **Career:** Teacher, Researcher & Res.Admin. CRRI & IARI 1954–72; DG ICAR and Sec.to Govt of India's DARE 1972–80; Sec.to Govt of India's Min.of Agric.& Irrigation 1979–80; Acting Dep.Chairman, Govt of India Planning Comm.1980; Memb.Govt of India Agric., Rural Dev., Sci.& Educ.Planning Comm.1980–82; DG IRRI 1982–88; Dir Centre for Res.on Sust.Agricl & Rural Dev.1989–. **Achievements:** elucidation of origin & differentiation of potato 'species'; understanding of genetic relationships among wheat 'species'; accomplishment of difficult crosses in potato 'species'; standardization of techniques for induction of polyploidy in several econ.plants; elucidation of factors influencing induction & recovery of mutations in wheat & rice and elaboration of relationships between secondary effects of food irradiation and assessment of the wholesomeness of irradiated food; identification of barriers to high yields in wheat and init.of the wheat breeding prog.involving the 'Norin' dwarfing genes obtained from Mexico; dev.of concept of 'crop cafeterias', 'mid-season corrections in crop-scheduling', risk distribn agron. & alternative cropping strats for diff.weather conditions; purposeful manipulation of genes in improving yield, qual., & stability, of performance of wheat, rice, and potato; dev.of whole village or watershed operational res.projects, disaster mgmt strats, and Nat.Demonstration and Lab.-to-Land progs; mgmt of disastrous drought of 1979; collection & cons.of plant genetic resources partic.of rice & wheat; orgn of coastal systems' res.and biovillages, and Genetic Resources Centres for sust.agric.and for adaptation to sea-level rise. **Memberships:** F.IAS, F. INSA, ISC (Gen.Pres.1976), SSA (Hon.F.) 1971, F.RS, US NAS (Foreign Assoc.1977), All-Union Acad.of Agricl Sci.(USSR, Foreign Memb.) 1978, RAAS (Foreign Memb.) 1992, TWAS (Founding F.), Pres.XV Intl Cong.of Genetics 1983, RSAAF (Foreign Memb.) 1983, NAAS (Mass. Foreign Hon.Memb.) 1984, NAS Italy (Foreign F.) 1985, F.RSA, Chinese AS (Hon.Res.Prof.1987, also in Genetics 1987), F.EAASH, F. Bangladesh AS, INAS (Pres. 1988–90 & Hon.F.1976), IUCN (Pres.1984–90), NAAS (Pres.1991–94); VP of INSONA; num. hon.positions on intl cttees & in orgns incl.(at present) WWF India & ISME, Chairman of Governing Bds of CABI & IIT, Chairman Bd of Trustees of IIMI & Commonwealth–Guyana Iwokrama Rain Forest Prog., Chairman ICPF & M.S.Swaminathan Res.Fndn, Chief Adv.to Chinese AS, Andrew D.White Prof.-at-Large, Cornell U. **Awards:** Mendel Mem.Award (Czech.AS), R.B.Bennett Commonwealth Prize (RSA) 1984, Bicentenary Medal (U.of Georgia) 1985, Albert Einstein World Sci.Award (WCC) 1986, Ramon Magsaysay Award 1971, AWD Award 1985, First World Food Prize 1987, The Golden Heart Pres.Award (Govt of Philippines) 1987, IRRI Award, Commander of Order of Golden Ark 1990, Tyler Prize 1991, Honda Prize,

Sasakawa Envt Prize (UNEP); 13 scientific, three nat., 33 Hon.DScs, seven Hon.Prof'ships. **Publications:** genetic cons.in potato, wheat & rice 1950–90: Elucidation of species relationships among tuber-bearing *Solanum* species and of the origin of *Solanum tuberosum* 1950–57, Intro.of Norin dwarfing genes in Indian Wheat varieties 1963–70, Discovery of indirect effects of radiations 1957–63, Biotech.applications in crop improvement 1980–88, Cons.of Mangrove ecosystems 1990. **Languages:** English, German, Hindi, Tamil. **Address:** M.S.Swaminathan Research Foundation, 3rd Cross Strcct, Taramani Institutional Area, Madras 600 113, Tamil Nadu, India. **Tel.**91 44 235 1229; **fax** 91 44 235 1319.

SWINGLAND, Professor Dr Ian Richard. Biodiversity management/conservation sciences. Founder & Research Director. *B.*2 Nov.1946, London, England, UK. British. *M.*Fiona Mairi: *s., d.* **Education:** Haberdashers' Aske's Sch.; U.of London, BSc(Hons)(Zool.) 1969, U.of Edinburgh PhD(Ecol., For., & Natural Resources) 1973, U.of Oxf.post-doctl res.in zool.1974–9. **Experience:** has taught world-wide, developed DICE which teaches & trains people from over 30 countries both in the UK & the tropics and which is now one of the leading res.& postgrad. training instns in cons.world-wide. **Career:** Rcs.Asst, Shell Rcs.Ltd 1969; Dem. U.of Edinburgh 1969–73; Regnl Tutor, Open U.1970–72; Wildlife Biol. Rep.of Zambia 1973–4; Vis.Sci. RS Res.Station 1974–6; Postdoctl Res.Asst, U.of Oxf.1974–8; Tutor in Ecol. Colls of U.of Oxf.1974–9; Lect.in Natural Scis 1979–85, Sr Lect.in Natural Scis Continuing Educ.1985–9, Dir 1989–91, Founder & Res.Dir 1991–, DICE, all at U.of Kent at Canterbury. **Achievements:** discovered envl sex determination in tortoises; founded DICE. **Memberships:** BES, BOS, IBiol. (F.1993), ZSL, BHS, Thc Zool.Club, SSAB, The Rain Forest Club, RURAL, FFPS, SEH, ASAB, SSAR, BCG, SCB, RGS (F.1992), RSA (F.1992). **Awards:** Throgmorton Trotman Sr Exhibition at Edinburgh U.1970–71; FCO (ODA) Scholarship at Edinburgh U. 1970–73; Disting.Guest, Soc.of Fellows (U.of Michigan) 1977; S.Dillon Ripley, Sec.to the Smithsonian, Guest Lect.1977; Disting.Lect.(Duke U.) 1977; Vis.Prof.of Biol.1986–7 and SRF Mus.of Zool.1986–7 (both U.of Michigan); Res.Assoc.(Smithsonian Instn) 1987–95; Hon.Life Memb. (BCG) 1989; 150th Anniversary Lect. RSPCA 1990, Prof.of Cons.Biol.& Biodiv.(U.of Oslo) 1993–. **Publications:** 150+ books, papers, & reports. Avoids pers.pub., favours news media support. **Languages:** Bahassa & Creole (spoken), English, French (fair), Spanish (passable). Willing to act as consult.etc. **Address:** The Durrell Trust for Conservation Biology, University of Kent, Canterbury, Kent CT2 7NX, England, UK. **Tel.** 44 1227 475480 or 764000; **fax** 44 1227 475481 or 459025; **telex** 965449; **e-mail** irs@ukc.ac.uk .

SYBESMA, Jeffrey. Natural marine resource management. Head of Management Authority.

*B.*21 Nov.1954, Jakarta, Indonesia. Dutch. **Education:** U.of Utrecht MSc(Marine Biol.) 1983; U.of The Netherlands Antilles BSc(Law) 1994. **Experience:** mgmt of trop.marine parks. **Career:** Mgr, Curaçao Underwater Park 1983– 92; Head, CITES Mgmt Auth.(Netherlands Antilles) 1992–. **Achievements:** mgmt plans, scientific & popular pubns, regular consultations on marine-park mgmt. **Publications:** *Guide to the Curaçao Underwater Park* (co-Author) 1989, *Complete Guide to Landside Diving & Snorkeling Locations in Curaçao* (co-Author) 1990; 15 papers. Indiff.to pers.pub.& news media support. **Languages:** Dutch, English, Papiamentu (written & spoken). Willing to act as consult. ctc. **Address:** POB 4465, Curaçao, Netherlands Antilles. **Tel.**(office) 5999 614555, **fax** 5999 612388.

SZILASSY, Dr Zoltán. Protected areas — categorization, management plans, and aesthetic evaluation; 'soft' tourism, birds. Deputy Head of Department. *B.*22 Dec.1942, Budapest, Hungary. Hungarian. *M.*Judith B.(resp.for PHARE projects, Min.of Envt & Regnl Policy): *d.* **Education:** U.for Silviculture & For.(Sopron, Hungary), Forest Engr's Dipl.1965, Spec.Postgrad.Dipl.in Envl Prot.& Landscape Mgmt 1990, PhD 1991. **Experience:** 27 yrs' in admin.and planning issues at c.orgns & instns (16 yrs at Nat.Auth.for Nature Cons.), practical ficld cxp.in most E. Euro.countries, comp.knowledge of Euro.wildlife. **Career:** Land Surveyor 1965 6, Planner in Forestplan Planning Office 1967–70, Min.of Agric.; Head, Planning Section, Melyepterv Planning Office, Min.for Housing & Urban Dev.1971–8; Dep.Head of Dept, Min.for Envt & Regnl Policy 1979–. **Achievements:** compiled WCMC's PADU documentation on Hungarian prot.areas, prep.of Report on Envl Status in Hungary for IUCN (identified priorities of long-term jt prog.and projects to be implemented). **Memberships:** IUCN CNPPA 1989– (later memb.of Euro.Steering Cttee), Council of Europe's Expert Group on Prot.Areas 1993–, IUCN (Regnl Counc.& VP 1994–), Hungarian Ornithl & Foresters' Socs. **Award:** Envl Award (Hungarian Govt) 1991. **Publications:** *Nature Cons.in Hungary* 1985, *Envl Status Report of Hungary* 1990, *The Problem of Nat.Parks in a Densely Populated Regn* (co-Author, contribn to Fourth World Cong.on Nat.Parks 1992 & FNNPE Assembly 1994). Dislikes pers.pub., indiff.to news media support. **Languages:** English, Hungarian. Willing to act as consult.etc. **Address:** Tulipán u. 15, 1022 Budapest, Hungary. **Tel.**(office) 36 1 155 1045, (home) 36 1 116 3258; **fax** 36 1 175 7457.

TAIT, Professor Elizabeth Joyce. Environmental management, technology management, risk, policy analysis. Deputy Director (Research & Advisory Services), Visiting Professor. *B.*19 Feb.1938, Edinburgh, Scotland, UK. British. *M.*Dr Alexander Dickson Tait (biochem.). **Education:** Glasgow U. BSc(1st Class Hons) 1959, Wolfson Coll.Camb. PhD 1976. **Experience:** res.& consult.— prod., regulation, & use, of pesticides; R&D in industry on new tech. partic.biotech.; public attitudes; regulation & risk assessment; admin.— course dev.(undergrad.& postgrad.), res.progs, res.& adv.work in public service; teaching envl & tech.mgmt. **Career:** Res.F. U.of Camb.1977–9; Lect.then Sr Lect. Tech.Fac.1979–91, Vis.Prof.1992–, Open U.; Prof. Strathclyde Grad.Business Sch.1991–2; Dep.Dir, Res.& Adv.Services, Scottish Natural Heritage 1992–. **Achievements:** res.on pesticide usage by farmers & its envl impact, and on interactions between industry, govt, & public, on implementation of biotech.innovations for agric.; postgrad.teaching progs in envl & tech. mgmt. **Memberships:** IEEM (Founder Memb. & ex-Counc.), F.RSA, SCI, SPS, IEM. **Awards:** T.H. Smith Prize for Pharmaceutical Chem.1959, Harold Samuel Studentship (Camb.U.), Huntington Res.Studentship (Wolfson Coll. Camb.), Rockefeller Fndn F'ship. **Publications:** Mgmt of Pests & Pesticides: Farmers' Perceptions & Practices (co-Author) 1987, Practical Cons.: Site Assessment & Mgmt Planning (co-Author) 1988, Practical Cons.: Woodland Mgmt (co-Author) 1990; 20+ refereed j.articles, num. contribns to books & consult.reports. Accepts pers. pub.& news media support. **Languages:** English, French (passable). Willing to act as consult. etc. **Address:** Research and Advisory Services, Scottish Natural Heritage, 2 Anderson Place, Edinburgh EH6 5NP, Scotland, UK. **Tel.** 44 131 446 2403; **fax** 44 131 446 2405.

TAN, Dr Koonlin. Tropical land-use, conservation of well-tried socio-economic systems; economic resources and appropriate technology in particular tropical environments, renewable & sustainable use of wetlands; women's contribution in developing world. *B.*19 Sept.1940, KL, Malaysia. Malaysian (Brit.Perm.Resident). *M.*Prof. W.Robert Stanton *qv.: s., d.* **Education:** U.of Malaya, BA(Hons) 1963, MA 1965, PhD 1974; Univs of Bonn, Giessen, & London. **Experience:** org., ed.& writer re.res.& planning activities in varied orgns for over 20 years. **Career:** Dir of Planning & Res./Consult. Fedn of Livestock Farmer Assns of Malaysia 1985–90, Adv./Chairman Socio-econ.Cttee on New Village Dev.of Malaysian Chinese Assn 1985–6, Consult.to Fedn of Family Planning Assns of Malaysia 1988–9. **Achievements:** polycultural or adaptive studied land-use systems in equatorial regn before they vanished under vast dev.schemes or from neglect, esp.of a wetland agrofor.economy producing industrial commodity. **Memberships:** RHS, AIM (former). **Awards:** Scholar, German Academic Exchange 1965–6, Agricl Council (NY) 1972, ASEAN Res.F.(first), Stiftung Volkswagenwerk (Inst.of SE Asian Studies, Singapore) 1978–9. **Publications:** 12 papers & books. Indiff.to pers.pub.& favours news media support. **Languages:** English, German (read), SE Chinese dialects (spoken). Willing to act as consult.etc. **Address:** 14 Friar Road, Orpington, Kent BR5 2BL, England, UK. **Tel.** (home) 44 1689 871590.

TAO, Professor Dr Kar-ling James. Strategy & technology on plant germ-plasm conservation; seed germination & dormancy mechanisms; seed testing; gene-bank standards, design & management. Agricultural Officer (Plant Genetic Resources). *B.*20 Aug.1941, Canton, Guangdong, China. American. *M.*Harriet Hoi-Yin: 2 *s.* **Education:** Chinese U.of HK, Dipl.in Biol. 1964; Tuskegee Inst. MSc(Biol.) 1968; U.of W–M PhD(Hort.& Bot.) 1971. **Experience:** res.— in-vitro protein synthesis, seed germination & vigour; admin.— project formulation, funding & monitoring; consult.— genebank design, plant germplasm cons.; teaching — high sch.biol.& chem., intl training course on germplasm cons.& mgmt. **Career:** high-sch. teacher 1965–6; Res.F. Tuskegee Inst.1966–8; Res. Asst, U.of Wisconsin 1968–71; Res.Assoc. Cornell U.1971–7; Plant Physiol. USDA 1977–84; Cons.& Res.Officer IBPGR 1984–92; Res. Prof.of Bot. Res.Inst. Academia Sinicae 1989–; Vis.Sci. UK 1989, Italy 1990, & USA 1991; Adv. Beijing Vegetable Res.Centre 1988– & Zhejiang Agricl U.1990–; Agricl Officer, FAO 1992–. **Achievements:** assisting many countries around the world to (i) develop strat.for cons.of plant germplasm and (ii) upgrade genebank cons.facilities; developing global network of base collections. **Memberships:** ASPP, CSSA, ASA, NYAS (1982), Chinese AS (Hon.Res. Prof.1989), Symposium Seed Storage (co-Chairman) 1989. **Awards:** Cert.for Tech. Recognition 1981, Gold Medal (Res.Inst.of Plant Prod.) 1988 & (ABI) 1991, Hon.Prof. Zhongsan U. 1991. **Publications:** *Seed Physiol.& Standards* 1981, *Genebank Mgmt & Seed Storage* 1986, *Applied Seed Physiol.*1990, *Seed Vigour* 1991, *Genebank Standards* 1994; 45+ scientific articles. Indiff.to pers.pub.& news media support. **Languages:** Chinese, English. Willing to act as consult.etc. **Address:** Via Joyce 46, B6, 00143 Rome, Italy. **Tel.**(office) 39 6 522 55347, (home) 39 6 500 4548; **fax** 39 6 522 56347; **e-mail** KarLing.Tao@FAO.ORG .

TARAK, Pedro. Environmental law. Executive Director. *B.*14 Dec.1952, Buenos Aires, Argentina. Argentinian. **Educaton:** U.of Buenos Aires LLB 1976, Indiana U. LLM 1980. **Experience:** training lawyers, advising govtl decision-makers & intl orgns, organizing instns. **Career:** Managing Ed. *Ambiente y Recursos Naturales* (j.on policy, law, & admin.) 1983–90, Senatorial Adv. 1984–6 & Adv.to VP 1987–9, Argentina; Consult.to OAS 1993– & Bolivian Govt 1992–, Exec.Dir FARN 1992–. **Achievements:** envl orgn dev., envl laws (species' prot., hazardous waste etc.), institutionalization of Public Hearings. **Memberships:** IUCN CEL, Fundacion Bariloche (Dir, Bd of Govs). **Award:** Albert Schweitzer Award. **Publications:** Intl law of migratory species 1980, Standing to sue in Argentina: the case of the Penguins 1983, Hazardous waste law 1985, Envl legis.in Argentina 1986. Indiff.to pers.pub.& news media support. **Languages:** Armenian (spoken), English, French (spoken), Spanish. Willing to act as consult.etc. **Address:** Fundacion Ambiente y Recursos Naturales, Monroe 2142, 1428 Buenos Aires, Argentina. **Tel.** office) 54 1 781 9171, (home) 54 1 784 1609; **fax** 54 1 781 6115.

TAYLOR, Professor Dr J.Mary. Conservation of mammals. Muscum Dircctor. *B.*30 May 1931, Portland, Oregon, USA. American. *W.* **Education:** Smith Coll. BA(Zool.) 1952; UCB MA (Zool.) 1953, PhD(Zool.) 1959. **Experience:** res.in mammalian repro., systematics, and ecol.; admin.leader of two museums of natural hist.; Prof.of Zool., SSC Chairman. **Career:** Instr.& Asst Prof. Dept of Zool.& Physiol. Wellesley Coll.1959–65; Assoc.Prof.of Zool.1965–74, Prof. of Zool.1974–82, Dir The Cowan Vertebrate Mus.1975–82, UCB; Collaborative Sci. Oregon Regnl Primate Res.Center 1983–7; Dir, The Cleveland Mus.of Natural Hist.1987–. **Achievements:** many res. pubns dealing with basic field biol.of mammals, some of which are endangered. **Memberships:** ASM (Past Pres., Bd of Dirs [Life]), ASMD (VP 3 yrs), Sigma Xi, IUCN SSC Rodent SG (Chairman). **Awards:** Fulbright Scholar (U.of Sydney 1954–5), Hartley H.T.Jackson Award (ASM) 1993. **Publications:** Reproductive biol. of the Australian Bush Rat, *Rattus assimilis* 1961, Results of the Archbold expedns, systematics of native Australian *Rattus* (co-Author) 1973, Amphibians, reptiles, & mammals of BC 1979, The Oxf.Guide to Mammals of Australia 1984, A revision of the genus *Rattus* (Rodentia: Muridae) in the New Guinea regn (co-Author) 1982. Indiff.to pers.pub. & news media support. **Language:** English. Willing to act as consult. etc. **Address:** The Cleveland Museum of Natural History, 1 Wade Oval, University Circle, Cleveland, Ohio 44106-1767, USA. **Tel.**1 216 231 4600; **fax** 1 216 231 5919.

TEEB'AKI, Katino (also called M'aere). Wildlife conservation, environmental management. Wildlife Warden. *B.*20 Nov.1955, Rep.of Kiribati. Nationality: 'I-Kiribati'. **Education:** Govt Sec.Sch.; NCC incl.For. Comm., Wildlife Trust, & ICBP; Wildlife Cons.Mgmt 1981. **Experience:** mgmt of wildlife cons.& prot.areas in the Line and Phoenix Islands (Rep. of Kiribati), adv.on project dev.& envl issues. **Career:** Accounts Clerk, Min.of Finance (Tarawa) 1976–8; Wildlife Warden, Min.of Line and Phoenix Dev. Kiritimati (Christmas Is.) 1978–. **Achievements:** mgmt of wildlife & prot.areas, helped initiate Nature tourism, increased public awareness and envl educ. **Memberships:** IUCN CNPPA (past) & SSC (for Australasia). **Publications:** incl. transl.of booklet on *Natural Hist.& Birdlife of Kiritimati Is.* Favours news media support. **Languages:** English (good), Kiribatese. **Address:** Ministry of Line and Phoenix Development, Kiritimati (Christmas Island), Republic of Kiribati, Central Pacific Ocean. **Tel.**686 81217; **fax** 686 81278; **cable address:** Wildlife Kiritimati .

TEJADHAMMO, Phra Ajahn Pongsak. Education in forest values & environmental awareness using Buddhist concept of SILATHAM. Foundation President. *B.*20 July 1932, Tannop Village, Nakorn Sawan, C.Thailand. Thai. **Education:** Ordination in 1951, Level 1 of Buddhist Study at Nakorn Sawan Monastery 1951–2 and level 2 at Mahatat Monastery 1953–5, Meditational Practice at Suab Mokh Monastery 1957–62, thereafter solitary meditational retreats (*Tudong*). **Experience:** *Tudong* in caves & forests of N. Thailand, estab.in Mae Soi Valley 1980 a Forest Meditation Centre which became a nat.one of recourse for envl problems (hardship of villagers due to forest destruction led to local, then national, teaching of forest values using Buddhist principles.). **Career:** estab.Tum Tu Bou Meditation Centre 1980 and Mae Soi Villagers' Assn for prot.of water-sheds and Dhammanaat Fndn to coordinate & fund Mae Soi Valley Project 1987 (Pres.of last 1987–); Abbot of Wat Palad 1983, founded Monks' Assn for Prot.of Life & Envt 1990. **Achievements:** through on-site educ.an understanding of forest values has been fostered together with the individual's resp.for mgmt of the envt. **Awards:** Exemplary Citizen's Award (Thai Rath Fndn) 1989, R.Forest Dept Award 1989, Global 500 Roll of Honour (UNEP) 1990. **Publications:** *First Stages in Meditation* 1985, *Buddhism & Cons.*1990. Favours pers.pub.& news media support. **Language:** Thai. **Address:** Dhammanaat Foundation for Conservation & Rural Development, POB 52, Chiangmai University, Chiangmai 50200, Thailand. **Tel.**66 53 248209; **fax** 66 53 223062.

TEMPLE, Professor Dr Stanley A. Endangered species especially of birds, conservation biology, ecology of birds of prey; landscape ecology especially issues of habitat fragmentation, island biogeography, and wildlife management. Professor of Conservation. *B.*26 Sept.1946, Cleveland, Ohio, USA. American. **Education:** Cornell U. BSc 1968, MSc 1970, PhD(Ecol.) 1973. **Experience:** res.on endangered species in N.& S.Amer., Carib., Indian & Pacific Oceans', regns; admin.as Pres., Chairman, Dir. **Career:** Res. Biol. WWF & ICBP 1972–5; Res.Assoc. Cornell Lab.of Ornith.1975–6; Asst Prof.1976–80, Assoc.Prof.1980–84, Prof.1984–, Dept of Widlife Ecol. Beers-Bascom Prof.in Cons.1984–, all at University of W–M; Bd of Dirs of Cornell Lab.of Ornith., Chairman of Bd of the [US] Nature Conservancy. **Achievements:** res.& mgmt of endangered birds; res.on habitat fragmentation; res.& design of natural areas; teaching, and training grad.students, in cons.& wildlife ecol.; contribns to formation of cons.biol. **Memberships:** AOU, AIBS, COS, Council of Biol Eds, ESA, Explorer's Club, ICBP, RRF, SCB (Pres.), The Wildlife Soc., WOS, WSO, ICF, BCI, IUCN SSC. **Awards:** Council Member AIBS, F. AOU, Chevron Cons.Award 1992, Res.F.Explorer's Club, Cons.F.WCI, Disting.Achievement Award (SCB), Excellence in Teaching Award (U.of Wisconsin), Golden Passenger Pigeon Award

(WSO). **Publications:** ten books incl.*Endangered Birds: Mgmt Techniques for Preserving Threatened Species* 1978; 175+ j.articles; Ed.of *The Passenger Pigeon and Bird Cons.;* Assoc. Ed. *Cons.Biol.*and *J.Field Ornith.* Favours pers. pub.& news media support. **Languages:** English, French (written), Spanish. Willing to act as consult.etc. **Address:** Department of Wildlife Ecology, University of Wisconsin, Madison, Wisconsin 53706, USA. **Tel.** (office) 1 608 263 6827, (home) 1 608 795 4226; **fax** 1 608 262 6099.

TERBLANCHE, Dr Petro. Environmental management & auditing with specialization in air pollution impacts. Services Manager. *B.*2 Feb.1959, SA. S.African. *M.*François H.Roux. **Education:** U.of Pretoria BSc(Bot.& Zool.), BSc(Hons)(Zool.)(Dist.in Biostats) 1981, MSc (Zool.)(*cum laude*) 1984, DSc 1987. **Experience:** envl health aspects of indoor & outdoor air poll., has conducted several large air poll. health studies in SA, and acts as co-worker on large studies in the USA through Harvard U. **Career:** Professional Officer, Dept of Med. Oncology, H.F.Verwoerd Hosp.1982; Res.Officer, Dept of Med.Oncology, U.of Pretoria 1988; Sr Med.Researcher 1988–90, Chief Med.Researcher 1990–91, Specialist Sci.1991, Res.Inst. for Envl Diseases, MRC; Vis.Sci. Harvard U. Sch.of Public Health 1989; Project Mgr, Atmos. Impact Assessment, Div.of Earth, Marine & Atmos.Techs 1992, Mgr Envl Health & Safety Mgmt Services, Envl Services 1993–6, Dir of Div.of Food Sci.and Tech.1996–, CSIR. **Achievements:** appointed as PI on the two largest air poll.health studies ever conducted in SA — Vaal Triangle Air Poll.Health Study and the Air Pollution Health Study in Kenyston Park, Edenvale and Modderfontein (AIRKEM). **Memberships:** AWMA, ISEE, ISEA, DSSA, S.African Oesophagus Cancer SG, SASMO, SAL SG, SAESF, NACA (Counc., Chairman Transvaal Branch & VC Indoor Envt Chapter), Organizing Cttee for Indoor Air '91 & '92 (Intl Confs on Indoor Air Poll.) and 1993 Annual NACA Conf., MRC Eval.Cttee on Envl Health & Toxicology 1990, Edl Bd *The Clean Air J.* **Awards:** Top Achiever Award (CSIR) 1983, Young Sci.Best Presentation Award (U.of Pretoria Med.Sch.) 1984. **Publications:** more than 100 since 1984 incl.Self-reported exertion levels on time/activity diaries: application to exposure assessment (co-Author) 1991, Self-reported activity levels and actual heart rates in teenagers (co-Author) 1991, Prelim.results of exposure measurements and health effects of the Vaal Triangle Air Poll.Health Study (co-Author) 1992, Exposure to air poll.from domestic fuels in a S.African pop.(co-Author) 1993. **Languages:** Afrikaans, English. Willing to act as consult.etc. **Address:** Foodtek, CSIR, POB 395, Pretoria 0001, South Africa. **Tel.**27 12 841 4220; **fax** 27 12 841 3865; **e-mail** pterblan@csir.co.za .

TERRASSON, François. Integrating Man & Nature; ecosystems' management: forest, rivers,

agriculture, wetlands; psychology of Nature, behaviour and communication about Nature philosophy; scientific research & application. Maître de Conférences. *B.*3 July 1939, Saint Bonnet Tronçais (Allier), France. French. **Education:** U.of Paris (Sorbonne), Licence Libre (pluridisciplinaire) 1962. **Experience:** res.& consult.on Man-managed ecosystems, bldg models for communication & changing behaviour, lectures & courses given in var.univs & high schools. **Career:** Maître de Conférences, Nat.Mus.of Natural Hist 1967–. **Achievements:** assisting several nat.& intl orgns in ecol mgmt & communication. **Memberships:** Biogeog.Soc., IUCN CEP, travellers' & explorers' clubs, CJNE. **Publications:** *La Peur de la Nature* 1988, *Cons.Strat.for Madagascar* 1985, Image of Nature in Urban Envts 1985; several papers. Favours pers.pub.& news media support. **Languages:** English (spoken), French; German & Spanish (understood & read). Willing to act as consult.etc. **Address:** 6 rue Scipion, 75005 Paris, France. **Tel.**(office) 33 40 793261 or 59, (home) 33 14 3319219; **fax** 33 40 793271.

TEWOLDE, Dr Assefaw. Sustainable agricultural production systems; domestic animal genetic resource conservation & management; animal evaluation in dairy & beef production systems; environmental education. International Programmes Director. *B.*21 Aug.1949, Addi-Uqri, Eritrea. Mexican. *M.*Maria (for. sci.): 3 *s.* **Education:** U.of Ethiopia, BSc(Animal Sci.) 1973; U.of Florida, MSc(Animal Breeding & Genetics) 1976; Oregon SU, PhD (Animal Breeding & Genetics) 1981. **Experience:** 15+ yrs in res.& educ.focused towards trop.envts; admin. **Career:** Grad.Coord.in Animal Sci. Universidad Autonoma de Chapingo 1982–5; Intl Staff 1985–95, Head of Grad. Sch.1992–3, Dir of Prog.on Educ.for Cons.& Devt 1994–5, CATIE; Intl Progs Dir, Universidad Autonoma de Tamaulipas 1995–. **Achievements:** Founder of Network on Animal Genetic Resources' Cons.& Mgmt in Latin Amer.1992, trained 18+ individuals at grad.level in prod.systems compatible with envl cons. **Memberships:** ASAS, BSAP, Latin Amer.Assn of Animal Prod.; Reviewer for *Agrociencia: Serie Ciencio Animal, Archives Latinoamericanos.* **Awards:** Scholarship (AID) 1974–6 and (Mexican Govt) 1978–81, Excellence in Teaching (CATIE) 1990. **Publications:** 35+ papers; Ed.*Newsletter on Animal Genetic Resources.* Indiff.to pers.pub.& news media support. **Languages:** Amharic, English; French & Portuguese (read & understood); Spanish, Tigrinya. Willing to act as consult.etc. **Address:** Facultad de Agronomia, Universidad Autonoma de Tamaulipas, Ciudad Victoria, Tamaulipas, Mexico. **Tel.**(office) 52 131 21738 or 27065, (home) 52 131 65998; **fax** 52 131 22461.

THAPA, Dr Gopal B. Regional environmental management, planning, natural resources' conservation; watershed management; sustainable agriculture. Assistant Professor. *B.*25 July 1955,

Dang, Nepal. Nepalese. **Education:** Tribhuwan U. MA(Geog.) 1981; AIT MSc(Regnl Planning) 1985, D.Tech.Sc.(Watershed Mgmt) 1990. **Experience:** res.& student theses, res. supervision exp.in natural resources' & watershed mgmt, GIS application to land-use planning & instnl capability-bldg for envl mgmt; consult. re.organizing training progs on envl mgmt, and for UNDP Nepal. **Career:** Asst Lect. Tribhuwan U.1981; Guest Lect. U.of Dortmund 1991; Res. Sci.& Affiliated Fac.Memb. 1992–5, Asst Prof. 1995–, AIT. **Achievements:** in-depth studies of watershed mgmt & private for.in Hills of Nepal. **Memberships:** AIT Alumni Assn, Nepal Geogl Soc. **Awards:** Gold Medal (Mahendra Vidya Bhusan), CIDA & AIT Scholarships. **Publications:** c.20 incl.*Watershed Mgmt* (monogr.) 1990 and j.articles. Dislikes pers.pub. & news media support. **Languages:** English, Hindi, Nepalese. Willing to act as consult.etc. **Address:** School of Environment, Resources & Development, Asian Institute of Technology, GPO Box 2754, Bangkok, Thailand. **Tel.**66 2 524 5624; **fax** 66 2 516 2126.

THEBAUD, Dr Christophe. Conservation biology especially of islands; population ecology & evolution especially of colonizing organisms; management & control of plant invasions in protected areas. Postdoctoral Researcher. *B.*31 May 1964, Auray, Morbihan, France. French. *M.*Véronique: *d.* **Education:** U.of Montpellier PhD(Biol.) 1993. **Experience:** res. fieldwork in Mascarene archipelago, genecology of invading Compositae; consult.for WWF in endemic plant cons.on La Réunion Is. **Career:** Consult. Conseil Régnl de La Réunion 1987–9, F.ICL & Griffiths U. **Achievements:** basic res. on pop.ecol.of invading plants & forest dynamics (La Réunion), dev.of cons.project aimed at estab.of prot.areas on La Réunion Is. **Memberships:** SFE, ESA, BSA, BOU. **Publications:** four scientific papers + one popular. Favours news media support. **Languages:** English, French, German (basic). Willing to act as consult.etc. **Address:** Centre d'Ecologie Fonctionnelle et Evolutive, Centre National de la Recherche Scientifique, BP 5051, F-34033 Montpellier Cedex, France. **Tel.**(office) 33 67 613311, (home) 33 67 610904; **fax** 33 67 412138.

THOM, David Alan. Conservation & environmental policy & management; reorientation of technology to achieve environmentally-sustainable development and its application. Committee Chairman. *B.*20 Oct.1924, Whakatane, NZ. New Zealander. **Education:** Mt Albert Grammar Sch.; Seddon Mem.Tech.Coll. ICE Exams 1954. **Experience:** engg consult.— roading, urban dev., industrial & major bldg contracts, water resource dev.and EIA & planning; envl policy; cons. admin. **Career:** Dir KRTA Ltd 1959–86; Pres. IPENZ 1979; Chairman — NZ Envl Council 1976–81, Nat.Parks and Reserves Auth.of NZ 1981–90, NZ Cons.Auth. 1990–93 and Cttee on Engg & Envt, World Fedn of Engg Orgns 1991–.

Endeavours: to estab.effective envl admin.& mgmt, to introduce high levels of envl performance into practice of engg, to enhance, expand, & protect, the NZ Cons.Estate. **Memberships:** F.ICE, F.IPENZ, F.RSA. **Awards:** Queen's Silver Jubilee Medal 1977, CBE 1982, Gold Award (Assn of Consulting Engrs) 1984, Maclean Citation (IPENZ) 1989, NZ Commem.Medal 1990. **Publications:** *Seacoast in the Seventies* (co-Author) 1973, *Heritage, the Parks of the People* 1987, *Selected Topics in Envl Mgmt* (co-Author) 1993; num.papers. Indiff.to pers.pub.& news media support. **Language:** English. Further details may be obtained from *Debrett's Handbook of Australia & NZ* 1982, *Who's Who in NZ* 1991. Willing to act as ref.or judge proposals. **Address:** 51 Evelyn Road, Howick, New Zealand. **Tel.**(office) 64 520 6069, (home) 64 534 7949; **fax** 64 520 4695.

THOMAS, Mrs Anamaria Angulo DE. Interpreter of conservation & wildlife topics; conservation outdoors. Managing Director. *B.*13 Jan. 1940, Lima, Perú. British. *M.*Norman V. Thomas: 3 *d.* **Education:** Universidad Catolica de Lima, courses in Liberal Arts 1957–8; Miami Dade Community Coll. courses in business 1971; one-yr intensive course (in Caracas) in simultaneous interpretation and written transl. 1976. **Experience:** 20 yrs' as simultaneous interpreter (English/Spanish) specializing in cons., wildlife, etc., topics. **Career:** co-Founder & MD, Simultaneous Interpretation (Venezuela) 1979–. **Achievements:** trans.for IUCN SSC at Costa Rica Cong.1988 and Parks Cong.Caracas 1992, and several specialized topics incl.crocodiles, Scarlet Ibis *(Eudocimis ruber)*, etc. **Membership:** SCAV (Bd of Dirs, Sec. 1984 8). Favours pers.pub.& news media support. **Languages:** English (good), Spanish. Willing to act as an interpreter. **Address:** Simultaneous Interpretation, c/o CCS 1002, POB 025323, Miami, Florida 33102-5323, USA. **Tel.**(office) 58 2 985 1868, (home) 58 2 986 5981; **fax** 58 2 985 2594 (all in Venezuela).

THOMAS, Dr John Donald. Freshwater biology: epidemiology of parasites including those of fish & Man (schistosomiasis), biochemical ecology and behaviour of snail hosts of schistosome parasites, use of bioengineering approaches for control of schistosomiasis; ecology of eutrophication and acid deposition in relation to water management. Emeritus Reader. *B.*8 June 1928, Tregaron, Wales, UK. British. *M.*Joy (biol.): 2 *s.*Neil Julian (biol. teacher & conservationist), Ian Justin (mgr of agrofor. estate); 2 *d.* **Education:** U.of Wales BSc (Chem., Bot. & Zool.) 1949, BSc(Hons) 1950, PhD 1954, DSc 1988. **Experience:** res.based on ecol.of brown trout, salmon, eels, and their parasites; from 1953–65 worked in Ghana (then Gold Coast) on taxonomy, epidemiology of parasites, and limnol.of Man-made lakes; admin.as Chairman & Head of Zool.Dept., Chief Examiner in Biol.for W.African Exam.Council;

init.& organized several courses at U.of Sussex whose unit of Biochem.& Bioengg Ecol.(aimed at control of snail host of schistosomiasis) was recognized as WHO collaborating centre 1964–93; supervision of 18 PhD & three MSc students, many from overseas. **Career:** Dem.in Zool. U. of Wales 1950–53; Lect.in Zool. UC of the Gold Coast 1953–9; Sr Lect.1959–63, Assoc. Prof.of Zool.1963–5, U.of Ghana; Vis.Prof. UCB (Carnegie Fndn) 1963–4; Lect.in Ecol. 1965–9, Dir Unit of Biochem.& Bioengg Ecol. 1964–93, Reader in Ecol.1969–93, Emer.1993–, U.of Sussex. **Achievements:** dev.of an interdisc. approach to study of interactions between snails, their conspecifics, water plants, and their epiphytic Bacteria and Algae — with biochemists, chemists, microbiologists, and engrs; these have helped to lay the fndns for bioengg strats not only to control or prevent schistosomiasis but also to alleviate effects of eutrophication & acid deposition; these studies in biochem. ecol.demonstrate importance of mutualisms — involving the exchange of nutrients between *living* organisms, and thus make it necessary to re-evaluate the food-web dogma in freshwater ecol. **Memberships:** FBA (Life), BES, F.IBiol., C.IBiol. **Publications:** An eval. of the interactions between freshwater pulmonate snails of human schistosomes & macrophytes 1987, The comparative ecol biochem.of sugar chemoreception and transport in freshwater snails and other aquatic organisms 1989, Mutualistic interactions in freshwater modular systems with molluscan components 1990. Indiff.to pers.pub. & news media support. **Languages:** English, Welsh. Willing to act as consult.etc.on selective basis. **Address:** School of Biological Sciences, University of Sussex, Biology Building, Falmer, Brighton BN1 9Q9, Sussex, England, UK. **Tel.**(office) 44 1273 606755 ext.2759, (home) 44 1273 473997; **fax** 44 1273 678433.

THOMAS, Dr Urs P. Political & institutional dimensions of international environmental affairs; global environmental governance particularly the trade–environment linkage. Research Associate. *B.*18 May 1944, Zürich, Switzerland. Canadian, Swiss. Father Prof.Dr E.A.Thomas-Pauli (1912–86), hydrobiol., pioneer in wastewater treatment and dedicated envl conservationist. *D.* **Education:** Concordia U. (Montreal) BSc(Envl Biol.) 1981, MBA(Intl Business) 1984; U.of Quebec at Montreal, PhD (Pol.Sci.) 1993. **Experience:** 15 yrs' work exp. in intl business followed by a reorientation towards intl envl affairs while teaching part-time at five univs in Quebec & Ont. **Career:** Res. Assoc. Interdisc.Res.Group in Envl Mgmt, U.of Quebec 1993–. **Achievement:** contributed to estab.of intl envl affairs as a distinct subdiscipline in particular to res.emphasis on organized global ecopolitical forces. **Memberships:** ISA (Envl Studies Section), Academic Council on the UN System, CPSA, SQSP. **Publications:** several papers, incl.Guest Editorial in *EC.* Indiff. to pers.pub.; interested in, but suspicious of,

news media support. **Languages:** English, French, German. Willing to act as consult.etc. **Address:** 6307 rue Beaulieu, Montréal H4E 3E9, Québec, Canada. **Tel.**(office & home) 1 514 767 6220; **fax** 1 514 767 1537.

THORSELL, Dr James Westvick. Conservation, parks' management; world heritage convention. Senior Adviser on Natural Heritage. *B.*5 Dec.1940, Alb., Canada. Canadian. **Education:** U.of Alb. BSc 1962, U.of Western Ont. MA 1967, UBC PhD 1971. **Experience:** worked in wildlife cons.& park mgmt in 75 countries since 1962 (researcher, teacher, project leader, planner, mgr, & scientific adv.), six yrs' consult., five yrs on field projects in Carib.& E.Africa (four yrs as Asst Prof.& Sr Lect.). **Career:** Ranger, Banff Nat.Park 1962–4; Private Consult. 1971–6; Asst Prof. U.of Alb. 1977–9; Wildlife Planning Unit (Kenya) 1980–81; Coll.of African Wildlife Mgmt (Tanzania) 1982–3; Sr Adv. Natural Heritage, IUCN 1984–. **Achievements:** training of *c.*500 students, involved in planning & mgmt of 400 prot.areas, author of 250 reports & pubns. **Memberships:** F.RGS, Adv.Bd Seychelles Islands Fndn, Adv.Ed.*EC.* **Award:** F.Envt & Policy E–W Centre. **Publications:** *Managing Prot.Areas in the Tropics* 1987, *Parks on the Borderline: Exp.in Transfrontier Cons.* 1990, *Nat.Parks & Nature Reserves in the Mtn Regns of the World* 1992, *World Heritage Twenty Yrs Later* 1992. Accepts pers.pub., favours news media support. **Language:** English. Further details may be obtained from *Canadian Who's Who* 1987–. Willing to act as consult.etc. **Address:** IUCN — The World Conservation Union, Rue Mauverney 28, 1196 Gland, Switzerland. **Tel.** 41 22 999 0159; **fax** 41 22 999 0015.

THRESHER, Philip Brian. Wildlife resource conservation & utilization including corals; land-use cost–benefit analysis, especially local community benefits; project preparation. Independent Consultant. *B.*22 June 1925, Sandown, Isle of Wight, England, UK. Canadian. *M.* Carolyn Dorothy (past-vol., African Parks): 2 *d.*incl.Valerie Anne, BA(Envl Econ.). **Education:** New Coll.Oxf. BA(Philos., Pol. & Econ.) 1949, MA 1950; McGill U. Hudson Bay Scholar (For.Taxation) 1950–51. **Experience:** ten yrs in forest products industry & investment banking; 24 yrs in Third World land-use & dev.planning; lead role in delineation/justification of num. nat.parks & wildlife preserves incl.marine; sometimes known as 'the ecologists' economist', aka Philcarol (intlly-published wildlife photographer & lect.). **Career:** Captain, The Rifle Brigade (UK) 1944–6; Asst to Pres. Bathurst Power & Paper Co.(Montreal) 1951–7; Investment Banker 1957–60; Consult. IUCN — Middle E.& S.Asia 1961–2 & E.Africa 1963–4; Planning Adv. Tanzania Nat.Parks 1964–72; Wildlife Resource Economist, FAO (Kenya) 1973–7; Economist, Investment Centre, FAO (Rome) 1978–81; Team Leader, Agricl Restructuring (Barbados) 1982–3; Pres. Santa Barbara Botanic Gdn 1986–8; Founding Bd Dir & Treas. Center for Study of Envt (Santa Barbara) 1991–3; Ind.Consult. African For.Comm. Working Party on Wildlife/Prot.Areas 1993–. **Achievements:** youngest memb.of HRH The Duke of Edinburgh's Study Conf.on Human Relations in Industry 1956, first IUCN field economist, dev.of computer modelling of econ.of renewable natural resources (model EARNEST), integrated wildlife parks & ecosystems into rangeland dev., pioneering rural income from wildlife to benefit ranchers. **Publications:** *Woodlots for Farmers* (popular handbook) 1956, j.articles incl.The present value of an Amboseli Lion 1980. Indiff. to pers.pub.& news media support. **Languages:** English; French & German (working); Italian & Spanish (comp.). Willing to act as consult.etc. **Address:** POB 50018, Santa Barbara, California 93150-0018, USA. **Tel.**(home) & **fax** 1 805 969 2337.

TICKELL, Sir Crispin Charles Cervantes. Climatology, palaeohistory, mountains. Diplomat, College Warden, Centre Director. *B.*25 Aug. 1930, England, UK. *D.*: 2 *s.*, *d.*; *M.*Penelope. **Education:** Westminster Sch.; Christ Church Oxf. 1st Class Hons (Modern Hist.) 1952. **Experience:** military, diplomatic, admin., co.dir. **Career:** Coldstream Guards 1952–4; HM Diplomatic Service 1954–: served at The Hague 1955–8, Mexico 1958–61, Paris 1964–70, Private Sec.to Chancellor of Duchy of Lancaster 1970–72, Head of Western Orgns Dept at FCO 1972–5, F.Center for Intl Affairs, Harvard U.1975–6, Chef de Cabinet to Pres.of CEC 1977–81, Vis.F. All Souls Coll.Oxf.1981, Amb.to Mexico 1981–3, Perm. Sec. ODA FCO 1981–7, Perm.Rep.of UK to UN 1987–90; Warden, Green Coll.Oxf.1990– and Dir, Green Coll.Centre for Envl Policy & Understanding 1992–, U.of Oxf. **Memberships:** MAIL, F. RGS, F.ZS. **Awards:** MVO 1958, Officer Order of Orange-Nassau 1958, KCVO 1983, GCMG 1989, Global 500 Roll of Honour (UNEP) 1991, num.hon.degrees. **Publications:** incl.*Climatic Change & World Affairs* 1977. Favours pers.pub.& news media support. **Languages:** English, French. Further details may be obtained from *International Who's Who* 1994–5, British *Who's Who* 1996. Willing to act as consult.etc. **Address:** Warden's Lodgings, Green College, Oxford OX2 6HG, England, UK.

TIKHOMIROV, Professor Dr Vadim N. Morphology & taxonomy of higher plants, floristics; Nature protection. Department Chairman. *B.*27 Jan.1932, Moscow, Russia. Russian. *M.*Dr Ljagina Tatiana (ichthyology): *s.* **Education:** Moscow SU Dipl.1954, PhD 1959, Dr Sci.1978. **Experience:** res.— morphology & taxonomy of Umbelliferae, the genus *Alchemilla*, and gen. questions of evol.of angiosperms; field-work mainly in c.Russia 1952–; teaching 1951–. **Career:** Asst & Docent 1957–79, Chairman 1976–, Prof.1980–, Dept of Higher Plants, Moscow SU; Dir 1967–82, Curator 1982–, Moscow

SU Botl Gdn. **Achievements:** orgn of geogl prot.territories, Red Data book of USSR & Russia, regnl cons.activities. **Memberships:** VP RBS & MSN, All-Russian SNP (Hon.), Botl Soc.of Bulgaria. **Awards:** several medals of All-Union Exposition of Success of Economy of USSR, Grand Medal of All-Russian SNP. **Publications:** *Cons.of Nature* (co-Author, in Russian) 1967, 450 scientific papers & popular books. Favours news media support. **Languages:** English, Russian. **Address:** Faculty of Biology, Moscow State University, Moscow 119 899, Russia. **Tel.**(office) 7 095 939 2820, (home) 7 095 434 1985; **fax** 7 095 939 4309.

TIMOSHENKO, Dr Alexandre. International environmental law & institutions. Chief. *B.*18 Sept.1939, Moscow, Russia. Russian. *M.*Elena: *d.*, *s.* **Education:** Moscow State Inst.of Intl Relations, Dipl.in Intl Econ.1961; Inst.of State & Law, PhD(Intl Law) 1972, Dr of Legal Scis 1984. **Experience:** extensive res.incl. coordn & supervision of res.workers & intl civil servants; coordn of negotiations of intl legal instruments; expert & consult.services in envl law to nat.& intl agencies; teaching from BSc to PhD levels; work in trade & diplomatic missions. **Career:** Econ.Analyst, USSR Min.for Foreign Trade 1961–5, and USSR Embassy to Somalia 1965–9; Sr Legal Researcher 1973–86, Dir Envl Law Dept 1987–91, USSR AS; Chief, Intl Legal Instruments, ELI/PAC, UNEP 1991–. **Achievements:** dev.of intl envl law doctrine through teaching, res. & pubns; active participation in elaboration of 1978 UNEP Guidelines on Shared Natural Resources, 1979 ECE Conv.on Long-range Transboundary Air Poll., 1992 Conv.on Biol Diversity; Promoting USSR–USA, –UK, & –Italy, bilateral coopn in envl law. **Memberships:** IUCN CEL, ICEL, various UNEP & ECE expert groups, WCED Legal Expert Group. **Awards:** Bronze & Silver Medals by all-Union (USSR) Exhibit of Econ.Achievements. **Publications:** *Intl Envl Coopn Within the UN System* (in Russian) 1981, *Formation & Dev.of Intl Envl Law* (in Russian) 1986; 70+ articles & essays in English, Italian, Japanese, Polish, and Russian. Favours pers.pub.& news media support. **Languages:** English, French (read), Italian, Russian, Spanish (read). Willing to act as consult.etc. **Address:** Environmental Law and Institutions/ Programme Activity Centre, United Nations Environment Programme, POB 47074, Nairobi, Kenya. **Tel.**(office) 254 2 623478; **fax** 254 2 230198.

TINKER, Jon. Sustainable development, information, aids. Senior Associate. *B.*19 Jan. 1940, Huddersfield, England, UK. British. **Education:** Charterhouse Sch.; U.of Camb. BA(Natural & Moral Scis) 1961. **Career:** Pers. Sec.to Bertrand Russell OM, FRS, 1961–2; Press Officer, UK Council for Nature 1964–6; Ed.*Wildlife & the Countryside* 1964–70; Envt & Dev.Edl Consult.to *New Scientist* 1969–76; Founder & Dir, Earthscan, IIED 1974–86; Founder & Pres. Panos Insts 1986–93; Sr Assoc. Sust.Dev.Res.Inst. UBC 1993–. **Achievements:** in many articles for *New Sci.*developed role of envl reporting & analysis, at Earthscan & Panos pioneered techniques for raising world-wide public understanding of sust.dev.*via* media & NGOs. **Awards:** Winston Churchill Mem. F'ship 1970, Memb.UK R.Comm.on Envl Poll. 1973–4, Glaxo F'ship (ABSW), Global 500 Roll of Honour (UNEP) 1992. Accepts pers.pub.& news media support. **Languages:** English, French (adequate), Spanish (some). Willing to act as consult.etc. **Address:** Sustainable Development Research Institute, B5-2202 Main Mall, University of British Columbia, Vancouver, British Columbia V6T 1Z4, Canada. **Tel.**1 604 822 8198; **fax** 1 604 822 9191.

TISDELL, Professor Dr Clement Allan. Economics of conservation; environmental economics; marine resource economics. Professor & Head of Economics and Deputy Director, School of Marine Science. *B.*18 Nov.1939, Taree, NSW, Australia. Australian. *M.*Marie Elisabeth: *d., s.* **Education:** U.of NSW BCom(ECS) 1961, ANU PhD 1964. **Experience:** in-depth res.on wild pigs and giant clams (tridacnids) from economic, envl, & cons., perspectives; involved in jt project on wildlife cons.in China 1994– and leader of project examining sust.& cons.in rural India & Bangladesh (1992–3); u.lecturing in envl econ. **Career:** Temp.Lect.in Econ.1964, Postdoctl Scholar 1975, Lect.in Econ.& subs.Reader in Econ.1966–72, ANU; Prof.of Econ. U.of Newcastle (Australia) 1972–89; Prof.of Econ.& Head of Dept and Dep.Dir, Sch.of Marine Sci. U.of Qld 1989–. **Achievement:** promotion of cons.of living things by strengthening bonds between econ.& cons. **Memberships:** ISEE, ESA, Western Economic Assn. **Awards:** U.Medal (U.of NSW), F.ASSA, Hon.Prof.(People's U., Beijing), Vis.F'ship (JSPS). **Publications:** *Wild Pigs* 1982, *Natural Resources, Growth & Dev.*1990, *Econ.of Envl Cons.*1991, *Envl Econ.*1993, *Giant Clams in the Sust.Dev.of the S.Pacific* 1993*; several hundred other pubns.* Favours pers.pub.& news media support. **Languages:** English, French (limited). Further details may be obtained from *Who's Who in the World* 1995, *Who's Who in Australia* 1995, *The Writer's Directory* 1995. Willing to act as consult.etc. **Address:** Department of Economics, University of Queensland, Brisbane 4072, Australia. **Tel.**(office) 61 7 365 6242, (home) 61 7 379 4802; **fax** 61 7 365 7299.

TOIT, Raoul Frederic DU. Conservation of African megafauna & habitats; land-use & environmental impact assessment in developing countries; field protection & management of Black Rhinoceros (*Diceros bicornis*); integration of commercial & community-based conservation activities in conservancies as models for sustainable economic development in Africa's semi-arid rangelands. Project Executant. *B.*6 June 1957, Marondera, Zimbabwe. Zimbabwean. *M.*

Delee: *d.* **Education:** U.of Rhodesia BSc(Hons) (Geog.& Biol Scis) 1979, U.of Cape Town MSc (Envl Studies) 1982. **Experience:** coordinated EIAs of two major proposed hydroelectric schemes; EIAs of oil pipeline, transport system, etc.; rural dev.& land-use planning, investigations into rural poverty & land-use problems in Zimbabwe; fuel-wood usage (rural & urban), rural afforestation, ecol monitoring & resource inventories; veg.mapping esp.of Zambesi Valley, aerial wildlife surveys, planning commercial wildlife ops; cons.biol.— res.on Black Rhinoceros, field prot., capture, translocation, & all aspects of mgmt. **Career:** Cadet Distr.Officer, Rhodesian Min.of Internal Affairs 1976; Military Service (Rhodesian Security Forces) 1976–9; Res.F. 'Dept of Land Mgmt, Biol Scis, Geol. and L.Kariba Res.Station', U.of Zimbabwe 1981–5; Scientific/Exec.Officer, IUCN Elephant & Rhino SGs 1985–7; Project Executant, WWF 1988– (seconded to Zimbabwe Nat.Parks as Tech.Coopn Officer, Conservancy Project 1991–). **Achievements:** undertaking first major EIA in Zimbabwe, coordn of baseline res.for Zimbabwe rural afforestation project, estab.of Zimbabwe conservancies as world's largest private game reserves and as models for the fusion of commercial & community-based cons.interests, developing viable Black Rhinoceros breeding projects. **Memberships:** IUCN African Rhino SG, ZSA. **Awards:** Three Feathers Scholarship 1978–9, Best BSc Student Award (U.of Rhodesia) 1977/8/9, SA Breweries Scholarship, C.Salomon Scholarship (U.of Cape Town) 1980. **Publications:** *c.*40 scientific papers & res.reports. Indiff.to pers.pub.& news media support. **Languages:** Afrikaans (basic), English, Shona (basic). Willing to act as consult.etc. **Address:** Rhino Conservancy Project, POB 1409, Causeway, Zimbabwe. **Tel.**263 4 882412; **fax** 263 4 730599.

TOLBA, Dr Mostafa Kamal. Philosophy of environmentally-sound development (Development without Destruction). Centre President. *B.* 8 Dec.1922, Gharbiah, Egypt. Egyptian. *M.* Saneya Zaki. **Education:** U.of Cairo, BSc 1943; U.of London PhD(Plant Pathol.) 1949, DIC 1988. **Career:** Asst Lect., Lect., Prof.of Microbiol. Cairo U., Egyptian Nat.Res.Centre, and Baghdad U. 1943–59; Asst Sec.-Gen., Sec.-Gen. Supreme Sci.Council (Egypt) 1959–63; Cultural Couns.& Dir, Egyptian Educ.Bur. (Washington, DC) 1963–5; Under-Sec.of State for Higher Educ.1965–71; Minister of Youth 1971; Pres. Acad.of Scientific Res.and Tech. 1971–3; Dep.Exec.Dir, UNEP 1973–5; Under-Sec.-Gen.UN & Exec.Dir UNEP 1976–92; Prof. Fac.of Sci. Cairo U.; Pres. ICED 1992–. **Memberships:** UN Adv.Bd on Sust.Dev., GEF (Adv. Group), Egyptian Adv.Councils on Prod., Services, and Scientific Res.& Educ. **Awards:** State Prize in Biol.1959, Hon.Prof.(Beijing U.), F.IC, Hon.Dr (Moscow U.), Hon.DSc (Seoul U.), (U.of Gembloux) 1985, and (U.of Nairobi) 1989, Hon.LLD (Williams Coll.) 1990, Sasakawa Envt

Prize (UNEP) 1993; other prizes and decorations from 21 countries. **Publications:** *Dev.without Destruction* 1982, *Earth Matters* 1983, *Sust.Dev.: Constraints and Opportunities* 1987, *Evolving Envl Perceptions: from Stockholm to Nairobi* 1988; 95 scientific papers. **Address:** International Centre for Environment and Development, Misr Construction Company Building–5, Sheraton Heliopolis Area, Cairo, Egypt, **tel.**20 2 266 5800 or 1267, **fax** 20 2 266 1267; *or* 8 Jules-Crosnier, CH-1206 Geneva, Switzerland, **tel.**41 22 346 9673, **fax** 41 22 347 5142.

TOLENTINO, Attorney Amado. Environmental law, legislative analysis; institutional development. Legal Consultant. *B.*28 Oct. 1942, Philippines. Filipino. *M.*Lourdes Eleazar: *d.* **Education:** U.of the Philippines LLB 1963, Universidad de Madrid 1969, U.of Texas 1974. **Experience:** consult.on envl law to UNEP, UN/ESCAP, ADB, private consult.firms, and in developing countries *e.g.*PNG, Tuvalu, Gambia; admin.as Dir Envl Mgmt Bur.and Coord. ASEAN Expert Group on Envt; conf.resource provision. **Career:** Dir Envl Mgmt Bur. 1987–9, Coord.ASEAN Expert Group on Envt 1987–9, Legal Consult. Fndn for Sust.Dev.Inc. 1990–. **Achievements:** pioneered envl law and spearheaded adoption of envt policy, code, & rules to implement EIA, in Philippines; introduced envl law course into curriculum of U.of Philippines and envt-oriented legis.& instns; co-Author of first Filipino envl law textbook; reviewed & eval.envl legis.& admin.in many developing countries; formulated & developed legal framework for EIA & hazardous waste control; assessed illegal traffic in toxic waste in Asia–Pacific. **Memberships:** Philippine & NY Bars, IUCN CEL (VC), ICEL (Regnl Gov.), IAWL. **Awards:** Elected Del. Philippines Constnl Conv.1971; Grantee (Envl Law), Intl Visitor Prog. US State Dept 1976, 1990; Vis.F. E–W Center 1983. **Publications:** Brave world of parks & wildlife legis.1982, Legislative response to marine threats in the Asian sub-regn 1988, Don't dump on the third world 1989, Legal & instnl arrangements for envt prot.& sust.dev.in developing countries 1991, Envl Law in the Philippines 1992; num.other papers. Favours pers.pub.& news media support. **Languages:** English, Filipino, Spanish. Willing to act as consult.etc. **Address:** 7 Mahiyain Street, Diliman, Quezon City 1100, Philippines. **Tel.**63 2 921 7878; **fax** 63 2 922 6397.

TÖLGYESI, Dr István. Appropriate management of the Kiskunság National Park and other comparable protected areas. Deputy Director. *B.*20 Feb.1947, Nagy Anizsa, Hungary. Hungarian. *M.*Maria Lendvai (envl educ.): 2 *s.*, *d.* **Education:** background education particularly in biology, botany, & phytocoenology; Eötvös Lóránd U.for Scis, PhD 1983. **Experience:** veg.and the selection of mgmt techniques on particular sites; direction of work of Nat.Park

professional staff. **Career:** Sec.Sch.Teacher 1972–4; Nat.Park Officer & Researcher 1975–89; Head of Nature Cons.Dept 1989–91, Deputy Dir 1992–, Kiskunság Nat.Park Directorate. **Achievements:** gathering info.re.wildlife in prot.areas and applying appropriate mgmt/maintenance techniques. **Memberships:** Hungarian AS (Nature Cons.Comm.1980–). **Awards:** Outstanding Worker's Prize (Min.for Envl Educ.) 1988 & 1990. **Publications:** Nat.Park in Kiskunság 1979, Res.work in Kiskunság Nat. Park during 1975–85 1986. Favours news media support. **Languages:** English, Hungarian. Willing to act as consult.etc. **Address:** Liszt Ferenc utca 19, 6000 Kecskemet, Hungary. **Tel.**36 76 482611; **fax** 36 76 481074.

TOMAR, Dr Sadachari Singh. Bio-energy & environmental pollution. Senior Scientist. *B.*10 July 1951, Satna, MP, India. Indian. *M.*Sarla. **Education:** Awadhesh Pratap Singh U. BSc, U.of Jabalpur BTech(Agricl Eng.) 1976; U.of Bhopal MTech(Engg Materials) 1985, PhD(Envl Eng.) 1993. **Experience:** 17 yrs' res.& admin. an agricl envt, conducted res.on bio-energy & envl poll., in charge of wasteland dev., biogas and remote sensing in MP, consult.to MP Consult.Orgn, Bhopal. **Career:** Res.F. (Agricl Eng.) C.Soil and Water Cons.Res.& Training Inst.1976–7; Training Asst, C Farm Machinery Training & Testing Inst.1977–8; Sci.1978–85, Sr Sci. Agricl Energy and Power Div.1985–, CIAE; Jt Dir, Govt of MP 1985–90. **Achievements:** completed res.project on pollutants from biogas plants & compost pits, PhD, pubns. **Memberships:** Inst.of Engrs (India), Bio-energy Soc.of India, ISAE, ARSF. **Awards:** Dr Rajendra Prasad Award on Energy (Govt of India) 1985, Pres.of India Prize on Energy & Envt 1991–2, Jawaharlal Nehru Award 1995, Book Award* (Min.of Health and Family Welfare) 1996; *c.*50 others. **Publications:** *Annotated Bibl.of Testing of Internal Combustion Engines with Alcohol Fuels* 1982, *Agricl Engg Directory* (Orange Book) *1984, Alternate Energy Sources for Agric.*1990, *Effect of Mechanical Dev.Work on Envt* 1992, **Soybean: Agric., Engg, Chem.and Nutrition* 1995; ten other books re.agricl energy & engg; *c.*74 papers incl.Scope of substitution of diesel by alcohol & biogas 1982. Favours pers. pub.& news media support. **Languages:** English, Hindi. Willing to act as consult.etc. **Address:** 86 Kothari Complex, Bhopal 462 016, Madhya Pradesh, India. **Tel.**91 755 554578 or 553224; **fax** 91 755 553929 or 554365; **e-mail** root%mpcost@sirnetdernetin .

TOMPSETT, Dr Paul Benjamin. Seed conservation; forest genetic resources research. Research Fellow. *B.*18 Dec.1944, Tunbridge Wells, Kent, England, UK. British. **Education:** King's Sch.(Canterbury); Hertford Coll. Oxf. MA 1966; U.of London, PhD 1972. **Experience:** res.on flowering mechanisms and seed physiol.; consult.on forest genetic resources' res. for IPGRI & ACIAR 1992–3. **Career:** Researcher, Chelsea Coll. U.of London –1975; Res.F. Long Ashton Res.Station, U.of Bristol –1979; Res.F. R.Botanic Gdns Kew 1979–. **Achievements:** completed consultancy to recommend res.agenda in forest genetic resources for relevant centres of consultative group in intl agric.res.1993; completed 16 yrs of res.on seed cons.physiol. **Memberships:** AAB, SEB. **Publications:** num.papers incl.Capture of genetic resources by collection and storage of seed: a physiol.approach 1994. Indiff.to pers. pub.& news media support. **Languages:** English, French, German (basic), Spanish, Thai (basic). Willing to act as consult.etc. **Address:** Royal Botanic Gardens Kew, Richmond, Surrey, England, UK. **Tel.**(office) 44 181 332 5087, (home & **fax**) 44 1444 452789; **fax** 44 181 332 5069.

TOORNSTRA, Franke Hendrik. Natural resource management in rural development; strategic environmental assessment; participatory approaches. Consultant, Programme Coordinator. *B.*19 Sept.1959, Heerenveen, The Netherlands. Dutch. **Education:** Agricl U. Wageningen, BSc (Soil & Water Cons.) 1980, MSc (Rural Engr & Agron.) 1984. **Experience:** res.on wetland functions & mgmt in trop.countries and on methodological dev.of participatory envl assessment; four yrs as dir of training & res.inst.; consults on natural resource mgmt in rural dev. **Career:** Researcher, Centre for Envl Sci. U.of Leiden 1984–8; Dir, Centre for Envt & Dev. Studies (Cameroon) 1988–92; Consult.& Coord. Envl Assessment Prog. AIDEnvt 1993–. **Achievements:** dev.of participatory envl assessment & planning methods; elaboration of legis.on EIA in several African countries. **Publications:** *c.*25 incl.LEARN: a methodological challenge for rapid envl assessment (co-Author) 1991, Intro.à la gestion des ressources naturelles dans le Département du Moyo Sava 1993, *Deforestation in a Context: A Cameroon Case Study* (report) 1994. Indiff.to pers.pub., favours news media support. **Languages:** Dutch, English, French, German, Portuguese (read). Willing to act as consult.etc. **Address:** AID Environment, Donker Curtinsstraat 7-523, 1051 JL Amsterdam, The Netherlands. **Tel.**(office) 31 20 6868 111, (home) 31 71 1556 57; **fax** 31 20 6866 251.

TORTELL, Dr Philip. Coastal resources' management; marine pollution control; environmental administration & law; environmental impact assessment, mitigation, & audit. Managing Director & Principal Consultant. *B.*16 Sept.1941, Balzan, Malta. Maltese, New Zealander. *M.* Dorothy: 2 *d.* **Education:** Malta Coll.of Educ. Dipl.in Teaching 1961; U.of Otago Dipl.in Phys. Educ.1965, U.of London BSc(Spec.) (Zool.) 1970; Vic.U.of Wellington BSc(Hons) (Zool.) 1971, PhD 1976. **Experience:** marine farming res.in NZ & SE Asia; public admin.& policy analysis; aid projects in Philippines, Indonesia, Fiji, Bangladesh, Iran, DPR of Korea, India, Bahrain, NW Pacific, Eastern Africa, and SE Asia regn; consult.for UNEP, UNDP, UNESCO,

FAO, IMO, GEF, and NZ, Maltese & Hungarian Govts; teaching primary- to adult-level; Planning Tribunal expert witness. **Career:** teaching in Malta & NZ at primary, sec., teachers' coll., & u., levels 1961–76; aid consult.to NZ Govt 1976–7; Investigating Sci.& Policy Analyst, NZ Comm.for the Envt 1977–85; Exec.Dir NZ NCC 1985–6; Coord.of unit setting up new Dept of Cons.1986–7; Dir, Prot. Ecosystems & Species, Dept of Cons.1987–9; MD & Prin.Consult. Envl Mgmt Ltd 1989–. **Achievements:** discovery of special rope for suspension farming of marine mussels; active contribn to dev.of envl law; admin.& procedures in NZ; collation & editing of *'NZ Atlas of Coastal Resources'* and dev.of methodology for coastal-zone mapping; var.assistance to developing countries & regns. **Memberships:** NZMSS, RSNZ, UN GESAMP, IUCN CEL, GEF Adv.Group on Intl Waters. **Awards:** Commonwealth Scholar 1963–5, Fulbright F.1976. **Publications:** *NZ Atlas of Coastal Resources* 1981, *Mangroves in NZ — Trees in the Tide* (co-Author) 1990, *Envl Guidelines for Dredging & River Improvement* (co-Author) 1992, *Review of the Envl & Legal Implications of Artificial Reefs* 1993; 80+ scientific & popular papers, consult.reports. Favours pers.pub.& news media support. **Languages:** Arabic (spoken), English, Italian, Maltese; some French, German, & Spanish. Willing to act as consult., project mgr, &/or envl adv. **Address:** Environmental Management Ltd, POB 17 391, Wellington, New Zealand. **Tel.**(office & home) 64 4 476 9276; **fax** 64 4 476 0000.

TRAPNELL, Colin Graham. Land & forest ecology in tropical Africa with particular reference to soil, vegetation, and land-use classification & cartography; applications of field research to conservation. Retired. *B.*10 April 1907, London, England, UK. British. *M.*Jeanne Mary: *s.*, 2 *d.* **Education:** Sedbergh Sch.; Trinity Coll. Oxf. BA (Lit.Hum.)1929, R.Coll.of Sci.1930. **Experience:** Oxf.U. Greenland Expedn 1928 (veg.survey), Ecol Survey of Zambia (then Northern Rhodesia) involving field survey of soils, veg.& agricl systems of the territory 1932–40; teaching & veg.survey work in E.Africa 1950–62; air photo interpretation of approx. 40,000 sq.miles for compilation of 1:250,000 veg.maps of SW Kenya. **Career:** Ecol. Dept of Agric. Northern Rhodesia 1931– 50; Officer in charge of Ecol Training, E. African Agric.& For. Res.Orgn 1950–62; post-retirement positions on W.of England cons. bodies. **Achievements:** dev. of ecol methods in agric.& land-use studies in Africa; estab.of Trapnell Fund for Envl Field Res.in Africa (U.of Oxf.); donor of several Nature Reserves in W.of England. **Memberships:** former of Bot. Soc.& Exchange Club of the Brit.Isles, BES, BSSS. **Award:** OBE. **Publications:** *The Soils, Veg.& Agricl Systems of N.Western Rhodesia* (co-Author)1937, *The Soils, Veg.& Agric.of Eastern Rhodesia* 1943, *Veg.– Soils Maps of Northern Rhodesia with accompanying Memorandum (1:1,000,000)* (co-Author)

1947, *Veg.& Climate Maps of S.Western Kenya (1:250,000)* (co-Author) 1987, The aims of pasture mgmt in Northern Rhodesia 1933, Ecol results of woodland burning experiments in Northern Rhodesia 1959, The Rainfall–altitude relation and its ecol sig.in Kenya (co-Author) 1960, The effects of fire & termites on a Zambian woodland soil 1976, Microaggregates in red earths & related soils in E.& c.Africa (co-Author) 1986. Indiff.to pers.pub.& news media support. **Languages:** English, Spanish (read, limited written). **Address:** Sunnyside, 2 Ivywell Road, Sneyd Park, Bristol BS9 1NX, England, UK. **Tel.**(home) 44 1272 685796.

TRENČIANSKA, Jana. Agricultural amelioration and irrigation systems; waste management. Waste Management Expert. *B.*7 Aug.1952, Nitra, Slovak Rep. Slovakian. *M.*Dr Roman S. Krajčovič *qv*: 2 *d.* **Education:** Agricl U.(Nitra), Dipl.Ing.1976. **Experience:** project designing (land readjustment); agricl amelioration; drainage systems, water supply and sewage systems; res.in ecol optimization of land-use planning in agricl landscapes; waste mgmt. **Career:** Project Designer, Res.and Project Inst.for Agric. (Zilina) 1976–9, Inst.for Urban Planning (Zilina) 1980–83, and Ministère de l'Hydraulique, de l'Environnement et des Forêts (Algeria) 1983–7; Sr Researcher, Inst.of Landscape Ecol, Slovak AS 1988–91; Head of Dept for Nature Cons.and Waste Mgmt, Regnl Government for Envt (Nitra) 1992–. **Achievement:** exec.search (legal, tech./techl, envl) for waste mgmt. **Publications:** several tech.reports. **Languages:** French, German, Russian, Slovak. Willing to act as consult.etc. **Address:** Regional Government for Environment, Stefanikova tr.69, 949 01 Nitra, Slovak Republic. **Tel.**42 87 522111; **fax** 42 87 413932.

TRESHOW, Professor Dr Michael. Air pollution biology. Emeritus Professor of Biology. *B.*14 July 1926, Copenhagen, Denmark. American. *M.*Jean Frances: 2 *s.* **Education:** UCD PhD 1954. **Experience:** consult.in envl systems; res.& teaching in biol., bot., & envl systems. **Career:** Prof.of Biol.1961–94, Emer.1994–, U.of Utah. **Achievements:** pubns. **Publications:** ten books incl.*Plant Stress from Air Poll.* 1991. Willing to act as consult.etc. **Address:** 3124 Emigration Canyon, Salt Lake City, Utah 84108, USA. **Tel.**(office & home) 1 801 582 0803.

TROMPF, Professor Dr Garry Winston. Research & writing on religions & environmental concerns. Professor in the History of Ideas, Visiting Fellow. *B.*27 Nov.1940, Melbourne, Australia. Australian. *M.*Dr Robyn R.(trop.medicine): 3 *d.*incl.Sharon Joya (green activist esp.for Wilderness Soc., Australia); son-in-law Dr Nicholas V.C.Polunin *qv*. **Education:** U.of Melbourne, BA(Hons) 1962, Dip. Ed. (Hons) 1963; Monash U. MA 1967; U.of Oxf. MA 1974; ANU PhD 1975. **Experience:** res. **Career:** Vis.Prof.in Hist.and Religious Studies,

UCSC 1975; F.Merrill Coll.UCSC 1975, 1982, 1988; Sr Lect.in Religious Studies 1975–7, Prof. of Hist.1983–5, U.of PNG (Port Moresby) 1975–7; Lect.1978–9, Sr Lect.1980–82, in Religious Studies, U.of Sydney; Vis.Prof. in Religion and the Social Scis, Rijskuniversiteit (The Netherlands) 1984; Assoc.Prof.in Religious Studies 1986–94, Prof.in the Hist.of Ideas 1995–, U.of Sydney; Vis.F. U.of Edinburgh 1996. **Achievements:** articles on religions & envl issues as work towards a monogr.on this subject. **Memberships:** AJRH, AASR, F. 1988– of Res. Inst.for Asia and the Pacific, and Counc.1991– of Centre for Peace and Conflict Studies (both U.of Sydney), Edl Bd *EC* 1995–. **Awards:** Dwight Prize in Educ.(U.of Melbourne) 1963, Brit.Free Passage Scholar (UK Govt) 1965, Fulbright Award (Australian– Amer.Fndn & US Govt) 1974–5, Charles Strong Lect.(Charles Strong Trust, Australia) 1980, Australian Res.Council Grant (Australian Govt) 1990–92, Res.Enablement Prog.Award (Pew Bequest) 1993–4. **Publications:** num.incl. *Friedrich Max Muller as a Theorist of Comparative Religion* 1978, *The Idea of Histl Recurrence in Western Thought* Vol.1 1979, *Melanesian Religion* 1991, *Payback: the Logic of Retribution in Melanesian Religions* 1994, *Religions of Oceania* (co-Author) 1995. Accepts pers.pub.& news media support. **Languages:** French, Italian, Neo-Melanesian Hiri Motu, Spanish; German, Greek, Hebrew, Latin, Portuguese (all spoken). Further details may be obtained from *Who's Who in the World* 1989. Willing to act as consult.etc. **Address:** School of Studies in Religion, University of Sydney, Sydney, New South Wales 2006, Australia. **Tel.**(office) 61 2 692 3650, (home) 61 2 489 6285; **fax** 61 2 552 1451.

TRZYNA, Dr Thaddeus 'Ted' Charles. Environmental policy. President, Director, Senior Associate. *B.*26 Oct.1939, Chicago, Illinois, USA. American. **Education:** USC BA (Intl Relations) 1961, Claremont Grad.Sch. PhD (Govt) 1975. **Experience:** consult.to USEPA, President's CEQ and other US fed.& Calif.state agencies; projects combining policy res.& discussion on energy, farmland prot., hazardous waste, & biol.diversity issues, EIA as policy tool, collaborative policy fora as a means of problem-solving in cons., improving links between res.& policy-making; writer, NGO leader, conf.org. **Career:** US Foreign Service Officer 1962–9; Pres. CIPA 1969–; Sr Assoc. Center for Politics & Policy, The Claremont Grad.Sch.1989–; Dir, Intl Center for the Envt & Public Policy 1993–. **Achievements:** promoting communication & coopn of envl problems across professions & sectors of soc.through a series of widely-used info.guides, mtgs, and res.& experimentation with collaborative decision-making. **Memberships:** ISA, SID, PIASA, HSSF, US Assn for Club of Rome, IUCN CESP (Chair), Sierra Club (past Chair). **Publications:** *The Calif.Envl Qual.Act* 1974, *The Calif.Handbook* (Ed.six edns) 1969–90, *World Directory of Envl Orgns*

(Ed.five edns) 1973–96, *The Power of Convening: Collaborative Policy Forums for Sust. Dev.*1990, *A Sustainable World: Defining and Measuring Sustainable Development* (co-Ed.) 1995. Favours pers.pub.& news media support. **Languages:** English, French (good). Willing to act as consult.etc. **Address:** California Institute of Public Affairs, POB 189040, Sacramento, California 95818, USA. **Tel.**1 916 442 2472; **fax** 1 916 442 2478.

TSHERNYSHEV, Professor Dr Wladimir B. Insect ecology, ecology of agro-ecosystems; ecological pest management; diurnal rhythms, influence of geomagnetic storms. Professor of Entomology. *B.*16 May 1936, Moscow, Russia. Russian. *M.*Valentina M.Afonina (entomol.): *s.* **Education:** Moscow SU, MSc 1958, PhD 1963, DSc 1978. **Experience:** widespread res.esp.in Karakum Desert (Turkmenistan). **Career:** Jr Sci.1961, Sr Sci.1975, Leading Sci.1986, Prof.of Entomol.1992–, Dept of Entomol. Fac.of Biol. Moscow SU. **Achievements:** proposed new strat.of ecol pest mgmt without chem.pesticides instead of integrated pest mgmt, some improvements in *Trichogramma* rearing (the main agent of biol pest control). **Memberships:** Russian Entomol.Soc.(C.Council), MSNH (C.Council), Council for Space Biol., Council for Industrial Entomol.(Chair). **Awards:** Prominent Scientist Scholarship, Veteran of Labour Medal, Prize (MSNH), Certs from Min.of Higher Educ.and on Scientific Problem Biodiv.(ISF). **Publications:** *Biol Rhythms* (co-Author) 1980, *Diurnal Rhythms of Activity in Insects* (co-Author) 1984, *Cultures of Insects & Mites in the USSR* (co-Author) 1988, *Insect Ecol.*(in press); *c.*200 scientific pubns. **Languages:** English (poor), French & German (read), Russian. Willing to act as consult.etc. **Address:** Department of Entomology, Faculty of Biology, Moscow State University, Moscow 119899, Russia. **Tel.**(office) 7 095 939 1695, (home) 7 095 246 6076; **fax** 7 095 939 5022.

TUBOKU-METZGER, Daphne Joan Adewomi. Conservation of biodiversity & wilderness in West Africa particularly Sierra Leone. School Head, NGO Founder & Chairman. *B.*15 Sept.1948, Freetown, Sierra Leone. Sierra Leonean. **Education:** St Agnes and St Michael (UK); St Hild's Coll. U.of Durham, BEd.1972. **Experience:** res.— status of Manatees *[Trichechus senegalensis]* in SL (1987) and propagation of indigenous forest trees (1987–94); teaching of biol.at primary & sec.levels; organized & initiated first field survey (1981) of forest elephant in SL. **Career:** Teacher, Port Loko Teachers' Coll.1972–3; Biol.& Art Teacher, Sec.Schools in SL 1973–5; Head of Kingharman Ind.Sch.(Freetown) 1975–; Founder and Exec.Memb. Council for Prot.of Nature (then SLENCA) 1976–. **Achievements:** founder of one of the first indigenous cons.NGOs in Africa, heightening public awareness in SL about need for cons.and care of envt, initiating & promoting scientific res.into status of species and habitats of

which little was known, bringing to an end uncontrolled trafficking of rare & endangered species out of SL, creation (through Council for Prot.of Nature) of first prot.area (Mamunta-Mayoso Nature Reserve) in SL 1977. **Membership:** IUCN SSC. **Publications:** incl.Why the Gola forests should be conserved 1977, an article calling for ban on the export of Chimpanzees [*Anthropopithecus troglodytes*] and other endangered species 1978, Wildlife utilization — an answer to protein deficiency in Africa 1979. Favours pers.pub.& news media support. **Languages:** English, Krio (SL). Willing to act as consult.etc. **Address:** Council for Protection of Nature, 17 Bath Street, Brookfields, Freetown, Sierra Leone. **Tel.** (office) 232 22 242277, (home) 232 22 240956.

TURIAN, Professor Gilbert. Microbiology and natural sciences. Professor of General Microbiology. *B.*5 Dec.1926, Geneva, Switzerland. Swiss. *M.*Yvonne: *s., d.* **Education:** U.of Geneva Lic.1948, DSc 1951, PD 1953. **Experience:** res.in fungal morphogenesis & bipolarity; envl bioindicators. **Career:** Bruce Post-doctl F.(Biol.), Johns Hopkins U.1951–2; Swiss Fed.Agricl Station 1952–4; Researcher, Swiss Nat.Fund 1954–8; Res.Asst Prof. (Mycology), Michigan SU 1958–9; Assoc.Prof.1961, Extraordinary Prof.1964, Full Prof.1971–, U.of Geneva. **Achievements:** first mapping of lichens as indicators of air poll.in Geneva (in *Saussurea* 1975, 1985). **Memberships:** NYAS, ASM, MSA, SHSN, BMS, SSPP, Geneva & Swiss Microbiol., Mycology, Botl, & Entomol., Socs. **Publications:** *Différenciation fongique* 1969, *The Fungal Spore* (co-Ed.) 1981, *Polarity* 1989–92; chapters in many intl journals & books. Indiff.to pers.pub., favours news media support. **Languages:** English, French, German. Willing to act as consult.etc. **Address:** Chemin Semailles 10, 1211 Grand-Lancy, Geneva, Switzerland. **Tel.**(office) 41 22 702 6755, (home) 41 22 794 0704; **fax** 41 22 781 1747.

TURNER, Professor Dr R.Eugene. Wetlands; biological oceanography; conservation, management. Professor of Oceanography and Coastal Sciences. *B.*7 April 1945, Niskayuna, NY, USA. *M.*Nancy Nash Rabalais (collab., ecol.): *d.* **Education:** Monmouth Coll. BA 1967; Drake U. MA 1969; U.of Georgia, PhD 1974. **Experience:** consult.to Indonesian Govt 1975, USAID, US Justice Dept; Chair, INTECOL Wetland WG and Dept of Oceanogr.and Coastal Scis, Louisiana SU; US NAS Exchange (Czech.); NRC Panel 1991–4; AGU Book Bd 1990–94; Ed.*Wetlands' Ecol.and Mgmt* 1992– and *Coastal and Estuarine Sci.Series* 1995–. **Career:** Asst Prof.1975–8 & Assoc.Prof. 1978– 83 of Marine Scis, Prof.of Oceanogr.and Coastal Scis 1983–, Chair of Dept of Marine Sci.1989–90 and of Dept of Oceanogr.and Coastal Sci.1990–92, Louisiana SU; Chair, INTECOL Wetland WG 1984–. **Achievement:** dev.of strong scientific basis for mgmt endeavours esp.of coastal ecosystems. **Memberships:** AAAS, ESA, ASLO, INTECOL, SWS, AGU, AFS, Soc.for Trop.Sci. **Awards:** F'ship (US NSF) 1972–4, Exchange Prog.(NAS) 1979, Nat.Resource Panel (US) 1991–4. **Publications:** seven books; 200+ scientific papers etc. Indiff.to pers.pub., favours news media support. **Languages:** English; Indonesian & Spanish (limited). Further details may be obtained from *Who's Who in Amer.Sci.*1995. Willing to act as consult.etc. **Address:** Department of Oceanography and Coastal Sciences, Louisiana State University, Baton Rouge, Louisiana 70803, USA. **Tel.**(office) 1 504 388 6454, (home) 1 504 752 4706; **fax** 1 504 388 6326.

UDVARDY, Professor Dr Miklos Dezso Ferenc. Biogeography, ornithology. Professor Emeritus of Biology. *B.*23 March 1919, Debrecen, Hungary. American. *M.*Maud E.: *s.*, 2 *d.* **Education:** U.of Debrecen PhD 1942. **Experience:** res.zool.& biogeog., writer, teacher, consult.to IUCN. **Career:** Asst Biol. Hungarian Inst.of Ornith.1942–5, Res.Assoc.in Biol. Hungarian AS 1945–8, Res.F.In Zool. Univs of Helsinki 1948–9 & Uppsala 1949–50; Asst Curator, Swedish Mus.of Natural Hist. 1951; Vis.Lect.in Ecol. U.of Toronto 1951–2, Lect.in Zool. UBC 1952–3, Asst Sci. Fisheries Res.Bd (Canada) 1952–5; Vis.Prof. Univs of Hawaii 1958–9 & Bonn 1970–71, Vis.Spec.Lect. UCLA 1963–4, Fulbright Lect.at U.of Honduras 1971–2; Summer Lect.at U.of Pasadena 1958, U.of Texas 1961, UCSB 1964, & U.of Arizona 1969; Asst Prof.1953–9, Assoc.Prof.1959–66, Prof.of Biol Sci.1966–83, Emer.1983–, Calif.SU. **Achievements:** the 'Udvardy System' of biogeogl realms & provinces of the Earth (on land) used by UNESCO, UNEP, WWF, IUCN. **Memberships:** AAAS, IUCN, CNPPA + 20 other socs & groups. **Awards:** F.AAAS, Corres.Memb. Finnish & Argentinian Ornithl Socs, Doctor *H.C.*(U.of Debrecen) 1989, Hungarian AS 1993. **Publications:** *Dynamic Zoogeogr.* 1969 (in Polish 1978 & Hungarian 1983), *A Class.of the Biogeogl Provinces of the World* 1975; *c.*180 papers, maps, & books. Accepts pers. pub.& news media support. **Languages:** English, German, Hungarian, Spanish, Swedish (all written); Danish, Dutch, Italian, Latin, Norwegian, Portuguese (all written & read). Further details may be obtained from *Who's Who in Sci.& Engg* (2nd edn). Willing to act as consult. etc. **Address:** Department of Biological Sciences, California State University, Sacramento, California 95819, USA. **Tel.** (office) 1 916 278 6535, (home) 1 916 487 1844; **fax** 1 916 278 6664.

UEXKÜLL, Carl Jakob Wolmar VON. Environment; sustainability; third world; economics; human rights. Chairman (Founder), Trustee. *B.* 19 Aug.1944, Uppsala, Sweden. German, Swedish. *M.*Sue: *s.* Grandfather Prof.Jakob von Uexküll, biol. **Education:** Christ Church Oxf. MA 1969. **Experience:** res.into & admin. of Right Livelihood Awards. **Career:** Journalist & Translator 1966–70, philately business 1970–

79, Founder & Chairman of Rt Livelihood Awards 1980–, Memb.of Euro.Parliament (Green Party) 1984–9. **Achievement:** founding Rt Livelihood Awards. **Membership:** F.RSA. **Publications:** *Il Premio Nobel Alternativo* 1988, *Projekte der Hoffnung* (co-Ed.) 1990. Favours pers.pub.& news media support. **Languages:** English, French, German, Swedish. Willing to act as consult.etc. **Address:** Right Livelihood Award, POB 15072, S-104 65 Stockholm, Sweden. **Tel.**46 8 702 0340; **fax** 46 8 702 0338.

UGWU, Christopher Ngwu. Conservation of biodiversity — stimulation of community-based conservation programmes & efforts; environmental impact assessment studies of governmental and non-governmental development projects. Programme Director & Research Fellow. *B.*11 Oct.1954, Nsukka, Enugu State, Nigeria. Nigerian. *M.*Faith O.(Coord. Women in Dev.Project of NSIRP): *s.*, 2 *d.* **Education:** U. of Nigeria, BSc(Hons)(Geog.) 1981, Postgrad. Dipl.in Educ.1987. **Experience:** res.— conducts adaptive res.aimed at rural improvement and regeneration; admin., consult.to UNDP & GEF, teaching. **Career:** Sch.Teacher, Christ High Sch.1975–7 and Edem Community Sec. Sch.1981–2; Sr Master, State Educ.Comm. 1982–90; Planning Officer, Min.of Finance & Planning 1990–91, Prog.Dir & Res.F. NSIRP 1991–. **Achievements:** being intl cttee memb. for pubn of a Guide*, and memb.of an Expert Group that articulated African Position on the Cons.of Biodiv.1994; having an opportunity to nominate an awardee for the 1994 Earth Day Intl Award. **Memberships:** Nigeria Geogl Soc., NCF, Envt Liaison Centre Intl (Nairobi, Memb./ Partner). **Awards:** Best Trickle Up Coord. (Trickle Up Prog.Inc. NY) 1992, training grants from Trickle Up Prog.Inc.1992 and UNDP 1993. **Publications:** The new Land Use Act in Nigeria — to be or not to be? 1990, *Partnership Guide for the Envt* (co-Author) 1993, two res.papers. Indiff.to pers.pub. **Languages:** English, French (poor). Willing to act as consult.&/or judge proposals. **Address:** Nigeria Society for the Improvement of Rural People, POB 3125, University of Nigeria, Nsukka, Enugu State, Nigeria. **Tel.** (office) 234 42 254968, (home) 234 42 259133; **fax** 234 42 258677 or 254811.

ULLUWISHEWA, Dr Rohana Kumarasiri. Biogeography; natural resource management; ethnobiology & indigenous knowledge systems in the tropics. Associate Professor, Consultant. *B.*5 Jan.1948, Bedigama, Sri Lanka. *M.*Nandanie (SO, Sri Lanka Natural Resources, Energy & Sci.Auth.). **Education:** U.of London MSc 1978, Kyushu U. Dr Agric.1985. **Experience:** res.— natural resources' mgmt, indigenous knowledge systems, agroecol.; admin.— centre dir & coord.of collaborative res.prog.; consults; teaching biogeog.& rural geog. **Career:** Lect. 1985–9, Sr Lect.1989–92, Assoc.Prof. 1993–, U.of Sri Jayewardenepura; Consult. Central Envl Auth.1986–7, Agrarian Res.& Training

Inst.1991–2, Min.of Envt 1993–. **Achievements:** estab.of Sri Lanka Resource Centre for Indigenous Knowledge, and Movement for Sust. Dev.; Org.first nat.symp.on Indigenous Knowledge & Sust.Dev. **Memberships:** IFOAM, IBG, SLAG. **Award:** Best Paper* Prize (FEC) 1991. **Publications:** *Polonnaruwa Distr.: An Envl Profile* 1990, *Dev.Planning, Envl Degradation & Rural Women: A Case Study of Kirindi Oya Irrigation & Settlement Project in Sri Lanka* 1993; *c.*14 papers incl.*Modernization v.*sust.: disintegrating village agroecocomplexes in the Dry Zone of Sri Lanka 1991. Favours pers.pub. & news media support. **Languages:** English, Japanese (spoken). Willing to act as consult.etc. **Address:** Nr 1B Right Circular Road, Jayanthipura, Battaramulla, Sri Lanka. **Tel.** (office) 94 1 852028, (home) 94 1 865178; **fax** 94 1 852604.

UNNI, Dr Nedunthuruthikonathu Variath MADHAVAN. Remote sensing applications for resources information system with special reference to forestry, ecology, ecosystem modelling, environment modelling, and related subjects. Terrestrial Environmental Services Manager. *B.*3 April 1938, Ker., India. Indian. *M.*Malini M.: 2 *d.* **Education:** Bombay U. MSc(Bot.) 1963, Gujarat U. PhD(Bot.) 1971; UN & CNES Summer Sch. training in remote sensing applications 1972, IMPE two wks' training 1973, and UNDP three months' training in US 1978–9. **Experience:** Tech.Coord.for Indo–German Tech. Coopn Prog.1977–93; admin.— Bd.Memb.of Nat.Forest Data Mgmt Centre, Standing Cttee on Bioresources, and several *ad hoc* nat.cttees dealing with for.& envt; consult.— memb.of jt Indo–Brit.team to prepare a pre-project report for ODA re.setting-up an image processing & GIS facility at Karnataka Forest Dept. **Career:** teaching 1963– 7; Res.Assoc. Phys.Res.Lab. and Sci. Space Applications Centre 1971–7; Sr Sci./Head, For. & Ecol.Div.1977–93 then Group Dir Remote Sensing Promotion 1993–5, NRSA; Mgr, Terr. Envl Services, Société Générale de Surveillance India Ltd 1995–. **Achievements:** pioneered intro.of remote sensing applications to veg. resources' studies in India, conducting first nat.remote sensing survey & change detection of forest cover in the country, campaigning for standardization & tech.transfer to State & C. Forest Depts, use of remote sensing for ecosystems' modelling, envt modelling, & monitoring processes in Nature. **Membership:** ISPRS (Life). **Publications:** 36 papers incl. Space & forest mgmt 1990, IRS-1A applications in for.(prin.Author) 1991, For.& ecol applications of IRS-1A data 1992, Applications of remote sensing for forest mgmt in developing countries — Indian example 1992. Indiff.to pers.pub.& news media support. **Languages:** English, Hindi, Malayalam. Willing to act as consult.etc. **Address:** Société Générale de Surveillance India Ltd, 43 Sarojini Devi Road, Secunderabad 500 003, Hyderabad, India. **Tel.**91 40 814039 or 840389; **fax** 91 40 802717.

UPRETI, Biswa Nath. Nature conservation, wildlife, biodiversity & protected areas; environment. Consultant, Executive Director. *B.*10 Aug. 1936, Kavre Palanchoke, Nepal. Nepali. *M.*Hari Kumari: 2 *s., d.* **Education:** IFC, Postgrad.Dipl. (For.)(Assoc.IFC) 1961; Tribhuvan U. LLB 1970; Michigan SU MS(Wildlife Mgmt) 1977. **Experience:** admin.& mgmt of nat.parks & prot. areas, wildlife mgmt activities such as control of dangerous animal translocation and CITES implementation in Nepal; consult.re.Cons.Area Mgmt through people's participation. **Career:** For.Officer 1961–70; Chief, Nat.Parks & Wildlife Office 1970–75 & 1979–80; Chief Warden Sagarmatha (Mt Everest) Nat.Park 1977–9; DG Dept of NPWC 1980–91; Sr Consult. Annapurna Cons.Area Project, King Mahendra Trust for Nature Cons.1992–3; Consult.1993–; Exec.Dir NAECAN-NEPAL 1996–. **Achievements:** as Head of Dept of NPWC was successful in establishing network of NPPAs in Nepal, instrumental in drafting an NPWC Act & five regs thereunder. **Memberships:** NHSN, NNCS, Foresters' Assn of Nepal, Nepal Forum of Envl Journalists (Assoc.). **Publications:** Nat.parks & prot.areas & wildlife mgmt 1988, Status of nat.parks & prot.areas in Nepal 1990, A background paper on biodiv.& prot.areas for Nepal Envl Policies & Action Plan 1993. Favours pers.pub.& indiff.to news media support. **Languages:** English, Nepali. Willing to act as consult.etc. **Address:** King Mahendra Trust for Nature Conservation, POB 3712, Kathmandu, Nepal. **Tel.**(office) 977 1 526573, (home) 977 1 410321; **fax** 977 1 526570.

URBAN, František. Nature conservation; protected areas & species; ecological forestry. Division Director. *B.*15 Nov.1937, Olomouc, Czech Rep. Czech. *M.*Irena: *s.* **Education:** Agricl U. Prague, Ing.(For.) 1961. **Experience:** forest mgmt (five yrs), regnl centre for Nature cons.(24 yrs), Min.of the Envt (four yrs). **Career:** Forest Mgmt Service, Inst.for Forest Mgmt Planning (ÚHÚL) 1961–6; Head of Dept of Nature Cons. in S.Bohemia 1966–90; postgrad.studies concurrently with Dir, Div.of Nature Cons. Min.of the Envt 1990–. **Achievements:** prot.areas' system plan for S.Bohemia (–1990) & Czech Rep., num.new Nature reserves & mgmt plans for Nature reserves & other prot.areas, new nat.parks & landscape prot.areas. **Memberships:** COS, CZS, CBS, CUNC, SSL (Prague), Union of Foresters. **Publications:** coopn on two books, papers, long collabn with radio & TV. Indiff.to pers.pub.& news media support. **Languages:** Czech, English, Russian, Slovak; German & Slavic languages understood. Willing to act as consult. etc. **Address:** Na Nábřeží 16, CZ 37001 Cěské Budéjovice, Czech Republic. **Tel.**(office) 42 2 6212 2410, (home) 42 38 55957; **fax** 42 2 6731 1388.

USHER, Professor Dr Michael B. Conservation biology; management of the natural heritage. Chief Scientific Adviser and Director of Research & Advisory Services. *B.*19 Nov.1941,

Old Colwyn, N.Wales, UK. British. *M*.Fionna: *s*.Graham Barham (ecol.), *d*. **Education:** U.of Edinburgh BSc(1st Class Hons)(For.) 1964, PhD(Pop.Dynamics of Soil Arthropods) 1967. **Experience:** u.res.& teaching; scientific admin. **Career:** Lect., Sr Lect., Reader, U.of York 1967– 91; Chief Scientific Adv. Scottish Natural Heritage 1991–; Hon.Chair of Zool. U.of Aberdeen 1993–. **Achievements:** dev.of cons.thinking esp.on eval., edl involvement with many scientific journals, contribn to Councils of Nat.Trust, English Nature, & vol.cons.orgns. **Memberships:** BES (*Bull*.Ed.1969–71, Sec. Math Ecol.Group 1973–9, Chairman Ecol Affairs Cttee 1979–85), F.RES, IEEM, BSBI, BAS. **Award:** Best Paper Prize (FEC) 1986. **Publications:** incl.*Biol.Mgmt & Cons*.1973, *Wildlife Cons.Eval*.1986, *Ecol Interactions in Soil* 1985, *Ecol Change in the Uplands* 1988, *The Islands of Scotland: a Living Marine Heritage* 1994. Dislikes pers.pub., indiff.to news media support. **Language:** English. Willing to act as consult.etc. **Address:** Scottish Natural Heritage, 2 Anderson Place, Edinburgh EH6 5NP, Scotland, UK. **Tel.**(office) 44 131 446 2401, (home) 44 131 662 0734; **fax** 44 131 446 2406.

USLU, Professor Dr Turhan. Coastal vegetation of Turkey & North Cyprus; effects of thermal power plants on flora & vegetation. Professor of Botany. *B*.21 April 1946, Ankara, Turkey. Turkish. *M*.Leyla: 2 *d*. **Education:** Atatürk High Sch.; U.of Ankara BSc 1968, PhD 1974. **Experience:** res.— coastal veg.of Turkey & N.Cyprus, effects of thermal power-plants on flora & veg.in Turkey; consult.— Adv.to Turkish Electricity Auth.1986 & 1991. **Career:** Assoc.Prof.1983–90, Prof.1990–, Dept of Biol. U.of Gazi. **Achievements:** finding & calling attention to endemic, rare & threatened, coastalplant assns; effects of thermal power-plants on plants (natural, agricl, etc.). **Memberships:** Assn Amicale Internationale de Phytosociologie (Bailleul), EUCC (Counc.); Cyprus Fndn, Assn of Biologists, TTKD, KAY (all in Ankara); Envl & Woodlands Prot.Soc.of Turkey, & DHKD (both in Istanbul); Turkish Nat.Cttee for Air Poll.Res.& Control. **Publications:** 66 scientific papers. **Languages:** English, Latin (poor), Turkish. Willing to act as consult.etc. **Address:** Tirebolu Sokak 22/10, TR 06550 Ankara, Turkey. **Tel.**(office) 90 312 212 6030, (home) 90 312 468 3242; **fax** 90 312 212 2279.

USUKI, Mitsuo. Geography, landscape architecture, and policy on environment & development — in particular Nature conservation & natural resources management. Deputy Regional Representative. *B*.3 July 1948, Kumamoto City, Japan. Japanese. *M*.Yuriko. **Education:** Tohoku U. BSc(Geo-sci.) 1972, MSc(Natural Geog.) 1974. **Experience:** consult.to UN– ESCAP, JICA, US–Japan jt design team in biodiv.cons. **Career:** Asst Warden, Nikko Nat. Park Office 1974–8, Intl Coopn Officer 1981–3, Coord.for Intl Affairs, Nature Cons.Bur. 1988–94, all at

JEA; Nat.Tourism–Policy Planning, PM's Office 1979–80; First Sec. Embassy of Japan in Kenya, and Dep.Perm.Rep.to UNEP & HABITAT 1984–7; Dep.Regnl Rep. UNEP (Thailand) 1994–. **Achievements:** compiled White Paper on Tourism 1979, 1980; compilation of monthly Envl Summary (in English) and yearly White Paper on Envt (in English) 1981–3; coopn with ESCAP to compile State of the Envt 1990 report for Asia and the Pacific; planned & expedited 4th Nat.Survey on Natural Envt from 1989–91. **Memberships:** Intl House Inst. Japan, IUCN SSC Regnl Memb.(E.Asia) & CNPPA, Japan Highway Landscape Assn (Cttee). **Publications:** *The Arc of E.Africa* 1989, *Global Envt* vol.2 (coAuthor) 1990, *Extinction* 1992, *Trop.Forest Cons*.(co-Author) 1992 (all in Japanese); mission & mtg reports, j.articles. Indiff.to pers.pub. & news media support. **Languages:** Chinese (some), English, German (some), Japanese. Willing to act as consult.etc.after retirement. **Address:** United Nations Environment Programme, Regional Office for Asia and the Pacific, United Nations Building, Rajdamnern Avenue, Bangkok 10200, Thailand. **Tel.** 66 2 282 9161 to 200 & 9381 to 9; **fax** 66 2 280 3829.

VALAORAS, Dr Georgia. Conservation in Greece. Director. *B*.16 Dec.1947, New York, NY, USA. American, Greek. Father Prof Vasilios G.Valaoras, hygiene & preventive medicine, UNFPA 1947–61. *M*.Gerhard Fischer. **Education:** Columbia U. BA(Chem.) 1968; U. of Penn. MS(Sci.Educ.) 1972; Washington U.(St Louis) MS(Envl Mgmt) & DSc(Envl Mgmt) 1984. **Experience:** teaching until 1979; res.& sci.policy on envl issues (pesticides & toxics, hazardous waste mgmt); cons.issues. **Career:** Industrial Food Chemist 1969–71; sec.Sch.Sci. Teacher 1972–9; Envl Policymaker, USEPA 1984–9; Fulbright Scholar, U.of The Aegean 1989–90; Dir WWF Greece 1990–. **Achievements:** estab.of WWF Greece, dev.& mgmt of over 20 cons.projects throughout Greece. **Memberships:** IUCN, EUCC, Sigma Xi. **Publications:** incl.On the contribn of motor vehicles to the Athenian 'Nephos': an application of factor signatures (co-Author) 1988. Indiff.to pers. pub., favours news media support. **Languages:** English, French (spoken), Greek. Willing to act as consult.etc. **Address:** WWF Greece, Asklepiou 14, Athens 10680, Greece. **Tel.**(office) 30 362 3342, (home) 30 360 9146; **fax** 30 362 3342.

VALDIYA, Professor Dr Khadga Singh. Neotectonics; hydrogeology of mountain springs; hazards of mass-movements & earthquakes. Professor of Geology & Head of Department. *B*.20 March 1937, Kalaw, Burma. Indian. *M*. Indira: *s*. **Education:** Lucknow U. BSc(Hons) 1956, MSc 1957, PhD 1963; Johns Hopkins U. Post-doctl Fulbright F.1965–6. **Experience:** res.during postgrad.period; admin.in academic positions; teaching throughout career. **Career:** Lect. Lucknow U.1957–69, Rajasthan U. 1969– 70, and Wadia Inst.of Himalayan Geol.(Delhi)

1970–73; SSO 1970–73, Dep.Dir 1973–6, Addit. Dir 1980, Wadia Inst.of Himalayan Geol. (Dehradun); Prof.of Geol.& Head of Dept 1976–, Dean Fac.Sci.1977–80, Acting V.-Chancellor 1981, 1985, 1992, Kumaun U. **Achievements:** founded an assn for preserv.of envt & pursuit of ecodev.in Himalaya, involved in developing spring sanctuaries in a watershed suffering from scarcity of water, orgn of annual meets of school-children & coll.students. **Memberships:** CHEA (Hon.Sec.1982–), GSI (VP 1993–), F. INSA & F.IAS 1980–, F.NAS 1985–. **Awards:** Bhatnagar Award (CSIR) 1976, Nat.Lect.(UGC) 1977–8, L.Rama Rao Gold Medal (GSI) 1979, Pant Nat.Envt F. Dept of Envt 1982–4, S.K.Mitra Award (INSA) 1992, SERC Lect.of Dept of Sci.& Tech.1991–2. **Publications:** *Envl Geol.: Indian Context* 1987; 70+ res. papers, two monogrs, three textbooks, six edited vols, 36 popular articles. Favours news media support. **Languages:** English, Hindi. Further details may be obtained from *Profiles of Fellows of the Acad.* (INSA). Willing to act as a consult.& judge proposals. **Address:** Longview, Tallital, Nainital 263002, Uttar Pradesh, India. **Tel.**(office) 91 5942 2114, (home) 91 5942 2283.

VALDRÈ, Professor Giovanni. Ethology; conservation of Nature & protected areas. Environmental Consultant. *B.*24 Feb.1928, Leghorn, Italy. Italian. *M.*Maria: *d.*Silvia (geog., consult. for prot.areas' projects), *s.*Andrea (vet.). **Education:** U.of Pisa, degree in Pol.Sci. 1954; ministerial qual.as u.teacher in social psych.and sci.of public relations. **Experience:** aetiological res.on social orgn of Wolves *(Canis lupus)* & Ravens *(Corvus corax)*; consult.in ecol.for Province Admin.of Florence; admin.re.prep.of world mtgs for IUCN & FNNPE, and as collab.at Appenino Center of Study of Abruzzo Nat.Park and Maremma Natural Park. **Career:** Assoc. Prof.of Social Psych.involving professional training courses for public bodies, U.of Pisa 1979–82; Coord. CEDIP 1982–. **Memberships:** IUCN CNPPA & CEC, FNNPE Pres. Italian Section, num.Comms on Nat.& Regnl Parks and Task Forces of public bodies for prot.areas' projects. **Publications:** seven books incl.*L'Alpinismo di Massa ed il Suo Impatto Ambientale sulle Aree Protette* 1990, *La Gestione dei Parchi e delle Aree Protette* 1991; *c.*200 papers & articles. **Languages:** English (read), French, Italian, Latin. Willing to act as consult.etc. **Address:** Centro Documentazione Internazionale Parchi, Via M.Melloni 8, 50133 Firenze, Italy. **Tel.**(office) 39 55 409051, (home) 39 55 573055; **fax** 39 55 476116.

VALENCIA DIAZ, Professor Dr José, *see* DIAZ, Professor Dr José VALENCIA.

VALLELY, Ms Bernadette Anne Marie. Writing; ecofeminism. Writer. *B.*9 Nov.1961, London, England, UK. British. *M.*Stewart T.Boyle (Dir, Euro.Intl Inst.of Energy Cons.): *d.* **Experience:** in intl delegations, public speaking, campaigning

training orgns; tech.— in life-cycle analysis, chlorine, and similar ecol problems; res.in ecofeminism, pulp & paper industry; consult.on ecol labelling, life-cycle assessment, & consumption of consumer goods. **Career:** Fundraiser, Anti-Apartheid Movement (London, UK) 1982–5; Asst to Dir FoE 1985–8; Dir, Scorpion Promotions 1988–9; Founder & Dir, WEN 1989–94; Writer 1994–. **Achievements:** brought women's issues into envl agenda; persuaded major multinat.cos to change prod. processes esp.re. chlorine-bleached paper, sanitary prot., packaging, chocolate, etc. **Memberships:** WEN (Trustee), London Ecol.Centre (Patron). **Awards:** Young Woman Achiever (*Cosmopolitan*) 1991 & 1994, Campaign of Yr (BEMA) 1993, Global 500 Roll of Honour (UNEP) 1994, 21st Anniv.Award (Schumacher Soc.) 1994. **Publications:** several incl.*1001 Ways to Save the Planet* 1990, *Young Person's Guide to Saving the Planet* 1990, *A Tissue of Lies, Disposable Paper and The Envt* 1991, *Ecofeminism — A Spiritual Approach* 1992. Accepts pers.pub.& news media support. **Language:** English. Further details may be obtained from *World Who's Who of Women* (12th & 13th edns). Willing to act as consult.etc. **Address:** POB 3724, London N16 6HY, England, UK. **Tel.**44 181 806 8872; **fax** 44 181 806 8572.

VALLENTYNE, Dr John R. aka 'Johnny Biosphere'*. Planetary ecology; environmental education. Research Scientist Emeritus, Adjunct Professor. *B.*31 July 1926, Toronto, Ont., Canada. Canadian. *M.*Ann V.: 3 *s.,* 2 *d.* **Education:** Queen's U. BA(Hons) 1949, Yale U. PhD 1953. **Experience:** res.& teaching in limnology, ecol., & evol.; sci.policy adv.to IJC on Gt Lakes issues; envl educ.as *'Johnny Biosphere'. **Career:** Asst Prof.of Biol. Queen's U.1952–8, Assoc.Prof.& Prof.of Zool. Cornell U.1958–66, Sci.Leader, Eutrophication Section, Freshwater Inst. Winnipeg 1966–72, Sr Sci. Dept of Fisheries & Oceans, Winnipeg & Burlington 1972–92, Res.Sci.Emer. Canada Centre for Inland Waters 1992–, Adjunct Prof. McMaster U. **Achievements:** control over levels of phosphates in detergents in The Gt Lakes, intro.of ecosystem approach to envl planning in The Gt Lakes Basin, scientific basis for 'sunsetting' industrial prod.& use of chlorine & chlorine-containing compounds. **Memberships:** ESA, ASLO (VP 1964–5), IAL (Pres.1974–80). **Awards:** J.Fund Award for learned pubn 1955–9, Award of Excellence & Merit (Canadian Dept of Fisheries & Oceans) 1992, Cert.of Recognition (Greenpeace) 1992, Rachel Carson Award (SETAC) 1992. **Publications:** incl.*The Algal Bowl: Lakes & Man* 1974, The ecosystem approach to transboundary problem-solving 1978, Managing the Gt Lakes Basin as a home 1986. Favours pers.pub.& news media support. **Languages:** English, French, German, Italian, Russian (limited read, written, spoken), Spanish. Further details in *Canadian Who's Who* 1995. Willing to act as consult.etc. **Address:** Department of

Fisheries and Oceans, Canada Centre for Inland Waters, POB 5050, Burlington, Ontario L7R 4A6, Canada. **Tel.**(office) 1 905 336 4586, (home) 1 905 527 4068; **fax** 1 905 336 6437.

VAN **BREE, Dr Peter J.H.,** *see* **BREE, Dr Peter J.H.** VAN.

VAN DER **MEULEN, Dr Frank,** *see* **MEULEN, Dr Frank** VAN DER.

VAN DER **WALT, Dr Pieter Toxopeus,** *see* **WALT, Dr Pieter Toxopeus** VAN DER.

VAN GUNDIA **NEEL, Dr James,** *see* **NEEL, Dr James** VAN GUNDIA.

VAN **LAVIEREN, Lambartus Piet,** *see* **LAVIEREN, Lambartus Piet** VAN.

VAN'T **HOF, Tom,** *see* **HOF, Tom** VAN'T.

VANTIER, Dr Lyndon Mark DE. Human & natural impacts on coral-reef ecosystems: particularly the effects of *Acanthaster* population outbreaks, coral bleaching, and reef symbioses associations. Coral Ecologist, Lecturer. *B.*14 May 1956, Brisbane, Australia. Australian. *M.* Janice M.Forbes (Reef Resource Mgr). **Education:** Qld Inst.of Tech, B.of Applied Sci.(Biol.) 1977; U.of Qld, BSc(Marine Zool., Marine Bot.) 1983, PhD (Zool.) 1994. **Experience:** res.— human & natural impacts on coral-reef ecosystems, coral pop.and community ecol.& dynamics; consult.— var.reef survey & monitoring contracts. **Career:** Experimental Sci. Coral Reef Ecol.Prog.1984–5, Crown-of-Thorns *(Acanthaster)* Study 1985–6 and Cooperative Res. Centre Reef Res.Centre 1994–, AIMS; Res. Officer, Dept of Zool. U.of Qld 1986–8; Consult.AIMS and GBRMPA 1988–94; Coral Ecol. Trop.Marine Ecosystem Project (Vietnam) 1994; Lect. UNESCO Intl Biodiv.Workshop 1994. **Achievements:** provision of data, reports, & advice, to mgmt agencies; lecturing and field training of SE Asian Marine Scis/Mgrs, assistance to UNESCO in such training. **Memberships:** ACRS, ISRS. **Publications:** *Studies in the Assessment of Coral Reef Ecosystems* (12 vols, co-Author) 1985. Indiff.to pers.pub., favours news media support. **Languages:** English, Indonesian (spoken). Willing to act as consult.etc. **Address:** Cooperative Research Centre Reef Research Centre, Australian Institute of Marine Science, PMB 3, Townsville MC, Queensland 4810, Australia. **Tel.**(office) 61 7 753 4334, (home) 61 7 778 5083; **fax** 61 7 772 5852.

VAOHITA, Dr Barthélémi. Protection of the environment; conservation; environmental education. Director, Lecturer. *B.*29 March 1937, Vohémar, Madagascar. Malagasy. *M.*Colette Andianarison (women & envt). **Education:** Certificat d'Ornithologie 1975; U.of Grenoble, Docteur en Sciences de l'Educ.1978; Jordanhill Coll.(Glasgow, Scotland, UK), Cert.in Educ.

1992. **Experience:** envl educ.& res., teaching. **Career:** Dir, WWF Madagascar 1979–, Lect.in Envl Educ. Jordanhill Coll.1992–. **Achievement:** res.into envl educ. **Award:** Chevalier de l'Ordre Nat.de la République Malgache. **Publications:** Resource-pack for Malagasy Teacher Training Colls & Primary Schools (*Intro.to Malagasy Biodiv., Envl Factors, Soil Erosion in Madagascar,* and *Trees*) 1988, some others. Favours pers.pub.& news media support. **Languages:** English, French (mother tongue). Willing to act as consult.etc. **Address:** POB 4373, Antananarivo 101, Madagascar. **Tel.**(office) 261 2 27446, (home) 261 2 40861.

VÁRALLYAY, Professor Dr György. Soil mapping, physics, and degradation processes. Institute Director, Department Head, Professor of Soil Science. *B.*17 July 1935, Debrecen, Hungary. Hungarian. *M.*Éva: *s., d.* **Education:** Gödöllő U.of Agricl Scis, Dipl.in Agricl Engg 1957, PhD 1964; Hungarian AS, Cand.of Agricl Scis (Soil Sci.) 1968, Dr of Agricl Scis (Soil Sci.) 1988, Corres.Memb.1993. **Experience:** res., admin., tech.— soil mapping; computerized soil info.systems (GIS), soil monitoring; hydrophysical properties and moisture regime of soils and their control; salinization–alkalization, acidification, structure destruction. **Career:** Soil Surveyor, Nat Inst for Agricl 1957–60; Scientific co-Worker, Dept of Salt-affected Soils 1960–76, Head of Soil Sci.Dept 1976–, Director 1981–, Res.Inst.for Soil Sci.& Agricl Chem. Hungarian AS; Vis.Prof. Ain Shams U. 1977; Prof.of Soil Sci.1988–, Head of Satellite Soil Sci.Dept 1992–, Gödöllő U.; Invited Prof. Eötvös Loránd U. **Achievements:** res.& study of envl aspects of land-use and soil mgmt; soil degradation process (salinization–alkalization, acidification, structure destruction & compaction); soil phys., hydrophysical properties of soils. **Memberships:** ISSS (Comm.VI [Soil Tech.] VP 1978–82, Pres.1982–6, Past-Pres. 1986–90; Cttees on Statute & Structure and Intl Progs), HSSS (Pres.1990–), scientific cttees of num.nat.& intl insts & progs, Edl Bds of num. nat.& intl journals incl.*Agrokemia es Talajtan, Geoderma, Soil Tech., Intl Agrophysics,* and *Land Degradation and Rehab.* **Awards:** Nat. Water Auth.1976, Labour Order of Merit Silver Degree 1985, Michal Oczapowski Medal (Polish AS) 1991. **Publications:** co-Author of 18 books incl.*Land Qualities in Space and Time* (co-Ed.) 1989, *Soils on Warmer Earth* (co-Ed.) 1990, *Soil Resilience and Sust.Land Use* (co-Ed.) 1994; seven sets of u.lecture notes, 261 scientific papers, 57 popular–scientific articles. **Languages:** English (good), German (fair), Hungarian, Russian. **Address:** Research Institute for Soil Science and Agricultural Chemistry, Hungarian Academy of Sciences, Herman Otto 15, H-1022 Budapest, Hungary. **Tel.**36 1 156 4682; **fax** 36 1 155 8839.

VARIAVA, Mrs Dilnavaz. Environmental education, institution-building, conservation of wild habitats & species, women & environment, campaign strategy, indigenous people (tribals). Company Director, Society Vice-President. *B.* 24 May 1944, Bombay, Mah., India. Indian. *M.* Justice S.N.Variava. **Education:** IIM MBA (Bus. Mgmt) 1966. **Experience:** ind.consult., admin. **Career:** sr mgmt positions in industry 1966–73, CEO WWF India 1973–8, VP BNHS, Dir of several cos incl.Grindwell Norton 1972– and Bharat Tiles & Marble Pvt Ltd 1991– apart from envl positions & activities. **Achievements:** helped estab.WWF India in its formative yrs and its Nature Clubs of India, Hon. Coord. Save Silent Valley Cttee, appointed to Nat.Cttee for Envl Planning and NCS Cttee. **Memberships:** BNHS, CSE, IUCN CNPPA & CEC. **Award:** Officer of Order of the Golden Ark. **Publications:** *Mgmt of Nat.Parks & Sanctuaries in India* (status Report, co-Author) 1989, num.conf. papers. Indiff.to pers.pub. **Languages:** English, French (fair), German (weak comp.), Gujarati, Hindi, Marathi. Willing to act as a consult. **Address:** Bharat Tiles & Marble Pvt.Ltd, 32 Bombay Samachar Marg, Bombay 400 001, Maharashtra, India. **Tel.**(office) 91 22 265 4837, 4965, or 5842, (home) 91 22 202 4759 or 283 0706; **fax** 91 22 265 1751.

VARUGHESE, George C. Environmental planning & management; impact assessment; community management institutions; microenterprises. Branch Manager. *B.*18 March 1957, Singapore. Indian. *M.*Dr Mary. **Education:** Rourkela Engg Coll. BSc(Civ.Eng.) 1980, Sch.of Planning & Arch.(New Delhi) MS(Urban & Regnl Planning) 1985. **Experience:** resp.for structuring a trans-disc.team capable of addressing issues of envt & dev., coordinates or actively participates in most of its activities; project mgmt in the field; res., admin., teaching, consult. **Career:** Construction Mgr 1980–83; Res.Assoc. Sch.of Planning & Arch.1985–6; Mgr Envt Systems Branch, Dev.Alternatives 1986–. **Achievement:** structuring a 20-memb.professional trans-disc.group with a social conscience. **Memberships:** IUCN CESP, IAIA M'ship Cttee (past). **Award:** Award for excellence & contribn to nat.sust.dev.(TARA). **Publications:** prin. author of *c.*20 project documents. Indiff.to pers. pub.& news media support. **Languages:** English, several Indian languages (mostly spoken). Willing to act as consult.etc. **Address:** Development Alternatives B-32 Tara Crescent, Qutab Institutional Area, New Delhi 110 016, Delhi, India. **Tel.**(office) 91 11 665370 & 657983, (home) 91 11 689 2098; **fax** 91 11 686 6031.

VASUDEVAN, Professor (Mrs) Padma. Rural development; polymer science–environment–sustainable development. Professor of Rural Development and Appropriate Technology, Adjunct Professor of Technical Education. *B.*6 Jan.1940, Calcutta, W.Bengal, India. Indian. Mother S.Rukmini, rural dev. *W.* **Education:** Madras U. PhD 1969; U.of Manchester, Postdoctl F.1974–5. **Experience:** res.& teaching,

admin.as Centre Chairperson, consult.in tech. transfer of biomass and renewable energy-based technologies, and women & dev. **Career:** Lect. in Chem.1968, Asst Prof.of Biomed.Engg 1977, Prof.of Rural Dev.and Appropriate Tech.1980–, IIT; Chairperson & Prof.of Rural Dev. Centre for Rural Dev.& Appropriate Tech.1984–91; Adjunct Prof.of Tech.Educ. W.Virginia U. 1995–. **Achievements:** res.& tech.transfer in rural areas and urban slums on waste recycling, waste mgmt, and organic & natural agric.; res.into use of biomass and renewable energy, water, sanitation, waste & dev., etc.; evolving courses and teaching on sust.dev.at under- & post-grad.levels; Edl Bds *J.Bioresources* 1994–, *J.of Scientific and Industrial Res.*1995–. **Memberships:** Bioenergy Soc.of India (elected VP), Biomaterial Soc.of India (past Pres.), Appropriate Tech.Assn of India (VP). **Awards:** F.of NYAS and INAS, Kshanika Oration Award (ICMR) 1983, Industrial Res.Award (VASVIK Fndn) 1985. **Publications:** nine vols of *Nat. Directory of Rural Tech.*1985–95, *Pioneers in Rural Dev.*1994; *c.*200 j.& abstracted papers. Indiff.to pers.pub., favours news media support for purpose of info.dissemination. **Languages:** English, Hindi, Tamil; French, German & Russian (all comp.). Willing to act as consult.etc. **Address:** 18 Minicampus, Indian Institute of Technology, Hauskhas, New Delhi 110016, Delhi, India. **Tel.**(office) 91 11 666979 ext. 3135, (home) 91 11 661427; **fax** 91 11 685 6884 & 696 6961.

VAVILOV, Andrey M. International aspects of environmental issues including within the United Nations system. Diplomat, currently Deputy Permanent Representative of Russia. *B.*26 April 1936, St Petersburg (then Leningrad), Russia. Russian. *M.*Marianna: *s.* **Education:** Moscow Inst.of Intl Relations 1960, Diplomatic Acad. Moscow 1982. **Experience:** multilateral negns, num. speaking engagements abroad, directed classes for young diplomats at Moscow Diplomatic Acad., occasional UN (Geneva) lectures. **Career:** professional diplomat, postings in India & UK at Russian Embassies; official interpreter at Foreign Min.at US–USSR summits; Couns.& Dep.Dir for Sci.& Tech. Russian Foreign Min. 1987–90; Head of Ext. Relations, UNCED 1990–92*; Spec.Adv. Secretariat INCD 1993–4; Sr Couns. Foreign Min.of Russia (Moscow) 1994–5; Dep.Perm.Rep.of Russia to UNEP and Habitat (Nairobi) 1995–. **Achievements:** negotiated envl modification conv.1988, *participation in UNCED with responsibilities for diplomatic liaison, intergovtl orgns, NGOs, media, and UN affairs focal point, chaired Working Party for Envl Educ.and Training for Agenda 21 1990–92. **Award:** Order of Merit (Govt, for Conf.on Security & Coopn in Europe) 1975. **Publications:** *Envl Consequences of the Arms Race* 1983, 1988; Ed.compilations of documents on disarmament. Indiff.to pers.pub. & news media support. **Languages:** English, French (written), Russian. Willing to act as consult.etc. **Address:** The Permanent Mission of the Russian Federation, POB 30049, Nairobi, Kenya. **Tel.**254 2 728700; fax 254 2 721888.

VAZQUEZ DE LA CERDA, Professor Dr Alberto Mariano, *see* **CERDA, Professor Dr Alberto Mariano VAZQUEZ DE LA.**

VENIZELOS, Mrs Lily Therese. Marine turtle conservation. President. *B.*10 April 1933, Athens, Greece. Greek. *M.*Lefteri Venizelos: *d.* **Education:** Lyceum, Athens 1951. **Experience:** admin.of MEDASSET 1988– and campaign leader since 1983; intl lecturing & project coordn. **Career:** campaign leader, marine turtle cons. 1983–; lect.on same and other Medit.problems 1986–; participation in intl mtgs etc. 1985–; founded MEDASSET 1988. **Achievements:** campaigning which has led to protective measures being taken to improve the cons.status of the Loggerhead Sea Turtle (*Caretta caretta*) in Laganas Bay, Zakynthos, Greece, the largest concentration of nesting sea turtles in the Medit.; founding of MEDASSET in 1988 two of whose projects have been submitted to & co-funded by EC (DGXIB), one survey project having been carried out in Egypt in 1993. **Memberships:** MEDASSET (Founder Pres.1988–), HSPN (Governing Council 1986– & VP 1993–), G500F (Regnl [Europe] rep., Governing Council 1992–), GAWF 1986–. **Awards:** Global 500 Roll of Honour (UNEP) 1987, Athens Acad. Award 1988. **Publications:** num. Indiff.to pers.pub., favours news media support. **Languages:** English, French, Greek. Willing to act as consult.etc. **Address:** MEDASSET, 1c Licavitou Street, Athens 10671, Greece, **tel.**(office) 30 1 361 3572, (home) 30 1 362 4971; **fax** 30 1 724 3007; or MEDASSET (UK), 24 Park Towers, 2 Brick Street, London W1Y 7DF, England, UK, **tel.& fax** 44 171 629 0654.

VERMA, Dr Sewa Ram. Research development in environment; Nature resource conservation. Lecturer in Zoology. *B.*4 Jan.1939, Seemli, Laksar, Hardwar, UP, India. Indian. *M.*Shukla: *s., d.* **Education:** Meerut U. BSc 1962, MSc (Zool.) 1964, PhD(Water Poll.& Ecol.) 1972. **Experience:** 28 yrs' teaching of ecol.& animal cons.; 28 yrs' res.on envl poll.& animal toxicology; admin.— Chief Investigator of Res. Projects, Hotel Warden, Coll.Proctor. **Career:** Sec.-Gen. Acad.of Envl Biol.1978–82; Coordinate Ed.*J.of Envl Biol.*1978–86; Sec.-Gen. Nature Conservators 1987–; Lect. Zool.Dept, Dayanand Anglo Vedic (DAV) Coll. **Achievements:** org.of several sems & symposia on envt & cons., and dir of four. **Memberships:** Soc.of Toxicology, Nature Cons., IAS. **Awards:** Gold Medal (undergrad.& grad.levels). **Publications:** *Envl Prot.— A Movement* (Ed.) 1989, *Animal Ecol.& Animal Behaviour* (Ed.) 1990, *Growth, Dev.& Natural Resource Cons.* (Ed.) 1990, *Threatened Fishes of India* (Ed.) 1995; Chief Ed.*J.of Nature Cons.* 1989–; 305 res. etc.papers. Dislikes pers.pub.& news media

support. **Languages:** English, German (basic), Hindi. Willing to act as consult.etc. **Address:** Department of Zoology, Dayanand Anglo Vedic College, Meerut University, Muzaffarnagar 251 001, Uttar Pradesh, India. **Tel.**(office & home) 91 131 401414.

VERNAUDON, Yolande. Marine & coastal management; parks & reserves. Scientific Officer. *B.*12 May 1963, Papeete, Tahiti. French. **Education:** Ecole Nat.Supérieure d'Agronomie de Toulouse, Ing.agronome 1986. **Experience:** admin.— coord.of res.for coastal & marine mgmt plan (Bora-Bora); Sec. Comm.des monuments naturels et des sites, French Polynesia 1989–91; drawing-up charts of territorial park (Tahiti) & territorial reserve (Scilly, Bellingshausen). **Career:** Officer, Chambre d'Agric.et d'Elevage 1988; Délégation à l'Environnement 1989–91, 1994–; SO, Service de la Mer et de l'Aquaculture 1992–4. **Achievements:** setting up first territorial (nat.) park of French Polynesia (Te Faaiti, Tahiti) and marine/coastal mgmt plans procedure. **Membership:** IUCN CNPPA. **Publication:** *Proposition de Plan d'Aménagement et de Gestion des Ressources du Lagon de Bora-Bora* 1991. Indiff.to pers.pub.& news media support. **Languages:** English, French, Spanish. **Address:** BP 4562, Papeete, Tahiti. **Tel.**689 432409, (home) 689 480882; **fax** 689 419252.

VERON, Dr John Edward Norwood. Coral taxonomy, biogeography, evolutionary mechanisms, systematics, & conservation. Senior Principal Research Scientist. *B.*16 Feb.1945, Sydney, Australia. Australian. *M.*Mary (coral envl res.): 2 *d.* **Education:** U.of New England MSc 1968, PhD 1972, DSc 1982. **Experience:** ref./ assessor for num.granting agencies, prog.leading, diving (3,000 hrs' SCUBA) and seaman's quals, conf.& workshop org., lecturing, lab.& field res. **Career:** Res.Asst 1967–8, Teaching F.1968–72, U.of New England; Res.F. James Cook U.of N.Qld 1972–5; Res.Sci.1975– 80, Sr Res.Sci.1980–82, Prin.Res.Sci.1982–7, Sr Prin. Res.Sci.1987–, AIMS. **Achievements:** raised issues re.envl degradation of coral reefs in early 1980, has written many articles on coral & coral reefs emphasizing envl issues. **Memberships:** ACRS (past-Pres., VP, & Counc.), AMSA, PSA, ICRS, SFC, F.AIB. **Award:** Whitley Medal 1987. **Publications:** *c.*50 incl.*Scleractinia of Eastern Australia* (co-author, five vols) 1976– 84. Dislikes pers.pub., encourages media involvement as essential to cons. **Language:** English. Willing to act as consult.etc. **Address:** Australian Institute of Marine Science, PMB 3, Townsville, Queensland 4810, Australia. **Tel.** (office) 61 77 534274; **fax** (office) 61 77 725852, (home) 61 77 784853.

VERSCHUREN, Dr Jacques C.F. General conservation & problems of environment; creation & management of national parks mainly in Africa, research in national parks; Ungulata & Chiroptera specialist. Biologist, Honorary Director-General. *B*.9 April 1926, Brussels, Belgium. Belgian. **Education:** Coll.Saint Michel, Humanités greco-latines 1943; U.of Louvain Lic.en Scis Zoologiques 1950, Dr en Scis Biologiques (Zool.) 1955. **Experience:** biol res.in lab.& field; consult.to var.nat.& intl orgns; intensive collabn with auths of 'new' countries; prospecting of num.prot.& unprot.areas for creation of nat.parks mainly, but not exclusively, in Africa, and resultant mgmt, admin., & res. **Career:** Sci. 1942–91 then Perm.Biol.1964–91 Institut R.des Scis Naturelles de Belgique; first leader & creator of Serengeti Res. Inst.1962–4; DG Nat. Parks of Zaire and creator of Institut Nat.pour la Cons.de la Nature 1969–74 (Hon.1974–); creation of Inst.for Nature Cons. Burundi 1976 and of Nat.Park, Liberia 1978–9. **Achievements:** creation of four nat. parks in Zaire incl.Salonga (the largest rainforest nat.park in the world); important contribn to save (and later reorganize) Zaire's parks incl.Virunga Park; contributed to save White Rhino *(Ceratotherium simus)*, Mtn Gorilla *(Gorilla gorilla)*, & Java's Rhino *(Rhinoceros sondaicus).* **Membership:** CITES Scientific Comm. **Awards:** Gold Medal (the first of WWF Intl), Order of the Golden Ark, var.hons. **Publications:** *Ecol.of Chiroptera Garamba Nat. Park* 1956, *Ecol.of Mammals of Albert Nat.Park* 1960, *Mourir pour les Eléphants* (ten edns in four languages) 1969–70, *Habitats & Fauna in Virunga Park after 65 yrs of Prot.*1993; 200 others + newspaper articles. Indiff.to pers.pub., favours news media support. **Languages:** Dutch & English (good), French, good knowledge of var.African languages. Willing to act as consult. etc. **Address:** (office) Institut Royal des Sciences Naturelles de Belgique, 29 rue Vautier, Brussels 1040, Belgium; (home) 82 Avenue Atlantique, Brussels 1150, Belgium. **Tel.**(office) 32 2 627 4211, (home) 32 2 7 708636; **fax** 32 2 646 4493.

VIDA, Professor Gabór. Genetics — cytogenetics, mutagen testing, genetic polymorphisms; evolutionary ecology — genetic diversity and population dynamics. Department Chairman, Professor of Genetics. *B*.24 March 1935, Budapest, Hungary. Hungarian. *M*. **Education:** Eötvös Loránd U.(Budapest), MSc(Biol.& Chem.) 1957, PhD(Ecol.) 1959; Hungarian AS, Cand.of Biol Sci.(Cytotaxonomy) 1966, Dr Sc.(Evol.Cytogenetics) 1973, Corres.Memb. 1985, Ordinary Memb.1993. **Experience:** since 1973 teaching gen.genetics, evol.genetics, pop.biol., cytogenetics, ecol genetics, evol.ecol. etc.; res.— 40 yrs in veg.mapping, taxonomy, cytogenetics, evol.& pop.biol. mainly at Inst.of Genetics (Hungarian AS), Dept of Bot. Leeds U.(UK), and Eötvös Loránd U.; Scientific Sec. Hungarian Nat.Cttee on Problems of the Envt 1972–86. **Career:** Professor of Genetics & Chairman, Genetics Dept, Eötvös Loránd U.1973–. **Memberships:** IBP (Scientific Sec. of Hungarian Nat.Cttee 1967–72), ESEB (VP 1987–9), UNESCO (VP, Hungarian Nat.Comm. 1989–93). **Publications:** ten books incl.*Orgnl*

Constraints on the Dynamics of Evol., Processes in Nonlinear Sci.(co-Ed.) 1990; chapters incl. Biodiv.from the Gene to the Species (co-Author) 1992, Genetic Resources 1993, Global Issues of Genetic Diversity 1994; 100+ res.papers. **Languages:** English, Hungarian. **Address:** Department of Genetics, Eötvös Loránd University, Muzeum korut 4/a, 1088 Budapest, Hungary. **Tel.**36 1 266 1296; **fax** 36 1 266 2694.

VIEJO MONTESINOS, Dr José Luis, *see* **MONTESINOS, Dr José Luis** VIEJO.

VISSER, Nicolaas Willem. Environment & development; wetlands & coastal-zone management; biodiversity; Nature conservation legislation; international conventions & treaties on the environment; sustainable agriculture. Attaché. *B*.24 Aug.1952, The Hague, The Netherlands. Dutch. *M*.Catherina Lucretia: 2 d., s. **Education:** Nederlansch Lyceum; Leiden U. BSc(Law) 1975, MSc(Ecol.) 1979, MSc(Law) 1980; Clingendael (The Hague), post-doctl course in intl relations 1989. **Experience:** Researcher at IUCN/WWF Indonesia Prog., IEEP (Asst), and Stichting Natuur en Milieu; mgmt consult. Min. of Tourism & Wildlife, Kenya; legal consult. UNEP Geneva & Kenya. **Career:** Intl Relations Officer, Directorate Gen.for the Envt, Min.of Housing, Phys.Planning & Envt 1981–4; Sr Intl Relations Officer, Dept of Nature, Envt & Forests, Min.of Agric., Nature Mgmt & Fisheries 1984–9; Attaché for Agric., Nature Mgmt, & Fisheries in E.Africa (mgmt of Netherlands-funded projects on Biodiv.) 1989–. Accredited in Kenya, Uganda, Tanzania, Rwanda, Ethiopia, & Mauritius as well as with UNEP 1989–. **Memberships:** IUCN CNPPA, EAWS, EANHS, NMKS. **Award:** Porteur de la Cravatte d'Honneur No 27 du Service des Parcs Nationaux de Sénégal. **Publications:** *Nature Prot.Legis.in Indonesia* 1979, Comparative study on envl legis.in Belgium & The Netherlands (in Dutch) 1981, *The Role of the Non-govtl Envl Orgns in the Decision-making Process in The Netherlands* (co-Author, in Dutch) 1982, *Intl Convs in the Field of the Envt* (co-Author, in Dutch) 1983, *Sawdust in Kenya* 1984, *Eén Aarde, één Milieu* (co-Author & Ed.) 1987, *Towards Sust.Coastal Tourism* (co-Author) 1991, *Envl Impacts of Tourism on the Kenya Coast* (co-Author) 1992; var.papers & articles. **Languages:** Dutch, English, French, German, Kiswahili (basic comp.& spoken). Willing to act as consult.etc. **Address:** Royal Netherlands Embassy, POB 41537, Nairobi, Kenya. **Tel.**254 2 227111 to 4; **fax** 254 2 339155.

VO, Professor Dr Quy. Ornithology, ecology; environmental conservation; national parks & protected areas; effects of defoliants on the environment during the Vietnam war; education, training in environmental science. Centre Director. *B*.31 Dec.1929, Ha Tinh, Vietnam. Vietnamese. *M*.Le Thanh (translator of envl documents): 2 *s*.Thanh Giang (memb.of EIA WG,

Centre for Natural Resource Management & Envl Studics), Thanh Son (cnvl sci.at samc Centre). **Education:** U.of Vietnam BSc 1953, U.of Moscow PhD(Zool.) 1955. **Experience:** res.— ornith., ecol., nat.utilization of natural resources, biodiv., cons.of Nature, effects of defoliants on envt; admin.— held admin.rank in some instns; chaired or presided over many scientific progs & socs; teaching — ecol., zool., ornith., cons. of Nature, from BSc–PhD levels. **Career:** Lect.then Prof. U.of Hanoi 1956– (incl.Head Dept of Zool., Dean Fac.of Biol., Dir Dept of Educ., Dir of Centre for Natural Resource and Envl Studies); Dir, Nat.Prog.on Rational Utilization of Natural Resources & Envl Prot.1980–90. **Achievements:** organizing activities on cons.of Nature, sust.use of natural resources, estab.of prot.areas, teaching as outlined above. **Memberships:** VC Soc.of Biologists of Vietnam, Soc.of Cons.of Nature & Envt, and MAB/UNESCO Cttee for Vietnam; IUCN SSC Steering Cttee, CNPPA, and Asian Wild Cattle SG (Chair). **Awards:** three Medals from Vietnamese Govt, Gold Medal (WWF) 1988, Global 500 Roll of Honour (UNEP) 1992, John C. Phillips Medal (IUCN) 1994. **Publications:** 70+ incl.*Birds of Vietnam* (two vols) 1975–81, *The Life of Birds* 1987, *Vietnam Nat.Cons. Strat.* 1985, Envt & Dev.in Vietnam 1993. Indiff.to pers.pub.& news media support. **Languages:** English, French, Russian, Vietnamese. Willing to act as consult.etc. **Address:** Centre for Natural Resource and Environmental Studies, University of Hanoi, Hanoi, Vietnam. **Tel.** (office) 84 42 53506, (home) 84 45 23625; **fax** 84 42 62932.

VOLLENWEIDER, Professor Dr Richard Albert. Limnology; environment. Senior Scientist Emeritus & Professor of Biology. *B.*27 June 1922, Zürich, Switzerland. Canadian (landed immigrant), Swiss. **Education:** High Sch. Luzern, teaching dipl.1942; U.of Zürich PhD 1951. **Experience:** res.— gen.limnol., primary prod., algal nutrition, water chem., modelling; tech.— water poll.& eutrophication (freshwater & marine), basin mgmt; admin.— res.& instnl mgmt; consult.— OECD, UNESCO/ FAO, WHO, PAHO, UNEP & envl admin.& instnl bodies of several countries. **Career:** Res.Asst & part-time Res.F. Hydrobiol.Inst. 1946–54 & 1959–66; Postdoctl F. Istituto Italiano di Idrobiologia 1954–5 & Limnol.Inst. U.of Uppsala 1955–7; UNESCO Field Expert to Inst.of Oceanogr.& Fisheries Res.(Min.of Agric. Egypt) 1957–9; Consult.to OECD 1966–8; Fisheries Res.Bd of Canada 1968–70; Sr Sci. NWRI 1980–88 whereafter Sr Sci.Emer.; Prof.of Biol. McMaster U. 1979–91. **Achievements:** organizing & developing early res.activities on Laurentian Gt Lakes & other limnol.studies in Canada; directed Canadian contribn to intlly-coordinated res.prog.on L.Ontario; studied primary prod.of Swiss, Italian, Swedish, and Egyptian, lakes using oxygen techniques & radioactive carbon (^{14}C); explored relationship betw-

een primary prod.and spectral correlation matrices and nutritional conditions over broad range of lakes; applied open-system concept to lakes relating their trophic conditions mathematically to nutrient loading, morphometry, & water renewal: these lines of res.became the frame for resolving question re.eutrophication; main contribn was result of integrated approach to conceive, delineate, & develop, a framework concerning our understanding of the process of Man-induced eutrophication of lakes & rivers, relating trophic conditions of bodies of water with catchment basin conditions, nutrient losses from agric., husbandry, human settlements, & industry (Dir Intl Cooperative Prog.on Eutrophication of 18 OECD countries 1972–80); coord. eutrophication res.on Adriatic Sea on behalf of Emilia-Romagna Regn (Italy) 1979–, coordinated assessment of Medit.eutrophication on behalf of UNEP (Athens) 1992–4; discovered acidification process of lakes due to industrial ammonia poll.(in L.Orta). **Memberships:** ILEC (Founder Memb., VC), ILEC Fndn (Counc.), Rawson Acad.of Aquatic Scis (Founder Memb., F.), Cervia Ambiente Fndn (Scientific Cttee), ECES (Tech.Scientific Cttee), ICAES (co-Chairman), SIL (Emer.). **Awards:** Cervia Ambiente Intl Prize 1979, Tyler Prize for Envl Achievement (co-Laureate) 1986, Frank Rigler Award (CSL) 1986, Naumann Thienemann Medal (SIL) 1987, Global 500 Roll of Honour (UNEP) 1988, F.RSC 1989; many hon. degrees & num.other awards; estab.by NWRI of Envt Canada of the 'R.A.Vollenweider Lectureship Award in Aquatic Scis' 1988. **Publications:** *Scientific Fundamentals of Eutrophication of Lakes and Flowing Waters, with Spec.Ref.to Phosphorus and Nitrogen* (OECD Tech.Report) 1968, *Primary Prod.in Aquatic Envts* (IBP Handbook) 1974, *Eutrophication of Inland Waters: Monitoring, Assessment & Control* (OECD Summary Report) 1982, *Intl Conf.on Marine Eutrophication* (1990 Conf. Proc., Prin.Ed.); Edl Adv.Bds of *Memorie, J.of Aquatic Ecosystem Health,* and *Environmetrics,* co-Ed.of ILEC/UNEP *Guideland Books on Lake Mgmt.* **Languages:** English, French, German (mother tongue), Italian, Portuguese (read), Spanish (read & understood), Swedish (read). Further details may be obtained from *The Canadian Enc.*1988, *Who's Who in Amer.*1972–3. Willing to act as consult.and/or ref. **Address:** 262 Townsend Avenue, Burlington, Ontario L7T 1Z6, Canada. **Tel.**(home) 1 905 632 8052.

VON DROSTE ZU HÜLSHOFF, Dr Bernd, *see* HÜLSHOFF, Dr Bernd VON DROSTE ZU.

VON MOLTKE, Dr Konrad, *see* MOLTKE, Dr Konrad VON.

VON UEXKÜLL, Carl Jakob Wolmar, see UEXKÜLL, Carl Jakob Wolmar VON.

VORONOV, Professor Dr Arkady Nicolaevich. Ecological (contaminant) hydrogeology, water

quality; oil & gas hydrogeology; isotopic composition of Helium & Argon; environment,
conservation, ecological education.   Head of
Department.   *B*.25 Dec.1936, Semipalatinsk,
Kazachstan. Russian. Father Nicolai Voronov,
geol.   *M*.Tatiana Voronova: *s*.Michael (oceanology), *d*.   **Education:** Leningrad (now St Petersburg) SU MSc(Hydrogeol.) 1959; All-Union
Petroleum Inst. PhD 1968, DSc(Geol.& Mineral-
ogy) 1977.   **Experience:** hydrogeol.of diff.parts
of Soviet Union;   oil & gas hydrogeol.in
Lithuania, Latvia, Russia, and other countries;
helium deposits in former Soviet Union & USA;
lect.on contaminant hydrogeol.;   ecol. & hydro-
geol.mapping in Russia, Turkmenistan, Poland,
and Mongolia; qual.of underground water and
mineral (medical) water; orgn of intl scientific
sems on geol.of Helium, ecol. hydrogeol.of
Baltic area.   **Career:** Hydrogeol.1959–63, Chief
of Dept 1963–82, All-Union Petroleum Inst.;
Prof. Hydr.& Met. Inst.1982–4; Lect. UNESCO
1990–95; Head, Dept of Hydr. St Petersburg U.
1984–.   **Achievements:** ecol & hydrogeol.maps
of Baltic area;   methods of economic & ecol
estimation of underground waters;   study of
ground-water flow contamination;   orgn of Conf.
'Ecol Hydrogeol.of Baltic Area' 1993;   lect.on
ecol hydrogeol.for UNESCO.   **Memberships:**
Russian AS (Scientific Council on Hydrogeol.&
Engg Geol., Ecol Council, Scientific Tech.
Soc.'Gornoe'), Educ. Council Proc.of St
Petersburg U., Scientific & Methodical Council
of Univs of Russia. **Publications:** six books and
c.200 scientific papers incl.*Natural Gases of
Deposit Thickness* 1976, *Analysis of Interaction
between Ground Water and Buried Pyrite Ends*
(Proc.) 1987, *The Role of Underground Hydro-
sphere in the Dev.of the Earth* (Ed.) 1990, *The
Actual Problems of Prot.Qual.of Underground
Water* (Ed.) 1992, *The Ecol.& Hydrogeol.
Mapping of Izhorskoe Plateau for the Purpose of
Rational Water Resources Usage* (Proc.) 1992,
The Trend of Geol Envt Evol.in St Petersburg
(Proc.) 1994. Favours pers.pub.& news media
support.   **Languages:** English (good), Polish,
Russian. Willing to act as consult.etc. **Address:**
Lunacharskogo Street 38-235, St Peters-
burg 194356, Russia.   **Tel.**(office) 7 812 218
9692, (home) 7 812 513 5307; **fax** 7 812 218
1346.

VOS, Dr Willem.   Applied physical geography,
landscape ecology & planning, in (sub-) Mediterranean zone. Head of Department, Lecturer.
B.12 June 1946, Amsterdam, The Netherlands.
Dutch.   *M*.Dieuwer E.: 3 *s*.   **Education:** Intl
Training Centre for Photogrammatic Interpretation and Aerial Survey, degree in air photointerpretation 1972;   U.of Amsterdam, MSc
(Phys.Geog.)(*cum laude*) 1974, PhD 1988. **Experience:** res.& consult.in landscape planning,
Nature cons., & forest mgmt.   **Career:** High
Sch.Teacher 1970–71; Asst, U.of Amsterdam
1970–74 and Euro.Parliament 1975; res.in land-
scape ecol.1975–80, Head of Dept of Landscape
Ecol.1981–8, Inst.for For.and Landscape Plann-

ing; Coord. For.Res.1988–93 and Head of Dept
of Natural Resources' Mgmt 1993–, Dutch
Inst.for For.and Nature Res.;   Lect.in Medit.
Landscape Ecol. Medit.Agronomy Inst. Chania
(Greece), 1991–.   **Achievements:** applied res.
for landscape planning & impact studies, integrated studies of landscape changes due to land-
use changes, scenario studies.   **Memberships:**
IUFRO, IALE, IUCN, WLO, NBV, De Levende
Natuur.   **Award:** Res.Award (Euro.Parliament)
1974.   **Publications:** *Vanishing Tuscan Landscapes* 1988, *The Farma R.Barrage Effect Study*
1988, *Forest Reserves Res.*1992;   70 articles &
reports. Dislikes pers.pub., favours news media
support.   **Languages:** Dutch, English, French,
German, Italian.   Willing to act as consult.
etc. **Address:** 7 Molenstreet, Wageningen 6701
DM, The Netherlands.   **Tel.**(office) 31 317 4
77826, (home) 31 317 4 16738; **fax** 31 317 4
24988.

WAAK, Ms Patricia Ann. Population, sustainable
development, biodiversity.   Department Director. *B*.1 Feb.1943, Muskogee, Oklahoma, USA.
American.   *M*.Kenneth John Strom (wildlife
biol.): 2 *d*.   **Education:** Mather Sch.of Nursing
(Tulane U.), RN 1964; U.of Houston, biol.
1964–6, govt & pol.1976–7; St Joseph Coll.
(Maine) BS(Psych.) 1995.   **Experience:** res.,
admin., tech., & consult., in fields of public health,
pop., envt, & women's dev., in US, China, Nepal,
Russia, Philippines, Bangladesh, Jordan, Egypt,
Uganda, Nigeria, Kenya, Zimbabwe, Mexico,
Costa Rica, Brazil, & Japan.   **Career:** Private
Health Practitioner 1964–6;   US Peace Corps
Vol.in Brazil 1966–8;   U.of Wisconsin Health
Practitioner 1968–70; Pol.Org.1970–72; Dir of
Counselling, Planned Parenthood of Metro-
politan Washington, DC 1973–5;   Dep.Dir,
Shriver for Pres.Campaign 1975–6;   Assoc.&
Dep.Dir, Office of Pop. US AID 1977–82; Asst
Dir, Center for Pop.& Family Health, Columbia
U.1982–5; Dir, Human Pop.and Resource Use
Dept, Nat.Audubon Soc.1985–. **Achievements:**
planning & design of widespread progs which
study human impacts on the natural world, and
communication & dissemination of findings.
Memberships: IUCN CESP, WorldWIDE,
AWD, Global Tomorrow Coalition (Bd of Dirs).
Awards: Roll of Honour (Friends of UNEP)
1988, Hon.Pop.F.(Pop.Ref.Bur.) 1993, Award as
Exec.Producer of video film '*Finding the Ba-
lance*' (Pop.Communications Intl) 1994.   **Pu-
blications:** num.incl.*Sharing the Earth: Cross
Cultural Experiences in Pop., Envt and Dev.*
1993;   Exec.Producer of such video films as
What is the Limit 1987, *Pop.and Wildlife* 1989,
Pop.: How to Make a Difference (co-Exec.
Producer) 1994. Favours pers.pub.& news me-
dia support.   **Languages:** English, Portuguese
(written & spoken), Spanish (read and spoken).
Willing to act as consult.etc. **Address:** National
Audubon Society, 4150 Darley Avenue Suite 7,
Boulder, Colorado 80303, USA. **Tel.**(office) 1
303 499 5155, (home) 1 303 828 0612; **fax** 1 303
499 0286; **internet** pwaak@audubon.org .

WADHAMS, Dr Peter. Climate change; Arctic & Antarctic ice & ocean research. Reader in Polar Studies. *B*.14 May 1948, Grays, Essex, England, UK. British. *M*.Maria Pia Casarini (polar hist.). **Education:** U.of Camb. BA (Phys.) 1969, PhD(Polar Oceanogr.) 1974, ScD 1994. **Experience:** res.— 25 yrs on polar oceans & ice incl.29 field expedns; admin.— five yrs as Inst.Dir, Coord. ESOP (large CEC-funded res.prog.in Greenland Sea). **Career:** Postdoctl F. Inst.of Ocean Scis (Vic. BC) 1974–5; Asst Dir of Res.1975–87, Dir 1988–92, Reader in Polar Studies 1992–, Scott Polar Res.Inst.(U.of Camb.). **Achievements:** study of mechanisms affecting global warming in polar regns esp.sea-ice thickness in Arctic & Antarctic, and deep convection in Greenland Sea. **Memberships:** AGU, F.RGS, IGS, Challenger Soc.(UK), Oceanogr.Soc.(USA). **Awards:** W.S.Bruce Prize (RSE) 1979, Polar Medal 1987, Prize for Envl Scis (Italgas) 1990. **Publications:** *c*.160 papers incl.sea ice thickness distribn in Frum Strait 1983, The underside of Arctic sea ice imaged by sidescan sonar 1988, Evidence for thinning of the Arctic ice cover north of Greenland 1990. Indiff.to pers.pub., favours news media support. **Languages:** English, Italian. Further details may be obtained from Brit.*Who's Who* 1995. Willing to act as consult.etc. **Address:** Scott Polar Research Institute, Lensfield Road, Cambridge CB2 1ER, England, UK. **Tel.**(office) 44 1223 336542, (home) 44 1223 359433; **fax** 44 1223 336549.

WAGER, Dr Jonathan Field. Landscape planning & management, teaching, consulting. Company Principal. *B*.29 April 1937, London, England, UK. British. Father the late Prof.L.R. Wager, geol. *M*.Eva Birgitta: 2 *s*., *d*. **Education:** Bootham Sch.; Fitzwilliam Coll.Camb. MA 1963, PhD 1966. **Experience:** res.into eval.& mgmt of British countryside & landscape; directing grad.& undergrad.professional courses in Town & Country Planning; teaching rural planning & envl mgmt, intl consult.in envl planning specializing in prot.areas' mgmt, cultural heritage, the coast, tourism, & EIA. **Career:** Sr Planning Officer, Durham Co.Council 1964–7; Lect./Sr Lect.in Town & Country Planning, U.of Manchester 1967–91; Partner, Cobham Resource Consults 1985–91; Prin. Jonathan Wager & Assocs 1991–. **Achievements:** memb.of IUCN CESP 1981–, Exec.& Council of Town & Country Planning Assn 1980–91, Chairman of Landscape Res.Group 1977–8 and Community Tech.Aid Centre 1984–9, Dir of 'Think Green' (UK nat.campaign) 1986–90. **Memberships:** IUCN (CESP 1981–), RTPI, F.Tourism Soc. **Publications:** num.reports & papers. Accepts pers.pub., favours news media support. **Languages:** English, Swedish (fair). Willing to act as consult.etc. **Address:** Jonathan Wager & Associates, Oaklands, 19 Langham Road, Bowdon, Cheshire WA14 2HX, England, UK. **Tel.**(office) 44 161 928 1287, (home) 44 161 928 1287; **fax** 44 161 928 8530.

WAHLSTEDT, Jens. Conservation of Nature; biological diversity; amateur ornithology. Secretary-General. *B*.2 March 1935, Vasteras, Sweden. Swedish. *M*.Kerstin. **Education:** U.of Gothenburg, degree in Econ.1975. **Experience:** res.& admin. **Career:** Officer in Swedish Army 1960–64, Exec.Dir/Marketing Dir in pharmaceutical industry 1964–83; Sec.-Gen. WWF Sweden 1983–. **Achievements:** expanding WWF Sweden from 2,000 to 170,000 members and attaining 175 cons.projects in Sweden per annum; projects in such regions or countries as Siberia, E.Africa, Ecuador (Galápagos), esp.on trop.forests, etc. **Publications:** *Ladrikets tåaglar* 1968, *Så länge solen går upp* 1993, hundreds of papers & articles. Favours pers.pub.& news media support. **Languages:** English, German, Swedish. Willing to act as consult.etc. **Address:** Worldwide Fund for Nature, Ulriksdals Slott, 171 71 Solna, Sweden. **Tel.**(office) 46 8 850120, (home) 46 8 851925; **fax** 46 8 851329.

WAJIH, Dr Shiraz A. Environmental education; sustainable agriculture; flood/waterlogging. Reader in Botany, Group Secretary. *B*.4 July 1954, Moradabad, Uttar Pradesh, India. Indian. *M*.Anjum Ara Khan: *s*. **Education:** Gorakhpur U.(UP), MSc 1974, PhD(Plant Ecol.) 1980. **Experience:** res.— academic, applied partic.to envl issues, admin.— mgmt of var.NGOs, consult.to Oxfam, UNICEF, NOVIB, PAN, etc.; u.lecturing. **Career:** with NGOs 1975–; Chairman, IYF for Envl Studies & Cons.1984–9; Reader in Bot.& Ecol. Mahatma Gandhi Postgrad.Coll.(UP) 1976–; Sec. Gorakhpur Envl Action Group 1986–. **Achievements:** achieving strong networking of NGOs, advocacy lobbying, practical demn of principles. **Memberships:** IUCN CEC, F.IBS, UP Vol.Health Assn. **Awards:** var.nat.prizes and f'ships. **Publications:** *c*.50 res.& allied papers. Favours pers.pub.& news media support. **Languages:** English, Hindi, Urdu. Willing to act as consult. etc. **Address:** 224 Purdilpur, Mahatma Gandhi Postgraduate College, Mahatma Gandhi College Road, Gorakhpur 273001, Uttar Pradesh, India. **Tel.**(office) 91 551 339774, (home) 91 551 334906; **fax** 91 551 339774.

WALKER, Brian Wilson. Directing a field science foundation. Foundation Executive Director. *B*.31 Oct.1930, Chipping Norton, Oxon., England, UK. British. *M*.Nancy Margaret: 2 *s*.Dr Peter Walker (soil sci.), Dorcas Walker (envlist). **Education:** Manchester U. Memb. IPM 1953. **Experience:** directed four major envl/devl agencies. **Career:** CEO Bridgeport Brass Ltd. 1961–73; DG Oxfam 1974–83; Dir Ind.Comm. on Intl Humanitarian Issues 1983–5; Pres.IIED 1983–9; Dir Earthwatch Europe 1989–. **Achievements:** established world's first comp.vegetable genebank; founded Earthwatch Europe 1989 and subs.Earth, Life, & Human Scis Support Prog.; directed Live Aid–Band Aid African Field Prog.; supported evol.of sust.devl insights & definition. **Memberships:** Green Coll.Oxf., Chairman SOS Sahel, Trustee Cambodia & Artizan Trusts. **Award:** MA *H.C.* (Oxf. U.). **Publications:** *Authentic Dev. in Africa* 1986, Edl Bd *World Resources Report.* Dislikes pers.pub.& news media support. **Languages:** English, French (some). Willing to act as consult.etc. **Address:** Earthwatch Europe, 57 Woodstock Road, Oxford OX2 6HU, England, UK. **Tel.**(office) 44 1865 311600, (home) 44 1865 515473; **fax** 44 1865 311383.

WALKER, Clive Hatton. Environmental education & ecotourism in the bush; wildlife painting. Managing Director, Professional Wildlife Artist, Foundation Chairman. *B.*19 June 1936, Johannesburg, SA. S.African. *M.*Conita: 2 *s.* incl. Anton (Game Ranger). **Education:** Treverton Coll., St Andrews; Johannesburg Art Sch.(SA); St Martin's Sch.of Fine Art (UK). **Experience:** game ranger & hunting, safari mgmt, wildlife painting, envl educ., cons.mgmt. **Career:** Overseas Visitors' Club (London, UK) 1959–63; Advertising Mgr, Herbert Evans & Co.1963–74; Game Ranger on private reserve in then Bechuanaland 1966–81; professional Wildlife Artist 1974–; MD, Lapalala Wilderness 1981–; Chairman, Rhino & Elephant Fndn 1986–. **Achievements:** Founder of Endangered Wildlife Trust 1973, Founder of Educl Wildlife Expedns 1975 to become Clive Walker Trails and (with son) Clive Walker Safaris 1994–, commenced envl prog.for children operating at Lapalala Wilderness (Nw Transvaal) 1981–, resp.for dev.of Rhino Prog.at Lapalala Wilderness 1990, advocated & pioneered estab. of Field Guides' Assn of Southern Africa, Founder Waterberg NC 1989, co-Founder Rhino & Elephant Fndn 1986. **Memberships:** IUCN Comm.on Educ.and SSC Elephant, Rhino, & Cat (Corres.) SGs, Game Rangers' Assn (Hon.), Field Guides' Assn of Southern Africa. **Award:** Paul Harris F.(Rotary Intl) 1984. **Publications:** num.books incl.*Okavango from the Air* 1990, *Savuti, the Vanishing River* 1901, *Dear Elephant, Sir* 1992; num.articles. Accepts pers.pub., favours news media support. **Language:** English. Willing to act as consult.etc. **Address:** Lapalala Wilderness Reserve, Northern Province, South Africa. **Tel.**(office) 27 11 453 7648, (home) 27 11 454 1647; **fax** 27 11 453 7649.

WALLÉN, Dr Carl-Christian. Climatology, global monitoring of environment; climate politics & change. Consultant. *B.*17 Aug.1917, Stockholm, Sweden. Swedish. Father Axel Wallén, DG of Swedish Met.Service 1918–35. *W.: d.* **Education:** U.of Stockholm, PhD 1949. **Experience:** u.-level lecturing, admin.; tech. coopn expert in Mexico 1954, Near E.1961–2, & Peru 1964–5; consult.re.climatology. **Career:** Assoc.Prof.of Phys.Geog. U.of Stockholm 1950–53; First State Meteorologist 1950–54, Asst Dir 1955–9, Dep.Dir 1960–68, SMHI; Chief of Div. WMO 1968–76; Dep.Dir UNEP/GEMS 1976–80; Consult. UNEP 1980–. **Achievements:** *c.*100 scientific articles on climatology, agricl met., & envl monitoring.

Memberships: SSAG (Chairman 1959–61, Ed.*Geografiska Annaler* 1950–65), SGS (Chair 1963–5), UNEP Scientific Adv.Cttee for Climate (Chair 1994–). **Award:** G.A.Wahlberg's Silver Medal (SSAG) 1965. **Publications:** *c.*100 incl. *Glacial-Met.Investigations in Northern Lappland* 1942–8 (doctl thesis) 1949, Variability of summer temps in Sweden 1953, A study of the agroclimatology of arid & semi-arid regns in the Near E., Impact of present-century climatic fluctuations in the n.hemisphere 1986. **Languages:** English, French; German & Spanish (spoken); Swedish. Further details may be obtained from *Who is Who in Intl Orgns* 1995. Willing to act as consult.etc. **Address:** World Meteorological Organization, CP 2300, 1211 Geneva 2, Switzerland. **Tel.**(office) 41 22 730 8111, (home) 33 59 50 428995 (France).

WALSH, Dr John Anthony. Plant virology & pathology especially of field vegetables. Research Leader. *B.*6 Aug.1954, Halifax, Yorks., England, UK. British. *M.*Lea Hultunen (plant path.): *d.* **Education:** Leeds U. BSc 1976, PhD 1981. **Experience:** res.— ultrastructural studies in plant parasitic nematodes and rickettsialike organisms infecting them; diagnosis, epidemiology, serology, & control, of plant viruses; studies on fungal transmission of plant viruses; virus/plant interactions, genetic control of resistance, and virus diversity/pathogenic variation & distribn. **Career:** Postdoctl, Nemotology Dept, Rothamsted Experimental Station 1979–82; Res. Leader, Plant Path.Dept, HRI 1983–. **Achievements:** proposed pathotype system for turnip mosaic potyvirus based on resistance genes in *Brassica napus* which is being used to study pathotypic variation in turnip mosaic virus worldwide. **Memberships:** AAB, M.IBiol., CBiol., ISHS Vegetable Virus WG (Sec.), Intl WG on Plant Viruses with Fungus Vectors. **Award:** Best Student Paper Award (Soc.of Nematologists) 1979. **Publications:** 40+. Indiff.to pers.pub.& news media support. **Languages:** English; Finnish & French (basic). **Address:** Department of Plant Pathology, Horticulture Research International, Wellesbourne, Warwickshire CV35 9EF, England, UK. **Tel.**(office) 44 1789 470382, (home) 44 1789 740915; **fax** 44 1789 470552.

WALT, Dr Pieter Toxopeus VAN DER. Arid plant ecology, park planning, ecological economics. Manager, Scientific Liaison. *B.*14 May 1941, Umtata, SA. S.African. *M.*Nicolette: 2 *s.* **Education:** Potchefstroom U. BSc 1962; Natal U. BSc(Hons) 1963, MSc 1965, PhD 1973. **Experience:** res.— ten yrs each as pasture sci.& Chief Res.Officer; admin.& consult.— seven yrs as Dep.Dir of Nature Cons.in Namibia, four yrs in scientific liaison. **Career:** Chief Res. Officer 1983–9, Mgr Scientific Liaison 1989–, Nat.Parks Bd; Dep.Dir Nature Cons.in Namibia 1983–9. **Achievements:** widespread exp.in negotiating new cons.areas — *c.*4 m.ha, getting to know arid-zone ecol., co-editing scientific j. **Membership:** Southern Africa Grassland Soc.

Publications: 12 scientific papers, 73 popular articles, co-Ed.*Koedoe* 1972–82. Indiff.to pers. pub., favours news media support. **Languages:** Afrikaans, English. Willing to act as consult.etc. **Address:** POB 787, Pretoria 0001, Republic of South Africa. **Tel.**(office) 27 12 343 9770, (home) 27 12 329 0037; **fax** 27 12 343 9958.

WALTON, Dr David Winston Harris. Ecology, conservation, and environmental management, especially of polar regions. Division Head, Honorary Reader. *B*.25 Aug.1945, St Anne's, Lancs., England, UK. British. *M*.Sharon Anne: *s*., 2 *d*. **Education:** U.of Edinburgh BSc(Hons) (Bot.) 1967; U.of Birmingham PhD 1975. **Experience:** res.in variety of antarctic biol.fields; extensive edl exp.; considerable exp. of writing scientific material for the public; scientific admin.& policy dev. **Career:** Antarctic Res. Sci.1967–79, PSO 1979–86, Head of Terr.& Freshwater Life Sci.Div.1986–, Brit.Antarctic Survey; Vis.Prof. U.of Colorado 1981; Hon. Reader, Robert Gordon U.(Aberdeen) 1990–. **Achievements:** Founding Ed. *Antarctic Sci.* 1989–; Chairman of Edl Bd of *Studies in Polar Res.* CUP; Convenor, Group of Specialists on Envl Affairs & Cons. SCAR. **Memberships:** BES (Counc. 1986–8 & 1990–, Chairman of Ecol Affairs Cttee 1990–, Sec.of Prod.& Decomposition Ecol.Group 1979–89), BLS, IAPT. **Award:** Polar Medal (UK) 1986. **Publications:** *Invertebrate–Microbial Interactions* 1984, *Key Environments — Antarctica* 1985, *Antarctic Sci.*1987, *Primary Succession on Land* 1993; Ed.-in-Chief *Antarctic Sci.*; *c*.150 scientific papers and articles. Accepts pers.pub., favours news media support. **Languages:** English, French (limited). **Address:** British Antarctic Survey, High Cross, Madingley Road, Cambridge CB3 0ET, England, UK. **Tel.**(office) 44 1223 251592, (home) 44 1487 840449; **fax** 44 1223 62616.

WALULYA-MUKASA, Joe. Environmental education; tree planting; energy conservation. Chief Security Officer, Chairman. *B*.25 March 1943, Mulago, Kampala, Uganda. Ugandan. *M*.Helen Kezia. **Education:** Makerere U.of E.Africa, Dipl.in Social Work 1966. **Experience:** over ten yrs in envl educ.and working with grassroot orgns in tree planting, soil erosion control, and improved cooking stoves. **Career:** Prin. Reformatory Sch.for Young Offenders, then Sr Prisons Officer 1968–82; Chief Security Officer, Uganda Grain Milling Co.1983–; Chairman, JEEP 1983–. **Achievements:** awards for leadership, as Founder/Chairman of JEEP, of campaigns for tree planting and desert.control in Uganda through heightening public awareness*. **Award:** *Global 500 Roll of Honour (UNEP) 1987. **Publications:** incl.*Tree Planting and How to Get Econ.Returns* 1992. Favours pers.pub. **Language:** English. **Address:** POB 1684, Jinja, Uganda. **Tel.**256 43 20054; **fax** 256 43 20060.

Wan Ru ZHANG, Professor, *see* ZHANG, **Professor Wan Ru.**

WANG, Professor Sung (also **Song**). Biodiversity; wildlife conservation & management; mammalian taxonomy & faunistics. Research Professor, Executive Vice-Chairman, Scientific Adviser, Committee Representative. *B*.11 July 1933, Jiangsu, PRC. Chinese. *M*.Chen Suang-Shuang: *d*.Jie (envl sci.), *s*. **Education:** Fudan U.(Shanghai), BA(Zool.) 1954. **Experience:** res.— mammalian systematics; fauna surveys in NE, SW, N, & S, China; wildlife prot.& mgmt, biodiv.cons.*e.g*.panda reserve survey, biodiv. inventory & database; admin.as deptl dir of Inst.of Zool. (Chinese AS) as well as Exec.VC of Endangered Species' Scientific Comm.(PRC); consult.— Scientific Adv. China's State Council Envl Prot.Comm.1991–; China Council for Intl Coopn on Envt & Dev.(Counc.& co-Chair, Biodiv.WG) 1991–; IUCN Regnl Counc.& SSC Regnl VC 1988–; Vice-Head of Expert Team for China's Nat.Biodiv.Action Plan, Academic Cttee Memb. Inst.of Zool. Kunmin Inst.of Zool.and Xinjiang Inst.of Biol., Pedology, and Desert; VC of Assessment Cttee for State Nature Reserves; teaching — mammalogy & wildlife cons.to BA & MA students; edl — Dep.Chief *Acta Zootaxonomica Sinica*, Chief Ed.*Acta Zoologica Sinica*, Dep.Chief *Chinese J.of Biodiv.*, Scientific Cttee Memb.*Cons.& Mgmt* (CITES). **Career:** Dep.Dir & Dir, Dept of Vertebrate Taxonomy & Faunistics 1980–88, Res.Prof. 1989–, Inst.of Zool. Chinese AS; Asian Rep.& Alternative Rep. for Animals Cttee 1989–95 and Nomenclature Cttee 1985 of CITES; Scientific Adv. Beijing Endangered Species Breeding Centre 1994–; Exec.VC, Endangered Species' Scientific Comm. (Scientific Auth.for CITES in China). **Achievements:** basic res.on Chinese mammalian fauna & taxonomy; init.of wildlife prot., mgmt, & legis., incl.Prot.Wildlife Species List by law; *in situ* cons.& Nature reserve planning, estab., & assessment; China's Red Data Books and endangered species status survey & action plans; CITES & Biodiv.Conv.implementation & enforcement; init.of pioneering biodiv.cons.in China. **Memberships:** Mammalogical Soc.of China (VP), China Zoo Assn (VP), China Nat. Cttee for IUBS, NYZS (Corres.), ASM (Checklist Cttee). **Awards:** Sci.& Tech.Award (Academia Sinica) 1987, Appreciation Cert.(NYZS) 1987, State Sci.& Tech. Award 1991. **Publications:** incl.Mammals of NE China 1958, Econ. Fauna Sinica — Mammals 1962, Mammals of S.Xinjiang 1965, China's NCS 1983, Fauna Sinica-Carnivora, Mammalia 1987, *Biodiv.in China* 1992, *China's Nat.Biodiv.Action Plan* 1994; 60+ others. **Languages:** Chinese (and var.native languages), English, Russian (read). Willing to act as consult.etc. **Address:** Institute of Zoology, Chinese Academy of Sciences, 19 Zhongguancun Lu, Haidian, Beijing 100080, People's Republic of China. **Tel.& fax** 86 10 256 2717.

WANG, Professor Xianpu. Vegetation ecology of tropical & subtropical regions; natural conservation, biodiversity. Professor of Vegetation Ecology. *B*.17 July 1929, Guangdong, China. Chinese. *M*.Yan Zhenglong (res.on *Malus* genetic resources): 2 *s*.Yang (geog.teacher), Shan (Genetic Inst. Academia Sinica). **Education:** Agricl Coll. Kwangsi U. M.(Forest Sci.) 1947–51; Forest Scis Lab. former USSR AS 1959–61. **Experience:** res.of veg.ecol.of trop. & subtrop.regns in China, and latterly of class.& effective mgmt of prot.areas and cons.& sust.utilization of biodiv. **Career:** Asst Researcher, Assoc.Prof., Prof.of Veg.Ecol., V.-Dir Lab.of Plant Ecol., 1951– and V.-Dir Inst.of Bot.1982–6, Academia Sinica. **Achievements:** giving great consideration to aspects of class.& dynamics of trop.& subtrop.veg.; class.& effective mgmt as well as cons.& sust.use of biodiv.in China. **Memberships:** Beijing Ecol Soc.(Hon.Chairman), Natural Cons.Comm.of China Envt Soc.(Dep.Chairman), IUCN CNPPA (VC), IUCN SSC Plant Cons.Task Force and China Plant SG (Chairman). **Awards:** Second Class Award Nat.Natural Scis 1987, Prof.Zhu Kezhen Award 1990. **Publications:** *The Veg.of China* 1980, *The Theory & Practice of Natural Prot.Areas* 1989, *The Theory & Practice of Biodiv.*1994; Nature cons.in China: the present situation 1980; Envl & socio-econ.aspects of trop.deforestation in China 1986, Prot.areas in China 1986, *Burretiodendron hsienmu*: its ecol. & its prot.1986, Floristic inventory of trop.China 1989. Favours pers.pub.& news media support. **Languages:** Chinese, English, Russian. Willing to act as consult.etc. **Address:** Institute of Botany, Academia Sinica, 141 Xizhimenwai Avenue, Beijing 100044, People's Republic of China. **Tel.**(office) 86 10 835 3831 ext.276, (home) 86 10 302 2293; **fax** 86 10 831 9534.

WARDEH, Dr Muhammad Fadel. Studies in animal production; research development in livestock & rangeland utilization; conservation of animal germ-plasm. Network Coordinator, Departmental Director. *B*.9 Jan.1943, Salamieh, Syria. Syrian. *M*.Rifaa: 2 *d*.incl.Rana (student of agric.), *s*. **Education:** Amer.U.of Beirut, BSc(Agric.) 1968, MSc(Breeding) 1969; Utah SU, PhD(Nutrition) 1981. **Experience:** res., consult., admin. **Career:** Nutritionist 1981–4, Prod.Specialist 1989–91; Dir Dept of Studies of Animal Wealth 1991–, ACSAD; Chairman, Intl Network of Feed Info.Centers 1984–9; Coord. Camel Applied Res.& Dev.Network 1991–. **Achievements:** estab.of cons.project of animal germ-plasm in Arab countries and a network of info.on feed resources. **Membership:** Phi Capa Phi (Utah). **Publications:** four books incl. *Arabian Horses and their Nutrition* (in Arabic) 1985, *Arabian Camels: Breed, Husbandry & Prod.*(in Arabic with English & French summaries) 1989; *c*.160 other. Indiff.to pers.pub.& news media support. **Languages:** Arabic, English. Willing to act as consult. **Address:** The Arab Center for the Studies of Arid Zones and Dry Lands, POB 2440, Damascus, Syrian Arab Republic. **Tel.**(office) 963 11 755713, (home) 963 11 212 3505; **fax** 963 11 755712.

WARNER, Professor Sir Frederick. Air & water pollution, risk, nuclear weapons' tests, movement of radionuclides, quality assurance. Visiting Professor, Institute Chairman, Committee Chairman, Consultant. *B*.31 March 1910, London, England, UK. British. *M*.Barbara (Lady Warner): 2 *s*., 2 *d*. **Education:** UCL BSc 1932. **Experience:** chem.engr in industry in prod., res., construction, & design; from 1956–80 covered problems of large-scale plant contracts, air & water poll., coal & oil gasification, applied fluid mechanics, risk assessment, and, generally, the educ.of engrs. **Career:** Partner, Cremer and Warner Consulting Chem.Engrs 1956–80; Court, Cranfield Inst.of Tech.1970–; Chairman, CEI/CSTI Working Party on Poll.1970–72; Memb. Adv. Cttee on Poll.of the Sea 1970–90; Vis.Prof.in Envl Engg, UCL 1970–86; Vis.Prof.in Chem. Engg, ICL 1970–76; Memb. Lord Zuckerman's Comm. on Mining and the Envt 1971–3; Chairman, Council of Sch.of Pharmacy, U.of London 1971–8; Vis.Prof. U.of Sydney 1972 & 1980; Memb. Adv.Council on Energy Cons. Dept of Energy 1974–80; Chairman, Study Group on Risk, RS 1978–83 & 1991–2; Vis. Prof.of Chem. 1983–, Vis.Prof.of Law 1988–94, Chairman of Inst.for Envl Res.1994–, U.of Essex; Memb. R.Comm.on Envl Poll.1973–6; Pro-Chancellor, Open U.1974–9; R.Comm.for the Exhibition of 1851, 1976–95; Assessor, Windscale Inquiry 1977–8; Chairman, SCOPE Project — Envl Consequences of Nuclear Warfare 1983–8; Chairman, Task Force on Qual.& Standards, NEDO 1983–5; Chairman, CSTI 1987–90; Pres. IQA 1987–90; Pres.BACIE 1979–89; Vis.Prof. R.Sch.of Mines, ICL 1993–; Chairman, Scientific Adv.Cttee, SCOPE–RADTEST/RADPATH 1988–; num.other appointments. **Achievements:** cleaning R.Thames; designing-out poll.; promoting integrated poll.control; dissemination of appeals for WWF 1961; Officer of SCOPE. **Memberships:** F.RS, F.Eng., F.IMechE, F. Chartered Inst.of Arbitrators, F.UCL, F.Academico Ordinario Tiberina, SCOPE (Hon.Treas. 1982–8), BHRA (Pres. 1980–87), MBA (Counc. 1975–8), IChemE (Pres. 1966–7), CEI (Bd, Cttees' Chairman), Fedn Européenne d'Assns Nationales d'Ingénieurs (Pres.1968–71), BSI (Chairman of Chem.Engg Industry Cttee 1970–73, Chairman of Exec.Bd 1973–6, Pres.1980–83, Dep.Pres. 1983–9), Delhi Inst.of Tech.Trust 1960–73. **Awards:** Osborne Reynolds Medal (IChemE) 1955, KB 1968, Gold Medal (Czechoslovak Soc.for Intl Relations) 1969, Medal (Insinooriliitto, Finland) 1969, Bronze Medal (Associazione Nationale Ingegneri e Architette d'Italia) 1971, Melchett Medal (Inst.of Fuel) 1973, Academico Correspondiente la Academia de Ingerieria (Mexico) 1971, Leverhulme Medal 1978 & Buchanan Medal 1982 (RS), Monckton Copeman Medal (Soc.of Apothecaries) 1980, W.M.Thornton Medal (Inst.of Mining, Elec., & Mech.Engrs) 1983, Rheinland Prize (Technische Übersichung Verein) 1984, Gerard Piel Award (*Scientific Amer.*for Service to Sci.) 1991, Gold Medal (WFEO) 1993; Hon.F. School of Pharmacy (U.of Lond.), Hon.F. UMIST, Hon.Memb. Koninklijk Instituut van Ingenieurs (The Hague), Euro.Ing., Hon.F.IChemE, num.hon. degrees. **Publications:** c.130 incl.*Risk Assessment* (Ed.) 1983, The Treatment and Handling of Wastes (co-Author) 1992, *Risk — Analysis, Perception and Mgmt* (Ed.) 1992, Sust.dev. 1994. **Languages:** English, French. Further details may be obtained from Brit.*Who's Who* 1995, *Intl Who's Who* 1995. Willing to act as consult.etc. **Address:** SCOPE–RADTEST, Department of Biological and Chemical Sciences, Main Campus, University of Essex, Wivenhoe Park, Colchester CO4 3SQ, England, UK. **Tel.**(office) 44 1206 873370, (home) 44 1636 816483; **fax** (office) 44 1206 873370, (home) 44 1636 816399.

WASAWO, Professor Dr David Peter Simon. Zoology; natural resources, conservation; environment & development. Development Consultant. *B*.17 May 1923, Gem, Kenya. Kenyan. *M*.Ruth P.(envlly-sound farming): 2 *s*., 2 *d*. **Education:** Alliance High Sch.; Makerere Coll.; St Peter's Coll.Oxf. MA 1953; U.of London PhD 1959. **Experience:** res.on swampworms and lungfish; u.admin.; intl civil servant; regnl dev., adv.services; consult.to UNEP, UNESCO, FAO, World Bank, etc. **Career:** Asst Lect. Lect. Sr Lect. Reader, Prof.& Head of Dept of Zool, VP, Makerere U. 1952–65; Dep.Prin.1965–8, Prof. & Head of Dept of Zool.and Dean Fac. Sci.1969–71, U.of Nairobi; Chairman of Working Party on Res.Priorities & Res.Admin. E.African Community (appointed jointly by Presidents of Kenya, Tanzania, & Uganda) 1969; Scientific Adv.to Govt of United Rep.of Tanzania, UNESCO 1971–3; Chief, Natural Resources Div. UNECA 1973–9; MD, Lake Basin Dev.Auth. 1979–82; Dev.Adv. Min.of Energy & Regnl Dev.1982–6; Dev.Consult. 1987–. **Achievements:** introduced students to problems of wildlife ecol.& cons.; contributed to African wildlife cons.and, in particular, to the dev.of Kenya Nat.Parks' System, and to world cons.through V.-Presidency of IUCN; Intl Trusteeship of WWF; membership of UNESCO's Adv.Cttee on Natural Resources Res.; SCOPE. **Awards:** Hon. DSc (Kenyatta U.), Chairman of Fifth Session of Second Intl Cong. of WWF, VP IUCN 1972–4. **Publications:** incl.overall Ed.of ten vols on *Strat.Resources Planning in Uganda* 1988– of which wrote vols I *Natural Resources and Envt in Uganda*, II *Wildlife & Prot.Areas*, III *Forests*, and VIII *Envl Educ*. Indiff.to pers.pub. & news media support. **Languages:** Dholuo, English, French (read), Kiswahili. Willing to act as consult.etc. **Address:** POB 41024, Nairobi, Kenya. **Tel.**(office & home) 254 2 724236.

WATSON, Charles St Denis, Jr. Ecology of United States of America's Bureau of Land Management; 'commons ecology' in Nevada. Company Director. *B*.14 Aug.1934, Cleveland, OH, USA. American. **Education:** Pasadena City Coll. AA 1952; U.of Nevada BSc(Geol.)

1960. **Experience:** began govt career with BLM, then cartographer for the Navy & USAF; as co-founder of NORA, pioneered concept of envl prot.of unappropriated govt lands, or 'commons', beginning on BLM public lands in Nevada. **Career:** Land Examiner, US BLM 1960–65; Cartographer, US Naval Oceanogr. Office 1965–7 and Air Force Chart & Info.Center 1967–72; Dir NORA (a Nat.Public Lands Task Force) 1972–. **Achievements:** compiled comp.natural areas' & wilderness inventory of BLM public lands in Nevada known as 'NORA Index & Survey', widely considered 'Father' of US Fed.Lands Policy & Mgmt Act 1976. **Memberships:** Sierra Club 1957–, NORA (Hon.Life) 1958–, The Wilderness Soc.1966–. **Awards:** Hilliard Mem.Award (Rocky Mtn Center for Envt) 1974, Desert Wilderness Conf. Award 1983, Envl Achievement Award (Desert Protective Council) 1987, Chevron Nat.Cons. Award 1989. **Publications:** *NORA Newsletter* (quarterly — the oldest 'commons ecol.' pubn in Amer.), *The Lands No One Knows* 1975. Favours pers.pub.& news media support. **Language:** English. Willing to act as consult.etc. **Address:** POB 1245, Carson City, Nevada 89702-1245, USA. **Tel.**1 702 883 1169.

WATSON, Dr John Richard. Land management, in particular conservation reserves, caves, mountains; Biosphere Reserves; recreation. Regional Manager. *B*.2 May 1946, Otley, Yorks., England, UK. Australian, British. *M*. Barbara: *s*., *d*. **Education:** Bradford Grammar Sch.; Durham U. BSc(Hons)(Chem.) 1967, Aberdeen U. PhD(Soil Sci.) 1970, U.of Western Australia (then Nedlands Coll.of Advanced Educ.) Grad.Dipl.in Rec.1978. **Experience:** res.in soil–water–pesticide relations, land-use planning & rec., cave mgmt & prot., nat.park mgmt, Nature cons.mgmt; spec.interests include cave prot.& mgmt, recreational impacts in prot.areas (Nat.Parks & cons.reserves), mtn prot.areas, Biosphere Reserves; experienced hill walker & rock climber, occasional caver; outdoor activities incl.many yrs in UK and Australia and visits to Europe, Africa, N Amer., Venezuela, SE Asia/Oceania. **Career:** Postdoctl F. U.of Western Australia 1970–76; Envl Officer, EPA (then Dept of Cons.& Envt) 1976–8, Southern Regnl Super.of Nat.Parks, Nat.Parks Auth. 1978–85, S.Coast Regnl Mgr, Dept of Cons.& Land Mgmt 1985–, all WA. **Achievements:** estab.first regnl office of nat.parks in S.WA 1978; resp.for declaration of many new prot.areas in S.WA; Chairman, WA WG on Cave Prot.& Mgmt 1978–; contribns to intl consult.on mtns 1991, 4th World Parks Cong. 1992, and inaugural SE Asia Pacific Mtn Symp.1993; Coord. IUCN CNPPA Network on Cave Prot.& Mgmt 1992–. **Memberships:** BSSS, ISSS, ACKMA, IUCN CNPPA Mtns, Biosphere Reserves WG (Australian Comm.for UNESCO). **Awards:** Graham Squance Mem. Award 1977, Winston Churchill Mem.F'ship 1984. **Publications:** *A Climber's Guide to the Stirling Range Western Australia*

1972, *100 years ago ... a spec.collection of papers on the background & sig.of the Fenian escape from Fremantle WA, Easter 1876* 1976; *c*.60 papers. **Languages:** English, French (poor). Willing to act as consult.etc. esp.through IUCN. **Address:** Department of Conservation and Land Management, 44 Serpentine Road, Albany, Western Australia 6330, Australia. **Tel.**(office) 61 98 417133, (home) 61 98 415373; **fax** 61 98 413329.

WATSON, Dr Richard. Wildlife conservation, especially birds of prey & their habitats. Conservation Programme Director. *B*.18 May 1957, Johannesburg, SA. American, British, South African. *M*.Christine (Prin.Investigator, study of impact of military training on birds of prey). **Education:** U.of N.Wales, BSc(Marine Zool.) 1978; U.of Witwatersrand, PhD(Raptor Ecol.) 1986. **Experience:** res.— ecol.of Bateleur Eagle *(Terathopius ecaudatus)*, desert ecophysiol. (insects), endangered raptor ecol.in Africa & Madagascar; consult.on Spotted Owls *(Strix occidentalis)* (USFS). **Career:** Post-doctl Desert Ecol.Res. Unit (Namibia) 1985–8, Adj.Fac. Boise SU 1990– & Idaho SU 1992–, Fac. Sch.for Field Studies (Kenya) 1989, Consult.USFS 1989, Prog.Dir for Cons.in Africa & Madagascar, The Peregrine Fund Inc.1990–. **Achievements:** estab.rainforest cons.monitoring prog. for Masoala Peninsula, Madagascar; created prog.to prevent extinction of Madagascar Fish Eagle. **Memberships:** SAZS, AOU. **Publications:** *c*.35 papers incl.Breeding biol.of the Bateleur 1990, Pop.dynamics of the Bateleur in the Kruger Nat.Park 1990, Cons.studies on the Madagascar Fish Eagle *(Haliaeetus vociferoides)* (co-Author) 1993; 30 others. Indiff.to pers.pub.& news media support. **Languages:** English, French (some spoken). Willing to act as consult. **Address:** The Peregrine Fund Inc., 5666 West Flying Hawk Lane, Boise, Idaho 83709, USA. **Tel.**1 208 362 3716; **fax** 1 208 362 2376.

WATT, Dr Trudy Alexandra. Grassland ecology; vegetation management; design & analysis of field experiments. University Lecturer. *B*.25 Jan.1953, London, England, UK. British. Father Hew Watt, sometime Council Memb.of UK NCC, farmer. *P*.Dr Keith J.Kirby *qv*. **Education:** Grays Convent; Somerville Coll. U.of Oxf. BA(Hons)(Agricl & Forest Scis) 1974, MA & DPhil(Grassland Ecol.) 1977; Open U. BA(Maths) 1990; Sheffield Hallam U. MSc (Applied Stats) 1994. **Experience:** res.— long-term changes in grassland composition, autecology of grassland weeds, hedgerow mgmt; admin.— coordn of undergrad.'Agric.and the Envt' degree; teaching — biol.stats and plant ecol.from BSc to PhD levels. **Career:** Res. Officer, Sports Turf Res.Inst.1977–9; Ernest Cook Res.F.in Envl Studies 1979–83, Lect.in Plant Scis 1984–90, Somerville Coll. U.of Oxf.; Res.Officer (Stats), Oxf.For.Inst.1986–8; Lect. in Stats in Biol. St John's Coll. U.of Oxf. 1988–90; Lect.in Applied Stats & Ecol. Wye

Coll. U.of London 1990–. **Achievements:** linking statl methods & envl studies in res.& teaching in higher educ.at under-/post-grad.& doctl levels. **Memberships:** AAB, BES, BGS, RSS, Biometrics Soc., IBiol., IEEM. **Publications:** *Introductory Stats for Biol.Students* 1993; *c*.40 papers. Indiff.to pers.pub.& news media support. **Languages:** English; French & Russian (poor). Willing to act as consult.etc. **Address:** Wye College, University of London, Wye, Ashford, Kent TN25 5AH, England, UK. **Tel.**(office) 44 1233 812401, (home) 44 1233 813364; **fax** 44 1233 812855.

WAYBURN, Dr Edgar. Conservation of Nature; parks and protected areas. Alliance, Trust, and Project, Director, Committee Chairman. *B*.17 Sept.1906, Macon, GA, USA. American. *M*.Cornelia T.: 3 *d., s*. **Education:** U.of Georgia, AB *magna cum laude* 1926, Harvard U. MD *cum laude* 1930. **Experience:** while serving as major, Med.Corps, US Army 1942–6, was officer in charge of mass chest X-ray service, for USAAF in Europe; played role in persuading AMA and other assns to accept idea of fed. Medicare; pioneer in convincing medical assns to use influence to get smoking banned in public places; pursued active career in med.both in private practice of internal med.and as a teacher at Stanford and U.of Calif.San Francisco Med. Sch.over a 50-yrs span; in second vocation as cons.activist, init.and led three of America's major cons.campaigns for — the Redwood Nat.Park, the Golden Gate Nat.Rec.Area, and the Alaska Nat.Interest Lands Cons.Act, which dedicated 104 m.acres as nat.parks, nat.wildlife refuges, and wilderness; recently has turned attention to global envl challenges. **Career:** In Med.— Asst in Pathology, U.of Berlin 1930–31; Med.House Officer, Columbia Presbyterian Med.Center 1931–3; Instr.in Med.1933–46, Asst Clin.Prof.of Med.1946–9, Assoc.Clin. Prof.of Med.1949–64, Adjunct Assoc.Clin.Prof.of Med. 1964–74, Stanford Med.Sch.; Epidemiologist, San Francisco Dept of Public Health 1937–71; Dir, Chronic Illness Service Center 1951–61; Chief, Endocrine Clinic 1959–72, V.Chief of Staff 1961–3, Hon.Staff 1985–, Pacific Presbyterian Med.Center; Assoc.Clin. Prof.1960–75, Emer.1975–, U.of Calif.Med. Sch.; Dir, Gdn Hosp.–Sullivan Rehab.Center 1963–78. In Cons. — Pres. Fedn of Western Outdoor Clubs 1953–5, Trustees for Cons.1958– 60, Sierra Club 1961–4 & 1967–9, Sierra Club Fndn 1971–8, and Small Wilderness Area Preserves 1970–77; VP Sierra Club 1959–61, 1964–7, 1969–71, 1991–3, NPPA 1983–91; Chairman, Sierra Club Alaska Task Force 1971– and Cons.Coord.Cttee 1991–3, People for a Golden Gate Nat.Rec.Area 1971–; VC Fourth World Wilderness Cong.1987; past-Chairman Sierra Club Cons.Cttee; Founding Trustee & Trustee for 27 yrs' Sierra Club Fndn; Dir 1957–93, Chairman of Intl Cttee 1993–, Sierra Club; Dir of Smith River Alliance 1989–, Yosemite Resto. Trust 1990–, and Antarctica Project 1992–. **Memberships:** Amer.and Calif.

Socs of Internal Med., AFCR, AMA, Calif.Med. Assn (Del.1958–83), Amer.Cancer Soc.(Dir SF Section 1964–6); San Francisco Med.Soc.(Pres. 1965), Mental Health Assn (Dir 1964–6), and Diabetes Assn (Dir 1964–71); Presbyterian Med.Center (Trustee 1978–86), ABIM (Diplomate), F.ACP (Life), Phi Beta Kappa, Phi Kappa Phi; Headlands Inc.1960–73, Sec.of Interior's Adv.Bd on Nat.Park System 1979–83, Citizens' Adv.Comm.on Golden Gate Nat.Rec.Area & Point Reyes Nat.Seashore 1974–, Adv.Bd Pacific Forest Trust, IUCN CNPPA 1984–. **Awards:** Calif.Cons.Council 1957, Amer.Motors Cons.1964, Cert.of Honor (City of San Francisco) 1967, Sierra Club John Muir 1972, San Francisco Bay Area Council Envl 1973, Phoebe Apperson Hearst for disting.community service San Francisco Bay Area 1974, Disting.Service (Calif.Med.Assn) 1986, Spec. Commendation (NPS) 1986, Marjorie Stoneman Douglas (NPCA) 1987, Citizen (Harvard Club of San Francisco) 1987, Starker Leopold (Calif. NC) 1988, Pop./Envl Annual 1993, Hon. Pres.(Sierra Club) 1993–, Fred Packer Award (IUCN CNPPA) 1994, Global 500 Roll of Honour (UNEP) 1994, First Cons.Award (Ecotrust) 1994. **Publications:** *The Last Redwoods* 1969, *Change in Alaska — People, Petroleum, & Politics* 1970, *Oil on Ice* 1971, *Alaska, the Great Land 1974, Alaska's Future 1986* (all as contributing Author); Ed.*Man, Med.& Ecol.* 1970 and *Bull.San Francisco Med.Soc.*1957–8; Edl Exec.Cttee of Edl Bd *Calif.Med.*1949–59; Edl Bd & Sr Ed.*Western J.Med.*1959–; num. articles and presentations of testimony. **Address:** (home) 314 30th Avenue, San Francisco, California 94121, USA, (office) 730 Polk Street, San Francisco, California 94109, USA. **Tel.** (office) 1 415 923 5579; **fax** 1 415 776 0350.

WEAVER, Dr Alex v.B. Environmental impact assessment. Manager. *B.*9 Aug.1953, Pinelands, SA. S.African. *M.*Meryl. Brothers John M.C. Weaver *qv,* Tony (envl journalist), and David (teacher of envl subjects). **Education:** Rhodes U. BA (Hons.) 1977, MA 1979, PhD 1986. **Experience:** res.in field of soil erosion hazard assessment, consult.; envl impact mgmt. **Career:** Res.Hydr. Dept of Water Affairs 1979–80; Sr Lect. Dept of Geog. Rhodes U. 1981–90; Consult.1991–3; Mgr CSIR Envl Services 1993–. **Achievement:** mgmt of two largest EIAs in S.Africa. **Membership:** IAIA, SAGS. **Publications:** over 30 incl.Continuous Measurement of Rainfall, Streamflow, and Suspended Sediment Concentration, in Semiarid Envts (co-Author) 1984, Soil erosion rates in the Roxeni Basin, Ciskei 1989, 2020 Running on Empty 1990. Indiff.to pers.pub.& news media support. **Languages:** Afrikaans, English. Willing to act as consult. **Address:** Council for Scientific and Industrial Research Environmental Services, POB 195, Pretoria 0001, Republic of South Africa. **Tel.**(office) 27 12 841 4684, (home) 27 12 667 2052; **fax** 27 12 841 2103; **e-mail** AWeaver@environ. CSIR.CO.ZA .

WEAVER, John Martin Cordwent. Pollution & management of ground-water resources. Projects Manager. *B.*13 Aug.1949, Manzini, Swaziland. S.African. *M.*Susan (horticulturalist, landscaper): *d.* Brothers Alex v.B.Weaver *qv,* Tony (envl journalism), and David (teacher of envl subjects). **Education:** U.of Witwatersrand, BSc (Hons) 1973. **Experience:** widespread res.& consult.esp.as project trouble-shooter; teaching, training courses, part-time u.lect. **Career:** Geol. gold & platinum mines 1974–80; Traveller 1981–2; Ground-water Consult.1983–7; Groundwater Researcher & Consult./Projects Mgr, CSIR 1987–. **Achievements:** provided water supplies to num.rural villages & towns; participated in EIAs & integrated envl mgmt rc.impact on ground-water; drafted S.African standards for test-pumping & ground-water sampling. **Memberships:** IAH, GSSA, IAHS (S.African Nat.Cttee). **Publications:** *Groundwater Sampling* 1992, *Test-pumping Standards for SA* 1994; 90 others. Favours pers.pub.& news media support. **Languages:** Afrikaans, English. Willing to act as consult.etc. **Address:** Council for Scientific and Industrial Research (CSIR), POB 320, Stellenbosch 7600, Republic of South Africa. **Tel.**(office) 27 21 887 5101, (home) 27 24 551221; **fax** 27 21 883 3086.

WEBB, Dr Leonard James. Research on rain forest ecology; Nature conservation; active interests in phytochemistry & ethnobotany, environmental education, ecophilosophy, & ecotheology. Retired (Honorary Professor of Rainforest Ecology). *B.*28 Oct.1920, Rockhampton, Qld, Australia. Australia. *M.*Doris Mary: *s., d.* **Education:** U.of Qld, BSc(1st Class Hons) 1947, MSc 1948, PhD 1956. **Experience:** much field-work and collabn with knowledgeable people, notably aboriginals; popular talks & activities with wildlife cons.bodies; brief trips to most regions (except Africa & N.Amer.) to see natural veg.and meet colleagues; bush excursions/camps to communicate ecol intuitions. **Career:** Clerk/Typist, Qld Dept of Agric.& Stock 1935–41; Shift Chemist (Supervisor), Munitions Supply Labs (Vic.& NSW) 1942–4; Field Bot. Australian Phytochemical Survey, CSIRO 1944–52; Tech. Officer–Res.Sci. 1952–74, Sr Prin.Res.Sci. 1975–80 (when retired), Australian Rainforest Ecol Surveys. **Achievements:** VP of WPSQ 1963–70, Fndn Counc. ACF 1965–, memb.of Australian Nat.MAB Cttee 1975–80 and IUCN Comm.on Ecol.1979–90; Vatican Study Week (May) 1990. **Memberships:** (mostly past) INTECOL, IUFRO, BES, Ecol Soc.of Australia, IFA, RSQ, ANZAAS, Australian Inst.of Aboriginal–Islander Studies. **Awards:** Inaugural Gold Medal (Ecol Soc.of Australia) 1983, Mueller Medal (ANZAAS) 1983, Pursuit of Excellence Award (Envt) (Broken Hill Pty) 1984, Australian Officer of the Gen.Order of Australia 1987; Hon.Res.F.1981–4 then Hon. Prof. 1985– (Griffith U.). **Publications:** incl. *Man & Envt* 1973, *Envl Boomerang* 1973; num.chapters and popular ecol articles;

c.100 solo & jt scientific papers. Indiff.to pers. pub., favours news media support. **Languages:** English, French (some read). Further details may be obtained from *Who's Who in Australia* 1995, *Debretts* (Australia & NZ) 1995. **Address:** POB 338, Alderley, Queensland 4051, Australia. **Tel.**(home) 61 7 3356 5782; **fax** (at Griffith U.) 61 7 387 57459.

WEBER, Dean Dr Karl E. Environmentally-sustainable development; regional environmental management (protected-area planning); research design, methods, & techniques (monitoring methodology). Professor & Founding Dean. *B.* 1 April 1939, Berlin, Germany. German. *s.* Phaibun Chuchailam (regnl planning & industrial econ. [envlly-sound & sust.dev.], Thailand Dev.Res. Inst.). **Education:** Ruperto-Carola U.(Heidelberg), MA(Ethnology) 1965, Dr Phil.(Sociol.) 1966. **Experience:** spatial diffusion of innovations, res.(SE Thailand); bush pasture dev./ monitoring of agricl prod.promotion (Thailand); strat.planning for water resources' dev.(NE Thailand), mtn watershed mgmt/prot.area planning & mgmt (Nepal), bldg productive communities (S & SE Asia); promoter, fundraiser, & contrib.to Studies on Human Settlements Dev.in Asia. **Career:** Acting Head *locum tenens,* Dept of Sociol. S.Asia Inst. Heidelberg U. 1968–76; Freelance Consult. 1976–7; Assoc.Prof.1978, Prof.1983–, Chair of Human Settlements Dev. Div.1982–6, Founding Dean of Sch.of Envt, Resources, and Dev.1993–, AIT. **Achievements:** intro.of Change and Dev. in Ecosystems course at AIT 1980–, init.of AIT Envl Forum 1990, supervision of 181 postgrad.student res.projects 1979–. **Memberships:** Deutsche Gesellschaft für Voelkerkunde 1962–, Gesellschaft für Sozialwissenschaften — Verein für Socialpolitik 1965–, Siam Soc.1968–. **Publications:** several incl.*Managing Mtn Watersheds* (co-Author) 1990, *Struggle for Existence: Park–People Conflict* (co-Author) 1993. Regards pers.pub.& news media support as essential to further the cause of envt & cons. **Languages:** English, French, German, Italian, Thai. Willing to act as consult.etc. **Address:** School of Environment, Resources, and Development, Asian Institute of Technology, GPO Box 2754, Bangkok 10501, Thailand. **Tel.**(office) 662 524 6072, (home) 662 311 3505 or 332 8519; **fax** 662 524 6071.

WEBSTER, Professor Dr Richard. Soil & land resource survey; statistical design and analysis of survey. Visiting Professor. *B.*6 May 1933, Derby, England, UK. British. *M.*Mary: 2 *d., s.* **Education:** U.of Sheffield, BSc(Chem.) 1954, DSc 1983; U.of Oxf. DPhil.(Soil Sci.) 1966. **Experience:** res.on land eval.of remote areas; consult.on soil poll.& land eval.; postgrad. student supervision, examining, lecturing. **Career:** Colonial Office Scholar, U.of London/Rothamsted Experimental Station 1956–7; Soil Chem. Northern Rhodesia (now Zambia) Govt; Res.Assoc. U.of Oxf.1961–8; SSO 1968–71, PSO 1971–9, Soil Survey of England & Wales; Sr Res.Sci.

CSIRO (Australia) Div.of Soils (by invitation) 1973–4; Sr PSO, Soils Dept, Rothamsted Experimental Station 1979–90; Maître de Recherche, Ecole Nationale Supérieure des Mines de Paris 1990; Directeur de Recherche, Institut Nat.de la Recherche Agronomique 1990–91; Vis.Sci.1991–2 & 1993–4, Ed.-in-Chief *Euro.J.of Soil Sci.*1995–, Rothamsted Experimental Station; Guest Prof. ETH 1992–3; Vis.Prof. EPFL & WSL 1994. **Achievements:** soil & physiographic mapping, chiefly in Zambia, Uganda & Kenya, incl.published land atlases of Uganda and w.Kenya; terrain eval.in remote areas; pedometrics — the application of stats & probability to soil; leader of res.on soil properties and composition at Rothamsted Experimental Station; successively Ed.of *Soil Use & Mgmt, Catena,* and *Euro.J.of Soil Sci.* **Memberships:** ISSS (Chairman, WG on Pedometrics), NERC (Terr.Life Scis & Spec.Arctic Cttees), F.RSA. **Publications:** *c*.175 books & papers incl.Estimating and mapping grass cover and biomass from low-level photographic sampling (co-Author) 1986, *Statl Methods for Soil and Land Resource Survey* (co-Author) 1990, *Soil Monitoring* (co-Ed.) 1993; Ed.*Soil Use & Mgmt,* Edl Bds *J.of Soil Sci.*and *Catena* (Chief Ed.). Indiff.to pers.pub.& news media support. **Languages:** English, French. Willing to act as consult.etc. **Address:** Rothamsted Experimental Station, Harpenden, Hertfordshire AL5 2JQ, England, UK. **Tel.**(office) 44 1582 763133, (home) 44 1727 851958; **fax** 44 1582 760981; **e-mail** richard.webster@afrc. ac.uk .

WEIR, David A. Writing, journalism, teaching. Investigative Editor. *B.*14 April 1947, Detroit, MI, USA. American. *M.*Constance: 2 *d., s.* **Education:** U.of Michigan, BA(Journalism) 1969. **Experience:** writing & edl. **Career:** Peace Corps (English teacher), Afghanistan 1969–71; Writer/Ed. *Rolling Stone* 1974–7; co-Founder/Exec.Dir 1977–89, Investigative Ed. 1993–, Center for Investigative Reporting; Instr. U.of Calif.Grad.Sch.of Journalism 1985–; Ed. *California* and *Mother Jones* magazines 1989–93. **Achievements:** founding participant Pesticide Action Network 1982–, best-selling book* (transl.into 12 languages). **Memberships:** Bd of Dirs — Pesticide Action Network, Rainforest Action Network, Center for Investigative Reporting, *The Nation* Magazine (NY). **Awards:** Nat.Magazine Award 1980, Investigative Reporters' & Eds' Award 1982, Sigma Delta Chi Award 1982, Global 500 Roll of Honour (UNEP) 1989. **Publications:** **Circle of Poison* (co-Author) 1981, *Raising Hell* (co-Author) 1983, *The Bhopal Syndrome* 1987; *c*.150 j./magazine/news stories; Ed.& writer — *Mother Jones, California,* and *Rolling Stone* magazines, *Pacific News* Service; writer for *The Nation, Omni, SF Examiner, NY Times, San José Mercury News,* etc. Indiff.to pers.pub.& news media support. **Languages:** English, Persian (weak), Spanish (moderate). **Address:** Center for Investigative Reporting, 568 Howard Street, San Francisco, California 94105, USA. **Tel.** 1 415 543 1200; **fax** 1 415 543 8311.

WELCOMME, Dr Robin Leon. Fisheries' ecology of large rivers, species' introductions; conservation of biological diversity; tropical inland fisheries; trends in inland fisheries & aquaculture. Service Chief. *B*.19 Aug.1938, London, England, UK. British. *M*.Valerie Anne: *s., d.* **Education:** Birkbeck Coll.London, BSc (Hons)(Zool.) 1st Class 1962; Makerere Coll. U.of E.Africa, PhD 1972. **Experience:** five yrs with EAFFRO conducting res.on fisheries of African Gt Lakes; five yrs as fisheries' expert with FAO in Benin; since 1971 progressively-resp.posts in FAO advising countries on inland fisheries' biol., dev., mgmt, & cons., involving visits to & work in 65+ countries. **Career:** Fishery Res.Officer, EAFFRO 1963–7; Fisheries' Expert 1967–71, Fishery Resources' Officer 1971–85, Sr Fishery Resources' Officer 1985–90, Chief FIRI 1990–, FAO. **Achievements:** studies & pubns on fisheries' ecol.of large rivers; collected, interpreted, & published, data on introduced species of fish; assisted in initial drafting of Biodiv.Conv. **Memberships:** Euro. Adv.Comm. (Sec.), AFS, FBA, Fisheries Soc.of UK, IFM. **Publications:** *Fisheries Ecol. of Floodplain Rivers* 1971, *River Fisheries* 1985; 70 addit. Indiff.to pers.pub.& news media support. **Languages:** English, French, Italian, Spanish. Willing to act as consult.etc. **Address:** Inland Fishery Resources and Aquaculture Service, Food and Agriculture Organization, Via delle Terme di Caracalla, Rome, Italy. **Tel.**(office) 39 6 522 55007, (home) 39 6 949 9739.

WELLS, Susan Mary. Coral-reef & invertebrate conservation. Freelance Environmental Consultant. *B*.12 Dec.1951, Bath, England, UK. British. **Education:** Downe House Sch.; New Hall, Camb.U. BA(Hons)(Zool.) 1973, MA 1978, MSc (Zool., Social Behaviour) 1979. **Experience:** wide range of cons.activities involving info.gathering & dissemination; consult. to IUCN, UNEP, WWF, EC, Greenpeace, etc. **Career:** Res.Asst. Mollusc Section, Natural Hist.Mus.London 1974; Researcher, Station Biologique de la Tour du Valat 1974–8 and IUCN 1980–87; Dev.Officer, ICBP (now BirdLife Intl) 1988–9; Freelance Envl Consult.1989–. **Achievements:** popular writing, promotion of reef & invertebrate cons. **Memberships:** ISRS, Unitas Malacologia, IUCN SSC Mollusc SG. **Award:** Sir Peter Kent Cons.Book (2nd) Prize 1993. **Publications:** *Coral Reefs of the World* Vols 1–3 1988/9, *IUCN Invertebrate Red Data* 1983, *Greenpeace Book of Coral Reefs* 1992. Favours pers.pub.& news media support. **Languages:** English, French (spoken). Willing to act as consult.etc. **Address:** 56 Oxford Road, Cambridge CB4 3PW, England, UK. **Tel.** (home) 44 1223 350409.

WEN, Professor Boping. Environmental law — national, comparative, & international. Emer-

itus Senior Research Fellow & Professor of Law. *B*.20 June 1927, Hunan, PRC. Chinese. *M*. Yazhong. **Education:** Beijing U. LLB 1951; Beijing Inst.of Light Industry, Sr Training Class of English 1987–8. **Experience:** widespread res.for 41 yrs, guide teacher and lect.of grad. students for 10 yrs, law consult.for 15 yrs, admin.as Dir of Envl Monitor Sci.for five yrs. **Career:** Beijing Municipal Public Security Bur.1952–72; Beijing Chang Gou Yu Coal Mine 1973; Beijing Inst.of Envl Monitor Sci.1974–8; Emer.SRF & Prof.of Law, Inst.of Law at CASS 1978–. **Achievements:** two books which filled the void of res.on envl law in China; joined expert groups for drafting Chinese envl laws, and Intl Conv.on Cons.of Biodiv.; trained many grad.students; participated in intl academic exchanges. **Memberships:** ICEL, IUCN CEL, CSLS, CSLL. **Award:** Spec.Contribn Sci.for Chinese Social Scis (State Council of PRC) 1992. **Publications:** *Intro.to Envl Law* 1982, *Envl Law of Western Countries* 1988 + ten others; num.papers incl.On major problems of revised envl prot.law of China 1990, How to strengthen intl envl law on cons.of biodiv.1991, New dev.of intl envl law (review to UN Framework Conv.on Climate Change) 1992, Suggestions relating to control climate warming 1993. Indiff.to pers.pub., favours news media support. **Languages:** Chinese, English. Further details may be obtained from *Dict.on Chinese Legal Scientists* 1991, *Big Dict.on Contemporary Chinese Scholars of Social Scis* 1990. Willing to act as consult.etc. **Address:** c/o Mr Liu Lei, Holiday Inn Lido BEIJING-F&B, Jichang Road, Jiang Tai Road, Beijing 100044, People's Republic of China. **Tel.**(office & home) 86 10 437 9122.

Wenhua LI, Professor Dr, *see* **LI, Professor Dr Wenhua.**

WENSLEY, Ambassador Penelope Anne. Environment and Mankind. Ambassador for the Environment. *B*.18 Oct.1946, Qld, Australia. Australian. *M*.Dr Thomas Stuart McCosken, BVSc, BEC, QDAH. **Education:** U.of Qld, BA(First Class Hons) 1967. **Career:** Diplomat 1968–, Amb.for the Envt 1992– & Perm.Rep.to UN in Geneva 1993–, Govt of Australia. **Achievements:** Leader of Australian delegations to negns for Convs on Climate Change, Desert., and Biodiv., to the Comm.on Sust.Dev.and UNEP Governing Council; VC Climate Change INC Bur.; Chairman of prep.process, and then main cttee, of the UN Global Conf.on the Sust.Dev.of Small Island Developing States 1993–4. **Award:** Alumnus of the Yr and Hon. Dr of Philos.(U.of Qld) 1994. **Languages:** English, French. Further details may be obtained from *Who's Who in Australia* 1995. **Address:** Australian Mission to the United Nations, 56 rue de Moillebeau, 1209 Petit-Saconnex, Geneva, Switzerland. **Tel.**(office) 41 22 918 2900.

WERIKHE, Michael Mayeku ('Rhino Man'). Rhinoceros conservation. Superintendent. *B*.25

May 1956, Mombasa, Kenya. Kenyan. *M*. Hellen: 2 *d*. **Education:** up to and incl.(then) O-level (Brit.) exams. **Experience:** knowledge of cons.and envl issues which has been acquired through yrs of self-taught observation, reading, working in the field, and learning from many well-established conservationists. **Career:** Freelance Conservationist, Kenya Game Dept 1976–7; Super. Associated Vehicle Assemblers Ltd 1978–. **Achievements:** in order to raise awareness of, and funds for, Rhino cons.projects in Africa, has walked from Mombasa to Nairobi (490 km), across E.Africa (2,300 kms), and in Taiwan 1982–1993, raising over US $1 million for Rhino cons.projects in six African countries. **Memberships:** WSPA (Adv.Dir), The Rhino Trust (Adv.Bd). **Awards:** Cert.of Appreciation (WSPA), Guinness Stout Award 1983, David Sheldrick Mem.Prize (*see* Sheldrick, Daphne M., *qv*) 1984, Boots Action Award 1985, Cons. Award (EAWS) 1985, Global 500 Roll of Honour (UNEP) 1989, Goldman Envt Prize (Goldman Envl Fndn) 1990, Eddie Bauer Heroes of the Earth Prize 1991, Cons.Medal (SDZS) 1991. Favours pers.pub.& news media support. **Languages:** English, Kiswahili. Willing to act as a consultant. **Address:** POB 80310, Mombasa, Kenya. **Tel.**(office) 254 433311, (home) 254 493496; **fax** 254 434461.

WESCOTT, Dr Geoffrey Charles. National park & protected area planning & management; coastal-zone management; marine conservation; ecotourism. Associate Professor of Environmental Management. *B*.9 Feb.1953, Melbourne, Australia. Australian. **Education:** U.of Melbourne BSc(Hons) 1974, MSc 1976; UCL MSc & Dipl.(Cons.) 1977; Deakin U. PhD 1989. **Experience:** admin.— Convener Nat.Parks Adv.Council, Memb.Ref. Area Adv.Cttee, Pres. Marine & Coastal Soc., former Dir, VP & Treas.of Cons.Council, Vic. **Career:** Dir Cons. Council of Vic.1977–81; acad.career (incl.part-time study) until appointment as Assoc.Prof.of Envl Mgmt, Deakin U.1992–. **Achievements:** major role in envl educ.& training through dev.of four tertiary courses as well as substantial role in series of vol.cons.groups (NGOs). **Memberships:** EIA, AMSA, IUCN CNPPA, AIB. **Awards:** Bryan F'ship (Melbourne U.) 1973, Cert.of Achievement (MESA) 1992. **Publications:** *Coastal Retreat: a Study of Coastal Mgmt in Vic.*(co-Author) 1977, *Energy to Burn?* 1980, *Rocky Shores of SE Australia* 1992; num. papers incl.Australia's distinctive Nat. Parks system 1992, Policy without implementation: Vic.coastal zone mgmt 1993. Favours pers.pub. & news media support. **Languages:** English, French (some read). Willing to act as consult. etc. **Address:** Deakin University, Rusden Campus, 662 Blackburn Road, Clayton 3168, Australia. **Tel.**(office) 61 3 244 7429, (home) 61 3 489 1087; **fax** 61 3 244 7480.

WESTING, Dr Arthur H. Environmental conservation; environmental security especially in relation to military activities & war. Consultant. *B*.18 July 1928, New York, NY, USA. American. *M*.Carol E.: *d*., *s*. **Education:** Columbia U. AB 1950; Yale U. MF 1954, PhD 1959. **Experience:** Sr Researcher SIPRI, Dean of Natural Sci. Hampshire Coll. **Career:** Prof.of Forest Ecol., Dean of Natural Sci., Sr Researcher in Envl Security; Consult.in Envl Security. **Achievements:** scholar of envl effects of military activities and of envl security. **Memberships:** F.AAAS, FFPS, IPRA, NYAS 1983. **Awards:** Hon.DSc (Windham Coll.VT) 1973, Guggenheim Fndn F.1973, Bulgarian Prot.of Nature Medal 1984, Global 500 Roll of Honour (UNEP) 1990. **Publications:** incl.*Ecol.Consequences of the Second Indochina War* 1976, *Weapons of Mass Destruction and the Envt* 1977, *Warfare in a Fragile World* 1980, *Herbicides in War* 1984, *Envl Warfare* 1984 & *Explosive Remnants of War* 1985 (Ed.& co-Author), *Global Resources and Intl Conflict* 1986, *Cultural Norms, War & the Envt* 1988, *Comp.Security for the Baltic* 1989, *Envl Hazards of War* 1990; 200+ addit. res.& other papers in professional journals. **Languages:** English, German (spoken). Further details may be obtained from *Amer.Men & Women of Sci., Who's Who in the World* (1993–94), *Who's Who in Sci.& Tech*. Willing to act as consult.etc. **Address:** Westing Associates in Environment, Security, & Education, RFD 2 Box 330H, Putney, Vermont 05346, USA. **Tel.**(office) 1 802 387 2152; **fax** 1 802 387 4001.

WESTREICHER, Antonio ANDALUZ. Environmental law especially in/of soil, forest, protected areas, and biodiversity. President. *B*.5 Nov. 1949, Pasco, Peru. Peruvian. *M*.Gemma: 2 *s*. **Education:** Universidad Nacional Mayor de San Marcos, B.of Law 1977; Tufts U. postgrad. in pol.econ., ethics, and envt 1991; Fletcher Sch.of Law & Diplomacy. **Experience:** teaching envl law; consult.to Bolivian Govt 1992–; contribns to num.sems & congs in Peru & Latin Amer. **Career:** Chief, Antoni Andaluz Lawyers & Assocs 1977–; Gen.Dir, Office of Legal Affairs 1979–80, V.Minister 1980–83, Nat.System of Social Property; Pres. PROTERRA 1983–. **Achievements:** Pres. Lima Ecol Belt 1990–91, VC for Latin Amer.& the Carib., IUCN CEL 1991–4. **Memberships:** ICEL, IUCN CEL, Colegio de Abogados de Lima, Comisión de Elaboración del Codigo del Medio Ambiente de Péru. **Publications:** four books incl.*Peruvian Envl Legis.Compilation* 1980–87, *Envl Law: Proposals & Essays* 1991, *The Yangunturo* 1993; num.articles. Indiff.to pers.pub., favours news media support. **Languages:** English, French (read), Spanish (mother tongue). Further details may be obtained from *Top People in Peru*. Willing to act as consult.etc. **Address:** Calle Zaipurú 128, Urbarí, Santa Cruz de la Sierra, Bolivia. **Tel.**(office & home) & **fax** 591 3 521796.

WHIPPS, Dr John M. Microbial ecology; disease biocontrol; mycoparasitism and release of genetically-modified microorganisms into the environment. Research Leader. *B*.10 July 1953, London, England, UK. British. *M*.Susan M.: *s.*, *d.* **Education:** U.of Sheffield BSc (Hons)(Bot.) 1974, PhD 1977, DSc 1994. **Experience:** res.— fungal–plant interactions, fungal–fungal interactions particularly concerned with biological disease control; interests in rhizosphere ecol., microbial biomass estimation, and monitoring microbial pops in the envt. **Career:** Researcher, U.of Sheffield 1974–82 and the now defunct AFRC Letcombe Lab. 1982–4; Res.Leader, Dept of Microbial Biotech. HRI (formerly GCRI) 1984–. **Achievements:** developing biol disease control methods, studying microbial ecol.and carrying out first release in UK of a free-living genetically-modified bacterium on wheat at HRI (Sussex) in collabn with IVEM Oxf. **Memberships:** BMS, BSPP, EFPP WG on Biol Disease Control. **Publications:** *Biotech.of Fungi for Improving Plant Growth* (co-Ed.) 1989, *Ecophysiol.of Fungi* (co-Author) 1993; 90+ scientific papers. **Language:** English. Willing to act as consult. etc. **Address:** Department of Microbial Biotechnology, Horticulture Research International, Wellesbourne, Warwickshire CV35 9EF, England, UK. **Tel.**44 1789 470382; **fax** 44 1789 470552.

WHITAKER, Romulus Earl Herpetology; wildlife management conservation; film-making. Director, Managing Director. *B*.23 May 1943, New York City, NY, USA. Indian. *M*. Zahida: 2 *s.* Father-in-law Zafar Futehally, noted Indian conservationist. **Education:** Pacific Western U. BSc Wildlife Mgmt 1986. **Experience:** res.since 1967, admin.for 23 yrs; consult.for FAO–UNDP, UNCTAD–GATT, IUCN–WWF, USAID, Govt of India, State Govts in India; making envl documentary films. **Career:** gen.herpetology, Venom Centre for Tribal People, Crocodile farming; consult.in Asia, Pacific, & Africa; Dir, Centre for Herpetology 1970–; MD, Whitaker Films Pty Ltd. 1991–. **Achievements:** set up India's first snake park, crocodile farm, sea-turtle rehab.prog., cooperative for tribal snake catchers, and cons.base in Andaman Islands. **Memberships:** IUCN SSCs — Crocodile SG (VC w.Asian regn), Freshwater Chelonian Group, Sea Turtle SG, Captive [now Cons.] Breeding SG, Indian Subcontinent Reptile & Amphibian Group, Sust.Use of Wild Species; BNHS; Indian Nat.Trust for Art & Cultural Heritage; Centre for Sci.& Envt. **Awards:** Cons.Merit (WWF Intl, jt) 1983, Rolex (hon.mention) 1984, Order of the Golden Ark 1985, Peter Scott (IUCN) 1986, Ashoka F'ship 1991. **Publications:** 100+ incl.*Common Indian Snakes* 1981, *Snakes Around Us* 1985, *Ecol.of the Mugger Crocodile* 1989, *Andaman Tribes, Cultural Survival* 1986; six documentary films, one children's envl feature film. Indiff.to pers. pub., favours news media support. **Languages:** Bahasa Indonesian (working knowledge), English, Hindi (spoken), Tamil (spoken). Willing to act as consult., etc. **Address:** Centre for Her-

petology, Madras Crocodile Bank, Post Bag 4, Mammallapuram 603104, Tamil Nadu, India. **Fax** 91 44 491 0910.

WHITE, Dr Alan Tyler. Coastal management, coastal resources' conservation; participatory management of natural resources. Consultant, Project Manager. *B*.4 June 1947, Merced, CA, USA. American. *M*.Evangeline: 2 *s.* **Education:** Sch.for Intl Training, M.Admin.1979; U.of Hawaii, PhD(Geog.) 1984. **Experience:** res.on coral reef, and coastal & marine prot.areas' mgmt; training in field survey techniques & info.analysis for mgmt; ten yrs' admin.on coastal mgmt projects. **Career:** worked on cons. project for Galápagos Islands 1970–75; owned business 1976 7; worked with Min.of Natural Resources (Philippines) 1978–80; Mgr of marine cons.project 1985–6; Tech.Adv. ASEAN–US CRMP (ICLARM–Manila) 1987–90, Consult. ADB 1991–; Mgr Coastal Resources Mgmt Project (Sri Lanka) 1992–. **Achievements:** successfully started several community-based coral-reef/coastal cons.progs which have endured over time in Philippines; published several books on coral-reef cons.& use. **Memberships:** ISRS, Western Soc.of Naturalists, Alumni of UCB & E–W Centre. **Awards:** Achievement in Sci. (Bank of Amer.) 1964, E–W Centre Award 1971–4. **Publications:** several books incl. *Galápagos Guide* 1971–4, *Philippine Coral Reefs: A Natural Hist.Guide* 1986; num.papers. Accepts pers.pub.& news media support. **Languages:** Bahasa Indonesia (limited spoken), English, Spanish, Tagalog (spoken). Willing to act as consult.etc. **Address:** 1 Gower Street, Colombo 5, Sri Lanka. **Tel.**(office) 94 1 500 207, (home) 94 1 580 302; **fax** 94 1 500 207.

WHITE, Professor Dr Gilbert F. Water management and associated environmental problems. Distinguished Professor Emeritus of Geography. *B*.26 Nov.1911, Chicago, Illinois, USA. American. *W*.Anne: *s.*, 2 *d.* **Education:** U.of Chicago, SB 1932, SM 1934, PhD 1942. **Experience:** res.on water resources, and appraisal of policy for envl mgmt; Officer of SCOPE–ICSU 1969–. **Career:** Resources' Planning Bd of Exec.Office of Pres.1934–42; Conscientious Objector to WWII 1942–6; Pres.Haverford Coll. 1946–55; Prof.of Geog. U.of Chicago 1956–69; Prof.of Geog.1969–78, Disting.Prof.Emer.of Geog.1979–, U.of Colorado at Boulder. **Achievement:** improvement of understanding & public action towards water & envt. **Memberships:** US NAS, Amer.AAS, APS, Russian AS. **Awards:** Tyler Prize 1987, Vautrin Lud Prize (Intl Geogl Festival) 1992, Hubbard Medal (NGS) 1994. **Publications:** incl.*Human Adjustment to Floods* 1942, *Sci.and the Future of Arid Lands* 1960, *Strats of Amer.Water Mgmt* 1969, *The World Envt 1973–82* (co-Ed.) 1982. **Languages:** English & French; German, Spanish & Russian (basic read). Further details may be obtained from *Who's Who in Amer.*1996, *Who's Who in the World* 1985, *Intl Who's Who* 1994–

95, etc. Willing to act as consult.etc. **Address:** Campus Box 482, University of Colorado, Boulder, Colorado 80309, USA. **Tel.** (office) 1 303 492 6311, (home) 1 303 444 0169; **fax** 1 303 492 2151.

WHITE, Dr James Geoffrey. Soil-borne plant pathogens particularly *Pythium* spp., biocontrol, detection by serological & molecular methods. Research Leader. *B.*10 May 1946, Ashton-in-Makerfield, England, UK. British. **Education:** Hull U. BSc(Bot.& Zool.) 1968, IC MSc (Mycology & Plant Path.) 1969, Reading U. PhD(Plant Path.) 1975. **Experience:** career res. worker, consult.to UK Min.of Defence 1986–8. **Career:** SO, Nat.Vegetable Res.Station 1973–5; Plant Path.Researcher, Inst.of Hortl Res.1975–84; Research Leader, HRI 1984–. **Achievement:** dev.of diagnostic systems to predict risk of soil-borne disease before crops are planted. **Memberships:** IBiol., BSPP, Edl Bd *Annals of Applied Biol.* **Award:** Innovation Prize (Brit. Growers Look Ahead) 1994. **Publications:** 28 refereed, 72 addit. Indiff.to pers.pub.& news media support. **Languages:** English, French (basic). Willing to act as consult.etc. **Address:** Horticulture Research International, Wellesbourne, Warwickshire CV35 9EF, England, UK. **Tel.**(office) 44 1789 470382, (home) 44 1926 882218; **fax** 44 1789 470552.

WHITE, Mrs Susan L. Coastal resource management; marine parks & protected areas with particular interest in environmental education & interpretation. Independent Consultant. *B.*12 July 1963, Okinawa, Japan. American. *M.* David G.White. **Education:** C.Michigan U. BSc 1986, Michigan Sec.Provisional Teaching Cert.1987. **Experience:** res.— fieldwork in coral reef monitoring, marine productivity monitoring, fish censusing; admin.— was solely resp.for complete admin.& mgmt of Saba Marine Park (Netherlands Antilles) and its one other employee; teaching — weekly interpretive presentations & daily educ.to park visitors, envl educ.progs for local schools, sec.sci.& biol.; consult.— dev.of Ref.Manual to complement Training Manual for Marine Park Mgr Trainers (UNEP 1994); complementary assistance to Florida Keys Nat.Marine Sanctuary. **Career:** Sec.Sci.& Substitute Teacher 1988, Dive Master 1989, Mgr Saba Marine Park 1989–94, Adv.to Saba Cons.Fndn 1989–94, Ind.Consult.1994–. **Achievements:** mgmt of Saba Marine Park (the first marine prot.area to achieve & sustain complete fin.independence); obtained & executed project proposals for res., educ.& equipment; close assn with local people & Saban Govt in resource prot.; implementation of continued envl educ.prog. **Memberships:** IUCN CNPPA, WWF, Intercoast Network, CARICOMP (Site Dir), Center for Marine Cons. Intl Coastal Clean-up (Country Coord.). **Award:** Outstanding Educator (Michigan Educators' Assn/NEA) 1988. **Publications:** *Guide to the Saba Marine Park* (co-Author) 1991; six papers. Indiff.to pers.pub.,

favours news media support. **Language:** English. Willing to act as consult. etc. **Address:** POB 420054, Summerland Key, Florida 33042, USA. **Tel.& fax** 1 305 745 2799.

WHITEHEAD, George Kenneth. Deer and their ecology. Retired. *B.*1913, Bury, Lancs., England, UK. British. **Education:** Uppingham Public Sch. 1927–32. **Experience:** acknowledged expertise on all species of the Cervidae and their pursuit. **Career:** Major, R.Artillery 1944–5; Mgr, Paper Mill 1945–65. **Membership:** IUCN SSC Deer SG. **Awards:** Prix Littéraire (Conseil Intl de la Chasse et de la Cons.du Gibier) 1975 & 1993, Sporting Writer of the Year* (BASC). **Publications:** *Deer and Their Mgmt* 1950, *Ancient White Cattle of Britain and Their Descendants* 1953, *Deerstalking Grounds of Gt Britain & Ireland* 1960, *Deer of Gt Britain & Ireland* 1964, *Deer Stalking in Scotland* 1964, *Wild Goats of Gt Britain & Ireland* 1972, *Deer of the World* 1972, *Hunting & Stalking Deer in Britain through the Ages* 1980, *The Game Trophies of the World* (co-Ed.& Compiler) 1981, *Hunting & Stalking Deer throughout the World* 1982, *Medal Categories for the Game Animals of the World* (Ed.& Compiler) 1986, *Practical Deerstalking* 1986, 1994 (paperback), *The Whitehead Enc.of Deer* 1993. No objection to pers.pub.& news media support. **Language:** English. Further details may be obtained from *The Naturalists' Directory* 1954, *Dict.of Intl Biog.*1963. Willing to act as consult.etc. **Address:** Old House, Withnell Fold, Chorley, Lancashire PR6 8AZ, England, UK. **Tel.**(home) 44 1254 830444.

WHITEHOUSE, John Frederick. Natural & cultural resources' management; environmental law; protected areas; environmental planning. Partner, Honorary Professorial Fellow. *B.*28 Mar.1952, Sydney, NSW, Australia. Australian. **Education:** Sydney U. LLB 1977, BA 1981; Macquarie U. BSc 1991; U.of Tech.(Sydney) Dipl.in Legal Practice 1991. **Experience:** res.— envl law, prot.areas' mgmt; tech.— lawyer & solicitor; admin.— public sector mgmt for 13 yrs, managing legal practice; consult.— envl policy & prot.area mgmt; teaching envl law & policy. **Career:** Spec.Adv.to NSW Minister for Planning & Envt 1976–80; Asst Chief Planner, NSW Planning & Envt Comm.1980; Head Envt Prot.Div.1980–84, Asst Dir 1984–5, NSW Dept of Envt & Planning; Dir, NSW NPWS 1985–9; Consult.1989–91, Partner 1991–, Dunhill Madden Butler; Hon.Professorial F. Centre for Natural Resources Law & Policy, U.of Wollongong 1994–. **Achievements:** prepared & drafted NSW legis.re.envl planning, impact assessment, & heritage cons., and assisted dev.of Govt policies on coastal prot., rainforest mgmt, & wilderness prot. **Memberships:** IUCN CNPPA & CEL, ICEL, RAIPR, RZS of NSW. **Award:** Advance Australia Award 1987. **Publications:** 12 incl.E.Australian rainforests: a case study in resource harvesting and cons.1991, Expert

Evidence in Envl Litigation 1992, *Managing Multiple Use in the Coastal Zone: a Rev.of the GBRMPA* 1993, Legislative Prot.for Wilderness in Australia 1994. Indiff.to pers. pub.& news media support. **Languages:** English, French (read), Latin. Willing to act as consult.etc. **Address:** 17 Mawson Street, St Ives, New South Wales 1075, Australia. **Tel.** (office) 61 2 224 9670, (home) 61 2 449 7151; **fax** 61 2 235 3099.

WHITMORE, Dr Timothy Charles. Tropical moist forest taxonomy, phytogeography, ecology, silviculture, management, sustainable utilization & conservation; palms, *Macaranga* (Euphorbiaceae). Visiting Scholar, Affiliated Lecturer. *B.*9 June 1935, Ruislip, Mx, England, UK. British. *M.* Wendy Ann: 2 *s., d.* **Education:** St John's Coll. Camb. BA(Hons)(Bot.) 1956, MA 1960, PhD 1961, ScD 1977; MA (by incorporation) & DSc Oxon.1978. **Experience:** extensive travel & res.in forests of Malesia & Melanesia, some exp.in Africa (Malawi, Ghana) & trop. Amer. (Brazil, Chile, Venezuela, Guyana, C.Amer.). **Career:** F.St John's Coll.Camb. 1960–63; Lect. U.of Southampton 1961–2; Forest Bot. Solomon Islands' Govt 1962–5 and Forest Res.Inst. Malaysia 1965–72; Prin.Res.F. Brit.Mus. (Natural Hist.) 1974–6; Sr Res.Officer, Oxford U. Commonwealth For.Inst. 1974–89; Vis.Scholar, Affiliated Lect. Geog.Dept, U.of Camb.1990–. **Memberships:** BES, MNS (Pres. 1971–2). **Awards:** Mark Medal (RGS) 1977, Hon.Dr (Ehime U., Japan) 1992. **Publications:** incl. *Guide to Forests Brit.Solomon Islands* 1966, *Tree Flora Malaya* 1972 & 1973, *Palms of Malaya* 1973, *Trop.Rain Forests of Far E.*1975 & 1984, *Intro.to Trop.Rain Forests* 1990, Jt Ed. *Oxf.Monogrs in Biogeog.* Indiff.to pers.pub.& news media support. **Languages:** English; French, German & Latin (written); Malay (modest), Spanish (written). **Address:** University Department of Geography, Downing Place, Cambridge CB2 3EN, England, UK. **Tel.**44 1223 315405; **fax** 44 1223 354419.

WHITTINGTON, Andrew Eric. Systematics, distribution, & conservation, of Afrotropical Diptera especially Syrphidae & Platystomatidae. Assistant Curator of Entomology. *B.*3 April 1963, Hampshire, England, UK. British. *M.: s., d.* **Education:** U.of Natal BSc 1989, BSc(Hons) 1990, MSc 1992. **Experience:** res.in African Diptera. **Career:** Res.Asst, Dept of Bot. 1982–3, u.training 1986–9, U.of Natal; Cons.Educ. Umgeni Valley Nature Reserve 1984–5; Res. Sci.& Sr Curator in Entomol. Natal Mus. 1990–93; self-employed Res.Sci.(Dipterist) 1993–5; Asst Curator of Entomol. Dept of Natural Hist., R.Mus.of Scotland, Nat.Museums of Scotland 1995–. **Membership:** Malloch Soc. **Awards:** five postgrad.bursaries & scholarships 1989–92, Fndn of Res.& Dev. Spec.Merit Award to Mus.Scientists 1993. **Publications:** ten papers incl.revision of Afrotrop.species of *Graptomyza* Wiedemann (Diptera: Syrphidae: Volucellini) 1992. Indiff.re.pers.pub.& news media

support. **Language:** English. Willing to act as consult. etc. **Address:** Department of Natural History, Royal Museum of Scotland, Chambers Street, Edinburgh EH1 1JF, Scotland, UK. **Tel.**44 131 225 7534; **fax** 44 131 220 4819.

WICKENS, Dr Gerald Ernest. Economic plants of arid & semi-arid regions. Retired. *B.* 18 Dec.1927, London, England, UK. British. *M.* Mimi M.: *s.* **Education:** UC of Wales (Aberystwyth) BSc 1961, MSc 1966; U.of Reading PhD 1972. **Experience:** land-use & veg.surveys in Zimbabwe, Zambia, & Sudan; soil & water cons.; init. Econ. & Cons.Section, R.Botanic Gdns; consult.to FAO on econ.plants; Counc.and Agricl & Bot. Adv. SOS Sahel UK, and Counc.& Ecol. Andes Project, Chile; Asst Ed.(Plants) *J.of Arid Envts* 1990–. **Career:** Brit.Army 1945–8; Tree Crops Officer, Min.of Agric. n.Nigeria 1953–5; Cons. Ext.Officer, Fed.Dept of Cons.& Ext. Fedn of Rhodesia & Nyasaland 1956–60; Dir Parc Cynog Farm Ltd (Wales) 1960–62; Ecol. Hunting Tech.Services (UK) 1962–6; Head, Econ.& Cons.Section, Herbarium, R. Botanic Gdns 1967–87. **Achievements:** recording changes in Sahel esp.Sudan and effect on rural pop.; veg.of N.Andes and their sust.utilization. **Memberships:** F.LS, SEB (Sec.UK Chapter), TAA. **Publications:** *Flora of Jebel Maara, Sudan Rep. and Its Geogl Affinities* (HMSO) 1970; 100+ papers. Indiff.to pers.pub., favours news media support. **Languages:** English, French (written), Spanish (written). Willing to act as consult.etc. **Address:** 50 Uxbridge Road, Hampton Hill, Middlesex TW12 3AD, England, UK. **Tel.** (home) 44 181 979 0036.

WIELGOLASKI, Professor Frans-Emil. Botanical ecology, plant phenology & productivity; studies of alpine & polar ecosystems, autecology of tundra plants; influence of acid precipitation. Professor of Botanical Ecology. *B.*9 April 1931, Oslo, Norway. Norwegian. *M.*C.Margrethe: *s., d.* **Education:** Norwegian Agricl U. Cand. hort.1957; U.of Oslo, Mag.scient.1964. **Experience:** res.— field-work partic.in alpine & polar regns; teaching — mainly ecol courses at var. levels for 30 yrs. **Career:** researcher & teacher at var.Norwegian univs & insts 1962–; Vis. Researcher, CSU 1972 & Utah SU 1973; Sec.-Gen.1968–75, Leader Intl Tundra Group 1973, Norwegian IBP. **Achievements:** Adv.to IUCN Comm.on Ecol., prepared ms on High Mtn Ecosystems for IUCN WCS Sourcebook. **Memberships:** NAE (co-Founder). **Publications:** eight books incl.*Fennoscandian Tundra Ecosystems* (two vols) 1975, *Plants and the Envt, a Botl Autecology* (in Norwegian) 1978, *Alpine and Polar Regns* ('Tundra') 1994; 100+ scientific papers. Indiff.to pers.pub.& news media support. **Languages:** English, German (poor), Norwegian. Willing to act as consult.etc. **Address:** Department of Biology, Division of Botany & Plant Physiology, University of Oslo, POB 1045 Blindern, 0316 Oslo, Norway. **Tel.**(office) 47 2285 4627, (home) 47 6753 4335; **fax** 47 2285 4664.

WIJESINGHE, Leslie. Forest conservation planning, biodiversity conservation. Country Representative. *B*.23 Aug.1931, Mt Lavinia, Sri Lanka. Sri Lankan. *M*.Yvonne. **Education:** U.of Ceylon, BSc 1955; U.of Oxf. BA(Hons) 1958, MA 1962. **Experience:** res.— investigative surveys of biomass fuel consumption and operational exp.in biogas in Sri Lanka; tech.& admin.— in field of for., and award of, monitoring, & evaluating, sci.grants; consult.— for., envt & dev. **Career:** Professional Forest Officer, Sri Lanka Forest Dept 1958–77; Dep. Sec.-Gen. Nat.Sci.Council 1977–80; Addit.DG, Natural Resources Energy & Sci.Auth.1981–90; UNDP Consult.on UNCED to Govt of Sri Lanka 1991–2; Country Rep. IUCN 1993–. **Achievements:** coordn of prep.of Sri Lanka Nat.Reports to UNCSTD & UNCED, carried out pioneering work on biomass consumption patterns in Sri Lanka, co-Author of nat.status report*. **Memberships:** SLAAS (past-Pres.of Section B), Sri Lanka NAS (F.& past-Gen.Sec.), Sri Lanka IBiol.(F.& past-Pres.). **Award:** Merit Award (NARESA) 1987. **Publications:** several incl. *Natural Resources of Sri Lanka — Conditions and Trends* (co-Author) 1990, *Nat.Report to UNCED* (co-Author) 1993, **Biol Cons.in Sri Lanka — a Nat.Status Report* (co-Author) 1993. Indiff.to pers.pub.& news media support. **Language:** English. Further details may be obtained from *Intl Directory of Human Ecologists* (SHE). Willing to act as consult.etc. **Address:** 5 Second Lane, Dehiwala, Sri Lanka. **Tel.**(office) 94 1 580202, (home) 94 1 732630; **fax** 94 1 580202.

WIJEWANSA, Ranjit Asoka. Environmental management & planning. Environmental Consultant. *B*.23 Aug.1936, Galle, Sri Lanka. Sri Lankan. *M*.Swarnamali: 2 *d*. **Education:** U.of Ceylon BSc(Agric.) 1960, U.of Colombo MSc (Envl Sci.) 1981. **Experience:** admin.— policy, orgn & mgmt of cons.progs., funding, EIA procedures, etc.; consult.to Bangladesh NCS 1987 & 1989–90, and Laos NCS & UNCED Nat.Report 1991; Convenor of inter-Ministerial WGs and Study Group on Soil Cons.; nat.& regnl training workshops on EIA. **Career:** Head of Agricl Sci.Dept, Hardy Sr Tech.Inst. 1963–9; Asst Adv.Officer, Rubber Res.Inst. 1969–76; Consult.to Maldivian Min.of Envt 1993 and JICA Study in Cambodia 1994. **Achievement:** intro.of envl thinking to public instns in Bangladesh through prep.of Bangladesh NCS. **Memberships:** SLAAS, SLIB, Ceylon Assn for Prevention of Tuberculosis (Hon.Sec. Ampara Branch 1968–9), Soil Cons.Soc. **Publications:** num.papers, reports & popular articles; Ed.*LORIS* (J.of SL Wildlife and Nature Prot.Soc.). Indiff.to pers.pub.& news media support. **Languages:** English, French (fair), Sinhala. Willing to act as consult.etc. **Address:** 33 Athula Mawatha, Mount Lavinia, Sri Lanka. **Tel.**(home) 94 1 716130; **fax** 94 1 712745.

WILKINSON, Dr Clive Robert. Tropical coastal resource management, coral-reef ecology. Principal Research Scientist. *B*.26 Feb. 1944, Sydney, Australia. Australian. *P*.Madeleine J.Nowak. **Education:** U.of Qld, BSc (Microbiol./Biochem.) 1966, BSc(Hons)(Marine Microbiol.) 1967, PhD(Zool.)(Marine Symbioses) 1976. **Experience:** res.— sponge ecol. & physiol.(Medit., Red Sea, GBR) 1971–90, and poll.of coral reefs and mgmt aspects (SE Asia, GBR) 1990–; admin.& consult.— Chief Tech. Adv.in ASEAN–Australia Marine Sci.Project (Living Coastal Resources) in Indonesia, Malaysia, Philippines, Singapore, & Thailand; consult.for UNDP in Sudan & India, and FAO; lecturing in industrial microbiol.& envl engg; Chairman, UNEP–IOC–IUCN–WMO Global Task Team on Coral Reefs 1992–. **Career:** Postdoctl F. Université Claude Bernard (Lyon) 1977; Leverhulme Vis.F. U.of Bristol 1978; Lect.in Envl Scis, Murdoch U.(Western Australia) 1979; Prin.Res.Sci. AIMS 1980–. **Achievements:** delivered Plenary Address at 7th Intl Coral Reef Symp.1992*, 60+ pubns, Biol.Ed. *Coral Reefs* 1987–92. **Memberships:** ISRS (Counc.), AMSA (Convenor, N.Qld Branch), ACRS, ASM, AIIA (past-Pres. N.Qld Branch). **Publications:** num.incl.**Coral Reefs are Facing Widespread Devastation: Can We Prevent This Through Sust.Mgmt Practices* 1992, Status of Coral Reefs in Southeast Asia: Threats and Responses (co-Author) 1993. **Languages:** English, French. Willing to act as consult.etc. **Address:** Australian Institute of Marine Science, Townsville MC, Queensland 4810, Australia. **Tel.**61 77 534372; **fax** 61 77 725852.

WILLIAMS, Professor Dr Martin A.J. Landforms, soils and climatic change in arid & semi-arid areas, desertification; environmental management in Africa, Australia, Asia. Foundation Professor & Centre Director. *B*.19 May 1941, Croxley Green, Herts., England, UK. Australian. *M*.Frances Mary (geol., geophys., Ethiopia): *s.*, *d.* **Education:** Lycée Hoche (Versailles), King Edward VII (Sheffield); U.of Camb. BA(Hons) 1962, MA 1966; ANU PhD 1969. **Experience:** 30+ yrs' res.in & field mapping of drylands in N.Africa, Australia, India, & China. **Career:** Reconnaissance Soil Surveyor, Hunting Tech. Services Ltd.(Sudan) 1962–4; Div.Land Res.& Regnl Surveyor, CSIRO (Canberra) 1964–6; Res.Scholar, ANU 1966–8; Lect.–Assoc.Prof. Sch.of Earth Scis, Macquarie U. 1969–84; Prof.of Geog.& Envl Sci. Monash U. 1985–92; Fndn Prof.& Dir, Mawson Grad.Centre for Envl Studies, Adelaide U. 1993–. **Achievements:** mapping & interpreting soils & landforms (Libya, Sudan, Ethiopia, Niger, Algeria, Tunisia, Egypt, Somalia, Australia, India, China) 1962–; monitoring hillslope erosion (trop.N.Australia & temperate SE Australia) 1965–; reconstruction of palaeoclimates & prehistoric envts (N.Africa esp.Sahara, Nile Valley, Ethiopia, Australia, India) 1962–; VP SWCAA Vic., State of Vic. Steering Cttee Decade of Land Care Plan; Dir UNEP–U.of Adelaide Intl Grad.Cert.course in Envl Mgmt 1993–; co-Author UNEP–WMO

Report on Interactions of Desert.& Climate. **Memberships:** SWCAA, ISSS, GSA, AQuA (Founding Memb.1982), A&NZGG, Victorian Inst.of Earth & Planetary Scis (Founding Memb. 1988), Victorian Soil Cons.Assn (VP 1989–90, Convener Land Degradation Study Group 1985–92). **Awards:** Cuthbert Peek Medal (RGS) 1973, Vis.Res.F. (CNRS) 1979, Professeur associé (U.Pierre et Marie Curie) 1978–9, Disting.Vis.Prof.(U.of Washington, Seattle) 1989, Miller Vis.Prof.(U.of Illinois) 1989. **Publications:** *Evol.of Australasian Landforms* 1978, *The Sahara and the Nile* 1980, *A Land between Two Niles: Quaternary Geol.& Biol.of the C.Sudan* 1982, *The Cainozoic in Australia* 1991, *Monsoonal Australia: Landscape, Ecol.and Man in the n.Lowlands* 1991, *Quaternary Envts* 1993; 120+ papers. Strongly favours pers.pub.& news media support if they promote better envl cons.& mgmt. **Languages:** English, French, German (fair), Sudanese Arabic (colloquial, spoken). Willing to act as consult.etc. **Address:** Mawson Graduate Centre for Environmental Studies, University of Adelaide, Adelaide, South Australia 5005, Australia. **Tel.**(office) 61 8 303 4170 or 5834; **fax** 61 8 303 4383.

WILLIAMS, Professor Dr William David. Water resources in dry lands; salt lakes. Private Consultant. *B.*21 Aug.1936, Liverpool, England, UK. Australian. *M.*Anne: 2 *s.* **Education:** U.of Liverpool BSc 1958, PhD 1961, DSc 1974. **Experience:** lect., admin., widely travelled to dry regns. **Career:** Lect., Sr Lect., Reader, in Zool. Monash U. 1961–74; Prof.of Zool. U.of Adelaide 1975–94; Private Consult. 1994–. **Achievement:** success in bringing intl attention & interest to importance of waters in dry regns. **Memberships:** AIB, RSSA, ILEC. **Awards:** F.AIB, Foreign F'ship (Russian Acad. of Natural Sci.). **Publications:** ten books incl. *Life in Inland Waters* 1983, *Limnol.in Australia* (co-Author) 1986; *c.*250 scientific papers. Favours pers.pub.as means of focusing attention on envl issues, & news media support. **Languages:** English, German (spoken). Further details may be obtained from *Who's Who in Australia* 1994. Willing to act as consult.etc. **Address:** Department of Zoology, University of Adelaide, Adelaide, South Australia 5005, Australia. **Tel.**61 8 303 5847; **fax** 61 8 303 4364.

WILLUMS, Dr Jan-Olaf. Environmental implications of petroleum industry. Executive Director. *B.*5 Aug.1946, Norway. Norwegian. *M.*Vera: 2 *s.* **Education:** ETH Dipl.Ing.1971; MIT DSc 1975. **Experience:** adv.to UN, EBRD, UNDP, UNEP. **Career:** Mgr Spec.Products, Saga Petroleum 1975–80; Mgr Corporate Planning, Volvo Energy AB 1980–82; Gen.Mgr, Volvo Petroleum AS 1981–2; Pres. Nordic Tech.Corpn 1985–90; Chairman, Nordic Enterprise AS 1990–; Exec.Dir, ICC Office of Envt 1990–92 and World Industry Council for the Envt 1993–. **Achievements:** positions as Sec.-Gen.of Second World Industry Conf.1991 and of Industry

Forum on Sust.Dev.at UNCED 1992. **Awards:** Gold Award (ETH) 1970, Emil Prize (Norway) 1993. **Publications:** incl.*From Ideas to Action* 1992. **Languages:** English, French, German, Norwegian. **Address:** 40 Cours Albert 1er, 75008 Paris, France. **Tel.**(office) 33 14 953 2891; **fax** 33 14 953 2889.

WILSON, Professor Dr Edward Osborne. Biodiversity, biogeography, sociobiology; entomology. Curator in Entomology, Pellegrino University Professor. *B.*10 June 1929, Birmingham, AL, USA. American. *M.*Irene Kelley: *d.* **Education:** U.of Alabama, BS 1949, MS 1950; Harvard U. PhD 1955. **Experience:** res.— field in N.Amer., New World tropics, Pacific Islands, Australia, and lab.in behavioural physiol.and mus.systematics of ants; bd & adv.cttee membership of many orgns and scientific journals. **Career:** Asst Prof.of Biol.1956–8, Assoc.Prof. of Zool.1958–76, Curator in Entomol.1972–, Baird Prof.of Sci.1976–94, Pellegrino U.Prof. 1994–, Mus.of Comparative Zool., all Harvard U. **Achievements:** res.on class.& biol.of ants 1949–; co-creator (with R.H.MacArthur) of theory of island biogeog.1963; first analysis of ant pheromones, and gen.theory of pheromone evol.1963; first synthesis & definition of sociobiology 1971–5; synthesis of biodiv.studies 1988–94. **Memberships:** NAS, RS, Russian Acad.of Natural Scis, Leopoldina, Amer.AAS, APS. **Awards:** Nat.Medal of Sci.1977, Crafoord Prize (RSAS), Tyler Prize for Envl Achievement 1984, Prix de l'Institut de la Vie, Pulitzer Prize for Gen.Non-fiction 1978 & 1991, Gold Medal (WWF) 1990, Intl Prize for Biol.(Govt of Japan) 1993, others. **Publications:** incl.*Sociobiology* 1975, *On Human Nature* 1978, *Biophilia* 1984, *Biodiv.*(Ed.) 1988, *The Ants* (co-Author) 1990, *The Diversity of Life* 1992, *Naturalist* 1994. Favours pers.pub.& news media support. **Address:** Museum of Comparative Zoology, Harvard University, Cambridge, Massachusetts 02138-2902, USA. **Tel.**1 617 495 2315; **fax** 1 617 495 5667.

WILSON, Dr George Robert. Wild animal conservation; sustainable development & strategic analysis; rangeland science, livestock production; endangered species, aerial surveys; Kangaroos — sustainable resource management & aerial surveys, multiple land-use; Aborigines — Aboriginal enterprise development, sustainable land-use, commercial use of wild-animal resources; quarantine & disease management — risk assessment, wild animal management. Research Consultant. *B.*4 March 1946, Sydney, Australia. Australian. *M.*Lynette Patricia: 3 *s.* **Education:** U.of Sydney BVSc 1970, MVSc 1975; U.of Aberdeen PhD 1979. **Experience:** res.— pop.dynamics, age structures of kangaroo & Red Grouse *[Lagopus lagopus scoticus]* pops, pop.estimations from aerial surveys, pathophysiol.of parasites; wildlife cons.esp.kangaroo mgmt throughout Australia, surveys of endangered macropods; policy dev.— leader of Australian Del.to CITES Conf.1981, prep.of NCS for Australia 1983, memb.of three intergovtl nat. cttees resp.for animal prod., health, & vertebrate pest control, direction of prog.on Aboriginal use of wild animal resources; aerial surveys — commercial pilot, low-level flying (Cessna aircraft). **Career:** Res.Sci. NSW NPWS 1970–74; Prin.Wildlife Officer, DoE 1974–6, Australian NPWS 1979–81; Dir NCS for Australia 1981–4; Sr Prin.Sci. Vertebrate Pest Mgmt 1984–8, Dir Animal Resources Branch 1988–92 and Head of Strat.Assessment Unit 1992–4 of Bur.of Resource Scis, all Dept of Primary Industries and Energy; Prin.Res. Consult. ACIL Econ.& Policy Pty Ltd 1994–. **Achievements:** res.into pop.ecol.& pop.assessment of kangaroos, role of diseases in pop. control in Red Grouse, dev.of NCS for Australia, improvements to mgmt of vertebrate pests partic. in exotic disease emergencies, increasing scientific component of resource mgmt of animal resources, use of wild animals by aboriginal people, pubn*. **Memberships:** AVA, AWMS, RSA, AMS, AAS (Fauna Cttee). **Awards:** Postgrad.Award (UK Game Conservancy) 1977, Scholarship (RCVS) 1978, Postgrad.Scholarship (Australian Public Service) 1978. **Publications:** *Pest Animals in Australia — a Survey of Introduced Wild Animals* 1992, *Wild Animal Resources and their Use by Aboriginal Communities* 1992, *Australian Horses as a Primary Industry* 1993, **Rural Industries Strat.for Aboriginal People* 1994; 50+ other chapters & papers. Willing to act as consult.etc. **Address:** 51 Stonehaven Crescent, Deakin, Western Australia 2600, Australia. **Tel.**61 6 281 2112; **fax** 61 6 257 4170.

WILSON, Dr Richard Trevor. African ornithology; conservation of genetic resources; maintenance of biodiversity; sustainable integrated production systems. Freelance Consultant. *B.*4 Sept.1938, Ossett, England, UK. British. *M.* Mary P.(ornith.). **Education:** U.of Wolverhampton PhD(Biol.) 1985, DSc(Trop.Animal Prod.) 1990. **Experience:** res.in ornith., cons.& trop.agricl systems; project design & mgmt; scientific mgmt; Ed. Proc.PanAfrican Ornithl Cong.1993; consult.to UN & several bilateral orgns; work exp.in over 25 countries. **Career:** Freelance Consult.working on rural dev.in trop. Africa; res.on trop.livestock prod.; African ornith.; design, orgn, & mgmt, of training/educ.in Africa, Asia, and S.Amer. **Achievements:** creation of sust.integrated prod.systems in tropics, cons.of genetic resources & biodiv. **Memberships:** F.IBiol., CBiol., F.LS, BOU. **Award:** Silver Medal (U.of Khartoum) 1988. **Publications:** *The Camel* 1984, *Ecophysiol.of the Camelidae and Desert Ruminants* 1989, *Small Ruminant Prod.Systems and the Small Ruminant Genetic Resource in Trop.Africa* 1994, *Livestock Prod.Systems in the Tropics* 1994; Ed.of several proc.; 100+ papers. Indiff.to pers.pub., favours news media support. **Languages:** Arabic (good); English, French, Kiswahili; German, Italian & Spanish (working knowledge). Willing to act as

consult.etc. **Address:** Bartridge House, Umberleigh, North Devon EX37 9AS, England, UK. **Tel.**(home) 44 1769 60244; **fax** 44 1769 60601.

WINGATE, David B. Restoration ecology; conservation; birds. Conservation Officer. *B.*11 Oct.1935, Bermuda. British. **Education:** Cornell U. BSc 1957. **Experience:** cons.biol.of Bermuda Petrel [*Pterodroma cahow*] (Cahow); resto.ecol.on Nonsuch Is.; Nature reserve mgmt for Govt & NGOs. **Career:** Pres.(periodically) Bermuda Audubon Soc.1964–90; Cons.Officer Dept of Agric. Fish & Parks, Govt of Bermuda 1966–. **Achievements:** successful cons.& increase of endangered Bermuda Petrel over 30 yrs; resto.of Nonsuch Is.as living mus.of pre-colonial Bermuda and of wetland habitats filled-in by garbage dumps. **Memberships:** F.AOU, BOU, Bermuda NT (Counc.1970–). **Awards:** MBE 1975, Ridder of Order of the Golden Ark 1978, Dr.Sci.*H.C.* (Clark U.) 1981, Global 500 Roll of Honour (UNEP) 1988, Kai Curry-Lindahl Award (Colonial Waterbird Soc.) 1993. **Publications:** several survey & status papers on flora & fauna of Bermuda incl.*Checklist & Guide to the Birds of Bermuda* 1973, Successful reintro.of the Yellow-crowned Night-Heron [*Nyctonassa violacea*] as a nesting resident of Bermuda 1982, The resto.of Nonsuch Is.as a living mus.of Bermuda's pre-colonial terr.biome 1985. Indiff.to pers.pub., favours news media support. **Language:** English. Willing to act as consult.etc. **Address:** POB DD 224, St David's DD BX, Bermuda. **Tel.**1 809 293 6153, (home) 1 809 297 2623; **fax** 1 809 236 3711.

WITT, Ronald George. Geography and remote sensing, geographic information systems, mapping & monitoring activities; environmental assessment, data & information management; capacity-building related to environment. Manager. *B.*12 Nov.1954, Philadelphia, PA, USA. American. *M.*Avinash K.Vadvae: 2 *d.* **Education:** Middlebury Coll.(VT) BA(Hist.) 1976; U.of Utah MA(Geog.) 1980. **Experience:** five yrs' remote sensing res.and tech.transfer for NASA, data mgmt & GIS applications for UNEP in Nairobi (Kenya) & Geneva (Switzerland) 1986–. **Career:** Researcher/Tech.Transfer Specialist, NASA (Goddard Space Flight Center) 1980–85; Systems Analyst, UNEP/GRID (Nairobi) 1986–7; Database Admin.1988–94, Mgr 1994–, UNEP/GRID (Geneva). **Achievements:** broad exp.in application & transfer of GIS & remote-sensing techs for envl problem-solving and related projects; database dev.at global & regnl scales; meta-database dev.for envl data contribn to knowledge, use, & understanding, of these tools. **Memberships:** AAG, ASPRS, AALS (all past). **Awards:** Bishop Atwood Memoriam (Middlebury Coll.), Phi Kappa Phi, Spec.Achievement & Group Achievement Awards (NASA). **Publications:** num.j. articles, scientific & non-scientific. Indiff.to pers.pub.& news media support. **Languages:** English, French (fair spoken), German (poor). Willing to act as consult.etc.

Address: United Nations Environment Programme/GRID Geneva, Geneva Executive Centre, 11 Chemin des Anémones, 1219 Châtelaine GE, Switzerland. **Tel.**41 22 979 9294; **fax** 41 22 979 9029.

WOLANSKI, Dr Eric J. Coastal, coral-reef, & mangrove, oceanography; Man's impact on tropical marine environments. Senior Principal Research Scientist. *B.*19 Oct.1946, Bukabu, Belgian Congo. *M.*Terry: 2 *s.* **Education:** U.of Louvain, BSc(Civil Eng.) 1969; Princeton U. MSc(Civil & Geol Eng.) 1970; Johns Hopkins U. PhD(Envl Eng.) 1972; CIT postdoctl course in hydraulics engg 1973. **Experience:** 20 yrs in res.; envl res.engg in coastal, coral-reef, & mangrove, oceanogr.; ocean disposal of mine waste, dredge spoils, & human waste in trop.waters (Australia, PNG, China, Indonesia, Thailand, Kenya, Mexico, Tanzania); combining field studies with modelling. **Career:** Water Qual.Engr, State Poll.Control Comm.1974–6; Hydr. Snowy Mtns Engg Corpn 1976–8; Sr Sci.then Sr Prin. Res.Sci. AIMS 1978–; Vis.Prof. U.of Louvain (Belgium) 1995. **Achievements:** pioneering field & modelling studies of the oceanog.of GBR coral-reefs & mangroves, of the dispersal of coral and fish eggs, and of envl impacts of mining & dredging in Australia (GBR), PNG, SE Asia, and E.Africa. **Memberships:** Sigma Xi, AIE. **Awards:** US$ 1 m.for modelling coral-reefs & mangroves for mgmt (IBM Intl Fndn) 1994, Edl Bds *Estuarine, Coastal & Shelf Sci.*, *Continental Shelf Res.*, *J.of Marine Systems*, *J.of Coastal Res.*, *Oceanogr.Lit.Review.* **Publications:** Phys.Oceanogr.Processes of the GBR 1994; 194 papers; Guest Ed.of spec.issues on mangrove oceanogr. 1990 and coral-reef oceanogr. 1992. Indiff.to pers.pub., favours news media support. **Languages:** English, French, Kiswahili (spoken). Willing to act as consult. etc. **Address:** Australian Institute of Marine Science, PMB Nr 3, Townsville MC, Queensland 4810, Australia. **Tel.**(office) 61 77 534243, (home) 61 77 795027; **fax** (office) 61 77 725852, (home) 61 77 790612.

WOLDHEK, Siegfried. Executive Director. *B.*14 May 1951, Emmen, The Netherlands. Dutch. **Education:** Free U.(Amsterdam, Holland) MSc(Biol.Theoretical Ecol.) 1977. **Career:** Coord. Migratory Bird Cttee, ICBP 1978–84; Biol. Dutch Soc.for the Prot.of Birds (Vogelbescherming) 1980–84; Dir 1985–90, Exec.Dir 1990–, WWF–Netherlands. Dislikes pers.pub., favours news media support. **Languages:** Dutch, English, French, German, Spanish (basic). **Address:** WWF–Netherlands, POB 7, 3700 AA Zeist, The Netherlands. **Tel.**(office) 313 404 37333, (home) 313 404 20407; **fax** 313 404 12064.

WOO, Professor Dr Bo-Myeong. Forest environment conservation. Professor. *B.*15 Nov.1938, Cheonyang, Chungnamdo, Korea. Korean. *M.*Soon-Bum: 3 *s.* **Education:** Seoul Nat.U. PhD 1976. **Experience:** res.in soil & water cons., watershed envt cons., forest envt. **Career:** Asst Prof.1973–7, Assoc.Prof.1977–82, Prof. Dept of Forest Resources 1982–, Seoul Nat.U. **Achievements:** pubn of three u.textbooks. **Memberships:** US SWCS, KFS (Bd). **Award:** for pubns (KFS) 1983. **Publications:** incl.*Soil and Water Cons.Engg* 1983, *Forest Engg* 1986 (both in Korean), *Landslides & Control Measures* 1991. Favours pers.pub.& news media support. **Languages:** English, Korean. Willing to act as consult.etc. **Address:** Dept of Forest Resources, College of Agriculture and Life Sciences, Seoul National University, Suwon 441744, Republic of South Korea. **Tel.**(office) 82 331 290 2324, (home) 88 2 543 4479; **fax** 82 331 293 1797.

WOOD, Professor Dr David Arthur. Physiology, biochemistry, & molecular genetics, of Basidiomycete Fungi, particularly edible Fungi; fungal biotechnology. Research Leader. *B.*18 April 1944, Wellington, TN, India. British. *M.*Janet Kathleen: *d., s.* **Education:** Southall Grammar Sch.; UCL BSc 1965, PhD 1968. **Experience:** res.— bacterial biochem.& cytology; teaching at several UK univs; Vis.Prof. King's Coll.London. **Career:** Postdoctl worker, Biochem.Dept, U.of Oxf.1968–72; Res.Leader, Dept of Microbial Biotech. HRI 1968 . **Achievements:** enzymology of nutrition of Basidiomycetes in complex substrates; dev.of methods for fungal biomass measurement; envl factors controlling fruiting of higher Fungi incl. CO_2 level. **Memberships:** SGM (Cells & Cell Surfaces Group), BMS (Ecol.& Physiol. Groups), SAB, Genetical Soc., IBiol., RMS, Save Brit. Sci.Soc., Edl Bd FEMS *Microbiol. Letters* and *J.Gen.Microbiol.* **Publications:** *The Biol.& Tech. of the Cultivated Mushroom* 1985, *Devl Biol.of Higher Fungi* 1985; 75+ papers mostly on biol. of edible Fungi. Indiff.to pers.pub.& news media support. **Languages:** English, French (better spoken). Willing to act as consult.etc. **Address:** Department of Microbial Biotechnology, Horticulture Research International, Wellesbourne, Warwickshire CV35 9EF, England, UK. **Tel.**44 1789 470382; **fax** 44 1789 470552.

WOODELL, Dr Stanley Reginald John. Ecology of extreme environments (desert, arctic, salt-marsh, serpentine); conservation of British vegetation; reproduction biology of plants. Emeritus Fellow, Fellow Librarian. *B.*15 Nov. 1928, London, England, UK. British. *M.*Rebecca (bird pop.censusing, butterfly cons., Nature sci.mgmt): 2 *s.* **Education:** Latymer Upper Sch.; Hatfield Coll.Durham BS(Hons) 1953, PhD(Dunelm) 1958; U.of Oxf. MA 1960. **Experience:** res.on Brit.Primulas, salt-marsh ecol., pattern in desert plants, reproductive biol.of plants in temperate & arctic envts; taught plant ecol.& plant geog.1959–88. **Career:** K. George VI Mem.F'ship (ESU), NC State Coll.; Asst. Lect. QMC 1957–9; Lect.in Bot. U.of Oxf.1959–88; Vis.Prof. UCLA 1965–6; Vis.Sr Lect. U.of

Sci.& Tech.Ghana 1970; Res.at RS Res.Station Aldabra 1974; Vis.Researcher, U.of Copenhagen 1974; Disting.Vis.Scholar, Adelaide U. 1983–4. **Achievements:** basic res.on distribn patterns in desert plants, reproductive biol.of arctic plants, ecol.of salt-marshes & serpentine soils, repro.in desert & trop.plants, tortoise–veg.interactions on Aldabra; campaigning for preserv.of veg.in SW Portugal; teaching aspects of cons.to undergrads & postgrads. **Memberships:** BES, BSBI, Plant Life, John Muir Trust, Field Studies Council (Exec.Cttee), SBNH. **Awards:** Scholarship for students in residence (Durham U.) 1951, K. George VI Mem.F'ship (ESU) 1956–7. **Publications:** *The English Landscape — Past, Present & Future* (Ed.) 1985; *c.*100 papers. Indiff.to pers.pub.& news media support. **Languages:** English, French (moderate). Willing to act as consult.etc. **Address:** Wolfson College, Linton Road, Oxford OX2 6UD, England, UK. **Tel.** (office) 44 1865 274075, (home) 44 1844 238399.

WOODFORD, Dr Michael Henry. All veterinary aspects of conservation: wild animal capture & translocation, management, disease, utilization especially meat production; national park management & biodiversity planning. Freelance Wildlife Veterinarian, Biodiversity Planner. *B.*27 Sept.1924, Easthampstead, Berkshire, England, UK. British. *M.*June Erica: 2 *d.* incl.Rosemary (wildlife artist); *s.*John Douglas (vet.epidemiologist). **Education:** Blundell's School; R.Vet.Coll.London, MRCVS 1946, F.RCVS 1977; U.of Zürich, Dr vet.med.1971. **Experience:** 21 yrs in agricl vet.practice in England, 15 yrs' employment by intl agencies (mainly FAO) on livestock & wildlife projects in E.Africa & Asia, 30 yrs as wildlife vet.consult.in 25 countries. **Career:** private vet.practice in England 1946–67; Admin./Vet.1967–9 and Dep. Dir 1969–71 Nuffield Unit of Trop.Animal Ecol. Queen Elizabeth Nat.Park, Uganda; Animal Health Officer, FAO Kenya Wildlife Mgmt Project 1971–6; Project Adv./Team Leader, FAO/ UNDP Animal Health Project, Kabul 1977–9; Team Leader FAO Animal Health Project, Maputo 1980–82, Vet.& Wildlife Consult.for intl agencies in 25 countries 1962–. **Achievements:** pioneer wildlife vet., init.of interest in wildlife disease on global scale. **Memberships:** AAWV, WDA, WAWV, IUCN SSC Vet.SG (Chairman 1984), OIE (Chairman WG on Wildlife Diseases) 1993–. **Award:** F.RCVS by thesis. **Publications:** *A Manual of Falconry* 1962, Ed. *IUCN SSC Vet.SG Newsletter*; several specialist book chapters; 30+ papers. Dislikes pers. pub., indiff.to news media support. **Languages:** English, French (read), Portuguese (read). Willing to act as consult.etc. **Address:** Apt B/709, 500 23rd St NW, Washington, DC 20037, USA. **Tel.**(home) & **fax** 1 202 331 9448.

WOODGATE, Dr Graham Roy. Nature–society relationships, 'coevolution'; rural-based livelihood systems especially agroforestry systems. Lecturer in Environmental Sociology,

Programme Coordinator. *B.*16 Sept.1960, Robertsbridge, Sussex, England, UK. British. **Education:** U.of London, PhD 1992. **Experience:** res.in Mexico 1987–; prog.coordn, coord. for undergrad.degrees in envt; consults with UK NRI & UN FAO. **Career:** Lect.in Envl Sociol. Wye Coll.(U.of London) 1992–; UK Coord. Brit.Council Higher Educ.Link Prog.for Sust. Rural Livelihoods with Mexico 1995–. **Endeavours:** to develop & extend understanding of relationships between soc.& envt, linking natural & social scis. **Membership:** IUCN CESP 1993–. **Awards:** Mgmt Trophy (RFS) 1984, Prize for best UK thesis on Mexico (Brit./ Mexican Soc.) 1992. **Publications:** *Concepts of the Envt in the Social Scis* (co-Author) 1993, *Sociol.of the Envt* (co-Ed., three vols) 1995. Indiff.to pers.pub.& news media support. **Languages:** English, Spanish. Further details may be obtained from *Intl Guide to Res.in Mexico* (UCSD) 1989. Willing to act as consult. etc. **Address:** Environment Section, Wye College, University of London, Wye, Kent TN25 5ES, England, UK. **Tel.** (office) 44 1233 812401 ext.436, (home & **fax**) 44 1233 813208; **fax** 44 1233 812855.

WOODRUFF, Professor Dr David S. Evolution & conservation of animal species; genetic management of free-ranging & captive populations; snail-transmitted diseases and development of hydropower & irrigation projects in Southeast Asia. Professor of Biology, Faculty Director. *B.*12 June 1943, Penrith, England, UK. Australian, American Resident Alien. *M.*Amy L.: 2 *d.* **Education:** U.of Melbourne BSc 1965, PhD 1973. **Experience:** res.— field-work in Australia, Bahamas, Thailand, and genetic studies of schistosomes, snails, Chimpanzees *(Anthropopithecus troglodytes)*, Gibbons *(Hylobates* spp.), birds; taught cons.biol.1973–; admin.— Dir U.of Calif./USAID Intl Course Animal Genetic Resource Cons.1992; consult.— memb. Animal Collection Cttee San Diego Zoo 1980–, NSF Cons.Resto.Biol.Panel 1991–3, IUCN SSC Cons.Breeding SG. **Career:** Postdoctl F.and Instr. Alexander Agassiz Lect.on Biogeog. 1971–4, Harvard U.; Asst Prof.of Biol Scis, Purdue U. 1974–9; Assoc.Prof.of Biol.1979–86, Prof.1986–, Fac.Dir of Educ.Abroad Prog. UCSD. **Achievements:** dev.of non-invasive methods of genotyping threatened species for cons.& mgmt using hair & feathers; documenting effects of habitat fragmentation on pop.viability of rainforest animals and promoting wildlife cons.in Thailand; Adv.to World Bank on ecol effects of hydroelectric projects in Mekong Basin; Assoc.Ed.*Zoo Biol., J.Envt & Dev.* **Memberships:** F.LS, F.AAAS, Sigma Xi, SCB, ESA, RSV (Sec.1967–9); six others. **Awards:** Exhibitioner in Zool.1964 and Howitt Natural Hist.Scholar 1965 (U.of Melbourne), Australian Commonwealth Postgrad.Scholar 1966–9, Frank Knox F.(Harvard U.) 1969–71. **Publications:** Ed.of three books/handbooks; 70 papers & 70 reports. Indiff.to pers.pub.& news media support. **Language:** English. Willing to act as consult.

etc. **Address:** Department of Biology 0116, University of California, San Diego, La Jolla, California 92093-0116, USA. **Tel.**1 619 534 2375; **fax** 1 619 534 7108.

WOODWELL, Dr George M. Ecology, structure & function of Nature; how the world works; biotic interactions in warming of Earth; role of forests, toxic substances, biotic impoverishment. Centre Director & President. *B.*23 Oct.1928, Camb., MA, USA. American. *M.*Katharine R. (admin. WHRC): 2 *d.*incl.Caroline A.(Open Space Inst., land cons.in Hudson Valley of NY), 2 *s.*incl.John C.(ecol econ.). **Education:** Dartmouth Coll. AB 1950; Duke U. AM 1957, PhD 1958. **Career:** Asst.then Assoc.Prof. U.of Maine 1957–61; Vis.Asst.Sci.to Sr Sci. Brookhaven Nat.Lab.1957–75; Founding Dir, Ecosystems Center, Marine Biol.Lab.1975–85, Dir & Pres. 1985–, WHRC. **Achievements:** fundamental res.on ecosystems, their structure, dev., metabolism; ecol efforts of toxins esp.ionizing radiation and pesticides; biotic interactions in the warming of the Earth; biotic impoverishment; 300+ pubns. **Memberships:** Amer. AAS, NAS, ESA (Founding Pres., VP). **Awards:** num.hon. degrees. **Publications:** incl.*The Earth in Transition: Patterns and Processes of Biotic Impoverishment* (Ed.) 1990, *World Forests for the Future, Their Use and Cons.*(co-Ed.) 1993, *Biotic Feedbacks in the Global Climate System: Will the Warming Feed the Warming?* (co-Author) 1995; Radiation and the patterns of Nature 1965, Toxic substances and ecol cycles 1967, Effects of poll.on the structure & physiol.of ecosystems 1970, The warming of industrialized middle latitudes 1985–2050: causes & consequences 1989. **Language:** English. Further details may be obtained from *Who's Who in Amer.* Willing to act as consult.etc. **Address:** Woods Hole Research Center, Woods Hole, Massachusetts 02543, USA. **Tel.**1 508 540 9900; **fax** 1 508 540 9700.

WORTHINGTON, Dr (Edgar) Barton. Environmental consulting; sheep- and trout-farmer; history of environmentalism; ecocomplex realism. Retired, Environmental Consultant. *B.*13 Jan.1905, London, England, UK. British. *M.*1. Stella: 3 *d.*incl. Martha (animal ethology); 2.Harriet. **Education:** Rugby Sch.; Gonville & Caius Coll. Camb.U. BA (1st Class Hons Zool.) 1927, PhD 1931. **Experience:** hydrobiol.& fisheries' res.; orgn of sci.esp. overseas & intl. **Career:** Asst, L.Victoria fishery survey 1927; Leader, Lakes Abert & Kiogo surveys 1928; Balfour student & Dem.in Zool. Camb.1930–36; Sci.to Lord Hanley's African Survey 1933–7; Dir FBA 1937–46; Adv. Middle E.Supply Council 1942–5; Dev.Adv. Uganda 1946; Scientific Sec.to Colonial Office & E. Africa High Comm. 1946–51; Sec.-Gen.to Scientific Council for Africa 1952–7; Dep.DG, Nature Conservancy (GB) 1952–62; Scientific Dir, IBP 1961–72; Envl Consult.1972–. **Achievements:** published results and follow-up in all the above. **Memberships:** RGS (Life & one-time Counc.), LS (Memb.of Honour & one-time

Counc.), IUCN (Memb.of Honour, one-time Counc.& VP), FFS (Memb.& one-time Counc.), F.IBiol., R.African Soc., CHEC (Gov.), Explorers' Club (USA). **Awards:** Gill Mem.(RGS) 1932, Mungo Park Medal (RSGS) 1937, CBE 1963, Ridder of Order of Golden Ark 1976. **Publications:** *Inland Waters of Africa* (co-Author) 1933, *Sci.in Africa* 1937, *Sci.in the Middle E.*1946, *Life on Lakes & Rivers* (co-Author) 1951, *Sci.in the Dev.of Africa* 1958, *IBP* (first of 25 vols) 1976, *The Ecol Century* 1983; *c.*100 main papers. Indiff. to pers.pub., favours news media support. **Languages:** English; French & Kiswahili (doubtful). Further details may be obtained from British *Who's Who* and *Intl Who's Who* 1994–95. Willing to act as consult.etc. **Address:** Colin Godmans, Furners Green, near Uckfield, East Sussex TN22 3RR, England, UK. **Tel.** (home) 44 1825 740322.

WRIGHT, Martin Paul William. Communications; environmental issues & solutions. Freelance Writer & Consultant, Editor, Contributing Editor, Producer. *B.*12 Dec.1958, London, England, UK. **Education:** U.of Exeter, BA 1980. **Experience:** widely-travelled as freelance writer, photographer, & film-maker; consult.to num. envl, official, & commercial, orgns incl.WWF, and English Nature. **Career:** Writer on Global Affairs, Longman Publishers 1982–7; Freelance Writer & Consult.1987–; Ed.*Envt Digest* 1990– and Contributing Ed.*Tomorrow* 1992–; Writer & Producer, *Go Global* and *Go Wild* (UK TV series) 1991–3; Founder, Still Pictures–Moving Words 1993 and The Ecosystem (Envl Info. Service on the Internet) 1995. **Achievements:** contribn to range of nat.newspapers & magazines incl.*New Scientist* & *Geogl Magazine*, on envl problems & solutions and the search for a sust.future; has broadcast on nat.radio; actively involved in search for solutions (in the widest sense of the word). **Memberships:** Envl Info. Forum, num.nat.envl orgns. **Award:** Science & Envt Journalist of the Yr (Envt Council) 1994. **Publications:** 15 books incl.*Countries in Crisis* (four vols) 1987–9, *Our Backyard: How to Challenge the Threats to Your Health and Envt* 1991, *Intro.to Envl Action* 1992. Generally favours pers.pub.& news media support. **Languages:** English, French (adequate). Willing to act as consult.etc. **Address:** 180 Albion Road, London N16 9JR, England, UK. **Tel.**44 171 275 7432; **e-mail** MartinW@Easynet.co.uk .

WRIGHT, Dr R.Michael. Addressing the linkage between poverty alleviation & environmental quality, community-based approaches to conservation; application of legal techniques in different cultural settings; issues of environmental justice. Programme Director. *B.*12 July 1943, Eugene, OR, USA. American. *M.* Peggy Ann: *s.*, *d.* **Education:** Stanford U. AB (Hist.) 1966, JD 1970. **Experience:** tech.assistance to countries developing resource policies — project eval.& country missions to design, assess, and undertake, field projects; admin.— manage all

WWF–USA field activities & field staff in Latin Amer., Asia, & Africa, fund-raising; legal — negns for land purchase (USA & overseas) and of govt agreements, tax issues for non-profits, trademark law; teaching intl envl affairs & peacekeeping at Stanford U. **Career:** Res.Assoc. Stanford Center for Res.in Intl Studies 1970–72; Western Regnl Counsel 1972–4, Dir Intl Prog.1972–9, Dir Compatible Dev.Programme 1994–, The Nature Conservancy; Asst Dir, Task Force on Global Resources, Pres.Carter's CEQ 1980; VP 1979–91 (Sr VP 1990–91), Sr F.1992–4, WWF–USA. **Achievements:** conceptualization & dev.of Wildlands & Human Needs prog.at WWF; dev.of Biodiv.Support Prog.(WRI–WWF–The Nature Conservancy jt venture); creation of intl prog.at The Nature Conservancy; negotiating & assisting with estab.of prot.areas in US, Canada, Dominica, Costa Rica, Dominican Rep., Colombia, Panama, Zambia, Nepal, Indonesia. **Memberships:** State Bar of CA 1970, Bar of US Supreme Court 1976, IUCN CNPPA 1983–, ICEL 1977–. **Awards:** Rockefeller Fndn Envl F.1979, Global 500 Roll of Honour (UNEP) 1988, ENRAC (Stanford Law Sch.), Woodrow Wilson Vis.F. 1992–3. **Publications:** Annapurna Cons.Area (co-Author) 1991, The Wildlands and Human Needs Prog.: Putting Rural Dev.to Work for Cons.(co-Author) 1992, Cons.& Dev.: The Donor's Dilemma 1993, *Community-based Cons.*(co-Ed.) in press. No objection to pers. pub., willing to deal with news media. **Languages:** English, French (modest). Further details may be obtained from *Nat. Leaders of Amer. Cons.*1985. Willing to act as consult.etc. **Address:** 4259 Vacation Lane, Arlington, Virginia 22207, USA. **Tel.**(office) 1 202 778 9615, (home) 1 703 243 0881; **fax** 1 703 841 1283.

WRIGHT, Dr Shane D.Tuatini. Forest regeneration dynamics, protected natural areas' survey & design, conservation biology. Lecturer in Ecology. *B.*20 Nov.1958, Wanganui, NZ. New Zealander (of Maori descent). *M.*Annette M. Lees *qv.* **Education:** U.of Auckland, PhD(Forest Ecol.) 1993. **Experience:** ten yrs in cons.& envl prot.in NZ & S.Pacific; field exp.in trop. S.Pacific in prot.area design & surveying; res. exp.in forest regeneration & dynamics. **Career:** Cons.Sci.for NGOs in NZ & Pacific 1988–94; Lect.in Ecol. U.of Auckland 1993–. **Achievement:** design & survey of first nat.prot.areas systems in Fiji & Soloman Islands. **Membership:** NZES. Indiff.to pers.pub.& news media support. **Languages:** English, Spanish (spoken), Tok Pidjin. Willing to act as consult.etc. **Address:** School of Biological Sciences, University of Auckland, Private Bag, Auckland, New Zealand. **Tel.**(office) 64 9 373 7999, (home) 64 9 810 9535.

Xianpu WANG, Professor, *see* **WANG, Professor Xianpu.**

XU, Professor Ouyong. Environmental science. University Professor. *B.*8 Feb.1931, Jiujiang, Jiangxi Province, PRC. Chinese. *M.*Yan Aizhen:

2 *d.* **Education:** Jinling U.(U.of Nanjing) BSc (Chem.) 1952. **Experience:** res., consult. **Career:** Lect.1956, Assoc.Prof.1981, Prof.1986–, Dep.Dir of Inst.of Envl Sci.1978– 84, Head Dept of Envl Sci.1984–92, Nanjing U. **Achievements:** developing strats & schemes for poll.control of urban areas; prep.for setting-up & mgmt of Dept of Envl Sci.at U.of Nanjing. **Memberships:** IUCN CEC, Directory Bd on Higher Envl Educ. State Educ.Cttee, Assoc. Chief Ed.*Envl Poll.& Control.* **Awards:** Progress Prize (3rd Class) of Sci.& Tech.(State Scientific & Techl Cttee), some prizes awarded by Sichuan 1981 & Jiangsu 1986 Provinces, and Nat.EPA. **Publications:** incl.*Coordinate Dev. of Economy & Envl Prot.in Cities: A Case Study* 1988, *The Prot.of Water Qual.of the Watershed of L.Taihu* 1992, Influence of particle sorption on the biodegradation rate of 2,4-D: an improvement model of Rao's 1992. **Languages:** Chinese, English (better written). Further details may be obtained from *Who's Who in Australasia and the Far E.*1989. Willing to act as consult. etc. **Address:** Department of Environmental Science and Engineering, Nanjing University, Nanjing 210093, People's Republic of China. **Tel.**86 25 663 7551 ext.3104; **fax** 86 25 330 7965.

YABLOKOV, Professor Dr Alexey V. Population biology; study of vertebrates, evolutionary theory; conservation biology, ecopolicies. Commission Chairman, Centre Chairman. *B.*3 Oct. 1933, Moscow, Russia. Russian. *M.* Dil'bar N. (ecol., TV journalist): *s.* **Education:** Moscow SU BA(Vertebrate Zool.) 1956; Inst.of Animal Morphology, Dr in Biol.(Marine Mammals) 1959; USSR AS Siberian Branch, Dr Sci.(Pop. Biol.) 1965. **Experience:** res., admin. **Career:** Head of Lab.of Postnatal Onthogenesis, N.K. Koltsov Inst.of Devl Biol. USSR AS 1969–91; Chairman, Comm.of Ichthyology, USSR Min.of Fisheries 1988–91; People's Dep. (MP) of USSR & Dep.Chairman, Cttee of Ecol. USSR Supreme Soviet 1989–91; Couns.to Pres.of Russian Fedn for Ecol.& Health 1991; Chairman, Ecol.Policy Council to Pres.of Russian Fedn 1992–3; Chairman, Interagency Comm.on Ecol Security, Nat.Security Council 1993–; Chairman, Center for Russian Envl Policy 1993–. **Achievements:** formulation of Living Nature Prot.Levels; work on prot.of marine mammals (Northern seals, Beluga [*Delphinapterus leucas*], big whales); dev.of non-invasive ('phenetics') methods of study of animals. **Memberships:** Greenpeace USSR (Chair), MSPA (Pres.), IUCN SSC, Russian AS (Corres.). **Awards:** A.N.Severtsov Award (USSR AS) 1976, Dr *H.C.* (VUB) 1991, Roll of Honour (IUCN) 1991, Sci.Award (SETAC) 1992, Intl Award (*Green House*, UK) 1993, Pew Award (Michigan U.) 1994. **Publications:** *Beluga* (Delphinapterus leucas) 1969, *Whales & Dolphins* 1974, *Variability of Mammals* 1974, *Grundriss der Populationslehre* 1977, *Phenetics* 1986, *Pop. Biol.*(in Russian) 1987, *Cons.of Living Nature & Resources: Problems, Trends & Prospects* 1991;

c.400 scientific books & papers. Indiff.to pers.pub., favours news media support. **Languages:** English, Russian. Further details may be obtained from *Who is Who in Russia* 1993, *Gt Soviet Enc.*(3rd edn), *Intl Who's Who* 1994–5. **Address:** 4 Staraya Pl., Moscow 103132, Russia. **Tel.**(office) 7 095 925 2327, (home) 7 095 134 4421; **fax** 7 095 206 0941.

YAHYA, Dr Hafiz Shaeque Ahmad. Avian ecology, ethology, conservation. Reader in Wildlife Ecology, Research Coordinator. *B*.27 Dec.1952, Nazramohamda, Via Sakri, Darbhanga Dist., Bihar, India. Indian. *M*.Nasreen Akhtar (Nature cons.): *d*.Tazeen F.(Nature cons.). **Education:** U.of Bombay, PhD(Field Ornith.) 1980. **Experience:** res., res.& teaching, res. coordn. **Career:** Res.Scholar 1977–80, Res. Biol.1980–82, BNHS; Lect.in Zool., Ram Krishna Coll.1983–5; Lect. 1986–93 & Reader 1993–, in Wildlife Ecol. Aligarh Muslim U.; Res. Coord. NCWCD 1994–. **Achievements:** supervision of five MPhil.and two PhD students, contribns to several books and tech.reports, teaching. **Memberships:** BNHS (Life), WPA (Life), Newsletter for Birdwatchers (Bangalore), Threatened Waterfowl Res.Group (UK). **Awards:** F'ship (BNHS) 1977–80, grant from BES 1993. **Publications:** several incl.thesis on ecol.& biol.of Indian Barbets *(Megalaima spp.)*, Roosting Behaviour of Barbets 1987, Habitat preference of birds in the Periyar Tiger Reserve 1990, Status of the Whitewinged Wood Duck, *Cairina scutulata*, and its cons.priorities in India 1994. Indiff.to pers.pub., favours news media support. **Languages:** Bengali (spoken), English, Hindi, Maithili, Urdu. Willing to act as consult.etc. **Address:** National Commission for Wildlife Conservation and Development, POB 61681, Riyadh 11575, Kingdom of Saudi Arabia. **Tel.**(office) 966 1 441 8700 ext.51; **fax** 966 1 405 4181.

YANSHIN, Academician Aleksandr Leonidovich. Geology; ecology. Presidium Counsellor, Consultant. *B*.28 March 1911, Smolensk, Russia. Russian. *M*.Fidan Taufikovna Yanshina (geol.). **Education:** Moscow Geol Prospection Inst.1932. **Experience:** scientific work in stratigraphy, tectonics, lithology, geomorph.; admin. **Career:** Scientific Worker, Geol Inst. USSR AS (Moscow) 1929–58; Dep.Dir, Inst.of Geol.& Geophys.(Novosibirsk) 1958–82; VP USSR AS and Dir Inst.of Lithosphere (Moscow) 1982–8; Consult.to AS 1988–; Counsellor of the Presidium of the Russian AS. **Achievements:** drew attention to decline of N.Rivers Transfer, and of New Volga Water River Reservoirs projects. **Memberships:** many scientific socs in Russia, Germany, Mongolia, Bulgaria. **Awards:** Karpinskii' Gold Medal 1973, S. Bubnov' Silver Medal (Germany) 1975; many USSR State prizes, medals, orders, & titles. **Publications:** *Lessons of Ecol Errors* (monogr.) 1991; many scientific articles. Positive attitude to pers.pub., favours news media support. **Languages:** English & French (both written & comp.), Russian.

Further details may be obtained from a bibl.book, *A.L.Yanshin*, Nauka, p.186, 1991. Willing to act as consult.etc. **Address:** Zvenigorodskaya ul.14, 1, Moscow 121433, Russia. **Tel.**(office) 7 095 237 7205, (home) 7 095 146 9473.

YAZGAN, Mrs Nergis. Nature conservation; endangered species. Director. *B*.21 Feb.1947, Istanbul, Turkey. Turkish. *M*.Gernant Magnin (BirdLife Intl, Turkey): *d*. **Education:** Inst.of Journalism & Public Relations (Paris), graduated 1971. **Experience:** worked as foreign corres. for newspaper *Milliyet;* Head of Public Relations, Eczacibasi Co. **Career:** Founding Memb. of WWF Turkey 1975–85; Pres.1985–9, Dir 1989–, Soc.for the Prot.of Nature. **Achievements:** leader in public awareness campaign to stop megatourism project in S.Turkey because of the importance of area to be developed to endangered Marine Turtles *(Caretta caretta),* and co-init.of estab.of this area as a Specially Prot.Area. **Memberships:** OSME (VP), IUCN SSC. **Awards:** Friend of the Envt Prize (Turkey) 1988, Global 500 Roll of Honour (UNEP, to Soc.for the Prot.of Nature) 1990. **Publications:** *Increasing Cons.Concern in Turkey* (ICBP Tech. Pubn Nr 21) 1991, *Goksu Delta, Integrated Wetland Mgmt Sem.* 1993; others. **Languages:** English, French, German, Spanish, Turkish. **Address:** Society for the Protection of Nature (DHKD), PK 18, 80810 Bebek, Istanbul, Turkey. **Tel.**90 1212 279 013940; **fax** 90 1212 279 5544.

Yearn Hong CHOI, Professor, *see* **CHOI, Professor Yearn Hong.**

YEROULANOS, Marinos. Environmental planning; aquaculture. Company Director. *B*.13 May 1930, Athens, Greece. Greek. *M*.Aimilia: 3 *d*., *s*. **Education:** Civil Engr, ETH 1954. **Experience:** former DG of Greek Min.of Coordn; former Envl Consult.to UNEP, Medit. Mtgs Chairman; Adv.to Cyprus Govt and to Greek Govt & Opposition on envl matters; high-level missions to S.Pacific, Indian Ocean, Kuwait Conv., and Medit.Sea, to evaluate envl progs. **Career:** Engr 1954–61; Greek R.Court 1961–73 (partly in exile); DG, Govt Envl Unit (first in Greece) 1975–81; Chairman, Phys. Planning and Envt Comm.1976–81; VP, Medit. States Signatories of Barcelona Conv.1979–81; Head, Greek Del.to UNEP Governing Councils, OECD and Council of Europe Envt Cttees, EEC Council and negns for Greek accession IUCN 1976–81; Chairman, Western Countries, UNEP Governing Council 1978 & 1980; Memb. Nat.Water Bd 1977–81, Nat.Coastal Planning Council & NRC 1979–81, Nat.Cttee for UNESCO 1977–82; Dir, Cephalonian Fisheries Ltd 1982–. **Achievements:** Head of Secretariat for Phys.Planning and the Envt (first envl unit) set up by Greek Govt, which achieved a turnaround in envl thinking and Govt decision-making, helped to develop envl awareness throughout the country, init.& passed array of envl legis., promoted & helped to accept a series of intl convs, promoted envl & regnl planning, was instrumental in acceptance of series of envl prot.measures in Greece incl.creation of a Min.of Envt. **Memberships:** Benaki Phytopathological Inst.(Benaki Mus.)(Pres.), Greek Chamber of Engrs, Yeroulanos Fndn, Greek Anticancer Inst., ASCE. **Awards:** Global 500 Roll of Honour (UNEP) 1987, several Greek & foreign decorations. **Publications:** several reviews for Ocean and Coastal Areas Div.of UNEP, articles on Greece and the Euro.Community, proposals to Greek Govt on envl matters. Indiff.to pers. pub.& news media support. **Languages:** English, French, German, Greek, Italian. **Address:** 10 Lykiou Street, Athens 106 74, Greece. **Tel.**(office) 30 1 620 5427, (home) 30 1 721 6600; **fax** 30 1 620 5905.

YONZON, Dr Pralad. Conservation biology in the Himalayan region and South & Southeast Asia. Team Leader. *B.*21 May 1951, Morang, Nepal. Nepalese. *M.*Binu: *s., d.* **Education:** U. of Maine, PhD 1989. **Experience:** biol res. (cons.& prot.areas); policymaking (envl); teaching, communication on indigenous knowledge & trad.systems. **Career:** Memb. Envt Prot.Council 1993, Project Coord.of Vietnam GEF Project 1994–5, Cons.Biol.Expert in Bhutan 1992–3, Wildlife Adv.1993, Govt of Nepal; Team Leader, Resources Nepal 1993–. **Achievements:** Red Panda cons., effective ban on selling of 'Gift Rhinos' from Nepal, intro.of Nepal's first ground census on Rhinos. **Memberships:** ZSN, Amer. Soc.of Mammalogists, Kathmandu Envt Educ. Project. **Awards:** Fulbright Scholar 1982, Crown Prince Award (R.Nepal Acad.of Sci.& Tech.) 1986. **Publications:** Cheese, Tourists, and Red Pandas, in Nepal–Himalaya (readings) 1995, Fighting the illegal fur trade in Kathmandu, Nepal (co-Author) 1995, *Habitat Himalaya* (quarterly factfile) 1993–. Favours pers. pub., indiff.to news media support. **Languages:** English, Nepali. Willing to act as consult.etc. **Address:** Resources Nepal, GPO Box 2448, Kathmandu, Nepal. **Tel.**977 1 523002; **fax** 977 1 412338.

YOUNG, Dr Raymond DE. Exploring the role of information & non-tangible motives in promoting conservation behaviour among individuals, and understanding the psychological aspects of common resource dilemmas *e.g.* 'tragedy of the commons'. Assistant Professor of Conservation Behaviour. *B.*24 Oct.1952, Paterson, NJ, USA. American. *M.* Noreen Fran: *d., s.* **Education:** Stevens Inst. of Tech. BE 1974, ME 1975; U.of Michigan PhD 1984. **Experience:** res.— psych. of durable behaviour change, using 'stories' as behaviour change techniques, the role of feedback & intrinsic satisfaction in cons.behaviour change; consult.— envl educ.& cons.behaviour change progs, dev., & eval.; teaching envl psych., cons.behaviour, recycling and source reduction, decentralism. **Career:** Envl Engr, Camp, Dresser & McKee 1976–80; Res.Asst/Assoc. 1980–84, Res.F.1984–90, Res.Sci.1990–91, Asst Prof.

1991–, Sch.of Natural Resources & Envt, U.of Michigan. **Achievements:** basic & applied res. on cons.motives, dev.of intrinsic satisfaction approach to understanding cons.behaviour of individual citizens. **Memberships:** APS, APA (Div.34), EDRA, NRC (USA). **Awards:** Pi Delta Epsilon (Stevens Inst.of Tech.) 1974, NJ Grad.& Professional Scholarship 1974–6, Horace H.Rackham Predoctoral F'ship 1983–4. **Publications:** over 25 tech. reports. Indiff.to pers.pub.& news media support. **Language:** English. Willing to act as consult. etc. **Address:** School of Natural Resources & Environment, University of Michigan, 430 East University Avenue, Ann Arbor, Michigan 48109-1115, USA. **Tel.**1 313 763 3129; **fax** 1 313 936 2195; **e-mail** RDEYOUNG@ UMICH. EDU .

YOUNG, Dr Steven Burr. Education in arctic environmental issues; research in Quaternary palaeoecology; biogeography. Centre Director. *B.*5 Sept.1938, New York, NY, USA. American. *B.*Dr Oran R.Young (arctic envl policy res.). **Education:** Middlebury Coll. AB(Biol.) 1960; U.of Alaska at Fairbanks MS(Biol.) 1965; Harvard U. PhD(Biol.) 1968. **Experience:** active in field res.& educ.in Arctic & sub-Arctic since early 1960s; admin.as Centre Dir.1971–. **Career:** Asst Prof.of Biol. Ohio SU 1968–72; Dir, Center for Northern Studies 1971–; Adjunct Prof.of Northern Studies, Middlebury Coll. 1977–87. **Achievements:** much basic res.on Nature and processes of arctic & sub-arctic envt; dev.of educ.prog.dealing with circumpolar envl issues. **Memberships:** AAAS, ESA, AINA. **Award:** Elected F.AINA 1973. **Publications:** *The Paleoecology of Beringia* (co-Author & -Ed.) 1982, *To the Arctic* 1989, 1994; num. papers & reports. Indiff.to pers.pub.& news media support. **Languages:** English, French (read), German (read). Willing to act as consult.etc. **Address:** The Center for Northern Studies, Wolcott, Vermont 05680, USA. **Tel.**(office) 1 802 888 4331, (home) 1 802 888 4803; **fax** 1 802 888 3969.

YOUSSEF, Professor Dr Abdullatif Kamel. Organic chemistry; marine & air environment. Professor of Organic Chemistry, Director. *B.*4 Dec.1939, Safita, Syria. Syrian. *M.*Hende: *d.* **Education:** Damascus U. BSc 1964; VPI PhD 1972. **Experience:** res.— polycyclic aromatic hydrocarbons, tobacco chem., polyarylated carbinols, air & sea poll., recycled oil; teaching chem. **Career:** Res.Assoc. Kentucky U.1969–70; Researcher 1972–4, V.Dean 1975–7 & Vis. Researcher 1985–6 VPI & SU; Dean Fac. Sci. 1978–80, Prof.of Organic Chem.& Dir Marine Res.Inst.1987–, Tishreen U.; Researcher, KISR 1980–87. **Achievements:** init.res.prog.on air poll.in Kuwait, chem.character of recycled oil, init.grad.prog.on marine envt. **Memberships:** [Syrian] Nat.Cttee for Prot.of Marine Envt, [Syrian] Nat.Contingency Plan, ACS, Sigma Xi, Phi Lamda Ypsilon. **Publications:** ten books incl.*Basic Gas Chromatography, Organic Chem.*

for Med.Students, Gen.Chem.for Med.Students, Organic Chem.& Spectroscopy; many other. **Languages:** Arabic, English, French, German (poor). Willing to act as consult.and to judge proposals. **Address:** Marine Research Institute, Tishreen University, Lattakia, Syria. **Tel.**(office) 963 41 225658, (home) 963 41 223525; **fax** 963 41 228504.

Yung JIM, Chi, Dr, *see* **JIM, Dr Chi Yung.**

ZABELINA, Dr Natalia M. Protected natural areas incl.national parks; geographical methods of their planning, design, and conservation. Chief Scientist. *B.*9 March 1937, Moscow, Russia. Russian. *D.: s.* **Education:** Moscow SU BSc (Geog.) 1960, PhD(Landscape Geog.) 1979, upgrading courses in Biogeog.& Bot. **Experience:** res.— geogl & biol diversity & prot.areas; tech.& consult.— nat.parks' planning & design; admin.— Chief, Sci.Info.Dept. **Career:** Sr Sci. 1980–90, Chief Sci.1990–, Res.Inst.on Nature Cons.& Reserves; State Expert on envl problems, Mins of Econ.and Construction. **Achievements:** developing the system of Nat.Parks for Russia, formulating policies & prescriptions in this field; designing rep.system of prot.areas for regns of Caucasus, Middle Asia, Siberia, etc. **Memberships:** Res. Inst.of Nature Cons.& Reserves (Scientific Bd) 1990–, All-Russian Cons. Soc.(C.Bd.), Sci.– Tech.Council), IUCN CNPPA 1991–, USSR Fndn of Culture (Council on Unique Areas) 1985–91. **Publications:** incl.*Nat. Parks* (in Russian) 1987, *Travel to Nat.Parks* (co-Author, in Russian) 1991; Ed.of several vols of articles & reports; 90+ scientific & review articles. Favours news media support. **Languages:** English (spoken), French (read), German (read), Russian. Willing to act as consult.&/or to judge proposals. **Address:** Znamenskoye Sadki (Research Institute on Nature Conservation and Reserves), Moscow 113628, Russia. **Tel.** (office) 7 095 423 0322 & 1301, (home) 7 095 311 9763; **fax** 7 095 423 2322.

ZALAORAS, Nicholas. Environment; ecology. Press Officer. *B.*8 Aug.1947, Athens, Greece. Greek. *M.*Elli. **Education:** Aristotelian U.of Thessaloniki, BSc(For.) 1972. **Career:** envl journalist on staff of daily newspaper 'AVGHI' 1979–90; Press Officer, Greek radio 1988– and WWF Greece 1992–. **Achievement:** first journalist resp.for perm.envl/ecol pp.in daily press which started in April 1980. **Membership:** Athenian Journalists' Assn. **Awards:** Global 500 Roll of Honour (UNEP) 1988. **Publications:** incl.The forests: the silent tragedy or the end of life 1991. **Languages:** English, Greek. Willing to act as consult.etc. **Address:** 52 Xanthou, Perissos, 142 32 Athens, Greece. **Tel.**(office) 30 1 363 4661, (home) 30 1 275 0763; **fax** 30 1 362 3342 (WWF Greece).

ZAMCHIYA, David Makhumbini. Environmental legislation. Director & Secretary, Partner. *B.*17 July 1940, Chipinge, Zimbabwe. Zimbab-

wean. *M.*Josephine T.: 2 *s.*, 3 *d.* **Education:** U.of Bristol, LLB 1964; LSE, LLM 1966; Gray's Inn (London) Barrister-at-Law 1966. **Experience:** drafting legis.; admin. **Career:** Perm.Sec. Min.of Justice 1982–9; Senator 1989–90; Dir/Sec. Envt Dev.Activities (ENDA) 1983–; Partner, Stumbles & Rowe 1993–, all in Zimbabwe. **Achievement:** co-Founder of Envt Dev.Activities (ENDA, Zimbabwe) 1983. **Memberships:** IUCN CEL, Perm.Court of Arbitration (The Hague), Hon. Soc.of Gray's Inn. Favours pers.pub.& news media support. **Language:** English. Willing to act as consult.etc. **Address:** 24 Elston Road, Chisipite, Harare, Zimbabwe. **Tel.**(office) 263 4 738903, (home) 263 4 494061; **fax** 263 4 738903.

ZHANG, Jia-shun. Growing flowers; planting trees; keeping birds. Vice-Director. *B.*10 June 1938, Yingshang Co., Anhui Prov., PRC. Chinese. *M.*Han Wei-ying: 2 *s.* **Education:** Yingshang U. Sr Agronomist 1993. **Career:** Head of Xiao Zhang Zhuang Village 1962–84 and of Xie Qiao Town Govt 1984–6; Dep. County Head, Yingshang Co.Govt 1986–. **Achievements:** in mid-1970s estab.model village based on comp. principles for integrated dev.of agric.incl.soil improvement, harnessing of water for irrigation, village planning and biol reconstruction through tree planting & animal husbandry. **Memberships:** IBA, ABI (Res.Bd of Advisers). **Awards:** Global 500 Roll of Honour (UNEP) 1992, Nat.Model Worker. **Publications:** incl.*Xiao Zhang Zhuang's Ecol Agric.* Favours pers.pub.& news media support. **Language:** Chinese. Willing to act as consult.etc. **Address:** Anhui, Yingshang County, People's Republic of China. **Tel.**(office) 86 5687 413646, (home) 86 5687 413648; **fax** 86 5687 413518.

ZHANG, Mrs Ping. National parks and protected areas; forest environment. Assistant Professor. *B.*21 Oct.1956, Beijing, PRC. Chinese. *F.*ather Zhang Wan-ru *qv.* *M.*Chen Kai: *d.* **Education:** He Bei Chem.Engg Coll. BSc 1982; Chinese Min.of For. English Training Centre, English Cert.1986, Math.Stats Training Course, Stats Cert.1987; U.of Edinburgh (UK), Vis. Scholar in Forest Site Sci.1993. **Experience:** res.— field-work in Chinese prot.and forest areas 1982–; teaching cons.training courses. **Career:** Asst.Lect.1982–7 & Asst Prof.1987–91, Dept of Forest Ecol., Asst Prof. Inst.of Forest Envt 1992–, all at CAF. **Achievements:** forecast of nat.envl qual.in China in AD 2000; cons. monitoring and database; analysis & assessment of forest envl background; air poll.and forest declining; forest soil class.system in China, ref. materials of forest soil. **Memberships:** IUCN CNPPA, CSE, CSF. **Awards:** Third Grade Award for an excellent thesis (Inst.of For. CAF) 1991; Scientific Award (Chinese Min.of For.) 1992. **Publications:** Studies on Estab.Chinese Monitoring System of Prot.Areas and Centre Database, 20+ papers. Indiff.to pers.pub.& news media support. **Languages:** Chinese, English.

Willing to act as consult.etc. **Address:** The Institute of Forest Environment, The Chinese Academy of Forestry, Beijing 100091, People's Republic of China. **Tel.**(office) 86 10 258 2211 ext.284, (home) 86 10 258 2211 ext.906; **fax** 86 10 258 2317.

ZHANG, Professor Wan Ru. Forest soil science, forest soil resources; ecology, environment; forest soil management. Emeritus Professor of Forest Soils. *B.*23 Oct.1926, Zhejiang, PRC. Chinese. *M.*Ding Shuiting (xylotomist): *s.*, 2 *d.*incl. Zhang Ping *qv.* **Education:** Shenyang Agricl U. BSc 1953. **Experience:** 40 yrs' forest soil res.in China; admin. **Career:** Min.of For.1953–7; Vis. Scholar, Moscow U.& USSR AS 1957–60; Prof.of Forest Soil Sci. CAF 1978–; VC Academic Cttee of Red-soil Ecol. Opening Experimental Station, Chinese AS 1990–. **Achievements:** basic res.on relation of forest & soil, Chief Ed.*Forest Soils in China and Nat.Standard Analysis Methods of Forest Soil*; forest site class.eval.& estab.of forest site class.system in China. **Memberships:** ISSS, CSSS (Standing Council Memb.& Chairman Forest Soil Comm.), CSF (Council & Chairman Forest Soil Comm.), Beijing SSS (VP). **Awards:** First & Second Prizes of Sci.& Tech. (Min.of For.); Sci.& Tech.Progressing Award (Nat.Tech. Supervisory Bur.); Honour of Spec. Subsidy (Nat.Council, PRC). **Publications:** 11 books incl.*Forest Soil in China* 1986, *Nat. Standard Analysis Methods of Forest Soil* 1987, *Long Term Researching Methods of Forest Soil* 1986, Forest site in China 1991, Ecol mgmt of forest soils 1994, *Forest & Soil* (vols 1–4) 1981, 1985, 1990, 1992; *c.*50 scientific papers; Ed. *Acta Pedologica Sinica* and *Scientia Silvae Sinicae*. **Languages:** Chinese; English & Russian (read & written). Willing to act as consult. etc. **Address:** Department of Forest Soils, Chinese Academy of Forestry, Wan Shou Shan, Beijing, People's Republic of China. **Tel.** (office) 86 10 258 2211, (home) 86 10 258 2211; **fax** 86 10 258 2317.

ZINKE, Alexander. Preservation of threatened ecosystems especially river systems; political lobbying & public awareness-raising. Officer for Central & Eastern Europe. *B.*28 Aug.1958, Saarbrucken, Germany. German. **Education:** Simon Fraser U.1983–4; U.of Saarland, Dipl. (Biogeog.) 1987. **Experience:** public communication of cons.& res.in floodplain ecol., seven yrs in public campaigns against river dev. projects and for rehab.of floodplains; consult.to NGOs in c.& e.Europe. **Career:** Communications Officer, WWF Inst.for Floodplains Ecol.1986–9; WWF campaign saving Austrian floodplains 1990; Officer for C.& Eastern Europe, WWF 1990–. **Achievements:** co-init. of 'Ecol Bricks for Our Common House of Europe' movement, co-Org.of intl campaigns against Loire & Danube hydro-dams. **Memberships:** WWF C.& Eastern Europe Adv.Group 1991–, IUCN CNPPA 1991–. **Publications:** *Ecol Bricks for Our Common House of Europe* (co-Author) 1990. Fa-

vours pers.pub.& news media support. **Languages:** English, French, German. Willing to act as consult.etc. **Address:** WWF Austria, POB 1, A-1162 Vienna, Austria. **Tel.**(office) 43 1 409 1641, (home) 43 1 822 0982; **fax** 43 1 409 164129.

ZLOTIN, Dr Roman Isaevich. Terrestrial ecology, biogeography; biodiversity conservation; degradation of environment by human activity. Head of Department. *B.*22 Nov.1940, Moscow, Russia. Russian. *M.*Sonja: *s.*Alexey (geog. student). **Education:** Moscow SU BSc(Geog.) 1963, Inst.of Geog. Russian AS PhD(Biogeog.& Soil Geog.) 1970–75. **Experience:** res.— field experimental terr.ecol., spatial structure & functioning of terr.ecosystems of diff.biomes (tundra, taiga, broad-leafed forests, steppes, deserts, mtns, rain- & trop.-forests); teaching. **Career:** Jr Researcher 1963–9, Main Researcher 1976–82, Head Dept of Biogeog.1983–, Inst.of Geog. Russian AS; Prof. Sch.of Public & Envl Affairs, Indiana U. 1992–93. **Achievements:** basic res.on spatial structure dynamic functioning on tundra, forest, steppe, deserts, high-mtn ecosystems; scientific approaches to biodiv. cons.in prot.natural areas. **Memberships:** IGBP SSC Core Project 'Global Change & Terr. Ecosystems', IUCN CNPPA. **Publications:** four monogrs incl.*Role of Animals in Functioning of Forest–Steppe Ecosystems* 1980; Edl Bds *INSTAAR* & *Isvestiya* (seriya Geographica); *c.*250 papers. Active re.pers.pub.& news media support. **Languages:** English, Russian. Willing to ref.papers. **Address:** Institute of Geography, Russian Academy of Sciences, Staromonetry 19, Moscow 17, Russia. **Tel.**(office) 7 095 131 9175, (home) 7 095 238 2727; **fax** 7 095 230 2090; **e-mail** <<Earth@ glas.ape.org>> .

ZOUHA, Sekkou. Desertification control: sand-dune fixation & reforestation of arid zones. Forestry Technician & Chief of District. *B.*5 Jan.1947, Morocco. Moroccan. *M.*Fadma: 2 *s.*, 4 *d.* **Education:** R.For.Sch. Dipl.1965. **Experience:** 26 yrs in desert.control of Draa 1965–87 and Ziz 1987– Valleys. **Career:** Forester & Field Dir, Eaux et Forêts 1965–. **Achievements:** prot.of Draa & Ziz Oases from desert. **Membership:** G500F. **Award:** Global 500 Roll of Honour (UNEP) 1987. Favours pers.pub.& news media support. **Languages:** Arabic, English (fair), French. Willing to act as consult.etc. **Address:** Eaux et Forêts, BP 41, Errchidia, Morocco. **Tel.**(office) 212 5 572147.

ZSÖGÖN, Dr Silvia JAQUENOD DE. Environmental law. Independent Adviser. *B.*1957, Córdoba, Argentina. Argentinian, Spanish. *M.* Esteban Zsögön Benczik (EIA and territorial planning). **Education:** Universidad Nacional de Córdoba, Lawyer & Procurator 1980; Universidad Complutense de Madrid, Doctorate in Law *cum laude* 1988, M(Envl Sci.) 1989. **Experience:** 14 yrs' res., consult., envl law training in developed & developing countries. **Career:**

Private Lawyer & Procurator 1980–, Legal Adv.to NGOs 1980–85 & Argentine Govt 1984, Private Consult.to NGOs & govtl agencies in Spain 1986–, Consult.in Envl Law for IUCN CEL 1988– & ICEL 1993–, Lect.of u.post-grad.courses 1988–, res.for Nature, Man & War (U.of Hawaii project) 1992–. **Achievements:** basic res.& divulgation in envl law (scholarship, postgrad.& u.levels). **Memberships:** IUCN CEL, IAIA, ICEL, EIA Trainers' Network Center, ELNI. **Awards:** Premio Príncipe de Asturias (Intl Award, for young investigators of Nature) 1984, Quinto Centenario (Natural Resources in Latin Amer.) 1990. **Publications:** incl.*Envl Law and Its Main Principles* 1988, 1989, 1991. Indiff. to pers.pub.& news media support. **Languages:** English (good), German (good), Spanish. Willing to act as consult.etc. **Address:** Princesa Nr 27-Planta 20-Apto 11, Iz 28008, Madrid, Spain. **Tel.** (office) 34 1 541 9244 ext.233, (home) & **fax** 34 1 559 1595.

zu **HÜLSHOFF, Dr Bernd** von **Droste,** *see* **HÜLSHOFF, Dr Bernd** von **Droste zu.**

ZWAHLEN, Dr Robert. Environmental impact assessment especially for water resources' development projects (hydropower, irrigation) in tropical & temperate environments. Lecturer, Head of Department. *B.*19 May 1947, Saanen, Switzerland. Swiss. *M.*Anna Rosa: *d., s.* **Education:** U.of Bern MSc(Biol.) 1972, PhD (Wild-life Ecol.) 1974; Swiss Trop.Inst. postgrad. course in vector- & water-borne trop. diseases 1981. **Experience:** consult.— envl impact studies on wide range of dev.& infrastructure projects, mostly as team leader, in Europe, Africa, Latin Amer., & Asia; teaching biol.at coll.level & EIA methodology at tech. high sch.level. **Career:** teacher in biol. 1970–77; specialist in terr.ecol., later Head of Ecol.Dept, in an intlly-active Swiss engg firm 1977–89; Partner, Ecosens 1989–94; Lect.in EIA at Tech. High Schools of Vaduz (Liechtenstein) & Chur (Switzerland) 1992–; Head of Dept of Ecol. Elektrowatt Ingenieurunternehmung (Electro-watt Engg Services) AG 1995–. **Achievements:** assisted in more envlly-friendly realization of nr of projects, contributed to abandonment of some projects for envl reasons. **Memberships:** BES, Wildlife Soc.(USA), Gesellschaft für Oekologie, INTECOL, IAIA, ISEE. **Publications:** *Tier-kunde* (= *Zool.*, sch.textbook Ed.) 1987, The ecol.of Rawa Aopa, a peat-swamp in Sulawesi, Indonesia 1992, Failure of irrigation projects & consequences for a diff.approach: a case study 1992; *c.*10 other papers. Positive attitude towards news media support. **Languages:** English, French, German, Indonesian (basic), Italian (basic), Spanish. Willing to act as consult.etc. **Address:** Elektrowatt Ingenieurunternehmung, POB, CH-8034 Zürich, Switzerland. **Tel.**(office) 41 1 385 3113, (home) 41 1 935 3057; **fax** 41 1 385 2653.

CLARK, Professor Dr William C. Environment and development, global environmental policy; adaptive management. Professor & Centre Director. *B.*20 Dec. 1948, Greenwick, CT, USA. American. *M.*Anna: 2 *s.* **Education:** Yale U. BSc 1971, U.of BC PhD 1979. **Experience:** res.and teaching. **Career:** Res. Scholar & Project Leader, IIASA 1973–4, 1978–9, 1984–7; Res.Sci. Inst.for Energy Analysis 1981–4, Prof.& Dir of Center for Sci.& Intl Affairs, Kennedy Sch. of Govt 1987–, Harvard U. **Award:** MacArthur Prize 1983. **Publications:** *Adaptive Envl Assessment & Mgmt* (co-Ed.) 1979, *Carbon Dioxide Review* 1982, *Sust.Dev.of the Biosphere* 1985, *The Earth as Transformed by Human Action* 1992; Ed. *Envt* magazine 1985–. Dislikes pers.pub.& news media support. **Languages:** English, German. **Address:** Kennedy School of Government, 79 Kennedy Street, Cambridge, Massachusetts 02138, USA. **Tel.**1 617 495 3981; **fax** 1 617 495 8963.

GRASSL, Professor Dr Hartmut. Climate research, global change research, remote sensing with satellites. World Climate Research Programme Director. *B.*18 March 1940, Salzburg, Berchtesgaden, Germany. German. *M.*Renate: *d.* **Education:** U.of Munich, Dipl.in Phys. 1966, PhD(Met.) 1970; U.of Hamburg, Habil. 1978. **Experience:** res.in radiative transfer, climate modelling, satellite remote-sensing; orgn of scientific expedns; dir of res.depts at Max-Planck Inst. **Career:** Jr Sci. U.of Mainz 1971–6; Sr Sci. Max-Planck Inst.for Met. (Hamburg) 1976–81; Prof.of Theoretical Met. U.of Kiel 1981–4; Dir, Inst.of Phys. GKSS Res.Centre (Geesthacht) 1984–8; Prof.of Met.& Dir, U.of Hamburg 1988–94; Dir, World Climate Res. Prog. WMO 1994–. **Achievements:** measurement of water vapour continuum in the atmos., gen. influence on radiation budget, measurement of cool skin of ocean; global aerosol modelling, surface energy fluxes from satellites; Chairman of Global Change Adv.Bd to German Govt*.

Memberships: Max-Planck Soc.(Scientific Memb.), German Met.Soc., *Global Change Adv. Bd (Govt of Germany, Chair 1992–4). **Awards:** Jr Sci.Award (German Met.Soc.) 1971, Max-Planck-Prize (Humboldt Fndn) 1991. **Publications:** num.since 1970 incl. Remote Sensing and Global Climate Change: Water Cycle and Energy Budget 1991, The measurement of turbulent surface-layer fluxes by use of bichromatic scintillation (co-Author) 1992, Envl Aspects of Orbital Transport 1993, *Warm Pool Heat Budget and Shortwave Cloud Forcing: A Missing Physics?* (co-Author) 1995. Indiff.to pers.pub. but favours news media support. **Languages:** English, French, German. Further details may be obtained from *Who's Who in Sci.& Tech.*1993, *Who's Who in Germany* 1994. Willing to act as consult.etc. **Address:** World Meteorological Organization, Case Postale 2300, CH-1211 Geneva 2, Switzerland. **Tel.** (office) 41 22 730 8246, (home) 49 40 422 9263; **fax** 41 22 734 0357.

Appendix I — by Country

ALGERIA

CHALABI, Bouzid — animal conservation; conservation & management of national parks & protected areas; conservation of water-birds & wetlands; legislation re.conservation of Nature & environment

DAMERDJI, M. Amine — afforestation & soil preservation against erosion, combatting desertification; leguminous, rhizobium, & mycorrhization, systems approaches for agricultural development in the Sahara; soil physics & improvement; traditional irrigation in oases and their rehabilitation; water harvesting & supply; water problems essentially in arid & semi-arid countries

ANTIGUA (Leeward Islands), West Indies

JAMES, Philmore A. — ecotourism; environmental studies

ARGENTINA

CANO, Guillermo J. — environmental law — national & international

CAPPATO, Jorge A. — environmental communication, education, information, & journalism

GOODALL, R. Natalie Prosser — flora, marine mammals (esp. cetaceans), & history, of southernmost South America

GRINBERG, Miguel — education; social ecology

HERKOVITS, Jorge — chemical safety, ecotoxicology

MORELLO, Jorge X. — ecological consequences of land-use changes in Latin America

OJEDA, Ricardo A. — biodiversity; ecology, biogeography, & conservation, of mammals; ecological management of watersheds; field biology

TARAK, Pedro — environmental law

AUSTRALIA

Australian Capital Territory

BRIDGEWATER, Peter — biodiversity conservation & management; conservation & management of mangrove & saltmarsh; landscape ecology & vegetation; seascape ecology

CULLEN, Peter W. — eutrophication; public involvement; state of environment reporting; water quality & catchment planning

FENNER, Frank — biological control of animal pests; conservation of biodiversity; infectious diseases of humans and animals

GOOD, Roger B. — alpine ecology (plant distributions & origins); biodiversity assessment & research; fire research (natural fire regimes and plant responses); land-use management & planning

HIBBERD, John K. — conservation resource assessment & planning; ecological survey; GIS & remote sensing; sustainable forest management

KENCHINGTON, Richard A. — coastal & marine resources' conservation & management; marine sciences

OVINGTON, John D. — aboriginal interests; environmental assessment & programmes; forest ecology; international aid; sustained natural-resource use

New South Wales

ARMSTRONG, Geoffrey J. — forest & national-park recreation, voluntary involvement in conservation issues & organizations

BENSON, John S. — environmental policy; research on threatened plant species; terrestrial plant ecology; vegetation survey & mapping

BIRCH, L. Charles — population ecology

BOER, Bernhard W. — environmental law

BOYD, William 'Bill' E. — archaeology; Australian Arboriginal studies; cultural heritage management; environmental archaeology, Quaternary environmental science

DORMAN, John — environmental planning & catchment management; Nature conservation

FOX, Allan M. — development of ecotourism programmes; education & training of Aboriginal natural-resource managers; environmental management plans for industrial projects; Nature reserve and park interpretation & management; writing & illustrating guide & natural-history books

FRY, Ian W. — environment & development assistance issues; environmental law advocacy, development, & training

LACY, Terry P. DE — heritage education; research in Nature conservation and protected area management; parks; tourism

SAENGER, Peter — coastal-zone management, coral-reef & mangrove ecology; environmental law; wetlands' management

SINCLAIR, John — conservation of Fraser Island; ecotactics, ecotourism; environmental strategies

SPATE, Andy P. — conservation & management of caves, Karst & cave biota, Antarctic geomorphology & limnology; impacts of human use of Antarctic & alpine environments

TROMPF, Garry W. — research & writing on religions & environmental concerns

WHITEHOUSE, John F.   environmental law & planning; natural & cultural resources' management; protected areas

Queensland

BAINES, Graham B.K.   sustainable resource management of tropical land & marine ecosystems with special interest in customary land & marine tenure and indigenous knowledge

BAKER, Joseph 'Joe' T.   coastal-zone management; ecologically-sustainable development; interdisciplinary studies and their application to human needs; marine natural product chemistry; total river catchment management

BARNES, David J.   calcification & growth in scleractian corals; environmental records stored in coral skeletons

BEETON, Robert J.S.   environmental policy esp.in context of managing fragmented landscapes; environmental problem-solving; protected area management; training

BOYLAND, Desmond E.   conservation administration; land use; organizational structures; wetlands

BRENNAN, Ngairetta J.   environment; landcare

BUCKLEY, Ralf C.   ecology, ecotourism, environment & trade; environmental economics, law, & management

COVACEVICH, Jeannette A.   aboriginal history, medicine (esp. following envenomation), and adaptations to life in deserts & in rain-forests; taxonomy & zoogeography of extant & extinct Australian reptiles — esp.those of deserts, heaths, & rain-forest

CRAIK, Wendy   community involvement in planning; marine areas and recreational-tourism management

DAVIE, James D.S.   conservation management, planning, & science, in tropical coastal environments esp.concerning issues of human use, development, application of law, environmental decision-making, & ethics

HOOPER, John N.A.   systematics, biogeography, ecology, and chemical ecology, of Porifera; tropical Porifera

INGRAM, Glen J.   biogeography, evolution, & systematics, of birds, frogs, reptiles, & slaters (woodlice etc.)

KETO, Aila   ecologically-sustainable use of native forests; Nature conservation esp.of rain-forests; world heritage

KOZLOWSKI, Jerzy (also under **POLAND**)   methodology of urban & environmental planning

MARSH, Helene D.   coastal-zone management, ecology of Dugongs & sea turtles and their habitats; wildlife management

MESSEL, Harry   Australian (northern) tidal waterways and their crocodile populations

PETER, Ian W.   computer communications re.environmental research, rain-forest, ecologically-sustainable development, information; information technology

PETR, Tomislav O.   inland-fisheries and interactions with environment

RAVEN, Robert J.   role of spiders, esp.Mygalomorphae, in questions of biodiversity, conservation, phylogeny, biogeography, & human envenomation

ROOM, Peter M.   biological control of weeds; insect–plant interactions; plant responses to damage

SATTLER, Paul S.   conservation policy development, establishment & selection of national park & protected area systems; Nature conservation planning, use of native wildlife (Kangaroos) to achieve ecologically-sustainable use of semi-arid lands

SPECHT, Raymond L.   biogeography; conservation; ethnobotany; history of Australian ecology; plant ecology

STANTON, James P.   habitat management in protected areas; surveys for assessment of natural resources

TISDELL, Clement A.   economics of conservation; environmental & marine resource economics

VANTIER, Lyndon M. DE   human & natural impacts on coral-reef ecosystems — particularly the effects of *Acanthaster* population outbreaks, coral bleaching, & reef symbioses associations

VERON, John E.N.   coral biogeography & taxonomy, evolutionary mechanisms, systematics, & conservation

WEBB, Leonard J.   research in ethnobotany & phytochemistry; Nature conservation; rainforest ecology; environmental education, ecophilosophy, & ecotheology

WILKINSON, Clive R.   coral-reef ecology; tropical coastal resource management

WOLANSKI, Eric J.   coastal, coral-reef, & mangrove, oceanography; Man's impact on tropical marine environment

South Australia

HEATHCOTE, Ronald L.   arid-land management; environmental perception; historical geography; natural hazards

WILLIAMS, Martin A.J.   desertification; environmental management in Africa, Asia, & Australia; landforms; soils & climatic change in arid & semi-arid areas

WILLIAMS, William D.   salt lakes; water resources in dry lands

Tasmania

DAVIS, Bruce W.   environmental management; natural resources' policy

JOHANNES, Robert E.   traditional marine ecological knowledge & resource management systems in the tropics, and their practical value today

MILNE, Christine   green politics

Victoria

CASWELL, Patricia J.   economy; environment; equity & management

KEAGE, Peter L.   alpine & polar environmental management; antarctic conservation; ecotourism; glaciology; natural resources' management & impact assessment

MOSLEY, John G.   Antarctica; landscape protection; national parks; national self-sufficiency; Nature conservation

NICHOLLS, Frank G.   environmental law

WESCOTT, Geoffrey C.   ecotourism; marine conservation; national park & protected area planning & management; coastal-zone management

Western Australia

BEARD, John S.   biogeography; ecological botany; vegetation mapping

BURBIDGE, Andrew A.   conservation of threatened species & ecosystems, mammals, & reptiles

HOBBS, Richard J.   biological invasions; conservation biology; fragmented ecosystems; restoration ecology; vegetation management

WATSON, John R.   Biosphere reserves, caves, conservation reserves; land management; mountains, recreation

WILSON, George R.   Aborigines — Aboriginal enterprise development, commercial use of wild animal resources, & sustainable land-use; aerial surveys; disease & quarantine management — risk assessment, wild animal management; endangered species; Kangaroos — aerial surveys, multiple land-use, & sustainable resource management; livestock production; rangeland science; strategic analysis and sustainable development; wild animal conservation

AUSTRIA

NILSSON, Sten   natural resources and their exploitation, environment (forest sector), policies, sustainability economics, & systems analysis

STOIBER, Hans H.   Nature conservation; description & evaluation of protected areas

ZINKE, Alexander   political lobbying, preservation of threatened ecosystems esp.river systems, public awareness-raising

BAHAMAS, West Indies

HOLOWESKO, Lynn P.   conservation of natural resources; environmental law; national parks; seabirds of the Bahamas; sustainable development

BAHRAIN, State of

ALNASER, Waheeb E.   environmental physics, estimating potential of solar, wind, tidal, water current, & wave, energy in Bahrain as these energies are pollution-free & non-depleting; correlating the climatic parameters with astronomical parameters such as cosmic radiation, ultraviolet solar radiation, and noise pollution

EKARATH, Raveendran   management of air, soil, waste, & water; environmental pollution monitoring; standards; legislation; laboratory management

OSMAN, Salih M.   environmental economics & management

BANGLADESH

HUQ, Saleemul   climate change impacts; environmental planning & management

MOUDUD, Hasna J.   coastal & cultural ecology; Law of the Sea; mangrove & coastal afforestation; marine environment, policy, planning, & environmental guidelines; sharing common river water; women & environment

SAMAD, Syed A.   community development, ecological development; economic reforms; information technology; planning; privatization; public finance; sustainable development; urban & regional economics

SHEIKH, Muhammad A.R.   environmental education; research; wetland management; wildlife conservation

BARBADOS, West Indies

BRERETON, Vera A.   human resource development; ecotourism

HOWELL, Calvin   environmental education; public awareness

BELGIUM

BOURDEAU, Philippe F.   ecology; environmental management

CHARLIER, Roger H.L.   coastal protection, coastal-zone management; alternative energies; environmental auditing

DUMONT, Henri J.   conservation of main aquatic biotopes of Arabian peninsula, Sahara, & Sahel; Odonata; zooplankton

DUNLOP, Nicholas J.   coordination of Earth Action Network
  (also under **UNITED KINGDOM, *England***)
HENS, Luc   human ecology
JUDGE, Anthony J.   organization of interdisciplinary information
LINET, Christiane   conservation
VERSCHUREN,   Chiroptera, conservation & problems of environment; creation & management
  Jacques C.F.   of national parks — Africa, research in national parks; * ungulates

BERMUDA
WINGATE, David B.   birds, conservation, restoration ecology

BOLIVIA
AUGSTBURGER, Franz   control of organic production, ecofarming
WESTREICHER,   environmental law — soil, forest, protected areas, biodiversity
  Antonio ANDALUZ

BRAZIL

Amazonas
CLEMENT, Charles R.   crop origins and biodiversity, plant genetic resources' conservation
FEARNSIDE, Philip M.   causes, rates, & impacts, of tropical deforestation; greenhouse gas emissions,
                               human carrying capacity; impacts of hydroelectric dams

Bahia
MARCOVALDI,   conservation & management of Marine Turtles off coast of Brazil
  Guy M.F. GUAGNI DEI &
MARCOVALDI,
  Maria Â. GUAGNI DEI

Brasilia DF
MARTINS,   Nature conservation, sustainable use of natural resources
  Edouardo DE SOUZA

Minas Gerais
FONSECA, Gustavo A.B.   biodiversity conservation, wildlife conservation & management, interdiscipli-
                               nary approaches to biodiversity conservation & sustainable development
FONSECA, Ivan C.M.DA   environment, Nature conservation, rain forest on Atlantic Coast of Brazil

Paraná
BRANDINI, Frederico   marine pelagic ecosystems of tropical & antarctic environments

Rio de Janeiro
CÂMARA, Ibsen de G.   conservation of natural ecosystems & protected areas
CORRAL, Thais   women — communication, environment, health
LACERDA, Luiz D.   biogeochemistry of coastal systems, heavy-metal contamination in tropical eco-
                               systems, Hg contamination in Amazon Basin

Rio Grande do Sul
LUTZENBERGER,   alternative sanitary engineering, environmental activism, landscaping, recycling
  José A.   of industrial waste, regenerative agriculture, sustainable development

Santa Catarina
FISCHER, Gert R.   autochthonous tropical forest management & conservation, environmental con-
                               servation, soil recovery agriculture and forestry; biological pest control

São Paulo
DIEGUES, Antonio C.S.   coastal planning, maritime anthropology, wetland inventories & studies
GOLDEMBERG, José   energy strategies & technology, environmental degradation & education; physics
MENDEZ,   environmental education, resource planning & policy, training park personnel
  Jesus M. DELGADO
PERES, Carlos A.   conservation biology, tropical ecology
  (also under **UNITED KINGDOM, *England***)
SILVA, Ricardo FREIRE DA   sustainable utilization of wildlife

BRITISH VIRGIN ISLANDS, West Indies
POTTER, Louis   development planning, project review, regulation development

---

* To have persisted, beyond this point in Appendix I and the corresponding Biographies, in substituting semi-colons for commas to indicate all major changes in subject, would have delayed publication unduly to correct a fault which we intend to remedy throughout the Second Edition. — Ed.

BRUNEI, SULTANATE OF
EATON, Peter P.   environmental management in Southeast Asia & South Pacific regions, national parks, protected areas

BURMA, *see* **MYANMAR**

BURUNDI
NTAHUGA, Laurent   biodiversity issues; environment & development; protection of wildlife

CAMEROON
NJE, Ngog   terrestrial animal ecology

CANADA

Alberta
BUTLER, James 'Jim' R.   conservation education, ecotourism, endangered species' conservation, interpretation, old-growth forest wildlife ecology, park & protected areas' management, teaching & research in parks, wildlife, & environmental conservation
FEICK, Jenny L.   ecosystem management, environmental citizenship, environmental education & heritage interpretation, protected areas' management, practical applications of ecologically-sustainable development
HERRERO, Stephen M.   conservation biology, special expertise re.ecology & management of carnivores esp.bears, management & planning of natural areas
HOLROYD, Geoffrey L.   avian ecology, temperate & tropical conservation
KUMAR, Prem   EIA and foreign aid, forest resource planning
MOORE, James W.   aquatic ecology esp. of arctic & subarctic waters, chemical contaminants of surface water, environmental management, large dams, regulatory toxicology

British Columbia
BENNETT, Sara L.   environmental aspects of international agriculture, water resources, transportation/navigation & sectoral/regional planning projects, preparation & management of project environmental components, field studies, impact assessments & EIA training, wetland & biodiversity resource assessments & management strategies
BLOOMFIELD, Michael I.   environmental education, philanthropy, sustainability, wilderness & wildlife
CRAMPTON, Colin B.   archaeology, forestry, geology, geomorphology, land classification, palynology, permafrost, soils, toxicology; ecological interactions of these earth sciences with *native* Canadian perceptions (oral traditions) of environmental conservation in western Canada related to *European* Canadian written traditions with their respect for organized science
DEARDEN, Philip   ecotourism, national parks, poverty, biodiversity & development in highland SE Asia, watershed management
GARDNER, Julia E.   adult environmental education, environmental NGOs, environmental planning & policy, public participation in environmental decision-making, sustainable development
HUSBAND, Vicky   old growth forests, wilderness, & wildlife, in British Columbia, temperate rainforest survival, educating federal & provincial governments and public
JOHNSTON, Douglas M.   Arctic, Asia–Pacific region, coastal & marine management, international environmental law, Law of the Sea
OKE, Timothy R.   urban climates & microclimates
TINKER, Jon   aids, information, sustainable development

Manitoba
BERKES, Fikret   common property resources
HARDI, Peter   central European environment, measuring indicators & performance, sustainable development including project design
SINGH, Naresh   ecosystem health, poverty and sustainable livelihoods, sustainable development
SMIL, Václav   interdisciplinary studies of environment–energy–food–economy interactions

Nova Scotia
BOARDMAN, Robert   environmental policy & law, Nature conservation
BORGESE, Elisabeth M.   Law of the Sea
DODDS, Donald G.   forest–wildlife relationships, integrated resource management, mammalian reproduction & behaviour, wildlife management & policy

Ontario
ARGUS, George W.   taxonomy of *Salix* in the New World, conservation of rare & endangered vascular plants in Canada
BEZANSON, Keith A.   environmental administration & education
CACCIA, Charles R.   adult education, forestry

FENGE, Terence A.E.	industrial development and environmental planning & management in Yukon, NWT, Nunavut, and the Arctic circumpolar world; rights and interests of aboriginal peoples; political development in the circumpolar Arctic, aboriginal self-government in Canada; protected areas, marine policy
FORBES, Bruce C.	arctic biogeography, disturbance ecology [now in Finland]
FUREDY, Christine	community-based environmental management in urban Asia, developing countries, ecology of cities, waste management in developing countries, waste recycling
GALLON, Gary T.	environmental assessment & policy development, environmental association- and organization-building, public participation
HACKMAN, Arlin C.	Canadian protected areas' system
HARE, F. Kenneth	climatology (northern & arid climates, heat & water balances) and environmental matters, energy policy, safety of nuclear power
HUMMEL, Solon L.	conservation
KEATING, Michael	conservation, environment
LUK, Shiu-hung	land degradation & management, management of environment in China, soil conservation & erosion
MacNEILL, James W.	environment, sustainable development
MALCOLM, Jay R.	conservation & ecology of mammals
MARSH, John	parks, sustainable development, tourism
McALLISTER, Donald E.	biodiversity, conservation, conservation of coral-reef ecosystems, environmental education, taxonomic ichthyology
McEACHERN, John D. (also under **NEPAL**)	coastal-zone management, economic impacts of large-capital projects (dams, pipelines, oil & gas exploration), field implementation of NCSs (planning & implementation)
NELSON, J. Gordon	assessment of human ecological perspective, coastal areas, environment, land-use resources (research & education), parks, protected areas
ROWLEY, Diana M.R.	arctic science esp.geography & history
ROWLEY, Graham W.	arctic regions, circumpolar peoples esp.Eskimos (Inuit & Yuit)
SLOCOMBE, D. Scott	ecosystem science, environmental planning & management, nonequilibrium systems theory, sustainability
STRONG, Maurice F.	environmental administration, farming
SVOBODA, Josef	arctic ecology: colonization & revegetation of polar deserts, ecosystems of polar oases, primary productivity, primary succession following deglaciation, toxic fallout
VALLENTYNE, John R.	environmental education, planetary ecology
VOLLENWEIDER, Richard A.	environment, limnology

Quebec

CLOUTIER, Antoine	park planning, regional integration
DUFOUR, Jules	environmental & peace education, establishment & management of protected areas, resource management
GRANDTNER, Miroslav M.	dendrology, forest ecology, international forestry
JACOBS, Peter D.A.	conservation & development of open-space systems, environmental assessment planning & management, landscape architecture, sustainable urban development
LEBLANC, Hubert	development, environment
PRESCOTT, Jacques	animal behaviour, biodiversity, mammalogy, wildlife conservation, zoobiology
REEVES, Randall R.	preservation of wild places & wildlife
THOMAS, Urs P.	global environmental governance particularly trade–environment linkage, institutional & political dimensions of international environmental affairs

Saskatchewan

CATANIA, Peter J.	energy & environment and international exchanges, systems engineering education, renewable energy
ROBARTS, Richard D.	freshwater & marine microbial ecology, impacts of UV radiation and microbial biogeochemical cycles in prairie saline lakes & prairie wetlands
STEWART, John W.B.	interrelationships between C/N/S/P biogeochemical cycles as influenced by anthropogenic activities

Canary Islands, see **SPAIN**

CAYMAN ISLANDS, *British West Indies*

JAMES, W. Clive	international agricultural research & development, transfer of agri-biotechnology applications

Channel Islands, see **UNITED KINGDOM**

CHILE

DIAZ, José VALENCIA — antarctic Penguins, ecology of feeding & reproduction of Chilean birds, reptiles & amphibians, and their conservation

DONOSO, Claudio — forest dynamics & ecology, variation, genecology, plantations with native Chilean species

NOVOA, Laura — education for democracy, environmental law, governability, human rights, implementation of Agenda 21, partnerships with civil society organizations, poverty, sustainable development, women

STUTZIN, Godofredo — conservation of fauna & flora, environmental law

CHINA, PEOPLE'S REPUBLIC OF

CHEN, Changdu — conservation, ecology

JIANG, Gaoming — environmental, plant, & pollution, ecology, urban ecology & botany

LI, Shuang Liang — harnessing & utilization of waste

LI, Wenhua — agroforestry, forest ecology, Nature conservation, sustainable development

LIU, Peitong — ecologically-sound & sustainable anthropocentric ecosystems, Man and environment

QU, Geping — environmental protection

SU, Jilan — coastal oceanography, marine environmental science

WANG, Sung — biodiversity, mammalian taxonomy, & faunistics, wildlife conservation & management

WANG, Xianpu — biodiversity, natural conservation, vegetation ecology of subtropical & tropical regions

WEN, Boping — comparative, national, & international, environmental law

XU, Ouyong — environmental science

ZHANG, Jia-Shun — growing flowers, keeping birds, planting trees

ZHANG, Ping — forest environment, national parks, protected areas

ZHANG, Wan Ru — forest-soil management, resource, & science; ecology, environment

COLOMBIA

RAMIREZ, José J. ESCOBAR — coastal & marine environments

SANCHEZ, Heliodoro — conservation of biodiversity, national parks, and protected areas

CONGO

NDINGA, Assitou — conservation of fauna, forest policy

N'SOSSO, Dominique — environmental conservation, protected areas' & parks' management

COSTA RICA

BARAHONA-ISRAEL, Rodrigo — environmental & natural-resource law & policy

BUDOWSKI, Gerardo — appropriate land-use including agroforestry, conservation of tropical forests, ecotourism, management of buffer zones & protected areas

CAMINO, Ronnie DE — natural resources' economics, management, & policy

CIFUENTES-ARIAS, Miguel — management & planning of protected areas, teaching re. and technical assistance to protected areas

GONZALEZ, Juan A. AGUIRRE — economics of agroforestry, environmental accounting, pricing, & valuation, project analysis, resource economics

LYNCH, James R. — community development & Nature conservation in the humid neo-tropics

CROATIA

LOVRIC, Andrija Z. — archaeo-ecology, coastal & Mediterranean ecology, palaeocenoses

PRAVDIĆ, Velimir — environmental management, marine environmental research, strategies for environmental management

CZECH REPUBLIC

ČEŘOVSKY, Jan — biodiversity conservation (threatened species, protected areas), environmental education, plant ecology

DEJMAL, Ivan — landscape ecology, territorial systems of ecological stability

MADAR, Zdeněk — European environmental law

MOLDAN, Bedřich — analytical chemistry, biogeochemistry, environment, environmental policy

RYCHNOVSKÁ, Milena — ecological function of grassland in landscape, grassland ecosystems, plant ecophysiology

URBAN, František — ecological forestry, Nature conservation, protected areas & species

DENMARK

HAMANN, Ole J. — botanic gardens, *in situ* & *ex situ* conservation of plants, Galápagos Islands, environmental conservation

KOESTER, Veit — national & international environmental law

MOESTRUP, Søren　　genetic conservation, seed procurement, and tree improvement, in developing countries

DOMINICA, COMMONWEALTH OF
CHRISTIAN, Colmore S.　　conservation, environmental education, EIA, natural resource management, reforestation, wildlife management (birds)

GREGOIRE, Felix W.　　environmental, forest, national park, & natural resources', management

DOMINICAN REPUBLIC
JAKOWSKA, Sophie　　environmental ethics & education, religion-motivated environmental action

ECUADOR
ARMIJOS, Mariano MONTAÑO　　coastal water quality, estuarine ecology, natural resources' management, research management, shrimp industry nutrition & management, technological applications

CANADAY, Christopher　　conservation biology
KAKABADSE, Yolanda　　public participation in sustainable development & environmental issues
SEVILLA, Rogue　　national parks, urban environment

EGYPT
ABDEL-GAWAAD, Ahmed A.-W.　　rural environmental pollution control

ABDELHADY, Abdelaziz (also under KUWAIT)　　national & international environmental law, legal aspects of natural protected areas & wildlife protection

ALI, Abd El moneim M.　　conservation of Nature, environment disinfection, pesticides, 'social' insects and vertebrate pests

BATANOUNY, Kamal H.　　arid lands' ecology, conservation, desert development, desertification, ethics, ethnobotany, human life in deserts, salinity problems in arid regions

GHABBOUR, Samir I.　　animal (soil fauna) & desert ecology, natural resources' conservation
HALIM, Youssef　　management & monitoring of coastal zones
KASSAS, Mohamed EL　　conservation of Nature, desert plant ecology
SPRINGUEL, Irina　　conservation of Nature, desert environment & plant ecology
TOLBA, Mostafa K.　　Development without Destruction, philosophy of environmentally-sound development

EL SALVADOR
ALVAREZ, Juan M.　　protected area management, environmental education, ecotourism
ROSE, Carlos R. HASBÚN　　protection of wildlands, sea-turtle conservation efforts with local communities, wildlife rescue & rehabilitation programmes

ESTONIA
KULL, Kalevi　　'biosemiotics', community modelling, ecology of meadow plants, evolutionary ecology, history of green philosophy, plant community diversity, semiotic mechanisms of biodiversity, theoretical ecology

KULL, Olevi　　pollution impacts on ecosystems & plants, research in plant community ecology
KÜLVIK, Mart　　environment, landscape biology, Nature conservation
MASING, Viktor　　biocoenology, biogeography, geobotany, mire conservation, peatland science (telmatology)

PUNNING, Jaan-Mati　　environmental management, palaeoecology, palaeogeography
RAUKAS, Anto　　environment, Quaternary geology
SEPP, Kalev　　landscape ecology & management in Nature conservation areas, Nature management

ETHIOPIA
ASFAW, Gedion　　policy & strategy development, monitoring, & evaluation, project preparation & appraisal

BAHRI, Ahmed　　development, environment, population
EGZIABHER, Tewolde B. GEBRE　　plant ecology & taxonomy, conservation, sustainable development, biodiversity, biosafety

FIJI
SINGH, Birandra B.　　conservation of ecotourism projects & sanctuaries, preservation of cultural sites and historic buildings & sites

FINLAND
FORBES, Bruce C.　　arctic biogeography, disturbance ecology
HOLLO, Erkki J.　　EIA, environmental, real estate, & water, law, comparative environmental law
HUTTUNEN, Satu　　air pollution/environmental ecology, forest tree ecophysiology
KOZLOV, Mikhail V.　　response of insect populations to industrial pollution, taxonomy & ecology of Lepidoptera

LINDSTRÖM, U.B.   ecological balance sheets, sustainable development esp.energy politics and sustainable agriculture

NUORTEVA, Pekka O.   bioaccumulation of metals in biota, effects of methyl mercury on health, environmental & forensic entomology, holistic aspects on environmental conservation (in a historical perspective of four thousand million years), role of metals in forest decline, subarctic biology

PIIROLA, Jouko   cartography, landscape evolution, Nature reserves, popularizing biological & geographical knowledge & information, wildlife management

FRANCE   *see also*, separately: **GUADELOUPE, LA RÉUNION, MARTINIQUE, ST BARTHÉLEMY**

AUSSEDAT, Nicole M.   island environments, marine conservation, plans for environmental management of human communities, protection of sites
(also under
ST BARTHÉLEMY)

BAKER, F.W.G. 'Mike'   ecology: horticulture, mycology, ornithology

BATISSE, Michel   biodiversity, Biosphere Reserves, environment & development, future studies, MAB programme, world heritage

BUÉ, Alain   geopolitical aspects of environment and protection policies

COLLIN, Gérard   heritage conservation, Man and Nature

COUSTEAU,   protection of rights of future generations; world economic, environmental, &
Jacques-Yves   social, issues

DÉCAMPS, Henri   landscape ecology of river floodplains

DORST, Jean   ecology & systematics of birds & mammals

DUNCAN, Patrick   ecology of mammalian herbivores; conservation of biodiversity (wetlands, rangelands)

EIDSVIK, Harold K.   biological diversity, national parks & protected areas, world heritage, policy, planning, management

FRANGI, Jean-Pierre   arid climates (Sahelian environment), atmospheric turbidity, botany, environmental physics, microclimatology, planetary boundary layer, solar energy, surface energy balance

FRIEDMAN, Yona   architecture, planning, self-help survival in developing countries

HOFFMANN, Luc   ecology, ornithology, wetland conservation & management

HOUÉROU, Henry N. LE   arid land ecology, bioclimatology, ecosystems dynamics

HÜLSHOFF,   conservation, ecology, forestry, heritage, hydrology, regional planning
Bernd VON DROSTE ZU

KLEMM, Cyrille DE   comparative & international Nature conservation law

LEBRETON, Philippe   bioconservation, biodiversity, natural areas, species' protection

LOURENÇO, Wilson R.   biogeography, evolutionary ecology, phylogeny, & reproduction, of scorpions; applied biogeography => conservation; public health problems resulting from scorpion stings

MONOD, Théodore A.   field natural history, zoology

PARKIN, Sara L.   campaigning, green politics

PICOUET, Michel R.   dynamics of demography, environment, & migration, in developing countries

PRIEUR, Michel   environmental law

RICHEZ, Gérard   protection of Nature re.tourism

SCLAVO, Jean-Pierre   botany (taxonomy of cycads), entomology

TERRASSON, François   behaviour & communication re.Nature philosophy, ecosystems management — forest, rivers, agriculture, & wetlands, integrating Man and Nature, psychology of Nature, scientific research & application

THEBAUD, Christophe   conservation biology esp. of islands, population ecology & evolution esp. of colonizing organisms, management & control of plant invasions in protected areas

WILLUMS, Jan-Olaf   environmental implications of petroleum industry

GERMANY

ADIS, Joaquim U.   holistic analysis of neotropical ecosystems

BALDUS, Rolf D.   community involvement in sustainable wildlife use, hunting as land-use, wildlife conservation & management in eastern & southern Africa

BOTHE, Michael   international & comparative international law & policy

BURHENNE, Wolfgang E.   Parliamentary & environmental law

DANIELS, Frederikus J.A.   lichens, species' diversity, vegetation ecology of Greenland

FREIBERG, Horst   Nature conservation, plant sociology, tropical silviculture

GÜNDLING, Lothar   comparative & international environmental law, Law of the Sea

HABER, Wolfgang   conservation ecology, ecosystem research, land-use ecology, landscape ecology, planning, & management

HEISS, Gerhard   evaluation methods for selection of natural & semi-natural forests, national park planning, forest & mountain ecology (boreal, temperate, and Mediterranean, regions of Europe), systems' planning for protected areas esp.national parks

HEMPEL, Gotthilf   marine & polar sciences, research management & policy

KELLER, Michael C.   environmental campaings & education, systematics of plants & birds of western
                          Europe
KELLERMANN, Adolf   early life-history of fish esp. antarctic fish, environmental monitoring & research,
 K.   environmental protection, national parks, polar marine ecology
KLINGEL, Hans   conservation, wildlife research
NIEMITZ, Carsten   evolution of communication, Nature conservation, primatology
PFADENHAUER, Jörg   restoration ecology, vegetation sciences
REHBINDER, Eckard   comparative & national environmental law & policy
SCHARMER, Klaus   biomass as energy resource, engine fuels from vegetable oils, feeding 6,000 m.
                          people, global warming, solar energy (cooling & water disinfection, medical
                          applications)
SEIBOLD, Eugen   marine geology
SIMONIS, Udo E.   environmental policy studies
SIOLI, Harald F.L.   cultures & fates of Amazonian Indians, tropical ecology mainly of Amazon
                          region

GHANA
ORGLE, Tetey K.   research in forest disturbance & recovery, tropical forest management

GREAT BRITAIN, *see* UNITED KINGDOM

GREECE
GOULANDRIS, Niki   environmental conservation & education
KASSIOUMIS,   biotopes and species' conservation, environmental forestry, outdoor recreation,
 Konstantinos   protected-area management & planning
LAVRENTIADES,   flora, plant identification & sociology, systematic botany & microbiology,
 George   vegetation
MALAMIDIS, George   conservation of the natural environment, evaluation & selection of natural areas
                          of Greece re.special protection
MARGARIS, Nickolas S.   teaching, research, & dissemination of information to mass media, on ecological
                          matters
PAPANASTASIS,   agroforestry, ecology & management of Mediterranean rangelands, landscape
 Vasilios P.   ecology
PYROVETSI, Myrto D.   Nature conservation, ornithology, wetland ecology, wildlife ecology & mana-
                          gement
SKOULIKIDIS, Theodore   catalysis, corrosion, & protection of metals, marbles, & monuments, kinetics,
                          liquid crystals
SOTIRIADOU, Victoria   physical & urban environment protection & improvement, regional develop-
                          ment policies (national & EEC)
VALAORAS, Georgia   conservation in Greece
VENIZELOS, Lily T.   marine turtle conservation
    (also under UNITED KINGDOM, *England*)
YEROULANOS, Marinos   aquaculture, environmental planning
ZALAORAS, Nicholas   ecology, environment

GUADELOUPE, *West Indies*
REDAUD, Louis R.M.   Caribbean region Nature conservation, protected area management, tropical
                          ecology
REDAUD, M. Gladys   bioindicators, environmental education, heavy-metal pollution, lichens
 BELANDRIA DE

GUATEMALA
ALVARADO,   management & development of protected areas
 Juan SKINNER
IBARRA, Jorge A.   environment, palaeontology, zoology
PONCIANO, Ismael   EIA, environmental legislation; policy, planification, & management, of protected
                          areas
SEVILLA,   design & planning of biological corridors, buffer zones, and extractive & mul-
 Lorenzo B. CARDENAL   tiple-use reserves, GIS, land-use planning, methodologies & techniques for
 (also under   strategic planning, planning & management of national parks and other pro-
 NICARAGUA)   tected wildlands and of *in situ* conservation systems, sustainable develop-
                          ment policy issues

GUINEA-BISSAU
MIRANDA, Ruiz   sustainable human development

HAITI
PARYSKI, Paul E.   biodiversity conservation, environmental protection & rehabilitation, sustain-
                          able development

HONG KONG

BOXALL, John E.   cleaner production, environmental control, environmental services project management

JIM, Chi Yung   soil and ecology, tropical biogeography & soils, urban vegetation and environmental impacts

LEE, Lawrence H.Y.   applied biology, Nature conservation

MacKINNON, John R.   biodiversity databases, conservation, ornithology, primatology

MORTON, Brian   marine science esp.malacology, coastal ecology, coastal-zone management, conservation, & pollution

NASH, Nancy   environmental ethics, public awareness, wildlife conservation

HUNGARY

BÁNDI, Gyula   environmental law & administration

BARCSAY, László   environmental impacts on Nature, landscape protection; masterplanning for protected areas, tourism, & conservation

FARAGÓ, Tibor   climate change, environmental science–policy, international environmental issues, natural hazards, societal problems of conservation & sustainability

FÜLEKY, György   reconstruction of former environmental conditions, soil fertility research, sustainable land-use

SZILASSY, Zoltán   aesthetic evaluation, categorization, & management plans, of protected areas, birds, soft tourism

TÖLGYESI, István   appropriate management of Kiskunság National Park, background education in biology, botany, & phytocoenology

VÁRALLYAY, György   soil mapping, physics, & degradation processes

VIDA, Gabór   evolutionary ecology — genetic diversity and population dynamics; genetics — mutagen testing, genetic polymorphisms, cytogenetics

ICELAND

FRIDRIKSSON, Sturla   ecology, genetics; biotic colonization of the volcanic island Surtsey

SCHRAM, Gunnar G.   human rights, international environmental law, Law of the Sea, promoting effectiveness of UN in these fields

INDIA

Andaman & Nicobar Islands

SINHA, Akhauri R.P.   environmental conservation; genecology & conservation of rare, endangered, & endemic, flora of A&N Islands

Andhra Pradesh

LAL, Piare   clonal technology applications for development of genetically-superior, high-yielding, & disease-resistant, clones of Poplars, Eucalypts, & Casuarina, farm forestry and reforestation projects, raw materials for wood-based industries, research & development work on tree improvement and vegetative propagation

MADDURI, V.B.N. Sastry   energy, environmental education

UNNI, N.V. MADHAVAN   remote sensing applications for resources information systems esp.re.forestry, ecology, ecosystem & environment modelling, and related subjects

Delhi

ABROL, Inder Pal   agroforestry, ecosystem productivity, desertification, land degradation & rehabilitation, natural resource management, soil & water management, sustainable agriculture

BISWAS, Dilip   EIA, pollution control

CHANDAK, Surya P.   air pollution control & energy management

CHATURVEDI, Amar N.   environment, forestry

DAVE, Jaydev M.   environmental pollution control & management

DEY, Subhash C.   conservation of biodiversity, environment, & wildlife

GOPAL, Brij   limnology, plant & wetland ecology

IYER, C.P. Jayalakshmi   environmental campaigning & NGO management & networking; project formulation, management, & evaluation

KHANDELWAL, Kailash C.   animal energy, biofertilizers, biomethanation, improved cookstoves, organic farming, rural energy planning, rural sanitation

KHOSHOO, Triloki N.   biodiversity, biomass energy, environmental management, wasteland development

KHOSLA, Ashok   development of innovative technologies for basic human needs, environmental planning & management, impact assessment and community management institutions

MATHUR, Harbansh B.   air pollution monitoring and control equipment design & development, control & monitoring of combustion-generated pollution, design of catalytic convertors for two- & four-stroke engine-powered two- and four-wheeled vehicles, EIA, vehicular emission control

MEHTA, Mahesh C.	environmental jurisprudence & law, grassroots action, human rights' issues
PACHAURI, Rajendra K.	energy, environment, sustainable development
RAMAKRISHNAN, P.S. 'Krishnan' or 'Ram'	agroecology, ecology, ecology of traditional societies, ecosystem dynamics, environmental sciences & sustainable development, linkages between ecological & social processes, population ecology
SAXENA, Anil K.	hazardous waste management, pollution monitoring & analysis
SHARMA, Sudhirendar	environmental journalism & consulting
SINGAL, Sagar P.	acoustic metrology & sounding (SODAR), air pollution modelling, atmospheric boundary layer, building acoustics, environmental pollution, noise measurement
SINGH, Hari Bansh	ecodevelopment programmes, environmental awareness through print media, environmental conservation activism
SINGH, Harjit	environmental information & education, natural resources' management
SINGH, Karan	advocacy of nexus between religion & Nature, environmental conservation, study of comparative religions & philosophy, sustainable development strategies, wildlife preservation
SINGH, Shekhar	biodiversity conservation, environmental planning & policy, wildlife management
VARUGHESE, George C.	community management institutions, EIA, environmental management & planning, microenterprises
VASUDEVAN, Padma	environment–sustainable development–polymer science, rural development

East Punjab

PRASAD, Basudeo	air, water, gas, noise, & consultation, programmes; research & development of environmental monitoring instruments

Goa

DESAI, Bhagirath N.	EIA, environmental conservation & management of marine environment, marine sciences pollution, outfalls, & resources; ocean policy

Gujarat

KASHYAP, Kant	occupational health, pesticide technology
OZA, Gunavant M. & OZA, Premlata	conservation, environmental movement, saving disappearing species; stressing Biosphere

Haryana

HAQUE, Mohammed A.	environmental awareness & education, environmental communication through electronic & print media; environmental pollution by heavy-metals

Jammu & Kashmir

PANDIT, Ashok K.	algology, ecosystem analysis & conservation of Himalayan ecosystems & natural resources, Himalayan lake ecology, limnology; fish & wildlife, plankton & benthic, production; trophic & wetland ecology

Karnataka

RAMPRASAD, Vanaja	environmental conservation, health, women

Kerala

NAYAR, M. Param	biodiversity, conservation, endangered plant species, endemism, mangroves, phytogeography, taxonomic botany, wetlands
PANDURANGAN, Alagramam G.	conservation biology, natural resource management for sustainable development, plant systematics and morphological studies
PRASAD, Manaparambil K.	conservation, environmental campaigning, informal environmental education
PULINKUNNEL, P.S. Easa	research, Nature education
PUSHPANGADAN, Palpu	ethnobiology, conservation biology and economic evaluation of biodiversity, conservation and sustainable utilization of biodiversity
SIVADAS, Ponathil	agriculture & aquaculture farms (personal), biodiversity protection programmes, eco-physiology, environmental conservation, environmental health hazards, HIV/AIDS eradication; natural history, promoting public awareness in social forestry

Madhya Pradesh

LAL, Jugal B.	forest ecology, forest sector development planning, sustainable forest use
MELKANIA, Niranjan P.	conservation ecology, ecodevelopment & biodiversity, ecosystem analysis, forest & integrated resource management, restoration ecology, tropical & mountain regions of India, valuation of Man–Nature relationships
RANJITSINH, M.K.	biodiversity, conservation of endangered species, management of ecosystems, natural resources, Nature conservation, protected areas; wildlife resources, tourism, & trade

SHYAM, Murari — biomass utilization for rural energy supply, biomass-based fuels for internal combustion engines, energy conservation in production agriculture

TOMAR, Sadachari S. — bio-energy and environmental pollution

Maharashtra

ARCEIVALA, Soli J. — EIA, reuse of water, wastewater treatment, water pollution control

KHANNA, Purushottam — environmental science & technology

KRISHNAYYA, Jaswant G. — GIS applied to sustainable development planning, multidisciplinary management analysis

MASCARENHAS, Anthony F. — biotechnology, conservation of endangered species, micropropagation, plant-tissue culture

PATIL, Rashmi S. — air pollution meteorology, air quality modelling & monitoring, EIA

VARIAVA, Dilnavaz — campaign strategy, conservation of wild habitats & species, environmental education, indigenous peoples, institution-building, tribals, women & environment

Mysore

SRINIVASAN, Kandadai — research & teaching in environmentally-acceptable refrigeration & air-conditioning

Punjab

DHINDSA, Manjit S. — behavioural ecology, bird management, research in & teaching of ornithology, wildlife conservation

KOHLI, Ravinder K. — allelopathy, chemical ecology, environmental botany, forestry

Sikkim

RAI, Suresh Chand — integrated rural area development, land & water resources' management, micro-level planning

Tamil Nadu

ABBASI, Shahid A. — alternative energy systems, aquatic ecology, environmental engineering

DANIELS, R.J. Ranjit — conservation biology — birds, amphibians, biodiversity

DAS, Indraneil — biodiversity assessment & conservation, herpetology

DAVIDAR, Reggie — wildlife biology & conservation

GUPTA, Brij K. — captive-breeding programmes, environmental awareness & education programmes, wildlife conservation

IGNACIMUTHU, Savarimuthu — biotechnology, botanical insecticides, environmental awareness & conservation, genetic resources, genetics, mutation breeding

ISMAIL, Sultan A. — organic farming, organic waste recycling using local species of earthworms, vermicomposting, vermiculture

KRISHNAMURTHY, Kothandaraman — biological oceanography, ecology, environmental conservation, estuaries, mangroves, plankton

LAKSHMANAN, Kalimedi K.g. — agroforestry, angiosperm embryology, coastal ecosystems with mangroves, seagrasses & seaweeds, ethnobotanical conservation, *in vitro* studies, plant anatomy, taxonomy of medicinal & biocidal plants

MATTHEW, Koyapillil M. — *in situ & ex situ* conservation on Palni Hills, environmental awareness generation among students & tribals, field botany of South India, taxonomic monography

MEHER-HOMJI, Vispy M. — arid zones, bioclimatology, conservation, ecology, plant geography, vegetation mapping

SUBRAMANIAN, Tarakad V. — clean technology, detoxification of hazardous wastes, environment (bio)technology, environmental engineering & preservation using biotechnology

SUNDARESAN, Bommaya B. — EIA of development projects, environmental protection

SWAMINATHAN, Monkombu S. — conservation of biodiversity, cytogenetics, ecological agriculture, economic ecology, genetics, plant breeding

WHITAKER, Romulus E. — film-making, herpetology, wildlife management & conservation

Uttar Pradesh

AMBASHT, Radhey S. — ecological research & writing

BAHUGUNA, Sunderlal — initiation of Chipko movement, opposition to construction of High Tehri Dam, social activism in Himalayan region, propaganda for environmental awareness

BHARGAVA, Devendra S. — environmental engineering, water pollution control technology & strategies, advanced water & wastewater treatment, remote sensing of water quality surveys, Modelling & Indexes, river classification & zoning, dissolved oxygen sag analysis, adsorption, sedimentation, filtration, aerobic digestion, use-oriented impact assessment, research teacher index evaluation, consultancy & design

JAIN, Sudhanshu K. — botanic gardens, conservation of endangered species & habitats, ethnobotany, floristic survey, formulation & administration of large research programmes, medicinal & psychoactive plants, plant resources, taxonomy of grasses & orchids

JARIWALA, C.M.   constitutional law, environmental law & education, law of education
JARIWALA, Savitri   research in biological control of some plant diseases through the antagonistic
                        activity of microorganisms
JAYAL, Nalni Dhar   conservation of natural heritage, 'Greening of the Himalaya' project
MISRA, Ramdeo   balancing conservation and consumption
PANDEYA, Satish C.   ecology — structure & functions of grazing land and forest ecosystems including
                        production ecology & bioenergetics; holistic environmental management,
                        process of desertification, systems analysis
RAHMANI, Asad Rafi   conservation, deserts, ornithology — bustards, cranes, storks, & francolins
SHARMA, Subrat   agroecology, forest & human ecology
SINGH, Jamuna S.   ecology of dry & wet tropical and Himalayan forests & savannas, ecophysio-
                        logy, restoration ecology
SINGH, Kaushalendra P. ecology of savannas, agroecosystems, & tropical forests
SINGH, O.N.   atmospheric chemistry esp.fibre optics, spectroscopy, & stratospheric pollution
VALDIYA, Khadga Singh   hazards of mass-movements and earthquakes, hydrogeology of mountain springs,
                        neotectonics
VERMA, Sewa R.   Nature resource conservation, research development in environment
WAJIH, Shiraz A.   environmental education, flood/waterlogging, sustainable agriculture

West Bengal
RAY, Prasanta K.   air & water pollution, environmental research esp.in toxicology, immunology,
                        & cancer
SHARMA, Archana   environmental mutagenesis
SHARMA, Arun K.   cell biology, cytochemistry, cytogenetics

INDONESIA
PRAWIROATMODJO,   conservation *in situ*, environmental education & protection
   Suryo W.
SABOGAL, Cesar A.   natural forest management, training activities, tropical silviculture
SALIM, Emil   economics, environment & development, population
SAYER, Jeffrey A.   terrestrial ecology & conservation, tropical forest conservation & management
SMITS, Willie   Dipterocarpaceae, mycorrhizae, Nature conservation, Orang-utans, tropical rain-
                        forests

IRAN, ISLAMIC REPUBLIC OF
ABBASPOUR, Madjid   air pollution in cities, marine pollution, energy policy, environmental safety,
                        ocean engineering, renewable energy, solid waste, transportation noise
MAKHDOUM, Majid F.   environmental evaluation, land-use planning

IRELAND, REPUBLIC OF
BARRY, James M.   diseases of the integument, non-vocal mammalian communication, hormonal
                        influences on mood, mammalian ecology (otter conservation, Red Fox ecology,
                        badger–bovine TB)
SCANNELL, Yvonne   land-use controls, liability for environmental damage, mineral exploitation &
                        development, pollution control
STRONACH, Neil R.H.   management of vegetation fire; wildlife, wildlands, & protected areas', conser-
                        vation management

ISRAEL
ALON, Azaria   Nature conservation: writing, photography, editing
COHEN, Yuval   marine pollution, environmental management, and policy
GOULDMAN, M. Dennis   environmental & planning law
LASTER, Richard E.   environmental law
MARINOV, Uri   environmental management
NAVEH, Zev   landscape conservation, ecology, management, & restoration
POR, Francis D.   aquatic biogeography, limnology (Israel & Brazil), macroevolution, mangrove
                        & salt lagoon ecology, meiobenthos, taxonomy of copepods

ITALY
ALLAVENA, Stefano   management of State natural reserves
ALLOTTA, Gaetano   environmental & marine protection
ANISHETTY,   conservation & utilization of plant genetic resources/biological diversity
   Narasimha M.
LAMBERTINI, Marco   education and awareness, NGO development; protected areas' organization,
                        development & management; species' action plans
LOVARI, Sandro   behavioural ecology of large mammals (Canidae, Caprinae, Cervidae), ethology
MEKOUAR, Mohamed A.   environmental law, forestry, wildlife legislation
MORELL, Merilio G.   institutional development, management of national parks & protected areas,
                        natural resources' policy analysis, public administration, strategic planning
                        for sustainable development

PALMBERG-LERCHE, Christel M. — biological diversity, conservation of genetic resources, deforestation, development & technical assistance to developing countries, forest genetic resources, forest tree improvement, forestry, forestry & environment, reforestation

PETRETTI, Francesco — conservation biology of agricultural & Mediterranean ecosystems, environmental restoration, ornithology — grassland & steppe birds

RADICELLA, Sandro M. — planning & organization of research & development projects & units particularly for developing countries, research & training for research in upper atmosphere physics & atmospheric system interactions with radiowaves environment

ROSSI, Patrizia — mountain environment, protected areas' management

TAO, Kar-ling J. — genebank standards, design, & management; seed germination and dormancy mechanisms, seed testing, strategy & technology of plant germplasm conservation

VALDRÈ, Giovanni — conservation of Nature & protected areas, ethology

WELCOMME, Robin L. — conservation of biological diversity, fisheries ecology of large rivers, species' introductions, trends in aquaculture and inland fisheries, tropical inland fisheries

JAMAICA, *West Indies*

HAYNES-SUTTON, Ann M. — ecology, wildlife conservation, national parks & protected areas, wetlands, seabirds, environmental education

McCALLA, Winston — environmental legislation & policy

ROYES, Veronica I.J. — use of manure & natural pesticides in organic farming; waste management & recycling

JAPAN

HARA, Takeshi — environment and resources, environmental news reporting

ISHI, Hiroyuki — desertification, Earth warming, rain-forest

KAWANABE, Hiroya — animal sociology & community ecology re.biodiversity

KIRA, Tatuo — forest ecosystem studies (carbon & nutrient cycling, geography, primary production), management of lake watersheds

KOBAYASHI, Osamu — environmental management re.emission control over power-plants

MOYER, Jack T. — conservation of biodiversity, coral reefs, marine wildlife

NISHIOKA, Shuzo — environmental systems analysis, global & regional environmental management

NUMATA, Makoto — bambooland & grassland ecology, Nature conservation and urban ecology, vegetation dynamics

OBARA, Hideo — evolutionary ecology and comparative ethology, evolutionary etho-ecology of Man, mammalogy

OJHA, Ek Raj — conservation of highland ecosystems

OKAJIMA, Shigeyuki — environmental journalism

SATOO, Taisitiroo — resource management

SHAPIRO, Harvey A. — coastal area management & planning, ecological planning in the Asia–Pacific region, impacts & policies of sea-level rise in Pacific Basin

SUGIMURA, Ken — forest landscape management particularly for conservation of ecosystems, wildlife conservation & ecology

SUZUKI, Kunio — environmental management, tropical ecology

JORDAN

ABU-RUBEIHA', Ali A. — mineral & natural resources

AL-ALAWNEH, Ziyad — environmental issues, public environmental campaigns

HATOUGH-BOURAN, Alia M.A. — conservation of arid & semi-arid ecosystems in coastal regions and in Jordan, role of reserves in ecological stability, reintroduction programmes of extinct species

KENYA

ANDRIANARIVO, Jonah A. — forestry in Madagascar, GIS, journalism

ASAVA, Wilfred W. — wildlife conservation

ATCHIA, Michael — environmental education & management training

BROUGH, Anthony T. — financial management of the environment

FITTER, Perin S. — catchment approach to soil conservation, promotion of tree nurseries in schools, tree planting

GAKAHU, Christopher G. — conservation biology, ecotourism; research, application, & policy development

GEBREMEDHIN, Naigzy — architecture, emergency response, environmental management, reconstruction, redevelopment, urban planning

HALLER, René D. — building economically-viable integrated ecosystems

LEAKEY, Richard R.B. — agroforestry systems esp. multi-strata agroforests, clonal selection of trees; domestication of tropical trees for forestry/agroforestry in humid, semi-arid, & montane, tropics; vegetative propagation of trees; weed biology

MERZ, Anna H. — rhinoceros

MILIMO, Patrick B.W. — genetics, molecular biology, plant physiology

ODULA, Michael A.N.	environmental conservation, protection, & restoration, of the Earth; environmental education, public awareness
ODUOL, Peter A.	arid ecosystems of Africa, wildlife management
OKIDI, Charles O.	environmental law (comparative & international), international water law, Law of the Sea
OKOTH-OGENDO, H. Wilfred O.	public law
PERTET, Fred O.	game watching, lecturing
PRICE, Mark R. STANLEY	African conservation: conservation & management of small biotic populations, involvement of rural human populations in conservation, reintroduction of animals & plants in theory and practices; wildlife utilization in all forms
RECKERS, Ute	arid lands, desertification, human ecology, nomads, range management & monitoring, semi-arid lands; sustainable land-use management, tropical ecology
SALM, Rodney V.	marine & coastal conservation & protected areas
SANCHEZ, Pedro A.	agroforestry, nutrient cycling, soil science; sustainable alternatives to slash-and-burn agriculture, tropical deforestation
SARMA, K. Madhava	environment & development issues; public administration
SHELDRICK, Daphne M.	animal psychology, wildlife — raising & rehabilitating orphaned animals back into wild
SUN, Lin	Earth's climate
TIMOSHENKO, Alexandre	international environmental institutions & law
VAVILOV, Andrey M.	international aspects of environmental issues including within the UN system
VISSER, Nicolaas W.	biodiversity, coastal-zone management, environment & development, international conventions & treaties on the environment, Nature conservation legislation, sustainable agriculture, wetlands' management
WASAWO, David P.S.	conservation, environment & development, natural resources; zoology
WERIKHE, Michael M.	Rhino conservation

KIRIBATI, REPUBLIC OF

TEEB'AKI, Katino	environmental management; wildlife conservation

KOREA, REPUBLIC OF SOUTH

RHO, Chae-Shik	atmospheric & environmental sciences
SHIN, Eung-Bai	water & wastewater management
WOO, Bo-Myeong	forest environment consevation

KUWAIT, STATE OF

ABDELHADY, Abdelaziz	*see* **EGYPT**
AL-HOUTY, Wasmia	fauna & insect surveys, protected areas
ASEM, Samira OMAR	desertification control, range ecology, wildlife conservation & management

LA RÉUNION, *Indian Ocean*

STRASBERG, Dominique	alien plants' invasion, conservation biology of rare plants, plant ecology

LATVIA

KRIKIS, Andris	environmentally-sound transport of dangerous goods, hazardous waste management, implementation of Helsinki Convention

LEBANON

SAOUMA, Edouard V.	sustainable development esp. agriculture, forestry, & fisheries
SERHAL, Assad	protected areas & wildlife esp.birds & mammals

LITHUANIA

BALČIAUSKAS, Linas	biodiversity, ecological diversity; ecology of hoofed, semi-aquatic, & small, mammals

LUXEMBURG

SINNER, Jean-Marie	Nature conservation & protection

MACAU

ESTÁCIO, Antônio J.E.	conservation and improvement of Macau Green Areas

MADAGASCAR

ANDRIAMAMPIANINA, Joseph	management of protected areas, Nature protection; research on Malagasy primates
BEHRA, Olivier	ecology of amphibians, crocodiles, & reptiles; sustainable conservation & development in third-world countries; wildlife management
VAOHITA, Barthélémy	conservation, environmental education, protection of the environment

MALAWI
   MKANDA, Francis X.   community involvement in wildlife management, research on vulnerability of wildlife to impacts of climate change, wildlife ecology

MALAYSIA
   ARIFFIN, Ishak BIN   natural resource & Nature park planning, strategies for sustainability, urban Nature conservation
   BENNETT, Elizabeth L.   training local graduates & government staff, wildlife conservation field research in South-east Asia esp.Sarawak & Sabah
   CH'NG, Kim-Looi   conservation & management of marine ecosystems, integrated coastal-zone & marine pollution management
   FAZAL, Anwar   community organizing, consumer protection, control of toxic chemicals, life-styles, networking, training, urban management
   HASAN,   animal behaviour, conservation biology, effects of habitat change on wildlife
      Mohammed NORDIN   ecology esp. due to logging, EIA, tropical zoology
   JUSOFF, Kamaruzaman   ecoengineering, forest conservation & management, rehabilitation of degraded forest & mining lands; satellite remote-sensing in forest conservation & management
   KIEW, Bong-Heang   biological conservation in tropical southeast Asia, EIA
   MARSH, Clive W.   conservation management of tropical forests, ecotourism, environmental impacts of tropical forestry, primate ecology
   PAYNE, Junaidi   conservation & management of Southeast Asian forests; mammals of Borneo
   SALLEH, Mohamed N.   forestry

MALDIVES, REPUBLIC OF
   DIDI, N.T. Hasen   fauna & Nature of Maldives esp.re. turtles
   GAYOOM,   astronomy
      Maumoon ABDUL

MALI
   OUEDRAOGO,   environment & development, migrations, natural resources' management,
      O. Dieudonné   population

MALTA
   SULTANA, Joe   Nature conservation, ornithology

MARTINIQUE, *West Indies*
   NOSEL, José   natural park development, protected areas

MEXICO
   ARIAS-CHAVEZ, Jesus   research in ecodevelopment (sustainable development & ecotechnologies) and applied physics, ecology, & biotechnology, re.recovery of refuse, and under-utilized resources
   BEZAURY-CREEL,   integrated conservation & development projects, protected areas' management
      Juan E.
   BYE, Robert   economic botany, edible plants, ethnobotany, flora of Sierra Madre Occidental of Mexico, history of botany & botanical exploration, medicinal, edible, & ornamental plants, plant taxonomy (*Datura* and related genera)
   CERDA, Alberto M.   research in physical oceanography in the Gulf of Mexico and protection of its
      VAZQUEZ DE LA   reefs & islands
   FRAZIER, John G.   biological conservation and quality control of training & ecological work re.people in the tropics; coastal ecosystems; ethics & politics in conservation of biotic & environmental resources; human ecology, island ecosystems; land tortoises, marine turtles
   IBARRA-OBANDO,   habitat preservation in coastal lagoons
      Silvia
   LEFF, Enrique   environmental education & training in Latin America & the Caribbean, theory on environment & sustainable development in underdeveloped regions
   MARQUEZ-MILLAN,   sea turtles' management, conservation, & population assessment
      René
   RUGE, Tiahoga   environmental communication & education
   TEWOLDE, Assefaw   animal evaluation in dairy & beef production systems, domestic animal genetic resource conservation & management, environmental education, sustainable agricultural production systems

MONACO, PRINCIPALITY OF
   DOUMENGE, François   aquariology, coastal & marine development, island ecology; tropical aqua-culture

MONGOLIA

JIGJ, Sonom — creation & management of national parks & protected areas, development of travel & tourism, economic & ecological regionalizations, educational & management aspects of environment, geodynamic processes of landscape of dryland regions, geoecological approaches re.human influence on Nature, Nature–economics–population model, prognosis of environmental changes, ecologically-sustainable development

MOROCCO

HADDANE, Brahim — conservation of endangered species of fauna, environmental education and public awareness re.conservation of Nature

HAFIDI, Moulay EL M. — prevention of desertification, natural resource conservation, wildlife protection

ZOUHA, Sekkou — desertification control, reforestation of arid zones, sand-dune fixation

MYANMAR (BURMA)

OHN — forestry, resources' planning, restoration ecology, socio-economic survey; wildlife conservation

NAMIBIA

KRAUS, Daniel* & MARKER-KRAUS, Laurie† — Cheeta[h] & predator conservation research & education, including non-lethal predator control methods, and livestock & wildlife management outside of protected reserves

SEELY, Mary K. — conservation, ecology of arid lands, environmental education, & research training

* also under **USA,** *California*
† also under **USA,** *District of Columbia*

NEPAL

BHATT, Dibya D. — ethnobotany; mass communication & world affairs particularly regarding interaction between environment & development; natural history

CHITRAKAR, Anil — communication, transfer of conservation skill & technology, education

DHUNGEL, Surya P.S. — environmental management, legislation formulation, policy issues

McEACHERN, John S. — *see* **CANADA,** *Ontario*

OLI, Krishna P. — community-based action research, coordinating governmental & non-governmental organizations, legal aspects of environmental management; planning of local areas, preparation of environmental action plans

RAI, Leghu D. — conservation of Himalayan ecology & environment

SHRESTHA, Aditya M. — environmental communications

UPRETI, Biswa N. — biodiversity & protected areas, environment, Nature conservation, wildlife

YONZON, Pralad — conservation biology in the Himalayan region and South & Southeast Asia

NETHERLANDS ANTILLES, *West Indies*

HOF, Tom VAN'T — marine conservation & sciences

SYBESMA, Jeffrey — natural marine resource management

NETHERLANDS, THE

BENTHEM, Roelof J. — creative conservation, envronmental planning

BOS, Luite — crop protection, ecology, plant virology

BREE, Peter J.H. VAN — international Nature conservation, taxonomy of marine mammals

DANKELMAN, Irene — environment–development, gender–environment–development

DOODY, James P. — coastal conservation management in Europe

DRIJVER, Carel A. — conservation & development in Cameroon, Indonesia, Surinam, & West African Sahel

GROOT, Wouter T. DE — deforestation, desertification, environment and development; theory for problem-oriented analysis & management

HESSELINK, Frederik J. — national & international environmental education & communication

JOOSTING, Peter E. — applied toxicology, criteria, epidemiology, medical environmentology, standard-setting

KUPER, Japp H. — forestry, Nature conservation

LAVIEREN, Lambartus P. VAN — EIA, protected areas', tropical forest, & wildlife, management

LEEFLANG, Sietz A. — ecological techniques (and ways of working, living, & building, on a human scale)

LEEMANS, Rik — biodiversity, ecological theory; vegetation dynamics & structure at different spatial & temporal scales

MEULEN, Frank VAN DER — geobotany, landscape ecology, Nature conservation; integrated coastal-zone management

OPDAM, Paul — conservation biology, landscape ecology

OPSCHOOR, Johannes B. — delinking growth from environment, environmental research planning, equity & environment, sustainable development, industrial metabolism; research on economic instruments

PERNETTA, John C.	cross-sectoral integrated coastal-zone management; environmental and climate change impact assessment
PRINS, Herbert H.T.	buffer-zone management, economic relation between Nature conservation & (local) human population; large mammal ecology, nomadism, & pastoral ecology; population dynamics, savanna & steppe ecology
REIJNDERS, Lucas	natural resources, pollution
REIJNDERS, Peter J.H.	marine mammals (Pinnipeds)
SALMAN, Albert H.P.M.	Nature conservation in coastal zones, sand-dune ecology & management, integrated coastal-zone management
SCHRIJVER, Nico J.	international environmental law, law of international institutions, North–South issues, peace research, public international law
TOORNSTRA, Franke H.	natural resource management in rural development, strategic environmental assessment, participatory approaches
VOS, Willem	applied physical geography, landscape ecology & planning, (sub-) Mediterranean zone
WOLDHEK, Siegfried	administration of Nature conservation

NEW ZEALAND

BURNS, Carolyn W.	freshwater ecology, Nature conservation
COCKLIN, Christopher R.	business and the environment, cumulative environmental change, EIA, environmental security & economics, GIS, Nature conservation, resources and environmental management & policy
GARRATT, Keith J.	environmental management policies, strategies, legislation, and institutional development; multidisciplinary environmental studies; environmental programme & project formulation & management; public participation and consultation procedures with particular emphasis on developing countries
GIVEN, David R.	arctic–alpine biology, conservation biology, ethics, ethnobotany, island biology; threatened species, vegetation, & species', recovery
LAIRD, Marshall	medical entomology & parasitology, esp.integrated control technologies for the amelioration of vector-borne diseases
LEES, Annette M.	design & implementation in tropical forests incorporating local & indigenous concerns; protected areas, sustainable logging of tropical forests
LUCAS, Percy H.C.	cultural & protected landscapes, national parks, protected areas, world heritage
PALMER, Geoffrey	international environmental law
PENNY, Stella F.	conservation management
SIMPSON, Philip G.	environmental education, ethnobotany, natural history of monocotyledons with secondary growth, restoration ecology
SMITH, Kevin D.	Nature conservation esp. forest, grassland, and marine & threatened species
THOM, David A.	conservation, environmental policy, management; reorientation of technology to achieve environmentally sustainable development
TORTELL, Philip	coastal resources' management; environmental administration, audit, impact assessment, law, & mitigation; marine pollution control
WRIGHT, Shane D.T.	conservation biology, forest regeneration dynamics; protected 'natural' areas' design & survey

NICARAGUA

SEVILLA, Lorenzo B. CARDENAL	*see* **GUATEMALA**

NIGER

ANADA, Tiega	natural resource management

NIGERIA

AJAYI, Seth S.	wildlife conservation
ANI, Olufemi	environmental policies & legislation, urban environmental planning
KUFORIJI-OLUBI, Bola	environment–demographic dynamics, environmentally-sound technology & cooperation in sub-Saharan Africa; hazardous waste, solid waste disposal management, toxic chemicals, waste pollution purification & control, waste recycling in plastics industry
OGUNDERE, Joseph D.	drafting of municipal & international environmental law or legislation
OLA-ADAMS, Bunyamin A.	bioproductivity, establishment & management of Nature Reserves, fire ecology in managed plantations & natural forests, nutrient cycling studies
OLOJEDE, Ayodele A.	environment and public administration, environmental strategies & planning; natural resource management
ONAYEMI, Olarotimi O.	alleviating environment-related poverty and creating sustainable development awareness & economies in the developing world; forest conservation in the tropics; human & animal rights
OSEMEOBO, Gbadebo J.	ecosystems & habitat conservation, land-use planning & policy, species' conservation & diversity, use of species' diversity by human societies

UGWU, Christopher N.   biodiversity conservation; EIA studies of governmental & non-governmental development projects; stimulation of community-based conservation programmes & efforts

NORWAY
BACKER, Inge L.   environmental law
BRUNDTLAND,   conservation; environment
  Gro Harlem
DAMMANN, Erik   conflict between free trade and competition for economic growth and a just distribution of the world's resources
FAEGRI, Knut   ecology, palynology
HAREIDE, Dag   consumption growth in rich societies; ecological economy in transition period to a sustainable society; life quality–material well-being
HEYERDAHL, Thor   anthropology, exploring, writing
LÅG, Jul   geomedicine; soil science
LARSEN, Thor   conservation & management of natural resources; population biology of large mammals
NORDERHAÜG, Magnar   ecology; global environmental trends; ornithology
PRESTRUD, Pål   arctic birds, foxes, & mammals; international environmental cooperation; polar research, protection of the arctic environment
SAKSHAUG, Egil   marine phytoplankton ecology; polar ecology
STEINNES, Eiliv   behaviour of trace elements in natural environment, chemical speciation; long-range atmospheric transport of metals & other pollutants, radioecology, soil chemistry
WIELGOLASKI,   alpine ecosystems, autecology of tundra plants, botanical ecology; influence of
  Frans-Emil   acid precipitation; plant phenology & productivity; polar ecosystems

OMAN, SULTANATE OF
AL-MANDHRY,   policy development; monitoring
  Abdullah R.
DALY, Ralph H.   captive breeding & conservation in wild of endangered species in Oman; conservation & development of the environment, habitat protection, management of Nature conservation areas & wildlife for the benefit of local people; reintroduction of Arabian Oryx to the wild in Oman
FRY, C.Hilary   African & Arabian ornithology, conservation, evolution, human biology
GARDNER, Andrew S.   biogeography; desert biology, ecology of desert mountains; ecology & evolution of geckos

Pacific Island Countries — see separately **FIJI, KIRIBATI, PALAU**

PAKISTAN
AKHTAR, Waseem   solid waste management research, environmental engineering
ALI, Iqbal   environmental conservation, environmental quality standards, water resources' engineering
ATAUR-RAHIM,   freshwater fishery — biology, culture, pollution, conservation
  Mohammed
BURNEY, M. Ilyas   microbiology, public health, and environment
DURRANI, Shakil   developing projects & programmes relating to conservation of wildlife & environment; narcotics drugs control
HASSAN, Parvez   conservation of Nature and environmental matters esp. law
KABRAJI, Aban M.   conservation; environment; management issues
QURESHI, Mohummad T.   management of mangrove ecosystems
QUTUB, Syed Ayub   conservation strategies, mobilizing rural communities for better common property management
REHMAN, Syed Ziaur   air pollution; hazardous & solid waste management; water & wastewater treatment

PALAU, REPUBLIC OF
IDECHONG, Noah   resource management

PANAMA, REPUBLIC OF
FLETCHER, Raúl E.   conservation, environmental planning in protected areas

PAPUA NEW GUINEA
JEFFERIES, Bruce E.   biodiversity & protected area conservation management

PERU
PONCE, Carlos F.   ، protected areas' management
PULIDO, Victor   wildlife conservation & protected areas

PHILIPPINES

KHUSH, Gurdev S. — plant biotechnology, breeding, cytogenetics, & genetics

LOHANI, Bindu N. — environmental planning & management; environmental pollution control; integration of environmental elements in development projects using EIA and other tools & techniques; regional & global environmental policies and concerns

MADULID, Domingo — botanical gardens, flora of the Philippines, plant conservation

NAYVE-ROSSI, Portia A. — bionutrition; ecology; health; sustainable agriculture

TOLENTINO, Amado — environmental law, institutional development, legislative analysis

POLAND

GŁOWACIŃSKI, Zbigniew A. — bird ecology, biodiversity, species' extinction, succession; wildlife protection & management

KORNAŚ, Jan — plant ecology (Man's impact on flora & vegetation), plant geography (Europe, tropical Africa) and taxonomy (pteridophytes & phanerogams)

KOZLOWSKI, Jerzy — *see* **AUSTRALIA,** *Queensland*

MEDWECKA-KORNAŚ, Anna M. — ecology (incl.plant sociology & vegetation mapping), Nature conservation (basic research), plant geography (esp.Africa & Europe)

OKOŁÓW, Czeslaw — ecology of bark beetles (Scolytidae); education; national parks, Nature conservation

PINOWSKI, Jan K. — applied ornithology, ecology of birds (*Passer* spp.); suburban ecosystems' management

PUCEK, Zdzislaw K. — conservation of mammals, fauna; population biology of shrews

SERAFIN, Rafal K. — business and the environment, economic restructuring and environmental change in Poland, environmental assessment, green tourism, heritage economics, parks, protected areas, regional & landscape planning

SKOLIMOWSKI, Henryk — eco-ethics, ecophilosophy, ecotheology

STAWICKI, Henryk — natural & cultural landscape conservation in spatial planning

PORTUGAL

CARVALHO, G. SOARES DE — evolution of coastal zones, Pleistocene–Holocene sedimentology & stratigraphy

GRANJA, Helena M. — impact study of anthropic processes in the coastal zone, sedimentology & geomorphology of coastal environments

MOURA, Robert MANNERS — ecological education; landscape ecology, design, & maintenance; protected areas' management, monitoring, & planning

PITTA, Luis CAEIRO — environmental legislation, access to justice, public participation, rights to information

RÉUNION, LA, *see* **LA RÉUNION**

ROMANIA

CIOCHIA, Victor — artificial breeding of entomophagous insects (*Trichogramma, Prospaltella, Coccinellidae*); Nature protection through biological control esp.with entomophagous insects; ornithology (structure, dynamics, bird protection); protection of Danube Delta & mountainous zone (Romania)

POPESCU, Dumitra — environmental law & policy

RUSSIA

AMIRKHANOV, Amirkhan M. — biodiversity protection, floristic research, Nature conservation; taxonomic botany

BARISHPOL, Ivan F. — forestry, Nature conservation

BOTCH, Marina S. — wetland ecology, Nature protection esp.protected areas and peatland

BRINCHUK, Mikhail M. — air pollution, environmental law, hazardous & solid waste, industrial safety, toxic chemicals

CHERKASOVA, Maria V. — conservation of natural & cultural heritage; environmental education, ecology, ecology & children's health; protection of human rights for a healthy environment, public environmental movement

DMITRIEVA, Vera A. — conservation of Nature, environmental policy & education

FEDOROV, Vadim D. — ecology, hydrobiology, physiology of microorganisms

FLINT, Vladimir E. — biology of birds & mammals, captive breeding; desert, steppe, taiga-forest, & tundra, in Siberia & Central Asia; endangered species, sustainable use of wildlife, wildlife conservation strategy

GALAZY, Grigori I. — ecology of land & water communities, geobotany, limnology

GALUSHIN, Vladimir M. — environmental education; study & conservation of birds esp.birds of prey

GOLUBEV, Genady N. — assessment & management of water resources; coordination & planning of environmental management world-wide and of global change research; glaciology

IZRAEL, Yuri — scientific research in anthropogenic and natural environmental sciences, ecology, geography, geophysics, oceanology, & physics of the atmosphere

KEFELI, Valentin   environment & physiology of plants
KOLBASOV, Oleg S.   environmental law & management
KONDRATYEV, Kirill Y.   global change [esp. of atmosphere–climatic phenomena]
KRASNOV, Eugene V.   marine biogeochemistry & geoecology, palaeoecology of coral reefs
LITVIN, Vladimir M.   cartography, ecology, geography, ocean geology
MARUSIK, Yuri M.   biogeography of Beringia & North Holarctic; principles of systematics; spider
                          taxonomy & zoogeography
MAXIMOV, Victor N.   marine ecology: ecological monitoring of coastal ecosystems, multidimen-
                          sional statistics in ecology
NIKULIN, Valery A.   applied mathematics; ecology & resource conservation; hydroaerodynamics
SINITSINA, Irene E.   aerohydrodynamics; civil engineering; environmental problems
SMIRNOV, Nikolai N.   ecology of catastrophic situations; limnology, morphology, & taxonomy, of
                          Cladocera (Crustacea)
SOKOLOV, Vladimir   biodiversity, Biosphere reserves, Nature conservation; protection of disappea-
                          ring & endangered species of mammals
TIKHOMIROV, Vadim N.   floristics, morphology, & taxonomy, of higher plants; Nature protection
TSHERNYSHEV,   diurnal rhythms, ecological pest management, ecology of agroecosystems;
   Wladimir B.   influence of geomagnetic storms; insect ecology
VORONOV, Arkady N.   conservation, ecological (contaminant) hydrogeology, ecological education,
                          environment, isotopic composition of Argon & Helium, oil & gas hydrogeo-
                          logy, water quality
YABLOKOV, Alexey V.   conservation biology, ecopolicies, evolutionary theory, population biology,
                          study of vertebrates
YANSHIN, Aleksandr L.   ecology, geology
ZABELINA, Natalia M.   national parks & protected natural areas: geographical methods of their plan-
                          ning, design, & conservation
ZLOTIN, Roman I.   biodiversity conservation, biogeography; degradation of environment by human
                          activity; terrestrial ecology

SALVADOR, EL, *see* EL SALVADOR

SAUDI ARABIA, KINGDOM OF
ABUZINADA, Abdul A.H. conservation management & research
AZIS, P.K. ABDUL   biodiversity of aquatic ecosystems, ecology, environmental conservation &
                          action plans
FAIZI, S.   biodiversity, international environmental policy
SULAYEM,   biodiversity conservation & management; conservation planning, protected
   Mohammad S.A.   areas' planning & management
YAHYA, Hafiz S.A.   avian ecology, conservation, ethology

SEYCHELLES
COLLIE, John S.   conservation, natural history
LIONNET, Joseph F.G.   agronomy, natural history; scientific bibliography

SIERRA LEONE
ALIEU, Emmanuel K.   energy, forestry development, environmental conservation
BANGURA, Kalie I.   antipoaching–protected areas, wildlife management & protection
BERETEH, Mohamed A.   forestry & wildlife conservation & management
COLE, Norman H.A.   conservation of biodiversity, ecophysiology of plants, environmental education,
                          environment & development (EIA); environmental legislation, sciences, &
                          training; research in tropical ecology
PALMER, Prince D.   equitable forest policies, forest conservation
TUBOKU-METZGER,   conservation of biodiversity & wilderness in West Africa esp. Sierra Leone
   Daphne J.A.

SINGAPORE, REPUBLIC OF
KOH, Tommy T.-B.   environmental law, Nature conservation, negotiations, sustainable development
POLUNIN, Ivan V.   research into general biology and synchronous displays by *Pteroptyx* fireflies;
                          floral conservation

SLOVAK REPUBLIC
BUBLINEC, Eduard   ecology, monitoring, soil science
ČABOUN, Vladimír   ecological & ecophysiological relations in forest ecosystems and their depen-
                          dence on dominant trees
DRDOŠ, Ján   environmental planning in national parks, environmental studies; landscape
                          ecology
HOLČÍK, Vladimír   hydraulic research on flows, river regulations, water management
HUBA, Mikuláš   coordination of environmental NGO activities, environmental geography, risks,
                          & hazards; implication of sustainable development concept; landscape planning
KADLEČÍK, Ján   conservation & ecology of carnivores, mammals; wetlands conservation &
                          management

KRAJČOVIČ, Roman S. — EIA, environmental management, land readjustment, landscape ecology, revitalization of abandoned & derelict landscapes, regional development
LISICKÝ, Mikuláš J. — ecosozology (conservation science), ecology of floodplains
MIKLÓS, Ladislav — ecological planning & politics; landscape ecology
TRENČIANSKA, Jana — agricultural amelioration, irrigation systems, waste management

SOUTH AFRICA, REPUBLIC OF

BATE, Guy C. — coastal ecophysiology — dunes, beaches, & estuaries; environmental management
BOUCHER, Charles — autecology, phytosociology, & restoration ecology, of Cape plants & vegetation
BROOKS, Peter M. — wildlife management; conservation of the African Rhinoceros
DIAB, Roseanne D. — atmospheric science — meteorology, ozone, wind energy
FERRAR, Tony — conservation organization administration; ecological research, environmental education, tropical (savanna) resource ecology; wildlife management
HUGHES, George R. — ecotourism & marine turtles, trout angling, wildlife management
MILLS, Gus — carnivore behavioural ecology & conservation biology; conservation of & research in arid & savanna ecosystems; mammalian predator–prey relationships
PLAYER, Ian C. — conservation issues, wilderness
PRESTON-WHYTE, Robert A. — atmospheric systems (southern Africa), environmental management policy issues
RYAN, Peter G. — biology & conservation of oceanic islands, evolutionary ecology, marine debris, ornithology
SAMWAYS, Michael J. — ecological landscaping; insect conservation biology, invertebrate conservation; landscape ecology
TERBLANCHE, Petro — environmental management & auditing esp.re.air pollution impacts
WALKER, Clive H. — ecotourism & environmental education in the bush, wildlife painting
WALT, Pieter T. VAN DER — arid plant ecology, ecological economics, park planning
WEAVER, Alex v.B. — EIA
WEAVER, John M.C. — management & pollution of groundwater resources

SOUTH KOREA, see KOREA, REPUBLIC OF SOUTH

SPAIN

ARAUJO, Joaquín — ecology, environment, organic farming
CROSBY, Arturo — environment — tourism, ecotourism, & rural tourism, planning & design; training programmes
MONTESINOS, José Luis VIEJO — conservation & ecology of insects, mainly Lepidoptera
MOREY, Miguel — island ecosystems, landscape ecology, Mediterranean ecosystems, vegetation dynamics
ZSÖGÖN, Silvia JAQUENOD DE — environmental law

Canary Islands

BRAMWELL, David — biogeography & evolution of Canarian flora, conservation biology & conservation ecology of endangered species, conservation of insular floras
CARRILLO, Antonio MACHADO — entomology (Carabid beetles); environmental policy (sustainable tourism), Nature conservation, protected areas, species recovery plans (terrestrial)

SRI LANKA (CEYLON)

FERNANDO, Ranjen L. — conservation of natural habitats, tropical forests and their fauna & flora, and the Sri Lankan wild elephant; creating awareness of significance & necessity to protect ecosystems & biodiversity; educating & encouraging youth on environmental protection
GUNAWARDENE, Nalaka J. — environmental journalism & education, public awareness
MUNASINGHE, Mohan — energy, environmental economics, sustainable development, water resources
NANAYAKKARA, Vitarana R. — agroforestry, ecology, forestry, Nature conservation; wood-based energy development
SILVA, Allenisheo L.M. DE — air & water pollution law, EIA, environmental law, human rights, land tenure, public interest litigation
ULLUWISHEWA, Rohana K. — biogeography, ethnobiology and indigenous knowledge systems in the tropics; natural resource management
WHITE, Alan T. — coastal management, coastal resources' conservation; participatory management of natural resources
WIJESINGHE, Leslie — biodiversity conservation, forest conservation planning
WIJEWANSA, Ranjit A. — environmental management & planning

ST BARTHÉLEMY, Guadeloupe, West Indies
AUSSEDAT, Nicole M.   see FRANCE

ST LUCIA, West Indies
BUTLER, Paul J.   environmental education, conservation marketing, resource management
JAMES, Brian   natural resources' management
ROMULUS, Giles   environmental management & planning, protected areas' planning and co-
                          management approaches to the environment

SUDAN
MOGHRABY, Asim I.EL   desertification & wildlife ecosystems' management & protection; freshwater
                          ecology
NOUR, Hassan O. ABDEL   biomass energy, environmental conservation & rehabilitation, ethnobotany, forest
                          entomology, forestry, gums, natural resource surveys; termites in forestry &
                          buildings

SURINAM
MALONE-JESSURUN,   environmental pollution, fisheries
Heidi Y.

SWAZILAND
ALLEN, Irma   environmental education & management, sustainable community development

SWEDEN
BOLIN, Bert R.   climate, climate change; interactions of environmental scientists and politi-
                          cians; global biogeochemical & carbon cycles
CHADWICK, Michael J.   arid zone ecology; quantitative measurement of comparative environmental
                          risk, restoration of degraded land
DAHL, R. Birgitta   development, environment, international affairs, social policy
HEDBERG, Inga M.M.   conservation of biodiversity, ethnobotany esp. of tropical plants, taxonomic
                          botany esp. of Africa
HEDBERG, K. Olov   conservation of biodiversity; ethnobotany; plant taxonomy & ecology esp.of
                          tropical high mountains
KERN, Berndt &   saving tropical forests, biological research, environmental education, local deve-
KERN, Eha   lopment & sustainable agroforestry; Nature awareness at home and in the
                          tropics, reforestation
LÖFGREN, Rolf   establishment & planning of national parks; forest conservation
MALMBERG, Ole   environmental & family medicine, human ecology
MALMBERG, Torsten   human ecology and conservation
ROSSWALL, Thomas   biogeochemical cycles, global environmental change, microbial ecology
SJÖGREN, Erik A.   bryophyte ecology & sociology, bryophytes as indicators of pollution, epiphyl-
                          lous bryophytes; Macaronesian vegetation, protection of natural forest vege-
                          tation
UEXKÜLL, Carl J.W. VON   economics, environment, human rights, sustainability, third world
WAHLSTEDT, Jens   biological diversity, Nature conservation

SWITZERLAND
BOJKOV, Rumen D.   international atmospheric environment esp.ozone studies
BÜTTIKER, William   desert animal ecology, medical zoology, zoological survey of Arabia
CHERIX, Daniel   biology, ecology, and protection, of ants (mainly Red Wood Ants)
COHEN, Maria L.   environment, environmental education & ethics; Nature conservation
DAHL, Arthur L.   biodiversity, coral-reef ecology; environmental assessment & monitoring;
                          environmental management & conservation of islands; marine Algae
DUGAN, Patrick J.   environmental policy, integrated management of natural ecosystems; wetland
                          conservation & management
EDWARDS, Peter J.   agroecology, environmental management; plant ecology
EGLI, Robert A.   chemistry of the atmosphere
FARID, Mohyeddin A.   malaria eradication; vector control programmes
FAULKNER, J. Hugh   development, environment
GIMINEZ-DIXON,   animal ecology, cervids; threatened species' management; wildlife conservation
Mariano
GRASSL, Hartmut   climate research, global change research; remote sensing with satellites
GRINEVALD, Jacques   environmental education, history of ecology; history & philosophy of global
                          ecology esp.the concept of The Biosphere
GRUCZMACHER,   environmental communications; evolutionary biology
Ricardo BAYÓN
HOECK, Hendrik N.   ecodevelopment & management of conservation areas, ecotourism; manage-
                          ment of research institutions; wildlife management
HUNKELER, Pierre   activities of NGOs, Nature conservation, relationships between agriculture &
                          conservation

HURNI, Hans	environment & development, geo-ecology, protection of Nature reserves; soil erosion & conservation; sustainable development of buffer zones, sustainable use of natural resources
INNES, John L.	biomonitoring, environment–forestry interactions, environmental change, forest health
LANG, Winfried	international environmental law — air pollution, climate change, nuclear accidents, protection of ozone layer
LANG-BEERMAN, Ernst M.	behaviour of animals, mammalogy, Nature protection, ornithology
LINDNER, Warren H.	implementation of action on sustainable development
MANSER, Bruno	customs, exploration of caves, flora & fauna in Switzerland & Sarawak, Nature medicine, traditional cultivation
MARTIN, Claude	conservation, environmental policy; tropical forests
MAYSTRE, Lucien Y.	environmental engineering & management
McCAMMON, Antony L.T.	application of financial experience and principles to 'The Commons'; fostering links between banking/finance & environment/development
McDOWELL, David K.	conservation
McNEELY, Jeffrey A	anthropology, biological diversity, conservation, economics; mammals of Southeast Asia
MESSERLI, Bruno	climate change, geoecology, mountain areas (Africa, Himalaya, Andes)
NEPAL, Sanjay K.	community-based tourism, ecotourism, parks, protected areas; regional environmental planning, rural development planning; wildlife & heritage conservation
OBASI, Godwin O.P.	climate change, global environmental issues; meteorology, operational hydrology and related fields; ozone layer depletion; sustainable development
PITT, David	anthropology, ecodevelopment, environmental security; health, islands, mountain ecosystems
POLUNIN, Nicholas	holistic ecological conservation; plant ecology/geography; public appreciation of The Biosphere and potentialities of the Noosphere/Homosphere
RUIZ-MURRIETA, Julio	conservation, indigenous peoples; sustainable use of forest ecosystems & species
RUMMEL-BULSKA, Iwona	environmental law
RYDÉN, Per A.	natural resource management, rural development
SCHLAEPFER, Rodolphe	climate change & forest, experimental design, forest biometry & decline; forest management in tropical forests
SCHWAB, Klaus	ecologically-sustainable development
STRAHM, Wendy A.	conservation, invasive species; Mascarene Island botany
THORSELL, James W.	conservation, parks' management; world heritage convention
TURIAN, Gilbert	microbiology; natural sciences
WALLÉN, Carl-Christian	climate change & politics, climatology, global monitoring of environment
WENSLEY, Penelope A.	environment and Mankind
WITT, Ronald G.	capacity-building re.environment, data and information management; environmental assessment, geography and remote sensing, GIS, mapping & monitoring activities
ZWAHLEN, Robert	EIA esp.for water resources' development projects, hydropower; irrigation in tropical & temperate environments

SYRIAN ARAB REPUBLIC

AWAD, Adel R.	wastewater systems & treatment, submarine outfalls, urban hydrology, solid waste management, regional & urban planning; seismic zonation in land-use planning
WARDEH, Muhammad Fadel	animal production, conservation of animal germplasm, research development in livestock & rangeland utilization
YOUSSEF, Abdullatif K.	air & marine environment; organic chemistry

TAHITI

VERNAUDON, Yolande	coastal & marine management, parks, reserves

TAIWAN

HSU, Kuo-Shih	endangered & rare plant species; national parks, Nature conservation

TANZANIA

MWALYOSI, Raphael B.B.	conservation biology, ecology, EIA; environmental & integrated resource management; limnology
MWASAGA, B.	conservation, ecotourism; wildlife ecology
STEPHENSON, Peter J.	conservation management planning, management of conservation & development projects; conservation biology of tropical mammals

THAILAND (SIAM)

AKSORNKOAE, Sanit	coastal-zone management, mangrove ecology

DEETES, Tuenjai	hill people in Thailand
MUTTAMARA, Samorn	EIA, hazardous & solid waste management; water and wastewater treatment, water supply & sanitation
PHORNPRAPHA, Phornthep	business & social activities
SOPHONPANICH, Chodchoy	anti-litter campaigning, community tree-planting, waste management, water pollution control
TEJADHAMMO, Pongsak	education in forest values, environmental awareness using concept of SILA-THAM
THAPA, Gopal B.	natural resources' conservation, regional environmental management planning, sustainable agriculture, watershed management
USUKI, Mitsuo	geography, landscape architecture & policy on development & environment esp. Nature conservation & natural resources' management
WEBER, Karl E.	environmentally-sustainable development; regional environmental management (protected-area planning); research design, methods, & techniques (monitoring methodology)

THE NETHERLANDS, *see* **NETHERLANDS, THE**

TRINIDAD & TOBAGO, REPUBLIC OF, *West Indies*

ADAMS, Aubrey	environmental activism, writing
LAYDOO, Richard S.	conservation; coral-reef ecology, biology, management, & monitoring; EIA, marine parks & protected areas; resource management

TUNISIA

ABROUGUI, Mohamed Ali	biodiversity, conservation of Nature, ecotourism; environment, environmental policy
KACEM, Slaheddine BEL	Nature protection; wild flora & fauna conservation incl. application of international agreements

TURKEY

ÖZTÜRK, Münir	plant ecology, pollution problems
SAVAS, M. Nizam	environmental matters; national parks, Nature conservation
USLU, Turhan	coastal vegetation of Turkey & N. Cyprus; effects of thermal power-plants on flora & vegetation
YAZGAN, Nergis	endangered species; Nature conservation

TURKMENISTAN

KHARIN, Nikolai	desert plant ecology; Nature conservation

UAE, *see* **UNITED ARAB EMIRATES**

UGANDA

NDYAKIRA, N. Amooti	environmental journalism
WALULYA-MUKASA, Joe	energy conservation; environmental education; tree-planting

UK, *see* **UNITED KINGDOM OF GREAT BRITAIN AND NORTHERN IRELAND**

UKRAINE

KOSTENKO, Yuriy I.	development of laws on environmental protection in Ukraine, national ecological reform concept & Nature protection programme
KUKHAR, Valery P.	bioorganic chemistry of natural compounds; chemical & technological aspects of environment protection; problems created by the Chernobyl disaster
SHEMSHUCHENKO, Yuri S.	environmental law & management

UNITED ARAB EMIRATES

KHAN, Niaz A.	industrial environmental pollution control, solid & hazardous waste evaluation, disposal, & management; environmental studies; noise assessment; industrial & sewage wastewater treatment & disposal

UNITED KINGDOM OF GREAT BRITAIN AND NORTHERN IRELAND

Channel Islands

DURRELL, Lee McG.	conservation of endangered species

England

AICKIN, R. Malcolm	environment policy, environmental insurance & security, environmental risk reduction; mechanisms of environmental degradation; social & cultural changes required by sustainable development

ALSTON, Frank H.	breeding & genetics of apples & pears, including introduction of pest- & disease-resistance
ANGEL, Martin V.	ecology of deep oceanic communities; marine biodiversity & zoogeography; taxonomy of pelagic Ostracods
APPLIN, David G.	comparative neuroendocrinology, conservation, evolution theory, insect biology, neurosecretory systems; wildlife photography
ASTLEY, David 'Dave'	conservation of genetic resources, particularly horticultural crops & related taxa
ATTENBOROUGH, David F.	broadcasting, Nature, writing
BARBARA, Derek J.	molecular plant pathology, mycology, plant virology
BARBIER, Edward B.	economics of environment & development, environmental & natural resource economics
BASS, Stephen M.J.	forest policy & environmental policy development esp. in tropical regions
BELL, J. Nigel B.	air pollution effects on plants & insects; business and the environment; pathways of radionuclides in the environment
BELLAMY, David J.	arid lands in western Australia, botany, broadcasting, business–environment, conservation, ecotourism, environment–human interaction; evolution of ecosystems esp.in coral reefs & wetlands, marine pollution, sustainable development, writing
BERRY, R.J. 'Sam'	conservation and ecological genetics, environmental ethics
BERTRAM, G. Colin L.	fisheries, population problems, seals, Sirenia
BIRNIE, Patricia W.	public international law esp.the Law of the Sea and international law & the environment
BISWAS, Asit K.	environmental policies (preparation of national environmental action plans), EIA; irrigation management, management of international waters; sustainable agricultural development
BISWAS, Margaret R.	environmental policies & issues, international relations; nutrition, sustainable agricultural development
BOA, Eric	Bamboos in rural development; forest pathology, tree health
BONNER, W. Nigel	Antarctic conservation; marine mammals
BOORMAN, Laurie A.	coastal-zone management. salt-marsh & sand-dune ecology
BOOTE, Robert E.	ageing society, environment
BOSWALL, Jeffery	popularization & teaching of biology & conservation through media of film, video, & television; bird protection
BOULTON, Mark N.	environmental education mainly in support of NGOs & governments in less-developed countries
BURKE, D.T. 'Tom'	politics of environment esp.re.business & environment, and energy policy
BURLEY, Jeffery	biodiversity, tree breeding, tropical forestry research & development; information and education
BURTON, John A.	history of natural history, identification guides, natural history; wildlife conservation
CAMPBELL, Kenneth L.I.	EIA, GIS, national park planning; remote sensing, wildlife surveys
CHEEK, Martin	conservation & taxonomic botany esp. of West & Central African forests; Malvales, Meliaceae, & carnivorous plants
CHEEK, Roy V.	plant conservation & cultivation; planting design & management, tree surgery
CLARK, Colin	causes of low flows, climatic effects of clouds, drainage basin management; effects of land-use change on climate & hydrology; rainfall frequency analysis
CLARK, Michael F.	field & molecular plant virology, mycoplasma-like organisms; plant pathology, serology
CLARK, Robert B.	marine pollution
CLARKE, Andrew	evolutionary history of polar regions; marine, polar, & thermal, ecology
CLOUDSLEY-THOMPSON, John L.	desert adaptations, diurnal rhythms, temperature & water relations of Arthropods & Reptiles
COBB, Stephen M.	tropical protected areas and their conservation
COHN-SHERBOK, Dan	Judaism and animals
COOPER, Jeffrey 'Jeff' C.	waste management, planning, recycling, & reduction
CROSS, Jeremy V.	crop & environment protection, horticultural entomology, horticulture and pesticide application
CROXALL, John P.	marine ecology esp.of seabirds & seals and of polar regions
CRUTE, Ian	genetics of plant–pathogen interactions in crop & natural ecosystems
CULLEN, James	plant taxonomy esp. of plants of horticultural interest
DARBY, Peter	hybridization & genetics of hops (*Humulus lupulus*) — resistance to pests & diseases
DAYSH, Zena	global interest in developing due understanding of human ecology
DRAKE, Christopher M.	forms of interaction and relationship with environment; ethical & moral elements of humanity's relationship with the environment; humanity's impact on environment, and each individual's potential for a constructive response to its present condition; judicious use of natural resources

DUFF, Keith L.   geological site protection, Nature conservation, research into Jurassic palaeontology

DUFFEY, Eric A.G.   invertebrtae ecology esp. of Araneida

DUNLOP, Nicholas J.   *see* **BELGIUM**

EARLL, Robert C.   coastal-zone management, environmental management systems; marine conservation (including benthos, rays, sharks, and protected areas)

EDINBURGH, Philip,   World Wildlife Fund — UK & International
Duke of

EDMUNDS, Malcolm   anti-predator defences of animals; biology & taxonomy of opisthobranch molluscs

EDWARDS, Mark   environmental photography

EKINS, Paul W.   ecological economics, ecologically-sustainable development

ELKINGTON, John B.   environmental consultancy; new technology esp.biotechnology, sustainable development

ELLIS, Peter R.   breeding pest-resistant varieties of horticultural crops, insect–plant relationships; non-chemical & integrated pest control

ELMES, Graham W.   ant–butterfly interactions, insect & rare species' conservation; population ecology, social insect ecology

ELTRINGHAM,   conservation & ecology of large mammals in East Africa; wildlife conservation
Stewart K.

ENTWISTLE, Andrew R.   epidemiology of soil-borne plant pathogens, plant pathology; ornamental horticulture

EVERETT, Rodney D.   gentle living on Earth, ecological farming & building; permaculture design, green living

FERMOR, Terence R.   bioremediation, composting, microbial ecology, mushroom science

FILHO, Walter L.   environmental education & information in industrialized & developing countries

FITTER, A Maisie S.   editing journals on wildlife conservation

FITTER, Julian R.   conservation of island & marine ecosystems & ecocomplexes

FITTER, Richard S.R.   field identification of, and writing field guides esp. on, birds and vascular plants

FOWLER, Sarah L.   coastal-zone management, Elasmobranch ecology & conservation; marine ecology & conservation, marine protected areas

FRAZER, John F.D.   animal populations esp.butterflies, mammals, & reptiles; wildlife conservation

GAMMELL, Alistair   organization & growth of a world bird conservation movement and the achievement of effective conservation

GANDY, Matthew   environmental philosophy & politics, interdisciplinary environmental research; urban environmental problems in developed economies

GATHORNE-HARDY,   Nature conservation, Southeast Asian rain-forests; worldwide sustainable development
Gathorne

GIRARDET, Herbert K.   cultural ecology research, writing, film-making

GITTINS, John W.E.H.   community environmental action, education for sustainability; environmental education, environmental philosophy & values through teaching, art & environment, research, & encouraging good practice both in Britain and overseas

GOLDSMITH, Edward   anthropology, ecology, environmental campaigning, life sciences

GOLDSMITH, Frank B.   Nature conservation esp. monitoring; plant ecology

GORDON, John K.   institutional & political aspects of sustainable development

GORIUP, Paul D.   Nature conservation planning, ornithological research esp.of Bustards (Otididae)

GOUDIE, Andrew S.   climatic change, desert environments, geomorphology

GREEN, Brynmor H.   agri-environmental policy, habitat management & restoration esp. on farmland; landscape protection

GRIFFITHS, Richard A.   amphibian & reptile biology & conservation; behavioural, community, & population, ecology

GRUBB, Peter J.   communities on calcareous soils of Europe, plant–soil relations; plants re.herbivores & dispersers, tropical rain-forests; vegetational dynamics, competition, & coexistence

GUBBAY, Susan   coastal-zone management, marine conservation, ecology, & protected areas

HAIGH, Martin J.   erosion control of lands affected by coal-mining, land reclamation; landslide research in central Himalaya

HAIGH, Nigel   European environmental policies

HAILES, Julia P.   environmental management, green consumerism

HAMBLER, Clive   conservation and ecology esp. of islands, succession in tropical & temperate regions

HAMBLER, David J.   plant ecology; grazing effects

HAMILTON, Alan   ethnobotany, plant conservation, tropical forest conservation

HANBURY-TENISON,   conservation, exploration, protection of indigenous peoples
A. Robin

HARRIS, Philip J.C.   organic agriculture & horticulture, plant biotechnology, sustainable forestry & agroforestry, tropical crop development

HARRISON, Paul A.   Africa, agriculture, development, environment, population

HAWKES, John G.	conservation of plant genetic resources, crop plant evolution; phylogeny & taxonomy of Solanaceae, taxonomy, evolution, & uses in plant breeding, of wild & cultivated potato species
HELLIWELL, D. Rodney	arboriculture, ecology, forestry, landscape management
HEMMING, John H.	Amazon, environmental conservation
HILL, Mark O.	bryophyte distributions, modelling, multivariate analysis, vegetation ecology
HOLDGATE, Martin W.	conservation & sustainable use of Nature & natural resources; ecology esp.of oceanic islands & polar regions; environmental trends & related social policies; pollution and its impacts
HOLDICH, David M.	environmental biology of aquatic Crustaceans, freshwater crayfish, Isopods, & Tanaids
HOLLIS, George E.	hydrology, sustainable development, water management, wetlands
HOUGHTON, John T.	climate policy & science; remote sensing from space
IMBODEN, Christoph N.	biodiversity, conservation, ornithology; ecologically sustainable development
JACOBSON, Robert J.	integrated pest management strategies re.protected crops
JAMES, David J.	genetic transformation of temperate fruit, plant biotechnology
JAMES, Roger D.	environmental coverage on broadcast television
JEWELL, Peter A.	conservation of rare breeds of British farm livestock, ecology of large African mammals
JOHNSON, Stanley P.	European environmental policy, population
JOHNSTON, Neil	biotechnology, cleaner technology, farming; waste minimization
JONES, Hamlyn G.	plant environmental micrometeorology & physiology, plant–water relations and ecology
JUEL-JENSEN, Bent E.	third-world development & medicine, tropical medicine
KEAY, Ronald W.J.	environmental biology & plant taxonomy of tropical areas esp.Nigeria
KELCEY, John G.	badgers, ecological engineering (habitat creation); industrial ecology, people, trees; urban ecology & landscape, paintings
KENDREW, John C.	national & international science policy, molecular biology
KENNEDY, Robert	epidemiology of foliar fungal pathogens of Brassicas, Alliums, *Citrus*, & Cashew; control of post-harvest moulds & mycotoxin production in stored-grain systems
KENT, Paul W.	biochemistry research, higher education
KILMARTIN, Marianne P.	hydrology & soil development of reclaimed lands after surface coal-mining in Wales
KING, Graham J.	molecular genetics as basis for crop improvement; structural & environmental constraints on DNA sequence variation; assessment of genetic diversity in crop plants
KIRBY, Keith J.	developing policies & practice for maintaining the biodiversity of managed forests, dynamics of woodland ground vegetation; extent of and changes in ancient woodland, forestry & woodland conservation, monitoring & survey of forests
KNIGHT, Peter T.	business–environment
KNILL, John	construction & environmental geology, earth science conservation; natural hazard reduction
KREBS, John R.	behavioural & population ecology, conservation biology
LAMB, Hubert H.	climate, human affairs, politics, weather
LAMB, Robert P.	environmental television
LAMBERT, Michael R.K.	ecotoxicology in amphibians, lizards, & reptiles, and their use as bioindicators of habitat contamination; Saharan & Sahelian herpetofaunal biodiversity; tortoise conservation and sustainable utilization
LAMPREY, Hugh F.	endangered natural ecosystems; national parks & protected areas' — establishment, management, & assessment
LANGSLOW, Derek R.	ecology, Nature conservation, ornithology
LEWIS-SMITH, Ronald I.	Antarctic conservation, environment, & plant ecology
LINZEY, Andrew	ethical & theological status of animals
LOCK, John M.	animal–plant interactions; classification of world vegetation; taxonomy of African Leguminosae & Zingiberaceae
LOVEJOY, Derek	environmental consulting, landscape architecture, town planning
LOVELOCK, James E.	Gaia research
MACDONALD, David W.	agroecology, carnivores, mammalian conservation
MACRORY, Richard B.	environmental law
MALLOCH, Andrew J.C.	animal–plant interactions, ecophysiology of maritime plants, phytosociology esp.of coastal environments
MALTBY, Edward	moorland, peatlands', soils', & wetlands', ecosystem functioning & management
MANSFIELD, Terence A.	plant physiology, responses of plants to abiotic stress
MOORE, Norman W.	wildlife conservation — research & policy-making esp.re.pollution control and conservation of Odonata
MORRIS, Michael G.	conservation & utilization of third-world resources esp. butterflies; conservation of British & European invertebrates; effects of conservation management on grassland invertebrates

MYERS, Norman	environment & development including agriculture, biodiversity, climate, energy, forests, population, & water — all within a context of environmentally-sustainable development and N–S relations
NEWMAN, Edward I.	research on sustainability of ecosystems esp. agricultural systems
NOBLE, Ralph	prevention of odour & water pollution from composting, controlled-environment composting for mushroom cultivation; cultivation of different *Agaricus* spp. mushrooms
NYE, Peter H.	soil–plant nutrient interactions, solute movement in soil; simulation modelling
O'RIORDAN, Timothy	EIA, environmental politics & management; interdisciplinary science & its role in policymaking; international environmental law & politics
OWEN, Denis F.	ecology, evolution, genetics; field studies on population genetics of lepidoptera & mollusca
PARRY, Martin L.	impacts of climate change
PAYNE, Roger S.	ocean toxicology, whale conservation
PEARCE, David W.	environmental economics
PEGLER, David N.	mycology: tropical macrofungi
PEREIRA, H. Charles	management of tropical watersheds, research in hydrological effects of land use; research organization
PERES, Carlos A.	*see* **BRAZIL, *São Paulo***
PETERKEN, George F.	ancient woodlands in Britain and rest of Europe; forest ecology, Nature conservation
PETTS, Geoffrey	environmental impacts of dams & water resource schemes, river regulation
PHILLIPS, Adrian	conservation esp.of protected areas, environmental protection
PHILLIPS, Cassandra F.E.	advocacy in international conventions; conservation of Antarctic, whale conservation
PINK, David A.C.	genetics of host–pathogen interactions in plant diseases, plant genetics; utilization of wild species in plant breeding
POLUNIN, Nicholas V.C.	marine and coastal ecology
PRANCE, Ghillean T.	Amazonian flora & conservation, economic botany, ethnobotany, plant systematics
PRICE, Martin F.	human dimensions of global environmental change; mountain peoples and their environments
RAMPHAL, Shridath	international affairs, international policy on sustainable development and the environment
RANDALL, Roland E.	coastal plant ecology, environmental management, Nature conservation
REYNOLDS, Fiona C.	environmental policy and its impact on countryside — UK & Europe
RICHARDSON, Paul N.	biological control of insects, conservation of insect fauna; reductions in pesticide usage
RIGGS, Timothy J.	genetics & plant breeding of horticultural crops
ROBERTS, Thomas M.	air pollution impacts, applied ecology; derelict land reclamation, research management
RODHOUSE, Paul G.K.	ecology & fisheries of marine molluscs, evolutionary biology, southern ocean Cephalopods
ROWLEY, John R.	Editor of international magazine re.environment, population, & sustainable development
ROWNTREE, Matthew J.W.	protected area management esp. re.subsistence community integration with protected-area authorities
SANDBROOK, J. Richard	sustainable development (environment/development)
SAYIGH, Ali M.	renewable energy
SHEPHERD, Alexander R. DAWSON	coastal-resource management, coastal-zone management, environmental education; management audit & information systems, reef fisheries, resource assessment (inventory & monitoring)
SHREEVE, David	The Conservation Foundation
SIMMONS, Ian	environmental history, books on environment
SISMAN, Richard 'Dick'	coastal processes; economics of rural tourism, sustainable tourism policies; travel and the environment
SOUTHWOOD, T. Richard E.	ecology, entomology, environmental policy & sciences
SPENCER, Jonathan W.	conservation of Nature & rare plants; forest ecology, historical ecology, & landscape history, silviculture
SPINAGE, Clive A.	African mammal ecology, development & planning of national parks & game reserves, wildlife legislation
STANTON, W. Robert	fermentation in tropical food & by-product recovery, nutritional improvement; waste treatment and pollution control; tropical Southeast Asian wetlands agroforestry for staple foods esp. starches
STEWART, John MASSEY	Russian, esp. Siberian, environment
STEWART, Philip J.	ecology of meaning & religion
STIRTON, Charles H.	biology of weeds, evolutionary biology of plants, and plant biogeography, conservation, & systematics (Leguminosae, petaloid monocotyledons, & Verbenaceae)

STONE, Peter B.	communication & international affairs; mountain conservation
SUETT, David L.	analytical & environmental chemistry; applied entomology
SULLIVAN, Francis	forest certification & conservation; sustainable forest management
SUNDERLAND, Keith D.	agroecology, arachnology, biological control
SWINGLAND, Ian R.	biodiversity management/conservation sciences
TAN, Koonlin	conservation of appropriate technology, economic resources, & socio-economic systems; renewable & sustainable use of wetlands; tropical environments & land-use, women's contribution in developing world
THOMAS, John D.	freshwater biology: epidemiology of parasites including those of fish & Man (schistosomiasis), biochemical ecology and behaviour of snail hosts of schistosome parasites, use of bioengineering approaches for control of schistosomiasis; ecology of eutrophication & acid deposition re.water management
TICKELL, Crispin C.C.	climatology, mountains, palaeohistory
TOMPSETT, Paul B.	forest genetic resources' research, seed conservation
TRAPNELL, Colin G.	applications of field research to conservation; land & forest ecology in tropical Africa — cartography, land-use classification, soil, & vegetation
VALLELY, Bernadette A.M.	ecofeminism, writing
VENIZELOS, Lily T.	see **GREECE**
WADHAMS, Peter	antarctic & arctic ice & ocean research, climate change
WAGER, Jonathan F.	consulting, landscape management & planning, teaching
WALKER, Brian W.	directing a field science foundation
WALSH, John A.	plant pathology & virology esp.of field vegetables
WALTON, David W.H.	conservation, ecology, & environmental management esp. in polar regions
WARNER, Frederick	air pollution, movement of radionuclides, nuclear weapons' tests, quality assurance, risk, water pollution
WATT, Trudy A.	design & analysis of field experiments; grassland ecology, vegetation management
WEBSTER, Richard	analysis & statistical design of survey, land & soil resource survey
WELLS, Susan M.	coral-reef & invertebrate conservation
WHIPPS, John M.	disease biocontrol, microbial ecology, mycoparasitism; release of genetically-modified microorganisms into environment
WHITE, James G.	soil-borne plant pathogens esp.*Pythium* spp.; biocontrol, detection by serological & molecular methods
WHITEHEAD, George K.	deer and their ecology
WHITMORE, Timothy C.	tropical moist forest taxonomy, phytogeography, ecology, silviculture, management, sustainable utilization & conservation; palms, *Macaranga* (Euphorbiaceae)
WICKENS, Gerald E.	economic plants of arid & semi-arid regions
WILSON, Richard T.	African ornithology, conservation of genetic resources, maintenance of biodiversity; sustainable integrated production systems
WOOD, David A.	physiology, biochemistry, & molecular genetics, of Basidiomycete Fungi esp.edible Fungi; fungal biotechnology
WOODELL, Stanley R.J.	conservation of British vegetation, ecology of extreme environments (arctic, desert, saltmarsh, serpentine); reproduction biology of plants
WOODGATE, Graham R.	'coevolution', Nature–society relationships; rural-based livelihood systems esp.agroforestry systems
WORTHINGTON, E. Barton	environmental consulting, ecocomplex realism; history of environmentalism; sheep- & trout-farming
WRIGHT, Martin P.W.	communication, environmental issues & solutions

Scotland

BOURNE, William R.P.	birds of sea & islands, petrels, pollution
BOYD, John M.	biology of Pinnipeds, ecology of Ungulates; environmental impacts of forest & electricity industries; island ecosystems, Nature conservation
BURBRIDGE, Peter R.	coastal zone management, environmental management & planning
CANNELL, Melvin G.R.	agroforestry, ecology, forestry; global environment
CLOUDSLEY, Timothy	Amazonian rain-forest (particularly in Peru) and indigenous native human societies; theories in the 'sociology of the environment' (or ecological sociology)
CORBET, Philip S.	carrying capacity, energy use in agricultural systems; environmental education, human population policies, medical entomology; wildlife conservation esp. of dragonflies
CROFTS, Roger	natural heritage, conservation
DAVIDSON, Donald A.	geoarchaeology, pedology, impact of ancient agriculture on soils; soil assessment for crops
DICK, Janet M.	domestication of tropical trees, tree physiology
DICKSON, James H.	archaeobotany, flora of Britain esp.Glasgow, oceanic islands (Tristan da Cunha, St Helena, Canary Islands), Papua New Guinea, Quaternary botany

DUNNET, George M. ecology of mammals & birds (esp. seabirds), environmental management, Nature conservation
FOSTER, John countryside, informal recreation
GRACE, John carbon & water relations of forest ecosystems, climatic change, environmental impacts on vegetation (wind, temperature, & drought stress); global carbon balance, tropical ecology
HAMMERTON, Desmond water pollution control, water quality management & monitoring
JENKINS, David zoology, environmental conservation, conservation of national & international wildlife esp.vertebrates
LAST, Frederick T. effects of atmospheric pollutants, integrated land-use, & tree biology — esp.role of mycorrhizas
LISTER-KAYE, John conservation lecturing & writing
LOENING, Ulrich E. ambient (renewable) energy technologies; academic studies on economic, & ethical, features of Humankind's place in the Biosphere; environmental & landscape photography, organic agriculture and ecologically-sound forestry
McINTYRE, Alasdair D. fisheries, marine ecology, pollution
MILLS, Derek H. conservation & ecology of Atlantic Salmon, effects of afforestation & agriculture on fisheries; effects of hydroelectric developments on aquatic fish & environment
MOFFATT, Ian environmental modelling incl.GIS; sustainable development in temperate & tropical environments
MOORE, Peter G. Amphipod Crustacea, marine biology, conservation, ecology, & systematics
NEWTON, Adrian C. forest conservation, genetic resources, resource ecology
PAGE, Christopher N. earth sciences, environmental evolution, taxonomy, evolution, & phytogeography, of Gymnosperms & Pteridophytes
POORE, M.E. Duncan ecology of land-use esp. in the tropics, mountains, & arid regions; Nature (biodiversity) conservation; principles of vegetational classification; science, philosophy, & policies, of environmental conservation, sustainable forestry
RACEY, Paul A. biology, ecology, & conservation of bats and other mammals
SMITH, Keith environmental hazards, hydroclimate variability
SMYTH, John C. environmental education esp.development of local & national strategies
TAIT, Elizabeth J. environmental management, policy analysis, risk, technology management
USHER, Michael B. conservation biology, management of the natural heritage
WHITTINGTON, Andrew E. distribution, systematics, & conservation, of Afrotropical Diptera esp. Platystomatidae & Syrdhidae,

Wales
FOGG, Gordon E. phytoplankton ecology, polar biology

UNITED STATES OF AMERICA

Alaska
DUFFY, David C. ecology, research on herbaceous biodiversity & forest harvesting, medical entomology, and seabird–fish interactions
KLEIN, David R. arctic ecology, effects of northern developments on wildlife & habitats, northern herbivory

Arizona
ANDERSON, Edward F. ethnobotany, systematics, & conservation, of Cacti
MAUGHAN, O. Eugene aquatic ecology & management
SHAW, William W. conservation biology, conservation in metropolitan environments, national parks, and protected areas; socio-political aspects of wildlife conservation

California
ALLEN, John P. biospherics, closed life-systems; ecology of ecobiomes in relation to Biosphere
ANGELO, Homer G. international law, communications, environmental protection
BAEZ, Albert V. environmental education
DASMANN, Raymond F. conservation biology, ecodevelopment
EHRLICH, Anne H. environmental consequences of nuclear war, environmental protection; population biology & control
EHRLICH, Paul R. biological sciences, population studies
FRANKIE, Gordon W. applied conservation biology, tropical ecology
GOLDBERG, Edward D. management of coastal zone, marine chemistry
HARDIN, Garrett H. ethics, population
HUNT, George L.,Jr biological oceanography, marine ornithology
JOHNSON, David W. international environmental law, policy, & philosophy
JOHNSTON, Harold S. chemistry of the stratosphere & troposphere; perturbation of natural global ozone balance by stratospheric aircraft, nuclear bombs, & other human activities
KETCHUM, Robert G. environmental photography & writing
KLEE, Gary A. coastal resource management, human ecology (cultural)

KRAUS, Daniel	*see* **NAMIBIA**
LaBUDDE, Samuel F.	prevention of illegal trading in wildlife and parts thereof; wildlife & species' protection
LEATHERWOOD, James S.	conservation & ecology of marine mammals
MacDONALD, Gordon J.F.	climate change, energy policy, geophysics; mathematical statistics, predictability
PEARLMAN, Nancy	environmental broadcasting
PEARMAN, Peter B.	amphibian & tropical ecology, ecology & conservation biology; experimental field biology evolution; development of science in developing countries
PURCELL, Arthur H.	preventive environmental management
ROWLAND, F.S. 'Sherry'	chemistry of the atmosphere esp.ozone & CFCs
SCHWARZSCHILD, B Shimon	environmental conservation, exploration/travel, Nature conservation, sustainable development
THRESHER, Philip B.	land-use cost–benefit analysis esp. of local community benefits, project preparation; wildlife resource conservation & utilization including corals
TRZYNA, Thaddeus C.	environmental policy
UDVARDY, Miklos D.F.	biogeography, ornithology
WAYBURN, Edgar	conservation of Nature; parks & protected areas
WEIR, David A.	investigative writing
WOODRUFF, David S.	conservation & evolution of animal species; development of natural resources (hydropower & irrigation projects) in Southeast Asia; genetic management of free-ranging & captive populations; snail-transmitted diseases in Southeast Asia

Colorado

BOYLE, Terence P.	aquatic ecology, conservation biology; ecological risk analysis, ecotoxicology; protected areas' research
DEMPSEY, Stanley	management of environmental conflict & impacts of mining operations
GLANTZ, Michael H.	climate–society interactions, third-world development
KELLOGG, William W.	atmospheric physics, climate theory, meteorological satellites
LOVINS, Amory B.	energy, resource efficiency, nuclear non-proliferation, hypercars, sustainability, electric utility policy
LOVINS, L. Hunter	corporate management, environment enhancement & restoration, resource efficiency, sustainability
MARTIN, Vance G.	conservation of wilderness & wildland values, indigenous knowledge, and natural resource management, cultural, psychological, & social, constructs & strategies for Nature conservation, trees and social forestry
PIELKE, Roger A.	air pollution modelling, atmospheric–ecological interactions, climate change & variability, mesoscale meteorology
SACKS, Arthur B.	environmental problems & policies in former Soviet Union, international environmental education, information, & training
WAAK, Patricia A.	biodiversity, population, sustainable development
WHITE, Gilbert F.	water management and associated environmental problems

Connecticut

ASHTON, Mark S.	agroforestry systems, forest restoration, regeneration ecology, silviculture
COHON, Jared L.	environmental management; systems analysis & modelling
EGLER, Frank E.	aesthetic landscape vegetation management, conservation, ecology, ecosystematics, environment, land preservation; right-of-way vegetation management
PELUSO, Nancy L.	development, environment, political ecology; social forestry, sociology of forestry

Delaware

PETERSON, Russell W.	environmental degradation and depletion of resources, influencing decision-makers re.such critical global issues as population growth

District of Columbia

AGARDY, M. Tündi	coastal management, fisheries' conservation, identification of critical marine ecological areas & processes; marine protected area planning, tropical marine ecology
AHMAD, Yusuf J.	environmental economics & management
BROWN, Lester R.	analysis of global environment & environmentally-related issues
BROWN, William Y.	natural history
CHALLINOR, David	forest ecology & soils, environmental conservation
EICHBAUM, William M.	biodiversity in the former Soviet Union; coastal & marine governance, pollution prevention
ENGELMAN, Robert	environment, natural resources, population, sustainable development
FULLER, Kathryn S.	World Wildlife Fund
FUTRELL, J. William	environmental law

GOODLAND, Robert J.A.   biodiversity conservation, ecology/economics interface; environmental aspects of agriculture, transport, & energy esp.big dams; environmental assessment & sustainability; tropical ecology & forests
HOYT, John A.   animal & environmental protection
JANSEN, Malcolm A.B.   biodiversity conservation, EIA, protected area management
LASH, Jonathan   environmental law & policy
MARKER-KRAUS, Laurie *see* **NAMIBIA**
McCLOSKEY, J. Michael   protection of the environment, particularly Nature
MITTERMEIER, Russell A.   biological diversity conservation, herpetology, primates
MORAN, Katy   applied anthropology, biocultural diversity, debt-for-Nature swaps; economic botany, environmental policy, ethnobiology
PELL, Claiborne   legislation & treaties re.oceans and environmental protection
PRESS, Frank   education, geophysics, science policy
PRITCHARD, Paul C.   national parks
REID, Walter V.   biological diversity, biotechnology, conservation, sustainable agriculture
SHAW, R. Paul   links between rapid population growth & environmental degradation; national sovereignty–warfaring propensities–environmental degradation; sustainable development through investments in human resources
WOODFORD, Michael H.   national park management and biodiversity planning; veterinary aspects of conservation — wild animal capture, disease, management, translocation, & utilization esp. in meat production

Florida
BJORNDAL, Karen A.   biology & conservation of marine turtles
BUSTAMANTE, Georgina   conservation & management of coastal ecosystems & fishery resources; tropical marine fish life-history, ecology, & ecophysiology
CLARK, John R.   environmental conservation esp.coastal-zone resources
CLEWELL, André F.   ecological restoration
GRUBER, Samuel H.   Elasmobranch (sharks, etc.) research, conservation, sensory physiology, & behaviour
HEINEN, Joel T.   conservation & ecology of terrestrial vertebrates, management of protected areas
RAY, Justina C.   ecology & conservation of African (and other tropical forest) carnivores & small mammals (rodents and shrews)
SMITH, Nigel J.H.   conservation & management of natural resources in humid tropics esp.agricultural resources, ethnobiology
THOMAS, Anamaria A.DE   interpreter of conservation & wildlife topics; outdoor conservation
WHITE, Susan L.   coastal resource management; environmental education & interpretation esp. re.marine parks & protected areas

Georgia
GOLLEY, Frank B.   ecology, ecosystems, human ecology
NORTON, Bryan G.   analysis of biodiversity policy; obligations to future generations, sustainability theory; valuation methodologies for policy analysis
SARMIENTO, Fausto O.   conservation ecology, environmental planning, landscape ecology; monitoring of environmental impacts on infrastructure development; restoration of 'tropandean' landscapes, sustainability

Hawaii
BREWBAKER, James L.   agriculture of tropics, crop & tree improvement
HOLTHUS, Paul F.   coastal/marine conservation & environmental management; islands in Asia/Pacific region — biodiversity conservation, coral reefs, ecosystem classification & inventory, marine parks, and sea-level rise impacts
MARAGOS, James E.   coastal-zone management, EIA; marine ecology in coastal areas in Asia–Pacific region and in tropical islands, protected areas' planning
POLOVINA, Jeffrey J.   marine climate & ecosystems, tropical marine population dynamics
RANDALL, Jack   classification of Indo–Pacific reef fishes esp.Acanthurid & Labroid fishes; marine conservation through parks & reserves, underwater guides to reef fishes

Idaho
MacFARLAND, Craig G.   management of protected areas: conservation & management of natural resources in developing countries using support of local people
WATSON, Richard   wildlife conservation esp.birds of prey and their habitats

Illinois
PETERSON, Claire McCARTHY   land-use law and zoning re.impacts of tourism on environmental & legal systems
PETERSON, Craig A.   land-use law esp. re.impacts of tourism on environmental & legal systems

Indiana
    CALDWELL, L. Keith   life sciences, public law & policy for the environment
    COHEN, Michael R.   children's concepts in science, technology, & the environment; experiential learning, teacher education

Iowa
    RAJAGOPAL,   environmental information systems, risk assessment, water pollution control,
      Rangaswamy   monitoring, and cost-effective regulation & policy

Kansas
    KIRKHAM, M.B.   plant–water–soil relations

Louisiana
    TURNER, R. Eugene   biological oceanography; conservation, management, wetlands

Maine
    DELOGU, Orlando E.   environmental land-use law
    LEMONS, John D., Jr   biological conservation, climate change; environmental education & ethics, national parks' management, nuclear waste
    SHORES, John N.   biodiversity, community participation, ecotourism; information systems, national parks, NGO development, protected areas; resource conservation & planning, sustainable development, wildland management

Maryland
    HAMED, Safei EL-DEEN   architecture and city planning in the Arab world, arid lands' development, ecotourism; environmental planning, assessments, & ethics, landscape analysis
    HOUGH, John L.   protected areas' policy & management; social dimensions of natural resource conservation & sustainable development
    McCLOSKEY, Maxine E.   arctic, coral reefs, marine mammals; marine protected areas esp. in the high seas, whale policy formation
    RITCHIE, Jerry C.   ecology, remote sensing, soil science
    SAUNIER, Richard E.   Biosphere reserves, environmental management planning & policy; identification & management of resource-use conflicts, *in situ* biodiversity conservation

Massachusetts
    ASHTON, Peter S.   impact of harvesting on biodiversity, maintenance of plant diversity in tropical forests
    BAZZAZ, Fakhri   biology of global change, recovery & regeneration of ecosystems
    CLARK, William C.   environment and development, global environmental policy; adaptive management
    COPPINGER, Raymond   canine behaviour & evolution, international agriculture and wildlife issues, non-lethal predator control
    EDSALL, John T.   continuing concern with environmental & population problems
    FIELD, Hermann H.   architecture, environmental planning, historic preservation, managing own wildlife protected area; public service at global & local levels in environmental issues
    GOLDMAN, Marshall I.   economics of Russia, environmental problems of former Soviet Union
    HOLLEMAN, Andrew D.   environmental education, wetlands' preservation
    LARSON, Joseph S.   application of wetland science to management & policy; beavers, wetland ecology, functions, & values
    MARGULIS, Lynn   cell evolution & biology, environmental evolution, Gaia theory, microbiology, symbiosis
    ORHUN-HEWSON,   environmental education, field research in ornithology; humpback whale iden-
      Canan   tification, oceanographic sampling (plankton tows, salinity, etc.)
    SCHULTES, Richard E.   economic & taxonomic botany, ethnobotanical conservation, ethnobotany of western Amazonia esp.of hallucinogenic, medicinal, & toxic, plants, rubber-yielding plants
    STOBAUGH, Robert B.   business education
    WILSON, Edward O.   biodiversity, biogeography, entomology, sociobiology
    WOODWELL, George M.   biotic impoverishment, biotic interactions in warming of Earth; ecology, how the world works, structure & function of Nature, toxic substances

Michigan
    GATES, David M.   biophysical (physiological) ecology, climate change
    NEEL, James VAN G.   population genetics
    STAPP, William B.   environmental education
    YOUNG, Raymond DE   exploring the role of information & non-tangible motives in promoting behaviour among individuals; understanding psychological aspects of common resource dilemmas *e.g.*tragedy of the commons

Minnesota
    MECH, L. David   population regulation, predator–prey relations, social ecology, Wolf ecology & behaviour

Mississippi
KUSHLAN, James A.   conservation of colonial waterbirds (herons, ibises, spoonbills, & storks), wet-
                               land ecology & conservation

Missouri
PHILLIPS, Oliver L.B.   ethnobotany, tropical forest ecology
RAVEN, Peter H.   biodiversity assessment & conservation esp.re.human population growth & tro-
                               pical forests; botanical gardens & scientific education; plant systematics &
                               evolution (evolutionary theory & biogeography)

Montana
GRITZNER, Jeffrey A.   environmental history, reconciliation of environmental rehabilitation with rural
                               livelihood systems
HENNING, Daniel H.   Asian national parks & tropical forests, biodiversity, interdisciplinary approaches,
                               public participation; Buddhism in Nature protection, ecotourism
PARSONS, David J.   ecosystem management, fire & plant ecology; global change, wilderness eco-
                               systems
PFEIFFER, Egbert W.   environmental physiology of mammals (adaptations to cold e.g.hibernation);
                               environmental problems of third world esp.re.war
STANFORD, Jack A.   groundwater ecology, limnology; river ecology and life histories of aquatic
                               insects

Nevada
WATSON, Charles St D. Jr 'commons ecology' in Nevada; ecology of USA's Bureau of Land Management

New Hampshire
CARROLL, John E.   environmental diplomacy, ecology; international environmental ethics & values,
                               religion
CROKER, Robert A.   coastal marine ecology, history of conservation & ecology; systematics-ecolo-
                               gy of marine Amphipoda

New Jersey
BURGER, Joanna   behavioural ecology of vertebrates, behavioural toxicology esp.lead in birds;
                               biomonitoring, effects of incubation temperature on development and beha-
                               viour of snakes; population dynamics and effects of people on coastal birds
                               esp.endangered and threatened species
GOCHFELD, Michael   occupational & environmental medicine, environmental toxicology, neuro-
                               behavioural toxicology of heavy-metals (esp.lead & mercury); medical sur-
                               veillance & biomonitoring, environmental biomonitoring, habitat & nest-site
                               selection, reproductive synchrony, growth and behavioural development;
                               global population and environmentally-sustainable development

New York
BALICK, Michael J.   economic botany, ethnobotany, palm taxonomy, plant domestication
BASSOW, Whitman   environmental communications & policy, industrial environmental manage-
                               ment, technical assistance & training
BRODEUR, Paul A.   journalism, writing
COHEN, Joel E.   demography, ecology, epidemiology, population biology & genetics
FORERO, Enrique   botanical gardens, floristics, neotropics, plant conservation, vascular plant
                               taxonomy
GRAD, Frank P.   environmental & public health law
KRATTIGER, Anatole F.   biodiversity, biotechnology, institution-building, international development,
                               technology transfer
LaBASTILLE, Anne   ecology, endangered species & extinction; land-use planning, wilderness
                               conservation
LIKENS, Gene E.   analysis of ecosystems, aquatic ecology, biogeochemistry, land–water inter-
                               actions, limnology, precipitation chemistry
LUSCOMBE, Bruce A.   animal behaviour, birds of prey, falcons; land-use strategies, natural resource
                               management, wildlife conservation
MATTHIESSEN, Peter   environment, Nature, social activism, writing, Zen teaching
MILBRATH, Lester W.   environmental beliefs & values, environmental policy; social change, sustain-
                               ability of society
RICHTER, Robert   documentary television/educational productions on environmental subjects
SCHALLER, George B.   conservation & field studies of vertebrates, esp.large mammals (Carnivores &
                               Ungulates)
SPETH, James G.   environmental sustainability, sustainable human development
STALTER, Richard   research in plant ecology

North Carolina
BILSBORROW,   environment & development in developing countries; population processes
   Richard E.

MALONE, Thomas F.	role of scientists in achieving sustainable human development world-wide while maintaining a healthy & biologically productive global environment in perpetuity
OKUN, Daniel A.	water quality management

Ohio

LAL, Rattan	ecological consequences of tropical deforestation and water management; teaching & research in soil conservation; soil processes and greenhouse gas emissions
TAYLOR, J. Mary	conservation of mammals

Oklahoma

KESSLER, Edwin	agriculture, environment, meteorology

Oregon

BONINE, John E.	environmental & public-interest law
SOLOMON, Allen M.	bioclimatology, global & plant ecology, palynology, Quaternary palaeoecology, vegetation geography

Pennsylvania

KIM, Ke Chung	biodiversity conservation, systematic/evolutionary biology (taxonomy, coevolution of Arthropods)

South Carolina

BURNETT, G. Wesley	biogeography; comparative philosophies & historical geography of conservation; conservation in developing countries, park planning, & management
McGREAL, Shirley	Primate conservation & protection

Tennessee

ABERNETHY, Virginia D.K.	population–immigration–environment
COUTANT, Charles C.	aquatic ecology, environment–energy issues; Pacific salmon & Striped Bass (*Roccus saxatilis*) biology, thermal effects
GORZULA, Stefan 'Steve'	environmental & social impact assessment of large dams; neotropical herpetology, wildlife conservation & management esp. of Crocodilians
MOORE, Alan W.	protected area planning & management, training of protected area personnel
PEINE, John D.	MAB, national park management, research in parks; strategies for sustainable development

Texas

PIANKA, Eric R.	biogeography, evolutionary biology; evolutionary community, landscape, & Lizard, ecology; phylogenetic systematics, remote sensing

Utah

BLAHNA, Dale J.	teaching & research in application of social science to natural resources' management & planning issues
CHAPMAN, Joseph A.	mammalogy specifically of Lagomorpha
KENNEDY, James J.	natural resources: environmental policy & administration
TRESHOW, Michael	air pollution biology

Vermont

DONOVAN, Richard Z.	forest management & certification; natural forest conservation & ecology
GADE, Daniel W.	past & present ecological relationships of peasant & folk societies, vegetation change esp.deforestation through historic time; process of plant & animal domestication, ethnobiology, settlement and disease
HAMILTON, Lawrence S.	forestry, protected area planning & management; sustainable use of mountain & small island environments
MOLTKE, Konrad VON	environmental policy, international environmental relations
WESTING, Arthur H.	environmental conservation, environmental security re.military activities & war
YOUNG, Steven B.	biogeography, education in arctic environmental issues, research in Quaternary palaeoecology

Virginia

BARNEY, Gerald O.	environment, future, strategic planning, sustainable development
CAHN, Robert	environmental writing
CARPENTER, Richard A.	EIA in developing countries; definition, measurement, & prediction, of sustainable development
CHOI, Yearn Hong	drinking-water, environmental management & policy, Potomac River Basin waste management, waste-water

DEAN, Faisal — protected areas' management, sustainable development, & wildlife conservation, in the Middle East

DOUROJEANNI, Marc J. — Amazon forest & wildlife management, environmental institution-building, protected areas' management; sustainable development in American humid tropics & tropical Andes

LUSIGI, Walter — natural resources' management, range ecology

McCARTHY, Gerald P. — education, environmental conservation, environmental law & public policy; environmental philanthropy, sustainable development

PERRY, John S. — atmospheric sciences, climatology, computer applications; environmental policy, international science

RAPPOLE, John H. — ecology of Nearctic migratory birds that winter in the Neotropics; effects of tropical habitat loss on vertebrate populations

RAY, G. Carleton — marine ecology esp.land–sea interactions in coastal zone; marine parks & protected areas; polar region ecology (marine mammals esp.Walrus)

SINGER, S. Fred — atmospheric chemistry & physics, energy economics & policy; environmental policy & science, global warming; space pollution (orbiting debris), stratospheric ozone

WRIGHT, R. Michael — community-based approaches to conservation, application of legal techniques in different cultural settings; environmental justice, poverty alleviation & environmental quality

Washington
BLISS, Lawrence C. — alpine & arctic ecology, development, structure, & functions, of arctic ecosystems; ecophysiology of plants in cold-stressed environments, patterning of plant communities, plant production; role of applied ecology in arctic development, role of soils in plant distribution

ORIANS, Gordon H. — conservation biology, ecology; science & environmental policy

West Virginia
ADAMS, Lowell W. — ecology & management of urban wildlife

Wisconsin
ARCHIBALD, George — preservation of cranes (Gruidae) and their habitats

BRYSON, Reid A. — climate change, climatology, interdisciplinary environmental studies

HASLER, Arthur D. — experimental limnology, migration of fishes esp. role of sense of smell in orientation (olfactory landscape imprinting); physiology of aquatic organisms, radioisotopes in lakes (under ice and transported by insects)

JORDAN III, William R. — ecological restoration

LANDFRIED, Steven E. — crane (Gruidae) conservation & migration, environmental education in rural areas, satellite tracking

TEMPLE, Stanley A. — conservation biology, ecology of birds of prey, endangered species esp. birds; island biogeography, landscape ecology esp. issues of habitat fragmentation; wildlife management

URUGUAY
DELPIANO, Jose P. CASTRO — cattle production, conservation & protection of natural resources, farming

MELLO, Mateo J. MAGARIÑOS-DE — environment in general; environmental economy, education, law, & policy

USA, *see* **UNITED STATES OF AMERICA**

VENEZUELA
DIAZ-MARTIN, Diego — communications, conservation, environmental education, management & planning of natural protected areas; scientific research, training of personnel

RODRIGUEZ, Andrés R. RODRIGUEZ — ichthyology, ecology, marine sciences; environmental education, journalism, writing

SALINAS, Pedro J. — animal ecology, environmental law & education, insect behaviour & ecology; protected areas' planning & management, wildlife management

VIETNAM
VO, Quy — ecology, education; effects of defoliants on environment during Vietnam war, environmental conservation, national parks and protected areas, ornithology, training in environmental science

WEST INDIES, *see separately* ***Antigua, Bahamas, Barbados, British Virgin Islands, Cayman Islands, Guadeloupe, Jamaica, Martinique, Netherlands Antilles, St Barthélemy, St Lucia, Trinidad & Tobago***

YUGOSLAVIA
   JOVANOVIĆ, Petar   desertification, environmental diseases, Man-made 'natural disasters'; ozone
                            depletion, satellite telemedicine

ZAMBIA
   ELLISON, Gabriel   conservation through art
   MUMBA, Wanga   environment & population issues, natural-resource use & management

ZIMBABWE
   CHILD, Graham P.T.   institutions & economics essential to effective resource conservation
   FÉRON, Eric M.   biodiversity, community-based conservation; rural & sustainable development,
                            wildlife conservation
   HUTTON, Jonathan M.   crocodylia in many areas of Africa, wildlife conservation & management
   NDUKU, Willie K.   national parks & wildlife management
   PANGETI, George N.   design & implementation of wildlife management and environmental conserva-
                            tion projects
   TOIT, Raoul F. DU   conservation of African megafauna & habitats, field protection & management
                            of Black Rhinoceros (*Diceros bicornis*); integration of commercial & com-
                            munity-based conservation activities in conservancies as models for sustain-
                            able economic development in Africa's semi-arid rangelands; land-use
                            planning and EIA in developing countries
   ZAMCHIYA, David M.   environmental legislation

Abandoned landscape, revitalization of
KRAJČOVIČ, Roman S. — Slovak Rep.
abiotic stress, responses of plants to
MANSFIELD, Terence A. — UK, England
aboriginal adaptations to life in deserts, and in rain-
forests*
— history
*COVACEVICH, Jeanette A. — Australia, Qld
— interests
OVINGTON, John D. — Australia, ACT
— natural-resource managers, training & education of
FOX, Allan M. — Australia, NSW
— peoples: rights, interests, & self-government
FENGE, Terence A.E. — Canada, Ont.
— studies, Australian
BOYD, William 'Bill' Edgar — Australia, NSW
Aborigines — Aboriginal enterprise development,
commercial use of wild animal resources,
sustainable land-use
WILSON, George R. — Australia, WA
Acanthaster population outbreaks (impact on coral-
reef ecosystems)
VANTIER, Lyndon M.DE — Australia, Qld
Acanthurid fishes
RANDALL, John 'Jack' — USA, HI
access to justice (environmental legislation)
PITTA, Luis CAEIRO — Portugal
accidents, nuclear (international environmental law)
LANG, Winfried — Switzerland
accounting, environmental
GONZÁLEZ, Juan A.AGUIRRE — Costa Rica
acid deposition, ecology of
THOMAS, John D. — UK, England
— precipitation, influence of
WIELGOLASKI, Frans-Emil — Norway
acoustic metrology, and sounding (SODAR)*
acoustics, building
*SINGAL, Sagar P. — India, Delhi
action, environmental, community
GITTINS, John W.E.H. — UK, England
—, —, religion-motivated
JAKOWSKA, Sophie — Dominican Rep.
—, grassroots
MEHTA, Mahesh C. — India, Delhi
—, implementation of, on sustainable development
LINDNER, Warren H. — Switzerland
— plans, environmental conservation and
AZIS, P.K.ABDUL — Saudi Arabia
— —, —, preparation of
OLI, Krishna P. — Nepal
— —, — — national
BISWAS, Asit K. — UK, England
— —, species'
LAMBERTINI, Marco — Italy
— research, community-based
OLI, Krishna P. — Nepal
activism, environmental
ADAMS, Aubrey — Trinidad
LUTZENBERGER, José A. — Brazil, RS
—, — conservation
SINGH, Hari B. — India, Delhi

—, social
MATTHIESSEN, Peter — USA, NY
—, —, in Himalayan region
BAHUGUNA, Sunderlal — India, UP
activities, antagonistic, of microorganisms
JARIWALA, Savitri — India, UP
—, anthropogenic, interrelationships between C/N/S/P
biogeochemical cycles as influenced by
STEWART, John W.B. — Canada, Sask.
—, human, effects of, on Caribou
BLOOMFIELD, Michael — Canada, BC
—, —, perturbation of natural global ozone balance
by
JOHNSTON, Harold S. — USA, CA
—, mapping & monitoring
WITT, Ronald G. — Switzerland
—, training
SABOGAL, Cesar A. — Indonesia
activity, human, degradation of environment by
ZLOTIN, Roman I. — Russia
adaptations, desert
CLOUDSLEY-THOMPSON, John L.
UK, England
— to life in deserts and in rain-forests — aboriginal
COVACEVICH, Jeanette A. — Australia, Qld
adaptive management
CLARK, William C. — USA, MA
administration, conservation
BOYLAND, Desmond E. — Australia, Qld
—, —, organization
FERRAR, Anthony A. — RSA
—, environmental
BÁNDI, Gyula — Hungary
BEZANSON, Keith A. — Canada, Ont.
KENNEDY, James J. — USA, UT
STRONG, Maurice F. — Canada, Ont.
TORTELL, Philip — NZ
— of Nature conservation
WOLDHEK, Siegfried — The Netherlands
—, public
MORELL, Merilio G. — Italy
SARMA, K.Madhava — Kenya
—, —, environment and
OLOJEDE, Ayodele A. — Nigeria
adult education
CACCIA, Charles L. — Canada, Ont.
— environmental education
GARDNER, Julia E. — Canada, BC
advocacy, environmental
FRY, Ian W. — Australia, NSW
— in international conventions
PHILLIPS, Cassandra F.E. — UK, England
— of nexus between religion and Nature
SINGH, Karan — India, Delhi
aerial surveys
WILSON, George R. — Australia, WA
aerohydrodynamics
SINITSINA, Irene E. — Russia
aesthetic evaluation, protected areas
SZILASSY, Zoltán — Hungary

---

† For fully effective use of this Appendix II it should be noted that some of the main subjects are reduced in complexity by being presented in two sets, both of which should be consulted before any search for a particular speciality is abandoned. Thus, as well as 'conservation' we have, *following its completion,* 'conservation of'; as well as 'development' we have, *following its completion,* 'development of'; as well as 'ecology' we have, *following its completion,* 'ecology of'; and as well as 'environment' we have, *following its completion,* 'environment of'. In these cases — as stated in the headings to the appropriate columns — the long dashes indicating repetition will refer to the preceding noun as well as the 'of'. Similarly treated in two sets are such paired groups as *e.g.* 'environment' and 'environmental', both of which alternatives (as cross-referenced *in situ*) should be consulted in cases of need.

* Indicates that the next-named and asterisk-marked Biographee is also responsible for this item. — Ed.

afforestation against erosion
  DAMERDJI, M.Amine   Algeria
—, coastal
  MOUDUD, Hasna J.   Bangladesh
—, effects of, on fisheries
  MILLS, Derek H.   UK, Scotland
—, mangrove
  MOUDUD, Hasna J.   Bangladesh
Africa
  HARRISON, Paul A.   UK, England
—, arid ecosystems of
  ODUOL, Peter A.   Kenya
—, creation & management of national parks esp.in
  VERSCHUREN, Jacques C.F.   Belgium
—, crocodiles in many areas of
  HUTTON, Jonathan M.   Zimbabwe
—, eastern & southern, wildlife conservation &
    management in
  BALDUS, Rolf D.   Germany
—, environmental management in
  WILLIAMS, Martin A.J.   Australia, SA
—, mountain areas of
  MESSERLI, Bruno   Switzerland
—, plant geography of
  MEDWECKA-KORNAŚ, Anna M.   Poland
—, southern, atmospheric systems of
  PRESTON-WHYTE, Robert A.   UK, England
—, sub-Saharan, environmentally-sound technology
    & cooperation in
  KUFORIJI-OLUBI, Bola   Nigeria
—, taxonomic botany of
  HEDBERG, Inga M.M.   Sweden
—, tropical, land & forest ecology in
  TRAPNELL, Colin G.   UK, England
—, tropical, plant geography of
  KORNAŚ, Jan   Poland
—, West, conservation of biodiversity & wilderness
    in
  TUBOKU-METZGER, Daphne J.A. Sierra Leone
African carnivores, ecology & conservation of
  RAY, Justina C.   USA, FL
— conservation
  PRICE, Mark R. STANLEY   Kenya
— forests, West & Central, taxonomic botany and
    conservation of
  CHEEK, Martin R.   UK, England
— Leguminosae, taxonomy of
  LOCK, John M.   UK, England
— mammal ecology
  SPINAGE, Clive A.   UK, England
— mammals, large
  ELTRINGHAM, Stewart K.   UK, England
— —, —, ecology of
  JEWELL, Peter A.   UK, England
— megafauna & habitats, conservation of
  TOIT, Raoul F.DU   Zimbabwe
— ornithology
  FRY, Charles H.   Oman
  WILSON, Richard T.   UK, England
— Rhinoceros, conservation of
  BROOKS, Peter M.   RSA
— Zingiberaceae, taxonomy of
  LOCK, John M.   UK, England
Africa's semi-arid rangelands, sustainable economic
    development in
  TOIT, Raoul F.DU   Zimbabwe
Afrotropical Diptera, distribution, conservation, &
    systematics, of
  WHITTINGTON, Andrew E.   UK, Scotland
Agaricus spp. mushrooms
  NOBLE, Ralph   UK, England

ageing society
  BOOTE, Robert E.   UK, England
Agenda 21, implementation of
  NOVOA, Laura   Chile
agreements, international, application of, re.wild flora
    & fauna
  KACEM, Slaheddine BEL   Tunisia
agri-biotechnology applications, transfer of (sustain-
    ability and a better environment)
  JAMES, W.Clive   Cayman Islands
— -environmental policy
  GREEN, Brynmor H.   UK, England
agricultural development in the Sahara
  DAMERDJI, M.Amine   Algeria
— —, international
  JAMES, W.Clive   Cayman Islands
— —, sustainable
  BISWAS, Asit K.   UK, England
  BISWAS, Margaret R.   UK, England
— ecosystems
  TERRASSON, François   France
— —, conservation biology of
  PETRETTI, Francesco   Italy
— melioration
  TRENČIANSKA, Jana   Slovak Rep.
— production systems, sustainable
  TEWOLDE, Assefaw   Mexico
— research, international
  JAMES, W.Clive   Cayman Islands
— resources in humid tropics
  SMITH, Nigel J.H.   USA, FL
— systems
  NEWMAN, Edward I.   UK, England
— —, energy use in
  CORBET, Philip S.   UK, Scotland
agriculture
  HARRISON, Paul A.   UK, England
  KESSLER, Edwin   USA, OK
—, ancient, impact of, on soils
  DAVIDSON, Donald A.   UK, Scotland
— and conservation, relationships between
  HUNKELER, Pierre   Switzerland
—, ecological
  SWAMINATHAN, Monkombu S.   India, TN
—, effects of, on fisheries
  MILLS, Derek H.   UK, Scotland
—, environmental aspects of
  GOODLAND, Robert J.A.   USA, DC
— farms
  SIVADAS, Ponathil   India, Ker.
—, impact of ancient, on soils
  DAVIDSON, Donald A.   UK, Scotland
—, international
  BENNETT, Sara L.   Canada, BC
—, —, & wildlife issues
  COPPINGER, Raymond   USA, MA
— of tropics
  BREWBAKER, James L.   USA, HI
—, organic
  HARRIS, Philip J.C.   UK, England
  LOENING, Ulrich E.   UK, Scotland
—, production, energy conservation in
  SHYAM, Murari   India, MP
—, regenerative
  LÜTZENBERGER, José A.   Brazil, RS
—, slash-and-burn, sustainable alternatives to
  SANCHEZ, Pedro A.   Kenya
—, soil recovery
  FISCHER, Gert R.   Brazil, SC
—, sustainable
  ABROL, Inder P.   India, Delhi

NAYVE-ROSSI, Portia A.   Philippines
REID, Walter V.   USA, DC
THAPA, Gopal B.   Thailand
VISSER, Nicolaas W.   Kenya
WAJIH, Shiraz A.   India, UP
—, —, and energy politics
LINDSTROM, U.B.   Finland
— (— development, N–S relations)
MYERS, Norman   UK, England
—, — — re.
SAOUMA, Edouard V.   Lebanon
agroecology
EDWARDS, Peter J.   Switzerland
MACDONALD, David W.   UK, England
RAMAKRISHNAN, P.S. ('Ram')   India, Delhi
SHARMA, Subrat   India, UP
SUNDERLAND, Keith D.   UK, England
agro-ecosystems, ecology of
SINGH, Kaushalendra P.   India, UP
TSHERNYSHEV, Wladimir B.   Russia
agroforestry
ABROL, Inder P.   India, Delhi
CANNELL, Melvin G.R.   UK, Scotland
LAKSHMANAN, Kalimedu K.   India, TN
LI, Wenhua   China
NANAYAKKARA, Vitarana R.   Sri Lanka
PAPANASTASIS, Vasilios P.   Greece
SANCHEZ, Pedro A.   Kenya
—, appropriate land-use including
BUDOWSKI, Gerardo   Costa Rica
—, economics of
GONZALEZ, Juan A AGUIRRE   Costa Rica
— /forestry in tropics, domestication of tropical trees
for
LEAKEY, Richard R.B.   Kenya
—, sustainable
HARRIS, Philip J.C.   UK, England
—, —, local development &
KERN, Berndt   Sweden
KERN, Eha   Sweden
— systems
ASHTON, Mark S.   USA, CT
WOODGATE, Graham R.   UK, England
— —, esp.multi-strata agroforests
LEAKEY, Richard R.B.   Kenya
—, tropical Southeast Asian wetlands, for staple
foods
STANTON, W.Robert   UK, England
agroforests, multi-strata, agroforestry systems esp.
LEAKEY, Richard R.B.   Kenya
agronomy
LIONNET, Joseph F.G.   Seychelles
aid, foreign
KUMAR, Prem   Canada, Alb.
—, international
OVINGTON, John D.   Australia, ACT
aids [information etc.]
TINKER, Jon   Canada, BC
AIDS eradication, HIV/
SIVADAS, Ponathil   India, Ker.
air-conditioning, environmentally-acceptable
SRINIVASAN, Kandadai   India, Mysore
— environment
YOUSSEF, Abdullatif K.   Syria
— management
EKARATH, Raveendran   Bahrain
— pollution
ABBASPOUR, Madjid   Iran
BRINCHUK, Mikhail M.   Russia
RAY, Prasanta K.   India, W. Bengal

REHMAN, Syed Z.   Pakistan
WARNER, Frederick   UK, England
— — biology
TRESHOW, Michael   USA, UT
— — control
CHANDAK, Surya P.   India, Delhi
— — effects on plants & insects
BELL, Nigel   UK, England
— — / environmental ecology
HUTTUNEN, Satu   Finland
— — impacts
ROBERTS, Thomas M.   UK, England
TERBLANCHE, Petro   RSA
— — (international environmental law)
LANG, Winfried   Switzerland
— — law
SILVA, Allenisheo L.M.DE   Sri Lanka
— meteorology
PATIL, Rashmi S.   India, Mah.
— — modelling
PIELKE, Roger A.   USA, CO
SINGAL, Sagar P.   India, Delhi
— — monitoring and control equipment design &
development
MATHUR, Harbansh B.   India, Delhi
— programmes (environmental monitoring
instruments)
PRASAD, Basudeo   India, E.Punjab
— quality modelling & monitoring
PATIL, Rashmi S.   India, Mah.
aircraft, stratospheric, perturbation of natural global
ozone balance by
JOHNSTON, Harold S.   USA, CA
Algae, marine
DAHL, Arthur L.   Switzerland
algology
PANDIT, Ashok K.   India, J&K
alien plants' invasion
STRASBERG, Dominique   La Réunion
allelopathy
KOHLI, Ravinder K.   India, Punjab
Alliums
KENNEDY, Robert   UK, England
alpine, arctic, biology
GIVEN, David R.   NZ
— ecology
BLISS, Lawrence C.   USA, WA
— — (plant distributions & origins)
GOOD, Roger B.   Australia, ACT
— ecosystems
WIELGOLASKI, Frans-Emil   Norway
— environmental management
KEAGE, Peter L.   Australia, Vic.
— environments, impacts of human use on
SPATE, Andrew 'Andy' P.   Australia, NSW
alternative energies
CHARLIER, Roger H.L.   Belgium
— energy systems
ABBASI, Shahid A.   India, TN
— sanitary engineering
LUTZENBERGER, José A.   Brazil, RS
Amazon
HEMMING, John H.   UK, England
— Basin, Hg contamination in
LACERDA, Luiz D.   Brazil, RJ
— forest management
DOUROJEANNI, Marc J.   USA, VA
— region, ecology of tropical
SIOLI, Harald F.L.   Germany
— wildlife management
DOUROJEANNI, Marc J.   USA, VA

Amazonian flora & conservation
  PRANCE, Ghillean T.   UK, England
— Indians, cultures & fates of
  SIOLI, Harald F.L.   Germany
— rain-forest esp.Peru and indigenous native human
    societies
  CLOUDSLEY, Timothy   UK, Scotland
ambient (renewable) energy technologies
  LOENING, Ulrich E.   UK, Scotland
American humid tropics, sustainable development in
  DOUROJEANNI, Marc J.   USA, VA
amphibian biology & conservation
  GRIFFITHS, Richard A.   UK, England
— ecology
  PEARMAN, Peter B.   USA, CA
amphibians, Chilean, ecology of feeding,
    reproduction, & conservation of
  DIAZ, José Valencia   Chile
—, conservation biology of
  DANIELS, R.L. Ranjit   India, TN
—, ecology of
  BEHRA, Olivier   Madagascar
—, research
  DIAZ, José Valencia   Chile
—, ecotoxicology in
  LAMBERT, Michael R.K.   UK, England
amphipod Crustacea
  MOORE, Peter G.   UK, Scotland
Amphipoda, marine, systematics-ecology of
  CROKER, Robert A.   USA, NH
analysis, ecological risk
  BOYLE, Terence P.   USA, CO
—, ecosystem
  MELKANIA, Niranjan P.   India, MP
  PANDIT, Ashok K.   India, J&K
—, environmental systems
  NISHIOKA, Shuzo   Japan
—, holistic, of neotropical ecosystems
  ADIS, Joachim U.   Germany
—, landscape
  HAMED, Safei El-Deen   USA, MA
—, land-use cost-benefit, esp.local community
  THRESHER, Philip B.   USA, CA
—, landscape
  HAMED, Safei El-Deen   USA, MD
—, legislative
  TOLENTINO, Amado   Philippines
—, multidisciplinary management
  KRISHNAYYA, Jaswant G.   India, Mah.
—, multivariate
  HILL, Mark O.   UK, England
—, natural resources policy
  MORELL, Merilio G.   Italy
— of biodiversity policy
  NORTON, Bryan G.   USA, GA
— — ecosystems
  LIKENS, Gene E.   USA, NY
— — field experiments
  WATT, Trudy A.   UK, England
— — global environment & environmentally-related
      issues
  BROWN, Lester R.   USA, DC
— — survey
  WEBSTER, Richard   UK, England
—, policy
  TAIT, Elizabeth J.   UK, Scotland
—, —, valuation methodologies for
  NORTON, Bryan G.   USA, GA
—, pollution (hazardous waste)
  SAXENA, Anil K.   India, Delhi

—, problem-oriented
  GROOT, Wouter T.de   The Netherlands
—, project
  GONZALEZ, Juan A.Aguirre   Costa Rica
—, rainfall frequency
  CLARK, Colin   UK, England
—, strategic, & sustainable development
  WILSON, George R.   Australia, WA
—, systems
  COHON, Jared L.   USA, CT
  NILSSON, Sten   Austria
  PANDEYA, Satish C.   India, UP
—, theory for problem-oriented
  GROOT, Wouter T.de   The Netherlands
analytical chemistry
  MOLDAN, Bedřich   Czech Rep.
  SUETT, David L.   UK, England
anatomy, plant
  LAKSHMANAN, Kalimedu K.   India, TN
ancient agriculture, impact of, on soils
  DAVIDSON, Donald A.   UK, Scotland
— woodland, extent of & changes in
  KIRBY, Keith J.   UK, England
— woodlands in Britain and rest of Europe
  PETERKEN, George F.   UK, England
Andaman & Nicobar Islands, conservation
    of endangered & endemic flora of
  SINHA, Akhauri R.P.   India, A&N Islands
Andes
  MESSERLI, Bruno   Switzerland
—, tropical, sustainable development in
  DOUROJEANNI, Marc J.   USA, VA
angiosperm embryology
  LAKSHMANAN, Kalimedu K.   India, TN
angling, trout
  HUGHES, George, R.   RSA
animal behaviour
  HASAN, Mohammed Nordin   Malaysia
  LUSCOMBE, Bruce A.   USA, NY
  PRESCOTT, Jacques   Canada, Que.
— capture, wild
  WOODFORD, Michael H.   USA, DC
— conservation
  CHALABI, Bouzid   Algeria
—, desert, ecology
  BÜTTIKER, William   Switzerland
— domestication, process of
  GADE, Daniel W.   USA, VT
— ecology
  GHABBOUR, Samir I.   Egypt
  GIMINEZ-DIXON, Mariano   Switzerland
  SALINAS, Pedro J.   Venezuela, NSW
— —, desert
  BÜTTIKER, William   Switzerland
— —, terrestrial
  NJE, Ngog   Cameroon
— energy
  KHANDELWAL, Kailash C.   India, Raj.
— evaluation in dairy & beef production systems*
— genetic resource, domestic, conservation &
      management of
  *TEWOLDE, Assefaw   Mexico
— germ-plasm, conservation of
  WARDEH, Muhammad Fadel   Syria
— pests, biological control of
  FENNER, Frank   Australia, ACT
— –plant interactions
  LOCK, John M.   UK, England
  MALLOCH, Andrew J.C.   UK, England

* See lower footnote on p. 409.

— populations
FRAZER, John F.D. UK, England
— production, studies in
WARDEH, Muhammad Fadel Syria
— protection
HOYT, John A. USA, DC
— psychology
SHELDRICK, Daphne M. Kenya
— rights
ONAYEMI, Olarotimi O. Nigeria
— sociology
KAWANABE, Hiroya Japan
— species, conservation & evolution of
WOODRUFF, David S. USA, CA
— translocation, wild
WOODFORD, Michael H. USA, DC
—, wild, conservation
WILSON, George R. Australia, WA
—, —: disease, management, & utilization, esp.meat
production
WOODFORD, Michael H. USA, DC
—, —, resources, commercial use of Aborigines
WILSON, George R. Australia, WA
animals, anti-predator defences of
EDMUNDS, Malcolm UK, England
—, behaviour of
LANG-BEERMAN, Ernst M. Switzerland
—, ethical status of
LINZEY, Andrew UK, England
—, infectious diseases of
FENNER, Frank Australia, ACT
—, Judaism and
COHN-SHERBOK, Dan UK, England
—, reintroduction of — Africa
PRICE, Mark R.Stanley Kenya
—, theological status of
LINZEY, Andrew UK, England
ant–butterfly interactions (see also ants)
ELMES, Graham W. UK, England
antagonistic activity of microorganisms
JARIWALA, Savitri India, UP
Antarctic (or antarctic) conservation
BONNER, W.Nigel UK, England
DIAZ, José Valencia Chile
KEAGE, Peter L. Australia, Vic.
LEWIS-SMITH, Ronald I. UK, England
PHILLIPS, Cassandra F.E. UK, England
— environment
LEWIS-SMITH, Ronald I. UK, England
— environments, impacts of human use of
SPATE, Andrew 'Andy' P. Australia, NSW
— —, marine pelagic ecosystems of
BRANDINI, Frederico Brazil, Par.
— fish, early life-history of
KELLERMANN, Adolf K. Germany
— geomorphology & limnology
SPATE, Andrew 'Andy' P. Australia, NSW
— ice & ocean research
WADHAMS, Peter UK, England
— Penguins
DIAZ, José Valencia Chile
— plant ecology
LEWIS-SMITH, Ronald I. UK, England
— research
DIAZ, José Valencia Chile
Antarctica
MOSLEY, John G. Australia, Vic.
anthropic processes, impact study of, in the coastal
zone
GRANJA, Helena M. Portugal

anthropogenic activities, interrelationships between
C/N/S/P biogeochemical cycles as influenced
by
STEWART, John B. Canada, Sask.
— sciences, scientific research in
IZRAEL, Yuri Russia
anthropology
GOLDSMITH, Edward UK, England
HEYERDAHL, Thor Norway
McNEELY, Jeffrey A. Switzerland
PITT, David Switzerland
—, applied
MORAN, Katy USA, DC
—, maritime
DIEGUES, Antonio C.S. Brazil, SP
anti-litter campaigning
SOPHONPANICH, Chodchoy Thailand
— -poaching–protected areas
BANGURA, Kalie I. Sierra Leone
ants (see also ant)
—, red wood, biology, ecology & protection of,
CHERIX, Daniel Switzerland
apples, genetics & breeding of
ALSTON, Frank H. UK, England
application of financial experience & principles to
'The Commons'
McCAMMON, Antony L.T. Switzerland
— — international agreements re.wild flora & fauna
KACEM, Slaheddine Bel Tunisia
— — law re.tropical coastal environments
DAVIE, James D.S. Australia, Qld
— — legal techniques in different cultural settings
WRIGHT, R.Michael USA, VA
— — satellite remote-sensing in forest management
& conservation
JUSOFF, Kamaruzaman Malaysia
— — social science to natural resource management
& planning issues
BLAHNA, Dale J. USA, UT
— — wetland science to policy & management
LARSON, Joseph S. USA, MA
—, pesticide, horticulture &
CROSS, Jeremy V. UK, England
—, scientific
TERRASSON, François France
applications, agri-biotechnology, transfer of (sustainability and a better environment)
JAMES, W.Clive Cayman Islands
—, clonal technology
LAL, Piare India, AP
—, computer
PERRY, John S. USA, VA
—, medical (solar energy)
SCHARMER, Klaus Germany
— of field research to conservation
TRAPNELL, Colin G. UK, England
—, technological
ARMIJOS, Mariano Montaño Ecuador
applied anthropology
MORAN, Katy USA, DC
— biogeography = conservation
LOURENÇO, Wilson R. France
— biology
LEE, Lawrence H.Y. Hong Kong
— conservation biology
FRANKIE, Gordon W. USA, CA
— ecology
ROBERTS, Thomas M. UK, England
— —, role of, in arctic development
BLISS, Lawrence C. USA, WA

applied (contd)
— entomology
SUETT, David L.   UK, England
— mathematics
NIKULIN, Valery A.   Russia
— ornithology
PINOWSKI, Jan K.   Poland
— physical geography in (sub-) Mediterranean zone
VOS, Willem   The Netherlands
— physics, research in, re.recovery of refuse, and
    underutilized resources
ARIAS-CHAVEZ, Jesus   Mexico
— toxicology
JOOSTING, Peter E.   The Netherlands
appropriate land-use including agroforestry
BUDOWSKI, Gerardo   Costa Rica
— management of Kiskunság National Park and
    other protected areas
TÖLGYESI, István   Hungary
— technology, conservation of well-tried
TAN, Koonlin   UK, England
aquaculture
YEROULANOS, Marinos   Greece
— farms
SIVADAS, Ponathil   India, Ker.
—, trends
WELCOMME, Robin L.   Italy
—, tropical
DOUMENGE, François   Monaco
aquariology
DOUMENGE, François   Monaco
aquatic biogeography
POR, Francis D.   Israel
— biotopes, main, of Arabian peninsula, Sahara, &
    Sahel
DUMONT, Henri J.   Belgium
— crustaceans, environmental biology of
HOLDICH, David M.   UK, England
— ecology
ABBASI, Shahid A.   India, TN
BOYLE, Terence P.   USA, CO
COUTANT, Charles C.   USA, TN
LIKENS, Gene E.   USA, NY
MAUGHAN, O.Eugene   USA, AZ
MOORE, James W.   Canada, Alb.
— ecosystems, biodiversity of
AZIS, P.K.Abdul   Saudi Arabia
— environment, effects of hydroelectric
    developments on
MILLS, Derek H.   UK, Scotland
— insects, life histories of, river ecology &
STANFORD, Jack A.   USA, MT
— management
MAUGHAN, O.Eugene   USA, AZ
— organisms, physiology of
HASLER, Arthur D.   USA, WI
—, semi-, mammals, ecology of
BALČIAUSKAS, Linas   Lithuania
Arab world, architecture & city planning in the
HAMED, Safei El-Deen   USA, MD
Arabia, zoological survey of
BÜTTIKER, William   Switzerland
Arabian ornithology
FRY, Charles H.   Oman
— Oryx, reintroduction of, to the wild in Oman
DALY, Ralph, H.   Oman
— peninsular, main aquatic biotopes of
DUMONT, Henri J.   Belgium
arachnology
SUNDERLAND, Keith D.   UK, England

Araneae, invertebrate ecology, esp.of
DUFFEY, Eric A.G.   UK, England
arboriculture
HELLIWELL, D.Rodney   UK, England
archaeobotany
DICKSON, James H.   UK, Scotland
archaeo-ecology
LOVRIC, Andrija Z.   Croatia
archaeology
BOYD, William 'Bill' Edgar   Australia, NSW
CRAMPTON, Colin B.   Canada, BC
—, environmental
BOYD, William 'Bill' Edgar   Australia, NSW
architecture
FIELD, Hermann H.   USA, MA
FRIEDMAN, Yona   France
GEBREMEDHIN, Naigzy   Kenya
— in the Arab World
HAMED, Safei El-Deen   USA, MD
—, landscape
JACOBS, Peter D.A.   Canada, Que.
LOVEJOY, Derek   UK, England
USUKI, Mitsuo   Thailand
Arctic (or arctic)
JOHNSTON, Douglas M.   Canada, BC
McCLOSKEY, Maxine E.   USA, MD
— alpine biology
GIVEN, David R.   NZ
— biogeography
FORBES, Bruce C.   Finland
— birds
PRESTRUD, Pål   Norway
— circumpolar flora
POLUNIN, Nicholas   Switzerland
—, —, political development in*
— — world, environmental management &
    planning, and industrial development, in
*FENGE, Terence A.E.   Canada, Ont.
— development, role of applied ecology
BLISS, Lawrence C.   USA, WA
— ecology
BLISS, Lawrence C.   USA, WA
KLEIN, David R.   USA, AK
SVOBODA, Josef   Canada, Ont.
WOODELL, Stanley R.J.   UK, England
— ecosystems
BLISS, Lawrence C.   USA, WA
— environment, protection of the
PRESTRUD, Pål   Norway
— environmental issues, education in
YOUNG, Steven B.   USA, VT
— foxes
PRESTRUD, Pål   Norway
— geography & history
ROWLEY, Diana M.R.   Canada, Ont.
— ice & ocean research
WADHAMS, Peter   UK, England
— mammals
PRESTRUD, Pål   Norway
— regions
ROWLEY, Graham W.   Canada, Ont.
— science
ROWLEY, Diana M.R.   Canada, Ont.
— vegetation
POLUNIN, Nicholas   Switzerland
— waters
MOORE, James W.   Canada, Alb.
area development, rural, integrated
RAI, Suresh Chand   India, Sikkim

* See lower footnote on p. 409.

—, marine protected, planning
  AGARDY, M.Tündi — USA, DC

—, protected, conservation management
  STRONACH, Neil R.H. — Ireland

—, —, management *see* protected area management

—, —, — & planning
  KASSIOUMIS, Konstantinos — Greece

—, —, personnel, training of*

—, —, planning
  *MOORE, Alan W. — USA, TN

—, —, research
  BOYLE, Terence P. — USA, CO

—, protection, planning & management
  WESCOTT, Geoffrey C. — Australia, Vic.

—, wildlife protected, own
  FIELD, Hermann H. — USA, MA

areas, arid & semi-arid, landforms, soils, & climatic change in
  WILLIAMS, Martin A.J. — Australia, SA

—, biodiversity & protected
  UPRETI, Biswa N. — Nepal

—, coastal, marine ecology in, in Pacific & Asia regions
  MARAGOS, James E. — USA, HI

—, conservation, ecodevelopment & management of
  HOECK, Hendrik N. — Switzerland

—, —, landscape management in Nature
  SEPP, Kalev — Estonia

—, local, planning of
  OLI, Krishna P. — Nepal

—, marine ecological, critical, identification of
  AGARDY, M. Tündi — USA, DC

—, —, management
  CRAIK, Wendy — Australia, Qld

—, — protected
  EARLL, Robert C. — UK, England
  FOWLER, Sarah L. — UK, England
  WHITE, Susan L. — USA, FL

—, — —, esp. in the high seas
  McCLOSKEY, Maxine E. — USA, MD

—, mountain (Africa, Himalaya, Andes)
  MESSERLI, Bruno — Switzerland

—, natural
  LEBRETON, Philippe — France

—, — protected, legal aspects of
  ABDELHADY, Abdelaziz — Egypt/Kuwait

—, — —, planning & management of
  DIAZ-MARTIN, Diego — Venezuela

—, —, planning & management of
  HERRERO, Stephen M. — Canada, Alb.

—, Nature conservation, management of
  DALY, Ralph H. — Oman

—, protected, *see* protected areas

—, — –anti-poaching
  BANGURA, Kalie I. — Sierra Leone

—, —, appropriate management of
  TÖLGYESI, István — Hungary

—, —, conservation of
  CÂMARA, Ibsen DE G. — Brazil, RJ
  CHALABI, Bouzid — Algeria
  PHILLIPS, Adrian — UK, England
  VALDRÈ, Giovanni — Italy
  WAYBURN, Edgar — USA, CA

—, —, coastal conservation &
  SALM, Rodney V. — Kenya

—, —, control of plant invasions in
  THEBAUD, Christophe — France

—, —, description of
  STOIBER, Hans H. — Austria

—, —, environmental planning in
  FLETCHER, Raúl E. — Panama

—, —, establishment, management & protection of
  LAMPREY, Hugh F. — UK, England

—, —, evaluation of
  STOIBER, Hans H. — Austria

—, —, in tropical forests incorporating local & indigenous concerns
  LEES, Annette M. — NZ

—, —, land–sea interactions in
  RAY, G.Carleton — USA, VA

—', —, management, *see* protected areas' management

—, —, — & control of plant invasions in
  THEBAUD, Christophe — France

—, —, — & development of
  ALVARADO, Juan SKINNER — Guatemala

—, — marine
  GUBBAY, Susan — UK, England

—, —, conservation &
  SALM, Rodney V. — Kenya

—, —, masterplanning for
  BARCSAY, László — Hungary

—, —, monitoring
  MOURA, Robert MANNERS — Portugal

—, —, national parks &
  HAYNES-SUTTON, Ann M. — Jamaica
  SANCHEZ, Heliodoro — Colombia
  VO, Quy — Vietnam

—, — natural
  ZABELINA, Natalia M. — Russia

—, — —, design & survey
  WRIGHT, Shane D.T. — NZ

—, —, organization, development, & management
  LAMBERTINI, Marco — Italy

—, —, planning, *see* protected areas' planning

—, —, policy
  HOUGH, John L. — USA, MD

—, —, —, planification, & management of
  PONCIANO, Ismael — Guatemala

—, —, systems planning for
  HEISS, Gerhard — Germany

—, —, tropical, and their conservation
  COBB, Stephen M. — UK, England

—, rural, environmental education in
  LANDFRIED, Steven E. — USA, WI

—, tropical, environmental biology and plant taxonomy
  KEAY, Ronald W.J. — UK, England

—, —, protected, conservation of
  COBB, Stephen M. — UK, England

—, —, voluntary work in
  MOURA, Robert MANNERS — Portugal

argon, isotopic composition of
  VORONOV, Arkady N. — Russia

arid & semi-arid areas, landforms, soils & climatic change in
  WILLIAMS, Martin A.J. — Australia, SA

— climates
  HARE, F.Kenneth — Canada, Ont.

— — (Sahelian environment)
  FRANGI, Jean-Pierre — France

— countries, water problems in
  DAMERDJI, M.Amine — Algeria

— ecosystems of Africa
  ODUOL, Peter A. — Kenya

— —, conservation of & research in
  MILLS, M.G.L. ('Gus') — RSA

* *See* lower footnote on p. 409.

arid ecosystems, conservation of (contd)
— —, — —, in coastal regions & in Jordan
  HATOUGH-BOURAN, Alia M.A.   Jordan
— -land management
  HEATHCOTE, Ronald L.   Australia, SA
— lands
  RECKERS, Ute   Kenya
— — development
  HAMED, Safei EL-DEEN   USA, MD
— — ecology
  BATANOUNY, Kamal H.   Egypt
  HOUÉROU, Henry N.LE   France
  SEELY, Mary K.   Namibia
— — in western Australia
  BELLAMY, David J.   UK, England
— plant ecology
  WALT, Pieter T.VAN DER   RSA
— regions, ecology of land-use in
  POORE, M.E.Duncan   UK, Scotland
— —, economic plants of
  WICKENS, Gerald E.   UK, England
— —, salinity problems in
  BATANOUNY, Kamal H.   Egypt
—, semi-, lands, ecological sustainable use of
  SATTLER, Paul S.   Australia, Qld
— zone ecology
  CHADWICK, Michael J.   Sweden
— zones
  MEHER-HOMJI, Vispy M.   India, TN
— —, reforestation of
  ZOUHA, Sekkou   Morocco
art, conservation through
  ELLISON, Gabriel   Zambia
—, environmental values & philosophy through
  GITTINS, John W.E.H.   UK, England
arthropods, coevolution of
  KIM, Ke Chung   USA, PA
—, temperature & water relations
  CLOUDSLEY-THOMPSON, John L.
                                     UK, England
artificial breeding of entomophagous insects
  CIOCHIA, Victor   Romania
Asia*
—, community-based environmental management in
    urban
  *FUREDY, Christine   Canada, Ont.
—, environmental management in
  WILLIAMS, Martin A.J.   Australia, SA
—, highland Southeast: poverty, biodiversity &
    development in
  DEARDEN, Philip   Canada, BC
— region, marine ecology in coastal areas in
  MARAGOS, James E.   USA, HI
—, South and Southeast, conservation biology in
  YONZON, Pralad   Nepal
—, Southeast, environmental management in Brunei
  EATON, Peter P.   Brunei
—, —, wildlife conservation field research in
  BENNETT, Elizabeth L.   Malaysia
—, —, mammals of
  McNEELY, Jeffrey A.   Switzerland
— –Pacific region
  JOHNSTON, Douglas M.   Canada, BC
— — — —, ecological planning in the
  SHAPIRO, Harvey A.   Japan
— — — —, islands in
  HOLTHUS, Paul F.   USA, HI

Asian national parks
  HENNING, Daniel H.   USA, MT
— rain-forest, Southeast
  GATHORNE-HARDY, Gathorne   UK, England
— tropical forests
  HENNING, Daniel H.   USA, MT
—, tropical Southeast, wetlands agroforestry for
    staple foods in
  STANTON, W.Robert   UK, England
assessment
  NELSON, J.Gordon   Canada, Ont.
—, biodiversity
  DAS, Indraneil   India, TN
  GOOD, Roger B.   Australia, ACT
  RAVEN, Peter H.   USA, MO
—, conservation resource
  HIBBERD, John K.   Australia, ACT
—, environmental
  DAHL, Arthur L.   Switzerland
  GALLON, Gary T.   Canada, Ont.
  GOODLAND, Robert J.A.   USA, DC
  HAMED, Safei EL-DEEN   USA, MA
  OVINGTON, John D.   Australia, ACT
  SERAFIN, Rafal K.   Poland
  WITT, Ronald G.   Switzerland
—, — impact see environmental impact assessment
—, —, impacts, of development projects
  SUNDARESAN, Bommaya B.   India, TN
—, —, of economic development projects
  GOODLAND, Robert J.A.   USA, DC
—, —, planning & management
  JACOBS, Peter D.A.   Canada, Que.
—, impact, climate change
  PERNETTA, John C.   The Netherlands
—, noise
  KHAN, Niaz A.   UAE
— of effects of northern development on wildlife &
    habitats
  KLEIN, David R.   USA, AK
— — national parks & protected areas
  LAMPREY, Hugh F.   England, UK
— — natural resources, surveys for
  STANTON, James P.   Australia, Qld
— — water resources
  GOLUBEV, Genady N.   Russia
—, population, sea-turtles'
  MARQUEZ-MILLAN, Rene   Mexico
—, resource (inventory & monitoring)
  SHEPHERD, Alexander R.DAWSON UK, England
—, risk
  RAJAGOPAL, Rangaswamy   USA, OH
—, soil, for crops
  DAVIDSON, Donald A.   UK, Scotland
—, strategic environmental
  TOORNSTRA, Franke H.   The Netherlands
assessments, environmental
  HAMED, Safei EL-DEEN   USA, MD
—, resource, wetland & biodiversity
  BENNETT, Sara L.   Canada, BC
—, social & environmental impact, of large dams
  GORZULA, Stefan   USA, TN
assistance, development
  PALMBERG-LERCHE, Christal M.   Italy
— issues, environment & development
  FRY, Ian W.   Australia, NSW
—, technical
  BASSOW, Whitman   USA, NY
—, —, to developing countries
  PALMBERG-LERCHE, Christel M.   Italy

association building, environmental
 GALLON, Gary T.   Canada, Ont.
associations
 VANTIER, Lyndon M.DE   Australia, Qld
assurance, quality
 WARNER, Frederick   UK, England
astronomy
 GAYOOM, Maumoon ABDUL   Maldives
Atlantic Salmon, ecology & conservation of
 MILLS, Derek H.   UK, Scotland
atmosphere, chemistry of the
 EGLI, Robert A.   Switzerland
 ROWLAND, F.Sherwood   USA, CA
—, physics of the, scientific research in
 IZRAEL, Yuri   Russia
—, upper, physics
 RADICELLA, Sandro M.   Italy
atmospheric boundary layer
 SINGAL, Sagar P.   India, Delhi
— chemistry
 SINGER, S.Fred   USA, VA
 SINGH, O.N.   India, UP
— –climatic phenomena
 KONDRATYEV, Kirill Y.   Russia
— –ecological interactions
 PIELKE, Roger A.   USA, CO
— environment, international
 BOJKOV, Rumen D.   Switzerland
— physics
 KELLOGG, William W.   USA, CO
 SINGER, S.Fred   USA, VA
— pollutants, effects of
 LAST, Frederick T.   UK, Scotland
— science
 DIAB, Roseanne D.   RSA
— sciences
 PERRY, John S.   USA, VA
 RHO, Chae-Shik   S.Korea
— system interactions
 RADICELLA, Sandro M.   Italy
— systems (southern Africa)
 PRESTON-WHYTE, Robert A.   UK, England
— transport, long-range, of metals & other pollutants
 STEINNES, Eiliv   Norway
— turbidity
 FRANGI, Jean-Pierre   France
audio productions
 GUNAWARDENE, Nalaka J.   Sri Lanka
audit, management
 SHEPHERD, Alexander R.DAWSON UK, England
auditing, environmental
 CHARLIER, Roger H.L.   Belgium
 TERBLANCHE, Petro   RSA
 TORTELL, Philip   NZ
Australia, arid lands in western
 BELLAMY, David J.   UK, England
—, environmental management in
 WILLIAMS, Martin A.J.   Australia, SA
Australian Arboriginal studies
 BOYD, William 'Bill' Edgar   Australia, NSW
— ecology, history of
 SPECHT, Raymond L.   Australia, Qld
— (northern) tidal waterways
 MESSEL, Harry   Australia, Qld
— reptiles: deserts, heaths, & rainforest; taxonomy &
     zoogeography of extant & extinct
 COVACEVICH, Jeanette A.   Australia, Qld
autecology of Cape plants & vegetation
 BOUCHER, Charles   RSA

— — tundra plants
 WIELGOLASKI, Frans-Emil   Norway
authorities, protected area, subsistence community
     integration with
 ROWNTREE, Matthew J.W.   UK, England
autochthonous tropical forest management &
     conservation
 FISCHER, Gert R.   Brazil, SC
avian ecology
 HOLROYD, Geoffrey L.   Canada, Alb.
 YAHYA, Hafiz S.A.   Saudi Arabia
awareness, education and
 LAMBERTINI, Marco   Italy
—, environmental
 IGNACIMUTHU, Savarimuthu   India, TN
 HAQUE, Mohammed A.   India, Har.
—, —, propaganda for
 BAHUGUNA, Sunderlal   India, UP
—, —, through print media
 SINGH, Hari B.   India, Delhi
—, —, using concept of SILATHAM
 TEJADHAMMO, Pongsak   Thailand
—, Nature, at home and in the tropics
 KERN, Berndt   Sweden
 KERN, Eha   Sweden
— programmes, environmental
 GUPTA, Brij K.   India , TN
—, promoting public, in social forestry
 SIVADAS, Ponathil   India, Ker.
—, public
 GUNAWARDENE, Nalaka J.   Sri Lanka
 HOWELL, Calvin A.   Barbados
 NASH, Nancy   Hong Kong
 ODULA, Michael A.N.   Kenya
 ,   , raising
 ZINKE, Alexander   Austria

badger–bovine TB
 BARRY, James M.   Ireland
badgers
 KELCEY, John G.   UK, England
Bahamas, sea birds of the
 HOLOWESKO, Lynn P.   Bahamas
balance, global carbon
 GRACE, John   UK, Scotland
—, heat & water
 HARE, F.Kenneth   Canada, Ont.
—, natural global ozone
 JOHNSTON, Harold S.   USA, CA
— sheets, ecological
 LINDSTRÖM, U.B.   Finland
— surface energy
 FRANGI, Jean-P.   France
balancing conservation & consumption
 MISRA, Ramdeo   India, UP
Bamboos in rural development
 BOA, Eric   UK, England
bambooland ecology
 NUMATA, Makoto   Japan
banking/finance–environment/development
 McCAMMON, Antony L.T.   Switzerland
bark beetles (Scolytidae), ecology of
 OKOŁÓW, Czeslaw   Poland
bass, striped, biology
 COUTANT, Charles C.   USA, TN

bats, conservation of
    RACEY, Paul A.   UK, Scotland
beaches
    BATE, Guy C.   RSA
bears, ecology & management of
    HERRERO, Stephen M.   Canada, Alb.
beavers
    LARSON, Joseph S.   USA, MA
beef production systems, animal evaluation in
    TEWOLDE, Assefaw   Mexico
beetles, bark (Scolytidae), ecology of
    OKOŁÓW, Czeslaw   Poland
—, Carabid
    CARRILLO, Antonio MACHADO   Canary Islands
behaviour, animal
    HASAN, Mohammed NORDIN   Malaysia
    LUSCOMBE, Bruce A.   USA, NY
    PRESCOTT, Jacques   Canada, Que.
—, canine
    COPPINGER, Raymond   USA, MA
—, conservation, among individuals
    YOUNG, Raymond DE   USA, MI
—, Elasmobranch
    GRUBER, Samuel H.   USA, FL
—, insect
    SALINAS, Pedro J.   Venezuela
—, mammalian
    DODDS, Donald G.   Canada, NS
— of animals
    LANG-BEERMAN, Ernst M.   Switzerland
— — snakes, effects of incubation temperature on
    BURGER, Joanna   USA, NJ
— — trace elements in natural environment
    STEINNES, Eiliv   Norway
— re.Nature philosophy
    TERRASSON, François   France
—, wolf
    MECH, L.David   USA, MN
behavioural development
    GOCHFELD, Michael   USA, NJ
— ecology
    DHINDSA, Manjit S.   India, Punjab
    GRIFFITHS, Richard A.   UK, England
    KREBS, John R.   UK, England
— — of large mammals
    LOVARI, Sandro   Italy
— — vertebrates
    BURGER, Joanna   USA, NJ
— —, carnivore
    MILLS, M.G.L. ('Gus')   RSA
— toxicology
    BURGER, Joanna   USA, NJ
beliefs, environmental
    MILBRATH, Lester W.   USA, NY
benthic ecology
    PANDIT, Ashok K.   India, J&K
benthos
    EARLL, Robert C.   UK, England
Beringia, biogeography of
    MARUSIK, Yuri M.   Russia
better environment, transfer of agri-biotechnology
    applications re.
    JAMES, W.Clive   Cayman Islands
bibliography, scientific
    LIONNET, Joseph F.G.   Seychelles
bioaccumulation of metals in biota
    NUORTEVA, Pekka O.   Finland
biochemistry
    WOOD, David A.   UK, England
— research
    KENT, Paul W.   UK, England

biocidal plants, taxonomy of
    LAKSHMANAN, Kalimedu K.   India, TN
bioclimatology
    HOUÉROU, Henry N.LE   France
    MEHER-HOMJI, Vispy M.   India, TN
    SOLOMON, Allen M.   USA, OR
biocoenology
    MASING, Viktor   Estonia
bioconservation
    LEBRETON, Philippe   France
biocontrol
    WHITE, James G.   UK, England
—, disease
    WHIPPS, John M.   UK, England
biocultural diversity
    MORAN, Katy   USA, DC
biodiversity
    ABROUGUI, Mohamed A.   Tunisia
    BALČIAUSKAS, Linas   Lithuania
    BATISSE, Michel   France
    BURLEY, Jeffery   UK, England
    DAHL, Arthur L.   Switzerland
    EGZIABHER, Tewolde B.GEBRE   Ethiopia
    FAIZI, Shahul   Saudi Arabia
    FÉRON, Eric M.   Zimbabwe
    GŁOWACIŃSKI, Zbigniew A.   Poland
    IMBODEN, Christoph N.   UK, England
    KAWANABE, Hiroya   Japan
    KHOSHOO, Triloki N.   India, Delhi
    KRATTIGER, Anatole F.   USA, NY
    LEBRETON, Philippe   France
    LEEMANS, Rik   The Netherlands
    McALLISTER, Donald E.   Canada, Ont.
    NAYAR, M.Param   India, Ker.
    OJEDA, Ricardo A.   Argentina
    PRESCOTT, Jacques   Canada, Que.
    RANJITSINH, M.K.   India, MP
    SHORES, John N.   USA, ME
    SOKOLOV, Vladimir   Russia
    VISSER, Nicolaas W.   Kenya
    WAAK, Patricia A.   USA, CO
    WANG, Sung   China
    WANG, Xianpu   China
    WILSON, Edward O.   USA, MA
— & protected areas
    UPRETI, Biswa N.   Nepal
— (Asian tropical forests and national parks)
    HENNING, Daniel H.   USA, MT
— assessment
    DAS, Indraneil   India, TN
    GOOD, Roger B.   Australia, ACT
    RAVEN, Peter H.   USA, MO
— conservation
    BRIDGEWATER, Peter   Australia, ACT
    ČEŘOVSKÝ, Jan   Czech Rep.
    COLE, Norman H.A.   Sierra Leone
    DANIELS, R.J.Ranjit   India, TN
    DEY, Subhash C.   India, Delhi
    DUNCAN, Patrick   France
    FENNER, Frank   Australia, ACT
    FONSECA, Gustavo A.B.   Brazil, MG
    GOODLAND, Robert J.A.   USA, DC
    HEDBERG, Inga M.M.   Sweden
    HEDBERG, K.Olov   Sweden
    JANSEN, Malcolm A.B.   USA, DC
    KIM, Ke Chung   USA, PA
    MOYER, Jack T.   Japan
    PARYSKI, Paul E.   Haiti
    RAVEN, Peter H.   USA, MO
    SANCHEZ, Heliodoro   Colombia
    SINGH, Shekhar   India, Delhi

SWAMINATHAN, Monkombu S. India, TN
UGWU, Christopher B. Nigeria
WIJESINGHE, Leslie Sri Lanka
ZLOTIN, Roman I. Russia
— — & management
SULAYEM, Mohammad S.A. Saudi Arabia
—, — biology
DANIELS, R.J.Ranjit India, TN
— —, in situ
SAUNIER, Richard E. USA, MD
— —, interdisciplinary approaches
FONSECA, Gustavo A.B. Brazil, MG
— —, islands in Asia–Pacific region
HOLTHUS, Paul F. USA, HI
— — management
JEFFERIES, Bruce E. Papua New Guinea
(—), —, Nature
POORE, M.E.Duncan UK, Scotland
—, — of, in West Africa esp.Sierra Leone
TUBOKU-METZGER, Daphne J.A. Sierra Leone
— databases
MacKINNON, John R. Hong Kong
—, ecodevelopment &
MELKANIA, Niranjan P. India, MP
—, economic evaluation of, conservation biology and
PUSHPANGADAN, Palpu India, Ker.
—, environmental law and
WESTREICHER, Antonio ANDALUZ Bolivia
—, herbaceous, & forest harvesting, research on
DUFFY, David C. USA, AK
—, herpetofaunal, Saharan & Sahelian
LAMBERT, Michael R.K. UK, England
—, Highland SE Asia
DEARDEN, Philip Canada, BC
—, impact of harvesting on
ASHTON, Peter S. USA, MA
— in the former Soviet Union
EICHBAUM, William M. USA, DC
— issues
NTAHUGA, Laurent Burundi
—, maintenance of
WILSON, Richard T. UK, England
— management
BRIDGEWATER, Peter Australia, ACT
SWINGLAND, Ian R. UK, England
—, marine
ANGEL, Martin V. UK, England
— of aquatic ecosystems
AZIS, P.K.ABDUL Saudi Arabia
— of managed forests, maintenance of
KIRBY, Keith J. UK, England
— planning
WOODFORD, Michael H. USA, DC
— policy, analysis of
NORTON, Bryan G. USA, GA
— protection
AMIRKHANOV, Amirkhan M. Russia
FERNANDO, Ranjen L. Sri Lanka
— — programmes
SIVADAS, Ponathil India, Ker.
— (rangelands), conservation of
DUNCAN, Patrick France
— research
GOOD, Roger B. Australia, ACT
— resource assessments & management strategies
BENNETT, Sara L. Canada, BC
—, semiotic mechanisms of
KULL, Kalevi Estonia
—, spiders re.
RAVEN, Robert J. Australia, Qld

— (sustainable development, North–South relations)
MYERS, Norman UK, England
—, — utilization of, conservation and
PUSHPANGADAN, Palpu India, Ker.
— (wetlands), conservation of
DUNCAN, Patrick France
bioenergetics
PANDEYA, Satish C. India, UP
bioengineering for control of schistosomiasis
THOMAS, John D. UK, England
biofertilizers
KHANDELWAL, Kailash C. India, Raj.
biogeochemical cycles
ROSSWALL, Thomas Sweden
— —, C/N/S/P, interrelationships between, as
influenced by anthropogenic activities
STEWART, John W.B. Canada, Sask.
— —, global
BOLIN, Bert R. Sweden
— —, microbial, in prairie saline lakes & prairie
wetlands
ROBARTS, Richard D. Canada, Sask.
biogeochemistry
LIKENS, Gene E. USA, NY
MOLDAN, Bedřich Czech Rep.
—, marine
KRASNOV, Eugene V. Russia
— of coastal systems
LACERDA, Luiz D. Brazil, RJ
biogeography
BEARD, John S. Australia, WA
BURNETT, G.Wesley USA, SC
GARDNER, Andrew S. Oman
INGRAM, Glen J. Australia, Qld
MASING, Viktor Estonia
PIANKA, Eric R. USA, TX
SPECHT, Raymond L. Australia, Qld
UDVARDY, Miklos D.F. USA, CA
ULLUWISHEWA, Rohana K. Sri Lanka
WILSON, Edward O. USA, MA
YOUNG, Steven B. USA, VT
ZLOTIN, Roman I. Russia
—, applied = conservation
LOURENÇO, Wilson R. France
—, aquatic
POR, Francis D. Israel
—, arctic
FORBES, Bruce C. Finland
—, coral
POLUNIN, Nicholas V.C. UK, England
VERON, John E.N. Australia, Qld
—, crop origins and
CLEMENT, Charles R. Brazil, Amaz.
—, evolutionary
RAVEN, Peter H. USA, MO
—, island
TEMPLE, Stanley A. USA, WI
— of Beringia
MARUSIK, Yuri M. Russia
— — Canarian flora
BRAMWELL, David Canary Islands
— — mammals
OJEDA, Ricardo A. Argentina
— — North Holarctic
MARUSIK, Yuri M. Russia
— — scorpions
LOURENÇO, Wilson R. France
—, spiders re.
RAVEN, Robert J. Australia, Qld
—, tropical
JIM, Chi Yung Hong Kong

biography, plant
STIRTON, Charles H.   UK, England
bioindicators
REDAUD, M.Gladys BELANDRIA DE   Guadeloupe
— of habitat contamination, ecotoxicology in reptiles
   as
LAMBERT, Michael R.F.   UK, England
biological conservation
LEMONS, John D., Jr   USA, ME
— — in tropical SE Asia
KIEW, Bong Heang   Malaysia
— — re.people in the tropics
FRAZIER, John G.   Mexico
— control
SUNDERLAND, Keith D.   UK, England
— —, Nature protection through
CIOCHIA, Victor   Romania
— — of animal pests
FENNER, Frank   Australia, ACT
— — — insects
RICHARDSON, Paul N.   UK, England
— — — some plant diseases
JARIWALA, Savitri   India, UP
— — — weeds
ROOM, Peter M.   Australia, Qld
— corridors, design of
SEVILLA, Lorenzo B.CARDENAL
   Nicaragua/Guatemala
— diversity
ANISHETTY, Narasimha M.   Italy
EIDSVIK, Harold K.   France
McNEELY, Jeffrey A.   Switzerland
PALMBERG-LERCHE, Christel M.   Italy
REID, Walter V.   USA, DC
WAHLSTEDT, Jens   Sweden
— — conservation
MITTERMEIER, Russell A.   USA, DC
WELCOMME, Robin L.   Italy
— features of Humankind's place in The Biosphere
LOENING, Ulrich E.   UK, Scotland
— knowledge & information, popularizing
PIIROLA, Jouko   Finland
— invasions
HOBBS, Richard J.   Australia, WA
— oceanography
HUNT, George L., Jr   USA, CA
KRISHNAMURTHY, Kothandaraman   India, TN
TURNER, R.Eugene   USA, LA
— pest control, forestry
FISCHER, Gert R.   Brazil, SC
— research
KERN, Berndt   Sweden
KERN, Eha   Sweden
— sciences
EHRLICH, Paul R.   USA, CA
biology
RACEY, Paul A.   UK, Scotland
—, air pollution
TRESHOW, Michael   USA, UT
— & conservation of oceanic islands
RYAN, Peter G.   RSA
—, applied
LEE, Lawrence H.Y.   Hong Kong
—, arctic-alpine
GIVEN, David R.   NZ
—, cell
MARGULIS, Lynn   USA, MA
SHARMA, Arun K.   India, W.Bengal
—, conservation, *see* conservation biology

—, —, and economic evaluation of biodiversity
PUSHPANGADAN, Palpu   India, Ker.
—, —, applied
FRANKIE, Gordon W.   USA, CA
—, —, carnivore
MILLS, M.G.L. ('Gus')   RSA
—, —, ecology &
PEARMAN, Peter B.   USA, CA
—, —, in South and Southeast Asia*
—, —, in the Himalayan region
*YONZON, Pralad   Nepal
—, —, of agricultural ecosystems
PETRETTI, Francesco   Italy
—, —, — endangered species
BRAMWELL, David   Canary Islands
—, —, — Mediterranean ecosystems
PETRETTI, Francesco   Italy
—, —, — rare plants
STRASBERG, Dominique   La Réunion
—, —, — tropical mammals
STEPHENSON, Peter J.   Tanzania
—, coral-reef
LAYDOO, Richard S.   Trinidad & Tobago
—, desert
GARDNER, Andrew S.   Oman
—, environmental, of aquatic crustaceans*
—, —, — freshwater crayfish
—, —, — isopods & tanaids
*HOLDICH, David M.   UK, England
—, —, — tropical areas esp.Nigeria
KEAY, Ronald W.J.   UK, England
—, evolutionary
GRUCZMACHER, Ricardo BAYÓN   Switzerland
KIM, Ke Chung   USA, PA
PIANKA, Eric R.   USA, TX
RODHOUSE, Paul G.K.   UK, England
—, —, of plants
STIRTON, Charles H.   UK, England
—, field
OJEDA, Ricardo A.   Argentina
—, field, experimental
PEARMAN, Peter B.   USA, CA
—, freshwater
THOMAS, John D.   UK, England
—, general, research into
POLUNIN, Ivan V.   Singapore
—, human
FRY, Charles H.   Oman
—, insect
APPLIN, David G.   UK, England
—, — conservation
SAMWAYS, Michael J.   RSA
—, island
GIVEN, David R.   NZ
—, land-use, integrated tree &
LAST, Frederick T.   UK, Scotland
—, landscape
KULVIK, Mart   Estonia
—, marine
MOORE, Peter G.   UK, Scotland
—, molecular
KENDREW, John C.   UK, England
MILIMO, Patrick B.W.   Kenya
— of bats
RACEY, Paul A.   UK, Scotland
— — birds
FLINT, Vladimir E.   Russia
— — freshwater fishery
ATAUR-RAHIM, Mohammed   Pakistan

* *See* lower footnote on p. 409.

— — global change
    BAZZAZ, Fakhri — USA, MA
— — mammals
    FLINT, Vladimir E. — Russia
    RACEY, Paul A. — UK, Scotland
— of marine turtles
    BJORNDAL, Karen A. — USA, FL
— — opisthobranch molluscs
    EDMUNDS, Malcolm — UK, England
— — pinnipeds
    BOYD, John M. — UK, Scotland
— — weeds
    STIRTON, Charles H. — UK, England
—, Pacific Salmon
    COUTANT, Charles C. — USA, TN
—, polar
    FOGG, Gordon E. — UK, Wales
—, popularization of, through media
    BOSWALL, Jeffery — UK, England
—, population
    COHEN, Joel E. — USA, NY
    EHRLICH, Anne H. — USA, CA
    YABLOKOV, Alexey V. — Russia
—, —, of large mammals
    LARSEN, Thor — Norway
—, —, of shrews
    PUCEK, Zdzislaw K. — Poland
—, reproduction, of plants
    WOODELL, Stanley R.J. — UK, England
—, reptile & amphibian
    GRIFFITHS, Richard A. — UK, England
—, striped bass
    COUTANT, Charles C. — USA, TN
—, subarctic
    NUORTEVA, Pekka O. — Finland
—, systematic/evolutionary
    KIM, Ke Chung — USA, PA
—, teaching of, through media
    BOSWALL, Jeffery — UK, England
—, tree, integrated land-use &
    LAST, Frederick T. — UK, Scotland
—, weed
    LEAKEY, Richard R.B. — Kenya
—, wildlife
    DAVIDAR, E.Reginald 'Reggie' C. — India, TN
biomass as energy resource
    SCHARMER, Klaus — Germany
— -based fuels for internal combustion engines
    SHYAM, Murari — India, MP
— energy
    KHOSHOO, Triloki N. — India, Delhi
    NOUR, Hassan O.ABDEL — Sudan
— utilization for rural energy supply
    SHYAM, Murari — India, MP
biomes, ecology of, in relation to Biosphere
    ALLEN, John P. — USA, CA
biomethanation
    KHANDELWAL, Kailash C. — India, Raj.
biometry, forest
    SCHLAEPFER, Rodolphe — Switzerland
biomonitoring
    BURGER, Joanna — USA, NJ
    INNES, John L. — Switzerland
—, medical & environmental
    GOCHFELD, Michael — USA, NJ
bionutrition
    NAYVE-ROSSI, Portia A. — Philippines
bioorganic chemistry of natural compounds
    KUKHAR, Valery P. — Ukraine
biophysical ecology
    GATES, David M. — USA, MI

bioproductivity
    OLA-ADAMS, Bunyamin A. — Nigeria
bioremediation
    FERMOR, Terence R. — UK, England
biosafety
    EGZIABHER, Tewolde B.GEBRE — Ethiopia
biosemiotics
    KULL, Kalevi — Estonia
Biosphere, ecology of biomes in relation to
    ALLEN, John P. — USA, CA
—, Humankind's place in The
    LOENING, Ulrich E. — UK, Scotland
— Reserves
    BATISSE, Michel — France
    SAUNIER, Richard E. — USA, MD
    SOKOLOV, Vladimir — Russia
    WATSON, John R. — Australia, WA
—, stressing theme of
    OZA, Gunavant M. — India, Guj.
    OZA, Premlata — India, Guj.
—, The, concept of
    GRINEVALD, Jacques — Switzerland
—, —, public appreciation & maintenance of
    POLUNIN, Nicholas — Switzerland
biospherics
    ALLEN, John P. — USA, CA
biota, bioaccumulation of metals in
    NUORTEVA, Pekka O. — Finland
—, cave & karst
    SPATE, Andrew 'Andy' P. — Australia, NSW
biotechnology
    ELKINGTON, John B. — UK, England
    IGNACIMUTHU, Savarimuthu — India, TN
    JOHNSTON, Neil — UK, England
    KRATTIGER, Anatole F. — USA, NY
    MASCARENHAS, Anthony F. — India, Mah.
    REID, Walter V. — USA, DC
    SUBRAMANIAN, Tarakad V. — India, TN
—, agri-, applications, transfer of (sustainability and a
    better environment)
    JAMES, W.Clive — Cayman Islands
—, environmental preservation using
    SUBRAMANIAN, Tarakad V. — India, TN
—, fungal
    WOOD, David A. — UK, England
—, plant
    HARRIS, Philip J.C. — UK, England
    JAMES, David J. — UK, England
    KHUSH, Gurdev S. — Philippines
—, research in, re.recovery of refuse and
    underutilized resources
    ARIAS-CHAVEZ, Jesus — Mexico
biotic colonization of the volcanic island Surtsey
    FRIDRIKSSON, Sturla — Iceland
— impoverishment*
— interactions in warming of Earth
    *WOODWELL, George M. — USA, MA
—, populations, small, conservation & management
    of
    PRICE, Mark R.STANLEY — Kenya
— resources, ethnics & politics in conservation of
    FRAZIER, John G. — Mexico
biotopes and species conservation
    KASSIOUMIS, Konstantinos — Greece
—, aquatic, of Arabian peninsula, Sahara, & Sahel
    DUMONT, Henri J. — Belgium
bird conservation movement, world, organization &
    growth of
    GAMMELL, Alistair — UK, England

* *See* lower footnote on p. 409.

bird (contd)
— ecology
    GŁOWACIŃSKI, Zbigniew A.   Poland
— management
    DHINDSA, Manjit S.   India, Punjab
— protection
    BOSWALL, Jeffery   UK, England
    CIOCHIA, Victor   Romania
birds
    CHRISTIAN, Colmore S.   Dominica
    SERHAL, Assad   Lebanon
    SZILASSY, Zoltán   Hungary
    WINGATE, David B.   Bermuda
—, arctic
    PRESTRUD, Pål   Norway
—, biology of
    FLINT, Vladimir E.   Russia
—, Chilean, ecology of feeding, reproduction &
    conservation of
    DIAZ, José VALENCIA   Chile
—, coastal, population dynamics and effects of people
    on
    BURGER, Joanna   USA, NJ
—, conservation biology of
    DANIELS, R.J.Ranjit   India, TN
—, — of colonial water
    KUSHLAN, James A.   USA, MS
—, ecology of
    DORST, Jean   France
    DUNNET, George M.   UK, Scotland
—, endangered species
    TEMPLE, Stanley A.   USA, WI
—, field identification of
    FITTER, Richard S.R.   UK, England
—, grassland
    PETRETTI, Francesco   Italy
—, keeping
    ZHANG, Jia-shun   China
—, lead in
    BURGER, Joanna   USA, NJ
—, Nearctic migratory, ecology of
    RAPPOLE, John H.   USA, VA
— of prey
    GALUSHIN, Vladimir M.   Russia
    LUSCOMBE, Bruce A.   USA, NY
— — — & their habitats
    WATSON, Richard   USA, ID
— — —, ecology of
    TEMPLE, Stanley A.   USA, WI
— — sea & islands
    BOURNE, William R.P.   UK, Scotland
— (Passer spp.), ecology of
    PINOWSKI, Jan K.   Poland
—, plants &, of western Europe, systematics of
    KELLER, Michael C.   Germany
—, research
    DIAZ, José VALENCIA   Chile
—, sea, of the Bahamas
    HOLOWESKO, Lynn P.   Bahamas
—, steppe
    PETRETTI, Francesco   Italy
—, study & conservation of
    GALUSHIN, Valdimir M.   Russia
—, systematics, biogeography, & evolution, of
    INGRAM, Glen J.   Australia, Qld
—, — of
    DORST, Jean   France
Black Rhinoceros, field protection & management of
    TOIT, Raoul F.DU   Zimbabwe
bleaching, coral (impact on coral-reef ecosystems)
    VANTIER, Lyndon M.DE   Australia, Qld

bombs, nuclear, perturbation of natural global ozone
    balance by
    JOHNSTON, Harold S.   USA, CA
books, guide & natural history, writer & illustrator of
    FOX, Allan M.   Australia, NSW
boreal regions of Europe, forest & mountain ecology
    HEISS, Gerhard   Germany
Borneo, mammals of
    PAYNE, Junaidi   Malaysia
botanic (see also botanical) gardens
    HAMANN, Ole J.   Denmark
    JAIN, Sudhanshu K.   India, UP
botanical ecology
    WIELGOLASKI, Frans-Emil   Norway
— exploration
    BYE, Robert   Mexico
— (see also botanic) gardens
    FORERO, Enrique   USA, NY
    MADULID, Domingo   Philippines
    RAVEN, Peter H.   USA, MO
— insecticides
    IGNACIMUTHU, Savarimuthu   India, TN
botany
    BELLAMY, David J.   UK, England
    SCLAVO, Jean-Pierre   France
—, ecological
    BEARD, John S.   Australia, WA
—, economic
    BALICK, Michael J.   USA, NY
    BYE, Robert   Mexico
    MORAN, Katy   USA, DC
    PRANCE, Ghillean T.   UK, England
    SCHULTES, Richard E.   USA, MA
—, environmental
    KOHLI, Ravinder K.   India, Punjab
—, field, of South India
    MATTHEW, Koyapillil M.   India, TN
—, history of
    BYE, Robert   Mexico
—, Quaternary
    DICKSON, James H.   UK, Scotland
—, systematic
    LAVRENTIADES, George   Greece
—, taxonomic
    AMIRKHANOV, Amirkhan M.   Russia
    CHEEK, Martin R.   UK, England
    HEDBERG, Inga M.M.   Sweden
    NAYAR, M.Param   India, Ker.
    SCHULTES, Richard E.   USA, MA
—, urban
    JIANG, Gaoming   China
boundary layer, atmospheric
    SINGAL, Sagar P.   India, Delhi
— —, planetary
    FRANGI, Jean-P.   France
bovine–badger TB
    BARRY, James M.   Ireland
Brassicas
    KENNEDY, Robert   UK England
Brazil, conservation & management of Marine
    Turtles off coast of
    MARCOVALDI, Guy M.F.GUAGNI DEI
                                      Brazil, Bahia
    MARCOVALDI, Maria Â.GUAGNI DEI
                                      Brazil, Bahia
—, limnology
    POR, Francis D.   Israel
breeding, artificial, of entomophagous insects
    CIOCHIA, Victor   Romania
—, captive
    FLINT, Vladimir E.   Russia

—, —, of endangered species in Oman
    DALY, Ralph H.   Oman
—, mutation
    IGNACIMUTHU, Savarimuthu   India, TN
— of apples & pears
    ALSTON, Frank H.   UK, England
— pest-resistant varieties of horticultural crops
    ELLIS, Peter R.   UK, England
—, plant
    KHUSH, Gurdev S.   Philippines
    SWAMINATHAN, Monkombu S.   India, TN
—, —, in horticultural crops
    RIGGS, Timothy J.   UK, England
—, —, uses in, of potato species
    HAWKES, John G.   UK, England
—, —, utilization of wild species in
    PINK, David A.C.   UK, England
— programmes, captive-
    GUPTA, Brij K.   India, TN
—, tree
    BURLEY, Jeffery   UK, England
breeds, rare, of British farm livestock
    JEWELL, Peter A.   UK, England
Britain, ancient woodlands in
    PETERKEN, George F.   UK, England
—, flora of, esp.Glasgow
    DICKSON, James H.   UK, Scotland
British Columbia — old-growth forests, wilderness, wildlife
    HUSBAND, Vicky   Canada, BC
— farm livestock, conservation of rare breeds
    JEWELL, Peter A.   UK, England
— invertebrates, conservation of
    MORRIS, Michael G.   UK England
— vegetation, conservation of
    WOODELL, Stanley R.J.   UK, England
— —, ecology & conservation of
    RICHARDS, Paul W.   UK, England
broadcasting
    ATTENBOROUGH, David F.   UK, England
    BELLAMY, David J.   UK, England
    PEARLMAN, Nancy   USA, CA
bryophyte distributions
    HILL, Mark O.   UK, England
— ecology & sociology
bryophytes as indicators of pollution*
—, epiphyllous
    *SJÖGREN, Erik A.   Sweden
Buddhism in Nature protection
    HENNING, Daniel H.   USA, MT
buffer-zone management
    PRINS, Herbert H.T.   The Netherlands
— zones, design of
    SEVILLA, Lorenzo B.CARDENAL
        Nicaragua/Guatemala
— —, management of
    BUDOWSKI, Gerardo   Costa Rica
— —, sustainable development of
    HURNI, Hans   Switzerland
building, ecological
    EVERETT, Rodney D.   UK, England
buildings, historic, preservation of
    SINGH, Birandra B.   Fiji
—, termites in
    NOUR, Hassan O.ABDEL   Sudan
Bureau of Land Management, USA's, ecology of
    WATSON, Charles St D., Jr   USA, NV
bush, environmental education & ecotourism in the
    WALKER, Clive H.   RSA

* *See* lower footnote on p. 409.

business and energy policy
    BURKE, David Thomas 'Tom'   UK, England
— — the environment
    BELL, J.Nigel B.   UK, England
    BURKE, David Thomas 'Tom'   UK, England
    COCKLIN, Christopher R.   NZ
    PHORNPRAPHA, Phornthep   Thailand
    SERAFIN, Rafal K.   Poland
— education
    STOBAUGH, Robert B.   USA, MA
— environment
    BELLAMY, David J.   UK, England
    KNIGHT, Peter T.   UK, England
bustards
    RAHMANI, Asad Rafi   India, UP
— (Otididae)
    GORIUP, Paul D.   UK, England
butterflies (third-world insect resources)
    MORRIS, Michael G.   UK, England
butterfly populations
    FRAZER, John F.D.   UK, England
— –ant interactions
    ELMES, Graham W.   UK, England
by-product recovery
    STANTON, W.Robert   UK, England

Cacti — conservation, ethnobotany, & systematics
    ANDERSON, Edward F.   USA, AZ
calcareous soils of Europe, communities of
    GRUBB, Peter J.   UK, England
calcification in scleractian corals
    BARNES, David J.   Australia, Qld
Cameroon, conservation & development in
    DRIJVER, Carel A.   The Netherlands
campaign, strategy
    VARIAVA, Dilnavaz   India, Mah.
campaigning
    PARKIN, Sara L.   France
—, anti-litter
    SOPHONPANICH, Chodchoy   Thailand
—, environmental
    GOLDSMITH, Edward   UK, England
    IYER, C.P.Jayalakshmi   India, Delhi
    KELLER, Michael C.   Germany
    PRASAD, Manaparambil K.   India, Ker.
—, public environmental
    AL-ALAWNEH, Ziyad   Jordan
Canada, conservation of rare & endangered vascular plants in
    ARGUS, George W.   Canada, Ont.
Canadian oral & written traditions
    CRAMPTON, Colin B.   Canada, BC
— protected areas' system
    HACKMAN, Arlin C.   Canada, Ont.
Canarian flora, biogeography & evolution of
    BRAMWELL, David   Canary Islands
cancer, environmental research in
    RAY, Prasanta K.   India, W.Bengal
Canidae
    LOVARI, Sandro   Italy
canine behaviour & evolution
    COPPINGER, Raymond   USA, MA
capacity-building related to environment
    WITT, Ronald, G.   Switzerland

Cape plants & vegetation, autecology,
    phytosociology, & restoration ecology, of
    BOUCHER, Charles   RSA
Caprinae
    LOVARI, Sandro   Italy
captive breeding
    FLINT, Vladimir E.   Russia
— — of endangered species in Oman
    DALY, Ralph H.   Oman
— -breeding programmes
    GUPTA, Brij K.   India, TN
— populations, genetic management of
    WOODRUFF, David S.   USA, CA
capture, Caribou
    BLOOMFIELD, Michael   Canada, BC
Carabid beetles
    CARILLO, Antonio MACHADO   Canary Islands
carbon & water relations of forest ecosystems*
— balance, global
    *GRACE, John   UK, Scotland
— cycle, global
    BOLIN, Bert R.   Sweden
— cycling (forest ecosystem studies)
    KIRA, Tatuo   Japan
Caribbean, environmental education & training in the
    LEFF, Enrique   Mexico
— region
    REDAUD, Louis R.M.   Guadeloupe
Caribou ecology, capture, and effects of human
    activity
    BLOOMFIELD, Michael   Canada, BC
carnivore behavioural ecology and conservation
    biology
    MILLS, M.G.L. ('Gus')   RSA
carnivores
    MACDONALD, David W.   UK, England
—, African, ecology & conservation of
    RAY, Justina C.   USA, FL
—, ecology & conservation of
    KADLEČÍK, Ján   Slovak Rep.
—, — & management of
    HERRERO, Stephen M.   Canada, Alb.
—, field studies & conservation
    SCHALLER, George B.   USA, NY
—, tropical forest, ecology & conservation of
    RAY, Justina C.   USA, FL
carnivorous plants
    CHEEK, Martin R.   UK, England
carrying capacity
    CORBET, Philip S.   UK, Scotland
— —, Human
    FEARNSIDE, Philip M.   Brazil, Amaz.
cartography
    LITVIN, Vladimir M.   Russia
    PIIROLA, Jouko   Finland
— : land & forest ecology in tropical Africa
    TRAPNELL, Colin G.   UK, England
Cashew (Anacardium occidentale)
    KENNEDY, Robert   UK, England
Casuarina, clones of
    LAL, Piare   India, AP
catalysis
    SKOULIKIDIS, Theodore   Greece
catastrophic situations, ecology of
    SMIRNOV, Nikolai N.   Russia
catchment management
    DORMAN, John   Australia, NSW
— planning, water quality and
    CULLEN, Peter W.   Australia, ACT

categorization of protected areas
    SZILASSY, Zoltán   Hungary
cattle production
    DELPIANO, José P.CASTRO   Uruguay
causes of low flows
    CLARK, Colin   UK, England
— — tropical deforestation
    FEARNSIDE, Philip M.   Brazil, Amaz.
cave biota
    SPATE, Andrew 'Andy' P.   Australia, NSW
caves
    WATSON, John R.   Australia, WA
—, conservation & management of
    SPATE, Andrew 'Andy' P.   Australia, NSW
—, exploration of
    MANSER, Bruno   Switzerland
cell biology
    SHARMA, Arun K.   India, W.Bengal
— evolution & biology
    MARGULIS, Lynn   USA, MA
Central African forests, taxonomic botany &
    conservation
    CHEEK, Martin R.   UK, England
— Asia: tundra, desert, taiga-forest, & steppe, in
    FLINT, Vladimir E.   Russia
— European environment
    HARDI, Peter   Canada, Man.
— Himalaya, landslide research in
    HAIGH, Martin J.   UK, England
Cephalopoda, southern ocean
    RODHOUSE, Paul G.K.   UK, England
certification, forest
    SULLIVAN, Francis   UK, England
—, forestry
    DONOVAN, Richard Z.   USA, VT
Cervidae
    LOVARI, Sandro   Italy
cervids
    GIMINEZ-DIXON, Mariano   Switzerland
Cetaceans of southernmost South America
    GOODALL, R.Natalie PROSSER   Argentina
CFCs
    ROWLAND, F.Sherwood   USA, CA
change, climate, see climate/climatic change
—, —, impact assessment
    PERNETTA, John C.   The Netherlands
—, —, impacts
    HUQ, Saleemul   Bangladesh
    PARRY, Martin L.   UK, England
—, environmental, in Poland
    SERAFIN, Rafal K.   Poland
—, global
    KONDRATYEV, Kirill Y.   Russia
    PARSONS, David J.   USA, MT
—, —, biology of
    BAZZAZ, Fakhri   USA, MA
—, — environmental
    PRICE, Martin F.   UK, England
    ROSSWALL, Thomas   Sweden
—, —, research
    GRASSL, Hartmut   Switzerland
—, —,—: coordination & planning of
    GOLUBEV, Genady N.   Russia
—, habitat, effects of, on wildlife ecology
    HASAN, Mohammed NORDIN   Malaysia
—, land-use, effects of, on hydrology & climate
    CLARK, Colin   UK, England
—, social
    MILBRATH, Lester W.   USA, NY
—, vegetation, esp.deforestation
    GADE, Daniel D.   USA, VT

* See lower footnote on p. 409.

changes, land-use, in Latin America, ecological
    consequences of
    MORELLO, Jorge X.   Argentina
—, social & cultural, required by sustainable
    development
    AICKIN, R. Malcolm   UK, England
Cheetah conservation
    KRAUS, Daniel   Namibia/USA, CA
    MARKER-KRAUS, Laurie   Namibia/USA, DC
chemical aspects of environment protection
    KUKHAR, Valery P.   Ukraine
— contaminants of surface water
    MOORE, James W.   Canada, Alb.
— ecology
    KOHLI, Ravinder K.   India, Punjab
— safety
    HERKOVITS, Jorge   Argentina
— speciation
    STEINNES, Eiliv   Norway
chemicals, toxic
    BRINCHUK, Mikhail M.   Russia
    KUFORIJI-OLUBI, Bola   Nigeria
—, —, control of
    FAZAL, Anwar   Malaysia
chemistry, analytical
    MOLDAN, Bedřich   Czech Rep.
    SUETT, David L.   UK, England
—, atmospheric
    SINGER, S.Fred   USA, VA
    SINGH, O.N.   India, UP
—, bioorganic, of natural compounds
    KUKHAR, Valery P.   Ukraine
—, environmental
    SUETT, David L.   UK, England
—, marine
    GOLDBERG, Edward D.   USA, CA
—, — natural product
    BAKER, Joseph 'Joe' T.   Australia, Qld
— of the atmosphere
    EGLI, Robert A.   Switzerland
    ROWLAND, F.Sherwood   USA, CA
— — — stratosphere & troposphere
    JOHNSTON, Harold S.   USA, CA
—, organic
    YOUSSEF, Abdullatif K.   Syria
—, precipitation
    LIKENS, Gene E.   USA, NY
—, soil
    STEINNES, Eiliv   Norway
Chernobyl disaster
    KUKHAR, Valery P.   Ukraine
children's concepts in science, technology, & the
    environment
    COHEN, Michael R.   USA, IN
— health, ecology and
    CHERKASOVA, Maria V.   Russia
Chilean amphibians, birds, & reptiles — ecology of
    feeding, reproduction & conservation of
    DIAZ, José VALENCIA   Chile
— species, plantations with native
    DONOSO, Claudio   Chile
China, management of environment in
    LUK, Shiu-hung   Canada, Ont.
Chipko movement, initiator of
    BAHUGUNA, Sunderlal   India, UP
Chiroptera
    VERSCHUREN, Jacques C.F.   Belgium
chlorofluorocarbons, see CFCs
circumpolar Arctic, political development in
    FENGE, Terence A.E.   Canada, Ont.

— peoples
    ROWLEY, Graham W.   Canada, Ont.
— world, Arctic, environmental management &
    planning, and industrial development in
    FENGE, Terence A.E.   Canada, Ont.
cities, air pollution in
    ABBASPOUR, Madjid   Iran
—, ecology of
    FUREDY, Christine   Canada, Ont.
citizenship, environmental
    FEICK, Jenny L.   Canada, Alb.
Citrus, foliar fungal pathogens of
    KENNEDY, Robert   UK, England
city planning in the Arab World
    HAMED, Safei EL-DEEN   USA, MD
civil engineering
    SINITSINA, Irene E.   Russia
— society organizations, partnerships with
    NOVOA, Laura   Chile
Cladocera (Crustacea), morphology & taxonomy of
    SMIRNOV, Nikolai N.   Russia
classification, ecosystems — islands in Asia–Pacific
    region
    HOLTHUS, Paul F.   USA, HI
—, land
    CRAMPTON, Colin B.   Canada, BC
—, — -use: tropical Africa
    TRAPNELL, Colin G.   UK, England
— of Indo–Pacific reef fishes
    RANDALL, John 'Jack'   USA, HI
— — world vegetation
    LOCK, John M.   UK, England
—, river
    BHARGAVA, Devendra S.   India, UP
—, vegetational, principles of
    POORE, M.E.Duncan   UK, Scotland
clean technology
    SUBRAMANIAN, Tarakad V.   India, TN
cleaner production
    BOXALL, John E.   Hong Kong
— technology & farming
    JOHNSTON, Neil   UK, England
climate
    BOLIN, Bert R.   Sweden
    LAMB, Hubert H.   UK, England
— change, see also climatic change
    BOLIN, Bert R.   Sweden
    BRYSON, Reid A.   USA, WI
    FARAGÓ, Tibor   Hungary
    GATES, David M.   USA, MI
    LEMONS, John D., Jr   USA, ME
    MacDONALD, Gordon J.F.   USA, CA
    MESSERLI, Bruno   Switzerland
    OBASI, Godwin O.P.   Switzerland
    PIELKE, Roger A.   USA, CO
    WADHAMS, Peter   UK, England
    WALLÉN, Carl-Christian   Switzerland
— — and energy
    ABROUGUI, Mohamed A.   Tunisia
— — & forest
    SCHLAEPFER, Rodolphe   Switzerland
— — impact assessment
    PERNETTA, John C.   The Netherlands
— — impacts
    HUQ, Saleemul   Bangladesh
    PARRY, Martin L.   UK, England
— — (international environmental law)
    LANG, Winfried   Switzerland
— —, research on vulnerability of wildlife to impacts
    of
    MKANDA, Francis X.   Malawi

climate (contd)
—, Earth's
  SUN, Lin   Kenya
—, effects of land-use change on
  CLARK, Colin   UK, England
—, marine
  POLOVINA, Jeffrey J.   USA, HI
— policy
  HOUGHTON, John T.   UK, England
— politics
  WALLÉN, Carl-Christian   Switzerland
— research
  GRASSL, Hartmut   Switzerland
— science
  HOUGHTON, John T.   UK, England
— –society interactions
  GLANTZ, Michael H.   USA, CO
— (sustainable development, N–S relations)
  MYERS, Norman   UK, England
— theory
  KELLOGG, William W.   USA, CO
— variability
  PIELKE, Roger A.   USA, CO
climates, arid
  HARE, F.Kenneth   Canada, Ont.
—, — (Sahelian environment)
  FRANGI, Jean-Pierre   France
—, northern
  HARE, F.Kenneth   Canada, Ont.
—, urban
  OKE, Timothy R.   Canada, BC
climatic change, see also climate change
  GOUDIE, Andrew S.   UK, England
  GRACE, John   UK, Scotland
— — in arid & semi-arid areas
  WILLIAMS, Martin A.J.   Australia, SA
— effect of clouds
  CLARK, Colin   UK, England
— phenomena, atmospheric–
  KONDRATYEV, Kirill Y.   Russia
climatology
  BRYSON, Reid A.   USA, WI
  HARE, F.Kenneth   Canada, Ont.
  PERRY, John S.   USA, VA
  TICKELL, Crispin C.C.   UK, England
  WALLÉN, Carl-Christian   Switzerland
clonal selection of trees
  LEAKEY, Richard R.B.   Kenya
— technology applications*
clones of Poplars, Eucalypts, & Casuarina
  *LAL, Piare   India, AP
closed life-systems
  ALLEN, John P.   USA, CA
clouds, climatic effect of
  CLARK, Colin   UK, England
C/N/S/P biogeochemical cycles, interrelationships
    between, as influenced by anthropogenic
    cycles
  STEWART, John W.B.   Canada, Sask.
co-existence, vegetational
  GRUBB, Peter J.   UK, England
co-management approaches to the environment
  ROMULUS, Giles   St Lucia
coal mining, erosion control of lands affected by
  HAIGH, Martin J.   UK, England
coastal afforestation
  MOUDUD, Hasna J.   Bangladesh
— area management & planning
  SHAPIRO, Harvey A.   Japan

— areas
  NELSON, J.Gordon   Canada, Ont.
— —, marine ecology in, Pacific & Asia regions
  MARAGOS, James E.   USA, HI
— birds, population dynamics, and effects of people
    on
  BURGER, Joanna   USA, NJ
— conservation
  HOLTHUS, Paul F.   USA, HI
— — & protected areas
  SALM, Rodney V.   Kenya
— — management in Europe
  DOODY, James P.   The Netherlands
— development
  DOUMENGE, François   Monaco
— ecology
  LOVRIC, Andrija Z.   Croatia
  MORTON, Brian   Hong Kong
  MOUDUD, Hasna J.   Bangladesh
  POLUNIN, Nicholas V.C.   UK, England
— ecophysiology
  BATE, Guy C.   RSA
— ecosystems
  FRAZIER, John G.   Mexico
  LAKSHMANAN, Kalimedu K.   India, TN
— —, conservation & management of
  BUSTAMANTE, Georgina   USA, FL
— —, ecological monitoring of
  MAXIMOV, Victor N.   Russia
— environment
  RAMIREZ, Jose J.Escobar   Colombia
— environmental management
  HOLTHUS, Paul F.   USA, HI
— environments, geomorphology of
  GRANJA, Helena M.   Portugal
— —, phytosociology of
  MALLOCH, Andrew J.C.   UK, England
— —, sedimentology of
  GRANJA, Helena M.   Portugal
— —, tropical: application of law re., and
    conservation science, planning, &
    management, in
  DAVIE, James D.S.   Australia, Qld
— governance
  EICHBAUM, William M.   USA, DC
— lagoons, habitat preservation in
  IBARRA-OBANDO, Silvia   Mexico
— management
  AGARDY, M.Tündi   USA, DC
  JOHNSTON, Douglas M.   Canada, BC
  VERNAUDON, Yolande   Tahiti
  WHITE, Alan T.   Sri Lanka
— marine ecology
  CROKER, Robert A.   USA, NH
  POLUNIN, Nicholas V.C.   UK, England
— oceanography
  SU, Jilan   China
  WOLANSKI, Eric J.   Australia, Qld
— planning
  DIEGUES, Antonio C.S.   Brazil, SP
— plant ecology
  RANDALL, Roland E.   UK, England
— processes
  SISMAN, Richard ('Dick')   UK, England
— protection
  CHARLIER, Roger H.L.   Belgium
— regions, conservation of arid & semi-arid
    ecosystems in
  HATOUGH-BOURAN, Alia M.A.   Jordan
— resource conservation
  KENCHINGTON, Richard A.   Australia, ACT

— — management
KENCHINGTON, Richard A.　Australia, ACT
KLEE, Gary A.　USA, CA
SHEPHERD, Alexander R.DAWSON　UK, England
TORTELL, Philip　NZ
WHITE, Susan L.　USA, FL
— — , tropical
WILKINSON, Clive R.　Australia, Qld
— resources conservation
WHITE, Alan T.　Sri Lanka
— systems, biogeochemistry of
LACERDA, Luiz D.　Brazil, RJ
— vegetation of Turkey & North Cyprus
USLU, Turhan　Turkey
— water quality
ARMIJOS, Mariano MONTAÑO　Ecuador
— zone, impact study of anthropic processes in the
GRANJA, Helena M.　Portugal
— —, land–sea interactions in
RAY, G.Carleton　USA, VA
coastal-zone management
AKSORNKOAE, Sanit　Thailand
BAKER, Joseph 'Joe' T.　Australia, Qld
BOORMAN, Laurie A.　UK, England
BURBRIDGE, Peter R.　UK, Scotland
CHARLIER, Roger H.L.　Belgium
CH'NG, Kim-Looi　Malaysia
EARLL, Robert C.　UK, England
FOWLER, Sarah L.　UK, England
GOLDBERG, Edward D.　USA, CA
GUBBAY, Susan　UK, England
HALIM, Youssef　Egypt
MARAGOS, James E.　USA, HI
MARSH, Helene D.　Australia, Qld
McEACHERN, John D.　Canada, Ont./Nepal
MORTON, Brian　Hong Kong
PERNETTA, John C.　The Netherlands
SAENGER, Peter　Australia, NSW
SHEPHERD, Alexander R.DAWSON　UK, England
VISSER, Nicolaas W.　Kenya
WESCOTT, Geoffrey C.　Australia, Vic.
— - — —, cross-sectoral integrated
PERNETTA, John C.　The Netherlands
— - — —, integrated
MEULEN, Frank VAN DER　The Netherlands
SALMAN, Albert H.P.M.　The Netherlands
— - — resources
CLARK, John R.　USA, FL
— zones, evolution of
CARVALHO, G.SOARES DE　Portugal
— —, monitoring of
HALIM, Youssef　Egypt
— —, Nature conservation in
SALMAN, Albert H.P.M.　The Netherlands
Coccinellidae
CIOCHIA, Victor　Romania
coevaluation
WOODGATE, Graham R.　UK, England
coevolution of arthropods
KIM, Ke C.　USA, PA
coexistence, vegetational
GRUBB, Peter J.　UK, England
colonial waterbirds, conservation of
KUSHLAN, James A.　USA, MS
colonization, biotic, of the volcanic island Surtsey
FRIDRIKSSON, Sturla　Iceland
— of polar deserts
SVOBODA, Josef　Canada, Ont.
colonizing organisms
THEBAUD, Christophe　France

combatting desertification
DAMERDJI, M.Amine　Algeria
commercial use of wild animal resources: Aborigines
WILSON, George R.　Australia, WA
common property management
QUTUB, Syed Ayub　Pakistan
— — resources
BERKES, Fikret　Canada, Man.
— resource dilemmas
YOUNG, Raymond DE　USA, MI
'commons ecology' in Nevada
WATSON, Charles St D., Jr　USA, NV
—' 'The, application of financial experience &
　principles to
McCAMMON, Antony L.T.　Switzerland
communication (see also communications)
CHITRAKAR, Anil　Nepal
—, environmental
CAPPATO, Jorge A.　Argentina
RUGE, Tiahoga　Mexico
—, —, national & international
HESSELINK, Frederik J.　The Netherlands
—, —, through electronic & print media
HAQUE, Mohammed A.　India, Har.
—, evolution of
NIEMITZ, Carsten　Germany
—, international
STONE, Peter B.　UK, England
—, mass, environment–development
BHATT, Dibya D.　Nepal
—, non-vocal mammalian
BARRY, James M　Ireland
— re.Nature philosophy
TERRASSON, François　France
— (women)
CORRAL, Thais　Brazil, RJ
communications (see also communication)
ANGELO, Homer G.　USA, CA
DIAZ-MARTIN, Diego　Venezuela
WRIGHT, Martin P.W.　UK, England
—, computer, re.environmental research, rainforest,
　sustainable development
PETER, Ian W.　Australia, Qld
—, environmental
BASSOW, Whitman　USA, NY
GRUCZMACHER, Ricardo BAYÓN　Switzerland
SHRESTHA, Aditya M.　Nepal
communities, ecology of deep oceanic
ANGEL, Martin V.　UK, England
—, human, plans for environmental management of
AUSSEDAT, Nicole M.　France/St Barthélemy
—, land, ecology of
GALAZY, Grigory I.　Russia
—, local, sea-turtle conservation efforts with
ROSE, Carlos R.HASBÚN　El Salvador
— of calcareous soils of Europe
GRUBB, Peter J.　UK, England
—, plant, patterning of
BLISS, Lawrence C.　USA, WA
—, rural, mobilizing, for better common property
　management
QUTUB, Syed Ayub　Pakistan
—, water, ecology of
GALAZY, Grigory I.　Russia
community-based action research
OLI, Krishna P.　Nepal
— - — approaches to conservation
WRIGHT, R.Michael　USA, VA
— - — conservation
FÉRON, Eric M.　Zimbabwe

community-based conservation (contd)
— - — — activities, interaction of commercial &
TOIT, Raoul F.DU   Zimbabwe
— - — — programmes & efforts, stimulation of
UGWU, Christopher N.   Nigeria
— - — environmental management in urban Asia
FUREDY, Christine   Canada, Ont.
— - — tourism
NEPAL, Sanjay K.   Switzerland
— development
SAMAD, Syed A.   Malaysia
— — in the humid neo-tropics
LYNCH, James R.   Costa Rica
— —, sustainable
ALLEN, Irma   Swaziland
— ecology
GRIFFITHS, Richard A.   UK, England
KAWANABE, Hiroya   Japan
— —, evolutionary
PIANKA, Eric R.   USA, TX
— —, plant, research in
KULL, Olevi   Estonia
— environmental action
GITTINS, John W.E.H.   UK, England
— integration, subsistence with protected area
    authorities
ROWNTREE, Matthew J.W.   UK, England
— involvement in planning
CRAIK, Wendy   Australia, Qld
— — — sustainable wildlife use
BALDUS, Rolf D.   Germany
— — — wildlife management
MKANDA, Francis X.   Malawi
— management institutions
KHOSLA, Ashok   India, Delhi
VARUGHESE, George C.   India, Delhi
— modelling
KULL, Kalevi   Estonia
— organizing
FAZAL, Anwar   Malaysia
— participation
SHORES, John N.   USA, ME
— , plant, diversity
KULL, Kalevi   Estonia
comparative environmental law
GÜNDLING, Lothar   Germany
— — — & policy
REHBINDER, Eckard   Germany
— — risk, quantitative measurement of
CHADWICK, Michael J.   Sweden
— ethology
OBARA, Hideo   Japan
— international law & policy
BOTHE, Michael   Germany
— Nature conservation law
KLEMM, Cyrille DE   France
— neuroendocrinology
APPLIN, David G.   UK, England
— philosophies of conservation
BURNETT, G. Wesley   USA, SC
— religions, study of
SINGH, Karan   India, Delhi
competition, vegetational
GRUBB, Peter J.   UK, England
composition, isotopic, of Helium and Argon
VORONOV, Arkady N.   Russia
composting
FERMOR, Terence R.   UK, England

—, controlled environment, for mushroom cultivation*
—, prevention of odour & water pollution from
*NOBLE, Ralph   UK, England
compounds, natural, bioorganic chemistry of
KUKHAR, Valery P.   Ukraine
computer applications
PERRY, John S.   USA, VA
— communications re.environmental research,
    rain-forest, sustainable development
PETER, Ian W.   Australia, Qld
concept, national ecological reform
KOSTENKO, Yuriy   Ukraine
concepts, children's, in science, technology, & the
    environment
COHEN, Michael R.   USA, IN
conflict between economic growth and a just
    distribution of resources
DAMMANN, Erik   Norway
—, environmental, management of
DEMPSEY, Stanley   USA, CO
conflicts, resource-use, identification & management
    of
SAUNIER, Richard E.   USA, MD
conservation, see also conservation of[†]
— activities, integration of commercial &
    community-based
TOIT, Raoul F.DU   Zimbabwe
— administration
BOYLAND, Desmond E.   Australia, Qld
—, African
PRICE, Mark R.STANLEY   Kenya
—, Amazonian
PRANCE, Ghillean T.   UK, England
—, amphibians
GRIFFITHS, Richard A.   UK, England
— & agriculture, relationships between
HUNKELER, Pierre   Switzerland
— — consumption, balancing
MISRA, Ramdeo   India, UP
— — development projects, integrated
BEZAURY-CREEL, Juan E.   Mexico
— — ethics
BATANOUNY, Kamal H.   Egypt
— — protection, primate
McGREAL, Shirley   USA, SC
— — sustainable utilization of biodiversity
PUSHPANGADAN, Palpu   India, Ker.
— — tourism
BARCSAY, László   Hungary
—, animal
CHALABI, Bouzid   Algeria
—, —, domestic, genetic resource
TEWOLDE, Assefaw   Mexico
—, —, wild
WILSON, George R.   Australia, WA
—, Antarctic
BONNER, W.Nigel   UK, England
DIAZ, José VALENCIA   Chile
KEAGE, Peter L.   Australia, Vic.
LEWIS-SMITH, Ronald I.   UK, England
PHILLIPS, Cassandra, F.E.   UK, England
—, applications of field research to
TRAPNELL, Colin G.   UK, England
—, applied biogeography =
LOURENÇO, Wilson R.   France
— areas, ecodevelopment & management of
HOECK, Hendrik N.   Switzerland

— —, landscape management in Nature
SEPP, Kalev   Estonia
— —, Nature, management of
DALY, Ralph H.   Oman
—, autochthonous tropical forest
FISCHER, Gert R.   Brazil, SC
— behaviour among individuals
YOUNG, Raymond DE   USA, MI
—, biodiversity *see* biodiversity conservation
—, —, & management
SULAYEM, Mohammad S.A.   Saudi Arabia
—, —, interdisciplinary approaches
FONSECA, Gustavo A.B.   Brazil, MG
—, —, islands in Asia–Pacific region
HOLTHUS, Paul F.   USA, HI
—, biogeography, applied, =
LOURENÇO, Wilson R.   France
—, biological
LEMONS, John D., Jr   USA, ME
—, — diversity
MITTERMEIER, Russell A.   USA, DC
—, —, in tropical SE Asia
KIEW, Bong-Heang   Malaysia
—, —, management
JEFFERIES, Bruce E.   Papua New Guinea
—, —, re.people in the tropics
FRAZIER, John G.   Mexico
— biology
BOYLE, Terence P.   USA, CO
CANADAY, Christopher   Ecuador
DANIELS, R.J.Ranjit   India, TN
DASMANN, Raymond F.   USA, CA
GAKAHU, Christopher G.   Kenya
GIVEN, David R.   NZ
HASAN, Mohammed NORDIN   Malaysia
HERRERO, Stephen M.   Canada, Alb.
HOBBS, Richard J.   Australia, WA
KREBS, John R.   UK, England
MWALYOSI, Raphael B.B.   Tanzania
OPDAM, Paul   The Netherlands
ORIANS, Gordon H.   USA, WA
PANDURANGAN, Alagramam G.   India, Ker.
PERES, Carlos A.   Brazil, SP/UK, England
SHAW, William W.   USA, AZ
TEMPLE, Stanley A.   USA, WI
THEBAUD, Christophe   France
USHER, Michael B.   UK, Scotland
WRIGHT, Shane D.T.   NZ
YABLOKOV, Alexey V.   Russia
— — and economic evaluation of biodiversity
PUSHPANGADAN, Palpu   India, Ker.
— —, applied
FRANKIE, Gordon W.   USA, CA
— —, carnivore
MILLS, M.G.L. ('Gus')   RSA
— —, ecology &
PEARMAN, Peter B.   USA, CA
— — in South and Southeast Asia*
— — — the Himalayan region
*YONZON, Pralad   Nepal
— —, insect
SAMWAYS, Michael J.   RSA
— — of agricultural ecosystems
PETRETTI, Francesco   Italy
— — — endangered species
BRAMWELL, David   Canary Islands
— — — Mediterranean ecosystems
PETRETTI, Francesco   Italy

* *See* lower footnote on p. 409.

— — — rare plants
STRASBERG, Dominique   La Réunion
— — — tropical mammals
STEPHENSON, Peter J.   Tanzania
—, biotopes
KASSIOUMIS, Konstantinos   Greece
—, bird, world, movement — organization & growth of
GAMMELL, Alistair   UK, England
—, Cheetah/predator
KRAUS, Daniel   Namibia/USA, CA
MARKER-KRAUS, Laurie   Namibia/USA, DC
—, coastal
HOLTHUS, Paul F.   USA, HI
POLUNIN, Nicholas V.C.   UK, England
—, —, & protected areas
SALM, Rodney V.   Kenya
—, — resource
KENCHINGTON, Richard A.   Australia, ACT
—, — resources
WHITE, Alan T.   Sri Lanka
—, community-based
FÉRON, Eric M.   Zimbabwe
—, — - — approaches to
WRIGHT, R.Michael   USA, VA
—, comparative philosophies of
BURNETT, G.Wesley   USA, SC
—, coral
VERON, John E.N.   Australia, Qld
—, coral-reef
WELLS, Susan M.   UK, England
—, crane
LANDFRIED, Steven E.   USA, WI
—, creative
BENTHEM, Roelof J.   The Netherlands
—, domestic animal genetic resource
TEWOLDE, Assefaw   Mexico
—, earth science
KNILL, John   UK, England
—, ecological, holistic
POLUNIN, Nicholas   Switzerland
— ecology
HABER, Wolfgang   Germany
MELKANIA, Niranjan P.   India, MP
NIKULIN, Valery A.   Russia
SARMIENTO, Fausto O.   USA, GA
— — of endangered species
BRAMWELL, David   Canary Islands
—, economics of
TISDELL, Clement A.   Australia, Qld
—, ecosystems
OSEMEOBO, Gbadebo J.   Nigeria
— education
BUTLER, James 'Jim' R.   Canada, Alb.
—, effective
GAMMELL, Alistair   UK, England
—, — resource
CHILD, Graham F.T.   Zimbabwe
—, elasmobranch
FOWLER, Sarah L.   UK, England
GRUBER, Samuel H.   USA, FL
—, endangered species
BUTLER, James 'Jim' R.   Canada, Alb.
—, energy
WALULYA-MUKASA, Joe   Uganda
—, —, in production agriculture
SHYAM, Murari   India, MP
—, environmental, *see* environmental conservation
—, —, activism
SINGH, Hari B.   India, Delhi

conservation, environmental (contd)
—, —, and action plans
    AZIS, P.K.ABDUL   Saudi Arabia
—, —, holistic aspects of
    NUORTEVA, Pekka O.   Finland
—, —, of marine environment
    DESAI, Bhagirath N.   India, Goa
—, —, — the Earth
    ODULA, Michael A.N.   Kenya
—, —: science, philosophy, & policies, of
    POORE, M.E.Duncan   UK, Scotland
—, —, projects, design & implementation
    PANGETI, George N.   Zimbabwe
—, —, teaching & research in
    BUTLER, James 'Jim' R.   Canada, Alb.
— esp.of polar regions
    WALTON, David W.H.   UK, England
—, ethnobotanical
    SCHULTES, Richard E.   USA, MA
    LAKSHMANAN, Kalimedu K.   India, TN
—, fisheries'
    AGARDY, M.Tündi   USA, DC
—, floral
    POLUNIN, Ivan V.   Singapore
—, forest
    JUSOFF, Kamaruzaman   Malaysia
    LÖFGREN, Rolf   Sweden
    NEWTON, Adrian C.   UK, Scotland
    PALMER, Prince Dowu   Sierra Leone
    SULLIVAN, Francis   UK, England
—, — environment
    WOO, Bo-Myeong   S.Korea
—, —, in the tropics
    ONAYEMI, Olarotimi O.   Nigeria
—, —, natural
    DONOVAN, Richard Z.   USA, VT
—, —, satellite remote-sensing in
    JUSOFF, Kamaruzaman   Malaysia
—, —, tropical autochthonous
    FISCHER, Gert R.   Brazil, SC
—, forestry
    BERETEH, Mohamed A.   Sierra Leone
    KIRBY, Keith J.   UK, England
— Foundation, The
    SHREEVE, David   UK, England
—, genetic, in developing countries
    MOESTRUP, Søren   Denmark
—, genetics
    BERRY, Robert James ('Sam')   UK, England
—, geographical methods of
    ZABELINA, Natalie M.   Russia
—, habitat
    OSEMEOBO, Gbadebo J.   Nigeria
—, heritage
    COLLIN, Gérard   France
    NEPAL, Sanjay K.   Switzerland
—, historical geography of
    BURNETT, G.Wesley   USA, SC
—, history of
    CROKER, Robert A.   USA, NH
—, human
    MALMBERG, Torsten   Sweden
— in Cameroon, Indonesia, Surinam, & W. African
    Sahel
    DRIJVER, Carel A.   The Netherlands
— — developing nations
    BURNETT, G.Wesley   USA, SC
— — Greece
    VALAORAS, Georgia   Greece

— — metropolitan environments
    SHAW, William W.   USA, AZ
— in situ
    PRAWIROATMODJO, Suryo W.   Indonesia
— — —, biodiversity
    SAUNIER, Richard E.   USA, MD
— — —, systems
    SEVILLA, Lorenzo B.CARDENAL
        Nicaragua/Guatemala
— in wild of endangered species in Oman
    DALY, Ralph H.   Oman
—, insect
    ELMES, Graham W.   UK, England
—, invertebrate
    SAMWAYS, Michael J.   RSA
    WELLS, Susan M.   UK, England
—, involvement of rural human populations in —
    Africa
    PRICE, Mark R. STANLEY   Kenya
—, island
    HAMBLER, Clive   UK, England
— issues
    PLAYER, Ian C.   RSA
— —, voluntary involvement in
    ARMSTRONG, Geoffrey J.   Australia, NSW
—, landscape
    NAVEH, Zev   Israel
—, —, natural & cultural, in spatial planning
    STAWICKI, Henryk   Poland
— lecturing
    LISTER-KAYE, John   UK, Scotland
—, mammalian
    MACDONALD, David W.   UK, England
— management
    ABUZINADA, Abdul A.H.   Saudi Arabia
    PENNY, Stella F.   NZ
— —, biodiversity
    JEFFERIES, Bruce E.   Papua New Guinea
— —, coastal, in Europe
    DOODY, James P.   The Netherlands
— —, effects of, on grassland invertebrates
    MORRIS, Michael G.   UK, England
— — in tropical coastal environments
    DAVIE, James D.S.   Australia, Qld
— — of tropical forests
    MARSH, Clive W.   Malaysia
— planning
    STEPHENSON, Peter J.   Tanzania
— —, protected area
    JEFFERIES, Bruce E.   Papua New Guinea
    STRONACH, Neil R.H.   Ireland
—, marine, see marine conservation
—, —, & protected areas
    SALM, Rodney V.   Kenya
—, — resource
    KENCHINGTON, Richard A.   Australia, ACT
—, (— science)
    MORTON, Brian   Hong Kong
—, — turtle
    VENIZELOS, Lily T.   Greece/UK, England
—, —, through parks & preserves
    RANDALL, John 'Jack'   USA, HI
—, marketing
    BUTLER, Paul J.   St Lucia
—, masterplanning for
    BARCSAY, László   Hungary
—, mire
    MASING, Viktor   Estonia
—, mountain
    STONE, Peter B.   UK, England

— movement, world bird — organization & growth of
GAMMELL, Alistair — UK, England
—, natural
WANG, Xianpu — China
—, — & cultural landscape, in spatial planning
STAWICKI, Henryk — Poland
—, — forest
DONOVAN, Richard Z. — USA, VT
—, — resource
HAFIDI, Moulay El M. — Morocco
—, — —, social dimensions of
HOUGH, John L. — USA, MD
—, — resources'
THAPA, Gopal B. — Thailand
—, Nature, see Nature Conservation
—, —, administration of
WOLDHEK, Siegfried — The Netherlands
—, —, & local human population — economic relation
PRINS, Herbert H.T. — The Netherlands
—, — (basic research)
MEDWECKA-KORNAŚ, Anna M. — Poland
—, — (biodiversity)
POORE, M.E.Duncan — UK, Scotland
—, —, cultural, social, psychological constructs, and strategies for
MARTIN, Vance G. — USA, CO
—, —, esp.monitoring
GOLDSMITH, Frank B. — UK, England
—, —, in coastal zones
SALMAN, Albert H.P.M. — The Netherlands
—, —, — the humid neo-tropics
LYNCH, James R. — Costa Rica
—, —, international
BREE, Peter J.H. VAN — The Netherlands
—, —, law, international & comparative
KLEMM, Cyrille DE — France
—, —, legislation
VISSER, Nicolaas W. — Kenya
—, —: policy
USUKI, Mitsuo — Thailand
—, — resource
VERMA, Sewa R. — India, UP
—, —, urban
ARIFFIN, Ishak BIN — Malaysia
— on Palni Hills
MATTHEW, Koyapillil M. — India, TN
— organization administration
FERRAR, Anthony A. — RSA
— organizations, voluntary involvement in
ARMSTRONG, Geoffrey J. — Australia, NSW
—, otters
BARRY, James M. — Ireland
— outdoors
THOMAS, Anamaria A.DE — USA, FL
— planning
SULAYEM, Mohammad S.A. — Saudi Arabia
— — in tropical coastal environments
DAVIE, James D.S. — Australia, Qld
— —, forest
WIJESINGHE, Leslie — Sri Lanka
— —, Nature
GORIUP, Paul D. — UK, England
SATTLER, Paul S. — Australia, Qld
—, plant(s')
CHEEK, Roy V. — UK, England
FORERO, Enrique — USA, NY
HAMILTON, Alan — UK, England
MADULID, Domingo — Philippines
STIRTON, Charles H. — UK, England

—, — genetic resources
CLEMENT, Charles R. — Brazil, Amaz.
—, — germ-plasm: strategy & technology
TAO, Kar-ling J. — Italy
— policy development
SATTLER, Paul S. — Australia, Qld
—, popularization of, through media
BOSWALL, Jeffery — UK, England
—, predator
MARKER-KRAUS, Laurie — Namibia/USA, DC
—, — /Cheetah
KRAUS, Daniel — Namibia/USA, CA
—, primate(s')
McGREAL, Shirley — USA, SC
— programmes & efforts, community-based, stimulation of
UGWU, Christopher N. — Nigeria
— projects, management of
STEPHENSON, Peter J. — Tanzania
—, rare species'
ELMES, Graham W. — UK, England
—, reptile(s)
GRIFFITHS, Richard A. — UK, England
— research
ABUZINADA, Adbul A.H. — Saudi Arabia
—, reserves'
WATSON, John R. — Australia, WA
—, resource(s')
SHORES, John N. — USA, ME
—, — assessment & planning
HIBBERD, John K. — Australia, ACT
—, —, coastal & marine
KENCHINGTON, Richard A. — Australia, ACT
—, — conservation (results)
NIKULIN, Valery A. — Russia
—, —, natural
HAFIDI, Moulay El M. — Morocco
—, —, —, social dimensions of
HOUGH, John L. — USA, MD
—, — —, economics & institutions essential to effective
CHILD, Graham P.T. — Zimbabwe
—, —, genetic, domestic animal
TEWOLDE, Assefaw — Mexico
— resources, coastal
WHITE, Alan T. — Sri Lanka
— —, natural
THAPA, Gopal B. — Thailand
—, rhino
WERIKHE, Michael M. — Kenya
— science (ecosozology)
LISICKÝ, Mikuláš J. — Slovak Rep.
— — in tropical coastal environments
DAVIE, James D.S. — Australia, Qld
— sciences
SWINGLAND, Ian R. — UK, England
—, sea-turtle(s)
MARQUEZ-MILLAN, René — Mexico
ROSE, Carlos R.HASBÚN — El Salvador
—, seed
TOMPSETT, Paul B. — UK, England
— skill, transfer of
CHITRAKAR, Anil — Nepal
—, societal problems of
FARAGÓ, Tibor — Hungary
—, soil
HURNI, Hans — Switzerland
LAL, Rattan — USA, OH
LUK, Shiu-hung — Canada, Ont.
—, species
KASSIOUMIS, Konstantinos — Greece
OSEMEOBO, Gbadebo J. — Nigeria

conservation, species (contd)
—, —, rare
    ELMES, Graham W.   UK, England
—, spiders, re.
    RAVEN, Robert J.   Australia, Qld
— strategies
    QUTUB, Syed Ayub   Pakistan
— strategy, wildlife
    FLINT, Vladimir E.   Russia
—, sustainable, in third-world countries
    BEHRA, Olivier   Madagascar
—, taxonomic botany &
    CHEEK, Martin R.   UK, England
—, teaching of, through media
    BOSWALL, Jeffery   UK, England
— technology, transfer of
    CHITRAKAR, Anil   Nepal
—, temperate
    HOLROYD, Geoffrey L.   Canada, Alb.
—, terrestrial ecology
    SAYER, Jeffrey A.   Indonesia
—, third-world countries, sustainable, in
    BEHRA, Olivier   Madagascar
— through art
    ELLISON, Gabriel   Zambia
— topics, interpreter of
    THOMAS, Anamaria A.DE   USA, FL
—, tortoise
    LAMBERT, Michael R.K.   UK, England
—, tropical avian ecology
    HOLROYD, Geoffrey L.   Canada, Alb.
—, — forest
    HAMILTON, Alan   UK, England
—, — —, autochthonous
    FISCHER, Gert R.   Brazil, SC
—, turtles, marine
    VENIZELOS, Lily T.   Greece/UK, England
—, —, sea
    MARQUEZ-MILLAN, René   Mexico
    ROSE, Carlos R.HASBÚN   El Salvador
—, urban Nature
    ARIFFIN, Ishak BIN   Malaysia
—, veterinary aspects of
    WOODFORD, Michael H.   USA, DC
—, wetland
    DUGAN, Patrick J.   Switzerland
    HOFFMANN, Luc   France
    KADLEČÍK, Ján   Slovak Rep.
    KUSHLAN, James A.   USA, MS
—, whale(s)
    PAYNE, Roger S.   UK, England
    PHILLIPS, Cassandra F.E.   UK, England
—, wild animal(s)
    WILSON, George R.   Australia, WA
—, — flora & fauna
    KACEM, Slaheddine BEL   Tunisia
—, wilderness
    LABASTILLE, Anne   USA, NY
—, wildlife, see wildlife conservation
—, —, & management
    WANG, Sung   China
—, —, editing journals on
    FITTER, A.Maisie S.   UK, England
—, —, field research in SE Asia esp.Sarawak
    & Sabah
    BENNETT, Elizabeth L.   Malaysia
—, —, in the Middle East
    DEAN, Faisal   USA, VA
—, —, resource, including corals
    THRESHER, Philip B.   USA, CA

—, —, socio-political aspects of
    SHAW, William W.   USA, AZ
—, —, strategy
    FLINT, Vladimir E.   Russia
—, woodland
    KIRBY, Keith J.   UK, England
—, writing about
    LISTER-KAYE, John   UK, Scotland
conservation of, see also conservation[†]
— African carnivores and small mammals
    RAY, Justina C.   USA, FL
— — megafauna & habitats
    TOIT, Raoul F.DU   Zimbabwe
— — Rhinoceros
    BROOKS, Peter M.   RSA
— Afrotropical Diptera
    WHITTINGTON, Andrew E.   UK, Scotland
— amphibians, Chilean
    DIAZ, José VALENCIA   Chile
— animal germ-plasm
    WARDEH, Muhammad Fadel   Syria
— — species
    WOODRUFF, David S.   USA, CA
— appropriate technology
    TAN, Koonlin   UK, England
— aquatic biotopes, main, in Sahara, Sahel, &
    Arabian peninsula
    DUMONT, Henri J.   Belgium
— arid ecosystems
    MILLS, M.G.L. ('Gus')   RSA
— — — in coastal regions & in Jordan
    HATOUGH-BOURAN, Alia M.A. Jordan
— Atlantic Salmon
    MILLS, Derek H.   UK, Scotland
— bats & other mammals
    RACEY, Paul A.   UK, Scotland
— biodiversity, see biodiversity conservation
— — in West Africa esp.Sierra Leone
    TUBOKU-METZGER, Daphne J.A. Sierra Leone
— biological diversity
    WELCOMME, Robin L.   Italy
— biotic resources, ethics & politics in
    FRAZIER, John G.   Mexico
— birds esp.birds of prey
    GALUSHIN, Vladimir M.   Russia
— —, Chilean [and other groups]
    DIAZ, José VALENCIA   Chile
— —, colonial water-
    KUSHLAN, James A.   USA, MS
— British farm livestock, rare breeds of
    JEWELL, Peter A.   UK, England
— — invertebrates
    MORRIS, Michael G.   UK, England
— — vegetation
    WOODELL, Stanley R.J.   UK, England
— Cacti
    ANDERSON, E.F.   USA, AZ
— carnivores
    KADLEČÍK, Ján   Slovak Rep.
— carnivorous plants
    CHEEK, Martin R.   UK, England
— caves
    SPATE, Andrew 'Andy' P. Australia, NSW
— Central African forests
    CHEEK, Martin R.   UK, England
— Chilean birds, reptiles, and amphibians
    DIAZ, José VALENCIA   Chile
— coastal ecosystems
    BUSTAMANTE, Georgina   USA, FL

[†] See upper footnote on p. 409.

— colonial waterbirds
KUSHLAN, James A. USA, MS
— coral-reef ecosystems
McALLISTER, Donald E. Canada, Ont.
— — reefs
MOYER, Jack T. Japan
— corals
THRESHER, Philip B. USA, CA
— cultural heritage
CHERKASOVA, Maria V. Russia
— ecology, Himalayan
RAI, Leghu D. Nepal
— economic resources
TAN, Koonlin UK, England
— ecosystems
SUGIMURA, Ken Japan
— —, arid & savanna
MILLS, M.G.L. ('Gus') RSA
— —, coastal
BUSTAMANTE, Georgina USA, FL
— —, coral-reef
McALLISTER, Donald E. Canada, Ont.
— —, highland
OJHA, Ek Raj Japan
— —, Himalayan
PANDIT, Ashok K. India, J&K
— —, island
FITTER, Julian R. UK, England
— —, marine
CH'NG, Kim-Looi Malaysia
FITTER, Julian R. UK, England
— —, natural
CÂMARA, Ibsen DE G. Brazil, RJ
— —, threatened
BURBIDGE, Andrew A. Australia, WA
— ecotourism projects
SINGH, Birandra B. Fiji
— endangered species
DURRELL, Lee McG. UK, Channel Islands
JAIN, Sudhanshu K. India, UP
MASCARENHAS, Anthony F. India, Mah.
RANJITSINH, M.K. India, MP
— — — of fauna
HADDANE, Brahim Morocco
— — vascular plants in Canada
ARGUS, George W. Canada, Ont.
— environment, Himalayan
RAI, Leghu D. Nepal
— —, legislation re.
CHALABI, Bouzid Algeria
— —, projects & programmes re.
DURRANI, Shakil Pakistan
— environmental resources, ethics & politics re.*
— ethics re.environmental resources
*FRAZIER, John G. Mexico
— European invertebrates
MORRIS, Michael G. UK, England
— farm livestock, British, rare breeds of
JEWELL, Peter A. UK, England
— fauna
NDINGA, Assitou Congo
— — & flora
FERNANDO, Ranjen L. Sri Lanka
STUTZIN, Godofredo Chile
— —, insect
RICHARDSON, Paul N. UK, England
— fishery, freshwater
ATAUR-RAHIM, Mohammed Pakistan

* See lower footnote on p. 409.

— resources
BUSTAMANTE, Georgina USA, FL
— flora, rare, endangered, & endemic, of Andaman
& Nicobar Islands
SINHA, Akhauri R.P. India, A&N Islands
— floras, insular
BRAMWELL, David Canary Islands
— forests, Southeast Asian
PAYNE, Junaidi Malaysia
— —, tropical
BUDOWSKI, Gerardo Costa Rica
SAYER, Jeffrey A. Indonesia
— —, West & Central African
CHEEK, Martin R. UK, England
— Fraser Island
SINCLAIR, John Australia, NSW
— freshwater fishery
ATAUR-RAHIM, Mohammed Pakistan
— genetic resources
ASTLEY, David 'Dave' UK, England
PALMBERG-LERCHE, Christel M. Italy
WILSON, Richard T. UK, England
— germ-plasm, animal
WARDEH, Muhammed Fadel Syria
— habitats, endangered
JAIN, Sudhanshu K. India, UP
— —, wild
VARIAVA, Dilnavaz India, Mah.
— herons
KUSHLAN, James A. USA, MS
— highland ecosystems
OJHA, Ek Raj Japan
— Himalayan ecology & environment
RAI, Leghu D. Nepal
— ecosystems & natural resources
PANDIT, Ashok K. India, J&K
— ibises
KUSHLAN, James A. USA, MS
— insect fauna
RICHARDSON, Paul N. UK, England
— resources, third world
MORRIS, Michael G. UK, England
— insects, mainly Lepidoptera
MONTESINOS, José Luis VIEJO Spain
— insular floras
BRAMWELL, David Canary Islands
— international wildlife
JENKINS, David UK, Scotland
— invertebrates, British & European
MORRIS, Michael G. UK, England
— island ecosystems & ecocomplexes
FITTER, Julian R. UK, England
— islands
DAHL, Arthur L. Switzerland
— Macau Green Areas
ESTÁCIO, Antônio J.E. Macau
— Malvales, Meliaceae
CHEEK, Martin R. UK, England
— mammals
BURBIDGE, Andrew A. Australia, WA
MALCOLM, Jay R. Canada, Ont.
OJEDA, Ricardo A. Argentina
PUCEK, Zdzislaw K. Poland
RACEY, Paul A. UK, Scotland
TAYLOR, J.Mary USA, OH
— —, large
LOVARI, Sandro Italy
— —, — (carnivores & ungulates)
SCHALLER, George B. USA, NY
— —, —, in E.Africa
ELTRINGHAM, Stewart K. UK, England

[conservation] of mammals (contd)
— —, marine
LEATHERWOOD, James S.   USA, CA
— mangrove
BRIDGEWATER, Peter   Australia, ACT
— marine ecosystems
CH'NG, Kim-Looi   Malaysia
— — & ecocomplexes
FITTER, Julian R.   UK, England
— — mammals
LEATHERWOOD, James S.   USA, CA
— — turtles
BJORNDAL, Karen A.   USA, FL
— — — off coast of Brazil
MARCOVALDI, Guy M.G.GUAGNI DEI
                                Brazil, Bahia
MARCOVALDI, Maria Â.GUAGNI DEI
                                Brazil, Bahia
— — wildlife
MOYER, Jack T.   Japan
— national parks
CHALABI, Bouzid   Algeria
— — wildlife
JENKINS, David   UK, Scotland
— natural ecosystems
CÃMARA, Ibsen DE G.   Brazil, RJ
— — environment
MALAMIDIS, George   Greece
— — habitats
FERNANDO, Ranjen L.   Sri Lanka
— — heritage
CHERKASOVA, Maria V.   Russia
JAYAL, Nalni Dhar   India, UP
— — resources
DELPIANO, José P.CASTRO   Uruguay
GHABBOUR, Samir I.   Egypt
HOLOWESKO, Lynn P.   Bahamas
LARSEN, Thor   Norway
— — —, Himalayan
PANDIT, Ashok K.   India, J&K
— — — in developing countries using support of
    local people
MacFARLAND, Craig G.   USA, ID
— — — — humid tropics
SMITH, Nigel J.H.   USA, FL
— Nature, see also Nature conservation
— — & natural resources
HOLDGATE, Martin W.   UK, England
— — — protected areas
VALDRÈ, Giovanni   Italy
— —, education & public awareness re.
HADDANE, Brahim   Morocco
— —, legislation re.
CHALABI, Bouzid   Algeria
— oceanic islands
RYAN, Peter G.   RSA
— Odonata, research & policy-making re.
MOORE, Norman W.   UK, England
— open space systems
JACOBS, Peter D.A.   Canada, Que.
— parks
WAYBURN, Edgar   USA, CA
— plant genetic resources
ANISHETTY, Narasimha   Italy
HAWKES, John G.   UK, England
— plants
CHEEK, Roy V.   UK, England
— —, carnivorous
CHEEK, Martin R.   UK, England
— —, in situ & ex situ
HAMANN, Ole J.   Denmark

— —, rare
SPENCER, Jonathan W.   UK, England
— politics re.environmental resources
FRAZIER, John G.   Mexico
— populations, small — Africa
PRICE, Mark R.STANLEY   Kenya
— protected areas
CÃMARA, Ibsen DE G.   Brazil, RJ
CHALABI, Bouzid   Algeria
PHILLIPS, Adrian   UK, England
VALDRÈ, Giovanni   Italy
WAYBURN, Edgar   USA, CA
— — —, tropical
COBB, Stephen M.   UK, England
— rare breeds of British farm livestock
JEWELL, Peter A.   UK, England
— — flora, endangered & endemic, of Andaman
    & Nicobar Islands
SINHA, Akhauri R.P.   India, A&N Islands
— — plants
SPENCER, Jonathan W.   UK, England
— — vascular plants in Canada
ARGUS, George W.   Canada, Ont.
— reefs, coral
MOYER, Jack T.   Japan
— reptiles
BURBIDGE, Andrew A.   Australia, WA
— —, Chilean
DIAZ, José VALENCIA   Chile
— resources, economic
TAN, Koonlin   UK, England
— —, environmental, ethics & politics in
FRAZIER, John G.   Mexico
— —, fishery
BUSTAMANTE, Georgina   USA, FL
— —, genetic
ASTLEY, David 'Dave'   UK, England
PALMBERG-LERCHE, Christel M.   Italy
WILSON, Richard T.   UK, England
— —, natural
LARSEN, Thor   Norway
— —, —, Himalayan
PANDIT, Ashok K.   India, J&K
— rodents & shrews
RAY, Justina C.   USA, FL
— Salmon, Atlantic
MILLS, Derek H.   UK, Scotland
— salt-marsh
BRIDGEWATER, Peter   Australia, ACT
— sanctuaries
SINGH, Birandra B.   Fiji
— savanna ecosystems
MILLS, M.G.L. ('Gus')   RSA
— semi-arid ecosystems in coastal regions & Jordan
HATOUGH-BOURAN, Alia M.A.   Jordan
— small biotic populations — Africa
PRICE, Mark R STANLEY   Kenya
— socio-economic systems
TAN, Koonlin   UK, England
— soil, catchment approach to
FITTER, Perin S.   Kenya
— Southeast Asian forests
PAYNE, Junaidi   Malaysia
— species, animal
WOODRUFF, David S.   USA, CA
— —, endangered
DURRELL, Lee McG.   UK, Channel Islands
JAIN, Sudhanshu K.   India, UP
MASCARENHAS, Anthony F.   India, Mah.
RANJITSINH, M.K.   India, MP

— —, threatened
BURBIDGE, Andrew A. — Australia, WA
— —, wild
VARIAVA, Dilnavaz — India, Mah.
— spoonbills & storks
KUSHLAN, James A. — USA, MS
— technology, appropriate
TAN, Koonlin — UK, England
— terrestrial vertebrates
HEINEN, Joel T. — USA, FL
— the environment
DALY, Ralph H. — Oman
— third-world insect resources
MORRIS, Michael G. — UK, England
— threatened species & ecosystems
BURBIDGE, Andrew A. — Australia, WA
— tropical forest carnivores
RAY, Justina C. — USA, FL
— — forests
BUDOWSKI, Gerardo — Costa Rica
SAYER, Jeffrey A. — Indonesia
— — protected areas
COBB, Stephen M. — UK, England
— Turtles, marine, off coast of Brazil
MARCOVALDI, Guy M.G.GUAGNI DEI
Brazil, Bahia
MARCOVALDI, Maria Â.GUAGNI DEI
Brazil, Bahia
— vegetation, British
WOODELL, Stanley R.J. — UK, England
— vertebrates
JENKINS, David — UK, Scotland
— —, terrestrial
HEINEN, Joel T. — USA, FL
— waterbirds
CHALABI, Bouzid — Algeria
— —, colonial
KUSHLAN, James A. — USA, MS
— West African forests
CHEEK, Martin R. — UK, England
— wetlands
CHALABI, Bouzid — Algeria
— wild habitats & species
VARIAVA, Dilnavaz — India, Mah.
— wilderness & wildland values
MARTIN, Vance G. — USA, CO
— — in West Africa esp.Sierra Leone
TUBOKU-METZGER, Daphne J.A. — Sierra Leone
— wildlife
DEY, Subhash C. — India, Delhi
JENKINS, David — UK, Scotland
— —, marine
MOYER, Jack T. — Japan
— —, projects & programmes re.
DURRANI, Shakil — Pakistan
constitutional law
JARIWALA, C.M. — India, UP
construction geology
KNILL, John — UK, England
constructs, cultural, social, & psychological, for
Nature conservation
MARTIN, Vance G. — USA, CO
consultation programmes
PRASAD, Basudeo — India, E.Punjab
consulting
WAGER, Jonathan F. — UK, England
—, environmental
ELKINGTON, John B. — UK, England
LOVEJOY, Derek — UK, England
MYERS, Norman — UK, England

SHARMA, Sudhirendar — India, Delhi
WORTHINGTON, E.Barton — UK, England
consumer protection
FAZAL, Anwar — Malaysia
consumerism, green
HAILES, Julia P. — UK, England
consumption growth in rich societies
HAREIDE, Dag — Norway
—, balancing conservation and
MISRA, Ramdeo — India, UP
(contaminant), ecological, hydrogeology
VORONOV, Arkady N. — Russia
contaminants, chemical, of surface water
MOORE, James W. — Canada, Alb.
contamination, habitat, bioindicators of,
ecotoxicology in reptiles as
LAMBERT, Michael R.K. — UK, England
—, heavy-metal, in tropical ecosystems*
—, Hg, in Amazon Basin
*LACERDA, Luiz D. — Brazil, RJ
control, air pollution
CHANDAK, Surya P. — India, Delhi
—, biological
SUNDERLAND, Keith D. — UK, England
—, —, Nature protection through
CIOCHIA, Victor — Romania
—, —, of animal pests
FENNER, Frank — Australia, ACT
—, —, — insects
RICHARDSON, Paul N. — UK, England
—, —, — some plant diseases
JARIWALA, Savitri — India, UP
—, —, — weeds
ROOM, Peter M. — Australia, Qld
—, desertification
ASEM, Samira ÔMAR — Kuwait
ZOUHA, Sekkou — Morocco
—, emission, over power-plants
KOBAYASHI, Osamu — Japan
—, environmental
BOXALL, John E. — Hong Kong
—, — pollution
DAVE, Jaydev M. — India, Delhi
—, erosion, of lands affected by coal-mining
HAIGH, Martin J. — UK, England
—, marine pollution
TORTELL, Philip — NZ
— methods, predator, non-lethal
KRAUS, Daniel — Namibia/USA, CA
MARKER-KRAUS, Laurie — Namibia/USA, DC
—, narcotic drugs'
DURRANI, Shakil — Pakistan
— of combustion-generated pollution
MATHUR, Harbansh B. — India, Delhi
— — foliar fungal pathogens
KENNEDY, Robert — UK, England
— — organic production
AUGSTBURGER, Franz — Bolivia
— — plant invasions in protected areas
THEBAUD, Christophe — France
— — post-harvest molds and mycotoxin production
KENNEDY, Robert — UK, England
— — toxic chemicals
FAZAL, Anwar — Malaysia
—, pest, non-chemical & integrated
ELLIS, Peter R. — UK, England
—, pollution
BISWAS, Dilip — India, Delhi
SCANNELL, Yvonne — Ireland

* *See* lower footnote on p. 409.

control, pollution (contd)
—, —, environmental
  DAVE, Jaydev M.   India, Delhi
  LOHANI, Bindu N.   Philippines
—, —, rural environmental
  ABDEL-GAWAAD, Ahmed A.-W.   Egypt
—, —, industrial environmental
  KHAN, Niaz A.   UAE
—, —, research & policymaking in
  MOORE, Norman W.   UK, England
—, predator, non-lethal
  COPPINGER, Raymond   USA, MA
— programmes, vector
  FARID, M.A.   Switzerland
—, quality, of training & ecological work re.people in
    the tropics
  FRAZIER, John G.   Mexico
—, toxic chemicals'
  FAZAL, Anwar   Malaysia
—, waste pollution
  KUFORIJI-OLUBI, Bola   Nigeria
—, water pollution
  ARCEIVALA, Soli J.   India, Mah.
  HAMMERTON, Desmond   UK, Scotland
  RAJAGOPAL, Rangaswamy   USA, OH
—, — —, technology and strategies
  BHARGAVA, Devendra S.   India, UP
controlled-environment composting for mushroom
    cultivation
  NOBLE, Ralph   UK, England
controls, land-use
  SCANNELL, Yvonne   Ireland
Convention, Helsinki, implementation of
  KRIKIS, Andris   Latvia
—, world heritage
  THORSELL, James W.   Switzerland
conventions, international, advocacy in
  PHILLIPS, Cassandra F.E.   UK, England
—, —, on the environment
  VISSER, Nicolaas W.   Kenya
cookstoves, improved
  KHANDELWAL, Kailash C.   India, Raj.
cooling (solar energy)
  SCHARMER, Klaus   Germany
cooperation, environmentally-sound, in sub-Saharan
    Africa
  KUFORIJI-OLUBI, Bola   Nigeria
—, international environmental
  PRESTRUD, Pål   Norway
coordination of EarthAction Network
  DUNLOP, Nicholas J.   Belgium/UK, England
— — environmental management*
— — global change research
  *GOLUBEV, Genady N.   Russia
Copepods, taxonomy of
  POR, Francis D.   Israel
coral biogeography, conservation, & evolutionary
    mechanisms
  VERON, John E.N.   Australia, Qld
— bleaching (impact on coral-reef ecosystems)
  VANTIER, Lyndon M.DE   Australia, Qld
— -reef conservation
  WELLS, Susan M.   UK, England
— - — ecology
  DAHL, Arthur L.   Switzerland
  SAENGER, Peter   Australia, NSW
  WILKINSON, Clive R.   Australia, Qld
— - — — & biology
  LAYDOO, Richard S.   Trinidad & Tobago

* See lower footnote on p. 409.

— - — ecosystems, conservation of
  McALLISTER, Donald E.   Canada, Ont.
— - — —, human & natural impacts on
  VANTIER, Lyndon M.DE   Australia, Qld
— - — management & monitoring
  LAYDOO, Richard S.   Trinidad & Tobago
— - — oceanography
  WOLANSKI, Eric J.   Australia, Qld
— reefs
  McCLOSKEY, Maxine E.   USA, MD
— —, conservation of
  MOYER, Jack T.   Japan
— —, evolution of
  BELLAMY, David J.   UK, England
— —, islands in Asia/Pacific region
  HOLTHUS, Paul F.   USA, HI
— —, palaeoecology of
  KRASNOV, Eugene V.   Russia
— skeletons, environmental records stored in
  BARNES, David J.   Australia, Qld
— systematics & taxonomy
  VERON, John E.N.   Australia, Qld
corals, conservation & utilization of
  THRESHER, Philip B.   USA, CA
—, scleractian, calcification & growth in
  BARNES, David J.   Australia, Qld
corporate management
  LOVINS, L.Hunter   USA, CO
corridors, biological, design of
  SEVILLA, Lorenzo B.CARDENAL
                   Nicaragua/Guatemala
corrosion of metals, marbles, & monuments
  SKOULIKIDIS, Theodore   Greece
cosmic radiation
  ALNASER, Waheeb E.   Bahrain
cost–benefit analysis, land-use, esp.local community
    benefits
  THRESHER, Philip B.   USA, CA
countries, developing, development of science in
  PEARMAN, Peter B.   USA, CA
—, —, EIA in
  CARPENTER, Richard A.   USA, VA
—, —, self-help survival in
  FRIEDMAN, Yona   France
countryside
  FOSTER, John   UK, Scotland
—, impact of environmental policy on
  REYNOLDS, Fiona C.   UK, England
crane (Gruidae) conservation & migration
  LANDFRIED, Steven E.   USA, WI
cranes (Gruidae)
  RAHMANI, Asad Rafi   India, UP
— & their habitats, preservation of
  ARCHIBALD, George   USA, WI
crayfish, freshwater, environmental biology of
  HOLDICH, David M.   UK, England
creation of national parks
  JIGJ, Sonom   Mongolia
— — — —, Africa
  VERSCHUREN, Jacques C.F.   Belgium
— — protected areas
  JIGJ, Sonom   Mongolia
creative conservation
  BENTHEM, Roelof J.   The Netherlands
criteria and standard-setting
  JOOSTING, Peter E.   The Netherlands
crocodile populations in Australian (northern) tidal
    waterways
  MESSEL, Harry   Australia, Qld
— ecology
  BEHRA, Olivier   Madagascar

crocodiles in many areas of Africa
  HUTTON, Jonathan M.   Zimbabwe
crocodilians (conservation & management)
  GORZULA, Stefan   USA, TN
crop ecosystems, genetics of plant–pathogen
  interactions in
  CRUTE, Ian   UK, England
— improvement
  BREWBAKER, James L.   USA, HI
  KING, Graham J.   UK, England
— origins and biogeography
  CLEMENT, Charles R.   Brazil, Amaz.
— plant evolution
  HAWKES, John G.   UK, England
— plants, genetic diversity in
  KING, Graham J.   UK, England
— protection
  BOS, Luitc   The Netherlands
  CROSS, Jeremy V.   UK, England
—, tropical, development
  HARRIS, Philip J.C.   UK, England
crops, horticultural, & related taxa
  ASTLEY, David 'Dave'   UK, England
—, —, breeding pest-resistant varieties of
  ELLIS, Peter R.   UK, England
—, —, plant breeding & genetics in
  RIGGS, Timothy J.   UK, England
—, protected, integrated pest management strategies
  in
  JACOBSON, Robert J.   UK, England
—, soil assessment for
  DAVIDSON, Donald A.   UK, Scotland
cross-sectoral integrated coastal-zone management
  PERNETTA, John C.   The Netherlands
Crustacea (Cladocera), morphology & taxonomy of
  SMIRNOV, Nikolai N.   Russia
Crustacea, amphipod
  MOORE, Peter G.   UK, Scotland
crustaceans, aquatic, environmental biology of
  HOLDICH, David M.   UK, England
crystals, liquid
  SKOULIKIDIS, Theodore   Greece
cultivated Potato
  HAWKES, John G.   UK, England
cultivation, mushroom
  NOBLE, Ralph   UK, England
— of plants
  CHEEK, Roy V.   UK, England
—, traditional
  MANSER, Bruno   Switzerland
cultural changes required by sustainable development
  AICKIN, R.Malcolm   UK, England
— constructs for Nature conservation
  MARTIN, Vance G.   USA, CO
— ecology
  KLEE, Gary A.   USA, CA
  MOUDUD, Hasna J.   Bangladesh
— — research, writing & film-making
  GIRARDET, Herbert K.   UK, England
— heritage, conservation of
  CHERKASOVA, Maria V.   Russia
— — management
  BOYD, William 'Bill' Edgar   Australia, NSW
— landscape conservation in spatial planning
  STAWICKI, Henryk   Poland
— landscapes
  LUCAS, Percy H.C. ('Bing')   NZ
— resources' management
  WHITEHOUSE, John F.   Australia, NSW

— settings, different, application of legal techniques
  in
  WRIGHT, R.Michael   USA, VA
— sites, preservation of
  SINGH, Birandra B.   Fiji
— strategies for Nature conservation
  MARTIN, Vance G.   USA, CO
culture, freshwater fishery
  ATAUR-RAHIM, Mohammed   Pakistan
—, plant-tissue
  MASCARENHAS, Anthony F.   India, Mah.
cultures & fates of Amazonian Indians
  SIOLI, Harald F.L.   Germany
customary land & marine tenure
  BAINES, Graham B.K.   Australia, Qld
customs
  MANSER, Bruno   Switzerland
Cycads, taxonomy of
  SCLAVO, Jean-Pierre   France
cycles, biogeochemical
  ROSSWALL, Thomas   Sweden
—, —, C/N/S/P, interrelationships between, as
  influenced by anthropogenic activities
  STEWART, John W.B.   Canada, Sask.
—, —, global
  BOLIN, Bert R.   Sweden
—, microbial biogeochemical, in prairie saline lakes
  & prairie wetlands
  ROBARTS, Richard D.   Canada, Sask.
cycling, nutrient
  SANCHEZ, Pedro A.   Kenya
studies, nutrient
  KIRA, Tatuo   Japan
  OLA-ADAMS, Bunyamin A.   Nigeria
cytochemistry
  SHARMA, Arun K.   India, W.Bengal
cytogenetics
  SHARMA, Arun K.   India, W.Bengal
  SWAMINATHAN, Monkombu S.   India, TN
  VIDA, Gabór   Hungary
—, plant
  KHUSH, Gurdev S.   Philippines

———————

dairy production systems, animal evaluation in
  TEWOLDE, Assefaw   Mexico
Dam, High Tehri, opposition to construction of
  BAHUGUNA, Sunderlal   India, UP
damage, environmental, liability for
  SCANNELL, Yvonne   Ireland
—, plant responses to
  ROOM, Peter M.   Australia, Qld
dams, big, environmental aspects of
  GOODLAND, Robert J.A.   USA, DC
—, economic impacts of
  McEACHERN, John D.   Canada, Ont./Nepal
—, environmental impacts of
  PETTS, Geoffrey   UK, England
—, hydroelectric, impacts of
  FEARNSIDE, Philip M.   Brazil, Amaz.
—, large
  MOORE, James W.   Canada, Alb.
—, —, social & environmental impact assessments of
  GORZULA, Stefan   USA, TN
dangerous goods, environmentally-sound transport of
  KRIKIS, Andris   Latvia

Danube Delta, protection of
   CIOCHIA, Victor — Romania
data management
   WITT, Ronald G. — Switzerland
databases, biodiversity
   MacKINNON, John R. — Hong Kong
Datura, taxonomy of (and related genera)
   BYE, Robert — Mexico
debris, marine
   RYAN, Peter, G. — RSA
—, orbiting
   SINGER, S.Fred — USA, VA
debt-for-Nature swaps
   MORAN, Katy — USA, DC
decision-makers, influencing
   PETERSON, Russell W. — USA, DE
— -making, environmental, public participation in
   GARDNER, Julia E. — Canada, BC
— - —, — re.tropical coastal environments
   DAVIE, James D.S. — Australia, Qld
deer and their ecology
   WHITEHEAD, George K. — UK, England
defences, anti-predator, of animals
   EDMUNDS, Malcolm — UK, England
defoliants, effects of, on environment during Vietnam war
   VO, Quy — Vietnam
deforestation
   GROOT, Wouter T.DE — The Netherlands
   PALMBERG-LERCHE, Christel M. — Italy
—, tropical
   SANCHEZ, Pedro A. — Kenya
—, —, causes, impacts & rates, of
   FEARNSIDE, Philip M. — Brazil, Amaz.
—, —, ecological consequences of
   LAL, Rattan — USA, OH
—, vegetation change through historic time
   GADE, Daniel W. — USA, VT
deglaciation, primary succession following
   SVOBODA, Josef — Canada, Ont.
degradation, environmental
   GOLDEMBERG, José — Brazil, SP
   PETERSON, Russell W. — USA, DE
—, —, mechanisms of
   AICKIN, R.Malcolm — UK, England
—, —, –national sovereignty–warfaring propensities*
—, —, –rapid population growth
   *SHAW, R.Paul — USA, DC
—, land
   ABROL, Inder P. — India, Delhi
   LUK, Shiu-hung — Canada, Ont.
— of environment by human activity
   ZLOTIN, Roman I. — Russia
—, soil, processes
   VÁRALLYAY, György — Hungary
degraded forest & mining lands, rehabilitation of
   JUSOFF, Kamaruzaman — Malaysia
— land, restoration of
   CHADWICK, Michael J. — Sweden
delinking growth from environment
   OPSCHOOR, Johannes B. — The Netherlands
Delta, Danube, protection of
   CIOCHIA, Victor — Romania
democracy, education for
   NOVOA, Laura — Chile
demographic dynamics–environment
   KUFORIJI-OLUBI, Bola — Nigeria
demography
   COHEN, Joel E. — USA, NY

—, dynamics of, in developing countries
   PICOUET, Michel R. — France
dendrology
   GRANDTNER, Miroslav M. — Canada, Que.
depletion of resources
   PETERSON, Russell W. — USA, DE
derelict land reclamation
   ROBERTS, Thomas M. — UK, England
— landscape, revitalization of
   KRAJČOVIČ, Roman S. — Slovak Rep.
desert adaptations
   CLOUDSLEY-THOMPSON, John L. — UK, England
— animal ecology
   BÜTTIKER, William — Switzerland
— biology
   GARDNER, Andrew S. — Oman
— development
   BATANOUNY, Kamal H. — Egypt
— ecology
   GHABBOUR, Samir I. — Egypt
   WOODELL, Stanley R.J. — UK, England
— environment
   SPRINGUEL, Irina — Egypt
— environments
   GOUDIE, Andrew S. — UK, England
— in Siberia & Central Asia
   FLINT, Vladimir E. — Russia
— mountains, ecology of
   GARDNER, Andrew S. — Oman
— plant ecology
   KASSAS, Mohamed EL — Egypt
   KHARIN, Nikolai — Turkmenistan
   SPRINGUEL, Irina — Egypt
desertification
   ABROL, Inder P. — India, Delhi
   BATANOUNY, Kamal H. — Egypt
   GROOT, Wouter T.DE — The Netherlands
   ISHI, Hiroyuki — Japan
   JOVANOVIĆ, Petar — Yugoslavia
   MOGHRABY, Asim I. — Sudan
   PANDEYA, Satish C. — India, UP
   RECKERS, Ute — Kenya
   WILLIAMS, Martin A.J. — Australia, SA
— control
   ASEM, Samira OMAR — Kuwait
   ZOUHA, Sekkou — Morocco
—, combatting
   DAMERDJI, M.Amine — Algeria
—, prevention of
   HAFIDI, Moulay El M. — Morocco
deserts
   RAHMANI, Asad Rafi — India, UP
—, adaption to life in, Aboriginal*
—: Australian reptiles
   *COVACEVICH, Jeanette A. — Australia, Qld
—, human life in
   BATANOUNY, Kamal H. — Egypt
—, polar, colonization & revegetation of
   SVOBODA, Josef — Canada, Ont.
design, air pollution monitoring & control equipment
   MATHUR, Harbansh B. — India, Delhi
—, environment–tourism
   CROSBY, Arturo — Spain
—, experimental, forest
   SCHLAEPFER, Rodolphe — Switzerland
—, gene-bank
   TAO, Kar-ling J. — Italy

—, geographical methods of
ZABELINA, Natalia M.   Russia
—, landscape
MOURA, Robert MANNERS   Portugal
— of biological corridors & buffer zones
SEVILLA, Lorenzo B.CARDENAL
Nicaragua/Guatemala
— — environmental conservation projects
PANGETI, George N.   Zimbabwe
— — extractive reserves
SEVILLA, Lorenzo B.CARDENAL
Nicaragua/Guatemala
— — field experiments
WATT, Trudy A.   UK, England
— — multiple-use reserves
SEVILLA, Lorenzo B.CARDENAL
Nicaragua/Guatemala
— — protected natural areas
WRIGHT, Shane D.T.   NZ
— — wildlife management projects
PANGETI, George N.   Zimbabwe
—, planting
CHEEK, Roy V.   UK, England
—, permaculture
EVERETT, Rodney D.   UK, England
—, research
WEBER, Karl E.   Thailand
—, sustainable development project
HARDI, Peter   Canada, Man.
Destruction, Development without
TOLBA, Mostafa K.   Egypt
detoxification of hazardous wastes
SUBRAMANIAN, Tarakad V.   India, TN
developed economies, urban environmental problems
in
GANDY, Matthew   UK, England
developing countries
FUREDY, Christine   Canada, Ont.
— —, conservation & management of natural
resources in, using support of local people
MacFARLAND, Craig G.   USA, ID
— —, development in
BILSBORROW, Richard E.   USA, NC
— —, — of science in
PEARMAN, Peter B.   USA, CA
— —, dynamics of demography, migration, &
environment, in
PICOUET, Michel R.   France
— —, EIA in
CARPENTER, Richard A.   USA, VA
TOIT, Raoul F.DU   Zimbabwe
— —, environment in
BILSBORROW, Richard E.   USA, NC
— —, genetic conservation in
MOESTRUP, Søren   Denmark
— —, planning of research & development projects
& units for
RADICELLA, Sandro M.   Italy
— —, public consultation & participation procedures
GARRATT, Keith J.   NZ
— —, seed procurement in
MOESTRUP, Søren   Denmark
— —, self-help survival
FRIEDMAN, Yona   France
— —, technical assistance to
PALMBERG-LERCHE, Christel M.   Italy
— —, tree improvement in
MOESTRUP, Søren   Denmark
— —, waste management in
FUREDY, Christine   Canada, Ont.

— nations, conservation in
BURNETT, G.Wesley   USA, SC
— world, alleviating environment-related poverty in*
— —, creating sustainable development awareness &
economies in
*ONAYEMI, Olarotimi O.   Nigeria
— —, women's contribution in
TAN, Koonlin   UK, England
development, see also development of†
BAHRI, Ahmed   Ethiopia
DAHL, R.Brigitta   Sweden
FAULKNER, J.Hugh   Switzerland
GROOT, Wouter T.DE   The Netherlands
HARRISON, Paul A.   UK, England
LEBLANC, Hubert   Canada, Que.
PELUSO, Nancy L.   USA, CT
SAMAD, Syed A.   Malaysia
VISSER, Nicolaas W.   Kenya
—, Aboriginal enterprise
WILSON, George R.   Australia, WA
—, agricultural, in the Sahara
DAMERDJI, M.Amine   Algeria
—, —, international
JAMES, W.Clive   Cayman Islands
—, air pollution monitoring & control equipment
MATHUR, Harbansh B.   India, Delhi
— & conservation projects, integrated
BEZAURY-CREEL, Juan E.   Mexico
—, arctic, role of applied ecology in
BLISS, Lawrence C.   USA, WA
—, arid lands'
HAMED, Safei EL-DEEN   USA, MA
— assistance
PALMBERG-LERCHE, Christel M.   Italy
, behavioural, growth &
GOCHFELD, Michael   USA, NJ
—, coastal
DOUMENGE, François   Monaco
—, community
SAMAD, Syed A.   Malaysia
—, —, in the humid neo-tropics
LYNCH, James R.   Costa Rica
—, conservation policy
SATTLER, Paul S.   Australia, Qld
—, desert
BATANOUNY, Kamal H.   Egypt
—, ecologically-sustainable
BAKER, Joseph 'Joe' T.   Australia, Qld
—, economics of
BARBIER, Edward B.   UK, England
—, environment &
BATISSE, Michel   France
CLARK, William C.   USA, MA
DANKELMAN, Irene   The Netherlands
HURNI, Hans   Switzerland
NTAHUGA, Laurent   Burundi
OUEDRAOGO, O.Dieudonné   Mali
SALIM, Emil   Indonesia
SANDBROOK, J.Richard   UK, England
WASAWO, David P.S.   Kenya
— /—-finance/banking
McCAMMON, Antony L.T.   Switzerland
— – – (mass communication & world affairs)
BHATT, Dibya D.   Nepal
— assistance issues*
—, environmental law
*FRY, Ian W.   Australia, NSW

* See lower footnote on p. 409.
† See upper footnote on p. 409.

development, environmental (contd)
—, — policy
   BASS, Stephen M.J.   UK, England
   GALLON, Gary T.   Canada, Ont.
—, environmentally-sound, philosophy of
   TOLBA, Mostafa K.   Egypt
—, — -sustainable
   WEBER, Karl E.   Thailand
—, forest policy
   BASS, Stephen M.J.   UK, England
—, forestry
   ALIEU, Emmanuel K.   Sierra Leone
— –gender–environment–
   DANKELMAN, Irene   The Netherlands
—, growth & behavioural
   GOCHFELD, Michael   USA, NJ
—, Highland Southeast Asia
   DEARDEN, Philip   Canada, BC
—, human resource
   BRERETON, Vera A.   Barbados
— in Cameroon, Indonesia, Surinam, & West
   African Sahel
   DRIJVER, Carel A.   The Netherlands
— — developing countries
   BILSBORROW, Richard E.   USA, NC
— — Highland Southeast Asia
   DEARDEN, Philip   Canada, BC
—, industrial, in Arctic circumpolar world, in
   Nunavut, & in Yukon and NWT
   FENGE, Terence A.E.   Canada, Ont.
— infrastructure, monitoring of environmental
   impacts on
   SARMIENTO, Fausto O.   USA, GA
—, institutional
   MORELL, Merillo G.   Italy
   TOLENTINO, Amado   Philippines
—, —, environmental management re.
   GARRATT, Keith J.   NZ
—, integrated rural area
   RAI, Suresh Chand   India, Sikkim
—, international
   KRATTIGER, Anatole F.   USA, NY
— issues
   SARMA, K.Madhava   Kenya
—, local, & sustainable agroforestry
   KERN, Berndt   Sweden
   KERN, Eha   Sweden
—, marine
   DOUMENGE, François   Monaco
—, mineral, liability for
   SCANNELL, Yvonne   Ireland
—, natural park
   NOSEL, José   Martinique
—, NGO
   LAMBERTINI, Marco   Italy
   SHORES, John N.   USA, ME
—, Noosphere
   POLUNIN, Nicholas   Switzerland
—, northern, assessment of effects of, on wildlife &
   habitats
   KLEIN, David R.   USA, AK
— planning
   POTTER, Louis   BVI
— —, forest sector
   LAL, Jugal B.   India, MP
— policies, regional (national & EEC)
   SOTIRIADOU, Victoria   Greece
— policy
   AL-MANDHRY, Abdullah R.   Oman
   ASFAW, Gedion   Ethiopia

   GAKAHU, Christopher G.   Kenya
   USUKI, Mitsuo   Thailand
— projects & units, planning of, for developing
   countries
   RADICELLA, Sandro M.   Italy
— —, economic, environmental assessment of
   GOODLAND, Robert J.A.   USA, DC
— —, EIA of
   SUNDARESAN, Bommaya B.   India, TN
— —, governmental & non-governmental, EIA
   studies of
   UGWU, Christopher N.   Nigeria
— —, integrated
   BEZAURY-CREEL, Juan E.   Mexico
— —, management of
   STEPHENSON, Peter J.   Tanzania
— —, water resources, re.tropical & temperate
   environments
   ZWAHLEN, Robert   Switzerland
—, regional environmental management
   KRAJČOVIČ, Roman S.   Slovak Rep.
— regulation
   POTTER, Louis   BVI
— research on environment
   VERMA, Sewa R.   India, UP
— — — livestock & rangeland utilization
   WARDEH, Muhammad Fadel   Syria
—, rural
   FÉRON, Eric M.   Zimbabwe
   RYDÉN, Per A.   Switzerland
   VASUDEVAN, Padma   India, Delhi
—, —, Bamboos in
   BOA, Eric   UK, England
—, —, natural resource management in
   TOORNSTRA, Franke H.   The Netherlands
— —, planning
   NEPAL, Sanjay K.   Switzerland
—, soil of reclaimed lands after surface coal-mining
   KILMARTIN, Marianne P.   UK, England
—, strategic planning for sustainable
   MORELL, Merilio G.   Italy
— strategies, sustainable
   SINGH, Karan   India, Delhi
— strategy
   ASFAW, Gedion   Ethiopia
—, sustainable *see* sustainable development
—, — agricultural
   BISWAS, Asit K.   UK, England
   BISWAS, Margaret R.   UK, England
—, —, & strategic analysis
   WILSON, George R.   Australia, WA
—, —, awareness in developing world
   ONAYEMI, Olarotimi O.   Nigeria
—, — community
   ALLEN, Irma   Swaziland
—, —, computer communications
   PETER, Ian W.   Australia, NSW
—, —, concept, implication of
   HUBA, Mikuláš   Slovak Rep.
—, —, definition of
   CARPENTER, Richard A.   USA, VA
—, — economic, in Africa's semi-arid rangelands
   TOIT, Raoul F.DU   Zimbabwe
—, —, esp.agriculture, forestry, & fisheries
   SAOUMA, Edouard V.   Lebanon
—, — human
   MIRANDA, Ruiz   Guinea-Bissau
   SPETH, James G.   USA, NY
—, —, implementation of action on
   LINDNER, Warren H.   Switzerland

—, —, in American humid tropics
DOUROJEANNI, Marc J.   USA, VA
—, —, — temperate environments
MOFFATT, Ian   UK, Scotland
—, —, — the Middle East
DEAN, Faisal   USA, VA
—, —, — third-world countries
BEHRA, Olivier   Madagascar
—, —, — tropical Andes
DOUROJEANNI, Marc J.   USA, VA
—, —, — — environments
MOFFATT, Ian   UK, Scotland
—, —, — underdeveloped regions, theory on
LEFF, Enrique   Mexico
—, —, interdisciplinary approaches to
FONSECA, Gustavo A.B.   Brazil, MG
—, —, international policy on
RAMPHAL, Shridath   UK, England
—, —, issues, public participation in
KAKABADSE, Yolanda   Ecuador
—, —, measurement of
CARPENTER, Richard A.   USA, VA
—, —, natural resources' management for
PANDURANGAN, Alagramam G.   India, Ker.
—, —, & N–S relations
MYERS, Norman   UK, England
—, —, of buffer zones
HURNI, Hans   Switzerland
—, —, planning, GIS applied to
KRISHNAYYA, Jaswant G.   India, Mah.
—, —, policy issues
SEVILLA, Lorenzo B. CARDENAL
                          Nicaragua/Guatemala
—, —, political & institutional aspects of
GORDON, John K.   UK, England
—, —, polymer science–environment–
VASUDEVAN, Padma   India, Delhi
—, —, practical applications of
FEICK, Jenny L.   Canada, Alb.
—, —, prediction of
CARPENTER, Richard A.   USA, VA
—, —, project design
HARDI, Peter   Canada, Man.
—, —, research in, re.recovery of refuse and
underutilized resources
ARIAS-CHAVEZ, Jesus   Mexico
—, —, social & cultural changes required by
AICKIN, R.Malcolm   UK, England
—, —, — dimensions of
HOUGH, John L.   USA, MD
—, —, strategic planning for
MORRELL, Merilio G.
—, —, strategies for
PEINE, John D.   USA, TN
—, —, through investments in human resources
SHAW, R.Paul   USA, DC
—, — urban
JACOBS, Peter D.A.   Canada, Que.
—, —, world-wide
GATHORNE-HARDY, Gathorne   UK, England
—, third world
GLANTZ, Michael H.   USA, CO
JUEL-JENSEN, Bent E.   UK, England
—, tropical crop
HARRIS, Philip J.C.   UK, England
—, wasteland
KHOSHOO, Triloki N.   India, Delhi
— without Destruction
TOLBA, Mostafa K.   Egypt
—, wood energy
NANAYAKKARA, Vitarana R.   Sri Lanka

development of (see also development)[†]
— arctic ecosystems
BLISS, Lawrence C.   USA, WA
— arid lands
HAMED, Safei EL-DEEN   USA, MD
— ecotourism programmes
FOX, Allan M.   Australia, NSW
— environmental monitoring instruments
PRASAD, Basudeo   India, E.Punjab
— disease resistant, genetically superior, & high-
yielding, clones of Poplars, Eucalypts, &
Casuarinas
LAL, Piare   India, AP
— human ecology
DAYSH, Zena   UK, England
— hydropower & irrigation projects in Southeast
Asia
WOODRUFF, David S.   USA, CA
— innovative technologies for basic human needs
KHOSLA, Ashok   India, Delhi
— law re.tropical coastal environments
DAVIE, James D.S.   Australia, Qld
— laws on environmental protection in Ukraine
KOSTENKO, Yuriy I.   Ukraine
— national parks & game reserves
SPINAGE, Clive A.   UK, England
— open space systems
JACOBS, Peter D.A.   Canada, Que.
— projects & programmes re.conservation of
wildlife & environment
DURRANI, Shakil   Pakistan
— protected areas
ALVARADO, Juan SKINNER   Guatemala
LAMBERTINI, Marco   Italy
— science in developing countries
PEARMAN, Peter B.   USA, CA
— the environment
DALY, Ralph H.   Oman
— travel & tourism
JIGJ, Sonom   Mongolia
— tree improvement
LAL, Piare   India, AP
— tropical forestry
BURLEY, Jeffery   UK, England
— vegetative propagation
LAL, Piare   India, AP
developments, effects of northern, on wildlife &
habitats
KLEIN, David R.   USA, AK
—, hydroelectric, effects of, on aquatic environment
and on fish
MILLS, Derek H.   UK, Scotland
Diceros bicornis, field protection & management of
TOIT, Raoul F.DU   Zimbabwe
dilemmas, common resource
YOUNG, Raymond DE   USA, MI
dimensions, human, of global environmental change
PRICE, Martin F.   UK, England
diplomacy, environmental
CARROLL, John E.   USA, NH
Diptera, Afrotropical, distribution, conservation, &
systematics, of
WHITTINGTON, Andrew E.   UK, Scotland
Dipterocarpaceae
SMITS, Willie   Indonesia
disappearing species, saving
OZA, Gunavant M.   India, Guj.
OZA, Premlata   India, Guj.

† *See* upper footnote on p. 409.

disaster, Chernobyl
   KUKHAR, Valery P. — Ukraine
disasters, 'natural', Man-made
   JOVANOVIĆ, Petar — Yugoslavia
disease biocontrol
   WHIPPS, John M. — UK, England
— management–risk assessment, wild animal
   management
   WILSON, George R. — Australia, WA
— resistance
   DARBY, Peter — UK, England
— —, introduction of
   ALSTON, Frank H. — UK, England
—, settlement &
   GADE, Daniel W. — USA, VT
—, wild animal
   WOODFORD, Michael H. — USA, DC
diseases, environmental
   JOVANOVIĆ, Petar — Yugoslavia
—, infectious, of animals & humans
   FENNER, Frank — Australia, ACT
— of the integument
   BARRY, James M. — Ireland
—, plant
   PINK, David A.C. — UK, England
— —, biological control of some
   JARIWALA, Savitri — India, UP
—, snail-transmitted, in Southeast Asia
   WOODRUFF, David S. — USA, CA
—, vector-borne
   LAIRD, Marshall — NZ
disinfection, environmental
   ALI, Abd 'El moneim' M. — Egypt
—, water (solar energy)
   SCHARMER, Klaus — Germany
dispersers & herbivores, plants in relation to
   GRUBB, Peter J. — UK, England
displays, synchronous, by *Pteroptyx* fireflies, research
   into
   POLUNIN, Ivan V. — Singapore
disposal, solid waste, management
   KUFORIJI-OLUBI, Bola — Nigeria
—, waste, solid/hazardous*
—, wastewater, industrial & sewage
   *KHAN, Niaz A. — UAE
dissemination of information to mass media on
   ecological matters
   MARGARIS, Nickolas S. — Greece
distribution & conservation of Afrotropical Diptera
   WHITTINGTON, Andrew E. — UK, Scotland
—, just, of world's resources
   DAMMANN, Erik — Norway
distributions, bryophyte
   HILL, Mark O. — UK, England
—, plant (alpine ecology)
   GOOD, Roger B. — Australia, ACT
disturbance ecology
   FORBES, Bruce C. — Finland
—, forest, & recovery, research in
   ORGLE, Tetey K. — Ghana
diurnal rhythms
   CLOUDSLEY-THOMPSON, John L.
         UK, England
   TSHERNYSHEV, Wladimir B. — Russia
diversity, biocultural
   MORAN, Katy — USA, DC
—, biological
   ANISHETTY, Narasimha M. — Italy
   EIDSVIK, Harold K. — France

McNEELY, Jeffrey A. — Switzerland
PALMBERG-LERCHE, Christel M. — Italy
REID, Walter V. — USA, DC
WAHLSTEDT, Jens — Sweden
—, —, conservation of
   MITTERMEIER, Russell A. — USA, DC
   WELCOMME, Robin L. — Italy
—, ecological
   BALČIAUSKAS, Linas — Lithuania
—, genetic, and population dynamics
   VIDA, Gabór — Hungary
—, plant community
   KULL, Kalevi — Estonia
—, —, maintenance of, in tropical forests
   ASHTON, Peter S. — USA, MA
—, species
   DANIELS, Frederikus J.A. — Germany
—, —, and use of by human societies
   OSEMEOBO, Gbadebo J. — Nigeria
DNA sequence variation
   KING, Graham J. — UK, England
documentary television
   RICHTER, Robert — USA, NY
domestic animal genetic resource conservation &
   management
   TEWOLDE, Assefaw — Mexico
domestication, animal, process of
   GADE, Daniel W. — USA, VT
— of tropical trees
   DICK, Janet M. — UK, Scotland
— — — — for forestry/agroforestry in tropics
   LEAKEY, Richard R.B. — Kenya
—, plant
   BALICK, Michael J. — USA, NY
dominant trees, ecological & ecophysiological
   relations in forest ecosystems and their
   dependence on
   ČABOUN, Vladimír — Slovak Rep.
dormancy mechanisms, seed germination &
   TAO, Kar-ling J. — Italy
drafting of municipal & international environmental
   law or legislation
   OGUNDERE, Joseph D. — Nigeria
dragonflies
   CORBET, Philip S. — UK, Scotland
drainage-basin management
   CLARK, Colin — UK, England
drinking-water
   CHOI, Yearn Hong — USA, VA
drought stress, impact of, on vegetation
   GRACE, John — UK, Scotland
drugs, narcotic, control
   DURRANI, Shakil — Pakistan
dry tropical forests, ecology of
   SINGH, Jamuna S. — India, UP
— lands, water resources in
   WILLIAMS, William D. — Australia, SA
dryland regions, geodynamic processes of landscape
   of
   JIGJ, Sonom — Mongolia
Dugongs, ecology of, and habitats
   MARSH, Helene D. — Australia, Qld
dune, sand-, ecology
   BOORMAN, Laurie A. — UK, England
dunes
   BATE, Guy C. — RSA
dynamics, demographic–environment
   KUFORIJI-OLUBI, Bola — Nigeria
—, ecosystems
   HOUÉROU, Henry N.LE — France
   RAMAKRISHNAN, P.S. ('Ram') — India, Delhi

—, forest regeneration
    WRIGHT, Shane D.T. — NZ
—, forest
    DONOSO, Claudio — Chile
— of demography, environment, & migration, in
    developing countries
    PICOUET, Michel R. — France
— — woodland ground vegetation
    KIRBY, Keith J. — UK, England
— (ornithology)
    CIOCHIA, Victor — Romania
—, population
    PRINS, Herbert H.T. — The Netherlands
—, —, of coastal birds
    BURGER, Joanna — USA, NJ
—, —, tropical marine
    POLOVINA, Jeffrey J. — USA, HI
—, vegetation
    LEEMANS, Rik — The Netherlands
    MOREY, Miguel — Spain
    NUMATA, Makoto — Japan
—, vegetational
    GRUBB, Peter J. — UK, England

---

early life-history of fish esp.antarctic fish
    KELLERMANN, Adolf K. — Germany
EarthAction Network
    DUNLOP, Nicholas — Belgium/UK, England
Earth, biotic interactions in warming of
    WOODWELL, George M. — USA, MA
—, environmental conservation, protection, &
    restoration, of the
    ODULA, Michael A.N. — Kenya
—, gentle living on
    EVERETT, Rodney D. — UK, England
— science conservation
    KNILL, John — UK, England
— sciences
    PAGE, Christopher N. — UK, Scotland
— —, ecological interactions of, with native
    Canadian perceptions
    CRAMPTON, Colin B. — Canada, BC
— warming
    ISHI, Hiroyuki — Japan
Earth's climate
    SUN, Lin — Kenya
earthquakes, hazards of
    VALDIYA, Khadga Singh — India, UP
earthworms, organic waste recycling using local
    species of
    ISMAIL, Sultan A. — India, TN
East Africa, conservation & ecology of large
    mammals
    ELTRINGHAM, Stewart K. — UK, England
eco-physiology, *see* ecophysiology
ecocomplex realism
    POLUNIN, Nicholas — Switzerland
    WORTHINGTON, E.Barton — UK, England
ecocomplexes, island & marine, conservation of
    FITTER, Julian R. — UK, England
ecodevelopment
    DASMANN, Raymond F. — USA, CA
    PITT, David — Switzerland
— & biodiversity
    MELKANIA, Niranjan P. — India, MP

— of conservation areas
    HOECK, Hendrik N. — Switzerland
— programmes
    SINGH, Hari B. — India, Delhi
—, research in, re.recovery of refuse and
    underutilized resources
    ARIAS-CHAVEZ, Jesus — Mexico
ecoengineering
    JUSOFF, Kamaruzaman — Malaysia
eco-ethics
    SKOLIMOWSKI, Henryk — Poland
ecofarming
    AUGSTBURGER, Franz — Bolivia
ecofeminism
    VALLELY, Bernadette A.M. — UK, England
ecological agriculture
    SWAMINATHAN, Monkombu S. — India, TN
— & social processes, linkages
    RAMAKRISHNAN, P.S. ('Ram') — India, Delhi
— –atmospheric interactions
    PIELKE, Roger A. — USA, CO
— balance sheets
    LINDSTROM, U.B. — Finland
— botany
    BEARD, John S. — Australia, WA
— consequences of land-use changes in Latin
    America
    MORELLO, Jorge X. — Argentina
— — — tropical deforestation & water management
    LAL, Rattan — USA, OH
— conservation, holistic
    POLUNIN, Nicholas — Switzerland
— (contaminant) hydrogeology
    VORONOV, Arkady N. — Russia
— diversity
    BALČIAUSKAS, Linas — Lithuania
— economics
    EKINS, Paul W. — UK, England
    WALT, Pieter T.van der — RSA
economy in transition period to a sustainable
    society
    HAREIDE, Dag — Norway
— education
    MOURA, Robert Manners — Portugal
    VORONOV, Arkady N. — Russia
— engineering
    KELCEY, John G. — UK, England
— farming & building
    EVERETT, Rodney D. — UK, England
— forestry
    URBAN, František — Czech Rep.
— function of grassland in landscape
    RYCHNOVSKÁ, Milena — Czech Rep.
— genetics
    BERRY, Robert James ('Sam') — UK, England
— hydrogeology (contaminant)
    VORONOV, Arkady N. — Russia
— interactions of certain earth sciences with *native*
    Canadian perceptions and *European* Canadian
    written traditions
    CRAMPTON, Colin B. — Canada, BC
— knowledge, traditional marine
    JOHANNES, Robert E. — Australia, Tas.
— landscaping
    SAMWAYS, Michael J. — RSA
— management of watersheds
    OJEDA, Ricardo A. — Argentina
— matters: teaching, research, & dissemination of
    information to mass media, on
    MARGARIS, Nickolas S. — Greece

ecological (contd)
— monitoring of coastal ecosystems
   MAXIMOV, Victor N. — Russia
— perspective, human
   NELSON, J.Gordon — Canada, Ont.
— pest management
   TSHERNYSHEV, Wladimir B. — Russia
— planning & politics
   MIKLÓS, Ladislav — Slovak Rep.
— — in the Asia–Pacific region
   SHAPIRO, Harvey A. — Japan
— — processes, marine
   AGARDY, M.Tündi — USA, DC
— reform concept, national
   KOSTENKO, Yuriy I. — Ukraine
— relations in forest ecosystems and their
     dependence on dominant trees
   ČABOUN, Vladimir — Slovak Rep.
— relationships — peasant & folk societies
   GADE, Daniel W. — USA, VT
— research
   AMBASHT, Radhey S. — India, UP
   FERRAR, Anthony A. — RSA
— restoration
   CLEWELL, Andre F. — USA, FL
   JORDAN III, William R. — USA, WI
— risk analysis
   BOYLE, Terence P. — USA, CO
— sociology
   CLOUDSLEY, Timothy — UK, Scotland
— stability, role of reserves in
   HATOUGH-BOURAN, Alia M.A. — Jordan
— —, territorial systems of
   DEJMAL, Ivan — Czech Rep.
— survey
   HIBBERD, John K. — Australia, ACT
— techniques
   LEEFLANG, Sietz A. — The Netherlands
— theory
   LEEMANS, Rik — The Netherlands
— work, quality control of, re.people in the tropics
   FRAZIER, John G. — Mexico
— writing
   AMBASHT, Radhey S. — India, UP
ecologically-sound anthropocentric ecosystem
   LIU, Peitong — China
— - — forestry
   LOENING, Ulrich E. — UK, Scotland
— -sustainable development
   BAKER, Joseph 'Joe' T. — Australia, Qld
— - — use of native forests
   KETO, Aila — Australia, Qld
— — — semi-arid lands
   SATTLER, Paul S. — Australia, Qld
ecology, *see also* ecology of[†]
   ARAUJO, Joaquín — Spain
   AZIS, P.K.Abdul — Saudi Arabia
   BAKER, F.W.G. ('Mike') — France
   BOS, Luite — The Netherlands
   BOURDEAU, Philippe F. — Belgium
   BUBLINEC, Eduard — Slovak Rep.
   BUCKLEY, Ralf C. — Australia, Qld
   CANNELL, Melvin G.R. — UK, Scotland
   CARROLL, John E. — USA, NH
   CHEN, Changdu — China
   CHERKASOVA, Maria V. — Russia
   COHEN, Joel E. — USA, NY
   DUFFY, David C. — USA, AK
   EGLER, Frank E. — USA, CT

[†] *See* upper footnote on p. 409.

FAEGRI, Knut — Norway
FEDOROV, Vadim D. — Russia
FRIDRIKSSON, Sturla — Iceland
GOLDSMITH, Edward — UK, England
GOLLEY, Frank B. — USA, GA
HAMBLER, Clive — UK, England
HAYNES-SUTTON, Ann M. — Jamaica
HELLIWELL, D.Rodney — UK, England
HOFFMANN, Luc — France
HOLDGATE, Martin W. — UK, England
HÜLSHOFF, Bernd von Droste zu — France
KRISHNAMURTHY, Kothandaraman — India, TN
LaBASTILLE, Anne — USA, NY
LANGSLOW, Derek R. — UK, England
LITVIN, Vladimir M. — Russia
MEHER-HOMJI, Vispy M. — India, TN
MWALYOSI, Raphael B.B. — Tanzania
NANAYAKKARA, Vitarana R. — Sri Lanka
NAYVE-ROSSI, Portia A. — Philippines
NORDERHAUG, Magnar — Norway
OJEDA, Ricardo A. — Argentina
ORIANS, Gordon H. — USA, WA
OWEN, Denis F. — UK, England
PANDEYA, Satish C. — India, UP
POLUNIN, Nicholas V.C. — UK, England
RACEY, Paul A. — UK, Scotland
RAMAKRISHNAN, P.S. ('Ram') — India, Delhi
RITCHIE, Jerry C. — USA, MD
RODRIGUEZ, Andrés R.Rodriguez — Venezuela
SOUTHWOOD, T.Richard E. — UK, England
UNNI, N.V.Madhavan — India, AP
VO, Quy — Vietnam
WHITMORE, Timothy C. — UK, England
WOODWELL, George M. — USA, MA
YANSHIN, Aleksandr L. — Russia
ZALAORAS, Nicholas — Greece
—, African mammal
   SPINAGE, Clive A. — UK, England
—, air pollution/environmental
   HUTTUNEN, Satu — Finland
—, alpine
   BLISS, Lawrence C. — USA, WA
—, — (plant distributions & origins)
   GOOD, Roger B. — Australia, ACT
—, amphibian
   PEARMAN, Peter B. — USA, CA
—, Amphipoda, marine, systematics-, of
   CROKER, Robert A. — USA, NH
— & conservation biology
   PEARMAN, Peter B. — USA, CA
— — children's health
   CHERKASOVA, Maria V. — Russia
—, animal
   GHABBOUR, Samir I. — Egypt
   GIMINEZ-DIXON, Mariano — Switzerland
   SALINAS, Pedro J. — Venezuela
—, —, desert
   BÜTTIKER, William — Switzerland
—, applied
   ROBERTS, Thomas M. — UK, England
—, —, in arctic development
   BLISS, Lawrence C. — USA, WA
—, aquatic
   ABBASI, Shahid A. — India, TN
   BOYLE, Terence P. — USA, CO
   COUTANT, Charles C. — USA, TN
   LIKENS, Gene E. — USA, NY
   MAUGHAN, O.Eugene — USA, AZ
   MOORE, James W. — Canada, Alb.
—, archaeo-
   LOVRIC, Andrija Z. — Croatia

—, arctic
BLISS, Lawrence C. — USA, WA
KLEIN, David R. — USA, AK
POLUNIN, Nicholas — Switzerland
SVOBODA, Josef — Canada, Ont.
WOODELL, Stanley R.J. — UK, England
—, arid lands'
BATANOUNY, Kamal H. — Egypt
HOUÉROU, Henry N.LE — France
—, — plant
WALT, Pieter T.VAN DER — RSA
—, — zone
CHADWICK, Michael J. — Sweden
—, Australian, history of
SPECHT, Raymond L. — Australia, Qld
—, avian
HOLROYD, Geoffrey L. — Canada, Alb.
YAHYA, Hafiz S.A. — Saudi Arabia
—, bambooland
NUMATA, Makoto — Japan
—, behavioural
DHINDSA, Manjit S. — India, Punjab
GRIFFITHS, Richard A. — UK, England
KREBS, John R. — UK, England
—, —, carnivore
MILLS, M.G.L. ('Gus') — RSA
—, —, of large mammals
LOVARI, Sandro — Italy
—, —, — vertebrates
BURGER, Joanna — USA, NJ
—, benthic
PANDIT, Ashok K. — India, J&K
—, biophysical (physiological)
GATES, David M. — USA, MI
—, bird
GŁOWACIŃSKI, Zbigniew A. — Poland
—, botanical
WIELGOLASKI, Frans-Emil — Norway
—, bryophyte
SJÖGREN, Erik A. — Sweden
—, caribou
BLOOMFIELD, Michael — Canada, BC
—, chemical
KOHLI, Ravinder K. — India, Punjab
—, coastal
LOVRIC, Andrija Z. — Croatia
MORTON, Brian — Hong Kong
MOUDUD, Hasna J. — Bangladesh
POLUNIN, Nicholas V.C. — UK, England
—, — marine
CROKER, Robert A. — USA, NH
—, — plant
RANDALL, Roland E. — UK, England
—, commons, in Nevada
WATSON, Charles St D., Jr — USA, NV
—, community
GRIFFITHS, Richard A. — UK, England
KAWANABE, Hiroya — Japan
—, —, evolutionary
PIANKA, Eric R. — USA, TX
—, conservation
HABER, Wolfgang — Germany
MELKANIA, Niranjan P. — India, MP
NIKULIN, Valery A. — Russia
SARMIENTO, Fausto O. — USA, GA
—, —, of endangered species
BRAMWELL, David — Canary Islands
—, coral-reef
DAHL, Arthur L. — Switzerland
LAYDOO, Richard S. — Trinidad & Tobago

SAENGER, Peter — Australia, NSW
WILKINSON, Clive R. — Australia, Qld
—, cultural
KLEE, Gary, A. — USA, CA
MOUDUD, Hasna J. — Bangladesh
—, —: research, writing, & film-making
GIRARDET, Herbert K. — UK, England
—, deer and their
WHITEHEAD, George K. — UK, England
—, desert
GHABBOUR, Samir I. — Egypt
—, — animal
BÜTTIKER, William — Switzerland
—, — plant
KASSAS, Mohamed EL — Egypt
KHARIN, Nikolai — Turkmenistan
SPRINGUEL, Irina — Egypt
—, disturbance
FORBES, Bruce C. — Finland
—, economic
SWAMINATHAN, Monkombu S. — India, TN
— –economics interface
GOODLAND, Robert J.A. — USA, DC
—, elasmobranch
FOWLER, Sarah L. — UK, England
—, environmental
JIANG, Gaoming — China
—, —/air pollution
HUTTUNEN, Satu — Finland
— esp.of polar regions
WALTON, David W.H. — UK, England
—, estuarine
ARMIJOS, Mariano MONTAÑO — Ecuador
—, evolutionary
KULL, Kalevi — Estonia
OBARA, Hideo — Japan
RYAN, Peter G. — RSA
VIDA, Gábor — Hungary
—, —, community*
—, —, lizard
*PIANKA, Eric R. — USA, TX
—, —, of scorpions
LOURENÇO, Wilson R. — France
—, fire
PARSONS, David J. — USA, MT
—, —, in managed plantations & natural forests
OLA-ADAMS, Bunyamin A. — Nigeria
—, fish
PANDIT, Ashok K. — India, J&K
—, fisheries, of large rivers
WELCOMME, Robin L. — Italy
—, forest
CHALLINOR, David — USA, DC
DONOSO, Claudio — Chile
GRANDTNER, Miroslav M. — Canada, Que.
HEISS, Gerhard — Germany
LAL, Jugal B. — India, MP
LI, Wenhua — China
OVINGTON, John D. — Australia, ACT
PETERKEN, George F. — UK, England
SHARMA, Subrat — India, UP
SPENCER, Jonathan W. — UK, England
—, —, in tropical Africa
TRAPNELL, Colin G. — UK, England
—, —, natural
DONOVAN, Richard Z. — USA, UT
—, —, old-growth, wildlife
BUTLER, James 'Jim' R. — Canada, Alb.

* *See* lower footnote on p. 409.

ecology, forest (contd)
—, — soil
   ZHANG, Wan Ru   China
—, — soils &
   CHALLINOR, David   USA, DC
—, forestry
   DONOSO, Claudio   Chile
—, Fox, Red
   BARRY, James M.   Ireland
—, freshwater
   BURNS, Carolyn W.   NZ
   MOGHRABY, Asim I.   Sudan
—, gene
   SINHA, Akhauri R.P.   India, A&N Islands
—, global
   SOLOMON, Allen M.   USA, OR
—, —, philosophy & history of
   GRINEVALD, Jacques   Switzerland
—, grassland
   NUMATA, Makoto   Japan
   WATT, Trudy A.   UK, England
—, ground-water
   STANFORD, Jack A.   USA, MT
—, Himalayan, conservation of
   RAI, Leghu D.   Nepal
—, — lake
   PANDIT, Ashok K.   India, J&K
—, historical
   SPENCER, Jonathan W.   UK, England
—, history of
   CROKER, Robert A.   USA, NH
   GRINEVALD, Jacques   Switzerland
—, — — global esp.The Biosphere
   GRINEVALD, Jacques   Switzerland
—, human
   DAYSH, Zena   UK, England
   FRAZIER, John G.   Mexico
   GOLLEY, Frank B.   USA, GA
   HENS, Luc   Belgium
   KLEE, Gary A.   USA, CA
   MALMBERG, Ole   Sweden
   MALMBERG, Torsten   Sweden
   RECKERS, Ute   Kenya
   SHARMA, Subrat   India, UP
—, industrial
   KELCEY, John G.   UK, England
—, insect
   SALINAS, Pedro J.   Venezuela
   TSHERNYSHEV, Wladimir B.   Russia
—, —, social
   ELMES, Graham W.   UK, England
—, invertebrate, esp.of Araneida
   DUFFEY, Eric A.G.   UK, England
—, island
   DOUMENGE, François   Monaco
   HAMBLER, Clive   UK, England
—, lagoon, salt
   POR, Francis D.   Israel
—, land, in tropical Africa
   TRAPNELL, Colin G.   UK, England
—, lands, arid
   BATANOUNY, Kamal H.   Egypt
   HOUÉROU, Henry N.le   France
—, landscape, see landscape ecology
—, —, conservation, land-use
   HABER, Wolfgang   Germany
—, —, evolutionary
   PIANKA, Eric R.   USA, TX
—, —, and vegetation
   BRIDGEWATER, Peter   Australia, ACT

—, — in (sub-) Mediterranean zone
   VOS, Willem   The Netherlands
—, —, of river floodplains
   DECAMPS, Henri   France
—, large mammal
   PRINS, Herbert H.T.   The Netherlands
—, lizard, evolutionary
   PIANKA, Eric R.   USA, TX
—, mammal, African
   SPINAGE, Clive A.   UK, England
—, mammalian
   BARRY, James M.   Ireland
—, mangrove
   AKSORNKOAE, Sanit   Thailand
   POR, Francis D.   Israel
   SAENGER, Peter   Australia, NSW
—, marine, see also marine ecology
—, — Amphipoda, systematics–, of*
—, —, coastal
   *CROKER, Robert A.   USA, NH
—, —, in coastal areas in Pacific & Asia regions, and
   in tropical islands
   MARAGOS, James E.   USA, HI
—, — phytoplankton
   SAKSHAUG, Egil   Norway
—, —, polar
   KELLERMANN, Adolf K.   Germany
—, —, tropical
   AGARDY, M.Tündi   USA, DC
—, Mediterranean
   LOVRIC, Andrija Z.   Croatia
—, microbial
   FERMOR, Terence R.   UK, England
   ROSSWALL, Thomas   Sweden
   WHIPPS, John M.   UK, England
—, —, freshwater & marine
   ROBARTS, Richard D.   Canada, Sask.
—, mountain
   HEISS, Gerhard   Germany
—, multidimensional statistics in
   MAXIMOV, Victor N.   Russia
—, natural forest
   DONOVAN, Richard Z.   USA, VT
—, old-growth forest wildlife
   BUTLER, James 'Jim' R.   Canada, Alb.
—, pastoral
   PRINS, Herbert H.T.   The Netherlands
—, philosophy of global
   GRINEVALD, Jacques   Switzerland
—, phytoplankton
   FOGG, Gordon E.   UK, Wales
—, planetary
   VALLENTYNE, John R.   Canada, Ont.
—, plankton
   PANDIT, Ashok K.   India, J&K
—, plant, see plant ecology
—, —, antarctic
   LEWIS-SMITH, Ronald I.   UK, England
—, —, arid
   WALT, Pieter T.van der   RSA
—, —, coastal
   RANDALL, Roland E.   UK, England
—, — community, research in
   KULL, Olevi   Estonia
—, —, research in
   STALTER, Richard   USA, NY
—, —, terrestrial
   BENSON, John S.   Australia, NSW

* See lower footnote on p. 409.

—, —water
    JONES, Hamlyn G.   UK, England
—, polar
    CLARKE, Andrew   UK, England
    SAKSHAUG, Egil   Norway
—, — marine
    KELLERMANN, Adolf K.   Germany
—, political
    PELUSO, Nancy L.   USA, CT
—, pollution
    JIANG, Gaoming   China
—, population
    BIRCH, L.Charles   Australia, NSW
    ELMES, Graham W.   UK, England
    GRIFFITHS, Richard A.   UK, England
    KREBS, John R.   UK, England
    RAMAKRISHNAN, P.S. ('Ram')   India, Delhi
—, —, & evolution
    THEBAUD, Christophe   France
—, primate
    MARSH, Clive W.   Malaysia
—, production
    PANDEYA, Satish C.   India, UP
    PANDIT, Ashok K.   India, J&K
—, rainforest, research in
    WEBB, Leonard J.   Australia, Qld
—, range
    ASEM, Samira OMAR   Kuwait
    LUSIGI, Walter   USA, VA
—, Red Fox
    BARRY, James M.   Ireland
—, regeneration
    ASHTON, Mark S.   USA, CT
—, research in, re.recovery of refuse and
    underutilized resources
    ARIAS-CHAVEZ, Jesus   Mexico
—, resource
    NEWTON, Adrian C.   UK, Scotland
—, restoration, see restoration ecology
—, —, of Cape plants & vegetation
    BOUCHER, Charles   RSA
—, river, & life-histories of aquatic insects
    STANFORD, Jack A.   USA, MT
—, salt lagoon
    POR, Francis D.   Israel
—, —-marsh
    BOORMAN, Laurie A.   UK, England
—, sand-dune
    BOORMAN, Laurie A.   UK, England
    SALMAN, Albert H.P.M.   The Netherlands
—, savanna
    PRINS, Herbert H.T.   The Netherlands
—, scientific research in
    IZRAEL, Yuri   Russia
—, scorpions, evolutionary, of
    LOURENÇO, Wilson R.   France
—, seascape
    BRIDGEWATER, Peter   Australia, ACT
—, social
    GRINBERG, Miguel   Argentina
    MECH, L.David   USA, MN
—, — insect
    ELMES, Graham W.   UK, England
—, soil and
    JIM, Chi Yung   Hong Kong
—, —, forest
    ZHANG, Wan Ru   China
—, soils, forests, &
    CHALLINOR, David   USA, DC
—, steppe
    PRINS, Herbert H.T.   The Netherlands

—, systematics–, of marine Amphipoda
    CROKER, Robert A.   USA, NH
—, terrestrial
    SAYER, Jeffrey A.   Indonesia
    ZLOTIN, Roman I.   Russia
—, — animal
    NJE, Ngog   Cameroon
—, — plant
    BENSON, John S.   Australia, NSW
—, theoretical
    KULL, Kalevi   Estonia
—, thermal
    CLARKE, Andrew   UK, England
—, trophic
    PANDIT, Ashok K.   India, J&K
—, tropical, see tropical ecology
—, — forest
    PHILLIPS, Oliver L.B.   USA, MO
—, — marine
    AGARDY, M.Tündi   USA, DC
—, —, of Amazon region
    SIOLI, Harald F.L.   Germany
—, — (savanna) resource
    FERRAR, Anthony A.   RSA
—, urban
    JIANG, Gaoming   China
    JIM, Chi Yung   Hong Kong
    KELCEY, John G.   UK, England
    NUMATA, Makoto   Japan
—, vegetation
    HILL, Mark O.   UK, England
—, —, of Greenland
    DANIELS, Fredericus J.A.   Germany
—, —, — tropical & subtropical regions
    WANG, Xianpu   China
—, wetland
    BOTCH, Marina S.   Russia
    GOPAL, Brij   India, Punjab
    KUSHLAN, James A.   USA, MS
    PANDIT, Ashok K.   India, J&K
    PYROVETSI, Myrto D.   Greece
—, —, functions & values
    LARSON, Joseph S.   USA, MA
—, wildlife
    MKANDA, Francis X.   Malawi
    MWASAGA, Belekebajobcgc   Tanzania
    PANDIT, Ashok K.   India, J&K
    PYROVETSI, Myrto D.   Greece
    SUGIMURA, Ken   Japan
—, —, effects of habitat change on
    HASAN, Mohammed NORDIN   Malaysia
—, —, old-growth forest
    BUTLER, James 'Jim' R.   Canada, Alb.
—, wolf
    MECH, L.David   USA, MN
ecology of, see also ecology[†]
— acid deposition
    THOMAS, John D.   UK, England
— African carnivores and small mammals
    RAY, Justina C.   USA, FL
— agro-ecosystems
    SINGH, Kaushalendra P.   India, UP
    TSHERNYSHEV, Wladimir B.   Russia
— amphibians
    BEHRA, Olivier   Madagascar
— animals, terrestrial
    NJE, Ngog   Cameroon
— arid lands
    SEELY, Mary K.   Namibia

[†] See upper footnote on p. 409.

[ecology] of (contd)
— Atlantic Salmon
   MILLS, Derek H.   UK, Scotland
— bark beetles (Scolytidae)
   OKOŁÓW, Czeslaw   Poland
— bats
   RACEY, Paul A.   UK, Scotland
— bears
   HERRERO, Stephen M.   Canada, Alb.
— biomes in relation to Biosphere
   ALLEN, John P.   USA, CA
— birds
   DORST, Jean   France
   DUNNET, George M.   UK, Scotland
— —, Nearctic migratory
   RAPPOLE, John H.   USA, VA
— — of prey
   TEMPLE, Stanley A.   USA, WI
— — (*Passer* spp.)
   PINOWSKI, Jan K.   Poland
— carnivores
   HERRERO, Stephen M.   Canada, Alb.
   KADLEČÍK, Ján   Slovak Rep.
— catastrophic situations
   SMIRNOV, Nikolai N.   Russia
— Chilean birds, reptiles, & amphibians,
   reproduction
   DIAZ, José VALENCIA   Chile
— cities
   FUREDY, Christine   Canada, Ont.
— crocodiles
   BEHRA, Olivier   Madagascar
— deep oceanic communities
   ANGEL, Martin V.   UK, England
— desert mountains
   GARDNER, Andrew S.   Oman
— Dugongs
   MARSH, Helene D.   Australia, Qld
— eutrophication
   THOMAS, John D.   UK, England
— extreme environments
   WOODELL, Stanley R.J.   UK, England
— feeding Chilean birds, reptiles, & amphibians
   DIAZ, José VALENCIA   Chile
— fish, tropical marine
   BUSTAMANTE, Georgina   USA, FL
— floodplains
   LISICKÝ, Mikuláš J.   Slovak Rep.
— forests
   SINGH, Jamuna S.   India, UP
— —, tropical
   SINGH, Kaushalendra P.   India, UP
— geckos
   GARDNER, Andrew S.   Oman
— hoofed animals
   BALČIAUSKAS, Linas   Lithuania
— insects, mainly Lepidoptera
   MONTESINOS, José Luis VIEJO   Spain
— islands, oceanic
   HOLDGATE, Martin W.   UK, England
— land communities
   GALAZY, Grigory I.   Russia
— lands, arid
   SEELY, Mary K.   Namibia
— land-use in the tropics, mountains, & arid regions
   POORE, M.E.Duncan   UK, Scotland
— Lepidoptera
   KOZLOV, Mikhail V.   Finland
— mammalian herbivores
   DUNCAN, Patrick   France

— mammals
   DORST, Jean   France
   DUNNET, George M.   UK, Scotland
   MALCOLM, Jay R.   Canada, Ont.
   RACEY, Paul A.   UK, Scotland
— —, hoofed, small, & semi-aquatic
   BALČIAUSKAS, Linas   Lithuania
— —, large African
   JEWELL, Peter A.   UK, England
— —, —, in E. Africa
   ELTRINGHAM, Stewart K.   UK, England
— —, marine
   LEATHERWOOD, James S.   USA, CA
— marine fish, tropical
   BUSTAMANTE, Georgina   USA, FL
— — molluscs
   RODHOUSE, Paul G.K.   UK, England
— meaning & religion
   STEWART, Philip J.   UK, England
— Mediterranean rangelands
   PAPANASTASIS, Vasilios P.   Greece
— mountains, desert
   GARDNER, Andrew S.   Oman
— Nearctic migratory birds
   RAPPOLE, John H.   USA, VA
— oceanic islands
   HOLDGATE, Martin W.   UK, England
— plants, meadow
   KULL, Kalevi   Estonia
— polar regions
   HOLDGATE, Martin W.   UK, England
— rangelands, Mediterranean
   PAPANASTASIS, Vasilios P.   Greece
— reproduction of Chilean birds, reptiles, &
   amphibians
   DIAZ, José VALENCIA   Chile
— reptiles
   BEHRA, Olivier   Madagascar
— rodents & shrews
   RAY, Justina C.   USA, FL
— Salmon, Atlantic
   MILLS, Derek H.   UK, Scotland
— savannas
   SINGH, Jamuna S.   India, UP
   SINGH, Kaushalendra P.   India, UP
— sea turtles
   MARSH, Helene D.   Australia, Qld
— seabirds
   DUNNET, George M.   UK, Scotland
— semi-aquatic & small mammals
   BALČIAUSKAS, Linas   Lithuania
— traditional societies
   RAMAKRISHNAN, P.S. ('Ram')   India, Delhi
— tropical forest carnivores
   RAY, Justina C.   USA, FL
— — forests
   SINGH, Kaushalendra P.   India, UP
— — marine fish
   BUSTAMANTE, Georgina   USA, FL
— turtles, sea
   MARSH, Helen D.   Australia, Qld
— ungulates
   BOYD, John M.   UK, Scotland
— urban wildlife
   ADAMS, Lowell W.   USA, WV
— USA's Bureau of Land Management
   WATSON, Charles St D., Jr   USA, NV
— vertebrates, terrestrial
   HEINEN, Joel T.   USA, FL
— water communities
   GALAZY, Grigory I.   Russia

— wildlife, urban
ADAMS, Lowell W. USA, WV
economic botany
BALICK, Michael J. USA, NY
BYE, Robert Mexico
MORAN, Katy USA, DC
PRANCE, Ghillean T. UK, England
SCHULTES, Richard E. USA, MA
— development, sustainable, in Africa's semi-arid
    rangelands
TOIT, Raoul F.DU Zimbabwe
— ecology
SWAMINATHAN, Monkombu S. India, TN
— evaluation of biodiversity, conservation biology,
    and sustainable utilization
PUSHPANGADAN, Palpu India, Ker.
— features on Humankind's place in The Biosphere
LOENING, Ulrich E. UK, Scotland
— growth and a just distribution of resources,
    conflict between
DAMMANN, Erik Norway
— impacts of large-capital projects
McEACHERN, John D. Canada, Ont./Nepal
— instruments
OPSCHOOR, Johannes B. The Netherlands
— issues, world
COUSTEAU, Jacques-Yves France
— plants of arid & semi-arid regions
WICKENS, Gerald E. UK, England
— reforms
SAMAD, Syed A. Malaysia
— resources, conservation of
TAN, Koonlin UK, England
— restructuring in Poland
SERAFIN, Rafal K. Poland
economically-viable integrated ecosystems
HALLER, René D. Kenya
economics
McNEELY, Jeffrey A. Switzerland
SALIM, Emil Indonesia
UEXKÜLL, Carl J.W.VON Sweden
—, ecological
EKINS, Paul W. UK, England
WALT, Pieter T.VAN DER RSA
— –ecology interface
GOODLAND, Robert J.A. USA, DC
JIGJ, Sonom Mongolia
—, energy
SINGER, S.Fred USA, VA
—, environmental, see environmental economics
— essential to effective resource conservation
CHILD, Graham P.T. Zimbabwe
—, heritage
SERAFIN, Rafal K. Poland
—, marine resource
TISDELL, Clement A. Australia, Qld
—, natural resource
BARBIER, Edward B. UK, England
CAMINO, Ronnie DE Costa Rica
— of agroforestry
GONZALEZ, Juan A.AGUIRRE Costa Rica
— — conservation
TISDELL, Clement A. Australia, Qld
— — environment & development
BARBIER, Edward B. UK, England
— — rural tourism
SISMAN, Richard ('Dick') UK, England
— — Russia
GOLDMAN, Marshall I. USA, MA
— –population–Nature model
JIGJ, Sonom Mongolia

—, regional
SAMAD, Syed A. Malaysia
—, resource
GONZALEZ, Juan A.AGUIRRE Costa Rica
—, sustainability
NILSSON, Sten Austria
—, urban
SAMAD, Syed A. Malaysia
economies, developed, urban environmental problems
    in
GANDY, Matthew UK, England
—, sustainable, in developing world
ONAYEMI, Olarotimi O. Nigeria
economy
CASWELL, Patricia J. Australia, Vic.
—, ecological, in transition period to a sustainable
    society
HAREIDE, Dag Norway
—, environmental
MELLO, Mateo J.MAGARIÑOS-DE Uruguay
— –environment–energy–food interactions
SMIL, Vaclav Canada, Man.
ecophilosophy
SKOLIMOWSKI, Henryk Poland
WEBB, Leonard J. Australia, Qld
ecophysiological relations in forest ecosystems and
    their dependence on dominant trees
ČABOUN, Vladimír Slovak Rep.
ecophysiology
SINGH, Jamuna S. India, UP
SIVADAS, Ponathil India, Ker.
—, coastal
DATE, Guy C. RSA
— of maritime plants
MALLOCH, Andrew J.C. UK, England
— — plants in cold, stressed environments
BLISS, Lawrence C. USA, WA
— — tropical marine fish
BUSTAMANTE, Georgina USA, FL
—, plant
COLE, Norman H.A. Sierra Leone
RYCHNOVSKÁ, Milena Czech Rep.
ecopolicies
YABLOKOV, Alexey V. Russia
ecosozology (conservation science)
LISICKÝ, Mikuláš J. Slovak Rep.
ecosystem analysis
MELKANIA, Niranjan P. India, MP
PANDIT, Ashok K. India, J&K
— classification, islands in Asia/Pacific region
HOLTHUS, Paul F. USA, HI
— dynamics
RAMAKRISHNAN, P.S. ('Ram') India, Delhi
— functioning
MALTBY, Edward UK, England
— health
SINGH, Naresh Canada, Man.
— inventory, islands in Asia/Pacific region
HOLTHUS, Paul F. USA, HI
— management
FEICK, Jenny L. Canada, Alb.
MALTBY, Edward UK, England
PARSONS, David J. USA, MT
— modelling
UNNI, N.V.MADHAVAN India, AP
— productivity
ABROL, Inder Pal India, Delhi
— research
HABER, Wolfgang Germany
— science
SLOCOMBE, D.Scott Canada, Ont.

ecosystem (contd)
— studies, forest
  KIRA, Tatuo — Japan
ecosystematics
  EGLER, Frank E. — USA, CT
ecosystems
  GOLLEY, Frank B. — USA, GA
—, agricultural, conservation biology of
  PETRETTI, Francesco — Italy
—, agriculture
  TERRASSON, François — France
—, alpine
  WIELGOLASKI, Frans-Emil — Norway
—, analysis of
  LIKENS, Gene E. — USA, NY
—, anthropocentric
  LIU, Peitong — China
—, aquatic, biodiversity of
  AZIS, P.K.ABDUL — Saudi Arabia
—, arctic
  BLISS, Lawrence C. — USA, WA
—, arid, conservation of
  MILLS, M.G.L. ('Gus') — RSA
—, biodiversity of aquatic
  AZIS, P.K.ABDUL — Saudi Arabia
—, building economically-viable integrated
  HALLER, René D. — Kenya
—, coastal
  FRAZIER, John G. — Mexico
  LAKSHMANAN, Kalimedu K. — India, TN
—, —, conservation & management of
  BUSTAMANTE, Georgina — USA, FL
—, —, ecological monitoring of
  MAXIMOV, Victor N. — Russia
—, conservation of
  OSEMEOBO, Gbadebo J. — Nigeria
  SUGIMURA, Ken — Japan
—, — — arid, in coastal regions & in Jordan
  HATOUGH-BOURAN, Alia M.A. — Jordan
—, — — natural
  CÂMARA, Ibsen DE G. — Brazil, RJ
—, — — threatened
  BURBIDGE, Andrew A. — Australia, WA
—, coral-reef, conservation of
  MCALLISTER, Donald E. — Canada, Ont.
—, — - —, human & natural impacts on
  VANTIER, Lyndon M.DE — Australia, Qld
—, crop, genetics of plant–pathogen interactions in
  CRUTE, Ian — UK, England
—, dynamics of
  HOUÉROU, Henry N.LE — France
—, ecologically-sound
  LIU, Peitong — China
—, economically-viable integrated
  HALLER, René D. — Kenya
—, endangered natural
  LAMPREY, Hugh F. — UK, England
—, evolution of
  BELLAMY, David J. — UK, England
—, forest
  TERRASSON, François — France
—, —, carbon, & water, relations of
  GRACE, John — UK, Scotland
—, —, ecological & ecophysiological relations in, and their dependence on dominant trees
  ČABOUN, Vladimír — Slovak Rep.
—, —, structure & functions of
  PANDEYA, Satish C. — India, UP
—, —, sustainable use of
  RUIZ-MURRIETA, Julio — Switzerland

—, fragmented
  HOBBS, Richard J. — Australia, WA
—, grassland
  RYCHNOVSKÁ, Milena — Czech Rep.
—, highland, conservation of
  OJHA, Ek Raj — Japan
—, Himalayan, conservation of
  PANDIT, Ashok K. — India, J&K
—, island
  BOYD, John M. — UK, Scotland
  FRAZIER, John G. — Mexico
  MOREY, Miguel — Spain
—, —, conservation of
  FITTER, Julian R. — UK, England
—' management
  FEICK, Jenny L. — Canada, Alb.
  MALTBY, Edward — UK, England
  MOGHRABY, Asim I. — Sudan
  PARSONS, David J. — USA, MT
  RANJITSINH, M.K. — India, MP
  TERRASSON, François — France
—' —, suburban
  PINOWSKI, Jan K. — Poland
—, mangrove, management of
  QURESHI, Mohummad T. — Pakistan
—, marine
  POLOVINA, Jeffrey J. — USA, HI
—, —, conservation of
  CH'NG, Kim-Looi — Malaysia
  FITTER, Julian R. — UK, England
—, —, management of
  CH'NG, Kim-Looi — Malaysia
—, marine pelagic, of tropical & antarctic environments
  BRANDINI, Frederico — Brazil, Par.
—, —, sustainable resource management of
  BAINES, Graham B.K. — Australia, Qld
—, Mediterranean
  MOREY, Miguel — Spain
—, —, conservation biology of
  PETRETTI, Francesco — Italy
—, mountain
  PITT, David — Switzerland
—, natural, conservation of
  CÂMARA, Ibsen DE G. — Brazil, RJ
—, —, endangered
  LAMPREY, Hugh F. — UK, England
—, —, genetics of plant–pathogen interactions in
  CRUTE, Ian — UK, England
—, —, integrated management of
  DUGAN, Patrick J. — Switzerland
—, neotropical, holistic analysis of
  ADIS, Joaquim U. — Germany
— of polar oases
  SVOBODA, Josef — Canada, Ont.
—, polar
  WIELGOLASKI, Frans-Emil — Norway
—, pollution impact on
  KULL, Olevi — Estonia
— protection
  FERNANDO, Ranjen L. — Sri Lanka
  MOGHRABY, Asim I. — Sudan
—, recovery & regeneration of
  BAZZAZ, Fakhri — USA, MA
—, [of] rivers
  TERRASSON, François — France
—, savanna, conservation of
  MILLS, M.G.L. ('Gus') — RSA
—, sustainability of, research on
  NEWMAN, Edward I. — UK, England

—, sustainable
    LIU, Peitong — China
—, threatened, conservation of
    BURBIDGE, Andrew A. — Australia, WA
—, —, preservation of
    ZINKE, Alexander — Austria
—, tropical, heavy-metal contamination in
    LACERDA, Luiz D. — Brazil RJ
—, wetlands
    TERRASSON, François — France
—, wilderness
    PARSONS, David J. — USA, MT
ecotactics
    SINCLAIR, John — Australia, NSW
ecotechnologies, research in, re.recovery of refuse
    and underutilized resources
    ARIAS-CHAVEZ, Jesus — Mexico
ecotheology
    SKOLIMOWSKI, Henryk — Poland
    WEBB, Leonard J. — Australia, Qld
ecotourism
    ABROUGUI, Mohamed A. — Tunisia
    ALVAREZ, Juan M. — El Salvador
    BELLAMY, David J. — UK, England
    BRERETON, Vera A. — Barbados
    BUCKLEY, Ralf C. — Australia, Qld
    BUDOWSKI, Gerardo — Costa Rica
    BUTLER, James 'Jim' R. — Canada, Alb.
    CROSBY, Arturo — Spain
    DEARDEN, Philip — Canada, BC
    GAKAHU, Christopher G. — Kenya
    HAMED, Safei EL-DEEN — USA, MD
    HENNING, Daniel H. — USA, MT
    HOECK, Hendrik N. — Switzerland
    JAMES, Philmore A. — Antigua, W.Indies
    KEAGE, Peter L. — Australia, Vic.
    MARSH, Clive W. — Malaysia
    MWASAGA, Belckebajobege — Tanzania
    NEPAL, Sanjay K. — Switzerland
    SHORES, John N. — USA, ME
    SINCLAIR, John — Australia, NSW
    WESCOTT, Geoffrey C. — Australia, Vic.
— & firefly-watching
    POLUNIN, Ivan V. — Singapore
— — marine turtles
    HUGHES, George R. — RSA
— in the bush
    WALKER, Clive H. — RSA
— programmes, development of
    FOX, Allan M. — Australia, NSW
— projects, conservation of
    SINGH, Birandra B. — Fiji
ecotoxicology
    BOYLE, Terence P. — USA, CO
    HERKOVITS, Jorge — Argentina
— in amphibians, lizards, & reptiles
    LAMBERT, Michael R.K. — UK, England
edible plants
    BYE, Robert — Mexico
editing, Nature conservation
    ALON, Azaria — Israel
educating federal & provincial governments
    HUSBAND, Vicky — Canada, BC
education, see also environmental education[†]
    ALON, Azaria — Israel
    CHITRAKAR, Anil — Nepal
    GRINBERG, Miguel — Argentina
    McCARTHY, Gerald P. — USA, VA
    OKOŁÓW, Czeslaw — Poland

PRESS, Frank — USA, DC
VO, Quy — Vietnam
—, adult
    CACCIA, Charles L. — Canada, Ont.
— and awareness
    LAMBERTINI, Marco — Italy
—, business
    STOBAUGH, Robert B. — USA, MA
—, Cheeta[h]/predator conservation
    KRAUS, Daniel — Namibia/USA, CA
    MARKER-KRAUS, Laurie — Namibia/USA, DC
—, conservation
    BUTLER, James 'Jim' R. — Canada, Alb.
—, ecological
    MOURA, Robert MANNERS — Portugal
    VORONOV, Arkady N. — Russia
—, environmental, see environmental education
—, — adult
    GARDNER, Julia F. — Canada, BC
—, —, & interpretations esp.in marine parks &
    protected areas
    WHITE, Susan L. — USA, FL
—, —, in Latin America & the Caribbean
    LEFF, Enrique — Mexico
—, —, — rural areas
    LANDFRIED, Steven E. — USA, WI
—, —, — the bush
    WALKER, Clive H. — RSA
—, —, informal
    PRASAD, Manaparambil K. — India, Ker.
—, —, international
    SACKS, Arthur B. — USA, CO
—, —, national & international
    HESSELINK, Frederik J. — The Netherlands
—, — (— & local strategies)
    SMYTH, John C. — UK, Scotland
—, —, programmes
    GUPTA, Brij K. — India, TN
—, protection
    FERNANDO, Ranjen L. — Sri Lanka
— for democracy
    NOVOA, Laura — Chile
— — sustainablilty
    GITTINS, John W.E.H. — UK, England
—, heritage
    LACY, Terry P.DE — Australia, NSW
—, higher
    KENT, Paul W. — UK, England
— in arctic environmental issues
    YOUNG, Steven B. — USA, VT
— — forest values
    TEJADHAMMO, Pongsak — Thailand
—, informal environmental
    PRASAD, Manaparambil K. — India, Ker.
—, international environmental
    SACKS, Arthur B. — USA, CO
—, land-use resources
    NELSON, James G. — Canada, Ont.
—, law of
    JARIWALA, C.M. — India, UP
—, Nature
    PULINKUNNEL, P.S.Easa — India, Ker.
— of Aboriginal natural-resource managers
    FOX, Allan M. — Australia, NSW
—, parks
    LACY, Terry P.DE — Australia, NSW
—, peace
    DUFOUR, Jules — Canada, Que.
—, predator/Cheeta[h] conservation
    KRAUS, Daniel — Namibia/USA, CA
    MARKER-KRAUS, Laurie — Namibia/USA, DC

[†] See upper footnote on p. 409.

education (contd)
—, programmes, environmental
    GUPTA, Brij K.   India, TN
— re.tropical forestry
    BURLEY, Jeffery   UK, England
—, scientific
    RAVEN, Peter H.   USA, MO
—, systems engineering
    CATANIA, Peter J.   Canada, Sask.
—, teacher
    COHEN, Michael R.   USA, IN
—, tourism
    LACY, Terry P.DE   Australia, NSW
—, training, environmental
    ATCHIA, Michael   Kenya
    ODULA, Michael A.N.   Kenya
educational aspects of environment
    JIGJ, Sonom   Mongolia
— productions on environmental subjects
    RICHTER, Robert   USA, NY
effective conservation
    GAMMELL, Alistair   UK, England
— resource conservation
    CHILD, Graham F.T.   Zimbabwe
effectiveness, promoting, of UN in his field
    SCHRAM, Gunnar G.   Iceland
effects, hydrological, of land-use
    PEREIRA, H.Charles   UK, England
— of afforestation & agriculture on fisheries
    MILLS, Derek H.   UK, Scotland
— — air pollution on plants & insects
    BELL, Nigel   UK, England
— — atmospheric pollutants
    LAST, Frederick T.   UK, Scotland
— — conservation management on grassland
    invertebrates
    MORRIS, Michael G.   UK, England
— — defoliants on environment during Vietnam war
    VO, Quy   Vietnam
— — human activity on Caribou
    BLOOMFIELD, Michael   Canada, BC
— — hydroelectric developments on fish & aquatic
    environment
    MILLS, Derek H.   UK, Scotland
— — incubation temperature on development &
    behaviour of snakes
    BURGER, Joanna   USA, NJ
— — methyl mercury on health
    NUORTEVA, Pekka O.   Finland
— — northern developments on wildlife & habitats
    KLEIN, David R.   USA, AK
— — people on coastal birds
    BURGER, Joanna   USA, NJ
— — thermal power-plants on flora & vegetation
    USLU, Turhan   Turkey
— — tropical habitat loss on vertebrate populations
    RAPPOLE, John H.   USA, VA
EIA, see environmental impact assessment
Elasmobranch ecology & conservation
    FOWLER, Sarah L.   UK, England
— research, conservation, sensory physiology, &
    behaviour
    GRUBER, Samuel H.   USA, FL
electric utility policy
    LOVINS, Amory B.   USA, CO
electricity industries, environmental impacts of
    BOYD, John M.   UK, Scotland
electronic media, environmental communication
    through
    HAQUE, Mohammed A.   India, Har.

elements, trace, behaviour of, in natural environment
    STEINNES, Eiliv   Norway
Elephant, Sri Lanka wild, conservation of
    FERNANDO, Ranjen L.   Sri Lanka
embryology, angiosperm
    LAKSHMANAN, Kalimedu K.   India, TN
emergency response
    GEBREMEDHIN, Naigzy   Kenya
emission control over power-plants
    KOBAYASHI, Osamu   Japan
— —, vehicular
    MATHUR, Harbansh B.   India, Delhi
emissions, greenhouse gas
    FEARNSIDE, Philip M.   Brazil, Amaz.
endangered & endemic flora of Andaman & Nicobar
    Islands, conservation of
    SINHA, Akhauri R.P.   India, A&N Islands
— habitats, conservation of
    JAIN, Sudhanshu   India, UP
— natural ecosystems
    LAMPREY, Hugh F.   UK, England
— plant species
    HSU, Kuo-Shih   Taiwan
    NAYAR, M.Param   India, Ker.
— species
    FLINT, Vladimir E.   Russia
    LaBASTILLE, Anne   USA, NY
    WILSON, George R.   Australia, WA
    YAZGAN, Nergis   Turkey
— — conservation
    BUTLER, James 'Jim' R.   Canada, Alb.
    DURRELL, Lee McG.   UK, Channel Islands
    JAIN, Sudhanshu K.   India, UP
    MASCARENHAS, Anthony F.   India, Mah.
    RANJITSINH, M.K.   India, MP
— —, — biology & conservation ecology of
    BRAMWELL, David   Canary Islands
— —, esp.birds
    TEMPLE, Stanley A.   USA, WI
— — in Oman, captive breeding & conservation in
    the wild of
    DALY, Ralph H.   Oman
— — of coastal birds
    BURGER, Joanna   USA, NJ
— — — fauna, conservation of
    HADDANE, Brahim   Morocco
— — — mammals, protection of
    SOKOLOV, Vladimir   Russia
— vascular plants, conservation of, in Canada
    ARGUS, George W.   Canada, Ont.
endemism
    NAYAR, M.Param   India, Ker.
energies
    ALNASER, Waheeb E.   Bahrain
—, alternative
    CHARLIER, Roger H.L.   Belgium
energy
    ALIEU, Emmanuel K.   Sierra Leone
    LOVINS, Amory B.   USA, CO
    MADDURI, V.B.N.Sastry   India, AP
    MUNASINGHE, Mohan   Sri Lanka
    PACHAURI, Rajendra K.   India, Delhi
— & environment and international exchanges
    CATANIA, Peter J.   Canada, Sask.
—, animal
    KHANDELWAL, Kailash C.   India, Raj.
—, bio-
    TOMAR, Sadachari S.   India, MP
—, biomass
    KHOSHOO, Triloki N.   India, Delhi
    NOUR, Hassan O.ABDEL   Sudan

—, climate change and
ABROUGUI, Mohamed A. — Tunisia
— conservation
WALULYA-MUKASA, Joe — Uganda
— — in production agriculture
SHYAM, Murari — India, MP
— development, wood
NANAYAKKARA, Vitarana R. — Sri Lanka
— economics
SINGER, S.Fred — USA, VA
— –environment issues
COUTANT, Charles C. — USA, TN
—, environmental aspects of
GOODLAND, Robert J.A. — USA, DC
— –food–economy–environment interactions
SMIL, Vaclav — Canada, Man.
— management
CHANDAK, Surya P. — India, Delhi
— planning, rural
KHANDELWAL, Kailash C. — India, Raj.
— policy
ABBASPOUR, Madjid — Iran
HARE, F.Kenneth — Canada, Ont.
MacDONALD, Gordon J.F. — USA, CA
SINGER, S.Fred — USA, VA
— — and business
BURKE, David Thomas 'Tom' — UK, England
— politics, sustainable agriculture and
LINDSTROM, U.B. — Finland
—, renewable
ABBASPOUR, Madjid — Iran
CATANIA, Peter J. — Canada, Sask.
SAYIGH, Ali M. — UK, England
— resource, biomass as
SCHARMER, Klaus — Germany
—, solar
FRANGI, Jean-Pierre — France
SCHARMER, Klaus — Germany
— strategies
GOLDEMBERG, José — Brazil, SP
— supply, rural, biomass utilization for
SHYAM, Murari — India, MP
—, surface, balance
FRANGI, Jean-Pierre — France
— (environmentally sustainable development, N–S relations)
MYERS, Norman — UK, England
— systems, alternative
ABBASI, Shahid A. — India, TN
— technologies, ambient (renewable)
LOENING, Ulrich E. — UK, Scotland
— technology
GOLDEMBERG, José — Brazil, SP
— use in agricultural systems
CORBET, Philip S. — UK, Scotland
—, wind
DIAB, Roseanne D. — RSA
engine fuels from vegetable oils
SCHARMER, Klaus — Germany
engineering, alternative sanitary
LUTZENBERGER, José A. — Brazil, RS
—, civil
SINITSINA, Irene E. — Russia
—, ecological
KELCEY, John G. — UK, England
—, environmental
ABBASI, Shahid A. — India, TN
AKHTAR, Wasem — Pakistan
BHARGAVA, Devendra S. — India, UP
MAYSTRE, Lucien Y. — Switzerland
SUBRAMANIAN, Tarakad V. — India, TN

—, ocean
ABBASPOUR, Madjid — Iran
—, systems, education
CATANIA, Peter J. — Canada, Sask.
—, water resources'
ALI, Iqbal — Pakistan
enterprise development: Aboriginal
WILSON, George R. — Australia, WA
entomology
CARRILLO, Antonio MACHADO — Canary Islands
SCLAVO, Jean-Pierre — France
SOUTHWOOD, T.Richard E. — UK, England
WILSON, Edward O. — USA, MA
—, applied
SUETT, David L. — UK, England
—, environmental & forensic
NUORTEVA, Pekka O. — Finland
—, forest
NOUR, Hassan O.ABDEL — Sudan
—, horticultural
CROSS, Jeremy V. — UK, England
—, medical
CORBET, Philip S. — UK, Scotland
LAIRD, Marshall — NZ
—, —, research on
DUFFY, David C. — USA, AK
entomophagous insects, artificial breeding of and biological control using
CIOCHIA, Victor — Romania
envenomation, Aboriginal medicine
COVACEVICH, Jeanette A. — Australia, Qld
—, human, spiders re.
RAVEN, Robert J. — Australia, Qld
environment, air
YOUSSEF, Abdullatif K. — Syria
— and business
BELL, Nigel — UK, England
BELLAMY, David J. — UK, England
BURKE, David Thomas 'Tom' — UK, England
KNIGHT, Peter T. — UK, England
PHORNPRAPHA, Phornthep — Thailand
SERAFIN, Rafal K. — Poland
— — development
BATISSE, Michel — France
CLARK, William C. — USA, MA
DANKELMAN, Irene — The Netherlands
HURNI, Hans — Switzerland
NTAHUGA, Laurent — Burundi
OUEDRAOGO, O.Dieudonné — Mali
SALIM, Emil — Indonesia
SANDBROOK, J.Richard — UK, England
WASAWO, David P.S. — Kenya
— — — assistance
FRY, Ian W. — Australia, NSW
— — —, interaction between
BHATT, Dibya D. — Nepal
— — equity
OPSCHOOR, Johannes B. — The Netherlands
— — Mankind
WENSLEY, Penelope A. — Switzerland
— — physiology of plants
KEFELI, Valentin — Russia
— — population issues
MUMBA, Wanga — Zambia
— — public administration
OLOJEDE, Ayodele A. — Nigeria
— — resources
HARA, Takeshi — Japan
— — trade
BUCKLEY, Ralf C. — Australia, Qld

environment (contd)
—, antarctic
    LEWIS-SMITH, Ronald I.   UK, England
—, aquatic, effect of hydroelectric developments on
    MILLS, Derek H.   UK, Scotland
—, arctic, protection of the
    PRESTRUD, Pål   Norway
—, assistance issues
    FRY, Ian W.   Australia, NSW
—, atmospheric, international
    BOJKOV, Rumen D.   Switzerland
—, better, transfer of agri-biotechnology applications
    JAMES, W.Clive   Cayman Islands
— (bio)technology
    SUBRAMANIAN, Tarakad V.   India, TN
—, capacity-building related to
    WITT, Ronald G.   Switzerland
—, central European
    HARDI, Peter   Canada, Man.
—, children's concepts in the
    COHEN, Michael R.   USA, IN
—, co-management approaches to the
    ROMULUS, Giles   St Lucia
—, coastal
    RAMIREZ, Jose J.ESCOBAR   Colombia
—, communication re.
    STONE, Peter B.   UK, England
—, conservation & development of
    DALY, Ralph H.   Oman
—, — — problems of
    VERSCHUREN, Jacques C.F.   Belgium
—, — of, legislation re.
    CHALABI, Bouzid   Algeria
—, — —, projects & programmes re.
    DURRANI, Shakil   Pakistan
—, degradation of, by human activity
    ZLOTIN, Roman I.   Russia
—, delinking growth from
    OPSCHOOR, Johannes B.   The Netherlands
— –demographic dynamics
    KUFORIJI-OLUBI, Bola   Nigeria
—, desert
    SPRINGUEL, Irina   Egypt
— /development–finance/banking
    McCAMMON, Antony L.T.   Switzerland
— — (mass communication & world affairs)
    BHATT, Dibya D.   Nepal
— –development–gender
    DANKELMAN, Irene   The Netherlands
— disinfection
    ALI, Abd 'El moneim' M.   Egypt
—, dynamics of, in developing countries
    PICOUET, Michel R.   France
—, economics of
    BARBIER, Edward B.   UK, England
—, educational aspects of
    JIGJ, Sonom   Mongolia
—, effects of defoliants on, during Vietnam war
    VO, Quy   Vietnam
—, energy, and international exchanges
    CATANIA, Peter J.   Canada, Sask.
— — — –food–economy interactions
    SMIL, Vaclav   Canada, Man.
— — – issues
    COUTANT, Charles C.   USA, TN
— enhancement
    LOVINS, L.Hunter   USA, CO
—, environmental values & philosophy through
    GITTINS, John W.E.H.   UK, England
—, fighting for and defending the
    FONSECA, Ivan C.M.DA   Brazil, MG

—, financial management of the
    BROUGH, Anthony T.   Kenya
—, forest
    ZHANG, Ping   China
—, —, conservation of
    WOO, Bo-Myeong   S.Korea
—, — soil
    ZHANG, Wan Ru   China
—, forestry &
    PALMBERG-LERCHE, Christel M.   Italy
    SALLEH, Mohamed N.   Malaysia
— – — interactions
    INNES, John L.   Switzerland
—, forms of interaction & of relationship with
    DRAKE, Christopher M.   UK, England
—, geopolitical aspects of
    BUÉ, Alain   France
—, global
    CANNELL, Melvin G.R.   UK, Scotland
—, — monitoring of
    WALLÉN, Carl-Christian   Switzerland
—, health, public, and
    BURNEY, M.Ilyas   Pakistan
—, healthy, protection of human rights for a
    CHERKASOVA, Maria V.   Russia
—, Himalayan, conservation of
    RAI, Leghu D.   Nepal
— –human interaction
    BELLAMY, David J.   UK, England
—, humanity's impact on and relationship with the
    DRAKE, Christopher M.   UK, England
— –inland fisheries
    PETR, Tomislav O.   Australia, Qld
— in developing countries
    BILSBORROW, Richard E.   USA, NC
—, international affairs re.
    STONE, Peter B.   UK, England
—, — atmospheric
    BOJKOV, Rumen D.   Switzerland
—, — conventions & treaties on
    VISSER, Nicolaas W.   Kenya
—, — law & the
    BIRNIE, Patricia W.   UK, England
—, — policy on the
    RAMPHAL, Shridath   UK, England
— in underdeveloped regions, theory on
    LEFF, Enrique   Mexico
—, Man and
    LIU, Peitong   China
—, management aspects of
    JIGJ, Sonom   Mongolia
—, — of, in China
    LUK, Shiu-hung   Canada, Ont.
—, marine
    MOUDUD, Hasna J.   Bangladesh
    RAMIREZ, Jose J.ESCOBAR   Colombia
    YOUSSEF, Abdullatif K.   Syria
—, —, environmental conservation & management of
    DESAI, Bhagirath N.   India, Goa
—, —, tropical, Man's impact on
    WOLANSKI, Eric J.   Australia, Qld
—, modelling
    UNNI, N.V.MADHAVAN   India, AP
—, mountain
    ROSSI, Patrizia   Italy
—, natural, behaviour of trace elements in
    STEINNES, Eiliv   Norway
—, —, conservation of
    MALAMIDIS, George   Greece
—, physical, protection & improvement
    SOTIRIADOU, Victoria   Greece

— policy
  AICKIN, R.Malcolm   UK, England
  CALDWELL, Lynton Keith   USA, IN
—, politics of
  BURKE, David Thomas 'Tom'   UK, England
— –population–immigration
  ABERNETHY, Virginia D.K.   USA, TN
—, protection of the arctic
  PRESTRUD, Pål   Norway
—, — — —, particularly Nature
  McCLOSKEY, J.Michael   USA, DC
—, public health and
  BURNEY, M.Ilyas   Pakistan
—, — law for
  CALDWELL, Lynton Keith   USA, IN
—, radionuclides in the, pathways of
  BELL, Nigel   UK, England
—, radiowaves
  RADICELLA, Sandro M.   Italy
— -related poverty, alleviating, in developing world
  ONAYEMI, Olarotimi O.   Nigeria
—, release of genetically-modified microorganisms
    into the
  WHIPPS, John M.   UK, England
—, reporting, state of
  CULLEN, Peter W.   Australia, ACT
—, restoration
  LOVINS, L.Hunter   USA, CO
—, Russian & Siberian
  STEWART, John MASSEY   UK, England
—, sociology of the, theories in
  CLOUDSLEY, Timothy   UK, Scotland
— (sustainable development, North South relations)
  MYERS, Norman   UK, England
— — — — –polymer science
  VASUDEVAN, Padma   India, Delhi
— –trade
  THOMAS, Urs P.   Canada, Que.
—, travel and the
  SISMAN, Richard ('Dick')   UK, England
—, tropical marine, Man's impact on
  WOLANSKI, Eric J.   Australia, Qld
—, urban
  SEVILLA, Rogue   Ecuador
—, —, protection & improvement
  SOTIRIADOU, Victoria   Greece
—, women &
  CORRAL, Thais   Brazil, RJ
  MOUDUD, Hasna J.   Bangladesh
  VARIAVA, Dilnavaz   India, Mah.
environmental, accounting
  GONZALEZ, Juan A.AGUIRRE   Costa Rica
— action plans
  AZIS, P.K.ABDUL   Saudi Arabia
— — —, preparation of
  OLI, Krishna P.   Nepal
— —, — — national
  BISWAS, Asit K.   UK, England
— —, community
  GITTINS, John W.E.H.   UK, England
— —, religion-motivated
  JAKOWSKA, Sophie   Dominican Rep.
— activism
  ADAMS, Aubrey   Trinidad
  LUTZENBERGER, José A.   Brazil, RS
— administration
  BÁNDI, Gyula   Hungary
  BEZANSON, Keith A.   Canada, Ont.
  KENNEDY, James J.   USA, UT
  STRONG, Maurice F.   Canada, Ont.
  TORTELL, Philip   NZ

— affairs, international, political & institutional
    dimensions of
  THOMAS, Urs P.   Canada, Que.
—, agri-, policy
  GREEN, Brynmor H.   UK, England
— archaeology
  BOYD, William 'Bill' Edgar   Australia, NSW
— aspects of agriculture, transport, & energy, esp.big
    dams
  GOODLAND, Robert J.A.   USA, DC
— — — international agriculture
  BENNETT, Sara L.   Canada, BC
— assessment
  DAHL, Arthur L.   Switzerland
  GALLON, Gary T.   Canada, Ont.
  HAMED, Safei EL-DEEN   USA, MD
  OVINGTON, John D.   Australia, ACT
  SERAFIN, Rafal K.   Poland
  WITT, Ronald G.   Switzerland
— — of economic development projects
  GOODLAND, Robert J.A.   USA, DC
— — planning & management
  JACOBS, Peter D.A.   Canada, Que.
— —, strategic
  TOORNSTRA, Franke H.   The Netherlands
— association-building
  GALLON, Gary T.   Canada, Ont.
— auditing
  CHARLIER, Roger H.L.   Belgium
  TERBLANCHE, Petro   RSA
  TORTELL, Philip   NZ
awareness
  HAQUE, Mohammed A.   India, Har.
  OZA, Gunavant M.   India, Guj.
  & conservation
  IGNACIMUTHU, Savarimuthu   India, TN
— — generation
  MATTHEW, Koyapillil M.   India, TN
— — programmes
  GUPTA, Brij K.   India, TN
— —, propaganda for
  BAHUGUNA, Sunderlal   India, UP
— — through print media
  SINGH, Hari B.   India, Delhi
— — using concept of SILATHAM
  TEJADHAMMO, Pongsak   Thailand
— beliefs & values
  MILBRATH, Lester W.   USA, NY
— biology of aquatic crustaceans & freshwater
    crayfish*
— — — isopods & tanaids
  *HOLDICH, David M.   UK, England
— — — tropical areas esp.Nigeria
  KEAY, Ronald W.J.   UK, England
— biomonitoring
  GOCHFELD, Michael   USA, NJ
— botany
  KOHLI, Ravinder K.   India, Punjab
— broadcasting
  PEARLMAN, Nancy   USA, CA
— campaigning
  GOLDSMITH, Edward   UK, England
  IYER, C.P.Jayalakshmi   India, Delhi
  PRASAD, Manaparambil K.   India, Ker.
— campaigns
  KELLER, Michael C.   Germany
— —, public
  AL-ALAWNEH, Ziyad   Jordan

* *See* lower footnote on p. 409.

environmental (contd)
— catchment management
DORMAN, John   Australia, NSW
— change
INNES, John L.   Switzerland
PERNETTA, John C.   The Netherlands
— —, cumulative
COCKLIN, Christopher R.   NZ
— —, global
ROSSWALL, Thomas   Sweden
— —, —, human dimensions of
PRICE, Martin F.   UK, England
— — in Poland
SERAFIN, Rafal K.   Poland
— changes, prognosis of
JIGJ, Sonom   Mongolia
— chemistry
SUETT, David L.   UK, England
— citizenship
FEICK, Jenny L.   Canada, Alb.
— communication (see also communications)
CAPPATO, Jorge A.   Argentina
RUGE, Tiahoga   Mexico
— — through electronic & print medias
HAQUE, Mohammed A.   India, Har.
— —, national & international
HESSELINK, Frederik J.   The Netherlands
— communications (see also communication)
BASSOW, Whitman   USA, NY
GRUCZMACHER, Ricardo Bayón   Switzerland
SHRESTHA, Aditya M.   Nepal
— concerns, research & writing on
TROMPF, Garry W.   Australia, NSW
— conditions, former, reconstruction of
FÜLEKY, György   Hungary
— conflict, management of
DEMPSEY, Stanley   USA, CO
— consequences of nuclear war
EHRLICH, Anne H.   USA, CA
— conservation
ALI, Iqbal   Pakistan
ALIEU, Emmanuel K.   Sierra Leone
AZIS, P.K.Abdul   Saudi Arabia
CHALLINOR, David   USA, DC
CLARK, John R.   USA, FL
DEY, Subhash C.   India, Delhi
GOULANDRIS, Niki   Greece
HAMANN, Ole J.   Denmark
JENKINS, David   UK, Scotland
KRISHNAMURTHY, Kothandaraman   India, TN
McCARTHY, Gerald P.   USA, VA
NOUR, Hassan O.Abdel   Sudan
N'SOSSO, Dominique   Congo
RAMPRASAD, Vanaja   India, Kar.
SCHWARZSCHILD, 'B' Shimon   USA, CA
SINGH, Karan   India, Delhi
SIVADAS, Ponathil   India, Ker.
VERSCHUREN, Jacques C.F.   Belgium
VO, Quy   Vietnam
WESTING, Arthur H.   USA, VT
— — activism
SINGH, Hari B.   India, Delhi
— —, holistic aspects on
NUORTEVA, Pekka O.   Finland
— — of marine environment
DESAI, Bhagirath N.   India, Goa
— — projects, design & implementation of
PANGETI, George N.   Zimbabwe
— —, protection, & restoration, of the Earth
ODULA, Michael A.N.   Kenya

— —: science, philosophy, & policies, of
POORE, M.E.Duncan   UK, Scotland
— —, teaching & research in
BUTLER, James 'Jim' R.   Canada, Alb.
— consulting
ELKINGTON, John B.   UK, England
LOVEJOY, Derek   UK, England
MYERS, Norman   UK, England
SHARMA, Sudhirendar   India, Delhi
WORTHINGTON, E.Barton   UK, England
— control
BOXALL, John E.   Hong Kong
— cooperation, international
PRESTRUD, Pål   Norway
— coverage on broadcast television
JAMES, Roger D.   UK, England
— damage, liability for
SCANNELL, Yvonne   Ireland
— decision-making, public participation in
GARDNER, Julia E.   Canada, BC
— — - — re.tropical coastal
DAVIE, James D.S.   Australia, Qld
— degradation
GOLDEMBERG, José   Brazil, SP
PETERSON, Russell W.   USA, DE
— —, mechanisms of
AICKIN, R.Malcolm   UK, England
— — –national sovereignty–warfaring propensities*
— — –rapid population growth
*SHAW, R.Paul   USA, DC
— diplomacy
CARROLL, John E.   USA, NH
— diseases
JOVANOVIĆ, Petar   Yugoslavia
— ecology
JIANG, Gaoming   China
— —/air pollution
HUTTUNEN, Satu   Finland
— economics
AHMAD, Yusuf   USA, DC
BARBIER, Edward B.   UK, England
BUCKLEY, Ralf C.   Australia, Qld
COCKLIN, Christopher R.   NZ
MUNASINGHE, Mohan   Sri Lanka
OSMAN, Salih M.   Kenya
PEARCE, David W.   UK, England
TISDELL, Clement A.   Australia, Qld
— economy
MELLO, Mateo J.Magariños–De   Uruguay
— education, see also education [adult, etc.]
ALLEN, Irma   Swaziland
ALVAREZ, Juan M.   El Salvador
ATCHIA, Michael   Kenya
BAEZ, Albert V.   USA, CA
BEZANSON, Keith A.   Canada, Ont.
BLOOMFIELD, Michael I.   Canada, BC
BOULTON, Mark N.   UK, England
BUTLER, Paul J.   St Lucia
CAPPATO, Jorge A.   Argentina
ČEŘOVSKY, Jan   Czech Rep.
CHERKASOVA, Maria V.   Russia
CHRISTIAN, Colmore S.   Dominica
COHEN, Maria L.   Switzerland
COLE, Norman H.A.   Sierra Leone
CORBET, Philip S.   UK, Scotland
DIAZ-MARTIN, Diego   Venezuela
DMITRIEVA, Vera A.   Russia
DUFOUR, Jules   Canada, Que.

* See lower footnote on p. 409.

FEICK, Jenny L. — Canada, Alb.
FERRAR, Anthony A. — RSA
FILHO, Walter L. — UK, England
GALUSHIN, Vladimir M. — Russia
GITTINS, John W.E.H. — UK, England
GOLDEMBERG, José — Brazil, SP
GOULANDRIS, Niki — Greece
GRINEVALD, Jacques — Switzerland
GUNAWARDENE, Nalaka J. — Sri Lanka
HADDANE, Brahim — Morocco
HAQUE, Mohammed A. — India, Har.
HAYNES-SUTTON, Ann M. — Jamaica
HOLLEMAN, Andrew D. — USA, MA
HOWELL, Calvin A. — Barbados
JAKOWSKA, Sophie — Dominican Rep.
JARIWALA, C.M. — India, UP
KELLER, Michael C. — Germany
KERN, Berndt — Sweden
KERN, Eha — Sweden
LEMONS, John D., Jr — USA, ME
MADDURI, V.B.N.Sastry — India, AP
MELLO, Mateo J.MAGARIÑOS–DE — Uruguay
McALLISTER, Donald E. — Canada, Ont.
MENDEZ, Jesus M.DELGADO — Brazil, SP
ORHUN-HEWSON, Canan — USA, MA
PRAWIROATMODJO, Suryo W. — Indonesia
REDAUD, M.Gladys BELANDRIA DE — Guadeloupe
RODRIGUEZ, Andrés R.RODRIGUEZ — Venezuela
RUGE, Tiahoga — Mexico
SALINAS, Pedro J. — Venezuela
SEELY, Mary K — Namibia
SHEIKH, Muhammad A.R. — Bangladesh
SHEPHERD, Alexander R.DAWSON — UK, England
SIMPSON, Philip G. — NZ
SINGH, Harjit — India, Delhi
SMYTH, John C. — UK, Scotland
STAPP, William B. — USA, MI
TEWOLDE, Assefaw — Mexico
VALLENTYNE, John R. — Canada, Ont.
VAOHITA, Barthélémi — Madagascar
VARIAVA, Dilnavaz — India, Mah.
WAJIH, Shiraz A. — India, UP
WALULYA-MUKASA, Joe — Uganda
WEBB, Leonard J. — Australia, Qld
— —, adult
GARDNER, Julia E. — Canada, BC
— — and interpretation esp.in marine parks &
   protected areas
WHITE, Susan L. — USA, FL
— — in Latin America
LEFF, Enrique — Mexico
— — — rural areas
LANDFRIED, Steven E. — USA, WI
— — — the bush
WALKER, Clive H. — RSA
— — — — Caribbean
LEFF, Enrique — Mexico
— —, informal
PRASAD, Manaparambil K. — India, Ker.
— —, international
SACKS, Arthur B. — USA, CO
— —, national & international
HESSELINK, Frederik J. — The Netherlands
— — (— — local strategies)
SMYTH, John C. — UK, Scotland
— — programmes
GUPTA, Brij K. — India, TN
— — training
ODULA, Michael A.N. — Kenya

— engineering
ABBASI, Shahid A. — India, TN
AKHTAR, Waseem — Pakistan
BHARGAVA, Devendra S. — India, UP
MAYSTRE, Lucien Y. — Switzerland
SUBRAMANIAN, Tarakad V. — India, TN
— entomology
NUORTEVA, Pekka O. — Finland
— ethics
BERRY, Robert James ('Sam') — UK, England
COHEN, Maria L. — Switzerland
HAMED, Safei EL-DEEN — USA, MD
JAKOWSKA, Sophie — Dominican Rep.
LEMONS, John D., Jr — USA, ME
NASH, Nancy — Hong Kong
— —, international
CARROLL, John E. — USA, NH
— evaluation
MAKHDOUM, Majid F. — Iran
— evolution
MARGULIS, Lynn — USA, MA
PAGE, Christopher N. — UK, Scotland
— forestry
KASSIOUMIS, Konstantinos — Greece
— geography
HUBA, Mikuláš — Slovak Rep.
— geology
KNILL, John — UK, England
— governance, global, particularly trade–
   environment linkage
THOMAS, Urs P. — Canada, Que.
— guidelines
MOUDUD, Hasna J. — Bangladesh
— hazards
HUBA, Mikuláš — Slovak Rep.
SMITH, Keith — UK, Scotland
— health hazards
SIVADAS, Ponathil — India, Ker.
— history
GRITZNER, Jeffrey A. — USA, MT
SIMMONS, Ian — UK, England
— impact assessment [EIA]
ARCEIVALA, Soli J. — India, Mah.
BENNETT, Sara L. — Canada, BC
BISWAS, Asit K. — UK, England
BISWAS, Dilip — India, Delhi
CAMPBELL, Kenneth L.I. — UK, England
CHRISTIAN, Colmore S. — Dominica
COCKLIN, Christopher R. — NZ
COLE, Norman H.A. — Sierra Leone
DESAI, Bhagirath — India, Goa
HASAN, Mohammed NORDIN — Malaysia
HOLLO, Erkki J. — Finland
JANSEN, Malcolm A.B. — USA, DC
KHOSLA, Ashok — India, Delhi
KIEW, Bong Heang — Malaysia
KRAJČOVIČ, Roman S. — Slovak Rep.
KUMAR, Prem — Canada, Alb.
LAVIEREN, Lambartus P.VAN — The Netherlands
LAYDOO, Richard S. — Trinidad & Tobago
LOHANI, Bindu N. — Philippines
MARAGOS, James E. — USA, HI
MATHUR, Harbansh B. — India, Delhi
MUTTAMARA, Samorn — Thailand
MWALYOSI, Raphael B.B. — Tanzania
O'RIORDAN, Timothy — UK, England
PATIL, Rashmi S. — India, Mah.
PERNETTA, John C. — The Netherlands
PONCIANO, Ismael — Guatemala

environmental impact assessment (contd)
SILVA, Allenisheo L.M.DE   Sri Lanka
TORTELL, Philip   NZ
VARUGHESE, George C.   India, Delhi
WEAVER, Alex v.B.   RSA
ZWAHLEN, Robert   Switzerland
— — — (environment and development)
COLE, Norman H.A.   Sierra Leone
— — — in developing countries
CARPENTER, Richard A.   USA, VA
TOIT, Raoul F.DU   Zimbabwe
— — — of development projects
SUNDARESAN, Boyamma B.   India, TN
— — — — large dams
GORZULA, Stefan   USA, TN
— — — studies of governmental & non-
   governmental development projects
UGWU, Christopher N.   Nigeria
— — — training
BENNETT, Sara L.   Canada, BC
— impacts, monitoring of, on infrastructure
   development
SARMIENTO, Fausto O.   USA, GA
— of dams
PETTS, Geoffrey   UK, England
— — — forest & electricity industries
BOYD, John M.   UK, Scotland
— — — mining operations & environmental
   conflict, management of
DEMPSEY, Stanley   USA, CO
— — — tropical forestry
MARSH, Clive W.   Malaysia
— — — water resource schemes
PETTS, Geoffrey   UK, England
— — on Nature
BARCSAY, László   Hungary
— — — vegetation (wind, temperature, & drought,
   stress)
GRACE, John   UK, Scotland
—, urban
JIM, Chi Yung   Hong Kong
— implications of petroleum industry
WILLUMS, Jan-Olaf   Norway
— information
CAPPATO, Jorge A.   Argentina
FILHO, Walter L.   UK, England
SINGH, Harjit   India, Delhi
— — systems
RAJAGOPAL, Rangaswamy   USA, OH
—, international
SACKS, Arthur B.   USA, CO
— institution-building
DOUROJEANNI, Marc J.   USA, VA
— institutions, international
TIMOSHENKO, Alexandre   Kenya
— insurance
AICKIN, R.Malcolm   UK, England
— issues
AL-ALAWNEH, Ziyad   Jordan
BISWAS, Margaret R.   UK, England
SARMA, K.MADHAVA   Kenya
WRIGHT, Martin P.W.   UK, England
— —, analysis of global
BROWN, Lester R.   USA, DC
— —, Arctic, education in
YOUNG, Steven B.   USA, VT
— —, global
FIELD, Hermann H.   USA, MA
OBASI, Godwin O.P.   Switzerland
— —, international
FARAGÓ, Tibor   Hungary

— —, — aspects of, including within the UN system
VAVILOV, Andrey M.   Kenya
— —, public participation in
KAKABADSE, Yolanda   Ecuador
— —, world
COUSTEAU, Jacques-Yves   France
— journalism
BRODEUR, Paul A.   USA, NY
CAPPATO, Jorge A.   Argentina
GUNAWARDENE, Nalaka J.   Sri Lanka
NDYAKIRA, N.Amooti   Uganda
OKAJIMA, Shigeyuki   Japan
SHARMA, Sudhirendar   India, Delhi
— jurisprudence
MEHTA, Mahesh C.   India, Delhi
— justice
WRIGHT, R.Michael   USA, VA
— land-use law
DELOGU, Orlando E.   USA, NE
— law
BACKER, Inge L.   Norway
BÁNDI, Gyula   Hungary
BARAHONA-ISRAEL, Rodrigo   Costa Rica
BOARDMAN, Robert   Canada, NS
BOER, Bernhard W.   Australia, NSW
BONINE, John E.   USA, OR
BRINCHUK, Mikhail M.   Russia
BUCKLEY, Ralf C.   Australia, Qld
BURHENNE, Wolfgang E.   Germany
FUTRELL, J.William   USA, DC
GOULDMAN, M.Dennis   Israel
GRAD, Frank P.   USA, NY
HASSAN, Parvez   Pakistan
HOLLO, Erkki J.   Finland
HOLOWESKO, Lynn P.   Bahamas
JARIWALA, C.M.   India, UP
KOH, Tommy T.-B.   Singapore
KOLBASOV, Oleg S.   Russia
LASH, Jonathan   USA, DC
LASTER, Richard E.   Israel
MACRORY, Richard B.   UK, England
MELLO, Mateo J.MAGARIÑOS–DE   Uruguay
MEHTA, Mahesh C.   India, Delhi
MEKOUAR, Mohamed A.   Italy
NICHOLLS, Frank G.   Australia, Vic.
NOVOA, Laura   Chile
POPESCU, Dumitra   Romania
PRIEUR, Michel   France
RUMMEL-BULSKA, Iwona   Switzerland
SAENGER, Peter   Australia, NSW
SALINAS, Pedro J.   Venezuela
SHEMSHUCHENKO, Yuri S.   Ukraine
SILVA, Allenisheo L.M.DE   Sri Lanka
STUTZIN, Godofredo   Chile
TARAK, Pedro   Argentina
TOLENTINO, Amado   Philippines
TORTELL, Philip   NZ
WHITEHOUSE, John F.   Australia, NSW
ZSÖGÖN, Silvia JAQUENOD DE   Spain
— — & policy, comparative & national
REHBINDER, Eckard   Germany
— — — public policy
McCARTHY, Gerald P.   USA, VA
— —: biodiversity
WESTREICHER, Antonio ANDALUZ   Bolivia
— —, comparative
GÜNDLING, Lothar   Germany
HOLLO, Erkki J.   Finland
OKIDI, Charles O.   Kenya
WEN, Boping   China

— — development
FRY, Ian W.   Australia, NSW
— —, European
MADAR, Zdeněk   Czech Rep.
— —: forest
WESTREICHER, Antonio ANDALUZ   Bolivia
— —, international, *see* international environmental law
— —, municipal & international, drafting of
OGUNDERE, Joseph D.   Nigeria
— —, national
ABDELHADY, Abdelaziz   Egypt/Kuwait
CANO, Guillermo J.   Argentina
KOESTER, Veit   Denmark
— —: protected areas*
— —: soil
*WESTREICHER, Antonio ANDALUZ   Bolivia
— —, training
FRY, Ian W.   Australia, NSW
— legislation
ANI, Olufemi   Nigeria
COLE, Norman H.A.   Sierra Leone
PITTA, Luis CAEIRO   Portugal
PONCIANO, Ismael   Guatemala
ZAMCHIYA, David M.   Zimbabwe
— — & policy
McCALLA, Winston   Jamaica
— management
AHMAD, Yusuf   USA, DC
ALLEN, Irma   Swaziland
BATE, Guy C.   RSA
BOURDEAU, Philippe F.   Belgium
BUCKLEY, Ralf C.   Australia, Qld
BURBRIDGE, Peter R.   UK, Scotland
CASWELL, Patricia J.   Australia, Vic.
CHOI, Yearn Hong   USA, VA
COCKLIN, Christopher   NZ
COHEN, Yuval   Israel
COHON, Jared L.   USA, CT
DAVIS, Bruce W.   Australia, Tas.
DHUNGEL, Surya P.S.   Nepal
DUNNET, George M.   UK, Scotland
EDWARDS, Peter J.   Switzerland
GEBREMEDHIN, Naigzy   Kenya
GREGOIRE, Felix W.   Dominica
HAILES, Julia P.   UK, England
HUQ, Saleemul   Bangladesh
KHOSHOO, Triloki N.   India, Delhi
KHOSLA, Ashok   India, Delhi
KOBAYASHI, Osamu   Japan
KOLBASOV, Oleg S.   Russia
KRAJČOVIČ, Roman S.   Slovak Rep.
LOHANI, Bindu N.   Philippines
MARINOV, Uri   Israel
MAYSTRE, Lucien Y.   Switzerland
MOORE, James W.   Canada, Alb.
MWALYOSI, Raphael B.B.   Tanzania
O'RIORDAN, Timothy   UK, England
OSMAN, Salih M.   Kenya
PRAVDIĆ, Velimir   Croatia
PUNNING, Jaan-Mati   Estonia
RANDALL, Roland E.   UK, England
ROMULUS, Giles   St Lucia
SHEMSHUCHENKO, Yuri S.   Ukraine
SLOCOMBE, D. Scott   Canada, Ont.
SUZUKI, Kunio   Japan
TAIT, Elizabeth J.   UK, Scotland
TEEB'AKI, Katino   Kiribati

TERBLANCHE, Petro   RSA
THOM, David A.   NZ
TURNER, R. Eugene   USA, CA
VARUGHESE, George C.   India, Delhi
WIJEWANSA, Ranjit A.   Sri Lanka
— —, alpine
KEAGE, Peter L.   Australia, Vic.
— —, coastal
HOLTHUS, Paul F.   USA, HI
— —, community-based, in urban Asia
FUREDY, Christine   Canada, Ont.
— —, coordination of
GOLUBEV, Genady N.   Russia
— —, esp.of polar regions
WALTON, David W.H.   UK, England
— —, global
NISHIOKA, Shuzo   Japan
— —, holistic
PANDEYA, Satish C.   India, UP
— — in Africa
WILLIAMS, Martin A.J.   Australia, SA
— — — Arctic circumpolar world
FENGE, Terence A.E.   Canada, Ont.
— — — Asia & Australia
WILLIAMS, Martin A.J.   Australia, SA
— — — Nunavut & Yukon, NWT
FENGE, Terence A.E.   Canada, Ont.
— —, industrial
BASSOW, Whitman   USA, NY
— —, legal aspects of
OLI, Krishna P.   Nepal
— — legislation
GARRATT, Keith J.   NZ
— —, marine
HOLTHUS, Paul F.   USA, HI
— — of human communities, plans for
AUSSEDAT, Nicole M.   France/St Barthélemy
— — — islands
DAHL, Arthur L.   Switzerland
— — — marine development
DESAI, Bhagirath N.   India, Goa
— — planning
GOLUBEV, Genady N.   Russia
SAUNIER, Richard E.   USA, MD
— — —, regional
THAPA, Gopal B.   Thailand
— — plans for industrial projects
FOX, Allan M.   Australia, NSW
— —, polar
KEAGE, Peter L.   Australia, Vic.
WALTON, David W.H.   UK, England
— — policies
GARRATT, Keith J.   NZ
— — policy
SAUNIER, Richard E.   USA, MD
— — — issues
PRESTON-WHYTE, Robert A.   UK, England
— —, preventive
PURCELL, Arthur H.   USA, CA
— — re.institutional development
GARRATT, Keith A.   NZ
— —, regional
NISHIOKA, Shuzo   Japan
WEBER, Karl E.   Thailand
— — (Southeast Asia & South Pacific regions)
EATON, Peter P.   Brunei
— — strategies
GARRATT, Keith J.   NZ
PRAVDIĆ, Velimir   Croatia
— — systems
EARLL, Robert C.   UK, England

environmental management (contd)
— — training
  ATCHIA, Michael   Kenya
— — world-wide
  GOLUBEV, Genady N.   Russia
— medicine
  GOCHFELD, Michael   USA, NJ
  MALMBERG, Ole   Sweden
— micrometeorology, plant
  JONES, Hamlyn G.   UK, England
— mitigation
  TORTELL, Philip   NZ
— modelling
  MOFFATT, Ian   UK, Scotland
— monitoring
  DAHL, Arthur L.   Switzerland
  KELLERMANN, Adolf K.   Germany
— — instruments, research & development of
  PRASAD, Basudeo   India, E.Punjab
— movement, the
  CHERKASOVA, Maria V.   Russia
  OZA, Gunavant M.   India, Guj.
  OZA, Premlata   India, Guj.
— mutagenesis
  SHARMA, Archana   India, W.Bengal
— news reporting
  HARA, Takeshi   Japan
— NGO activities, coordination of
  HUBA, Mikuláš   Slovak Rep.
— — management & networking
  IYER, C.P.Jayalakshmi   India, Delhi
— NGOs
  GARDNER, Julia E.   Canada, BC
— organization-building
  GALLON, Gary T.   Canada, Ont.
— perception
  HEATHCOTE, Ronald L.   Australia, SA
— philanthropy
  McCARTHY, Gerald P.   USA, VA
— philosophy
  GANDY, Matthew   UK, England
— —, international
  JOHNSON, David W.   USA, CA
— — through teaching, art, and environment
  GITTINS, John W.E.H.   UK, England
— photography
  EDWARDS, Mark   UK, England
  KETCHUM, Robert G.   USA, CA
  LOENING, Ulrich E.   UK, Scotland
— physics
  ALNASER, Waheeb E.   Bahrain
  FRANGI, Jean-Pierre   France
— physiology of mammals
  PFEIFFER, Egbert W.   USA, MT
— —, plant
  JONES, Hamlyn G.   UK, England
— planning
  BENTHEM, Roelof J. The Netherlands
  BURBRIDGE, Peter R.   UK, Scotland
  DORMAN, John   Australia, NSW
  FIELD, Hermann H.   USA, MA
  GARDNER, Julia E.   Canada, BC
  HAMED, Safei EL-DEEN   USA, MD
  HUQ, Saleemul   Bangladesh
  KHOSLA, Ashok   India, Delhi
  LOHANI, Bindu N.   Philippines
  OLOJEDI, Ayodele A.   Nigeria
  ROMULUS, Giles   St Lucia
  SARMIENTO, Fausto O.   USA, GA
  SINGH, Shekhar   India, Delhi

  SLOCOMBE, D.Scott   Canada, Ont.
  VARUGHESE, George C.   India, Delhi
  WHITEHOUSE, John F.   Australia, NSW
  WIJEWANSA, Ranjit A.   Sri Lanka
  YEROULANOS, Marinos   Greece
— — in Arctic circumpolar world
  FENGE, Terence A.E.   Canada, Ont.
— — — national parks
  DRDOŠ, Ján   Slovak Rep.
— — — Nunavut
  FENGE, Terence A.E.   Canada, Ont.
— — — protected areas
  FLETCHER M., Raul   Panama
— — — Yukon, NWT
  FENGE, Terence A.E.   Canada, Ont.
— —, methodology of
  KOZLOWSKI, Jerzy Australia, Qld/Poland
— —, regional
  BISWAS, Asit K.   UK, England
  NEPAL, Sanjay K.   Switzerland
— —, urban
  ANI, Olufemi   Nigeria
— policies, *see also* environmental policy
  ANI, Olufemi   Nigeria
  BISWAS, Margaret   UK, England
  COLE, Norman H.A.   Sierra Leone
— —, European
  HAIGH, Nigel   UK, England
— — in former Soviet Union
  SACKS, Arthur B.   USA, CO
— — re.national environmental action plans
  BISWAS, Asit K.   UK, England
— —, regional & global
  LOHANI, Bindu N.   Philippines
— policy, *see also* environmental policies
  ABROUGUI, Mohamed A.   Tunisia
  AICKIN, R.Malcolm   UK, England
  BARAHONA-ISRAEL, Rodrigo Costa Rica
  BASSOW, Whitman   USA, NY
  BENSON, John S.   Australia, NSW
  BOARDMAN, Robert   Canada, NS
  CALDWELL, Lynton Keith   USA, IN
  CARRILLO, Antonio MACHADO Canary Islands
  CHOI, Yearn Hong   USA, VA
  COCKLIN, Christopher R.   NZ
  COHEN, Yuval   Israel
  DMITRIEVA, Vera A.   Russia
  DUGAN, Patrick J.   Switzerland
  GARDNER, Julia E.   Canada, BC
  KENNEDY, James J.   USA, UT
  LASH, Jonathan   USA, DC
  MELLO, Mateo J.MAGARIÑOS–DE Uruguay
  MARTIN, Claude   Switzerland
  McCALLA, Winston   Jamaica
  MILBRATH, Lester W.   USA, NY
  MOLDAN, Bedřich   Czech Rep.
  MOLTKE, Konrad VON   USA, VT
  MORAN, Katy   USA, DC
  PERRY, John S.   USA, VA
  POPESCU, Dumitra   Romania
  REHBINDER, Eckard   Germany
  SINGER, S.Fred   USA, VA
  SINGH, Shekhar   India, Delhi
  SOUTHWOOD, T.Richard E.   UK, England
  THOM, David A.   NZ
  TRZYNA, Thaddeus C.   USA, CA
  USUKI, Mitsuo   Thailand
— — at UK & European levels — impact on
    countryside
  REYNOLDS, Fiona C.   UK, England

— — development
| BASS, Stephen M.J. | UK, England |
| GALLON, Gary T. | UK, England |

— —, European
| JOHNSON, Stanley P. | UK, England |

— —, global
| CLARK, William C. | USA, MA |

— — impact on countryside
| REYNOLDS, Fiona C. | UK, England |

— —, international
| FAIZI, Shahul | Saudi Arabia |
| JOHNSON, David W. | USA, CA |

— — re.management of fragmented landscapes
| BEETON, Robert J.S. | Australia, Qld |

— —, science &
| ORIANS, Gordon H. | USA, WA |

— — studies
| SIMONIS, Udo E. | Germany |

— politics
| GANDY, Matthew | UK, England |
| O'RIORDAN, Timothy | UK, England |

— —, international
| O'RIORDAN, Timothy | UK, England |

— pollution
MALONE-JESSURUN, Heidi Y	Surinam
SINGAL, Sagar P.	India, Delhi
TOMAR, Sadachari S.	India, MP

— — by heavy metals
| HAQUE, Mohammed A. | India, Har. |

— — control
| DAVE, Jaydev M. | India, Delhi |
| LOHANI, Bindu N | Philippines |

— — —, industrial
| KHAN, Niaz A. | UAE |

— — —, rural
| ABDEL-GAWAAD, Ahmed A.-W. | Egypt |

— — management
| DAVE, Jaydev M. | India, Delhi |

— — monitoring
| EKARATH, Raveendran | Bahrain |

— preservation using biotechnology
| SUBRAMANIAN, Tarakad V. | India, TN |

— pricing
| GONZALEZ, Juan A.AGUIRRE | Costa Rica |

— problem-solving
| BEETON, Robert J.S. | Australia, Qld |

— problems
| SINITSINA, Irene E. | Russia |

— —, continuing concern with
| EDSALL, John T. | USA, MA |

— — of former Soviet Union
| GOLDMAN, Marshall I. | USA, MA |
| SACKS, Arthur B. | USA, CO |

— — — third world re.war
| PFEIFFER, Egbert W. | USA, MT |

— —, urban, in developed economies
| GANDY, Matthew | UK, England |

— —, water management and associated
| WHITE, Gilbert F. | USA, CO |

— programme & project formulation & management
| GARRATT, Keith J. | NZ |

— programmes
| OVINGTON, John D. | Australia, ACT |

— protection
ALLOTTA, Gaetano	Italy
ANGELO, Homer G.	USA, CA
CROSS, Jeremy V.	UK, England
EHRLICH, Anne H.	USA, CA
HOYT, John A.	USA, DC
KELLERMANN, Adolf K.	Germany

PARYSKI, Paul E.	Haiti
PHILLIPS, Adrian	UK, England
PRAWIROATMODJO, Suryo W.	Indonesia
QU, Geping	China
SUNDARESAN, Bommaya B.	India, TN
VAOHITA, Barthélémi	Madagascar

— — education
| FERNANDO, Ranjen L. | Sri Lanka |

— —, legislation & treaties
| PELL, Claiborne | USA, DC |

— —, chemical & technological aspects
| KUKHAR, Valery P. | Ukraine |

— —, development of laws on, in Ukraine
| KOSTENKO, Yuriy I. | Ukraine |

— quality, poverty alleviation &
| WRIGHT, R.Michael | USA, VA |

— — standards
| ALI, Iqbal | Pakistan |

— records stored in coral skeletons
| BARNES, David J. | Australia, Qld |

— rehabilitation
GRITZNER, Jeffrey A.	USA, MT
NOUR, Hassan O.ABDEL	Sudan
PARYSKI, Paul E.	Haiti

— relations, international
| MOLTKE, Konrad VON | USA, VT |

— research–computer communications
| PETER, Ian W. | Australia, Qld |

— — esp.in toxicology, immunology, & cancer
| RAY, Prasanta K. | India, W.Bengal |

— —, interdisciplinary
| GANDY, Matthew | UK, England |

— —, marine
| PRAVDIĆ, Velimir | Croatia |

— planning
| OPSCHOOR, Johannes B. | The Netherlands |

— training
| SEELY, Mary K. | Namibia |

— resources, ethics & politics in conservation of
| FRAZIER, John G. | Mexico |

— restoration
| PETRETTI, Francesco | Italy |

— risk reduction
| AICKIN, R.Malcolm | UK, England |

— —, comparative, quantitative measurement of
| CHADWICK, Michael J. | Sweden |

— risks
| HUBA, Mikuláš | Slovak Rep. |

— safety
| ABBASPOUR, Madjid | Iran |

— science (see also environmental sciences)
KHANNA, Purushottam	India, MP
SINGER, S.Fred	USA, VA
XU, Ouyong	China

— & technology
| KHANNA, Purushottam | India, MP |

— —, marine
| SU, Jilan | China |

— —, Quaternary
| BOYD, William 'Bill' Edgar | Australia, NSW |

— —, training in
| VO, Quy | Vietnam |

— — –policy
| FARAGÓ, Tibor | Hungary |

— sciences (see also environmental science)
COLE, Norman H.A.	Sierra Leone
RAMAKRISHNAN, P.S. ('Ram')	India, Delhi
RHO, Chae-Shik	S.Korea
SOUTHWOOD, T.Richard E.	UK, England

environmental sciences (contd)
— —, natural, scientific research in
 IZRAEL, Yuri   Russia
— scientists and politicians, interactions of
 BOLIN, Bert R.   Sweden
— security
 AICKIN, R.Malcolm   UK, England
 COCKLIN, Christopher R.   NZ
 PITT, David   Switzerland
— — re.military activities & war
 WESTING, Arthur H.   USA, VT
— services project management
 BOXALL, John E.   Hong Kong
— solutions
 WRIGHT, Martin P.W.   UK, England
— strategies
 OLOJEDE, Ayodele A.   Nigeria
 SINCLAIR, John   Australia, NSW
— studies
 DRDOŠ, Ján   Slovak Rep.
 JAMES, Philmore A.   Antigua
 KHAN, Niaz A.   UAE
— —, interdisciplinary
 BRYSON, Reid A.   USA, WI
— —, multidisciplinary
 GARRATT, Keith J.   NZ
— subjects, educational productions on
 RICHTER, Robert   USA, NY
— sustainability
 GOODLAND, Robert J.A.   USA, DC
 SPETH, James G.   USA, NY
— systems analysis
 NISHIOKA, Shuzo   Japan
— —, impacts of tourism on (land-use law)
 PETERSON, Craig A.   USA, IL
— —, — — — — (— - — & zoning)
 PETERSON, Claire McCARTHY   USA, IL
— television
 LAMB, Robert P.   UK, England
— toxicology
 GOCHFELD, Michael   USA, NJ
— training
 COLE, Norman H.A.   Sierra Leone
— — in Latin America & the Caribbean
 LEFF, Enrique   Mexico
— —, international
 SACKS, Arthur B.   USA, CO
— trends & related social policies
 HOLDGATE, Martin W.   UK, England
— —, global
 NORDERHAÜG, Magnar   Norway
— valuation
 GONZALEZ, Juan A.AGUIRRE   Costa Rica
— values, international
 CARROLL, John E.   USA, NH
— — through teaching, art & environment
 GITTINS, John W.E.H.   UK, England
— writing
 BRODEUR, Paul A.   USA, NY
 CAHN, Robert   USA, VA
 KETCHUM, Robert G.   USA, CA
environmentalism, history of
 WORTHINGTON, E.Barton   UK, England
environmentally-related issues, analysis of global
 BROWN, Lester R.   USA, DC
— -sound development, philosophy of
 TOLBA, Mostafa K.   Egypt
— - — technology & cooperation in sub-Saharan
 Africa
 KUFORIJI-OLUBI, Bola   Nigeria

— - — transport of dangerous goods
 KRIKIS, Andris   Latvia
— -sustainable development
 WEBER, Karl E.   Thailand
environmentology, medical
 JOOSTING, Peter E.   The Netherlands
environments, alpine & antarctic, impacts of human
 use of
 SPATE, Andrew 'Andy' P.   Australia, NSW
—, antarctic, marine pelagic ecosystems of
 BRANDINI, Frederico   Brazil, Par.
—, coastal, geomorphology of
 GRANJA, Helena M.   Portugal
—, —, phytosociology of
 MALLOCH, Andrew J.C.   UK, England
—, —, sedimentology of
 GRANJA, Helena M.   Portugal
—, desert
 GOUDIE, Andrew S.   UK, England
—, ecology of extreme
 WOODELL, Stanley R.J.   UK, England
—, impacts of human use of antarctic & alpine
 SPATE, Andrew 'Andy' P.   Australia, NSW
—, island
 AUSSEDAT, Nicole M.   France/St Barthélemy
—, metropolitan, conservation in
 SHAW, Willam W.   USA, AZ
—, oceanic & shelf, marine pelagic ecosystems of
 BRANDINI, Frederico   Brazil, Par.
—, tropical
 TAN, Koonlin   UK, England
—, — & temperate, hydropower, irrigation, & water
 resources development projects, in
 ZWAHLEN, Robert   Switzerland
—, — — —, sustainable development in
 MOFFATT, Ian   UK, Scotland
—, — coastal: application of law re., and conservation
 science, planning, & management, in
 DAVIE, James D.S.   Australia, Qld
—, —, marine pelagic ecosystems of
 BRANDINI, Frederico   Brazil, Par.
epidemiology
 COHEN, Joel E.   USA, NY
 JOOSTING, Peter E.   The Netherlands
— of foliar fungal pathogens
 KENNEDY, Robert   UK, England
— — parasites
 THOMAS, John D.   UK, England
— — soil-borne plant pathogens
 ENTWISTLE, Andrew R.   UK, England
epiphyllous bryophytes
 SJÖGREN, Erik A.   Sweden
equitable forest policies
 PALMER, Prince Dowu   Sierra Leone
equity
 CASWELL, Patricia J.   Australia, Vic.
— and environment
 OPSCHOOR, Johannes B.   The Netherlands
erosion, afforestation against
 DAMERDJI, M.Amine   Algeria
— control of lands affected by coal-mining
 HAIGH, Martin J.   UK, England
—, soil
 HURNI, Hans   Switzerland
 LUK, Shiu-hung   Canada, Ont.
—, —, preservation against
 DAMERDJI, M.Amine   Algeria
Eskimos (Inuit & Yuit)
 ROWLEY, Graham W.   Canada, Ont.

establishment of national park and protected area
  systems
  SATTLER, Paul S.   Australia, Qld
— — — parks
  LAMPREY, Hugh F.   UK, England
  LÖFGREN, Rolf   Sweden
— — Nature reserves
  OLA-ADAMS, Bunyamin A.   Nigeria
— — — areas
  DUFOUR, Jules   Canada, Que.
  LAMPREY, Hugh F.   UK, England
estuaries
  BATE, Guy C.   RSA
  KRISHNAMURTHY, Kothandaraman   India, TN
estuarine ecology
  ARMIJOS, Mariano MONTAÑO   Ecuador
ethical elements of human relationships
  DRAKE, Christopher M.   UK, England
— features of Humankind's place in The Biosphere
  LOENING, Ulrich E.   UK, Scotland
— status of animals
  LINZEY, Andrew   UK, England
ethics
  BATANOUNY, Kamal H.   Egypt
  GIVEN, David R.   NZ
  HAMED, Safei EL-DEEN   USA, MD
  HARDIN, Garrett H.   USA, CA
—, environmental
  BERRY, Robert James ('Sam')   UK, England
  COHEN, Maria L.   Switzerland
  JAKOWSKA, Sophie   Dominican Rep.
  LEMONS, John D., Jr   USA, ME
  NASH, Nancy   Hong Kong
— in conservation of biotic & environmental
  resources
  FRAZIER, John G.   Mexico
—, international environmental
  CARROLL, John E.   USA, NH
— re.tropical coastal environments
  DAVIE, James D.S.   Australia, Qld
ethnobiology
  GADE, Daniel W.   USA, VT
  MORAN, Katy   USA, DC
  PUSHPANGADAN, Palpu   India, Ker.
  SMITH, Nigel J.H.   USA, FL
— in the tropics
  ULLUWISHEWA, Rohana K.   Sri Lanka
ethnobotanical conservation
  LAKSHMANAN, Kalimedu K.   India, TN
  SCHULTES, Richard E.   USA, MA
ethnobotany
  BALICK, Michael J.   USA, NY
  BATANOUNY, Kamal H.   Egypt
  BHATT, Dibya D.   Nepal
  BYE, Robert   Mexico
  GIVEN, David R.   NZ
  HAMILTON, Alan   UK, England
  HEDBERG, K.Olov   Sweden
  JAIN, Sudhanshu K.   India, UP
  NOUR, Hassan O.ABDEL   Sudan
  PHILLIPS, Oliver L.B.   USA, MO
  PRANCE, Ghillean T.   UK, England
  SIMPSON, Philip G.   NZ
  SPECHT, Raymond L.   Australia, Qld
  WEBB, Leonard J.   Australia, Qld
— of Cacti
  ANDERSON, Edward F.   USA, AZ
— — plants
  HEDBERG, Inga M.M.   Sweden
— — western Amazonia
  SCHULTES, Richard E.   USA, MA

etho-ecology of Man, evolutionary
  OBARA, Hideo   Japan
ethology
  LOVARI, Sandro   Italy
  VALDRÉ, Giovanni   Italy
  YAHYA, Hafiz S.A.   Saudi Arabia
—, comparative
  OBARA, Hideo   Japan
Eucalypts, clones of
  LAL, Piare   India, AP
Europe, ancient woodlands in
  PETERKEN, George F.   UK, England
—, coastal conservation management in
  DOODY, James P.   The Netherlands
—, communities on calcareous soils of
  GRUBB, Peter J.   UK, England
—, forest & mountain ecology
  HEISS, Gerhard   Germany
—, plant geography
  KORNAŚ, Jan   Poland
  MEDWECKA-KORNAŚ, Anna M.   Poland
—, plants & birds of western, systematics of
  KELLER, Michael C.   Germany
European, central, environment
  HARDI, Peter   Canada, Man.
— environmental law
  MADAR, Zdeněk   Czech Rep.
— — policy
  HAIGH, Nigel   UK, England
  JOHNSON, Stanley P.   UK, England
— invertebrates, conservation of
  MORRIS, Michael G.   UK, England
eutrophication
  CULLEN, Peter W.   Australia, ACT
—, ecology of
  THOMAS, John D.   UK, England
evaluation, aesthetic, protected areas'
  SZILASSY, Zoltán   Hungary
—, animal, in dairy & beef production systems
  TEWOLDE, Assefaw   Mexico
—, economic, of biodiversity, conservation biology
  and
  PUSHPANGADAN, Palpu   India, Ker.
—, environmental
  MAKHDOUM, Majid F.   Iran
— methods for selection of natural & seminatural
  forests
  HEISS, Gerhard   Germany
— of natural areas of Greece
  MALAMIDES, George   Greece
— — protected areas
  STOIBER, Hans H.   Austria
—, policy & strategy
  ASFAW, Gedion   Ethiopia
—, project
  IYER, C.P.Jayalakshmi   India, Ker.
—, waste, solid/hazardous
  KHAN, Niaz A.   UAE
evolution (see also evolution of)[†]
  FRY, Charles H.   Oman
  OWEN, Denis F.   UK, England
  PEARMAN, Peter B.   USA, CA
—, canine
  COPPINGER, Raymond   USA, MA
—, cell
  MARGULIS, Lynn   USA, MA
—, crop plant
  HAWKES, John G.   UK, England

[†] See upper footnote on p. 409.

evolution (contd)
—, environmental
    MARGULIS, Lynn   USA, MA
    PAGE, Christopher N.   UK, Scotland
—, landscape
    PIIROLA, Jouko   Finland
—, plant
    RAVEN, Peter H.   USA, MO
—, population ecology &
    THEBAUD, Christophe   France
— theory
    APPLIN, David G.   UK, England
evolution of (*see also* evolution)[†]
— animal species
    WOODRUFF, David S.   USA, CA
— birds
    INGRAM, Glen J.   Australia, Qld
— Canarian flora
    BRAMWELL, David   Canary Islands
— coastal zones
    CARVALHO, G.Soares de   Portugal
— communication
    NIEMITZ, Carsten   Germany
— coral reefs, and ecosystems
    BELLAMY, David J.   UK, England
— frogs
    INGRAM, Glen J.   Australia, Qld
— geckos
    GARDNER, Andrew S.   Oman
— gymnosperms & pteridophytes
    PAGE, Christopher N.   UK, Scotland
— potato species
    HAWKES, John G.   UK, England
— reptiles & slaters (wood-lice etc.)
    INGRAM, Glen J.   Australia, Qld
— wetlands
    BELLAMY, David J.   UK, England
evolutionary biogeography
    RAVEN, Peter H.   USA, MO
— biology
    GRUCZMACHER, Ricardo Bayón   Switzerland
    KIM, Ke Chung   USA, PA
    PIANKA, Eric R.   USA, TX
    RODHOUSE, Paul G.K.   UK, England
— — of plants
    STIRTON, Charles H.   UK, England
— community ecology
    PIANKA, Eric R.   USA, TX
— ecology
    KULL, Kalevi   Estonia
    OBARA, Hideo   Japan
    RYAN, Peter G.   RSA
    VIDA, Gábor   Hungary
— — of scorpions
    LOURENÇO, Wilson R.   France
— etho-ecology of Man
    OBARA, Hideo   Japan
— history of polar regions
    CLARKE, Andrew   UK, England
— landscape ecology*
— lizard ecology
    *PIANKA, Eric R.   USA, TX
— mechanisms of coral
    VERON, John E.N.   Australia, Qld
— theory
    RAVEN, Peter H.   USA, MO
    YABLOKOV, Alexey V.   Russia

[†] *See* upper footnote on p. 409.
* *See* lower footnote on p. 409.

ex situ conservation of plants
    HAMANN, Ole   Denmark
exchanges, international, energy & environment and
    CATANIA, Peter J.   Canada, Sask.
experience, financial, application of, to 'The
    Commons'
    McCAMMON, Antony L.T.   Switzerland
experiential learning
    COHEN, Michael R.   USA, IN
experimental field biology
    PEARMAN, Peter B.   USA, CA
— limnology
    HASLER, Arthur D.   USA, WI
experiments, field, design & analysis of
    WATT, Trudy A.   UK, England
exploitation of natural resources
    NILSSON, Sten   Austria
—, mineral, liability for
    SCANNELL, Yvonne   Ireland
exploration
    HANBURY-TENISON, A.Robin UK, England
    HEYERDAHL, Thor   Norway
—, botanical
    BYE, Robert   Mexico
— of caves
    MANSER, Bruno   Switzerland
—, oil & gas, economic impacts of
    McEACHERN, John D.   Canada, Ont./Nepal
— /travel
    SCHWARZSCHILD, 'B' Shimon   USA, CA
exploring role of information & non-tangible motives
    in promoting conservation behaviour
    YOUNG, Raymond de   USA, MI
extinct species, reintroduction programmes of
    HATOUGH-BOURAN, Alia M.A.   Jordan
extinction
    LaBASTILLE, Anne   USA, NY
—, species'
    GŁOWACIŃSKI, Zbigniew A.   Poland
extractive reserves, design of
    SEVILLA, Lorenzo B.Cardenal
                Nicaragua/Guatemala

---

falcons
    LUSCOMBE, Bruce A.   USA, NY
fallout, toxic
    SVOBODA, Josef   Canada, Ont.
family medicine
    MALMBERG, Ole   Sweden
farm forestry & reforestation projects
    LAL, Piare   India, AP
— livestock, British, rare breeds of
    JEWELL, Peter A.   UK, England
farming
    DELPIANO, José P.Castro   Uruguay
    STRONG, Maurice F.   Canada, Ont.
—, cleaner
    JOHNSTON, Neil   UK, England
—, ecological
    EVERETT, Rodney D.   UK, England
—, organic
    ISMAIL, Sultan A.   India, TN
    KHANDELWAL, Kailash C.   India, Raj.
    ARAUJO, Joaquín   Spain
—, — (natural pesticides & manure)
    ROYES, Veronica I.J.   Jamaica

, sheep & trout
WORTHINGTON, E.Barton — UK, England
farmland, habitat restoration & management of
GREEN, Brynmor H. — UK, England
farms, agriculture, and aquaculture
SIVADAS, Ponathil — India, Ker.
fates, cultures &, of Amazonian Indians
SIOLI, Harald F.L. — Germany
fauna
PUCEK, Zdzislaw K. — Poland
—, conservation of
FERNANDO, Ranjen L. — Sri Lanka
NDINGA, Assitou — Congo
STUTZIN, Godofredo — Chile
—, — — endangered species of
HADDANE, Brahim — Morocco
—, —, wild
KACEM, Slaheddine BEL — Tunisia
—, flora &, in Switzerland and Sarawak
MANSER, Bruno — Switzerland
—, insect, conservation of
RICHARDSON, Paul N. — UK, England
— of Maldives
DIDI, N.T.Hasen — Maldives
— — tropical forests, conservation of
FERNANDO, Ranjen L. — Sri Lanka
—, soil
GHABBOUR, Samir I. — Egypt
— surveys
AL-HOUTY, Wasmia — Kuwait
—, wild, conservation
KACEM, Slaheddine BEL — Tunisia
faunistics
WANG, Sung — China
feeding 6,000 m.people
SCHARMER, Klaus — Germany
—, ecology of, Chilean birds, reptiles, & amphibians
DIAZ, José VALENCIA — Chile
fermentation in tropical food & by-product recovery,
     nutritional improvement waste treatment, and
     pollution control
STANTON, W.Robert — UK, England
fertility, soil, research
FÜLEKY, György — Hungary
fibre optics
SINGH, O.N. — India, UP
field biology
OJEDA, Ricardo A. — Argentina
— biology, experimental
PEARMAN, Peter B. — USA, CA
— botany of South India
MATTHEW, Koyapillil M. — India, TN
— experiments, design & analysis of
WATT, Trudy A. — UK, England
— guides, writing*
— identification of birds & vascular plants
*FITTER, Richard S.R. — UK, England
— implementation of NCSs (planning &
     implementation)
McEACHERN, John D. — Canada, Ont./Nepal
— natural history
MONOD, Théodore A. — France
— protection of Black Rhinoceros (Diceros bicornis)
TOIT, Raoul F.DU — Zimbabwe
— research, applications of, to conservation
TRAPNELL, Colin G. — UK, England
— —, wildlife conservation, in Southeast Asia
     esp.Sarawak & Sabah
BENNETT, Elizabeth L. — Malaysia

— science foundation, directing
WALKER, Brian W. — UK, England
— studies
BENNETT, Sara L. — Canada, BC
— — of vertebrates
SCHALLER, George B. — USA, NY
— — on population genetics of Lepidoptera &
     Mollusca
OWEN, Denis F. — UK, England
— vegetables, plant virology & pathology of
WALSH, John A. — UK, England
— virology
CLARK, Michael F. — UK, England
film-making
WHITAKER, Romulus E. — India, TN
—, popularization & teaching of biology &
     conservation via
BOSWALL, Jeffery — UK, England
finance/banking–environment/development
McCAMMON, Antony L.T. — Switzerland
—, public
SAMAD, Syed A. — Malaysia
financial experience & principles, application of, to
     'The Commons'
McCAMMON, Antony L.T. — Switzerland
— management of the environment
BROUGH, Anthony T. — Kenya
fire ecology
PARSONS, David J. — USA, MT
— — in managed plantations & natural forests
OLA-ADAMS, Bunyamin A. — Nigeria
— regimes, natural, and plant responses (fire
     research)
GOOD, Roger B. — Australia, ACT
—, vegetation, management of
STRONACH, Neil R.H. — Ireland
fireflies, Pteroptyx, synchronous displays by, research
     into
POLUNIN, Ivan V. — Singapore
fish, early life-history of, esp.antarctic fish
KELLERMANN, Adolf K. — Germany
— ecology
PANDIT, Ashok K. — India, J&K
—, effects of hydroelectric developments on
MILLS, Derek H. — UK, Scotland
— –seabird interactions, research on
DUFFY, David C. — USA, AK
—, tropical marine — ecology, ecophysiology, & life
     history
BUSTAMANTE, Georgina — USA, FL
fisheries
BERTRAM, G.Colin L. — UK, England
MALONE-JESSURUN, Heidi Y. — Surinam
McINTYRE, Alasdair D. — UK, Scotland
— conservation
AGARDY, M.Tündi — USA, DC
— ecology of large rivers
WELCOMME, Robin L. — Italy
—, effects of afforestation & agriculture on
MILLS, Derek H. — UK, Scotland
—, inland–environment interaction
PETR, Tomislav O. — Australia, Qld
—, — trends in*
—, —, tropical
*WELCOMME, Robin L. — Italy
— of marine molluscs
RODHOUSE, Paul G.K. — UK, England

fisheries (contd)
—, reef
    POLUNIN, Nicholas V.C.   UK, England
    SHEPHERD, Alexander R.DAWSON UK, England
—, sustainable development re.
    SAOUMA, Edouard V.   Lebanon
fishery, freshwater
    ATAUR-RAHIM, Mohammed   Pakistan
— resources, conservation & management of
    BUSTAMANTE, Georgina   USA, FL
fishes, Acanthurid and Labroid
    RANDALL, John 'Jack'   USA, HI
—, migration of
    HASLER, Arthur D.   USA, WI
—, reef, Indo–Pacific, classification of*
—, —, underwater guides to
    *RANDALL, John 'Jack'   USA, HI
flood/waterlogging
    WAJIH, Shiraz A.   India, UP
floodplains, ecology of
    LISICKÝ, Mikuláš J.   Slovak Rep.
—, river, landscape ecology of
    DECAMPS, Henri   France
flora
    LAVRENTIADES, George   Greece
—, Amazonian
    PRANCE, Ghillean T.   UK, England
— & fauna in Switzerland and Sarawak
    MANSER, Bruno   Switzerland
—, Canarian, biogeography & evolution of
    BRAMWELL, David   Canary Islands
—, conservation of
    FERNANDO, Ranjen L.   Sri Lanka
    POLUNIN, Ivan V.   Singapore
    STUTZIN, Godofredo   Chile
—, effects of thermal power-plants on
    USLU, Turhan   Turkey
—, endangered & endemic, of Andaman & Nicobar
    Islands, conservation of
    SINHA, Akhauri R.P.   India, A&N Islands
— (Man's impact on)
    KORNAŚ, Jan   Poland
— of Britain esp.Glasgow
    DICKSON, James H.   UK, Scotland
— — Sierra Madre Occidental of Mexico
    BYE, Robert   Mexico
— — southernmost South America
    GOODALL, R.Natalie PROSSER   Argentina
— — the Philippines
    MADULID, Domingo   Philippines
— — tropical forests, conservation of
    FERNANDO, Ranjen L.   Sri Lanka
—, wild, conservation
    KACEM, Slaheddine BEL   Tunisia
floras, conservation of insular
    BRAMWELL, David   Canary Islands
floristic research
    AMIRKHANOV, Amirkhan M.   Russia
— survey
    JAIN, Sudhanshu K.   India, UP
floristics
    FORERO, Enrique   USA, NY
    TIKHOMIROV, Vadim N.   Russia
flowers, growing
    ZHANG, Jia-Shun   China
flows, hydraulic research of
    HOLČIK, Vladimír   Slovak Rep.
—, low, causes of
    CLARK, Colin   UK, England

foliar fungal pathogens
    KENNEDY, Robert   UK, England
folk societies, ecological relationships of
    GADE, Daniel W.   USA, VT
food, tropical, fermentation in
    STANTON, W.Robert   UK, England
food–economy–environment–energy interactions
    SMIL, Vaclav   Canada, Man.
foods, staple, tropical Southeast Asian wetlands
    agroforestry for
    STANTON, W.Robert   UK, England
foreign aid
    KUMAR, Prem   Canada, Alb.
forensic entomology
    NUORTEVA, Pekka O.   Finland
forest, *see also* forests[†]
    NILSSON, Sten   Austria
—, Amazon, management
    DOUROJEANNI, Marc J.   USA, VA
— biometry
    SCHLAEPFER, Rodolphe   Switzerland
— certification
    SULLIVAN, Francis   UK, England
—, climate change &
    SCHLAEPFER, Rodolphe   Switzerland
— conservation
    JUSOFF, Kamaruzaman   Malaysia
    LÖFGREN, Rolf   Sweden
    NEWTON, Adrian C.   UK, Scotland
    PALMER, Prince Dowu   Sierra Leone
    SULLIVAN, Francis   UK, England
— — in the tropics
    ONAYEMI, Olarotimi O.   Nigeria
— — planning
    WIJESINGHE, Leslie   Sri Lanka
— —, satellite remote-sensing in
    JUSOFF, Kamaruzaman   Malaysia
— —, tropical, autochthonous
    FISCHER, Gert R.   Brazil, SC
— decline
    SCHLAEPFER, Rodolphe   Switzerland
— —, role of metals in
    NUORTEVA, Pekka O.   Finland
—, degraded, rehabilitation of
    JUSOFF, Kamaruzaman   Malaysia
— disturbance & recovery, research in
    ORGLE, Tetey K.   Ghana
— dynamics
    DONOSO, Claudio   Chile
— ecology
    CHALLINOR, David   USA, DC
    DONOSO, Claudio   Chile
    GRANDTNER, Miroslav M.   Canada, Que.
    HEISS, Gerhard   Germany
    LAL, Jugal B.   India, MP
    LI, Wenhua   China
    OVINGTON, John D.   Australia, Qld
    PETERKEN, George F.   UK, England
    SHARMA, Subrat   India, UP
    SPENCER, Jonathan W.   UK, England
— — in tropical Africa
    TRAPNELL, Colin G.   UK, England
— —, tropical
    PHILLIPS, Oliver L.B.   USA, MO
— ecosystem studies
    KIRA, Tatuo   Japan
— ecosystems
    TERRASSON, François   France

---

* *See* lower footnote on p. 409.   [†] *See* upper footnote on p. 409.

— —, carbon & water relations of
GRACE, John — UK, Scotland
— —, ecological & ecophysiological relations in, and their dependence on dominant trees
ČABOUN, Vladimír — Slovak Rep.
— —, structure & functions of
PANDEYA, Satish C. — India, UP
— —, sustainable use of
RUIZ-MURRIETA, Julio — Switzerland
— entomology
NOUR, Hassan O.ABDEL — Sudan
— environment
ZHANG, Ping — China
— — conservation
WOO, Bo-Myeong — S.Korea
— environmental law
WESTREICHER, Antonio ANDALUZ — Bolivia
— genetic resources
PALMBERG-LERCHE, Christel M. — Italy
— — — research
TOMPSETT, Paul B. — UK, England
— harvesting, research on herbaceous biodiversity &
DUFFY, David C. — USA, AK
— health
INNES, John L. — Switzerland
— industries, environmental impacts of
BOYD, John M. — UK, Scotland
— landscape management
SUGIMURA, Ken — Japan
— management
DONOVAN, Richard Z. — USA, VT
GRÉGOIRE, Felix W. — Dominica
JUSOFF, Kamaruzaman — Malaysia
MELKANIA, Niranjan P. — India, MP
— —, Amazon
DOUROJEANNI, Marc J. — USA, VA
— — in tropical forests
SCHLAEPFER, Rodolphe — Switzerland
— —, natural
SABOGAL, Cesar A. — Indonesia
— —, satellite remote-sensing in
JUSOFF, Kamaruzaman — Malaysia
— —, sustainable
HIBBERD, John K. — Australia, ACT
SULLIVAN, Francis — UK, England
— —, tropical
ORGLE, Tetey K. — Ghana
— —, —, autochthonous
FISCHER, Gert R. — Brazil, SC
—, natural, conservation & ecology
DONOVAN, Richard Z. — USA, VT
—, Nature conservation
SMITH, Kevin D. — NZ
—, old-growth, wildlife ecology
BUTLER, James 'Jim' R. — Canada, Alb.
— pathology
BOA, Eric — UK, England
— policies, equitable
PALMER, Prince Dowu — Sierra Leone
— policy
BASS, Stephen M.J. — UK, England
NDINGA, Assitou — Congo
— recreation
ARMSTRONG, Geoffrey J. — Australia, NSW
— regeneration dynamics
WRIGHT, Shane D.T. — NZ
— resource planning
KUMAR, Prem — Canada
— restoration
ASHTON, Mark S. — USA, CT

— sector development planning
LAL, Jugal B. — India, MP
— soil ecology & development*
— — management, resource, & science
*ZHANG, Wan Ru — China
— soils & ecology
CHALLINOR, David — USA, DC
— species, sustainable use of
RUIZ-MURRIETA, Julio — Switzerland
— tree ecophysiology
HUTTUNEN, Satu — Finland
— — improvement
PALMBERG-LERCHE, Christel M. — Italy
—, tropical, autochthonous, management & conservation
FISCHER, Gert R. — Brazil, SC
—, —, carnivores, ecology & conservation of
RAY, Justina C. — USA, FL
—, —, conservation
HAMILTON, Alan — UK, England
SAYER, Jeffrey A. — Indonesia
—, —, management
LAVIEREN, Lambartus P.VAN — The Netherlands
ORGLE, Tetey K. — Ghana
SAYER, Jeffrey A. — Indonesia
—, — moist, taxonomy
WHITMORE, Timothy C. — UK, England
— use, sustainable
LAL, Jugal B. — India, MP
— values, education in
TEJADHAMMO, Pongsak — Thailand
vegetation, natural, protection of
SJÖGREN, Erik A. — Sweden
— –wildlife relationships
DODDS, Donald G. — Canada, NS
forestry
BARISHPOL, Ivan F. — Russia
CACCIA, Charles L. — Canada, Ont.
CANNELL, Melvin G.R. — UK, Scotland
CHATURVEDI, Amar N. — India, Delhi
CRAMPTON, Colin B. — Canada, BC
HAMILTON, Lawrence S. — USA, VT
HELLIWELL, D.Rodney — UK, England
HÜLSHOFF, Bernd VON DROSTE ZU — France
KOHLI, Ravinder K. — India, Punjab
KUPER, Jaap H. — The Netherlands
NANAYAKKARA, Vitarana R. — Sri Lanka
NOUR, Hassan O.ABDEL — Sudan
OHN — Myanmar
PALMBERG-LERCHE, Christel M. — Italy
SALLEH, Mohamed N. — Malaysia
UNNI, N.V.MADHAVAN — India, AP
— /agroforestry in tropics, domestication of tropical trees for
LEAKEY, Richard R.B. — Kenya
— & environment
PALMBERG-LERCHE, Christel M. — Italy
SALLEH, Mohamed N. — Malaysia
— biological pest control
FISCHER, Gert R. — Brazil, SC
— certification
DONOVAN, Richard Z. — USA, VT
— conservation
BERETEH, Mohamed A. — Sierra Leone
KIRBY, Keith J. — UK, England
— development
ALIEU, Emmanuel K. — Sierra Leone
—, ecological
URBAN, František — Czech Rep.

* *See* lower footnote on p. 409.

forestry (contd)
—, ecologically-sound
LOENING, Ulrich E.   UK, Scotland
— –environment interactions
INNES, John L.   Switzerland
—, environmental
KASSIOUMIS, Konstantinos   Greece
—, farm, & reforestation projects
LAL, Piare   India, AP
— in Madagascar
ANDRIANARIVO, Jonah A.   Kenya
—, international
GRANDTNER, Miroslav M.   Canada, Que.
— legislation
MEKOUAR, Mohamed A.   Italy
— management
BERETEH, Mohamed A.   Sierra Leone
—, social
MARTIN, Vance G.   USA, CO
PELUSO, Nancy L.   USA, CT
—, —, promoting public awareness in
SIVADAS, Ponathil   India, Ker.
—, sociology of
PELUSO, Nancy L.   USA, CT
—, sustainable
HARRIS, Philip J.C.   UK, England
POORE, M.E.Duncan   UK, Scotland
—, — development re.
SAOUMA, Edouard V.   Lebanon
—, termites in
NOUR, Hassan O.ABDEL   Sudan
—, tropical, environmental impacts of
MARSH, Clive W.   Malaysia
—, —: research, development, information, &
education
BURLEY, Jeffery   UK, England
forests, *see also* forest[†]
—, Asian tropical
HENNING, Daniel H.   USA, MT
—, biodiversity of managed, maintenance of
KIRBY, Keith J.   UK, England
—, conservation of SE Asian
PAYNE, Junaidi   Malaysia
—, — — West & Central African
CHEEK, Martin R.   UK, England
—, dry & wet tropical, ecology of*
—, ecology of Himalayan
*SINGH, Jamuna S.   India, UP
—, experimental design
SCHLAEPFER, Rodolphe   Switzerland
—, Himalayan, saving
BAHUGUNA, Sunderlal   India, UP
—, managed, maintaining biodiversity of
KIRBY, Keith J.   UK, England
—, management of SE Asian
PAYNE, Junaidi   Malaysia
—, monitoring of
KIRBY, Keith J.   UK, England
—, native, ecologically-sustainable use of
KETO, Aila   Australia, Qld
—, natural, evaluation methods for selection of
HEISS, Gerhard   Germany
—, —, fire ecology in
OLA-ADAMS, Bunyamin A.   Nigeria
—, old-growth, in British Columbia
HUSBAND, Vicky   Canada, BC
—, rain-, tropical
GRUBB, Peter J.   UK, England

—, role of
WOODWELL, George M.   USA, MA
—, seminatural, evaluation methods for selection of
HEISS, Gerhard   Germany
—, surveys of
KIRBY, Keith J.   UK, England
— (sustainable development, North–South relations)
MYERS, Norman   UK, England
—, taxonomic botany of West & Central African
CHEEK, Martin R.   UK, England
—, tropical
GOODLAND, Robert J.A.   USA, DC
MARTIN, Claude   Switzerland
—, —, biodiversity assessment & conservation esp.re.
RAVEN, Peter H.   USA, MO
—, —, conservation management of
MARSH, Clive W.   Malaysia
—, —, — of
BUDOWSKI, Gerardo   Costa Rica
FERNANDO, Ranjen L.   Sri Lanka
—, —, ecology of
SINGH, Kaushalendra P.   India, UP
—, —, environmental impacts of
MARSH, Clive W.   Malaysia
—, —, flora & fauna of, conservation of
FERNANDO, Ranjen L.   Sri Lanka
—, —, forest management in
SCHLAEPFER, Rodolphe   Switzerland
—, —, maintenance of plant diversity in
ASHTON, Peter S.   USA, MA
—, —, protected areas in, incorporating local &
indigenous concerns
LEES, Annette M.   NZ
—, — rain-
SMITS, Willie   Indonesia
—, —, saving
KERN, Berndt   Sweden
KERN, Eha   Sweden
—, —, sustainable logging of
LEES, Annette M.   NZ
forms of interaction & relationship with environment
DRAKE, Christopher M.   UK, England
formulation, legislation
DHUNGEL, Surya P.S.   Nepal
—, project
IYER, C.P.Jayalakshmi   India, Delhi
fostering links between banking/finance and
environment/development
McCAMMON, Antony L.T.   Switzerland
Fox, Red, ecology
BARRY, James M.   Ireland
foxes, arctic
PRESTRUD, Pål   Norway
fragmentation, habitat (landscape ecology)
TEMPLE, Stanley A.   USA, WI
fragmented ecosystems
HOBBS, Richard J.   Australia, WA
— landscapes, environmental policy re.
BEETON, Robert J.S.   Australia, Qld
francolins
RAHMANI, Asad Rafi   India, UP
Fraser Island, conservation of
SINCLAIR, John   Australia, NSW
free-ranging populations, genetic management of
WOODRUFF, David S.   USA, CA
— trade/economic growth *v.* just distribution of
world's resources
DAMMANN, Erik   Norway
freshwater biology
THOMAS, John D.   UK, England

[†] *See* upper footnote on p. 409.
* *See* lower footnote on p. 409.

crayfish, environmental biology of
HOLDICH, David M.   UK, England
— ecology
BURNS, Carolyn W.   NZ
MOGHRABY, Asim I.   Sudan
— fishery
ATAUR-RAHIM, Mohammed   Pakistan
— microbial ecology
ROBARTS, Richard D.   Canada, Sask.
frogs, systematics, biogeography, & evolution, of
INGRAM, Glen J.   Australia, Qld
fruit, temperate, genetic transformation of
JAMES, David J.   UK, England
fuels, biomass-based, for internal combustion engines
SHYAM, Murari   India, MP
—, engine, from vegetable oils
SCHARMER, Klaus   Germany
function of arctic ecosystems
BLISS, Lawrence C.   USA, WA
— — Nature
WOODWELL, George M.   USA, MA
functioning, ecosystem
MALTBY, Edward   UK, England
functions of forest ecosystems & grazing land
PANDEYA, Satish C.   India, UP
fungal biotechnology
WOOD, David A.   UK, England
— pathogens, foliar
KENNEDY, Robert   UK, England
future, [the]
BARNEY, Gerald O.   USA, VA
— generations, obligations to
NORTON, Bryan G.   USA, GA
— —, protection of rights of
COUSTEAU, Jacques-Yves   France
— studies
BATISSE, Michel   France

Gaia research
LOVELOCK, James E.   UK, England
— theory
MARGULIS, Lynn   USA, MA
Galápagos Islands
HAMANN, Ole J.   Denmark
game reserves, planning & development of
SPINAGE, Clive A.   UK, England
— watching
PERTET, Fred O.   Kenya
gardens, botanic
HAMANN, Ole J.   Denmark
JAIN, Sudhanshu K.   India, UP
—, botanical
FORERO, Enrique   USA, NY
MADULID, Domingo   Philippines
RAVEN, Peter H.   USA, MO
gas exploration, economic impacts of
McEACHERN, John D.   Canada, Ont./Nepal
—, greenhouse, emissions
FEARNSIDE, Philip M.   Brazil, Amaz.
LAL, Rattan   USA, OH
— hydrogeology
VORONOV, Arkady N.   Russia
— programmes
PRASAD, Basudeo   India, E.Punjab

geckos, ecology & evolution of
GARDNER, Andrew S.   Oman
gender–environment–development
DANKELMAN, Irene   The Netherlands
gene-bank standards, design & management
TAO, Kar-ling J.   Italy
genecology
DONOSO, Claudio   Chile
SINHA, Akhauri R.P.   India, A&N Islands
generations, future, obligations to
NORTON, Bryan G.   USA, GA
—, —, protection of rights of
COUSTEAU, Jacques-Yves   France
genetic conservation in developing countries
MOESTRUP, Søren   Denmark
— diversity and population dynamics
VIDA, Gábor   Hungary
— — in crop plants
KING, Graham J.   UK, England
— management of free-ranging & captive
    populations
WOODRUFF, David S.   USA, CA
— polymorphisms
VIDA, Gábor   Hungary
— resource conservation & management, domestic
    animal
TEWOLDE, Assefaw   Mexico
— resources
IGNACIMUTHU, Savarimuthu   India, TN
NEWTON, Adrian C.   UK, Scotland
— —, conservation (of)
ASTLEY, David 'Dave'   UK, England
PALMBERG-LERCHE, Christel M.   Italy
WILSON, Richard T.   UK, England
— —, forest
PALMBERG-LERCHE, Christel M.   Italy
— —', plant, conservation
CLEMENT, Charles R.   Brazil, Amaz.
HAWKES, John G.   UK, England
— —, —, & utilization of
ANISHETTY, Narasimha M.   Italy
— — research, forest
TOMPSETT, Paul B.   UK, England
— transformation of temperate fruit
JAMES, David J.   UK, England
genetics
FRIDRIKSSON, Sturla   Iceland
IGNACIMUTHU, Savarimuthu   India, TN
MILIMO, Patrick B.W.   Kenya
OWEN, Denis F.   UK, England
SWAMINATHAN, Monkombu S.   India, TN
VIDA, Gábor   Hungary
—, conservation*
—, ecological
*BERRY, Robert James ('Sam')   UK, England
—, horticultural crops
RIGGS, Timothy J.   UK, England
—, molecular
WOOD, David A.   UK, England
—, —: crop improvement
KING, Graham G.   UK, England
— of apple & pears
ALSTON, Frank H.   UK, England
— — hops
DARBY, Peter   UK, England
— — host–pathogen interactions in plant diseases
PINK, David A.C.   UK, England

* *See* lower footnote on p. 409.

genetics of (contd)
— — plant–pathogen interactions in crop & natural
  ecosystems
  CRUTE, Ian   UK, England
—, plant
  KHUSH, Gurdev S.   Philippines
  PINK, David A.C.   UK, England
—, population
  COHEN, Joel E.   USA, NY
  NEEL, James VAN G.   USA, MI
—, —, of Lepidoptera & Mollusca
  OWEN, Denis F.   UK, England
geoarchaeology
  DAVIDSON, Donald A.   UK, Scotland
geobotany
  GALAZY, Grigory I.   Russia
  MASING, Viktor   Estonia
  MEULEN, Frank VAN DER   The Netherlands
geochemical cycles, global
  BOLIN, Bert R.   Sweden
geodynamic processes of landscape of dryland
  regions*
geoecological approaches re.human influence on
  Nature
  *JIGJ, Sonom   Mongolia
geoecology
  HURNI, Hans   Switzerland
  MESSERLI, Bruno   Switzerland
—, marine
  KRASNOV, Eugene V.   Russia
geographical information systems (GIS)
  ANDRIANARIVO, Jonah A.   Kenya
  CAMPBELL, Kenneth L.I.   UK, England
  COCKLIN, Christopher R.   NZ
  HIBBERD, John K.   Australia, ACT
  MOFFATT, Ian   UK, Scotland
  SEVILLA, Lorenzo B.CARDENAL
                                    Nicaragua/Guatemala
  WITT, Ronald G.   Switzerland
— — — applied to sustainable development
  planning
  KRISHNAYYA, Jaswant G.   India, Mah.
— knowledge & information, popularizing
  PIIROLA, Jouko   Finland
— methods of planning, design, & conservation, of
  national parks & protected natural areas
  ZABELINA, Natalia M.   Russia
geography
  LITVIN, Vladimir M.   Russia
  USUKI, Mitsuo   Thailand
  WITT, Ronald G.   Switzerland
—, applied physical, in (sub-) Mediterranean zone
  VOS, Willem   The Netherlands
—, environmental
  HUBA, Mikuláš   Slovak Rep.
— (forest ecosystem studies)
  KIRA, Tatuo   Japan
—, historical
  HEATHCOTE, Ronald L.   Australia, SA
—, —, of conservation
  BURNETT, G.Wesley   USA, SC
— of arctic science
  ROWLEY, Diana M.R.   Canada, Ont.
—, plant
  KORNAŚ, Jan   Poland
  MEDWECKA-KORNAŚ, Anna M.   Poland
  MEHER-HOMJI, Vispy M.   India, TN
  POLUNIN, Nicholas   Switzerland

* See lower footnote on p. 409.

—, scientific research in
  IZRAEL, Yuri   Russia
—, vegetation
  SOLOMON, Allen M.   USA, OR
geological site protection
  DUFF, Keith L.   UK, England
geology
  CRAMPTON, Colin B.   Canada, BC
  YANSHIN, Aleksandr L.   Russia
—, construction & environmental
  KNILL, John   UK, England
—, marine
  SIEBOLD, Eugen   Germany
—, ocean
  LITVIN, Vladimir M.   Russia
—, Quaternary
  RAUKAS, Anto   Estonia
geomagnetic storms, influence of
  TSHERNYSHEV, Wladimir B.   Russia
geomedicine
  LÅG, Jul   Norway
geomorphology
  CRAMPTON, Colin B.   Canada, BC
  GOUDIE, Andrew S.   UK, England
—, antarctic
  SPATE, Andrew 'Andy' P.   Australia, NSW
— of coastal environments
  GRANJA, Helena M.   Portugal
geophysics
  MACDONALD, Gordon J.F.   USA, CA
  PRESS, Frank   USA, DC
—, scientific research in
  IZRAEL, Yuri   Russia
geopolitical aspects of environment and protection
  policies
  BUÉ, Alain   France
germination, seed, & dormancy mechanisms
  TAO, Kar-ling J.   Italy
germ-plasm, animal, conservation of
  WARDEH, Muhammad Fadel   Syria
— - —, plant: conservation, strategy, & technology
  TAO, Kar-ling J.   Italy
GIS, see geographical information systems
glaciology
  GOLUBEV, Genady N.   Russia
  KEAGE, Peter L.   Australia, Vic.
Glasgow, flora of
  DICKSON, James H.   UK, Scotland
global biogeochemical cycles
  BOLIN, Bert R.   Sweden
— carbon balance
  GRACE, John   UK, Scotland
— — cycle
  BOLIN, Bert R.   Sweden
— change
  KONDRATYEV, Kirill Y.   Russia
  PARSONS, David J.   USA, MT
— —, biology of
  BAZZAZ, Fakhri   USA, MA
— — research
  GRASSL, Hartmut   Switzerland
— — —, coordination & planning of
  GOLUBEV, Genady N.   Russia
— ecology
  SOLOMON, Allen M.   USA, OR
—, philosophy & history of
  GRINEVALD, Jacques   Switzerland
— environment
  CANNELL, Melvin G.R.   UK, Scotland
— environmental change
  ROSSWALL, Thomas   Sweden

— — —, human dimensions of
  PRICE, Martin F.   UK, England
— — governance particularly trade–environment
    linkage
  THOMAS, Urs P.   Canada, Que.
— — issues
  BROWN, Lester R.   USA, DC
  OBASI, Godwin O.P.   Switzerland
— — management
  NISHIOKA, Shuzo   Japan
— — policy
  CLARK, William C.   USA, MA
— — trends
  NORDERHAÜG, Magnar   Norway
— issues, critical, influencing decision-makers re.
  PETERSON, Russell W.   USA, DE
— monitoring of environment
  WALLÉN, Carl-Christian   Switzerland
— ozone balance, natural
  JOHNSTON, Harold S.   USA, CA
— population
  GOCHFELD, Michael   USA, NJ
— warming
  SCHARMER, Klaus   Germany
  SINGER, S.Fred   USA, VA
good practice, encouraging
  GITTINS, John W.E.H.   UK, England
governability
  NOVOA, Laura   Chile
governance, coastal
  EICHBAUM, William M.   USA, DC
—, global environmental, particularly trade–
    environment linkage
  THOMAS, Urs P.   Canada, Que.
—, marine
  EICHBAUM, William M.   USA, DC
governmental organizations, coordinating
  OLI, Krishna P.   Nepal
— development projects, EIA studies of
  UGWU, Christopher N.   Nigeria
governments, federal & provincial, educating
  HUSBAND, Vicky   Canada, BC
— in less-developed countries, environmental
    education in support of
  BOULTON, Mark N.   UK, England
grain systems, stored
  KENNEDY, Robert   UK, England
grasses, taxonomy of
  JAIN, Sudhanshu K.   India, UP
grassland birds
  PETRETTI, Francesco   Italy
— ecology
  NUMATA, Makoto   Japan
  WATT, Trudy A.   UK, England
— ecosystems*
— in landscape, ecological function of
  *RYCHNOVSKÁ, Milena   Czech Rep.
— invertebrates, effects of conservation management
  MORRIS, Michael G.   UK, England
—: Nature conservation
  SMITH, Kevin D.   NZ
grassroots action
  MEHTA, Mahesh C.   India, Delhi
grazing effects
  HAMBLER, David J.   UK, England
— land, structure & functions of
  PANDEYA, Satish C.   India, UP
Greece, conservation in
  VALAORAS, Georgia   Greece

—, natural areas of
  MALAMIDIS, George   Greece
green consumerism
  HAILES, Julia P.   UK, England
— living
  EVERETT, Rodney D.   UK, England
— philosophy, history of
  KULL, Kalevi   Estonia
— politics
  MILNE, Christine   Australia, Tas.
  PARKIN, Sara L.   France
— tourism
  SERAFIN, Rafal K.   Poland
greenhouse gas emissions
  FEARNSIDE, Philip M.   Brazil, Amaz.
  LAL, Rattan   USA, OH
Greening of the Himalaya project
  JAYAL, Nalni Dhar   India, UP
Greenland, vegetation ecology of
  DANIELS, Frederikus J.A.   Germany
ground vegetation, woodland, dynamics of
  KIRBY, Keith J.   UK, England
— -water ecology
  STANFORD, Jack A.   USA, MT
growth, consumption, in rich societies
  HAREIDE, Dag   Norway
—, delinking, from environment
  OPSCHOOR, Johannes B.   The Netherlands
— development
  GOCHFELD, Michael   USA, NJ
—, economic/free trade
  DAMMANN, Erik   Norway
— in scleractian corals
  BARNES, David J.   Australia, Qld
— of world bird conservation movement
  GAMMELL, Alistair   UK, England
—, population
  PETERSON, Russell W.   USA, DE
—, rapid population, –environmental degradation
  SHAW, R.Paul   USA, DC
guide books, writer & illustrator of
  FOX, Allan M.   Australia, Qld
guidelines, environmental
  MOUDUD, Hasna J.   Bangladesh
guides, identification
  BURTON, John A.   UK, England
—, underwater, to reef fishes
  RANDALL, John 'Jack'   USA, HI
Gulf of Mexico, research in physical oceanography in
    the, and protection of its reefs & islands
  CERDA, Alberto M.VAZQUEZ DE LA   Mexico
gums
  NOUR, Hassan O.ABDEL   Sudan
gymnosperms, taxonomy, evolution, &
    phytogeography, of
  PAGE, Christopher N.   UK, Scotland

---

habitat change, effects of, on wildlife ecology
  HASAN, Mohammed NORDIN   Malaysia
— conservation
  OSEMEOBO, Gbadebo J.   Nigeria
— contamination, bioindicators of, ecotoxicology in
    reptiles as
  LAMBERT, Michael R.K.   UK, England
— creation
  KELCEY, John G.   UK, England

habitat (contd)
— fragmentation
  TEMPLE, Stanley A.   USA, WI
— loss, effects of tropical, on vertebrate populations
  RAPPOLE, John H.   USA, VA
— management in protected areas
  STANTON, James P.   Australia, Qld
— — particularly on farmland
  GREEN, Brynmor H.   UK, England
— preservation in coastal lagoons
  IBARRA-OBANDO, Silvia   Mexico
— protection
  DALY, Ralph H.   Oman
— restoration particularly on farmland
  GREEN, Brynmor H.   UK, England
— selection
  GOCHFELD, Michael   USA, NJ
habitats, birds of prey and their
  WATSON, Richard   USA, ID
—, conservation of African megafauna &
  TOIT, Raoul F.DU   Zimbabwe
—, cranes'
  ARCHIBALD, George   USA, WI
—, Dugongs'
  MARSH, Helene D.   Australia, Qld
—, effects of northern development on, assessment of
  KLEIN, David R.   USA, AK
—, endangered, conservation of
  JAIN, Sudhanshu K.   India, UP
—, natural, conservation of
  FERNANDO, Ranjen L.   Sri Lanka
—, sea turtles'
  MARSH, Helene D.   Australia, Qld
—, wild, conservation of
  VARIAVA, Dilnavaz   India, Mah.
hallucinogenic plants
  SCHULTES, Richard E.   USA, MA
harnessing of waste
  LI, Shuang Liang   China
harvesting, impact of, on biodiversity
  ASHTON, Peter S.   USA, MA
hazard, natural, reduction
  KNILL, John   UK, England
hazardous waste
  BRINCHUK, Mikhail M.   Russia
  KHAN, Niaz A.   UAE
  KUFORIJI-OLUBI, Bola   Nigeria
— — management
  KRIKIS, Andris   Latvia
  MUTTAMARA, Samorn   Thailand
  REHMAN, Syed Z.   Pakistan
  SAXENA, Anil K.   India, Delhi
— wastes, detoxification of
  SUBRAMANIAN, Tarakad V.   India, TN
hazards of mass-movements and earthquakes
  VALDIYA, Khadga Singh   India, UP
—, environmental
  HUBA, Mikuláš   Slovak Rep.
  SMITH, Keith   UK, Scotland
—, environmental health
  SIVADAS, Ponathil   India, Ker.
—, natural
  FARAGÓ, Tibor   Hungary
  HEATHCOTE, Ronald L.   Australia, SA
health
  NAYVE-ROSSI, Portia A.   Philippines
  PITT, David   Switzerland
  RAMPRASAD, Vanaja   India, Kar.
—, children's, ecology and
  CHERKASOVA, Maria V.   Russia

—, ecosystem
  SINGH, Naresh   Canada, Man.
—, effects of methyl mercury on
  NUORTEVA, Pekka O.   Finland
—, forest
  INNES, John L.   Switzerland
— hazards, environmental
  SIVADAS, Ponathil   India, Ker.
—, occupational
  KASHYAP, Kant   India, Guj.
— problems, public, resulting from scorpion stings
  LOURENÇO, Wilson R.   France
—, public
  BURNEY, M.Ilyas   Pakistan
—, —, law
  GRAD, Frank P.   USA, NY
—, tree
  BOA, Eric   UK, England
— (women)
  CORRAL, Thais   Brazil, RJ
healthy environment, protection of human rights for a
  CHERKASOVA, Maria V.   Russia
heat & water balance
  HARE, F.Kenneth   Canada, Ont.
heaths: Australian reptiles
  COVACEVICH, Jeanette A.   Australia, Qld
heavy-metal pollution
  REDAUD, M.Gladys BELANDRIA DE   Guadeloupe
— — — contamination in tropical ecosystems
  LACERDA, Luiz D.   Brazil, RJ
Helium, isotopic composition of
  VORONOV, Arkady N.   Russia
Helsinki Convention, implementation of
  KRIKIS, Andris   Latvia
herbaceous biodiversity & forest harvesting, research
  on
  DUFFY, David C.   USA, AK
herbivores & dispersers, plants in relation to
  GRUBB, Peter J.   UK, England
—, mammalian, ecology of
  DUNCAN, Patrick   France
herbivory, northern
  KLEIN, David R.   USA, AK
heritage
  HÜLSHOFF, Bernd VON DROSTE ZU   France
— conservation
  COLLIN, Gérard   France
  NEPAL, Sanjay K.   Switzerland
— convention, world
  THORSELL, James W.   Switzerland
—, cultural, conservation of
  CHERKASOVA, Maria V.   Russia
— economics
  SERAFIN, Rafal K.   Poland
— education
  LACY, Terry P.DE   Australia, NSW
— interpretation
  FEICK, Jenny L.   Canada, Alb.
— management, cultural
  BOYD, William 'Bill' Edgar   Australia, NSW
—, natural
  CROFTS, Roger   UK, Scotland
—, —, conservation of
  CHERKASOVA, Maria V.   Russia
  JAYAL, Nalni Dhar   India, UP
—, —, management of the
  USHER, Michael B.   UK, Scotland
—, world
  BATISSE, Michel   France
  KETO, Aila   Australia, Qld
  LUCAS, Percy H.C. ('Bing')   NZ

—, —: policy, planning, & management
EIDSVIK, Harold K. — France
herons, conservation of
KUSHLAN, James A. — USA, MS
herpetofaunal biodiversity, Saharan & Sahelian
LAMBERT, Michael R.K. — UK, England
herpetology
DAS, Indraneil — India, TN
MITTERMEIER, Russell A. — USA, DC
WHITAKER, Romulus E. — India, TN
—, neotropical
GORZULA, Stefan — USA, TN
Hg contamination in Amazon basin
LACERDA, Luiz D. — Brazil, RJ
hibernation (environmental physiology of mammals)
PFEIFFER, Egbert W. — USA, MT
High Tehri Dam, opposition to
BAHUGUNA, Sunderlal — India, UP
higher education
KENT, Paul W. — UK, England
highland ecosystems, conservation of
OJHA, Ek Raj — Japan
hill people in Thailand
DEETES, Tuenjai — Thailand
Himalaya
MESSERLI, Bruno — Thailand
—, central, landslide research in
HAIGH, Martin J. — UK, England
—, Greening of the, project
JAYAL, Nalni Dhar — India, UP
Himalayan ecology, conservation of
RAI, Leghu D. — Nepal
ecosystems (and ecocomplexes), conservation of
PANDIT, Ashok K. — India, J&K
— environment, conservation of
RAI, Leghu D. — Nepal
— forests, ecology of
SINGH, Jamuna S. — India, UP
— —, saving of
BAHUGUNA, Sunderlal — India, UP
— lake ecology*
— natural resources, conservation of
*PANDIT, Ashok K. — India, J&K
— region, conservation biology in the
YONZON, Pralad — Nepal
Himalayas, social activism in region of
BAHUGUNA, Sunderlal — India, UP
historic buildings, preservation of
SINGH, Birandra B. — Fiji
— preservation
FIELD, Hermann H. — USA, MA
— sites, preservation of
SINGH, Birandra B. — Fiji
historical ecology
SPENCER, Jonathan W. — UK, England
— geography
HEATHCOTE, Ronald L. — Australia, SA
— — of conservation
BURNETT, G.Wesley — USA, SC
histories, life, of aquatic insects, river ecology &
STANFORD, Jack A. — USA, MT
history, Aboriginal
COVACEVICH, Jeanette A. — Australia, Qld
—, early life-, of fish esp.antarctic fish
KELLERMANN, Adolf K. — Germany
—, environmental
GRITZNER, Jeffrey A. — USA, MT
SIMMONS, Ian — UK, England

* See lower footnote on p. 409.

—, evolutionary, of polar regions
CLARKE, Andrew — UK, England
—, landscape
SPENCER, Jonathan — UK, England
—, life-, of tropical marine fish
BUSTAMANTE, Georgina — USA, FL
—, natural
BHATT, Dibya D. — Nepal
BROWN, William Y. — USA, DC
BURTON, John A. — UK, England
COLLIE, John S. — Seychelles
LIONNET, Joseph F.G. — Seychelles
SIVADAS, Ponathil — India, Ker.
—, —, field
MONOD, Théodore A. — France
—, —, history of
BURTON, John A. — UK, England
—, —, of monocotyledons with secondary growth
SIMPSON, Philip G. — NZ
— of arctic science
ROWLEY, Diana M.R. — Canada, Ont.
— — Australian ecology
SPECHT, Raymond L. — Australia, Qld
— — botany & botanical exploration
BYE, Robert — Mexico
— — conservation & ecology
CROKER, Robert A. — USA, NH
— — ecology & global ecology
GRINEVALD, Jacques — Switzerland
— — environmentalism
WORTHINGTON, E.Barton — UK, England
— — green philosophy
KULL, Kalevi — Estonia
— — natural history
BURTON, John A. — UK, England
— — southernmost South Africa
GOODALL, R.Natalie PROSSER — Argentina
HIV/AIDS eradication
SIVADAS, Ponathil — India, Ker.
holistic analysis of neotropical ecosystems
ADIS, Joachim U. — Germany
— aspects on environmental conservation
NUORTEVA, Pekka O. — Finland
— ecological conservation
POLUNIN, Nicholas — Switzerland
— environmental management
PANDEYA, Satish C. — India, UP
Holocene, Pleistocene-, sedimentology & stratigraphy
CARVALHO, G.SOARES DE — Portugal
Homosphere potentialities
POLUNIN, Nicholas — Switzerland
hoofed mammals, ecology of
BALČIAUSKAS, Linas — Lithuania
hops (Humulus lupulus)
DARBY, Peter — UK, Scotland
hormonal influences on mood
BARRY, James M. — Ireland
horticultural crops & related taxa
ASTLEY, David 'Dave' — UK, England
— —, breeding pest-resistant varieties of
ELLIS, Peter R. — UK, England
— —, plant breeding & genetics of
RIGGS, Timothy J. — UK, England
— entomology
CROSS, Jeremy V. — UK, England
— interest, plants of
CULLEN, James — UK, England
horticulture
BAKER, F.W.G. ('Mike') — France
CROSS, Jeremy V. — UK, England

horticulture (contd)
—, organic
    HARRIS, Philip J.C.   UK, England
—, ornamental
    ENTWISTLE, Andrew R.   UK, England
host–pathogen interactions
    PINK, David A.C.   UK, England
human activities, perturbation of natural global ozone
    balance by
    JOHNSTON, Harold S.   USA, CA
— activity, degradation of environment by
    ZLOTIN, Roman I.   Russia
— —, effects of, on Caribou
    BLOOMFIELD, Michael   Canada, BC
— affairs & politics
    LAMB, Hubert H.   UK, England
— biology
    FRY, Charles H.   Oman
— carrying capacity
    FEARNSIDE, Philip M.   Brazil, Amaz.
— communities, plans for environmental
    management of
    AUSSEDAT, Nicole M.   France/St Barthélemy
— conservation
    MALMBERG, Torsten   Sweden
— development, sustainable
    MIRANDA, Ruiz   Guinea-Bissau
    SPETH, James G.   USA, NY
— dimensions of global environmental change
    PRICE, Martin F.   UK, England
— ecological perspective
    NELSON, J.Gordon   Canada, Ont.
— ecology
    DAYSH, Zena   UK, England
    FRAZIER, John G.   Mexico
    GOLLEY, Frank B.   USA, GA
    HENS, Luc   Belgium
    MALMBERG, Ole   Sweden
    MALMBERG, Torsten   Sweden
    RECKERS, Ute   Kenya
    SHARMA, Subrat   India, UP
— — (cultural)
    KLEE, Gary A.   USA, CA
— envenomation, spiders re.
    RAVEN, Robert J.   Australia, Qld
— –environment interaction
    BELLAMY, David J.   UK, England
— impacts on coral-reef ecosystems
    VANTIER, Lyndon M.DE   Australia, Qld
— influence on Nature, geoecological approach for
    studying
    JIGJ, Sonom   Mongolia
— life in deserts
    BATANOUNY, Kamal H.   Egypt
— needs, interdisciplinary studies and their
    application to
    BAKER, Joseph 'Joe' T.   Australia, Qld
— population growth, biodiversity assessment, and
    conservation
    RAVEN, Peter H.   USA, MO
— —, local, & Nature conservation, economic
    relation between
    PRINS, Herbert H.T.   The Netherlands
— — policies
    CORBET, Philip S.   UK, Scotland
— populations in conservation, involvement of rural
    PRICE, Mark R.STANLEY   Kenya
— resource development
    BRERETON, Vera A.   Barbados, W.Indies

— resources, investments in, sustainable development
    through
    SHAW, R.Paul   USA, DC
— rights
    MEHTA, Mahesh C.   India Delhi
    NOVOA, Laura   Chile
    ONAYEMI, Olarotimi O.   Nigeria
    SCHRAM, Gunnar G.   Iceland
    SILVA, Allenisheo L.M.DE   Sri Lanka
    UEXKÜLL, Carl J.W.VON   Sweden
— —, protection of, for a healthy environment
    CHERKASOVA, Maria V.   Russia
— societies, indigenous native: Amazonian rain-forest
    CLOUDSLEY, Timothy   UK, Scotland
— —, use of species diversity by
    OSEMEOBO, Gbadebo J.   Nigeria
— use, impacts of, of antarctic & alpine
    environments
    SPATE, Andrew 'Andy' P.   Australia, NSW
— — re.tropical coastal environments
    DAVIE, James D.S.   Australia, Qld
humanity's impact on, & relationship with, the
    environment and use of natural resources
    DRAKE, Christopher M.   UK, England
humankind's place in The Biosphere
    LOENING, Ulrich E.   UK, Scotland
humans, infectious diseases of
    FENNER, Frank   Australia, ACT
humid tropics, agricultural resources in
    SMITH, Nigel J.H.   USA, FL
— —, American, sustainable development in
    DOUROJEANNI, Marc J.   USA, VA
— —, conservation & management of natural
    resources in
    SMITH, Nigel J.H.   USA, FL
— —, domestication of tropical trees for
    forestry/agroforestry in
    LEAKEY, Richard R.B.   Kenya
humpback whale (*Megaptera* spp.) identification
    ORHUN-HEWSON, Canan   USA, MA
Humulus lupulus, hybridization & genetics of
    DARBY, Peter   UK, England
hunting as a form of land-use
    BALDUS, Rolf D.   Germany
hybridization of hops
    DARBY, Peter   UK, England
hydraulic research of flows
    HOLČIK, Vladímír   Slovak Rep.
hydroaerodynamics
    NIKULIN, Valery A.   Russia
hydrobiology
    FEDOROV, Vadim D.   Russia
hydroclimate variability
    SMITH, Keith   UK, Scotland
hydroelectric dams, impacts of
    FEARNSIDE, Philip M.   Brazil, Amaz.
— developments on aquatic environment & fish,
    effects of
    MILLS, Derek H.   UK, Scotland
hydrogeology, ecological (contaminant)*
—, gas & oil
    *VORONOV, Arkady N.   Russia
— of mountain springs
    VALDIYA, Khadga Singh   India, UP
hydrological effects of land-use, research in
    PEREIRA, H.Charles   UK, England
hydrology
    HOLLIS, George E.   UK, England
    HÜLSHOFF, Bernd VON DROSTE ZU France

* *See* lower footnote on p. 409.

—, effects of land-use change on
CLARK, Colin UK, England
— of reclaimed lands after surface coal-mining
KILMARTIN, Marianne P. UK, England
—, operational
OBASI, Godwin O.P. Switzerland
—, urban
AWAD, Adel R. Syria
hydropower & irrigation projects, development of, in
Southeast Asia
WOODRUFF, David S. USA, CA
— in tropical & temperate environments
ZWAHLEN, Robert Switzerland
hypercars
LOVINS, Amory B. USA, CO

ibises, conservation of
KUSHLAN, James A. USA, MS
ice, arctic & antarctic, & ocean research
WADHAMS, Peter UK, England
—, radioisotopes in lakes under
HASLER, Arthur D. USA, WI
ichthyology
RODRÍGUEZ, Andrés R.RODRIGUEZ Venezuela
—, taxonomic
McALLISTER, Donald E. Canada, Ont.
identification guides
BURTON, John A. UK, England
— of critical marine ecological processes & areas
AGARDY, M Tiindi USA, DC
— — resource-use conflicts
SAUNIER, Richard E. USA, MD
—, plant
LAVRENTIADES, George Greece
illegal trading in wildlife and parts thereof,
prevention of
LaBUDDE, Samuel F. USA, CA
immigration environment–population
ABERNETHY, Virginia D.K. USA, TN
immunology, environmental research in
RAY, Prasanta K. India, W.Bengal
impact assessment, environmental, *see* environmental
impact assessment
— —, climate change
PERNETTA, John C. The Netherlands
— —, natural resources management &
KEAGE, Peter L. Australia, Vic.
— — of large dams, social & environmental
GORZULA, Stefan USA, TN
—, humanity's, on the environment
DRAKE, Christopher M. UK, England
—, Man's, on flora & vegetation
KORNAŚ, Jan Poland
—, —, — tropical marine environments
WOLANSKI, Eric J. Australia, Qld
— of ancient agriculture on soils
DAVIDSON, Donald A. UK, Scotland
— — drought stress on vegetation
GRACE, John UK, Scotland
— — environmental policy on countryside
REYNOLDS, Fiona C. UK, England
— — harvesting on biodiversity
ASHTON, Peter S. USA, MA
—, pollution, on ecosystems & plants
KULL, Olevi Estonia
— study of anthropic processes in the coastal zone
GRÁNJA, Helena M. Portugal

impacts, air pollution
ROBERTS, Thomas M. UK, England
TERBLANCHE, Petro RSA
—, climate change
HUQ, Saleemul Bangladesh
—, economic, of large-capital projects
McEACHERN, John D. Canada, Ont./Nepal
—, environmental, of mining, management of
DEMPSEY, Stanley USA, CO
—, —, monitoring of, on infrastructure development
SARMIENTO, Fausto O. USA, GA
—, —, of dams & water resource schemes
PETTS, Geoffrey UK, England
— —, — forest & electrical industries
BOYD, John M. UK, Scotland
—, —, — tropical forestry
MARSH, Clive W. Malaysia
—, —, on Nature
BARCSAY, László Hungary
—, —, — vegetation (wind, temperature, & drought,
stress)
GRACE, John UK, Scotland
—, human & natural, on coral-reef ecosystems
VANTIER, Lyndon M.DE Australia, Qld
— of climate change
PARRY, Martin L. UK, England
— — — —, research on vulnerability of wildlife
MKANDA, Francis X. Malawi
— — human use of antarctic & alpine environments
SPATE, Andrew 'Andy' P. Australia, NSW
— — hydroelectric dams
FEARNSIDE, Philip M. Brazil, Amaz.
— — sea-level rise in Pacific Basin
SHAPIRO, Harvey A. Japan
— — tourism on environmental & legal systems
incl.land-use law
PETERSON, Claire McCARTHY USA, IL
PETERSON, Craig A. USA, IL
— — tropical deforestation
FEARNSIDE, Philip M. Brazil, Amaz.
— — UV radiation in prairie saline lakes and prairie
wetlands
ROBARTS, Richard D. Canada, Sask.
—, pollution and its
HOLDGATE, Martin W. UK, England
—, sea-level rise: islands in Asia–Pacific region
HOLTHUS, Paul F. USA, HI
—, urban environmental
JIM, Chi Y. Hong Kong
implementation, field, of NCSs
McEACHERN, John D. Canada, Ont./Nepal
— of action on sustainable development
LINDNER, Warren H. Switzerland
— — Agenda 21
NOVOA, Laura Chile
— — environmental conservation & wildlife
management projects
PANGETI, George N. Zimbabwe
— — Helsinki Convention
KRIKIS, Andris Latvia
impoverishment, biotic
WOODWELL, George M. USA, MA
imprinting, olfactory landscape (migration of fishes)
HASLER, Arthur D. USA, MI
improvement, crop & tree
BREWBAKER, James L. USA, HI
—, physical & urban environmental protection &
SOTIRIADOU, Victoria Greece
in situ conservation
PRAWIROATMODJO, Suryo W. Indonesia

in situ conservation (contd)
— — — of plants
  HAMANN, Ole J.   Denmark
— — — systems
  SEVILLA, Lorenzo B.CARDENAL
                        Nicaragua/Guatemala
— *vitro* studies
  LAKSHMANAN, Kalimedu K.   India, TN
incubation temperature — snakes
  BURGER, Joanna   USA, NJ
India, mountain & tropical regions of
  MELKANIA, Niranjan P.   India, MP
—, South, field botany of
  MATTHEW, Koyapillil M.   India, TN
Indians, Amazonian, cultures & fates of
  SIOLI, Harald F.L.   Germany
indicators, measuring
  HARDI, Peter   Canada, Man.
— of pollution, bryophytes as
  SJÖGREN, Erik A.   Sweden
indigenous knowledge
  BAINES, Graham B.K.   Australia, Qld
— — & natural resource management
  MARTIN, Vance G.   USA, CO
— — systems in the tropics
  ULLUWISHEWA, Rohana K.   Sri Lanka
— native human societies of Amazonian rain-forest
  particularly in Peru
  CLOUDSLEY, Timothy   UK, Scotland
— peoples
  RUIZ-MURRIETA, Julio   Switzerland
  VARIAVA, Dilnavaz   India, Mah.
— —, protection of
  HANBURY-TENISON, A.Robin   UK, England
Indo–Pacific reef fishes, classification of
  RANDALL, John 'Jack'   USA, MI
Indonesia, conservation & development in
  DRIJVER, Carel A.   The Netherlands
industrial development in Arctic circumpolar world,
  Nunavut, & Yukon, NWT
  FENGE, Terence A.E.   Canada, Ont.
— ecology
  KELCEY, John G.   UK, England
— environmental management
  BASSOW, Whitman   USA, NY
— — pollution control
  KHAN, Niaz A.   UAE
— metabolism
  OPSCHOOR, Johannes B.   The Netherlands
— pollution, response of insect populations to
  KOZLOV, Mikhail V.   Finland
— projects, environmental management plans for
  FOX, Allan M.   Australia, NSW
— safety
  BRINCHUK, Mikhail M.   Russia
— waste, recycling of
  LUTZENBERGER, José A.   Brazil, RS
— wastewater treatment & disposal
  KHAN, Niaz A.   UAE
industries, forest & electricity, environmental impacts
  of
  BOYD, John M.   UK, Scotland
—, wood-based, raw materials for
  LAL, Piare   India, AP
industry, petroleum, environmental implications of the
  WILLUMS, Jan-Olaf   France
—, plastics, waste recycling in
  KUFORIJI-OLUBI, Bola   Nigeria
infectious diseases of animals & humans
  FENNER, Frank   Australia, ACT

influence of acid precipitation
  WIELGOLASKI, Frans-Emil   Norway
— — geomagnetic storms
  TSHERNYSHEV, Wladimir B.   Russia
influencing decision-makers re.critical global issues
  PETERSON, Russell W.   USA, DE
informal environmental education
  PRASAD, Manaparambil K.   India, Ker.
information, biological & geographical, popularizing
  PIIROLA, Jouko   Finland
—, environmental
  CAPPATO, Jorge A.   Argentina
  FILHO, Walter L.   UK, England
  PETER, Ian W.   Australia, Qld
  SINGH, Harjit   India, Delhi
—, interdisciplinary, organization of
  JUDGE, Anthony J.   Germany
—, international environmental
  SACKS, Arthur B.   USA, CO
— management
  WITT, Ronald G.   Switzerland
— on tropical forestry
  BURLEY, Jeffery   UK, England
—, right to (environmental legislation)
  PITTA, Luis CAEIRO   Portugal
—, role of, re.promoting conservation behaviour
  YOUNG, Raymond DE   USA, MI
— systems
  SHEPHERD, Alexander R.DAWSON UK, England
  SHORES, John N.   USA, ME
— —, environmental
  RAJAGOPAL, Rangaswamy   USA, OH
— — for resources
  UNNI, N.V.MADHAVAN   India, AP
— —, geographical, *see* geographical information
  systems
— technology
  PETER, Ian W.   Australia, Qld
  SAMAD, Syed A.   Malaysia
infrastructure development, monitoring of
  environmental impacts on
  SARMIENTO, Fausto O.   USA, GA
inland fisheries–environment
  PETR, Tomislav O.   Australia, Qld
— — –trends*
— —, tropical
  *WELCOMME, Robin L.   Italy
innovative technologies, development of
  KHOSLA, Ashok   India, Delhi
insect behaviour
  SALINAS, Pedro J.   Venezuela
— biology
  APPLIN, David G.   UK, England
— conservation
  ELMES, Graham W.   UK, England
— — biology
  SAMWAYS, Michael J.   RSA
— ecology
  SALINAS, Pedro J.   Venezuela
  TSHERNYSHEV, Wladimir B.   Russia
— —, social
  ELMES, Graham W.   UK, England
— fauna, conservation of
  RICHARDSON, Paul N.   UK, England
— –plant interactions
  ROOM, Peter M.   Australia, Qld
— — — relationships
  ELLIS, Peter R.   UK, England

* *See* lower footnote on p. 409.

— populations, response of, to industrial pollution
KOZLOV, Mikhail V.   Finland
— resources, conservation & utilization of third-
world, esp.butterflies
MORRIS, Michael G.   UK, England
— surveys
AL-HOUTY, Wasmia   Kuwait
insecticides, botanical
IGNACIMUTHU, Savarimuthu   India, TN
insects, aquatic, life histories of, river ecology &
STANFORD, Jack A.   USA, MT
—, biological control of
RICHARDSON, Paul N.   UK, England
—, ecology & conservation of, mainly Lepidoptera
MONTESINOS, José Luis VIEJO   Spain
—, effects of air pollution on
BELL, Nigel   UK, England
—, entomophagous, artificial breeding of, and
biological control using
CIOCHIA, Victor   Romania
—, radioisotopes in lakes, transport by
HASLER, Arthur D.   USA, WI
—, 'social'
ALI, Abd 'El moneim' M.   Egypt
institution-building
KRATTIGER, Anatole F.   USA, NY
VARIAVA, Dilnavaz   India, Mah.
— – –, environmental
DOUROJEANNI, Marc J.   USA, VA
institutional aspects of sustainable development
GORDON, John K.   UK, England
development
MORELL, Merilio G.   Italy
TOLENTINO, Amado   Philippines
— dimensions of international environmental affairs
THOMAS, Urs P.   Canada, Que.
institutions, community management
KHOSLA, Ashok   India, Delhi
VARUGHESE, George C.   India, Delhi
— essential to effective resource conservation
CHILD, Graham P.T.   Zimbabwe
—, international environmental
TIMOSHENKO, Alexandre   Kenya
—, —, law of
SCHRIJVER, Nico J.   The Netherlands
—, research, management of
HOECK, Hendrik N.   Switzerland
instruments, economic
OPSCHOOR, Johannes B.   The Netherlands
—, environmental monitoring
PRASAD, Basudeo   India, E.Punjab
insular floras, conservation of
BRAMWELL, David   Canary Islands
insurance, environmental
AICKIN, R.Malcolm   UK, England
integrated coastal-zone management
MEULEN, Frank VAN DER   The Netherlands
— – – – –, cross-sectoral
PERNETTA, John C.   The Netherlands
— conservation & development projects
BEZAURY-CREEL, Juan E.   Mexico
— ecosystems, economically viable
HALLER, René D.   Kenya
— land-use and tree biology
LAST, Frederick T.   UK, Scotland
— management of natural ecosystems
DUGAN, Patrick F.   Switzerland
— pest control
ELLIS, Peter R.   UK, England
— — management strategies
JACOBSON, Robert J.   UK, England

— resource management
DODDS, Donald G.   Canada, NS
MELKANIA, Niranjan P.   India, MP
MWALYOSI, Raphael B.B.   Tanzania
— rural area development
RAI, Suresh Chand   India, Sikkim
integrating Man and Nature
TERRASSON, François   France
integration of commercial & community-based
conservation activities
TOIT, Raoul F.DU   Zimbabwe
—, regional
CLOUTIER, Antoine   Canada, Que.
—, subsistence community, with protected area
authorities
ROWNTREE, Matthew J.W.   UK, England
integument, diseases of the
BARRY, James M.   Ireland
interaction between environment & development
BHATT, Dibya D.   Nepal
interactions, atmospheric system
RADICELLA, Sandro M.   Italy
—, — –ecological
PIELKE, Roger A.   USA, CO
—, biotic, in warming of Earth
WOODWELL, George M.   USA, MA
—, ecological, of certain earth sciences with *native*
Canadian perceptions and *European* Canadian
written traditions
CRAMPTON, Colin B.   Canada, BC
—, environment–energy–food–economy,
interdisciplinary studies of
SMIL, Václav   Canada, Man.
—, — –forestry
INNES, John L.   Switzerland
—, environmental scientists–politicians'
BOLIN, Bert R.   Sweden
—, host–pathogen, genetics of
PINK, David A.C.   UK England
—, insect–plant
ROOM, Peter M.   Australia, Qld
—, land–water
LIKENS, Gene E.   USA, NY
—, plant–animal
MALLOCH, Andrew J.C.   UK, England
—, — –pathogen, genetics of, in crop & natural
ecosystems
CRUTE, Ian   UK, England
—, society–climate
GLANTZ, Michael H.   USA, CO
—, soil–plant nutrient
NYE, Peter H.   UK, England
interdisciplinary approaches (asian tropical forests
and national parks)
HENNING, Daniel H.   USA, MT
— environmental research
GANDY, Matthew   UK, England
— — studies
BRYSON, Reid A.   USA, WI
— information, organization of
JUDGE, Anthony J.   Germany
— science and its role in policymaking
O'RIORDAN, Timothy   UK, England
— studies and their application to human needs
BAKER, Joseph 'Joe' T.   Australia, Qld
— — of environment–energy–food–economy
interactions
SMIL, Václav   Canada, Man.
internal combustion engines, biomass-based fuels for
SHYAM, Murari   India, MP

international affairs
DAHL, R.Birgitta — Sweden
RAMPHAL, Shridath — UK, England
— — & communications
STONE, Peter B. — UK, England
— agreements, application of, re.wild flora & fauna
KACEM, Slaheddine BEL — Tunisia
— agricultural research & development
JAMES, W.Clive — Cayman Islands
— agriculture
BENNETT, Sara L. — Canada, BC
— — & wildlife issues
COPPINGER, Raymond — USA, MA
— aid
OVINGTON, John D. — Australia, ACT
— aspects of environmental issues including within
  the UN system
VAVILOV, Andrey M. — Kenya
— atmospheric environment
BOJKOV, Rumen D. — Switzerland
— conventions, advocacy in
PHILLIPS, Cassandra F.E. — UK, England
— development
KRATTIGER, Anatole F. — USA, NY
— environmental affairs, political & institutional
  dimensions of
THOMAS, Urs P. — Canada, Que.
— — communication
HESSELINK, Frederik J. — The Netherlands
— — cooperation
PRESTRUD, Pål — Norway
— — education
HESSELINK, Frederik J. — The Netherlands
SACKS, Arthur B. — USA, CO
— — ethics & values
CARROLL, John E. — USA, NH
— — information
SACKS, Arthur B. — USA, CO
— — institutions
TIMOSHENKO, Alexandre — Kenya
— — issues
FARAGÓ, Tibor — Hungary
— — law
ABDELHADY, Abdelaziz — Egypt/Kuwait
CANO, Guillermo J. — Argentina
GÜNDLING, Lothar — Germany
JOHNSON, David W. — USA, CA
JOHNSTON, Douglas M. — Canada, BC
KOESTER, Veit — Denmark
LANG, Winfried — Switzerland
OKIDI, Charles O. — Kenya
O'RIORDAN, Timothy — UK, England
PALMER, Geoffrey — NZ
SCHRAM, Gunnar G. — Iceland
SCHRIJVER, Nico J. — The Netherlands
TIMOSHENKO, Alexandre — Kenya
WEN, Boping — China
— — — (or legislation), drafting of
OGUNDERE, Joseph D. — Nigeria
— — philosophy
JOHNSON, David W. — USA, CA
— — policy
FAIZI, Shahul — Saudi Arabia
JOHNSON, David W. — USA, CA
— — politics
O'RIORDAN, Timothy — UK, England
— — relations
MOLTKE, Konrad VON — USA, VT
— — training
SACKS, Arthur B. — USA, CO

— exchanges, energy & environment and
CATANIA, Peter J. — Canada, Sask.
— forestry
GRANDTNER, Miroslav M. — Canada, Que.
— institutions, law of
SCHRIJVER, Nico J. — The Netherlands
— law
ANGELO, Homer G. — USA, CA
— — & policy*
— — — —, comparative
*BOTHE, Michael — Germany
— — & the environment
BIRNIE, Patricia W. — UK, England
— —, public
BIRNIE, Patricia W. — UK, England
SCHRIJVER, Nico J. — The Netherlands
— Nature conservation
BREE, Peter J.H. VAN — The Netherlands
— — law
KLEMM, Cyrille DE — France
— — on sustainable development & the environment
RAMPHAL, Shridath — UK, England
— relations
BISWAS, Margaret R. — UK, England
— science
PERRY, John S. — USA, VA
— policy
KENDREW, John C. — UK, England
— water law
OKIDI, Charles O. — Kenya
— waters
BISWAS, Asit K. — UK, England
— wildlife, conservation of
JENKINS, David — UK, Scotland
interpretation
BUTLER, James 'Jim' R. — Canada, Alb.
—, environmental education and, esp.in marine parks
  & protected areas
WHITE, Susan L. — USA, FL
—, Nature reserve & park
FOX, Allan M. — Australia, NSW
interpreter of conservation & wildlife topics
THOMAS, Anamaria A.DE — USA, FL
introduction of pest & disease resistance
ALSTON, Frank H. — UK, England
introductions, species
WELCOMME, Robin L. — Italy
Inuit (Eskimos)
ROWLEY, Graham W. — Canada, Ont.
invasion, alien plants'
STRASBERG, Dominique — La Réunion
invasions, biological
HOBBS, Richard J. — Australia, WA
—, plant, control of, in protected areas
THEBAUD, Christophe — France
invasive species
STRAHM, Wendy A. — Switzerland
inventories, wetland
DIEGUES, Antonio C.S. — Brazil, SP
inventory, ecosystem, islands in Asia/Pacific region
HOLTHUS, Paul F. — USA, HI
— of resources
SHEPHERD, Alexander R.DAWSON — UK, England
invertebrate conservation
SAMWAYS, Michael J. — RSA
WELLS, Susan M. — UK, England
— ecology esp.of Araneae
DUFFEY, Eric A.G. — UK, England

* See lower footnote on p. 409.

invertebrates, conservation of British & European*
  , grassland, effects of conservation management on
  *MORRIS, Michael G.   UK, England
investigative writing
  WEIR, David A.   USA, CA
investments in human resources, sustainable
  development through
  SHAW, R.Paul   USA, DC
involvement of rural human populations in
  conservation — Africa
  PRICE, Mark R.STANLEY   Kenya
irrigation & hydropower projects, development of, in
  Southeast Asia
  WOODRUFF, David S.   USA, CA
— in tropical & temperate environments
  ZWAHLEN, Robert   Switzerland
— management
  BISWAS, Asit K.   UK, England
— systems
  TRENČIANSKA, Jana   Slovak Rep.
—, traditional, in oases and their rehabilitation
  DAMERDJI, M.Amine   Algeria
island biogeography
  TEMPLE, Stanley A.   USA, WI
— biology
  GIVEN, David R.   NZ
— conservation & ecology
  HAMBLER, Clive   UK, England
— ecology
  DOUMENGE, François   Monaco
— ecosystems
  BOYD, John M   UK, Scotland
  FRAZIER, John G.   Mexico
  MOREY, Miguel   Spain
— — & ecocomplexes, conservation of
  FITTER, Julian R.   UK, England
— environments
  AUSSEDAT, Nicole M.   France/St Barthélemy
— —, sustainable use of small-
  HAMILTON, Lawrence S.   USA, VT
—, volcanic, Surtsey, biotic colonization of
  FRIDRIKSSON, Sturla   Iceland
islands
  PITT, David   Switzerland
—, birds
  BOURNE, William R.P.   UK, Scotland
—, conservation biology of
  THEBAUD, Christophe   France
—, environmental management & conservation of
  DAHL, Arthur L.   Switzerland
—, Galápagos
  HAMANN, Ole J.   Denmark
— in Asia–Pacific region
  HOLTHUS, Paul F.   USA, HI
—, oceanic
  DICKSON, James H.   UK, Scotland
—, —, biology & conservation of
  RYAN, Peter G.   RSA
—, —, ecology of
  HOLDGATE, Martin W.   UK, England
—, protection of, in Gulf of Mexico
  CERDA, Alberto M.VAZQUEZ DE LA   Mexico
—, tropical, marine ecology [around]
  MARAGOS, James E.   USA, HI
isopods, environmental biology of
  HOLDICH, David M.   UK, England
isotopic composition of Argon & Helium
  VORONOV, Arkady N.   Russia

* See lower footnote on p. 409.

Israel — limnology
  POR, Francis D.   Israel
issues, agriculture, international
  COPPINGER, Raymond   USA, MA
—, arctic environmental, education in
  YOUNG, Steven B.   USA, VT
—, assistance, environment & development
  FRY, Ian W.   Australia, NSW
—, conservation, voluntary involvement in
  ARMSTRONG, Geoffrey J.   Australia, NSW
—, —: wildlife
  PLAYER, Ian C.   RSA
—: development & environment
  SARMA, K.Madhava   Kenya
—, energy–environment
  COUTANT, Charles C.   USA, TN
—, environment/conservation
  KABRAJI, Aban M.   Pakistan
—, /population
  MUMBA, Wanga   Zambia
—, environmental
  AL-ALAWNEH, Ziyad   Jordan
  KAKABADSE, Yolanda   Ecuador
  SARMA, K.Madhava   Kenya
  WRIGHT, Martin P.W.   UK, England
—, — management
  PRESTON-WHYTE, Robert A.   UK, England
—, global, critical, influencing decision-makers re.
  PETERSON, Russell W.   USA, DE
—, — environmental
  OBASI, Godwin O.P.   Switzerland
—, — —, analysis of
  BROWN, Lester R.   USA, DC
—, human rights
  MEHTA, Mahesh C.   India, Delhi
—, international aspects of environmental, including
  within the UN system
  VAVILOV, Andrey M.   Kenya
—, — environmental
  FARAGÓ, Tibor   Hungary
—, management
  KABRAJI, Aban M.   Pakistan
—, — & planning, natural resource
  BLAHNA, Dale J.   USA, UT
—, North–South
  MYERS, Norman   UK, England
  SCHRIJVER, Nico J.   The Netherlands
— of environmental justice
  WRIGHT, R.Michael   USA, VA
—, policy
  DHUNGEL, Surya P.S.   Nepal
—, sustainable development
  KAKABADSE, Yolanda   Ecuador
—, — — policy
  SEVILLA, Lorenzo B.CARDENAL
               Nicaragua/Guatemala
—, wildlife, international
  COPPINGER, Raymond   USA, MA
—, world economic
  COUSTEAU, Jacques-Y.   France

Jordan, conservation of arid & semi-arid ecosystems in
  HATOUGH-BOURAN, Alia M.A.   Jordan
journalism
  ANDRIANARIVO, Jonah A.   Kenya
  RODRIGUEZ, Andrés R.RODRIGUEZ Venezuela

journalism (contd)
—, environmental
  CAPPATO, Jorge A.   Argentina
  GUNAWARDENE, Nalaka J.   Sri Lanka
  NDYAKIRA, N.Amooti   Uganda
  OKAJIMA, Shigeyuki   Japan
  SHARMA, Sudhirendar   India, Delhi
Judaism and animals
  COHN-SHERBOK, Dan   UK, England
Jurassic palaeontology, research into
  DUFF, Keith L.   UK, England
jurisprudence, environmental
  MEHTA, Mahesh C.   India, Delhi
just distribution of world's resources
  DAMMANN, Erik   Norway
justice, access to (environmental legislation)
  PITTA, Luis Caeiro   Portugal
—, environmental
  WRIGHT, R.Michael   USA, VA

Kangaroos — aerial surveys, multiple land-use, &
  sustainable resource management
  WILSON, George R.   Australia, WA
—, native wildlife
  SATTLER, Paul S.   Australia, Qld
Karst biota
  SPATE, Andrew 'Andy' P.   Australia, NSW
kinetics & catalysis
  SKOULIKIDIS, Theodore   Greece
Kiskunság National Park, appropriate management of
  TÖLGYESI, István   Hungary
knowledge, biological & geographical, popularizing
  PIIROLA, Jouko   Finland
—, indigenous
  BAINES, Graham B.K.   Australia, Qld
—, —, & natural resource management
  MARTIN, Vance G.   USA, CO
— systems, indigenous, in the tropics
  ULLUWISHEWA, Rohana K.   Sri Lanka
—, traditional marine ecological
  JOHANNES, Robert E.   Australia, Tas.

Labroid fishes
  RANDALL, John 'Jack'   USA, HI
Lagomorpha
  CHAPMAN, Joseph A.   USA, UT
lagoon, salt, ecology
  POR, Francis D.   Israel
lagoons, coastal, habitat preservation in
  IBARRA-OBANDO, Silvia   Mexico
lake ecology, Himalayan
  PANDIT, Ashok K.   India, J&K
— watersheds, management of
  KIRA,Tatuo   Japan
lakes, radioisotopes in
  HASLER, Arthur D.   USA, WI
—, saline, prairie, impacts of UV radiation in*
—, —, —, microbial biogeochemical cycles in
  *ROBARTS, Richard D.   Canada, Sask.

*See lower footnote on p. 409.

—, salt
  WILLIAMS, William D.   Australia, SA
land, arid, ecology
  HOUÉROU, Henry N.le   France
—, —, management
  HEATHCOTE, Ronald L.   Australia, SA
— classification
  CRAMPTON, Colin B.   Canada, BC
— communities, ecology of
  GALAZY, Grigory I.   Russia
— degradation
  ABROL, Inder P.   India, Delhi
  LUK, Shiu-hung   Canada, Ont.
—, degraded, restoration of
  CHADWICK, Michael J.   Sweden
— ecology in tropical Africa
  TRAPNELL, Colin G.   UK, England
—, grazing, structure & functions of
  PANDEYA, Satish C.   India, UP
— management
  LUK, Shiu-hung   Canada, Ont.
  WATSON, John R.   Australia, WA
— Management, Bureau of, USA's, ecology of
  WATSON, Charles St D., Jr   USA, NV
— preservation
  EGLER, Frank E.   USA, CT
— readjustment
  KRAJČOVIČ, Roman S.   Slovak Rep.
— reclamation
  HAIGH, Martin J.   UK, England
— —, derelict
  ROBERTS, Thomas M.   UK, England
— rehabilitation
  ABROL, Inder P.   India, Delhi
— resource management
  RAI, Suresh Chand   India, Sikkim
— — survey
  WEBSTER, Richard   UK, England
— –sea interactions in coastal zone, marine parks, &
  protected areas
  RAY, G.Carleton   USA, VA
— tenure
  SILVA, Allenisheo L.M.de   Sri Lanka
— —, customary
  BAINES, Graham B.K.   Australia, Qld
— tortoises
  FRAZIER, John G.   Mexico
—, tropical, sustainable resource management of
  BAINES, Graham B.K.   Australia, Qld
— -use
  BOYLAND, Desmond E.   Australia, Qld
— - —, appropriate, including agroforestry
  BUDOWSKI, Gerardo   Costa Rica
— - — change, effects of, on climate & hydrology
  CLARK, Colin   UK, England
— - — changes, ecological consequences of, in Latin
  America
  MORELLO, Jorge X.   Argentina
— - — classification re.land & forest ecology in
  tropical Africa
  TRAPNELL, Colin G.   UK, England
— - — controls
  SCANNELL, Yvonne   Ireland
— - — cost–benefit analysis, esp. local community
  benefits
  THRESHER, Philip B.   USA, CA
— - — ecology
  HABER, Wolfgang   Germany
— - —, — of, in the tropics, mountains, & arid
  regions
  POORE, M.E.Duncan   UK, Scotland

— - —, hunting as a form of
BALDUS, Rolf D.   Germany
— - —, hydrological effects of, research in
PEREIRA, H.Charles   UK, England
— - —, integrated, & tree biology
LAST, Frederick T.   UK, Scotland
— - — law
PETERSON, Craig A.   USA, IL
— — - — and zoning re.impacts of tourism on
    environmental & legal systems
PETERSON, Claire MCCARTHY   USA, IL
— - — —, environmental
DELOGU, Orlando E.   USA, NE
— - — management & planning
GOOD, Roger B.   Australia, ACT
— - — —, sustainable
RECKERS, Ute   Kenya
— - — planning
GOOD, Roger B   Australia, ACT
LaBASTILLE, Anne   USA, NY
MAKHDOUM, Majid F.   Iran
OSEMEOBO, Gbadebo J.   Nigeria
SEVILLA, Lorenzo B.CARDENAL
    Nicaragua/Guatemala
TOIT, Raoul F.DU   Zimbabwe
— - — —, seismic zonation in
AWAD, Adel R.   Syria
— - — policy
OSEMEOBO, Gbadebo J.   Nigeria
— - — resources, research & education re.
NELSON, J.Gordon   Canada, Ont.
    strategies
LUSCOMBE, Bruce A.   USA, NY
— - —, sustainable
FULEKY, György   Hungary
— - —, —: Aborigines
WILSON, George R.   Australia, WA
— - —, tropical
TAN, Koonlin   UK, England
— —water interactions
LIKENS, Gene E.   USA, NY
landcare
BRENNAN, Ngairetta J.   Australia, Qld
landforms in arid & semi-arid areas
WILLIAMS, Martin A.J.   Australia, SA
lands affected by coal-mining, erosion control of
HAIGH, Martin J.   UK, England
—, arid, development
HAMED, Safei EL-DEEN   USA, MD
—, —, in western Australia
BELLAMY, David J.   UK, England
—, dry, water resources in
WILLIAMS, William D.   Australia, SA
—, ecological sustainable use of semi-arid
SATTLER, Paul S.   Australia, Qld
—, reclaimed, hydrology of, after surface coal-mining
KILMARTIN, Marianne P.   UK, England
landscape, abandoned, revitalization of
KRAJČOVIČ, Roman S.   Slovak Rep.
— analysis
HAMED, Safei EL-DEEN   USA, MD
— architecture
JACOBS, Peter D.A.   Canada, Que.
LOVEJOY, Derek   UK, England
USUKI, Mitsuo   Thailand
— biology
KULVIK, Mart   Estonia
— conservation
NAVEH, Zev   Israel
— —, natural & cultural, in spatial planning
STAWICKI, Henryk   Poland

—, derelict, revitalization of
KRAJČOVIČ, Roman S.   Slovak Rep.
— design
MOURA, Robert MANNERS   Portugal
—, ecological function of grassland in
RYCHNOVSKÁ, Milena   Czech Rep.
— ecology
DEJMAL, Ivan   Czech Rep.
DRDOŠ, Ján   Slovak Rep.
HABER, Wolfgang   Germany
KRAJČOVIČ, Roman S.   Slovak Rep.
MEULEN, Frank VAN DER   The Netherlands
MIKLÓS, Ladislav   Slovak Rep.
MOREY, Miguel   Spain
MOURA, Robert MANNERS   Portugal
NAVEH, Zev   Israel
OPDAM, Paul   The Netherlands
PAPANASTASIS, Vasilios P.   Greece
SAMWAYS, Michael J.   RSA
SARMIENTO, Fausto O.   USA, GA
SEPP, Kalev   Estonia
TEMPLE, Stanley A.   USA, WI
— — and vegetation
BRIDGEWATER, Peter   Australia, ACT
— —, design & maintenance
MOURA, Robert MANNERS   Portugal
— —, evolutionary
PIANKA, Eric R.   USA, TX
— — in (sub-) Mediterranean zone
VOS, Willem   The Netherlands
— — of river floodplains
DECAMPS, Henri   France
— evolution
PIIROLA, Jouko   Finland
— history
SPENCER, Jonathan W.   UK, England
— imprinting, olfactory (migration of fishes)
HASLER, Arthur D.   USA, WI
— maintenance
MOURA, Robert MANNERS   Portugal
— management
HABER, Wolfgang   Germany
HELLIWELL, D.Rodney   UK, England
NAVEH, Zev   Israel
WAGER, Jonathan F.   UK, England
— —, forest
SUGIMURA, Ken   Japan
— — in Nature conservation areas
SEPP, Kalev   Estonia
— of dryland regions, geodynamic processes
JIGJ, Sonom   Mongolia
— paintings, urban
KELCEY, John G.   UK, England
— photography
LOENING, Ulrich E.   UK, Scotland
— planning
HABER, Wolfgang   Germany
HUBA, Mikuláš   Slovak Rep.
SERAFIN, Rafal K.   Poland
WAGER, Jonathan F.   UK, England
— — in (sub-) Mediterranean zone
VOS, Willem   The Netherlands
— protection
BARCSAY, László   Hungary
GREEN, Brynmor H.   UK, England
MOSLEY, John G.   Australia, Vic.
— restoration
NAVEH, Zev   Israel
— vegetation (and ecology)
BRIDGEWATER, Peter   Australia, ACT

landscape vegetation (contd)
— — management, aesthetic
　EGLER, Frank E.　　　　　　　USA, CT
landscapes, cultural & protected
　LUCAS, Percy H.C. ('Bing')　　NZ
—, fragmented, management of
　BEETON, Robert J.S.　　　Australia, Qld
—, 'tropandean', restoration of
　SARMIENTO, Fausto O.　　　USA, GA
landscaping
　LUTZENBERGER, José A.　　Brazil, RS
—, ecological
　SAMWAYS, Michael J.　　　　RSA
landslide research in central Himalaya
　HAIGH, Martin J.　　　UK, England
large dams
　MOORE, James W.　　　Canada, Alb.
— mammal ecology
　PRINS, Herbert H.T.　　The Netherlands
— mammals (carnivores & ungulates)
　SCHALLER, George B.　　　USA, NY
— —, population biology of
　LARSEN, Thor　　　　　　Norway
Latin America, ecological consequences of land-use
　changes in
　MORELLO, Jorge X.　　　Argentina
— —, environmental education & training in
　LEFF, Enrique　　　　　Mexico
law, air pollution
　SILVA, Allenisheo L.M.DE　　Sri Lanka
—, application of, re.tropical coastal environments
　DAVIE, James D.S.　　　Australia, Qld
—, comparative international, & policy
　BOTHE, Michael　　　　Germany
—, constitutional
　JARIWALA, C.M.　　　　India, UP
—, development & application of, re.tropical coastal
　environments
　DAVIE, James D.S.　　　Australia, Qld
—, environmental, see environmental law
—, —, and public policy
　McCARTHY, Gerald P.　　　USA, VA
—, —, comparative
　GÜNDLING, Lothar　　　Germany
　HOLLO, Erkki J.　　　　Finland
—, —, (— & international)
　OKIDI, Charles O.　　　Kenya
—, —, — — national
　REHBINDER, Eckard　　　Germany
—, —, development
　FRY, Ian W.　　　Australia, NSW
—, —, — & municipal drafting of
　OGUNDERE, Joseph D.　　　Nigeria
—, —, European
　MADAR, Zdeněk　　　Czech Rep.
—, —, national & international
　ABDELHADY, Abdelaziz　　Egypt/Kuwait
　CANO, Guillermo J.　　　Argentina
　KOESTER, Veit　　　　Denmark
—, —, —: comparative
　WEN, Boping　　　　　China
—, —, international, see international environmental
　law
—, —, training
　FRY, Ian W.　　　Australia, NSW
—, international
　ANGELO, Homer G.　　　USA, CA
—, —, & policy
　BOTHE, Michael　　　　Germany
—, —, and the environment
　BIRNIE, Patricia W.　　　England, UK

—, — environmental, see international environmental
　law
—, — water
　OKIDI, Charles O.　　　Kenya
—, land-use
　PETERSON, Craig A.　　　USA, IL
—, — - —, and zoning re.impacts of tourism on
　environment & legal systems
　PETERSON, Claire McCARTHY　　USA, IL
—, — - —, environmental
　DELOGU, Orlando E.　　　USA, ME
—, natural-resource
　BARAHONA-ISRAEL, Rodrigo　Costa Rica
—, Nature conservation, international & comparative
　KLEMM, Cyrille DE　　　France
— of education
　JARIWALA, C.M.　　　India, UP
— — international institutions
　SCHRIJVER, Nico J.　　The Netherlands
— — the Sea
　BIRNIE, Patricia W.　　　UK, England
　BORGESE, Elisabeth M.　　Canada, NS
　GÜNDLING, Lothar　　　Germany
　JOHNSTON, Douglas M.　　Canada, BC
　MOUDUD, Hasna J.　　　Bangladesh
　OKIDI, Charles O.　　　Kenya
　SCHRAM, Gunnar G.　　　Iceland
—, Parliamentary
　BURHENNE, Wolfgang E.　　Germany
—, planning
　GOULDMAN, M.Dennis　　Israel
—, public
　CALDWELL, Lynton Keith　　USA, IN
　OKOTH-OGENDO, H.Wilfred O.　Kenya
—, — health
　GRAD, Frank P.　　　　USA, NY
—, — interest
　BONINE, John E.　　　USA, OR
—, — international
　BIRNIE, Patricia W.　　　UK, England
　SCHRIJVER, Nico J.　　The Netherlands
—, real estate*
—, water
　*HOLLO, Erkki J.　　　　Finland
—, — pollution
　SILVA, Allenisheo L.M.DE　　Sri Lanka
laws, development of, on environmental protection in
　Ukraine
　KOSTENKO, Yuriy I.　　　Ukraine
layer, boundary, atmospheric
　SINGAL, Sagar P.　　　India, Delhi
lead in birds
　BURGER, Joanna　　　USA, NJ
—, neurobehavioural toxicology of
　GOCHFELD, Michael　　　USA, NJ
learning, experiential
　COHEN, Michael R.　　　USA, IN
legal aspects of environmental management
　OLI, Krishna P.　　　　Nepal
— — — natural protected areas & wildlife protection
　ABDELHADY, Abdelaziz　　Egypt/Kuwait
— systems, impacts of tourism on (land-use law &
　zoning)
　PETERSON, Claire McCARTHY　　USA, IL
— —, — — — —, land-use law
　PETERSON, Craig A.　　　USA, IL
— techniques, application of, in difficult cultural
　settings
　WRIGHT, R.Michael　　　USA, VA

* See lower footnote on p. 409.

legislation, environmental
 ANI, Olufemi — Nigeria
 COLE, Norman H.A. — Sierra Leone
 McCALLA, Winston — Jamaica
 PITTA, Luis CAEIRO — Portugal
 PONCIANO, Ismael — Guatemala
 ZAMCHIYA, David M. — Zimbabwe
—, — management
 GARRATT, Keith J. — NZ
—, — protection
 PELL, Claiborne — USA, DC
—, forestry
 MEKOUAR, Mohamed A. — Italy
— formulation
 DHUNGEL, Surya P.S. — Nepal
—, international & municipal, drafting of
 OGUNDERE, Joseph D. — Nigeria
—, oceans and environmental protection
 PELL, Claiborne — USA, DC
— re.conservation of environment & Nature
 CHALABI, Bouzid — Algeria
—, wildlife
 MEKOUAR, Mohamed A. — Italy
 SPINAGE, Clive A. — UK, England
legislative analysis
 TOLENTINO, Amado — Philippines
Leguminosae — plant systematics
 STIRTON, Charles H. — UK, England
—, African, taxonomy of
 LOCK, John M. — UK, England
leguminous systems approaches — Sahara
 HAMERDJI, M.Amine — Algeria
Lepidoptera
 MONTESINOS, Jose Luis VIEJO — Spain
—, ecology & taxonomy of
 KOZLOV, Mikhail V. — Finland
—, population genetics of
 OWEN, Denis F. — UK, England
less-developed countries, environmental education in
 BOULTON, Mark N. — UK, England
liability for environmental damage*
— — mineral exploitation & development
 *SCANNELL, Yvonne — Ireland
lichens
 DANIELS, Frederikus J.A. — Germany
 REDAUD, M.Gladys BELANDRIA DE — Guadeloupe
life-histories of aquatic insects, river ecology &
 STANFORD, Jack A. — USA, MT
— -history, early, of fish esp.antarctic fish
 KELLERMANN, Adolf K. — Germany
— - —, tropical marine fish
 BUSTAMANTE, Georgina — USA, FL
—, human, in deserts
 BATANOUNY, Kamal H. — Egypt
— quality–material well-being
 HAREIDE, Dag — Norway
— sciences
 CALDWELL, Lynton Keith — USA, IN
 GOLDSMITH, Edward — UK, England
— -systems, closed
 ALLEN, John P. — USA, CA
lifestyles
 FAZAL, Anwar — Malaysia
limnology
 GALAZY, Grigory O. — Russia
 GOPAL, Brij — India, Punjab
 LIKENS, Gene E. — USA, NY
 MWALYOSI, Raphael B.B. — Tanzania

* See lower footnote on p. 409.

PANDIT, Ashok K. — India, J&K
SMIRNOV, Nikolai N. — Russia
STANFORD, Jack A. — USA, MT
VOLLENWEIDER, Richard A. — Canada, Ont.
—, antarctic
 SPATE, Andrew 'Andy' P. — Australia, NSW
—, experimental
 HASLER, Arthur D. — USA, WI
— (Israel and Brazil)
 POR, Francis D. — Israel
liquid crystals
 SKOULIKIDIS, Theodore — Greece
litigation, public interest
 SILVA, Allenisheo L.M.DE — Sri Lanka
litter, anti-
 SOPHONPANICH, Chodchoy — Thailand
livelihood systems, rural
 GRITZNER, Jeffrey A. — USA, MT
—, rural-based
 WOODGATE, Graham R. — UK, England
livelihoods, sustainable, poverty and
 SINGH, Naresh — Canada, Man.
livestock, British farm, rare breeds of
 JEWELL, Peter A. — UK, England
— management outside of protected reserves
 KRAUS, Daniel — Namibia/USA, CA
 MARKER-KRAUS, Laurie — Namibia/USA, DC
— production
 WILSON, George R. — Australia, WA
— utilization, research development in
 WARDEH, Muhammad Fadel — Syria
lizard ecology, evolutionary
 PIANKA, Eric R. — USA, TX
lizards, ecotoxicology in
 LAMBERT, Michael R.K. — UK, England
local communities, sea-turtle conservation efforts with
 ROSE, Carlos R.HASBÚN — El Salvador
— community benefits
 THRESHER, Philip B. — USA, CA
— development & sustainable agroforestry
 KERN, Berndt — Sweden
 KERN, Eha — Sweden
logging
 HASAN, Mohammed NORDIN — Malaysia
—, sustainable, of tropical forests
 LEES, Annette M. — NZ
long-range atmospheric transport of metals & other pollutants
 STEINNES, Eiliv — Norway
low flows, causes of
 CLARK, Colin — UK, England

—

MAB
 BATISSE, Michel — France
 PEINE, John D. — USA, TN
Macaranga (Euphorbiaceae)
 WHITMORE, Timothy C. — UK, England
'Macaronesian' vegetation
 SJÖGREN, Erik A. — Sweden
Macau Green Areas
 ESTÁCIO, Antônio J.E. — Macau
macroevolution
 POR, Francis D. — Israel
macrofungi, tropical
 PEGLER, David N. — UK, England

Madagascar, forestry in
  ANDRIANARIVO, Jonah A.   Kenya
maintenance, landscape
  MOURA, Robert Manners   Portugal
— of plant diversity in tropical forests
  ASHTON, Peter S.   USA, MA
— — The Biosphere
  POLUNIN, Nicholas   Switzerland
malacology
  MORTON, Brian   Hong Kong
Malagasy primates, research on
  ANDRIAMAMPIANINA, Joseph   Madagascar
malaria eradication
  FARID, Mohyeddin A.   Switzerland
Maldives, Nature & fauna of*
— turtles
  *DIDI, N.T.Hasen   Maldives
Malvales' Meliaceae
  CHEEK, Martin R.   UK, England
mammal, *see also* mammals
—, ecology, African
  SPINAGE, Clive A.   UK, England
— populations
  FRAZER, John F.D.   UK, England
—, large, ecology
  PRINS, Herbert H.T.   The Netherlands
mammalian communication, non-vocal
  BARRY, James M.   Ireland
— conservation
  MACDONALD, David W.   UK, England
— ecology
  BARRY, James M.   Ireland
— herbivores, ecology of
  DUNCAN, Patrick   France
— predator–prey relationships
  MILLS, M.G.L. ('Gus')   RSA
— reproduction & behaviour
  DODDS, Donald G.   Canada, NS
— taxonomy
  WANG, Sung   China
mammalogy
  LANG-BEERMAN, Ernst M.   Switzerland
  PRESCOTT, Jacques   Canada, Que.
— specifically of Lagomorpha
  CHAPMAN, Joseph A.   USA, UT
—, general
  OBARA, Hideo   Japan
mammals, *see also* mammal
  KADLEČÍK, Ján   Slovak Rep.
  SERHAL, Assad   Lebanon
—, adaptation to cold (hibernation)
  PFEIFFER, Egbert W.   USA, MT
—, African, large, ecology of
  JEWELL, Peter A.   UK, England
—, arctic
  PRESTRUD, Pål   Norway
—, biogeography of
  OJEDA, Ricardo A.   Argentina
—, biology of
  FLINT, Vladimir E.   Russia
—, conservation biology of tropical
  STEPHENSON, Peter J.   Tanzania
—, — of
  BURBIDGE, Andrew A.   Australia, WA
  MALCOLM, Jay R.   Canada, Ont.
  OJEDA, Ricardo   Argentina
  PUCEK, Zdzislaw K.   Poland
  RACEY, Paul A.   UK, Scotland
  TAYLOR, J.Mary   USA, OH

—, ecology of
  DORST, Jean   France
  DUNNET, George M.   UK, Scotland
  MALCOLM, Jay R.   Canada, Ont.
—, — — hoofed, semi-aquatic, & small
  BALČIAUSKAS, Linas   Lithuania
—, environmental physiology of
  PFEIFFER, Egbert W.   USA, MT
—, hoofed, ecology of
  BALČIAUSKAS, Linas   Lithuania
—, large, behavioural ecology & conservation of
  LOVARI, Sandro   Italy
—, — (carnivores & ungulates)
  SCHALLER, George B.   USA, NY
—, —, conservation & ecology of, in East Africa
  ELTRINGHAM, Stewart W.   UK, England
—, —, population biology of
  LARSEN, Thor   Norway
—, marine
  BONNER, W.Nigel   UK, England
  McCLOSKEY, Maxine E.   USA, MD
  RAY, G.Carleton   USA, VA
—, —, ecology and conservation of
  LEATHERWOOD, James S.   USA, CA
—, —, of southernmost South America
  GOODALL, R.Natalie Prosser   Argentina
—, — (pinnipeds)
  REIJNDERS, Peter J.H.   The Netherlands
—, —, taxonomy of
  BREE, Peter J.H.van   The Netherlands
— of Borneo
  PAYNE, Junaidi   Malaysia
— — Southeast Asia
  McNEELY, Jeffrey A.   Switzerland
—, protection of endangered & disappearing species of
  SOKOLOV, Vladimir   Russia
—, semi-aquatic & small, ecology of
  BALČIAUSKAS, Linas   Lithuania
—, small, ecology & conservation of
  RAY, Justina C.   USA, FL
—, systematics of
  DORST, Jean   France
—, tropical, conservation biology of
  STEPHENSON, Peter J.   Tanzania
Man and environment
  LIU, Peitong   China
— & Nature
  COLLIN, Gérard   France
— — —, integrating
  TERRASSON, François   France
—, evolutionary etho-ecology of
  OBARA, Hideo   Japan
— –Nature interrelationships, valuation of
  MELKANIA, Niranjan P.   India, MP
— -made 'natural' disasters
  JOVANOVIĆ, Petar   Yugoslavia
Man's, *see* page 490.
managed forest, maintaining biodiversity of
  KIRBY, Keith J.   UK, England
— plantations, fire ecology in
  OLA-ADAMS, Bunyamin A.   Nigeria
management (*see also* management of —)†
—, adaptive
  CLARK, William C.   USA, MA
—, alpine environmental
  KEAGE, Peter L.   Australia, Vic.
—, Amazon forest & wildlife
  DOUROJEANNI, Marc J.   USA, VA

—, analysis, multidisciplinary
  KRISHNAYYA, Jaswant G.   India, Mah.
—, animal, domestic, genetic resource
  TEWOLDE, Assefaw   Mexico
—, —, wild
  WOODFORD, Michael H.   USA, DC
—, application of wetland science to
  LARSON, Joseph F.   USA, MA
—, appropriate, of Kiskunság National Park and
    other protected areas
  TÖLGYESI, István   Hungary
—, aquatic ecology &
  MAUGHAN, O.Eugene   USA, AZ
—, area, coastal
  SHAPIRO, Harvey A.   Japan
—, —, protected, conservation
  JEFFERIES, Bruce E.   Papua New Guinea
  STRONACH, Neil R.H.   Ireland
—, areas', protected, see protected areas' management
—, —, —, habitat, in
  STANTON, James P.   Australia, Qld
—, —', —, in the Middle East
  DEAN, Faizal   USA, VA
—, —, —, plans
  SZILASSY, Zoltán   Hungary
—, arid-land
  HEATHCOTE, Ronald L.   Australia, SA
—, aspect of environment
  JIGJ, Sonom   Mongolia
—, assessment, impact, & natural resources'
  KEAGE, Peter L.   Australia, Vic.
—, audit
  SHEPHERD, Alexander R.Dawson   UK, England
—, autochthonous tropical forest
  FISCHER, Gert R.   Brazil, SC
—, basin, drainage-
  CLARK, Colin   UK, England
—, biodiversity
  BRIDGEWATER, Peter   Australia, ACT
  SWINGLAND, Ian R.   UK, England
—, — conservation
  JEFFERIES, Bruce E.   Papua New Guinea
—, — — &
  SULAYEM, Mohammad S.A.   Saudi Arabia
—, — strategies
  BENNETT, Sara L.   Canada, BC
—, bird
  DHINDSA, Manjit S.   India, Mah.
—, buffer-zone
  PRINS, Herbert H.T.   The Netherlands
—, catchment
  DORMAN, John   Australia, NSW
—, co-, approaches to the environment
  ROMULUS, Giles   St Lucia
—, coastal
  AGARDY, M.Tündi   USA, DC
  JOHNSTON, Douglas M.   Canada, BC
  VERNAUDON, Yolande   Tahiti
  WHITE, Alan T.   Sri Lanka
—, — area
  SHAPIRO, Harvey A.   Japan
—, — conservation, in Europe
  DOODY, James P.   The Netherlands
—, — environmental
  HOLTHUS, Paul F.   USA, HI
—, —, tropical, environments
  DAVIE, James D.S.   Australia, Qld
—, — resource, see coastal resource management
—, — —, tropical
  WILKINSON, Clive R.   Australia, Qld

—, coastal-zone, see coastal-zone management
—, - -, integrated
  MEULEN, Frank van der   The Netherlands
  SALMAN, Albert H.P.M.   The Netherlands
—, common property
  QUTUB, Syed Ayub   Pakistan
—, conservation
  ABUZINADA, Abdul A.H.   Saudi Arabia
  PENNY, Stella F.   NZ
—, —, coastal, in Europe
  DOODY, James P.   The Netherlands
—, —, in tropical coastal environments
  DAVIE, James D.S.   Australia, Qld
—, —, of tropical forests
  MARSH, Clive W.   Malaysia
—, —, planning
  STEPHENSON, Peter J.   Tanzania
—, —, protected area
  JEFFERIES, Bruce E.   Papua New Guinea
  STRONACH, Neil R.H.   Ireland
—, coral-reef
  LAYDOO, Richard S.   Trinidad & Tobago
—, corporate
  LOVINS, L.Hunter   USA, CO
—, cross-sectoral integrated coastal-zone
  PERNETTA, John C.   The Netherlands
—, cultural heritage
  BOYD, William 'Bill' Edgar   Australia, NSW
—, data
  WITT, Ronald G.   Switzerland
—, disease, quarantine & — risk assessment, wild
  animal management
  WILSON, George R.   Australia, WA
—, domestic animal genetic resource
  TEWOLDE, Assefaw   Mexico
—, drainage-basin
  CLARK, Colin   UK, England
—, ecological, of watersheds
  OJEDA, Ricardo A.   Argentina
—, — pest
  TSHERNYSHEV, Wladimir B.   Russia
—, — consequences of water
  LAL, Rattan   USA, OH
—, ecosystems'
  FEICK, Jenny L.   Canada, Alb.
  MALTBY, Edward   UK, England
  MOGHRABY, Asim I.   Sudan
  PARSONS, David J.   USA, MT
  RANJITSINH, M.K.   India, MP
  TERRASSON, François   France
—, —, suburban
  PINOWSKI, Jan K.   Poland
—, effects of, on grassland invertebrates
  MORRIS, Michael G.   UK, England
—, energy
  CHANDAK, Surya P.   India, Delhi
—, environmental, see environmental management
—, —, alpine
  KEAGE, Peter L.   Australia, Vic.
—, — assessment
  JACOBS, Peter D.A.   Canada, Que.
—, — catchment
  DORMAN, John   Australia, NSW
—, —, coastal
  HOLTHUS, Paul F.   USA, HI
—, —, community-based, in urban Asia
  FUREDY, Christine   Canada, Ont.
—, —, coordination of
  GOLUBEV, Genady N.   Russia
—, —, esp.of polar regions
  WALTON, David W.H.   UK, England

management, environmental (contd)
—, —, global
  NISHIOKA, Shuzo   Japan
—, —, holistic
  PANDEYA, Satish C.   India, UP
—, —, legislation
  GARRATT, Keith J.   NZ
—, —, in Africa
  WILLIAMS, Martin A.J.   Australia, SA
—, —, — arctic circumpolar world
  FENGE, Terence A.E.   Canada, Ont.
—, —, — Asia & Australia
  WILLIAMS, Martin A.J.   Australia, SA
—, —, — Nunavut*
—, —, — Yukon, NWT
  *FENGE, Terence A.E.   Canada, Ont.
—, —, industrial
  BASSOW, Whitman   USA, NY
—, —, legal aspects of
  OLI, Krishna P.   Nepal
—, —, marine
  HOLTHUS, Paul F.   USA, HI
—, — NGO
  IYER, C.P.Jayalakshmi   India, Delhi
—, —, of human communities, plans for
  AUSSEDAT, Nicole M.   France/St Barthélemy
—, —, — islands
  DAHL, Arthur L.   Switzerland
—, —, planning of
  GOLUBEV, Genady N.   Russia
—, — —, regional
  THAPA, Gopal B.   Thailand
—, — planning
  SAUNIER, Richard E.   USA, MD
—, —, plans for industrial projects
  FOX, Allan M.   Australia, NSW
—, —, polar
  KEAGE, Peter L.   Australia, Vic.
—, — policies'
  GARRATT, Keith J.   NZ
—, — policy
  SAUNIER, Richard E.   USA, MD
—, — — issues
  PRESTON-WHYTE, Robert A.   UK, England
—, — pollution
  DAVE, Jaydev M.   India, Delhi
—, —, preventive
  PURCELL, Arthur H.   USA, CA
—, —, re.institutional development
  GARRATT, Keith J.   NZ
—, —, regional
  NISHIOKA, Shuzo   Japan
  WEBER, Karl E.   Thailand
—, — services project
  BOXALL, John E.   Hong Kong
—, — (Southeast Asia & South Pacific regions)
  EATON, Peter P.   Brunei
—, — strategies'
  GARRATT, Keith J.   NZ
—, — systems'
  EARLL, Robert C.   UK, England
—, — training
  ATCHIA, Michael   Kenya
—, —, world-wide
  GOLUBEV, Genady N.   Russia
—, Europe, coastal conservation in
  DOODY, James P.   The Netherlands
—, financial, of the environment
  BROUGH, Anthony T.   Kenya

—, forest
  DONOVAN, Richard Z.   USA, VT
  GREGOIRE, Felix W.   Dominica
  JUSOFF, Kamaruzaman   Malaysia
  MELKANIA, Niranjan P.   India, MP
—, —, Amazon
  DOUROJEANNI, Marc J.   USA, VA
—, — landscape
  SUGIMURA, Ken   Japan
—, —, natural
  SABOGAL, Cesar A.   Indonesia
—, — soil
  ZHANG, Wan Ru   China
—, —, satellite remote-sensing in
  JUSOFF, Kamaruzaman   Malaysia
—, —, sustainable
  HIBBERD, John K.   Australia, ACT
  SULLIVAN, Francis   UK, England
—, —, tropical
  LAVIEREN, Lambartus P.VAN   The Netherlands
  ORGLE, Tetey K.   Ghana
—, —, —, autochthonous
  FISCHER, Gert R.   Brazil, SC
—, forestry
  BERETEH, Mohamed A.   Sierra Leone
—, forests, tropical, conservation, of
  MARSH, Clive W.   Malaysia
—, gene-bank
  TAO, Kar-ling J.   Italy
—, genetic, of free-ranging & captive populations
  WOODRUFF, David S.   USA, CA
—, — resource, domestic animal
  TEWOLDE, Assefaw   Mexico
—, global environmental
  NISHIOKA, Shuzo   Japan
—, grassland invertebrates, effects of, on
  MORRIS, Michael G.   UK, England
—, habitat, in protected areas
  STANTON, James P.   Australia, Qld
—, hazardous waste
  KHAN, Niaz A.   UAE
  KRIKIS, Andris   Latvia
  MUTTAMARA, Samorn   Thailand
  REHMAN, Syed Z.   Pakistan
  SAXENA, Anil K.   India, Delhi
—, heritage, cultural
  BOYD, William 'Bill' Edgar   Australia, NSW
—, impact assessment, & natural resources
  KEAGE, Peter L.   Australia, Vic.
—, industrial environmental
  BASSOW, Whitman   USA, NY
—, information
  WITT, Ronald G.   Switzerland
—, institutions, community
  KHOSLA, Ashok   India, Delhi
  VARUGHESE, George C.   India, Delhi
—, integrated coastal-zone
  CH'NG, Kim-Looi   Malaysia
  MEULEN, Frank VAN DER   The Netherlands
  SALMAN, Albert H.P.M.   The Netherlands
—, —, of natural ecosystems
  DUGAN, Patrick J.   Switzerland
—, — resource
  MELKANIA, Niranjan P.   India, MP
  MWALYOSI, Raphael B.B.   Tanzania
—, international waters'
  BISWAS, Asit K.   UK, England
—, invertebrates, grassland, effects of, on
  MORRIS, Michael G.   UK, England
—, irrigation
  BISWAS, Asit K.   UK, England

* See lower footnote on p. 409.

— issues
    KABRAJI, Aban M.   Pakistan
—, land
    LUK, Shiu-hung   Canada, Ont.
    WATSON, John R.   Australia, WA
—, Land, Bureau of, USA's, ecology of
    WATSON, Charles St D., Jr   USA, NV
—, land-use
    GOOD, Roger B.   Australia, ACT
—, — - —, sustainable
    RECKERS, Ute   Kenya
—, landscape
    HABER, Wolfgang   Germany
    HELLIWELL, D.Rodney   UK, England
    NAVEH, Zev   Israel
    WAGER, Jonathan F.   UK, England
—, —, forest
    SUGIMURA, Ken   Japan
—, —, in Nature conservation areas
    SEPP, Kalev   Estonia
—, (—), soil
    ZHANG, Wan Ru   China
—, — vegetation, aesthetic
    EGLER, Frank E.   USA, CT
—, legislation, environmental
    GARRATT, Keith J.   NZ
—, livestock, outside of protected reserves
    KRAUS, Daniel   Namibia/USA, CA
    MARKER-KRAUS, Laurie   Namibia/USA, DC
—, marine
    JOHNSTON, Douglas M.   Canada, BC
    VERNAUDON, Yolande   Tahiti
—, — environmental
    HOLTHUS, Paul F.   USA, HI
—, — pollution
    CH'NG, Kim-Looi   Malaysia
—, — resource
    KENCHINGTON, Richard A.   Australia, ACT
—, —, natural
    SYBESMA, Jeffrey   Netherlands Antilles
—, Middle East, protected areas', in the
    DEAN, Faisal   USA, VA
—, national parks', see national parks' management
—, natural forest
    SABOGAL, Cesar A.   Indonesia
—, — marine resource
    SYBESMA, Jeffrey   Netherlands Antilles
—, — resource, indigenous knowledge &
    MARTIN, Vance G.   USA, CO
—, — resource, see natural resources' management
—, — resources', see natural resources' management
—, — —, & impact assessment
    KEAGE, Peter L.   Australia, Vic.
—, — —, application of social science to
    BLAHNA, Dale J.   USA, UT
—, — —, for sustainable development
    PANDURANGAN, Alagramam G.   India, Ker.
—, — —, in rural development
    TOORNSTRA, Franke H.   The Netherlands
—, — —, participatory of
    WHITE, Alan T.   Sri Lanka
—, Nature reserve
    FOX, Allan M.   Australia, NSW
—, parks
    BURNETT, G.Wesley   USA, SC
    BUTLER, James 'Jim' R.   Canada, Alb.
    FOX, Allan M.   Australia, NSW
    N'SOSSO, Dominique   Congo
    THORSELL, James W.   Switzerland
—, —, national, see national parks' management

—, participatory, of natural resources
    WHITE, Alan T.   Sri Lanka
—, pest, ecological
    TSHERNYSHEV, Wladimir B.   Russia
—, —, strategies, integrated
    JACOBSON, Robert J.   UK, England
— planning, conservation
    STEPHENSON, Peter J.   Tanzania
— —, environmental
    SAUNIER, Richard E.   USA, MD
— —, regional environmental
    THAPA, Gopal B.   Thailand
— plans, environmental, for industrial projects
    FOX, Allan M.   Australia, NSW
— —, protected areas'
    SZILASSY, Zoltán   Hungary
—, planting
    CHEEK, Roy V.   UK, England
—, polar environmental
    KEAGE, Peter L.   Australia, Vic.
— policies, environmental
    GARRATT, Keith J.   NZ
— policy, environmental
    SAUNIER, Richard E.   USA, MD
— — issues, environmental
    PRESTON-WHYTE, Robert A.   UK, England
—, pollution, marine
    CH'NG, Kim-Looi   Malaysia
—, populations, free-ranging & captive, genetic, of
    WOODRUFF, David S.   USA, CA
—, problem-oriented, theory for
    GROOT, Wouter T, De   The Netherlands
—, project
    IYER, C.P.Jayalakshmi   India, Delhi
—, projects, wildlife, design & implementation of
    PANGETI, George N.   Zimbabwe
—, protected area, see protected areas' management
—, — — conservation
    JEFFERIES, Bruce E.   Papua New Guinea
    STRONACH, Neil R.H.   Ireland
—, — areas', see protected areas' management
—, — —, habitat, in
    STANTON, James P.   Australia, Qld
—, — —, in the Middle East
    DEAN, Faisal   USA, VA
—, — —, plans
    SZILASSY, Zoltán   Hungary
—, quarantine & disease — risk assessment, wild
    animal management
    WILSON, George R.   Australia, WA
—, range
    RECKERS, Ute   Kenya
—, recreational tourism
    CRAIK, Wendy   Australia, Qld
—, regional environmental
    NISHIOKA, Shuzo   Japan
    WEBER, Karl E.   Thailand
—, — — planning
    THAPA, Gopal B.   Thailand
—, research
    ARMIJOS, Mariano MONTAÑO   Ecuador
    HEMPEL, Gotthilf   Germany
    ROBERTS, Thomas M.   UK, England
— —, solid waste
    AKHTAR, Waseem   Pakistan
—, reserve, Nature
    FOX, Allan M.   Australia, NSW
—, resource
    BUTLER, Paul J.   St Lucia
    DUFOUR, Jules   Canada, Que.
    IDECHONG, Noah   Palau

management, resource (contd)
LAYDOO, Richard S.   Trinidad & Tobago
SATOO, Taisitiroo   Japan
—, —, coastal, *see* coastal resource management
—, —, tropical
WILKINSON, Clive R.   Australia, Qld
—, —, genetic, domestic animal
TEWOLDE, Assefaw   Mexico
—, —, integrated
DODDS, Donald G.   Canada, NS
MELKANIA, Niranjan P.   India, MP
MWALYOSI, Raphael B.B.   Tanzania
—, —, marine
KENCHINGTON, Richard A.   Australia, ACT
—, —, natural, application of social science to
BLAHNA, Dale J.   USA, UT
—, —, — marine
SYBESMA, Jeffrey   Netherlands Antilles
—, —, sustainable
BAINES, Graham B.K.   Australia, Qld
—, — systems', in the tropics
JOHANNES, Robert E.   Australia, Tas.
—, —', natural, *see* natural resources' management
—, —', —, & impact assessment
KEAGE, Peter L.   Australia, Vic.
—, —', —, application of social science to
BLAHNA, Dale J.   USA, UT
—, —', —, for sustainable development
PANDURANGAN, Alagramam G.   India, Ker.
—, —', —, in rural development
TOORNSTRA, Franke H.   The Netherlands
—, —', —, participatory, of
WHITE, Alan T.   Sri Lanka
—, river catchment, total
BAKER, Joseph 'Joe' T.   Australia, Qld
—, sand-dune
SALMAN, Albert H.P.M.   The Netherlands
—, sea turtles'
MARQUEZ-MILLAN, René   Mexico
—, shrimp industry
ARMIJOS, Mariano MONTAÑO   Ecuador
—, soil (resource)
ABROL, Inder P.   India, Delhi
—, solid waste
AWAD, Adel R.   Syria
KHAN, Niaz A.   UAE
MUTTAMARA, Samorn   Thailand
REHMAN, Syed Z.   Pakistan
—, — — disposal
KUFORIJI-OLUBI, Bola   Nigeria
—, — — research
AKHTAR, Waseem   Pakistan
—, species', threatened
GIMENEZ-DIXON, Mariano   Switzerland
—, strategies', environmental
GARRATT, Keith J.   NZ
—, —', integrated pest
JACOBSON, Robert J.   UK, England
—, —', wetland & biodiversity
BENNETT, Sara L.   Canada, BC
—, suburban ecosystems'
PINOWSKI, Jan K.   Poland
—, sustainable forest
HIBBERD, John K.   Australia, ACT
SULLIVAN, Francis   UK, England
—, — land-use
RECKERS, Ute   Kenya
—, — resource
BAINES, Graham B.K.   Australia, Qld
—, systems', environmental
EARLL, Robert C.   UK, England

—, —', resource, in the tropics
JOHANNES, Robert E.   Australia, Tas.
—, technology
TAIT, Elizabeth J.   UK, Scotland
—, theory for problem-oriented analysis &
GROOT, Wouter T.DE   The Netherlands
—, threatened species'
GIMINEZ-DIXON, Mariano   Switzerland
—, total river catchment
BAKER, Joseph 'Joe' T.   Australia, Qld
—, tourism, recreational
CRAIK, Wendy   Australia, Qld
—, training, environmental
ATCHIA, Michael   Kenya
—, tropical coastal environments, conservation, in
DAVIE, James D.S.   Australia, Qld
—, — — resource
WILKINSON, Clive R.   Australia, Qld
—, — forest
LAVIEREN, Lambartus P.VAN   The Netherlands
ORGLE, Tetey K.   Ghana
—, —, autochthonous
FISCHER, Gert R.   Brazil, SC
—, — forests, conservation, of
MARSH, Clive W.   Malaysia
—, tropics, resource systems', in the
JOHANNES, Robert E.   Australia, Tas.
—, urban (life-quality)
FAZAL, Anwar   Malaysia
—, vegetation
HOBBS, Richard J.   Australia, WA
WATT, Trudy A.   UK, England
—, —, landscape, aesthetic*
—, —, right-of-way
*EGLER, Frank E.   USA, CT
—, waste
CHOI, Yearn Hong   USA, VA
COOPER, Jeffrey C.   UK, England
EKARATH, Raveendran   Bahrain
ROYES, Veronica I.J.   Jamaica
SOPHONPANICH, Chodchoy   Thailand
TRENČIANSKA, Jana   Slovak Rep.
—, —, hazardous
KHAN, Niaz A.   UAE
KRIKIS, Andris   Latvia
MUTTAMARA, Samorn   Thailand
REHMAN, Syed Z.   Pakistan
SAXENA, Anil K.   India, Delhi
—, —, in developing countries
FUREDY, Christine   Canada, Ont.
—, —, solid
AWAD, Adel R.   Syria
KHAN, Niaz A.   UAE
MUTTAMARA, Samorn   Thailand
REHMAN, Syed Z.   Pakistan
—, —, —, disposal
KUFORIJI-OLUBI, Bola   Nigeria
—, wastewater
SHIN, Eung-Bai   S.Korea
—, water
ABROL, Inder Pal   India, Delhi
HOLČIK, Vladímir   Slovak Rep.
HOLLIS, George E.   UK, England
SHIN, Eung-Bai   S.Korea
THOMAS, John D.   UK, England
—, — quality
HAMMERTON, Desmond   UK, Scotland
OKUN, Daniel A.   USA, NC

* *See* lower footnote on p. 409.

—, —, and associated environmental problems
   WHITE, Gilbert F.   USA, CO
—, —, ecological consequences of
   LAL, Rattan   USA, OH
—, waters', international
   BISWAS, Asit K.   UK, England
—, watershed
   DEARDEN, Philip   Canada, BC
   THAPA, Gopal B.   Thailand
—, watersheds, ecological, of
   OJEDA, Ricardo A.   Argentina
—, wetland science, application of, to
   LARSON, Joseph F.   USA, MA
—, — strategies'
   BENNETT, Sara L.   Canada, BC
—, wetlands'
   DUGAN, Patrick J.   Switzerland
   HOFFMANN, Luc   France
   KADLEČÍK, Ján   Slovak Rep.
   SAENGER, Peter   Australia, NSW
   SHEIKH, Muhammad A.R.   Bangladesh
—, wild animal
   WOODFORD, Michael H.   USA, DC
—, wildland
   SHORES, John N.   USA, ME
—, wildlife see wildlife management
—, —, Amazon
   DOUROJEANNI, Marc J.   USA, VA
—, — (birds)
   CHRISTIAN, Colmore S.   Dominica
—, —, community involvement in
   MKANDA, Francis X.   Malawi
—, —, in eastern & southern Africa
   BALDUS, Rolf D.   Germany
—, —, outside of protected reserves
   KRAUS, Daniel   Namibia/USA, CA
   MARKER-KRAUS, Laurie   Namibia/USA, DC
management of — (see also management —)[†]
—, African, national parks
   VERSCHUREN, Jacques C.F.   Belgium
— — small biotic populations
   PRICE, Mark R. STANLEY   Kenya
— air
   EKARATH, Raveendran   Bahrain
— areas, conservation
   HOECK, Hendrik N.   Switzerland
— —, natural
   HERRERO, Stephen M.   Canada, Alb.
—, —', protected, see protected areas' management
— —, —, natural
   DIAZ-MARTIN, Diego   Venezuela
— —, Nature conservation
   DALY, Ralph H.   Oman
— bears
   HERRERO, Stephen M.   Canada, Alb.
— Black Rhinoceros (Diceros bicornis)
   TOIT, Raoul F.DU   Zimbabwe
—, Brazil, marine Turtles off coast of
   MARCOVALDI, Guy M.F.GUAGNI DEI
    Brazil, Bahia
   MARCOVALDI, Maria Â.GUAGNI DEI
    Brazil, Bahia
— buffer zones
   BUDOWSKI, Gerardo   Costa Rica
— carnivores
   HERRERO, Stephen M.   Canada, Alb.
— caves
   SPATE, Andrew 'Andy' P.   Australia, NSW

—, China, environment in
   LUK, Shiu-hung   Canada, Ont.
— coastal ecosystems
   BUSTAMANTE, Georgina   USA, FL
— — zones
   GOLDBERG, Edward D.   USA, CA
   HALIM, Youssef   Egypt
— conflict, environmental
   DEMPSEY, Stanley   USA, CO
— conflicts, resource-use
   SAUNIER, Richard E.   USA, MD
— conservation areas
   HOECK, Hendrik N.   Switzerland
— — —, Nature
   DALY, Ralph H.   Oman
— — & development projects
   STEPHENSON, Peter J.   Tanzania
— ecosystems
   RANJITSINH, M.K.   India, MP
— —, coastal
   BUSTAMANTE, Georgina   USA, FL
— —, mangrove
   QURESHI, Mohummad T.   Pakistan
— —, marine
   CH'NG, Kim Looi   Malaysia
— —, natural
   DUGAN, Patrik J.   Switzerland
— environment in China
   LUK, Shiu-hung   Canada, Ont.
— —, marine
   DESAI, Bhagirath N.   India, Kar.
— environmental impacts of mining operations &
    environmental conflict
   DEMPSEY, Stanley   USA, CO
— fires, vegetation
   STRONACH, Neil R.H.   Ireland
— fishery resources
   BUSTAMANTE, Georgina   USA, FL
— forests, Southeast Asian
   PAYNE, Junaidi   Malaysia
— —, tropical
   SAYER, Jeffrey A.   Indonesia
— fragmented landscapes
   BEETON, Robert J.S.   Australia, Qld
— heritage, natural
   USHER, Michael B.   UK, Scotland
— ground-water resources
   WEAVER, John M.C.   RSA
— humid tropics, natural resources in
   SMITH, Nigel J.H.   USA FL
— international waters
   BISWAS, Asit K.   UK, England
— islands, environmental
   DAHL, Arthur L.   Switzerland
— lake watersheds
   KIRA, Tatuo   Japan
— landscapes, fragmented
   BEETON, Robert J.S.   Australia, Qld
— mangrove
   BRIDGEWATER, Peter   Australia, ACT
— — ecosystems
   QURESHI, Mohummad T.   Pakistan
— marine ecosystems
   CH'NG, Kim-Looi   Malaysia
— — environment
   DESAI, Bhagirath N.   India, Kar.
— — turtles off coast of Brazil
   MARCOVALDI, Guy M.F.GUAGNI DEI
    Brazil, Bahia
   MARCOVALDI, Maria Â.GUAGNI DEI
    Brazil, Bahia

[management] of (contd)
— Mediterranean rangelands
PAPANASTASIS, Vasilios P.   Greece
— mining operations, environmental impacts of
DEMPSEY, Stanley   USA, CO
— national parks, see national parks' management
— — —, Africa
VERSCHUREN, Jacques C.F.   Belgium
— natural areas
HERRERO, Stephen M.   Canada, Alb.
— — ecosystems, integrated
DUGAN, Patrick J.   Switzerland
— — heritage
USHER, Michael B.   UK, Scotland
— — protected areas
DIAZ-MARTIN, Diego   Venezuela
— — reserves, State
ALLAVENA, Stefano   Italy
— — resources in developing countries using
  support of local people
MacFARLAND, Craig G.   USA, ID
— — — humid tropics
SMITH, Nigel J.H.   USA, FL
— Nature conservation areas
DALY, Ralph H.   Oman
— — Reserves
OLA-ADAMS, Bunyamin A.   Nigeria
— parks, National, see National parks' management
— plant invasions in protected areas
THEBAUD, Christophe   France
— populations, small, Africa
PRICE, Mark R. STANLEY   Kenya
— projects, conservation & development
STEPHENSON, Peter J.   Tanzania
— protected areas, see protected areas' management
— — —, natural
DIAZ-MARTIN, Diego   Venezuela
— — —, plant invasions in
THEBAUD, Christophe   France
— — wildlands
SEVILLA, Lorenzo B.CARDENAL
                              Nicaragua/Guatemala
— rangelands, Mediterranean
PAPANASTASIS, Vasilios P.   Greece
— research institutions
HOECK, Hendrik N.   Switzerland
— Reserves, Nature
OLA-ADAMS, Bunyamin A.   Nigeria
— —, State, natural
ALLAVENA, Stefano   Italy
— resource-use conflicts
SAUNIER, Richard E.   USA, MD
— resources, fishery
BUSTAMANTE, Georgina   USA, FL
— —, ground-water
WEAVER, John M.C.   RSA
— —, natural, in developing countries
MacFARLAND, Craig G.   USA, ID
— —, —,— humid tropics
SMITH, Nigel J.H.
— —, water
GOLUBEV, Genedy   Russia
— Rhinoceros, Black (Diceros bicornis)
TOIT, Raoul F.DU   Zimbabwe
— salt marsh
BRIDGEWATER, Peter   Australia, ACT
— Southeast Asian forests
PAYNE, Junaidi   Malaysia
— small biotic populations — Africa
PRICE, Mark R.STANLEY   Kenya

— soil
EKARATH, Raveendran   Bahrain
— State natural reserves
ALLAVENA, Stefano   Italy
— tropical forests
SAYER, Jeffrey A.   Indonesia
— — watersheds
PEREIRA, H.Charles   UK, England
— tropics, humid, natural resources in
SMITH, Nigel J.H.   USA, FL
— turtles, marine, off coast of Brazil
MARCOVALDI, Guy M.F.GUAGNI DEI
                                    Brazil, Bahia
MARCOVALDI, Maria Â.GUAGNI DEI
                                    Brazil, Bahia
— urban wildlife
ADAMS, Lowell W.   USA, WV
— vegetation fires
STRONACH, Neil R.H.   Ireland
— waste*
— water
*EKARATH, Raveendran   Bahrain
— — resources
GOLUBEV, Genady N.   Russia
— waters, international
BISWAS, Asit K.   UK, England
— watersheds, lake
KIRO, Tatuo   Japan
— wildlife
DALY, Ralph H.   Oman
— —, urban
ADAMS, Lowell W.   USA, WV
— wildlands, protected
SEVILLA, Lorenzo B.CARDENAL
                              Nicaragua/Guatemala
— —, tropical
PEREIRA, H.Charles   UK, England
— zones, buffer
BUDOWSKI, Gerardo   Costa Rica
— —, coastal
GOLDBERG, Edward D.   USA, CA
HALIM, Youssef   Egypt
managers, natural-resource, training & education of
FOX, Allan M.   Australia, NSW
mangrove afforestation
MOUDUD, Hasna J.   Bangladesh
—, conservation & management of
BRIDGEWATER, Peter   Australia, ACT
— ecology
AKSORNKOAE, Sanit   Thailand
POR, Francis D.   Israel
SAENGER, Peter   Australia, NSW
— ecosystems, management of
QURESHI, Mohummad T.   Pakistan
— oceanography
WOLANSKI, Eric J.   Australia, Qld
mangroves
KRISHNAMURTHY, Kothandaraman   India, TN
LAKSHMANAN, Kalimedu K.   India, TN
NAYAR, M.Param   India, Ker.
Mankind, environment and
WENSLEY, Penelope A.   Switzerland
Man's impact on flora & vegetation
KORNAŚ, Jan   Poland
— — — tropical marine environments
WOLANSKI, Eric J.   Australia, Qld
manure, use of, in organic farming
ROYES, Veronica I.J.   Jamaica

* See lower footnote on p. 409.

mapping activities
  WITT, Ronald G.   Switzerland
—, soil
  VÁRALLYAY, György   Hungary
—, vegetation
  BEARD, John S.   Australia, WA
  BENSON, John S.   Australia, NSW
  MEDWECKA-KORNAŚ, Anna M.   Poland
  MEHER-HOMJI, Vispy M.   India, TN
marble corrosion & protection
  SKOULIKIDIS, Theodore   Greece
marine Algae
  DAHL, Arthur L.   Switzerland
— Amphipoda, systematics–ecology of
  CROKER, Robert A.   USA, NH
— areas (tourism management etc.)
  CRAIK, Wendy   Australia, Qld
— biodiversity
  ANGEL, Martin V.   UK, England
— biogeochemistry
  KRASNOV, Eugene V.   Russia
— biology (systematics & ecology)
  MOORE, Peter G.   UK, Scotland
— chemistry (particularly micro-)
  GOLDBERG, Edward D.   USA, CA
— climate
  POLOVINA, Jeffrey J.   USA, HI
— conservation
  AUSSEDAT, Nicole M.   France/St Barthélemy
  EARLL, Robert C.   UK, England
  FOWLER, Sarah L.   UK, England
  GUBBAY, Susan   UK, England
  HOF, Tom VAN'T   Netherlands Antilles
  HOLTHUS, Paul F.   USA, HI
  MOORE, Peter G.   UK, Scotland
  WESCOTT, Geoffrey C.   Australia, Vic.
— — & protected areas
  SALM, Rodney V.   Kenya
— — through parks & preserves
  RANDALL, John 'Jack'   USA, HI
— debris
  RYAN, Peter G.   RSA
— development
  DOUMENGE, François   Monaco
— ecological areas & processes
  AGARDY, M.Tündi   USA, DC
— — knowledge, traditional
  JOHANNES, Robert E.   Australia, Tas.
— ecology
  CLARKE, Andrew   UK, England
  CROXALL, John P.   UK, England
  FOWLER, Sarah L.   UK, England
  GUBBAY, Susan   UK, England
  MAXIMOV, Victor N.   Russia
  McINTYRE, Alasdair D.   UK, Scotland
  MOORE, Peter G.   UK, Scotland
  POLUNIN, Nicholas V.C.   UK, England
  RAY, G.Carleton   USA, VA
— —, coastal
  CROKER, Robert A.   USA, NH
— — in coastal areas in Pacific & Asian regions*
— — of tropical islands
  *MARAGOS, James E.   USA, HI
— —, polar
  KELLERMANN, Adolf K.   Germany
— —, tropical
  AGARDY, M.Tündi   USA, DC

— ecosystems
  POLOVINA, Jeffrey J.   USA, HI
— —, conservation & management of
  CH'NG, Kim-Looi   Malaysia
— ecocomplexes, conservation of
  FITTER, Julian R.   UK, England
— —, sustainable resource management of
  BAINES, Graham B.K.   Australia, Qld
— environment
  MOUDUD, Hasna J.   Bangladesh
  RAMIREZ, Jose J.ESCOBAR   Colombia
  YOUSSEF, Abdullatif K.   Syria
— —, management of
  DESAI, Bhagirath N.   India, Goa
— —, tropical, Man's impact on
  WOLANSKI, Eric J.   Australia, Qld
— environmental management
  HOLTHUS, Paul F.   USA, HI
— — research
  PRAVDIĆ, Velimir   Croatia
— — science
  SU, Jilan   China
— fish, tropical — ecology, ecophysiology, & life-
  history
  BUSTAMANTE, Georgina   USA, FL
— geoecology
  KRASNOV, Eugene V.   Russia
— geology
  SIEBOLD, Eugen   Germany
— governance
  EICHBAUM, William M.   USA, DC
— mammals
  BONNER, W.Nigel   UK, England
  McCLOSKEY, Maxine E.   USA, MD
  RAY, G.Carleton   USA, VA
— —, ecology & conservation of
  LEATHERWOOD, James S.   USA, CA
— — (pinnipeds)
  REIJNDERS, Peter J.H.   The Netherlands
— — of southernmost South America
  GOODALL, R.Natalie PROSSER   Argentina
— —, taxonomy of
  BREE, Peter J.H.VAN   The Netherlands
— management
  JOHNSTON, Douglas M.   Canada, BC
  VERNAUDON, Yolande   Tahiti
— microbial ecology
  ROBARTS, Richard D.   Canada, Sask.
— molluscs, ecology & fisheries of
  RODHOUSE, Paul G.K.   UK, England
— natural product chemistry
  BAKER, Joseph 'Joe' T.   Australia, Qld
— ornithology
  HUNT, George L., Jr   USA, CA
— outfalls (and EIAs)
  DESAI, Bhagirath N.   India, Goa
— parks
  LAYDOO, Richard S.   Trinidad & Tobago
  WHITE, Susan L.   USA, FL
— —, islands in Asia–Pacific region
  HOLTHUS, Paul F.   USA, HI
— —, land–sea interactions in
  RAY, G.Carleton   USA, VA
— pelagic ecosystems of tropical & antarctic
  environments
  BRANDINI, Frederico   Brazil, Par.
— phytoplankton ecology
  SAKSHAUG, Egil   Norway
— policy
  FENGE, Terence A.E.   Canada, Ont.

* See lower footnote on p. 409.

marine (contd)
— pollution
  ABBASPOUR, Madjid   Iran
  BELLAMY, David J.   UK, England
  CLARK, Robert B.   UK, England
  COHEN, Yuval   Israel
  DESAI, Bhagirath N.   India, Goa
— — control
  TORTELL, Philip   NZ
— — management
  CH'NG, Kim-Looi   Malaysia
— population dynamics, tropical
  POLOVINA, Jeffrey J.   USA, HI
— protected area planning
  AGARDY, M.Tündi   USA, DC
— — areas
  EARLL, Robert C.   UK, England
  FOWLER, Sarah L.   UK, England
  GUBBAY, Susan   UK, England
  LAYDOO, Richard S.   Trinidad & Tobago
  WHITE, Susan L.   USA, FL
— — — esp.in the high seas
  McCLOSKEY, Maxine E.   USA, MD
— protection
  ALLOTTA, Gaetano   Italy
— resource conservation & management
  KENCHINGTON, Richard A.   Australia, ACT
— — economics
  TISDELL, Clement A.   Australia, Qld
— — management, natural
  SYBESMA, Jeffrey   Netherlands Antilles
— resources
  DESAI, Bhagirath N.   India, Goa
— sciences
  DESAI, Bhagirath N.   India, Goa
  HEMPEL, Gotthilf   Germany
  HOF, Tom van't   Netherlands Antilles
  KENCHINGTON, Richard A.   Australia, ACT
  MORTON, Brian   Hong Kong
  RODRIGUEZ, Andrés R.Rodriguez   Venezuela
— species — Nature conservation
  SMITH, Kevin D.   NZ
— systematics
  MOORE, Peter G.   UK, Scotland
— tenure, customary
  BAINES, Graham B.K.   Australia, Qld
— turtle conservation
  VENIZELOS, Lily T.   Greece/UK, England
— turtles
  FRAZIER, John G.   Mexico
— — & ecotourism
  HUGHES, George R.   RSA
— —, biology & conservation of
  BJORNDAL, Karen A.   USA, FL
— —, conservation & management of, off coast of
  Brazil
  MARCOVALDI, Guy M.F.Guagni dei
                     Brazil, Bahia
  MARCOVALDI, Maria Â.Guagni dei
                     Brazil, Bahia
— wildlife, conservation of
  MOYER, Jack T.   Japan
— zoogeography
  ANGEL, Martin V.   UK, England
maritime anthropology
  DIEGUES, Antonio C.S.   Brazil, SP
— plants, ecophysiology of
  MALLOCH, Andrew J.C.   UK, England
marketing, conservation
  BUTLER, Paul J.   St Lucia

marsh, salt-, ecology
  BOORMAN, Laurie A.   UK, England
Mascarene Island botany
  STRAHM, Wendy A.   Switzerland
mass communication (environment–development)
  BHATT, Dibya D.   Nepal
— -movements, hazards of
  VALDIYA, Khadga Singh   India, UP
masterplanning for protected areas, tourism, &
  conservation
  BARCSAY, László   Hungary
material well-being–life quality
  HAREIDE, Dag   Norway
materials, raw, for wood-based industries
  LAL, Piare   India, AP
mathematical statistics
  MacDONALD, Gordon J.F.   USA, CA
mathematics, applied
  NIKULIN, Valery A.   Russia
meadow plants, ecology of
  KULL, Kalevi   Estonia
meaning, ecology of
  STEWART, Philip J.   UK, England
measurement, noise
  SINGAL, Sagar P.   India, Delhi
—, quantitative, of comparative environmental risk
  CHADWICK, Michael J.   Sweden
measuring indicators & performance
  HARDI, Peter   Canada, Man.
meat production, wild animal utilization for
  WOODFORD, Michael H.   USA, DC
mechanisms of environmental degradation
  AICKIN, R.Malcolm   UK, England
—, evolutionary, of coral
  VERON, John E.N.   Australia, Qld
—, semiotic, of biodiversity
  KULL, Kalevi   Estonia
—, understanding, by which plant diversity is
  maintained in tropical forests
  ASHTON, Peter S.   USA, MA
media, mass, dissemination of information to, on
  ecological matters
  MARGARIS, Nickolas S.   Greece
—, popularization & teaching of biology &
  conservation via
  BOSWALL, Jeffery   UK, England
—, print, environmental awareness through
  SINGH, Hari B.   India, Delhi
medias, electronic & print, environmental
  communication through
  HAQUE, Mohammed A.   India, Har.
medical applications of solar energy
  SCHARMER, Klaus   Germany
— entomology
  CORBET, Philip S.   UK, Scotland
  LAIRD, Marshall   NZ
— —, research on
  DUFFY, David C.   USA, AK
— environmentology
  JOOSTING, Peter E.   The Netherlands
— parasitology
  LAIRD, Marshall   NZ
— surveillance & biomonitoring
  GOCHFELD, Michael   USA, NJ
— zoology
  BÜTTIKER, William   Switzerland
medicinal plants
  BYE, Robert   Mexico
  JAIN, Sudhanshu K.   India, UP
  SCHULTES, Richard E.   USA, MA

— —, taxonomy of
LAKSHMANAN, Kalimedu K.   India, TN
medicine, Aboriginal, esp.envenomation
COVACEVICH, Jeanette A.   Australia, Qld
—, environmental
GOCHFELD, Michael   USA, NJ
MALMBERG, Ole   Sweden
—, family
MALMBERG, Ole   Sweden
—, Nature (well-being)
MANSER, Bruno   Switzerland
—, occupational
GOCHFELD, Michael   USA, NJ
—, third-world & tropical
JUEL-JENSEN, Bent E.   UK, England
Mediterranean ecology
LOVRIC, Andrija Z.   Croatia
— ecosystems (& ecocomplexes)
MOREY, Miguel   Spain
— —, conservation biology of
PETRETTI, Francesco   Italy
— rangelands, ecology & management of
PAPANASTASIS, Vasilios P.   Greece
— region, forest & mountain ecology
HEISS, Gerhard   Germany
—, (sub-), zone: applied physical geography,
landscape ecology, & landscape planning, in
VOS, Willem   The Netherlands
megafauna, African & habitats, conservation of
TOIT, Raoul F.DU   Zimbabwe
meiobenthos
POR, Francis D.   Israel
Meliaceae, Malvales
CHEEK, Martin R   UK, England
mercury, methyl, effects of, on health
NUORTEVA, Pekka O.   Finland
—, neurobehavioural toxicology of
GOCHFELD, Michael   USA, NJ
mesoscale meteorology
PIELKE, Roger A.   USA, CO
metabolism, industrial
OPSCHOOR, Johannes B.   The Netherlands
metal corrosion & protection
SKOULIKIDIS, Theodore   Greece
—, heavy-, contamination in tropical ecosystems
LACERDA, Luis D.   Brazil, RJ
—, — -, pollution
REDAUD, M.Gladys BELANDRIA DE   Guadeloupe
metals, bioaccumulation of, in biota
NUORTEVA, Pekka O.   Finland
—, heavy-, environmental pollution by
HAQUE, Mohammed A.   India, Har.
—, long-range atmospheric transport of
STEINNES, Eiliv   Norway
—, role of, in forest decline
NUORTEVA, Pekka O.   Finland
meteorological satellites
KELLOGG, William W.   USA, CO
meteorology
DIAB, Roseanne D.   RSA
KESSLER, Edwin   USA, OK
OBASI, Godwin O.P.   Switzerland
—, air pollution
PATIL, Rashmi S.   India, Mah.
—, mesoscale
PIELKE, Roger A.   USA, CO
methodologies for strategic planning
SEVILLA, Lorenzo B.CARDENAL
    Nicaragua/Guatemala

—, valuation, for policy analysis
NORTON, Bryan G.   USA, GA
methodology of environmental & urban planning
KOZLOWSKI, Jerzy   Australia, Qld/Poland
—, monitoring
WEBER, Karl E.   Thailand
methods, evaluation, for selection of natural & semi-
natural forests
HEISS, Gerhard   Germany
—, geographical, re.national parks and protected
natural areas
ZABELINA, Natalia M.   Russia
—, non-lethal predator control
KRAUS, Daniel   Namibia/USA, CA
MARKER-KRAUS, Laurie   Namibia/USA, DC
—, research (& design)
WEBER, Karl E.   Thailand
—, serological & molecular, detection by
WHITE, James G.   UK, England
methyl mercury, effects of, on health
NUORTEVA, Pekka O.   Finland
metrology, acoustic
SINGAL, Sagar P.   India, Delhi
metropolitan environments, conservation in
SHAW, William W.   USA, AZ
Mexico, flora of Sierra Madre Occidental of
BYE, Robert   Mexico
—, Gulf of, research in physical oceanography in the,
and protection of its reefs & islands
CERDA, Alberto M.VAZQUEZ DE LA   Mexico
micro-level planning
RAI, Suresh Chand   India, Sikkim
microbial biogeochemical cycles in prairie saline
lakes & prairie wetlands
ROBARTS, Richard D.   Canada, Sask.
— ecology
FERMOR, Terence R.   UK, England
ROSSWALL, Thomas   Sweden
WHIPPS, John M.   UK, England
— —, freshwater & marine
ROBARTS, Richard D.   Canada, Sask.
microbiology
BURNEY, M.Ilyas   Pakistan
MARGULIS, Lynn   USA, MA
TURIAN, Gilbert   Switzerland
—, systematic
LAVRENTIADES, George   Greece
microclimates, urban
OKE, Timothy R.   Canada, BC
microclimatology
FRANGI, Jean-Pierre   France
microenterprises
VARUGHESE, George C.   India, Delhi
micrometeorology, plant environmental
JONES, Hamlyn G.   UK, England
microorganisms, antagonistic activity of
JARIWALA, Savitri   India, UP
—, physiology of
FEDOROV, Vadim D.   Russia
—, release of genetically-modified, into environment
WHIPPS, John M.   UK, England
micropropagation
MASCARENHAS, Anthony F.   India, Mah.
Middle East: protected areas' management,
sustainable development, & wildlife
conservation, in the
DEAN, Faisal   USA, VA
migration, crane (Gruidae)
LANDFRIED, Steven E.   USA, WI

migration (contd)
—, dynamics of, in developing countries
PICOUET, Michel R.   France
— of fishes
HASLER, Arthur D.   USA, WI
migrations
OUEDRAOGO, O.Dieudonné   Mali
migratory birds, Nearctic, ecology of
RAPPOLE, John H.   USA, VA
military activities, environmental security re.
WESTING, Arthur H.   USA, VT
mineral exploitation & development, liability for
SCANNELL, Yvonne   Ireland
— resources
ABU-RUBEIHA', Ali A.   Jordan
minimization, waste
JOHNSTON, Neil   UK, England
mining, coal, erosion control on lands affected by
HAIGH, Martin J.   UK, England
— lands, degraded, rehabilitation of
JUSOFF, Kamaruzaman   Malaysia
— operations, management of environmental impacts
of
DEMPSEY, Stanley   USA, CO
mire conservation
MASING, Viktor   Estonia
mitigation, environmental
TORTELL, Philip   NZ
mobilizing rural communities for better common
property management
QUTUB, Syed Ayub   Pakistan
modelling
BHARGAVA, Devendra S.   India, UP
HILL, Mark O.   UK, England
—, air pollution
PIELKE, Roger A.   USA, CO
SINGAL, Sagar P.   India, Delhi
—, — quality
PATIL, Rashmi S.   India, Mah.
—, community (meadow plants etc.)
KULL, Kalevi   Estonia
—, ecosystem
UNNI, N.V.MADHAVAN   India, AP
—, environmental
MOFFATT, Ian   UK, Scotland
UNNI, N.V.MADHAVAN   India, AP
—, simulation
NYE, Peter H.   UK, England
—, systems'
COHON, Jared L.   USA, CT
molecular biology
KENDREW, John C.   UK, England
MILIMO, Patrick B.W.   Kenya
— genetics
KING, Graham J.   UK, England
WOOD, David A.   UK, England
— plant pathology
BARBARA, Derek J.   UK, England
— — virology
CLARK Michael F.   UK, England
Mollusca, population genetics of
OWEN, Denis F.   UK, England
molluscs, opisthobranch, biology & taxonomy of
EDMUNDS, Malcolm   UK, England
monitoring
AL-MANDHRY, Abdullah R.   Oman
BUBLINEC, Eduard   Slovak Rep.
— activities
WITT, Ronald G.   Switzerland
—, air quality
PATIL, Rashmi S.   India, Mah.

— coastal zones
HALIM, Youssef   Egypt
—, coral-reef
LAYDOO, Richard S.   Trinidad & Tobago
—, ecological, of coastal ecosystems
MAXIMOV, Victor N.   Russia
—, environmental
DAHL, Arthur L.   Switzerland
KELLERMANN, Adolf K.   Germany
—, — pollution
EKARATH, Raveendran   Bahrain
— methodology
WEBER, Karl E.   Thailand
— (Nature conservation)
GOLDSMITH, Frank B.   UK, England
— of combustion-generated pollution
MATHUR, Harbansh B.   India, Delhi
— — environment, global
WALLÉN, Carl-Christian   Switzerland
— — environmental impacts on infrastructure
development
SARMIENTO, Fausto O.   USA, GA
— — forests
KIRBY, Keith J.   UK, England
— — resources
SHEPHERD, Alexander R.DAWSON UK, England
—, policy & strategy
ASFAW, Gedion   Ethiopia
—, pollution (hazardous waste)
SAXENA, Anil K.   India, Delhi
—, protected areas
MOURA, Robert MANNERS   Portugal
—, range
RECKERS, Ute   Kenya
—, water pollution
RAJAGOPAL, Rangaswamy   USA, OH
—, — quality
HAMMERTON, Desmond   UK, Scotland
monocotyledons with secondary growth, natural
history of
SIMPSON, Philip G.   NZ
monography, taxonomic
MATTHEW, Koyapillil M.   India, TN
montane tropics, domestication of tropical trees for
forestry/agroforestry in
LEAKEY, Richard R.B.   Kenya
monuments, corrosion & protection
SKOULIKIDIS, Theodore   Greece
mood, hormonal influences on
BARRY, James M.   Ireland
moorland (ecosystems' functioning & management)
MALTBY, Edward   UK, England
moral elements of human relationships
DRAKE, Christopher M.   UK, England
morphological studies, plant systematics and
PANDURANGAN, Alagramam G.   India, Ker.
morphology of Cladocera (Crustacea)
SMIRNOV, Nikolai N.   Russia
— — higher plants
TIKHOMIROV, Vadim N.   Russia
motives, non-tangible, role of, re.promoting
conservation behaviour
YOUNG, Raymond DE   USA, MI
moulds in stored grain systems
KENNEDY, Robert   UK, England
mountain areas (Africa, Himalaya, Andes)
MESSERLI, Bruno   Switzerland
— conservation
STONE, Peter B.   UK, England
— ecology
HEISS, Gerhard   Germany

— ecosystems
PITT, David — Switzerland
— environment
ROSSI, Patrizia — Italy
— environments, sustainable use of
HAMILTON, Lawrence S. — USA, VT
— peoples and their environments
PRICE, Martin F. — UK, England
— regions of India
MELKANIA, Niranjan P. — India, MP
— springs, hydrogeology of
VALDIYA, Khadga Singh — India, UP
mountainous zone, protection of (Romania)
CIOCHIA, Victor — Romania
mountains
TICKELL, Crispin C.C. — UK, England
WATSON, John R. — Australia, Vic.
—, desert, ecology of
GARDNER, Andrew S. — Oman
—, ecology of land-use in the
POORE, M.E.Duncan — UK, Scotland
—, tropical high, plant taxonomy & ecology of
HEDBERG, K.Olov — Sweden
movement, environmental
CHERKASOVA, Maria V. — Russia
OZA, Gunavant M. — India, Guj.
OZA, Premlata — India, Guj.
— of radionuclides
WARNER, Frederick — UK, England
—, solute, in soil
NYE, Peter H. — UK, England
multidimensional statistics in ecology
MAXIMOV, Victor N. — Russia
multidisciplinary environmental studies
GARRATT, Keith J. — NZ
— management analysis
KRISHNAYYA, Jaswant G. — India, Mah.
multiple-use reserves, design of
SEVILLA, Lorenzo B.Cardenal — Nicaragua/Guatemala
multi-strata agroforests, agroforestry systems esp.
LEAKEY, Richard R.B. — Kenya
multivariate analysis
HILL, Mark O. — UK, England
municipal environmental law or legislation, drafting of
OGUNDERE, Joseph D. — Nigeria
mushroom cultivation
NOBLE, Ralph — UK, England
— science
FERMOR, Terence R. — UK, England
mutagen testing
VIDA, Gábor — Hungary
mutagenesis, environmental
SHARMA, Archana — India, W.Bengal
mutation breeding
IGNACIMUTHU, Savarimuthu — India, TN
mycology
BAKER, F.W.G. ('Mike') — France
BARBARA, Derek J. — UK, England
PEGLER, David N. — UK, England
mycoparasitism
WHIPPS, John M. — UK, England
mycoplasma-like organisms
CLARK, Michael F. — UK, England
mycorrhizae
SMITS, Willie — Indonesia
mycorrhizas
LAST, Frederick T. — UK, Scotland
mycorrhization systems approaches — Sahara
DAMERDJI, M.Amine — Algeria

mycotoxin production in stored grain systems
KENNEDY, Robert — UK, England
Mygalomorphae in questions of conservation
RAVEN, Robert J. — Australia, Qld

narcotic drugs control
DURRANI, Shakil — Pakistan
National Conservation Strategies, field implementation
of (planning & implementation)
McEACHERN, John D. — Canada, Ont./Nepal
— ecological reform concept
KOSTENKO, Yuriy I. — Ukraine
— environmental action plans
BISWAS, Asit K. — UK, England
— — communication & education
HESSELINK, Frederik J. — The Netherlands
— — law
ABDELHADY, Abdelaziz — Egypt/Kuwait
CANO, Guillermo J. — Argentina
KOESTER, Veit — Denmark
— — — & policy
REHBINDER, Eckard — Germany
— Nature protection programme
KOSTENKO, Yuriy I. — Ukraine
— Park, Kiskunság, appropriate management of
TÖLGYESI, István — Hungary
— — management
GREGOIRE, Felix W. — Dominica
PEINE, John D. — USA, TN
WOODFORD, Michael H. — USA, DC
— — planning
CAMPBELL, Kenneth L.I. — UK, England
HEISS, Gerhard — Germany
WESCOTT, Geoffrey C. — Australia, Vic.
— — systems, selection & establishment of
SATTLER, Paul S. — Australia, Qld
— parks
DEARDEN, Philip — Canada, BC
EATON, Peter P. — Brunei
EIDSVIK, Harold K. — France
HOLOWESKO, Lynn P. — Bahamas
HSU, Kuo-Shih — Taiwan
KELLERMANN, Adolf K. — Germany
LUCAS, Percy H.C. ('Bing') — NZ
MOSLEY, John G. — Australia, Vic.
OKOŁÓW, Czeslaw — Poland
PRITCHARD, Paul C. — USA, DC
SAVAS, M.Nizam — Turkey
SEVILLA, Rogue — Ecuador
SHORES, John N. — USA, ME
ZABELINA, Natalia M. — Russia
ZHANG, Ping — China
— — & game reserves, planning & development of
SPINAGE, Clive A. — UK, England
— — — protected areas
HAYNES-SUTTON, Ann M. — Jamaica
SANCHEZ, Heliodoro — Colombia
SHAW, William W. — USA, AZ
VO, Quy — Vietnam
— — — —, establishment, management, &
assessment, of
LAMPREY, Hugh F. — UK, England
— —, Asian
HENNING, Daniel H. — USA, MT
— —, conservation of
CHALABI, Bouzid — Algeria

national parks (contd)
— —, creation & management of — Africa
VERSCHUREN, Jacques C.F.   Belgium
— —, — of
JIGJ, Sonom   Mongolia
— —, environmental management in
EATON, Peter P.   Brunei
— —, — planning in
DRDOŠ, Ján   Slovak Rep.
— —' management
CHALABI, Bouzid   Algeria
GREGOIRE, Felix W.   Dominica
JIGJ, Sonom   Mongolia
LEMONS, John D., Jr   USA, ME
MORELL, Merilio G.   Italy
NDUKU, Willie K.   Zimbabwe
PEINE, John D.   USA, TN
SEVILLA, Lorenzo B.Cardenal
    Nicaragua/Guatemala
WOODFORD, Michael H.   USA, DC
— —, planning & establishment of
LÖFGREN, Rolf   Sweden
— —, — of
SEVILLA, Lorenzo B.Cardenal
    Nicaragua/Guatemala
— — recreation
ARMSTRONG, Geoffrey J.   Australia, NSW
— —, research in
VERSHUREN, Jacques C.F.   Belgium
— —, systems planning for
HEISS, Gerhard   Germany
— science policy
KENDREW, John C.   UK, England
— self-sufficiency
MOSLEY, John G.   Australia, Vic.
— sovereignty–warfaring propensities–
    environmental degradation
SHAW, R.Paul   USA, DC
— wildlife, conservation of
JENKINS, David   UK, Scotland
nations, developing, conservation in
BURNETT, G.Wesley   USA, SC
native forests, ecologically-sustainable use of
KETO, Aila   Australia, Qld
— human societies, indigenous, Amazonian
    rain-forest particularly in Peru
CLOUDLSEY, Timothy   UK, Scotland
natural areas
LEBRETON, Philippe   France
— — of Greece, evaluation & selection of
MALAMIDIS, George   Greece
— —, planning & management of
HERRERO, Stephen M.   Canada, Alb.
— —, protected
ABDELHADY, Abdelaziz   Egypt/Kuwait
ZABELINA, Natalia M.   Russia
— —, —, design & survey of
WRIGHT, Shane D.T.   NZ
— compounds, bioorganic chemistry of
KUKHAR, Valery P.   Ukraine
— conservation
WANG, Xianpu   China
'—' disasters, Man-made
JOVANOVIĆ, Petar   Yugoslavia
— ecosystems, conservation of
CÂMARA, Ibsen de G.   Brazil RJ
— —, endangered
LAMPREY, Hugh F.   UK, England
— —, genetics of plant–pathogen interactions in
CRUTE, Ian   UK, England

— —, integrated management of
DUGAN, Patrick J.   Switzerland
— environment, behaviour of trace-elements in the
STEINNES, Eiliv   Norway
— —, conservation of the
MALAMIDIS, George   Greece
— environmental sciences, scientific research in
IZRAEL, Yuri   Russia
— fire regimes and plant responses (fire research)
GOOD, Roger B.   Australia, ACT
— forest conservation & ecology
DONOVAN, Richard Z.   USA, VT
— — management
SABOGAL, Cesar A.   Indonesia
— — vegetation, protection of
SJÖGREN, Erik A.   Sweden
— forests, evaluation methods for selection of
HEISS, Gerhard   Germany
— global ozone balance, perturbation of
JOHNSTON, Harold S.   USA, CA
— habitats, conservation of
FERNANDO, Ranjen L.   Sri Lanka
— hazard reduction
KNILL, John   UK, England
— hazards
FARAGÓ, Tibor   Hungary
HEATHCOTE, Ronald L.   Australia, SA
— heritage
CROFTS, Roger   UK, Scotland
— —, conservation of
CHERKASOVA, Maria V.   Russia
JAYAL, Nalni Dhar   India, UP
— —, management of the
USHER, Michael B.   UK, Scotland
— history
BHATT, Dibya D.   Nepal
BROWN, William Y.   USA, DC
BURTON, John A.   UK, England
COLLIE, John S.   Seychelles
LIONNET, Joseph F.G.   Seychelles
SIVADAS, Ponathil   India, Ker.
— — books, writer & illustrator of
FOX, Allan M.   Australia, NSW
— —, field [esp. desert]
MONOD, Théodore A.   France
— —, history of
BURTON, John A.   UK, England
— — of monocotyledons with secondary growth
SIMPSON, Philip G.   NZ
— impacts on coral-reef ecosystems
VANTIER, Lyndon M.de   Australia, Qld
— landscape conservation in spatial planning
STAWICKI, Henryk   Poland
— marine resource management
SYBESMA, Jeffrey   Netherlands Antilles
— park development
NOSEL, José   Martinique
— product chemistry, marine
BAKER, Joseph 'Joe' T.   Australia, Qld
— protected areas, planning & management of
DIAZ-MARTIN, Diego   Venezuela
— reserves, State, management of
ALLAVENA, Stefano   Italy
— resource, see also [natural] resources[†]
—* conservation
HAFIDI, Moulay El M.   Morocco
—* —, social dimensions of
HOUGH, John L.   USA, MD

[†] See upper footnote on p. 409.
* [natural] resource or resources

—* economics
BARBIER, Edward B. — UK, England
CAMINO, Ronnie DE — Costa Rica
—* law
BARAHONA-ISRAEL, Rodrigo — Costa Rica
—* management, *see* natural resources' management
—* —,application of social science to
BLAHNA, Dale J. — USA, UT
—* — for sustainable development
PANDURANGAN, Alagramam G. — India, Ker.
—* — in rural development
TOORNSTRA, Franke H. — The Netherlands
—* —, indigenous knowledge and
MARTIN, Vance G. — USA, CO
—* managers, training & education of
FOX, Allan M. — Australia, NSW
—* planning
ARIFFIN, Ishak BIN — Malaysia
—* policy
BARAHONA-ISRAEL, Rodrigo — Costa Rica
CAMINO, Ronnie DE — Costa Rica
—* surveys
NOUR, Hassan O.ABDEL — Sudan
—* use
DRAKE, Christopher M. — UK, England
MUMBA, Wanga — Zambia
—* —, sustained
OVINGTON, John D. — Australia, ACT
— resources, *see also* [natural] resource[†]
ABU-RUBEIHA, Ali A. — Jordan
ENGELMAN, Robert — USA, DC
KENNEDY, James J. — USA, UT
NILSSON, Sten — Austria
RANJITSINH, M.K. — India, MP
REIJNDERS, Lucas — The Netherlands
WASAWO, David P.S. — Kenya
—*' conservation
GHABBOUR, Samir I. — Egypt
HOLOWESKO, Lynn P. — Bahamas
LARSEN, Thor — Norway
THAPA, Gopal B. — Thailand
—*, exploitation of
NILSSON, Sten — Austria
—*, Himalayan, conservation of
PANDIT, Ashok K. — India, J&K
—*, humanity's use of
DRAKE, Christopher M. — UK, England
—* in developing countries, conservation &
management of, using support of local people
MacFARLAND, Craig G. — USA, ID
—* — humid tropics, conservation & management of
SMITH, Nigel J.H. — USA, FL
—* management
ABROL, Inder P. — India, Delhi
ANADA, Tiega — Niger
ARMIJOS, Mariano MONTAÑO — Ecuador
CAMINO, Ronnie DE — Costa Rica
CHRISTIAN, Colmore S. — Dominica
GREGOIRE, Felix W. — Dominica
JAMES, Brian — St Lucia
LARSEN, Thor — Norway
LUSCOMBE, Bruce A. — USA, NY
LUSIGI, Walter — USA, VA
MARTIN, Vance G. — USA, CO
MUMBA, Wanga — Zambia
OLOJEDE, Ayodele A. — Nigeria
OUEDRAOGO, O.Dieudonné — Mali
RYDÉN, Per A. — Switzerland

SINGH, Harjit — India, Delhi
ULLUWISHEWA, Rohana K. — Sri Lanka
USUKI, Mitsuo — Thailand
WHITEHOUSE, John F. — Australia, NSW
—* — and impact assessment
KEAGE, Peter L. — Australia, Vic.
—*, Nature &, conservation & sustainable use of
HOLDGATE, Martin W. — UK, England
—*, participatory management of
WHITE, Alan T. — Sri Lanka
—*' policy
CAMINO, Ronnie DE — Costa Rica
DAVIS, Bruce W. — Australia, Tas.
USUKI, Mitsuo — Thailand
—*' — analysis
MORELL, Merilio G. — Italy
—*, protection of
DELPIANO, José P.CASTRO — Uruguay
—*, surveys for assessment of
STANTON, James P. — Australia, Qld
—*, sustainable use of
HURNI, Hans — Switzerland
MARTINS, Edouardo DE SOUZA — Brazil
natural sciences
TURIAN, Gilbert — Switzerland
Nature, *see also* Nature conservation[†]
ATTENBOROUGH, David F. — UK, England
COLLIN, Gérard — France
MATTHIESSEN, Peter — USA, NY
— and Man
COLLIN, Gérard — France
— — —, integrating
TERRASSON, François — France
— & natural resources, conservation & sustainable
use of
HOLDGATE, Martin W. — UK, England
— awareness at home and in the tropics
KERN, Berndt — Sweden
KERN, Eha — Sweden
— (biodiversity) conservation
POORE, M.E.Duncan — UK, Scotland
— conservation
ABROUGUI, Mohamed A. — Tunisia
ALI, Abd 'El moneim' M. — Egypt
AMIRKHANOV, Amirkhan M. — Russia
ALON, Azaria — Israel
BARISHPOL, Ivan F. — Russia
BOARDMAN, Robert — Canada, NS
BOYD, John M. — UK, Scotland
BURNS, Carolyn W. — NZ
CARRILLO, Antonio MACHADO — Canary Islands
COCKLIN, Christopher R. — NZ
COHEN, Maria L. — Switzerland
DMITRIEVA, Vera A. — Russia
DORMAN, John — Australia, NSW
DUFF, Keith L. — UK, England
DUNNET, George M. — UK, Scotland
FONSECA, Ivan C.M.DA — Brazil, MG
FREIBERG, Horst — Germany
GATHORNE-HARDY, Gathorne — UK, England
HASSAN, Parvez — Pakistan
HSU, Kuo-Shih — Taiwan
HUNKELER, Pierre — Switzerland
KASSAS, Mohamed EL — Egypt
KETO, Aila — Australia, Qld
KHARIN, Nikolai — Turkmenistan
KOH, Tommy T.-B. — Singapore
KÜLVIK, Mart — Estonia

---

* [natural] resource or resources
[†] *See* upper footnote on p. 409.

* [natural] resource or resources
[†] *See* upper footnote on p. 409.

Nature conservation (contd)
KUPER, Jaap H. — The Netherlands
LACY, Terry P.DE — Australia, NSW
LANGSLOW, Derek R. — UK, England
LEE, Lawrence H.Y. — Hong Kong
LI, Wenhua — China
MARTINS, Edouardo DE SOUZA — Brazil, Bras.DF
MEULEN, Frank VAN DER — The Netherlands
MOSLEY, John G. — Australia, Vic.
NANAYAKKARA, Vitarana R. — Sri Lanka
NIEMITZ, Carsten — Germany
NUMATA, Makoto — Japan
OKOŁÓW, Czeslaw — Poland
PETERKEN, George F. — UK, England
PYROVETSI, Myrto D. — Greece
RANDALL, Roland E. — UK, England
RANJITSINH, M.K. — India, MP
REDAUD, Louis R.M. — Guadeloupe
SAVAS, M.Nizam — Turkey
SCHWARZSCHILD, 'B' Shimon — USA, CA
SEPP, Kalev — Estonia
SINNER, Jean-Marie — Luxemburg
SMITH, Kevin D. — NZ
SMITS, Willie — Indonesia
SOKOLOV, Vladimir — Russia
SPENCER, Jonathan W. — UK, England
SPRINGUEL, Irina — Egypt
STOIBER, Hans H. — Austria
SULTANA, Joe — Malta
UPRETI, Biswa N. — Nepal
URBAN, František — Czech Rep.
VALDRÈ, Giovanni — Italy
WAHLSTEDT, Jens — Sweden
WAYBURN, Edgar — USA, CA
WEBB, Leonard J. — Australia, Qld
YAZGAN, Nergis — Turkey
— —, administration of
WOLDHEK, Siegfried — The Netherlands
—* & local human population, economic relation
PRINS, Herbert H.T. — The Netherlands
—* areas, management of
DALY, Ralph H. — Oman
—* basic research
MEDWECKA-KORNAŚ, Anna M. — Poland
—*, cultural, social, & psychological, constructs &
strategies, for
MARTIN, Vance G. — USA, CO
—*, education & public awareness re.
HADDANE, Brahim — Morocco
—* esp.monitoring
GOLDSMITH, Frank B. — UK, England
—* in coastal zones
SALMAN, Albert H.P.M. — The Netherlands
—* — the humid neotropics
LYNCH, James R. — Costa Rica
—*, international
BREE, Peter J.H.VAN — The Netherlands
—* law, international & comparative
KLEMM, Cyrille DE — France
—* legislation
CHALABI, Bouzid — Algeria
VISSER, Nicolaas W. — Kenya
—* planning
GORIUP, Paul D. — UK, England
SATTLER, Paul S. — Australia, Qld
—* policy
USUKI, Mitsuo — Thailand
—*, urban
ARIFFIN, Ishak BIN — Malaysia

—, debt-for-, swaps
MORAN, Katy — USA, DC
— –economics–population model
JIGJ, Sonom — Mongolia
— education
PULINKUNNEL, P.S.Easa — India, Ker.
—, environmental impacts on
BARCSAY, László — Hungary
—, geoecological approach for studying human
influence on
JIGJ, Sonom — Mongolia
—, Man &
COLLIN, Gérard — France
— – — interrelationships, valuation for
MELKANIA, Niranjan P. — India, MP
— medicine (contemplation for well-being)
MANSER, Bruno — Switzerland
— of Maldives
DIDI, N.T.Hasen — Maldives
— park planning
ARIFFIN, Ishak BIN — Malaysia
— philosophy, behaviour & communication re.
TERRASSON, François — France
— protection
ANDRIAMAMPIANINA, Joseph — Madagascar
KACEM, Slaheddine BEL — Tunisia
LANG-BEERMAN, Ernst M. — Switzerland
SINNER, Jean-Marie — Luxemburg
TIKHOMIROV, Vadim N. — Russia
— —, Buddhism, role in
HENNING, Daniel H. — USA, MT
— — esp.protected areas and peatland protection
BOTCH, Marina S. — Russia
— — of the environment, particularly
McCLOSKEY, J.Michael — USA, DC
— — programme, national
KOSTENKO, Yuriy I. — Ukraine
— —, re.tourism
RICHEZ, Gérard — France
— — through biological control
CIOCHIA, Victor — Romania
—, psychology of
TERRASSON, François — France
—, religion and, advocacy of nexus between
SINGH, Karan — India, Delhi
— reserve interpretation & management
FOX, Allan M. — Australia, NSW
— reserves
HURNI, Hans — Switzerland
PIIROLA, Jouko — Finland
— —, establishment & management of
OLA-ADAMS, Bunyamin A. — Nigeria
— resource conservation
VERMA, Sewa R. — India, UP
— –society relationships
WOODGATE, Graham R. — UK, England
—, structure & function of
WOODWELL, George M. — USA, MA
navigation/transportation planning projects
BENNETT, Sara L. — Canada, BC
Nearctic migratory birds, ecology of
RAPPOLE, John H. — USA, VA
negotiations
KOH, Tommy T.-B. — Singapore
neotectonics
VALDIYA, Khadga Singh — India, UP
neotropical ecosystems, holistic analysis of
ADIS, Joaquim U. — Germany
— herpetology
GORZULA, Stefan — USA, TN

* [Nature] conservation

neotropics
    FORERO, Enrique   USA, NY
—, ecology of Nearctic migratory birds that winter in the
    RAPPOLE, John H.   USA, VA
—, humid, community development*
— Nature conservation in the
    *LYNCH, James R.   Costa Rica
nest-site selection
    GOCHFELD, Michael   USA, NJ
Network, EarthAction
    DUNLOP, Nicholas J.   Belgium/UK, England
networking
    FAZAL, Anwar   Malaysia
—, environmental NGO
    IYER, C.P.Jayalakshmi   India, Delhi
neurobehavioural toxicology of heavy-metals
    GOCHFELD, Michael   USA, NJ
neuroendocrinology, comparative*
neurosecretory systems
    *APPLIN, David G.   UK, England
Nevada, 'commons ecology' in
    WATSON, Charles St D., Jr   USA, NV
news reporting, environmental
    HARA, Takeshi   Japan
nexus between religion and Nature, advocacy of
    SINGH, Karan   India, Delhi
NGO(s), see nongovernmental organization(s)
Nigeria, environmental biology & plant taxonomy of
    KEAY, Ronald W.J.   UK, England
noise assessment
    KHAN, Niaz A.   UAE
— measurement
    SINGAL, Sagar P.   India, New Delhi
— pollution
    ALNASER, Waheeb E.   Bahrain
— programmes
    PRASAD, Basudeo   India, E.Punjab
—, transportation
    ABBASPOUR, Madjid   Iran
nomadism
    PRINS, Herbert H.T.   The Netherlands
nomads
    RECKERS, Ute   Kenya
non-chemical pest control
    ELLIS, Peter R.   UK, England
— -lethal predator control
    COPPINGER, Raymond   USA, MA
    KRAUS, Daniel   Namibia/USA, CA
    MARKER-KRAUS, Laurie   Namibia/USA, DC
— -proliferation, nuclear
    LOVINS, Amory B.   USA, CO
— -vocal mammalian communication
    BARRY, James M.   Ireland
nonequilibrium systems theory
    SLOCOMBE, D.Scott   Canada, Ont.
nongovernmental organization activities,
    environmental, coordination of
    HUBA, Mikuláš   Slovak Rep.
— organizations, activities of
    HUNKELER, Pierre   Switzerland
— —, coordinating
    OLI, Krishna P.   Nepal
— —' development
    LAMBERTINI, Marco   Italy
    SHORES, John N.   USA, ME
— —' — projects, EIA studies of
    UGWU, Christopher N.   Nigeria
— —, environmental
    GARDNER, Julia E.   Canada, BC

— —, —, networking & management
    IYER, C P Jayalakshmi   India, Delhi
— — in less-developed countries, environmental
    education in support of
    BOULTON, Mark N.   UK, England
Noosphere/Homosphere potentialities
    POLUNIN, Nicholas   Switzerland
North Cyprus, coastal vegetation of
    USLU, Turhan   Turkey
— Holarctic, biogeography of
    MARUSIK, Yuri M.   Russia
— –South issues
    MYERS, Norman   UK, England
    SCHRIJVER, Nico J.   The Netherlands
northern climates
    HARE, F.Kenneth   Canada, Ont.
— development, assessment of effects of, on wildlife
    & habitats,*
— herbivory
    *KLEIN, David R.   USA, AK
N/S/P/C biogeochemical cycles, see C/N/S/P
    biogeochemical cycles ...
nuclear accidents (international environmental law)
    LANG, Winfried   Switzerland
— bombs, perturbation of natural global ozone
    balance by
    JOHNSTON, Harold S.   USA, CA
— non-proliferation
    LOVINS, Amory B.   USA, CO
— power, safety of
    HARE, F.Kenneth   Canada, Ont.
— war, environmental consequences of
    EHRLICH, Anne H.   USA, CA
— waste, research & writing on
    LEMONS, John D., Jr   USA, ME
— weapons' tests
    WARNER, Frederick   UK, England
Nunavut, environmental management & planning in*
—, industrial development in
    *FENGE, Terence A.E.   Canada, Ont.
nurseries, tree, promotion of, in schools
    FITTER, Perin S.   Kenya
nutrient cycling
    OLA-ADAMS, Bunyamin A.   Nigeria
    SANCHEZ, Pedro A.   Kenya
— — (forest ecosystem studies)
    KIRA, Tatuo   Japan
— interactions, soil–plant
    NYE, Peter H.   UK, England
nutrition (and development issues)
    BISWAS, Margaret R.   UK, England
—, shrimp industry
    ARMIJOS, Mariano MONTAÑO   Ecuador
nutritional improvement (and) waste treatment,
    fermentation in
    STANTON, W.Robert   UK, England
NWT, Yukon, environmental planning &
    management in*
—, —, industrial development in
    *FENGE, Terence A.E.   Canada, Ont.

oases, polar, ecosystems of
    SVOBODA, Josef   Canada, Ont.
—, traditional irrigation in, and their rehabilitation
    DAMERDJI, M.Amine   Algeria

obligations to future generations
  NORTON, Bryan G. — USA, GA
occupational health
  KASHYAP, Kant — India, Guj.
— medicine
  GOCHFELD, Michael — USA, NJ
ocean engineering
  ABBASPOUR, Madjid — Iran
— geology
  LITVIN, Vladimir M. — Russia
— legislation
  PELL, Claiborne — USA, DC
— policy
  DESAI, Bhagirath N. — India, Goa
— research, arctic & antarctic ice and
  WADHAMS, Peter — UK, England
—, southern, Cephalopoda
  RODHOUSE, Paul G.K. — UK, England
— toxicology
  PAYNE, Roger S. — UK, England
— treaties
  PELL, Claiborne — USA, DC
oceanic communities, ecology of deep
  ANGEL, Martin V. — UK, England
— islands
  DICKSON, James H. — UK, Scotland
— —, biology & conservation of
  RYAN, Peter G. — RSA
— —, ecology of
  HOLDGATE, Martin W. — UK, England
oceanographic sampling
  ORHUN-HEWSON, Canan — USA, MA
oceanography, biological
  HUNT, George L., Jr — USA, CA
  KRISHNAMURTHY, Kothandaraman — India, TN
  TURNER, R.Eugene — USA, LA
—, coastal
  SU, Jilan — China
  WOLANSKI, Eric J. — Australia, Qld
—, coral-reef & mangrove
  WOLANSKI, Eric J. — Australia, Qld
—, physical, research in, in the Gulf of Mexico
  CERDA, Alberto M.VAZQUEZ DE LA — Mexico
oceanology, scientific research in
  IZRAEL, Yuri — Russia
oceans, legislation & treaties
  PELL, Claiborne — USA, DC
Odonata
  DUMONT, Henri J. — Belgium
—, conservation of, research & policy-making in
  MOORE, Norman W. — UK, England
odour, prevention of, from composting
  NOBLE, Ralph — UK, England
oil exploration, economic impacts of
  McEACHERN, John D. — Canada, Ont./Nepal
— hydrogeology
  VORONOV, Arkady N. — Russia
oils, vegetable, engine fuels from
  SCHARMER, Klaus — Germany
old-growth forest wildlife ecology
  BUTLER, James 'Jim' R. — Canada, Alb.
— - — forests in British Columbia
  HUSBAND, Vicky — Canada, BC
olfactory landscape imprinting (migration of fishes)
  HASLER, Arthur D. — USA, WI
Oman, captive breeding & conservation in the wild of
  endangered species in*
—, reintroduction of Arabian Oryx to the wild in
  *DALY, Ralph H. — Oman

* See lower footnote on p. 409.

open-space systems, conservation & development of
  JACOBS, Peter D.A. — Canada, Que.
operational hydrology
  OBASI, Godwin O.P. — Switzerland
opisthobranch molluscs, biology & taxonomy of
  EDMUNDS, Malcolm — UK, England
Orangutans
  SMITS, Willie — Indonesia
orchids, taxonomy of
  JAIN, Sudhanshu K. — India, UP
organic agriculture
  LOENING, Ulrich E. — UK, Scotland
— — & horticulture
  HARRIS, Philip J.C. — UK, England
— chemistry (marine etc. aspects)
  YOUSSEF, Abdullatif K. — Syria
— farming
  ARAUJO, Joaquín — Spain
  ISMAIL, Sultan A. — India, TN
  KHANDELWAL, Kailash C. — India, Raj.
— — (natural pesticides & manure)
  ROYES, Veronica I.J. — Jamaica
— production control
  AUGSTBURGER, Franz — Bolivia
— waste recycling using local species of earthworms
  ISMAIL, Sultan A. — India, TN
organisms, aquatic, physiology of
  HASLER, Arthur D. — USA, WI
—, colonizing
  THEBAUD, Christophe — France
—, mycoplasma-like
  CLARK, Michael F. — UK, England
organization activities, environmental
  nongovernmental, coordination of
  HUBA, Mikuláš — Slovak Rep.
— -building, environmental
  GALLON, Gary T. — Canada, Ont.
— of interdisciplinary information
  JUDGE, Anthony J. — Germany
— — world bird conservation movement
  GAMMELL, Alistair — UK, England
—, protected areas'
  LAMBERTINI, Marco — Italy
—, research
  PEREIRA, H.Charles — UK, England
organizational structures (conservation
  administration)
  BOYLAND, Desmond E. — Australia, Qld
organizations, conservation, voluntary involvement in
  ARMSTRONG, Geoffrey J. — Australia, NSW
—, governmental & nongovernmental, coordinating
  OLI, Krishna P. — Nepal
—, nongovernmental, see nongovernmental
  organizations
orientation, role of sense of smell in (migration of
  fishes)
  HASLER, Arthur D. — USA, WI
origins, crop, and biogeography
  CLEMENT, Charles R. — Brazil
—, plant (alpine ecology)
  GOOD, Roger B. — Australia, ACT
ornamental plants
  BYE, Robert — Mexico
ornithological research
  GORIUP, Paul D. — UK, England
ornithology
  BAKER, F.W.G. ('Mike') — France
  CIOCHIA, Victor — Romania
  HOFFMANN, Luc — France
  IMBODEN, Christoph N. — UK, England
  LANG-BEERMAN, Ernst M. — Switzerland

LANGSLOW, Derek R. — UK, England
MacKINNON, John R. — Hong Kong
NORDERHAUG, Magnar — Norway
PETRETTI, Francesco — Italy
PYROVETSI, Myrto D. — Greece
RYAN, Peter G. — RSA
SULTANA, Joe — Malta
UDVARDY, Miklos D.F. — USA, CA
VO, Quy — Vietnam
—, African
WILSON, Richard T. — UK, England
—, — & Arabian
FRY, Charles H. — Oman
—, amateur
WAHLSTEDT, Jens — Sweden
—, applied
PINOWSKI, Jan K. — Poland
—: bustards, cranes, storks, and francolins
RAHMANI, Asad Rafi — India, UP
—, field research in
ORHUN-HEWSON, Canan — USA, MA
—, marine
HUNT, George L., Jr — USA, CA
—, research & teaching
DHINDSA, Manjit S. — India, Mah.
Oryx, Arabian, reintroduction of, to the wild in Oman
DALY, Ralph H. — Oman
ostracods, taxonomy of pelagic
ANGEL, Martin V. — UK, England
Otididae, bustards
GORIUP, Paul D. — UK, England
Otter conservation
BARRY, James M. — Ireland
outdoor recreation
KASSIOUMIS, Konstantinos — Greece
outdoors, conservation
THOMAS, Anamaria A.DE — USA, FL
outfalls, marine
DESAI, Bhagirath N. — India, Kar.
—, submarine
AWAD, Adel R. — Syria
oxygen sag analysis, dissolved
BHARGAVA, Devendra S. — India, UP
ozone
DIAB, Roseanne D. — RSA
ROWLAND, F.Sherwood — USA, CA
— balance, natural global
JOHNSTON, Harold S. — USA, CA
— depletion
JOVANOVIĆ, Petar — Yugoslavia
— layer depletion
OBASI, Godwin O.P. — Switzerland
— —, protection of (international environmental
law)
LANG, Winfried — Switzerland
—, stratospheric
SINGER, S.Fred — USA, VA
— studies
BOJKOV, Rumen D. — Switzerland

Pacific–Asia region
JOHNSTON, Douglas M. — Canada, BC
— – – —, ecological planning in the
SHAPIRO, Harvey A. — Japan
—, Indo-, reef fishes, classification of
RANDALL, John 'Jack' — USA, HI

— region, marine ecology in coastal areas in
MARAGOS, James E. — USA, HI
—, South, region, environmental management in
EATON, Peter P. — Brunei
— salmon biology
COUTANT, Charles C. — USA, TN
painting, wildlife
WALKER, Clive H. — RSA
paintings, urban landscape
KELCEY, John G. — UK, England
palaeobiocenoses
LOVRIC, Andrija Z. — Croatia
palaeoecology
PUNNING, Jaan-Mati — Estonia
— of coral reefs
KRASNOV, Eugene V. — Russia
—, Quaternary
SOLOMON, Allen M. — USA, OR
—, —, research in
YOUNG, Steven B. — USA, VT
palaeogeography
PUNNING, Jann-Mati — Estonia
palaeohistory
TICKELL, Crispin C.C. — UK, England
palaeontology
IBARRA, Jorge A. — Guatemala
—, Jurassic, research into
DUFF, Keith L. — UK, England
palm taxonomy
BALICK, Michael J. — USA, NY
Palni Hills, conservation on
MATTHEW, Koyapillil — India, TN
palynology
CRAMPTON, Colin B. — Canada, BC
FAEGRI, Knut — Norway
Papua New Guinea
DICKSON, James H. — UK, Scotland
parasites, epidemiology of
THOMAS, John D. — UK, England
parasitology, medical
LAIRD, Marshall — NZ
park development, natural
NOSEL, José — Martinique
— interpretation & management
FOX, Allan M. — Australia, NSW
—, Kiskunság National, appropriate management of
TÖLGYESI, István — Hungary
— management, national, see national parks'
management
—, national, planning
CAMPBELL, Kenneth L.I. — UK, England
HEISS, Gerhard — Germany
WESCOTT, Geoffrey C. — Australia, Vic.
—, Nature, planning
ARIFFIN, Ishak BIN — Malaysia
— personnel, training of
MENDEZ, Jesus M.DELGADO — Brazil
— planning
CLOUTIER, Antoine — Canada, Que.
WALT, Pieter T.VAN DER — RSA
— — & management
BURNETT, G.Wesley — USA, SC
— systems, selection & establishment of
SATTLER, Paul S. — Australia, Qld
parks
LACY, Terry P.DE — Australia, NSW
MARSH, John — Canada, Ont.
NELSON, J.Gordon — Canada, Ont.
NEPAL, Sanjay K. — Switzerland
SERAFIN, Rafal K. — Poland
VERNAUDON, Yolande — Tahiti
WAYBURN, Edgar — USA, CA

parks (contd)
— and preserves, marine conservation through
RANDALL, John 'Jack'   USA, HI
—, Asian national
HENNING, Daniel H.   USA, MT
—, conservation of
WAYBURN, Edgar   USA, CA
—' education
LACY, Terry P.DE   Australia, NSW
—' management
BURNETT, G.Wesley   USA, SC
BUTLER, James 'Jim' R.   Canada, Alb.
FOX, Allan M.   Australia, NSW
N'SOSSO, Dominique   Congo
THORSELL, James W.   Switzerland
—, marine
LAYDOO, Richard S.   Trinidad & Tobago
WHITE, Susan L.   USA, FL
—, —, islands in Asian–Pacific region
HOLTHUS, Paul F.   USA, HI
—, —, land–sea interactions in
RAY, G.Carleton   USA, VA
—, national, see national parks
—, —, & protected areas
HAYNES-SUTTON, Ann M.   Jamaica
SANCHEZ, Heliodoro   Colombia
SHAW, William W.   USA, AZ
VO, Quy   Vietnam
—, —, creation & management of — Africa
VERSCHUREN, Jacques C.F.   Belgium
—, —, environmental management in
EATON, Peter P.   Brunei
—, —, — planning in
DRDOŠ, Ján   Slovak Rep.
—', —, establishment, management, and assessment
LAMPREY, Hugh F.   UK, England
—', —, management, see national parks'
management
—, —, planning & development of
SPINAGE, Clive A.   UK, England
—, —, — — establishment of
LÖFGREN, Rolf   Sweden
—, —, — of
SEVILLA, Lorenzo B.CARDENAL
                                    Nicaragua/Guatemala
—, —, recreation (in)
ARMSTRONG, Geoffrey J.   Australia, NSW
—, —, research in
VERSCHUREN, Jacques C.F.   Belgium
—, —, systems planning for
HEISS, Gerhard   Germany
—, research in
PEINE, John D.   USA, TN
—, teaching & research in
BUTLER, James 'Jim' R.   Canada, Alb.
Parliamentary law
BURHENNE, Wolfgang   Germany
participation, community
SHORES, John N.   USA, ME
—, public, in environmental decision-making
GARDNER, Julia E.   Canada, BC
—, —, — sustainable development & environmental
issues
KAKABADSE, Yolanda   Ecuador
participatory management of natural resources
WHITE, Alan T.   Sri Lanka
partnerships with civil society organizations
NOVOA, Laura   Chile
Passer spp., ecology of
PINOWSKI, Jan K.   Poland

pastoral ecology
PRINS, Herbert H.T.   The Netherlands
pathogen–host interactions
PINK, David A.C.   UK, England
— –plant interactions, genetics of, in crop & natural
ecosystems
CRUTE, Ian   UK, England
pathogens, foliar fungal
KENNEDY, Robert   UK, England
—, plant, epidemiology of soil-borne
ENTWISTLE, Andrew R.   UK, England
—, —, soil-borne
WHITE, James G.   UK, England
pathology, forest
BOA, Eric   UK, England
—, plant
CLARK, Michael F.   UK, England
ENTWISTLE, Andrew R.   UK, England
WALSH, John A.   UK, England
—, —, molecular
BARBARA, Derek J.   UK, England
P/C/N/S biogeochemical cycles, see C/N/S/P
biogeochemical cycles ...
peace education
DUFOUR, Jules   Canada, Que.
— research
SCHRIJVER, Nico J.   The Netherlands
pears, genetics & breeding of
ALSTON, Frank H.   UK, England
peasant societies, ecological relationships of
GADE, Daniel W.   USA, VT
peatland protection
BOTCH, Marina S.   Russia
— science (telmatology)
MASING, Viktor   Estonia
peatlands
MALTBY, Edward   UK, England
pedology (incl.impact of ancient agriculture on soils)
DAVIDSON, Donald A.   UK, Scotland
pelagic ecosystems, marine, of tropical & antarctic
environments
BRANDINI, Frederico   Brazil, Par.
— ostracods, taxonomy of
ANGEL, Martin V.   UK, England
Penguins, antarctic
DIAZ, José VALENCIA   Chile
people [needs and effects etc.of]
KELCEY, John G.   UK, England
—, effects of, on coastal birds
BURGER, Joanna   USA, NJ
—, feeding 6,000 m.
SCHARMER, Klaus   Germany
—, local, conservation & management of natural
resources in developing countries, using
support of
MACFARLAND, Craig G.   USA, ID
peoples, Aboriginal: rights, interests, & self-
government
FENGE, Terence A.E.   Canada, Ont.
—, circumpolar
ROWLEY, Graham W.   Canada, Ont.
—, indigenous
RUIZ-MURRIETA, Julio   Switzerland
VARIAVA, Dilnavaz   India, Mah.
—, —, protection of
HANBURY-TENISON, A.Robin   UK, England
—, mountain, and their environments
PRICE, Martin F.   UK, England
perception, environmental
HEATHCOTE, Ronald L.   Australia, SA

performance, measuring
  HARDI, Peter   Canada, Man.
permaculture design & teaching
  EVERETT, Rodney D.   UK, England
permafrost
  CRAMPTON, Colin B.   Canada, BC
perturbation of natural global ozone balance by
    human activities, nuclear bombs, &
    stratospheric aircraft
  JOHNSTON, Harold S.   USA, CA
Peru, Amazonian rainforest particularly
  CLOUDSLEY, Timothy   UK, Scotland
pest control, biological
  FISCHER, Gert R.   Brazil, SC
— —, non-chemical & integrated
  ELLIS, Peter R.   UK, England
— management, ecological
  TSHERNYSHEV, Wladimir B.   Russia
— — strategies, integrated
  JACOBSON, Robert J.   UK, England
— resistance
  DARBY, Peter   UK, England
— —, introduction of
  ALSTON, Frank H.   UK, England
— -resistant varieties of horticultural crops, breeding
  ELLIS, Peter R.   UK, England
pesticide application
  CROSS, Jeremy V.   UK, England
— technology
  KASHYAP, Kant   India, Guj.
— usage, reductions in
  RICHARDSON, Paul N.   UK, England
pesticides
  ALI, Abd 'El moneim' M.   Egypt
—, natural, use of, in organic farming
  ROYES, Veronica I.J.   Jamaica
pests, animal, biological control of
  FENNER, Frank   Australia, ACT
—, vertebrate
  ALI, Abd 'El moneim' M.   Egypt
petaloid monocotyledons — plant systematics
  STIRTON, Charles H.   UK, England
petrels
  BOURNE, William R.P.   UK, Scotland
petroleum industry, environmental implications of the
  WILLUMS, Jan-Olaf   France
phanerogams
  KORNAŚ, Jan   Poland
phenology, plant
  WIELGOLASKI, Frans-Emil   Norway
phenomena, atmospheric–climatic
  KONDRATYEV, Kirill Y.   Russia
philanthropy
  BLOOMFIELD, Michael I.   Canada, BC
—, environmental
  McCARTHY, Gerald P.   USA, VA
Philippines, flora of the
  MADULID, Domingo   Philippines
philosophies, comparative, of conservation
  BURNETT, G.Wesley   USA, SC
philosophy, environmental
  GANDY, Matthew   UK, England
—, —, international
  JOHNSON, David W.   USA, CA
—, —, through teaching, art, & environment
  GITTINS, John W.E.H.   UK, England
—, green, history of
  KULL, Kalevi   Estonia
— international environmental
  JOHNSON, David W.   USA, CA

—, Nature, behaviour and communication about
  TERRASSON, François   France
— of environmental conservation
  POORE, M.E.Duncan   UK, Scotland
— — environmentally-sound development
  TOLBA, Mostafa K.   Egypt
— — global ecology
  GRINEVALD, Jacques   Switzerland
—, study of comparative religions and
  SINGH, Karan   India, Delhi
photography, environmental
  EDWARDS, Mark   UK, England
  KETCHUM, Robert G.   USA, CA
  LOENING, Ulrich E.   UK, Scotland
—, landscape
  LOENING, Ulrich E.   UK, Scotland
—, Nature conservation
  ALON, Azaria   Israel
—, wildlife
  APPLIN, David G.   UK, England
phylogenetic systematics
  PIANKA, Eric R.   USA, TX
phylogeny of scorpions
  LOURENÇO, Wilson R.   France
— — Solonaceae
  HAWKES, John G.   UK, England
—, spiders re.
  RAVEN, Robert J.   Australia, Qld
physical environment protection & improvement
  SOTIRIADOU, Victoria   Greece
— geography, applied in (sub-) Mediterranean zone
  VOS, Willem   The Netherlands
— oceanography, research in, in the Gulf of Mexico
  CERDA, Alberto M.VAZQUEZ DE LA   Mexico
physics (of) energy technology & strategies
  GOLDEMBERG, José   Brazil, SP
—, applied, research in, re.recovery of refuse and
    underutilized resources
  ARIAS-CHAVEZ, Jesus   Mexico
—, atmospheric
  KELLOGG, William W.   USA, CO
  SINGER, S.Fred   USA, VA
—, environmental
  ALNASER, Waheeb E.   Bahrain
  FRANGI, Jean-Pierre   France
— of the atmosphere, scientific reserach in
  IZRAEL, Yuri   Russia
—, soil
  DAMERDJI, M.Amine   Algeria
  VÁRALLYAY, György   Hungary
—, upper atmosphere
  RADICELLA, Sandro M.   Italy
physiological ecology
  GATES, David M.   USA, MI
physiology & environment of plants
  KEFELI, Valentin   Russia
—, environmental, of mammals
  PFEIFFER, Egbert W.   USA, MT
— of aquatic organisms
  HASLER, Arthur D.   USA, WI
— — Basidiomycete Fungi
  WOOD, David A.   UK, England
— — microorganisms
  FEDOROV, Vadim D.   Russia
—, plant
  MANSFIELD, Terence A.   UK, England
  MILIMO, Patrick B.W.   Kenya
—, — environmental
  JONES, Hamlyn G.   UK, England
—, sensory, elasmobranch
  GRUBER, Samuel H.   USA, FL

physiology (contd)
—, tree
  DICK, Janet M.   UK, Scotland
phytochemistry
  WEBB, Leonard J.   Australia, Qld
phytogeography
  NAYAR, M.Param   India, Ker.
  WHITMORE, Timothy C.   UK, England
— of gymnosperms & pteridophytes
  PAGE, Christopher N.   UK, Scotland
phytoplankton ecology
  FOGG, Gordon E.   UK, Wales
— —, marine
  SAKSHAUG, Egil   Norway
phytosociology
  MALLOCH, Andrew J.C.   UK, England
— of Cape plants & vegetation
  BOUCHER, Charles   RSA
pinnepeds, biology of
  BOYD, John M.   UK, Scotland
— (marine mammals)
  REIJNDERS, Peter J.H.   The Netherlands
pipelines, economic impacts of
  McEACHERN, John D.   Canada, Ont./Nepal
planetary boundary layer
  FRANGI, Jean-Pierre   France
— ecology
  VALLENTYNE, John R.   Canada, Ont.
planification of protected areas
  PONCIANO, Ismael   Guatemala
plankton
  KRISHNAMURTHY, Kothandaraman   India, TN
— ecology
  PANDIT, Ashok K.   India, J&K
— tows
  ORHUN-HEWSON, Canan   USA, MA
planning, see also [planning] of[†]
  FRIEDMAN, Yona   France
  SAMAD, Syed A.   Malaysia
—, biodiversity
  WOODFORD, Michael H.   USA, DC
—, catchment, water quality and
  CULLEN, Peter W.   Australia, ACT
—, city, in the Arab World
  HAMED, Safei EL-DEEN   USA, MD
—, coastal
  DIEGUES, Antonio C.S.   Brazil, SP
—, — area
  SHAPIRO, Harvey A.   Japan
—, community involvement in
  CRAIK, Wendy   Australia, Qld
—, conservation
  SULAYEM, Mohammad S.A.   Saudi Arabia
—, —, in tropical coastal environments
  DAVIE, James D.S.   Australia, Qld
—, — management
  STEPHENSON, Peter J.   Tanzania
—, — resource
  HIBBERD, John K.   Australia, ACT
—, development
  POTTER, Louis   BVI
—, —, forest sector
  LAL, Jugal B.   India, MP
—, ecological, & politics
  MIKLÓS, Ladislav   Slovak Rep.
—, —, in the Asia–Pacific region
  SHAPIRO, Harvey A.   Japan
— environment–tourism
  CROSBY, Arturo   Spain

—, environmental, see environmental planning
—, — assessment
  JACOBS, Peter D.A.   Canada, Que.
—, —, in Arctic circumpolar world
  FENGE, Terence A.E.   Canada, Ont.
—, —, — national parks
  DRDOŠ, Ján   Slovak Rep.
—, —, — Nunavut & Yukon, NWT
  FENGE, Terence A.E.   Canada, Ont.
—, — management
  SAUNIER, Richard E.   USA, MD
—, —, methodology of
  KOZLOWSKI, Jerzy   Australia, Qld/Poland
—, — research
  OPSCHOOR, Johannes B.   The Netherlands
—, —, urban
  ANI, Olufemi   Nigeria
—, forest conservation
  WIJESINGHE, Leslie   Sri Lanka
—, — resource
  KUMAR, Prem   Canada, Alb.
—, — sector development
  LAL, Jugal B.   India, MP
—, geographical methods of
  ZABELINA, Natalia M.   Russia
— issues, application of social science to
  BLAHNA, Dale J.   USA, UT
—, land-use
  GOOD, Roger B.   Australia, ACT
  LaBASTILLE, Anne   USA, NY
  MAKHDOUM, Majid F.   Iran
  OSEMEOBO, Gbadebo J.   Nigeria
  SEVILLA, Lorenzo B.CARDENAL
                            Nicaragua/Guatemala
  TOIT, Raoul F.DU   Zimbabwe
—, — - —, seismic zonation in
  AWAD, Adel R.   Syria
—, landscape
  HABER, Wolfgang   Germany
  HUBA, Mikuláš   Slovak Rep.
  SERAFIN, Rafal K.   Poland
  WAGER, Jonathan F.   UK, England
—, —, natural & cultural, conservation in spatial
  STAWICKI, Henryk   Poland
—, law (environmental)
  GOULDMAN, M.Dennis   Israel
—, marine protected area
  AGARDY, M.Tündi   USA, DC
—, micro-level
  RAI, Suresh Chand   India, Sikkim
—, national parks'
  CAMPBELL, Kenneth L.I.   UK, England
  HEISS, Gerhard   Germany
  WESCOTT, Geoffrey C.   Australia, Vic.
—, natural resource
  ARIFFIN, Ishak BIN   Malaysia
—, Nature conservation
  GORIUP, Paul D.   UK, England
  SATTLER, Paul S.   Australia, Qld
—, — park
  ARIFFIN, Ishak BIN   Malaysia
—, park
  ARIFFIN, Ishak BIN   Malaysia
  BURNETT, G.Wesley   USA, SC
  CLOUTIER, Antoine   Canada, Que.
  WALT, Pieter T.VAN DER   RSA
— projects, transportation/navigation &
     sectoral/regional
  BENNETT, Sara L.   Canada, BC
—, protected areas', see protected areas' planning

† See upper footnote on p. 409.

—, — —, national
CAMPBELL, Kenneth L.I. — UK, England
HEISS, Gerhard — Germany
WESCOTT, Geoffrey C. — Australia, Vic.
—, regional
AWAD, Adel R. — Syria
BENNETT, Sara L. — Canada, BC
HÜLSHOFF, Bernd VON DROSTE ZU — France
SERAFIN, Rafal K. — Poland
—, — environmental
NEPAL, Sanjay K. — Switzerland
—, — — management
THAPA, Gopal B. — Thailand
—, research
OPSCHOOR, Johannes B. — The Netherlands
—, resources'
MENDEZ, Jesus M.DELGADO — Brazil
OHN — Myanmar
SHORES, John N. — USA, ME
—, rural development
NEPAL, Sanjay K. — Switzerland
—, — energy
KHANDELWAL, Kailash C. — India, Raj.
—, sectoral
BENNETT, Sara L. — Canada, BC
—, spatial, natural & cultural landscape conservation
in
STAWICKI, Henryk — Poland
—, strategic
BARNEY, Gerald O. — USA
—, —, for sustainable development
MORELL, Merilio G. — Italy
—, sustainable development, GIS applied to
KRISHNAYYA, Jaswant G. — India, Mah.
—, systems for national parks & protected areas
HEISS, Gerhard — Germany
—, tourism–environment
CROSBY, Arturo — Spain
—, town (environmental)
LOVEJOY, Derek — UK, England
—, urban (and regional)
AWAD, Adel — Syria
—, — environmental
ANI, Olufemi — Nigeria
—, —, methodology of
KOZLOWSKI, Jerzy — Australia, Qld/Poland
—, waste (management, reduction, & recycling)
COOPER, Jeffrey C. — UK, England
—, water quality & catchment
CULLEN, Peter W. — Australia, ACT
— of, see also planning[†]
— environmental management
GOLUBEV, Genady N. — Russia
— game reserves
SPINAGE, Clive A. — UK, England
— global change research
GOLUBEV, Genady N. — Russia
— local areas
OLI, Krishna P. — Nepal
— national parks
LÖFGREN, Rolf — Sweden
SEVILLA, Lorenzo B.CARDENAL
— Nicaragua/Guatemala
SPINAGE, Clive A. — UK, England
— natural areas
HERRERO, Stephen M. — Canada, Alb.
— — protected areas
DIAZ-MARTIN, Diego — Venezuela

— protected wildlands
SEVILLA, Lorenzo B.CARDENAL
— Nicaragua/Guatemala
— research & development projects & units for
developing countries
RADICELLA, Sandro M. — Italy
plans, action, environmental
AZIS, P.K.ABDUL — Saudi Arabia
OLI, Krishna P. — Nepal
—, —, species'
LAMBERTINI, Marco — Italy
—, environmental management, for industrial projects
FOX, Allan M. — Australia, NSW
— for environmental management of human
communities
AUSSEDAT, Nicole M. — France/St Barthélemy
—, management, protected areas'
SZILASSY, Zoltán — Hungary
—, national environmental action
BISWAS, Asit K. — UK, England
—, species' recovery (terrestrial)
CARRILLO, Antonio MACHADO — Canary Islands
plant, see also plants[†]
— anatomy
LAKSHMANAN, Kalimedu K. — India, TN
— –animal interactions
LOCK, John M. — UK, England
MALLOCH, Andrew J.C. — UK, England
— biography
STIRTON, Charles H. — UK, England
— biotechnology
HARRIS, Philip J.C. — UK, England
JAMES, David J. — UK, England
KHUSH, Gurdev S. — Philippines
— breeding (for crops' improvement etc.)
KHUSH, Gurdev S. — Philippines
SWAMINATHAN, Monkombu S. — India, TN
—, —, horticultural crops'
RIGGS, Timothy J. — UK, England
—, —, use in, of potato species
HAWKES, John G. — UK, England
—, —, utilization of wild species in
PINK, David A.C. — UK, England
— communities, patterning of
BLISS, Lawrence C. — USA, WA
— community diversity*
— ecology, research in
*KULL, Olevi — Estonia
— conservation
CHEEK, Roy V. — UK, England
FORERO, Enrique — USA, NY
HAMILTON, Alan — UK, England
MADULID, Domingo — Philippines
STIRTON, Charles H. — UK, England
— cultivation
CHEEK, Roy V. — UK, England
— cytogenetics
KHUSH, Gurdev S. — Philippines
—, desert, ecology of
KASSAS, Mohamed EL — Egypt
KHARIN, Nikolai — Turkmenistan
— diseases
PINK, David A.C. — UK, England
—, some, biological control of
JARIWALA, Savitri — India, UP
— distribution, role of soils in
BLISS, Lawrence C. — USA, WA

[†] See also upper footnote on p. 409.
[*] See also lower footnote on p. 409.

plant (contd)
— distributions (alpine ecology)
GOOD, Roger B.   Australia, ACT
— diversity, maintenance of, in tropical forests
ASHTON, Peter S.   USA, MA
— domestication
BALICK, Michael J.   USA, NY
— —, process of
GADE, Daniel W.   USA, VT
— ecology
ČEŘOVSKÝ, Jan   Czech Rep.
EDWARDS, Peter J.   Switzerland
EGZIABHER, Tewolde B.GEBRE   Ethiopia
GOLDSMITH, Frank B.   UK, England
GOPAL, Brij   India, Punjab
HAMBLER, David J.   UK, England
HEDBERG, K.Olov   Sweden
JIANG, Gaoming   China
KORNAŚ, Jan   Poland
ÖZTÜRK, Münir   Turkey
PARSONS, David J.   USA, MT
POLUNIN, Nicholas   Switzerland
SOLOMON, Allen M.   USA, OR
SPECHT, Raymond L.   Australia, Qld
STRASBERG, Dominique   La Réunion
— —, antarctic
LEWIS-SMITH, Ronald I.   UK, England
— —, arid (regions)
WALT, Pieter T.VAN DER   RSA
— —, coastal
RANDALL, Roland E.   UK, England
— —, desert
KASSAS, Mohamed EL   Egypt
KHARIN, Nikolai   Turkmenistan
SPRINGUEL, Irina   Egypt
— —, research in
STALTER, Richard   USA, NY
— —, terrestrial
BENSON, John S.   Australia, NSW
— ecophysiology
RYCHNOVSKÁ, Milena   Czech Rep.
— environmental micrometeorology & physiology
JONES, Hamlyn G.   UK, England
— evolution
RAVEN, Peter H.   USA, MO
— —, crop
HAWKES, John G.   UK, England
— genetic resources' conservation
CLEMENT, Charles R.   Brazil, Amaz.
HAWKES, John G.   UK, England
— —, — & utilization of
ANISHETTY, Narasimha M.   Italy
— genetics
KHUSH, Gurdev S.   Philippines
PINK, David A.C.   UK, England
— geography
MEDWECKA-KORNAŚ, Anna M.   Poland
MEHER-HOMJI, Vispy M.   India, TN
POLUNIN, Nicholas   Switzerland
— — (including Europe, tropical Africa)
KORNAŚ, Jan   Poland
— germ-plasm conservation, strategy, and
technology
TAO, Kar-ling J.   Italy
— identification
LAVRENTIADES, George   Greece
— –insect interactions
ROOM, Peter M.   Australia, Qld
— — — relationships
ELLIS, Peter R.   UK, England

— invasions, management & control of, in protected
areas
THEBAUD, Christophe   France
—, molecular, virology
CLARK, Michael F.   UK, England
— morphological studies
PANDURANGAN, Alagramam G.   India, Ker.
— origins (alpine ecology)
GOOD, Roger B.   Australia, ACT
— –pathogen interactions, genetics of, in crop &
natural ecosystems
CRUTE, Ian   UK, England
— pathogens, epidemiology of soil-borne
ENTWISTLE, Andrew R.   UK, England
— —, soil-borne
WHITE, James G.   UK, England
— pathology
CLARK, Michael F.   UK, England
ENTWISTLE, Andrew R.   UK, England
WALSH, John A.   UK, England
— —, molecular
BARBARA, Derek J.   UK, England
— phenology
WIELGOLASKI, Frans-Emil   Norway
— physiology
MANSFIELD, Terence A.   UK, England
MILIMO, Patrick B.W.   Kenya
— production
BLISS, Lawrence C.   USA, WA
— productivity
WIELGOLASKI, Frans-Emil   Norway
— resources
JAIN, Sudhanshu K.   India, UP
— responses to damage
ROOM, Peter M.   Australia, Qld
— —, natural fire regimes and (fire research)
GOOD, Roger B.   Australia, ACT
— sociology
FREIBERG, Horst   Germany
LAVRENTIADES, George   Greece
MEDWECKA-KORNAŚ, Anna M.   Poland
— soil, nutrient interactions
NYE, Peter H.   UK, England
— –soil relations
GRUBB, Peter J.   UK, England
— species, endangered
NAYAR, M.Param   India, Ker.
— —, rare & endangered
HSU, Kuo-Shih   Taiwan
— —, threatened, research on
BENSON, John S.   Australia, NSW
— systematics
PANDURANGAN, Alagramam G.   India, Ker.
PRANCE, Ghillean T.   UK, England
RAVEN, Peter H.   USA, MO
STIRTON, Charles H.   UK, England
— taxonomy
CULLEN, James   UK, England
EGZIABHER, Tewolde B.GEBRE   Ethiopia
HEDBERG, K.Olov   Sweden
KORNAŚ, Jan   Poland
— — (Datura & related plants)
BYE, Robert   Mexico
— — of tropical areas esp.Nigeria
KEAY, Ronald W.J.   UK, England
— —, vascular
FORERO, Enrique   USA, NY
— -tissue culture
MASCARENHAS, Anthony F.   India, Mah.

— virology
  BARBARA, Derek J.   UK, England
  BOS, Luite   The Netherlands
  WALSH, John A.   UK, England
— —, molecular
  CLARK, Michael F.   UK, England
— –water relations & ecology
  JONES, Hamlyn G.   UK, England
— – — –soil relations
  KIRKHAM, M.B.   USA, KS
plantations, managed, fire ecology in
  OLA-ADAMS, Bunyamin A.   Nigeria
— with native Chilean species
  DONOSO, Claudio   Chile
planting design & management
  CHEEK, Roy V.   UK, England
—, tree
  FITTER, Perin S.   Kenya
  WALULYA-MUKASA, Joe   Uganda
plants, *see also* plant[†]
—, air pollution, effects of, on
  BELL, Nigel   UK, England
— & birds of western Europe, systematics of
  KELLER, Michael C.   Germany
— — vegetation, Cape, autecology, phytosociology,
    & restoration ecology, of
  BOUCHER, Charles   RSA
—, biocidal, taxonomy of
  LAKSHMANAN, Kalimedu K.   India, TN
—, carnivorous
  CHEEK, Martin R.   UK, England
, conservation & cultivation of
  CHEEK, Roy V.   UK, England
—, — of, *in situ* & *ex situ*
  HAMANN, Ole J.   Denmark
—, crop, genetic diversity in
  KING, Graham J.   UK, England
—, ecology of meadow
  KULL, Kalevi   Estonia
—, economic, of arid & semi arid regions
  WICKENS, Gerald E.   UK, England
—, ecophysiology of
  COLE, Norman H.A.   Sierra Leone
—, — —, in cold stressed environments
  BLISS, Lawrence C.   USA, WA
—, — — maritime
  MALLOCH, Andrew J.C.   UK, England
—, edible, medicinal, etc.
  BYE, Robert   Mexico
—, endangered vascular, conservation of, in Canada
  ARGUS, George W.   Canada, Ont.
—, environment of
  KEFELI, Valentin   Russia
—, ethnobotany
  HEDBERG, Inga M.M.   Sweden
—, evolutionary biology of
  STIRTON, Charles H.   UK, England
—, higher, morphology & taxonomy of
  TIKHOMIROV, Vadim N.   Russia
—' invasion, alien
  STRASBERG, Dominique   La Réunion
—' —, maritime, ecophysiology of
  MALLOCH, Andrew J.C.   UK, England
—' —, meadow, ecology of
  KULL, Kalevi   Estonia
—, medicinal
  BYE, Robert   Mexico
  JAIN, Sudhanshu K.   India, UP

[†] *See* upper footnote on p. 409.

—, —, hallucinogenic & toxic
  SCHULTES, Richard E.   USA, MA
—, —, taxonomy of
  LAKSHMANAN, Kalimedu K.   India, TN
— of horticultural interest
  CULLEN, James   UK, England
—, ornamental
  BYE, Robert   Mexico
—, physiology of
  KEFELI, Valentin   Russia
—, pollution, air, effects of, on
  BELL, Nigel   UK, England
—, — impact on
  KULL, Olevi   Estonia
—, psychoactive
  JAIN, Sudhanshu K.   India, UP
—, rare, conservation of
  SPENCER, Jonathan W.   UK, England
—, —, — biology of
  STRASBERG, Dominique   La Réunion
—, — vascular, conservation of, in Canada
  ARGUS, George W.   Canada, Ont.
— re.herbivores & dispersers
  GRUBB, Peter J.   UK, England
—, reintroduction of — Africa
  PRICE, Mark R.STANLEY   Kenya
—, reproduction biology of
  WOODELL, Stanley R.J.   UK, England
—, responses of, to abiotic stress
  MANSFIELD, Terence A.   UK, England
—, rubber-yielding
  SCHULTES, Richard E.   USA, MA
—, taxonomy of medicinal & biocidal
  LAKSHMANAN, Kalimedu K.   India, TN
—, tundra, autecology of
  WIELGOLASKI, Frans-Emil   Norway
—, vascular, conservation of rare & endangered, in
  Canada
  ARGUS, George W.   Canada, Ont.
—, —, field identification of
  FITTER, Richard S.R.   UK, England
plastics industry, waste recycling in
  KUFORIJI-OLUBI, Bola   Nigeria
Platystomatidae
  WHITTINGTON, Andrew E.   UK, Scotland
Pleistocene–Holocene sedimentology & stratigraphy
  CARVALHO, G.SOARES DE   Portugal
Poland, economic restructuring & environmental
  change in
  SERAFIN, Rafal K.   Poland
polar biology
  FOGG, Gordon E.   UK, Wales
— deserts, colonization & revegetation of
  SVOBODA, Josef   Canada, Ont.
— ecology
  CLARKE, Andrew   UK, England
  SAKSHAUG, Egil   Norway
— —, marine
  KELLERMANN, Adolf K.   Germany
— ecosystems
  WIELGOLASKI, Frans-Emil   Norway
— environmental management
  KEAGE, Peter L.   Australia, Vic.
— marine ecology
  KELLERMANN, Adolf K.   Germany
— oases, ecosystems of
  SVOBODA, Josef   Canada, Ont.
— region (esp. marine)
  RAY, G.Carleton   USA, VA
— regions
  WALTON, David W.H.   UK, England

polar regions (contd)
— —, ecology of
    HOLDGATE, Martin W.   UK, England
— —, evolutionary history of
    CLARKE, Andrew   UK, England
— —, marine ecology esp.of
    CROXALL, John P.   UK, England
— research
    PRESTRUD, Pål   Norway
— sciences
    HEMPEL, Gotthilf   Germany
policies, *see also* policy[†]
    NILSSON, Sten   Austria
—, environmental
    ANI, Olufemi   Nigeria
    BISWAS, Asit K.   UK, England
    BISWAS, Margaret R.   UK, England
    COLE, Norman H.A.   Sierra Leone
—, —, in former Soviet Union
    SACKS, Arthur B.   USA, CO
—, — management
    GARRATT, Keith J.   NZ
—, —, regional & global
    LOHANI, Bindu N.   Philippines
—, equitable forest
    PALMER, Prince Dowu   Sierra Leone
—, European environmental
    HAIGH, Nigel   UK, England
— for maintaining biodiversity of managed forests
    KIRBY, Keith J.   UK, England
—, human population
    CORBET, Philip S.   UK, Scotland
— of environmental conservation
    POORE, M.E.Duncan   UK, Scotland
— — sea-level rise in Pacific Basin
    SHAPIRO, Harvey A.   Japan
—, protection, geopolitical aspects of
    BUÉ, Alain   France
—, regional development (national & EEC)
    SOTIRIADOU, Victoria   Greece
—, social, environmental trends & related
    HOLDGATE, Martin W.   UK, England
—, sustainable tourism
    SISMAN, Richard ('Dick')   UK, England
policy, *see also* policies[†]
—, administration
    KENNEDY, James J.   USA, UT
—, agri-environmental
    GREEN, Brynmor H.   UK, England
— analysis
    TAIT, Elizabeth J.   UK, Scotland
—, —, natural resources'
    MORELL, Merilio G.   Italy
—, —, valuation methodologies for
    NORTON, Bryan G.   USA, GA
— & law, environmental, comparative, & national
    REHBINDER, Eckard   Germany
—, application of wetland science to
    LARSON, Joseph S.   USA, MA
—, biodiversity, analysis of
    NORTON, Bryan G.   USA, GA
—, climate
    HOUGHTON, John T.   UK, England
—, comparative
    REHBINDER, Eckard   Germany
— development
    AL-MANDHRY, Abdullah R.   Oman
    GAKAHU, Christopher G.   Kenya
    USUKI, Mitsuo   Thailand

— —, conservation
    SATTLER, Paul S.   Australia, Qld
— —, environmental
    BASS, Stephen M.J.   UK, England
    GALLON, Gary T.   Canada, Ont.
    GARDNER, Julia E.   Canada, BC
— —, monitoring & evaluation
    ASFAW, Gedion   Ethiopia
—, electric utility
    LOVINS, Amory B.   USA, CO
—, energy
    ABBASPOUR, Madjid   Iran
    HARE, F.Kenneth   Canada, Ont.
    MacDONALD, Gordon J.F.   USA, CA
    SINGER, S.Fred   USA, VA
—, —, and business
    BURKE, David Thomas 'Tom'   UK, England
—, — economics &
    SINGER, S.Fred   USA, VA
—, environmental, *see* environmental policy
—, —, at European & UK levels — impact on
    countryside
    REYNOLDS, Fiona C.   UK, England
—, —, comparative & national
    REHBINDER, Eckard   Germany
—, —, global
    CLARK, William C.   USA, MA
—, —, international
    FAIZI, Shahul   Saudi Arabia
    JOHNSON, David W.   USA, CA
—, — management
    SAUNIER, Richard E.   USA, MD
—, —, re.management of fragmented landscapes
    BEETON, Robert J.S.   Australia, Qld
—, — studies
    SIMONIS, Udo E.   Germany
—, European environmental
    JOHNSON, Stanley P.   UK, England
—, forest
    BASS, Stephen M.J.   UK, England
    NDINGA, Assitou   Congo
— formation, whale
    McCLOSKEY, Maxine E.   USA, MD
—, global environmental
    CLARK, William C.   USA, MA
— international, on sustainable development & the
    environment
    RAMPHAL, Shridath   UK, England
— issues
    DHUNGEL, Surya P.S.   Nepal
— —, environmental management
    PRESTON-WHYTE, Robert A.   UK, England
— —, sustainable development
    SEVILLA, Lorenzo B.CARDENAL
        Nicaragua/Guatemala
—, land-use
    OSEMEOBO, Gbadebo J.   Nigeria
—, landscape
    USUKI, Mitsuo   Japan
—, law &, comparative international*
—, — —, international
    *BOTHE, Michael   Germany
—, national (environmental law)
    REHBINDER, Eckard   Germany
—, marine (Canadian arctic)
    FENGE, Terence A.E.   Canada, Ont.
—, natural resource
    BARAHONA-ISRAEL, Rodrigo   Costa Rica
    CAMINO, Ronnie DE   Costa Rica
    DAVIS, Bruce W.   Australia, Tas.

[†] *See* upper footnote on p. 409.

* *See* lower footnote on p. 409.

—, — — management
USUKI, Mitsuo — Japan
—, ocean
DESAI, Bhagirath N. — India, Goa
—, protected areas'
HOUGH, John L. — USA, MD
PONCIANO, Ismael — Guatemala
—, public, for the environment
CALDWELL, Lynton Keith — USA, IN
—, —, environmental law and
McCARTHY, Gerald P. — USA, VA
—, research (marine & polar)
HEMPEL, Gotthilf — Germany
—, resource
MENDEZ, Jesus M.DELGADO — Brazil
—, science
PRESS, Frank — USA, DC
—, — & environmental
ORIANS, Gordon H. — USA, WA
—, —, environmental
FARAGÓ, Tibor — Hungary
—, —, national & international
KENDREW, John C. — UK, England
—, social (re.environment & development)
DAHL, R.Birgitta — Sweden
—, utility, electric
LOVINS, Amory B. — USA, CO
—, water pollution cost-effective
RAJAGOPAL, Rangaswamy — USA, OH
—, whale, formation
McCLOSKEY, Maxine E. — USA, MD
—, wildlife
DODDS, Donald G. — Canada, NS
policymaking, conservation of Odonata
MOORE, Norman W. — UK, England
—, interdisciplinary science & its role in
O'RIORDAN, Timothy — UK, England
—, pollution control
MOORE, Norman W. — UK, England
political aspects of sustainable development
GORDON, John K. — UK, England
— development in the circumpolar Arctic
FENGE, Terence A.E. — Canada, Ont.
— dimensions of international environmental affairs
THOMAS, Urs P. — Canada, Que.
— ecology
PELUSO, Nancy L. — USA, CT
— lobbying & public awareness-raising
ZINKE, Alexander — Austria
—, socio-, aspects of wildlife conservation
SHAW, William W. — USA, AZ
politicians–environmental scientists, interactions
BOLIN, Bert R. — Sweden
politics, climate
WALLÉN, Carl-Christian — Switzerland
—, ecological planning &
MIKLÓS, Ladislav — Slovak Rep.
—, environmental
GANDY, Matthew — UK, England
O'RIORDAN, Timothy — UK, England
—, —, international
O'RIORDAN, Timothy — UK, England
—, green (ecologically concerned)
MILNE, Christine — Australia, Tas.
PARKIN, Sara L. — France
—, human affairs &
LAMB, Hubert H. — UK, England
— in conservation of biotic & environmental
resources
FRAZIER, John G. — Mexico

— of environment
BURKE, David Thomas 'Tom' — UK, England
—, sustainable agriculture and energy
LINDSTROM, U.B. — Finland
pollutants, atmospheric, effects of
LAST, Frederick T. — UK, Scotland
—, long-range atmospheric transport of
STEINNES, Eiliv — Norway
pollution, air
ABBASPOUR, Madjid — Iran
BRINCHUK, Mikhail M. — Russia
RAY, Prasanta K. — India, W.Bengal
REHMAN, Syed Z. — Pakistan
WARNER, Frederick — UK, England
—, —, effects of, on plants & insects
BELL, Nigel — UK, England
—, —, biology
TRESHOW, Michael — USA, UT
—, —, control
CHANDAK, Surya P. — India, Delhi
—, —/environmental ecology
HUTTUNEN, Satu — Finland
—, —, impacts
TERBLANCHE, Petro — RSA
—, — (international environmental law)
LANG, Winfried — Switzerland
—, —, meteorology
PATIL, Rashmi S. — India, Mah.
—, —, modelling
PIELKE, Roger A. — USA, CO
SINGAL, Sagar P. — India, Delhi
—, —, monitoring & control equipment design &
development
MATHUR, Harbansh B. — India, Delhi
—, analysis (hazardous waste)
SAXENA, Anil K. — India, Delhi
— and its impacts
HOLDGATE, Martin W. — UK, England
—, bio-energy
TOMAR, Sadachari S. — India, MP
—, bryophytes as indicators of
SJÖGREN, Erik A. — Sweden
—, combustion generated, monitoring, and control
MATHUR, Harbansh D. — India, Delhi
— control
BISWAS, Dilip — India, Delhi
SCANNELL, Yvonne — Ireland
—, —, air
CHANDAK, Surya P. — India, Delhi
— —, environmental
DAVE, Jaydev M. — India, Delhi
LOHANI, Bindu N. — Philippines
— —, fermentation &
STANTON, W.Robert — UK, England
— —, industrial environmental
KHAN, Niaz A. — UAE
— —, marine
TORTELL, Philip — NZ
— —, research & policy-making in
MOORE, Norman W. — UK, England
— —, rural environmental
ABDEL-GAWAAD, Ahmed A.-W. — Egypt
— —, water
ARCEIVALA, Soli J. — India, Mah.
BHARGAVA, Devendra S. — India, UP
HAMMERTON, Desmond — UK, Scotland
RAJAGOPAL, Rangaswamy — USA, OH
— ecology
JIANG, Gaoming — China
— effects, air, on insects & plants
BELL, J.Nigel B. — UK, England

pollution (contd)
—, environmental
   MALONE-JESSURUN, Heidi Y.   Surinam
   SINGAL, Sagar P.   India, Delhi
   TOMAR, Sadachari S.   India, MP
—, —, by heavy-metals
   HAQUE, Mohammed A.   India, Har.
—, —, control & management
   DAVE, Jaydev M.   India, Delhi
—, freshwater fishery
   ATAUR-RAHIM, Mohammed   Pakistan
—, ground-water resources'
   WEAVER, John M.C.   RSA
—, heavy-metal
   REDAUD, M.Gladys BELANDRIA DE   Guadeloupe
— impact on ecosystems & plants
   KULL, Olevi   Estonia
— impacts, air
   ROBERTS, Thomas M.   UK, England
—, industrial, response of insect populations to
   KOZLOV, Mikhail V.   Finland
— law, air & water
   SILVA, Allenisheo L.M.DE   Sri Lanka
— management, environmental
   DAVE, Jaydev M.   India, Delhi
—, marine
   ABBASPOUR, Madjid   Iran
   BELLAMY, David J.   UK, England
   BOURNE, William R.P.   UK, Scotland
   CLARK, Robert B.   UK, England
   COHEN, Yuval   Israel
   DESAI, Bhagirath N.   India, Kar.
   McINTYRE, Alasdair D.   UK, Scotland
—, —, control
   TORTELL, Philip   NZ
—, —, management
   CH'NG, Kim Looi   Malaysia
— (— science)
   MORTON, Brian   Hong Kong
—, —, environmental
   EKARATH, Raveendran   Bahrain
— monitoring (hazardous waste)
   SAXENA, Anil K.   India, Delhi
—, —, water
   RAJAGOPAL, Rangaswamy   USA, OH
—: natural resources'
   REIJNDERS, Lucas   The Netherlands
—, noise
   ALNASER, Waheeb E.   Bahrain
— prevention
   EICHBAUM, William M.   USA, DC
— problems
   ÖZTÜRK, Münir   Turkey
—, space, orbiting debris
   SINGER, S.Fred   USA, VA
—, stratospheric
   SINGH, O.N.   India, UP
—, waste, purification & control
   KUFORIJI-OLUBI, Bola   Nigeria
—, water
   RAY, Prasanta K.   India, W.Bengal
   SOPHONPANICH, Chodchoy   Thailand
   WARNER, Frederick   UK, England
—, —, control technology & strategies
   BHARGAVA, Devendra S.   India, UP
—, —, cost-effective regulation & policy
   RAJAGOPAL, Rangaswamy   USA, OH
—, —, prevention of, from composting
   NOBLE, Ralph   UK, England

polymer science–environment–sustainable
   development
   VASUDEVAN, Padma   India, Delhi
polymorphisms, genetic
   VIDA, Gabór   Hungary
polynology
   SOLOMON, Allen M.   USA, OR
Poplars, clones of
   LAL, Piare   India, AP
popularization of biology & conservation through
   media
   BOSWALL, Jeffery   UK, England
popularizing biological & geographical knowledge &
   information
   PIIROLA, Jouko   Finland
population, *see also* populations
   BAHRI, Ahmed   Ethiopia
   ENGELMAN, Robert   USA, DC
   HARDIN, Garrett H.   USA, CA
   HARRISON, Paul A.   UK, England
   JOHNSON, Stanley P.   UK, England
   OUEDRAOGO, O.Dieudonné   Mali
   ROWLEY, John R.   UK, England
   SALIM, Emil   Indonesia
   WAAK, Patricia A.   USA, CO
— assessment, sea turtles'
   MARQUEZ-MILLAN, René   Mexico
— biology
   COHEN, Joel E.   USA, NY
   EHRLICH, Anne H.   USA, CA
   YABLOKOV, Alexey V.   Russia
— — of large mammals
   LARSEN, Thor   Norway
— — — shrews
   PUCEK, Zdzislaw K.   Poland
— control
   EHRLICH, Anne H.   USA, CA
— dynamics
   PRINS, Herbert H.T.   The Netherlands
— —, genetic diversity and
   VIDA, Gabór   Hungary
— — of coastal birds
   BURGER, Joanna   USA, NJ
— —, tropical marine
   POLOVINA, Jeffrey J.   USA, HI
— ecology
   BIRCH, L.Charles   Australia, NSW
   ELMES, Graham W.   UK, England
   GRIFFITHS, Richard A.   UK, England
   KREBS, John R.   UK, England
   RAMAKRISHNAN, P.S. ('Ram')   India, Delhi
— — & evolution
   THEBAUD, Christophe   France
—, environment &, issues
   MUMBA, Wanga   Zambia
— genetics
   COHEN, Joel E.   USA, NY
   NEEL, James van G.   USA, MI
— — of Lepidoptera & Mollusca
   OWEN, Denis F.   UK, England
—, global
   GOCHFELD, Michael   USA, NJ
— growth
   PETERSON, Russell W.   USA, DE
— —, human, biodiversity assessment &
   conservation re.
   RAVEN, Peter H.   USA, MO
— —, rapid–environmental degradation
   SHAW, R.Paul   USA, DC
— –immigration–environment
   ABERNETHY, Virginia D.K.   USA, TN

—, local human, & Nature conservation, economic
    relation between
    PRINS, Herbert H.T. — The Netherlands
— –Nature–economics model
    JIGJ, Sonom — Mongolia
— policies, human
    CORBET, Philip S. — UK, Scotland
— problems
    BERTRAM, G.Colin L. — UK, England
    EDSALL, John T. — USA, MA
— processes
    BILSBORROW, Richard E. — USA, NC
— regulation
    MECH, L.David — USA, MN
— studies
    EHRLICH, Paul R. — USA, CA
— (sustainable development, North–South relations)
    MYERS, Norman — UK, England
populations, *see also* population
—, animal*
—, butterfly
    *FRAZER, John F.D. — UK, England
—, conservation & management of small biotic —
    Africa
    PRICE, Mark R.Stanley — Kenya
—, crocodile, Australian (northern) tidal waterways
    MESSEL, Harry — Australia, Qld
—, free-ranging & captive, genetic management of
    WOODRUFF, David S. — USA, CA
—, insect, response of, to industrial pollution
    KOZLOV, Mikhail V. — Finland
, mammal*
—, reptile
    *FRAZER, John F.D. — UK, England
—, rural human, involvement of, in conservation —
    Africa
    PRICE, Mark R.Stanley — Kenya
—, vertebrate, effects of tropical habitat loss on
    RAPPOLE, John H. — USA, VA
Porifera, tropical
    HOOPER, John N.A. — Australia, Qld
potato species, wild & cultivated — evolution &
    taxonomy of, and uses in plant breeding
    HAWKES, John G. — UK, England
Potomac River Basin
    CHOI, Yearn Hong — USA, VA
poverty
    NOVOA, Laura — Chile
—, alleviating environment-related, in developing
    world
    ONAYEMI, Olarotimi O. — Nigeria
— alleviation & environmental quality
    WRIGHT, R.Michael — USA, VA
— and sustainable livelihoods
    SINGH, Naresh — Canada, Man.
—, Highland SE Asia
    DEARDEN, Philip — Canada, BC
power plants, emission control over
    KOBAYASHI, Osamu — Japan
—, nuclear, safety of
    HARE, F.Kenneth — Canada, Ont.
prairie saline lakes & wetlands, impacts of UV radiation
    & microbial biogeochemical cycles in
    ROBARTS, Richard D. — Canada, Sask.
precipitation, acid, influence of
    WIELGOLASKI, Frans-Emil — Norway
— chemistry (re. land–water interactions)
    LIKENS, Gene E. — USA, NY

predator, anti-, defences of animals
    EDMUNDS, Malcolm — UK, England
— conservation & non-lethal control methods
    KRAUS, Daniel — Namibia/USA, CA
    MARKER-KRAUS, Laurie — Namibia/USA, DC
— control, non-lethal
    COPPINGER, Raymond — USA, MA
— –prey relations, wolf
    MECH, L.David — USA, MN
— – – relationships, mammalian
    MILLS, M.G.L. ('Gus') — RSA
predictability (climate)
    MacDONALD, Gordon, J.F. — USA, CA
preparation of environmental action plans
    OLI, Krishna P. — Nepal
preservation, environmental, using biotechnology
    (for)
    SUBRAMANIAN, Tarakad V. — India, TN
—, habitat, in coastal lagoons
    IBARRA-OBANDO, Silvia — Mexico
—, historic
    FIELD, Hermann H. — USA, MA
—, land
    EGLER, Frank E. — USA, CT
— of cranes & their habitats
    ARCHIBALD, George — USA, WI
— — cultural sites and historic buildings & sites
    SINGH, Birandra B. — Fiji
— — threatened ecosystems
    ZINKE, Alexander — Austria
— — wild places & wildlife
    REEVES, Randall R. — Canada, Que.
—, soil, against erosion
    DAMERDJI, M.Amine — Algeria
—, wetlands
    HOLLEMAN, Andrew D. — USA, MA
—, wildlife
    SINGH, Karan — India, Delhi
preserves, parks &, marine conservation through
    RANDALL, John 'Jack' — USA, HI
prevention of illegal trading in wildlife and parts
    thereof
    LaBUDDE, Samuel F. — USA, CA
— — odour & water pollution from composting
    NOBLE, Ralph — UK, England
—, pollution (esp. marine and coastal)
    EICHBAUM, William M. — USA, DC
preventive environmental management
    PURCELL, Arthur H. — USA, CA
prey, birds of
    GALUSHIN, Vladimir M. — Russia
    LUSCOMBE, Bruce A. — USA, NY
—, — —, & their habitats
    WATSON, Richard — USA, ID
— –predator relations
    MECH, L.David — USA, MN
— – – —, mammalian
    MILLS, M.G.L. ('Gus') — RSA
pricing, environmental
    GONZALEZ, Juan A.Aguirre — Costa Rica
primary production (forest ecosystem studies)
    KIRA, Tatuo — Japan
— productivity (esp. in the Arctic)*
— succession following deglaciation
    *SVOBODA, Josef — Canada, Ont.
primate conservation & protection
    McGREAL, Shirley — USA, SC
— ecology
    MARSH, Clive W. — Malaysia

See lower footnote on p. 409.

See lower footnote on p. 409.

primates
    MITTERMEIER, Russell A.   USA, DC
—, Malagasy, research on
    ANDRIAMAMPIANINA, Joseph   Madagascar
primatology
    MacKINNON, John R.   Hong Kong
    NIEMITZ, Carsten   Germany
principles, financial, application of, to 'The
    Commons'
    McCAMMON, Antony L.T.   Switzerland
— of systematics
    MARUSIK, Yuri M.   Russia
— — vegetational classification
    POORE, M.E.Duncan   UK, Scotland
print media, environmental awareness through
    SINGH, Hari B.   India, Delhi
— —, communication through
    HAQUE, Mohammed A.   India, Har.
privatization
    SAMAD, Syed A.   Malaysia
problem-oriented analysis & management
    GROOT, Wouter T.DE   The Netherlands
— -solving, environmental
    BEETON, Robert J.S.   Australia, Qld
problems, environmental
    EDSALL, John T.   USA, MA
    SINITSINA, Irene E.   Russia
    VERSCHUREN, Jacques C.F.   Belgium
—, —, in former Soviet Union
    SACKS, Arthur B.   USA, CO
—, —, water management and associated
    WHITE, Gilbert F.   USA, CO
—, population
    BERTRAM, George C.L.   UK, England
    EDSALL, John T.   USA, MA
—, public health, resulting from scorpion stings
    LOURENÇO, Wilson R.   France
—, salinity, in arid regions
    BATANOUNY, Kamal H.   Egypt
—, urban environmental, in developed economies
    GANDY, Matthew   UK, England
processes, anthropic, impact study of, in the coastal
    zone
    GRANJA, Helena M.   Portugal
—, coastal
    SISMAN, Richard ('Dick')   UK, England
—, ecological & social, linkages between
    RAMAKRISHNAN, P.S. ('Ram')   India, Delhi
—, —, identification of critical marine
    AGARDY, M.Tündi   USA, DC
—, geodynamic, of landscape of dryland regions
    JIGJ, Sonom   Mongolia
—, population
    BILSBORROW, Richard E.   USA, NC
—, soil
    LAL, Rattan   USA, OH
product chemistry, marine natural
    BAKER, Joseph 'Joe' T.   Australia, Qld
production, cattle
    DELPIANO, José P.CASTRO   Uruguay
—, cleaner
    BOXALL, John E.   Hong Kong
— ecology & bioenergetics
    PANDEYA, Satish C.   India, UP
— — (wetland etc.)
    PANDIT, Ashok K.   India, J&K
—, mycotoxin, control of
    KENNEDY, Robert   UK, England
—, organic, control of
    AUGSTBURGER, Franz   Bolivia

—, primary (forest ecosystem studies)
    KIRA, Tatuo   Japan
— systems, dairy & beef, animal evaluation in*
— —, sustainable agricultural
    *TEWOLDE, Assefaw   Mexico
— —, — integrated
    WILSON, Richard T.   UK, England
productivity, plant
    WIELGOLASKI, Frans-Emil   Norway
—, primary
    SVOBODA, Josef   Canada, Ont.
programme formulation & management,
    environmental
    GARRATT, Keith J.   NZ
—, Nature protection
    KOSTENKO, Yuriy   Ukraine
programmes — air, water, gas, noise, consultation
    PRASAD, Basudeo   India, E.Punjab
—, biodiversity protection
    SIVADAS, Ponathil   India, Ker.
—, captive-breeding
    GUPTA, Brij K.   India, TN
—, conservation, community-based, stimulation of
    UGWU, Christopher N.   Nigeria
—, ecodevelopment
    SINGH, Hari B.   India, Delhi
—, ecotourism, development of
    FOX, Allan M.   Australia, NSW
—, environmental
    OVINGTON, John D.   Australia, ACT
— re.conservation of wildlife & environment
    DURRANI, Shakil   Pakistan
—, reintroduction, of extinct species
    HATOUGH-BOURAN, Alia M.A.   Jordan
—, research, formulation & administration of
    JAIN, Sudhanshu K.   India, UP
—, training
    CROSBY, Arturo   Spain
—, vector control
    FARID, M.A.   Switzerland
—, wildlife rescue & rehabilitation
    ROSE, Carlos R.HASBÚN   El Salvador
project analysis
    GONZALEZ, Juan A.AGUIRRE   Costa Rica
— design, sustainable development
    HARDI, Peter   Canada, Man.
— environmental components, management &
    preparation of
    BENNETT, Sara L.   Canada, BC
— formulation & management, environmental
    GARRATT, Keith J.   NZ
— —, management, & evaluation
    IYER, C.P.Jayalakshmi   India, Delhi
— management, environmental services
    BOXALL, John E.   Hong Kong
— preparation
    THRESHER, Philip B.   USA, CA
— — & appraisal
    ASFAW, Gedion   Ethiopia
— review
    POTTER, Louis   BVI
projects, arid & semi-arid lands'
    RECKERS, Ute   Kenya
—, conservation & development, management of
    STEPHENSON, Peter J.   Tanzania
—, development, EIA of
    SUNDARESAN, Bommaya B.   India, TN

* See lower footnote on p. 409.

—, environmental conservation, design &
    implementation of
    PANGETI, George N.   Zimbabwe
—, farm forestry & reforestation
    LAL, Piare   India, AP
—, industrial, environmental management plans for
    FOX, Allan M.   Australia, NSW
—, integrated conservation & management
    BEZAURY-CREEL, Juan E.   Mexico
—, large-capital, economic impacts of
    McEACHERN, John D.   Canada, Ont./Nepal
— re.conservation of wildlife & environment
    DURRANI, Shakil   Pakistan
—, research & development, planning & organization
    RADICELLA, Sandro M.   Italy
—, water resources' development, re.tropical &
    temperate environments
    ZWAHLEN, Robert   Switzerland
—, wildlife management, design & implementation of
    PANGETI, George N.   Zimbabwe
promoting conservation behaviour
    YOUNG, Raymond DE   USA, MI
— effectiveness of UN in his fields
    SCHRAM, Gunnar G.   Iceland
— public awareness in social forestry
    SIVADAS, Ponathil   India, Ker.
propaganda for environmental awareness
    BAHUGUNA, Sunderlal   India, UP
propagation, vegetative, of trees
    LEAKEY, Richard R.B.   Kenya
—, —, research & development work on
    LAL, Piare   India, AP
property, common, management
    QUTUB, Syed Ayub   Pakistan
—, —, resources
    BERKES, Fikret   Canada
Prospaltella
    CIOCHIA, Victor   Romania
protected area, *see also* [protected] areas†
— — authorities, subsistence community integration
    with
    ROWNTREE, Matthew J.W.   UK, England
— — conservation management
    JEFFERIES, Bruce E.   Papua New Guinea
    STRONACH, Neil R.H.   Ireland
— — management, *see also* [protected] areas'
    management†
    ALVAREZ, Juan M.   El Salvador
    BEETON, Robert J.S.   Australia, Qld
    JANSEN, Malcolm A.B.   USA, DC
    KASSIOUMIS, Konstantinos   Greece
    LACY, Terry P.DE   Australia, NSW
    MOORE, Alan W.   USA, TN
    REDAUD, Louis R.M.   Guadeloupe
    ROWNTREE, Matthew J.W.   UK, England
— — personnel, training of
    MOORE, Alan W.   USA, TN
— — planning
    KASSIOUMIS, Konstantinos   Greece
    MOORE, Alan W.   USA, TN
    WEBER, Karl E.   Thailand
— — — & management
    HAMILTON, Lawrence S.   USA, VT
    WESCOTT, Geoffrey C.   Australia, Vic.
— —, marine
    AGARDY, M.Tündi   USA, DC
— — research
    BOYLE, Terence P.   USA, CO

— — systems, selection & establishment of
    SATTLER, Paul S.   Australia, Qld
— — wildlife, own
    FIELD, Hermann H.   USA, MA
[protected] areas, *see also* protected area†
    AL-HOUTY, Wasmia   Kuwait
    BOTCH, Marina S.   Russia
    CARRILLO, Antonio MACHADO   Canary Islands
    ČEŘOVSKY, Jan   Czech Rep.
    EATON, Peter P.   Brunei
    EIDSVIK, Harold K.   France
    FENGE, Terence A.E.   Canada, Ont.
    LAYDOO, Richard S.   Trinidad & Tobago
    LUCAS, Percy H.C. ('Bing')   NZ
    NELSON, J.Gordon   Canada, Ont.
    NEPAL, Sanjay K.   Switzerland
    NOSEL, José   Martinique
    PULIDO, Victor   Peru
    RANJITSINH, M.K.   India, MP
    SERAFIN, Rafal K.   Poland
    SERHAL, Assad   Lebanon
    SHORES, John N.   USA, ME
    SZILASSY, Zoltán   Hungary
    URBAN, František   Czech Rep.
    WAYBURN, Edgar   USA, CA
    WHITEHOUSE, John F.   Australia, NSW
    ZHANG, Ping   China
— and wildlife
    SERHAL, Assad   Lebanon
— –anti-poaching
    BANGURA, Kalie I.   Sierra Leone
, appropriate management of
    TÖLGYESI, István   Hungary
—, biodiversity and
    UPRETI, Biswa N.   Nepal
—, coastal conservation &
    SALM, Rodney V.   Kenya
—' conservation
    CÂMARA, Ibsen DE G.   Brazil, RJ
    CHALABI, Bouzid   Algeria
    PHILLIPS, Adrian   UK, England
    VALDRÈ, Giovanni   Italy
    WAYBURN, Edgar   USA, CA
—, control of plant invasions in
    THEBAUD, Christophe   France
—, creation of
    JIGJ, Sonom   Mongolia
—, description of
    STOIBER, Hans H.   Austria
— development
    LAMBERTINI, Marco   Italy
—, environmental law
    WESTREICHER, Antonio ANDALUZ   Bolivia
—, — management in
    EATON, Peter P.   Brunei
—, — planning in
    FLETCHER, Raúl E.   Panama
—, establishment, management, & assessment of
    LAMPREY, Hugh F.   UK, England
—, — of
    DUFOUR, Jules   Canada, Que.
—, evaluation of
    STOIBER, Hans H.   Austria
—, habitat management in
    STANTON, James P.   Australia, Qld
— in tropical forests incorporating local &
    indigenous concerns
    LEES, Annette M.   NZ

† *See* upper footnote on p. 409, except that, here, pluraliz-
ation to 'areas' replaces the usual 'of' as the alternative.

† *See* upper footnote on p. 409, except that, here, pluraliz-
ation to 'areas' replaces the usual 'of' as the alternative.

[protected] areas (contd)
—, land–sea interactions in
   RAY, G.Carleton — USA, VA
—' management, *see also* protected area management
   ANDRIAMAMPIANINA, Joseph — Madagascar
   BEZAURY-CREEL, Juan E. — Mexico
   BUDOWSKI, Gerardo — Costa Rica
   BUTLER, James 'Jim' R. — Canada, Alb.
   CHALABI, Bouzid — Algeria
   CIFUENTES-ARIAS, Miguel — Costa Rica
   DOUROJEANNI, Marc J. — USA, VA
   DUFOUR, Jules — Canada, Que.
   FEICK, Jenny L. — Canada, Alb.
   HAMILTON, Lawrence S. — USA, VT
   HEINEN, Joel T. — USA, FL
   HOUGH, John L. — USA, MD
   JIGJ, Sonom — Mongolia
   LAMBERTINI, Marco — Italy
   LAMPREY, Hugh F. — UK, England
   LAVIEREN, Lambartus P.VAN — The Netherlands
   MacFARLAND, Craig G. — USA, ID
   MORELL, Merilio G. — Italy
   MOURA, Robert MANNERS — Portugal
   N'SOSSO, Dominique — Congo
   PONCE, Carlos F. — Peru
   ROSSI, Patrizia — Italy
   SALINAS, Pedro J. — Venezuela
   SULAYEM, Mohammad S.A. — Saudi Arabia
   WESCOTT, Geoffrey C. — Australia, Vic.
—', — & control of plant invasions in
   THEBAUD, Christophe — France
—', — & development of
   ALVARADO, Juan SKINNER — Guatemala
—' — in the Middle East
   DEAN, Faisal — USA, VA
—, marine
   EARLL, Robert C. — UK, England
   FOWLER, Sarah L. — UK, England
   GUBBAY, Susan — UK, England
   LAYDOO, Richard S. — Trinidad & Tobago
   WHITE, Susan L. — USA, FL
—, —, esp.in the high seas
   McCLOSKEY, Maxine E. — USA, MD
—, —, conservation &
   SALM, Rodney V. — Kenya
—, master-planning for
   BARCSAY, László — Hungary
—, monitoring
   MOURA, Robert MANNERS — Portugal
—, national parks &
   HAYNES-SUTTON, Ann M. — Jamaica
   SANCHEZ, Heliodoro — Colombia
   SHAW, William W. — USA, AZ
   VO, Quy — Vietnam
—, natural
   ZABELINA, Natalia M. — Russia
—, —, legal aspects of
   ABDELHADY, Abdelaziz — Egypt/Kuwait
—, —, planning & management of
   DIAZ-MARTIN, Diego — Venezuela
—' organization
   LAMBERTINI, Marco — Italy
—' planning
   CIFUENTES-ARIAS, Miguel — Costa Rica
   FLETCHER, Raúl E. — Panama
   HAMILTON, Lawrence S. — USA, VT
   KASSIOUMIS, Konstantinos — Greece
   MARAGOS, James E. — USA, HI
   MOORE, Alan W. — USA, TN
   MOURA, Robert MANNERS — Portugal

   ROMULUS, Giles — St Lucia
   SALINAS, Pedro J. — Venezuela
   SULAYEM, Mohammad S.A. — Saudi Arabia
   WEBER, Karl E. — Thailand
   WESCOTT, Geoffrey C. — Australia, Vic.
—' policy
   HOUGH, John L. — USA, MD
—' —, planification, & management
   PONCIANO, Ismael — Guatemala
—' system, Canadian
   HACKMAN, Arlin C. — Canada, Ont.
—, systems planning for
   HEISS, Gerhard — Germany
—, teaching & technical assistance
   CIFUENTES-ARIAS, Miguel — Costa Rica
—, tropical, and their conservation
   COBB, Stephen M. — UK, England
—, voluntary work in
   MOURA, Robert MANNERS — Portugal
protected crops, integrated pest management
   strategies in
   JACOBSON, Robert J. — UK, England
— landscapes
   LUCAS, Percy H.C. ('Bing') — NZ
— natural areas' design & survey
   WRIGHT, Shane D.T. — NZ
— reserves, wildlife & livestock management
   outside of
   KRAUS, Daniel — Namibia/USA, CA
   MARKER-KRAUS, Laurie — Namibia/USA, DC
— species
   URBAN, František — Czech Rep.
— wildlands, management & planning of
   SEVILLA, Lorenzo B.CARDENAL
        Nicaragua/Guatemala
protection, animal
   HOYT, John A. — USA, DC
—, biodiversity
   AMIRKHANOV, Amirkhan M. — Russia
   SIVADAS, Ponathil — India, Ker.
—, bird
   BOSWALL, Jeffery — UK, England
   CIOCHIA, Victor — Romania
—, coastal
   CHARLIER, Roger H.L. — Belgium
—, consumer
   FAZAL, Anwar — Malaysia
—, crop
   BOS, Luite — The Netherlands
   CROSS, Jeremy V. — UK, England
—, ecosystems'
   MOGHRABY, Asim I. — Sudan
—, environmental, *see* environmental protection
—, —, chemical & technological aspects of
   KUKHAR, Valery P. — Ukraine
—, —, development of laws on, in Ukraine
   KOSTENKO, Yuriy I. — Ukraine
—, —, legislation & treaties dealing with oceans &
   PELL, Claiborne — USA, DC
—, geological site
   DUFF, Keith L. — UK, England
—, habitat
   DALY, Ralph H. — Oman
—, landscape
   BARCSAY, László — Hungary
   GREEN, Brynmor H. — UK, England
   MOSLEY, John G. — Australia, Vic.
—, marine
   ALLOTTA, Gaetano — Italy

—, Nature
  ΛNDRIAMAMPIANINA, Joseph   Madagascar
  KACEM, Slaheddine BEL   Tunisia
  LANG-BEERMAN, Ernst M.   Switzerland
  SINNER, Jean-Marie   Luxemburg
  TIKHOMIROV, Vadim N.   Russia
—, —, Buddhism in
  HENNING, Daniel H.   USA, MT
—, —, esp.protected areas and peatland
  BOTCH, Marina S.   Russia
—, — re. tourism
  RICHEZ, Gérard   France
—, —, through biological control of Danube Delta
  CIOCHIA, Victor   Romania
— of disappearing & endangered species of mammals
  SOKOLOV, Vladimir   Russia
— — indigenous peoples
  HANBURY-TENISON, A.Robin   UK, England
— — islands in Gulf of Mexico
  CERDA, Alberto M.VAZQUEZ DE LA   Mexico
— — metals, marbles, & monuments
  SKOULIKIDIS, Theodore   Greece
— — mountainous zone (Romania)
  CIOCHIA, Victor   Romania
— — natural forest vegetation
  SJÖGREN, Erik A.   Sweden
— — — resources
  DELPIANO, José P.CASTRO   Uruguay
— — Nature reserves
  HURNI, Hans   Switzerland
— — human rights for a healthy environment
  CHERKASOVA, Maria V.   Russia
— — the Earth
  ODULA, Michael A.N.   Kenya
— — ozone layer, international environmental law
  LANG, Winfried   Switzerland
— — reefs in Gulf of Mexico
  CERDA, Alberto M.VAZQUEZ DE LA   Mexico
— — rights of future generations
  COUSTEAU, Jacques-Yves   France
— — sites (in island environments)
  AUSSEDAT, Nicole M.   France/St Barthélemy
— — the Arctic environment
  PRESTRUD, Pål   Norway
— — — environment, particularly Nature
  McCLOSKEY, J.Michael   USA, DC
— — wildlands
  ROSE, Carlos R.HASBÚN   El Salvador
—, peatland
  BOTCH, Marina S.   Russia
—, physical environment, & improvement
  SOTIRIADOU, Victoria   Greece
—, plant, *see* plant conservation, etc.
—, policies, geopolitical aspects of
  BUÉ, Alain   France
—, primate
  McGREAL, Shirley   USA, SC
— programme, national Nature
  KOSTENKO, Yuriy I.   Ukraine
—, species'
  LABUDDE, Samuel F.   USA, CA
  LEBRETON, Philippe   France
—, urban environment, & improvement
  SOTIRIADOU, Victoria   Greece
—, wildlife
  BANGURA, Kalie I.   Sierra Leone
  GŁOWACIŃSKI, Zbigniew A.   Poland
  HAFIDI, Moulay El M.   Morocco
  LABUDDE, Samuel F.   USA, CA
  NTAHUGA, Laurent   Burundi

—, —, legal aspects of
  ABDELHADY, Abdelaziz   Egypt/Kuwait
psychoactive plants
  JAIN, Sudhanshu K.   India, UP
psychological aspects, understanding, re.common
  resource dilemmas
  YOUNG, Raymond DE   USA, MI
— constructs & strategies for Nature conservation
  MARTIN, Vance G.   USA, CO
psychology, animal
  SHELDRICK, Daphne M.   Kenya
— of Nature
  TERRASSON, François   France
pteridophytes
  KORNAŚ, Jan   Poland
—: taxonomy, evolution, & phytogeography, of
  PAGE, Christopher N.   UK, Scotland
Pteroptyx fireflies, synchronous displays by, research
  into
  POLUNIN, Ivan V.   Singapore
public administration
  MORELL, Merilio G.   Italy
  SARMA, K.Madhava   Kenya
—, environment and
  OLOJEDE, Ayodele A   Nigeria
— appreciaton of The Biosphere
  POLUNIN, Nicholas   Switzerland
— awareness
  GUNAWARDENE, Nalaka J.   Sri Lanka
  HOWELL, Calvin A.   Barbados
  NASH, Nancy   Hong Kong
  ODULA, Michael A N   Kenya
— -raising
  ZINKE, Alexander   Austria
— — re.conservation of Nature
  HADDANE, Brahim   Morocco
— consultation including developing countries
  GARRATT, Keith J.   NZ
—, educating (governments, etc.)
  HUSBAND, Vicky   Canada, BC
— environmental campaigns
  AL-ALAWNEH, Ziyad   Jordan
— — movement
  CHERKASOVA, Maria V.   Russia
— finance
  SAMAD, Syed A.   Malaysia
— health and environment
  BURNEY, M.Ilyas   Pakistan
— — law
  GRAD, Frank P.   USA, NY
— — problems resulting from scorpion stings
  LOURENÇO, Wilson R.   France
— interest law
  BONINE, John E.   USA, OR
  SILVA, Allenisheo L.M.DE   Sri Lanka
— international law
  BIRNIE, Patricia W.   UK, England
  SCHRIJVER, Nico J.   The Netherlands
— involvement
  CULLEN, Peter W.   Australia, ACT
— law
  CALDWELL, Lynton Keith   USA, IN
  OKOTH-OGENDO, H.Wilfred O.   Kenya
— participation
  GALLON, Gary T.   Canada, Ont.
  PITTA, Luis CAEIRO   Portugal
— — (Asian tropical forests and national parks)
  HENNING, Daniel H.   USA, MT
— — in environmental decision-making
  GARDNER, Julia E.   Canada, BC

public participation in (contd)
— — — sustainable development & environmental
   issues
   KAKABADSE, Yolanda   Ecuador
— — including developing countries
   GARRATT, Keith J.   NZ
— policy
   CALDWELL, Lynton Keith   USA, IN
— —, environmental law and
   McCARTHY, Gerald P.   USA, VA
— relations
   SHREEVE, David   UK, England
purification, waste pollution
   KUFORIJI-OLUBI, Bola   Nigeria
Pythium spp.
   WHITE, James G.   UK, England

quality, air, monitoring & modelling
   PATIL, Rashmi S.   India, Mah.
— assurance
   WARNER, Frederick   UK, England
—, coastal water
   ARMIJOS, Mariano Montaño   Ecuador
— control of training & ecological work re.people in
   the tropics
   FRAZIER, John G.   Mexico
—, environmental, poverty alleviation &
   WRIGHT, R.Michael   USA, VA
—, life–material well-being and
   HAREIDE, Dag   Norway
— standards, environmental
   ALI, Iqbal   Pakistan
—, water, and catchment planning
   CULLEN, Peter W.   Australia, ACT
—, —, (fresh)
   BHARGAVA, Devendra S.   India, UP
   VORONOV, Arkady N.   Russia
—, —, management
   OKUN, Daniel A.   USA, NC
—, —, — & monitoring
   HAMMERTON, Desmond   UK, Scotland
quantitative measurement of comparative
   environmental risk
   CHADWICK, Michael J.   Sweden
quarantine management — risk assessment, wild
   animal management
   WILSON, George R.   Australia, WA
Quaternary botany
   DICKSON, James H.   UK, Scotland
— environmental science
   BOYD, William 'Bill' Edgar   Australia, NSW
— geology
   RAUKAS, Anto   Estonia
— palaeoecology
   SOLOMON, Allen M.   USA, OR
— —, research in
   YOUNG, Steven B.   USA, VT

radiation, cosmic
   ALNASER, Waheeb E.   Bahrain

—, UV, impacts of, in prairie saline lakes and prairie
   wetlands
   ROBARTS, Richard D.   Canada, Sask.
—, — solar
   ALNASER, Waheeb E.   Bahrain
radioecology
   STEINNES, Eiliv   Norway
radioisotopes in lakes
   HASLER, Arthur D.   USA, WI
radionuclides, movement of
   WARNER, Frederick   UK, England
—, pathways of
   BELL, J.Nigel B.   UK, England
radiowaves environment
   RADICELLA, Sandro M.   Italy
rainfall frequency analysis
   CLARK, Colin   UK, England
rain-forest
   ISHI, Hiroyuki   Japan
— - —, Amazonian, particularly Peru and indigenous
   native human societies
   CLOUDSLEY, Timothy   UK, Scotland
— - —: computer communications
   PETER, Ian W.   Australia, Qld
— - — ecology, research in
   WEBB, Leonard J.   Australia, Qld
— - — survival, temperate
   HUSBAND, Vicky   Canada, BC
— -forests
   KETO, Aila   Australia, Qld
— - —, adaptation to life in, Aboriginal*
— - —: Australian reptiles
   *COVACEVICH, Jeannette A.   Australia, Qld
— - —, South–East Asian (biotic conservation)
   GATHORNE-HARDY, Gathorne   UK, England
— - —, tropical
   GRUBB, Peter J.   UK, England
   SMITS, Willie   Indonesia
range ecology
   ASEM, Samira Omar   Kuwait
   LUSIGI, Walter   USA, VA
— management & monitoring
   RECKERS, Ute   Kenya
rangeland science
   WILSON, George R.   Australia, WA
— utilization, research development in
   WARDEH, Muhammad Fadel   Syria
rangelands, Africa's semi-arid, sustainable economic
   development in
   TOIT, Raoul F.du   Zimbabwe
—: conservation of biodiversity
   DUNCAN, Patrick   France
—, Mediterranean, ecology & management of
   PAPANASTASIS, Vasilios P.   Greece
rare breeds of British farm livestock, conservation of
   JEWELL, Peter A.   UK, England
— flora of Andaman & Nicobar Islands,
   conservation of
   SINHA, Akhauri R.P.   India, A&N Islands
— plant species
   HSU, Kuo-Shih   Taiwan
— plants' conservation
   SPENCER, Jonathan W.   UK, England
— —, conservation biology of
   STRASBERG, Dominique   La Réunion
— vascular plants, conservation of, in Canada
   ARGUS, George W.   Canada, Ont.
rates of tropical deforestation
   FEARNSIDE, Philip M.   Brazil, Amaz.

* *See* lower footnote on p. 409.

raw materials for wood-based industries
  LAL, Piare   India, AP
rays (& sharks, conservation of)
  EARLL, Robert C.   UK, England
real estate law
  HOLLO, Erkki J.   Finland
realism, ecocomplex
  POLUNIN, Nicholas   Switzerland
  WORTHINGTON, E.Barton   UK, England
reclaimed lands, hydrology & soil development of,
    after surface coal-mining
  KILMARTIN, Marianne P.   UK, England
reclamation, derelict land
  ROBERTS, Thomas M.   UK, England
— , land (after mining etc.)
  HAIGH, Martin J.   UK, England
reconstruction (environmental)
  GEBREMEDHIN, Naigzy   Kenya
— of former environmental conditions
  FÜLEKY, György   Hungary
records, environmental, stored in coral skeletons
  BARNES, David J.   Australia, Qld
recovery, forest disturbance &, research in
  ORGLE, Tetey K.   Ghana
— of ecosystems
  BAZZAZ, Fakhri   USA, MA
— plans, species (terrestrial)
  CARRILLO, A.MACHADO   Canary Islands
— , refuse (and underutilized resources)
  ARIAS-CHAVEZ, Jesus   Mexico
— , vegetation & species
  GIVEN, David R.   NZ
recreation
  MARTIN, Vance G.   USA, CO
  WATSON, John R.   Australia, WA
— , forest & national parks
  ARMSTRONG, Geoffrey J.   Australia, NSW
— , informal
  FOSTER, John   UK, Scotland
— , outdoor
  KASSIOUMIS, Konstantinos   Greece
recreational tourism management
  CRAIK, Wendy   Australia, Qld
recycling (waste etc.)
  ROYES, Veronica I.J.   Jamaica
— of industrial waste
  LUTZENBERGER, José A.   Brazil, RS
— , organic waste, using local species of earthworms
  ISMAIL, Sultan A.   India, TN
— , waste
  COOPER, Jeffrey C.   UK, England
  FUREDY, Christine   Canada, Ont.
— , — , in plastics industry
  KUFORIJI-OLUBI, Bola   Nigeria
Red Fox ecology
  BARRY, James M.   Ireland
— wood ants
  CHERIX, Daniel   Switzerland
redevelopment
  GEBREMEDHIN, Naigzy   Kenya
reduction, environmental risk
  AICKIN, Robert M.   UK, England
— , natural hazard
  KNILL, John   UK, England
— , waste (recycling etc.)
  COOPER, Jeffrey C.   UK, England
reductions in pesticide usage
  RICHARDSON, Paul N.   UK, England
reef fisheries
  SHEPHERD, Alexander R.DAWSON UK, England

— fishes, classification of Indo–Pacific*
— — , underwater guides to
  *RANDALL, John 'Jack'   USA, HI
— symbioses associations (impact on coral-reef
    ecosystems)
  VANTIER, Lyndon M.DE   Australia, Qld
reefs, coral
  McCLOSKEY, Maxine E.   USA, MD
— , — , conservation of
  MOYER, Jack T.   Japan
— , — : islands in Asia/Pacific region
  HOLTHUS, Paul F.   USA, HI
— , — , palaeoecology of
  KRASNOV, Eugene V.   Russia
— , protection of, in Gulf of Mexico
  CERDA, Alberto M.VAZQUEZ DE LA   Mexico
reforestation
  CHRISTIAN, Colmore S.   Dominica
  KERN, Berndt   Sweden
  KERN, Eha   Sweden
  PALMBERG-LERCHE, Christel M.   Italy
— of arid zones
  ZOUHA, Sekkou   Morocco
— projects, farm forestry &
  LAL, Piare   India, AP
reform concept, national ecological
  KOSTENKO, Yuriy I.   Ukraine
reforms, economic
  SAMAD, Syed A.   Malaysia
refrigeration, environmentally-acceptable
  SRINIVASAN, Kandadai   India, Mysore
refuse, recovery of
  ARIAS-CHAVEZ, Jesus   Mexico
regeneration dynamics, forest
  WRIGHT, Shane D.T.   NZ
— ecology (for forest restoration)
  ASHTON, Mark S.   USA, CT
— of ecosystems
  BAZZAZ, Fakhri   USA, MA
regenerative agriculture
  LUTZENBERGER, José A.   Brazil, RS
regimes, natural fire, and plant responses (fire
    research)
  GOOD, Roger B.   Australia, ACT
region, Asia–Pacific
  JOHNSTON, Douglas M.   Canada, BC
— , Caribbean (Nature conservation in)
  REDAUD, Louis H.M.   Guadeloupe
regional development
  KRAJČOVIČ, Roman S.   Slovak Rep.
— — policies (national & EEC)
  SOTIRIADOU, Victoria   Greece
— economics
  SAMAD, Syed A.   Malaysia
— environmental management
  NISHIOKA, Shuzo   Japan
  WEBER, Karl E.   Thailand
— — planning
  NEPAL, Sanjay K.   Switzerland
— integration
  CLOUTIER, Antoine   Canada, Que.
— planning
  AWAD, Adel R.   Syria
  HÜLSHOFF, Bernd VON DROSTE ZU   France
  SERAFIN, Rafal K.   Poland
— — projects
  BENNETT, Sara L.   Canada, BC
regionalizations, ecological & economic
  JIGJ, Sonom   Mongolia

* *See* lower footnote on p. 409.

regions, arctic
ROWLEY, Graham W.   Canada, Ont.
—, arid & semi-arid, economic plants of
WICKENS, Gerald E.   UK, England
—, —, ecology of land-use in
POORE, M.E.Duncan   UK, Scotland
—, —, salinity problems in
BATANOUNY, Kamal H.   Egypt
—, coastal, conservation of arid & semi-arid
ecosystems in
HATOUGH-BOURAN, Alia M.A.   Jordan
—, dryland, geodynamic processes of landscape of
JIGJ, Sonom   Mongolia
—, economic plants of arid & semi-arid
WICKENS, Gerald A.   UK, England
—, mountain, of India
MELKANIA, Niranjan P.   India, MP
—, polar (esp. southern)
WALTON, David W.H.   UK, England
—, —, ecology of (esp. southern)
HOLDGATE, Martin W.   UK, England
—, —, evolutionary history of
CLARKE, Andrew   UK, England
—, —, marine ecology esp.of
CROXALL, John P.   UK, England
—, Southeast Asia & South Pacific, environmental
management in
EATON, Peter P.   Brunei
—, temperate & tropical
HAMBLER, Clive   UK, England
—, tropical & sub-tropical, vegetation ecology of
WANG, Xianpu   China
—, —: forest policy/environmental policy
development
BASS, Stephen M.J.   UK, England
—, —, of India
MELKANIA, Niranjan P.   India, MP
—, underdeveloped, sustainable development in
LEFF, Enrique   Mexico
regulation development (planning etc.)
POTTER, Louis   BVI
—, wolf population
MECH, L.David   USA, MN
—, river
HOLČIK, Vladimír   Slovak Rep.
PETTS, Geoffrey   UK, England
—, water pollution, cost-effective
RAJAGOPAL, Rangaswamy   USA, OH
regulatory toxicology
MOORE, James W.   Canada, Alb.
rehabilitation, environmental
GRITZNER, Jeffrey A.   USA, MT
NOUR, Hassan O.ABDEL   Sudan
PARYSKI, Paul E.   Haiti
—, land degradation &
ABROL, Inder Pal   India, Delhi
—, oases and their, traditional irrigation in
DAMERDJI, M.Amine   Algeria
— of degraded forest & mining lands
JUSOFF, Kamaruzaman   Malaysia
— programmes, wildlife
ROSE, Carlos R.HASBÚN   El Salvador
reintroduction of Arabian Oryx to the wild in Oman
DALY, Ralph H.   Oman
— programmes of extinct species
HATOUGH-BOURAN, Alia M.A.   Jordan
reintroductions of plants & animals — Africa
PRICE, Mark R.STANLEY   Kenya
relations, ecological & ecophysiological, in forest ecosystems and their dependence on dominant trees
ČABOUN, Vladimír   Slovak Rep.

—, plant–water
JONES, Hamlyn G.   UK, England
—, temperature–water, of Arthropods & Reptiles
CLOUDSLEY-THOMPSON, John L.
                                     UK, England
relationships, forest–wildlife
DODDS, Donald G.   Canada, NS
—, mammalian predator–prey
MILLS, M.G.L. ('Gus')   RSA
—, Nature–society
WOODGATE, Graham R.   UK, England
release of genetically-modified microorganisms into
the environment
WHIPPS, John M.   UK, England
religion
CARROLL, John E.   USA, NH
— and Nature, advocacy of nexus between
SINGH, Karan   India, Delhi
—, ecology of
STEWART, Philip J.   UK, England
— -motivated environmental action
JAKOWSKA, Sophie   Dominican Rep.
religions, research & writing on
TROMPF, Garry W.   Australia, NSW
—, study of comparative
SINGH, Karan   India, Delhi
remote sensing
CAMPBELL, Kenneth L.I.   UK, England
HIBBERD, John K.   Australia, ACT
PIANKA, Eric R.   USA, TX
RITCHIE, Jerry C.   USA, MD
WITT, Ronald G.   Switzerland
— — applications
UNNI, N.V.MADHAVAN   India, AP
— — from space
HOUGHTON, John T.   UK, England
— — of water quality surveys
BHARGAVA, Devendra S.   India, UP
— —, satellite
GRASSL, Hartmut   Switzerland
— —, —, in forest conservation & management
JUSOFF, Kamaruzaman   Malaysia
renewable use of wetlands
TAN, Koonlin   UK, England
— energy
ABBASPOUR, Madjid   Iran
CATANIA, Peter J.   Canada, Sask.
SAYIGH, Ali M.   UK, England
— — technologies
LOENING, Ulrich E.   UK, Scotland
reporting, environment, state of
CULLEN, Peter W.   Australia, ACT
reproduction biology of plants
WOODELL, Stanley R.J.   UK, England
—, ecology of, re.Chilean birds, reptiles, &
amphibians
DIAZ, José VALENCIA   Chile
—, mammalian
DODDS, Donald G.   Canada, NS
— of scorpions
LOURENÇO, Wilson R.   France
reproductive synchrony
GOCHFELD, Michael   USA, NJ
reptile biology & conservation
GRIFFITHS, Richard A.   UK, England
— populations
FRAZER, John F.D.   UK, England
reptiles, Australian, extant & extinct, taxonomy &
zoogeography of
COVACEVICH, Jeanette A.   Australia, Qld

—, Chilean, ecology of feeding, reproduction, &
    conservation, of
    DIAZ, José VALENCIA   Chile
—, conservation of
    BURBIDGE, Andrew A.   Australia, WA
—, ecology of
    BEHRA, Olivier   Madagascar
—, ecotoxicology of
    LAMBERT, Michael R.K.   UK, England
—, research into ecology of feeding & reproduction
    of Chilean
    DIAZ, José VALENCIA   Chile
—, systematics, biogeography, & evolution, of
    INGRAM, Glen J.   Australia, Qld
—: temperature & water relations
    CLOUDSLEY-THOMPSON, John L.
                                       UK, England
rescue programmes, wildlife
    ROSE, Carlos R.HASBÚN   El Salvador
research, see also research in, research into, research on†
    GAKAHU, Christopher G.   Kenya
— action, community-based
    OLI, Krishna P.   Nepal
—, agricultural, international
    JAMES, W.Clive   Cayman Islands
—, basic, Nature conservation
    MEDWECKA-KORNAŚ, Anna M.   Poland
—, biochemistry
    KENT, Paul W.   UK, England
—, biodiversity
    GOOD, Roger B.   Australia, ACT
—, biological (tropical reforestation etc.)
    KERN, Berndt   Sweden
    KERN, Eha   Sweden
—, Cheetah/predator conservation
    KRAUS, Daniel   Namibia/USA, CA
    MARKER-KRAUS, Laurie   Namibia/USA, DC
—, climate (esp. global change)
    GRASSL, Hartmut   Switzerland
—, conservation management and
    ABUZINADA, Abdul A.H.   Saudi Arabia
—, —, elasmobranch
    GRUBER, Samuel H.   USA, FL
—, cultural ecology
    GIRARDET, Herbert K.   UK, England
—, design of
    WEBER, Karl E.   Thailand
—, development in environment[al]
    VERMA, Sewa R.   India, UP
—, — — livestock & rangeland utilization
    WARDEH, Muhammad Fadel   Syria
—, ecological
    AMBASHT, Radhey S.   India, UP
    FERRAR, Anthony A.   RSA
    MARGARIS, Nickolas S.   Greece
—, ecosystem
    HABER, Wolfgang   Germany
—, environmental monitoring &
    KELLERMANN, Adolf K.   Germany
—, — — computer communications
    PETER, Ian W.   Australia, Qld
—, —, esp.in toxicology, immunology, & cancer
    RAY, Prasanta K.   India, W.Bengal
—, —, interdisciplinary
    GANDY, Matthew   UK, England
—, —, marine
    PRAVDIĆ, Velimir   Croatia
—, —, planning
    OPSCHOOR, Johannes B.   The Netherlands

—, —, training (for)
    SEELY, Mary K.   Namibia
—, — values & philosophy through
    GITTINS, John W.E.H.   UK, England
—, field, applications of, to conservation
    TRAPNELL, Colin G.   UK, England
—, —, in ornithology
    ORHUN-HEWSON, Canan   USA, MA
—, —, wildlife conservation, in SE Asia esp.Sarawak
    & Sabah
    BENNETT, Elizabeth L.   Malaysia
—, fire (natural fire regimes and plant responses)
    GOOD, Roger B.   Australia, ACT
—, floristic
    AMIRKHANOV, Amirkhan M.   Russia
—, forest genetic resources
    TOMPSETT, Paul B.   UK, England
—, Gaia
    LOVELOCK, James E.   UK, England
—, global change
    GRASSL, Hartmut   Switzerland
—, — —, coordination & planning of
    GOLUBEV, Genady N.   Russia
—, hydraulic, on flows
    HOLČÍK, Vladimír   Slovak Rep.
— in, see also research, research into, research on
— — amphibians & birds
    DIAZ, José VALENCIA   Chile
— — application of social science to natural
    resource management & planning issues
    BLAHNA, Dale J.   USA, UT
— — arid ecosystems
    MILLS, M.G.L. ('Gus')   RSA
— — biological control of some plant diseases
    JARIWALA, Savitri   India, UP
— — conservation of Odonata
    MOORE, Norman W.   UK, England
— — ecodevelopment (applied physics, ecology, &
    biotechnology), re.recovery of refuse and
    underutilized resources
    ARIAS-CHAVEZ, Jesus   Mexico
— — environmental conservation
    BUTLER, James 'Jim' R.   Canada, Alb.
— — forest disturbance & recovery
    ORGLE, Tetey K.   Ghana
— — hydrological effects of land-use
    PEREIRA, H.Charles   UK, England
— — national parks
    VERSCHUREN, Jacques C.F.   Belgium
— — Nature conservation
    LACY, Terry P.DE   Australia, NSW
— — ornithology
    DHINDSA, Manjit S.   India, Mah.
— — —, field
    ORHUN-HEWSON, Canan   USA, MA
— — parks
    BUTLER, James 'Jim' R.   Canada, Alb.
    PEINE, John D.   USA, TN
— — physical oceanography in the Gulf of Mexico
    CERDA, Alberto M.VAZQUEZ DE LA   Mexico
— — plant community ecology
    KULL, Olevi   Estonia
— — — ecology
    STALTER, Richard   USA, NY
— — pollution control
    MOORE, Norman W.   UK, England
— — protected area management
    LACY, Terry P.DE   Australia, NSW
— — Quaternary palaeoecology
    YOUNG, Steven B.   USA, VT

† See upper footnote on p. 409.

research in (contd)
— — rainforest ecology
    WEBB, Leonard J.   Australia, Qld
— — reptiles
    DIAZ, José VALENCIA   Chile
— — savanna ecosystems
    MILLS, M.G.L. ('Gus')   RSA
— — soil conservation
    LAL, Rattan   USA, OH
— — — fertility
    FÜLECKY, György   Hungary
— — sustainable development
    ARIAS-CHAVEZ, Jesus   Mexico
— — tropical ecology
    COLE, Norman H.A.   Sierra Leone
— — — forestry
    BURLEY, Jeffery   UK, England
— — radiowaves environment*
— — upper atmosphere physics–atmospheric system
    interactions
    *RADICELLA, Sandro M.   Italy
— — wildlife
    BUTLER, James 'Jim' R.   Canada, Alb.
—, institutions, management of
    HOECK, Hendrik N.   Switzerland
—, interdisciplinary environmental
    GANDY, Matthew   UK, England
—, international agricultural
    JAMES, W.Clive   Cayman Islands
— into, see also research, research in, research on
— — ecology of feeding & reproduction of Chilean
    reptiles, amphibians, & birds
    DIAZ, José VALENCIA   Chile
— — effects of air pollution on plants & insects
    BELL, Nigel   UK, England
— — general biology
    POLUNIN, Ivan V.   Singapore
— — Jurassic palaeontology
    DUFF, Keith L.   UK, England
— — synchronous displays by *Pteroptyx* fireflies
    POLUNIN, Ivan V.   Singapore
—, land-use resources'
    NELSON, J.Gordon   Canada, Ont.
—, landslide, in central Himalaya
    HAIGH, Martin J.   England, UK
—, management
    ARMIJOS, Mariano MONTAÑO   Ecuador
    HEMPEL, Gotthilf   Germany
    ROBERTS, Thomas M.   UK, England
—, marine environmental
    PRAVDIĆ, Velimir   Croatia
—, methods
    WEBER, Karl E.   Thailand
—, ocean, arctic & antarctic ice and
    WADHAMS, Peter   UK, England
— on, see also research, research in, research into
— — ecological matters
    MARGARIS, Nickolas S.   Greece
— — economic instruments
    OPSCHOOR, Johannes B.   The Netherlands
— — environmental concerns
    TROMPF, Garry W.   Australia, NSW
— — environmental monitoring instruments
    PRASAD, Basudeo   India, E.Punjab
— — fish–seabird interactions*
— — herbaceous biodiversity & forest harvesting
    *DUFFY, David C.   USA, AK
— — Malagasy primates
    ANDRIAMAMPIANINA, Joseph   Madagascar

— — medical entomology
    DUFFY, David C.   USA, AK
— — nuclear waste
    LEMONS, John D., Jr   USA, ME
— — religions & environmental concerns
    TROMPF, Garry W.   Australia, NSW
— — seabird–fish interactions
    DUFFY, David C.   USA, AK
— — sustainability of ecosystems
    NEWMAN, Edward I.   UK, England
— — threatened plant species
    BENSON, John S.   Australia, NSW
— — tree improvement*
— — vegetative propagation
    *LAL, Piare   India, AP
— — vulnerability of wildlife to impacts of climate
    change
    MKANDA, Francis X.   Malawi
— organization
    PEREIRA, H.Charles   UK, England
    RADICELLA, Sandro M.   Italy
—, ornithological
    GORIUP, Paul D.   UK, England
—, peace, and North–South issues
    SCHRIJVER, Nico J.   The Netherlands
—, planning
    OPSCHOOR, Johannes B.   The Netherlands
    RADICELLA, Sandro M.   Italy
—, polar, protection of arctic environment
    PRESTRUD, Pål   Norway
— policy & management
    HEMPEL, Gotthilf   Germany
—, predator/Cheetah conservation
    KRAUS, Daniel   Namibia/USA, CA
    MARKER-KRAUS, Laurie   Namibia/USA, DC
— programmes, formulation & administration of
    JAIN, Sudhanshu K.   India, UP
— projects & units, planning of, for developing
    countries
    RADICELLA, Sandro M.   Italy
—, protected areas'
    BOYLE, Terence P.   USA, CO
—, scientific (for application/management)
    DIAZ-MARTIN, Diego   Venezuela
    TERRASSON, François   France
—, —, & application
    TERRASSON, François   France
—, —, in anthropogenic sciences: ecology, geography,
    geophysics, natural environmental sciences,
    oceanology, physics of the atmosphere
    IZRAEL, Yuri   Russia
—, solid waste management
    AKHTAR, Waseem   Pakistan
— techniques
    WEBER, Karl E.   Thailand
— training, environmental
    SEELY, Mary K.   Namibia
—, wildlife
    KLINGEL, Hans   Germany
—, — conservation field, in South–east Asia
    esp.Sarawak & Sabah
    BENNETT, Elizabeth L.   Malaysia
reserves
    VERNAUDON, Yolande   Tahiti
—, Biosphere
    BATISSE, Michel   France
    SAUNIER, Richard E.   USA, MD
    SOKOLOV, Vladimir   Russia
    WATSON, John R.   Australia, WA

—, conservation
WATSON, John R.   Australia, WA
—, extractive & multiple-use, design of
SEVILLA, Lorenzo B.CARDENAL
                          Nicaragua/Guatemala
—, game, planning & development of
SPINAGE, Clive A.   UK, England
—, natural, management of State
ALLAVENA, Stefano   Italy
—, Nature
PIIROLA, Jouko   Finland
—, protected, wildlife & livestock management
    outside of
KRAUS, Daniel   Namibia/USA, CA
MARKER-KRAUS, Laurie   Namibia/USA, DC
—, role of, in ecological stability
HATOUGH-BOURAN, Alia M.A.   Jordan
resistance, introduction of pest & disease
ALSTON, Frank H.   UK, England
— to pest & diseases: Hops (*Humulus lupulus*)
DARBY, Peter   UK, England
resource, *see also* resources[†]
— assessment (inventory & monitoring)
SHEPHERD, Alexander R.DAWSON   UK, England
— —, conservation
HIBBERD, John K.   Australia, ACT
— assessments, wetland & biodiversity
BENNETT, Sara L.   Canada, BC
—, coastal, management
WHITE, Susan L.   USA, FL
— conservation
NIKULIN, Valery A   Russia
SHORES, John N.   USA, ME
— — & management, genetic, domestic animal
TEWOLDE, Assefaw   Mexico
— —, economics & institutions essential to effective
CHILD, Graham P.T.   Zimbabwe
— —, marine & coastal
KENCHINGTON, Richard A.   Australia, ACT
— —, natural, social dimensions of
HOUGH, John L.   USA, MD
— —, Nature
VERMA, Sewa R.   India, UP
— development, human
BRERETON, Vera A.   Barbados
— dilemmas, common
YOUNG, Raymond DE   USA, MI
— ecology (esp. of forests)
NEWTON, Adrian C.   UK, Scotland
— —, tropical (savanna)
FERRAR, Anthony A.   RSA
— economics (incl.of agroforestry)
GONZALEZ, Juan A.AGUIRRE   Costa Rica
— efficiency (incl.use of energy)
LOVINS, Amory B.   USA, CO
LOVINS, L.Hunter   USA, CO
—, energy, biomass as
SCHARMER, Klaus   Germany
—, forest soil
ZHANG, Wan Ru   China
— management, *see also* resources' management
BUTLER, Paul J.   St Lucia
DUFOUR, Jules   Canada, Que.
IDECHONG, Noah   Palau
LAYDOO, Richard S.   Trinidad & Tobago
SATOO, Taisitiroo   Japan
— —, coastal
KLEE, Gary A.   USA, CA
SHEPHERD, Alexander R.DAWSON   UK, England

— —, integrated
DODDS, Donald G.   Canada, NS
MELKANIA, Niranjan P.   India, MP
MWALYOSI, Raphael B.B.   Tanzania
— —, land & water
RAI, Suresh Chand   India, Sikkim
— —, marine & coastal
KENCHINGTON, Richard A.   Australia, ACT
— —, natural, *see* [natural] resources' management
— —, —, for sustainable development
PANDURANGAN, Alagramam G.   India, Ker.
— —, —, in rural development
TOORNSTRA, Franke H.   The Netherlands
— —, — marine
SYBESMA, Jeffrey   Netherlands Antilles
— —, sustainable, of tropical land & marine
    ecosystems
BAINES, Graham B.K.   Australia, Qld
— — systems in the tropics
JOHANNES, Robert E.   Australia, Tas.
— —, tropical coastal
WILKINSON, Clive R.   Australia, Qld
— —, water
RAI, Suresh Chand   India, Sikkim
—, marine, economics
TISDELL, Clement A.   Australia, Qld
—, natural, economics
BARBIER, Edward B.   UK, England
CAMINO, Ronnie DE   Costa Rica
—', —, management, *see* natural resources'
    management
—, ,   & planning issues, application of social
    science to
BLAHNA, Dale J.   USA, UT
—, — — use
MUMBA, Wanga   Zambia
—, —, planning
ARIFFIN, Ishak BIN   Malaysia
—, —, policy
CAMINO, Ronnie DE   Costa Rica
—, —, — and law
BARAHONA-ISRAEL, Rodrigo   Costa Rica
—, —, surveys
NOUR, Hassan O.ABDEL   Sudan
— planning
MENDEZ, Jesus M.DELGADO   Brazil
SHORES, John N.   USA, ME
— —, conservation
HIBBERD, John K.   Australia, ACT
— —, forest
KUMAR, Prem   Canada, Alb.
— policy
MENDEZ, Jesus M.DELGADO   Brazil
— schemes, water, environmental impacts of
PETTS, Geoffrey   UK, England
— survey, soil & land
WEBSTER, Richard   UK, England
— -use conflicts, identification & management of
SAUNIER, Richard E.   USA, MD
— use, natural
DRAKE, Christopher M.   UK, England
— —, — sustained
OVINGTON, John D.   Australia, ACT
—, wildlife, conservation & utilization including
    corals
THRESHER, Philip B.   USA, CA
resources, *see also* resource[†]
—, agricultural, in humid tropics
SMITH, Nigel J.H.   USA, FL

resources (contd)
— and environmental management & policy
   COCKLIN, Christopher R.   NZ
—, biotic, ethics & politics in conservation of
   FRAZIER, John G.   Mexico
—, coastal, management
   TORTELL, Philip   NZ
—, coastal-zone
   CLARK, John R.   USA, FL
—, common property
   BERKES, Fikret   Canada, Man.
—' conservation, coastal
   WHITE, Alan T.   Sri Lanka
—' —, natural
   LARSEN, Thor   Norway
   THAPA, Gopal B.   Thailand
—, — of Nature & natural
   HOLDGATE, Martin W.   UK, England
—, — — plant genetic
   CLEMENT, Charles R.   Brazil, Amaz.
   HAWKES, John G.   UK, England
—, depletion of
   PETERSON, Russell W.   USA, DE
—, economic, conservation of
   TAN, Koonlin   UK, England
—, environment and
   HARA, Takeshi   Japan
—, environmental, ethics & politics in conservation of
   FRAZIER, John G.   Mexico
—, fishery, conservation & management of
   BUSTAMANTE, Georgina   USA, FL
—, genetic
   IGNACIMUTHU, Savarimuthu   India, TN
   NEWTON, Adrian C.   UK, Scotland
—, —, conservation
   ASTLEY, David 'Dave'   UK, England
   PALMBERG-LERCHE, Christel M.   Italy
   WILSON, Richard T.   UK, England
—, —, forest
   PALMBERG-LERCHE, Christel M.   Italy
—, —, —, research
   TOMPSETT, Paul B.   UK, England
—, —, plant
   ANISHETTY, Narasimha M.   Italy
   HAWKES, John G.   UK, England
—, ground-water, pollution & management
   WEAVER, John M.C.   RSA
—, Himalayan natural, conservation of
   PANDIT, Ashok K.   India, J&K
—, human, investments in, sustainable development
   through
   SHAW, R.Paul   USA, DC
—, information systems
   UNNI, N.V.Madhavan   India, AP
—, insect, conservation & utilization of third-world
   MORRIS, Michael G.   UK, England
—, land-use, research & education
   NELSON, J.Gordon   Canada, Ont.
—' management, cultural
   WHITEHOUSE, John F.   Australia, NSW
—' —, natural, see natural resources' management
—' —, —, & impact assessment
   KEAGE, Peter L.   Australia, Vic.
—, marine
   DESAI, Bhagirath N.   India, Kar.
—, mineral
   ABU-RUBEIHA', Ali A.   Jordan
—, natural, see also [natural] resources
—, —, conservation of
   GHABBOUR, Samir I.   Egypt

   HOLDGATE, Martin W.   UK, England
   HOLOWESKO, Lynn P.   Bahamas
—, —, exploitation of
   NILSSON, Sten   Austria
—, —, humanity's use of
   DRAKE, Christopher M.   UK, England
—, —, in developing countries, conservation &
   management of, using support of local
   people
   MacFARLAND, Craig G.   USA, ID
—, —, management, see natural resources'
   management
—, —, participatory management of
   WHITE, Alan T.   Sri Lanka
—', —, policy
   DAVIS, Bruce W.   Australia, Tas.
—', —, — analysis
   MORELL, Merilio G.   Italy
—, —, protection of
   DELPIANO, José P.Castro   Uruguay
—, —, surveys for assessment of
   STANTON, James P.   Australia, Qld
—, —, sustainable use of
   HOLDGATE, Martin W.   UK, England
   HURNI, Hans   Switzerland
   MARTINS, Edouardo de Souza   Brazil, Bras.DF
—' planning
   OHN   Myanmar
—, plant
   JAIN, Sudhanshu K.   India, UP
—, — genetic, conservation of
   CLEMENT, Charles R.   Brazil, Amaz.
   HAWKES, John G.   UK, England
—' policy, natural
   DAVIS, Bruce W.   Australia, Tas.
—, pollution & management of ground-water
   WEAVER, John M.C.   RSA
—' research, forest genetic
   TOMPSETT, Paul B.   UK, England
—, sustainable use of Nature &
   HOLDGATE, Martin W.   UK, England
—, underutilized
   ARIAS-CHAVEZ, Jesus   Mexico
—, water, assessment & management
   GOLUBEV, Genady N.   Russia
—, —, development projects re.tropical & temperate
   environments
   ZWAHLEN, Robert   Switzerland
—, —, engineering
   ALI, Iqbal   Pakistan
—, — [fresh]
   BENNETT, Sara L.   Canada, BC
   MUNASINGHE, Mohan   Sri Lanka
—, —, in dry lands
   WILLIAMS, William D.   Australia, SA
—, wild animal, commercial use of
   WILSON, George R.   Australia, WA
—, wildlife
   RANJITSINH, M.K.   India, MP
—, world's, just distribution of, v.free trade/economic
   growth
   DAMMANN, Erik   Norway
response, emergency
   GEBREMEDHIN, Naigzy   Kenya
— of insect populations to industrial pollution
   KOZLOV, Mikhail V.   Finland
responses, plant, natural fire regimes and (fire
   research)
   GOOD, Roger B.   Australia, ACT

—, —, to abiotic stress
   MANSFIELD, Terence A.   UK, England
—, —, — damage
   ROOM, Peter M.   Australia, Qld
restoration, ecological
   CLEWELL, Andre F.   USA, FL
   JORDAN III, William R.   USA, WI
— ecology
   HOBBS, Richard J.   Australia, WA
   MELKANIA, Niranjan P.   India, MP
   OHN   Myanmar
   PFADENHAUER, Jörg   Germany
   SIMPSON, Philip G.   NZ
   SINGH, Jamuna S.   India, UP
   WINGATE, David B.   Bermuda
— — of Cape plants & vegetation
   BOUCHER, Charles   RSA
—, environmental
   LOVINS, L.Hunter   USA, CO
   PETRETTI, Francesco   Italy
—, —, of the Earth
   ODULA, Michael A.N.   Kenya
—, forest
   ASHTON, Mark S.   USA, CT
—, landscape
   NAVEH, Zev   Israel
— of degraded land
   CHADWICK, Michael J.   Sweden
— — 'tropandean' landscapes
   SARMIENTO, Fausto O.   USA, GA
restructuring, economic, in Poland
   SERAFIN, Rafal K.   Poland
reuse of water
   ARCEIVALA, Soli J.   India, Mah.
revegetation of polar deserts
   SVOBODA, Josef   Canada, Ont.
review, project
   POTTER, Louis   BVI
revitalization of abandoned & derelict landscape
   KRAJČOVIČ, Roman S.   Slovak Rep.
rhino conservation
   WERIKHE, Michael M.   Kenya
rhinoceros (protection and conservation)
   MERZ, Anna H.   Kenya
—, conservation of the African
   BROOKS, Peter M.   RSA
rhizobium systems approaches — Sahara
   DAMERDJI, M.Amine   Algeria
rhythms, diurnal
   CLOUDSLEY-THOMPSON, John L.
        UK, England
right to information (environmental legislation)
   PITTA, Luis CAEIRO   Portugal
right-of-way vegetation management
   EGLER, Frank E.   USA, CT
rights, human
   NOVOA, Laura   Chile
   SCHRAM, Gunnar G.   Iceland
   SILVA, Allenisheo L.M.DE   Sri Lanka
   UEXKÜLL, Carl J.W.VON   Sweden
—, — & animal
   ONAYEMI, Olarotimi O.   Nigeria
—, —, issues
   MEHTA, Mahesh C.   India, Delhi
—, —, protection of, for a healthy environment
   CHERKASOVA, Maria V.   Russia
— of future generations, protection of
   COUSTEAU, Jacques-Yves   France
rise, sea-level, in Pacific Basin
   SHAPIRO, Harvey A.   Japan

risk (environmental etc.)
   TAIT, Elizabeth J.   UK, Scotland
   WARNER, Frederick   UK, England
— analysis, ecological
   BOYLE, Terence P.   USA, CO
— assessment
   RAJAGOPAL, Rangaswamy   USA, OH
—, comparative environmental, quantitative
   measurement of
   CHADWICK, Michael J.   Sweden
— reduction, environmental
   AICKIN, R.Malcolm   UK, England
risks, environmental
   HUBA, Mikuláš   Slovak Rep.
river catchment management, total
   BAKER, Joseph 'Joe' T.   Australia, Qld
— classification & zoning
   BHARGAVA, Devendra S.   India, UP
— ecology & life histories of aquatic insects
   STANFORD, Jack A.   USA, MT
— ecosystems' management
   TERRASSON, François   France
— floodplains, landscape ecology of
   DECAMPS, Henri   France
— regulation
   HOLČIK, Vladímír   Slovak Rep.
   PETTS, Geoffrey   UK, England
— systems, preservation of
   ZINKE, Alexander   Austria
— water, sharing common, between countries
   MOUDUD, Hasna J.   Bangladesh
rivers, large, fisheries ecology of
   WELCOMME, Robin L.   Italy
rodents, ecology & conservation of
   RAY, Justina C.   USA, FL
rubber-yielding plants
   SCHULTES, Richard E.   USA, MA
rural area development, integrated
   RAI, Suresh Chand   India, Sikkim
— areas, environmental education in
   LANDFRIED, Steven E.   USA, WI
— communities, mobilizing, for better common
   property management
   QUTUB, Syed Ayub   Pakistan
— development
   FÉRON, Eric M.   Zimbabwe
   RYDÉN, Per A.   Switzerland
   VASUDEVAN, Padma   India, Delhi
— —, Bamboo in
   BOA, Eric   UK, England
— —, natural resource management in
   TOORNSTRA, Franke H.   The Netherlands
— — planning
   NEPAL, Sanjay K.   Switzerland
— energy planning
   KHANDELWAL, Kailash C.   India, Raj.
— environmental pollution control
   ABDEL-GAWAAD, Ahmed A.-W.   Egypt
— human populations, involvement of, in
   conservation
   PRICE, Mark R.STANLEY   Kenya
— livelihood systems
   GRITZNER, Jeffrey A.   USA, MT
— sanitation
   KHANDELWAL, Kailash C.   India, Raj.
— tourism
   CROSBY, Arturo   Spain
— —, economics of
   SISMAN, Richard ('Dick')   UK, England
— -based livelihood systems
   WOODGATE, Graham R.   UK, England

Russia, economics of
GOLDMAN, Marshall I.   USA, MA
Russian environment
STEWART, John MASSEY   UK, England

Sabah, wildlife conservation field research in
BENNETT, Elizabeth L.   Malaysia
safety, chemical
HERKOVITS, Jorge   Argentina
—, environmental
ABBASPOUR, Madjid   Iran
—, industrial
BRINCHUK, Mikhail M.   Russia
— of nuclear power
HARE, F.Kenneth   Canada, Ont.
Sahara, agricultural development in the
DAMERDJI, M.Amine   Algeria
—, conservation of main aquatic biotopes of
DUMONT, Henri J.   Belgium
Saharan herpetofaunal biodiversity
LAMBERT, Michael R.K.   UK, England
Sahel
FRANGI, Jean-Pierre   France
—, conservation of main aquatic biotopes of
DUMONT, Henri J.   Belgium
—, West African, conservation & development in
DRIJVER, Carel A.   The Netherlands
Sahelian herpetofaunal biodiversity
LAMBERT, Michael R.K.   UK, England
saline lakes, prairie, impacts of UV radiation &
    microbial biogeochemical cycles in
ROBARTS, Richard D.   Canada, Sask.
salinity
ORHUN-HEWSON, Canan   USA, MA
— problems in arid regions
BATANOUNY, Kamal H.   Egypt
Salix, taxonomy of, in the New World
ARGUS, George W.   Canada, Ont.
Salmon, Atlantic, ecology & conservation of
MILLS, Derek H.   UK, Scotland
—, Pacific, biology
COUTANT, Charles C.   USA, TN
salt lagoon ecology
POR, Francis D.   Israel
— lakes
WILLIAMS, William D.   Australia, SA
— marsh, conservation & management of
BRIDGEWATER, Peter   Australia, ACT
— — ecology
BOORMAN, Laurie A.   UK, England
WOODELL, Stanley R.J.   UK, England
sampling, oceanographic
ORHUN-HEWSON, Canan   USA, MA
sanctuaries, conservation of
SINGH, Birandra B.   Fiji
sand-dune ecology
BOORMAN, Laurie A.   UK, England
SALMAN, Albert H.P.M.   The Netherlands
— - — fixation
ZOUHA, Sekkou   Morocco
— - — management
SALMAN, Albert H.P.M.   The Netherlands
sanitary engineering, alternative
LUTZENBERGER, José A.   Brazil, RS
sanitation
MUTTAMARA, Samorn   Thailand

—, rural
KHANDELWAL, Kailash C.   India, Raj.
Sarawak, flora & fauna of
MANSER, Bruno   Switzerland
—, wildlife conservation field research in
BENNETT, Elizabeth L.   Malaysia
satellite remote-sensing
GRASSL, Hartmut   Switzerland
— — - — in forest conservation & management
JUSOFF, Kamaruzaman   Malaysia
— telemedicine
JOVANOVIĆ, Petar   Yugoslavia
— tracking
LANDFRIED, Steven E.   USA, WI
satellites, meteorological
KELLOGG, William W.   USA, CO
savanna ecology
PRINS, Herbert H.T.   The Netherlands
SINGH, Jamuna S.   India, UP
SINGH, Kaushalendra P.   India, UP
— ecosystems, conservation of and research in
MILLS, M.G.L. ('Gus')   RSA
—, tropical, resource ecology
FERRAR, Anthony A.   RSA
schistosomiasis
THOMAS, John D.   UK, England
schools, promotion of tree nurseries in
FITTER, Perin S.   Kenya
science, *see also* sciences
— & environmental policy
ORIANS, Gordon H.   USA, WA
—, arctic, esp.geography & history
ROWLEY, Diana M.R.   Canada, Ont.
—, atmospheric
DIAB, Roseanne D.   RSA
—, children's concepts in
COHEN, Michael R.   USA, IN
—, climate
HOUGHTON, John T.   UK, England
— conservation, earth
KNILL, John   UK, England
—, — (ecosozology)
LISICKÝ, Mikuláš J.   Slovak Rep.
—, —, in tropical coastal environments
DAVIE, James D.S.   Australia, Qld
—, development of, in developing countries
PEARMAN, Peter B.   USA, CA
—, ecosystem
SLOCOMBE, D.Scott   Canada, Ont.
—, environmental, *see also* sciences, environmental
KHANNA, Purushottam   India, MP
SINGER, S.Fred   USA, VA
XU, Ouyong   China
—, —, & policy
FARAGÓ, Tibor   Hungary
—, —, Quaternary
BOYD, William 'Bill' Edgar   Australia, NSW
—, field, foundation, directing a
WALKER, Brian W.   UK, England
—, forest soil
ZHANG, Wan Ru   China
—, interdisciplinary, & its role in policymaking
O'RIORDAN, Timothy   UK, England
—, international (atmospheric etc.)
PERRY, John S.   USA, VA
—, marine, *see also* sciences, marine
HOF, Tom VAN'T   Netherlands Antilles
MORTON, Brian   Hong Kong
—, — environmental
SU, Jilan   China

—, mushroom
 FERMOR, Terence R. UK, England
— of environmental conservation
 POORE, M.E.Duncan UK, Scotland
—, peatland (telmatology)
 MASING, Viktor Estonia
— policy
 PRESS, Frank USA, DC
— —, national & international
 KENDREW, John C. UK, England
—, polymer–environment–sustainable development
 VASUDEVAN, Padma India, Delhi
—, rangeland
 WILSON, George R. Australia, WA
—, social, application of, to natural resource
  management & planning issues
 BLAHNA, Dale J. USA, UT
—, soil
 BUBLINEC, Eduard Slovak Rep.
 LÅG, Jul Norway
 RITCHIE, Jerry C. USA, MD
 SANCHEZ, Pedro A. Kenya
—, wetland, applied to policy & management
 LARSON, Joseph S. USA, MA
sciences, see also science
—, atmospheric
 PERRY, John S. USA, VA
 RHO, Chae-Shik S.Korea
—, biological
 EHRLICH, Paul R. USA, CA
—, conservation
 SWINGLAND, Ian R. UK, England
—, earth
 PAGE, Christopher N. UK, Scotland
—, environmental, see also science, environmental
 COLE, Norman H.A. Sierra Leone
 RAMAKRISHNAN, P.S. ('Ram') India, Delhi
 RHO, Chae-Shik S.Korea
 SOUTHWOOD, T.Richard E. UK, England
—, life
 CALDWELL, Lynton Keith USA, IN
 GOLDSMITH, Edward UK, England
—, marine, see also science, marine
 DESAI, Bhagirath N. India, Goa
 HEMPEL, Gotthilf Germany
 KENCHINGTON, Richard A. Australia, ACT
 RODRIGUEZ, Andrés R.RODRIGUEZ Venezuela
—, — & polar
 HEMPEL, Gotthilf Germany
—, natural (esp. Fungi)
 TURIAN, G. Switzerland
—, scientific research in anthropogenic & natural
  environmental
 IZRAEL, Yuri Russia
—, vegetation
 PFADENHAUER, Jörg Germany
scientific bibliography
 LIONNET, Joseph F.G. Seychelles
— education (esp. from botanical gardens)
 RAVEN, Peter H. USA, MO
— research (esp. for conservation)
 DIAZ-MARTIN, Diego Venezuela
— — & application
 TERRASSON, François France
— — in anthropogenic ecology, geophysics, physics
  of the atmosphere, oceanology, & geography
 IZRAEL, Yurii Russia
scientists, environmental–politicians, interactions of
 BOLIN, Bert R. Sweden
—' role re.sustainable human development
 MALONE, Thomas F. USA, NC

scleractian corals, calcification & growth in
 BARNES, David J. Australia, Qld
scorpion stings, public health problems resulting from
scorpions: phylogeny, evolutionary ecology,
  biogeography, & reproduction, of
 LOURENÇO, Wilson R. France
Scolytidae (bark beetles), ecology of
 OKOŁÓW, Czeslaw Poland
— –land interactions in coastal zone, marine parks,
  & protected areas
 RAY, G.Carleton USA, VA
Sea, Law of the, see Law of the Sea
— -level rise impacts, islands in Asia–Pacific region
 HOLTHUS, Paul F. USA, HI
— - — — in Pacific Basin
 SHAPIRO, Harvey A. Japan
— -turtle conservation
 ROSE, Carlos R.HASBÚN El Salvador
— turtles, ecology of, and habitats
 MARSH, Helene D. Australia, Qld
— - —' management, conservation, & population
  assessment
 MARQUEZ-MILLAN, René Mexico
seabird–fish interactions, research on
 DUFFY, David C. USA, AK
seabirds
 BOURNE, William R.P. UK, Scotland
 HAYNES-SUTTON, Ann M. Jamaica
—, ecology of
 DUNNET, George M. UK, Scotland
—, marine ecology esp.of
 CROXALL, John P. UK, England
— of the Bahamas
 HOLOWESKO, Lynn P. Bahamas
seagrasses
 LAKSHMANAN, Kalimedu K. India, TN
seals
 BERTRAM, G.Colin L. UK, England
—, marine ecology esp.of
 CROXALL, John P. UK, England
seas, high, marine protected areas esp.in the
 McCLOSKEY, Maxine E. USA, MD
seascape ecology
 BRIDGEWATER, Peter Australia, ACT
seaweeds
 LAKSHMANAN, Kalimedu K. India, TN
sectoral planning projects
 BENNETT, Sara L. Canada, BC
security, environmental
 AICKIN, R.Malcolm UK, England
 COCKLIN, Christopher R. NZ
 PITT, David Switzerland
—, —, re.military activities & war
 WESTING, Arthur H. USA, VT
sedimentology of coastal environments
 GRANJA, Helena M. Portugal
—, Pleistocene–Holocene
 CARVALHO, G.SOARES DE Portugal
seed conservation
 TOMPSETT, Paul B. UK, England
— germination & dormancy mechanisms
 TAO, Kar-ling J. Italy
— procurement in developing countries
 MOESTRUP, Søren Denmark
— testing
 TAO, Kar-ling J. Italy
seismic zonation in land-use planning
 AWAD, Adel R. Syria
selection, clonal, of trees
 LEAKEY, Richard R.B. Kenya

selection (contd)
—, evaluation methods for, of natural & semi-natural
forests
 HEISS, Gerhard   Germany
— of national park & protected area systems
 SATTLER, Paul S.   Australia, Qld
— — natural areas of Greece
 MALAMIDES, George   Greece
self-help survival in developing countries
 FRIEDMAN, Yona   France
— -sufficiency, national
 MOSLEY, John G.   Australia, Vic.
semi-aquatic mammals, ecology of
 BALČIAUSKAS, Linas   Lithuania
— -arid areas, landforms, soils, & climatic change, in
 WILLIAMS, Martin A.J. Australia, SA
— - — countries, water problems in
 DAMERDJI, M.Amine   Algeria
— - — ecosystems, conservation of, in coastal
regions & in Jordan
 HATOUGH-BOURAN, Alia M.A. Jordan
— - — forests, evaluation methods for selection of
 HEISS, Gerhard   Germany
— - — lands
 RECKERS, Ute   Kenya
— - — rangelands, sustainable economic
development in Africa's
 TOIT, Raoul F.DU   Zimbabwe
— - — regions, economic plants of
 WICKENS, Gerald E. UK, England
— - — tropics, domestication of tropical trees for
forestry/agroforestry in
 LEAKEY, Richard R.B. Kenya
semiotic mechanisms of biodiversity
 KULL, Kalevi   Estonia
sense of smell, role of, in orientation (migration of
fishes)
 HASLER, Arthur D.   USA, WI
sensing, remote see remote sensing
sensory physiology, elasmobranch
 GRUBER, Samuel H.   USA, FL
serology
 CLARK, Michael F.   UK, England
serpentine ecology
 WOODELL, Stanley R.J. UK, England
settlement & disease
 GADE, Daniel W.   USA, VT
sewage wastewater treatment & disposal
 KHAN, Niaz A.   UAE
sharks & rays
 EARLL, Robert C.   UK, England
—, conservation, research, sensory physiology, &
behaviour, of
 GRUBER, Samuel H.   USA, FL
sheep-farming
 WORTHINGTON, E.Barton UK, England
shrews, ecology & conservation of
 RAY, Justina C.   USA, FL
—, population biology of
 PUCEK, Zdzislaw K.   Poland
shrimp industry nutrition & management
 ARMIJOS, Mariano MONTAÑO Ecuador
Siberia: tundra, desert, taiga-forest, & steppe, in
 FLINT, Vladimir E.   Russia
Siberian environment
 STEWART, John MASSEY UK, England
Sierra Leone, conservation of biodiversity &
wilderness in
 TUBOKU-METZGER, Daphne J.A. Sierra Leone
— Madre Occidental of Mexico, flora of
 BYE, Robert   Mexico

SILATHAM, environmental awareness using concept
of
 TEJADHAMMO, Pongsak Thailand
silviculture
 ASHTON, Mark S.   USA, CT
 SPENCER, Jonathan W. UK, England
 WHITMORE, Timothy C. UK, England
—, tropical
 FREIBERG, Horst   Germany
 SABOGAL, Cesar A.   Indonesia
simulation modelling
 NYE, Peter H.   UK, England
sirenia
 BERTRAM, G.Colin L. UK, England
site protection, geological
 DUFF, Keith L.   UK, England
sites, cultural & historic, preservation of
 SINGH, Birandra B.   Fiji
—, protection of
 AUSSEDAT, Nicole M. France/St Barthélemy
skeletons, coral, environmental records stored in
 BARNES, David J.   Australia, Qld
skill, conservation, and technology, transfer of
 CHITRAKAR, Anil   Nepal
slash-and-burn agriculture, sustainable alternatives to
 SANCHEZ, Pedro A.   Kenya
slaters (wood-lice etc.), systematics, biogeography, &
evolution, of
 INGRAM, Glen J.   Australia, Qld
small biotic populations, conservation & management
of
 PRICE, Mark R.STANLEY Kenya
— mammals, ecology of
 BALČIAUSKAS, Linas   Lithuania
smell, role of sense of, in orientation (migration of
fishes)
 HASLER, Arthur D.   USA, WI
snail hosts of schistosome parasites
 THOMAS, John D.   UK, England
— -transmitted diseases in Southeast Asia
 WOODRUFF, David S. USA, CA
snakes, development & behaviour of
 BURGER, Joanna   USA, NJ
social activism
 MATHIESSEN, Peter   USA, NY
— — in Himalayan region
 BAHUGUNA, Sunderlal India, UP
— & ecological processes, linkages between
 RAMAKRISHNAN, P.S. ('Ram') India, Delhi
— change
 MILBRATH, Lester W. USA, NY
— changes required by sustainable development
 AICKIN, R.Malcolm UK, England
— constructs & strategies for Nature conservation
 MARTIN, Vance G.   USA, CO
— dimensions of natural resource conservation &
(environmentally) sustainable development
 HOUGH, John L.   USA, MD
— ecology
 GRINBERG, Miguel   Argentina
— —, wolf
 MECH, L.David   USA, MN
— forestry
 MARTIN, Vance G.   USA, CO
 PELUSO, Nancy L.   USA, CT
— —, promoting public awareness in
 SIVADAS, Ponathil   India, Ker.
— impact assessment of large dams
 GORZULA, Stefan   USA, TN
'—' insects
 ALI, Abd 'El moneim' M. Egypt

— issues, world
COUSTEAU, Jacques-Yves — France
— policies, environmental trends and related
HOLDGATE, Martin W. — UK, England
— policy
DAHL, R.Birgitta — Sweden
— science, application of, to natural resource management & planning issues
BLAHNA, Dale J. — USA, UT
societal problems of conservation & sustainability
FARAGÓ, Tibor — Hungary
societies', human, use of species diversity
OSEMEOBO, Gbadebo J. — Nigeria
—, indigenous native human, Amazonian rain-forest particularly
CLOUDSLEY, Timothy — UK, England
—, peasant & folk, ecological relationships of
GADE, Daniel W. — USA, VT
—, rich, consumption growth in
HAREIDE, Dag — Norway
—, traditional, ecology of
RAMAKRISHNAN, P.S. ('Ram') — India, Delhi
society, ageing
BOOTE, Robert E. — UK, England
— –climate interactions
GLANTZ, Michael H. — USA, CO
—, Nature–, relationships
WOODGATE, Graham R. — UK, England
—, sustainability of
MILBRATH, Lester W. — USA, NY
—, sustainable, ecological economy in transition period to a
HAREIDE, Dag — Norway
socio-economic survey
OHN — Myanmar
— - — systems, conservation of
TAN, Koonlin — UK, England
— -political aspects of wildlife conservation
SHAW, William W. — USA, AZ
sociobiology
WILSON, Edward O. — USA, MA
sociology, animal
KAWANABE, Hiroya — Japan
—, bryophyte
SJÖGREN, Erik A. — Sweden
—, ecological
CLOUDSLEY, Timothy — UK, Scotland
— of forestry
PELUSO, Nancy L. — USA, CT
'— — the Environment', theories in
CLOUDSLEY, Timothy — UK, England
—, plant
FREIBERG, Horst — Germany
LAVRENTIADES, George — Greece
MEDWECKA-KORNAŚ, Anna M. — Poland
SODAR (acoustic sounding)
SINGAL, Sagar P. — India, Delhi
soil and ecology
JIM, Chi Yung — Hong Kong
— assessment for crops
DAVIDSON, Donald A. — UK, Scotland
— -borne plant pathogens
WHITE, James G. — UK, England
— chemistry
STEINNES, Eiliv — Norway
— conservation
LAL, Rattan — USA, OH
LUK, Shiu-hung — Canada, Ont.
— —, catchment approach to
FITTER, Perin S. — Kenya

— degradation processes
VÁRALLYAY, György — Hungary
— development of reclaimed lands after surface coal-mining
KILMARTIN, Marianne P. — UK, England
—, environmental law
WESTREICHER, Antonio ANDALUZ — Bolivia
— erosion
LUK, Shiu-hung — Canada, Ont.
— — & conservation
HURNI, Hans — Switzerland
— fauna
GHABBOUR, Samir I. — Egypt
— fertility research
FÜLEKY, György — Hungary
—, forest, ecology & environment*
—, —, management & resource
*ZHANG, Wan Ru — China
— improvement (combatting desertification)
DAMERDJI, M.Amine — Algeria
— management
ABROL, Inder P. — India, Delhi
EKARATH, Raveendran — Bahrain
— mapping
VÁRALLYAY, György — Hungary
— physics
DAMERDJI, M.Amine — Algeria
VÁRALLYAY, György — Hungary
— –plant nutrient interactions
NYE, Peter H. — UK, England
— — relations
GRUBB, Peter J. — UK, England
— — –water relations
KIRKHAM, M.B. — USA, KS
— preservation against erosion
DAMERDJI, M.Amine — Algeria
— processes and 'greenhouse' gas emissions
LAL, Rattan — USA, OH
— re.land & forest ecology in tropical Africa
TRAPNELL, Colin G. — UK, England
— recovery agriculture
FISCHER, Gert R. — Brazil, SC
— resource survey
WEBSTER, Richard — UK, England
— science
BUBLINEC, Eduard — Slovak Rep.
LÅG, Jul — Norway
RITCHIE, Jerry C. — USA, MD
SANCHEZ, Pedro A. — Kenya
— —, forest
ZHANG, Wan Ru — China
—, solute movement in
NYE, Peter H. — UK, England
soils (general references)
CRAMPTON, Colin B. — Canada, BC
MALTBY, Edward — UK, England
—, calcareous, communities of, in Europe
GRUBB, Peter J. — UK, England
—, forest, & ecology
CHALLINOR, David — USA, DC
—, impact of ancient agriculture on
DAVIDSON, Donald A. — UK, Scotland
— in arid & semi-arid areas
WILLIAMS, Martin A.J. — Australia, SA
—, role of, in plant distribution
BLISS, Lawrence C. — USA, WA
—, tropical
JIM, Chi Yung — Hong Kong

* See lower footnote on p. 409.

Solanaceae, taxonomy & phylogeny of
   HAWKES, John G.   UK, England
solar energy
   FRANGI, Jean-Pierre   France
   SCHARMER, Klaus   Germany
— — in Bahrain*
— radiation, UV
   *ALNASER, Waheeb E.   Bahrain
solid waste
   ABBASPOUR, Madjid   Iran
   BRINCHUK, Mikhail M.   Russia
   KHAN, Niaz A.   UAE
— — disposal management
   KUFORIJI-OLUBI, Bola   Nigeria
— — management
   AWAD, Adel R.   Syria
   MUTTAMARA, Samorn   Thailand
   REHMAN, Syed Z.   Pakistan
— — — research
   AKHTAR, Waseem   Pakistan
solute movement in soil
   NYE, Peter H.   UK, England
solutions, environmental
   WRIGHT, Martin P.W.   UK, England
South America, cetaceans & flora of southernmost*
— —, history & marine mammals of southernmost
   *GOODALL, R.Natalie PROSSER   Argentina
— and Southeast Asia, conservation biology in
   YONZON, Pralad   Nepal
— Pacific regions, environmental management in
   EATON, Peter P.   Brunei
Southeast Asia, biological conservation in tropical
   KIEW, Bong Heang   Malaysia
— —, conservation & management of forests
   PAYNE, Junaidi   Malaysia
— —, development of hydropower & irrigation
   projects in
   WOODRUFF, David S.   USA, CA
— —, environmental management in
   EATON, Peter P.   Brunei
— —: poverty, biodiversity, & development in
   Highland
   DEARDEN, Philip   Canada, BC
— —, snail-transmitted diseases in
   WOODRUFF, David S.   USA, CA
— —, wildlife conservation field research in
   BENNETT, Elizabeth L.   Malaysia
— Asian rain-forests
   GATHORNE-HARDY, Gathorne   UK, England
southern ocean Cephalopoda
   RODHOUSE, Paul G.K.   UK, England
sovereignty, national, –warfaring propensities–
   environmental degradation
   SHAW, R.Paul   USA, DC
Soviet Union, former, biodiversity in the
   EICHBAUM, William M.   USA, DC
— —, —, environmental problems & policies in
   SACKS, Arthur B.   USA, CO
— —, —, — — of
   GOLDMAN, Marshall I.   USA, MA
space pollution, orbiting debris
   SINGER, S.Fred   USA, VA
—, remote sensing from
   HOUGHTON, John T.   UK, England
spatial planning, natural & cultural landscape
   conservation in
   STAWICKI, Henryk   Poland
— scales
   LEEMANS, Rik   The Netherlands

S/P/C/N biogeochemical cycles, see C/N/S/P
   biogeochemical cycles ...
speciation, chemical
   STEINNES, Eiliv   Norway
species action plans
   LAMBERTINI, Marco   Italy
— and vegetation recovery
   GIVEN, David R.   NZ
—, animal, conservation & evolution of
   WOODRUFF, David S.   USA, CA
—' conservation
   KASSIOUMIS, Konstantinos   Greece
   OSEMEOBO, Gbadebo J.   Nigeria
—, disappearing, saving
   OZA, Gunavant M.   India, Guj.
   OZA, Premlata   India, Guj.
—' diversity
   DANIELS, Frederikus J.A.   Germany
—' —, use of, by human societies
   OSEMEOBO, Gbadebo J.   Nigeria
—, endangered, see also species, endangered,
   conservation
   FLINT, Vladimir E.   Russia
   LaBASTILLE, Anne   USA, NY
   WILSON, George R.   Australia, WA
   YAZGAN, Nergis   Turkey
—, & disappearing, of mammals, protection of
   SOKOLOV, Vladimir   Russia
—, —, conservation
   BUTLER, James 'Jim' R.   Canada, Alb.
   DURRELL, Lee McG. UK, Channel Islands
   JAIN, Sudhanshu K.   India, UP
   MASCARENHAS, Anthony F. India, Mah.
   RANJITSINH, M.K.   India, MP
—, —, — biology & ecology of
   BRAMWELL, David   Canary Islands
—, —, esp.birds
   TEMPLE, Stanley A.   USA, WI
—, —, in Oman, conservation in wild and captive
   breeding of
   DALY, Ralph H.   Oman
—, —, of coastal birds
   BURGER, Joanna   USA, NJ
—, extinct, reintroduction programmes of
   HATOUGH-BOURAN, Alia M.A. Jordan
— extinction
   GŁOWACIŃSKI, Zbigniew A.   Poland
—, forest, sustainable use of
   RUIZ-MURRIERA, Julio   Switzerland
— introductions
   WELCOMME, Robin L.   Italy
—, invasive
   STRAHM, Wendy A.   Switzerland
—' management, threatened
   GIMINEZ-DIXON, Mariano Switzerland
—, marine — Nature conservation
   SMITH, Kevin D.   NZ
—, native Chilean, plantations of
   DONOSO, Claudio   Chile
— of fauna, endangered, conservation of
   HADDANE, Brahim   Morocco
—, plant, endangered
   NAYAR, M.Param   India, Ker.
—, —, rare & endangered
   HSU, Kuo-Shih   Taiwan
—, potato, wild & cultivated — use in plant breeding
   HAWKES, John G.   UK, England
—, protected
   URBAN, František   Czech Rep.

* See lower footnote on p. 409.

—' protection
  LABUDDE, Samuel F.   USA, CA
  LEBRETON, Philippe   France
—, rare, conservation
  ELMES, Graham W.   UK, England
— recovery
  GIVEN, David R.   NZ
— — plans (terrestrial)
  CARRILLO, Antonio MACHADO   Canary Islands
—, threatened
  ČEŘOVSKY, Jan   Czech Rep.
  GIVEN, David R.   NZ
—, —, conservation of
  BURBIDGE, Andrew A.   Australia, WA
—, —, management of
  GIMENEZ-DIXON, Mariano   Switzerland
—, —: Nature conservation
  SMITH, Kevin D.   NZ
—, —, of coastal birds
  BURGER, Joanna   USA, NJ
—, — plant, research on
  BENSON, John S.   Australia, NSW
—, utilization of wild, in plant breeding
  PINK, David A.C.   UK, England
—, wild, conservation of
  VARIAVA, Dilnavaz   India, Mah.
spectroscopy & fine optics
  SINGH, O.N.   India, UP
spider taxonomy & zoogeography
  MARUSIK, Yuri M.   Russia
spiders, role of, in questions of biodiversity,
    conservation, phylogeny, biogeography, &
    human envenomation
  RAVEN, Robert J.   Australia, Qld
spoonbills, conservation of
  KUSHLAN, James A.   USA, MS
Sri Lankan wild elephant, conservation of
  FERNANDO, Ranjen L.   Sri Lanka
stability, ecological, role of reserves in
  HATOUGH-BOURAN, Alia M.A.   Jordan
—, —, territorial systems of
  DEJMAL, Ivan   Czech Rep.
standard-setting
  JOOSTING, Peter E.   The Netherlands
standards, gene-bank
  TAO, Kar-ling J.   Italy
—, quality, environmental
  ALI, Iqbal   Pakistan
starches (staple foods)
  STANTON, W.Robert   UK, England
state of environment reporting
  CULLEN, Peter W.   Australia, ACT
statistical design and analysis of survey
  WEBSTER, Richard   UK, England
statistics, mathematical
  MacDONALD, Gordon J.F.   USA, CA
—, multidimensional, in ecology
  MAXIMOV, Victor N.   Russia
steppe birds
  PETRETTI, Francesco   Italy
— ecology
  PRINS, Herbert H.T.   The Netherlands
— in Siberia & Central Asia
  FLINT, Vladimir E.   Russia
stimulation of community-based conservation
    programmes & efforts
  UGWU, Christopher N.   Nigeria
stings, scorpion, public health problems resulting
    from
  LOURENÇO, Wilson R.   France

stored-grain systems
  KENNEDY, Robert   UK, England
storks [Cicoonidae]
  RAHMANI, Asad Rafi   India, UP
—, conservation of
  KUSHLAN, James A.   USA, MS
strategic analysis & sustainable development
  WILSON, George R.   Australia, WA
— environmental assessment
  TOORNSTRA, Franke H.   The Netherlands
— planning
  BARNEY, Gerald O.   USA, VA
— — for sustainable development
  MORELL, Merilio G.   Italy
— —, methodologies & techniques for
  SEVILLA, Lorenzo B.CARDENAL
    Nicaragua/Guatemala
strategies, conservation
  QUTUB, Syed Ayub   Pakistan
—, cultural, social, & psychological, for Nature
    conservation
  MARTIN, Vance G.   USA, CO
—, development of national & local, re.environmental
    education
  SMYTH, John C.   UK, Scotland
—, energy technology &
  GOLDEMBERG, José   Brazil, SP
—, environmental
  OLOJEDE, Ayodele A.   Nigeria
  SINCLAIR, John   Australia, NSW
—, — management
  GARRATT, Keith J.   NZ
  PRAVDIĆ, Velimir   Croatia
—, [environmentally] sustainable development
  SINGH, Karan   India, Delhi
— for sustainability
  ARIFFIN, Ishak BIN   Malaysia
— — sustainable development
  PEINE, John D.   USA, TN
—, integrated pest management
  JACOBSON, Robert J.   UK, England
—, land-use
  LUSCOMBE, Bruce A.   USA, NY
—, management, wetland & biodiversity
  BENNETT, Sara L.   Canada, BC
strategy, campaign
  VARIAVA, Dilnavaz   India, Mah.
— development, monitoring & evaluation
  ASFAW, Gedion   Ethiopia
stratigraphy, Pleistocene–Holocene
  CARVALHO, G.SOARES DE   Portugal
stratosphere, chemistry of the*
stratospheric aircraft, perturbation of natural global
    ozone balance by
  *JOHNSTON, Harold S.   USA, CA
— ozone
  SINGER, S.Fred   USA, VA
— pollution
  SINGH, O.N.   India, UP
stress, abiotic, responses of plants to
  MANSFIELD, Terence A.   UK, England
—, drought, impact of, on vegetation
  GRACE, John   UK, Scotland
Striped Bass biology
  COUTANT, Charles C.   USA, TN
structure of arctic ecosystems
  BLISS, Lawrence C.   USA, WA
— — forest ecosystems & grazing land
  PANDEYA, Satish C.   India, UP

* See lower footnote on p. 409.

structure of (contd)
— — Nature [& its function]
   WOODWELL, George M.   USA, MA
(—) ornithology (incl. bird protection)
   CIOCHIA, Victor   Romania
—, vegetation
   LEEMANS, Rik   The Netherlands
structures, organizational
   BOYLAND, Desmond E.   Australia, Qld
studies, Australian Aboriginal
   BOYD, William 'Bill' Edgar   Australia, NSW
—, EIA, of governmental & nongovernmental
   development projects
   UGWU, Christopher N.   Nigeria
—, environmental
   DRDOŠ, Ján   Slovak Rep.
   JAMES, Philmore A.   Antigua
   KHAN, Niaz A.   UAE
—, — policy
   SIMONIS, Udo E.   Germany
—, field [of environmental components, etc.]
   BENNETT, Sara L.   Canada, BC
—, —, of vertebrates
   SCHALLER, George B.   USA, NY
—, —, on population genetics of Lepidoptera &
   Mollusca
   OWEN, Denis F.   UK, England
—, forest ecosystem
   KIRA, Tatuo   Japan
—, future
   BATISSE, Michel   France
—, in vitro
   LAKSHMANAN, Kalimedu K.   India, TN
—, interdisciplinary, and their application to human
   needs
   BAKER, Joseph 'Joe' T.   Ausralia, Qld
—, — environmental
   BRYSON, Reid A.   USA, WI
—, — (environment–energy–food–economy)
   interactions
   SMIL, Václav   Canada, Man.
—, morphological, plant systematics and
   PANDURANGAN, Alagramam G.   India, Ker.
—, multidisciplinary environmental
   GARRATT, Keith J.   NZ
—, nutrient cycling, bioproductivity and
   OLA-ADAMS, Bunyamin A.   Nigeria
— of alpine & polar ecosystems
   WIELGOLASKI, Frans-Emil   Norway
— — atmospheric boundary layer
   SINGAL, Sagar P.   India, Delhi
—, ozone, see also ozone
   BOJKOV, Rumen D.   Switzerland
—, population
   EHRLICH, Paul R.   USA, CA
—, wetlands (& inventories)
   DIEGUES, Antonio C.S.   Brazil, SP
study, impact, of anthropic processes in coastal zone
   GRANJA, Helena M.   Portugal
— of birds esp.birds of prey
   GALUSHIN, Vladimir M.   Russia
— — comparative religions & philosophy
   SINGH, Karan   India, Delhi
— — vertebrates
   YABLOKOV, Alexey V.   Russia
sub-Saharan Africa, environmentally-sound
   technology & cooperation in
   KUFORIJI-OLUBI, Bola   Nigeria
subarctic biology
   NUORTEVA, Pekka O.   Finland

— waters
   MOORE, James W.   Canada, Alb.
submarine outfalls
   AWAD, Adel R.   Syria
subsistence community integration with protected
   area authorities
   ROWNTREE, Matthew J.W.   UK, England
substances, toxic
   WOODWELL, George M.   USA, MA
subtropical regions, vegetation ecology of
   WANG, Xianpu   China
suburban ecosystems' management
   PINOWSKI, Jan K.   Poland
succession [ecological]
   GŁOWACIŃSKI, Zbigniew A.   Poland
— in tropical & temperate regions
   HAMBLER, Clive   UK, England
—, primary, following deglaciation
   SVOBODA, Josef   Canada, Ont.
superecocomplex, sustainable anthropocentric
   LIU, Peitong   China
support of local people, garnering
   MacFARLAND, Craig G.   USA, ID
surface energy balance
   FRANGI, Jean-Pierre   France
— water, chemical contaminants of
   MOORE, James W.   Canada, Alb.
surgery, tree
   CHEEK, Roy V.   UK, England
Surinam, conservation & development in
   DRIJVER, Carel A.   The Netherlands
Surtsey, biotic colonization of the volcanic island
   FRIDRIKSSON, Sturla   Iceland
survey, floristic
   JAIN, Sudhanshu K.   India, UP
— of forests
   KIRBY, Keith J.   UK, England
— — protected natural areas
   WRIGHT, Shane D.T.   NZ
—, socio-economic
   OHN   Myanmar
—, soil & land resource, statistical design & analysis
   of
   WEBSTER, Richard   UK, England
—, vegetation
   BENSON, John S.   Australia, NSW
—, zoological, of Arabia
   BÜTTIKER, William   Switzerland
surveys, aerial
   WILSON, George R.   Australia, WA
—, fauna & insect
   AL-HOUTY, Wasmia   Kuwait
— for assessment of natural resources
   STANTON, James P.   Australia, Qld
—, natural resource
   NOUR, Hassan O.ABDEL   Sudan
—, water quality, remote sensing of
   BHARGAVA, Devendra S.   India, UP
—, wildlife
   CAMPBELL, Kenneth L.I.   UK, England
survival, self-help, in developing countries
   FRIEDMAN, Yona   France
sustainability
   BLOOMFIELD, Michael I.   Canada, BC
   LOVINS, Amory B.   USA, CO
   LOVINS, L.Hunter   USA, CO
   SARMIENTO, Fausto O.   USA, GA
   SLOCOMBE, D.Scott   Canada, Ont.
   UEXKÜLL, Carl J.W.VON   Sweden
— economics
   NILSSON, Sten   Austria

—, education for
  GITTINS, John W.E.H   UK, England
—, environmental
  GOODLAND, Robert J.A.   USA, DC
  SPETH, James G.   USA, NY
— of ecosystems, research on
  NEWMAN, Edward I.   UK, England
— — society
  MILBRATH, Lester W.   USA, NY
—, societal problems of
  FARAGÓ, Tibor   Hungary
—, strategies for
  ARIFFIN, Ishak BIN   Malaysia
— theory
  NORTON, Bryan G.   USA, GA
—, transfer of agri-biotechnology applications re.
  JAMES, W.Clive   Cayman Islands
sustainable agricultural development
  BISWAS, Asit K.   UK, England
  BISWAS, Margaret R.   UK, England
— — production systems
  TEWOLDE, Assefaw   Mexico
— agriculture
  ABROL, Inder P.   India, Delhi
  NAYVE-ROSSI, Portia A.   Philippines
  REID, Walter V.   USA, DC
  THAPA, Gopal B.   Thailand
  VISSER, Nicolaas W.   Kenya
  WAJIH, Shiraz A.   India, UP
— — and energy politics
  LINDSTROM, U.B.   Finland
— agroforestry
  HARRIS, Philip J.C.   UK, England
— —, local development &
  KERN, Berndt   Sweden
  KERN, Eha   Sweden
— alternatives to slash-and-burn agriculture
  SANCHEZ, Pedro A.   Kenya
— anthropocentric superecocomplex
  LIU, Peitong   China
— community development
  ALLEN, Irma   Swaziland
— conservation in third-world countries
  BEHRA, Olivier   Madagascar
— —: tropical moist forest
  WHITMORE, Timothy C.   UK, England
— development [ecologically, environmentally]
  BARNEY, Gerald O.   USA
  BELLAMY, David J.   UK, England
  EGZIABHER, Tewolde B.GEBRE   Ethiopia
  EKINS, Paul W.   UK, England
  ELKINGTON, John B.   UK, England
  ENGELMAN, Robert   USA, DC
  FÉRON, Eric M.   Zimbabwe
  GARDNER, Julia E.   Canada, BC
  GOCHFELD, Michael   USA, NJ
  HARDI, Peter   Canada, Man.
  HOLLIS, George E.   UK, England
  HOLOWESKO, Lynn P.   Bahamas
  IMBODEN, Christoph N.   UK, England
  JIGJ, Sonom   Mongolia
  KOH, Tommy T.-B.   Singapore
  LI, Wenhua   China
  LINDSTROM, U.B.   Finland
  LUTZENBERGER, José A.   Brazil, RS
  MacNEILL, James W.   Canada, Ont.
  MARSH, John   Canada, Ont.
  McCARTHY, Gerald P.   USA, VA
  MUNASINGHE, Mohan   Sri Lanka
  NOVOA, Laura   Chile

  OBASI, Godwin O.P.   Switzerland
  OPSCHOOR, Johannes B.   The Netherlands
  PACHAURI, Rajendra K.   India, Delhi
  PARYSKI, Paul E.   Haiti
  RAMAKRISHNAN, P.S. ('Ram')   India, Delhi
  ROWLEY, John R.   UK, England
  SAMAD, Syed A.   Malaysia
  SANDBROOK, J.Richard   UK, England
  SCHWAB, Klaus   Switzerland
  SCHWARZSCHILD, 'B' Shimon   USA, CA
  SHORES, John N.   USA, ME
  SINGH, Naresh   Canada, Man.
  THOM, David A.   NZ
  TINKER, Jon   Canada, BC
  WAAK, Patricia A.   USA, CO
— — and strategic analysis
  WILSON, George R.   Australia, WA
— — awareness in developing world
  ONAYEMI, Olarotimi O.   Nigeria
— —–computer communications
  PETER, Ian W.   Australia, Qld
— concept, implication of
  HUBA, Mikuláš   Slovak Rep.
— —, definition of
  CARPENTER, Richard A.   USA, VA
— — esp.agriculture, forestry, & fisheries
  SAOUMA, Edouard V.   Lebanon
— —, implementation of action on
  LINDNER, Warren H.   Switzerland
— — in American humid tropics
  DOUROJEANNI, Marc J.   USA, VA
— — — temperate environments
  MOFFATT, Ian   UK, Scotland
— — — the Middle East
  DEAN, Faisal   USA, VA
— — — third-world countries
  BEHRA, Olivier   Madagascar
— — — tropical Andes
  DOUROJEANNI, Marc J.   USA, VA
— — — — environments
  MOFFATT, Ian   UK, Scotland
— — — underdeveloped regions, theory on
  LEFF, Enrique   Mexico
— —, interdisciplinary approaches to
  FONSECA, Gustavo A.B.   Brazil, MG
— —, international policy on
  RAMPHAL, Shridath   UK, England
— — issues, public participation in
  KAKABADSE, Yolanda   Ecuador
— —, measurement of
  CARPENTER, Richard A.   USA, VA
— —, natural resource management for
  PANDURANGAN, Alagramam G.   India, Ker.
— — of buffer zones
  HURNI, Hans   Switzerland
— — planning, GIS applied to
  KRISHNAYYA, Jaswant G.   India, Mah.
— — policy issues
  SEVILLA, Lorenzo B.CARDENAL
                    Nicaragua/Guatemala
— —, political & institutional aspects of
  GORDON, John K.   UK, England
— —–polymer science–environment
  VASUDEVAN, Padma   India, Delhi
— —, practical applications of
  FEICK, Jenny L.   Canada, Alb.
— —, prediction of
  CARPENTER, Richard A.   USA, VA
— — project design
  HARDI, Peter   Canada, Man.

sustainable development (contd)
— —, research in, re.recovery of refuse and
    underutilized resources
    ARIAS-CHAVEZ, Jesus   Mexico
— —, social & cultural changes required by
    AICKIN, R.Malcolm   UK, England
— —, — dimensions of
    HOUGH, John L.   USA, MD
— —, strategic planning for
    MORELL, Merilio G.   Italy
— — strategies
    PEINE, John D.   USA, TN
    SINGH, Karan   India, Delhi
— — through investments in human resources
    SHAW, R.Paul   USA, DC
— —, utilization of biodiversity, conservation and
    PUSHPANGADAN, Palpu   India, Ker.
— — world-wide
    GATHORNE-HARDY, Gathorne   UK, England
— economic development in Africa's semi-arid
    rangelands
    TOIT, Raoul F.DU   Zimbabwe
— economies in developing world
    ONAYEMI, Olarotimi O.   Nigeria
— forest management
    HIBBERD, John K.   Australia, ACT
    SULLIVAN, Francis   UK, England
— — use
    LAL, Jugal B.   India, MP
— forestry
    HARRIS, Philip J.C.   UK, England
    POORE, M.E.Duncan   UK, Scotland
— human development
    MIRANDA, Ruiz   Guinea-Bissau
    SPETH, James G.   USA, NY
— — — world-wide
    MALONE, Thomas F.   USA, NC
— integrated production systems
    WILSON, Richard T.   UK, England
— land-use
    FÜLEKY, György   Hungary
— — - — management
    RECKERS, Ute   Kenya
— — - —, Aborigines'
    WILSON, George R.   Australia, WA
— livelihoods, poverty and
    SINGH, Naresh   Canada, Man.
— logging of tropical forests
    LEES, Annette M.   NZ
— resource management of tropical land & marine
    ecosystems
    BAINES, Graham B.K.   Australia, Qld
— society, ecological economy in transition period to
    HAREIDE, Dag   Norway
— tourism
    CARRILLO, Antonio Machado   Canary Islands
— — policies
    SISMAN, Richard ('Dick')   UK, England
— urban development
    JACOBS, Peter D.A.   Canada, Que.
— use, ecological, of semi-arid lands
    SATTLER, Paul S.   Australia, Qld
— — of forest ecosystems & forest species
    RUIZ-MURRIETA, Julio   Switzerland
— — — mountain environments
    HAMILTON, Lawrence S.   USA, VT
— — — natural resources
    HURNI, Hans   Switzerland
    MARTINS, Edouardo de Souza   Brazil, Bras.DF
— — — Nature & natural resources
    HOLDGATE, Martin W.   UK, England

— — small island environments
    HAMILTON, Lawrence S.   USA, VT
— — wetlands
    TAN, Koonlin   UK, England
— — wildlife
    BALDUS, Rolf D.   Germany
    FLINT, Vladimir E.   Russia
— utilization of wildlife
    SILVA, Ricardo Freire da   Brazil, SP
— —: tropical moist forest
    WHITMORE, Timothy C.   UK, England
— —, tortoise
    LAMBERT, Michael R.K.   UK, England
sustained natural resource-use
    OVINGTON, John D.   Australia, ACT
Switzerland, flora & fauna in
    MANSER, Bruno   Switzerland
symbioses associations, reef (impact on coral-reef
    ecosystems)
    VANTIER, Lyndon M.de   Australia, Qld
symbiosis
    MARGULIS, Lynn   USA, MA
synchronous displays by *Pteroptyx* fireflies, research
    into
    POLUNIN, Ivan V.   Singapore
Syrdhidae
    WHITTINGTON, Andrew E.   UK, Scotland
system, atmospheric, interactions
    RADICELLA, Sandro M.   Italy
—, protected areas, Canadian
    HACKMAN, Arlin C.   Canada, Ont.
—, UN, international aspects of
    VAVILOV, Andrey M.   Kenya
systematic biology
    KIM, Ke Chung   USA, PA
— botany & microbiology
    LAVRENTIADES, George   Greece
systematics–ecology of marine Amphipoda
    CROKER, Robert A.   USA, NH
—, marine amphipod Crustacea
    MOORE, Peter G.   UK, Scotland
— of Afrotropical Diptera
    WHITTINGTON, Andrew E.   UK, Scotland
— birds & mammals
    DORST, Jean   France
— —, reptiles, frogs, and slaters
    INGRAM, Glen J.   Australia, Qld
— Cacti
    ANDERSON, Edward F.   USA, AZ
— — coral[s]
    VERON, John E.N.   Australia, Qld
— — plants & birds of western Europe
    KELLER, Michael C.   Germany
—, phylogenetic
    PIANKA, Eric R.   USA, TX
—, plant
    PRANCE, Ghillean T.   UK, England
    RAVEN, Peter H.   USA, MO
    STIRTON, Charles H.   UK, England
—, —, and morphological studies
    PANDURANGAN, Alagramam G.   India, Ker.
—, principles of
    MARUSIK, Yuri M.   Russia
systems, agricultural
    NEWMAN, Edward I.   UK, England
—, —, energy use in
    CORBET, Philip S.   UK, Scotland
—, agroforestry
    ASHTON, Mark S.   USA, CT
    WOODGATE, Graham R.   UK, England

—, —, esp.multi-strata agroforests
  LEAKEY, Richard R.B.   Kenya
—, alternative energy
  ABBASI, Shahid A.   India, TN
— analysis
  COHON, Jared L.   USA, CT
  NILSSON, Sten   Austria
  PANDEYA, Satish C.   India, UP
— —, environmental
  NISHIOKA, Shuzo   Japan
—, atmospheric (southern Africa)
  PRESTON-WHYTE, Robert A.   UK, England
—, coastal, biogeochemistry of
  LACERDA, Luiz D.   Brazil, RJ
—, engineering education
  CATANIA, Peter J.   Canada, Sask.
—, environmental, impacts of tourism on — land-use
    law
  PETERSON, Claire McCARTHY   USA, IL
  PETERSON, Craig A.   USA, IL
—, — information
  RAJAGOPAL, Rangaswamy   USA, OH
—, — management
  EARLL, Robert C.   UK, England
—, geographical information, see geographical
    information systems
—, in situ conservation
  SEVILLA, Lorenzo B.CARDENAL
                         Nicaragua/Guatemala
—, indigenous knowledge, in the tropics
  ULLUWISHEWA, Rohana K.   Sri Lanka
—, information
  SHEPHERD, Alexander R.DAWSON UK, England
  SHORES, John N.   USA, ME
—, legal, impacts of tourism on — land-use law
  PETERSON, Claire McCARTHY   USA, IL
  PETERSON, Craig A.   USA, IL
— modelling (& analysis)
  COHON, Jared L.   USA, CT
—, national parks', selection & establishment of
  SATTLER, Paul S.   Australia, Qld
—, neurosecretory
  APPLIN, David G.   UK, England
—, open space, conservation & development of
  JACOBS, Peter D.A.   Canada, Que.
— planning for national parks & protected areas
  HEISS, Gerhard   Germany
—, production, dairy & beef, animal evaluation in
  TEWOLDE, Assefaw   Mexico
—, —, sustainable agricultural
  TEWOLDE, Assefaw   Mexico
—, —, — integrated
  WILSON, Richard T.   UK, England
—, protected areas', selection & establishment of
  SATTLER, Paul S.   Australia, Qld
—, resource management, in the tropics
  JOHANNES, Robert E.   Australia, Tas.
—, resources information
  UNNI, N.V.MADHAVAN   India, AP
—, river, preservation of
  ZINKE, Alexander   Austria
—, rural livelihood–environmental rehabilitation
  GRITZNER, Jeffrey A.   USA, MT
—, — -based livelihood (esp.agroforestry)
  WOODGATE, Graham R.   UK, England
—, socio-economic, conservation of
  TAN, Koonlin   UK, England
—, stored-grain
  KENNEDY, Robert   UK, England
—, sustainable agricultural production
  TEWOLDE, Assefaw   Mexico

—, — integrated production
  WILSON, Richard T.   UK, England
—, territorial, of ecological stability
  DEJMAL, Ivan   Czech Rep.
— theory, nonequilibrium
  SLOCOMBE, D.Scott   Canada, Ont.
—, wastewater
  AWAD, Adel R.   Syria

----

taiga–forest in Siberia & Central Asia
  FLINT, Vladimir E.   Russia
tanaids, environmental biology of
  HOLDICH, David M.   UK, England
taxa, genetic resources conservation esp.horticultural
    crops and related
  ASTLEY, David 'Dave'   UK, England
taxonomic botany
  AMIRKHANOV, Amirkhan M.   Russia
  HEDBERG, Inga M.M.   Sweden
  NAYAR, M.Param   India, Ker.
  SCHULTES, Richard E.   USA, MA
— — of West & Central African forests
  CHEEK, Martin R.   UK, England
— ichthyology
  McALLISTER, Donald E.   Canada, Ont.
— monography
  MATTHEW, Koyapillil M.   India, TN
taxonomy, see also [taxonomy] of†
—, coral
  VERON, John E.N.   Australia, Qld
—, mammalian
  WANG, Sung   China
—, palm
  BALICK, Michael J.   USA, NY
—, plant
  CULLEN, James   UK, England
  EGZIABHER, Tewolde B.GEBRE   Ethiopia
  HEDBERG, K.Olov   Sweden
  KORNAŚ, Jan   Poland
—, — (Datura & related plants)
  BYE, Robert   Mexico
—, —, of tropical areas esp.Nigeria
  KEAY, Ronald W.J.   UK, England
—, spider
  MARUSIK, Yuri M.   Russia
—, tropical moist forest
  WHITMORE, Timothy C.   UK, England
—, vascular plant
  FORERO, Enrique   USA, NY
taxonomy of, see also taxonomy†
— African Leguminosae
  LOCK, John M.   UK, England
— Australian reptiles, extant & extinct
  COVACEVICH, Jeannette A.   Australia, Qld
— biocidal plants
  LAKSHMANAN, Kalimedu K.   India, TN
— Cladocera (Crustacea)
  SMIRNOV, Nikolai N.   Russia
— copepods
  POR, Francis D.   Israel
— cycads
  SCLAVO, Jean-Pierre   France
— grasses & orchids
  JAIN, Sudhanshu K.   India, UP

† See upper footnote on p. 409.

[taxonomy] of (contd)
— gymnosperms
PAGE, Christopher N.   UK, Scotland
— higher plants
TIKHOMIROV, Vadim N.   Russia
— Lepidoptera
KOZLOV, Mikhail V.   Finland
— marine mammals
BREE, Peter J.H.van   The Netherlands
— medicinal plants
LAKSHMANAN, Kalimedu K.   India, TN
— opisthobranch molluscs
EDMUNDS, Malcolm   UK, England
— pelagic ostracods
ANGEL, Martin V.   UK, England
— potato species
HAWKES, John G.   UK, England
— pteridophytes
PAGE, Christopher N.   UK, Scotland
— Salix in the New World
ARGUS, George W.   Canada, Ont.
— Solanaceae
HAWKES, John G.   UK, England
— Zingiberaceae
LOCK, John M.   UK, England
TB, badger–bovine
BARRY, James M.   Ireland
teacher education
COHEN, Michael R.   USA, IN
teaching
WAGER, Jonathan F.   UK, England
— biology & conservation through the media
BOSWALL, Jeffery   UK, England
—, environmental values & philosophy through
GITTINS, John W.E.H.   UK, England
— in application of social science to natural resource
    management & planning issues
BLAHNA, Dale J.   USA, UT
— on ecological matters
MARGARIS, Nickolas S.   Greece
— — ornithology
DHINDSA, Manjit S.   India, Mah.
— — parks, wildlife, & environmental conservation
BUTLER, James 'Jim' R.   Canada, Alb.
— — soil conservation
LAL, Rattan   USA, OH
—, permaculture
EVERETT, Rodney D.   UK, England
— re.protected areas
CIFUENTES-ARIAS, Miguel   Costa Rica
technical assistance
BASSOW, Whitman   USA, NY
— — to developing countries
PALMBERG-LERCHE, Christel M.   Italy
— — to protected areas
CIFUENTES-ARIAS, Miguel   Costa Rica
— training
BASSOW, Whitman   USA, NY
techniques, application of legal, in different cultural
    settings
WRIGHT, R.Michael   USA, VA
—, ecological
LEEFLANG, Sietz A.   The Netherlands
— for strategic planning
SEVILLA, Lorenzo B.Cardenal
                                Nicaragua/Guatemala
—, research
WEBER, Karl E.   Thailand
technological applications
ARMIJOS, Mariano Montaño   Ecuador
— aspects of environment protection
KUKHAR, Valery P.   Ukraine

technologies, innovative, development of
KHOSLA, Ashok   India, Delhi
technology, appropriate, conservation of
TAN, Koonlin   UK, England
—, children's concepts in
COHEN, Michael R.   USA, IN
—, clean
SUBRAMANIAN, Tarakad V.   India, TN
—, cleaner
JOHNSTON, Neil   UK, England
—, clonal, applications
LAL, Piare   India, AP
—, conservation
CHITRAKAR, Anil   Nepal
—, energy
GOLDEMBERG, José   Brazil, SP
—, environment (bio-)
SUBRAMANIAN, Tarakad V.   India, TN
—, environmental
KHANNA, Purushottam   India, MP
—, environmentally-sound, in sub-Saharan Africa
KUFORIJI-OLUBI, Bola   Nigeria
—, information
PETER, Ian W.   Australia, Qld
SAMAD, Syed A.   Malaysia
—, management
TAIT, Elizabeth J.   UK, Scotland
—, new
ELKINGTON, John B.   UK, England
—, pesticide
KASHYAP, Kant   India, Guj.
—, reorientation of
THOM, David A.   NZ
—, transfer
KRATTIGER, Anatole F.   USA, NY
—, — of conservation skill and
CHITRAKAR, Anil   Nepal
telemedicine, satellite
JOVANOVIĆ, Petar   Yugoslavia
television, documentary
RICHTER, Robert   USA, NY
—, environmental
LAMB, Robert P.   UK, England
—, — coverage on broadcast
JAMES, Roger D.   UK, England
—, popularization & teaching of biology &
    conservation via
BOSWALL, Jeffery   UK, England
telmatology (peatland science)
MASING, Viktor   Estonia
temperate conservation
HOLROYD, Geoffrey L.   Canada, Alb.
— environments, hydropower & irrigation in
ZWAHLEN, Robert   Switzerland
— —, sustainable development in
MOFFATT, Ian   UK, Scotland
— —, water resources' development projects in
ZWAHLEN, Robert   Switzerland
— fruit, genetic transformation of
JAMES, David J.   UK, England
— rainforest survival
HUSBAND, Vicky   Canada, BC
— regions of Europe, forest & mountain ecology of
HEISS, Gerhard   Germany
— —, succession in
HAMBLER, Clive   UK, England
temperature, impact of, on vegetation
GRACE, John   UK, Scotland
— –water relations re.Arthropods & Reptiles
CLOUDSLEY-THOMPSON, John L.
                                    UK, England

temporal scales
  LEEMANS, Rik				The Netherlands
termites in forestry & buildings
  NOUR, Hassan O.ABDEL			Sudan
terrestrial animal ecology
  NJE, Ngog					Cameroon
— ecology
  ZLOTIN, Roman I.				Russia
— — & conservation
  SAYER, Jeffrey A.				Indonesia
— plant ecology
  BENSON, John S.				Australia, NSW
— vertebrates, ecology & conservation of
  HEINEN, Joel T.				USA, FL
territorial systems of ecological stability
  DEJMAL, Ivan					Czech Rep.
testing, seed
  TAO, Kar-ling J.				Italy
tests, nuclear weapons
  WARNER, Frederick			UK, England
Thailand, hill people in
  DEETES, Tuenjai				Thailand
theological status of animals
  LINZEY, Andrew				UK, England
theoretical ecology
  KULL, Kalevi					Estonia
theories in the 'Sociology of the Environment'
  CLOUDSLEY, Timothy			UK, England
theory, climate
  KELLOGG, William W.			USA, CO
—, ecological
  LEEMANS, Rik				The Netherlands
—, evolution
  APPLIN, David G.				UK, England
—, evolutionary
  RAVEN, Peter H.				USA, MO
  YABLOKOV, Alexey V.			Russia
— for problem-oriented analysis and management
  GROOT, Wouter T.DE			The Netherlands
—, Gaia
  MARGULIS, Lynn				USA, MA
—, nonequilibrium systems
  SLOCOMBE, D.Scott			Canada, Ont.
— on environment & sustainable development in
    underdeveloped regions
  LEFF, Enrique				Mexico
—, sustainability
  NORTON, Bryan G.				USA, GA
thermal ecology
  CLARKE, Andrew				UK, England
— effects
  COUTANT, Charles C.			USA, TN
— power-plant, effects of, on flora & vegetation
  USLU, Turhan				Turkey
third world
  UEXKÜLL, Carl J.W.VON			Sweden
— — countries, sustainable conservation &
    development in
  BEHRA, Olivier				Madagascar
— — development
  GLANTZ, Michael H.			USA, CO
  JUEL-JENSEN, Bent E.			UK, England
— —, environmental problems re.war
  PFEIFFER, Egbert W.			USA, MT
— — medicine
  JUEL-JENSEN, Bent E.			UK, England
threatened ecosystems, conservation of
  BURBIDGE, Andrew A.			Australia, WA
— —, preservation of
  ZINKE, Alexander				Austria
— plant species, research on
  BENSON, John S.				Australia, NSW

— species
  ČEROVSKY, Jan				Czech Rep.
  GIVEN, David R.				NZ
— —, conservation of
  BURBIDGE, Andrew A.			Australia, WA
— —' management
  GIMINEZ-DIXON, Mariano			Switzerland
— —: Nature conservation
  SMITH, Kevin D.				NZ
— — of coastal birds
  BURGER, Joanna				USA, NJ
tidal waterways, Australian (northern)
  MESSEL, Harry				Australia, Qld
tortoise conservation & sustainable utilization
  LAMBERT, Michael R.K.			UK, England
tortoises, land
  FRAZIER, John G.				Mexico
total river catchment management
  BAKER, Joseph 'Joe' T.			Australia, Qld
tourism, see also ecotourism
  CROSBY, Arturo				Spain
  MARSH, John				Canada, Ont.
  MARTIN, Vance G.				USA, CO
—, community-based
  NEPAL, Sanjay K.				Switzerland
—, development
  JIGJ, Sonom				Mongolia
—, economics of rural
  SISMAN, Richard ('Dick')			UK, England
— education
  LACY, Terry P.DE				Australia, NSW
—, green
  SERAFIN, Rafal K.				Poland
—, impacts of, on environmental & legal systems
  PETERSON, Claire McCARTHY		USA, IL
—, — —, — — — — —: land-use law
  PETERSON, Craig A.			USA, IL
— management, recreational
  CRAIK, Wendy				Australia, Qld
—, masterplanning for
  BARCSAY, László				Hungary
— policies, sustainable
  SISMAN, Richard ('Dick')			UK, England
—, protection of Nature re.
  RICHEZ, Gérard				France
—, rural
  CROSBY, Arturo				Spain
—, soft
  SZILASSY, Zoltán				Hungary
—, sustainable
  CARRILLO, Antonio MACHADO		Canary Islands
—, wildlife trade &
  RANJITSINH, M.K.				India, MP
town planning
  LOVEJOY, Derek				UK, England
toxic chemicals
  BRINCHUK, Mikhail M.			Russia
  KUFORIJI-OLUBI, Bola			Nigeria
— —' control
  FAZAL, Anwar				Malaysia
— fallout
  SVOBODA, Josef				Canada, Ont.
— plants
  SCHULTES, Richard E.			USA, MA
— substances
  WOODWELL, George M.			USA, MA
toxicology
  CRAMPTON, Colin B.			Canada, BC
—, applied
  JOOSTING, Peter E.			The Netherlands

toxicology (contd)
—, behavioural
　BURGER, Joanna   USA, NJ
—, environmental
　GOCHFELD, Michael   USA, NJ
—, — research in
　RAY, Prasanta K.   India, W.Bengal
—, neurobehavioural, of heavy-metals
　GOCHFELD, Michael   USA, NJ
—, ocean
　PAYNE, Roger S.   UK, England
—, regulatory
　MOORE, James W.   Canada, Alb.
trace elements, behaviour of, in natural environment
　STEINNES, Eiliv   Norway
trade & environment
　BUCKLEY, Ralf C.   Australia, Qld
　THOMAS, Urs P.   Canada, Que.
—, free/economic growth
　DAMMANN, Erik   Norway
—, wildlife
　RANJITSINH, M.K.   India, MP
trading, illegal, in wildlife and parts thereof,
　prevention of
　LaBUDDE, Samuel F.   USA, CA
traditional cultivation
　MANSER, Bruno   Switzerland
— irrigation in oases and their rehabilitation
　DAMERDJI, M.Amine   Algeria
— marine ecological knowledge in the tropics
　JOHANNES, Robert E.   Australia, Tas.
— societies, ecology of
　RAMAKRISHNAN, P.S. ('Ram')   India, Delhi
traditions, Canadian oral & written
　CRAMPTON, Colin B.   Canada, BC
tragedy of the commons
　YOUNG, Raymond DE   USA, MI
training
　BEETON, Robert J.S.   Australia, Qld
　BENNETT, Elizabeth L.   Malaysia
　FAZAL, Anwar   Malaysia
　FRY, Ian W.   Australia, NSW
— activities
　SABOGAL, Cesar A.   Indonesia
—, environmental
　COLE, Norman H.A.   Sierra Leone
—, — education
　ATCHIA, Michael   Kenya
　ODULA, Michael A.N.   Kenya
—, EIA
　BENNETT, Sara L.   Canada, BC
—, — management
　ATCHIA, Michael   Kenya
—, — research
　SEELY, Mary K.   Namibia
—, —, in Latin America & the Caribbean
　LEFF, Enrique   Mexico
— in environmental science
　VO, Quy   Vietnam
—, international environmental
　SACKS, Arthur B.   USA, CO
— of Aboriginal natural-resource managers
　FOX, Allan M.   Australia, NSW
— — personnel
　DIAZ-MARTIN, Diego   Venezuela
— — protected area personnel
　MOORE, Alan W.   USA, TN
— park personnel
　MENDEZ, Jesus M.DELGADO   Brazil, SP
— programmes, environment–tourism
　CROSBY, Arturo   Spain

—, quality control of, re.people in the tropics
　FRAZIER, John G.   Mexico
—, technical
　BASSOW, Whitman   USA, NY
transfer of agri-biotechnology applications
　(sustainability and a better environment)
　JAMES, W.Clive   Cayman Islands
— — conservation skill and technology
　CHITRAKAR, Anil   Nepal
—, technology
　KRATTIGER, Anatole F.   USA, NY
transformation, genetic, of temperate fruit
　JAMES, David J.   UK, England
transport, environmental aspects of
　GOODLAND, Robert J.A.   USA, DC
—, environmentally-sound, of dangerous goods
　KRIKIS, Andris   Latvia
—, long-range atmospheric, of metals & other
　pollutants
　STEINNES, Eiliv   Norway
transportation noise
　ABBASPOUR, Madjid   Iran
— /navigation planning projects
　BENNETT, Sara L.   Canada, BC
travel and the environment
　SISMAN, Richard ('Dick')   UK, England
—, development
　JIGJ, Sonom   Mongolia
— /exploration
　SCHWARZSCHILD, 'B' Shimon   USA, CA
treaties, international, on the environment
　VISSER, Nicolaas W.   Kenya
—, oceans and environmental protection
　PELL, Claiborne   USA, DC
treatment, water & wastewater
　BHARGAVA, Devendra S.   India, UP
　MUTTAMARA, Samorn   Thailand
　REHMAN, Syed Z.   Pakistan
—, wastewater
　ARCEIVALA, Soli J.   India, Mah.
　AWAD, Adel R.   Syria
— —, industrial & sewage
　KHAN, Niaz A.   UAE
tree biology, integrated land-use &
　LAST, Frederick T.   UK, Scotland
— breeding
　BURLEY, Jeffery   UK, England
— ecophysiology
　HUTTUNEN, Satu   Finland
— health
　BOA, Eric   UK, England
— improvement
　BREWBAKER, James L.   USA, HI
　LAL, Piare   India, AP
— —, forest
　PALMBERG-LERCHE, Christel M.   Italy
— — in developing countries
　MOESTRUP, Søren   Denmark
— —, research & development work on
　LAL, Piare   India, AP
— nurseries, promotion of, in schools
　FITTER, Perin S.   Kenya
— physiology
　DICK, Janet M.   UK, Scotland
— planting
　FITTER, Perin S.   Kenya
　MALULYA-MUKASA, Joe   Uganda
— - —, community
　SOPHONPANICH, Chodchoy   Thailand
— surgery
　CHEEK, Roy V.   UK, England

trees
  KELCEY, John G.   UK, England
  MARTIN, Vance G.   USA, CO
—, clonal selection of
  LEAKEY, Richard R.B.   Kenya
—, dominant, ecological & ecophysiological relations
    in forest ecosystems and their dependence on
  ČABOUN, Vladimír   Slovak Rep.
—, planting
  ZHANG, Jia-Shun   China
—, tropical, domestication of
  DICK, Janet M.   UK, Scotland
—, —, — —, for forestry/agroforestry in tropics*
—, vegetative propagation of
  *LEAKEY, Richard R.B.   Kenya
trends, environmental, & related social policies
  HOLDGATE, Martin W.   UK, England
—, global environmental
  NORDERHAÜG, Magnar   Norway
— in inland fisheries & aquaculture
  WELCOMME, Robin L.   Italy
tribals (indigenous people)
  VARIAVA, Dilnavaz   India, Mah.
Trichogramma
  CIOCHIA, Victor   Romania
'tropandean' landscapes, restoration of
  SARMIENTO, Fausto O.   USA, GA
trophic ecology
  PANDIT, Ashok K.   India, J&K
tropical Africa, land & forest ecology in
  TRAPNELL, Colin G.   UK, England
— —, plant geography [of]
  KORNAŚ, Jan   Poland
— Andes, sustainable development in
  DOUROJEANNI, Marc J.   USA, VA
— aquaculture
  DOUMENGE, François   Monaco
— areas, environmental biology & plant taxonomy of
  KEAY, Ronald W.K.   UK, England
— biogeography
  JIM, Chi Yung   Hong Kong
— coastal environments: application of law re., and
    conservation science, planning, &
    management, in
  DAVIE, James D.S.   Australia, Qld
— — resource management
  WILKINSON, Clive R.   Australia, Qld
— conservation
  HOLROYD, Geoffrey L.   Canada, Alb.
— crop development
  HARRIS, Philip J.C.   UK, England
— deforestation
  SANCHEZ, Pedro A.   Kenya
— —, causes of
  FEARNSIDE, Philip M.   Brazil, Amaz.
— —, ecological consequences of
  LAL, Rattan   USA, OH
— —, impacts of & rates of
  FEARNSIDE, Philip M.   Brazil, Amaz.
— ecology
  COLE, Norman H.A.   Sierra Leone
  FRANKIE, Gordon W.   USA, CA
  GOODLAND, Robert J.A.   USA, DC
  GRACE, John   UK, Scotland
  PEARMAN, Peter B.   USA, CA
  PERES, Carlos A.   Brazil, SP/UK, England
  RECKERS, Ute   Kenya
  REDAUD, Louis R.M.   Guadeloupe
  SUZUKI, Kunio   Japan

— — of Amazon region
  SIOLI, Harald F.L.   Germany
— ecosystems, heavy-metal contamination in
  LACERDA, Luiz D.   Brazil, RJ
— environments
  TAN, Koonlin   UK, England
— —, hydropower & irrigation in
  ZWAHLEN, Robert   Switzerland
— —, marine pelagic ecosystems of
  BRANDINI, Frederico   Brazil, Par.
— —, sustainable development in
  MOFFATT, Ian   UK, Scotland
— —, water resources development projects in
  ZWAHLEN, Robert   Switzerland
— fisheries, inland
  WELCOMME, Robin L.   Italy
— food, fermentation in
  STANTON, W.Robert   UK, England
— forest carnivores, ecology & conservation of
  RAY, Justina C.   USA, FL
— — conservation
  HAMILTON, Alan   UK, England
  SAYER, Jeffrey A.   Indonesia
— — —, autochthonous
  FISCHER, Gert R.   Brazil, SC
— — ecology
  PHILLIPS, Oliver L.B.   USA, MO
  SINGH, Kaushalendra P.   India, UP
— — management
  LAVIEREN, Lambartus P.van   The Netherlands
  ORGLE, Tetey K.   Ghana
  SAYER, Jeffrey A.   Indonesia
  SCHLAEPFER, Rodolphe   Switzerland
— — —, autochthonous
  FISCHER, Gert R.   Brazil, SC
— —, moist, taxonomy
  WHITMORE, Timothy C.   UK, England
— forestry — research, development, information, &
    education
  BURLEY, Jeffery   UK, England
— —, environmental impacts of
  MARSH, Clive W.   Malaysia
— forests
  GOODLAND, Robert J.A.   USA, DC
  MARTIN, Claude   Switzerland
— —, Asian
  HENNING, Daniel H.   USA, MT
— —, biodiversity assessment & conservation
  RAVEN, Peter H.   USA, MO
— —, conservation management of
  MARSH, Clive W.   Malaysia
— —, — of
  BUDOWSKI, Gerardo   Costa Rica
  FERNANDO, Ranjen L.   Sri Lanka
— —, fauna & flora of, conservation of
  FERNANDO, Ranjen L.   Sri Lanka
— —, maintenance of plant diversity in
  ASHTON, Peter S.   USA, MA
— —, protected areas in, incorporating local &
    indigenous concerns
  LEES, Annette M.   NZ
— —, saving
  KERN, Berndt   Sweden
  KERN, Eha   Sweden
— —, sustainable logging of
  LEES, Annette M.   NZ
— —, wet & dry, ecology of
  SINGH, Jamuna S.   India, UP
— habitat loss, effects of, on vertebrate populations
  RAPPOLE, John H.   USA, VA

* *See* lower footnote on p. 409.

tropical (contd)
— high mountains, plant taxonomy & ecology of
   HEDBERG, K.Olov   Sweden
— inland fisheries
   WELCOMME, Robin L.   Italy
— islands, marine ecology of, & coastal areas
   MARAGOS, James E.   USA, HI
— land ecosystems, sustainable resource
   management of
   BAINES, Graham B.K.   Australia, Qld
— — -use
   TAN, Koonlin   UK, England
— macrofungi
   PEGLER, David N.   UK, England
— mammals, conservation biology of
   STEPHENSON, Peter J.   Tanzania
— marine ecology
   AGARDY, M.Tündi   USA, DC
— — — of islands and coastal areas
   MARAGOS, James E.   USA, HI
— — ecosystems, sustainable resource management
   of
   BAINES, Graham B.K.   Australia, Qld
— — environment, Man's impact on
   WOLANSKI, Eric J.   Australia, Qld
— — fish ecology, fish ecophysiology, & fish
   life-history
   BUSTAMANTE, Georgina   USA, FL
— — population dynamics
   POLOVINA, Jeffrey J.   USA, HI
— medicine
   JUEL-JENSEN, Bent E.   UK, England
— moist forest taxonomy
   WHITMORE, Timothy C.   UK, England
— mountains, high, plant taxonomy & ecology of
   HEDBERG, K.Olov   Sweden
— plants, ethnobotany of
   HEDBERG, Inga M.M.   Sweden
— Porifera
   HOOPER, John N.A.   Australia, Qld
— protected areas and their conservation
   COBB, Stephen M.   UK, England
— — forests
   GRUBB, Peter J.   UK, England
   SMITS, Willie   Indonesia
— regions — forest policy & environmental policy
   development
   BASS, Stephen M.J.   UK, England
— — of India
   MELKANIA, Niranjan P.   India, MP
— —, succession in
   HAMBLER, Clive   UK, England
— —, vegetation ecology of
   WANG, Xianpu   China
— (savanna) resource ecology
   FERRAR, Anthony A.   RSA
— silviculture
   FREIBERG, Horst   Germany
   SABOGAL, Cesar A.   Indonesia
— soils
   JIM, Chi Yung   Hong Kong
— Southeast Asian wetlands agroforestry for staple
   foods
   STANTON, W.Robert   UK, England
— trees, domestication of
   DICK, Janet M.   UK, Scotland
— —, — —, for forestry/agroforestry in tropics
   LEAKEY, Richard R.B.   Kenya
— watersheds, management of
   PEREIRA, H.Charles   UK, England

— zoology
   HASAN, Mohammed NORDIN   Malaysia
tropics, agriculture of
   BREWBAKER, James L.   USA, HI
—, American humid, sustainable development in
   DOUROJEANNI, Marc J.   USA, VA
—, ecology of land-use in the
   POORE, M.E.Duncan   UK, Scotland
—, ethnobiology & indigenous knowledge systems in
   ULLUWISHEWA, Rohana K.   Sri Lanka
—, forest conservation in the
   ONAYEMI, Olarotimi O.   Nigeria
—, forestry/agroforestry in, domestication of tropical
   trees for
   LEAKEY, Richard R.B.   Kenya
—, humid, agricultural resources in the*
—, —, conservation & management of natural
   resources in the
   *SMITH, Nigel J.H.   USA, FL
—, Nature awareness in the
   KERN, Berndt   Sweden
   KERN, Eha   Sweden
—, resource management systems in the*
—, traditional marine ecological knowledge in the
   *JOHANNES, Robert E.   Australia, Tas.
troposphere, chemistry of the
   JOHNSTON, Harold S.   USA, CA
trout angling
   HUGHES, George R.   RSA
— farming
   WORTHINGTON, E.Barton   UK, England
tundra in Siberia & Central Asia
   FLINT, Vladimir E.   Russia
— plants, autecology of
   WIELGOLASKI, Frans-Emil   Norway
turbidity, atmospheric
   FRANGI, Jean-Pierre   France
Turkey, coastal vegetation of
   USLU, Turhan   Turkey
turtle, Maldives
   DIDI, N.T.Hasen   Maldives
—, marine, conservation
   VENIZELOS, Lily T.   Greece/UK, England
—, sea-, conservation
   ROSE, Carlos R.HASBÚN   El Salvador
turtles, marine
   FRAZIER, John G.   Mexico
—, —, & ecotourism
   HUGHES, George R.   RSA
—, —, biology & conservation
   BJORNDAL, Karen A.   USA, FL
—, —, conservation & management of, off coast of
   Brazil
   MARCOVALDI, Guy M.F.GUAGNI DEI
       Brazil, Bahia
   MARCOVALDI, Maria Â.GUAGNI DEI
       Brazil, Bahia
—, sea, ecology of, and their habitats
   MARSH, Helene D.   Australia, Qld
TV, see television

Ukraine, development of laws on environmental
   protection in
   KOSTENKO, Yuriy I.   Ukraine

* See lower footnote on p. 409.

ultra-violet, see UV
UN, see United Nations
underdeveloped regions, theory on environment and
    sustainable development of
    LEFF, Enrique   Mexico
underutilized resources
    ARIAS-CHAVEZ, Jesus   Mexico
underwater guides to reef fishes
    RANDALL, John 'Jack'   USA, HI
ungulates
    VERSCHUREN, Jacques C.F.   Belgium
—, ecology of
    BOYD, John M.   UK, Scotland
—, field studies & conservation of
    SCHALLER, George B.   USA, NY
United Nations system, international aspects of
    environmental issues in
    VAVILOV, Andrey M.   Kenya
— —, promoting effectiveness of, in his fields
    SCHRAM, Gunnar G.   Iceland
upper atmosphere physics
    RADICELLA, Sandro M.   Italy
urban botany
    JIANG, Gaoming   China
— climates & microclimates
    OKE, Timothy R.   Canada, BC
— development, sustainable
    JACOBS, Peter D.A.   Canada, Que.
urban ecology
    JIANG, Gaoming   China
    KELCEY, John G.   UK, England
    NUMATA, Makoto   Japan
— economics
    SAMAD, Syed A.   Malaysia
— environment
    SEVILLA, Rogue   Ecuador
— environmental impacts
    JIM, Chi Yung   Hong Kong
— — planning
    ANI, Olufeml   Nigeria
— — problems in developed economies
    GANDY, Matthew   UK, England
— — protection & improvement
    SOTIRIADOU, Victoria   Greece
— hydrology
    AWAD, Adel R.   Syria
— landscape paintings
    KELCEY, John G.   UK, England
— management
    FAZAL, Anwar   Malaysia
— Nature conservation
    ARIFFIN, Ishak BIN   Malaysia
— planning
    AWAD, Adel R.   Syria
    GEBREMEDHIN, Naigzy   Kenya
— —, methodology of
    KOZLOWSKI, Jerzy   Australia, Qld/Poland
— vegetation
    JIM, Chi Yung   Hong Kong
— wildlife, ecology & management
    ADAMS, Lowell W.   USA, WV
USA's Bureau of Land Management, ecology of
    WATSON, Charles St D., Jr   USA, NV
use, energy, in agricultural systems
    CORBET, Philip S.   UK, Scotland
—, human, impacts of, of antarctic & alpine
    environments
    SPATE, Andrew 'Andy' P.   Australia, NSW
—, —, re.tropical coastal environments
    DAVIE, James D.S.   Australia, Qld

— of reptiles as bioindicators of habitat
    contamination
    LAMBERT, Michael R.K.   UK, England
—, sustainable forest
    LAL, Jugal B.   India, MP
—, —, of forest species & ecosystems
    RUIZ-MURRIETA, Julio   Switzerland
—, —, — natural resources
    HURNI, Hans   Switzerland
—, —, — small island & mountain environments
    HAMILTON, Lawrence S.   USA, VT
—, sustained natural resource
    OVINGTON, John D.   Australia, ACT
utilization, biomass, for rural energy supply
    SHYAM, Murari   India, MP
— of corals
    THRESHER, Philip B.   USA, CA
— — plant genetic resources
    ANISHETTY, Narasimha M.   Italy
— — third-world insect resources esp.butterflies
    MORRIS, Michael G.   UK, England
— — waste
    LI, Shuang Liang   China
— — wildlife, sustainable
    SILVA, Ricardo FREIRE DA   Brazil, SP
—, sustainable, conservation and, of biodiversity
    PUSHPANGADAN, Palpu   India, Ker.
—, —, tortoise conservation &
    LAMBERT, Michael R.K.   UK, England
—, —: tropical moist forest
    WHITMORE, Timothy C.   UK, England
—, wild animal, esp meat production
    WOODFORD, Michael H.   USA, DC
—, wildlife
    PRICE, Mark R.STANLEY   Kenya
—, — resource, including corals
    THRESHER, Philip B.   USA, CA
UV radiation, impacts of, in prairie saline lakes and
    prairie wetlands
    ROBARTS, Richard D.   Canada, Sask.
— solar radiation
    ALNASER, Waheeb E.   Bahrain

valuation methodologies for policy analysis
    NORTON, Bryan G.   USA, GA
—, environmental
    GONZALEZ, Juan A.AGUIRRE   Costa Rica
values, environmental
    MILBRATH, Lester W.   USA, NY
—, —, through teaching, art, & environment
    GITTINS, John W.E.H.   UK, England
—, international environmental
    CARROLL, John E.   USA, NH
—, wilderness & wildland
    MARTIN, Vance G.   USA, CO
variability, climate
    PIELKE, Roger A.   USA, CO
—, hydroclimate
    SMITH, Keith   UK, Scotland
variation (in Chilean forests)
    DONOSO, Claudio   Chile
vascular plant taxonomy
    FORERO, Enrique   USA, NY
— plants, field identification of
    FITTER, Richard S.R.   UK, England

vascular plants (contd)
— —, rare & endangered, conservation of, in Canada
    ARGUS, George W.   Canada, Ont.
vector control programmes
    FARID, Mohyeddin A.   Switzerland
vegetable oils, engine fuels from
    SCHARMER, Klaus   Germany
vegetables, field, plant virology & pathology of
    WALSH, John A.   UK, England
vegetation (esp. Greek)
    LAVRENTIADES, George   Greece
—, British, conservation of
    WOODELL, Stanley R.J.   UK, England
—, Cape plants &, autecology, phytosociology, &
    restoration ecology of
    BOUCHER, Charles   RSA
— change through historic time
    GADE, Daniel W.   USA, VT
— dynamics
    LEEMANS, Rik   The Netherlands
    MOREY, Miguel   Spain
    NUMATA, Makoto   Japan
— ecology
    HILL, Mark O.   UK, England
— — of Greenland
    DANIELS, Frederikus J.A.   Germany
— — of tropical & subtropical regions
    WANG, Xianpu   China
—, effects of thermal power-plants on
    USLU, Turhan   Turkey
—, environmental impacts on (wind, temperature, &
    drought stress)
    GRACE, John   UK, Scotland
— fire, management of
    STRONACH, Neil R.H.   Ireland
— geography
    SOLOMON, Allen M.   USA, OR
—, impacts of wind, temperature, & drought stress on,
    GRACE, John   UK, Scotland
—, landscape ecology and
    BRIDGEWATER, Peter   Australia, ACT
— 'Macaronesian'
    SJÖGREN, Erik A.   Sweden
— management
    HOBBS, Richard J.   Australia, WA
    WATT, Trudy A.   UK, England
— —, landscape, aesthetic*
— —, right-of-way
    *EGLER, Frank E.   USA, CT
—, Man's impact on
    KORNAŚ, Jan   Poland
—, mapping
    BEARD, John S.   Australia, WA
    BENSON, John S.   Australia, NSW
    MEDWECKA-KORNAŚ, Anna M.   Poland
    MEHER-HOMJI, Vispy M.   India, TN
—, natural forest, protection of
    SJÖGREN, Erik A.   Sweden
— re.land & forest ecology in tropical Africa
    TRAPNELL, Colin G.   UK, England
— recovery
    GIVEN, David R.   NZ
— sciences
    PFADENHAUER, Jörg   Germany
— structure
    LEEMANS, Rik   The Netherlands
— survey
    BENSON, John S.   Australia, NSW

—, urban
    JIM, Chi Yung   Hong Kong
—, woodland ground, dynamics of
    KIRBY, Keith J.   UK, England
—, world, classification of
    LOCK, John M.   UK, England
vegetational classification, principles of
    POORE, M.E.Duncan   UK, Scotland
— dynamics, competition, & coexistence
    GRUBB, Peter J.   UK, England
vegetative propagation of trees
    LEAKEY, Richard R.B.   Kenya
— —, research & development work on
    LAL, Piare   India, AP
vehicular emission control
    MATHUR, Harbansh B.   India, Delhi
Verbenaceae — plant systematics
    STIRTON, Charles H.   UK, England
vermicomposting*
vermiculture
    *ISMAIL, Sultan A.   India, TN
vertebrate conservation
    JENKINS, David   UK, Scotland
— pests
    ALI, Abd 'El moneim' M.   Egypt
— populations, effects of tropical habitat loss on
    RAPPOLE, John H.   USA, VA
vertebrates, behavioural ecology of
    BURGER, Joanna   USA, NJ
—, conservation of
    JENKINS, David   UK, Scotland
—, field studies of
    SCHALLER, George B.   USA, NY
—, study of
    YABLOKOV, Alexey V.   Russia
—, terrestrial, ecology & conservation of
    HEINEN, Joel T.   USA, FL
veterinary aspects of conservation
    WOODFORD, Michael H.   USA, DC
video, popularization & teaching of biology &
    conservation via
    BOSWALL, Jeffery   UK, England
— productions
    GUNAWARDENE, Nalaka J.   Sri Lanka
Vietnam war, effects of defoliants on environment
    during
    VO, Quy   Vietnam
virology, plant
    BARBARA, Derek J.   UK, England
    BOS, Luite   The Netherlands
    WALSH, John A.   UK, England
—, —, field & molecular
    CLARK, Michael F.   UK, England
—, —: — vegetables
    WALSH, John A.   UK, England
voluntary involvement in conservation issues &
    organizations
    ARMSTRONG, Geoffrey J.   Australia, NSW
— work in protected areas
    MOURA, Robert MANNERS   Portugal

Wales, hydrology & soil development of reclaimed
    lands after surface coal-mining in
    KILMARTIN, Marianne P.   UK, England

Walrus
   RAY, G.Carleton   USA, VA
war, environmental problems of third world re.
   PFEIFFER, Egbert W.   USA, MT
—, — security re.
   WESTING, Arthur H.   USA, VT
warfaring propensities–environmental
   degradation–national sovereignty
   SHAW, R.Paul   USA, DC
warming, Earth
   ISHI, Hiroyuki   Japan
—, global
   SINGER, S.Fred   USA, VA
— of the Earth, biotic interactions in
   WOODWELL, George M.   USA, MA
waste, harnessing of
   LI, Shuang Liang   China
, hazardous
   BRINCHUK, Mikhail M.   Russia
   KHAN, Niaz A.   UAE
   KUFORIJI-OLUBI, Bola   Nigeria
—, —, management
   KRIKIS, Andris   Latvia
   MUTTAMARA, Samorn   Thailand
   REHMAN, Syed Z.   Pakistan
   SAXENA, Anil K.   India, Delhi
—, industrial, recycling of
   LUTZENBERGER, José A.   Brazil, RS
— management
   CHOI, Yearn Hong   USA, VA
   COOPER, Jeffrey C.   UK, England
   EKARATH, Raveendran   Bahrain
   ROYES, Veronica I.J.   Jamaica
   SOPHONPANICH, Chodchoy Thailand
   TRENČIANSKA, Jana   Slovak Rep.
— — in developing countries
   FUREDY, Christine   Canada, Ont.
— —, solid
   AWAD, Adel R.   Syria
   MUTTAMARA, Samorn   Thailand
— —, — research
   AKHTAR, Waseem   Pakistan
— minimization
   JOHNSTON, Neil   UK, England
—, nuclear, research & writing
   LEMONS, John D., Jr   USA, ME
— planning
   COOPER, Jeffrey C.   UK, England
— pollution purification & control
   KUFORIJI-OLUBI, Bola   Nigeria
— recycling
   COOPER, Jeffrey C.   UK, England
   FUREDY, Christine   Canada, Ont.
— — in plastics industry
   KUFORIJI-OLUBI, Bola   Nigeria
—, — of industrial
   LUTZENBERGER, José A.   Brazil, RS
— —, organic, using local species of earthworms
   ISMAIL, Sultan A.   India, TN
— reduction
   COOPER, Jeffrey C.   UK, England
—, solid
   ABBASPOUR, Madjid   Iran
   BRINCHUK, Mikhail M.   Russia
   KHAN, Niaz A.   UAE
—, —, disposal management
   KUFORIJI-OLUBI, Bola   Nigeria
—, —, management
   REHMAN, Syed Z.   Pakistan

—, —, — research
   AKHTAR, Waseem   Pakistan
— treatment, nutritional improvement, fermentation
   in
   STANTON, W.Robert   UK, England
—, utilization of
   LI, Shuang Liang   China
— water, see also adjectival 'wastewater'
   CHOI, Yearn Hong   USA, VA
wasteland development
   KHOSHOO, Triloki N.   India, Delhi
wastes, hazardous, detoxification of
   SUBRAMANIAN, Tarakad V. India, YN
wastewater management
   SHIN, Eung-Bai   S.Korea
— treatment
   ARCEIVALA, Soil J.   India, Mah.
   BHARGAVA, Devendra S.   India, UP
   MUTTAMARA, Samorn   Thailand
   REHMAN, Syed Z.   Pakistan
—, industrial and sewage — treatment & disposal
   KHAN, Niaz A.   UAE
— systems & treatment
   AWAD, Adel R.   Syria
water, carbon &, relations of forest ecosystems
   GRACE, John   UK, Scotland
— catchment planning
   CULLEN, Peter W.   Australia, ACT
— communities, ecology of
   GALAZY, Grigory I.   Russia
— current energy in Bahrain
   ALNASER, Waheeb E.   Bahrain
— disinfection (solar energy)
   SCHARMER, Klaus   Germany
—, drinking-
   CHOI, Yearn Hong   USA, VA
— harvesting & supply
   DAMERDJI, M.Amine   Algeria
—, heat &, balances
   HARE, F.Kenneth   Canada, Ont.
— –land interactions
   LIKENS, Gene E.   USA, NY
— law
   HOLLO, Erkki J.   Finland
—, international
   OKIDI, Charles O.   Kenya
— management
   ABROL, Inder P.   India, Delhi
   EKARATH, Raveendran   Bahrain
   HOLČIK, Vladimír   Slovak Rep.
   HOLLIS, George E.   UK, England
   SHIN, Eung-Bai   S.Korea
   THOMAS, John D.   UK, England
— — and associated environmental problems
   WHITE, Gilbert F.   USA, CO
— —, ecological consequences of
   LAL, Rattan   USA, OH
— –plant relations & ecology
   JONES, Hamlyn G.   UK, England
— pollution
   RAY, Prasanta K.   India, W.Bengal
   SOPHONPANICH, Chodchoy Thailand
   WARNER, Frederick   UK, England
— — control
   ARCEIVALA, Soli J.   India, Mah.
   HAMMERTON, Desmond UK, Scotland
   RAJAGOPAL, Rangaswamy   USA, OH
— — technology & strategies
   BHARGAVA, Devendra S.   India, UP

water pollution (contd)
— —, cost-effective regulation & policy
  RAJAGOPAL, Rangaswamy   USA, OH
— — law
  SILVA, Allenisheo L.M.DE   Sri Lanka
— — monitoring
  RAJAGOPAL, Rangaswamy   USA, OH
— —, prevention of, from composting
  NOBLE, Ralph   UK, England
— problems in arid & semi-arid countries
  DAMERDJI, M.Amine   Algeria
— programmes
  PRASAD, Basudeo   India, E.Punjab
— quality
  CULLEN, Peter W.   Australia, ACT
  VORONOV, Arkady N.   Russia
— —, coastal
  ARMIJOS, Mariano MONTAÑO   Ecuador
— — management
  OKUN, Daniel A.   USA, NC
— — — & monitoring
  HAMMERTON, Desmond   UK, Scotland
— — surveys, remote sensing of
  BHARGAVA, Devendra S.   India, UP
— resource management
  RAI, Suresh Chand   India, Sikkim
— — schemes, environmental impacts of
  PETTS, Geoffrey   UK, England
— resources
  BENNETT, Sara L.   Canada, BC
  MUNASINGHE, Mohan   Sri Lanka
— —, assessment & management of
  GOLUBEV, Genady N.   Russia
— — development projects re.tropical & temperate
    environments
  ZWAHLEN, Robert   Switzerland
— — engineering
  ALI, Iqbal   Pakistan
— — in dry lands
  WILLIAMS, William D.   Australia, SA
—, reuse of
  ARCEIVALA, Soli J.   India, Mah.
—, river, sharing common, between countries
  MOUDUD, Hasna J.   Bangladesh
— –soil–plant relations
  KIRKHAM, M.B.   USA, KS
— supply
  DAMERDJI, M.Amine   Algeria
  MUTTAMARA, Samorn   Thailand
—, surface, chemical contaminants of
  MOORE, James W.   Canada, Alb.
— (sustainable development, North–South
    relations)
  MYERS, Norman   UK, England
— –temperature relations re.Arthropods & Reptiles
  CLOUDSLEY-THOMPSON, John L.
                                 UK, England
— treatment
  BHARGAVA, Devendra S.   India, UP
  MUTTAMARA, Samorn   Thailand
  REHMAN, Syed Z.   Pakistan
—, waste-
  CHOI, Yearn Hong   USA, VA
waterbirds, conservation of
  CHALABI, Bouzid   Algeria
—, — — colonial
  KUSHLAN, Norman   UK, England
waterlogging/flood
  WAJIH, Shiraz A.   India, UP

waters, arctic & subarctic
  MOORE, James W.   Canada, Alb.
—, international management of
  BISWAS, Asit K.   UK, England
watershed management
  DEARDEN, Philip   Canada, BC
  THAPA, Gopal B.   Thailand
watersheds, ecological management of
  OJEDA, Ricardo A.   Argentina
—, lake, management of
  KIRA, Tatuo   Japan
—, tropical, management of
  PEREIRA, H.Charles   UK, England
waterways, tidal, Australian (northern)
  MESSEL, Harry   Australia, Qld
wave energy in Bahrain
  ALNASER, Waheeb E.   Bahrain
weapons, nuclear, tests
  WARNER, Frederick   UK, England
weather (& climate)
  LAMB, Hubert H.   UK, England
weed biology
  LEAKEY, Richard R.B.   Kenya
weeds, biological control of
  ROOM, Peter M.   Australia, Qld
—, biology of
  STIRTON, Charles H.   UK, England
well-being, material–life quality
  HAREIDE, Dag   Norway
West Africa, conservation of biodiversity &
    wilderness in
  TUBOKU-METZGER, Daphne J.A. Sierra Leone
— African Sahel, conservation & development in
  DRIJVER, Carel A.   The Netherlands
western Australia, arid lands in
  BELLAMY, David J.   UK, England
wet tropical forests, ecology of
  SINGH, Jamuna S.   India, UP
wetland (see also wetlands) conservation
  DUGAN, Patrick J.   Switzerland
  HOFFMANN, Luc   France
  KADLEČÍK, Ján   Slovak Rep.
  KUSHLAN, James A.   USA, MS
— ecology
  BOTCH, Marina S.   Russia
  GOPAL, Brij   India, Punjab
  PANDIT, Ashok K.   India, J&K
  PYROVETSI, Myrto D.   Greece
— — & conservation
  KUSHLAN, James A.   USA, MS
— —, functions & values (of)
  LARSON, Joseph S.   USA, MA
— ecosystems
  TERRASSON, François   France
— inventories
  DIEGUES, Antonio C.S.   Brazil, SP
— management
  DUGAN, Patrick J.   Switzerland
  HOFFMANN, Luc   France
  SHEIKH, Muhammad A.R.   Bangladesh
— resource assessment & management strategy
  BENNETT, Sara L.   Canada, BC
— science applied to policy & management
  LARSON, Joseph S.   USA, MA
wetlands
  BOYLAND, Desmond E.   Australia, Qld
  HAYNES-SUTTON, Ann M.   Jamaica
  HOLLIS, George E.   UK, England
  MALTBY, Edward   UK, England
  NAYAR, M.Param   India, Ker.
  TURNER, R.Eugene   USA, LA
  VISSER, Nicolaas W.   Kenya

— agroforestry, tropical Southeast Asian, for staple foods
STANTON, W.Robert — UK, England
—' conservation
CHALABI, Bouzid — Algeria
KADLEČÍK, Ján — Slovak Rep.
—: — of biodiversity
DUNCAN, Patrick — France
—, evolution of
BELLAMY, David J. — UK, England
—' management
KADLEČÍK, Ján — Slovak Rep.
SAENGER, Peter — Australia, NSW
—, prairie, impacts of UV radiation in*
—, —, microbial biogeochemical cycles in
*ROBARTS, Richard D. — Canada, Sask.
— preservations
HOLLEMAN, Andrew D. — USA, MA
—, renewable & sustainable use of
TAN, Koonlin — UK, England
— studies (and inventories)
DIEGUES, Antonio C.S. — Brazil, SP
whale conservation
PAYNE, Roger S. — UK, England
PHILLIPS, Cassandra F.E. — UK, England
—, humpback, identification
ORHUN-HEWSON, Canan — USA, MA
— policy formation
McCLOSKEY, Maxine E. — USA, MD
wild animal capture
WOODFORD, Michael H. — USA, DC
— conservation
WILSON, George R. — Australia, WA
— — disease, management, & translocation
WOODFORD, Michael H. — USA, DC
— — resources, commercial use of
WILSON, George R. — Australia, WA
— — utilization, esp.meat production
WOODFORD, Michael H. — USA, DC
—, conservation in, of endangered species in Oman
DALY, Ralph H. — Oman
— fauna & flora conservation
KACEM, Slaheddine BEL — Tunisia
— habitats, conservation of
VARIAVA, Dilnavaz — India, Mah.
— places (preservation of)
REEVES, Randall R. — Canada, Que.
— potato species
HAWKES, John G. — UK, England
— species, conservation of
VARIAVA, Dilnavaz — India, Mah.
— —, utilization of, in plant breeding
PINK, David A.C. — UK, England
wilderness
BLOOMFIELD, Michael I. — Canada, BC
PLAYER, Ian C. — RSA
— conservation
LaBASTILLE, Anne — USA, NY
MARTIN, Vance G. — USA, CO
—, — of, in West Africa esp.Sierra Leone
TUBOKU-METZGER, Daphne J.A. — Sierra Leone
— ecosystems (management)
PARSONS, David J. — USA, MT
— in British Columbia
HUSBAND, Vicky — Canada, BC
— values, conservation of
MARTIN, Vance G. — USA, CO

wildland management
SHORES, John N. — USA, ME
— values, conservation of
MARTIN, Vance G. — USA, CO
wildlands
STRONACH, Neil R.H. — Ireland
—, protected, management & planning of
SEVILLA, Lorenzo B. CARDENAL — Nicaragua/Guatemala
—, protection of
ROSE, Carlos R.HASBÚN — El Salvador
wildlife [plant and/or animal]
BLOOMFIELD, Michael I. — Canada, BC
MOGHRABY, Asim I. — Sudan
REEVES, Randall R. — Canada, Que.
SHELDRICK, Daphne M. — Kenya
STRONACH, Neil R.H. — Ireland
UPRETI, Biswa N. — Nepal
— and parts thereof, prevention of illegal trading in
LaBUDDE, Samuel F. — USA, CA
—, assessment of effects of northern development on
KLEIN, David R. — USA, AK
— biology (& conservation)
DAVIDAR, E.Reginald 'Reggie' C. — India, TN
— conservation
AJAYI, Seth S. — Nigeria
ASAVA, Wilfred W. — Kenya
ASEM, Samira OMAR — Kuwait
BALDUS, Rolf D. — Germany
BERETEH, Mohamed A. — Sierra Leone
BURTON, John A. — UK, England
CORBET, Philip S. — UK, Scotland
DAVIDAR, E.Reginald 'Reggie' C. — India, TN
DEY, Subhash C. — India, Delhi
DHINDSA, Manjit S. — India, Mah.
ELTRINGHAM, Stewart K. — UK, England
FÉRON, Eric M. — Zimbabwe
FONSECA, Gustavo A.A. — Brazil, MG
FRAZER, John F.D. — UK, England
GIMINEZ-DIXON, Mariano — Switzerland
GORZULA, Stefan — USA, TN
GUPTA, Brij K. — India, TN
HAYNES-SUTTON, Ann M. — Jamaica
HUTTON, Jonathan M. — Zimbabwe
JENKINS, David — UK, Scotland
LUSCOMBE, Bruce A. — USA, NY
MOORE, Norman W. — UK, England
NASH, Nancy — Hong Kong
NEPAL, Sanjay K. — Switzerland
OHN — Myanmar
PRESCOTT, Jacques — Canada, Que.
PULIDO, Victor — Peru
SHEIKH, Muhammad A.R. — Bangladesh
SUGIMURA, Ken — Japan
TEEB'AKI, Katino — Kiribati
WANG, Sung — China
WATSON, Richard — USA, ID
WHITAKER, Romulus E. — India, TN
— —, editing journals on
FITTER, A.Maisie S. — UK, England
— — field research in South-East Asia esp.Sarawak & Sabah
BENNETT, Elizabeth L. — Malaysia
— — in the Middle East
DEAN, Faisal — USA, VA
—, — of national & international (esp.vertebrates)
JENKINS, David — UK, Scotland
—, — projects & programmes re.
DURRANI, Shakil — Pakistan
— —, socio-political aspects of
SHAW, William W. — USA, AZ

* See lower footnote on p. 409.

wildlife conservation (contd)
— — strategy
    FLINT, Vladimir E. — Russia
— ecology
    MKANDA, Francis X. — Malawi
    MWASAGA, Belekebajobege — Tanzania
    PANDIT, Ashok K. — India, J&K
    PYROVETSI, Myrto D. — Greece
    SUGIMURA, Ken — Japan
— —, effects of habitat change on
    HASAN, Mohammed NORDIN — Malaysia
— —, old-growth forest
    BUTLER, James 'Jim' R. — Canada, Alb.
—, effects of northern development of
    KLEIN, David R. — USA, AK
— –forest relationships
    DODDS, Donald G. — Canada, NS
— Fund, World
    EDINBURGH, Philip Duke of — UK, England
    FULLER, Kathryn S. — USA, DC
— in British Columbia
    HUSBAND, Vicky — Canada, BC
—, international, conservation of
    JENKINS, David — UK, Scotland
— issues, international, agriculture &
    COPPINGER, Raymond — USA, MA
— legislation
    MEKOUAR, Mohamed A. — Italy
    SPINAGE, Clive A. — UK, England
— management
    ASEM, Samira OMAR — Kuwait
    BANGURA, Kalie I. — Sierra Leone
    BEHRA, Olivier — Madagascar
    BERETEH, Mohamed A. — Sierra Leone
    BROOKS, Peter M. — RSA
    DALY, Ralph H. — Oman
    DODDS, Donald G. — Canada, NS
    FERRAR, Anthony A. — RSA
    FONSECA, Gustavo A.B. — Brazil, MG
    GŁOWACIŃSKI, Zbigniew A. — Poland
    GORZULA, Stefan — USA, TN
    HOECK, Hendrik N. — Switzerland
    HUGHES, George R. — RSA
    HUTTON, Jonathan M. — Zimbabwe
    KRAUS, Daniel — Namibia/USA, CA
    LAVIEREN, Lambartus P.VAN — The Netherlands
    MARSH, Helene D. — Australia, Qld
    NDUKU, Willie K. — Zimbabwe
    ODUOL, Peter A. — Kenya
    PIIROLA, Jouko — Finland
    PYROVETSI, Myrto D. — Greece
    SALINAS, Pedro J. — Venezuela
    SINGH, Shekhar — India, Delhi
    TEMPLE, Stanley A. — USA, WI
    WANG, Sung — China
    WHITAKER, Romulus E. — India, TN
— —, Amazon (and forest)
    DOUROJEANNI, Marc J. — USA, VA
— — (birds)
    CHRISTIAN, Colmore S. — Dominica
— —, community involvement in
    MKANDA, Francis X. — Malawi
— — in eastern & southern Africa
    BALDUS, Rolf D. — Germany
— — outside of protected reserves
    KRAUS, Daniel — Namibia/USA, CA
    MARKER-KRAUS, Laurie — Namibia/USA, DC
— — projects, design & implementation of
    PANGETI, George N. — Zimbabwe

—, marine, conservation of
    MOYER, Jack T. — Japan
—, national, conservation of
    JENKINS, David — UK, Scotland
—, native (Kangaroos)
    SATTLER, Paul S. — Australia, Qld
— painting
    WALKER, Clive H. — RSA
— photography
    APPLIN, David G. — UK, England
— policy & management
    DODDS, Donald G. — Canada, NS
— preservation
    SINGH, Karan — India, Delhi
— protected area, own
    FIELD, Hermann H. — USA, MA
—, — areas &
    SERHAL, Assad — Lebanon
— protection
    BANGURA, Kalie I. — Sierra Leone
    GŁOWACIŃSKI, Zbigniew A. — Poland
    HAFIDI, Moulay El M. — Morocco
    LaBUDDE, Samuel F. — USA, CA
    NTAHUGA, Laurent — Burundi
— —, legal aspects of
    ABDELHADY, Abdelaziz — Egypt/Kuwait
— rehabilitation programmes*
— rescue
    *ROSE, Carlos R.HASBÚN — El Salvador
— research
    BUTLER, James 'Jim' R. — Canada, Alb.
    KLINGEL, Hans — Germany
— resource conservation & utilization incl. corals
    THRESHER, Philip B. — USA, CA
— resources (& natural)
    RANJITSINH, M.K. — India, MP
— surveys
    CAMPBELL, Kenneth L.I. — UK, England
—, sustainable use of
    FLINT, Vladimir E. — Russia
—, — utilization of
    SILVA, Ricardo FREIRE DA — Brazil, SP
—, teaching in (& research in parks)
    BUTLER, James 'Jim' R. — Canada, Alb.
— topics, interpreter of
    THOMAS, Anamaria A.DE — USA, FL
— tourism*
— trade
    *RANJITSINH, M.K. — India, MP
—, urban, ecology & management [of]
    ADAMS, Lowell W. — USA, WV
— use, sustainable, community involvement in
    BALDUS, Rolf D. — Germany
—, —, —, of
    FLINT, Vladimir E. — Russia
— utilization
    PRICE, Mark R.STANLEY — Kenya
—, vulnerability of, to impacts of climate change,
    research on
    MKANDA, Francis X. — Malawi
wind energy
    DIAB, Roseanne D. — RSA
— — in Bahrain
    ALNASER, Waheeb E. — Bahrain
—, impact of, on vegetation
    GRACE, John — UK, Scotland
wolf ecology & behaviour
    MECH, L.David — USA, MN

* *See* lower footnote on p. 409.

women
NOVOA, Laura — Chile
RAMPRASAD, Vanaja — India, Kar.
— & environment
MOUDUD, Hasna J. — Bangladesh
VARIAVA, Dilnavaz — India, Mah.
—: communication, environment, health
CORRAL, Thais — Brazil, RJ
women's contribution in developing world
TAN, Koonlin — UK, England
wood-based industries, raw materials for
LAL, Piare — India, AP
— - — energy development
NANAYAKKARA, Vitarana R. — Sri Lanka
— -lice, evolution of
INGRAM, Glen J. — Australia, Qld
woodland, ancient, extent of & changes in*
— conservation, forestry and
— ground vegetation, dynamics of
*KIRBY, Keith J. — UK, England
woodlands, ancient, in Britain and rest of Europe
PETERKEN, George F. — UK, England
world affairs (environment–development)
BHATT, Dibya D. — Nepal
— economic & environmental issues
COUSTEAU, Jacques-Yves — France
— heritage
BATISSE, Michel — France
KETO, Aila — Australia, Qld
LUCAS, Percy H.C. ('Bing') — NZ
— — convention
THORSELL, James W. — Switzerland
— —: policy, planning, & management
EIDSVIK, Harold K. — France
— social issues
COUSTEAU, Jacques-Yves — France
— vegetation, classification of
LOCK, John M. — UK, England
— Wildlife Fund (WWF), now partly 'World Wide
Fund for Nature'
FULLER, Kathryn S. — USA, DC
— — —, UK & International
EDINBURGH, Philip Duke of — UK, England
—, how it works
WOODWELL, George M. — USA, MA
world's resources, just distribution of
DAMMANN, Erik — Norway
world-wide sustainable development
GATHORNE-HARDY, Gathorne — UK, England
writing (on environment and/or conservation)
ADAMS, Aubrey — Trinidad
ATTENBOROUGH, David F. — UK, England
BELLAMY, David J. — UK, England
BRODEUR, Paul A. — USA, NY
CAHN, Robert — USA, VA
GUNAWARDENE, Nalaka J. — Sri Lanka
HEYERDAHL, Thor — Norway
KETCHUM, Robert G. — USA, CA
MATTHIESSEN, Peter — USA, NY
POLUNIN, Nicholas — Switzerland
RODRIGUEZ, Andrés R.RODRIGUEZ — Venezuela
VALLELY, Bernadette A.M. — UK, England
—, ecological research &
AMBASHT, Radhey S. — India, UP
—, —: investigative editor
WEIR, David A. — USA, CA
—, Nature conservation, photography, editing
ALON, Azaria — Israel

— on environmental concerns & on religions
TROMPF, Garry W. — Australia, NSW
— — nuclear waste (& research on)
LEMONS, John D., Jr — USA, ME

———

Yuit (Eskimos) aka Inuit
ROWLEY, Graham W. — Canada, Ont.
Yukon, NWT, environmental management &
planning in*
—, —, industrial development in
*FENGE, Terence A.E. — Canada, Ont.

———

Zen teaching
MATTHIESSEN, Peter — USA, NY
Zingiberaceae, African, taxonomy of
LOCK, John M. — UK, England
zonation, seismic, in land-use planning
AWAD, Adel R. — Syria
zone, arid, ecology (of)
CHADWICK, Michael J. — Sweden
—, coastal, impact study of anthropic processes in the
GRANJA, Helena M. — Portugal
—, —, land–sea interactions in protected areas
RAY, G.Carleton — USA, VA
—, mountainous, protection of (Romania)
CIOCHIA, Victor — Romania
zones, arid, conservation
MEHER-HOMJI, Vispy M. — India, TN
—, —, sand-dune fixation & reforestation
ZOUHA, Sekkou — Morocco
—, buffer, design of
SEVILLA, Lorenzo B.CARDENAL — Nicaragua/Guatemala
—, —, management of
BUDOWSKI, Gerardo — Costa Rica
—, coastal, evolution of
CARVALHO, G.SOARES DE — Portugal
—, —, management & monitoring of
HALIM, Youssef — Egypt
zoning, land-use law and, re.impacts of tourism on
environmental & legal systems
PETERSON, Claire McCARTHY — USA, IL
—, river classification &
BHARGAVA, Devendra S. — India, UP
zoobiology (biodiversity)
PRESCOTT, Jacques — Canada, Que.
zoogeography, marine
ANGEL, Martin V. — UK, England
— of Australian reptiles, extant & extinct
COVACEVICH, Jeanette A. — Australia, Qld
—, spider
MARUSIK, Yuri M. — Russia
zoological survey of Arabia
BÜTTIKER, William — Switzerland
zoology
IBARRA, Jorge A. — Guatemala
JENKINS, David — UK, Scotland

zoology (contd)
  MONOD, Théodore   France
  WASAWO, David P.S.   Kenya
—, medical
  BÜTTIKER, William   Switzerland

—, tropical (& conservation biology)
  HASAN, Mohammed NORDIN   Malaysia
zooplankton
  DUMONT, Henri J.   Belgium

APPENDIX III — ABBREVIATIONS, ACRONYMS, CONTRACTIONS, AND SOME EXPLANATIONS*

AA	Arboricultural Association, Associate in Arts[†]
AAA	American Anthropological Association, Australian Archaeological Association
AAAL	American Academy of Arts and Letters
AAAS	American Association for the Advancement of Science
AAAV	American Association of Avian Veterinarians
AAB	Alberta Association of Biologists, Association of Applied Biologists
AABGA	American Association for Botanical Gardens and Arboreta
AABNF	African Association for Biological Nitrogen Fixation
AACR	American Association of Cancer Research
AAEE	American Academy of Environmental Engineers, Australian Association for Environmental Education
AAERE	American Association for Environment & Resource Economics
AAG	Association of American Geographers
AAGB	Arboricultural Association of Great Britain
AAGG	Argentine Association of Geophysicists & Geodesists
AAK	Architectural Association of Kenya
AALS	Association of Arid Land Studies
AAM	American Association of Museums
A&N	Andaman & Nicobar (Islands)
AAP	American Association of Planners, Association of American Physicians
AAPT	American Association of Physics Teachers
AAR	American Academy of Religion
AAS	Academy for Arts and Sciences, American Arachnological Society, Association for the Advancement of Science, Association of Astronautical Societies, Australasian Arachnological Society, Australian Academy of Sciences
AASR	Australian Association for the Study of Religions
AATSE	Australian Academy of Technical Sciences & Engineering
AAUP	American Association of University Professors
AAUW	American Association of University Women
AAWV	American Association of Wildlife Veterinarians
AAZV	American Association of Zoo Veterinarians
AB	Artrium Baccalaureus (Bachelor of Arts), company name ending such as 'Limited'
ABA	American Bar Association
ABC	Australian Broadcasting Commission
ABDIL	Agri–biotech & Development International Ltd
ABEN	Association of Biologists & Ecologists of Nicaragua
ABI	American Biographical Institute
ABIM	American Board of Internal Medicine
ABQ	Association des Biologistes du Québec
ABS	Animal Behavior Society
ABSW	Association of British Science Writers
AC	Asociación Civil (= non-profit organization), Companion of the Order of Australia
ACA	Institute of Chartered Accountants of England & Wales
Acad.	Academician, Academy
ACBM	Asociación Colombiana de Biologos Marino (Colombian Association of Marine Biologists)
ACCA	Chartered Association of Certified Accountants
ACCT	Agence de Coopération Culturelle et Technique (an INGO)
ACE	Caribbean Conservation Association
ACEL	Australian Centre for Environmental Law
ACF	Australian Conservation Foundation
ACFOD	Asian Cultural Forum on Development (Bangkok, Thailand)
ACHA	American College Health Association
ACIAR	Australian Centre for International Agricultural Research
ACIC	American Committee for International Conservation
ACIF	Asociación Colombiana de Ingenieros Forestales (Colombian Association of Forest Engineers)

---

* Any punctuation, etc., has been ignored in arranging the order alphabetically.
[†] The order of two or more items having the same acronym etc. is given alphabetically.

ACIL	Agricultural Consulting International Ltd (was once known as)
ACIS	Chartered Institute of Company Secretaries (UK)
ACKMA	Australasian Cave & Karst Management Association (Inc.)
ACLS	American Council of Learned Societies
ACLU	American Civil Liberties Union
ACN	Agricultural Council of Norway
ACOEM	American College of Occupational & Environmental Medicine
ACP	American College of Physicians
ACRS	Australian Coral Reef Society
ACS	American Cetacean Society, American Chemical Society, Association for Canadian Studies
ACSAD	Arab Centre for the Studies of Arid Zones & Drylands
ACSANZ	Australian–Canadian Studies Association (including NZ)
ACT	Australian Capital Territory (Australia)
ACUNS	Association of Canadian Universities for Northern Studies
ACW	Association for Conservation of Wildlife (Bangkok, Thailand)
ADAS	Agricultural Development and Advisory Service (UK Government Extension Service of MAFF)
ADB	Asian Development Bank
addit.	additional
ADELF	Association des Ecrivains de la Langue Française
ADENA	Asociación para la Defensa de la Naturaleza (Spanish section of WWF)
ADIPA	Association of Development, Research, and Training Institutes of Asia and the Pacific
Adj.	Adjunct
A/admin.*	Administrator, administration, administrative
ADSTW	Association for the Development of Science in the Third World
Adv.	Adviser(s), Advisory
AEA	American Economic Association, Association for Environmental Archaeology
AEAC	American Energy Assurance Council
AEB	Association of Environmental Biologists
AEE	Asociación Española de Entomología (Spanish Association of Entomology), Association for Evolutionary Economics
AEEH	Association of European Environmental History
AEEP	Association of Environmental Engineering Professors
AEI	Asian Energy Institute
AEL	Association of Environmental Law
AEM	Asociación Etnobiológica Mexicana (Mexican Ethnobiological Association)
AEP	Asia Environmental Partnership (*see also* US–AEP)
AERA	American Education Research Association
AERC	Association of Environmental and Research Chemists
AERO	*see* ISAR AERO
AEROMech	name of the College — no other explanation
AES	American Elasmobranch Society, Australian Ecological Society, Australian Entomological Society
AFAS	American–French Academy of Sciences
AFCR	American Federation of Clinical Research
AFHVS	Agriculture, Food, & Human Values Society
AFL	Association Française de Lichenologie
AFO	Association of Field Ornithologists
AFP	Association of Friends of Parks
AFRC	Agriculture & Food Research Council
AFS	American Fern Society, American Fisheries Society, American Forestry Society, Australian Forest School
AFT	Australian Frog Trust
AG	Aktiengesellschaft (joint-stock company)
AGA	American Genetics Association
AGAPAN	Associacáo Gaucha para de Proteção as Ambiente Natural
Agric.spec.Hort.	Agriculture specializing in Horticulture
agric., agricl	agriculture, agricultural
agrofor.	agroforestry
A/agron.*	Agronomist, agronomy

* The capitalized (or decapitalized) initial letter and slash ('solidus') in such situations indicate alternative treatments in the Biographies but for simplicity are usually not upheld in the right-hand columns of this terminal Appendix.

AGS	American Geographical Society
AGU	American Geophysical Union
AHA	American Humanists' Association
A&I	Arts & Industries
AIA	Alberta Institute of Agrologists, American Institute of Architects
AIAA	American Institute for Aeronautics & Astronautics
AIAPP	Asociación de Investigadores Agricolas y Pecuarias del Peru
AIAS	Australian Institute of Agricultural Science
AIB	Australian Institute of Biology (Inc.)
AIBS	American Institute of Biological Sciences (Inc.)
AIC	American Institute of Chemists
AIChE	American Institute of Chemical Engineers
AICP	American Institute of Certified Planners
AID	Agency for International Development
AIDA	Association Internationale de Droit d'Assurance (International Association of Insurance Law)
AIDAB	Australian International Development Assistance Bureau
AIDEnvt	Advice and Research for Development and Environment
AIDIS	Inter-American Association of Sanitary Engineers
AIDS	Auto Immune Deficiency Syndrome
AIE	Australian Institute of Engineers
AIFC	Associate of Indian Forest College
AIFRB	American Institute of Fisheries Research Biologists
AIIA	Australian Institute of International Affairs
AILA	American Institute of Landscape Architects
AIM	Agricultural Institute of Malaysia
AIMM	Australian Institute of Mining and Metallurgy
AIMS	Australian Institute of Marine Science
AINA	Arctic Institute of North America
AIP	Australian Institute of Physics
AIPS	Association Internationale de Phyto-Sociologie
AIT	Asian Institute of Technology (Bangkok, Thailand)
AIU	Association of Indian Universities (New Delhi, India)
AIVF	Association of Independent Video and Filmmakers
AJRH	Association for the Journal of Religious History
AK	Alaska (USA)
aka	also known as
Akademia Nauk	Academy of Sciences (USSR)
AKC	Associate of King's College (theological qualification gained by examination)
AKUR	Arbeitskreis für Umweltrecht (German Council for Environmental Law)
AL	Alabama (USA)
ALA	American Library Association, Asociación Latinoamericana de Acultura (LatinAmerican Association of Aquaculture)
Alb.	Alberta (Canada)
ALCA	Asociación Latinoamericana de Ciencias Agricolas
ALCPP	Asociación Latinoamericana de Ciencias Pecuarias del Peru
ALECSO	Arab League Educational, Cultural, & Scientific, Organization
ALI	American Law Institute
ALS	Australian Littoral Society
alt.	altitude
AM	Master of Arts, Member of Order of Australia
AMA	American Medical Association
AMAX	Company name
Amaz.	Amazonas (Brazil)
AMBIFORUM	private-consultancy-company index of all environmental regulations in Portugal and references to EU-regulations on environment
Amb.	Ambassador
AMCA	American Mosquito Control Association
AMDEL	Australian Mineral Development Laboratories (became Amdel Ltd)
Amer.	America, American
AMNH	American Museum of Natural History
AMPLA	Australian Mining & Petroleum Law Association
AMQUA	American Quaternary Association (*but see also* AQA)
AMS	African Meteorological Society, American Mammal Society, American Meteorological Society, Australian Mammal Society
AMSA	Australian Marine Sciences Association (Inc.)

AMWA	Association of Metropolitan Water Agencies
A&N	Andaman & Nicobar (Islands)
ANAI	name, not an acronym
ANC	Australian National Commission
ANCA	Australian Nature Conservation Agency
ANCON	Asociación Nacional para la Conservación de la Naturaleza
ANCT	Association of Nature Conservation of Turkey
ANEE	*see* SASEANEE
anniv.	anniversary
Ann.Biol.	Annals of Biology
ANPC	Australian Network for Plant Conservation
ANS	Academy of Natural Sciences, Audubon Naturalists' Society
ANSA	American Nature Study Association
ANSS	American Nature Study Society
A/anthrop.; anthropl	Anthropologist, anthropology; anthropological
ANU	Australian National University
ANZAAS	Australia and New Zealand Association for the Advancement of Science
A&NZGG	Australia & New Zealand Geomorphology Group
AO	Order of Australia
AOS	Academy of Overseas Sciences (Belgium)
AOU	American Ornithologists' Union
AP; A/ap.	Andhra Pradesh (India), Apartado Postal; Apartamento (apartment)
APA	American Planning Association, American Potato Association, American Psychological Association, Association of Polish Architects (*see also* SARP)
APDC	Asia and Pacific Development Centre (KL, Malaysia)
Apdo, *see also* Apto	Apartado, Apartamento (apartment)
APECO	Asociación Peruana de la Conservación de la Naturaleza
APEQ	Associação Portuguesa paro o Estudo do Quaternário
APG	Associação Portuguesa de Geólogos
APHA	American Public Health Association
APhS	American Philosophical Society (*see also* APS)
APO	Asian Productivity Organization
approx.	approximate, approximately
APPS	Australasian Plant Pathological Society, Australian Plant Physiology Society
APQS	Association for Prehistoric and Quaternary Studies
APRL	Atmospheric Physics & Radiopropagation Laboratory
APROFA	Asociación Chilena de Protección e la Familia
APS	American Philosophical Society (oldest scholarly Society in USA, *see also* APhS), American Physical Society, American Phytopathological Society, American Psychological Society, Association of Pacific Systematists
APSA	Australian Political Studies Association
APSI	Academy of Plant Sciences of India
A/apt	apartment
APTI	Air Pollution Training Institute (US EPA)
A/apto	Apartamento (apartment)
APWA	American Public Works Association
AQA	American Quaternary Association (*see also* AMQUA)
AQuA	Australasian Quaternary Association
AR	Arkansas (USA)
arach.	arachnology, arachnological
ARAS	Australian Royal Agricultural Society
ARC	Agricultural Research Council
A/arch.	Architect, architecture
archaeobot.	archaeobotany, archaeobotanist
archaeol.	archaeology, archaeologist
archl	archaeological
ARC/INFO	computer-aided processing
ARCS	Achievement Rewards for College Scientists (Hawaii, USA)
ARIAS	Associate Royal Incorporation of Architects in Scotland
ARIBA	Associate Royal Institute of British Architects
Arq.	Arquitecto (Architect)
ARS	Agricultural Research Service Station
ARSF	Agricultural Research Scientist Forum
ARTI	Agrarian Research and Training Institute

ARVO	Association for Research in Vision & Ophthalmology
Arz.	Arzobispo (Archbishop)
AS	Academy of Science(s), company ending (Norwegian, as 'Limited' or 'Incorporated')
ASA	American Society of Agronomy
ASAB	Association for the Study of Animal Behaviour
ASABP	Australian Society of Aquatic Botany & Physiology
ASAS	American Society of Animal Science, Romanian Academy of Forest & Agriculture
ASB	American Society of Botany
ASBMB	American Society for Biochemistry and Molecular Biology
ASBS	Australian Systematic Botany Society
ASBPA	American Shore & Beach Preservation Association
ASCB	American Society for Conservation Biology
ASCE	American Society of Civil Engineers
ASEAMS	Association of Southeast Asian Marine Scientists
ASEAN	Association of South East Asian Nations (involves Thailand, Indonesia, Singapore, Philippines, & Malaysia)
ASEH	American Society for Environmental History
ASEP	Asian Society for Environmental Protection
ASF	American Society of Forestry, Australian Speliological Federation (Inc.)
ASFB	Australian Society for Fish Biology
ASH	Australian Society of Herpetologists
ASHG	American Society of Human Genetics
ASHOKA	international organization based in Washington, DC, whose programme is mainly in Asia and America
ASHRAE	international organization based in Washington, DC
ASHS	American Society of Horticultural Science
ASI	Acoustical Society of India
ASIH	American Society of Ichthyologists & Herpetologists
ASIL	American Society of International Law
ASIS	American Society for Information Science
ASL	Australian Society for Limnology
ASLA	American Society of Landscape Architects
ASLO	American Society of Limnology and Oceanography
ASM	American Society of Mammalogists, American Society of Microbiology, Australian Society for Microbiology
ASMA	American Standard Methods Association
ASMAPE	Association Marocaine pour la Protection de l'Environnement
ASMD	Association of Science Museum Directors
ASME	American Society of Mechanical Engineers
ASN	American Society of Naturalists
ASP	American Society of Pharmacognosy
ASPA	American Society for Public Administration
ASPCA	American Society for the Prevention of Cruelty to Animals
ASPCC	American Society of Primatologists Conservation Committee
ASPP	American Society of Plant Physiologists, American Society of Plant Physiology
ASPRS	American Society for Photogrammetry and Remote Sensing
ASPT	American Society of Plant Taxonomists
ASRCT	Applied Scientific Research Corporation of Thailand
ASSA	Academy of Social Science in Australia
ASSE	American Society of Safety Engineers
Assn(s)	Association(s)
Assoc., Assocs	Associate, Associates
Asst, Asstship	Assistant, Assistantship
ASSWC	American Society of Soil & Water Conservation (*see also* SWCS)
AST	Association of Science Teachers
ASTD	American Society for Training and Development
ASTeR	Atmospheric Simulation, Testing & Research (company name)
ASTM	American Society for Testing and Materials
ASU	Association of Scientific Unions
ASZ	American Society of Zoologists
ATA	Alberta Teachers' Association, Argentine Toxicology Association
ATAS	Academy of Television Arts and Sciences
ATB	Association for Tropical Biology (USA)

ATF	Association of Tropical Foresters
ATL	Association for Tropical Lepidoptera, Association of Tropical Lepidopterists
ATLA	American Trial Lawyers' Association
atmos.	atmosphere, atmospheric
ATSE	Academy of Technological Sciences and Engineering
ATV	Associated Television
AUDA	Asociación Uruguaya de Derecho Ambiental
Aug.	August
AUL	Association of Ukrainian Lawyers
AUSIMM	Australian Institute of Mining & Metallurgy
Auth., Auths	Authority, Authorities
AVA	Australian Veterinary Association
AVCC	Australian Vice-Chancellors' Committee
Av.	Avenida, Avenue
AWB	Asian Wetland Bureau
AWD	Association for Women in Development
AWMA	Air & Waste Management Association (USA)
AWMS	Australian Wildlife Management Society
AWRA	American Water Resources Association
AWWA	American Water Works Association, Australian Water & Wastewater Association
AZ	Arizona (USA)
AZA	American Association of Zoological Parks & Aquariums
AZL	Company name
B.; *B.*	Bachelor; Born, Brother
BA	Bachelor of Arts, British Association
BAAS	British Association for the Advancement of Science
Bacc.	Baccalauréat
BACIE	British Association for Commercial & Industrial Education
BAFTA	British Academy of Film & TV Arts (formerly SFTA)
BAgr.	Bachelor of Agriculture Science
BAgrSc	Bachelor of Agricultural Science
BAgrSci	Bachelor of Agricultural Sciences
BANC	British Association of Nature Conservationists
BANCORP	name of Bank
BAO	Baccalaureatus in Arte Obstetricus (Bachelor of Obstetrics)
BAPT	British Association of Physical Training
BArch.	Bachelor of Architecture
BAS	Bachelor of Applied Science, Bangladesh Academy of Sciences, British Arachnological Society, Bulgarian Astronautical Society
BASA	Barcelona Academy of Sciences & Arts
BASC	British Association for Shooting and Conservation
BASF	Bayerische Anilin und Soda Fabrik
BASL	Bar Association of Sri Lanka
Bât.	Bâtiment (building)
BAZ	Brazilian Association of Zoos
BBA	Bachelor of Business Administration, Bahamas Bar Association
BBC	British Broadcasting Corporation
BBS	British Biochemistry Society, British Bryological Society
BC	British Columbia (Canada)
BCAS	Bangladesh Centre for Advanced Studies
BCG	British Chelonia Group
BCh	Baccalaureatus in Chirurgeae (Bachelor of Surgery)
BCI	Bat Conservation International
BCL	Bachelor of Civil Law
BCom	Bachelor of Commerce
BCom (ECS)	Bachelor of Commerce (in Economics)
BCRA	Britsh Cave Research Association
BCS	Brazilian College of Surgeons
BCSD	Business Council For Sustainable Development (WBCSD *qv* from 1.1.95)
Bd	Board
BD	Bachelor of Divinity
BDS	British Dragonfly Society
BE	Bachelor of Engineering
BEc, BEC	Bachelor of Economics

B.Ed.	Bachelor of Education
BEE	Bachelor of Electrical Engineering
BEMA	British Environmental Media Awards
B.Eng.	Bachelor of Engineering
Berks.	Berkshire (England, UK)
BES	British Ecological Society, British Entomological Society
BGCI	Botanic Gardens Conservation International
BGRG	British Geomorphological Research Group
BGS	British Geomorphological Society, British Grassland Society
BHL	Bachelor of Hebrew Letters
BHRA	British Hydromechanics Research Association
BHS	British Herpetological Society, British Hydrological Society
BHU	Banaras Hindu University (UP, India)
BHyd.S.	British Hydrological Society
BI	Balearic Islands (Spain)
bibl., bibl	bibliography, bibliographical
BILA	British Insurance Law Association
BIM	British Institute of Management
biochem.	biochemistry, biochemical
BIODEV	BIOdiversité et DEVeloppement
biodiv.	biodiversity
bioengg	bioengineering
biogeochem.	biogeochemical, biogeochemistry
biogeog., biogeogl	biogeography, biogeographical
biog., biogl	biography, biographical
biol.; biol	biology, biologist; biological
BIOMASS	Biological Investigations of Marine Antarctic Systems & Stocks
biomed.	biomedical
BioNet	US NGOs on biodiversity conservation
bioregnl	bioregional
BIOS	trademark (name of enterprise)
Bioscis	Biological Sciences, Biosciences
biostats	biostatistics
biotech.	biotechnology
BIS	Bachelor of Independent Studies (in Integrated Studies), British Institute of Statisticians
BITS	Birla Institute of Technology & Science (Rajasthan, India)
BL	Barrister-at-Law
BLD	Bachelor of Landscape Design
bldg	building
BLitt.	Bachelor of Letters
BLM	Bureau of Land Management
BLS	British Lichen Society
BLV	no-longer-used abbreviation for the publication
BM	Bachelor of Medicine; British Museum
BMil.Sc.	Bachelor of Military Science
BMNH	British Museum of Natural History
BMS	British Mycological Society
BM, BCh	Baccaeleurus Medicinae, Baccaeleurus Chirurgiae (two degrees granted together, U.of Oxford, England, UK)
BNA	British Naturalists' Association
BNHS	Bombay Natural History Society (Hornbill House)
BNT	Bahamas National Trust
BOC	British Ornithologists' Club
BOLSA	Bank of London and South America
BOS	British Ornithological Society
Bot., bot.; B/botl	Botanist, botany; botanical
BOU	British Ornithologists' Union
BP	Boîte Postale, British Petroleum
BPS	British Phycological Society
Bras.DF	Brasilia Distrito Federal (Brazil)
BRC	Borneo Research Council
Brit.	British
B/bro(s)	brother(s)
BS	Bachelor of Science, Bachelor of Surgery
BSA	Botanical Society of America

BSAP	British Society of Animal Production
BSAS	Brazilian Society for the Advancement of Science
BSB	Botanical Society of Brazil
BSBI	Botanical Society of the British Isles
BSc	Bachelor of Science
BSC	British Society for Chronobiology
BSCB	Belgian Society for Cell Biology
BScF	Bachelor of Science of Forestry
BSI	British Standards Institution
BSJ	Botanical Society of Japan
BSL	Brazilian Society for Limnology
BSM	Belgian Society for Mutagenesis
BSN	Botanic Society of Natal
BSPP	British Society for Plant Pathology
BSPS	Brazilian Society for the Promotion of Science
BSS	Botanical Society of Scotland
BSSA	Botanical Society of South Africa
BSSFF	Brazilian Society for the Study of Flora & Fauna
BSSS	British Society of Soil Science
BSTA	Brazil Seed Technologies Association
BSZ	Brazilian Society of Zoology
Bt	Baronet (title of Sir and wife Lady)
BTCV	British Trust for Conservation Volunteers
BTech	Bachelor of Technology
BTO	British Trust for Ornithology
BTS	Brazil Technicians' Standards
Bucks.	Buckinghamshire (England, UK)
Bull.	Bulletin
Bur.	Bureau
Bus.	Business
BVI	British Virgin Islands
BVSc	Bachelor of Veterinary Science
BWEA	British Wind Energy Association
BZS	Belgian Zoological Society (*see also* RBZS, same organization)
C, C./c., c.; ©	Carbon, C/central, *circa* (= approximately); copyright
CA	California (USA)
CABI	Commonwealth Agricultural Bureaux International
CACGP	Commission on Atmospheric Chemistry & Global Pollution
CADIC	Centro Austral de Investigaciónes Cientificas (Ushuaia, Argentina)
CAE	Chinese Association of Ecology
CAES	Chinese Academy for Environmental Sciences
CAF	Chinese Academy of Forestry
CAG	Canadian Association of Geographers
CAJ	Canadian Association of Journalists
CALACS	Canadian Association of Latin American & Caribbean Studies
Calif.	California (USA), Californian
Camb., Cambs.	Cambridge, Cambridgeshire (England, UK)
CAMPFIRE	Programme name
CANARI	Caribbean Natural Resources Institute
cand.	candidate
Cand.agric.	Candidatus agriculturae
Cand.hort.	Candidatus horticulturae
Cand.jur.	Candidatus juris
Cand.real.	Candidatus Realis, Candidatus realium (*c.* MSc)
Cand.Sc.	Candidate of Science
CANR	Chinese Association of Natural Resources
Cantab.	Cantabrigiensis (= of Cambridge University)
CAPE	Children's Alliance for the Protection of the Environment
CAPS	Californians for Population Stabilization
Capt.	Captain
CARC	Canadian Arctic Resources Committee
CARE	Cooperation American Relief Everywhere
Carib.	Caribbean
CARICOMP	Caribbean Coastal Marine Productivity
CAS	Chinese Academy of Sciences (Academia Sineca), Czechoslovakian Academy of Sciences

CASA	Croatian Academy of Sciences & Arts
CASAFA	Committee on Application of Science to Agriculture, Forestry & Aquaculture
CASS	Chinese Academy of Social Sciences
CASTASIA	Conference for the Application of Science & Technology in Asia
CATIE	Centro Agronómico Tropical de Investigación y Enseñanza (Tropical, Agricultural, Research & Education Centre, Costa Rica)
CAWC	Chinese Association for Wildlife Conservation
CAZPA	Canadian Association of Zoological Parks & Aquariums
CB	Campus Box; Commander of the Bath (UK)
CBA	Canadian Botanical Association, Colorado Bar Association
CBC	Canadian Broadcasting Corporation
CBDC	Community Biodiversity Development & Conservation
CBE	Commander, Order of the British Empire
CBiol., C.Biol.	Chartered Biologist, Chartered Consultant in Biology
CBPCWP	Central Board for the Prevention & Control of Water Pollution
CBS	California, Chinese, or Czech, Botanical Society; Columbia Broadcasting System
CC	Casilla Correo (POB), Commander of Canada, Consultative Committee
CC2	Courier's internal code
CCA	Caribbean Conservation Association
CCAMLR	Commission for the Conservation of Antarctic Marine Living Resources
CCAR	Canadian Coalition on Acid Rain, Central Conference of American Rabbis
CCC	Contact Commission on Conservation
CCEA	Canadian Council on Ecological Areas
CCED	China Council on Environment & Development
CCESR	Committee on Critical Environmental Situations and Regions
CChem, C.Chem	Chartered Chemist
CCNY	City College of New York
CCS	Courier Company Service, Croatian Chemistry Society
CCSK	Communication Centre of Scientific Knowledge for Self Reliance
CDA	College Diploma in Agriculture
CEAC	Canadian Environmental Advisory Council
CEARC	Canadian Environmental Assessment Research Council
CEC	Commission of European Communities, Commission on Education and Communication (IUCN)
CECIA	Consejo Ecuatoriano para la Conservación e Investigación de las Aves
CEDA	Centre for Economic Development & Administration (Kathmandu, Nepal)
CEDIP	Centro Documentazione Internazionale Parchi
CEEC	Commission of the Economic European Community
CEFAT	Centro Europeo de Formación Ambiental y Turistica (European Centre for Professional Training in Environment & Tourism)
CEGB	Central Electricity Generating Board (UK)
CEI	Council of Engineering Institutions
CEIA	Canadian Environment Industry Association
CEIS	Center for Environmental Information Science
CEL	Commission on Environmental Law (IUCN)
CEO	Chief Executive Officer
CEP	Certified Environmental Professional (The Academy of Board Certified Environmental Professionals), Commission on Environmental Planning (IUCN)
CEPAL	Comición Economica para Americano Latine (Economic Commission for Latin America)
CEPLA	Commission on Environmental Policy, Law & Administration (IUCN)
CEQ	Council on Environmental Quality
cert., certs	certificate, certificates
CES	Colombian Ecology Society
CESP	Commission on Environmental Strategy and Planning (IUCN)
CEST	Centre for Exploitation of Science and Technology
CET	Commission for Education & Training (IUCN)
CFA	Caribbean Foresters' Association, Commonwealth Forestry Association
CFC	chlorofluorocarbon
CFI	Commonwealth Forestry Institute (Oxford, England, UK)
CFO	Chief Financial Officer
CFR	Council on Foreign Relations
CGIAR	Consultative Group on International Agricultural Research
CGO	Central Government Office
CGS	Czech Geographical Society

CH	Confédération Helvétique (= Switzerland)
Chargé(e) de Cours	Lecturer
CHEA	Central Himalayan Environment Association
CHEC	Commonwealth Human Ecology Council (London HQ, England, UK)
chem.	chemistry, chemical
Chem.Eng.	Chemical Engineering
CIAE	Central Institute of Agricultural Engineering
CIArb.	Chartered Institute of Arbitrators
CIAT	Centro Internacional de Agricultura Tropical (Colombia)
C.IBiol.	Chartered Member of Institute of Biology
CICAR	Cooperative Investigation of the Caribbean & Adjacent Regions
CICESE	Center of Scientific Research and Higher Education of Ensenada
CIDA	Canadian International Development Agency, Centre International de Documentation Arachnologique (France)
CIDYAA	Comite Interamericano de Derecho y Administracion 'del Ambiente
CIEC	Centre International des Engrais Chimiques
CIEL	Council of International Environmental Law
CIEL-US	Center for International Environmental Law (US)
CIESM	Commission Internationale pour l'Exploration Scientifique de la Méditerranée
CIF	Canadian Institute of Forestry
CIFOR	Centre for International Forestry Research (research and centre of CGIAR system)
CII	Chartered Insurance Institute
CIIA	Canadian Institute for International Affairs
CILSS	Comité Inter-Etats de Lutte contre la Sécheresse, Pays Sahel (InterState Committee for Fight against Drought in Sahelian countries)
CIM	Chartered Institute of Marketing, Centre International de Myriapodologie (France)
CIME	Comite Internacional Migraciónes Europeas
CIMMYT	Centro Internacional de Mejoramiento de Maiz y Trigo (International Maize & Wheat Improvement Centre)
CIP	Canadian Institute of Planners
CIPA	California Institute of Public Affairs
CIPRA	Commission Internationale pour la Protection des Régions Alpines
circs	circumstances
CIS	Community of Independent States
CIT	California Institute of Technology, Central Independent Television
CITES	Convention on International Trade in Endangered Species of Wild Fauna & Flora (The Washington Convention)
Civ.Eng.	Civil Engineering
CJNE	Council of Journalists for Nature and Ecology
class.	classification
clin.	clinical
C&M	Conservation & Management
CMEA	Council of Mutual Economic Assistance (can also be COMECON) — main economic organization within former socialist states
CMG	Companion of the Order of St Michael & St George
CMOS	Canadian Meteorological & Oceanographic Society
CMS	Canadian Meteorological Service (which became CMOS, *qv*), Colombian Meteorological Society, Convention on the Conservation of Migratory Species of Wild Animals
CNEEC	Canadian Network for Environmental Education & Communication
CNES	Centre National d'Etudes Spatiales
CNF	Canadian Nature Federation
CNPPA	Commission on National Parks and Protected Areas (IUCN)
CNR	Commission on Natural Resources
CNRC	Canadian National Research Council
CNRI	Caribbean Natural Resources Institute
CNRS	Centre National de la Recherche Scientifique
CNU	Conseil National des Universités
c/Co.;c/Cos	County, c/Company; c/Companies
%	(in) care of
CO	Colorado (USA)
COBSEA	Coordinating Body of the Seas of East Asia
CODEFF	Comite Nacional pro Defensa de la Fauna y Flora (Chile)

coevol.	coevolution
collab., collabn	collaborator, collaboration
Coll., Colls	College, Colleges
Col.	Colonia (= suburb)
Comb. Hons.	Combined Honours
COMECON	Council of Mutual Economic Assistance (can also be CMEA, *qv*)
Comm., Comms	Commission, Commissions
Commem.	Commemoration
comp.	comprehensive, comprehension
CONACYT	Consejo Nacional de Ciencia y Tecnología (National Council of Sciences & Technologies)
Cong.	Congress
CONICET	Consejo Nacional de Ciencia y Tecnología (Argentinian National Science Foundation)
CONICIT	Centro Nacional de Investigaciónes Cientificas y Technologicas (Venezuela)
Conn.	Connecticut (USA)
cons.	conservation
constn, constnl	constitution, constitutional
C/consult.; C/consults	Consultant, consulting, consultative, consultancy; consultancies
contd	continued
contrib., contribn(s)	contributor, contribution(s)
c/Conv., c/Convs	c/Convention, c/Conventions
coopn	cooperation
Coord., coordn	Coordinator, coordination
COPERNICUS	Cooperation Programme in Europe for Research on Nature and Industry through Coordinated University Studies
CORINE	COoRdination INformation Environment (an EC project)
Corp., Corpn	Corporation
Corres.	Correspondence, Correspondent, Corresponding
COS	Cooper Ornithological Society, Czech Ornithological Society
Co.Sec.	Company Secretary
COSPAR	Committee on Space Research (ICSU)
COSTI	Centro Organizzativo Scuole Tecniche Italiane (Italian Community Adult Training Centre)
COU	Chilean Ornithological Union
Counc.	Councillor
Couns.	Counsellor
CP	Campus Post, Case Postale, Central Provinces (India), Codigo Postal
CPESC	Certified Professional in Erosion and Sediment Control (ASA Registry)
CPRE	Council for the Protection of Rural England
CPRI	Colombian Potato Research Institute
CPS	College of Physicians & Surgeons
CPSA	Canadian Political Science Association
CPWS	Canadian Parks & Wilderness Society
CRBC	Centre de Recherches Biologiques de Chizé
CRF	Cancer Research Foundation
CRICYT	Centro Regional de Investigaciónes Cientificas y Tecnologicas (Regional Centre for Science & Technology)
CRIOMM	Centre for Research on Indian Ocean Marine Mammals
CRMP	Coastal Resources Management Project
CRRI	Central Rice Research Institute
CSA	Current Science Association
CSAS	Czech Society for Arts & Science
CSB	Chilean Society of Biology
CSBS	Cuban Society of Biological Sciences
CSc	Candidatus Sciencia (Candidate of Sciences)
CSE	Chinese Society of Environment
CSEB	Canadian Society of Environmental Biology
CSF	Chinese Society of Forestry
CSFR	Czech & Slovak Federal Republic (until 1992)
CSFRI	Citrus and Subtropical Fruit Research Institute
CSI	Cetacean Society International
CSIC	Consejo Superior de Investigaciones Cientificas
CSIR	Council for Scientific and Industrial Research
CSIRO	Commonwealth Scientific & Industrial Research Organization (Australia)
CSL	Canadian Society of Limnologists

CSLA	Canadian Society of Landscape Architects
CSLL	China Society on Land Law
CSLS	China Society on Legal Science
CSME	Canadian Society for Mechanical Engineering
CSNS	Croatian Society of Natural Sciences
CSO	Chinese Society of Oceanography
CSPE	Canadian Society of Professional Engineers
CSRD	Centre for Sustainable Regional Development
CSRI	Central Scientific Research Institute
CSSA	Cactus & Succulent Society of America, Crop Science Society of America
CSSS	Chinese Society of Soil Science
CSTI	Council of Science and Technology Institutes
CSU	Colorado State University
CSWA	Canadian Science Writers' Association
CT	Connecticut (USA)
C.Theol.	Certificate in Theology
Cttee	Committee
CUNC	Czech Union of Nature Conservation (largest Czech NGO)
CUNY	City University of New York
CUP	Cambridge University Press
curr.	curriculum, curricular
CVO	Commander, Royal Victorian Order
CWF	Canadian Wildlife Federation
CWNG	Canadian Western Natural Gas
CWS	Canadian Wildlife Service, Colonial Waterbird Society (USA)
CYCAD	name of international conferences on Cycads
Czech.	Czechoslovak, Czechoslovakia(n)
CZS	Czech Zoological Society
D., d., d.	Divorced, daughter(s), dom (Russian = house)
DAAD	Deutscher Akademischer Austauschdienst
DANIDA	Danish International Development Agency
DARE	Department of Agricultural Research and Education
DAS	Dutch Anthropogenetic Society
Dato'	Royal decoration
DBS	Danish Botanical Society
DC	District of Columbia (USA), Distrito Capital
DC/PAC	Desertification Control/Programme Activity Centre
DD	Doctor of Divinity
DDT	Dichloro-diphenyl-trichloroethane
DE	Delaware (USA), Doctor of Engineering
DEA	Diplôme d'Etudes Approfondies
Dec.	December
DEH	Swiss Society of Technology and Humanitarian Help
D/del.	D/delegate, D/delegation
Dem., demn	Demonstrator, demonstration
Dept, Deptl	Department, Departmental
Dep.	Deputy
Derbys.	Derbyshire (England, UK)
DES	Dutch Ecological Society
desert.	desertification
D/dev., devs, devl	D/development, developments, developmental
DF	Distrito Federal
DFC	Desert Fishes Council, Distinguished Flying Cross
DG	Director-General
DGE	Deutsche Gesellschaft für allgemeine und angewandte Entomologie
DGIC	Directorate-General for International Cooperation (Netherlands Ministry of Foreign Affairs)
DGIS	Directoraat Generaal voor Internationale Samenwerking, *see also* DGIC
DGIX (Envt)	Commission of the European Communities
DGT	Deutsche Gesellschaft für Tropenökologie
DGXI	Directorate General for the Environment, Nuclear Safety, and Civil Protection of the European Union
DGXIB	Directorate General of the Commission of the European Communities which deals with the environment
DGXII	Directorate General XII — Science Research & Development (EC)

DHF	Dengue Haemorrhagic Fever
DHKD	The Society for the Protection of Nature (Istanbul, Turkey)
DHV	company name
DIAND	Department of Indian Affairs & Northern Development (Canada)
DIC	Diploma of Imperial College (London, UK)
DICE	Durrell Institute of Conservation & Ecology (University of Kent, England, UK)
Dict.	Dictionary
diff.	different
DINAC	Dirección Nacional de Aeronautica Civil
Dip.Ag.Econ.	Diploma in Agricultural Economics
Dip.Ed.	Diploma in Education
Dip.Eng.	Diploma in Engineering
Dip.For.	Diploma in Forestry
Dip.in Adv.Studies	Diploma in Advanced Studies
DipM	Diploma in Marketing
Dip.Perm.DES	Diploma in Permaculture Design
Dip.Ph.Ed.	Diploma in Physical Education
Dip.P.Admin.	Diploma in Public Administration
Dip.Str.Eng.	Diploma in Structural Engineering
Dipl.	Diploma
Dipl.-Forstwirt	Diplom-Forstwirt (title received after four years' study, German)
Dipl.Ing.	Diplomierte Ingénieur
Dir	Director
disc.	discipline, disciplinary
Dist.	Distinction
Disting.	Distinguished
Distr.	District
distribn	distribution
DIVERSITAS	International Biodiversity Research Programme (IUBS/SCOPE/UNESCO)
div., divs.; divl	division, divisions; divisional
DLitt	Dr of Letters (Oxf., UK), Dr of Literature (Aberdeen, UK)
DM	Doctor of Medicine
DNA	Desoxyribunucleic Acid
DNHS	Danish Natural History Society
DoA	Department of Agriculture
Docent	University Lecturer
doct., doctl	doctorate, doctoral
DoE	Department of the Environment
DOLE	Dutch Organization of Landscape Ecology
DOS	Dutch Ornithological Society
Dozent	University Lecturer
DPh	Doctor of Philosophy
D.Phil.	Doctor of Philosophy
DPIE	Department of Primary Industries & Energy
DPR	Democratic People's Republic
Dr	Doctor, Docteur
Dr Agric.	Doctor of Agriculture
Dr Biol.	Doctor of Biology
Drh.	Dokter hewan (veterinarian, Indonesia)
Dr habil.	Doktor habilitowary (= Dozent = approx. Associate Professor)
Dr hab.	Doctor habilitatus (Polish higher doctorate), Doctor of Science
Dr-Ing.	Doctor Engineer
Dr I/iur.	Doctor I/iuris (= Doctor of Law)
Dr iur.habil.	Doctor of Law qualified to teach
Dr Jr, Dr Jur.	Doctor Juris, Doctor of Jurisprudence
Dr med.vet.	Doctor of Veterinary Medicine
DrPH	Doctor of Public Health
Dr philos.	Doctor philosophiae (PhD)
Dr rer.nat.	Doctor rerum naturalium
Dr rer.silv.	Doctor rerum silvarum/silvae (title for forest affairs, Latin)
Drs/drs	Doctorandus (degree between MSc & PhD)
DrSc	Doctor of Sciences
Dr Scient.	Doctor Scientarum (= Doctor's degree in natural scences)
Dr Sci.	Doctor of Science (higher than PhD)
Dr U.	Doctor of the University (special Hungarian scientific degree)

Dr Vet.Med.	Doctor of Veterinary Medicine
DRMS	Dominican Republic Meteorological Society
DSc, D.Sci.	Doctor of Science
DSF	Dendrological Society of Finland
DSIR	Dept of Scientific & Industrial Research
DSMES	Dutch Society for Medical Environmental Sciences
DSSA	Dendrological Society of South Africa
D.Tech.Sc.	Doctor of Technical Science
Dunelm	Latin for Durham (England, UK)
DVM	Doctor of Veterinary Medicine
DWK	Deutsche Wissenschaftliche Kommission für Meeresforschung (German Scientific Commission for Marine Research)
DZG	Deutsche Zoologisches Gesellschaft
e., E., E	eastern, East, building identification
EAAE	Ethiopian Association of Architects and Engineers
EAAFRO	East African Agriculture & Forest Research Organization
EAASH	European Academy of Arts, Sciences, and Humanities
EACNR	Egyptian Association for Conservation of Natural Resources
EAEE	European Association of Environmental Economists
EAEL	European Association for Environmental Law
EAEPE	European Association for Evolutionary Political Economy
EAER	European Arctic Ecological Research
EAERE	European Association of Environmental & Resource Economics
EAFFRO	East African Freshwater Fisheries Research Organization
EANHS	East African Natural History Society
EAPR	European Association for Potato Research
EAR	Ecological Academy of Russia
EARNEST	Economic Analysis of Rangeland Numerations Ecologically Structured
EAS	Egyptian Academy of Science, Eurasian Arachnological Society, European Arachnological Society
EASA	European Academy of Sciences & Art
EASRT	Egyptian Academy of Scientific Research and Technology
EAVRO	East African Virus Research Organization
EAWS	East African Wildlife Society
EBCD	European Bureau for Conservation & Development
EBRD	European Bank for Reconstruction & Development
EBS	Egyptian Botanical Society
EC; EC	*Environmental Conservation;* European Commission, European Community
ECA	Economic Commission for Africa
ECCA	Environmental Camps for Conservation Awareness
ECCO	Asociación de Ecologia y Conservación
ECE	Economic Commission for Europe
ECES	European Centre of Environmental Studies
ECFT	Environmental Conservation Fund of Turkey
ECLA	Economic Commission for Latin America
ECNC	European Centre for Nature Conservation (Tilburg, The Netherlands)
ecocomplex	A complex of ecosystems
ECOCRISIS	title of Publication by Rodriguez Rodriguez (*qv*)
ecodev.	ecodevelopment
e/Ecol.; ecol; ecolly	ecology, Ecologist; ecological; ecologically
ECONAT	name of company (Studies in Applied Ecology)
ECONET	regional UNDP Network
econ.	economic(s)
ECOPATH	name of a computer programme
ecophysiol.	ecophysiology
ECOPS	European Committee on Ocean & Polar Sciences
ECOROPA	Association écologique européenne
ECOSOC	Economic and Social Council
ECS	European Cetacean Society, 'in Economics' in case of B.Com(ECS)
ECSA	Estuarine and Coastal Sciences Association
ECTF	Edinburgh Centre of Tropical Forests
e/Ed.	Editor [= edited by]
Ed.D.	Doctor of Education
EDF	Environmental Defense Fund (USA), European Development Fund (EU, DGVIII)

EDGI	Environment and Development Group International
E/edl	E/editorial
edn	edition
EDRA	Environmental Design Research Association
educ., educl	education, educational
EEA	Egyptian Engineering Academy
EEASA	Environmental Education Association of Southern Africa
EEC	European Economic Community, European Environmental Commission
EEF	European Ecological Federation
EELA	European Environmental Law Association
EEPA	Ethiopian Environmental Protection Agency
EES	Egyptian Entomology Society
EESJ	Environmental Education Society of Japan
EEZ	Exclusive Economic Zone
EFNNP	European Federation of Nature and Natural Parks
EFPP	European Foundation for Plant Pathology
EFTA	European Free Trade Association
e.g.	*exempli gratia* (for example)
EGF	European Grassland Federation
EGS	European Geophysical Society
EIA	Environment Institute of Australia, environmental impact assessment
EIS	European Invertebrate Survey (Centre in ITE)
EKO	native name for Lagos City, former capital of Nigeria
EKOFILM	International Festival of Environmental Films & TV Programmes
ELA	Environmental Law Association
E-LAW	Environmental Law Alliance Worldwide
ELC	Environmental Law Commission, Environment Liaison Centre (Nairobi, Kenya)
ELCI	Environment Liaison Centre International
elec.	electrical
Elec.Eng.	Electrical engineering
ELF	Environmental Law Foundation
ELI	Environmental Law & Institutions, Environmental Law Institute
ELI/PAC	Environmental Law & Institutions Programme Activity Centre
ELISA	enzyme-linked immunosorbent assay
ELNI	Environmental Law Network International
EMBRAPA	Empresa Braziliera de Pesquisa Agropecuaria (Brazilian agricultural research company)
EMDI	Environmental Management Development in Indonesia
Emer.	Emeritus
EMLA	Environmental Management and Law Association
EMMY	no explanation so far, just a name
EMRAM	Environmental Management and Research Association of Malaysia
EMS	Ecuadorian Meteorological Society
Enc.	Encyclopaedia
ENDA	Environment Development Activities (Zimbabwe)
ENDS	Environmental Data Services
E/engg	E/engineering (except when 'Eng.' as in degrees)
English Nature	*see* NCC
Eng.Lit.	English Literature
Engr(s)	Engineer(s)
ENRAC	Environmental and Nature Resources Advisory Council
ENSEARCH	Environmental Management and Research Association
ENSERC	Natural Sciences & Engineering Research Council of Canada (E added at beginning to make it pronounceable, *see also* NSERC)
entomol.	entomology, entomologist, entomological
ENVIRAC	Environmental Action Committee (University of Natal, SA)
ENVIS	Environment Information System
envl, envlism	environmental, environmentalism
envlist(s)	environmentalist(s)
envlly	environmentally
envt	environment
EO	Experimental Officer
EOHSI	Environmental and Occupational Health Sciences Institute
EPA	Environmental Protection Authority/Agency (US, etc.)
EPC	Environmental Protection Committee

EPFL	Ecole polytechnique fédérale de Lausanne
EPS	Environmental Protection Service (Israel)
EPSOP	Environmental Protection Society of Pakistan
EQ	Entre-Quadras
equiv.	equivalence, equivalent
ERA	environmental risk assessment
ERC	Environment Research Council
ERF	Estuarine Research Federation
ERIM	Environmental Research Institute of Michigan
EROPA	Eastern Regional Organization for Public Administration
ERS	Estuarine Research Society
ESA	Ecological Society of America, Ecological Society of Australia, Economics Society of Australia, Entomological Society of America
ESAL	Escola Superior de Agricultura de Lavras
ESC	Ecological Society of China, Entomological Society of Canada
ESCAP	Economic & Social Commission for Asia and the Pacific (UN)
ESCWA	Economic & Social Commission for Western Asia (UN)
ESEB	European Society for Evolutionary Biology
ESES	Egyptian Society for Environmental Sciences
ESF	European Science Foundation (Strasbourg)
ESHG	European Society for Human Genetics
ESHRE	European Society of Human Reproduction & Embryology
ESI	Ecological Society of Israel, Ethological Society of India
ESIL	Egyptian Society of International Law
ESJ	Ecological Society of Japan
ESK	Ecotourism Society of Kenya
ESN	European Society of Nematologists
ESNZ	Entomological Society of New Zealand
ESOP	European Subpolar Ocean Programme (large CEC-funded research programme in Greenland Sea)
E SOURCE	Source of technical information on advanced electric efficiency
ESP	Entomological Society of Peru
ESPOL	Escuela Superior Politecnica del Litoral
esp.	especially
ESQ	Entomological Society of Queensland
ESRC	Economic and Social Research Council
ESSA	Entomological Society of South Africa (*see also* SAES)
EST	Egyptian Society of Toxicology
estab.	establish, established, establishment
ESU	English Speaking Union
ESW	Entomological Society of Washington
et seq.	*et sequen(s)* (= and the following)
ETBA	European Tropical Biology Association
etc.	*et cetera* (= and so on)
ETFRN	European Tropical Forest Research Network
ETH	Eidgenossische Technische Hochschule (Swiss Federal Institute of Technology)
ethnobiol.	ethnobiology
ethnobot., ethnobotl	ethnobotany, ethnobotanical
EU	European Union
EUCARPIA	European Association for Research in Plant Breeding
EUCC	European Union for Coastal Conservation (The Netherlands)
EUI	European Union of Ichthyology
EUROCOAST	European Coastal Zone Federation
EUROSITE	International NGO
Euro.	European
EVA	environmental education, Czech.
eval.	evaluation, evaluating, evaluated
evol.	evolution, evolutionary
E–W	East–West
exam., exams	examination, examinations
Exec.Dir.	Executive Director
EXNORA	NGO in Madras, India (EXcellence, NOvel, RAdical)
exp.	experience
expedn(s)	expedition(s)
E/ext.	E/external, extension

F.	Fellow
FAA	Federal Aeronautic Administration, Federal Aviation Administration
Fac.	Faculty
FAEAB	Federacao das Associacaoes de Engenheiros Agronomos do Brasil
FAF	Finnish Association of Foresters
FAIR	Federation for American Immigration Reform
FAO	Food and Agriculture Organization (UN)
FARN	Fundación Ambiente y Recursos Naturales
FAS	Federation of American Scientists, Finnish Academy of Sciences
FASAS	Federation of Asian Scientific Academies and Societies
FBA	Freshwater Biological Association (UK)
FCIArb.	Fellow, Chartered Institute of Arbitrators
FCO	Foreign and Commonwealth Office
FD	Franklin Delano (Roosevelt)
Feb.	February
FEC	Foundation for Environmental Conservation
Fedn	Federation
Fed.	Federal
FEEE	Foundation for Environmental Education in Europe
FEES	Federation of European Ecological Societies
FEMS	Federation of European Microbiological Societies
F.Eng.	Fellow of the Royal Academy of Engineering
FEPA	Forestry Economic Policy Analysis
FERRO	Far Eastern Regional Research Organization
FESPP	Federation of European Societies of Plant Physiologists
FFA	Forum Fisheries Agency
FFI	Flora & Fauna International
FFPS	Flora and Fauna Preservation Society (UK)
FFS	Fauna & Flora Society (then called)
FHGO	Fundación Herpetologica Gustavo Orces (Ecuador)
FIAP	Federation International d'Arte Photographique
FICCI	Federation of Indian Chamber of Commerce and Industry
FIEF	Fuel Instruments & Engineers' Foundation
Fil.Dr.(*Hon. Causa*)	Honorary Doctor of Philosophy
F/fin.	finance, financial
FINNIDA	Finnish International Development Agency
FIRI	Inland Fisheries Resources & Agriculture Service
FL	Florida (USA)
FLACSO	Latin American Faculty of Social Sciences (an international intergovernmental organization)
FMNH	Field Museum of Natural History (Chicago)
Fndn(s)	Foundation(s)
FNNPE	Federation of Nature and National Parks of Europe
FOA	Friends of Animals
FOE, FoE	Friends of the Earth
FOM	Fundamenteel Onderzoek der Materie (Instituut voor Atoom-en Molecuul-fysica (Amsterdam)
F/for.	Forestry
FORTRAN	FORmula TRANslation, early computer language
foster-d.	foster-daughter
foster-s.	foster-son
FPS	Fauna Preservation Society
FRB	Fisheries Research Board
FRG	Federal Republic of Germany
FRIM	Forest Research Institute Malaysia
FSBI	Fisheries Society of the British Isles
FSEL	French Society for Environmental Law
f/F'ship(s)	Fellowship(s)
FSL	Swiss Federal Institute for Forest, Snow & Landscape Research
f.s.p.	forms in a single species
FUDENA	Fundación para la defensa de la naturaleza
FUNEP	Friends of the UN Environment Programme
FVS	Foundation for Nature Conservation (Stiftung FVS, Hamburg, Germany)
FWAG	Farming and Wildlife Advisory Group
FWS	Fish and Wildlife Service

G500F	Global 500 Forum
GA	General Assembly, Georgia (USA)
GAEL	German Association of Environmental Law
GAIA	Goddess of Earth
GARP	Global Atmospheric Research Programme
GASA	Guinness Award for Scientific Achievements (London, UK)
GATE	Global Atmospheric Research Programme Atlantic Tropical Experiment
GATT	General Agreement on Tariffs and Trade
GAWF	Greek Animal Welfare Fund
GB	Great Britain
GBPIHED	G.(obind) B.(allabh) Pant Institute of Himalayan Environment & Development
GBR	Great Barrier Reef
GBRMAC	Great Barrier Reef Monitoring Advisory Committee
GBRMPA	Great Barrier Reef Marine Park Authority
GCMG	Knight Grand Cross of the Most Distinguished Order of St Michael & St George
GCRI	Glasshouse Crops Research Institute (UK)
GCVO	Grand Commander of the Victorian Order
gdns	gardens
GEF	Global Environment Facility, Global Environmental Fund
GEMS	global environment monitoring system
gen.	general
GEO	a German environmental magazine, part of street address
geobot., geobotl	geobotany, geobotanical
geochem.	geochemistry
geoecol.	geoecology, geoecological
geog.; geogl	geography, geographic; geographical
geol.; geol	geology, geologist; geological
geomorph.; geomorphl	geomorphology, geomorphologist; geomorphological
geophys.; geophysl	geophysics, geophysicist; geophysical
geosci.	geoscience
GES	German Ecological Society
GESAMP	Group of Experts on the Scientific Aspects of Marine Pollution
GFCEA	German Federal Council of Environmental Advisers
GIPRI	Geneva International Peace Research Institute
GIS	geographical information systems
GKSS	Gesellschaft für Kernenenergieverwertung in Schiffbau und Schiffahrt (no longer used but well-known old abbreviation)
GLOBEC	Global Ecosystem Changes Programme
Glos.	Gloucestershire (England, UK)
GmbH	Gesellschaft mit beschränkter Haftung
GNHS	Glasgow National History Society
GOOS	Global Ocean Observing System
Gov., G/govt; G/govtl	Governor, Government; governmental
GPO	General Post Office
grad., grads	graduate, graduates
GRC	German Research Council
GREEN	Global Rivers Environmental Education Network
GRID	Global Resource Information Database
GRO-ACT	UK pome fruit quality assurance company
GS	Geological Society
GSA	Genetic Society of America, Geological Society of America
GSC	Geographical Society of China
GSFC	Goddard Space Flight Center
GSI	Geological Society of India
GSSA	Geological Society of South Africa
gt.; Gt	gate (= street, Swedish); Great
GTZ	Gesellschaft für Technische Zusammenarbeit (German Foreign Development Agency/Society of Technical Cooperation)
Guj.	Gujarat (India)
ha	hectare(s)
Habil.	Habilitation (second scientific work *eg* PhD conditional in German universities for getting a Professorship, qualification to teach)
HABITAT	UN Centre for Human Settlements (UNCHS-HABITAT)
Hadj	*see* Hj.

Hants	Hampshire (England, UK)
Har.	Haryana (India)
HAS	Hungarian Academy of Sciences
HC, *h.c./H.C.*	High Commissioner, *h/Honoris c/Causa*
HCS	Himalayan Conservation Society
HCT	Herpetological Conservation Trust
HDP	Human Dimensions Programme
HDRA	Henry Doubleday Research Association
HE	His Excellency
Herts	Hertfordshire (England, UK)
Hg	Mercury
HHD	Doctor of Humanities
HI	Hawaii (USA)
hist., histl	history, historical
HIV	Human Immunodeficiency Virus
Hj.	Haji (title given to someone who has made the Islamic pilgrimage to Mecca)
IIK	Hong Kong
HKIE	Hong Kong Institution of Engineers
HL	Herpetologists' League
HLA	Hungarian Lawyers' Association
HM	His (or Her) Majesty('s)
HMOCS	His/Her Majesty's Overseas Civil Service
HMS	Hungarian Meteorological Society
HMSO	His/Her Majesty's Stationery Office (UK)
HNC	Higher National Certificate
HND	Higher National Diploma
HOLIS	Society for a Sustainable Future
Hons	Honours
Hon.	Honorary, Honorable, Honourable
hon.caus.	*honoris causa* (see also *h.c.*)
hort., hortl	horticulture, horticultural
hosp	hospital
HP	Himachal Pradesh (India)
HQ	Headquarters
HRH	His/Her Royal Highness
HRI	Horticulture Research International (formerly in Sussex GCRI *qv*, in Kent formerly East Malling Research Station, in Warwickshire AFRC *qv* Inst. of Horticultural Research & National Vegetable Research Station)
HSHK	Horticultural Society of Hong Kong
HSI	Humane Society International
HSPN	Hellenic Society for the Protection of Nature
HSSF	Holistic Society for a Sustainable Future
HSSS	Hungarian Soil Science Society
HSUS	Humane Society of the United States
HTL	Chemical Engineering School (CH)
hydrobiol.	hydrobiology, hydrobiological
hydrogeol.	hydrogeology, hydrogeological, hydrogeologist
hydr.	hydrology, hydrologist, hydrological
i.a.	*inter alia* (= among other things)
IA	Iowa (USA)
IAA	International Academy of Architecture, International Academy of Astronautics (Paris, France), International Association of Astacology
IAAAM	International Association for Aquatic Animal Medicine
IAABG	International Association of Alpine Botanical Gardens
IAAPC	Indian Association of Air Pollution Control
IAAS	Indian Academy of Agricultural Sciences
IAAT	Indian Association of Angiosperm Taxonomy
IABRM	International Association for Bear Research & Management
IABS	Indian Association of Biological Sciences
IAC	International Advisory Council
IACIS	International Association of Colloid & Interface Scientists
IACT	International Association for Clean Technology
IADIZA	Instituto Argentino de Investigaciones de las Zonas Aridas
IADS	International Agricultural Development Service

IAE	Indian Academy of Engineering, Institute of Environmental Assessment, Institution of Agricultural Engineers, Institution of Automobile Engineers, International Academy of The Environment (Geneva, Switzerland)
IAEA	International Atomic Energy Agency (Vienna, Austria)
IAEB	Indian Academy of Environmental Biology
IAEC	International Agricultural Engineering Corporation
IAEE	International Association of Ecological Economics, International Association for Energy Economics, International Association of Energy Economists
IAEL	Irish Association of Environmental Lawyers
IAEM	Indian Association for Environmental Management
IAF	International Astronautical Federation
IAG	Institute of Australian Geographers, International Association of Geomorphologists
IAGLR	International Association for Great Lakes Research
IAgrE	Institution of Agricultural Engineers (UK)
IAH	International Association of Hydrogeologists
IAHO	International Association for the History of Oceanography
IAHS	International Association of Hydrological Sciences
IAIA	International Association for Impact Assessment (USA)
IAL	International Association of Limnology, *see also* SIL, IATAL, ISL
IALE	International Association of Landscape Ecologists
IAM	International Association of Meiobenthologists
IAMAP	International Association of Meteorology & Atmospheric Physics
IAMAT	International Association of Marine Animal Trainers
IAMP	Institute of Atomic and Molecular Physics (Instituut voor Atoom-en Molecuulfysica, Amsterdam, *see also* FOM)
IANIGLA	Instituto Argentino de Nivologia y Glaciologia
IAP	International Association of Pteridology, *see also* IAPterid
IAPA	Inter American Press Association
IAPCB	Indian Association of Pollution Chemists & Biologists
IAPPP	International Association of Public Participation Practitioners
IAPT	International Association for Plant Taxonomy
IAPTC	International Association for Plant Tissue Culture
IAPterid.	International Association of Pteridologists, *see also* IAP
IARI	Indian Agricultural Research Institute (New Delhi, India)
IAS	Indian National Academy of Science (*see also* INAS & INSA), Institute of Aerospace Sciences, International Association of Sedimentologists (The Netherlands), Israel Academy of Sciences
IASC	International Arctic Science Committee
IASCP	International Association for the Study of Common Property (Minnesota, USA)
IASE	International Association for the Study of Ecology
IASF	International Atlantic Salmon Foundation
IASFCP	International Association for the Study of Fossil Cnidaria and Porifera
IASL	International Academy of Sciences 'Leopoldina'
IASTA	Indian Aerosol Science & Technology Association
IASTAM	Indian Association for the Study of Traditional Asian Medicine
IASWS	International Association for Sediment Water Science
IATAL	International Association for Theoretical & Applied Limnology (*see also* SIL etc.)
IAVS	International/Indian Association for Vegetation Science
IAWL	International Association of Water Law
IAWPC	Indian Association for Water Pollution Control
IAWPR	International Association for Water Pollution & Research
IAWPRC	International Association for Water Pollution Research & Control (now IAWQ *qv*)
IAWQ	International Association on Water Quality (was IAWPRC *qv*)
IAZ	Indian Academy of Zoology
IBA	International Bar Association, International Biographical Association, Italian Biologists' Association
IBAMA	Instituto Brasileiro do Meio Ambiente e dos Recursos Naturais Renóvaveis (Brazilian Federal Institute for Environment)
IBC	International Botanical Congress
IBDF	Instituto Brasileiro de Desenvolvimento Florestal (Brazilian Institute for Forest Development)
IBF	Indonesian Biodiversity Foundation

IBG	Institute of British Geographers
IBiol.	Institute of Biology
IBM	International Business Machines
IBP	International Biological Programme
IBPGR	International Board for Plant Genetic Resources (FAO, Rome)
IBPW	Indian Board for Preservation of Wildlife
IBRA	International Bee Research Association
IBRD	International Bank for Reconstruction & Development
IBS	Indian Botanical Society, International Biometric Society, Italian Botanical Society
IBSRAM	International Board for Soil Research & Management
IC	Imperial College (University of London), *see also* ICL
ICA	Institute of Canarian Studies, Institute of Chartered Accountants, International Conservation Agency (Italy), International Council of Archives, Israel Chamber of Advocates
ICAAI	Indian College of Allergy & Applied Immunology
ICAE	International Centre for Alpine Environments
ICAES	International Centre for Advanced Environmental Studies
ICAEW	Institute of Chartered Accountants England & Wales
ICALPE	International Centre for Alpine Environments
ICAN	Institute of Chartered Accountants of Nigeria
ICAR	Indian Council of Agricultural Research
ICARDA	International Centre for Agricultural Research in Dry Areas
ICBD	International Convention on Biological Diversity
ICBP	International Council for Bird Preservation (now BirdLife International)
ICC	International Chamber of Commerce, International Commission on Climate
ICCD	International Commission for Culture & Development
ICCE	International Centre for Conservation Education
ICCEL	International Centre of Comparative Environmental Law
ICCLE	International Centre for Comparative Law of the Environment
ICD	Institute of Company Directors
ICE	Institution of Civil Engineers
ICED	International Centre of Environment and Development
ICEL	International Council of Environmental Law (founded in Geneva, Switzerland), International Council of Environmental Lawyers (founded in New Delhi, India)
ICELA	Indian Council for Enviro-Legal Action
ICES	International Council for the Exploration of the Seas
ICF	Institute of Chartered Foresters, International Crane Foundation
ICFRE	Indian Council of Forest Research & Education
ICG	International Crisis Group
IChemE	Institution of Chemical Engineers
ICHG	International Congress of Human Genetics
ICHGC	International Council of Hunting and Game Conservation
ICIMOD	International Centre for Integrated Mountain Development (Kathmandu, Nepal)
ICL	Imperial College London (England, UK)
ICLARM	International Centre for Living Aquatic Resources Management (a network of tropical aquaculture scientists)
ICLPS	International Centre for Land Policy Studies
ICME	Indian Council of Management Executives
ICMR	Indian Council of Medical Research
ICOH	International Commission on Occupational Health
ICOM	International Council of Museums
ICOMOS	International Council on Monuments and Sites
ICONA	Spanish Institute for Nature Conservation
ICPAM	International Committee for the Preservation of Ancient Monuments
ICPB	International Council for the Protection of Birds
ICPD	International Conference on Population and Development
ICPF	International Commission on Peace and Food
ICPL	International Centre for Protected Landscapes
ICPM	International Committee for the Preservation of Monuments
ICPP	International Congress of Plant Protection
ICRAF	International Centre for Research in Agroforestry
ICRISAT	International Crops Research Institute for the Semi-Arid Tropics
ICRO	International Cell Research Organization (UN-supported body, HQ Paris)

ICRS	International Coral Reef Society
ICS	Indian Chemical Society
ICSEM	International Commission for the Scientific Exploration of the Mediterranean Sea (Intergovernmental Agency founded 1921, 21 member states in 1993)
ICSU	International Council of Scientific Unions
ICTAE	International Centre for Theoretical & Applied Ecology
ICTE	International Centre for Tropical Ecology
ICTF	International Commission on the Taxonomy of Fungi
ICTP	International Centre for Theoretical Physics (Trieste, Italy)
ID	Idaho (USA), Institute of Directors
IDA	International Documentary Association, International Diatom Association
IDB	Interamerican Development Bank
IDEA	Innovators for DEvelopment Association
ident.	identification
IDRC	International Development Research Centre
IDS	International Dendrology Society
IDSA	Institute for Defence Studies & Analysis
IDU	International Dendrology Union
i.e.	*id est* (that is)
IE	Institution of Engineers
IEA	Institute for Environmental Assessment
IEAust.	Institution of Engineers Australia
IEE	Institution of Electrical Engineering
IEEE	Institute of Electrical and Electronic Engineering
IEEM	Institute of Ecology & Environmental Management
IEEP	Institute of European Environmental Policy (UK)
IEES	Institute of Energy & Environmental Studies
IEF	International Energy Foundation
IEI	International Energy Initiative
IELA	Israel Environmental Law Association
IEM	Institute of Environmental Managers
IEMS	Indian Environmental Monitoring Society
IERM	Institute of Ecology and Resource Management
IES	Indian Ecological Society, Indian Environmental Society
IESANZ	Illuminating Engineering Societies of Australia & New Zealand
IETC	International Environment Technology Centre (Osaka, Japan)
IETE	Institute of Electronics & Telecommunication Engineers
IEU	International Ecological Union
IFA	Institute of Foresters of Australia
IFAD	International Fund for Agricultural Development
IFC	Indian Forest College
IFDA	International Foundation for Development Alternatives
IFERM	International Forest Environment, Research & Management
IFIAS	International Federation of Institutes for Advanced Study (Stockholm)
IFLA	International Federation of Landscape Architects
IFM	Institute of Fisheries Management
IFMBE	International Federation for Medical and Biological Engineering
IFNR	Institute for Forestry and Nature Research
IFOAM	International Federation for Organic Agricultural Movements
IFPRA	International Federation of Park & Recreation Administration
IFS	International Federation of Scientists, International Foundation for Science
IFSI	Inland Fisheries Society of India
IFST	Institute of Food Science & Technology
IFWST	International Foundation for Water Science and Technology
IGA	Indian Geographers' Association
IGADD	InterGovernmental Authority on Drought & Desertification
IGBP	International Geosphere-Biosphere Programme (on Global Change, of ICSU *qv*)
IGES	International Genetic Epidemiology Society
IGR	insect growth regulator
IGS	International Gecko Society, International Glaciology Society
IGSAC	Independent Group for South Asian Cooperation
IGU	Indian Geophysical Union, International Geographical Union, International Geophysical Union
IHE	Institute of Human Ecology

IHort.	Institute of Horticulture
IHS	Indian Herpetological Society, International Horticultural Society
IIAC	Interamerican Institute for Agricultural Cooperation, *see also* IICA
IIAS	International Institute of Agricultural Science (Costa Rica)
IIASA	International Institute for Applied Systems Analysis
IIASES	International Institute for Aerospace Survey & Earth Sciences (The Netherlands)
IICA	Instituto Interamericano de Ciencias Agricolas, Interamerican Institute for Cooperation on Agriculture (HQ, Costa Rica), *see also* IIAC
IICAL	Institute of International & Comparative Agrarian Law
IICE	Indian Institute of Chemical Engineers
IIDB	International Institute of Developmental Biology (Utrecht, The Netherlands)
IIE	Indian Institute of Engineers, Institute of International Education (NY, USA)
IIED	International Institute for Environment & Development (UK)
IIFM	Indian Institute of Forest Management
IIM	Indian Institute of Management (Ahmedabad, Gujarat, India)
IIMC	Indian Institute of Mass Communication
IIMI	International Irrigation Management Institute
IIOE	International Indian Ocean Expedition
IIPA	Indian Institute of Public Administration
IIR	International Institute of Refrigeration
IISc	Indian Institute of Science
IISD	International Institute for Sustainable Development
IIT	Indian Institute of Technology (*e.g.* at Bombay, Maharashtra, India)
IITA	International Institute of Tropical Agriculture
IJC	International Joint Commission
IL	Illinois (USA)
ILA	Institute of Landscape Architects, International Law Association
ILAM	Institute of Leisure and Amenity Management
ILCA	International Livestock Centre for Africa
ILEC	International Lake Environment Committee (Tokyo, Japan)
ILEIA	Information Centre for Low-External Input and Sustainable Agriculture
ILI	Indian Law Institute
illustr., illustrs	illustrated. illustrations
ILO	International Labour Office
IMA	International Mycological Association
IMAGE	Integrated Model to Assess the Greenhouse Effect
IMCG	International Mire Conservation Group
IMD	International Institute for Management Development
I.MechE	Institution of Mechanical Engineers
IMI	International Management Institute (Geneva, Switzerland), International Mycological Institute
IMO	International Maritime Organization
impt	important
IMS	International Mountain Society
IN	Indiana (USA)
INAE	Indian National Academy of Engineers
INAS	Indian National Academy of Sciences, *see also* IAS & INSA,
Inc.	Incorporated
INC	Intergovernmental Negotiating Committee
INCD	Intergovernmental Negotiating Committee for a Convention on Desertification
INCFCCC	Intergovernmental Negotiating Committee for a Framework Convention on Climate Change
incl.	including
i/Ind.	i/Independent
indiff.	indifferent
info.	information
INFORMS	merging of ORSA and Institute for Management Sciences
INFOTERRA	Global Information Systems on Environment (INFOrmation for the Earth (TERRA))
Ing.	Ingenieur (= MSc)
INGO	international nongovernmental organization
INIPA	Instituto Nacional de Investigación y Promoción Agropercuaria
init.	initiator, initiated, initiating, initiation

INPA	Instituto Nacional de Pesquisas da Amazónia (National Institute for Research in the Amazon)
INPE	Instituto Nacional de Pesquisas Espaciais
INRA	Institut National de Recherches Agronomiques, International Network for Religion and Animals
INRD	Institute of Natural Resources Development
INSA	Indian National Science Academy (*see also* IAS, INAS, NAS)
INSONA	International Society of Naturalists (formerly Indian Society of Naturalists)
INSTAAR	Institute of Arctic & Alpine Research
I/inst., I/insts	Institute, Institutes
I/instn; I/instnl	Institution; institutional
Instr.	Instructor
INSULA	Latin for island — International Scientific Council for Island Development, a scientific association of MAB (UNESCO, Paris)
INTACH	Indian National Trust for Art & Cultural Heritage
INTECOL	International Association for Ecology
interdisc.	interdisciplinary
intergovtl	intergovernmental
intl, intlly, intlist	international, internationally, internationalist
intro.	introduction, introductory
IOBC	International Organization for Biological Control
IOC	Intergovernmental Oceanographic Commission (UNESCO), International Ornithological Committee/Congress
IOCU	International Organization of Consumer Unions
IOJ	International Organization of Journalists
IOLR	Israel Oceanographic and Limnological Research
IOM	Institute of Medicine
IOP	Institute of Oriental Philosophy
IOPB	International Organization of Plant Biosystematics
IOS	Indian Ornithological Society, International Odonatological Society
IOSPS	International Organization for Succulent Plant Study
IPA	International Permafrost Association, Indian Potato Association
IPAC	Institute of Public Administration of Canada
IPC	International Potato Centre
IPCC	Intergovernmental Panel on Climate Change
IPCS	International Programme on Chemical Safety
IPE	International Phytogeographical Excursion
IPENZ	Institution of Professional Engineers of New Zealand
IPGRI	International Plant Genetic Resources Institute
IPHA	Indian Public Health Association
IPHE	Institution of Public Health Engineers
IPM	Institute of Personnel Management
IPMA	Indian Paper Makers' Association
IPN	Instituto Politécnico Nacional
IPPF	International Planned Parenthood Federation
IPPL	International Primate Protection League
IPPTA	Indian Pulp & Paper Technical Association
IPRA	International Peace Research Association
IPS	Indian Palynological Society, International Palm Society, International Phycological Society, International Primatological Society
IPSCC	International Primatology Society Conservation Committee
IPSS	Institute of Professional Soil Scientists (UK)
IQA	Institute of Quality Assurance
Ir	Ingenieur
IRCSA	International Rainwater Catchment Systems Association
IRPA	Intensification of Research in Priority Areas
IRRI	International Rice Research Institute
IRRS	International Root Research Society
IRS	Indian Rangeland Society
IRS–1A	first of Indian Remote Sensing Satellite Series
IRSAC	Institut pour la Recherche Scientifique en Afrique Centrale
IRSIA	Institut pour l'Encouragement de la Recherche Scientifique dans l'Industrie et l'Agriculture
IS; I/is.; i/Iss	Institution of Surveyors; I/island; i/Islands
ISA	International Studies Association

ISAAA	International Service for the Acquisition of Agri-biotech Applications (a not-for profit organization based in Cayman Islands, British West Indies, & Cornell U.)
ISACF	International Society of Arctic Char Fanatics
ISAE	Indian Society of Agricultural Engineers
ISAR	Institute for Soviet–American Relations, Institute of Scientific Applied Research, a clearinghouse on grassroots cooperation in Eurasia
ISAR AERO	clearinghouse + its name
ISARS	International Society on Acoustic Remote Sensing
ISB	International Society for Biometeorology
ISBE	International Society of Behavioural Ecology
ISC	Indian Science Congress, International Science Committee, International Solanaceae Committee
ISCA	Indian Science Congress Association
ISCB	Indian Society for Conservation Biology
ISCG	Indian Society of Cytologists & Geneticists
ISCO	International Soil Conservation Organization
ISDE	International Society of Doctors for the Environment
ISE	International Society of Ecology, International Society of Ethnobiology (Brazil), Israel Society of Engineers
ISEA	International Society for Exposure Analysis
ISEE	International Society for Ecological Economics, International Society for Environmental Education, International Society for Environmental Epidemiology, International Society for Environmental Ethics
ISEEQS	Israel Society for Ecological & Environmental Quality Sciences
ISEM	International Society for Ecological Modelling
ISEP	International Society for Environmental Protistology
ISES	International Solar Energy Society
ISF	International Science Foundation
ISGPB	Indian Society of Genetics and Plant Breeding
ISHE	International Society for Human Ecology
ISHS	International Society for Horticultural Science
ISI	International Statistical Institute
ISIS	International Species Inventory System
ISJ	Ichthyological Society of Japan, see also JIS
ISL	International Society of Limnology , see also SIL
ISME	International Society for Mediterranean Ecosystems
ISME	International Society for Mangrove Ecosystems
ISN	Indian Society of Naturalists
ISNA	Indian Science News Association
ISNAB	Indian Society for Nuclear Agriculture & Biology
ISNE	Indian Society for Nature & Environment
ISOMED	International Society for the Study of Mediterranean Ecology, International Society of Mediterranean Ecologists
ISPAN	Institut de Sauvegarde du Patrimoine National
ISPE	International Society for Philosophical Enquiry
ISPGR	Indian Society of Plant Genetic Resources
ISPMB	International Society of Plant Molecular Biology
ISPP	International Society of Plant Pathology
ISPRS	Indian Society for Photointerpretation and Remote Sensing
ISRO	Indian Space Research Organization
ISRS	International Society for Reef Studies
ISSBE	Indian Society of Soil Biology and Ecology
ISSC	International Social Science Council
ISSCP	International Society for the Study of Common Property
ISSOL	International Society for the Study of the Origin of Life
ISSS	International Society of Soil Science
ISTAL	International Society of Theoretical & Applied Limnology
ISTB	International Society for Tropical Biology
ISTE	International Society for Tropical Ecology (Varanasi, Uttar Pradesh, India), Indian Society of Technical Education
ISTF	International Society of Tropical Foresters (Inc.)
ISTRO	International Soil or Tillage Research Organization
ISTS	Indian Society of Tree Scientists
ISWA	Indian Science Writers' Association, International Science Writers' Association, International Solid Waste Association

ISWF	International Society for Wildland Fire
ITAC	International Trade Advisory Committee
ITAS	Istituto Trentino Assicurazioni
ITB	Institute of Tree Biology (Edinburgh, Scotland, UK),
ITC	Indian Tobacco Company
ITE	Institute of Terrestrial Ecology (UK)
ITEX	International Tundra Experiment
ITP	International Teachers' Programme
ITRC	Industrial Toxicology Research Centre
ITTO	International Tropical Timber Organization
IUAPPA	International Union of Air Pollution Prevention Associations
IUBS	International Union of Biological Sciences
IUC	Inter-University Council
IUCN	International Union for Conservation of Nature and Natural Resources — now The World Conservation Union
IUDZG	International Union of Directors of Zoological Gardens
IUFRO	International Union of Forestry Research Organizations
IUGG	International Union of Geodesy & Geophysics
IUGS	International Union of Geological Sciences
IUHEI	Institut Universitaire de Hautes Etudes Internationales
IUNS	International Union of Nutritional Sciences
IUPAB	International Union for Pure and Applied Biophysics
IUPAC	International Union of Pure & Applied Chemistry
IUPN	International Union for the Protection of Nature (now IUCN)
IUR; Iur.	International Union of Radioecologists; Iuris (= Jurisprudence = Law)
IURS	International Union of Radio Science
IUSSI	International Union for the Study of Social Insects
IUSSP	International Union for Scientific Study of Population
IVEM	Institute of Virology & Environmental Microbiology
IWA	Institute of World Affairs (Connecticut, USA)
IWAPCA	Indian Water & Air Pollution Control Association
IWC	International Whaling Commission
IWEM	Institution of Water & Environmental Management (London, UK)
IWF	International Wildlife Federation
IWGIA	International Working Group for Indigenous Affairs (Copenhagen, Denmark)
IWM	Institute of Wastes Management (UK)
IWPT	International Wildlife Preservation Trust
IWQA	International Water Quality Association
IWRA	International Water Resources Association
IWRB	International Waterfowl and Wetlands Research Bureau (UK)
IWRS	Indian Water Resources Society
IWSA	International Water Supply Association
IWWA	Indian Water Works Association
IYF	International Youth Federation (for Environmental Studies and Conservation)
IZS	Israel Zoological Society, Italian Zoological Society
J./j.	J/journal
JANC	Japanese Association for Nature Conservation
Jan.	January
J.B.	James Buchanan [Duke] (donor to Duke University)
JBA	Jamaica Bar Assn
JCCI	Japanese Chamber of Commerce & Industry
JD	Juris Doctor
JDS	Japan Desert Society
JEA	Japan Environmental Agency/Association
JEC	Japan Environmental Council
JEEP	Joint Energy and Environment Projects
JES	Japanese Ethological Society
JFEJ	Japanese Forum of Environmental Journalists
JFS	Japanese Forestry Society
JGA	Japan Geography Association
JICA	Japan International Cooperation Agency
JIS	Japanese Ichthyological Society (*see also* ISJ)
J&K	Jammu & Kashmir (India)
JNCC	Joint Nature Conservation Committee
JNCS	Japanese Nature Conservation Society

JNE	Journalistes pour la Nature et Environnement (Paris, France)
JNIFS	Japan National Institute of Forest Sciences
jnl(s)	journal(s)
JNU	Jawaharlal Nehru University (Delhi, India)
JOS	Japanese Oceanographic Society
JP	Justice of the Peace
Jr	Junior
JSC	Japan Science Council
JSCE	Japanese Society of Civil Engineering
JSCP	Jordanian Society for the Control of Pollution
JSD	Juris Scientis Doctor
JSES	Japanese Society of Environmental Science
JSI	Japanese Society of Ichthyology
JSPE	Japanese Society of Population Ecology
JSPS	Japan Society for the Promotion of Science
JSTE	Japan Society for Tropical Ecology
Jt	Joint
JUDr	Doctor of Law
Jur.	Jurisprudence (skill in law)
JWBS	Japan Wild Bird Society
JWPT	Jersey Wildlife Preservation Trust
JWRC	Japan Wildlife Research Centre
k.; K.	katu (= street, Finnish); King, Kingdom
KAA	Kenya Association of Architects
KAERI	Korea Atomic Energy Research Institute
KAPRA	Korea Air Pollution Research Association
KARP	Korean Association of Radiological Protection
Kar.	Karnataka (India)
KAWPRC	Korean Association of Water Pollution Research & Control
KAY	Turkish National Committee on Coastal Zone Management
KB	Knight Bachelor
KCMG	Knight Commander of the Most Honourable St Michael and St George
KCSI	Knight Commander of the Star of India
KCVO	Knight Commander of the Royal Victorian Order
KEEO	Kenya Energy and Environment Organization
Ker.	Kerala (India)
KETRI	Korea Environmental Technology Research Institute
KFA	Kenya Forest Association
KFS	Korea Forestry Society
KICE, KIChE	Korea Institute of Chemical Engineers
KINS	Korea Institute of Nuclear Safety
KISR	Kuwait Institute for Scientific Research
KIST	Korea Institute of Science & Technology
KL	Kuala Lumpur (Malaysia)
km(s), KMS	kilometre(s), Korean Meteorological Society
KNAW	Koninklijke Nederlandse Akademie van Wetenschappen (Royal Netherlands Academy of Sciences)
KNS	Korean Nuclear Society
KORA	Reserve in East Africa (not an acronym)
KORCES	Korean Research Council on Environmental Sciences
KPS	Korean Physical Society
KRTA	company name (consulting engineers, architects, planners)
KS	Kansas (USA)
KSCE	Korean Society of Civil Engineers
KSEE	Korean Society of Environmental Engineers
KSL	name of Mortgage Bankers in Nigeria
KSS	Kent, Surrey, & Sussex (branches of IBiol.)
Kv	apartment
KWWA	Korean Water Works Association
KY	Kentucky (USA)
L.	Lake
LA	Louisiana (USA)
lab.	laboratory
LAFTA	Latin America Free Trade Association

Lancs.	Lancashire (England, UK)
LANDEP	Landscape Ecological Planning
LANDSAT	satellite imagery (name)
LCA	Life Cycle Analysis
LEAD	Leadership in Environment and Development
LEARN	a methodological challenge for rapid environmental assessment
Lect.	Lector, Lecturer
LEEC	London Environmental Economics Centre
legis.	legislation, legislator
Lic.	Licentiate, Licencie (Belgium), Licenciado (Spain) = MS (approx. equiv.)
LICC–LERM	Landscape Ecological Impact of Climate Change–Longterm Ecological Research & Monitoring (a European network)
Lic.iur.	Licencie Iuris (Master of Laws)
limnol.	limnological, limnologist, limnology
Lincs.	Lincolnshire (England, UK)
LIPU	Lega Italiana Protezione Uccelli (Italian Society for the Protection of Birds)
LITA	Literary Agency of Slovakia
Litt.D.	Dr of Letters
L/lit.	literary, literature
Lit.Hum.	Literae Humaniores
LLB	Bachelor of Laws
LLD	Doctor of Laws
LLM	Master of Laws
LMB	Locked Mail Bag
LNP	League of Nature Protection
LOICZ	Land–Ocean Interactions in the Coastal Zone
LOP	League for Nature Protection (Poland)
LPO	Ligue pour la Protection des Oiseaux
LS	Linnean Society of London (Britain's premier biological outfit)
LSE	London School of Economics
LSHTM	London School of Hygiene and Tropical Medicine
LSJ	Limnological Society of Japan
LSSR	London Society for the Study of Religion
Lt	Lieutenant
Ltd, Ltda	Limited
LTER	Long Term Ecological Research
M or M.; *M.;* m.	Master; Married; million(s) or metre(s)/meter(s)
MA	Massachusetts (USA), Master of Arts
MAB	Man and Biosphere
MACC	Massachusetts Association of Conservation Commissions
macroevol.	macroevolution
MAFF	Ministry of Agriculture, Fisheries & Food (UK)
Magister	Master *e.g.* MSc
Magister scientiarum	MSc (Venezuela)
M.Agr.	Master of Agriculture
M.Agr.Sci.	Master of Agricultural Science
Mag.scient.	Magister scientiarum
MAHL	Master of Hebrew Letters
Mah.	Maharashtra (India)
MAIL	Mexican Academy of International Law
Man.	Manitoba (Canada)
MAPA	Marine Affairs & Policy Association
MArch or M.Arch.	Master of Architecture
Mar.	March
MASc	Master of Applied Sciences
Mass.	Massachusetts (USA)
MAT	Master of Arts in Teaching
math; maths	mathematical; mathematics
MB	Bachelor of Medicine, Medicae Baccalaureatus
MBA	Marine Biological Association, Marine Biological Association of the United Kingdom, Master of Business Administration
MB BS	Bachelor of Medicine and of Surgery
MBE	Member of the Most Excellent Order of the British Empire
MBE (Mil.)	Member of the Order of the British Empire (Military Division)
mbH	mit beschränkter Haftung (usually GmbH, *qv*)

M.Biol.	Master of Biology
MBS	Master of Biological Sciences
MC	Mail Center
MCE	Master of Civil Engineering
MCL	Master of Civil Law
MCP	Master of City Planning, Member College of Pathologists
MCS	Marine Conservation Society (UK)
MD	Doctor of Medicine, Managing Director, Maryland (USA)
MDiv	Master of Divinity
MDRA	Ministério do Desenvolvimento Rural e Agricultura (Ministry of Rural Development and Agriculture)
ME	Maine (USA), Master of Engineering
MEA	Malaysian Ecological Association
mech.	mechanical
med.	medical, medicine
MEd.or M.Ed.	Master of Education
MEDASSET	Mediterranean Association to Save the Sea Turtles
Medit.	Mediterranean
Mem.	Memorial
M/memb.	member
MEng.	Master of Engineering
MES	Master of Environmental Studies
MESA	Marine Education Society of Australasia
MESAEP	Mediterranean Scientific Association for Environmental Protection
M/met.	meteorological, meteorology
MF	Master of Forestry
MFA	Master of Fine Arts
MG	Minas Gerais (Brazil)
mgmt	management
Mgr(s)	Manager(s)
MGS	Mongolian Geographical Society
MH	*Mencion Honorifica* (hon.degree)
M.Hort.	Master of Horticulture
MI	Michigan (USA)
MIBiol.	Member of Institute of Biology
Mich.	Michigan (USA)
microbiol.	microbiology, microbiological
microevol.	microevolution
M.IHort.	Member of the Institute of Horticulture
MIMgmt	Member of Institute of Management
Min.; Mins	Ministry; Ministries
M(Info.Sci.)	Master of Information Science
Minn.	Minnesota (USA)
mismgmt	mismanagement
MIT	Massachusetts Institute of Technology
MLArch	Master of Landscape Architecture
MLitt	Master of Letters, Master of Literature
MLS	Master of Liberal Sciences
MMAP	Marine Mammal Action Plan
MME	Mongolian Ministry of Environment
MMRP	Marine Mammal Research Programme
MMS	Mineral Management Service
MN	Minnesota (USA)
M.Nat.Res.	Master of Natural Resources
MNS	Malayan Nature Society
MO	Missouri (USA)
MO A	Middelbaar onderwys (secondary-school teacher, Dutch)
MO B	Middelbaar onderwys (high-school teacher, Dutch)
Mods	Moderatores
monogr., monogrs	monograph, monographs
MP	Madhya Pradesh (India), Member of Parliament
MPA	Master of Public Administration or Affairs
MPH	Master of Public Health
M.Phil.	Master of Philosophy
MPRT	Master of Parks, Recreation and Tourism
MPS	Master of Professional Studies

MRC	Medical Research Council
MRCGP	Member of Royal College of General Practitioners
MRCP	Member of Royal College of Physicians
MRCVS	Member of the Royal College of Veterinary Surgeons
MRME	Ministry of Regional Municipalities & Environment
MRP	Master of Regional Planning
MRSC	Member of Royal Society of Chemistry
MRSH	Member of Royal Society of Health
ms(s)/MS(s)	m/Manuscript(s)
MS	Malacological Society, Mammal Society, Master of Science (USA), Meteorological Society, Mississippi (USA)
M.S.	Monkombu Sambasivan (Swaminathan, *qv*)
MSA	Mycological Society of America
MSAB	Malaysian Society of Applied Biology
MSBI	Mammal Society of the British Isles
MSc	Master of Science (UK, etc.)
MScF	Master of Science in Forestry
MSE	Master of Science in Nuclear Engineering
MSEL	Moroccan Society for Environmental Law
MSGBI	Mammal Society of Great Britain and Ireland
m/M'ship(s)	Membership(s)
MSI	Meteorological Society of India, Mutagen Society of India
MSJ	Mammalogical Society of Japan
MSL	Malacological Society of London
MSN	Moscow Society of Naturalists
MSNE	Mongolian Society of Nature and Environment
MSNH	Moscow Society for Natural History
MSP	Master of Science Planning
MSPA	Moscow Society for the Protection of Animals
MST	Master of Science for Teachers
Mt	Mount
MT	Montana (USA)
MTech or M.Tech	Master of Technology
mtg(s)	meeting(s)
mtn(s)	mountain(s)
multidisc.	multidisciplinary
multinat.	multinational
Mus.	Museum
MVO	Member (of Fourth or Fifth Class) of Royal Victorian Order
MVSc	Master of Veterinary Science
Mx	Middlesex (UK)
MZS	Minnesota Zoological Society
n., N., N	northern, North, Nitrogen
NA	Indian National Science Academy (*qv*), other national academies colloquially
NAAEE	North American Association for Environmental Education
NAAS	National Academy of Agricultural Sciences, National Academy of Arts & Sciences
nabr.Gen.	Quay of General
NABS	North American Benthological Society
NAC	National Agroforestry Committee
NACA	National Association for Clean Air
NACEC	North American Commission for Environmental Cooperation
NACTA	North American College Teaching Association
NAE	National Academy of Engineering, Norwegian Association for Ecology
NAECAN-NEPAL	National Academy for Environmental Conservation, Population, and Development (based in Kathmandu, Nepal)
NAEE	National Association for Environmental Education, National Association of Environmental Educators
NAEP	National Association of Environmental Professionals (USA)
NAGT	National Association of Geology Teachers (USA)
NAPA	National Academy of Public Administration
NARC	National Avian Research Centre
NARESA	Natural Resources, Energy, and Science, Authority
NARF	National Agricultural Research Foundation
NAS	National Academy of Science(s)

NASA	National Aeronautics & Space Administration (USA)
NASC; NASc	National Academy Science Committee; National Academy of Sciences India
NASL	Norwegian Academy of Science & Letters
NASPAA	National Association of Schools of Public Affairs & Administration
nat.	national
NATAS	National Academy of Television Arts and Sciences
NATO	North Atlantic Treaty Organization
NATOUR	title of publication — NAture and TOURism
NATS	Norwegian Academy of Technical Sciences
NBS	National Bureau of Standards
NBV	Dutch Soil Science Society
NC	Nature Conservancy ('Council' added later in UK), North Carolina (USA)
NCAR	National Center for Atmospheric Research
NCB	National Conservation Bureau (UK)
NCC	Nature Conservancy Council (UK, split into separate agencies for England, Scotland, & Wales, on 1 April 1981; English part became NCC for England — English Nature in popular usage), Nature Conservation Council
NCCP	National College of Chest Physicians
NCCPB	National Council of Commercial Plant Breeders
NCCPG	National Council for Conservation of Plants and Gardens
NCCS	Nature Conservancy Council for Scotland
NCCW	National Council for Conservation of Wildlife
NCEP	National Council for Environmental Protection
NCEPC	National Committee on Environmental Planning & Coordination
NCF	Nigeria Conservation Foundation
NCIS	National Chemical Industries Society
NCNEC	National Committee for Natural Environment Conservation
NCPPG	National Council for the Preservation of Plants and Gardens
NCPV	Netherlands Circle of Plant Virologists
NCRC	Nature Conservation Research Centre
NCS(s)	National Conservation Strategy(Strategies)
NC3J	Nature Conservation Society of Japan
NCSN	Nature Conservation Society of Nepal
NCSSA	Nature Conservation Society of South Australia
NCST	National Council for Science & Technology
NCSTRA	National Council of Scientific & Technological Research of Argentina
NCSU	North Carolina State University
NCVO	National Council for Voluntary Organizations (UK)
NCWA	Norwegian Church Workers' Associations
NCWCD	National Commission for Wildlife Conservation and Development (Riyadh, Government of Saudi Arabia)
ND	North Dakota (USA)
NDA	National Diploma in Agriculture (Royal Agricultural Society of England)
NDEA	National Defense Education Act
NDRC	National Defence Research Council
Ne	Northeastern
NE	New England (USA)
NEA	National Educators' Association
NEAC	National Environmental Awards Council
NEBC	New England Botanical Club
Nebr.	Nebraska (USA)
NEC	National Environmental Council
NED-Net	Nigerian Environment & Development Network
NEDO	National Economic Development Office
NEERI	National Environmental Engineering Research Institute
NEF	National Environment Fellow, New Economics Foundation
negn(s)	negotiation(s)
NELA	National Environmental Law Association
NEN	Nigerian Environment Network
neotrop.	neotropical
NEPA	National Environmental Policy Act
NERC	Natural Environment Research Council
NESPAK	National Engineering Service Pakistan
NEST	National Environmental Societies Trust
NEXUS	project at World Bank

NFA	Nigerian Forestry Association
NFS	Nigerian Forest Service
NGO	nongovernmental organization
NGS	National Geographic Society
NGWA	National Groundwater Association
NH	New Hampshire (USA)
NHSN	Natural History Society of Nepal
NI	Northern Ireland
NIDC	National Industrial Development Corporation
NIE	National Institute of Ecology
NIES	National Institute of Environmental Sciences
NIH	National Institute of Health
NIHS	National Institute of Health & Security
NILI	Netherlands Institute of Agricultural Science
NIMR	National Institute for Medical Research
NIO	National Institute of Oceanography
NISSAT	National Information System on Science & Technology
NJ	New Jersey (USA)
NLC	National Liberal Caucus
NM	New Mexico (USA)
NMFS	National Marine Fisheries Service
NMIS–MMS	National Management Information System–Mineral Management Service
NMKS	National Museums of Kenya Society
NMMRP	Navy Marine Mammal Research Programme (USA)
NMS	Nigerian Meteorological Society
NNA	Norwegian–Namibia Association
NNCS	Nepal Nature Conservation Society
no	number (French *numéro*), *see also* nr (preferred) and #
NOAA	National Oceanic & Atmospheric Administration (USA)
NORA	Nevada Outdoor Recreation Association, Inc.
NORAD	Norwegian Agency for Development Corporation
NORAGRIC	amalgamation in 1995 of Norwegian Centre for International Agricultural Development and other units in the Agricultural University of Norway to form Centre for International Environment and Development Studies
Norconsult.	Company name
Northants.	Northamptonshire (England, UK)
Notts.	Nottinghamshire (England, UK)
NOU	Netherlands Ornithological Union
NOVIB	Nederlandse Organisatie voor Internationale Ontwikkelingssamenwer-king (Netherlands Organization for International Development Cooperation)
Nov.	November
NPA	National Parks Association
NPAC	National Plan Advisory Committee
NPC	National Parks Commission, National Productivity Council
NPCA	National Park & Conservation Authority (USA)
NPL	National Physical Laboratory
NPPA	National Parks and Protected Areas
NPPAC	National and Provincial Parks Association of Canada
NPPP	National Project Professional Personnel (FAO term for local consultant)
NPRA	National Programme of Radiopropagation of Argentina
NPS	National Park Service
NPWC	National Parks & Wildlife Conservation
NPWS	National Parks and Wildlife Service
NQ	North Queensland (Australia)
NQPS	North Queensland Palm Society
nr(s)	number(s), *see also* no and #
NRC	National Recycling Coalition, National Research Council
NRCC	National Research Council of Canada
NRDC	Natural Resources Defense Council
NRI	Natural Resources Institute (UK Ministry of Overseas Development)
NRPB	National Radiological Protection Board
NRSA	National Remote Sensing Agency
NS	Nova Scotia (Canada)
N–S	North–South
NSA	Norwegian Scientific Academy
NSB	National Science Board

NSC	National Science Council
NSCBA	National Sweet Corn Breeders' Association
NSCN	Norwegian Society for Conservation of Nature
NSCNC	Norwegian State Council of Nature Conservation
NSERC	Natural Sciences & Engineering Research Council of Canada, *see also* ENSERC
NSF	National Science Foundation
NSF RANN	NSF Research Applied to Nations' Needs
NSHE	Nordic Society for Human Ecology
NSIL	Nigerian Society of International Law
NSIRP	Nigeria Society for the Improvement of Rural People
NSLA	Netherlands Society for Landscape Architects
NSMR	Norwegian Society of Marine Researchers
NSSS	Norwegian Society of Soil Science
NSTA	National Science Teachers' Association
NSW	New South Wales (Australia)
NSWA	National Small Woods Association
NT	National Trust, Northern Territory (Australia)
NTU	Northern Territories University
num.	numerous
NUPAUB	Nucleo de Apoio a Pesquisa sobre Populacoes Humanas e Areas Umidas Brasileiras (Centre for Research on Human Population and Wetlands in Brazil)
NV	Nevada (USA)
NWF	National Wildlife Federation (USA)
NWFTI	Naiwasha Wildlife & Fisheries Training Institute
NWFP	North West Frontier Province (Pakistan)
NWRI	National Water Research Institute
NWSC	National Wetlands Steering Committee
NWT	Northwest Territories (Canada)
NY	New York (USA)
NYAS	New York Academy of Sciences
NYBG	New York Botanical Garden
NYC	New York City (NY, USA)
NYSC	New York Safari Club
NYZS	New York Zoological Society (now Wildlife Conservation Society)
NZ	New Zealand
NZAEE	New Zealand Association for Environmental Education
NZBS	New Zealand Botanical Society
NZCA	New Zealand Conservation Authority
NZDC	New Zealand Department of Conservation
NZDS	New Zealand Demographic Society
NZEC	New Zealand Electricity Corporation
NZES	New Zealand Ecological Society
NZIP	New Zealand Institute of Parks
NZLS	New Zealand Limnological Society
NZMSS	New Zealand Marine Sciences Society
NZPI	New Zealand Planning Institute
NZS	Netherlands Zoological Society
NZWS	New Zealand Wildlife Service
OA	Order of Australia
OAS	Organization of American States
OAU	Organization for African Unity
OBB	Offical Bar of Biologist
OBE	Officer of Order of the British Empire
OBMS	Outward Bound Mountain School (UK)
obs., Obs.	observation, Observatory
OBU	Oxford Brookes University (UK)
OC	Order of Canada
oceanogr.	oceanography, oceanographical
OCED	Organización para Co-operación y Desarrollo (*see also* OECD)
Oct.	October
ODA	Overseas Development Administration/Agency (UK)
ODC	Overseas Development Council
OECD	Organization for Economic Cooperation & Development

OECS	Organization for Eastern Caribbean States
OEP	Order of Engineering of Peru
OFFS	Oman Flora & Fauna Surveys
OH	Ohio (USA)
OIE	Office International des Epizooties
OK	Oklahoma (USA)
O-level	Ordinary-level
OM	Order of Merit (UK)
ONC	Ordinary National Certificate
OND	Ordinary National Diploma
Ont.	Ontario (Canada)
OPCA	Overseas Press Club of America
open lit.	open literature (UNESCO term to describe openly accessible scientific & technical journals)
OPTIMA	Organization for the Phytotaxonomic Investigation of the Mediterranean Area
op., ops	operation, operations
OR	Oregon (USA)
ORA	Overseas Research Award
Org., orgn(s), orgnl	Organizer, organization(s), organizational
ORMP	Ocean Resource Management Programme
ornith.; ornithl	ornithology, ornithologist; ornithological
ORNL	Oak Ridge National Laboratory (USA)
ORSA	Operations Research Society of America
ORSI	Operational Research Society of India
ORSTOM	Institut Français de Recherche Scientifique pour le Développement en Coopération
OSA	Optical Society of America
OSC	Ornithological Society of China
OSI	Ornithological Society of India
OSLR	Ocean Sciences and Living Resources [one of the scientific programmes of IOC (UNESCO)]
OSME	Ornithological Society of the Middle East
OSNZ	Ornithological Society of New Zealand
OTS	Organization for Tropical Studies
Ott.	Ottawa (Canada)
OUEC	Oxford University Exploration Club
Oxf.	Oxford (UK)
Oxfam.	NGO
Oxon.	Oxonia (= Oxford or Oxfordshire, England, UK); Oxoniensis (= of Oxford University)
P.; P.; P	Partner; Public; Phosphorus
PA	Pennsylvania (USA)
PAA	Population Association of America
PAAF	name of building
PAAZAB	Pan African Association of Zoos, Aquariums and Botanical Gardens
PAC	Programme Activity Centre
PADU	Protected Areas Data Units
PAEL	Portuguese Association of Environmental Law
PAHO	PanAmerican Health Organization
Pak.	Pakistan
PALA	Portuguese Association of Landscape Architects
paleoenvts	paleoenvironments
PAMS	Pakistan Academy of Medical Sciences
PAN	Pesticide Action Network
PAOC	Pan African Ornithological Congress
PAP	Pakistan Association of Pathologists
Par.	Paraná (Brazil)
PARC	Pakistan Agricultural Research Council
partic.	particularly
Participa	a non-profit organization for promotion of democracy
PAS	Polish Agricultural Society
PASA	Phycological Association of South Africa
path.	pathology
PAU	Punjab Agricultural University

PB	Post Box, Private Bag
PBS	Polish Botanical Society, Public Broadcasting Service
PC	Privy Council
PCRW	Production Credit for Rural Women
PCSA	Palm and Cycad Society of Australia
PD	Privat-Docent (Swiss equivalent of Associate Professorship, permanent tenure), or -Dozent
PDN	Pastoral Development Network (UK)
PDNP	Peak District National Park
PDR	People's Democratic Republic
PEA	Peruvian Engineers' Association
PEC	Pakistan Engineering Council
Penn.	Pennsylvania (USA)
PEPC	Pakistan Environmental Protection Council
per.	pereulok (Russian, side street)
Perm.	Permanent
PERS	Pacific Estuarine Research Society
pers.	personal
pers.corres.	personal correspondence
PES	Polish Entomological Society
PFEA	Peruvian Forestry Engineers' Association
PFNC	Peruvian Foundation for Nature Conservancy
PFS	Polish Forester Society, Punjab Forest Service
PGR/pgr	P/plant G/genetic R/resources
PGS	Portugal Geography Society
PHA	Public Health Association
PHARE	Polish–Hungarian Aid for Reconstruction of Economy (EU)
pharm.	pharmacology, pharmacological
PhB	Bachelor of Philosophy
PhD	Doctor of Philosophy ('first doctorate', regardless of subject)
phil.; Phil.	philosophy, philosophical; Philadelphia (USA)
philos.	philosophy
photochem.	photochemistry
PHS	Public Health Service
physiol.	physiological, physiologist, physiology
phys.	physics, physical
phytochem.	phytochemistry
phytogeog., phytogeogl	phytogeography, phytogeographical
phytopath.	phytopathology
phytosoc.	phytosociology
PI	Principal Investigator
PIASA	Polish Institute of Arts & Sciences of America
PIEDAR	Pakistan Institute for Environment–Development Action Research
pl	ploshchad (= square, as in an address)
PL	Post Box (Sweden)
PLC	Private Limited Company
PLNP	Portuguese League for Nature Protection
ploshchad	square (as in an address)
PM	Prime Minister
PMB	Private/Public Postal Mail Bag
PNCNC	Polish National Council for Nature Conservation
PNG	Papua New Guinea
Pnt.	Poniente (= West)
PO	Post Office
POB	Post Office Box
pol.	politics, political
poll.	pollution
Poly.	Polytechnic
pop., pops	population, populations
postdoctl	postdoctoral (*i.e.* after first doctorate, commonly working towards higher)
postgrad., postgrads	postgraduate, postgraduates
pp.	pages
PPAZ	Planned Parenthood Association of Zambia
PPLH	Pusat Pendidikan Lingkungan Hidup (environmental education centre)
PR	Puerto Rico
PRC	People's Republic of China

precip.	precipitation
prelim.	preliminary
prep.	preparation, preparatory
PrepCom	Preparatory Committee
preserv.	preservation
Pres.	President
PRI	Potato Research Institute
P/prin.	Principal
PRO	Public Relations Officer
PROCITROPICOS	network of agricultural research centres of the Amazon countries
Proc., Procs	Proceeding(s)
prod.	production
Profors	bilateral programme of German GTZ
Prof., Profs; Prof'ship(s)	Professor, Professors; Professorship(s)
prog., progs	program(me), program(me)s
prop.	propulsion
PROTERRA	in favour of the Earth
prot.	protected, protection
Prov.	Province
PSA	Pacific Science Association, Phycological Society of America
PSF	Pakistan Science Foundation, Peruvian Society of Foresters
PSG	Pacific Seabird Group
PSGB	Primate Society of Great Britain
PSO	Principal Scientific Officer
PSWAB	Punjab State Wildlife Advisory Board
psych.	psychology
PSZN	Pubblicazioni Stazione Zoologia di Napoli
Pty	Proprietary
pub.	publicity
pubn(s)	publication(s)
Pvt.	Private
PZS	Polish Zoological Society
QAB	Quebec Association of Biologists
QAPG	Quebec Association for Professional Geographers
QCC	Queensland Conservation Council
QCM	Queensland Conservation Movement
QCMCC	Queensland Catchment Management Coordinating Committee
QDAH	Queensland Diploma of Animal Husbandry
QICMC	Queensland Integrated Catchment Management Committee
QJ	Quarterly Journal
QL	Quadra do Lago
Qld	Queensland (Australia)
QMC	Queen Mary College (University of London, England, UK)
QMWC	Queen Mary & Westfield College (University of London, England, UK)
QOS	Queensland Ornithological Society
QRA	Quaternary Research Association
QSOPC	Queensland State Oil Pollution Committee
Q/qual.; qual(s)	quality; qualification(s)
Que.	Québec (Canada)
QUT	Queensland University of Technology
qv	*quod vide* (which (or who) see)
QWC	Quebec Wildlife Council
R.	River, Royal
RAA	Royal Academy of Arts
RAAS	Russian Academy of Agricultural Sciences
RACI	Royal Australian Chemical Institute
rad	street (Slovak)
RADPATH	RADionuclide biogeochemical PATHways
RADTEST	RADiation from nuclear TEST explosions
RAE	Royal Academy of Engineering, Russian Academy of Engineering
RAI	Royal Anthropological Institute
RAIPA	Royal Australian Institute of Public Administration
RAIPR	Royal Australian Institute of Parks & Recreation
Raj.	Rajasthan (India)

RAMC	Royal Army Medical College
RAMSAR	Ramsar Convention (Ramsar being a town in Iran which agreed to host an IUCN Conference on Migratory Bird Species' Survival)
RANA	Restoring Australian Native Amphibia
RANS	Russian Academy of Natural Sciences
RAPI	Royal Australian Planning Institute
Rapp.	Rapporteur
RARE	now a name, not an acronym (initially Rare Animal Relief Effort)
RAS	Royal African Society, Royal Anthropological Society, Royal Astronomical Society, Russian Academy of Sciences
RASA	Royal Academy of Sciences and Arts
RASE	Royal Agricultural Society of England
RASEW	Royal Agricultural Society of England and Wales
RBS	Russian Botanical Society
RBSGS	Royal Belgian Society for Geographical Studies
RBZS	Royal Belgian Zoological Society (*see also* BZS)
r/c	ground floor
RCA	Royal College of Anaesthetists
RCEP	Royal Commission on Environmental Pollution
RCGP	Royal College of General Practitioners
RCGS	Royal Canadian Geographical Society
RCP	Royal College of Pathologists, Royal College of Physicians
RCS	Royal College of Science, Royal Commonwealth Society
RCVS	Royal College of Veterinary Surgeons (UK)
R&D	R/research & D/development
RD	Rural Delivery
RDX	company name, no meaning
re.	regarding, relating to
REA	Russian Ecological Academy
R/rec	Recreation
redev.	redevelopment
R/redistribn	redistribution
ref.	referee, reference
Regis.	Registered
regn(s); regnl	region(s); regional
regs	regulations
rehab.	rehabilitation
reintro.	reintroduction
RENRIC	Regional Environment & Natural Resources Information Centre
reorgn	reorganization
R/rep., R/reps; Repub.	R/representative, R/representatives; Republic
repro.	reproduction
Rer.Nat.	Rerum Naturalium
RES	Royal Entomological Society of London
res.	research
RESA	Research Society of America
Res.Assoc.	Research Associate
resp.	responsible, responsibility
resto.	restoration
rev.	review
RFDN	Rural Forestry Development Network (UK)
RFS	Royal Forestry Society (of England, Wales & Northern Ireland)
RGN	Registered General Nurse
RGS	Royal Geographical Society (UK)
RHS	Royal Horticultural Society (UK)
RI	Rhode Island (USA)
RIAM	Royal Irish Academy of Medicine
RIAS	Royal Incorporation of Architects in Scotland
RIBA	Royal Institute of British Architects
RICCA	InterAmerican Network Against Environmental Pollution
RICS	Royal Institution of Chartered Surveyors
RIIA	Royal Institute for International Affairs
RIPA	Royal Institute for Public Administration
RIVM	National Institute for Public Health and the Environment
RJ	Rio de Janeiro (Brazil)
RMB	Roadside Mail Box

RMIT	Royal Melbourne Institute of Technology
RMS	Royal Meteorological Society, Royal Microscopical Society
RN	Registered Nurse, Royal Navy
RNAS	Royal Netherlands Academy of Sciences
RNASL	Royal Norwegian Academy of Science and Letters
RNBS	Royal Netherlands Botanical Society
RNDr	Rerum Naturalium/Naturale Doctor
RNS	Royal Numismatic Society
RNSAS	Royal Netherlands Society of Agricultural Sciences
RNSPP	Royal Netherlands Society of Plant Pathology
RNSSL	Royal Norwegian Society of Science & Letters
RNZAF	Royal New Zealand Air Force
RNZIH	Royal New Zealand Institute of Horticulture
RoyMetS	Royal Meteorological Society
RPPS	Russian Plant Physiological Society
RPS	Royal Photographic Society (GB)
RPT	name of planning firm
RR	Rural Route
RRF	Raptor Research Foundation
RS	Rio Grande do Sul (southern State of Brazil), (The) Royal Society (of London)
RSA	Rangelands Society of Australia, Republic of South Africa
RSA	actually Royal Society for the Encouragement of Arts, Manufactures & Commerce but commonly known as Royal Society of Arts
RSAA	Royal Society for Asian Affairs
RSAAF	Royal Swedish Academy of Agriculture and Forestry
RSAAS	Royal Swedish Academy of Agricultural Sciences
RSAP	Russian Society for Animals' Protection
RSAS	Royal Society of Arts & Sciences, Royal Swedish Academy of Sciences
RSC	Royal Society of Canada, Royal Society of Chemistry (UK)
RSCN	Royal Society for the Conservation of Nature (Jordan)
RSD	Road Side Delivery
RSE	Royal Society of Edinburgh
RSEL	Romanian Society of Environmental Law
RSFS	Royal Scottish Forestry Society
RSGS	Royal Scottish Geographical Society, Royal Swedish Geographical Society
RSM	Royal Society of Medicine
RSNC	Royal Society for Nature Conservation (UK), *see also* WATCH
RSNZ	Royal Society of New Zealand
RSPB	Royal Society for the Protection of Birds (UK)
RSPCA	Royal Society for the Prevention of Cruelty to Animals (UK)
RSQ	Royal Society of Queensland
RSS	Royal Statistical Society
RSSA	Royal Society of South Africa, Royal Society of South Australia
RSTMH	Royal Society of Tropical Medicine and Hygiene
RSV	Royal Society of Victoria
RSWA	Royal Society of Western Australia
Rt	Right
RT	Rural Route
RTPI	Royal Town Planning Institute
RTS	Royal Television Society
RUKH	Ukrainian Popular Movement
RURAL	Responsible Use of Resource in Agriculture and on the Land
RZS	Royal Zoological Society
RZSS	Royal Zoological Society of Scotland
s., s.	son(s), southern
S.; S., S	Single, Separated; South, Sulphur
SA	Société Anonyme, South Africa, South Australia
SAA	Society for American Archaeology, Society for Applied Anthropology
SAAAS	South African Association for the Advancement of Science
SAAB	South African Association of Botanists
SAAEES	South Africa Association of Ecologists and Environmental Scientists
SAARC	South Asian Association for Regional Cooperation
SAAR CLAW	South Asian Association of Regional Cooperation Lawyers
SAB	Society for Advancement of Botany (Meerut, India), Society for Applied Bacteriology

sabb., sabbs	sabbatical, sabbaticals
SAC	Scientific Advisory Committee
SACEP	South Asia Cooperative Environment Programme
SACNAS	South African Council for Natural Scientists
SADC	South Africa Development Committee
SAE	Spanish Association of Entomology
SAES	Swedish Academy of Engineering Sciences
SAES	South African Entomological Society
SAESF	South African Environmental Scientific Forum
SAF	Society of American Foresters
SAGS	South African Geographical Society
SAIE	South African Institute of Ecologists
SAIEES	South African Institute of Ecologists & Environmental Scientists
SAL	Society of Antiquaries of London, South African Lymphoma
SAMS	Scottish Association of Marine Science
SAN	Society of American Naturalists
SANZ	Systematics Association of New Zealand
San.Eng., San.Engr	Sanitary Engineering, Sanitary Engineer
SAOS	Southern African Ornithological Society
SAPS	Society for Advances in Plant Science
SAREM	Argentine Society for the Study of Mammals
SARP	Stowarzyszenic Architektow Polskich (Association of Polish Architects)
SAS	Society of Antiquaries of Scotland
SASAS	South African Society for Atmospheric Sciences
SASE	Southern Africa Society of Ecologists
SASEANEE	South Asia & SouthEast Asia Network for Environmental Education (based in Centre for Environmental Education, Ahmedabad, India)
Sask.	Saskatchewan (Canada)
SASMO	South African Society of Medical Oncology
SASQR	South African Society of Quaternary Research
SATIS	World Union of Appropriate Technology (Amsterdam)
SAWH	South African Wildlife Heritage
SAWMA	Southern African Wildlife Management Association
SAZS	South African Zoological Society
SB	Bachelor of Science (*see also* BS)
SBB	Sociedade Brasileira de Biología
SBCI	Society of Biological Chemists India
SBM	Sociedad Botánica de Mexico
SBNH	Society for the Bibliography of Natural History
SC	Santa Catarina (Brazil), South Carolina (USA)
SCAI	Scientific Committee of Academia Istropolitana
SCAR	Scientific Committee on Antarctic Research
SCAV	Sociedad Conservacionista Audubon de Venezuela
ScB	Bachelor of Science (*see also* BSc, BS, SB)
SCB	Society for Conservation Biology
SCCS	Sociedad Colombiana de la Ciencia del Suelo
ScD	Doctor of Science (U.of Cambridge and MIT form), *see also* DSc
Sc.Dr	Doctor of Science (*see also* DSc etc.)
SCE	Society for Conservation Ecology
SCES	Society for Chinese Environmental Sciences
SCG	Society of Cytologists & Geneticists
s/Sch.	s/School
SCI	Society of Chemical Industry
s/Sci.; s/Scis	s/Science, s/Scientist, scientific; s/Sciences
SCN	Society for Conservation of Nature
SCOPE	Scientific Committee on Problems of the Environment (of ICSU)
SCOR	Scientific Committee on Oceanic Research
SCUBA	Self-Contained Underwater Breathing Apparatus
SD	South Dakota (USA)
SDE	Swedish Doctors for the Environment
Sdn Bhd	Sendirian Berhad (Private Ltd)
SDPI	Sustainable Development Policy Institute
SDZS	San Diego Zoological Society (*see also* ZSSD)
Se	Southeastern, Selenium
SE	Society of Ethnobiology
SEAPOL	Southeast Asia Programme in Ocean Law, Policy, & Management

SEB	Society for Economic Botany (USA), Society for Experimental Biology
SECS	Sudan Environment Conservation Society
SECT	Society for Environmental Chemistry & Toxicology
S/sec.	Secretary, secondary
Sec.-Gen.	Secretary-General
SEE	Society for Ecological Economics, Society of Environmental Engineers (UK)
SEEC	Scottish Environmental Education Council
SEEDS	Society for Environment, Eco-sociology, and Development of Science
SEES	Society of Ecotoxicology & Environmental Safety
SEF	Société d'Ecologie Française
SEH	Society of European Herpetologists
SEI	Stockholm Environment Institute
SEJ	Society of Environmental Journalists
SEL	Societas Europaea Lepidopterologica, Society of Environmental Law
S/sem., S/sems	S/seminar, S/seminars
SEP	Society for Environmental Protistology
SEPA	Science Education Programme for Africa (US AID-sponsored)
SEPM	Society of Economic Paleontologists & Mineralogists (USA)
Sept.	September
SER	Society for Ecological Restoration
SERC	Science & Engineering Research Council
SERMISA	office name
SES	Swiss Entomological Society
SESC	Solar Energy Society of Canada
SESI	Solar Energy Society of India
SESJ	Society for Environmental Science, Japan
SETAC	Society for Environmental Toxicology and Chemistry (USA)
SF	San Francisco (USA)
SFC	Society of Fossil Cnidaria
SFE	Société Française d'Ecologie
SFECA	Société Française de l'Etude du Comportement Animal
SFI	Société Française d'Ichthyologie
SFSF	Society for Forestry Sciences in Finland
SFTA	Society of Film & TV Arts (became BAFTA)
SG(s)/sg(s)	S/specialist G/group(s)
SGF	Société Géologique de France
SGL	Sociedade Geografia de Lisboa
SGM	Society for General Microbiology
SGP	Sociedade Geologica de Portugal
SGS	Scottish Geographical Society, Slovak Geographical Society, Swedish Geophysical Society
SHE	Society for Human Ecology (USA)
SHIS	Setor de Habitacoes Individuais Sul
SHSN	Swiss Academy of Sciences
SID	Society for International Development
SIDA	Swedish International Development Authority
SIENT	name of journal
SIF	Society of Indian Foresters
sig.	significant, significance
SIL	International Association for Theoretical & Applied Limnology (*see also* IATAL), Schweizerische Ingenieurschule für Landwirtschaft, Societas Internationalis Limnologiae (*see also* ISL)
SILATHAM	a concept — a locally-familiar Buddhist principle meaning the maintenance of the correct balance of Nature, within the individual, society, & environment
SIP	Society of Invertebrate Pathology
SIPI	Scientists' Institute for Public Information (NY, USA)
SIPRI	Stockholm International Peace Research Institute
SIRATAC	first computer system for cotton-pest management in Australia
SIRO	Scientific & Industrial Research Organization
SISI	Swedish Institute for Social Improvements
SL	Sierra Leone
SLAAS	Sri Lanka Association for the Advancement of Science
SLAG	Sri Lanka Association of Geographers
SLCS	Sociedad Latinoamericana de la Ciencia del Suelo

SLENCA	Sierra Leone Environment & Conservation Association (now known as Council for the Protection of Nature)
SLIB	Sri Lanka Institute of Biology
SLT	Schweiz-Landwirtschaft Technikum (Swiss Agricultural College, became SIL, *qv,* in 1991)
SM	Master of Science (*see also* MS, MSc, etc.)
SMA	Swedish Medical Association
SMCS	Sudan Marine Conservation Society
SME	Society of Mining Engineers
SMF	Société Mycologique de France
SMHI	Swedish Meteorological & Hydrological Institute
SMM	Society for Marine Mammalogy
S/N, S–N	Sin Numeros (= without number), South–North
SNCB	Swedish National Committee for Biology
SNH	Scottish Natural Heritage
SNP	Society for Nature Protection
SO	Scientific Officer
SOC	Scottish Ornithologists' Club
sociol.	sociology, sociological
SOCLEEN	Society of Clean Environment
Soc., S/socs	Society, S/societies
SODAR	Sonic Detection and Ranging
SOS	Save Our Souls (alarm), Swedish Ornithological Society
SP	São Paulo (Brazil)
sp.; spp.	species (singular); species (plural)
SPA	specially protected area
SPAE	Sociedade Portuguesa de Antyropologia e Etnografia
SPANA	Society for the Protection of Animals in North Africa
SPCS	Sociedad Peruana de la Ciencia del Suelo
SPEC	Society for the Promotion of Environmental Conservation
spec., specn	special, specialist; specialization
SPIE	International Society for Optical Engineering
SPNI	Society for the Protection of Nature in Israel
SPNL	Society for the Protection of Nature In Lebanon
SPREP	South Pacific Regional Environment Programme
SPS	Strategic Planning Society
SQ, sq.	part of address, square (measurement)
SQSP	Société Québecoise de Science Politique
Sr	Senior
SRC	Speliological Research Council
SRE	Society for Restoration Ecology
SRF	Senior Research Fellow
SRL	Society of Rural Law
SRM	Society for Range Management (North America)
SSA	Seismological Society of America, Swedish Seed Association
SSAB	Society for the Study of Animal Behaviour
SSAG	Swedish Society for Anthropology & Geography
SSAR	Society for the Study of Amphibians & Reptiles
SSB	Society of Systematic Biologists
SSC	Species Survival Commission (IUCN)
SSE	Society for the Study of Evolution (USA)
SSHRCC	Social Sciences & Humanities Research Council of Canada
SSL	Society for Sustainable Living
SSM	Swedish Society of Medicine
SSMR	Swedish Society of Marine Researchers
SSNP	Swedish Society for Nature Protection
SSO	Senior Scientific Officer
SSPN	Swedish Society for Nature Protection
SSPP	Scandinavian Society of Plant Physiology
S/sr	S/senior
SSR	Soviet Socialist Republic
SSRC	Social Sciences Research Council
SSS	Society of Soil Science
SSSA	Soil Science Society of America
SSSG	Soil Science Society of Germany
SSSI	Sites of Special Scientific Interest
SSTMP	Swiss Society for Tropical Medicine & Parasitology

SSZ	Society of Systematic Zoology
stab.	stability, stabilization
Staffs.	Staffordshire (England, UK)
STAR	Science Teaching And Research Training
START	Global Change System for Analysis, Research, & Training
stats, statl	statistics, statistical
STB	Society for Tropical Biology
step-d.	step-daughter
step-s.	step-son
STF	Society of Tropical Forests
STI	Society of Toxicologists of India
STM	Society of Tropical Medicine (Switzerland)
strat., strats	strategy, strategies
St, Ste	Saint
SU	State University
S/subcttee	subcommittee
subs.	subsequent, subsequently
subtrop.	subtropical
SUNY	State University of New York
Super.	Superintendent
sust.	sustainable, sustainability
SUT	Society for Underwater Technology
SVOO	Schweizerischer Verband der Oekologuinen und Oekologen (Swiss Association for Professional Ecologists)
SVP	Society of Vertebrate Paleobiology
Sw, SW	Southwestern, South West
SWC	Society of Wetland Scientists
SWCAA	Soil & Water Conservation Association of Australia/Australasia
SWCS	Soil and Water Conservation Society (USA), Sudan Wildlife Conservation Society
SWG	Society of Woman Geographers
SWS	Society of Wetland Scientists
symp.	symposium
SZG	Schweizerischer Zoologische Gesellschaft (Swiss Zoological Society)
SZOPK	Slovak Union of Nature and Landscape Protectors
SZS	Swiss Zoological Society
TAA	Tropical Agriculture Association (UK)
TAMAR	Tartarugas Marinhas (sea-turtles)
TANAPA	Tanzania National Parks
TARA	Technology and Action for Rural Advancement
Tas.	Tasmania (Australia)
TB	tuberculosis
TBS	Turkish Biological Society
TECHSULT	name of company
tech.; techs; techl	technical, technology; technologies; technological
TEK	initials of original Directors of Company
telecomm., telecomms	telecommunication, telecommunications
temp., temps	temperature, temperatures
TEPA	Turkish Environmental Protection Agency
TERI	Tata Energy Research Institute (New Delhi, India)
terr.	terrestrial
TEST	Transport and Environment Studies
TFAP	Tropical Forest Action Plan
THEMAPS	name of software package
T/theol.	T/theology, theological
TIGER	Terrestrial Impacts of Global Environmental Change
tm	trade mark
TMAG	Trilateral Monitoring and Assessment Group
TMEG	Trilateral Monitoring Expert Group
TN	Tamil Nadu (India), Tennessee (USA)
TNC	The Nature Conservancy (USA)
TNCS	Turkish Nature Conservation Society
TR	Turkey (part of postal code)
tr.	trieda (Slovak, avenue or boulevard); transfer(red), transport(ed)
trad.	traditional

TRAFFIC	Trade Records Analysis of Flora & Fauna in Commerce
Trans.	Transactions
transl.	translated, translation, translator
trop.	tropical
TROPENBOS	Foundation for world-wide research on tropical forests (The Netherlands' Government)
TSES	Territorial System of Ecological Stability
TTKD	Turkish Association for Conservation of Nature & Natural Resources
TUP	Towarzystwo Urbanistòw Polskich (Society of Polish Town Planners)
TV	television
TVE	Television Trust for the Environment
TWAS	Third World Academy of Sciences (Italy)
TWOW	Third World Organization for Women
TWWAS	Third World Women Academy of Science
TX	Texas (USA)
u.; U./u.	ulitsa, utca (= street); U/university
UAE	United Arab Emirates
UAPS	Union of African Population Studies
UBC	University of British Columbia
UC, UCL	University College (London, England, UK)
UCB	University of California at Berkeley
UCD	University of California at Davis
UCI	University of California at Irvine
UCL	University College London (England, UK)
UCLA	University of California at Los Angeles
UCNW	University College of North Wales (Bangor)
UCR	University of California at Riverside
UCSB	University of California at Santa Barbara
UCSC	University of California at Santa Cruz
UCSD	University of California at San Diego
UCWOS	Universities' Consortium for World Order Studies
UET	University of Engineering & Technology (Lahore, Pakistan)
UGC	University Grants Commission
UHH	University of Hawaii at Honolulu
ÚHÚL	Ústav pro Hospodarskou Úpravu Lesu (Czech Institute for Forest Management Planning)
UIA	Union of International Associations (Brussels, Belgium)
UK	United Kingdom
UKAEA	United Kingdom Atomic Energy Authority
UKM	Universiti Kebangsaan Malaysie
UKSEE	United Kingdom Society of Environmental Engineers
ULB	Université Libre de Bruxelles (actually VUB)
ul.	ulica, ulitsa (= street)
UMBSM	University Marine Biological Station Millport (Scotland, UK — jointly run as a College by Universities of Glasgow & London)
UMC	University Mail Code
UMIST	University of Manchester Institute for Science & Technology
UN	United Nations
UNAM	Universidad Nacional Autonoma de Mexico (National Autonomous University of Mexico)
UNASL	United Nations Association of Sri Lanka
UNCED	United Nations Conference on Environment and Development
UNCHE	United Nations Conference on the Human Environment
UNCHS	United Nations Conference on Human Settlements
UNCRD	United Nations Centre for Regional Development (Japan)
UNCSTD	United Nations Conference on Science & Technology for Development
UNCTAD	United Nations Conference on Trade & Development
undergrad., undergrads	undergraduate, undergraduates
Undersec.	Undersecretary
UNDP	United Nations Development Programme
UNECA	United Nations Economic Commission for Africa
UNED	United Nations Environment & Development
UNEP	United Nations Environment Programme
UNESCO	United Nations Educational, Scientific, & Cultural Organization
UNFAO	United Nations Food and Agriculture Organization

UNFPA	United Nations Population Fund (formerly UN Fund for Population Activities)
UNGA	United Nations General Assembly
UNHCR	United Nations High Commision for Refugees
UNICEF	United Nations International Children's Fund
UNIDO	United Nations Industrial Development Organization
UNIDROIT	International Institute for the Unification of Private Law (Rome, Italy)
UNIFEM	United Nations Fund for Women
UNITAR	United Nations Institute for Training & Research
UNITAS	International Union of Malacologists
U/univs	U/universities
Univ.	Universitatis (or other-language form)
UNOLS	University National Oceanographic Laboratory System
UNRISD	United Nations Research Institute for Social Development
UNU	United Nations University (HQ in Tokyo)
UP	Uttar Pradesh (India)
UPI	United Press International
UPM	Universiti Pertanian Malaysia
URI	University of Rhode Island
URL	Universal Resource Locator
US	United States (commonly meaning 'of America')
USA	United States of America
USAAF	United States Army Air Force
USAEC	United States Atomic Energy Commission (now US Dept of Energy *qv*)
USAEE	United States Association of Environmental Economists
US–AEP	United States–Asia Environmental Partnership
USAF	United States Air Force
US AID, USAID	United States Agency for International Development
USC	University of Southern California
USDA	United States Department of Agriculture
USDC	United States Department of Commerce
USDE	United States Department of Energy (formerly USAEC)
USDI	United States Department of the Interior
USEDA	United States Energy & Development Administration
USEPA	United States Environmental Protection Agency
USFS	United States Forest Service
USI	Ultrasonic Society of India
USIA	United States Information Agency
USVI	United States Virgin Islands
UT	Utah (USA)
UTM	Universal Transverse Mercator
UV	ultraviolet
v., V.	*versus*, Vice
VA	Virginia (USA)
var.	variety, various
VASVIK	Vividhlaxi Audyogik Samshodhan Vikas Kendra
VC	Vice-Chairman
VEE	Virginia Environmental Endowment
veg.	vegetation
Venia Legendi	the right of reading own university lectures
VERMITECH	Vermi (worms) Tech.(technology)
vet.	veterinary, veterinarian
Vic.	Victoria (Australia)
Vis.	Visiting
viz.	*videlicet* (= namely)
vol.; vols	volunteer, voluntary, volume; volunteers, volumes
VP	Vice-President
VPI	Virginia Polytechnic Institute & State University
VSE	Venezuelan Society of Entomology
VSEcol.	Venezuelan Society of Ecology
VSL	Venezuelan Society of Lepidopterology
VT	Vermont (USA)
VTEE	Virginia Transportation Environmental Enhancement
VUB	Vrije Universiteit Brussel (Free University of Brussels)
VWC [AB]	Virginia Water Centre [Advisory Board]

W.; W., w.	Widow(er); West, western
WA	Washington (USA), Western Australia (Australia)
WAAS	World Academy of Art & Sciences
WAC	World Association of Copepodologists
WANC	Western Australian Naturalists' Club
Warks.	Warwickshire (England, UK)
WASWC	World Association of Soil & Water Conservation
WATCH	Junior Section of RSNC
WAWF	World Association of World Federalists
WAWV	World Association of Wildlife Veterinarians
WBCSD	World Business Council for Sustainable Development
WCB	World Council For The Biosphere
WCC	World Climate Conference, World Cultural Council
WCCD	World Commission for Culture & Development
WCED	World Commission on Environment & Development
WCF	World Conservation Fellowship
WCI	Wildlife Conservation International
WCK	Wildlife Clubs of Kenya
WCMC	World Conservation Monitoring Centre
WCRP	World Climate Research Programme
WCRPS	World Coral Reef Protection Society
WCS	Wildlife Conservation Society (was NYZS), World Conservation Strategy
WCU	World Conservation Union (IUCN, as formerly International Union for Conservation of Nature & Natural Resources)
WDA	Wildlife Disease Association
WEC	World Energy Council
WEDO	Women, Environment & Development Organization, Women in Development Organization
WEF	Water Environment Federation (formerly WPCF)
WEN	Women's Environmental Network
WESTPAC	Sub-Commission for the Western Pacific
WFARP	World Foundation Aids Research and Prevention
WFEO	World Federation of Engineering Organizations
WFP	World Food Programme
WFSF	World Future Studies Federation
WFT	Wildlife Fund of Turkey
WG	Working Group
WHII	World Heritage Interpretation International
WHO	World Health Organization
WHOI	Woods Hole Oceanographic Institution
WHRC	Woods Hole Research Center
WHS	World Heritage Site
WHSNR	Western Hemisphere Shorebird Nature Reserve
WI	Wisconsin (USA)
WIDECAST	Wider Caribbean Network for Sea Turtle Conservation (UNEP)
WII	Wildlife Institute of India
Win.	Winnipeg (Canada)
WIPAC	Womens' International Policy Action Committee
WLNPS	Wild Life and Nature Protection Society
WLO	Dutch Association of Landscape Ecologists
W–M	Wisconsin–Madison
WMA	Wildlife Management Association
WMO	World Meteorological Organization (was International Meteorological Organization)
WMRT	name of firm
WNA	World Nature Association
WNPS	Wildlife & Nature Protection Society
WNWED	WorldWIDE Network of Women in Environment & Development
WOCAT	World Overview of Conservation Approaches & Technologies
Worcs.	Worcestershire (England, UK)
WorldWIDE	World Women in Development and Environment
WOS	Wilson Ornithological Society
WOTRO	Stichting Weten Schappelijk Onderzoek in de Tropen (Netherlands Foundation for the Advancement of Tropical Research)
WPA	World Pheasant Association
WPCA	Water Pollution Control Association

WPCF	Water Pollution Control Federation (now WEF)
WPRSA	Western and Pacific Regional Science Association
WPSI	Wildlife Preservation Society of India
WPSQ	Wildlife Preservation Society of Queensland
WPTC	Wildlife Preservation Trust Canada
WPTI	Wildlife Preservation Trust International
WREN	World Renewable Energy Network
WRI	World Resources Institute
WSB	Wildlife Society of Bangladesh
WSL	Eidgenossische Forschungsanstalt für Wald, Schnee, und Landschaft
WSN	Western Society of Naturalists
WSO	Wisconsin Society for Ornithology
WSPA	World Society for the Protection of Animals
WSSA	Wildlife Society of South Africa
WSSJ	Weed Science Society of Japan
WST	Wildlife Society of Tanzania
WSU	Washington State University
WTO	World Trade Organization
WV	West Virginia (USA)
WWF	World Wildlife Fund International (changed in 1987 in most countries to World Wide Fund for Nature)
WWII	World War II
WY	Wyoming (USA)
Xerox	photocopying machine (product of Rank Xerox, 'The Document Company') most helpful in completing this work
XL	Forty
YHA	Youth Hostels Association (UK)
Yorks.	Yorkshire (England, UK)
yr(s)	year(s)
ZAIKS	Association of Polish Authors
ZCOG	Zoo Conservation Outreach Group
ZMT	Centre for Tropical Marine Ecology
zoogeog.	zoogeography
zool.; zool	zoology; zoological
ZS	Zoological Society
ZSA	Zimbabwe Scientific Association
ZSF	Zoological Society of France
ZSJ	Zoological Society of Japan
ZSL	Zoological Society of London
ZSN	Zoological Society of Nepal
ZSP	Zoological Society of Pakistan
ZSSA	Zoological Society of Southern Africa
ZSSD	Zoological Society of San Diego (*see also* SDZS)
ZWO	Nederlandse Organisatie voor Zuiver-Wetenschappelijk Onderzoek (Netherlands Organization for the Advancement of Pure Research)
@; @	at; sign used in E-mail 'numbers'
©	Copyright (with holder and year added)
#, #	number, *see also* no and (preferred) nr; can also indicate a space
=	sign indicating equality or meaning